W9-BSN-579

Collins

BESTSELLING BILINGUAL DICTIONARIES

Spanish Dictionary

Collins

HarperCollins Publishers
Westerhill Road
Bishopbriggs
Glasgow
G64 2QT
Great Britain

Fifth Edition 2008

Reprint 10 9 8 7 6 5 4 3 2 1

© HarperCollins Publishers 1997, 2000, 2004, 2006, 2008

ISBN 978-0-00-726054-6

Collins® and Bank of English® are registered trademarks of HarperCollins Publishers Limited

www.collinslanguage.com

A catalogue record for this book is available from the British Library

HarperCollins Publishers,
10 East 53rd Street,
New York, NY 10022

COLLINS SPANISH CONCISE DICTIONARY.
Fifth US Edition 2008

ISBN 978-0-06-114184-3

Library of Congress Cataloging-in-Publication Data has been applied for

www.harpercollins.com

HarperCollins books may be purchased for educational, business, or sales promotional use. For information, please write to:
Special Markets Department,
HarperCollins Publishers,
10 East 53rd Street,
New York, NY 10022

Typeset by Davidson Pre-Press, Glasgow

Printed in Italy by
LEGO Spa, Lavis (Trento), ITALY

Acknowledgements
We would like to thank those authors and publishers who kindly gave permission for copyright material to be used in the Collins Word Web. We would also like to thank Times Newspapers Ltd for providing valuable data.

All rights reserved.

Entered words that we have reason to believe constitute trademarks have been designated as such. However, neither the presence nor absence of such designation should be regarded as affecting the legal status of any trademark.

When you buy a Collins dictionary or thesaurus and register on www.collinslanguage.com for the free online and digital services, you will not be charged by HarperCollins for access to Collins free Online Dictionary content or Collins free Online Thesaurus content on that website. However, your operator's charges for using the internet on your computer will apply. Costs vary from operator to operator. HarperCollins is not responsible for any charges levied by online service providers for accessing Collins free Online Dictionary or Collins free Online Thesaurus on www.collinslanguage.com using these services.

HarperCollins does not warrant that the functions contained in www.collinslanguage.com content will be uninterrupted or error free, that defects will be corrected, or that www.collinslanguage.com or the server that makes it available are free of viruses or bugs. HarperCollins is not responsible for any access difficulties that may be experienced due to problems with network, web, online or mobile phone connections.

PUBLISHING DIRECTOR
Catherine Love

MANAGING EDITOR
Gaëlle Amiot-Cadey

PROJECT MANAGEMENT
Carol McCann

CONTRIBUTORS
Jeremy Butterfield, Mike González, Gerry Breslin, Teresa Álvarez García, Brian Steel, Ana Cristina Llompart, José Miguel Galván Déniz, Val McNulty, Sharon Hunter, Tracy Lomas, Enrique González Sandinero, Caitlin McMahon, Genevieve Gerrard

TECHNICAL SUPPORT
Thomas Callan

SERIES EDITOR
Rob Scriven

Índice de materias

Contents

MARCAS REGISTRADAS
Las marcas que creemos que constituyen marcas registradas las denominamos como tales. Sin embargo, no debe considerarse que la presencia o la ausencia de esta designación tenga que ver con la situatión legal de ninguna marca.

NOTE ON TRADEMARKS
Words which we have reason to believe constitute registered trademarks have been designated as such. However, neither the presence nor the absence of such designation should be regarded as affecting the legal status of any trademark.

William Collins' dream of knowledge for all began with the publication of his first book in 1819. A self-educated mill worker, he not only enriched millions of lives, but also founded a flourishing publishing house. Today, staying true to this spirit, Collins books are packed with inspiration, innovation, and practical expertise. They place you at the centre of a world of possibility and give you exactly what you need to explore it.

Language is the key to this exploration, and at the heart of Collins Dictionaries is language as it is really used. New words, phrases, and meanings spring up every day, and all of them are captured and analysed by the Collins Word Web. Constantly updated, and with over 2.5 billion entries, this living language resource is unique to our dictionaries.

Words are tools for life. And a Collins Dictionary makes them work for you.

Collins. Do more.

Introduction

You may be starting Spanish for the first time, or you may wish to extend your knowledge of the language. Perhaps you want to read and study Spanish books, newspapers and magazines, or perhaps simply have a conversation with Spanish speakers. Whatever the reason, whether you're a student, a tourist or want to use Spanish for business, this is the ideal book to help you understand and communicate. This modern, user-friendly dictionary gives priority to everyday vocabulary and the language of current affairs, business, computing and tourism, and, as in all Collins dictionaries, the emphasis is firmly placed on contemporary language and expressions.

How to use the dictionary

Below you will find an outline of how information is presented in your dictionary. Our aim is to give you the maximum amount of detail in the clearest and most helpful way.

Entries

A typical entry in your dictionary will be made up of the following elements:

Phonetic transcription

Phonetics appear in square brackets immediately after the headword. They are shown using the International Phonetic Alphabet (IPA), and a complete list of the symbols used in this system can be found on page x. The pronunciation given is for Castilian Spanish except where a word is solely used in Latin America, when we give the Latin American pronunciation. A further guide to the differences in types of Spanish pronunciation is given on page x.

Grammatical information

All words belong to one of the following parts of speech: noun, verb, adjective, adverb, pronoun, article, conjunction, preposition, abbreviation. Nouns can be singular or plural and, in Spanish, masculine or feminine. Verbs can be transitive, intransitive, reflexive or impersonal. Parts of speech appear in *italics* immediately after the phonetic spelling of the headword. The gender of the translation also appears in *italics* immediately following the key element of the translation, except where this is a regular masculine singular noun ending in "o", or a regular feminine singular noun ending in "a".

Often a word can have more than one part of speech. Just as the English word **chemical** can be an adjective or a noun, the Spanish word **conocido** can be an adjective ("(well-) known") or a noun ("acquaintance"). In the same way the verb **to walk** is sometimes transitive, ie it takes an object ("to walk the dog") and sometimes intransitive, ie it doesn't take an object ("to walk to school"). To help you find the meaning you are looking for quickly and for clarity of presentation, the different part of speech categories are separated by a shaded square ■.

Meaning divisions

Most words have more than one meaning. Take, for example, **punch** which can be, amongst other things, a blow with the fist or an object used for making holes. Other words are translated differently depending on the context in which they are used. The transitive verb **to put on**, for example, can be translated by "ponerse", "encender" etc depending on *what* it is you are putting on. To help you select the most appropriate translation in every context, entries are divided according to meaning. Each different meaning is introduced by an "indicator" in *italics* and in brackets. Thus, the examples given above will be shown as follows:

> **punch** [pʌntʃ] *n* (*blow*) golpe *m*, puñetazo; (*tool*) punzón *m*

Likewise, some words can have a different meaning when used to talk about a specific subject area or field. For example **bishop**, which in a religious context means a high-ranking clergyman, is also the name of a chess piece. To show English speakers which translation to use, we have added "subject field labels" in brackets, in this case *(Chess)*:

> **bishop** [ˈbɪʃəp] *n* obispo; (*Chess*) alfil *m*

Field labels are often shortened to save space. You will find a complete list of abbreviations used in the dictionary on pages viii and ix.

Translations

Most English words have a direct translation in Spanish and vice versa, as shown in the examples given above. Sometimes, however, no exact equivalent exists in the target language. In such cases we have given an approximate equivalent, indicated by the sign ≈. An example is **Health Service**, the Spanish equivalent of which is "Insalud". There is no exact equivalent since the bodies in the two countries are quite different:

> **Health Service** *n* (*Brit*) servicio de salud pública, ≈ Insalud *m* (*SP*)

On occasion it is impossible to find even an approximate equivalent. This may be the case, for example, with the names of types of food:

> **fabada** [faˈβaða] *nf* *bean and sausage stew*

Here the translation (which doesn't exist) is replaced by an explanation. For increased clarity, the explanation, or "gloss", is shown in *italics*.

It is often the case that a word, or a particular meaning of a word, cannot be translated in isolation. The translation of **Dutch**, for example, is "holandés/esa". However, the phrase **to go Dutch** is rendered by "pagar cada uno lo suyo". Even an expression as simple as **washing powder** needs a separate translation since it translates as "detergente (en polvo)", not "polvo para lavar". This is where your dictionary will prove to be particularly informative and useful since it contains an abundance of compounds, phrases and idiomatic expressions.

Levels of formality and familiarity

In English you instinctively know when to say **I'm broke** or **I'm a bit short of cash** and when to say **I don't have any money**. When you are trying to understand someone who is speaking Spanish, however, or when you yourself try to speak Spanish, it is important to know what is polite and what is less so, and what you can say in a relaxed situation but not in a formal context. To help you with this, on the Spanish-English side we have added the label (*fam*) to show that a Spanish meaning or expression is colloquial, while those meanings or expressions which are vulgar are given an exclamation mark (*fam!*), warning you they can cause serious offence. Note also that on the English-Spanish side, translations which are vulgar are followed by an exclamation mark in brackets.

Keywords

Words labelled in the text as KEYWORDS, such as **have** and **do** or their Spanish equivalents **tener** and **hacer**, have been given special treatment because they form the basic elements of the language. This extra help will ensure that you know how to use these complex words with confidence.

Cultural information

Entries which are marked in the main text by a column of dots explain aspects of culture in Spanish and English-speaking countries. Subject areas covered include politics, education, media and national festivals.

Spanish alphabetical order

In 1994 the **Real Academia Española** and the Spanish American language academies jointly decided to stop treating CH and LL as separate letters in Spanish, thereby bringing it into line with European spelling norms. This means that **chapa** and **lluvia** will appear in letters C and L respectively. Of course, it should also be remembered that words like **cancha** and **callar**, with **ch** and **ll** in the middle of the words, will also have changed places alphabetically, now being found after **cáncer** and **cáliz** respectively. Spanish, however still has one more letter than English with Ñ treated separately, between N and O.

Abreviaturas		Abbreviations
abreviatura	*ab(b)r*	abbreviation
adjetivo, locución adjetiva	*adj*	adjective, adjectival phrase
administración, lenguaje administrativo	*Admin*	administration
adverbio, locución adverbial	*adv*	adverb, adverbial phrase
agricultura	*Agr*	agriculture
alguien	*algn*	
América Latina	*Am*	Latin America
anatomía	*Anat*	anatomy
arquitectura	*Arq, Arch*	architecture
astrología, astronomía	*Astro*	astrology, astronomy
el automóvil	*Aut(o)*	the motor car and motoring
aviación, viajes en avión	*Aviat*	flying, air travel
biología	*Bio(l)*	biology
botánica, flores	*Bot*	botany
inglés británico	*Brit*	British English
química	*Chem*	chemistry
cine	*Cine*	cinema
lenguaje familiar (! vulgar)	*col (!)*	colloquial usage (! particularly offensive)
comercio, finanzas, banca	*Com(m)*	commerce, finance, banking
informática	*Comput*	computing
conjunción	*conj*	conjunction
construcción	*Constr*	building
compuesto	*cpd*	compound element
cocina	*Culin*	cookery
economía	*Econ*	economics
electricidad, electrónica	*Elec*	electricity, electronics
enseñanza, sistema escolar	*Escol*	schooling, schools
España	*Esp*	Spain
especialmente	*esp*	especially
exclamación, interjección	*excl*	exclamation, interjection
femenino	*f*	feminine
lenguaje familiar (! vulgar)	*fam (!)*	colloquial usage (! particularly offensive)
ferrocarril	*Ferro*	railways
uso figurado	*fig*	figurative use
fotografía	*Foto*	photography
(verbo inglés) del cual la partícula es inseparable	*fus*	(phrasal verb) where the particle is inseparable
generalmente	*gen*	generally
geografía, geología	*Geo*	geography, geology
geometría	*Geom*	geometry
informática	*Inform*	computing
invariable	*inv*	invariable
irregular	*irreg*	irregular
lo jurídico	*Jur*	law
América Latina	*LAm*	Latin America
gramática, lingüística	*Ling*	grammar, linguistics

literatura	*Lit*	literature
masculino	*m*	masculine
matemáticas	*Mat(h)*	mathematics
medicina	*Med*	medical term, medicine
masculino/femenino	*m/f*	masculine/feminine
lo militar, el ejército	*Mil*	military matters
música	*Mus*	music
sustantivo	*n*	noun
navegación, náutica	*Naut*	sailing, navigation
sustantivo no empleado en el plural	*no pl*	collective (uncountable) noun, not used in plural
sustantivo numérico	*num*	numeral noun
complemento	*obj*	(grammatical) object
	o.s.	oneself
peyorativo	*pey, pej*	derogatory, pejorative
fotografía	*Phot*	photography
fisiología	*Physiol*	physiology
plural	*pl*	plural
política	*Pol*	politics
participio de pasado	*pp*	past participle
prefijo	*pref*	prefix
preposición	*prep*	preposition
pronombre	*pron*	pronoun
psicología, psiquiatría	*Psico, Psych*	psychology, psychiatry
tiempo pasado	*pt*	past tense
ferrocarril	*Rail*	railways
religión, lo eclesiástico	*Rel*	religion, church service
	sb	somebody
enseñanza, sistema escolar	*Scol*	schooling, schools
singular	*sg*	singular
España	*SP*	Spain
	sth	something
subjuntivo	*subjun*	subjunctive
sujeto	*su(b)j*	(grammatical) subject
sufijo	*suff*	suffix
tauromaquia	*Taur*	bullfighting
también	*tb*	also
teatro	*Teat*	
técnica, tecnología	*Tec(h)*	technical term, technology
telecomunicaciones	*Telec, Tel*	telecommunications
	Theat	theatre
imprenta, tipografía	*Tip, Typ*	typography, printing
televisión	*TV*	television
sistema universitario	*Univ*	universities
inglés norteamericano	*US*	American English
verbo	*vb*	verb
verbo intransitivo	*vi*	intransitive verb
verbo pronominal	*vr*	reflexive verb
verbo transitivo	*vt*	transitive verb
zoología, animales	*Zool*	zoology
marca registrada	®	registered trademark
indica un equivalente cultural	≈	introduces a cultural equivalent

Spanish Pronunciation

Consonants

b	[b] [β]	See notes on *v* below	*b*om*b*a la*b*or
c	[k]	*c* before *a*, *o* or *u* is pronounced as in *c*at	*c*aja
ce, ci	[θe,θi] [se,si']	*c* before *e* or *i* is pronounced as in *th*in and as *s* in *s*in in Latin America and parts of Spain	*ce*ro, *ci*elo vo*ce*ro, noti*ci*ero
ch	[tʃ]	*ch* is pronounced as *ch* in *ch*air	*ch*iste
d	[d] [ð]	at the beginning of a word or after *l* or *n*, *d* is pronounced as in English. In any other position it is like *th* in *th*e	*d*anés ciu*d*a*d*
g	[g] [ɣ]	*g* before *a*, *o* or *u* is pronounced as in *g*ap if at the beginning of a word or after *n*. In other positions the sound is softened.	*g*afas, *g*uerra pa*g*a
ge, gi	[xe, xi]	*g* before *e* or *i* is pronounced similar to *ch* in Scottish lo*ch*	*ge*nte, *gi*rar
h		*h* is always silent in Spanish	*h*aber
j	[x]	*j* is pronounced like *ch* in Scottish lo*ch*	jugar
ll	[ʎ]	*ll* is pronounced like the *lli* in mi*lli*on	ta*ll*e
ñ	[ɲ]	*ñ* is pronounced like the *ni* in o*ni*on	niño
q	[k]	*q* is pronounced as *k* in *k*ing	*q*ue
r, rr	[r] [rr]	*r* is always pronounced in Spanish, unlike the *r* in dancer. *rr* and *r* at the beginning of a word are trilled, like a Scottish *r*	quita*r* ga*rr*a
s	[s] [z]	*s* is usually pronounced as in pass, but before *b*, *d*, *g*, *l*, *m* or *n* it is pronounced as in rose	quizá*s* i*s*la
v	[b] [β]	*v* is pronounced something like *b*. At the beginning of a word or after *m* or *n* it is pronounced as *b* in *b*oy. In any other position it is pronounced with the lips in position to pronounce *b* of *b*oy, but not meeting	*v*ía di*v*idir
w	[b] [w]	pronounced either like Spanish *b*, or like English *w*	*w*áter *wh*iskey

z	[θ] [s']	*z* is pronounced as *th* in *th*in and as *s* in *s*in in Latin America and parts of Spain	tenaz izada
	[ks] [s]	*x* is pronounced as in to*x*in except in informal Spanish or at the beginning of a word	tó*x*ico *x*enofobia

f, k, l, m, n, p and *t* are pronounced as in English
' Only shown in Latin American entries.

Vowels

a	[a]	Not as long as *a* in f*a*r. When followed by a consonant in the same syllable (ie in a closed syllable), as in am*a*nte, the *a* is short as in b*a*t	p*a*ta
e	[e]	like *e* in th*e*y. In a closed syllable, as in g*e*nte, the *e* is short as in p*e*t	m*e*
i	[i]	as in m*ea*n or mach*i*ne	p*i*no
o	[o]	as in l*o*cal. In a closed syllable, as in c*o*ntr*o*l, the *o* is short as in c*o*t	l*o*
u	[u]	As in r*u*le. It is silent after *q*, and in *gue*, *gui*, unless marked *güe*, *güi* eg anti*güe*dad, when it is pronounced like *w* in *w*olf	l*u*nes

Semi-vowels

i, y	[j]	pronounced like *y* in *y*es	b*i*en, h*i*elo, *y*unta
u	[w]	unstressed *u* between consonant and vowel is pronounced like *w* in *w*ell. See also notes on *u* above	h*u*evo, f*u*ente, antig*ü*edad

Diphthongs

ai, ay	[ai]	as *i* in r*i*de	b*ai*le
au	[au]	as *ou* in sh*ou*t	*au*to
ei, ey	[ei]	as *ey* in gr*ey*	bu*ey*
eu	[eu]	both elements pronounced independently [e] + [u]	d*eu*da
oi, oy	[oi]	as *oy* in t*oy*	h*oy*

Stress

The rules of stress in Spanish are as follows:

(a) when a word ends in a vowel or in *n* or *s*, the second last syllable is stressed: pat*a*ta, pat*a*tas, *co*me, *co*men

(b) when a word ends in a consonant other than *n* or *s*, the stress falls on the last syllable: pa*red*, ha*blar*

(c) when the rules set out in (a) and (b) are not applied, an acute accent appears over the stressed vowel: com*ú*n, geograf*í*a, ingl*é*s

In the phonetic transcription, the symbol ['] precedes the syllable on which the stress falls.

In general, we give the pronunciation of each entry in square brackets after the word in question.

Spanish Verb Forms

1 Gerund **2** Imperative **3** Present **4** Preterite **5** Future **6** Present subjunctive **7** Imperfect subjunctive **8** Past participle **9** Imperfect

acertar 2 acierta **3** acierto, aciertas, acierta, aciertan **6** acierte, aciertes, acierte, acierten
acordar 2 acuerda **3** acuerdo, acuerdas, acuerda, acuerdan **6** acuerde, acuerdes, acuerde, acuerden
advertir 1 advirtiendo **2** advierte **3** advierto, adviertes, advierte, advierten **4** advirtió, advirtieron **6** advierta, adviertas, advierta, advirtamos, advirtáis, adviertan **7** advirtiera *etc*
agradecer 3 agradezco **6** agradezca *etc*
andar 4 anduve, anduviste, anduvo, anduvimos, anduvisteis, anduvieron **7** anduviera *or* anduviese *etc*
aparecer 3 aparezco **6** aparezca *etc*
aprobar 2 aprueba **3** apruebo, apruebas, aprueba, aprueban **6** apruebe, apruebes, apruebe, aprueben
atravesar 2 atraviesa **3** atravieso, atraviesas, atraviesa, atraviesan **6** atraviese, atravieses, atraviese, atraviesen
caber 3 quepo **4** cupe, cupiste, cupo, cupimos, cupisteis, cupieron **5** cabré *etc* **6** quepa *etc* **7** cupiera *etc*
caer 1 cayendo **3** caigo **4** cayó, cayeron **6** caiga *etc* **7** cayera *etc*
calentar 2 calienta **3** caliento, calientas, calienta, calientan **6** caliente, calientes, caliente, calienten
cerrar 2 cierra **3** cierro, cierras, cierra, cierran **6** cierre, cierres, cierre, cierren
COMER 1 comiendo **2** come, comed **3** como, comes, come, comemos, coméis, comen **4** comí, comiste, comió, comimos, comisteis, comieron **5** comeré, comerás, comerá, comeremos, comeréis, comerán **6** coma, comas, coma, comamos, comáis, coman **7** comiera, comieras, comiera, comiéramos, comierais, comieran **8** comido **9** comía, comías, comía, comíamos, comíais, comían
conocer 3 conozco **6** conozca *etc*
contar 2 cuenta **3** cuento, cuentas, cuenta, cuentan **6** cuente, cuentes, cuente, cuenten
costar 2 cuesta **3** cuesto, cuestas, cuesta, cuestan **6** cueste, cuestes, cueste, cuesten
dar 3 doy **4** di, diste, dio, dimos, disteis, dieron **7** diera *etc*
decir 2 di **3** digo **4** dije, dijiste, dijo, dijimos, dijisteis, dijeron **5** diré *etc* **6** diga *etc* **7** dijera *etc* **8** dicho
despertar 2 despierta **3** despierto, despiertas, despierta, despiertan **6** despierte, despiertes, despierte, despierten
divertir 1 divirtiendo **2** divierte **3** divierto, diviertes, divierte, divierten **4** divirtió, divirtieron **6** divierta, diviertas, divierta, divirtamos, divirtáis, diviertan **7** divirtiera *etc*
dormir 1 durmiendo **2** duerme **3** duermo, duermes, duerme, duermen **4** durmió, durmieron **6** duerma, duermas, duerma, durmamos, durmáis, duerman **7** durmiera *etc*
empezar 2 empieza **3** empiezo, empiezas, empieza, empiezan **4** empecé **6** empiece, empieces, empiece, empecemos, empecéis, empiecen
entender 2 entiende **3** entiendo, entiendes, entiende, entienden **6** entienda, entiendas, entienda, entiendan
ESTAR 2 está **3** estoy, estás, está, están **4** estuve, estuviste, estuvo, estuvimos, estuvisteis, estuvieron **6** esté, estés, esté, estén **7** estuviera *etc*
HABER 3 he, has, ha, hemos, habéis, han **4** hube, hubiste, hubo, hubimos, hubisteis, hubieron **5** habré *etc* **6** haya *etc* **7** hubiera *etc*
HABLAR 1 hablando **2** habla, hablad **3** hablo, hablas, habla, hablamos, habláis, hablan **4** hablé, hablaste, habló, hablamos, hablasteis, hablaron **5** hablaré, hablarás, hablará, hablaremos, hablaréis, hablarán **6** hable, hables, hable, hablemos, habléis, hablen **7** hablara *or* hablase, hablaras *or* hablases, habláramos *or* hablásemos, hablarais *or* hablaseis, hablaran *or* hablasen **8** hablado **9** hablaba, hablabas, hablaba, hablábamos, hablabais, hablaban
hacer 2 haz **3** hago **4** hice, hiciste, hizo, hicimos, hicisteis, hicieron **5** haré *etc* **6** haga *etc* **7** hiciera *etc* **8** hecho
instruir 1 instruyendo **2** instruye **3** instruyo, instruyes, instruye, instruyen **4** instruyó, instruyeron **6** instruya *etc* **7** instruyera *etc*
ir 1 yendo **2** ve **3** voy, vas, va, vamos, vais, van **4** fui, fuiste, fue, fuimos, fuisteis, fueron **6** vaya, vayas, vaya, vayamos, vayáis, vayan **7** fuera *etc* **9** iba, ibas, iba, íbamos, ibais, iban

jugar **2** juega **3** juego, juegas, juega, juegan **4** jugué **6** juegue *etc*
leer **1** leyendo **4** leyó, leyeron **7** leyera *etc*
morir **1** muriendo **2** muere **3** muero, mueres, muere, mueren **4** murió, murieron **6** muera, mueras, muera, muramos, muráis, mueran **7** muriera *etc* **8** muerto
mostrar **2** muestra **3** muestro, muestras, muestra, muestran **6** muestre, muestres, muestre, muestren
mover **2** mueve **3** muevo, mueves, mueve, mueven **6** mueva, muevas, mueva, muevan
negar **2** niega **3** niego, niegas, niega, niegan **4** negué **6** niegue, niegues, niegue, neguemos, neguéis, nieguen
ofrecer **3** ofrezco **6** ofrezca *etc*
oír **1** oyendo **2** oye **3** oigo, oyes, oye, oyen **4** oyó, oyeron **6** oiga *etc* **7** oyera *etc*
oler **2** huele **3** huelo, hueles, huele, huelen **6** huela, huelas, huela, huelan
parecer **3** parezco **6** parezca *etc*
pedir **1** pidiendo **2** pide **3** pido, pides, pide, piden **4** pidió, pidieron **6** pida *etc* **7** pidiera *etc*
pensar **2** piensa **3** pienso, piensas, piensa, piensan **6** piense, pienses, piense, piensen
perder **2** pierde **3** pierdo, pierdes, pierde, pierden **6** pierda, pierdas, pierda, pierdan
poder **1** pudiendo **2** puede **3** puedo, puedes, puede, pueden **4** pude, pudiste, pudo, pudimos, pudisteis, pudieron **5** podré *etc* **6** pueda, puedas, pueda, puedan **7** pudiera *etc*
poner **2** pon **3** pongo **4** puse, pusiste, puso, pusimos, pusisteis, pusieron **5** pondré *etc* **6** ponga *etc* **7** pusiera *etc* **8** puesto
preferir **1** prefiriendo **2** prefiere **3** prefiero, prefieres, prefiere, prefieren **4** prefirió, prefirieron **6** prefiera, prefieras, prefiera, prefiramos, prefiráis, prefieran **7** prefiriera *etc*
querer **2** quiere **3** quiero, quieres, quiere, quieren **4** quise, quisiste, quiso, quisimos, quisisteis, quisieron **5** querré *etc* **6** quiera, quieras, quiera, quieran **7** quisiera *etc*
reír **2** ríe **3** río, ríes, ríe, ríen **4** rió, rieron **6** ría, rías, ría, riamos, riáis, rían **7** riera *etc*
repetir **1** repitiendo **2** repite **3** repito, repites, repite, repiten **4** repitió, repitieron **6** repita *etc* **7** repitiera *etc*
rogar **2** ruega **3** ruego, ruegas, ruega, ruegan **4** rogué **6** ruegue, ruegues, ruegue, roguemos, roguéis, rueguen
saber **3** sé **4** supe, supiste, supo, supimos, supisteis, supieron **5** sabré *etc* **6** sepa *etc* **7** supiera *etc*
salir **2** sal **3** salgo **5** saldré *etc* **6** salga *etc*
seguir **1** siguiendo **2** sigue **3** sigo, sigues, sigue, siguen **4** siguió, siguieron **6** siga *etc* **7** siguiera *etc*
sentar **2** sienta **3** siento, sientas, sienta, sientan **6** siente, sientes, siente, sienten
sentir **1** sintiendo **2** siente **3** siento, sientes, siente, sienten **4** sintió, sintieron **6** sienta, sientas, sienta, sintamos, sintáis, sientan **7** sintiera *etc*
SER **2** sé **3** soy, eres, es, somos, sois, son **4** fui, fuiste, fue, fuimos, fuisteis, fueron **6** sea *etc* **7** fuera *etc* **9** era, eras, era, éramos, erais, eran
servir **1** sirviendo **2** sirve **3** sirvo, sirves, sirve, sirven **4** sirvió, sirvieron **6** sirva *etc* **7** sirviera *etc*
soñar **2** sueña **3** sueño, sueñas, sueña, sueñan **6** sueñe, sueñes, sueñe, sueñen
tener **2** ten **3** tengo, tienes, tiene, tienen **4** tuve, tuviste, tuvo, tuvimos, tuvisteis, tuvieron **5** tendré *etc* **6** tenga *etc* **7** tuviera *etc*
traer **1** trayendo **3** traigo **4** traje, trajiste, trajo, trajimos, trajisteis, trajeron **6** traiga *etc* **7** trajera *etc*
valer **2** val **3** valgo **5** valdré *etc* **6** valga *etc*
venir **2** ven **3** vengo, vienes, viene, vienen **4** vine, viniste, vino, vinimos, vinisteis, vinieron **5** vendré *etc* **6** venga *etc* **7** viniera *etc*
ver **3** veo **6** vea *etc* **8** visto **9** veía *etc*
vestir **1** vistiendo **2** viste **3** visto, vistes, viste, visten **4** vistió, vistieron **6** vista *etc* **7** vistiera *etc*
VIVIR **1** viviendo **2** vive, vivid **3** vivo, vives, vive, vivimos, vivís, viven **4** viví, viviste, vivió, vivimos, vivisteis, vivieron **5** viviré, vivirás, vivirá, viviremos, viviréis, vivirán **6** viva, vivas, viva, vivamos, viváis, vivan **7** viviera *or* viviese, vivieras *or* vivieses, viviera *or* viviese, viviéramos *or* viviésemos, vivierais *or* vivieseis, vivieran *or* viviesen **8** vivido **9** vivía, vivías, vivía, vivíamos, vivías, vivían
volcar **2** vuelca **3** vuelco, vuelcas, vuelca, vuelcan **4** volqué **6** vuelque, vuelques, vuelque, volquemos, volquéis, vuelquen
volver **2** vuelve **3** vuelvo, vuelves, vuelve, vuelven **6** vuelva, vuelvas, vuelva, vuelvan **8** vuelto

For additional information on Spanish verb formation, see pp 6 – 161 of the Grammar section.

Números / Numbers

Números		Numbers
uno (un, una)*	1	one
dos	2	two
tres	3	three
cuatro	4	four
cinco	5	five
seis	6	six
siete	7	seven
ocho	8	eight
nueve	9	nine
diez	10	ten
once	11	eleven
doce	12	twelve
trece	13	thirteen
catorce	14	fourteen
quince	15	fifteen
dieciséis	16	sixteen
diecisiete	17	seventeen
dieciocho	18	eighteen
diecinueve	19	nineteen
veinte	20	twenty
veintiuno(-un, -una)*	21	twenty-one
veintidós	22	twenty-two
treinta	30	thirty
treinta y uno(un, una)*	31	thirty-one
treinta y dos	32	thirty-two
cuarenta	40	forty
cincuenta	50	fifty
sesenta	60	sixty
setenta	70	seventy
ochenta	80	eighty
noventa	90	ninety
cien(ciento)**	100	a hundred, one hundred
ciento uno(un, una)*	101	a hundred and one
ciento dos	102	a hundred and two
ciento cincuenta y seis	156	a hundred and fifty-six
doscientos(-as)	200	two hundred
trescientos(-as)	300	three hundred
quinientos(-as)	500	five hundred
mil	1,000	a thousand
mil tres	1,003	a thousand and three
dos mil	2,000	two thousand
un millón	1,000,000	a million

*'uno' (+ 'veintiuno' etc) agrees in gender (but not number) with its noun: **treinta y una personas**; the masculine form is shortened to 'un' unless it stands alone: **veintiún caballos, veintiuno**.

'ciento' is used in compound numbers, except when it multiplies: **ciento diez, but **cien mil**. 'Cien' is used before nouns: **cien hombres, cien casas**.

Números	Numbers
primero (primer, primera) 1º, 1er/1ª, 1^{era}	first, 1st
segundo(-a) 2º/2ª	second, 2nd
tercero (tercer, tercera) 3º, 3er/3ª, 3^{era}	third, 3rd
cuarto(-a) 4º/4ª	fourth, 4th
quinto(-a)	fifth, 5th
sexto(-a)	sixth, 6th
séptimo(-a)	seventh
octavo(-a)	eighth
noveno(-a); nono(-a)	ninth
décimo(-a)	tenth
undécimo(-a)	eleventh
duodécimo(-a)	twelfth
decimotercero(-a)	thirteenth
decimocuarto(-a)	fourteenth
decimoquinto(-a)	fifteenth
decimosexto(-a)	sixteenth
decimoséptimo(-a)	seventeenth
decimoctavo(-a)	eighteenth
decimonoveno(-a)	nineteenth
vigésimo(-a)	twentieth
vigésimo(-a) primero(-a)	twenty-first
vigésimo(-a) segundo(-a)	twenty-second
trigésimo(-a)	thirtieth
trigésimo(-a) primero(-a)	thirty-first
trigésimo(-a) segundo(-a)	thirty-second
cuadragésimo(-a)	fortieth
quincuagésimo(-a)	fiftieth
sexagésimo(-a)	sixtieth
septuagésimo(-a)	seventieth
octogésimo(-a)	eightieth
nonagésimo(-a)	ninetieth
centésimo(-a)	hundredth
centésimo(-a) primero(-a)	hundred-and-first
milésimo(-a)	thousandth

La hora / The time

La hora	The time
¿qué hora es?	*what time is it?*
es la una	it's one o'clock
son las cuatro	it's four o'clock
medianoche, las doce de la noche	midnight
la una (de la madrugada)	one o'clock (in the morning), one (a.m.)
la una y cinco	five past one
la una y diez	ten past one
la una y cuarto *or* quince	a quarter past one, one fifteen
la una y veinticinco	twenty-five past one, one twenty-five
la una y media *or* treinta	half past one, one thirty
las dos menos veinticinco, la una treinta y cinco	twenty-five to two, one thirty-five
las dos menos veinte, la una cuarenta	twenty to two, one forty
las dos menos cuarto, la una cuarenta y cinco	a quarter to two, one forty-five
las dos menos diez, la una cincuenta	ten to two, one fifty
mediodía, las doce (de la mañana)	twelve o'clock, midday, noon
la dos (de la tarde)	
two o'clock (in the afternoon)	two (p.m.)
la siete (de la tarde), seven o'clock (in the evening)	seven (p.m.)
¿a qué hora?	*at what time?*
a medianoche	at midnight
a las siete	at seven o'clock
a la una	at one o'clock
en veinte minutos	in twenty minutes
hace diez minutos	ten minutes ago

La fecha / The date

La fecha	The date
hoy	today
mañana	tomorrow
pasado mañana	the day after tomorrow
ayer	yesterday
antes de ayer, anteayer	the day before yesterday
la víspera	the day before, the previous day
el día siguiente	the next *or* following day
la mañana	morning
la tarde	evening
esta mañana	this morning
esta tarde	this evening, this afternoon
ayer por la mañana	yesterday morning
ayer por la tarde	yesterday evening

mañana por la mañana	tomorrow morning
mañana por la tarde	tomorrow evening, tomorrow afternoon
en la noche del sábado al domingo	during Saturday night, during the night of Saturday to Sunday
vendrá el sábado	he's coming on Saturday
los sábados	on Saturdays
todos los sábados	every Saturday
el sábado pasado	last Saturday
el sábado que viene, el próximo sábado	next Saturday
ocho días a partir del sábado	a week on Saturday
quince días a partir del sábado	a fortnight *or* two weeks on Saturday
de lunes a sábado	from Monday to Saturday
todos las días	every day
una vez a la semana	once a week
una vez a la mes	once a month
dos veces a la semana	twice a week
hace una semana *u* ocho días	a week ago
hace quince días	a fortnight *or* two weeks ago
el año pasado	last year
dentro de dos días	in two days
dentro de ocho días *o* una semana	in a week
dentro de quince días	in a fortnight *or* two weeks
el mes que viene, el próximo mes	next month
el año que viene, el próximo año	next year
¿a qué o a cuántos estamos?	*what day is it?*
el 1/22 octubre de 2008	the 1st/22nd of October 2008, October 1st/22nd 2008
en 2008	in 2008
mil novicientos noventa y cinco	nineteen ninety-five
44 a. de J.C.	44 BC
14 d. de J.C.	14 AD
en el (siglo) XIX	in the nineteenth century
en los años treinta	in the thirties
érase una vez ...	once upon a time ...

Aa

A, a [a] *nf* (*letra*) A, a; **A de Antonio** A for Andrew (*Brit*) *o* Able (*US*)
A. *abr* (*Escol*: = *aprobado*) pass

PALABRA CLAVE

a [a] *prep* (**a + el = al**) **1** (*dirección*) to; **fueron a Madrid/Grecia** they went to Madrid/Greece; **me voy a casa** I'm going home
2 (*distancia*): **está a 15 km de aquí** it's 15 kms from here
3 (*posición*): **estar a la mesa** to be at table; **al lado de** next to, beside; **a la derecha/izquierda** on the right/left; *ver tb* **puerta**
4 (*tiempo*): **a las 10/a medianoche** at 10/midnight; **¿a qué hora?** (at) what time?; **a la mañana siguiente** the following morning; **a los pocos días** after a few days; **estamos a 9 de julio** it's the 9th of July; **a los 24 años** at the age of 24; **ocho horas al día** eight hours a day; **al año/a la semana** (*Am*) a year/week later
5 (*manera*): **a la francesa** the French way; **a caballo** on horseback; **a oscuras** in the dark; **a rayas** striped; **le echaron a patadas** they kicked him out
6 (*medio, instrumento*): **a lápiz** in pencil; **a mano** by hand; **cocina a gas** gas stove
7 (*razón*): **a dos euros el kilo** at two euros a kilo; **a más de 50 kms por hora** at more than 50 kms per hour; **poco a poco** little by little
8 (*dativo*): **se lo di a él** I gave it to him; **se lo compré a él** I bought it from him
9 (*complemento directo*): **vi al policía** I saw the policeman
10 (*tras ciertos verbos*): **voy a verle** I'm going to see him; **empezó a trabajar** he started working *o* to work; **sabe a queso** it tastes of cheese
11 (*+infin*): **al verle, le reconocí inmediatamente** when I saw him I recognized him at once; **el camino a recorrer** the distance we (*etc*) have to travel; **¡a callar!** keep quiet!; **¡a comer!** let's eat!
12 (*a+que*): **¡a que llueve!** I bet it's going to rain!; **¿a qué viene eso?** what's the meaning of this?; **¿a que sí va a venir?** he IS coming, isn't he?; **¿a que no lo haces? — ¡a que sí!** bet you don't do it! — yes, I WILL!

AA *nfpl abr* = **Aerolíneas Argentinas**
AA EE *abr* (= *Asuntos Exteriores*): **Min. de ~** ≈ FO (*Brit*)
ab. *abr* (= *abril*) Apr
abad, esa [a'βað, 'ðesa] *nm/f* abbot/abbess
abadía [aβa'ðia] *nf* abbey
abajo [a'βaxo] *adv* (*situación*) (down) below, underneath; (*en edificio*) downstairs; (*dirección*) down, downwards; **~ de** *prep* below, under; **el piso de ~** the downstairs flat; **la parte de ~** the lower part; **¡~ el gobierno!** down with the government!; **cuesta/río ~** downhill/downstream; **de arriba ~** from top to bottom; **el ~ firmante** the undersigned; **más ~** lower *o* further down
abalance *etc* [aβa'lanθe] *vb ver* **abalanzarse**
abalanzarse [aβalan'θarse] *vr*: **~ sobre** *o* **contra** to throw o.s. at
abalear [aβale'ar] *vt* (*Am fam*) to shoot
abalorios [aβa'lorjos] *nmpl* (*chucherías*) trinkets
abanderado [aβande'raðo] *nm* standard bearer
abandonado, -a [aβando'naðo, a] *adj* derelict; (*desatendido*) abandoned; (*desierto*) deserted; (*descuidado*) neglected
abandonar [aβando'nar] *vt* to leave; (*persona*) to abandon, desert; (*cosa*) to abandon, leave behind; (*descuidar*) to neglect; (*renunciar a*) to give up; (*Inform*) to quit; **abandonarse** *vr*: **abandonarse a** to abandon o.s. to; **abandonarse al alcohol** to take to drink
abandono [aβan'dono] *nm* (*acto*) desertion, abandonment; (*estado*) abandon, neglect;

(*renuncia*) withdrawal, retirement; **ganar por ~** to win by default
abanicar [aβani'kar] *vt* to fan
abanico [aβa'niko] *nm* fan; (*Naut*) derrick; **en ~** fan-shaped
abanique *etc* [aβa'nike] *vb ver* **abanicar**
abaratar [aβara'tar] *vt* to lower the price of ■ *vi*, **abaratarse** *vr* to go *o* come down in price
abarcar [aβar'kar] *vt* to include, embrace; (*contener*) to comprise; (*Am*) to monopolize; **quien mucho abarca poco aprieta** don't bite off more than you can chew
abarque *etc* [a'βarke] *vb ver* **abarcar**
abarrotado, -a [aβarro'taðo, a] *adj* packed; **~ de** packed *o* bursting with
abarrote [aβa'rrote] *nm* packing; **abarrotes** *nmpl* (*Am*) groceries, provisions
abarrotería [aβarrote'ria] *nf* (*Am*) grocery store
abarrotero, -a [aβarro'tero, a] *nm/f* (*Am*) grocer
abastecedor, a [aβasteθe'ðor, a] *adj* supplying ■ *nm/f* supplier
abastecer [aβaste'θer] *vt*: **~ (de)** to supply (with)
abastecimiento [aβasteθi'mjento] *nm* supply
abastezca *etc* [aβas'teθka] *vb ver* **abastecer**
abasto [a'βasto] *nm* supply; (*abundancia*) abundance; **no dar ~ a algo** not to be able to cope with sth
abatible [aβa'tiβle] *adj*: **asiento ~** tip-up seat
abatido, -a [aβa'tiðo, a] *adj* dejected, downcast; **estar muy ~** to be very depressed
abatimiento [aβati'mjento] *nm* (*depresión*) dejection, depression
abatir [aβa'tir] *vt* (*muro*) to demolish; (*pájaro*) to shoot *o* bring down; (*fig*) to depress; **abatirse** *vr* to get depressed; **abatirse sobre** to swoop *o* pounce on
abdicación [aβðika'θjon] *nf* abdication
abdicar [aβði'kar] *vi* to abdicate; **~ en algn** to abdicate in favour of sb
abdique *etc* [aβ'ðike] *vb ver* **abdicar**
abdomen [aβ'ðomen] *nm* abdomen
abdominal [aβðomi'nal] *adj* abdominal ■ *nm*: **abdominales** (*Deporte*) abdominals; (*Anat*) abdominals, stomach muscles
abecedario [aβeθe'ðarjo] *nm* alphabet
abedul [aβe'ðul] *nm* birch
abeja [a'βexa] *nf* bee; (*fig: hormiguita*) hard worker
abejorro [aβe'xorro] *nm* bumblebee
aberración [aβerra'θjon] *nf* aberration
aberrante [aβe'rrante] *adj* (*disparatado*) ridiculous
abertura [aβer'tura] *nf* = **apertura**
abertzale [aβer'tʃale] *adj, nm/f* Basque nationalist
abeto [a'βeto] *nm* fir
abierto, -a [a'βjerto, a] *pp de* **abrir** ■ *adj* open; (*fig: carácter*) frank
abigarrado, -a [aβiɣa'rraðo, a] *adj* multicoloured; (*fig*) motley
abismal [aβis'mal] *adj* (*fig*) vast, enormous
abismar [aβis'mar] *vt* to humble, cast down; **abismarse** *vr* to sink; (*Am*) to be amazed; **abismarse en** (*fig*) to be plunged into
abismo [a'βismo] *nm* abyss; **de sus ideas a las mías hay un ~** our views are worlds apart
abjurar [aβxu'rar] *vt* to abjure, forswear ■ *vi*: **~ de** to abjure, forswear
ablandar [aβlan'dar] *vt* to soften up; (*conmover*) to touch; (*Culin*) to tenderize ■ *vi*, **ablandarse** *vr* to get softer
abnegación [aβneɣa'θjon] *nf* self-denial
abnegado, -a [aβne'ɣaðo, a] *adj* self-sacrificing
abobado, -a [aβo'βaðo, a] *adj* silly
abobamiento [aβoβa'mjento] *nm* (*asombro*) bewilderment
abocado, -a [aβo'kaðo, a] *adj*: **verse ~ al desastre** to be heading for disaster
abochornar [aβotʃor'nar] *vt* to embarrass; **abochornarse** *vr* to get flustered; (*Bot*) to wilt; **abochornarse de** to get embarrassed about
abofetear [aβofete'ar] *vt* to slap (in the face)
abogacía [aβoɣa'θia] *nf* legal profession; (*ejercicio*) practice of the law
abogado, -a [aβo'ɣaðo, a] *nm/f* lawyer; (*notario*) solicitor; (*asesor*) counsel; (*en tribunal*) barrister, advocate, attorney (*US*); **~ defensor** defence lawyer *o* attorney (*US*); **~ del diablo** devil's advocate
abogar [aβo'ɣar] *vi*: **~ por** to plead for; (*fig*) to advocate
abogue *etc* [a'βoɣe] *vb ver* **abogar**
abolengo [aβo'lengo] *nm* ancestry, lineage
abolición [aβoli'θjon] *nf* abolition
abolir [aβo'lir] *vt* to abolish; (*cancelar*) to cancel
abolladura [aβoʎa'ðura] *nf* dent
abollar [aβo'ʎar] *vt* to dent
abominable [aβomi'naβle] *adj* abominable
abominación [aβomina'θjon] *nf* abomination
abonado, -a [aβo'naðo, a] *adj* (*deuda*) paid (-up) ■ *nm/f* subscriber
abonar [aβo'nar] *vt* to pay; (*deuda*) to settle; (*terreno*) to fertilize; (*idea*) to endorse; **abonarse** *vr* to subscribe; **~ dinero en una cuenta** to pay money into an account, credit

money to an account
abono [a'βono] *nm* payment; fertilizer; subscription
abordable [aβor'ðaβle] *adj* (*persona*) approachable
abordar [aβor'ðar] *vt* (*barco*) to board; (*asunto*) to broach; (*individuo*) to approach
aborigen [aβo'rixen] *nm/f* aborigine
aborrecer [aβorre'θer] *vt* to hate, loathe
aborrezca *etc* [aβo'rreθka] *vb ver* **aborrecer**
abortar [aβor'tar] *vi* (*malparir*) to have a miscarriage; (*deliberadamente*) to have an abortion
aborto [a'βorto] *nm* miscarriage; abortion
abotagado, -a [aβota'ɣaðo, a] *adj* swollen
abotonar [aβoto'nar] *vt* to button (up), do up
abovedado, -a [aβoβe'ðaðo, a] *adj* vaulted, domed
abr. *abr* (= *abril*) Apr
abrace *etc* [a'βraθe] *vb ver* **abrazar**
abrasar [aβra'sar] *vt* to burn (up); (*Agr*) to dry up, parch
abrazadera [aβraθa'ðera] *nf* bracket
abrazar [aβra'θar] *vt* to embrace, hug; **abrazarse** *vr* to embrace, hug each other
abrazo [a'βraθo] *nm* embrace, hug; **un ~** (*en carta*) with best wishes
abrebotellas [aβreβo'teʎas] *nm inv* bottle opener
abrecartas [aβre'kartas] *nm inv* letter opener
abrelatas [aβre'latas] *nm inv* tin (*Brit*) *o* can (*US*) opener
abrevadero [aβreβa'ðero] *nm* watering place
abreviar [aβre'βjar] *vt* to abbreviate; (*texto*) to abridge; (*plazo*) to reduce ■ *vi*: **bueno, para ~** well, to cut a long story short
abreviatura [aβreβja'tura] *nf* abbreviation
abridor [aβri'ðor] *nm* (*de botellas*) bottle opener; (*de latas*) tin (*Brit*) *o* can (*US*) opener
abrigar [aβri'ɣar] *vt* (*proteger*) to shelter; (*suj: ropa*) to keep warm; (*fig*) to cherish; **abrigarse** *vr* (*con ropa*) to cover (o.s.) up; **abrigarse (de)** to take shelter (from), protect o.s. (from); **¡abrígate bien!** wrap up well!
abrigo [a'βriɣo] *nm* (*prenda*) coat, overcoat; (*lugar protegido*) shelter; **al ~ de** in the shelter of
abrigue *etc* [a'βriɣe] *vb ver* **abrigar**
abril [a'βril] *nm* April; *ver tb* **julio**
abrillantar [aβriʎan'tar] *vt* (*pulir*) to polish; (*fig*) to enhance
abrir [a'βrir] *vt* to open (up); (*camino etc*) to open up; (*apetito*) to whet; (*lista*) to head ■ *vi* to open; **abrirse** *vr* to open (up); (*extenderse*) to open out; (*cielo*) to clear; **~ un negocio** to start up a business; **en un ~ y cerrar de ojos** in the twinkling of an eye; **abrirse paso** to find *o* force a way through
abrochar [aβro'tʃar] *vt* (*con botones*) to button (up); (*zapato, con broche*) to do up; **abrocharse** *vr*: **abrocharse los zapatos** to tie one's shoelaces
abrogación [aβroɣa'θjon] *nf* repeal
abrogar [aβro'ɣar] *vt* to repeal
abrumador, a [aβruma'ðor, a] *adj* (*mayoría*) overwhelming
abrumar [aβru'mar] *vt* to overwhelm; (*sobrecargar*) to weigh down
abrupto, -a [a'βrupto, a] *adj* abrupt; (*empinado*) steep
absceso [aβs'θeso] *nm* abscess
absentismo [aβsen'tismo] *nm* (*de obreros*) absenteeism
absolución [aβsolu'θjon] *nf* (*Rel*) absolution; (*Jur*) acquittal
absoluto, -a [aβso'luto, a] *adj* absolute; (*total*) utter, complete; **en ~** *adv* not at all
absolver [aβsol'βer] *vt* to absolve; (*Jur*) to pardon; (*: acusado*) to acquit
absorbente [aβsor'βente] *adj* absorbent; (*interesante*) absorbing, interesting; (*exigente*) demanding
absorber [aβsor'βer] *vt* to absorb; (*embeber*) to soak up; **absorberse** *vr* to become absorbed
absorción [aβsor'θjon] *nf* absorption; (*Com*) takeover
absorto, -a [aβ'sorto, a] *pp de* **absorber** ■ *adj* absorbed, engrossed
abstemio, -a [aβs'temjo, a] *adj* teetotal
abstención [aβsten'θjon] *nf* abstention
abstendré *etc* [aβsten'dre] *vb ver* **abstenerse**
abstenerse [aβste'nerse] *vr*: **~ (de)** to abstain *o* refrain (from)
abstenga *etc* [aβs'tenga] *vb ver* **abstenerse**
abstinencia [aβsti'nenθja] *nf* abstinence; (*ayuno*) fasting
abstracción [aβstrak'θjon] *nf* abstraction
abstracto, -a [aβ'strakto, a] *adj* abstract; **en ~** in the abstract
abstraer [aβstra'er] *vt* to abstract; **abstraerse** *vr* to be *o* become absorbed
abstraído, -a [aβstra'iðo, a] *adj* absent-minded
abstraiga *etc* [aβs'traiɣa], **abstraje** *etc* [aβs'traxe], **abstrayendo** *etc* [aβstra'jendo] *vb ver* **abstraer**
abstuve *etc* [aβs'tuβe] *vb ver* **abstenerse**
absuelto [aβ'swelto] *pp de* **absolver**
absurdo, -a [aβ'surðo, a] *adj* absurd; **lo ~ es que ...** the ridiculous thing is that ... ■ *nm* absurdity
abuchear [aβutʃe'ar] *vt* to boo
abucheo [aβu'tʃeo] *nm* booing; **ganarse un ~** (*Teat*) to be booed
abuela [a'βwela] *nf* grandmother;

¡cuéntaselo a tu ~! (*fam!*) do you think I was born yesterday? (*fam*); **no tener/necesitar ~** (*fam*) to be full of o.s./blow one's own trumpet
abuelita [aβwe'lita] *nf* granny
abuelo [a'βwelo] *nm* grandfather; (*antepasado*) ancestor; **abuelos** *nmpl* grandparents
abulense [aβu'lense] *adj* of Ávila ■ *nm/f* native *o* inhabitant of Ávila
abulia [a'βulja] *nf* lethargy
abúlico, -a [a'βuliko, a] *adj* lethargic
abultado, -a [aβul'taðo, a] *adj* bulky
abultar [aβul'tar] *vt* to enlarge; (*aumentar*) to increase; (*fig*) to exaggerate ■ *vi* to be bulky
abundancia [aβun'danθja] *nf*: **una ~ de** plenty of; **en ~** in abundance
abundante [aβun'dante] *adj* abundant, plentiful
abundar [aβun'dar] *vi* to abound, be plentiful; **~ en una opinión** to share an opinion
aburguesarse [aβurɣe'sarse] *vr* to become middle-class
aburrido, -a [aβu'rriðo, a] *adj* (*hastiado*) bored; (*que aburre*) boring
aburrimiento [aβurri'mjento] *nm* boredom, tedium
aburrir [aβu'rrir] *vt* to bore; **aburrirse** *vr* to be bored, get bored; **aburrirse como una almeja** *u* **ostra** to be bored stiff
abusar [aβu'sar] *vi* to go too far; **~ de** to abuse
abusivo, -a [aβu'siβo, a] *adj* (*precio*) exorbitant
abuso [a'βuso] *nm* abuse; **~ de confianza** betrayal of trust
abyecto, -a [aβ'jekto, a] *adj* wretched, abject
a. C. *abr* (= *antes de Cristo*) B.C.
a/c *abr* (= *al cuidado de*) c/o; (= *a cuenta*) on account
acá [a'ka] *adv* (*lugar*) here; **pasearse de acá para allá** to walk up and down; **¡vente para acá!** come over here!; **¿de cuándo acá?** since when?
acabado, -a [aka'βaðo, a] *adj* finished, complete; (*perfecto*) perfect; (*agotado*) worn out; (*fig*) masterly ■ *nm* finish
acabar [aka'βar] *vt* (*llevar a su fin*) to finish, complete; (*consumir*) to use up; (*rematar*) to finish off ■ *vi* to finish, end; (*morir*) to die; **acabarse** *vr* to finish, stop; (*terminarse*) to be over; (*agotarse*) to run out; **~ con** to put an end to; **~ mal** to come to a sticky end; **esto ~á conmigo** this will be the end of me; **~ de llegar** to have just arrived; **acababa de hacerlo** I had just done it; **~ haciendo** *o* **por hacer algo** to end up (by) doing sth; **¡se acabó!** (*¡basta!*) that's enough!; (*se terminó*) it's all over!; **se me acabó el tabaco** I ran out of cigarettes
acabóse [aka'βose] *nm*: **esto es el ~** this is the limit
acacia [a'kaθja] *nf* acacia
academia [aka'ðemja] *nf* academy; (*Escol*) private school; *ver tb* **colegio**
académico, -a [aka'ðemiko, a] *adj* academic
acaecer [akae'θer] *vi* to happen, occur
acaezca *etc* [aka'eθka] *vb ver* **acaecer**
acallar [aka'ʎar] *vt* (*silenciar*) to silence; (*calmar*) to pacify
acalorado, -a [akalo'raðo, a] *adj* (*discusión*) heated
acalorarse [akalo'rarse] *vr* (*fig*) to get heated
acampada [akam'paða] *nf*: **ir de ~** to go camping
acampanado, -a [akampa'naðo, a] *adj* flared
acampar [akam'par] *vi* to camp
acanalado, -a [akana'laðo, a] *adj* (*hierro*) corrugated
acanalar [akana'lar] *vt* to groove; (*ondular*) to corrugate
acantilado [akanti'laðo] *nm* cliff
acaparador, a [akapara'ðor, a] *nm/f* monopolizer
acaparar [akapa'rar] *vt* to monopolize; (*acumular*) to hoard
acápite [a'kapite] *nm* (*Am*) paragraph; **punto ~** full stop, new paragraph
acaramelado, -a [akarame'laðo, a] *adj* (*Culin*) toffee-coated; (*fig*) sugary
acariciar [akari'θjar] *vt* to caress; (*esperanza*) to cherish
acarrear [akarre'ar] *vt* to transport; (*fig*) to cause, result in; **le acarreó muchos disgustos** it brought him lots of problems
acaso [a'kaso] *adv* perhaps, maybe ■ *nm* chance; **¿~ es mi culpa?** (*Am fam*) what makes you think it's my fault?; **(por) si ~** (just) in case
acatamiento [akata'mjento] *nm* respect; (*de la ley*) observance
acatar [aka'tar] *vt* to respect; (*ley*) to obey, observe
acatarrarse [akata'rrarse] *vr* to catch a cold
acaudalado, -a [akauða'laðo, a] *adj* well-off
acaudillar [akauði'ʎar] *vt* to lead, command
acceder [akθe'ðer] *vi* to accede, agree; **~ a** (*Inform*) to access
accesible [akθe'siβle] *adj* accessible; **~ a** open to
accésit [ak'θesit] (*pl* **accésits** [ak'θesits]) *nm* consolation prize
acceso [ak'θeso] *nm* access, entry; (*camino*)

access road; (*Med*) attack, fit; (*de cólera*) fit; (*Pol*) accession; (*Inform*) access; **~ aleatorio/directo/secuencial** *o* **en serie** (*Inform*) random/direct/sequential *o* serial access; **de ~ múltiple** multi-access
accesorio, -a [akθe'sorjo, a] *adj* accessory ■ *nm* accessory; **accesorios** *nmpl* (*Auto*) accessories, extras; (*Teat*) props
accidentado, -a [akθiðen'taðo, a] *adj* uneven; (*montañoso*) hilly; (*azaroso*) eventful ■ *nm/f* accident victim
accidental [akθiðen'tal] *adj* accidental; (*empleo*) temporary
accidentarse [akθiðen'tarse] *vr* to have an accident
accidente [akθi'ðente] *nm* accident; **por ~** by chance; **accidentes** *nmpl* unevenness *sg*, roughness *sg*
acción [ak'θjon] *nf* action; (*acto*) action, act; (*Teat*) plot; (*Com*) share; (*Jur*) action, lawsuit; **capital en acciones** share capital; **~ liberada/ordinaria/preferente** fully-paid/ordinary/preference share
accionamiento [akθjona'mjento] *nm* (*de máquina*) operation
accionar [akθjo'nar] *vt* to work, operate
accionista [akθjo'nista] *nm/f* shareholder
acebo [a'θeβo] *nm* holly; (*árbol*) holly tree
acechanza [aθe'tʃanθa] *nf* = **acecho**
acechar [aθe'tʃar] *vt* to spy on; (*aguardar*) to lie in wait for
acecho [a'θetʃo] *nm*: **estar al ~ (de)** to lie in wait (for)
acedera [aθe'ðera] *nf* sorrel
aceitar [aθei'tar] *vt* to oil, lubricate
aceite [a'θeite] *nm* oil; (*de oliva*) olive oil; **~ de hígado de bacalao** cod-liver oil
aceitera [aθei'tera] *nf* oilcan
aceitoso, -a [aθei'toso, a] *adj* oily
aceituna [aθei'tuna] *nf* olive
aceitunado, -a [aθeitu'naðo, a] *adj* olive *cpd*; **de tez aceitunada** olive-skinned
acelerador [aθelera'ðor] *nm* accelerator
acelerar [aθele'rar] *vt* to accelerate; **acelerarse** *vr* to hurry
acelga [a'θelɣa] *nf* chard, beet
acendrado, -a [aθen'draðo, a] *adj*: **de ~ carácter español** typically Spanish
acendrar [aθen'drar] *vt* to purify
acento [a'θento] *nm* accent; (*acentuación*) stress; **~ cerrado** strong *o* thick accent
acentuar [aθen'twar] *vt* to accent; to stress; (*fig*) to accentuate
acepción [aθep'θjon] *nf* meaning
aceptación [aθepta'θjon] *nf* acceptance; (*aprobación*) approval
aceptar [aθep'tar] *vt* to accept; to approve
acequia [a'θekja] *nf* irrigation ditch
acera [a'θera] *nf* pavement (*Brit*), sidewalk (*US*)
acerado, -a [aθe'raðo, a] *adj* steel; (*afilado*) sharp; (*fig: duro*) steely; (*: mordaz*) biting
acerbo, -a [a'θerβo, a] *adj* bitter; (*fig*) harsh
acerca [a'θerka]: **~ de** *prep* about, concerning
acercar [aθer'kar] *vt* to bring *o* move nearer; **acercarse** *vr* to approach, come near
acerico [aθe'riko] *nm* pincushion
acero [a'θero] *nm* steel; **~ inoxidable** stainless steel
acerque *etc* [a'θerke] *vb ver* **acercar**
acérrimo, -a [a'θerrimo, a] *adj* (*partidario*) staunch; (*enemigo*) bitter
acertado, -a [aθer'taðo, a] *adj* correct; (*apropiado*) apt; (*sensato*) sensible
acertar [aθer'tar] *vt* (*blanco*) to hit; (*solución*) to get right; (*adivinar*) to guess ■ *vi* to get it right, be right; **~ a** to manage to; **~ con** to happen *o* hit on
acertijo [aθer'tixo] *nm* riddle, puzzle
acervo [a'θerβo] *nm* heap; **~ común** undivided estate
achacar [atʃa'kar] *vt* to attribute
achacoso, -a [atʃa'koso, a] *adj* sickly
achantar [atʃan'tar] *vt* (*fam*) to scare, frighten; **achantarse** *vr* to back down
achaque *etc* [a'tʃake] *vb ver* **achacar** ■ *nm* ailment
achatar [atʃa'tar] *vt* to flatten
achicar [atʃi'kar] *vt* to reduce; (*humillar*) to humiliate; (*Naut*) to bale out; **achicarse** *vr* (*ropa*) to shrink; (*fig*) to humble o.s.
achicharrar [atʃitʃa'rrar] *vt* to scorch, burn
achicoria [atʃi'korja] *nf* chicory
achinado, -a [atʃi'naðo, a] *adj* (*ojos*) slanting; (*Am*) half-caste
achique *etc* [a'tʃike] *vb ver* **achicar**
acholado, -a [atʃo'laðo, a] *adj* (*Am*) half-caste
achuchar [atʃu'tʃar] *vt* to crush
achuchón [atʃu'tʃon] *nm* shove; **tener un ~** (*Med*) to be poorly
achuras [a'tʃuras] *nf* (*Am, Culin*) offal
aciago, -a [a'θjaɣo, a] *adj* ill-fated, fateful
acicalar [aθika'lar] *vt* to polish; (*adornar*) to bedeck; **acicalarse** *vr* to get dressed up
acicate [aθi'kate] *nm* spur; (*fig*) incentive
acidez [aθi'ðeθ] *nf* acidity
ácido, -a ['aθiðo, a] *adj* sour, acid ■ *nm* acid; (*fam: droga*) LSD
acierto *etc* [a'θjerto] *vb ver* **acertar** ■ *nm* success; (*buen paso*) wise move; (*solución*) solution; (*habilidad*) skill, ability; (*al adivinar*) good guess; **fue un ~ suyo** it was a sensible choice on his part
aclamación [aklama'θjon] *nf* acclamation; (*aplausos*) applause

aclamar [akla'mar] *vt* to acclaim; to applaud
aclaración [aklara'θjon] *nf* clarification, explanation
aclarar [akla'rar] *vt* to clarify, explain; (*ropa*) to rinse ■ *vi* to clear up; **aclararse** *vr* (*suj: persona: explicarse*) to understand; (*fig: asunto*) to become clear; **aclararse la garganta** to clear one's throat
aclaratorio, -a [aklara'torjo, a] *adj* explanatory
aclimatación [aklimata'θjon] *nf* acclimatization
aclimatar [aklima'tar] *vt* to acclimatize; **aclimatarse** *vr* to become *o* get acclimatized; **aclimatarse a algo** to get used to sth
acné [ak'ne] *nm* acne
ACNUR *nm abr* (= *Alto Comisionado de las Naciones Unidas para los Refugiados*) UNHCR *f*
acobardar [akoβar'ðar] *vt* to daunt, intimidate; **acobardarse** *vr* (*atemorizarse*) to be intimidated; (*echarse atrás*): **acobardarse (ante)** to shrink back (from)
acodarse [ako'ðarse] *vr*: ~ **en** to lean on
acogedor, a [akoxe'ðor, a] *adj* welcoming; (*hospitalario*) hospitable
acoger [ako'xer] *vt* to welcome; (*abrigar*) to shelter; **acogerse** *vr* to take refuge; **acogerse a** (*pretexto*) to take refuge in; (*ley*) to resort to
acogida [ako'xiða] *nf* reception; refuge
acoja *etc* [a'koxa] *vb ver* **acoger**
acojonante [akoxo'nante] *adj* (*Esp fam*) tremendous
acolchar [akol'tʃar] *vt* to pad; (*fig*) to cushion
acólito [a'kolito] *nm* (*Rel*) acolyte; (*fig*) minion
acometer [akome'ter] *vt* to attack; (*emprender*) to undertake
acometida [akome'tiða] *nf* attack, assault
acomodado, -a [akomo'ðaðo, a] *adj* (*persona*) well-to-do
acomodador, a [akomoða'ðor, a] *nm/f* usher(ette)
acomodar [akomo'ðar] *vt* to adjust; (*alojar*) to accommodate; **acomodarse** *vr* to conform; (*instalarse*) to install o.s.; (*adaptarse*) to adapt o.s.; **¡acomódese a su gusto!** make yourself comfortable!
acomodaticio, -a [akomoða'tiθjo, a] *adj* (*pey*) accommodating, obliging; (*manejable*) pliable
acompañamiento [akompaɲa'mjento] *nm* (*Mus*) accompaniment
acompañante, -a [akompa'ɲante, a] *nm/f* companion
acompañar [akompa'ɲar] *vt* to accompany, go with; (*documentos*) to enclose; **¿quieres que te acompañe?** do you want me to come with you?; ~ **a algn a la puerta** to see sb to the door *o* out; **le acompaño en el sentimiento** please accept my condolences
acompasar [akompa'sar] *vt* (*Mus*) to mark the rhythm of
acomplejado, -a [akomple'xaðo, a] *adj* neurotic
acomplejar [akomple'xar] *vt* to give a complex to; **acomplejarse** *vr*: **acomplejarse (con)** to get a complex (about)
acondicionado, -a [akondiθjo'naðo, a] *adj* (*Tec*) in good condition
acondicionador [akondiθjona'ðor] *nm* conditioner
acondicionar [akondiθjo'nar] *vt* to get ready, prepare; (*pelo*) to condition
acongojar [akongo'xar] *vt* to distress, grieve
aconsejable [akonse'xaβle] *adj* advisable
aconsejar [akonse'xar] *vt* to advise, counsel; **aconsejarse** *vr*: **aconsejarse con** *o* **de** to consult
acontecer [akonte'θer] *vi* to happen, occur
acontecimiento [akonteθi'mjento] *nm* event
acontezca *etc* [akon'teθka] *vb ver* **acontecer**
acopiar [ako'pjar] *vt* (*recoger*) to gather; (*Com*) to buy up
acopio [a'kopjo] *nm* store, stock
acoplador [akopla'ðor] *nm*: ~ **acústico** (*Inform*) acoustic coupler
acoplamiento [akopla'mjento] *nm* coupling, joint
acoplar [ako'plar] *vt* to fit; (*Elec*) to connect; (*vagones*) to couple
acoquinar [akoki'nar] *vt* to scare; **acoquinarse** *vr* to get scared
acorazado, -a [akora'θaðo, a] *adj* armour-plated, armoured ■ *nm* battleship
acordar [akor'ðar] *vt* (*resolver*) to agree, resolve; **acordarse** *vr* to agree; **acordarse (de algo)** to remember (sth)
acorde [a'korðe] *adj* (*Mus*) harmonious; ~ **con** (*medidas etc*) in keeping with ■ *nm* chord
acordeón [akorðe'on] *nm* accordion
acordonado, -a [akorðo'naðo, a] *adj* (*calle*) cordoned-off
acorralar [akorra'lar] *vt* to round up, corral; (*fig*) to intimidate
acortar [akor'tar] *vt* to shorten; (*duración*) to cut short; (*cantidad*) to reduce; **acortarse** *vr* to become shorter
acosar [ako'sar] *vt* to pursue relentlessly; (*fig*) to hound, pester; ~ **a algn a preguntas** to pester sb with questions
acoso [a'koso] *nm* relentless pursuit; (*fig*) hounding; ~ **sexual** sexual harassment

acostar [akos'tar] *vt* (*en cama*) to put to bed; (*en suelo*) to lay down; (*barco*) to bring alongside; **acostarse** *vr* to go to bed; to lie down
acostumbrado, -a [akostum'braðo, a] *adj* (*habitual*) usual; **estar ~ a (hacer) algo** to be used to (doing) sth
acostumbrar [akostum'brar] *vt*: **~ a algn a algo** to get sb used to sth ■ *vi*: **~ (a hacer algo)** to be in the habit (of doing sth); **acostumbrarse** *vr*: **acostumbrarse a** to get used to
acotación [akota'θjon] *nf* (*apunte*) marginal note; (*Geo*) elevation mark; (*de límite*) boundary mark; (*Teat*) stage direction
acotar [ako'tar] *vt* (*terreno*) to mark out; (*fig*) to limit; (*caza*) to protect
acotejar [akote'xar] *vt* (*Am*) to put in order, arrange
ácrata ['akrata] *adj, nm/f* anarchist
acre ['akre] *adj* (*sabor*) sharp, bitter; (*olor*) acrid; (*fig*) biting ■ *nm* acre
acrecentar [akreθen'tar] *vt* to increase, augment
acreciente *etc* [akre'θjente] *vb ver* **acrecentar**
acreditado, -a [akreði'taðo, a] *adj* (*Pol*) accredited; (*Com*): **una casa acreditada** a reputable firm
acreditar [akreði'tar] *vt* (*garantizar*) to vouch for, guarantee; (*autorizar*) to authorize; (*dar prueba de*) to prove; (*Com: abonar*) to credit; (*embajador*) to accredit; **acreditarse** *vr* to become famous; (*demostrar valía*) to prove one's worth; **acreditarse de** to get a reputation for
acreedor, a [akree'ðor, a] *adj*: **~ a** worthy of ■ *nm/f* creditor; **~ común/diferido/con garantía** (*Com*) unsecured/deferred/secured creditor
acribillar [akriβi'ʎar] *vt*: **~ a balazos** to riddle with bullets
acrimonia [akri'monja], **acritud** [akri'tuð] *nf* acrimony
acrobacia [akro'βaθja] *nf* acrobatics; **~ aérea** aerobatics
acróbata [a'kroβata] *nm/f* acrobat
acta ['akta] *nf* certificate; (*de comisión*) minutes *pl*, record; **~ de nacimiento/de matrimonio** birth/marriage certificate; **~ notarial** affidavit; **levantar ~** (*Jur*) to make a formal statement *o* deposition
actitud [akti'tuð] *nf* attitude; (*postura*) posture; **adoptar una ~ firme** to take a firm stand
activar [akti'βar] *vt* to activate; (*acelerar*) to speed up
actividad [aktiβi'ðað] *nf* activity; **estar en plena ~** to be in full swing
activo, -a [ak'tiβo, a] *adj* active; (*vivo*) lively ■ *nm* (*Com*) assets *pl*; **~ y pasivo** assets and liabilities; **~ circulante/fijo/inmaterial/invisible** (*Com*) current/fixed/intangible/invisible assets; **~ realizable** liquid assets; **activos congelados** *o* **bloqueados** frozen assets; **estar en ~** (*Mil*) to be on active service
acto ['akto] *nm* act, action; (*ceremonia*) ceremony; (*Teat*) act; **en el ~** immediately; **hacer ~ de presencia** (*asistir*) to attend (formally)
actor [ak'tor] *nm* actor; (*Jur*) plaintiff
actora [ak'tora] *adj*: **parte ~** prosecution; (*demandante*) plaintiff
actriz [ak'triθ] *nf* actress
actuación [aktwa'θjon] *nf* action; (*comportamiento*) conduct, behaviour; (*Jur*) proceedings *pl*; (*desempeño*) performance
actual [ak'twal] *adj* present(-day), current; **el 6 del ~** the 6th of this month
actualice *etc* [aktwa'liθe] *vb ver* **actualizar**
actualidad [aktwali'ðað] *nf* present; **actualidades** *nfpl* news *sg*; **en la ~** nowadays, at present; **ser de gran ~** to be current
actualización [aktwaliθa'θjon] *nf* updating, modernization
actualizar [aktwali'θar] *vt* to update, modernize
actualmente [aktwal'mente] *adv* at present; (*hoy día*) nowadays
actuar [ak'twar] *vi* (*obrar*) to work, operate; (*actor*) to act, perform ■ *vt* to work, operate; **~ de** to act as
actuario, -a [ak'twarjo, a] *nm/f* clerk; (*Com*) actuary
acuarela [akwa'rela] *nf* watercolour
acuario [a'kwarjo] *nm* aquarium; **A~** (*Astro*) Aquarius
acuartelar [akwarte'lar] *vt* (*Mil: alojar*) to quarter
acuático, -a [a'kwatiko, a] *adj* aquatic
acuchillar [akutʃi'ʎar] *vt* (*Tec*) to plane (down), smooth
acuciar [aku'θjar] *vt* to urge on
acuclillarse [akukli'ʎarse] *vr* to crouch down
ACUDE [a'kuðe] *nf abr* = **Asociación de Consumidores y Usuarios de España**
acudir [aku'ðir] *vi* to attend, turn up; **~ a** to turn to; **~ en ayuda de** to go to the aid of; **~ a una cita** to keep an appointment; **~ a una llamada** to answer a call; **no tener a quién ~** to have nobody to turn to
acuerdo *etc* [a'kwerðo] *vb ver* **acordar** ■ *nm* agreement; (*Pol*) resolution; **~ de**

pago respectivo (*Com*) knock-for-knock agreement; **A~ general sobre aranceles aduaneros y comercio** (*Com*) General Agreement on Tariffs and Trade; **tomar un ~** to pass a resolution; **¡de ~!** agreed!; **de ~ con** (*persona*) in agreement with; (*acción, documento*) in accordance with; **de común ~** by common consent; **estar de ~** (*persona*) to agree; **llegar a un ~** to come to an understanding

acueste *etc* [a'kweste] *vb ver* **acostar**

acullá [aku'ʎa] *adv* over there

acumular [akumu'lar] *vt* to accumulate, collect

acunar [aku'nar] *vt* to rock (to sleep)

acuñar [aku'ɲar] *vt* (*moneda*) to mint; (*frase*) to coin

acuoso, -a [a'kwoso, a] *adj* watery

acupuntura [akupun'tura] *nf* acupuncture

acurrucarse [akurru'karse] *vr* to crouch; (*ovillarse*) to curl up

acurruque *etc* [aku'rruke] *vb ver* **acurrucarse**

acusación [akusa'θjon] *nf* accusation

acusado, -a [aku'saðo, a] *adj* (*Jur*) accused; (*marcado*) marked; (*acento*) strong

acusar [aku'sar] *vt* to accuse; (*revelar*) to reveal; (*denunciar*) to denounce; (*emoción*) to show; **~ recibo** to acknowledge receipt; **su rostro acusó extrañeza** his face registered surprise; **acusarse** *vr*: **acusarse (de)** to confess (to)

acuse [a'kuse] *nm*: **~ de recibo** acknowledgement of receipt

acústico, -a [a'kustiko, a] *adj* acoustic ■ *nf* (*de una sala etc*) acoustics *pl*; (*ciencia*) acoustics *sg*

ADA ['aða] *nf abr* (*Esp*: = *Ayuda del Automovilista*) ≈ AA, RAC (*Brit*), AAA (*US*)

adagio [a'ðaxjo] *nm* adage; (*Mus*) adagio

adalid [aða'lið] *nm* leader, champion

adaptación [aðapta'θjon] *nf* adaptation

adaptador [aðapta'ðor] *nm* (*Elec*) adapter; **~ universal** universal adapter

adaptar [aðap'tar] *vt* to adapt; (*acomodar*) to fit; (*convertir*): **~ (para)** to convert (to)

adecentar [aðeθen'tar] *vt* to tidy up

adecuado, -a [aðe'kwaðo, a] *adj* (*apto*) suitable; (*oportuno*) appropriate; **el hombre ~ para el puesto** the right man for the job

adecuar [aðe'kwar] *vt* (*adaptar*) to adapt; (*hacer apto*) to make suitable

adefesio [aðe'fesjo] *nm* (*fam*): **estaba hecha un ~** she looked a sight

a. de J.C. *abr* (= *antes de Jesucristo*) B.C.

adelantado, -a [aðelan'taðo, a] *adj* advanced; (*reloj*) fast; **pagar por ~** to pay in advance

adelantamiento [aðelanta'mjento] *nm* advance, advancement; (*Auto*) overtaking

adelantar [aðelan'tar] *vt* to move forward; (*avanzar*) to advance; (*acelerar*) to speed up; (*Auto*) to overtake ■ *vi* (*ir delante*) to go ahead; (*progresar*) to improve; **adelantarse** *vr* (*tomar la delantera*) to go forward, advance; **adelantarse a algn** to get ahead of sb; **adelantarse a los deseos de algn** to anticipate sb's wishes

adelante [aðe'lante] *adv* forward(s), onward(s), ahead ■ *excl* come in!; **de hoy en ~** from now on; **más ~** later on; (*más allá*) further on

adelanto [aðe'lanto] *nm* advance; (*mejora*) improvement; (*progreso*) progress; (*dinero*) advance; **los adelantos de la ciencia** the advances of science

adelgace *etc* [aðel'ɣaθe] *vb ver* **adelgazar**

adelgazar [aðelɣa'θar] *vt* to thin (down); (*afilar*) to taper ■ *vi* to get thin; (*con régimen*) to slim down, lose weight

ademán [aðe'man] *nm* gesture; **ademanes** *nmpl* manners; **en ~ de** as if to

además [aðe'mas] *adv* besides; (*por otra parte*) moreover; (*también*) also; **~ de** besides, in addition to

ADENA [a'ðena] *nf abr* (*Esp*: = *Asociación para la Defensa de la Naturaleza*) *organization for nature conservation*

adentrarse [aðen'trarse] *vr*: **~ en** to go into, get inside; (*penetrar*) to penetrate (into)

adentro [a'ðentro] *adv* inside, in; **mar ~** out at sea; **tierra ~** inland ■ *nm*: **dijo para sus adentros** he said to himself

adepto, -a [a'ðepto, a] *nm/f* supporter

aderece *etc* [aðe'reθe] *vb ver* **aderezar**

aderezar [aðere'θar] *vt* (*ensalada*) to dress; (*comida*) to season

aderezo [aðe'reθo] *nm* dressing; seasoning

adeudar [aðeu'ðar] *vt* to owe; **adeudarse** *vr* to run into debt; **~ una suma en una cuenta** to debit an account with a sum

adherirse [aðe'rirse] *vr*: **~ a** to adhere to; (*fig*) to follow

adhesión [aðe'sjon] *nf* adhesion; (*fig*) adherence

adhesivo, -a [aðe'siβo, a] *adj* adhesive ■ *nm* sticker

adhiera *etc* [a'ðjera], **adhiriendo** *etc* [aði'rjendo] *vb ver* **adherirse**

adicción [aðik'θion] *nf* addiction

adición [aði'θjon] *nf* addition

adicional [aðiθjo'nal] *adj* additional; (*Inform*) add-on

adicionar [aðiθjo'nar] *vt* to add

adicto, -a [a'ðikto, a] *adj*: **~ a** (*droga etc*) addicted to; (*dedicado*) devoted to ■ *nm/f*

supporter, follower; (*toxicómano etc*) addict
adiestrar [aðjes'trar] *vt* to train, teach; (*conducir*) to guide, lead; **adiestrarse** *vr* to practise; (*aprender*) to train o.s.
adinerado, -a [aðine'raðo, a] *adj* wealthy
adiós [a'ðjos] *excl* (*para despedirse*) goodbye!, cheerio!; (*al pasar*) hello!
aditivo [aði'tiβo] *nm* additive
adivinanza [aðiβi'nanθa] *nf* riddle
adivinar [aðiβi'nar] *vt* (*profetizar*) to prophesy; (*conjeturar*) to guess
adivino, -a [aði'βino, a] *nm/f* fortune-teller
adj *abr* (= *adjunto*) encl; (= *adjetivo*) adj
adjetivo [aðxe'tiβo] *nm* adjective
adjudicación [aðxuðika'θjon] *nf* award; (*Com*) adjudication
adjudicar [aðxuði'kar] *vt* to award; **adjudicarse** *vr*: **adjudicarse algo** to appropriate sth
adjudique *etc* [aðxu'ðike] *vb ver* **adjudicar**
adjuntar [aðxun'tar] *vt* to attach, enclose
adjunto, -a [að'xunto, a] *adj* attached, enclosed ▪ *nm/f* assistant
adminículo [aðmi'nikulo] *nm* gadget
administración [aðministra'θjon] *nf* administration; (*dirección*) management; **~ pública** civil service; **A~ de Correos** General Post Office
administrador, a [aðministra'ðor, a] *nm/f* administrator; manager(ess)
administrar [aðminis'trar] *vt* to administer
administrativo, -a [aðministra'tiβo, a] *adj* administrative
admirable [aðmi'raβle] *adj* admirable
admiración [aðmira'θjon] *nf* admiration; (*asombro*) wonder; (*Ling*) exclamation mark
admirar [aðmi'rar] *vt* to admire; (*extrañar*) to surprise; **admirarse** *vr* to be surprised; **se admiró de saberlo** he was amazed to hear it; **no es de ~ que ...** it's not surprising that ...
admisible [aðmi'siβle] *adj* admissible
admisión [aðmi'sjon] *nf* admission; (*reconocimiento*) acceptance
admitir [aðmi'tir] *vt* to admit; (*aceptar*) to accept; (*dudas*) to leave room for; **esto no admite demora** this must be dealt with immediately
admón. *abr* (= *administración*) admin
admonición [aðmoni'θjon] *nf* warning
ADN *nm abr* (= *acido desoxirribonucleico*) DNA
adobar [aðo'βar] *vt* (*preparar*) to prepare; (*cocinar*) to season
adobe [a'ðoβe] *nm* adobe, sun-dried brick
adocenado, -a [aðoθe'naðo, a] *adj* (*fam*) mediocre
adoctrinar [aðoktri'nar] *vt* to indoctrinate
adolecer [aðole'θer] *vi*: **~ de** to suffer from
adolescente [aðoles'θente] *nm/f* adolescent, teenager ▪ *adj* adolescent, teenage
adolezca *etc* [aðo'leθka] *vb ver* **adolecer**
adonde [a'ðonde] *adv* (to) where
adónde [a'ðonde] *adv* = **dónde**
adondequiera [aðonde'kjera] *adv* wherever
adopción [aðop'θjon] *nf* adoption
adoptar [aðop'tar] *vt* to adopt
adoptivo, -a [aðop'tiβo, a] *adj* (*padres*) adoptive; (*hijo*) adopted
adoquín [aðo'kin] *nm* paving stone
adorar [aðo'rar] *vt* to adore
adormecer [aðorme'θer] *vt* to put to sleep; **adormecerse** *vr* to become sleepy; (*dormirse*) to fall asleep
adormezca *etc* [aðor'meθka] *vb ver* **adormecer**
adormilarse [aðormi'larse] *vr* to doze
adornar [aðor'nar] *vt* to adorn
adorno [a'ðorno] *nm* adornment; (*decoración*) decoration
adosado, -a [aðo'saðo, a] *adj* (*casa*) semidetached
adquiera *etc* [að'kjera] *vb ver* **adquirir**
adquirir [aðki'rir] *vt* to acquire, obtain
adquisición [aðkisi'θjon] *nf* acquisition; (*compra*) purchase
adrede [a'ðreðe] *adv* on purpose
Adriático [að'rjatiko] *nm*: **el (Mar) ~** the Adriatic (Sea)
adscribir [aðskri'βir] *vt* to appoint; **estuvo adscrito al servicio de ...** he was attached to ...
adscrito [að'skrito] *pp de* **adscribir**
aduana [a'ðwana] *nf* customs *pl*; (*impuesto*) (customs) duty
aduanero, -a [aðwa'nero, a] *adj* customs *cpd* ▪ *nm/f* customs officer
aducir [aðu'θir] *vt* to adduce; (*dar como prueba*) to offer as proof
adueñarse [aðwe'ɲarse] *vr*: **~ de** to take possession of
adulación [aðula'θjon] *nf* flattery
adular [aðu'lar] *vt* to flatter
adulterar [aðulte'rar] *vt* to adulterate ▪ *vi* to commit adultery
adulterio [aðul'terjo] *nm* adultery
adúltero, -a [a'ðultero, a] *adj* adulterous ▪ *nm/f* adulterer/adulteress
adulto, -a [a'ðulto, a] *adj, nm/f* adult
adusto, -a [a'ðusto, a] *adj* stern; (*austero*) austere
aduzca *etc* [a'ðuθka] *vb ver* **aducir**
advenedizo, -a [aðβene'ðiθo, a] *nm/f* upstart
advenimiento [aðβeni'mjento] *nm* arrival; (*al trono*) accession

adverbio [að'βerβjo] *nm* adverb
adversario, -a [aðβer'sarjo, a] *nm/f* adversary
adversidad [aðβersi'ðað] *nf* adversity; (*contratiempo*) setback
adverso, -a [að'βerso, a] *adj* adverse; (*suerte*) bad
advertencia [aðβer'tenθja] *nf* warning; (*prefacio*) preface, foreword
advertir [aðβer'tir] *vt* (*observar*) to notice; (*avisar*): ~ **a algn de** to warn sb about *o* of
Adviento [að'βjento] *nm* Advent
advierta *etc* [að'βjerta], **advirtiendo** *etc* [aðβir'tjendo] *vb ver* **advertir**
adyacente [aðja'θente] *adj* adjacent
aéreo, -a [a'ereo, a] *adj* aerial; (*tráfico*) air *cpd*
aerobic [ae'roβik] *nm* aerobics *sg*
aerodeslizador [aeroðesliθa'ðor] *nm* hovercraft
aerodinámico, -a [aeroði'namiko, a] *adj* aerodynamic
aeródromo [ae'roðromo] *nm* aerodrome
aerograma [aero'ɣrama] *nm* airmail letter
aeromodelismo [aeromoðe'lismo] *nm* model aircraft making, aeromodelling
aeromozo, -a [aero'moso, a] *nm/f* (*Am*) flight attendant, air steward(ess)
aeronáutico, -a [aero'nautiko, a] *adj* aeronautical
aeronave [aero'naβe] *nm* spaceship
aeroplano [aero'plano] *nm* aeroplane
aeropuerto [aero'pwerto] *nm* airport
aerosol [aero'sol] *nm* aerosol, spray
a/f *abr* (= *a favor*) in favour
afabilidad [afaβili'ðað] *nf* affability, pleasantness
afable [a'faβle] *adj* affable, pleasant
afamado, -a [afa'maðo, a] *adj* famous
afán [a'fan] *nm* hard work; (*deseo*) desire; **con** ~ keenly
afanar [afa'nar] *vt* to harass; (*fam*) to pinch; **afanarse** *vr*: **afanarse por** to strive to
afanoso, -a [afa'noso, a] *adj* (*trabajo*) hard; (*trabajador*) industrious
AFE ['afe] *nf abr* (= *Asociación de Futbolistas Españoles*) ≈ F.A
afear [afe'ar] *vt* to disfigure
afección [afek'θjon] *nf* affection; (*Med*) disease
afectación [afekta'θjon] *nf* affectation
afectado, -a [afek'taðo, a] *adj* affected
afectar [afek'tar] *vt* to affect, have an effect on; (*Am: dañar*) to hurt; **por lo que afecta a esto** as far as this is concerned
afectísimo, -a [afek'tisimo, a] *adj* affectionate; **suyo** ~ yours truly
afectivo, -a [afek'tiβo, a] *adj* affective
afecto, -a [a'fekto, a] *adj*: ~ **a** fond of; (*Jur*) subject to ■ *nm* affection; **tenerle ~ a algn** to be fond of sb
afectuoso, -a [afek'twoso, a] *adj* affectionate
afeitar [afei'tar] *vt* to shave; **afeitarse** *vr* to shave
afeminado, -a [afemi'naðo, a] *adj* effeminate
aferrar [afe'rrar] *vt* to moor; (*fig*) to grasp ■ *vi* to moor; **aferrarse** *vr* (*agarrarse*) to cling on; **aferrarse a un principio** to stick to a principle; **aferrarse a una esperanza** to cling to a hope
Afganistán [afɣanis'tan] *nm* Afghanistan
afgano, -a [af'ɣano, a] *adj, nm/f* Afghan
afiance *etc* [a'fjanθe] *vb ver* **afianzar**
afianzamiento [afjanθa'mjento] *nm* strengthening; security
afianzar [afjan'θar] *vt* to strengthen, secure; **afianzarse** *vr* to steady o.s.; (*establecerse*) to become established
afiche [a'fitʃe] *nm* (*Am*) poster
afición [afi'θjon] *nf*: ~ **a** fondness *o* liking for; **la** ~ the fans *pl*; **pinto por** ~ I paint as a hobby
aficionado, -a [afiθjo'naðo, a] *adj* keen, enthusiastic; (*no profesional*) amateur ■ *nm/f* enthusiast, fan; amateur
aficionar [afiθjo'nar] *vt*: ~ **a algn a algo** to make sb like sth; **aficionarse** *vr*: **aficionarse a algo** to grow fond of sth
afilado, -a [afi'laðo, a] *adj* sharp
afilador [afila'ðor] *nm* knife grinder
afilalápices [afila'lapiθes] *nm inv* pencil sharpener
afilar [afi'lar] *vt* to sharpen; **afilarse** *vr* (*cara*) to grow thin
afiliación [afilja'θjon] *nf* (*de sindicatos*) membership
afiliado, -a [afi'ljaðo, a] *adj* subsidiary ■ *nm/f* affiliate
afiliarse [afi'ljarse] *vr* to affiliate
afín [a'fin] *adj* (*parecido*) similar; (*conexo*) related
afinar [afi'nar] *vt* (*Tec*) to refine; (*Mus*) to tune ■ *vi* to play/sing in tune
afincarse [afin'karse] *vr* to settle
afinidad [afini'ðað] *nf* affinity; (*parentesco*) relationship; **por** ~ by marriage
afirmación [afirma'θjon] *nf* affirmation
afirmar [afir'mar] *vt* to affirm, state; (*sostener*) to strengthen; **afirmarse** *vr* (*recuperar el equilibrio*) to steady o.s.; **afirmarse en lo dicho** to stand by what one has said
afirmativo, -a [afirma'tiβo, a] *adj* affirmative

aflicción [aflik'θjon] *nf* affliction; (*dolor*) grief
afligir [afli'xir] *vt* to afflict; (*apenar*) to distress; **afligirse** *vr*: **afligirse (por** *o* **con** *o* **de)** to grieve (about *o* at); **no te aflijas tanto** you must not let it affect you like this
aflija *etc* ['aflixa] *vb ver* **afligir**
aflojar [aflo'xar] *vt* to slacken; (*desatar*) to loosen, undo; (*relajar*) to relax ■ *vi* (*amainar*) to drop; (*bajar*) to go down; **aflojarse** *vr* to relax
aflorar [aflo'rar] *vi* (*Geo, fig*) to come to the surface, emerge
afluencia [aflu'enθja] *nf* flow
afluente [aflu'ente] *adj* flowing ■ *nm* (*Geo*) tributary
afluir [aflu'ir] *vi* to flow
afluya *etc* [a'fluja], **afluyendo** *etc* [aflu'jendo] *vb ver* **afluir**
afmo., -a. *abr* (= *afectísimo, a suyo, a*) Yours
afónico, -a [a'foniko, a] *adj*: **estar ~** to have a sore throat; to have lost one's voice
aforar [afo'rar] *vt* (*Tec*) to gauge; (*fig*) to value
aforo [a'foro] *nm* (*Tec*) gauging; (*de teatro etc*) capacity; **el teatro tiene un ~ de 2,000** the theatre can seat 2,000
afortunado, -a [afortu'naðo, a] *adj* fortunate, lucky
afrancesado, -a [afranθe'saðo, a] *adj* francophile; (*pey*) Frenchified
afrenta [a'frenta] *nf* affront, insult; (*deshonra*) dishonour (*Brit*), dishonor (*US*), shame
afrentoso, -a [afren'toso, a] *adj* insulting; shameful
África ['afrika] *nf* Africa; **África del Sur** South Africa
africano, -a [afri'kano, a] *adj, nm/f* African
afrontar [afron'tar] *vt* to confront; (*poner cara a cara*) to bring face to face
after ['after] (*pl* **afters** *o* **~**) *nm*, **afterhours** ['afterauars] *nm inv* after-hours club
afuera [a'fwera] *adv* out, outside; **por ~** on the outside; **afueras** *nfpl* outskirts
ag. *abr* (= *agosto*) Aug
agachar [aɣa'tʃar] *vt* to bend, bow; **agacharse** *vr* to stoop, bend
agalla [a'ɣaʎa] *nf* (*Zool*) gill; **agallas** *nfpl* (*Med*) tonsillitis *sg*; (*Anat*) tonsils; **tener agallas** (*fam*) to have guts
agarradera [aɣarra'ðera] *nf* (*Am*), **agarradero** [aɣarra'ðero] *nm* handle; **agarraderas** *nfpl* pull *sg*, influence *sg*
agarrado, -a [aɣa'rraðo, a] *adj* mean, stingy
agarrar [aɣa'rrar] *vt* to grasp, grab; (*Am*) to take, catch ■ *vi* (*planta*) to take root; **agarrarse** *vr* to hold on (tightly); (*meterse uno con otro*) to grapple (with each other); **agarrársela con algn** (*Am*) to pick on sb; **agarró y se fue** (*esp Am fam*) he upped and went
agarrotar [aɣarro'tar] *vt* (*lío*) to tie tightly; (*persona*) to squeeze tightly; (*reo*) to garrotte; **agarrotarse** *vr* (*motor*) to seize up; (*Med*) to stiffen
agasajar [aɣasa'xar] *vt* to treat well, fête
agave [a'ɣaβe] *nf* agave
agazapar [aɣaθa'par] *vt* (*coger*) to grab hold of; **agazaparse** *vr* (*agacharse*) to crouch down
agencia [a'xenθja] *nf* agency; **~ de créditos/publicidad/viajes** credit/advertising/travel agency; **~ inmobiliaria** estate agent's (office) (*Brit*), real estate office (*US*); **~ matrimonial** marriage bureau
agenciar [axen'θjar] *vt* to bring about; **agenciarse** *vr* to look after o.s.; **agenciarse algo** to get hold of sth
agenda [a'xenda] *nf* diary; **~ electrónica** PDA; **~ telefónica** telephone directory
agente [a'xente] *nm* agent; (*de policía*) policeman; **~ femenino** policewoman; **~ de bolsa** stockbroker; **~ inmobiliario** estate agent (*Brit*), realtor (*US*); **~ de negocios** (*Com*) business agent; **~ de seguros** insurance broker; **~ de viajes** travel agent; **agentes sociales** social partners
ágil ['axil] *adj* agile, nimble
agilidad [axili'ðað] *nf* agility, nimbleness
agilizar [axili'θar] *vt* to speed up
agitación [axita'θjon] *nf* (*de mano etc*) shaking, waving; (*de líquido etc*) stirring; agitation
agitar [axi'tar] *vt* to wave, shake; (*líquido*) to stir; (*fig*) to stir up, excite; **agitarse** *vr* to get excited; (*inquietarse*) to get worried *o* upset
aglomeración [aɣlomera'θjon] *nf*: **~ de tráfico/gente** traffic jam/mass of people
aglomerar [aɣlome'rar] *vt*, **aglomerarse** *vr* to crowd together
agnóstico, -a [aɣ'nostiko, a] *adj, nm/f* agnostic
agobiante [aɣo'βjante] *adj* (*calor*) oppressive
agobiar [aɣo'βjar] *vt* to weigh down; (*oprimir*) to oppress; (*cargar*) to burden; **sentirse agobiado por** to be overwhelmed by
agobio [a'ɣoβjo] *nm* (*peso*) burden; (*fig*) oppressiveness
agolpamiento [aɣolpa'mjento] *nm* crush
agolparse [aɣol'parse] *vr* to crowd together
agonía [aɣo'nia] *nf* death throes *pl*; (*fig*) agony, anguish
agonice *etc* [aɣo'niθe] *vb ver* **agonizar**
agonizante [aɣoni'θante] *adj* dying
agonizar [aɣoni'θar] *vi* (*tb*: **estar**

agonizando) to be dying
agorero, -a [aγo'rero, a] *adj* ominous ■ *nm/f* soothsayer; **ave agorera** bird of ill omen
agostar [aγo'star] *vt* (*quemar*) to parch; (*fig*) to wither
agosto [a'γosto] *nm* August; (*fig*) harvest; **hacer su ~** to make one's pile; *ver tb* **julio**
agotado, -a [aγo'taðo, a] *adj* (*persona*) exhausted; (*acabado*) finished; (*Com*) sold out; (*: libros*) out of print; (*pila*) flat
agotador, a [aγota'ðor, a] *adj* exhausting
agotamiento [aγota'mjento] *nm* exhaustion
agotar [aγo'tar] *vt* to exhaust; (*consumir*) to drain; (*recursos*) to use up, deplete; **agotarse** *vr* to be exhausted; (*acabarse*) to run out; (*libro*) to go out of print
agraciado, -a [aγra'θjaðo, a] *adj* (*atractivo*) attractive; (*en sorteo etc*) lucky
agraciar [aγra'θjar] *vt* (*Jur*) to pardon; (*con premio*) to reward; (*hacer más atractivo*) to make more attractive
agradable [aγra'ðaβle] *adj* pleasant, nice
agradar [aγra'ðar] *vt, vi* to please; **agradarse** *vr* to like each other
agradecer [aγraðe'θer] *vt* to thank; (*favor etc*) to be grateful for; **le ~ía me enviara ...** I would be grateful if you would send me ...; **agradecerse** *vr*: **¡se agradece!** much obliged!
agradecido, -a [aγraðe'θiðo, a] *adj* grateful; **¡muy ~!** thanks a lot!
agradecimiento [aγraðeθi'mjento] *nm* thanks *pl*; gratitude
agradezca *etc* [aγra'ðeθka] *vb ver* **agradecer**
agrado [a'γraðo] *nm*: **ser de tu** *etc* **~** to be to your *etc* liking
agrandar [aγran'dar] *vt* to enlarge; (*fig*) to exaggerate; **agrandarse** *vr* to get bigger
agrario, -a [a'γrarjo, a] *adj* agrarian, land *cpd*; (*política*) agricultural, farming *cpd*
agravante [aγra'βante] *adj* aggravating ■ *nf* complication; **con la ~ de que ...** with the further difficulty that ...
agravar [aγra'βar] *vt* (*pesar sobre*) to make heavier; (*irritar*) to aggravate; **agravarse** *vr* to worsen, get worse
agraviar [aγra'βjar] *vt* to offend; (*ser injusto con*) to wrong; **agraviarse** *vr* to take offence
agravio [a'γraβjo] *nm* offence; wrong; (*Jur*) grievance
agraz [a'γraθ] *nm* (*uva*) sour grape; **en ~** (*fig*) immature
agredir [aγre'ðir] *vt* to attack
agregado [aγre'γaðo] *nm* aggregate; (*persona*) attaché; (*profesor*) assistant professor
agregar [aγre'γar] *vt* to gather; (*añadir*) to add; (*persona*) to appoint
agregue *etc* [a'γreγe] *vb ver* **agregar**
agresión [aγre'sjon] *nf* aggression; (*ataque*) attack
agresivo, -a [aγre'siβo, a] *adj* aggressive
agreste [a'γreste] *adj* (*rural*) rural; (*fig*) rough
agriar [a'γrjar] *vt* (*fig*) to (turn) sour; **agriarse** *vr* to turn sour
agrícola [a'γrikola] *adj* farming *cpd*, agricultural
agricultor, a [aγrikul'tor, a] *nm/f* farmer
agricultura [aγrikul'tura] *nf* agriculture, farming
agridulce [aγri'ðulθe] *adj* bittersweet; (*Culin*) sweet and sour
agrietarse [aγrje'tarse] *vr* to crack; (*la piel*) to chap
agrimensor, a [aγrimen'sor, a] *nm/f* surveyor
agringado, -a [aγrin'gaðo, a] *adj* gringolike
agrio, -a ['aγrjo, a] *adj* bitter
agronomía [aγrono'mia] *nf* agronomy, agriculture
agrónomo, -a [a'γronomo, a] *nm/f* agronomist, agricultural expert
agropecuario, -a [aγrope'kwarjo, a] *adj* farming *cpd*, agricultural
agrupación [aγrupa'θjon] *nf* group; (*acto*) grouping
agrupar [aγru'par] *vt* to group; (*Inform*) to block; **agruparse** *vr* (*Pol*) to form a group; (*juntarse*) to gather
agua ['aγwa] *nf* water; (*Naut*) wake; (*Arq*) slope of a roof; **aguas** *nfpl* (*de joya*) water *sg*, sparkle *sg*; (*Med*) water *sg*, urine *sg*; (*Naut*) waters; **aguas abajo/arriba** downstream/upstream; **~ bendita/destilada/potable** holy/distilled/drinking water; **~ caliente** hot water; **~ corriente** running water; **~ de colonia** eau de cologne; **~ mineral (con/sin gas)** (fizzy/non-fizzy) mineral water; **aguas jurisdiccionales** territorial waters; **aguas mayores** excrement *sg*; **~ pasada no mueve molino** it's no use crying over spilt milk; **estar con el ~ al cuello** to be up to one's neck; **venir como ~ de mayo** to be a godsend
aguacate [aγwa'kate] *nm* avocado (pear)
aguacero [aγwa'θero] *nm* (heavy) shower, downpour
aguachirle [aγwa'tʃirle] *nm* (*bebida*) slops *pl*
aguado, -a [a'γwaðo, a] *adj* watery, watered down ■ *nf* (*Agr*) watering place; (*Naut*) water supply; (*Arte*) watercolour
aguafiestas [aγwa'fjestas] *nm/f inv* spoilsport
aguafuerte [aγwa'fwerte] *nf* etching
aguaitar [aγwai'tar] *vt* (*Am*) to watch
aguanieve [aγwa'njeβe] *nf* sleet

aguantable [aɣwan'taβle] *adj* bearable, tolerable
aguantar [aɣwan'tar] *vt* to bear, put up with; (*sostener*) to hold up ■ *vi* to last; **aguantarse** *vr* to restrain o.s.; **no sé cómo aguanta** I don't know how he can take it
aguante [a'ɣwante] *nm* (*paciencia*) patience; (*resistencia*) endurance; (*Deporte*) stamina
aguar [a'ɣwar] *vt* to water down; (*fig*): ~ **la fiesta a algn** to spoil sb's fun
aguardar [aɣwar'ðar] *vt* to wait for
aguardentoso, -a [aɣwarðen'toso, a] *adj* (*pey: voz*) husky, gruff
aguardiente [aɣwar'ðjente] *nm* brandy, liquor
aguarrás [aɣwa'rras] *nm* turpentine
aguce *etc* [a'ɣuθe] *vb ver* **aguzar**
agudeza [aɣu'ðeθa] *nf* sharpness; (*ingenio*) wit
agudice *etc* [aɣu'ðiθe] *vb ver* **agudizar**
agudizar [aɣuði'θar] *vt* to sharpen; (*crisis*) to make worse; **agudizarse** *vr* to worsen, deteriorate
agudo, -a [a'ɣuðo, a] *adj* sharp; (*voz*) high-pitched, piercing; (*dolor, enfermedad*) acute
agüe *etc* ['aɣwe] *vb ver* **aguar**
agüero [a'ɣwero] *nm*: **buen/mal** ~ good/bad omen; **ser de buen** ~ to augur well; **pájaro de mal** ~ bird of ill omen
aguerrido, -a [aɣe'rriðo, a] *adj* hardened; (*fig*) experienced
aguijar [aɣi'xar] *vt* to goad; (*incitar*) to urge on ■ *vi* to hurry along
aguijón [aɣi'xon] *nm* sting; (*fig*) spur
aguijonear [aɣixone'ar] *vt* = **aguijar**
águila ['aɣila] *nf* eagle; (*fig*) genius
aguileño, -a [aɣi'leɲo, a] *adj* (*nariz*) aquiline; (*rostro*) sharp-featured
aguinaldo [aɣi'naldo] *nm* Christmas box
aguja [a'ɣuxa] *nf* needle; (*de reloj*) hand; (*Arq*) spire; (*Tec*) firing-pin; **agujas** *nfpl* (*Zool*) ribs; (*Ferro*) points
agujerear [aɣuxere'ar] *vt* to make holes in; (*penetrar*) to pierce
agujero [aɣu'xero] *nm* hole; (*Com*) deficit
agujetas [aɣu'xetas] *nfpl* stitch *sg*; (*rigidez*) stiffness *sg*
aguzar [aɣu'θar] *vt* to sharpen; (*fig*) to incite; ~ **el oído** to prick up one's ears
aherrumbrarse [aerrum'brarse] *vr* to get rusty
ahí [a'i] *adv* there; (*allá*) over there; **de ahí que** so that, with the result that; **ahí llega** here he comes; **por ahí** (*dirección*) that way; **¡hasta ahí hemos llegado!** so it has come to this!; **¡ahí va!** (*objeto*) here it comes!; (*individuo*) there he goes!; **ahí donde le ve** as sure as he's standing there
ahijado, -a [ai'xaðo, a] *nm/f* godson/ daughter
ahijar [ai'xar] *vt*: ~ **algo a algn** (*fig*) to attribute sth to sb
ahínco [a'inko] *nm* earnestness; **con** ~ eagerly
ahíto, -a [a'ito, a] *adj*: **estoy** ~ I'm full up
ahogado, -a [ao'ɣaðo, a] *adj* (*en agua*) drowned; (*emoción*) pent-up; (*grito*) muffled
ahogar [ao'ɣar] *vt* (*en agua*) to drown; (*asfixiar*) to suffocate, smother; (*fuego*) to put out; **ahogarse** *vr* (*en agua*) to drown; (*por asfixia*) to suffocate
ahogo [a'oɣo] *nm* (*Med*) breathlessness; (*fig*) distress; (*problema económico*) financial difficulty
ahogue *etc* [a'oɣe] *vb ver* **ahogar**
ahondar [aon'dar] *vt* to deepen, make deeper; (*fig*) to go deeply into ■ *vi*: ~ **en** to go deeply into
ahora [a'ora] *adv* now; (*hace poco*) a moment ago, just now; (*dentro de poco*) in a moment; ~ **voy** I'm coming; ~ **mismo** right now; ~ **bien** now then; **por** ~ for the present
ahorcado, -a [aor'kaðo, a] *nm/f* hanged person
ahorcar [aor'kar] *vt* to hang; **ahorcarse** *vr* to hang o.s.
ahorita [ao'rita], **ahoritita** [aori'tita] *adv* (*esp Am: fam*) right now
ahorque *etc* [a'orke] *vb ver* **ahorcar**
ahorrar [ao'rrar] *vt* (*dinero*) to save; (*esfuerzos*) to save, avoid; **ahorrarse** *vr*: **ahorrarse molestias** to save o.s. trouble
ahorrativo, -a [aorra'tiβo, a] *adj* thrifty
ahorro [a'orro] *nm* (*acto*) saving; (*frugalidad*) thrift; **ahorros** *nmpl* savings
ahuecar [awe'kar] *vt* to hollow (out); (*voz*) to deepen ■ *vi*: **¡ahueca!** (*fam*) beat it! (*fam*); **ahuecarse** *vr* to give o.s. airs
ahueque *etc* [a'weke] *vb ver* **ahuecar**
ahumar [au'mar] *vt* to smoke, cure; (*llenar de humo*) to fill with smoke ■ *vi* to smoke; **ahumarse** *vr* to fill with smoke
ahuyentar [aujen'tar] *vt* to drive off, frighten off; (*fig*) to dispel
AI *nf abr* (= *Amnistía Internacional*) AI
aimara [ai'mara], **aimará** [aima'ra] *adj, nm/f* Aymara
aindiado, -a [aindi'aðo, a] *adj* (*Am*) Indian-like
airado, -a [ai'raðo, a] *adj* angry
airar [ai'rar] *vt* to anger; **airarse** *vr* to get angry
aire ['aire] *nm* air; (*viento*) wind; (*corriente*) draught; (*Mus*) tune; **aires** *nmpl*: **darse**

aires to give o.s. airs; **al ~ libre** in the open air; **~ acondicionado** air conditioning; **tener ~ de** to look like; **estar de buen/mal ~** to be in a good/bad mood; **estar en el ~** (*Radio*) to be on the air; (*fig*) to be up in the air
airear [aire'ar] *vt* to ventilate; (*fig: asunto*) to air; **airearse** *vr* to take the air
airoso, -a [ai'roso, a] *adj* windy; draughty; (*fig*) graceful
aislado, -a [ais'laðo, a] *adj* (*remoto*) isolated; (*incomunicado*) cut off; (*Elec*) insulated
aislante [ais'lante] *nm* (*Elec*) insulator
aislar [ais'lar] *vt* to isolate; (*Elec*) to insulate; **aislarse** *vr* to cut o.s. off
ajar [a'xar] *vt* to spoil; (*fig*) to abuse; **ajarse** *vr* to get crumpled; (*fig: piel*) to get wrinkled
ajardinado, -a [axarði'naðo, a] *adj* landscaped
ajedrez [axe'ðreθ] *nm* chess
ajenjo [a'xenxo] *nm* (*bebida*) absinth(e)
ajeno, -a [a'xeno, a] *adj* (*que pertenece a otro*) somebody else's; **~ a** foreign to; **~ de** free from, devoid of; **por razones ajenas a nuestra voluntad** for reasons beyond our control
ajetreado, -a [axetre'aðo, a] *adj* busy
ajetrearse [axetre'arse] *vr* (*atarearse*) to bustle about; (*fatigarse*) to tire o.s. out
ajetreo [axe'treo] *nm* bustle
ají [a'xi] *nm* chil(l)i, red pepper; (*salsa*) chil(l)i sauce
ajiaco [axi'ako] *nm* (*Am*) potato and chil(l)i stew
ajilimoje [axili'moxe] *nm* sauce of garlic and pepper; **ajilimojes** *nmpl* (*fam*) odds and ends
ajo ['axo] *nm* garlic; **~ porro** *o* **puerro** leek; **(tieso) como un ~** (*fam*) snobbish; **estar en el ~** to be mixed up in it
ajorca [a'xorka] *nf* bracelet
ajuar [a'xwar] *nm* household furnishings *pl*; (*de novia*) trousseau; (*de niño*) layette
ajustado, -a [axus'taðo, a] *adj* (*tornillo*) tight; (*cálculo*) right; (*ropa*) tight(-fitting); (*Deporte: resultado*) close
ajustar [axus'tar] *vt* (*adaptar*) to adjust; (*encajar*) to fit; (*Tec*) to engage; (*Tip*) to make up; (*apretar*) to tighten; (*concertar*) to agree (on); (*reconciliar*) to reconcile; (*cuenta*) to settle ■ *vi* to fit
ajuste [a'xuste] *nm* adjustment; (*Costura*) fitting; (*acuerdo*) compromise; (*de cuenta*) settlement
al [al] = **a+el**; *ver* **a**
ala ['ala] *nf* wing; (*de sombrero*) brim; (*futbolista*) winger; **~ delta** hang-glider; **andar con el ~ caída** to be downcast; **cortar las alas a algn** to clip sb's wings; **dar alas a algn** to encourage sb
alabanza [ala'βanθa] *nf* praise
alabar [ala'βar] *vt* to praise
alacena [ala'θena] *nf* cupboard (*Brit*), closet (*US*)
alacrán [ala'kran] *nm* scorpion
ALADI [a'laði] *nf abr* = **Asociación Latinoamericana de Integración**
alado, -a [a'laðo, a] *adj* winged
ALALC [a'lalk] *nf abr* (= *Asociación Latinoamericana de Libre Comercio*) LAFTA
alambicado, -a [alambi'kaðo, a] *adj* distilled; (*fig*) affected
alambicar [alambi'kar] *vt* to distil
alambique *etc* [alam'bike] *vb ver* **alambicar** ■ *nm* still
alambrada [alam'braða] *nf*, **alambrado** [alam'braðo] *nm* wire fence; (*red*) wire netting
alambre [a'lambre] *nm* wire; **~ de púas** barbed wire
alambrista [alam'brista] *nm/f* tightrope walker
alameda [ala'meða] *nf* (*plantío*) poplar grove; (*lugar de paseo*) avenue, boulevard
álamo ['alamo] *nm* poplar; **álamo temblón** aspen
alano [a'lano] *nm* mastiff
alarde [a'larðe] *nm* show, display; **hacer ~ de** to boast of
alardear [alarðe'ar] *vi* to boast
alargador [alarɣa'ðor] *nm* extension cable *o* lead
alargar [alar'ɣar] *vt* to lengthen, extend; (*paso*) to hasten; (*brazo*) to stretch out; (*cuerda*) to pay out; (*conversación*) to spin out; **alargarse** *vr* to get longer
alargue *etc* [a'larɣe] *vb ver* **alargar**
alarido [ala'riðo] *nm* shriek
alarma [a'larma] *nf* alarm; **voz de ~** warning note; **dar la ~** to raise the alarm
alarmante [alar'mante] *adj* alarming
alarmar [alar'mar] *vt* to alarm; **alarmarse** *vr* to get alarmed
alavés, -esa [ala'βes, esa] *adj* of Álava ■ *nm/f* native *o* inhabitant of Álava
alazán [ala'θan] *nm* sorrel
alba ['alβa] *nf* dawn
albacea [alβa'θea] *nm/f* executor/executrix
albaceteño, -a [alβaθe'teɲo, a] *adj* of Albacete ■ *nm/f* native *o* inhabitant of Albacete
albahaca [al'βaka] *nf* (*Bot*) basil
Albania [al'βanja] *nf* Albania
albañal [alβa'ɲal] *nm* drain, sewer
albañil [alβa'ɲil] *nm* bricklayer; (*cantero*) mason

albarán [alβa'ran] *nm* (*Com*) invoice
albarda [al'βarða] *nf* packsaddle
albaricoque [alβari'koke] *nm* apricot
albedrío [alβe'ðrio] *nm*: **libre ~** free will
alberca [al'βerka] *nf* reservoir; (*Am*) swimming pool
albergar [alβer'ɣar] *vt* to shelter; (*esperanza*) to cherish; **albergarse** *vr* (*refugiarse*) to shelter; (*alojarse*) to lodge
albergue *etc* [al'βerɣe] *vb ver* **albergar** ▪ *nm* shelter, refuge; **~ de juventud** youth hostel
albis ['alβis] *adv*: **quedarse en ~** not to have a clue
albóndiga [al'βondiɣa] *nf* meatball
albor [al'βor] *nm* whiteness; (*amanecer*) dawn
alborada [alβo'raða] *nf* dawn; (*diana*) reveille
alborear [alβore'ar] *vi* to dawn
albornoz [alβor'noθ] *nm* (*de los árabes*) burnous; (*para el baño*) bathrobe
alboroce *etc* [alβo'roθe] *vb ver* **alborozar**
alborotar [alβoro'tar] *vi* to make a row ▪ *vt* to agitate, stir up; **alborotarse** *vr* to get excited; (*mar*) to get rough
alboroto [alβo'roto] *nm* row, uproar
alborozar [alβoro'θar] *vt* to gladden; **alborozarse** *vr* to rejoice, be overjoyed
alborozo [alβo'roθo] *nm* joy
albricias [al'βriθjas] *nfpl*: **¡~!** good news!
álbum ['alβum] (*pl* **álbums** *o* **álbumes**) *nm* album
albumen [al'βumen] *nm* egg white, albumen
alcabala [alka'βala] *nf* (*Am*) roadblock
alcachofa [alka'tʃofa] *nf* (globe) artichoke; (*Tip*) golf ball; (*de ducha*) shower head
alcahueta [alka'weta] *nf* procuress
alcahuete [alka'wete] *nm* pimp
alcalde, -esa [al'kalde, alkal'desa] *nm/f* mayor(ess)
alcaldía [alkal'dia] *nf* mayoralty; (*lugar*) mayor's office
álcali ['alkali] *nm* (*Química*) alkali
alcance *etc* [al'kanθe] *vb ver* **alcanzar** ▪ *nm* (*Mil: Radio*) range; (*fig*) scope; (*Com*) adverse balance, deficit; **estar al/fuera del ~ de algn** to be within/beyond one's reach; (*fig*) to be within one's powers/over one's head; **de gran ~** (*Mil*) long-range; (*fig*) far-reaching
alcancía [alkan'θia] *nf* money box
alcanfor [alkan'for] *nm* camphor
alcantarilla [alkanta'riʎa] *nf* (*de aguas cloacales*) sewer; (*en la calle*) gutter
alcanzar [alkan'θar] *vt* (*algo: con la mano, el pie*) to reach; (*alguien: en el camino etc*) to catch up (with); (*autobús*) to catch; (*suj: bala*) to hit, strike ▪ *vi* (*ser suficiente*) to be enough; **~ algo a algn** to hand sth to sb; **alcánzame la sal, por favor** pass the salt please; **~ a hacer** to manage to do
alcaparra [alka'parra] *nf* (*Bot*) caper
alcatraz [alka'traθ] *nm* gannet
alcayata [alka'jata] *nf* hook
alcázar [al'kaθar] *nm* fortress; (*Naut*) quarter-deck
alce *etc* ['alθe] *vb ver* **alzar**
alcista [al'θista] *adj* (*Com: Econ*): **mercado ~** bull market; **la tendencia ~** the upward trend ▪ *nm* speculator
alcoba [al'koβa] *nf* bedroom
alcohol [al'kol] *nm* alcohol; **no bebe ~** he doesn't drink (alcohol)
alcoholemia [alkoo'lemia] *nf* blood alcohol level; **prueba de la ~** breath test
alcoholice *etc* [alko'liθe] *vb ver* **alcoholizarse**
alcohólico, -a [al'koliko, a] *adj, nm/f* alcoholic
alcoholímetro [alko'limetro] *nm* Breathalyser®, drunkometer (US)
alcoholismo [alko'lismo] *nm* alcoholism
alcoholizarse [alkoli'θarse] *vr* to become an alcoholic
alcornoque [alkor'noke] *nm* cork tree; (*fam*) idiot
alcotana [alko'tana] *nf* pickaxe; (*Deporte*) ice-axe
alcurnia [al'kurnja] *nf* lineage
alcuza [al'kusa] *nf* (*Am*) cruet
aldaba [al'daβa] *nf* (door) knocker
aldea [al'dea] *nf* village
aldeano, -a [alde'ano, a] *adj* village *cpd* ▪ *nm/f* villager
ale ['ale] *excl* come on!, let's go!
aleación [alea'θjon] *nf* alloy
aleatorio, -a [alea'torjo, a] *adj* random, contingent; **acceso ~** (*Inform*) random access
aleccionador, a [alekθjona'ðor, a] *adj* instructive
aleccionar [alekθjo'nar] *vt* to instruct; (*adiestrar*) to train
aledaño, -a [ale'ðaɲo, a] *adj*: **~ a** bordering on ▪ *nmpl*: **aledaños** outskirts
alegación [aleɣa'θjon] *nf* allegation
alegar [ale'ɣar] *vt* (*dificultad etc*) to plead; (*Jur*) to allege ▪ *vi* (*Am*) to argue; **~ que ...** to give as an excuse that ...
alegato [ale'ɣato] *nm* (*Jur*) allegation; (*escrito*) indictment; (*declaración*) statement; (*Am*) argument
alegoría [aleɣo'ria] *nf* allegory
alegrar [ale'ɣrar] *vt* (*causar alegría*) to cheer (up); (*fuego*) to poke; (*fiesta*) to liven up; **alegrarse** *vr* (*fam*) to get merry *o* tight; **alegrarse de** to be glad about
alegre [a'leɣre] *adj* happy, cheerful; (*fam*) merry, tight; (*licencioso*) risqué, blue

alegría [ale'ɣria] *nf* happiness; merriment; **~ vital** joie de vivre
alegrón [ale'ɣron] *nm (fig)* sudden joy
alegue *etc* [a'leɣe] *vb ver* **alegar**
alejamiento [alexa'mjento] *nm* removal; *(distancia)* remoteness
alejar [ale'xar] *vt* to move away, remove; *(fig)* to estrange; **alejarse** *vr* to move away
alelado, -a [ale'laðo, a] *adj (bobo)* foolish
alelar [ale'lar] *vt* to bewilder
aleluya [ale'luja] *nm (canto)* hallelujah
alemán, -ana [ale'man, ana] *adj, nm/f* German ■ *nm (lengua)* German
Alemania [ale'manja] *nf* Germany; **~ Occidental/Oriental** West/East Germany
alentador, a [alenta'ðor, a] *adj* encouraging
alentar [alen'tar] *vt* to encourage
alergia [a'lerxja] *nf* allergy
alero [a'lero] *nm (de tejado)* eaves *pl*; *(de foca, Deporte)* flipper; *(Auto)* mudguard
alerta [a'lerta] *adj inv, nm* alert
aleta [a'leta] *nf (de pez)* fin; *(de ave)* wing; *(de coche)* mudguard
aletargar [aletar'ɣar] *vt* to make drowsy; *(entumecer)* to make numb; **aletargarse** *vr* to grow drowsy; to become numb
aletargue *etc* [ale'tarɣe] *vb ver* **aletargar**
aletear [alete'ar] *vi* to flutter; *(ave)* to flap its wings; *(individuo)* to wave one's arms
alevín [ale'βin] *nm* fry, young fish
alevosía [aleβo'sia] *nf* treachery
alfabetización [alfaβetiθa'θjon] *nf*: **campaña de ~** literacy campaign
alfabeto [alfa'βeto] *nm* alphabet
alfajor [alfa'xor] *nm (Esp: polvorón) cake eaten at Christmas time*
alfalfa [al'falfa] *nf* alfalfa, lucerne
alfaque [al'fake] *nm (Naut)* bar, sandbank
alfar [al'far] *nm (taller)* potter's workshop; *(arcilla)* clay
alfarería [alfare'ria] *nf* pottery; *(tienda)* pottery shop
alfarero [alfa'rero] *nm* potter
alféizar [al'feiθar] *nm* window-sill
alférez [al'fereθ] *nm (Mil)* second lieutenant; *(Naut)* ensign
alfil [al'fil] *nm (Ajedrez)* bishop
alfiler [alfi'ler] *nm* pin; *(broche)* clip; *(pinza)* clothes peg *(Brit) o* pin *(US)*; **~ de gancho** *(Am)* safety pin; **prendido con alfileres** shaky
alfiletero [alfile'tero] *nm* needle case
alfombra [al'fombra] *nf* carpet; *(más pequeña)* rug
alfombrar [alfom'brar] *vt* to carpet
alfombrilla [alfom'briʎa] *nf* rug, mat; *(Inform)* mouse mat *o* pad
alforja [al'forxa] *nf* saddlebag
alforza [al'forθa] *nf* pleat
algarabía [alɣara'βia] *nf (fam)* gibberish; *(griterío)* hullabaloo
algarada [alɣa'raða] *nf* outcry; **hacer** *o* **levantar una ~** to kick up a tremendous fuss
Algarbe [al'ɣarβe] *nm*: **el ~** the Algarve
algarroba [alɣa'rroβa] *nf* carob
algarrobo [alɣa'rroβo] *nm* carob tree
algas ['alɣas] *nfpl* seaweed *sg*
algazara [alɣa'θara] *nf* din, uproar
álgebra ['alxeβra] *nf* algebra
álgido, -a ['alxiðo, a] *adj* icy; *(momento etc)* crucial, decisive
algo ['alɣo] *pron* something; *(en frases interrogativas)* anything ■ *adv* somewhat, rather; **por ~ será** there must be some reason for it; **es ~ difícil** it's a bit awkward
algodón [alɣo'ðon] *nm* cotton; *(planta)* cotton plant; **~ de azúcar** candy floss *(Brit)*, cotton candy *(US)*; **~ hidrófilo** cotton wool *(Brit)*, absorbent cotton *(US)*
algodonero, -a [alɣoðo'nero, a] *adj* cotton *cpd* ■ *nm/f* cotton grower ■ *nm* cotton plant
algoritmo [alɣo'ritmo] *nm* algorithm
alguacil [alɣwa'θil] *nm* bailiff; *(Taur)* mounted official
alguien ['alɣjen] *pron* someone, somebody; *(en frases interrogativas)* anybody
alguno, -a [al'ɣuno, a] *adj (antes de nmsg* **algún**) some; *(después de n)*: **no tiene talento ~** he has no talent, he hasn't any talent ■ *pron (alguien)* someone, somebody; **algún que otro libro** some book or other; **algún día iré** I'll go one *o* some day; **sin interés ~** without the slightest interest; **~ que otro** an occasional one; **algunos piensan** some (people) think; **~ de ellos** one of them
alhaja [a'laxa] *nf* jewel; *(tesoro)* precious object, treasure
alhelí [ale'li] *nm* wallflower, stock
aliado, -a [a'ljaðo, a] *adj* allied
alianza [a'ljanθa] *nf (Pol etc)* alliance; *(anillo)* wedding ring
aliar [a'ljar] *vt* to ally; **aliarse** *vr* to form an alliance
alias ['aljas] *adv* alias
alicaído, -a [alika'iðo, a] *adj (Med)* weak; *(fig)* depressed
alicantino, -a [alikan'tino, a] *adj* of Alicante ■ *nm/f* native *o* inhabitant of Alicante
alicatar [alika'tar] *vt* to tile
alicate [ali'kate] *nm*, **alicates** [ali'kates] *nmpl* pliers *pl*; **~(s) de uñas** nail clippers
aliciente [ali'θjente] *nm* incentive; *(atracción)* attraction
alienación [aljena'θjon] *nf* alienation

aliento *etc* [a'ljento] *vb ver* **alentar** ■ *nm* breath; (*respiración*) breathing; **sin ~** breathless; **de un ~** in one breath; (*fig*) in one go
aligerar [alixe'rar] *vt* to lighten; (*reducir*) to shorten; (*aliviar*) to alleviate; (*mitigar*) to ease
alijo [a'lixo] *nm* (*Naut*) unloading; (*contrabando*) smuggled goods
alimaña [ali'maɲa] *nf* pest
alimentación [alimenta'θjon] *nf* (*comida*) food; (*acción*) feeding; (*tienda*) grocer's (shop); **~ continua** (*en fotocopiadora etc*) stream feed
alimentador [alimenta'ðor] *nm*: **~ de papel** sheet-feeder
alimentar [alimen'tar] *vt* to feed; (*nutrir*) to nourish; **alimentarse** *vr*: **alimentarse (de)** to feed (on)
alimenticio, -a [alimen'tiθjo, a] *adj* food *cpd*; (*nutritivo*) nourishing, nutritious
alimento [ali'mento] *nm* food; (*nutrición*) nourishment; **alimentos** *nmpl* (*Jur*) alimony *sg*
alimón [ali'mon]: **al ~** *adv* jointly, together
alineación [alinea'θjon] *nf* alignment; (*Deporte*) line-up
alineado, -a [aline'aðo, a] *adj* (*Tip*): **(no) ~** (un)justified; **~ a la izquierda/derecha** ranged left/right
alinear [aline'ar] *vt* to align; (*Tip*) to justify; **alinearse** *vr* to line up; **alinearse en** to fall in with
aliñar [ali'ɲar] *vt* (*Culin*) to dress
aliño [a'liɲo] *nm* (*Culin*) dressing
alisar [ali'sar] *vt* to smooth
aliso [a'liso] *nm* alder
alistamiento [alista'mjento] *nm* recruitment
alistar [ali'star] *vt* to recruit; **alistarse** *vr* to enlist; (*inscribirse*) to enrol; (*Am: prepararse*) to get ready
aliviar [ali'βjar] *vt* (*carga*) to lighten; (*persona*) to relieve; (*dolor*) to relieve, alleviate
alivio [a'liβjo] *nm* alleviation, relief; **~ de luto** half-mourning
aljibe [al'xiβe] *nm* cistern
allá [a'ʎa] *adv* (*lugar*) there; (*por ahí*) over there; (*tiempo*) then; **allá abajo** down there; **más allá** further on; **más allá de** beyond; **¡allá tú!** that's your problem!
allanamiento [aʎana'mjento] *nm* (*Am Policía*) raid, search; **~ de morada** housebreaking
allanar [aʎa'nar] *vt* to flatten, level (out); (*igualar*) to smooth (out); (*fig*) to subdue; (*Jur*) to burgle, break into; (*Am Policía*) to raid, search; **allanarse** *vr* to fall down; **allanarse a** to submit to, accept
allegado, -a [aʎe'ɣaðo, a] *adj* near, close ■ *nm/f* relation
allende [a'ʎenðe] *adv* on the other side ■ *prep*: **~ los mares** beyond the seas
allí [a'ʎi] *adv* there; **allí mismo** right there; **por allí** over there; (*por ese camino*) that way
alma ['alma] *nf* soul; (*persona*) person; (*Tec*) core; **se le cayó el ~ a los pies** he became very disheartened; **entregar el ~** to pass away; **estar con el ~ en la boca** to be scared to death; **lo siento en el ~** I am truly sorry; **tener el ~ en un hilo** to have one's heart in one's mouth; **estar como ~ en pena** to suffer; **ir como ~ que lleva el diablo** to go at breakneck speed
almacén [alma'θen] *nm* (*depósito*) warehouse, store; (*Mil*) magazine; (*Am*) grocer's shop, food store, grocery store (*US*); **(grandes) almacenes** *nmpl* department store *sg*; **~ depositario** (*Com*) depository
almacenaje [almaθe'naxe] *nm* storage; **~ secundario** backup storage
almacenamiento [almaθena'mjento] *nm* (*Inform*) storage; **~ temporal en disco** disk spooling
almacenar [almaθe'nar] *vt* to store, put in storage; (*Inform*) to store; (*proveerse*) to stock up with
almacenero [almaθe'nero] *nm* warehouseman; (*Am*) grocer, shopkeeper
almanaque [alma'nake] *nm* almanac
almeja [al'mexa] *nf* clam
almenas [al'menas] *nfpl* battlements
almendra [al'mendra] *nf* almond
almendro [al'mendro] *nm* almond tree
almeriense [alme'rjense] *adj* of Almería ■ *nm/f* native *o* inhabitant of Almería
almiar [al'mjar] *nm* haystack
almíbar [al'miβar] *nm* syrup
almidón [almi'ðon] *nm* starch
almidonado, -a [almiðo'naðo, a] *adj* starched
almidonar [almiðo'nar] *vt* to starch
almirantazgo [almiran'taθɣo] *nm* admiralty
almirante [almi'rante] *nm* admiral
almirez [almi'reθ] *nm* mortar
almizcle [al'miθkle] *nm* musk
almizclero [almiθ'klero] *nm* musk deer
almohada [almo'aða] *nf* pillow; (*funda*) pillowcase
almohadilla [almoa'ðiʎa] *nf* cushion; (*Tec*) pad; (*Am*) pincushion; (*Inform*) hash key
almohadillado, -a [almoaði'ʎaðo, a] *adj* (*acolchado*) padded
almohadón [almoa'ðon] *nm* large pillow
almorcé [almor'θe], **almorcemos** *etc* [almor'θemos] *vb ver* **almorzar**
almorranas [almo'rranas] *nfpl* piles, haemorrhoids (*Brit*), hemorrhoids (*US*)

almorzar [almor'θar] *vt*: **~ una tortilla** to have an omelette for lunch ■ *vi* to (have) lunch
almuerce *etc* [al'mwerθe] *vb ver* **almorzar**
almuerzo *etc* [al'mwerθo] *vb ver* **almorzar** ■ *nm* lunch
aló [a'lo] *excl* (*esp Am Telec*) hello!
alocado, -a [alo'kaðo, a] *adj* crazy
alojamiento [aloxa'mjento] *nm* lodging(s) (*pl*); (*viviendas*) housing
alojar [alo'xar] *vt* to lodge; **alojarse** *vr*: **alojarse en** to stay at; (*bala*) to lodge in
alondra [a'londra] *nf* lark, skylark
alpaca [al'paka] *nf* alpaca
alpargata [alpar'ɣata] *nf* espadrille
Alpes ['alpes] *nmpl*: **los ~** the Alps
alpinismo [alpi'nismo] *nm* mountaineering, climbing
alpinista [alpi'nista] *nm/f* mountaineer, climber
alpino, -a [al'pino, a] *adj* alpine
alpiste [al'piste] *nm* (*semillas*) birdseed; (*Am fam: dinero*) dough; (*fam: alcohol*) booze
alquería [alke'ria] *nf* farmhouse
alquilar [alki'lar] *vt* (*suj: propietario: inmuebles*) to let, rent (out); (*: coche*) to hire out; (*: TV*) to rent (out); (*suj: alquilador: inmuebles, TV*) to rent; (*: coche*) to hire; **"se alquila casa"** "house to let (*Brit*) *o* to rent (*US*)"
alquiler [alki'ler] *nm* renting, letting; hiring; (*arriendo*) rent; hire charge; **de ~** for hire; **~ de automóviles** car hire
alquimia [al'kimja] *nf* alchemy
alquitrán [alki'tran] *nm* tar
alrededor [alreðe'ðor] *adv* around, about; **alrededores** *nmpl* surroundings; **~ de** *prep* around, about; **mirar a su ~** to look (round) about one
Alsacia [al'saθja] *nf* Alsace
alta ['alta] *nf* (certificate of) discharge; **dar a algn de ~** to discharge sb; **darse de ~** (*Mil*) to join, enrol; (*Deporte*) to declare o.s. fit
altanería [altane'ria] *nf* haughtiness, arrogance
altanero, -a [alta'nero, a] *adj* haughty, arrogant
altar [al'tar] *nm* altar
altavoz [alta'βoθ] *nm* loudspeaker; (*amplificador*) amplifier
alteración [altera'θjon] *nf* alteration; (*alboroto*) disturbance; **~ del orden público** breach of the peace
alterar [alte'rar] *vt* to alter; to disturb; **alterarse** *vr* (*persona*) to get upset
altercado [alter'kaðo] *nm* argument
alternar [alter'nar] *vt* to alternate ■ *vi*, **alternarse** *vr* to alternate; (*turnar*) to take turns; **~ con** to mix with
alternativo, -a [alterna'tiβo, a] *adj* alternative; (*alterno*) alternating ■ *nf* alternative; (*elección*) choice; **alternativas** *nfpl* ups and downs; **tomar la alternativa** (*Taur*) to become a fully-qualified bullfighter
alterno, -a [al'terno, a] *adj* (*Bot: Mat*) alternate; (*Elec*) alternating
alteza [al'teθa] *nf* (*tratamiento*) highness
altibajos [alti'βaxos] *nmpl* ups and downs
altillo [al'tiʎo] *nm* (*Geo*) small hill; (*Am*) attic
altiplanicie [altipla'niθje] *nf*, **altiplano** [alti'plano] *nm* high plateau
altisonante [altiso'nante] *adj* high-flown, high-sounding
altitud [alti'tuð] *nf* altitude, height; **a una ~ de** at a height of
altivez [alti'βeθ] *nf* haughtiness, arrogance
altivo, -a [al'tiβo, a] *adj* haughty, arrogant
alto, -a ['alto, a] *adj* high; (*persona*) tall; (*sonido*) high, sharp; (*noble*) high, lofty; (*Geo, clase*) upper ■ *nm* halt; (*Mus*) alto; (*Geo*) hill; (*Am*) pile ■ *adv* (*estar*) high; (*hablar*) loud, loudly ■ *excl* halt!; **la pared tiene dos metros de ~** the wall is two metres high; **en alta mar** on the high seas; **en voz alta** in a loud voice; **las altas horas de la noche** the small (*Brit*) *o* wee (*US*) hours; **en lo ~ de** at the top of; **pasar por ~** to overlook; **altos y bajos** ups and downs; **poner la radio más ~** to turn the radio up; **¡más ~, por favor!** louder, please!
altoparlante [altopar'lante] *nm* (*Am*) loudspeaker
altramuz [altra'muθ] *nm* lupin
altruismo [al'truismo] *nm* altruism
altura [al'tura] *nf* height; (*Naut*) depth; (*Geo*) latitude; **la pared tiene 1.80 de ~** the wall is 1 metre 80 (cm) high; **a esta ~ del año** at this time of the year; **estar a la ~ de las circunstancias** to rise to the occasion; **ha sido un partido de gran ~** it has been a terrific match
alubia [a'luβja] *nf* French bean, kidney bean
alucinación [aluθina'θjon] *nf* hallucination
alucinante [aluθi'nante] *adj* (*fam: estupendo*) great, super
alucinar [aluθi'nar] *vi* to hallucinate ■ *vt* to deceive; (*fascinar*) to fascinate
alud [a'luð] *nm* avalanche; (*fig*) flood
aludir [alu'ðir] *vi*: **~ a** to allude to; **darse por aludido** to take the hint; **no te des por aludido** don't take it personally
alumbrado [alum'braðo] *nm* lighting
alumbramiento [alumbra'mjento] *nm* lighting; (*Med*) childbirth, delivery
alumbrar [alum'brar] *vt* to light (up) ■ *vi* (*iluminar*) to give light; (*Med*) to give birth

aluminio [alu'minjo] *nm* aluminium (*Brit*), aluminum (*US*)
alumnado [alum'naðo] *nm* (*Univ*) student body; (*Escol*) pupils *pl*
alumno, -a [a'lumno, a] *nm/f* pupil, student
alunice *etc* [alu'niθe] *vb ver* **alunizar**
alunizar [aluni'θar] *vi* to land on the moon
alusión [alu'sjon] *nf* allusion
alusivo, -a [alu'siβo, a] *adj* allusive
aluvión [alu'βjon] *nm* (*Geo*) alluvium; (*fig*) flood; **~ de improperios** torrent of abuse
alvéolo [al'βeolo] *nm* (*Anat*) alveolus; (*fig*) network
alza ['alθa] *nf* rise; (*Mil*) sight; **alzas fijas/graduables** fixed/adjustable sights; **al** *o* **en ~** (*precio*) rising; **jugar al ~** to speculate on a rising *o* bull market; **cotizarse** *o* **estar en ~** to be rising
alzado, -a [al'θaðo, a] *adj* (*gen*) raised; (*Com*: *precio*) fixed; (: *quiebra*) fraudulent; **por un tanto ~** for a lump sum ■ *nf* (*de caballos*) height; (*Jur*) appeal
alzamiento [alθa'mjento] *nm* (*aumento*) rise, increase; (*acción*) lifting, raising; (*mejor postura*) higher bid; (*rebelión*) rising; (*Com*) fraudulent bankruptcy
alzar [al'θar] *vt* to lift (up); (*precio, muro*) to raise; (*cuello de abrigo*) to turn up; (*Agr*) to gather in; (*Tip*) to gather; **alzarse** *vr* to get up, rise; (*rebelarse*) to revolt; (*Com*) to go fraudulently bankrupt; (*Jur*) to appeal; **alzarse con el premio** to carry off the prize
a.m. *abr* (*Am*: = *ante meridiem*) a.m.
ama ['ama] *nf* lady of the house; (*dueña*) owner; (*institutriz*) governess; (*madre adoptiva*) foster mother; **~ de casa** housewife; **~ de cría** *o* **de leche** wet-nurse; **~ de llaves** housekeeper
amabilidad [amaβili'ðað] *nf* kindness; (*simpatía*) niceness
amabilísimo, -a [amaβi'lisimo, a] *adj superlativo de* **amable**
amable [a'maβle] *adj* kind; nice
amaestrado, -a [amaes'traðo, a] *adj* (*animal*) trained; (: *en circo etc*) performing
amaestrar [amaes'trar] *vt* to train
amagar [ama'ɣar] *vt, vi* to threaten
amago [a'maɣo] *nm* threat; (*gesto*) threatening gesture; (*Med*) symptom
amague *etc* [a'maɣe] *vb ver* **amagar**
amainar [amai'nar] *vt* (*Naut*) to lower, take in; (*fig*) to calm ■ *vi*, **amainarse** *vr* to drop, die down; **el viento amaina** the wind is dropping
amalgama [amal'ɣama] *nf* amalgam
amalgamar [amalɣa'mar] *vt* to amalgamate; (*combinar*) to combine, mix
amamantar [amaman'tar] *vt* to suckle, nurse
amancebarse [amanθe'βarse] *vr* (*pareja*) to live together
amanecer [amane'θer] *vi* to dawn; (*fig*) to appear, begin to show ■ *nm* dawn; **el niño amaneció afiebrado** the child woke up with a fever
amanerado, -a [amane'raðo, a] *adj* affected
amanezca *etc* [ama'neθka] *vb ver* **amanecer**
amansar [aman'sar] *vt* to tame; (*persona*) to subdue; **amansarse** *vr* (*persona*) to calm down
amante [a'mante] *adj*: **~ de** fond of ■ *nm/f* lover
amanuense [ama'nwense] *nm* (*escribiente*) scribe; (*copista*) copyist; (*Pol*) secretary
amañar [ama'ɲar] *vt* (*gen*) to do skilfully; (*pey*: *resultado*) to alter
amaño [a'maɲo] *nm* (*habilidad*) skill; **amaños** *nmpl* (*Tec*) tools; (*fig*) tricks
amapola [ama'pola] *nf* poppy
amar [a'mar] *vt* to love
amargado, -a [amar'ɣaðo, a] *adj* bitter; embittered
amargar [amar'ɣar] *vt* to make bitter; (*fig*) to embitter; **amargarse** *vr* to become embittered
amargo, -a [a'marɣo, a] *adj* bitter
amargor [amar'ɣor] *nm* (*sabor*) bitterness; (*fig*) grief
amargue *etc* [a'marɣe] *vb ver* **amargar**
amargura [amar'ɣura] *nf* = **amargor**
amarillento, -a [amari'ʎento, a] *adj* yellowish; (*tez*) sallow
amarillismo [amari'ʎismo] *nm* (*de prensa*) sensationalist journalism
amarillo, -a [ama'riʎo, a] *adj, nm* yellow
amarra [a'marra] *nf* (*Naut*) mooring line; **amarras** *nfpl* (*fig*) protection *sg*; **tener buenas amarras** to have good connections; **soltar amarras** to set off
amarrar [ama'rrar] *vt* to moor; (*sujetar*) to tie up
amartillar [amarti'ʎar] *vt* (*fusil*) to cock
amasar [ama'sar] *vt* to knead; (*mezclar*) to mix, prepare; (*confeccionar*) to concoct
amasijo [ama'sixo] *nm* kneading; mixing; (*fig*) hotchpotch
amateur ['amatur] *nm/f* amateur
amatista [ama'tista] *nf* amethyst
amazacotado, -a [amaθako'taðo, a] *adj* (*terreno, arroz etc*) lumpy
amazona [ama'θona] *nf* horsewoman
Amazonas [ama'θonas] *nm*: **el (Río) ~** the Amazon
ambages [am'baxes] *nmpl*: **sin ~** in plain language

ámbar ['ambar] *nm* amber
Amberes [am'beres] *nm* Antwerp
ambición [ambi'θjon] *nf* ambition
ambicionar [ambiθjo'nar] *vt* to aspire to
ambicioso, -a [ambi'θjoso, a] *adj* ambitious
ambidextro, -a [ambi'ðekstro, a] *adj* ambidextrous
ambientación [ambjenta'θjon] *nf* (*Cine: Lit etc*) setting; (*Radio etc*) sound effects *pl*
ambientador [ambjenta'ðor] *nm* air freshener
ambientar [ambjen'tar] *vt* (*gen*) to give an atmosphere to; (*Lit etc*) to set
ambiente [am'bjente] *nm* (*tb fig*) atmosphere; (*medio*) environment; (*Am*) room
ambigüedad [ambiɣwe'ðað] *nf* ambiguity
ambiguo, -a [am'biɣwo, a] *adj* ambiguous
ámbito ['ambito] *nm* (*campo*) field; (*fig*) scope
ambos, -as ['ambos, as] *adj pl, pron pl* both
ambulancia [ambu'lanθja] *nf* ambulance
ambulante [ambu'lante] *adj* travelling, itinerant; (*biblioteca*) mobile
ambulatorio [ambula'torio] *nm* state health-service clinic
ameba [a'meβa] *nf* amoeba
amedrentar [ameðren'tar] *vt* to scare
amén [a'men] *excl* amen; **~ de** *prep* besides, in addition to; **en un decir ~** in the twinkling of an eye; **decir ~ a todo** to have no mind of one's own
amenace *etc* [ame'naθe] *vb ver* **amenazar**
amenaza [ame'naθa] *nf* threat
amenazar [amena'θar] *vt* to threaten ■ *vi*: **~ con hacer** to threaten to do
amenidad [ameni'ðað] *nf* pleasantness
ameno, -a [a'meno, a] *adj* pleasant
América [a'merika] *nf* (*continente*) America, the Americas; (*EEUU*) America; (*Hispanoamérica*) Latin *o* South America; **~ del Norte/del Sur** North/South America; **~ Central/Latina** Central/Latin America
americanismo [amerika'nismo] *nm* Americanism
americano, -a [ameri'kano, a] *adj, nm/f ver* **América** American; Latin *o* South American ■ *nf* coat, jacket
americe *etc* [ame'riθe] *vb ver* **amerizar**
amerindio, -a [ame'rindjo, a] *adj, nm/f* Amerindian, American Indian
amerizaje [ameri'θaxe] *nm* (*Aviat*) landing (on the sea)
amerizar [ameri'θar] *vi* (*Aviat*) to land (on the sea)
ametralladora [ametraʎa'ðora] *nf* machine gun
amianto [a'mjanto] *nm* asbestos
amigable [ami'ɣaβle] *adj* friendly
amígdala [a'miɣðala] *nf* tonsil
amigdalitis [amiɣða'litis] *nf* tonsillitis
amigo, -a [a'miɣo, a] *adj* friendly ■ *nm/f* friend; (*amante*) lover; **~ de lo ajeno** thief; **~ corresponsal** penfriend; **hacerse amigos** to become friends; **ser ~ de** to like, be fond of; **ser muy amigos** to be close friends
amigote [ami'ɣote] *nm* mate (*Brit*), buddy
amilanar [amila'nar] *vt* to scare; **amilanarse** *vr* to get scared
aminorar [amino'rar] *vt* to diminish; (*reducir*) to reduce; **~ la marcha** to slow down
amistad [amis'tað] *nf* friendship; **amistades** *nfpl* friends
amistoso, -a [ami'stoso, a] *adj* friendly
amnesia [am'nesja] *nf* amnesia
amnistía [amnis'tia] *nf* amnesty
amnistiar [amni'stjar] *vt* to amnesty, grant an amnesty to
amo ['amo] *nm* owner; (*jefe*) boss
amodorrarse [amoðo'rrarse] *vr* to get sleepy
amolar [amo'lar] *vt* to annoy
amoldar [amol'dar] *vt* to mould; (*adaptar*) to adapt
amonestación [amonesta'θjon] *nf* warning; **amonestaciones** *nfpl* marriage banns
amonestar [amone'star] *vt* to warn; to publish the banns of
amoniaco [amo'njako] *nm* ammonia
amontonar [amonto'nar] *vt* to collect, pile up; **amontonarse** *vr* (*gente*) to crowd together; (*acumularse*) to pile up; (*datos*) to accumulate; (*desastres*) to come one on top of another
amor [a'mor] *nm* love; (*amante*) lover; **hacer el ~** to make love; **~ interesado** cupboard love; **~ propio** self-respect; **por (el) ~ de Dios** for God's sake; **estar al ~ de la lumbre** to be close to the fire
amoratado, -a [amora'taðo, a] *adj* purple, blue with cold; (*con cardenales*) bruised
amordace *etc* [amor'ðaθe] *vb ver* **amordazar**
amordazar [amorða'θar] *vt* to muzzle; (*fig*) to gag
amorfo, -a [a'morfo, a] *adj* amorphous, shapeless
amorío [amo'rio] *nm* (*fam*) love affair
amoroso, -a [amo'roso, a] *adj* affectionate, loving
amortajar [amorta'xar] *vt* (*fig*) to shroud
amortice *etc* [amor'tiθe] *vb ver* **amortizar**
amortiguador [amortiɣwa'ðor] *nm* shock absorber; (*parachoques*) bumper; (*silenciador*) silencer; **amortiguadores** *nmpl* (*Auto*) suspension *sg*
amortiguar [amorti'ɣwar] *vt* to deaden; (*ruido*) to muffle; (*color*) to soften

amortigüe *etc* [amor'tiɣwe] *vb ver* **amortiguar**
amortización [amortiθa'θjon] *nf* redemption; repayment; (*Com*) capital allowance
amortizar [amorti'θar] *vt* (*Econ: bono*) to redeem; (*: capital*) to write off; (*: préstamo*) to pay off
amoscarse [amos'karse] *vr* to get cross
amosque *etc* [a'moske] *vb ver* **amoscarse**
amotinar [amoti'nar] *vt* to stir up, incite (to riot); **amotinarse** *vr* to mutiny
amparar [ampa'rar] *vt* to protect; **ampararse** *vr* to seek protection; (*de la lluvia etc*) to shelter
amparo [am'paro] *nm* help, protection; **al ~ de** under the protection of
amperímetro [ampe'rimetro] *nm* ammeter
amperio [am'perjo] *nm* ampère, amp
ampliable [am'pljaβle] *adj* (*Inform*) expandable
ampliación [amplja'θjon] *nf* enlargement; (*extensión*) extension
ampliar [am'pljar] *vt* to enlarge; to extend
amplificación [amplifika'θjon] *nf* enlargement
amplificador [amplifika'ðor] *nm* amplifier
amplificar [amplifi'kar] *vt* to amplify
amplifique *etc* [ampli'fike] *vb ver* **amplificar**
amplio, -a ['ampljo, a] *adj* spacious; (*falda etc*) full; (*extenso*) extensive; (*ancho*) wide
amplitud [ampli'tuð] *nf* spaciousness; extent; (*fig*) amplitude; **~ de miras** broadmindedness; **de gran ~** far-reaching
ampolla [am'poʎa] *nf* blister; (*Med*) ampoule
ampolleta [ampo'ʎeta] *nf* (*Am*) (light) bulb
ampuloso, -a [ampu'loso, a] *adj* bombastic, pompous
amputar [ampu'tar] *vt* to cut off, amputate
amueblar [amwe'βlar] *vt* to furnish
amuleto [amu'leto] *nm* (lucky) charm
amurallar [amura'ʎar] *vt* to wall up *o* in
anacarado, -a [anaka'raðo, a] *adj* mother-of-pearl *cpd*
anacardo [ana'karðo] *nm* cashew (nut)
anaconda [ana'konda] *nf* anaconda
anacronismo [anakro'nismo] *nm* anachronism
ánade ['anaðe] *nm* duck
anagrama [ana'ɣrama] *nm* anagram
anales [a'nales] *nmpl* annals
analfabetismo [analfaβe'tismo] *nm* illiteracy
analfabeto, -a [analfa'βeto, a] *adj, nm/f* illiterate
analgésico [anal'xesiko] *nm* painkiller, analgesic
analice *etc* [ana'liθe] *vb ver* **analizar**
análisis [a'nalisis] *nm inv* analysis; **~ de costos-beneficios** cost-benefit analysis; **~ de mercados** market research; **~ de sangre** blood test
analista [ana'lista] *nm/f* (*gen*) analyst; (*Pol: Historia*) chronicler; **~ de sistemas** (*Inform*) systems analyst
analizar [anali'θar] *vt* to analyse
analogía [analo'xia] *nf* analogy; **por ~ con** on the analogy of
analógico, -a [ana'loxico, a] *adj* analogue
análogo, -a [a'naloɣo, a] *adj* analogous, similar
ananá [ana'na], **ananás** [ana'nas] *nm* pineapple
anaquel [ana'kel] *nm* shelf
anaranjado, -a [anaran'xaðo, a] *adj* orange (-coloured)
anarquía [anar'kia] *nf* anarchy
anarquismo [anar'kismo] *nm* anarchism
anarquista [anar'kista] *nm/f* anarchist
anatematizar [anatemati'θar] *vt* (*Rel*) to anathematize; (*fig*) to curse
anatemice *etc* [anate'miθe] *vb ver* **anatemizar**
anatomía [anato'mia] *nf* anatomy
anca ['anka] *nf* rump, haunch; **ancas** *nfpl* (*fam*) behind *sg*; **llevar a algn en ancas** to carry sb behind one
ancestral [anθes'tral] *adj* (*costumbre*) age-old
ancho, -a ['antʃo, a] *adj* wide; (*falda*) full; (*fig*) liberal ▪ *nm* width; (*Ferro*) gauge; **le viene muy ~ el cargo** (*fig*) the job is too much for him; **ponerse ~** to get conceited; **quedarse tan ~** to go on as if nothing had happened; **estar a sus anchas** to be at one's ease
anchoa [an'tʃoa] *nf* anchovy
anchura [an'tʃura] *nf* width; (*amplitud*) wideness
anchuroso, -a [antʃu'roso, a] *adj* wide
anciano, -a [an'θjano, a] *adj* old, aged ▪ *nm/f* old man/woman ▪ *nm* elder
ancla ['ankla] *nf* anchor; **levar anclas** to weigh anchor
ancladero [ankla'ðero] *nm* anchorage
anclar [an'klar] *vi* to (drop) anchor
andadas [an'daðas] *nfpl* (*aventuras*) adventures; **volver a las ~** to backslide
andaderas [anda'ðeras] *nfpl* baby-walker *sg*
andadura [anda'ðura] *nf* gait; (*de caballo*) pace
Andalucía [andalu'θia] *nf* Andalusia
andaluz, a [anda'luθ, a] *adj, nm/f* Andalusian
andamio [an'damjo] *nm*, **andamiaje** [anda'mjaxe] *nm* scaffold(ing)
andanada [anda'naða] *nf* (*fig*) reprimand;

soltarle a algn una ~ to give sb a rocket
andante [an'dante] *adj*: **caballero ~** knight errant
andar [an'dar] *vt* to go, cover, travel ■ *vi* to go, walk, travel; (*funcionar*) to go, work; (*estar*) to be ■ *nm* walk, gait, pace; **andarse** *vr* (*irse*) to go away *o* off; **~ a pie/a caballo/en bicicleta** to go on foot/on horseback/by bicycle; **¡anda!** (*sorpresa*) go on!; **anda en** *o* **por los 40** he's about 40; **¿en qué andas?** what are you up to?; **andamos mal de dinero/tiempo** we're badly off for money/ we're short of time; **andarse por las ramas** to beat about the bush; **no andarse con rodeos** to call a spade a spade (*fam*); **todo se ~á** all in good time; **anda por aquí** it's round here somewhere; **~ haciendo algo** to be doing sth
andariego, -a [anda'rjeɣo, a] *adj* fond of travelling
andas ['andas] *nfpl* stretcher *sg*
andén [an'den] *nm* (*Ferro*) platform; (*Naut*) quayside; (*Am*: *acera*) pavement (*Brit*), sidewalk (*US*)
Andes ['andes] *nmpl*: **los ~** the Andes
andinismo [andin'ismo] *nm* (*Am*) mountaineering, climbing
andino, -a [an'dino, a] *adj* Andean, of the Andes
Andorra [an'dorra] *nf* Andorra
andrajo [an'draxo] *nm* rag
andrajoso, -a [andra'xoso, a] *adj* ragged
andurriales [andu'rrjales] *nmpl* out-of-the-way place *sg*, the sticks; **en esos ~** in that godforsaken spot
anduve [an'duβe], **anduviera** *etc* [andu'βjera] *vb ver* **andar**
anécdota [a'nekðota] *nf* anecdote, story
anegar [ane'ɣar] *vt* to flood; (*ahogar*) to drown; **anegarse** *vr* to drown; (*hundirse*) to sink
anegue *etc* [a'neɣe] *vb ver* **anegar**
anejo, -a [a'nexo, a] *adj* attached ■ *nm* (*Arq*) annexe
anemia [a'nemja] *nf* anaemia
anestesia [anes'tesja] *nf* anaesthetic; **~ general/local** general/local anaesthetic
anestesiar [aneste'sjar] *vt* to anaesthetize (*Brit*), anesthetize (*US*)
anestésico [anes'tesiko] *nm* anaesthetic
anexar [anek'sar] *vt* to annex; (*documento*) to attach; (*Inform*) to append
anexión [anek'sjon] *nf*, **anexionamiento** [aneksjona'mjento] *nm* annexation
anexionar [aneksjo'nar] *vt* to annex; **anexionarse** *vr*: **anexionarse un país** to annex a country
anexo, -a [a'nekso, a] *adj* attached ■ *nm* annexe
anfetamina [anfeta'mina] *nf* amphetamine
anfibio, -a [an'fiβjo, a] *adj* amphibious ■ *nm* amphibian
anfiteatro [anfite'atro] *nm* amphitheatre; (*Teat*) dress circle
anfitrión, -ona [anfi'trjon, ona] *nm/f* host(ess)
ángel ['anxel] *nm* angel; **ángel de la guarda** guardian angel; **tener ángel** to have charm
Ángeles ['anxeles] *nmpl*: **los Ángeles** Los Angeles
angélico, -a [an'xeliko, a], **angelical** [anxeli'kal] *adj* angelic(al)
angina [an'xina] *nf* (*Med*): **~ de pecho** angina; **tener anginas** to have a sore throat *o* throat infection
anglicano, -a [angli'kano, a] *adj*, *nm/f* Anglican
anglicismo [angli'θismo] *nm* anglicism
anglosajón, -ona [anglosa'xon, 'xona] *adj*, *nm/f* Anglo-Saxon
Angola [an'gola] *nf* Angola
angoleño, -a [ango'leɲo, a] *adj*, *nm/f* Angolan
angosto, -a [an'gosto, a] *adj* narrow
anguila [an'gila] *nf* eel; **anguilas** *nfpl* slipway *sg*
angula [an'gula] *nf* elver, baby eel
ángulo ['angulo] *nm* angle; (*esquina*) corner; (*curva*) bend
angustia [an'gustja] *nf* anguish
angustiar [angus'tjar] *vt* to distress, grieve; **angustiarse** *vr*: **angustiarse (por)** to be distressed (at, on account of)
anhelante [ane'lante] *adj* eager; (*deseoso*) longing
anhelar [ane'lar] *vt* to be eager for; to long for, desire ■ *vi* to pant, gasp
anhelo [a'nelo] *nm* eagerness; desire
anhídrido [a'niðriðo] *nm*: **~ carbónico** carbon dioxide
anidar [ani'ðar] *vt* (*acoger*) to take in, shelter ■ *vi* to nest; (*fig*) to make one's home
anilina [ani'lina] *nf* aniline
anilla [a'niʎa] *nf* ring; **(las) anillas** (*Deporte*) the rings
anillo [a'niʎo] *nm* ring; **~ de boda** wedding ring; **~ de compromiso** engagement ring; **venir como ~ al dedo** to suit to a tee
ánima ['anima] *nf* soul; **las ánimas** the Angelus (bell) *sg*
animación [anima'θjon] *nf* liveliness; (*vitalidad*) life; (*actividad*) bustle
animado, -a [ani'maðo, a] *adj* (*vivo*) lively; (*vivaz*) animated; (*concurrido*) bustling; (*alegre*) in high spirits; **dibujos animados** cartoon *sg*

animador, a [anima'ðor, a] *nm/f* (*TV*) host(ess) ■ *nf* (*Deporte*) cheerleader
animadversión [animaðβer'sjon] *nf* ill-will, antagonism
animal [ani'mal] *adj* animal; (*fig*) stupid ■ *nm* animal; (*fig*) fool; (*bestia*) brute
animalada [anima'laða] *nf* (*gen*) silly thing (to do *o* say); (*ultraje*) disgrace
animar [ani'mar] *vt* (*Bio*) to animate, give life to; (*fig*) to liven up, brighten up, cheer up; (*estimular*) to stimulate; **animarse** *vr* to cheer up, feel encouraged; (*decidirse*) to make up one's mind
ánimo ['animo] *nm* soul, mind; (*valentía*) courage ■ *excl* cheer up!; **cobrar ánimo** to take heart; **dar ánimo(s) a** to encourage
animoso, -a [ani'moso, a] *adj* brave; (*vivo*) lively
aniñado, -a [ani'ɲaðo, a] *adj* (*facción*) childlike; (*carácter*) childish
aniquilar [aniki'lar] *vt* to annihilate, destroy
anís [a'nis] *nm* (*grano*) aniseed; (*licor*) anisette
aniversario [aniβer'sarjo] *nm* anniversary
Ankara [an'kara] *nf* Ankara
ano ['ano] *nm* anus
anoche [a'notʃe] *adv* last night; **antes de ~** the night before last
anochecer [anotʃe'θer] *vi* to get dark ■ *nm* nightfall, dark; **al ~** at nightfall
anochezca *etc* [ano'tʃeθka] *vb ver* **anochecer**
anodino, -a [ano'ðino, a] *adj* dull, anodyne
anomalía [anoma'lia] *nf* anomaly
anonadado, -a [anona'ðaðo, a] *adj* stunned
anonimato [anoni'mato] *nm* anonymity
anónimo, -a [a'nonimo, a] *adj* anonymous; (*Com*) limited ■ *nm* (*carta*) anonymous letter; (*: maliciosa*) poison-pen letter
anorak [ano'rak] (*pl* **anoraks**) *nm* anorak
anorexia [ano'reksja] *nf* anorexia
anormal [anor'mal] *adj* abnormal
anotación [anota'θjon] *nf* note; annotation
anotar [ano'tar] *vt* to note down; (*comentar*) to annotate
anquilosado, -a [ankilo'saðo, a] *adj* (*fig*) stale, out of date
anquilosamiento [ankilosa'mjento] *nm* (*fig*) paralysis, stagnation
ansia ['ansja] *nf* anxiety; (*añoranza*) yearning
ansiar [an'sjar] *vt* to long for
ansiedad [ansje'ðað] *nf* anxiety
ansioso, -a [an'sjoso, a] *adj* anxious; (*anhelante*) eager; **~ de** *o* **por algo** greedy for sth
antagónico, -a [anta'ɣoniko, a] *adj* antagonistic; (*opuesto*) contrasting
antagonista [antaɣo'nista] *nm/f* antagonist
antaño [an'taɲo] *adv* long ago
Antártico [an'tartiko] *nm*: **el (océano) ~** the Antarctic (Ocean)
Antártida [an'tartiða] *nf* Antarctica
ante ['ante] *prep* before, in the presence of; (*encarado con*) faced with ■ *nm* suede; **~ todo** above all
anteanoche [antea'notʃe] *adv* the night before last
anteayer [antea'jer] *adv* the day before yesterday
antebrazo [ante'βraθo] *nm* forearm
antecámara [ante'kamara] *nf* (*Arq*) anteroom; (*antesala*) waiting room; (*Pol*) lobby
antecedente [anteθe'ðente] *adj* previous ■ *nm*: **antecedentes** *nmpl* (*profesionales*) background *sg*; **antecedentes penales** criminal record; **no tener antecedentes** to have a clean record; **estar en antecedentes** to be well-informed; **poner a algn en antecedentes** to put sb in the picture
anteceder [anteθe'ðer] *vt* to precede, go before
antecesor, a [anteθe'sor, a] *nm/f* predecessor
antedicho, -a [ante'ðitʃo, a] *adj* aforementioned
antelación [antela'θjon] *nf*: **con ~** in advance
antemano [ante'mano]: **de ~** *adv* beforehand, in advance
antena [an'tena] *nf* antenna; (*de televisión etc*) aerial
anteojeras [anteo'xeras] *nfpl* blinkers (*Brit*), blinders (*US*)
anteojo [ante'oxo] *nm* eyeglass; **anteojos** *nmpl* (*esp Am*) glasses, spectacles
antepasados [antepa'saðos] *nmpl* ancestors
antepecho [ante'petʃo] *nm* guardrail, parapet; (*repisa*) ledge, sill
antepondré *etc* [antepon'dre] *vb ver* **anteponer**
anteponer [antepo'ner] *vt* to place in front; (*fig*) to prefer
anteponga *etc* [ante'ponɣa] *vb ver* **anteponer**
anteproyecto [antepro'jekto] *nm* preliminary sketch; (*fig*) blueprint; (*Pol*): **~ de ley** draft bill
antepuesto, -a [ante'pwesto, a] *pp de* **anteponer**
antepuse *etc* [ante'puse] *vb ver* **anteponer**
anterior [ante'rjor] *adj* preceding, previous
anterioridad [anterjori'ðað] *nf*: **con ~ a** prior to, before
anteriormente [anterjor'mente] *adv* previously, before
antes ['antes] *adv* sooner; (*primero*) first; (*con anterioridad*) before; (*hace tiempo*) previously, once; (*más bien*) rather ■ *prep*: **~ de** before

■ *conj*: **~ (de) que** before; **~ bien** (but) rather; **dos días ~** two days before *o* previously; **mucho/poco ~** long/shortly before; **~ muerto que esclavo** better dead than enslaved; **tomo el avión ~ que el barco** I take the plane rather than the boat; **cuanto ~, lo ~ posible** as soon as possible; **cuanto ~ mejor** the sooner the better
antesala [ante'sala] *nf* anteroom
antiadherente [antiaðe'rente] *adj* non-stick
antiaéreo, -a [antia'ereo, a] *adj* anti-aircraft
antialcohólico, -a [antial'koliko, a] *adj*: **centro ~** (*Med*) detoxification unit
antibalas [anti'βalas] *adj inv*: **chaleco ~** bulletproof jacket
antibiótico [anti'βjotiko] *nm* antibiotic
anticiclón [antiθi'klon] *nm* (*Meteorología*) anti-cyclone
anticipación [antiθipa'θjon] *nf* anticipation; **con 10 minutos de ~** 10 minutes early
anticipado, -a [antiθi'paðo, a] *adj* (in) advance; **por ~** in advance
anticipar [antiθi'par] *vt* to anticipate; (*adelantar*) to bring forward; (*Com*) to advance; **anticiparse** *vr*: **anticiparse a su época** to be ahead of one's time
anticipo [anti'θipo] *nm* (*Com*) advance; *ver tb* **anticipación**
anticonceptivo, -a [antikonθep'tiβo, a] *adj, nm* contraceptive; **métodos anticonceptivos** methods of birth control
anticongelante [antikonxe'lante] *nm* antifreeze
anticonstitucional [antikonstituθjo'nal] *adj* unconstitutional
anticuado, -a [anti'kwaðo, a] *adj* out-of-date, old-fashioned; (*desusado*) obsolete
anticuario [anti'kwarjo] *nm* antique dealer
anticuerpo [anti'kwerpo] *nm* (*Med*) antibody
antidemocrático, -a [antiðemo'kratiko, a] *adj* undemocratic
antideportivo, -a [antiðepor'tiβo, a] *adj* unsporting
antidepresivo [antiðepre'siβo] *nm* antidepressant
antideslumbrante [antiðeslum'brante] *adj* (*Inform*) anti-dazzle
antidoping [anti'ðopin] *adj inv* anti-drug
antídoto [an'tiðoto] *nm* antidote
antidroga [anti'ðroɣa] *adj inv* anti-drug; **brigada ~** drug squad
antiestético, -a [anties'tetiko, a] *adj* unsightly
antifaz [anti'faθ] *nm* mask; (*velo*) veil
antigás [anti'gas] *adj inv*: **careta ~** gas mask
antiglobalización [antiglobaliθa'θjon] *n* anti-globalization; **manifestantes ~** anti-globalization protesters
antigualla [anti'ɣwaʎa] *nf* antique; (*reliquia*) relic; **antiguallas** *nfpl* old things
antiguamente [antiɣwa'mente] *adv* formerly; (*hace mucho tiempo*) long ago
antigüedad [antiɣwe'ðað] *nf* antiquity; (*artículo*) antique; (*rango*) seniority
antiguo, -a [an'tiɣwo, a] *adj* old, ancient; (*que fue*) former; **a la antigua** in the old-fashioned way
antihigiénico, -a [anti'xjeniko, a] *adj* unhygienic
antihistamínico, -a [antista'miniko, a] *adj, nm* antihistamine
antiinflacionista [antinflaθjo'nista] *adj* anti-inflationary, counter-inflationary
antillano, -a [anti'ʎano, a] *adj, nm/f* West Indian
Antillas [an'tiʎas] *nfpl*: **las ~** the West Indies, the Antilles; **el mar de las ~** the Caribbean Sea
antílope [an'tilope] *nm* antelope
antimonopolios [antimono'poljos] *adj inv*: **ley ~** anti-trust law
antinatural [antinatu'ral] *adj* unnatural
antiparras [anti'parras] *nfpl* (*fam*) specs
antipatía [antipa'tia] *nf* antipathy, dislike
antipático, -a [anti'patiko, a] *adj* disagreeable, unpleasant
Antípodas [an'tipoðas] *nfpl*: **las ~** the Antipodes
antiquísimo, -a [anti'kisimo, a] *adj* ancient
antirreglamentario, -a [antirreɣlamen'tarjo, a] *adj* (*gen*) unlawful; (*Pol etc*) unconstitutional
antirrobo [anti'rroβo] *nm* (*tb*: **dispositivo antirrobo**: *para casas etc*) burglar alarm; (*para coches*) car alarm
antisemita [antise'mita] *adj* anti-Semitic ■ *nm/f* anti-Semite
antiséptico, -a [anti'septiko, a] *adj, nm* antiseptic
antiterrorista [antiterro'rista] *adj* antiterrorist; **la lucha ~** the fight against terrorism
antítesis [an'titesis] *nf inv* antithesis
antojadizo, -a [antoxa'ðiθo, a] *adj* capricious
antojarse [anto'xarse] *vr* (*desear*): **se me antoja comprarlo** I have a mind to buy it; (*pensar*): **se me antoja que** I have a feeling that
antojo [an'toxo] *nm* caprice, whim; (*rosa*) birthmark; (*lunar*) mole; **hacer a su ~** to do as one pleases
antología [antolo'xia] *nf* anthology
antonomasia [antono'masja] *nf*: **por ~** par excellence

antorcha [an'tortʃa] *nf* torch
antro ['antro] *nm* cavern; **~ de corrupción** (*fig*) den of iniquity
antropófago, -a [antro'pofaɣo, a] *adj, nm/f* cannibal
antropología [antropolo'xia] *nf* anthropology
antropólogo, -a [antro'poloɣo, a] *nm/f* anthropologist
anual [a'nwal] *adj* annual
anualidad [anwali'ðað] *nf* annuity, annual payment; **~ vitalicia** life annuity
anuario [a'nwarjo] *nm* yearbook
anudar [anu'ðar] *vt* to knot, tie; (*unir*) to join; **anudarse** *vr* to get tied up; **se me anudó la voz** I got a lump in my throat
anulación [anula'θjon] *nf* annulment; cancellation; repeal
anular [anu'lar] *vt* to annul, cancel; (*suscripción*) to cancel; (*ley*) to repeal ■ *nm* ring finger
anunciación [anunθja'θjon] *nf* announcement; **A~** (*Rel*) Annunciation
anunciante [anun'θjante] *nm/f* (*Com*) advertiser
anunciar [anun'θjar] *vt* to announce; (*proclamar*) to proclaim; (*Com*) to advertise
anuncio [a'nunθjo] *nm* announcement; (*señal*) sign; (*Com*) advertisement; (*cartel*) poster; (*Teat*) bill; **anuncios por palabras** classified ads
anverso [am'berso] *nm* obverse
anzuelo [an'θwelo] *nm* hook; (*para pescar*) fish hook; **tragar el ~** to swallow the bait
añadido [aɲa'ðiðo] *nm* addition
añadidura [aɲaði'ðura] *nf* addition, extra; **por ~** besides, in addition
añadir [aɲa'ðir] *vt* to add
añejo, -a [a'ɲexo, a] *adj* old; (*vino*) vintage; (*jamón*) well-cured
añicos [a'ɲikos] *nmpl*: **hacer ~** to smash, shatter; **hacerse ~** to smash, shatter
añil [a'ɲil] *nm* (*Bot, color*) indigo
año ['aɲo] *nm* year; **¡Feliz A~ Nuevo!** Happy New Year!; **tener 15 años** to be 15 (years old); **los años 80** the eighties; **~ bisiesto/escolar** leap/school year; **~ fiscal** fiscal *o* tax year; **estar de buen ~** to be in good shape; **en el ~ de la nana** in the year dot; **el ~ que viene** next year
añoranza [aɲo'ranθa] *nf* nostalgia; (*anhelo*) longing
añorar [aɲo'rar] *vt* to long for
añoso, -a [a'ɲoso, a] *adj* ancient, old
aovado, -a [ao'βaðo, a] *adj* oval
aovar [ao'βar] *vi* to lay eggs
apabullar [apaβu'ʎar] *vt* (*lit: fig*) to crush
apacentar [apaθen'tar] *vt* to pasture, graze
apacible [apa'θiβle] *adj* gentle, mild
apaciente *etc* [apa'θjente] *vb ver* **apacentar**
apaciguar [apaθi'ɣwar] *vt* to pacify, calm (down)
apacigüe *etc* [apa'θiɣwe] *vb ver* **apaciguar**
apadrinar [apaðri'nar] *vt* to sponsor, support; (*Rel*) to act as godfather to
apagado, -a [apa'ɣaðo, a] *adj* (*volcán*) extinct; (*color*) dull; (*voz*) quiet; (*sonido*) muted, muffled; (*persona: apático*) listless; **estar ~** (*fuego, luz*) to be out; (*radio, TV etc*) to be off
apagar [apa'ɣar] *vt* to put out; (*color*) to tone down; (*sonido*) to silence, muffle; (*sed*) to quench; (*Inform*) to toggle off; **apagarse** *vr* (*luz, fuego*) to go out; (*sonido*) to die away; (*pasión*) to wither; **~ el sistema** (*Inform*) to close *o* shut down
apagón [apa'ɣon] *nm* blackout, power cut
apague *etc* [a'paɣe] *vb ver* **apagar**
apaisado, -a [apai'saðo, a] *adj* (*papel*) landscape *cpd*
apalabrar [apala'βrar] *vt* to agree to; (*obrero*) to engage
Apalaches [apa'latʃes] *nmpl*: **(Montes) ~** Appalachians
apalear [apale'ar] *vt* to beat, thrash; (*Agr*) to winnow
apañado, -a [apa'ɲaðo, a] *adj* (*mañoso*) resourceful; (*arreglado*) tidy; (*útil*) handy
apañar [apa'ɲar] *vt* to pick up; (*asir*) to take hold of, grasp; (*reparar*) to mend, patch up; **apañarse** *vr* to manage, get along; **apañárselas por su cuenta** to look after number one (*fam*)
apaño [a'paɲo] *nm* (*Costura*) patch; (*maña*) skill; **esto no tiene ~** there's no answer to this one
aparador [apara'ðor] *nm* sideboard; (*escaparate*) shop window
aparato [apa'rato] *nm* apparatus; (*máquina*) machine; (*doméstico*) appliance; (*boato*) ostentation; (*Inform*) device; **~ de facsímil** facsimile (machine), fax; **~ respiratorio** respiratory system; **aparatos de mando** (*Aviat etc*) controls
aparatoso, -a [apara'toso, a] *adj* showy, ostentatious
aparcamiento [aparka'mjento] *nm* car park (*Brit*), parking lot (*US*)
aparcar [apar'kar] *vt, vi* to park
aparear [apare'ar] *vt* (*objetos*) to pair, match; (*animales*) to mate; **aparearse** *vr* to form a pair; to mate
aparecer [apare'θer] *vi*, **aparecerse** *vr* to appear; **apareció borracho** he turned up drunk

aparejado, -a [apare'xaðo, a] *adj* fit, suitable; **ir ~ con** to go hand in hand with; **llevar** *o* **traer ~** to involve
aparejador, a [aparexa'ðor, a] *nm/f* (*Arq*) quantity surveyor
aparejar [apare'xar] *vt* to prepare; (*caballo*) to saddle, harness; (*Naut*) to fit out, rig out
aparejo [apa'rexo] *nm* preparation; (*de caballo*) harness; (*Naut*) rigging; (*de poleas*) block and tackle
aparentar [aparen'tar] *vt* (*edad*) to look; (*fingir*): **~ tristeza** to pretend to be sad
aparente [apa'rente] *adj* apparent; (*adecuado*) suitable
aparezca *etc* [apa'reθka] *vb ver* **aparecer**
aparición [apari'θjon] *nf* appearance; (*de libro*) publication; (*de fantasma*) spectre
apariencia [apa'rjenθja] *nf* (outward) appearance; **en ~** outwardly, seemingly
aparque *etc* [a'parke] *vb ver* **aparcar**
apartado, -a [apar'taðo, a] *adj* separate; (*lejano*) remote ■ *nm* (*tipográfico*) paragraph; **~ (de correos)** post office box
apartamento [aparta'mento] *nm* apartment, flat (*Brit*)
apartamiento [aparta'mjento] *nm* separation; (*aislamiento*) remoteness; (*Am*) apartment, flat (*Brit*)
apartar [apar'tar] *vt* to separate; (*quitar*) to remove; (*Mineralogía*) to extract; **apartarse** *vr* (*separarse*) to separate, part; (*irse*) to move away; (*mantenerse aparte*) to keep away
aparte [a'parte] *adv* (*separadamente*) separately; (*además*) besides ■ *prep*: **~ de** apart from ■ *nm* (*Teat*) aside; (*tipográfico*) new paragraph; **"punto y ~"** "new paragraph"
apasionado, -a [apasjo'naðo, a] *adj* passionate; (*pey*) biassed, prejudiced ■ *nm/f* admirer
apasionante [apasjo'nante] *adj* exciting
apasionar [apasjo'nar] *vt* to arouse passion in; **apasionarse** *vr* to get excited; **le apasiona el fútbol** she's crazy about football
apatía [apa'tia] *nf* apathy
apático, -a [a'patiko, a] *adj* apathetic
apátrida [a'patriða] *adj* stateless
Apdo. *nm abr* (= *Apartado (de Correos)*) P.O. Box
apeadero [apea'ðero] *nm* halt, stopping place
apearse [ape'arse] *vr* (*jinete*) to dismount; (*bajarse*) to get down *o* out; (*de coche*) to get out, alight; **no ~ del burro** to refuse to climb down
apechugar [apetʃu'ɣar] *vi*: **~ con algo** to face up to sth
apechugue *etc* [ape'tʃuɣe] *vb ver* **apechugar**
apedrear [apeðre'ar] *vt* to stone
apegarse [ape'ɣarse] *vr*: **~ a** to become attached to
apego [a'peɣo] *nm* attachment, devotion
apegue *etc* [a'peɣe] *vb ver* **apegarse**
apelación [apela'θjon] *nf* appeal
apelar [ape'lar] *vi* to appeal; **~ a** (*fig*) to resort to
apelativo [apela'tiβo] *nm* (*Ling*) appellative; (*Am*) surname
apellidar [apeʎi'ðar] *vt* to call, name; **apellidarse** *vr*: **se apellida Pérez** her (sur)name's Pérez
apellido [ape'ʎiðo] *nm* surname; *see note*

APELLIDO

In the Spanish-speaking world most people use two *apellidos*, the first being their father's first surname, and the second their mother's first surname: eg the children of Juan García López, married to Carmen Pérez Rodríguez would have as their surname García Pérez. Married women retain their own surname(s) and sometimes add their husband's first surname on to theirs: eg Carmen Pérez de García. She could also be referred to as (la) Señora de García. In Latin America it is usual for the second surname to be shortened to an initial in correspondence eg: Juan García L.

apelmazado, -a [apelma'θaðo, a] *adj* compact, solid
apelotonar [apeloto'nar] *vt* to roll into a ball; **apelotonarse** *vr* (*gente*) to crowd together
apenar [ape'nar] *vt* to grieve, trouble; (*Am: avergonzar*) to embarrass; **apenarse** *vr* to grieve; (*Am*) to be embarrassed
apenas [a'penas] *adv* scarcely, hardly ■ *conj* as soon as, no sooner
apéndice [a'pendiθe] *nm* appendix
apendicitis [apendi'θitis] *nf* appendicitis
Apeninos [ape'ninos] *nmpl* Apennines
apercibimiento [aperθiβi'mjento] *nm* (*aviso*) warning
apercibir [aperθi'βir] *vt* to prepare; (*avisar*) to warn; (*Jur*) to summon; (*Am*) to notice, see; **apercibirse** *vr* to get ready; **apercibirse de** to notice
aperitivo [aperi'tiβo] *nm* (*bebida*) aperitif; (*comida*) appetizer
apero [a'pero] *nm* (*Agr*) implement; **aperos** *nmpl* farm equipment *sg*
apertura [aper'tura] *nf* (*gen*) opening;

(*Pol*) openness, liberalization; (*Teat etc*) beginning; **~ de un juicio hipotecario** (*Com*) foreclosure
aperturismo [apertu'rismo] *nm* (*Pol*) (policy of) liberalization
apesadumbrar [apesaðum'brar] *vt* to grieve, sadden; **apesadumbrarse** *vr* to distress o.s.
apestar [apes'tar] *vt* to infect ■ *vi*: **~ (a)** to stink (of)
apestoso, -a [apes'toso, a] *adj* (*hediondo*) stinking; (*asqueroso*) sickening
apetecer [apete'θer] *vt*: **¿te apetece una tortilla?** do you fancy an omelette?
apetecible [apete'θiβle] *adj* desirable; (*comida*) tempting
apetezca *etc* [ape'teθka] *vb ver* **apetecer**
apetito [ape'tito] *nm* appetite
apetitoso, -a [apeti'toso, a] *adj* (*gustoso*) appetizing; (*fig*) tempting
apiadarse [apja'ðarse] *vr*: **~ de** to take pity on
ápice ['apiθe] *nm* apex; (*fig*) whit, iota; **ni un ápice** not a whit; **no ceder un ápice** not to budge an inch
apicultor, a [apikul'tor, a] *nm/f* beekeeper, apiarist
apicultura [apikul'tura] *nf* beekeeping
apiladora [apila'ðora] *nf* (*para máquina impresora*) stacker
apilar [api'lar] *vt* to pile *o* heap up; **apilarse** *vr* to pile up
apiñado, -a [api'ɲaðo, a] *adj* (*apretado*) packed
apiñar [api'ɲar] *vt* to crowd; **apiñarse** *vr* to crowd *o* press together
apio ['apjo] *nm* celery
apisonadora [apisona'ðora] *nf* (*máquina*) steamroller
aplacar [apla'kar] *vt* to placate; **aplacarse** *vr* to calm down
aplace *etc* [a'plaθe] *vb ver* **aplazar**
aplanamiento [aplana'mjento] *nm* smoothing, levelling
aplanar [apla'nar] *vt* to smooth, level; (*allanar*) to roll flat, flatten; **aplanarse** *vr* (*edificio*) to collapse; (*persona*) to get discouraged
aplaque *etc* [a'plake] *vb ver* **aplacar**
aplastar [aplas'tar] *vt* to squash (flat); (*fig*) to crush
aplatanarse [aplata'narse] *vr* to get lethargic
aplaudir [aplau'ðir] *vt* to applaud
aplauso [a'plauso] *nm* applause; (*fig*) approval, acclaim
aplazamiento [aplaθa'mjento] *nm* postponement
aplazar [apla'θar] *vt* to postpone, defer
aplicación [aplika'θjon] *nf* application; (*esfuerzo*) effort; **aplicaciones de gestión** business applications
aplicado, -a [apli'kaðo, a] *adj* diligent, hard-working
aplicar [apli'kar] *vt* (*gen*) to apply; (*poner en vigor*) to put into effect; (*esfuerzos*) to devote; **aplicarse** *vr* to apply o.s.
aplique *etc* [a'plike] *vb ver* **aplicar** ■ *nm* wall light *o* lamp
aplomo [a'plomo] *nm* aplomb, self-assurance
apocado, -a [apo'kaðo, a] *adj* timid
apocamiento [apoka'mjento] *nm* timidity; (*depresión*) depression
apocarse [apo'karse] *vr* to feel small *o* humiliated
apocopar [apoko'par] *vt* (*Ling*) to shorten
apócope [a'pokope] *nf* apocopation; **gran es ~ de grande** "gran" is the shortened form of "grande"
apócrifo, -a [a'pokrifo, a] *adj* apocryphal
apodar [apo'ðar] *vt* to nickname
apoderado [apoðe'raðo] *nm* agent, representative
apoderar [apoðe'rar] *vt* to authorize, empower; (*Jur*) to grant (a) power of attorney to; **apoderarse** *vr*: **apoderarse de** to take possession of
apodo [a'poðo] *nm* nickname
apogeo [apo'xeo] *nm* peak, summit
apolillado, -a [apoli'ʎaðo, a] *adj* moth-eaten
apolillarse [apoli'ʎarse] *vr* to get moth-eaten
apología [apolo'xia] *nf* eulogy; (*defensa*) defence
apoltronarse [apoltro'narse] *vr* to get lazy
apoplejía [apople'xia] *nf* apoplexy, stroke
apoque *etc* [a'poke] *vb ver* **apocarse**
apoquinar [apoki'nar] *vt* (*fam*) to cough up, fork out
aporrear [aporre'ar] *vt* to beat (up)
aportación [aporta'θjon] *nf* contribution
aportar [apor'tar] *vt* to contribute ■ *vi* to reach port
aposentar [aposen'tar] *vt* to lodge, put up
aposento [apo'sento] *nm* lodging; (*habitación*) room
apósito [a'posito] *nm* (*Med*) dressing
aposta [a'posta] *adv* on purpose
apostar [apos'tar] *vt* to bet, stake; (*tropas etc*) to station, post ■ *vi* to bet
apostatar [aposta'tar] *vi* (*Rel*) to apostatize; (*fig*) to change sides
a posteriori [aposte'rjori] *adv* at a later date *o* stage; (*Lógica*) a posteriori
apostilla [apos'tiʎa] *nf* note, comment
apóstol [a'postol] *nm* apostle
apóstrofo [a'postrofo] *nm* apostrophe

apostura [apos'tura] *nf* neatness, elegance
apoteósico, -a [apote'osiko, a] *adj* tremendous
apoyar [apo'jar] *vt* to lean, rest; (*fig*) to support, back; **apoyarse** *vr*: **apoyarse en** to lean on
apoyo [a'pojo] *nm* support, backing
apreciable [apre'θjaβle] *adj* considerable; (*fig*) esteemed
apreciación [apreθja'θjon] *nf* appreciation; (*Com*) valuation
apreciar [apre'θjar] *vt* to evaluate, assess; (*Com*) to appreciate, value ■ *vi* (*Econ*) to appreciate
aprecio [a'preθjo] *nm* valuation, estimate; (*fig*) appreciation
aprehender [apreen'der] *vt* to apprehend, detain; (*ver*) to see, observe
aprehensión [apreen'sjon] *nf* detention, capture
apremiante [apre'mjante] *adj* urgent, pressing
apremiar [apre'mjar] *vt* to compel, force ■ *vi* to be urgent, press
apremio [a'premjo] *nm* urgency; **~ de pago** demand note
aprender [apren'der] *vt, vi* to learn; **~ a conducir** to learn to drive; **aprenderse** *vr*: **aprenderse algo** to learn sth (off) by heart
aprendiz, a [apren'diθ, a] *nm/f* apprentice; (*principiante*) learner, trainee; **~ de comercio** business trainee
aprendizaje [aprendi'θaxe] *nm* apprenticeship
aprensión [apren'sjon] *nm* apprehension, fear
aprensivo, -a [apren'siβo, a] *adj* apprehensive
apresar [apre'sar] *vt* to seize; (*capturar*) to capture
aprestar [apres'tar] *vt* to prepare, get ready; (*Tec*) to prime, size; **aprestarse** *vr* to get ready
apresto [a'presto] *nm* (*gen*) preparation; (*sustancia*) size
apresurado, -a [apresu'raðo, a] *adj* hurried, hasty
apresuramiento [apresura'mjento] *nm* hurry, haste
apresurar [apresu'rar] *vt* to hurry, accelerate; **apresurarse** *vr* to hurry, make haste; **me apresuré a sugerir que ...** I hastily suggested that ...
apretado, -a [apre'taðo, a] *adj* tight; (*escritura*) cramped
apretar [apre'tar] *vt* to squeeze, press; (*mano*) to clasp; (*dientes*) to grit; (*Tec*) to tighten; (*presionar*) to press together, pack ■ *vi* to be too tight; **apretarse** *vr* to crowd together; **~ la mano a algn** to shake sb's hand; **~ el paso** to quicken one's step
apretón [apre'ton] *nm* squeeze; **~ de manos** handshake
aprieto *etc* [a'prjeto] *vb ver* **apretar** ■ *nm* squeeze; (*dificultad*) difficulty, jam; **estar en un ~** to be in a jam; **ayudar a algn a salir de un ~** to help sb out of trouble
a priori [apri'ori] *adv* beforehand; (*Lógica*) a priori
aprisa [a'prisa] *adv* quickly, hurriedly
aprisionar [aprisjo'nar] *vt* to imprison
aprobación [aproβa'θjon] *nf* approval
aprobado [apro'βaðo] *nm* (*nota*) pass mark
aprobar [apro'βar] *vt* to approve (of); (*examen, materia*) to pass ■ *vi* to pass
apropiación [apropja'θjon] *nf* appropriation
apropiado, -a [apro'pjaðo, a] *adj* appropriate
apropiarse [apro'pjarse] *vr*: **~ de** to appropriate
aprovechado, -a [aproβe'tʃaðo, a] *adj* industrious, hardworking; (*económico*) thrifty; (*pey*) unscrupulous
aprovechamiento [aproβetʃa'mjento] *nm* use, exploitation
aprovechar [aproβe'tʃar] *vt* to use; (*explotar*) to exploit; (*experiencia*) to profit from; (*oferta, oportunidad*) to take advantage of ■ *vi* to progress, improve; **aprovecharse** *vr*: **aprovecharse de** to make use of; (*pey*) to take advantage of; **¡que aproveche!** enjoy your meal!
aprovisionar [aproβisjo'nar] *vt* to supply
aproximación [aproksima'θjon] *nf* approximation; (*de lotería*) consolation prize
aproximadamente [aproksimaða'mente] *adv* approximately
aproximado, -a [aproksi'maðo, a] *adj* approximate
aproximar [aproksi'mar] *vt* to bring nearer; **aproximarse** *vr* to come near, approach
apruebe *etc* [a'prweβe] *vb ver* **aprobar**
aptitud [apti'tuð] *nf* aptitude; (*capacidad*) ability; **~ para los negocios** business sense
apto, -a ['apto, a] *adj* (*hábil*) capable; (*apropiado*): **~ (para)** fit (for), suitable (for); **~/no ~ para menores** (*Cine*) suitable/unsuitable for children
apuesto, -a *etc* [a'pwesto, a] *vb ver* **apostar** ■ *adj* neat, elegant ■ *nf* bet, wager
apuntador [apunta'ðor] *nm* prompter
apuntalar [apunta'lar] *vt* to prop up
apuntar [apun'tar] *vt* (*con arma*) to aim at; (*con dedo*) to point at *o* to; (*anotar*) to note (down); (*datos*) to record; (*Teat*) to prompt;

apuntarse *vr* (*Deporte: tanto, victoria*) to score; (*Escol*) to enrol; **~ una cantidad en la cuenta de algn** to charge a sum to sb's account; **apuntarse en un curso** to enrol on a course; **¡yo me apunto!** count me in!
apunte [a'punte] *nm* note; (*Teat: voz*) prompt; (*: texto*) prompt book
apuñalar [apuɲa'lar] *vt* to stab
apurado, -a [apu'raðo, a] *adj* needy; (*difícil*) difficult; (*peligroso*) dangerous; (*Am*) hurried, rushed; **estar en una situación apurada** to be in a tight spot; **estar ~** to be in a hurry
apurar [apu'rar] *vt* (*agotar*) to drain; (*recursos*) to use up; (*molestar*) to annoy; **apurarse** *vr* (*preocuparse*) to worry; (*esp Am: darse prisa*) to hurry
apuro [a'puro] *nm* (*aprieto*) fix, jam; (*escasez*) want, hardship; (*vergüenza*) embarrassment; (*Am*) haste, urgency
aquejado, -a [ake'xaðo, a] *adj*: **~ de** (*Med*) afflicted by
aquejar [ake'xar] *vt* (*afligir*) to distress; **le aqueja una grave enfermedad** he suffers from a serious disease
aquel, aquella, aquellos, -as [a'kel, a'keʎa, a'keʎos, as] *adj* that, those *pl*
aquél, aquélla, aquéllos, -as [a'kel, a'keʎa, a'keʎos, as] *pron* that (one), those (ones) *pl*
aquello [a'keʎo] *pron* that, that business
aquí [a'ki] *adv* (*lugar*) here; (*tiempo*) now; **aquí arriba** up here; **aquí mismo** right here; **aquí yace** here lies; **de aquí a siete días** a week from now
aquietar [akje'tar] *vt* to quieten (down), calm (down)
Aquisgrán [akis'ɣran] *nm* Aachen, Aix-la-Chapelle
A.R. *abr* (= *Alteza Real*) R.H.
ara ['ara] *nf* (*altar*) altar; **en aras de** for the sake of
árabe ['araβe] *adj* Arab, Arabian, Arabic ■ *nm/f* Arab ■ *nm* (*Ling*) Arabic
Arabia [a'raβja] *nf* Arabia; **~ Saudí** *o* **Saudita** Saudi Arabia
arábigo, -a [a'raβiɣo, a] *adj* Arab, Arabian, Arabic
arácnido [a'rakniðo] *nm* arachnid
arado [a'raðo] *nm* plough
aragonés, -esa [araɣo'nes, esa] *adj, nm/f* Aragonese ■ *nm* (*Ling*) Aragonese
arancel [aran'θel] *nm* tariff, duty; **~ de aduanas** (customs) duty
arandela [aran'dela] *nf* (*Tec*) washer; (*chorrera*) frill
araña [a'raɲa] *nf* (*Zool*) spider; (*lámpara*) chandelier
arañar [ara'ɲar] *vt* to scratch
arañazo [ara'ɲaθo] *nm* scratch
arar [a'rar] *vt* to plough, till
araucano, -a [arau'kano, a] *adj, nm/f* Araucanian
arbitraje [arβi'traxe] *nm* arbitration
arbitrar [arβi'trar] *vt* to arbitrate in; (*recursos*) to bring together; (*Deporte*) to referee ■ *vi* to arbitrate
arbitrariedad [arβitrarje'ðað] *nf* arbitrariness; (*acto*) arbitrary act
arbitrario, -a [arβi'trarjo, a] *adj* arbitrary
arbitrio [ar'βitrjo] *nm* free will; (*Jur*) adjudication, decision; **dejar al ~ de algn** to leave to sb's discretion
árbitro ['arβitro] *nm* arbitrator; (*Deporte*) referee; (*Tenis*) umpire
árbol ['arβol] *nm* (*Bot*) tree; (*Naut*) mast; (*Tec*) axle, shaft
arbolado, -a [arβo'laðo, a] *adj* wooded; (*camino*) tree-lined ■ *nm* woodland
arboladura [arβola'ðura] *nf* rigging
arbolar [arβo'lar] *vt* to hoist, raise
arboleda [arβo'leða] *nf* grove, plantation
arbusto [ar'βusto] *nm* bush, shrub
arca ['arka] *nf* chest, box; **A~ de la Alianza** Ark of the Covenant; **A~ de Noé** Noah's Ark
arcada [ar'kaða] *nf* arcade; (*de puente*) arch, span; **arcadas** *nfpl* retching *sg*
arcaico, -a [ar'kaiko, a] *adj* archaic
arce ['arθe] *nm* maple tree
arcén [ar'θen] *nm* (*de autopista*) hard shoulder; (*de carretera*) verge
archiconocido, -a [artʃikono'θiðo, a] *adj* extremely well-known
archipiélago [artʃi'pjelaɣo] *nm* archipelago
archisabido, -a [artʃisa'βiðo, a] *adj* extremely well-known
archivador [artʃiβa'ðor] *nm* filing cabinet; **~ colgante** suspension file
archivar [artʃi'βar] *vt* to file (away); (*Inform*) to archive
archivo [ar'tʃiβo] *nm* archive(s) (*pl*); (*Inform*) file; **A~ Nacional** Public Record Office; **archivos policíacos** police files; **nombre de ~** (*Inform*) filename; **~ adjunto** (*Inform*) attachment; **~ de seguridad** (*Inform*) backup file
arcilla [ar'θiʎa] *nf* clay
arco ['arko] *nm* arch; (*Mat*) arc; (*Mil: Mus*) bow; (*Am Deporte*) goal; **~ iris** rainbow
arcón [ar'kon] *nm* large chest
arder [ar'ðer] *vt* to burn; **~ sin llama** to smoulder; **estar que arde** (*persona*) to fume
ardid [ar'ðið] *nm* ruse
ardiente [ar'ðjente] *adj* ardent
ardilla [ar'ðiʎa] *nf* squirrel
ardor [ar'ðor] *nm* (*calor*) heat, warmth; (*fig*)

ardour; **~ de estómago** heartburn
ardoroso, -a [arðo'roso, a] *adj* passionate
arduo, -a ['arðwo, a] *adj* arduous
área ['area] *nf* area; (*Deporte*) penalty area
arena [a'rena] *nf* sand; (*de una lucha*) arena
arenal [are'nal] *nm* (*arena movediza*) quicksand
arenga [a'renga] *nf* (*fam*) sermon
arengar [aren'gar] *vt* to harangue
arengue *etc* [a'renge] *vb ver* **arengar**
arenillas [are'niʎas] *nfpl* (*Med*) stones
arenisca [are'niska] *nf* sandstone; (*cascajo*) grit
arenoso, -a [are'noso, a] *adj* sandy
arenque [a'renke] *nm* herring
arepa [a'repa] *nf* (*Am*) corn pancake
arete [a'rete] *nm* earring
argamasa [arɣa'masa] *nf* mortar, plaster
Argel [ar'xel] *n* Algiers
Argelia [ar'xelja] *nf* Algeria
argelino, -a [arxe'lino, a] *adj, nm/f* Algerian
Argentina [arxen'tina] *nf*: **(la) ~** the Argentine, Argentina
argentino, -a [arxen'tino, a] *adj* Argentinian; (*de plata*) silvery ■ *nm/f* Argentinian
argolla [ar'ɣoʎa] *nf* (large) ring; (*Am: de matrimonio*) wedding ring
argot [ar'ɣo] *nm* (*pl* **argots** [ar'ɣo, ar'ɣos]) slang
argucia [ar'ɣuθja] *nf* subtlety, sophistry
argüir [ar'ɣwir] *vt* to deduce; (*discutir*) to argue; (*indicar*) to indicate, imply; (*censurar*) to reproach ■ *vi* to argue
argumentación [arɣumenta'θjon] *nf* (line of) argument
argumentar [arɣumen'tar] *vt, vi* to argue
argumento [arɣu'mento] *nm* argument; (*razonamiento*) reasoning; (*de novela etc*) plot; (*Cine: TV*) storyline
arguyendo *etc* [arɣu'jendo] *vb ver* **argüir**
aria ['arja] *nf* aria
aridez [ari'ðeθ] *nf* aridity, dryness
árido, -a ['ariðo, a] *adj* arid, dry; **áridos** *nmpl* dry goods
Aries ['arjes] *nm* Aries
ariete [a'rjete] *nm* battering ram
ario, -a ['arjo, a] *adj* Aryan
arisco, -a [a'risko, a] *adj* surly; (*insociable*) unsociable
aristocracia [aristo'kraθja] *nf* aristocracy
aristócrata [aris'tokrata] *nm/f* aristocrat
aristocrático, -a [aristo'kratiko, a] *adj* aristocratic
aritmética [arit'metika] *nf* arithmetic
aritmético, -a [arit'metiko, a] *adj* arithmetic(al) ■ *nm/f* arithmetician
arma ['arma] *nf* arm; **armas** *nfpl* arms; **~ blanca** blade, knife; (*espada*) sword; **~ de fuego** firearm; **armas cortas** small arms; **armas de destrucción masiva** weapons of mass destruction; **rendir las armas** to lay down one's arms; **ser de armas tomar** to be somebody to be reckoned with
armada [ar'maða] *nf* armada; (*flota*) fleet; *ver tb* **armado**
armadillo [arma'ðiʎo] *nm* armadillo
armado, -a [ar'maðo, a] *adj* armed; (*Tec*) reinforced
armador [arma'ðor] *nm* (*Naut*) shipowner
armadura [arma'ðura] *nf* (*Mil*) armour; (*Tec*) framework; (*Zool*) skeleton; (*Física*) armature
armamentista [armamen'tista], **armamentístico, a** [armamen'tistiko, a] *adj* arms *cpd*
armamento [arma'mento] *nm* armament; (*Naut*) fitting-out
armar [ar'mar] *vt* (*soldado*) to arm; (*máquina*) to assemble; (*navío*) to fit out; **armarla, ~ un lío** to start a row; **armarse** *vr*: **armarse de valor** to summon up one's courage
armario [ar'marjo] *nm* wardrobe; **salir del ~** to come out (of the closet)
armatoste [arma'toste] *nm* (*mueble*) monstrosity; (*máquina*) contraption
armazón [arma'θon] *nf o m* body, chassis; (*de mueble etc*) frame; (*Arq*) skeleton
Armenia [ar'menja] *nf* Armenia
armería [arme'ria] *nf* (*museo*) military museum; (*tienda*) gunsmith's
armiño [ar'miɲo] *nm* stoat; (*piel*) ermine
armisticio [armis'tiθjo] *nm* armistice
armonía [armo'nia] *nf* harmony
armónica [ar'monika] *nf* harmonica; *ver tb* **armónico**
armonice *etc* [armo'niθe] *vb ver* **armonizar**
armónico, -a [ar'moniko, a] *adj* harmonic
armonioso, -a [armo'njoso, a] *adj* harmonious
armonizar [armoni'θar] *vt* to harmonize; (*diferencias*) to reconcile ■ *vi* to harmonize; **~ con** (*fig*) to be in keeping with; (*colores*) to tone in with
arnés [ar'nes] *nm* armour; **arneses** *nmpl* harness *sg*
aro ['aro] *nm* ring; (*tejo*) quoit; (*Am: pendiente*) earring; **entrar por el ~** to give in
aroma [a'roma] *nm* aroma
aromaterapia [aromate'rapja] *nf* aromatherapy
aromático, -a [aro'matiko, a] *adj* aromatic
arpa ['arpa] *nf* harp
arpegio [ar'pexjo] *nm* (*Mus*) arpeggio
arpía [ar'pia] *nf* (*fig*) shrew
arpillera [arpi'ʎera] *nf* sacking, sackcloth

arpón [ar'pon] *nm* harpoon
arquear [arke'ar] *vt* to arch, bend; **arquearse** *vr* to arch, bend
arqueo [ar'keo] *nm* (*gen*) arching; (*Naut*) tonnage
arqueología [arkeolo'xia] *nf* archaeology
arqueológico, -a [arkeo'loxiko, a] *adj* archaeological
arqueólogo, -a [arke'oloɣo, a] *nm/f* archaeologist
arquero [ar'kero] *nm* archer, bowman; (*Am Deporte*) goalkeeper
arquetipo [arke'tipo] *nm* archetype
arquitecto, -a [arki'tekto, a] *nm/f* architect; **~ paisajista** *o* **de jardines** landscape gardener
arquitectónico, -a [arkitek'toniko, a] *adj* architectural
arquitectura [arkitek'tura] *nf* architecture
arrabal [arra'βal] *nm* suburb; **arrabales** *nmpl* outskirts
arrabalero, -a [arraβa'lero, a] *adj* (*fig*) common, coarse
arracimarse [arraθi'marse] *vr* to cluster together
arraigado, -a [arrai'ɣaðo, a] *adj* deep-rooted; (*fig*) established
arraigar [arrai'ɣar] *vt* to establish ■ *vi*, **arraigarse** *vr* to take root; (*persona*) to settle
arraigo [a'rraiɣo] *nm* (*raíces*) roots *pl*; (*bienes*) property; (*influencia*) hold; **hombre de ~** man of property
arraigue *etc* [a'rraiɣe] *vb ver* **arraigar**
arrancada [arran'kaða] *nf* (*arranque*) sudden start
arrancar [arran'kar] *vt* (*sacar*) to extract, pull out; (*arrebatar*) to snatch (away); (*pedazo*) to tear off; (*página*) to rip out; (*suspiro*) to heave; (*Auto*) to start; (*Inform*) to boot; (*fig*) to extract ■ *vi* (*Auto, máquina*) to start; (*ponerse en marcha*) to get going; **~ información a algn** to extract information from sb; **~ de** to stem from
arranque *etc* [a'rranke] *vb ver* **arrancar** ■ *nm* sudden start; (*Auto*) start; (*fig*) fit, outburst
arras ['arras] *nfpl* pledge *sg*, security *sg*
arrasar [arra'sar] *vt* (*aplanar*) to level, flatten; (*destruir*) to demolish
arrastrado, -a [arras'traðo, a] *adj* poor, wretched
arrastrador [arrastra'ðor] *nm* (*en máquina impresora*) tractor
arrastrar [arras'trar] *vt* to drag (along); (*fig*) to drag down, degrade; (*suj: agua, viento*) to carry away ■ *vi* to drag, trail on the ground; **arrastrarse** *vr* to crawl; (*fig*) to grovel; **llevar algo arrastrado** to drag sth along
arrastre [a'rrastre] *nm* drag, dragging; (*Deporte*) crawl; **estar para el ~** (*fig*) to have had it
array [a'rrai] *nm* (*Inform*) array; **~ empaquetado** (*Inform*) packed array
arrayán [arra'jan] *nm* myrtle
arre ['arre] *excl* gee up!
arrear [arre'ar] *vt* to drive on, urge on ■ *vi* to hurry along
arrebañar [arreβa'ɲar] *vt* (*juntar*) to scrape together
arrebatado, -a [arreβa'taðo, a] *adj* rash, impetuous; (*repentino*) sudden, hasty
arrebatar [arreβa'tar] *vt* to snatch (away), seize; (*fig*) to captivate; **arrebatarse** *vr* to get carried away, get excited
arrebato [arre'βato] *nm* fit of rage, fury; (*éxtasis*) rapture; **en un ~ de cólera** in an outburst of anger
arrebolar [arreβo'lar] *vt* to redden; **arrebolarse** *vr* (*enrojecer*) to blush
arrebujar [arreβu'xar] *vt* (*objetos*) to jumble together; **arrebujarse** *vr* to wrap o.s. up
arrechar [arre'tʃar] (*Am*) *vt* to arouse, excite; **arrecharse** *vr* to become aroused
arrechucho [arre'tʃutʃo] *nm* (*Med*) turn
arreciar [arre'θjar] *vi* to get worse; (*viento*) to get stronger
arrecife [arre'θife] *nm* reef
arredrar [arre'ðrar] *vt* (*hacer retirarse*) to drive back; **arredrarse** *vr* (*apartarse*) to draw back; **arredrarse ante algo** to shrink away from sth
arreglado, -a [arre'ɣlaðo, a] *adj* (*ordenado*) neat, orderly; (*moderado*) moderate, reasonable
arreglar [arre'ɣlar] *vt* (*poner orden*) to tidy up; (*algo roto*) to fix, repair; (*problema*) to solve; **arreglarse** *vr* to reach an understanding; **arreglárselas** (*fam*) to get by, manage
arreglo [a'rreɣlo] *nm* settlement; (*orden*) order; (*acuerdo*) agreement; (*Mus*) arrangement, setting; (*Inform*) array; **con ~ a** in accordance with; **llegar a un ~** to reach a compromise
arrellanarse [arreʎa'narse] *vr* to sprawl; **~ en el asiento** to lie back in one's chair
arremangar [arreman'gar] *vt* to roll up, turn up; **arremangarse** *vr* to roll up one's sleeves
arremangue *etc* [arre'mange] *vb ver* **arremangar**
arremeter [arreme'ter] *vt* to attack, assault; **~ contra algn** to attack sb
arremetida [arreme'tiða] *nf* assault
arremolinarse [arremoli'narse] *vr* to crowd around, mill around; (*corriente*) to swirl, eddy
arrendador, a [arrenda'ðor, a] *nm/f* landlord/lady

arrendamiento [arrenda'mjento] *nm* letting; (*el alquilar*) hiring; (*contrato*) lease; (*alquiler*) rent
arrendar [arren'dar] *vt* to let; to hire; to lease; to rent
arrendatario, -a [arrenda'tarjo, a] *nm/f* tenant
arreos [a'rreos] *nmpl* harness *sg*, trappings
arrepentido, -a [arrepen'tiðo, a] *nm/f* (*Pol*) reformed terrorist
arrepentimiento [arrepenti'mjento] *nm* regret, repentance
arrepentirse [arrepen'tirse] *vr* to repent; **~ de (haber hecho) algo** to regret (doing) sth
arrepienta *etc* [arre'pjenta], **arrepintiendo** *etc* [arrepin'tjendo] *vb ver* **arrepentirse**
arrestar [arres'tar] *vt* to arrest; (*encarcelar*) to imprison
arresto [a'rresto] *nm* arrest; (*Mil*) detention; (*audacia*) boldness, daring; **~ domiciliario** house arrest
arriar [a'rrjar] *vt* (*velas*) to haul down; (*bandera*) to lower, strike; (*un cable*) to pay out
arriate [a'rrjate] *nm* (*Bot*) bed; (*camino*) road

PALABRA CLAVE

arriba [a'rriβa] *adv* **1** (*posición*) above; **desde arriba** from above; **arriba del todo** at the very top, right on top; **Juan está arriba** Juan is upstairs; **lo arriba mencionado** the aforementioned; **aquí/allí arriba** up here/there; **está hasta arriba de trabajo** (*fam*) he's up to his eyes in work (*fam*)
2 (*dirección*) up, upwards; **más arriba** higher *o* further up; **calle arriba** up the street
3: **de arriba abajo** from top to bottom; **mirar a algn de arriba abajo** to look sb up and down
4: **para arriba**: **de 50 euros para arriba** from 50 euros up(wards); **de la cintura (para) arriba** from the waist up
■ *adj*: **de arriba**: **el piso de arriba** the upstairs flat (*Brit*) *o* apartment; **la parte de arriba** the top *o* upper part
■ *prep*: **arriba de** (*Am*) above; **arriba de 200 dólares** more than 200 dollars
■ *excl*: **¡arriba!** up!; **¡manos arriba!** hands up!; **¡arriba España!** long live Spain!

arribar [arri'βar] *vi* to put into port; (*esp Am*: *llegar*) to arrive
arribista [arri'βista] *nm/f* parvenu(e), upstart
arribo [a'rriβo] *nm* (*esp Am*) arrival
arriendo *etc* [a'rrjendo] *vb ver* **arrendar** ■ *nm* = **arrendamiento**
arriero [a'rrjero] *nm* muleteer
arriesgado, -a [arrjes'ɣaðo, a] *adj* (*peligroso*) risky; (*audaz*) bold, daring
arriesgar [arrjes'ɣar] *vt* to risk; (*poner en peligro*) to endanger; **arriesgarse** *vr* to take a risk
arriesgue *etc* [a'rrjesɣe] *vb ver* **arriesgar**
arrimar [arri'mar] *vt* (*acercar*) to bring close; (*poner de lado*) to set aside; **arrimarse** *vr* to come close *o* closer; **arrimarse a** to lean on; (*fig*) to keep company with; (*buscar ayuda*) to seek the protection of; **arrímate a mí** cuddle up to me
arrinconado, -a [arrinko'naðo, a] *adj* forgotten, neglected
arrinconar [arrinko'nar] *vt* to put in a corner; (*fig*) to put on one side; (*abandonar*) to push aside
arriscado, -a [arris'kaðo, a] *adj* (*Geo*) craggy; (*fig*) bold, resolute
arroba [a'rroβa] *nf* (*peso*) 25 pounds; (*Inform*: *en dirección electrónica*) at sign, @; **tiene talento por arrobas** he has loads *o* bags of talent
arrobado, -a [arro'βaðo, a] *adj* entranced, enchanted
arrobamiento [arroβa'mjento] *nm* ecstasy
arrobar [arro'βar] *vt* to enchant; **arrobarse** *vr* to be enraptured; (*místico*) to go into a trance
arrodillarse [arroði'ʎarse] *vr* to kneel (down)
arrogancia [arro'ɣanθja] *nf* arrogance
arrogante [arro'ɣante] *adj* arrogant
arrojar [arro'xar] *vt* to throw, hurl; (*humo*) to emit, give out; (*Com*) to yield, produce; **arrojarse** *vr* to throw *o* hurl o.s.
arrojo [a'rroxo] *nm* daring
arrollador, a [arroʎa'ðor, a] *adj* crushing, overwhelming
arrollar [arro'ʎar] *vt* (*enrollar*) to roll up; (*suj*: *inundación*) to wash away; (*Auto*) to run over; (*Deporte*) to crush
arropar [arro'par] *vt* to cover (up), wrap up; **arroparse** *vr* to wrap o.s. up
arrostrar [arros'trar] *vt* to face (up to); **arrostrarse** *vr*: **arrostrarse con algn** to face up to sb
arroyo [a'rrojo] *nm* stream; (*de la calle*) gutter; **poner a algn en el ~** to turn sb onto the streets
arroz [a'rroθ] *nm* rice; **~ con leche** rice pudding
arrozal [arro'θal] *nm* paddy field
arruga [a'rruɣa] *nf* fold; (*de cara*) wrinkle; (*de vestido*) crease
arrugar [arru'ɣar] *vt* to fold; to wrinkle; to crease; **arrugarse** *vr* to get wrinkled; to get creased
arrugue *etc* [a'rruɣe] *vb ver* **arrugar**

arruinar [arrwi'nar] *vt* to ruin, wreck; **arruinarse** *vr* to be ruined
arrullar [arru'ʎar] *vi* to coo ■ *vt* to lull to sleep
arrumaco [arru'mako] *nm* (*caricia*) caress; (*halago*) piece of flattery
arrumbar [arrum'bar] *vt* (*objeto*) to discard; (*individuo*) to silence
arrurruz [arru'rruθ] *nm* arrowroot
arsenal [arse'nal] *nm* naval dockyard; (*Mil*) arsenal
arsénico [ar'seniko] *nm* arsenic
arte ['arte] *nm* (*gen m en sg, f en pl*) art; (*maña*) skill, guile; **por ~ de magia** (as if) by magic; **no tener ~ ni parte en algo** to have nothing whatsoever to do with sth; **artes** *nfpl* arts; **Bellas Artes** Fine Art *sg*; **artes y oficios** arts and crafts
artefacto [arte'fakto] *nm* appliance; (*Arqueología*) artefact
arteria [ar'terja] *nf* artery
arterial [arte'rjal] *adj* arterial; (*presión*) blood *cpd*
arterioesclerosis [arterjoeskle'rosis], **arteriosclerosis** [arterjoskle'rosis] *nf inv* hardening of the arteries, arteriosclerosis
artesa [ar'tesa] *nf* trough
artesanía [artesa'nia] *nf* craftsmanship; (*artículos*) handicrafts *pl*
artesano, -a [arte'sano, a] *nm/f* artisan, craftsman/woman
ártico, -a ['artiko, a] *adj* Arctic ■ *nm*: **el (océano) Ártico** the Arctic (Ocean)
articulación [artikula'θjon] *nf* articulation; (*Med: Tec*) joint
articulado, -a [artiku'laðo, a] *adj* articulated; jointed
articular [artiku'lar] *vt* to articulate; to join together
articulista [artiku'lista] *nm/f* columnist, contributor (to a newspaper)
artículo [ar'tikulo] *nm* article; (*cosa*) thing, article; (*TV*) feature, report; **~ de fondo** leader, editorial; **artículos** *nmpl* goods; **artículos de marca** (*Com*) proprietary goods
artífice [ar'tifiθe] *nm* artist, craftsman; (*fig*) architect
artificial [artifi'θjal] *adj* artificial
artificio [arti'fiθjo] *nm* art, skill; (*artesanía*) craftsmanship; (*astucia*) cunning
artillería [artiʎe'ria] *nf* artillery
artillero [arti'ʎero] *nm* artilleryman, gunner
artilugio [arti'luxjo] *nm* gadget
artimaña [arti'maɲa] *nf* trap, snare; (*astucia*) cunning
artista [ar'tista] *nm/f* (*pintor*) artist, painter; (*Teat*) artist, artiste
artístico, -a [ar'tistiko, a] *adj* artistic
artritis [ar'tritis] *nf* arthritis
artrosis [ar'trosis] *nf* osteoarthritis
arveja [ar'βexa] *nf* (*Am*) pea
Arz. *abr* (= *Arzobispo*) Abp
arzobispo [arθo'βispo] *nm* archbishop
as [as] *nm* ace; **as del fútbol** star player
asa ['asa] *nf* handle; (*fig*) lever
asado [a'saðo] *nm* roast (meat); (*Am: barbacoa*) barbecue
asador [asa'ðor] *nm* (*varilla*) spit; (*aparato*) spit roaster
asadura [asa'ðura] *nf*, **asaduras** [asa'ðuras] *nfpl* entrails *pl*, offal *sg*; (*Culin*) chitterlings *pl*
asaetear [asaete'ar] *vt* (*fig*) to bother
asalariado, -a [asala'rjaðo, a] *adj* paid, wage-earning, salaried ■ *nm/f* wage earner
asaltador, a [asalta'ðor, a], **asaltante** [asal'tante] *nm/f* assailant
asaltar [asal'tar] *vt* to attack, assault; (*fig*) to assail
asalto [a'salto] *nm* attack, assault; (*Deporte*) round
asamblea [asam'blea] *nf* assembly; (*reunión*) meeting
asar [a'sar] *vt* to roast; **~ al horno/a la parrilla** to bake/grill; **asarse** *vr* (*fig*): **me aso de calor** I'm roasting; **aquí se asa uno vivo** it's boiling hot here
asbesto [as'βesto] *nm* asbestos
ascendencia [asθen'denθja] *nf* ancestry; **de ~ francesa** of French origin
ascender [asθen'der] *vi* (*subir*) to ascend, rise; (*ser promovido*) to gain promotion ■ *vt* to promote; **~ a** to amount to
ascendiente [asθen'djente] *nm* influence ■ *nm/f* ancestor
ascensión [asθen'sjon] *nf* ascent; **la A~** the Ascension
ascenso [as'θenso] *nm* ascent; (*promoción*) promotion
ascensor [asθen'sor] *nm* lift (*Brit*), elevator (*US*)
ascético, -a [as'θetiko, a] *adj* ascetic
ascienda *etc* [as'θjenda] *vb ver* **ascender**
asco ['asko] *nm*: **el ajo me da ~** I hate *o* loathe garlic; **hacer ascos de algo** to turn up one's nose at sth; **estar hecho un ~** to be filthy; **poner a algn de ~** to call sb all sorts of names *o* every name under the sun; **¡qué ~!** how revolting *o* disgusting!
ascua ['askwa] *nf* ember; **arrimar el ~ a su sardina** to look after number one; **estar en ascuas** to be on tenterhooks
aseado, -a [ase'aðo, a] *adj* clean; (*arreglado*) tidy; (*pulcro*) smart
asear [ase'ar] *vt* (*lavar*) to wash; (*ordenar*) to tidy (up)

asechanza [ase'tʃanθa] *nf* trap, snare
asediar [ase'ðjar] *vt* (*Mil*) to besiege, lay siege to; (*fig*) to chase, pester
asedio [a'seðjo] *nm* siege; (*Com*) run
asegurado, a [aseɣu'raðo, a] *adj* insured
asegurador, -a [aseɣura'ðor, a] *nm/f* insurer
asegurar [aseɣu'rar] *vt* (*consolidar*) to secure, fasten; (*dar garantía de*) to guarantee; (*preservar*) to safeguard; (*afirmar: dar por cierto*) to assure, affirm; (*tranquilizar*) to reassure; (*hacer un seguro*) to insure; **asegurarse** *vr* to assure o.s., make sure
asemejarse [aseme'xarse] *vr* to be alike; ~ **a** to be like, resemble
asentado, -a [asen'taðo, a] *adj* established, settled
asentar [asen'tar] *vt* (*sentar*) to seat, sit down; (*poner*) to place, establish; (*alisar*) to level, smooth down *o* out; (*anotar*) to note down ■ *vi* to be suitable, suit
asentimiento [asenti'mjento] *nm* assent, agreement
asentir [asen'tir] *vi* to assent, agree
aseo [a'seo] *nm* cleanliness; **aseos** *nmpl* toilet *sg* (*Brit*), restroom *sg* (*US*), cloakroom *sg*
aséptico, -a [a'septiko, a] *adj* germ-free, free from infection
asequible [ase'kiβle] *adj* (*precio*) reasonable; (*meta*) attainable; (*persona*) approachable
aserradero [aserra'ðero] *nm* sawmill
aserrar [ase'rrar] *vt* to saw
asesinar [asesi'nar] *vt* to murder; (*Pol*) to assassinate
asesinato [asesi'nato] *nm* murder; assassination
asesino, -a [ase'sino, a] *nm/f* murderer, killer; (*Pol*) assassin
asesor, a [ase'sor, a] *nm/f* adviser, consultant; (*Com*) assessor, consultant; ~ **administrativo** management consultant
asesorar [aseso'rar] *vt* (*Jur*) to advise, give legal advice to; (*Com*) to act as consultant to; **asesorarse** *vr*: **asesorarse con** *o* **de** to take advice from, consult
asesoría [aseso'ria] *nf* (*cargo*) consultancy; (*oficina*) consultant's office
asestar [ases'tar] *vt* (*golpe*) to deal; (*arma*) to aim; (*tiro*) to fire
aseverar [aseβe'rar] *vt* to assert
asfaltado, -a [asfal'taðo, a] *adj* asphalted ■ *nm* (*pavimiento*) asphalt
asfalto [as'falto] *nm* asphalt
asfixia [as'fiksja] *nf* asphyxia, suffocation
asfixiar [asfik'sjar] *vt* to asphyxiate, suffocate
asga *etc* ['asɣa] *vb ver* **asir**
así [a'si] *adv* (*de esta manera*) in this way, like this, thus; (*aunque*) although; (*tan pronto como*) as soon as; **así que** so; **así como** as well as; **así y todo** even so; **¿no es así?** isn't it?, didn't you? *etc*; **así de grande** this big; **¡así sea!** so be it!; **así es la vida** such is life, that's life
Asia ['asja] *nf* Asia
asiático, -a [a'sjatiko, a] *adj, nm/f* Asian, Asiatic
asidero [asi'ðero] *nm* handle
asiduidad [asiðwi'ðað] *nf* assiduousness
asiduo, -a [a'siðwo, a] *adj* assiduous; (*frecuente*) frequent ■ *nm/f* regular (customer)
asiento *etc* [a'sjento] *vb ver* **asentar; asentir** ■ *nm* (*mueble*) seat, chair; (*de coche, en tribunal etc*) seat; (*localidad*) seat, place; (*fundamento*) site; ~ **delantero/trasero** front/back seat
asierre *etc* [a'sjerre] *vb ver* **aserrar**
asignación [asiɣna'θjon] *nf* (*atribución*) assignment; (*reparto*) allocation; (*Com*) allowance; ~ **(semanal)** pocket money; ~ **de presupuesto** budget appropriation
asignar [asiɣ'nar] *vt* to assign, allocate
asignatura [asiɣna'tura] *nf* subject; (*curso*) course; ~ **pendiente** (*fig*) matter pending
asilado, -a [asi'laðo, a] *nm/f* refugee
asilo [a'silo] *nm* (*refugio*) asylum, refuge; (*establecimiento*) home, institution; ~ **político** political asylum
asimilación [asimila'θjon] *nf* assimilation
asimilar [asimi'lar] *vt* to assimilate
asimismo [asi'mismo] *adv* in the same way, likewise
asintiendo *etc* [asin'tjendo] *vb ver* **asentir**
asir [a'sir] *vt* to seize, grasp; **asirse** *vr* to take hold; **asirse a** *o* **de** to seize
asistencia [asis'tenθja] *nf* presence; (*Teat*) audience; (*Med*) attendance; (*ayuda*) assistance; ~ **social** social *o* welfare work
asistente, -a [asis'tente, a] *nm/f* assistant ■ *nm* (*Mil*) orderly ■ *nf* daily help; **los asistentes** those present; ~ **social** social worker
asistido, -a [asis'tiðo, a] *adj* (*Auto: dirección*) power-assisted; ~ **por ordenador** computer-assisted
asistir [asis'tir] *vt* to assist, help ■ *vi*: ~ **a** to attend, be present at
asma ['asma] *nf* asthma
asno ['asno] *nm* donkey; (*fig*) ass
asociación [asoθja'θjon] *nf* association; (*Com*) partnership
asociado, -a [aso'θjaðo, a] *adj* associate ■ *nm/f* associate; (*Com*) partner
asociar [aso'θjar] *vt* to associate; **asociarse** *vr* to become partners

asolar [aso'lar] *vt* to destroy
asolear [asole'ar] *vt* to put in the sun; **asolearse** *vr* to sunbathe
asomar [aso'mar] *vt* to show, stick out ■ *vi* to appear; **asomarse** *vr* to appear, show up; **~ la cabeza por la ventana** to put one's head out of the window
asombrar [asom'brar] *vt* to amaze, astonish; **asombrarse** *vr*: **asombrarse (de)** (*sorprenderse*) to be amazed (at); (*asustarse*) to be frightened (at)
asombro [a'sombro] *nm* amazement, astonishment
asombroso, -a [asom'broso, a] *adj* amazing, astonishing
asomo [a'somo] *nm* hint, sign; **ni por ~** by no means
asonancia [aso'nanθja] *nf* (*Lit*) assonance; (*fig*) connection; **no tener ~ con** to bear no relation to
asorocharse [asoro'tʃarse] *vr* (*Am*) to get mountain sickness
aspa ['aspa] *nf* (*cruz*) cross; (*de molino*) sail; **en ~** X-shaped
aspaviento [aspa'βjento] *nm* exaggerated display of feeling; (*fam*) fuss
aspecto [as'pekto] *nm* (*apariencia*) look, appearance; (*fig*) aspect; **bajo ese ~** from that point of view
aspereza [aspe'reθa] *nf* roughness; (*de fruta*) sharpness; (*de carácter*) surliness
áspero, -a ['aspero, a] *adj* rough; sharp; harsh
aspersión [asper'sjon] *nf* sprinkling; (*Agr*) spraying
aspersor [asper'sor] *nm* sprinkler
aspiración [aspira'θjon] *nf* breath, inhalation; (*Mus*) short pause; **aspiraciones** *nfpl* aspirations
aspiradora [aspira'ðora] *nf* vacuum cleaner, Hoover®
aspirante [aspi'rante] *nm/f* (*candidato*) candidate; (*Deporte*) contender
aspirar [aspi'rar] *vt* to breathe in ■ *vi*: **~ a** to aspire to
aspirina [aspi'rina] *nf* aspirin
asquear [aske'ar] *vt* to sicken ■ *vi* to be sickening; **asquearse** *vr* to feel disgusted
asquerosidad [askerosi'ðað] *nf* (*suciedad*) filth; (*dicho*) obscenity; (*faena*) dirty trick
asqueroso, -a [aske'roso, a] *adj* disgusting, sickening
asta ['asta] *nf* lance; (*arpón*) spear; (*mango*) shaft, handle; (*Zool*) horn; **a media ~** at half mast
astado, -a [as'taðo, a] *adj* horned ■ *nm* bull
asterisco [aste'risko] *nm* asterisk
asteroide [aste'roiðe] *nm* asteroid
astigmatismo [astiɣma'tismo] *nm* astigmatism
astilla [as'tiʎa] *nf* splinter; (*pedacito*) chip; **astillas** *nfpl* firewood *sg*
astillarse [asti'ʎarse] *vr* to splinter; (*fig*) to shatter
astillero [asti'ʎero] *nm* shipyard
astringente [astrin'xente] *adj, nm* astringent
astro ['astro] *nm* star
astrología [astrolo'xia] *nf* astrology
astrólogo, -a [as'troloɣo, a] *nm/f* astrologer
astronauta [astro'nauta] *nm/f* astronaut
astronave [astro'naβe] *nm* spaceship
astronomía [astrono'mia] *nf* astronomy
astronómico, -a [astro'nomiko, a] *adj* (*tb fig*) astronomical
astrónomo, -a [as'tronomo, a] *nm/f* astronomer
astroso, -a [as'troso, a] *adj* (*desaliñado*) untidy; (*vil*) contemptible
astucia [as'tuθja] *nf* astuteness; (*destreza*) clever trick
asturiano, -a [astu'rjano, a] *adj, nm/f* Asturian
Asturias [as'turjas] *nfpl* Asturias; **Príncipe de ~** crown prince
astuto, -a [as'tuto, a] *adj* astute; (*taimado*) cunning
asueto [a'sweto] *nm* holiday; (*tiempo libre*) time off; **día de ~** day off; **tarde de ~** (*trabajo*) afternoon off; (*Escol*) half-holiday
asumir [asu'mir] *vt* to assume
asunción [asun'θjon] *nf* assumption
asunto [a'sunto] *nm* (*tema*) matter, subject; (*negocio*) business; **¡eso es ~ mío!** that's my business!; **asuntos exteriores** foreign affairs; **asuntos a tratar** agenda *sg*
asustadizo, -a [asusta'ðiθo, a] *adj* easily frightened
asustar [asus'tar] *vt* to frighten; **asustarse** *vr* to be/become frightened
atacante [ata'kante] *nm/f* attacker
atacar [ata'kar] *vt* to attack
atadura [ata'ðura] *nf* bond, tie
atajar [ata'xar] *vt* (*gen*) to stop; (*ruta de fuga*) to cut off; (*discurso*) to interrupt ■ *vi* to take a short cut
atajo [a'taxo] *nm* short cut; (*Deporte*) tackle
atalaya [ata'laja] *nf* watchtower
atañer [ata'ɲer] *vi*: **~ a** to concern; **en lo que atañe a eso** with regard to that
ataque *etc* [a'take] *vb ver* **atacar** ■ *nm* attack; **~ cardíaco** heart attack
atar [a'tar] *vt* to tie, tie up; **~ la lengua a algn** (*fig*) to silence sb
atardecer [atarðe'θer] *vi* to get dark ■ *nm*

evening; (*crepúsculo*) dusk
atardezca *etc* [atar'ðeθka] *vb ver* **atardecer**
atareado, -a [atare'aðo, a] *adj* busy
atascar [atas'kar] *vt* to clog up; (*obstruir*) to jam; (*fig*) to hinder; **atascarse** *vr* to stall; (*cañería*) to get blocked up; (*fig*) to get bogged down; (*en discurso*) to dry up
atasco [a'tasko] *nm* obstruction; (*Auto*) traffic jam
atasque *etc* [a'taske] *vb ver* **atascar**
ataúd [ata'uð] *nm* coffin
ataviar [ata'βjar] *vt* to deck, array; **ataviarse** *vr* to dress up
atavío [ata'βio] *nm* attire, dress; **atavíos** *nmpl* finery *sg*
ateísmo [ate'ismo] *nm* atheism
atemorice *etc* [atemo'riθe] *vb ver* **atemorizar**
atemorizar [atemori'θar] *vt* to frighten, scare; **atemorizarse** *vr* to get frightened *o* scared
Atenas [a'tenas] *nf* Athens
atención [aten'θjon] *nf* attention; (*bondad*) kindness ■ *excl* (be) careful!, look out!; **en ~ a esto** in view of this
atender [aten'der] *vt* to attend to, look after; (*Tec*) to service; (*enfermo*) to care for; (*ruego*) to comply with ■ *vi* to pay attention; **~ a** to attend to; (*detalles*) to take care of
atendré *etc* [aten'dre] *vb ver* **atenerse**
atenerse [ate'nerse] *vr*: **~ a** to abide by, adhere to
atenga *etc* [a'tenga] *vb ver* **atenerse**
ateniense [ate'njense] *adj, nm/f* Athenian
atentado [aten'taðo] *nm* crime, illegal act; (*asalto*) assault; (*terrorista*) attack; **~ contra la vida de algn** attempt on sb's life; **~ golpista** attempted coup; **~ suicida** suicide bombing, suicide attack
atentamente [atenta'mente] *adv*: **le saluda ~** Yours faithfully
atentar [aten'tar] *vi*: **~ a** *o* **contra** to commit an outrage against
atento, -a [a'tento, a] *adj* attentive, observant; (*cortés*) polite, thoughtful; **su atenta (carta)** (*Com*) your letter
atenuante [ate'nwante] *adj*: **circunstancias atenuantes** extenuating *o* mitigating circumstances ■ *nfpl*: **atenuantes** extenuating *o* mitigating circumstances
atenuar [ate'nwar] *vt* to attenuate; (*disminuir*) to lessen, minimize
ateo, -a [a'teo, a] *adj* atheistic ■ *nm/f* atheist
aterciopelado, -a [aterθjope'laðo, a] *adj* velvety
aterido, -a [ate'riðo, a] *adj*: **~ de frío** frozen stiff
aterrador, a [aterra'ðor, a] *adj* frightening
aterrar [ate'rrar] *vt* to frighten; (*aterrorizar*) to terrify; **aterrarse** *vr* to be frightened; to be terrified
aterrice *etc* [ate'rriθe] *vb ver* **aterrizar**
aterrizaje [aterri'θaxe] *nm* landing; **~ forzoso** forced landing
aterrizar [aterri'θar] *vi* to land
aterrorice *etc* [aterro'riθe] *vb ver* **aterrorizar**
aterrorizar [aterrori'θar] *vt* to terrify
atesorar [ateso'rar] *vt* to hoard, store up
atestado, -a [ates'taðo, a] *adj* packed ■ *nm* (*Jur*) affidavit
atestar [ates'tar] *vt* to pack, stuff; (*Jur*) to attest, testify to
atestiguar [atesti'ɣwar] *vt* to testify to, bear witness to
atestigüe *etc* [ates'tiɣwe] *vb ver* **atestiguar**
atiborrar [atiβo'rrar] *vt* to fill, stuff; **atiborrarse** *vr* to stuff o.s.
atice *etc* [a'tiθe] *vb ver* **atizar**
ático ['atiko] *nm* attic; **~ de lujo** penthouse flat
atienda *etc* [a'tjenda] *vb ver* **atender**
atildar [atil'dar] *vt* to criticize; (*Tip*) to put a tilde over; **atildarse** *vr* to spruce o.s. up
atinado, -a [ati'naðo, a] *adj* correct; (*sensato*) sensible
atinar [ati'nar] *vi* (*acertar*) to be right; **~ con** *o* **en** (*solución*) to hit upon; **~ a hacer** to manage to do
atípico, -a [a'tipiko, a] *adj* atypical
atiplado, -a [ati'plaðo, a] *adj* (*voz*) high-pitched
atisbar [atis'βar] *vt* to spy on; (*echar ojeada*) to peep at
atizar [ati'θar] *vt* to poke; (*horno etc*) to stoke; (*fig*) to stir up, rouse
atlántico, -a [at'lantiko, a] *adj* Atlantic ■ *nm*: **el (océano) A~** the Atlantic (Ocean)
atlas ['atlas] *nm inv* atlas
atleta [at'leta] *nm/f* athlete
atlético, -a [at'letiko, a] *adj* athletic
atletismo [atle'tismo] *nm* athletics *sg*
atmósfera [at'mosfera] *nf* atmosphere
atmosférico, -a [atmos'feriko, a] *adj* atmospheric
atol [a'tol], **atole** [a'tole] *nm* (*Am*) cornflour drink
atolladero [atoʎa'ðero] *nm*: **estar en un ~** to be in a jam
atollarse [ato'ʎarse] *vr* to get stuck; (*fig*) to get into a jam
atolondrado, -a [atolon'draðo, a] *adj* scatterbrained
atolondramiento [atolondra'mjento] *nm* bewilderment; (*insensatez*) silliness
atómico, -a [a'tomiko, a] *adj* atomic

atomizador [atomiθa'ðor] *nm* atomizer
átomo ['atomo] *nm* atom
atónito, -a [a'tonito, a] *adj* astonished, amazed
atontado, -a [aton'taðo, a] *adj* stunned; (*bobo*) silly, daft
atontar [aton'tar] *vt* to stun; **atontarse** *vr* to become confused
atorar [ato'rar] *vt* to obstruct; **atorarse** *vr* (*atragantarse*) to choke
atormentar [atormen'tar] *vt* to torture; (*molestar*) to torment; (*acosar*) to plague, harass
atornillar [atorni'ʎar] *vt* to screw on *o* down
atorón [ato'ron] *nm* (*Am*) traffic jam
atosigar [atosi'ɣar] *vt* to harass
atosigue *etc* [ato'siɣe] *vb ver* **atosigar**
atrabiliario, -a [atraβi'ljarjo, a] *adj* bad-tempered
atracadero [atraka'ðero] *nm* pier
atracador, a [atraka'ðor, a] *nm/f* robber
atracar [atra'kar] *vt* (*Naut*) to moor; (*robar*) to hold up, rob ■ *vi* to moor; **atracarse** *vr* (*hartarse*) to stuff o.s.
atracción [atrak'θjon] *nf* attraction
atraco [a'trako] *nm* holdup, robbery
atracón [atra'kon] *nm*: **darse** *o* **pegarse un ~ (de)** (*fam*) to pig out (on)
atractivo, -a [atrak'tiβo, a] *adj* attractive ■ *nm* attraction; (*belleza*) attractiveness
atraer [atra'er] *vt* to attract; **dejarse ~ por** to be tempted by
atragantarse [atraɣan'tarse] *vr*: **~ (con algo)** to choke (on sth); **se me ha atragantado el chico ese/el inglés** I don't take to that boy/English
atraiga *etc* [a'traiɣa], **atraje** *etc* [a'traxe] *vb ver* **atraer**
atrancar [atran'kar] *vt* (*con tranca, barra*) to bar, bolt
atranque *etc* [a'tranke] *vb ver* **atrancar**
atrapar [atra'par] *vt* to trap; (*resfriado etc*) to catch
atraque *etc* [a'trake] *vb ver* **atracar**
atrás [a'tras] *adv* (*movimiento*) back(wards); (*lugar*) behind; (*tiempo*) previously; **ir hacia ~** to go back(wards); to go to the rear; **estar ~** to be behind *o* at the back
atrasado, -a [atra'saðo, a] *adj* slow; (*pago*) overdue, late; (*país*) backward
atrasar [atra'sar] *vi* to be slow; **atrasarse** *vr* to remain behind; (*llegar tarde*) to arrive late
atraso [a'traso] *nm* slowness; lateness, delay; (*de país*) backwardness; **atrasos** *nmpl* arrears
atravesado, -a [atraβe'saðo, a] *adj*: **un tronco ~ en la carretera** a tree trunk lying across the road
atravesar [atraβe'sar] *vt* (*cruzar*) to cross (over); (*traspasar*) to pierce; (*período*) to go through; (*poner al través*) to lay *o* put across; **atravesarse** *vr* to come in between; (*intervenir*) to interfere
atraviese *etc* [atra'βjese] *vb ver* **atravesar**
atrayendo [atra'jendo] *vb ver* **atraer**
atrayente [atra'jente] *adj* attractive
atreverse [atre'βerse] *vr* to dare; (*insolentarse*) to be insolent
atrevido, -a [atre'βiðo, a] *adj* daring; insolent
atrevimiento [atreβi'mjento] *nm* daring; insolence
atribución [atriβu'θjon] *nf* (*Lit*) attribution; **atribuciones** *nfpl* (*Pol*) functions; (*Admin*) responsibilities
atribuir [atriβu'ir] *vt* to attribute; (*funciones*) to confer
atribular [atriβu'lar] *vt* to afflict, distress
atributo [atri'βuto] *nm* attribute
atribuya *etc* [atri'βuja], **atribuyendo** *etc* [atriβu'jendo] *vb ver* **atribuir**
atril [a'tril] *nm* lectern; (*Mus*) music stand
atrincherarse [atrintʃe'rarse] *vr* (*Mil*) to dig (o.s.) in; **~ en** (*fig*) to hide behind
atrio ['atrjo] *nm* (*Rel*) porch
atrocidad [atroθi'ðað] *nf* atrocity, outrage
atrofiado, -a [atro'fjaðo, a] *adj* (*extremidad*) withered
atrofiarse [atro'fjarse] *vr* (*tb fig*) to atrophy
atronador, a [atrona'ðor, a] *adj* deafening
atropellar [atrope'ʎar] *vt* (*derribar*) to knock over *o* down; (*empujar*) to push (aside); (*Auto*) to run over *o* down; (*agraviar*) to insult; **atropellarse** *vr* to act hastily
atropello [atro'peʎo] *nm* (*Auto*) accident; (*empujón*) push; (*agravio*) wrong; (*atrocidad*) outrage
atroz [a'troθ] *adj* atrocious, awful
A.T.S. *nm/f abr* (= *Ayudante Técnico Sanitario*) nurse
attrezzo [a'treθo] *nm* props *pl*
atuendo [a'twendo] *nm* attire
atufar [atu'far] *vt* (*suj: olor*) to overcome; (*molestar*) to irritate; **atufarse** *vr* (*fig*) to get cross
atún [a'tun] *nm* tuna, tunny
aturdir [atur'ðir] *vt* to stun; (*suj: ruido*) to deafen; (*fig*) to dumbfound, bewilder
aturrullar, aturullar [atur(r)u'ʎar] *vt* to bewilder
atusar [atu'sar] *vt* (*cortar*) to trim; (*alisar*) to smooth (down)
atuve *etc* [a'tuβe] *vb ver* **atenerse**
audacia [au'ðaθja] *nf* boldness, audacity
audaz [au'ðaθ] *adj* bold, audacious

audible [au'ðiβle] *adj* audible
audición [auði'θjon] *nf* hearing; (*Teat*) audition; ~ **radiofónica** radio concert
audiencia [au'ðjenθja] *nf* audience; (*Jur*) high court; (*Pol*): ~ **pública** public inquiry
audífono [au'ðifono] *nm* hearing aid
audiovisual [auðjoβi'swal] *adj* audio-visual
auditivo, -a [auði'tiβo, a] *adj* hearing *cpd*; (*conducto, nervio*) auditory
auditor [auði'tor] *nm* (*Jur*) judge-advocate; (*Com*) auditor
auditoría [auðito'ria] *nf* audit; (*profesión*) auditing
auditorio [auði'torjo] *nm* audience; (*sala*) auditorium
auge ['auxe] *nm* boom; (*clímax*) climax; (*Econ*) expansion; **estar en** ~ to thrive
augurar [auɣu'rar] *vt* to predict; (*presagiar*) to portend
augurio [au'ɣurjo] *nm* omen
aula ['aula] *nf* classroom
aullar [au'ʎar] *vi* to howl, yell
aullido [au'ʎiðo] *nm* howl, yell
aumentar [aumen'tar] *vt* to increase; (*precios*) to put up; (*producción*) to step up; (*con microscopio, anteojos*) to magnify ■ *vi*, **aumentarse** *vr* to increase, be on the increase
aumento [au'mento] *nm* increase; rise
aún [a'un] *adv* still, yet
aun [a'un] *adv* even
aunque [a'unke] *conj* though, although, even though
aúpa [a'upa] *excl* up!, come on!; (*fam*): **una función de** ~ a slap-up do; **una paliza de** ~ a good hiding
aupar [au'par] *vt* (*levantar*) to help up; (*fig*) to praise
aura ['aura] *nf* (*atmósfera*) aura
aureola [aure'ola] *nf* halo
auricular [auriku'lar] *nm* earpiece, receiver; **auriculares** *nmpl* headphones
aurora [au'rora] *nf* dawn; ~ **boreal(is)** northern lights *pl*
auscultar [auskul'tar] *vt* (*Med: pecho*) to listen to, sound
ausencia [au'senθja] *nf* absence
ausentarse [ausen'tarse] *vr* to go away; (*por poco tiempo*) to go out
ausente [au'sente] *adj* absent ■ *nm/f* (*Escol*) absentee; (*Jur*) missing person
auspiciar [auspi'sjar] *vt* (*Am*) to back, sponsor
auspicios [aus'piθjos] *nmpl* auspices; (*protección*) protection *sg*
austeridad [austeri'ðað] *nf* austerity
austero, -a [aus'tero, a] *adj* austere
austral [aus'tral] *adj* southern ■ *nm monetary unit of Argentina (1985-1991)*
Australia [aus'tralja] *nf* Australia
australiano, -a [austra'ljano, a] *adj, nm/f* Australian
Austria ['austrja] *nf* Austria
austriaco, -a [aus'trjako, a], **austríaco a** [aus'triako, a] *adj, nm/f* Austrian
autenticar [autenti'kar] *vt* to authenticate
auténtico, -a [au'tentiko, a] *adj* authentic
autentificar [autentifi'kar] *vt* to authenticate
autentique *etc* [auten'tike] *vb ver* **autenticar**
auto ['auto] *nm* (*coche*) car; (*Jur*) edict, decree; (*: orden*) writ; **autos** *nmpl* (*Jur*) proceedings; (*: acta*) court record *sg*; ~ **de comparecencia** summons, subpoena; ~ **de ejecución** writ of execution
autoadhesivo, -a [autoaðe'siβo, a] *adj* self-adhesive; (*sobre*) self-sealing
autoalimentación [autoalimenta'θjon] *nf* (*Inform*): ~ **de hojas** automatic paper feed
autobiografía [autoβjoɣra'fia] *nf* autobiography
autobronceador [autoβronθea'ðor] *adj* self-tanning
autobús [auto'βus] *nm* bus (*Brit*), (passenger) bus (*US*)
autocar [auto'kar] *nm* coach; ~ **de línea** intercity coach
autocomprobación [autokomproβa'θjon] *nf* (*Inform*) self-test
autóctono, -a [au'toktono, a] *adj* native, indigenous
autodefensa [autoðe'fensa] *nf* self-defence
autodeterminación [autoðetermina'θjon] *nf* self-determination
autodidacta [autoði'ðakta] *adj* self-taught ■ *nm/f*: **ser un(a)** ~ to be self-taught
autoescuela [autoes'kwela] *nf* driving school
autofinanciado, -a [autofinan'θjaðo, a] *adj* self-financing
autogestión [autoxes'tjon] *nf* self-management
autógrafo [au'toɣrafo] *nm* autograph
automación [automa'θjon] *nf* = **automatización**
autómata [au'tomata] *nm* automaton
automáticamente [auto'matikamente] *adv* automatically
automatice *etc* [automa'tiθe] *vb ver* **automatizar**
automático, -a [auto'matiko, a] *adj* automatic ■ *nm* press stud
automatización [automatiθa'θjon] *nf*: ~ **de fábricas** factory automation; ~ **de oficinas** office automation

automatizar [automati'θar] *vt* to automate
automontable [automon'taʙle] *adj* self-assembly
automotor, -triz [automo'tor, 'triz] *adj* self-propelled ■ *nm* diesel train
automóvil [auto'moβil] *nm* (motor) car (*Brit*), automobile (*US*)
automovilismo [automoβi'lismo] *nm* (*Deporte*) (sports) car racing
automovilista [automoβi'lista] *nm/f* motorist, driver
automovilístico, -a [automoβi'listiko, a] *adj* (*industria*) car *cpd*
autonomía [autono'mia] *nf* autonomy; (*Esp Pol*) autonomy, self-government; (: *comunidad*) autonomous region
autonómico, -a [auto'nomiko, a] *adj* (*Esp Pol*) relating to autonomy, autonomous; **gobierno ~** autonomous government
autónomo, -a [au'tonomo, a] *adj* autonomous; (*Inform*) stand-alone, offline
autopista [auto'pista] *nf* motorway (*Brit*), freeway (*US*)
autopsia [au'topsja] *nf* autopsy
autor, a [au'tor, a] *nm/f* author; **los autores del atentado** those responsible for the attack
autorice *etc* [auto'riθe] *vb ver* **autorizar**
autoridad [autori'ðað] *nf* authority; **~ local** local authority
autoritario, -a [autori'tarjo, a] *adj* authoritarian
autorización [autoriθa'θjon] *nf* authorization
autorizado, -a [autori'θaðo, a] *adj* authorized; (*aprobado*) approved
autorizar [autori'θar] *vt* to authorize; to approve
autorretrato [autorre'trato] *nm* self-portrait
autoservicio [autoser'βiθjo] *nm* self-service shop *o* store; (*restaurante*) self-service restaurant
autostop [auto'stop] *nm* hitch-hiking; **hacer ~** to hitch-hike
autostopista [autosto'pista] *nm/f* hitch-hiker
autosuficiencia [autosufi'θjenθja] *nf* self-sufficiency
autosuficiente [autosufi'θjente] *adj* self-sufficient; (*pey*) smug
autosugestión [autosuxes'tjon] *nf* autosuggestion
autovía [auto'βia] *nf* ≈ dual carriageway (*Brit*), ≈ separated highway (*US*)
auxiliar [auksi'ljar] *vt* to help ■ *nm/f* assistant
auxilio [auk'siljo] *nm* assistance, help; **primeros auxilios** first aid *sg*
Av *abr* (= *Avenida*) Av(e)
a/v *abr* (*Com*: = *a vista*) at sight
aval [a'βal] *nm* guarantee; (*persona*) guarantor
avalancha [aβa'lantʃa] *nf* avalanche
avalar [aβa'lar] *vt* (*Com etc*) to underwrite; (*fig*) to endorse
avalista [aβa'lista] *nm* (*Com*) endorser
avance *etc* [a'βanθe] *vb ver* **avanzar** ■ *nm* advance; (*pago*) advance payment; (*Cine*) trailer
avanzado, -a [aβan'θaðo, a] *adj* advanced; **de edad avanzada, ~ de edad** elderly
avanzar [aβan'θar] *vt, vi* to advance
avaricia [aβa'riθja] *nf* avarice, greed
avaricioso, -a [aβari'θjoso, a] *adj* avaricious, greedy
avaro, -a [a'βaro, a] *adj* miserly, mean ■ *nm/f* miser
avasallar [aβasa'ʎar] *vt* to subdue, subjugate
avatar [aβa'tar] *nm* change; **avatares** ups and downs
Avda *abr* (= *Avenida*) Av(e)
AVE ['aβe] *nm abr* (= *Alta Velocidad Española*) ≈ Bullet train
ave ['aβe] *nf* bird; **~ de rapiña** bird of prey
avecinarse [aβeθi'narse] *vr* (*tormenta, fig*) to approach, be on the way
avejentar [aβexen'tar] *vt, vi*, **avejentarse** *vr* to age
avellana [aβe'ʎana] *nf* hazelnut
avellano [aβe'ʎano] *nm* hazel tree
avemaría [aβema'ria] *nm* Hail Mary, Ave Maria
avena [a'βena] *nf* oats *pl*
avendré *etc* [aβen'dre], **avenga** *etc* [a'βenga] *vb ver* **avenir**
avenida [aβe'niða] *nf* (*calle*) avenue
avenir [aβe'nir] *vt* to reconcile; **avenirse** *vr* to come to an agreement, reach a compromise
aventado, -a [aβen'taðo, a] *adj* (*Am*) daring
aventajado, -a [aβenta'xaðo, a] *adj* outstanding
aventajar [aβenta'xar] *vt* (*sobrepasar*) to surpass, outstrip
aventar [aβen'tar] *vt* to fan, blow; (*grano*) to winnow; (*Am fam: echar*) to chuck out
aventón [aβen'ton] *nm* (*Am*) push; **pedir ~** to hitch a lift
aventura [aβen'tura] *nf* adventure; **~ sentimental** love affair
aventurado, -a [aβentu'raðo, a] *adj* risky
aventurar [aβentu'rar] *vt* to risk; **aventurarse** *vr* to dare; **aventurarse a hacer algo** to venture to do sth
aventurero, -a [aβentu'rero, a] *adj* adventurous

avergoncé [aβerɣon'θe], **avergoncemos** *etc* [aβerɣon'θemos] *vb ver* **avergonzar**
avergonzar [aβerɣon'θar] *vt* to shame; (*desconcertar*) to embarrass; **avergonzarse** *vr* to be ashamed; to be embarrassed
avergüence *etc* [aβer'ɣwenθe] *vb ver* **avergonzar**
avería [aβe'ria] *nf* (*Tec*) breakdown, fault
averiado, -a [aβe'rjaðo, a] *adj* broken-down
averiar [aβe'rjar] *vt* to break; **averiarse** *vr* to break down
averiguación [aβeriɣwa'θjon] *nf* investigation
averiguar [aβeri'ɣwar] *vt* to investigate; (*descubrir*) to find out, ascertain
averigüe *etc* [aβe'riɣwe] *vb ver* **averiguar**
aversión [aβer'sjon] *nf* aversion, dislike; **cobrar ~ a** to take a strong dislike to
avestruz [aβes'truθ] *nm* ostrich
aviación [aβja'θjon] *nf* aviation; (*fuerzas aéreas*) air force
aviado, -a [a'βjaðo, a] *adj*: **estar ~** to be in a mess
aviador, a [aβja'ðor, a] *nm/f* aviator, airman/woman
aviar [a'βjar] *vt* to prepare, get ready
avícola [a'βikola] *adj* poultry *cpd*
avicultura [aβikul'tura] *nf* poultry farming
avidez [aβi'ðeθ] *nf* avidity, eagerness
ávido, -a ['aβiðo, a] *adj* avid, eager
aviente *etc* [a'βjente] *vb ver* **aventar**
avieso, -a [a'βjeso, a] *adj* (*torcido*) distorted; (*perverso*) wicked
avinagrado, -a [aβina'ɣraðo, a] *adj* sour, acid
avinagrarse [aβina'ɣrarse] *vr* to go *o* turn sour
avine *etc* [a'βine] *vb ver* **avenir**
Aviñón [aβi'ɲon] *nm* Avignon
avío [a'βio] *nm* preparation; **avíos** *nmpl* gear *sg*, kit *sg*
avión [a'βjon] *nm* aeroplane; (*ave*) martin; **~ de reacción** jet (plane); **por ~** (*Correos*) by air mail
avioneta [aβjo'neta] *nf* light aircraft
avisar [aβi'sar] *vt* (*advertir*) to warn, notify; (*informar*) to tell; (*aconsejar*) to advise, counsel
aviso [a'βiso] *nm* warning; (*noticia*) notice; (*Com*) demand note; (*Inform*) prompt; **~ escrito** notice in writing; **sin previo ~** without warning; **estar sobre ~** to be on the look-out
avispa [a'βispa] *nf* wasp
avispado, -a [aβis'paðo, a] *adj* sharp, clever
avispero [aβis'pero] *nm* wasp's nest
avispón [aβis'pon] *nm* hornet
avistar [aβis'tar] *vt* to sight, spot
avitaminosis [aβitami'nosis] *nf inv* vitamin deficiency
avituallar [aβitwa'ʎar] *vt* to supply with food
avivar [aβi'βar] *vt* to strengthen, intensify; **avivarse** *vr* to revive, acquire new life
avizor [aβi'θor] *adj*: **estar ojo ~** to be on the alert
avizorar [aβiθo'rar] *vt* to spy on
axila [ak'sila] *nf* armpit
axioma [ak'sjoma] *nm* axiom
ay [ai] *excl* (*dolor*) ow!, ouch!; (*aflicción*) oh!, oh dear!; **¡ay de mí!** poor me!
aya ['aja] *nf* governess; (*niñera*) nanny
ayer [a'jer] *adv, nm* yesterday; **antes de ~** the day before yesterday; **~ por la tarde** yesterday afternoon/evening
aymara, aymará [ai'mara] [aima'ra] *adj, nm/f* Aymara
ayo ['ajo] *nm* tutor
ayote [a'jote] *nm* (*Am*) pumpkin
Ayto. *abr* = **Ayuntamiento**
ayuda [a'juða] *nf* help, assistance; (*Med*) enema ■ *nm* page; **~ humanitaria** humanitarian aid
ayudante, -a [aju'ðante, a] *nm/f* assistant, helper; (*Escol*) assistant; (*Mil*) adjutant
ayudar [aju'ðar] *vt* to help, assist
ayunar [aju'nar] *vi* to fast
ayunas [a'junas] *nfpl*: **estar en ~** (*no haber comido*) to be fasting; (*ignorar*) to be in the dark
ayuno [a'juno] *nm* fasting
ayuntamiento [ajunta'mjento] *nm* (*consejo*) town/city council; (*edificio*) town/city hall; (*cópula*) sexual intercourse
azabache [aθa'βatʃe] *nm* jet
azada [a'θaða] *nf* hoe
azafata [aθa'fata] *nf* air hostess (*Brit*) *o* stewardess
azafate [asa'fate] *nm* (*Am*) tray
azafrán [aθa'fran] *nm* saffron
azahar [aθa'ar] *nm* orange/lemon blossom
azalea [aθa'lea] *nf* azalea
azar [a'θar] *nm* (*casualidad*) chance, fate; (*desgracia*) misfortune, accident; **por ~** by chance; **al ~** at random
azaroso, -a [aθa'roso, a] *adj* (*arriesgado*) risky; (*vida*) eventful
Azerbaiyán [aθerba'jan] *nm* Azerbaijan
azerbaiyano, -a [aθerba'jano, a], **azerí** [aθe'ri] *adj, nm/f* Azerbaijani, Azeri
azogue [a'θoɣe] *nm* mercury
azor [a'θor] *nm* goshawk
azoramiento [aθora'mjento] *nm* alarm; (*confusión*) confusion
azorar [aθo'rar] *vt* to alarm; **azorarse** *vr* to get alarmed

Azores [a'θores] *nfpl*: **las (Islas)** ~ the Azores
azotaina [aθo'taina] *nf* beating
azotar [aθo'tar] *vt* to whip, beat; (*pegar*) to spank
azote [a'θote] *nm* (*látigo*) whip; (*latigazo*) lash, stroke; (*en las nalgas*) spank; (*calamidad*) calamity
azotea [aθo'tea] *nf* (flat) roof
azteca [aθ'teka] *adj, nm/f* Aztec
azúcar [a'θukar] *nm* sugar
azucarado, -a [aθuka'raðo, a] *adj* sugary, sweet
azucarero, -a [aθuka'rero, a] *adj* sugar *cpd* ■ *nm* sugar bowl
azuce *etc* [a'θuθe] *vb ver* **azuzar**
azucena [aθu'θena] *nf* white lily
azufre [a'θufre] *nm* sulphur
azul [a'θul] *adj, nm* blue; **~ celeste/marino** sky/navy blue
azulejo [aθu'lexo] *nm* tile
azulgrana [aθul'ɣrana] *adj inv* of Barcelona Football Club ■ *nm*: **los A~** the Barcelona F.C. players *o* team
azuzar [aθu'θar] *vt* to incite, egg on

Bb

B, b *(Esp)* [be] *(Am)* [be'laɾɣa] *nf (letra)* B, b; **B de Barcelona** B for Benjamin *(Brit)* *o* Baker *(US)*
baba ['baβa] *nf* spittle, saliva; **se le caía la ~** *(fig)* he was thrilled to bits
babear [baβe'ar] *vi (echar saliva)* to slobber; *(niño)* to dribble; *(fig)* to drool, slaver
babel [ba'βel] *nm o f* bedlam
babero [ba'βero] *nm* bib
Babia ['baβja] *nf*: **estar en ~** to be daydreaming
bable ['baβle] *nm* Asturian (dialect)
babor [ba'βor] *nm* port (side); **a ~** to port
babosada [baβo'saða] *nf*: **decir babosadas** *(Am fam)* to talk rubbish
baboso, -a [ba'βoso, a] *adj* slobbering; *(Zool)* slimy; *(Am)* silly ■ *nm/f (Am)* fool
babucha [ba'βutʃa] *nf* slipper
baca ['baka] *nf (Auto)* luggage *o* roof rack
bacalao [baka'lao] *nm* cod(fish)
bacanal [baka'nal] *nf* orgy
bache ['batʃe] *nm* pothole, rut; *(fig)* bad patch
bachillerato [batʃiʎe'rato] *nm two-year secondary school course*; *ver tb* **sistema educativo**
bacilo [ba'θilo] *nm* bacillus, germ
bacinica [baθi'nika] *nf*, **bacinilla** [baθi'niʎa] *nf* chamber pot
bacteria [bak'terja] *nf* bacterium, germ
bacteriológico, -a [bakterjo'loxico, a] *adj* bacteriological; **guerra bacteriológica** germ warfare
báculo ['bakulo] *nm* stick, staff; *(fig)* support
badajo [ba'ðaxo] *nm* clapper *(of a bell)*
bádminton ['baðminton] *nm* badminton
bafle ['bafle], **baffle** ['baffle] *nm (Elec)* speaker
bagaje [ba'ɣaxe] *nm* baggage; *(fig)* background
bagatela [baɣa'tela] *nf* trinket, trifle
Bahama [ba'ama]: **las (Islas) ~, las Bahamas** *nfpl* the Bahamas
bahía [ba'ia] *nf* bay
bailar [bai'lar] *vt, vi* to dance
bailarín, -ina [baila'rin, ina] *nm/f* dancer; *(de ballet)* ballet dancer
baile ['baile] *nm* dance; *(formal)* ball
baja ['baxa] *nf* drop, fall; *(Econ)* slump; *(Mil)* casualty; *(paro)* redundancy; **dar de ~** *(soldado)* to discharge; *(empleado)* to dismiss, sack; **darse de ~** *(retirarse)* to drop out; *(Med)* to go sick; *(dimitir)* to resign; **estar de ~** *(enfermo)* to be off sick; *(Bolsa)* to be dropping *o* falling; **jugar a la ~** *(Econ)* to speculate on a fall in prices; *ver tb* **bajo**
bajada [ba'xaða] *nf* descent; *(camino)* slope; *(de aguas)* ebb
bajamar [baxa'mar] *nf* low tide
bajar [ba'xar] *vi* to go *o* come down; *(temperatura, precios)* to drop, fall ■ *vt (cabeza)* to bow; *(escalera)* to go *o* come down; *(radio etc)* to turn down; *(precio, voz)* to lower; *(llevar abajo)* to take down; **bajarse** *vr (de vehículo)* to get out; *(de autobús)* to get off; **~ de** *(coche)* to get out of; *(autobús)* to get off; **bajarle los humos a algn** *(fig)* to cut sb down to size; **bajarse algo de Internet** to download sth from the Internet
bajeza [ba'xeθa] *nf* baseness; *(una bajeza)* vile deed
bajío [ba'xio] *nm* shoal, sandbank; *(Am)* lowlands *pl*
bajista [ba'xista] *nm/f (Mus)* bassist ■ *adj (Bolsa)* bear *cpd*
bajo, -a ['baxo, a] *adj (terreno)* low(-lying); *(mueble, número, precio)* low; *(piso)* ground *cpd*; *(de estatura)* small, short; *(color)* pale; *(sonido)* faint, soft, low; *(voz, tono)* deep; *(metal)* base ■ *adv (hablar)* softly, quietly; *(volar)* low ■ *prep* under, below, underneath ■ *nm (Mus)* bass; **hablar en voz baja** to whisper; **~ la lluvia** in the rain
bajón [ba'xon] *nm* fall, drop
bajura [ba'xura] *nf*: **pesca de ~** coastal fishing
bakalao [baka'lao] *nm (Mus)* rave music
bala ['bala] *nf* bullet; **~ de goma** plastic bullet

balacera [bala'sera] *nf* (*Am*) shoot-out
balada [ba'laða] *nf* ballad
baladí [bala'ði] *adj* trivial
baladronada [balaðro'naða] *nf* (*dicho*) boast, brag; (*hecho*) piece of bravado
balance [ba'lanθe] *nm* (*Com*) balance; (: *libro*) balance sheet; (: *cuenta general*) stocktaking; **~ de comprobación** trial balance; **~ consolidado** consolidated balance sheet; **hacer ~** to take stock
balancear [balanθe'ar] *vt* to balance ■ *vi*, **balancearse** *vr* to swing (to and fro); (*vacilar*) to hesitate
balanceo [balan'θeo] *nm* swinging
balandro [ba'landro] *nm* yacht
balanza [ba'lanθa] *nf* scales *pl*, balance; **~ comercial** balance of trade; **~ de pagos/de poder(es)** balance of payments/of power; (*Astro*): **B~** Libra
balar [ba'lar] *vi* to bleat
balaustrada [balaus'traða] *nf* balustrade; (*pasamanos*) banister
balazo [ba'laθo] *nm* (*tiro*) shot; (*herida*) bullet wound
balboa [bal'βoa] *nf Panamanian currency unit*
balbucear [balβuθe'ar] *vi, vt* to stammer, stutter
balbuceo [balβu'θeo] *nm* stammering, stuttering
balbucir [balβu'θir] *vi, vt* to stammer, stutter
balbuzca *etc* [bal'βuθka] *vb ver* **balbucir**
Balcanes [bal'kanes] *nmpl*: **los (Montes) ~** the Balkans, the Balkan Mountains; **la Península de los ~** the Balkan Peninsula
balcánico, -a [bal'kaniko, a] *adj* Balkan
balcón [bal'kon] *nm* balcony
balda ['balda] *nf* (*estante*) shelf
baldar [bal'dar] *vt* to cripple; (*agotar*) to exhaust
balde ['balde] *nm* (*esp Am*) bucket, pail; **de ~** *adv* (for) free, for nothing; **en ~** *adv* in vain
baldío, -a [bal'dio, a] *adj* uncultivated; (*terreno*) waste; (*inútil*) vain ■ *nm* wasteland
baldosa [bal'dosa] *nf* (*azulejo*) floor tile; (*grande*) flagstone
baldosín [baldo'sin] *nm* wall tile
balear [bale'ar] *adj* Balearic, of the Balearic Islands ■ *nm/f* native *o* inhabitant of the Balearic Islands ■ *vt* (*Am*) to shoot (at)
Baleares [bale'ares] *nfpl*: **las (Islas) ~** the Balearics, the Balearic Islands
balido [ba'liðo] *nm* bleat, bleating
balín [ba'lin] *nm* pellet; **balines** *nmpl* buckshot *sg*
balística [ba'listika] *nf* ballistics *pl*
baliza [ba'liθa] *nf* (*Aviat*) beacon; (*Naut*) buoy
ballena [ba'ʎena] *nf* whale
ballenero, -a [baʎe'nero, a] *adj*: **industria ballenera** whaling industry ■ *nm* (*pescador*) whaler; (*barco*) whaling ship
ballesta [ba'ʎesta] *nf* crossbow; (*Auto*) spring
ballet (*pl* **ballets**) [ba'le] [ba'les] *nm* ballet
balneario, -a [balne'arjo, a] *adj*: **estación balnearia** (bathing) resort ■ *nm* spa, health resort
balompié [balom'pje] *nm* football
balón [ba'lon] *nm* ball
baloncesto [balon'θesto] *nm* basketball
balonmano [balon'mano] *nm* handball
balonvolea [balombo'lea] *nm* volleyball
balsa ['balsa] *nf* raft; (*Bot*) balsa wood
bálsamo ['balsamo] *nm* balsam, balm
balsón [bal'son] *nm* (*Am*) swamp, bog
báltico, -a ['baltiko, a] *adj* Baltic; **el (Mar) B~** the Baltic (Sea)
baluarte [ba'lwarte] *nm* bastion, bulwark
bambolearse [bambole'arse] *vr* to swing, sway; (*silla*) to wobble
bamboleo [bambo'leo] *nm* swinging, swaying; wobbling
bambú [bam'bu] *nm* bamboo
banal [ba'nal] *adj* banal, trivial
banana [ba'nana] *nf* (*Am*) banana
bananal [bana'nal] *nm* (*Am*) banana plantation
banano [ba'nano] *nm* (*Am*) banana tree
banasta [ba'nasta] *nf* large basket, hamper
banca ['banka] *nf* (*asiento*) bench; (*Com*) banking
bancario, -a [ban'karjo, a] *adj* banking *cpd*, bank *cpd*; **giro ~** bank draft
bancarrota [banka'rrota] *nf* bankruptcy; **declararse en** *o* **hacer ~** to go bankrupt
banco ['banko] *nm* bench; (*Escol*) desk; (*Com*) bank; (*Geo*) stratum; **~ comercial** *o* **mercantil** commercial bank; **~ por acciones** joint-stock bank; **~ de crédito/de ahorros** credit/savings bank; **~ de arena** sandbank; **~ de datos** (*Inform*) data bank; **~ de hielo** iceberg
banda ['banda] *nf* band; (*cinta*) ribbon; (*pandilla*) gang; (*Mus*) brass band; (*Naut*) side, edge; **la ~ ancha** broadband; **la B~ Oriental** Uruguay; **~ sonora** soundtrack; **~ transportadora** conveyor belt
bandada [ban'daða] *nf* (*de pájaros*) flock; (*de peces*) shoal
bandazo [ban'daθo] *nm*: **dar bandazos** (*coche*) to veer from side to side
bandeja [ban'dexa] *nf* tray; **~ de entrada/salida** in-tray/out-tray
bandera [ban'dera] *nf* (*de tela*) flag; (*estandarte*) banner; **izar la ~** to hoist the flag

banderilla [bande'riʎa] *nf* banderilla; *(tapa) savoury appetizer (served on a cocktail stick)*
banderín [bande'rin] *nm* pennant, small flag
banderola [bande'rola] *nf (Mil)* pennant
bandido [ban'diðo] *nm* bandit
bando ['bando] *nm (edicto)* edict, proclamation; *(facción)* faction; **pasar al otro ~** to change sides; **los bandos** *(Rel)* the banns
bandolera [bando'lera] *nf*: **bolsa de ~** shoulder bag
bandolero [bando'lero] *nm* bandit, brigand
bandoneón [bandone'on] *nm (Am)* large accordion
banquero [ban'kero] *nm* banker
banqueta [ban'keta] *nf* stool; *(Am: acera)* pavement *(Brit)*, sidewalk *(US)*
banquete [ban'kete] *nm* banquet; *(para convidados)* formal dinner; **~ de boda** wedding breakfast
banquillo [ban'kiʎo] *nm (Jur)* dock, prisoner's bench; *(banco)* bench; *(para los pies)* footstool
bañadera [baɲa'ðera] *nf (Am)* bath(tub)
bañado [ba'ɲaðo] *nm (Am)* swamp
bañador [baɲa'ðor] *nm* swimming costume *(Brit)*, bathing suit *(US)*
bañar [ba'ɲar] *vt (niño)* to bath, bathe; *(objeto)* to dip; *(de barniz)* to coat; **bañarse** *vr (en el mar)* to bathe, swim; *(en la bañera)* to have a bath
bañero, -a [ba'ɲero, a] *nm/f* lifeguard ▪ *nf* bath(tub)
bañista [ba'ɲista] *nm/f* bather
baño ['baɲo] *nm (en bañera)* bath; *(en río, mar)* dip, swim; *(cuarto)* bathroom; *(bañera)* bath(tub); *(capa)* coating; **ir a tomar los baños** to take the waters
baptista [bap'tista] *nm/f* Baptist
baqueano, -a, baquiano, -a [bake'ano, a] [baki'ano, a] *nm/f (Am)* guide
baqueta [ba'keta] *nf (Mus)* drumstick
bar [bar] *nm* bar
barahúnda [bara'unda] *nf* uproar, hubbub
baraja [ba'raxa] *nf* pack (of cards); *see note*

BARAJA ESPAÑOLA

The *baraja española* is the traditional Spanish deck of cards and differs from a standard poker deck. The four *palos* (suits) are *oros* (golden coins), *copas* (goblets), *espadas* (swords), and *bastos* ("clubs", but not like the clubs in a poker pack). Every suit has 9 numbered cards, although for certain games only 7 are used, and 3 face cards: *sota* (Jack), *caballo* (queen) and *rey* (king).

barajar [bara'xar] *vt (naipes)* to shuffle; *(fig)* to jumble up
baranda [ba'randa], **barandilla** [baran'diʎa] *nf* rail, railing
baratija [bara'tixa] *nf* trinket; *(fig)* trifle; **baratijas** *nfpl (Com)* cheap goods
baratillo [bara'tiʎo] *nm (tienda)* junk shop; *(subasta)* bargain sale; *(conjunto de cosas)* second-hand goods *pl*
barato, -a [ba'rato, a] *adj* cheap ▪ *adv* cheap, cheaply
baratura [bara'tura] *nf* cheapness
baraúnda [bara'unda] *nf* = **barahúnda**
barba ['barβa] *nf (mentón)* chin; *(pelo)* beard; **tener ~** to be unshaven; **hacer algo en las barbas de algn** to do sth under sb's very nose; **reírse en las barbas de algn** to laugh in sb's face
barbacoa [barβa'koa] *nf (parrilla)* barbecue; *(carne)* barbecued meat
barbaridad [barβari'ðað] *nf* barbarity; *(acto)* barbarism; *(atrocidad)* outrage; **una ~ de** *(fam)* loads of; **¡qué ~!** *(fam)* how awful!; **cuesta una ~** *(fam)* it costs a fortune
barbarie [bar'βarje] *nf*, **barbarismo** [barβa'rismo] *nm* barbarism; *(crueldad)* barbarity
bárbaro, -a ['barβaro, a] *adj* barbarous, cruel; *(grosero)* rough, uncouth ▪ *nm/f* barbarian ▪ *adv*: **lo pasamos ~** *(fam)* we had a great time; **¡qué ~!** *(fam)* how marvellous!; **un éxito ~** *(fam)* a terrific success; **es un tipo ~** *(fam)* he's a great bloke
barbecho [bar'βetʃo] *nm* fallow land
barbero [bar'βero] *nm* barber, hairdresser
barbilampiño [barβilam'piɲo] *adj* smooth-faced; *(fig)* inexperienced
barbilla [bar'βiʎa] *nf* chin, tip of the chin
barbitúrico [barβi'turiko] *nm* barbiturate
barbo ['barβo] *nm*: **~ de mar** red mullet
barbotar [barβo'tar], **barbotear** [barβote'ar] *vt, vi* to mutter, mumble
barbudo, -a [bar'βuðo, a] *adj* bearded
barbullar [barβu'ʎar] *vi* to jabber away
barca ['barka] *nf* (small) boat; **~ pesquera** fishing boat; **~ de pasaje** ferry
barcaza [bar'kaθa] *nf* barge; **~ de desembarco** landing craft
Barcelona [barθe'lona] *nf* Barcelona
barcelonés, -esa [barθelo'nes, esa] *adj* of *o* from Barcelona ▪ *nm/f* native *o* inhabitant of Barcelona
barco ['barko] *nm* boat; *(buque)* ship; *(Com etc)* vessel; **~ de carga** cargo boat; **~ de guerra** warship; **~ de vela** sailing ship; **ir en ~** to go by boat
baremo [ba'remo] *nm* scale; *(tabla de cuentas)*

ready reckoner
barítono [ba'ritono] *nm* baritone
barman ['barman] *nm* barman
Barna *abr* = **Barcelona**
barnice *etc* [bar'niθe] *vb ver* **barnizar**
barniz [bar'niθ] *nm* varnish; (*en la loza*) glaze; (*fig*) veneer
barnizar [barni'θar] *vt* to varnish; (*loza*) to glaze
barómetro [ba'rometro] *nm* barometer
barón [ba'ron] *nm* baron
baronesa [baro'nesa] *nf* baroness
barquero [bar'kero] *nm* boatman
barquilla [bar'kiʎa] *nf* (*Naut*) log
barquillo [bar'kiʎo] *nm* cone, cornet
barra ['barra] *nf* bar, rod; (*Jur*) rail; (: *banquillo*) dock; (*de un bar, café*) bar; (*de pan*) French loaf; (*palanca*) lever; **~ de carmín** *o* **de labios** lipstick; **~ de herramientas** (*Inform*) toolbar; **~ de espaciado** (*Inform*) space bar; **~ inversa** backslash; **~ libre** free bar; **no pararse en barras** to stick *o* stop at nothing
barrabasada [barraβa'saða] *nf* (piece of) mischief
barraca [ba'rraka] *nf* hut, cabin; (*en Valencia*) thatched farmhouse; (*en feria*) booth
barracón [barra'kon] *nm* (*caseta*) big hut
barragana [barra'ɣana] *nf* concubine
barranca [ba'rranka] *nf* ravine, gully
barranco [ba'rranko] *nm* ravine; (*fig*) difficulty
barrena [ba'rrena] *nf* drill
barrenar [barre'nar] *vt* to drill (through), bore
barrendero, -a [barren'dero, a] *nm/f* street-sweeper
barreno [ba'rreno] *nm* large drill
barreño [ba'rreɲo] *nm* washing-up bowl
barrer [ba'rrer] *vt* to sweep; (*quitar*) to sweep away; (*Mil: Naut*) to sweep, rake (with gunfire) ▪ *vi* to sweep up
barrera [ba'rrera] *nf* barrier; (*Mil*) barricade; (*Ferro*) crossing gate; **poner barreras a** to hinder; **~ arancelaria** (*Com*) tariff barrier; **~ comercial** (*Com*) trade barrier
barriada [ba'rrjaða] *nf* quarter, district
barricada [barri'kaða] *nf* barricade
barrida [ba'rriða] *nf*, **barrido** [ba'rriðo] *nm* sweep, sweeping
barriga [ba'rriɣa] *nf* belly; (*panza*) paunch; (*vientre*) guts *pl*; **echar ~** to get middle-age spread
barrigón, -ona [barri'ɣon, ona], **barrigudo, -a** [barri'ɣuðo, a] *adj* potbellied
barril [ba'rril] *nm* barrel, cask; **cerveza de ~** draught beer
barrio ['barrjo] *nm* (*vecindad*) area, neighborhood (*US*); (*en las afueras*) suburb; **barrios bajos** poor quarter *sg*; **~ chino** red-light district
barriobajero, -a [barrjobβa'xero, a] *adj* (*vulgar*) common
barro ['barro] *nm* (*lodo*) mud; (*objetos*) earthenware; (*Med*) pimple
barroco, -a [ba'rroko, a] *adj* Baroque; (*fig*) elaborate ▪ *nm* Baroque
barrote [ba'rrote] *nm* (*de ventana etc*) bar
barruntar [barrun'tar] *vt* (*conjeturar*) to guess; (*presentir*) to suspect
barrunto [ba'rrunto] *nm* guess; suspicion
bartola [bar'tola]: **a la ~** *adv*: **tirarse a la ~** to take it easy, be lazy
bártulos ['bartulos] *nmpl* things, belongings
barullo [ba'ruʎo] *nm* row, uproar
basa ['basa] *nf* (*Arq*) base
basamento [basa'mento] *nm* base, plinth
basar [ba'sar] *vt* to base; **basarse** *vr*: **basarse en** to be based on
basca ['baska] *nf* nausea
báscula ['baskula] *nf* (platform) scales *pl*
base ['base] *nf* base; **a ~ de** on the basis of, based on; (*mediante*) by means of; **a ~ de bien** in abundance; **~ de conocimiento** knowledge base; **~ de datos** database
básico, -a ['basiko, a] *adj* basic
Basilea [basi'lea] *nf* Basle
basílica [ba'silika] *nf* basilica
basilisco [basi'lisco] *nm* (*Am*) iguana; **estar hecho un ~** to be hopping mad
basket, básquet ['basket] *nm* basketball

PALABRA CLAVE

bastante [bas'tante] *adj* **1** (*suficiente*) enough; **bastante dinero** enough *o* sufficient money; **bastantes libros** enough books
2 (*valor intensivo*): **bastante gente** quite a lot of people; **tener bastante calor** to be rather hot; **hace bastante tiempo que ocurrió** it happened quite *o* rather a long time ago
▪ *adv*: **bastante bueno/malo** quite good/ rather bad; **bastante rico** pretty rich; **(lo) bastante inteligente (como) para hacer algo** clever enough *o* sufficiently clever to do sth; **voy a tardar bastante** I'm going to be a while *o* quite some time

bastar [bas'tar] *vi* to be enough *o* sufficient; **bastarse** *vr* to be self-sufficient; **~ para** to be enough to; **¡basta!** (that's) enough!
bastardilla [bastar'ðiʎa] *nf* italics *pl*
bastardo, -a [bas'tarðo, a] *adj, nm/f* bastard
bastidor [basti'ðor] *nm* frame; (*de coche*) chassis; (*Arte*) stretcher; (*Teat*) wing; **entre**

bastidores behind the scenes
basto, -a ['basto, a] *adj* coarse, rough ■ *nmpl*: **bastos** (*Naipes*) *one of the suits in the Spanish card deck*; *ver tb* **baraja española**
bastón [bas'ton] *nm* stick, staff; (*para pasear*) walking stick; **~ de mando** baton
bastonazo [basto'naθo] *nm* blow with a stick
bastoncillo [baston'θiʎo] *nm* (*tb*: **bastoncillo de algodón**) cotton bud
basura [ba'sura] *nf* rubbish, refuse (*Brit*), garbage (*US*) ■ *adj*: **comida/televisión ~** junk food/TV
basurero [basu'rero] *nm* (*hombre*) dustman (*Brit*), garbage collector *o* man (*US*); (*lugar*) rubbish dump; (*cubo*) (rubbish) bin (*Brit*), trash can (*US*)
bata ['bata] *nf* (*gen*) dressing gown; (*cubretodo*) smock, overall; (*Med: Tec etc*) lab(oratory) coat
batacazo [bata'kaθo] *nm* bump
batalla [ba'taʎa] *nf* battle; **de ~** for everyday use
batallar [bata'ʎar] *vi* to fight
batallón [bata'ʎon] *nm* battalion
batata [ba'tata] *nf* (*Am: Culin*) sweet potato
bate ['bate] *nm* (*Deporte*) bat
batea [ba'tea] *nf* (*Am*) washing trough
bateador [batea'ðor] *nm* (*Deporte*) batter, batsman
batería [bate'ria] *nf* battery; (*Mus*) drums *pl*; (*Teat*) footlights *pl*; **~ de cocina** kitchen utensils *pl*
batiburrillo [batiβu'rriʎo] *nm* hotchpotch
batido, -a [ba'tiðo, a] *adj* (*camino*) beaten, well-trodden ■ *nm* (*Culin*) batter; **~ (de leche)** milk shake ■ *nf* (*Am*) (police) raid
batidora [bati'ðora] *nf* beater, mixer; **~ eléctrica** food mixer, blender
batir [ba'tir] *vt* to beat, strike; (*vencer*) to beat, defeat; (*revolver*) to beat, mix; (*pelo*) to back-comb; **batirse** *vr* to fight; **~ palmas** to clap, applaud
baturro, -a [ba'turro, a] *nm/f* Aragonese peasant
batuta [ba'tuta] *nf* baton; **llevar la ~** (*fig*) to be the boss
baudio ['bauðjo] *nm* (*Inform*) baud
baúl [ba'ul] *nm* trunk; (*Am Auto*) boot (*Brit*), trunk (*US*)
bautice *etc* [bau'tiθe] *vb ver* **bautizar**
bautismo [bau'tismo] *nm* baptism, christening
bautista [bau'tista] *adj, nm/f* Baptist
bautizar [bauti'θar] *vt* to baptize, christen; (*fam: diluir*) to water down; (*dar apodo*) to dub
bautizo [bau'tiθo] *nm* baptism, christening
bávaro, -a ['baβaro, a] *adj, nm/f* Bavarian
Baviera [ba'βjera] *nf* Bavaria
baya ['baja] *nf* berry; *ver tb* **bayo**
bayeta [ba'jeta] *nf* (*trapo*) floor cloth; (*Am: pañal*) nappy (*Brit*), diaper (*US*)
bayo, -a ['bajo, a] *adj* bay
bayoneta [bajo'neta] *nf* bayonet
baza ['baθa] *nf* trick; **meter ~** to butt in
bazar [ba'θar] *nm* bazaar
bazo ['baθo] *nm* spleen
bazofia [ba'θofja] *nf* pigswill (*Brit*), hogwash (*US*); (*libro etc*) trash
BCE *nm abr* (= *Banco Central Europeo*) ECB
beatificar [beatifi'kar] *vt* to beatify
beato, -a [be'ato, a] *adj* blessed; (*piadoso*) pious
bebe (*Am*) (*pl* **bebes**) ['beβe, 'beβes], **bebé** (*pl* **bebés**) [be'βe, be'βes] *nm* baby; **~ de diseño** designer baby
bebedero, -a [beβe'ðero, a] *nm* (*para animales*) drinking trough
bebedizo, -a [beβe'ðiθo, a] *adj* drinkable ■ *nm* potion
bebedor, a [beβe'ðor, a] *adj* hard-drinking
bebé-probeta [be'βe-pro'βeta] (*pl* **bebés-probeta**) *nm/f* test-tube baby
beber [be'βer] *vt, vi* to drink; **~ a sorbos/tragos** to sip/gulp; **se lo bebió todo** he drank it all up
bebido, -a [be'βiðo, a] *adj* drunk ■ *nf* drink
beca ['beka] *nf* grant, scholarship
becado, -a [be'kaðo, a] *nm/f*, **becario, a** [be'karjo, a] *nm/f* scholarship holder
becerro [be'θerro] *nm* yearling calf
bechamel [betʃa'mel] *nf* = **besamel**
becuadro [be'kwaðro] *nm* (*Mus*) natural sign
bedel [be'ðel] *nm* porter, janitor
beduino, -a [be'ðwino, a] *adj, nm/f* Bedouin
befarse [be'farse] *vr*: **~ de algo** to scoff at sth
beige ['beix], **beis** ['beis] *adj, nm* beige
béisbol ['beisβol] *nm* baseball
bejuco [be'juko] *nm* (*Am*) reed, liana
beldad [bel'dað] *nf* beauty
Belén [be'len] *nm* Bethlehem; **belén** (*de Navidad*) nativity scene, crib
belga ['belɣa] *adj, nm/f* Belgian
Bélgica ['belxika] *nf* Belgium
Belgrado [bel'ɣraðo] *nm* Belgrade
Belice [be'liθe] *nm* Belize
bélico, -a ['beliko, a] *adj* (*actitud*) warlike
belicoso, -a [beli'koso, a] *adj* (*guerrero*) warlike; (*agresivo*) aggressive, bellicose
beligerante [belixe'rante] *adj* belligerent
bellaco, -a [be'ʎako, a] *adj* sly, cunning ■ *nm* villain, rogue
belladona [beʎa'ðona] *nf* deadly nightshade
bellaquería [beʎake'ria] *nf* (*acción*) dirty trick; (*calidad*) wickedness
belleza [be'ʎeθa] *nf* beauty

bello, -a ['beʎo, a] *adj* beautiful, lovely; **Bellas Artes** Fine Art *sg*
bellota [be'ʎota] *nf* acorn
bemol [be'mol] *nm* (*Mus*) flat; **esto tiene bemoles** (*fam*) this is a tough one
bencina [ben'sina] *nf* (*Am*) petrol (*Brit*), gas (*US*)
bendecir [bende'θir] *vt* to bless; **~ la mesa** to say grace
bendición [bendi'θjon] *nf* blessing
bendiga *etc* [ben'diɣa], **bendije** *etc* [ben'dixe] *vb ver* **bendecir**
bendito, -a [ben'dito, a] *pp de* **bendecir** ■ *adj* (*santo*) blessed; (*agua*) holy; (*afortunado*) lucky; (*feliz*) happy; (*sencillo*) simple ■ *nm/f* simple soul; **¡~ sea Dios!** thank goodness!; **es un ~** he's sweet; **dormir como un ~** to sleep like a log
benedictino, -a [beneðik'tino, a] *adj, nm* Benedictine
benefactor, a [benefak'tor, a] *nm/f* benefactor/benefactress
beneficencia [benefi'θenθja] *nf* charity
beneficiar [benefi'θjar] *vt* to benefit, be of benefit to; **beneficiarse** *vr* to benefit, profit
beneficiario, -a [benefi'θjarjo, a] *nm/f* beneficiary; (*de cheque*) payee
beneficio [bene'fiθjo] *nm* (*bien*) benefit, advantage; (*Com*) profit, gain; **a ~ de** for the benefit of; **en ~ propio** to one's own advantage; **~ bruto/neto** gross/net profit; **~ por acción** earnings *pl* per share
beneficioso, -a [benefi'θjoso, a] *adj* beneficial
benéfico, -a [be'nefiko, a] *adj* charitable; **sociedad benéfica** charity (organization)
benemérito, -a [bene'merito, a] *adj* meritorious ■ *nf*: **la Benemérita** (*Esp*) the Civil Guard; *ver tb* **Guardia Civil**
beneplácito [bene'plaθito] *nm* approval, consent
benevolencia [beneβo'lenθja] *nf* benevolence, kindness
benévolo, -a [be'neβolo, a] *adj* benevolent, kind
Bengala [ben'gala] *nf* Bengal; **el Golfo de ~** the Bay of Bengal
bengala [ben'gala] *nf* (*Mil*) flare; (*fuego*) Bengal light; (*materia*) rattan
bengalí [benga'li] *adj, nm/f* Bengali
benignidad [beniɣni'ðað] *nf* (*afabilidad*) kindness; (*suavidad*) mildness
benigno, -a [be'niɣno, a] *adj* kind; (*suave*) mild; (*Med: tumor*) benign, non-malignant
benjamín [benxa'min] *nm* youngest child
beodo, -a [be'oðo, a] *adj* drunk ■ *nm/f* drunkard
berberecho [berβe'retʃo] *nm* cockle
berenjena [beren'xena] *nf* aubergine (*Brit*), eggplant (*US*)
berenjenal [berenxe'nal] *nm* (*Agr*) aubergine bed; (*fig*) mess; **en buen ~ nos hemos metido** we've got ourselves into a fine mess
bergantín [berɣan'tin] *nm* brig(antine)
Berlín [ber'lin] *nm* Berlin
berlinés, -esa [berli'nes, esa] *adj* of o from Berlin ■ *nm/f* Berliner
bermejo, -a [ber'mexo, a] *adj* red
bermellón [berme'ʎon] *nm* vermilion
bermudas [ber'muðas] *nfpl* Bermuda shorts
berrear [berre'ar] *vi* to bellow, low
berrido [be'rriðo] *nm* bellow(ing)
berrinche [be'rrintʃe] *nm* (*fam*) temper, tantrum
berro ['berro] *nm* watercress
berza ['berθa] *nf* cabbage; **~ lombarda** red cabbage
besamel [besa'mel], **besamela** [besa'mela] *nf* (*Culin*) white sauce, bechamel sauce
besar [be'sar] *vt* to kiss; (*fig: tocar*) to graze; **besarse** *vr* to kiss (one another)
beso ['beso] *nm* kiss
bestia ['bestja] *nf* beast, animal; (*fig*) idiot; **~ de carga** beast of burden; **¡~!** you idiot!; **¡no seas ~!** (*bruto*) don't be such a brute!; (*idiota*) don't be such an idiot!
bestial [bes'tjal] *adj* bestial; (*fam*) terrific
bestialidad [bestjali'ðað] *nf* bestiality; (*fam*) stupidity
besugo [be'suɣo] *nm* sea bream; (*fam*) idiot
besuguera [besu'ɣera] *nf* (*Culin*) fish pan
besuquear [besuke'ar] *vt* to cover with kisses; **besuquearse** *vr* to kiss and cuddle
bético, -a ['betiko, a] *adj* Andalusian
betún [be'tun] *nm* shoe polish; (*Química*) bitumen, asphalt
Bib. *abr* = **Biblioteca**
biberón [biβe'ron] *nm* feeding bottle
Biblia ['biβlja] *nf* Bible
bíblico, -a ['biβliko, a] *adj* biblical
bibliografía [biβljoɣra'fia] *nf* bibliography
biblioteca [biβljo'teka] *nf* library; (*estantes*) bookcase, bookshelves *pl*; **~ de consulta** reference library
bibliotecario, -a [biβljote'karjo, a] *nm/f* librarian
B.I.C. [bik] *nf abr* (= *Brigada de Investigación Criminal*) ≈ CID (*Brit*), FBI (*US*)
bicarbonato [bikarβo'nato] *nm* bicarbonate
bíceps ['biθeps] *nm inv* biceps
bicho ['bitʃo] *nm* (*animal*) small animal; (*sabandija*) bug, insect; (*Taur*) bull; **~ raro** (*fam*) queer fish
bici ['biθi] *nf* (*fam*) bike

bicicleta [biθi'kleta] *nf* bicycle, cycle; **~ estática/de montaña** exercise/mountain bike
bicoca [bi'koka] *nf* (*Esp fam*) cushy job
bidé [bi'ðe] *nm* bidet
bidireccional [biðirekθjo'nal] *adj* bidirectional
bidón [bi'ðon] *nm* (*grande*) drum; (*pequeño*) can
Bielorrusia [bjelo'rrusja] *nf* Belarus, Byelorussia
bielorruso, -a [bjelo'rruso, a] *adj, nm/f* Belarussian, Belorussian ■ *nm* (*Ling*) Belarussian, Belorussian

PALABRA CLAVE

bien [bjen] *nm* **1** (*bienestar*) good; **te lo digo por tu bien** I'm telling you for your own good; **el bien y el mal** good and evil
2 (*posesión*): **bienes** goods; **bienes de consumo/equipo** consumer/capital goods; **bienes inmuebles** *o* **raíces/bienes muebles** real estate *sg*/personal property *sg*
■ *adv* **1** (*de manera satisfactoria, correcta etc*) well; **trabaja/come bien** she works/eats well; **contestó bien** he answered correctly; **oler bien** to smell nice *o* good; **me siento bien** I feel fine; **no me siento bien** I don't feel very well; **se está bien aquí** it's nice here
2 (*frases*): **hiciste bien en llamarme** you were right to call me
3 (*valor intensivo*) very; **un cuarto bien caliente** a nice warm room; **bien de veces** lots of times; **bien se ve que ...** it's quite clear that ...
4: **estar bien**: **estoy muy bien aquí** I feel very happy here; **¿te encuentras bien?** are you all right?; **te está bien la falda** (*ser la talla*) the skirt fits you; (*sentar*) the skirt suits you; **el libro está muy bien** the book is really good; **está bien que vengan** it's all right for them to come; **¡está bien! lo haré** oh all right, I'll do it; **ya está bien de quejas** that's quite enough complaining
5 (*de buena gana*): **yo bien que iría pero ...** I'd gladly go but ...
■ *excl*: **¡bien!** (*aprobación*) OK!; **¡muy bien!** well done!; **¡qué bien!** great!; **bien, gracias, ¿y usted?** fine thanks, and you?
■ *adj inv*: **niño bien** rich kid; **gente bien** posh people
■ *conj* **1**: **bien ... bien**: **bien en coche bien en tren** either by car or by train
2: **no bien** (*esp Am*): **no bien llegue te llamaré** as soon as I arrive I'll call you
3: **si bien** even though; *ver tb* **más**

bienal [bje'nal] *adj* biennial
bienaventurado, -a [bjenaβentu'raðo, a] *adj* (*feliz*) happy; (*afortunado*) fortunate; (*Rel*) blessed
bienestar [bjenes'tar] *nm* well-being; **estado de ~** welfare state
bienhechor, a [bjene'tʃor, a] *adj* beneficent ■ *nm/f* benefactor/benefactress
bienio ['bjenjo] *nm* two-year period
bienvenido, -a [bjembe'niðo, a] *adj* welcome ■ *excl* welcome! ■ *nf* welcome; **dar la bienvenida a algn** to welcome sb
bies ['bjes] *nm*: **falda al ~** bias-cut skirt; **cortar al ~** to cut on the bias
bifásico, -a [bi'fasiko, a] *adj* (*Elec*) two-phase
bife ['bife] *nm* (*Am*) steak
bifocal [bifo'kal] *adj* bifocal
bifurcación [bifurka'θjon] *nf* fork; (*Ferro: Inform*) branch
bifurcarse [bifur'karse] *vr* to fork
bigamia [bi'ɣamja] *nf* bigamy
bígamo, -a ['biɣamo, a] *adj* bigamous ■ *nm/f* bigamist
bígaro ['biɣaro] *nm* winkle
bigote [bi'ɣote] *nm* (*tb*: **bigotes**) moustache
bigotudo, -a [biɣo'tuðo, a] *adj* with a big moustache
bigudí [biɣu'ði] *nm* (hair-)curler
bikini [bi'kini] *nm* bikini; (*Culin*) toasted cheese and ham sandwich
bilateral [bilate'ral] *adj* bilateral
bilbaíno, -a [bilβa'ino, a] *adj* of *o* from Bilbao ■ *nm/f* native *o* inhabitant of Bilbao
bilingüe [bi'lingwe] *adj* bilingual
bilis ['bilis] *nf inv* bile
billar [bi'ʎar] *nm* billiards *sg*; (*lugar*) billiard hall; (*galería de atracciones*) amusement arcade; **~ americano** pool
billete [bi'ʎete] *nm* ticket; (*de banco*) banknote (*Brit*), bill (*US*); (*carta*) note; **~ sencillo, ~ de ida solamente/~ de ida y vuelta** single (*Brit*) *o* one-way (*US*) ticket/return (*Brit*) *o* round-trip (*US*) ticket; **sacar (un) ~** to get a ticket; **un ~ de cinco libras** a five-pound note
billetera [biʎe'tera] *nf*, **billetero** [biʎe'tero] *nm* wallet
billón [bi'ʎon] *nm* billion
bimensual [bimen'swal] *adj* twice monthly
bimestral [bimes'tral] *adj* bimonthly
bimestre [bi'mestre] *nm* two-month period
bimotor [bimo'tor] *adj* twin-engined ■ *nm* twin-engined plane
binario, -a [bi'narjo, a] *adj* (*Inform*) binary
bingo ['bingo] *nm* (*juego*) bingo; (*sala*) bingo hall
binóculo [bi'nokulo] *nm* pince-nez
binomio [bi'nomjo] *nm* (*Mat*) binomial

biodegradable [bioðeɣra'ðaβle] *adj* biodegradable
biodiversidad [bioðiβersi'ðað] *nf* biodiversity
biografía [bjoɣra'fia] *nf* biography
biográfico, -a [bio'ɣrafiko, a] *adj* biographical
biógrafo, -a [bi'oɣrafo, a] *nm/f* biographer
biología [biolo'xia] *nf* biology
biológico, -a [bio'loxiko, a] *adj* biological; (*cultivo, producto*) organic; **guerra biológica** biological warfare
biólogo, -a [bi'oloɣo, a] *nm/f* biologist
biombo ['bjombo] *nm* (folding) screen
biopsia [bi'opsja] *nf* biopsy
bioquímico, -a [bio'kimiko, a] *adj* biochemical ■ *nm/f* biochemist ■ *nf* biochemistry
biosfera [bios'fera] *nf* biosphere
bioterrorismo [bioterro'rismo] *nm* bioterrorism
bióxido [bi'oksiðo] *nm* dioxide
bipartidismo [biparti'ðismo] *nm* (*Pol*) two-party system
biquini [bi'kini] *nm* = **bikini**
birlar [bir'lar] *vt* (*fam*) to pinch
birlibirloque [birliβir'loke] *nm*: **por arte de ~** (as if) by magic
Birmania [bir'manja] *nf* Burma
birmano, -a [bir'mano, a] *adj, nm/f* Burmese
birrete [bi'rrete] *nm* (*Jur*) judge's cap
birria ['birrja] *nf* (*fam*): **ser una ~** to be rubbish; **ir hecho una ~** to be *o* look a sight
bis [bis] *excl* encore! ■ *nm* encore ■ *adv* (*dos veces*) twice; **viven en el 27 ~** they live at 27a
bisabuelo, -a [bisa'βwelo, a] *nm/f* great-grandfather/mother; **bisabuelos** *nmpl* great-grandparents
bisagra [bi'saɣra] *nf* hinge
bisbisar [bisβi'sar], **bisbisear** [bisβise'ar] *vt* to mutter, mumble
bisbiseo [bisβi'seo] *nm* muttering
biselar [bise'lar] *vt* to bevel
bisexual [bisek'swal] *adj, nm/f* bisexual
bisiesto [bi'sjesto] *adj*: **año ~** leap year
bisnieto, -a [bis'njeto, a] *nm/f* great-grandson/daughter; **bisnietos** *nmpl* great-grandchildren
bisonte [bi'sonte] *nm* bison
bisoñé [biso'ɲe] *nm* toupée
bisoño, -a [bi'soɲo, a] *adj* green, inexperienced
bistec [bis'tek], **bisté** [bis'te] *nm* steak
bisturí [bistu'ri] *nm* scalpel
bisutería [bisute'ria] *nf* imitation *o* costume jewellery
bit [bit] *nm* (*Inform*) bit; **~ de parada** stop bit; **~ de paridad** parity bit
bitácora [bi'takora] *nf*: **cuaderno de ~** logbook, ship's log
bizantino, -a [biθan'tino, a] *adj* Byzantine; (*fig*) pointless
bizarría [biθa'rria] *nf* (*valor*) bravery; (*generosidad*) generosity
bizarro, -a [bi'θarro, a] *adj* brave; generous
bizco, -a ['biθko, a] *adj* cross-eyed
bizcocho [biθ'kotʃo] *nm* (*Culin*) sponge cake
biznieto, -a [biθ'nieto, a] *nm/f* = **bisnieto**
bizquear [biθke'ar] *vi* to squint
blanco, -a ['blanko, a] *adj* white ■ *nm/f* white man/woman, white ■ *nm* (*color*) white; (*en texto*) blank; (*Mil, fig*) target ■ *nf* (*Mus*) minim; **en ~** blank; **cheque en ~** blank cheque; **votar en ~** to spoil one's vote; **quedarse en ~** to be disappointed; **noche en ~** sleepless night; **ser el ~ de las burlas** to be the butt of jokes; **estar sin blanca** to be broke
blancura [blan'kura] *nf* whiteness
blandengue [blan'denge] *adj* (*fam*) soft, weak
blandir [blan'dir] *vt* to brandish
blando, -a ['blando, a] *adj* soft; (*tierno*) tender, gentle; (*carácter*) mild; (*fam*) cowardly ■ *nm/f* (*Pol etc*) soft-liner
blandura [blan'dura] *nf* softness; tenderness; mildness
blanquear [blanke'ar] *vt* to whiten; (*fachada*) to whitewash; (*paño*) to bleach; (*dinero*) to launder ■ *vi* to turn white
blanquecino, -a [blanke'θino, a] *adj* whitish
blanqueo [blan'keo] *nm* (*de pared*) whitewashing; (*de dinero*) laundering
blasfemar [blasfe'mar] *vi* to blaspheme; (*fig*) to curse
blasfemia [blas'femja] *nf* blasphemy
blasfemo, -a [blas'femo, a] *adj* blasphemous ■ *nm/f* blasphemer
blasón [bla'son] *nm* coat of arms; (*fig*) honour
blasonar [blaso'nar] *vt* to emblazon ■ *vi* to boast, brag
bledo ['bleðo] *nm*: **(no) me importa un ~** I couldn't care less
blindado, -a [blin'daðo, a] *adj* (*Mil*) armour-plated; (*antibalas*) bulletproof; **coche** *o* (*Am*) **carro ~** armoured car; **puertas blindadas** security doors
blindaje [blin'daxe] *nm* armour, armour-plating
bloc (*pl* **blocs**) [blok, blos] *nm* writing pad; (*Escol*) jotter; **~ de dibujos** sketch pad
bloque ['bloke] *nm* (*tb Inform*) block; (*Pol*) bloc; **~ de cilindros** cylinder block
bloquear [bloke'ar] *vt* (*Naut etc*) to blockade; (*aislar*) to cut off; (*Com: Econ*) to freeze; **fondos bloqueados** frozen assets

bloqueo [blo'keo] *nm* blockade; (*Com*) freezing, blocking
bluejean [blu'jin] *nm* (*Am*) jeans *pl*, denims *pl*
blusa ['blusa] *nf* blouse
B.° *abr* (*Finanzas: = banco*) bank; (*Com: = beneficiario*) beneficiary
boa ['boa] *nf* boa
boato [bo'ato] *nm* show, ostentation
bobada [bo'βaða] *nf* foolish action (*o* statement); **decir bobadas** to talk nonsense
bobalicón, -ona [boβali'kon, ona] *adj* utterly stupid
bobería [boβe'ria] *nf* = **bobada**
bobina [bo'βina] *nf* (*Tec*) bobbin; (*Foto*) spool; (*Elec*) coil, winding
bobo, -a ['boβo, a] *adj* (*tonto*) daft, silly; (*cándido*) naïve ■ *nm/f* fool, idiot ■ *nm* (*Teat*) clown, funny man
boca ['boka] *nf* mouth; (*de crustáceo*) pincer; (*de cañón*) muzzle; (*entrada*) mouth, entrance; **bocas** *nfpl* (*de río*) mouth *sg*; **~ abajo/arriba** face down/up; **a ~ jarro** point-blank; **se me hace la ~ agua** my mouth is watering; **todo salió a pedir de ~** it all turned out perfectly; **en ~ de** (*esp Am*) according to; **la cosa anda de ~ en ~** the story is going the rounds; **¡cállate la ~!** (*fam*) shut up!; **quedarse con la ~ abierta** to be dumbfounded; **no abrir la ~** to keep quiet; **~ del estómago** pit of the stomach; **~ de metro** tube (*Brit*) *o* subway (*US*) entrance
bocacalle [boka'kaʎe] *nf* side street; **la primera ~** the first turning *o* street
bocadillo [boka'ðiʎo] *nm* sandwich
bocado [bo'kaðo] *nm* mouthful, bite; (*de caballo*) bridle; **~ de Adán** Adam's apple
bocajarro [boka'xarro]: **a ~** *adv* (*Mil*) at point-blank range; **decir algo a ~** to say sth bluntly
bocanada [boka'naða] *nf* (*de vino*) mouthful, swallow; (*de aire*) gust, puff
bocata [bo'kata] *nm* (*fam*) sandwich
bocazas [bo'kaθas] *nm/f inv* (*fam*) bigmouth
boceto [bo'θeto] *nm* sketch, outline
bocha ['botʃa] *nf* bowl; **bochas** *nfpl* bowls *sg*
bochinche [bo'tʃintʃe] *nm* (*fam*) uproar
bochorno [bo'tʃorno] *nm* (*vergüenza*) embarrassment; (*calor*): **hace ~** it's very muggy
bochornoso, -a [botʃor'noso, a] *adj* muggy; embarrassing
bocina [bo'θina] *nf* (*Mus*) trumpet; (*Auto*) horn; (*para hablar*) megaphone; **tocar la ~** (*Auto*) to sound *o* blow one's horn
bocinazo [boθi'naθo] *nm* (*Auto*) toot
bocio ['boθjo] *nm* (*Med*) goitre
boda ['boða] *nf* (*tb*: **bodas**) wedding, marriage; (*fiesta*) wedding reception; **bodas de plata/de oro** silver/golden wedding *sg*
bodega [bo'ðeɣa] *nf* (*de vino*) (wine) cellar; (*bar*) bar; (*restaurante*) restaurant; (*depósito*) storeroom; (*de barco*) hold
bodegón [boðe'ɣon] *nm* (*Arte*) still life
bodrio [bo'ðrio] *nm*: **el libro es un ~** the book is awful *o* rubbish
B.O.E. ['boe] *nm abr* = **Boletín Oficial del Estado**
bofe ['bofe] *nm* (*tb*: **bofes**: *de res*) lights *pl*; **echar los bofes** to slave (away)
bofetada [bofe'taða] *nf* slap (in the face); **dar de bofetadas a algn** to punch sb
bofetón [bofe'ton] *nm* = **bofetada**
boga ['boɣa] *nf*: **en ~** in vogue
bogar [bo'ɣar] *vi* (*remar*) to row; (*navegar*) to sail
bogavante [boɣa'βante] *nm* (*Naut*) stroke, first rower; (*Zool*) lobster
Bogotá [boɣo'ta] *n* Bogota
bogotano, -a [boɣo'tano, a] *adj* of *o* from Bogota ■ *nm/f* native *o* inhabitant of Bogota
bogue *etc* ['boɣe] *vb ver* **bogar**
bohemio, -a [bo'emjo, a] *adj, nm/f* Bohemian
boicot [boi'ko(t)] (*pl* **boicots**) *nm* boycott
boicotear [boikote'ar] *vt* to boycott
boicoteo [boiko'teo] *nm* boycott
boina ['boina] *nf* beret
bola ['bola] *nf* ball; (*canica*) marble; (*Naipes*) (grand) slam; (*betún*) shoe polish; (*mentira*) tale, story; **bolas** *nfpl* (*Am*) bolas; **~ de billar** billiard ball; **~ de nieve** snowball
bolchevique [boltʃe'βike] *adj, nm/f* Bolshevik
boleadoras [bolea'ðoras] *nfpl* (*Am*) bolas *sg*
bolera [bo'lera] *nf* skittle *o* bowling alley
bolero [bo'lero] *nm* bolero
boleta [bo'leta] *nf* (*Am: permiso*) pass, permit; (*: para votar*) ballot
boletería [bolete'ria] *nf* (*Am*) ticket office
boletero, -a [bole'tero, a] *nm/f* (*Am*) ticket seller
boletín [bole'tin] *nm* bulletin; (*periódico*) journal, review; **~ escolar** (*Esp*) school report; **~ de noticias** news bulletin; **~ de pedido** application form; **~ de precios** price list; **~ de prensa** press release; *see note*

BOLETÍN

The *Boletín Oficial del Estado*, abbreviated to BOE, is the official government record of all laws and resolutions passed by *las Cortes* (Spanish Parliament). It is widely consulted, mainly because it also publishes the announcements for the *oposiciones* (public competitive examinations).

boleto [bo'leto] *nm* (*esp Am*) ticket; **~ de apuestas** betting slip
boli ['boli] *nm* Biro®
boliche [bo'litʃe] *nm* (*bola*) jack; (*juego*) bowls *sg*; (*lugar*) bowling alley; (*Am: tienda*) small grocery store
bólido ['boliðo] *nm* meteorite; (*Auto*) racing car
bolígrafo [bo'liɣrafo] *nm* ball-point pen, Biro®
bolillo [bo'liʎo] *nm* (*Costura*) bobbin (for lacemaking)
bolívar [bo'liβar] *nm monetary unit of Venezuela*
Bolivia [bo'liβja] *nf* Bolivia
boliviano, -a [boli'βjano, a] *adj, nm/f* Bolivian
bollo ['boʎo] *nm* (*de pan*) roll; (*dulce*) scone; (*chichón*) bump, lump; (*abolladura*) dent; **bollos** *nmpl* (*Am*) troubles
bolo ['bolo] *nm* skittle; (*píldora*) (large) pill; **(juego de) bolos** skittles *sg*
Bolonia [bo'lonja] *nf* Bologna
bolsa ['bolsa] *nf* (*cartera*) purse; (*saco*) bag; (*Am*) pocket; (*Anat*) cavity, sac; (*Com*) stock exchange; (*Minería*) pocket; **~ de agua caliente** hot water bottle; **~ de aire** air pocket; **~ de (la) basura** bin-liner; **~ de dormir** (*Am*) sleeping bag; **~ de papel** paper bag; **~ de plástico** plastic (*o* carrier) bag; **"B~ de la propiedad"** "Property Mart"; **~ de trabajo** employment bureau; **jugar a la ~** to play the market
bolsillo [bol'siʎo] *nm* pocket; (*cartera*) purse; **de ~** pocket *cpd*; **meterse a algn en el ~** to get sb eating out of one's hand
bolsista [bol'sista] *nm/f* stockbroker
bolso ['bolso] *nm* (*bolsa*) bag; (*de mujer*) handbag
boludo, -a [bo'luðo, a] (*Am fam!*) *adj* stupid ■ *nm/f* prat (*!*)
bomba ['bomba] *nf* (*Mil*) bomb; (*Tec*) pump; (*Am: borrachera*) drunkenness ■ *adj* (*fam*): **noticia ~** bombshell ■ *adv* (*fam*): **pasarlo ~** to have a great time; **~ atómica/de humo/de retardo** atomic/smoke/time bomb; **~ de gasolina** petrol pump; **~ de incendios** fire engine
bombacho, -a [bom'batʃo, a] *adj* baggy
bombardear [bombarðe'ar] *vt* to bombard; (*Mil*) to bomb
bombardeo [bombar'ðeo] *nm* bombardment; bombing
bombardero [bombar'ðero] *nm* bomber
bombear [bombe'ar] *vt* (*agua*) to pump (out *o* up); (*Mil*) to bomb; (*Fútbol*) to lob; **bombearse** *vr* to warp
bombero [bom'bero] *nm* fireman; **(cuerpo de) bomberos** fire brigade
bombilla [bom'biʎa] *nf* (*Esp*), **bombillo** [bom'biʎo] *nm* (*Am*) (light) bulb
bombín [bom'bin] *nm* bowler hat
bombo ['bombo] *nm* (*Mus*) bass drum; (*Tec*) drum; (*fam*) exaggerated praise; **hacer algo a ~ y platillo** to make a great song and dance about sth; **tengo la cabeza hecha un ~** I've got a splitting headache
bombón [bom'bon] *nm* chocolate; (*belleza*) gem
bombona [bom'bona] *nf*: **~ de butano** gas cylinder
bombonería [bombone'ria] *nf* sweetshop
bonachón, -ona [bona'tʃon, ona] *adj* good-natured
bonaerense [bonae'rense] *adj* of *o* from Buenos Aires ■ *nm/f* native *o* inhabitant of Buenos Aires
bonancible [bonan'θiβle] *adj* (*tiempo*) fair, calm
bonanza [bo'nanθa] *nf* (*Naut*) fair weather; (*fig*) bonanza; (*Minería*) rich pocket *o* vein
bondad [bon'dað] *nf* goodness, kindness; **tenga la ~ de** (please) be good enough to
bondadoso, -a [bonda'ðoso, a] *adj* good, kind
bongo ['bonɣo] *nm* large canoe
boniato [bo'njato] *nm* sweet potato, yam
bonificación [bonifika'θjon] *nf* (*Com*) allowance, discount; (*pago*) bonus; (*Deporte*) extra points *pl*
bonito, -a [bo'nito, a] *adj* (*lindo*) pretty; (*agradable*) nice ■ *adv* (*Am fam*) well ■ *nm* (*atún*) tuna (fish)
bono ['bono] *nm* voucher; (*Finanzas*) bond; **~ de billetes de metro** booklet of metro tickets; **~ del Tesoro** treasury bill
bonobús [bono'βus] *nm* (*Esp*) bus pass
Bono Loto, bonoloto [bono'loto] *nm o f* (*Esp*) *state-run weekly lottery; ver tb* **lotería**
boom (*pl* **booms**) [bum, bums] *nm* boom
boquear [boke'ar] *vi* to gasp
boquerón [boke'ron] *nm* (*pez*) (kind of) anchovy; (*agujero*) large hole
boquete [bo'kete] *nm* gap, hole
boquiabierto, -a [bokia'βjerto, a] *adj* open-mouthed (in astonishment); **quedar ~** to be left aghast
boquilla [bo'kiʎa] *nf* (*de riego*) nozzle; (*de cigarro*) cigarette holder; (*Mus*) mouthpiece
borbollar [borβo'ʎar], **borbollear** [borβoʎe'ar] *vi* to bubble
borbollón [borβo'ʎon] *nm* bubbling; **hablar a borbollones** to gabble; **salir a borbollones** (*agua*) to gush out
borbotar [borβo'tar] *vi* = **borbollar**
borbotón [borβo'ton] *nm*: **salir a borbotones** to gush out

borda ['borða] *nf* (*Naut*) gunwale; **echar** *o* **tirar algo por la ~** to throw sth overboard
bordado [bor'ðaðo] *nm* embroidery
bordar [bor'ðar] *vt* to embroider
borde ['borðe] *nm* edge, border; (*de camino etc*) side; (*en la costura*) hem; **al ~ de** (*fig*) on the verge *o* brink of; **ser ~** (*Esp fam*) to be a pain in the neck
bordear [borðe'ar] *vt* to border
bordillo [bor'ðiʎo] *nm* kerb (*Brit*), curb (*US*)
bordo ['borðo] *nm* (*Naut*) side; **a ~** on board
Borgoña [bor'ɣoɲa] *nf* Burgundy
borgoña [bor'ɣoɲa] *nm* burgundy
boricua [bo'rikwa], **borinqueño, -a** [borin'keɲo, a] *adj, nm/f* Puerto Rican
borla ['borla] *nf* (*gen*) tassel; (*de gorro*) pompon
borra ['borra] *nf* (*pelusa*) fluff; (*sedimento*) sediment
borrachera [borra'tʃera] *nf* (*ebriedad*) drunkenness; (*orgía*) spree, binge
borracho, -a [bo'rratʃo, a] *adj* drunk ▪ *nm/f* (*que bebe mucho*) drunkard, drunk; (*temporalmente*) drunk, drunk man/woman ▪ *nm* (*Culin*) *cake soaked in liqueur or spirit*
borrador [borra'ðor] *nm* (*escritura*) first draft, rough sketch; (*cuaderno*) scribbling pad; (*goma*) rubber (*Brit*), eraser; (*Com*) daybook; (*para pizarra*) duster; **hacer un nuevo ~ de** (*Com*) to redraft
borrar [bo'rrar] *vt* to erase, rub out; (*tachar*) to delete; (*cinta*) to wipe out; (*Inform: archivo*) to delete, erase; (*Pol etc: eliminar*) to deal with
borrasca [bo'rraska] *nf* (*Meteorología*) storm
borrascoso, -a [borras'koso, a] *adj* stormy
borrego, -a [bo'rreɣo, a] *nm/f* lamb; (*oveja*) sheep; (*fig*) simpleton
borricada [borri'kaða] *nf* foolish action/statement
borrico, -a [bo'rriko, a] *nm* donkey; (*fig*) stupid man ▪ *nf* she-donkey; (*fig*) stupid woman
borrón [bo'rron] *nm* (*mancha*) stain; **~ y cuenta nueva** let bygones be bygones
borroso, -a [bo'rroso, a] *adj* vague, unclear; (*escritura*) illegible; (*escrito*) smudgy; (*Foto*) blurred
Bósforo ['bosforo] *nm*: **el (Estrecho del) ~** the Bosp(h)orus
Bosnia ['bosnja] *nf* Bosnia
bosnio, -a ['bosnjo, a] *adj, nm/f* Bosnian
bosque ['boske] *nm* wood; (*grande*) forest
bosquejar [boske'xar] *vt* to sketch
bosquejo [bos'kexo] *nm* sketch
bosta ['bosta] *nf* dung, manure
bostece *etc* [bos'teθe] *vb ver* **bostezar**
bostezar [boste'θar] *vi* to yawn
bostezo [bos'teθo] *nm* yawn
bota ['bota] *nf* (*calzado*) boot; (*de vino*) leather wine bottle; **ponerse las botas** (*fam*) to strike it rich
botadura [bota'ðura] *nf* launching
botanas [bo'tanas] *nfpl* (*Am*) hors d'œuvres
botánico, -a [bo'taniko, a] *adj* botanical ▪ *nm/f* botanist ▪ *nf* botany
botar [bo'tar] *vt* to throw, hurl; (*Naut*) to launch; (*esp Am fam*) to throw out ▪ *vi* to bounce
botarate [bota'rate] *nm* (*imbécil*) idiot
bote ['bote] *nm* (*salto*) bounce; (*golpe*) thrust; (*vasija*) tin, can; (*embarcación*) boat; **de ~ en ~** packed, jammed full; **~ salvavidas** lifeboat; **dar un ~** to jump; **dar botes** (*Auto etc*) to bump; **~ de la basura** (*Am*) dustbin (*Brit*), trash can (*US*)
botella [bo'teʎa] *nf* bottle; **~ de vino** (*contenido*) bottle of wine; (*recipiente*) wine bottle
botellero [bote'ʎero] *nm* wine rack
botellín [bote'ʎin] *nm* small bottle
botellón [bote'ʎon] *nm* (*Esp: fam*) outdoor drinking session (*involving groups of young people*)
botica [bo'tika] *nf* chemist's (shop) (*Brit*), pharmacy
boticario, -a [boti'karjo, a] *nm/f* chemist (*Brit*), pharmacist
botijo [bo'tixo] *nm* (earthenware) jug; (*tren*) excursion train
botín [bo'tin] *nm* (*calzado*) half boot; (*polaina*) spat; (*Mil*) booty; (*de ladrón*) loot
botiquín [boti'kin] *nm* (*armario*) medicine chest; (*portátil*) first-aid kit
botón [bo'ton] *nm* button; (*Bot*) bud; (*de florete*) tip; **~ de arranque** (*Auto etc*) starter; **~ de oro** buttercup; **pulsar el ~** to press the button
botones [bo'tones] *nm inv* bellboy, bellhop (*US*)
botulismo [botu'lismo] *nm* botulism, food poisoning
bóveda ['boβeða] *nf* (*Arq*) vault
bovino, -a [bo'βino, a] *adj* bovine; (*Agr*): **ganado ~** cattle
box [boks] *nm* (*Am*) boxing
boxeador [boksea'ðor] *nm* boxer
boxear [bokse'ar] *vi* to box
boxeo [bok'seo] *nm* boxing
boya ['boja] *nf* (*Naut*) buoy; (*flotador*) float
boyante [bo'jante] *adj* (*Naut*) buoyant; (*feliz*) buoyant; (*próspero*) prosperous
bozal [bo'θal] *nm* (*de caballo*) halter; (*de perro*) muzzle
bozo ['boθo] *nm* (*pelusa*) fuzz; (*boca*) mouth
bracear [braθe'ar] *vi* (*agitar los brazos*) to wave one's arms

bracero [bra'θero] *nm* labourer; (*en el campo*) farmhand
braga ['braɣa] *nf* (*cuerda*) sling, rope; (*de bebé*) nappy, diaper (*US*); **bragas** *nfpl* (*de mujer*) panties
braguero [bra'ɣero] *nm* (*Med*) truss
bragueta [bra'ɣeta] *nf* fly (*Brit*), flies *pl* (*Brit*), zipper (*US*)
braguetazo [braɣe'taθo] *nm* marriage of convenience
braille [breil] *nm* braille
bramante [bra'mante] *nm* twine, string
bramar [bra'mar] *vi* to bellow, roar
bramido [bra'miðo] *nm* bellow, roar
branquias ['brankjas] *nfpl* gills
brasa ['brasa] *nf* live *o* hot coal; **carne a la ~** grilled meat; **dar la ~** (*col: dar la lata, molestar*) to be a pain (*col*); **dar la ~ a algn** to go on at sb (*col*); **¡deja de darme la ~!** stop going on at me! (*col*)
brasero [bra'sero] *nm* brazier; (*Am: chimenea*) fireplace
Brasil [bra'sil] *nm*: **(el) ~** Brazil
brasileño, -a [brasi'leɲo, a] *adj, nm/f* Brazilian
bravata [bra'βata] *nf* boast
braveza [bra'βeθa] *nf* (*valor*) bravery; (*ferocidad*) ferocity
bravío, -a [bra'βio, a] *adj* wild; (*feroz*) fierce
bravo, -a ['braβo, a] *adj* (*valiente*) brave; (*bueno*) fine, splendid; (*feroz*) ferocious; (*salvaje*) wild; (*mar etc*) rough, stormy; (*Culin*) hot, spicy ▪ *excl* bravo!
bravucón, -ona [braβu'kon, ona] *adj* swaggering ▪ *nm/f* braggart
bravura [bra'βura] *nf* bravery; ferocity; (*pey*) boast
braza ['braθa] *nf* fathom; **nadar a la ~** to swim (the) breast-stroke
brazada [bra'θaða] *nf* stroke
brazalete [braθa'lete] *nm* (*pulsera*) bracelet; (*banda*) armband
brazo ['braθo] *nm* arm; (*Zool*) foreleg; (*Bot*) limb, branch; **brazos** *nmpl* (*braceros*) hands, workers; **~ derecho** (*fig*) right-hand man; **a ~ partido** hand-to-hand; **cogidos** *etc* **del ~** arm in arm; **no dar su ~ a torcer** not to give way easily; **huelga de brazos caídos** sit-down strike
brea ['brea] *nf* pitch, tar
brebaje [bre'βaxe] *nm* potion
brecha ['bretʃa] *nf* breach; (*hoyo vacío*) gap, opening
brécol ['brekol] *nm* broccoli
brega ['breɣa] *nf* (*lucha*) struggle; (*trabajo*) hard work
bregar [bre'ɣar] *vi* (*luchar*) to struggle; (*trabajar mucho*) to slog away
bregue *etc* ['breɣe] *vb ver* **bregar**
breña ['breɲa] *nf* rough ground
Bretaña [bre'taɲa] *nf* Brittany
brete ['brete] *nm* (*cepo*) shackles *pl*; (*fig*) predicament; **estar en un ~** to be in a jam
breteles [bre'teles] *nmpl* (*Am*) straps
bretón, -ona [bre'ton, ona] *adj, nm/f* Breton
breva ['breβa] *nf* (*Bot*) early fig; (*puro*) flat cigar; **¡no caerá esa ~!** no such luck!
breve ['breβe] *adj* short, brief; **en ~** (*pronto*) shortly; (*en pocas palabras*) in short ▪ *nf* (*Mus*) breve
brevedad [breβe'ðað] *nf* brevity, shortness; **con** *o* **a la mayor ~** as soon as possible
breviario [bre'βjarjo] *nm* (*Rel*) breviary
brezal [bre'θal] *nm* moor(land), heath
brezo ['breθo] *nm* heather
bribón, -ona [bri'βon, ona] *adj* idle, lazy ▪ *nm/f* (*vagabundo*) vagabond; (*pícaro*) rascal, rogue
bricolaje [briko'laxe] *nm* do-it-yourself, DIY
brida ['briða] *nf* bridle, rein; (*Tec*) clamp; **a toda ~** at top speed
bridge [britʃ] *nm* (*Naipes*) bridge
brigada [bri'ɣaða] *nf* (*unidad*) brigade; (*trabajadores*) squad, gang ▪ *nm* warrant officer
brigadier [briɣa'ðjer] *nm* brigadier(-general)
brillante [bri'ʎante] *adj* brilliant; (*color*) bright; (*joya*) sparkling ▪ *nm* diamond
brillantez [briʎan'teθ] *nf* (*de color etc*) brightness; (*fig*) brilliance
brillar [bri'ʎar] *vi* (*tb fig*) to shine; (*joyas*) to sparkle; **~ por su ausencia** to be conspicuous by one's absence
brillo ['briʎo] *nm* shine; (*brillantez*) brilliance; (*fig*) splendour; **sacar ~ a** to polish
brilloso, -a [bri'ʎoso, a] *adj* (*Am*) = **brillante**
brincar [brin'kar] *vi* to skip about, hop about, jump about; **está que brinca** he's hopping mad
brinco ['brinko] *nm* jump, leap; **a brincos** by fits and starts; **de un ~** at one bound
brindar [brin'dar] *vi*: **~ a** *o* **por** to drink (a toast) to ▪ *vt* to offer, present; **le brinda la ocasión de** it offers *o* affords him the opportunity to; **brindarse** *vr*: **brindarse a hacer algo** to offer to do sth
brindis ['brindis] *nm inv* toast; (*Taur*) (ceremony of) dedication
brinque *etc* ['brinke] *vb ver* **brincar**
brío ['brio] *nm* spirit, dash
brioso, -a [bri'oso, a] *adj* spirited, dashing
brisa ['brisa] *nf* breeze
británico, -a [bri'taniko, a] *adj* British ▪ *nm/f* Briton, British person; **los británicos** the British

brizna ['briθna] *nf* *(hebra)* strand, thread; *(de hierba)* blade; *(trozo)* piece
broca ['broka] *nf* *(Costura)* bobbin; *(Tec)* drill bit; *(clavo)* tack
brocado [bro'kaðo] *nm* brocade
brocal [bro'kal] *nm* rim
brocha ['brotʃa] *nf* (large) paintbrush; **~ de afeitar** shaving brush; **pintor de ~ gorda** painter and decorator; *(fig)* poor painter
brochazo [bro'tʃaθo] *nm* brush-stroke; **a grandes brochazos** *(fig)* in general terms
broche ['brotʃe] *nm* brooch
broma ['broma] *nf* joke; *(inocentada)* practical joke; **en ~** in fun, as a joke; **gastar una ~ a algn** to play a joke on sb; **tomar algo a ~** to take sth as a joke
bromear [brome'ar] *vi* to joke
bromista [bro'mista] *adj* fond of joking ■ *nm/f* joker, wag
bromuro [bro'muro] *nm* bromide
bronca ['bronka] *nf* row; *(regañada)* ticking-off; **armar una ~** to kick up a fuss; **echar una ~ a algn** to tell sb off
bronce ['bronθe] *nm* bronze; *(latón)* brass
bronceado, -a [bronθe'aðo, a] *adj* bronze *cpd*; *(por el sol)* tanned ■ *nm* (sun)tan; *(Tec)* bronzing
bronceador [bronθea'ðor] *nm* suntan lotion
broncearse [bronθe'arse] *vr* to get a suntan
bronco, -a ['bronko, a] *adj* *(manera)* rude, surly; *(voz)* harsh
bronquios ['bronkjos] *nmpl* bronchial tubes
bronquitis [bron'kitis] *nf inv* bronchitis
brotar [bro'tar] *vt* *(tierra)* to produce ■ *vi* *(Bot)* to sprout; *(aguas)* to gush (forth); *(lágrimas)* to well up; *(Med)* to break out
brote ['brote] *nm* *(Bot)* shoot; *(Med, fig)* outbreak
broza ['broθa] *nf* *(Bot)* dead leaves *pl*; *(fig)* rubbish
bruces ['bruθes]: **de ~** *adv*: **caer** *o* **dar de ~** to fall headlong, fall flat
bruja ['bruxa] *nf* witch
Brujas ['bruxas] *nf* Bruges
brujería [bruxe'ria] *nf* witchcraft
brujo ['bruxo] *nm* wizard, magician
brújula ['bruxula] *nf* compass
bruma ['bruma] *nf* mist
brumoso, -a [bru'moso, a] *adj* misty
bruñendo *etc* [bru'ɲenðo] *vb ver* **bruñir**
bruñido [bru'ɲiðo] *nm* polish
bruñir [bru'ɲir] *vt* to polish
brusco, -a ['brusko, a] *adj* *(súbito)* sudden; *(áspero)* brusque
Bruselas [bru'selas] *nf* Brussels
brusquedad [bruske'ðað] *nf* suddenness; brusqueness
brutal [bru'tal] *adj* brutal
brutalidad [brutali'ðað] *nf* brutality
bruto, -a ['bruto, a] *adj* *(idiota)* stupid; *(bestial)* brutish; *(peso)* gross ■ *nm* brute; **a la bruta, a lo ~** roughly; **en ~** raw, unworked
Bs. *abr* = **bolívares**
Bs.As. *abr* = **Buenos Aires**
bucal [bu'kal] *adj* oral; **por vía ~** orally
bucanero [buka'nero] *nm* buccaneer
bucear [buθe'ar] *vi* to dive ■ *vt* to explore
buceo [bu'θeo] *nm* diving; *(fig)* investigation
buche ['butʃe] *nm* *(de ave)* crop; *(Zool)* maw; *(fam)* belly
bucle ['bukle] *nm* curl; *(Inform)* loop
budín [bu'ðin] *nm* pudding
budismo [bu'ðismo] *nm* Buddhism
budista [bu'ðista] *adj, nm/f* Buddhist
buen [bwen] *adj ver* **bueno**
buenamente [bwena'mente] *adv* *(fácilmente)* easily; *(voluntariamente)* willingly
buenaventura [bwenaβen'tura] *nf* *(suerte)* good luck; *(adivinación)* fortune; **decir** *o* **echar la ~ a algn** to tell sb's fortune

PALABRA CLAVE

bueno, -a ['bweno, a] *(antes de nmsg* **buen***)* *adj*
1 *(excelente etc)* good; *(Med)* well; **es un libro bueno, es un buen libro** it's a good book; **hace bueno, hace buen tiempo** the weather is fine, it is fine; **es buena persona** he's a good sort; **el bueno de Paco** good old Paco; **fue muy bueno conmigo** he was very nice *o* kind to me; **ya está bueno** he's fine now
2 *(apropiado)*: **ser bueno para** to be good for; **creo que vamos por buen camino** I think we're on the right track
3 *(irónico)*: **le di un buen rapapolvo** I gave him a good *o* real ticking off; **¡buen conductor estás hecho!** some driver *o* a fine driver you are!; **¡estaría bueno que ...!** a fine thing it would be if ...!
4 *(atractivo, sabroso)*: **está bueno este bizcocho** this sponge is delicious; **Julio está muy bueno** *(fam)* Julio is a bit of alright
5 *(grande)* good, big; **un buen número de ...** a good number of ...; **un buen trozo de ...** a nice big piece of ...
6 *(saludos)*: **¡buen día!** *(Am)*, **¡buenos días!** (good) morning!; **¡buenas (tardes)!** good afternoon!; *(más tarde)* good evening!; **¡buenas noches!** good night!
7 *(otras locuciones)*: **estar de buenas** to be in a good mood; **por las buenas o por las malas** by hook or by crook; **de buenas a primeras** all of a sudden

■ *excl*: **¡bueno!** all right!; **bueno, ¿y qué?** well, so what?; **bueno, lo que pasa es que ...** well, the thing is ...; **pero ¡bueno!** well, I like that!; **bueno, pues ...** right, (then) ...

Buenos Aires [bweno'saires] *nm* Buenos Aires
buey [bwei] *nm* ox
búfalo ['bufalo] *nm* buffalo
bufanda [bu'fanda] *nf* scarf
bufar [bu'far] *vi* to snort
bufete [bu'fete] *nm* (*despacho de abogado*) lawyer's office; **establecer su ~** to set up in legal practice
buffer ['bufer] *nm* (*Inform*) buffer
bufón [bu'fon] *nm* clown
bufonada [bufo'naða] *nf* (*dicho*) jest; (*hecho*) piece of buffoonery; (*Teat*) farce
buhardilla [buar'ðiʎa] *nf* attic
búho ['buo] *nm* owl; (*fig*) hermit, recluse
buhonero [buo'nero] *nm* pedlar
buitre ['bwitre] *nm* vulture
bujía [bu'xia] *nf* (*vela*) candle; (*Elec*) candle (power); (*Auto*) spark plug
bula ['bula] *nf* (papal) bull
bulbo ['bulβo] *nm* (*Bot*) bulb
bulevar [bule'βar] *nm* boulevard
Bulgaria [bul'ɣarja] *nf* Bulgaria
búlgaro, -a ['bulɣaro, a] *adj, nm/f* Bulgarian
bulimia [bu'limja] *nf* bulimia
bulla ['buʎa] *nf* (*ruido*) uproar; (*de gente*) crowd; **armar** *o* **meter ~** to kick up a row
bullendo *etc* [bu'ʎendo] *vb ver* **bullir**
bullicio [bu'ʎiθjo] *nm* (*ruido*) uproar; (*movimiento*) bustle
bullicioso, -a [buʎi'θjoso, a] *adj* (*ruidoso*) noisy; (*calle*) busy; (*situación*) turbulent
bullir [bu'ʎir] *vi* (*hervir*) to boil; (*burbujear*) to bubble; (*moverse*) to move, stir; (*insectos*) to swarm; **~ de** (*fig*) to teem *o* seethe with
bulo ['bulo] *nm* false rumour
bulto ['bulto] *nm* (*paquete*) package; (*fardo*) bundle; (*tamaño*) size, bulkiness; (*Med*) swelling, lump; (*silueta*) vague shape; (*estatua*) bust, statue; **hacer ~** to take up space; **escurrir el ~** to make o.s. scarce; (*fig*) to dodge the issue
buñuelo [bu'ɲwelo] *nm* ≈ doughnut, ≈ donut (*US*)
buque ['buke] *nm* ship, vessel; **~ de guerra** warship; **~ mercante** merchant ship; **~ de vela** sailing ship
burbuja [bur'βuxa] *nf* bubble; **hacer burbujas** to bubble; (*gaseosa*) to fizz
burbujear [burβuxe'ar] *vi* to bubble
burdel [bur'ðel] *nm* brothel
Burdeos [bur'ðeos] *nm* Bordeaux
burdo, -a ['burðo, a] *adj* coarse, rough
burgalés, -esa [burɣa'les, esa] *adj* of *o* from Burgos ■ *nm/f* native *o* inhabitant of Burgos
burgués, -esa [bur'ɣes, esa] *adj* middle-class, bourgeois; **pequeño ~** lower middle-class; (*Pol, pey*) petty bourgeois
burguesía [burɣe'sia] *nf* middle class, bourgeoisie
burla ['burla] *nf* (*mofa*) gibe; (*broma*) joke; (*engaño*) trick; **hacer ~ de** to make fun of
burladero [burla'ðero] *nm* (bullfighter's) refuge
burlador, a [burla'ðor, a] *adj* mocking ■ *nm/f* mocker; (*bromista*) joker ■ *nm* (*libertino*) seducer
burlar [bur'lar] *vt* (*engañar*) to deceive; (*seducir*) to seduce ■ *vi*, **burlarse** *vr* to joke; **burlarse de** to make fun of
burlesco, -a [bur'lesko, a] *adj* burlesque
burlón, -ona [bur'lon, ona] *adj* mocking
buró [bu'ro] *nm* bureau
burocracia [buro'kraθja] *nf* bureaucracy
burócrata [bu'rokrata] *nm/f* bureaucrat
buromática [buro'matika] *nf* office automation
burrada [bu'rraða] *nf* stupid act; **decir burradas** to talk nonsense
burro, -a ['burro, a] *nm/f* (*Zool*) donkey; (*fig*) ass, idiot ■ *adj* stupid; **caerse del ~** to realise one's mistake; **no ver tres en un ~** to be as blind as a bat
bursátil [bur'satil] *adj* stock-exchange *cpd*
bus [bus] *nm* bus
busca ['buska] *nf* search, hunt ■ *nm* bleeper, pager; **en ~ de** in search of
buscador, a [buska'ðor, a] *nm/f* searcher ■ *nm* (*Internet*) search engine
buscapiés [buska'pjes] *nm inv* jumping jack (*Brit*), firecracker (*US*)
buscapleitos [buska'pleitos] *nm/f inv* troublemaker
buscar [bus'kar] *vt* to look for; (*objeto perdido*) to have a look for; (*beneficio*) to seek; (*enemigo*) to seek out; (*traer*) to bring, fetch; (*provocar*) to provoke; (*Inform*) to search ■ *vi* to look, search, seek; **ven a buscarme a la oficina** come and pick me up at the office; **buscarle 3** *o* **4 pies al gato** to split hairs; **"~ y reemplazar"** (*Inform*) "search and replace"; **se busca secretaria** secretary wanted; **se la buscó** he asked for it
buscavidas [buska'βiðas] *nm/f inv* snooper; (*persona ambiciosa*) go-getter
buscona [bus'kona] *nf* whore
busilis [bu'silis] *nm inv* (*fam*) snag
busque *etc* ['buske] *vb ver* **buscar**

búsqueda ['buskeðа] *nf* = **busca**
busto ['busto] *nm* (*Anat: Arte*) bust
butaca [bu'taka] *nf* armchair; (*de cine, teatro*) stall, seat
butano [bu'tano] *nm* butane (gas); **bombona de ~** gas cylinder
butifarra [buti'farra] *nf* Catalan sausage
buzo ['buθo] *nm* diver; (*Am: chandal*) tracksuit
buzón [bu'θon] *nm* (*gen*) letter box; (*en la calle*) pillar box (*Brit*); (*Telec*) mailbox; **echar al ~** to post
buzonear [buθone'ar] *vt* to leaflet
byte [bait] *nm* (*Inform*) byte

Cc

C, c [θe] [se] *(esp Am) nf (letra)* C, c; **C de Carmen** C for Charlie
C. *abr (= centígrado)* C.; *(= compañía)* Co
c. *abr (= capítulo)* ch
C/ *abr (= calle)* St, Rd
c/ *abr (Com: = cuenta)* a/c
ca [ka] *excl* not a bit of it!
c.a. *abr (= corriente alterna)* A.C.
cabal [ka'βal] *adj (exacto)* exact; *(correcto)* right, proper; *(acabado)* finished, complete; **cabales** *nmpl*: **estar en sus cabales** to be in one's right mind
cábala ['kaβala] *nf (Rel)* cab(b)ala; *(fig)* cabal, intrigue; **cábalas** *nfpl* guess *sg*, supposition *sg*
cabalgadura [kaβalɣa'ðura] *nf* mount, horse
cabalgar [kaβal'ɣar] *vt, vi* to ride
cabalgata [kaβal'ɣata] *nf* procession; *ver tb* **Reyes Magos**
cabalgue *etc* [ka'βalɣe] *vb ver* **cabalgar**
cabalístico, -a [kaβa'listiko, a] *adj (fig)* mysterious
caballa [ka'βaʎa] *nf* mackerel
caballeresco, -a [kaβaʎe'resko, a] *adj* noble, chivalrous
caballería [kaβaʎe'ria] *nf* mount; *(Mil)* cavalry
caballeriza [kaβaʎe'riθa] *nf* stable
caballerizo [kaβaʎe'riθo] *nm* groom, stableman
caballero [kaβa'ʎero] *nm* gentleman; *(de la orden de caballería)* knight; *(trato directo)* sir; **"Caballeros"** "Gents"
caballerosidad [kaβaʎerosi'ðað] *nf* chivalry
caballete [kaβa'ʎete] *nm (Agr)* ridge; *(Arte)* easel
caballito [kaβa'ʎito] *nm (caballo pequeño)* small horse, pony; *(juguete)* rocking horse; **caballitos** *nmpl* merry-go-round *sg*; **~ de mar** seahorse; **~ del diablo** dragonfly
caballo [ka'βaʎo] *nm* horse; *(Ajedrez)* knight; *(Naipes)* ≈ queen; **~ de vapor** *o* **de fuerza** horsepower; **es su ~ de batalla** it's his hobby-horse; **~ blanco** *(Com)* backer; *ver tb* **Baraja Española**
cabaña [ka'βaɲa] *nf (casita)* hut, cabin
cabaré, cabaret *(pl* **cabarets***)* [kaβa're, kaβa'res] *nm* cabaret
cabecear [kaβeθe'ar] *vi* to nod
cabecera [kaβe'θera] *nf (gen)* head; *(de distrito)* chief town; *(de cama)* headboard; *(Imprenta)* headline
cabecilla [kaβe'θiʎa] *nm* ringleader
cabellera [kaβe'ʎera] *nf* (head of) hair; *(de cometa)* tail
cabello [ka'βeʎo] *nm (tb:* **cabellos***)* hair *sg*
cabelludo [kaβe'ʎuðo] *adj ver* **cuero**
caber [ka'βer] *vi (entrar)* to fit, go; **caben tres más** there's room for three more; **cabe preguntar si…** one might ask whether…; **cabe que venga más tarde** he may come later
cabestrillo [kaβes'triʎo] *nm* sling
cabestro [ka'βestro] *nm* halter
cabeza [ka'βeθa] *nf* head; *(Pol)* chief, leader ■ *nm/f*: **~ rapada** skinhead; **caer de ~** to fall head first; **sentar la ~** to settle down; **~ de lectura/escritura** read/write head; **~ impresora** *o* **de impresión** printhead
cabezada [kaβe'θaða] *nf (golpe)* butt; **dar una ~** to nod off
cabezal [kaβe'θal] *nm*: **~ impresor** print head
cabezazo [kaβe'θaθo] *nm (golpe)* headbutt; *(Fútbol)* header
cabezón, -ona [kaβe'θon, ona] *adj* with a big head; *(vino)* heady; *(obstinado)* obstinate, stubborn
cabezota [kaβe'θota] *adj inv* obstinate, stubborn
cabezudo, -a [kaβe'θuðo, a] *adj* with a big head; *(obstinado)* obstinate, stubborn
cabida [ka'βiða] *nf* space; **dar ~ a** to make room for; **tener ~ para** to have room for
cabildo [ka'βildo] *nm (de iglesia)* chapter; *(Pol)* town council

cabina [ka'βina] *nf* (*de camión*) cabin; **~ telefónica** (tele)phone box (*Brit*) *o* booth
cabizbajo, -a [kaβiθ'βaxo, a] *adj* crestfallen, dejected
cable ['kaβle] *nm* cable; (*de aparato*) lead; **~ aéreo** (*Elec*) overhead cable; **conectar con ~** (*Inform*) to hardwire
cabo ['kaβo] *nm* (*de objeto*) end, extremity; (*Mil*) corporal; (*Naut*) rope, cable; (*Geo*) cape; (*Tec*) thread; **al ~ de tres días** after three days; **de ~ a rabo** *o* **~** from beginning to end; (*libro: leer*) from cover to cover; **llevar a ~** to carry out; **atar cabos** to tie up the loose ends; **C~ de Buena Esperanza** Cape of Good Hope; **C~ de Hornos** Cape Horn; **las Islas de C~ Verde** the Cape Verde Islands
cabra ['kaβra] *nf* goat; **estar como una ~** (*fam*) to be nuts
cabré *etc* [ka'βre] *vb ver* **caber**
cabrear [kaβre'ar] *vt* to annoy; **cabrearse** *vr* to fly off the handle
cabrío, -a [ka'βrio, a] *adj* goatish; **macho ~** (he-)goat, billy goat
cabriola [ka'βrjola] *nf* caper
cabritilla [kaβri'tiʎa] *nf* kid, kidskin
cabrito [ka'βrito] *nm* kid
cabrón [ka'βron] *nm* (*fig: fam!*) bastard (*!*)
cabronada [kaβro'naða] *nf* (*fam!*): **hacer una ~ a algn** to be a bastard to sb
caca ['kaka] *nf* (*palabra de niños*) pooh ■ *excl*: **no toques, ¡~!** don't touch, it's dirty!
cacahuete [kaka'wete] *nm* (*Esp*) peanut
cacao [ka'kao] *nm* cocoa; (*Bot*) cacao
cacarear [kakare'ar] *vi* (*persona*) to boast; (*gallina*) to cackle
cacatúa [kaka'tua] *nf* cockatoo
cacereño, -a [kaθe'reɲo, a] *adj* of *o* from Cáceres ■ *nm/f* native *o* inhabitant of Cáceres
cacería [kaθe'ria] *nf* hunt
cacerola [kaθe'rola] *nf* pan, saucepan
cacha ['katʃa] *nf* (*mango*) handle; (*nalga*) buttock
cachalote [katʃa'lote] *nm* sperm whale
cacharro [ka'tʃarro] *nm* (*cazo*) pot; (*cerámica*) piece of pottery; (*fam*) useless object; **cacharros** *nmpl* pots and pans
cachear [katʃe'ar] *vt* to search, frisk
cachemir [katʃe'mir] *nm* cashmere
cacheo [ka'tʃeo] *nm* searching, frisking
cachete [ka'tʃete] *nm* (*Anat*) cheek; (*bofetada*) slap (in the face)
cachimba [ka'tʃimba] *nf*, **cachimbo** [ka'tʃimbo] *nm* (*Am*) pipe
cachiporra [katʃi'porra] *nf* truncheon
cachivache [katʃi'βatʃe] *nm* piece of junk; **cachivaches** *nmpl* trash *sg*, junk *sg*
cacho ['katʃo] *nm* (small) bit; (*Am: cuerno*) horn
cachondearse [katʃonde'arse] *vr*: **~ de algn** to tease sb
cachondeo [katʃon'deo] *nm* (*fam*) farce, joke; (*guasa*) laugh
cachondo, -a [ka'tʃondo, a] *adj* (*Zool*) on heat; (*caliente*) randy, sexy; (*gracioso*) funny
cachorro, -a [ka'tʃorro, a] *nm/f* (*de perro*) pup, puppy; (*de león*) cub
cacique [ka'θike] *nm* chief, local ruler; (*Pol*) local party boss; (*fig*) despot
caco ['kako] *nm* pickpocket
cacofonía [kakofo'nia] *nf* cacophony
cacto ['kakto] *nm*, **cactus** ['kaktus] *nm inv* cactus
cada ['kaða] *adj inv* each; (*antes de número*) every; **~ día** each day, every day; **~ dos días** every other day; **~ uno/a** each one, every one; **~ vez más/menos** more and more/less and less; **uno de ~ diez** one out of every ten; **¿~ cuánto?** how often?
cadalso [ka'ðalso] *nm* scaffold
cadáver [ka'ðaβer] *nm* (dead) body, corpse
cadavérico, -a [kaða'βeriko, a] *adj* cadaverous; (*pálido*) deathly pale
cadena [ka'ðena] *nf* chain; (*TV*) channel; **reacción en ~** chain reaction; **trabajo en ~** assembly line work; **~ midi/mini** (*Mus*) midi/mini system; **~ perpetua** (*Jur*) life imprisonment; **~ de caracteres** (*Inform*) character string
cadencia [ka'ðenθja] *nf* cadence, rhythm
cadera [ka'ðera] *nf* hip
cadete [ka'ðete] *nm* cadet
Cádiz ['kaðiθ] *nm* Cadiz
caducar [kaðu'kar] *vi* to expire
caducidad [kaðuθi'ðað] *nf*: **fecha de ~** expiry date; (*de comida*) sell-by date
caduco, -a [ka'ðuko, a] *adj* (*idea etc*) outdated, outmoded; **de hoja caduca** deciduous
caduque *etc* [ka'ðuke] *vb ver* **caducar**
caer [ka'er] *vi* to fall; (*premio*) to go; (*sitio*) to be, lie; (*pago*) to fall due; **caerse** *vr* to fall (down); **dejar ~** to drop; **estar al ~** to be due to happen; (*persona*) to be about to arrive; **me cae bien/mal** I like/don't like him; **~ en la cuenta** to catch on; **su cumpleaños cae en viernes** her birthday falls on a Friday; **se me ha caído el guante** I've dropped my glove
café (*pl* **~s**) [ka'fe, ka'fes] *nm* (*bebida, planta*) coffee; (*lugar*) café ■ *adj* (*color*) brown; **café con leche** white coffee; **café solo, café negro** (*Am*) (small) black coffee
cafeína [kafe'ina] *nf* caffein(e)
cafetal [kafe'tal] *nm* coffee plantation
cafetera [kafe'tera] *nf ver* **cafetero**

cafetería [kafete'ria] *nf* cafe
cafetero, -a [kafe'tero, a] *adj* coffee *cpd* ■ *nf* coffee pot; **ser muy ~** to be a coffee addict
cafre ['kafre] *nm/f*: **como cafres** (*fig*) like savages
cagalera [kaɣa'lera] *nf* (*fam!*): **tener ~** to have the runs
cagar [ka'ɣar] (*fam!*) *vt* to shit (*!*); (*fig*) to bungle, mess up ■ *vi* to have a shit (*!*); **cagarse** *vr*: **¡me cago en diez** *etc*! Christ! (*!*)
cague *etc* ['kaɣe] *vb ver* **cagar**
caído, -a [ka'iðo, a] *adj* fallen; (*Inform*) down ■ *nf* fall; (*declive*) slope; (*disminución*) fall, drop; **~ del cielo** out of the blue; **a la caída del sol** at sunset; **sufrir una caída** to have a fall
caiga *etc* ['kaiɣa] *vb ver* **caer**
caimán [kai'man] *nm* alligator
Cairo ['kairo] *nm*: **el ~** Cairo
caja ['kaxa] *nf* box; (*ataúd*) coffin, casket (*US*); (*para reloj*) case; (*de ascensor*) shaft; (*Com*) cash box; (*Econ*) fund; (*donde se hacen los pagos*) cashdesk; (*en supermercado*) checkout, till; (*Tip*) case; (*de parking*) pay station; **~ de ahorros** savings bank; **~ de cambios** gearbox; **~ fuerte, ~ de caudales** safe, strongbox; **ingresar en ~** to be paid in
cajero, -a [ka'xero, a] *nm/f* cashier; (*en banco*) (bank) teller ■ *nm*: **~ automático** cash dispenser, automatic telling machine, A.T.M.
cajetilla [kaxe'tiʎa] *nf* (*de cigarrillos*) packet
cajista [ka'xista] *nm/f* typesetter
cajón [ka'xon] *nm* big box; (*de mueble*) drawer
cal [kal] *nf* lime; **cerrar algo a ~ y canto** to shut sth firmly
cal. *abr* (= *caloría(s)*) cal. (= *calorie(s)*)
cala ['kala] *nf* (*Geo*) cove, inlet; (*de barco*) hold
calabacín [kalaβa'θin] *nm* (*Bot*) baby marrow, courgette, zucchini (*US*)
calabaza [kala'βaθa] *nf* (*Bot*) pumpkin; **dar calabazas a** (*candidato*) to fail
calabozo [kala'βoθo] *nm* (*cárcel*) prison; (*celda*) cell
calado, -a [ka'laðo, a] *adj* (*prenda*) lace *cpd* ■ *nm* (*Tec*) fretwork; (*Naut*) draught ■ *nf* (*de cigarrillo*) puff; **estar ~ (hasta los huesos)** to be soaked (to the skin)
calamar [kala'mar] *nm* squid
calambre [ka'lambre] *nm* (*tb*: **calambres**) cramp
calamidad [kalami'ðað] *nf* calamity, disaster; (*persona*): **es una ~** he's a dead loss
calamina [kala'mina] *nf* calamine
cálamo ['kalamo] *nm* (*Bot*) stem; (*Mus*) reed
calaña [ka'laɲa] *nf* model, pattern; (*fig*) nature, stamp
calar [ka'lar] *vt* to soak, drench; (*penetrar*) to pierce, penetrate; (*comprender*) to see through; (*vela, red*) to lower; **calarse** *vr* (*Auto*) to stall; **calarse las gafas** to stick one's glasses on
calavera [kala'βera] *nf* skull
calcañal [kalka'ɲal], **calcañar** [kalka'ɲar] *nm* heel
calcar [kal'kar] *vt* (*reproducir*) to trace; (*imitar*) to copy
calce *etc* ['kalθe] *vb ver* **calzar**
cal. cen. *abr* = **calefacción central**
calceta [kal'θeta] *nf* (knee-length) stocking; **hacer ~** to knit
calcetín [kalθe'tin] *nm* sock
calcinar [kalθi'nar] *vt* to burn, blacken
calcio ['kalθjo] *nm* calcium
calco ['kalko] *nm* tracing
calcomanía [kalkoma'nia] *nf* transfer
calculador, a [kalkula'ðor, a] *adj* calculating ■ *nf* calculator
calcular [kalku'lar] *vt* (*Mat*) to calculate, compute; **~ que ...** to reckon that ...
cálculo ['kalkulo] *nm* calculation; (*Med*) (gall)stone; (*Mat*) calculus; **~ de costo** costing; **~ diferencial** differential calculus; **obrar con mucho ~** to act cautiously
caldear [kalde'ar] *vt* to warm (up), heat (up); (*metales*) to weld
caldera [kal'dera] *nf* boiler
calderero [kalde'rero] *nm* boilermaker
calderilla [kalde'riʎa] *nf* (*moneda*) small change
caldero [kal'dero] *nm* small boiler
caldo ['kaldo] *nm* stock; (*consomé*) consommé; **~ de cultivo** (*Bio*) culture medium; **poner a ~ a algn** to tear sb off a strip; **los caldos jerezanos** sherries
caldoso, -a [kal'doso, a] *adj* (*guisado*) juicy; (*sopa*) thin
calé [ka'le] *adj* gipsy *cpd*
calefacción [kalefak'θjon] *nf* heating; **~ central** central heating
caleidoscopio [kaleiðos'kopjo] *nm* kaleidoscope
calendario [kalen'darjo] *nm* calendar
calentador [kalenta'ðor] *nm* heater
calentamiento [kalenta'mjento] *nm* (*Deporte*) warm-up
calentar [kalen'tar] *vt* to heat (up); (*fam*: *excitar*) to turn on; (*Am*: *enfurecer*) to anger; **calentarse** *vr* to heat up, warm up; (*fig*: *discusión etc*) to get heated
calentura [kalen'tura] *nf* (*Med*) fever, (high) temperature; (*de boca*) mouth sore
calenturiento, -a [kalentu'rjento, a] *adj* (*mente*) overactive

calibrar [kali'βrar] *vt* to gauge, measure
calibre [ka'liβre] *nm* (*de cañón*) calibre, bore; (*diámetro*) diameter; (*fig*) calibre
calidad [kali'ðað] *nf* quality; **de ~** quality *cpd*; **~ de borrador** (*Inform*) draft quality; **~ de carta** *o* **de correspondencia** (*Inform*) letter quality; **~ texto** (*Inform*) text quality; **~ de vida** quality of life; **en ~ de** in the capacity of
cálido, -a ['kaliðo, a] *adj* hot; (*fig*) warm
caliente *etc* [ka'ljente] *vb ver* **calentar** ■ *adj* hot; (*fig*) fiery; (*disputa*) heated; (*fam: cachondo*) randy
califa [ka'lifa] *nm* caliph
calificación [kalifika'θjon] *nf* qualification; (*de alumno*) grade, mark; **~ de sobresaliente** first-class mark
calificar [kalifi'kar] *vt* to qualify; (*alumno*) to grade, mark; **~ de** to describe as
calificativo, -a [kalifika'tiβo, a] *adj* qualifying ■ *nm* qualifier, epithet
califique *etc* [kali'fike] *vb ver* **calificar**
californiano, -a [kalifor'njano, a] *adj, nm/f* Californian
caligrafía [kaliɣra'fia] *nf* calligraphy
calima [ka'lima] *nf* mist
calina [ka'lina] *nf* haze
cáliz ['kaliθ] *nm* (*Bot*) calyx; (*Rel*) chalice
caliza [ka'liθa] *nf* limestone
callado, -a [ka'ʎaðo, a] *adj* quiet, silent
callar [ka'ʎar] *vt* (*asunto delicado*) to keep quiet about, say nothing about; (*omitir*) to pass over in silence; (*persona, oposición*) to silence ■ *vi*, **callarse** *vr* to keep quiet, be silent; (*dejar de hablar*) to stop talking; **¡calla!** be quiet!; **¡cállate!**, **¡cállese!** shut up!; **¡cállate la boca!** shut your mouth!
calle ['kaʎe] *nf* street; (*Deporte*) lane; **~ arriba/abajo** up/down the street; **~ de sentido único** one-way street; **poner a algn (de patitas) en la ~** to kick sb out
calleja [ka'ʎexa] *nf* alley, narrow street
callejear [kaʎexe'ar] *vi* to wander (about) the streets
callejero, -a [kaʎe'xero, a] *adj* street *cpd* ■ *nm* street map
callejón [kaʎe'xon] *nm* alley, passage; (*Geo*) narrow pass; **~ sin salida** cul-de-sac; (*fig*) blind alley
callejuela [kaʎe'xwela] *nf* side-street, alley
callista [ka'ʎista] *nm/f* chiropodist
callo ['kaʎo] *nm* callus; (*en el pie*) corn; **callos** *nmpl* (*Culin*) tripe *sg*
callosidad [kaʎosi'ðað] *nf* (*de pie*) corn; (*de mano*) callus
calloso, -a [ka'ʎoso, a] *adj* horny, rough
calma ['kalma] *nf* calm; (*pachorra*) slowness; (*Com: Econ*) calm, lull; **~ chicha** dead calm; **¡~!**, **¡con ~!** take it easy!
calmante [kal'mante] *adj* soothing ■ *nm* sedative, tranquillizer
calmar [kal'mar] *vt* to calm, calm down; (*dolor*) to relieve ■ *vi*, **calmarse** *vr* (*tempestad*) to abate; (*mente etc*) to become calm
calmoso, -a [kal'moso, a] *adj* calm, quiet
caló [ka'lo] *nm* (*de gitanos*) gipsy language, Romany; (*argot*) slang
calor [ka'lor] *nm* heat; (*calor agradable*) warmth; **entrar en ~** to get warm; **tener ~** to be *o* feel hot
caloría [kalo'ria] *nf* calorie
calorífero, -a [kalo'rifero, a] *adj* heat-producing, heat-giving ■ *nm* heating system
calque *etc* ['kalke] *vb ver* **calcar**
calumnia [ka'lumnja] *nf* slander; (*por escrito*) libel
calumniar [kalum'njar] *vt* to slander; to libel
calumnioso, -a [kalum'njoso, a] *adj* slanderous; libellous
caluroso, -a [kalu'roso, a] *adj* hot; (*sin exceso*) warm; (*fig*) enthusiastic
calva ['kalβa] *nf* bald patch; (*en bosque*) clearing
calvario [kal'βarjo] *nm* stations *pl* of the cross; (*fig*) cross, heavy burden
calvicie [kal'βiθje] *nf* baldness
calvo, -a ['kalβo, a] *adj* bald; (*terreno*) bare, barren; (*tejido*) threadbare ■ *nm* bald man
calza ['kalθa] *nf* wedge, chock
calzado, -a [kal'θaðo, a] *adj* shod ■ *nm* footwear ■ *nf* roadway, highway
calzador [kalθa'ðor] *nm* shoehorn
calzar [kal'θar] *vt* (*zapatos etc*) to wear; (*un mueble*) to put a wedge under; (*Tec: rueda etc*) to scotch; **calzarse** *vr*: **calzarse los zapatos** to put on one's shoes; **¿qué (número) calza?** what size do you take?
calzón [kal'θon] *nm* (*tb:* **calzones**) shorts *pl*; (*Am: de hombre*) pants *pl*; (*: de mujer*) panties *pl*
calzoncillos [kalθon'θiʎos] *nmpl* underpants
cama ['kama] *nf* bed; (*Geo*) stratum; **~ individual/de matrimonio** single/double bed; **guardar ~** to be ill in bed
camada [ka'maða] *nf* litter; (*de personas*) gang, band
camafeo [kama'feo] *nm* cameo
camaleón [kamale'on] *nm* chameleon
cámara ['kamara] *nf* (*Pol etc*) chamber; (*habitación*) room; (*sala*) hall; (*Cine*) cine camera; (*fotográfica*) camera; **~ de aire** inner tube; **~ alta/baja** upper/lower house; **~ de comercio** chamber of commerce; **~ digital** digital camera; **~ de gas** gas chamber; **~ de video** video camera; **a ~ lenta** in slow motion

camarada [kama'raða] *nm* comrade, companion
camaradería [kamaraðe'ria] *nf* comradeship
camarero, -a [kama'rero, a] *nm* waiter ■ *nf* (*en restaurante*) waitress; (*en casa, hotel*) maid
camarilla [kama'riʎa] *nf* (*clan*) clique; (*Pol*) lobby
camarín [kama'rin] *nm* (*Teat*) dressing room
camarón [kama'ron] *nm* shrimp
camarote [kama'rote] *nm* (*Naut*) cabin
cambiable [kam'bjaβle] *adj* (*variable*) changeable, variable; (*intercambiable*) interchangeable
cambiante [kam'bjante] *adj* variable
cambiar [kam'bjar] *vt* to change; (*trocar*) to exchange ■ *vi* to change; **cambiarse** *vr* (*mudarse*) to move; (*de ropa*) to change; **~(se) de ...** to change one's ...; **~ de idea/de ropa** to change one's mind/clothes
cambiazo [kam'bjaθo] *nm*: **dar el ~ a algn** to swindle sb
cambio ['kambjo] *nm* change; (*trueque*) exchange; (*Com*) rate of exchange; (*oficina*) bureau de change; (*dinero menudo*) small change; **en ~** on the other hand; (*en lugar de eso*) instead; **~ de divisas** (*Com*) foreign exchange; **~ de línea** (*Inform*) line feed; **~ de página** (*Inform*) form feed; **~ a término** (*Com*) forward exchange; **~ de velocidades** gear lever; **~ de vía** points *pl*
cambista [kam'bista] *nm* (*Com*) exchange broker
Camboya [kam'boja] *nf* Cambodia, Kampuchea
camboyano, -a [kambo'jano, a] *adj, nm/f* Cambodian, Kampuchean
camelar [kame'lar] *vt* (*con mujer*) to flirt with; (*persuadir*) to cajole
camelia [ka'melia] *nf* camellia
camello [ka'meʎo] *nm* camel; (*fam: traficante*) pusher
camelo [ka'melo] *nm*: **me huele a ~** it smells fishy
camerino [kame'rino] *nm* (*Teat*) dressing room
camilla [ka'miʎa] *nf* (*Med*) stretcher
caminante [kami'nante] *nm/f* traveller
caminar [kami'nar] *vi* (*marchar*) to walk, go; (*viajar*) to travel, journey ■ *vt* (*recorrer*) to cover, travel
caminata [kami'nata] *nf* long walk
camino [ka'mino] *nm* way, road; (*sendero*) track; **a medio ~** halfway (there); **en el ~** on the way, en route; **~ de** on the way to; **~ particular** private road; **~ vecinal** country road; **Caminos, Canales y Puertos** (*Univ*) Civil Engineering; **ir por buen ~** (*fig*) to be on the right track; **C~ de Santiago** *see note*

CAMINO DE SANTIAGO

The *Camino de Santiago* is a medieval pilgrim route stretching from the Pyrenees to Santiago de Compostela in north-west Spain, where tradition has it the body of the Apostle James is buried. Nowadays it is a popular tourist route as well as a religious one. The *concha* (cockleshell) is a symbol of the *Camino de Santiago*, because it is said that when St James' body was found it was covered in shells.

camión [ka'mjon] *nm* lorry, truck (*US*); (*Am: autobús*) bus; **~ de bomberos** fire engine
camionero [kamjo'nero] *nm* lorry *o* truck (*US*) driver, trucker (*esp US*)
camioneta [kamjo'neta] *nf* van, transit®
camisa [ka'misa] *nf* shirt; (*Bot*) skin; **~ de dormir** nightdress; **~ de fuerza** straitjacket
camisería [kamise'ria] *nf* outfitter's (shop)
camiseta [kami'seta] *nf* tee-shirt; (*ropa interior*) vest; (*de deportista*) top
camisón [kami'son] *nm* nightdress, nightgown
camomila [kamo'mila] *nf* camomile
camorra [ka'morra] *nf*: **armar ~** to kick up a row; **buscar ~** to look for trouble
camorrista [kamo'rrista] *nm/f* thug
camote [ka'mote] *nm* (*Am*) sweet potato
campal [kam'pal] *adj*: **batalla ~** pitched battle
campamento [kampa'mento] *nm* camp
campana [kam'pana] *nf* bell
campanada [kampa'naða] *nf* peal
campanario [kampa'narjo] *nm* belfry
campanilla [kampa'niʎa] *nf* (*campana*) small bell
campante [kam'pante] *adj*: **siguió tan ~** he went on as if nothing had happened
campaña [kam'paɲa] *nf* (*Mil: Pol*) campaign; **hacer ~ (en pro de/contra)** to campaign (for/against); **~ de venta** sales campaign
campechano, -a [kampe'tʃano, a] *adj* open
campeón, -ona [kampe'on, ona] *nm/f* champion
campeonato [kampeo'nato] *nm* championship
campesino, -a [kampe'sino, a] *adj* country *cpd*, rural; (*gente*) peasant *cpd* ■ *nm/f* countryman/woman; (*agricultor*) farmer
campestre [kam'pestre] *adj* country *cpd*, rural
camping ['kampin] *nm* camping; (*lugar*) campsite; **ir de** *o* **hacer ~** to go camping
campiña [kam'piɲa] *nf* countryside

campista [kam'pista] *nm/f* camper
campo ['kampo] *nm* (*fuera de la ciudad*) country, countryside; (*Agr: Elec: Inform*) field; (*de fútbol*) pitch; (*de golf*) course; (*Mil*) camp; **~ de batalla** battlefield; **~ de minas** minefield; **~ petrolífero** oilfield; **~ visual** field of vision; **~ de concentración/de internación/de trabajo** concentration/internment/labour camp
camposanto [kampo'santo] *nm* cemetery
campus ['kampus] *nm inv* (*Univ*) campus
camuflaje [kamu'flaxe] *nm* camouflage
camuflar [kamu'flar] *vt* to camouflage
can [kan] *nm* dog, mutt (*fam*)
cana ['kana] *nf ver* **cano**
Canadá [kana'ða] *nm* Canada
canadiense [kana'ðjense] *adj, nm/f* Canadian ■ *nf* fur-lined jacket
canal [ka'nal] *nm* canal; (*Geo*) channel, strait; (*de televisión*) channel; (*de tejado*) gutter; **C~ de la Mancha** English Channel; **C~ de Panamá** Panama Canal
canalice *etc* [kana'liθe] *vb ver* **canalizar**
canalizar [kanali'θar] *vt* to channel
canalla [ka'naʎa] *nf* rabble, mob ■ *nm* swine
canallada [kana'ʎaða] *nf* (*hecho*) dirty trick
canalón [kana'lon] *nm* (*conducto vertical*) drainpipe; (*del tejado*) gutter; **canalones** *nmpl* (*Culin*) cannelloni
canapé (*pl* **~s**) [kana'pe, kana'pes] *nm* sofa, settee; (*Culin*) canapé
Canarias [ka'narjas] *nfpl*: **las (Islas) ~** the Canaries, the Canary Isles
canario, -a [ka'narjo, a] *adj* of *o* from the Canary Isles ■ *nm/f* native *o* inhabitant of the Canary Isles ■ *nm* (*Zool*) canary
canasta [ka'nasta] *nf* (round) basket
canastilla [kanas'tiʎa] *nf* small basket; (*de niño*) layette
canasto [ka'nasto] *nm* large basket
cancela [kan'θela] *nf* (wrought-iron) gate
cancelación [kanθela'θjon] *nf* cancellation
cancelar [kanθe'lar] *vt* to cancel; (*una deuda*) to write off
cáncer ['kanθer] *nm* (*Med*) cancer; **C~** (*Astro*) Cancer
cancerígeno, -a [kanθe'rixeno, a] *adj* carcinogenic
cancha ['kantʃa] *nf* (*de baloncesto, tenis etc*) court; (*Am: de fútbol etc*) pitch
canciller [kanθi'ʎer] *nm* chancellor; **C~** (*Am*) Foreign Minister, ≈ Foreign Secretary (*Brit*)
Cancillería [kansiʎe'ria] *nf* (*Am*) Foreign Ministry, ≈ Foreign Office (*Brit*)
canción [kan'θjon] *nf* song; **~ de cuna** lullaby
cancionero [kanθjo'nero] *nm* song book
candado [kan'daðo] *nm* padlock
candela [kan'dela] *nf* candle
candelabro [kande'laβro] *nm* candelabra
candelero [kande'lero] *nm* (*para vela*) candlestick; (*de aceite*) oil lamp
candente [kan'dente] *adj* red-hot; (*tema*) burning
candidato, -a [kandi'ðato, a] *nm/f* candidate; (*para puesto*) applicant
candidatura [kandiða'tura] *nf* candidature
candidez [kandi'ðeθ] *nf* (*sencillez*) simplicity; (*simpleza*) naiveté
cándido, -a ['kandiðo, a] *adj* simple; naive
candil [kan'dil] *nm* oil lamp
candilejas [kandi'lexas] *nfpl* (*Teat*) footlights
candor [kan'dor] *nm* (*sinceridad*) frankness; (*inocencia*) innocence
canela [ka'nela] *nf* cinnamon
canelo [ka'nelo] *nm*: **hacer el ~** to act the fool
canelones [kane'lones] *nmpl* cannelloni
cangrejo [kan'grexo] *nm* crab
canguro [kan'guro] *nm* (*Zool*) kangaroo; (*de niños*) baby-sitter; **hacer de ~** to baby-sit
caníbal [ka'niβal] *adj, nm/f* cannibal
canica [ka'nika] *nf* marble
caniche [ka'nitʃe] *nm* poodle
canícula [ka'nikula] *nf* midsummer heat
canijo, -a [ka'nixo, a] *adj* frail, sickly
canilla [ka'niʎa] *nf* (*Tec*) bobbin
canino, -a [ka'nino, a] *adj* canine ■ *nm* canine (tooth)
canje [kan'xe] *nm* exchange; (*trueque*) swap
canjear [kanxe'ar] *vt* to exchange; (*trocar*) to swap
cano, -a ['kano, a] *adj* grey-haired, white-haired ■ *nf* (*tb*: **canas**) white *o* grey hair; **tener canas** to be going grey
canoa [ka'noa] *nf* canoe
canon ['kanon] *nm* canon; (*pensión*) rent; (*Com*) tax
canonice *etc* [kano'niθe] *vb ver* **canonizar**
canónico, -a [ka'noniko, a] *adj*: **derecho ~** canon law
canónigo [ka'noniɣo] *nm* canon
canonizar [kanoni'θar] *vt* to canonize
canoro, -a [ka'noro, a] *adj* melodious
canoso, -a [ka'noso, a] *adj* (*pelo*) grey (*Brit*), gray (*US*); (*persona*) grey-haired
cansado, -a [kan'saðo, a] *adj* tired, weary; (*tedioso*) tedious, boring; **estoy ~ de hacerlo** I'm sick of doing it
cansancio [kan'sanθjo] *nm* tiredness, fatigue
cansar [kan'sar] *vt* (*fatigar*) to tire, tire out; (*aburrir*) to bore; (*fastidiar*) to bother; **cansarse** *vr* to tire, get tired; (*aburrirse*) to get bored

cantábrico, -a [kan'taβriko, a] *adj* Cantabrian; **Mar C~** Bay of Biscay; **(Montes) Cantábricos, Cordillera Cantábrica** Cantabrian Mountains
cántabro, -a ['kantaβro, a] *adj, nm/f* Cantabrian
cantante [kan'tante] *adj* singing ■ *nm/f* singer
cantaor, a [kanta'or, a] *nm/f* Flamenco singer
cantar [kan'tar] *vt* to sing ■ *vi* to sing; (*insecto*) to chirp; (*rechinar*) to squeak; (*fam: criminal*) to squeal ■ *nm* (*acción*) singing; (*canción*) song; (*poema*) poem; **~ a algn las cuarenta** to tell sb a few home truths; **~ a dos voces** to sing a duet
cántara ['kantara] *nf* large pitcher
cántaro ['kantaro] *nm* pitcher, jug
cantautor, a [kantau'tor, a] *nm/f* singer-songwriter
cante ['kante] *nm*: **~ jondo** flamenco singing
cantera [kan'tera] *nf* quarry
cántico ['kantiko] *nm* (*Rel*) canticle; (*fig*) song
cantidad [kanti'ðað] *nf* quantity, amount; (*Econ*) sum ■ *adv* (*fam*) a lot; **~ alzada** lump sum; **~ de** lots of
cantilena [kanti'lena] *nf* = **cantinela**
cantimplora [kantim'plora] *nf* water bottle, canteen
cantina [kan'tina] *nf* canteen; (*de estación*) buffet; (*esp Am*) bar
cantinela [kanti'nela] *nf* ballad, song
canto ['kanto] *nm* singing; (*canción*) song; (*borde*) edge, rim; (*de un cuchillo*) back; **~ rodado** boulder
cantón [kan'ton] *nm* canton
cantor, a [kan'tor, a] *nm/f* singer
canturrear [kanturre'ar] *vi* to sing softly
canutas [ka'nutas] *nfpl*: **pasarlas ~** (*fam*) to have a rough time (of it)
canuto [ka'nuto] *nm* (*tubo*) small tube; (*fam: porro*) joint
caña ['kaɲa] *nf* (*Bot: tallo*) stem, stalk; (*carrizo*) reed; (*vaso*) tumbler; (*de cerveza*) glass of beer; (*Anat*) shinbone; (*Am: aguardiente*) cane liquor; **~ de azúcar** sugar cane; **~ de pescar** fishing rod
cañada [ka'ɲaða] *nf* (*entre dos montañas*) gully, ravine; (*camino*) cattle track
cáñamo ['kaɲamo] *nm* (*Bot*) hemp
cañaveral [kaɲaβe'ral] *nm* (*Bot*) reedbed; (*Agr*) sugar-cane field
cañería [kaɲe'ria] *nf* piping; (*tubo*) pipe
caño ['kaɲo] *nm* (*tubo*) tube, pipe; (*de aguas servidas*) sewer; (*Mus*) pipe; (*Naut*) navigation channel; (*de fuente*) jet
cañón [ka'ɲon] *nm* (*Mil*) cannon; (*de fusil*) barrel; (*Geo*) canyon, gorge
cañonazo [kaɲo'naθo] *nm* (*Mil*) gunshot
cañonera [kaɲo'nera] *nf* (*tb*: **lancha cañonera**) gunboat
caoba [ka'oβa] *nf* mahogany
caos ['kaos] *nm* chaos
caótico, -a [ka'otiko, a] *adj* chaotic
C.A.P. *nm abr* (= *Certificado de Aptitud Pedagógica*) *teaching certificate*
cap. *abr* (= *capítulo*) ch.
capa ['kapa] *nf* cloak, cape; (*Culin*) coating; (*Geo*) layer, stratum; (*de pintura*) coat; **de ~ y espada** cloak-and-dagger; **so ~ de** under the pretext of; **~ de ozono** ozone layer; **capas sociales** social groups
capacho [ka'patʃo] *nm* wicker basket
capacidad [kapaθi'ðað] *nf* (*medida*) capacity; (*aptitud*) capacity, ability; **una sala con ~ para 900** a hall seating 900; **~ adquisitiva** purchasing power
capacitación [kapaθita'θjon] *nf* training
capacitar [kapaθi'tar] *vt*: **~ a algn para algo** to qualify sb for sth; (*Tec*) to train sb for sth
capar [ka'par] *vt* to castrate, geld
caparazón [kapara'θon] *nm* (*Zool*) shell
capataz [kapa'taθ] *nm* foreman, charge hand
capaz [ka'paθ] *adj* able, capable; (*amplio*) capacious, roomy; **es ~ que venga mañana** (*Am*) he'll probably come tomorrow
capcioso, -a [kap'θjoso, a] *adj* wily, deceitful; **pregunta capciosa** trick question
capea [ka'pea] *nf* (*Taur*) bullfight with young bulls
capear [kape'ar] *vt* (*dificultades*) to dodge; **~ el temporal** to weather the storm
capellán [kape'ʎan] *nm* chaplain; (*sacerdote*) priest
caperuza [kape'ruθa] *nf* hood; (*de bolígrafo*) cap
capi ['kapi] *nf* (*esp Am fam*) capital (city)
capicúa [kapi'kua] *nf* *reversible number, e.g. 1441*
capilar [kapi'lar] *adj* hair *cpd*
capilla [ka'piʎa] *nf* chapel
capital [kapi'tal] *adj* capital ■ *nm* (*Com*) capital ■ *nf* (*de nación*) capital (city); (*tb*: **capital de provincia**) provincial capital, ≈ county town; **~ activo/en acciones** working/share *o* equity capital; **~ arriesgado** venture capital; **~ autorizado** *o* **social** authorised capital; **~ emitido** issued capital; **~ improductivo** idle money; **~ invertido** *o* **utilizado** capital employed; **~ pagado** paid-up capital; **~ de riesgo** risk capital; **~ social** equity *o* share capital; **inversión de capitales** capital investment; *ver tb* **provincia**
capitalice *etc* [kapita'liθe] *vb ver* **capitalizar**

capitalino, -a [kapita'lino, a] *adj* (*Am*) of *o* from the capital ■ *nm/f* native *o* inhabitant of the capital
capitalismo [kapita'lismo] *nm* capitalism
capitalista [kapita'lista] *adj, nm/f* capitalist
capitalizar [kapitali'θar] *vt* to capitalize
capitán [kapi'tan] *nm* captain; (*fig*) leader
capitana [kapi'tana] *nf* flagship
capitanear [kapitane'ar] *vt* to captain
capitanía [kapita'nia] *nf* captaincy
capitel [kapi'tel] *nm* (*Arq*) capital
capitolio [kapi'toljo] *nm* capitol
capitulación [kapitula'θjon] *nf* (*rendición*) capitulation, surrender; (*acuerdo*) agreement, pact; **capitulaciones matrimoniales** marriage contract *sg*
capitular [kapitu'lar] *vi* to come to terms, make an agreement; (*Mil*) to surrender
capítulo [ka'pitulo] *nm* chapter
capo [ka'po] *nm* drugs baron
capó [ka'po] *nm* (*Auto*) bonnet (*Brit*), hood (*US*)
capón [ka'pon] *nm* capon
caporal [kapo'ral] *nm* chief, leader
capota [ka'pota] *nf* (*de mujer*) bonnet; (*Auto*) hood (*Brit*), top (*US*)
capote [ka'pote] *nm* (*abrigo: de militar*) greatcoat; (*de torero*) cloak
capricho [ka'pritʃo] *nm* whim, caprice
caprichoso, -a [kapri'tʃoso, a] *adj* capricious
Capricornio [kapri'kornjo] *nm* Capricorn
cápsula ['kapsula] *nf* capsule; **~ espacial** space capsule
captar [kap'tar] *vt* (*comprender*) to understand; (*Radio*) to pick up; (*atención, apoyo*) to attract
captura [kap'tura] *nf* capture; (*Jur*) arrest
capturar [kaptu'rar] *vt* to capture; (*Jur*) to arrest; (*datos*) to input
capucha [ka'putʃa] *nf* hood, cowl
capullo [ka'puʎo] *nm* (*Zool*) cocoon; (*Bot*) bud; (*fam!*) berk (*Brit*), jerk (*US*)
caqui ['kaki] *nm* khaki
cara ['kara] *nf* (*Anat, de moneda*) face; (*aspecto*) appearance; (*de disco*) side; (*fig*) boldness; (*descaro*) cheek, nerve ■ *prep*: **~ a** facing; **de ~ a** opposite, facing; **dar la ~** to face the consequences; **echar algo en ~ a algn** to reproach sb for sth; **¿~ o cruz?** heads or tails?; **¡qué ~ más dura!** what a nerve!; **de una ~** (*disquete*) single-sided
carabina [kara'βina] *nf* carbine, rifle; (*persona*) chaperone
carabinero [karaβi'nero] *nm* (*de aduana*) customs officer; (*Am*) gendarme
Caracas [ka'rakas] *nm* Caracas
caracol [kara'kol] *nm* (*Zool*) snail; (*concha*) (sea)shell; **escalera de ~** spiral staircase
caracolear [karakole'ar] *vi* (*caballo*) to prance about
carácter (*pl* **caracteres**) [ka'rakter, karak'teres] *nm* character; **caracteres de imprenta** (*Tip*) type(face) *sg*; **~ libre** (*Inform*) wildcard character; **tener buen/mal ~** to be good-natured/bad tempered
caracterice *etc* [karakte'riθe] *vb ver* **caracterizar**
característico, -a [karakte'ristiko, a] *adj* characteristic ■ *nf* characteristic
caracterizar [karakteri'θar] *vt* (*distinguir*) to characterize, typify; (*honrar*) to confer a distinction on
caradura [kara'ðura] *nm/f* cheeky person; **es un ~** he's got a nerve
carajillo [kara'xiʎo] *nm* *black coffee with brandy*
carajo [ka'raxo] *nm* (*esp Am fam!*): **¡~!** shit! (*!*); **¡qué ~!** what the hell!; **me importa un ~** I don't give a damn
caramba [ka'ramba] *excl* well!, good gracious!
carámbano [ka'rambano] *nm* icicle
carambola [karam'bola] *nf*: **por ~** by a fluke
caramelo [kara'melo] *nm* (*dulce*) sweet; (*azúcar fundido*) caramel
carantoñas [karan'toɲas] *nfpl*: **hacer ~ a algn** to (try to) butter sb up
caraqueño, -a [kara'keɲo, a] *adj* of *o* from Caracas ■ *nm/f* native *o* inhabitant of Caracas
carátula [ka'ratula] *nf* (*máscara*) mask; (*Teat*): **la ~** the stage
caravana [kara'βana] *nf* caravan; (*fig*) group; (*de autos*) tailback
carbón [kar'βon] *nm* coal; **~ de leña** charcoal; **papel ~** carbon paper
carbonatado, -a [karβono'taðo, a] *adj* carbonated
carbonato [karβo'nato] *nm* carbonate; **~ sódico** sodium carbonate
carboncillo [karβon'θiʎo] *nm* (*Arte*) charcoal
carbonice *etc* [karβo'niθe] *vb ver* **carbonizar**
carbonilla [karβo'niʎa] *nf* coal dust
carbonizar [karβoni'θar] *vt* to carbonize; (*quemar*) to char; **quedar carbonizado** (*Elec*) to be electrocuted
carbono [kar'βono] *nm* carbon
carburador [karβura'ðor] *nm* carburettor
carburante [karβu'rante] *nm* fuel
carca ['karka] *adj, nm/f inv* reactionary
carcajada [karka'xaða] *nf* (loud) laugh, guffaw
carcajearse [karkaxe'arse] *vr* to roar with laughter
cárcel ['karθel] *nf* prison, jail; (*Tec*) clamp
carcelero, -a [karθe'lero, a] *adj* prison *cpd* ■ *nm/f* warder

carcoma [kar'koma] *nf* woodworm
carcomer [karko'mer] *vt* to bore into, eat into; *(fig)* to undermine; **carcomerse** *vr* to become worm-eaten; *(fig)* to decay
carcomido, -a [karko'miðo, a] *adj* worm-eaten; *(fig)* rotten
cardar [kar'ðar] *vt (Tec)* to card, comb
cardenal [karðe'nal] *nm (Rel)* cardinal; *(Med)* bruise
cárdeno, -a ['karðeno, a] *adj* purple; *(lívido)* livid
cardiaco, -a [kar'ðjako, a], **cardíaco, a** [kar'ðiako, a] *adj* cardiac; *(ataque)* heart *cpd*
cardinal [karði'nal] *adj* cardinal
cardiólogo, -a [karðj'oloɣo, a] *nm/f* cardiologist
cardo ['karðo] *nm* thistle
carear [kare'ar] *vt* to bring face to face; *(comparar)* to compare; **carearse** *vr* to come face to face, meet
carecer [kare'θer] *vi*: **~ de** to lack, be in need of
carencia [ka'renθja] *nf* lack; *(escasez)* shortage; *(Med)* deficiency
carente [ka'rente] *adj*: **~ de** lacking in, devoid of
carestía [kares'tia] *nf (escasez)* scarcity, shortage; *(Com)* high cost; **época de ~** period of shortage
careta [ka'reta] *nf* mask
carey [ka'rei] *nm (tortuga)* turtle; *(concha)* tortoiseshell
carezca *etc* [ka'reθka] *vb ver* **carecer**
carga ['karɣa] *nf (peso, Elec)* load; *(de barco)* cargo, freight; *(Finanzas)* tax, duty; *(Mil)* charge; *(Inform)* loading; *(obligación, responsabilidad)* duty, obligation; **~ aérea** *(Com)* air cargo; **~ útil** *(Com)* payload; **la ~ fiscal** the tax burden
cargadero [karɣa'ðero] *nm* goods platform, loading bay
cargado, -a [kar'ɣaðo, a] *adj* loaded; *(Elec)* live; *(café, té)* strong; *(cielo)* overcast
cargador, a [karɣa'ðor, a] *nm/f* loader; *(Naut)* docker ■ *nm (Inform)*: **~ de discos** disk pack; *(Telec: del móvil)* charger
cargamento [karɣa'mento] *nm (acción)* loading; *(mercancías)* load, cargo
cargante [kar'ɣante] *adj (persona)* trying
cargar [kar'ɣar] *vt (barco, arma)* to load; *(Elec)* to charge; *(impuesto)* to impose; *(Com: algo en cuenta)* to charge, debit; *(Mil: enemigo)* to charge ■ *vi (Auto)* to load (up); *(inclinarse)* to lean; *(Inform)* to load, feed in; **~ con** to pick up, carry away; **cargarse** *vr (fam: estropear)* to break; *(: matar)* to bump off; *(Elec)* to become charged
cargo ['karɣo] *nm (Com etc)* charge, debit; *(puesto)* post, office; *(responsabilidad)* duty, obligation; *(fig)* weight, burden; *(Jur)* charge; **altos cargos** high-ranking officials; **una cantidad en ~ a algn** a sum chargeable to sb; **hacerse ~ de** to take charge of *o* responsibility for
cargue *etc* ['karɣe] *vb ver* **cargar**
carguero [kar'ɣero] *nm* freighter, cargo boat; *(avión)* freight plane
Caribe [ka'riβe] *nm*: **el ~** the Caribbean
caribeño, -a [kari'βeɲo, a] *adj* Caribbean
caricatura [karika'tura] *nf* caricature
caricia [ka'riθja] *nf* caress; *(a animal)* pat, stroke
caridad [kari'ðað] *nf* charity
caries ['karjes] *nf inv (Med)* tooth decay
cariño [ka'riɲo] *nm* affection, love; *(caricia)* caress; *(en carta)* love ...
cariñoso, -a [kari'ɲoso, a] *adj* affectionate
carioca [ka'rjoka] *adj (Am)* of *o* from Rio de Janeiro ■ *nm/f* native *o* inhabitant of Rio de Janeiro
carisma [ka'risma] *nm* charisma
carismático, -a [karis'matiko, a] *adj* charismatic
caritativo, -a [karita'tiβo, a] *adj* charitable
cariz [ka'riθ] *nm*: **tener** *o* **tomar buen/mal ~** to look good/bad
carmesí [karme'si] *adj, nm* crimson
carmín [kar'min] *nm (color)* carmine; **~ (de labios)** lipstick
carnal [kar'nal] *adj* carnal; **primo ~** first cousin
carnaval [karna'βal] *nm* carnival; *see note*

CARNAVAL

The 3 days before *miércoles de ceniza* (Ash Wednesday), when fasting traditionally starts, are the time for *carnaval*, an exuberant celebration which dates back to pre-Christian times. Although in decline during the Franco years, the *carnaval* has grown in popularity recently in Spain, Cádiz and Tenerife being particularly well-known for their celebrations. *El martes de carnaval* (Shrove Tuesday) is the biggest day, with colourful street parades, fancy dress, fireworks and a general party atmosphere.

carne ['karne] *nf* flesh; *(Culin)* meat; **~ de cerdo/de cordero/de ternera/de vaca** pork/lamb/veal/beef; **~ picada** mince; **~ de gallina** *(fig)* gooseflesh
carné [kar'ne] *nm* = **carnet**

carnero [kar'nero] *nm* sheep, ram; (*carne*) mutton
carnet (*pl* **carnets**) [kar'ne, kar'nes] *nm*: ~ **de conducir** driving licence; ~ **de identidad** identity card; *ver tb* **Documento Nacional de Identidad**
carnicería [karniθe'ria] *nf* butcher's (shop); (*fig: matanza*) carnage, slaughter
carnicero, -a [karni'θero, a] *adj* carnivorous ▪ *nm/f* (*tb fig*) butcher ▪ *nm* carnivore
carnívoro, -a [kar'niβoro, a] *adj* carnivorous ▪ *nm* carnivore
carnoso, -a [kar'noso, a] *adj* beefy, fat
caro, -a ['karo, a] *adj* dear; (*Com*) dear, expensive ▪ *adv* dear, dearly; **vender** ~ to sell at a high price
carpa ['karpa] *nf* (*pez*) carp; (*de circo*) big top; (*Am: de camping*) tent
carpeta [kar'peta] *nf* folder, file
carpintería [karpinte'ria] *nf* carpentry
carpintero [karpin'tero] *nm* carpenter; **pájaro** ~ woodpecker
carraca [ka'rraka] *nf* (*Deporte*) rattle
carraspear [karraspe'ar] *vi* (*aclararse la garganta*) to clear one's throat
carraspera [karras'pera] *nf* hoarseness
carrera [ka'rrera] *nf* (*acción*) run(ning); (*espacio recorrido*) run; (*certamen*) race; (*trayecto*) course; (*profesión*) career; (*Escol: Univ*) course; (*de taxi*) ride; (*en medias*) ladder; **a la** ~ at (full) speed; **caballo de ~(s)** racehorse; ~ **de armamentos** arms race
carrerilla [karre'riʎa] *nf*: **decir algo de** ~ to reel sth off; **tomar** ~ to get up speed
carreta [ka'rreta] *nf* wagon, cart
carrete [ka'rrete] *nm* reel, spool; (*Tec*) coil
carretera [karre'tera] *nf* (main) road, highway; ~ **nacional** ≈ A road (*Brit*), ≈ state highway (*US*); ~ **de circunvalación** ring road
carretilla [karre'tiʎa] *nf* trolley; (*Agr*) (wheel)barrow
carril [ka'rril] *nm* furrow; (*de autopista*) lane; (*Ferro*) rail
carril bici [karil'βiθi] (*pl* **carriles bici** [kariles'βiθi]) *nm* cycle lane, bikeway (*US*)
carrillo [ka'rriʎo] *nm* (*Anat*) cheek; (*Tec*) pulley
carro ['karro] *nm* cart, wagon; (*Mil*) tank; (*Am: coche*) car; (*Tip*) carriage; ~ **blindado** armoured car
carrocería [karroθe'ria] *nf* body, bodywork *no pl* (*Brit*)
carroña [ka'rroɲa] *nf* carrion *no pl*
carroza [ka'rroθa] *nf* (*vehículo*) coach ▪ *nm/f* (*fam*) old fogey
carruaje [ka'rrwaxe] *nm* carriage
carrusel [karru'sel] *nm* merry-go-round, roundabout (*Brit*)
carta ['karta] *nf* letter; (*Culin*) menu; (*naipe*) card; (*mapa*) map; (*Jur*) document; ~ **de crédito** credit card; ~ **de crédito documentaria** (*Com*) documentary letter of credit; ~ **de crédito irrevocable** (*Com*) irrevocable letter of credit; ~ **certificada/urgente** registered/special delivery letter; ~ **marítima** chart; ~ **de pedido** (*Com*) order; ~ **verde** (*Auto*) green card; ~ **de vinos** wine list; **echar una ~ al correo** to post a letter; **echar las cartas a algn** to tell sb's fortune
cartabón [karta'βon] *nm* set square
cartearse [karte'arse] *vr* to correspond
cartel [kar'tel] *nm* (*anuncio*) poster, placard; (*Escol*) wall chart; (*Com*) cartel
cartelera [karte'lera] *nf* hoarding, billboard; (*en periódico etc*) listings *pl*, entertainments guide; **"en ~"** "showing"
cartera [kar'tera] *nf* (*de bolsillo*) wallet; (*de colegial, cobrador*) satchel; (*Am: de señora*) handbag (*Brit*), purse (*US*); (*para documentos*) briefcase; **ministro sin** ~ (*Pol*) minister without portfolio; **ocupa la ~ de Agricultura** he is Minister of Agriculture; ~ **de pedidos** (*Com*) order book; **efectos en** ~ (*Econ*) holdings
carterista [karte'rista] *nm/f* pickpocket
cartero [kar'tero] *nm* postman
cartílago [kar'tilaɣo] *nm* cartilage
cartilla [kar'tiʎa] *nf* (*Escol*) primer, first reading book; ~ **de ahorros** bank book
cartografía [kartoɣra'fia] *nf* cartography
cartón [kar'ton] *nm* cardboard
cartucho [kar'tutʃo] *nm* (*Mil*) cartridge; (*bolsita*) paper cone; ~ **de datos** (*Inform*) data cartridge; ~ **de tinta** ink cartridge
cartulina [kartu'lina] *nf* fine cardboard, card
CASA ['kasa] *nf abr* (*Esp Aviat*) = **Construcciones Aeronáuticas S.A.**
casa ['kasa] *nf* house; (*hogar*) home; (*edificio*) building; (*Com*) firm, company; ~ **consistorial** town hall; ~ **de huéspedes** ≈ guest house; ~ **de socorro** first aid post; ~ **de citas** (*fam*) brothel; ~ **rural** (*de alquiler*) holiday cottage; (*pensión*) rural B&B; **ir a** ~ to go home; **salir de** ~ to go out; (*para siempre*) to leave home; **echar la ~ por la ventana** (*gastar*) to spare no expense; *ver tb* **hotel**
casadero, -a [kasa'ðero, a] *adj* marriageable
casado, -a [ka'saðo, a] *adj* married ▪ *nm/f* married man/woman
casamiento [kasa'mjento] *nm* marriage, wedding
casar [ka'sar] *vt* to marry; (*Jur*) to quash, annul; **casarse** *vr* to marry, get married;

casarse por lo civil to have a civil wedding, get married in a registry office (*Brit*)
cascabel [kaska'βel] *nm* (small) bell; (*Zool*) rattlesnake
cascada [kas'kaða] *nf* waterfall
cascajo [kas'kaxo] *nm* gravel, stone chippings *pl*
cascanueces [kaska'nweθes] *nm inv*: **un ~** a pair of nutcrackers
cascar [kas'kar] *vt* to split; (*nuez*) to crack ▪ *vi* to chatter; **cascarse** *vr* to crack, split, break (open)
cáscara ['kaskara] *nf* (*de huevo, fruta seca*) shell; (*de fruta*) skin; (*de limón*) peel
cascarón [kaska'ron] *nm* (broken) eggshell
cascarrabias [kaska'raβjas] *nm/f inv* (*fam*) hothead
casco ['kasko] *nm* (*de bombero, soldado*) helmet; (*cráneo*) skull; (*Naut: de barco*) hull; (*Zool: de caballo*) hoof; (*botella*) empty bottle; (*de ciudad*): **el ~ antiguo** the old part; **el ~ urbano** the town centre; **los cascos azules** the UN peace-keeping force, the blue helmets
cascote [kas'kote] *nm* piece of rubble; **cascotes** *nmpl* rubble *sg*
caserío [kase'rio] *nm* hamlet, group of houses; (*casa*) country house
casero, -a [ka'sero, a] *adj*: **ser muy ~** (*persona*) to be homeloving; **"comida casera"** "home cooking" ▪ *nm/f* (*propietario*) landlord/lady; (*Com*) house agent
caserón [kase'ron] *nm* large (ramshackle) house
caseta [ka'seta] *nf* hut; (*para bañista*) cubicle; (*de feria*) stall
casete [ka'sete] *nm o f* cassette; **~ digital** digital audio tape, DAT
casi ['kasi] *adv* almost; **~ nunca** hardly ever, almost never; **~ nada** next to nothing; **~ te caes** you almost *o* nearly fell
casilla [ka'siʎa] *nf* (*casita*) hut, cabin; (*Teat*) box office; (*para cartas*) pigeonhole; (*Ajedrez*) square; **C~ postal** *o* **de Correo(s)** (*Am*) P.O. Box; **sacar a algn de sus casillas** to drive sb round the bend (*fam*), make sb lose his temper
casillero [kasi'ʎero] *nm* pigeonholes
casino [ka'sino] *nm* club; (*de juego*) casino
caso ['kaso] *nm* case; (*suceso*) event; **en ~ de ...** in case of ...; **el ~ es que** the fact is that; **en el mejor de los casos** at best; **en ese ~** in that case; **en todo ~** in any case; **en último ~** as a last resort; **hacer ~ a** to pay attention to; **hacer ~ omiso de** to fail to mention, pass over; **hacer** *o* **venir al ~** to be relevant
caspa ['kaspa] *nf* dandruff
Caspio ['kaspjo] *adj*: **Mar ~** Caspian Sea
casque *etc* ['kaske] *vb ver* **cascar**
casquillo [kas'kiʎo] *nm* (*de bombilla*) fitting; (*de bala*) cartridge case
cassette [ka'set] *nf o m* = **casete**
casta ['kasta] *nf* caste; (*raza*) breed
castaña [kas'taɲa] *nf ver* **castaño**
castañetear [kastaɲete'ar] *vi* (*dientes*) to chatter
castaño, -a [kas'taɲo, a] *adj* chestnut (-coloured), brown ▪ *nm* chestnut tree ▪ *nf* chestnut; (*fam: golpe*) punch; **~ de Indias** horse chestnut tree
castañuelas [kasta'ɲwelas] *nfpl* castanets
castellano, -a [kaste'ʎano, a] *adj* Castilian; (*fam*) Spanish ▪ *nm/f* Castilian; (*fam*) Spaniard ▪ *nm* (*Ling*) Castilian, Spanish; *see note*

CASTELLANO

The term *castellano* is now the most widely used term in Spain and Spanish America to refer to the Spanish language, since español is too closely associated with Spain as a nation. Of course some people maintain that *castellano* should only refer to the type of Spanish spoken in Castilla.

castellonense [kasteʎo'nense] *adj* of *o* from Castellón de la Plana ▪ *nm/f* native *o* inhabitant of Castellón de la Plana
castidad [kasti'ðað] *nf* chastity, purity
castigar [kasti'ɣar] *vt* to punish; (*Deporte*) to penalize; (*afligir*) to afflict
castigo [kas'tiɣo] *nm* punishment; (*Deporte*) penalty
castigue *etc* [kas'tiɣe] *vb ver* **castigar**
Castilla [kas'tiʎa] *nf* Castile
castillo [kas'tiʎo] *nm* castle
castizo, -a [kas'tiθo, a] *adj* (*Ling*) pure; (*de buena casta*) purebred, pedigree; (*auténtico*) genuine
casto, -a ['kasto, a] *adj* chaste, pure
castor [kas'tor] *nm* beaver
castrar [kas'trar] *vt* to castrate; (*gato*) to doctor; (*Bot*) to prune
castrense [kas'trense] *adj* army *cpd*, military
casual [ka'swal] *adj* chance, accidental
casualidad [kaswali'ðað] *nf* chance, accident; (*combinación de circunstancias*) coincidence; **¡qué ~!** what a coincidence!
casualmente [kaswal'mente] *adv* by chance
cataclismo [kata'klismo] *nm* cataclysm
catador [kata'ðor] *nm* taster
catadura [kata'ðura] *nf* (*aspecto*) looks *pl*
catalán, -ana [kata'lan, ana] *adj, nm/f*

Catalan ■ *nm* (*Ling*) Catalan; *ver tb* **lenguas cooficiales**
catalejo [kata'lexo] *nm* telescope
catalizador [kataliθa'ðor] *nm* catalyst; (*Auto*) catalytic converter
catalogar [katalo'ɣar] *vt* to catalogue; ~ **(de)** (*fig*) to classify as
catálogo [ka'taloɣo] *nm* catalogue
catalogue *etc* [kata'loɣe] *vb ver* **catalogar**
Cataluña [kata'luɲa] *nf* Catalonia
cataplasma [kata'plasma] *nf* (*Med*) poultice
catapulta [kata'pulta] *nf* catapult
catar [ka'tar] *vt* to taste, sample
catarata [kata'rata] *nf* (*Geo*) (water)fall; (*Med*) cataract
catarro [ka'tarro] *nm* catarrh; (*constipado*) cold
catarsis [ka'tarsis] *nf* catharsis
catastro [ka'tastro] *nm* property register
catástrofe [ka'tastrofe] *nf* catastrophe
catear [kate'ar] *vt* (*fam*) to flunk
catecismo [kate'θismo] *nm* catechism
cátedra ['kateðra] *nf* (*Univ*) chair, professorship; (*Escol*) principal teacher's post; **sentar ~ sobre un argumento** to take one's stand on an argument
catedral [kate'ðral] *nf* cathedral
catedrático, -a [kate'ðratiko, a] *nm/f* professor; (*Escol*) principal teacher
categoría [kateɣo'ria] *nf* category; (*rango*) rank, standing; (*calidad*) quality; **de ~** (*hotel*) top-class; **de baja ~** (*oficial*) low-ranking; **de segunda ~** second-rate; **no tiene ~** he has no standing
categórico, -a [kate'ɣoriko, a] *adj* categorical
catequesis [kate'kesis] *nf* catechism lessons
caterva [ka'terβa] *nf* throng, crowd
cateto, -a [ka'teto, a] *nm/f* yokel
cátodo ['katoðo] *nm* cathode
catolicismo [katoli'θismo] *nm* Catholicism
católico, -a [ka'toliko, a] *adj, nm/f* Catholic
catorce [ka'torθe] *num* fourteen
catre ['katre] *nm* camp bed (*Brit*), cot (*US*); (*fam*) pit
Cáucaso ['kaukaso] *nm* Caucasus
cauce ['kauθe] *nm* (*de río*) riverbed; (*fig*) channel
caucho ['kautʃo] *nm* rubber; (*Am: llanta*) tyre
caución [kau'θjon] *nf* bail
caucionar [kauθjo'nar] *vt* (*Jur*) to bail (out), go bail for
caudal [kau'ðal] *nm* (*de río*) volume, flow; (*fortuna*) wealth; (*abundancia*) abundance
caudaloso, -a [kauða'loso, a] *adj* (*río*) large; (*persona*) wealthy, rich
caudillaje [kauði'ʎaxe] *nm* leadership
caudillo [kau'ðiʎo] *nm* leader, chief
causa ['kausa] *nf* cause; (*razón*) reason; (*Jur*) lawsuit, case; **a** *o* **por ~ de** because of, on account of
causar [kau'sar] *vt* to cause
cáustico, -a ['kaustiko, a] *adj* caustic
cautela [kau'tela] *nf* caution, cautiousness
cauteloso, -a [kaute'loso, a] *adj* cautious, wary
cautivar [kauti'βar] *vt* to capture; (*fig*) to captivate
cautiverio [kauti'βerjo] *nm*, **cautividad** [kautiβi'ðað] *nf* captivity
cautivo, -a [kau'tiβo, a] *adj, nm/f* captive
cauto, -a ['kauto, a] *adj* cautious, careful
cava ['kaβa] *nf* (*bodega*) (wine) cellar ■ *nm* (*vino*) *champagne-type wine*
cavar [ka'βar] *vt* to dig; (*Agr*) to dig over
caverna [ka'βerna] *nf* cave, cavern
cavernoso, -a [kaβer'noso, a] *adj* cavernous; (*voz*) resounding
caviar [ka'βjar] *nm* caviar(e)
cavidad [kaβi'ðað] *nf* cavity
cavilación [kaβila'θjon] *nf* deep thought
cavilar [kaβi'lar] *vt* to ponder
cayado [ka'jaðo] *nm* (*de pastor*) crook; (*de obispo*) crozier
cayendo *etc* [ka'jendo] *vb ver* **caer**
caza ['kaθa] *nf* (*acción: gen*) hunting; (*: con fusil*) shooting; (*una caza*) hunt, chase; (*animales*) game; **coto de ~** hunting estate ■ *nm* (*Aviat*) fighter
cazabe [ka'saβe] *nm* (*Am*) cassava bread *o* flour
cazador, a [kaθa'ðor, a] *nm/f* hunter/ huntress ■ *nf* jacket
cazaejecutivos [kaθaexeku'tiβos] *nm inv* (*Com*) headhunter
cazar [ka'θar] *vt* to hunt; (*perseguir*) to chase; (*prender*) to catch; **cazarlas al vuelo** to be pretty sharp
cazasubmarinos [kaθasuβma'rinos] *nm inv* (*Naut*) destroyer; (*Aviat*) anti-submarine craft
cazo ['kaθo] *nm* saucepan
cazuela [ka'θwela] *nf* (*vasija*) pan; (*guisado*) casserole
cazurro, -a [ka'θurro, a] *adj* surly
CC *nm abr* (*Pol: = Comité Central*) Central Committee
c/c. *abr* (*Com: = cuenta corriente*) current account
CCAA *abr* (*Esp*) = **Comunidades Autónomas**
CCI *nf abr* (*Com: = Cámara de Comercio Internacional*) ICC
CC.OO. *nfpl abr* = **Comisiones Obreras**
c/d *abr* (*= en casa de*) c/o, care of
CD *nm abr* (*= compact disc*) CD ■ *abr* (*Pol: = Cuerpo Diplomático*) CD (= Diplomatic Corps)

CDN *nm abr* (= *Centro Dramático Nacional*) ≈ RADA (*Brit*)
CD-Rom *nm abr* CD-Rom
CE *nm abr* (= *Consejo de Europa*) Council of Europe ■ *nf abr* (= *Comunidad Europea*) EC
cebada [θe'βaða] *nf* barley
cebar [θe'βar] *vt* (*animal*) to fatten (up); (*anzuelo*) to bait; (*Mil: Tec*) to prime; **cebarse** *vr*: **cebarse en** to vent one's fury on, take it out on
cebo ['θeβo] *nm* (*gen: para animales*) feed, food; (*para peces, fig*) bait; (*de arma*) charge
cebolla [θe'βoʎa] *nf* onion
cebolleta [θebo'ʎeta] *nf* spring onion
cebollino [θeβo'ʎino] *nm* spring onion
cebón, -ona [θe'βon, ona] *adj* fat, fattened
cebra ['θeβra] *nf* zebra; **paso de ~** zebra crossing
CECA ['θeka] *nf abr* (= *Comunidad Europea del Carbón y del Acero*) ECSC
ceca ['θeka] *nf*: **andar** *o* **ir de la ~ a la Meca** to chase about all over the place
cecear [θeθe'ar] *vi* to lisp
ceceo [θe'θeo] *nm* lisp
cecina [θe'θina] *nf* cured *o* smoked meat
cedazo [θe'ðaθo] *nm* sieve
ceder [θe'ðer] *vt* (*entregar*) to hand over; (*renunciar a*) to give up, part with ■ *vi* (*renunciar*) to give in, yield; (*disminuir*) to diminish, decline; (*romperse*) to give way; (*viento*) to drop; (*fiebre etc*) to abate; **"ceda el paso"** (*Auto*) "give way"
cedro ['θeðro] *nm* cedar
cédula ['θeðula] *nf* certificate, document; **~ de identidad** (*Am*) identity card; **~ en blanco** blank cheque; *ver tb* **Documento Nacional de Identidad**
CEE *nf abr* (= *Comunidad Económica Europea*) EEC
cegar [θe'ɣar] *vt* to blind; (*tubería etc*) to block up, stop up ■ *vi* to go blind; **cegarse** *vr*: **cegarse (de)** to be blinded (by)
cegué *etc* [θe'ɣe] *vb ver* **cegar**
ceguemos *etc* [θe'ɣemos] *vb ver* **cegar**
ceguera [θe'ɣera] *nf* blindness
CEI *nf abr* (= *Comunidad de Estados Independientes*) CIS
Ceilán [θei'lan] *nm* Ceylon, Sri Lanka
ceja ['θexa] *nf* eyebrow; **cejas pobladas** bushy eyebrows; **arquear las cejas** to raise one's eyebrows; **fruncir las cejas** to frown
cejar [θe'xar] *vi* (*fig*) to back down; **no ~** to keep it up, stick at it
cejijunto, -a [θexi'xunto, a] *adj* with bushy eyebrows; (*fig*) scowling
celada [θe'laða] *nf* ambush, trap
celador, a [θela'ðor, a] *nm/f* (*de edificio*) watchman; (*de museo etc*) attendant; (*de cárcel*) warder
celda ['θelda] *nf* cell
celebérrimo, -a [θele'βerrimo, a] *adj superlativo de* **célebre**
celebración [θeleβra'θjon] *nf* celebration
celebrar [θele'βrar] *vt* to celebrate; (*alabar*) to praise ■ *vi* to be glad; **celebrarse** *vr* to occur, take place
célebre ['θeleβre] *adj* celebrated, renowned
celebridad [θeleβri'ðað] *nf* fame; (*persona*) celebrity
celeridad [θeleri'ðað] *nf*: **con ~** promptly
celeste [θe'leste] *adj* sky-blue; (*cuerpo etc*) heavenly ■ *nm* sky blue
celestial [θeles'tjal] *adj* celestial, heavenly
celibato [θeli'βato] *nm* celibacy
célibe ['θeliβe] *adj, nm/f* celibate
celo ['θelo] *nm* zeal; (*Rel*) fervour; (*pey*) envy; **celos** *nmpl* jealousy *sg*; **dar celos a algn** to make sb jealous; **tener celos de algn** to be jealous of sb; **en ~** (*animales*) on heat
celofán [θelo'fan] *nm* Cellophane®
celosía [θelo'sia] *nf* lattice (window)
celoso, -a [θe'loso, a] *adj* (*envidioso*) jealous; (*trabajador*) zealous; (*desconfiado*) suspicious
celta ['θelta] *adj* Celtic ■ *nm/f* Celt
célula ['θelula] *nf* cell
celular [θelu'lar] *adj*: **tejido ~** cell tissue
celulitis [θelu'litis] *nf* (*enfermedad*) cellulitis; (*grasa*) cellulite
celuloide [θelu'loiðe] *nm* celluloid
celulosa [θelu'losa] *nf* cellulose
cementerio [θemen'terjo] *nm* cemetery, graveyard; **~ de coches** scrap yard
cemento [θe'mento] *nm* cement; (*hormigón*) concrete; (*Am: cola*) glue
CEN *nm abr* (*Esp*) = **Consejo de Economía Nacional**
cena ['θena] *nf* evening meal, dinner
cenagal [θena'ɣal] *nm* bog, quagmire
cenar [θe'nar] *vt* to have for dinner, dine on ■ *vi* to have dinner, dine
cencerro [θen'θerro] *nm* cowbell; **estar como un ~** (*fam*) to be round the bend
cenicero [θeni'θero] *nm* ashtray
ceniciento, -a [θeni'θjento, a] *adj* ash-coloured, ashen
cenit [θe'nit] *nm* zenith
ceniza [θe'niθa] *nf* ash, ashes *pl*
censar [θen'sar] *vt* to take a census of
censo ['θenso] *nm* census; **~ electoral** electoral roll
censor [θen'sor] *nm* censor; **~ de cuentas** (*Com*) auditor; **~ jurado de cuentas** chartered (*Brit*) *o* certified public (*US*) accountant
censura [θen'sura] *nf* (*Pol*) censorship; (*moral*) censure, criticism

censurable [θensu'raβle] *adj* reprehensible
censurar [θensu'rar] *vt* (*idea*) to censure; (*cortar: película*) to censor
centavo [θen'taβo] *nm* hundredth (part); (*Am*) cent
centella [θen'teʎa] *nf* spark
centellear [θenteʎe'ar] *vi* (*metal*) to gleam; (*estrella*) to twinkle; (*fig*) to sparkle
centelleo [θente'ʎeo] *nm* gleam(ing); twinkling; sparkling
centena [θen'tena] *nf* hundred
centenar [θente'nar] *nm* hundred
centenario, -a [θente'narjo, a] *adj* one hundred years old ■ *nm* centenary
centeno [θen'teno] *nm* rye
centésimo, -a [θen'tesimo, a] *adj, nm* hundredth
centígrado [θen'tiɣraðo] *adj* centigrade
centigramo [θenti'ɣramo] *nm* centigramme
centilitro [θenti'litro] *nm* centilitre (*Brit*), centiliter (*US*)
centímetro [θen'timetro] *nm* centimetre (*Brit*), centimeter (*US*)
céntimo, -a ['θentimo, a] *adj* hundredth ■ *nm* cent
centinela [θenti'nela] *nm* sentry, guard
centollo, -a [θen'toʎo, a] *nm/f* large (*o* spider) crab
central [θen'tral] *adj* central ■ *nf* head office; (*Tec*) plant; (*Telec*) exchange; ~ **nuclear** nuclear power station
centralice *etc* [θentra'liθe] *vb ver* **centralizar**
centralita [θentra'lita] *nf* switchboard
centralización [θentraliθa'θjon] *nf* centralization
centralizar [θentrali'θar] *vt* to centralize
centrar [θen'trar] *vt* to centre
céntrico, -a ['θentriko, a] *adj* central
centrifugar [θentrifu'ɣar] *vt* (*ropa*) to spin-dry
centrífugo, -a [θent'rifuɣo, a] *adj* centrifugal
centrifugue *etc* [θentri'fuɣe] *vb ver* **centrifugar**
centrista [θen'trista] *adj* centre *cpd*
centro ['θentro] *nm* centre; **ser de** ~ (*Pol*) to be a moderate; ~ **de acogida (para niños)** children's home; ~ **de beneficios** (*Com*) profit centre; ~ **cívico** community centre; ~ **comercial** shopping centre; ~ **de informática** computer centre; ~ **(de determinación) de costos** (*Com*) cost centre; ~ **delantero** (*Deporte*) centre forward; ~ **docente** teaching institution; ~ **juvenil** youth club; ~ **de llamadas** call centre; ~ **social** community centre
centroafricano, -a [θentroafri'kano, a] *adj*: **la República Centroafricana** the Central African Republic
centroamericano, -a [θentroameri'kano, a] *adj, nm/f* Central American
centrocampista [θentrokam'pista] *nm/f* (*Deporte*) midfielder
ceñido, -a [θe'ɲiðo, a] *adj* tight
ceñir [θe'ɲir] *vt* (*rodear*) to encircle, surround; (*ajustar*) to fit (tightly); (*apretar*) to tighten; **ceñirse** *vr*: **ceñirse algo** to put sth on; **ceñirse al asunto** to stick to the matter in hand
ceño ['θeɲo] *nm* frown, scowl; **fruncir el** ~ to frown, knit one's brow
CEOE *nf abr* (= *Confederación Española de Organizaciones Empresariales*) ≈ CBI (*Brit*)
cepa ['θepa] *nf* (*de vid, fig*) stock; (*Bio*) strain
CEPAL [θe'pal] *nf abr* (= *Comisión Económica de las Naciones Unidas para la América Latina*) ECLA
cepillar [θepi'ʎar] *vt* to brush; (*madera*) to plane (down)
cepillo [θe'piʎo] *nm* brush; (*para madera*) plane; (*Rel*) poor box, alms box; ~ **de dientes** toothbrush
cepo ['θepo] *nm* (*de caza*) trap
CEPSA ['θepsa] *nf abr* (*Com*) = **Compañía Española de Petróleos, S.A.**
CEPYME *nf abr* = **Confederación Española de la Pequeña y Mediana Empresa**
cera ['θera] *nf* wax; ~ **de abejas** beeswax
cerámica [θe'ramika] *nf* pottery; (*arte*) ceramics *sg*
ceramista [θera'mista] *nm/f* potter
cerbatana [θerβa'tana] *nf* blowpipe
cerca ['θerka] *nf* fence ■ *adv* near, nearby, close; **por aquí** ~ nearby ■ *prep*: ~ **de** (*cantidad*) nearly, about; (*distancia*) near, close to ■ *nmpl*: **cercas** foreground *sg*
cercado [θer'kaðo] *nm* enclosure
cercanía [θerka'nia] *nf* nearness, closeness; **cercanías** *nfpl* outskirts, suburbs; **tren de cercanías** commuter *o* local train
cercano, -a [θer'kano, a] *adj* close, near; (*pueblo etc*) nearby; **C~ Oriente** Near East
cercar [θer'kar] *vt* to fence in; (*rodear*) to surround
cerciorar [θerθjo'rar] *vt* (*asegurar*) to assure; **cerciorarse** *vr*: **cerciorarse (de)** (*descubrir*) to find out (about); (*asegurarse*) to make sure (of)
cerco ['θerko] *nm* (*Agr*) enclosure; (*Am*) fence; (*Mil*) siege
cerda ['θerða] *nf* (*de cepillo*) bristle; (*Zool*) sow
cerdada [θer'ðaða] *nf* (*fam*): **hacer una ~ a algn** to play a dirty trick on sb
Cerdeña [θer'ðeɲa] *nf* Sardinia
cerdo ['θerðo] *nm* pig; **carne de** ~ pork
cereal [θere'al] *nm* cereal; **cereales** *nmpl* cereals, grain *sg*

cerebral [θere'βral] *adj* (*tb fig*) cerebral; (*tumor*) brain *cpd*
cerebro [θe'reβro] *nm* brain; (*fig*) brains *pl*; **ser un ~** (*fig*) to be brilliant
ceremonia [θere'monja] *nf* ceremony; **reunión de ~** formal meeting; **hablar sin ~** to speak plainly
ceremonial [θeremo'njal] *adj, nm* ceremonial
ceremonioso, -a [θeremo'njoso, a] *adj* ceremonious; (*cumplido*) formal
cereza [θe'reθa] *nf* cherry
cerezo [θe'reθo] *nm* cherry tree
cerilla [θe'riʎa] *nf*, **cerillo** [se'riʎo] *nm* (*Am*) match
cerner [θer'ner] *vt* to sift, sieve; **cernerse** *vr* to hover
cero ['θero] *nm* nothing, zero; (*Deporte*) nil; **8 grados bajo ~** 8 degrees below zero; **a partir de ~** from scratch
cerque *etc* ['θerke] *vb ver* **cercar**
cerrado, -a [θe'rraðo, a] *adj* closed, shut; (*con llave*) locked; (*tiempo*) cloudy, overcast; (*curva*) sharp; (*acento*) thick, broad; **a puerta cerrada** (*Jur*) in camera
cerradura [θerra'ðura] *nf* (*acción*) closing; (*mecanismo*) lock
cerrajería [θerraxe'ria] *nf* locksmith's craft; (*tienda*) locksmith's (shop)
cerrajero, -a [θerra'xero, a] *nm/f* locksmith
cerrar [θe'rrar] *vt* to close, shut; (*paso, carretera*) to close; (*grifo*) to turn off; (*trato, cuenta, negocio*) to close ■ *vi* to close, shut; (*la noche*) to come down; **~ con llave** to lock; **~ el sistema** (*Inform*) to close *o* shut down the system; **~ un trato** to strike a bargain; **cerrarse** *vr* to close, shut; (*herida*) to heal
cerro ['θerro] *nm* hill; **andar por las cerros de Úbeda** to wander from the point, digress
cerrojo [θe'rroxo] *nm* (*herramienta*) bolt; (*de puerta*) latch
certamen [θer'tamen] *nm* competition, contest
certero, -a [θer'tero, a] *adj* accurate
certeza [θer'teθa], **certidumbre** [θerti'ðumbre] *nf* certainty
certificación [θertifika'θjon] *nf* certification; (*Jur*) affidavit
certificado, -a [θertifi'kaðo, a] *adj* certified; (*Correos*) registered ■ *nm* certificate
certificar [θertifi'kar] *vt* (*asegurar, atestar*) to certify
certifique *etc* [θerti'fike] *vb ver* **certificar**
cervatillo [θerβa'tiʎo] *nm* fawn
cervecería [θerβeθe'ria] *nf* (*fábrica*) brewery; (*taberna*) public house
cerveza [θer'βeθa] *nf* beer; **~ de barril** draught beer
cervical [θerβi'kal] *adj* cervical
cerviz [θer'βiθ] *nf* nape of the neck
cesación [θesa'θjon] *nf* cessation, suspension
cesante [θe'sante] *adj* redundant; (*Am*) unemployed; (*ministro*) outgoing; (*diplomático*) recalled ■ *nm/f* redundant worker
cesantía [θesan'tia] *nf* (*Am*) unemployment
cesar [θe'sar] *vi* to cease, stop; (*de un trabajo*) to leave ■ *vt* (*en el trabajo*) to dismiss; (*alto cargo*) to remove from office
cesárea [θe'sarea] *nf* Caesarean (section)
cese ['θese] *nm* (*de trabajo*) dismissal; (*de pago*) suspension
CESID [θe'sið] *nm abr* (*Esp*: = *Centro Superior de Investigación de la Defensa Nacional*) *military intelligence service*
cesión [θe'sjon] *nf*: **~ de bienes** surrender of property
césped ['θespeð] *nm* grass, lawn
cesta ['θesta] *nf* basket
cesto ['θesto] *nm* (large) basket, hamper
cetrería [θetre'ria] *nf* falconry
cetrino, -a [θe'trino, a] *adj* (*tez*) sallow
cetro ['θetro] *nm* sceptre
Ceuta [θe'uta] *nf* Ceuta
ceutí [θeu'ti] *adj* of *o* from Ceuta ■ *nm/f* native *o* inhabitant of Ceuta
C.F. *nm abr* (= *Club de Fútbol*) F.C.
CFC *nm abr* (= *clorofluorocarbono*) CFC
cfr *abr* (= *confróntese, compárese*) cf
cg *abr* (= *centígramo*) cg
CGPJ *nm abr* (= *Consejo General del Poder Judicial*) *governing body of Spanish legal system*
CGS *nf abr* (*Guatemala: El Salvador*) = **Confederación General de Sindicatos**
CGT *nf abr* (*Colombia: México: Nicaragua: Esp*: = **Confederación General de Trabajadores**) (*Argentina*: = **Confederación General del Trabajo**)
Ch, ch [tʃe] *nf former letter in the Spanish alphabet*
chabacano, -a [tʃaβa'kano, a] *adj* vulgar, coarse
chabola [tʃa'βola] *nf* shack; **chabolas** *nfpl* shanty town *sg*
chabolismo [tʃaβo'lismo] *nm*: **el problema del ~** the problem of substandard housing, the shanty town problem
chacal [tʃa'kal] *nm* jackal
chacarero [tʃaka'rero] *nm* (*Am*) small farmer
chacha ['tʃatʃa] *nf* (*fam*) maid
cháchara ['tʃatʃara] *nf* chatter; **estar de ~** to chatter away
chacra ['tʃakra] *nf* (*Am*) smallholding
chafar [tʃa'far] *vt* (*aplastar*) to crush, flatten; (*arruinar*) to ruin

chaflán [tʃa'flan] *nm (Tec)* bevel
chal [tʃal] *nm* shawl
chalado, -a [tʃa'laðo, a] *adj (fam)* crazy
chalé *(pl* **~s**) [tʃa'le, tʃa'les] *nm* = **chalet**
chaleco [tʃa'leko] *nm* waistcoat, vest *(US)*; **~ antibala** bulletproof vest; **~ salvavidas** life jacket; **~ reflectante** *(Aut)* high-visibility vest
chalet *(pl* **chalets**) [tʃa'le, tʃa'les] *nm* villa, ≈ detached house; **~ adosado** semi-detached house
chalupa [tʃa'lupa] *nf* launch, boat
chamaco, -a [tʃa'mako, a] *nm/f (Am)* boy/girl
chamarra [tʃa'marra] *nf* sheepskin jacket; *(Am: poncho)* blanket
champán [tʃam'pan] *nm*, **champaña** [tʃam'paɲa] *nm* champagne
champiñón [tʃampi'ɲon] *nm* mushroom
champú [tʃam'pu] *(pl* **~es** *o* **~s**) *nm* shampoo
chamuscar [tʃamus'kar] *vt* to scorch, singe
chamusque *etc* [tʃa'muske] *vb ver* **chamuscar**
chamusquina [tʃamus'kina] *nf* singeing
chance ['tʃanθe] *nm (a veces nf) (Am)* chance, opportunity
chanchada [tʃan'tʃaða] *nf (Am fam)* dirty trick
chancho, -a ['tʃantʃo, a] *nm/f (Am)* pig
chanchullo [tʃan'tʃuʎo] *nm (fam)* fiddle, wangle
chancla ['tʃankla] *nf*, **chancleta** [tʃan'kleta] *nf* flip-flop; *(zapato viejo)* old shoe
chandal [tʃan'dal] *nm* tracksuit; **~ (de tactel)** shellsuit
chantaje [tʃan'taxe] *nm* blackmail; **hacer ~ a uno** to blackmail sb
chanza ['tʃanθa] *nf* joke
chao [tʃao] *excl (fam)* cheerio
chapa ['tʃapa] *nf (de metal)* plate, sheet; *(de madera)* board, panel; *(de botella)* bottle top; *(insignia)* (lapel) badge; *(Am: Auto: tb:* **chapa de matrícula**) number *(Brit) o* license *(US)* plate; *(Am: cerradura)* lock; **de 3 chapas** *(madera)* 3-ply
chapado, -a [tʃa'paðo, a] *adj (metal)* plated; *(muebles etc)* finished
chaparro, -a [tʃa'parro, a] *adj* squat; *(Am: bajito)* short
chaparrón [tʃapa'rron] *nm* downpour, cloudburst
chapotear [tʃapote'ar] *vt* to sponge down ■ *vi (fam)* to splash about
chapucero, -a [tʃapu'θero, a] *adj* rough, crude ■ *nm/f* bungler
chapurrar [tʃapurr'ar], **chapurrear** [tʃapurre'ar] *vt (idioma)* to speak badly
chapuza [tʃa'puθa] *nf* botched job
chapuzón [tʃapu'θon] *nm*: **darse un ~** to go for a dip
chaqué [tʃa'ke] *nm* morning coat
chaqueta [tʃa'keta] *nf* jacket; **cambiar la ~** *(fig)* to change sides
chaquetón [tʃake'ton] *nm* three-quarter-length coat
charca ['tʃarka] *nf* pond, pool
charco ['tʃarko] *nm* pool, puddle
charcutería [tʃarkute'ria] *nf (tienda) shop selling chiefly pork meat products*; *(productos)* cooked pork meats *pl*
charla ['tʃarla] *nf* talk, chat; *(conferencia)* lecture
charlar [tʃar'lar] *vi* to talk, chat
charlatán, -ana [tʃarla'tan, ana] *nm/f* chatterbox; *(estafador)* trickster
charol[1] [tʃa'rol] *nm* varnish; *(cuero)* patent leather
charol[2] [tʃa'rol] *nm (Am)*, **charola** [tʃa'rola] *nf (Am)* tray
charqui ['tʃarki] *nm (Am)* dried beef, jerky *(US)*
charro, -a ['tʃarro, a] *adj* Salamancan; *(Am)* Mexican; *(ropa)* loud, gaudy; *(Am: costumbres)* traditional ■ *nm/f* Salamancan; Mexican
chárter ['tʃarter] *adj inv*: **vuelo ~** charter flight
chascarrillo [tʃaska'rriʎo] *nm (fam)* funny story
chasco ['tʃasko] *nm (broma)* trick, joke; *(desengaño)* disappointment
chasis ['tʃasis] *nm inv (Auto)* chassis; *(Foto)* plate holder
chasquear [tʃaske'ar] *vt (látigo)* to crack; *(lengua)* to click
chasquido [tʃas'kiðo] *nm (de lengua)* click; *(de látigo)* crack
chat [tʃat] *nm (Internet)* chat room
chatarra [tʃa'tarra] *nf* scrap (metal)
chatero, -a [tʃa'tero, a] *adj* chat *cpd* ■ *nm/f* chat-room user
chato, -a ['tʃato, a] *adj* flat; *(nariz)* snub ■ *nm* wine tumbler; **beber unos chatos** to have a few drinks
chau [tʃau], **chaucito** [tʃau'sito] *excl (fam)* cheerio
chauvinismo [tʃoβi'nismo] *nm* chauvinism
chauvinista [tʃoβi'nista] *adj, nm/f* chauvinist
chaval, a [tʃa'βal, a] *nm/f* kid *(fam)*, lad/lass
chavo ['tʃaβo] *nm (Am: fam)* bloke *(Brit)*, guy
checo, -a ['tʃeko, a] *adj, nm/f* Czech ■ *nm (Ling)* Czech
checoeslovaco, -a [tʃekoeslo'βako, a], **checoslovaco, -a** [tʃekoslo'βako, a] *adj, nm/f* Czech, Czechoslovak
Checoeslovaquia [tʃekoeslo'βakja], **Checoslovaquia** [tʃekoslo'βakja] *nf* Czechoslovakia
chepa ['tʃepa] *nf* hump

cheque ['tʃeke] *nm* cheque (*Brit*), check (*US*); **~ abierto/en blanco/cruzado** open/blank/ crossed cheque; **~ al portador** cheque payable to bearer; **~ de viajero** traveller's cheque
chequeo [tʃe'keo] *nm* (*Med*) check-up; (*Auto*) service
chequera [tʃe'kera] *nf* (*Am*) chequebook (*Brit*), checkbook (*US*)
chévere ['tʃeβere] *adj* (*Am*) great, fabulous (*fam*)
chicano, -a [tʃi'kano, a] *adj, nm/f* chicano, Mexican-American
chicha ['tʃitʃa] *nf* (*Am*) maize liquor
chícharo ['tʃitʃaro] *nm* (*Am*) pea
chicharra [tʃi'tʃarra] *nf* harvest bug, cicada
chicharrón [tʃitʃa'rron] *nm* (pork) crackling
chichón [tʃi'tʃon] *nm* bump, lump
chicle ['tʃikle] *nm* chewing gum
chico, -a ['tʃiko, a] *adj* small, little ■ *nm/f* child; (*muchacho*) boy; (*muchacha*) girl
chicote [tʃi'kote] *nm* (*Am*) whip
chiflado, -a [tʃi'flaðo, a] *adj* (*fam*) crazy, round the bend ■ *nm/f* nutcase
chiflar [tʃi'flar] *vt* to hiss, boo ■ *vi* (*esp Am*) to whistle
Chile ['tʃile] *nm* Chile
chile ['tʃile] *nm* chilli, pepper
chileno, -a [tʃi'leno, a] *adj, nm/f* Chilean
chillar [tʃi'ʎar] *vi* (*persona*) to yell, scream; (*animal salvaje*) to howl; (*cerdo*) to squeal; (*puerta*) to creak
chillido [tʃi'ʎiðo] *nm* (*de persona*) yell, scream; (*de animal*) howl; (*de frenos*) screech(ing)
chillón, -ona [tʃi'ʎon, ona] *adj* (*niño*) noisy; (*color*) loud, gaudy
chimenea [tʃime'nea] *nf* chimney; (*hogar*) fireplace
chimpancé (*pl* **~s**) [tʃimpan'θe, tʃimpan'θes] *nm* chimpanzee
China ['tʃina] *nf*: **(la) ~** China
china ['tʃina] *nf* pebble
chinchar [tʃin'tʃar] (*fam*) *vt* to pester, annoy; **chincharse** *vr* to get cross; **¡chínchate!** tough!
chinche ['tʃintʃe] *nf* bug; (*Tec*) drawing pin (*Brit*), thumbtack (*US*) ■ *nm/f* nuisance, pest
chincheta [tʃin'tʃeta] *nf* drawing pin (*Brit*), thumbtack (*US*)
chinchorro [tʃin'tʃorro] *nm* (*Am*) hammock
chingado, -a [tʃin'gaðo, a] *adj* (*esp Am fam!*) lousy, bloody (*!*); **hijo de la chingada** bastard (*!*), son of a bitch (*US!*)
chingar [tʃin'gar] *vt* (*Am: fam!*) to fuck (up) (*!*), screw (up) (*!*); **chingarse** *vr* (*Am: emborracharse*) to get pissed (*Brit*), get plastered; (*: fracasar*) to fail
chingue *etc* ['tʃinge] *vb ver* **chingar**
chino, -a ['tʃino, a] *adj, nm/f* Chinese ■ *nm* (*Ling*) Chinese; (*Culin*) chinois, conical strainer
chip [tʃip] *nm* (*Inform*) chip
chipirón [tʃipi'ron] *nm* squid
Chipre ['tʃipre] *nf* Cyprus
chipriota [tʃi'prjota], **chipriote** [tʃi'prjote] *adj* Cypriot, Cyprian ■ *nm/f* Cypriot
chiquillada [tʃiki'ʎada] *nf* childish prank; (*Am: chiquillos*) kids *pl*
chiquillo, -a [tʃi'kiʎo, a] *nm/f* kid (*fam*), youngster, child
chiquito, -a [tʃi'kito, a] *adj* very small, tiny ■ *nm/f* kid (*fam*)
chirigota [tʃiri'ɣota] *nf* joke
chirimbolo [tʃirim'bolo] *nm* thingummyjig (*fam*)
chirimoya [tʃiri'moja] *nf* custard apple
chiringuito [tʃirin'gito] *nm* refreshment stall *o* stand
chiripa [tʃi'ripa] *nf* fluke; **por ~** by chance
chirona [tʃi'rona], **chirola** (*Am*) [tʃi'rola] *nf* (*fam*) clink, jail
chirriar [tʃi'rrjar] *vi* (*goznes*) to creak, squeak; (*pájaros*) to chirp, sing
chirrido [tʃi'rriðo] *nm* creak(ing), squeak(ing); (*de pájaro*) chirp(ing)
chis [tʃis] *excl* sh!
chisme ['tʃisme] *nm* (*habladurías*) piece of gossip; (*fam: objeto*) thingummyjig
chismoso, -a [tʃis'moso, a] *adj* gossiping ■ *nm/f* gossip
chispa ['tʃispa] *nf* spark; (*fig*) sparkle; (*ingenio*) wit; (*fam*) drunkenness
chispeante [tʃispe'ante] *adj* (*tb fig*) sparkling
chispear [tʃispe'ar] *vi* to spark; (*lloviznar*) to drizzle
chisporrotear [tʃisporrote'ar] *vi* (*fuego*) to throw out sparks; (*leña*) to crackle; (*aceite*) to hiss, splutter
chistar [tʃis'tar] *vi*: **no ~** not to say a word
chiste ['tʃiste] *nm* joke, funny story; **~ verde** blue joke
chistera [tʃis'tera] *nf* top hat
chistoso, -a [tʃis'toso, a] *adj* (*gracioso*) funny, amusing; (*bromista*) witty
chistu ['tʃistu] *nm* = **txistu**
chivarse [tʃi'βarse] *vr* (*fam*) to grass
chivatazo [tʃiβa'taθo] *nm* (*fam*) tip-off; **dar ~** to inform
chivo, -a ['tʃiβo, a] *nm/f* (billy/nanny-)goat; **~ expiatorio** scapegoat
chocante [tʃo'kante] *adj* startling; (*extraño*) odd; (*ofensivo*) shocking
chocar [tʃo'kar] *vi* (*coches etc*) to collide, crash; (*Mil, fig*) to clash ■ *vt* to shock; (*sorprender*)

to startle; **~ con** to collide with; *(fig)* to run into, run up against; **¡chócala!** *(fam)* put it there!
chochear [tʃotʃe'ar] *vi* to dodder, be senile
chocho, -a ['tʃotʃo, a] *adj* doddering, senile; *(fig)* soft, doting
chocolate [tʃoko'late] *adj* chocolate ■ *nm* chocolate; *(fam)* dope, marijuana
chocolatería [tʃokolate'ria] *nf* chocolate factory (*o* shop)
chófer ['tʃofer], **chofer** [tʃo'fer] *(esp Am) nm* driver
chollo ['tʃoʎo] *nm (fam)* bargain, snip
chomba ['tʃomba], **chompa** ['tʃompa] *nf (Am)* jumper, sweater
chopo ['tʃopo] *nm* black poplar
choque *etc* ['tʃoke] *vb ver* **chocar** ■ *nm (impacto)* impact; *(golpe)* jolt; *(Auto)* crash; *(fig)* conflict
chorizo [tʃo'riθo] *nm hard pork sausage (type of salami)*; *(ladrón)* crook
chorra ['tʃorra] *nf* luck
chorrada [tʃo'rraða] *nf (fam)*: **¡es una ~!** that's crap! (*!*); **decir chorradas** to talk crap (*!*)
chorrear [tʃorre'ar] *vt* to pour ■ *vi* to gush (out), spout (out); *(gotear)* to drip, trickle
chorreras [tʃo'rreras] *nfpl (adorno)* frill *sg*
chorro ['tʃorro] *nm* jet; *(caudalito)* dribble, trickle; *(fig)* stream; **salir a chorros** to gush forth; **con propulsión a ~** jet-propelled
chotearse [tʃote'arse] *vr* to joke
choto ['tʃoto] *nm (cabrito)* kid
chovinismo [tʃoβi'nismo] *nm* = **chauvinismo**
chovinista [tʃoβi'nista] *adj, nm/f* = **chauvinista**
choza ['tʃoθa] *nf* hut, shack
chubasco [tʃu'βasko] *nm* squall
chubasquero [tʃuβas'kero] *nm* oilskins *pl*
chuchería [tʃutʃe'ria] *nf* trinket
chucho ['tʃutʃo] *nm (Zool)* mongrel
chufa ['tʃufa] *nf* chufa, earth almond, tiger nut; **horchata de chufas** *drink made from chufas*
chuleta [tʃu'leta] *nf* chop, cutlet; *(Escol etc: fam)* crib
chulo, -a ['tʃulo, a] *adj (encantador)* charming; *(aire)* proud; *(pey)* fresh; *(fam: estupendo)* great, fantastic ■ *nm (pícaro)* rascal; *(madrileño)* working-class Madrilenian; *(rufián: tb:* **chulo de putas**) pimp
chumbera [tʃum'bera] *nf* prickly pear
chungo, -a ['tʃungo, a] *(fam) adj* lousy ■ *nf*: **estar de chunga** to be in a merry mood
chupa ['tʃupa] *nf (fam)* jacket
chupado, -a [tʃu'paðo, a] *adj (delgado)* skinny, gaunt; **está ~** *(fam)* it's simple, it's dead easy
chupar [tʃu'par] *vt* to suck; *(absorber)* to absorb; **chuparse** *vr* to grow thin; **para chuparse los dedos** mouthwatering
chupatintas [tʃupa'tintas] *nm inv* penpusher
chupe ['tʃupe] *nm (Am)* stew
chupete [tʃu'pete] *nm* dummy *(Brit)*, pacifier *(US)*
chupetón [tʃupe'ton] *nm* suck
churrasco [tʃu'rrasko] *nm (Am)* barbecue, barbecued meat
churrería [tʃurre'ria] *nf stall or shop which sells "churros"*
churrete [tʃu'rrete] *nm* grease spot
churretón [tʃurre'ton] *nm* stain
churrigueresco, -a [tʃurrige'resko, a] *adj (Arq)* baroque; *(fig)* excessively ornate
churro, -a ['tʃurro, a] *adj* coarse ■ *nm (Culin)* (type of) fritter; *see note*; *(chapuza)* botch, mess

CHURRO

Churros, long fritters made with flour and water, are very popular in much of Spain and are often eaten with thick hot chocolate, either for breakfast or as a snack. In Madrid, they eat a thicker variety of *churro* called *porra*.

churruscar [tʃurrus'kar] *vt* to fry crisp
churrusque *etc* [tʃu'rruske] *vb ver* **churruscar**
churumbel [tʃurum'bel] *nm (fam)* kid
chus [tʃus] *excl*: **no decir ni ~ ni mus** not to say a word
chusco, -a ['tʃusko, a] *adj* funny
chusma ['tʃusma] *nf* rabble, mob
chutar [tʃu'tar] *vi (Deporte)* to shoot (at goal); **esto va que chuta** it's going fine
chuzo ['tʃuθo] *nm*: **llueve a chuzos, llueven chuzos de punta** it's raining cats and dogs
C.I. *nm abr* = **coeficiente intelectual** *o* **de inteligencia**
Cía *abr (= compañía)* Co.
cianuro [θja'nuro] *nm* cyanide
ciática ['θjatika] *nf* sciatica
cibercafé [θiβerka'fe] *nm* cybercafé
ciberespacio [θiβeres'paθjo] *nm* cyberspace
cibernauta [θiβer'nauta] *nmf* cybernaut
cibernética [θiβer'netika] *nf* cybernetics *sg*
cicatrice *etc* [θika'triθe] *vb ver* **cicatrizar**
cicatriz [θika'triθ] *nf* scar
cicatrizar [θikatri'θar] *vt* to heal; **cicatrizarse** *vr* to heal (up), form a scar
cíclico, -a ['θikliko, a] *adj* cyclical
ciclismo [θi'klismo] *nm* cycling
ciclista [θi'klista] *nm/f* cyclist
ciclo ['θiklo] *nm* cycle
ciclomotor [θiklomo'tor] *nm* moped

ciclón [θi'klon] *nm* cyclone
cicloturismo [θiklotu'rismo] *nm* touring by bicycle
cicuta [θi'kuta] *nf* hemlock
ciego, -a *etc* ['θjeɣo, a] *vb ver* **cegar** ■ *adj* blind ■ *nm/f* blind man/woman; **a ciegas** blindly; **me puse ciega mariscos** (*fam*) I stuffed myself with seafood
ciegue *etc* ['θjeɣe] *vb ver* **cegar**
cielo ['θjelo] *nm* sky; (*Rel*) heaven; (*Arq*: *tb*: **cielo raso**) ceiling; **¡cielos!** good heavens!; **ver el ~ abierto** to see one's chance
ciempiés [θjem'pjes] *nm inv* centipede
cien [θjen] *num ver* **ciento**
ciénaga ['θjenaɣa] *nf* marsh, swamp
ciencia ['θjenθja] *nf* science; **ciencias** *nfpl* science *sg*; **saber algo a ~ cierta** to know sth for certain
ciencia-ficción ['θjenθjafik'θjon] *nf* science fiction
cieno ['θjeno] *nm* mud, mire
científico, -a [θjen'tifiko, a] *adj* scientific ■ *nm/f* scientist
ciento ['θjento], **cien** *num* hundred; **pagar al 10 por ~** to pay at 10 per cent
cierne *etc* ['θjerne] *vb ver* **cerner** ■ *nm*: **en ~** in blossom; **en ~(s)** (*fig*) in its infancy
cierre *etc* ['θjerre] *vb ver* **cerrar** ■ *nm* closing, shutting; (*con llave*) locking; (*Radio*: *TV*) close-down; **~ de cremallera** zip (fastener); **precios de ~** (*Bolsa*) closing prices; **~ del sistema** (*Inform*) system shutdown
cierto, -a ['θjerto, a] *adj* sure, certain; (*un tal*) a certain; (*correcto*) right, correct; **~ hombre** a certain man; **ciertas personas** certain *o* some people; **sí, es ~** yes, that's correct; **por ~** by the way; **lo ~ es que ...** the fact is that ...; **estar en lo ~** to be right
ciervo ['θjerβo] *nm* (*Zool*) deer; (: *macho*) stag
cierzo ['θjerθo] *nm* north wind
CIES *nm abr* = **Consejo Interamericano Económico y Social**
cifra ['θifra] *nf* number, figure; (*cantidad*) number, quantity; (*secreta*) code; **~ global** lump sum; **~ de negocios** (*Com*) turnover; **en cifras redondas** in round figures; **~ de referencia** (*Com*) bench mark; **~ de ventas** (*Com*) sales figures
cifrado, -a [θi'fraðo, a] *adj* in code
cifrar [θi'frar] *vt* to code, write in code; (*resumir*) to abridge; (*calcular*) to reckon
cigala [θi'ɣala] *nf* Norway lobster
cigarra [θi'ɣarra] *nf* cicada
cigarrera [θiɣa'rrera] *nf* cigar case
cigarrillo [θiɣa'rriʎo] *nm* cigarette
cigarro [θi'ɣarro] *nm* cigarette; (*puro*) cigar
cigüeña [θi'ɣweɲa] *nf* stork
cilíndrico, -a [θi'lindriko, a] *adj* cylindrical
cilindro [θi'lindro] *nm* cylinder
cima ['θima] *nf* (*de montaña*) top, peak; (*de árbol*) top; (*fig*) height
címbalo ['θimbalo] *nm* cymbal
cimbrear [θimbre'ar] *vt* to brandish; **cimbrearse** *vr* to sway
cimentar [θimen'tar] *vt* to lay the foundations of; (*fig*: *reforzar*) to strengthen; (: *fundar*) to found
cimiento *etc* [θi'mjento] *vb ver* **cimentar** ■ *nm* foundation
cinc [θink] *nm* zinc
cincel [θin'θel] *nm* chisel
cincelar [θinθe'lar] *vt* to chisel
cincha ['θintʃa] *nf* girth, saddle strap
cincho ['θintʃo] *nm* sash, belt
cinco ['θinko] *num* five; (*fecha*) fifth; **las ~** five o'clock; **no estar en sus ~** (*fam*) to be off one's rocker
cincuenta [θin'kwenta] *num* fifty
cincuentón, -ona [θinkwen'ton, ona] *adj, nm/f* fifty-year-old
cine ['θine] *nm* cinema; **el ~ mudo** silent films *pl*; **hacer ~** to make films
cineasta [θine'asta] *nm/f* (*director de cine*) film-maker *o* director
cine-club ['θine'klub] *nm* film club
cinéfilo, -a [θi'nefilo, a] *nm/f* film buff
cinematográfico, -a [θinemato'ɣrafiko, a] *adj* cine-, film *cpd*
cínico, -a ['θiniko, a] *adj* cynical; (*descarado*) shameless ■ *nm/f* cynic
cinismo [θi'nismo] *nm* cynicism
cinta ['θinta] *nf* band, strip; (*de tela*) ribbon; (*película*) reel; (*de máquina de escribir*) ribbon; (*métrica*) tape measure; (*magnetofónica*) tape; **~ adhesiva** sticky tape; **~ aislante** insulating tape; **~ de carbón** carbon ribbon; **~ magnética** (*Inform*) magnetic tape; **~ métrica** tape measure; **~ de múltiples impactos** (*en impresora*) multistrike ribbon; **~ de tela** (*para máquina de escribir*) fabric ribbon; **~ transportadora** conveyor belt
cinto ['θinto] *nm* belt, girdle
cintura [θin'tura] *nf* waist; (*medida*) waistline
cinturón [θintu'ron] *nm* belt; (*fig*) belt, zone; **~ salvavidas** lifebelt; **~ de seguridad** safety belt
ciña *etc* ['θiɲa], **ciñendo** *etc* [θi'ɲenðo] *vb ver* **ceñir**
ciprés [θi'pres] *nm* cypress (tree)
circo ['θirko] *nm* circus
circuito [θir'kwito] *nm* circuit; (*Deporte*) lap; **TV por ~ cerrado** closed-circuit TV; **~ experimental** (*Inform*) breadboard; **~ impreso** printed circuit; **~ lógico** (*Inform*)

logical circuit
circulación [θirkula'θjon] *nf* circulation; (*Auto*) traffic; **"cerrado a la ~ rodada"** "closed to vehicles"
circular [θirku'lar] *adj, nf* circular ▪ *vt* to circulate ▪ *vi* to circulate; (*dinero*) to be in circulation; (*Auto*) to drive; (*autobús*) to run
círculo ['θirkulo] *nm* circle; (*centro*) clubhouse; (*Pol*) political group
circuncidar [θirkunθi'dar] *vt* to circumcise
circunciso, -a [θrikun'θiso, a] *pp de* **circuncidar**
circundante [θirkun'dante] *adj* surrounding
circundar [θirkun'dar] *vt* to surround
circunferencia [θirkunfe'renθja] *nf* circumference
circunloquio [θirkun'lokjo] *nm* circumlocution
circunscribir [θirkunskri'βir] *vt* to circumscribe; **circunscribirse** *vr* to be limited
circunscripción [θirkunskrip'θjon] *nf* division; (*Pol*) constituency
circunscrito [θirkuns'krito] *pp de* **circunscribir**
circunspección [θirkunspek'θjon] *nf* circumspection, caution
circunspecto, -a [θirkuns'pekto, a] *adj* circumspect, cautious
circunstancia [θirkuns'tanθja] *nf* circumstance; **circunstancias agravantes/ extenuantes** aggravating/extenuating circumstances; **estar a la altura de las circunstancias** to rise to the occasion
circunvalación [θirkumbala'θjon] *nf*: **carretera de ~** ring road
cirio ['θirjo] *nm* (wax) candle
cirrosis [θi'rrosis] *nf* cirrhosis (of the liver)
ciruela [θi'rwela] *nf* plum; **~ pasa** prune
ciruelo [θi'rwelo] *nm* plum tree
cirugía [θiru'xia] *nf* surgery; **~ estética** *o* **plástica** plastic surgery
cirujano [θiru'xano] *nm* surgeon
cisco ['θisko] *nm*: **armar un ~** to kick up a row; **estar hecho ~** to be a wreck
cisma ['θisma] *nm* schism; (*Pol etc*) split
cisne ['θisne] *nm* swan; **canto de ~** swan song
cisterna [θis'terna] *nf* cistern, tank
cistitis [θis'titis] *nf* cystitis
cita ['θita] *nf* appointment, meeting; (*de novios*) date; (*referencia*) quotation; **acudir/ faltar a una ~** to turn up for/miss an appointment
citación [θita'θjon] *nf* (*Jur*) summons *sg*
citadino, -a [sita'ðino, a] (*Am*) *adj* urban ▪ *nm/f* urban *o* city dweller
citar [θi'tar] *vt* to make an appointment with, arrange to meet; (*Jur*) to summons; (*un autor, texto*) to quote; **citarse** *vr*: **citarse con algn** to arrange to meet sb; **se citaron en el cine** they arranged to meet at the cinema
cítara ['θitara] *nf* zither
citología [θitolo'xia] *nf* smear test
cítrico, -a ['θitriko, a] *adj* citric ▪ *nm*: **cítricos** citrus fruits
CiU *nm abr* (*Pol*) = **Convergència i Unió**
ciudad [θju'ðað] *nf* town; (*capital de país etc*) city; **~ universitaria** university campus; **C~ del Cabo** Cape Town; **la C~ Condal** Barcelona
ciudadanía [θjuðaða'nia] *nf* citizenship
ciudadano, -a [θjuða'ðano, a] *adj* civic ▪ *nm/f* citizen
ciudadrealeño, -a [θjuðaðrea'leɲo, a] *adj* of *o* from Ciudad Real ▪ *nm/f* native *o* inhabitant of Ciudad Real
cívico, -a ['θiβiko, a] *adj* civic; (*fig*) public-spirited
civil [θi'βil] *adj* civil ▪ *nm* (*guardia*) policeman
civilice *etc* [θiβi'liθe] *vb ver* **civilizar**
civilización [θiβiliθa'θjon] *nf* civilization
civilizar [θiβili'θar] *vt* to civilize
civismo [θi'βismo] *nm* public spirit
cizaña [θi'θaɲa] *nf* (*fig*) discord; **sembrar ~** to sow discord
cl *abr* (= *centilitro*) cl.
clamar [kla'mar] *vt* to clamour for, cry out for ▪ *vi* to cry out, clamour
clamor [kla'mor] *nm* (*grito*) cry, shout; (*fig*) clamour, protest
clamoroso, -a [klamo'roso, a] *adj* (*éxito etc*) resounding
clan [klan] *nm* clan; (*de gángsters*) gang
clandestinidad [klandestini'ðað] *nf* secrecy
clandestino, -a [klandes'tino, a] *adj* clandestine; (*Pol*) underground
clara ['klara] *nf* (*de huevo*) egg white
claraboya [klara'βoja] *nf* skylight
clarear [klare'ar] *vi* (*el día*) to dawn; (*el cielo*) to clear up, brighten up; **clarearse** *vr* to be transparent
clarete [kla'rete] *nm* rosé (wine)
claridad [klari'ðað] *nf* (*del día*) brightness; (*de estilo*) clarity
clarificar [klarifi'kar] *vt* to clarify
clarifique *etc* [klari'fike] *vb ver* **clarificar**
clarín [kla'rin] *nm* bugle
clarinete [klari'nete] *nm* clarinet
clarividencia [klariβi'ðenθja] *nf* clairvoyance; (*fig*) far-sightedness
claro, -a ['klaro, a] *adj* clear; (*luminoso*) bright; (*color*) light; (*evidente*) clear, evident; (*poco espeso*) thin ▪ *nm* (*en bosque*) clearing

■ *adv* clearly ■ *excl* of course!; **hablar ~** (*fig*) to speak plainly; **a las claras** openly; **no sacamos nada en ~** we couldn't get anything definite
clase ['klase] *nf* class; (*tipo*) kind, sort; (*Escol etc*) class; (*: aula*) classroom; **~ alta/media/obrera** upper/middle/working class; **dar clases** to teach
clásico, -a ['klasiko, a] *adj* classical; (*fig*) classic
clasificable [klasifi'kaβle] *adj* classifiable
clasificación [klasifika'θjon] *nf* classification; (*Deporte*) league (table); (*Com*) ratings *pl*
clasificador [klasifika'ðor] *nm* filing cabinet
clasificar [klasifi'kar] *vt* to classify; (*Inform*) to sort; **clasificarse** *vr* (*Deporte: en torneo*) to qualify
clasifique *etc* [klasi'fike] *vb ver* **clasificar**
clasista [kla'sista] *adj* (*fam: actitud*) snobbish
claudicar [klauði'kar] *vi* (*fig*) to back down
claudique *etc* [klau'ðike] *vb ver* **claudicar**
claustro ['klaustro] *nm* cloister; (*Univ*) staff; (*junta*) senate
claustrofobia [klaustro'foβja] *nf* claustrophobia
cláusula ['klausula] *nf* clause; **~ de exclusión** (*Com*) exclusion clause
clausura [klau'sura] *nf* closing, closure
clausurar [klausu'rar] *vt* (*congreso etc*) to close, bring to a close; (*Pol etc*) to adjourn; (*cerrar*) to close (down)
clavado, -a [kla'βaðo, a] *adj* nailed ■ *excl* exactly!, precisely!
clavar [kla'βar] *vt* (*tablas etc*) to nail (together); (*con alfiler*) to pin; (*clavo*) to hammer in; (*cuchillo*) to stick, thrust; (*mirada*) to fix; (*fam: estafar*) to cheat
clave ['klaβe] *nf* key; (*Mus*) clef ■ *adj inv* key *cpd*; **~ de acceso** password
clavel [kla'βel] *nm* carnation
clavicémbalo [klaβi'θembalo] *nm* harpsichord
clavicordio [klaβikor'ðjo] *nm* clavicord
clavícula [kla'βikula] *nf* collar bone
clavija [kla'βixa] *nf* peg, pin; (*Mus*) peg; (*Elec*) plug
clavo ['klaβo] *nm* (*de metal*) nail; (*Bot*) clove; **dar en el ~** (*fig*) to hit the nail on the head
claxon ['klakson] (*pl* **claxons**) *nm* horn; **tocar el ~** to sound one's horn
clemencia [kle'menθja] *nf* mercy, clemency
clemente [kle'mente] *adj* merciful, clement
cleptómano, -a [klep'tomano, a] *nm/f* kleptomaniac
clerical [kleri'kal] *adj* clerical
clérigo ['kleriɣo] *nm* priest, clergyman
clero ['klero] *nm* clergy
clic [klik] *nm* click; **hacer ~/doble ~ en algo** to click/double-click on sth
clicar [kli'kar] *vi* (*Inform*) to click; **clica en el icono** click on the icon
cliché [kli'tʃe] *nm* cliché; (*Tip*) stencil; (*Foto*) negative
cliente, -a ['kljente, a] *nm/f* client, customer
clientela [kljen'tela] *nf* clientele, customers *pl*; (*Com*) goodwill; (*Med*) patients *pl*
clima ['klima] *nm* climate
climatizado, -a [klimati'θaðo, a] *adj* air-conditioned
clímax ['klimaks] *nm inv* climax
clínico, -a ['kliniko, a] *adj* clinical ■ *nf* clinic; (*particular*) private hospital
clip (*pl* **clips**) [klip, klis] *nm* paper clip
cliquear [klike'ar] *vi* (*Inform*) to click; **cliquea en el icono** click on the icon
clítoris ['klitoris] *nm inv* clitoris
cloaca [klo'aka] *nf* sewer, drain
clonación [klona'θjon] *nf* cloning
clorhídrico, -a [klo'ridriko, a] *adj* hydrochloric
cloro ['kloro] *nm* chlorine
clorofila [kloro'fila] *nf* chlorophyl(l)
cloroformo [kloro'formo] *nm* chloroform
cloruro [klo'ruro] *nm* chloride; **~ sódico** sodium chloride
club (*pl* **clubs** *o* **clubes**) [klub, klus, 'kluβes] *nm* club; **~ de jóvenes** youth club
cm *abr* (*= centímetro*) cm
C.N.T. *nf abr* (*Esp: = Confederación Nacional de Trabajo*) *Anarchist Union Confederation*; (*Am*) = **Confederación Nacional de Trabajadores**
coacción [koak'θjon] *nf* coercion, compulsion
coaccionar [koakθjo'nar] *vt* to coerce, compel
coagular [koaɣu'lar] *vt*, **coagularse** *vr* (*sangre*) to clot; (*leche*) to curdle
coágulo [ko'aɣulo] *nm* clot
coalición [koali'θjon] *nf* coalition
coartada [koar'taða] *nf* alibi
coartar [koar'tar] *vt* to limit, restrict
coba ['koβa] *nf*: **dar ~ a algn** to soft-soap sb
cobarde [ko'βarðe] *adj* cowardly ■ *nm/f* coward
cobardía [koβar'ðia] *nf* cowardice
cobaya [ko'βaja] *nf* guinea pig
cobertizo [koβer'tiθo] *nm* shelter
cobertor [koβer'tor] *nm* bedspread
cobertura [koβer'tura] *nf* cover; (*Com*) coverage; **~ de dividendo** (*Com*) dividend cover; **estar fuera de ~** (*Telec*) to be out of range; **no tengo ~** (*Telec*) I'm out of range
cobija [ko'βixa] *nf* (*Am*) blanket

cobijar [koβi'xar] *vt* (*cubrir*) to cover; (*abrigar*) to shelter; **cobijarse** *vr* to take shelter
cobijo [ko'βixo] *nm* shelter
cobra ['koβra] *nf* cobra
cobrador, a [koβra'ðor, a] *nm/f* (*de autobús*) conductor/conductress; (*de impuestos, gas*) collector
cobrar [ko'βrar] *vt* (*cheque*) to cash; (*sueldo*) to collect, draw; (*objeto*) to recover; (*precio*) to charge; (*deuda*) to collect ■ *vi* to draw one's pay; **cobrarse** *vr* to recover, get on well; **cóbrese al entregar** cash on delivery (COD) (*Brit*), collect on delivery (COD) (*US*); **a ~** (*Com*) receivable; **cantidades por ~** sums due
cobre ['koβre] *nm* copper; (*Am fam*) cent
cobrizo, -a [ko'βriθo, a] *adj* coppery
cobro ['koβro] *nm* (*de cheque*) cashing; (*pago*) payment; **presentar al ~** to cash; *ver tb* **llamada**
coca ['koka] *nf* coca; (*droga*) coke
cocaína [koka'ina] *nf* cocaine
cocainómano, -a [kokai'nomano, a] *nm/f* cocaine addict
cocción [kok'θjon] *nf* (*Culin*) cooking; (*el hervir*) boiling
cocear [koθe'ar] *vi* to kick
cocer [ko'θer] *vt, vi* to cook; (*en agua*) to boil; (*en horno*) to bake
coche ['kotʃe] *nm* (*Auto*) car, automobile (*US*); (*de tren, de caballos*) coach, carriage; (*para niños*) pram (*Brit*), baby carriage (*US*); **~ de bomberos** fire engine; **~ celular** Black Maria, prison van; **~ (comedor)** (*Ferro*) (dining) car; **~ fúnebre** hearse
coche-bomba ['kotʃe'βomba] (*pl* **coches-bomba**) *nm* car bomb
coche-cama ['kotʃe'kama] (*pl* **coches-cama**) *nm* (*Ferro*) sleeping car, sleeper
cochera [ko'tʃera] *nf* garage; (*de autobuses, trenes*) depot
coche-restaurante ['kotʃerestau'rante] (*pl* **coches-restaurante**) *nm* (*Ferro*) dining-car, diner
cochinada [kotʃi'naða] *nf* dirty trick
cochinillo [kotʃi'niʎo] *nm* piglet, suckling pig
cochino, -a [ko'tʃino, a] *adj* filthy, dirty ■ *nm/f* pig
cocido, -a [ko'θiðo, a] *adj* boiled; (*fam*) plastered ■ *nm* stew
cociente [ko'θjente] *nm* quotient
cocina [ko'θina] *nf* kitchen; (*aparato*) cooker, stove; (*actividad*) cookery; **~ casera** home cooking; **~ eléctrica** electric cooker; **~ francesa** French cuisine; **~ de gas** gas cooker
cocinar [koθi'nar] *vt, vi* to cook
cocinero, -a [koθi'nero, a] *nm/f* cook
coco ['koko] *nm* coconut; (*fantasma*) bogeyman; (*fam: cabeza*) nut; **comer el ~ a algn** (*fam*) to brainwash sb
cocodrilo [koko'ðrilo] *nm* crocodile
cocotero [koko'tero] *nm* coconut palm
cóctel ['koktel] *nm* (*bebida*) cocktail; (*reunión*) cocktail party; **~ Molotov** Molotov cocktail, petrol bomb
coctelera [kokte'lera] *nf* cocktail shaker
cod. *abr* (= *código*) code
codazo [ko'ðaθo] *nm*: **dar un ~ a algn** to nudge sb
codear [koðe'ar] *vi* to elbow, jostle; **codearse** *vr*: **codearse con** to rub shoulders with
códice ['koðiθe] *nm* manuscript, codex
codicia [ko'ðiθja] *nf* greed; (*fig*) lust
codiciar [koði'θjar] *vt* to covet
codicioso, -a [koði'θjoso, a] *adj* covetous
codificador [koðifika'ðor] *nm* (*Inform*) encoder; **~ digital** digitizer
codificar [koðifi'kar] *vt* (*mensaje*) to (en)code; (*leyes*) to codify
código ['koðiɣo] *nm* code; **~ de barras** (*Com*) bar code; **~ binario** binary code; **~ de caracteres** (*Inform*) character code; **~ de (la) circulación** highway code; **~ civil** common law; **~ de control** (*Inform*) control code; **~ máquina** (*Inform*) machine code; **~ militar** military law; **~ de operación** (*Inform*) operational *o* machine code; **~ penal** penal code; **~ de práctica** code of practice
codillo [ko'ðiʎo] *nm* (*Zool*) knee; (*Tec*) elbow (joint)
codo ['koðo] *nm* (*Anat, de tubo*) elbow; (*Zool*) knee; **hablar por los codos** to talk nineteen to the dozen
codorniz [koðor'niθ] *nf* quail
coeficiente [koefi'θjente] *nm* (*Mat*) coefficient; (*Econ etc*) rate; **~ intelectual** *o* **de inteligencia** I.Q.
coerción [koer'θjon] *nf* coercion
coercitivo, -a [koerθi'tiβo, a] *adj* coercive
coetáneo, -a [koe'taneo, a] *nm/f*: **coetáneos** contemporaries
coexistencia [koeksis'tenθja] *nf* coexistence
coexistir [koeksis'tir] *vi* to coexist
cofia ['kofja] *nf* (*de enfermera*) (white) cap
cofradía [kofra'ðia] *nf* brotherhood, fraternity; *ver tb* **Semana Santa**
cofre ['kofre] *nm* (*baúl*) trunk; (*de joyas*) box; (*Am AUTO*) bonnet (*Brit*), hood (*US*)
cogedor [koxe'ðor] *nm* dustpan
coger [ko'xer] *vt* (*Esp*) to take (hold of); (*objeto caído*) to pick up; (*frutas*) to pick, harvest; (*resfriado, ladrón, pelota*) to catch; (*Am fam!*) to lay (*!*) ■ *vi*: **~ por el buen camino** to take the right road; **cogerse** *vr* (*el dedo*) to catch;

~ a algn desprevenido to take sb unawares; **cogerse a algo** to get hold of sth
cogida [ko'xiða] *nf* gathering, harvesting; (*de peces*) catch; (*Taur*) goring
cogollo [ko'ɣoʎo] *nm* (*de lechuga*) heart; (*fig*) core, nucleus
cogorza [ko'ɣorθa] *nf* (*fam*): **agarrar una ~** to get smashed
cogote [ko'ɣote] *nm* back *o* nape of the neck
cohabitar [koaβi'tar] *vi* to live together, cohabit
cohecho [ko'etʃo] *nm* (*acción*) bribery; (*soborno*) bribe
coherencia [koe'renθja] *nf* coherence
coherente [koe'rente] *adj* coherent
cohesión [koe'sjon] *nm* cohesion
cohete [ko'ete] *nm* rocket
cohibido, -a [koi'βiðo, a] *adj* (*Psico*) inhibited; (*tímido*) shy; **sentirse ~** to feel embarrassed
cohibir [koi'βir] *vt* to restrain, restrict; **cohibirse** *vr* to feel inhibited
COI *nm abr* (= *Comité Olímpico Internacional*) IOC
coima ['koima] *nf* (*Am fam*) bribe
coincidencia [koinθi'ðenθja] *nf* coincidence
coincidir [koinθi'ðir] *vi* (*en idea*) to coincide, agree; (*en lugar*) to coincide
coito ['koito] *nm* intercourse, coitus
cojear [koxe'ar] *vi* (*persona*) to limp, hobble; (*mueble*) to wobble, rock
cojera [ko'xera] *nf* lameness; (*andar cojo*) limp
cojín [ko'xin] *nm* cushion
cojinete [koxi'nete] *nm* small cushion, pad; (*Tec*) (ball) bearing
cojo, -a *etc* ['koxo, a] *vb ver* **coger** ■ *adj* (*que no puede andar*) lame, crippled; (*mueble*) wobbly ■ *nm/f* lame person, cripple
cojón [ko'xon] *nm* (*fam!*) ball (*!*), testicle; **¡cojones!** shit! (*!*)
cojonudo, -a [koxo'nuðo, a] *adj* (*Esp fam*) great, fantastic
col [kol] *nf* cabbage; **coles de Bruselas** Brussels sprouts
cola ['kola] *nf* tail; (*de gente*) queue; (*lugar*) end, last place; (*para pegar*) glue, gum; (*de vestido*) train; **hacer ~** to queue (up)
colaboración [kolaβora'θjon] *nf* (*gen*) collaboration; (*en periódico*) contribution
colaborador, a [kolaβora'ðor, a] *nm/f* collaborator; contributor
colaborar [kolaβo'rar] *vi* to collaborate
colación [kola'θjon] *nf*: **sacar a ~** to bring up
colado, -a [ko'laðo, a] *adj* (*metal*) cast ■ *nf*: **hacer la colada** to do the washing
colador [kola'ðor] *nm* (*de té*) strainer; (*para verduras etc*) colander
colapsar [kolap'sar] *vt* (*tráfico etc*) to bring to a standstill
colapso [ko'lapso] *nm* collapse; **~ nervioso** nervous breakdown
colar [ko'lar] *vt* (*líquido*) to strain off; (*metal*) to cast ■ *vi* to ooze, seep (through); **colarse** *vr* to jump the queue; (*en mitin*) to sneak in; (*equivocarse*) to slip up; **colarse en** to get into without paying; (*en una fiesta*) to gatecrash
colateral [kolate'ral] *nm* collateral
colcha ['koltʃa] *nf* bedspread
colchón [kol'tʃon] *nm* mattress; **~ inflable** inflatable mattress
colchoneta [coltʃo'neta] *nf* (*en gimnasio*) mattress; **~ hinchable** airbed
colear [kole'ar] *vi* (*perro*) to wag its tail
colección [kolek'θjon] *nf* collection
coleccionar [kolekθjo'nar] *vt* to collect
coleccionista [kolekθjo'nista] *nm/f* collector
colecta [ko'lekta] *nf* collection
colectivo, -a [kolek'tiβo, a] *adj* collective, joint ■ *nm* (*Am: autobús*) (small) bus; (*taxi*) collective taxi
colector [kolek'tor] *nm* collector; (*sumidero*) sewer
colega [ko'leɣa] *nm/f* colleague
colegiado, -a [kole'xjaðo, a] *adj* (*profesional*) registered ■ *nm/f* referee
colegial, a [kole'xjal, a] *adj* (*Escol etc*) school *cpd*, college *cpd* ■ *nm/f* schoolboy/girl
colegio [ko'lexjo] *nm* college; (*escuela*) school; (*de abogados etc*) association; **~ de internos** boarding school; **ir al ~** to go to school; *see note*

COLEGIO

A *colegio* is normally a private primary or secondary school. In the state system it means a primary school although these are also called *escuela*. State secondary schools are called *institutos*. Extracurricular subjects, such as computing or foreign languages, are offered in private schools called *academias*.

colegir [kole'xir] *vt* (*juntar*) to collect, gather; (*deducir*) to infer, conclude
cólera ['kolera] *nf* (*ira*) anger; **montar en ~** to get angry ■ *nm* (*Med*) cholera
colérico, -a [ko'leriko, a] *adj* angry, furious
colesterol [koleste'rol] *nm* cholesterol
coleta [ko'leta] *nf* pigtail
coletazo [kole'taθo] *nm*: **dar un ~** (*animal*) to flap its tail; **los últimos coletazos** death throes
coletilla [kole'tiʎa] *nf* (*en carta*) postscript; (*en conversación*) filler phrase
colgado, -a [kol'ɣaðo, a] *pp de* **colgar** ■ *adj*

hanging; *(ahorcado)* hanged; **dejar ~ a algn** to let sb down
colgajo [kol'ɣaxo] *nm* tatter
colgante [kol'ɣante] *adj* hanging; *ver* **puente** ■ *nm (joya)* pendant
colgar [kol'ɣar] *vt* to hang (up); *(tender: ropa)* to hang out ■ *vi* to hang; *(teléfono)* to hang up
colgué [kol'ɣe], **colguemos** *etc* [kol'ɣemos] *vb ver* **colgar**
colibrí [koli'βri] *nm* hummingbird
cólico ['koliko] *nm* colic
coliflor [koli'flor] *nf* cauliflower
coligiendo *etc* [koli'xjenðo] *vb ver* **colegir**
colija *etc* [ko'lixa] *vb ver* **colegir**
colilla [ko'liʎa] *nf* cigarette end, butt
colina [ko'lina] *nf* hill
colindante [kolin'dante] *adj* adjacent, neighbouring
colindar [kolin'dar] *vi* to adjoin, be adjacent
colisión [koli'sjon] *nf* collision; **~ de frente** head-on crash
colitis [ko'litis] *nf inv*: **tener ~** to have diarrhoea
collar [ko'ʎar] *nm* necklace; *(de perro)* collar
colmado, -a [kol'maðo, a] *adj* full ■ *nm* grocer's (shop) *(Brit)*, grocery store *(US)*
colmar [kol'mar] *vt* to fill to the brim; *(fig)* to fulfil, realize
colmena [kol'mena] *nf* beehive
colmillo [kol'miʎo] *nm (diente)* eye tooth; *(de elefante)* tusk; *(de perro)* fang
colmo ['kolmo] *nm* height, summit; **para ~ de desgracias** to cap it all; **¡eso es ya el ~!** that's beyond a joke!
colocación [koloka'θjon] *nf (acto)* placing; *(empleo)* job, position; *(situación)* place, position; *(Com)* placement
colocar [kolo'kar] *vt* to place, put, position; *(poner en empleo)* to find a job for; **~ dinero** to invest money; **colocarse** *vr* to place o.s.; *(conseguir trabajo)* to find a job
colofón [kolo'fon] *nm*: **como ~ de las conversaciones** as a sequel to *o* following the talks
Colombia [ko'lombja] *nf* Colombia
colombiano, -a [kolom'bjano, a] *adj, nm/f* Colombian
colon ['kolon] *nm* colon
colón [ko'lon] *nm (Am) monetary unit of Costa Rica and El Salvador*
Colonia [ko'lonja] *nf* Cologne
colonia [ko'lonja] *nf* colony; *(de casas)* housing estate; *(agua de colonia)* cologne; **~ escolar** summer camp (for schoolchildren)
colonice *etc* [kolo'niθe] *vb ver* **colonizar**
colonización [koloniθa'θjon] *nf* colonization
colonizador, a [koloniθa'ðor, a] *adj* colonizing ■ *nm/f* colonist, settler
colonizar [koloni'θar] *vt* to colonize
colono [ko'lono] *nm (Pol)* colonist, settler; *(Agr)* tenant farmer
coloque *etc* [ko'loke] *vb ver* **colocar**
coloquial [kolo'kjal] *adj* colloquial
coloquio [ko'lokjo] *nm* conversation; *(congreso)* conference
color [ko'lor] *nm* colour; **a todo ~** in full colour; **verlo todo ~ de rosa** to see everything through rose-coloured spectacles; **le salieron los colores** she blushed
colorado, -a [kolo'raðo, a] *adj (rojo)* red; *(Am: chiste)* rude, blue; **ponerse ~** to blush
colorante [kolo'rante] *nm* colouring (matter)
colorar [kolo'rar] *vt* to colour; *(teñir)* to dye
colorear [kolore'ar] *vt* to colour
colorete [kolo'rete] *nm* blusher
colorido [kolo'riðo] *nm* colour(ing)
coloso [ko'loso] *nm* colossus
columbrar [kolum'brar] *vt* to glimpse, spy
columna [ko'lumna] *nf* column; *(pilar)* pillar; *(apoyo)* support; **~ blindada** *(Mil)* armoured column; **~ vertebral** spine, spinal column
columpiar [kolum'pjar] *vt*, **columpiarse** *vr* to swing
columpio [ko'lumpjo] *nm* swing
colza ['kolθa] *nf* rape; **aceite de ~** rapeseed oil
coma ['koma] *nf* comma ■ *nm (Med)* coma
comadre [ko'maðre] *nf (madrina)* godmother; *(vecina)* neighbour; *(chismosa)* gossip
comadrear [komaðre'ar] *vi (esp Am)* to gossip
comadreja [koma'ðrexa] *nf* weasel
comadrona [koma'ðrona] *nf* midwife
comandancia [koman'danθja] *nf* command
comandante [koman'dante] *nm* commandant; *(grado)* major
comandar [koman'dar] *vt* to command
comando [ko'mando] *nm (Mil: mando)* command; *(: grupo)* commando unit; *(Inform)* command; **~ de búsqueda** search command
comarca [ko'marka] *nf* region; *ver tb* **provincia**
comarcal [komar'kal] *adj* local
comba ['komba] *nf (curva)* curve; *(en viga)* warp; *(cuerda)* skipping rope; **saltar a la ~** to skip
combar [kom'bar] *vt* to bend, curve
combate [kom'bate] *nm* fight; *(fig)* battle; **fuera de ~** out of action
combatiente [komba'tjente] *nm* combatant
combatir [komba'tir] *vt* to fight, combat
combatividad [kombatiβi'ðað] *nf (actitud)* fighting spirit; *(agresividad)* aggressiveness

combativo, -a [komba'tiβo, a] *adj* full of fight
combi ['kombi] *nm* fridge-freezer
combinación [kombina'θjon] *nf* combination; (*Química*) compound; (*bebida*) cocktail; (*plan*) scheme, setup; (*prenda*) slip
combinado, -a [kombi'naðo, a] *adj*: **plato ~** *main course served with vegetables*
combinar [kombi'nar] *vt* to combine; (*colores*) to match
combustible [kombus'tiβle] *nm* fuel
combustión [kombus'tjon] *nf* combustion
comedia [ko'meðja] *nf* comedy; (*Teat*) play, drama; (*fig*) farce
comediante [kome'ðjante] *nm/f* (comic) actor/actress
comedido, -a [kome'ðiðo, a] *adj* moderate
comedirse [kome'ðirse] *vr* to behave moderately; (*ser cortés*) to be courteous
comedor, a [kome'ðor, a] *nm/f* (*persona*) glutton ■ *nm* (*habitación*) dining room; (*restaurante*) restaurant; (*cantina*) canteen
comencé [komen'θe], **comencemos** *etc* [komen'θemos] *vb ver* **comenzar**
comensal [komen'sal] *nm/f* fellow guest/diner
comentar [komen'tar] *vt* to comment on; (*fam*) to discuss; **comentó que...** he made the comment that...
comentario [komen'tarjo] *nm* comment, remark; (*Lit*) commentary; **comentarios** *nmpl* gossip *sg*; **dar lugar a comentarios** to cause gossip
comentarista [komenta'rista] *nm/f* commentator
comenzar [komen'θar] *vt, vi* to begin, start, commence; **~ a hacer algo** to begin *o* start doing *o* to do sth
comer [ko'mer] *vt* to eat; (*Damas: Ajedrez*) to take, capture ■ *vi* to eat; (*almorzar*) to have lunch; **comerse** *vr* to eat up; (*párrafo etc*) to skip; **~ el coco a** (*fam*) to brainwash; **¡a ~!** food's ready!
comercial [komer'θjal] *adj* commercial; (*relativo al negocio*) business *cpd*
comerciante [komer'θjante] *nm/f* trader, merchant; (*tendero*) shopkeeper; **~ exclusivo** (*Com*) sole trader
comerciar [komer'θjar] *vi* to trade, do business
comercio [ko'merθjo] *nm* commerce, trade; (*negocio*) business; (*grandes empresas*) big business; (*fig*) dealings *pl*; **~ autorizado** (*Com*) licensed trade; **~ electrónico** e-commerce; **~ exterior** foreign trade
comestible [komes'tiβle] *adj* eatable, edible ■ *nm*: **comestibles** food *sg*, foodstuffs; (*Com*) groceries
cometa [ko'meta] *nm* comet ■ *nf* kite
cometer [kome'ter] *vt* to commit
cometido [kome'tiðo] *nm* (*misión*) task, assignment; (*deber*) commitment
comezón [kome'θon] *nf* itch, itching
cómic (*pl* **cómics**) ['komik, 'komiks] *nm* comic
comicios [ko'miθjos] *nmpl* elections; (*voto*) voting *sg*
cómico, -a ['komiko, a] *adj* comic(al) ■ *nm/f* comedian; (*de teatro*) (comic) actor/actress
comida *etc* [ko'miða] *vb ver* **comedirse** ■ *nf* (*alimento*) food; (*almuerzo, cena*) meal; (*de mediodía*) lunch; (*Am*) dinner
comidilla [komi'ðiʎa] *nf*: **ser la ~ de la ciudad** to be the talk of the town
comience *etc* [ko'mjenθe] *vb ver* **comenzar**
comienzo *etc* [ko'mjenθo] *vb ver* **comenzar** ■ *nm* beginning, start; **dar ~ a un acto** to begin a ceremony; **~ del archivo** (*Inform*) top-of-file
comillas [ko'miʎas] *nfpl* quotation marks
comilón, -ona [komi'lon, ona] *adj* greedy ■ *nf* (*fam*) blow-out
comino [ko'mino] *nm* cumin (seed); **no me importa un ~** I don't give a damn!
comisaría [komisa'ria] *nf* police station, precinct (*US*); (*Mil*) commissariat
comisario [komi'sarjo] *nm* (*Mil etc*) commissary; (*Pol*) commissar
comisión [komi'sjon] *nf* (*Com: pago*) commission, rake-off (*fam*); (*: junta*) board; (*encargo*) assignment; **~ mixta/permanente** joint/standing committee; **Comisiones Obreras** (*Esp*) *formerly Communist Union Confederation*
comisura [komi'sura] *nf*: **~ de los labios** corner of the mouth
comité (*pl* **~s**) *nm* [komi'te, komi'tes] committee; **comité de empresa** works council
comitiva [komi'tiβa] *nf* suite, retinue
como ['komo] *adv* as; (*tal como*) like; (*aproximadamente*) about, approximately ■ *conj* (*ya que, puesto que*) as, since; (*en seguida que*) as soon as; (*si: +subjun*) if; **¡~ no!** of course!; **~ no lo haga hoy** unless he does it today; **~ si** as if; **es tan alto ~ ancho** it is as high as it is wide
cómo ['komo] *adv* how?, why? ■ *excl* what?, I beg your pardon? ■ *nm*: **el ~ y el porqué** the whys and wherefores; **¿~ está Ud?** how are you?; **¿~ no?** why not?; **¡~ no!** (*esp Am*) of course!; **¿~ son?** what are they like?
cómoda ['komoða] *nf* chest of drawers
comodidad [komoði'ðað] *nf* comfort; **venga a su ~** come at your convenience

comodín [komo'ðin] *nm* joker; (*Inform*) wild card; **símbolo ~** wild-card character
cómodo, -a ['komoðo, a] *adj* comfortable; (*práctico, de fácil uso*) convenient
comodón, -ona [komo'ðon, ona] *adj* comfort-loving ■ *nm/f*: **ser un(a) ~/ona** to like one's home comforts
comoquiera [como'kjera] *conj*: **~ que** (*+subjun*) in whatever way; **~ que sea eso** however that may be
comp. *abr* (= *compárese*) cp
compacto, -a [kom'pakto, a] *adj* compact
compadecer [kompaðe'θer] *vt* to pity, be sorry for; **compadecerse** *vr*: **compadecerse de** to pity, be sorry for
compadezca *etc* [kompa'ðeθka] *vb ver* **compadecer**
compadre [kom'paðre] *nm* (*padrino*) godfather; (*esp Am: amigo*) friend, pal
compaginar [kompaxi'nar] *vt*: **~ A con B** to bring A into line with B; **compaginarse** *vr*: **compaginarse con** to tally with, square with
compañerismo [kompaɲe'rismo] *nm* comradeship
compañero, -a [kompa'ɲero, a] *nm/f* companion; (*novio*) boyfriend/girlfriend; **~ de clase** classmate
compañía [kompa'ɲia] *nf* company; **~ afiliada** associated company; **~ concesionaria** franchiser; **~ (no) cotizable** (un)listed company; **~ inversionista** investment trust; **hacer ~ a algn** to keep sb company
comparación [kompara'θjon] *nf* comparison; **en ~ con** in comparison with
comparar [kompa'rar] *vt* to compare
comparativo, -a [kompara'tiβo, a] *adj* comparative
comparecencia [kompare'θenθja] *nf* (*Jur*) appearance (in court); **orden de ~** summons *sg*
comparecer [kompare'θer] *vi* to appear (in court)
comparezca *etc* [kompa'reθka] *vb ver* **comparecer**
comparsa [kom'parsa] *nm/f* extra
compartimento [komparti'mento], **compartimiento** [komparti'mjento] *nm* (*Ferro*) compartment; (*de mueble, cajón*) section; **~ estanco** (*fig*) watertight compartment
compartir [kompar'tir] *vt* to divide (up), share (out)
compás [kom'pas] *nm* (*Mus*) beat, rhythm; (*Mat*) compasses *pl*; (*Naut etc*) compass; **al ~** in time
compasión [kompa'sjon] *nf* compassion, pity
compasivo, -a [kompa'siβo, a] *adj* compassionate
compatibilidad [kompatiβili'ðað] *nf* (*tb Inform*) compatibility
compatible [kompa'tiβle] *adj* compatible
compatriota [kompa'trjota] *nm/f* compatriot, fellow countryman/woman
compendiar [kompen'djar] *vt* to summarize; (*libro*) to abridge
compendio [kom'pendjo] *nm* summary; abridgement
compenetración [kompenetra'θjon] *nf* (*fig*) mutual understanding
compenetrarse [kompene'trarse] *vr* (*fig*): **~ (muy) bien** to get on (very) well together
compensación [kompensa'θjon] *nf* compensation; (*Jur*) damages *pl*; (*Com*) clearing
compensar [kompen'sar] *vt* to compensate; (*pérdida*) to make up for
competencia [kompe'tenθja] *nf* (*incumbencia*) domain, field; (*Com*) receipt; (*Jur, habilidad*) competence; (*rivalidad*) competition
competente [kompe'tente] *adj* (*Jur, persona*) competent; (*conveniente*) suitable
competer [kompe'ter] *vi*: **~ a** to be the responsibility of, fall to
competición [kompeti'θjon] *nf* competition
competidor, a [kompeti'ðor, a] *nm/f* competitor
competir [kompe'tir] *vi* to compete
competitivo, -a [kompeti'tiβo, a] *adj* competitive
compilación [kompila'θjon] *nf* compilation; **tiempo de ~** (*Inform*) compile time
compilador [kompila'ðor] *nm* compiler
compilar [kompi'lar] *vt* to compile
compinche [kom'pintʃe] *nm/f* (*fam*) crony
compita *etc* [kom'pita] *vb ver* **competir**
complacencia [kompla'θenθja] *nf* (*placer*) pleasure; (*satisfacción*) satisfaction; (*buena voluntad*) willingness
complacer [kompla'θer] *vt* to please; **complacerse** *vr* to be pleased
complaciente [kompla'θjente] *adj* kind, obliging, helpful
complazca *etc* [kom'plaθka] *vb ver* **complacer**
complejo, -a [kom'plexo, a] *adj, nm* complex
complementario, -a [komplemen'tarjo, a] *adj* complementary
complemento [komple'mento] *nm* (*de moda, diseño*) accessory; (*Ling*) complement
completar [komple'tar] *vt* to complete
completo, -a [kom'pleto, a] *adj* complete; (*perfecto*) perfect; (*lleno*) full ■ *nm* full complement

complexión [komple'ksjon] *nf* constitution
complicación [komplika'θjon] *nf* complication
complicado, -a [kompli'kaðo, a] *adj* complicated; **estar ~ en** to be involved in
complicar [kompli'kar] *vt* to complicate
cómplice ['kompliθe] *nm/f* accomplice
complique *etc* [kom'plike] *vb ver* **complicar**
complot (*pl* **complots**) [kom'plo(t), kom'plos] *nm* plot; (*conspiración*) conspiracy
compondré *etc* [kompon'dre] *vb ver* **componer**
componenda [kompo'nenda] *nf* compromise; (*pey*) shady deal
componente [kompo'nente] *adj, nm* component
componer [kompo'ner] *vt* to make up, put together; (*Mus: Lit: Imprenta*) to compose; (*algo roto*) to mend, repair; (*adornar*) to adorn; (*arreglar*) to arrange; (*reconciliar*) to reconcile; **componerse** *vr*: **componerse de** to consist of; **componérselas para hacer algo** to manage to do sth
componga *etc* [kom'ponga] *vb ver* **componer**
comportamiento [komporta'mjento] *nm* behaviour, conduct
comportarse [kompor'tarse] *vr* to behave
composición [komposi'θjon] *nf* composition
compositor, a [komposi'tor, a] *nm/f* composer
compostelano, -a [komposte'lano, a] *adj* of *o* from Santiago de Compostela ▪ *nm/f* native *o* inhabitant of Santiago de Compostela
compostura [kompos'tura] *nf* (*reparación*) mending, repair; (*composición*) composition; (*acuerdo*) agreement; (*actitud*) composure
compota [kom'pota] *nf* compote, preserve
compra ['kompra] *nf* purchase; **compras** *nfpl* purchases, shopping *sg*; **hacer la ~/ir de compras** to do the/go shopping; **~ a granel** (*Com*) bulk buying; **~ proteccionista** (*Com*) support buying
comprador, a [kompra'ðor, a] *nm/f* buyer, purchaser
comprar [kom'prar] *vt* to buy, purchase; **~ deudas** (*Com*) to factor
compraventa [kompra'βenta] *nf* (*Jur*) contract of sale
comprender [kompren'der] *vt* to understand; (*incluir*) to comprise, include
comprensible [kompren'siβle] *adj* understandable
comprensión [kompren'sjon] *nf* understanding; (*totalidad*) comprehensiveness
comprensivo, -a [kompren'siβo, a] *adj* comprehensive; (*actitud*) understanding
compresa [kom'presa] *nf* compress; **~ higiénica** sanitary towel (*Brit*) *o* napkin (*US*)
compresión [kompre'sjon] *nf* compression
comprimido, -a [kompri'miðo, a] *adj* compressed ▪ *nm* (*Med*) pill, tablet; **en caracteres comprimidos** (*Tip*) condensed
comprimir [kompri'mir] *vt* to compress; (*fig*) to control; (*Inform*) to pack
comprobación [komproβa'θjon] *nf*: **~ general de cuentas** (*Com*) general audit
comprobante [kompro'βante] *nm* proof; (*Com*) voucher; **~ (de pago)** receipt
comprobar [kompro'βar] *vt* to check; (*probar*) to prove; (*Tec*) to check, test
comprometedor, a [kompromete'ðor, a] *adj* compromising
comprometer [komprome'ter] *vt* to compromise; (*exponer*) to endanger; **comprometerse** *vr* to compromise o.s.; (*involucrarse*) to get involved
comprometido, -a [komprome'tiðo, a] *adj* (*situación*) awkward; (*escritor etc*) committed
compromiso [kompro'miso] *nm* (*obligación*) obligation; (*cita*) engagement, date; (*cometido*) commitment; (*convenio*) agreement; (*dificultad*) awkward situation; **libre de ~** (*Com*) without obligation
comprueba *etc* [kom'prweβa] *vb ver* **comprobar**
compuerta [kom'pwerta] *nf* (*en canal*) sluice, floodgate; (*Inform*) gate
compuesto, -a [kom'pwesto, a] *pp de* **componer** ▪ *adj*: **~ de** composed of, made up of ▪ *nm* compound; (*Med*) preparation
compulsar [kompul'sar] *vt* (*cotejar*) to collate, compare; (*Jur*) to make an attested copy of
compulsivo, -a [kompul'siβo, a] *adj* compulsive
compungido, -a [kompun'xiðo, a] *adj* remorseful
compuse *etc* [com'puse] *vb ver* **componer**
computador [komputa'ðor] *nm*, **computadora** [komputa'ðora] *nf* computer; **~ central** mainframe computer; **~ especializado** dedicated computer; **~ personal** personal computer
computar [kompu'tar] *vt* to calculate, compute
cómputo ['komputo] *nm* calculation
comulgar [komul'ɣar] *vi* to receive communion
comulgue *etc* [ko'mulɣe] *vb ver* **comulgar**
común [ko'mun] *adj* (*gen*) common; (*corriente*) ordinary; **por lo ~** generally ▪ *nm*: **el ~** the community
comuna [ko'muna] *nf* commune; (*Am*) district

comunicación [komunika'θjon] *nf* communication; (*informe*) report
comunicado [komuni'kaðo] *nm* announcement; **~ de prensa** press release
comunicar [komuni'kar] *vt* to communicate; (*Arq*) to connect ■ *vi* to communicate; to send a report; **comunicarse** *vr* to communicate; **está comunicando** (*Telec*) the line's engaged (*Brit*) *o* busy (*US*)
comunicativo, -a [komunika'tiβo, a] *adj* communicative
comunidad [komuni'ðað] *nf* community; **~ autónoma** autonomous region; **~ de vecinos** residents' association; **C~ Económica Europea (CEE)** European Economic Community (EEC); *see note*

COMUNIDAD

The 1978 Constitution provides for a degree of self-government for the 19 regions, called *comunidades autónomas* or *autonomías*. Some, such as Catalonia and the Basque Country, with their own language, history and culture, have long felt separate from the rest of Spain. This explains why some of the autonomías have more devolved powers than others, in all matters except foreign affairs and national defence. The regions are: Andalucía, Aragón, Asturias, Islas Baleares, Canarias, Cantabria, Castilla y León, Castilla-La Mancha, Cataluña, Extremadura, Galicia, Madrid, Murcia, Navarra, País Vasco, La Rioja, Comunidad Valenciana, Ceuta, Melilla.

comunión [komu'njon] *nf* communion
comunique *etc* [komu'nike] *vb ver* **comunicar**
comunismo [komu'nismo] *nm* communism
comunista [komu'nista] *adj, nm/f* communist
comunitario, -a [komuni'tarjo, a] *adj* (*de la* CE) Community *cpd*, EC *cpd*

PALABRA CLAVE

con [kon] *prep* **1** (*medio, compañía, modo*) with; **comer con cuchara** to eat with a spoon; **café con leche** white coffee; **estoy con un catarro** I've got a cold; **pasear con algn** to go for a walk with sb; **con habilidad** skilfully
2 (*a pesar de*): **con todo, merece nuestros respetos** all the same *o* even so, he deserves our respect
3 (*para con*): **es muy bueno para con los niños** he's very good with (the) children
4 (*+infin*): **con llegar tan tarde se quedó sin comer** by arriving *o* because he arrived so late he missed out on eating; **con estudiar un poco apruebas** with a bit of studying you should pass
5 (*queja*): **¡con las ganas que tenía de ir!** and I really wanted to go (too)!
■ *conj*: **con que**: **será suficiente con que le escribas** it will be enough if you write to her

conato [ko'nato] *nm* attempt; **~ de robo** attempted robbery
cóncavo, -a ['konkaβo, a] *adj* concave
concebir [konθe'βir] *vt* to conceive; (*imaginar*) to imagine ■ *vi* to conceive
conceder [konθe'ðer] *vt* to concede
concejal, a [konθe'xal, a] *nm/f* town councillor
concejo [kon'θexo] *nm* council
concentración [konθentra'θjon] *nf* concentration
concentrar [konθen'trar] *vt*, **concentrarse** *vr* to concentrate
concéntrico, -a [kon'θentriko, a] *adj* concentric
concepción [konθep'θjon] *nf* conception
concepto [kon'θepto] *nm* concept; **por ~ de** as, by way of; **tener buen ~ de algn** to think highly of sb; **bajo ningún ~** under no circumstances
conceptuar [konθep'twar] *vt* to judge
concernir [konθer'nir] *vi*: **en lo que concierne a** concerning
concertar [konθer'tar] *vt* (*Mus*) to harmonize; (*acordar: precio*) to agree; (*: tratado*) to conclude; (*trato*) to arrange, fix up; (*combinar: esfuerzos*) to coordinate; (*reconciliar: personas*) to reconcile ■ *vi* to harmonize, be in tune
concesión [konθe'sjon] *nf* concession; (*Com: fabricación*) licence
concesionario, -a [konθesjo'narjo, a] *nm/f* (*Com*) (licensed) dealer, agent, concessionaire; (*: de venta*) franchisee; (*: de transportes etc*) contractor
concha ['kontʃa] *nf* shell; (*Am fam!*) cunt (*!*)
conchabarse [kontʃa'βarse] *vr*: **~ contra** to gang up on
conciencia [kon'θjenθja] *nf* (*moral*) conscience; (*conocimiento*) awareness; **libertad de ~** freedom of worship; **tener/tomar ~ de** to be/become aware of; **tener la ~ limpia** *o* **tranquila** to have a clear conscience; **tener plena ~ de** to be fully aware of
concienciar [konθjen'θjar] *vt* to make aware; **concienciarse** *vr* to become aware

concienzudo, -a [konθjen'θuðo, a] *adj* conscientious
concierne *etc* [kon'θjerne] *vb ver* **concernir**
concierto *etc* [kon'θjerto] *vb ver* **concertar** ■ *nm* concert; *(obra)* concerto
conciliación [konθilja'θjon] *nf* conciliation
conciliar [konθi'ljar] *vt* to reconcile ■ *adj* *(Rel)* of a council; **~ el sueño** to get to sleep
concilio [kon'θiljo] *nm* council
concisión [konθi'sjon] *nf* conciseness
conciso, -a [kon'θiso, a] *adj* concise
conciudadano, -a [konθjuða'ðano, a] *nm/f* fellow citizen
concluir [konklu'ir] *vt* *(acabar)* to conclude; *(inferir)* to infer, deduce ■ *vi*, **concluirse** *vr* to conclude; **todo ha concluido** it's all over
conclusión [konklu'sjon] *nf* conclusion; **llegar a la ~ de que ...** to come to the conclusion that ...
concluya *etc* [kon'kluja] *vb ver* **concluir**
concluyente [konklu'jente] *adj* *(prueba, información)* conclusive
concordancia [konkor'ðanθja] *nf* agreement
concordar [konkor'ðar] *vt* to reconcile ■ *vi* to agree, tally
concordia [kon'korðja] *nf* harmony
concretamente [konkreta'mente] *adv* specifically, to be exact
concretar [konkre'tar] *vt* to make concrete, make more specific; *(problema)* to pinpoint; **concretarse** *vr* to become more definite
concreto, -a [kon'kreto, a] *adj, nm* *(Am)* concrete; **en ~** *(en resumen)* to sum up; *(específicamente)* specifically; **no hay nada en ~** there's nothing definite
concubina [konku'βina] *nf* concubine
concuerde *etc* [kon'kwerðe] *vb ver* **concordar**
concupiscencia [konkupis'θenθja] *nf* *(avaricia)* greed; *(lujuria)* lustfulness
concurrencia [konku'rrenθja] *nf* turnout
concurrido, -a [konku'rriðo, a] *adj* *(calle)* busy; *(local: reunión)* crowded
concurrir [konku'rrir] *vi* *(juntarse: ríos)* to meet, come together; *(: personas)* to gather, meet
concursante [konkur'sante] *nm* competitor
concursar [konkur'sar] *vi* to compete
concurso [kon'kurso] *nm* *(de público)* crowd; *(Escol: Deporte, competición)* competition; *(Com)* invitation to tender; *(examen)* open competition; *(TV etc)* quiz; *(ayuda)* help, cooperation
condado [kon'daðo] *nm* county
condal [kon'dal] *adj*: **la ciudad ~** Barcelona
conde ['konde] *nm* count
condecoración [kondekora'θjon] *nf* *(Mil)* medal, decoration
condecorar [kondeko'rar] *vt* to decorate
condena [kon'dena] *nf* sentence; **cumplir una ~** to serve a sentence
condenación [kondena'θjon] *nf* condemnation; *(Rel)* damnation
condenado, -a [konde'naðo, a] *adj* *(Jur)* condemned; *(fam: maldito)* damned ■ *nm/f* *(Jur)* convicted person
condenar [konde'nar] *vt* to condemn; *(Jur)* to convict; **condenarse** *vr* *(Jur)* to confess (one's guilt); *(Rel)* to be damned
condensar [konden'sar] *vt* to condense
condesa [kon'desa] *nf* countess
condescendencia [kondesθen'denθja] *nf* condescension; **aceptar algo por ~** to accept sth so as not to hurt feelings
condescender [kondesθen'der] *vi* to acquiesce, comply
condescienda *etc* [kondes'θjenda] *vb ver* **condescender**
condición [kondi'θjon] *nf* *(gen)* condition; *(rango)* social class; **condiciones** *nfpl* *(cualidades)* qualities; *(estado)* condition; **a ~ de que ...** on condition that ...; **las condiciones del contrato** the terms of the contract; **condiciones de trabajo** working conditions; **condiciones de venta** conditions of sale
condicional [kondiθjo'nal] *adj* conditional
condicionamiento [kondiθjona'mjento] *nm* conditioning
condicionar [kondiθjo'nar] *vt* *(acondicionar)* to condition; **~ algo a algo** to make sth conditional *o* dependent on sth
condimento [kondi'mento] *nm* seasoning
condiscípulo, -a [kondis'θipulo, a] *nm/f* fellow student
condolerse [kondo'lerse] *vr* to sympathize
condominio [kondo'minjo] *nm* *(Com)* joint ownership; *(Am)* condominium, apartment
condón [kon'don] *nm* condom
condonar [kondo'nar] *vt* *(Jur: reo)* to reprieve; *(Com: deuda)* to cancel
cóndor ['kondor] *nm* condor
conducente [kondu'θente] *adj*: **~ a** conducive to, leading to
conducir [kondu'θir] *vt* to take, convey; *(Elec etc)* to carry; *(Auto)* to drive; *(negocio)* to manage ■ *vi* to drive; *(fig)* to lead; **conducirse** *vr* to behave
conducta [kon'dukta] *nf* conduct, behaviour
conducto [kon'dukto] *nm* pipe, tube; *(fig)* channel; *(Elec)* lead; **por ~ de** through
conductor, a [konduk'tor, a] *adj* leading, guiding ■ *nm* *(Física)* conductor; *(de vehículo)* driver
conduela *etc* [kon'dwela] *vb ver* **condolerse**

conduje *etc* [kon'duxe] *vb ver* **conducir**
conduzca *etc* [kon'duθka] *vb ver* **conducir**
conectado, -a [konek'taðo, a] *adj* (*Elec*) connected, plugged in; (*Inform*) on-line
conectar [konek'tar] *vt* to connect (up), plug in; (*Inform*) to toggle on; **conectarse** *vr* (*Inform*) to log in *or* on
conejillo [kone'xiʎo] *nm*: ~ **de Indias** guinea pig
conejo [ko'nexo] *nm* rabbit
conexión [konek'sjon] *nf* connection; (*Inform*) logging in *or* on
confabularse [konfaβu'larse] *vr*: ~ **(para hacer algo)** to plot *o* conspire (to do sth)
confección [konfek'θjon] *nf* (*preparación*) preparation, making-up; (*industria*) clothing industry; (*producto*) article; **de** ~ (*ropa*) off-the-peg
confeccionar [konfe(k)θjo'nar] *vt* to make (up)
confederación [konfeðera'θjon] *nf* confederation
conferencia [konfe'renθja] *nf* conference; (*lección*) lecture; (*Telec*) call; ~ **de cobro revertido** (*Telec*) reversed-charge (*Brit*) *o* collect (*US*) call; ~ **cumbre** summit (conference)
conferenciante [konferen'θjante] *nm/f* lecturer
conferir [konfe'rir] *vt* to award
confesar [konfe'sar] *vt* (*admitir*) to confess, admit; (*error*) to acknowledge; (*crimen*) to own up to
confesión [konfe'sjon] *nf* confession
confesionario [konfesjo'narjo] *nm* confessional
confeso, -a [kon'feso, a] *adj* (*Jur etc*) self-confessed
confeti [kon'feti] *nm* confetti
confiado, -a [kon'fjaðo, a] *adj* (*crédulo*) trusting; (*seguro*) confident; (*presumido*) conceited, vain
confianza [kon'fjanθa] *nf* trust; (*aliento, confidencia*) confidence; (*familiaridad*) intimacy, familiarity; (*pey*) vanity, conceit; **margen de** ~ credibility gap; **tener** ~ **con algn** to be on close terms with sb
confiar [kon'fjar] *vt* to entrust ▪ *vi* (*fiarse*) to trust; (*contar con*) to rely; **confiarse** *vr* to put one's trust in
confidencia [konfi'ðenθja] *nf* confidence
confidencial [konfiðen'θjal] *adj* confidential
confidente [konfi'ðente] *nm/f* confidant/confidante; (*policial*) informer
confiera *etc* [kon'fjera] *vb ver* **conferir**
confiese *etc* [kon'fjese] *vb ver* **confesar**
configuración [konfiɣura'θjon] *nf* (*tb Inform*) configuration; **la** ~ **del terreno** the lie of the land; ~ **de bits** (*Inform*) bit pattern
configurar [konfiɣu'rar] *vt* to shape, form
confín [kon'fin] *nm* limit; **confines** *nmpl* confines, limits
confinar [konfi'nar] *vi* to confine; (*desterrar*) to banish
confiriendo *etc* [konfi'rjendo] *vb ver* **conferir**
confirmación [konfirma'θjon] *nf* confirmation; (*Rel*) Confirmation
confirmar [konfir'mar] *vt* to confirm; (*Jur etc*) to corroborate; **la excepción confirma la regla** the exception proves the rule
confiscar [konfis'kar] *vt* to confiscate
confisque *etc* [kon'fiske] *vb ver* **confiscar**
confitado, -a [konfi'taðo, a] *adj*: **fruta confitada** crystallized fruit
confite [kon'fite] *nm* sweet (*Brit*), candy (*US*)
confitería [konfite'ria] *nf* confectionery; (*tienda*) confectioner's (shop)
confitura [konfi'tura] *nf* jam
conflagración [konflaɣra'θjon] *nf* conflagration
conflictivo, -a [konflik'tiβo, a] *adj* (*asunto, propuesta*) controversial; (*país, situación*) troubled
conflicto [kon'flikto] *nm* conflict; (*fig*) clash; (*: dificultad*): **estar en un** ~ to be in a jam; ~ **laboral** labour dispute
confluir [konflu'ir] *vi* (*ríos etc*) to meet; (*gente*) to gather
confluya *etc* [kon'fluja] *vb ver* **confluir**
conformar [konfor'mar] *vt* to shape, fashion ▪ *vi* to agree; **conformarse** *vr* to conform; (*resignarse*) to resign o.s.
conforme [kon'forme] *adj* alike, similar; (*de acuerdo*) agreed, in agreement; (*satisfecho*) satisfied ▪ *adv* as ▪ *excl* agreed! ▪ *nm* agreement ▪ *prep*: ~ **a** in accordance with
conformidad [konformi'ðað] *nf* (*semejanza*) similarity; (*acuerdo*) agreement; (*resignación*) resignation; **de/en** ~ **con** in accordance with; **dar su** ~ to consent
conformismo [konfor'mismo] *nm* conformism
conformista [konfor'mista] *nm/f* conformist
confort (*pl* **conforts**) [kon'for, kon'for(t)s] *nm* comfort
confortable [konfor'taβle] *adj* comfortable
confortar [konfor'tar] *vt* to comfort
confraternidad [konfraterni'ðað] *nf* brotherhood; **espíritu de** ~ feeling of unity
confraternizar [konfraterni'θar] *vi* to fraternize
confrontación [konfronta'θjon] *nf* confrontation
confrontar [konfron'tar] *vt* to confront; (*dos personas*) to bring face to face; (*cotejar*) to

compare ■ *vi* to border
confundir [konfun'dir] *vt* (*borrar*) to blur; (*equivocar*) to mistake, confuse; (*mezclar*) to mix; (*turbar*) to confuse; **confundirse** *vr* (*hacerse borroso*) to become blurred; (*turbarse*) to get confused; (*equivocarse*) to make a mistake; (*mezclarse*) to mix
confusión [konfu'sjon] *nf* confusion
confusionismo [konfusjo'nismo] *nm* confusion, uncertainty
confuso, -a [kon'fuso, a] *adj* (*gen*) confused; (*recuerdo*) hazy; (*estilo*) obscure
congelación [konxela'θjon] *nf* freezing; **~ de créditos** credit freeze
congelado, -a [konxe'laðo, a] *adj* frozen ■ *nmpl*: **congelados** frozen food *sg o* foods
congelador [konxela'ðor] *nm* freezer, deep freeze
congelar [konxe'lar] *vt* to freeze; **congelarse** *vr* (*sangre, grasa*) to congeal
congénere [kon'xenere] *nm/f*: **sus congéneres** his peers
congeniar [konxe'njar] *vi* to get on (*Brit*) *o* along (*US*) (well)
congénito, -a [kon'xenito, a] *adj* congenital
congestión [konxes'tjon] *nf* congestion
congestionado, -a [konxestjo'naðo, a] *adj* congested
congestionar [konxestjo'nar] *vt* to congest; **congestionarse** *vr* to become congested; **se le congestionó la cara** his face became flushed
conglomerado [konglome'raðo] *nm* conglomerate
Congo ['kongo] *nm*: **el ~** the Congo
congoja [kon'goxa] *nf* distress, grief
congraciarse [kongra'θjarse] *vr* to ingratiate o.s.
congratular [kongratu'lar] *vt* to congratulate
congregación [kongreɣa'θjon] *nf* congregation
congregar [kongre'ɣar] *vt*, **congregarse** *vr* to gather together
congregue *etc* [kon'greɣe] *vb ver* **congregar**
congresista [kongre'sista] *nm/f* delegate, congressman/woman
congreso [kon'greso] *nm* congress; **C~ de los Diputados** (*Esp Pol*) ≈ House of Commons (*Brit*), House of Representatives (*US*); *ver tb* **Las Cortes (españolas)**
congrio ['kongrjo] *nm* conger (eel)
congruente [kon'grwente] *adj* congruent, congruous
conífera [ko'nifera] *nf* conifer
conjetura [konxe'tura] *nf* guess; (*Com*) guesstimate
conjeturar [konxetu'rar] *vt* to guess
conjugación [konxuɣa'θjon] *nf* conjugation
conjugar [konxu'ɣar] *vt* to combine, fit together; (*Ling*) to conjugate
conjugue *etc* [kon'xuɣe] *vb ver* **conjugar**
conjunción [konxun'θjon] *nf* conjunction
conjunctivitis [konxunti'βitis] *nf* conjunctivitis
conjunto, -a [kon'xunto, a] *adj* joint, united ■ *nm* whole; (*Mus*) band; (*de ropa*) ensemble; (*Inform*) set; **en ~** as a whole; **~ integrado de programas** (*Inform*) integrated software suite
conjura [kon'xura] *nf* plot, conspiracy
conjurar [konxu'rar] *vt* (*Rel*) to exorcise; (*peligro*) to ward off ■ *vi* to plot
conjuro [kon'xuro] *nm* spell
conllevar [konʎe'βar] *vt* to bear; (*implicar*) to imply, involve
conmemoración [konmemora'θjon] *nf* commemoration
conmemorar [konmemo'rar] *vt* to commemorate
conmigo [kon'miɣo] *pron* with me
conminar [konmi'nar] *vt* to threaten
conmiseración [konmisera'θjon] *nf* pity, commiseration
conmoción [konmo'θjon] *nf* shock; (*Pol*) disturbance; (*fig*) upheaval; **~ cerebral** (*Med*) concussion
conmovedor, a [konmoβe'ðor, a] *adj* touching, moving; (*emocionante*) exciting
conmover [konmo'βer] *vt* to shake, disturb; (*fig*) to move; **conmoverse** *vr* (*fig*) to be moved
conmueva *etc* [kon'mweβa] *vb ver* **conmover**
conmutación [konmuta'θjon] *nf* (*Inform*) switching; **~ de mensajes** message switching; **~ por paquetes** packet switching
conmutador [konmuta'ðor] *nm* switch; (*Am Telec*) switchboard
conmutar [konmu'tar] *vt* (*Jur*) to commute
connivencia [konni'βenθja] *nf*: **estar en ~ con** to be in collusion with
connotación [konnota'θjon] *nf* connotation
cono ['kono] *nm* cone; **C~ Sur** Southern Cone
conocedor, a [konoθe'ðor, a] *adj* expert, knowledgeable ■ *nm/f* expert, connoisseur
conocer [kono'θer] *vt* to know; (*por primera vez*) to meet, get to know; (*entender*) to know about; (*reconocer*) to recognize; **conocerse** *vr* (*una persona*) to know o.s.; (*dos personas*) to (get to) know each other; **darse a ~** (*presentarse*) to make o.s. known; **se conoce que ...** (*parece*) apparently ...
conocido, -a [kono'θiðo, a] *adj* (well-)known ■ *nm/f* acquaintance

conocimiento [konoθi'mjento] *nm* knowledge; (*Med*) consciousness; (*Naut*: *tb*: **conocimiento de embarque**) bill of lading; **conocimientos** *nmpl* (*personas*) acquaintances; (*saber*) knowledge *sg*; **hablar con ~ de causa** to speak from experience; **~ (de embarque) aéreo** (*Com*) air waybill
conozca *etc* [ko'noθka] *vb ver* **conocer**
conque ['konke] *conj* and so, so then
conquense [kon'kense] *adj* of *o* from Cuenca ■ *nm/f* native *o* inhabitant of Cuenca
conquista [kon'kista] *nf* conquest
conquistador, a [konkista'ðor, a] *adj* conquering ■ *nm* conqueror
conquistar [konkis'tar] *vt* (*Mil*) to conquer; (*puesto, simpatía*) to win; (*enamorar*) to win the heart of
consabido, -a [konsa'βiðo, a] *adj* (*frase etc*) old; (*pey*): **las consabidas excusas** the same old excuses
consagrado, -a [konsa'ɣraðo, a] *adj* (*Rel*) consecrated; (*actor*) established
consagrar [konsa'ɣrar] *vt* (*Rel*) to consecrate; (*fig*) to devote
consciente [kons'θjente] *adj* conscious; **ser** *o* **estar ~ de** to be aware of
consecución [konseku'θjon] *nf* acquisition; (*de fin*) attainment
consecuencia [konse'kwenθja] *nf* consequence, outcome; (*firmeza*) consistency; **de ~** of importance
consecuente [konse'kwente] *adj* consistent
consecutivo, -a [konseku'tiβo, a] *adj* consecutive
conseguir [konse'ɣir] *vt* to get, obtain; (*sus fines*) to attain
consejería [konsexe'ria] *nf* (*Pol*) ministry (*in a regional government*)
consejero, -a [konse'xero, a] *nm/f* adviser, consultant; (*Pol*) minister (*in a regional government*); (*Com*) director; (*en comisión*) member
consejo [kon'sexo] *nm* advice; (*Pol*) council; (*Com*) board; **un ~** a piece of advice; **~ de administración** board of directors; **~ de guerra** court-martial; **C~ de Europa** Council of Europe
consenso [kon'senso] *nm* consensus
consentido, -a [konsen'tiðo, a] *adj* (*mimado*) spoiled
consentimiento [konsenti'mjento] *nm* consent
consentir [konsen'tir] *vt* (*permitir, tolerar*) to consent to; (*mimar*) to pamper, spoil ■ *vi* to agree, consent; **~ que algn haga algo** to allow sb to do sth
conserje [kon'serxe] *nm* caretaker; (*portero*) porter
conserva [kon'serβa] *nf*: **en ~** (*alimentos*) tinned (*Brit*), canned; **conservas** tinned *o* canned foods
conservación [konserβa'θjon] *nf* conservation; (*de alimentos, vida*) preservation
conservador, a [konserβa'ðor, a] *adj* (*Pol*) conservative ■ *nm/f* conservative
conservadurismo [konserβaðu'rismo] *nm* (*Pol etc*) conservatism
conservante [konser'βante] *nm* preservative
conservar [konser'βar] *vt* (*gen*) to preserve; (*recursos*) to conserve, keep; (*alimentos, vida*) to preserve; **conservarse** *vr* to survive
conservas [kon'serβas] *nfpl*: **~ (alimenticias)** tinned (*Brit*) *o* canned goods
conservatorio [konserβa'torjo] *nm* (*Mus*) conservatoire; (*Am*) greenhouse
considerable [konsiðe'raβle] *adj* considerable
consideración [konsiðera'θjon] *nf* consideration; (*estimación*) respect; **de ~** important; **De mi** *o* **nuestra (mayor) ~** (*Am*) Dear Sir(s) *o* Madam; **tomar en ~** to take into account
considerado, -a [konsiðe'raðo, a] *adj* (*atento*) considerate; (*respetado*) respected
considerar [konsiðe'rar] *vt* (*gen*) to consider; (*meditar*) to think about; (*tener en cuenta*) to take into account
consienta *etc* [kon'sjenta] *vb ver* **consentir**
consigna [kon'siɣna] *nf* (*orden*) order, instruction; (*para equipajes*) left-luggage office (*Brit*), checkroom (*US*)
consignación [konsiɣna'θjon] *nf* consignment; **~ de créditos** allocation of credits
consignador [konsiɣna'ðor] *nm* (*Com*) consignor
consignar [konsiɣ'nar] *vt* (*Com*) to send; (*créditos*) to allocate
consignatario, -a [konsiɣna'tarjo, a] *nm/f* (*Com*) consignee
consigo *etc* [kon'siɣo] *vb ver* **conseguir** ■ *pron* (*m*) with him; (*f*) with her; (*usted*) with you; (*reflexivo*) with o.s.
consiguiendo *etc* [konsi'ɣjendo] *vb ver* **conseguir**
consiguiente [konsi'ɣjente] *adj* consequent; **por ~** and so, therefore, consequently
consintiendo *etc* [konsin'tjendo] *vb ver* **consentir**
consistente [konsis'tente] *adj* consistent; (*sólido*) solid, firm; (*válido*) sound; **~ en** consisting of
consistir [konsis'tir] *vi*: **~ en** (*componerse de*)

to consist of; (*ser resultado de*) to be due to
consola [kon'sola] *nf* console, control panel; (*mueble*) console table; **~ de juegos** games console; **~ de mandos** (*Inform*) control console; **~ de visualización** visual display console
consolación [konsola'θjon] *nf* consolation
consolar [konso'lar] *vt* to console
consolidar [konsoli'ðar] *vt* to consolidate
consomé (*pl* **~s**) [konso'me, konso'mes] *nm* consommé, clear soup
consonancia [konso'nanθja] *nf* harmony; **en ~ con** in accordance with
consonante [konso'nante] *adj* consonant, harmonious ■ *nf* consonant
consorcio [kon'sorθjo] *nm* (*Com*) consortium, syndicate
consorte [kon'sorte] *nm/f* consort
conspicuo, -a [kons'pikwo, a] *adj* conspicuous
conspiración [konspira'θjon] *nf* conspiracy
conspirador, a [konspira'ðor, a] *nm/f* conspirator
conspirar [konspi'rar] *vi* to conspire
constancia [kons'tanθja] *nf* (*gen*) constancy; (*certeza*) certainly; **dejar ~ de algo** to put sth on record
constante [kons'tante] *adj, nf* constant
constar [kons'tar] *vi* (*evidenciarse*) to be clear *o* evident; **~ (en)** to appear (in); **~ de** to consist of; **hacer ~** to put on record; **me consta que ...** I have evidence that ...; **que conste que lo hice por ti** believe me, I did it for your own good
constatar [konsta'tar] *vt* (*controlar*) to check; (*observar*) to note
constelación [konstela'θjon] *nf* constellation
consternación [konsterna'θjon] *nf* consternation
constipado, -a [konsti'paðo, a] *adj*: **estar ~** to have a cold ■ *nm* cold
constiparse [konsti'parse] *vr* to catch a cold
constitución [konstitu'θjon] *nf* constitution; **Día de la C~** (*Esp*) Constitution Day (*6th December*)
constitucional [konstituθjo'nal] *adj* constitutional
constituir [konstitu'ir] *vt* (*formar, componer*) to constitute, make up; (*fundar, erigir, ordenar*) to constitute, establish; (*ser*) to be; **constituirse** *vr* (*Pol etc: cuerpo*) to be composed; (*: fundarse*) to be established
constitutivo, -a [konstitu'tiβo, a] *adj* constitutive, constituent
constituya *etc* [konsti'tuja] *vb ver* **constituir**
constituyente [konstitu'jente] *adj* constituent
constreñir [konstre'ɲir] *vt* (*obligar*) to compel, oblige; (*restringir*) to restrict
constriño *etc* [kons'triɲo], **constriñendo** *etc* [konstri'ɲendo] *vb ver* **constreñir**
construcción [konstruk'θjon] *nf* construction, building
constructivo, -a [konstruk'tiβo, a] *adj* constructive
constructor, a [konstruk'tor, a] *nm/f* builder
construir [konstru'ir] *vt* to build, construct
construyendo *etc* [konstru'jendo] *vb ver* **construir**
consuelo *etc* [kon'swelo] *vb ver* **consolar** ■ *nm* consolation, solace
consuetudinario, -a [konswetuði'narjo, a] *adj* customary; **derecho ~** common law
cónsul ['konsul] *nm* consul
consulado [konsu'laðo] *nm* (*sede*) consulate; (*cargo*) consulship
consulta [kon'sulta] *nf* consultation; (*Med: consultorio*) consulting room; (*Inform*) enquiry; **horas de ~** surgery hours; **obra de ~** reference book
consultar [konsul'tar] *vt* to consult; **~ un archivo** (*Inform*) to interrogate a file
consultor, a [konsul'tor, a] *nm*: **~ en dirección de empresas** management consultant
consultorio [konsul'torjo] *nm* (*Med*) surgery
consumado, -a [konsu'maðo, a] *adj* perfect; (*bribón*) out-and-out
consumar [konsu'mar] *vt* to complete, carry out; (*crimen*) to commit; (*sentencia*) to carry out
consumición [konsumi'θjon] *nf* consumption; (*bebida*) drink; (*comida*) food; **~ mínima** cover charge
consumido, -a [konsu'miðo, a] *adj* (*flaco*) skinny
consumidor, a [konsumi'ðor, a] *nm/f* consumer
consumir [konsu'mir] *vt* to consume; **consumirse** *vr* to be consumed; (*persona*) to waste away
consumismo [konsu'mismo] *nm* (*Com*) consumerism
consumo [kon'sumo] *nm* consumption; **bienes de ~** consumer goods
contabilice *etc* [kontaβi'liθe] *vb ver* **contabilizar**
contabilidad [kontaβili'ðað] *nf* accounting, book-keeping; (*profesión*) accountancy; (*Com*): **~ analítica** variable costing; **~ de costos** cost accounting; **~ de doble partida** double-entry book-keeping; **~ de gestión** management accounting; **~ por partida simple** single-entry book-keeping

contabilizar [kontaβi'liθar] *vt* to enter in the accounts
contable [kon'taβle] *nm/f* bookkeeper; (*licenciado*) accountant; **~ de costos** (*Com*) cost accountant
contactar [kontak'tar] *vi*: **~ con algn** to contact sb
contacto [kon'takto] *nm* contact; **lentes de ~** contact lenses; **estar en ~ con** to be in touch with
contado, -a [kon'taðo, a] *adj*: **contados** (*escasos*) numbered, scarce, few ■ *nm*: **al ~** for cash; **pagar al ~** to pay (in) cash; **precio al ~** cash price
contador [konta'ðor] *nm* (*aparato*) meter; (*Am: contable*) accountant
contaduría [kontaðu'ria] *nf* accountant's office
contagiar [konta'xjar] *vt* (*enfermedad*) to pass on, transmit; (*persona*) to infect; **contagiarse** *vr* to become infected
contagio [kon'taxjo] *nm* infection
contagioso, -a [konta'xjoso, a] *adj* infectious; (*fig*) catching
contaminación [kontamina'θjon] *nf* (*gen*) contamination; (*del ambiente etc*) pollution
contaminar [kontami'nar] *vt* (*gen*) to contaminate; (*aire, agua*) to pollute; (*fig*) to taint
contante [kon'tante] *adj*: **dinero ~ (y sonante)** hard cash
contar [kon'tar] *vt* (*páginas, dinero*) to count; (*anécdota etc*) to tell ■ *vi* to count; **contarse** *vr* to be counted, figure; **~ con** to rely on, count on; **sin ~** not to mention; **le cuento entre mis amigos** I reckon him among my friends
contemplación [kontempla'θjon] *nf* contemplation; **no andarse con contemplaciones** not to stand on ceremony
contemplar [kontem'plar] *vt* to contemplate; (*mirar*) to look at
contemporáneo, -a [kontempo'raneo, a] *adj, nm/f* contemporary
contemporizar [kontempori'θar] *vi*: **~ con** to keep in with
contención [konten'θjon] *nf* (*Jur*) suit; **muro de ~** retaining wall
contencioso, -a [konten'θjoso, a] *adj* (*Jur etc*) contentious ■ *nm* (*Pol*) conflict, dispute
contender [konten'der] *vi* to contend; (*en un concurso*) to compete
contendiente [konten'djente] *nm/f* contestant
contendrá *etc* [konten'dra] *vb ver* **contener**
contenedor [kontene'ðor] *nm* container; (*de escombros*) skip; **~ de (la) basura** wheelie-bin (*Brit*); **~ de vidrio** bottle bank
contener [konte'ner] *vt* to contain, hold; (*risa etc*) to hold back, contain; **contenerse** *vr* to control *o* restrain o.s.
contenga *etc* [kon'tenga] *vb ver* **contener**
contenido, -a [konte'niðo, a] *adj* (*moderado*) restrained; (*risa etc*) suppressed ■ *nm* contents *pl*, content
contentar [konten'tar] *vt* (*satisfacer*) to satisfy; (*complacer*) to please; (*Com*) to endorse; **contentarse** *vr* to be satisfied
contento, -a [kon'tento, a] *adj* contented, content; (*alegre*) pleased; (*feliz*) happy
contestación [kontesta'θjon] *nf* answer, reply; **~ a la demanda** (*Jur*) defence plea
contestador [kontesta'ðor] *nm*: **~ automático** answering machine
contestar [kontes'tar] *vt* to answer (back), reply; (*Jur*) to corroborate, confirm
contestatario, -a [kontesta'tarjo, a] *adj* anti-establishment, nonconformist
contexto [kon'teksto] *nm* context
contienda [kon'tjenda] *nf* contest, struggle
contiene *etc* [kon'tjene] *vb ver* **contener**
contigo [kon'tiɣo] *pron* with you
contiguo, -a [kon'tiɣwo, a] *adj* (*de al lado*) next; (*vecino*) adjacent, adjoining
continental [kontinen'tal] *adj* continental
continente [konti'nente] *adj, nm* continent
contingencia [kontin'xenθja] *nf* contingency; (*riesgo*) risk; (*posibilidad*) eventuality
contingente [kontin'xente] *adj* contingent ■ *nm* contingent; (*Com*) quota
continuación [kontinwa'θjon] *nf* continuation; **a ~** then, next
continuamente [kon'tinwamente] *adv* (*sin interrupción*) continuously; (*a todas horas*) constantly
continuar [konti'nwar] *vt* to continue, go on with; (*reanudar*) to resume ■ *vi* to continue, go on; **~ hablando** to continue talking *o* to talk
continuidad [kontinwi'ðað] *nf* continuity
continuo, -a [kon'tinwo, a] *adj* (*sin interrupción*) continuous; (*acción perseverante*) continual
contonearse [kontone'arse] *vr* (*hombre*) to swagger; (*mujer*) to swing one's hips
contorno [kon'torno] *nm* outline; (*Geo*) contour; **contornos** *nmpl* neighbourhood *sg*, surrounding area *sg*
contorsión [kontor'sjon] *nf* contortion
contra ['kontra] *prep* against; (*Com: giro*) on ■ *adv* against ■ *adj, nm/f* (*Pol fam*) counter-revolutionary ■ *nm* con ■ *nf*: **la C~ (nicaragüense)** the Contras *pl*

contraalmirante [kontraalmi'rante] *nm* rear admiral
contraanálisis [kontraa'nalisis] *nm* follow-up test, countertest
contraataque [kontraa'take] *nm* counterattack
contrabajo [kontra'βaxo] *nm* double bass
contrabandista [kontraβan'dista] *nm/f* smuggler
contrabando [kontra'βando] *nm* (*acción*) smuggling; (*mercancías*) contraband; **~ de armas** gun-running
contracción [kontrak'θjon] *nf* contraction
contrachapado [kontratʃa'paðo] *nm* plywood
contracorriente [kontrako'rrjente] *nf* cross-current
contradecir [kontraðe'θir] *vt* to contradict
contradicción [kontraðik'θjon] *nf* contradiction; **espíritu de ~** contrariness
contradicho [kontra'ðitʃo] *pp de* **contradecir**
contradiciendo *etc* [kontraði'θjendo] *vb ver* **contradecir**
contradictorio, -a [kontraðik'torjo, a] *adj* contradictory
contradiga *etc* [kontra'ðiɣa], **contradije** [kontra'ðixe], **contradirá** *etc* [kontraði'ra] *vb ver* **contradecir**
contraer [kontra'er] *vt* to contract; (*hábito*) to acquire; (*limitar*) to restrict; **contraerse** *vr* to contract; (*limitarse*) to limit o.s.
contraespionage [kontraespjo'naxe] *nm* counter-espionage
contrafuerte [kontra'fwerte] *nm* (*Arq*) buttress
contragolpe [kontra'ɣolpe] *nm* backlash
contrahacer [kontraa'θer] *vb* (*copiar*) to copy, imitate; (*moneda*) to conterfeit; (*documento*) to forge, fake; (*libro*) to pirate
contrahaga *etc* [kontra'aɣa], **contraharé** *etc* [kontraa're] *vb ver* **contrahacer**
contrahecho, -a [kontra'etʃo, a] *pp de* **contrahacer** ■ *adj* fake; (*Anat*) hunchbacked
contrahice *etc* [kontra'iθe] *vb ver* **contrahacer**
contraiga *etc* [kon'traiɣa] *vb ver* **contraer**
contraindicaciones [kontraindika'θjones] *nfpl* (*Med*) contraindications
contraje *etc* [kon'traxe] *vb ver* **contraer**
contralor [kontra'lor] *nm* (*Am*) government accounting inspector
contraluz [kontra'luθ] *nf* (*Foto etc*) back lighting; **a ~** against the light
contramaestre [kontrama'estre] *nm* foreman
contraofensiva [kontraofen'siβa] *nf* counteroffensive
contraorden [kontra'orðen] *nf* counter-order, countermand
contrapartida [kontrapar'tiða] *nf* (*Com*) balancing entry; **como ~ (de)** in return (for), as *o* in compensation (for)
contrapelo [kontra'pelo]: **a ~** *adv* the wrong way
contrapesar [kontrape'sar] *vt* to counterbalance; (*fig*) to offset
contrapeso [kontra'peso] *nm* counterweight; (*fig*) counterbalance; (*Com*) makeweight
contrapondré *etc* [kontrapon'dre] *vb ver* **contraponer**
contraponer [kontrapo'ner] *vt* (*cotejar*) to compare; (*oponer*) to oppose
contraponga *etc* [kontra'ponga] *vb ver* **contraponer**
contraportada [kontrapor'taða] *nf* (*de revista*) back page
contraproducente [kontraproðu'θente] *adj* counterproductive
contrapuesto [kontra'pwesto] *pp de* **contraponer**
contrapunto [kontra'punto] *nm* counterpoint
contrapuse *etc* [kontra'puse] *vb ver* **contraponer**
contrariar [kontra'rjar] *vt* (*oponerse*) to oppose; (*poner obstáculo*) to impede; (*enfadar*) to vex
contrariedad [kontrarje'ðað] *nf* (*oposición*) opposition; (*obstáculo*) obstacle, setback; (*disgusto*) vexation, annoyance
contrario, -a [kon'trarjo, a] *adj* contrary; (*persona*) opposed; (*sentido, lado*) opposite ■ *nm/f* enemy, adversary; (*Deporte*) opponent; **al ~, por el ~** on the contrary; **de lo ~** otherwise
Contrarreforma [kontrarre'forma] *nf* Counter-Reformation
contrarreloj [kontrarre'lo(x)] *nf* (*tb*: **prueba contrarreloj**) time trial
contrarrestar [kontrarres'tar] *vt* to counteract
contrarrevolución [kontrarreβolu'θjon] *nf* counter-revolution
contrasentido [kontrasen'tiðo] *nm* contradiction; **es un ~ que él ...** it doesn't make sense for him to ...
contraseña [kontra'seɲa] *nf* countersign; (*frase*) password
contrastar [kontras'tar] *vt* to resist ■ *vi* to contrast
contraste [kon'traste] *nm* contrast
contrata [kon'trata] *nf* (*Jur*) written contract; (*empleo*) hiring

contratar [kontra'tar] *vt* (*firmar un acuerdo para*) to contract for; (*empleados, obreros*) to hire, engage; (*Deporte*) to sign up; **contratarse** *vr* to sign on
contratiempo [kontra'tjempo] *nm* (*revés*) setback; (*accidente*) mishap; **a ~** (*Mus*) off-beat
contratista [kontra'tista] *nm/f* contractor
contrato [kon'trato] *nm* contract; **~ de compraventa** contract of sale; **~ a precio fijo** fixed-price contract; **~ a término** forward contract; **~ de trabajo** contract of employment *o* service
contravalor [kontraβa'lor] *nm* exchange value
contravención [kontraβen'θjon] *nf* contravention, violation
contravendré *etc* [kontraβen'dre], **contravenga** *etc* [kontra'βenga] *vb ver* **contravenir**
contravenir [kontraβe'nir] *vi*: **~ a** to contravene, violate
contraventana [kontraβen'tana] *nf* shutter
contraviene *etc* [kontra'βjene], **contraviniendo** *etc* [kontraβi'njendo] *vb ver* **contravenir**
contrayendo [kontra'jendo] *vb ver* **contraer**
contribución [kontriβu'θjon] *nf* (*municipal etc*) tax; (*ayuda*) contribution; **exento de contribuciones** tax-free
contribuir [kontriβu'ir] *vt, vi* to contribute; (*Com*) to pay (in taxes)
contribuyendo *etc* [kontriβu'jendo] *vb ver* **contribuir**
contribuyente [kontriβu'jente] *nm/f* (*Com*) taxpayer; (*que ayuda*) contributor
contrincante [kontrin'kante] *nm* opponent, rival
control [kon'trol] *nm* control; (*inspección*) inspection, check; (*Com*): **~ de calidad** quality control; **~ de cambios** exchange control; **~ de costos** cost control; **~ de créditos** credit control; **~ de existencias** stock control; **~ de precios** price control
controlador, a [kontrola'ðor, a] *nm/f* controller; **~ aéreo** air-traffic controller
controlar [kontro'lar] *vt* to control; to inspect, check; (*Com*) to audit
controversia [kontro'βersja] *nf* controversy
contubernio [kontu'βernjo] *nm* ring, conspiracy
contumaz [kontu'maθ] *adj* obstinate, stubbornly disobedient
contundente [kontun'dente] *adj* (*prueba*) conclusive; (*fig: argumento*) convincing; **instrumento ~** blunt instrument
contusión [kontu'sjon] *nf* bruise
contuve *etc* [kon'tuβe] *vb ver* **contener**
convalecencia [kombale'θenθja] *nf* convalescence
convalecer [kombale'θer] *vi* to convalesce, get better
convaleciente [kombale'θjente] *adj, nm/f* convalescent
convalezca *etc* [komba'leθka] *vb ver* **convalecer**
convalidar [kombali'ðar] *vt* (*título*) to recognize
convencer [komben'θer] *vt* to convince; (*persuadir*) to persuade
convencimiento [kombenθi'mjento] *nm* (*acción*) convincing; (*persuasión*) persuasion; (*certidumbre*) conviction; **tener el ~ de que ...** to be convinced that ...
convención [komben'θjon] *nf* convention
convencional [kombenθjo'nal] *adj* conventional
convendré *etc* [komben'dre], **convenga** *etc* [kom'benga] *vb ver* **convenir**
conveniencia [kombe'njenθja] *nf* suitability; (*conformidad*) agreement; (*utilidad, provecho*) usefulness; **conveniencias** *nfpl* conventions; (*Com*) property *sg*; **ser de la ~ de algn** to suit sb
conveniente [kombe'njente] *adj* suitable; (*útil*) useful; (*correcto*) fit, proper; (*aconsejable*) advisable
convenio [kom'benjo] *nm* agreement, treaty; **~ de nivel crítico** threshold agreement
convenir [kombe'nir] *vi* (*estar de acuerdo*) to agree; (*ser conveniente*) to suit, be suitable; **"sueldo a ~"** "salary to be agreed"; **conviene recordar que ...** it should be remembered that ...
convento [kom'bento] *nm* monastery; (*de monjas*) convent
convenza *etc* [kom'benθa] *vb ver* **convencer**
convergencia [komber'xenθja] *nf* convergence
converger [komber'xer], **convergir** [komber'xir] *vi* to converge; **sus esfuerzos convergen a un fin común** their efforts are directed towards the same objective
converja *etc* [kom'berxa] *vb ver* **converger**; **convergir**
conversación [kombersa'θjon] *nf* conversation
conversar [komber'sar] *vi* to talk, converse
conversión [komber'sjon] *nf* conversion
converso, -a [kom'berso, a] *nm/f* convert
convertir [komber'tir] *vt* to convert; (*transformar*) to transform, turn; (*Com*) to (ex)change; **convertirse** *vr* (*Rel*) to convert
convexo, -a [kom'bekso, a] *adj* convex

convicción [kombik'θjon] *nf* conviction
convicto, -a [kom'bikto, a] *adj* convicted; (*condenado*) condemned
convidado, -a [kombi'ðaðo, a] *nm/f* guest
convidar [kombi'ðar] *vt* to invite
conviene *etc* [kom'bjene] *vb ver* **convenir**
convierta *etc* [kom'bjerta] *vb ver* **convertir**
convincente [kombin'θente] *adj* convincing
conviniendo *etc* [kombi'njendo] *vb ver* **convenir**
convirtiendo *etc* [kombir'tjendo] *vb ver* **convertir**
convite [kom'bite] *nm* invitation; (*banquete*) banquet
convivencia [kombi'βenθja] *nf* coexistence, living together
convivir [kombi'βir] *vi* to live together; (*Pol*) to coexist
convocar [kombo'kar] *vt* to summon, call (together)
convocatoria [komboka'torja] *nf* summons *sg*; (*anuncio*) notice of meeting; (*Escol*) examination session
convoque *etc* [kom'boke] *vb ver* **convocar**
convoy [kom'boj] *nm* (*Ferro*) train
convulsión [kombul'sjon] *nf* convulsion; (*Pol etc*) upheaval
conyugal [konju'ɣal] *adj* conjugal; **vida ~** married life
cónyuge ['konyuxe] *nm/f* spouse, partner
coña ['koɲa] *nf*: **tomar algo a ~** (*fam!*) to take sth as a joke
coñac (*pl* **coñacs**) ['koɲa(k), 'koɲas] *nm* cognac, brandy
coñazo [ko'ɲaθo] *nm* (*fam*) pain; **dar el ~** to be a real pain
coño ['koɲo] (*fam!*) *nm* cunt (*!*); (*Am pey*) Spaniard ■ *excl* (*enfado*) shit (*!*); (*sorpresa*) bloody hell (*!*); **¡qué ~!** what a pain in the arse! (*!*)
cooperación [koopera'θjon] *nf* cooperation
cooperar [koope'rar] *vi* to cooperate
cooperativo, -a [koopera'tiβo, a] *adj* cooperative ■ *nf* cooperative
coordenada [koorðe'naða] *nf* (*Mat*) coordinate; (*fig*): **coordenadas** *nfpl* guidelines, framework *sg*
coordinación [koorðina'θjon] *nf* coordination
coordinador, a [koorðina'ðor, a] *nm/f* coordinator ■ *nf* coordinating committee
coordinar [koorði'nar] *vt* to coordinate
copa ['kopa] *nf* (*tb Deporte*) cup; (*vaso*) glass; (*de árbol*) top; (*de sombrero*) crown; **copas** *nfpl* (*Naipes*) *one of the suits in the Spanish card deck*; **(tomar una) ~** (to have a) drink; **ir de copas** to go out for a drink; *ver tb* **Baraja Española**
copar [ko'par] *vt* (*puestos*) to monopolize
coparticipación [kopartiθipa'θjon] *nf* (*Com*) co-ownership
COPE *nf abr* (= *Cadena de Ondas Populares Españolas*) *Spanish radio network*
Copenhague [kope'naɣe] *n* Copenhagen
copete [ko'pete] *nm* tuft (of hair); **de alto ~** aristocratic, upper-crust (*fam*)
copia ['kopja] *nf* copy; (*Arte*) replica; (*Com etc*) duplicate; (*Inform*): **~ impresa** hard copy; **~ de respaldo** *o* **de seguridad** backup copy; **hacer ~ de seguridad** to back up; **~ de trabajo** working copy
copiadora [kopja'ðora] *nf* photocopier; **~ al alcohol** spirit duplicator
copiar [ko'pjar] *vt* to copy; **~ al pie de la letra** to copy word for word
copiloto [kopi'loto] *nm* (*Aviat*) co-pilot; (*Auto*) co-driver
copioso, -a [ko'pjoso, a] *adj* copious, plentiful
copita [ko'pita] *nf* (small) glass; (*Golf*) tee
copla ['kopla] *nf* verse; (*canción*) (popular) song
copo ['kopo] *nm*: **copos de maíz** cornflakes; **~ de nieve** snowflake
coprocesador [koproθesa'ðor] *nm* (*Inform*) co-processor
coproducción [koproðuk'θjon] *nf* (*Cine etc*) joint production
copropietarios [kopropje'tarjos] *nmpl* (*Com*) joint owners
cópula ['kopula] *nf* copulation
copular [kopu'lar] *vi* to copulate
coqueta [ko'keta] *adj* flirtatious, coquettish ■ *nf* (*mujer*) flirt
coquetear [kokete'ar] *vi* to flirt
coraje [ko'raxe] *nm* courage; (*ánimo*) spirit; (*ira*) anger
coral [ko'ral] *adj* choral ■ *nf* choir ■ *nm* (*Zool*) coral
Corán [ko'ran] *nm*: **el ~** the Koran
coraza [ko'raθa] *nf* (*armadura*) armour; (*blindaje*) armour-plating
corazón [kora'θon] *nm* heart; (*Bot*) core; **corazones** *nmpl* (*Naipes*) hearts; **de buen ~** kind-hearted; **de todo ~** wholeheartedly; **estar mal del ~** to have heart trouble
corazonada [koraθo'naða] *nf* impulse; (*presentimiento*) presentiment, hunch
corbata [kor'βata] *nf* tie
corbeta [kor'βeta] *nf* corvette
Córcega ['korθeɣa] *nf* Corsica
corcel [kor'θel] *nm* steed
corchea [kor'tʃea] *nf* quaver
corchete [kor'tʃete] *nm* catch, clasp; **corchetes** *nmpl* (*Tip*) square brackets

corcho ['kortʃo] *nm* cork; (*Pesca*) float
corcovado, -a [korko'βaðo, a] *adj* hunchbacked ■ *nm/f* hunchback
cordel [kor'ðel] *nm* cord, line
cordero [kor'ðero] *nm* lamb; (*piel*) lambskin
cordial [kor'ðjal] *adj* cordial ■ *nm* cordial, tonic
cordialidad [korðjali'ðað] *nf* warmth, cordiality
cordillera [korði'ʎera] *nf* range (of mountains)
Córdoba ['korðoβa] *nf* Cordova
cordobés, -esa [korðo'βes, esa] *adj, nm/f* Cordovan
cordón [kor'ðon] *nm* (*cuerda*) cord, string; (*de zapatos*) lace; (*Elec*) flex, wire (*US*); (*Mil etc*) cordon
cordura [kor'ðura] *nf* (*Med*) sanity; (*fig*) good sense
Corea [ko'rea] *nf* Korea; **~ del Norte/Sur** North/South Korea
coreano, -a [kore'ano, a] *adj, nm/f* Korean
corear [kore'ar] *vt* to chorus
coreografía [koreoɣra'fia] *nf* choreography
corista [ko'rista] *nf* (*Teat etc*) chorus girl
cornada [kor'naða] *nf* (*Taur etc*) butt, goring
córner (*pl* **córners**) ['korner, 'korners] *nm* corner (kick)
corneta [kor'neta] *nf* bugle
cornisa [kor'nisa] *nf* cornice
Cornualles [kor'nwaʎes] *nm* Cornwall
cornudo, -a [kor'nuðo, a] *adj* (*Zool*) horned; (*marido*) cuckolded
coro ['koro] *nm* chorus; (*conjunto de cantores*) choir
corolario [koro'larjo] *nm* corollary
corona [ko'rona] *nf* crown; (*de flores*) garland
coronación [korona'θjon] *nf* coronation
coronar [koro'nar] *vt* to crown
coronel [koro'nel] *nm* colonel
coronilla [koro'niʎa] *nf* (*Anat*) crown (of the head); **estar hasta la ~ (de)** to be utterly fed up (with)
corpiño [korpiɲo] *nm* bodice; (*Am: sostén*) bra
corporación [korpora'θjon] *nf* corporation
corporal [korpo'ral] *adj* corporal, bodily
corporativo, -a [korpora'tiβo, a] *adj* corporate
corpulento, -a [korpu'lento, a] *adj* (*persona*) well-built
corral [ko'rral] *nm* (*patio*) farmyard; (*Agr: de aves*) poultry yard; (*redil*) pen
correa [ko'rrea] *nf* strap; (*cinturón*) belt; (*de perro*) lead, leash; **~ transportadora** conveyor belt
correaje [korre'axe] *nm* (*Agr*) harness
corrección [korrek'θjon] *nf* correction; (*reprensión*) rebuke; (*cortesía*) good manners; (*Inform*): **~ por líneas** line editing; **~ en pantalla** screen editing; **~ (de pruebas)** (*Tip*) proofreading
correccional [korrekθjo'nal] *nm* reformatory
correcto, -a [ko'rrekto, a] *adj* correct; (*persona*) well-mannered
corrector, a [korrek'tor, a] *nm/f*: **~ de pruebas** proofreader
corredera [korre'ðera] *nf*: **puerta de ~** sliding door
corredizo, -a [korre'ðiθo, a] *adj* (*puerta etc*) sliding; (*nudo*) running
corredor, a [korre'ðor, a] *adj* running; (*rápido*) fast ■ *nm/f* (*Deporte*) runner ■ *nm* (*pasillo*) corridor; (*balcón corrido*) gallery; (*Com*) agent, broker; **~ de bienes raíces** real-estate broker; **~ de bolsa** stockbroker; **~ de seguros** insurance broker
corregir [korre'xir] *vt* (*error*) to correct; (*amonestar, reprender*) to rebuke, reprimand; **corregirse** *vr* to reform
correo [ko'rreo] *nm* post, mail; (*persona*) courier; **Correos** *nmpl* Post Office *sg*; **~ aéreo** airmail; **~ basura** (*por carta*) junk mail; (*por Internet*) spam; **~ certificado** registered mail; **~ electrónico** e-mail, electronic mail; **~ urgente** special delivery; **a vuelta de ~** by return (of post)
correr [ko'rrer] *vt* to run; (*viajar*) to cover, travel; (*riesgo*) to run; (*aventura*) to have; (*cortinas*) to draw; (*cerrojo*) to shoot ■ *vi* to run; (*líquido*) to run, flow; (*rumor*) to go round; **correrse** *vr* to slide, move; (*colores*) to run; (*fam: tener orgasmo*) to come; **echar a ~** to break into a run; **~ con los gastos** to pay the expenses; **eso corre de mi cuenta** I'll take care of that
correspondencia [korrespon'denθja] *nf* correspondence; (*Ferro*) connection; (*reciprocidad*) return; **~ directa** (*Com*) direct mail
corresponder [korrespon'der] *vi* to correspond; (*convenir*) to be suitable; (*pertenecer*) to belong; (*tocar*) to concern; (*favor*) to repay; **corresponderse** *vr* (*por escrito*) to correspond; (*amarse*) to love one another; **"a quien corresponda"** "to whom it may concern"
correspondiente [korrespon'djente] *adj* corresponding; (*respectivo*) respective
corresponsal [korrespon'sal] *nm/f* (newspaper) correspondent; (*Com*) agent
corretaje [korre'taxe] *nm* (*Com*) brokerage
corretear [korrete'ar] *vi* to loiter
corrido, -a [ko'rriðo, a] *adj* (*avergonzado*) abashed; (*fluido*) fluent ■ *nf* run, dash;

(*de toros*) bullfight; **de ~** fluently; **tres noches corridas** three nights running; **un kilo ~** a good kilo
corriente [ko'rrjente] *adj* (*agua*) running; (*fig*) flowing; (*dinero, cuenta etc*) current; (*común*) ordinary, normal ■ *nf* current; (*fig: tendencia*) course ■ *nm* current month; **~ de aire** draught; **~ eléctrica** electric current; **las corrientes modernas del arte** modern trends in art; **estar al ~ de** to be informed about
corrigiendo *etc* [korri'xjendo] *vb ver* **corregir**
corrija *etc* [ko'rrixa] *vb ver* **corregir**
corrillo [ko'rriʎo] *nm* ring, circle (of people); (*fig*) clique
corro ['korro] *nm* ring, circle (of people); (*baile*) ring-a-ring-a-roses; **la gente hizo ~** the people formed a ring
corroborar [korroβo'rar] *vt* to corroborate
corroer [korro'er] *vt* (*tb fig*) to corrode, eat away; (*Geo*) to erode
corromper [korrom'per] *vt* (*madera*) to rot; (*fig*) to corrupt
corrompido, -a [korrom'piðo, a] *adj* corrupt
corrosivo, -a [korro'siβo, a] *adj* corrosive
corroyendo *etc* [korro'jendo] *vb ver* **corroer**
corrupción [korrup'θjon] *nf* rot, decay; (*fig*) corruption
corrupto, -a [ko'rrupto, a] *adj* corrupt
corsario [kor'sarjo] *nm* privateer, corsair
corsé [kor'se] *nm* corset
corso, -a ['korso, a] *adj, nm/f* Corsican
cortacésped [korta'θespeð] *nm* lawn mower
cortado, -a [kor'taðo, a] *adj* (*con cuchillo*) cut; (*leche*) sour; (*confuso*) confused; (*desconcertado*) embarrassed; (*tímido*) shy ■ *nm* white coffee (with a little milk)
cortadora [korta'ðora] *nf* cutter, slicer
cortadura [korta'ðura] *nf* cut
cortante [kor'tante] *adj* (*viento*) biting; (*frío*) bitter
cortapisa [korta'pisa] *nf* (*restricción*) restriction; (*traba*) snag
cortar [kor'tar] *vt* to cut; (*suministro*) to cut off; (*un pasaje*) to cut out; (*comunicación, teléfono*) to cut off ■ *vi* to cut; (*Am Telec*) to hang up; **cortarse** *vr* (*turbarse*) to become embarrassed; (*leche*) to turn, curdle; **~ por lo sano** to settle things once and for all; **cortarse el pelo** to have one's hair cut; **se cortó la línea** *o* **el teléfono** I got cut off
cortauñas [korta'uɲas] *nm inv* nail clippers *pl*
corte ['korte] *nm* cut, cutting; (*filo*) edge; (*de tela*) piece, length; (*Costura*) tailoring ■ *nf* (*real*) (royal) court; **~ y confección** dressmaking; **~ de corriente** *o* **luz** power cut; **~ de pelo** haircut; **me da ~ pedírselo** I'm embarrassed to ask him for it; **¡qué ~ le di!** I left him with no comeback!; **C~ Internacional de Justicia** International Court of Justice; **las Cortes** the Spanish Parliament *sg*; **hacer la ~ a** to woo, court; *see note*

CORTE

The Spanish Parliament, *Las Cortes (Españolas)*, has a Lower and an Upper Chamber, the *Congreso de los Diputados* and the *Senado* respectively. Members of Parliament are called *diputados* and are elected in national elections by proportional representation. Some Senate members, *senadores*, are chosen by being voted in during national elections and others are appointed by the regional parliaments.

cortejar [korte'xar] *vt* to court
cortejo [kor'texo] *nm* entourage; **~ fúnebre** funeral procession, cortège
cortés [kor'tes] *adj* courteous, polite
cortesano, -a [korte'sano, a] *adj* courtly
cortesía [korte'sia] *nf* courtesy
corteza [kor'teθa] *nf* (*de árbol*) bark; (*de pan*) crust; (*de fruta*) peel, skin; (*de queso*) rind
cortijo [kor'tixo] *nm* farmhouse
cortina [kor'tina] *nf* curtain; **~ de humo** smoke screen
corto, -a ['korto, a] *adj* (*breve*) short; (*tímido*) bashful; **~ de luces** not very bright; **~ de oído** hard of hearing; **~ de vista** short-sighted; **estar ~ de fondos** to be short of funds
cortocircuito [kortoθir'kwito] *nm* short-circuit
cortometraje [kortome'traxe] *nm* (*Cine*) short
Coruña [ko'ruɲa] *nf*: **La ~** Corunna
coruñés, -esa [koru'ɲes, esa] *adj* of *o* from Corunna ■ *nm/f* native *o* inhabitant of Corunna
corvo, -a ['korβo, a] *adj* curved; (*nariz*) hooked ■ *nf* back of knee
cosa ['kosa] *nf* thing; (*asunto*) affair; **~ de** about; **eso es ~ mía** that's my business; **es poca ~** it's not important; **¡qué ~ más rara!** how strange!
cosaco, -a [ko'sako, a] *adj, nm/f* Cossack
coscorrón [kosko'rron] *nm* bump on the head
cosecha [ko'setʃa] *nf* (*Agr*) harvest; (*acto*) harvesting; (*de vino*) vintage; (*producción*) yield

cosechadora [kosetʃa'ðora] *nf* combine harvester
cosechar [kose'tʃar] *vt* to harvest, gather (in)
coser [ko'ser] *vt* to sew; (*Med*) to stitch (up)
cosido [ko'siðo] *nm* sewing
cosmético, -a [kos'metiko, a] *adj, nm* cosmetic ▪ *nf* cosmetics *pl*
cosmopolita [kosmopo'lita] *adj* cosmopolitan
cosmos ['kosmos] *nm* cosmos
coso ['koso] *nm* bullring
cosquillas [kos'kiʎas] *nfpl*: **hacer ~** to tickle; **tener ~** to be ticklish
cosquilleo [koski'ʎeo] *nm* tickling (sensation)
costa ['kosta] *nf* (*Geo*) coast; **C~ Brava** Costa Brava; **C~ Cantábrica** Cantabrian Coast; **C~ de Marfil** Ivory Coast; **C~ del Sol** Costa del Sol; **a ~** (*Com*) at cost; **a ~ de** at the expense of; **a toda ~** at any price
costado [kos'taðo] *nm* side; **de ~** (*dormir*) on one's side; **español por los 4 costados** Spanish through and through
costal [kos'tal] *nm* sack
costalada [kosta'laða] *nf* bad fall
costanera [kosta'nera] *nf* (*Am*) (seaside) promenade
costar [kos'tar] *vt* (*valer*) to cost; **me cuesta hablarle** I find it hard to talk to him; **¿cuánto cuesta?** how much does it cost?
Costa Rica [kosta'rika] *nf* Costa Rica
costarricense [kostarri'θense], **costarriqueño, -a** [kostarri'keɲo, a] *adj, nm/f* Costa Rican
coste ['koste] *nm* (*Com*): **~ promedio** average cost; **costes fijos** fixed costs; *ver tb* **costo**
costear [koste'ar] *vt* to pay for; (*Com etc*) to finance; (*Naut*) to sail along the coast of; **costearse** *vr* (*negocio*) to pay for itself, cover its costs
costeño, -a [kos'teɲo, a] *adj* coastal
costero [kos'tero, a] *adj* coastal, coast *cpd*
costilla [kos'tiʎa] *nf* rib; (*Culin*) cutlet
costo ['kosto] *nm* cost, price; **~ directo** direct cost; **~ de expedición** shipping charges; **~ de sustitución** replacement cost; **~ unitario** unit cost; **~ de la vida** cost of living
costoso, -a [kos'toso, a] *adj* costly, expensive
costra ['kostra] *nf* (*corteza*) crust; (*Med*) scab
costumbre [kos'tumbre] *nf* custom, habit; **como de ~** as usual
costura [kos'tura] *nf* sewing, needlework; (*confección*) dressmaking; (*zurcido*) seam
costurera [kostu'rera] *nf* dressmaker
costurero [kostu'rero] *nm* sewing box *o* case
cota ['kota] *nf* (*Geo*) height above sea level; (*fig*) height
cotarro [ko'tarro] *nm*: **dirigir el ~** (*fam*) to rule the roost
cotejar [kote'xar] *vt* to compare
cotejo [ko'texo] *nm* comparison
cotice *etc* [ko'tiθe] *vb ver* **cotizar**
cotidiano, -a [koti'ðjano, a] *adj* daily, day to day
cotilla [ko'tiʎa] *nf* busybody, gossip
cotillear [kotiʎe'ar] *vi* to gossip
cotilleo [koti'ʎeo] *nm* gossip(ing)
cotización [kotiθa'θjon] *nf* (*Com*) quotation, price; (*de club*) dues *pl*
cotizado, -a [koti'θaðo, a] *adj* (*fig*) highly-prized
cotizar [koti'θar] *vt* (*Com*) to quote, price; **cotizarse** *vr* (*fig*) to be highly prized; **cotizarse a** to sell at, fetch; (*Bolsa*) to stand at, be quoted at
coto ['koto] *nm* (*terreno cercado*) enclosure; (*de caza*) reserve; (*Com*) price-fixing agreement; **poner ~ a** to put a stop to
cotorra [ko'torra] *nf* (*Zool: loro*) parrot; (*fam: persona*) windbag
coyote [ko'jote] *nm* coyote, prairie wolf
coyuntura [kojun'tura] *nf* (*Anat*) joint; (*fig*) juncture, occasion; **esperar una ~ favorable** to await a favourable moment
coz [koθ] *nf* kick
CP *nm abr* (= *computador personal*) PC
C.P. *abr* (*Esp*) = **Caja Postal**
C.P.A. *nf abr* (= *Caja Postal de Ahorros*) Post Office Savings Bank
CP/M *nm abr* (= *Programa de control para microprocesadores*) CP/M
CPN *nm abr* (*Esp*) = **Cuerpo de la Policía Nacional**
cps *abr* (= *caracteres por segundo*) c.p.s.
crac [krak] *nm* (*Econ*) crash
cráneo ['kraneo] *nm* skull, cranium
crápula ['krapula] *nf* drunkenness
cráter ['krater] *nm* crater
creación [krea'θjon] *nf* creation
creador, a [krea'ðor, a] *adj* creative ▪ *nm/f* creator
crear [kre'ar] *vt* to create, make; (*originar*) to originate; (*Inform: archivo*) to create; **crearse** *vr* (*comité etc*) to be set up
creativo, -a [krea'tiβo, a] *adj* creative
crecer [kre'θer] *vi* to grow; (*precio*) to rise; **crecerse** *vr* (*engreírse*) to get cocky
creces ['kreθes]: **con ~** *adv* amply, fully
crecido, -a [kre'θiðo, a] *adj* (*persona, planta*) full-grown; (*cantidad*) large ▪ *nf* (*de río*) spate, flood
creciente [kre'θjente] *adj* growing; (*cantidad*) increasing; (*luna*) crescent ▪ *nm* crescent
crecimiento [kreθi'mjento] *nm* growth;

(*aumento*) increase; (*Com*) rise
credenciales [kreðen'θjales] *nfpl* credentials
crédito ['kreðito] *nm* credit; **a ~** on credit; **dar ~ a** to believe (in); **~ al consumidor** consumer credit; **~ rotativo** *o* **renovable** revolving credit
credo ['kreðo] *nm* creed
crédulo, -a ['kreðulo, a] *adj* credulous
creencia [kre'enθja] *nf* belief
creer [kre'er] *vt, vi* to think, believe; (*considerar*) to think, consider; **creerse** *vr* to believe o.s. (to be); **~ en** to believe in; **¡ya lo creo!** I should think so!
creíble [kre'iβle] *adj* credible, believable
creído, -a [kre'iðo, a] *adj* (*engreído*) conceited
crema ['krema] *adj inv* cream (coloured) ■ *nf* cream; (*natillas*) custard; **la ~ de la sociedad** the cream of society
cremallera [krema'ʎera] *nf* zip (fastener) (*Brit*), zipper (*US*)
crematorio [krema'torjo] *nm* crematorium (*Brit*), crematory (*US*)
cremoso, -a [kre'moso, a] *adj* creamy
crepitar [krepi'tar] *vi* (*fuego*) to crackle
crepúsculo [kre'puskulo] *nm* twilight, dusk
crespo, -a ['krespo, a] *adj* (*pelo*) curly
crespón [kres'pon] *nm* crêpe
cresta ['kresta] *nf* (*Geo: Zool*) crest
Creta ['kreta] *nf* Crete
cretino, -a [kre'tino, a] *adj* cretinous ■ *nm/f* cretin
creyendo *etc* [kre'jendo] *vb ver* **creer**
creyente [kre'jente] *nm/f* believer
crezca *etc* ['kreθka] *vb ver* **crecer**
cría *etc* ['kria] *vb ver* **criar** ■ *nf ver* **crío, a**
criada [kri'aða] *nf ver* **criado, a**
criadero [kria'ðero] *nm* nursery; (*Zool*) breeding place
criadillas [kria'ðiʎas] *nfpl* (*Culin*) bull's (*o* sheep's) testicles
criado, -a [kri'aðo, a] *nm* servant ■ *nf* servant, maid
criador [kria'ðor] *nm* breeder
crianza [kri'anθa] *nf* rearing, breeding; (*fig*) breeding; (*Med*) lactation
criar [kri'ar] *vt* (*amamantar*) to suckle, feed; (*educar*) to bring up; (*producir*) to grow, produce; (*animales*) to breed; **criarse** *vr* to grow (up); **~ cuervos** to nourish a viper in one's bosom; **Dios los cría y ellos se juntan** birds of a feather flock together
criatura [kria'tura] *nf* creature; (*niño*) baby, (small) child
criba ['kriβa] *nf* sieve
cribar [kri'βar] *vt* to sieve
crimen ['krimen] *nm* crime; **~ pasional** crime of passion
criminal [krimi'nal] *adj, nm/f* criminal
crin [krin] *nf* (*tb:* **crines**) mane
crío, -a ['krio, a] *nm/f* (*fam: chico*) kid ■ *nf* (*de animales*) rearing, breeding; (*animal*) young
criollo, -a [kri'oʎo, a] *adj* (*gen*) Creole; (*Am*) native (to America), national ■ *nm/f* (*gen*) Creole; (*Am*) native American
cripta ['kripta] *nf* crypt
crisis ['krisis] *nf inv* crisis; **~ nerviosa** nervous breakdown
crisma ['krisma] *nf*: **romperle la ~ a algn** (*fam*) to knock sb's block off
crisol [kri'sol] *nm* (*Tec*) crucible; (*fig*) melting pot
crispación [krispa'θjon] *nf* tension
crispar [kris'par] *vt* (*músculo*) to cause to contract; (*nervios*) to set on edge
cristal [kris'tal] *nm* crystal; (*de ventana*) glass, pane; (*lente*) lens; **de ~** glass *cpd*; **~ ahumado/tallado** smoked/cut glass
cristalería [kristale'ria] *nf* (*tienda*) glassware shop; (*objetos*) glassware
cristalice *etc* [krista'liθe] *vb ver* **cristalizar**
cristalino, -a [krista'lino, a] *adj* crystalline; (*fig*) clear ■ *nm* lens of the eye
cristalizar [kristali'θar] *vt, vi* to crystallize
cristiandad [kristjan'dað] *nf*, **cristianismo** [kristja'nismo] *nm* Christianity
cristiano, -a [kris'tjano, a] *adj, nm/f* Christian; **hablar en ~** to speak proper Spanish; (*fig*) to speak clearly
Cristo ['kristo] *nm* (*dios*) Christ; (*crucifijo*) crucifix
Cristóbal [kris'toβal] *nm*: **~ Colón** Christopher Columbus
criterio [kri'terjo] *nm* criterion; (*juicio*) judgement; (*enfoque*) attitude, approach; (*punto de vista*) view, opinion; **~ de clasificación** (*Inform*) sort criterion
criticar [kriti'kar] *vt* to criticize
crítico, -a ['kritiko, a] *adj* critical ■ *nm* critic ■ *nf* criticism; (*Teat etc*) review, notice; **la crítica** the critics *pl*
critique *etc* [kri'tike] *vb ver* **criticar**
Croacia [kro'aθja] *nf* Croatia
croar [kro'ar] *vi* to croak
croata [kro'ata] *adj, nm/f* Croat(ian) ■ *nm* (*Ling*) Croat(ian)
croissan, croissant [krwa'san] *nm* croissant
crol ['krol] *nm* crawl
cromado [kro'maðo] *nm* chromium plating, chrome
cromo ['kromo] *nm* chrome; (*Tip*) coloured print
cromosoma [kromo'soma] *nm* chromosome
crónico, -a ['kroniko, a] *adj* chronic ■ *nf* chronicle, account; (*de periódico*) feature, article

cronología [kronolo'xia] *nf* chronology
cronológico, -a [krono'loxiko, a] *adj* chronological
cronometraje [kronome'traxe] *nm* timing
cronometrar [kronome'trar] *vt* to time
cronómetro [kro'nometro] *nm* (*Deporte*) stopwatch; (*Tec etc*) chronometer
croqueta [kro'keta] *nf* croquette, rissole
croquis ['krokis] *nm inv* sketch
cruce *etc* ['kruθe] *vb ver* **cruzar** ■ *nm* crossing; (*de carreteras*) crossroads; (*Auto etc*) junction, intersection; (*Bio: proceso*) crossbreeding; **luces de ~** dipped headlights
crucero [kru'θero] *nm* (*Naut: barco*) cruise ship; (*: viaje*) cruise
crucial [kru'θjal] *adj* crucial
crucificar [kruθifi'kar] *vt* to crucify; (*fig*) to torment
crucifijo [kruθi'fixo] *nm* crucifix
crucifique *etc* [kruθi'fike] *vb ver* **crucificar**
crucigrama [kruθi'ɣrama] *nm* crossword (puzzle)
crudeza [kru'ðeθa] *nf* (*rigor*) harshness; (*aspereza*) crudeness
crudo, -a ['kruðo, a] *adj* raw; (*no maduro*) unripe; (*petróleo*) crude; (*rudo, cruel*) cruel; (*agua*) hard; (*clima etc*) harsh ■ *nm* crude (oil)
cruel [krwel] *adj* cruel
crueldad [krwel'ðað] *nf* cruelty
cruento, -a ['krwento, a] *adj* bloody
crujido [kru'xiðo] *nm* (*de madera etc*) creak
crujiente [kru'xjente] *adj* (*galleta etc*) crunchy
crujir [kru'xir] *vi* (*madera etc*) to creak; (*dedos*) to crack; (*dientes*) to grind; (*nieve, arena*) to crunch
cruz [kruθ] *nf* cross; (*de moneda*) tails *sg*; (*fig*) burden; **~ gamada** swastika; **C~ Roja** Red Cross
cruzado, -a [kru'θaðo, a] *adj* crossed ■ *nm* crusader ■ *nf* crusade
cruzar [kru'θar] *vt* to cross; (*palabras*) to exchange; **cruzarse** *vr* (*líneas etc*) to cross, intersect; (*personas*) to pass each other; **cruzarse de brazos** to fold one's arms; (*fig*) not to lift a finger to help; **cruzarse con algn en la calle** to pass sb in the street
CSIC [θe'sik] *nm abr* (*Esp Escol*) = **Consejo Superior de Investigaciones Científicas**
cta, c.ta *nf abr* (= *cuenta*) a/c
cta. cto. *abr* (= *carta de crédito*) L.C.
cte. *abr* (= *corriente, de los corrientes*) inst.
CTNE *nf abr* (*Telec*) = **Compañía Telefónica Nacional de España**
c/u *abr* (= *cada uno*) ea
cuaco ['kwako] *nm* (*Am*) nag
cuaderno [kwa'ðerno] *nm* notebook; (*de escuela*) exercise book; (*Naut*) logbook
cuadra ['kwaðra] *nf* (*caballeriza*) stable; (*Am*) (city) block
cuadrado, -a [kwa'ðraðo, a] *adj* square ■ *nm* (*Mat*) square
cuadragésimo, -a [kwaðra'xesimo, a] *num* fortieth
cuadrángulo [kwa'ðrangulo] *nm* quadrangle
cuadrante [kwa'ðrante] *nm* quadrant
cuadrar [kwa'ðrar] *vt* to square; (*Tip*) to justify ■ *vi*: **~ con** (*cuenta*) to square with, tally with; **cuadrarse** *vr* (*soldado*) to stand to attention; **~ por la derecha/izquierda** to right-/left-justify
cuadrícula [kwa'ðrikula] *nf* (*Tip etc*) grid, ruled squares
cuadriculado, -a [kwaðriku'laðo, a] *adj*: **papel ~** squared *o* graph paper
cuadrilátero [kwaðri'latero] *nm* (*Deporte*) boxing ring; (*Geom*) quadrilateral
cuadrilla [kwa'ðriʎa] *nf* (*de amigos*) party, group; (*de delincuentes*) gang; (*de obreros*) team
cuadro ['kwaðro] *nm* square; (*Pintura*) painting; (*Teat*) scene; (*diagrama*: *tb*: **cuadro sinóptico**) chart, table, diagram; (*Deporte: Med*) team; (*Pol*) executive; **~ de mandos** control panel; **a cuadros** check *cpd*
cuadruplicarse [kwaðrupli'karse] *vr* to quadruple
cuádruplo, -a ['kwaðruplo, a], **cuádruple** ['kwaðruple] *adj* quadruple
cuajado, -a [kwa'xaðo, a] *adj*: **~ de** (*fig*) full of ■ *nf* (*de leche*) curd
cuajar [kwa'xar] *vt* to thicken; (*leche*) to curdle; (*sangre*) to congeal; (*adornar*) to adorn; (*Culin*) to set ■ *vi* (*nieve*) to lie; (*fig*) to become set, become established; (*idea*) to be received, be acceptable; **cuajarse** *vr* to curdle; to congeal; (*llenarse*) to fill up
cuajo ['kwaxo] *nm*: **arrancar algo de ~** to tear sth out by its roots
cual [kwal] *adv* like, as ■ *pron*: **el ~** *etc* which; (*persona: sujeto*) who; (*: objeto*) whom; **lo ~** (*relativo*) which; **allá cada ~** every man to his own taste; **son a ~ más gandul** each is as idle as the other; **cada ~** each one ■ *adj* such as; **tal ~** just as it is
cuál [kwal] *pron interrogativo* which (one), what
cualesquier [kwales'kjer], **cualesquiera** [kwales'kjera] *adj pl, pron pl de* **cualquier**; **cualquiera**
cualidad [kwali'ðað] *nf* quality
cualificado, -a [kwalifi'kaðo, a] *adj* (*obrero*) skilled, qualified
cualquiera [kwal'kjera], **cualquier** [kwal'kjer] (*pl* **cualesquier(a)**) *adj* any ■ *pron* anybody, anyone; (*quienquiera*) whoever;

en cualquier momento any time; **en cualquier parte** anywhere; **~ que sea** whichever it is; *(persona)* whoever it is
cuán ['kwan] *adv* how
cuando ['kwando] *adv* when; *(aún si)* if, even if ■ *conj (puesto que)* since ■ *prep*: **yo, ~ niño ...** when I was a child *o* as a child I ...; **~ no sea así** even if it is not so; **~ más** at (the) most; **~ menos** at least; **~ no** if not, otherwise; **de ~ en ~** from time to time; **ven ~ quieras** come when(ever) you like
cuándo ['kwando] *adv* when; **¿desde ~?, ¿de ~ acá?** since when?
cuantía [kwan'tia] *nf (alcance)* extent; *(importancia)* importance
cuantioso, -a [kwan'tjoso, a] *adj* substantial

PALABRA CLAVE

cuanto, -a ['kwanto, a] *adj* **1** *(todo)*: **tiene todo cuanto desea** he's got everything he wants; **le daremos cuantos ejemplares necesite** we'll give him as many copies as *o* all the copies he needs; **cuantos hombres la ven** all the men who see her
2: **unos cuantos**: **había unos cuantos periodistas** there were (quite) a few journalists
3 *(+más)*: **cuanto más vino bebas peor te sentirás** the more wine you drink the worse you'll feel; **cuantos más, mejor** the more the merrier
■ *pron*: **tiene cuanto desea** he has everything he wants; **tome cuanto/cuantos quiera** take as much/many as you want
■ *adv*: **en cuanto**: **en cuanto profesor** as a teacher; **en cuanto a mí** as for me; *ver tb* **antes**
■ *conj* **1**: **cuanto más gana menos gasta** the more he earns the less he spends; **cuanto más joven se es más se es confiado** the younger you are the more trusting you are
2: **en cuanto**: **en cuanto llegue/llegué** as soon as I arrive/arrived

cuánto, -a ['kwanto, a] *adj (exclamación)* what a lot of; *(interrogativo: sg)* how much?; *(: pl)* how many? ■ *pron, adv* how; *(interrogativo: sg)* how much?; *(: pl)* how many? ■ *excl*: **¡~ me alegro!** I'm so glad!; **¡~ gente!** what a lot of people!; **¿~ tiempo?** how long?; **¿~ cuesta?** how much does it cost?; **¿a ~s estamos?** what's the date?; **¿~ hay de aquí a Bilbao?** how far is it from here to Bilbao?; **Señor no sé ~s** Mr. So-and-So
cuarenta [kwa'renta] *num* forty
cuarentena [kwaren'tena] *nf (Med etc)* quarantine; *(conjunto)* forty(-odd)
cuarentón, -ona [kwaren'ton, ona] *adj* forty-year-old, fortyish ■ *nm/f* person of about forty
cuaresma [kwa'resma] *nf* Lent
cuarta ['kwarta] *nf ver* **cuarto**
cuartear [kwarte'ar] *vt* to quarter; *(dividir)* to divide up; **cuartearse** *vr* to crack, split
cuartel [kwar'tel] *nm (de ciudad)* quarter, district; *(Mil)* barracks *pl*; **~ general** headquarters *pl*
cuartelazo [kwarte'laθo] *nm* coup, military uprising
cuarteto [kwar'teto] *nm* quartet
cuartilla [kwar'tiʎa] *nf (hoja)* sheet (of paper); **cuartillas** *nfpl (Tip)* copy *sg*
cuarto, -a ['kwarto, a] *adj* fourth ■ *nm (Mat)* quarter, fourth; *(habitación)* room ■ *nf (Mat)* quarter, fourth; *(palmo)* span; **~ de baño** bathroom; **~ de estar** living room; **~ de hora** quarter (of an) hour; **~ de kilo** quarter kilo; **no tener un ~** to be broke *(fam)*
cuarzo ['kwarθo] *nm* quartz
cuatrero [kwa'trero] *nm (Am)* rustler, stock thief
cuatrimestre [kwatri'mestre] *nm* four-month period
cuatro ['kwatro] *num* four; **las ~** four o'clock; **el ~ de octubre** (on) the fourth of October; *ver tb* **seis**
cuatrocientos, -as [kwatro'θjentos, as] *num* four hundred; *ver tb* **seiscientos**
Cuba ['kuβa] *nf* Cuba
cuba ['kuβa] *nf* cask, barrel; **estar como una ~** *(fam)* to be sloshed
cubalibre [kuβa'liβre] *nm* (white) rum and coke®
cubano, -a [ku'βano, a] *adj, nm/f* Cuban
cubata [ku'βata] *nm* = **cubalibre**
cubertería [kuβerte'ria] *nf* cutlery
cúbico, -a ['kuβiko, a] *adj* cubic
cubierto, -a [ku'βjerto, a] *pp de* **cubrir** ■ *adj* covered; *(cielo)* overcast ■ *nm* cover; *(en la mesa)* place ■ *nf* cover, covering; *(neumático)* tyre; *(Naut)* deck; **cubiertos** *nmpl* cutlery *sg*; **a ~ de** covered with *o* in; **precio del ~** cover charge
cubil [ku'βil] *nm* den
cubilete [kuβi'lete] *nm (en juegos)* cup
cubito [ku'βito] *nm*: **~ de hielo** ice cube
cubo ['kuβo] *nm* cube; *(balde)* bucket, tub; *(Tec)* drum; **~ de (la) basura** dustbin
cubrecama [kuβre'kama] *nm* bedspread
cubrir [ku'βrir] *vt* to cover; *(vacante)* to fill; *(Bio)* to mate with; *(gastos)* to meet; **cubrirse** *vr (cielo)* to become overcast; *(Com: gastos)* to

be met *o* paid; (*: deuda*) to be covered; **~ las formas** to keep up appearances; **lo cubrieron las aguas** the waters closed over it; **el agua casi me cubría** I was almost out of my depth

cucaracha [kuka'ratʃa] *nf* cockroach

cuchara [ku'tʃara] *nf* spoon; (*Tec*) scoop

cucharada [kutʃa'raða] *nf* spoonful; **~ colmada** heaped spoonful

cucharadita [kutʃara'ðita] *nf* teaspoonful

cucharilla [kutʃa'riʎa] *nf* teaspoon

cucharita [kutʃa'rita] *nf* teaspoon

cucharón [kutʃa'ron] *nm* ladle

cuchichear [kutʃitʃe'ar] *vi* to whisper

cuchicheo [kutʃi'tʃeo] *nm* whispering

cuchilla [ku'tʃiʎa] *nf* (large) knife; (*de arma blanca*) blade; **~ de afeitar** razor blade; **pasar a ~** to put to the sword

cuchillada [kutʃi'ʎaða] *nf* (*golpe*) stab; (*herida*) knife *o* stab wound

cuchillo [ku'tʃiʎo] *nm* knife

cuchitril [kutʃi'tril] *nm* hovel; (*habitación etc*) pigsty

cuclillas [ku'kliʎas] *nfpl*: **en ~** squatting

cuco, -a ['kuko, a] *adj* pretty; (*astuto*) sharp ■ *nm* cuckoo

cucurucho [kuku'rutʃo] *nm* paper cone, cornet

cuece *etc* ['kweθe] *vb ver* **cocer**

cuele *etc* ['kwele] *vb ver* **colar**

cuelgue *etc* ['kwelɣe] *vb ver* **colgar**

cuello ['kweʎo] *nm* (*Anat*) neck; (*de vestido, camisa*) collar

cuenca ['kwenka] *nf* (*Anat*) eye socket; (*Geo: valle*) bowl, deep valley; (*: fluvial*) basin

cuenco ['kwenko] *nm* (earthenware) bowl

cuenta *etc* ['kwenta] *vb ver* **contar** ■ *nf* (*cálculo*) count, counting; (*en café, restaurante*) bill; (*Com*) account; (*de collar*) bead; (*fig*) account; **a fin de ~s** in the end; **en resumidas ~s** in short; **caer en la ~** to catch on; **dar ~ a algn de sus actos** to account to sb for one's actions; **darse ~ de** to realize; **tener en ~** to bear in mind; **echar ~s** to take stock; **~ atrás** countdown; **~ corriente/de ahorros/a plazo (fijo)** current/savings/deposit account; **~ de caja** cash account; **~ de capital** capital account; **~ por cobrar** account receivable; **~ de correo** (*Internet*) e-mail account; **~ de crédito** credit *o* loan account; **~ de gastos e ingresos** income and expenditure account; **~ por pagar** account payable; **abonar una cantidad en ~ a algn** to credit a sum to sb's account; **ajustar** *o* **liquidar una ~** to settle an account; **pasar la ~** to send the bill

cuentagotas [kwenta'ɣotas] *nm inv* (*Med*) dropper; **a** *o* **con ~** (*fam, fig*) drop by drop, bit by bit

cuentakilómetros [kwentaki'lometros] *nm inv* (*de distancias*) ≈ milometer, clock; (*velocímetro*) speedometer

cuentista [kwen'tista] *nm/f* gossip; (*Lit*) short-story writer

cuento *etc* ['kwento] *vb ver* **contar** ■ *nm* story; (*Lit*) short story; **~ de hadas** fairy story; **es el ~ de nunca acabar** it's an endless business; **eso no viene a ~** that's irrelevant

cuerda ['kwerða] *nf* rope; (*hilo*) string; (*de reloj*) spring; (*Mus: de violín etc*) string; (*Mat*) chord; (*Anat*) cord; **~ floja** tightrope; **cuerdas vocales** vocal cords; **dar ~ a un reloj** to wind up a clock

cuerdo, -a ['kwerðo, a] *adj* sane; (*prudente*) wise, sensible

cuerear [kwere'ar] *vt* (*Am*) to skin

cuerno ['kwerno] *nm* (*Zool: gen*) horn; (*: de ciervo*) antler; **poner los cuernos a** (*fam*) to cuckold; **saber a ~ quemado** to leave a nasty taste

cuero ['kwero] *nm* (*Zool*) skin, hide; (*Tec*) leather; **en cueros** stark naked; **~ cabelludo** scalp

cuerpo ['kwerpo] *nm* body; (*cadáver*) corpse; (*fig*) main part; **~ de bomberos** fire brigade; **~ diplomático** diplomatic corps; **luchar ~ a ~** to fight hand-to-hand; **tomar ~** (*plan etc*) to take shape

cuervo ['kwerβo] *nm* (*Zool*) raven, crow; *ver* **criar**

cuesta *etc* ['kwesta] *vb ver* **costar** ■ *nf* slope; (*en camino etc*) hill; **~ arriba/abajo** uphill/downhill; **a ~s** on one's back

cuestión [kwes'tjon] *nf* matter, question, issue; (*riña*) quarrel, dispute; **eso es otra ~** that's another matter

cuestionar [kwestjo'nar] *vt* to question

cuestionario [kwestjo'narjo] *nm* questionnaire

cueva ['kweβa] *nf* cave

cueza *etc* ['kweθa] *vb ver* **cocer**

cuidado [kwi'ðaðo] *nm* care, carefulness; (*preocupación*) care, worry ■ *excl* careful!, look out!; **eso me tiene sin ~** I'm not worried about that

cuidadoso, -a [kwiða'ðoso, a] *adj* careful; (*preocupado*) anxious

cuidar [kwi'ðar] *vt* (*Med*) to care for; (*ocuparse de*) to take care of, look after; (*detalles*) to pay attention to ■ *vi*: **~ de** to take care of, look after; **cuidarse** *vr* to look after o.s.; **cuidarse de hacer algo** to take care to do something

cuita ['kwita] *nf* (*preocupación*) worry, trouble; (*pena*) grief
culata [ku'lata] *nf* (*de fusil*) butt
culatazo [kula'taθo] *nm* kick, recoil
culebra [ku'leβra] *nf* snake; **~ de cascabel** rattlesnake
culebrear [kuleβre'ar] *vi* to wriggle along; (*río*) to meander
culebrón [kule'βron] *nm* (*fam*) soap (opera)
culinario, -a [kuli'narjo, a] *adj* culinary, cooking *cpd*
culminación [kulmina'θjon] *nf* culmination
culminante [kulmi'nante] *adj*: **momento ~** climax, highlight, highspot
culminar [kulmi'nar] *vi* to culminate
culo ['kulo] *nm* (*fam: asentaderas*) bottom, backside, bum (*Brit*); (*: ano*) arse(hole) (*Brit!*), ass(hole) (*US!*); (*de vaso*) bottom
culpa ['kulpa] *nf* fault; (*Jur*) guilt; **culpas** *nfpl* sins; **por ~ de** through, because of; **tener la ~ (de)** to be to blame (for)
culpabilidad [kulpaβili'ðað] *nf* guilt
culpable [kul'paβle] *adj* guilty ■ *nm/f* culprit; **confesarse ~** to plead guilty; **declarar ~ a algn** to find sb guilty
culpar [kul'par] *vt* to blame; (*acusar*) to accuse
cultivadora [kultiβa'ðora] *nf* cultivator
cultivar [kulti'βar] *vt* to cultivate; (*cosecha*) to raise; (*talento*) to develop
cultivo [kul'tiβo] *nm* (*acto*) cultivation; (*plantas*) crop; (*Bio*) culture
culto, -a ['kulto, a] *adj* (*cultivado*) cultivated; (*que tiene cultura*) cultured, educated ■ *nm* (*homenaje*) worship; (*religión*) cult; (*Pol etc*) cult
cultura [kul'tura] *nf* culture
cultural [kultu'ral] *adj* cultural
culturismo [kultu'rismo] *nm* body-building
cumbre ['kumbre] *nf* summit, top; (*fig*) top, height; **conferencia (en la) ~** summit (conference)
cumpleaños [kumple'aɲos] *nm inv* birthday
cumplido, -a [kum'pliðo, a] *adj* complete, perfect; (*abundante*) plentiful; (*cortés*) courteous ■ *nm* compliment; **visita de ~** courtesy call
cumplidor, a [kumpli'ðor, a] *adj* reliable
cumplimentar [kumplimen'tar] *vt* to congratulate; (*órdenes*) to carry out
cumplimiento [kumpli'mjento] *nm* (*de un deber*) fulfilment, execution, performance; (*acabamiento*) completion; (*Com*) expiry, end
cumplir [kum'plir] *vt* (*orden*) to carry out, obey; (*promesa*) to carry out, fulfil; (*condena*) to serve; (*años*) to reach, attain ■ *vi* (*pago*) to fall due; (*plazo*) to expire; **cumplirse** *vr* (*plazo*) to expire; (*plan etc*) to be fulfilled; (*vaticinio*) to come true; **hoy cumple dieciocho años** he is eighteen today; **~ con** (*deber*) to carry out, fulfil
cúmulo ['kumulo] *nm* (*montón*) heap; (*nube*) cumulus
cuna ['kuna] *nf* cradle, cot; **canción de ~** lullaby
cundir [kun'dir] *vi* (*noticia, rumor, pánico*) to spread; (*rendir*) to go a long way
cuneta [ku'neta] *nf* ditch
cuña ['kuɲa] *nf* (*Tec*) wedge; (*Com*) advertising spot; (*Med*) bedpan; **tener cuñas** to have influence
cuñado, -a [ku'ɲaðo, a] *nm/f* brother/sister-in-law
cuño ['kuɲo] *nm* (*Tec*) die-stamp; (*fig*) stamp
cuota ['kwota] *nf* (*parte proporcional*) share; (*cotización*) fee, dues *pl*; **~ inicial** (*Com*) down payment
cupo *etc* ['kupo] *vb ver* **caber** ■ *nm* quota, share; (*Com*): **~ de importación** import quota; **~ de ventas** sales quota
cupón [ku'pon] *nm* coupon; **~ de la ONCE** *o* **de los ciegos** ONCE lottery ticket; *ver tb* **lotería**
cúpula ['kupula] *nf* (*Arq*) dome
cura ['kura] *nf* (*curación*) cure; (*método curativo*) treatment ■ *nm* priest; **~ de emergencia** emergency treatment
curación [kura'θjon] *nf* cure; (*acción*) curing
curado, -a [ku'raðo, a] *adj* (*Culin*) cured; (*pieles*) tanned
curandero, -a [kuran'dero, a] *nm/f* healer
curar [ku'rar] *vt* (*Med: herida*) to treat, dress; (*: enfermo*) to cure; (*Culin*) to cure, salt; (*cuero*) to tan ■ *vi*, **curarse** *vr* to get well, recover
curda ['kurða] (*fam*) *nm* drunk ■ *nf*: **agarrar una/estar ~** to get/be sloshed
curiosear [kurjose'ar] *vt* to glance at, look over ■ *vi* to look round, wander round; (*explorar*) to poke about
curiosidad [kurjosi'ðað] *nf* curiosity
curioso, -a [ku'rjoso, a] *adj* curious; (*aseado*) neat ■ *nm/f* bystander, onlooker; **¡qué ~!** how odd!
curita [ku'rita] *nf* (*Am*) sticking plaster
currante [ku'rrante] *nm/f* (*fam*) worker
currar [ku'rrar] *vi* (*fam*), **currelar** [kurre'lar] *vi* (*fam*) to work
currículo [ku'rrikulo] *nm*, **currículum** [ku'rrikulum] *nm* curriculum vitae
curro ['kurro] *nm* (*fam*) work, job
cursar [kur'sar] *vt* (*Escol*) to study
cursi ['kursi] *adj* (*fam*) pretentious; (*: amanerado*) affected
cursilada [kursi'laða] *nf*: **¡qué ~!** how tacky!
cursilería [kursile'ria] *nf* (*vulgaridad*) bad taste; (*amaneramiento*) affectation

cursillo [kur'siʎo] *nm* short course
cursiva [kur'siβa] *nf* italics *pl*
curso ['kurso] *nm* (*dirección*) course; (*fig*) progress; (*Escol*) school year; (*Univ*) academic year; **en ~** (*año*) current; (*proceso*) going on, under way; **moneda de ~ legal** legal tender
cursor [kur'sor] *nm* (*Inform*) cursor; (*Tec*) slide
curtido, -a [kur'tiðo, a] *adj* (*cara etc*) weather-beaten; (*fig: persona*) experienced
curtir [kur'tir] *vt* (*piel*) to tan; (*fig*) to harden
curvo, -a ['kurβo, a] *adj* (*gen*) curved; (*torcido*) bent ■ *nf* (*gen*) curve, bend; **curva de rentabilidad** (*Com*) break-even chart
cúspide ['kuspiðe] *nf* (*Geo*) summit, peak; (*fig*) top, pinnacle
custodia [kus'toðja] *nf* (*cuidado*) safekeeping; (*Jur*) custody
custodiar [kusto'ðjar] *vt* (*conservar*) to keep, take care of; (*vigilar*) to guard
custodio [kus'toðjo] *nm* guardian, keeper
cutáneo, -a [ku'taneo, a] *adj* skin *cpd*
cutícula [ku'tikula] *nf* cuticle
cutis ['kutis] *nm inv* skin, complexion
cutre ['kutre] *adj* (*fam: lugar*) grotty; (*: persona*) naff
cuyo, -a ['kujo, a] *pron* (*de quien*) whose; (*de que*) whose, of which; **la señora en cuya casa me hospedé** the lady in whose house I stayed; **el asunto cuyos detalles conoces** the affair the details of which you know; **por ~ motivo** for which reason
C.V. *abr* (= *Curriculum Vitae*) CV; (= *caballos de vapor*) H.P.

Dd

D, d [de] *nf* (*letra*) D, d; **D de Dolores** D for David (*Brit*), D for Dog (*US*)
D. *abr* = **Don**
D.ª *abr* = **Doña**
dactilar [dakti'lar] *adj*: **huellas dactilares** fingerprints
dactilógrafo, -a [dakti'loɣrafo, a] *nm/f* typist
dádiva ['daðiβa] *nf* (*donación*) donation; (*regalo*) gift
dadivoso, -a [daði'βoso, a] *adj* generous
dado, -a ['daðo, a] *pp de* **dar** ■ *nm* die; **dados** *nmpl* dice ■ *adj*: **en un momento ~** at a certain point; **ser ~ a (hacer algo)** to be very fond of (doing sth); **~ que** *conj* given that
daga ['daɣa] *nf* dagger
daltónico, -a [dal'toniko, a] *adj* colour-blind
daltonismo [dalto'nismo] *nm* colour blindness
dama ['dama] *nf* (*gen*) lady; (*Ajedrez*) queen; **damas** *nfpl* draughts; **primera ~** (*Teat*) leading lady; (*Pol*) president's wife, first lady (*US*); **~ de honor** (*de reina*) lady-in-waiting; (*de novia*) bridesmaid
damasco [da'masko] *nm* (*tela*) damask; (*Am*: *árbol*) apricot tree; (: *fruta*) apricot
damnificado, -a [damnifi'kaðo, a] *nm/f*: **los damnificados** the victims
damnificar [damnifi'kar] *vt* to harm; (*persona*) to injure
damnifique *etc* [damni'fike] *vb ver* **damnificar**
dance *etc* ['danθe] *vb ver* **danzar**
danés, -esa [da'nes, esa] *adj* Danish ■ *nm/f* Dane ■ *nm* (*Ling*) Danish
Danubio [da'nuβjo] *nm* Danube
danza ['danθa] *nf* (*gen*) dancing; (*una danza*) dance
danzar [dan'θar] *vt, vi* to dance
danzarín, -ina [danθa'rin, ina] *nm/f* dancer
dañar [da'ɲar] *vt* (*objeto*) to damage; (*persona*) to hurt; (*estropear*) to spoil; **dañarse** *vr* (*objeto*) to get damaged
dañino, -a [da'ɲino, a] *adj* harmful
daño ['daɲo] *nm* (*a un objeto*) damage; (*a una persona*) harm, injury; **daños y perjuicios** (*Jur*) damages; **hacer ~ a** to damage; (*persona*) to hurt, injure; **hacerse ~** to hurt o.s.
DAO *abr* (= *Diseño Asistido por Ordenador*) CAD

PALABRA CLAVE

dar [dar] *vt* **1** (*gen*) to give; (*obra de teatro*) to put on; (*film*) to show; (*fiesta*) to have; **dar algo a algn** to give sb sth *o* sth to sb; **dar una patada a algn/algo** to kick sb/sth, give sb/sth a kick; **dar un susto a algn** to give sb a fright; **dar de beber a algn** to give sb a drink
2 (*producir: intereses*) to yield; (: *fruta*) to produce
3 (*locuciones +n*): **da gusto escucharle** it's a pleasure to listen to him; **me da pena/asco** it frightens/sickens me; *ver tb* **paseo** *y otros sustantivos*
4 (*considerar*): **dar algo por descontado/entendido** to take sth for granted/as read; **dar algo por concluido** to consider sth finished; **le dieron por desaparecido** they gave him up as lost
5 (*hora*): **el reloj dio las seis** the clock struck six (o'clock)
6: **me da lo mismo** it's all the same to me; *ver tb* **igual; más**
7: **¡y dale!** (*¡otra vez!*) not again!; **estar/seguir dale que dale** *o* **dale que te pego** *o* (*Am*) **dale y dale** to go/keep on and on
■ *vi* **1**: **dar a** (*habitación*) to overlook, look on to; (*accionar: botón etc*) to press, hit
2: **dar con**: **dimos con él dos horas más tarde** we came across him two hours later; **al final di con la solución** I eventually came up with the answer
3: **dar en** (*blanco, suelo*) to hit; **el sol me da en la cara** the sun is shining (right) in my face
4: **dar de sí** (*zapatos etc*) to stretch, give
5: **dar para** to be enough for; **nuestro**

presupuesto no da para más our budget's really tight
6: **dar por**: **le ha dado por estudiar música** now he's into studying music
7: **dar que hablar** to set people talking; **una película que da que pensar** a thought-provoking film
darse *vr* 1: **darse un baño** to have a bath; **darse un golpe** to hit o.s.
2: **darse por vencido** to give up; **con eso me doy por satisfecho** I'd settle for that
3 (*ocurrir*): **se han dado muchos casos** there have been a lot of cases
4: **darse a**: **se ha dado a la bebida** he's taken to drinking
5: **se me dan bien/mal las ciencias** I'm good/bad at science
6: **dárselas de**: **se las da de experto** he fancies himself *o* poses as an expert

dardo ['darðo] *nm* dart
dársena ['darsena] *nf* (*Naut*) dock
datar [da'tar] *vi*: ~ **de** to date from
dátil ['datil] *nm* date
dativo [da'tiβo] *nm* (*Ling*) dative
dato ['dato] *nm* fact, piece of information; (*Mat*) datum; **datos** *nmpl* (*Inform*) data; **datos de entrada/salida** input/output data; **datos personales** personal particulars
dcha. *abr* (= *derecha*) r (= *right*)
d. de J. C. *abr* (= *después de Jesucristo*) A.D. (= *Anno Domini*)

PALABRA CLAVE

de [de] *prep* (*de+el = del*) 1 (*posesión, pertenencia*) of; **la casa de Isabel/mis padres** Isabel's/my parents' house; **es de ellos/ella** it's theirs/hers; **un libro de Unamuno** a book by Unamuno
2 (*origen, distancia, con números*) from; **soy de Gijón** I'm from Gijón; **de 8 a 20** from 8 to 20; **5 metros de largo** 5 metres long; **salir del cine** to go out of *o* leave the cinema; **de ... en ...** from ... to ...; **de 2 en 2** 2 by 2, 2 at a time; **9 de cada 10** 9 out of every 10
3 (*valor descriptivo*): **una copa de vino** a glass of wine; **una silla de madera** a wooden chair; **la mesa de la cocina** the kitchen table; **un viaje de dos días** a two-day journey; **un billete de 50 euros** a 50-euro note; **un niño de tres años** a three-year-old (child); **una máquina de coser** a sewing machine; **la ciudad de Madrid** the city of Madrid; **el tonto de Juan** that idiot Juan; **ir vestido de gris** to be dressed in grey; **la niña del vestido azul** the girl in the blue dress; **la chica del pelo largo** the girl with long hair; **trabaja de profesora** she works as a teacher; **de lado** sideways; **de atrás/delante** rear/front
4 (*hora, tiempo*): **a las 8 de la mañana** at 8 o'clock in the morning; **de día/noche** by day/night; **de hoy en ocho días** a week from now; **de niño era gordo** as a child he was fat
5 (*comparaciones*): **más/menos de cien personas** more/less than a hundred people; **el más caro de la tienda** the most expensive in the shop; **menos/más de lo pensado** less/more than expected
6 (*causa*): **del calor** from the heat; **de puro tonto** out of sheer stupidity
7 (*tema*) about; **clases de inglés** English classes; **¿sabes algo de él?** do you know anything about him?; **un libro de física** a physics book
8 (*adj+de+infin*): **fácil de entender** easy to understand
9 (*oraciones pasivas*): **fue respetado de todos** he was loved by all
10 (*condicional+infin*) if; **de ser posible** if possible; **de no terminarlo hoy** if I *etc* don't finish it today

dé [de] *vb ver* **dar**
deambular [deambu'lar] *vi* to stroll, wander
debajo [de'βaxo] *adv* underneath; ~ **de** below, under; **por ~ de** beneath
debate [de'βate] *nm* debate
debatir [deβa'tir] *vt* to debate; **debatirse** *vr* to struggle
debe ['deβe] *nm* (*en cuenta*) debit side; ~ **y haber** debit and credit
deber [de'βer] *nm* duty ■ *vt* to owe ■ *vi*: **debe (de)** it must, it should; **deberse** *vr*: **deberse a** to be owing *o* due to; **deberes** *nmpl* (*Escol*) homework *sg*; **debo hacerlo** I must do it; **debe de ir** he should go; **¿qué** *o* **cuánto le debo?** how much is it?
debidamente [deβiða'mente] *adv* properly; (*rellenar*) duly
debido, -a [de'βiðo, a] *adj* proper, due; ~ **a** due to, because of; **en debida forma** duly
débil ['deβil] *adj* weak; (*persona: físicamente*) feeble; (*salud*) poor; (*voz, ruido*) faint; (*luz*) dim
debilidad [deβili'ðað] *nf* weakness; feebleness; dimness; **tener ~ por algn** to have a soft spot for sb
debilitar [deβili'tar] *vt* to weaken; **debilitarse** *vr* to grow weak
débito ['deβito] *nm* debit; (*deuda*) debt
debutante [deβu'tante] *nm/f* beginner
debutar [deβu'tar] *vi* to make one's debut

década ['dekaðа] *nf* decade
decadencia [deka'ðenθja] *nf* (*estado*) decadence; (*proceso*) decline, decay
decadente [deca'ðente] *adj* decadent
decaer [deka'er] *vi* (*declinar*) to decline; (*debilitarse*) to weaken; (*salud*) to fail; (*negocio*) to fall off
decaído, -a [deka'iðo, a] *adj*: **estar ~** (*persona*) to be down
decaiga *etc* [de'kaiɣa] *vb ver* **decaer**
decaimiento [dekai'mjento] *nm* (*declinación*) decline; (*desaliento*) discouragement; (*Med: depresión*) depression
decanato [deka'nato] *nm* (*cargo*) deanship; (*despacho*) dean's office
decano, -a [de'kano, a] *nm/f* (*Univ etc*) dean; (*de grupo*) senior member
decantar [dekan'tar] *vt* (*vino*) to decant
decapitar [dekapi'tar] *vt* to behead
decayendo *etc* [deca'jendo] *vb ver* **decaer**
decena [de'θena] *nf*: **una ~** ten (or so)
decencia [de'θenθja] *nf* (*modestia*) modesty; (*honestidad*) respectability
decenio [de'θenjo] *nm* decade
decente [de'θente] *adj* (*correcto*) proper; (*honesto*) respectable
decepción [deθep'θjon] *nf* disappointment
decepcionante [deθepθjo'nante] *adj* disappointing
decepcionar [deθepθjo'nar] *vt* to disappoint
decibelio [deθi'βeljo] *nm* decibel
decidido, -a [deθi'ðiðo, a] *adj* decided; (*resuelto*) resolute
decidir [deθi'ðir] *vt* (*persuadir*) to convince, persuade; (*resolver*) to decide ▪ *vi* to decide; **decidirse** *vr*: **decidirse a** to make up one's mind to; **decidirse por** to decide *o* settle on, choose
decimal [deθi'mal] *adj, nm* decimal
décimo, -a ['deθimo, a] *num* tenth ▪ *nf* (*Mat*) tenth; **tiene unas décimas de fiebre** he has a slight temperature
decimoctavo, -a [deθimok'taβo, a] *num* eighteenth; *ver tb* **sexto**
decimocuarto, -a [deθimo'kwarto, a] *num* fourteenth; *ver tb* **sexto**
decimonoveno, -a [deθimono'βeno, a] *num* nineteenth; *ver tb* **sexto**
decimoquinto, -a [deθimo'kinto, a] *num* fifteenth; *ver tb* **sexto**
decimoséptimo, -a [deθimo'septimo, a] *num* seventeenth; *ver tb* **sexto**
decimosexto, -a [deθimo'seksto, a] *num* sixteenth; *ver tb* **sexto**
decimotercero, -a [deθimoter'θero, a] *num* thirteenth; *ver tb* **sexto**
decir [de'θir] *vt* (*expresar*) to say; (*contar*) to tell; (*hablar*) to speak; (*indicar*) to show; (*revelar*) to reveal; (*fam: nombrar*) to call ▪ *nm* saying; **decirse** *vr*: **se dice** it is said, they say; (*se cuenta*) the story goes; **¿cómo se dice en inglés "cursi"?** what's the English for "cursi"?; **~ para** *o* **entre sí** to say to o.s.; **~ por ~** to talk for talking's sake; **dar que ~ (a la gente)** to make people talk; **querer ~** to mean; **es ~** that is to say, namely; **ni que ~ tiene que ...** it goes without saying that ...; **como quien dice** so to speak; **¡quién lo diría!** would you believe it!; **el qué dirán** gossip; **¡diga!, ¡dígame!** (*en tienda etc*) can I help you?; (*Telec*) hello?; **le dije que fuera más tarde** I told her to go later; **es un ~** it's just a phrase
decisión [deθi'sjon] *nf* decision; (*firmeza*) decisiveness; (*voluntad*) determination
decisivo, -a [deθi'siβo, a] *adj* decisive
declamar [dekla'mar] *vt, vi* to declaim; (*versos etc*) to recite
declaración [deklara'θjon] *nf* (*manifestación*) statement; (*explicación*) explanation; (*Jur: testimonio*) evidence; **~ de derechos** (*Pol*) bill of rights; **~ de impuestos** (*Com*) tax return; **~ de ingresos** *o* **de la renta** income tax return; **~ jurada** affidavit; **falsa ~** (*Jur*) misrepresentation
declarar [dekla'rar] *vt* to declare ▪ *vi* to declare; (*Jur*) to testify; **declararse** *vr* (*a una chica*) to propose; (*guerra, incendio*) to break out; **~ culpable/inocente a algn** to find sb guilty/not guilty; **declararse culpable/inocente** to plead guilty/not guilty
declinación [deklina'θjon] *nf* (*decaimiento*) decline; (*Ling*) declension
declinar [dekli'nar] *vt* (*gen, Ling*) to decline; (*Jur*) to reject ▪ *vi* (*el día*) to draw to a close
declive [de'kliβe] *nm* (*cuesta*) slope; (*inclinación*) incline; (*fig*) decline; (*Com: tb:* **declive económico**) slump
decodificador [dekoðifika'ðor] *nm* (*Inform*) decoder
decolorarse [dekolo'rarse] *vr* to become discoloured
decomisar [dekomi'sar] *vt* to seize, confiscate
decomiso [deko'miso] *nm* seizure
decoración [dekora'θjon] *nf* decoration; (*Teat*) scenery, set; **~ de escaparates** window dressing
decorado [deko'raðo] *nm* (*Cine, Teat*) scenery, set
decorador, a [dekora'ðor, a] *nm/f* (*de interiores*) (interior) decorator; (*Teat*) stage *o* set designer
decorar [deko'rar] *vt* to decorate

decorativo, -a [dekora'tiβo, a] *adj* ornamental, decorative
decoro [de'koro] *nm* (*respeto*) respect; (*dignidad*) decency; (*recato*) propriety
decoroso, -a [deko'roso, a] *adj* (*decente*) decent; (*modesto*) modest; (*digno*) proper
decrecer [dekre'θer] *vi* to decrease, diminish; (*nivel de agua*) to go down; (*días*) to draw in
decrépito, -a [de'krepito, a] *adj* decrepit
decretar [dekre'tar] *vt* to decree
decreto [de'kreto] *nm* decree; (*Pol*) act
decreto-ley [dekreto'lei] (*pl* **decretos-leyes**) *nm* decree
decrezca *etc* [de'kreθka] *vb ver* **decrecer**
decúbito [de'kuβito] *nm* (*Med*): **~ prono/supino** prone/supine position
dedal [de'ðal] *nm* thimble
dedalera [deða'lera] *nf* foxglove
dédalo ['deðalo] *nm* (*laberinto*) labyrinth; (*fig*) tangle, mess
dedicación [deðika'θjon] *nf* dedication; **con ~ exclusiva** *o* **plena** full-time
dedicar [deði'kar] *vt* (*libro*) to dedicate; (*tiempo, dinero*) to devote; **dedicarse** *vr*: **dedicarse a (hacer algo)** to devote o.s. to (doing sth); (*carrera, estudio*) to go in for (doing sth), take up (doing sth); **¿a qué se dedica usted?** what do you do (for a living)?
dedicatoria [deðika'torja] *nf* (*de libro*) dedication
dedillo [de'ðiʎo] *nm*: **saber algo al ~** to have sth at one's fingertips
dedique *etc* [de'ðike] *vb ver* **dedicar**
dedo ['deðo] *nm* finger; (*de vino etc*) drop; **~ (del pie)** toe; **~ pulgar** thumb; **~ índice** index finger; **~ mayor** *o* **cordial** middle finger; **~ anular** ring finger; **~ meñique** little finger; **contar con los dedos** to count on one's fingers; **comerse los dedos** to get very impatient; **entrar a ~** to get a job by pulling strings; **hacer ~** (*fam*) to hitch (a lift); **poner el ~ en la llaga** to put one's finger on it; **no tiene dos dedos de frente** he's pretty dim
deducción [deðuk'θjon] *nf* deduction
deducir [deðu'θir] *vt* (*concluir*) to deduce, infer; (*Com*) to deduct
deduje *etc* [de'ðuxe], **dedujera** *etc* [deðu'xera], **deduzca** *etc* [de'ðuθka] *vb ver* **deducir**
defección [defek'θjon] *nf* defection, desertion
defecto [de'fekto] *nm* defect, flaw; (*de cara*) imperfection; **~ de pronunciación** speech defect; **por ~** (*Inform*) default; **~ latente** (*Com*) latent defect
defectuoso, -a [defek'twoso, a] *adj* defective, faulty
defender [defen'der] *vt* to defend; (*ideas*) to uphold; (*causa*) to champion; (*amigos*) to stand up for; **defenderse** *vr* to defend o.s.; **defenderse bien** to give a good account of o.s.; **me defiendo en inglés** (*fig*) I can get by in English
defendible [defen'diβle] *adj* defensible
defensa [de'fensa] *nf* defence; (*Naut*) fender ■ *nm* (*Deporte*) back; **en ~ propia** in self-defence
defensivo, -a [defen'siβo, a] *adj* defensive ■ *nf*: **a la defensiva** on the defensive
defensor, -a [defen'sor, a] *adj* defending ■ *nm/f* (*abogado defensor*) defending counsel; (*protector*) protector; **~ del pueblo** (*Esp*) ≈ ombudsman
deferente [defe'rente] *adj* deferential
deferir [defe'rir] *vt* (*Jur*) to refer, delegate ■ *vi*: **~ a** to defer to
deficiencia [defi'θjenθja] *nf* deficiency
deficiente [defi'θjente] *adj* (*defectuoso*) defective; **~ en** lacking *o* deficient in ■ *nm/f*: **ser un ~ mental** to be mentally handicapped
déficit (*pl* **déficits**) ['defiθit] *nm* (*Com*) deficit; (*fig*) lack, shortage; **~ presupuestario** budget deficit
deficitario, -a [defiθi'tarjo, a] *adj* (*Com*) in deficit; (*: empresa*) loss-making
defienda *etc* [de'fjenda] *vb ver* **defender**
defiera *etc* [de'fjera] *vb ver* **deferir**
definición [defini'θjon] *nf* definition; (*Inform: de pantalla*) resolution
definido, -a [defi'niðo, a] *adj* (*tb Ling*) definite; **bien ~** well *o* clearly defined; **~ por el usuario** (*Inform*) user-defined
definir [defi'nir] *vt* (*determinar*) to determine, establish; (*decidir, Inform*) to define; (*aclarar*) to clarify
definitivo, -a [defini'tiβo, a] *adj* (*edición, texto*) definitive; (*fecha*) definite; **en definitiva** definitively; (*en conclusión*) finally; (*en resumen*) in short
defiriendo *etc* [defi'rjendo] *vb ver* **deferir**
deflacionario, -a [deflaθjo'narjo, a], **deflacionista** [deflaθjo'nista] *adj* deflationary
deflector [deflek'tor] *nm* (*Tec*) baffle
deforestación [deforesta'θjon] *nf* deforestation
deformación [deforma'θjon] *nf* (*alteración*) deformation; (*Radio etc*) distortion
deformar [defor'mar] *vt* (*gen*) to deform; **deformarse** *vr* to become deformed
deforme [de'forme] *adj* (*informe*) deformed; (*feo*) ugly; (*mal hecho*) misshapen

deformidad [deformi'ðað] *nf* (*forma anormal*) deformity; (*fig: defecto*) (moral) shortcoming
defraudar [defrau'ðar] *vt* (*decepcionar*) to disappoint; (*estafar*) to cheat; to defraud; **~ impuestos** to evade tax
defunción [defun'θjon] *nf* decease, demise
degeneración [dexenera'θjon] *nf* (*de las células*) degeneration; (*moral*) degeneracy
degenerar [dexene'rar] *vi* to degenerate; (*empeorar*) to get worse
deglutir [deɣlu'tir] *vt, vi* to swallow
degolladero [deɣoʎa'ðero] *nm* (*Anat*) throat; (*cadalso*) scaffold; (*matadero*) slaughterhouse
degollar [deɣo'ʎar] *vt* to slaughter
degradar [deɣra'ðar] *vt* to debase, degrade; (*Inform: datos*) to corrupt; **degradarse** *vr* to demean o.s.
degüelle *etc* [de'ɣweʎe] *vb ver* **degollar**
degustación [deɣusta'θjon] *nf* sampling, tasting
deificar [deifi'kar] *vt* (*persona*) to deify
deifique *etc* [dei'fike] *vb ver* **deificar**
dejadez [dexa'ðeθ] *nf* (*negligencia*) neglect; (*descuido*) untidiness, carelessness
dejado, -a [de'xaðo, a] *adj* (*desaliñado*) slovenly; (*negligente*) careless; (*indolente*) lazy
dejar [de'xar] *vt* (*gen*) to leave; (*permitir*) to allow, let; (*abandonar*) to abandon, forsake; (*actividad, empleo*) to give up; (*beneficios*) to produce, yield ■ *vi*: **~ de** (*parar*) to stop; **dejarse** *vr* (*abandonarse*) to let o.s. go; **no puedo ~ de fumar** I can't give up smoking; **no dejes de visitarles** don't fail to visit them; **no dejes de comprar un billete** make sure you buy a ticket; **~ a un lado** to leave *o* set aside; **~ caer** to drop; **~ entrar/salir** to let in/out; **~ pasar** to let through; **¡déjalo!** (*no te preocupes*) don't worry about it; **te dejo en tu casa** I'll drop you off at your place; **deja mucho que desear** it leaves a lot to be desired; **dejarse persuadir** to allow o.s. to *o* let o.s. be persuaded; **¡déjate de tonterías!** stop messing about!
deje ['dexe] *nm* (trace of) accent
dejo ['dexo] *nm* (*Ling*) accent
del [del] **= de + el**; *ver* **de**
del. *abr* (*Admin: = Delegación*) district office
delantal [delan'tal] *nm* apron
delante [de'lante] *adv* in front; (*enfrente*) opposite; (*adelante*) ahead ■ *prep*: **~ de** in front of, before; **la parte de ~** the front part; **estando otros ~** with others present
delantero, -a [delan'tero, a] *adj* front; (*patas de animal*) fore ■ *nm* (*Deporte*) forward ■ *nf* (*de vestido, casa etc*) front part; (*Teat*) front row; (*Deporte*) forward line; **llevar la delantera (a algn)** to be ahead (of sb)
delatar [dela'tar] *vt* to inform on *o* against, betray; **los delató a la policía** he reported them to the police
delator, -a [dela'tor, a] *nm/f* informer
delegación [deleɣa'θjon] *nf* (*acción: delegados*) delegation; (*Com: oficina*) district office, branch; **~ de poderes** (*Pol*) devolution; **~ de policía** police station
delegado, -a [dele'ɣaðo, a] *nm/f* delegate; (*Com*) agent
delegar [dele'ɣar] *vt* to delegate
delegue *etc* [de'leɣe] *vb ver* **delegar**
deleitar [delei'tar] *vt* to delight; **deleitarse** *vr*: **deleitarse con** *o* **en** to delight in, take pleasure in
deleite [de'leite] *nm* delight, pleasure
deletrear [deletre'ar] *vt* (*tb fig*) to spell (out)
deletreo [dele'treo] *nm* spelling; (*fig*) interpretation, decipherment
deleznable [deleθ'naβle] *adj* (*frágil*) fragile; (*fig: malo*) poor; (*: excusa*) feeble
delfín [del'fin] *nm* dolphin
delgadez [delɣa'ðeθ] *nf* thinness, slimness
delgado, -a [del'ɣaðo, a] *adj* thin; (*persona*) slim, thin; (*tierra*) poor; (*tela etc*) light, delicate ■ *adv*: **hilar (muy) ~** (*fig*) to split hairs
deliberación [deliβera'θjon] *nf* deliberation
deliberar [deliβe'rar] *vt* to debate, discuss ■ *vi* to deliberate
delicadeza [delika'ðeθa] *nf* delicacy; (*refinamiento, sutileza*) refinement
delicado, -a [deli'kaðo, a] *adj* delicate; (*sensible*) sensitive; (*rasgos*) dainty; (*gusto*) refined; (*situación: difícil*) tricky; (*: violento*) embarrassing; (*punto, tema*) sore; (*persona: difícil de contentar*) hard to please; (*: sensible*) touchy, hypersensitive; (*: atento*) considerate
delicia [de'liθja] *nf* delight
delicioso, -a [deli'θjoso, a] *adj* (*gracioso*) delightful; (*exquisito*) delicious
delictivo, -a [delik'tiβo, a] *adj* criminal *cpd*
delimitar [delimi'tar] *vt* to delimit
delincuencia [delin'kwenθja] *nf*: **~ juvenil** juvenile delinquency; **cifras de la ~** crime rate
delincuente [delin'kwente] *nm/f* delinquent; (*criminal*) criminal; **~ sin antecedentes** first offender; **~ habitual** hardened criminal
delineante [deline'ante] *nm/f* draughtsman
delinear [deline'ar] *vt* to delineate; (*dibujo*) to draw; (*contornos, fig*) to outline; **~ un proyecto** to outline a project
delinquir [delin'kir] *vi* to commit an offence
delirante [deli'rante] *adj* delirious
delirar [deli'rar] *vi* to be delirious, rave; (*fig: desatinar*) to talk nonsense

delirio [de'lirjo] *nm* (*Med*) delirium; (*palabras insensatas*) ravings *pl*; **~ de grandeza** megalomania; **~ de persecución** persecution mania; **con ~** (*fam*) madly; **¡fue el ~!** (*fam*) it was great!

delito [de'lito] *nm* (*gen*) crime; (*infracción*) offence

delta ['delta] *nm* delta

demacrado, -a [dema'kraðo, a] *adj* emaciated

demagogia [dema'ɣoxja] *nf* demagogy, demagoguery

demagogo [dema'ɣoɣo] *nm* demagogue

demanda [de'manda] *nf* (*pedido, Com*) demand; (*petición*) request; (*pregunta*) inquiry; (*reivindicación*) claim; (*Jur*) action, lawsuit; (*Teat*) call; (*Elec*) load; **~ de pago** demand for payment; **escribir en ~ de ayuda** to write asking for help; **entablar ~** (*Jur*) to sue; **presentar ~ de divorcio** to sue for divorce; **~ final** final demand; **~ indirecta** derived demand; **~ de mercado** market demand

demandado, -a [deman'daðo, a] *nm/f* defendant; (*en divorcio*) respondent

demandante [deman'dante] *nm/f* claimant; (*Jur*) plaintiff

demandar [deman'dar] *vt* (*gen*) to demand; (*Jur*) to sue, file a lawsuit against, start proceedings against; **~ a algn por calumnia/daños y perjuicios** to sue sb for libel/damages

demarcación [demarka'θjon] *nf* (*de terreno*) demarcation

demás [de'mas] *adj*: **los ~ niños** the other children, the remaining children ■ *pron*: **los/las ~** the others, the rest (of them); **lo ~** the rest (of it); **por ~** moreover; (*en vano*) in vain; **y ~** etcetera

demasía [dema'sia] *nf* (*exceso*) excess, surplus; **comer en ~** to eat to excess

demasiado, -a [dema'sjaðo, a] *adj*: **~ vino** too much wine ■ *adv* (*antes de adj, adv*) too; **demasiados libros** too many books; **¡es ~!** it's too much!; **es ~ pesado para levantar** it is too heavy to lift; **~ lo sé** I know it only too well; **hace ~ calor** it's too hot

demencia [de'menθja] *nf* (*locura*) madness

demencial [demen'θjal] *adj* crazy

demente [de'mente] *adj* mad, insane ■ *nm/f* lunatic

democracia [demo'kraθja] *nf* democracy

demócrata [de'mokrata] *nm/f* democrat

democratacristiano, -a [demokratakris'tjano, a], **democristiano, -a** [demokris'tjano, a] *adj, nm/f* Christian Democrat

democrático, -a [demo'kratiko, a] *adj* democratic

demográfico, -a [demo'ɣrafiko, a] *adj* demographic, population *cpd*; **la explosión demográfica** the population explosion

demoledor, a [demole'ðor, a] *adj* (*fig: argumento*) overwhelming; (*: ataque*) shattering

demoler [demo'ler] *vt* to demolish; (*edificio*) to pull down

demolición [demoli'θjon] *nf* demolition

demonio [de'monjo] *nm* devil, demon; **¡demonios!** hell!; **¿cómo demonios?** how the hell?; **¿qué demonios será?** what the devil can it be?; **¿dónde ~ lo habré dejado?** where the devil can I have left it?; **tener el ~ en el cuerpo** (*no parar*) to be always on the go

demora [de'mora] *nf* delay

demorar [demo'rar] *vt* (*retardar*) to delay, hold back; (*dilatar*) to hold up ■ *vi* to linger, stay on; **demorarse** *vr* to linger, stay on; (*retrasarse*) to take a long time; **demorarse en hacer algo** (*esp Am*) to take time doing sth

demos ['demos] *vb ver* **dar**

demostración [demostra'θjon] *nf* (*gen, Mat*) demonstration; (*de cariño, fuerza*) show; (*de teorema*) proof; (*de amistad*) gesture; (*de cólera, gimnasia*) display; **~ comercial** commercial exhibition

demostrar [demos'trar] *vt* (*probar*) to prove; (*mostrar*) to show; (*manifestar*) to demonstrate

demostrativo, -a [demostra'tiβo, a] *adj* demonstrative

demudado, -a [demu'ðaðo, a] *adj* (*rostro*) pale; (*fig*) upset; **tener el rostro ~** to look pale

demudar [demu'ðar] *vt* to change, alter; **demudarse** *vr* (*expresión*) to alter; (*perder color*) to change colour

demuela *etc* [de'mwela] *vb ver* **demoler**

demuestre *etc* [de'mwestre] *vb ver* **demostrar**

den [den] *vb ver* **dar**

denegación [deneɣa'θjon] *nf* refusal

denegar [dene'ɣar] *vt* (*rechazar*) to refuse; (*negar*) to deny; (*Jur*) to reject

denegué [dene'ɣe], **deneguemos** *etc* [dene'ɣemos], **deniego** *etc* [de'njeɣo], **deniegue** *etc* [de'njeɣe] *vb ver* **denegar**

dengue ['denɣe] *nm* dengue *o* breakbone fever

denigrante [deni'ɣrante] *adj* (*injurioso*) insulting; (*deshonroso*) degrading

denigrar [deni'ɣrar] *vt* (*desacreditar*) to denigrate; (*injuriar*) to insult

denodado, -a [deno'ðaðo, a] *adj* bold, brave

denominación [denomina'θjon] *nf* (*acto*) naming; (*clase*) denomination; *see note*

DENOMINACIÓN

The *denominación de origen*, often abbreviated to *D.O.*, is a prestigious product classification given to designated regions by the awarding body, the *Consejo Regulador de la Denominación de Origen*, when their produce meets the required quality and production standards. It is often associated with *manchego* cheeses and many of the wines from the Rioja and Ribera de Duero regions.

denominador [denomina'ðor] *nm*: **~ común** common denominator
denostar [denos'tar] *vt* to insult
denotar [deno'tar] *vt* (*indicar*) to indicate, denote
densidad [densi'ðað] *nf* (*Física*) density; (*fig*) thickness
denso, -a ['denso, a] *adj* (*apretado*) solid; (*espeso, pastoso*) thick; (*fig*) heavy
dentado, -a [den'taðo, a] *adj* (*rueda*) cogged; (*filo*) jagged; (*sello*) perforated; (*Bot*) dentate
dentadura [denta'ðura] *nf* (set of) teeth *pl*; **~ postiza** false teeth *pl*
dental [den'tal] *adj* dental
dentellada [dente'ʎaða] *nf* (*mordisco*) bite, nip; (*señal*) tooth mark; **partir algo a dentelladas** to sever sth with one's teeth
dentera [den'tera] *nf* (*sensación desgradable*) the shivers *pl*
dentición [denti'θjon] *nf* (*acto*) teething; (*Anat*) dentition; **estar con la ~** to be teething
dentífrico, -a [den'tifriko, a] *adj* dental, tooth *cpd* ▪ *nm* toothpaste; **pasta dentífrica** toothpaste
dentista [den'tista] *nm/f* dentist
dentro ['dentro] *adv* inside ▪ *prep*: **~ de** in, inside, within; **allí ~** in there; **mirar por ~** to look inside; **~ de lo posible** as far as possible; **~ de todo** all in all; **~ de tres meses** within three months
denuedo [de'nweðo] *nm* boldness, daring
denuesto [de'nwesto] *nm* insult
denuncia [de'nunθja] *nf* (*delación*) denunciation; (*acusación*) accusation; (*de accidente*) report; **hacer** *o* **poner una ~** to report an incident to the police
denunciable [denun'θjaβle] *adj* indictable, punishable
denunciante [denun'θjante] *nm/f* accuser; (*delator*) informer
denunciar [denun'θjar] *vt* to report; (*delatar*) to inform on *o* against
Dep. *abr* (= *Departamento*) Dept.; (= *Depósito*) dep.
deparar [depa'rar] *vt* (*brindar*) to provide *o* furnish with; (*futuro, destino*) to have in store for; **los placeres que el viaje nos deparó** the pleasures which the trip afforded us
departamento [departa'mento] *nm* (*sección*) department, section; (*Am: piso*) flat (*Brit*), apartment (*US*); (*distrito*) department, province; **~ de envíos** (*Com*) dispatch department; **~ de máquinas** (*Naut*) engine room
departir [depar'tir] *vi* to talk, converse
dependencia [depen'denθja] *nf* dependence; (*Pol*) dependency; (*Com*) office, section; (*sucursal*) branch office; (*Arq: cuarto*) room; **dependencias** *nfpl* outbuildings
depender [depen'der] *vi*: **~ de** to depend on; (*contar con*) to rely on; (*autoridad*) to be under, be answerable to; **depende** it (all) depends; **no depende de mí** it's not up to me
dependienta [depen'djenta] *nf* saleswoman, shop assistant
dependiente [depen'djente] *adj* dependent ▪ *nm* salesman, shop assistant
depilación [depila'θjon] *nf* hair removal
depilar [depi'lar] *vt* (*con cera: piernas*) to wax; (*cejas*) to pluck
depilatorio, -a [depila'torjo, a] *adj* depilatory ▪ *nm* hair remover
deplorable [deplo'raβle] *adj* deplorable
deplorar [deplo'rar] *vt* to deplore
depondré *etc* [depon'dre] *vb ver* **deponer**
deponer [depo'ner] *vt* (*armas*) to lay down; (*rey*) to depose; (*gobernante*) to oust; (*ministro*) to remove from office ▪ *vi* (*Jur*) to give evidence; (*declarar*) to make a statement
deponga *etc* [de'ponga] *vb ver* **deponer**
deportación [deporta'θjon] *nf* deportation
deportar [depor'tar] *vt* to deport
deporte [de'porte] *nm* sport
deportista [depor'tista] *adj* sports *cpd* ▪ *nm/f* sportsman(-woman)
deportivo, -a [depor'tiβo, a] *adj* (*club, periódico*) sports *cpd* ▪ *nm* sports car
deposición [deposi'θjon] *nf* (*de funcionario etc*) removal from office; (*Jur: testimonio*) evidence
depositante [deposi'tante] *nm/f* depositor
depositar [deposi'tar] *vt* (*dinero*) to deposit; (*mercaderías*) to put away, store; **depositarse** *vr* to settle; **~ la confianza en algn** to place one's trust in sb
depositario, -a [deposi'tarjo, a] *nm/f* trustee; **~ judicial** official receiver
depósito [de'posito] *nm* (*gen*) deposit; (*de mercaderías*) warehouse, store; (*de animales, coches*) pound; (*de agua, gasolina etc*) tank; (*en retrete*) cistern; **~ afianzado** bonded warehouse; **~ bancario** bank deposit; **~ de**

cadáveres mortuary; ~ **de maderas** timber yard; ~ **de suministro** feeder bin
depravar [depra'βar] *vt* to deprave, corrupt; **depravarse** *vr* to become depraved
depreciación [depreθja'θjon] *nf* depreciation
depreciar [depre'θjar] *vt* to depreciate, reduce the value of; **depreciarse** *vr* to depreciate, lose value
depredador, a [depreða'ðor, a] (*Zool*) *adj* predatory ■ *nm* predator
depredar [depre'ðar] *vt* to pillage
depresión [depre'sjon] *nf* (*gen, Med*) depression; (*hueco*) hollow; (*en horizonte, camino*) dip; (*merma*) drop; (*Econ*) slump, recession; ~ **nerviosa** nervous breakdown
deprimente [depri'mente] *adj* depressing
deprimido, -a [depri'miðo, a] *adj* depressed
deprimir [depri'mir] *vt* to depress; **deprimirse** *vr* (*persona*) to become depressed
deprisa [de'prisa] *adv ver* **prisa**
depuesto [de'pwesto] *pp de* **deponer**
depuración [depura'θjon] *nf* purification; (*Pol*) purge
depurador [depura'ðor] *nm* purifier
depuradora [depura'ðora] *nf* (*de agua*) water-treatment plant; (*tb*: **depuradora de aguas residuales**) sewage farm
depurar [depu'rar] *vt* to purify; (*purgar*) to purge
depuse *etc* [de'puse] *vb ver* **deponer**
der., der.° *abr* (= *derecho*) r
der.ª *abr* (= *derecha*) r
derecha [de'retʃa] *nf ver* **derecho, a**
derechazo [dere'tʃaθo] *nm* (*Boxeo*) right; (*Tenis*) forehand drive; (*Taur*) *a pass with the cape*
derechista [dere'tʃista] (*Pol*) *adj* right-wing ■ *nm/f* right-winger
derecho, -a [de'retʃo, a] *adj* right, right-hand ■ *nm* (*privilegio*) right; (*título*) claim, title; (*lado*) right(-hand) side; (*leyes*) law ■ *nf* right(-hand) side ■ *adv* straight, directly; **derechos** *nmpl* dues; (*profesionales*) fees; (*impuestos*) taxes; (*de autor*) royalties; **la(s) derecha(s)** (*Pol*) the Right; **derechos civiles** civil rights; **derechos de patente** patent rights; **derechos portuarios** (*Com*) harbour dues; ~ **de propiedad literaria** copyright; ~ **de timbre** (*Com*) stamp duty; ~ **de votar** right to vote; ~ **a voto** voting right; **Facultad de D~** Faculty of Law; **a derechas** rightly, correctly; **de derechas** (*Pol*) right-wing; **"reservados todos los derechos"** "all rights reserved"; **¡no hay ~!** it's not fair!; **tener ~ a** to have a right to; **a la derecha** on the right; (*dirección*) to the right; **siga todo ~** carry *o* (*Brit*) go straight on
deriva [de'riβa] *nf*: **ir** *o* **estar a la ~** to drift, be adrift
derivación [deriβa'θjon] *nf* derivation
derivado, -a [deri'βaðo, a] *adj* derived ■ *nm* (*Ling*) derivative; (*Industria, Química*) by-product
derivar [deri'βar] *vt* to derive; (*desviar*) to direct ■ *vi*, **derivarse** *vr* to derive, be derived; **~(se) de** (*consecuencia*) to spring from
dermatólogo, -a [derma'toloɣo, a] *nm/f* dermatologist
dérmico, -a ['dermiko, a] *adj* skin *cpd*
dermoprotector, a [dermoprotek'tor, a] *adj* protective
derogación [deroɣa'θjon] *nf* repeal
derogar [dero'ɣar] *vt* (*ley*) to repeal; (*contrato*) to revoke
derogue *etc* [de'roɣe] *vb ver* **derogar**
derramamiento [derrama'mjento] *nm* (*dispersión*) spilling; (*fig*) squandering; ~ **de sangre** bloodshed
derramar [derra'mar] *vt* to spill; (*verter*) to pour out; (*esparcir*) to scatter; **derramarse** *vr* to pour out; ~ **lágrimas** to weep
derrame [de'rrame] *nm* (*de líquido*) spilling; (*de sangre*) shedding; (*de tubo etc*) overflow; (*pédida*) leakage; (*Med*) discharge; (*declive*) slope; ~ **cerebral** brain haemorrhage; ~ **sinovial** water on the knee
derrapar [derra'par] *vi* to skid
derredor [derre'ðor] *adv*: **al** *o* **en ~ de** around, about
derrengado, -a [derren'gaðo, a] *adj* (*torcido*) bent; (*cojo*) crippled; **estar ~** (*fig*) to ache all over; **dejar ~ a algn** (*fig*) to wear sb out
derretido, -a [derre'tiðo, a] *adj* melted; (*metal*) molten; **estar ~ por algn** (*fig*) to be crazy about sb
derretir [derre'tir] *vt* (*gen*) to melt; (*nieve*) to thaw; (*fig*) to squander; **derretirse** *vr* to melt
derribar [derri'βar] *vt* to knock down; (*construcción*) to demolish; (*persona, gobierno, político*) to bring down
derribo [de'rriβo] *nm* (*de edificio*) demolition; (*Lucha*) throw; (*Aviat*) shooting down; (*Pol*) overthrow; **derribos** *nmpl* rubble *sg*, debris *sg*
derrita *etc* [de'rrita] *vb ver* **derretir**
derrocar [derro'kar] *vt* (*gobierno*) to bring down, overthrow; (*ministro*) to oust
derrochador, a [derrotʃa'ðor, a] *adj, nm/f* spendthrift
derrochar [derro'tʃar] *vt* (*dinero, recursos*) to squander; (*energía, salud*) to be bursting with *o* full of
derroche [de'rrotʃe] *nm* (*despilfarro*) waste, squandering; (*exceso*) extravagance; **con un**

~ **de buen gusto** with a fine display of good taste
derroque *etc* [de'rroke] *vb ver* **derrocar**
derrota [de'rrota] *nf* (*Naut*) course; (*Mil*) defeat, rout; **sufrir una grave ~** (*fig*) to suffer a grave setback
derrotar [derro'tar] *vt* (*gen*) to defeat
derrotero [derro'tero] *nm* (*rumbo*) course; **tomar otro ~** (*fig*) to adopt a different course
derrotista [derro'tista] *adj, nm/f* defeatist
derruir [derru'ir] *vt* to demolish, tear down
derrumbamiento [derrumba'mjento] *nm* (*caída*) plunge; (*demolición*) demolition; (*desplome*) collapse; ~ **de tierra** landslide
derrumbar [derrum'bar] *vt* to throw down; (*despeñar*) to fling *o* hurl down; (*volcar*) to upset; **derrumbarse** *vr* (*hundirse*) to collapse; (*: techo*) to fall in, cave in; (*fig: esperanzas*) to collapse
derrumbe [de'rrumbe] *nm* = **derrumbamiento**
derruyendo *etc* [derru'jendo] *vb ver* **derruir**
des [des] *vb ver* **dar**
desabastecido, -a [desaβaste'θiðo, a] *adj*: **estar ~ de algo** to be short of *o* out of sth
desabotonar [desaβoto'nar] *vt* to unbutton, undo ■ *vi* (*flores*) to blossom; **desabotonarse** *vr* to come undone
desabrido, -a [desa'βriðo, a] *adj* (*comida*) insipid, tasteless; (*persona: soso*) dull; (*: antipático*) rude, surly; (*respuesta*) sharp; (*tiempo*) unpleasant
desabrigado, -a [desaβri'ɣaðo, a] *adj* (*sin abrigo*) not sufficiently protected; (*fig*) exposed
desabrigar [desaβri'ɣar] *vt* (*quitar ropa a*) to remove the clothing of; (*descubrir*) to uncover; (*fig*) to deprive of protection; **desabrigarse** *vr*: **me desabrigué en la cama** the bedclothes came off
desabrigue *etc* [desa'βriɣe] *vb ver* **desabrigar**
desabrochar [desaβro'tʃar] *vt* (*botones, broches*) to undo, unfasten; **desabrocharse** *vr* (*ropa etc*) to come undone
desacatar [desaka'tar] *vt* (*ley*) to disobey
desacato [desa'kato] *nm* (*falta de respeto*) disrespect; (*Jur*) contempt
desacertado, -a [desaθer'taðo, a] *adj* (*equivocado*) mistaken; (*inoportuno*) unwise
desacierto [desa'θjerto] *nm* (*error*) mistake, error; (*dicho*) unfortunate remark
desaconsejable [desakonse'xaβle] *adj* inadvisable
desaconsejado, -a [desakonse'xaðo, a] *adj* ill-advised
desaconsejar [desakonse'xar] *vt*: ~ **algo a algn** to advise sb against sth
desacoplar [desako'plar] *vt* (*Elec*) to disconnect; (*Tec*) to take apart
desacorde [desa'korðe] *adj* (*Mus*) discordant; (*fig: opiniones*) conflicting; **estar ~ con algo** to disagree with sth
desacreditar [desakreði'tar] *vt* (*desprestigiar*) to discredit, bring into disrepute; (*denigrar*) to run down
desactivar [desakti'βar] *vt* to deactivate; (*bomba*) to defuse
desacuerdo [desa'kwerðo] *nm* (*conflicto*) disagreement, discord; (*error*) error, blunder; **en ~** out of keeping
desafiante [desa'fjante] *adj* (*insolente*) defiant; (*retador*) challenging ■ *nm/f* challenger
desafiar [desa'fjar] *vt* (*retar*) to challenge; (*enfrentarse a*) to defy
desafilado, -a [desafi'laðo, a] *adj* blunt
desafinado, -a [desafi'naðo, a] *adj*: **estar ~** to be out of tune
desafinar [desafi'nar] *vi* to be out of tune; **desafinarse** *vr* to go out of tune
desafío [desa'fio] *nm* (*reto*) challenge; (*combate*) duel; (*resistencia*) defiance
desaforadamente [desaforaða'mente] *adv*: **gritar ~** to shout one's head off
desaforado, -a [desafo'raðo, a] *adj* (*grito*) ear-splitting; (*comportamiento*) outrageous
desafortunadamente [desafortunaða'mente] *adv* unfortunately
desafortunado, -a [desafortu'naðo, a] *adj* (*desgraciado*) unfortunate, unlucky
desagradable [desaɣra'ðaβle] *adj* (*fastidioso, enojoso*) unpleasant; (*irritante*) disagreeable; **ser ~ con algn** to be rude to sb
desagradar [desaɣra'ðar] *vi* (*disgustar*) to displease; (*molestar*) to bother
desagradecido, -a [desaɣraðe'θiðo, a] *adj* ungrateful
desagrado [desa'ɣraðo] *nm* (*disgusto*) displeasure; (*contrariedad*) dissatisfaction; **con ~** unwillingly
desagraviar [desaɣra'βjar] *vt* to make amends to
desagravio [desa'ɣraβjo] *nm* (*satisfacción*) amends; (*compensación*) compensation
desaguadero [desaɣwa'ðero] *nm* drain
desagüe [de'saɣwe] *nm* (*de un líquido*) drainage; (*cañería: tb:* **tubo de desagüe**) drainpipe; (*salida*) outlet, drain
desaguisado, -a [desaɣi'saðo, a] *adj* illegal ■ *nm* outrage
desahogado, -a [desao'ɣaðo, a] *adj* (*holgado*) comfortable; (*espacioso*) roomy
desahogar [desao'ɣar] *vt* (*aliviar*) to ease, relieve; (*ira*) to vent; **desahogarse** *vr* (*distenderse*) to relax; (*desfogarse*) to let off steam (*fam*); (*confesarse*) to confess, get sth off one's chest (*fam*)

desahogo [desa'oɣo] *nm* (*alivio*) relief; (*comodidad*) comfort, ease; **vivir con ~** to be comfortably off
desahogue *etc* [desa'oɣe] *vb ver* **desahogar**
desahuciado, -a [desau'θjaðo, a] *adj* hopeless
desahuciar [desau'θjar] *vt* (*enfermo*) to give up hope for; (*inquilino*) to evict
desahucio [de'sauθjo] *nm* eviction
desairado, -a [desai'raðo, a] *adj* (*menospreciado*) disregarded; (*desgarbado*) shabby; (*sin éxito*) unsuccessful; **quedar ~** to come off badly
desairar [desai'rar] *vt* (*menospreciar*) to slight, snub; (*cosa*) to disregard; (*Com*) to default on
desaire [des'aire] *nm* (*menosprecio*) slight; (*falta de garbo*) unattractiveness; **dar** *o* **hacer un ~ a algn** to offend sb; **¿me va usted a hacer ese ~?** I won't take no for an answer!
desajustar [desaxus'tar] *vt* (*desarreglar*) to disarrange; (*desconcertar*) to throw off balance; (*fig: planes*) to upset; **desajustarse** *vr* to get out of order; (*aflojarse*) to loosen
desajuste [desa'xuste] *nm* (*de máquina*) disorder; (*avería*) breakdown; (*situación*) imbalance; (*desacuerdo*) disagreement
desalentador, -a [desalenta'ðor, a] *adj* discouraging
desalentar [desalen'tar] *vt* (*desanimar*) to discourage; **desalentarse** *vr* to get discouraged
desaliento *etc* [desa'ljento] *vb ver* **desalentar** ■ *nm* discouragement; (*abatimiento*) depression
desaliñado, -a [desali'ɲaðo, a] *adj* (*descuidado*) slovenly; (*raído*) shabby; (*desordenado*) untidy; (*negligente*) careless
desaliño [desa'liɲo] *nm* (*descuido*) slovenliness; (*negligencia*) carelessness
desalmado, -a [desal'maðo, a] *adj* (*cruel*) cruel, heartless
desalojar [desalo'xar] *vt* (*gen*) to remove, expel; (*expulsar, echar*) to eject; (*abandonar*) to move out of ■ *vi* to move out; **la policía desalojó el local** the police cleared people out of the place
desalquilar [desalki'lar] *vt* to vacate, move out; **desalquilarse** *vr* to become vacant
desamarrar [desama'rrar] *vt* to untie; (*Naut*) to cast off
desamor [desa'mor] *nm* (*frialdad*) indifference; (*odio*) dislike
desamparado, -a [desampa'raðo, a] *adj* (*persona*) helpless; (*lugar: expuesto*) exposed; (: *desierto*) deserted
desamparar [desampa'rar] *vt* (*abandonar*) to desert, abandon; (*Jur*) to leave defenceless; (*barco*) to abandon
desamparo [desam'paro] *nm* (*acto*) desertion; (*estado*) helplessness
desamueblado, -a [desamwe'βlaðo, a] *adj* unfurnished
desandar [desan'dar] *vt*: **~ lo andado** *o* **el camino** to retrace one's steps
desanduve *etc* [desan'duβe], **desanduviera** *etc* [desandu'βjera] *vb ver* **desandar**
desangelado, -a [desanxe'laðo, a] *adj* (*habitación, edificio*) lifeless
desangrar [desan'grar] *vt* to bleed; (*fig: persona*) to bleed dry; (*lago*) to drain; **desangrarse** *vr* to lose a lot of blood; (*morir*) to bleed to death
desanimado, -a [desani'maðo, a] *adj* (*persona*) downhearted; (*espectáculo, fiesta*) dull
desanimar [desani'mar] *vt* (*desalentar*) to discourage; (*deprimir*) to depress; **desanimarse** *vr* to lose heart
desánimo [de'sanimo] *nm* despondency; (*abatimiento*) dejection; (*falta de animación*) dullness
desanudar [desanu'ðar] *vt* to untie; (*fig*) to clear up
desapacible [desapa'θiβle] *adj* unpleasant
desaparecer [desapare'θer] *vi* to disappear; (*el sol, la luz*) to vanish; (*desaparecer de vista*) to drop out of sight; (*efectos, señales*) to wear off ■ *vt* (*esp Am Pol*) to cause to disappear; (: *eufemismo*) to murder
desaparecido, -a [desapare'θiðo, a] *adj* missing; (*especie*) extinct ■ *nm/f* (*Am Pol*) kidnapped *o* missing person
desaparezca *etc* [desapa'reθka] *vb ver* **desaparecer**
desaparición [desapari'θjon] *nf* disappearance; (*de especie etc*) extinction
desapasionado, -a [desapasjo'naðo, a] *adj* dispassionate, impartial
desapego [desa'peɣo] *nm* (*frialdad*) coolness; (*distancia*) detachment
desapercibido, -a [desaperθi'βiðo, a] *adj* unnoticed; (*desprevenido*) unprepared; **pasar ~** to go unnoticed
desaplicado, -a [desapli'kado, a] *adj* slack, lazy
desaprensivo, -a [desapren'siβo, a] *adj* unscrupulous
desaprobar [desapro'βar] *vt* (*reprobar*) to disapprove of; (*condenar*) to condemn; (*no consentir*) to reject
desaprovechado, -a [desaproβe'tʃaðo, a] *adj* (*oportunidad, tiempo*) wasted; (*estudiante*) slack
desaprovechar [desaproβe'tʃar] *vt* to waste; (*talento*) not to use to the full ■ *vi* (*perder terreno*) to lose ground

desapruebe *etc* [desa'prweβe] *vb ver* **desaprobar**
desarmar [desar'mar] *vt* (*Mil, fig*) to disarm; (*Tec*) to take apart, dismantle
desarme [de'sarme] *nm* disarmament
desarraigado, -a [desarrai'ɣaðo, a] *adj* (*persona*) without roots, rootless
desarraigar [desarrai'ɣar] *vt* to uproot; (*fig*: *costumbre*) to root out; (: *persona*) to banish
desarraigo [desa'rraiɣo] *nm* uprooting
desarraigue *etc* [desa'rraiɣe] *vb ver* **desarraigar**
desarrapado, -a [desarra'paðo, a] *adj* ragged; **(de aspecto)** ~ shabby
desarreglado, -a [desarre'ɣlaðo, a] *adj* (*desordenado*) disorderly, untidy; (*hábitos*) irregular
desarreglar [desarre'ɣlar] *vt* to mess up; (*desordenar*) to disarrange; (*trastocar*) to upset, disturb
desarreglo [desa'rreɣlo] *nm* (*de casa, persona*) untidiness; (*desorden*) disorder; (*Tec*) trouble; (*Med*) upset; **viven en el mayor ~** they live in complete chaos
desarrollado, -a [desarro'ʎaðo, a] *adj* developed
desarrollar [desarro'ʎar] *vt* (*gen*) to develop; (*extender*) to unfold; (*teoría*) to explain; **desarrollarse** *vr* to develop; (*extenderse*) to open (out); (*film*) to develop; (*fig*) to grow; (*tener lugar*) to take place; **aquí desarrollan un trabajo muy importante** they carry on o out very important work here; **la acción se desarrolla en Roma** (*Cine etc*) the scene is set in Rome
desarrollo [desa'rroʎo] *nm* development; (*de acontecimientos*) unfolding; (*de industria, mercado*) expansion, growth; **país en vías de ~** developing country; **la industria está en pleno ~** industry is expanding steadily; **~ sostenible** sustainable development
desarrugar [desarru'ɣar] *vt* (*alisar*) to smooth (out); (*ropa*) to remove the creases from
desarrugue *etc* [desa'rruɣe] *vb ver* **desarrugar**
desarticulado, -a [desartiku'laðo, a] *adj* disjointed
desarticular [desartiku'lar] *vt* (*huesos*) to dislocate, put out of joint; (*objeto*) to take apart; (*grupo terrorista etc*) to break up
desaseado, -a [desase'aðo, a] *adj* (*sucio*) dirty; (*desaliñado*) untidy
desaseo [desa'seo] *nm* (*suciedad*) dirtiness; (*desarreglo*) untidiness
desasga *etc* [de'sasɣa] *vb ver* **desasir**
desasir [desa'sir] *vt* to loosen; **desasirse** *vr* to extricate o.s.; **desasirse de** to let go, give up
desasosegar [desasose'ɣar] *vt* (*inquietar*) to disturb, make uneasy; **desasosegarse** *vr* to become uneasy
desasosegué [desasose'ɣe], **desasoseguemos** *etc* [desasose'ɣemos] *vb ver* **desasosegar**
desasosiego *etc* [desaso'sjeɣo] *vb ver* **desasosegar** ■ *nm* (*intranquilidad*) uneasiness, restlessness; (*ansiedad*) anxiety; (*Pol etc*) unrest
desasosiegue *etc* [desaso'sjeɣe] *vb ver* **desasosegar**
desastrado, -a [desas'traðo, a] *adj* (*desaliñado*) shabby; (*sucio*) dirty
desastre [de'sastre] *nm* disaster; **¡un ~!** how awful!; **la función fue un ~** the show was a shambles
desastroso, -a [desas'troso, a] *adj* disastrous
desatado, -a [desa'taðo, a] *adj* (*desligado*) untied; (*violento*) violent, wild
desatar [desa'tar] *vt* (*nudo*) to untie; (*paquete*) to undo; (*perro, odio*) to unleash; (*misterio*) to solve; (*separar*) to detach; **desatarse** *vr* (*zapatos*) to come untied; (*tormenta*) to break; (*perder control de sí mismo*) to lose self-control; **desatarse en injurias** to pour out a stream of insults
desatascar [desatas'kar] *vt* (*cañería*) to unblock, clear
desatasque *etc* [desa'taske] *vb ver* **desatascar**
desatención [desaten'θjon] *nf* (*descuido*) inattention; (*distracción*) absent-mindedness
desatender [desaten'der] *vt* (*no prestar atención a*) to disregard; (*abandonar*) to neglect
desatento, -a [desa'tento, a] *adj* (*distraído*) inattentive; (*descortés*) discourteous
desatienda *etc* [desa'tjenda] *vb ver* **desatender**
desatinado, -a [desati'naðo, a] *adj* foolish, silly
desatino [desa'tino] *nm* (*idiotez*) foolishness, folly; (*error*) blunder; **desatinos** *nmpl* nonsense *sg*; **¡qué ~!** how silly!, what rubbish!
desatornillar [desatorni'ʎar] *vt* to unscrew
desatrancar [desatran'kar] *vt* (*puerta*) to unbolt; (*cañería*) to unblock
desatranque *etc* [desa'tranke] *vb ver* **desatrancar**
desautorice *etc* [desauto'riθe] *vb ver* **desautorizar**
desautorizado, -a [desautori'θaðo, a] *adj* unauthorized
desautorizar [desautori'θar] *vt* (*oficial*) to deprive of authority; (*informe*) to deny
desavendré *etc* [desaβen'dre] *vb ver* **desavenir**
desavenencia [desaβe'nenθja] *nf* (*desacuerdo*) disagreement; (*discrepancia*) quarrel

desavenga *etc* [desa'βenga] *vb ver* **desavenir**
desavenido, -a [desaβe'niðo, a] *adj (opuesto)* contrary; *(reñido)* in disagreement; **ellos están desavenidos** they are at odds
desavenir [desaβe'nir] *vt (enemistar)* to make trouble between; **desavenirse** *vr* to fall out
desaventajado, -a [desaβenta'xaðo, a] *adj (inferior)* inferior; *(poco ventajoso)* disadvantageous
desaviene *etc* [desa'βjene], **desaviniendo** *etc* [desaβi'njendo] *vb ver* **desavenir**
desayunar [desaju'nar] *vi*, **desayunarse** *vr* to have breakfast ■ *vt* to have for breakfast; **~ con café** to have coffee for breakfast; **~ con algo** *(fig)* to get the first news of sth
desayuno [desa'juno] *nm* breakfast
desazón [desa'θon] *nf (angustia)* anxiety; *(Med)* discomfort; *(fig)* annoyance
desazonar [desaθo'nar] *vt (fig)* to annoy, upset; **desazonarse** *vr (enojarse)* to be annoyed; *(preocuparse)* to worry, be anxious
desbancar [desβan'kar] *vt (quitar el puesto a)* to oust; *(suplantar)* to supplant (in sb's affections)
desbandada [desβan'daða] *nf* rush; **~ general** mass exodus; **a la ~** in disorder
desbandarse [desβan'darse] *vr (Mil)* to disband; *(fig)* to flee in disorder
desbanque *etc* [des'βanke] *vb ver* **desbancar**
desbarajuste [desβara'xuste] *nm* confusion, disorder; **¡qué ~!** what a mess!
desbaratar [desβara'tar] *vt (gen)* to mess up; *(plan)* to spoil; *(deshacer, destruir)* to ruin ■ *vi* to talk nonsense; **desbaratarse** *vr (máquina)* to break down; *(persona: irritarse)* to fly off the handle *(fam)*
desbarrar [desβa'rrar] *vi* to talk nonsense
desbloquear [desβloke'ar] *vt (negociaciones, tráfico)* to get going again; *(Com: cuenta)* to unfreeze
desbocado, -a [desβo'kaðo, a] *adj (caballo)* runaway; *(herramienta)* worn
desbocar [desβo'kar] *vt (vasija)* to break the rim of; **desbocarse** *vr (caballo)* to bolt; *(persona: soltar injurias)* to let out a stream of insults
desboque *etc* [des'βoke] *vb ver* **desbocar**
desbordamiento [desβorða'mjento] *nm (de río)* overflowing; *(Inform)* overflow; *(de cólera)* outburst; *(de entusiasmo)* upsurge
desbordar [desβor'ðar] *vt (sobrepasar)* to go beyond; *(exceder)* to exceed ■ *vi*, **desbordarse** *vr (líquido, río)* to overflow; *(entusiasmo)* to erupt; *(persona: exaltarse)* to get carried away
desbravar [desβra'βar] *vt (caballo)* to break in; *(animal)* to tame
descabalgar [deskaβal'γar] *vi* to dismount
descabalgue *etc* [deska'βalγe] *vb ver* **descabalgar**
descabellado, -a [deskaβe'ʎaðo, a] *adj (disparatado)* wild, crazy; *(insensato)* preposterous
descabellar [deskaβe'ʎar] *vt* to ruffle; *(Taur: toro)* to give the coup de grace to
descabezado, -a [deskaβe'θaðo, a] *adj (sin cabeza)* headless; *(insensato)* wild
descafeinado, -a [deskafei'naðo, a] *adj* decaffeinated ■ *nm* decaffeinated coffee, de-caff
descalabrar [deskala'βrar] *vt* to smash; *(persona)* to hit; *(: en la cabeza)* to hit on the head; *(Naut)* to cripple; *(dañar)* to harm, damage; **descalabrarse** *vr* to hurt one's head
descalabro [deska'laβro] *nm* blow; *(desgracia)* misfortune
descalce *etc* [des'kalθe] *vb ver* **descalzar**
descalificación [deskalifika'θjon] *nf* disqualification; **descalificaciones** *nfpl* discrediting *sg*
descalificar [deskalifi'kar] *vt* to disqualify; *(desacreditar)* to discredit
descalifique *etc* [deskali'fike] *vb ver* **descalificar**
descalzar [deskal'θar] *vt (persona)* to take the shoes off
descalzo, -a [des'kalθo, a] *adj* barefoot(ed); *(fig)* destitute; **estar (con los pies) ~(s)** to be barefooted
descambiar [deskam'bjar] *vt* to exchange
descaminado, -a [deskami'naðo, a] *adj (equivocado)* on the wrong road; *(fig)* misguided; **en eso no anda usted muy ~** you're not far wrong there
descamisado, -a [deskami'saðo, a] *adj* bare-chested
descampado [deskam'paðo] *nm* open space, piece of empty ground; **comer al ~** to eat in the open air
descansado, -a [deskan'saðo, a] *adj (gen)* rested; *(que tranquiliza)* restful
descansar [deskan'sar] *vt (gen)* to rest; *(apoyar)*: **~ (sobre)** to lean (on) ■ *vi* to rest, have a rest; *(echarse)* to lie down; *(cadáver, restos)* to lie; **¡que usted descanse!** sleep well!; **~ en** *(argumento)* to be based on
descansillo [deskan'siʎo] *nm (de escalera)* landing
descanso [des'kanso] *nm (reposo)* rest; *(alivio)* relief; *(pausa)* break; *(Deporte)* interval, half time; **día de ~** day off; **~ de enfermedad/maternidad** sick/maternity leave; **tomarse unos días de ~** to take a few days' leave *o* rest
descapitalizado, -a [deskapitali'θaðo, a] *adj* undercapitalized

descapotable [deskapo'taβle] *nm* (*tb*: **coche descapotable**) convertible
descarado, -a [deska'raðo, a] *adj* (*sin vergüenza*) shameless; (*insolente*) cheeky
descarga [des'karɣa] *nf* (*Arq, Elec, Mil*) discharge; (*Naut*) unloading
descargador [deskarɣa'ðor] *nm* (*de barcos*) docker
descargar [deskar'ɣar] *vt* to unload; (*golpe*) to let fly; (*arma*) to fire; (*Elec*) to discharge; (*pila*) to run down; (*conciencia*) to relieve; (*Com*) to take up; (*persona*: *de una obligación*) to release; (: *de una deuda*) to free; (*Jur*) to clear ■ *vi* (*río*): **~ (en)** to flow (into); **descargarse** *vr* to unburden o.s.; **descargarse de algo** to get rid of sth; **descargarse algo de Internet** to download sth from the Internet
descargo [des'karɣo] *nm* (*de obligación*) release; (*Com*: *recibo*) receipt; (: *de deuda*) discharge; (*Jur*) evidence; **~ de una acusación** acquittal on a charge
descargue *etc* [des'karɣe] *vb ver* **descargar**
descarnado, -a [deskar'naðo, a] *adj* scrawny; (*fig*) bare; (*estilo*) straightforward
descaro [des'karo] *nm* nerve
descarriar [deska'rrjar] *vt* (*descaminar*) to misdirect; (*fig*) to lead astray; **descarriarse** *vr* (*perderse*) to lose one's way; (*separarse*) to stray; (*pervertirse*) to err, go astray
descarrilamiento [deskarrila'mjento] *nm* (*de tren*) derailment
descarrilar [deskarri'lar] *vi* to be derailed
descartable [deskar'taβle] *adj* (*Inform*) temporary
descartar [deskar'tar] *vt* (*rechazar*) to reject; (*eliminar*) to rule out; **descartarse** *vr* (*Naipes*) to discard; **descartarse de** to shirk
descascarar [deskaska'rar] *vt* (*naranja, limón*) to peel; (*nueces, huevo duro*) to shell; **descascararse** *vr* to peel (off)
descascarillado, -a [deskaskari'ʎaðo, a] *adj* (*paredes*) peeling
descendencia [desθen'denθja] *nf* (*origen*) origin, descent; (*hijos*) offspring; **morir sin dejar ~** to die without issue
descendente [desθen'dente] *adj* (*cantidad*) diminishing; (*Inform*) top-down
descender [desθen'der] *vt* (*bajar*: *escalera*) to go down ■ *vi* to descend; (*temperatura, nivel*) to fall, drop; (*líquido*) to run; (*cortina etc*) to hang; (*fuerzas, persona*) to fail, get weak; **~ de** to be descended from
descendiente [desθen'djente] *nm/f* descendant
descenso [des'θenso] *nm* descent; (*de temperatura*) drop; (*de producción*) downturn; (*de calidad*) decline; (*Minería*) collapse; (*bajada*) slope; (*fig*: *decadencia*) decline; (*de empleado etc*) demotion
descentrado, -a [desθen'traðo, a] *adj* (*pieza de una máquina*) off-centre; (*rueda*) out of true; (*persona*) bewildered; (*desequilibrado*) unbalanced; (*problema*) out of focus; **todavía está algo ~** he is still somewhat out of touch
descentralice *etc* [desθentra'liθe] *vb ver* **descentralizar**
descentralizar [desθentrali'θar] *vt* to decentralize
descerrajar [desθerra'xar] *vt* (*puerta*) to break open
descienda *etc* [des'θjenda] *vb ver* **descender**
descifrable [desθi'fraβle] *adj* (*gen*) decipherable; (*letra*) legible
descifrar [desθi'frar] *vt* (*escritura*) to decipher; (*mensaje*) to decode; (*problema*) to puzzle out; (*misterio*) to solve
descocado, -a [desko'kaðo, a] *adj* (*descarado*) cheeky; (*desvergonzado*) brazen
descoco [des'koko] *nm* (*descaro*) cheek; (*atrevimiento*) brazenness
descodificador [deskoðifika'ðor] *nm* decoder
descodificar [deskoðifi'kar] *vt* to decode
descolgar [deskol'ɣar] *vt* (*bajar*) to take down; (*desde una posición alta*) to lower; (*de una pared etc*) to unhook; (*teléfono*) to pick up; **descolgarse** *vr* to let o.s. down; **descolgarse por** (*bajar escurriéndose*) to slip down; (*pared*) to climb down; **dejó el teléfono descolgado** he left the phone off the hook
descolgué [deskol'ɣe], **descolguemos** *etc* [deskol'ɣemos] *vb ver* **descolgar**
descollar [desko'ʎar] *vi* (*sobresalir*) to stand out; (*montaña etc*) to rise; **la obra que más descuella de las suyas** his most outstanding work
descolocado, -a [deskolo'kaðo, a] *adj*: **estar ~** (*cosa*) to be out of place; (*criada*) to be unemployed
descolorido, -a [deskolo'riðo, a] *adj* (*color, tela*) faded; (*pálido*) pale; (*fig*: *estilo*) colourless
descompaginar [deskompaxi'nar] *vt* (*desordenar*) to disarrange, mess up
descompasado, -a [deskompa'saðo, a] *adj* (*sin proporción*) out of all proportion; (*excesivo*) excessive; (*hora*) unearthly
descompensar [deskompen'sar] *vt* to unbalance
descompondré *etc* [deskompon'dre] *vb ver* **descomponer**
descomponer [deskompo'ner] *vt* (*gen, Ling, Mat*) to break down; (*desordenar*) to disarrange, disturb; (*materia orgánica*) to rot, decompose; (*Tec*) to put out of order; (*facciones*) to distort; (*estómago etc*) to upset;

(: *planes*) to mess up; (*persona: molestar*) to upset; (*irritar*) to annoy; **descomponerse** *vr* (*corromperse*) to rot, decompose; (*estómago*) to get upset; (*el tiempo*) to change (for the worse); (*Tec*) to break down
descomponga *etc* [deskom'ponga] *vb ver* **descomponer**
descomposición [deskomposi'θjon] *nf* (*gen*) breakdown; (*de fruta etc*) decomposition; (*putrefacción*) rotting; (*de cara*) distortion; **~ de vientre** (*Med*) stomach upset, diarrhoea
descompostura [deskompos'tura] *nf* (*Tec*) breakdown; (*desorganización*) disorganization; (*desorden*) untidiness
descompuesto, -a [deskom'pwesto, a] *pp de* **descomponer** ▪ *adj* (*corrompido*) decomposed; (*roto*) broken (down)
descompuse *etc* [deskom'puse] *vb ver* **descomponer**
descomunal [deskomu'nal] *adj* (*enorme*) huge; (*fam: excelente*) fantastic
desconcertado, -a [deskonθer'taðo, a] *adj* disconcerted, bewildered
desconcertar [deskonθer'tar] *vt* (*confundir*) to baffle; (*incomodar*) to upset, put out; (*orden*) to disturb; **desconcertarse** *vr* (*turbarse*) to be upset; (*confundirse*) to be bewildered
desconchado, -a [deskon'tʃaðo, a] *adj* (*pintura*) peeling
desconchar [deskon'tʃar] *vt* (*pared*) to strip off; (*loza*) to chip off
desconcierto *etc* [deskon'θjerto] *vb ver* **desconcertar** ▪ *nm* (*gen*) disorder; (*desorientación*) uncertainty; (*inquietud*) uneasiness; (*confusión*) bewilderment
desconectado, -a [deskonek'taðo, a] *adj* (*Elec*) disconnected, switched off; (*Inform*) offline; **estar ~ de** (*fig*) to have no contact with
desconectar [deskonek'tar] *vt* to disconnect; (*desenchufar*) to unplug; (*radio, televisión*) to switch off; (*Inform*) to toggle off
desconfiado, -a [deskon'fjaðo, a] *adj* suspicious
desconfianza [deskon'fjanθa] *nf* distrust
desconfiar [deskon'fjar] *vi* to be distrustful; **~ de** (*sospechar*) to mistrust, suspect; (*no tener confianza en*) to have no faith *o* confidence in; **desconfío de ello** I doubt it; **desconfíe de las imitaciones** (*Com*) beware of imitations
desconforme [deskon'forme] *adj* = **disconforme**
descongelar [deskonxe'lar] *vt* (*nevera*) to defrost; (*comida*) to thaw; (*Auto*) to de-ice; (*Com, Pol*) to unfreeze
descongestionar [desconxestjo'nar] *vt* (*cabeza, tráfico*) to clear; (*calle, ciudad*) to relieve congestion in; (*fig: despejar*) to clear
desconocer [deskono'θer] *vt* (*ignorar*) not to know, be ignorant of; (*no aceptar*) to deny; (*repudiar*) to disown
desconocido, -a [deskono'θiðo, a] *adj* unknown; (*que no se conoce*) unfamiliar; (*no reconocido*) unrecognized ▪ *nm/f* stranger; (*recién llegado*) newcomer; **está ~** he is hardly recognizable
desconocimiento [deskonoθi'mjento] *nm* (*falta de conocimientos*) ignorance; (*repudio*) disregard
desconozca *etc* [desko'noθka] *vb ver* **desconocer**
desconsiderado, -a [deskonsiðe'raðo, a] *adj* inconsiderate; (*insensible*) thoughtless
desconsolado, -a [deskonso'laðo, a] *adj* (*afligido*) disconsolate; (*cara*) sad; (*desanimado*) dejected
desconsolar [deskonso'lar] *vt* to distress; **desconsolarse** *vr* to despair
desconsuelo *etc* [deskon'swelo] *vb ver* **desconsolar** ▪ *nm* (*tristeza*) distress; (*desesperación*) despair
descontado, -a [deskon'taðo, a] *adj*: **por ~** of course; **dar por ~ (que)** to take it for granted (that)
descontar [deskon'tar] *vt* (*deducir*) to take away, deduct; (*rebajar*) to discount
descontento, -a [deskon'tento, a] *adj* dissatisfied ▪ *nm* dissatisfaction, discontent
descontrol [deskon'trol] *nm* (*fam*) lack of control
descontrolado, -a [deskontro'laðo, a] *adj* uncontrolled
descontrolarse [deskontro'larse] *vr* (*persona*) to lose control
desconvenir [deskombe'nir] *vi* (*personas*) to disagree; (*no corresponder*) not to fit; (*no convenir*) to be inconvenient
desconvocar [deskombo'kar] *vt* to call off
descorazonar [deskoraθo'nar] *vt* to discourage, dishearten; **descorazonarse** *vr* to get discouraged, lose heart
descorchador [deskortʃa'ðor] *nm* corkscrew
descorchar [deskor'tʃar] *vt* to uncork, open
descorrer [desko'rrer] *vt* (*cortina, cerrojo*) to draw back; (*velo*) to remove
descortés [deskor'tes] *adj* (*mal educado*) discourteous; (*grosero*) rude
descortesía [deskorte'sia] *nf* discourtesy; (*grosería*) rudeness
descoser [desko'ser] *vt* to unstitch; **descoserse** *vr* to come apart (at the seams); (*fam: descubrir un secreto*) to blurt out a secret; **descoserse de risa** to split one's sides laughing

descosido, -a [desko'siðo, a] *adj* (*costura*) unstitched; (*desordenado*) disjointed ■ *nm*: **como un ~** (*obrar*) wildly; (*beber, comer*) to excess; (*estudiar*) like mad
descoyuntar [deskojun'tar] *vt* (*Anat*) to dislocate; (*hechos*) to twist; **descoyuntarse** *vr*: **descoyuntarse un hueso** (*Anat*) to put a bone out of joint; **descoyuntarse de risa** (*fam*) to split one's sides laughing; **estar descoyuntado** (*persona*) to be double-jointed
descrédito [des'kreðito] *nm* discredit; **caer en ~** to fall into disrepute; **ir en ~ de** to be to the discredit of
descreído, -a [deskre'iðo, a] *adj* (*incrédulo*) incredulous; (*falto de fe*) unbelieving
descremado, -a [deskre'maðo, a] *adj* skimmed
descremar [deskre'mar] *vt* (*leche*) to skim
describir [deskri'βir] *vt* to describe
descripción [deskrip'θjon] *nf* description
descrito [des'krito] *pp de* **describir**
descuajar [deskwa'xar] *vt* (*disolver*) to melt; (*planta*) to pull out by the roots; (*extirpar*) to eradicate, wipe out; (*desanimar*) to dishearten
descuajaringarse [deskwaxarin'garse] *vr* to fall to bits
descuajaringue *etc* [deskwaxa'ringe] *vb ver* **descuajaringarse**
descuartice *etc* [deskwar'tiθe] *vb ver* **descuartizar**
descuartizar [deskwarti'θar] *vt* (*animal*) to carve up, cut up; (*fig: hacer pedazos*) to tear apart
descubierto, -a [desku'βjerto, a] *pp de* **descubrir** ■ *adj* uncovered, bare; (*persona*) bare-headed; (*cielo*) clear; (*coche*) open; (*campo*) treeless ■ *nm* (*lugar*) open space; (*Com: en el presupuesto*) shortage; (*: bancario*) overdraft; **al ~** in the open; **poner al ~** to lay bare; **quedar al ~** to be exposed; **estar en ~** to be overdrawn
descubridor, a [deskuβri'ðor, a] *nm/f* discoverer
descubrimiento [deskuβri'mjento] *nm* (*hallazgo*) discovery; (*de criminal, fraude*) detection; (*revelación*) revelation; (*de secreto etc*) disclosure; (*de estatua etc*) unveiling
descubrir [desku'βrir] *vt* to discover, find; (*petróleo*) to strike; (*inaugurar*) to unveil; (*vislumbrar*) to detect; (*sacar a luz: crimen*) to bring to light; (*revelar*) to reveal, show; (*poner al descubierto*) to expose to view; (*naipes*) to lay down; (*quitar la tapa de*) to uncover; (*cacerola*) to take the lid off; (*enterarse de: causa, solución*) to find out; (*divisar*) to see, make out; (*delatar*) to give away, betray; **descubrirse** *vr* to reveal o.s.; (*quitarse sombrero*) to take off one's hat; (*confesar*) to confess; (*fig: salir a luz*) to come out o to light
descuelga *etc* [des'kwelɣa], **descuelgue** *etc* [des'kwelɣe] *vb ver* **descolgar**
descuelle *etc* [des'kweʎe] *vb ver* **descollar**
descuento *etc* [des'kwento] *vb ver* **descontar** ■ *nm* discount; **~ del 3%** 3% off; **con ~** at a discount; **~ por pago al contado** (*Com*) cash discount; **~ por volumen de compras** (*Com*) volume discount
descuidado, -a [deskwi'ðaðo, a] *adj* (*sin cuidado*) careless; (*desordenado*) untidy; (*olvidadizo*) forgetful; (*dejado*) neglected; (*desprevenido*) unprepared
descuidar [deskwi'ðar] *vt* (*dejar*) to neglect; (*olvidar*) to overlook ■ *vi*, **descuidarse** *vr* (*distraerse*) to be careless; (*estar desaliñado*) to let o.s. go; (*desprevenirse*) to drop one's guard; **¡descuida!** don't worry!
descuido [des'kwiðo] *nm* (*dejadez*) carelessness; (*olvido*) negligence; (*un descuido*) oversight; **al ~** casually; (*sin cuidado*) carelessly; **al menor ~** if my *etc* attention wanders for a minute; **con ~** thoughtlessly; **por ~** by an oversight

PALABRA CLAVE

desde ['desðe] *prep* **1** (*lugar*) from; **desde Burgos hasta mi casa hay 30 km** it's 30 kms from Burgos to my house; **desde lejos** from a distance
2 (*posición*): **hablaba desde el balcón** she was speaking from the balcony
3 (*tiempo: +adv, n*): **desde ahora** from now on; **desde entonces/la boda** since then/the wedding; **desde niño** since I *etc* was a child; **desde tres años atrás** since three years ago
4 (*tiempo: +vb*) since; for; **nos conocemos desde 1978/desde hace 20 años** we've known each other since 1978/for 20 years; **no le veo desde 1983/desde hace 5 años** I haven't seen him since 1983/for 5 years; **¿desde cuándo vives aquí?** how long have you lived here?
5 (*gama*): **desde los más lujosos hasta los más económicos** from the most luxurious to the most reasonably priced
6: **desde luego (que no)** of course (not)
■ *conj*: **desde que**: **desde que recuerdo** for as long as I can remember; **desde que llegó no ha salido** he hasn't been out since he arrived

desdecir [desðe'θir] *vi*: **~ de** (*no merecer*) to be unworthy of; (*no corresponder*) to clash with; **desdecirse** *vr*: **desdecirse de** to go back on

desdén [des'ðen] *nm* scorn
desdentado, -a [desðen'taðo, a] *adj* toothless
desdeñable [desðe'ɲaβle] *adj* contemptible; **nada ~** far from negligible, considerable
desdeñar [desðe'ɲar] *vt* (*despreciar*) to scorn
desdeñoso, -a [desðe'ɲoso, a] *adj* scornful
desdibujar [desðiβu'xar] *vt* to blur (the outlines of); **desdibujarse** *vr* to get blurred, fade (away); **el recuerdo se ha desdibujado** the memory has become blurred
desdichado, -a [desði'tʃaðo, a] *adj* (*sin suerte*) unlucky; (*infeliz*) unhappy; (*día*) ill-fated ■ *nm/f* (*pobre desgraciado*) poor devil
desdicho, -a [des'ðitʃo, a] *pp de* **desdecir** ■ *nf* (*desgracia*) misfortune; (*infelicidad*) unhappiness
desdiciendo *etc* [desði'θjendo] *vb ver* **desdecir**
desdiga *etc* [des'ðiɣa], **desdije** *etc* [des'dixe] *vb ver* **desdecir**
desdoblado, -a [desðo'βlaðo, a] *adj* (*personalidad*) split
desdoblar [desðo'βlar] *vt* (*extender*) to spread out; (*desplegar*) to unfold
deseable [dese'aβle] *adj* desirable
desear [dese'ar] *vt* to want, desire, wish for; **¿qué desea la señora?** (*tienda etc*) what can I do for you, madam?; **estoy deseando que esto termine** I'm longing for this to finish
desecar [dese'kar] *vt*, **desecarse** *vr* to dry up
desechable [dese'tʃaβle] *adj* (*envase etc*) disposable
desechar [dese'tʃar] *vt* (*basura*) to throw out *o* away; (*ideas*) to reject, discard; (*miedo*) to cast aside; (*plan*) to drop
desecho [de'setʃo] *nm* (*desprecio*) contempt; (*lo peor*) dregs *pl*; **desechos** *nmpl* rubbish *sg*, waste *sg*; **de ~** (*hierro*) scrap; (*producto*) waste; (*ropa*) cast-off
desembalar [desemba'lar] *vt* to unpack
desembarace *etc* [desemba'raθe] *vb ver* **desembarazar**
desembarazado, -a [desembara'θaðo, a] *adj* (*libre*) clear, free; (*desenvuelto*) free and easy
desembarazar [desembara'θar] *vt* (*desocupar*) to clear; (*desenredar*) to free; **desembarazarse** *vr*: **desembarazarse de** to free o.s. of, get rid of
desembarazo [desemba'raθo] *nm* (*acto*) clearing; (*Am: parto*) birth; (*desenfado*) ease
desembarcadero [desembarka'ðero] *nm* quay
desembarcar [desembar'kar] *vt* (*personas*) to land; (*mercancías etc*) to unload ■ *vi*, **desembarcarse** *vr* (*de barco, avión*) to disembark
desembarco [desem'barko] *nm* landing
desembargar [desembar'ɣar] *vt* (*gen*) to free; (*Jur*) to remove the embargo on
desembargue *etc* [desem'βarɣe] *vb ver* **desembargar**
desembarque *etc* [desem'barke] *vb ver* **desembarcar** ■ *nm* disembarkation; (*de pasajeros*) landing; (*de mercancías*) unloading
desembocadura [desemboka'ðura] *nf* (*de río*) mouth; (*de calle*) opening
desembocar [desembo'kar] *vi*: **~ en** to flow into; (*fig*) to result in
desemboce *etc* [desem'boθe] *vb ver* **desembozar**
desembolsar [desembol'sar] *vt* (*pagar*) to pay out; (*gastar*) to lay out
desembolso [desem'bolso] *nm* payment
desemboque *etc* [desem'boke] *vb ver* **desembocar**
desembozar [desembo'θar] *vt* to unmask
desembragar [desembra'ɣar] *vt* (*Tec*) to disengage, release ■ *vi* (*Auto*) to declutch
desembrague *etc* [desem'βraɣe] *vb ver* **desembragar**
desembrollar [desembro'ʎar] *vt* (*madeja*) to unravel; (*asunto, malentendido*) to sort out
desembuchar [desembu'tʃar] *vt* to disgorge; (*fig*) to come out with ■ *vi* (*confesar*) to spill the beans (*fam*); **¡desembucha!** out with it!
desemejante [deseme'xante] *adj* dissimilar; **~ de** different from, unlike
desemejanza [deseme'xanθa] *nf* dissimilarity
desempacar [desempa'kar] *vt* (*esp Am*) to unpack
desempañar [desempa'ɲar] *vt* (*cristal*) to clean, demist
desempaque *etc* [desem'pake] *vb ver* **desempacar**
desempaquetar [desempake'tar] *vt* to unpack, unwrap
desempatar [desempa'tar] *vi* to break a tie; **volvieron a jugar para ~** they held a play-off
desempate [desem'pate] *nm* (*Fútbol*) play-off; (*Tenis*) tie-break(er)
desempeñar [desempe'ɲar] *vt* (*cargo*) to hold; (*papel*) to play; (*deber, función*) to perform, carry out; (*lo empeñado*) to redeem; **desempeñarse** *vr* to get out of debt; **~ un papel** (*fig*) to play (a role)
desempeño [desem'peɲo] *nm* occupation; (*de lo empeñado*) redeeming; **de mucho ~** very capable
desempleado, -a [desemple'aðo, a] *adj* unemployed, out of work ■ *nm/f* unemployed person
desempleo [desem'pleo] *nm* unemployment
desempolvar [desempol'βar] *vt* (*muebles etc*)

to dust; (*lo olvidado*) to revive
desencadenar [desenkaðe'nar] *vt* to unchain; (*ira*) to unleash; (*provocar*) to cause, set off; **desencadenarse** *vr* to break loose; (*tormenta*) to burst; (*guerra*) to break out; **se desencadenó una lucha violenta** a violent struggle ensued
desencajar [desenka'xar] *vt* (*hueso*) to put out of joint; (*mandíbula*) to dislocate; (*mecanismo, pieza*) to disconnect, disengage
desencantar [desenkan'tar] *vt* to disillusion, disenchant
desencanto [desen'kanto] *nm* disillusionment, disenchantment
desenchufar [desentʃu'far] *vt* to unplug, disconnect
desenfadado, -a [desenfa'ðaðo, a] *adj* (*desenvuelto*) uninhibited; (*descarado*) forward; (*en el vestir*) casual
desenfado [desen'faðo] *nm* (*libertad*) freedom; (*comportamiento*) free and easy manner; (*descaro*) forwardness; (*desenvoltura*) self-confidence
desenfocado, -a [desenfo'kaðo, a] *adj* (*Foto*) out of focus
desenfrenado, -a [desenfre'naðo, a] *adj* (*descontrolado*) uncontrolled; (*inmoderado*) unbridled
desenfrenarse [desenfre'narse] *vr* (*persona: desmandarse*) to lose all self-control; (*multitud*) to run riot; (*tempestad*) to burst; (*viento*) to rage
desenfreno [desen'freno] *nm* (*vicio*) wildness; (*falta de control*) lack of self-control; (*de pasiones*) unleashing
desenganchar [desengan'tʃar] *vt* (*gen*) to unhook; (*Ferro*) to uncouple; (*Tec*) to disengage
desengañar [desenga'ɲar] *vt* to disillusion; (*abrir los ojos a*) to open the eyes of; **desengañarse** *vr* to become disillusioned; **¡desengáñate!** don't you believe it!
desengaño [desen'gaɲo] *nm* disillusionment; (*decepción*) disappointment; **sufrir un ~ amoroso** to be disappointed in love
desengrasar [desengra'sar] *vt* to degrease
desenlace *etc* [desen'laθe] *vb ver* **desenlazar** ▪ *nm* outcome; (*Lit*) ending
desenlazar [desenla'θar] *vt* (*desatar*) to untie; (*problema*) to solve; (*aclarar: asunto*) to unravel; **desenlazarse** *vr* (*desatarse*) to come undone; (*Lit*) to end
desenmarañar [desenmara'ɲar] *vt* (*fig*) to unravel
desenmascarar [desenmaska'rar] *vt* to unmask, expose
desenredar [desenre'ðar] *vt* to resolve
desenrollar [desenro'ʎar] *vt* to unroll, unwind
desenroscar [desenros'kar] *vt* (*tornillo etc*) to unscrew
desenrosque *etc* [desen'roske] *vb ver* **desenroscar**
desentenderse [desenten'derse] *vr*: **~ de** to pretend not to know about; (*apartarse*) to have nothing to do with
desentendido, -a [desenten'diðo, a] *adj*: **hacerse el ~** to pretend not to notice; **se hizo el ~** he didn't take the hint
desenterrar [desente'rrar] *vt* to exhume; (*tesoro, fig*) to unearth, dig up
desentierre *etc* [desen'tjerre] *vb ver* **desenterrar**
desentonar [desento'nar] *vi* (*Mus*) to sing (*o* play) out of tune; (*no encajar*) to be out of place; (*color*) to clash
desentorpecer [desentorpe'θer] *vt* (*miembro*) to stretch; (*fam: persona*) to polish up
desentorpezca *etc* [desentor'peθka] *vb ver* **desentorpecer**
desentrañar [desentra'ɲar] *vt* (*misterio*) to unravel
desentrenado, -a [desentre'naðo, a] *adj* out of training
desentumecer [desentume'θer] *vt* (*pierna etc*) to stretch; (*Deporte*) to loosen up
desentumezca *etc* [desentu'meθka] *vb ver* **desentumecer**
desenvainar [desembai'nar] *vt* (*espada*) to draw, unsheathe
desenvoltura [desembol'tura] *nf* (*libertad, gracia*) ease; (*descaro*) free and easy manner; (*al hablar*) fluency
desenvolver [desembol'βer] *vt* (*paquete*) to unwrap; (*fig*) to develop; **desenvolverse** *vr* (*desarrollarse*) to unfold, develop; (*suceder*) to go off; (*prosperar*) to prosper; (*arreglárselas*) to cope
desenvolvimiento [desembolβi'mjento] *nm* (*desarrollo*) development; (*de idea*) exposition
desenvuelto, -a [desem'bwelto, a] *pp de* **desenvolver** ▪ *adj* (*suelto*) easy; (*desenfadado*) confident; (*al hablar*) fluent; (*pey*) forward
desenvuelva *etc* [desem'buelβa] *vb ver* **desenvolver**
deseo [de'seo] *nm* desire, wish; **~ de saber** thirst for knowledge; **buen ~** good intentions *pl*; **arder en deseos de algo** to yearn for sth
deseoso, -a [dese'oso, a] *adj*: **estar ~ de hacer** to be anxious to do
deseque *etc* [de'seke] *vb ver* **desecar**
desequilibrado, -a [desekili'βraðo, a] *adj* unbalanced ▪ *nm/f* unbalanced person; **~ mental** mentally disturbed person

desequilibrar [desekili'βrar] *vt* (*mente*) to unbalance; (*objeto*) to throw out of balance; (*persona*) to throw off balance
desequilibrio [deseki'liβrio] *nm* (*mental*) unbalance; (*entre cantidades*) imbalance; (*Med*) unbalanced mental condition
desertar [deser'tar] *vt* (*Jur: derecho de apelación*) to forfeit ■ *vi* to desert; ~ **de sus deberes** to neglect one's duties
desértico, -a [de'sertiko, a] *adj* desert *cpd*; (*vacío*) deserted
desertor, a [deser'tor, a] *nm/f* deserter
desesperación [desespera'θjon] *nf* desperation, despair; (*irritación*) fury; **es una** ~ it's maddening; **es una ~ tener que ...** it's infuriating to have to ...
desesperado, -a [desespe'raðo, a] *adj* (*persona: sin esperanza*) desperate; (*caso, situación*) hopeless; (*esfuerzo*) furious ■ *nm*: **como un** ~ like mad ■ *nf*: **hacer algo a la desesperada** to do sth as a last resort *o* in desperation
desesperance *etc* [desespe'ranθe] *vb ver* **desesperanzar**
desesperante [desespe'rante] *adj* (*exasperante*) infuriating; (*persona*) hopeless
desesperanzar [desesperan'θar] *vt* to drive to despair; **desesperanzarse** *vr* to lose hope, despair
desesperar [desespe'rar] *vt* to drive to despair; (*exasperar*) to drive to distraction ■ *vi*: ~ **de** to despair of; **desesperarse** *vr* to despair, lose hope
desespero [deses'pero] *nm* (*Am*) despair
desestabilice *etc* [desestaβi'liθe] *vb ver* **desestabilizar**
desestabilizar [desestaβili'θar] *vt* to destabilize
desestimar [desesti'mar] *vt* (*menospreciar*) to have a low opinion of; (*rechazar*) to reject
desfachatez [desfatʃa'teθ] *nf* (*insolencia*) impudence; (*descaro*) rudeness
desfalco [des'falko] *nm* embezzlement
desfallecer [desfaʎe'θer] *vi* (*perder las fuerzas*) to become weak; (*desvanecerse*) to faint
desfallecido, -a [desfaʎe'θiðo, a] *adj* (*débil*) weak
desfallezca *etc* [desfa'ʎeθka] *vb ver* **desfallecer**
desfasado, -a [desfa'saðo, a] *adj* (*anticuado*) old-fashioned; (*Tec*) out of phase
desfasar [desfa'sar] *vt* to phase out
desfase [des'fase] *nm* (*diferencia*) gap
desfavorable [desfaβo'raβle] *adj* unfavourable
desfavorecer [desfaβore'θer] *vt* (*sentar mal*) not to suit
desfavorezca *etc* [desfaβo'reθka] *vb ver* **desfavorecer**
desfiguración [desfiɣura'θjon] *nf*, **desfiguramiento** [desfiɣura'mjento] *nm* (*de persona*) disfigurement; (*de monumento*) defacement; (*Foto*) blurring
desfigurar [desfiɣu'rar] *vt* (*cara*) to disfigure; (*cuerpo*) to deform; (*cuadro, monumento*) to deface; (*Foto*) to blur; (*sentido*) to twist; (*suceso*) to misrepresent
desfiladero [desfila'ðero] *nm* gorge, defile
desfilar [desfi'lar] *vi* to parade; **desfilaron ante el general** they marched past the general
desfile [des'file] *nm* procession; (*Mil*) parade; ~ **de modelos** fashion show
desflorar [desflo'rar] *vt* (*mujer*) to deflower; (*arruinar*) to tarnish; (*asunto*) to touch on
desfogar [desfo'ɣar] *vt* (*fig*) to vent ■ *vi* (*Naut: tormenta*) to burst; **desfogarse** *vr* (*fig*) to let off steam
desfogue *etc* [des'foɣe] *vb ver* **desfogar**
desgajar [desɣa'xar] *vt* (*arrancar*) to tear off; (*romper*) to break off; (*naranja*) to split into segments; **desgajarse** *vr* to come off
desgana [des'ɣana] *nf* (*falta de apetito*) loss of appetite; (*renuencia*) unwillingness; **hacer algo a** ~ to do sth unwillingly
desganado, -a [desɣa'naðo, a] *adj*: **estar** ~ (*sin apetito*) to have no appetite; (*sin entusiasmo*) to have lost interest
desgañitarse [desɣaɲi'tarse] *vr* to shout o.s. hoarse
desgarbado, -a [desɣar'βaðo, a] *adj* (*sin gracia*) clumsy, ungainly
desgarrador, a [desɣarra'ðor, a] *adj* heartrending
desgarrar [desɣa'rrar] *vt* to tear (up); (*fig*) to shatter
desgarro [des'ɣarro] *nm* (*en tela*) tear; (*aflicción*) grief; (*descaro*) impudence
desgastar [desɣas'tar] *vt* (*deteriorar*) to wear away *o* down; (*estropear*) to spoil; **desgastarse** *vr* to get worn out
desgaste [des'ɣaste] *nm* wear (and tear); (*de roca*) erosion; (*de cuerda*) fraying; (*de metal*) corrosion; ~ **económico** drain on one's resources
desglosar [desɣlo'sar] *vt* to detach
desgobernar [desɣoβer'nar] *vb* (*Pol*) to misgovern, misrule; (*asunto*) to handle badly; (*Anat*) to dislocate
desgobierno *etc* [desɣo'βjerno] *vb ver* **desgobernar** ■ *nm* (*Pol*) misgovernment, misrule
desgracia [des'ɣraθja] *nf* misfortune; (*accidente*) accident; (*vergüenza*) disgrace;

(*contratiempo*) setback; **por ~** unfortunately; **en el accidente no hay que lamentar desgracias personales** there were no casualties in the accident; **caer en ~** to fall from grace; **tener la ~ de** to be unlucky enough to

desgraciadamente [desɣraθjaða'mente] *adv* unfortunately

desgraciado, -a [desɣra'θjaðo, a] *adj* (*sin suerte*) unlucky, unfortunate; (*miserable*) wretched; (*infeliz*) miserable ■ *nm/f* (*malvado*) swine; (*infeliz*) poor creature; **¡esa radio desgraciada!** (*esp Am*) that lousy radio!

desgraciar [desɣra'θjar] *vt* (*estropear*) to spoil; (*ofender*) to displease

desgranar [desɣra'nar] *vt* (*trigo*) to thresh; (*guisantes*) to shell; **~ un racimo** to pick the grapes from a bunch; **~ mentiras** to come out with a string of lies

desgravación [desɣraβa'θjon] *nf* (*Com*): **~ de impuestos** tax relief; **~ personal** personal allowance

desgravar [desɣra'βar] *vt* (*producto*) to reduce the tax *o* duty on

desgreñado, -a [desɣre'ɲaðo, a] *adj* dishevelled

desguace [des'ɣwaθe] *nm* (*de coches*) scrapping; (*lugar*) scrapyard

desguazar [desɣwa'θar] *vt* (*coche*) to scrap

deshabitado, -a [desaβi'taðo, a] *adj* uninhabited

deshabitar [desaβi'tar] *vt* (*casa*) to leave empty; (*despoblar*) to depopulate

deshacer [desa'θer] *vt* (*lo hecho*) to undo, unmake; (*proyectos: arruinar*) to spoil; (*casa*) to break up; (*Tec*) to take apart; (*enemigo*) to defeat; (*diluir*) to melt; (*contrato*) to break; (*intriga*) to solve; (*cama*) to strip; (*maleta*) to unpack; (*paquete*) to unwrap; (*nudo*) to untie; (*costura*) to unpick; **deshacerse** *vr* (*desatarse*) to come undone; (*estropearse*) to be spoiled; (*descomponerse*) to fall to pieces; (*disolverse*) to melt; (*despedazarse*) to come apart *o* undone; **deshacerse de** to get rid of; (*Com*) to dump, unload; **deshacerse en** (*cumplidos, elogios*) to be lavish with; **deshacerse en lágrimas** to burst into tears; **deshacerse por algo** to be crazy about sth

deshaga *etc* [de'saɣa], **desharé** *etc* [desa're] *vb ver* **deshacer**

desharrapado, -a [desarra'paðo, a] *adj* = **desarrapado**

deshecho, -a [de'setʃo, a] *pp de* **deshacer** ■ *adj* (*lazo, nudo*) undone; (*roto*) smashed; (*despedazado*) in pieces; (*cama*) unmade; (*Med: persona*) weak, emaciated; (*: salud*) broken; **estoy ~** I'm shattered

deshelar [dese'lar] *vt* (*cañería*) to thaw; (*heladera*) to defrost

desheredar [desere'ðar] *vt* to disinherit

deshice *etc* [de'siθe] *vb ver* **deshacer**

deshidratación [desiðrata'θjon] *nf* dehydration

deshidratar [desiðra'tar] *vt* to dehydrate

deshielo *etc* [des'jelo] *vb ver* **deshelar** ■ *nm* thaw

deshilachar [desila'tʃar] *vt*, **deshilacharse** *vr* to fray

deshilar [desi'lar] *vt* (*tela*) to unravel

deshilvanado, -a [desilβa'naðo, a] *adj* (*fig*) disjointed, incoherent

deshinchar [desin'tʃar] *vt* (*neumático*) to let down; (*herida etc*) to reduce (the swelling of); **deshincharse** *vr* (*neumático*) to go flat; (*hinchazón*) to go down

deshojar [deso'xar] *vt* (*árbol*) to strip the leaves off; (*flor*) to pull the petals off; **deshojarse** *vr* to lose its leaves *etc*

deshollinar [desoʎi'nar] *vt* (*chimenea*) to sweep

deshonesto, -a [deso'nesto, a] *adj* (*no honrado*) dishonest; (*indecente*) indecent

deshonor [deso'nor] *nm* dishonour, disgrace; (*un deshonor*) insult, affront

deshonra [de'sonra] *nf* (*deshonor*) dishonour; (*vergüenza*) shame

deshonrar [deson'rar] *vt* to dishonour

deshonroso, -a [deson'roso, a] *adj* dishonourable, disgraceful

deshora [de'sora]: **a ~** *adv* at the wrong time; (*llegar*) unexpectedly; (*acostarse*) at some unearthly hour

deshuesar [deswe'sar] *vt* (*carne*) to bone; (*fruta*) to stone

desidia [de'siðja] *nf* (*pereza*) idleness

desierto, -a [de'sjerto, a] *adj* (*casa, calle, negocio*) deserted; (*paisaje*) bleak ■ *nm* desert

designación [desiɣna'θjon] *nf* (*para un cargo*) appointment; (*nombre*) designation

designar [desiɣ'nar] *vt* (*nombrar*) to designate; (*indicar*) to fix

designio [de'siɣnjo] *nm* plan; **con el ~ de** with the intention of

desigual [desi'ɣwal] *adj* (*lucha*) unequal; (*diferente*) different; (*terreno*) uneven; (*tratamiento*) unfair; (*cambiadizo: tiempo*) changeable; (*: carácter*) unpredictable

desigualdad [desiɣwal'dað] *nf* (*Econ, Pol*) inequality; (*de carácter, tiempo*) unpredictability; (*de escritura*) unevenness; (*de terreno*) roughness

desilusión [desilu'sjon] *nf* disillusionment; (*decepción*) disappointment

desilusionar [desilusjo'nar] *vt* to disillusion;

(*decepcionar*) to disappoint; **desilusionarse** *vr* to become disillusioned
desinencia [desi'nenθja] *nf* (*Ling*) ending
desinfectar [desinfek'tar] *vt* to disinfect
desinfestar [desinfes'tar] *vt* to decontaminate
desinflación [desinfla'θjon] *nf* (*Com*) disinflation
desinflar [desin'flar] *vt* to deflate; **desinflarse** *vr* (*neumático*) to go down *o* flat
desintegración [desinteɣra'θjon] *nf* disintegration; **~ nuclear** nuclear fission
desintegrar [desinte'ɣrar] *vt* (*gen*) to disintegrate; (*átomo*) to split; (*grupo*) to break up; **desintegrarse** *vr* to disintegrate; to split; to break up
desinterés [desinte'res] *nm* (*objetividad*) disinterestedness; (*altruismo*) unselfishness
desinteresado, -a [desintere'saðo, a] *adj* (*imparcial*) disinterested; (*altruista*) unselfish
desintoxicar [desintoksi'kar] *vt* to detoxify; **desintoxicarse** *vr* (*drogadicto*) to undergo treatment for drug addiction; **desintoxicarse de** (*rutina, trabajo*) to get away from
desintoxique *etc* [desintok'sike] *vb ver* **desintoxicar**
desistir [desis'tir] *vi* (*renunciar*) to stop, desist; **~ de** (*empresa*) to give up; (*derecho*) to waive
deslavazado, -a [deslaβa'θaðo, a] *adj* (*lacio*) limp; (*desteñido*) faded; (*insípido*) colourless; (*incoherente*) disjointed
desleal [desle'al] *adj* (*infiel*) disloyal; (*Com: competencia*) unfair
deslealtad [desleal'tað] *nf* disloyalty
desleído, -a [desle'iðo, a] *adj* weak, woolly
desleír [desle'ir] *vt* (*líquido*) to dilute; (*sólido*) to dissolve
deslenguado, -a [deslen'gwaðo, a] *adj* (*grosero*) foul-mouthed
deslía *etc* [des'lia] *vb ver* **desleír**
desliar [des'ljar] *vt* (*desatar*) to untie; (*paquete*) to open; **desliarse** *vr* to come undone
deslice *etc* [des'liθe] *vb ver* **deslizar**
desliendo *etc* [desli'endo] *vb ver* **desleír**
desligar [desli'ɣar] *vt* (*desatar*) to untie, undo; (*separar*) to separate; **desligarse** *vr* (*de un compromiso*) to extricate o.s.
desligue *etc* [des'liɣe] *vb ver* **desligar**
deslindar [deslin'dar] *vt* (*señalar las lindes de*) to mark out, fix the boundaries of; (*fig*) to define
desliz [des'liθ] *nm* (*fig*) lapse; **~ de lengua** slip of the tongue; **cometer un ~** to slip up
deslizar [desli'θar] *vt* to slip, slide; **deslizarse** *vr* (*escurrirse: persona*) to slip, slide; (*: coche*) to skid; (*aguas mansas*) to flow gently; (*error*) to creep in; (*tiempo*) to pass; (*persona: irse*) to slip away; **deslizarse en un cuarto** to slip into a room
deslomar [deslo'mar] *vt* (*romper el lomo de*) to break the back of; (*fig*) to wear out; **deslomarse** *vr* (*fig, fam*) to work one's guts out
deslucido, -a [deslu'θiðo, a] *adj* dull; (*torpe*) awkward, graceless; (*deslustrado*) tarnished; (*fracasado*) unsuccessful; **quedar ~** to make a poor impression
deslucir [deslu'θir] *vt* (*deslustrar*) to tarnish; (*estropear*) to spoil, ruin; (*persona*) to discredit; **la lluvia deslució el acto** the rain ruined the ceremony
deslumbrar [deslum'brar] *vt* (*con la luz*) to dazzle; (*cegar*) to blind; (*impresionar*) to dazzle; (*dejar perplejo a*) to puzzle, confuse
deslustrar [deslus'trar] *vt* (*vidrio*) to frost; (*quitar lustre a*) to dull; (*reputación*) to sully
desluzca *etc* [des'luθka] *vb ver* **deslucir**
desmadrarse [desma'ðrarse] *vr* (*fam*) to run wild
desmadre [des'maðre] *nm* (*fam: desorganización*) chaos; (*: jaleo*) commotion
desmán [des'man] *nm* (*exceso*) outrage; (*abuso de poder*) abuse
desmandarse [desman'darse] *vr* (*portarse mal*) to behave badly; (*excederse*) to get out of hand; (*caballo*) to bolt
desmano [des'mano]: **a ~** *adv*: **me coge** *o* **pilla a desmano** it's out of my way
desmantelar [desmante'lar] *vt* (*deshacer*) to dismantle; (*casa*) to strip; (*organización*) to disband; (*Mil*) to raze; (*andamio*) to take down; (*Naut*) to unrig
desmaquillador [desmakiʎa'ðor] *nm* make-up remover
desmaquillarse [desmaki'ʎarse] *vr* to take off one's make-up
desmarcarse [desmar'karse] *vr*: **~ de** (*Deporte*) to get clear of; (*fig*) to distance o.s. from
desmayado, -a [desma'jaðo, a] *adj* (*sin sentido*) unconscious; (*carácter*) dull; (*débil*) faint, weak; (*color*) pale
desmayar [desma'jar] *vi* to lose heart; **desmayarse** *vr* (*Med*) to faint
desmayo [des'majo] *nm* (*Med: acto*) faint; (*estado*) unconsciousness; (*depresión*) dejection; (*de voz*) faltering; **sufrir un ~** to have a fainting fit
desmedido, -a [desme'ðiðo, a] *adj* excessive; (*ambición*) boundless
desmejorado, -a [desmexo'raðo, a] *adj*: **está muy desmejorada** (*Med*) she's not looking too well

desmejorar [desmexo'rar] *vt* (*dañar*) to impair, spoil; (*Med*) to weaken
desmembración [desmembra'θjon] *nf* dismemberment; (*fig*) break-up
desmembrar [desmem'brar] *vt* (*Med*) to dismember; (*fig*) to separate
desmemoriado, -a [desmemo'rjaðo, a] *adj* forgetful, absent-minded
desmentir [desmen'tir] *vt* (*contradecir*) to contradict; (*refutar*) to deny; (*rumor*) to scotch ■ *vi*: **~ de** to refute; **desmentirse** *vr* to contradict o.s.
desmenuce *etc* [desme'nuθe] *vb ver* **desmenuzar**
desmenuzar [desmenu'θar] *vt* (*deshacer*) to crumble; (*carne*) to chop; (*examinar*) to examine closely
desmerecer [desmere'θer] *vt* to be unworthy of ■ *vi* (*deteriorarse*) to deteriorate
desmerezca *etc* [desme'reθka] *vb ver* **desmerecer**
desmesurado, -a [desmesu'raðo, a] *adj* (*desmedido*) disproportionate; (*enorme*) enormous; (*ambición*) boundless; (*descarado*) insolent
desmiembre *etc* [des'mjembre] *vb ver* **desmembrar**
desmienta *etc* [des'mjenta] *vb ver* **desmentir**
desmigajar [desmiɣa'xar], **desmigar** [desmi'ɣar] *vt* to crumble
desmigue *etc* [des'miɣe] *vb ver* **desmigar**
desmilitarice *etc* [desmilita'riθe] *vb ver* **desmilitarizar**
desmilitarizar [desmilitari'θar] *vt* to demilitarize
desmintiendo *etc* [desmin'tjendo] *vb ver* **desmentir**
desmochar [desmo'tʃar] *vt* (*árbol*) to lop; (*texto*) to cut, hack about
desmontable [desmon'taβle] *adj* (*que se quita*) detachable; (*en compartimientos*) sectional; (*que se puede plegar etc*) collapsible
desmontar [desmon'tar] *vt* (*deshacer*) to dismantle; (*motor*) to strip down; (*máquina*) to take apart; (*escopeta*) to uncock; (*tienda de campaña*) to take down; (*tierra*) to level; (*quitar los árboles a*) to clear; (*jinete*) to throw ■ *vi* to dismount
desmonte [des'monte] *nm* (*de tierra*) levelling; (*de árboles*) clearing; (*terreno*) levelled ground; (*Ferro*) cutting
desmoralice *etc* [desmora'liθe] *vb ver* **desmoralizar**
desmoralizador, a [desmoraliθa'ðor, a] *adj* demoralizing
desmoralizar [desmorali'θar] *vt* to demoralize
desmoronado, -a [desmoro'naðo, a] *adj* (*casa, edificio*) dilapidated
desmoronamiento [desmorona'mjento] *nm* (*tb fig*) crumbling
desmoronar [desmoro'nar] *vt* to wear away, erode; **desmoronarse** *vr* (*edificio, dique*) to fall into disrepair; (*economía*) to decline
desmovilice *etc* [desmoβi'liθe] *vb ver* **desmovilizar**
desmovilizar [desmoβili'θar] *vt* to demobilize
desnacionalización [desnaθjonaliθa'θjon] *nf* denationalization
desnacionalizado, -a [desnaθjonali'θaðo, a] *adj* (*industria*) denationalized; (*persona*) stateless
desnatado, -a [desna'taðo, a] *adj* skimmed; (*yogur*) low-fat
desnatar [desna'tar] *vt* (*leche*) to skim; **leche sin ~** whole milk
desnaturalice *etc* [desnatura'liθe] *vb ver* **desnaturalizar**
desnaturalizado, -a [desnaturali'θaðo, a] *adj* (*persona*) unnatural; **alcohol ~** methylated spirits
desnaturalizar [desnaturali'θar] *vt* (*Química*) to denature; (*corromper*) to pervert; (*sentido de algo*) to distort; **desnaturalizarse** *vr* (*perder la nacionalidad*) to give up one's nationality
desnivel [desni'βel] *nm* (*de terreno*) unevenness; (*Pol*) inequality; (*diferencia*) difference
desnivelar [desniβe'lar] *vt* (*terreno*) to make uneven; (*fig: desequilibrar*) to unbalance; (*balanza*) to tip
desnuclearizado, -a [desnukleari'θaðo, a] *adj*: **región desnuclearizada** nuclear-free zone
desnudar [desnu'ðar] *vt* (*desvestir*) to undress; (*despojar*) to strip; **desnudarse** *vr* (*desvestirse*) to get undressed
desnudez [desnu'ðeθ] *nf* (*de persona*) nudity; (*fig*) bareness
desnudo, -a [des'nuðo, a] *adj* (*cuerpo*) naked; (*árbol, brazo*) bare; (*paisaje*) flat; (*estilo*) unadorned; (*verdad*) plain ■ *nm/f* nude; **~ de** devoid *o* bereft of; **la retrató al ~** he painted her in the nude; **poner al ~** to lay bare
desnutrición [desnutri'θjon] *nf* malnutrition
desnutrido, -a [desnu'triðo, a] *adj* undernourished
desobedecer [desoβeðe'θer] *vt, vi* to disobey
desobedezca *etc* [desoβe'ðeθka] *vb ver* **desobedecer**
desobediencia [desoβe'ðjenθja] *nf* disobedience

desocupación [desokupa'θjon] *nf (Am)* unemployment
desocupado, -a [desoku'paðo, a] *adj* at leisure; *(desempleado)* unemployed; *(deshabitado)* empty, vacant
desocupar [desoku'par] *vt* to vacate; **desocuparse** *vr (quedar libre)* to be free; **se ha desocupado aquella mesa** that table's free now
desodorante [desoðo'rante] *nm* deodorant
desoiga *etc* [de'soiɣa] *vb ver* **desoír**
desoír [deso'ir] *vt* to ignore, disregard
desolación [desola'θjon] *nf (de lugar)* desolation; *(fig)* grief
desolar [deso'lar] *vt* to ruin, lay waste
desollar [deso'ʎar] *vt (quitar la piel a)* to skin; *(criticar)*: **~ vivo a** to criticize unmercifully
desorbitado, -a [desorβi'taðo, a] *adj (excesivo)* excessive; *(precio)* exorbitant; **con los ojos desorbitados** pop-eyed
desorbitar [desorβi'tar] *vt (exagerar)* to exaggerate; *(interpretar mal)* to misinterpret; **desorbitarse** *vr (persona)* to lose one's sense of proportion; *(asunto)* to get out of hand
desorden [de'sorðen] *nm* confusion; *(de casa, cuarto)* mess; *(político)* disorder; **desórdenes** *nmpl (alborotos)* disturbances; *(excesos)* excesses; **en ~** *(gente)* in confusion
desordenado, -a [desorðe'naðo, a] *adj (habitación, persona)* untidy; *(objetos revueltos)* in a mess, jumbled; *(conducta)* disorderly
desordenar [desorðe'nar] *vt (gen)* to disarrange; *(pelo)* to mess up; *(cuarto)* to make a mess in; *(causar confusión a)* to throw into confusion
desorganice *etc* [desorɣa'niθe] *vb ver* **desorganizar**
desorganizar [desorɣani'θar] *vt* to disorganize
desorientar [desorjen'tar] *vt (extraviar)* to mislead; *(confundir, desconcertar)* to confuse; **desorientarse** *vr (perderse)* to lose one's way
desovar [deso'βar] *vi (peces)* to spawn; *(insectos)* to lay eggs
desoyendo *etc* [deso'jendo] *vb ver* **desoír**
despabilado, -a [despaβi'laðo, a] *adj (despierto)* wide-awake; *(fig)* alert, sharp
despabilar [despaβi'lar] *vt (despertar)* to wake up; *(fig: persona)* to liven up; *(trabajo)* to get through quickly ■ *vi*, **despabilarse** *vr* to wake up; *(fig)* to get a move on
despachar [despa'tʃar] *vt (negocio)* to do, complete; *(resolver: problema)* to settle; *(correspondencia)* to deal with; *(fam: comida)* to polish off; *(: bebida)* to knock back; *(enviar)* to send, dispatch; *(vender)* to sell, deal in; *(Com: cliente)* to attend to; *(billete)* to issue; *(mandar ir)* to send away ■ *vi (decidirse)* to get things settled; *(apresurarse)* to hurry up; **despacharse** *vr* to finish off; *(apresurarse)* to hurry up; **despacharse de algo** to get rid of sth; **despacharse a su gusto con algn** to give sb a piece of one's mind; **¿quién despacha?** is anybody serving?
despacho [des'patʃo] *nm (oficina)* office; *(: en una casa)* study; *(de paquetes)* dispatch; *(Com: venta)* sale (of goods); *(comunicación)* message; **~ de billetes** *o* **boletos** *(Am)* booking office; **~ de localidades** box office; **géneros sin ~** unsaleable goods; **tener buen ~** to find a ready sale
despachurrar [despatʃu'rrar] *vt (aplastar)* to crush; *(persona)* to flatten
despacio [des'paθjo] *adv (lentamente)* slowly; *(esp Am: en voz baja)* softly; **¡~!** take it easy!
despacito [despa'θito] *adv (fam)* slowly; *(suavemente)* softly
despampanante [despampa'nante] *adj (fam: chica)* stunning
desparejado, -a [despare'xaðo, a] *adj* odd
desparpajo [despar'paxo] *nm (desenvoltura)* self-confidence; *(pey)* nerve
desparramar [desparra'mar] *vt (esparcir)* to scatter; *(líquido)* to spill
despatarrarse [despata'rrarse] *vr (abrir las piernas)* to open one's legs wide; *(caerse)* to tumble; *(fig)* to be flabbergasted
despavorido, -a [despaβo'riðo, a] *adj* terrified
despecho [des'petʃo] *nm* spite; **a ~ de** in spite of; **por ~** out of (sheer) spite
despectivo, -a [despek'tiβo, a] *adj (despreciativo)* derogatory; *(Ling)* pejorative
despedace *etc* [despe'ðaθe] *vb ver* **despedazar**
despedazar [despeða'θar] *vt* to tear to pieces
despedida [despe'ðiða] *nf (adiós)* goodbye, farewell; *(antes de viaje)* send-off; *(en carta)* closing formula; *(de obrero)* sacking; *(Inform)* logout; **cena/función de ~** farewell dinner/performance; **regalo de ~** parting gift; **~ de soltero/soltera** stag/hen party
despedir [despe'ðir] *vt (visita)* to see off, show out; *(empleado)* to dismiss; *(inquilino)* to evict; *(objeto)* to hurl; *(olor etc)* to give out *o* off; **despedirse** *vr (dejar un empleo)* to give up one's job; *(Inform)* to log out *o* off; **despedirse de** to say goodbye to; **se despidieron** they said goodbye to each other
despegado, -a [despe'ɣaðo, a] *adj (separado)* detached; *(persona: poco afectuoso)* cold, indifferent ■ *nm/f*: **es un ~** he has cut himself off from his family
despegar [despe'ɣar] *vt* to unstick; *(sobre)* to open ■ *vi (avión)* to take off; *(cohete)* to blast

off; **despegarse** *vr* to come loose, come unstuck; **sin ~ los labios** without uttering a word
despego [des'peɣo] *nm* detachment
despegue *etc* [des'peɣe] *vb ver* **despegar** ■ *nm* takeoff; (*de cohete*) blast-off
despeinado, -a [despei'naðo, a] *adj* dishevelled, unkempt
despeinar [despei'nar] *vt* (*pelo*) to ruffle; **¡me has despeinado todo!** you've completely ruined my hairdo!
despejado, -a [despe'xaðo, a] *adj* (*lugar*) clear, free; (*cielo*) clear; (*persona*) wide-awake, bright
despejar [despe'xar] *vt* (*gen*) to clear; (*misterio*) to clarify, clear up; (*Mat: incógnita*) to find ■ *vi* (*el tiempo*) to clear; **despejarse** *vr* (*tiempo, cielo*) to clear (up); (*misterio*) to become clearer; (*cabeza*) to clear; **¡despejen!** (*moverse*) move along!; (*salirse*) everybody out!
despeje [des'pexe] *nm* (*Deporte*) clearance
despellejar [despeʎe'xar] *vt* (*animal*) to skin; (*criticar*) to criticize unmercifully; (*fam: arruinar*) to fleece
despelotarse [despelo'tarse] *vr* (*fam*) to strip off; (*fig*) to let one's hair down
despelote [despe'lote] *nm* (*Am: fam: lío*) mess; **¡qué** *o* **vaya ~!** what a riot *o* laugh!
despenalizar [despenali'θar] *vt* to decriminalize
despensa [des'pensa] *nf* (*armario*) larder; (*Naut*) storeroom; (*provisión de comestibles*) stock of food
despeñadero [despeɲa'ðero] *nm* (*Geo*) cliff, precipice
despeñar [despe'ɲar] *vt* (*arrojar*) to fling down; **despeñarse** *vr* to fling o.s. down; (*caer*) to fall headlong
desperdiciar [desperði'θjar] *vt* (*comida, tiempo*) to waste; (*oportunidad*) to throw away
desperdicio [desper'ðiθjo] *nm* (*despilfarro*) squandering; (*residuo*) waste; **desperdicios** *nmpl* (*basura*) rubbish *sg*, refuse *sg*, garbage *sg* (US); (*residuos*) waste *sg*; **desperdicios de cocina** kitchen scraps; **el libro no tiene ~** the book is excellent from beginning to end
desperdigar [desperði'ɣar] *vt* (*esparcir*) to scatter; (*energía*) to dissipate; **desperdigarse** *vr* to scatter
desperdigue *etc* [desper'ðiɣe] *vb ver* **desperdigar**
desperece *etc* [despe'reθe] *vb ver* **desperezarse**
desperezarse [despere'θarse] *vr* to stretch
desperfecto [desper'fekto] *nm* (*deterioro*) slight damage; (*defecto*) flaw, imperfection
despertador [desperta'ðor] *nm* alarm clock; **~ de viaje** travelling clock
despertar [desper'tar] *vt* (*persona*) to wake up; (*recuerdos*) to revive; (*esperanzas*) to raise; (*sentimiento*) to arouse ■ *vi*, **despertarse** *vr* to awaken, wake up ■ *nm* awakening; **despertarse a la realidad** to wake up to reality
despiadado a [despja'ðaðo, a] *adj* (*ataque*) merciless; (*persona*) heartless
despido *etc* [des'piðo] *vb ver* **despedir** ■ *nm* dismissal, sacking; **~ improcedente** *o* **injustificado** wrongful dismissal; **~ injusto** unfair dismissal; **~ libre** right to hire and fire; **~ voluntario** voluntary redundancy
despierto, -a [des'pjerto, a] *pp de* **despertar** ■ *adj* awake; (*fig*) sharp, alert
despilfarrar [despilfa'rrar] *vt* (*gen*) to waste; (*dinero*) to squander
despilfarro [despil'farro] *nm* (*derroche*) squandering; (*lujo desmedido*) extravagance
despintar [despin'tar] *vt* (*quitar pintura a*) to take the paint off; (*hechos*) to distort ■ *vi*: **A no despinta a B** A is in no way inferior to B; **despintarse** *vr* (*desteñir*) to fade
despiojar [despjo'xar] *vt* to delouse
despistado, -a [despis'taðo, a] *adj* (*distraído*) vague, absent-minded; (*poco práctico*) unpractical; (*confuso*) confused; (*desorientado*) off the track ■ *nm/f* (*persona distraída*) scatterbrain, absent-minded person
despistar [despis'tar] *vt* to throw off the track *o* scent; (*fig*) to mislead, confuse; **despistarse** *vr* to take the wrong road; (*fig*) to become confused
despiste [des'piste] *nm* (*Auto etc*) swerve; (*error*) slip; (*distracción*) absent-mindedness; **tiene un terrible ~** he's terribly absent-minded
desplace *etc* [des'plaθe] *vb ver* **desplazar**
desplante [des'plante] *nm*: **hacer un ~ a algn** to be rude to sb
desplazado, -a [despla'θaðo, a] *adj* (*pieza*) wrongly placed ■ *nm/f* (*inadaptado*) misfit; **sentirse un poco ~** to feel rather out of place
desplazamiento [desplaθa'mjento] *nm* displacement; (*viaje*) journey; (*de opinión, votos*) shift, swing; (*Inform*) scrolling; **~ hacia arriba/abajo** (*Inform*) scroll up/down
desplazar [despla'θar] *vt* (*gen*) to move; (*Física, Naut, Tec*) to displace; (*tropas*) to transfer; (*suplantar*) to take the place of; (*Inform*) to scroll; **desplazarse** *vr* (*persona, vehículo*) to travel, go; (*objeto*) to move, shift; (*votos, opinión*) to shift, swing
desplegar [desple'ɣar] *vt* (*tela, papel*) to unfold, open out; (*bandera*) to unfurl; (*alas*) to spread; (*Mil*) to deploy; (*manifestar*) to display

desplegué [desple'ɣe], **despleguemos** *etc* [desple'ɣemos] *vb ver* **desplegar**
despliegue *etc* [des'pljeɣe] *vb ver* **desplegar** ■ *nm* unfolding, opening; deployment, display
desplomarse [desplo'marse] *vr* (*edificio, gobierno, persona*) to collapse; (*derrumbarse*) to topple over; (*precios*) to slump; **se ha desplomado el techo** the ceiling has fallen in
desplumar [desplu'mar] *vt* (*ave*) to pluck; (*fam: estafar*) to fleece
despoblado, -a [despo'βlaðo, a] *adj* (*sin habitantes*) uninhabited; (*con pocos habitantes*) depopulated; (*con insuficientes habitantes*) underpopulated ■ *nm* deserted spot
despojar [despo'xar] *vt* (*a alguien: de sus bienes*) to divest of, deprive of; (*casa*) to strip, leave bare; (*de su cargo*) to strip of; **despojarse** *vr* (*desnudarse*) to undress; **despojarse de** (*ropa, hojas*) to shed; (*poderes*) to relinquish
despojo [des'poxo] *nm* (*acto*) plundering; (*objetos*) plunder, loot; **despojos** *nmpl* (*de ave, res*) offal *sg*
desposado, -a [despo'saðo, a] *adj, nm/f* newly-wed
desposar [despo'sar] *vt* (*sacerdote: pareja*) to marry; **desposarse** *vr* (*casarse*) to marry, get married
desposeer [despose'er] *vt* (*despojar*) to dispossess; **~ a algn de su autoridad** to strip sb of his authority
desposeído, -a [despose'iðo, a] *nm/f*: **los desposeídos** the have-nots
desposeyendo *etc* [despose'jendo] *vb ver* **desposeer**
desposorios [despo'sorjos] *nmpl* (*esponsales*) betrothal *sg*; (*boda*) marriage ceremony *sg*
déspota ['despota] *nm/f* despot
despotismo [despo'tismo] *nm* despotism
despotricar [despotri'kar] *vi*: **~ contra** to moan *o* complain about
despotrique *etc* [despo'trike] *vb ver* **despotricar**
despreciable [despre'θjaβle] *adj* (*moralmente*) despicable; (*objeto*) worthless; (*cantidad*) negligible
despreciar [despre'θjar] *vt* (*desdeñar*) to despise, scorn; (*afrentar*) to slight
despreciativo, -a [despreθja'tiβo, a] *adj* (*observación, tono*) scornful, contemptuous; (*comentario*) derogatory
desprecio [des'preθjo] *nm* scorn, contempt; slight
desprender [despren'der] *vt* (*soltar*) to loosen; (*separar*) to separate; (*desatar*) to unfasten; (*olor*) to give off; **desprenderse** *vr* (*botón: caerse*) to fall off; (*: abrirse*) to unfasten; (*olor, perfume*) to be given off; **desprenderse de** to follow from; **desprenderse de algo** (*ceder*) to give sth up; (*desembarazarse*) to get rid of sth; **se desprende que ...** it transpires that ...
desprendido, -a [despren'dido, a] *adj* (*pieza*) loose; (*sin abrochar*) unfastened; (*desinteresado*) disinterested; (*generoso*) generous
desprendimiento [desprendi'mjento] *nm* (*gen*) loosening; (*generosidad*) disinterestedness; (*indiferencia*) detachment; (*de gas*) leak; (*de tierra, rocas*) landslide
despreocupado, -a [despreoku'paðo, a] *adj* (*sin preocupación*) unworried, unconcerned; (*tranquilo*) nonchalant; (*en el vestir*) casual; (*negligente*) careless
despreocuparse [despreoku'parse] *vr* to be carefree; (*dejar de inquietarse*) to stop worrying; (*ser indiferente*) to be unconcerned; **~ de** to have no interest in
desprestigiar [despresti'xjar] *vt* (*criticar*) to run down, disparage; (*desacreditar*) to discredit
desprestigio [despres'tixjo] *nm* (*denigración*) disparagement; (*impopularidad*) unpopularity
desprevenido, -a [despreβe'niðo, a] *adj* (*no preparado*) unprepared, unready; **coger** (*Esp*) *o* **agarrar** (*Am*) **a algn ~** to catch sb unawares
desproporción [despropor'θjon] *nf* disproportion, lack of proportion
desproporcionado, -a [desproporθjo'naðo, a] *adj* disproportionate, out of proportion
despropósito [despro'posito] *nm* (*salida de tono*) irrelevant remark; (*disparate*) piece of nonsense
desprovisto, -a [despro'βisto, a] *adj*: **~ de** devoid of; **estar ~ de** to lack
después [des'pwes] *adv* afterwards, later; (*desde entonces*) since (then); (*próximo paso*) next; **poco ~** soon after; **un año ~** a year later; **~ se debatió el tema** next the matter was discussed ■ *prep*: **~ de** (*tiempo*) after, since; (*orden*) next (to); **~ de comer** after lunch; **~ de corregido el texto** after the text had been corrected; **~ de esa fecha** (*pasado*) since that date; (*futuro*) from *o* after that date; **~ de todo** after all; **~ de verlo** after seeing it, after I *etc* saw it; **mi nombre está ~ del tuyo** my name comes next to yours ■ *conj*: **~ (de) que** after; **~ (de) que lo escribí** after *o* since I wrote it, after writing it
despuntar [despun'tar] *vt* (*lápiz*) to blunt ■ *vi* (*Bot: plantas*) to sprout; (*: flores*) to bud; (*alba*) to break; (*día*) to dawn; (*persona: descollar*) to stand out
desquiciar [deski'θjar] *vt* (*puerta*) to take off its hinges; (*descomponer*) to upset; (*persona: turbar*) to disturb; (*: volver loco a*) to unhinge

desquitarse [deski'tarse] *vr* to obtain satisfaction; (*Com*) to recover a debt; (*fig: vengarse de*) to get one's own back; **~ de una pérdida** to make up for a loss

desquite [des'kite] *nm* (*satisfacción*) satisfaction; (*venganza*) revenge

Dest. *abr* = **destinatario**

destacado, -a [desta'kaðo, a] *adj* outstanding

destacamento [destaka'mento] *nm* (*Mil*) detachment

destacar [desta'kar] *vt* (*Arte: hacer resaltar*) to make stand out; (*subrayar*) to emphasize, point up; (*Mil*) to detach, detail; (*Inform*) to highlight ■ *vi*, **destacarse** *vr* (*resaltarse*) to stand out; (*persona*) to be outstanding *o* exceptional; **quiero ~ que...** I wish to emphasize that...; **~(se) contra** *o* **en** *o* **sobre** to stand out *o* be outlined against

destajo [des'taxo] *nm*: **a ~** (*por pieza*) by the job; (*con afán*) eagerly; **trabajar a ~** to do piecework; (*fig*) to work one's fingers to the bone

destapar [desta'par] *vt* (*botella*) to open; (*cacerola*) to take the lid off; (*descubrir*) to uncover; **destaparse** *vr* (*descubrirse*) to get uncovered; (*revelarse*) to reveal one's true character

destape [des'tape] *nm* nudity; (*fig*) permissiveness; **el ~ español** *the process of liberalization in Spain after Franco's death*

destaque *etc* [des'take] *vb ver* **destacar**

destartalado, -a [destarta'laðo, a] *adj* (*desordenado*) untidy; (*casa etc: grande*) rambling; (*: ruinoso*) tumbledown

destellar [deste'ʎar] *vi* (*diamante*) to sparkle; (*metal*) to glint; (*estrella*) to twinkle

destello [des'teʎo] *nm* (*de diamante*) sparkle; (*de metal*) glint; (*de estrella*) twinkle; (*de faro*) signal light; **no tiene un ~ de verdad** there's not a grain of truth in it

destemplado, -a [destem'plaðo, a] *adj* (*Mus*) out of tune; (*voz*) harsh; (*Med*) out of sorts; (*Meteorología*) unpleasant, nasty

destemplar [destem'plar] *vt* (*Mus*) to put out of tune; (*alterar*) to upset; **destemplarse** *vr* (*Mus*) to lose its pitch; (*descomponerse*) to get out of order; (*persona: irritarse*) to get upset; (*Med*) to get out of sorts

desteñir [deste'ɲir] *vt* to fade ■ *vi*, **desteñirse** *vr* to fade; **esta tela no destiñe** this fabric will not run

desternillarse [desterni'ʎarse] *vr*: **~ de risa** to split one's sides laughing

desterrado, -a [deste'rraðo, a] *nm/f* (*exiliado*) exile

desterrar [deste'rrar] *vt* (*exilar*) to exile; (*fig*) to banish, dismiss

destetar [deste'tar] *vt* to wean

destiempo [des'tjempo]: **a ~** *adv* at the wrong time

destierro *etc* [des'tjerro] *vb ver* **desterrar** ■ *nm* exile; **vivir en el ~** to live in exile

destilar [desti'lar] *vt* to distil; (*pus, sangre*) to ooze; (*fig: rebosar*) to exude; (*: revelar*) to reveal ■ *vi* (*gotear*) to drip

destilería [destile'ria] *nf* distillery; **~ de petróleo** oil refinery

destinar [desti'nar] *vt* (*funcionario*) to appoint, assign; (*fondos*) to set aside; **es un libro destinado a los niños** it is a book (intended *o* meant) for children; **una carta que viene destinada a usted** a letter for you, a letter addressed to you

destinatario, -a [destina'tarjo, a] *nm/f* addressee; (*Com*) payee

destino [des'tino] *nm* (*suerte*) destiny; (*de viajero*) destination; (*función*) use; (*puesto*) post, placement; **~ público** public appointment; **salir con ~ a** to leave for; **con ~ a Londres** (*avión, barco*) (bound) for London; (*carta*) to London

destiña *etc* [des'tiɲa], **destiñendo** *etc* [desti'ɲenðo] *vb ver* **desteñir**

destitución [destitu'θjon] *nf* dismissal, removal

destituir [destitu'ir] *vt* (*despedir*) to dismiss; (*: ministro, funcionario*) to remove from office

destituyendo *etc* [destitu'jendo] *vb ver* **destituir**

destornillador [destorniʎa'ðor] *nm* screwdriver

destornillar [destorni'ʎar] *vt*, **destornillarse** *vr* (*tornillo*) to unscrew

destreza [des'treθa] *nf* (*habilidad*) skill; (*maña*) dexterity

destripar [destri'par] *vt* (*animal*) to gut; (*reventar*) to mangle

destroce *etc* [de'stroθe] *vb ver* **destrozar**

destronar [destro'nar] *vt* (*rey*) to dethrone; (*fig*) to overthrow

destroncar [destron'kar] *vt* (*árbol*) to chop off, lop; (*proyectos*) to ruin; (*discurso*) to interrupt

destronque *etc* [des'tronke] *vb ver* **destroncar**

destrozar [destro'θar] *vt* (*romper*) to smash, break (up); (*estropear*) to ruin; (*nervios*) to shatter; **~ a algn en una discusión** to crush sb in an argument

destrozo [des'troθo] *nm* (*acción*) destruction; (*desastre*) smashing; **destrozos** *nmpl* (*pedazos*) pieces; (*daños*) havoc *sg*

destrucción [destruk'θjon] *nf* destruction

destructor, a [destruk'tor, a] *adj* destructive ■ *nm* (*Naut*) destroyer

destruir [destru'ir] *vt* to destroy; (*casa*) to demolish; (*equilibrio*) to upset; (*proyecto*) to spoil; (*esperanzas*) to dash; (*argumento*) to demolish
destruyendo *etc* [destru'jendo] *vb ver* **destruir**
desuelle *etc* [de'sweʎe] *vb ver* **desollar**
desueve *etc* [de'sweβe] *vb ver* **desovar**
desunión [desu'njon] *nf* (*separación*) separation; (*discordia*) disunity
desunir [desu'nir] *vt* to separate; (*Tec*) to disconnect; (*fig*) to cause a quarrel *o* rift between
desuso [de'suso] *nm* disuse; **caer en ~** to fall into disuse, become obsolete; **una expresión caída en ~** an obsolete expression
desvaído, -a [desβa'iðo, a] *adj* (*color*) pale; (*contorno*) blurred
desvalido, -a [desβa'liðo, a] *adj* (*desprotegido*) destitute; (*sin fuerzas*) helpless; **niños desvalidos** waifs and strays
desvalijar [desβali'xar] *vt* (*persona*) to rob; (*casa, tienda*) to burgle; (*coche*) to break into
desvalorice *etc* [desβalo'riθe] *vb ver* **desvalorizar**
desvalorizar [desβalori'θar] *vt* to devalue
desván [des'βan] *nm* attic
desvanecer [desβane'θer] *vt* (*disipar*) to dispel; (*recuerdo, temor*) to banish; (*borrar*) to blur; **desvanecerse** *vr* (*humo etc*) to vanish, disappear; (*duda*) to be dispelled; (*color*) to fade; (*recuerdo, sonido*) to fade away; (*Med*) to pass out
desvanecido, -a [desβane'θiðo, a] *adj* (*Med*) faint; **caer ~** to fall in a faint
desvanecimiento [desβaneθi'mjento] *nm* (*desaparición*) disappearance; (*de dudas*) dispelling; (*de colores*) fading; (*evaporación*) evaporation; (*Med*) fainting fit
desvanezca *etc* [desβa'neθka] *vb ver* **desvanecer**
desvariar [desβa'rjar] *vi* (*enfermo*) to be delirious; (*delirar*) to talk nonsense
desvarío [desβa'rio] *nm* delirium; (*desatino*) absurdity; **desvaríos** *nmpl* ravings
desvelar [desβe'lar] *vt* to keep awake; **desvelarse** *vr* (*no poder dormir*) to stay awake; (*vigilar*) to be vigilant *o* watchful; **desvelarse por algo** (*inquietarse*) to be anxious about sth; (*poner gran cuidado*) to take great care over sth
desvelo [des'βelo] *nm* lack of sleep; (*insomnio*) sleeplessness; (*fig*) vigilance; **desvelos** *nmpl* (*preocupación*) anxiety *sg*, effort *sg*
desvencijado, -a [desβenθi'xaðo, a] *adj* (*silla*) rickety; (*máquina*) broken-down
desvencijar [desβenθi'xar] *vt* (*romper*) to break; (*soltar*) to loosen; (*persona: agotar*) to exhaust; **desvencijarse** *vr* to come apart
desventaja [desβen'taxa] *nf* disadvantage; (*inconveniente*) drawback
desventajoso, -a [desβenta'xoso, a] *adj* disadvantageous, unfavourable
desventura [desβen'tura] *nf* misfortune
desventurado, -a [desβentu'raðo, a] *adj* (*desgraciado*) unfortunate; (*de poca suerte*) ill-fated
desvergonzado, -a [desβerɣon'θaðo, a] *adj* (*sin vergüenza*) shameless; (*descarado*) insolent ■ *nm/f* shameless person
desvergüenza [desβer'ɣwenθa] *nf* (*descaro*) shamelessness; (*insolencia*) impudence; (*mala conducta*) effrontery; **esto es una ~** this is disgraceful; **¡qué ~!** what a nerve!
desvestir [desβes'tir] *vt*, **desvestirse** *vr* to undress
desviación [desβja'θjon] *nf* deviation; (*Auto: rodeo*) diversion, detour; (*: carretera de circunvalación*) ring road (*Brit*), circular route (*US*); **~ de la circulación** traffic diversion; **es una ~ de sus principios** it is a departure from his usual principles
desviar [des'βjar] *vt* to turn aside; (*balón, flecha, golpe*) to deflect; (*pregunta*) to parry; (*ojos*) to avert, turn away; (*río*) to alter the course of; (*navío*) to divert, re-route; (*conversación*) to sidetrack; **desviarse** *vr* (*apartarse del camino*) to turn aside; (*: barco*) to go off course; (*Auto: dar un rodeo*) to make a detour; **desviarse de un tema** to get away from the point
desvincular [desβinku'lar] *vt* to free, release; **desvincularse** *vr* (*aislarse*) to be cut off; (*alejarse*) to cut o.s. off
desvío *etc* [des'βio] *vb ver* **desviar** ■ *nm* (*desviación*) detour, diversion; (*fig*) indifference
desvirgar [desβir'ɣar] *vt* to deflower
desvirtuar [desβir'twar] *vt* (*estropear*) to spoil; (*argumento, razonamiento*) to detract from; (*efecto*) to counteract; (*sentido*) to distort; **desvirtuarse** *vr* to spoil
desvistiendo *etc* [desβis'tjendo] *vb ver* **desvestir**
desvitalizar [desβitali'θar] *vt* (*nervio*) to numb
desvivirse [desβi'βirse] *vr*: **~ por** to long for, crave for; **~ por los amigos** to do anything for one's friends
detalladamente [detaʎaða'mente] *adv* (*en detalle*) in detail; (*extensamente*) at great length
detallar [deta'ʎar] *vt* to detail; (*asunto por asunto*) to itemize
detalle [de'taʎe] *nm* detail; (*fig*) gesture,

token; **al ~** in detail; (*Com*) retail *cpd*; **comercio al ~** retail trade; **vender al ~** to sell retail; **no pierde ~** he doesn't miss a trick; **me observaba sin perder ~** he watched my every move; **tiene muchos detalles** she is very considerate

detallista [deta'ʎista] *nm/f* retailer ■ *adj* (*meticuloso*) meticulous; **comercio ~** retail trade

detectar [detek'tar] *vt* to detect

detective [detek'tiβe] *nm/f* detective; **~ privado** private detective

detector [detek'tor] *nm* (*Naut, Tec etc*) detector; **~ de mentiras/de minas** lie/mine detector

detención [deten'θjon] *nf* (*acción*) stopping; (*estancamiento*) stoppage; (*retraso*) holdup, delay; (*Jur: arresto*) arrest; (*cuidado*) care; **~ de juego** (*Deporte*) stoppage of play; **~ ilegal** unlawful detention

detendré *etc* [deten'dre] *vb ver* **detener**

detener [dete'ner] *vt* (*gen*) to stop; (*Jur: arrestar*) to arrest; (*: encarcelar*) to detain; (*objeto*) to keep; (*retrasar*) to hold up, delay; (*aliento*) to hold; **detenerse** *vr* to stop; **detenerse en** (*demorarse*) to delay over, linger over

detenga *etc* [de'tenga] *vb ver* **detener**

detenidamente [deteniða'mente] *adv* (*minuciosamente*) carefully; (*extensamente*) at great length

detenido, -a [dete'niðo, a] *adj* (*arrestado*) under arrest; (*minucioso*) detailed; (*examen*) thorough; (*tímido*) timid ■ *nm/f* person under arrest, prisoner

detenimiento [deteni'mjento] *nm* care; **con ~** thoroughly

detentar [deten'tar] *vt* to hold; (*sin derecho: título*) to hold unlawfully; (*: puesto*) to occupy unlawfully

detergente [deter'xente] *adj, nm* detergent

deteriorado, -a [deterjo'raðo, a] *adj* (*estropeado*) damaged; (*desgastado*) worn

deteriorar [deterjo'rar] *vt* to spoil, damage; **deteriorarse** *vr* to deteriorate

deterioro [dete'rjoro] *nm* deterioration

determinación [determina'θjon] *nf* (*empeño*) determination; (*decisión*) decision; (*de fecha, precio*) settling, fixing

determinado, -a [determi'naðo, a] *adj* (*preciso*) fixed, set; (*Ling: artículo*) definite; (*persona: resuelto*) determined; **un día ~** on a certain day; **no hay ningún tema ~** there is no particular theme

determinar [determi'nar] *vt* (*plazo*) to fix; (*precio*) to settle; (*daños, impuestos*) to assess; (*pleito*) to decide; (*causar*) to cause; **determinarse** *vr* to decide; **el reglamento determina que ...** the rules lay it down *or* state that ...; **aquello determinó la caída del gobierno** that brought about the fall of the government; **esto le determinó** this decided him

detestable [detes'taβle] *adj* (*persona*) hateful; (*acto*) detestable

detestar [detes'tar] *vt* to detest

detonación [detona'θjon] *nf* detonation; (*sonido*) explosion

detonante [deto'nante] *nm* (*fig*) trigger

detonar [deto'nar] *vi* to detonate

detractor, a [detrak'tor, a] *adj* disparaging ■ *nm/f* detractor

detrás [de'tras] *adv* behind; (*atrás*) at the back ■ *prep*: **~ de** behind; **por ~ de algn** (*fig*) behind sb's back; **salir de ~** to come out from behind; **por ~** behind

detrasito [detra'sito] *adv* (*Am fam*) behind

detrimento [detri'mento] *nm*: **en ~ de** to the detriment of

detuve *etc* [de'tuβe] *vb ver* **detener**

deuda [de'uða] *nf* (*condición*) indebtedness, debt; (*cantidad*) debt; **~ a largo plazo** long-term debt; **~ exterior/pública** foreign/ national debt; **~ incobrable** *o* **morosa** bad debt; **deudas activas/pasivas** assets/ liabilities; **contraer deudas** to get into debt

deudor, a [deu'ðor, a] *nm/f* debtor; **~ hipotecario** mortgager; **~ moroso** slow payer

devaluación [deβalwa'θjon] *nf* devaluation

devaluar [deβalu'ar] *vt* to devalue

devanar [deβa'nar] *vt* (*hilo*) to wind; **devanarse** *vr*: **devanarse los sesos** to rack one's brains

devaneo [deβa'neo] *nm* (*Med*) delirium; (*desatino*) nonsense; (*fruslería*) idle pursuit; (*amorío*) flirtation

devastar [deβas'tar] *vt* (*destruir*) to devastate

devendré *etc* [deβen'dre], **devenga** *etc* [de'βenga] *vb ver* **devenir**

devengar [deβen'gar] *vt* (*salario: ganar*) to earn; (*: tener que cobrar*) to be due; (*intereses*) to bring in, accrue, earn

devengue *etc* [de'βenge] *vb ver* **devengar**

devenir [deβe'nir] *vi*: **~ en** to become, turn into ■ *nm* (*movimiento progresivo*) process of development; (*transformación*) transformation

deviene *etc* [de'βjene], **deviniendo** *etc* [deβi'njendo] *vb ver* **devenir**

devoción [deβo'θjon] *nf* devotion; (*afición*) strong attachment

devolución [deβolu'θjon] *nf* (*reenvío*) return, sending back; (*reembolso*) repayment; (*Jur*) devolution

devolver [deβol'βer] *vt* *(lo extraviado, prestado)* to give back; *(a su sitio)* to put back; *(carta al correo)* to send back; *(Com)* to repay, refund; *(visita, la palabra)* to return; *(salud, vista)* to restore; *(fam: vomitar)* to throw up ■ *vi* *(fam)* to be sick; **devolverse** *vr* *(Am)* to return; **~ mal por bien** to return ill for good; **~ la pelota a algn** to give sb tit for tat
devorar [deβo'rar] *vt* to devour; *(comer ávidamente)* to gobble up; *(fig: fortuna)* to run through; **todo lo devoró el fuego** the fire consumed everything; **le devoran los celos** he is consumed with jealousy
devoto, -a [de'βoto, a] *adj* *(Rel: persona)* devout; *(: obra)* devotional; *(amigo)*: **~ (de algn)** devoted (to sb) ■ *nm/f* admirer; **los devotos** *nmpl* *(Rel)* the faithful; **su muy ~** your devoted servant
devuelto [de'βwelto], **devuelva** *etc* [de'βwelβa] *vb ver* **devolver**
D.F. *abr* *(México)* = **Distrito Federal**
dg *abr* *(= decigramo)* dg
D.G. *abr* *(= Dirección General, Director General)* DG
DGT *nf abr* *(= Dirección General de Tráfico)* = **Dirección General de Turismo**
di [di] *vb ver* **dar**; **decir**
día ['dia] *nm* day; **~ de asueto** day off; **~ feriado** *(Am)* *o* **festivo** (public) holiday; **~ hábil/inhábil** working/non-working day; **~ lunes** *(Am)* Monday; **~ lectivo** teaching day; **~ libre** day off; **D~ de Reyes** Epiphany *(6 January)*; **¿qué ~ es?** what's the date?; **estar/poner al ~** to be/keep up to date; **el ~ de hoy/de mañana** today/tomorrow; **el ~ menos pensado** when you least expect it; **al ~ siguiente** on the following day; **todos los días** every day; **un ~ sí y otro no** every other day; **vivir al ~** to live from hand to mouth; **de ~** during the day, by day; **es de ~** it's daylight; **del ~** *(estilos)* fashionable; *(menú)* today's; **de un ~ para otro** any day now; **en pleno ~** in full daylight; **en su ~** in due time; **¡hasta otro ~!** so long!
diabetes [dja'betes] *nf* diabetes *sg*
diabético, -a [dja'betiko, a] *adj, nm/f* diabetic
diablo ['djaβlo] *nm* *(tb fig)* devil; **pobre ~** poor devil; **hace un frío de todos los diablos** it's hellishly cold
diablura [dja'βlura] *nf* prank; *(travesura)* mischief
diabólico, -a [dja'βoliko, a] *adj* diabolical
diadema [dja'ðema] *nf* *(para el pelo)* Alice band, headband; *(joya)* tiara
diáfano, -a ['djafano, a] *adj* *(tela)* diaphanous; *(agua)* crystal-clear
diafragma [dja'fraɣma] *nm* diaphragm
diagnosis [djaɣ'nosis] *nf inv*, **diagnóstico** [diaɣ'nostiko] *nm* diagnosis
diagnosticar [djaɣnosti'kar] *vt* to diagnose
diagonal [djaɣo'nal] *adj* diagonal ■ *nf* *(Geom)* diagonal; **en ~** diagonally
diagrama [dja'ɣrama] *nm* diagram; **~ de barras** *(Com)* bar chart; **~ de dispersión** *(Com)* scatter diagram; **~ de flujo** *(Inform)* flowchart
dial [di'al] *nm* dial
dialecto [dja'lekto] *nm* dialect
dialogar [djalo'ɣar] *vt* to write in dialogue form ■ *vi* *(conversar)* to have a conversation; **~ con** *(Pol)* to hold talks with
diálogo ['djaloɣo] *nm* dialogue
dialogue *etc* [dja'loɣe] *vb ver* **dialogar**
diamante [dja'mante] *nm* diamond
diametralmente [djametral'mente] *adv* diametrically; **~ opuesto a** diametrically opposed to
diámetro [di'ametro] *nm* diameter; **~ de giro** *(Auto)* turning circle; **faros de gran ~** wide-angle headlights
diana ['djana] *nf* *(Mil)* reveille; *(de blanco)* centre, bull's-eye
diantre ['djantre] *nm*: **¡~!** *(fam)* oh hell!
diapasón [djapa'son] *nm* *(instrumento)* tuning fork; *(de violín etc)* fingerboard; *(de voz)* tone
diapositiva [djaposi'tiβa] *nf* *(Foto)* slide, transparency
diario, -a ['djarjo, a] *adj* daily ■ *nm* newspaper; *(libro diario)* diary; *(: Com)* daybook; *(Com: gastos)* daily expenses; **~ de navegación** *(Naut)* logbook; **~ hablado** *(Radio)* news (bulletin); **~ de sesiones** parliamentary report; **a ~** daily; **de *o* para ~** everyday
diarrea [dja'rrea] *nf* diarrhoea
diatriba [dja'triβa] *nf* diatribe, tirade
dibujante [diβu'xante] *nm/f* *(de bosquejos)* sketcher; *(de dibujos animados)* cartoonist; *(de moda)* designer; **~ de publicidad** commercial artist
dibujar [diβu'xar] *vt* to draw, sketch; **dibujarse** *vr* *(emoción)* to show; **dibujarse contra** to be outlined against
dibujo [di'βuxo] *nm* drawing; *(Tec)* design; *(en papel, tela)* pattern; *(en periódico)* cartoon; *(fig)* description; **dibujos animados** cartoons; **~ del natural** drawing from life
dic., dic.[e] *abr* *(= diciembre)* Dec.
diccionario [dikθjo'narjo] *nm* dictionary
dicharachero, -a [ditʃara'tʃero, a] *adj* talkative ■ *nm/f* *(con ingenio)* wit; *(parlanchín)* chatterbox
dicho, -a ['ditʃo, a] *pp de* **decir** ■ *adj* *(susodicho)* aforementioned ■ *nm* saying; *(proverbio)* proverb; *(ocurrencia)* bright remark

■ *nf* (*buena suerte*) good luck; **mejor ~** rather; **~ y hecho** no sooner said than done
dichoso, -a [di'tʃoso, a] *adj* (*feliz*) happy; (*afortunado*) lucky; **¡aquel ~ coche!** (*fam*) that blessed car!
diciembre [di'θjembre] *nm* December; *ver tb* **julio**
diciendo *etc* [di'θjendo] *vb ver* **decir**
dictado [dik'taðo] *nm* dictation; **escribir al ~** to take dictation; **los dictados de la conciencia** (*fig*) the dictates of conscience
dictador [dikta'ðor] *nm* dictator
dictadura [dikta'ðura] *nf* dictatorship
dictáfono® [dik'tafono] *nm* Dictaphone®
dictamen [dik'tamen] *nm* (*opinión*) opinion; (*informe*) report; **~ contable** auditor's report; **~ facultativo** (*Med*) medical report
dictar [dik'tar] *vt* (*carta*) to dictate; (*Jur: sentencia*) to pass; (*decreto*) to issue; (*Am: clase*) to give; (*: conferencia*) to deliver
didáctico, -a [di'ðaktiko, a] *adj* didactic; (*material*) teaching *cpd*; (*juguete*) educational
diecinueve [djeθinu'eβe] *num* nineteen; (*fecha*) nineteenth; *ver tb* **seis**
dieciochesco, -a [djeθio'tʃesko, a] *adj* eighteenth-century
dieciocho [djeθi'otʃo] *num* eighteen; (*fecha*) eighteenth; *ver tb* **seis**
dieciséis [djeθi'seis] *num* sixteen; (*fecha*) sixteenth; *ver tb* **seis**
diecisiete [djeθi'sjete] *num* seventeen; (*fecha*) seventeenth; *ver tb* **seis**
diente ['djente] *nm* (*Anat, Tec*) tooth; (*Zool*) fang; (*: de elefante*) tusk; (*de ajo*) clove; **~ de león** dandelion; **dientes postizos** false teeth; **enseñar los dientes** (*fig*) to show one's claws; **hablar entre dientes** to mutter, mumble; **hincar el ~ en** (*comida*) to bite into
diera *etc* ['djera] *vb ver* **dar**
diéresis [di'eresis] *nf* diaeresis
dieron ['djeron] *vb ver* **dar**
diesel ['disel] *adj*: **motor ~** diesel engine
diestro, -a ['djestro, a] *adj* (*derecho*) right; (*hábil*) skilful; (*: con las manos*) handy ■ *nm* (*Taur*) matador ■ *nf* right hand; **a ~ y siniestro** (*sin método*) wildly
dieta ['djeta] *nf* diet; **dietas** *nfpl* expenses; **estar a ~** to be on a diet
dietético, -a [dje'tetiko, a] *adj* dietetic ■ *nm/f* dietician ■ *nf* dietetics *sg*
dietista [dje'tista] *nm/f* dietician
diez [djeθ] *num* ten; (*fecha*) tenth; **hacer las ~ de últimas** (*Naipes*) to sweep the board; *ver tb* **seis**
diezmar [djeθ'mar] *vt* to decimate
difamación [difama'θjon] *nf* slander; libel
difamar [difa'mar] *vt* (*Jur: hablando*) to slander; (*: por escrito*) to libel
difamatorio, -a [difama'torjo, a] *adj* slanderous; libellous
diferencia [dife'renθja] *nf* difference; **a ~ de** unlike; **hacer ~ entre** to make a distinction between; **~ salarial** (*Com*) wage differential
diferencial [diferen'θjal] *nm* (*Auto*) differential
diferenciar [diferen'θjar] *vt* to differentiate between ■ *vi* to differ; **diferenciarse** *vr* to differ, be different; (*distinguirse*) to distinguish o.s.
diferente [dife'rente] *adj* different
diferido [dife'riðo] *nm*: **en ~** (*TV etc*) recorded
diferir [dife'rir] *vt* to defer
difícil [di'fiθil] *adj* difficult; (*tiempos, vida*) hard; (*situación*) delicate; **es un hombre ~** he's a difficult man to get on with
difícilmente [di'fiθilmente] *adv* (*con dificultad*) with difficulty; (*apenas*) hardly
dificultad [difikul'tað] *nf* difficulty; (*problema*) trouble; (*objeción*) objection
dificultar [difikul'tar] *vt* (*complicar*) to complicate, make difficult; (*estorbar*) to obstruct; **las restricciones dificultan el comercio** the restrictions hinder trade
dificultoso, -a [difikul'toso, a] *adj* (*difícil*) difficult, hard; (*fam: cara*) odd, ugly; (*persona: exigente*) fussy
difiera *etc* [di'fjera], **difiriendo** *etc* [difi'rjendo] *vb ver* **diferir**
difuminar [difumi'nar] *vt* to blur
difundir [difun'dir] *vt* (*calor, luz*) to diffuse; (*Radio*) to broadcast; **difundirse** *vr* to spread (out); **~ una noticia** to spread a piece of news
difunto, a [di'funto, a] *adj* dead, deceased ■ *nm/f*: **el ~** the deceased
difusión [difu'sjon] *nf* (*de calor, luz*) diffusion; (*de noticia, teoría*) dissemination; (*de programa*) broadcasting; (*programa*) broadcast
difuso, -a [di'fuso, a] *adj* (*luz*) diffused; (*conocimientos*) widespread; (*estilo, explicación*) wordy
diga *etc* ['diɣa] *vb ver* **decir**
digerir [dixe'rir] *vt* to digest; (*fig*) to absorb; (*reflexionar sobre*) to think over
digestión [dixes'tjon] *nf* digestion; **corte de ~** indigestion
digestivo, -a [dixes'tiβo, a] *adj* digestive ■ *nm* (*bebida*) liqueur, digestif
digiera *etc* [di'xjera], **digiriendo** *etc* [dixi'rjenðo] *vb ver* **digerir**
digital [dixi'tal] *adj* (*Inform*) digital; (*dactilar*) finger *cpd* ■ *nf* (*Bot*) foxglove; (*droga*) digitalis

digitalizador [dixitaliθa'ðor] *nm* (*Inform*) digitizer
dignarse [diɣ'narse] *vr* to deign to
dignidad [diɣni'ðað] *nf* dignity; (*honra*) honour; (*rango*) rank; (*persona*) dignitary; **herir la ~ de algn** to hurt sb's pride
dignificar [diɣnifi'kar] *vt* to dignify
dignifique *etc* [diɣni'fike] *vb ver* **dignificar**
digno, -a ['diɣno, a] *adj* worthy; (*persona: honesto*) honourable; **~ de elogio** praiseworthy; **~ de mención** worth mentioning; **es ~ de verse** it is worth seeing; **poco ~** unworthy
digresión [diɣre'sjon] *nf* digression
dije *etc* ['dixe], **dijera** *etc* [di'xera] *vb ver* **decir**
dilación [dila'θjon] *nf* delay; **sin ~** without delay, immediately
dilapidar [dilapi'ðar] *vt* to squander, waste
dilatación [dilata'θjon] *nf* (*expansión*) dilation
dilatado, -a [dila'taðo, a] *adj* dilated; (*período*) long drawn-out; (*extenso*) extensive
dilatar [dila'tar] *vt* (*gen*) to dilate; (*prolongar*) to prolong; (*aplazar*) to delay; **dilatarse** *vr* (*pupila etc*) to dilate; (*agua*) to expand
dilema [di'lema] *nm* dilemma
diligencia [dili'xenθja] *nf* diligence; (*rapidez*) speed; (*ocupación*) errand, job; (*carruaje*) stagecoach; **diligencias** *nfpl* (*Jur*) formalities; **diligencias judiciales** judicial proceedings; **diligencias previas** inquest *sg*
diligente [dili'xente] *adj* diligent; **poco ~** slack
dilucidar [diluθi'ðar] *vt* (*aclarar*) to elucidate, clarify; (*misterio*) to clear up
diluir [dilu'ir] *vt* to dilute; (*aguar, fig*) to water down
diluviar [dilu'βjar] *vi* to pour with rain
diluvio [di'luβjo] *nm* deluge, flood; **un ~ de cartas** (*fig*) a flood of letters
diluyendo *etc* [dilu'jendo] *vb ver* **diluir**
dimanar [dima'nar] *vi*: **~ de** to arise *o* spring from
dimensión [dimen'sjon] *nf* dimension; **dimensiones** *nfpl* size *sg*; **tomar las dimensiones de** to take the measurements of
dimes ['dimes] *nmpl*: **andar en ~ y diretes con algn** to bicker *o* squabble with sb
diminutivo [diminu'tiβo] *nm* diminutive
diminuto, -a [dimi'nuto, a] *adj* tiny, diminutive
dimisión [dimi'sjon] *nf* resignation
dimitir [dimi'tir] *vt* (*cargo*) to give up; (*despedir*) to sack ■ *vi* to resign
dimos ['dimos] *vb ver* **dar**
Dinamarca [dina'marka] *nf* Denmark
dinamarqués, -esa [dinamar'kes, esa] *adj* Danish ■ *nm/f* Dane ■ *nm* (*Ling*) Danish
dinámico, -a [di'namiko, a] *adj* dynamic ■ *nf* dynamics *sg*
dinamita [dina'mita] *nf* dynamite
dinamitar [dinami'tar] *vt* to dynamite
dinamo [di'namo], **dínamo** ['dinamo] *nf, nm en AM* dynamo
dinastía [dinas'tia] *nf* dynasty
dineral [dine'ral] *nm* fortune
dinero [di'nero] *nm* money; (*dinero en circulación*) currency; **~ caro** (*Com*) dear money; **~ contante (y sonante)** hard cash; **~ de curso legal** legal tender; **~ efectivo** cash, ready cash; **es hombre de ~** he is a man of means; **andar mal de ~** to be short of money; **ganar ~ a espuertas** to make money hand over fist
dinosaurio [dino'saurjo] *nm* dinosaur
dintel [din'tel] *nm* lintel; (*umbral*) threshold
diñar [di'ɲar] *vt* (*fam*) to give; **diñarla** to kick the bucket
dio [djo] *vb ver* **dar**
diócesis ['djoθesis] *nf inv* diocese
Dios [djos] *nm* God; **~ mediante** God willing; **a ~ gracias** thank heaven; **a la buena de ~** any old how; **una de ~ es Cristo** an almighty row; **~ los cría y ellos se juntan** birds of a feather flock together; **como ~ manda** as is proper; **¡~ mío!** (oh) my God!; **¡por ~!** for God's sake!; **¡válgame ~!** bless my soul!
dios [djos] *nm* god
diosa ['djosa] *nf* goddess
Dip. *abr* (= *Diputación*) ≈ CC
diploma [di'ploma] *nm* diploma
diplomacia [diplo'maθja] *nf* diplomacy; (*fig*) tact
diplomado, -a [diplo'maðo, a] *adj* qualified ■ *nm/f* holder of a diploma; (*Univ*) graduate; *ver tb* **licenciado**
diplomático, -a [diplo'matiko, a] *adj* (*cuerpo*) diplomatic; (*que tiene tacto*) tactful ■ *nm/f* diplomat
diptongo [dip'tongo] *nm* diphthong
diputación [diputa'θjon] *nf* deputation; **~ permanente** (*Pol*) standing committee; **~ provincial** ≈ county council
diputado, -a [dipu'taðo, a] *nm/f* delegate; (*Pol*) ≈ member of parliament (*Brit*), ≈ representative (*US*); *ver tb* **Corte**
dique ['dike] *nm* dyke; (*rompeolas*) breakwater; **~ de contención** dam
Dir. *abr* = **dirección**; (= *director*) Mgr
diré *etc* [di're] *vb ver* **decir**
dirección [direk'θjon] *nf* direction; (*fig: tendencia*) trend; (*señas, tb Inform*) address; (*Auto*) steering; (*gerencia*) management; (*de periódico*) editorship; (*en escuela*)

headship; (*Pol*) leadership; (*junta*) board of directors; (*despacho*) director's/manager's/headmaster's/editor's office; **~ administrativa** office management; **~ asistida** power-assisted steering; **D~ General de Seguridad/Turismo** State Security/Tourist Office; **~ única** *o* **prohibida** one-way; **tomar la ~ de una empresa** to take over the running of a company

direccionamiento [direkθjona'mjento] *nm* (*Inform*) addressing

directivo, -a [direk'tiβo, a] *adj* (*junta*) managing; (*función*) administrative ■ *nm/f* (*Com*) manager ■ *nf* (*norma*) directive; (*tb*: **junta directiva**) board of directors

directo, -a [di'rekto, a] *adj* direct; (*línea*) straight; (*inmediato*) immediate; (*tren*) through; (*TV*) live; **programa en ~** live programme; **transmitir en ~** to broadcast live

director, a [direk'tor, a] *adj* leading ■ *nm/f* director; (*Escol*) head (teacher) (*Brit*), principal (*US*); (*gerente*) manager/manageress; (*de compañía*) president; (*jefe*) head; (*Prensa*) editor; (*de prisión*) governor; (*Mus*) conductor; **~ adjunto** assistant manager; **~ de cine** film director; **~ comercial** marketing manager; **~ ejecutivo** executive director; **~ de empresa** company director; **~ general** general manager; **~ gerente** managing director; **~ de sucursal** branch manager

directorio [direk'torjo] *nm* (*Inform*) directory

directrices [direk'triθes] *nfpl* guidelines

dirigente [diri'xente] *adj* leading ■ *nm/f* (*Pol*) leader; **los dirigentes del partido** the party leaders

dirigible [diri'xiβle] *adj* (*Aviat, Naut*) steerable ■ *nm* airship

dirigir [diri'xir] *vt* to direct; (*acusación*) to level; (*carta*) to address; (*obra de teatro, film*) to direct; (*Mus*) to conduct; (*comercio*) to manage; (*expedición*) to lead; (*sublevación*) to head; (*periódico*) to edit; (*guiar*) to guide; **dirigirse** *vr*: **dirigirse a** to go towards, make one's way towards; (*hablar con*) to speak to; **dirigirse a algn solicitando algo** to apply to sb for sth; **"diríjase a ..."** "apply to ..."

dirigismo [diri'xismo] *nm* management, control; **~ estatal** state control

dirija *etc* [di'rixa] *vb ver* **dirigir**

dirimir [diri'mir] *vt* (*contrato, matrimonio*) to dissolve

discado [dis'kaðo] *nm*: **~ automático** autodial

discernir [disθer'nir] *vt* to discern ■ *vi* to distinguish

discierna *etc* [dis'θjerna] *vb ver* **discernir**

disciplina [disθi'plina] *nf* discipline

disciplinar [disθipli'nar] *vt* to discipline; (*enseñar*) to school; (*Mil*) to drill; (*azotar*) to whip

discípulo, -a [dis'θipulo, a] *nm/f* disciple; (*seguidor*) follower; (*Escol*) pupil

Discman® ['diskman] *nm* Discman®, personal CD player

disco ['disko] *nm* disc (*Brit*), disk (*US*); (*Deporte*) discus; (*Telec*) dial; (*Auto: semáforo*) light; (*Mus*) record; (*Inform*) disk; **~ de arranque** boot disk; **~ compacto** compact disc; **~ de densidad sencilla/doble** single/double density disk; **~ de larga duración** long-playing record (LP); **~ flexible** *o* **floppy** floppy disk; **~ de freno** brake disc; **~ maestro** master disk; **~ de reserva** backup disk; **~ rígido** hard disk; **~ de una cara/dos caras** single-/double-sided disk; **~ virtual** RAMdisk

discóbolo [dis'koβolo] *nm* discus thrower

discográfico, -a [disko'ɣrafiko, a] *adj* record *cpd*; **casa discográfica** record company; **sello ~** label

díscolo, -a ['diskolo, a] *adj* (*rebelde*) unruly

disconforme [diskon'forme] *adj* differing; **estar ~ (con)** to be in disagreement (with)

discontinuo, -a [diskon'tinwo, a] *adj* discontinuous; (*Auto: línea*) broken

discordar [diskor'ðar] *vi* (*Mus*) to be out of tune; (*estar en desacuerdo*) to disagree; (*colores, opiniones*) to clash

discorde [dis'korðe] *adj* (*sonido*) discordant; (*opiniones*) clashing

discordia [dis'korðja] *nf* discord

discoteca [disko'teka] *nf* disco(theque)

discreción [diskre'θjon] *nf* discretion; (*reserva*) prudence; **¡a ~!** (*Mil*) stand easy!; **añadir azúcar a ~** (*Culin*) add sugar to taste; **comer a ~** to eat as much as one wishes

discrecional [diskreθjo'nal] *adj* (*facultativo*) discretionary; **parada ~** request stop

discrepancia [diskre'panθja] *nf* (*diferencia*) discrepancy; (*desacuerdo*) disagreement

discrepante [diskre'pante] *adj* divergent; **hubo varias voces discrepantes** there were some dissenting voices

discrepar [diskre'par] *vi* to disagree

discreto, -a [dis'kreto, a] *adj* (*diplomático*) discreet; (*sensato*) sensible; (*reservado*) quiet; (*sobrio*) sober; (*mediano*) fair, fairly good; **le daremos un plazo ~** we'll allow him a reasonable time

discriminación [diskrimina'θjon] *nf* discrimination

discriminar [diskrimi'nar] *vt* to discriminate

against; (*diferenciar*) to discriminate between
discuerde *etc* [dis'kwerðe] *vb ver* **discordar**
disculpa [dis'kulpa] *nf* excuse; (*pedir perdón*) apology; **pedir disculpas a/por** to apologize to/for
disculpar [diskul'par] *vt* to excuse, pardon; **disculparse** *vr* to excuse o.s.; to apologize
discurrir [disku'rrir] *vt* to contrive, think up ■ *vi* (*pensar, reflexionar*) to think, meditate; (*recorrer*) to roam, wander; (*río*) to flow; (*el tiempo*) to pass, flow by
discurso [dis'kurso] *nm* speech; **~ de clausura** closing speech; **pronunciar un ~** to make a speech; **en el ~ del tiempo** with the passage of time
discusión [disku'sjon] *nf* (*diálogo*) discussion; (*riña*) argument; **tener una ~** to have an argument
discutible [disku'tiβle] *adj* debatable; **de mérito ~** of dubious worth
discutido, -a [disku'tiðo, a] *adj* controversial
discutir [disku'tir] *vt* (*debatir*) to discuss; (*pelear*) to argue about; (*contradecir*) to argue against ■ *vi* to discuss; (*disputar*) to argue; **~ de política** to argue about politics; **¡no discutas!** don't argue!
disecar [dise'kar] *vt* (*para conservar: animal*) to stuff; (*: planta*) to dry
diseminar [disemi'nar] *vt* to disseminate, spread
disentir [disen'tir] *vi* to dissent, disagree
diseñador, a [diseɲa'dor, a] *nm/f* designer
diseñar [dise'ɲar] *vt* to design
diseño [di'seɲo] *nm* (*Tec*) design; (*Arte*) drawing; (*Costura*) pattern; **de ~ italiano** Italian-designed; **~ asistido por ordenador** computer-assisted design, CAD
diseque *etc* [di'seke] *vb ver* **disecar**
disertar [diser'tar] *vi* to speak
disfrace *etc* [dis'fraθe] *vb ver* **disfrazar**
disfraz [dis'fraθ] *nm* (*máscara*) disguise; (*traje*) fancy dress; (*excusa*) pretext; **bajo el ~ de** under the cloak of
disfrazado, -a [disfra'θaðo, a] *adj* disguised; **ir ~ de** to masquerade as
disfrazar [disfra'θar] *vt* to disguise; **disfrazarse** *vr* to dress (o.s.) up; **disfrazarse de** to disguise o.s. as
disfrutar [disfru'tar] *vt* to enjoy ■ *vi* to enjoy o.s.; **¡que disfrutes!** have a good time!; **~ de** to enjoy, possess; **~ de buena salud** to enjoy good health
disfrute [dis'frute] *nm* (*goce*) enjoyment; (*aprovechamiento*) use
disgregar [disɣre'ɣar] *vt* (*desintegrar*) to disintegrate; (*manifestantes*) to disperse; **disgregarse** *vr* to disintegrate, break up
disgregue *etc* [dis'ɣreɣe] *vb ver* **disgregar**
disgustar [disɣus'tar] *vt* (*no gustar*) to displease; (*contrariar, enojar*) to annoy; to upset; **disgustarse** *vr* to be annoyed; (*dos personas*) to fall out; **estaba muy disgustado con el asunto** he was very upset about the affair
disgusto [dis'ɣusto] *nm* (*repugnancia*) disgust; (*contrariedad*) annoyance; (*desagrado*) displeasure; (*tristeza*) grief; (*riña*) quarrel; (*desgracia*) misfortune; **hacer algo a ~** to do sth unwillingly; **matar a algn a disgustos** to drive sb to distraction
disidente [disi'ðente] *nm* dissident
disienta *etc* [di'sjenta] *vb ver* **disentir**
disimulado, -a [disimu'laðo, a] *adj* (*solapado*) furtive, underhand; (*oculto*) covert; **hacerse el ~** to pretend not to notice
disimular [disimu'lar] *vt* (*ocultar*) to hide, conceal ■ *vi* to dissemble
disimulo [disi'mulo] *nm* (*fingimiento*) dissimulation; **con ~** cunningly
disipar [disi'par] *vt* (*duda, temor*) to dispel; (*esperanza*) to destroy; (*fortuna*) to squander; **disiparse** *vr* (*nubes*) to vanish; (*dudas*) to be dispelled; (*indisciplinarse*) to dissipate
diskette [dis'ket] *nm* (*Inform*) diskette, floppy disk
dislate [dis'late] *nm* (*absurdo*) absurdity; **dislates** *nmpl* nonsense *sg*
dislexia [dis'leksja] *nf* dyslexia
dislocar [dislo'kar] *vt* (*gen*) to dislocate; (*tobillo*) to sprain
disloque *etc* [dis'loke] *vb ver* **dislocar** ■ *nm*: **es el ~** (*fam*) it's the last straw
disminución [disminu'θjon] *nf* diminution
disminuido, -a [disminu'iðo, a] *nm/f*: **~ mental/físico** mentally/physically-handicapped person
disminuir [disminu'ir] *vt* to decrease, diminish; (*estrechar*) to lessen; (*temperatura*) to lower; (*gastos, raciones*) to cut down; (*dolor*) to relieve; (*autoridad, prestigio*) to weaken; (*entusiasmo*) to damp ■ *vi* (*días*) to grow shorter; (*precios, temperatura*) to drop, fall; (*velocidad*) to slacken; (*población*) to decrease; (*beneficios, número*) to fall off; (*memoria, vista*) to fail
disminuyendo *etc* [disminu'jendo] *vb ver* **disminuir**
disociar [diso'θjar] *vt* to disassociate; **disociarse** *vr* to disassociate o.s.
disoluble [diso'luβle] *adj* soluble
disolución [disolu'θjon] *nf* (*acto*) dissolution; (*Química*) solution; (*Com*) liquidation; (*moral*) dissoluteness
disoluto, -a [diso'luto, a] *adj* dissolute

disolvente [disol'βente] *nm* solvent, thinner
disolver [disol'βer] *vt* (*gen*) to dissolve; (*manifestación*) to break up; **disolverse** *vr* to dissolve; (*Com*) to go into liquidation
disonar [diso'nar] *vb* (*Mus*) to be out of tune; (*no armonizar*) to lack harmony; **~ con** to be out of keeping with, clash with
dispar [dis'par] *adj* (*distinto*) different; (*irregular*) uneven
disparado, -a [dispa'raðo, a] *adj*: **entrar ~** to shoot in; **salir ~** to shoot out; **ir ~** to go like mad
disparador [dispara'ðor] *nm* (*de arma*) trigger; (*Foto, Tec*) release; **~ atómico** aerosol; **~ de bombas** bomb release
disparar [dispa'rar] *vt, vi* to shoot, fire; **dispararse** *vr* (*arma de fuego*) to go off; (*persona: marcharse*) to rush off; (*: enojarse*) to lose control; (*caballo*) to bolt
disparatado, -a [dispara'taðo, a] *adj* crazy
disparate [dispa'rate] *nm* (*tontería*) foolish remark; (*error*) blunder; **decir disparates** to talk nonsense; **¡qué ~!** how absurd!; **costar un ~** to cost a hell of a lot
disparo [dis'paro] *nm* shot; (*acto*) firing; **disparos** *nmpl* shooting *sg*, exchange *sg* of shots, shots; **~ inicial** (*de cohete*) blast-off
dispendio [dis'pendjo] *nm* waste
dispensar [dispen'sar] *vt* to dispense; (*ayuda*) to give; (*honores*) to grant; (*disculpar*) to excuse; **¡usted dispense!** I beg your pardon!; **~ a algn de hacer algo** to excuse sb from doing sth
dispensario [dispen'sarjo] *nm* (*clínica*) community clinic; (*de hospital*) outpatients' department
dispersar [disper'sar] *vt* to disperse; (*manifestación*) to break up; **dispersarse** *vr* to scatter
disperso, -a [dis'perso, a] *adj* scattered
displicencia [displi'θenθja] *nf* (*mal humor*) peevishness; (*desgana*) lack of enthusiasm
displicente [displi'θente] *adj* (*malhumorado*) peevish; (*poco entusiasta*) unenthusiastic
dispondré *etc* [dispon'dre] *vb ver* **disponer**
disponer [dispo'ner] *vt* (*arreglar*) to arrange; (*ordenar*) to put in order; (*preparar*) to prepare, get ready ■ *vi*: **~ de** to have, own; **disponerse** *vr*: **disponerse para** to prepare to, prepare for; **la ley dispone que ...** the law provides that ...; **no puede ~ de esos bienes** she cannot dispose of those properties
disponga *etc* [dis'ponga] *vb ver* **disponer**
disponibilidad [disponiβili'ðað] *nf* availability; **disponibilidades** *nfpl* (*Com*) resources, financial assets
disponible [dispo'niβle] *adj* available; (*tiempo*) spare; (*dinero*) on hand
disposición [disposi'θjon] *nf* arrangement, disposition; (*de casa, Inform*) layout; (*ley*) order; (*cláusula*) provision; (*aptitud*) aptitude; **~ de ánimo** attitude of mind; **última ~** last will and testament; **a la ~ de** at the disposal of; **a su ~** at your service
dispositivo [disposi'tiβo] *nm* device, mechanism; **~ de alimentación** hopper; **~ de almacenaje** storage device; **~ periférico** peripheral (device); **~ de seguridad** safety catch; (*fig*) security measure
dispuesto, -a [dis'pwesto, a] *pp de* **disponer** ■ *adj* (*arreglado*) arranged; (*preparado*) disposed; (*persona: dinámico*) bright; **estar ~/poco ~ a hacer algo** to be inclined/reluctant to do sth
dispuse *etc* [dis'puse] *vb ver* **disponer**
disputa [dis'puta] *nf* (*discusión*) dispute, argument; (*controversia*) controversy
disputar [dispu'tar] *vt* (*discutir*) to dispute, question; (*contender*) to contend for ■ *vi* to argue
disquete [dis'kete] *nm* (*Inform*) diskette, floppy disk
disquetera [diske'tera] *nf* disk drive
Dist. *abr* (= *Distrito*) dist.
distancia [dis'tanθja] *nf* distance; (*de tiempo*) interval; **~ de parada** braking distance; **~ del suelo** (*Auto etc*) height off the ground; **a gran** *o* **a larga ~** long-distance; **mantenerse a ~** to keep one's distance; (*fig*) to remain aloof; **guardar las distancias** to keep one's distance
distanciado, -a [distan'θjaðo, a] *adj* (*remoto*) remote; (*fig: alejado*) far apart; **estamos distanciados en ideas** our ideas are poles apart
distanciamiento [distanθja'mjento] *nm* (*acto*) spacing out; (*estado*) remoteness; (*fig*) distance
distanciar [distan'θjar] *vt* to space out; **distanciarse** *vr* to become estranged
distante [dis'tante] *adj* distant
distar [dis'tar] *vi*: **dista 5 kms de aquí** it is 5 kms from here; **¿dista mucho?** is it far?; **dista mucho de la verdad** it's very far from the truth
diste ['diste], **disteis** ['disteis] *vb ver* **dar**
distensión [disten'sjon] *nf* distension; (*Pol*) détente; **~ muscular** (*Med*) muscular strain
distinción [distin'θjon] *nf* distinction; (*elegancia*) elegance; (*honor*) honour; **a ~ de** unlike; **sin ~** indiscriminately; **sin ~ de edades** irrespective of age
distinga *etc* [dis'tinga] *vb ver* **distinguir**
distinguido, -a [distin'giðo, a] *adj*

distinguished; (*famoso*) prominent, well-known; (*elegante*) elegant
distinguir [distin'gir] *vt* to distinguish; (*divisar*) to make out; (*escoger*) to single out; (*caracterizar*) to mark out; **distinguirse** *vr* to be distinguished; (*destacarse*) to distinguish o.s.; **a lo lejos no se distingue** it's not visible from a distance
distintivo, -a [distin'tiβo, a] *adj* distinctive; (*signo*) distinguishing ■ *nm* (*de policía etc*) badge; (*fig*) characteristic
distinto, -a [dis'tinto, a] *adj* different; (*claro*) clear; **distintos** several, various
distorsión [distor'sjon] *nf* (*Anat*) twisting; (*Radio etc*) distortion
distorsionar [distorsjo'nar] *vt, vi* to distort
distracción [distrak'θjon] *nf* distraction; (*pasatiempo*) hobby, pastime; (*olvido*) absent-mindedness, distraction
distraer [distra'er] *vt* (*atención*) to distract; (*divertir*) to amuse; (*fondos*) to embezzle ■ *vi* to be relaxing; **distraerse** *vr* (*entretenerse*) to amuse o.s.; (*perder la concentración*) to allow one's attention to wander; **~ a algn de su pensamiento** to divert sb from his train of thought; **el pescar distrae** fishing is a relaxation
distraído, -a [distra'iðo, a] *adj* (*gen*) absent-minded; (*desatento*) inattentive; (*entretenido*) amusing ■ *nm*: **hacerse el ~** to pretend not to notice; **con aire ~** idly; **me miró distraída** she gave me a casual glance
distraiga *etc* [dis'traiɣa], **distraje** *etc* [dis'traxe], **distrajera** *etc* [distra'xera], **distrayendo** [distra'jendo] *vb ver* **distraer**
distribución [distriβu'θjon] *nf* distribution; (*entrega*) delivery; (*en estadística*) distribution, incidence; (*Arq*) layout; **~ de premios** prize giving; **la ~ de los impuestos** the incidence of taxes
distribuidor, a [distriβui'ðor, a] *nm/f* (*persona: gen*) distributor; (*: Correos*) sorter; (*: Com*) dealer; **su ~ habitual** your regular dealer
distribuir [distriβu'ir] *vt* to distribute; (*prospectos*) to hand out; (*cartas*) to deliver; (*trabajo*) to allocate; (*premios*) to award; (*dividendos*) to pay; (*peso*) to distribute; (*Arq*) to plan
distribuyendo *etc* [distriβu'jendo] *vb ver* **distribuir**
distrito [dis'trito] *nm* (*sector, territorio*) region; (*barrio*) district; **~ electoral** constituency; **~ postal** postal district
disturbio [dis'turβjo] *nm* disturbance; (*desorden*) riot; **los disturbios** *nmpl* the troubles
disuadir [diswa'ðir] *vt* to dissuade
disuasión [diswa'sjon] *nf* dissuasion; (*Mil*) deterrent; **~ nuclear** nuclear deterrent
disuasivo, -a [diswa'siβo, a] *adj* dissuasive; **arma disuasiva** deterrent
disuasorio, -a [diswa'sorjo, a] *adj* = **disuasivo**
disuelto [di'swelto] *pp de* **disolver**
disuelva *etc* [di'swelβa] *vb ver* **disolver**
disuene *etc* [di'swene] *vb ver* **disonar**
disyuntiva [disjun'tiβa] *nf* (*dilema*) dilemma
DIU ['diu] *nm abr* (= *dispositivo intrauterino*) IUD
diurno, -a ['djurno, a] *adj* day *cpd*, diurnal
diva ['diβa] *nf* prima donna
divagar [diβa'ɣar] *vi* (*desviarse*) to digress
divague *etc* [di'βaɣe] *vb ver* **divagar**
diván [di'βan] *nm* divan
divergencia [diβer'xenθja] *nf* divergence
divergir [diβer'xir] *vi* (*líneas*) to diverge; (*opiniones*) to differ; (*personas*) to disagree
diverja *etc* [di'βerxa] *vb ver* **divergir**
diversidad [diβersi'ðað] *nf* diversity, variety
diversificación [diβersifika'θjon] *nf* (*Com*) diversification
diversificar [diβersifi'kar] *vt* to diversify
diversifique *etc* [diβersi'fike] *vb ver* **diversificar**
diversión [diβer'sjon] *nf* (*gen*) entertainment; (*actividad*) hobby, pastime
diverso, -a [di'βerso, a] *adj* diverse; (*diferente*) different ■ *nm*: **diversos** (*Com*) sundries; **diversos libros** several books
divertido, -a [diβer'tiðo, a] *adj* (*chiste*) amusing, funny; (*fiesta etc*) enjoyable; (*película, libro*) entertaining; **está ~** (*irónico*) this is going to be fun
divertir [diβer'tir] *vt* (*entretener, recrear*) to amuse, entertain; **divertirse** *vr* (*pasarlo bien*) to have a good time; (*distraerse*) to amuse o.s.
dividendo [diβi'ðendo] *nm* (*Com*): **dividendos** *nmpl* dividends; **dividendos por acción** earnings per share; **~ definitivo** final dividend
dividir [diβi'ðir] *vt* (*gen*) to divide; (*separar*) to separate; (*distribuir*) to distribute, share out
divierta *etc* [di'βjerta] *vb ver* **divertir**
divinidad [diβini'ðað] *nf* (*esencia divina*) divinity; **la D~** God
divino, -a [di'βino, a] *adj* divine; (*fig*) lovely
divirtiendo *etc* [diβir'tjendo] *vb ver* **divertir**
divisa [di'βisa] *nf* (*emblema*) emblem, badge; **divisas** *nfpl* currency *sg*; (*Com*) foreign exchange *sg*; **control de divisas** exchange control; **~ de reserva** reserve currency
divisar [diβi'sar] *vt* to make out
división [diβi'sjon] *nf* division; (*de partido*) split; (*de país*) partition

divisorio, -a [diβi'sorjo, a] *adj* (*línea*) dividing; **línea divisoria de las aguas** watershed
divorciado, -a [diβor'θjaðo, a] *adj* divorced; (*opinión*) split ■ *nm/f* divorcé(e)
divorciar [diβor'θjar] *vt* to divorce; **divorciarse** *vr* to get divorced
divorcio [di'βorθjo] *nm* divorce; (*fig*) split
divulgación [diβulγa'θjon] *nf* (*difusión*) spreading; (*popularización*) popularization
divulgar [diβul'γar] *vt* (*desparramar*) to spread; (*popularizar*) to popularize; (*hacer circular*) to divulge, circulate; **divulgarse** *vr* (*secreto*) to leak out; (*rumor*) to get about
divulgue *etc* [di'βulγe] *vb ver* **divulgar**
dizque ['diske] *adv* (*Am fam*) apparently
Dls., dls *abr* (*Am*) = **dólares**
dm *abr* (= *decímetro*) dm
DNI *nm abr* (*Esp*) = **Documento Nacional de Identidad**
Dña. *abr* (= *Doña*) Mrs
do [do] *nm* (*Mus*) C
D.O. *abr* = **Denominación de Origen**; *ver* **denominación**
dobladillo [doβla'ðiʎo] *nm* (*de vestido*) hem; (*de pantalón: vuelta*) turn-up (*Brit*), cuff (*US*)
doblaje [do'βlaxe] *nm* (*Cine*) dubbing
doblar [do'βlar] *vt* to double; (*papel*) to fold; (*caño*) to bend; (*la esquina*) to turn, go round; (*film*) to dub ■ *vi* to turn; (*campana*) to toll; **doblarse** *vr* (*plegarse*) to fold (up), crease; (*encorvarse*) to bend
doble ['doβle] *adj* (*gen*) double; (*de dos aspectos*) dual; (*cuerda*) thick; (*fig*) two-faced ■ *nm* double ■ *nm/f* (*Teat*) double, stand-in; **dobles** *nmpl* (*Deporte*) doubles *sg*; **~ o nada** double or quits; **~ página** double-page spread; **con ~ sentido** with a double meaning; **el ~** twice the quantity *o* as much; **su sueldo es el ~ del mío** his salary is twice (as much as) mine; (*Inform*): **~ cara** double-sided; **~ densidad** double density; **~ espacio** double spacing
doblegar [doβle'γar] *vt* to fold, crease; **doblegarse** *vr* to yield
doblegue *etc* [do'βleγe] *vb ver* **doblegar**
doblez [do'βleθ] *nm* (*pliegue*) fold, hem ■ *nf* (*falsedad*) duplicity
doc. *abr* (= *docena*) doz.; (= *documento*) doc.
doce ['doθe] *num* twelve; (*fecha*) twelfth; **las ~** twelve o'clock; *ver tb* **seis**
docena [do'θena] *nf* dozen; **por docenas** by the dozen
docente [do'θente] *adj*: **centro/personal ~** teaching institution/staff
dócil ['doθil] *adj* (*pasivo*) docile; (*manso*) gentle; (*obediente*) obedient
docto, -a ['dokto, a] *adj* learned, erudite ■ *nm/f* scholar
doctor, a [dok'tor, a] *nm/f* doctor; **~ en filosofía** Doctor of Philosophy
doctorado [dokto'raðo] *nm* doctorate
doctorarse [dokto'rarse] *vr* to get a doctorate
doctrina [dok'trina] *nf* doctrine, teaching
documentación [dokumenta'θjon] *nf* documentation; (*de identidad etc*) papers *pl*
documental [dokumen'tal] *adj, nm* documentary
documentar [dokumen'tar] *vt* to document; **documentarse** *vr* to gather information
documento [doku'mento] *nm* (*certificado*) document; (*Jur*) exhibit; **documentos** *nmpl* papers; **~ adjunto** (*Inform*) attachment; **~ justificativo** voucher; **D~ Nacional de Identidad** national identity card; *see note*

DOCUMENTO

A laminated plastic ID card with the holder's personal details and photograph, the *Documento Nacional de Identidad* is renewed every 10 years. People are required to carry it at all times and to produce it on request for the police. In Spain it is commonly known as the DNI or *carnet de identidad*. In Spanish America a similar card is called the *cédula (de identidad)*.

dogma ['doγma] *nm* dogma
dogmático, -a [doγ'matiko, a] *adj* dogmatic
dogo ['doγo] *nm* bulldog
dólar ['dolar] *nm* dollar
dolencia [do'lenθja] *nf* (*achaque*) ailment; (*dolor*) ache
doler [do'ler] *vt, vi* to hurt; (*fig*) to grieve; **dolerse** *vr* (*de su situación*) to grieve, feel sorry; (*de las desgracias ajenas*) to sympathize; (*quejarse*) to complain; **me duele el brazo** my arm hurts; **no me duele el dinero** I don't mind about the money; **¡ahí le duele!** you've put your finger on it!
doliente [do'ljente] *adj* (*enfermo*) sick; (*dolorido*) aching; (*triste*) sorrowful; **la familia ~** the bereaved family
dolor [do'lor] *nm* pain; (*fig*) grief, sorrow; **~ de cabeza** headache; **~ de estómago** stomach ache; **~ de oídos** earache; **~ sordo** dull ache
dolorido, -a [dolo'riðo, a] *adj* (*Med*) sore; **la parte dolorida** the part which hurts
doloroso, -a [dolo'roso, a] *adj* (*Med*) painful; (*fig*) distressing
dom. *abr* (= *domingo*) Sun.
domar [do'mar] *vt* to tame

domesticado, -a [domesti'kaðo, a] *adj* (*amansado*) tame
domesticar [domesti'kar] *vt* to tame
doméstico, -a [do'mestiko, a] *adj* domestic ■ *nm/f* servant; **economía doméstica** home economy; **gastos domésticos** household expenses
domestique *etc* [domes'tike] *vb ver* **domesticar**
domiciliación [domiθilja'θjon] *nf*: **~ de pagos** (*Com*) direct debit
domiciliar [domiθi'ljar] *vt* to domicile; **domiciliarse** *vr* to take up (one's) residence
domiciliario, -a [domiθi'ljarjo, a] *adj*: **arresto ~** house arrest
domicilio [domi'θiljo] *nm* home; **~ particular** private residence; **~ social** (*Com*) head office, registered office; **servicio a ~** delivery service; **sin ~ fijo** of no fixed abode
dominante [domi'nante] *adj* dominant; (*person*) domineering
dominar [domi'nar] *vt* (*gen*) to dominate; (*países*) to rule over; (*adversario*) to overpower; (*caballo, nervios, emoción*) to control; (*incendio, epidemia*) to bring under control; (*idiomas*) to be fluent in ■ *vi* to dominate, prevail; **dominarse** *vr* to control o.s.
domingo [do'mingo] *nm* Sunday; **D~ de Ramos** Palm Sunday; **D~ de Resurrección** Easter Sunday; *ver tb* **sábado**; **Semana Santa**
dominguero, -a [domin'gero, a] *adj* Sunday *cpd*
dominical [domini'kal] *adj* Sunday *cpd*; **periódico ~** Sunday newspaper
dominicano, -a [domini'kano, a] *adj, nm/f* Dominican
dominio [do'minjo] *nm* (*tierras*) domain; (*Pol*) dominion; (*autoridad*) power, authority; (*supremacía*) supremacy; (*de las pasiones*) grip, hold; (*de idioma*) command; **ser del ~ público** to be widely known
dominó [domi'no] *nm* (*pieza*) domino; (*juego*) dominoes
don [don] *nm* (*talento*) gift; **D~ Juan Gómez** Mr Juan Gómez, Juan Gómez Esq. (*Brit*); **tener ~ de gentes** to know how to handle people; **~ de lenguas** gift for languages; **~ de mando** (qualities of) leadership; **~ de palabra** gift of the gab; *see note*

DON

Don or *doña* is a term used before someone's first name – eg Don Diego, Doña Inés – when showing respect or being polite to someone of a superior social standing or to an older person. It is becoming somewhat rare, but it does however continue to be used with names and surnames in official documents and in correspondence: eg Sr. D. Pedro Rodríguez Hernández, Sra. Dña Inés Rodríguez Hernández.

donación [dona'θjon] *nf* donation
donaire [do'naire] *nm* charm
donante [do'nante] *nm/f* donor; **~ de sangre** blood donor
donar [do'nar] *vt* to donate
donativo [dona'tiβo] *nm* donation
doncella [don'θeʎa] *nf* (*criada*) maid
donde ['donde] *adv* where ■ *prep*: **el coche está allí ~ el farol** the car is over there by the lamppost *o* where the lamppost is; **por ~** through which; **a ~** to where, to which; **en ~** where, in which; **es a ~ vamos nosotros** that's where we're going
dónde ['donde] *adv interrogativo* where?; **¿a ~ vas?** where are you going (to)?; **¿de ~ vienes?** where have you come from?; **¿en ~?** where?; **¿por ~?** where?, whereabouts?; **¿por ~ se va al estadio?** how do you get to the stadium?
dondequiera [donde'kjera] *adv* anywhere ■ *conj*: **~ que** wherever; **por ~** everywhere, all over the place
donostiarra [donos'tjarra] *adj* of *o* from San Sebastián ■ *nm/f* native *o* inhabitant of San Sebastián
doña ['doɲa] *nf*: **D~ Carmen Gómez** Mrs Carmen Gómez; *ver tb* **don**
dopar [do'par] *vt* to dope, drug
doping ['dopin] *nm* doping, drugging
doquier [do'kjer] *adv*: **por ~** all over, everywhere
dorado, -a [do'raðo, a] *adj* (*color*) golden; (*Tec*) gilt
dorar [do'rar] *vt* (*Tec*) to gild; (*Culin*) to brown, cook lightly; **~ la píldora** to sweeten the pill
dormilón, -ona [dormi'lon, ona] *adj* fond of sleeping ■ *nm/f* sleepyhead
dormir [dor'mir] *vt*: **~ la siesta por la tarde** to have an afternoon nap ■ *vi* to sleep; **dormirse** *vr* (*persona, brazo, pierna*) to fall asleep; **dormirla** (*fam*) to sleep it off; **~ la mona** (*fam*) to sleep off a hangover; **~ como un lirón** *o* **tronco** to sleep like a log; **~ a pierna suelta** to sleep soundly
dormitar [dormi'tar] *vi* to doze
dormitorio [dormi'torjo] *nm* bedroom; **~ común** dormitory
dorsal [dor'sal] *adj* dorsal ■ *nm* (*Deporte*) number
dorso ['dorso] *nm* back; **escribir algo al ~** to write sth on the back; **"vease al ~"** "see

other side", "please turn over"
DOS *nm abr (= sistema operativo de disco)* DOS
dos [dos] *num* two; *(fecha)* second; **los ~** the two of them, both of them; **cada ~ por tres** every five minutes; **de ~ en ~** in twos; **estamos a ~** *(Tenis)* the score is deuce; *ver tb* **seis**
doscientos, -as [dos'θjentos, as] *num* two hundred
dosel [do'sel] *nm* canopy
dosificar [dosifi'kar] *vt (Culin, Med, Química)* to measure out; *(no derrochar)* to be sparing with
dosifique *etc* [dosi'fike] *vb ver* **dosificar**
dosis ['dosis] *nf inv* dose, dosage
dossier [do'sjer] *nm* dossier, file
dotación [dota'θjon] *nf (acto, dinero)* endowment; *(plantilla)* staff; *(Naut)* crew; **la ~ es insuficiente** we are understaffed
dotado, -a [do'taðo, a] *adj* gifted; **~ de** *(persona)* endowed with; *(máquina)* equipped with
dotar [do'tar] *vt* to endow; *(Tec)* to fit; *(barco)* to man; *(oficina)* to staff
dote ['dote] *nf (de novia)* dowry; **dotes** *nfpl (talentos)* gifts
doy [doj] *vb ver* **dar**
Dpto. *abr (= Departamento)* dept.
Dr., Dra. *abr (= Doctor, Doctora)* Dr
draga ['draɣa] *nf* dredge
dragado [dra'ɣaðo] *nm* dredging
dragar [dra'ɣar] *vt* to dredge; *(minas)* to sweep
dragón [dra'ɣon] *nm* dragon
drague *etc* ['draɣe] *vb ver* **dragar**
drama ['drama] *nm* drama; *(obra)* play
dramático, -a [dra'matiko, a] *adj* dramatic ■ *nm/f* dramatist; *(actor)* actor; **obra dramática** play
dramaturgo, -a [drama'turɣo, a] *nm/f* dramatist, playwright
dramón [dra'mon] *nm (Teat)* melodrama; **¡qué ~!** what a scene!
drástico, -a ['drastiko, a] *adj* drastic
drenaje [dre'naxe] *nm* drainage
drenar [dre'nar] *vt* to drain
droga ['droɣa] *nf* drug; *(Deporte)* dope; **el problema de la ~** the drug problem
drogadicto, -a [droɣa'ðikto, a] *nm/f* drug addict
drogar [dro'ɣar] *vt* to drug; *(Deporte)* to dope; **drogarse** *vr* to take drugs
drogodependencia [droɣoðepen'denθja] *nf* drug addiction
drogue *etc* ['droɣe] *vb ver* **drogar**
droguería [droɣe'ria] *nf* ≈ hardware shop *(Brit) o* store *(US)*
dromedario [drome'ðarjo] *nm* dromedary
Dto. *abr* = **descuento**
Dtor., Dtora. *abr (= Director, Directora)* Dir.
ducado [du'kaðo] *nm* duchy, dukedom
ducha ['dutʃa] *nf (baño)* shower; *(Med)* douche
ducharse [du'tʃarse] *vr* to take a shower
ducho, -a ['dutʃo, a] *adj*: **~ en** *(experimentado)* experienced in; *(hábil)* skilled at
dúctil ['duktil] *adj (metal)* ductile; *(persona)* easily influenced
duda ['duða] *nf* doubt; **sin ~** no doubt, doubtless; **¡sin ~!** of course!; **no cabe ~** there is no doubt about it; **no le quepa ~** make no mistake about it; **no quiero poner en ~ su conducta** I don't want to call his behaviour into question; **sacar a algn de la ~** to settle sb's doubts; **tengo una ~** I have a query
dudar [du'ðar] *vt* to doubt ■ *vi* to doubt, have doubts; **~ acerca de algo** to be uncertain about sth; **dudó en comprarlo** he hesitated to buy it; **dudan que sea verdad** they doubt whether *o* if it's true
dudoso, -a [du'ðoso, a] *adj (incierto)* hesitant; *(sospechoso)* doubtful; *(conducta)* dubious
duelo *etc* ['dwelo] *vb ver* **doler** ■ *nm (combate)* duel; *(luto)* mourning; **batirse en** *etc* to fight a duel
duende ['dwende] *nm* imp, goblin; **tiene ~** he's got real soul
dueño, -a ['dweɲo, a] *nm/f (propietario)* owner; *(de pensión, taberna)* landlord(-lady); *(de casa, perro)* master/mistress; *(empresario)* employer; **ser ~ de sí mismo** to have self-control; *(libre)* to be one's own boss; **eres ~ de hacer como te parezca** you're free to do as you think fit; **hacerse ~ de una situación** to take command of a situation
duerma *etc* ['dwerma] *vb ver* **dormir**
duermevela [dwerme'βela] *nf (fam)* nap, snooze
Duero ['dwero] *nm* Douro
dulce ['dulθe] *adj* sweet; *(carácter, clima)* gentle, mild ■ *adv* gently, softly ■ *nm* sweet
dulcificar [dulθifi'kar] *vt (fig)* to soften
dulcifique *etc* [dulθi'fike] *vb ver* **dulcificar**
dulzón, -ona [dul'θon, ona] *adj (alimento)* sickly-sweet, too sweet; *(canción etc)* gooey
dulzura [dul'θura] *nf* sweetness; *(ternura)* gentleness
duna ['duna] *nf* dune
Dunquerque [dun'kerke] *nm* Dunkirk
dúo ['duo] *nm* duet, duo
duodécimo, -a [duo'deθimo, a] *adj* twelfth; *ver tb* **sexto, a**
dup., dup.do *abr (= duplicado)* duplicated
dúplex ['dupleks] *nm inv (piso)* duplex (apartment); *(Telec)* link-up; *(Inform)*: **~ integral** full duplex
duplicar [dupli'kar] *vt (hacer el doble de)* to duplicate; *(cantidad)* to double; **duplicarse** *vr* to double

duplique *etc* [du'plike] *vb ver* **duplicar**
duque ['duke] *nm* duke
duquesa [du'kesa] *nf* duchess
duración [dura'θjon] *nf* duration, length; (*de máquina*) life; **~ media de la vida** average life expectancy; **de larga ~** (*enfermedad*) lengthy; (*pila*) long-life; (*disco*) long-playing; **de poca ~** short
duradero, -a [dura'ðero, a] *adj* (*tela*) hard-wearing; (*fe, paz*) lasting
durante [du'rante] *adv* during; **~ toda la noche** all night long; **habló ~ una hora** he spoke for an hour
durar [du'rar] *vi* (*permanecer*) to last; (*recuerdo*) to remain; (*ropa*) to wear (well)
durazno [du'rasno] *nm* (*Am: fruta*) peach; (*: árbol*) peach tree
durex ['dureks] *nm* (*Am: tira adhesiva*) Sellotape® (*Brit*), Scotch tape® (*US*)
dureza [du'reθa] *nf* (*cualidad*) hardness; (*de carácter*) toughness
durmiendo *etc* [dur'mjendo] *vb ver* **dormir**
durmiente [dur'mjente] *adj* sleeping ▪ *nm/f* sleeper
duro, -a ['duro, a] *adj* hard; (*carácter*) tough; (*pan*) stale; (*cuello, puerta*) stiff; (*clima, luz*) harsh ▪ *adv* hard ▪ *nm* (*moneda*) five peseta coin; **el sector ~ del partido** the hardliners *pl* in the party; **ser ~ con algn** to be tough with *o* hard on sb; **~ de mollera** (*torpe*) dense; **~ de oído** hard of hearing; **trabajar ~** to work hard; **estar sin un ~** to be broke
DVD *nm abr* (*= disco de vídeo digital*) DVD

Ee

E, e [e] *nf* (*letra*) E, e; **E de Enrique** E for Edward (*Brit*) *o* Easy (*US*)
E *abr* (= *este*) E
e [e] *conj* (*delante de* **i-** *e* **hi-** *pero no* **hie-**) and; *ver tb* **y**
e/ *abr* (*Com:* = *envío*) shpt.
EA *abr* = **Ejército del Aire**
EAU *nmpl abr* (= *Emiratos Árabes Unidos*) UAE
ebanista [eβa'nista] *nm/f* cabinetmaker
ébano ['eβano] *nm* ebony
ebrio, -a ['eβrjo, a] *adj* drunk
Ebro ['eβro] *nm* Ebro
ebullición [eβuʎi'θjon] *nf* boiling; **punto de ~** boiling point
eccema [ek'θema] *nm* (*Med*) eczema
echar [e'tʃar] *vt* to throw; (*agua, vino*) to pour (out); (*Culin*) to put in, add; (*dientes*) to cut; (*discurso*) to give; (*empleado: despedir*) to fire, sack; (*hojas*) to sprout; (*cartas*) to post; (*humo*) to emit, give out; (*reprimenda*) to deal out; (*cuenta*) to make up; (*freno*) to put on ■ *vi*: **~ a correr/llorar** to break into a run/burst into tears; **~ a reír** to burst out laughing; **echarse** *vr* to lie down; **~ abajo** (*gobierno*) to overthrow; (*edificio*) to demolish; **~ la buenaventura a algn** to tell sb's fortune; **~ la culpa a** to lay the blame on; **~ de menos** to miss; **echarse atrás** to throw o.s. back(wards); (*fig*) to go back on what one has said; **echarse una novia** to get o.s. a girlfriend; **echarse una siestecita** to have a nap
echarpe [e'tʃarpe] *nm* (woman's) stole
eclesiástico, -a [ekle'sjastiko, a] *adj* ecclesiastical; (*autoridades etc*) church *cpd* ■ *nm* clergyman
eclipsar [eklip'sar] *vt* to eclipse; (*fig*) to outshine, overshadow
eclipse [e'klipse] *nm* eclipse
eco ['eko] *nm* echo; **encontrar un ~ en** to produce a response from; **hacerse ~ de una opinión** to echo an opinion; **tener ~** to catch on
ecografía [ekoɣra'fia] *nf* ultrasound
ecología [ekolo'xia] *nf* ecology
ecológico, -a [eko'loxiko, a] *adj* ecological; (*producto, método*) environmentally-friendly; (*agricultura*) organic
ecologista [ekolo'xista] *adj* environmental, conservation *cpd* ■ *nm/f* environmentalist
economato [ekono'mato] *nm* cooperative store
economía [ekono'mia] *nf* (*sistema*) economy; (*cualidad*) thrift; **~ dirigida** planned economy; **~ doméstica** housekeeping; **~ de mercado** market economy; **~ mixta** mixed economy; **~ sumergida** black economy; **hacer economías** to economize; **economías de escala** economies of scale
economice *etc* [ekono'miθe] *vb ver* **economizar**
económico, -a [eko'nomiko, a] *adj* (*barato*) cheap, economical; (*persona*) thrifty; (*Com: año etc*) financial; (*: situación*) economic
economista [ekono'mista] *nm/f* economist
economizar [ekonomi'θar] *vt* to economize on ■ *vi* (*ahorrar*) to save up; (*pey*) to be miserly
ecosistema [ekosis'tema] *nm* ecosystem
ecu ['eku] *nm* ecu
ecuación [ekwa'θjon] *nf* equation
ecuador [ekwa'ðor] *nm* equator; **(el) E~** Ecuador
ecuánime [e'kwanime] *adj* (*carácter*) level-headed; (*estado*) calm
ecuatorial [ekwato'rjal] *adj* equatorial
ecuatoriano, -a [ekwato'rjano, a] *adj, nm/f* Ecuador(i)an
ecuestre [e'kwestre] *adj* equestrian
eczema [ek'θema] *nm* = **eccema**
ed. *abr* (= *edición*) ed.
edad [e'ðað] *nf* age; **¿qué ~ tienes?** how old are you?; **tiene ocho años de ~** he is eight (years old); **de ~ corta** young; **ser de ~ mediana/avanzada** to be middle-aged/getting on; **ser mayor de ~** to be of age; **llegar a mayor ~** to come of age; **ser menor**

de ~ to be under age; **la E~ Media** the Middle Ages; **la E~ de Oro** the Golden Age
Edén [e'ðen] *nm* Eden
edición [eði'θjon] *nf* (*acto*) publication; (*ejemplar*) edition; **"al cerrar la ~"** (*Tip*) "stop press"
edicto [e'ðikto] *nm* edict, proclamation
edificante [eðifi'kante] *adj* edifying
edificar [edifi'kar] *vt* (*Arq*) to build
edificio [eði'fiθjo] *nm* building; (*fig*) edifice, structure
edifique *etc* [eði'fike] *vb ver* **edificar**
Edimburgo [eðim'burɣo] *nm* Edinburgh
editar [eði'tar] *vt* (*publicar*) to publish; (*preparar textos, tb Inform*) to edit
editor, a [eði'tor, a] *nm/f* (*que publica*) publisher; (*redactor*) editor ■ *adj*: **casa editora** publishing company
editorial [eðito'rjal] *adj* editorial ■ *nm* leading article, editorial ■ *nf* (*tb*: **casa editorial**) publisher
editorialista [eðitorja'lista] *nm/f* leader-writer
edredón [eðre'ðon] *nm* eiderdown, quilt; **~ nórdico** continental quilt, duvet
educación [eðuka'θjon] *nf* education; (*crianza*) upbringing; (*modales*) (good) manners *pl*; (*formación*) training; **sin ~** ill-mannered; **¡qué falta de ~!** how rude!
educado, -a [eðu'kaðo, a] *adj* well-mannered; **mal ~** ill-mannered
educar [eðu'kar] *vt* to educate; (*criar*) to bring up; (*voz*) to train
educativo, -a [eðuka'tiβo, a] *adj* educational; (*política*) education *cpd*
eduque *etc* [e'ðuke] *vb ver* **educar**
EE UU *nmpl abr* (= *Estados Unidos*) USA
efectista [efek'tista] *adj* sensationalist
efectivamente [efektiβa'mente] *adv* (*como respuesta*) exactly, precisely; (*verdaderamente*) really; (*de hecho*) in fact
efectivo, -a [efek'tiβo, a] *adj* effective; (*real*) actual, real ■ *nm*: **pagar en ~** to pay (in) cash; **hacer ~ un cheque** to cash a cheque
efecto [e'fekto] *nm* effect, result; (*objetivo*) purpose, end; **efectos** *nmpl* (*personales*) effects; (*bienes*) goods; (*Com*) assets; (*Econ*) bills, securities; **~ 2000** millennium bug; **~ invernadero** greenhouse effect; **efectos de consumo** consumer goods; **efectos a cobrar** bills receivable; **efectos especiales** special effects; **efectos personales** personal effects; **efectos secundarios** (*Com*) spin-off effects; **efectos sonoros** sound effects; **hacer** *o* **surtir ~** to have the desired effect; **hacer ~** (*impresionar*) to make an impression; **llevar algo a ~** to carry sth out; **en ~** in fact; (*respuesta*) exactly, indeed
efectuar [efek'twar] *vt* to carry out; (*viaje*) to make
efervescente [eferβes'θente] *adj* (*bebida*) fizzy, bubbly
eficacia [efi'kaθja] *nf* (*de persona*) efficiency; (*de medicamento etc*) effectiveness
eficaz [efi'kaθ] *adj* (*persona*) efficient; (*acción*) effective
eficiencia [efi'θjenθja] *nf* efficiency
eficiente [efi'θjente] *adj* efficient
efigie [e'fixje] *nf* effigy
efímero, -a [e'fimero, a] *adj* ephemeral
EFTA *sigla f* = **Asociación Europea de Libre Comercio**
efusión [efu'sjon] *nf* outpouring; (*en el trato*) warmth; **con ~** effusively
efusivo, -a [efu'siβo, a] *adj* effusive; **mis más efusivas gracias** my warmest thanks
EGB *nf abr* (*Esp Escol*: = *Educación General Básica*) *primary education for six- to fourteen-year olds*; *ver tb* **sistema educativo**
Egeo [e'xeo] *nm*: **(Mar) ~** Aegean (Sea)
egipcio, -a [e'xipθjo, a] *adj, nm/f* Egyptian
Egipto [e'xipto] *nm* Egypt
egocéntrico, -a [eɣo'θentriko, a] *adj* self-centred
egoísmo [eɣo'ismo] *nm* egoism
egoísta [eɣo'ista] *adj* egoistical, selfish ■ *nm/f* egoist
ególatra [e'ɣolatra] *adj* big-headed
egregio, -a [e'ɣrexjo, a] *adj* eminent, distinguished
egresado, -a [eɣre'saðo, a] *nm/f* (*Am*) graduate
egresar [eɣre'sar] *vi* (*Am*) to graduate
eh [e] *excl* hey!, hi!
Eire ['eire] *nm* Eire
ej. *abr* (= *ejemplo*) ex.
eje ['exe] *nm* (*Geo, Mat*) axis; (*Pol, fig*) axis, main line; (*de rueda*) axle; (*de máquina*) shaft, spindle
ejecución [exeku'θjon] *nf* execution; (*cumplimiento*) fulfilment; (*actuación*) performance; (*Jur*: *embargo de deudor*) attachment
ejecutar [exeku'tar] *vt* to execute, carry out; (*matar*) to execute; (*cumplir*) to fulfil; (*Mus*) to perform; (*Jur*: *embargar*) to attach, distrain; (*deseos*) to fulfil; (*Inform*) to run
ejecutivo, -a [exeku'tiβo, a] *adj, nm/f* executive; **el (poder) ~** the Executive (Power)
ejecutor [exeku'tor] *nm* (*tb*: **ejecutor testamentario**) executor
ejecutoria [exeku'torja] *nf* (*Jur*) final judgment
ejemplar [exem'plar] *adj* exemplary ■ *nm* example; (*Zool*) specimen; (*de libro*) copy;

(*de periódico*) number, issue; **~ de regalo** complimentary copy; **sin ~** unprecedented
ejemplificar [exemplifi'kar] *vt* to exemplify, illustrate
ejemplifique *etc* [exempli'fike] *vb ver* **ejemplificar**
ejemplo [e'xemplo] *nm* example; (*caso*) instance; **por ~** for example; **dar ~** to set an example
ejercer [exer'θer] *vt* to exercise; (*funciones*) to perform; (*negocio*) to manage; (*influencia*) to exert; (*un oficio*) to practise; (*poder*) to wield ■ *vi*: **~ de** to practise as
ejercicio [exer'θiθjo] *nm* exercise; (*Mil*) drill; (*Com*) fiscal *o* financial year; (*período*) tenure; **~ acrobático** (*Aviat*) stunt; **~ comercial** business year; **ejercicios espirituales** (*Rel*) retreat *sg*; **hacer ~** to take exercise
ejercitar [exerθi'tar] *vt* to exercise; (*Mil*) to drill
ejército [e'xerθito] *nm* army; **E~ del Aire/de Tierra** Air Force/Army; **~ de ocupación** army of occupation; **~ permanente** standing army; **entrar en el ~** to join the army, join up
ejerza *etc* [e'xerθa] *vb ver* **ejercer**
ejote [e'xote] *nm* (*Am*) green bean

PALABRA CLAVE

el, la, lo [el, la] (*pl* **los, las**) *artículo definido*
1 the; **el libro/la mesa/los estudiantes/las flores** the book/table/students/flowers; **me gusta el fútbol** I like football; **está en la cama** she's in bed
2 (*con n abstracto o propio: no se traduce*): **el amor/la juventud** love/youth; **el Conde Drácula** Count Dracula
3 (*posesión: se traduce a menudo por adj posesivo*): **romperse el brazo** to break one's arm; **levantó la mano** he put his hand up; **se puso el sombrero** she put her hat on
4 (*valor descriptivo*): **tener la boca grande/los ojos azules** to have a big mouth/blue eyes
5 (*con días*) on; **me iré el viernes** I'll leave on Friday; **los domingos suelo ir a nadar** on Sundays I generally go swimming
6 (*lo + adj*): **lo difícil/caro** what is difficult/expensive; (*cuán*): **no se da cuenta de lo pesado que es** he doesn't realize how boring he is
■ *pron demostrativo* 1: **mi libro y el de usted** my book and yours; **las de Pepe son mejores** Pepe's are better; **no la(s) blanca(s) sino la(s) gris(es)** not the white one(s) but the grey one(s)
2: **lo de**: **lo de ayer** what happened yesterday; **lo de las facturas** that business about the invoices
■ *pron relativo*: **el que** *etc* 1 (*indef*): **el (los) que quiera(n) que se vaya(n)** anyone who wants to can leave; **llévese el/la que más le guste** take the one you like best
2 (*def*): **el que compré ayer** the one I bought yesterday; **los que se van** those who leave
3: **lo que**: **lo que pienso yo/más me gusta** what I think/like most
■ *conj*: **el que**: **el que lo diga** the fact that he says so; **el que sea tan vago me molesta** his being so lazy bothers me
■ *excl*: **¡el susto que me diste!** what a fright you gave me!
■ *pron personal* 1 (*persona: m*) him; (*: f*) her; (*: pl*) them; **lo/las veo** I can see him/them
2 (*animal, cosa: sg*) it; (*: pl*) them; **lo (*o* la) veo** I can see it; **los (*o* las) veo** I can see them
3: **lo** (*como sustituto de frase*): **no lo sabía** I didn't know; **ya lo entiendo** I understand now

él [el] *pron* (*persona*) he; (*cosa*) it; (*después de prep: persona*) him; (*: cosa*) it; **mis libros y los de él** my books and his
elaboración [elaβora'θjon] *nf* (*producción*) manufacture; **~ de presupuestos** (*Com*) budgeting
elaborar [elaβo'rar] *vt* (*producto*) to make, manufacture; (*preparar*) to prepare; (*madera, metal etc*) to work; (*proyecto etc*) to work on *o* out
elasticidad [elastiθi'ðað] *nf* elasticity
elástico, -a [e'lastiko, a] *adj* elastic; (*flexible*) flexible ■ *nm* elastic; (*gomita*) elastic band
elección [elek'θjon] *nf* election; (*selección*) choice, selection; **elecciones parciales** by-election *sg*; **elecciones generales** general election *sg*
electo, -a [e'lekto, a] *adj* elect; **el presidente ~** the president-elect
electorado [elekto'raðo] *nm* electorate, voters *pl*
electoral [elekto'ral] *adj* electoral
electrice *etc* [elek'triθe] *vb ver* **electrizar**
electricidad [elektriθi'ðað] *nf* electricity
electricista [elektri'θista] *nm/f* electrician
eléctrico, -a [e'lektriko, a] *adj* electric
electrificar [elektrifi'kar] *vt* to electrify
electrizar [elektri'θar] *vt* (*Ferro, fig*) to electrify
electro... [elektro] *pref* electro...
electrocardiograma [elektrokarðjo'ɣrama] *nm* electrocardiogram
electrocución [elektroku'θjon] *nf* electrocution
electrocutar [elektroku'tar] *vt* to electrocute
electrodo [elek'troðo] *nm* electrode

electrodomésticos [elektroðo'mestikos] *nmpl* (electrical) household appliances; (*Com*) white goods
electroimán [electroi'man] *nm* electromagnet
electromagnético, -a [elektromaɣ'netiko, a] *adj* electromagnetic
electrón [elek'tron] *nm* electron
electrónico, -a [elek'troniko, a] *adj* electronic ■ *nf* electronics *sg*
electrotecnia [elektro'teknja] *nf* electrical engineering
electrotécnico, -a [elektro'tekniko, a] *nm/f* electrical engineer
elefante [ele'fante] *nm* elephant
elegancia [ele'ɣanθja] *nf* elegance, grace; (*estilo*) stylishness
elegante [ele'ɣante] *adj* elegant, graceful; (*traje etc*) smart, fashionable; (*decoración*) tasteful
elegía [ele'xia] *nf* elegy
elegir [ele'xir] *vt* (*escoger*) to choose, select; (*optar*) to opt for; (*presidente*) to elect
elemental [elemen'tal] *adj* (*claro, obvio*) elementary; (*fundamental*) elemental, fundamental
elemento [ele'mento] *nm* element; (*fig*) ingredient; (*Am*) person, individual; (*tipo raro*) odd person; (*de pila*) cell; **elementos** *nmpl* elements, rudiments; **estar en su ~** to be in one's element; **vino a verle un ~** someone came to see you
elenco [e'lenko] *nm* catalogue, list; (*Teat*) cast; (*Am: equipo*) team
elepé [ele'pe] *nm* LP
elevación [eleβa'θjon] *nf* elevation; (*acto*) raising, lifting; (*de precios*) rise; (*Geo etc*) height, altitude
elevador [eleβa'ðor] *nm* (*Am*) lift (*Brit*), elevator (*US*)
elevar [ele'βar] *vt* to raise, lift (up); (*precio*) to put up; (*producción*) to step up; (*informe etc*) to present; **elevarse** *vr* (*edificio*) to rise; (*precios*) to go up; (*transportarse, enajenarse*) to get carried away; **la cantidad se eleva a ...** the total amounts to ...
eligiendo *etc* [eli'xjenðo], **elija** *etc* [e'lixa] *vb ver* **elegir**
eliminar [elimi'nar] *vt* to eliminate, remove; (*olor, persona*) to get rid of; (*Deporte*) to eliminate, knock out
eliminatoria [elimina'torja] *nf* heat, preliminary (round)
elite [e'lite], **élite** ['elite] *nf* elite, élite
elitista [eli'tista] *adj* elitist
elixir [elik'sir] *nm* elixir; (*tb:* **elixir bucal**) mouthwash
ella ['eʎa] *pron* (*persona*) she; (*cosa*) it; (*después de prep: persona*) her; (*cosa*) it; **de ~** hers
ellas ['eʎas] *pron ver* **ellos**
ello ['eʎo] *pron neutro* it; **es por ~ que ...** that's why ...
ellos, -as ['eʎos, as] *pron personal pl* they; (*después de prep*) them; **de ~** theirs
elocuencia [elo'kwenθja] *nf* eloquence
elocuente [elo'kwente] *adj* eloquent; (*fig*) significant; **un dato ~** a fact which speaks for itself
elogiar [elo'xjar] *vt* to praise, eulogize
elogio [e'loxjo] *nm* praise; **queda por encima de todo ~** it's beyond praise; **hacer ~ de** to sing the praises of
elote [e'lote] *nm* (*Am*) corn on the cob
El Salvador *nm* El Salvador
eludir [elu'ðir] *vt* (*evitar*) to avoid, evade; (*escapar*) to escape, elude
E.M. *abr* (*Mil*) = **Estado Mayor**
Em.ª *abr* (= *Eminencia*) Mgr
email ['imeil] *nm* (*gen*) e-mail *m*; (*dirección*) e-mail address; **mandar un ~ a algn** to e-mail sb, send sb an e-mail
emanar [ema'nar] *vi*: **~ de** to emanate from, come from; (*derivar de*) to originate in
emancipar [emanθi'par] *vt* to emancipate; **emanciparse** *vr* to become emancipated, free o.s.
embadurnar [embaður'nar] *vt* to smear
embajada [emba'xaða] *nf* embassy
embajador, a [embaxa'ðor, a] *nm/f* ambassador/ambassadress
embaladura [embala'ðura] *nf* (*Am*), **embalaje** [emba'laxe] *nm* packing
embalar [emba'lar] *vt* (*envolver*) to parcel, wrap (up); (*envasar*) to package ■ *vi* to sprint
embalsamar [embalsa'mar] *vt* to embalm
embalsar [embal'sar] *vt* (*río*) to dam (up); (*agua*) to retain
embalse [em'balse] *nm* (*presa*) dam; (*lago*) reservoir
embarace *etc* [emba'raθe] *vb ver* **embarazar**
embarazada [embara'θaða] *adj f* pregnant ■ *nf* pregnant woman
embarazar [embara'θar] *vt* to obstruct, hamper; **embarazarse** *vr* (*aturdirse*) to become embarrassed; (*confundirse*) to get into a mess
embarazo [emba'raθo] *nm* (*de mujer*) pregnancy; (*impedimento*) obstacle, obstruction; (*timidez*) embarrassment
embarazoso, -a [embara'θoso, a] *adj* (*molesto*) awkward; (*violento*) embarrassing
embarcación [embarka'θjon] *nf* (*barco*) boat, craft; (*acto*) embarkation; **~ de arrastre** trawler; **~ de cabotaje** coasting vessel

embarcadero [embarka'ðero] *nm* pier, landing stage
embarcar [embar'kar] *vt* (*cargamento*) to ship, stow; (*persona*) to embark, put on board; (*fig*): ~ **a algn en una empresa** to involve sb in an undertaking; **embarcarse** *vr* to embark, go on board; (*marinero*) to sign on; (*Am: en tren etc*) to get on, get in
embargar [embar'ɣar] *vt* (*frenar*) to restrain; (*sentidos*) to overpower; (*Jur*) to seize, impound
embargo [em'barɣo] *nm* (*Jur*) seizure; (*Com etc*) embargo; **sin** ~ still, however, nonetheless
embargue *etc* [em'barɣe] *vb ver* **embargar**
embarque *etc* [em'barke] *vb ver* **embarcar** ■ *nm* shipment, loading
embarrancar [embarran'kar] *vt, vi* (*Naut*) to run aground; (*Auto etc*) to run into a ditch
embarranque *etc* [emba'rranke] *vb ver* **embarrancar**
embarullar [embaru'ʎar] *vt* to make a mess of
embate [em'bate] *nm* (*de mar, viento*) beating, violence
embaucador, a [embauka'ðor, a] *nm/f* (*estafador*) trickster; (*impostor*) impostor
embaucar [embau'kar] *vt* to trick, fool
embauque *etc* [em'bauke] *vb ver* **embaucar**
embeber [embe'βer] *vt* (*absorber*) to absorb, soak up; (*empapar*) to saturate ■ *vi* to shrink; **embeberse** *vr*: **embeberse en un libro** to be engrossed *o* absorbed in a book
embelesado, -a [embele'saðo, a] *adj* spellbound
embelesar [embele'sar] *vt* to enchant; **embelesarse** *vr*: **embelesarse (con)** to be enchanted (by)
embellecer [embeʎe'θer] *vt* to embellish, beautify
embellezca *etc* [embe'ʎeθka] *vb ver* **embellecer**
embestida [embes'tiða] *nf* attack, onslaught; (*carga*) charge
embestir [embes'tir] *vt* to attack, assault; to charge, attack ■ *vi* to attack
embistiendo *etc* [embis'tjendo] *vb ver* **embestir**
emblanquecer [emblanke'θer] *vt* to whiten, bleach; **emblanquecerse** *vr* to turn white
emblanquezca *etc* [emblan'keθka] *vb ver* **emblanquecer**
emblema [em'blema] *nm* emblem
embobado, -a [embo'βaðo, a] *adj* (*atontado*) stunned, bewildered
embobar [embo'βar] *vt* (*asombrar*) to amaze; (*fascinar*) to fascinate; **embobarse** *vr*: **embobarse con** *o* **de** *o* **en** to be amazed at; to be fascinated by
embocadura [emboka'ðura] *nf* narrow entrance; (*de río*) mouth; (*Mus*) mouthpiece
embolado [embo'laðo] *nm* (*Teat*) bit part, minor role; (*fam*) trick
embolia [em'bolja] *nf* (*Med*) embolism; ~ **cerebral** clot on the brain
émbolo ['embolo] *nm* (*Auto*) piston
embolsar [embol'sar] *vt* to pocket
emboquillado, -a [emboki'ʎaðo, a] *adj* (*cigarrillo*) tipped, filter *cpd*
emborrachar [emborra'tʃar] *vt* to make drunk; **emborracharse** *vr* to get drunk
emboscada [embos'kaða] *nf* (*celada*) ambush
embotar [embo'tar] *vt* to blunt, dull; **embotarse** *vr* (*adormecerse*) to go numb
embotellamiento [emboteʎa'mjento] *nm* (*Auto*) traffic jam
embotellar [embote'ʎar] *vt* to bottle; **embotellarse** *vr* (*circulación*) to get into a jam
embozo [em'boθo] *nm* muffler, mask; (*de sábana*) turnover
embragar [embra'ɣar] *vt* (*Auto, Tec*) to engage; (*partes*) to connect ■ *vi* to let in the clutch
embrague *etc* [em'braɣe] *vb ver* **embragar** ■ *nm* (*tb*: **pedal de embrague**) clutch
embravecer [embraβe'θer] *vt* to enrage, infuriate; **embravecerse** *vr* to become furious; (*mar*) to get rough; (*tormenta*) to rage
embravecido, -a [embraβe'θiðo, a] *adj* (*mar*) rough; (*persona*) furious
embriagador, a [embrjaɣa'ðor, a] *adj* intoxicating
embriagar [embrja'ɣar] *vt* (*emborrachar*) to make drunk; (*alegrar*) to delight; **embriagarse** *vr* (*emborracharse*) to get drunk
embriague *etc* [em'brjaɣe] *vb ver* **embriagar**
embriaguez [embrja'ɣeθ] *nf* (*borrachera*) drunkenness
embrión [em'brjon] *nm* embryo
embrionario, -a [embrjo'narjo, a] *adj* embryonic
embrollar [embro'ʎar] *vt* (*asunto*) to confuse, complicate; (*persona*) to involve, embroil; **embrollarse** *vr* (*confundirse*) to get into a muddle *o* mess
embrollo [em'broʎo] *nm* (*enredo*) muddle, confusion; (*aprieto*) fix, jam
embromado, -a [embro'maðo, a] *adj* (*Am fam*) tricky, difficult
embromar [embro'mar] *vt* (*burlarse de*) to tease, make fun of; (*Am fam: molestar*) to annoy
embrujado, -a [embru'xaðo, a] *adj* (*persona*) bewitched; **casa embrujada** haunted house

embrujo [em'bruxo] *nm* *(de mirada etc)* charm, magic
embrutecer [embrute'θer] *vt* *(atontar)* to stupefy; **embrutecerse** *vr* to be stupefied
embrutezca *etc* [embru'teθka] *vb ver* **embrutecer**
embudo [em'buðo] *nm* funnel
embuste [em'buste] *nm* trick; *(mentira)* lie; *(humorístico)* fib
embustero, -a [embus'tero, a] *adj* lying, deceitful ■ *nm/f* *(tramposo)* cheat; *(mentiroso)* liar; *(humorístico)* fibber
embutido [embu'tiðo] *nm* *(Culin)* sausage
embutir [embu'tir] *vt* to insert; *(Tec)* to inlay; *(llenar)* to pack tight, cram
emergencia [emer'xenθja] *nf* emergency; *(surgimiento)* emergence
emergente [emer'xente] *adj* resultant, consequent; *(nación)* emergent; *(Inform)* pop-up *cpd*; **menú/ventana ~** pop-up menu/window
emerger [emer'xer] *vi* to emerge, appear
emeritense [emeri'tense] *adj* of *o* from Mérida ■ *nm/f* native *o* inhabitant of Mérida
emerja *etc* [e'merxa] *vb ver* **emerger**
emigración [emiɣra'θjon] *nf* emigration; *(de pájaros)* migration
emigrado, -a [emi'ɣraðo, a] *nm/f* emigrant; *(Pol etc)* émigré(e)
emigrante [emi'ɣrante] *adj, nm/f* emigrant
emigrar [emi'ɣrar] *vi* *(personas)* to emigrate; *(pájaros)* to migrate
eminencia [emi'nenθja] *nf* eminence; *(en títulos)*: **Su E~** His Eminence; **Vuestra E~** Your Eminence
eminente [emi'nente] *adj* eminent, distinguished; *(elevado)* high
emisario [emi'sarjo] *nm* emissary
emisión [emi'sjon] *nf* *(acto)* emission; *(Com etc)* issue; *(Radio, TV: acto)* broadcasting; *(: programa)* broadcast, programme, program (US); **~ de acciones** *(Com)* share issue; **~ gratuita de acciones** *(Com)* rights issue; **~ de valores** *(Com)* flotation
emisor, a [emi'sor, a] *nm* transmitter ■ *nf* radio *o* broadcasting station
emitir [emi'tir] *vt* *(olor etc)* to emit, give off; *(moneda etc)* to issue; *(opinión)* to express; *(voto)* to cast; *(señal)* to send out; *(Radio)* to broadcast; **~ una señal sonora** to beep
emoción [emo'θjon] *nf* emotion; *(excitación)* excitement; *(sentimiento)* feeling; **¡qué ~!** how exciting!; *(irónico)* what a thrill!
emocionado, -a [emoθjo'naðo, a] *adj* deeply moved, stirred
emocionante [emoθjo'nante] *adj* *(excitante)* exciting, thrilling
emocionar [emoθjo'nar] *vt* *(excitar)* to excite, thrill; *(conmover)* to move, touch; *(impresionar)* to impress; **emocionarse** *vr* to get excited
emoticón [emoti'kon] *nm* smiley, emoticon
emotivo, -a [emo'tiβo, a] *adj* emotional
empacar [empa'kar] *vt* *(gen)* to pack; *(en caja)* to bale, crate
empacharse [empa'tʃarse] *vr* *(Med)* to get indigestion
empacho [em'patʃo] *nm* *(Med)* indigestion; *(fig)* embarrassment
empadronamiento [empaðrona'mjento] *nm* census; *(de electores)* electoral register
empadronarse [empaðro'narse] *vr* *(Pol: como elector)* to register
empalagar [empala'ɣar] *vt* *(comida)* to cloy; *(hartar)* to pall on ■ *vi* to pall
empalagoso, -a [empala'ɣoso, a] *adj* cloying; *(fig)* tiresome
empalague *etc* [empa'laɣe] *vb ver* **empalagar**
empalizada [empali'θaða] *nf* fence; *(Mil)* palisade
empalmar [empal'mar] *vt* to join, connect ■ *vi* *(dos caminos)* to meet, join
empalme [em'palme] *nm* joint, connection; *(de vías)* junction; *(de trenes)* connection
empanada [empa'naða] *nf* pie, pasty
empanar [empa'nar] *vt* *(Culin)* to cook *o* roll in breadcrumbs *o* pastry
empantanarse [empanta'narse] *vr* to get swamped; *(fig)* to get bogged down
empañarse [empa'ɲarse] *vr* *(nublarse)* to get misty, steam up
empapar [empa'par] *vt* *(mojar)* to soak, saturate; *(absorber)* to soak up, absorb; **empaparse** *vr*: **empaparse de** to soak up
empapelar [empape'lar] *vt* *(paredes)* to paper
empaque *etc* [em'pake] *vb ver* **empacar**
empaquetar [empake'tar] *vt* to pack, parcel up; *(Com)* to package
emparedado [empare'ðaðo] *nm* sandwich
emparejar [empare'xar] *vt* to pair ■ *vi* to catch up
emparentar [emparen'tar] *vi*: **~ con** to marry into
empariente *etc* [empa'rjente] *vb ver* **emparentar**
empastar [empas'tar] *vt* *(embadurnar)* to paste; *(diente)* to fill
empaste [em'paste] *nm* *(de diente)* filling
empatar [empa'tar] *vi* to draw, tie
empate [em'pate] *nm* draw, tie; **un ~ a cero** a no-score draw
empecé [empe'θe], **empecemos** *etc* [empe'θemos] *vb ver* **empezar**
empecinado, -a [empeθi'naðo, a] *adj* stubborn

empedernido, -a [empeðer'niðo, a] *adj* hard, heartless; (*fijado*) hardened, inveterate; **un fumador ~** a heavy smoker
empedrado, -a [empe'ðraðo, a] *adj* paved ■ *nm* paving
empedrar [empe'ðrar] *vt* to pave
empeine [em'peine] *nm* (*de pie, zapato*) instep
empellón [empe'ʎon] *nm* push, shove; **abrirse paso a empellones** to push *o* shove one's way past *o* through
empeñado, -a [empe'ɲaðo, a] *adj* (*persona*) determined; (*objeto*) pawned
empeñar [empe'ɲar] *vt* (*objeto*) to pawn, pledge; (*persona*) to compel; **empeñarse** *vr* (*obligarse*) to bind o.s., pledge o.s.; (*endeudarse*) to get into debt; **empeñarse en hacer** to be set on doing, be determined to do
empeño [em'peɲo] *nm* (*determinación*) determination; (*cosa prendada*) pledge; **casa de empeños** pawnshop; **con ~** insistently; (*con celo*) eagerly; **tener ~ en hacer algo** to be bent on doing sth
empeoramiento [empeora'mjento] *nm* worsening
empeorar [empeo'rar] *vt* to make worse, worsen ■ *vi* to get worse, deteriorate
empequeñecer [empekeɲe'θer] *vt* to dwarf; (*fig*) to belittle
empequeñezca *etc* [empeke'ɲeθka] *vb ver* **empequeñecer**
emperador [empera'ðor] *nm* emperor
emperatriz [empera'triθ] *nf* empress
emperrarse [empe'rrarse] *vr* to get stubborn; **~ en algo** to persist in sth
empezar [empe'θar] *vt, vi* to begin, start; **empezó a llover** it started to rain; **bueno, para ~** well, to start with
empiece *etc* [em'pjeθe] *vb ver* **empezar**
empiedre *etc* [em'pjeðre] *vb ver* **empedrar**
empiezo *etc* [em'pjeθo] *vb ver* **empezar**
empinado, -a [empi'naðo, a] *adj* steep
empinar [empi'nar] *vt* to raise; (*botella*) to tip up; **empinarse** *vr* (*persona*) to stand on tiptoe; (*animal*) to rear up; (*camino*) to climb steeply; **~ el codo** to booze (*fam*)
empingorotado, -a [empingoro'taðo, a] *adj* (*fam*) stuck-up
empírico, -a [em'piriko, a] *adj* empirical
emplace *etc* [em'plaθe] *vb ver* **emplazar**
emplaste [em'plaste], **emplasto** [em'plasto] *nm* (*Med*) plaster
emplazamiento [emplaθa'mjento] *nm* site, location; (*Jur*) summons *sg*
emplazar [empla'θar] *vt* (*ubicar*) to site, place, locate; (*Jur*) to summons; (*convocar*) to summon
empleado, -a [emple'aðo, a] *nm/f* (*gen*) employee; (*de banco etc*) clerk; **~ público** civil servant
emplear [emple'ar] *vt* (*usar*) to use, employ; (*dar trabajo a*) to employ; **emplearse** *vr* (*conseguir trabajo*) to be employed; (*ocuparse*) to occupy o.s.; **~ mal el tiempo** to waste time; **¡te está bien empleado!** it serves you right!
empleo [em'pleo] *nm* (*puesto*) job; (*puestos: colectivamente*) employment; (*uso*) use, employment; **"modo de ~"** "instructions for use"
emplumar [emplu'mar] *vt* (*estafar*) to swindle
empobrecer [empoβre'θer] *vt* to impoverish; **empobrecerse** *vr* to become poor *o* impoverished
empobrecimiento [empoβreθi'mjento] *nm* impoverishment
empobrezca *etc* [empo'βreθka] *vb ver* **empobrecer**
empollar [empo'ʎar] *vt* to incubate; (*Escol fam*) to swot (up) ■ *vi* (*gallina*) to brood; (*Escol fam*) to swot
empollón, -ona [empo'ʎon, ona] *nm/f* (*Escol fam*) swot
empolvar [empol'βar] *vt* (*cara*) to powder; **empolvarse** *vr* to powder one's face; (*superficie*) to get dusty
emponzoñar [emponθo'ɲar] *vt* (*esp fig*) to poison
emporio [em'porjo] *nm* emporium, trading centre; (*Am: gran almacén*) department store
empotrado, -a [empo'traðo, a] *adj* (*armario etc*) built-in
empotrar [empo'trar] *vt* to embed; (*armario etc*) to build in
emprendedor, a [emprende'ðor, a] *adj* enterprising
emprender [empren'der] *vt* to undertake; (*empezar*) to begin, embark on; (*acometer*) to tackle, take on; **~ marcha a** to set out for
empresa [em'presa] *nf* enterprise; (*Com: sociedad*) firm, company; (*: negocio*) business; (*esp Teat*) management; **~ filial** (*Com*) affiliated company; **~ matriz** (*Com*) parent company
empresarial [empresa'rjal] *adj* (*función, clase*) managerial; **sector ~** business sector
empresariales [empresa'rjales] *nfpl* business studies
empresario, -a [empre'sarjo, a] *nm/f* (*Com*) businessman(-woman), entrepreneur; (*Tec*) manager; (*Mus: de ópera etc*) impresario; **~ de pompas fúnebres** undertaker (*Brit*), mortician (*US*)
empréstito [em'prestito] *nm* (public) loan; (*Com*) loan capital

empujar [empu'xar] *vt* to push, shove
empuje [em'puxe] *nm* thrust; (*presión*) pressure; (*fig*) vigour, drive
empujón [empu'xon] *nm* push, shove; **abrirse paso a empujones** to shove one's way through
empuñadura [empuɲa'ðura] *nf* (*de espada*) hilt; (*de herramienta etc*) handle
empuñar [empu'ɲar] *vt* (*asir*) to grasp, take (firm) hold of; **~ las armas** (*fig*) to take up arms
emulación [emula'θjon] *nf* emulation
emular [emu'lar] *vt* to emulate; (*rivalizar*) to rival
émulo, -a ['emulo, a] *nm/f* rival, competitor
emulsión [emul'sjon] *nf* emulsion

PALABRA CLAVE

en [en] *prep* **1** (*posición*) in; (: *sobre*) on; **está en el cajón** it's in the drawer; **en Argentina/La Paz** in Argentina/La Paz; **en el colegio/la oficina** at school/the office; **en casa** at home; **está en el suelo/quinto piso** it's on the floor/the fifth floor; **en el periódico** in the paper
2 (*dirección*) into; **entró en el aula** she went into the classroom; **meter algo en el bolso** to put sth into one's bag; **ir de puerta en puerta** to go from door to door
3 (*tiempo*) in; on; **en 1605/3 semanas/invierno** in 1605/3 weeks/winter; **en (el mes de) enero** in (the month of) January; **en aquella ocasión/época** on that occasion/at that time
4 (*precio*) for; **lo vendió en 20 dólares** he sold it for 20 dollars
5 (*diferencia*) by; **reducir/aumentar en una tercera parte/un 20 por ciento** to reduce/increase by a third/20 per cent
6 (*manera, forma*): **en avión/autobús** by plane/bus; **escrito en inglés** written in English; **en serio** seriously; **en espiral/círculo** in a spiral/circle
7 (*después de vb que indica gastar etc*) on; **han cobrado demasiado en dietas** they've charged too much to expenses; **se le va la mitad del sueldo en comida** half his salary goes on food
8 (*tema, ocupación*): **experto en la materia** expert on the subject; **trabaja en la construcción** he works in the building industry
9 (*adj + en + infin*): **lento en reaccionar** slow to react

enagua [enaɣwa] *nf*, **enaguas** [enaɣwas] *nfpl* (*esp Am*) petticoat
enajenación [enaxena'θjon] *nf*, **enajenamiento** [enaxena'mjento] ■ *nm* alienation; (*fig: distracción*) absent-mindedness; (: *embelesamiento*) rapture, trance; **~ mental** mental derangement
enajenar [enaxe'nar] *vt* to alienate; (*fig*) to carry away
enamorado, -a [enamo'raðo, a] *adj* in love ■ *nm/f* lover; **estar ~ (de)** to be in love (with)
enamorar [enamo'rar] *vt* to win the love of; **enamorarse** *vr*: **enamorarse (de)** to fall in love (with)
enano, -a [e'nano, a] *adj* tiny, dwarf ■ *nm/f* dwarf; (*pey*) runt
enarbolar [enarβo'lar] *vt* (*bandera etc*) to hoist; (*espada etc*) to brandish
enardecer [enarðe'θer] *vt* (*pasiones*) to fire, inflame; (*persona*) to fill with enthusiasm; **enardecerse** *vr* to get excited; **enardecerse por** to get enthusiastic about
enardezca *etc* [enar'deθka] *vb ver* **enardecer**
encabece *etc* [enka'βeθe] *vb ver* **encabezar**
encabezado [enkaβe'θaðo] *nm* (*Com*) header
encabezamiento [enkaβeθa'mjento] *nm* (*de carta*) heading; (*Com*) billhead, letterhead; (*de periódico*) headline; (*preámbulo*) foreword, preface; **~ normal** (*Tip etc*) running head
encabezar [enkaβe'θar] *vt* (*movimiento, revolución*) to lead, head; (*lista*) to head; (*carta*) to put a heading to; (*libro*) to entitle
encadenar [enkaðe'nar] *vt* to chain (together); (*poner grilletes a*) to shackle
encajar [enka'xar] *vt* (*ajustar*): **~ en** to fit (into); (*meter a la fuerza*) to push in; (*máquina etc*) to house; (*partes*) to join; (*fam: golpe*) to give, deal; (*entremeter*) to insert ■ *vi* to fit (well); (*fig: corresponder a*) to match; **encajarse** *vr*: **encajarse en un sillón** to squeeze into a chair
encaje [en'kaxe] *nm* (*labor*) lace
encajonar [enkaxo'nar] *vt* to box (up), put in a box
encalar [enka'lar] *vt* (*pared*) to whitewash
encallar [enka'ʎar] *vi* (*Naut*) to run aground
encaminado, -a [enkami'naðo, a] *adj*: **medidas encaminadas a ...** measures designed to *o* aimed at ...
encaminar [enkami'nar] *vt* to direct, send; **encaminarse** *vr*: **encaminarse a** to set out for; **~ por** (*expedición etc*) to route via
encandilar [enkandi'lar] *vt* to dazzle; (*persona*) to daze, bewilder
encanecer [enkane'θer] *vi*, **encanecerse** *vr* (*pelo*) to go grey
encanezca *etc* [enka'neθka] *vb ver* **encanecer**

encantado, -a [enkan'taðo, a] *adj* delighted; **¡~!** how do you do!, pleased to meet you
encantador, a [enkanta'ðor, a] *adj* charming, lovely ■ *nm/f* magician, enchanter/enchantress
encantar [enkan'tar] *vt* to charm, delight; (*cautivar*) to fascinate; (*hechizar*) to bewitch, cast a spell on
encanto [en'kanto] *nm* (*magia*) spell, charm; (*fig*) charm, delight; (*expresión de ternura*) sweetheart; **como por ~** as if by magic
encapotado, -a [enkapo'taðo, a] *adj* (*cielo*) overcast
encapricharse [enkapri'tʃarse] *vr*: **se ha encaprichado con ir** he's taken it into his head to go; **se ha encaprichado** he's digging his heels in
encaramar [enkara'mar] *vt* (*subir*) to raise, lift up; **encaramarse** *vr* (*subir*) to perch; **encaramarse a** (*árbol etc*) to climb
encararse [enka'rarse] *vr*: **~ a** *o* **con** to confront, come face to face with
encarcelar [enkarθe'lar] *vt* to imprison, jail
encarecer [enkare'θer] *vt* to put up the price of ■ *vi*, **encarecerse** *vr* to get dearer
encarecidamente [enkareθiða'mente] *adv* earnestly
encarecimiento [enkareθi'mjento] *nm* price increase
encarezca *etc* [enka'reθka] *vb ver* **encarecer**
encargado, -a [enkar'ɣaðo, a] *adj* in charge ■ *nm/f* agent, representative; (*responsable*) person in charge
encargar [enkar'ɣar] *vt* to entrust; (*Com*) to order; (*recomendar*) to urge, recommend; **encargarse** *vr*: **encargarse de** to look after, take charge of; **~ algo a algn** to put sb in charge of sth
encargo [en'karɣo] *nm* (*pedido*) assignment, job; (*responsabilidad*) responsibility; (*recomendación*) recommendation; (*Com*) order
encargue *etc* [en'karɣe] *vb ver* **encargar**
encariñarse [enkari'ɲarse] *vr*: **~ con** to grow fond of, get attached to
encarnación [enkarna'θjon] *nf* incarnation, embodiment
encarnado, -a [enkar'naðo, a] *adj* (*color*) red; **ponerse ~** to blush
encarnar [enkar'nar] *vt* to personify; (*Teat: papel*) to play ■ *vi* (*Rel etc*) to become incarnate
encarnizado, -a [enkarni'θaðo, a] *adj* (*lucha*) bloody, fierce
encarrilar [enkarri'lar] *vt* (*tren*) to put back on the rails; (*fig*) to correct, put on the right track
encasillar [enkasi'ʎar] *vt* (*Teat*) to typecast; (*clasificar: pey*) to pigeonhole
encasquetar [enkaske'tar] *vt* (*sombrero*) to pull down *o* on; **encasquetarse** *vr*: **encasquetarse el sombrero** to pull one's hat down *o* on; **~ algo a algn** to offload sth onto sb
encauce *etc* [en'kauθe] *vb ver* **encauzar**
encausar [enkau'sar] *vt* to prosecute, sue
encauzar [enkau'θar] *vt* to channel; (*fig*) to direct
encendedor [enθende'ðor] *nm* lighter
encender [enθen'der] *vt* (*con fuego*) to light; (*incendiar*) to set fire to; (*luz, radio*) to put on, switch on; (*Inform*) to toggle on, switch on; (*avivar: pasiones etc*) to inflame; (*despertar: entusiasmo*) to arouse; (*odio*) to awaken; **encenderse** *vr* to catch fire; (*excitarse*) to get excited; (*de cólera*) to flare up; (*el rostro*) to blush
encendidamente [enθendiða'mente] *adv* passionately
encendido, -a [enθen'diðo, a] *adj* alight; (*aparato*) (switched) on; (*mejillas*) glowing; (*cara: por el vino etc*) flushed; (*mirada*) passionate ■ *nm* (*Auto*) ignition; (*de faroles*) lighting
encerado, -a [enθe'raðo, a] *adj* (*suelo*) waxed, polished ■ *nm* (*Escol*) blackboard; (*hule*) oilcloth
encerar [enθe'rar] *vt* (*suelo*) to wax, polish
encerrar [enθe'rrar] *vt* (*confinar*) to shut in *o* up; (*con llave*) to lock in *o* up; (*comprender, incluir*) to include, contain; **encerrarse** *vr* to shut *o* lock o.s. up *o* in
encerrona [enθe'rrona] *nf* trap
encestar [enθes'tar] *vi* to score a basket
encharcar [entʃar'kar] *vt* to swamp, flood; **encharcarse** *vr* to become flooded
encharque *etc* [en'tʃarke] *vb ver* **encharcar**
enchufar [entʃu'far] *vt* (*Elec*) to plug in; (*Tec*) to connect, fit together; (*Com*) to merge
enchufe [en'tʃufe] *nm* (*Elec: clavija*) plug; (*: toma*) socket; (*de dos tubos*) joint, connection; (*fam: influencia*) contact, connection; (*puesto*) cushy job; **~ de clavija** jack plug; **tiene un ~ en el ministerio** he can pull strings at the ministry
encía [en'θia] *nf* (*Anat*) gum
enciclopedia [enθiklo'peðja] *nf* encyclopaedia
encienda *etc* [en'θjenda] *vb ver* **encender**
encierro *etc* [en'θjerro] *vb ver* **encerrar** ■ *nm* shutting in *o* up; (*calabozo*) prison; (*Agr*) pen; (*Taur*) penning
encima [en'θima] *adv* (*sobre*) above, over; (*además*) besides; **~ de** (*en*) on, on top of; (*sobre*) above, over; (*además de*) besides, on top

of; **por ~ de** over; **¿llevas dinero ~?** have you (got) any money on you?; **se me vino ~** it took me by surprise
encina [en'θina] *nf* (holm) oak
encinta [en'θinta] *adj f* pregnant
enclave [en'klaβe] *nm* enclave
enclenque [en'klenke] *adj* weak, sickly
encoger [enko'xer] *vt* (*gen*) to shrink, contract; (*fig: asustar*) to scare; (*: desanimar*) to discourage; **encogerse** *vr* to shrink, contract; (*fig*) to cringe; **encogerse de hombros** to shrug one's shoulders
encoja *etc* [en'koxa] *vb ver* **encoger**
encolar [enko'lar] *vt* (*engomar*) to glue, paste; (*pegar*) to stick down
encolerice *etc* [enkole'riθe] *vb ver* **encolerizar**
encolerizar [enkoleri'θar] *vt* to anger, provoke; **encolerizarse** *vr* to get angry
encomendar [enkomen'dar] *vt* to entrust, commend; **encomendarse** *vr*: **encomendarse a** to put one's trust in
encomiar [enko'mjar] *vt* to praise, pay tribute to
encomienda *etc* [enko'mjenda] *vb ver* **encomendar** ■ *nf* (*encargo*) charge, commission; (*elogio*) tribute; (*Am*) parcel, package; **~ postal** (*Am*) parcel post
encomio [en'komjo] *nm* praise, tribute
encono [en'kono] *nm* (*rencor*) rancour, spite
encontrado, -a [enkon'traðo, a] *adj* (*contrario*) contrary, conflicting; (*hostil*) hostile
encontrar [enkon'trar] *vt* (*hallar*) to find; (*inesperadamente*) to meet, run into; **encontrarse** *vr* to meet (each other); (*situarse*) to be (situated); (*persona*) to find o.s., be; (*entrar en conflicto*) to crash, collide; **encontrarse con** to meet; **encontrarse bien (de salud)** to feel well; **no se encuentra aquí en este momento** he's not in at the moment
encontronazo [enkontro'naθo] *nm* collision, crash
encorvar [enkor'βar] *vt* to curve; (*inclinar*) to bend (down); **encorvarse** *vr* to bend down, bend over
encrespado, -a [enkres'paðo, a] *adj* (*pelo*) curly; (*mar*) rough
encrespar [enkres'par] *vt* (*cabellos*) to curl; (*fig*) to anger, irritate; **encresparse** *vr* (*el mar*) to get rough; (*fig*) to get cross *o* irritated
encrucijada [enkruθi'xaða] *nf* crossroads *sg*; (*empalme*) junction
encuadernación [enkwaðerna'θjon] *nf* binding; (*taller*) binder's
encuadernador, a [enkwaðerna'ðor, a] *nm/f* bookbinder
encuadrar [enkwa'ðrar] *vt* (*retrato*) to frame; (*ajustar*) to fit, insert; (*encerrar*) to contain
encubierto [enku'βjerto] *pp de* **encubrir**
encubrir [enku'βrir] *vt* (*ocultar*) to hide, conceal; (*criminal*) to harbour, shelter; (*ayudar*) to be an accomplice in
encuentro *etc* [en'kwentro] *vb ver* **encontrar** ■ *nm* (*de personas*) meeting; (*Auto etc*) collision, crash; (*Deporte*) match, game; (*Mil*) encounter
encuesta [en'kwesta] *nf* inquiry, investigation; (*sondeo*) public opinion poll; **~ judicial** post-mortem
encumbrado, -a [enkum'braðo, a] *adj* eminent, distinguished
encumbrar [enkum'brar] *vt* (*persona*) to exalt; **encumbrarse** *vr* (*fig*) to become conceited
endeble [en'deβle] *adj* (*argumento, excusa, persona*) weak
endémico, -a [en'demiko, a] *adj* endemic
endemoniado, -a [endemo'njaðo, a] *adj* possessed (of the devil); (*travieso*) devilish
enderece *etc* [ende'reθe] *vb ver* **enderezar**
enderezar [endere'θar] *vt* (*poner derecho*) to straighten (out); (*: verticalmente*) to set upright; (*fig*) to straighten *o* sort out; (*dirigir*) to direct; **enderezarse** *vr* (*persona sentada*) to sit up straight
endeudarse [endeu'ðarse] *vr* to get into debt
endiablado, -a [endja'βlaðo, a] *adj* devilish, diabolical; (*humorístico*) mischievous
endibia [en'diβja] *nf* endive
endilgar [endil'ɣar] *vt* (*fam*): **~ algo a algn** to lumber sb with sth; **~ un sermón a algn** to give sb a lecture
endilgue *etc* [en'dilɣe] *vb ver* **endilgar**
endiñar [endi'ɲar] *vt*: **~ algo a algn** to land sth on sb
endomingarse [endomin'garse] *vr* to dress up, put on one's best clothes
endomingue *etc* [endo'minge] *vb ver* **endomingarse**
endosar [endo'sar] *vt* (*cheque etc*) to endorse
endulce *etc* [en'dulθe] *vb ver* **endulzar**
endulzar [endul'θar] *vt* to sweeten; (*suavizar*) to soften
endurecer [endure'θer] *vt* to harden; **endurecerse** *vr* to harden, grow hard
endurecido, -a [endure'θiðo, a] *adj* (*duro*) hard; (*fig*) hardy, tough; **estar ~ a algo** to be hardened *o* used to sth
endurezca *etc* [endu'reθka] *vb ver* **endurecer**
ene. *abr* (= *enero*) Jan.
enemigo, -a [ene'miɣo, a] *adj* enemy, hostile ■ *nm/f* enemy ■ *nf* enmity, hostility; **ser ~ de** (*persona*) to dislike; (*tendencia*) to be inimical to

enemistad [enemis'tað] *nf* enmity
enemistar [enemis'tar] *vt* to make enemies of, cause a rift between; **enemistarse** *vr* to become enemies; (*amigos*) to fall out
energético, -a [ener'xetiko, a] *adj*: **política energética** energy policy
energía [ener'xia] *nf* (*vigor*) energy, drive; (*Tec, Elec*) energy, power; **~ atómica/eléctrica/eólica** atomic/electric/wind power; **energías renovables** renewable energy sources
enérgico, -a [e'nerxiko, a] *adj* (*gen*) energetic; (*ataque*) vigorous; (*ejercicio*) strenuous; (*medida*) bold; (*voz, modales*) forceful
energúmeno, -a [ener'ɣumeno, a] *nm/f* madman(-woman); **ponerse como un ~ con algn** to get furious with sb
enero [e'nero] *nm* January; *ver tb* **julio**
enervar [ener'βar] *vt* (*poner nervioso a*) to get on sb's nerves
enésimo, -a [e'nesimo, a] *adj* (*Mat*) nth; **por enésima vez** (*fig*) for the umpteenth time
enfadado, -a [enfa'ðaðo, a] *adj* angry, annoyed
enfadar [enfa'ðar] *vt* to anger, annoy; **enfadarse** *vr* to get angry *o* annoyed
enfado [en'faðo] *nm* (*enojo*) anger, annoyance; (*disgusto*) trouble, bother
énfasis ['enfasis] *nm* emphasis, stress; **poner énfasis en** to stress
enfático, -a [en'fatiko, a] *adj* emphatic
enfatizado, -a [enfati'θaðo, a] *adj*: **en caracteres enfatizados** (*Inform*) emphasized
enfermar [enfer'mar] *vt* to make ill ■ *vi* to fall ill, be taken ill; **su actitud me enferma** his attitude makes me sick; **~ del corazón** to develop heart trouble
enfermedad [enferme'ðað] *nf* illness; **~ venérea** venereal disease
enfermera [enfer'mera] *nf ver* **enfermero**
enfermería [enferme'ria] *nf* infirmary; (*de colegio etc*) sick bay
enfermero, -a [enfer'mero, a] *nm* (male) nurse ■ *nf* nurse; **enfermera jefa** matron
enfermizo, -a [enfer'miθo, a] *adj* (*persona*) sickly, unhealthy; (*fig*) unhealthy
enfermo, -a [en'fermo, a] *adj* ill, sick ■ *nm/f* invalid, sick person; (*en hospital*) patient
enfilar [enfi'lar] *vt* (*aguja*) to thread; (*calle*) to go down
enflaquecer [enflake'θer] *vt* (*adelgazar*) to make thin; (*debilitar*) to weaken
enflaquezca *etc* [enfla'keθka] *vb ver* **enflaquecer**
enfocar [enfo'kar] *vt* (*foto etc*) to focus; (*problema etc*) to consider, look at
enfoque *etc* [en'foke] *vb ver* **enfocar** ■ *nm* focus; (*acto*) focusing; (*óptica*) approach
enfrascado, -a [enfras'kaðo, a] *adj*: **estar ~ en algo** (*fig*) to be wrapped up in sth
enfrascarse [enfras'karse] *vr*: **~ en un libro** to bury o.s. in a book
enfrasque *etc* [en'fraske] *vb ver* **enfrascarse**
enfrentamiento [enfrenta'mjento] *nm* confrontation
enfrentar [enfren'tar] *vt* (*peligro*) to face (up to), confront; (*oponer*) to bring face to face; **enfrentarse** *vr* (*dos personas*) to face *o* confront each other; (*Deporte: dos equipos*) to meet; **enfrentarse a** *o* **con** to face up to, confront
enfrente [en'frente] *adv* opposite; **~ de** *prep* opposite, facing; **la casa de ~** the house opposite, the house across the street
enfriamiento [enfria'mjento] *nm* chilling, refrigeration; (*Med*) cold, chill
enfriar [enfri'ar] *vt* (*alimentos*) to cool, chill; (*algo caliente*) to cool down; (*habitación*) to air, freshen; (*entusiasmo*) to dampen; **enfriarse** *vr* to cool down; (*Med*) to catch a chill; (*amistad*) to cool
enfurecer [enfure'θer] *vt* to enrage, madden; **enfurecerse** *vr* to become furious, fly into a rage; (*mar*) to get rough
enfurezca *etc* [enfu'reθka] *vb ver* **enfurecer**
engalanar [engala'nar] *vt* (*adornar*) to adorn; (*ciudad*) to decorate; **engalanarse** *vr* to get dressed up
enganchar [engan'tʃar] *vt* to hook; (*ropa*) to hang up; (*dos vagones*) to hitch up; (*Tec*) to couple, connect; (*Mil*) to recruit; (*fam: atraer: persona*) to rope into; **engancharse** *vr* (*Mil*) to enlist, join up; **engancharse (a)** (*drogas*) to get hooked (on)
enganche [en'gantʃe] *nm* hook; (*Tec*) coupling, connection; (*acto*) hooking (up); (*Mil*) recruitment, enlistment; (*Am: depósito*) deposit
engañar [enga'ɲar] *vt* to deceive; (*estafar*) to cheat, swindle ■ *vi*: **las apariencias engañan** appearances are deceptive; **engañarse** *vr* (*equivocarse*) to be wrong; (*asimismo*) to deceive *o* kid o.s.; **engaña a su mujer** he's unfaithful to *o* cheats on his wife
engaño [en'gaɲo] *nm* deceit; (*estafa*) trick, swindle; (*error*) mistake, misunderstanding; (*ilusión*) delusion
engañoso, -a [enga'ɲoso, a] *adj* (*tramposo*) crooked; (*mentiroso*) dishonest, deceitful; (*aspecto*) deceptive; (*consejo*) misleading
engarce *etc* [en'garθe] *vb ver* **engarzar**
engarzar [engar'θar] *vt* (*joya*) to set, mount; (*fig*) to link, connect
engatusar [engatu'sar] *vt* (*fam*) to coax

engendrar [enxen'drar] *vt* to breed; (*procrear*) to beget; (*fig*) to cause, produce
engendro [en'xendro] *nm* (*Bio*) foetus; (*fig*) monstrosity; (*: idea*) brainchild
englobar [englo'βar] *vt* (*comprender*) to include, comprise; (*incluir*) to lump together
engomar [engo'mar] *vt* to glue, stick
engordar [engor'ðar] *vt* to fatten ■ *vi* to get fat, put on weight
engorro [en'gorro] *nm* bother, nuisance
engorroso, -a [engo'rroso, a] *adj* bothersome, trying
engranaje [engra'naxe] *nm* (*Auto*) gear; (*juego*) gears *pl*
engrandecer [engrande'θer] *vt* to enlarge, magnify; (*alabar*) to praise, speak highly of; (*exagerar*) to exaggerate
engrandezca *etc* [engran'deθka] *vb ver* **engrandecer**
engrasar [engra'sar] *vt* (*Tec: poner grasa*) to grease; (*: lubricar*) to lubricate, oil; (*manchar*) to make greasy
engrase [en'grase] *nm* greasing, lubrication
engreído, -a [engre'iðo, a] *adj* vain, conceited
engrosar [engro'sar] *vt* (*ensanchar*) to enlarge; (*aumentar*) to increase; (*hinchar*) to swell
engrudo [en'gruðo] *nm* paste
engruese *etc* [en'grwese] *vb ver* **engrosar**
engullir [engu'ʎir] *vt* to gobble, gulp (down)
enhebrar [ene'βrar] *vt* to thread
enhiesto, -a [e'njesto, a] *adj* (*derecho*) erect; (*bandera*) raised; (*edificio*) lofty
enhorabuena [enora'βwena] *excl* congratulations
enigma [e'niɣma] *nm* enigma; (*problema*) puzzle; (*misterio*) mystery
enigmático, -a [eniɣ'matiko, a] *adj* enigmatic
enjabonar [enxaβo'nar] *vt* to soap; (*barba*) to lather; (*fam: adular*) to soft-soap; (*: regañar*) to tick off
enjalbegar [enxalβe'ɣar] *vt* (*pared*) to whitewash
enjalbegue *etc* [enxal'βeɣe] *vb ver* **enjalbegar**
enjambre [en'xambre] *nm* swarm
enjaular [enxau'lar] *vt* to (put in a) cage; (*fam*) to jail, lock up
enjuagar [enxwa'ɣar] *vt* (*ropa*) to rinse (out)
enjuague *etc* [en'xwaɣe] *vb ver* **enjuagar** ■ *nm* (*Med*) mouthwash; (*de ropa*) rinse, rinsing
enjugar [enxu'ɣar] *vt* to wipe (off); (*lágrimas*) to dry; (*déficit*) to wipe out
enjugue *etc* [en'xuɣe] *vb ver* **enjugar**
enjuiciar [enxwi'θjar] *vt* (*Jur: procesar*) to prosecute, try; (*fig*) to judge
enjuto, -a [en'xuto, a] *adj* dry, dried up; (*fig*) lean, skinny
enlace *etc* [en'laθe] *vb ver* **enlazar** ■ *nm* link, connection; (*relación*) relationship; (*tb*: **~ matrimonial**) marriage; (*de trenes*) connection; **~ de datos** data link; **~ sindical** shop steward; **~ telefónico** telephone link-up
enlazar [enla'θar] *vt* (*unir con lazos*) to bind together; (*atar*) to tie; (*conectar*) to link, connect; (*Am*) to lasso
enlodar [enlo'ðar] *vt* to cover in mud; (*fig: manchar*) to stain; (*: rebajar*) to debase
enloquecer [enloke'θer] *vt* to drive mad ■ *vi*, **enloquecerse** *vr* to go mad
enloquezca *etc* [enlo'keθka] *vb ver* **enloquecer**
enlutado, -a [enlu'taðo, a] *adj* (*persona*) in mourning
enlutar [enlu'tar] *vt* to dress in mourning; **enlutarse** *vr* to go into mourning
enmarañar [enmara'ɲar] *vt* (*enredar*) to tangle up, entangle; (*complicar*) to complicate; (*confundir*) to confuse; **enmarañarse** *vr* (*enredarse*) to become entangled; (*confundirse*) to get confused
enmarcar [enmar'kar] *vt* (*cuadro*) to frame; (*fig*) to provide a setting for
enmarque *etc* [en'marke] *vb ver* **enmarcar**
enmascarar [enmaska'rar] *vt* to mask; (*intenciones*) to disguise; **enmascararse** *vr* to put on a mask
enmendar [enmen'dar] *vt* to emend, correct; (*constitución etc*) to amend; (*comportamiento*) to reform; **enmendarse** *vr* to reform, mend one's ways
enmienda *etc* [en'mjenda] *vb ver* **enmendar** ■ *nf* correction; amendment; reform
enmohecerse [enmoe'θerse] *vr* (*metal*) to rust, go rusty; (*muro, plantas*) to go mouldy
enmohezca *etc* [enmo'eθka] *vb ver* **enmohecerse**
enmudecer [enmuðe'θer] *vt* to silence ■ *vi*, **enmudecerse** *vr* (*perder el habla*) to fall silent; (*guardar silencio*) to remain silent; (*por miedo*) to be struck dumb
enmudezca *etc* [enmu'ðeθka] *vb ver* **enmudecer**
ennegrecer [enneɣre'θer] *vt* (*poner negro*) to blacken; (*oscurecer*) to darken; **ennegrecerse** *vr* to turn black; (*oscurecerse*) to get dark, darken
ennegrezca *etc* [enne'ɣreθka] *vb ver* **ennegrecer**
ennoblecer [ennoβle'θer] *vt* to ennoble
ennoblezca *etc* [enno'βleθka] *vb ver* **ennoblecer**

en.° *abr* (*= enero*) Jan.
enojadizo, -a [enoxa'ðiθo, a] *adj* irritable, short-tempered
enojar [eno'xar] (*esp Am*) *vt* (*encolerizar*) to anger; (*disgustar*) to annoy, upset; **enojarse** *vr* to get angry; to get annoyed
enojo [e'noxo] *nm* (*esp Am: cólera*) anger; (*irritación*) annoyance; **enojos** *nmpl* trials, problems
enojoso, -a [eno'xoso, a] *adj* annoying
enorgullecerse [enorɣuʎe'θerse] *vr* to be proud; **~ de** to pride o.s. on, be proud of
enorgullezca *etc* [enorɣu'ʎeθka] *vb ver* **enorgullecerse**
enorme [e'norme] *adj* enormous, huge; (*fig*) monstrous
enormidad [enormi'ðað] *nf* hugeness, immensity
enraice *etc* [en'raiθe] *vb ver* **enraizar**
enraizar [enrai'θar] *vi* to take root
enrarecido, -a [enrare'θiðo, a] *adj* rarefied
enredadera [enreða'ðera] *nf* (*Bot*) creeper, climbing plant
enredar [enre'ðar] *vt* (*cables, hilos etc*) to tangle (up), entangle; (*situación*) to complicate, confuse; (*meter cizaña*) to sow discord among *o* between; (*implicar*) to embroil, implicate; **enredarse** *vr* to get entangled, get tangled (up); (*situación*) to get complicated; (*persona*) to get embroiled
enredo [en'reðo] *nm* (*maraña*) tangle; (*confusión*) mix-up, confusion; (*intriga*) intrigue; (*apuro*) jam; (*amorío*) love affair
enrejado [enre'xaðo] *nm* grating; (*de ventana*) lattice; (*en jardín*) trellis
enrevesado, -a [enreβe'saðo, a] *adj* (*asunto*) complicated, involved
enriquecer [enrike'θer] *vt* to make rich; (*fig*) to enrich; **enriquecerse** *vr* to get rich
enriquezca *etc* [enri'keθka] *vb ver* **enriquecer**
enrojecer [enroxe'θer] *vt* to redden ▪ *vi*, **enrojecerse** *vr* (*persona*) to blush
enrojezca *etc* [enro'xeθka] *vb ver* **enrojecer**
enrolar [enro'lar] *vt* (*Mil*) to enlist; (*reclutar*) to recruit; **enrolarse** *vr* (*Mil*) to join up; (*afiliarse*) to enrol, sign on
enrollar [enro'ʎar] *vt* to roll (up), wind (up); **enrollarse** *vr*: **enrollarse con algn** to get involved with sb
enroque [en'roke] *nm* (*Ajedrez*) castling
enroscar [enros'kar] *vt* (*torcer, doblar*) to twist; (*arrollar*) to coil (round), wind; (*tornillo, rosca*) to screw in; **enroscarse** *vr* to coil, wind
enrosque *etc* [en'roske] *vb ver* **enroscar**
ensalada [ensa'laða] *nf* salad; (*lío*) mix-up
ensaladilla [ensala'ðiʎa] *nf* (*tb*: **ensaladilla rusa**) ≈ Russian salad
ensalce *etc* [en'salθe] *vb ver* **ensalzar**
ensalzar [ensal'θar] *vt* (*alabar*) to praise, extol; (*exaltar*) to exalt
ensamblador [ensambla'ðor] *nm* (*Inform*) assembler
ensambladura [ensambla'ðura] *nf*, **ensamblaje** [ensam'blaxe] *nm* assembly; (*Tec*) joint
ensamblar [ensam'blar] *vt* (*montar*) to assemble; (*madera etc*) to join
ensanchar [ensan'tʃar] *vt* (*hacer más ancho*) to widen; (*agrandar*) to enlarge, expand; (*Costura*) to let out; **ensancharse** *vr* to get wider, expand; (*pey*) to give o.s. airs
ensanche [en'santʃe] *nm* (*de calle*) widening; (*de negocio*) expansion
ensangrentado, -a [ensangren'taðo, a] *adj* bloodstained, covered with blood
ensangrentar [ensangren'tar] *vt* to stain with blood
ensangriente *etc* [ensan'grjente] *vb ver* **ensangrentar**
ensañarse [ensa'ɲarse] *vr*: **~ con** to treat brutally
ensartar [ensar'tar] *vt* (*gen*) to string (together); (*carne*) to spit, skewer
ensayar [ensa'jar] *vt* to test, try (out); (*Teat*) to rehearse
ensayista [ensa'jista] *nm/f* essayist
ensayo [en'sajo] *nm* test, trial; (*Química*) experiment; (*Teat*) rehearsal; (*Deporte*) try; (*Escol, Lit*) essay; **pedido de ~** (*Com*) trial order; **~ general** (*Teat*) dress rehearsal; (*Mus*) full rehearsal
enseguida [ense'ɣuiða] *adv* at once, right away; **~ termino** I've nearly finished, I shan't be long now
ensenada [ense'naða] *nf* inlet, cove
enseña [en'seɲa] *nf* ensign, standard
enseñante [ense'ɲante] *nm/f* teacher
enseñanza [ense'ɲanθa] *nf* (*educación*) education; (*acción*) teaching; (*doctrina*) teaching, doctrine; **~ primaria/secundaria/superior** primary/secondary/higher education
enseñar [ense'ɲar] *vt* (*educar*) to teach; (*instruir*) to teach, instruct; (*mostrar, señalar*) to show
enseres [en'seres] *nmpl* belongings
ensillar [ensi'ʎar] *vt* to saddle (up)
ensimismarse [ensimis'marse] *vr* (*abstraerse*) to become lost in thought; (*estar absorto*) to be lost in thought; (*Am*) to become conceited
ensopar [enso'par] *vt* (*Am*) to soak
ensordecer [ensorðe'θer] *vt* to deafen ▪ *vi* to go deaf
ensordezca *etc* [ensor'ðeθka] *vb ver* **ensordecer**

ensortijado, -a [ensorti'xaðo, a] *adj* (*pelo*) curly
ensuciar [ensu'θjar] *vt* (*manchar*) to dirty, soil; (*fig*) to defile; **ensuciarse** *vr* (*mancharse*) to get dirty; (*niño*) to dirty (*o* wet) o.s.
ensueño [en'sweɲo] *nm* (*sueño*) dream, fantasy; (*ilusión*) illusion; (*soñando despierto*) daydream; **de ~** dream-like
entablado [enta'βlaðo] *nm* (*piso*) floorboards *pl*; (*armazón*) boarding
entablar [enta'βlar] *vt* (*recubrir*) to board (up); (*Ajedrez, Damas*) to set up; (*conversación*) to strike up; (*Jur*) to file ■ *vi* to draw
entablillar [entaβli'ʎar] *vt* (*Med*) to (put in a) splint
entallado, -a [enta'ʎaðo, a] *adj* waisted
entallar [enta'ʎar] *vt* (*traje*) to tailor ■ *vi*: **el traje entalla bien** the suit fits well
ente ['ente] *nm* (*organización*) body, organization; (*compañía*) company; (*fam: persona*) odd character; (*ser*) being; **~ público** (*Esp*) state(-owned) body
entender [enten'der] *vt* (*comprender*) to understand; (*darse cuenta*) to realize; (*querer decir*) to mean ■ *vi* to understand; (*creer*) to think, believe ■ *nm*: **a mi ~** in my opinion; **~ de** to know all about; **~ algo de** to know a little about; **~ en** to deal with, have to do with; **entenderse** *vr* (*comprenderse*) to be understood; (*2 personas*) to get on together; (*ponerse de acuerdo*) to agree, reach an agreement; **dar a ~ que ...** to lead to believe that ...; **entenderse mal** to get on badly; **¿entiendes?** (do you) understand?
entendido, -a [enten'diðo, a] *adj* (*comprendido*) understood; (*hábil*) skilled; (*inteligente*) knowledgeable ■ *nm/f* (*experto*) expert ■ *excl* agreed!
entendimiento [entendi'mjento] *nm* (*comprensión*) understanding; (*inteligencia*) mind, intellect; (*juicio*) judgement
enterado, -a [ente'raðo, a] *adj* well-informed; **estar ~ de** to know about, be aware of; **no darse por ~** to pretend not to understand
enteramente [entera'mente] *adv* entirely, completely
enterarse [ente'rarse] *vr*: **~ (de)** to find out (about); **para que te enteres ...** (*fam*) for your information ...
entereza [ente'reθa] *nf* (*totalidad*) entirety; (*fig: de carácter*) strength of mind; (*honradez*) integrity
enternecedor, a [enterneθe'ðor, a] *adj* touching
enternecer [enterne'θer] *vt* (*ablandar*) to soften; (*apiadar*) to touch, move; **enternecerse** *vr* to be touched, be moved
enternezca *etc* [enter'neθka] *vb ver* **enternecer**
entero, -a [en'tero, a] *adj* (*total*) whole, entire; (*fig: recto*) honest; (*: firme*) firm, resolute ■ *nm* (*Mat*) integer; (*Com: punto*) point; (*Am: pago*) payment; **las acciones han subido dos enteros** the shares have gone up two points
enterrador [enterra'ðor] *nm* gravedigger
enterrar [ente'rrar] *vt* to bury; (*fig*) to forget
entibiar [enti'βjar] *vt* (*enfriar*) to cool; (*calentar*) to warm; **entibiarse** *vr* (*fig*) to cool
entidad [enti'ðað] *nf* (*empresa*) firm, company; (*organismo*) body; (*sociedad*) society; (*Filosofía*) entity
entienda *etc* [en'tjenda] *vb ver* **entender**
entierro *etc* [en'tjerro] *vb ver* **enterrar** ■ *nm* (*acción*) burial; (*funeral*) funeral
entomología [entomolo'xia] *nf* entomology
entomólogo, -a [ento'moloɣo, a] *nm/f* entomologist
entonación [entona'θjon] *nf* (*Ling*) intonation; (*fig*) conceit
entonar [ento'nar] *vt* (*canción*) to intone; (*colores*) to tone; (*Med*) to tone up ■ *vi* to be in tune; **entonarse** *vr* (*engreírse*) to give o.s. airs
entonces [en'tonθes] *adv* then, at that time; **desde ~** since then; **en aquel ~** at that time; **(pues) ~** and so; **el ~ embajador de España** the then Spanish ambassador
entornar [entor'nar] *vt* (*puerta, ventana*) to half close, leave ajar; (*los ojos*) to screw up
entorno [en'torno] *nm* setting, environment; **~ de redes** (*Inform*) network environment
entorpecer [entorpe'θer] *vt* (*entendimiento*) to dull; (*impedir*) to obstruct, hinder; (*: tránsito*) to slow down, delay
entorpezca *etc* [entor'peθka] *vb ver* **entorpecer**
entrado, -a [en'traðo, a] *adj*: **~ en años** elderly; **(una vez) ~ el verano** in the summer(time), when summer comes ■ *nf* (*acción*) entry, access; (*sitio*) entrance, way in; (*principio*) beginning; (*Com*) receipts *pl*, takings *pl*; (*Culin*) entrée; (*Deporte*) innings *sg*; (*Teat*) house, audience; (*para el cine etc*) ticket; (*Inform*) input; (*Econ*): **entradas** *nfpl* income *sg*; **entradas brutas** gross receipts; **entradas y salidas** (*Com*) income and expenditure; **entrada de aire** (*Tec*) air intake *o* inlet; **de entrada** right away; **"entrada gratis"** "admission free"; **tiene entradas** he's losing his hair
entrante [en'trante] *adj* next, coming; (*Pol*) incoming ■ *nm* inlet; (*Culin*) starter; **mes/año ~** next month/year

entraña [en'traɲa] *nf* (*fig: centro*) heart, core; (*raíz*) root; **entrañas** *nfpl* (*Anat*) entrails; (*fig*) heart *sg*
entrañable [entra'ɲaβle] *adj* (*persona, lugar*) dear; (*relación*) close; (*acto*) intimate
entrañar [entra'ɲar] *vt* to entail
entrar [en'trar] *vt* (*introducir*) to bring in; (*persona*) to show in; (*Inform*) to input ■ *vi* (*meterse*) to go *o* come in, enter; (*comenzar*): **~ diciendo** to begin by saying; **entré en** *o* **a** (*Am*) **la casa** I went into the house; **le entraron ganas de reír** he felt a sudden urge to laugh; **no me entra** I can't get the hang of it
entre ['entre] *prep* (*dos*) between; (*en medio de*) among(st); (*por*): **se abrieron paso ~ la multitud** they forced their way through the crowd; **~ una cosa y otra** what with one thing and another; **~ más estudia más aprende** (*Am*) the more he studies the more he learns
entreabierto [entrea'βjerto] *pp de* **entreabrir**
entreabrir [entrea'βrir] *vt* to half-open, open halfway
entreacto [entre'akto] *nm* interval
entrecano, -a [entre'kano, a] *adj* greying; **ser ~** (*persona*) to be going grey
entrecejo [entre'θexo] *nm*: **fruncir el ~** to frown
entrechocar [entretʃo'kar] *vi* (*dientes*) to chatter
entrechoque *etc* [entre'tʃoke] *vb ver* **entrechocar**
entrecomillado, -a [entrekomi'ʎaðo, a] *adj* in inverted commas
entrecortado, -a [entrekor'taðo, a] *adj* (*respiración*) laboured, difficult; (*habla*) faltering
entrecot [entre'ko(t)] *nm* (*Culin*) sirloin steak
entrecruce *etc* [entre'kruθe] *vb ver* **entrecruzarse**
entrecruzarse [entrekru'θarse] *vr* (*Bio*) to interbreed
entredicho [entre'ðitʃo] *nm* (*Jur*) injunction; **poner en ~** to cast doubt on; **estar en ~** to be in doubt
entrega [en'treɣa] *nf* (*de mercancías*) delivery; (*de premios*) presentation; (*de novela etc*) instalment; **"~ a domicilio"** "door-to-door delivery service"
entregar [entre'ɣar] *vt* (*dar*) to hand (over), deliver; (*ejercicios*) to hand in; **entregarse** *vr* (*rendirse*) to surrender, give in, submit; **entregarse a** (*dedicarse*) to devote o.s. to; **a ~** (*Com*) to be supplied
entregue *etc* [en'treɣe] *vb ver* **entregar**
entrelace *etc* [entre'laθe] *vb ver* **entrelazar**
entrelazar [entrela'θar] *vt* to entwine
entremedias [entre'meðjas] *adv* (*en medio*) in between, halfway
entremeses [entre'meses] *nmpl* hors d'œuvres
entremeter [entreme'ter] *vt* to insert, put in; **entremeterse** *vr* to meddle, interfere
entremetido, -a [entreme'tiðo, a] *adj* meddling, interfering
entremezclar [entremeθ'klar] *vt*, **entremezclarse** *vr* to intermingle
entrenador, a [entrena'ðor, a] *nm/f* trainer, coach
entrenamiento [entrena'mjento] *nm* training
entrenar [entre'nar] *vt* (*Deporte*) to train; (*caballo*) to exercise ■ *vi*, **entrenarse** *vr* to train
entrepierna [entre'pjerna] *nf* (*tb*: **entrepiernas**) crotch, crutch
entresacar [entresa'kar] *vt* to pick out, select
entresaque *etc* [entre'sake] *vb ver* **entresacar**
entresuelo [entre'swelo] *nm* mezzanine, entresol; (*Teat*) dress *o* first circle
entretanto [entre'tanto] *adv* meanwhile, meantime
entretejer [entrete'xer] *vt* to interweave
entretela [entre'tela] *nf* (*de ropa*) interlining; **entretelas** *nfpl* heartstrings
entretención [entreten'sjon] *nf* (*Am*) entertainment
entretendré *etc* [entreten'dre] *vb ver* **entretener**
entretener [entrete'ner] *vt* (*divertir*) to entertain, amuse; (*detener*) to hold up, delay; (*mantener*) to maintain; **entretenerse** *vr* (*divertirse*) to amuse o.s.; (*retrasarse*) to delay, linger; **no le entretengo más** I won't keep you any longer
entretenga *etc* [entre'tenga] *vb ver* **entretener**
entretenido, -a [entrete'niðo, a] *adj* entertaining, amusing
entretenimiento [entreteni'mjento] *nm* entertainment, amusement; (*mantenimiento*) upkeep, maintenance
entretiempo [entre'tjempo] *nm*: **ropa de ~** *clothes for spring and autumn*
entretiene *etc* [entre'tjene], **entretuve** *etc* [entre'tuβe] *vb ver* **entretener**
entreveía *etc* [entreβe'ia] *vb ver* **entrever**
entrever [entre'βer] *vt* to glimpse, catch a glimpse of
entrevista [entre'βista] *nf* interview
entrevistar [entreβis'tar] *vt* to interview; **entrevistarse** *vr*: **entrevistarse con** to have an interview with, see; **el ministro**

se entrevistó con el Rey ayer the minister had an audience with the King yesterday
entrevisto [entre'βisto] *pp de* **entrever**
entristecer [entriste'θer] *vt* to sadden, grieve; **entristecerse** *vr* to grow sad
entristezca *etc* [entris'teθka] *vb ver* **entristecer**
entrometerse [entrome'terse] *vr*: ~ **(en)** to interfere (in *o* with)
entrometido, -a [entrome'tiðo, a] *adj* interfering, meddlesome
entroncar [entron'kar] *vi* to be connected *o* related
entronque *etc* [en'tronke] *vb ver* **entroncar**
entuerto [en'twerto] *nm* wrong, injustice; **entuertos** *nmpl* (*Med*) afterpains
entumecer [entume'θer] *vt* to numb, benumb; **entumecerse** *vr* (*por el frío*) to go *o* become numb
entumecido, -a [entume'θiðo, a] *adj* numb, stiff
entumezca *etc* [entu'meθka] *vb ver* **entumecer**
enturbiar [entur'βjar] *vt* (*el agua*) to make cloudy; (*fig*) to confuse; **enturbiarse** *vr* (*oscurecerse*) to become cloudy; (*fig*) to get confused, become obscure
entusiasmar [entusjas'mar] *vt* to excite, fill with enthusiasm; (*gustar mucho*) to delight; **entusiasmarse** *vr*: **entusiasmarse con** *o* **por** to get enthusiastic *o* excited about
entusiasmo [entu'sjasmo] *nm* enthusiasm; (*excitación*) excitement
entusiasta [entu'sjasta] *adj* enthusiastic ■ *nm/f* enthusiast
enumerar [enume'rar] *vt* to enumerate
enunciación [enunθja'θjon] *nf*, **enunciado** [enun'θjaðo] *nm* enunciation; (*declaración*) declaration, statement
enunciar [enun'θjar] *vt* to enunciate; to declare, state
envainar [embai'nar] *vt* to sheathe
envalentonar [embalento'nar] *vt* to give courage to; **envalentonarse** *vr* (*pey: jactarse*) to boast, brag
envanecer [embane'θer] *vt* to make conceited; **envanecerse** *vr* to grow conceited
envanezca *etc* [emba'neθka] *vb ver* **envanecer**
envasar [emba'sar] *vt* (*empaquetar*) to pack, wrap; (*enfrascar*) to bottle; (*enlatar*) to can; (*embolsar*) to pocket
envase [em'base] *nm* packing, wrapping; bottling; canning; pocketing; (*recipiente*) container; (*paquete*) package; (*botella*) bottle; (*lata*) tin (*Brit*), can
envejecer [embexe'θer] *vt* to make old, age ■ *vi*, **envejecerse** *vr* (*volverse viejo*) to grow old; (*parecer viejo*) to age
envejecido, -a [embexe'θiðo, a] *adj* old, aged; (*de aspecto*) old-looking
envejezca *etc* [embe'xeθka] *vb ver* **envejecer**
envenenar [embene'nar] *vt* to poison; (*fig*) to embitter
envergadura [emberɣa'ðura] *nf* (*expansión*) expanse; (*Naut*) breadth; (*fig*) scope; **un programa de gran** ~ a wide-ranging programme
envés [em'bes] *nm* (*de tela*) back, wrong side
enviado, -a [em'bjaðo, a] *nm/f* (*Pol*) envoy; ~ **especial** (*de periódico, TV*) special correspondent
enviar [em'bjar] *vt* to send; ~ **un mensaje a algn** (*por móvil*) to text sb, send sb a text message
enviciar [embi'θjar] *vt* to corrupt ■ *vi* (*trabajo etc*) to be addictive; **enviciarse** *vr*: **enviciarse (con** *o* **en)** to get addicted (to)
envidia [em'biðja] *nf* envy; **tener ~ a** to envy, be jealous of
envidiar [embi'ðjar] *vt* (*desear*) to envy; (*tener celos de*) to be jealous of
envidioso, -a [embi'ðjoso, a] *adj* envious, jealous
envío [em'bio] *nm* (*acción*) sending; (*de mercancías*) consignment; (*de dinero*) remittance; (*en barco*) shipment; **gastos de ~** postage and packing; **~ contra reembolso** COD shipment
enviudar [embju'ðar] *vi* to be widowed
envoltura [embol'tura] *nf* (*cobertura*) cover; (*embalaje*) wrapper, wrapping
envolver [embol'βer] *vt* to wrap (up); (*cubrir*) to cover; (*enemigo*) to surround; (*implicar*) to involve, implicate
envuelto [em'bwelto], **envuelva** *etc* [em'bwelβa] *vb ver* **envolver**
enyesar [enje'sar] *vt* (*pared*) to plaster; (*Med*) to put in plaster
enzarzarse [enθar'θarse] *vr*: ~ **en algo** to get mixed up in sth
epa ['epa], **épale** ['epale] (*Am*) *excl* hey!, wow!
E.P.D. *abr* (= *en paz descanse*) RIP
epicentro [epi'θentro] *nm* epicentre
épico, -a ['epiko, a] *adj* epic ■ *nf* epic (poetry)
epidemia [epi'ðemja] *nf* epidemic
epidémico, -a [epi'ðemiko, a] *adj* epidemic
epidermis [epi'ðermis] *nf* epidermis
epifanía [epifa'nia] *nf* Epiphany
epilepsia [epi'lepsja] *nf* epilepsy
epiléptico, -a [epi'leptiko, a] *adj, nm/f* epileptic
epílogo [e'piloɣo] *nm* epilogue

episcopado [episko'paðo] *nm* (*cargo*) bishopric; (*obispos*) bishops *pl* (*collectively*)
episodio [epi'soðjo] *nm* episode; (*suceso*) incident
epístola [e'pistola] *nf* epistle
epitafio [epi'tafjo] *nm* epitaph
epíteto [e'piteto] *nm* epithet
época ['epoka] *nf* period, time; (*temporada*) season; (*Historia*) age, epoch; **hacer ~** to be epoch-making
equidad [eki'ðað] *nf* equity, fairness
equilibrar [ekili'βrar] *vt* to balance
equilibrio [eki'liβrjo] *nm* balance, equilibrium; **~ político** balance of power
equilibrista [ekili'βrista] *nm/f* (*funámbulo*) tightrope walker; (*acróbata*) acrobat
equinoccio [eki'nokθjo] *nm* equinox
equipaje [eki'paxe] *nm* luggage (*Brit*), baggage (*US*); (*avíos*) equipment, kit; **~ de mano** hand luggage; **hacer el ~** to pack
equipar [eki'par] *vt* (*proveer*) to equip
equiparar [ekipa'rar] *vt* (*igualar*) to put on the same level; (*comparar*): **~ con** to compare with; **equipararse** *vr*: **equipararse con** to be on a level with
equipo [e'kipo] *nm* (*conjunto de cosas*) equipment; (*Deporte, grupo*) team; (*de obreros*) shift; (*de máquinas*) plant; (*turbinas etc*) set; **~ de caza** hunting gear; **~ físico** (*Inform*) hardware; **~ médico** medical team; **~ de música** music centre
equis ['ekis] *nf* (the letter) X
equitación [ekita'θjon] *nf* (*acto*) riding; (*arte*) horsemanship
equitativo, -a [ekita'tiβo, a] *adj* equitable, fair
equivaldré *etc* [ekiβal'dre] *vb ver* **equivaler**
equivalencia [ekiβa'lenθja] *nf* equivalence
equivalente [ekiβa'lente] *adj, nm* equivalent
equivaler [ekiβa'ler] *vi*: **~ a** to be equivalent *o* equal to; (*en rango*) to rank as
equivalga *etc* [eki'βalɣa] *vb ver* **equivaler**
equivocación [ekiβoka'θjon] *nf* mistake, error; (*malentendido*) misunderstanding
equivocado, -a [ekiβo'kaðo, a] *adj* wrong, mistaken
equivocarse [ekiβo'karse] *vr* to be wrong, make a mistake; **~ de camino** to take the wrong road
equívoco, -a [e'kiβoko, a] *adj* (*dudoso*) suspect; (*ambiguo*) ambiguous ■ *nm* ambiguity; (*malentendido*) misunderstanding
equivoque *etc* [eki'βoke] *vb ver* **equivocarse**
era ['era] *vb ver* **ser** ■ *nf* era, age; (*Agr*) threshing floor
erais ['erais], **éramos** ['eramos], **eran** ['eran] *vb ver* **ser**
erario [e'rarjo] *nm* exchequer, treasury
eras ['eras], **eres** ['eres] *vb ver* **ser**
erección [erek'θjon] *nf* erection
ergonomía [erɣono'mia] *nf* ergonomics *sg*, human engineering
erguir [er'ɣir] *vt* to raise, lift; (*poner derecho*) to straighten; **erguirse** *vr* to straighten up
erice *etc* [e'riθe] *vb ver* **erizarse**
erigir [eri'xir] *vt* to erect, build; **erigirse** *vr*: **erigirse en** to set o.s. up as
erija *etc* [e'rixa] *vb ver* **erigir**
erizado, -a [eri'θaðo, a] *adj* bristly
erizarse [eri'θarse] *vr* (*pelo: de perro*) to bristle; (*: de persona*) to stand on end
erizo [e'riθo] *nm* hedgehog; **~ de mar** sea urchin
ermita [er'mita] *nf* hermitage
ermitaño, -a [ermi'taɲo, a] *nm/f* hermit
erosión [ero'sjon] *nf* erosion
erosionar [erosjo'nar] *vt* to erode
erótico, -a [e'rotiko, a] *adj* erotic
erotismo [ero'tismo] *nm* eroticism
erradicar [erraði'kar] *vt* to eradicate
erradique *etc* [erra'ðike] *vb ver* **erradicar**
errado, -a [e'rraðo, a] *adj* mistaken, wrong
errante [e'rrante] *adj* wandering, errant
errar [e'rrar] *vi* (*vagar*) to wander, roam; (*equivocarse*) to be mistaken ■ *vt*: **~ el camino** to take the wrong road; **~ el tiro** to miss
errata [e'rrata] *nf* misprint
erre ['erre] *nf* (the letter) R; **~ que ~** stubbornly
erróneo, -a [e'rroneo, a] *adj* (*equivocado*) wrong, mistaken; (*falso*) false, untrue
error [e'rror] *nm* error, mistake; (*Inform*) bug; **~ de imprenta** misprint; **~ de lectura/escritura** (*Inform*) read/write error; **~ sintáctico** syntax error; **~ judicial** miscarriage of justice
Ertzaintza [er'tʃantʃa] *nf* Basque police; *ver tb* **policía**
eructar [eruk'tar] *vt* to belch, burp
eructo [e'rukto] *nm* belch
erudición [eruði'θjon] *nf* erudition, learning
erudito, -a [eru'ðito, a] *adj* erudite, learned ■ *nm/f* scholar; **los eruditos en esta materia** the experts in this field
erupción [erup'θjon] *nf* eruption; (*Med*) rash; (*de violencia*) outbreak; (*de ira*) outburst
es [es] *vb ver* **ser**
E/S *abr* (*Inform*: = *entrada/salida*) I/O
esa ['esa], **esas** ['esas] *adj demostrativo ver* **ese**
ésa ['esa], **ésas** ['esas] *pron ver* **ése**
esbelto, -a [es'βelto, a] *adj* slim, slender
esbirro [es'βirro] *nm* henchman
esbozar [esβo'θar] *vt* to sketch, outline
esbozo [es'βoθo] *nm* sketch, outline

escabeche [eska'βetʃe] *nm* brine; (*de aceitunas etc*) pickle; **en ~** pickled
escabechina [eskaβe'tʃina] *nf* (*batalla*) massacre; **hacer una ~** (*Escol*) to fail a lot of students
escabroso, -a [eska'βroso, a] *adj* (*accidentado*) rough, uneven; (*fig*) tough, difficult; (*: atrevido*) risqué
escabullirse [eskaβu'ʎirse] *vr* to slip away; (*largarse*) to clear out
escacharrar [eskatʃa'rrar] *vt* (*fam*) to break; **escacharrarse** *vr* to get broken
escafandra [eska'fandra] *nf* (*buzo*) diving suit; (*escafandra espacial*) spacesuit
escala [es'kala] *nf* (*proporción, Mus*) scale; (*de mano*) ladder; (*Aviat*) stopover; (*de colores etc*) range; **~ de tiempo** time scale; **~ de sueldos** salary scale; **una investigación a ~ nacional** a nationwide inquiry; **reproducir a ~** to reproduce to scale; **hacer ~ en** to stop off *o* over at
escalada [eska'laða] *nf* (*de montaña*) climb; (*de pared*) scaling
escalafón [eskala'fon] *nm* (*escala de salarios*) salary scale, wage scale
escalar [eska'lar] *vt* to climb, scale ■ *vi* (*Mil, Pol*) to escalate
escaldar [eskal'dar] *vt* (*quemar*) to scald; (*escarmentar*) to teach a lesson
escalera [eska'lera] *nf* stairs *pl*, staircase; (*escala*) ladder; (*Naipes*) run; (*de camión*) tailboard; **~ mecánica** escalator; **~ de caracol** spiral staircase; **~ de incendios** fire escape
escalerilla [eskale'riʎa] *nf* (*de avión*) steps *pl*
escalfar [eskal'far] *vt* (*huevos*) to poach
escalinata [eskali'nata] *nf* staircase
escalofriante [eskalo'frjante] *adj* chilling
escalofrío [eskalo'frio] *nm* (*Med*) chill; **escalofríos** *nmpl* (*fig*) shivers
escalón [eska'lon] *nm* step, stair; (*de escalera*) rung; (*fig: paso*) step; (*al éxito*) ladder
escalonar [eskalo'nar] *vt* to spread out; (*tierra*) to terrace; (*horas de trabajo*) to stagger
escalope [eska'lope] *nm* (*Culin*) escalope
escama [es'kama] *nf* (*de pez, serpiente*) scale; (*de jabón*) flake; (*fig*) resentment
escamar [eska'mar] *vt* (*pez*) to scale; (*producir recelo*) to make wary
escamotear [eskamote'ar] *vt* (*fam: robar*) to lift, swipe; (*hacer desaparecer*) to make disappear
escampar [eskam'par] *vb impersonal* to stop raining
escanciar [eskan'θjar] *vt* (*vino*) to pour (out)
escandalice *etc* [eskanda'liθe] *vb ver* **escandalizar**
escandalizar [eskandali'θar] *vt* to scandalize, shock; **escandalizarse** *vr* to be shocked; (*ofenderse*) to be offended
escándalo [es'kandalo] *nm* scandal; (*alboroto, tumulto*) row, uproar; **armar un ~** to make a scene; **¡es un ~!** it's outrageous!
escandaloso, -a [eskanda'loso, a] *adj* scandalous, shocking; (*risa*) hearty; (*niño*) noisy
Escandinavia [eskandi'naβja] *nf* Scandinavia
escandinavo, -a [eskandi'naβo, a] *adj, nm/f* Scandinavian
escaneo [es'kaneo] *nm* scanning
escáner [es'kaner] *nm* scanner
escaño [es'kaɲo] *nm* bench; (*Pol*) seat
escapada [eska'paða] *nf* (*huida*) escape, flight; (*Deporte*) breakaway; (*viaje*) quick trip
escapar [eska'par] *vi* (*gen*) to escape, run away; (*Deporte*) to break away; **escaparse** *vr* to escape, get away; (*agua, gas, noticias*) to leak (out); **se me escapa su nombre** his name escapes me
escaparate [eskapa'rate] *nm* shop window; (*Com*) showcase
escapatoria [eskapa'torja] *nf*: **no tener ~** (*fig*) to have no way out
escape [es'kape] *nm* (*huida*) escape; (*de agua, gas*) leak; (*de motor*) exhaust; **salir a ~** to rush out
escapismo [eska'pismo] *nm* escapism
escaquearse [eskake'arse] *vr* (*fam*) to duck out
escarabajo [eskara'βaxo] *nm* beetle
escaramuza [eskara'muθa] *nf* skirmish; (*fig*) brush
escarbar [eskar'βar] *vt* (*gallina*) to scratch; (*fig*) to inquire into, investigate
escarceos [eskar'θeos] *nmpl*: **en sus ~ con la política** in his occasional forays into politics; **~ amorosos** flirtations
escarcha [es'kartʃa] *nf* frost
escarlata [eskar'lata] *adj inv* scarlet
escarlatina [eskarla'tina] *nf* scarlet fever
escarmentar [eskarmen'tar] *vt* to punish severely ■ *vi* to learn one's lesson; **¡para que escarmientes!** that'll teach you!
escarmiento *etc* [eskar'mjento] *vb ver* **escarmentar** ■ *nm* (*ejemplo*) lesson; (*castigo*) punishment
escarnio [es'karnjo] *nm* mockery; (*injuria*) insult
escarola [eska'rola] *nf* (*Bot*) endive
escarpado, -a [eskar'paðo, a] *adj* (*pendiente*) sheer, steep; (*rocas*) craggy
escasamente [eskasa'mente] *adv* (*insuficientemente*) scantily; (*apenas*) scarcely

escasear [eskase'ar] *vi* to be scarce
escasez [eska'seθ] *nf* (*falta*) shortage, scarcity; (*pobreza*) poverty; **vivir con ~** to live on the breadline
escaso, -a [es'kaso, a] *adj* (*poco*) scarce; (*raro*) rare; (*ralo*) thin, sparse; (*limitado*) limited; (*recursos*) scanty; (*público*) sparse; (*posibilidad*) slim; (*visibilidad*) poor
escatimar [eskati'mar] *vt* (*limitar*) to skimp (on), be sparing with; **no ~ esfuerzos (para)** to spare no effort (to)
escayola [eska'jola] *nf* plaster
escayolar [eskajo'lar] *vt* to put in plaster
escena [es'θena] *nf* scene; (*decorado*) scenery; (*escenario*) stage; **poner en ~** to put on
escenario [esθe'narjo] *nm* (*Teat*) stage; (*Cine*) set; (*fig*) scene; **el ~ del crimen** the scene of the crime; **el ~ político** the political scene
escenografía [esθenoɣra'fia] *nf* set *o* stage design
escepticismo [esθepti'θismo] *nm* scepticism
escéptico, -a [es'θeptiko, a] *adj* sceptical ■ *nm/f* sceptic
escindir [esθin'dir] *vt* to split; **escindirse** *vr* (*facción*) to split off; **escindirse en** to split into
escisión [esθi'sjon] *nf* (*Med*) excision; (*fig, Pol*) split; **~ nuclear** nuclear fission
esclarecer [esklare'θer] *vt* (*iluminar*) to light up, illuminate; (*misterio, problema*) to shed light on
esclarezca *etc* [eskla'reθka] *vb ver* **esclarecer**
esclavice *etc* [eskla'βiθe] *vb ver* **esclavizar**
esclavitud [esklaβi'tuð] *nf* slavery
esclavizar [esklaβi'θar] *vt* to enslave
esclavo, -a [es'klaβo, a] *nm/f* slave
esclusa [es'klusa] *nf* (*de canal*) lock; (*compuerta*) floodgate
escoba [es'koβa] *nf* broom; **pasar la ~** to sweep up
escobazo [esko'βaθo] *nm* (*golpe*) blow with a broom; **echar a algn a escobazos** to kick sb out
escobilla [esko'βiʎa] *nf* brush
escocer [esko'θer] *vi* to burn, sting; **escocerse** *vr* to chafe, get chafed
escocés, -esa [esko'θes, esa] *adj* Scottish; (*whisky*) Scotch ■ *nm/f* Scotsman(-woman), Scot ■ *nm* (*Ling*) Scots *sg*; **tela escocesa** tartan
Escocia [es'koθja] *nf* Scotland
escoger [esko'xer] *vt* to choose, pick, select
escogido, -a [esko'xiðo, a] *adj* chosen, selected; (*calidad*) choice, select; (*persona*): **ser muy ~** to be very fussy
escoja *etc* [es'koxa] *vb ver* **escoger**
escolar [esko'lar] *adj* school *cpd* ■ *nm/f* schoolboy(-girl), pupil
escolaridad [eskolari'ðað] *nf* schooling; **libro de ~** school record
escolarización [eskolariθa'θjon] *nf*: **~ obligatoria** compulsory education
escolarizado, -a [eskolari'θaðo, a] *adj, nm/f*: **los escolarizados** those in *o* attending school
escollo [es'koʎo] *nm* (*arrecife*) reef, rock; (*fig*) pitfall
escolta [es'kolta] *nf* escort
escoltar [eskol'tar] *vt* to escort; (*proteger*) to guard
escombros [es'kombros] *nmpl* (*basura*) rubbish *sg*; (*restos*) debris *sg*
esconder [eskon'der] *vt* to hide, conceal; **esconderse** *vr* to hide
escondidas [eskon'diðas] *nfpl* (*Am*) hide-and-seek *sg*; **a ~** secretly; **hacer algo a ~ de algn** to do sth behind sb's back
escondite [eskon'dite] *nm* hiding place; (*juego*) hide-and-seek
escondrijo [eskon'drixo] *nm* hiding place, hideout
escopeta [esko'peta] *nf* shotgun; **~ de aire comprimido** air gun
escoria [es'korja] *nf* (*desecho mineral*) slag; (*fig*) scum, dregs *pl*
Escorpio [es'korpjo] *nm* (*Astro*) Scorpio
escorpión [eskor'pjon] *nm* scorpion
escotado, -a [esko'taðo, a] *adj* low-cut
escotar [esko'tar] *vt* (*vestido: ajustar*) to cut to fit; (*cuello*) to cut low
escote [es'kote] *nm* (*de vestido*) low neck; **pagar a ~** to share the expenses
escotilla [esko'tiʎa] *nf* (*Naut*) hatchway
escotillón [eskoti'ʎon] *nm* trapdoor
escozor [esko'θor] *nm* (*dolor*) sting(ing)
escribano, -a [eskri'βano, a], **escribiente** [eskri'βjente] *nm/f* clerk; (*secretario judicial*) court *o* lawyer's clerk
escribir [eskri'βir] *vt, vi* to write; **~ a máquina** to type; **¿cómo se escribe?** how do you spell it?
escrito, -a [es'krito, a] *pp de* **escribir** ■ *adj* written, in writing; (*examen*) written ■ *nm* (*documento*) document; (*manuscrito*) text, manuscript; **por ~** in writing
escritor, a [eskri'tor, a] *nm/f* writer
escritorio [eskri'torjo] *nm* desk; (*oficina*) office
escritura [eskri'tura] *nf* (*acción*) writing; (*caligrafía*) (hand)writing; (*Jur: documento*) deed; (*Com*) indenture; **~ de propiedad** title deed; **Sagrada E~** (Holy) Scripture; **~ social** articles *pl* of association
escroto [es'kroto] *nm* scrotum
escrúpulo [es'krupulo] *nm* scruple; (*minuciosidad*) scrupulousness

escrupuloso, -a [eskrupu'loso, a] *adj* scrupulous
escrutar [eskru'tar] *vt* to scrutinize, examine; (*votos*) to count
escrutinio [eskru'tinjo] *nm* (*examen atento*) scrutiny; (*Pol: recuento de votos*) count(ing)
escuadra [es'kwaðra] *nf* (*Tec*) square; (*Mil etc*) squad; (*Naut*) squadron; (*de coches etc*) fleet
escuadrilla [eskwa'ðriʎa] *nf* (*de aviones*) squadron
escuadrón [eskwa'ðron] *nm* squadron
escuálido, -a [es'kwaliðo, a] *adj* skinny, scraggy; (*sucio*) squalid
escucha [es'kutʃa] *nf* (*acción*) listening ■ *nm* (*Telec: sistema*) monitor; (*oyente*) listener; **estar a la ~** to listen in; **estar de ~** to spy; **escuchas telefónicas** (phone)tapping *sg*
escuchar [esku'tʃar] *vt* to listen to; (*consejo*) to heed; (*esp Am: oír*) to hear ■ *vi* to listen; **escucharse** *vr*: **se escucha muy mal** (*Telec*) it's a very bad line
escudarse [esku'ðarse] *vr*: **~ en** (*fig*) to hide behind
escudería [eskuðe'ria] *nf*: **la ~ Ferrari** the Ferrari team
escudero [esku'ðero] *nm* squire
escudilla [esku'ðiʎa] *nf* bowl, basin
escudo [es'kuðo] *nm* shield; **~ de armas** coat of arms
escudriñar [eskuðri'ɲar] *vt* (*examinar*) to investigate, scrutinize; (*mirar de lejos*) to scan
escuece *etc* [es'kweθe] *vb ver* **escocer**
escuela [es'kwela] *nf* (*tb fig*) school; **~ normal** teacher training college; **~ técnica superior** *university offering five-year courses in engineering and technical subjects*; **~ universitaria** *university offering three-year diploma courses*; **~ de párvulos** kindergarten; *ver tb* **colegio**
escueto, -a [es'kweto, a] *adj* plain; (*estilo*) simple; (*explicación*) concise
escueza *etc* [es'kweθa] *vb ver* **escocer**
escuincle [es'kwinkle] *nm* (*Am fam*) kid
esculpir [eskul'pir] *vt* to sculpt; (*grabar*) to engrave; (*tallar*) to carve
escultor, a [eskul'tor, a] *nm/f* sculptor
escultura [eskul'tura] *nf* sculpture
escupidera [eskupi'ðera] *nf* spittoon
escupir [esku'pir] *vt* to spit (out) ■ *vi* to spit
escupitajo [eskupi'taxo] *nm* (*fam*) gob of spit
escurreplatos [eskurre'platos] *nm inv* plate rack
escurridizo, -a [eskurri'ðiθo, a] *adj* slippery
escurrir [esku'rrir] *vt* (*ropa*) to wring out; (*verduras, platos*) to drain ■ *vi* (*los líquidos*) to drip; **escurrirse** *vr* (*secarse*) to drain; (*resbalarse*) to slip, slide; (*escaparse*) to slip away
ese¹ ['ese] *nf* (the letter) S; **hacer eses** (*carretera*) to zigzag; (*borracho*) to reel about
ese² ['ese], **esa** ['esa], **esos** ['esos], **esas** ['esas] *adj demostrativo* that *sg*, those *pl*
ése ['ese], **ésa** ['esa], **ésos** ['esos], **ésas** ['esas] *pron* that (one) *sg*, those (ones) *pl*; **ése ... éste ...** the former ... the latter ...; **¡no me vengas con ésas!** don't give me any more of that nonsense!
esencia [e'senθja] *nf* essence
esencial [esen'θjal] *adj* essential; (*principal*) chief; **lo ~** the main thing
esfera [es'fera] *nf* sphere; (*de reloj*) face; **~ de acción** scope; **~ terrestre** globe
esférico, -a [es'feriko, a] *adj* spherical
esfinge [es'finxe] *nf* sphinx
esforcé [esfor'θe], **esforcemos** *etc* [esfor'θemos] *vb ver* **esforzarse**
esforzado, -a [esfor'θaðo, a] *adj* (*enérgico*) energetic, vigorous
esforzarse [esfor'θarse] *vr* to exert o.s., make an effort
esfuerce *etc* [es'fwerθe] *vb ver* **esforzarse**
esfuerzo *etc* [es'fwerθo] *vb ver* **esforzarse** ■ *nm* effort; **sin ~** effortlessly
esfumarse [esfu'marse] *vr* (*apoyo, esperanzas*) to fade away; (*persona*) to vanish
esgrima [es'ɣrima] *nf* fencing
esgrimidor [esɣrimi'ðor] *nm* fencer
esgrimir [esɣri'mir] *vt* (*arma*) to brandish; (*argumento*) to use ■ *vi* to fence
esguince [es'ɣinθe] *nm* (*Med*) sprain
eslabón [esla'βon] *nm* link; **~ perdido** (*Bio, fig*) missing link
eslabonar [eslaβo'nar] *vt* to link, connect
eslálom [es'lalom] *nm* slalom
eslavo, -a [es'laβo, a] *adj* Slav, Slavonic ■ *nm/f* Slav ■ *nm* (*Ling*) Slavonic
eslogan [es'loɣan] *nm* (*pl* **eslogans**) slogan
eslora [es'lora] *nf* (*Naut*) length
eslovaco, -a [eslo'βako, a] *adj, nm/f* Slovak, Slovakian ■ *nm* (*Ling*) Slovak, Slovakian
Eslovaquia [eslo'βakja] *nf* Slovakia
Eslovenia [eslo'βenja] *nf* Slovenia
esloveno, -a [eslo'βeno, a] *adj, nm/f* Slovene, Slovenian ■ *nm* (*Ling*) Slovene, Slovenian
esmaltar [esmal'tar] *vt* to enamel
esmalte [es'malte] *nm* enamel; **~ de uñas** nail varnish *o* polish
esmerado, -a [esme'raðo, a] *adj* careful, neat
esmeralda [esme'ralda] *nf* emerald
esmerarse [esme'rarse] *vr* (*aplicarse*) to take great pains, exercise great care; (*afanarse*) to work hard; (*hacer lo mejor*) to do one's best
esmero [es'mero] *nm* (great) care
esmirriado, -a [esmi'rrjaðo, a] *adj* puny
esmoquin [es'mokin] *nm* dinner jacket (*Brit*), tuxedo (*US*)

esnob [es'nob] *adj inv* (*persona*) snobbish; (*coche etc*) posh ■ *nm/f* snob
esnobismo [esno'βismo] *nm* snobbery
eso ['eso] *pron* that, that thing *o* matter; **~ de su coche** that business about his car; **~ de ir al cine** all that about going to the cinema; **a ~ de las cinco** at about five o'clock; **en ~** thereupon, at that point; **por ~** therefore; **~ es** that's it; **nada de ~** far from it; **¡~ sí que es vida!** now this is really living!; **por ~ te lo dije** that's why I told you; **y ~ que llovía** in spite of the fact it was raining
esófago [e'sofaɣo] *nm* (*Anat*) oesophagus
esos ['esos] *adj demostrativo ver* **ese**
ésos ['esos] *pron ver* **ése**
esotérico, -a [eso'teriko, a] *adj* esoteric
esp. *abr* (= *español*) Sp., Span.; = **especialmente**
espabilado, -a [espaβi'laðo, a] *adj* quick-witted
espabilar [espaβi'lar] *vt*, **espabilarse** *vr* = **despabilar(se)**
espachurrar [espatʃu'rrar] *vt* to squash; **espachurrarse** *vr* to get squashed
espaciado [espa'θjaðo] *nm* (*Inform*) spacing
espacial [espa'θjal] *adj* (*del espacio*) space *cpd*
espaciar [espa'θjar] *vt* to space (out)
espacio [es'paθjo] *nm* space; (*Mus*) interval; (*Radio, TV*) programme, program (*US*); **el ~** space; **ocupar mucho ~** to take up a lot of room; **a dos espacios, a doble ~** (*Tip*) double-spaced; **por ~ de** during, for
espacioso, -a [espa'θjoso, a] *adj* spacious, roomy
espada [es'paða] *nf* sword ■ *nm* swordsman; (*Taur*) matador; **espadas** *nfpl* (*Naipes*) *one of the suits in the Spanish card deck*; **estar entre la ~ y la pared** to be between the devil and the deep blue sea; *ver tb* **baraja española**
espadachín [espaða'tʃin] *nm* (*esgrimidor*) skilled swordsman
espaguetis [espa'ɣetis] *nmpl* spaghetti *sg*
espalda [es'palda] *nf* (*gen*) back; (*Natación*) backstroke; **espaldas** *nfpl* (*hombros*) shoulders; **a espaldas de algn** behind sb's back; **estar de espaldas** to have one's back turned; **tenderse de espaldas** to lie (down) on one's back; **volver la ~ a algn** to cold-shoulder sb
espaldarazo [espalda'raθo] *nm* (*tb fig*) slap on the back
espaldilla [espal'ðiʎa] *nf* shoulder blade
espantadizo, -a [espanta'ðiθo, a] *adj* timid, easily frightened
espantajo [espan'taxo] *nm*, **espantapájaros** [espanta'paxaros] *nm inv* scarecrow
espantar [espan'tar] *vt* (*asustar*) to frighten, scare; (*ahuyentar*) to frighten off; (*asombrar*) to horrify, appal; **espantarse** *vr* to get frightened *o* scared; to be appalled
espanto [es'panto] *nm* (*susto*) fright; (*terror*) terror; (*asombro*) astonishment; **¡qué ~!** how awful!
espantoso, -a [espan'toso, a] *adj* frightening, terrifying; (*ruido*) dreadful
España [es'paɲa] *nf* Spain; **la ~ de pandereta** touristy Spain
español, a [espa'ɲol, a] *adj* Spanish ■ *nm/f* Spaniard ■ *nm* (*Ling*) Spanish; *ver tb* **castellano**
españolice *etc* [espaɲo'liθe] *vb ver* **españolizar**
españolizar [espaɲoli'θar] *vt* to make Spanish, Hispanicize; **españolizarse** *vr* to adopt Spanish ways
esparadrapo [espara'ðrapo] *nm* (sticking) plaster, Band-Aid® (*US*)
esparcido, -a [espar'θiðo, a] *adj* scattered
esparcimiento [esparθi'mjento] *nm* (*dispersión*) spreading; (*derramamiento*) scattering; (*fig*) cheerfulness
esparcir [espar'θir] *vt* to spread; (*derramar*) to scatter; **esparcirse** *vr* to spread (out); to scatter; (*divertirse*) to enjoy o.s.
espárrago [es'parraɣo] *nm* (*tb*: **espárragos**) asparagus; **estar hecho un ~** to be as thin as a rake; **¡vete a freír espárragos!** (*fam*) go to hell!
esparto [es'parto] *nm* esparto (grass)
esparza *etc* [es'parθa] *vb ver* **esparcir**
espasmo [es'pasmo] *nm* spasm
espátula [es'patula] *nf* (*Med*) spatula; (*Arte*) palette knife; (*Culin*) fish slice
especia [es'peθja] *nf* spice
especial [espe'θjal] *adj* special
especialidad [espeθjali'ðað] *nf* speciality, specialty (*US*); (*Escol: ramo*) specialism
especialista [espeθja'lista] *nm/f* specialist; (*Cine*) stuntman(-woman)
especializado, -a [espeθjali'θaðo, a] *adj* specialized; (*obrero*) skilled
especialmente [espeθjal'mente] *adv* particularly, especially
especie [es'peθje] *nf* (*Bio*) species; (*clase*) kind, sort; **pagar en ~** to pay in kind
especificar [espeθifi'kar] *vt* to specify
específico, -a [espe'θifiko, a] *adj* specific
especifique *etc* [espeθi'fike] *vb ver* **especificar**
espécimen [es'peθimen] (*pl* **especímenes**) *nm* specimen
espectáculo [espek'takulo] *nm* (*gen*) spectacle; (*Teat etc*) show; (*función*) performance; **dar un ~** to make a scene
espectador, a [espekta'ðor, a] *nm/f* spectator; (*de incidente*) onlooker; **los**

espectadores *nmpl (Teat)* the audience *sg*
espectro [es'pektro] *nm* ghost; *(fig)* spectre
especulación [espekula'θjon] *nf* speculation; **~ bursátil** speculation on the Stock Market
especular [espeku'lar] *vt, vi* to speculate
especulativo, -a [espekula'tiβo, a] *adj* speculative
espejismo [espe'xismo] *nm* mirage
espejo [es'pexo] *nm* mirror; *(fig)* model; **~ retrovisor** rear-view mirror; **mirarse al ~** to look (at o.s.) in the mirror
espeleología [espeleolo'xia] *nf* potholing
espeluznante [espeluθ'nante] *adj* horrifying, hair-raising
espera [es'pera] *nf (pausa, intervalo)* wait; *(Jur: plazo)* respite; **en ~ de** waiting for; *(con expectativa)* expecting; **en ~ de su contestación** awaiting your reply
esperance *etc* [espe'ranθe] *vb ver* **esperanzar**
esperanza [espe'ranθa] *nf (confianza)* hope; *(expectativa)* expectation; **hay pocas esperanzas de que venga** there is little prospect of his coming
esperanzador, a [esperanθa'ðor, a] *adj* hopeful, encouraging
esperanzar [esperan'θar] *vt* to give hope to
esperar [espe'rar] *vt (aguardar)* to wait for; *(tener expectativa de)* to expect; *(desear)* to hope for ■ *vi* to wait; to expect; to hope; **esperarse** *vr*: **como podía esperarse** as was to be expected; **hacer ~ a uno** to keep sb waiting; **ir a ~ a uno** to go and meet sb; **~ un bebé** to be expecting (a baby)
esperma [es'perma] *nf* sperm
espermatozoide [espermato'θoiðe] *nm* spermatozoid
esperpento [esper'pento] *nm (persona)* sight *(fam)*; *(disparate)* (piece of) nonsense
espesar [espe'sar] *vt* to thicken; **espesarse** *vr* to thicken, get thicker
espeso, -a [es'peso, a] *adj* thick; *(bosque)* dense; *(nieve)* deep; *(sucio)* dirty
espesor [espe'sor] *nm* thickness; *(de nieve)* depth
espesura [espe'sura] *nf (de bosque)* thicket
espetar [espe'tar] *vt (reto, sermón)* to give
espía [es'pia] *nm/f* spy
espiar [espi'ar] *vt (observar)* to spy on ■ *vi*: **~ para** to spy for
espiga [es'piɣa] *nf (Bot: de trigo etc)* ear; *(: de flores)* spike
espigado, -a [espi'ɣaðo, a] *adj (Bot)* ripe; *(fig)* tall, slender
espigón [espi'ɣon] *nm (Bot)* ear; *(Naut)* breakwater
espina [es'pina] *nf* thorn; *(de pez)* bone; **~ dorsal** *(Anat)* spine; **me da mala ~** I don't like the look of it
espinaca [espi'naka] *nf (tb:* **espinacas***)* spinach
espinar [espi'nar] *nm (matorral)* thicket
espinazo [espi'naθo] *nm* spine, backbone
espinilla [espi'niʎa] *nf (Anat: tibia)* shin(bone); *(: en la piel)* blackhead
espino [es'pino] *nm* hawthorn
espinoso, -a [espi'noso, a] *adj (planta)* thorny, prickly; *(fig)* bony; *(problema)* knotty
espionaje [espjo'naxe] *nm* spying, espionage
espiral [espi'ral] *adj, nf* spiral; **la ~ inflacionista** the inflationary spiral
espirar [espi'rar] *vt, vi* to breathe out, exhale
espiritista [espiri'tista] *adj, nm/f* spiritualist
espíritu [es'piritu] *nm* spirit; *(mente)* mind; *(inteligencia)* intelligence; *(Rel)* spirit, soul; **E~ Santo** Holy Ghost; **con ~ amplio** with an open mind
espiritual [espiri'twal] *adj* spiritual
espita [es'pita] *nf* tap *(Brit)*, faucet *(US)*
esplendidez [esplendi'ðeθ] *nf (abundancia)* lavishness; *(magnificencia)* splendour
espléndido, -a [es'plendiðo, a] *adj (magnífico)* magnificent, splendid; *(generoso)* generous, lavish
esplendor [esplen'dor] *nm* splendour
espliego [es'pljeɣo] *nm* lavender
espolear [espole'ar] *vt* to spur on
espoleta [espo'leta] *nf (de bomba)* fuse
espolvorear [espolβore'ar] *vt* to dust, sprinkle
esponja [es'ponxa] *nf* sponge; *(fig)* sponger
esponjoso, -a [espon'xoso, a] *adj* spongy
esponsales [espon'sales] *nmpl* betrothal *sg*
espontaneidad [espontanei'ðað] *nf* spontaneity
espontáneo, -a [espon'taneo, a] *adj* spontaneous; *(improvisado)* impromptu; *(persona)* natural
espora [es'pora] *nf* spore
esporádico, -a [espo'raðiko, a] *adj* sporadic
esposa [es'posa] *nf ver* **esposo**
esposar [espo'sar] *vt* to handcuff
esposo, -a [es'poso, a] *nm* husband ■ *nf* wife; **esposas** *nfpl* handcuffs
espuela [es'pwela] *nf* spur; *(fam: trago)* one for the road
espuerta [es'pwerta] *nf* basket, pannier
espuma [es'puma] *nf* foam; *(de cerveza)* froth, head; *(de jabón)* lather; *(de olas)* surf
espumadera [espuma'ðera] *nf* skimmer
espumarajo [espuma'raxo] *nm* froth, foam; **echar espumarajos (de rabia)** to splutter with rage

espumoso, -a [espu'moso, a] *adj* frothy, foamy; (*vino*) sparkling
esputo [es'puto] *nm* (*de saliva*) spit; (*Med*) sputum
esqueje [es'kexe] *nm* (*Bot*) cutting
esquela [es'kela] *nf*: **~ mortuoria** announcement of death
esquelético, -a [eske'letiko, a] *adj* (*fam*) skinny
esqueleto [eske'leto] *nm* skeleton; (*lo esencial*) bare bones (of a matter); **en ~** unfinished
esquema [es'kema] *nm* (*diagrama*) diagram; (*dibujo*) plan; (*plan*) scheme; (*Filosofía*) schema
esquemático, -a [eske'matiko, a] *adj* schematic; **un resumen ~** a brief outline
esquí [es'ki] (*pl* **~s**) *nm* (*objeto*) ski; (*deporte*) skiing; **~ acuático** water-skiing; **hacer ~** to go skiing
esquiador, a [eskja'ðor, a] *nm/f* skier
esquiar [es'kjar] *vi* to ski
esquila [es'kila] *nf* (*campanilla*) small bell; (*encerro*) cowbell
esquilar [eski'lar] *vt* to shear
esquimal [eski'mal] *adj, nm/f* Eskimo
esquina [es'kina] *nf* corner; **doblar la ~** to turn the corner
esquinazo [eski'naθo] *nm*: **dar ~ a algn** to give sb the slip
esquirla [es'kirla] *nf* splinter
esquirol [eski'rol] *nm* blackleg
esquivar [eski'βar] *vt* to avoid; (*evadir*) to dodge, elude
esquivo, -a [es'kiβo, a] *adj* (*altanero*) aloof; (*desdeñoso*) scornful, disdainful
esquizofrenia [eskiθo'frenja] *nf* schizophrenia
esta ['esta] *adj demostrativo ver* **este**
ésta ['esta] *pron ver* **éste**
está [es'ta] *vb ver* **estar**
estabilice *etc* [estaβi'liθe] *vb ver* **estabilizar**
estabilidad [estaβili'ðað] *nf* stability
estabilización [estaβiliθa'θjon] *nf* (*Com*) stabilization
estabilizar [estaβili'θar] *vt* to stabilize; (*fijar*) to make steady; (*precios*) to peg; **estabilizarse** *vr* to become stable
estable [es'taβle] *adj* stable
establecer [estaβle'θer] *vt* to establish; (*fundar*) to set up; (*colonos*) to settle; (*récord*) to set (up); **establecerse** *vr* to establish o.s.; (*echar raíces*) to settle (down); (*Com*) to start up
establecimiento [estaβleθi'mjento] *nm* establishment; (*fundación*) institution; (*de negocio*) start-up; (*de colonias*) settlement; (*local*) establishment; **~ comercial** business house
establezca *etc* [esta'βleθka] *vb ver* **establecer**
establo [es'taβlo] *nm* (*Agr*) stall; (*: esp Am*) barn
estaca [es'taka] *nf* stake, post; (*de tienda de campaña*) peg
estacada [esta'kaða] *nf* (*cerca*) fence, fencing; (*palenque*) stockade; **dejar a algn en la ~** to leave sb in the lurch
estación [esta'θjon] *nf* station; (*del año*) season; **~ de autobuses/ferrocarril** bus/railway station; **~ balnearia (de turistas)** seaside resort; **~ de servicio** service station; **~ terminal** terminus; **~ de trabajo** (*Com*) work station; **~ transmisora** transmitter; **~ de visualización** display unit
estacionamiento [estaθjona'mjento] *nm* (*Auto*) parking; (*Mil*) stationing
estacionar [estaθjo'nar] *vt* (*Auto*) to park; (*Mil*) to station
estacionario, -a [estaθjo'narjo, a] *adj* stationary; (*Com: mercado*) slack
estada [es'taða], **estadía** [esta'ðia] *nf* (*Am*) stay
estadio [es'taðjo] *nm* (*fase*) stage, phase; (*Deporte*) stadium
estadista [esta'ðista] *nm* (*Pol*) statesman; (*Estadística*) statistician
estadística [esta'ðistika] *nf* (*una estadística*) figure, statistic; (*ciencia*) statistics *sg*
estado [es'taðo] *nm* (*Pol: condición*) state; **~ civil** marital status; **~ de cuenta(s)** bank statement, statement of accounts; **~ de excepción** (*Pol*) state of emergency; **~ financiero** (*Com*) financial statement; **~ mayor** (*Mil*) staff; **~ de pérdidas y ganancias** (*Com*) profit and loss statement, operating statement; **Estados Unidos (EE. UU.)** United States (of America) (USA); **estar en ~ (de buena esperanza)** to be pregnant
estadounidense [estaðouni'ðense] *adj* United States *cpd*, American ■ *nm/f* United States citizen, American
estafa [es'tafa] *nf* swindle, trick; (*Com etc*) racket
estafar [esta'far] *vt* to swindle, defraud
estafeta [esta'feta] *nf* (*oficina de correos*) post office; **~ diplomática** diplomatic bag
estalactita [estalak'tita] *nf* stalactite
estalagmita [estalaɣ'mita] *nf* stalagmite
estallar [esta'ʎar] *vi* to burst; (*bomba*) to explode, go off; (*volcán*) to erupt; (*vidrio*) to shatter; (*látigo*) to crack; (*epidemia, guerra, rebelión*) to break out; **~ en llanto** to burst into tears
estallido [esta'ʎiðo] *nm* explosion; (*de látigo, trueno*) crack; (*fig*) outbreak
estambre [es'tambre] *nm* (*tela*) worsted; (*Bot*) stamen

Estambul [estam'bul] *nm* Istanbul
estamento [esta'mento] *nm* (social) class
estampa [es'tampa] *nf* (*impresión, imprenta*) print, engraving; (*imagen, figura: de persona*) appearance
estampado, -a [estam'paðo, a] *adj* printed ■ *nm* (*impresión: acción*) printing; (*: efecto*) print; (*marca*) stamping
estampar [estam'par] *vt* (*imprimir*) to print; (*marcar*) to stamp; (*metal*) to engrave; (*poner sello en*) to stamp; (*fig*) to stamp, imprint
estampida [estam'piða] *nf* stampede
estampido [estam'piðo] *nm* bang, report
estampilla [estam'piʎa] *nf* (*sello de goma*) (rubber) stamp; (*Am*) (postage) stamp
están [es'tan] *vb ver* **estar**
estancado, -a [estan'kaðo, a] *adj* (*agua*) stagnant
estancamiento [estanka'mjento] *nm* stagnation
estancar [estan'kar] *vt* (*aguas*) to hold up, hold back; (*Com*) to monopolize; (*fig*) to block, hold up; **estancarse** *vr* to stagnate
estancia [es'tanθja] *nf* (*permanencia*) stay; (*sala*) room; (*Am*) farm, ranch
estanciero [estan'sjero] *nm* (*Am*) farmer, rancher
estanco, -a [es'tanko, a] *adj* watertight ■ *nm* tobacconist's (shop); *see note*

ESTANCO

Cigarettes, tobacco, postage stamps and official forms are all sold under state monopoly and usually through a shop called an *estanco*. Tobacco products are also sold in *quioscos* and bars but are generally more expensive. The number of *estanco* licences is regulated by the state.

estándar [es'tandar] *adj, nm* standard
estandarice *etc* [estanda'riθe] *vb ver* **estandarizar**
estandarizar [estandari'θar] *vt* to standardize
estandarte [estan'darte] *nm* banner, standard
estanque *etc* [es'tanke] *vb ver* **estancar** ■ *nm* (*lago*) pool, pond; (*Agr*) reservoir
estanquero, -a [estan'kero, a] *nm/f* tobacconist
estante [es'tante] *nm* (*armario*) rack, stand; (*biblioteca*) bookcase; (*anaquel*) shelf; (*Am*) prop
estantería [estante'ria] *nf* shelving, shelves *pl*
estaño [es'taɲo] *nm* tin

PALABRA CLAVE

estar [es'tar] *vi* **1** (*posición*) to be; **está en la plaza** it's in the square; **¿está Juan?** is Juan in?; **estamos a 30 km de Junín** we're 30 kms from Junín
2 (*+ adj o adv: estado*) to be; **estar enfermo** to be ill; **está muy elegante** he's looking very smart; **estar lejos** to be far (away); **¿cómo estás?** how are you keeping?
3 (*+ gerundio*) to be; **estoy leyendo** I'm reading
4 (*uso pasivo*): **está condenado a muerte** he's been condemned to death; **está envasado en ...** it's packed in ...
5: **estar a**: **¿a cuántos estamos?** what's the date today?; **estamos a 9 de mayo** it's the 9th of May; **las manzanas están a 1,50 euros** apples are (selling at) 1.5 euros; **estamos a 25 grados** it's 25 degrees today
6 (*locuciones*): **¿estamos?** (*¿de acuerdo?*) okay?; (*¿listo?*) ready?; **¡ya está bien!** that's enough!; **¿está la comida?** is dinner ready?; **¡ya está!**, **¡ya estuvo!** (*Am*) that's it!
7: **estar con**: **está con gripe** he's got (the) flu
8: **estar de**: **estar de vacaciones/viaje** to be on holiday/away *o* on a trip; **está de camarero** he's working as a waiter
9: **estar para**: **está para salir** he's about to leave; **no estoy para bromas** I'm not in the mood for jokes
10: **estar por** (*propuesta etc*) to be in favour of; (*persona etc*) to support, side with; **está por limpiar** it still has to be cleaned; **¡estoy por dejarlo!** I think I'm going to leave this!
11 (*+ que*): **está que rabia** (*fam*) he's hopping mad (*fam*); **estoy que me caigo de sueño** I'm terribly sleepy, I can't keep my eyes open
12: **estar sin**: **estar sin dinero** to have no money; **está sin terminar** it isn't finished yet
estarse *vr*: **se estuvo en la cama toda la tarde** he stayed in bed all afternoon; **¡estáte quieto!** stop fidgeting!

estárter [es'tarter] *nm* (*Auto*) choke
estas ['estas] *adj demostrativo ver* **este**
éstas ['estas] *pron ver* **éste**
estás [es'tas] *vb ver* **estar**
estatal [esta'tal] *adj* state *cpd*
estático, -a [es'tatiko, a] *adj* static
estatua [es'tatwa] *nf* statue
estatura [esta'tura] *nf* stature, height
estatus [es'tatus] *nm inv* status
estatutario, -a [estatu'tarjo, a] *adj* statutory
estatuto [esta'tuto] *nm* (*Jur*) statute; (*de*

ciudad) bye-law; (*de comité*) rule; **estatutos sociales** (*Com*) articles of association
este¹ ['este] *adj* (*lado*) east; (*dirección*) easterly ■ *nm* east; **en la parte del ~** in the eastern part
este² ['este], **esta** ['esta], **estos** ['estos], **estas** ['estas] *adj demostrativo* this *sg*, these *pl*; (*Am: como muletilla*) er, um
éste ['este], **ésta** ['esta], **éstos** ['estos], **éstas** ['estas] *pron* this (one) *sg*, these (ones) *pl*; **ése ... éste ...** the former ... the latter ...
esté [es'te] *vb ver* **estar**
estela [es'tela] *nf* wake, wash; (*fig*) trail
estelar [este'lar] *adj* (*Astro*) stellar; (*Teat*) star *cpd*
estén [es'ten] *vb ver* **estar**
estenografía [estenoɣra'fia] *nf* shorthand
estentóreo, -a [esten'toreo, a] *adj* (*sonido*) strident; (*voz*) booming
estepa [es'tepa] *nf* (*Geo*) steppe
estera [es'tera] *nf* (*alfombra*) mat; (*tejido*) matting
estercolero [esterko'lero] *nm* manure heap, dunghill
estéreo [es'tereo] *adj inv, nm* stereo
estereofónico, -a [estereo'foniko, a] *adj* stereophonic
estereotipar [estereoti'par] *vt* to stereotype
estereotipo [estereo'tipo] *nm* stereotype
estéril [es'teril] *adj* sterile, barren; (*fig*) vain, futile
esterilice *etc* [esteri'liθe] *vb ver* **esterilizar**
esterilizar [esterili'θar] *vt* to sterilize
esterilla [este'riʎa] *nf* (*alfombrilla*) small mat
esterlina [ester'lina] *adj*: **libra ~** pound sterling
esternón [ester'non] *nm* breastbone
estero [es'tero] *nm* (*Am*) swamp
estertor [ester'tor] *nm* death rattle
estés [es'tes] *vb ver* **estar**
esteta [es'teta] *nm/f* aesthete
esteticienne [esteti'θjen] *nf* beautician
estético, -a [es'tetiko, a] *adj* aesthetic ■ *nf* aesthetics *sg*
estetoscopio [estetos'kopjo] *nm* stethoscope
estibador [estiβa'ðor] *nm* stevedore
estibar [esti'βar] *vt* (*Naut*) to stow
estiércol [es'tjerkol] *nm* dung, manure
estigma [es'tiɣma] *nm* stigma
estigmatice *etc* [estiɣma'tiθe] *vb ver* **estigmatizar**
estigmatizar [estiɣmati'θar] *vt* to stigmatize
estilarse [esti'larse] *vr* (*estar de moda*) to be in fashion; (*usarse*) to be used
estilice *etc* [esti'liθe] *vb ver* **estilizar**
estilizar [estili'θar] *vt* to stylize; (*Tec*) to design
estilo [es'tilo] *nm* style; (*Tec*) stylus; (*Natación*) stroke; **~ de vida** lifestyle; **al ~ de** in the style of; **algo por el ~** something along those lines
estilográfica [estilo'ɣrafika] *nf* fountain pen
estima [es'tima] *nf* esteem, respect
estimación [estima'θjon] *nf* (*evaluación*) estimation; (*aprecio, afecto*) esteem, regard
estimado, -a [esti'maðo, a] *adj* esteemed; **"E~ Señor"** "Dear Sir"
estimar [esti'mar] *vt* (*evaluar*) to estimate; (*valorar*) to value; (*apreciar*) to esteem, respect; (*pensar, considerar*) to think, reckon
estimulante [estimu'lante] *adj* stimulating ■ *nm* stimulant
estimular [estimu'lar] *vt* to stimulate; (*excitar*) to excite; (*animar*) to encourage
estímulo [es'timulo] *nm* stimulus; (*ánimo*) encouragement
estío [es'tio] *nm* summer
estipendio [esti'pendjo] *nm* salary; (*Com*) stipend
estipulación [estipula'θjon] *nf* stipulation, condition
estipular [estipu'lar] *vt* to stipulate
estirado, -a [esti'raðo, a] *adj* (*tenso*) (stretched *o* drawn) tight; (*fig: persona*) stiff, pompous; (*engreído*) stuck-up
estirar [esti'rar] *vt* to stretch; (*dinero, suma etc*) to stretch out; (*cuello*) to crane; (*discurso*) to spin out; **~ la pata** (*fam*) to kick the bucket; **estirarse** *vr* to stretch
estirón [esti'ron] *nm* pull, tug; (*crecimiento*) spurt, sudden growth; **dar un ~** (*niño*) to shoot up
estirpe [es'tirpe] *nf* stock, lineage
estival [esti'βal] *adj* summer *cpd*
esto ['esto] *pron* this, this thing *o* matter; (*como muletilla*) er, um; **~ de la boda** this business about the wedding; **en ~** at this *o* that point; **por ~** for this reason
estocada [esto'kaða] *nf* (*acción*) stab; (*Taur*) death blow
Estocolmo [esto'kolmo] *nm* Stockholm
estofa [es'tofa] *nf*: **de baja ~** poor-quality
estofado [esto'faðo] *nm* stew
estofar [esto'far] *vt* (*bordar*) to quilt; (*Culin*) to stew
estoico, -a [es'toiko, a] *adj* (*Filosofía*) stoic(al); (*fig*) cold, indifferent
estomacal [estoma'kal] *adj* stomach *cpd*; **trastorno ~** stomach upset
estómago [es'tomaɣo] *nm* stomach; **tener ~** to be thick-skinned
Estonia [es'tonja] *nf* Estonia
estonio, -a [es'tonjo, a] *adj, nm/f* Estonian ■ *nm* (*Ling*) Estonian

estoque [es'toke] *nm* rapier, sword
estorbar [estor'βar] *vt* to hinder, obstruct; (*fig*) to bother, disturb ■ *vi* to be in the way
estorbo [es'torβo] *nm* (*molestia*) bother, nuisance; (*obstáculo*) hindrance, obstacle
estornino [estor'nino] *nm* starling
estornudar [estornu'ðar] *vi* to sneeze
estornudo [estor'nuðo] *nm* sneeze
estos ['estos] *adj demostrativo ver* **este**
éstos ['estos] *pron ver* **éste**
estoy [es'toi] *vb ver* **estar**
estrabismo [estra'βismo] *nm* squint
estrado [es'traðo] *nm* (*tarima*) platform; (*Mus*) bandstand; **estrados** *nmpl* law courts
estrafalario, -a [estrafa'larjo, a] *adj* odd, eccentric; (*desarreglado*) slovenly, sloppy
estrago [es'traɣo] *nm* ruin, destruction; **hacer estragos en** to wreak havoc among
estragón [estra'ɣon] *nm* (*Culin*) tarragon
estrambótico, -a [estram'botiko, a] *adj* odd, eccentric
estrangulación [estrangula'θjon] *nf* strangulation
estrangulador, -a [estrangula'ðor, a] *nm/f* strangler ■ *nm* (*Tec*) throttle; (*Auto*) choke
estrangulamiento [estrangula'mjento] *nm* (*Auto*) bottleneck
estrangular [estrangu'lar] *vt* (*persona*) to strangle; (*Med*) to strangulate
estraperlista [estraper'lista] *nm/f* black marketeer
estraperlo [estra'perlo] *nm* black market
estratagema [estrata'xema] *nf* (*Mil*) stratagem; (*astucia*) cunning
estratega [estra'teɣa] *nm/f* strategist
estrategia [estra'texja] *nf* strategy
estratégico, -a [estra'texiko, a] *adj* strategic
estratificar [estratifi'kar] *vt* to stratify
estratifique *etc* [estrati'fike] *vb ver* **estratificar**
estrato [es'trato] *nm* stratum, layer
estratosfera [estratos'fera] *nf* stratosphere
estrechar [estre'tʃar] *vt* (*reducir*) to narrow; (*vestido*) to take in; (*persona*) to hug, embrace; **estrecharse** *vr* (*reducirse*) to narrow, grow narrow; (*2 personas*) to embrace; **~ la mano** to shake hands
estrechez [estre'tʃeθ] *nf* narrowness; (*de ropa*) tightness; (*intimidad*) intimacy; (*Com*) want *o* shortage of money; **estrecheces** *nfpl* financial difficulties
estrecho, -a [es'tretʃo, a] *adj* narrow; (*apretado*) tight; (*íntimo*) close, intimate; (*miserable*) mean ■ *nm* strait; **~ de miras** narrow-minded; **E~ de Gibraltar** Straits of Gibraltar
estrella [es'treʎa] *nf* star; **~ fugaz** shooting star; **~ de mar** starfish; **tener (buena)/ mala** ~ to be lucky/unlucky
estrellado, -a [estre'ʎaðo, a] *adj* (*forma*) star-shaped; (*cielo*) starry; (*huevos*) fried
estrellar [estre'ʎar] *vt* (*hacer añicos*) to smash (to pieces); (*huevos*) to fry; **estrellarse** *vr* to smash; (*chocarse*) to crash; (*fracasar*) to fail
estrellato [estre'ʎato] *nm* stardom
estremecer [estreme'θer] *vt* to shake; **estremecerse** *vr* to shake, tremble; **~ de** (*horror*) to shudder with; (*frío*) to shiver with
estremecimiento [estremeθi'mjento] *nm* (*temblor*) trembling, shaking
estremezca *etc* [estre'meθka] *vb ver* **estremecer**
estrenar [estre'nar] *vt* (*vestido*) to wear for the first time; (*casa*) to move into; (*película, obra de teatro*) to present for the first time; **estrenarse** *vr* (*persona*) to make one's début; (*película*) to have its première; (*Teat*) to open
estreno [es'treno] *nm* (*primer uso*) first use; (*Cine etc*) première
estreñido, -a [estre'ɲiðo, a] *adj* constipated
estreñimiento [estreɲi'mjento] *nm* constipation
estreñir [estre'ɲir] *vt* to constipate
estrépito [es'trepito] *nm* noise, racket; (*fig*) fuss
estrepitoso, -a [estrepi'toso, a] *adj* noisy; (*fiesta*) rowdy
estrés [es'tres] *nm* stress
estresante [estre'sante] *adj* stressful
estría [es'tria] *nf* groove; **estrías (en el cutis)** stretchmarks
estribación [estriβa'θjon] *nf* (*Geo*) spur; **estribaciones** *nfpl* foothills
estribar [estri'βar] *vi*: **~ en** to rest on, be supported by; **la dificultad estriba en el texto** the difficulty lies in the text
estribillo [estri'βiʎo] *nm* (*Lit*) refrain; (*Mus*) chorus
estribo [es'triβo] *nm* (*de jinete*) stirrup; (*de coche, tren*) step; (*de puente*) support; (*Geo*) spur; **perder los estribos** to fly off the handle
estribor [estri'βor] *nm* (*Naut*) starboard
estricnina [estrik'nina] *nf* strychnine
estricto, -a [es'trikto, a] *adj* (*riguroso*) strict; (*severo*) severe
estridente [estri'ðente] *adj* (*color*) loud; (*voz*) raucous
estro ['estro] *nm* inspiration
estrofa [es'trofa] *nf* verse
estropajo [estro'paxo] *nm* scourer
estropeado, -a [estrope'aðo, a] *adj*: **está ~** it's not working
estropear [estrope'ar] *vt* (*arruinar*) to spoil;

(*dañar*) to damage; (*: máquina*) to break; **estropearse** *vr* (*objeto*) to get damaged; (*coche*) to break down; (*la piel etc*) to be ruined
estropicio [estro'piθjo] *nm* (*rotura*) breakage; (*efectos*) harmful effects *pl*
estructura [estruk'tura] *nf* structure
estruendo [es'trwendo] *nm* (*ruido*) racket, din; (*fig: alboroto*) uproar, turmoil
estrujar [estru'xar] *vt* (*apretar*) to squeeze; (*aplastar*) to crush; (*fig*) to drain, bleed
estuario [es'twarjo] *nm* estuary
estuche [es'tutʃe] *nm* box, case
estudiante [estu'ðjante] *nm/f* student
estudiantil [estuðjan'til] *adj inv* student *cpd*
estudiantina [estuðjan'tina] *nf* student music group
estudiar [estu'ðjar] *vt* to study; (*propuesta*) to think about *o* over; **~ para abogado** to study to become a lawyer
estudio [es'tuðjo] *nm* study; (*encuesta*) research; (*proyecto*) plan; (*piso*) studio flat; (*Cine, Arte, Radio*) studio; **estudios** *nmpl* studies; (*erudición*) learning *sg*; **cursar** *o* **hacer estudios** to study; **~ de casos prácticos** case study; **~ de desplazamientos y tiempos** (*Com*) time and motion study; **estudios de motivación** motivational research *sg*; **~ del trabajo** (*Com*) work study; **~ de viabilidad** (*Com*) feasibility study
estudioso, -a [estu'ðjoso, a] *adj* studious
estufa [es'tufa] *nf* heater, fire
estulticia [estul'tiθja] *nf* foolishness
estupefaciente [estupefa'θjente] *adj, nm* narcotic
estupefacto, -a [estupe'fakto, a] *adj* speechless, thunderstruck
estupendamente [estupenda'mente] *adv* (*fam*): **estoy ~** I feel great; **le salió ~** he did it very well
estupendo, -a [estu'pendo, a] *adj* wonderful, terrific; (*fam*) great; **¡~!** that's great!, fantastic!
estupidez [estupi'ðeθ] *nf* (*torpeza*) stupidity; (*acto*) stupid thing (to do); **fue una ~ mía** that was a silly thing for me to do *o* say
estúpido, -a [es'tupiðo, a] *adj* stupid, silly
estupor [estu'por] *nm* stupor; (*fig*) astonishment, amazement
estupro [es'tupro] *nm* rape
estuve *etc* [es'tuβe], **estuviera** *etc* [estu'βjera] *vb ver* **estar**
esvástica [es'βastika] *nf* swastika
ET *abr* = **Ejército de Tierra**
ETA ['eta] *nf abr* (*Pol: = Euskadi Ta Askatasuna*) ETA
etapa [e'tapa] *nf* (*de viaje*) stage; (*Deporte*) leg; (*parada*) stopping place; (*fig*) stage, phase; **por etapas** gradually, in stages
etarra [e'tarra] *adj* ETA *cpd* ■ *nm/f* member of ETA
etc. *abr* (*= etcétera*) etc
etcétera [et'θetera] *adv* etcetera
etéreo, -a [e'tereo, a] *adj* ethereal
eternice *etc* [eter'niθe] *vb ver* **eternizarse**
eternidad [eterni'ðað] *nf* eternity
eternizarse [eterni'θarse] *vr*: **~ en hacer algo** to take ages to do sth
eterno, -a [e'terno, a] *adj* eternal, everlasting; (*despectivo*) never-ending
ético, -a ['etiko, a] *adj* ethical ■ *nf* ethics
etimología [etimolo'xia] *nf* etymology
etiqueta [eti'keta] *nf* (*modales*) etiquette; (*rótulo*) label, tag; **de ~** formal
etnia ['etnja] *nf* ethnic group
étnico, -a ['etniko, a] *adj* ethnic
ETS *sigla f* (*= Enfermedad de Transmisión Sexual*) STD
EU(A) *nmpl abr* (*esp Am: = Estados Unidos (de América)*) US(A)
eucalipto [euka'lipto] *nm* eucalyptus
Eucaristía [eukaris'tia] *nf* Eucharist
eufemismo [eufe'mismo] *nm* euphemism
euforia [eu'forja] *nf* euphoria
eufórico, -a [eu'foriko, a] *adj* euphoric
eunuco [eu'nuko] *nm* eunuch
euro ['euro] *nm* (*moneda*) euro
eurodiputado, -a [euroðipu'taðo, a] *nm/f* Euro MP, MEP
Eurolandia [euro'landja] *nf* Euroland
Europa [eu'ropa] *nf* Europe
europeice *etc* [euro'peiθe] *vb ver* **europeizar**
europeizar [europei'θar] *vt* to Europeanize; **europeizarse** *vr* to become Europeanized
europeo, -a [euro'peo, a] *adj, nm/f* European
Eurotúnel [euro'tunel] *nm* (*estructura*) Channel Tunnel
eurozona [euro'θona] *nf* Eurozone
Euskadi [eus'kaði] *nm* the Basque Provinces *pl*
euskera, eusquera [eus'kera] *nm* (*Ling*) Basque; *ver tb* **Lengua**
eutanasia [euta'nasja] *nf* euthanasia
evacuación [eβakwa'θjon] *nf* evacuation
evacuar [eβa'kwar] *vt* to evacuate
evadir [eβa'ðir] *vt* to evade, avoid; **evadirse** *vr* to escape
evaluación [eβalwa'θjon] *nf* evaluation, assessment
evaluar [eβa'lwar] *vt* to evaluate, assess
evangélico, -a [eβan'xeliko, a] *adj* evangelical
evangelio [eβan'xeljo] *nm* gospel
evaporación [eβapora'θjon] *nf* evaporation
evaporar [eβapo'rar] *vt* to evaporate;

evaporarse *vr* to vanish
evasión [eβa'sjon] *nf* escape, flight; (*fig*) evasion; **~ fiscal** *o* **tributaria** tax evasion
evasivo, -a [eβa'siβo, a] *adj* evasive, non-committal ■ *nf* (*pretexto*) excuse; **contestar con evasivas** to avoid giving a straight answer
evento [e'βento] *nm* event; (*eventualidad*) eventuality
eventual [eβen'twal] *adj* possible, conditional (upon circumstances); (*trabajador*) casual, temporary
Everest [eβe'rest] *nm*: **el (Monte) ~** (Mount) Everest
evidencia [eβi'ðenθja] *nf* evidence, proof; **poner en ~** to make clear; **ponerse en ~** (*persona*) to show o.s. up
evidenciar [eβiðen'θjar] *vt* (*hacer patente*) to make evident; (*probar*) to prove, show; **evidenciarse** *vr* to be evident
evidente [eβi'ðente] *adj* obvious, clear, evident
evitar [eβi'tar] *vt* (*evadir*) to avoid; (*impedir*) to prevent; (*peligro*) to escape; (*molestia*) to save; (*tentación*) to shun; **si puedo evitarlo** if I can help it
evocador, a [eβoka'ðor, a] *adj* (*sugestivo*) evocative
evocar [eβo'kar] *vt* to evoke, call forth
evolución [eβolu'θjon] *nf* (*desarrollo*) evolution, development; (*cambio*) change; (*Mil*) manoeuvre
evolucionar [eβoluθjo'nar] *vi* to evolve; (*Mil, Aviat*) to manoeuvre
evoque *etc* [e'βoke] *vb ver* **evocar**
ex [eks] *adj* ex-; **el ex ministro** the former minister, the ex-minister
exabrupto [eksa'βrupto] *nm* interjection
exacción [eksak'θjon] *nf* (*acto*) exaction; (*de impuestos*) demand
exacerbar [eksaθer'βar] *vt* to irritate, annoy
exactamente [eksakta'mente] *adv* exactly
exactitud [eksakti'tuð] *nf* exactness; (*precisión*) accuracy; (*puntualidad*) punctuality
exacto, -a [ek'sakto, a] *adj* exact; accurate; punctual; **¡~!** exactly!; **eso no es del todo ~** that's not quite right; **para ser ~** to be precise
exageración [eksaxera'θjon] *nf* exaggeration
exagerado, -a [eksaxe'raðo, a] *adj* (*relato*) exaggerated; (*precio*) excessive; (*persona*) over-demonstrative; (*gesto*) theatrical
exagerar [eksaxe'rar] *vt* to exaggerate; (*exceder*) to overdo
exaltado, -a [eksal'taðo, a] *adj* (*apasionado*) over-excited, worked up; (*exagerado*) extreme; (*fanático*) hot-headed; (*discurso*) impassioned ■ *nm/f* (*fanático*) hothead; (*Pol*) extremist
exaltar [eksal'tar] *vt* to exalt, glorify; **exaltarse** *vr* (*excitarse*) to get excited *o* worked up
examen [ek'samen] *nm* examination; (*de problema*) consideration; **~ de** (*encuesta*) inquiry into; **~ de ingreso** entrance examination; **~ de conducir** driving test; **~ eliminatorio** qualifying examination
examinar [eksami'nar] *vt* to examine; (*poner a prueba*) to test; (*inspeccionar*) to inspect; **examinarse** *vr* to be examined, take an examination
exánime [ek'sanime] *adj* lifeless; (*fig*) exhausted
exasperar [eksaspe'rar] *vt* to exasperate; **exasperarse** *vr* to get exasperated, lose patience
Exc.ª *abr* = **Excelencia**
excarcelar [ekskarθe'lar] *vt* to release (from prison)
excavador, a [ekskaβa'ðor, a] *nm/f* (*persona*) excavator ■ *nf* (*Tec*) digger
excavar [ekska'βar] *vt* to excavate, dig (out)
excedencia [eksθe'ðenθja] *nf* (*Mil*) leave; (*Escol*) sabbatical
excedente [eksθe'ðente] *adj, nm* excess, surplus
exceder [eksθe'ðer] *vt* to exceed, surpass; **excederse** *vr* (*extralimitarse*) to go too far; (*sobrepasarse*) to excel o.s.
excelencia [eksθe'lenθja] *nf* excellence; **E~** Excellency; **por ~** par excellence
excelente [eksθe'lente] *adj* excellent
excelso, -a [eks'θelso, a] *adj* lofty, sublime
excentricidad [eksθentriθi'ðað] *nf* eccentricity
excéntrico, -a [eks'θentriko, a] *adj, nm/f* eccentric
excepción [eksθep'θjon] *nf* exception; **la ~ confirma la regla** the exception proves the rule
excepcional [eksθepθjo'nal] *adj* exceptional
excepto [eks'θepto] *adv* excepting, except (for)
exceptuar [eksθep'twar] *vt* to except, exclude
excesivo, -a [eksθe'siβo, a] *adj* excessive
exceso [eks'θeso] *nm* excess; (*Com*) surplus; **~ de equipaje/peso** excess luggage/weight; **~ de velocidad** speeding; **en** *o* **por ~** excessively
excitación [eksθita'θjon] *nf* (*sensación*) excitement; (*acción*) excitation
excitado, -a [eksθi'taðo, a] *adj* excited; (*emociones*) aroused

excitante [eksθi'tante] *adj* exciting; (*Med*) stimulating ■ *nm* stimulant
excitar [eksθi'tar] *vt* to excite; (*incitar*) to urge; (*emoción*) to stir up; (*esperanzas*) to raise; (*pasión*) to arouse; **excitarse** *vr* to get excited
exclamación [eksklama'θjon] *nf* exclamation
exclamar [ekskla'mar] *vi* to exclaim; **exclamarse** *vr*: **exclamarse (contra)** to complain (about)
excluir [eksklu'ir] *vt* to exclude; (*dejar fuera*) to shut out; (*solución*) to reject; (*posibilidad*) to rule out
exclusión [eksklu'sjon] *nf* exclusion
exclusiva [eksklu'siβa] *nf ver* **exclusivo**
exclusive [eksklu'siβe] *prep* exclusive of, not counting
exclusivo, -a [eksklu'siβo, a] *adj* exclusive ■ *nf* (*Prensa*) exclusive, scoop; (*Com*) sole right *o* agency; **derecho ~** sole *o* exclusive right
excluyendo *etc* [eksklu'jendo] *vb ver* **excluir**
Excma., Excmo. *abr* (= *Excelentísima, Excelentísimo*) *courtesy title*
excombatiente [ekskomba'tjente] *nm* ex-serviceman, war veteran (*US*)
excomulgar [ekskomul'ɣar] *vt* (*Rel*) to excommunicate
excomulgue *etc* [eksko'mulɣe] *vb ver* **excomulgar**
excomunión [ekskomu'njon] *nf* excommunication
excoriar [eksko'rjar] *vt* to flay, skin
excremento [ekskre'mento] *nm* excrement
exculpar [ekskul'par] *vt* to exonerate; (*Jur*) to acquit; **exculparse** *vr* to exonerate o.s.
excursión [ekskur'sjon] *nf* excursion, outing; **ir de ~** to go (off) on a trip
excursionista [ekskursjo'nista] *nm/f* (*turista*) sightseer
excusa [eks'kusa] *nf* excuse; (*disculpa*) apology; **presentar sus excusas** to excuse o.s.
excusado, -a [eksku'saðo, a] *adj* unnecessary; (*disculpado*) excused, forgiven
excusar [eksku'sar] *vt* to excuse; (*evitar*) to avoid, prevent; **excusarse** *vr* (*disculparse*) to apologize
execrable [ekse'kraβle] *adj* appalling
exención [eksen'θjon] *nf* exemption
exento, -a [ek'sento, a] *pp de* **eximir** ■ *adj* exempt
exequias [ek'sekjas] *nfpl* funeral rites
exfoliar [eksfo'ljar] *vt* to exfoliate
exhalación [eksala'θjon] *nf* (*del aire*) exhalation; (*de vapor*) fumes *pl*, vapour; (*rayo*) shooting star; **salir como una ~** to shoot out
exhalar [eksa'lar] *vt* to exhale, breathe out; (*olor etc*) to give off; (*suspiro*) to breathe, heave
exhaustivo, -a [eksaus'tiβo, a] *adj* exhaustive
exhausto, -a [ek'sausto, a] *adj* exhausted, worn-out
exhibición [eksiβi'θjon] *nf* exhibition; (*demostración*) display, show; (*de película*) showing; (*de equipo*) performance
exhibicionista [eksiβiθjo'nista] *adj, nm/f* exhibitionist
exhibir [eksi'βir] *vt* to exhibit; to display, show; (*cuadros*) to exhibit; (*artículos*) to display; (*pasaporte*) to show; (*película*) to screen; (*mostrar con orgullo*) to show off; **exhibirse** *vr* (*mostrarse en público*) to show o.s. off; (*fam: indecentemente*) to expose o.s.
exhortación [eksorta'θjon] *nf* exhortation
exhortar [eksor'tar] *vt*: **~ a** to exhort to
exhumar [eksu'mar] *vt* to exhume
exigencia [eksi'xenθja] *nf* demand, requirement
exigente [eksi'xente] *adj* demanding; (*profesor*) strict; **ser ~ con algn** to be hard on sb
exigir [eksi'xir] *vt* (*gen*) to demand, require; (*impuestos*) to exact, levy; **~ el pago** to demand payment
exiguo, -a [ek'siɣwo, a] *adj* (*cantidad*) meagre; (*objeto*) tiny
exija *etc* [e'ksixa] *vb ver* **exigir**
exiliado, -a [eksi'ljaðo, a] *adj* exiled, in exile ■ *nm/f* exile
exiliar [eksi'ljar] *vt* to exile; **exiliarse** *vr* to go into exile
exilio [ek'siljo] *nm* exile
eximio, -a [ek'simjo, a] *adj* (*eminente*) distinguished, eminent
eximir [eksi'mir] *vt* to exempt
existencia [eksis'tenθja] *nf* existence; **existencias** *nfpl* stock *sg*; **~ de mercancías** (*Com*) stock-in-trade; **tener en ~** to have in stock; **amargar la ~ a algn** to make sb's life a misery
existir [eksis'tir] *vi* to exist, be
éxito ['eksito] *nm* (*resultado*) result, outcome; (*triunfo*) success; (*Mus, Teat*) hit; **éxito editorial** bestseller; **éxito rotundo** smash hit; **tener éxito** to be successful
exitoso, -a [eksi'toso, a] *adj* (*esp Am*) successful
éxodo ['eksoðo] *nm* exodus; **el éxodo rural** the drift from the land
ex oficio [ekso'fiθjo] *adj, adv* ex officio
exonerar [eksone'rar] *vt* to exonerate; **~ de una obligación** to free from an obligation
exorcice *etc* [eksor'θiθe] *vb ver* **exorcizar**
exorcismo [eksor'θismo] *nm* exorcism

exorcizar [eksorθi'θar] *vt* to exorcize
exótico, -a [ek'sotiko, a] *adj* exotic
expandido, -a [ekspan'diðo, a] *adj*: **en caracteres expandidos** (*Inform*) double width
expandir [ekspan'dir] *vt* to expand; (*Com*) to expand, enlarge; **expandirse** *vr* to expand, spread
expansión [ekspan'sjon] *nf* expansion; (*recreo*) relaxation; **la ~ económica** economic growth; **economía en ~** expanding economy
expansionarse [ekspansjo'narse] *vr* (*dilatarse*) to expand; (*recrearse*) to relax
expansivo, -a [ekspan'siβo, a] *adj* expansive; (*efusivo*) communicative
expatriado, -a [ekspa'trjaðo, a] *nm/f* (*emigrado*) expatriate; (*exiliado*) exile
expatriarse [ekspa'trjarse] *vr* to emigrate; (*Pol*) to go into exile
expectación [ekspekta'θjon] *nf* (*esperanza*) expectation; (*ilusión*) excitement
expectativa [ekspekta'tiβa] *nf* (*espera*) expectation; (*perspectiva*) prospect; **~ de vida** life expectancy; **estar a la ~** to wait and see (what will happen)
expedición [ekspeði'θjon] *nf* (*excursión*) expedition; **gastos de ~** shipping charges
expedientar [ekspeðjen'tar] *vt* to open a file on; (*funcionario*) to discipline, start disciplinary proceedings against
expediente [ekspe'ðjente] *nm* expedient; (*Jur: procedimento*) action, proceedings *pl*; (*: papeles*) dossier, file, record; **~ judicial** court proceedings *pl*; **~ académico** (student's) record
expedir [ekspe'ðir] *vt* (*despachar*) to send, forward; (*pasaporte*) to issue; (*cheque*) to make out
expedito, -a [ekspe'ðito, a] *adj* (*libre*) clear, free
expeler [ekspe'ler] *vt* to expel, eject
expendedor, a [ekspende'ðor, a] *nm/f* (*vendedor*) dealer; (*Teat*) ticket agent ■ *nm* (*aparato*) (vending) machine; **~ de cigarrillos** cigarette machine
expendeduría [ekspendedu'ria] *nf* (*estanco*) tobacconist's (shop) (*Brit*), cigar store (*US*)
expendio [eks'pendjo] *nm* (*Am*) small shop (*Brit*) *o* store (*US*)
expensas [eks'pensas] *nfpl* (*Jur*) costs; **a ~ de** at the expense of
experiencia [ekspe'rjenθja] *nf* experience
experimentado, -a [eksperimen'taðo, a] *adj* experienced
experimentar [eksperimen'tar] *vt* (*en laboratorio*) to experiment with; (*probar*) to test, try out; (*notar, observar*) to experience; (*deterioro, pérdida*) to suffer; (*aumento*) to show; (*sensación*) to feel
experimento [eksperi'mento] *nm* experiment
experto, -a [eks'perto, a] *adj* expert ■ *nm/f* expert
expiar [ekspi'ar] *vt* to atone for
expida *etc* [eks'piða] *vb ver* **expedir**
expirar [ekspi'rar] *vi* to expire
explanada [ekspla'naða] *nf* (*paseo*) esplanade; (*a orillas del mar*) promenade
explayarse [ekspla'jarse] *vr* (*en discurso*) to speak at length; **~ con algn** to confide in sb
explicación [eksplika'θjon] *nf* explanation
explicar [ekspli'kar] *vt* to explain; (*teoría*) to expound; (*Univ*) to lecture in; **explicarse** *vr* to explain (o.s.); **no me lo explico** I can't understand it
explícito, -a [eks'pliθito, a] *adj* explicit
explique *etc* [eks'plike] *vb ver* **explicar**
exploración [eksplora'θjon] *nf* exploration; (*Mil*) reconnaissance
explorador, a [eksplora'ðor, a] *nm/f* (*pionero*) explorer; (*Mil*) scout ■ *nm* (*Med*) probe; (*radar*) (radar) scanner
explorar [eksplo'rar] *vt* to explore; (*Med*) to probe; (*radar*) to scan
explosión [eksplo'sjon] *nf* explosion
explosivo, -a [eksplo'siβo, a] *adj* explosive
explotación [eksplota'θjon] *nf* exploitation; (*de planta etc*) running; (*de mina*) working; (*de recurso*) development; **~ minera** mine; **gastos de ~** operating costs
explotar [eksplo'tar] *vt* to exploit; (*planta*) to run, operate; (*mina*) to work ■ *vi* (*bomba etc*) to explode, go off
expondré *etc* [ekspon'dre] *vb ver* **exponer**
exponer [ekspo'ner] *vt* to expose; (*cuadro*) to display; (*vida*) to risk; (*idea*) to explain; (*teoría*) to expound; (*hechos*) to set out; **exponerse** *vr*: **exponerse a (hacer) algo** to run the risk of (doing) sth
exponga *etc* [eks'ponga] *vb ver* **exponer**
exportación [eksporta'θjon] *nf* (*acción*) export; (*mercancías*) exports *pl*
exportador, a [eksporta'ðor, a] *adj* (*país*) exporting ■ *nm/f* exporter
exportar [ekspor'tar] *vt* to export
exposición [eksposi'θjon] *nf* (*gen*) exposure; (*de arte*) show, exhibition; (*Com*) display; (*feria*) show, fair; (*explicación*) explanation; (*de teoría*) exposition; (*narración*) account, statement
exprés [eks'pres] *adj inv* (*café*) espresso ■ *nm* (*Ferro*) express (train)
expresamente [ekspresa'mente] *adv* (*concretamente*) expressly; (*a propósito*) on purpose

expresar [ekspre'sar] *vt* to express; (*redactar*) to phrase, put; (*emoción*) to show; **expresarse** *vr* to express o.s.; (*dato*) to be stated; **como abajo se expresa** as stated below
expresión [expre'sjon] *nf* expression; **~ familiar** colloquialism
expresivo, -a [ekspre'siβo, a] *adj* expressive; (*cariñoso*) affectionate
expreso, -a [eks'preso, a] *adj* (*explícito*) express; (*claro*) specific, clear; (*tren*) fast ■ *nm* (*Ferro*) fast train ■ *adv*: **mandar ~** to send by express (delivery)
exprimidor [eksprimi'ðor] *nm* (lemon) squeezer
exprimir [ekspri'mir] *vt* (*fruta*) to squeeze; (*zumo*) to squeeze out
ex profeso [ekspro'feso] *adv* expressly
expropiar [ekspro'pjar] *vt* to expropriate
expuesto, -a [eks'pwesto, a] *pp de* **exponer** ■ *adj* exposed; (*cuadro etc*) on show, on display; **según lo ~ arriba** according to what has been stated above
expulsar [ekspul'sar] *vt* (*echar*) to eject, throw out; (*alumno*) to expel; (*despedir*) to sack, fire; (*Deporte*) to send off
expulsión [ekspul'sjon] *nf* expulsion; sending-off
expurgar [ekspur'ɣar] *vt* to expurgate
expuse *etc* [eks'puse] *vb ver* **exponer**
exquisito, -a [ekski'sito, a] *adj* exquisite; (*comida*) delicious; (*afectado*) affected
Ext. *abr* (= *Exterior*) ext.; (= *Extensión*) ext.
éxtasis ['ekstasis] *nm* (*tb droga*) ecstasy
extemporáneo, -a [ekstempo'raneo, a] *adj* unseasonal
extender [eksten'der] *vt* to extend; (*los brazos*) to stretch out, hold out; (*mapa, tela*) to spread (out), open (out); (*mantequilla*) to spread; (*certificado*) to issue; (*cheque, recibo*) to make out; (*documento*) to draw up; **extenderse** *vr* to extend; (*terreno*) to stretch *o* spread (out); (*persona: en el suelo*) to stretch out; (*en el tiempo*) to extend, last; (*costumbre, epidemia*) to spread; (*guerra*) to escalate; **extenderse sobre un tema** to enlarge on a subject
extendido, -a [eksten'diðo, a] *adj* (*abierto*) spread out, open; (*brazos*) outstretched; (*costumbre etc*) widespread
extensible [eksten'siβle] *adj* extending
extensión [eksten'sjon] *nf* (*de terreno, mar*) expanse, stretch; (*Mus*) range; (*de conocimientos*) extent; (*de programa*) scope; (*de tiempo*) length, duration; (*Telec*) extension; **~ de plazo** (*Com*) extension; **en toda la ~ de la palabra** in every sense of the word; **de ~** (*Inform*) add-on
extenso, -a [eks'tenso, a] *adj* extensive
extenuar [ekste'nwar] *vt* (*debilitar*) to weaken
exterior [ekste'rjor] *adj* (*de fuera*) external; (*afuera*) outside, exterior; (*apariencia*) outward; (*deuda, relaciones*) foreign ■ *nm* exterior, outside; (*aspecto*) outward appearance; (*Deporte*) wing(er); (*países extranjeros*) abroad; **asuntos exteriores** foreign affairs; **al ~** outwardly, on the outside; **en el ~** abroad; **noticias del ~** foreign *o* overseas news
exteriorice *etc* [eksterjo'riθe] *vb ver* **exteriorizar**
exteriorizar [eksterjori'θar] *vt* (*emociones*) to show, reveal
exteriormente [eksterjor'mente] *adv* outwardly
exterminar [ekstermi'nar] *vt* to exterminate
exterminio [ekster'minjo] *nm* extermination
externo, -a [eks'terno, a] *adj* (*exterior*) external, outside; (*superficial*) outward ■ *nm/f* day pupil
extienda *etc* [eks'tjenda] *vb ver* **extender**
extinción [ekstin'θjon] *nf* extinction
extinga *etc* [eks'tinga] *vb ver* **extinguir**
extinguido, -a [ekstin'giðo, a] *adj* (*animal, volcán*) extinct; (*fuego*) out, extinguished
extinguir [ekstin'gir] *vt* (*fuego*) to extinguish, put out; (*raza, población*) to wipe out; **extinguirse** *vr* (*fuego*) to go out; (*Bio*) to die out, become extinct
extinto, -a [eks'tinto, a] *adj* extinct
extintor [ekstin'tor] *nm* (fire) extinguisher
extirpar [ekstir'par] *vt* (*vicios*) to eradicate, stamp out; (*Med*) to remove (surgically)
extorsión [ekstor'sjon] *nf* blackmail
extra ['ekstra] *adj inv* (*tiempo*) extra; (*vino*) vintage; (*chocolate*) good-quality; (*gasolina*) high-octane ■ *nm/f* extra ■ *nm* (*bono*) bonus; (*periódico*) special edition
extracción [ekstrak'θjon] *nf* extraction; (*en lotería*) draw; (*de carbón*) mining
extracto [eks'trakto] *nm* extract
extractor [ekstrak'tor] *nm* (*tb*: **extractor de humos**) extractor fan
extradición [ekstraði'θjon] *nf* extradition
extraditar [ekstraði'tar] *vt* to extradite
extraer [ekstra'er] *vt* to extract, take out
extrafino, -a [ekstra'fino, a] *adj* extra-fine; **azúcar ~** caster sugar
extraiga *etc* [eks'traiɣa], **extraje** *etc* [eks'traxe], **extrajera** *etc* [ekstra'xera] *vb ver* **extraer**
extralimitarse [ekstralimi'tarse] *vr* to go too far
extranjerismo [ekstranxe'rismo] *nm* foreign word *o* phrase *etc*

extranjero, -a [ekstran'xero, a] *adj* foreign ■ *nm/f* foreigner ■ *nm* foreign lands *pl*; **en el ~** abroad
extrañamiento [ekstraɲa'mjento] *nm* estrangement
extrañar [ekstra'ɲar] *vt* (*sorprender*) to find strange *o* odd; (*echar de menos*) to miss; **extrañarse** *vr* (*sorprenderse*) to be amazed, be surprised; (*distanciarse*) to become estranged, grow apart; **me extraña** I'm surprised
extrañeza [ekstra'ɲeθa] *nf* (*rareza*) strangeness, oddness; (*asombro*) amazement, surprise
extraño, -a [eks'traɲo, a] *adj* (*extranjero*) foreign; (*raro, sorprendente*) strange, odd
extraoficial [ekstraofi'θjal] *adj* unofficial, informal
extraordinario, -a [ekstraorði'narjo, a] *adj* extraordinary; (*edición, número*) special ■ *nm* (*de periódico*) special edition; **horas extraordinarias** overtime *sg*
extrarradio [ekstra'rraðjo] *nm* suburbs *pl*
extrasensorial [ekstrasenso'rjal] *adj*: **percepción ~** extrasensory perception
extraterrestre [ekstrate'rrestre] *adj* of *o* from outer space ■ *nm/f* creature from outer space
extravagancia [ekstraβa'ɣanθja] *nf* oddness; outlandishness; (*rareza*) peculiarity; **extravagancias** *nfpl* (*tonterías*) nonsense *sg*
extravagante [ekstraβa'ɣante] *adj* (*excéntrico*) eccentric; (*estrafalario*) outlandish
extraviado, -a [ekstra'βjaðo, a] *adj* lost, missing
extraviar [ekstra'βjar] *vt* to mislead, misdirect; (*perder*) to lose, misplace; **extraviarse** *vr* to lose one's way, get lost; (*objeto*) to go missing, be mislaid
extravío [ekstra'βio] *nm* loss; (*fig*) misconduct
extrayendo [ekstra'jendo] *vb ver* **extraer**
extremado, -a [ekstre'maðo, a] *adj* extreme, excessive
Extremadura [ekstrema'ðura] *nf* Estremadura
extremar [ekstre'mar] *vt* to carry to extremes; **extremarse** *vr* to do one's utmost, make every effort
extremaunción [ekstremaun'θjon] *nf* extreme unction, last rites *pl*
extremidad [ekstremi'ðað] *nf* (*punta*) extremity; (*fila*) edge; **extremidades** *nfpl* (*Anat*) extremities
extremista [ekstre'mista] *adj, nm/f* extremist
extremo, -a [eks'tremo, a] *adj* extreme; (*más alejado*) furthest; (*último*) last ■ *nm* end; (*situación*) extreme; **E~ Oriente** Far East; **en último ~** as a last resort; **pasar de un ~ a otro** (*fig*) to go from one extreme to the other; **con ~** in the extreme; **la extrema derecha** (*Pol*) the far right; **~ derecho/ izquierdo** (*Deporte*) outside right/left
extrínseco, -a [eks'trinseko, a] *adj* extrinsic
extrovertido, -a [ekstroβer'tiðo, a] *adj* extrovert, outgoing ■ *nm/f* extrovert
exuberancia [eksuβe'ranθja] *nf* exuberance
exuberante [eksuβe'rante] *adj* exuberant; (*fig*) luxuriant, lush
exudar [eksu'ðar] *vt, vi* to exude
exultar [eksul'tar] *vi*: **~ (en)** to exult (in); (*pey*) to gloat (over)
exvoto [eks'βoto] *nm* votive offering
eyaculación [ejakula'θjon] *nf* ejaculation
eyacular [ejaku'lar] *vt, vi* to ejaculate

Ff

F, f ['efe] *nf* (*letra*) F, f; **F de Francia** F for Frederick (*Brit*), F for Fox (*US*)
fa [fa] *nm* (*Mus*) F
f.ª *abr* (*Com:* = *factura*) Inv.
fabada [fa'βaða] *nf bean and sausage stew*
fábrica ['faβrika] *nf* factory; **~ de moneda** mint; **marca de ~** trademark; **precio de ~** factory price
fabricación [faβrika'θjon] *nf* (*manufactura*) manufacture; (*producción*) production; **de ~ casera** home-made; **de ~ nacional** home produced; **~ en serie** mass production
fabricante [faβri'kante] *nm/f* manufacturer
fabricar [faβri'kar] *vt* (*manufacturar*) to manufacture, make; (*construir*) to build; (*cuento*) to fabricate, devise; **~ en serie** to mass-produce
fabril [fa'βril] *adj*: **industria ~** manufacturing industry
fabrique *etc* [fa'βrike] *vb ver* **fabricar**
fábula ['faβula] *nf* (*cuento*) fable; (*chisme*) rumour; (*mentira*) fib
fabuloso, -a [faβu'loso, a] *adj* fabulous, fantastic
facción [fak'θjon] *nf* (*Pol*) faction; **facciones** *nfpl* (*del rostro*) features
faceta [fa'θeta] *nf* facet
facha ['fatʃa] (*fam*) *nm/f* fascist, right-wing extremist ■ *nf* (*aspecto*) look; (*cara*) face; **¡qué ~ tienes!** you look a sight!
fachada [fa'tʃaða] *nf* (*Arq*) façade, front; (*Tip*) title page; (*fig*) façade, outward show
facial [fa'θjal] *adj* facial
fácil ['faθil] *adj* (*simple*) easy; (*sencillo*) simple, straightforward; (*probable*) likely; (*respuesta*) facile; **~ de usar** (*Inform*) user-friendly
facilidad [faθili'ðað] *nf* (*capacidad*) ease; (*sencillez*) simplicity; (*de palabra*) fluency; **facilidades** *nfpl* facilities; **"facilidades de pago"** (*Com*) "credit facilities", "payment terms"
facilitar [faθili'tar] *vt* (*hacer fácil*) to make easy; (*proporcionar*) to provide; (*documento*) to issue; **le agradecería me facilitara ...** I would be grateful if you could let me have ...
fácilmente ['faθilmente] *adv* easily
facsímil [fak'simil] *nm* (*documento*) facsimile; **enviar por ~** to fax
factible [fak'tiβle] *adj* feasible
factor [fak'tor] *nm* factor; (*Com*) agent; (*Ferro*) freight clerk
factoría [fakto'ria] *nf* (*Com: fábrica*) factory
factura [fak'tura] *nf* (*cuenta*) bill; (*nota de pago*) invoice; (*hechura*) manufacture; **presentar ~ a** to invoice
facturación [faktura'θjon] *nf* (*Com*) invoicing; (*: ventas*) turnover; **~ de equipajes** luggage check-in; **~ online** online check-in
facturar [faktu'rar] *vt* (*Com*) to invoice, charge for; (*Aviat*) to check in; (*equipaje*) to register, check (*US*)
facultad [fakul'tað] *nf* (*aptitud, Escol etc*) faculty; (*poder*) power
facultativo, -a [fakulta'tiβo, a] *adj* optional; (*de un oficio*) professional; **prescripción facultativa** medical prescription
FAD *nm abr* (*Esp*) = **Fondo de Ayuda y Desarrollo**
faena [fa'ena] *nf* (*trabajo*) work; (*quehacer*) task, job; **faenas domésticas** housework *sg*
faenar [fae'nar] *vi* to fish
fagot [fa'ɣot] *nm* (*Mus*) bassoon
faisán [fai'san] *nm* pheasant
faja ['faxa] *nf* (*para la cintura*) sash; (*de mujer*) corset; (*de tierra*) strip
fajo ['faxo] *nm* (*de papeles*) bundle; (*de billetes*) role, wad
falange [fa'lanxe] *nf*: **la F~** (*Pol*) the Falange
falda ['falda] *nf* (*prenda de vestir*) skirt; (*Geo*) foothill; **~ escocesa** kilt
fálico, -a ['faliko, a] *adj* phallic
falla ['faʎa] *nf* (*defecto*) fault, flaw
fallar [fa'ʎar] *vt* (*Jur*) to pronounce sentence on; (*Naipes*) to trump ■ *vi* (*memoria*) to fail; (*plan*) to go wrong; (*motor*) to miss; **~ a algn** to let sb down
Fallas ['faʎas] *nfpl see note*

Fallas

In the week of the 19th of March (the feast of St Joseph, San José), Valencia honours its patron saint with a spectacular *fiesta* called *las Fallas*. The *Fallas* are huge sculptures, made of wood, cardboard, paper and cloth, depicting famous politicians and other targets for ridicule, which are set alight and burned by the *falleros*, members of the competing local groups who have just spent months preparing them.

fallecer [faʎe'θer] *vi* to pass away, die
fallecido, -a [faʎe'θiðo, a] *adj* late ■ *nm/f* deceased
fallecimiento [faʎeθi'mjento] *nm* decease, demise
fallero, -a [fa'ʎero, a] *nm/f* maker of "Fallas"
fallezca *etc* [fa'ʎeθka] *vb ver* **fallecer**
fallido, -a [fa'ʎiðo, a] *adj* vain; (*intento*) frustrated, unsuccessful
fallo ['faʎo] *nm* (*Jur*) verdict, ruling; (*decisión*) decision; (*de jurado*) findings; (*fracaso*) failure; (*Deporte*) miss; (*Inform*) bug
falo ['falo] *nm* phallus
falsear [false'ar] *vt* to falsify; (*firma etc*) to forge ■ *vi* (*Mus*) to be out of tune
falsedad [false'ðað] *nf* falseness; (*hipocresía*) hypocrisy; (*mentira*) falsehood
falsificación [falsifika'θjon] *nf* (*acto*) falsification; (*objeto*) forgery
falsificar [falsifi'kar] *vt* (*firma etc*) to forge; (*voto etc*) to rig; (*moneda*) to counterfeit
falsifique *etc* [falsi'fike] *vb ver* **falsificar**
falso, -a ['falso, a] *adj* false; (*erróneo*) wrong, mistaken; (*firma, documento*) forged; (*moneda etc*) fake; **en ~** falsely; **dar un paso en ~** to trip; (*fig*) to take a false step
falta ['falta] *nf* (*defecto*) fault, flaw; (*privación*) lack, want; (*ausencia*) absence; (*carencia*) shortage; (*equivocación*) mistake; (*Jur*) default; (*Deporte*) foul; (*Tenis*) fault; **~ de ortografía** spelling mistake; **~ de respeto** disrespect; **echar en ~** to miss; **hacer ~ hacer algo** to be necessary to do sth; **me hace ~ una pluma** I need a pen; **sin ~** without fail; **por ~ de** through *o* for lack of
faltar [fal'tar] *vi* (*escasear*) to be lacking, be wanting; (*ausentarse*) to be absent, be missing; **¿falta algo?** is anything missing?; **falta mucho todavía** there's plenty of time yet; **¿falta mucho?** is there long to go?; **faltan dos horas para llegar** there are two hours to go till arrival; **~ (al respeto) a algn** to be disrespectful to sb; **~ a una cita** to miss an appointment; **~ a la verdad** to lie; **¡no faltaba más!** that's the last straw!
falto, -a ['falto, a] *adj* (*desposeído*) deficient, lacking; (*necesitado*) poor, wretched; **estar ~ de** to be short of
fama ['fama] *nf* (*renombre*) fame; (*reputación*) reputation
famélico, -a [fa'meliko, a] *adj* starving
familia [fa'milja] *nf* family; **~ política** in-laws *pl*
familiar [fami'ljar] *adj* (*relativo a la familia*) family *cpd*; (*conocido, informal*) familiar; (*estilo*) informal; (*Ling*) colloquial ■ *nm/f* relative, relation
familiarice *etc* [familja'riθe] *vb ver* **familiarizarse**
familiaridad [familjari'ðað] *nf* familiarity; (*informalidad*) homeliness
familiarizarse [familjari'θarse] *vr*: **~ con** to familiarize o.s. with
famoso, -a [fa'moso, a] *adj* (*renombrado*) famous
fan (*pl* **fans**) [fan, fans] *nm* fan
fanático, -a [fa'natiko, a] *adj* fanatical ■ *nm/f* fanatic; (*Cine, Deporte etc*) fan
fanatismo [fana'tismo] *nm* fanaticism
fanfarrón, -ona [fanfa'rron, ona] *adj* boastful; (*pey*) showy
fanfarronear [fanfarrone'ar] *vi* to boast
fango ['fango] *nm* mud
fangoso, -a [fan'goso, a] *adj* muddy
fantasear [fantase'ar] *vi* to fantasize; **~ con una idea** to toy with an idea
fantasía [fanta'sia] *nf* fantasy, imagination; (*Mus*) fantasia; (*capricho*) whim; **joyas de ~** imitation jewellery *sg*
fantasma [fan'tasma] *nm* (*espectro*) ghost, apparition; (*presumido*) show-off
fantástico, -a [fan'tastiko, a] *adj* (*irreal, fam*) fantastic
fanzine [fan'θine] *nm* fanzine
FAO ['fao] *nf abr* (= *Organización de las Naciones Unidas para la Agricultura y la Alimentación*) FAO
faquir [fa'kir] *nm* fakir
faraón [fara'on] *nm* Pharaoh
faraónico, -a [fara'oniko, a] *adj* Pharaonic; (*fig*) grandiose
fardar [far'ðar] *vi* to show off; **~ de** to boast about
fardo ['farðo] *nm* bundle; (*fig*) burden
faringe [fa'rinxe] *nf* pharynx
faringitis [farin'xitis] *nf* pharyngitis
farmacéutico, -a [farma'θeutiko, a] *adj* pharmaceutical ■ *nm/f* chemist (*Brit*), pharmacist
farmacia [far'maθja] *nf* (*ciencia*) pharmacy; (*tienda*) chemist's (shop) (*Brit*), pharmacy,

drugstore (*US*); **~ de turno** duty chemist
fármaco ['farmako] *nm* medicine, drug
faro ['faro] *nm* (*Naut: torre*) lighthouse; (*señal*) beacon; (*Auto*) headlamp; **faros antiniebla** fog lamps; **faros delanteros/traseros** headlights/rear lights
farol [fa'rol] *nm* (*luz*) lantern, lamp; (*Ferro*) headlamp; (*poste*) lamppost; **echarse un ~** (*fam*) to show off
farola [fa'rola] *nf* street lamp (*Brit*) *o* light (*US*), lamppost
farruco, -a [fa'rruko, a] *adj* (*fam*): **estar** *o* **ponerse ~** to get aggressive
farsa ['farsa] *nf* farce
farsante [far'sante] *nm/f* fraud, fake
FASA ['fasa] *nf abr* (*Esp Auto*) = **Fábrica de Automóviles, S.A.**
fascículo [fas'θikulo] *nm* part, instalment (*Brit*), installment (*US*)
fascinante [fasθi'nante] *adj* fascinating
fascinar [fasθi'nar] *vt* to fascinate; (*encantar*) to captivate
fascismo [fas'θismo] *nm* fascism
fascista [fas'θista] *adj, nm/f* fascist
fase ['fase] *nf* phase
fastidiar [fasti'ðjar] *vt* (*disgustar*) to annoy, bother; (*estropear*) to spoil; **fastidiarse** *vr* (*disgustarse*) to get annoyed *o* cross; **¡no fastidies!** you're joking!; **¡que se fastidie!** (*fam*) he'll just have to put up with it!
fastidio [fas'tiðjo] *nm* (*disgusto*) annoyance
fastidioso, -a [fasti'ðjoso, a] *adj* (*molesto*) annoying
fastuoso, -a [fas'twoso, a] *adj* (*espléndido*) magnificent; (*banquete etc*) lavish
fatal [fa'tal] *adj* (*gen*) fatal; (*desgraciado*) ill-fated; (*fam: malo, pésimo*) awful ■ *adv* terribly; **lo pasó ~** he had a terrible time (of it)
fatalidad [fatali'ðað] *nf* (*destino*) fate; (*mala suerte*) misfortune
fatídico, -a [fa'tiðiko, a] *adj* fateful
fatiga [fa'tiγa] *nf* (*cansancio*) fatigue, weariness; **fatigas** *nfpl* hardships
fatigar [fati'γar] *vt* to tire, weary; **fatigarse** *vr* to get tired
fatigoso, -a [fati'γoso, a] *adj* (*que cansa*) tiring
fatigue *etc* [fa'tiγe] *vb ver* **fatigar**
fatuo, -a ['fatwo, a] *adj* (*vano*) fatuous; (*presuntuoso*) conceited
fauces ['fauθes] *nfpl* (*Anat*) gullet *sg*; (*fam*) jaws
fauna ['fauna] *nf* fauna
favor [fa'βor] *nm* favour (*Brit*), favor (*US*); **haga el ~ de ...** would you be so good as to ..., kindly ...; **por ~** please; **a ~** in favo(u)r; **a ~ de** in favo(u)r of; (*Com*) to the order of
favorable [faβo'raβle] *adj* favourable (*Brit*), favorable (*US*); (*condiciones etc*) advantageous
favorecer [faβore'θer] *vt* to favour (*Brit*), favor (*US*); (*amparar*) to help; (*vestido etc*) to become, flatter; **este peinado le favorece** this hairstyle suits him
favorezca *etc* [faβo'reθka] *vb ver* **favorecer**
favorito, -a [faβo'rito, a] *adj, nm/f* favourite (*Brit*), favorite (*US*)
fax [faks] *nm inv* fax; **mandar por ~** to fax
faz [faθ] *nf* face; **la ~ de la tierra** the face of the earth
FBI *nm abr* FBI
F.C., f.c. *abr* = **ferrocarril**; (= *Fútbol Club*) FC
FE *nf abr* = **Falange Española**
fe [fe] *nf* (*Rel*) faith; (*confianza*) belief; (*documento*) certificate; **de buena fe** (*Jur*) bona fide; **prestar fe a** to believe, credit; **actuar con buena/mala fe** to act in good/bad faith; **dar fe de** to bear witness to; **fe de erratas** errata
fealdad [feal'dað] *nf* ugliness
feb., feb.° *abr* (= *febrero*) Feb.
febrero [fe'βrero] *nm* February; *ver tb* **julio**
febril [fe'βril] *adj* feverish; (*movido*) hectic
fecha ['fetʃa] *nf* date; **~ límite** *o* **tope** closing *o* last date; **~ límite de venta** (*de alimentos*) sell-by date; **~ de caducidad** (*de alimentos*) sell-by date; (*de contrato*) expiry date; **en ~ próxima** soon; **hasta la ~** to date, so far; **~ de vencimiento** (*Com*) due date; **~ de vigencia** (*Com*) effective date
fechar [fe'tʃar] *vt* to date
fechoría [fetʃo'ria] *nf* misdeed
fécula ['fekula] *nf* starch
fecundación [fekunda'θjon] *nf* fertilization; **~ in vitro** in vitro fertilization, I.V.F.
fecundar [fekun'dar] *vt* (*generar*) to fertilize, make fertile
fecundidad [fekundi'ðað] *nf* fertility; (*fig*) productiveness
fecundo, -a [fe'kundo, a] *adj* (*fértil*) fertile; (*fig*) prolific; (*productivo*) productive
FED *nm abr* (= *Fondo Europeo de Desarrollo*) EDF
FEDER *nm abr* (= *Fondo Europeo de Desarrollo Regional*) ERDF
federación [feðera'θjon] *nf* federation
federal [feðe'ral] *adj* federal
federalismo [feðera'lismo] *nm* federalism
FEF [fef] *nf abr* = **Federación Española de Fútbol**
felicidad [feliθi'ðað] *nf* (*satisfacción, contento*) happiness; **felicidades** *nfpl* best wishes, congratulations
felicitación [feliθita'θjon] *nf* (*tarjeta*) greetings card; **felicitaciones** *nfpl* (*enhorabuena*) congratulations; **~ navideña** *o* **de Navidad** Christmas Greetings

felicitar [feliθi'tar] *vt* to congratulate
feligrés, -esa [feli'ɣres, esa] *nm/f* parishioner
felino, -a [fe'lino, a] *adj* cat-like; (*Zool*) feline ■ *nm* feline
feliz [fe'liθ] *adj* (*contento*) happy; (*afortunado*) lucky
felonía [felo'nia] *nf* felony, crime
felpa ['felpa] *nf* (*terciopelo*) plush; (*toalla*) towelling
felpudo [fel'puðo] *nm* doormat
femenino, -a [feme'nino, a] *adj* feminine; (*Zool etc*) female ■ *nm* (*Ling*) feminine
feminismo [femi'nismo] *nm* feminism
feminista [femi'nista] *adj, nm/f* feminist
fenomenal [fenome'nal] *adj* phenomenal; (*fam*) great, terrific
fenómeno [fe'nomeno] *nm* phenomenon; (*fig*) freak, accident ■ *adv*: **lo pasamos ~** we had a great time ■ *excl* great!, marvellous!
feo, -a ['feo, a] *adj* (*gen*) ugly; (*desagradable*) bad, nasty ■ *nm* insult; **hacer un ~ a algn** to offend sb; **más ~ que Picio** as ugly as sin
féretro ['feretro] *nm* (*ataúd*) coffin; (*sarcófago*) bier
feria ['ferja] *nf* (*gen*) fair; (*Am*: *mercado*) market; (*descanso*) holiday, rest day; (*Am*: *cambio*) small change; **~ comercial** trade fair; **~ de muestras** trade show
feriado, -a [fe'rjaðo, a] (*Am*) *adj*: **día ~** (public) holiday ■ *nm* (public) holiday
fermentar [fermen'tar] *vi* to ferment
fermento [fer'mento] *nm* leaven, leavening
ferocidad [feroθi'ðað] *nf* fierceness, ferocity
ferocísimo, -a [fero'θisimo, a] *adj superlativo de* **feroz**
feroz [fe'roθ] *adj* (*cruel*) cruel; (*salvaje*) fierce
férreo, -a ['ferreo, a] *adj* iron *cpd*; (*Tec*) ferrous; (*fig*) (of) iron
ferretería [ferrete'ria] *nf* (*tienda*) ironmonger's (shop) (*Brit*), hardware store
ferrocarril [ferroka'rril] *nm* railway, railroad (*US*); **~ de vía estrecha/única** narrow-gauge/single-track railway *o* line
ferroviario, -a [ferrovja'rjo, a] *adj* rail *cpd*, railway *cpd* (*Brit*), railroad *cpd* (*US*) ■ *nm*: **ferroviarios** railway (*Brit*) *o* railroad (*US*) workers
fértil ['fertil] *adj* (*productivo*) fertile; (*rico*) rich
fertilice *etc* [ferti'liθe] *vb ver* **fertilizar**
fertilidad [fertili'ðað] *nf* (*gen*) fertility; (*productividad*) fruitfulness
fertilizante [fertili'θante] *nm* fertilizer
fertilizar [fertili'θar] *vt* to fertilize
ferviente [fer'βjente] *adj* fervent
fervor [fer'βor] *nm* fervour (*Brit*), fervor (*US*)
fervoroso, -a [ferβo'roso, a] *adj* fervent
festejar [feste'xar] *vt* (*agasajar*) to wine and dine, fête; (*galantear*) to court; (*celebrar*) to celebrate
festejo [fes'texo] *nm* (*diversión*) entertainment; (*galanteo*) courtship; (*fiesta*) celebration
festín [fes'tin] *nm* feast, banquet
festival [festi'βal] *nm* festival
festividad [festiβi'ðað] *nf* festivity
festivo, -a [fes'tiβo, a] *adj* (*de fiesta*) festive; (*fig*) witty; (*Cine, Lit*) humorous; **día ~** holiday
fetiche [fe'titʃe] *nm* fetish
fetichista [feti'tʃista] *adj* fetishistic ■ *nm/f* fetishist
fétido, -a ['fetiðo, a] *adj* (*hediondo*) foul-smelling
feto ['feto] *nm* foetus; (*fam*) monster
F.E.V.E. *nf abr* (= *Ferrocarriles Españoles de Vía Estrecha*) *Spanish narrow-gauge railways*
FF.AA. *nfpl abr* (*Mil*) = **Fuerzas Armadas**
FF.CC. *nmpl abr* (= *Ferrocarriles*) *ver* **ferrocarril**
fiable [fi'aβle] *adj* (*persona*) trustworthy; (*máquina*) reliable
fiado [fi'aðo] *nm*: **comprar al ~** to buy on credit; **en ~** on bail
fiador, a [fia'ðor, a] *nm/f* (*Jur*) surety, guarantor; (*Com*) backer; **salir ~ por algn** to stand bail for sb
fiambre ['fjambre] *adj* (*Culin*) served cold ■ *nm* (*Culin*) cold meat (*Brit*), cold cut (*US*); (*fam*) corpse, stiff
fiambrera [fjam'brera] *nf* ≈ lunch box, ≈ dinner pail (*US*)
fianza ['fjanθa] *nf* surety; (*Jur*): **libertad bajo ~** release on bail
fiar [fi'ar] *vt* (*salir garante de*) to guarantee; (*Jur*) to stand bail *o* bond (*US*) for; (*vender a crédito*) to sell on credit; (*secreto*) to confide ■ *vi*: **~ (de)** to trust (in); **ser de ~** to be trustworthy; **fiarse** *vr*: **fiarse de** to trust (in), rely on
fiasco ['fjasko] *nm* fiasco
fibra ['fiβra] *nf* fibre (*Brit*), fiber (*US*); (*fig*) vigour (*Brit*), vigor (*US*); **~ óptica** (*Inform*) optical fibre (*Brit*) *o* fiber (*US*)
ficción [fik'θjon] *nf* fiction
ficha ['fitʃa] *nf* (*Telec*) token; (*en juegos*) counter, marker; (*en casino*) chip; (*Com, Econ*) tally, check (*US*); (*Inform*) file; (*tarjeta*) (index) card; (*Elec*) plug; (*en hotel*) registration form; **~ policíaca** police dossier
fichaje [fi'tʃaxe] *nm* signing(-up)
fichar [fi'tʃar] *vt* (*archivar*) to file, index; (*Deporte*) to sign (up) ■ *vi* (*deportista*) to sign (up); (*obrero*) to clock in *o* on; **estar fichado** to have a record
fichero [fi'tʃero] *nm* card index; (*archivo*) filing cabinet; (*Com*) box file; (*Inform*) file, archive; (*de policía*) criminal records; **~ activo**

(*Inform*) active file; ~ **archivado** (*Inform*) archived file; ~ **indexado** (*Inform*) index file; ~ **de reserva** (*Inform*) backup file; ~ **de tarjetas** card index; **nombre de** ~ filename
ficticio, -a [fik'tiθjo, a] *adj* (*imaginario*) fictitious; (*falso*) fabricated
ficus ['fikus] *nm inv* (*Bot*) rubber plant
fidedigno, -a [fiðe'ðiɣno, a] *adj* reliable
fideicomiso [fiðeiko'miso] *nm* (*Com*) trust
fidelidad [fiðeli'ðað] *nf* (*lealtad*) fidelity, loyalty; (*exactitud: de dato etc*) accuracy; **alta** ~ high fidelity, hi-fi
fidelísimo, -a [fiðe'lisimo, a] *adj superlativo de* **fiel**
fideos [fi'ðeos] *nmpl* noodles
fiduciario, -a [fiðu'θjarjo, a] *nm/f* fiduciary
fiebre ['fjeβre] *nf* (*Med*) fever; (*fig*) fever, excitement; ~ **amarilla/del heno** yellow/hay fever; ~ **palúdica** malaria; **tener** ~ to have a temperature
fiel [fjel] *adj* (*leal*) faithful, loyal; (*fiable*) reliable; (*exacto*) accurate ■ *nm* (*aguja*) needle, pointer; **los fieles** *nmpl* the faithful
fieltro ['fjeltro] *nm* felt
fiera ['fjera] *nf ver* **fiero**
fiereza [fje'reθa] *nf* (*Zool*) wildness; (*bravura*) fierceness
fiero, -a ['fjero, a] *adj* (*cruel*) cruel; (*feroz*) fierce; (*duro*) harsh ■ *nm/f* (*fig*) fiend ■ *nf* (*animal feroz*) wild animal *o* beast; (*fig*) dragon
fierro ['fjerro] *nm* (*Am*) iron
fiesta ['fjesta] *nf* party; (*de pueblo*) festival; **la ~ nacional** bullfighting; **(día de)** ~ (public) holiday; **mañana es** ~ it's a holiday tomorrow; ~ **de guardar** (*Rel*) day of obligation; *see note*

FIESTA

Fiestas can be official public holidays (such as the *Día de la Constitución*), or special holidays for each *comunidad autónoma*, many of which are religious feast days. All over Spain there are also special local *fiestas* for a patron saint or the Virgin Mary. These often last several days and can include religious processions, carnival parades, bullfights, dancing and feasts of typical local produce.

FIFA *nf abr* (= *Federación Internacional de Fútbol Asociación*) FIFA
figura [fi'ɣura] *nf* (*gen*) figure; (*forma, imagen*) shape, form; (*Naipes*) face card
figurado, -a [fiɣu'raðo, a] *adj* figurative
figurante [fiɣu'rante] *nm/f* (*Teat*) walk-on part; (*Cine*) extra
figurar [fiɣu'rar] *vt* (*representar*) to represent; (*fingir*) to feign ■ *vi* to figure; **figurarse** *vr* (*imaginarse*) to imagine; (*suponer*) to suppose; **ya me lo figuraba** I thought as much
fijador [fixa'ðor] *nm* (*Foto etc*) fixative; (*de pelo*) gel
fijar [fi'xar] *vt* (*gen*) to fix; (*cartel*) to post, put up; (*estampilla*) to affix, stick (on); (*pelo*) to set; (*fig*) to settle (on), decide; **fijarse** *vr*: **fijarse en** to notice; **¡fíjate!** just imagine!; **¿te fijas?** see what I mean?
fijo, -a ['fixo, a] *adj* (*gen*) fixed; (*firme*) firm; (*permanente*) permanent; (*trabajo*) steady; (*colorfast*) fast ■ *adv*: **mirar** ~ to stare
fila ['fila] *nf* row; (*Mil*) rank; (*cadena*) line; (*en marcha*) file; ~ **india** single file; **ponerse en** ~ to line up, get into line; **primera** ~ front row
filántropo, -a [fi'lantropo, a] *nm/f* philanthropist
filarmónico, a [filar'moniko, a] *adj, nf* philharmonic
filatelia [fila'telja] *nf* philately, stamp collecting
filatelista [filate'lista] *nm/f* philatelist, stamp collector
filete [fi'lete] *nm* (*de carne*) fillet steak; (*de cerdo*) tenderloin; (*pescado*) fillet; (*Mecánica: rosca*) thread
filiación [filja'θjon] *nf* (*Pol etc*) affiliation; (*señas*) particulars *pl*; (*Mil, Policía*) records *pl*
filial [fi'ljal] *adj* filial ■ *nf* subsidiary; (*sucursal*) branch
Filipinas [fili'pinas] *nfpl*: **las (Islas)** ~ the Philippines
filipino, -a [fili'pino, a] *adj, nm/f* Philippine
film [film] (*pl* **films**) *nm* = **filme**
filmación [filma'θjon] *nf* filming, shooting
filmar [fil'mar] *vt* to film, shoot
filme ['filme] *nm* film, movie (US)
filmoteca [filmo'teka] *nf* film library
filo ['filo] *nm* (*gen*) edge; **sacar ~ a** to sharpen; **al ~ del medio día** at about midday; **de doble** ~ double-edged
filología [filolo'xia] *nf* philology
filólogo, -a [fi'loloɣo, a] *nm/f* philologist
filón [fi'lon] *nm* (*Minería*) vein, lode; (*fig*) gold mine
filoso, -a [fi'loso, a] *adj* (*Am*) sharp
filosofía [filoso'fia] *nf* philosophy
filosófico, -a [filo'sofiko, a] *adj* philosophic(al)
filósofo, -a [fi'losofo, a] *nm/f* philosopher
filtración [filtra'θjon] *nf* (*Tec*) filtration; (*Inform*) sorting; (*fig: de fondos*) misappropriation; (*de datos*) leak
filtrar [fil'trar] *vt, vi* to filter, strain; (*información*) to leak; **filtrarse** *vr* to filter;

(*fig: dinero*) to dwindle
filtro ['filtro] *nm* (*Tec, utensilio*) filter
filudo, -a [fi'luðo, a] *adj* (*Am*) sharp
fin [fin] *nm* end; (*objetivo*) aim, purpose; **a ~ de cuentas** at the end of the day; **al ~ y al cabo** when all's said and done; **a ~ de** in order to; **por ~** finally; **en ~** (*resumiendo*) in short; **¡en ~!** (*resignación*) oh, well!; **~ de archivo** (*Inform*) end-of-file; **~ de semana** weekend; **sin ~** endless(ly)
final [fi'nal] *adj* final ■ *nm* end, conclusion ■ *nf* (*Deporte*) final
finalice *etc* [fina'liθe] *vb ver* **finalizar**
finalidad [finali'ðað] *nf* finality; (*propósito*) purpose, aim
finalista [fina'lista] *nm/f* finalist
finalizar [finali'θar] *vt* to end, finish ■ *vi* to end, come to an end; **~ la sesión** (*Inform*) to log out *o* off
financiación [finanθja'θjon] *nf* financing
financiar [finan'θjar] *vt* to finance
financiero, -a [finan'θjero, a] *adj* financial ■ *nm/f* financier
financista [finan'sista] *nm/f* (*Am*) financier
finanzas [fi'nanθas] *nfpl* finances
finca ['finka] *nf* country estate
finde ['finde] *nm abbr* (*fam: = fin de semana*) weekend
fineza [fi'neθa] *nf* (*cualidad*) fineness; (*de modales*) refinement
fingir [fin'xir] *vt* (*simular*) to simulate, feign; (*pretextar*) to sham, fake ■ *vi* (*aparentar*) to pretend; **fingirse** *vr*: **fingirse dormido** to pretend to be asleep
finiquitar [finiki'tar] *vt* (*Econ: cuenta*) to settle and close
Finisterre [finis'terre] *nm*: **el cabo de ~** Cape Finisterre
finja *etc* ['finxa] *vb ver* **fingir**
finlandés, -esa [finlan'des, esa] *adj* Finnish ■ *nm/f* Finn ■ *nm* (*Ling*) Finnish
Finlandia [fin'landja] *nf* Finland
fino, -a ['fino, a] *adj* fine; (*delgado*) slender; (*de buenas maneras*) polite, refined; (*inteligente*) shrewd; (*punta*) sharp; (*gusto*) discriminating; (*oído*) sharp; (*jerez*) fino, dry ■ *nm* (*jerez*) dry sherry
finura [fi'nura] *nf* (*calidad*) fineness; (*cortesía*) politeness; (*elegancia*) elegance; (*agudeza*) shrewdness
FIP [fip] *nf abr* (*Esp*) = **Formación Intensiva Profesional**
firma ['firma] *nf* signature; (*Com*) firm, company
firmamento [firma'mento] *nm* firmament
firmante [fir'mante] *adj, nm/f* signatory; **los abajo firmantes** the undersigned
firmar [fir'mar] *vt* to sign; **~ un contrato** (*Com: colocarse*) to sign on; **firmado y sellado** signed and sealed
firme ['firme] *adj* firm; (*estable*) stable; (*sólido*) solid; (*constante*) steady; (*decidido*) resolute; (*duro*) hard; **¡firmes!** (*Mil*) attention!; **oferta en ~** (*Com*) firm offer ■ *nm* road (surface)
firmemente [firme'mente] *adv* firmly
firmeza [fir'meθa] *nf* firmness; (*constancia*) steadiness; (*solidez*) solidity
fiscal [fis'kal] *adj* fiscal ■ *nm* (*Jur*) ≈ Crown Prosecutor, ≈ Procurator Fiscal (*Escocia*), ≈ district attorney (*US*)
fiscalice *etc* [fiska'liθe] *vb ver* **fiscalizar**
fiscalizar [fiskali'θar] *vt* (*controlar*) to control; (*registrar*) to inspect (officially); (*fig*) to criticize
fisco ['fisko] *nm* (*hacienda*) treasury, exchequer; **declarar algo al ~** to declare sth for tax purposes
fisgar [fis'ɣar] *vt* to pry into
fisgón, -ona [fis'ɣon, ona] *adj* nosey
fisgue *etc* ['fisɣe] *vb ver* **fisgar**
físico, -a ['fisiko, a] *adj* physical ■ *nm* physique; (*aspecto*) appearance, looks *pl* ■ *nm/f* physicist ■ *nf* physics *sg*
fisioterapeuta [fisjotera'peuta] *nm/f* physiotherapist
fisioterapia [fisjote'rapja] *nf* physiotherapy
fisioterapista [fisjotera'pista] *nm/f* (*Am*) physiotherapist
fisonomía [fisono'mia] *nf* physiognomy, features *pl*
fisonomista [fisono'mista] *nm/f*: **ser buen ~** to have a good memory for faces
flaccidez [flakθi'ðeθ], **flacidez** [flaθi'ðeθ] *nf* softness, flabbiness
fláccido, -a ['flakθiðo, a], **flácido, -a** ['flaθiðo, a] *adj* flabby
flaco, -a ['flako, a] *adj* (*muy delgado*) skinny, thin; (*débil*) weak, feeble
flagrante [fla'ɣrante] *adj* flagrant
flamante [fla'mante] *adj* (*fam*) brilliant; (*: nuevo*) brand-new
flamear [flame'ar] *vt* (*Culin*) to flambé
flamenco, -a [fla'menko, a] *adj* (*de Flandes*) Flemish; (*baile, música*) gipsy ■ *nm/f* Fleming; **los flamencos** the Flemish ■ *nm* (*Ling*) Flemish; (*baile, música*) flamenco; (*Zool*) flamingo
flan [flan] *nm* creme caramel
flanco ['flanko] *nm* side; (*Mil*) flank
Flandes ['flandes] *nm* Flanders
flanquear [flanke'ar] *vt* to flank; (*Mil*) to outflank
flaquear [flake'ar] *vi* (*debilitarse*) to weaken; (*persona*) to slack

flaqueza [fla'keθa] *nf* (*delgadez*) thinness, leanness; (*fig*) weakness
flaquísimo, -a [fla'kisimo, a] *adj superlativo de* **flaco**
flash [flas] (*pl* **flashes**) [flas] *nm* (*Foto*) flash
flato ['flato] *nm*: **el (*o* un)** ~ the (*o* a) stitch
flauta ['flauta] (*Mus*) *nf* flute ■ *nm/f* flautist, flute player; **¡la gran ~!** (*Am*) my God!; **hijo de la gran ~** (*Am fam!*) bastard (*!*), son of a bitch (*US!*)
flecha ['fletʃa] *nf* arrow
flechazo [fle'tʃaθo] *nm* (*acción*) bowshot; (*fam*): **fue un ~** it was love at first sight
fleco ['fleko] *nm* fringe
flema ['flema] *nm* phlegm
flemático, -a [fle'matiko, a] *adj* phlegmatic; (*tono etc*) matter-of-fact
flemón [fle'mon] *nm* (*Med*) gumboil
flequillo [fle'kiʎo] *nm* (*de pelo*) fringe, bangs (*US*)
fletar [fle'tar] *vt* (*Com*) to charter; (*embarcar*) to load; (*Auto*) to lease(-purchase)
flete ['flete] *nm* (*carga*) freight; (*alquiler*) charter; (*precio*) freightage; **~ debido** (*Com*) freight forward; **~ sobre compras** (*Com*) freight inward
flexible [flek'siβle] *adj* flexible; (*individuo*) compliant
flexión [flek'sjon] *nf* (*Deporte*) bend; (*: en el suelo*) press-up
flexo ['flekso] *nm* adjustable table lamp
flipper ['fliper] *nm* pinball machine
flirtear [flirte'ar] *vi* to flirt
FLN *nm abr* (*Pol: Esp, Perú, Venezuela: = Frente de Liberación Nacional*) *political party*
flojear [floxe'ar] *vi* (*piernas: al andar*) to give way; (*alumno*) to do badly; (*cosecha, mercado*) to be poor
flojera [flo'xera] *nf* (*Am*) laziness; **me da ~** I can't be bothered
flojo, -a ['floxo, a] *adj* (*gen*) loose; (*sin fuerzas*) limp; (*débil*) weak; (*viento*) light; (*bebida*) weak; (*trabajo*) poor; (*actitud*) slack; (*precio*) low; (*Com: mercado*) dull, slack; (*Am*) lazy
flor [flor] *nf* flower; (*piropo*) compliment; **la ~ y nata de la sociedad** (*fig*) the cream of society; **en la ~ de la vida** in the prime of life; **a ~ de** on the surface of
flora ['flora] *nf* flora
florecer [flore'θer] *vi* (*Bot*) to flower, bloom; (*fig*) to flourish
floreciente [flore'θjente] *adj* (*Bot*) in flower, flowering; (*fig*) thriving
Florencia [flo'renθja] *nf* Florence
florero [flo'rero] *nm* vase
florezca *etc* [flo'reθka] *vb ver* **florecer**
florista [flo'rista] *nm/f* florist
floristería [floriste'ria] *nf* florist's (shop)
flota ['flota] *nf* fleet
flotación [flota'θjon] *nf* (*Com*) flotation
flotador [flota'ðor] *nm* (*gen*) float; (*para nadar*) rubber ring; (*de cisterna*) ballcock
flotante [flo'tante] *adj* floating; (*Inform*): **de coma ~** floating-point
flotar [flo'tar] *vi* to float
flote ['flote] *nm*: **a ~** afloat; **ponerse a ~** (*fig*) to get back on one's feet
FLS *nm abr* (*Pol: Nicaragua*) = **Frente de Liberación Sandinista**
fluctuación [fluktwa'θjon] *nf* fluctuation
fluctuante [fluk'twante] *adj* fluctuating
fluctuar [fluk'twar] *vi* (*oscilar*) to fluctuate
fluidez [flui'ðeθ] *nf* fluidity; (*fig*) fluency
fluido, -a ['flwiðo, a] *adj* fluid; (*lenguaje*) fluent; (*estilo*) smooth ■ *nm* (*líquido*) fluid
fluir [flu'ir] *vi* to flow
flujo ['fluxo] *nm* flow; (*Pol*) swing; (*Naut*) rising tide; **~ y reflujo** ebb and flow; **~ de sangre** (*Med*) haemorrhage (*Brit*), hemorrhage (*US*); **~ positivo/negativo de efectivo** (*Com*) positive/negative cash flow
flúor ['fluor] *nm* fluorine; (*en dentífrico*) fluoride
fluorescente [flwores'θente] *adj* fluorescent ■ *nm* (*tb:* **tubo fluorescente**) fluorescent tube
fluoruro [flwo'ruro] *nm* fluoride
fluvial [fluβi'al] *adj* fluvial, river *cpd*
fluyendo *etc* [flu'jendo] *vb ver* **fluir**
FM *nf abr* (*= Frecuencia Modulada*) FM
FMI *nm abr* (*= Fondo Monetario Internacional*) IMF
F.N. *nf abr* (*Esp Pol*) = **Fuerza Nueva** ■ *nm abr* = **Frente Nacional**
f.º *abr* (*= folio*) fo., fol.
foca ['foka] *nf* seal
foco ['foko] *nm* focus; (*centro*) focal point; (*fuente*) source; (*de incendio*) seat; (*Elec*) floodlight; (*Teat*) spotlight; (*Am*) (light) bulb, light
fofo, -a ['fofo, a] *adj* (*esponjoso*) soft, spongy; (*músculo*) flabby
fogata [fo'ɣata] *nf* (*hoguera*) bonfire
fogón [fo'ɣon] *nm* (*de cocina*) ring, burner
fogoso, -a [fo'ɣoso, a] *adj* spirited
foja ['foxa] *nf* (*Am*) sheet (of paper); **~ de servicios** record (file)
fol. *abr* (*= folio*) fo., fol.
folder, fólder ['folder] *nm* (*Am*) folder
folio ['foljo] *nm* folio; (*hoja*) leaf
folklore [fol'klore] *nm* folklore
folklórico, -a [fol'kloriko, a] *adj* traditional
follaje [fo'ʎaxe] *nm* foliage
follar [fo'ʎar] *vt, vi* (*fam!*) to fuck (*!*)
folletinesco, -a [foʎetin'esko, a] *adj* melodramatic

folleto [fo'ʎeto] *nm* pamphlet; (*Com*) brochure; (*prospecto*) leaflet; (*Escol etc*) handout
follón [fo'ʎon] *nm* (*fam: lío*) mess; (*: conmoción*) fuss, rumpus, shindy; **armar un ~** to kick up a fuss; **se armó un ~** there was a hell of a row
fomentar [fomen'tar] *vt* (*Med*) to foment; (*fig: promover*) to promote, foster; (*odio etc*) to stir up
fomento [fo'mento] *nm* (*fig: ayuda*) fostering; (*promoción*) promotion
fonda ['fonda] *nf* ≈ guest house; *ver tb* **hotel**
fondear [fonde'ar] *vt* (*Naut: sondear*) to sound; (*barco*) to search
fondo ['fondo] *nm* (*de caja etc*) bottom; (*medida*) depth; (*de coche, sala*) back; (*Arte etc*) background; (*reserva*) fund; (*fig: carácter*) nature; **fondos** *nmpl* (*Com*) funds, resources; **~ de escritorio** (*Inform*) wallpaper; **F~ Monetario Internacional** International Monetary Fund; **~ del mar** sea bed *o* floor; **una investigación a ~** a thorough investigation; **en el ~** at bottom, deep down; **tener buen ~** to be good-natured
fonética [fo'netika] *nf* phonetics *sg*
fono ['fono] *nm* (*Am*) telephone (number)
fonobuzón [fonoβu'θon] *nm* voice mail
fonógrafo [fo'noɣrafo] *nm* (*esp Am*) gramophone, phonograph (*US*)
fonología [fonolo'xia] *nf* phonology
fontanería [fontane'ria] *nf* plumbing
fontanero [fonta'nero] *nm* plumber
footing ['futin] *nm* jogging; **hacer ~** to jog
F.O.P. [fop] *nfpl abr* (*Esp*) = **Fuerza del Orden Público**
forajido [fora'xiðo] *nm* outlaw
foráneo, -a [fo'raneo, a] *adj* foreign ▪ *nm/f* outsider
forastero, -a [foras'tero, a] *nm/f* stranger
forcé [for'θe] *vb ver* **forzar**
forcejear [forθexe'ar] *vi* (*luchar*) to struggle
forcemos *etc* [for'θemos] *vb ver* **forzar**
fórceps ['forθeps] *nm inv* forceps *pl*
forense [fo'rense] *adj* forensic ▪ *nm/f* pathologist
forestal [fores'tal] *adj* forest *cpd*
forjar [for'xar] *vt* to forge; (*formar*) to form
forma ['forma] *nf* (*figura*) form, shape; (*molde*) mould, pattern; (*Med*) fitness; (*método*) way, means; **estar en ~** to be fit; **~ de pago** (*Com*) method of payment; **las formas** the conventions; **de ~ que ...** so that ...; **de todas formas** in any case
formación [forma'θjon] *nf* (*gen*) formation; (*enseñanza*) training; **~ profesional** vocational training; **~ fuera del trabajo** off-the-job training; **~ en el trabajo** *o* **sobre la práctica** on-the-job training
formal [for'mal] *adj* (*gen*) formal; (*fig: persona*) serious; (*: de fiar*) reliable; (*conducta*) steady
formalice *etc* [forma'liθe] *vb ver* **formalizar**
formalidad [formali'ðað] *nf* formality; seriousness; reliability; steadiness
formalizar [formali'θar] *vt* (*Jur*) to formalize; (*plan*) to draw up; (*situación*) to put in order, regularize; **formalizarse** *vr* (*situación*) to be put in order, be regularized
formar [for'mar] *vt* (*componer*) to form, shape; (*constituir*) to make up, constitute; (*Escol*) to train, educate ▪ *vi* (*Mil*) to fall in; (*Deporte*) to line up; **formarse** *vr* (*Escol*) to be trained (*o* educated); (*cobrar forma*) to form, take form; (*desarrollarse*) to develop
formatear [formate'ar] *vt* (*Inform*) to format
formateo [forma'teo] *nm* (*Inform*) formatting
formato [for'mato] *nm* (*Inform*): **sin ~** (*disco, texto*) unformatted; **~ de registro** record format
formidable [formi'ðaβle] *adj* (*temible*) formidable; (*asombroso*) tremendous
fórmula ['formula] *nf* formula
formular [formu'lar] *vt* (*queja*) to lodge; (*petición*) to draw up; (*pregunta*) to pose, formulate; (*idea*) to formulate
formulario [formu'larjo] *nm* form; **~ de solicitud/de pedido** (*Com*) application/order form; **llenar un ~** to fill in a form; **~ continuo desplegable** (*Inform*) fanfold paper
fornicar [forni'kar] *vi* to fornicate
fornido, -a [for'niðo, a] *adj* well-built
fornique *etc* [for'nike] *vb ver* **fornicar**
foro ['foro] *nm* (*gen*) forum; (*Jur*) court; **~ de discusión** (*Internet*) discussion forum
forofo, -a [fo'rofo, a] *nm/f* fan
FORPPA ['forpa] *nm abr* (*Esp*) = **Fondo de Ordenación y Regulación de Productos y Precios Agrarios**
FORPRONU [for'pronu] *nf abr* (= *Fuerza de Protección de las Naciones Unidas*) UNPROFOR
forrado, -a [fo'rraðo, a] *adj* (*ropa*) lined; (*fam*) well-heeled
forrar [fo'rrar] *vt* (*abrigo*) to line; (*libro*) to cover; (*coche*) to upholster; **forrarse** *vr* (*fam*) to line one's pockets
forro ['forro] *nm* (*de cuaderno*) cover; (*costura*) lining; (*de sillón*) upholstery; **~ polar** fleece
fortalecer [fortale'θer] *vt* to strengthen; **fortalecerse** *vr* to fortify o.s.; (*opinión etc*) to become stronger
fortaleza [forta'leθa] *nf* (*Mil*) fortress, stronghold; (*fuerza*) strength; (*determinación*) resolution

fortalezca *etc* [forta'leθka] *vb ver* **fortalecer**
fortificar [fortifi'kar] *vt* to fortify; (*fig*) to strengthen
fortifique *etc* [forti'fike] *vb ver* **fortificar**
fortísimo, -a [for'tisimo, a] *adj superlativo de* **fuerte**
fortuito, -a [for'twito, a] *adj* accidental, chance *cpd*
fortuna [for'tuna] *nf* (*suerte*) fortune, (good) luck; (*riqueza*) fortune, wealth
forzar [for'θar] *vt* (*puerta*) to force (open); (*compeler*) to compel; (*violar*) to rape; (*ojos etc*) to strain
forzoso, -a [for'θoso, a] *adj* necessary; (*inevitable*) inescapable; (*obligatorio*) compulsory
forzudo, -a [for'θuðo, a] *adj* burly
fosa ['fosa] *nf* (*sepultura*) grave; (*en tierra*) pit; (*Med*) cavity; **fosas nasales** nostrils
fosfato [fos'fato] *nm* phosphate
fosforescente [fosfores'θente] *adj* phosphorescent
fósforo ['fosforo] *nm* (*Química*) phosphorus; (*esp Am: cerilla*) match
fósil ['fosil] *adj* fossil, fossilized ■ *nm* fossil
foso ['foso] *nm* ditch; (*Teat*) pit; (*Auto*): ~ **de reconocimiento** inspection pit
foto ['foto] *nf* photo, snap(shot); **sacar una ~** to take a photo *o* picture
fotocopia [foto'kopja] *nf* photocopy
fotocopiadora [fotokopja'ðora] *nf* photocopier
fotocopiar [fotoko'pjar] *vt* to photocopy
fotogénico, -a [foto'xeniko, a] *adj* photogenic
fotografía [fotoɣra'fia] *nf* (*arte*) photography; (*una fotografía*) photograph
fotografiar [fotoɣra'fjar] *vt* to photograph
fotógrafo, -a [fo'toɣrafo, a] *nm/f* photographer
fotomatón [fotoma'ton] *nm* (*cabina*) photo booth
fotómetro [fo'tometro] *nm* (*Foto*) light meter
fotonovela [fotono'βela] *nf* photo-story
foulard [fu'lar] *nm* (head)scarf
FP *nf abr* (*Esp: Escol, Com*) = **Formación Profesional** ■ *nm abr* (*Pol*) = **Frente Popular**
FPLP *nm abr* (*Pol: = Frente Popular para la Liberación de Palestina*) PFLP
Fr. *abr* (= *Fray*) Fr.
fra. *abr* = **factura**
frac (*pl* **fracs** *o* **fraques**) [frak, 'frakes] *nm* dress coat, tails
fracasar [fraka'sar] *vi* (*gen*) to fail; (*plan etc*) to fall through
fracaso [fra'kaso] *nm* (*desgracia, revés*) failure; (*de negociaciones etc*) collapse, breakdown
fracción [frak'θjon] *nf* fraction; (*Pol*) faction, splinter group
fraccionamiento [fraksjona'mjento] *nm* (*Am*) housing estate
fractura [frak'tura] *nf* fracture, break
fragancia [fra'ɣanθja] *nf* (*olor*) fragrance, perfume
fragante [fra'ɣante] *adj* fragrant, scented
fraganti [fra'ɣanti]: **in ~** *adv*: **coger a algn in fraganti** to catch sb red-handed
fragata [fra'ɣata] *nf* frigate
frágil ['fraxil] *adj* (*débil*) fragile; (*Com*) breakable; (*fig*) frail, delicate
fragilidad [fraxili'ðað] *nf* fragility; (*de persona*) frailty
fragmento [fraɣ'mento] *nm* fragment; (*pedazo*) piece; (*de discurso*) excerpt; (*de canción*) snatch
fragor [fra'ɣor] *nm* (*ruido intenso*) din
fragua ['fraɣwa] *nf* forge
fraguar [fra'ɣwar] *vt* to forge; (*fig*) to concoct ■ *vi* to harden
fragüe *etc* ['fraɣwe] *vb ver* **fraguar**
fraile ['fraile] *nm* (*Rel*) friar; (*: monje*) monk
frambuesa [fram'bwesa] *nf* raspberry
francés, -esa [fran'θes, esa] *adj* French ■ *nm/f* Frenchman(-woman) ■ *nm* (*Ling*) French
Francia ['franθja] *nf* France
franco, -a ['franko, a] *adj* (*cándido*) frank, open; (*Com: exento*) free ■ *nm* (*moneda*) franc; ~ **de derechos** duty-free; **~ al costado del buque** (*Com*) free alongside ship; **~ puesto sobre vagón** (*Com*) free on rail; **~ a bordo** free on board
francotirador, a [frankotira'ðor, a] *nm/f* sniper
franela [fra'nela] *nf* flannel
franja ['franxa] *nf* fringe; (*de uniforme*) stripe; (*de tierra etc*) strip
franquear [franke'ar] *vt* (*camino*) to clear; (*carta, paquete*) to frank, stamp; (*obstáculo*) to overcome; (*Com etc*) to free, exempt
franqueo [fran'keo] *nm* postage
franqueza [fran'keθa] *nf* frankness
franquicia [fran'kiθja] *nf* exemption; **~ aduanera** exemption from customs duties
franquismo [fran'kismo] *nm*: **el ~** (*sistema*) the Franco system; (*período*) the Franco years; *see note*

FRANQUISMO

The political reign and style of government of Francisco Franco (from the end of the Spanish Civil War in 1939 until his death in 1975) are commonly called *franquismo*. He was a powerful, authoritarian, right-wing dictator, who promoted a traditional, Catholic and self-sufficient country. From the 1960s Spain gradually opened its doors to the international community, coinciding with a rise in economic growth and internal political opposition. On his death Spain became a democratic constitutional monarchy.

franquista [fran'kista] *adj* pro-Franco ■ *nm/f* supporter of Franco
frasco ['frasko] *nm* bottle, flask; **~ al vacio** (vacuum) flask
frase ['frase] *nf* sentence; (*locución*) phrase, expression; **~ hecha** set phrase
fraternal [frater'nal] *adj* brotherly, fraternal
fraude ['frauðe] *nm* (*cualidad*) dishonesty; (*acto*) fraud, swindle
fraudulento, -a [frauðu'lento, a] *adj* fraudulent
frazada [fra'saða] *nf* (*Am*) blanket
frecuencia [fre'kwenθja] *nf* frequency; **con ~** frequently, often; **~ de red** (*Inform*) mains frequency; **~ del reloj** (*Inform*) clock speed; **~ telefónica** voice frequency
frecuentar [frekwen'tar] *vt* (*lugar*) to frequent; (*persona*) to see frequently *o* often; **~ la buena sociedad** to mix in high society
frecuente [fre'kwente] *adj* frequent; (*costumbre*) common; (*vicio*) rife
fregadero [freɣa'ðero] *nm* (kitchen) sink
fregado, -a [fre'gaðo, a] *adj* (*Am fam!*) damn, bloody (*!*)
fregar [fre'ɣar] *vt* (*frotar*) to scrub; (*platos*) to wash (up); (*Am*) to annoy
fregón, -ona [fre'ɣon, ona] *adj* = **fregado** ■ *nf* (*utensilio*) mop; (*pey: sirvienta*) skivvy
fregué [fre'ɣe], **freguemos** *etc* [fre'ɣemos] *vb ver* **fregar**
freidora [frei'ðora] *nf* deep-fat fryer
freír [fre'ir] *vt* to fry
fréjol ['frexol] *nm* = **fríjol**
frenar [fre'nar] *vt* to brake; (*fig*) to check
frenazo [fre'naθo] *nm*: **dar un ~** to brake sharply
frenesí [frene'si] *nm* frenzy
frenético, -a [fre'netiko, a] *adj* frantic; **ponerse ~** to lose one's head
freno ['freno] *nm* (*Tec, Auto*) brake; (*de cabalgadura*) bit; (*fig*) check
frente ['frente] *nm* (*Arq, Mil, Pol*) front; (*de objeto*) front part ■ *nf* forehead, brow; **~ de batalla** battle front; **hacer ~ común con algn** to make common cause with sb; **~ a** in front of; (*en situación opuesta a*) opposite; **chocar de ~** to crash head-on; **hacer ~ a** to face up to
fresa ['fresa] *nf* (*Esp: fruta*) strawberry; (*de dentista*) drill
fresco, -a ['fresko, a] *adj* (*nuevo*) fresh; (*huevo*) newly-laid; (*frío*) cool; (*descarado*) cheeky, bad-mannered ■ *nm* (*aire*) fresh air; (*Arte*) fresco; (*Am: bebida*) fruit juice *o* drink ■ *nm/f* (*fam*) shameless person; (*persona insolente*) impudent person; **tomar el ~** to get some fresh air; **¡qué ~!** what a cheek!
frescor [fres'kor] *nm* freshness
frescura [fres'kura] *nf* freshness; (*descaro*) cheek, nerve; (*calma*) calmness
fresno ['fresno] *nm* ash (tree)
fresón [fre'son] *nm* strawberry
frialdad [frjal'dað] *nf* (*gen*) coldness; (*indiferencia*) indifference
fricción [frik'θjon] *nf* (*gen*) friction; (*acto*) rub(bing); (*Med*) massage; (*Pol, fig etc*) friction, trouble
friega *etc* ['frjeɣa], **friegue** *etc* ['frjeɣe] *vb ver* **fregar**
friendo *etc* [fri'endo] *vb ver* **freír**
frigidez [frixi'ðeθ] *nf* frigidity
frígido, -a ['frixiðo, a] *adj* frigid
frigorífico, -a [friɣo'rifiko, a] *adj* refrigerating ■ *nm* refrigerator; (*camión*) freezer lorry *o* truck (*US*); **instalación frigorífica** cold-storage plant
frijol [fri'xol], **fríjol** ['frixol] *nm* kidney bean
friki (*col*) *adj* weird (*col*); **me pasó una cosa muy ~** something really weird (*col*) happened to me; **¡qué tío más ~!** What a weirdo! (*col*) ■ *nmf* weirdo (*col*)
frió [fri'o] *vb ver* **freír**
frío, -a *etc* ['frio, a] *vb ver* **freír** ■ *adj* cold; (*fig: indiferente*) unmoved, indifferent; (*poco entusiasta*) chilly ■ *nm* cold(ness); indifference; **¡qué ~!** how cold it is!
friolento, -a [frjo'lento, a], (*Am*) **friolero, -a** [frjo'lero, a] *adj* sensitive to cold
frito, -a ['frito, a] *pp de* **freír** ■ *adj* fried ■ *nm* fry; **me trae ~ ese hombre** I'm sick and tired of that man; **fritos variados** mixed grill
frívolo, -a ['friβolo, a] *adj* frivolous
frondoso, -a [fron'doso, a] *adj* leafy
frontal [fron'tal] *nm*: **choque ~** head-on collision
frontera [fron'tera] *nf* frontier; (*línea divisoria*) border; (*zona*) frontier area
fronterizo, -a [fronte'riθo, a] *adj* frontier *cpd*; (*contiguo*) bordering
frontón [fron'ton] *nm* (*Deporte: cancha*) pelota court; (*: juego*) pelota
frotar [fro'tar] *vt* to rub; (*fósforo*) to strike;

frotarse *vr*: **frotarse las manos** to rub one's hands
frs. *abr* (*Historia*: = *francos*) fr.
fructífero, -a [fruk'tifero, a] *adj* productive, fruitful
frugal [fru'ɣal] *adj* frugal
fruncir [frun'θir] *vt* (*Costura*) to gather; (*ceño*) to frown; (*labios*) to purse
frunza *etc* ['frunθa] *vb ver* **fruncir**
frustración [frustra'θjon] *nf* frustration
frustrar [frus'trar] *vt* to frustrate; **frustrarse** *vr* to be frustrated; (*plan etc*) to fail
fruta ['fruta] *nf* fruit
frutal [fru'tal] *adj* fruit-bearing, fruit *cpd* ▪ *nm*: **(árbol) ~** fruit tree
frutería [frute'ria] *nf* fruit shop
frutero, -a [fru'tero, a] *adj* fruit *cpd* ▪ *nm/f* fruiterer ▪ *nm* fruit dish *o* bowl
frutilla [fru'tiʎa] *nf* (*Am*) strawberry
fruto ['fruto] *nm* (*Bot*) fruit; (*fig*: *resultado*) result, outcome; **frutos secos** ≈ nuts and raisins
FSLN *nm abr* (*Pol*: *Nicaragua*) = **Frente Sandinista de Liberación Nacional**
fue [fwe] *vb ver* **ser; ir**
fuego ['fweɣo] *nm* (*gen*) fire; (*Culin*: *gas*) burner, ring; (*Mil*) fire; (*fig*: *pasión*) fire, passion; **~ amigo** friendly fire; **fuegos artificiales** *o* **de artificio** fireworks; **prender ~ a** to set fire to; **a ~ lento** on a low flame *o* gas; **¡alto el ~!** cease fire!; **estar entre dos fuegos** to be in the crossfire; **¿tienes ~?** have you (got) a light?
fuelle ['fweʎe] *nm* bellows *pl*
fuel-oil [fuel'oil] *nm* paraffin (*Brit*), kerosene (*US*)
fuente ['fwente] *nf* fountain; (*manantial, fig*) spring; (*origen*) source; (*plato*) large dish; **~ de alimentación** (*Inform*) power supply; **de ~ desconocida/fidedigna** from an unknown/reliable source
fuera *etc* ['fwera] *vb ver* **ser; ir** ▪ *adv* out(side); (*en otra parte*) away; (*excepto, salvo*) except, save ▪ *prep*: **~ de** outside; (*fig*) besides; **~ de alcance** out of reach; **~ de combate** out of action; (*boxeo*) knocked out; **~ de sí** beside o. s.; **por ~** (on the) outside; **los de ~** strangers, newcomers; **estar ~** (*en el extranjero*) to be abroad
fuera-borda [fwera'βorða] *nm inv* outboard engine *o* motor
fuerce *etc* ['fwerθe] *vb ver* **forzar**
fuereño, -a [fwe'reɲo, a] *nm/f* (*Am*) outsider
fuero ['fwero] *nm* (*carta municipal*) municipal charter; (*leyes locales*) local *o* regional law code; (*privilegio*) privilege; (*autoridad*) jurisdiction; (*fig*): **en mi** *etc* **~ interno ...** in my *etc* heart of hearts ..., deep down ...
fuerte ['fwerte] *adj* strong; (*golpe*) hard; (*ruido*) loud; (*comida*) rich; (*lluvia*) heavy; (*dolor*) intense ▪ *adv* strongly; hard; loud(ly) ▪ *nm* (*Mil*) fort, strongpoint; (*fig*): **el canto no es mi ~** singing is not my strong point
fuerza *etc* ['fwerθa] *vb ver* **forzar** ▪ *nf* (*fortaleza*) strength; (*Tec, Elec*) power; (*coacción*) force; (*violencia*) violence; (*Mil*: *tb*: **fuerzas**) forces *pl*; **~ de arrastre** (*Tec*) pulling power; **~ de brazos** manpower; **~ mayor** force majeure; **~ bruta** brute force; **F~ Armadas (FF.AA.)** armed forces; **F~ del Orden Público (F.O.P.)** police (forces); **~ vital** vitality; **a ~ de** by (dint of); **cobrar ~s** to recover one's strength; **tener ~s para** to have the strength to; **hacer algo a la ~** to be forced to do sth; **con ~ legal** (*Com*) legally binding; **a la ~, por ~** of necessity; **~ de voluntad** willpower
fuete ['fwete] *nm* (*Am*) whip
fuga ['fuɣa] *nf* (*huida*) flight, escape; (*de enamorados*) elopement; (*de gas etc*) leak; **~ de cerebros** (*fig*) brain drain
fugarse [fu'ɣarse] *vr* to flee, escape
fugaz [fu'ɣaθ] *adj* fleeting
fugitivo, -a [fuxi'tiβo, a] *adj* fugitive, fleeing ▪ *nm/f* fugitive
fugue *etc* ['fuɣe] *vb ver* **fugarse**
fui *etc* [fwi] *vb ver* **ser; ir**
fulano, -a [fu'lano, a] *nm/f* so-and-so, what's-his-name/what's-her-name
fulgor [ful'ɣor] *nm* brilliance
fulminante [fulmi'nante] *adj* (*pólvora*) fulminating; (*fig*: *mirada*) withering; (*Med*) fulminant; (*fam*) terrific, tremendous
fulminar [fulmi'nar] *vt*: **caer fulminado por un rayo** to be struck down by lightning; **~ a algn con la mirada** to look daggers at sb
fumador, a [fuma'ðor, a] *nm/f* smoker; **no ~** non-smoker
fumar [fu'mar] *vt, vi* to smoke; **fumarse** *vr* (*disipar*) to squander; **~ en pipa** to smoke a pipe
fumigar [fumi'ɣar] *vt* to fumigate
funámbulo, -a [fu'nambulo, a], **funambulista** [funambu'lista] *nm/f* tightrope walker
función [fun'θjon] *nf* function; (*de puesto*) duties *pl*; (*Teat etc*) show; **entrar en funciones** to take up one's duties; **~ de tarde/de noche** matinée/evening performance
funcional [funθjo'nal] *adj* functional
funcionamiento [funθjona'mjento] *nm* functioning; (*Tec*) working; **en ~** (*Com*) on stream; **entrar en ~** to come into operation

funcionar [funθjo'nar] *vi* (*gen*) to function; (*máquina*) to work; **"no funciona"** "out of order"
funcionario, -a [funθjo'narjo, a] *nm/f* official; (*público*) civil servant
funda ['funda] *nf* (*gen*) cover; (*de almohada*) pillowcase; **~ protectora del disco** (*Inform*) disk-jacket
fundación [funda'θjon] *nf* foundation
fundado, -a [fun'daðo, a] *adj* (*justificado*) well-founded
fundamental [fundamen'tal] *adj* fundamental, basic
fundamentalismo [fundamenta'lismo] *nm* fundamentalism
fundamentalista [fundamenta'lista] *adj, nm/f* fundamentalist
fundamentar [fundamen'tar] *vt* (*poner base*) to lay the foundations of; (*establecer*) to found; (*fig*) to base
fundamento [funda'mento] *nm* (*base*) foundation; (*razón*) grounds *pl*; **eso carece de ~** that is groundless
fundar [fun'dar] *vt* to found; (*crear*) to set up; (*fig: basar*): **~ (en)** to base *o* found (on); **fundarse** *vr*: **fundarse en** to be founded on
fundición [fundi'θjon] *nf* (*acción*) smelting; (*fábrica*) foundry; (*Tip*) fount (*Brit*), font
fundir [fun'dir] *vt* (*gen*) to fuse; (*metal*) to smelt, melt down; (*Com*) to merge; (*estatua*) to cast; **fundirse** *vr* (*colores etc*) to merge, blend; (*unirse*) to fuse together; (*Elec: fusible, lámpara etc*) to blow; (*nieve etc*) to melt
fúnebre ['funeβre] *adj* funeral *cpd*, funereal
funeral [fune'ral] *nm* funeral
funeraria [fune'rarja] *nf* undertaker's (*Brit*), mortician's (*US*)
funesto, -a [fu'nesto, a] *adj* ill-fated; (*desastroso*) fatal
fungir [fun'xir] *vi*: **~ de** (*Am*) to act as
furgón [fur'ɣon] *nm* wagon
furgoneta [furɣo'neta] *nf* (*Auto, Com*) (transit) van (*Brit*), pickup (truck) (*US*)
furia ['furja] *nf* (*ira*) fury; (*violencia*) violence
furibundo, -a [furi'βundo, a] *adj* furious
furioso, -a [fu'rjoso, a] *adj* (*iracundo*) furious; (*violento*) violent
furor [fu'ror] *nm* (*cólera*) rage; (*pasión*) frenzy, passion; **hacer ~** to be a sensation
furtivo, -a [fur'tiβo, a] *adj* furtive ■ *nm* poacher
furúnculo [fu'runkulo] *nm* (*Med*) boil
fuselaje [fuse'laxe] *nm* fuselage
fusible [fu'siβle] *nm* fuse
fusil [fu'sil] *nm* rifle
fusilamiento [fusila'mjento] *nm* (*Jur*) execution by firing squad
fusilar [fusi'lar] *vt* to shoot
fusión [fu'sjon] *nf* (*gen*) melting; (*unión*) fusion; (*Com*) merger, amalgamation
fusionar [fusjo'nar] *vt* to fuse (together); (*Com*) to merge; **fusionarse** *vr* (*Com*) to merge, amalgamate
fusta ['fusta] *nf* (*látigo*) riding crop
fútbol ['futβol] *nm* football
futbolín [futβo'lin] *nm* table football
futbolista [futβo'lista] *nm/f* footballer
fútil ['futil] *adj* trifling
futilidad [futili'ðað], **futileza** [futi'leθa] *nf* triviality
futón [fu'ton] *nm* futon
futuro, -a [fu'turo, a] *adj* future ■ *nm* future; (*Ling*) future tense; **futuros** *nmpl* (*Com*) futures

Gg

G, g [xe] *nf* (*letra*) G, g; **G de Gerona** G for George
gabacho, -a [ga'βatʃo, a] *adj* Pyrenean; (*fam*) Frenchified ■ *nm/f* Pyrenean villager; (*fam*) Frenchy
gabán [ga'βan] *nm* overcoat
gabardina [gaβar'ðina] *nf* (*tela*) gabardine; (*prenda*) raincoat
gabinete [gaβi'nete] *nm* (*Pol*) cabinet; (*estudio*) study; (*de abogados etc*) office; ~ **de consulta/de lectura** consulting/reading room
gacela [ga'θela] *nf* gazelle
gaceta [ga'θeta] *nf* gazette
gacetilla [gaθe'tiʎa] *nf* (*en periódico*) news in brief; (*de personalidades*) gossip column
gachas ['gatʃas] *nfpl* porridge *sg*
gacho, -a ['gatʃo, a] *adj* (*encorvado*) bent down; (*orejas*) drooping
gaditano, -a [gaði'tano, a] *adj* of *o* from Cadiz ■ *nm/f* native *o* inhabitant of Cadiz
gaélico, -a [ga'eliko, a] *adj* Gaelic ■ *nm/f* Gael ■ *nm* (*Ling*) Gaelic
gafar [ga'far] *vt* (*fam: traer mala suerte*) to put a jinx on
gafas ['gafas] *nfpl* glasses; ~ **oscuras** dark glasses; ~ **de sol** sunglasses
gafe ['gafe] *adj*: **ser** ~ to be jinxed ■ *nm* (*fam*) jinx
gaita ['gaita] *nf* flute; (*tb:* **gaita gallega**) bagpipes *pl*; (*dificultad*) bother; (*cosa engorrosa*) tough job
gajes ['gaxes] *nmpl* (*salario*) pay *sg*; **los ~ del oficio** occupational hazards; ~ **y emolumentos** perquisites
gajo ['gaxo] *nm* (*gen*) bunch; (*de árbol*) bough; (*de naranja*) segment
gala ['gala] *nf* full dress; (*fig: lo mejor*) cream, flower; **galas** *nfpl* finery *sg*; **estar de** ~ to be in one's best clothes; **hacer ~ de** to display, show off; **tener algo a** ~ to be proud of sth
galaico, -a [ga'laiko, a] *adj* Galician
galán [ga'lan] *nm* lover, gallant; (*hombre atractivo*) ladies' man; (*Teat*): **primer** ~ leading man
galante [ga'lante] *adj* gallant; (*atento*) charming; (*cortés*) polite
galantear [galante'ar] *vt* (*hacer la corte a*) to court, woo
galanteo [galan'teo] *nm* (*coqueteo*) flirting; (*de pretendiente*) wooing
galantería [galante'ria] *nf* (*caballerosidad*) gallantry; (*cumplido*) politeness; (*piropo*) compliment
galápago [ga'lapaɣo] *nm* (*Zool*) freshwater tortoise
galardón [galar'ðon] *nm* award, prize
galardonar [galarðo'nar] *vt* (*premiar*) to reward; (*una obra*) to award a prize for
galaxia [ga'laksja] *nf* galaxy
galbana [gal'βana] *nf* (*pereza*) sloth, laziness
galeote [gale'ote] *nm* galley slave
galera [ga'lera] *nf* (*nave*) galley; (*carro*) wagon; (*Med*) hospital ward; (*Tip*) galley
galería [gale'ria] *nf* (*gen*) gallery; (*balcón*) veranda(h); (*de casa*) corridor; (*fam: público*) audience; ~ **secreta** secret passage
Gales ['gales] *nm*: **(el País de)** ~ Wales
galés, -esa [ga'les, esa] *adj* Welsh ■ *nm/f* Welshman(-woman) ■ *nm* (*Ling*) Welsh
galgo, -a ['galɣo, a] *nm/f* greyhound
Galia ['galja] *nf* Gaul
Galicia [ga'liθja] *nf* Galicia
galicismo [gali'θismo] *nm* gallicism
Galilea [gali'lea] *nf* Galilee
galimatías [galima'tias] *nm inv* (*asunto*) rigmarole; (*lenguaje*) gibberish, nonsense
gallardía [gaʎar'ðia] *nf* (*galantería*) dash; (*gracia*) gracefulness; (*valor*) bravery; (*elegancia*) elegance; (*nobleza*) nobleness
gallego, -a [ga'ʎeɣo, a] *adj* Galician; (*Am pey*) Spanish ■ *nm/f* Galician; (*Am pey*) Spaniard ■ *nm* (*Ling*) Galician; *ver tb* **Lengua**
galleta [ga'ʎeta] *nf* biscuit; (*fam: bofetada*) whack, slap
gallina [ga'ʎina] *nf* hen ■ *nm* (*fam*) coward; ~ **ciega** blind man's buff; ~ **llueca** broody hen

gallinazo [gaʎi'naso] *nm* (*Am*) turkey buzzard
gallinero [gaʎi'nero] *nm* (*criadero*) henhouse; (*Teat*) gods *sg*, top gallery; (*voces*) hubbub
gallo ['gaʎo] *nm* cock, rooster; (*Mus*) false *o* wrong note; (*cambio de voz*) break in the voice; **en menos que canta un ~** in an instant
galo, -a ['galo, a] *adj* Gallic; (*= francés*) French ■ *nm/f* Gaul
galón [ga'lon] *nm* (*Costura*) braid; (*Mil*) stripe; (*medida*) gallon
galopante [galo'pante] *adj* galloping
galopar [galo'par] *vi* to gallop
galope [ga'lope] *nm* gallop; **al ~** (*fig*) in great haste; **a ~ tendido** at full gallop
galvanice *etc* [galβa'niθe] *vb ver* **galvanizar**
galvanizar [galβani'θar] *vt* to galvanize
gama ['gama] *nf* (*Mus*) scale; (*fig*) range; (*Zool*) doe
gamba ['gamba] *nf* prawn
gamberrada [gambe'rraða] *nf* act of hooliganism
gamberro, -a [gam'berro, a] *nm/f* hooligan, lout
gamo ['gamo] *nm* (*Zool*) buck
gamuza [ga'muθa] *nf* chamois; (*bayeta*) duster; (*Am: piel*) suede
gana ['gana] *nf* (*deseo*) desire, wish; (*apetito*) appetite; (*voluntad*) will; (*añoranza*) longing; **de buena ~** willingly; **de mala ~** reluctantly; **me dan ganas de** I feel like, I want to; **tener ganas de** to feel like; **no me da la (real) ~** I don't (damned well) want to; **son ganas de molestar** they're just trying to be awkward
ganadería [ganaðe'ria] *nf* (*ganado*) livestock; (*ganado vacuno*) cattle *pl*; (*cría, comercio*) cattle raising
ganadero, -a [gana'ðero, a] *adj* stock *cpd* ■ *nm* stockman
ganado [ga'naðo] *nm* livestock; **~ caballar/cabrío** horses *pl*/goats *pl*; **~ lanar** *u* **ovejuno** sheep *pl*; **~ porcino/vacuno** pigs *pl*/cattle *pl*
ganador, -a [gana'ðor, a] *adj* winning ■ *nm/f* winner; (*Econ*) earner
ganancia [ga'nanθja] *nf* (*lo ganado*) gain; (*aumento*) increase; (*beneficio*) profit; **ganancias** *nfpl* (*ingresos*) earnings; (*beneficios*) profit *sg*, winnings; **ganancias y pérdidas** profit and loss; **~ bruta/líquida** gross/net profit; **ganancias de capital** capital gains; **sacar ~ de** to draw profit from
ganapán [gana'pan] *nm* (*obrero casual*) odd-job man; (*individuo tosco*) lout
ganar [ga'nar] *vt* (*obtener*) to get, obtain; (*sacar ventaja*) to gain; (*Com*) to earn; (*Deporte, premio*) to win; (*derrotar*) to beat; (*alcanzar*) to reach; (*Mil: objetivo*) to take; (*apoyo*) to gain, win ■ *vi* (*Deporte*) to win; **ganarse** *vr*: **ganarse la vida** to earn one's living; **se lo ha ganado** he deserves it; **~ tiempo** to gain time
ganchillo [gan'tʃiʎo] *nm* (*para croché*) crochet hook; (*arte*) crochet work
gancho ['gantʃo] *nm* (*gen*) hook; (*colgador*) hanger; (*pey: revendedor*) tout; (*fam: atractivo*) sex appeal; (*Boxeo: golpe*) hook
gandul, -a [gan'dul, a] *adj, nm/f* good-for-nothing
ganga ['ganga] *nf* (*cosa*) bargain; (*chollo*) cushy job
Ganges ['ganxes] *nm*: **el (Río) ~** the Ganges
ganglio ['gangljo] *nm* (*Anat*) ganglion; (*Med*) swelling
gangrena [gan'grena] *nf* gangrene
gansada [gan'saða] *nf* (*fam*) stupid thing (to do)
ganso, -a ['ganso, a] *nm/f* (*Zool*) gander/goose; (*fam*) idiot
Gante ['gante] *nm* Ghent
ganzúa [gan'θua] *nf* skeleton key ■ *nm/f* burglar
gañán [ga'ɲan] *nm* farmhand, farm labourer
garabatear [garaβate'ar] *vt* to scribble, scrawl
garabato [gara'βato] *nm* (*gancho*) hook; (*garfio*) grappling iron; (*escritura*) scrawl, scribble; (*fam*) sex appeal
garaje [ga'raxe] *nm* garage
garante [ga'rante] *adj* responsible ■ *nm/f* guarantor
garantía [garan'tia] *nf* guarantee; (*seguridad*) pledge; (*compromiso*) undertaking; (*Jur: caución*) warranty; **de máxima ~** absolutely guaranteed; **~ de trabajo** job security
garantice *etc* [garan'tiθe] *vb ver* **garantizar**
garantizar [garanti'θar] *vt* (*hacerse responsable de*) to vouch for; (*asegurar*) to guarantee
garbanzo [gar'βanθo] *nm* chickpea
garbeo [gar'βeo] *nm*: **darse un ~** to go for a walk
garbo ['garβo] *nm* grace, elegance; (*desenvoltura*) jauntiness; (*de mujer*) glamour; **andar con ~** to walk gracefully
garboso, -a [gar'βoso, a] *adj* graceful, elegant
garete [ga'rete] *nm*: **irse al ~** to go to the dogs
garfio ['garfjo] *nm* grappling iron; (*gancho*) hook; (*Alpinismo*) climbing iron
gargajo [gar'ɣaxo] *nm* phlegm, sputum
garganta [gar'ɣanta] *nf* (*interna*) throat; (*externa, de botella*) neck; (*Geo: barranco*) ravine; (*desfiladero*) narrow pass
gargantilla [garɣan'tiʎa] *nf* necklace
gárgara ['garɣara] *nf* gargle, gargling; **hacer gárgaras** to gargle; **¡vete a hacer gárgaras!** (*fam*) go to blazes!

gárgola ['garɣola] *nf* gargoyle
garita [ga'rita] *nf* cabin, hut; (*Mil*) sentry box; (*puesto de vigilancia*) lookout post
garito [ga'rito] *nm* (*lugar*) gaming house *o* den
garra ['garra] *nf* (*de gato, Tec*) claw; (*de ave*) talon; (*fam*) hand, paw; (*fig: de canción etc*) bite; **caer en las garras de algn** to fall into sb's clutches
garrafa [ga'rrafa] *nf* carafe, decanter
garrafal [garra'fal] *adj* enormous, terrific; (*error*) terrible
garrapata [garra'pata] *nf* (*Zool*) tick
garrotazo [garro'taθo] *nm* blow with a stick *o* club
garrote [ga'rrote] *nm* (*palo*) stick; (*porra*) club, cudgel; (*suplicio*) garrotte
garza ['garθa] *nf* heron
gas [gas] *nm* gas; (*vapores*) fumes *pl*; **gases de escape** exhaust (fumes)
gasa ['gasa] *nf* gauze; (*de pañal*) nappy liner
gaseoso, -a [gase'oso, a] *adj* gassy, fizzy ■ *nf* lemonade, pop (*fam*)
gasoducto [gaso'ðukto] *nm* gas pipeline
gasoil [ga'soil], **gasóleo** [ga'soleo] *nm* diesel (oil)
gasolina [gaso'lina] *nf* petrol, gas(oline) (*US*); **~ sin plomo** unleaded petrol
gasolinera [gasoli'nera] *nf* petrol (*Brit*) *o* gas (*US*) station
gastado, -a [gas'taðo, a] *adj* (*ropa*) worn out; (*usado: frase etc*) trite
gastar [gas'tar] *vt* (*dinero, tiempo*) to spend; (*consumir*) to use (up), consume; (*desperdiciar*) to waste; (*llevar*) to wear; **gastarse** *vr* to wear out; (*terminarse*) to run out; (*estropearse*) to waste; **~ bromas** to crack jokes; **¿qué número gastas?** what size (shoe) do you take?
gasto ['gasto] *nm* (*desembolso*) expenditure, spending; (*cantidad gastada*) outlay, expense; (*consumo, uso*) use; (*desgaste*) waste; **gastos** *nmpl* (*desembolsos*) expenses; (*cargos*) charges, costs; **~ corriente** (*Com*) revenue expenditure; **~ fijo** (*Com*) fixed charge; **gastos bancarios** bank charges; **gastos corrientes** running expenses; **gastos de distribución** (*Com*) distribution costs; **gastos generales** overheads; **gastos de mantenimiento** maintenance expenses; **gastos operacionales** operating costs; **gastos de tramitación** (*Com*) handling charge *sg*; **gastos vencidos** (*Com*) accrued charges; **cubrir gastos** to cover expenses; **meterse en gastos** to incur expense
gastronomía [gastrono'mia] *nf* gastronomy
gata ['gata] *nf* (*Zool*) she-cat; **andar a gatas** to go on all fours
gatear [gate'ar] *vi* to go on all fours
gatillo [ga'tiʎo] *nm* (*de arma de fuego*) trigger; (*de dentista*) forceps
gato ['gato] *nm* (*Zool*) cat; (*Tec*) jack; **~ de Angora** Angora cat; **~ montés** wildcat; **dar a algn ~ por liebre** to take sb in; **aquí hay ~ encerrado** there's something fishy here
GATT [gat] *sigla m* (= *Acuerdo General sobre Aranceles Aduaneros y Comercio*) GATT
gatuno, -a [ga'tuno, a] *adj* feline
gaucho, -a ['gautʃo, a] *adj, nm/f* gaucho
gaveta [ga'βeta] *nf* drawer
gavilán [gaβi'lan] *nm* sparrowhawk
gavilla [ga'βiʎa] *nf* sheaf
gaviota [ga'βjota] *nf* seagull
gay [ge] *adj, nm* gay, homosexual
gazapo [ga'θapo] *nm* young rabbit
gaznate [gaθ'nate] *nm* (*pescuezo*) gullet; (*garganta*) windpipe
gazpacho [gaθ'patʃo] *nm* gazpacho
gel [xel] *nm* gel
gelatina [xela'tina] *nf* jelly; (*polvos etc*) gelatine
gema ['xema] *nf* gem
gemelo, -a [xe'melo, a] *adj, nm/f* twin; **gemelos** *nmpl* (*de camisa*) cufflinks; **gemelos de campo** field glasses, binoculars; **gemelos de teatro** opera glasses
gemido [xe'miðo] *nm* (*quejido*) moan, groan; (*lamento*) wail, howl
Géminis ['xeminis] *nm* (*Astro*) Gemini
gemir [xe'mir] *vi* (*quejarse*) to moan, groan; (*animal*) to whine; (*viento*) to howl
gen [xen] *nm* gene
gen. *abr* (*Ling*) = **género**; **genitivo**
gendarme [xen'darme] *nm* (*Am*) policeman
genealogía [xenealo'xia] *nf* genealogy
generación [xenera'θjon] *nf* generation; **primera/segunda/tercera/cuarta ~** (*Inform*) first/second/third/fourth generation
generado, -a [xene'raðo, a] *adj* (*Inform*): **~ por ordenador** computer generated
generador [xenera'ðor] *nm* generator; **~ de programas** (*Inform*) program generator
general [xene'ral] *adj* general; (*común*) common; (*pey: corriente*) rife; (*frecuente*) usual ■ *nm* general; **~ de brigada/de división** brigadier-/major-general; **por lo** *o* **en ~** in general
generalice *etc* [xenera'liθe] *vb ver* **generalizar**
generalidad [xenerali'ðað] *nf* generality
Generalitat [jenerali'tat] *nf regional government of Catalonia*; **~ Valenciana** *regional government of Valencia*
generalización [xeneraliθa'θjon] *nf* generalization
generalizar [xenerali'θar] *vt* to generalize;

generalizarse *vr* to become generalized, spread; (*difundirse*) to become widely known
generalmente [xeneral'mente] *adv* generally
generar [xene'rar] *vt* to generate
genérico, -a [xe'neriko, a] *adj* generic
género ['xenero] *nm* (*clase*) kind, sort; (*tipo*) type; (*Bio*) genus; (*Ling*) gender; (*Com*) material; **géneros** *nmpl* (*productos*) goods; **~ humano** human race; **~ chico** (*zarzuela*) Spanish operetta; **géneros de punto** knitwear *sg*
generosidad [xenerosi'ðað] *nf* generosity
generoso, -a [xene'roso, a] *adj* generous
genético, -a [xe'netiko, a] *adj* genetic ■ *nf* genetics *sg*
genial [xe'njal] *adj* inspired; (*idea*) brilliant; (*afable*) genial
genialidad [xenjali'ðað] *nf* (*singularidad*) genius; (*acto genial*) stroke of genius; **es una ~ suya** it's one of his brilliant ideas
genio ['xenjo] *nm* (*carácter*) nature, disposition; (*humor*) temper; (*facultad creadora*) genius; **mal ~** bad temper; **~ vivo** quick *o* hot temper; **de mal ~** bad-tempered
genital [xeni'tal] *adj* genital ■ *nm*: **genitales** genitals, genital organs
genitivo [xeni'tiβo] *nm* (*Ling*) genitive
genocidio [xeno'θiðjo] *nm* genocide
Génova ['xenoβa] *nf* Genoa
genovés, -esa [xeno'βes, esa] *adj, nm/f* Genoese
gente ['xente] *nf* (*personas*) people *pl*; (*raza*) race; (*nación*) nation; (*parientes*) relatives *pl*; **~ bien/baja** posh/lower-class people *pl*; **~ menuda** (*niños*) children *pl*; **es buena ~** (*fam: esp Am*) he's a good sort; **una ~ como Vd** (*Am*) a person like you
gentil [xen'til] *adj* (*elegante*) graceful; (*encantador*) charming; (*Rel*) gentile
gentileza [xenti'leθa] *nf* grace; charm; (*cortesía*) courtesy; **por ~ de** by courtesy of
gentilicio, -a [xenti'liθjo, a] *adj* (*familiar*) family *cpd*
gentío [xen'tio] *nm* crowd, throng
gentuza [xen'tuθa] *nf* (*pey: plebe*) rabble; (*: chusma*) riffraff
genuflexión [xenuflek'sjon] *nf* genuflexion
genuino, -a [xe'nwino, a] *adj* genuine
GEO ['xeo] *nmpl abr* (*Esp: = Grupos Especiales de Operaciones*) *Special Police Units used in anti-terrorist operations etc*
geografía [xeoɣra'fia] *nf* geography
geográfico, -a [xeo'ɣrafiko, a] *adj* geographic(al)
geología [xeolo'xia] *nf* geology
geólogo, -a [xe'oloɣo, a] *nm/f* geologist
geometría [xeome'tria] *nf* geometry
geométrico, -a [xeo'metriko, a] *adj* geometric(al)
Georgia [xe'orxja] *nf* Georgia
georgiano, -a [xeor'xjano, a] *adj, nm/f* Georgian ■ *nm* (*Ling*) Georgian
geranio [xe'ranjo] *nm* (*Bot*) geranium
gerencia [xe'renθja] *nf* management; (*cargo*) post of manager; (*oficina*) manager's office
gerente [xe'rente] *nm/f* (*supervisor*) manager; (*jefe*) director
geriatría [xerja'tria] *nf* (*Med*) geriatrics *sg*
geriátrico, -a [xer'jatriko, a] *adj* geriatric
germano, -a [xer'mano, a] *adj* German, Germanic ■ *nm/f* German
germen ['xermen] *nm* germ
germinar [xermi'nar] *vi* to germinate; (*brotar*) to sprout
gerundense [xerun'dense] *adj* of *o* from Gerona ■ *nm/f* native *o* inhabitant of Gerona
gerundio [xe'rundjo] *nm* (*Ling*) gerund
gestación [xesta'θjon] *nf* gestation
gesticulación [xestikula'θjon] *nf* (*ademán*) gesticulation; (*mueca*) grimace
gesticular [xestiku'lar] *vi* (*con ademanes*) to gesture; (*con muecas*) to make faces
gestión [xes'tjon] *nf* management; (*diligencia, acción*) negotiation; **hacer las gestiones preliminares** to do the groundwork; **~ de cartera** (*Com*) portfolio management; **~ financiera** (*Com*) financial management; **~ interna** (*Inform*) housekeeping; **~ de personal** personnel management; **~ de riesgos** (*Com*) risk management
gestionar [xestjo'nar] *vt* (*tratar de arreglar*) to try to arrange; (*llevar*) to manage
gesto ['xesto] *nm* (*mueca*) grimace; (*ademán*) gesture; **hacer gestos** to make faces
gestor, a [xes'tor, a] *adj* managing ■ *nm/f* manager; (*promotor*) promoter; (*agente*) business agent
gestoría [xesto'ria] *nf agency undertaking business with government departments, insurance companies etc*
Gibraltar [xiβral'tar] *nm* Gibraltar
gibraltareño, -a [xiβralta'reɲo, a] *adj* of *o* from Gibraltar ■ *nm/f* native *o* inhabitant of Gibraltar
gigante [xi'ɣante] *adj, nm/f* giant
gijonés, -esa [xixo'nes, esa] *adj* of *o* from Gijón ■ *nm/f* native *o* inhabitant of Gijón
gilipollas [xili'poʎas] (*fam*) *adj inv* daft ■ *nm/f* berk
gilipollez [xilipo'ʎez] *nf* (*fam*): **es una ~** that's a load of crap (*!*); **decir gilipolleces** to talk crap (*!*)
gima *etc* ['xima] *vb ver* **gemir**

gimnasia [xim'nasja] *nf* gymnastics *pl*; **confundir la ~ con la magnesia** to get things mixed up
gimnasio [xim'nasjo] *nm* gym(nasium)
gimnasta [xim'nasta] *nm/f* gymnast
gimotear [ximote'ar] *vi* to whine, whimper; *(lloriquear)* to snivel
Ginebra [xi'neβra] *n* Geneva
ginebra [xi'neβra] *nf* gin
ginecología [xinekolo'xia] *nf* gyn(a)ecology
ginecológico, -a [xineko'loxiko, a] *adj* gyn(a)ecological
ginecólogo, -a [xine'koloɣo, a] *nm/f* gyn(a)ecologist
gira ['xira] *nf* tour, trip
girar [xi'rar] *vt* *(dar la vuelta)* to turn (around); (: *rápidamente)* to spin; *(Com: giro postal)* to draw; *(comerciar: letra de cambio)* to issue ■ *vi* to turn (round); *(dar vueltas)* to rotate; *(rápido)* to spin; **la conversación giraba en torno a las elecciones** the conversation centred on the election; **~ en descubierto** to overdraw
giratorio, -a [xira'torjo, a] *adj* *(gen)* revolving; *(puente)* swing *cpd*; *(silla)* swivel *cpd*
giro ['xiro] *nm* *(movimiento)* turn, revolution; *(Ling)* expression; *(Com)* draft; *(de sucesos)* trend, course; **~ bancario** money order, bank giro; **~ de existencias** *(Com)* stock turnover; **~ postal** postal order
gis [xis] *nm* *(Am)* chalk
gitano, -a [xi'tano, a] *adj, nm/f* gypsy
glacial [gla'θjal] *adj* icy, freezing
glaciar [gla'θjar] *nm* glacier
glándula ['glandula] *nf* *(Anat, Bot)* gland
glicerina [gliθe'rina] *nf* *(Tec)* glycerin(e)
global [glo'βal] *adj* *(en conjunto)* global; *(completo)* total; *(investigación)* full; *(suma)* lump *cpd*
globalización [gloβaliθa'θjon] *nf* globalization
globo ['gloβo] *nm* *(esfera)* globe, sphere; *(aeróstato, juguete)* balloon
glóbulo ['gloβulo] *nm* globule; *(Anat)* corpuscle; **~ blanco/rojo** white/red corpuscle
gloria ['glorja] *nf* glory; *(fig)* delight; *(delicia)* bliss
glorieta [glo'rjeta] *nf* *(de jardín)* bower, arbour, arbor *(US)*; *(Auto)* roundabout *(Brit)*, traffic circle *(US)*; *(plaza redonda)* circus; *(cruce)* junction
glorificar [glorifi'kar] *vt* *(enaltecer)* to glorify, praise
glorifique *etc* [glori'fike] *vb ver* **glorificar**
glorioso, -a [glo'rjoso, a] *adj* glorious
glosa ['glosa] *nf* comment; *(explicación)* gloss
glosar [glo'sar] *vt* *(comentar)* to comment on
glosario [glo'sarjo] *nm* glossary
glotón, -ona [glo'ton, ona] *adj* gluttonous, greedy ■ *nm/f* glutton
glotonería [glotone'ria] *nf* gluttony, greed
glúteo ['gluteo] *nm* *(fam: nalga)* buttock
G.N. *abr* *(Nicaragua, Panama: = Guardia Nacional)* police
gnomo ['nomo] *nm* gnome
gobernación [goβerna'θjon] *nf* government, governing; *(Pol)* Provincial Governor's office; **Ministro de la G~** Minister of the Interior, Home Secretary *(Brit)*
gobernador, -a [goβerna'ðor, a] *adj* governing ■ *nm/f* governor
gobernanta [goβer'nanta] *nf* *(esp Am: niñera)* governess
gobernante [goβer'nante] *adj* governing ■ *nm* ruler, governor ■ *nf* *(en hotel etc)* housekeeper
gobernar [goβer'nar] *vt* *(dirigir)* to guide, direct; *(Pol)* to rule, govern ■ *vi* to govern; *(Naut)* to steer; **~ mal** to misgovern
gobierno *etc* [go'βjerno] *vb ver* **gobernar** ■ *nm* *(Pol)* government; *(gestión)* management; *(dirección)* guidance, direction; *(Naut)* steering; *(puesto)* governorship
goce *etc* ['goθe] *vb ver* **gozar** ■ *nm* enjoyment
godo, -a ['goðo, a] *nm/f* Goth; *(Am pey)* Spaniard
gol [gol] *nm* goal
golear [gole'ar] *vt* *(marcar)* to score a goal against
golf [golf] *nm* golf
golfo, -a ['golfo, a] *nm/f* *(pilluelo)* street urchin; *(vagabundo)* tramp; *(gorrón)* loafer; *(gamberro)* lout ■ *nm* *(Geo)* gulf ■ *nf* *(fam: prostituta)* slut, whore, hooker *(US)*
golondrina [golon'drina] *nf* swallow
golosina [golo'sina] *nf* titbit; *(dulce)* sweet
goloso, -a [go'loso, a] *adj* sweet-toothed; *(fam: glotón)* greedy
golpe ['golpe] *nm* blow; *(de puño)* punch; *(de mano)* smack; *(de remo)* stroke; *(Fútbol)* kick; *(Tenis etc)* hit, shot; *(mala suerte)* misfortune; *(fam: atraco)* job, heist *(US)*; *(fig: choque)* clash; **no dar ~** to be bone idle; **de un ~** with one blow; **de ~** suddenly; **~ (de estado)** coup (d'état); **~ de gracia** coup de grâce *(tb fig)*; **~ de fortuna/maestro** stroke of luck/genius; **cerrar una puerta de ~** to slam a door
golpear [golpe'ar] *vt, vi* to strike, knock; *(asestar)* to beat; *(de puño)* to punch; *(golpetear)* to tap; *(mesa)* to bang
golpista [gol'pista] *adj*: **intentona ~** coup attempt ■ *nm/f* participant in a coup (d'état)
golpiza [gol'pisa] *nf*: **dar una ~ a algn** *(Am)* to beat sb up

goma ['goma] *nf* (*caucho*) rubber; (*elástico*) elastic; (*tira*) rubber *o* elastic (*Brit*) band; (*fam: preservativo*) condom; (*droga*) hashish; (*explosivo*) plastic explosive; **~ (de borrar)** eraser, rubber (*Brit*); **~ de mascar** chewing gum; **~ de pegar** gum, glue
goma-espuma [gomaes'puma] *nf* foam rubber
gomina [go'mina] *nf* hair gel
gomita [go'mita] *nf* rubber *o* elastic (*Brit*) band
góndola ['gondola] *nf* (*barco*) gondola; (*de tren*) goods wagon
gordo, -a ['gorðo, a] *adj* (*gen*) fat; (*persona*) plump; (*agua*) hard; (*fam*) enormous ■ *nm/f* fat man *o* woman; **el (premio) ~** (*en lotería*) first prize; **¡~!** (*fam*) fatty!
gordura [gor'ðura] *nf* fat; (*corpulencia*) fatness, stoutness
gorgojo [gor'ɣoxo] *nm* (*insecto*) grub
gorgorito [gorɣ'rito] *nm* (*gorjeo*) trill, warble
gorila [go'rila] *nm* gorilla; (*fam*) tough, thug; (*guardaespaldas*) bodyguard
gorjear [gorxe'ar] *vi* to twitter, chirp
gorjeo [gor'xeo] *nm* twittering, chirping
gorra ['gorra] *nf* (*gen*) cap; (*de niño*) bonnet; (*militar*) bearskin; **~ de montar/de paño/de punto/de visera** riding/cloth/knitted/peaked cap; **andar** *o* **ir** *o* **vivir de ~** to sponge, scrounge; **entrar de ~** (*fam*) to gatecrash
gorrión [go'rrjon] *nm* sparrow
gorro ['gorro] *nm* cap; (*de niño, mujer*) bonnet; **estoy hasta el ~** I am fed up
gorrón, -ona [go'rron, ona] *nm* pebble; (*Tec*) pivot ■ *nm/f* scrounger
gorronear [gorrone'ar] *vi* (*fam*) to sponge, scrounge
gota ['gota] *nf* (*gen*) drop; (*de pintura*) blob; (*de sudor*) bead; (*Med*) gout; **~ a ~** drop by drop; **caer a gotas** to drip
gotear [gote'ar] *vi* to drip; (*escurrir*) to trickle; (*salirse*) to leak; (*cirio*) to gutter; (*lloviznar*) to drizzle
gotera [go'tera] *nf* leak
gótico, -a ['gotiko, a] *adj* Gothic
gozar [go'θar] *vi* to enjoy o.s.; **~ de** (*disfrutar*) to enjoy; (*poseer*) to possess; **~ de buena salud** to enjoy good health
gozne ['goθne] *nm* hinge
gozo ['goθo] *nm* (*alegría*) joy; (*placer*) pleasure; **¡mi ~ en el pozo!** that's torn it!, just my luck!
g.p. *nm abr* (= *giro postal*) m.o.
gr *abr* (= *gramo(s)*) g
grabación [graβa'θjon] *nf* recording
grabado, -a [gra'βaðo, a] *adj* (*Mus*) recorded; (*en cinta*) taped, on tape ■ *nm* print, engraving; **~ al agua fuerte** etching; **~ al aguatinta** aquatint; **~ en cobre** copperplate; **~ en madera** woodcut; **~ rupestre** rock carving
grabador, -a [graβa'ðor, a] *nm/f* engraver ■ *nf* tape-recorder; **grabadora de cassettes** cassette recorder
grabar [gra'βar] *vt* to engrave; (*discos, cintas*) to record; (*impresionar*) to impress
gracejo [gra'θexo] *nm* (*ingenio*) wit, humour; (*elegancia*) grace
gracia ['graθja] *nf* (*encanto*) grace, gracefulness; (*Rel*) grace; (*chiste*) joke; (*humor*) humour, wit; **¡muchas gracias!** thanks very much!; **gracias a** thanks to; **tener ~** (*chiste etc*) to be funny; **¡qué ~!** how funny!; (*irónico*) what a nerve!; **no me hace ~** (*broma*) it's not funny; (*plan*) I am not too keen; **con gracias anticipadas/repetidas** thanking you in advance/again; **dar las gracias a algn por algo** to thank sb for sth
grácil ['graθil] *adj* (*sutil*) graceful; (*delgado*) slender; (*delicado*) delicate
gracioso, -a [gra'θjoso, a] *adj* (*garboso*) graceful; (*chistoso*) funny; (*cómico*) comical; (*agudo*) witty; (*título*) gracious ■ *nm/f* (*Teat*) comic character, fool; **su graciosa Majestad** His/Her Gracious Majesty
grada ['graða] *nf* (*de escalera*) step; (*de anfiteatro*) tier, row; **gradas** *nfpl* (*de estadio*) terraces
gradación [graða'θjon] *nf* gradation; (*serie*) graded series
gradería [graðe'ria] *nf* (*gradas*) (flight of) steps *pl*; (*de anfiteatro*) tiers *pl*, rows *pl*; **~ cubierta** covered stand
grado ['graðo] *nm* degree; (*etapa*) stage, step; (*nivel*) rate; (*de parentesco*) order of lineage; (*de aceite, vino*) grade; (*grada*) step; (*Escol*) class, year, grade (*US*); (*Univ*) degree; (*Ling*) degree of comparison; (*Mil*) rank; **de buen ~** willingly; **en sumo ~, en ~ superlativo** in the highest degree
graduación [graðwa'θjon] *nf* (*acto*) gradation; (*clasificación*) rating; (*del alcohol*) proof, strength; (*Escol*) graduation; (*Mil*) rank; **de alta ~** high-ranking
gradual [gra'ðwal] *adj* gradual
graduar [gra'ðwar] *vt* (*gen*) to graduate; (*medir*) to gauge; (*Tec*) to calibrate; (*Univ*) to confer a degree on; (*Mil*) to commission; **graduarse** *vr* to graduate; **graduarse la vista** to have one's eyes tested
grafía [gra'fia] *nf* (*escritura*) writing; (*ortografía*) spelling
gráfico, -a ['grafiko, a] *adj* graphic; (*fig: vívido*) vivid, lively ■ *nm* diagram ■ *nf* graph; **~ de barras** (*Com*) bar chart;

~ de sectores *o* **de tarta** (*Com*) pie chart; **gráficos** *nmpl* (*tb Inform*) graphics; **gráficos empresariales** (*Com*) business graphics
grafito [gra'fito] *nm* (*Tec*) graphite, black lead
grafología [grafolo'xia] *nf* graphology
gragea [gra'xea] *nf* (*Med*) pill; (*caramelo*) dragée
grajo ['graxo] *nm* rook
Gral. *abr* (*Mil*: = *General*) Gen.
gramático, -a [gra'matiko, a] *nm/f* (*persona*) grammarian ▪ *nf* grammar
gramo ['gramo] *nm* gramme (*Brit*), gram (*US*)
gran [gran] *adj ver* **grande**
grana ['grana] *nf* (*Bot*) seedling; (*color*) scarlet; **ponerse como la ~** to go as red as a beetroot
granada [gra'naða] *nf* pomegranate; (*Mil*) grenade; **~ de mano** hand grenade; **~ de metralla** shrapnel shell
granadilla [grana'ðiʎa] *nf* (*Am*) passion fruit
granadino, -a [grana'ðino, a] *adj* of *o* from Granada ▪ *nm/f* native *o* inhabitant of Granada ▪ *nf* grenadine
granar [gra'nar] *vi* to seed
granate [gra'nate] *adj inv* maroon ▪ *nm* garnet; (*color*) maroon
Gran Bretaña [grambre'taɲa] *nf* Great Britain
Gran Canaria [granka'narja] *nf* Grand Canary
grancanario, -a [granka'narjo, a] *adj* of *o* from Grand Canary ▪ *nm/f* native *o* inhabitant of Grand Canary
grande ['grande], **gran** *adj* (*de tamaño*) big, large; (*alto*) tall; (*distinguido*) great; (*impresionante*) grand ▪ *nm* grandee; **¿cómo es de ~?** how big is it?, what size is it?; **pasarlo en ~** to have a tremendous time
grandeza [gran'deθa] *nf* greatness; (*tamaño*) bigness; (*esplendor*) grandness; (*nobleza*) nobility
grandioso, -a [gran'djoso, a] *adj* magnificent, grand
grandullón, -ona [granðu'ʎon, ona] *adj* oversized
granel [gra'nel] *nm* (*montón*) heap; **a ~** (*Com*) in bulk
granero [gra'nero] *nm* granary, barn
granice *etc* [gra'niθe] *vb ver* **granizar**
granito [gra'nito] *nm* (*Agr*) small grain; (*roca*) granite
granizada [grani'θaða] *nf* hailstorm; (*fig*) hail; **una ~ de balas** a hail of bullets
granizado [grani'θaðo] *nm* iced drink; **~ de café** iced coffee
granizar [grani'θar] *vi* to hail
granizo [gra'niθo] *nm* hail
granja ['granxa] *nf* (*gen*) farm; **~ avícola** chicken *o* poultry farm
granjear [granxe'ar] *vt* (*cobrar*) to earn; (*ganar*) to win; (*avanzar*) to gain; **granjearse** *vr* (*amistad etc*) to gain for o.s.
granjero, -a [gran'xero, a] *nm/f* farmer
grano ['grano] *nm* grain; (*semilla*) seed; (*baya*) berry; (*Med*) pimple, spot; (*partícula*) particle; (*punto*) speck; **granos** *nmpl* cereals; **~ de café** coffee bean; **ir al ~** to get to the point
granuja [gra'nuxa] *nm* rogue; (*golfillo*) urchin
grapa ['grapa] *nf* staple; (*Tec*) clamp; (*sujetador*) clip, fastener; (*Arq*) cramp
grapadora [grapa'ðora] *nf* stapler
GRAPO ['grapo] *nm abr* (*Esp Pol*) = **Grupo de Resistencia Antifascista Primero de Octubre**
grasa ['grasa] *nf ver* **graso**
grasiento, -a [gra'sjento, a] *adj* greasy; (*de aceite*) oily; (*mugriento*) filthy
graso, -a ['graso, a] *adj* fatty; (*aceitoso*) greasy, oily ▪ *nf* (*gen*) grease; (*de cocina*) fat, lard; (*sebo*) suet; (*mugre*) filth; (*Auto*) oil; (*lubricante*) grease; **grasa de ballena** blubber; **grasa de pescado** fish oil
grasoso, -a [gra'soso, a] *adj* (*Am*) greasy, sticky
gratificación [gratifika'θjon] *nf* (*propina*) tip; (*aguinaldo*) gratuity; (*bono*) bonus; (*recompensa*) reward
gratificar [gratifi'kar] *vt* (*dar propina*) to tip; (*premiar*) to reward; **"se ~á"** "a reward is offered"
gratifique *etc* [grati'fike] *vb ver* **gratificar**
gratinar [grati'nar] *vt* to cook au gratin
gratis ['gratis] *adv* free, for nothing
gratitud [grati'tuð] *nf* gratitude
grato, -a ['grato, a] *adj* (*agradable*) pleasant, agreeable; (*bienvenido*) welcome; **nos es ~ informarle que ...** we are pleased to inform you that ...
gratuito, -a [gra'twito, a] *adj* (*gratis*) free; (*sin razón*) gratuitous; (*acusación*) unfounded
grava ['graβa] *nf* (*guijos*) gravel; (*piedra molida*) crushed stone; (*en carreteras*) road metal
gravamen [gra'βamen] *nm* (*carga*) burden; (*impuesto*) tax; **libre de ~** (*Econ*) free from encumbrances
gravar [gra'βar] *vt* to burden; (*Com*) to tax; (*Econ*) to assess for tax; **~ con impuestos** to burden with taxes
grave ['graβe] *adj* heavy; (*fig, Med*) grave, serious; (*importante*) important; (*herida*) severe; (*Mus*) low, deep; (*Ling*: *acento*) grave; **estar ~** to be seriously ill
gravedad [graβe'ðað] *nf* gravity; (*fig*) seriousness; (*grandeza*) importance; (*dignidad*) dignity; (*Mus*) depth

grávido, -a ['graβiðo, a] *adj* (*preñada*) pregnant
gravilla [gra'βiʎa] *nf* gravel
gravitación [graβita'θjon] *nf* gravitation
gravitar [graβi'tar] *vi* to gravitate; **~ sobre** to rest on
gravoso, -a [gra'βoso, a] *adj* (*pesado*) burdensome; (*costoso*) costly
graznar [graθ'nar] *vi* (*cuervo*) to squawk; (*pato*) to quack; (*hablar ronco*) to croak
graznido [graθ'niðo] *nm* squawk; croak
Grecia ['greθja] *nf* Greece
gregario, -a [gre'ɣarjo, a] *adj* gregarious; **instinto ~** herd instinct
gremio ['gremjo] *nm* (*asociación*) professional association, guild
greña ['greɲa] *nf* (*cabellos*) shock of hair; (*maraña*) tangle; **andar a la ~** to bicker, squabble
greñudo, -a [gre'ɲuðo, a] *adj* (*persona*) dishevelled; (*pelo*) tangled
gresca ['greska] *nf* uproar; (*trifulca*) row
griego, -a ['grjeɣo, a] *adj* Greek, Grecian ▪ *nm/f* Greek ▪ *nm* (*Ling*) Greek
grieta ['grjeta] *nf* crack; (*hendidura*) chink; (*quiebra*) crevice; (*Med*) chap; (*Pol*) rift
grifa ['grifa] *nf* (*fam: droga*) marijuana
grifo ['grifo] *nm* tap (*Brit*), faucet (*US*); (*Am*) petrol (*Brit*) *o* gas (*US*) station
grilletes [gri'ʎetes] *nmpl* fetters, shackles
grillo ['griʎo] *nm* (*Zool*) cricket; (*Bot*) shoot; **grillos** *nmpl* shackles, irons
grima ['grima] *nf* (*horror*) loathing; (*desagrado*) reluctance; (*desazón*) uneasiness; **me da ~** it makes me sick
gringo, -a ['gringo, a] (*Am*) *adj* (*pey: extranjero*) foreign; (*: norteamericano*) Yankee; (*idioma*) foreign ▪ *nm/f* foreigner; Yank
gripa ['gripa] *nf* (*Am*) flu, influenza
gripe ['gripe] *nf* flu, influenza
gris [gris] *adj* grey
grisáceo, -a [gri'saθeo, a] *adj* greyish
grisoso, -a [gri'soso, a] *adj* (*Am*) greyish, grayish (*esp US*)
gritar [gri'tar] *vt, vi* to shout, yell; **¡no grites!** stop shouting!
grito ['grito] *nm* shout, yell; (*de horror*) scream; **a ~ pelado** at the top of one's voice; **poner el ~ en el cielo** to scream blue murder; **es el último ~** (*de moda*) it's all the rage
groenlandés, -esa [groenlan'des, esa] *adj* Greenland *cpd* ▪ *nm/f* Greenlander
Groenlandia [groen'landja] *nf* Greenland
grosella [gro'seʎa] *nf* (red)currant; **~ negra** blackcurrant
grosería [grose'ria] *nf* (*actitud*) rudeness; (*comentario*) vulgar comment; (*palabrota*) swearword
grosero, -a [gro'sero, a] *adj* (*poco cortés*) rude, bad-mannered; (*ordinario*) vulgar, crude
grosor [gro'sor] *nm* thickness
grotesco, -a [gro'tesko, a] *adj* grotesque; (*absurdo*) bizarre
grúa ['grua] *nf* (*Tec*) crane; (*de petróleo*) derrick; **~ corrediza** *o* **móvil/de pescante/puente/de torre** travelling/jib/overhead/tower crane
grueso, -a ['grweso, a] *adj* thick; (*persona*) stout; (*calidad*) coarse ▪ *nm* bulk; (*espesor*) thickness; (*densidad*) density; (*de gente*) main body, mass; **el ~ de** the bulk of
grulla ['gruʎa] *nf* (*Zool*) crane
grumete [gru'mete] *nm* (*Naut*) cabin *o* ship's boy
grumo ['grumo] *nm* (*coágulo*) clot, lump; (*masa*) dollop
gruñido [gru'ɲiðo] *nm* grunt, growl; (*fig*) grumble
gruñir [gru'ɲir] *vi* (*animal*) to grunt, growl; (*fam*) to grumble
gruñón, -ona [gru'ɲon, ona] *adj* grumpy ▪ *nm/f* grumbler
grupa ['grupa] *nf* (*Zool*) rump
grupo ['grupo] *nm* group; (*Tec*) unit, set; (*de árboles*) cluster; **~ sanguíneo** blood group
gruta ['gruta] *nf* grotto
Gta. *abr* (*Auto*) = **Glorieta**
guaca ['gwaka] *nf* Indian tomb
guacamole [gwaka'mole] *nm* (*Am*) avocado salad
guachimán [gwatʃi'man] *nm* (*Am*) night watchman
guadalajareño, -a [gwaðalaxa'reɲo, a] *adj* of *o* from Guadalajara ▪ *nm/f* native *o* inhabitant of Guadalajara
Guadalquivir [gwaðalki'βir] *nm*: **el (Río) ~** the Guadalquivir
guadaña [gwa'ðaɲa] *nf* scythe
guadañar [gwaða'ɲar] *vt* to scythe, mow
Guadiana [gwa'ðjana] *nm*: **el (Río) ~** the Guadiana
guagua ['gwaɣwa] *nf* (*Am, Canarias*) bus; (*Am: criatura*) baby
guajolote [gwajo'lote] *nm* (*Am*) turkey
guano ['gwano] *nm* guano
guantada [gwan'taða] *nf*, **guantazo** [gwan'taθo] *nm* slap
guante ['gwante] *nm* glove; **se ajusta como un ~** it fits like a glove; **echar el ~ a algn** to catch hold of sb; (*fig: policía*) to catch sb
guapo, -a ['gwapo, a] *adj* good-looking; (*mujer*) pretty, attractive; (*hombre*) handsome; (*elegante*) smart ▪ *nm* lover, gallant; (*Am fam*) tough guy, bully
guaraní [gwara'ni] *adj, nm/f* Guarani ▪ *nm* (*moneda*) *monetary unit of Paraguay*

guarapo [gwa'rapo] *nm (Am)* fermented cane juice
guarda ['gwarða] *nm/f (persona)* warden, keeper ■ *nf (acto)* guarding; *(custodia)* custody; *(Tip)* flyleaf, endpaper; ~ **forestal** game warden
guardaagujas [gwarda'ɣuxas] *nm inv (Ferro)* switchman
guardabarros [gwarða'βarros] *nm inv* mudguard *(Brit)*, fender *(US)*
guardabosques [gwarda'βoskes] *nm inv* gamekeeper
guardacoches [gwarða'kotʃes] *nm/f inv (celador)* parking attendant
guardacostas [gwarda'kostas] *nm inv* coastguard vessel
guardador, a [gwarða'ðor, a] *adj* protective; *(tacaño)* mean, stingy ■ *nm/f* guardian, protector
guardagujas [gwarda'ɣuxas] *nm inv* = **guardaagujas**
guardaespaldas [gwardaes'paldas] *nm/f inv* bodyguard
guardameta [gwarða'meta] *nm* goalkeeper
guardapolvo [gwarda'polβo] *nm* dust cover; *(prenda de vestir)* overalls *pl*
guardar [gwar'ðar] *vt (gen)* to keep; *(vigilar)* to guard, watch over; *(conservar)* to put away; *(dinero: ahorrar)* to save; *(promesa etc)* to keep; *(ley)* to observe; *(rencor)* to bear, harbour; *(Inform: archivo)* to save; **guardarse** *vr (preservarse)* to protect o.s.; **guardarse de algo** *(evitar)* to avoid sth; *(abstenerse)* to refrain from sth; **guardarse de hacer algo** to be careful not to do sth; **guardársela a algn** to have it in for sb
guardarropa [gwarða'rropa] *nm (armario)* wardrobe; *(en establecimiento público)* cloakroom
guardería [gwarðe'ria] *nf* nursery
guardia ['gwarðja] *nf (Mil)* guard; *(cuidado)* care, custody ■ *nm/f* guard; *(policía)* policeman(-woman); **estar de** ~ to be on guard; **montar** ~ to mount guard; **la G~ Civil** the Civil Guard; ~ **municipal** *o* **urbana** municipal police; **un ~ civil** a Civil Guard(sman); **un(a) ~ nacional** a policeman(-woman); ~ **urbano** traffic policeman; *see note*

GUARDIA

The *Guardia Civil* is a branch of the *Ejército de Tierra* (Army) run along military lines, which fulfils a policing role outside large urban communities and is under the joint control of the Spanish Ministry of Defence and the Ministry of the Interior. It is also known as *La Benemérita*.

guardián, -ana [gwar'ðjan, ana] *nm/f (gen)* guardian, keeper
guarecer [gware'θer] *vt (proteger)* to protect; *(abrigar)* to shelter; **guarecerse** *vr* to take refuge
guarezca *etc* [gwa'reθka] *vb ver* **guarecer**
guarida [gwa'riða] *nf (de animal)* den, lair; *(de persona)* haunt, hideout; *(refugio)* refuge
guarnecer [gwarne'θer] *vt (equipar)* to provide; *(adornar)* to adorn; *(Tec)* to reinforce
guarnezca *etc* [gwar'neθka] *vb ver* **guarnecer**
guarnición [gwarni'θjon] *nf (de vestimenta)* trimming; *(de piedra)* mount; *(Culin)* garnish; *(arneses)* harness; *(Mil)* garrison
guarrada [gwa'rraða] *(fam) nf (cosa sucia)* dirty mess; *(acto o dicho obsceno)* obscenity; **hacer una ~ a algn** to do the dirty on sb
guarrería [gwarre'ria] *nf* = **guarrada**
guarro, -a ['gwarro, a] *nm/f (fam)* pig; *(fig)* dirty *o* slovenly person
guasa ['gwasa] *nf* joke; **con** *o* **de** ~ jokingly, in fun
guasón, -ona [gwa'son, ona] *adj* witty; *(bromista)* joking ■ *nm/f* wit; joker
Guatemala [gwate'mala] *nf* Guatemala
guatemalteco, -a [gwatemal'teko, a] *adj, nm/f* Guatemalan
guateque [gwa'teke] *nm (fiesta)* party
guay [gwai] *adj (fam)* super, great
guayaba [gwa'jaβa] *nf (Bot)* guava
Guayana [gwa'jana] *nf* Guyana, Guiana
gubernamental [guβernamen'tal], **gubernativo, -a** [guβerna'tiβo, a] *adj* governmental
guedeja [ge'ðexa] *nf* long hair
guerra ['gerra] *nf* war; *(arte)* warfare; *(pelea)* struggle; ~ **atómica/bacteriológica/nuclear/de guerrillas** atomic/germ/nuclear/guerrilla warfare; **Primera/Segunda G~ Mundial** First/Second World War; ~ **de precios** *(Com)* price war; ~ **civil/fría** civil/cold war; ~ **a muerte** fight to the death; **de** ~ military, war *cpd*; **estar en** ~ to be at war; **dar** ~ to be annoying
guerrear [gerre'ar] *vi* to wage war
guerrero, -a [ge'rrero, a] *adj* fighting; *(carácter)* warlike ■ *nm/f* warrior
guerrilla [ge'rriʎa] *nf* guerrilla warfare; *(tropas)* guerrilla band *o* group
guerrillero, -a [gerri'ʎero, a] *nm/f* guerrilla (fighter); *(contra invasor)* partisan
gueto ['geto] *nm* ghetto
guía *etc* ['gia] *vb ver* **guiar** ■ *nm/f (persona)* guide ■ *nf (libro)* guidebook; *(manual)* handbook; ~ **de ferrocarriles** railway timetable; ~ **telefónica** telephone directory; ~ **del turista/del viajero** tourist/traveller's guide

guiar [gi'ar] *vt* to guide, direct; (*dirigir*) to lead; (*orientar*) to advise; (*Auto*) to steer; **guiarse** *vr*: **guiarse por** to be guided by
guijarro [gi'xarro] *nm* pebble
guillotina [giʎo'tina] *nf* guillotine
guinda ['ginda] *nf* morello cherry; (*licor*) cherry liqueur
guindar [gin'dar] *vt* to hoist; (*fam: robar*) to nick
guindilla [gin'diʎa] *nf* chil(l)i pepper
Guinea [gi'nea] *nf* Guinea
guineo, -a [gi'neo, a] *adj* Guinea *cpd*, Guinean ■ *nm/f* Guinean
guiñapo [gi'ɲapo] *nm* (*harapo*) rag; (*persona*) rogue
guiñar [gi'ɲar] *vi* to wink
guiño ['giɲo] *nm* (*parpadeo*) wink; (*muecas*) grimace; **hacer guiños a** (*enamorados*) to make eyes at
guiñol [gi'ɲol] *nm* (*Teat*) puppet theatre
guión [gi'on] *nm* (*Ling*) hyphen, dash; (*esquema*) summary, outline; (*Cine*) script
guionista [gjo'nista] *nm/f* scriptwriter
guipuzcoano, -a [gipuθko'ano, a] *adj* of *o* from Guipúzcoa ■ *nm/f* native *o* inhabitant of Guipúzcoa
guiri ['giri] *nm/f* (*fam, pey*) foreigner
guirigay [giri'gai] *nm* (*griterío*) uproar; (*confusión*) chaos
guirnalda [gir'nalda] *nf* garland
guisa ['gisa] *nf*: **a ~ de** as, like
guisado [gi'saðo] *nm* stew
guisante [gi'sante] *nm* pea
guisar [gi'sar] *vt, vi* to cook; (*fig*) to arrange
guiso ['giso] *nm* cooked dish
guita ['gita] *nf* twine; (*fam: dinero*) dough
guitarra [gi'tarra] *nf* guitar
guitarrista [gita'rrista] *nm/f* guitarist
gula ['gula] *nf* gluttony, greed
gusano [gu'sano] *nm* maggot, worm; (*de mariposa, polilla*) caterpillar; (*fig*) worm; (*ser despreciable*) creep; **~ de seda** silk-worm
gustar [gus'tar] *vt* to taste, sample ■ *vi* to please, be pleasing; **~ de algo** to like *o* enjoy sth; **me gustan las uvas** I like grapes; **le gusta nadar** she likes *o* enjoys swimming; **¿gusta Ud?** would you like some?; **como Ud guste** as you wish
gusto ['gusto] *nm* (*sentido, sabor*) taste; (*agrado*) liking; (*placer*) pleasure; **tiene un ~ amargo** it has a bitter taste; **tener buen ~** to have good taste; **sobre gustos no hay nada escrito** there's no accounting for tastes; **de buen/mal ~** in good/bad taste; **sentirse a ~** to feel at ease; **¡mucho *o* tanto ~ (en conocerle)!** how do you do?, pleased to meet you; **el ~ es mío** the pleasure is mine; **tomar ~ a** to take a liking to; **con ~** willingly, gladly
gustoso, -a [gus'toso, a] *adj* (*sabroso*) tasty; (*agradable*) pleasant; (*con voluntad*) willing, glad; **lo hizo ~** he did it gladly
gutural [gutu'ral] *adj* guttural
guyanés, -esa [gwaja'nes, esa] *adj, nm/f* Guyanese

Hh

H, h ['atʃe] *nf* (*letra*) H, h; **H de Historia** H for Harry (*Brit*) *o* How (*US*)
H. *abr* (*Química*: = *Hidrógeno*) H; (= *Hectárea(s)*) ha.
h. *abr* (= *hora(s)*) h., hr(s). ■ *nmpl abr* (= *habitantes*) pop.
ha[1] [a] *vb ver* **haber**
ha[2] *abr* (= *Hectárea(s)*) ha.
haba ['aβa] *nf* bean; **son habas contadas** it goes without saying; **en todas partes cuecen habas** it's the same (story) the whole world over
Habana [a'βana] *nf*: **la ~** Havana
habanero, -a [aβa'nero, a] *adj* of *o* from Havana ■ *nm/f* native *o* inhabitant of Havana ■ *nf* (*Mus*) habanera
habano [a'βano] *nm* Havana cigar
habeas corpus [a'βeas'korpus] *nm* (*Law*) habeas corpus

PALABRA CLAVE

haber [a'βer] *vb auxiliar* **1** (*tiempos compuestos*) to have; **había comido** I have/had eaten; **antes/después de haberlo visto** before seeing/after seeing *o* having seen it; **si lo hubiera sabido habría ido** if I had known I would have gone
2: **¡haberlo dicho antes!** you should have said so before!; **¿habráse visto (cosa igual)?** have you ever seen anything like it?
3: **haber de**: **he de hacerlo** I must do it; **ha de llegar mañana** it should arrive tomorrow
■ *vb impersonal* **1** (*existencia*: *sg*) there is; (: *pl*) there are; **hay un hermano/dos hermanos** there is one brother/there are two brothers; **¿cuánto hay de aquí a Sucre?** how far is it from here to Sucre?; **habrá unos 4 grados** it must be about 4 degrees; **no hay quien te entienda** there's no understanding you
2 (*obligación*): **hay que hacer algo** something must be done; **hay que apuntarlo para acordarse** you have to write it down to remember
3: **¡hay que ver!** well I never!
4: **¡no hay de** *o* **por** (*Am*) **qué!** don't mention it!, not at all!
5: **¿qué hay?** (*¿qué pasa?*) what's up?, what's the matter?; (*¿qué tal?*) how's it going?
■ *vt*: **he aquí unas sugerencias** here are some suggestions; **todos los inventos habidos y por haber** all inventions present and future; **en el encuentro habido ayer** in yesterday's game
haberse *vr*: **habérselas con algn** to have it out with sb
■ *nm* (*en cuenta*) credit side
haberes *nmpl* assets; **¿cuánto tengo en el haber?** how much do I have in my account?; **tiene varias novelas en su haber** he has several novels to his credit

habichuela [aβi'tʃwela] *nf* kidney bean
hábil ['aβil] *adj* (*listo*) clever, smart; (*capaz*) fit, capable; (*experto*) expert; **día ~** working day
habilidad [aβili'ðað] *nf* (*gen*) skill, ability; (*inteligencia*) cleverness; (*destreza*) expertness, expertise; (*Jur*) competence; **~ (para)** fitness (for); **tener ~ manual** to be clever with one's hands
habilitación [aβilita'θjon] *nf* qualification; (*colocación de muebles*) fitting out; (*financiamiento*) financing; (*oficina*) paymaster's office
habilitado [aβili'taðo] *nm* paymaster
habilitar [aβili'tar] *vt* to qualify; (*autorizar*) to authorize; (*capacitar*) to enable; (*dar instrumentos*) to equip; (*financiar*) to finance
hábilmente [aβil'mente] *adv* skilfully, expertly
habitable [aβi'taβle] *adj* inhabitable
habitación [aβita'θjon] *nf* (*cuarto*) room; (*casa*) dwelling, abode; (*Bio*: *morada*) habitat; **~ sencilla** *o* **individual** single room; **~ doble** *o* **de matrimonio** double room

habitante [aβi'tante] *nm/f* inhabitant
habitar [aβi'tar] *vt* (*residir en*) to inhabit; (*ocupar*) to occupy ■ *vi* to live
hábitat (*pl* **hábitats**) ['aβitat, 'aβitats] *nm* habitat
hábito ['aβito] *nm* habit; **tener el ~ de hacer algo** to be in the habit of doing sth
habitual [aβi'twal] *adj* habitual
habituar [aβi'twar] *vt* to accustom;
habituarse *vr*: **habituarse a** to get used to
habla ['aβla] *nf* (*capacidad de hablar*) speech; (*idioma*) language; (*dialecto*) dialect; **perder el ~** to become speechless; **de ~ francesa** French-speaking; **estar al ~** to be in contact; (*Telec*) to be on the line; **¡González al ~!** (*Telec*) Gonzalez speaking!
hablador, a [aβla'ðor, a] *adj* talkative ■ *nm/f* chatterbox
habladuría [aβlaðu'ria] *nf* rumour;
habladurías *nfpl* gossip *sg*
hablante [a'βlante] *adj* speaking ■ *nm/f* speaker
hablar [a'βlar] *vt* to speak, talk ■ *vi* to speak;
hablarse *vr* to speak to each other; **~ con** to speak to; **¡hable!, ¡puede ~!** (*Telec*) you're through!; **de eso ni ~** no way, that's not on; **~ alto/bajo/claro** to speak loudly/quietly/ plainly *o* bluntly; **~ de** to speak of *o* about; **"se habla inglés"** "English spoken here"; **no se hablan** they are not on speaking terms
habré *etc* [a'βre] *vb ver* **haber**
hacedor, a [aθe'ðor, a] *nm/f* maker
hacendado, -a [aθen'daðo, a] *adj* property-owning ■ *nm* (*terrateniente*) large landowner
hacendoso, -a [aθen'doso, a] *adj* industrious, hard-working

PALABRA CLAVE

hacer [a'θer] *vt* **1** (*fabricar, producir, conseguir*) to make; (*construir*) to build; **hacer una película/un ruido** to make a film/noise; **el guisado lo hice yo** I made *o* cooked the stew; **hacer amigos** to make friends
2 (*ejecutar: trabajo etc*) to do; **hacer la colada** to do the washing; **hacer la comida** to do the cooking; **¿qué haces?** what are you doing?; **¡eso está hecho!** you've got it!; **hacer el tonto/indio** to act the fool/clown; **hacer el malo** *o* **el papel del malo** (*Teat*) to play the villain
3 (*estudios, algunos deportes*) to do; **hacer español/económicas** to do *o* study Spanish/ economics; **hacer yoga/gimnasia** to do yoga/go to the gym
4 (*transformar, incidir en*): **esto lo hará más difícil** this will make it more difficult; **salir te hará sentir mejor** going out will make you feel better; **te hace más joven** it makes you look younger
5 (*cálculo*): **2 y 2 hacen 4** 2 and 2 make 4; **éste hace 100** this one makes 100
6 (*+ sub*): **esto hará que ganemos** this will make us win; **harás que no quiera venir** you'll stop him wanting to come
7 (*como sustituto de vb*) to do; **él bebió y yo hice lo mismo** he drank and I did likewise
8: **no hace más que criticar** all he does is criticize
■ *vb semi-auxiliar* (*+ infin*) **1** (*directo*): **les hice venir** I made *o* had them come; **hacer trabajar a los demás** to get others to work
2 (*por intermedio de otros*): **hacer reparar algo** to get sth repaired
■ *vi* **1**: **haz como que no lo sabes** act as if you don't know; **hiciste bien en decírmelo** you were right to tell me
2 (*ser apropiado*): **si os hace** if it's alright with you
3: **hacer de**: **hacer de madre para uno** to be like a mother to sb; (*Teat*): **hacer de Otelo** to play Othello; **la tabla hace de mesa** the board does as a table
■ *vb impersonal* **1**: **hace calor/frío** it's hot/ cold; *ver tb* **bueno**; **sol**; **tiempo**
2 (*tiempo*): **hace tres años** three years ago; **hace un mes que voy/no voy** I've been going/I haven't been for a month; **no le veo desde hace mucho** I haven't seen him for a long time
3: **¿cómo has hecho para llegar tan rápido?** how did you manage to get here so quickly?
hacerse *vr* **1** (*volverse*) to become; **se hicieron amigos** they became friends; **hacerse viejo** to get *o* grow old; **se hace tarde** it's getting late
2: **hacerse algo**: **me hice un traje** I got a suit made
3 (*acostumbrarse*): **hacerse a** to get used to; **hacerse a la idea** to get used to the idea
4: **se hace con huevos y leche** it's made out of eggs and milk; **eso no se hace** that's not done
5 (*obtener*): **hacerse de** *o* **con algo** to get hold of sth
6 (*fingirse*): **hacerse el sordo/sueco** to turn a deaf ear/pretend not to notice

hacha ['atʃa] *nf* axe; (*antorcha*) torch
hachazo [a'tʃaθo] *nm* axe blow
hache ['atʃe] *nf* (the letter) H; **llámele usted ~** call it what you will
hachís [a'tʃis] *nm* hashish

hacia ['aθja] *prep* (*en dirección de, actitud*) towards; (*cerca de*) near; ~ **arriba/abajo** up(wards)/down(wards); ~ **mediodía** about noon
hacienda [a'θjenda] *nf* (*propiedad*) property; (*finca*) farm; (*Am*) ranch; ~ **pública** public finance; **(Ministerio de) H~** Exchequer (*Brit*), Treasury Department (*US*)
hacinar [aθi'nar] *vt* to pile (up); (*Agr*) to stack; (*fig*) to overcrowd
hada ['aða] *nf* fairy; ~ **madrina** fairy godmother
hado ['aðo] *nm* fate, destiny
haga *etc* ['aɣa] *vb ver* **hacer**
Haití [ai'ti] *nm* Haiti
haitiano, -a [ai'tjano, a] *adj, nm/f* Haitian
hala ['ala] *excl* (*vamos*) come on!; (*anda*) get on with it!
halagar [ala'ɣar] *vt* (*lisonjear*) to flatter
halago [a'laɣo] *nm* (*adulación*) flattery
halague *etc* [a'laɣe] *vb ver* **halagar**
halagüeño, -a [ala'ɣweɲo, a] *adj* flattering
halcón [al'kon] *nm* falcon, hawk
hálito ['alito] *nm* breath
halitosis [ali'tosis] *nf* halitosis, bad breath
hallar [a'ʎar] *vt* (*gen*) to find; (*descubrir*) to discover; (*toparse con*) to run into; **hallarse** *vr* to be (situated); (*encontrarse*) to find o.s.; **se halla fuera** he is away; **no se halla** he feels out of place
hallazgo [a'ʎaθɣo] *nm* discovery; (*cosa*) find
halo ['alo] *nm* halo
halógeno, a [a'loxeno, a] *adj*: **faro** ~ halogen lamp
halterofilia [altero'filja] *nf* weightlifting
hamaca [a'maka] *nf* hammock
hambre ['ambre] *nf* hunger; (*carencia*) famine; (*inanición*) starvation; (*fig*) longing; **tener** ~ to be hungry
hambriento, -a [am'brjento, a] *adj* hungry, starving ▪ *nm/f* starving person; **los hambrientos** the hungry; ~ **de** hungry *o* longing for
hambruna [am'bruna] *nf* famine
Hamburgo [am'burɣo] *nm* Hamburg
hamburguesa [ambur'ɣesa] *nf* hamburger, burger
hampa ['ampa] *nf* underworld
hampón [am'pon] *nm* thug
han [an] *vb ver* **haber**
haragán, -ana [ara'ɣan, ana] *adj, nm/f* good-for-nothing
haraganear [araɣane'ar] *vi* to idle, loaf about
harapiento, -a [ara'pjento, a] *adj* tattered, in rags
harapo [a'rapo] *nm* rag
hardware ['xardwer] *nm* (*Inform*) hardware
haré *etc* [a're] *vb ver* **hacer**
harén [a'ren] *nm* harem
harina [a'rina] *nf* flour; **eso es ~ de otro costal** that's another kettle of fish
harinero, -a [ari'nero, a] *nm/f* flour merchant
harinoso, -a [ari'noso, a] *adj* floury
hartar [ar'tar] *vt* to satiate, glut; (*fig*) to tire, sicken; **hartarse** *vr* (*de comida*) to fill o.s., gorge o.s.; (*cansarse*): **hartarse de** to get fed up with
hartazgo [ar'taθɣo] *nm* surfeit, glut
harto, -a ['arto, a] *adj* (*lleno*) full; (*cansado*) fed up ▪ *adv* (*bastante*) enough; (*muy*) very; **estar ~ de** to be fed up with; **¡estoy ~ de decírtelo!** I'm sick and tired of telling you (so)!
hartura [ar'tura] *nf* (*exceso*) surfeit; (*abundancia*) abundance; (*satisfacción*) satisfaction
has[1] [as] *vb ver* **haber**
has[2] *abr* (= *Hectáreas*) ha.
hasta ['asta] *adv* even ▪ *prep* (*alcanzando a*) as far as, up/down to; (*de tiempo: a tal hora*) till, until; (*: antes de*) before ▪ *conj*: ~ **que** until; ~ **luego** *o* **ahora/el sábado** (*fam*) see you soon/ on Saturday; ~ **la fecha** (up) to date; ~ **nueva orden** until further notice; ~ **en Valencia hiela a veces** even in Valencia it freezes sometimes
hastiar [as'tjar] *vt* (*gen*) to weary; (*aburrir*) to bore; **hastiarse** *vr*: **hastiarse de** to get fed up with
hastío [as'tio] *nm* weariness; boredom
hatajo [a'taxo] *nm*: **un ~ de gamberros** a bunch of hooligans
hatillo [a'tiʎo] *nm* belongings *pl*, kit; (*montón*) bundle, heap
Hawai [a'wai] *nm* (*tb*: **las Islas Hawai**) Hawaii
hawaianas [awa'janas] *nfpl* (*esp Am*) flip-flops (*Brit*), thongs
hawaiano, -a [awa'jano, a] *adj, nm/f* Hawaian
hay [ai] *vb ver* **haber**
Haya ['aja] *nf*: **la** ~ The Hague
haya *etc* ['aja] *vb ver* **haber** ▪ *nf* beech tree
hayal [a'jal] *nm* beech grove
haz [aθ] *vb ver* **hacer** ▪ *nm* bundle, bunch; (*rayo: de luz*) beam ▪ *nf*: ~ **de la tierra** face of the earth
hazaña [a'θaɲa] *nf* feat, exploit; **sería una ~** it would be a great achievement
hazmerreír [aθmerre'ir] *nm inv* laughing stock
he [e] *vb ver* **haber** ▪ *adv*: **he aquí** here is, here are; **he aquí por qué ...** that is why ...
hebilla [e'βiʎa] *nf* buckle, clasp
hebra ['eβra] *nf* thread; (*Bot: fibra*) fibre, grain

hebreo, -a [e'βreo, a] *adj, nm/f* Hebrew ■ *nm* (*Ling*) Hebrew
Hébridas ['eβriðas] *nfpl*: **las ~** the Hebrides
hechice *etc* [e'tʃiθe] *vb ver* **hechizar**
hechicero, -a [etʃi'θero, a] *nm/f* sorcerer/ sorceress
hechizar [etʃi'θar] *vt* to cast a spell on, bewitch
hechizo [e'tʃiθo] *nm* witchcraft, magic; (*acto de magia*) spell, charm
hecho, -a ['etʃo, a] *pp de* **hacer** ■ *adj* complete; (*maduro*) mature; (*Costura*) ready-to-wear ■ *nm* deed, act; (*dato*) fact; (*cuestión*) matter; (*suceso*) event ■ *excl* agreed!, done!; **¡bien ~!** well done!; **de ~** in fact, as a matter of fact; (*Pol etc*: *adj, adv*) de facto; **de ~ y de derecho** de facto and de jure; **~ a la medida** made-to-measure; **a lo ~, pecho** it's no use crying over spilt milk
hechura [e'tʃura] *nf* making, creation; (*producto*) product; (*forma*) form, shape; (*de persona*) build; (*Tec*) craftsmanship
hectárea [ek'tarea] *nf* hectare
heder [e'ðer] *vi* to stink, smell; (*fig*) to be unbearable
hediondez [eðjon'deθ] *nf* stench, stink; (*cosa*) stinking thing
hediondo, -a [e'ðjondo, a] *adj* stinking
hedor [e'ðor] *nm* stench
hegemonía [exemo'nia] *nf* hegemony
helada [e'laða] *nf* frost
heladera [ela'ðera] *nf* (*Am*: *refrigerador*) refrigerator
heladería [elaðe'ria] *nf* ice-cream stall (*o* parlour)
helado, -a [e'laðo, a] *adj* frozen; (*glacial*) icy; (*fig*) chilly, cold ■ *nm* ice-cream; **dejar ~ a algn** to dumbfound sb
helador, a [ela'ðor, a] *adj* (*viento etc*) icy, freezing
helar [e'lar] *vt* to freeze, ice (up); (*dejar atónito*) to amaze; (*desalentar*) to discourage ■ *vi*, **helarse** *vr* to freeze; (*Aviat, Ferro etc*) to ice (up), freeze up; (*líquido*) to set
helecho [e'letʃo] *nm* bracken, fern
helénico, -a [e'leniko, a] *adj* Hellenic, Greek
heleno, -a [e'leno, a] *nm/f* Hellene, Greek
hélice ['eliθe] *nf* spiral; (*Tec*) propeller; (*Mat*) helix
helicóptero [eli'koptero] *nm* helicopter
helio ['eljo] *nm* helium
helmántico, -a [el'mantiko, a] *adj* of *o* from Salamanca
helvético, -a [el'βetiko, a] *adj, nm/f* Swiss
hematoma [ema'toma] *nm* bruise
hembra ['embra] *nf* (*Bot, Zool*) female; (*mujer*) woman; (*Tec*) nut; **un elefante ~** a she-elephant
hemeroteca [emero'teka] *nf* newspaper library
hemiciclo [emi'θiklo] *nm*: **el ~** (*Pol*) the floor
hemisferio [emis'ferjo] *nm* hemisphere
hemofilia [emo'filja] *nf* haemophilia (*Brit*), hemophilia (*US*)
hemorragia [emo'rraxja] *nf* haemorrhage (*Brit*), hemorrhage (*US*)
hemorroides [emo'rroiðes] *nfpl* haemorrhoids (*Brit*), hemorrhoids (*US*)
hemos ['emos] *vb ver* **haber**
henar [e'nar] *nm* meadow, hayfield
henchir [en'tʃir] *vt* to fill, stuff; **henchirse** *vr* (*llenarse de comida*) to stuff o.s. (with food); (*inflarse*) to swell (up)
Hendaya [en'daja] *nf* Hendaye
hender [en'der] *vt* to cleave, split
hendidura [endi'ðura] *nf* crack, split; (*Geo*) fissure
henequén [ene'ken] *nm* (*Am*) henequen
heno ['eno] *nm* hay
hepatitis [epa'titis] *nf inv* hepatitis
herbario, -a [er'βarjo, a] *adj* herbal ■ *nm* (*colección*) herbarium; (*especialista*) herbalist; (*botánico*) botanist
herbicida [erβi'θiða] *nm* weedkiller
herbívoro, -a [er'βiβoro, a] *adj* herbivorous
herboristería [erβoriste'ria] *nf* herbalist's shop
heredad [ere'ðað] *nf* landed property; (*granja*) farm
heredar [ere'ðar] *vt* to inherit
heredero, -a [ere'ðero, a] *nm/f* heir(ess); **~ del trono** heir to the throne
hereditario, -a [ereði'tarjo, a] *adj* hereditary
hereje [e'rexe] *nm/f* heretic
herejía [ere'xia] *nf* heresy
herencia [e'renθja] *nf* inheritance; (*fig*) heritage; (*Bio*) heredity
herético, -a [e'retiko, a] *adj* heretical
herido, -a [e'riðo, a] *adj* injured, wounded; (*fig*) offended ■ *nm/f* casualty ■ *nf* wound, injury
herir [e'rir] *vt* to wound, injure; (*fig*) to offend; (*conmover*) to touch, move
hermana [er'mana] *nf ver* **hermano**
hermanar [erma'nar] *vt* to match; (*unir*) to join; (*ciudades*) to twin
hermanastro, -a [erma'nastro, a] *nm/f* stepbrother(-sister)
hermandad [erman'dað] *nf* brotherhood; (*de mujeres*) sisterhood; (*sindicato etc*) association
hermano, -a [er'mano, a] *adj* similar ■ *nm* brother ■ *nf* sister; **~ gemelo** twin brother; **~ político** brother-in-law; **~ primo** first cousin; **mis hermanos** my brothers, my brothers and sisters; **hermana política** sister-in-law

hermético, -a [er'metiko, a] *adj* hermetic; (*fig*) watertight
hermoso, -a [er'moso, a] *adj* beautiful, lovely; (*estupendo*) splendid; (*guapo*) handsome
hermosura [ermo'sura] *nf* beauty; (*de hombre*) handsomeness
hernia ['ernja] *nf* hernia, rupture; ~ **discal** slipped disc
herniarse [er'njarse] *vr* to rupture o.s.; (*fig*) to break one's back
héroe ['eroe] *nm* hero
heroicidad [eroiθi'ðað] *nf* heroism; (*una heroicidad*) heroic deed
heroico, -a [e'roiko, a] *adj* heroic
heroína [ero'ina] *nf* (*mujer*) heroine; (*droga*) heroin
heroinómano, -a [eroi'nomano, a] *nm/f* heroin addict
heroísmo [ero'ismo] *nm* heroism
herpes ['erpes] *nmpl o nfpl* (*Med: gen*) herpes *sg*; (*: de la piel*) shingles *sg*
herradura [erra'ðura] *nf* horseshoe
herraje [e'rraxe] *nm* (*trabajos*) ironwork
herramienta [erra'mjenta] *nf* tool
herrería [erre'ria] *nf* smithy; (*Tec*) forge
herrero [e'rrero] *nm* blacksmith
herrumbre [e'rrumbre] *nf* rust
herrumbroso, -a [errum'broso, a] *adj* rusty
hervidero [erβi'ðero] *nm* (*fig*) swarm; (*Pol etc*) hotbed
hervir [er'βir] *vi* to boil; (*burbujear*) to bubble; (*fig*): ~ **de** to teem with; ~ **a fuego lento** to simmer
hervor [er'βor] *nm* boiling; (*fig*) ardour, fervour
heterogéneo, -a [etero'xeneo, a] *adj* heterogeneous
heterosexual [eterosek'swal] *adj, nm/f* heterosexual
hez [eθ] *nf* (*tb:* **heces**) dregs
hibernar [iβer'nar] *vi* to hibernate
híbrido, -a ['iβriðo, a] *adj* hybrid
hice *etc* ['iθe] *vb ver* **hacer**
hidalgo, -a [i'ðalɣo, a] *adj* noble; (*honrado*) honourable (*Brit*), honorable (*US*) ■ *nm/f* noble(man(-woman))
hidratante [iðra'tante] *adj*: **crema ~** moisturizing cream, moisturizer
hidratar [iðra'tar] *vt* to moisturize
hidrato [i'ðrato] *nm* hydrate; ~ **de carbono** carbohydrate
hidráulico, -a [i'ðrauliko, a] *adj* hydraulic ■ *nf* hydraulics *sg*
hidro... [iðro] *pref* hydro..., water-...
hidroavión [iðroa'βjon] *nm* seaplane
hidroeléctrico, -a [iðroe'lektriko, a] *adj* hydroelectric
hidrófilo, -a [i'ðrofilo, a] *adj* absorbent; **algodón ~** cotton wool (*Brit*), absorbent cotton (*US*)
hidrofobia [iðro'foβja] *nf* hydrophobia, rabies
hidrófugo, -a [i'ðrofuɣo, a] *adj* damp-proof
hidrógeno [i'ðroxeno] *nm* hydrogen
hieda *etc* ['jeða] *vb ver* **heder**
hiedra ['jeðra] *nf* ivy
hiel [jel] *nf* gall, bile; (*fig*) bitterness
hielo *etc* ['jelo] *vb ver* **helar** ■ *nm* (*gen*) ice; (*escarcha*) frost; (*fig*) coldness, reserve; **romper el ~** (*fig*) to break the ice
hiena ['jena] *nf* (*Zool*) hyena
hiera *etc* ['jera] *vb ver* **herir**
hierba ['jerβa] *nf* (*pasto*) grass; (*Culin, Med: planta*) herb; **mala ~** weed; (*fig*) evil influence
hierbabuena [jerβa'βwena] *nf* mint
hierro ['jerro] *nm* (*metal*) iron; (*objeto*) iron object; ~ **acanalado** corrugated iron; ~ **colado** *o* **fundido** cast iron; **de ~** iron *cpd*
hierva *etc* ['jerβa] *vb ver* **hervir**
hígado ['iɣaðo] *nm* liver; **hígados** *nmpl* (*fig*) guts; **echar los hígados** to wear o.s. out
higiene [i'xjene] *nf* hygiene
higiénico, -a [i'xjeniko, a] *adj* hygienic
higo ['iɣo] *nm* fig; ~ **seco** dried fig; ~ **chumbo** prickly pear; **de higos a brevas** once in a blue moon
higuera [i'gera] *nf* fig tree
hijastro, -a [i'xastro, a] *nm/f* stepson(-daughter)
hijo, -a ['ixo, a] *nm/f* son/daughter, child; (*uso vocativo*) dear; **hijos** *nmpl* children, sons and daughters; **sin hijos** childless; **~/hija político/a** son-/daughter-in-law; ~ **pródigo** prodigal son; ~ **de papá/mamá** daddy's/mummy's boy; ~ **de puta** (*fam!*) bastard (*!*), son of a bitch (*!*); **cada ~ de vecino** any Tom, Dick or Harry
hilacha [i'latʃa] *nf* ravelled thread; ~ **de acero** steel wool
hilado, -a [i'laðo, a] *adj* spun
hilandero, -a [ilan'dero, a] *nm/f* spinner
hilar [i'lar] *vt* to spin; (*fig*) to reason, infer; ~ **delgado** to split hairs
hilera [i'lera] *nf* row, file
hilo ['ilo] *nm* thread; (*Bot*) fibre; (*tela*) linen; (*de metal*) wire; (*de agua*) trickle, thin stream; (*de luz*) beam, ray; (*de conversación*) thread, theme; (*de pensamientos*) train; ~ **dental** dental floss; **colgar de un ~** (*fig*) to hang by a thread; **traje de ~** linen suit
hilvanar [ilβa'nar] *vt* (*Costura*) to tack (*Brit*), baste (*US*); (*fig*) to do hurriedly
Himalaya [ima'laja] *nm*: **el ~, los Montes Himalaya** the Himalayas

himno ['imno] *nm* hymn; ~ **nacional** national anthem
hincapié [inka'pje] *nm*: **hacer hincapié en** to emphasize, stress
hincar [in'kar] *vt* to drive (in), thrust (in); (*diente*) to sink; **hincarse** *vr*: **hincarse de rodillas** (*esp Am*) to kneel down
hincha ['intʃa] *nm/f* (*fam: Deporte*) fan
hinchado, -a [in'tʃaðo, a] *adj* (*gen*) swollen; (*persona*) pompous ■ *nf* (group of) supporters *o* fans
hinchar [in'tʃar] *vt* (*gen*) to swell; (*inflar*) to blow up, inflate; (*fig*) to exaggerate; **hincharse** *vr* (*inflarse*) to swell up; (*fam: llenarse*) to stuff o.s.; (*fig*) to get conceited; **hincharse de reír** to have a good laugh
hinchazón [intʃa'θon] *nf* (*Med*) swelling; (*protuberancia*) bump, lump; (*altivez*) arrogance
hindú [in'du] *adj, nm/f* Hindu
hinojo [i'noxo] *nm* fennel
hinque *etc* ['inke] *vb ver* **hincar**
hipar [i'par] *vi* to hiccup
hiper... [iper] *pref* hyper...
hiperactivo, -a [iperak'tiβo, a] *adj* hyperactive
hipermercado [ipermer'kaðo] *nm* hypermarket, superstore
hipersensible [ipersen'siβle] *adj* hypersensitive
hipertensión [iperten'sjon] *nf* high blood pressure, hypertension
hípico, -a ['ipiko, a] *adj* horse *cpd*, equine; **club** ~ riding club
hipnosis [ip'nosis] *nf inv* hypnosis
hipnotice *etc* [ipno'tiθe] *vb ver* **hipnotizar**
hipnotismo [ipno'tismo] *nm* hypnotism
hipnotizar [ipnoti'θar] *vt* to hypnotize
hipo ['ipo] *nm* hiccups *pl*; **quitar el ~ a algn** to cure sb's hiccups
hipocondría [ipokon'dria] *nf* hypochondria
hipocondríaco, -a [ipokon'driako, a] *adj, nm/f* hypochondriac
hipocresía [ipokre'sia] *nf* hypocrisy
hipócrita [i'pokrita] *adj* hypocritical ■ *nm/f* hypocrite
hipodérmico, -a [ipo'ðermiko, a] *adj*: **aguja hipodérmica** hypodermic needle
hipódromo [i'poðromo] *nm* racetrack
hipopótamo [ipo'potamo] *nm* hippopotamus
hipoteca [ipo'teka] *nf* mortgage; **redimir una** ~ to pay off a mortgage
hipotecar [ipote'kar] *vt* to mortgage; (*fig*) to jeopardize
hipotecario, -a [ipote'karjo, a] *adj* mortgage *cpd*
hipótesis [i'potesis] *nf inv* hypothesis; **es una ~ (nada más)** that's just a theory
hipotético, -a [ipo'tetiko, a] *adj* hypothetic(al)
hiriendo *etc* [i'rjendo] *vb ver* **herir**
hiriente [i'rjente] *adj* offensive, wounding
hirsuto, -a [ir'suto, a] *adj* hairy
hirviendo *etc* [ir'βjendo] *vb ver* **hervir**
hisopo [i'sopo] *nm* (*Rel*) sprinkler; (*Bot*) hyssop; (*de algodón*) swab
hispánico, -a [is'paniko, a] *adj* Hispanic, Spanish
hispanidad [ispani'ðað] *nf* (*cualidad*) Spanishness; (*Pol*) Spanish *o* Hispanic world
hispanista [ispa'nista] *nm/f* (*Univ etc*) Hispan(ic)ist
hispano, -a [is'pano, a] *adj* Hispanic, Spanish, Hispano- ■ *nm/f* Spaniard
Hispanoamérica [ispanoa'merika] *nf* Spanish *o* Latin America
hispanoamericano, -a [ispanoameri'kano, a] *adj, nm/f* Spanish *o* Latin American
hispanohablante [ispanoa'βlante], **hispanoparlante** [ispanopar'lante] *adj* Spanish-speaking
histeria [is'terja] *nf* hysteria
histérico, -a [is'teriko, a] *adj* hysterical
histerismo [iste'rismo] *nm* (*Med*) hysteria; (*fig*) hysterics
histograma [isto'ɣrama] *nm* histogram
historia [is'torja] *nf* history; (*cuento*) story, tale; **historias** *nfpl* (*chismes*) gossip *sg*; **dejarse de historias** to come to the point; **pasar a la ~** to go down in history
historiador, a [istorja'ðor, a] *nm/f* historian
historial [isto'rjal] *nm* record; (*profesional*) curriculum vitae, c.v., résumé (*US*); (*Med*) case history
histórico, -a [is'toriko, a] *adj* historical; (*fig*) historic
historieta [isto'rjeta] *nf* tale, anecdote; (*de dibujos*) comic strip
histrionismo [istrjo'nismo] *nm* (*Teat*) acting; (*fig*) histrionics *pl*
hito ['ito] *nm* (*fig*) landmark; (*objetivo*) goal, target; (*fig*) milestone
hizo ['iθo] *vb ver* **hacer**
Hna., Hnas. *abr* (= *Hermana(s)*) Sr(s).
Hno., Hnos. *abr* (= *Hermano(s)*) Bro(s).
hocico [o'θiko] *nm* snout; (*fig*) grimace
hockey ['xoki] *nm* hockey; **~ sobre hielo** ice hockey
hogar [o'ɣar] *nm* fireplace, hearth; (*casa*) home; (*vida familiar*) home life
hogareño, -a [oɣa'reɲo, a] *adj* home *cpd*; (*persona*) home-loving
hogaza [o'ɣaθa] *nf* (*de pan*) large loaf
hoguera [o'ɣera] *nf* (*gen*) bonfire; (*para herejes*) stake

hoja ['oxa] *nf* *(gen)* leaf; *(de flor)* petal; *(de hierba)* blade; *(de papel)* sheet; *(página)* page; *(formulario)* form; *(de puerta)* leaf; **~ de afeitar** razor blade; **~ de cálculo electrónica** spreadsheet; **~ de ruta** road map; **~ de trabajo** *(Inform)* worksheet; **de ~ ancha** broad-leaved; **de ~ caduca/perenne** deciduous/evergreen

hojalata [oxa'lata] *nf* tin(plate)

hojaldre [o'xaldre] *nm* *(Culin)* puff pastry

hojarasca [oxa'raska] *nf* *(hojas)* dead *o* fallen leaves *pl*; *(fig)* rubbish

hojear [oxe'ar] *vt* to leaf through, turn the pages of

hola ['ola] *excl* hello!

Holanda [o'landa] *nf* Holland

holandés, -esa [olan'des, esa] *adj* Dutch ▪ *nm/f* Dutchman(-woman); **los holandeses** the Dutch ▪ *nm* *(Ling)* Dutch

holgado, -a [ol'ɣaðo, a] *adj* loose, baggy; *(rico)* well-to-do

holgar [ol'ɣar] *vi* *(descansar)* to rest; *(sobrar)* to be superfluous; **huelga decir que** it goes without saying that

holgazán, -ana [olɣa'θan, ana] *adj* idle, lazy ▪ *nm/f* loafer

holgazanear [olɣaθane'ar] *vi* to laze *o* loaf around

holgura [ol'ɣura] *nf* looseness, bagginess; *(Tec)* play, free movement; *(vida)* comfortable living, luxury

hollar [o'ʎar] *vt* to tread (on), trample

hollín [o'ʎin] *nm* soot

hombre ['ombre] *nm* man; *(raza humana)*: **el ~** man(kind) ▪ *excl*: **¡sí ~!** *(claro)* of course!; *(para énfasis)* man, old chap; **~ de negocios** businessman; **~-rana** frogman; **~ de bien** *o* **pro** honest man; **~ de confianza** right-hand man; **~ de estado** statesman; **el ~ medio** the average man

hombrera [om'brera] *nf* shoulder strap

hombro ['ombro] *nm* shoulder; **arrimar el ~** to lend a hand; **encogerse de hombros** to shrug one's shoulders

hombruno, -a [om'bruno, a] *adj* mannish

homenaje [ome'naxe] *nm* *(gen)* homage; *(tributo)* tribute; **un partido ~** a benefit match

homeopatía [omeopa'tia] *nf* hom(o)eopathy

homeopático, -a [omeo'patiko, a] *adj* hom(o)eopathic

homicida [omi'θiða] *adj* homicidal ▪ *nm/f* murderer

homicidio [omi'θiðjo] *nm* murder, homicide; *(involuntario)* manslaughter

homologación [omoloɣa'θjon] *nf* *(de sueldo, condiciones)* parity

homologar [omolo'ɣar] *vt* *(Com)* to standardize; *(Escol)* to officially approve; *(Deporte)* to officially recognize; *(sueldos)* to equalize

homólogo, -a [o'moloɣo, a] *nm/f* counterpart, opposite number

homónimo [o'monimo] *nm* *(tocayo)* namesake

homosexual [omosek'swal] *adj, nm/f* homosexual

hondo, -a ['ondo, a] *adj* deep; **lo ~** the depth(s) *(pl)*, the bottom; **con ~ pesar** with deep regret

hondonada [ondo'naða] *nf* hollow, depression; *(cañón)* ravine; *(Geo)* lowland

hondura [on'dura] *nf* depth, profundity

Honduras [on'duras] *nf* Honduras

hondureño, -a [ondu'reɲo, a] *adj, nm/f* Honduran

honestidad [onesti'ðað] *nf* purity, chastity; *(decencia)* decency

honesto, -a [o'nesto, a] *adj* chaste; decent, honest; *(justo)* just

hongo ['ongo] *nm* *(Bot: gen)* fungus; *(: comestible)* mushroom; *(: venenoso)* toadstool; *(sombrero)* bowler (hat) *(Brit)*, derby *(US)*; **hongos del pie** foot rot *sg*, athlete's foot *sg*

honor [o'nor] *nm* *(gen)* honour *(Brit)*, honor *(US)*; *(gloria)* glory; **~ profesional** professional etiquette; **en ~ a la verdad** to be fair

honorable [ono'raβle] *adj* honourable *(Brit)*, honorable *(US)*

honorario, -a [ono'rarjo, a] *adj* honorary ▪ *nm*: **honorarios** fees

honorífico, -a [ono'rifiko, a] *adj* honourable *(Brit)*, honorable *(US)*; **mención honorífica** hono(u)rable mention

honra ['onra] *nf* *(gen)* honour *(Brit)*, honor *(US)*; *(renombre)* good name; **honras fúnebres** funeral rites; **tener algo a mucha ~** to be proud of sth

honradez [onra'ðeθ] *nf* honesty; *(de persona)* integrity

honrado, -a [on'raðo, a] *adj* honest, upright

honrar [on'rar] *vt* to honour *(Brit)* *o* honor *(US)*; **honrarse** *vr*: **honrarse con algo/de hacer algo** to be honoured by sth/to do sth

honroso, -a [on'roso, a] *adj* *(honrado)* honourable *(Brit)*, honorable *(US)*; *(respetado)* respectable

hora ['ora] *nf* hour; *(tiempo)* time; **¿qué ~ es?** what time is it?; **¿a qué ~?** at what time?; **media ~** half an hour; **a la ~ de comer/de recreo** at lunchtime/at playtime; **a primera ~** first thing (in the morning); **a última ~** at the last moment; **"última ~"** "stop press"; **noticias de última ~** last-minute news; **a altas horas** in the small hours; **a la ~ en punto** on the dot; **¡a buena ~!** about time, too!; **en mala ~** unluckily; **dar la ~** to strike the hour; **poner el reloj en ~** to set one's watch; **horas de oficina/de trabajo** office/ working hours; **horas de visita** visiting times; **horas extras** *o* **extraordinarias** overtime *sg*; **horas punta** rush hours; **no ver la ~ de** to look forward to; **¡ya era ~!** and about time too!

horadar [ora'ðar] *vt* to drill, bore

horario, -a [o'rarjo, a] *adj* hourly, hour *cpd* ■ *nm* timetable; **~ comercial** business hours

horca ['orka] *nf* gallows *sg*; (*Agr*) pitchfork

horcajadas [orka'xaðas]: **a ~** *adv* astride

horchata [or'tʃata] *nf cold drink made from tiger nuts and water*, tiger nut milk

horda ['orða] *nf* horde

horizontal [oriθon'tal] *adj* horizontal

horizonte [ori'θonte] *nm* horizon

horma ['orma] *nf* mould; **~ (de calzado)** last; **~ de sombrero** hat block

hormiga [or'miɣa] *nf* ant; **hormigas** *nfpl* (*Med*) pins and needles

hormigón [ormi'ɣon] *nm* concrete; **~ armado/pretensado** reinforced/prestressed concrete

hormigueo [ormi'ɣeo] *nm* (*comezón*) itch; (*fig*) uneasiness

hormiguero [ormi'ɣero] *nm* (*Zool*) ant's nest; **era un ~** it was swarming with people

hormona [or'mona] *nf* hormone

hornada [or'naða] *nf* batch of loaves (*etc*)

hornillo [or'niʎo] *nm* (*cocina*) portable stove

horno ['orno] *nm* (*Culin*) oven; (*Tec*) furnace; (*para cerámica*) kiln; **~ microondas** microwave (oven); **alto ~** blast furnace; **~ crematorio** crematorium

horóscopo [o'roskopo] *nm* horoscope

horquilla [or'kiʎa] *nf* hairpin; (*Agr*) pitchfork

horrendo, -a [o'rrendo, a] *adj* horrendous, frightful

horrible [o'rriβle] *adj* horrible, dreadful

horripilante [orripi'lante] *adj* hair-raising, horrifying

horripilar [orripi'lar] *vt*: **~ a algn** to horrify sb; **horripilarse** *vr* to be horrified

horror [o'rror] *nm* horror, dread; (*atrocidad*) atrocity; **¡qué ~!** (*fam*) how awful!; **estudia horrores** he studies a hell of a lot

horrorice *etc* [orro'riθe] *vb ver* **horrorizar**

horrorizar [orrori'θar] *vt* to horrify, frighten; **horrorizarse** *vr* to be horrified

horroroso, -a [orro'roso, a] *adj* horrifying, ghastly

hortaliza [orta'liθa] *nf* vegetable

hortelano, -a [orte'lano, a] *nm/f* (market) gardener

hortera [or'tera] *adj* (*fam*) vulgar, naff

horterada [orte'raða] *nf* (*fam*): **es una ~** it's really naff

hortícola [or'tikola] *adj* horticultural

horticultura [ortikul'tura] *nf* horticulture

hortofrutícola [ortofru'tikola] *adj* fruit and vegetable *cpd*

hosco, -a ['osko, a] *adj* dark; (*persona*) sullen, gloomy

hospedaje [ospe'ðaxe] *nm* (cost of) board and lodging

hospedar [ospe'ðar] *vt* to put up; **hospedarse** *vr*: **hospedarse (con/en)** to stay *o* lodge (with/at)

hospedería [ospeðe'ria] *nf* (*edificio*) inn; (*habitación*) guest room

hospicio [os'piθjo] *nm* (*para niños*) orphanage

hospital [ospi'tal] *nm* hospital

hospitalario, -a [ospita'larjo, a] *adj* (*acogedor*) hospitable

hospitalice *etc* [ospita'liθe] *vb ver* **hospitalizar**

hospitalidad [ospitali'ðað] *nf* hospitality

hospitalizar [ospitali'θar] *vt* to send *o* take to hospital, hospitalize

hosquedad [oske'ðað] *nf* sullenness

hostal [os'tal] *nm* small hotel; *ver tb* **hotel**

hostelería [ostele'ria] *nf* hotel business *o* trade

hostia ['ostja] *nf* (*Rel*) host, consecrated wafer; (*fam: golpe*) whack, punch ■ *excl*: **¡~(s)!** (*fam!*) damn!

hostigar [osti'ɣar] *vt* to whip; (*fig*) to harass, pester

hostigue *etc* [os'tiɣe] *vb ver* **hostigar**

hostil [os'til] *adj* hostile

hostilidad [ostili'ðað] *nf* hostility

hotel [o'tel] *nm* hotel; *see note*

HOTEL

In Spain you can choose from the following categories of accommodation, in descending order of quality and price: hotel (from 5 stars to 1), *hostal, pensión, casa de huéspedes, fonda*. Quality can vary widely even within these categories. The State also runs luxury hotels called *paradores*, which are usually sited in places of particular historical interest and are often historic buildings themselves.

hotelero, -a [ote'lero, a] *adj* hotel *cpd* ■ *nm/f* hotelier

hoy [oi] *adv* (*este día*) today; (*en la actualidad*) now(adays) ■ *nm* present time; **~ (en) día** now(adays); **el día de ~**, **~ día** (*Am*) this very day; **~ por ~** right now; **de ~ en ocho días** a week today; **de ~ en adelante** from now on
hoya ['oja] *nf* pit; (*sepulcro*) grave; (*Geo*) valley
hoyo ['ojo] *nm* hole, pit; (*tumba*) grave; (*Golf*) hole; (*Med*) pockmark
hoyuelo [oj'welo] *nm* dimple
hoz [oθ] *nf* sickle
hube *etc* ['uβe] *vb ver* **haber**
hucha ['utʃa] *nf* money box
hueco, -a ['weko, a] *adj* (*vacío*) hollow, empty; (*resonante*) booming; (*sonido*) resonant; (*persona*) conceited; (*estilo*) pompous ■ *nm* hollow, cavity; (*agujero*) hole; (*de escalera*) well; (*de ascensor*) shaft; (*vacante*) vacancy; **~ de la mano** hollow of the hand
huela *etc* ['wela] *vb ver* **oler**
huelga *etc* ['welɣa] *vb ver* **holgar** ■ *nf* strike; **declararse en ~** to go on strike, come out on strike; **~ general** general strike; **~ de hambre** hunger strike; **~ oficial** official strike
huelgue *etc* ['welɣe] *vb ver* **holgar**
huelguista [wel'ɣista] *nm/f* striker
huella ['weʎa] *nf* (*acto de pisar, pisada*) tread(ing); (*marca del paso*) footprint, footstep; (*: de animal, máquina*) track; **~ digital** fingerprint; **sin dejar ~** without leaving a trace
huérfano, -a ['werfano, a] *adj* orphan(ed); (*fig*) unprotected ■ *nm/f* orphan
huerta ['werta] *nf* market garden (*Brit*), truck farm (*US*); (*de Murcia, Valencia*) irrigated region
huerto ['werto] *nm* kitchen garden; (*de árboles frutales*) orchard
hueso ['weso] *nm* (*Anat*) bone; (*de fruta*) stone, pit (*US*); **sin ~** (*carne*) boned; **estar en los huesos** to be nothing but skin and bone; **ser un ~** (*profesor*) to be terribly strict; **un ~ duro de roer** a hard nut to crack
huesoso, -a [we'soso, a] *adj* (*esp Am*) bony
huésped, a ['wespeð, a] *nm/f* (*invitado*) guest; (*habitante*) resident; (*anfitrión*) host(ess)
huesudo, -a [we'suðo, a] *adj* bony, big-boned
huevas ['weβas] *nfpl* eggs, roe *sg*; (*Am: fam!*) balls (*!*)
huevera [we'βera] *nf* eggcup
huevo ['weβo] *nm* egg; (*fam!*) ball (*!*), testicle; **~ duro/escalfado/estrellado** *o* **frito/pasado por agua** hard-boiled/poached/fried/soft-boiled egg; **huevos revueltos** scrambled eggs; **me costó un ~** (*fam!*) it was hard work; **tener huevos** (*fam!*) to have guts
huevón, -ona [we'βon, ona] *nm/f* (*Am fam!*) stupid bastard (*!*), stupid idiot
huida [u'iða] *nf* escape, flight; **~ de capitales** (*Com*) flight of capital
huidizo, -a [ui'ðiθo, a] *adj* (*tímido*) shy; (*pasajero*) fleeting
huir [u'ir] *vt* (*escapar*) to flee, escape; (*evadir*) to avoid ■ *vi* to flee, run away
hule ['ule] *nm* (*encerado*) oilskin; (*esp Am*) rubber
hulla ['uʎa] *nf* bituminous coal
humanice *etc* [uma'niθe] *vb ver* **humanizar**
humanidad [umani'ðað] *nf* (*género humano*) man(kind); (*cualidad*) humanity; (*fam: gordura*) corpulence
humanitario, -a [umani'tarjo, a] *adj* humanitarian; (*benévolo*) humane
humanizar [umani'θar] *vt* to humanize; **humanizarse** *vr* to become more human
humano, -a [u'mano, a] *adj* (*gen*) human; (*humanitario*) humane ■ *nm* human; **ser ~** human being
humareda [uma'reða] *nf* cloud of smoke
humeante [ume'ante] *adj* smoking, smoky
humedad [ume'ðað] *nf* (*del clima*) humidity; (*de pared etc*) dampness; **a prueba de ~** damp-proof
humedecer [umeðe'θer] *vt* to moisten, wet; **humedecerse** *vr* to get wet
humedezca *etc* [ume'ðeθka] *vb ver* **humedecer**
húmedo, -a ['umeðo, a] *adj* (*mojado*) damp, wet; (*tiempo etc*) humid
humildad [umil'dað] *nf* humility, humbleness
humilde [u'milde] *adj* humble, modest; (*clase etc*) low, modest
humillación [umiʎa'θjon] *nf* humiliation
humillante [umi'ʎante] *adj* humiliating
humillar [umi'ʎar] *vt* to humiliate; **humillarse** *vr* to humble o.s., grovel
humo ['umo] *nm* (*de fuego*) smoke; (*gas nocivo*) fumes *pl*; (*vapor*) steam, vapour; **humos** *nmpl* (*fig*) conceit *sg*; **irse todo en ~** (*fig*) to vanish without trace; **bajar los humos a algn** to take sb down a peg or two
humor [u'mor] *nm* (*disposición*) mood, temper; (*lo que divierte*) humour; **de buen/mal ~** in a good/bad mood
humorismo [umo'rismo] *nm* humour
humorista [umo'rista] *nm/f* comic
humorístico, -a [umo'ristiko, a] *adj* funny, humorous
hundimiento [undi'mjento] *nm* (*gen*) sinking; (*colapso*) collapse
hundir [un'dir] *vt* to sink; (*edificio, plan*) to ruin, destroy; **hundirse** *vr* to sink, collapse; (*fig: arruinarse*) to be ruined; (*desaparecer*) to

disappear; **se hundió la economía** the economy collapsed; **se hundieron los precios** prices slumped
húngaro, -a ['ungaro, a] *adj, nm/f* Hungarian ■ *nm* (*Ling*) Hungarian, Magyar
Hungría [un'gria] *nf* Hungary
huracán [ura'kan] *nm* hurricane
huraño, -a [u'raɲo, a] *adj* shy; (*antisocial*) unsociable
hurgar [ur'ɣar] *vt* to poke, jab; (*remover*) to stir (up); **hurgarse** *vr*: **hurgarse (las narices)** to pick one's nose
hurgonear [urɣone'ar] *vt* to poke
hurgue *etc* ['urɣe] *vb ver* **hurgar**
hurón [u'ron] *nm* (*Zool*) ferret
hurra ['urra] *excl* hurray!, hurrah!
hurtadillas [urta'ðiʎas]: **a ~** *adv* stealthily, on the sly
hurtar [ur'tar] *vt* to steal; **hurtarse** *vr* to hide, keep out of the way
hurto ['urto] *nm* theft, stealing; (*lo robado*) (piece of) stolen property, loot
husmear [usme'ar] *vt* (*oler*) to sniff out, scent; (*fam*) to pry into ■ *vi* to smell bad
huso ['uso] *nm* (*Tec*) spindle; (*de torno*) drum
huy ['ui] *excl* (*dolor*) ow!, ouch!; (*sorpresa*) well!; (*alivio*) phew!; **¡~, perdona!** oops, sorry!
huyendo *etc* [u'jendo] *vb ver* **huir**

Ii

I, i [i] *nf (letra)* I, i; **I de Inés** I for Isaac *(Brit)* o Item *(US)*
IA *abr* = **inteligencia artificial**
iba *etc* ['iβa] *vb ver* **ir**
Iberia [i'βerja] *nf* Iberia
ibérico, -a [i'βeriko, a] *adj* Iberian; **la Península ibérica** the Iberian Peninsula
ibero, -a [i'βero, a], **íbero, -a** ['iβero, a] *adj, nm/f* Iberian
iberoamericano, -a [iβeroameri'kano, a] *adj, nm/f* Latin American
íbice ['iβiθe] *nm* ibex
ibicenco, -a [iβi'θenko, a] *adj* of o from Ibiza ■ *nm/f* native o inhabitant of Ibiza
Ibiza [i'βiθa] *nf* Ibiza
ice *etc* ['iθe] *vb ver* **izar**
iceberg [iθe'ber] *nm* iceberg
ICONA [i'kona] *nm abr (Esp)* = **Instituto Nacional para la Conservación de la Naturaleza**
icono [i'kono] *nm (tb Inform)* icon
iconoclasta [ikono'klasta] *adj* iconoclastic ■ *nm/f* iconoclast
ictericia [ikte'riθja] *nf* jaundice
íd. *abr* = **ídem**
I+D *nf abr (= Investigación y Desarrollo)* R&D
ida ['iða] *nf* going, departure; **~ y vuelta** round trip, return; **idas y venidas** comings and goings
IDE ['iðe] *nf abr (= Iniciativa de Defensa Estratégica)* SDI
idea [i'ðea] *nf* idea; *(impresión)* opinion; *(propósito)* intention; **~ genial** brilliant idea; **a mala ~** out of spite; **no tengo la menor ~** I haven't a clue
ideal [iðe'al] *adj, nm* ideal
idealice *etc* [iðea'liθe] *vb ver* **idealizar**
idealista [iðea'lista] *adj* idealistic ■ *nm/f* idealist
idealizar [iðeali'θar] *vt* to idealize
idear [iðe'ar] *vt* to think up; *(aparato)* to invent; *(viaje)* to plan
ídem ['iðem] *pron* ditto
idéntico, -a [i'ðentiko, a] *adj* identical
identidad [iðenti'ðað] *nf* identity; **~ corporativa** corporate identity o image
identificación [iðentifika'θjon] *nf* identification
identificador de llamadas [iðentifika'ðor-] *nm* caller ID
identificar [iðentifi'kar] *vt* to identify; **identificarse** *vr*: **identificarse con** to identify with
identifique *etc* [iðenti'fike] *vb ver* **identificar**
ideología [iðeolo'xia] *nf* ideology
ideológico, -a [iðeo'loxiko, a] *adj* ideological
idílico, -a [i'ðiliko, a] *adj* idyllic
idilio [i'ðiljo] *nm* love affair
idioma [i'ðjoma] *nm* language
idiomático, -a [iðjo'matiko, a] *adj* idiomatic
idiota [i'ðjota] *adj* idiotic ■ *nm/f* idiot
idiotez [iðjo'teθ] *nf* idiocy
idolatrar [iðola'trar] *vt (fig)* to idolize
ídolo ['iðolo] *nm (tb fig)* idol
idoneidad [iðonei'ðað] *nf* suitability; *(capacidad)* aptitude
idóneo, -a [i'ðoneo, a] *adj* suitable
I.E.S. *nm abr* = **Instituto de Enseñanza Secundaria**
iglesia [i'ɣlesja] *nf* church; **~ parroquial** parish church; **¡con la ~ hemos topado!** now we're really up against it!
iglú [i'ɣlu] *nm* igloo; *(contenedor)* bottle bank
IGME *nm abr* = **Instituto Geográfico y Minero**
ignición [iɣni'θjon] *nf* ignition
ignominia [iɣno'minja] *nf* ignominy
ignominioso, -a [iɣnomi'njoso, a] *adj* ignominious
ignorado, -a [iɣno'raðo, a] *adj* unknown; *(dato)* obscure
ignorancia [iɣno'ranθja] *nf* ignorance; **por ~** through ignorance
ignorante [iɣno'rante] *adj* ignorant, uninformed ■ *nm/f* ignoramus
ignorar [iɣno'rar] *vt* not to know, be ignorant of; *(no hacer caso a)* to ignore; **ignoramos su**

paradero we don't know his whereabouts
ignoto, -a [iɣ'noto, a] *adj* unknown
igual [i'ɣwal] *adj* equal; *(similar)* like, similar; *(mismo)* (the) same; *(constante)* constant; *(temperatura)* even ■ *nm/f* equal; **al ~ que** *prep, conj* like, just like; **~ que** the same as; **sin ~** peerless; **me da** *o* **es ~** I don't care, it makes no difference; **no tener ~** to be unrivalled; **son iguales** they're the same
iguala [i'ɣwala] *nf* equalization; *(Com)* agreement
igualada [iɣwa'laða] *nf* equalizer
igualar [iɣwa'lar] *vt* *(gen)* to equalize, make equal; *(terreno)* to make even; *(Com)* to agree upon; **igualarse** *vr* *(platos de balanza)* to balance out; **igualarse (a)** *(equivaler)* to be equal (to)
igualdad [iɣwal'dað] *nf* equality; *(similaridad)* sameness; *(uniformidad)* uniformity; **en ~ de condiciones** on an equal basis
igualmente [iɣwal'mente] *adv* equally; *(también)* also, likewise ■ *excl* the same to you!
iguana [i'ɣwana] *nf* iguana
ikurriña [iku'rriɲa] *nf* Basque flag
ilegal [ile'ɣal] *adj* illegal
ilegitimidad [ilexitimi'ðað] *nf* illegitimacy
ilegítimo, -a [ile'xitimo, a] *adj* illegitimate
ileso, -a [i'leso, a] *adj* unhurt, unharmed
ilícito, -a [i'liθito, a] *adj* illicit
ilimitado, -a [ilimi'taðo, a] *adj* unlimited
Ilma., Ilmo. *abr (= Ilustrísima, Ilustrísimo) courtesy title*
ilógico, -a [i'loxiko, a] *adj* illogical
iluminación [ilumina'θjon] *nf* illumination; *(alumbrado)* lighting; *(fig)* enlightenment
iluminar [ilumi'nar] *vt* to illuminate, light (up); *(fig)* to enlighten
ilusión [ilu'sjon] *nf* illusion; *(quimera)* delusion; *(esperanza)* hope; *(emoción)* excitement, thrill; **hacerse ilusiones** to build up one's hopes; **no te hagas ilusiones** don't build up your hopes *o* get too excited
ilusionado, -a [ilusjo'naðo, a] *adj* excited
ilusionar [ilusjo'nar] *vt*: **~ a algn** *(falsamente)* to build up sb's hopes; **ilusionarse** *vr* *(falsamente)* to build up one's hopes; *(entusiasmarse)* to get excited; **me ilusiona mucho el viaje** I'm really excited about the trip
ilusionista [ilusjo'nista] *nm/f* conjurer
iluso, -a [i'luso, a] *adj* gullible, easily deceived ■ *nm/f* dreamer, visionary
ilusorio, -a [ilu'sorjo, a] *adj* *(de ilusión)* illusory, deceptive; *(esperanza)* vain
ilustración [ilustra'θjon] *nf* illustration; *(saber)* learning, erudition; **la I~** the Enlightenment
ilustrado, -a [ilus'traðo, a] *adj* illustrated; learned
ilustrar [ilus'trar] *vt* to illustrate; *(instruir)* to instruct; *(explicar)* to explain, make clear; **ilustrarse** *vr* to acquire knowledge
ilustre [i'lustre] *adj* famous, illustrious
imagen [i'maxen] *nf* *(gen)* image; *(dibujo, TV)* picture; *(Rel)* statue; **ser la viva ~ de** to be the spitting *o* living image of; **a su ~** in one's own image
imaginación [imaxina'θjon] *nf* imagination; *(fig)* fancy; **ni por ~** on no account; **no se me pasó por la ~ que ...** it never even occurred to me that ...
imaginar [imaxi'nar] *vt* *(gen)* to imagine; *(idear)* to think up; *(suponer)* to suppose; **imaginarse** *vr* to imagine; **¡imagínate!** just imagine!, just fancy!; **imagínese que ...** suppose that ...; **me imagino que sí** I should think so
imaginario, -a [imaxi'narjo, a] *adj* imaginary
imaginativo, -a [imaxina'tiβo, a] *adj* imaginative ■ *nf* imagination
imán [i'man] *nm* magnet
imanar [ima'nar], **imantar** [ima'ntar] *vt* to magnetize
imbécil [im'beθil] *nm/f* imbecile, idiot
imbecilidad [imbeθili'ðað] *nf* imbecility, stupidity
imberbe [im'berβe] *adj* beardless
imborrable [imbo'rraβle] *adj* indelible; *(inolvidable)* unforgettable
imbuir [imbu'ir] *vi* to imbue
imbuyendo *etc* [imbu'jendo] *vb ver* **imbuir**
imitación [imita'θjon] *nf* imitation; *(parodia)* mimicry; **a ~ de** in imitation of; **desconfíe de las imitaciones** *(Com)* beware of copies *o* imitations
imitador, a [imita'ðor, a] *adj* imitative ■ *nm/f* imitator; *(Teat)* mimic
imitar [imi'tar] *vt* to imitate; *(parodiar, remedar)* to mimic, ape; *(copiar)* to follow
impaciencia [impa'θjenθja] *nf* impatience
impacientar [impaθjen'tar] *vt* to make impatient; *(enfadar)* to irritate; **impacientarse** *vr* to get impatient; *(inquietarse)* to fret
impaciente [impa'θjente] *adj* impatient; *(nervioso)* anxious
impacto [im'pakto] *nm* impact; *(esp Am: fig)* shock
impagado, -a [impa'ɣaðo, a] *adj* unpaid, still to be paid
impar [im'par] *adj* odd ■ *nm* odd number
imparable [impa'raβle] *adj* unstoppable
imparcial [impar'θjal] *adj* impartial, fair

imparcialidad [imparθjali'ðað] *nf* impartiality, fairness
impartir [impar'tir] *vt* to impart, give
impasible [impa'siβle] *adj* impassive
impávido, -a [im'paβiðo, a] *adj* fearless, intrepid
IMPE ['impe] *nm abr (Esp, Com)* = **Instituto de la Mediana y Pequeña Empresa**
impecable [impe'kaβle] *adj* impeccable
impedido, -a [impe'ðiðo, a] *adj*: **estar ~** to be an invalid ■ *nm/f*: **ser un ~ físico** to be an invalid
impedimento [impeði'mento] *nm* impediment, obstacle
impedir [impe'ðir] *vt (obstruir)* to impede, obstruct; *(estorbar)* to prevent; **~ el tráfico** to block the traffic
impeler [impe'ler] *vt* to drive, propel; *(fig)* to impel
impenetrabilidad [impenetraβili'ðað] *nf* impenetrability
impenetrable [impene'traβle] *adj* impenetrable; *(fig)* incomprehensible
impensable [impen'saβle] *adj* unthinkable
impepinable [impepi'naβle] *adj (fam)* certain, inevitable
imperante [impe'rante] *adj* prevailing
imperar [impe'rar] *vi (reinar)* to rule, reign; *(fig)* to prevail, reign; *(precio)* to be current
imperativo, -a [impera'tiβo, a] *adj (persona)* imperious; *(urgente, Ling)* imperative
imperceptible [imperθep'tiβle] *adj* imperceptible
imperdible [imper'ðiβle] *nm* safety pin
imperdonable [imperðo'naβle] *adj* unforgivable, inexcusable
imperecedero, -a [impereθe'ðero, a] *adj* undying
imperfección [imperfek'θjon] *nf* imperfection; *(falla)* flaw, fault
imperfecto, -a [imper'fekto, a] *adj* faulty, imperfect ■ *nm (Ling)* imperfect tense
imperial [impe'rjal] *adj* imperial
imperialismo [imperja'lismo] *nm* imperialism
imperialista [imperja'lista] *adj* imperialist(ic) ■ *nm/f* imperialist
impericia [impe'riθja] *nf (torpeza)* unskilfulness; *(inexperiencia)* inexperience
imperio [im'perjo] *nm* empire; *(autoridad)* rule, authority; *(fig)* pride, haughtiness; **vale un ~** *(fig)* it's worth a fortune
imperioso, -a [impe'rjoso, a] *adj* imperious; *(urgente)* urgent; *(imperativo)* imperative
impermeable [imperme'aβle] *adj (a prueba de agua)* waterproof ■ *nm* raincoat, mac *(Brit)*
impersonal [imperso'nal] *adj* impersonal
impertérrito, -a [imper'territo, a] *adj* undaunted
impertinencia [imperti'nenθja] *nf* impertinence
impertinente [imperti'nente] *adj* impertinent
imperturbable [impertur'βaβle] *adj* imperturbable; *(sereno)* unruffled; *(impasible)* impassive
ímpetu ['impetu] *nm (impulso)* impetus, impulse; *(impetuosidad)* impetuosity; *(violencia)* violence
impetuosidad [impetwosi'ðað] *nf* impetuousness; *(violencia)* violence
impetuoso, -a [impe'twoso, a] *adj* impetuous; *(río)* rushing; *(acto)* hasty
impida *etc* [im'piða] *vb ver* **impedir**
impío, -a [im'pio, a] *adj* impious, ungodly; *(cruel)* cruel, pitiless
implacable [impla'kaβle] *adj* implacable, relentless
implantación [implanta'θjon] *nf* introduction; *(Bio)* implantation
implantar [implan'tar] *vt (costumbre)* to introduce; *(Bio)* to implant; **implantarse** *vr* to be introduced
implicar [impli'kar] *vt* to involve; *(entrañar)* to imply; **esto no implica que ...** this does not mean that ...
implícito, -a [im'pliθito, a] *adj (tácito)* implicit; *(sobreentendido)* implied
implique *etc* [im'plike] *vb ver* **implicar**
implorar [implo'rar] *vt* to beg, implore
impondré *etc* [impon'dre] *vb ver* **imponer**
imponente [impo'nente] *adj (impresionante)* impressive, imposing; *(solemne)* grand ■ *nm/f (Com)* depositor
imponer [impo'ner] *vt (gen)* to impose; *(tarea)* to set; *(exigir)* to exact; *(miedo)* to inspire; *(Com)* to deposit; **imponerse** *vr* to assert o.s.; *(prevalecer)* to prevail; *(costumbre)* to grow up; **imponerse un deber** to assume a duty
imponga *etc* [im'ponga] *vb ver* **imponer**
imponible [impo'niβle] *adj (Com)* taxable, subject to tax; *(importación)* dutiable, subject to duty; **no ~** tax-free, tax-exempt *(US)*
impopular [impopu'lar] *adj* unpopular
importación [importa'θjon] *nf (acto)* importing; *(mercancías)* imports *pl*
importancia [impor'tanθja] *nf* importance; *(valor)* value, significance; *(extensión)* size, magnitude; **no dar ~ a** to consider unimportant; *(fig)* to make light of; **no tiene ~** it's nothing
importante [impor'tante] *adj* important; valuable, significant
importar [impor'tar] *vt (del extranjero)* to

import; (*costar*) to amount to; (*implicar*) to involve ■ *vi* to be important, matter; **me importa un bledo** I don't give a damn; **¿le importa que fume?** do you mind if I smoke?; **¿te importa prestármelo?** would you mind lending it to me?; **¿qué importa?** what difference does it make?; **no importa** it doesn't matter; **no le importa** he doesn't care, it doesn't bother him; **"no importa precio"** "cost no object"
importe [im'porte] *nm* (*cantidad*) amount; (*valor*) value
importunar [importu'nar] *vt* to bother, pester
importuno, -a [impor'tuno, a] *adj* (*inoportuno, molesto*) inopportune; (*indiscreto*) troublesome
imposibilidad [imposiβili'ðað] *nf* impossibility; **mi ~ para hacerlo** my inability to do it
imposibilitado, -a [imposiβili'taðo, a] *adj*: **verse ~ para hacer algo** to be unable to do sth
imposibilitar [imposiβili'tar] *vt* to make impossible, prevent
imposible [impo'siβle] *adj* impossible; (*insoportable*) unbearable, intolerable; **es ~** it's out of the question; **es ~ de predecir** it's impossible to forecast *o* predict
imposición [imposi'θjon] *nf* imposition; (*Com*) tax; (*inversión*) deposit; **efectuar una ~** to make a deposit
impostor, a [impos'tor, a] *nm/f* impostor
impostura [impos'tura] *nf* fraud, imposture
impotencia [impo'tenθja] *nf* impotence
impotente [impo'tente] *adj* impotent
impracticable [imprakti'kaβle] *adj* (*irrealizable*) impracticable; (*intransitable*) impassable
imprecar [impre'kar] *vi* to curse
imprecisión [impreθi'sjon] *nf* lack of precision, vagueness
impreciso, -a [impre'θiso, a] *adj* imprecise, vague
impredecible [impreðe'θiβle], **impredictible** [impreðik'tiβle] *adj* unpredictable
impregnar [imprey'nar] *vt* to impregnate; (*fig*) to pervade; **impregnarse** *vr* to become impregnated
imprenta [im'prenta] *nf* (*acto*) printing; (*aparato*) press; (*casa*) printer's; (*letra*) print
impreque *etc* [im'preke] *vb ver* **imprecar**
imprescindible [impresθin'diβle] *adj* essential, vital
impresión [impre'sjon] *nf* impression; (*Imprenta*) printing; (*edición*) edition; (*Foto*) print; (*marca*) imprint; **~ digital** fingerprint
impresionable [impresjo'naβle] *adj* (*sensible*) impressionable
impresionado, -a [impresjo'naðo, a] *adj* impressed; (*Foto*) exposed
impresionante [impresjo'nante] *adj* impressive; (*tremendo*) tremendous; (*maravilloso*) great, marvellous
impresionar [impresjo'nar] *vt* (*conmover*) to move; (*afectar*) to impress, strike; (*película fotográfica*) to expose; **impresionarse** *vr* to be impressed; (*conmoverse*) to be moved
impresionista [impresjo'nista] *adj* impressionist(ic); (*Arte*) impressionist ■ *nm/f* impressionist
impreso, -a [im'preso, a] *pp de* **imprimir** ■ *adj* printed ■ *nm* printed paper/book *etc*; **impresos** *nmpl* printed matter *sg*; **~ de solicitud** application form
impresora [impre'sora] *nf* (*Inform*) printer; **~ de chorro de tinta** ink-jet printer; **~ (por) láser** laser printer; **~ de línea** line printer; **~ de matriz (de agujas)** dot-matrix printer; **~ de rueda** *o* **de margarita** daisy-wheel printer
imprevisible [impreβi'siβle] *adj* unforeseeable; (*individuo*) unpredictable
imprevisión [impreβi'sjon] *nf* short-sightedness; (*irreflexión*) thoughtlessness
imprevisto, -a [impre'βisto, a] *adj* unforeseen; (*inesperado*) unexpected ■ *nm*: **imprevistos** (*dinero*) incidentals, unforeseen expenses
imprimir [impri'mir] *vt* to stamp; (*textos*) to print; (*Inform*) to output, print out
improbabilidad [improβaβili'ðað] *nf* improbability, unlikelihood
improbable [impro'βaβle] *adj* improbable; (*inverosímil*) unlikely
improcedente [improθe'ðente] *adj* inappropriate; (*Jur*) inadmissible
improductivo, -a [improðuk'tiβo, a] *adj* unproductive
impronunciable [impronun'θjaβle] *adj* unpronounceable
improperio [impro'perjo] *nm* insult; **improperios** *nmpl* abuse *sg*
impropiedad [impropje'ðað] *nf* impropriety (of language)
impropio, -a [im'propjo, a] *adj* improper; (*inadecuado*) inappropriate
improvisación [improβisa'θjon] *nf* improvization
improvisado, -a [improβi'saðo, a] *adj* improvised, impromptu
improvisar [improβi'sar] *vt* to improvise; (*comida*) to rustle up ■ *vi* to improvise; (*Mus*) to extemporize; (*Teat etc*) to ad-lib

improviso [impro'βiso] *adv*: **de ~** unexpectedly, suddenly; *(Mus etc)* impromptu
imprudencia [impru'ðenθja] *nf* imprudence; *(indiscreción)* indiscretion; *(descuido)* carelessness
imprudente [impru'ðente] *adj* imprudent; indiscreet
Impte. *abr (= Importe)* amt.
impúdico, -a [im'puðiko, a] *adj* shameless; *(lujurioso)* lecherous
impudor [impu'ðor] *nm* shamelessness; *(lujuria)* lechery
impuesto, -a [im'pwesto, a] *pp de* **imponer** ▪ *adj* imposed ▪ *nm* tax; **anterior al ~** pre-tax; **sujeto a ~** taxable; **~ de lujo** luxury tax; **~ de plusvalía** capital gains tax; **~ sobre la propiedad** property tax; **~ sobre la renta** income tax; **~ sobre la renta de las personas físicas (IRPF)** personal income tax; **~ sobre la riqueza** wealth tax; **~ de transferencia de capital** capital transfer tax; **~ de venta** sales tax; **~ sobre el valor añadido (IVA)** value added tax (VAT)
impugnar [impuɣ'nar] *vt* to oppose, contest; *(refutar)* to refute, impugn
impulsar [impul'sar] *vt* to promote
impulsivo, -a [impul'siβo, a] *adj* impulsive
impulso [im'pulso] *nm* impulse; *(fuerza, empuje)* thrust, drive; *(fig: sentimiento)* urge, impulse; **a impulsos del miedo** driven on by fear
impune [im'pune] *adj* unpunished
impunemente [impune'mente] *adv* with impunity
impureza [impu'reθa] *nf* impurity; *(fig)* lewdness
impuro, -a [im'puro, a] *adj* impure; lewd
impuse *etc* [im'puse] *vb ver* **imponer**
imputación [imputa'θjon] *nf* imputation
imputar [impu'tar] *vt*: **~ a** to attribute to, to impute to
inabordable [inaβor'ðaβle] *adj* unapproachable
inacabable [inaka'βaβle] *adj (infinito)* endless; *(interminable)* interminable
inaccesible [inakθe'siβle] *adj* inaccessible; *(fig: precio)* beyond one's reach, prohibitive; *(individuo)* aloof
inacción [inak'θjon] *nf* inactivity
inaceptable [inaθep'taβle] *adj* unacceptable
inactividad [inaktiβi'ðað] *nf* inactivity; *(Com)* dullness
inactivo, -a [inak'tiβo, a] *adj* inactive; *(Com)* dull; *(población)* non-working
inadaptación [inaðapta'θjon] *nf* maladjustment
inadaptado, -a [inaðap'taðo, a] *adj* maladjusted ▪ *nm/f* misfit
inadecuado, -a [inaðe'kwaðo, a] *adj (insuficiente)* inadequate; *(inapto)* unsuitable
inadmisible [inaðmi'siβle] *adj* inadmissible
inadvertido, -a [inaðβer'tiðo, a] *adj (no visto)* unnoticed
inagotable [inaɣo'taβle] *adj* inexhaustible
inaguantable [inaɣwan'taβle] *adj* unbearable
inalámbrico, -a [ina'lambriko, a] *adj* cordless
inalcanzable [inalkan'θaβle] *adj* unattainable
inalterable [inalte'raβle] *adj* immutable, unchangeable
inamovible [inamo'βiβle] *adj* fixed, immovable; *(Tec)* undetachable
inanición [inani'θjon] *nf* starvation
inanimado, -a [inani'maðo, a] *adj* inanimate
inapelable [inape'laβle] *adj (Jur)* unappealable; *(fig)* irremediable
inapetencia [inape'tenθja] *nf* lack of appetite
inaplicable [inapli'kaβle] *adj* not applicable
inapreciable [inapre'θjaβle] *adj* invaluable
inarrugable [inarru'ɣaβle] *adj* crease-resistant
inasequible [inase'kiβle] *adj* unattainable
inaudito, -a [inau'ðito, a] *adj* unheard-of
inauguración [inauɣura'θjon] *nf* inauguration; *(de exposición)* opening
inaugurar [inauɣu'rar] *vt* to inaugurate; to open
I.N.B.A. *abr (Am)* = **Instituto Nacional de Bellas Artes**
inca ['inka] *nm/f* Inca
INCAE [in'kae] *nm abr* = **Instituto Centroamericano de Administración de Empresas**
incaico, -a [in'kaiko, a] *adj* Inca
incalculable [inkalku'laβle] *adj* incalculable
incandescente [inkandes'θente] *adj* incandescent
incansable [inkan'saβle] *adj* tireless, untiring
incapacidad [inkapaθi'ðað] *nf* incapacity; *(incompetencia)* incompetence; **~ física/mental** physical/mental disability
incapacitar [inkapaθi'tar] *vt (inhabilitar)* to incapacitate, handicap; *(descalificar)* to disqualify
incapaz [inka'paθ] *adj* incapable; **~ de hacer algo** unable to do sth
incautación [inkauta'θjon] *nf* seizure, confiscation

incautarse [inkau'tarse] *vr*: ~ **de** to seize, confiscate
incauto, -a [in'kauto, a] *adj* (*imprudente*) incautious, unwary
incendiar [inθen'djar] *vt* to set fire to; (*fig*) to inflame; **incendiarse** *vr* to catch fire
incendiario, -a [inθen'djarjo, a] *adj* incendiary ■ *nm/f* fire-raiser, arsonist
incendio [in'θendjo] *nm* fire; ~ **intencionado** arson
incentivo [inθen'tiβo] *nm* incentive
incertidumbre [inθerti'ðumbre] *nf* (*inseguridad*) uncertainty; (*duda*) doubt
incesante [inθe'sante] *adj* incessant
incesto [in'θesto] *nm* incest
incidencia [inθi'ðenθja] *nf* (*Mat*) incidence; (*fig*) effect
incidente [inθi'ðente] *nm* incident
incidir [inθi'ðir] *vi*: ~ **en** (*influir*) to influence; (*afectar*) to affect; ~ **en un error** to be mistaken
incienso [in'θjenso] *nm* incense
incierto, -a [in'θjerto, a] *adj* uncertain
incineración [inθinera'θjon] *nf* incineration; (*de cadáveres*) cremation
incinerar [inθine'rar] *vt* to burn; to cremate
incipiente [inθi'pjente] *adj* incipient
incisión [inθi'sjon] *nf* incision
incisivo, -a [inθi'siβo, a] *adj* sharp, cutting; (*fig*) incisive
inciso [in'θiso] *nm* (*Ling*) clause, sentence; (*coma*) comma; (*Jur*) subsection
incitante [inθi'tante] *adj* (*estimulante*) exciting; (*provocativo*) provocative
incitar [inθi'tar] *vt* to incite, rouse
incivil [inθi'βil] *adj* rude, uncivil
inclemencia [inkle'menθja] *nf* (*severidad*) harshness, severity; (*del tiempo*) inclemency
inclemente [inkle'mente] *adj* harsh, severe; inclement
inclinación [inklina'θjon] *nf* (*gen*) inclination; (*de tierras*) slope, incline; (*de cabeza*) nod, bow; (*fig*) leaning, bent
inclinado, -a [inkli'naðo, a] *adj* (*objeto*) leaning; (*superficie*) sloping
inclinar [inkli'nar] *vt* to incline; (*cabeza*) to nod, bow; **inclinarse** *vr* to lean, slope; (*en reverencia*) to bow; (*encorvarse*) to stoop; **inclinarse a** (*parecerse*) to take after, resemble; **inclinarse ante** to bow down to; **me inclino a pensar que ...** I'm inclined to think that ...
incluir [inklu'ir] *vt* to include; (*incorporar*) to incorporate; (*meter*) to enclose; **todo incluido** (*Com*) inclusive, all-in
inclusive [inklu'siβe] *adv* inclusive ■ *prep* including
incluso, -a [in'kluso, a] *adj* included ■ *adv* inclusively; (*hasta*) even
incluyendo *etc* [inklu'jendo] *vb ver* **incluir**
incobrable [inko'βraβle] *adj* irrecoverable; (*deuda*) bad
incógnita [in'koɣnita] *nf* (*fig*) mystery
incógnito [in'koɣnito]: **de** ~ *adv* incognito
incoherencia [inkoe'renθja] *nf* incoherence; (*falta de conexión*) disconnectedness
incoherente [inkoe'rente] *adj* incoherent
incoloro, -a [inko'loro, a] *adj* colourless
incólume [in'kolume] *adj* safe; (*indemne*) unhurt, unharmed
incombustible [inkombus'tiβle] *adj* (*gen*) fire-resistant; (*telas*) fireproof
incomodar [inkomo'ðar] *vt* to inconvenience; (*molestar*) to bother, trouble; (*fastidiar*) to annoy; **incomodarse** *vr* to put o.s. out; (*fastidiarse*) to get annoyed; **no se incomode** don't bother
incomodidad [inkomoði'ðað] *nf* inconvenience; (*fastidio, enojo*) annoyance; (*de vivienda*) discomfort
incómodo, -a [in'komoðo, a] *adj* (*inconfortable*) uncomfortable; (*molesto*) annoying; (*inconveniente*) inconvenient; **sentirse** ~ to feel ill at ease
incomparable [inkompa'raβle] *adj* incomparable
incomparecencia [inkompare'θenθja] *nf* (*Jur etc*) failure to appear
incompatible [inkompa'tiβle] *adj* incompatible
incompetencia [inkompe'tenθja] *nf* incompetence
incompetente [inkompe'tente] *adj* incompetent
incompleto, -a [inkom'pleto, a] *adj* incomplete, unfinished
incomprendido, -a [inkompren'diðo, a] *adj* misunderstood
incomprensible [inkompren'siβle] *adj* incomprehensible
incomunicado, -a [inkomuni'kaðo, a] *adj* (*aislado*) cut off, isolated; (*confinado*) in solitary confinement
incomunicar [inkomuni'kar] *vt* (*gen*) to cut off; (*preso*) to put into solitary confinement; **incomunicarse** *vr* (*fam*) to go into one's shell
incomunique *etc* [inkomu'nike] *vb ver* **incomunicar**
inconcebible [inkonθe'βiβle] *adj* inconceivable
inconcluso, -a [inkon'kluso, a] *adj* (*inacabado*) unfinished
incondicional [inkondiθjo'nal] *adj* unconditional; (*apoyo*) wholehearted; (*partidario*) staunch

inconexo, -a [inko'nekso, a] *adj* unconnected; (*desunido*) disconnected; (*incoherente*) incoherent
inconfeso, -a [inkon'feso, a] *adj* unconfessed; **un homosexual** ~ a closet homosexual
inconformista [inkonfor'mista] *adj, nm/f* nonconformist
inconfundible [inkonfun'diβle] *adj* unmistakable
incongruente [inkon'grwente] *adj* incongruous
inconmensurable [inkonmensu'raβle] *adj* immeasurable, vast
inconsciencia [inkons'θjenθja] *nf* unconsciousness; (*fig*) thoughtlessness
inconsciente [inkons'θjente] *adj* unconscious; thoughtless; (*ignorante*) unaware; (*involuntario*) unwitting
inconsecuencia [inkonse'kwenθja] *nf* inconsistency
inconsecuente [inkonse'kwente] *adj* inconsistent
inconsiderado, -a [inkonsiðe'raðo, a] *adj* inconsiderate
inconsistente [inkonsis'tente] *adj* inconsistent; (*Culin*) lumpy; (*endeble*) weak; (*tela*) flimsy
inconstancia [inkons'tanθja] *nf* inconstancy; (*de tiempo*) changeability; (*capricho*) fickleness
inconstante [inkons'tante] *adj* inconstant; changeable; fickle
incontable [inkon'taβle] *adj* countless, innumerable
incontestable [inkontes'taβle] *adj* unanswerable; (*innegable*) undeniable
incontinencia [inkonti'nenθja] *nf* incontinence
incontrolado, -a [inkontro'laðo, a] *adj* uncontrolled
incontrovertible [inkontroβer'tiβle] *adj* undeniable, incontrovertible
inconveniencia [inkombe'njenθja] *nf* unsuitability, inappropriateness; (*falta de cortesía*) impoliteness
inconveniente [inkombe'njente] *adj* unsuitable; impolite ■ *nm* obstacle; (*desventaja*) disadvantage; **el ~ es que ...** the trouble is that ...; **no hay ~ en** *o* **para hacer eso** there is no objection to doing that; **no tengo** ~ I don't mind
incordiar [inkor'ðjar] *vt* (*fam*) to hassle
incorporación [inkorpora'θjon] *nf* incorporation; (*fig*) inclusion
incorporado, -a [inkorpo'raðo, a] *adj* (*Tec*) built-in
incorporar [inkorpo'rar] *vt* to incorporate; (*abarcar*) to embody; (*Culin*) to mix; **incorporarse** *vr* to sit up; **incorporarse a** to join
incorrección [inkorrek'θjon] *nf* incorrectness, inaccuracy; (*descortesía*) bad-mannered behaviour
incorrecto, -a [inko'rrekto, a] *adj* incorrect, wrong; (*comportamiento*) bad-mannered
incorregible [inkorre'xiβle] *adj* incorrigible
incorruptible [inkorrup'tiβle] *adj* incorruptible
incorrupto, -a [inko'rrupto, a] *adj* uncorrupted; (*fig*) pure
incredulidad [inkreðuli'ðað] *nf* incredulity; (*escepticismo*) scepticism
incrédulo, -a [in'kreðulo, a] *adj* incredulous, unbelieving; sceptical
increíble [inkre'iβle] *adj* incredible
incrementar [inkremen'tar] *vt* (*aumentar*) to increase; (*alzar*) to raise; **incrementarse** *vr* to increase
incremento [inkre'mento] *nm* increment; (*aumento*) rise, increase; **~ de precio** rise in price
increpar [inkre'par] *vt* to reprimand
incriminar [inkrimi'nar] *vt* (*Jur*) to incriminate
incruento, -a [in'krwento, a] *adj* bloodless
incrustar [inkrus'tar] *vt* to incrust; (*piedras: en joya*) to inlay; (*fig*) to graft; (*Tec*) to set
incubar [inku'βar] *vt* to incubate; (*fig*) to hatch
incuestionable [inkwestjo'naβle] *adj* unchallengeable
inculcar [inkul'kar] *vt* to inculcate
inculpar [inkul'par] *vt*: **~ de** (*acusar*) to accuse of; (*achacar, atribuir*) to charge with, blame for
inculque *etc* [in'kulke] *vb ver* **inculcar**
inculto, -a [in'kulto, a] *adj* (*persona*) uneducated, uncultured; (*fig: grosero*) uncouth ■ *nm/f* ignoramus
incumbencia [inkum'benθja] *nf* obligation; **no es de mi ~** it is not my field
incumbir [inkum'bir] *vi*: **~ a** to be incumbent upon; **no me incumbe a mí** it is no concern of mine
incumplimiento [inkumpli'mjento] *nm* non-fulfilment; (*Com*) repudiation; **~ de contrato** breach of contract; **por ~** by default
incurable [inku'raβle] *adj* (*enfermedad*) incurable; (*paciente*) incurably ill
incurrir [inku'rrir] *vi*: **~ en** to incur; (*crimen*) to commit; **~ en un error** to make a mistake
indagación [indaɣa'θjon] *nf* investigation; (*búsqueda*) search; (*Jur*) inquest

indagar [inda'ɣar] *vt* to investigate; to search; (*averiguar*) to ascertain
indague *etc* [in'daɣe] *vb ver* **indagar**
indebido, -a [inde'βiðo, a] *adj* undue; (*dicho*) improper
indecencia [inde'θenθja] *nf* indecency; (*dicho*) obscenity
indecente [inde'θente] *adj* indecent, improper; (*lascivo*) obscene
indecible [inde'θiβle] *adj* unspeakable; (*indescriptible*) indescribable
indeciso, -a [inde'θiso, a] *adj* (*por decidir*) undecided; (*vacilante*) hesitant
indefenso, -a [inde'fenso, a] *adj* defenceless
indefinido, -a [indefi'niðo, a] *adj* indefinite; (*vago*) vague, undefined
indeleble [inde'leβle] *adj* indelible
indemne [in'demne] *adj* (*objeto*) undamaged; (*persona*) unharmed, unhurt
indemnice *etc* [indem'niθe] *vb ver* **indemnizar**
indemnización [indemniθa'θjon] *nf* (*acto*) indemnification; (*suma*) indemnity; **~ de cese** redundancy payment; **~ de despido** severance pay; **doble ~** double indemnity
indemnizar [indemni'θar] *vt* to indemnify; (*compensar*) to compensate
independencia [indepen'denθja] *nf* independence
independice *etc* [indepen'diθe] *vb ver* **independizar**
independiente [indepen'djente] *adj* (*libre*) independent; (*autónomo*) self-sufficient; (*Inform*) stand-alone
independizar [independi'θar] *vt* to make independent; **independizarse** *vr* to become independent
indescifrable [indesθi'fraβle] *adj* (*Mil: código*) indecipherable; (*fig: misterio*) impenetrable
indeseable [indese'aβle] *adj, nm/f* undesirable
indeterminado, -a [indetermi'naðo, a] *adj* (*tb Ling*) indefinite; (*desconocido*) indeterminate
India ['indja] *nf*: **la ~** India
indiano, -a [in'djano, a] *adj* (Spanish-) American ■ *nm Spaniard who has made good in America*
indicación [indika'θjon] *nf* indication; (*dato*) piece of information; (*señal*) sign; (*sugerencia*) suggestion, hint; **indicaciones** *nfpl* (*Com*) instructions
indicado, -a [indi'kaðo, a] *adj* (*apto*) right, appropriate
indicador [indika'ðor] *nm* indicator; (*Tec*) gauge, meter; (*aguja*) hand, pointer; (*de carretera*) roadsign; **~ de encendido** (*Inform*) power-on indicator
indicar [indi'kar] *vt* (*mostrar*) to indicate, show; (*suj: termómetro etc*) to read, register; (*señalar*) to point to
indicativo, -a [indika'tiβo, a] *adj* indicative ■ *nm* (*Radio*) call sign; **~ de nacionalidad** (*Auto*) national identification plate
índice ['indiθe] *nm* index; (*catálogo*) catalogue; (*Anat*) index finger, forefinger; **~ del coste de (la) vida** cost-of-living index; **~ de crédito** credit rating; **~ de materias** table of contents; **~ de natalidad** birth rate; **~ de precios al por menor (IPM)** (*Com*) retail price index (RPI)
indicio [in'diθjo] *nm* indication, sign; (*en pesquisa etc*) clue
indiferencia [indife'renθja] *nf* indifference; (*apatía*) apathy
indiferente [indife'rente] *adj* indifferent; **me es ~** it makes no difference to me
indígena [in'dixena] *adj* indigenous, native ■ *nm/f* native
indigencia [indi'xenθja] *nf* poverty, need
indigenista [indixe'nista] (*Am*) *adj* pro-Indian ■ *nm/f* (*estudiante*) student of Indian cultures; (*Pol etc*) promoter of Indian cultures
indigestar [indixes'tar] *vt* to cause indigestion to; **indigestarse** *vr* to get indigestion
indigestión [indixes'tjon] *nf* indigestion
indigesto, -a [indi'xesto, a] *adj* undigested; (*indigerible*) indigestible; (*fig*) turgid
indignación [indiɣna'θjon] *nf* indignation
indignante [indiɣ'nante] *adj* outrageous, infuriating
indignar [indiɣ'nar] *vt* to anger, make indignant; **indignarse** *vr*: **indignarse por** to get indignant about
indigno, -a [in'diɣno, a] *adj* (*despreciable*) low, contemptible; (*inmerecido*) unworthy
indio, -a ['indjo, a] *adj, nm/f* Indian
indique *etc* [in'dike] *vb ver* **indicar**
indirecto, -a [indi'rekto, a] *adj* indirect ■ *nf* insinuation, innuendo; (*sugerencia*) hint
indisciplina [indisθi'plina] *nf* (*gen*) lack of discipline; (*Mil*) insubordination
indiscreción [indiskre'θjon] *nf* (*imprudencia*) indiscretion; (*irreflexión*) tactlessness; (*acto*) gaffe, faux pas; **..., si no es ~** ..., if I may say so
indiscreto, -a [indis'kreto, a] *adj* indiscreet
indiscriminado, -a [indiskrimi'naðo, a] *adj* indiscriminate
indiscutible [indisku'tiβle] *adj* indisputable, unquestionable
indispensable [indispen'saβle] *adj* indispensable

indispondré *etc* [indispon'dre] *vb ver* **indisponer**
indisponer [indispo'ner] *vt* to spoil, upset; (*salud*) to make ill; **indisponerse** *vr* to fall ill; **indisponerse con algn** to fall out with sb
indisponga *etc* [indis'ponga] *vb ver* **indisponer**
indisposición [indisposi'θjon] *nf* indisposition; (*desgana*) unwillingness
indispuesto, -a [indis'pwesto, a] *pp de* **indisponer** ■ *adj* indisposed; **sentirse ~** to feel unwell *o* indisposed
indispuse *etc* [indis'puse] *vb ver* **indisponer**
indistinto, -a [indis'tinto, a] *adj* indistinct; (*vago*) vague
individual [indiβi'ðwal] *adj* individual; (*habitación*) single ■ *nm* (*Deporte*) singles *sg*
individuo, -a [indi'βiðwo, a] *adj* individual ■ *nm* individual
Indochina [indo'tʃina] *nf* Indochina
indocumentado, -a [indokumen'taðo, a] *adj* without identity papers
indoeuropeo, -a [indoeuro'peo, a] *adj, nm/f* Indo-European
índole ['indole] *nf* (*naturaleza*) nature; (*clase*) sort, kind
indolencia [indo'lenθja] *nf* indolence, laziness
indoloro, -a [in'doloro, a] *adj* painless
indomable [indo'maβle] *adj* (*animal*) untameable; (*espíritu*) indomitable
indómito, -a [in'domito, a] *adj* indomitable
Indonesia [indo'nesja] *nf* Indonesia
indonesio, -a [indo'nesjo, a] *adj, nm/f* Indonesian
inducción [induk'θjon] *nf* (*Filosofía, Elec*) induction; **por ~** by induction
inducir [indu'θir] *vt* to induce; (*inferir*) to infer; (*persuadir*) to persuade; **~ a algn en el error** to mislead sb
indudable [indu'ðaβle] *adj* undoubted; (*incuestionable*) unquestionable; **es ~ que ...** there is no doubt that ...
indulgencia [indul'xenθja] *nf* indulgence; (*Jur etc*) leniency; **proceder sin ~ contra** to proceed ruthlessly against
indultar [indul'tar] *vt* (*perdonar*) to pardon, reprieve; (*librar de pago*) to exempt
indulto [in'dulto] *nm* pardon; exemption
indumentaria [indumen'tarja] *nf* (*ropa*) clothing, dress
industria [in'dustrja] *nf* industry; (*habilidad*) skill; **~ agropecuaria** farming and fishing; **~ pesada** heavy industry; **~ petrolífera** oil industry
industrial [indus'trjal] *adj* industrial ■ *nm* industrialist
industrializar [industrjali'θar] *vt* to industrialize; **industrializarse** *vr* to become industrialized
INE ['ine] *nm abr* (*Esp*) = **Instituto Nacional de Estadística**
inédito, -a [i'neðito, a] *adj* (*libro*) unpublished; (*nuevo*) unheard-of
inefable [ine'faβle] *adj* ineffable, indescribable
ineficacia [inefi'kaθja] *nf* (*de medida*) ineffectiveness; (*de proceso*) inefficiency
ineficaz [inefi'kaθ] *adj* (*inútil*) ineffective; (*ineficiente*) inefficient
ineludible [inelu'ðiβle] *adj* inescapable, unavoidable
INEM [i'nem] *nm abr* (*Esp*: = *Instituto Nacional de Empleo*) ≈ Department of Employment (*Brit*)
INEN ['inen] *nm abr* (*México*) = **Instituto Nacional de Energía Nuclear**
inenarrable [inena'rraβle] *adj* inexpressible
ineptitud [inepti'tuð] *nf* ineptitude, incompetence
inepto, -a [i'nepto, a] *adj* inept, incompetent
inequívoco, -a [ine'kiβoko, a] *adj* unequivocal; (*inconfundible*) unmistakable
inercia [i'nerθja] *nf* inertia; (*pasividad*) passivity
inerme [i'nerme] *adj* (*sin armas*) unarmed; (*indefenso*) defenceless
inerte [i'nerte] *adj* inert; (*inmóvil*) motionless
inescrutable [ineskru'taβle] *adj* inscrutable
inesperado, -a [inespe'raðo, a] *adj* unexpected, unforeseen
inestable [ines'taβle] *adj* unstable
inestimable [inesti'maβle] *adj* inestimable; **de valor ~** invaluable
inevitable [ineβi'taβle] *adj* inevitable
inexactitud [ineksakti'tuð] *nf* inaccuracy
inexacto, -a [inek'sakto, a] *adj* inaccurate; (*falso*) untrue
inexistente [ineksis'tente] *adj* non-existent
inexorable [inekso'raβle] *adj* inexorable
inexperiencia [inekspe'rjenθja] *nf* inexperience, lack of experience
inexperto, -a [ineks'perto, a] *adj* (*novato*) inexperienced
inexplicable [inekspli'kaβle] *adj* inexplicable
inexpresable [inekspre'saβle] *adj* inexpressible
inexpresivo, -a [inekspre'siβo, a] *adj* inexpressive; (*ojos*) dull; (*cara*) wooden
inexpugnable [inekspuɣ'naβle] *adj* (*Mil*) impregnable; (*fig*) firm
infalible [infa'liβle] *adj* infallible; (*indefectible*) certain, sure; (*plan*) foolproof
infame [in'fame] *adj* infamous
infamia [in'famja] *nf* infamy; (*deshonra*) disgrace

infancia [in'fanθja] *nf* infancy, childhood; **jardín de la ~** nursery school
infanta [in'fanta] *nf* (*hija del rey*) infanta, princess
infante [in'fante] *nm* (*hijo del rey*) infante, prince
infantería [infante'ria] *nf* infantry
infantil [infan'til] *adj* child's, children's; (*pueril, aniñado*) infantile; (*cándido*) childlike
infarto [in'farto] *nm* (*tb*: **infarto de miocardio**) heart attack
infatigable [infati'ɣaβle] *adj* tireless, untiring
infección [infek'θjon] *nf* infection
infeccioso, -a [infek'θjoso, a] *adj* infectious
infectar [infek'tar] *vt* to infect; **infectarse** *vr*: **infectarse (de)** (*tb fig*) to become infected (with)
infecundidad [infekundi'ðað] *nf* (*de tierra*) infertility, barrenness; (*de mujer*) sterility
infecundo, -a [infe'kundo, a] *adj* infertile, barren; sterile
infeliz [infe'liθ] *adj* (*desgraciado*) unhappy, wretched; (*inocente*) gullible ■ *nm/f* (*desgraciado*) wretch; (*inocentón*) simpleton
inferior [infe'rjor] *adj* inferior; (*situación, Mat*) lower ■ *nm/f* inferior, subordinate; **cualquier número ~ a nueve** any number less than *o* under *o* below nine; **una cantidad ~** a lesser quantity
inferioridad [inferjori'ðað] *nf* inferiority; **estar en ~ de condiciones** to be at a disadvantage
inferir [infe'rir] *vt* (*deducir*) to infer, deduce; (*causar*) to cause
infernal [infer'nal] *adj* infernal
infértil [in'fertil] *adj* infertile
infestar [infes'tar] *vt* to infest
infidelidad [infiðeli'ðað] *nf* infidelity, unfaithfulness
infiel [in'fjel] *adj* unfaithful, disloyal; (*falso*) inaccurate ■ *nm/f* infidel, unbeliever
infiera *etc* [in'fjera] *vb ver* **inferir**
infierno [in'fjerno] *nm* hell; **¡vete al ~!** go to hell; **está en el quinto ~** it's at the back of beyond
infiltrar [infil'trar] *vt* to infiltrate; **infiltrarse** *vr* to infiltrate, filter; (*líquidos*) to percolate
ínfimo, -a ['infimo, a] *adj* (*vil*) vile, mean; (*más bajo*) lowest; (*peor*) worst; (*miserable*) wretched
infinidad [infini'ðað] *nf* infinity; (*abundancia*) great quantity; **~ de** vast numbers of; **~ de veces** countless times
infinitivo [infini'tiβo] *nm* infinitive
infinito, -a [infi'nito, a] *adj* infinite; (*fig*) boundless ■ *adv* infinitely ■ *nm* infinite; (*Mat*) infinity; **hasta lo ~** ad infinitum
infiriendo *etc* [infi'rjendo] *vb ver* **inferir**
inflación [infla'θjon] *nf* (*hinchazón*) swelling; (*monetaria*) inflation; (*fig*) conceit
inflacionario, -a [inflaθjo'narjo, a] *adj* inflationary
inflacionismo [inflaθjo'nismo] *nm* (*Econ*) inflation
inflacionista [inflaθjo'nista] *adj* inflationary
inflamar [infla'mar] *vt* to set on fire; (*Med, fig*) to inflame; **inflamarse** *vr* to catch fire; to become inflamed
inflar [in'flar] *vt* (*hinchar*) to inflate, blow up; (*fig*) to exaggerate; **inflarse** *vr* to swell (up); (*fig*) to get conceited
inflexible [inflek'siβle] *adj* inflexible; (*fig*) unbending
infligir [infli'xir] *vt* to inflict
inflija *etc* [in'flixa] *vb ver* **infligir**
influencia [in'flwenθja] *nf* influence
influenciar [inflwen'θjar] *vt* to influence
influir [influ'ir] *vt* to influence ■ *vi* to have influence, carry weight; **~ en** *o* **sobre** to influence, affect; (*contribuir a*) to have a hand in
influjo [in'fluxo] *nm* influence; **~ de capitales** (*Econ etc*) capital influx
influyendo *etc* [influ'jendo] *vb ver* **influir**
influyente [influ'jente] *adj* influential
información [informa'θjon] *nf* information; (*noticias*) news *sg*; (*informe*) report; (*Inform: datos*) data; (*Jur*) inquiry; **I~** (*oficina*) Information; (*Telec*) Directory Enquiries (*Brit*), Directory Assistance (*US*); (*mostrador*) Information Desk; **una ~** a piece of information; **abrir una ~** (*Jur*) to begin proceedings; **~ deportiva** (*en periódico*) sports section
informal [infor'mal] *adj* informal
informante [infor'mante] *nm/f* informant
informar [infor'mar] *vt* (*gen*) to inform; (*revelar*) to reveal, make known ■ *vi* (*Jur*) to plead; (*denunciar*) to inform; (*dar cuenta de*) to report on; **informarse** *vr* to find out; **informarse de** to inquire into
informática [infor'matika] *nf ver* **informático**
informatice *etc* [informa'tiθe] *vb ver* **informatizar**
informático, -a [infor'matiko, a] *adj* computer *cpd* ■ *nf* (*Tec*) information technology; computing; (*Escol*) computer science *o* studies; **~ de gestión** commercial computing
informativo, -a [informa'tiβo, a] *adj* (*libro*) informative; (*folleto*) information *cpd*;

(*Radio, TV*) news *cpd* ■ *nm* (*Radio, TV*) news programme
informatización [informatiθa'θjon] *nf* computerization
informatizar [informati'θar] *vt* to computerize
informe [in'forme] *adj* shapeless ■ *nm* report; (*dictamen*) statement; (*Mil*) briefing; (*Jur*) plea; **informes** *nmpl* information *sg*; (*datos*) data; **~ anual** annual report; **~ del juez** summing-up
infortunio [infor'tunjo] *nm* misfortune
infracción [infrak'θjon] *nf* infraction, infringement; (*Auto*) offence
infraestructura [infraestruk'tura] *nf* infrastructure
in fraganti [infra'ɣanti] *adv*: **pillar a algn ~** to catch sb red-handed
infranqueable [infranke'aβle] *adj* impassable; (*fig*) insurmountable
infrarrojo, -a [infra'rroxo, a] *adj* infrared
infravalorar [infraβalo'rar] *vt* to undervalue; (*Finanzas*) to underestimate
infringir [infrin'xir] *vt* to infringe, contravene
infrinja *etc* [in'frinxa] *vb ver* **infringir**
infructuoso, -a [infruk'twoso, a] *adj* fruitless, unsuccessful
infundado, -a [infun'daðo, a] *adj* groundless, unfounded
infundir [infun'dir] *vt* to infuse, instil; **~ ánimo a algn** to encourage sb; **~ miedo a algn** to intimidate sb
infusión [infu'sjon] *nf* infusion; **~ de manzanilla** camomile tea
Ing. *abr* (*Am*) = **Ingeniero**
ingeniar [inxe'njar] *vt* to think up, devise; **ingeniarse** *vr* to manage; **ingeniarse para** to manage to
ingeniería [inxenje'ria] *nf* engineering; **~ genética** genetic engineering; **~ de sistemas** (*Inform*) systems engineering
ingeniero, -a [inxe'njero, a] *nm/f* engineer; (*Am*) *courtesy title*; **~ de sonido** sound engineer; **~ de caminos** civil engineer
ingenio [in'xenjo] *nm* (*talento*) talent; (*agudeza*) wit; (*habilidad*) ingenuity, inventiveness; (*Tec*): **~ azucarero** sugar refinery
ingenioso, -a [inxe'njoso, a] *adj* ingenious, clever; (*divertido*) witty
ingente [in'xente] *adj* huge, enormous
ingenuidad [inxenwi'ðað] *nf* ingenuousness; (*sencillez*) simplicity
ingenuo, -a [in'xenwo, a] *adj* ingenuous
ingerir [inxe'rir] *vt* to ingest; (*tragar*) to swallow; (*consumir*) to consume
ingiera *etc* [in'xjera], **ingiriendo** *etc* [inxi'rjenðo] *vb ver* **ingerir**
Inglaterra [ingla'terra] *nf* England
ingle ['ingle] *nf* groin
inglés, -esa [in'gles, esa] *adj* English ■ *nm/f* Englishman(-woman) ■ *nm* (*Ling*) English; **los ingleses** the English
ingratitud [ingrati'tuð] *nf* ingratitude
ingrato, -a [in'grato, a] *adj* ungrateful; (*tarea*) thankless
ingravidez [ingraβi'ðeθ] *nf* weightlessness
ingrediente [ingre'ðjente] *nm* ingredient; **ingredientes** *nmpl* (*Am: tapas*) titbits
ingresar [ingre'sar] *vt* (*dinero*) to deposit ■ *vi* to come *o* go in; **~ a** (*esp Am*) to enter; **~ en** (*club*) to join; (*Mil, Escol*) to enrol in; **~ en el hospital** to go into hospital
ingreso [in'greso] *nm* (*entrada*) entry; (*: en hospital etc*) admission; (*Mil, Escol*) enrolment; **ingresos** *nmpl* (*dinero*) income *sg*; (*: Com*) takings *pl*; **~ gravable** taxable income *sg*; **ingresos accesorios** fringe benefits; **ingresos brutos** gross receipts; **ingresos devengados** earned income *sg*; **ingresos exentos de impuestos** non-taxable income *sg*; **ingresos personales disponibles** disposable personal income *sg*
íngrimo, -a ['ingrimo, a] *adj* (*Am: tb:* **íngrimo y solo**) all alone
inhábil [i'naβil] *adj* unskilful, clumsy
inhabilitar [inaβili'tar] *vt* (*Pol, Med*): **~ a algn (para hacer algo)** to disqualify sb (from doing sth)
inhabitable [inaβi'taβle] *adj* uninhabitable
inhabituado, -a [inaβi'twaðo, a] *adj* unaccustomed
inhalador [inala'ðor] *nm* (*Med*) inhaler
inhalar [ina'lar] *vt* to inhale
inherente [ine'rente] *adj* inherent
inhibición [iniβi'θjon] *nf* inhibition
inhibir [ini'βir] *vt* to inhibit; (*Rel*) to restrain; **inhibirse** *vr* to keep out
inhospitalario, -a [inospita'larjo, a], **inhóspito, -a** [i'nospito, a] *adj* inhospitable
inhumación [inuma'θjon] *nf* burial, interment
inhumano, -a [inu'mano, a] *adj* inhuman
INI ['ini] *nm abr* = **Instituto Nacional de Industria**
inicial [ini'θjal] *adj, nf* initial
inicialice *etc* [iniθja'liθe] *vb ver* **inicializar**
inicializar [iniθjali'θar] *vt* (*Inform*) to initialize
iniciar [ini'θjar] *vt* (*persona*) to initiate; (*empezar*) to begin, commence; (*conversación*) to start up; **~ a algn en un secreto** to let sb into a secret; **~ la sesión** (*Inform*) to log in *o* on

iniciativa [iniθja'tiβa] *nf* initiative; *(liderazgo)* leadership; **la ~ privada** private enterprise
inicio [i'niθjo] *nm* start, beginning
inicuo, -a [i'nikwo, a] *adj* iniquitous
inigualado, -a [iniɣwa'laðo, a] *adj* unequalled
ininteligible [ininteli'xiβle] *adj* unintelligible
ininterrumpido, -a [ininterrum'piðo, a] *adj* uninterrupted; *(proceso)* continuous; *(progreso)* steady
injerencia [inxe'renθja] *nf* interference
injertar [inxer'tar] *vt* to graft
injerto [in'xerto] *nm* graft; **~ de piel** skin graft
injuria [in'xurja] *nf (agravio, ofensa)* offence; *(insulto)* insult; **injurias** *nfpl* abuse *sg*
injuriar [inxu'rjar] *vt* to insult
injurioso, -a [inxu'rjoso, a] *adj* offensive; insulting
injusticia [inxus'tiθja] *nf* injustice, unfairness; **con ~** unjustly
injusto, -a [in'xusto, a] *adj* unjust, unfair
inmaculado, -a [inmaku'laðo, a] *adj* immaculate, spotless
inmadurez [inmaðu'reθ] *nf* immaturity
inmaduro, -a [inma'ðuro, a] *adj* immature; *(fruta)* unripe
inmediaciones [inmeðja'θjones] *nfpl* neighbourhood *sg*, environs
inmediatez [inmeðja'teθ] *nf* immediacy
inmediato, -a [inme'ðjato, a] *adj* immediate; *(contiguo)* adjoining; *(rápido)* prompt; *(próximo)* neighbouring, next; **de ~** *(esp Am)* immediately
inmejorable [inmexo'raβle] *adj* unsurpassable; *(precio)* unbeatable
inmemorable [inmemo'raβle], **inmemorial** [inmemo'rjal] *adj* immemorial
inmenso, -a [in'menso, a] *adj* immense, huge
inmerecido, -a [inmere'θiðo, a] *adj* undeserved
inmersión [inmer'sjon] *nf* immersion; *(buzo)* dive
inmigración [inmiɣra'θjon] *nf* immigration
inmigrante [inmi'ɣrante] *adj, nm/f* immigrant
inminente [inmi'nente] *adj* imminent, impending
inmiscuirse [inmisku'irse] *vr* to interfere, meddle
inmiscuyendo *etc* [inmisku'jendo] *vb ver* **inmiscuirse**
inmobiliario, -a [inmoβi'ljarjo, a] *adj* real-estate *cpd*, property *cpd* ■ *nf* estate agency
inmolar [inmo'lar] *vt* to immolate, sacrifice
inmoral [inmo'ral] *adj* immoral
inmortal [inmor'tal] *adj* immortal
inmortalice *etc* [inmorta'liθe] *vb ver* **inmortalizar**
inmortalizar [inmortali'θar] *vt* to immortalize
inmotivado, -a [inmoti'βaðo, a] *adj* motiveless; *(sospecha)* groundless
inmóvil [in'moβil] *adj* immobile
inmovilizar [inmoβili'θar] *vt* to immobilize; *(paralizar)* to paralyse; **inmovilizarse** *vr*: **se le ha inmovilizado la pierna** her leg was paralysed
inmueble [in'mweβle] *adj*: **bienes inmuebles** real estate *sg*, landed property *sg* ■ *nm* property
inmundicia [inmun'diθja] *nf* filth
inmundo, -a [in'mundo, a] *adj* filthy
inmune [in'mune] *adj (Med)* immune
inmunidad [inmuni'ðað] *nf* immunity; *(fisco)* exemption; **~ diplomática/parlamentaria** diplomatic/parliamentary immunity
inmunitario, -a [inmuni'tarjo, a] *adj*: **sistema ~** immune system
inmunización [inmuniθa'θjon] *nf* immunization
inmunizar [inmuni'θar] *vt* to immunize
inmutable [inmu'taβle] *adj* immutable; **permaneció ~** he didn't flinch
inmutarse [inmu'tarse] *vr*: **siguió sin ~** he carried on unperturbed
innato, -a [in'nato, a] *adj* innate
innecesario, -a [inneθe'sarjo, a] *adj* unnecessary
innegable [inne'ɣaβle] *adj* undeniable
innoble [in'noβle] *adj* ignoble
innovación [innoβa'θjon] *nf* innovation
innovador, a [innoβa'ðor, a] *adj* innovatory, innovative ■ *nm/f* innovator
innovar [inno'βar] *vt* to introduce
innumerable [innume'raβle] *adj* countless
inocencia [ino'θenθja] *nf* innocence
inocentada [inoθen'taða] *nf* practical joke
inocente [ino'θente] *adj (ingenuo)* naive, innocent; *(no culpable)* innocent; *(sin malicia)* harmless ■ *nm/f* simpleton; **día de los (Santos) Inocentes** ≈ April Fool's Day; *see note*

INOCENTE

The 28th December, *el día de los (Santos) Inocentes*, is when the Church commemorates the story of Herod's slaughter of the innocent children of Judea in the time of Christ. On this day

Spaniards play *inocentadas* (practical jokes) on each other, much like our April Fools' Day pranks, eg typically sticking a *monigote* (cut-out paper figure) on someone's back, or broadcasting unlikely news stories.

inocuidad [inokwi'ðað] *nf* harmlessness
inocular [inoku'lar] *vt* to inoculate
inocuo, -a [i'nokwo, a] *adj* (*sustancia*) harmless
inodoro, -a [ino'ðoro, a] *adj* odourless ■ *nm* toilet (*Brit*), lavatory (*Brit*), washroom (*US*)
inofensivo, -a [inofen'siβo, a] *adj* inoffensive
inolvidable [inolβi'ðaβle] *adj* unforgettable
inoperante [inope'rante] *adj* ineffective
inopinado, -a [inopi'naðo, a] *adj* unexpected
inoportuno, -a [inopor'tuno, a] *adj* untimely; (*molesto*) inconvenient; (*inapropiado*) inappropriate
inoxidable [inoksi'ðaβle] *adj* stainless; **acero ~** stainless steel
inquebrantable [inkeβran'taβle] *adj* unbreakable; (*fig*) unshakeable
inquiera *etc* [in'kjera] *vb ver* **inquirir**
inquietante [inkje'tante] *adj* worrying
inquietar [inkje'tar] *vt* to worry, trouble; **inquietarse** *vr* to worry, get upset
inquieto, -a [in'kjeto, a] *adj* anxious, worried; **estar ~ por** to be worried about
inquietud [inkje'tuð] *nf* anxiety, worry
inquilino, -a [inki'lino, a] *nm/f* tenant; (*Com*) lessee
inquiriendo *etc* [inki'rjendo] *vb ver* **inquirir**
inquirir [inki'rir] *vt* to enquire into, investigate
insaciable [insa'θjaβle] *adj* insatiable
insalubre [insa'luβre] *adj* unhealthy; (*condiciones*) insanitary
INSALUD [insa'luð] *nm abr* (*Esp*) = **Instituto Nacional de la Salud**
insano, -a [in'sano, a] *adj* (*loco*) insane; (*malsano*) unhealthy
insatisfacción [insatisfak'θjon] *nf* dissatisfaction
insatisfecho, -a [insatis'fetʃo, a] *adj* (*condición*) unsatisfied; (*estado de ánimo*) dissatisfied
inscribir [inskri'βir] *vt* to inscribe; (*en lista*) to put; (*en censo*) to register; **inscribirse** *vr* to register; (*Escol etc*) to enrol
inscripción [inskrip'θjon] *nf* inscription; (*Escol etc*) enrolment; (*en censo*) registration
inscrito [ins'krito] *pp de* **inscribir**
insecticida [insekti'θiða] *nm* insecticide
insecto [in'sekto] *nm* insect
inseguridad [inseɣuri'ðað] *nf* insecurity
inseguro, -a [inse'ɣuro, a] *adj* insecure; (*inconstante*) unsteady; (*incierto*) uncertain
inseminación [insemina'θjon] *nf*: **~ artificial** artificial insemination (A.I.)
inseminar [insemi'nar] *vt* to inseminate, fertilize
insensato, -a [insen'sato, a] *adj* foolish, stupid
insensibilice *etc* [insensiβi'liθe] *vb ver* **insensibilizar**
insensibilidad [insensiβili'ðað] *nf* (*gen*) insensitivity; (*dureza de corazón*) callousness
insensibilizar [insensiβili'θar] *vt* to desensitize; (*Med*) to anaesthetize (*Brit*), anesthetize (*US*); (*eufemismo*) to knock out *o* unconscious
insensible [insen'siβle] *adj* (*gen*) insensitive; (*movimiento*) imperceptible; (*sin sensación*) numb
inseparable [insepa'raβle] *adj* inseparable
INSERSO [in'serso] *nm abr* (= *Instituto Nacional de Servicios Sociales*) *branch of social services*
insertar [inser'tar] *vt* to insert
inservible [inser'βiβle] *adj* useless
insidioso, -a [insi'ðjoso, a] *adj* insidious
insigne [in'siɣne] *adj* distinguished; (*famoso*) notable
insignia [in'siɣnja] *nf* (*señal distintiva*) badge; (*estandarte*) flag
insignificante [insiɣnifi'kante] *adj* insignificant
insinuar [insi'nwar] *vt* to insinuate, imply; **insinuarse** *vr*: **insinuarse con algn** to ingratiate o.s. with sb
insípido, -a [in'sipiðo, a] *adj* insipid
insistencia [insis'tenθja] *nf* insistence
insistir [insis'tir] *vi* to insist; **~ en algo** to insist on sth; (*enfatizar*) to stress sth
in situ [in'situ] *adv* on the spot, in situ
insobornable [insoβor'naβle] *adj* incorruptible
insociable [inso'θjaβle] *adj* unsociable
insolación [insola'θjon] *nf* (*Med*) sunstroke
insolencia [inso'lenθja] *nf* insolence
insolente [inso'lente] *adj* insolent
insólito, -a [in'solito, a] *adj* unusual
insoluble [inso'luβle] *adj* insoluble
insolvencia [insol'βenθja] *nf* insolvency
insomne [in'somne] *adj* sleepless ■ *nm/f* insomniac
insomnio [in'somnjo] *nm* insomnia
insondable [inson'daβle] *adj* bottomless
insonorización [insonoriθa'θjon] *nf* soundproofing
insonorizado, -a [insonori'θaðo, a] *adj* (*cuarto etc*) soundproof

insoportable [insopor'taβle] *adj* unbearable
insoslayable [insosla'jaβle] *adj* unavoidable
insospechado, -a [insospe'tʃaðo, a] *adj* (*inesperado*) unexpected
insostenible [insoste'niβle] *adj* untenable
inspección [inspek'θjon] *nf* inspection, check; **I~** inspectorate; **~ técnica (de vehículos)** ≈ MOT (test) (*Brit*)
inspeccionar [inspekθjo'nar] *vt* (*examinar*) to inspect, examine; (*controlar*) to check
inspector, a [inspek'tor, a] *nm/f* inspector
inspectorado [inspekto'raðo] *nm* inspectorate
inspiración [inspira'θjon] *nf* inspiration
inspirador, a [inspira'ðor, a] *adj* inspiring
inspirar [inspi'rar] *vt* to inspire; (*Med*) to inhale; **inspirarse** *vr*: **inspirarse en** to be inspired by
instalación [instala'θjon] *nf* (*equipo*) fittings *pl*, equipment; **~ eléctrica** wiring
instalar [insta'lar] *vt* (*establecer*) to instal; (*erguir*) to set up, erect; **instalarse** *vr* to establish o.s.; (*en una vivienda*) to move into
instancia [ins'tanθja] *nf* (*solicitud*) application; (*ruego*) request; (*Jur*) petition; **a ~ de** at the request of; **en última ~** in the last resort
instantáneo, -a [instan'taneo, a] *adj* instantaneous ■ *nf* snap(shot); **café ~** instant coffee
instante [ins'tante] *nm* instant, moment; **en un ~** in a flash
instar [ins'tar] *vt* to press, urge
instaurar [instau'rar] *vt* (*establecer*) to establish, set up
instigador, a [instiɣa'ðor, a] *nm/f* instigator; **~ de un delito** (*Jur*) accessory before the fact
instigar [insti'ɣar] *vt* to instigate
instigue *etc* [ins'tiɣe] *vb ver* **instigar**
instintivo, -a [instin'tiβo, a] *adj* instinctive
instinto [ins'tinto] *nm* instinct; **por ~** instinctively
institución [institu'θjon] *nf* institution, establishment; **~ benéfica** charitable foundation
instituir [institu'ir] *vt* to establish; (*fundar*) to found
instituto [insti'tuto] *nm* (*gen*) institute; **I~ Nacional de Enseñanza** (*Esp*) ≈ comprehensive (*Brit*) *o* high (*US*) school; **I~ Nacional de Industria (INI)** (*Esp Com*) ≈ National Enterprise Board (*Brit*)
institutriz [institu'triθ] *nf* governess
instituyendo *etc* [institu'jendo] *vb ver* **instituir**
instrucción [instruk'θjon] *nf* instruction; (*enseñanza*) education, teaching; (*Jur*) proceedings *pl*; (*Mil*) training; (*Deporte*) coaching; (*conocimientos*) knowledge; (*Inform*) statement; **instrucciones para el uso** directions for use; **instrucciones de funcionamiento** operating instructions
instructivo, -a [instruk'tiβo, a] *adj* instructive
instruir [instru'ir] *vt* (*gen*) to instruct; (*enseñar*) to teach, educate; (*Jur: proceso*) to prepare, draw up; **instruirse** *vr* to learn, teach o.s.
instrumento [instru'mento] *nm* (*gen, Mus*) instrument; (*herramienta*) tool, implement; (*Com*) indenture; (*Jur*) legal document; **~ de percusión/cuerda/viento** percussion/string(ed)/wind instrument
instruyendo *etc* [instru'jendo] *vb ver* **instruir**
insubordinarse [insuβorði'narse] *vr* to rebel
insuficiencia [insufi'θjenθja] *nf* (*carencia*) lack; (*inadecuación*) inadequacy; **~ cardíaca/renal** heart/kidney failure
insuficiente [insufi'θjente] *adj* (*gen*) insufficient; (*Escol: nota*) unsatisfactory
insufrible [insu'friβle] *adj* insufferable
insular [insu'lar] *adj* insular
insulina [insu'lina] *nf* insulin
insulso, -a [in'sulso, a] *adj* insipid; (*fig*) dull
insultar [insul'tar] *vt* to insult
insulto [in'sulto] *nm* insult
insumisión [insumi'sjon] *nf* *refusal to do military service or community service*
insumiso, -a [insu'miso, a] *adj* (*rebelde*) rebellious ■ *nm/f* (*Pol*) *person who refuses to do military service or community service*; *ver tb* **mili**
insuperable [insupe'raβle] *adj* (*excelente*) unsurpassable; (*problema etc*) insurmountable
insurgente [insur'xente] *adj, nm/f* insurgent
insurrección [insurrek'θjon] *nf* insurrection, rebellion
insustituible [insusti'twiβle] *adj* irreplaceable
intachable [inta'tʃaβle] *adj* irreproachable
intacto, -a [in'takto, a] *adj* (*sin tocar*) untouched; (*entero*) intact
integrado, -a [inte'ɣraðo, a] *adj* (*Inform*): **circuito ~** integrated circuit
integral [inte'ɣral] *adj* integral; (*completo*) complete; (*Tec*) built-in; **pan ~** wholemeal bread
integrante [inte'ɣrante] *adj* integral ■ *nm/f* member
integrar [inte'ɣrar] *vt* to make up, compose; (*Mat, fig*) to integrate
integridad [inteɣri'ðað] *nf* wholeness; (*carácter, tb Inform*) integrity; **en su ~** completely

integrismo [inte'ɣrismo] *nm* fundamentalism
integrista [inte'ɣrista] *adj, nm/f* fundamentalist
íntegro, -a ['inteɣro, a] *adj* whole, entire; (*texto*) uncut, unabridged; (*honrado*) honest
intelectual [intelek'twal] *adj, nm/f* intellectual
intelectualidad [intelektwali'ðað] *nf* intelligentsia, intellectuals *pl*
inteligencia [inteli'xenθja] *nf* intelligence; (*ingenio*) ability; **~ artificial** artificial intelligence
inteligente [inteli'xente] *adj* intelligent
inteligible [inteli'xiβle] *adj* intelligible
intemperancia [intempe'ranθja] *nf* excess, intemperance
intemperie [intem'perje] *nf*: **a la ~** outdoors, in the open air
intempestivo, -a [intempes'tiβo, a] *adj* untimely
intención [inten'θjon] *nf* intention, purpose; **con segundas intenciones** maliciously; **con ~** deliberately
intencionado, -a [intenθjo'naðo, a] *adj* deliberate; **bien ~** well-meaning; **mal ~** ill-disposed, hostile
intendencia [inten'denθja] *nf* management, administration; (*Mil*: *tb*: **cuerpo de intendencia**) ≈ service corps
intensidad [intensi'ðað] *nf* (*gen*) intensity; (*Elec, Tec*) strength; (*de recuerdo*) vividness; **llover con ~** to rain hard
intensificar [intensifi'kar] *vt*, **intensificarse** *vr* to intensify
intensifique *etc* [intensi'fike] *vb ver* **intensificar**
intensivo, -a [inten'siβo, a] *adj* intensive; **curso ~** crash course
intenso, -a [in'tenso, a] *adj* intense; (*impresión*) vivid; (*sentimiento*) profound, deep
intentar [inten'tar] *vt* (*tratar*) to try, attempt
intento [in'tento] *nm* (*intención*) intention, purpose; (*tentativa*) attempt
intentona [inten'tona] *nf* (*Pol*) attempted coup
interaccionar [interakθjo'nar] *vi* (*Inform*) to interact
interactivo, -a [interak'tiβo, a] *adj* interactive; (*Inform*): **computación interactiva** interactive computing
intercalación [interkala'θjon] *nf* (*Inform*) merging
intercalar [interka'lar] *vt* to insert; (*Inform*: *archivos, texto*) to merge
intercambiable [interkam'bjaβle] *adj* interchangeable
intercambio [inter'kambjo] *nm* (*canje*) exchange; (*trueque*) swap
interceder [interθe'ðer] *vi* to intercede
interceptar [interθep'tar] *vt* to intercept, cut off; (*Auto*) to hold up
interceptor [interθep'tor] *nm* interceptor; (*Tec*) trap
intercesión [interθe'sjon] *nf* intercession
interés [inte'res] *nm* (*gen, Com*) interest; (*importancia*) concern; (*parte*) share, part; (*pey*) self-interest; **~ compuesto** compound interest; **~ simple** simple interest; **con un ~ de 9 por ciento** at an interest of 9%; **dar a ~** to lend at interest; **tener ~ en** (*Com*) to hold a share in; **intereses acumulados** accrued interest *sg*; **intereses por cobrar** interest receivable *sg*; **intereses creados** vested interests; **intereses por pagar** interest payable *sg*
interesado, -a [intere'saðo, a] *adj* interested; (*prejuiciado*) prejudiced; (*pey*) mercenary, self-seeking ■ *nm/f* person concerned; (*firmante*) the undersigned
interesante [intere'sante] *adj* interesting
interesar [intere'sar] *vt* to interest, be of interest to ■ *vi* to interest, be of interest; (*importar*) to be important; **interesarse** *vr*: **interesarse en** *o* **por** to take an interest in; **no me interesan los toros** bullfighting does not appeal to me
interestatal [interesta'tal] *adj* inter-state
interface [inter'faθe], **interfase** [inter'fase] *nm* (*Inform*) interface; **~ hombre/máquina/por menús** man/machine/menu interface
interfaz [inter'faθ] *nm* = **interface**
interferencia [interfe'renθja] *nf* interference
interferir [interfe'rir] *vt* to interfere with; (*Telec*) to jam ■ *vi* to interfere
interfiera *etc* [inter'fjera], **interfiriendo** *etc* [interfi'rjendo] *vb ver* **interferir**
interfono [inter'fono] *nm* intercom
ínterin ['interin] *adv* meanwhile ■ *nm* interim; **en el ínterin** in the meantime
interino, -a [inte'rino, a] *adj* temporary; (*empleado etc*) provisional ■ *nm/f* temporary holder of a post; (*Med*) locum; (*Escol*) supply teacher; (*Teat*) stand-in
interior [inte'rjor] *adj* inner, inside; (*Com*) domestic, internal ■ *nm* interior, inside; (*fig*) soul, mind; (*Deporte*) inside forward; **Ministerio del I~** ≈ Home Office (*Brit*), Ministry of the Interior; **dije para mi ~** I said to myself
interjección [interxek'θjon] *nf* interjection
interlínea [inter'linea] *nf* (*Inform*) line feed
interlocutor, a [interloku'tor, a] *nm/f*

speaker; (*al teléfono*) person at the other end (of the line); **mi** ~ the person I was speaking to
intermediario, -a [interme'ðjarjo, a] *adj* (*mediador*) mediating ■ *nm/f* intermediary, go-between; (*mediador*) mediator
intermedio, -a [inter'meðjo, a] *adj* intermediate; (*tiempo*) intervening ■ *nm* interval; (*Pol*) recess
interminable [intermi'naβle] *adj* endless, interminable
intermitente [intermi'tente] *adj* intermittent ■ *nm* (*Auto*) indicator
internacional [internaθjo'nal] *adj* international
internado [inter'naðo] *nm* boarding school
internamiento [interna'mjento] *nm* internment
internar [inter'nar] *vt* to intern; (*en un manicomio*) to commit; **internarse** *vr* (*penetrar*) to penetrate; **internarse en** to go into *o* right inside; **internarse en un estudio** to study a subject in depth
internauta [inter'nauta] *nmf* Internet user
Internet [inter'net] *nm o nf* Internet
interno, -a [in'terno, a] *adj* internal, interior; (*Pol etc*) domestic ■ *nm/f* (*alumno*) boarder
interpelación [interpela'θjon] *nf* appeal, plea
interpelar [interpe'lar] *vt* (*rogar*) to implore; (*hablar*) to speak to; (*Pol*) to ask for explanations, question formally
interpondré *etc* [interpon'dre] *vb ver* **interponer**
interponer [interpo'ner] *vt* to interpose, put in; **interponerse** *vr* to intervene
interponga *etc* [inter'ponga] *vb ver* **interponer**
interposición [interposi'θjon] *nf* insertion
interpretación [interpreta'θjon] *nf* interpretation; (*Mus, Teat*) performance; **mala** ~ misinterpretation
interpretar [interpre'tar] *vt* to interpret
intérprete [in'terprete] *nm/f* (*Ling*) interpreter, translator; (*Mus, Teat*) performer, artist(e)
interpuesto [inter'pwesto], **interpuse** *etc* [inter'puse] *vb ver* **interponer**
interrogación [interroɣa'θjon] *nf* interrogation; (*Ling*: *tb*: **signo de interrogación**) question mark; (*Telec*) polling
interrogante [interro'ɣante] *adj* questioning ■ *nm* question mark; (*fig*) question mark, query
interrogar [interro'ɣar] *vt* to interrogate, question
interrogatorio [interroɣa'torjo] *nm* interrogation; (*Mil*) debriefing; (*Jur*) examination
interrogue *etc* [inte'rroɣe] *vb ver* **interrogar**
interrumpir [interrum'pir] *vt* to interrupt; (*vacaciones*) to cut short; (*servicio*) to cut off; (*tráfico*) to block
interrupción [interrup'θjon] *nf* interruption
interruptor [interrup'tor] *nm* (*Elec*) switch
intersección [intersek'θjon] *nf* intersection; (*Auto*) junction
interurbano, -a [interur'βano, a] *adj* inter-city; (*Telec*) long-distance
intervalo [inter'βalo] *nm* interval; (*descanso*) break; **a intervalos** at intervals, every now and then
intervención [interβen'θjon] *nf* supervision; (*Com*) audit(ing); (*Med*) operation; (*Telec*) tapping; (*participación*) intervention; ~ **quirúrgica** surgical operation; **la política de no** ~ the policy of non-intervention
intervencionista [interβenθjo'nista] *adj*: **no** ~ (*Com*) laissez-faire
intervendré *etc* [interβen'dre], **intervenga** *etc* [inter'βenga] *vb ver* **intervenir**
intervenir [interβe'nir] *vt* (*controlar*) to control, supervise; (*Com*) to audit; (*Med*) to operate on; (*Telec*) to tap ■ *vi* (*participar*) to take part, participate; (*mediar*) to intervene
interventor, a [interβen'tor, a] *nm/f* inspector; (*Com*) auditor
interviniendo *etc* [interβi'njendo] *vb ver* **intervenir**
interviú [inter'βju] *nf* interview
intestino [intes'tino] *nm* intestine
inti ['inti] *nm monetary unit of Peru*
intimar [inti'mar] *vt* to intimate, announce; (*mandar*) to order ■ *vi*, **intimarse** *vr* to become friendly
intimidad [intimi'ðað] *nf* intimacy; (*familiaridad*) familiarity; (*vida privada*) private life; (*Jur*) privacy
intimidar [intimi'ðar] *vt* to intimidate, scare
íntimo, -a ['intimo, a] *adj* intimate; (*pensamientos*) innermost; (*vida*) personal, private; **una boda íntima** a quiet wedding
intolerable [intole'raβle] *adj* intolerable, unbearable
intolerancia [intole'ranθja] *nf* intolerance
intoxicación [intoksika'θjon] *nf* poisoning; ~ **alimenticia** food poisoning
intraducible [intraðu'θiβle] *adj* untranslatable
intranet [intra'net] *nf* intranet
intranquilice *etc* [intranki'liθe] *vb ver* **intranquilizarse**
intranquilizarse [intrankili'θarse] *vr* to get worried *o* anxious
intranquilo, -a [intran'kilo, a] *adj* worried
intranscendente [intransθen'dente] *adj* unimportant

intransferible [intransfe'riβle] *adj* not transferable
intransigente [intransi'xente] *adj* intransigent
intransitable [intransi'taβle] *adj* impassable
intransitivo, -a [intransi'tiβo, a] *adj* intransitive
intratable [intra'taβle] *adj* (*problema*) intractable; (*dificultad*) awkward; (*individuo*) unsociable
intrepidez [intrepi'ðeθ] *nf* courage, bravery
intrépido, -a [in'trepiðo, a] *adj* intrepid, fearless
intriga [in'triɣa] *nf* intrigue; (*plan*) plot
intrigar [intri'ɣar] *vt, vi* to intrigue
intrigue *etc* [in'triɣe] *vb ver* **intrigar**
intrincado, -a [intrin'kaðo, a] *adj* intricate
intrínseco, -a [in'trinseko, a] *adj* intrinsic
introducción [introðuk'θjon] *nf* introduction; (*de libro*) foreword; (*Inform*) input
introducir [introðu'θir] *vt* (*gen*) to introduce; (*moneda*) to insert; (*Inform*) to input, enter
introduje *etc* [intro'ðuxe], **introduzca** *etc* [intro'ðuθka] *vb ver* **introducir**
intromisión [intromi'sjon] *nf* interference, meddling
introvertido, -a [introβer'tiðo, a] *adj, nm/f* introvert
intruso, -a [in'truso, a] *adj* intrusive ■ *nm/f* intruder
intuición [intwi'θjon] *nf* intuition
intuir [intu'ir] *vt* to know by intuition, intuit
intuyendo *etc* [intu'jendo] *vb ver* **intuir**
inundación [inunda'θjon] *nf* flood(ing)
inundar [inun'dar] *vt* to flood; (*fig*) to swamp, inundate
inusitado, -a [inusi'taðo, a] *adj* unusual
inútil [i'nutil] *adj* useless; (*esfuerzo*) vain, fruitless
inutilice *etc* [inuti'liθe] *vb ver* **inutilizar**
inutilidad [inutili'ðað] *nf* uselessness
inutilizar [inutili'θar] *vt* to make unusable, put out of action; (*incapacitar*) to disable; **inutilizarse** *vr* to become useless
invadir [imba'ðir] *vt* to invade
invalidar [imbali'ðar] *vt* to invalidate
invalidez [imbali'ðeθ] *nf* (*Med*) disablement; (*Jur*) invalidity
inválido, -a [im'baliðo, a] *adj* invalid; (*Jur*) null and void ■ *nm/f* invalid
invariable [imba'rjable] *adj* invariable
invasión [imba'sjon] *nf* invasion
invasor, a [imba'sor, a] *adj* invading ■ *nm/f* invader
invencible [imben'θiβle] *adj* invincible; (*timidez, miedo*) unsurmountable
invención [imben'θjon] *nf* invention
inventar [imben'tar] *vt* to invent
inventario [imben'tarjo] *nm* inventory; (*Com*) stocktaking
inventiva [imben'tiβa] *nf* inventiveness
invento [im'bento] *nm* invention; (*fig*) brainchild; (*pey*) silly idea
inventor, a [imben'tor, a] *nm/f* inventor
invernadero [imberna'ðero] *nm* greenhouse
invernal [imber'nal] *adj* wintry, winter *cpd*
invernar [imber'nar] *vi* (*Zool*) to hibernate
inverosímil [imbero'simil] *adj* implausible
inversión [imber'sjon] *nf* (*Com*) investment; ~ **de capitales** capital investment; **inversiones extranjeras** foreign investment *sg*
inverso, a [im'berso, a] *adj* inverse, opposite; **en el orden ~** in reverse order; **a la inversa** inversely, the other way round
inversor, -a [imber'sor, a] *nm/f* (*Com*) investor
invertebrado, -a [imberte'βraðo, a] *adj, nm* invertebrate
invertido, -a [imber'tiðo, a] *adj* inverted; (*al revés*) reversed; (*homosexual*) homosexual ■ *nm/f* homosexual
invertir [imber'tir] *vt* (*Com*) to invest; (*volcar*) to turn upside down; (*tiempo etc*) to spend
investigación [imbestiɣa'θjon] *nf* investigation; (*indagación*) inquiry; (*Univ*) research; ~ **y desarrollo** (*Com*) research and development (R & D); ~ **de los medios de publicidad** media research; ~ **del mercado** market research
investigador, a [imbestiɣa'ðor, a] *nm/f* investigator; (*Univ*) research fellow
investigar [imbesti'ɣar] *vt* to investigate; (*estudiar*) to do research into
investigue *etc* [imbes'tiɣe] *vb ver* **investigar**
investir [imbes'tir] *vt*: ~ **a algn con algo** to confer sth on sb; **fue investido Doctor Honoris Causa** he was awarded an honorary doctorate
invicto, -a [im'bikto, a] *adj* unconquered
invidente [imbi'ðente] *adj* sightless ■ *nm/f* blind person; **los invidentes** the sightless
invierno [im'bjerno] *nm* winter
invierta *etc* [im'bjerta] *vb ver* **invertir**
inviolabilidad [imbjolaβili'ðað] *nf* inviolability; ~ **parlamentaria** parliamentary immunity
invirtiendo *etc* [imbir'tjendo] *vb ver* **invertir**
invisible [imbi'siβle] *adj* invisible; **exportaciones/importaciones invisibles** invisible exports/imports
invitación [imbita'θjon] *nf* invitation
invitado, -a [imbi'taðo, a] *nm/f* guest

invitar [imbi'tar] *vt* to invite; (*incitar*) to entice; **~ a algn a hacer algo** to invite sb to do sth; **~ a algo** to pay for sth; **nos invitó a cenar fuera** she took us out for dinner; **invito yo** it's on me
in vitro [im'bitro] *adv* in vitro
invocar [imbo'kar] *vt* to invoke, call on
involucrar [imbolu'krar] *vt*: **~ algo en un discurso** to bring something irrelevant into a discussion; **~ a algn en algo** to involve sb in sth; **involucrarse** *vr* (*interesarse*) to get involved
involuntario, -a [imbolun'tarjo, a] *adj* involuntary; (*ofensa etc*) unintentional
invoque *etc* [im'boke] *vb ver* **invocar**
inyección [injek'θjon] *nf* injection
inyectar [injek'tar] *vt* to inject
ión [i'on] *nm* ion
IPC *nm abr* (*Esp*: = *índice de precios al consumo*) CPI
IPM *nm abr* (= *índice de precios al por menor*) RPI

PALABRA CLAVE

ir [ir] *vi* **1** to go; (*a pie*) to walk; (*viajar*) to travel; **ir caminando** to walk; **fui en tren** I went *o* travelled by train; **voy a la calle** I'm going out; **ir en coche/en bicicleta** to drive/cycle; **ir a pie** to walk, go on foot; **ir de pesca** to go fishing; **¡(ahora) voy!** (I'm just) coming!
2: **ir (a) por**: **ir (a) por el médico** to fetch the doctor
3 (*progresar*: *persona, cosa*) to go; **el trabajo va muy bien** work is going very well; **¿cómo te va?** how are things going?; **me va muy bien** I'm getting on very well; **le fue fatal** it went awfully badly for him
4 (*funcionar*): **el coche no va muy bien** the car isn't running very well
5 (*sentar*): **me va estupendamente** (*ropa, color*) it suits me really well; (*medicamento*) it works really well for me; **ir bien con algo** to go well with sth
6 (*aspecto*): **iba muy bien vestido** he was very well dressed; **ir con zapatos negros** to wear black shoes
7 (*locuciones*): **¿vino? — ¡que va!** did he come? — of course not!; **vamos, no llores** come on, don't cry; **¡vaya coche!** (*admiración*) what a car!, that's some car!; (*desprecio*) that's a terrible car!; **¡vaya!** (*regular*) so so; (*desagrado*) come on!; **¡vamos!** come on!; **¡que le vaya bien!** (*adiós*) take care!
8: **no vaya a ser**: **tienes que correr, no vaya a ser que pierdas el tren** you'll have to run so as not to miss the train
9: **no me** *etc* **va ni me viene** I *etc* don't care
■ *vb auxiliar* **1**: **ir a**: **voy/iba a hacerlo hoy** I am/was going to do it today
2 (*+gerundio*): **iba anocheciendo** it was getting dark; **todo se me iba aclarando** everything was gradually becoming clearer to me
3 (*+pp = pasivo*) **van vendidos 300 ejemplares** 300 copies have been sold so far
irse *vr* **1**: **¿por dónde se va al zoológico?** which is the way to the zoo?
2 (*marcharse*) to leave; **ya se habrán ido** they must already have left *o* gone; **¡vámonos!**, **¡nos fuimos!** (*Am*) let's go!; **¡vete!** go away!; **¡vete a saber!** your guess is as good as mine!, who knows!

IRA ['ira] *nm abr* (= *Irish Republican Army*) IRA
ira ['ira] *nf* anger, rage
iracundo, -a [ira'kundo, a] *adj* irascible
Irak [i'rak] *nm* = **Iraq**
Irán [i'ran] *nm* Iran
iraní [ira'ni] *adj, nm/f* Iranian
Iraq [i'rak] *nm* Iraq
iraquí [ira'ki] *adj, nm/f* Iraqi
irascible [iras'θiβle] *adj* irascible
irguiendo *etc* [ir'ɣjendo] *vb ver* **erguir**
iris ['iris] *nm inv* (*arco iris*) rainbow; (*Anat*) iris
Irlanda [ir'landa] *nf* Ireland; **~ del Norte** Northern Ireland, Ulster
irlandés, -esa [irlan'des, esa] *adj* Irish ■ *nm/f* Irishman(-woman) ■ *nm* (*Ling*) Gaelic, Irish; **los irlandeses** *nmpl* the Irish
ironía [iro'nia] *nf* irony
irónico, -a [i'roniko, a] *adj* ironic(al)
IRPF *nm abr* (*Esp*) = **impuesto sobre la renta de las personas físicas**
irracional [irraθjo'nal] *adj* irrational
irrazonable [irraθo'naβle] *adj* unreasonable
irreal [irre'al] *adj* unreal
irrealizable [irreali'θaβle] *adj* (*gen*) unrealizable; (*meta*) unrealistic
irrebatible [irreβa'tiβle] *adj* irrefutable
irreconocible [irrekono'θiβle] *adj* unrecognizable
irrecuperable [irrekupe'raβle] *adj* irrecoverable, irretrievable
irreembolsable [irreembol'saβle] *adj* (*Com*) non-returnable
irreflexión [irreflek'sjon] *nf* thoughtlessness; (*ímpetu*) rashness
irregular [irreɣu'lar] *adj* irregular; (*situación*) abnormal, anomalous; **margen izquierdo/derecho ~** (*texto*) ragged left/right (margin)
irregularidad [irreɣulari'ðað] *nf* irregularity
irremediable [irreme'ðjaβle] *adj* irremediable; (*vicio*) incurable
irreprochable [irrepro'tʃaβle] *adj*

irreproachable
irresistible [irresis'tiβle] *adj* irresistible
irresoluto, -a [irreso'luto, a] *adj* irresolute, hesitant; (*sin resolver*) unresolved
irrespetuoso, -a [irrespe'twoso, a] *adj* disrespectful
irresponsable [irrespon'saβle] *adj* irresponsible
irreverente [irreβe'rente] *adj* disrespectful
irreversible [irreβer'siβle] *adj* irreversible
irrevocable [irreβo'kaβle] *adj* irrevocable
irrigar [irri'ɣar] *vt* to irrigate
irrigue *etc* [i'rriɣe] *vb ver* **irrigar**
irrisorio, -a [irri'sorjo, a] *adj* derisory, ridiculous; (*precio*) bargain *cpd*
irritación [irrita'θjon] *nf* irritation
irritar [irri'tar] *vt* to irritate, annoy; **irritarse** *vr* to get angry, lose one's temper
irrompible [irrom'piβle] *adj* unbreakable
irrumpir [irrum'pir] *vi*: **~ en** to burst *o* rush into
irrupción [irrup'θjon] *nf* irruption; (*invasión*) invasion
IRTP *nm abr* (*Esp: = impuesto sobre el rendimiento del trabajo personal*) ≈ PAYE
ISBN *nm abr* (*= International Standard Book Number*) ISBN
isla ['isla] *nf* (*Geo*) island; **Islas Británicas** British Isles; **Islas Filipinas/Malvinas/Canarias** Philippines/Falklands/Canaries
Islam [is'lam] *nm* Islam
islámico, -a [is'lamiko, a] *adj* Islamic
islandés, -esa [islan'des, esa] *adj* Icelandic ▪ *nm/f* Icelander ▪ *nm* (*Ling*) Icelandic
Islandia [is'landja] *nf* Iceland
isleño, -a [is'leɲo, a] *adj* island *cpd* ▪ *nm/f* islander
islote [is'lote] *nm* small island
isotónico, -a [iso'toniko, a] *adj* isotonic
isótopo [i'sotopo] *nm* isotope
Israel [isra'el] *nm* Israel
israelí [israe'li] *adj, nm/f* Israeli
istmo ['istmo] *nm* isthmus; **el I~ de Panamá** the Isthmus of Panama
Italia [i'talja] *nf* Italy
italiano, -a [ita'ljano, a] *adj, nm/f* Italian ▪ *nm* (*Ling*) Italian
itinerante [itine'rante] *adj* travelling; (*embajador*) roving
itinerario [itine'rarjo] *nm* itinerary, route
ITV *nf abr* (*= Inspección Técnica de Vehículos*) ≈ MOT (test) (*Brit*)
IVA ['iβa] *nm abr* (*Esp Com: = Impuesto sobre el Valor Añadido*) VAT
IVP *nm abr* = **Instituto Venezolano de Petroquímica**
izada [i'saða] *nf* (*Am*) lifting, raising
izar [i'θar] *vt* to hoist
izda, izq.ª *abr* (*= izquierda*) L, l
izdo, izq.º *abr* (*= izquierdo*) L, l
izquierda [iθ'kjerða] *nf ver* **izquierdo**
izquierdista [iθkjer'ðista] *adj* leftist, left-wing ▪ *nm/f* left-winger, leftist
izquierdo, -a [iθ'kjerðo, a] *adj* left ▪ *nf* left; (*Pol*) left (wing); **a la izquierda** on the left; **es un cero a la izquierda** (*fam*) he is a nonentity; **conducción por la izquierda** left-hand drive

Jj

J, j ['xota] *nf* (*letra*) J, j; **J de José** J for Jack (*Brit*) *o* Jig (*US*)
J *abr* (= *julio(s)*) J
jabalí [xaβa'li] *nm* wild boar
jabalina [xaβa'lina] *nf* javelin
jabato, -a [xa'βato, a] *adj* brave, bold ■ *nm* young wild boar
jabón [xa'βon] *nm* soap; (*fam: adulación*) flattery; **~ de afeitar** shaving soap; **~ de tocador** toilet soap; **dar ~ a algn** to soft-soap sb
jabonar [xaβo'nar] *vt* to soap
jaca ['xaka] *nf* pony
jacinto [xa'θinto] *nm* hyacinth
jactancia [xak'tanθja] *nf* boasting, boastfulness
jactarse [xak'tarse] *vr*: **~ (de)** to boast *o* brag (about *o* of)
jadear [xaðe'ar] *vi* to pant, gasp for breath
jadeo [xa'ðeo] *nm* panting, gasping
jaguar [xa'ɣwar] *nm* jaguar
jalar [xa'lar] *vt* (*Am*) to pull
jalbegue [xal'βeɣe] *nm* whitewash
jalea [xa'lea] *nf* jelly
jaleo [xa'leo] *nm* racket, uproar; **armar un ~** to kick up a racket
jalón [xa'lon] *nm* (*Am*) tug
jalonar [xalo'nar] *vt* to stake out; (*fig*) to mark
Jamaica [xa'maika] *nf* Jamaica
jamaicano, -a [xamai'kano, a] *adj, nm/f* Jamaican
jamás [xa'mas] *adv* never, not ... ever; (*interrogativo*) ever; **¿~ se vio tal cosa?** did you ever see such a thing?
jamón [xa'mon] *nm* ham; **~ (de) York** boiled ham; **~ dulce/serrano** boiled/cured ham
Japón [xa'pon] *nm*: **el ~** Japan
japonés, -esa [xapo'nes, esa] *adj, nm/f* Japanese ■ *nm* (*Ling*) Japanese
jaque ['xake] *nm*: **~ mate** checkmate
jaqueca [xa'keka] *nf* (very bad) headache, migraine
jarabe [xa'raβe] *nm* syrup; **~ para la tos** cough syrup *o* mixture
jarana [xa'rana] *nf* (*juerga*) spree (*fam*); **andar/ir de ~** to be/go on a spree
jarcia ['xarθja] *nf* (*Naut*) ropes *pl*, rigging
jardín [xar'ðin] *nm* garden; **~ botánico** botanical garden; **~ de (la) infancia** (*Esp*) *o* **de niños** (*Am*) *o* **infantil** (*Am*) kindergarten, nursery school
jardinería [xarðine'ria] *nf* gardening
jardinero, -a [xarði'nero, a] *nm/f* gardener
jarra ['xarra] *nf* jar; (*jarro*) jug; (*de leche*) churn; (*de cerveza*) mug; **de** *o* **en jarras** with arms akimbo
jarro ['xarro] *nm* jug
jarrón [xa'rron] *nm* vase; (*Arqueología*) urn
jaspeado, -a [xaspe'ado, a] *adj* mottled, speckled
jaula ['xaula] *nf* cage; (*embalaje*) crate
jauría [xau'ria] *nf* pack of hounds
jazmín [xaθ'min] *nm* jasmine
J. C. *abr* = **Jesucristo**
jeep® (*pl* **jeeps**) [jip, jips] *nm* jeep®
jefa ['xefa] *nf ver* **jefe**
jefatura [xefa'tura] *nf* (*liderazgo*) leadership; (*sede*) central office; **J~ de la aviación civil** ≈ Civil Aviation Authority; **~ de policía** police headquarters *sg*
jefazo [xe'faθo] *nm* bigwig
jefe, -a ['xefe, a] *nm/f* (*gen*) chief, head; (*patrón*) boss; (*Pol*) leader; (*Com*) manager(ess); **~ de camareros** head waiter; **~ de cocina** chef; **~ ejecutivo** (*Com*) chief executive; **~ de estación** stationmaster; **~ de estado** head of state; **~ de oficina** (*Com*) office manager; **~ de producción** (*Com*) production manager; **~ supremo** commander-in-chief; **ser el ~** (*fig*) to be the boss
JEN [xen] *nf abr* (*Esp*) = **Junta de Energía Nuclear**
jengibre [xen'xiβre] *nm* ginger
jeque ['xeke] *nm* sheik(h)

jerarquía [xerar'kia] *nf* (*orden*) hierarchy; (*rango*) rank
jerárquico, -a [xe'rarkiko, a] *adj* hierarchic(al)
jerez [xe'reθ] *nm* sherry; **J~ de la Frontera** Jerez
jerezano, -a [xere'θano, a] *adj* of *o* from Jerez ■ *nm/f* native *o* inhabitant of Jerez
jerga ['xerɣa] *nf* (*tela*) coarse cloth; (*lenguaje*) jargon; **~ informática** computer jargon
jerigonza [xeri'ɣonθa] *nf* (*jerga*) jargon, slang; (*galimatías*) nonsense, gibberish
jeringa [xe'ringa] *nf* syringe; (*Am*) annoyance, bother; **~ de engrase** grease gun
jeringar [xerin'gar] *vt* to annoy, bother
jeringue *etc* [xe'ringe] *vb ver* **jeringar**
jeringuilla [xerin'guiʎa] *nf* hypodermic (syringe)
jeroglífico [xero'ɣlifiko] *nm* hieroglyphic
jersey [xer'sei] (*pl* **jerseys**) *nm* jersey, pullover, jumper
Jerusalén [xerusa'len] *n* Jerusalem
Jesucristo [xesu'kristo] *nm* Jesus Christ
jesuita [xe'swita] *adj, nm* Jesuit
Jesús [xe'sus] *nm* Jesus; **¡~!** good heavens!; (*al estornudar*) bless you!
jet (*pl* **jets**) [jet, jet] *nm* jet (plane) ■ *nf*: **la ~** the jet set
jeta ['xeta] *nf* (*Zool*) snout; (*fam: cara*) mug; **¡que ~ tienes!** (*fam: insolencia*) you've got a nerve!
jíbaro, -a ['xiβaro, a] *adj, nm/f* Jibaro (Indian)
jícara ['xikara] *nf* small cup
jiennense [xjen'nense] *adj* of *o* from Jaén ■ *nm/f* native *o* inhabitant of Jaén
jilguero [xil'ɣero] *nm* goldfinch
jinete, -a [xi'nete, a] *nm/f* horseman(-woman)
jipijapa [xipi'xapa] *nm* (*Am*) straw hat
jira ['xira] *nf* (*de tela*) strip; (*excursión*) picnic
jirafa [xi'rafa] *nf* giraffe
jirón [xi'ron] *nm* rag, shred
JJ.OO. *nmpl abr* = **Juegos Olímpicos**
jocosidad [xokosi'ðað] *nf* humour; (*chiste*) joke
jocoso, -a [xo'koso, a] *adj* humorous, jocular
joder [xo'ðer] (*fam!*) *vt* to fuck (*!*), screw (*!*); (*fig: fastidiar*) to piss off (*!*), bug; **joderse** *vr* (*fracasar*) to fail; **¡~!** damn it!; **se jodió todo** everything was ruined
jodido, -a [xo'ðiðo, a] *adj* (*fam!: difícil*) awkward; **estoy ~** I'm knackered
jofaina [xo'faina] *nf* washbasin
jojoba [xo'xoβa] *nf* jojoba
jolgorio [xol'ɣorjo] *nm* (*juerga*) fun, revelry
jonrón [xon'ron] *nm* home run
Jordania [xor'ðanja] *nf* Jordan
jornada [xor'naða] *nf* (*viaje de un día*) day's journey; (*camino o viaje entero*) journey; (*día de trabajo*) working day; **~ de 8 horas** 8-hour day; **(trabajar a) ~ partida** (to work a) split shift
jornal [xor'nal] *nm* (day's) wage
jornalero, -a [xorna'lero, a] *nm/f* (day) labourer
joroba [xo'roβa] *nf* hump
jorobado, -a [xoro'βaðo, a] *adj* hunchbacked ■ *nm/f* hunchback
jorobar [xoro'βar] *vt* to annoy, pester, bother; **jorobarse** *vr* to get cross; **¡hay que jorobarse!** to hell with it!; **esto me joroba!** ¡I'm fed up with this!
jota ['xota] *nf* letter J; (*danza*) *Aragonese dance*; (*fam*) jot, iota; **no saber ni ~** to have no idea
joven ['xoβen] *adj* young ■ *nm* young man, youth ■ *nf* young woman, girl
jovencito, -a [xoβen'θito, a] *nm/f* youngster
jovial [xo'βjal] *adj* cheerful, jolly
jovialidad [xoβjali'ðað] *nf* cheerfulness
joya ['xoja] *nf* jewel, gem; (*fig: persona*) gem; **joyas de fantasía** imitation jewellery *sg*
joyería [xoje'ria] *nf* (*joyas*) jewellery; (*tienda*) jeweller's (shop)
joyero [xo'jero] *nm* (*persona*) jeweller; (*caja*) jewel case
Juan [xwan] *nm*: **Noche de San ~** *see note*

JUAN

The *Noche de San Juan* (evening of the Feast of Saint John) on the 24th June is a *fiesta* coinciding with the summer solstice, and which has taken the place of other ancient pagan festivals. Traditionally fire plays a major part in these festivities, which can last for days in certain areas. Celebrations and dancing take place around *hogueras* (bonfires) in towns and villages across the country.

juanete [xwa'nete] *nm* (*del pie*) bunion
jubilación [xuβila'θjon] *nf* (*retiro*) retirement
jubilado, -a [xuβi'lado, a] *adj* retired ■ *nm/f* retired person, pensioner (*Brit*), senior citizen
jubilar [xuβi'lar] *vt* to pension off, retire; (*fam*) to discard; **jubilarse** *vr* to retire
jubileo [xuβi'leo] *nm* jubilee
júbilo ['xuβilo] *nm* joy, rejoicing
jubiloso, -a [xuβi'loso, a] *adj* jubilant
judaísmo [xuða'ismo] *nm* Judaism
judía [xu'ðia] *nf ver* **judío**
judicatura [xuðika'tura] *nf* (*cargo de juez*) office of judge; (*cuerpo de jueces*) judiciary

judicial [xuði'θjal] *adj* judicial
judío, -a [xu'ðio, a] *adj* Jewish ■ *nm* Jew ■ *nf* Jewess, Jewish woman; (*Culin*) bean; **judía blanca** haricot bean; **judía verde** French *o* string bean
juego *etc* ['xweɣo] *vb ver* **jugar** ■ *nm* (*gen*) play; (*pasatiempo, partido*) game; (*en casino*) gambling; (*deporte*) sport; (*conjunto*) set; (*herramientas*) kit; **~ de azar** game of chance; **~ de café** coffee set; **~ de caracteres** (*Inform*) font; **~ limpio/sucio** fair/foul *o* dirty play; **J~s Olímpicos** Olympic Games; **~ de programas** (*Inform*) suite of programs; **fuera de ~** (*Deporte: persona*) offside; (*: pelota*) out of play; **por ~** in fun, for fun
juegue *etc* ['xweɣe] *vb ver* **jugar**
juerga ['xwerɣa] *nf* binge; (*fiesta*) party; **ir de ~** to go out on a binge
juerguista [xwer'ɣista] *nm/f* reveller
jueves ['xweβes] *nm inv* Thursday; *ver tb* **sábado**
juez [xweθ] *nm/f* judge; (*Tenis*) umpire; **~ de línea** linesman; **~ de paz** justice of the peace; **~ de salida** starter
jueza [xweθa] *nf ver* **juez**
jugada [xu'ɣaða] *nf* play; **buena ~** good move (*o* shot *o* stroke) *etc*
jugador, a [xuɣa'ðor, a] *nm/f* player; (*en casino*) gambler
jugar [xu'ɣar] *vt* to play; (*en casino*) to gamble; (*apostar*) to bet ■ *vi* to play; to gamble; (*Com*) to speculate; **jugarse** *vr* to gamble (away); **jugarse el todo por el todo** to stake one's all, go for bust; **¿quién juega?** whose move is it?; **¡me la han jugado!** (*fam*) I've been had!
jugarreta [xuɣa'rreta] *nf* (*mala jugada*) bad move; (*trampa*) dirty trick; **hacer una ~ a algn** to play a dirty trick on sb
juglar [xu'ɣlar] *nm* minstrel
jugo ['xuɣo] *nm* (*Bot, de fruta*) juice; (*fig*) essence, substance; **~ de naranja** (*esp Am*) orange juice
jugoso, -a [xu'ɣoso, a] *adj* juicy; (*fig*) substantial, important
jugué [xu'ɣe], **juguemos** *etc* [xu'ɣemos] *vb ver* **jugar**
juguete [xu'ɣete] *nm* toy
juguetear [xuɣete'ar] *vi* to play
juguetería [xuɣete'ria] *nf* toyshop
juguetón, -ona [xuɣe'ton, ona] *adj* playful
juicio ['xwiθjo] *nm* judgement; (*sana razón*) sanity, reason; (*opinión*) opinion; (*Jur: proceso*) trial; **estar fuera de ~** to be out of one's mind; **a mi ~** in my opinion
juicioso, -a [xwi'θjoso, a] *adj* wise, sensible
JUJEM [xu'xem] *nf abr* (*Esp Mil*) = **Junta de Jefes del Estado Mayor**
jul. *abr* (= *julio*) Jul.
julio ['xuljo] *nm* July; **el uno** *o* **el primero de ~** the first of July; **en el mes de ~** during July; **en ~ del año que viene** in July of next year
jumento, -a [xu'mento, a] *nm/f* donkey
jun. *abr* (= *junio*) Jun.
junco ['xunko] *nm* rush, reed
jungla ['xungla] *nf* jungle
junio ['xunjo] *nm* June; *ver tb* **julio**
junta ['xunta] *nf ver* **junto**
juntar [xun'tar] *vt* to join, unite; (*maquinaria*) to assemble, put together; (*dinero*) to collect; **juntarse** *vr* to join, meet; (*reunirse: personas*) to meet, assemble; (*arrimarse*) to approach, draw closer; **juntarse con algn** to join sb
junto, -a ['xunto, a] *adj* joined; (*unido*) united; (*anexo*) near, close; (*contiguo, próximo*) next, adjacent ■ *nf* (*asamblea*) meeting, assembly; (*comité, consejo*) board, council, committee; (*Mil, Pol*) junta; (*articulación*) joint ■ *adv*: **todo ~** all at once ■ *prep*: **~ a** near (to), next to; **juntos** together; **junta constitutiva** (*Com*) statutory meeting; **junta directiva** (*Com*) board of management; **junta general extraordinaria** (*Com*) extraordinary general meeting
juntura [xun'tura] *nf* (*punto de unión*) join, junction; (*articulación*) joint
jura ['xura] *nf* oath, pledge; **~ de bandera** (ceremony of taking the) oath of allegiance
jurado [xu'raðo] *nm* (*Jur: individuo*) juror; (*: grupo*) jury; (*de concurso: grupo*) panel (of judges); (*: individuo*) member of a panel
juramentar [xuramen'tar] *vt* to swear in, administer the oath to; **juramentarse** *vr* to be sworn in, take the oath
juramento [xura'mento] *nm* oath; (*maldición*) oath, curse; **bajo ~** on oath; **prestar ~** to take the oath; **tomar ~ a** to swear in, administer the oath to
jurar [xu'rar] *vt, vi* to swear; **~ en falso** to commit perjury; **jurárselas a algn** to have it in for sb
jurídico, -a [xu'riðiko, a] *adj* legal, juridical
jurisdicción [xurisðik'θjon] *nf* (*poder, autoridad*) jurisdiction; (*territorio*) district
jurisprudencia [xurispru'ðenθja] *nf* jurisprudence
jurista [xu'rista] *nm/f* jurist
justamente [xusta'mente] *adv* justly, fairly; (*precisamente*) just, exactly
justicia [xus'tiθja] *nf* justice; (*equidad*) fairness, justice; **de ~** deservedly
justiciero, -a [xusti'θjero, a] *adj* just, righteous
justificable [xustifi'kaβle] *adj* justifiable

justificación [xustifika'θjon] *nf* justification; **~ automática** (*Inform*) automatic justification
justificado, -a [xustifi'kaðo, a] *adj* (*Tip*): **(no) ~** (un)justified
justificante [xustifi'kante] *nm* voucher; **~ médico** sick note
justificar [xustifi'kar] *vt* (*tb Tip*) to justify; (*probar*) to verify
justifique *etc* [xusti'fike] *vb ver* **justificar**
justo, -a ['xusto, a] *adj* (*equitativo*) just, fair, right; (*preciso*) exact, correct; (*ajustado*) tight ■ *adv* (*precisamente*) exactly, precisely; (*apenas a tiempo*) just in time; **¡~!** that's it!, correct!; **llegaste muy ~** you just made it; **vivir muy ~** to be hard up
juvenil [xuβe'nil] *adj* youthful
juventud [xuβen'tuð] *nf* (*adolescencia*) youth; (*jóvenes*) young people *pl*
juzgado [xuθ'ɣaðo] *nm* tribunal; (*Jur*) court
juzgar [xuθ'ɣar] *vt* to judge; **a ~ por ...** to judge by ..., judging by ...; **~ mal** to misjudge; **júzguelo usted mismo** see for yourself

Kk

K, k [ka] *nf* *(letra)* K, k; **K de Kilo** K for King
K *abr* (= 1.000) K; *(Inform:* = 1.024) K
Kampuchea [kampu'tʃea] *nf* Kampuchea
karaoke [kara'oke] *nm* karaoke
kárate ['karate], **karate** [ka'rate] *nm* karate
KAS *nf abr* (= *Koordinadora Abertzale Sozialista)* *Basque nationalist umbrella group*
Kazajstán [kaθaxs'tan] *nm* Kazakhstan
k/c. *abr* (= *kilociclos)* kc.
Kenia ['kenja] *nf* Kenya
keniata [ke'njata] *adj, nm/f* Kenyan
kepí, kepis [ke'pi, 'kepis] *nm* *(esp Am)* kepi, military hat
kerosene [kero'sene] *nm* kerosene
Kg, kg *abr* (= *kilogramo(s))* K, kg
KGB *sigla m* KGB
kilate [ki'late] *nm* = **quilate**
kilo ['kilo] *nm* kilo
kilobyte ['kiloβait] *nm* *(Inform)* kilobyte
kilogramo [kilo'ɣramo] *nm* kilogramme *(Brit)*, kilogram *(US)*
kilolitro [kilo'litro] *nm* kilolitre *(Brit)*, kiloliter *(US)*
kilometraje [kilome'traxe] *nm* distance in kilometres, ≈ mileage
kilométrico, -a [kilo'metriko, a] *adj* kilometric; *(fam)* very long; **(billete) ~** *(Ferro)* mileage ticket
kilómetro [ki'lometro] *nm* kilometre *(Brit)*, kilometer *(US)*
kiloocteto [kilook'teto] *nm* *(Inform)* kilobyte
kilovatio [kilo'βatjo] *nm* kilowatt
kiosco ['kjosko] *nm* = **quiosco**
Kirguizistán [kirɣiθis'tan] *nm* Kirghizia
kiwi ['kiwi] *nm* kiwi (fruit)
km *abr* (= *kilómetro(s))* km
km/h *abr* (= *kilómetros por hora)* km/h
knock-out ['nokau], **K.O.** ['kao] *nm* knockout; *(golpe)* knockout blow; **dejar** *o* **poner a algn ~** to knock sb out
kosovar [koso'βar] *adj* Kosovan
Kosovo [koso'βo] *nm* Kosovo
k.p.h. *abr* (= *kilómetros por hora)* km/h
k.p.l. *abr* (= *kilómetros por litro)* ≈ mpg
kurdo, -a ['kurðo, a] *adj* Kurdish ■ *nm/f* Kurd ■ *nm* *(Ling)* Kurdish
kuwaití [kuβai'ti] *adj, nm/f* Kuwaiti
kv *abr* (= *kilovatio)* kw
kv/h *abr* (= *kilovatios-hora)* kw-h

L

L, l ['ele] *nf (letra)* L, l; **L de Lorenzo** L for Lucy *(Brit) o* Love *(US)*
l *abr* (= *litro(s)*) l; (= *libro*) bk
L/ *abr (Com)* = **letra**
la [la] *artículo definido fsg* the ■ *pron* her; *(en relación a usted)* you; *(en relación a una cosa)* it ■ *nm (Mus)* A; **está en la cárcel** he's in jail; **la del sombrero rojo** the woman/girl/one in the red hat
laberinto [laβe'rinto] *nm* labyrinth
labia ['laβja] *nf* fluency; *(pey)* glibness; **tener mucha ~** to have the gift of the gab
labial [la'βjal] *adj* labial
labio ['laβjo] *nm* lip; *(de vasija etc)* edge, rim; **~ inferior/superior** lower/upper lip
labor [la'βor] *nf* labour; *(Agr)* farm work; *(tarea)* job, task; *(Costura)* needlework, sewing; *(punto)* knitting; **~ de equipo** teamwork; **~ de ganchillo** crochet
laborable [laβo'raβle] *adj (Agr)* workable; **día ~** working day
laboral [laβo'ral] *adj (accidente, conflictividad)* industrial; *(jornada)* working; *(derecho, relaciones)* labour *cpd*
laboralista [laβora'lista] *adj*: **abogado ~** labour lawyer
laborar [laβo'rar] *vi* to work
laboratorio [laβora'torjo] *nm* laboratory
laborioso, -a [laβo'rjoso, a] *adj (persona)* hard-working; *(trabajo)* tough
laborista [laβo'rista] *(Pol) adj*: **Partido L~** Labour Party ■ *nm/f* Labour Party member *o* supporter
labrado, -a [la'βraðo, a] *adj* worked; *(madera)* carved; *(metal)* wrought ■ *nm (Agr)* cultivated field
Labrador [laβra'ðor] *nm* Labrador
labrador, a [laβra'ðor, a] *nm/f* farmer
labranza [la'βranθa] *nf (Agr)* cultivation
labrar [la'βrar] *vt (gen)* to work; *(madera etc)* to carve; *(fig)* to cause, bring about
labriego, -a [la'βrjeɣo, a] *nm/f* peasant
laca ['laka] *nf* lacquer; *(de pelo)* hairspray; **~ de uñas** nail varnish
lacayo [la'kajo] *nm* lackey
lacerar [laθe'rar] *vt* to lacerate
lacio, -a ['laθjo, a] *adj (pelo)* lank, straight
lacón [la'kon] *nm* shoulder of pork
lacónico, -a [la'koniko, a] *adj* laconic
lacra ['lakra] *nf (defecto)* blemish; **~ social** social disgrace
lacrar [la'krar] *vt (cerrar)* to seal (with sealing wax)
lacre ['lakre] *nm* sealing wax
lacrimógeno, -a [lakri'moxeno, a] *adj (fig)* sentimental; **gas ~** tear gas
lacrimoso, -a [lakri'moso, a] *adj* tearful
lactancia [lak'tanθja] *nf* breast-feeding
lactar [lak'tar] *vt, vi* to suckle, breast-feed
lácteo, -a ['lakteo, a] *adj*: **productos lácteos** dairy products
ladear [laðe'ar] *vt* to tip, tilt ■ *vi* to tilt; **ladearse** *vr* to lean; *(Deporte)* to swerve; *(Aviat)* to bank, turn
ladera [la'ðera] *nf* slope
ladino, -a [la'ðino, a] *adj* cunning
lado ['laðo] *nm (gen)* side; *(fig)* protection; *(Mil)* flank; **~ izquierdo** left(-hand) side; **~ a ~** side by side; **al ~ de** next to, beside; **hacerse a un ~** to stand aside; **poner de ~** to put on its side; **poner a un ~** to put aside; **me da de ~** I don't care; **por un ~ ..., por otro ~ ...** on the one hand ..., on the other (hand) ...; **por todos lados** on all sides, all round *(Brit)*
ladrar [la'ðrar] *vi* to bark
ladrido [la'ðriðo] *nm* bark, barking
ladrillo [la'ðriʎo] *nm (gen)* brick; *(azulejo)* tile
ladrón, -ona [la'ðron, ona] *nm/f* thief
lagar [la'ɣar] *nm* (wine/oil) press
lagartija [laɣar'tixa] *nf* (small) lizard, wall lizard
lagarto [la'ɣarto] *nm (Zool)* lizard; *(Am)* alligator
lago ['laɣo] *nm* lake
Lagos ['laɣos] *nm* Lagos

lágrima ['laɣrima] *nf* tear
lagrimal [laɣri'mal] *nm* (inner) corner of the eye
lagrimear [laɣrime'ar] *vi* to weep; (*ojos*) to water
laguna [la'ɣuna] *nf* (*lago*) lagoon; (*en escrito, conocimientos*) gap
laico, -a ['laiko, a] *adj* lay ■ *nm/f* layman(-woman)
laja ['laxa] *nf* rock
lamber [lam'ber] *vt* (*Am*) to lick
lambiscón, -ona [lambis'kon, ona] *adj* flattering ■ *nm/f* flatterer
lameculos [lame'kulos] *nm/f inv* (*fam*) arse licker (*!*), crawler
lamentable [lamen'taβle] *adj* lamentable, regrettable; (*miserable*) pitiful
lamentación [lamenta'θjon] *nf* lamentation; **ahora no sirven lamentaciones** it's no good crying over spilt milk
lamentar [lamen'tar] *vt* (*sentir*) to regret; (*deplorar*) to lament; **lamentarse** *vr* to lament; **lo lamento mucho** I'm very sorry
lamento [la'mento] *nm* lament
lamer [la'mer] *vt* to lick
lámina ['lamina] *nf* (*plancha delgada*) sheet; (*para estampar, estampa*) plate; (*grabado*) engraving
laminar [lami'nar] *vt* (*en libro*) to laminate; (*Tec*) to roll
lámpara ['lampara] *nf* lamp; **~ de alcohol/gas** spirit/gas lamp; **~ de pie** standard lamp
lamparilla [lampa'riʎa] *nf* night-light
lamparón [lampa'ron] *nm* (*Med*) scrofula; (*mancha*) (large) grease spot
lampiño, -a [lam'piɲo, a] *adj* (*sin pelo*) hairless
lana ['lana] *nf* wool; (*tela*) woollen (*Brit*) *o* woolen (*US*) cloth; (*Am fam: dinero*) dough; **(hecho) de ~** wool *cpd*
lance *etc* ['lanθe] *vb ver* **lanzar** ■ *nm* (*golpe*) stroke; (*suceso*) event, incident
lanceta [lan'seta] *nf* (*Am*) sting
lancha ['lantʃa] *nf* launch; **~ motora** motorboat; **~ de pesca** fishing boat; **~ salvavidas/torpedera** lifeboat/torpedo boat; **~ neumática** rubber dinghy
lanero, -a [la'nero, a] *adj* wool *cpd*
langosta [lan'gosta] *nf* (*insecto*) locust; (*crustáceo*) lobster; (*: de río*) crayfish
langostino [langos'tino] *nm* prawn; (*de agua dulce*) crayfish
languidecer [langiðe'θer] *vi* to languish
languidez [langi'ðeθ] *nf* languor
languidezca *etc* [langi'ðeθka] *vb ver* **languidecer**
lánguido, -a ['langiðo, a] *adj* (*gen*) languid; (*sin energía*) listless
lanilla [la'niʎa] *nf* nap; (*tela*) thin flannel cloth
lanolina [lano'lina] *nf* lanolin(e)
lanudo, -a [la'nuðo, a] *adj* woolly, fleecy
lanza ['lanθa] *nf* (*arma*) lance, spear; **medir lanzas** to cross swords
lanzacohetes [lanθako'etes] *nm inv* rocket launcher
lanzadera [lanθa'ðera] *nf* shuttle
lanzado, -a [lan'θaðo, a] *adj* (*atrevido*) forward; (*decidido*) determined; **ir ~** (*rápido*) to fly along
lanzallamas [lanθa'ʎamas] *nm inv* flamethrower
lanzamiento [lanθa'mjento] *nm* (*gen*) throwing; (*Naut, Com*) launch, launching; **~ de pesos** putting the shot
lanzar [lan'θar] *vt* (*gen*) to throw; (*con violencia*) to fling; (*Deporte: pelota*) to bowl, to pitch (*US*) (*Naut, Com*) to launch; (*Jur*) to evict; (*grito*) to give, utter; **lanzarse** *vr* to throw o.s.; (*fig*) to take the plunge; **lanzarse a** (*fig*) to embark upon
Lanzarote [lanθa'rote] *nm* Lanzarote
lanzatorpedos [lanθator'peðos] *nm inv* torpedo tube
lapa ['lapa] *nf* limpet
La Paz *nf* La Paz
lapicero [lapi'θero] *nm* pencil; (*Am*) propelling (*Brit*) *o* mechanical (*US*) pencil; (*: bolígrafo*) Biro®
lápida ['lapiða] *nf* stone; **~ conmemorativa** memorial stone; **~ mortuoria** headstone
lapidar [lapi'ðar] *vt* to stone; (*Tec*) to polish, lap
lapidario, -a [lapi'ðarjo, a] *adj, nm* lapidary
lápiz ['lapiθ] *nm* pencil; **~ de color** coloured pencil; **~ de labios** lipstick; **~ óptico** *o* **luminoso** light pen
lapón, -ona [la'pon, ona] *adj* Lapp ■ *nm/f* Laplander, Lapp ■ *nm* (*Ling*) Lapp
Laponia [la'ponja] *nf* Lapland
lapso ['lapso] *nm* lapse; (*error*) error; **~ de tiempo** interval of time
lapsus ['lapsus] *nm inv* error, mistake
LAR [lar] *nf abr* (*Esp Jur*) = **Ley de Arrendamientos Rústicos**
largamente [larɣa'mente] *adv* for a long time; (*relatar*) at length
largar [lar'ɣar] *vt* (*soltar*) to release; (*aflojar*) to loosen; (*lanzar*) to launch; (*fam*) to let fly; (*velas*) to unfurl; (*Am*) to throw; **largarse** *vr* (*fam*) to beat it; **largarse a** (*Am*) to start to
largo, -a ['larɣo, a] *adj* (*longitud*) long; (*tiempo*) lengthy; (*persona: alta*) tall; (*: fig*) generous

■ *nm* length; (*Mus*) largo; **dos años largos** two long years; **a ~ plazo** in the long term; **tiene nueve metros de ~** it is nine metres long; **a lo ~** (*posición*) lengthways; **a lo ~ de** along; (*tiempo*) all through, throughout; **a la larga** in the long run; **me dio largas con una promesa** she put me off with a promise; **¡~ de aquí!** (*fam*) clear off!
largometraje [laryome'traxe] *nm* full-length *o* feature film
largue *etc* ['larye] *vb ver* **largar**
larguero [lar'yero] *nm* (*Arq*) main beam, chief support; (*de puerta*) jamb; (*Deporte*) crossbar; (*de cama*) bolster
largueza [lar'yeθa] *nf* generosity
larguirucho, -a [laryi'rutʃo, a] *adj* lanky, gangling
larguísimo, -a [lar'yisimo, a] *adj superlativo de* **largo**
largura [lar'yura] *nf* length
laringe [la'rinxe] *nf* larynx
laringitis [larin'xitis] *nf* laryngitis
larva ['larβa] *nf* larva
las [las] *artículo definido fpl* the ■ *pron* them; **~ que cantan** the ones/women/girls who sing
lasaña [la'saɲa] *nf* lasagne, lasagna
lasca ['laska] *nf* chip of stone
lascivia [las'θiβja] *nf* lewdness; (*lujuria*) lust; (*fig*) playfulness
lascivo, -a [las'θiβo, a] *adj* lewd
láser ['laser] *nm* laser
Las Palmas *nf* Las Palmas
lástima ['lastima] *nf* (*pena*) pity; **dar ~** to be pitiful; **es una ~ que** it's a pity that; **¡qué ~!** what a pity!; **estar hecho una ~** to be a sorry sight
lastimar [lasti'mar] *vt* (*herir*) to wound; (*ofender*) to offend; **lastimarse** *vr* to hurt o.s.
lastimero, -a [lasti'mero, a] *adj* pitiful, pathetic
lastre ['lastre] *nm* (*Tec, Naut*) ballast; (*fig*) dead weight
lata ['lata] *nf* (*metal*) tin; (*envase*) tin, can; (*fam*) nuisance; **en ~** tinned; **dar (la) ~** to be a nuisance
latente [la'tente] *adj* latent
lateral [late'ral] *adj* side, lateral ■ *nm* (*Teat*) wings *pl*
latido [la'tiðo] *nm* (*del corazón*) beat; (*de herida*) throb(bing)
latifundio [lati'fundjo] *nm* large estate
latifundista [latifun'dista] *nm/f* owner of a large estate
latigazo [lati'yaθo] *nm* (*golpe*) lash; (*sonido*) crack; (*fig: regaño*) dressing-down
látigo ['latiyo] *nm* whip
latiguillo [lati'yiʎo] *nm* (*Teat*) hamming
latín [la'tin] *nm* Latin; **saber (mucho) ~** (*fam*) to be pretty sharp
latinajo [lati'naxo] *nm* dog Latin; **echar latinajos** to come out with Latin words
latino, -a [la'tino, a] *adj* Latin
Latinoamérica [latinoa'merika] *nf* Latin America
latinoamericano, -a [latinoameri'kano, a] *adj, nm/f* Latin American
latir [la'tir] *vi* (*corazón, pulso*) to beat
latitud [lati'tuð] *nf* (*Geo*) latitude; (*fig*) breadth, extent
lato, -a ['lato, a] *adj* broad
latón [la'ton] *nm* brass
latoso, -a [la'toso, a] *adj* (*molesto*) annoying; (*aburrido*) boring
latrocinio [latro'θinjo] *nm* robbery
LAU *nf abr* (*Esp Jur*) = **Ley de Arrendamientos Urbanos**
laúd [la'uð] *nm* lute
laudatorio, -a [lauða'torjo, a] *adj* laudatory
laudo ['lauðo] *nm* (*Jur*) decision, finding
laurear [laure'ar] *vt* to honour, reward
laurel [lau'rel] *nm* (*Bot*) laurel; (*Culin*) bay
Lausana [lau'sana] *nf* Lausanne
lava ['laβa] *nf* lava
lavable [la'βaβle] *adj* washable
lavabo [la'βaβo] *nm* (*jofaina*) washbasin; (*retrete*) lavatory (*Brit*), toilet (*Brit*), washroom (*US*)
lavadero [laβa'ðero] *nm* laundry
lavado [la'βaðo] *nm* washing; (*de ropa*) wash, laundry; (*Arte*) wash; **~ de cerebro** brainwashing
lavadora [laβa'ðora] *nf* washing machine
lavanda [la'βanda] *nf* lavender
lavandería [laβande'ria] *nf* laundry; **~ automática** launderette
lavaparabrisas [laβapara'βrisas] *nm inv* windscreen washer
lavaplatos [laβa'platos] *nm inv* dishwasher
lavar [la'βar] *vt* to wash; (*borrar*) to wipe away; **lavarse** *vr* to wash o.s.; **lavarse las manos** to wash one's hands; (*fig*) to wash one's hands of it; **~ y marcar** (*pelo*) to shampoo and set; **~ en seco** to dry-clean
lavativa [laβa'tiβa] *nf* (*Med*) enema
lavavajillas [laβaβa'xiʎas] *nm inv* dishwasher
laxante [lak'sante] *nm* laxative
laxitud [laksi'tuð] *nf* laxity, slackness
lazada [la'θaða] *nf* bow
lazarillo [laθa'riʎo] *nm*: **perro de ~** guide dog
lazo ['laθo] *nm* knot; (*lazada*) bow; (*para animales*) lasso; (*trampa*) snare; (*vínculo*) tie; **~ corredizo** slipknot
LBE *nf abr* (*Esp Jur*) = **Ley Básica de Empleo**

lb *abr* = **libra**
lbs *abr* = **libras**
L/C *abr* (= *Letra de Crédito*) B/E
Lda., Ldo. *abr* = **Licenciado, a**
le [le] *pron* (*directo*) him (*o* her); (*: en relación a usted*) you; (*indirecto*) to him (*o* her *o* it); (*: a usted*) to you
leal [le'al] *adj* loyal
lealtad [leal'tað] *nf* loyalty
lebrel [le'βrel] *nm* greyhound
lección [lek'θjon] *nf* lesson; **~ práctica** object lesson; **dar lecciones** to teach, give lessons; **dar una ~ a algn** (*fig*) to teach sb a lesson
leche ['letʃe] *nf* milk; (*fam!*) semen, spunk (*!*); **dar una ~ a algn** (*fam*) to belt sb; **estar de mala ~** (*fam*) to be in a foul mood; **tener mala ~** (*fam*) to be a nasty piece of work; **~ condensada/en polvo** condensed/powdered milk; **~ desnatada** skimmed milk; **~ de magnesia** milk of magnesia; **¡~!** hell!
lechera [le'tʃera] *nf ver* **lechero**
lechería [letʃe'ria] *nf* dairy
lechero, -a [le'tʃero, a] *adj* milk *cpd* ■ *nm* milkman ■ *nf* (*vendedora*) milkwoman; (*recipiente*) milk pan; (*para servir*) milk churn
lecho ['letʃo] *nm* (*cama, de río*) bed; (*Geo*) layer; **~ mortuorio** deathbed
lechón [le'tʃon] *nm* sucking (*Brit*) *o* suckling (*US*) pig
lechoso, -a [le'tʃoso, a] *adj* milky
lechuga [le'tʃuɣa] *nf* lettuce
lechuza [le'tʃuθa] *nf* (barn) owl
lectivo, -a [lek'tiβo, a] *adj* (*horas*) teaching *cpd*; **año** *o* **curso ~** (*Escol*) school year; (*Univ*) academic year
lector, a [lek'tor, a] *nm/f* reader; (*Escol, Univ*) (conversation) assistant ■ *nm*: **~ óptico de caracteres** (*Inform*) optical character reader ■ *nf*: **lectora de fichas** (*Inform*) card reader
lectura [lek'tura] *nf* reading; **~ de marcas sensibles** (*Inform*) mark sensing
leer [le'er] *vt* to read; **~ entre líneas** to read between the lines
legación [leɣa'θjon] *nf* legation
legado [le'ɣaðo] *nm* (*don*) bequest; (*herencia*) legacy; (*enviado*) legate
legajo [le'ɣaxo] *nm* file, bundle (of papers)
legal [le'ɣal] *adj* legal, lawful; (*persona*) trustworthy
legalice *etc* [leɣa'liθe] *vb ver* **legalizar**
legalidad [leɣali'ðað] *nf* legality
legalizar [leɣali'θar] *vt* to legalize; (*documento*) to authenticate
legaña [le'ɣaɲa] *nf* sleep (*in eyes*)
legar [le'ɣar] *vt* to bequeath, leave
legatario, -a [leɣa'tarjo, a] *nm/f* legatee
legendario, -a [lexen'darjo, a] *adj* legendary
legible [le'xiβle] *adj* legible; **~ por máquina** (*Inform*) machine-readable
legión [le'xjon] *nf* legion
legionario, -a [lexjo'narjo, a] *adj* legionary ■ *nm* legionnaire
legislación [lexisla'θjon] *nf* legislation; (*leyes*) laws *pl*; **~ antimonopolio** (*Com*) anti-trust legislation
legislar [lexis'lar] *vt* to legislate
legislativo, -a [lexisla'tiβo, a] *adj*: **(elecciones) legislativas** ≈ general election
legislatura [lexisla'tura] *nf* (*Pol*) period of office
legitimar [lexiti'mar] *vt* to legitimize
legítimo, -a [le'xitimo, a] *adj* (*genuino*) authentic; (*legal*) legitimate, rightful
lego, -a ['leɣo, a] *adj* (*Rel*) secular; (*ignorante*) ignorant ■ *nm* layman
legua ['leɣwa] *nf* league; **se ve** (*o* **nota**) **a la ~** you can tell (it) a mile off
legue *etc* ['leɣe] *vb ver* **legar**
leguleyo [leɣu'lejo] *nm* (*pey*) petty *o* shyster (*US*) lawyer
legumbres [le'ɣumbres] *nfpl* pulses
leído, -a [le'iðo, a] *adj* well-read
lejanía [lexa'nia] *nf* distance
lejano, -a [le'xano, a] *adj* far-off; (*en el tiempo*) distant; (*fig*) remote; **L~ Oriente** Far East
lejía [le'xia] *nf* bleach
lejísimos [le'xisimos] *adv* a long, long way
lejos ['lexos] *adv* far, far away; **a lo ~** in the distance; **de** *o* **desde ~** from a distance; **está muy ~** it's a long way (away); **¿está ~?** is it far?; **~ de** *prep* far from
lelo, -a ['lelo, a] *adj* silly ■ *nm/f* idiot
lema ['lema] *nm* motto; (*Pol*) slogan
lencería [lenθe'ria] *nf* (*telas*) linen, drapery; (*ropa interior*) lingerie
lendakari [lenda'kari] *nm* *head of the Basque Autonomous Government*
lengua ['lengwa] *nf* tongue; **~ materna** mother tongue; **~ de tierra** (*Geo*) spit *o* tongue of land; **dar a la ~** to chatter; **morderse la ~** to hold one's tongue; **sacar la ~ a algn** (*fig*) to cock a snook at sb; *see note*

LENGUA

Under the Spanish constitution *lenguas cooficiales* or *oficiales* enjoy the same status as *castellano* in those regions which have retained their own distinct language, ie in Galicia, *gallego*; in the Basque Country, *euskera*; in Catalonia and the Balearic Islands, *catalán*. The regional governments actively promote their own language through the media and the education system. Of the three regions with their own language, Catalonia has the highest number of people who speak the *lengua cooficial*.

lenguado [len'gwaðo] *nm* sole
lenguaje [len'gwaxe] *nm* language; (*forma de hablar*) (mode of) speech; **~ comercial** business language; **~ ensamblador** *o* **de alto nivel** (*Inform*) high-level language; **~ máquina** (*Inform*) machine language; **~ original** source language; **~ periodístico** journalese; **~ de programación** (*Inform*) programming language; **en ~ llano** ≈ in plain English
lenguaraz [lengwa'raθ] *adj* talkative; (*pey*) foul-mouthed
lengüeta [len'gweta] *nf* (*Anat*) epiglottis; (*de zapatos, Mus*) tongue
lenidad [leni'ðað] *nf* lenience
Leningrado [lenin'graðo] *nm* Leningrad
lente ['lente] *nm o nf* lens; (*lupa*) magnifying glass; **lentes** *nmpl* glasses; **lentes de contacto** contact lenses; **lentes progresivas** varifocal lenses
lenteja [len'texa] *nf* lentil
lentejuela [lente'xwela] *nf* sequin
lentilla [len'tiʎa] *nf* contact lens
lentitud [lenti'tuð] *nf* slowness; **con ~** slowly
lento, -a ['lento, a] *adj* slow
leña ['leɲa] *nf* firewood; **dar ~ a** to thrash; **echar ~ al fuego** to add fuel to the flames
leñador, a [leɲa'ðor, a] *nm/f* woodcutter
leño ['leɲo] *nm* (*trozo de árbol*) log; (*madera*) timber; (*fig*) blockhead
Leo ['leo] *nm* (*Astro*) Leo
león [le'on] *nm* lion; **~ marino** sea lion
leonera [leo'nera] *nf* (*jaula*) lion's cage; **parece una ~** it's shockingly dirty
leonés, -esa [leo'nes, esa] *adj, nm/f* Leonese ■ *nm* (*Ling*) Leonese
leonino, -a [leo'nino, a] *adj* leonine
leopardo [leo'parðo] *nm* leopard
leotardos [leo'tarðos] *nmpl* tights
lepra ['lepra] *nf* leprosy
leprosería [leprose'ria] *nf* leper colony
leproso, -a [le'proso, a] *nm/f* leper
lerdo, -a ['lerðo, a] *adj* (*lento*) slow; (*patoso*) clumsy
leridano, -a [leri'ðano, a] *adj* of *o* from Lérida ■ *nm/f* native *o* inhabitant of Lérida
les [les] *pron* (*directo*) them; (*: en relación a ustedes*) you; (*indirecto*) to them; (*: a ustedes*) to you
lesbiana [les'βjana] *nf* lesbian
lesión [le'sjon] *nf* wound, lesion; (*Deporte*) injury
lesionado, -a [lesjo'naðo, a] *adj* injured ■ *nm/f* injured person
lesionar [lesjo'nar] *vt* (*dañar*) to hurt; (*herir*) to wound; **lesionarse** *vr* to get hurt
letal [le'tal] *adj* lethal
letanía [leta'nia] *nf* litany; (*retahíla*) long list
letárgico, -a [le'tarxiko, a] *adj* lethargic
letargo [le'tarɣo] *nm* lethargy
letón, -ona [le'ton, ona] *adj, nm/f* Latvian ■ *nm* (*Ling*) Latvian
Letonia [le'tonja] *nf* Latvia
letra ['letra] *nf* letter; (*escritura*) handwriting; (*Com*) letter, bill, draft; (*Mus*) lyrics *pl*; **letras** *nfpl* (*Univ*) arts; **~ bastardilla/negrilla** italics *pl*/bold type; **~ de cambio** bill of exchange; **~ de imprenta** print; **~ inicial/mayúscula/minúscula** initial/capital/small letter; **lo tomó al pie de la ~** he took it literally; **~ bancaria** (*Com*) bank draft; **~ de patente** (*Com*) letters patent *pl*; **escribir cuatro letras a algn** to drop a line to sb
letrado, -a [le'traðo, a] *adj* learned; (*fam*) pedantic ■ *nm/f* lawyer
letrero [le'trero] *nm* (*cartel*) sign; (*etiqueta*) label
letrina [le'trina] *nf* latrine
leucemia [leu'θemja] *nf* leukaemia
leucocito [leuko'θito] *nm* white blood cell, leucocyte
leva ['leβa] *nf* (*Naut*) weighing anchor; (*Mil*) levy; (*Tec*) lever
levadizo, -a [leβa'ðiθo, a] *adj*: **puente ~** drawbridge
levadura [leβa'ðura] *nf* yeast, leaven; **~ de cerveza** brewer's yeast
levantamiento [leβanta'mjento] *nm* raising, lifting; (*rebelión*) revolt, rising; (*Geo*) survey; **~ de pesos** weightlifting
levantar [leβan'tar] *vt* (*gen*) to raise; (*del suelo*) to pick up; (*hacia arriba*) to lift (up); (*plan*) to make, draw up; (*mesa*) to clear; (*campamento*) to strike; (*fig*) to cheer up, hearten; **levantarse** *vr* to get up; (*enderezarse*) to straighten up; (*rebelarse*) to rebel; (*sesión*) to be adjourned; (*niebla*) to lift; (*viento*) to rise; **levantarse (de la cama)** to get up, get out of bed; **~ el ánimo** to cheer up
levante [le'βante] *nm* east; (*viento*) east wind; **el L~** *region of Spain extending from Castellón to Murcia*
levantino, -a [leβan'tino, a] *adj* of *o* from the *Levante* ■ *nm/f*: **los levantinos** the people of the *Levante*
levar [le'βar] *vi* to weigh anchor
leve ['leβe] *adj* light; (*fig*) trivial; (*mínimo*) slight
levedad [leβe'ðað] *nf* lightness; (*fig*) levity

levita [le'βita] *nf* frock coat
léxico, -a ['leksiko, a] *adj* lexical ■ *nm* (*vocabulario*) vocabulary; (*Ling*) lexicon
ley [lei] *nf* (*gen*) law; (*metal*) standard; **decreto-~** decree law; **de buena ~** (*fig*) genuine; **según la ~** in accordance with the law, by law, in law
leyenda [le'jenda] *nf* legend; (*Tip*) inscription
leyendo *etc* [le'jendo] *vb ver* **leer**
liar [li'ar] *vt* to tie (up); (*unir*) to bind; (*envolver*) to wrap (up); (*enredar*) to confuse; (*cigarrillo*) to roll; **liarse** *vr* (*fam*) to get involved; (*confundirse*) to get mixed up; **liarse a palos** to get involved in a fight
lib. *abr* (= *libro*) bk.
libanés, -esa [liβa'nes, esa] *adj, nm/f* Lebanese
Líbano ['liβano] *nm*: **el ~** the Lebanon
libar [li'βar] *vt* to suck
libelo [li'βelo] *nm* satire, lampoon; (*Jur*) petition
libélula [li'βelula] *nf* dragonfly
liberación [liβera'θjon] *nf* liberation; (*de la cárcel*) release
liberado, -a [liβe'raðo, a] *adj* liberated; (*Com*) paid-up, paid-in (*US*)
liberal [liβe'ral] *adj, nm/f* liberal
liberar [liβe'rar] *vt* to liberate
libertad [liβer'tað] *nf* liberty, freedom; **~ de asociación/de culto/de prensa/de comercio/de palabra** freedom of association/of worship/of the press/of trade/of speech; **~ condicional** probation; **~ bajo palabra** parole; **~ bajo fianza** bail; **estar en ~** to be free; **poner a algn en ~** to set sb free
libertador, a [liβerta'ðor, a] *adj* liberating ■ *nm/f* liberator; **El L~** (*Am*) The Liberator
libertar [liβer'tar] *vt* (*preso*) to set free; (*de una obligación*) to release; (*eximir*) to exempt
libertinaje [liβerti'naxe] *nm* licentiousness
libertino, -a [liβer'tino, a] *adj* permissive ■ *nm/f* permissive person
Libia ['liβja] *nf* Libya
libidinoso, -a [liβiði'noso, a] *adj* lustful; (*viejo*) lecherous
libido [li'βiðo] *nf* libido
libio, -a ['liβjo, a] *adj, nm/f* Libyan
libra ['liβra] *nf* pound; **L~** (*Astro*) Libra; **~ esterlina** pound sterling
librador, a [liβra'ðor, a] *nm/f* drawer
libranza [li'βranθa] *nf* (*Com*) draft; (*letra de cambio*) bill of exchange
librar [li'βrar] *vt* (*de peligro*) to save; (*batalla*) to wage, fight; (*de impuestos*) to exempt; (*cheque*) to make out; (*Jur*) to exempt; **librarse** *vr*: **librarse de** to escape from, free o.s. from; **de buena nos hemos librado** we're well out of that
libre ['liβre] *adj* (*gen*) free; (*lugar*) unoccupied; (*tiempo*) spare; (*asiento*) vacant; (*Com*): **~ a bordo** free on board; **~ de franqueo** post-free; **~ de impuestos** free of tax; **tiro ~** free kick; **los 100 metros ~** the 100 metres freestyle (race); **al aire ~** in the open air; **¿estás ~?** are you free?
librecambio [liβre'kambjo] *nm* free trade
librecambista [liβrekam'bista] *adj* free-trade *cpd* ■ *nm* free-trader
librería [liβre'ria] *nf* (*tienda*) bookshop; (*estante*) bookcase; **~ de ocasión** secondhand bookshop
librero, -a [li'βrero, a] *nm/f* bookseller
libreta [li'βreta] *nf* notebook; (*pan*) one-pound loaf; **~ de ahorros** savings book
libro ['liβro] *nm* book; **~ de actas** minute book; **~ de bolsillo** paperback; **~ de cabecera** bedside book; **~ de caja** (*Com*) cashbook; **~ de caja auxiliar** (*Com*) petty cash book; **~ de cocina** cookery book (*Brit*), cookbook (*US*); **~ de consulta** reference book; **~ de cuentas** account book; **~ de cuentos** storybook; **~ de cheques** cheque (*Brit*) *o* check (*US*) book; **~ diario** journal; **~ de entradas y salidas** (*Com*) daybook; **~ de honor** visitors' book; **~ electrónico** e-book; **~ mayor** (*Com*) general ledger; **~ de reclamaciones** complaints book; **~ de texto** textbook
Lic. *abr* = **Licenciado, a**
licencia [li'θenθja] *nf* (*gen*) licence; (*permiso*) permission; **~ por enfermedad/con goce de sueldo** sick/paid leave; **~ de armas/de caza** gun/game licence; **~ de exportación** (*Com*) export licence; **~ poética** poetic licence
licenciado, -a [liθen'θjaðo, a] *adj* licensed ■ *nm/f* graduate; **L~ en Filosofía y Letras** ≈ Bachelor of Arts; *see note*

LICENCIADO

When students finish University after an average of five years they receive the degree of *licenciado*. If the course is only three years such as Nursing, or if they choose not to do the optional two-year specialization, they are awarded the degree of *diplomado*. *Cursos de posgrado*, postgraduate courses, are becoming increasingly popular, especially one-year specialist courses called *masters*.

licenciar [liθen'θjar] *vt* (*empleado*) to dismiss; (*permitir*) to permit, allow; (*soldado*) to

discharge; *(estudiante)* to confer a degree upon; **licenciarse** *vr*: **licenciarse en letras** to get an arts degree
licenciatura [liθenθja'tura] *nf (título)* degree; *(estudios)* degree course
licencioso, -a [liθen'θjoso, a] *adj* licentious
liceo [li'θeo] *nm (esp Am)* (high) school
licitación [liθita'θjon] *nf* bidding; *(oferta)* tender, offer
licitador [liθita'ðor] *nm* bidder
licitar [liθi'tar] *vt* to bid for ■ *vi* to bid
lícito, -a ['liθito, a] *adj (legal)* lawful; *(justo)* fair, just; *(permisible)* permissible
licor [li'kor] *nm* spirits *pl (Brit)*, liquor (US); *(con hierbas etc)* liqueur
licra® ['likra] *nf* Lycra®
licuadora [likwa'ðora] *nf* blender
licuar [li'kwar] *vt* to liquidize
lid [lið] *nf* combat; *(fig)* controversy
líder ['liðer] *nm/f* leader
liderato [liðe'rato] *nm* = **liderazgo**
liderazgo [liðe'raθɣo] *nm* leadership
lidia ['liðja] *nf* bullfighting; *(una lidia)* bullfight; **toros de ~** fighting bulls
lidiar [li'ðjar] *vt, vi* to fight
liebre ['ljeβre] *nf* hare; **dar gato por ~** to con
Lieja ['ljexa] *nf* Liège
lienzo ['ljenθo] *nm* linen; *(Arte)* canvas; *(Arq)* wall
lifting ['liftin] *nm* facelift
liga ['liɣa] *nf (de medias)* garter, suspender; *(confederación)* league; *(Am: gomita)* rubber band
ligadura [liɣa'ðura] *nf* bond, tie; *(Med, Mus)* ligature
ligamento [liɣa'mento] *nm (Anat)* ligament; *(atadura)* tie; *(unión)* bond
ligar [li'ɣar] *vt (atar)* to tie; *(unir)* to join; *(Med)* to bind up; *(Mus)* to slur; *(fam)* to get off with, pick up ■ *vi* to mix, blend; *(fam)* to get off with sb; *(2 personas)* to get off with one another; **ligarse** *vr (fig)* to commit o.s.; **~ con** *(fam)* to get off with, pick up; **ligarse a algn** to get off with *o* pick up sb
ligereza [lixe'reθa] *nf* lightness; *(rapidez)* swiftness; *(agilidad)* agility; *(superficialidad)* flippancy
ligero, -a [li'xero, a] *adj (de peso)* light; *(tela)* thin; *(rápido)* swift, quick; *(ágil)* agile, nimble; *(de importancia)* slight; *(de carácter)* flippant, superficial ■ *adv* quickly, swiftly; **a la ligera** superficially; **juzgar a la ligera** to jump to conclusions
light ['lait] *adj inv (cigarrillo)* low-tar; *(comida)* diet *cpd*
ligón [li'ɣon] *nm (fam)* Romeo
ligue *etc* ['liɣe] *vb ver* **ligar** ■ *nm/f* boyfriend/girlfriend ■ *nm (persona)* pick-up
liguero [li'ɣero] *nm* suspender *(Brit) o* garter (US) belt
lija ['lixa] *nf (Zool)* dogfish; **(papel de) ~** sandpaper
lijar [li'xar] *vt* to sand
lila ['lila] *adj inv, nf* lilac ■ *nm (fam)* twit
lima ['lima] *nf* file; *(Bot)* lime; **~ de uñas** nail file; **comer como una ~** to eat like a horse
limar [li'mar] *vt* to file; *(alisar)* to smooth over; *(fig)* to polish up
limbo ['limbo] *nm (Rel)* limbo; **estar en el ~** to be on another planet
limitación [limita'θjon] *nf* limitation, limit; **~ de velocidad** speed limit
limitado, -a [limi'taðo, a] *adj* limited; **sociedad limitada** *(Com)* limited company
limitar [limi'tar] *vt* to limit; *(reducir)* to reduce, cut down ■ *vi*: **~ con** to border on; **limitarse** *vr*: **limitarse a** to limit *o* confine o.s. to
límite ['limite] *nm (gen)* limit; *(fin)* end; *(frontera)* border; **como ~** at (the) most; *(fecha)* at the latest; **no tener límites** to know no bounds; **~ de crédito** *(Com)* credit limit; **~ de página** *(Inform)* page break; **~ de velocidad** speed limit
limítrofe [li'mitrofe] *adj* bordering, neighbouring
limón [li'mon] *nm* lemon ■ *adj*: **amarillo ~** lemon-yellow
limonada [limo'naða] *nf* lemonade
limonero [limo'nero] *nm* lemon tree
limosna [li'mosna] *nf* alms *pl*; **pedir ~** to beg; **vivir de ~** to live on charity
limpiabotas [limpja'βotas] *nm/f inv* bootblack *(Brit)*, shoeshine boy/girl
limpiacristales [limpjakris'tales] *nm inv (detergente)* window cleaner
limpiador, a [limpja'ðor, a] *adj* cleaning, cleansing ■ *nm/f* cleaner
limpiaparabrisas [limpjapara'βrisas] *nm inv* windscreen *(Brit) o* windshield (US) wiper
limpiar [lim'pjar] *vt* to clean; *(con trapo)* to wipe; *(quitar)* to wipe away; *(zapatos)* to shine, polish; *(casa)* to tidy up; *(fig)* to clean up; *(: purificar)* to cleanse, purify; *(Mil)* to mop up; **~ en seco** to dry-clean
limpieza [lim'pjeθa] *nf (estado)* cleanliness; *(acto)* cleaning; *(: de las calles)* cleansing; *(: de zapatos)* polishing; *(habilidad)* skill; *(fig: Policía)* clean-up; *(pureza)* purity; *(Mil)*: **operación de ~** mopping-up operation; **~ étnica** ethnic cleansing; **~ en seco** dry cleaning
limpio, -a ['limpjo, a] *adj* clean; *(moralmente)* pure; *(ordenado)* tidy; *(despejado)* clear; *(Com)* clear, net; *(fam)* honest ■ *adv*: **jugar ~** to play fair; **pasar a ~** to make a fair copy; **sacar**

algo en ~ to get benefit from sth; **~ de** free from
linaje [li'naxe] *nm* lineage, family
linaza [li'naθa] *nf* linseed; **aceite de ~** linseed oil
lince ['linθe] *nm* lynx; **ser un ~** (*fig: observador*) to be very observant; (*: astuto*) to be shrewd
linchar [lin'tʃar] *vt* to lynch
lindante [lin'dante] *adj* adjoining; **~ con** bordering on
lindar [lin'dar] *vi* to adjoin; **~ con** to border on; (*Arq*) to abut on
linde ['linde] *nm o nf* boundary
lindero, -a [lin'dero, a] *adj* adjoining ■ *nm* boundary
lindo, -a ['lindo, a] *adj* pretty, lovely ■ *adv* (*esp Am: fam*) nicely, very well; **canta muy ~** (*Am*) he sings beautifully; **se divertían de lo ~** they enjoyed themselves enormously
línea ['linea] *nf* (*gen, moral, Pol etc*) line; (*talle*) figure; (*Inform*): **en ~** on line; **fuera de ~** off line; **~ de estado** status line; **~ de formato** format line; **~ aérea** airline; **~ de alto el fuego** ceasefire line; **~ de fuego** firing line; **~ de meta** goal line; (*de carrera*) finishing line; **~ de montaje** assembly line; **~ dura** (*Pol*) hard line; **~ recta** straight line; **la ~ de 2008** (*moda*) the 2008 look
lineal [line'al] *adj* linear
lingote [lin'gote] *nm* ingot
lingüista [lin'gwista] *nm/f* linguist
lingüística [lin'gwistika] *nf* linguistics *sg*
linimento [lini'mento] *nm* liniment
lino ['lino] *nm* linen; (*Bot*) flax
linóleo [li'noleo] *nm* lino, linoleum
linterna [lin'terna] *nf* lantern, lamp; **~ eléctrica** *o* **a pilas** torch (*Brit*), flashlight (*US*)
lío ['lio] *nm* bundle; (*desorden*) muddle, mess; (*fam: follón*) fuss; (*: relación amorosa*) affair; **armar un ~** to make a fuss; **meterse en un ~** to get into a jam; **tener un ~ con algn** to be having an affair with sb
lipotimia [lipo'timja] *nf* blackout
liquen ['liken] *nm* lichen
liquidación [likiða'θjon] *nf* liquidation; (*de cuenta*) settlement; **venta de ~** clearance sale
liquidar [liki'ðar] *vt* (*Química*) to liquefy; (*Com*) to liquidate; (*deudas*) to pay off; (*empresa*) to wind up; **~ a algn** to bump sb off, rub sb out (*fam*)
liquidez [liki'ðeθ] *nf* liquidity
líquido, -a ['likiðo, a] *adj* liquid; (*ganancia*) net ■ *nm* liquid; (*Com: efectivo*) ready cash *o* money; (*: ganancia*) net amount *o* profit; **~ imponible** net taxable income
lira ['lira] *nf* (*Mus*) lyre; (*moneda*) lira
lírico, -a ['liriko, a] *adj* lyrical
lirio ['lirjo] *nm* (*Bot*) iris
lirismo [li'rismo] *nm* lyricism; (*sentimentalismo*) sentimentality
lirón [li'ron] *nm* (*Zool*) dormouse; (*fig*) sleepyhead
Lisboa [lis'βoa] *nf* Lisbon
lisboeta [lisβo'eta] *adj* of *o* from Lisbon ■ *nm/f* native *o* inhabitant of Lisbon
lisiado, -a [li'sjaðo, a] *adj* injured ■ *nm/f* cripple
lisiar [li'sjar] *vt* to maim; **lisiarse** *vr* to injure o.s.
liso, -a ['liso, a] *adj* (*terreno*) flat; (*cabello*) straight; (*superficie*) even; (*tela*) plain; **lisa y llanamente** in plain language, plainly
lisonja [li'sonxa] *nf* flattery
lisonjear [lisonxe'ar] *vt* to flatter; (*fig*) to please
lisonjero, -a [lison'xero, a] *adj* flattering; (*agradable*) gratifying, pleasing ■ *nm/f* flatterer
lista ['lista] *nf* list; (*de alumnos*) school register; (*de libros*) catalogue; (*de correos*) poste restante; (*de platos*) menu; (*de precios*) price list; **pasar ~** to call the roll; (*Escol*) to call the register; **~ de correos** poste restante; **~ de direcciones** mailing list; **~ electoral** electoral roll; **~ de espera** waiting list; **tela a listas** striped material
listado, -a [lis'taðo, a] *adj* striped ■ *nm* (*Com, Inform*) listing; **~ paginado** (*Inform*) paged listing
listar [lis'tar] *vt* (*Inform*) to list
listo, -a ['listo, a] *adj* (*perspicaz*) smart, clever; (*preparado*) ready; **~ para usar** ready-to-use; **¿estás ~?** are you ready?; **pasarse de ~** to be too clever by half
listón [lis'ton] *nm* (*de tela*) ribbon; (*de madera, metal*) strip
litera [li'tera] *nf* (*en barco, tren*) berth; (*en dormitorio*) bunk, bunk bed
literal [lite'ral] *adj* literal
literario, -a [lite'rarjo, a] *adj* literary
literato, -a [lite'rato, a] *nm/f* writer
literatura [litera'tura] *nf* literature
litigante [liti'ɣante] *nm/f* litigant, claimant
litigar [liti'ɣar] *vt* to fight ■ *vi* (*Jur*) to go to law; (*fig*) to dispute, argue
litigio [li'tixjo] *nm* (*Jur*) lawsuit; (*fig*): **en ~ con** in dispute with
litigue *etc* [li'tiɣe] *vb ver* **litigar**
litografía [litoɣra'fia] *nf* lithography; (*una litografía*) lithograph
litoral [lito'ral] *adj* coastal ■ *nm* coast, seaboard
litro ['litro] *nm* litre, liter (*US*)
Lituania [li'twanja] *nf* Lithuania

lituano, -a [li'twano, a] *adj, nm/f* Lithuanian ■ *nm* (*Ling*) Lithuanian
liturgia [li'turxja] *nf* liturgy
liviano, -a [li'βjano, a] *adj* (*persona*) fickle; (*cosa, objeto*) trivial; (*Am*) light
lívido, -a ['liβiðo, a] *adj* livid
living ['liβin] (*pl* **livings**) *nm* (*esp Am*) sitting room
Ll, ll ['eʎe] *nf former letter in the Spanish alphabet*
llaga ['ʎaɣa] *nf* wound
llagar [ʎa'ɣar] *vt* to make sore; (*herir*) to wound
llague *etc* ['ʎaɣe] *vb ver* **llagar**
llama ['ʎama] *nf* flame; (*fig*) passion; (*Zool*) llama; **en llamas** burning, ablaze
llamada [ʎa'maða] *nf* call; (*a la puerta*) knock; (*: al timbre*) ring; **~ a cobro revertido** reverse-charge call; **~ al orden** call to order; **~ a pie de página** reference note; **~ a procedimiento** (*Inform*) procedure call; **~ interurbana** trunk call
llamado [ʎa'maðo] *nm* (*Am*) (telephone) call; (*llamamiento*) appeal, call
llamamiento [ʎama'mjento] *nm* call; **hacer un ~ a algn para que haga algo** to appeal to sb to do sth
llamar [ʎa'mar] *vt* to call; (*convocar*) to summon; (*invocar*) to invoke; (*atraer con gesto*) to beckon; (*atención*) to attract; (*Telec: tb*: **llamar por teléfono**) to call, ring up, telephone; (*Mil*) to call up ■ *vi* (*por teléfono*) to phone; (*a la puerta*) to knock (*o* ring); (*por señas*) to beckon; **llamarse** *vr* to be called, be named; **¿cómo se llama usted?** what's your name?; **¿quién llama?** (*Telec*) who's calling?, who's that?; **no me llama la atención** (*fam*) I don't fancy it
llamarada [ʎama'raða] *nf* (*llamas*) blaze; (*rubor*) flush; (*fig*) flare-up
llamativo, -a [ʎama'tiβo, a] *adj* showy; (*color*) loud
llamear [ʎame'ar] *vi* to blaze
llanamente [ʎana'mente] *adv* (*lisamente*) smoothly; (*sin ostentaciones*) plainly; (*sinceramente*) frankly; *ver tb* **liso**
llaneza [ʎa'neθa] *nf* (*gen*) simplicity; (*honestidad*) straightforwardness, frankness
llano, -a ['ʎano, a] *adj* (*superficie*) flat; (*persona*) straightforward; (*estilo*) clear ■ *nm* plain, flat ground
llanta ['ʎanta] *nf* (wheel) rim; (*Am: neumático*) tyre; (*: cámara*) (inner) tube
llanto ['ʎanto] *nm* weeping; (*fig*) lamentation; (*canción*) dirge, lament
llanura [ʎa'nura] *nf* (*lisura*) flatness, smoothness; (*Geo*) plain
llave ['ʎaβe] *nf* key; (*de gas, agua*) tap (*Brit*), faucet (*US*); (*Mecánica*) spanner; (*de la luz*) switch; (*Mus*) key; **~ inglesa** monkey wrench; **~ maestra** master key; **~ de contacto** (*Auto*) ignition key; **~ de paso** stopcock; **echar ~ a** to lock up
llavero [ʎa'βero] *nm* keyring
llavín [ʎa'βin] *nm* latchkey
llegada [ʎe'ɣaða] *nf* arrival
llegar [ʎe'ɣar] *vt* to bring up, bring over ■ *vi* to arrive; (*bastar*) to be enough; **llegarse** *vr*: **llegarse a** to approach; **~ a** (*alcanzar*) to reach; to manage to, succeed in; **~ a saber** to find out; **~ a ser famoso/el jefe** to become famous/the boss; **~ a las manos** to come to blows; **~ a las manos de** to come into the hands of; **no llegues tarde** don't be late; **esta cuerda no llega** this rope isn't long enough
llegue *etc* ['ʎeɣe] *vb ver* **llegar**
llenar [ʎe'nar] *vt* to fill; (*superficie*) to cover; (*espacio, tiempo*) to fill, take up; (*formulario*) to fill in *o* out; (*fig*) to heap; **llenarse** *vr* to fill (up); **llenarse de** (*fam*) to stuff o.s. with
lleno, -a ['ʎeno, a] *adj* full, filled; (*repleto*) full up ■ *nm* (*abundancia*) abundance; (*Teat*) full house; **dar de ~ contra un muro** to hit a wall head-on
llevadero, -a [ʎeβa'ðero, a] *adj* bearable, tolerable
llevar [ʎe'βar] *vt* to take; (*ropa*) to wear; (*cargar*) to carry; (*quitar*) to take away; (*en coche*) to drive; (*transportar*) to transport; (*ruta*) to follow, keep to; (*traer: dinero*) to carry; (*suj: camino etc*): **~ a** to lead to; (*Mat*) to carry; (*aguantar*) to bear; (*negocio*) to conduct, direct; to manage; **llevarse** *vr* to carry off, take away; **llevamos dos días aquí** we have been here for two days; **él me lleva dos años** he's two years older than me; **~ adelante** (*fig*) to carry forward; **~ por delante a uno** (*en coche etc*) to run sb over; (*fig*) to ride roughshod over sb; **~ la ventaja** to be winning *o* in the lead; **~ los libros** (*Com*) to keep the books; **llevo las de perder** I'm likely to lose; **no las lleva todas consigo** he's not all there; **nos llevó a cenar fuera** she took us out for a meal; **llevarse a uno por delante** (*atropellar*) to run sb over; **llevarse bien** to get on well (together)
llorar [ʎo'rar] *vt* to cry, weep ■ *vi* to cry, weep; (*ojos*) to water; **~ a moco tendido** to sob one's heart out; **~ de risa** to cry with laughter
lloriquear [ʎorike'ar] *vi* to snivel, whimper
lloro ['ʎoro] *nm* crying, weeping
llorón, -ona [ʎo'ron, ona] *adj* tearful ■ *nm/f* cry-baby
lloroso, -a [ʎo'roso, a] *adj* (*gen*) weeping,

tearful; (*triste*) sad, sorrowful
llover [ʎo'βer] *vi* to rain; **~ a cántaros** *o* **a cubos** *o* **a mares** to rain cats and dogs, pour (down); **ser una cosa llovida del cielo** to be a godsend; **llueve sobre mojado** it never rains but it pours
llovizna [ʎo'βiθna] *nf* drizzle
lloviznar [ʎoβiθ'nar] *vi* to drizzle
llueve *etc* ['ʎweβe] *vb ver* **llover**
lluvia ['ʎuβja] *nf* rain; (*cantidad*) rainfall; (*fig: de balas etc*) hail, shower; **~ radioactiva** radioactive fallout; **día de ~** rainy day; **una ~ de regalos** a shower of gifts
lluvioso, -a [ʎu'βjoso, a] *adj* rainy
lo [lo] *artículo definido neutro*: **lo bueno** the good ■ *pron* (*en relación a una persona*) him; (*en relación a una cosa*) it; **lo mío** what is mine; **lo difícil es que ...** the difficult thing about it is that ...; **no saben lo aburrido que es** they don't know how boring it is; **viste a lo americano** he dresses in the American style; **lo de** that matter of; **lo que** what, that which; **toma lo que quieras** take what(ever) you want; **lo que sea** whatever; **¡toma lo que he dicho!** I stand by what I said!
loa ['loa] *nf* praise
loable [lo'aβle] *adj* praiseworthy
LOAPA [lo'apa] *nf abr* (*Esp Jur*) = **Ley Orgánica de Armonización del Proceso Autónomo**
loar [lo'ar] *vt* to praise
lobato [lo'βato] *nm* (*Zool*) wolf cub
lobo ['loβo] *nm* wolf; **~ de mar** (*fig*) sea dog; **~ marino** seal
lóbrego, -a ['loβreɣo, a] *adj* dark; (*fig*) gloomy
lóbulo ['loβulo] *nm* lobe
LOC *nm abr* (= *lector óptico de caracteres*) OCR
local [lo'kal] *adj* local ■ *nm* place, site; (*oficinas*) premises *pl*
localice *etc* [loka'liθe] *vb ver* **localizar**
localidad [lokali'ðað] *nf* (*barrio*) locality; (*lugar*) location; (*Teat*) seat, ticket
localizador *nm* (*de un vuelo*) booking reference, reservation code
localizar [lokali'θar] *vt* (*ubicar*) to locate, find; (*encontrar*) to find, track down; (*restringir*) to localize; (*situar*) to place
loción [lo'θjon] *nf* lotion, wash
loco, -a ['loko, a] *adj* mad; (*fig*) wild, mad ■ *nm/f* lunatic, madman(-woman); **~ de atar, ~ de remate, ~ rematado** raving mad; **a lo ~** without rhyme or reason; **ando ~ con el examen** the exam is driving me crazy; **estar ~ de alegría** to be overjoyed *o* over the moon
locomoción [lokomo'θjon] *nf* locomotion
locomotora [lokomo'tora] *nf* engine, locomotive
locuaz [lo'kwaθ] *adj* loquacious, talkative
locución [loku'θjon] *nf* expression
locura [lo'kura] *nf* madness; (*acto*) crazy act
locutor, a [loku'tor, a] *nm/f* (*Radio*) announcer; (*comentarista*) commentator; (*TV*) newscaster, newsreader
locutorio [loku'torjo] *nm* (*Telec*) telephone box *o* booth; (*negocio*) *shop or internet café providing telephone services*
lodo ['lodo] *nm* mud
logia ['loxja] *nf* (*Mil, de masones*) lodge; (*Arq*) loggia
lógico, -a ['loxiko, a] *adj* logical; (*correcto*) natural; (*razonable*) reasonable ■ *nm* logician ■ *nf* logic; **es ~ que ...** it stands to reason that ...; **ser de una lógica aplastante** to be as clear as day
logístico, -a [lo'xistiko, a] *adj* logistical ■ *nf* logistics *pl*
logotipo [loɣo'tipo] *nm* logo
logrado, -a [lo'ɣraðo, a] *adj* accomplished
lograr [lo'ɣrar] *vt* (*obtener*) to get, obtain; (*conseguir*) to achieve, attain; **~ hacer** to manage to do; **~ que algn venga** to manage to get sb to come; **~ acceso a** (*Inform*) to access
logro ['loɣro] *nm* achievement, success; (*Com*) profit
logroñés, -esa [logro'ɲes, esa] *adj* of *o* from Logroño ■ *nm/f* native *o* inhabitant of Logroño
Loira ['loira] *nm* Loire
loma ['loma] *nf* hillock, low ridge
Lombardía [lombar'ðia] *nf* Lombardy
lombriz [lom'briθ] *nf* (earth)worm
lomo ['lomo] *nm* (*de animal*) back; (*Culin: de cerdo*) pork loin; (*: de vaca*) rib steak; (*de libro*) spine
lona ['lona] *nf* canvas
loncha ['lontʃa] *nf* = **lonja**
lonche ['lontʃe] *nm* (*Am*) lunch
lonchería [lontʃe'ria] *nf* (*Am*) snack bar, diner (*US*)
londinense [londi'nense] *adj* London *cpd*, of *o* from London ■ *nm/f* Londoner
Londres ['londres] *nm* London
longaniza [longa'niθa] *nf* pork sausage
longevidad [lonxeβi'ðað] *nf* longevity
longitud [lonxi'tuð] *nf* length; (*Geo*) longitude; **tener tres metros de ~** to be three metres long; **~ de onda** wavelength; **salto de ~** long jump
longitudinal [lonxituði'nal] *adj* longitudinal
lonja ['lonxa] *nf* slice; (*de tocino*) rasher; (*Com*) market, exchange; **~ de pescado** fish market
lontananza [lonta'nanθa] *nf* background; **en ~** far away, in the distance
Lorena [lo'rena] *nf* Lorraine

loro ['loro] *nm* parrot
los [los] *artículo definido mpl* the ▪ *pron* them; *(en relación a ustedes)* you; **mis libros y ~ de usted** my books and yours
losa ['losa] *nf* stone; **~ sepulcral** gravestone
lote ['lote] *nm* portion, share; (*Com*) lot; (*Inform*) batch
lotería [lote'ria] *nf* lottery; *(juego)* lotto; **le tocó la ~** he won a big prize in the lottery; (*fig*) he struck lucky; **~ nacional** national lottery; **~ primitiva** (*Esp*) *type of state-run lottery; see note*

LOTERÍA

Millions of pounds are spent every year on *loterías*, lotteries. There is the weekly *Lotería Nacional* which is very popular especially at Christmas. Other weekly lotteries are the *Bono Loto* and the *(Lotería) Primitiva*. One of the most famous lotteries is run by the wealthy and influential society for the blind, *la* ONCE, and the form is called *el cupón de la* ONCE or *el cupón de los ciegos*.

lotero, -a [lo'tero, a] *nm/f* seller of lottery tickets
Lovaina [lo'βaina] *nf* Louvain
loza ['loθa] *nf* crockery; **~ fina** china
lozanía [loθa'nia] *nf* (*lujo*) luxuriance
lozano, -a [lo'θano, a] *adj* luxuriant; (*animado*) lively
LPA *sigla f* (= *Ley del Proceso Autonómico*) *law for the autonomy of the regions*
LRA *sigla f* = **Ley de Reforma Agraria**
LRU *sigla f* = **Ley de Reforma Universitaria**
LSD *sigla m* (= *Dietilamida del Acido Lisérgico*) LSD
lubina [lu'βina] *nf* (*Zool*) sea bass
lubricante [luβri'kante] *adj, nm* lubricant
lubricar [luβri'kar], **lubrificar** [luβrifi'kar] *vt* to lubricate
lubrique *etc* [lu'βrike] *vb ver* **lubricar**
lucense [lu'θense] *adj* of *o* from Lugo ▪ *nm/f* native *o* inhabitant of Lugo
Lucerna [lu'θerna] *nf* Lucerne
lucero [lu'θero] *nm* (*Astro*) bright star; (*fig*) brilliance; **~ del alba/de la tarde** morning/evening star
luces ['luθes] *nfpl de* **luz**
lucha ['lutʃa] *nf* fight, struggle; **~ de clases** class struggle; **~ libre** wrestling
luchar [lu'tʃar] *vi* to fight
lucidez [luθi'ðeθ] *nf* lucidity
lucido, -a [lu'θiðo, a] *adj* (*espléndido*) splendid, brilliant; (*elegante*) elegant; (*exitoso*) successful
lúcido, -a ['luθiðo, a] *adj* lucid
luciérnaga [lu'θjernaγa] *nf* glow-worm
lucimiento [luθi'mjento] *nm* (*brillo*) brilliance; (*éxito*) success
lucio ['luθjo] *nm* (*Zool*) pike
lucir [lu'θir] *vt* to illuminate, light (up); (*ostentar*) to show off ▪ *vi* (*brillar*) to shine; (*Am: parecer*) to look, seem; **lucirse** *vr* (*irónico*) to make a fool of o.s.; (*presumir*) to show off; **la casa luce limpia** the house looks clean
lucrativo, -a [lukra'tiβo, a] *adj* lucrative, profitable; **institución no lucrativa** non profit-making institution
lucro ['lukro] *nm* profit, gain; **lucros y daños** (*Com*) profit and loss *sg*
luctuoso, -a [luk'twoso, a] *adj* mournful
lúdico, -a ['luðiko, a] *adj* playful; (*actividad*) recreational
ludopatía [luðopa'tia] *nf* addiction to gambling (*o* videogames)
luego ['lweγo] *adv* (*después*) next; (*más tarde*) later, afterwards; (*Am fam: en seguida*) at once, immediately; **desde ~** of course; **¡hasta ~!** see you later!, so long!; **¿y ~?** what next?
lugar [lu'γar] *nm* place; (*sitio*) spot; (*pueblo*) village, town; **en ~ de** instead of; **en primer ~** in the first place, firstly; **dar ~ a** to give rise to; **hacer ~** to make room; **fuera de ~** out of place; **tener ~** to take place; **~ común** commonplace; **yo en su ~** if I were him; **no hay ~ para preocupaciones** there is no cause for concern
lugareño, -a [luγa'reɲo, a] *adj* village *cpd* ▪ *nm/f* villager
lugarteniente [luγarte'njente] *nm* deputy
lúgubre ['luγuβre] *adj* mournful
lujo ['luxo] *nm* luxury; (*fig*) profusion, abundance; **de ~** luxury *cpd*, de luxe
lujoso, -a [lu'xoso, a] *adj* luxurious
lujuria [lu'xurja] *nf* lust
lumbago [lum'baγo] *nm* lumbago
lumbre ['lumbre] *nf* (*luz*) light; (*fuego*) fire; **cerca de la ~** near the fire, at the fireside; **¿tienes ~?** (*para cigarro*) have you got a light?
lumbrera [lum'brera] *nf* luminary; (*fig*) leading light
luminoso, -a [lumi'noso, a] *adj* luminous, shining; (*idea*) bright, brilliant
luna ['luna] *nf* moon; (*vidrio: escaparate*) plate glass; (*: de un espejo*) glass; (*: de gafas*) lens; (*fig*) crescent; **~ creciente/llena/menguante/nueva** crescent/full/waning/new moon; **~ de miel** honeymoon; **estar en la ~** to have one's head in the clouds
lunar [lu'nar] *adj* lunar ▪ *nm* (*Anat*) mole; **tela a lunares** spotted material
lunes ['lunes] *nm inv* Monday; *ver tb* **sábado**

luneta [lu'neta] *nf* lens
lupa ['lupa] *nf* magnifying glass
lusitano, -a [lusi'tano, a], **luso, -a** ['luso, a] *adj, nm/f* Portuguese
lustrador [lustra'ðor] *nm* (*Am*) bootblack
lustrar [lus'trar] *vt* (*esp Am*: *mueble*) to polish; (*zapatos*) to shine
lustre ['lustre] *nm* polish; (*fig*) lustre; **dar ~ a** to polish
lustro ['lustro] *nm* period of five years
lustroso, -a [lus'troso, a] *adj* shining
luterano, -a [lute'rano, a] *adj* Lutheran
luto ['luto] *nm* mourning; (*congoja*) grief, sorrow; **llevar el** *o* **vestirse de ~** to be in mourning
luxación [luksa'θjon] *nf* (*Med*) dislocation; **tener una ~ de tobillo** to have a dislocated ankle
Luxemburgo [luksem'buryo] *nm* Luxembourg
luz [luθ] (*pl* **luces**) *nf* (*tb fig*) light; (*fam*) electricity; **dar a ~ un niño** to give birth to a child; **sacar a la ~** to bring to light; **dar la ~** to switch on the light; **encender** (*Esp*) *o* **prender** (*Am*)**/apagar la ~** to switch the light on/off; **les cortaron la ~** their (electricity) supply was cut off; **a la ~ de** in the light of; **a todas luces** by any reckoning; **hacer la ~ sobre** to shed light on; **tener pocas luces** to be dim *o* stupid; **~ de la luna/del sol** *o* **solar** moonlight/sunlight; **~ eléctrica** electric light; **~ roja/verde** red/green light; **~ de cruce** (*Auto*) dipped headlight; **~ de freno** brake light; **~ intermitente/trasera** flashing/rear light; **luces de tráfico** traffic lights; **el Siglo de las Luces** the Age of Enlightenment; **traje de luces** bullfighter's costume

Mm

M, m ['eme] *nf* (*letra*) M, m; **M de Madrid** M for Mike
M. *abr* (*Ferro*) = **Metro**; (= *mujer*) F
m *abr* (= *metro(s)*) m; (= *minuto(s)*) min., m; (= *masculino*) m., masc
M.ª *abr* = **María**
macabro, -a [ma'kaβro, a] *adj* macabre
macaco [ma'kako] *nm* (*Zool*) rhesus monkey; (*fam*) runt, squirt
macana [ma'kana] *nf* (*Am*: *porra*) club; (: *mentira*) lie, fib; (: *tontería*) piece of nonsense
macanudo, -a [maka'nuðo, a] *adj* (*Am fam*) great
macarra [ma'karra] *nm* (*fam*) thug
macarrones [maka'rrones] *nmpl* macaroni *sg*
Macedonia [maθe'ðonja] *nf* Macedonia
macedonia [maθe'ðonja] *nf*: **~ de frutas** fruit salad
macedonio [maθe'ðonjo] *adj, nm/f* Macedonian ■ *nm* (*Ling*) Macedonian
macerar [maθe'rar] *vt* (*Culin*) to soak, macerate; **macerarse** *vr* to soak, soften
maceta [ma'θeta] *nf* (*de flores*) pot of flowers; (*para plantas*) flowerpot
macetero [maθe'tero] *nm* flowerpot stand *o* holder
machacar [matʃa'kar] *vt* to crush, pound; (*moler*) to grind (up); (*aplastar*) to mash ■ *vi* (*insistir*) to go on, keep on
machacón, -ona [matʃa'kon, ona] *adj* (*pesado*) tiresome; (*insistente*) insistent; (*monótono*) monotonous
machamartillo [matʃamar'tiʎo]: **a ~** *adv*: **creer a machamartillo** (*firmemente*) to believe, firmly
machaque *etc* [ma'tʃake] *vb ver* **machacar**
machete [ma'tʃete] *nm* machete, (large) knife
machismo [ma'tʃismo] *nm* sexism; male chauvinism
machista [ma'tʃista] *adj, nm* sexist; male chauvinist
macho ['matʃo] *adj* male; (*fig*) virile ■ *nm* male; (*fig*) he-man, tough guy (*US*); (*Tec*: *perno*) pin, peg; (*Elec*) pin, plug; (*Costura*) hook
macilento, -a [maθi'lento, a] *adj* (*pálido*) pale; (*ojeroso*) haggard
macizo, -a [ma'θiθo, a] *adj* (*grande*) massive; (*fuerte, sólido*) solid ■ *nm* mass, chunk; (*Geo*) massif
macramé [makra'me] *nm* macramé
macrobiótico, -a [makro'βjotiko, a] *adj* macrobiotic
macrocomando [makroko'mando] *nm* (*Inform*) macro (command)
macroeconomía [makroekono'mia] *nf* (*Com*) macroeconomics *sg*
mácula ['makula] *nf* stain, blemish
macuto [ma'kuto] *nm* (*Mil*) knapsack
Madagascar [maðaɣas'kar] *nm* Madagascar
madeja [ma'ðexa] *nf* (*de lana*) skein, hank
madera [ma'ðera] *nf* wood; (*fig*) nature, character; (: *aptitud*) aptitude; **una ~** a piece of wood; **~ contrachapada** *o* **laminada** plywood; **tiene buena ~** he's made of solid stuff; **tiene ~ de futbolista** he's got the makings of a footballer
maderaje [maðe'raxe], **maderamen** [maðe'ramen] *nm* timber; (*trabajo*) woodwork, timbering
maderero [maðe'rero] *nm* timber merchant
madero [ma'ðero] *nm* beam; (*fig*) ship
madrastra [ma'ðrastra] *nf* stepmother
madre ['maðre] *adj* mother *cpd*; (*Am*) tremendous ■ *nf* mother; (*de vino etc*) dregs *pl*; **~ adoptiva/política/soltera** foster mother/mother-in-law/unmarried mother; **la M~ Patria** the Mother Country; **sin ~** motherless; **¡~ mía!** oh dear!; **¡tu ~!** (*fam!*) fuck off! (*!*); **salirse de ~** (*río*) to burst its banks; (*persona*) to lose all self-control
madreperla [maðre'perla] *nf* mother-of-pearl
madreselva [maðre'selβa] *nf* honeysuckle
Madrid [ma'ðrið] *n* Madrid
madriguera [maðri'ɣera] *nf* burrow

madrileño, -a [maðri'leɲo, a] *adj* of *o* from Madrid ■ *nm/f* native *o* inhabitant of Madrid
Madriles [ma'ðriles] *nmpl*: **Los ~** (*fam*) Madrid *sg*
madrina [ma'ðrina] *nf* godmother; (*Arq*) prop, shore; (*Tec*) brace; **~ de boda** bridesmaid
madroño [ma'ðroɲo] *nm* (*Bot*) strawberry tree, arbutus
madrugada [maðru'ɣaða] *nf* early morning, small hours; (*alba*) dawn, daybreak; **a las cuarto de la ~** at four o'clock in the morning
madrugador, a [maðruɣa'ðor, a] *adj* early-rising
madrugar [maðru'ɣar] *vi* to get up early; (*fig*) to get a head start
madrugue *etc* [ma'ðruɣe] *vb ver* **madrugar**
madurar [maðu'rar] *vt, vi* (*fruta*) to ripen; (*fig*) to mature
madurez [maðu'reθ] *nf* ripeness; (*fig*) maturity
maduro, -a [ma'ðuro, a] *adj* ripe; (*fig*) mature; **poco ~** unripe
MAE *nm abr* (*Esp Pol*) = **Ministerio de Asuntos Exteriores**
maestra [ma'estra] *nf ver* **maestro**
maestría [maes'tria] *nf* mastery; (*habilidad*) skill, expertise; (*Am*) Master's Degree
maestro, -a [ma'estro, a] *adj* masterly; (*perito*) skilled, expert; (*principal*) main; (*educado*) trained ■ *nm/f* master/mistress; (*profesor*) teacher ■ *nm* (*autoridad*) authority; (*Mus*) maestro; (*obrero*) skilled workman; **~ albañil** master mason; **~ de obras** foreman
mafia ['mafja] *nf* mafia; **la M~** the Mafia
mafioso [ma'fjoso] *nm* gangster
Magallanes [maɣa'ʎanes] *nm*: **Estrecho de ~** Strait of Magellan
magia ['maxja] *nf* magic
mágico, -a ['maxiko, a] *adj* magic(al) ■ *nm/f* magician
magisterio [maxis'terjo] *nm* (*enseñanza*) teaching; (*profesión*) teaching profession; (*maestros*) teachers *pl*
magistrado [maxis'traðo] *nm* magistrate; **Primer M~** (*Am*) President, Prime Minister
magistral [maxis'tral] *adj* magisterial; (*fig*) masterly
magistratura [maxistra'tura] *nf* magistracy; **M~ del Trabajo** (*Esp*) ≈ Industrial Tribunal
magnánimo, -a [maɣ'nanimo, a] *adj* magnanimous
magnate [maɣ'nate] *nm* magnate, tycoon; **~ de la prensa** press baron
magnesio [maɣ'nesjo] *nm* (*Química*) magnesium
magnetice *etc* [maɣne'tiθe] *vb ver* **magnetizar**
magnético, -a [maɣ'netiko, a] *adj* magnetic
magnetismo [maɣne'tismo] *nm* magnetism
magnetizar [maɣneti'θar] *vt* to magnetize
magnetofón [maɣneto'fon], **magnetófono** [maɣne'tofono] *nm* tape recorder
magnetofónico, -a [maɣneto'fonico, a] *adj*: **cinta magnetofónica** recording tape
magnicidio [maɣni'θiðjo] *nm* assassination (*of an important person*)
magnífico, -a [maɣ'nifiko, a] *adj* splendid, magnificent
magnitud [maɣni'tuð] *nf* magnitude
mago, -a ['maɣo, a] *nm/f* magician, wizard; **los Reyes Magos** the Magi, the Three Wise Men; *ver tb* **Reyes Magos**
magrear [maɣre'ar] *vt* (*fam*) to touch up
magro, -a ['maɣro, a] *adj* (*persona*) thin, lean; (*carne*) lean
maguey [ma'ɣei] *nm* (*Bot*) agave
magulladura [maɣuʎa'ðura] *nf* bruise
magullar [maɣu'ʎar] *vt* (*amoratar*) to bruise; (*dañar*) to damage; (*fam: golpear*) to bash, beat
Maguncia [ma'ɣunθja] *nf* Mainz
mahometano, -a [maome'tano, a] *adj* Mohammedan
mahonesa [mao'nesa] *nf* = **mayonesa**
maicena [mai'θena] *nf* cornflour, corn starch (*US*)
mail [meil] *nm* (*fam*) email
maillot [ma'jot] *nm* swimming costume; (*Deporte*) vest
maître ['metre] *nm* head waiter
maíz [ma'iθ] *nm* maize (*Brit*), corn (*US*); sweet corn
maizal [mai'θal] *nm* maize field, cornfield
majadero, -a [maxa'ðero, a] *adj* silly, stupid
majar [ma'xar] *vt* to crush, grind
majareta [maxa'reta] *adj* (*fam*) cracked, potty
majestad [maxes'tað] *nf* majesty; **Su M~** His/Her Majesty; **(Vuestra) M~** Your Majesty
majestuoso, -a [maxes'twoso, a] *adj* majestic
majo, -a ['maxo, a] *adj* nice; (*guapo*) attractive, good-looking; (*elegante*) smart
mal [mal] *adv* badly; (*equivocadamente*) wrongly; (*con dificultad*) with difficulty ■ *adj* = **malo, a** ■ *nm* evil; (*desgracia*) misfortune; (*daño*) harm, damage; (*Med*) illness ■ *conj*: **~ que le pese** whether he likes it or not; **me entendió ~** he misunderstood me; **hablar ~ de algn** to speak ill of sb; **huele ~** it smells bad; **ir de ~ en peor** to go from bad to worse; **oigo/veo ~** I can't hear/see very well; **si ~ no recuerdo** if my memory serves me right;

¡menos ~! just as well!; **~ que bien** rightly or wrongly; **no hay ~ que por bien no venga** every cloud has a silver lining; **~ de ojo** evil eye

malabarismo [malaβa'rismo] *nm* juggling

malabarista [malaβa'rista] *nm/f* juggler

malaconsejado, -a [malakonse'xaðo, a] *adj* ill-advised

malacostumbrado, -a [malakostum'braðo, a] *adj* (*consentido*) spoiled

malacostumbrar [malakostum'brar] *vt*: **~ a algn** to get sb into bad habits

malagueño, -a [mala'ɣeɲo, a] *adj* of *o* from Málaga ■ *nm/f* native *o* inhabitant of Málaga

Malaisia [ma'laisja] *nf* Malaysia

malaria [ma'larja] *nf* malaria

Malasia [ma'lasja] *nf* Malaysia

malavenido, -a [malaβe'niðo, a] *adj* incompatible

malayo, -a [ma'lajo, a] *adj* Malay(an) ■ *nm/f* Malay ■ *nm* (*Ling*) Malay

Malaysia [ma'laisia] *nf* Malaysia

malcarado, -a [malka'raðo, a] *adj* ugly, grim-faced

malcriado, -a [mal'krjaðo, a] *adj* (*consentido*) spoiled

malcriar [mal'krjar] *vt* to spoil, pamper

maldad [mal'dað] *nf* evil, wickedness

maldecir [malde'θir] *vt* to curse ■ *vi*: **~ de** to speak ill of

maldiciendo *etc* [maldi'θjendo] *vb ver* **maldecir**

maldición [maldi'θjon] *nf* curse; **¡~!** curse it!, damn!

maldiga *etc* [mal'diɣa], **maldije** *etc* [mal'dixe] *vb ver* **maldecir**

maldito, -a [mal'dito, a] *adj* (*condenado*) damned; (*perverso*) wicked ■ *nm*: **el ~** the devil; **¡~ sea!** damn it!; **no le hace ~ (el) caso** he doesn't take a blind bit of notice

maleable [male'aβle] *adj* malleable

maleante [male'ante] *adj* wicked ■ *nm/f* criminal, crook

malecón [male'kon] *nm* pier, jetty

maledicencia [maleði'θenθja] *nf* slander, scandal

maleducado, -a [maleðu'kaðo, a] *adj* bad-mannered, rude

maleficio [male'fiθjo] *nm* curse, spell

malentendido [malenten'diðo] *nm* misunderstanding

malestar [males'tar] *nm* (*gen*) discomfort; (*enfermedad*) indisposition; (*fig: inquietud*) uneasiness; (*Pol*) unrest; **siento un ~ en el estómago** my stomach is upset

maleta [ma'leta] *nf* case, suitcase; (*Auto*) boot (*Brit*), trunk (*US*); **hacer la ~** to pack

maletera [male'tera] *nf* (*Am Auto*) boot (*Brit*), trunk (*US*)

maletero [male'tero] *nm* (*Auto*) boot (*Brit*), trunk (*US*); (*persona*) porter

maletín [male'tin] *nm* small case, bag; (*portafolio*) briefcase

malevolencia [maleβo'lenθja] *nf* malice, spite

malévolo, -a [ma'leβolo, a] *adj* malicious, spiteful

maleza [ma'leθa] *nf* (*malas hierbas*) weeds *pl*; (*arbustos*) thicket

malgache [mal'ɣatʃe] *adj* of *o* from Madagascar ■ *nm/f* native *o* inhabitant of Madagascar

malgastar [malɣas'tar] *vt* (*tiempo, dinero*) to waste; (*recursos*) to squander; (*salud*) to ruin

malhaya [ma'laja] *excl* (*esp Am: fam!*) damn (it)! (*!*); **¡~ sea/sean!** damn it/them! (*!*)

malhechor, a [male'tʃor, a] *nm/f* delinquent; (*criminal*) criminal

malherido, -a [male'riðo, a] *adj* badly injured

malhumorado, -a [malumo'raðo, a] *adj* bad-tempered

malicia [ma'liθja] *nf* (*maldad*) wickedness; (*astucia*) slyness, guile; (*mala intención*) malice, spite; (*carácter travieso*) mischievousness

malicioso, -a [mali'θjoso, a] *adj* wicked, evil; sly, crafty; malicious, spiteful; mischievous

malignidad [maliɣni'ðað] *nf* (*Med*) malignancy; (*malicia*) malice

maligno, -a [ma'liɣno, a] *adj* evil; (*dañino*) pernicious, harmful; (*malévolo*) malicious; (*Med*) malignant ■ *nm*: **el ~** the devil

malintencionado, -a [malintenθjo'naðo, a] *adj* (*comentario*) hostile; (*persona*) malicious

malla ['maʎa] *nf* (*de una red*) mesh; (*red*) network; (*Am: de baño*) swimsuit; (*de ballet, gimnasia*) leotard; **mallas** *nfpl* tights; **~ de alambre** wire mesh

Mallorca [ma'ʎorka] *nf* Majorca

mallorquín, -ina [maʎor'kin, ina] *adj, nm/f* Majorcan ■ *nm* (*Ling*) Majorcan

malnutrido, -a [malnu'triðo, a] *adj* undernourished

malo, -a ['malo, a] *adj* (**mal** *before nmsg*) bad; (*calidad*) poor; (*falso*) false; (*espantoso*) dreadful; (*niño*) naughty ■ *nm/f* villain ■ *nm* (*Cine fam*) bad guy ■ *nf* spell of bad luck; **estar ~** to be ill; **andar a malas con algn** to be on bad terms with sb; **estar de malas** (*mal humor*) to be in a bad mood; **lo ~ es que ...** the trouble is that ...

malograr [malo'ɣrar] *vt* to spoil; (*plan*) to upset; (*ocasión*) to waste; **malograrse** *vr*

(*plan etc*) to fail, come to grief; (*persona*) to die before one's time
maloliente [malo'ljente] *adj* stinking, smelly
malparado, -a [malpa'raðo, a] *adj*: **salir ~** to come off badly
malpensado, -a [malpen'saðo, a] *adj* evil-minded
malquerencia [malke'renθja] *nf* dislike
malquistar [malkis'tar] *vt*: **~ a dos personas** to cause a rift between two people; **malquistarse** *vr* to fall out
malsano, -a [mal'sano, a] *adj* unhealthy
malsonante [malso'nante] *adj* (*palabra*) nasty, rude
Malta ['malta] *nf* Malta
malta ['malta] *nf* malt
malteada [malte'aða] *nf* (*Am*) milk shake
maltés, -esa [mal'tes, esa] *adj, nm/f* Maltese
maltraer [maltra'er] *vt* (*abusar*) to insult, abuse; (*maltratar*) to ill-treat
maltratar [maltra'tar] *vt* to ill-treat, mistreat
maltrecho, -a [mal'tretʃo, a] *adj* battered, damaged
malva ['malβa] *nf* mallow; **~ loca** hollyhock; **(de color de) ~** mauve
malvado, -a [mal'βaðo, a] *adj* evil, villainous
malvavisco [malβa'βisko] *nm* marshmallow
malvender [malβen'der] *vt* to sell off cheap *o* at a loss
malversación [malβersa'θjon] *nf* embezzlement, misappropriation
malversar [malβer'sar] *vt* to embezzle, misappropriate
Malvinas [mal'βinas] *nfpl*: **Islas ~** Falkland Islands
mama ['mama] (*pl* **mamás**) *nf* (*de animal*) teat; (*de mujer*) breast
mamá [ma'ma] *nf* (*fam*) mum, mummy
mamacita [mama'sita] *nf* (*Am fam*) mum, mummy
mamadera [mama'dera] *nf* (*Am*) baby's bottle
mamagrande [mama'grande] *nf* (*Am*) grandmother
mamar [ma'mar] *vt* (*pecho*) to suck; (*fig*) to absorb, assimilate ■ *vi* to suck; **dar de ~** to (breast-)feed; (*animal*) to suckle
mamarracho [mama'rratʃo] *nm* sight, mess
mambo ['mambo] *nf* (*Mus*) mambo
mamífero, -a [ma'mifero, a] *adj* mammalian, mammal *cpd* ■ *nm* mammal
mamón, -ona [ma'mon, ona] *adj* small, baby *cpd* ■ *nm/f* small baby; (*fam!*) wanker (*!*)
mamotreto [mamo'treto] *nm* hefty volume; (*fam*) whacking great thing
mampara [mam'para] *nf* (*entre habitaciones*) partition; (*biombo*) screen
mamporro [mam'porro] *nm* (*fam*): **dar un ~ a** to clout
mampostería [mamposte'ria] *nf* masonry
mamut [ma'mut] *nm* mammoth
maná [ma'na] *nm* manna
manada [ma'naða] *nf* (*Zool*) herd; (*: de leones*) pride; (*: de lobos*) pack; **llegaron en manadas** (*fam*) they came in droves
Managua [ma'naɣwa] *n* Managua
manantial [manan'tjal] *nm* spring; (*fuente*) fountain; (*fig*) source
manar [ma'nar] *vt* to run with, flow with ■ *vi* to run, flow; (*abundar*) to abound
manaza [ma'naθa] *nf* big hand ■ *adj, nm/f inv*: **manazas**: **ser un manazas** to be clumsy
mancebo [man'θeβo] *nm* (*joven*) young man
mancha ['mantʃa] *nf* stain, mark; (*de tinta*) blot; (*de vegetación*) patch; (*imperfección*) stain, blemish, blot; (*boceto*) sketch, outline; **la M~** La Mancha
manchado, -a [man'tʃaðo, a] *adj* (*sucio*) dirty; (*animal*) spotted; (*ave*) speckled; (*de tinta*) smudged
manchar [man'tjar] *vt* to stain, mark; (*Zool*) to patch; (*ensuciar*) to soil, dirty; **mancharse** *vr* to get dirty; (*fig*) to dirty one's hands
manchego, -a [man'tʃeɣo, a] *adj* of *o* from La Mancha ■ *nm/f* native *o* inhabitant of La Mancha
mancilla [man'θiʎa] *nf* stain, blemish
mancillar [manθi'ʎar] *vt* to stain, sully
manco, -a ['manko, a] *adj* one-armed; one-handed; (*fig*) defective, faulty; **no ser ~** to be useful *o* active
mancomunar [mankomu'nar] *vt* to unite, bring together; (*recursos*) to pool; (*Jur*) to make jointly responsible
mancomunidad [mankomuni'ðað] *nf* union, association; (*comunidad*) community; (*Jur*) joint responsibility
mandado [man'daðo] *nm* (*orden*) order; (*recado*) commission, errand
mandamás [manda'mas] *adj, nm/f inv* boss; **ser un ~** to be very bossy
mandamiento [manda'mjento] *nm* (*orden*) order, command; (*Rel*) commandment; **~ judicial** warrant
mandar [man'dar] *vt* (*ordenar*) to order; (*dirigir*) to lead, command; (*país*) to rule over; (*enviar*) to send; (*pedir*) to order, ask for ■ *vi* to be in charge; (*pey*) to be bossy; **mandarse** *vr*: **mandarse mudar** (*Am fam*) to go away, clear off; **¿mande?** pardon?, excuse me? (*US*); **¿manda usted algo más?** is there anything else?; **~ a algn a paseo** *o* **a la porra** to tell sb

to go to hell; **se lo mandaremos por correo** we'll post it to you; ~ **hacer un traje** to have a suit made
mandarín [manda'rin] *nm* petty bureaucrat
mandarina [manda'rina] *nf* (*fruta*) tangerine, mandarin (orange)
mandatario, -a [manda'tarjo, a] *nm/f* (*representante*) agent; **primer ~** (*esp Am*) head of state
mandato [man'dato] *nm* (*orden*) order; (*Pol: período*) term of office; (*: territorio*) mandate; ~ **judicial** (search) warrant
mandíbula [man'diβula] *nf* jaw
mandil [man'dil] *nm* (*delantal*) apron
Mandinga [man'dinɣa] *nm* (*Am*) Devil
mandioca [man'djoka] *nf* cassava
mando ['mando] *nm* (*Mil*) command; (*de país*) rule; (*el primer lugar*) lead; (*Pol*) term of office; (*Tec*) control; ~ **a la izquierda** left-hand drive; **los altos mandos** the high command *sg*; ~ **por botón** push-button control; **al ~ de** in charge of; **tomar el ~** to take the lead
mandolina [mando'lina] *nf* mandolin(e)
mandón, -ona [man'don, ona] *adj* bossy, domineering
manecilla [mane'θiʎa] *nf* (*Tec*) pointer; (*de reloj*) hand
manejable [mane'xaβle] *adj* manageable; (*fácil de usar*) handy
manejar [mane'xar] *vt* to manage; (*máquina*) to work, operate; (*caballo etc*) to handle; (*casa*) to run, manage; (*Am Auto*) to drive ■ *vi* (*Am Auto*) to drive; **manejarse** *vr* (*comportarse*) to act, behave; (*arreglárselas*) to manage; **"~ con cuidado"** "handle with care"
manejo [ma'nexo] *nm* management; handling; running; driving; (*facilidad de trato*) ease, confidence; (*de idioma*) command; **manejos** *nmpl* intrigues; **tengo ~ del francés** I have a good command of French
manera [ma'nera] *nf* way, manner, fashion; (*Arte, Lit etc: estilo*) manner, style; **maneras** *nfpl* (*modales*) manners; **su ~ de ser** the way he is; (*aire*) his manner; **de mala ~** (*fam*) badly, unwillingly; **de ninguna ~** no way, by no means; **de otra ~** otherwise; **de todas maneras** at any rate; **en gran ~** to a large extent; **sobre ~** exceedingly; **a mi ~ de ver** in my view; **no hay ~ de persuadirle** there's no way of convincing him
manga ['manga] *nf* (*de camisa*) sleeve; (*de riego*) hose; **de ~ corta/larga** short-/long-sleeved; **andar ~ por hombro** (*desorden*) to be topsy-turvy; **tener ~ ancha** to be easy-going
mangante [man'gante] *adj* (*descarado*) brazen ■ *nm* (*mendigo*) beggar
mangar [man'gar] *vt* (*unir*) to plug in; (*fam: birlar*) to pinch, nick, swipe; (*mendigar*) to beg
mango ['mango] *nm* handle; (*Bot*) mango; ~ **de escoba** broomstick
mangonear [mangone'ar] *vt* to boss about ■ *vi* to be bossy
mangue *etc* ['mange] *vb ver* **mangar**
manguera [man'gera] *nf* (*de riego*) hose; (*tubo*) pipe; ~ **de incendios** fire hose
maní [ma'ni] *nm* (*pl* **~es** *o* **manises**) (*Am: cacahuete*) peanut; (*: planta*) groundnut plant
manía [ma'nia] *nf* (*Med*) mania; (*fig: moda*) rage, craze; (*disgusto*) dislike; (*malicia*) spite; **tiene manías** she's a bit fussy; **tener ~ a algn** to dislike sb
maníaco, -a [ma'niako, a] *adj* maniac(al) ■ *nm/f* maniac
maniatar [manja'tar] *vt* to tie the hands of
maniático, -a [ma'njatiko, a] *adj* maniac(al); (*loco*) crazy; (*tiquismiquis*) fussy ■ *nm/f* maniac
manicomio [mani'komjo] *nm* mental hospital (*Brit*), insane asylum (*US*)
manicuro, -a [mani'kuro, a] *nm/f* manicurist ■ *nf* manicure
manido, -a [ma'niðo, a] *adj* (*tema etc*) trite, stale
manifestación [manifesta'θjon] *nf* (*declaración*) statement, declaration; (*demostración*) show, display; (*Pol*) demonstration
manifestante [manifes'tante] *nm/f* demonstrator
manifestar [manifes'tar] *vt* to show, manifest; (*declarar*) to state, declare; **manifestarse** *vr* to show, become apparent; (*Pol: desfilar*) to demonstrate; (*: reunirse*) to hold a mass meeting
manifiesto, -a *etc* [mani'fjesto, a] *vb ver* **manifestar** ■ *adj* clear, manifest ■ *nm* manifesto; (*Anat, Naut*) manifest; **poner algo de ~** (*aclarar*) to make sth clear; (*revelar*) to reveal sth; **quedar ~** to be plain *o* clear
manija [ma'nixa] *nf* handle
manilla [ma'niʎa] *nf* (*de reloj*) hand; (*Am*) handle, lever; **manillas (de hierro)** *nfpl* handcuffs
manillar [mani'ʎar] *nm* handlebars *pl*
maniobra [ma'njoβra] *nf* manœuvring; (*manejo*) handling; (*fig: movimiento*) manœuvre, move; (*: estratagema*) trick, stratagem; **maniobras** *nfpl* manœuvres
maniobrar [manio'βrar] *vt* to manœuvre; (*manejar*) to handle ■ *vi* to manœuvre
manipulación [manipula'θjon] *nf* manipulation; (*Com*) handling
manipular [manipu'lar] *vt* to manipulate; (*manejar*) to handle

maniquí [mani'ki] *nm/f* model ▪ *nm* dummy
manirroto, -a [mani'rroto, a] *adj* lavish, extravagant ▪ *nm/f* spendthrift
manita [ma'nita] *nf* little hand; **manitas de plata** artistic hands
manitas [ma'nitas] *adj inv* good with one's hands ▪ *nm/f inv*: **ser un ~** to be very good with one's hands
manito [ma'nito] *nm* (*Am: en conversación*) mate (*fam*), chum
manivela [mani'βela] *nf* crank
manjar [man'xar] *nm* (tasty) dish
mano¹ ['mano] *nf* hand; (*Zool*) foot, paw; (*de pintura*) coat; (*serie*) lot, series; **a ~** by hand; **a ~ derecha/izquierda** on (*o* to) the right(-hand side)/left(-hand side); **hecho a ~** handmade; **a manos llenas** lavishly, generously; **de primera ~** (at) first hand; **de segunda ~** (at) second hand; **robo a ~ armada** armed robbery; **Pedro es mi ~ derecha** Pedro is my right-hand man; **~ de obra** labour, manpower; **~ de santo** sure remedy; **darse la(s) ~(s)** to shake hands; **echar una ~** to lend a hand; **echar una ~ a** to lay hands on; **echar ~ de** to make use of; **estrechar la ~ a algn** to shake sb's hand; **traer** *o* **llevar algo entre manos** to deal *o* be busy with sth; **está en tus manos** it's up to you; **se le fue la ~** his hand slipped; (*fig*) he went too far; **¡manos a la obra!** to work!
mano² ['mano] *nm* (*Am fam*) friend, mate
manojo [ma'noxo] *nm* handful, bunch; **~ de llaves** bunch of keys
manómetro [ma'nometro] *nm* (pressure) gauge
manopla [ma'nopla] *nf* (*paño*) flannel; **manoplas** *nfpl* mittens
manoseado, -a [manose'aðo, a] *adj* well-worn
manosear [manose'ar] *vt* (*tocar*) to handle, touch; (*desordenar*) to mess up, rumple; (*insistir en*) to overwork; (*acariciar*) to caress, fondle; (*pey: persona*) to feel *o* touch up
manotazo [mano'taθo] *nm* slap, smack
mansalva [man'salβa]: **a ~** *adv* indiscriminately
mansedumbre [manse'ðumbre] *nf* gentleness, meekness; (*de animal*) tameness
mansión [man'sjon] *nf* mansion
manso, -a ['manso, a] *adj* gentle, mild; (*animal*) tame
manta ['manta] *nf* blanket; (*Am*) poncho
manteca [man'teka] *nf* fat; (*Am*) butter; **~ de cacahuete/cacao** peanut/cocoa butter; **~ de cerdo** lard
mantecado [mante'kaðo] *nm* ice cream
mantecoso, -a [mante'koso, a] *adj* fat, greasy; **queso ~** soft cheese
mantel [man'tel] *nm* tablecloth
mantelería [mantele'ria] *nf* table linen
mantendré *etc* [manten'dre] *vb ver* **mantener**
mantener [mante'ner] *vt* to support, maintain; (*alimentar*) to sustain; (*conservar*) to keep; (*Tec*) to maintain, service; **mantenerse** *vr* (*seguir de pie*) to be still standing; (*no ceder*) to hold one's ground; (*subsistir*) to sustain o.s., keep going; **~ algo en equilibrio** to keep sth balanced; **mantenerse a distancia** to keep one's distance; **mantenerse firme** to hold one's ground
mantenga *etc* [man'tenga] *vb ver* **mantener**
mantenimiento [manteni'mjento] *nm* maintenance; sustenance; (*sustento*) support
mantequería [manteke'ria] *nf* (*ultramarinos*) grocer's (shop)
mantequilla [mante'kiʎa] *nf* butter
mantilla [man'tiʎa] *nf* mantilla; **mantillas** *nfpl* baby clothes; **estar en mantillas** (*persona*) to be terribly innocent; (*proyecto*) to be in its infancy
manto ['manto] *nm* (*capa*) cloak; (*de ceremonia*) robe, gown
mantón [man'ton] *nm* shawl
mantuve *etc* [man'tuβe] *vb ver* **mantener**
manual [ma'nwal] *adj* manual ▪ *nm* manual, handbook; **habilidad ~** manual skill
manubrio [ma'nuβrio] *nm* (*Am Auto*) steering wheel
manufactura [manufak'tura] *nf* manufacture; (*fábrica*) factory
manufacturado, -a [manufaktu'raðo, a] *adj* manufactured
manuscrito, -a [manus'krito, a] *adj* handwritten ▪ *nm* manuscript
manutención [manuten'θjon] *nf* maintenance; (*sustento*) support
manzana [man'θana] *nf* apple; (*Arq*) block; **~ de la discordia** (*fig*) bone of contention
manzanal [manθa'nal] *nm* apple orchard
manzanilla [manθa'niʎa] *nf* (*planta*) camomile; (*infusión*) camomile tea; (*vino*) manzanilla
manzano [man'θano] *nm* apple tree
maña ['maɲa] *nf* (*gen*) skill, dexterity; (*pey*) guile; (*costumbre*) habit; (*una maña*) trick, knack; **con ~** craftily
mañana [ma'ɲana] *adv* tomorrow ▪ *nm* future ▪ *nf* morning; **de** *o* **por la ~** in the morning; **¡hasta ~!** see you tomorrow!; **pasado ~** the day after tomorrow; **~ por la ~** tomorrow morning
mañanero, -a [maɲa'nero, a] *adj* early-rising
maño, -a ['maɲo, a] *adj* Aragonese ▪ *nm/f*

native *o* inhabitant of Aragon
mañoso, -a [ma'ɲoso, a] *adj* *(hábil)* skilful; *(astuto)* smart, clever
mapa ['mapa] *nm* map
mapuche, -a [ma'putʃe, a] *adj, nm/f* Mapuche, Araucanian
maqueta [ma'keta] *nf* (scale) model
maquiavélico, -a [makja'βeliko, a] *adj* Machiavellian
maquillador, a [makiʎa'ðor, a] *nm/f* *(Teat etc)* make-up artist
maquillaje [maki'ʎaxe] *nm* make-up; *(acto)* making up
maquillar [maki'ʎar] *vt* to make up; **maquillarse** *vr* to put on (some) make-up
máquina ['makina] *nf* machine; *(de tren)* locomotive, engine; *(Foto)* camera; *(Am: coche)* car; *(fig)* machinery; *(: proyecto)* plan, project; **a toda ~** at full speed; **escrito a ~** typewritten; **~ de escribir** typewriter; **~ de coser/lavar** sewing/washing machine; **~ de facsímil** facsimile (machine), fax; **~ de franqueo** franking machine; **~ tragaperras** fruit machine; *(Com)* slot machine
maquinación [makina'θjon] *nf* machination, plot
maquinal [maki'nal] *adj* *(fig)* mechanical, automatic
maquinar [maki'nar] *vt, vi* to plot
maquinaria [maki'narja] *nf* *(máquinas)* machinery; *(mecanismo)* mechanism, works *pl*
maquinilla [maki'niʎa] *nf* small machine; *(torno)* winch; **~ de afeitar** razor; **~ eléctrica** electric razor
maquinista [maki'nista] *nm* *(Ferro)* engine driver *(Brit)*, engineer *(US)*; *(Tec)* operator; *(Naut)* engineer
mar [mar] *nm* sea; **~ de fondo** groundswell; **~ llena** high tide; **~ adentro** *o* **afuera** out at sea; **en alta ~** on the high seas; **por ~** by sea *o* boat; **hacerse a la ~** to put to sea; **a mares** in abundance; **un ~ de** lots of; **es la ~ de guapa** she is ever so pretty; **el M~ Negro/Báltico** the Black/Baltic Sea; **el M~ Muerto/Rojo** the Dead/Red Sea; **el M~ del Norte** the North Sea
mar. *abr* *(= marzo)* Mar.
maraca [ma'raka] *nf* maraca
maraña [ma'raɲa] *nf* *(maleza)* thicket; *(confusión)* tangle
maravilla [mara'βiʎa] *nf* marvel, wonder; *(Bot)* marigold; **hacer maravillas** to work wonders; **a (las mil) maravillas** wonderfully well
maravillar [maraβi'ʎar] *vt* to astonish, amaze; **maravillarse** *vr* to be astonished, be amazed
maravilloso, -a [maraβi'ʎoso, a] *adj* wonderful, marvellous
marbellí [marβe'ʎi] *adj* of *o* from Marbella ■ *nm/f* native *o* inhabitant of Marbella
marca ['marka] *nf* mark; *(sello)* stamp; *(Com)* make, brand; *(de ganado)* brand; *(: acto)* branding; *(Naut)* seamark; *(: boya)* marker; *(Deporte)* record; **de ~** excellent, outstanding; **~ de fábrica** trademark; **~ propia** own brand; **~ registrada** registered trademark
marcación [marka'θjon] *nf* *(Telec)*: **~ automática** autodial
marcado, -a [mar'kaðo, a] *adj* marked, strong
marcador [marka'ðor] *nm* marker; *(rotulador)* marker (pen); *(de libro)* bookmark; *(Deporte)* scoreboard; *(: persona)* scorer
marcapasos [marka'pasos] *nm inv* pacemaker
marcar [mar'kar] *vt* to mark; *(número de teléfono)* to dial; *(gol)* to score; *(números)* to record, keep a tally of; *(el pelo)* to set; *(ganado)* to brand; *(suj: termómetro)* to read, register; *(: reloj)* to show; *(tarea)* to assign; *(Com)* to put a price on ■ *vi* *(Deporte)* to score; *(Telec)* to dial; **mi reloj marca las dos** it's two o'clock by my watch; **~ el compás** *(Mus)* to keep time; **~ el paso** *(Mil)* to mark time
marcha ['martʃa] *nf* march; *(Deporte)* walk; *(Tec)* running, working; *(Auto)* gear; *(velocidad)* speed; *(fig)* progress; *(curso)* course; **dar ~ atrás** to reverse, put into reverse; **estar en ~** to be under way, be in motion; **hacer algo sobre la ~** to do sth as you *etc* go along; **poner en ~** to put into gear; **ponerse en ~** to start, get going; **a marchas forzadas** *(fig)* with all speed; **¡en ~!** *(Mil)* forward march!; *(fig)* let's go!; **"~ moderada"** *(Auto)* "drive slowly"; **que tiene** *o* **de mucha ~** *(fam)* very lively
marchante, -a [mar'tʃante, a] *nm/f* dealer, merchant
marchar [mar'tʃar] *vi* *(ir)* to go; *(funcionar)* to work, go; *(fig)* to go, proceed; **marcharse** *vr* to go (away), leave; **todo marcha bien** everything is going well
marchitar [martʃi'tar] *vt* to wither, dry up; **marchitarse** *vr* *(Bot)* to wither; *(fig)* to fade away
marchito, -a [mar'tʃito, a] *adj* withered, faded; *(fig)* in decline
marchoso, -a [mar'tʃoso, a] *adj* *(fam: animado)* lively; *(: moderno)* modern
marcial [mar'θjal] *adj* martial, military
marciano, -a [mar'θjano, a] *adj* Martian, of *o* from Mars
marco ['marko] *nm* frame; *(Deporte)* goalposts

pl; (*moneda*) mark; (*fig*) setting; (*contexto*) framework; ~ **de chimenea** mantelpiece
marea [ma'rea] *nf* tide; (*llovizna*) drizzle; ~ **alta/baja** high/low tide; ~ **negra** oil slick
mareado, -a [mare'aðo, a] *adj*: **estar** ~ (*con náuseas*) to feel sick; (*aturdido*) to feel dizzy
marear [mare'ar] *vt* (*fig: irritar*) to annoy, upset; (*Med*): ~ **a algn** to make sb feel sick; **marearse** *vr* (*tener náuseas*) to feel sick; (*desvanecerse*) to feel faint; (*aturdirse*) to feel dizzy; (*fam: emborracharse*) to get tipsy
marejada [mare'xaða] *nf* (*Naut*) swell, heavy sea
maremágnum [mare'maɣnum] *nm* (*fig*) ocean, abundance
maremoto [mare'moto] *nm* tidal wave
mareo [ma'reo] *nm* (*náusea*) sick feeling; (*aturdimiento*) dizziness; (*fam: lata*) nuisance
marfil [mar'fil] *nm* ivory
margarina [marɣa'rina] *nf* margarine
margarita [marɣa'rita] *nf* (*Bot*) daisy; **(rueda)** ~ (*en máquina impresora*) daisy wheel
margen ['marxen] *nm* (*borde*) edge, border; (*fig*) margin, space ■ *nf* (*de río etc*) bank; ~ **de beneficio** *o* **de ganancia** profit margin; ~ **comercial** mark-up; ~ **de confianza** credibility gap; **dar ~ para** to give an opportunity for; **dejar a algn al ~** to leave sb out (in the cold); **mantenerse al ~** to keep out (of things); **al ~ de lo que digas** despite what you say
marginado, -a [marxi'naðo, a] *nm/f* outcast
marginal [marxi'nal] *adj* (*tema, error*) minor; (*grupo*) fringe *cpd*; (*anotación*) marginal
marginar [marxi'nar] *vt* to exclude
maría [ma'ria] *nf* (*fam: mujer*) housewife
mariachi [ma'rjatʃi] *nm* (*música*) mariachi music; (*grupo*) mariachi band; (*persona*) mariachi player
marica [ma'rika] *nm* (*fam*) sissy; (*homosexual*) queer
Maricastaña [marikas'taɲa] *nf*: **en los días** *o* **en tiempos de ~** way back, in the good old days
maricón [mari'kon] *nm* (*fam*) queer
marido [ma'riðo] *nm* husband
marihuana [mari'wənə] *nf* marijuana, cannabis
marimacho [mari'matʃo] *nf* (*fam*) mannish woman
marimorena [marimo'rena] *nf* fuss, row; **armar una ~** to kick up a row
marina [ma'rina] *nf* navy; ~ **mercante** merchant navy
marinero, -a [mari'nero, a] *adj* sea *cpd*; (*barco*) seaworthy ■ *nm* sailor, seaman
marino, -a [ma'rino, a] *adj* sea *cpd*, marine ■ *nm* sailor; ~ **de agua dulce/de cubierta/de primera** landlubber/deckhand/able seaman
marioneta [marjo'neta] *nf* puppet
mariposa [mari'posa] *nf* butterfly
mariposear [maripose'ar] *vi* (*revolotear*) to flutter about; (*ser inconstante*) to be fickle; (*coquetear*) to flirt
mariquita [mari'kita] *nm* (*fam*) sissy; (*homosexual*) queer ■ *nf* (*Zool*) ladybird (*Brit*), ladybug (*US*)
marisco [ma'risko] *nm* (*tb*: **mariscos**) shellfish, seafood
marisma [ma'risma] *nf* marsh, swamp
marisquería [mariske'ria] *nf* shellfish bar, seafood restaurant
marítimo, -a [ma'ritimo, a] *adj* sea *cpd*, maritime
marmita [mar'mita] *nf* pot
mármol ['marmol] *nm* marble
marmóreo, -a [mar'moreo, a] *adj* marble
marmota [mar'mota] *nf* (*Zool*) marmot; (*fig*) sleepyhead
maroma [ma'roma] *nf* rope
marque *etc* ['marke] *vb ver* **marcar**
marqués, -esa [mar'kes, esa] *nm/f* marquis/marchioness
marquesina [marke'sina] *nf* (*de parada*) bus-shelter
marquetería [markete'ria] *nf* marquetry, inlaid work
marranada [marra'naða] *nf* (*fam*): **es una ~** that's disgusting; **hacer una ~ a algn** to do the dirty on sb
marrano, -a [ma'rrano, a] *adj* filthy, dirty ■ *nm* (*Zool*) pig; (*malo*) swine; (*sucio*) dirty pig
marras ['marras]: **de ~** *adv*: **es el problema de ~** it's the same old problem
marrón [ma'rron] *adj* brown
marroquí [marro'ki] *adj, nm/f* Moroccan ■ *nm* Morocco (leather)
Marruecos [ma'rrwekos] *nm* Morocco
marta ['marta] *nf* (*animal*) (pine) marten; (*piel*) sable
Marte ['marte] *nm* Mars
martes ['martes] *nm inv* Tuesday; ~ **de carnaval** Shrove Tuesday; *ver tb* **Carnaval; sábado**
martillar [marti'ʎar], **martillear** [martiʎe'ar] *vt* to hammer
martilleo [marti'ʎeo] *nm* hammering
martillo [mar'tiʎo] *nm* hammer; (*de presidente de asamblea, comité*) gavel; ~ **neumático** pneumatic drill (*Brit*), jackhammer (*US*)
Martinica [marti'nika] *nf* Martinique
mártir ['martir] *nm/f* martyr
martirice *etc* [marti'riθe] *vb ver* **martirizar**

martirio [mar'tirjo] *nm* martyrdom; (*fig*) torture, torment
martirizar [martiri'θar] *vt* (*Rel*) to martyr; (*fig*) to torture, torment
maruja [ma'ruxa] *nf* (*fam*) = **maría**
marxismo [mark'sismo] *nm* Marxism
marxista [mark'sista] *adj, nm/f* Marxist
marzo ['marθo] *nm* March; **11-M** (= *11 de marzo*) *the Madrid train bombings of 11th March 2004*; *ver tb* **julio**
mas [mas] *conj* but

PALABRA CLAVE

más [mas] *adj, adv* **1**: **~ (que, de)** (*compar*) more (than), ...+ er (than); **~ grande/inteligente** bigger/more intelligent; **trabaja ~ (que yo)** he works more (than me); **~ de seis** more than six; **es ~ de medianoche** it's after midnight; **durar ~** to last longer; *ver tb* **cada**
2 (*superl*): **el ~** the most, ...+ est; **el ~ grande/inteligente (de)** the biggest/most intelligent (in)
3 (*negativo*): **no tengo ~ dinero** I haven't got any more money; **no viene ~ por aquí** he doesn't come round here any more; **no sé ~** I don't know any more, that's all I know
4 (*adicional*): **un kilómetro ~** one more kilometre; **no le veo ~ solución que ...** I see no other solution than to ...; **¿algo ~?** anything else?; (*en tienda*) will that be all?; **¿quién ~?** anybody else?
5 (*+ adj: valor intensivo*): **¡qué perro ~ sucio!** what a filthy dog!; **¡es ~ tonto!** he's so stupid!
6 (*locuciones*): **~ o menos** more or less; **los ~** most people; **es ~** in fact, furthermore; **~ bien** rather; **¡qué ~ da!** what does it matter!; *ver tb* **no**
7: **por ~**: **por más que lo intento** no matter how much *o* hard I try; **por ~ que quisiera ayudar** much as I should like to help
8: **de ~**: **veo que aquí estoy de más** I can see I'm not needed here; **tenemos uno de ~** we've got one extra
9 (*Am*): **no ~** only, just; **ayer no ~** just yesterday ■ *prep*: **2 ~ 2 son 4** 2 and *o* plus 2 are 4
■ *nm inv*: **este trabajo tiene sus ~ y sus menos** this job's got its good points and its bad points

masa ['masa] *nf* (*mezcla*) dough; (*volumen*) volume, mass; (*Física*) mass; **en ~** en masse; **las masas** (*Pol*) the masses
masacrar [masa'krar] *vt* to massacre
masacre [ma'sakre] *nf* massacre
masaje [ma'saxe] *nm* massage; **dar ~ a** to massage
masajista [masa'xista] *nm/f* masseur/masseuse
mascar [mas'kar] *vt, vi* to chew; (*fig*) to mumble, mutter
máscara ['maskara] *nf* (*tb Inform*) mask ■ *nm/f* masked person; **~ antigás** gas mask
mascarada [maska'raða] *nf* masquerade
mascarilla [maska'riʎa] *nf* mask; (*vaciado*) deathmask; (*de maquillaje*) face pack
mascarón [maska'ron] *nm* large mask; **~ de proa** figurehead
mascota [mas'kota] *nf* mascot
masculino, -a [masku'lino, a] *adj* masculine; (*Bio*) male ■ *nm* (*Ling*) masculine
mascullar [masku'ʎar] *vt* to mumble, mutter
masificación [masifika'θjon] *nf* overcrowding
masilla [ma'siʎa] *nf* putty
masivo, -a [ma'siβo, a] *adj* (*en masa*) mass
masón [ma'son] *nm* (free)mason
masonería [masone'ria] *nf* (free)masonry
masoquista [maso'kista] *adj* masochistic ■ *nm/f* masochist
masque *etc* ['maske] *vb ver* **mascar**
mastectomía [mastekto'mia] *nf* mastectomy
máster (*pl* **masters**) ['master, 'masters] *nm* postgraduate degree; *ver tb* **licenciado**
masticar [masti'kar] *vt* to chew; (*fig*) to ponder over
mástil ['mastil] *nm* (*de navío*) mast; (*de guitarra*) neck
mastín [mas'tin] *nm* mastiff
mastique *etc* [mas'tike] *vb ver* **masticar**
masturbación [masturβa'θjon] *nf* masturbation
masturbarse [mastur'βarse] *vr* to masturbate
Mat. *abr* = **Matemáticas**
mata ['mata] *nf* (*arbusto*) bush, shrub; (*de hierbas*) tuft; (*campo*) field; (*manojo*) tuft, blade; **matas** *nfpl* scrub *sg*; **~ de pelo** mop of hair; **a salto de ~** (*día a día*) from day to day; (*al azar*) haphazardly
matadero [mata'ðero] *nm* slaughterhouse, abattoir
matador, a [mata'ðor, a] *adj* killing ■ *nm/f* killer ■ *nm* (*Taur*) matador, bullfighter
matamoscas [mata'moskas] *nm inv* (*palo*) fly swat
matanza [ma'tanθa] *nf* slaughter
matar [ma'tar] *vt* to kill; (*tiempo, pelota*) to kill ■ *vi* to kill; **matarse** *vr* (*suicidarse*) to kill o.s., commit suicide; (*morir*) to be *o* get killed;

(*gastarse*) to wear o.s. out; **~ el hambre** to stave off hunger; **~ a algn a disgustos** to make sb's life a misery; **matarlas callando** to go about things slyly; **matarse trabajando** to kill o.s. with work; **matarse por hacer algo** to struggle to do sth
matarife [mata'rife] *nm* slaughterman
matasanos [mata'sanos] *nm inv* quack
matasellos [mata'seʎos] *nm inv* postmark
mate ['mate] *adj* (*sin brillo: color*) dull, matt ■ *nm* (*en ajedrez*) (check)mate; (*Am: hierba*) maté; (*: vasija*) gourd
matemático, -a [mate'matiko, a] *adj* mathematical ■ *nm/f* mathematician; **matemáticas** *nfpl* mathematics *sg*
materia [ma'terja] *nf* (*gen*) matter; (*Tec*) material; (*Escol*) subject; **en ~ de** on the subject of; (*en cuanto a*) as regards; **~ prima** raw material; **entrar en ~** to get down to business
material [mate'rjal] *adj* material; (*dolor*) physical; (*real*) real; (*literal*) literal ■ *nm* material; (*Tec*) equipment; **~ de construcción** building material; **materiales de derribo** rubble *sg*
materialismo [materja'lismo] *nm* materialism
materialista [materja'lista] *adj* materialist(ic)
materialmente [materjal'mente] *adv* materially; (*fig*) absolutely
maternal [mater'nal] *adj* motherly, maternal
maternidad [materni'ðað] *nf* motherhood, maternity
materno, -a [ma'terno, a] *adj* maternal; (*lengua*) mother *cpd*
matice *etc* [ma'tiθe] *vb ver* **matizar**
matinal [mati'nal] *adj* morning *cpd*
matiz [ma'tiθ] *nm* shade; (*de sentido*) shade, nuance; (*de ironía etc*) touch
matizar [mati'θar] *vt* (*variar*) to vary; (*Arte*) to blend; **~ de** to tinge with
matón [ma'ton] *nm* bully
matorral [mato'rral] *nm* thicket
matraca [ma'traka] *nf* rattle; (*fam*) nuisance
matraz [ma'traθ] *nm* (*Química*) flask
matriarcado [matrjar'kaðo] *nm* matriarchy
matrícula [ma'trikula] *nf* (*registro*) register; (*Escol: inscripción*) registration; (*Auto*) registration number; (*: placa*) number plate
matricular [matriku'lar] *vt* to register, enrol
matrimonial [matrimo'njal] *adj* matrimonial
matrimonio [matri'monjo] *nm* (*pareja*) (married) couple; (*acto*) marriage; **~ civil/clandestino** civil/secret marriage; **contraer ~ (con)** to marry
matriz [ma'triθ] *nf* (*Anat*) womb; (*Tec*) mould; (*Mat*) matrix; **casa ~** (*Com*) head office
matrona [ma'trona] *nf* (*mujer de edad*) matron
matutino, -a [matu'tino, a] *adj* morning *cpd*
maula ['maula] *adj* (*persona*) good-for-nothing ■ *nm/f* (*vago*) idler, slacker ■ *nf* (*persona*) dead loss (*fam*)
maullar [mau'ʎar] *vi* to mew, miaow
maullido [mau'ʎiðo] *nm* mew(ing), miaow(ing)
Mauricio [mau'riθjo] *nm* Mauritius
Mauritania [mauri'tanja] *nf* Mauritania
mausoleo [mauso'leo] *nm* mausoleum
max. *abr* (= *máximo*) max.
maxilar [maksi'lar] *nm* jaw(bone)
máxima ['maksima] *nf ver* **máximo**
máxime ['maksime] *adv* especially
máximo, -a ['maksimo, a] *adj* maximum; (*más alto*) highest; (*más grande*) greatest ■ *nm* maximum ■ *nf* maxim; **~ jefe** *o* **líder** (*Am*) President, leader; **como ~** at most; **al ~** to the utmost
maxisingle [maksi'singel] *nm* twelve-inch (single)
maya ['maja] *adj* Mayan ■ *nm/f* Maya(n)
mayo ['majo] *nm* May; *ver tb* **julio**
mayonesa [majo'nesa] *nf* mayonnaise
mayor [ma'jor] *adj* main, chief; (*adulto*) grown-up, adult; (*Jur*) of age; (*de edad avanzada*) elderly; (*Mus*) major; (*comparativo: de tamaño*) bigger; (*: de edad*) older; (*superlativo: de tamaño*) biggest; (*tb fig*) greatest; (*: de edad*) oldest ■ *nm* chief, boss; (*adulto*) adult; **al por ~** wholesale; **~ de edad** adult; *ver tb* **mayores**
mayoral [majo'ral] *nm* foreman
mayordomo [major'ðomo] *nm* butler
mayoreo [majo'reo] *nm* (*Am*) wholesale (trade)
mayores [ma'jores] *nmpl* grown-ups; **llegar a ~** to get out of hand
mayoría [majo'ria] *nf* majority, greater part; **en la ~ de los casos** in most cases; **en su ~** on the whole
mayorista [majo'rista] *nm/f* wholesaler
mayoritario, -a [majori'tarjo, a] *adj* majority *cpd*; **gobierno ~** majority government
mayúsculo, -a [ma'juskulo, a] *adj* (*fig*) big, tremendous ■ *nf* capital (letter); **mayúsculas** *nfpl* capitals; (*Tip*) upper case *sg*
maza ['maθa] *nf* (*arma*) mace; (*Deporte*) bat; (*Polo*) stick
mazacote [maθa'kote] *nm* hard mass; (*Culin*) dry doughy food; (*Arte, Lit etc*) mess, hotchpotch
mazapán [maθa'pan] *nm* marzipan
mazmorra [maθ'morra] *nf* dungeon

mazo ['maθo] *nm* (*martillo*) mallet; (*de mortero*) pestle; (*de flores*) bunch; (*Deporte*) bat
mazorca [ma'θorka] *nf* (*Bot*) spike; (*de maíz*) cob, ear
Mb *abr* (= *megabyte*) Mb
MCAC *nm abr* = **Mercado Común de la América Central**
m.c.d. *abr* (= *mínimo común denominador*) lcd
MCI *nm abr* = **Mercado Común Iberoamericano**
m.c.m. *abr* = **mínimo común múltiplo**
me [me] *pron* (*directo*) me; (*indirecto*) (to) me; (*reflexivo*) (to) myself; **¡dámelo!** give it to me!; **me lo compró** (*de mí*) he bought it from me; (*para mí*) he bought it for me
meandro [me'andro] *nm* meander
mear [me'ar] (*fam*) *vt* to piss on (*!*) ■ *vi* to pee, piss (*!*), have a piss (*!*); **mearse** *vr* to wet o.s.
Meca ['meka] *nf*: **La ~** Mecca
mecánica [me'kanika] *nf ver* **mecánico**
mecanice *etc* [meka'niθe] *vb ver* **mecanizar**
mecánico, -a [me'kaniko, a] *adj* mechanical; (*repetitivo*) repetitive ■ *nm/f* mechanic ■ *nf* (*estudio*) mechanics *sg*; (*mecanismo*) mechanism
mecanismo [meka'nismo] *nm* mechanism; (*engranaje*) gear
mecanizar [mekani'θar] *vt* to mechanize
mecanografía [mekanoɣra'fia] *nf* typewriting
mecanografiado, -a [mekanoɣra'fjaðo, a] *adj* typewritten ■ *nm* typescript
mecanógrafo, -a [meka'noɣrafo, a] *nm/f* (copy) typist
mecate [me'kate] *nm* (*Am*) rope
mecedor [mese'ðor] *nm* (*Am*), **mecedora** [meθe'ðora] *nf* rocking chair
mecenas [me'θenas] *nm inv* patron
mecenazgo [meθe'naθɣo] *nm* patronage
mecer [me'θer] *vt* (*cuna*) to rock; **mecerse** *vr* to rock; (*rama*) to sway
mecha ['metʃa] *nf* (*de vela*) wick; (*de bomba*) fuse; **a toda ~** at full speed; **ponerse mechas** to streak one's hair
mechero [me'tʃero] *nm* (cigarette) lighter
mechón [me'tʃon] *nm* (*gen*) tuft; (*manojo*) bundle; (*de pelo*) lock
medalla [me'ðaʎa] *nf* medal
media ['meðja] *nf ver* **medio**
mediación [meða'θjon] *nf* mediation; **por ~ de** through
mediado, -a [me'ðjaðo, a] *adj* half-full; (*trabajo*) half-completed; **a mediados de** in the middle of, halfway through
medianamente [meðjana'mente] *adv* (*moderadamente*) moderately, fairly; (*regularmente*) moderately well
mediano, -a [me'ðjano, a] *adj* (*regular*) medium, average; (*mediocre*) mediocre ■ *nf* (*Aut*) central reservation, median (*US*); **(de tamaño) ~** medium-sized
medianoche [meðja'notʃe] *nf* midnight
mediante [me'ðjante] *adv* by (means of), through
mediar [me'ðjar] *vi* (*tiempo*) to elapse; (*interceder*) to mediate, intervene; (*existir*) to exist; **media el hecho de que ...** there is the fact that ...
medicación [meðika'θjon] *nf* medication, treatment
medicamento [meðika'mento] *nm* medicine, drug
medicina [meði'θina] *nf* medicine
medicinal [meðiθi'nal] *adj* medicinal
medición [meði'θjon] *nf* measurement
médico, -a ['meðiko, a] *adj* medical ■ *nm/f* doctor; **~ de cabecera** family doctor; **~ pediatra** paediatrician; **~ residente** house physician, intern (*US*)
medida [me'ðiða] *nf* measure; (*medición*) measurement; (*de camisa, zapato etc*) size, fitting; (*moderación*) moderation, prudence; **en cierta/gran ~** up to a point/to a great extent; **un traje a la ~** made-to-measure suit; **~ de cuello** collar size; **a ~ de** in proportion to; (*de acuerdo con*) in keeping with; **con ~** with restraint; **sin ~** immoderately; **a ~ que ...** (at the same time) as ...; **tomar medidas** to take steps
medieval [meðje'βal] *adj* medieval
medio, -a ['meðjo, a] *adj* half (a); (*punto*) mid, middle; (*promedio*) average ■ *adv* half-; (*esp Am: un tanto*) rather, quite ■ *nm* (*centro*) middle, centre; (*método*) means, way; (*ambiente*) environment ■ *nf* (*prenda de vestir*) stocking; (*Am*) sock; (*promedio*) average; **medias** *nfpl* tights; **media hora** half an hour; **~ litro** half a litre; **las tres y media** half past three; **M~ Oriente** Middle East; **a ~ camino** halfway (there); **~ dormido** half asleep; **~ enojado** (*esp Am*) rather annoyed; **lo dejó a medios** he left it half-done; **ir a medios** to go fifty-fifty; **a ~ terminar** half finished; **en ~** in the middle; (*entre*) in between; **por ~ de** by (means of), through; **en los medios financieros** in financial circles; **encontrarse en su ~** to be in one's element; **~ ambiente** environment; **~ circulante** (*Com*) money supply; *ver tb* **medios**
medioambiental [meðjoambjen'tal] *adj* environmental
mediocre [me'ðjokre] *adj* middling, average; (*pey*) mediocre

mediocridad [meðjokri'ðað] *nf* middling quality; *(pey)* mediocrity
mediodía [meðjo'ðia] *nm* midday, noon
mediopensionista [meðjopensjo'nista] *nm/f* day boy (girl)
medios ['meðjos] *nmpl* means, resources; **los ~ de comunicación** the media
medir [me'ðir] *vt (gen)* to measure ■ *vi* to measure; **medirse** *vr (moderarse)* to be moderate, act with restraint; **¿cuánto mides? — mido 1.50 m** how tall are you? — I am 1.50 m tall
meditabundo, -a [meðita'βundo, a] *adj* pensive
meditar [meði'tar] *vt* to ponder, think over, meditate on; *(planear)* to think out ■ *vi* to ponder, think, meditate
mediterráneo, -a [meðite'rraneo, a] *adj* Mediterranean ■ *nm*: **el (mar) M~** the Mediterranean (Sea)
medrar [me'ðrar] *vi* to increase, grow; *(mejorar)* to improve; *(prosperar)* to prosper, thrive; *(animal, planta etc)* to grow
medroso, -a [me'ðroso, a] *adj* fearful, timid
médula ['meðula] *nf (Anat)* marrow; *(Bot)* pith; **~ espinal** spinal cord; **hasta la ~** *(fig)* to the core
medusa [me'ðusa] *nf (Esp)* jellyfish
megabyte ['meɣaβait] *nm (Inform)* megabyte
megafonía [meɣgafo'nia] *nf* PA *o* public address system
megáfono [me'ɣafono] *nm* public address system
megalomanía [meɣaloma'nia] *nf* megalomania
megalómano, -a [meɣa'lomano, a] *nm/f* megalomaniac
megaocteto [meɣaok'teto] *nm (Inform)* megabyte
mejicano, -a [mexi'kano, a] *adj, nm/f* Mexican
Méjico ['mexiko] *nm* Mexico
mejilla [me'xiʎa] *nf* cheek
mejillón [mexi'ʎon] *nm* mussel
mejor [me'xor] *adj, adv (comparativo)* better; *(superlativo)* best; **lo ~** the best thing; **lo ~ de la vida** the prime of life; **a lo ~** probably; *(quizá)* maybe; **~ dicho** rather; **tanto ~** so much the better; **es el ~ de todos** he's the best of all
mejora [me'xora] *nf*, **mejoramiento** [mexora'mjento] *nm* improvement
mejorar [mexo'rar] *vt* to improve, make better ■ *vi*, **mejorarse** *vr* to improve, get better; *(Com)* to do well, prosper; **~ a** to be better than; **los negocios mejoran** business is picking up
mejoría [mexo'ria] *nf* improvement; *(restablecimiento)* recovery
mejunje [me'xunxe] *nm (pey)* concoction
melancolía [melanko'lia] *nf* melancholy
melancólico, -a [melan'koliko, a] *adj (triste)* sad, melancholy; *(soñador)* dreamy
melena [me'lena] *nf (de persona)* long hair; *(Zool)* mane
melillense [meli'ʎense] *adj* of *o* from Melilla ■ *nm/f* native *o* inhabitant of Melilla
mella ['meʎa] *nf (rotura)* notch, nick; **hacer ~** *(fig)* to make an impression
mellizo, -a [me'ʎiθo, a] *adj, nm/f* twin
melocotón [meloko'ton] *nm (Esp)* peach
melodía [melo'ðia] *nf* melody; *(tonada)* tune; *(de móvil)* ringtone
melodrama [melo'ðrama] *nm* melodrama
melodramático, -a [meloðra'matiko, a] *adj* melodramatic
melón [me'lon] *nm* melon
melopea [melo'pea] *nf (fam)*: **tener una ~** to be sloshed
meloso, -a [me'loso, a] *adj* honeyed, sweet; *(empalagoso)* sickly, cloying; *(voz)* sweet; *(zalamero)* smooth
membrana [mem'brana] *nf* membrane
membrete [mem'brete] *nm* letterhead; **papel con ~** headed notepaper
membrillo [mem'briʎo] *nm* quince; **carne de ~** quince jelly
memo, -a ['memo, a] *adj* silly, stupid ■ *nm/f* idiot
memorable [memo'raβle] *adj* memorable
memorándum [memo'randum] *nm (libro)* notebook; *(comunicación)* memorandum
memoria [me'morja] *nf (gen)* memory; *(artículo)* (learned) paper; **memorias** *nfpl (de autor)* memoirs; **~ anual** annual report; **aprender algo de ~** to learn sth by heart; **si tengo buena ~** if my memory serves me right; **venir a la ~** to come to mind; *(Inform)*: **~ de acceso aleatorio** random access memory, RAM; **~ auxiliar** backing storage; **~ fija** read-only memory, ROM; **~ del teclado** keyboard memory
memorice *etc* [memo'riθe] *vb ver* **memorizar**
memorizar [memori'θar] *vt* to memorize
menaje [me'naxe] *nm (muebles)* furniture; *(utensilios domésticos)* household equipment; **~ de cocina** kitchenware
mención [men'θjon] *nf* mention; **digno de ~** noteworthy; **hacer ~ de** to mention
mencionar [menθjo'nar] *vt* to mention; *(nombrar)* to name; **sin ~ ...** let alone ...
mendicidad [mendiθi'ðað] *nf* begging
mendigar [mendi'ɣar] *vt* to beg (for)
mendigo, -a [men'diɣo, a] *nm/f* beggar

mendigue *etc* [men'diɣe] *vb ver* **mendigar**
mendrugo [men'druɣo] *nm* crust
menear [mene'ar] *vt* to move; (*cola*) to wag; (*cadera*) to swing; (*fig*) to handle; **menearse** *vr* to shake; (*balancearse*) to sway; (*moverse*) to move; (*fig*) to get a move on
menester [menes'ter] *nm* (*necesidad*) necessity; **menesteres** *nmpl* (*deberes*) duties; **es ~ hacer algo** it is necessary to do sth, sth must be done
menestra [me'nestra] *nf*: **~ de verduras** vegetable stew
mengano, -a [men'gano, a] *nm/f* Mr (*o* Mrs *o* Miss) So-and-so
mengua ['mengwa] *nf* (*disminución*) decrease; (*falta*) lack; (*pobreza*) poverty; (*fig*) discredit; **en ~ de** to the detriment of
menguante [men'gwante] *adj* decreasing, diminishing; (*luna*) waning; (*marea*) ebb *cpd*
menguar [men'gwar] *vt* to lessen, diminish; (*fig*) to discredit ■ *vi* to diminish, decrease; (*fig*) to decline
mengüe *etc* ['mengwe] *vb ver* **menguar**
menopausia [meno'pausja] *nf* menopause
menor [me'nor] *adj* (*más pequeño: comparativo*) smaller; (*número*) less, lesser; (*: superlativo*) smallest; (*número*) least; (*más joven: comparativo*) younger; (*: superlativo*) youngest; (*Mus*) minor ■ *nm/f* (*joven*) young person, juvenile; **Juanito es ~ que Pepe** Juanito is younger than Pepe; **ella es la ~ de todas** she is the youngest of all; **no tengo la ~ idea** I haven't the faintest idea; **al por ~** retail; **~ de edad** under age
Menorca [me'norka] *nf* Minorca
menorquín, -ina [menor'kin, ina] *adj, nm/f* Minorcan

PALABRA CLAVE

menos [menos] *adj* **1**: **~ (que/de)** (*compar: cantidad*) less (than); (*: número*) fewer (than); **con ~ entusiasmo** with less enthusiasm; **~ gente** fewer people; *ver tb* **cada**
2 (*superl*): **es el que ~ culpa tiene** he is the least to blame; **donde ~ problemas hay** where there are fewest problems
■ *adv* **1** (*compar*): **~ (que/de)** less (than); **me gusta ~ que el otro** I like it less than the other one; **~ de cinco** less than five; **~ de lo que piensas** less than you think
2 (*superl*): **es el ~ listo (de su clase)** he's the least bright (in his class); **de todas ellas es la que ~ me agrada** out of all of them she's the one I like least; **(por) lo ~** at (the very) least; **es lo ~ que puedo hacer** it's the least I can do; **lo ~ posible** as little as possible
3 (*locuciones*): **no quiero verle y ~ visitarle** I don't want to see him let alone visit him; **tenemos siete (de) ~** we're seven short; **eso es lo de ~** that's the least of it; **¡todo ~ eso!** anything but that!; **al/por lo ~** at (the very) least; **si al ~** if only
■ *prep* except; (*cifras*) minus; **todos ~ él** everyone except (for) him; **5 ~ 2** 5 minus 2; **las 7 ~ 20** (*hora*) 20 to 7
■ *conj*: **a ~ que**: **a menos que venga mañana** unless he comes tomorrow

menoscabar [menoska'βar] *vt* (*estropear*) to damage, harm; (*fig*) to discredit
menospreciar [menospre'θjar] *vt* to underrate, undervalue; (*despreciar*) to scorn, despise
menosprecio [menos'preθjo] *nm* (*subestimación*) underrating, undervaluation; (*desdén*) scorn, contempt
mensaje [men'saxe] *nm* message; **~ de error** (*Inform*) error message; **~ de texto** text message
mensajero, -a [mensa'xero, a] *nm/f* messenger
menstruación [menstrwa'θjon] *nf* menstruation
menstruar [mens'trwar] *vi* to menstruate
mensual [men'swal] *adj* monthly; **10 euros mensuales** 10 euros a month
mensualidad [menswali'ðað] *nf* (*salario*) monthly salary; (*Com*) monthly payment *o* instalment
menta ['menta] *nf* mint
mentado, -a [men'taðo, a] *adj* (*mencionado*) aforementioned; (*famoso*) well-known ■ *nf*: **hacerle una mentada a algn** (*Am fam*) to (seriously) insult sb
mental [men'tal] *adj* mental
mentalidad [mentali'ðað] *nf* mentality
mentalizar [mentali'θar] *vt* (*sensibilizar*) to make aware; (*convencer*) to convince; (*preparar mentalmente*) to psych up; **mentalizarse** *vr* (*concienciarse*) to become aware; (*prepararse mentalmente*) to get psyched up; **mentalizarse de que ...** (*convencerse*) to get it into one's head that ...
mentar [men'tar] *vt* to mention, name; **~ la madre a algn** to swear at sb
mente ['mente] *nf* mind; (*inteligencia*) intelligence; **no tengo en ~ hacer eso** it is not my intention to do that
mentecato, -a [mente'kato, a] *adj* silly, stupid ■ *nm/f* fool, idiot
mentir [men'tir] *vi* to lie; **¡miento!** sorry, I'm wrong!
mentira [men'tira] *nf* (*una mentira*) lie; (*acto*)

lying; *(invención)* fiction; **~ piadosa** white lie; **una ~ como una casa** a whopping great lie *(fam)*; **parece ~ que ...** it seems incredible that ..., I can't believe that ...
mentiroso, -a [menti'roso, a] *adj* lying; *(falso)* deceptive ■ *nm/f* liar
mentís [men'tis] *nm inv* denial; *(tb:* **dar el mentís a**) to deny
mentón [men'ton] *nm* chin
menú [me'nu] *nm (tb Inform)* menu; *(tb:* **menú del día**) set meal; **guiado por menú** *(Inform)* menu-driven
menudear [menuðe'ar] *vt (repetir)* to repeat frequently ■ *vi (ser frecuente)* to be frequent; *(detallar)* to go into great detail
menudencia [menu'ðenθja] *nf (bagatela)* trifle; **menudencias** *nfpl* odds and ends
menudeo [menu'ðeo] *nm* retail sales *pl*
menudillos [menu'ðiʎos] *nmpl* giblets
menudo, -a [me'nuðo, a] *adj (pequeño)* small, tiny; *(sin importancia)* petty, insignificant; **¡~ negocio!** *(fam)* some deal!; **a ~** often, frequently
meñique [me'ɲike] *nm* little finger
meollo [me'oʎo] *nm (fig)* essence, core
mequetrefe [meke'trefe] *nm* good-for-nothing, whippersnapper
mercader [merka'ðer] *nm* merchant
mercadería [merkaðe'ria] *nf* commodity; **mercaderías** *nfpl* goods, merchandise *sg*
mercado [mer'kaðo] *nm* market; **~ en baja** falling market; **M~ Común** Common Market; **~ de demanda/de oferta** seller's/buyer's market; **~ laboral** labour market; **~ objetivo** target market; **~ de productos básicos** commodity market; **~ de valores** stock market; **~ exterior/interior** *o* **nacional/libre** overseas/home/free market
mercancía [merkan'θia] *nf* commodity; **mercancías** *nfpl* goods, merchandise *sg*; **mercancías en depósito** bonded goods; **mercancías perecederas** perishable goods
mercancías [merkan'θias] *nm inv* goods train, freight train *(US)*
mercantil [merkan'til] *adj* mercantile, commercial
mercenario, -a [merθe'narjo, a] *adj, nm* mercenary
mercería [merθe'ria] *nf (artículos)* haberdashery *(Brit)*, notions *pl (US)*; *(tienda)* haberdasher's shop *(Brit)*, drapery *(Brit)*, notions store *(US)*
Mercosur [merko'sur] *nm abr (Argentina, Brasil, Paraguay, Uruguay)* = **Mercado Común del Sur**
mercurio [mer'kurjo] *nm* mercury
merecedor, a [mereθe'ðor, a] *adj* deserving; **~ de confianza** trustworthy
merecer [mere'θer] *vt* to deserve, merit ■ *vi* to be deserving, be worthy; **merece la pena** it's worthwhile
merecido, -a [mere'θiðo, a] *adj* (well) deserved; **llevarse su ~** to get one's deserts
merendar [meren'dar] *vt* to have for tea ■ *vi* to have tea; *(en el campo)* to have a picnic
merendero [meren'dero] *nm (café)* tearoom; *(en el campo)* picnic spot
merengue [me'renge] *nm* meringue
merezca *etc* [me'reθka] *vb ver* **merecer**
meridiano [meri'ðjano] *nm (Astro, Geo)* meridian; **la explicación es de una claridad meridiana** the explanation is as clear as day
meridional [meriðjo'nal] *adj* Southern ■ *nm/f* Southerner
merienda *etc* [me'rjenda] *vb ver* **merendar** ■ *nf* (light) tea, afternoon snack; *(de campo)* picnic; **~ de negros** free-for-all
mérito ['merito] *nm* merit; *(valor)* worth, value; **hacer méritos** to make a good impression; **restar ~ a** to detract from
meritorio, -a [meri'torjo, a] *adj* deserving
merluza [mer'luθa] *nf* hake; **coger una ~** *(fam)* to get sozzled
merma ['merma] *nf* decrease; *(pérdida)* wastage
mermar [mer'mar] *vt* to reduce, lessen ■ *vi* to decrease, dwindle
mermelada [merme'laða] *nf* jam; **~ de naranja** marmalade
mero, -a ['mero, a] *adj* mere, simple; *(Am fam)* real ■ *adv (Am)* just, right ■ *nm (Zool)* grouper; **el ~ ~** *(Am fam)* the boss
merodear [meroðe'ar] *vi (Mil)* to maraud; *(de noche)* to prowl (about); *(curiosear)* to snoop around
mes [mes] *nm* month; *(salario)* month's pay; **el ~ corriente** this *o* the current month
mesa ['mesa] *nf* table; *(de trabajo)* desk; *(Com)* counter; *(en mitin)* platform; *(Geo)* plateau; *(Arq)* landing; **~ de noche/de tijera/de operaciones** *u* **operatoria** bedside/folding/operating table; **~ redonda** *(reunión)* round table; **~ digitalizadora** *(Inform)* graph pad; **~ directiva** board; **~ y cama** bed and board; **poner/quitar la ~** to lay/clear the table
mesarse [me'sarse] *vr*: **~ el pelo** *o* **los cabellos** to tear one's hair
mesera [me'sera] *nf (Am)* waitress
mesero [me'sero] *nm (Am)* waiter
meseta [me'seta] *nf (Geo)* tableland; *(Arq)* landing
mesilla [me'siʎa], **mesita** [me'sita] *nf*: **~ de noche** bedside table
mesón [me'son] *nm* inn

mestizo, -a [mes'tiθo, a] *adj* half-caste, of mixed race; (*Zool*) crossbred ■ *nm/f* half-caste
mesura [me'sura] *nf* (*calma*) calm; (*moderación*) moderation, restraint; (*cortesía*) courtesy
mesurar [mesu'rar] *vt* (*contener*) to restrain; **mesurarse** *vr* to restrain o.s.
meta ['meta] *nf* goal; (*de carrera*) finish; (*fig*) goal, aim, objective
metabolismo [metaβo'lismo] *nm* metabolism
metafísico, -a [meta'fisiko, a] *adj* metaphysical ■ *nf* metaphysics *sg*
metáfora [me'tafora] *nf* metaphor
metafórico, -a [meta'foriko, a] *adj* metaphorical
metal [me'tal] *nm* (*materia*) metal; (*Mus*) brass
metálico, -a [me'taliko, a] *adj* metallic; (*de metal*) metal ■ *nm* (*dinero contante*) cash
metalurgia [meta'lurxja] *nf* metallurgy
metalúrgico, -a [meta'lurxiko, a] *adj* metallurgic(al); **industria metalúrgica** engineering industry
metamorfosear [metamorfose'ar] *vt*: **~ (en)** to metamorphose *o* transform (into)
metamorfosis [metamor'fosis] *nf inv* metamorphosis, transformation
metedura [mete'ðura] *nf*: **~ de pata** (*fam*) blunder
meteorito [meteo'rito] *nm* meteorite
meteoro [mete'oro] *nm* meteor
meteorología [meteorolo'xia] *nf* meteorology
meteorólogo, -a [meteo'roloɣo, a] *nm/f* meteorologist; (*Radio, TV*) weather reporter
meter [me'ter] *vt* (*colocar*) to put, place; (*introducir*) to put in, insert; (*involucrar*) to involve; **meterse** *vr*: **meterse en** to go into, enter; (*fig*) to interfere in, meddle in; **meterse a** to start; **meterse a escritor** to become a writer; **meterse con algn** to provoke sb, pick a quarrel with sb; **~ prisa a algn** to hurry sb up
meticuloso, -a [metiku'loso, a] *adj* meticulous, thorough
metido, -a [me'tiðo, a] *adj*: **estar muy ~ en un asunto** to be deeply involved in a matter; **~ en años** elderly; **~ en carne** plump
metódico, -a [me'toðiko, a] *adj* methodical
metodismo [meto'ðismo] *nm* Methodism
método ['metoðo] *nm* method
metodología [metoðolo'xia] *nf* methodology
metomentodo [metomen'toðo] *nm inv* meddler, busybody
metraje [me'traxe] *nm* (*Cine*) length; **cinta de largo/corto ~** full-length film/short
metralla [me'traʎa] *nf* shrapnel
metralleta [metra'ʎeta] *nf* sub-machine-gun
métrico, -a ['metriko, a] *adj* metric ■ *nf* metrics *pl*; **cinta métrica** tape measure
metro ['metro] *nm* metre; (*tren*: *tb*: **metropolitano**) underground (*Brit*), subway (*US*); (*instrumento*) rule; **~ cuadrado/cúbico** square/cubic metre
metrópoli [me'tropoli], **metrópolis** [me'tropolis] *nf* (*ciudad*) metropolis; (*colonial*) mother country
mexicano, -a [mexi'kano, a] *adj, nm/f* (*Am*) Mexican
México ['mexiko] *nm* (*Am*) Mexico; **Ciudad de ~** Mexico City
mezcla ['meθkla] *nf* mixture; (*fig*) blend
mezclar [meθ'klar] *vt* to mix (up); (*armonizar*) to blend; (*combinar*) to merge; **mezclarse** *vr* to mix, mingle; **~ en** to get mixed up in, get involved in
mezcolanza [meθko'lanθa] *nf* hotchpotch, jumble
mezquindad [meθkin'dað] *nf* (*cicatería*) meanness; (*miras estrechas*) pettiness; (*acto*) mean action
mezquino, -a [meθ'kino, a] *adj* (*cicatero*) mean ■ *nm/f* (*avaro*) mean person; (*miserable*) petty individual
mezquita [meθ'kita] *nf* mosque
mg *abr* (= *miligramo(s)*) mg
mi [mi] *adj posesivo* my ■ *nm* (*Mus*) E
mí [mi] *pron* me, myself; **¿y a mí qué?** so what?
miaja ['mjaxa] *nf* crumb; **ni una ~** (*fig*) not the least little bit
miau [mjau] *nm* miaow
michelín [mitʃe'lin] *nm* (*fam*) spare tyre
mico ['miko] *nm* monkey
micro ['mikro] *nm* (*Radio*) mike, microphone; (*Am*: *pequeño*) minibus; (*: grande*) coach, bus
microbio [mi'kroβjo] *nm* microbe
microbús [mikro'βus] *nm* minibus
microchip [mikro'tʃip] *nm* microchip
microcomputador [mikrokomputa'ðor] *nm*, **microcomputadora** [mikrokomputa'ðora] *nf* micro(computer)
microeconomía [mikroekono'mia] *nf* microeconomics *sg*
microficha [mikro'fitʃa] *nf* microfiche
microfilm (*pl* **microfilms**) [mikro'film, mikro'films] *nm* microfilm
micrófono [mi'krofono] *nm* microphone
microinformática [mikroinfor'matika] *nf* microcomputing
micrómetro [mi'krometro] *nm* micrometer
microonda [mikro'onda] *nf* microwave;

(horno) microondas microwave (oven)
microordenador [mikroordena'ðor] *nm* microcomputer
micropastilla [mikropas'tiʎa], **microplaqueta** [mikropla'keta] *nf* (*Inform*) chip, wafer
microplaquita [mikropla'kita] *nf*: **~ de silicio** silicon chip
microprocesador [mikroprocesa'ðor] *nm* microprocessor
microscópico, -a [mikros'kopiko, a] *adj* microscopic
microscopio [mikros'kopjo] *nm* microscope
midiendo *etc* [mi'ðjendo] *vb ver* **medir**
miedo ['mjeðo] *nm* fear; (*nerviosismo*) apprehension, nervousness; **meter ~ a** to scare, frighten; **tener ~** to be afraid; **de ~** wonderful, marvellous; **¡qué ~!** (*fam*) how awful!; **me da ~** it scares me; **hace un frío de ~** (*fam*) it's terribly cold
miedoso, -a [mje'ðoso, a] *adj* fearful, timid
miel [mjel] *nf* honey; **no hay ~ sin hiel** there's no rose without a thorn
miembro ['mjembro] *nm* limb; (*socio*) member; (*de institución*) fellow; **~ viril** penis
mientes *etc* ['mjentes] *vb ver* **mentar; mentir** ■ *nfpl*: **no parar ~ en** to pay no attention to; **traer a las ~** to recall
mientras ['mjentras] *conj* while; (*duración*) as long as ■ *adv* meanwhile; **~ (que)** whereas; **~ tanto** meanwhile; **~ más tiene, más quiere** the more he has, the more he wants
miércoles ['mjerkoles] *nm inv* Wednesday; **~ de ceniza** Ash Wednesday; *ver tb* **Carnaval; sábado**
mierda ['mjerða] *nf* (*fam!*) shit (*!*), crap (*!*); (*fig*) filth, dirt; **¡vete a la ~!** go to hell!
mies [mjes] *nf* (ripe) corn, wheat, grain
miga ['miɣa] *nf* crumb; (*fig: meollo*) essence; **hacer buenas migas** (*fam*) to get on well; **esto tiene su ~** there's more to this than meets the eye
migaja [mi'ɣaxa] *nf*: **una ~ de** (*un poquito*) a little; **migajas** *nfpl* crumbs; (*pey*) left-overs
migración [miɣra'θjon] *nf* migration
migratorio, -a [miɣra'torjo, a] *adj* migratory
mil [mil] *num* thousand; **dos ~ libras** two thousand pounds
milagro [mi'laɣro] *nm* miracle; **hacer milagros** (*fig*) to work wonders
milagroso, -a [mila'ɣroso, a] *adj* miraculous
Milán [mi'lan] *nm* Milan
milenario, -a [mile'narjo, a] *adj* millennial; (*fig*) very ancient
milenio [mi'lenjo] *nm* millennium
milésimo, -a [mi'lesimo, a] *num* thousandth
mileurista *nmf person earning around a thousand euros or less*; **un ~ no puede comprar ese piso** no one on a salary of a thousand euros could afford that flat ■ *adj* of (around) a thousand euros; **un sueldo ~** a salary of (around) a thousand euros
mili ['mili] *nf*: **hacer la ~** (*fam*) to do one's military service; *see note*

MILI

La mili, military service, is compulsory in Spain although the number of months' service has been reduced and recruits are now posted close to their home town. There continues to be strong opposition from *objetores de conciencia*, conscientious objectors, who are obliged to do *Prestación Social Sustitutoria* in place of military service; this usually involves doing community service and lasts longer. Those who refuse to do either of these, *los insumisos*, can be sent to prison.

milicia [mi'liθja] *nf* (*Mil*) militia; (*servicio militar*) military service
miligramo [mili'ɣramo] *nm* milligram
milímetro [mi'limetro] *nm* millimetre (*Brit*), millimeter (*US*)
militante [mili'tante] *adj* militant
militar [mili'tar] *adj* military ■ *nm/f* soldier ■ *vi* to serve in the army; (*fig*) to militate, fight
militarismo [milita'rismo] *nm* militarism
milla ['miʎa] *nf* mile; **~ marina** nautical mile
millar [mi'ʎar] *num* thousand; **a millares** in thousands
millón [mi'ʎon] *num* million
millonario, -a [miʎo'narjo, a] *nm/f* millionaire
millonésimo, -a [miʎo'nesimo, a] *num* millionth
mimado, -a [mi'maðo, a] *adj* spoiled
mimar [mi'mar] *vt* to spoil, pamper
mimbre ['mimbre] *nm* wicker; **de ~** wicker *cpd*, wickerwork
mimetismo [mime'tismo] *nm* mimicry
mímica ['mimika] *nf* (*para comunicarse*) sign language; (*imitación*) mimicry
mimo ['mimo] *nm* (*caricia*) caress; (*de niño*) spoiling; (*Teat*) mime; (*: actor*) mime artist
mina ['mina] *nf* mine; (*pozo*) shaft; (*de lápiz*) lead refill; **hullera** *o* **~ de carbón** coalmine
minar [mi'nar] *vt* to mine; (*fig*) to undermine
mineral [mine'ral] *adj* mineral ■ *nm* (*Geo*) mineral; (*mena*) ore
minería [mine'ria] *nf* mining
minero, -a [mi'nero, a] *adj* mining *cpd* ■ *nm/f* miner

miniatura [minja'tura] *adj inv, nf* miniature
minicadena [minika'ðena] *nf* (*Mus*) mini hi-fi
minicomputador [minikomputa'ðor] *nm* minicomputer
MiniDisc® [mini'disk] *nm* MiniDisc®
minidisco [mini'ðisko] *nm* diskette
minifalda [mini'falda] *nf* miniskirt
minifundio [mini'fundjo] *nm* smallholding, small farm
minimizar [minimi'θar] *vt* to minimize
mínimo, -a ['minimo, a] *adj* minimum; (*insignificante*) minimal ▪ *nm* minimum; **precio/salario ~** minimum price/wage; **lo ~ que pueden hacer** the least they can do
minino, -a [mi'nino, a] *nm/f* (*fam*) puss, pussy
ministerio [minis'terjo] *nm* ministry (*Brit*), department (*US*); **M~ de Asuntos Exteriores** Foreign Office (*Brit*), State Department (*US*); **M~ del Comercio e Industria** Department of Trade and Industry; **M~ de (la) Gobernación** *o* **del Interior** ≈ Home Office (*Brit*), Ministry of the Interior; **M~ de Hacienda** Treasury (*Brit*), Treasury Department (*US*)
ministro, -a [mi'nistro, a] *nm/f* minister, secretary (*esp US*); **M~ de Hacienda** Chancellor of the Exchequer, Secretary of the Treasury (*US*); **M~ de (la) Gobernación** *o* **del Interior** ≈ Home Secretary (*Brit*), Secretary of the Interior (*US*)
minoría [mino'ria] *nf* minority
minorista [mino'rista] *nm* retailer
mintiendo *etc* [min'tjendo] *vb ver* **mentir**
minucia [mi'nuθja] *nf* (*detalle insignificante*) trifle; (*bagatela*) mere nothing
minuciosidad [minuθjosi'ðað] *nf* (*meticulosidad*) thoroughness, meticulousness
minucioso, -a [minu'θjoso, a] *adj* thorough, meticulous; (*prolijo*) very detailed
minúsculo, -a [mi'nuskulo, a] *adj* tiny, minute ▪ *nf* small letter; **minúsculas** *nfpl* (*Tip*) lower case *sg*
minusvalía [minusβa'lia] *nf* physical handicap; (*Com*) depreciation, capital loss
minusválido, -a [minus'βaliðo, a] *adj* (physically) handicapped *o* disabled ▪ *nm/f* disabled person
minuta [mi'nuta] *nf* (*de comida*) menu; (*de abogado etc*) fee
minutero [minu'tero] *nm* minute hand
minuto [mi'nuto] *nm* minute
Miño ['miɲo] *nm*: **el (río) ~** the Miño
mío, -a ['mio, a] *adj, pron*: **el ~** mine; **un amigo ~** a friend of mine; **lo ~** what is mine; **los míos** my people, my relations
miope ['mjope] *adj* short-sighted
miopía [mjo'pia] *nf* near- *o* short-sightedness
MIR [mir] *nm abr* (*Pol*) = **Movimiento de Izquierda Revolucionaria**; (*Esp Med*) = **Médico Interno y Residente**
mira ['mira] *nf* (*de arma*) sight(s) *pl*; (*fig*) aim, intention; **de amplias/estrechas miras** broad-/narrow-minded
mirada [mi'raða] *nf* look, glance; (*expresión*) look, expression; **~ de soslayo** sidelong glance; **~ fija** stare, gaze; **~ perdida** distant look; **echar una ~ a** to glance at; **levantar/bajar la ~** to look up/down; **resistir la ~ de algn** to stare sb out
mirado, -a [mi'raðo, a] *adj* (*sensato*) sensible; (*considerado*) considerate; **bien/mal ~** well/not well thought of
mirador [mira'ðor] *nm* viewpoint, vantage point
miramiento [mira'mjento] *nm* (*consideración*) considerateness; **tratar sin miramientos a algn** to ride roughshod over sb
mirar [mi'rar] *vt* to look at; (*observar*) to watch; (*considerar*) to consider, think over; (*vigilar, cuidar*) to watch, look after ▪ *vi* to look; (*Arq*) to face; **mirarse** *vr* (*dos personas*) to look at each other; **~ algo/a algn de reojo** *o* **de través** to look askance at sth/sb; **~ algo/a algn por encima del hombro** to look down on sth/sb; **~ bien/mal** to think highly of/have a poor opinion of; **~ fijamente** to stare *o* gaze at; **~ por** (*fig*) to look after; **~ por la ventana** to look out of the window; **mirarse al espejo** to look at o.s. in the mirror; **mirarse a los ojos** to look into each other's eyes
mirilla [mi'riʎa] *nf* (*agujero*) spyhole, peephole
mirlo ['mirlo] *nm* blackbird
misa ['misa] *nf* mass; **~ del gallo** midnight mass (*on Christmas Eve*); **~ de difuntos** requiem mass; **como en ~** in dead silence; **estos datos van a ~** (*fig*) these facts are utterly trustworthy
misántropo [mi'santropo] *nm* misanthrope, misanthropist
miscelánea [misθe'lanea] *nf* miscellany
miserable [mise'raβle] *adj* (*avaro*) mean, stingy; (*nimio*) miserable, paltry; (*lugar*) squalid; (*fam*) vile, despicable ▪ *nm/f* (*malvado*) rogue
miseria [mi'serja] *nf* misery; (*pobreza*) poverty; (*tacañería*) meanness, stinginess; (*condiciones*) squalor; **una ~** a pittance
misericordia [miseri'korðja] *nf* (*compasión*) compassion, pity; (*perdón*) forgiveness, mercy
misil [mi'sil] *nm* missile
misión [mi'sjon] *nf* mission; (*tarea*) job,

duty; *(Pol)* assignment; **misiones** *nfpl* *(Rel)* overseas missions
misionero, -a [misjo'nero, a] *nm/f* missionary
mismamente [misma'mente] *adv* *(fam: sólo)* only, just
mismísimo, -a [mis'misimo, a] *adj superlativo* selfsame, very (same)
mismo, -a ['mismo, a] *adj* *(semejante)* same; *(después de pronombre)* -self; *(para énfasis)* very ■ *adv*: **aquí/ayer/hoy ~** right here/only yesterday/this very day; **ahora ~** right now ■ *conj*: **lo ~ que** just like, just as; **por lo ~** for the same reason; **el ~ traje** the same suit; **en ese ~ momento** at that very moment; **vino el ~ Ministro** the Minister himself came; **yo ~ lo vi** I saw it myself; **lo hizo por sí ~** he did it by himself; **lo ~** the same (thing); **da lo ~** it's all the same; **quedamos en las mismas** we're no further forward
misógino [mi'soxino] *nm* misogynist
miss [mis] *nf* beauty queen
misterio [mis'terjo] *nm* mystery; *(lo secreto)* secrecy
misterioso, -a [miste'rjoso, a] *adj* mysterious; *(inexplicable)* puzzling
misticismo [misti'θismo] *nm* mysticism
místico, -a ['mistiko, a] *adj* mystic(al) ■ *nm/f* mystic ■ *nf* mysticism
mitad [mi'tað] *nf* *(medio)* half; *(centro)* middle; **~ (y) ~** half-and-half; *(fig)* yes and no; **a ~ de precio** (at) half-price; **en** *o* **a ~ del camino** halfway along the road; **cortar por la ~** to cut through the middle
mítico, -a ['mitiko, a] *adj* mythical
mitigar [miti'ɣar] *vt* to mitigate; *(dolor)* to relieve; *(sed)* to quench; *(ira)* to appease; *(preocupación)* to allay; *(soledad)* to alleviate
mitigue *etc* [mi'tiɣe] *vb ver* **mitigar**
mitin ['mitin] *nm* *(esp Pol)* meeting
mito ['mito] *nm* myth
mitología [mitolo'xia] *nf* mythology
mitológico, -a [mito'loxiko, a] *adj* mythological
mixto, -a ['miksto, a] *adj* mixed; *(comité)* joint
ml *abr* (= *mililitro(s)*) ml
mill. *abr* (= *millón, millones*) M
mm *abr* (= *milímetro(s)*) mm
MMS *nm abr* (= *multimedia message service*) MMS *m*
M.N. *(Am)*, **m/n** *abr* *(Econ)* = **moneda nacional**
M.° *abr* *(Pol: = Ministerio)* Min
m/o *abr* *(Com)* = **mi orden**
mobiliario [moβi'ljarjo] *nm* furniture
mocasín [moka'sin] *nm* moccasin
mocedad [moθe'ðað] *nf* youth
mochila [mo'tʃila] *nf* rucksack *(Brit)*, backpack
moción [mo'θjon] *nf* motion; **~ compuesta** *(Pol)* composite motion
moco ['moko] *nm* mucus; **limpiarse los mocos** to blow one's nose; **no es ~ de pavo** it's no trifle
mocoso, -a [mo'koso, a] *adj* snivelling; *(fig)* ill-bred ■ *nm/f* *(fam)* brat
moda ['moða] *nf* fashion; *(estilo)* style; **de** *o* **a la ~** in fashion, fashionable; **pasado de ~** out of fashion; **vestido a la última ~** trendily dressed
modal [mo'ðal] *adj* modal ■ *nm*: **modales** manners
modalidad [moðali'ðað] *nf* *(clase)* kind, variety; *(manera)* way; *(Inform)* mode; **~ de texto** *(Inform)* text mode
modelar [moðe'lar] *vt* to model
modelo [mo'ðelo] *adj inv* model ■ *nm/f* model ■ *nm* *(patrón)* pattern; *(norma)* standard
módem ['moðem] *nm* *(Inform)* modem
moderado, -a [moðe'raðo, a] *adj* moderate
moderar [moðe'rar] *vt* to moderate; *(violencia)* to restrain, control; *(velocidad)* to reduce; **moderarse** *vr* to restrain o.s., control o.s
modernice *etc* [moðer'niθe] *vb ver* **modernizar**
modernizar [moðerni'θar] *vt* to modernize; *(Inform)* to upgrade
moderno, -a [mo'ðerno, a] *adj* modern; *(actual)* present-day; *(equipo etc)* up-to-date
modestia [mo'ðestja] *nf* modesty
modesto, -a [mo'ðesto, a] *adj* modest
módico, -a ['moðiko, a] *adj* moderate, reasonable
modificar [moðifi'kar] *vt* to modify
modifique *etc* [moði'fike] *vb ver* **modificar**
modismo [mo'ðismo] *nm* idiom
modisto, -a [mo'ðisto, a] *nm/f* dressmaker
modo ['moðo] *nm* *(manera, forma)* way, manner; *(Inform, Mus)* mode; *(Ling)* mood; **modos** *nmpl* manners; **"~ de empleo"** "instructions for use"; **~ de gobierno** form of government; **a ~ de** like; **de este ~** in this way; **de ningún ~** in no way; **de todos modos** at any rate; **de un ~ u otro** (in) one way or another
modorra [mo'ðorra] *nf* drowsiness
modoso, -a [mo'ðoso, a] *adj* *(educado)* quiet, well-mannered
modulación [moðula'θjon] *nf* modulation; **~ de frecuencia** *(Radio)* frequency modulation, FM

módulo ['moðulo] *nm* module; (*de mueble*) unit
mofarse [mo'farse] *vr*: **~ de** to mock, scoff at
moflete [mo'flete] *nm* fat cheek, chubby cheek
mogollón [moɣo'ʎon] (*fam*) *nm*: **~ de discos** *etc* loads of records *etc* ■ *adv*: **un ~** a hell of a lot
mohín [mo'in] *nm* (*mueca*) (wry) face; (*pucheros*) pout
mohíno, -a [mo'ino, a] *adj* (*triste*) gloomy, depressed; (*enojado*) sulky
moho ['moo] *nm* (*Bot*) mould, mildew; (*en metal*) rust
mohoso, -a [mo'oso, a] *adj* mouldy; rusty
mojado, -a [mo'xaðo, a] *adj* wet; (*húmedo*) damp; (*empapado*) drenched
mojar [mo'xar] *vt* to wet; (*humedecer*) to damp(en), moisten; (*calar*) to soak; **mojarse** *vr* to get wet; **~ el pan en el café** to dip *o* dunk one's bread in one's coffee
mojigato, -a [moxi'ɣato, a] *adj* (*hipócrita*) hypocritical; (*santurrón*) sanctimonious; (*gazmoño*) prudish ■ *nm/f* hypocrite; sanctimonious person; prude
mojón [mo'xon] *nm* (*hito*) landmark; (*en un camino*) signpost; (*tb*: **mojón kilométrico**) milestone
mol. *abr* (= *molécula*) mol
molar [mo'lar] *nm* molar ■ *vt* (*fam*): **lo que más me mola es ...** what I'm really into is ...; **¿te mola un pitillo?** do you fancy a smoke?
Moldavia [mol'ðaβja], **Moldova** [mol'ðoβa] *nf* Moldavia, Moldova
moldavo, -a [mol'ðaβo, a] *adj, nm/f* Moldavian, Moldovan
molde ['molde] *nm* mould; (*vaciado*) cast; (*de costura*) pattern; (*fig*) model
moldear [molde'ar] *vt* to mould; (*en yeso etc*) to cast
mole ['mole] *nf* mass, bulk; (*edificio*) pile
molécula [mo'lekula] *nf* molecule
moler [mo'ler] *vt* to grind, crush; (*pulverizar*) to pound; (*trigo etc*) to mill; (*cansar*) to tire out, exhaust; **~ a algn a palos** to give sb a beating
molestar [moles'tar] *vt* to bother; (*fastidiar*) to annoy; (*incomodar*) to inconvenience, put out; (*perturbar*) to trouble, upset ■ *vi* to be a nuisance; **molestarse** *vr* to bother; (*incomodarse*) to go to a lot of trouble; (*ofenderse*) to take offence; **¿le molesta el ruido?** do you mind the noise?; **siento molestarle** I'm sorry to trouble you
molestia [mo'lestja] *nf* bother, trouble; (*incomodidad*) inconvenience; (*Med*) discomfort; **no es ninguna ~** it's no trouble at all
molesto, -a [mo'lesto, a] *adj* (*que fastidia*) annoying; (*incómodo*) inconvenient; (*inquieto*) uncomfortable, ill at ease; (*enfadado*) annoyed; **estar ~** (*Med*) to be in some discomfort; **estar ~ con algn** (*fig*) to be cross with sb; **me sentí ~** I felt embarrassed
molido, -a [mo'liðo, a] *adj* (*machacado*) ground; (*pulverizado*) powdered; **estar ~** (*fig*) to be exhausted *o* dead beat
molinero [moli'nero] *nm* miller
molinillo [moli'niʎo] *nm* hand mill; **~ de carne/café** mincer/coffee grinder
molino [mo'lino] *nm* (*edificio*) mill; (*máquina*) grinder
mollera [mo'ʎera] *nf* (*Anat*) crown of the head; (*fam*: *seso*) brains *pl*; **duro de ~** (*estúpido*) thick
Molucas [mo'lukas] *nfpl*: **las (Islas) ~** the Moluccas, the Molucca Islands
molusco [mo'lusko] *nm* mollusc
momentáneo, -a [momen'taneo, a] *adj* momentary
momento [mo'mento] *nm* (*gen*) moment; (*Tec*) momentum; **de ~** at the moment, for the moment; **en ese ~** at that moment, just then; **por el ~** for the time being
momia ['momja] *nf* mummy
mona ['mona] *nf ver* **mono**
Mónaco ['monako] *nm* Monaco
monada [mo'naða] *nf* (*gracia*) charming habit; (*cosa primorosa*) lovely thing; (*chica*) pretty girl; **¡qué ~!** isn't it cute?
monaguillo [mona'ɣiʎo] *nm* altar boy
monarca [mo'narka] *nm/f* monarch, ruler
monarquía [monar'kia] *nf* monarchy
monárquico, -a [mo'narkiko, a] *nm/f* royalist, monarchist
monasterio [monas'terjo] *nm* monastery
Moncloa [mon'kloa] *nf*: **la ~** *official residence of the Spanish Prime Minister*
monda ['monda] *nf* (*poda*) pruning; (*: de árbol*) lopping; (*: de fruta*) peeling; (*cáscara*) skin; **¡es la ~!** (*fam*: *fantástico*) it's great!; (*: el colmo*) it's the limit!; (*: persona: gracioso*) he's a knockout!
mondadientes [monda'ðjentes] *nm inv* toothpick
mondar [mon'dar] *vt* (*limpiar*) to clean; (*pelar*) to peel; **mondarse** *vr*: **mondarse de risa** (*fam*) to split one's sides laughing
moneda [mo'neða] *nf* (*tipo de dinero*) currency, money; (*pieza*) coin; **una ~ de 50 céntimos** a 50-cent coin; **~ de curso** legal tender; **~ extranjera** foreign exchange; **~ única** single currency; **es ~ corriente** (*fig*) it's common knowledge
monedero [mone'ðero] *nm* purse
monegasco, -a [mone'ɣasko, a] *adj* of *o* from

Monaco, Monegasque ■ *nm/f* Monegasque
monetario, -a [mone'tarjo, a] *adj* monetary, financial
monetarista [moneta'rista] *adj, nm/f* monetarist
mongólico, -a [mon'goliko, a] *adj, nm/f* Mongol
monigote [moni'ɣote] *nm* (*dibujo*) doodle; (*de papel*) cut-out figure; (*pey*) wimp; *ver tb* **inocente**
monitor [moni'tor] *nm* (*Inform*) monitor; **~ en color** colour monitor
monja ['monxa] *nf* nun
monje ['monxe] *nm* monk
mono, -a ['mono, a] *adj* (*bonito*) lovely, pretty; (*gracioso*) nice, charming ■ *nm/f* monkey, ape ■ *nm* dungarees *pl*; (*traje de faena*) overalls *pl*; (*fam: de drogadicto*) cold turkey; **una chica muy mona** a very pretty girl; **dormir la ~** to sleep it off
monóculo [mo'nokulo] *nm* monocle
monografía [monoɣra'fia] *nf* monograph
monolingüe [mono'lingwe] *adj* monolingual
monólogo [mo'noloɣo] *nm* monologue
monomando [mono'mando] *nm* (*tb*: **grifo monomando**) mixer tap
monoparental [monoparen'tal] *adj*: **familia ~** single-parent family
monopatín [monopa'tin] *nm* skateboard
monopolice *etc* [monopo'liθe] *vb ver* **monopolizar**
monopolio [mono'poljo] *nm* monopoly; **~ total** absolute monopoly
monopolista [monopo'lista] *adj, nm/f* monopolist
monopolizar [monopoli'θar] *vt* to monopolize
monosílabo, -a [mono'silaβo, a] *adj* monosyllabic ■ *nm* monosyllable
monotonía [monoto'nia] *nf* (*sonido*) monotone; (*fig*) monotony
monótono, -a [mo'notono, a] *adj* monotonous
mono-usuario, -a [monou'swarjo, a] *adj* (*Inform*) single-user
monóxido [mo'noksiðo] *nm* monoxide; **~ de carbono** carbon monoxide
Mons. *abr* (*Rel*) = **Monseñor**
monseñor [monse'ɲor] *nm* monsignor
monserga [mon'serɣa] *nf* (*lenguaje confuso*) gibberish; (*tonterías*) drivel
monstruo ['monstrwo] *nm* monster ■ *adj inv* fantastic
monstruoso, -a [mons'trwoso, a] *adj* monstrous
monta ['monta] *nf* total, sum; **de poca ~** unimportant, of little account
montacargas [monta'karɣas] *nm inv* service lift (*Brit*), freight elevator (*US*)
montador [monta'ðor] *nm* (*para montar*) mounting block; (*profesión*) fitter; (*Cine*) film editor
montaje [mon'taxe] *nm* assembly; (*organización*) fitting up; (*Teat*) décor; (*Cine*) montage
montante [mon'tante] *nm* (*poste*) upright; (*soporte*) stanchion; (*Arq: de puerta*) transom; (*: de ventana*) mullion; (*suma*) amount, total
montaña [mon'taɲa] *nf* (*monte*) mountain; (*sierra*) mountains *pl*, mountainous area; (*Am: selva*) forest; **~ rusa** roller coaster
montañero, -a [monta'ɲero, a] *adj* mountain *cpd* ■ *nm/f* mountaineer, climber
montañés, -esa [monta'ɲes, esa] *adj* mountain *cpd*; (*de Santander*) of *o* from the Santander region ■ *nm/f* highlander; native *o* inhabitant of the Santander region
montañismo [monta'ɲismo] *nm* mountaineering, climbing
montañoso, -a [monta'ɲoso, a] *adj* mountainous
montar [mon'tar] *vt* (*subir a*) to mount, get on; (*caballo etc*) to ride; (*Tec*) to assemble, put together; (*negocio*) to set up; (*colocar*) to lift on to; (*Cine: película*) to edit; (*Teat: obra*) to stage, put on; (*Culin: batir*) to whip, beat ■ *vi* to mount, get on; (*sobresalir*) to overlap; **~ en cólera** to get angry; **~ un número** *o* **numerito** to make a scene; **tanto monta** it makes no odds
montaraz [monta'raθ] *adj* mountain *cpd*, highland *cpd*; (*pey*) uncivilized
monte ['monte] *nm* (*montaña*) mountain; (*bosque*) woodland; (*área sin cultivar*) wild area, wild country; **~ de piedad** pawnshop; **~ alto** forest; **~ bajo** scrub(land)
montera [mon'tera] *nf* (*sombrero*) cloth cap; (*de torero*) bullfighter's hat
monto ['monto] *nm* total, amount
montón [mon'ton] *nm* heap, pile; **un ~ de** (*fig*) heaps of, lots of; **a montones** by the score, galore
montura [mon'tura] *nf* (*cabalgadura*) mount; (*silla*) saddle; (*arreos*) harness; (*de joya*) mounting; (*de gafas*) frame
monumental [monumen'tal] *adj* (*tb fig*) monumental; **zona ~** area of historical interest
monumento [monu'mento] *nm* monument; (*de conmemoración*) memorial
monzón [mon'θon] *nm* monsoon
moña ['moɲa] *nf* hair ribbon
moño ['moɲo] *nm* (*de pelo*) bun; **estar hasta**

el ~ (*fam*) to be fed up to the back teeth
MOPTMA *nm abr* = **Ministerio de Obras Públicas, Transporte y Medio Ambiente**
moqueta [mo'keta] *nf* fitted carpet
moquillo [mo'kiʎo] *nm* (*enfermedad*) distemper
mora ['mora] *nf* (*Bot*) mulberry; (*: zarzamora*) blackberry; (*Com*): **en** ~ in arrears
morado, -a [mo'raðo, a] *adj* purple, violet ■ *nm* bruise ■ *nf* (*casa*) dwelling, abode; **pasarlas moradas** to have a tough time of it
moral [mo'ral] *adj* moral ■ *nf* (*ética*) ethics *pl*; (*moralidad*) morals *pl*, morality; (*ánimo*) morale; **tener baja la** ~ to be in low spirits
moraleja [mora'lexa] *nf* moral
moralice *etc* [mora'liθe] *vb ver* **moralizar**
moralidad [morali'ðað] *nf* morals *pl*, morality
moralizar [morali'θar] *vt* to moralize
morar [mo'rar] *vi* to live, dwell
moratón [mora'ton] *nm* bruise
moratoria [mora'torja] *nf* moratorium
morbo ['morβo] *nm* (*fam*) morbid pleasure
morbosidad [morβosi'ðað] *nf* morbidity
morboso, -a [mor'βoso, a] *adj* morbid
morcilla [mor'θiʎa] *nf* blood sausage, ≈ black pudding (*Brit*)
mordaz [mor'ðaθ] *adj* (*crítica*) biting, scathing
mordaza [mor'ðaθa] *nf* (*para la boca*) gag; (*Tec*) clamp
morder [mor'ðer] *vt* to bite; (*mordisquear*) to nibble; (*fig: consumir*) to eat away, eat into ■ *vi*, **morderse** *vr* to bite; **está que muerde** he's hopping mad; **morderse la lengua** to hold one's tongue
mordida [mor'ðiða] *nf* (*Am fam*) bribe
mordisco [mor'ðisko] *nm* bite
mordisquear [morðiske'ar] *vt* to nibble at
moreno, -a [mo'reno, a] *adj* (*color*) (dark) brown; (*de tez*) dark; (*de pelo moreno*) dark-haired; (*negro*) black ■ *nm/f* (*de tez*) dark-skinned man/woman; (*de pelo*) dark-haired man/woman
morfina [mor'fina] *nf* morphine
morfinómano, -a [morfi'nomano, a] *adj* addicted to hard drugs ■ *nm/f* drug addict
morgue ['morgue] *nf* (*Am*) mortuary (*Brit*), morgue (*US*)
moribundo, -a [mori'βundo, a] *adj* dying ■ *nm/f* dying person
morir [mo'rir] *vi* to die; (*fuego*) to die down; (*luz*) to go out; **morirse** *vr* to die; (*fig*) to be dying; (*Ferro etc: vías*) to end; (*calle*) to come out; **fue muerto a tiros/en un accidente** he was shot (dead)/was killed in an accident; ~ **de frío/hambre** to die of cold/starve to death; **¡me muero de hambre!** (*fig*) I'm starving!; **morirse por algo** to be dying for sth; **morirse por algn** to be crazy about sb
mormón, -ona [mor'mon, ona] *nm/f* Mormon
moro, -a ['moro, a] *adj* Moorish ■ *nm/f* Moor; **¡hay moros en la costa!** watch out!
moroso, -a [mo'roso, a] *adj* (*lento*) slow ■ *nm* (*Com*) bad debtor, defaulter; **deudor** ~ (*Com*) slow payer
morral [mo'rral] *nm* haversack
morriña [mo'rriɲa] *nf* homesickness; **tener** ~ to be homesick
morro ['morro] *nm* (*Zool*) snout, nose; (*Auto, Aviat*) nose; (*fam: labio*) (thick) lip; **beber a** ~ to drink from the bottle; **caer de** ~ to nosedive; **estar de morros (con algn)** to be in a bad mood (with sb); **tener** ~ to have a nerve
morrocotudo, -a [morroko'tuðo, a] *adj* (*fam: fantástico*) smashing; (*riña, golpe*) tremendous; (*fuerte*) strong; (*pesado*) heavy; (*difícil*) awkward
morsa ['morsa] *nf* walrus
morse ['morse] *nm* Morse (code)
mortadela [morta'ðela] *nf* mortadella, bologna sausage
mortaja [mor'taxa] *nf* shroud; (*Tec*) mortise; (*Am*) cigarette paper
mortal [mor'tal] *adj* mortal; (*golpe*) deadly
mortalidad [mortali'ðað], **mortandad** [mortan'dað] *nf* mortality
mortecino, -a [morte'θino, a] *adj* (*débil*) weak; (*luz*) dim; (*color*) dull
mortero [mor'tero] *nm* mortar
mortífero, -a [mor'tifero, a] *adj* deadly, lethal
mortificar [mortifi'kar] *vt* to mortify; (*atormentar*) to torment
mortifique *etc* [morti'fike] *vb ver* **mortificar**
mortuorio, -a [mor'tworjo, a] *adj* mortuary, death *cpd*
Mosa ['mosa] *nm*: **el (Río)** ~ the Meuse
mosaico [mo'saiko] *nm* mosaic
mosca ['moska] *nf* fly; **por si las moscas** just in case; **estar** ~ (*desconfiar*) to smell a rat; **tener la** ~ **en** *o* **detrás de la oreja** to be wary
moscovita [mosko'βita] *adj* Muscovite, Moscow *cpd* ■ *nm/f* Muscovite
Moscú [mos'ku] *nm* Moscow
mosquear [moske'ar] (*fam*) *vt* (*hacer sospechar*) to make suspicious; (*fastidiar*) to annoy; **mosquearse** *vr* (*enfadarse*) to get annoyed; (*ofenderse*) to take offence
mosquita [mos'kita] *nf*: **parece una** ~ **muerta** he looks as though butter wouldn't melt in his mouth
mosquitero [moski'tero] *nm* mosquito net

mosquito [mos'kito] *nm* mosquito
Mossos ['mosos] *nmpl*: **~ d'Esquadra** Catalan police; *ver tb* **policía**
mostaza [mos'taθa] *nf* mustard
mosto ['mosto] *nm* unfermented grape juice
mostrador [mostra'ðor] *nm* (*de tienda*) counter; (*de café*) bar
mostrar [mos'trar] *vt* to show; (*exhibir*) to display, exhibit; (*explicar*) to explain; **mostrarse** *vr*: **mostrarse amable** to be kind; to prove to be kind; **no se muestra muy inteligente** he doesn't seem (to be) very intelligent; **~ en pantalla** (*Inform*) to display
mota ['mota] *nf* speck, tiny piece; (*en diseño*) dot
mote ['mote] *nm* (*apodo*) nickname
motín [mo'tin] *nm* (*del pueblo*) revolt, rising; (*del ejército*) mutiny
motivación [motiβa'θjon] *nf* motivation
motivar [moti'βar] *vt* (*causar*) to cause, motivate; (*explicar*) to explain, justify
motivo [mo'tiβo] *nm* motive, reason; (*Arte, Mus*) motif; **con ~ de** (*debido a*) because of; (*en ocasión de*) on the occasion of; (*con el fin de*) in order to; **sin ~** for no reason at all
moto ['moto] *nf*, **motocicleta** [motoθi'kleta] *nf* motorbike (*Brit*), motorcycle
motoneta [moto'neta] *nf* (*Am*) Vespa®
motor, a [mo'tor, a] *adj* (*Tec*) motive; (*Anat*) motor ■ *nm* motor, engine; **~ a chorro** *o* **de reacción/de explosión** jet engine/internal combustion engine; **~ de búsqueda** (*Internet*) search engine ■ *nf* motorboat
motorismo [moto'rismo] *nm* motorcycling
motorista [moto'rista] *nm/f* (*esp Am: automovilista*) motorist; (*: motociclista*) motorcyclist
motorizado, -a [motori'θaðo, a] *adj* motorized
motosierra [moto'sjerra] *nf* mechanical saw
motriz [mo'triz] *adj*: **fuerza ~** motive power; (*fig*) driving force
movedizo, -a [moβe'ðiθo, a] *adj* (*inseguro*) unsteady; (*fig*) unsettled, changeable; (*persona*) fickle
mover [mo'βer] *vt* to move; (*cambiar de lugar*) to shift; (*cabeza: para negar*) to shake; (*: para asentir*) to nod; (*accionar*) to drive; (*fig*) to cause, provoke; **moverse** *vr* to move; (*mar*) to get rough; (*viento*) to rise; (*fig: apurarse*) to get a move on; (*: transformarse*) to be on the move
movible [mo'βiβle] *adj* (*no fijo*) movable; (*móvil*) mobile; (*cambiadizo*) changeable
movido, -a [mo'βiðo, a] *adj* (*Foto*) blurred; (*persona: activo*) active; (*mar*) rough; (*día*) hectic ■ *nf* move; **la movida madrileña** the Madrid scene
móvil ['moβil] *adj* mobile; (*pieza de máquina*) moving; (*mueble*) movable ■ *nm* (*motivo*) motive; (*teléfono*) mobile
movilice *etc* [moβi'liθe] *vb ver* **movilizar**
movilidad [moβili'ðað] *nf* mobility
movilizar [moβili'θar] *vt* to mobilize
movimiento [moβi'mjento] *nm* (*gen, Lit, Pol*) movement; (*Tec*) motion; (*actividad*) activity; (*Mus*) tempo; **el M~** the Falangist Movement; **~ de bloques** (*Inform*) block move; **~ de mercancías** (*Com*) turnover, volume of business; **~ obrero/sindical** workers'/trade union movement; **~ sísmico** earth tremor
Mozambique [moθam'bike] *nm* Mozambique
mozambiqueño, -a [moθambi'keɲo, a] *adj, nm/f* Mozambican
mozo, -a ['moθo, a] *adj* (*joven*) young; (*soltero*) single, unmarried ■ *nm/f* (*joven*) youth, young man (girl); (*camarero*) waiter; (*camarera*) waitress; **~ de estación** porter
MP3 *nm* MP3; **reproductor (de) ~** MP3 player
MPAIAC [emepa'jak] *nm abr* (*Esp Pol*) = **Movimiento para la Autodeterminación y la Independencia del Archipiélago Canario**
mucama [mu'kama] *nf* (*Am*) maid
muchacho, -a [mu'tʃatʃo, a] *nm/f* (*niño*) boy/girl; (*criado*) servant/servant *o* maid
muchedumbre [mutʃe'ðumbre] *nf* crowd
muchísimo, -a [mu'tʃisimo, a] *adj superlativo de* **mucho** lots and lots of, ever so much ■ *adv* ever so much

PALABRA CLAVE

mucho, -a ['mutʃo, a] *adj* **1** (*cantidad*) a lot of, much; (*número*) lots of, a lot of, many; **~ dinero** a lot of money; **hace ~ calor** it's very hot; **muchas amigas** lots *o* a lot of *o* many friends
2 (*sg: fam*): **ésta es mucha casa para él** this house is much too big for him; **había ~ borracho** there were a lot *o* lots of drunks
■ *pron*: **tengo ~ que hacer** I've got a lot to do; **muchos dicen que ...** a lot of people say that ...; *ver tb* **tener**
■ *adv* **1**: **me gusta ~** I like it a lot *o* very much; **lo siento ~** I'm very sorry; **come ~** he eats a lot; **trabaja ~** he works hard; **¿te vas a quedar ~?** are you going to be staying long?; **~ más/menos** much *o* a lot more/less
2 (*respuesta*) very; **¿estás cansado? — ¡~!** are you tired? — very!
3 (*locuciones*): **como ~** at (the) most; **el mejor**

con ~ by far the best; **¡ni ~ menos!** far from it!; **no es rico ni ~ menos** he's far from being rich
4: **por ~ que**: **por mucho que le creas** however much *o* no matter how much you believe him

muda ['muða] *nf* (*de ropa*) change of clothing; (*Zool*) moult; (*de serpiente*) slough
mudanza [mu'ðanθa] *nf* (*cambio*) change; (*de casa*) move; **estar de ~** to be moving
mudar [mu'ðar] *vt* to change; (*Zool*) to shed ▪ *vi* to change; **mudarse** *vr* (*la ropa*) to change; **mudarse de casa** to move house
mudo, -a ['muðo, a] *adj* dumb; (*callado: película*) silent; (*Ling: letra*) mute; (*: consonante*) voiceless; **quedarse ~ (de)** (*fig*) to be dumb with; **quedarse ~ de asombro** to be speechless
mueble ['mweβle] *nm* piece of furniture; **muebles** *nmpl* furniture *sg*
mueble-bar [mweβle'βar] *nm* cocktail cabinet
mueca ['mweka] *nf* face, grimace; **hacer muecas a** to make faces at
muela *etc* ['mwela] *vb ver* **moler** ▪ *nf* (*diente*) tooth; (*: de atrás*) molar; (*de molino*) millstone; (*de afilar*) grindstone; **~ del juicio** wisdom tooth
muelle ['mweʎe] *adj* (*blando*) soft; (*fig*) soft, easy ▪ *nm* spring; (*Naut*) wharf; (*malecón*) jetty
muera *etc* ['mwera] *vb ver* **morir**
muerda *etc* ['mwerða] *vb ver* **morder**
muermo ['mwermo] *nm* (*fam*) wimp
muerte ['mwerte] *nf* death; (*homicidio*) murder; **dar ~ a** to kill; **de mala ~** (*fam*) lousy, rotten; **es la ~** (*fam*) it's deadly boring
muerto, -a ['mwerto, a] *pp de* **morir** ▪ *adj* dead; (*color*) dull ▪ *nm/f* dead man(-woman); (*difunto*) deceased; (*cadáver*) corpse; **cargar con el ~** (*fam*) to carry the can; **echar el ~ a algn** to pass the buck; **hacer el ~** (*nadando*) to float; **estar ~ de cansancio** to be dead tired
muesca ['mweska] *nf* nick
muestra *etc* ['mwestra] *vb ver* **mostrar** ▪ *nf* (*señal*) indication, sign; (*demostración*) demonstration; (*prueba*) proof; (*estadística*) sample; (*modelo*) model, pattern; (*testimonio*) token; **dar ~s de** to show signs of; **~ al azar** (*Com*) random sample
muestrario [mwes'trarjo] *nm* collection of samples; (*exposición*) showcase
muestreo [mwes'treo] *nm* sample, sampling
mueva *etc* [mweβa] *vb ver* **mover**
mugir [mu'xir] *vi* (*vaca*) to moo
mugre ['muɣre] *nf* dirt, filth, muck
mugriento, -a [mu'ɣrjento, a] *adj* dirty, filthy, mucky
mugroso, -a [muɣ'roso, a] *adj* (*Am*) filthy, grubby
muja *etc* ['muxa] *vb ver* **mugir**
mujer [mu'xer] *nf* woman; (*esposa*) wife
mujeriego [muxe'rjeɣo] *nm* womaniser
mula ['mula] *nf* mule
mulato, -a [mu'lato, a] *adj, nm/f* mulatto
muleta [mu'leta] *nf* (*para andar*) crutch; (*Taur*) *stick with red cape attached*
muletilla [mule'tiʎa] *nf* (*palabra*) pet word, tag; (*de cómico*) catch phrase
mullido, -a [mu'ʎiðo, a] *adj* (*cama*) soft; (*hierba*) soft, springy
multa ['multa] *nf* fine; **echar** *o* **poner una ~ a** to fine
multar [mul'tar] *vt* to fine; (*Deporte*) to penalize
multiacceso [multjak'θeso] *adj* (*Inform*) multi-access
multicine [multi'θine] *nm* multiscreen cinema
multicolor [multiko'lor] *adj* multicoloured
multimillonario, -a [multimiʎo'narjo, a] *adj* (*contrato*) multimillion pound *o* dollar *cpd* ▪ *nm/f* multimillionaire/-millionairess
multinacional [multinaθjo'nal] *adj, nf* multinational
múltiple ['multiple] *adj* multiple, many *pl*, numerous; **de tarea ~** (*Inform*) multi-tasking; **de usuario ~** (*Inform*) multi-user
multiplicar [multipli'kar] *vt* (*Mat*) to multiply; (*fig*) to increase; **multiplicarse** *vr* (*Bio*) to multiply; (*fig*) to be everywhere at once
multiplique *etc* [multi'plike] *vb ver* **multiplicar**
múltiplo ['multiplo] *adj, nm* multiple
multitud [multi'tuð] *nf* (*muchedumbre*) crowd; **~ de** lots of
multitudinario, -a [multituði'narjo, a] *adj* (*numeroso*) multitudinous; (*de masas*) mass *cpd*
mundanal [munda'nal] *adj* worldly; **alejarse del ~ ruido** to get away from it all
mundano, -a [mun'dano, a] *adj* worldly; (*de moda*) fashionable
mundial [mun'djal] *adj* world-wide, universal; (*guerra, récord*) world *cpd*
mundialización [mundjaliθa'θjon] *nf* globalization
mundialmente [mundjal'mente] *adv* worldwide; **~ famoso** world-famous
mundo ['mundo] *nm* world; (*ámbito*) world, circle; **el otro ~** the next world; **el ~ del espectáculo** show business; **todo el ~** everybody; **tener ~** to be experienced, know

one's way around; **el ~ es un pañuelo** it's a small world; **no es nada del otro ~** it's nothing special; **se le cayó el ~ (encima)** his world fell apart

Munich ['munitʃ] *nm* Munich

munición [muni'θjon] *nf* (*Mil: provisiones*) stores *pl*, supplies *pl*; (*: de armas*) ammunition

municipal [muniθi'pal] *adj* (*elección*) municipal; (*concejo*) town *cpd*, local; (*piscina etc*) public ■ *nm* (*guardia*) policeman

municipio [muni'θipjo] *nm* (*ayuntamiento*) town council, corporation; (*territorio administrativo*) town, municipality

muñeca [mu'ɲeka] *nf* (*Anat*) wrist; (*juguete*) doll

muñeco [mu'ɲeko] *nm* (*figura*) figure; (*marioneta*) puppet; (*fig*) puppet, pawn; (*niño*) pretty little boy; **~ de nieve** snowman

muñequera [muɲe'kera] *nf* wristband

muñón [mu'ɲon] *nm* (*Anat*) stump

mural [mu'ral] *adj* mural, wall *cpd* ■ *nm* mural

muralla [mu'raʎa] *nf* (city) wall(s) *pl*

murciano, -a [mur'θjano, a] *adj* of *o* from Murcia ■ *nm/f* native *o* inhabitant of Murcia

murciélago [mur'θjelaɣo] *nm* bat

murga ['murɣa] *nf* (*banda*) band of street musicians; **dar la ~** to be a nuisance

murmullo [mur'muʎo] *nm* murmur(ing); (*cuchicheo*) whispering; (*de arroyo*) murmur, rippling; (*de hojas, viento*) rustle, rustling; (*ruido confuso*) hum(ming)

murmuración [murmura'θjon] *nf* gossip; (*críticas*) backbiting

murmurador, a [murmura'ðor, a] *adj* gossiping; (*criticón*) backbiting ■ *nm/f* gossip; backbiter

murmurar [murmu'rar] *vi* to murmur, whisper; (*criticar*) to criticize; (*cotillear*) to gossip

muro ['muro] *nm* wall; **~ de contención** retaining wall

mus [mus] *nm card game*

musaraña [musa'raɲa] *nf* (*Zool*) shrew; (*insecto*) creepy-crawly; **pensar en las musarañas** to daydream

muscular [musku'lar] *adj* muscular

músculo ['muskulo] *nm* muscle

musculoso, -a [musku'loso, a] *adj* muscular

museo [mu'seo] *nm* museum; **~ de arte** *o* **de pintura** art gallery; **~ de cera** waxworks

musgo ['musɣo] *nm* moss

musical [musi'kal] *adj, nm* musical

músico, -a ['musiko, a] *adj* musical ■ *nm/f* musician ■ *nf* music; **irse con la música a otra parte** to clear off

musitar [musi'tar] *vt, vi* to mutter, mumble

muslo ['muslo] *nm* thigh; (*de pollo*) leg, drumstick

mustio, -a ['mustjo, a] *adj* (*persona*) depressed, gloomy; (*planta*) faded, withered

musulmán, -ana [musul'man, ana] *nm/f* Moslem, Muslim

mutación [muta'θjon] *nf* (*Bio*) mutation; (*: cambio*) (sudden) change

mutilar [muti'lar] *vt* to mutilate; (*a una persona*) to maim

mutis ['mutis] *nm inv* (*Teat*) exit; **hacer ~** (*Teat: retirarse*) to exit, go off; (*fig*) to say nothing

mutismo [mu'tismo] *nm* silence

mutualidad [mutwali'ðað] *nf* (*reciprocidad*) mutual character; (*asociación*) friendly *o* benefit (US) society

mutuamente [mutwa'mente] *adv* mutually

mutuo, -a ['mutwo, a] *adj* mutual

muy [mwi] *adv* very; (*demasiado*) too; **M~ Señor mío** Dear Sir; **~ bien** (*de acuerdo*) all right; **~ de noche** very late at night; **eso es ~ de él** that's just like him; **eso es ~ español** that's typically Spanish

Nn

N, n ['ene] *nf* *(letra)* N, n; **N de Navarra** N for Nellie *(Brit)* *o* Nan *(US)*
N *abr* *(= norte)* N
N. *abr* = **carretera nacional** *(Am: = moneda nacional)* local currency; **le entregaron sólo N.$2.000** they only gave him $2000 pesos
N.° *abr* *(= número)* No
n. *abr* *(Ling: = nombre)* n; = **nacido, a**
n/ *abr* = **nuestro, a**
nabo ['naβo] *nm* turnip
nácar ['nakar] *nm* mother-of-pearl
nacer [na'θer] *vi* to be born; *(huevo)* to hatch; *(vegetal)* to sprout; *(río)* to rise; *(fig)* to begin, originate, have its origins; **nació para poeta** he was born to be a poet; **nadie nace enseñado** we all have to learn; **nació una sospecha en su mente** a suspicion formed in her mind
nacido, -a [na'θiðo, a] *adj* born; **recién ~** newborn
naciente [na'θjente] *adj* new, emerging; *(sol)* rising
nacimiento [naθi'mjento] *nm* birth; *(fig)* birth, origin; *(de Navidad)* Nativity; *(linaje)* descent, family; *(de río)* source; **ciego de ~** blind from birth
nación [na'θjon] *nf* nation; *(pueblo)* people; **Naciones Unidas** United Nations
nacional [naθjo'nal] *adj* national; *(Com, Econ)* domestic, home *cpd*
nacionalice *etc* [naθjona'liθe] *vb ver* **nacionalizar**
nacionalidad [naθjonali'ðað] *nf* nationality; *(Esp, Pol)* autonomous region
nacionalismo [naθjona'lismo] *nm* nationalism
nacionalista [naθjona'lista] *adj, nm/f* nationalist
nacionalizar [naθjonali'θar] *vt* to nationalize; **nacionalizarse** *vr* *(persona)* to become naturalized
nada ['naða] *pron* nothing ▪ *adv* not at all, in no way ▪ *nf* nothingness; **no decir ~ (más)** to say nothing (else), not to say anything (else); **¡~ más!** that's all; **de ~** don't mention it; **~ de eso** nothing of the kind; **antes de ~** right away; **como si ~** as if it didn't matter; **no ha sido ~** it's nothing; **la ~** the void
nadador, a [naða'ðor, a] *nm/f* swimmer
nadar [na'ðar] *vi* to swim; **~ en la abundancia** *(fig)* to be rolling in money
nadie ['naðje] *pron* nobody, no-one; **~ habló** nobody spoke; **no había ~** there was nobody there, there wasn't anybody there; **es un don ~** he's a nobody *o* nonentity
nadita [na'ðita] *(esp Am: fam)* = **nada**
nado ['naðo]: **a ~** *adv*: **pasar a ~** to swim across
nafta ['nafta] *nf* *(Am)* petrol *(Brit)*, gas(oline) *(US)*
naftalina [nafta'lina] *nf*: **bolas de ~** mothballs
náhuatl ['nawatl] *adj, nm* Nahuatl
naipe ['naipe] *nm* (playing) card; **naipes** *nmpl* cards
nal. *abr* *(= nacional)* nat
nalgas ['nalɣas] *nfpl* buttocks
Namibia [na'miβja] *nf* Namibia
nana ['nana] *nf* lullaby
napias ['napjas] *nfpl* *(fam)* conk *sg*
Nápoles ['napoles] *nf* Naples
napolitano, -a [napoli'tano, a] *adj* of *o* from Naples, Neapolitan ▪ *nm/f* Neapolitan
naranja [na'ranxa] *adj inv, nf* orange; **media ~** *(fam)* better half; **¡naranjas de la China!** nonsense!
naranjada [naran'xaða] *nf* orangeade
naranjo [na'ranxo] *nm* orange tree
Narbona [nar'βona] *nf* Narbonne
narcisista [narθi'sista] *adj* narcissistic
narciso [nar'θiso] *nm* narcissus
narcotice *etc* [narko'tiθe] *vb ver* **narcotizar**
narcótico, -a [nar'kotiko, a] *adj, nm* narcotic
narcotizar [narkoti'θar] *vt* to drug
narcotraficante [narkotrafi'kante] *nm/f* narcotics *o* drug trafficker

narcotráfico [narko'trafiko] *nm* narcotics *o* drug trafficking
nardo ['narðo] *nm* lily
narices [na'riθes] *nfpl ver* **nariz**
narigón, -ona [nari'ɣon, ona], **narigudo, a** [nari'ɣuðo, a] *adj* big-nosed
nariz [na'riθ] *nf* nose; **narices** *nfpl* nostrils; **¡narices!** (*fam*) rubbish!; **delante de las narices de algn** under one's (very) nose; **estar hasta las narices** to be completely fed up; **meter las narices en algo** to poke one's nose into sth
narración [narra'θjon] *nf* narration
narrador, a [narra'ðor, a] *nm/f* narrator
narrar [na'rrar] *vt* to narrate, recount
narrativo, -a [narra'tiβo, a] *adj* narrative ▪ *nf* narrative, story
nasal [na'sal] *adj* nasal
N.ª *abr* = **Nuestra Señora**
nata ['nata] *nf* cream (*tb fig*); (*en leche cocida etc*) skin; **~ batida** whipped cream
natación [nata'θjon] *nf* swimming
natal [na'tal] *adj* natal; (*país*) native; **ciudad ~** home town
natalicio [nata'liθjo] *nm* birthday
natalidad [natali'ðað] *nf* birth rate
natillas [na'tiʎas] *nfpl* (egg) custard *sg*
natividad [natiβi'ðað] *nf* nativity
nativo, -a [na'tiβo, a] *adj, nm/f* native
nato, -a ['nato, a] *adj* born; **un músico ~** a born musician
natural [natu'ral] *adj* natural; (*fruta etc*) fresh ▪ *nm/f* native ▪ *nm* disposition, temperament; **buen ~** good nature; **fruta al ~** fruit in its own juice
naturaleza [natura'leθa] *nf* nature; (*género*) nature, kind; **~ muerta** still life
naturalice *etc* [natura'liθe] *vb ver* **naturalizarse**
naturalidad [naturali'ðað] *nf* naturalness
naturalización [naturaliθa'θjon] *nf* naturalization
naturalizarse [naturali'θarse] *vr* to become naturalized; (*aclimatarse*) to become acclimatized
naturalmente [natural'mente] *adv* naturally; **¡~!** of course!
naturista [natu'rista] *adj* (*Med*) naturopathic ▪ *nm/f* naturopath
naufragar [naufra'ɣar] *vi* (*barco*) to sink; (*gente*) to be shipwrecked; (*fig*) to fail
naufragio [nau'fraxjo] *nm* shipwreck
náufrago, -a ['naufraɣo, a] *nm/f* castaway, shipwrecked person
naufrague *etc* [nau'fraɣe] *vb ver* **naufragar**
náusea ['nausea] *nf* nausea; **me da náuseas** it makes me feel sick
nauseabundo, -a [nausea'βundo, a] *adj* nauseating, sickening
náutico, -a ['nautiko, a] *adj* nautical; **club ~** sailing *o* yacht club ▪ *nf* navigation, seamanship
navaja [na'βaxa] *nf* (*cortaplumas*) clasp knife (*Brit*), penknife; **~ (de afeitar)** razor
navajazo [naβa'xaθo] *nm* (*herida*) gash; (*acto*) slash
naval [na'βal] *adj* (*Mil*) naval; **construcción ~** shipbuilding; **sector ~** shipbuilding industry
Navarra [na'βarra] *nf* Navarre
navarro, -a [na'βarro, a] *adj* of *o* from Navarre, Navarrese ▪ *nm/f* Navarrese ▪ *nm* (*Ling*) Navarrese
nave ['naβe] *nf* (*barco*) ship, vessel; (*Arq*) nave; **~ espacial** spaceship; **quemar las naves** to burn one's boats
navegación [naβeɣa'θjon] *nf* navigation; (*viaje*) sea journey; **~ aérea** air traffic; **~ costera** coastal shipping; **~ fluvial** river navigation
navegador [naβeɣa'ðor] *nm* (*Inform*) browser; (*de coche*) sat nav
navegante [naβe'ɣante] *nm/f* navigator
navegar [naβe'ɣar] *vi* (*barco*) to sail; (*avión*) to fly ▪ *vt* to sail; to fly; (*dirigir el rumbo de*) to navigate
navegue *etc* [na'βeɣe] *vb ver* **navegar**
navidad [naβi'ðað] *nf* Christmas; **navidades** *nfpl* Christmas time *sg*; **día de ~** Christmas Day; **por navidades** at Christmas (time); **¡felices navidades!** Merry Christmas
navideño, -a [naβi'ðeɲo, a] *adj* Christmas *cpd*
navío [na'βio] *nm* ship
nazi ['naθi] *adj, nm/f* Nazi
nazismo [na'θismo] *nm* Nazism
N. de la R. *abr* (= *nota de la redacción*) editor's note
N. de la T./del T. *abr* (= *nota de la traductora/del traductor*) translator's note
NE *abr* (= *nor(d)este*) NE
neblina [ne'βlina] *nf* mist
nebuloso, -a [neβu'loso, a] *adj* foggy; (*calinoso*) misty; (*indefinido*) nebulous, vague ▪ *nf* nebula
necedad [neθe'ðað] *nf* foolishness; (*una necedad*) foolish act
necesario, -a [neθe'sarjo, a] *adj* necessary; **si fuera** *o* **fuese ~** if need(s) be
neceser [neθe'ser] *nm* vanity case; (*bolsa grande*) holdall
necesidad [neθesi'ðað] *nf* need; (*lo inevitable*) necessity; (*miseria*) poverty, need; **en caso de ~** in case of need *o* emergency; **hacer sus necesidades** to relieve o.s.

necesitado, -a [neθesi'taðo, a] *adj* needy, poor; **~ de** in need of
necesitar [neθesi'tar] *vt* to need, require ■ *vi*: **~ de** to have need of; **necesitarse** *vr* to be needed; *(en anuncios)*: **"necesítase coche"** "car wanted"
necio, -a ['neθjo, a] *adj* foolish ■ *nm/f* fool
necrología [nekrolo'xia] *nf* obituary
necrópolis [ne'kropolis] *nf inv* cemetery
néctar ['nektar] *nm* nectar
nectarina [nekta'rina] *nf* nectarine
neerlandés, -esa [neerlan'des, esa] *adj* Dutch ■ *nm/f* Dutchman(-woman) ■ *nm* *(Ling)* Dutch; **los neerlandeses** the Dutch
nefando, -a [ne'fando, a] *adj* unspeakable
nefasto, -a [ne'fasto, a] *adj* ill-fated, unlucky
negación [neɣa'θjon] *nf* negation; *(Ling)* negative; *(rechazo)* refusal, denial
negado, -a [ne'ɣaðo, a] *adj*: **~ para** inept at, unfitted for
negar [ne'ɣar] *vt* *(renegar, rechazar)* to refuse; *(prohibir)* to refuse, deny; *(desmentir)* to deny; **negarse** *vr*: **negarse a hacer algo** to refuse to do sth
negativo, -a [neɣa'tiβo, a] *adj* negative ■ *nm* *(Foto)* negative; *(Mat)* minus ■ *nf* *(gen)* negative; *(rechazo)* refusal, denial; **negativa rotunda** flat refusal
negligencia [neɣli'xenθja] *nf* negligence
negligente [neɣli'xente] *adj* negligent
negociable [neɣo'θjaβle] *adj* negotiable
negociación [neɣoθja'θjon] *nf* negotiation
negociado [neɣo'θjaðo] *nm* department, section
negociante [neɣo'θjante] *nm/f* businessman(-woman)
negociar [neɣo'θjar] *vt, vi* to negotiate; **~ en** to deal in, trade in
negocio [ne'ɣoθjo] *nm* *(Com)* business; *(asunto)* affair, business; *(operación comercial)* deal, transaction; *(Am)* shop, store; *(lugar)* place of business; **los negocios** business *sg*; **hacer ~** to do business; **el ~ del libro** the book trade; **~ autorizado** licensed trade; **hombre de negocios** businessman; **~ sucio** shady deal; **hacer un buen ~** to pull off a profitable deal; **¡mal ~!** it looks bad!
negra ['neɣra] *nf ver* **negro** ■ *nf* *(Mus)* crotchet
negrita [ne'ɣrita] *nf* *(Tip)* bold face; **en ~** in bold (type)
negro, -a ['neɣro, a] *adj* black; *(suerte)* awful, atrocious; *(humor etc)* sad; *(lúgubre)* gloomy ■ *nm* *(color)* black ■ *nm/f* Negro/Negress, black ■ *nf* *(Mus)* crotchet; **~ como la boca del lobo** pitch-black; **estoy ~ con esto** I'm getting desperate about it; **ponerse ~** *(fam)* to get cross
negrura [ne'ɣrura] *nf* blackness
negué [ne'ɣe], **neguemos** *etc* [ne'ɣemos] *vb ver* **negar**
nene, -a ['nene, a] *nm/f* baby, small child
nenúfar [ne'nufar] *nm* water lily
neologismo [neolo'xismo] *nm* neologism
neón [ne'on] *nm* neon
neoyorquino, -a [neojor'kino, a] *adj* New York *cpd* ■ *nm/f* New Yorker
neozelandés, -esa [neoθelan'des, esa] *adj* New Zealand *cpd* ■ *nm/f* New Zealander
nepotismo [nepo'tismo] *nm* nepotism
nervio ['nerβjo] *nm* *(Anat)* nerve; *(: tendón)* tendon; *(fig)* vigour; *(Tec)* rib; **crispar los nervios a algn, poner los nervios de punta a algn** to get on sb's nerves
nerviosismo [nerβjo'sismo] *nm* nervousness, nerves *pl*
nervioso, -a [ner'βjoso, a] *adj* nervous; *(sensible)* nervy, highly-strung; *(impaciente)* restless; **¡no te pongas ~!** take it easy!
nervudo, -a [ner'βuðo, a] *adj* tough; *(mano)* sinewy
neto, -a ['neto, a] *adj* clear; *(limpio)* clean; *(Com)* net
neumático, -a [neu'matiko, a] *adj* pneumatic ■ *nm* *(Esp)* tyre *(Brit)*, tire *(US)*; **~ de recambio** spare tyre
neumonía [neumo'nia] *nf* pneumonia; **~ asiática** SARS
neura ['neura] *(fam)* *nm/f* *(persona)* neurotic ■ *nf* *(obsesión)* obsession
neuralgia [neu'ralxja] *nf* neuralgia
neurálgico, -a [neu'ralxiko, a] *adj* neuralgic; *(fig: centro)* nerve *cpd*
neurastenia [neuras'tenja] *nf* neurasthenia; *(fig)* excitability
neurasténico, -a [neuras'teniko, a] *adj* neurasthenic; excitable
neurólogo, -a [neu'roloɣo, a] *nm/f* neurologist
neurona [neu'rona] *nf* neuron
neurosis [neu'rosis] *nf inv* neurosis
neurótico, -a [neu'rotiko, a] *adj, nm/f* neurotic
neutral [neu'tral] *adj* neutral
neutralice *etc* [neutra'liθe] *vb ver* **neutralizar**
neutralizar [neutrali'θar] *vt* to neutralize; *(contrarrestar)* to counteract
neutro, -a ['neutro, a] *adj* *(Bio, Ling)* neuter
neutrón [neu'tron] *nm* neutron
nevado, -a [ne'βaðo, a] *adj* snow-covered; *(montaña)* snow-capped; *(fig)* snowy, snow-white ■ *nf* snowstorm; *(caída de nieve)* snowfall
nevar [ne'βar] *vi* to snow ■ *vt* *(fig)* to whiten
nevera [ne'βera] *nf* *(Esp)* refrigerator *(Brit)*, icebox *(US)*

nevisca [ne'βiska] *nf* flurry of snow
nexo ['nekso] *nm* link, connection
n/f *abr* (*Com*) = **nuestro favor**
ni [ni] *conj* nor, neither; (*tb*: **ni siquiera**) not even; **ni que** not even if; **ni blanco ni negro** neither white nor black; **ni el uno ni el otro** neither one nor the other
Nicaragua [nika'raɣwa] *nf* Nicaragua
nicaragüense [nikara'ɣwense] *adj, nm/f* Nicaraguan
nicho ['nitʃo] *nm* niche
nick [nik] *nm* (*Internet*) nickname, user name, nick
nicotina [niko'tina] *nf* nicotine
nido ['niðo] *nm* nest; (*fig*) hiding place; **~ de ladrones** den of thieves
niebla ['njeβla] *nf* fog; (*neblina*) mist; **hay ~** it is foggy
niego *etc* ['njeɣo], **niegue** *etc* ['njeɣe] *vb ver* **negar**
nieto, -a ['njeto, a] *nm/f* grandson/granddaughter; **nietos** *nmpl* grandchildren
nieve *etc* ['njeβe] *vb ver* **nevar** ■ *nf* snow; (*Am*) ice cream; **copo de ~** snowflake
N.I.F. *nm abr* (= *Número de Identificación Fiscal*) *ID number used for tax purposes*
Nigeria [ni'xerja] *nf* Nigeria
nigeriano, -a [nixe'rjano, a] *adj, nm/f* Nigerian
nigromancia [niɣro'manθja] *nf* necromancy, black magic
nihilista [nii'lista] *adj* nihilistic ■ *nm* nihilist
Nilo ['nilo] *nm*: **el (Río) ~** the Nile
nimbo ['nimbo] *nm* (*aureola*) halo; (*nube*) nimbus
nimiedad [nimje'ðað] *nf* small-mindedness; (*trivialidad*) triviality; (*una nimiedad*) trifle, tiny detail
nimio, -a ['nimjo, a] *adj* trivial, insignificant
ninfa ['ninfa] *nf* nymph
ninfómana [nin'fomana] *nf* nymphomaniac
ninguno, -a [nin'guno, a] *adj* (*antes de nmsg* **ningún**) no ■ *pron* (*nadie*) nobody; (*ni uno*) none, not one; (*ni uno ni otro*) neither; **de ninguna manera** by no means, not at all; **no voy a ninguna parte** I'm not going anywhere
niña ['niɲa] *nf ver* **niño**
niñera [ni'ɲera] *nf* nursemaid, nanny
niñería [niɲe'ria] *nf* childish act
niñez [ni'ɲeθ] *nf* childhood; (*infancia*) infancy
niño, -a ['niɲo, a] *adj* (*joven*) young; (*inmaduro*) immature ■ *nm* (*chico*) boy, child ■ *nf* girl, child; (*Anat*) pupil; **los niños** the children; **~ bien** rich kid; **~ expósito** foundling; **~ de pecho** babe-in-arms; **~ prodigio** child prodigy; **de ~** as a child; **ser el ~ mimado de algn** to be sb's pet; **ser la niña de los ojos de algn** to be the apple of sb's eye
nipón, -ona [ni'pon, ona] *adj, nm/f* Japanese; **los nipones** the Japanese
níquel ['nikel] *nm* nickel
niquelar [nike'lar] *vt* (*Tec*) to nickel-plate
níspero ['nispero] *nm* medlar
nitidez [niti'ðeθ] *nf* (*claridad*) clarity; (*: de atmósfera*) brightness; (*: de imagen*) sharpness
nítido, -a ['nitiðo, a] *adj* bright; (*fig*) pure; (*imagen*) clear, sharp
nitrato [ni'trato] *nm* nitrate
nitrógeno [ni'troxeno] *nm* nitrogen
nitroglicerina [nitroɣliθe'rina] *nf* nitroglycerine
nivel [ni'βel] *nm* (*Geo*) level; (*norma*) level, standard; (*altura*) height; **~ de aceite** oil level; **~ de aire** spirit level; **~ de vida** standard of living; **al ~ de** on a level with, at the same height as; (*fig*) on a par with; **a 900m sobre el ~ del mar** at 900m above sea level
nivelado, -a [niβe'laðo, a] *adj* level, flat; (*Tec*) flush
nivelar [niβe'lar] *vt* to level out; (*fig*) to even up; (*Com*) to balance
Niza ['niθa] *nf* Nice
n/l. *abr* (*Com*) = **nuestra letra**
NNE *abr* (= *nornordeste*) NNE
NNO *abr* (= *nornoroeste*) NNW
NN. UU. *nfpl abr* (= *Naciones Unidas*) UN *sg*
NO *abr* (= *noroeste*) NW
no [no] *adv* no; (*con verbo*) not ■ *excl* no!; **no tengo nada** I don't have anything, I have nothing; **no es el mío** it's not mine; **ahora no** not now; **¿no lo sabes?** don't you know?; **no mucho** not much; **no bien termine, lo entregaré** as soon as I finish I'll hand it over; **¡a que no lo sabes!** I bet you don't know!; **¡cómo no!** of course!; **pacto de no agresión** non-aggression pact; **los países no alineados** the non-aligned countries; **el no va más** the ultimate; **la no intervención** non-intervention
n/o *abr* (*Com*) = **nuestra orden**
noble ['noβle] *adj, nm/f* noble; **los nobles** the nobility *sg*
nobleza [noβ'leθa] *nf* nobility
noche ['notʃe] *nf* night, night-time; (*la tarde*) evening; (*fig*) darkness; **de ~, por la ~** at night; **ayer por la ~** last night; **esta ~** tonight; **(en) toda la ~** all night; **hacer ~ en un sitio** to spend the night in a place; **se hace de ~** it's getting dark
Nochebuena [notʃe'βwena] *nf* Christmas Eve; *see note*

NOCHEBUENA

On *Nochebuena* in Spanish homes there is normally a large supper when family members come from all over to be together. The more religiously inclined attend *la misa del gallo* at midnight. The tradition of receiving Christmas presents from Santa Claus that night is becoming more and more widespread and gradually replacing the tradition of *los Reyes Magos* (The Three Wise Men) on the 6th of January.

Nochevieja [notʃe'βjexa] *nf* New Year's Eve; *ver tb* **uvas**
noción [no'θjon] *nf* notion; **nociones** *nfpl* elements, rudiments
nocivo, -a [no'θiβo, a] *adj* harmful
noctambulismo [noktambu'lismo] *nm* sleepwalking
noctámbulo, -a [nok'tambulo, a] *nm/f* sleepwalker
nocturno, -a [nok'turno, a] *adj* (*de la noche*) nocturnal, night *cpd*; (*de la tarde*) evening *cpd* ■ *nm* nocturne
Noé [no'e] *nm* Noah
nogal [no'ɣal] *nm* walnut tree; (*madera*) walnut
nómada ['nomaða] *adj* nomadic ■ *nm/f* nomad
nomás [no'mas] *adv* (*Am: gen*) just; (*: tan sólo*) only; **así ~** (*Am fam*) just like that; **ayer ~** only yesterday ■ *conj* (*Am: en cuanto*): **~ se fue se acordó** no sooner had she left than she remembered
nombramiento [nombra'mjento] *nm* naming; (*para un empleo*) appointment; (*Pol etc*) nomination; (*Mil*) commission
nombrar [nom'brar] *vt* (*gen*) to name; (*mencionar*) to mention; (*designar*) to appoint, nominate; (*Mil*) to commission
nombre ['nombre] *nm* name; (*sustantivo*) noun; (*fama*) renown; **~ y apellidos** name in full; **~ común/propio** common/proper noun; **~ de pila/de soltera** Christian/ maiden name; **~ de fichero** (*Inform*) file name; **en ~ de** in the name of, on behalf of; **sin ~** nameless; **su conducta no tiene ~** his behaviour is utterly despicable
nomenclatura [nomenkla'tura] *nf* nomenclature
nomeolvides [nomeol'βiðes] *nm inv* forget-me-not
nómina ['nomina] *nf* (*lista*) list; (*Com: tb:* **nóminas**) payroll
nominal [nomi'nal] *adj* nominal; (*valor*) face *cpd*; (*Ling*) noun *cpd*, substantival
nominar [nomi'nar] *vt* to nominate
nominativo, -a [nomina'tiβo, a] *adj* (*Ling*) nominative; (*Com*): **un cheque ~ a X** a cheque made out to X
non [non] *adj* odd, uneven ■ *nm* odd number; **pares y nones** odds and evens
nonagésimo, -a [nona'xesimo, a] *num* ninetieth
nono, -a ['nono, a] *num* ninth
nordeste [nor'ðeste] *adj* north-east, north-eastern, north-easterly ■ *nm* north-east; (*viento*) north-east wind, north-easterly
nórdico, -a ['norðiko, a] *adj* (*del norte*) northern, northerly; (*escandinavo*) Nordic, Norse ■ *nm/f* northerner; (*escandinavo*) Norseman/-woman ■ *nm* (*Ling*) Norse
noreste [no'reste] *adj, nm* = **nordeste**
noria ['norja] *nf* (*Agr*) waterwheel; (*de carnaval*) big (*Brit*) *o* Ferris (*US*) wheel
norma ['norma] *nf* standard, norm, rule; (*patrón*) pattern; (*método*) method
normal [nor'mal] *adj* (*corriente*) normal; (*habitual*) usual, natural; (*Tec*) standard; **Escuela N~** teacher training college; **(gasolina) ~** two-star petrol
normalice *etc* [norma'liθe] *vb ver* **normalizar**
normalidad [normali'ðað] *nf* normality
normalización [normaliθa'θjon] *nf* (*Com*) standardization
normalizar [normali'θar] *vt* (*reglamentar*) to normalize; (*Com, Tec*) to standardize; **normalizarse** *vr* to return to normal
normalmente [normal'mente] *adv* (*con normalidad*) normally; (*habitualmente*) usually
Normandía [norman'dia] *nf* Normandy
normando, -a [nor'mando, a] *adj, nm/f* Norman
normativo, -a [norma'tiβo, a] *adj*: **es ~ en todos los coches nuevos** it is standard in all new cars ■ *nf* regulations *pl*
noroeste [noro'este] *adj* north-west, north-western, north-westerly ■ *nm* north-west; (*viento*) north-west wind, north-westerly
norte ['norte] *adj* north, northern, northerly ■ *nm* north; (*fig*) guide
Norteamérica [nortea'merika] *nf* North America
norteamericano, -a [norteameri'kano, a] *adj, nm/f* (North) American
norteño, -a [nor'teɲo, a] *adj* northern ■ *nm/f* northerner
Noruega [no'rweɣa] *nf* Norway
noruego, -a [no'rweɣo, a] *adj, nm/f* Norwegian ■ *nm* (*Ling*) Norwegian
nos [nos] *pron* (*directo*) us; (*indirecto*) (to) us; (*reflexivo*) (to) ourselves; (*recíproco*) (to) each

other; **~ levantamos a las siete** we get up at seven
nosocomio [noso'komio] *nm* (*Am*) hospital
nosotros, -as [no'sotros, as] *pron* (*sujeto*) we; (*después de prep*) us; **~ (mismos)** ourselves
nostalgia [nos'talxja] *nf* nostalgia, homesickness
nostálgico, -a [nos'talxiko, a] *adj* nostalgic, homesick
nota ['nota] *nf* note; (*Escol*) mark; (*de fin de año*) report; (*Univ etc*) footnote; (*Com*) account; **~ de aviso** advice note; **~ de crédito/débito** credit/debit note; **~ de gastos** expenses claim; **~ de sociedad** gossip column; **tomar notas** to take notes
notable [no'taβle] *adj* noteworthy, notable; (*Escol etc*) outstanding ■ *nm/f* notable
notar [no'tar] *vt* to notice, note; (*percibir*) to feel; (*ver*) to see; **notarse** *vr* to be obvious; **se nota que ...** one observes that ...
notaría [nota'ria] *nf* (*profesión*) profession of notary; (*despacho*) notary's office
notarial [nota'rjal] *adj* (*estilo*) legal; **acta ~** affidavit
notario [no'tarjo] *nm* notary; (*abogado*) solicitor
noticia [no'tiθja] *nf* (*información*) piece of news; (*TV etc*) news item; **las noticias** the news *sg*; **según nuestras noticias** according to our information; **tener noticias de algn** to hear from sb
noticiario [noti'θjarjo] *nm* (*Cine*) newsreel; (*TV*) news bulletin
noticiero [noti'θjero] *nm* newspaper, gazette; (*Am*: *tb*: **noticiero telediario**) news bulletin
notificación [notifika'θjon] *nf* notification
notificar [notifi'kar] *vt* to notify, inform
notifique *etc* [noti'fike] *vb ver* **notificar**
notoriedad [notorje'ðað] *nf* fame, renown
notorio, -a [no'torjo, a] *adj* (*público*) well-known; (*evidente*) obvious
nov. *abr* (= *noviembre*) Nov.
novatada [noβa'taða] *nf* (*burla*) teasing, hazing (*US*); **pagar la ~** to learn the hard way
novato, -a [no'βato, a] *adj* inexperienced ■ *nm/f* beginner, novice
novecientos, -as [noβe'θjentos, as] *num* nine hundred
novedad [noβe'ðað] *nf* (*calidad de nuevo*) newness, novelty; (*noticia*) piece of news; (*cambio*) change, (new) development; (*sorpresa*) surprise; **novedades** *nfpl* (*noticia*) latest (news) *sg*
novedoso, -a [noβe'ðoso, a] *adj* novel
novel [no'βel] *adj* new; (*inexperto*) inexperienced ■ *nm/f* beginner
novela [no'βela] *nf* novel; **~ policíaca** detective story
novelero, -a [noβe'lero, a] *adj* highly imaginative
novelesco, -a [noβe'lesko, a] *adj* fictional; (*romántico*) romantic; (*fantástico*) fantastic
novelista [noβe'lista] *nm/f* novelist
novelística [noβe'listika] *nf*: **la ~** fiction, the novel
noveno, -a [no'βeno, a] *num* ninth
noventa [no'βenta] *num* ninety
novia ['noβja] *nf ver* **novio**
noviazgo [no'βjaθɣo] *nm* engagement
novicio, -a [no'βiθjo, a] *nm/f* novice
noviembre [no'βjembre] *nm* November; *ver tb* **julio**
novilla [no'βiʎa] *nf* heifer
novillada [noβi'ʎaða] *nf* (*Taur*) *bullfight with young bulls*
novillero [noβi'ʎero] *nm* novice bullfighter
novillo [no'βiʎo] *nm* young bull, bullock; **hacer novillos** (*fam*) to play truant (*Brit*) *o* hooky (*US*)
novio, -a ['noβjo, a] *nm/f* boyfriend/girlfriend; (*prometido*) fiancé/fiancée; (*recién casado*) bridegroom/bride; **los novios** the newly-weds
novísimo, -a [no'βisimo, a] *adj superlativo de* **nuevo, a**
NPI *nm abr* (*Inform*: = *número personal de identificación*) PIN
N. S. *abr* = **Nuestro Señor**
ns/nc *abr* = **no sabe(n)/no contesta(n)**
ntra., ntro. *abr* = **nuestra, nuestro**
Ntro. Sr. *abr* = **Nuestro Señor**
NU *nfpl abr* (= *Naciones Unidas*) UN *sg*
nubarrón [nuβa'rron] *nm* storm cloud
nube ['nuβe] *nf* cloud; (*Med*: *ocular*) cloud, film; (*fig*) mass; **una ~ de críticas** a storm of criticism; **los precios están por las nubes** prices are sky-high; **estar en las nubes** to be away with the fairies
nublado, -a [nu'βlaðo, a] *adj* cloudy ■ *nm* storm cloud
nublar [nu'βlar] *vt* (*oscurecer*) to darken; (*confundir*) to cloud; **nublarse** *vr* to cloud over
nuca ['nuka] *nf* nape of the neck
nuclear [nukle'ar] *adj* nuclear
nuclearizado, -a [nukleari'θaðo, a] *adj*: **países nuclearizados** countries possessing nuclear weapons
núcleo ['nukleo] *nm* (*centro*) core; (*Física*) nucleus
nudillo [nu'ðiʎo] *nm* knuckle
nudista [nu'ðista] *adj, nm/f* nudist
nudo ['nuðo] *nm* knot; (*unión*) bond; (*de problema*) crux; (*Ferro*) junction; (*fig*) lump;

~ **corredizo** slipknot; **con un ~ en la garganta** with a lump in one's throat
nudoso, -a [nu'ðoso, a] *adj* knotty; (*tronco*) gnarled; (*bastón*) knobbly
nueces ['nweθes] *nfpl de* **nuez**
nuera ['nwera] *nf* daughter-in-law
nuestro, -a ['nwestro, a] *adj posesivo* our ■ *pron* ours; ~ **padre** our father; **un amigo** ~ a friend of ours; **es el** ~ it's ours; **los nuestros** our people; (*Deporte*) our *o* the local team *o* side
nueva ['nweβa] *nf ver* **nuevo**
Nueva Escocia *nf* Nova Scotia
nuevamente [nweβa'mente] *adv* (*otra vez*) again; (*de nuevo*) anew
Nueva York [-'jork] *nf* New York
Nueva Zelanda [-θe'landa], **Nueva Zelandia** [-θe'landja] *nf* New Zealand
nueve ['nweβe] *num* nine
nuevo, -a ['nweβo, a] *adj* (*gen*) new ■ *nf* piece of news; **¿qué hay de ~?** (*fam*) what's new?; **de** ~ again
Nuevo Méjico *nm* New Mexico
nuez [nweθ] (*pl* **nueces**) *nf* nut; (*del nogal*) walnut; ~ **de Adán** Adam's apple; ~ **moscada** nutmeg
nulidad [nuli'ðað] *nf* (*incapacidad*) incompetence; (*abolición*) nullity; (*individuo*) nonentity; **es una** ~ he's a dead loss
nulo, -a ['nulo, a] *adj* (*inepto, torpe*) useless; (*inválido*) (null and) void; (*Deporte*) drawn, tied
núm. *abr* (= *número*) no.
numen ['numen] *nm* inspiration
numeración [numera'θjon] *nf* (*cifras*) numbers *pl*; (*arábiga, romana etc*) numerals *pl*; ~ **de línea** (*Inform*) line numbering
numerador [numera'ðor] *nm* (*Mat*) numerator
numeral [nume'ral] *nm* numeral
numerar [nume'rar] *vt* to number; **numerarse** *vr* (*Mil etc*) to number off
numerario, -a [nume'rarjo, a] *adj* numerary; **profesor** ~ permanent *o* tenured member of teaching staff ■ *nm* hard cash
numérico, -a [nu'meriko, a] *adj* numerical
número ['numero] *nm* (*gen*) number; (*tamaño: de zapato*) size; (*ejemplar: de diario*) number, issue; (*Teat etc*) turn, act, number; **sin** ~ numberless, unnumbered; ~ **binario** (*Inform*) binary number; ~ **de matrícula/de teléfono** registration/telephone number; ~ **personal de identificación** (*Inform etc*) personal identification number; ~ **de serie** (*Com*) serial number; ~ **atrasado** back number
numeroso, -a [nume'roso, a] *adj* numerous; **familia numerosa** large family
numerus ['numerus] *nm*: ~ **clausus** (*Univ*) restricted *o* selective entry
nunca ['nunka] *adv* (*jamás*) never; (*con verbo negativo*) ever; ~ **lo pensé** I never thought it; **no viene** ~ he never comes; ~ **más** never again
nuncio ['nunθjo] *nm* (*Rel*) nuncio
nupcial [nup'θjal] *adj* wedding *cpd*
nupcias ['nupθjas] *nfpl* wedding *sg*, nuptials
nutria ['nutrja] *nf* otter
nutrición [nutri'θjon] *nf* nutrition
nutrido, -a [nu'triðo, a] *adj* (*alimentado*) nourished; (*fig: grande*) large; (*abundante*) abundant; **mal** ~ undernourished; ~ **de** full of
nutrir [nu'trir] *vt* to feed, nourish; (*fig*) to feed, strengthen
nutritivo, -a [nutri'tiβo, a] *adj* nourishing, nutritious
nylon [ni'lon] *nm* nylon

Ññ

Ñ, ñ ['eɲe] *nf* (*letra*) Ñ ñ
ñato, -a ['ɲato, a] *adj* (*Am*) snub-nosed
ñoñería [ɲoɲe'ria], **ñoñez** [ɲo'ɲeθ] *nf* insipidness
ñoño, -a ['ɲoɲo, a] *adj* (*soso*) insipid; (*persona: débil*) spineless
ñoquis ['ɲokis] *nmpl* (*Culin*) gnocchio

Oo

O, o [o] *nf* (*letra*) O, o; **O de Oviedo** O for Oliver (*Brit*) *o* Oboe (*US*)
O *abr* (= *oeste*) W
o [o] *conj* or; **o ... o** either ... or; **o sea** that is
ó [o] *conj* (*en números para evitar confusión*) or; **cinco ó seis** five or six
o/ *nm* (*Com*: = *orden*) o
OACI *nf abr* (= *Organización de la Aviación Civil Internacional*) ICAO
oasis [o'asis] *nm inv* oasis
obcecado, -a [oβθe'kaðo, a] *adj* blind; (*terco*) stubborn
obcecarse [oβθe'karse] *vr* to be obstinate; **~ en hacer** to insist on doing
obceque *etc* [oβ'θeke] *vb ver* **obcecarse**
obedecer [oβeðe'θer] *vt* to obey; **~ a** (*Med etc*) to yield to; (*fig*): **~ a ..., ~ al hecho de que ...** to be due to ..., arise from ...
obedezca *etc* [oβe'ðeθka] *vb ver* **obedecer**
obediencia [oβe'ðjenθja] *nf* obedience
obediente [oβe'ðjente] *adj* obedient
obertura [oβer'tura] *nf* overture
obesidad [oβesi'ðað] *nf* obesity
obeso, -a [o'βeso, a] *adj* obese
óbice ['oβiθe] *nm* obstacle, impediment
obispado [oβis'paðo] *nm* bishopric
obispo [o'βispo] *nm* bishop
óbito ['oβito] *nm* demise
objeción [oβxe'θjon] *nf* objection; **hacer una ~, poner objeciones** to raise objections, object
objetar [oβxe'tar] *vt, vi* to object
objetivo, -a [oβxe'tiβo, a] *adj* objective ■ *nm* objective; (*fig*) aim; (*Foto*) lens
objeto [oβ'xeto] *nm* (*cosa*) object; (*fin*) aim
objetor, a [oβxe'tor, a] *nm/f* objector; **~ de conciencia** conscientious objector; *ver tb* **mili**
oblea [o'βlea] *nf* (*Rel, fig*) wafer
oblicuo, -a [o'βlikwo, a] *adj* oblique; (*mirada*) sidelong
obligación [oβliɣa'θjon] *nf* obligation; (*Com*) bond, debenture
obligar [oβli'ɣar] *vt* to force; **obligarse** *vr*: **obligarse a** to commit o.s. to
obligatorio, -a [oβliɣa'torjo, a] *adj* compulsory, obligatory
obligue *etc* [o'βliɣe] *vb ver* **obligar**
oboe [o'βoe] *nm* oboe; (*músico*) oboist
Ob.º *abr* (= *Obispo*) Bp
obra ['oβra] *nf* work; (*producción*) piece of work; (*Arq*) construction, building; (*libro*) book; (*Mus*) opus; (*Teat*) play; **~ de arte** work of art; **~ maestra** masterpiece; **~ de consulta** reference book; **obras completas** complete works; **~ benéfica** charity; **"obras"** (*en carretera*) "men at work"; **obras públicas** public works; **por ~ de** thanks to (the efforts of); **obras son amores y no buenas razones** actions speak louder than words
obrar [o'βrar] *vt* to work; (*tener efecto*) to have an effect on ■ *vi* to act, behave; (*tener efecto*) to have an effect; **la carta obra en su poder** the letter is in his/her possession
Ob.po *abr* = **obispo**
obr. cit. *abr* (= *obra citada*) op. cit.
obrero, -a [o'βrero, a] *adj* working; (*movimiento*) labour *cpd*; **clase obrera** working class ■ *nm/f* (*gen*) worker; (*sin oficio*) labourer
obscenidad [oβsθeni'ðað] *nf* obscenity
obsceno, -a [oβs'θeno, a] *adj* obscene
obscu... *pref* = **oscu...**
obsequiar [oβse'kjar] *vt* (*ofrecer*) to present; (*agasajar*) to make a fuss of, lavish attention on
obsequio [oβ'sekjo] *nm* (*regalo*) gift; (*cortesía*) courtesy, attention
obsequioso, -a [oβse'kjoso, a] *adj* attentive
observación [oβserβa'θjon] *nf* observation; (*reflexión*) remark; (*objeción*) objection
observador, a [oβserβa'ðor, a] *adj* observant ■ *nm/f* observer
observancia [oβser'βanθja] *nf* observance
observar [oβser'βar] *vt* to observe; (*notar*) to notice; (*leyes*) to observe, respect; (*reglas*) to abide by

observatorio [oβserβa'torjo] *nm* observatory; **~ del tiempo** weather station
obsesión [oβse'sjon] *nf* obsession
obsesionar [oβsesjo'nar] *vt* to obsess
obseso, -a [oβ'seso, a] *nm/f* (*sexual*) sex maniac
obsolescencia [oβsoles'θenθja] *nf*: **~ incorporada** (*Com*) built-in obsolescence
obsoleto, -a [oβso'leto, a] *adj* obsolete
obstaculice *etc* [oβstaku'liθe] *vb ver* **obstaculizar**
obstaculizar [oβstakuli'θar] *vt* (*dificultar*) to hinder, hamper
obstáculo [oβs'takulo] *nm* (*gen*) obstacle; (*impedimento*) hindrance, drawback
obstante [oβs'tante]: **no ~** *adv* nevertheless; (*de todos modos*) all the same *prep* in spite of
obstetra [oβs'tetra] *nm/f* obstetrician
obstetricia [oβste'triθja] *nf* obstetrics *sg*
obstinado, -a [oβsti'naðo, a] *adj* (*gen*) obstinate; (*terco*) stubborn
obstinarse [oβsti'narse] *vr* to dig one's heels in; **~ en** to persist in
obstrucción [oβstruk'θjon] *nf* obstruction
obstruir [oβstru'ir] *vt* to obstruct; (*bloquear*) to block; (*estorbar*) to hinder
obstruyendo *etc* [oβstru'jendo] *vb ver* **obstruir**
obtención [oβten'θjon] *nf* (*Com*) procurement
obtendré *etc* [oβten'dre] *vb ver* **obtener**
obtener [oβte'ner] *vt* (*conseguir*) to obtain; (*ganar*) to gain
obtenga *etc* [oβ'tenga] *vb ver* **obtener**
obturación [oβtura'θjon] *nf* plugging, stopping; (*Foto*): **velocidad de ~** shutter speed
obturador [oβtura'ðor] *nm* (*Foto*) shutter
obtuso, -a [oβ'tuso, a] *adj* (*filo*) blunt; (*Mat, fig*) obtuse
obtuve *etc* [oβ'tuβe] *vb ver* **obtener**
obús [o'βus] *nm* (*Mil*) shell
obviar [oβ'βjar] *vt* to obviate, remove
obvio, -a ['oββjo, a] *adj* obvious
oca ['oka] *nf* goose; (*tb*: **juego de la oca**) ≈ snakes and ladders
ocasión [oka'sjon] *nf* (*oportunidad*) opportunity, chance; (*momento*) occasion, time; (*causa*) cause; **de ~** secondhand; **con ~ de** on the occasion of; **en algunas ocasiones** sometimes; **aprovechar la ~** to seize one's opportunity
ocasionar [okasjo'nar] *vt* to cause
ocaso [o'kaso] *nm* sunset; (*fig*) decline
occidental [okθiðen'tal] *adj* western ■ *nm/f* westerner ■ *nm* west
occidente [okθi'ðente] *nm* west; **el O~** the West
occiso, -a [ok'θiso, a] *nm/f*: **el ~** the deceased; (*de asesinato*) the victim
O.C.D.E. *nf abr* (= *Organización de Cooperación y Desarrollo Económicos*) OECD
océano [o'θeano] *nm* ocean; **el ~ Índico** the Indian Ocean
ochenta [o'tʃenta] *num* eighty
ocho ['otʃo] *num* eight; (*fecha*) eighth; **~ días** a week
ochocientos, -as [otʃo'θjentos, as] *num* eight hundred
OCI ['oθi] *nf abr* (*Pol: Venezuela, Perú*) = **Oficina Central de Información**
ocio ['oθjo] *nm* (*tiempo*) leisure; (*pey*) idleness; **"guía del ~"** "what's on"
ociosidad [oθjosi'ðað] *nf* idleness
ocioso, -a [o'θjoso, a] *adj* (*inactivo*) idle; (*inútil*) useless
oct. *abr* (= *octubre*) Oct.
octanaje [okta'naxe] *nm*: **de alto ~** high octane
octano [ok'tano] *nm* octane
octavilla [okta'βiʎa] *nm* leaflet, pamphlet
octavo, -a [ok'taβo, a] *num* eighth
octeto [ok'teto] *nm* (*Inform*) byte
octogenario, -a [oktoxe'narjo, a] *adj, nm/f* octogenarian
octubre [ok'tuβre] *nm* October; *ver tb* **julio**
OCU ['oku] *nf abr* (*Esp:* = *Organización de Consumidores y Usuarios*) ≈ Consumers' Association
ocular [oku'lar] *adj* ocular, eye *cpd*; **testigo ~** eyewitness
oculista [oku'lista] *nm/f* oculist
ocultar [okul'tar] *vt* (*esconder*) to hide; (*callar*) to conceal; (*disfrazar*) to screen; **ocultarse** *vr* to hide (o.s.); **ocultarse a la vista** to keep out of sight
oculto, -a [o'kulto, a] *adj* hidden; (*fig*) secret
ocupación [okupa'θjon] *nf* occupation; (*tenencia*) occupancy
ocupado, -a [oku'paðo, a] *adj* (*persona*) busy; (*plaza*) occupied, taken; (*teléfono*) engaged; **¿está ocupada la silla?** is that seat taken?
ocupar [oku'par] *vt* (*gen*) to occupy; (*puesto*) to hold, fill; (*individuo*) to engage; (*obreros*) to employ; (*confiscar*) to seize; **ocuparse** *vr*: **ocuparse de** *o* **en** to concern o.s. with; (*cuidar*) to look after; **ocuparse de lo suyo** to mind one's own business
ocurrencia [oku'rrenθja] *nf* (*ocasión*) occurrence; (*agudeza*) witticism
ocurrir [oku'rrir] *vi* to happen; **ocurrirse** *vr*: **se me ocurrió que ...** it occurred to me that ...; **¿se te ocurre algo?** can you think of *o* come up with anything?; **¿qué ocurre?** what's going on?

oda ['oða] *nf* ode
ODECA [o'ðeka] *nf abr* = **Organización de Estados Centroamericanos**
odiar [o'ðjar] *vt* to hate
odio ['oðjo] *nm* (*gen*) hate, hatred; (*disgusto*) dislike
odioso, -a [o'ðjoso, a] *adj* (*gen*) hateful; (*malo*) nasty
odisea [oði'sea] *nf* odyssey
odontología [oðontolo'xia] *nf* dentistry, dental surgery
odontólogo, -a [oðon'toloɣo, a] *nm/f* dentist, dental surgeon
odre ['oðre] *nm* wineskin
O.E.A. *nf abr* (= *Organización de Estados Americanos*) O.A.S.
OECE *nf abr* (= *Organización Europea de Cooperación Económica*) OEEC
OELA [o'ela] *nf abr* = **Organización de Estados Latinoamericanos**
oeste [o'este] *nm* west; **una película del ~** a western
ofender [ofen'der] *vt* (*agraviar*) to offend; (*insultar*) to insult; **ofenderse** *vr* to take offence
ofensa [o'fensa] *nf* offence; (*insulto*) slight
ofensivo, -a [ofen'siβo, a] *adj* (*insultante*) insulting; (*Mil*) offensive ■ *nf* offensive
oferta [o'ferta] *nf* offer; (*propuesta*) proposal; (*para contrato*) bid, tender; **la ~ y la demanda** supply and demand; **artículos en ~** goods on offer; **~ excedentaria** (*Com*) excess supply; **~ monetaria** money supply; **~ pública de adquisición (OPA)** (*Com*) takeover bid; **ofertas de trabajo** (*en periódicos*) situations vacant column
offset ['ofset] *nm* offset
oficial [ofi'θjal] *adj* official ■ *nm* official; (*Mil*) officer
oficialista [ofisja'lista] *adj* (*Am*) (pro-) government; **el candidato ~** the governing party's candidate
oficiar [ofi'θjar] *vt* to inform officially ■ *vi* (*Rel*) to officiate
oficina [ofi'θina] *nf* office; **~ de empleo** employment agency; **~ de información** information bureau; **~ de objetos perdidos** lost property office (*Brit*), lost-and-found department (*US*); **~ de turismo** tourist office; **~ principal** (*Com*) head office, main branch
oficinista [ofiθi'nista] *nm/f* clerk; **los oficinistas** white-collar workers
oficio [o'fiθjo] *nm* (*profesión*) profession; (*puesto*) post; (*Rel*) service; (*función*) function; (*comunicado*) official letter; **ser del ~** to be an old hand; **tener mucho ~** to have a lot of experience; **~ de difuntos** funeral service; **de ~** officially
oficioso, -a [ofi'θjoso, a] *adj* (*pey*) officious; (*no oficial*) unofficial, informal
ofimática [ofi'matika] *nf* office automation
ofrecer [ofre'θer] *vt* (*dar*) to offer; (*proponer*) to propose; **ofrecerse** *vr* (*persona*) to offer o.s., volunteer; (*situación*) to present itself; **¿qué se le ofrece?, ¿se le ofrece algo?** what can I do for you?, can I get you anything?
ofrecimiento [ofreθi'mjento] *nm* offer, offering
ofrendar [ofren'dar] *vt* to offer, contribute
ofrezca *etc* [o'freθka] *vb ver* **ofrecer**
oftalmología [oftalmolo'xia] *nf* ophthalmology
oftalmólogo, -a [oftal'moloɣo, a] *nm/f* ophthalmologist
ofuscación [ofuska'θjon] *nf*, **ofuscamiento** [ofuska'mjento] *nm* (*fig*) bewilderment
ofuscar [ofus'kar] *vt* (*confundir*) to bewilder; (*enceguecer*) to dazzle, blind
ofusque *etc* [o'fuske] *vb ver* **ofuscar**
ogro ['oɣro] *nm* ogre
OIC *nf abr* (= *Organización Interamericana del Café: Com*) = **Organización Internacional del Comercio**
oída [o'iða] *nf*: **de oídas** by hearsay
oído [o'iðo] *nm* (*Anat, Mus*) ear; (*sentido*) hearing; **~ interno** inner ear; **de ~** by ear; **apenas pude dar crédito a mis oídos** I could scarcely believe my ears; **hacer oídos sordos a** to turn a deaf ear to
OIEA *nm abr* (= *Organismo Internacional de Energía Atómica*) IAEA
oiga *etc* ['oiɣa] *vb ver* **oír**
OIR [o'ir] *nf abr* (= *Organización Internacional para los Refugiados*) IRO; = **Organización Internacional de Radiodifusión**
oír [o'ir] *vt* (*gen*) to hear; (*esp Am: escuchar*) to listen to; **¡oye!** (*sorpresa*) I say!, say! (US); **¡oiga!** (*Telec*) hullo?; **~ misa** to attend mass; **como quien oye llover** without paying (the slightest) attention
O.I.T. *nf abr* (= *Organización Internacional del Trabajo*) ILO
ojal [o'xal] *nm* buttonhole
ojalá [oxa'la] *excl* if only (it were so)!, some hope! ■ *conj* if only...!, would that...!; **ojalá que venga hoy** I hope he comes today; **¡ojalá pudiera!** I wish I could!
ojeada [oxe'aða] *nf* glance; **echar una ~ a** to take a quick look at
ojera [o'xera] *nf*: **tener ojeras** to have bags under one's eyes
ojeriza [oxe'riθa] *nf* ill-will; **tener ~ a** to have a grudge against, have it in for

ojeroso, -a [oxe'roso, a] *adj* haggard
ojete [o'xete] *nm* eye(let)
ojo ['oxo] *nm* eye; (*de puente*) span; (*de cerradura*) keyhole ■ *excl* careful!; **tener ~ para** to have an eye for; **ojos saltones** bulging *o* goggle eyes; **~ de buey** porthole; **~ por ~** an eye for an eye; **en un abrir y cerrar de ojos** in the twinkling of an eye; **a ojos vistas** openly; (*crecer etc*) before one's (very) eyes; **a ~ (de buen cubero)** roughly; **ojos que no ven, corazón que no siente** out of sight, out of mind; **ser el ~ derecho de algn** (*fig*) to be the apple of sb's eye
okupa [o'kupa] *nm/f* (*fam*) squatter
OL *abr* (= *onda larga*) LW, long wave
ola ['ola] *nf* wave; **~ de calor/frío** heatwave/cold spell; **la nueva ~** the latest fashion; (*Cine, Mus*) (the) new wave
OLADE [o'laðe] *nf abr* = **Organización Latinoamericana de Energía**
olé [o'le] *excl* bravo!, olé!
oleada [ole'aða] *nf* big wave, swell; (*fig*) wave
oleaje [ole'axe] *nm* swell
óleo ['oleo] *nm* oil
oleoducto [oleo'ðukto] *nm* (oil) pipeline
oler [o'ler] *vt* (*gen*) to smell; (*inquirir*) to pry into; (*fig: sospechar*) to sniff out ■ *vi* to smell; **~ a** to smell of; **huele mal** it smells bad, it stinks
olfatear [olfate'ar] *vt* to smell; (*fig: sospechar*) to sniff out; (*inquirir*) to pry into
olfato [ol'fato] *nm* sense of smell
oligarquía [oliɣar'kia] *nf* oligarchy
olimpiada [olim'piaða] *nf*: **la ~** *o* **las olimpiadas** the Olympics
olímpicamente [o'limpikamente] *adv*: **pasar ~ de algo** to totally ignore sth
olímpico, -a [o'limpiko, a] *adj* Olympian; (*deportes*) Olympic
oliva [o'liβa] *nf* (*aceituna*) olive; **aceite de ~** olive oil
olivar [oli'βar] *nm* olive grove *o* plantation
olivo [o'liβo] *nm* olive tree
olla ['oʎa] *nf* pan; (*para hervir agua*) kettle; (*comida*) stew; **~ a presión** pressure cooker
olmo ['olmo] *nm* elm (tree)
olor [o'lor] *nm* smell
oloroso, -a [olo'roso, a] *adj* scented
OLP *nf abr* (= *Organización para la Liberación de Palestina*) PLO
olvidadizo, -a [olβiða'ðiθo, a] *adj* (*desmemoriado*) forgetful; (*distraído*) absent-minded
olvidar [olβi'ðar] *vt* to forget; (*omitir*) to omit; (*abandonar*) to leave behind; **olvidarse** *vr* (*fig*) to forget o.s.; **se me olvidó** I forgot
olvido [ol'βiðo] *nm* oblivion; (*acto*) oversight; (*descuido*) slip; **caer en el ~** to fall into oblivion
O.M. *abr* (= *onda media*) MW, medium wave; (= *Oriente Medio*) Middle East; (*Pol*) = **Orden Ministerial**
ombligo [om'bliɣo] *nm* navel
OMI *nf abr* (= *Organización Marítima Internacional*) IMO
ominoso, -a [omi'noso, a] *adj* ominous
omisión [omi'sjon] *nf* (*abstención*) omission; (*descuido*) neglect
omiso, -a [o'miso, a] *adj*: **hacer caso ~ de** to ignore, pass over
omitir [omi'tir] *vt* to leave *o* miss out, omit
ómnibus ['omniβus] *nm* (*Am*) bus
omnipotente [omnipo'tente] *adj* omnipotent
omnipresente [omnipre'sente] *adj* omnipresent
omnívoro, -a [om'niβoro, a] *adj* omnivorous
omoplato [omo'plato], **omóplato** [o'moplato] *nm* shoulder-blade
OMS *nf abr* (= *Organización Mundial de la Salud*) WHO
ONCE ['onθe] *nf abr* (= *Organización Nacional de Ciegos Españoles*) *charity for the blind*
once ['onθe] *num* eleven ■ *nm* (*Am*); **onces** *nfpl* tea break *sg*
onda ['onda] *nf* wave; **~ corta/larga/media** short/long/medium wave; **ondas acústicas/hertzianas** acoustic/Hertzian waves; **~ sonora** sound wave
ondear [onde'ar] *vi* to wave; (*tener ondas*) to be wavy; (*agua*) to ripple; **ondearse** *vr* to swing, sway
ondulación [ondula'θjon] *nf* undulation
ondulado, -a [ondu'laðo, a] *adj* wavy ■ *nm* wave
ondulante [ondu'lante] *adj* undulating
ondular [ondu'lar] *vt* (*el pelo*) to wave ■ *vi*, **ondularse** *vr* to undulate
oneroso, -a [one'roso, a] *adj* onerous
ONG *nf abr* (= *organización no gubernamental*) NGO
onomástico, -a [ono'mastiko, a] *adj*: **fiesta onomástica** saint's day ■ *nm* saint's day
ONU ['onu] *nf abr ver* **Organización de las Naciones Unidas**
onubense [onu'βense] *adj* of *o* from Huelva ■ *nm/f* native *o* inhabitant of Huelva
ONUDI [o'nuði] *nf abr* (= *Organización de las Naciones Unidas para el Desarrollo Industrial*) UNIDO (= *United Nations Industrial Development Organization*)
onza ['onθa] *nf* ounce
O.P. *nfpl abr* = **Obras Públicas**; (*Com*) = **Oficina Principal**

OPA ['opa] *nf abr* (= *Oferta Pública de Adquisición*) takeover bid
opaco, -a [o'pako, a] *adj* opaque; (*fig*) dull
ópalo ['opalo] *nm* opal
opción [op'θjon] *nf* (*gen*) option; (*derecho*) right, option; **no hay ~** there is no alternative
opcional [opθjo'nal] *adj* optional
O.P.E.P. [o'pep] *nf abr* (= *Organización de Países Exportadores de Petróleo*) OPEC
ópera ['opera] *nf* opera; **ópera bufa** *o* **cómica** comic opera
operación [opera'θjon] *nf* (*gen*) operation; (*Com*) transaction, deal; **~ a plazo** (*Com*) forward transaction; **operaciones accesorias** (*Inform*) housekeeping; **operaciones a término** (*Com*) futures
operador, a [opera'ðor, a] *nm/f* operator; (*Cine: proyección*) projectionist; (*: rodaje*) cameraman
operar [ope'rar] *vt* (*producir*) to produce, bring about; (*Med*) to operate on ▪ *vi* (*Com*) to operate, deal; **operarse** *vr* to occur; (*Med*) to have an operation; **se han operado grandes cambios** great changes have been made *o* have taken place
operario, -a [ope'rarjo, a] *nm/f* worker
opereta [ope'reta] *nf* operetta
opinar [opi'nar] *vt* (*estimar*) to think ▪ *vi* (*enjuiciar*) to give one's opinion; **~ bien de** to think well of
opinión [opi'njon] *nf* (*creencia*) belief; (*criterio*) opinion; **la ~ pública** public opinion
opio ['opjo] *nm* opium
opíparo, -a [o'piparo, a] *adj* sumptuous
opondré *etc* [opon'dre] *vb ver* **oponer**
oponente [opo'nente] *nm/f* opponent
oponer [opo'ner] *vt* (*resistencia*) to put up, offer; (*negativa*) to raise; **oponerse** *vr* (*objetar*) to object; (*estar frente a frente*) to be opposed; (*dos personas*) to oppose each other; **~ A a B** to set A against B; **me opongo a pensar que ...** I refuse to believe *o* think that ...
oponga *etc* [o'ponga] *vb ver* **oponer**
Oporto [o'porto] *nm* Oporto
oporto [o'porto] *nm* port
oportunidad [oportuni'ðað] *nf* (*ocasión*) opportunity; (*posibilidad*) chance
oportunismo [oportu'nismo] *nm* opportunism
oportunista [oportu'nista] *nm/f* opportunist; (*infección*) opportunistic
oportuno, -a [opor'tuno, a] *adj* (*en su tiempo*) opportune, timely; (*respuesta*) suitable; **en el momento ~** at the right moment
oposición [oposi'θjon] *nf* opposition; **oposiciones** *nfpl* public examinations; **ganar un puesto por oposiciones** to win a post by public competitive examination; **hacer oposiciones a, presentarse a unas oposiciones a** to sit a competitive examination for; *see note*

OPOSICIÓN

The *oposiciones* are exams held every year for posts nationally and locally in the public sector, State education, the Judiciary etc. These posts are permanent and the number of candidates is high so the exams are tough. The candidates, *opositores*, have to study a great number of subjects relating to their field and also the Constitution. People can spend years studying and resitting exams.

opositar [oposi'tar] *vi* to sit a public entrance examination
opositor, -a [oposi'tor, a] *nm/f* (*Admin*) candidate to a public examination; (*adversario*) opponent
opresión [opre'sjon] *nf* oppression
opresivo, -a [opre'siβo, a] *adj* oppressive
opresor, a [opre'sor, a] *nm/f* oppressor
oprimir [opri'mir] *vt* to squeeze; (*asir*) to grasp; (*pulsar*) to press; (*fig*) to oppress
optar [op'tar] *vi* (*elegir*) to choose; **~ a** *o* **por** to opt for
optativo, -a [opta'tiβo, a] *adj* optional
óptico, -a ['optiko, a] *adj* optic(al) ▪ *nm/f* optician ▪ *nf* optics *sg*; (*fig*) viewpoint
optimismo [opti'mismo] *nm* optimism
optimista [opti'mista] *nm/f* optimist
óptimo, -a ['optimo, a] *adj* (*el mejor*) very best
opuesto, -a [o'pwesto, a] *pp de* **oponer** ▪ *adj* (*contrario*) opposite; (*antagónico*) opposing
opulencia [opu'lenθja] *nf* opulence
opulento, -a [opu'lento, a] *adj* opulent
opuse *etc* [o'puse] *vb ver* **oponer**
ora ['ora] *adv*: **~ tú ~ yo** now you, now me
oración [ora'θjon] *nf* (*Rel*) prayer; (*Ling*) sentence
oráculo [o'rakulo] *nm* oracle
orador, a [ora'ðor, a] *nm/f* orator; (*conferenciante*) speaker
oral [o'ral] *adj* oral; **por vía ~** (*Med*) orally
orangután [orangu'tan] *nm* orang-utan
orar [o'rar] *vi* (*Rel*) to pray
oratoria [ora'torja] *nf* oratory
orbe ['orβe] *nm* orb, sphere; (*fig*) world; **en todo el ~** all over the globe
órbita ['orβita] *nf* orbit; (*Anat: ocular*) (eye-) socket
orden ['orðen] *nm* (*gen*) order; (*Inform*)

command; **~ público** public order, law and order; (*números*): **del ~ de** about; **de primer ~** first-rate; **en ~ de prioridad** in order of priority ■ *nf* (*gen*) order; **~ bancaria** banker's order; **~ de compra** (*Com*) purchase order; **~ del día** agenda; **eso ahora está a la ~ del día** that is now the order of the day; **a la ~ de usted** at your service; **dar la ~ de hacer algo** to give the order to do sth

ordenación [orðena'θjon] *nf* (*estado*) order; (*acto*) ordering; (*Rel*) ordination

ordenado, -a [orðe'naðo, a] *adj* (*metódico*) methodical; (*arreglado*) orderly

ordenador [orðena'ðor] *nm* computer; **~ central** mainframe computer; **~ de gestión** business computer; **~ portátil** laptop (computer); **~ de sobremesa** desktop computer

ordenamiento [orðena'mjento] *nm* legislation

ordenanza [orðe'nanθa] *nf* ordinance; **ordenanzas municipales** by-laws ■ *nm* (*Com etc*) messenger; (*Mil*) orderly; (*bedel*) porter

ordenar [orðe'nar] *vt* (*mandar*) to order; (*poner orden*) to put in order, arrange; **ordenarse** *vr* (*Rel*) to be ordained

ordeñadora [orðeɲa'ðora] *nf* milking machine

ordeñar [orðe'ɲar] *vt* to milk

ordinariez [orðina'rjeθ] *nf* (*cualidad*) coarseness, vulgarity; (*una ordinariez*) coarse remark *o* joke *etc*

ordinario, -a [orði'narjo, a] *adj* (*común*) ordinary, usual; (*vulgar*) vulgar, common

ordinograma [orðino'ɣrama] *nm* flowchart

orear [ore'ar] *vt* to air; **orearse** *vr* (*ropa*) to air

orégano [o'reɣano] *nm* oregano

oreja [o'rexa] *nf* ear; (*Mecánica*) lug, flange

orensano, -a [oren'sano, a] *adj* of *o* from Orense ■ *nm/f* native *o* inhabitant of Orense

orfanato [orfa'nato] *nm*, **orfanatorio** [orfana'torjo] *nm* orphanage

orfandad [orfan'dað] *nf* orphanhood

orfebre [or'feβre] *nm* gold-/silversmith

orfebrería [orfeβre'ria] *nf* gold/silver work

orfelinato [orfeli'nato] *nm* orphanage

orfeón [orfe'on] *nm* (*Mus*) choral society

organice *etc* [orɣa'niθe] *vb ver* **organizar**

orgánico, -a [or'ɣaniko, a] *adj* organic

organigrama [orɣani'ɣrama] *nm* flow chart; (*de organización*) organization chart

organillo [orɣa'niʎo] *nm* barrel organ

organismo [orɣa'nismo] *nm* (*Bio*) organism; (*Pol*) organization; **O~ Internacional de Energía Atómica** International Atomic Energy Agency

organista [orɣa'nista] *nm/f* organist

organización [orɣaniθa'θjon] *nf* organization; **O~ de las Naciones Unidas (ONU)** United Nations Organization; **O~ del Tratado del Atlántico Norte (OTAN)** North Atlantic Treaty Organization (NATO)

organizador, a [orɣaniθa'ðor, a] *adj* organizing; **el comité ~** the organizing committee ■ *nm/f* organizer

organizar [orɣani'θar] *vt* to organize

órgano ['orɣano] *nm* organ

orgasmo [or'ɣasmo] *nm* orgasm

orgía [or'xia] *nf* orgy

orgullo [or'ɣuʎo] *nm* (*altanería*) pride; (*autorespeto*) self-respect

orgulloso, -a [orɣu'ʎoso, a] *adj* (*gen*) proud; (*altanero*) haughty

orientación [orjenta'θjon] *nf* (*posición*) position; (*dirección*) direction; **~ profesional** occupational guidance

oriental [orjen'tal] *adj* oriental; (*región etc*) eastern ■ *nm/f* oriental

orientar [orjen'tar] *vt* (*situar*) to orientate; (*señalar*) to point; (*dirigir*) to direct; (*guiar*) to guide; **orientarse** *vr* to get one's bearings; (*decidirse*) to decide on a course of action

oriente [o'rjente] *nm* east; **el O~** the East, the Orient; **Cercano/Medio/Lejano O~** Near/Middle/Far East

orificio [ori'fiθjo] *nm* orifice

origen [o'rixen] *nm* origin; (*nacimiento*) lineage, birth; **dar ~ a** to cause, give rise to

original [orixi'nal] *adj* (*nuevo*) original; (*extraño*) odd, strange ■ *nm* original; (*Tip*) manuscript; (*Tec*) master (copy)

originalidad [orixinali'ðað] *nf* originality

originar [orixi'nar] *vt* to originate; **originarse** *vr* to originate

originario, -a [orixi'narjo, a] *adj* (*nativo*) native; (*primordial*) original; **ser ~ de** to originate from; **país ~** country of origin

orilla [o'riʎa] *nf* (*borde*) border; (*de río*) bank; (*de bosque, tela*) edge; (*de mar*) shore; **a orillas de** on the banks of

orillar [ori'ʎar] *vt* (*bordear*) to skirt, go round; (*Costura*) to edge; (*resolver*) to wind up; (*tocar: asunto*) to touch briefly on; (*dificultad*) to avoid

orín [o'rin] *nm* rust

orina [o'rina] *nf* urine

orinal [ori'nal] *nm* (chamber) pot

orinar [ori'nar] *vi* to urinate; **orinarse** *vr* to wet o.s.

orines [o'rines] *nmpl* urine *sg*

oriundo, -a [o'rjundo, a] *adj*: **~ de** native of

orla ['orla] *nf* edge, border; (*Escol*) graduation photograph

ornamentar [ornamen'tar] *vt* (*adornar,*

ataviar) to adorn; (*revestir*) to bedeck
ornar [or'nar] *vt* to adorn
ornitología [ornitolo'xia] *nf* ornithology, bird watching
ornitólogo, -a [orni'toloɣo, a] *nm/f* ornithologist
oro ['oro] *nm* gold; **~ en barras** gold ingots; **de ~** gold, golden; **no es ~ todo lo que reluce** all that glitters is not gold; **hacerse de ~** to make a fortune; *ver tb* **oros**
orondo, -a [o'rondo, a] *adj* (*vasija*) rounded; (*individuo*) smug, self-satisfied
oropel [oro'pel] *nm* tinsel
oros ['oros] *nmpl* (*Naipes*) *one of the suits in the Spanish card deck*; *ver tb* **Baraja Española**
orquesta [or'kesta] *nf* orchestra; **~ de cámara/sinfónica** chamber/symphony orchestra; **~ de jazz** jazz band
orquestar [orkes'tar] *vt* to orchestrate
orquídea [or'kiðea] *nf* orchid
ortiga [or'tiɣa] *nf* nettle
ortodoncia [orto'ðonθja] *nf* orthodontics *sg*
ortodoxo, -a [orto'ðokso, a] *adj* orthodox
ortografía [ortoɣra'fia] *nf* spelling
ortopedia [orto'peðja] *nf* orthop(a)edics *sg*
ortopédico, -a [orto'peðiko, a] *adj* orthop(a)edic
oruga [o'ruɣa] *nf* caterpillar
orujo [o'ruxo] *nm* *type of strong grape liqueur made from grape pressings*
orzuelo [or'θwelo] *nm* (*Med*) stye
os [os] *pron* (*gen*) you; (*a vosotros*) (to) you; (*reflexivo*) (to) yourselves; (*mutuo*) (to) each other; **vosotros os laváis** you wash yourselves; **¡callaros!** (*fam*) shut up!
osa ['osa] *nf* (she-)bear; **O~ Mayor/Menor** Great/Little Bear, Ursa Major/Minor
osadía [osa'ðia] *nf* daring; (*descaro*) impudence
osamenta [osa'menta] *nf* skeleton
osar [o'sar] *vi* to dare
oscense [os'θense] *adj* of *o* from Huesca ■ *nm/f* native *o* inhabitant of Huesca
oscilación [osθila'θjon] *nf* (*movimiento*) oscillation; (*fluctuación*) fluctuation; (*vacilación*) hesitation; (*de columpio*) swinging, movement to and fro
oscilar [osθi'lar] *vi* to oscillate; to fluctuate; to hesitate
ósculo ['oskulo] *nm* kiss
oscurecer [oskure'θer] *vt* to darken ■ *vi* to grow dark; **oscurecerse** *vr* to grow *o* get dark
oscurezca *etc* [osku'reθka] *vb ver* **oscurecer**
oscuridad [oskuri'ðað] *nf* obscurity; (*tinieblas*) darkness
oscuro, -a [os'kuro, a] *adj* dark; (*fig*) obscure; (*indefinido*) confused; (*cielo*) overcast, cloudy; (*futuro etc*) uncertain; **a oscuras** in the dark
óseo, -a ['oseo, a] *adj* bony; (*Med etc*) bone *cpd*
oso ['oso] *nm* bear; **~ blanco/gris/pardo** polar/grizzly/brown bear; **~ de peluche** teddy bear; **~ hormiguero** anteater; **hacer el ~** to play the fool
Ostende [os'tende] *nm* Ostend
ostensible [osten'siβle] *adj* obvious
ostensiblemente [ostensiβle'mente] *adv* perceptibly, visibly
ostentación [ostenta'θjon] *nf* (*gen*) ostentation; (*acto*) display
ostentar [osten'tar] *vt* (*gen*) to show; (*pey*) to flaunt, show off; (*poseer*) to have, possess
ostentoso, -a [osten'toso, a] *adj* ostentatious, showy
osteópata [oste'opata] *nm/f* osteopath
ostra ['ostra] *nf* oyster ■ *excl*: **¡ostras!** (*fam*) sugar!
ostracismo [ostra'θismo] *nm* ostracism
OTAN ['otan] *nf abr ver* **Organización del Tratado del Atlántico Norte**
OTASE [o'tase] *nf abr* (= *Organización del Tratado del Sudeste Asiático*) SEATO
otear [ote'ar] *vt* to observe; (*fig*) to look into
otero [o'tero] *nm* low hill, hillock
otitis [o'titis] *nf* earache
otoñal [oto'ɲal] *adj* autumnal
otoño [o'toɲo] *nm* autumn, fall (*US*)
otorgamiento [otorɣa'mjento] *nm* conferring, granting; (*Jur*) execution
otorgar [otor'ɣar] *vt* (*conceder*) to concede; (*dar*) to grant; (*poderes*) to confer; (*premio*) to award
otorgue *etc* [o'torɣe] *vb ver* **otorgar**
otorrinolaringólogo, -a [otorrinolarin'go loɣo, a] *nm/f* (*Med*: *tb*: **otorrino**) ear, nose and throat specialist

PALABRA CLAVE

otro, -a ['otro, a] *adj* **1** (*distinto*: *sg*) another; (: *pl*) other; **otra cosa/persona** something/someone else; **con otros amigos** with other *o* different friends; **a/en otra parte** elsewhere, somewhere else
2 (*adicional*): **tráigame ~ café (más), por favor** can I have another coffee please; **otros 10 días más** another 10 days
■ *pron* **1** (*sg*) another one; **el ~** the other one; **(los) otros** (the) others; **¡otra!** (*Mus*) more!; **de ~** somebody *o* someone else's; **que lo haga ~** let somebody *o* someone else do it; **ni uno ni ~** neither one nor the other
2 (*recíproco*): **se odian (la) una a (la) otra** they hate one another *o* each other

3: **~ tanto**: **comer otro tanto** to eat the same *o* as much again; **recibió una decena de telegramas y otras tantas llamadas** he got about ten telegrams and as many calls

otrora [o'trora] *adv* formerly; **el ~ señor del país** the one-time ruler of the country
OUA *nf abr* (= *Organización de la Unidad Africana*) OAU
ovación [oβa'θjon] *nf* ovation
ovacionar [oβaθjo'nar] *vt* to cheer
oval [o'βal], **ovalado, a** [oβa'laðo, a] *adj* oval
óvalo ['oβalo] *nm* oval
ovario [o'βarjo] *nm* ovary
oveja [o'βexa] *nf* sheep; **~ negra** (*fig*) black sheep (of the family)
overol [oβe'rol] *nm* (*Am*) overalls *pl*
ovetense [oβe'tense] *adj* of *o* from Oviedo ■ *nm/f* native *o* inhabitant of Oviedo
ovillo [o'βiʎo] *nm* (*de lana*) ball; (*fig*) tangle; **hacerse un ~** to curl up (into a ball)
OVNI ['oβni] *nm abr* (= *objeto volante (o volador) no identificado*) UFO
ovulación [oβula'θjon] *nf* ovulation
óvulo ['oβulo] *nm* ovum
oxidación [oksiða'θjon] *nf* rusting
oxidar [oksi'ðar] *vt* to rust; **oxidarse** *vr* to go rusty; (*Tec*) to oxidize
óxido ['oksiðo] *nm* oxide
oxigenado, -a [oksixe'naðo, a] *adj* (*Química*) oxygenated; (*pelo*) bleached
oxigenar [oksixe'nar] *vt* to oxygenate; **oxigenarse** *vr* to become oxygenated; (*fam*) to get some fresh air
oxígeno [ok'sixeno] *nm* oxygen
oyendo *etc* [o'jendo] *vb ver* **oír**
oyente [o'jente] *nm/f* listener, hearer; (*Escol*) unregistered *o* occasional student

Pp

P, p [pe] *nf* (*letra*) P, p; **P de París** P for Peter
P *abr* (*Rel:* = *padre*) Fr.; = **papa**; (= *pregunta*) Q
p. *abr* (= *página*) p; (*Costura*) = **punto**
p.a. *abr* = **por autorización; por ausencia**
pabellón [paβe'ʎon] *nm* bell tent; (*Arq*) pavilion; (*de hospital etc*) block, section; (*bandera*) flag; **~ de conveniencia** (*Com*) flag of convenience; **~ de la oreja** outer ear
pábilo ['paβilo] *nm* wick
pábulo ['paβulo] *nm* food; **dar ~ a** to feed, encourage
PAC *nf abr* (= *Política Agrícola Común*) CAP
pacense [pa'θense] *adj* of *o* from Badajoz ■ *nm/f* native *o* inhabitant of Badajoz
paceño, -a [pa'θeɲo, a] *adj* of *o* from La Paz ■ *nm/f* native *o* inhabitant of La Paz
pacer [pa'θer] *vi* to graze ■ *vt* to graze on
pachá [pa'tʃa] *nm*: **vivir como un pachá** to live like a king
pachanguero, -a [patʃan'gero, a] *adj* (*pey: música*) *noisy and catchy*
pachorra [pa'tʃorra] *nf* (*indolencia*) slowness; (*tranquilidad*) calmness
pachucho, -a [pa'tʃutʃo, a] *adj* (*fruta*) overripe; (*persona*) off-colour, poorly
paciencia [pa'θjenθja] *nf* patience; **¡~!** be patient!; **¡~ y barajar!** don't give up!; **perder la ~** to lose one's temper
paciente [pa'θjente] *adj, nm/f* patient
pacificación [paθifika'θjon] *nf* pacification
pacificar [paθifi'kar] *vt* to pacify; (*tranquilizar*) to calm
pacífico, -a [pa'θifiko, a] *adj* peaceful; (*persona*) peace-loving; (*existencia*) pacific; **el (Océano) P~** the Pacific (Ocean)
pacifique *etc* [paθi'fike] *vb ver* **pacificar**
pacifismo [paθi'fismo] *nm* pacifism
pacifista [paθi'fista] *nm/f* pacifist
pack [pak] *nm* (*de yogures, latas*) pack; (*de vacaciones*) package
pacotilla [pako'tiʎa] *nf* trash; **de ~** shoddy
pactar [pak'tar] *vt* to agree to, agree on ■ *vi* to come to an agreement
pacto ['pakto] *nm* (*tratado*) pact; (*acuerdo*) agreement
padecer [paðe'θer] *vt* (*sufrir*) to suffer; (*soportar*) to endure, put up with; (*ser víctima de*) to be a victim of ■ *vi*: **~ de** to suffer from
padecimiento [paðeθi'mjento] *nm* suffering
pádel ['paðel] *nm* paddle tennis
padezca *etc* [pa'ðeθka] *vb ver* **padecer**
padrastro [pa'ðrastro] *nm* stepfather
padre ['paðre] *nm* father ■ *adj* (*fam*): **un éxito ~** a tremendous success; **padres** *nmpl* parents; **~ espiritual** confessor; **P~ Nuestro** Lord's Prayer; **~ político** father-in-law; **García ~** García senior; **¡tu ~!** (*fam!*) up yours! (!)
padrino [pa'ðrino] *nm* godfather; (*fig*) sponsor, patron; **padrinos** *nmpl* godparents; **~ de boda** best man
padrón [pa'ðron] *nm* (*censo*) census, roll; (*de socios*) register
paella [pa'eʎa] *nf* paella,, *dish of rice with meat, shellfish etc*
paga ['paɣa] *nf* (*dinero pagado*) payment; (*sueldo*) pay, wages *pl*
pagadero, -a [paɣa'ðero, a] *adj* payable; **~ a la entrega/a plazos** payable on delivery/in instalments
pagano, -a [pa'ɣano, a] *adj, nm/f* pagan, heathen
pagar [pa'ɣar] *vt* (*gen*) to pay; (*las compras, crimen*) to pay for; (*deuda*) to pay (off); (*fig: favor*) to repay ■ *vi* to pay; **pagarse** *vr*: **pagarse con algo** to be content with sth; **¡me las ~ás!** I'll get you for this!
pagaré [paɣa're] *nm* I.O.U
página ['paxina] *nf* page; **~ de inicio** (*Inform*) home page; **~ personal** (*Internet*) personal web page
páginas amarillas *nfpl* Yellow Pages®; **página web** web page
paginación [paxina'θjon] *nf* (*Inform, Tip*) pagination
paginar [paxi'nar] *vt* (*Inform, Tip*) to paginate

pago ['paɣo] *nm* *(dinero)* payment; *(fig)* return; **~ anticipado/a cuenta/a la entrega/en especie/inicial** advance payment/payment on account/cash on delivery/payment in kind/down payment; **~ a título gracioso** ex gratia payment; **en ~ de** in return for
pág(s). *abr* (= *página(s)*) p(p)
pague *etc* ['paɣe] *vb ver* **pagar**
paila ['paila] *nf* *(Am)* frying pan
país [pa'is] *nm* *(gen)* country; *(región)* land; **los Paises Bajos** the Low Countries; **el P~ Vasco** the Basque Country
paisaje [pai'saxe] *nm* countryside, landscape; *(vista)* scenery
paisano, -a [pai'sano, a] *adj* of the same country ■ *nm/f* *(compatriota)* fellow countryman(-woman); **vestir de ~** *(soldado)* to be in civilian clothes; *(guardia)* to be in plain clothes
paja ['paxa] *nf* straw; *(fig)* trash, rubbish; *(en libro, ensayo)* padding, waffle; **riñeron por un quítame allá esas pajas** they quarrelled over a trifle
pajar [pa'xar] *nm* hay loft
pajarita [paxa'rita] *nf* bow tie
pájaro ['paxaro] *nm* bird; *(fam: astuto)* clever fellow; **tener la cabeza a pájaros** to be featherbrained
pajita [pa'xita] *nf* (drinking) straw
pajizo, -a [pa'xiθo, a] *adj* *(de paja)* straw *cpd*; *(techo)* thatched; *(color)* straw-coloured
pakistaní [pakista'ni] *adj, nm/f* Pakistani
pala ['pala] *nf* *(de mango largo)* spade; *(de mango corto)* shovel; *(raqueta etc)* bat; *(: de tenis)* racquet; *(Culin)* slice; **~ matamoscas** fly swat
palabra [pa'laβra] *nf* *(gen, promesa)* word; *(facultad)* (power of) speech; *(derecho de hablar)* right to speak; **faltar a su ~** to go back on one's word; **quedarse con la ~ en la boca** to stop short; *(en reunión, comité etc)*: **tomar la ~** to speak, take the floor; **pedir la ~** to ask to be allowed to speak; **tener la ~** to have the floor; **no encuentro palabras para expresarme** words fail me
palabrería [palaβre'ria] *nf* hot air
palabrota [pala'βrota] *nf* swearword
palacio [pa'laθjo] *nm* palace; *(mansión)* mansion, large house; **~ de justicia** courthouse; **~ municipal** town/city hall
palada [pa'laða] *nf* shovelful, spadeful; *(de remo)* stroke
paladar [pala'ðar] *nm* palate
paladear [palaðe'ar] *vt* to taste
palanca [pa'lanka] *nf* lever; *(fig)* pull, influence; **~ de cambio** *(Auto)* gear lever, gearshift (US); **~ de freno** *(Auto)* brake lever; **~ de gobierno** *o* **de control** *(Inform)* joystick
palangana [palan'gana] *nf* washbasin
palco ['palko] *nm* box
palenque [pa'lenke] *nm* *(cerca)* stockade, fence; *(área)* arena, enclosure; *(de gallos)* pit
palentino, -a [palen'tino, a] *adj* of *o* from Palencia ■ *nm/f* native *o* inhabitant of Palencia
paleolítico, -a [paleo'litiko, a] *adj* paleolithic
paleontología [paleontolo'xia] *nf* paleontology
Palestina [pales'tina] *nf* Palestine
palestino, -a [pales'tino, a] *adj, nm/f* Palestinian
palestra [pa'lestra] *nf*: **salir** *o* **saltar a la ~** to come into the spotlight
paleto, -a [pa'leto, a] *nm/f* yokel, hick (US) ■ *nf* *(pala)* small shovel; *(Arte)* palette; *(Anat)* shoulder blade; *(Am)* ice lolly
paliar [pa'ljar] *vt* *(mitigar)* to mitigate; *(disfrazar)* to conceal
paliativo [palja'tiβo] *nm* palliative
palidecer [paliðe'θer] *vi* to turn pale
palidez [pali'ðeθ] *nf* paleness
palidezca *etc* [pali'ðeθka] *vb ver* **palidecer**
pálido, -a ['paliðo, a] *adj* pale
palillo [pa'liʎo] *nm* small stick; *(para dientes)* toothpick; **palillos (chinos)** chopsticks; **estar hecho un ~** to be as thin as a rake
palio ['paljo] *nm* canopy
palique [pa'like] *nm*: **estar de ~** *(fam)* to have a chat
paliza [pa'liθa] *nf* beating, thrashing; **dar** *o* **propinar > una ~ a algn** *(fam)* to give sb a thrashing
palma ['palma] *nf* *(Anat)* palm; *(árbol)* palm tree; **batir** *o* **dar palmas** to clap, applaud; **llevarse la ~** to triumph, win
palmada [pal'maða] *nf* slap; **palmadas** *nfpl* clapping *sg*, applause *sg*
Palma de Mallorca *nf* Palma
palmar [pal'mar] *vi* (*tb*: **palmarla**) to die, kick the bucket
palmarés [palma'res] *nm* *(lista)* list of winners; *(historial)* track record
palmear [palme'ar] *vi* to clap
palmero, -a [pal'mero, a] *adj* of the island of Palma ■ *nm/f* native *o* inhabitant of the island of Palma ■ *nm* *(Am)* ■ *nf* palm tree
palmo ['palmo] *nm* *(medida)* span; *(fig)* small amount; **~ a ~** inch by inch
palmotear [palmote'ar] *vi* to clap, applaud
palmoteo [palmo'teo] *nm* clapping, applause
palo ['palo] *nm* stick; *(poste)* post, pole; *(mango)* handle, shaft; *(golpe)* blow, hit; *(de golf)* club; *(de béisbol)* bat; *(Naut)* mast; *(Naipes)* suit; **vermut a ~ seco** straight vermouth; **de tal ~ tal astilla** like father like son

paloma [pa'loma] *nf* dove, pigeon; ~ **mensajera** carrier *o* homing pigeon
palomilla [palo'miʎa] *nf* moth; (*Tec: tuerca*) wing nut; (*soporte*) bracket
palomitas [palo'mitas] *nfpl* popcorn *sg*
palpable [pal'paβle] *adj* palpable; (*fig*) tangible
palpar [pal'par] *vt* to touch, feel
palpitación [palpita'θjon] *nf* palpitation
palpitante [palpi'tante] *adj* palpitating; (*fig*) burning
palpitar [palpi'tar] *vi* to palpitate; (*latir*) to beat
palta ['palta] *nf* (*Am*) avocado
palúdico, -a [pa'luðiko, a] *adj* marshy
paludismo [palu'ðismo] *nm* malaria
palurdo, -a [pa'lurðo, a] *adj* coarse, uncouth ■ *nm/f* yokel, hick (US)
pamela [pa'mela] *nf* sun hat
pampa ['pampa] *nf* (*Am*) pampa(s), prairie
pamplinas [pam'plinas] *nfpl* nonsense *sg*
pamplonés, -esa [pamplo'nes, esa], **pamplonica** [pamplo'nika] *adj* of *o* from Pamplona ■ *nm/f* native *o* inhabitant of Pamplona
pan [pan] *nm* bread; (*una barra*) loaf; **~ de molde** sliced loaf; **~ integral** wholemeal bread; **~ rallado** breadcrumbs *pl*; **eso es ~ comido** it's a cinch; **llamar al ~ ~ y al vino vino** to call a spade a spade
pana ['pana] *nf* corduroy
panadería [panaðe'ria] *nf* baker's (shop)
panadero, -a [pana'ðero, a] *nm/f* baker
panal [pa'nal] *nm* honeycomb
Panamá [pana'ma] *nm* Panama
panameño, -a [pana'meɲo, a] *adj* Panamanian
pancarta [pan'karta] *nf* placard, banner
pancho, -a ['pantʃo, a] *adj*: **estar tan ~** to remain perfectly calm
pancito [pan'sito] *nm* (*Am*) (bread) roll
páncreas ['pankreas] *nm* pancreas
panda ['panda] *nm* panda ■ *nf* gang
pandereta [pande'reta] *nf* tambourine
pandilla [pan'diʎa] *nf* set, group; (*de criminales*) gang; (*pey*) clique
pando, -a ['pando, a] *adj* sagging
panecillo [pane'θiʎo] *nm* (bread) roll
panel [pa'nel] *nm* panel; **~ acústico** acoustic screen
panera [pa'nera] *nf* bread basket
panfleto [pan'fleto] *nm* (*Pol etc*) pamphlet; lampoon
pánico ['paniko] *nm* panic
panificadora [panifika'ðora] *nf* bakery
panorama [pano'rama] *nm* panorama; (*vista*) view
panqué [pan'ke] *nm* (*Am*) pancake
pantaletas [panta'letas] *nfpl* (*Am*) panties
pantalla [pan'taʎa] *nf* (*de cine*) screen; (*cubreluz*) lampshade; (*Inform*) screen, display; **servir de ~ a** to be a blind for; **~ de cristal líquido** liquid crystal display; **~ táctil** touch-sensitive screen; **~ de ayuda** help screen
pantalón [panta'lon] *nm*, **pantalones** [panta'lones] *nmpl* trousers *pl*, pants *pl* (US); **pantalones cortos** shorts *pl*; **pantalones vaqueros** jeans *pl*
pantano [pan'tano] *nm* (*ciénaga*) marsh, swamp; (*depósito: de agua*) reservoir; (*fig*) jam, fix, difficulty
pantera [pan'tera] *nf* panther
pantis ['pantis] *nmpl* tights
pantomima [panto'mima] *nf* pantomime
pantorrilla [panto'rriʎa] *nf* calf (of the leg)
pantufla [pan'tufla] *nf* slipper
panty ['panti] *nm* = **pantis**
panza ['panθa] *nf* belly, paunch
panzón, -ona [pan'θon, ona], **panzudo, -a** [pan'θuðo, a] *adj* fat, potbellied
pañal [pa'ɲal] *nm* nappy, diaper (US); **estar todavía en pañales** to be still wet behind the ears
pañería [paɲe'ria] *nf* (*artículos*) drapery; (*tienda*) draper's (shop), dry-goods store (US)
paño ['paɲo] *nm* (*tela*) cloth; (*pedazo de tela*) (piece of) cloth; (*trapo*) duster, rag; **~ de cocina** dishcloth; **~ higiénico** sanitary towel; **paños menores** underclothes; **paños calientes** (*fig*) half-measures; **no andarse con paños calientes** to pull no punches
pañuelo [pa'ɲwelo] *nm* handkerchief, hanky (*fam*); (*para la cabeza*) (head)scarf
papa ['papa] *nf* (*Am*) potato ■ *nm*: **el P~** the Pope
papá [pa'pa] *nm* (*pl* **~s**) (*fam*) dad, daddy, pop (US); **papás** *nmpl* parents; **hijo de papá** Hooray Henry (*fam*)
papada [pa'paða] *nf* double chin
papagayo [papa'ɣajo] *nm* parrot
papanatas [papa'natas] *nm inv* (*fam*) sucker, simpleton
paparrucha [papa'rrutʃa] *nf* (*tontería*) piece of nonsense
papaya [pa'paja] *nf* papaya
papear [pape'ar] *vt, vi* (*fam*) to eat
papel [pa'pel] *nm* (*gen*) paper; (*hoja de papel*) sheet of paper; (*Teat*) part, role; **papeles** *nmpl* identification papers; **~ de calco/carbón/de cartas** tracing paper/carbon paper/stationery; **~ continuo** (*Inform*) continuous stationery; **~ de envolver/de**

empapelar brown paper/wrapping paper/ wallpaper; **~ de aluminio/higiénico** tinfoil/ toilet paper; **~ del** *o* **de pagos al Estado** government bonds *pl*; **~ de lija** sandpaper; **~ moneda** paper money; **~ plegado (en abanico** *o* **en acordeón)** fanfold paper; **~ secante** blotting paper; **~ térmico** thermal paper
papeleo [pape'leo] *nm* red tape
papelera [pape'lera] *nf* (*cesto*) wastepaper basket; (*escritorio*) desk; **~ de reciclaje** (*Inform*) wastebasket
papelería [papele'ria] *nf* (*tienda*) stationer's (shop)
papeleta [pape'leta] *nf* (*pedazo de papel*) slip *o* bit of paper; (*Pol*) ballot paper; (*Escol*) report; **¡vaya ~!** this is a tough one!
paperas [pa'peras] *nfpl* mumps *sg*
papilla [pa'piʎa] *nf* (*de bebé*) baby food; (*pey*) mush; **estar hecho ~** to be dog-tired
paquete [pa'kete] *nm* (*caja*) packet; (*bulto*) parcel; (*Am fam*) nuisance, bore; (*Inform*) package (*of software*); (*de vacaciones*) package tour; **~ de aplicaciones** (*Inform*) applications package; **~ integrado** (*Inform*) integrated package; **~ de gestión integrado** combined management suite; **paquetes postales** parcel post *sg*
paquistaní [pakista'ni] = **pakistaní**
par [par] *adj* (*igual*) like, equal; (*Mat*) even ▪ *nm* equal; (*de guantes*) pair; (*de veces*) couple; (*título*) peer; (*Golf, Com*) par ▪ *nf* par; **pares o nones** odds or evens; **abrir de ~ en ~** to open wide; **a la ~** par; **sobre/bajo la ~** above/ below par
para ['para] *prep* for; **no es ~ comer** it's not for eating; **decir ~ sí** to say to o.s.; **¿~ qué lo quieres?** what do you want it for?; **se casaron ~ separarse otra vez** they married only to separate again; **~ entonces** by then *o* that time; **lo tendré ~ mañana** I'll have it for tomorrow; **ir ~ casa** to go home, head for home; **~ profesor es muy estúpido** he's very stupid for a teacher; **¿quién es usted ~ gritar así?** who are you to shout like that?; **tengo bastante ~ vivir** I have enough to live on
parabellum [paraβe'lum] *nm* (automatic) pistol
parabién [para'βjen] *nm* congratulations *pl*
parábola [pa'raβola] *nf* parable; (*Mat*) parabola
parabólica [para'βolika] *nf* (*tb*: **antena parabólica**) satellite dish
parabrisas [para'βrisas] *nm inv* windscreen, windshield (*US*)
paracaídas [paraka'iðas] *nm inv* parachute
paracaidista [parakai'ðista] *nm/f* parachutist; (*Mil*) paratrooper
parachoques [para'tʃokes] *nm inv* bumper, fender (*US*); shock absorber
parada [pa'raða] *nf ver* **parado**
paradero [para'ðero] *nm* stopping-place; (*situación*) whereabouts
parado, -a [pa'raðo, a] *adj* (*persona*) motionless, standing still; (*fábrica*) closed, at a standstill; (*coche*) stopped; (*Am*: *de pie*) standing (up); (*sin empleo*) unemployed, idle; (*confuso*) confused ▪ *nf* (*gen*) stop; (*acto*) stopping; (*de industria*) shutdown, stoppage; (*lugar*) stopping-place; **salir bien ~** to come off well; **parada de autobús** bus stop; **parada discrecional** request stop; **parada en seco** sudden stop; **parada de taxis** taxi rank
paradoja [para'ðoxa] *nf* paradox
paradójico, -a [para'ðoxiko, a] *adj* paradoxical
parador [para'ðor] *nm* (luxury) hotel
parafrasear [parafrase'ar] *vt* to paraphrase
paráfrasis [pa'rafrasis] *nf inv* paraphrase
paraguas [pa'raɣwas] *nm inv* umbrella
Paraguay [para'ɣwai] *nm*: **el ~** Paraguay
paraguayo, -a [para'ɣwajo, a] *adj, nm/f* Paraguayan
paraíso [para'iso] *nm* paradise, heaven; **~ fiscal** (*Com*) tax haven
paraje [pa'raxe] *nm* place, spot
paralelo, -a [para'lelo, a] *adj, nm* parallel; **en ~** (*Elec, Inform*) (in) parallel
paralice *etc* [para'liθe] *vb ver* **paralizar**
parálisis [pa'ralisis] *nf inv* paralysis; **~ cerebral** cerebral palsy; **~ progresiva** creeping paralysis
paralítico, -a [para'litiko, a] *adj, nm/f* paralytic
paralizar [parali'θar] *vt* to paralyse; **paralizarse** *vr* to become paralysed; (*fig*) to come to a standstill
parámetro [pa'rametro] *nm* parameter
paramilitar [paramili'tar] *adj* paramilitary
páramo ['paramo] *nm* bleak plateau
parangón [paran'gon] *nm*: **sin ~** incomparable
paraninfo [para'ninfo] *nm* (*Escol*) assembly hall
paranoia [para'noia] *nf* paranoia
paranoico, -a [para'noiko, a] *adj, nm/f* paranoid
paranormal [paranor'mal] *adj* paranormal
parapetarse [parape'tarse] *vr* to shelter
parapléjico, -a [para'plexiko, a] *adj, nm/f* paraplegic
parar [pa'rar] *vt* to stop; (*progreso etc*) to

check, halt; *(golpe)* to ward off ■ *vi* to stop; *(hospedarse)* to stay, put up; **pararse** *vr* to stop; *(Am)* to stand up; **no ~ de hacer algo** to keep on doing sth; **ha parado de llover** it has stopped raining; **van a ~ en la comisaría** they're going to end up in the police station; **no sabemos en qué va a ~ todo esto** we don't know where all this is going to end; **pararse a hacer algo** to stop to do sth; **pararse en** to pay attention to
pararrayos [para'rrajos] *nm inv* lightning conductor
parásito, -a [pa'rasito, a] *nm/f* parasite
parasol [para'sol] *nm* parasol, sunshade
parcela [par'θela] *nf* plot, piece of ground, smallholding
parche ['partʃe] *nm* patch
parchís [par'tʃis] *nm* ludo
parcial [par'θjal] *adj (pago)* part-; *(eclipse)* partial; *(juez)* prejudiced, biased
parcialidad [parθjali'ðað] *nf (prejuicio)* prejudice, bias
parco, -a ['parko, a] *adj (frugal)* sparing; *(moderado)* moderate
pardillo, -a [par'ðiʎo, a] *adj (pey)* provincial ■ *nm/f (pey)* country bumpkin ■ *nm (Zool)* linnet
pardo, -a ['parðo, a] *adj (color)* brown; *(cielo)* overcast; *(voz)* flat, dull
parear [pare'ar] *vt (juntar, hacer par)* to match, put together; *(calcetines)* to put into pairs; *(Bio)* to mate, pair
parecer [pare'θer] *nm (opinión)* opinion, view; *(aspecto)* looks *pl* ■ *vi (tener apariencia)* to seem, look; *(asemejarse)* to look like, seem like; *(aparecer, llegar)* to appear; **parecerse** *vr* to look alike, resemble each other; **parecerse a** to look like, resemble; **al ~** apparently; **me parece que** I think (that), it seems to me that
parecido, -a [pare'θiðo, a] *adj* similar ■ *nm* similarity, likeness, resemblance; **~ a** like, similar to; **bien ~** good-looking, nice-looking
pared [pa'reð] *nf* wall; **~ divisoria/ medianera** dividing/party wall; **subirse por las paredes** *(fam)* to go up the wall
paredón [pare'ðon] *nm*: **llevar a algn al ~** to put sb up against a wall, shoot sb
parejo, -a [pa'rexo, a] *adj (igual)* equal; *(liso)* smooth, even ■ *nf (dos)* pair; *(: de personas)* couple; *(el otro: de un par)* other one (of a pair); *(: persona)* partner; *(de Guardias)* Civil Guard patrol
parentela [paren'tela] *nf* relations *pl*
parentesco [paren'tesko] *nm* relationship
paréntesis [pa'rentesis] *nm inv* parenthesis; *(digresión)* digression; *(en escrito)* bracket
parezca *etc* [pa'reθka] *vb ver* **parecer**
parida [pa'riða] *nf*: **~ mental** *(fam)* dumb idea
paridad [pari'ðað] *nf (Econ)* parity
pariente, -a [pa'rjente, a] *nm/f* relative, relation
parihuela [pari'wela] *nf* stretcher
paripé [pari'pe] *nm*: **hacer el ~** to put on an act
parir [pa'rir] *vt* to give birth to ■ *vi (mujer)* to give birth, have a baby; *(yegua)* to foal; *(vaca)* to calve
París [pa'ris] *nm* Paris
parisiense [pari'sjense] *adj, nm/f* Parisian
paritario, -a [pari'tarjo, a] *adj* equal
parking ['parkin] *nm* car park, parking lot (US)
parlamentar [parlamen'tar] *vi (negociar)* to parley
parlamentario, -a [parlamen'tarjo, a] *adj* parliamentary ■ *nm/f* member of parliament
parlamento [parla'mento] *nm (Pol)* parliament; *(Jur)* speech
parlanchín, -ina [parlan'tʃin, ina] *adj* loose-tongued, indiscreet ■ *nm/f* chatterbox
parlante [par'lante] *nm (Am)* loudspeaker
parlar [par'lar] *vi* to chatter (away)
parlotear [parlote'ar] *vi* to chatter, prattle
parloteo [parlo'teo] *nm* chatter, prattle
paro ['paro] *nm (huelga)* stoppage (of work), strike; *(desempleo)* unemployment; **~ cardiaco** cardiac arrest; **subsidio de ~** unemployment benefit; **hay ~ en la industria** work in the industry is at a standstill; **~ del sistema** *(Inform)* system shutdown
parodia [pa'roðja] *nf* parody
parodiar [paro'ðjar] *vt* to parody
parpadear [parpaðe'ar] *vi (los ojos)* to blink; *(luz)* to flicker
parpadeo [parpa'ðeo] *nm (de ojos)* blinking, winking; *(de luz)* flickering
párpado ['parpaðo] *nm* eyelid
parque ['parke] *nm (lugar verde)* park; **~ de atracciones/de bomberos/zoológico** fairground/fire station/zoo; **~ infantil** children's playground; **~ temático** theme park
parqué, parquet [par'ke] *nm* parquet
parqueadero [parkea'ðero] *nm (Am)* car park, parking lot (US)
parquímetro [par'kimetro] *nm* parking meter
parra ['parra] *nf* grapevine
párrafo ['parrafo] *nm* paragraph; **echar un ~** *(fam)* to have a chat

parranda [pa'rranda] *nf* (*fam*) spree, binge
parrilla [pa'rriʎa] *nf* (*Culin*) grill; (*Am Auto*) roof-rack; **~ (de salida)** (*Auto*) starting grid; **carne a la ~** grilled meat
parrillada [parri'ʎaða] *nf* barbecue
párroco ['parroko] *nm* parish priest
parroquia [pa'rrokja] *nf* parish; (*iglesia*) parish church; (*Com*) clientele, customers *pl*
parroquiano, -a [parro'kjano, a] *nm/f* parishioner; client, customer
parsimonia [parsi'monja] *nf* (*frugalidad*) sparingness; (*calma*) deliberateness; **con ~** calmly
parte ['parte] *nm* message; (*informe*) report; **~ meteorológico** weather forecast ■ *nf* part; (*lado, cara*) side; (*de reparto*) share; (*Jur*) party; **en alguna ~ de Europa** somewhere in Europe; **en cualquier ~** anywhere; **por ahí no se va a ninguna ~** that leads nowhere; (*fig*) this is getting us nowhere; **en** *o* **por todas partes** everywhere; **en gran ~** to a large extent; **la mayor ~ de los españoles** most Spaniards; **de algún tiempo a esta ~** for some time past; **de ~ de algn** on sb's behalf; **¿de ~ de quién?** (*Telec*) who is speaking?; **por ~ de** on the part of; **yo por mi ~** I for my part; **por una ~ ... por otra ~** on the one hand, ... on the other (hand); **dar ~ a algn** to report to sb; **tomar ~** to take part
partera [par'tera] *nf* midwife
parterre [par'terre] *nm* (flower)bed
partición [parti'θjon] *nf* division, sharing-out; (*Pol*) partition
participación [partiθipa'θjon] *nf* (*acto*) participation, taking part; (*parte*) share; (*Com*) share, stock (US); (*de lotería*) shared prize; (*aviso*) notice, notification; **~ en los beneficios** profit-sharing; **~ minoritaria** minority interest
participante [partiθi'pante] *nm/f* participant
participar [partiθ'par] *vt* to notify, inform ■ *vi* to take part, participate; **~ en una empresa** (*Com*) to invest in an enterprise; **le participo que ...** I have to tell you that ...
partícipe [par'tiθipe] *nm/f* participant; **hacer ~ a algn de algo** to inform sb of sth
participio [parti'θipjo] *nm* participle; **~ de pasado/presente** past/present participle
partícula [par'tikula] *nf* particle
particular [partiku'lar] *adj* (*especial*) particular, special; (*individual, personal*) private, personal ■ *nm* (*punto, asunto*) particular, point; (*individuo*) individual; **tiene coche ~** he has a car of his own; **no dijo mucho sobre el ~** he didn't say much about the matter
particularice *etc* [partikula'riθe] *vb ver* **particularizar**
particularidad [partikulari'ðað] *nf* peculiarity; **tiene la ~ de que ...** one of its special features is (that) ...
particularizar [partikulari'θar] *vt* to distinguish; (*especificar*) to specify; (*detallar*) to give details about
partida [par'tiða] *nf* (*salida*) departure; (*Com*) entry, item; (*juego*) game; (*grupo, bando*) band, group; **mala ~** dirty trick; **~ de nacimiento/matrimonio/defunción** birth/marriage/death certificate; **echar una ~** to have a game
partidario, -a [parti'ðarjo, a] *adj* partisan ■ *nm/f* (*Deporte*) supporter; (*Pol*) partisan
partidismo [parti'ðismo] *nm* (*Jur*) partisanship, bias; (*Pol*) party politics
partido [par'tiðo] *nm* (*Pol*) party; (*encuentro*) game, match; (*apoyo*) support; (*equipo*) team; **~ amistoso** (*Deporte*) friendly (game); **~ de fútbol** football match; **sacar ~ de** to profit from, benefit from; **tomar ~** to take sides
partir [par'tir] *vt* (*dividir*) to split, divide; (*compartir, distribuir*) to share (out), distribute; (*romper*) to break open, split open; (*rebanada*) to cut (off); (*vi: ponerse en camino*) to set off, set out; (*comenzar*) to start (off *o* out); **partirse** *vr* to crack *o* split *o* break (in two *etc*); **a ~ de** (starting) from; **partirse de risa** to split one's sides (laughing)
partitura [parti'tura] *nf* score
parto ['parto] *nm* birth, delivery; (*fig*) product, creation; **estar de ~** to be in labour
parvulario [parβu'larjo] *nm* nursery school, kindergarten
párvulo, -a ['parβulo, a] *nm/f* infant
pasa ['pasa] *nf ver* **paso**
pasable [pa'saβle] *adj* passable
pasada [pa'saða] *nf ver* **pasado**
pasadizo [pasa'ðiθo] *nm* (*pasillo*) passage, corridor; (*callejuela*) alley
pasado, -a [pa'saðo, a] *adj* past; (*malo: comida, fruta*) bad; (*muy cocido*) overdone; (*anticuado*) out of date ■ *nm* past; (*Ling*) past (tense) ■ *nf* passing, passage; (*acción de pulir*) rub, polish; **~ mañana** the day after tomorrow; **el mes ~** last month; **pasados dos días** after two days; **lo ~, ~** let bygones be bygones; **~ de moda** old-fashioned; **~ por agua** (*huevo*) boiled; **estar ~ de vueltas** *o* **de rosca** (*grifo, tuerca*) to be worn; **de pasada** in passing, incidentally; **una mala pasada** a dirty trick
pasador [pasa'ðor] *nm* (*gen*) bolt; (*de pelo*) pin, grip, slide; **pasadores** *nmpl* (*Am: cordones*) shoelaces
pasaje [pa'saxe] *nm* (*gen*) passage; (*pago de*

viaje) fare; (*los pasajeros*) passengers *pl*; (*pasillo*) passageway
pasajero, -a [pasa'xero, a] *adj* passing; (*ave*) migratory ■ *nm/f* passenger; (*viajero*) traveller
pasamanos [pasa'manos] *nm inv* rail, handrail; (*de escalera*) banister
pasamontañas [pasamon'taɲas] *nm inv* balaclava (helmet)
pasaporte [pasa'porte] *nm* passport
pasar [pa'sar] *vt* (*gen*) to pass; (*tiempo*) to spend; (*durezas*) to suffer, endure; (*noticia*) to give, pass on; (*película*) to show; (*persona*) to take, conduct; (*río*) to cross; (*barrera*) to pass through; (*falta*) to overlook, tolerate; (*contrincante*) to surpass, do better than; (*coche*) to overtake; (*contrabando*) to smuggle (in/out); (*enfermedad*) to give, infect with ■ *vi* (*gen*) to pass, go; (*terminarse*) to be over; (*ocurrir*) to happen; **pasarse** *vr* (*efectos*) to pass, be over; (*flores*) to fade; (*comida*) to go bad, go off; (*fig*) to overdo it, go too far *o* over the top; **~ de** to go beyond, exceed; **¡pase!** come in!; **nos hicieron ~** they showed us in; **~ por** to fetch; **~ por alto** to skip; **~ por una crisis** to go through a crisis; **se hace ~ por médico** he passes himself off as a doctor; **pasarlo bien/bomba** *o* **de maravilla** to have a good/great time; **pasarse al enemigo** to go over to the enemy; **pasarse de la raya** to go too far; **¡no te pases!** don't try me!; **se me pasó** I forgot; **se me pasó el turno** I missed my turn; **no se le pasa nada** nothing escapes him, he misses nothing; **ya se te ~á** you'll get over it; **¿qué pasa?** what's happening?, what's going on?, what's up?; **¡cómo pasa el tiempo!** time just flies!; **pase lo que pase** come what may; **el autobús pasa por nuestra casa** the bus goes past our house
pasarela [pasa'rela] *nf* footbridge; (*en barco*) gangway
pasatiempo [pasa'tjempo] *nm* pastime, hobby; (*distracción*) amusement
Pascua, pascua ['paskwa] *nf*: **~ (de Resurrección)** Easter; **~ de Navidad** Christmas; **Pascuas** *nfpl* Christmas time *sg*; **¡felices Pascuas!** Merry Christmas!; **de Pascuas a Ramos** once in a blue moon; **hacer la ~ a** (*fam*) to annoy, bug
pase ['pase] *nm* pass; (*Cine*) performance, showing; (*Com*) permit; (*Jur*) licence
pasear [pase'ar] *vt* to take for a walk; (*exhibir*) to parade, show off ■ *vi*, **pasearse** *vr* to walk, go for a walk; **~ en coche** to go for a drive
paseo [pa'seo] *nm* (*avenida*) avenue; (*distancia corta*) short walk; **~ marítimo** promenade; **dar un ~** to go for a walk; **~ en bicicleta** (bike) ride; **~ en barco** boat trip; **mandar a algn a ~** to tell sb to go to blazes; **¡vete a ~!** get lost!
pasillo [pa'siʎo] *nm* passage, corridor
pasión [pa'sjon] *nf* passion
pasional [pasjo'nal] *adj* passionate; **crimen ~** crime of passion
pasivo, -a [pa'siβo, a] *adj* passive; (*inactivo*) inactive ■ *nm* (*Com*) liabilities *pl*, debts *pl*; (*de cuenta*) debit side; **~ circulante** current liabilities
pasma ['pasma] *nm* (*fam*) cop
pasmado, -a [pas'maðo, a] *adj* (*asombrado*) astonished; (*atontado*) bewildered
pasmar [pas'mar] *vt* (*asombrar*) to amaze, astonish; **pasmarse** *vr* to be amazed *o* astonished
pasmo ['pasmo] *nm* amazement, astonishment; (*fig*) wonder, marvel
pasmoso, -a [pas'moso, a] *adj* amazing, astonishing
paso, -a ['paso, a] *adj* dried ■ *nm* (*gen, de baile*) step; (*modo de andar*) walk; (*huella*) footprint; (*rapidez*) speed, pace, rate; (*camino accesible*) way through, passage; (*cruce*) crossing; (*pasaje*) passing, passage; (*Rel*) *religious float or sculpture*; (*Geo*) pass; (*estrecho*) strait; (*fig*) step, measure; (*apuro*) difficulty ■ *nf* raisin; **pasa de Corinto/de Esmirna** currant/sultana; **~ a ~** step by step; **a ese ~** (*fig*) at that rate; **salir al ~ de** *o* **a** to waylay; **salir del ~** to get out of trouble; **dar un ~ en falso** to trip; (*fig*) to take a false step; **estar de ~** to be passing through; **~ atrás** step backwards; (*fig*) backward step; **~ elevado/subterráneo** flyover/subway, underpass (US); **prohibido el ~** no entry; **ceda el ~** give way; *ver tb* **Semana Santa**
pasota [pa'sota] *adj, nm/f* (*fam*) ≈ dropout; **ser un (tipo) ~** to be a bit of a dropout; (*ser indiferente*) not to care about anything
pasotismo [paso'tismo] *nm* underground *o* alternative culture
pasta ['pasta] *nf* (*gen*) paste; (*Culin: masa*) dough; (*: de bizcochos etc*) pastry; (*fam*) money, dough; (*encuadernación*) hardback; **pastas** *nfpl* (*bizcochos*) pastries, small cakes; (*espaguetis etc*) pasta *sg*; **~ de dientes** *o* **dentífrica** toothpaste; **~ de madera** wood pulp
pastar [pas'tar] *vt, vi* to graze
pastel [pas'tel] *nm* (*dulce*) cake; (*de carne*) pie; (*Arte*) pastel; (*fig*) plot; **pasteles** *nmpl* pastry *sg*, confectionery *sg*
pastelería [pastele'ria] *nf* cake shop, pastry shop

pasteurizado, -a [pasteuri'θaðo, a] *adj* pasteurized
pastilla [pas'tiʎa] *nf* (*de jabón, chocolate*) cake, bar; (*píldora*) tablet, pill
pastizal [pasti'θal] *nm* pasture
pasto ['pasto] *nm* (*hierba*) grass; (*lugar*) pasture, field; (*fig*) food, nourishment
pastor, a [pas'tor, a] *nm/f* shepherd(ess) ■ *nm* clergyman, pastor; (*Zool*) sheepdog; **~ alemán** Alsatian
pastoso, -a [pas'toso, a] *adj* (*material*) doughy, pasty; (*lengua*) furry; (*voz*) mellow
pat. *abr* (= *patente*) pat
pata ['pata] *nf* (*pierna*) leg; (*pie*) foot; (*de muebles*) leg; **patas arriba** upside down; **a cuatro patas** on all fours; **meter la ~** to put one's foot in it; **~ de cabra** (*Tec*) crowbar; **patas de gallo** crow's feet; **tener buena/mala ~** to be lucky/unlucky
patada [pa'taða] *nf* stamp; (*puntapié*) kick; **a patadas** in abundance; (*trato*) roughly; **echar a algn a patadas** to kick sb out
patagón, -ona [pata'ɣon, ona] *adj, nm/f* Patagonian
Patagonia [pata'ɣonja] *nf*: **la ~** Patagonia
patalear [patale'ar] *vi* to stamp one's feet
pataleo [pata'leo] *nm* stamping
patán [pa'tan] *nm* rustic, yokel
patata [pa'tata] *nf* potato; **patatas fritas** *o* **a la española** chips, French fries; **patatas a la inglesa** crisps; **ni ~** (*fam*) nothing at all; **no entendió ni ~** he didn't understand a single word
paté [pa'te] *nm* pâté
patear [pate'ar] *vt* (*pisar*) to stamp on, trample (on); (*pegar con el pie*) to kick ■ *vi* to stamp (with rage), stamp one's foot
patentar [paten'tar] *vt* to patent
patente [pa'tente] *adj* obvious, evident; (*Com*) patent ■ *nf* patent
patera [pa'tera] *nf* boat
paternal [pater'nal] *adj* fatherly, paternal
paternalista [paterna'lista] *adj* (*tono, actitud etc*) patronizing
paternidad [paterni'ðað] *nf* fatherhood, parenthood; (*Jur*) paternity
paterno, -a [pa'terno, a] *adj* paternal
patético, -a [pa'tetiko, a] *adj* pathetic, moving
patíbulo [pa'tiβulo] *nm* scaffold, gallows *sg*
patilla [pa'tiʎa] *nf* (*de gafas*) arm; (*de pelo*) sideburn
patín [pa'tin] *nm* skate; (*de tobogán*) runner; **~ de hielo** ice skate; **~ de ruedas** roller skate
patinaje [pati'naxe] *nm* skating
patinar [pati'nar] *vi* to skate; (*resbalarse*) to skid, slip; (*fam*) to slip up, blunder
patinazo [pati'naθo] *nm* (*Auto*) skid; **dar un ~** (*fam*) to blunder
patio ['patjo] *nm* (*de casa*) patio, courtyard; **~ de recreo** playground
pato ['pato] *nm* duck; **pagar el ~** (*fam*) to take the blame, carry the can
patológico, -a [pato'loxiko, a] *adj* pathological
patoso, -a [pa'toso, a] *adj* awkward, clumsy
patraña [pa'traɲa] *nf* story, fib
patria ['patrja] *nf* native land, mother country; **~ chica** home town
patrimonio [patri'monjo] *nm* inheritance; (*fig*) heritage; (*Com*) net worth
patriota [pa'trjota] *nm/f* patriot
patriotero, -a [patrjo'tero, a] *adj* chauvinistic
patriótico, -a [pa'trjotiko, a] *adj* patriotic
patriotismo [patrjo'tismo] *nm* patriotism
patrocinador, a [patroθina'ðor, a] *nm/f* sponsor
patrocinar [patroθi'nar] *vt* to sponsor; (*apoyar*) to back, support
patrocinio [patro'θinjo] *nm* sponsorship; backing, support
patrón, -ona [pa'tron, ona] *nm/f* (*jefe*) boss, chief, master/mistress; (*propietario*) landlord(-lady); (*Rel*) patron saint ■ *nm* (*Costura*) pattern; (*Tec*) standard; **~ oro** gold standard
patronal [patro'nal] *adj*: **la clase ~** management; **cierre ~** lockout
patronato [patro'nato] *nm* sponsorship; (*acto*) patronage; (*Com*) employers' association; (*fundación*) trust; **el ~ de turismo** the tourist board
patrulla [pa'truʎa] *nf* patrol
patrullar [patru'ʎar] *vi* to patrol
paulatino, -a [paula'tino, a] *adj* gradual, slow
paupérrimo, -a [pau'perrimo, a] *adj* very poor, poverty-stricken
pausa ['pausa] *nf* pause; (*intervalo*) break; (*interrupción*) interruption; (*Tec: en videograbadora*) hold; **con ~** slowly
pausado, -a [pau'saðo, a] *adj* slow, deliberate
pauta ['pauta] *nf* line, guide line
pavimento [paβi'mento] *nm* (*Arq*) flooring
pavo ['paβo] *nm* turkey; (*necio*) silly thing, idiot; **~ real** peacock; **¡no seas ~!** don't be silly!
pavonearse [paβone'arse] *vr* to swagger, show off
pavor [pa'βor] *nm* dread, terror
payasada [paja'saða] *nf* ridiculous thing (to do); **payasadas** *nfpl* clowning *sg*
payaso, -a [pa'jaso, a] *nm/f* clown

payo, -a ['pajo, a] *adj, nm/f* non-gipsy
paz [paθ] *nf* peace; (*tranquilidad*) peacefulness, tranquillity; **dejar a algn en ~** to leave sb alone *o* in peace; **hacer las paces** to make peace; (*fig*) to make up; **¡haya ~!** stop it!
pazca *etc* ['paθka] *vb ver* **pacer**
PC *nm abr* (*Pol*: = *Partido Comunista*) CP
P.C.E. *nm abr* = **Partido Comunista Español**
PCL *nf abr* (= *pantalla de cristal líquido*) LCD
P.D. *abr* (= *posdata*) P.S.
pdo. *abr* (= *pasado*) ult.
peaje [pe'axe] *nm* toll; **autopista de ~** toll motorway, turnpike (US)
peatón [pea'ton] *nm* pedestrian; **paso de peatones** pedestrian crossing, crosswalk (US)
peca ['peka] *nf* freckle
pecado [pe'kaðo] *nm* sin
pecador, a [peka'ðor, a] *adj* sinful ■ *nm/f* sinner
pecaminoso, -a [pekami'noso, a] *adj* sinful
pecar [pe'kar] *vi* (*Rel*) to sin; (*fig*): **~ de generoso** to be too generous
pecera [pe'θera] *nf* goldfish bowl
pecho ['petʃo] *nm* (*Anat*) chest; (*de mujer*) breast(s) *pl*, bosom; (*corazón*) heart, breast; (*valor*) courage, spirit; **dar el ~ a** to breast-feed; **tomar algo a ~** to take sth to heart; **no le cabía en el ~** he was bursting with happiness
pechuga [pe'tʃuɣa] *nf* breast (of chicken *etc*)
pecoso, -a [pe'koso, a] *adj* freckled
peculiar [peku'ljar] *adj* special, peculiar; (*característico*) typical, characteristic
peculiaridad [pekuljari'ðað] *nf* peculiarity; special feature, characteristic
pedagogía [peðaɣo'ɣia] *nf* education
pedagogo [peða'ɣoɣo] *nm* pedagogue, teacher
pedal [pe'ðal] *nm* pedal; **~ de embrague** clutch (pedal); **~ de freno** footbrake
pedalear [peðale'ar] *vi* to pedal
pedante [pe'ðante] *adj* pedantic ■ *nm/f* pedant
pedantería [peðante'ria] *nf* pedantry
pedazo [pe'ðaθo] *nm* piece, bit; **hacerse pedazos** to fall to pieces; (*romperse*) to smash, shatter; **un ~ de pan** a scrap of bread; (*fig*) a terribly nice person
pedernal [peðer'nal] *nm* flint
pedestal [peðes'tal] *nm* base; **tener/poner a algn en un ~** to put sb on a pedestal
pedestre [pe'ðestre] *adj* pedestrian; **carrera ~** foot race
pediatra [pe'ðjatra] *nm/f* paediatrician (*Brit*), pediatrician (US)
pediatría [peðja'tria] *nf* paediatrics *sg* (*Brit*), pediatrics *sg* (US)
pedicuro, -a [peði'kuro, a] *nm/f* chiropodist (*Brit*), podiatrist (US)
pedido [pe'ðiðo] *nm* (*Com*: *mandado*) order; (*petición*) request; **pedidos en cartera** (*Com*) backlog *sg*
pedigrí [peði'ɣri] *nm* pedigree
pedir [pe'ðir] *vt* to ask for, request; (*comida, Com*: *mandar*) to order; (*exigir*: *precio*) to ask; (*necesitar*) to need, demand, require ■ *vi* to ask; **~ prestado** to borrow; **~ disculpas** to apologize; **me pidió que cerrara la puerta** he asked me to shut the door; **¿cuánto piden por el coche?** how much are they asking for the car?
pedo ['peðo] (*fam*) *adj inv*: **estar ~** to be pissed (!) ■ *nm* fart (!)
pedrada [pe'ðraða] *nf* throw of a stone; (*golpe*) blow from a stone; **herir a algn de una ~** to hit sb with a stone
pedrea [pe'ðrea] *nf* (*granizada*) hailstorm; (*de lotería*) minor prizes
pedrisco [pe'ðrisko] *nm* (*granizo*) hail; (*granizada*) hailstorm
Pedro ['peðro] *nm* Peter; **entrar como ~ por su casa** to come in as if one owned the place
pega ['peɣa] *nf* (*dificultad*) snag; **de ~** false, dud; **poner pegas** to raise objections
pegadizo, -a [peɣa'ðiθo, a] *adj* (*canción etc*) catchy
pegajoso, -a [peɣa'xoso, a] *adj* sticky, adhesive
pegamento [peɣa'mento] *nm* gum
pegar [pe'ɣar] *vt* (*papel, sellos*) to stick (on); (*con cola*) to glue; (*cartel*) to post, stick up; (*coser*) to sew (on); (*unir*: *partes*) to join, fix together; (*Inform*) to paste; (*Med*) to give, infect with; (*dar*: *golpe*) to give, deal ■ *vi* (*adherirse*) to stick, adhere; (*Inform*) to paste; (*ir juntos*: *colores*) to match, go together; (*golpear*) to hit; (*quemar*: *el sol*) to strike hot, burn; (*fig*); **pegarse** *vr* (*gen*) to stick; (*dos personas*) to hit each other, fight; **pegarle a algo** to be a great one for sth; **~ un grito** to let out a yell; **~ un salto** to jump (with fright); **~ fuego** to catch fire; **~ en** to touch; **pegarse un tiro** to shoot o.s.; **no pega** that doesn't seem right; **ese sombrero no pega con el abrigo** that hat doesn't go with the coat
pegatina [peɣa'tina] *nf* (*Pol etc*) sticker
pego ['peɣo] *nm*: **dar el ~** (*pasar por verdadero*) to look like the real thing
pegote [pe'ɣote] *nm* (*fig*) patch, ugly mend; **tirarse pegotes** (*fam*) to come on strong
pegue *etc* ['peɣe] *vb ver* **pegar**
peinado [pei'naðo] *nm* (*en peluquería*) hairdo; (*estilo*) hair style

peinar [pei'nar] *vt* to comb sb's hair; (*con un cierto estilo*) to style; **peinarse** *vr* to comb one's hair
peine ['peine] *nm* comb
peineta [pei'neta] *nf* ornamental comb
p.ej. *abr* (= *por ejemplo*) e.g.
Pekín [pe'kin] *n* Peking
pela ['pela] *nf* (*Esp fam*) peseta; *ver tb* **pelas**
pelado, -a [pe'laðo, a] *adj* (*cabeza*) shorn; (*fruta*) peeled; (*campo, fig*) bare; (*fam: sin dinero*) broke
pelaje [pe'laxe] *nm* (*Zool*) fur, coat; (*fig*) appearance
pelambre [pe'lambre] *nm* long hair, mop
pelar [pe'lar] *vt* (*fruta, patatas*) to peel; (*cortar el pelo a*) to cut the hair of; (*quitar la piel: animal*) to skin; (*ave*) to pluck; (*habas etc*) to shell; **pelarse** *vr* (*la piel*) to peel off; **corre que se las pela** (*fam*) he runs like nobody's business
pelas ['pelas] *nfpl* (*Esp fam*) dough
peldaño [pel'daɲo] *nm* step; (*de escalera portátil*) rung
pelea [pe'lea] *nf* (*lucha*) fight; (*discusión*) quarrel, row
peleado, -a [pele'aðo, a] *adj*: **estar ~ (con algn)** to have fallen out (with sb)
pelear [pele'ar] *vi* to fight; **pelearse** *vr* to fight; (*reñir*) to fall out, quarrel
pelele [pe'lele] *nm* (*figura*) guy, dummy; (*fig*) puppet
peletería [pelete'ria] *nf* furrier's, fur shop
peliagudo, -a [pelja'ɣuðo, a] *adj* tricky
pelícano [pe'likano] *nm* pelican
película [pe'likula] *nf* (*Cine*) film, movie (*US*); (*cobertura ligera*) film, thin covering; (*Foto: rollo*) roll *o* reel of film; **~ de dibujos (animados)** cartoon film; **~ muda** silent film; **de ~** (*fam*) astonishing, out of this world
peligrar [peli'ɣrar] *vi* to be in danger
peligro [pe'liɣro] *nm* danger; (*riesgo*) risk; **"~ de muerte"** "danger"; **correr ~ de** to be in danger of; **con ~ de la vida** at the risk of one's life
peligrosidad [peliɣrosi'ðað] *nf* danger, riskiness
peligroso, -a [peli'ɣroso, a] *adj* dangerous; risky
pelirrojo, -a [peli'rroxo, a] *adj* red-haired, red-headed
pellejo [pe'ʎexo] *nm* (*de animal*) skin, hide; **salvar el ~** to save one's skin
pellizcar [peʎiθ'kar] *vt* to pinch, nip
pellizco [pe'ʎiθko] *nm* pinch
pellizque *etc* [pe'ʎiθke] *vb ver* **pellizcar**
pelma ['pelma] *nm/f*, **pelmazo** [pel'maθo] *nm* (*fam*) pest
pelo ['pelo] *nm* (*cabellos*) hair; (*de barba, bigote*) whisker; (*de animal: piel*) fur, coat; (*de perro etc*) hair, coat; (*de ave*) down; (*de tejido*) nap; (*Tec*) fibre; **a ~** bareheaded; (*desnudo*) naked; **al ~** just right; **venir al ~** to be exactly what one needs; **por los pelos** by the skin of one's teeth; **escaparse por un ~** to have a close shave; **se me pusieron los pelos de punta** my hair stood on end; **no tener pelos en la lengua** to be outspoken, not mince words; **tomar el ~ a algn** to pull sb's leg
pelón, -ona [pe'lon, ona] *adj* hairless, bald
pelota [pe'lota] *nf* ball; (*fam: cabeza*) nut (*fam*); **en ~(s)** stark naked; **~ vasca** pelota; **devolver la ~ a algn** (*fig*) to turn the tables on sb; **hacer la ~ (a algn)** to creep (to sb)
pelotera [pelo'tera] *nf* (*fam*) barney
pelotón [pelo'ton] *nm* (*Mil*) squad, detachment
peluca [pe'luka] *nf* wig
peluche [pe'lutʃe] *nm*: **muñeco de ~** soft toy
peludo, -a [pe'luðo, a] *adj* hairy, shaggy
peluquería [peluke'ria] *nf* hairdresser's; (*para hombres*) barber's (shop)
peluquero, -a [pelu'kero, a] *nm/f* hairdresser; barber
peluquín [pelu'kin] *nm* toupée
pelusa [pe'lusa] *nf* (*Bot*) down; (*Costura*) fluff
pelvis ['pelβis] *nf* pelvis
PEMEX [pe'meks] *nm abr* = **Petróleos Mejicanos**
PEN [pen] *nm abr* (*Esp:* = *Plan Energético Nacional: Arg*) = **Poder Ejecutivo Nacional**
pena ['pena] *nf* (*congoja*) grief, sadness; (*remordimiento*) regret; (*dificultad*) trouble; (*dolor*) pain; (*Am: vergüenza*) shame; (*Jur*) sentence; (*Deporte*) penalty; **~ capital** capital punishment; **~ de muerte** death penalty; **~ pecuniaria** fine; **merecer** *o* **valer la ~** to be worthwhile; **a duras penas** with great difficulty; **so ~ de** on pain of; **me dan ~** I feel sorry for them; **¿no te da ~ hacerlo?** (*Am*) aren't you embarrassed doing that?; **¡qué ~!** what a shame *o* pity!
penal [pe'nal] *adj* penal ▪ *nm* (*cárcel*) prison
penalidad [penali'ðað] *nf* (*problema, dificultad*) trouble, hardship; (*Jur*) penalty, punishment
penalizar [penali'θar] *vt* to penalize
penalti, penalty [pe'nalti] *nm* (*Deporte*) penalty
penar [pe'nar] *vt* to penalize; (*castigar*) to punish ▪ *vi* to suffer
pendejo, -a [pen'dexo, a] *nm/f* (*Am fam!*) wanker (*Brit*) (!), jerk (*US*) (!)
pender [pen'der] *vi* (*colgar*) to hang; (*Jur*) to be pending
pendiente [pen'djente] *adj* pending,

unsettled ■ *nm* earring ■ *nf* hill, slope; **tener una asignatura ~** to have to resit a subject
pendón [pen'don] *nm* banner, standard
péndulo ['pendulo] *nm* pendulum
pene ['pene] *nm* penis
penene [pe'nene] *nm/f* = **PNN**
penetración [penetra'θjon] *nf* (*acto*) penetration; (*agudeza*) sharpness, insight
penetrante [pene'trante] *adj* (*herida*) deep; (*persona, arma*) sharp; (*sonido*) penetrating, piercing; (*mirada*) searching; (*viento, ironía*) biting
penetrar [pene'trar] *vt* to penetrate, pierce; (*entender*) to grasp ■ *vi* to penetrate, go in; (*líquido*) to soak in; (*emoción*) to pierce
penicilina [peniθi'lina] *nf* penicillin
península [pe'ninsula] *nf* peninsula; **P~ Ibérica** Iberian Peninsula
peninsular [peninsu'lar] *adj* peninsular
penique [pe'nike] *nm* penny; **peniques** *nmpl* pence
penitencia [peni'tenθja] *nf* (*remordimiento*) penitence; (*castigo*) penance; **en ~** as a penance
penitencial [peniten'θjal] *adj* penitential
penitenciaría [penitenθja'ria] *nf* prison, penitentiary
penitenciario, -a [peniten'θjarjo, a] *adj* prison *cpd*
penoso, -a [pe'noso, a] *adj* laborious, difficult
pensado, -a [pen'saðo, a] *adj*: **bien/mal ~** well intentioned/cynical; **en el momento menos ~** when least expected
pensador, a [pensa'ðor, a] *nm/f* thinker
pensamiento [pensa'mjento] *nm* (*gen*) thought; (*mente*) mind; (*idea*) idea; (*Bot*) pansy; **no se le pasó por el ~** it never occurred to him
pensar [pen'sar] *vt* to think; (*considerar*) to think over, think out; (*proponerse*) to intend, plan, propose; (*imaginarse*) to think up, invent ■ *vi* to think; **~ en** to think of *o* about; (*anhelar*) to aim at, aspire to; **dar que ~ a algn** to give sb food for thought
pensativo, -a [pensa'tiβo, a] *adj* thoughtful, pensive
pensión [pen'sjon] *nf* (*casa*) ≈ guest house; (*dinero*) pension; (*cama y comida*) board and lodging; **~ de jubilación** retirement pension; **~ escalada** graduated pension; **~ completa** full board; **media ~** half board
pensionista [pensjo'nista] *nm/f* (*jubilado*) (old-age) pensioner; (*el que vive en una pensión*) lodger; (*Escol*) boarder
pentágono [pen'taɣono] *nm* pentagon; **el P~** the Pentagon
pentagrama [penta'ɣrama] *nm* (*Mus*) stave, staff
penúltimo, -a [pe'nultimo, a] *adj* penultimate, second last
penumbra [pe'numbra] *nf* half-light, semi-darkness
penuria [pe'nurja] *nf* shortage, want
peña ['peɲa] *nf* (*roca*) rock; (*acantilado*) cliff, crag; (*grupo*) group, circle; (*Deporte*) supporters' club
peñasco [pe'ɲasko] *nm* large rock, boulder
peñón [pe'ɲon] *nm* crag; **el P~** the Rock (of Gibraltar)
peón [pe'on] *nm* labourer; (*Am*) farm labourer, farmhand; (*Tec*) spindle, shaft; (*Ajedrez*) pawn
peonza [pe'onθa] *nf* spinning top
peor [pe'or] *adj* (*comparativo*) worse; (*superlativo*) worst ■ *adv* worse; worst; **de mal en ~** from bad to worse; **tanto ~** so much the worse; **A es ~ que B** A is worse than B; **Z es el ~ de todos** Z is the worst of all
pepenar [pepe'nar] *vi* (*Am*) to sift through rubbish *o* garbage
pepinillo [pepi'niʎo] *nm* gherkin
pepino [pe'pino] *nm* cucumber; **(no) me importa un ~** I don't care two hoots
pepita [pe'pita] *nf* (*Bot*) pip; (*Minería*) nugget
pepito [pe'pito] *nm* meat sandwich
peque *etc* ['peke] *vb ver* **pecar**
pequeñez [peke'ɲeθ] *nf* smallness, littleness; (*trivialidad*) trifle, triviality
pequeño, -a [pe'keɲo, a] *adj* small, little; (*cifra*) small, low; (*bajo*) short; **~ burgués** lower middle-class
pequinés, -esa [peki'nes, esa] *adj, nm/f* Pekinese
pera ['pera] *adj inv* classy; **niño ~** spoiled upper-class brat ■ *nf* pear; **eso es pedir peras al olmo** that's asking the impossible
peral [pe'ral] *nm* pear tree
percance [per'kanθe] *nm* setback, misfortune
per cápita [per'kapita] *adj*: **renta ~** per capita income
percatarse [perka'tarse] *vr*: **~ de** to notice, take note of
percebe [per'θeβe] *nm* (*Zool*) barnacle; (*fam*) idiot
percepción [perθep'θjon] *nf* (*vista*) perception; (*idea*) notion, idea; (*Com*) collection
perceptible [perθep'tiβle] *adj* perceptible, noticeable; (*Com*) payable, receivable
percha ['pertʃa] *nf* (*poste*) pole, support; (*gancho*) peg; (*de abrigos*) coat stand; (*colgador*) coat hanger; (*de ave*) perch

perchero [per'tʃero] *nm* clothes rack
percibir [perθi'βir] *vt* to perceive, notice; (*ver*) to see; (*peligro etc*) to sense; (*Com*) to earn, receive, get
percusión [perku'sjon] *nf* percussion
percusor [perku'sor], **percutor** [perku'tor] *nm* (*Tec*) hammer; (*de arma*) firing pin
perdedor, a [perðe'ðor, a] *adj* losing ▪ *nm/f* loser
perder [per'ðer] *vt* to lose; (*tiempo, palabras*) to waste; (*oportunidad*) to lose, miss; (*tren*) to miss ▪ *vi* to lose; **perderse** *vr* (*extraviarse*) to get lost; (*desaparecer*) to disappear, be lost to view; (*arruinarse*) to be ruined; **echar a ~** (*comida*) to spoil, ruin; (*oportunidad*) to waste; **tener buen ~** to be a good loser; **¡no te lo pierdas!** don't miss it!; **he perdido la costumbre** I have got out of the habit
perdición [perði'θjon] *nf* perdition; (*fig*) ruin
pérdida ['perðiða] *nf* loss; (*de tiempo*) waste; (*Com*) net loss; **pérdidas** *nfpl* (*Com*) losses; **¡no tiene ~!** you can't go wrong!; **~ contable** (*Com*) book loss
perdido, -a [per'ðiðo, a] *adj* lost; **estar ~ por** to be crazy about; **es un caso ~** he is a hopeless case
perdigón [perði'ɣon] *nm* pellet
perdiz [per'ðiθ] *nf* partridge
perdón [per'ðon] *nm* (*disculpa*) pardon, forgiveness; (*clemencia*) mercy; **¡~!** sorry!, I beg your pardon!; **con ~** if I may, if you don't mind
perdonar [perðo'nar] *vt* to pardon, forgive; (*la vida*) to spare; (*excusar*) to exempt, excuse ▪ *vi* to pardon, forgive; **¡perdone (usted)!** sorry!, I beg your pardon!; **perdone, pero me parece que ...** excuse me, but I think ...
perdurable [perðu'raβle] *adj* lasting; (*eterno*) everlasting
perdurar [perðu'rar] *vi* (*resistir*) to last, endure; (*seguir existiendo*) to stand, still exist
perecedero, -a [pereθe'ðero, a] *adj* perishable
perecer [pere'θer] *vi* to perish, die
peregrinación [pereɣrina'θjon] *nf* (*Rel*) pilgrimage
peregrino, -a [pere'ɣrino] *adj* (*extraño*) strange; (*singular*) rare ▪ *nm/f* pilgrim
perejil [pere'xil] *nm* parsley
perenne [pe'renne] *adj* perennial
perentorio, -a [peren'torjo, a] *adj* (*urgente*) urgent; (*terminante*) peremptory; (*fijo*) set, fixed
pereza [pe'reθa] *nf* (*flojera*) laziness; (*lentitud*) sloth, slowness
perezca *etc* [pe'reθka] *vb ver* **perecer**
perezoso, -a [pere'θoso, a] *adj* lazy; slow, sluggish
perfección [perfek'θjon] *nf* perfection; **a la ~** to perfection
perfeccionar [perfekθjo'nar] *vt* to perfect; (*acabar*) to complete, finish
perfecto, -a [per'fekto, a] *adj* perfect ▪ *nm* (*Ling*) perfect (tense)
perfidia [per'fiðja] *nf* perfidy, treachery
pérfido, -a ['perfiðo, a] *adj* perfidious, treacherous
perfil [per'fil] *nm* (*parte lateral*) profile; (*silueta*) silhouette, outline; (*Tec*) (cross) section; **perfiles** *nmpl* features; (*fig*) social graces; **~ del cliente** (*Com*) customer profile; **en ~** from the side, in profile
perfilado, -a [perfi'laðo, a] *adj* (*bien formado*) well-shaped; (*largo: cara*) long
perfilar [perfi'lar] *vt* (*trazar*) to outline; (*dar carácter a*) to shape, give character to; **perfilarse** *vr* to be silhouetted (*en* against); **el proyecto se va perfilando** the project is taking shape
perforación [perfora'θjon] *nf* perforation; (*con taladro*) drilling
perforadora [perfora'ðora] *nf* drill; **~ de fichas** card-punch
perforar [perfo'rar] *vt* to perforate; (*agujero*) to drill, bore; (*papel*) to punch a hole in ▪ *vi* to drill, bore
perfumar [perfu'mar] *vt* to scent, perfume
perfume [per'fume] *nm* perfume, scent
perfumería [perfume'ria] *nf* perfume shop
pergamino [perɣa'mino] *nm* parchment
pericia [pe'riθja] *nf* skill, expertise
periferia [peri'ferja] *nf* periphery; (*de ciudad*) outskirts *pl*
periférico, -a [peri'feriko, a] *adj* peripheral ▪ *nm* (*Inform*) peripheral; (*Am: Auto*) ring road; **barrio ~** outlying district
perilla [pe'riʎa] *nf* goatee
perímetro [pe'rimetro] *nm* perimeter
periódico, -a [pe'rjoðiko, a] *adj* periodic(al) ▪ *nm* (news)paper; **~ dominical** Sunday (news)paper
periodismo [perjo'ðismo] *nm* journalism
periodista [perjo'ðista] *nm/f* journalist
periodístico, -a [perjo'ðistiko, a] *adj* journalistic
periodo [pe'rjoðo], **período** [pe'rioðo] *nm* period; **~ contable** (*Com*) accounting period
peripecias [peri'peθjas] *nfpl* adventures
peripuesto, -a [peri'pwesto, a] *adj* dressed up; **tan ~** all dressed up (to the nines)
periquito [peri'kito] *nm* budgerigar, budgie (*fam*)
perito, -a [pe'rito, a] *adj* (*experto*) expert; (*diestro*) skilled, skilful ▪ *nm/f* expert; skilled worker; (*técnico*) technician

perjudicar [perxuði'kar] *vt* (*gen*) to damage, harm; (*fig*) to prejudice
perjudicial [perxuði'θjal] *adj* damaging, harmful; (*en detrimento*) detrimental
perjudique *etc* [perxu'ðike] *vb ver* **perjudicar**
perjuicio [per'xwiθjo] *nm* damage, harm; **en/sin ~ de** to the detriment of/without prejudice to
perjurar [perxu'rar] *vi* to commit perjury
perla ['perla] *nf* pearl; **me viene de perlas** it suits me fine
permanecer [permane'θer] *vi* (*quedarse*) to stay, remain; (*seguir*) to continue to be
permanencia [perma'nenθja] *nf* (*duración*) permanence; (*estancia*) stay
permanente [perma'nente] *adj* (*que queda*) permanent; (*constante*) constant; (*comisión etc*) standing ■ *nf* perm; **hacerse una ~** to have one's hair permed
permanezca *etc* [perma'neθka] *vb ver* **permanecer**
permisible [permi'siβle] *adj* permissible, allowable
permiso [per'miso] *nm* permission; (*licencia*) permit, licence (*Brit*), license (*US*); **con ~** excuse me; **estar de ~** (*Mil*) to be on leave; **~ de conducir** *o* **conductor** driving licence (*Brit*), driver's license (*US*); **~ de exportación/importación** export/import licence; **~ por asuntos familiares** compassionate leave
permitir [permi'tir] *vt* to permit, allow; **permitirse** *vr*: **permitirse algo** to allow o.s. sth; **no me puedo ~ ese lujo** I can't afford that; **¿me permite?** may I?; **si lo permite el tiempo** weather permitting
permuta [per'muta] *nf* exchange
permutar [permu'tar] *vt* to switch, exchange; **~ destinos con algn** to swap *o* exchange jobs with sb
pernicioso, -a [perni'θjoso, a] *adj* (*maligno*, *Med*) pernicious; (*persona*) wicked
perno ['perno] *nm* bolt
pernoctar [pernok'tar] *vi* to stay for the night
pero ['pero] *conj* but; (*aún*) yet ■ *nm* (*defecto*) flaw, defect; (*reparo*) objection; **¡no hay ~ que valga!** there are no buts about it
perogrullada [peroɣru'ʎaða] *nf* platitude, truism
perol [pe'rol] *nm*, **perola** [pe'rola] *nf* pan
peronista [pero'nista] *adj*, *nm/f* Peronist
perorata [pero'rata] *nf* long-winded speech
perpendicular [perpendiku'lar] *adj* perpendicular; **el camino es ~ al río** the road is at right angles to the river
perpetrar [perpe'trar] *vt* to perpetrate
perpetuamente [perpetwa'mente] *adv* perpetually
perpetuar [perpe'twar] *vt* to perpetuate
perpetuo, -a [per'petwo, a] *adj* perpetual; (*Jur etc: condena*) life *cpd*
Perpiñán [perpi'ɲan] *nm* Perpignan
perplejo, -a [per'plexo, a] *adj* perplexed, bewildered
perra ['perra] *nf* bitch; (*fam: dinero*) money; (*: manía*) mania, crazy idea; (*: rabieta*) tantrum; **estar sin una ~** to be flat broke
perrera [pe'rrera] *nf* kennel
perro ['perro] *nm* dog; **~ caliente** hot dog; **"~ peligroso"** "beware of the dog"; **ser ~ viejo** to be an old hand; **tiempo de perros** filthy weather; **~ que ladra no muerde** his bark is worse than his bite
persa ['persa] *adj*, *nm/f* Persian ■ *nm* (*Ling*) Persian
persecución [perseku'θjon] *nf* pursuit, hunt, chase; (*Rel*, *Pol*) persecution
perseguir [perse'ɣir] *vt* to pursue, hunt; (*cortejar*) to chase after; (*molestar*) to pester, annoy; (*Rel*, *Pol*) to persecute; (*Jur*) to prosecute
perseverante [perseβe'rante] *adj* persevering, persistent
perseverar [perseve'rar] *vi* to persevere, persist; **~ en** to persevere in, persist with
persiana [per'sjana] *nf* (Venetian) blind
persiga *etc* [per'siɣa] *vb ver* **perseguir**
persignarse [persiɣ'narse] *vr* to cross o.s.
persiguiendo *etc* [persi'ɣjenðo] *vb ver* **perseguir**
persistente [persis'tente] *adj* persistent
persistir [persis'tir] *vi* to persist
persona [per'sona] *nf* person; **10 personas** 10 people; **tercera ~** third party; (*Ling*) third person; **en ~** in person *o* the flesh; **por ~** a head; **es buena ~** he's a good sort
personaje [perso'naxe] *nm* important person, celebrity; (*Teat*) character
personal [perso'nal] *adj* (*particular*) personal; (*para una persona*) single, for one person ■ *nm* (*plantilla*) personnel, staff; (*Naut*) crew; (*fam: gente*) people
personalidad [personali'ðað] *nf* personality; (*Jur*) status
personalizar [personali'θar] *vt* to personalize ■ *vi* (*al hablar*) to name names
personarse [perso'narse] *vr* to appear in person; **~ en** to present o.s. at, report to
personero, -a [perso'nero, a] *nm/f* (*Am*) (government) official
personificar [personifi'kar] *vt* to personify
personifique *etc* [personi'fike] *vb ver* **personificar**

perspectiva [perspek'tiβa] *nf* perspective; (*vista, panorama*) view, panorama; (*posibilidad futura*) outlook, prospect; **tener algo en ~** to have sth in view
perspicacia [perspi'kaθja] *nf* discernment, perspicacity
perspicaz [perspi'kaθ] *adj* shrewd
persuadir [perswa'ðir] *vt* (*gen*) to persuade; (*convencer*) to convince; **persuadirse** *vr* to become convinced
persuasión [perswa'sjon] *nf* (*acto*) persuasion; (*convicción*) conviction
persuasivo, -a [perwa'siβo, a] *adj* persuasive; convincing
pertenecer [pertene'θer] *vi*: **~ a** to belong to; (*fig*) to concern
perteneciente [pertene'θjente] *adj*: **~ a** belonging to
pertenencia [perte'nenθja] *nf* ownership; **pertenencias** *nfpl* possessions, property *sg*
pertenezca *etc* [perte'neθka] *vb ver* **pertenecer**
pértiga ['pertiɣa] *nf* pole; **salto de ~** pole vault
pertinaz [perti'naθ] *adj* (*persistente*) persistent; (*terco*) obstinate
pertinente [perti'nente] *adj* relevant, pertinent; (*apropiado*) appropriate; **~ a** concerning, relevant to
pertrechar [pertre'tʃar] *vt* (*gen*) to supply; (*Mil*) to supply with ammunition and stores; **pertrecharse** *vr*: **pertrecharse de algo** to provide o.s. with sth
pertrechos [per'tretʃos] *nmpl* (*gen*) implements; (*Mil*) supplies and stores
perturbación [perturβa'θjon] *nf* (*Pol*) disturbance; (*Med*) upset, disturbance; **~ del orden público** breach of the peace
perturbador, a [perturβa'ðor, a] *adj* (*que perturba*) perturbing, disturbing; (*subversivo*) subversive
perturbar [pertur'βar] *vt* (*el orden*) to disturb; (*Med*) to upset, disturb; (*mentalmente*) to perturb
Perú [pe'ru] *nm*: **el Perú** Peru
peruano, -a [pe'rwano, a] *adj, nm/f* Peruvian
perversión [perβer'sjon] *nf* perversion
perverso, -a [perβerso, a] *adj* perverse; (*depravado*) depraved
pervertido, -a [perβer'tiðo, a] *adj* perverted ■ *nm/f* pervert
pervertir [perβer'tir] *vt* to pervert, corrupt
pervierta *etc* [per'βjerta], **pervirtiendo** *etc* [perβir'tjendo] *vb ver* **pervertir**
pesa ['pesa] *nf* weight; (*Deporte*) shot
pesadez [pesa'ðeθ] *nf* (*calidad de pesado*) heaviness; (*lentitud*) slowness; (*aburrimiento*) tediousness; **es una ~ tener que ...** it's a bind having to ...
pesadilla [pesa'ðiʎa] *nf* nightmare, bad dream; (*fig*) worry, obsession
pesado, -a [pe'saðo, a] *adj* (*gen*) heavy; (*lento*) slow; (*difícil, duro*) tough, hard; (*aburrido*) tedious, boring; (*bochornoso*) sultry ■ *nm/f* bore; **tener el estómago ~** to feel bloated; **¡no seas ~!** come off it!
pesadumbre [pesa'ðumbre] *nf* grief, sorrow
pésame ['pesame] *nm* expression of condolence, message of sympathy; **dar el ~** to express one's condolences
pesar [pe'sar] *vt* to weigh; (*fig*) to weigh heavily on; (*afligir*) to grieve ■ *vi* to weigh; (*ser pesado*) to weigh a lot, be heavy; (*fig: opinión*) to carry weight ■ *nm* (*sentimiento*) regret; (*pena*) grief, sorrow; **a ~ de (que)** in spite of, despite; **no me pesa haberlo hecho** I'm not sorry I did it
pesca ['peska] *nf* (*acto*) fishing; (*cantidad de pescado*) catch; **~ de altura/en bajura** deep sea/coastal fishing; **ir de ~** to go fishing
pescadería [peskaðe'ria] *nf* fish shop, fishmonger's
pescadilla [peska'ðiʎa] *nf* whiting
pescado [pes'kaðo] *nm* fish
pescador, a [peska'ðor, a] *nm/f* fisherman(-woman)
pescar [pes'kar] *vt* (*coger*) to catch; (*tratar de coger*) to fish for; (*fam: lograr*) to get hold of, land; (*conseguir: trabajo*) to manage to get; (*sorprender*) to catch unawares ■ *vi* to fish, go fishing
pescuezo [pes'kweθo] *nm* neck
pese ['pese] *prep*: **~ a** despite, in spite of
pesebre [pe'seβre] *nm* manger
peseta [pe'seta] *nf* peseta
pesetero, -a [pese'tero, a] *adj* money-grubbing
pesimismo [pesi'mismo] *nm* pessimism
pesimista [pesi'mista] *adj* pessimistic ■ *nm/f* pessimist
pésimo, -a ['pesimo, a] *adj* abominable, vile
peso ['peso] *nm* weight; (*balanza*) scales *pl*; (*Am Com*) *monetary unit*; (*moneda*) peso; (*Deporte*) shot; **~ bruto/neto** gross/net weight; **~ mosca/pesado** fly-/heavyweight; **de poco ~** light(weight); **levantamiento de pesos** weightlifting; **vender a ~** to sell by weight; **argumento de ~** weighty argument; **eso cae de su ~** that goes without saying
pesque *etc* ['peske] *vb ver* **pescar**
pesquero, -a [pes'kero, a] *adj* fishing *cpd*
pesquisa [pes'kisa] *nf* inquiry, investigation
pestaña [pes'taɲa] *nf* (*Anat*) eyelash; (*borde*) rim

pestañear [pestaɲe'ar] *vi* to blink
peste ['peste] *nf* plague; (*fig*) nuisance; (*mal olor*) stink, stench; ~ **negra** Black Death; **echar pestes** to swear, fume
pesticida [pesti'θiða] *nm* pesticide
pestilencia [pesti'lenθja] *nf* (*mal olor*) stink, stench
pestillo [pes'tiʎo] *nm* bolt, latch; (*cerrojo*) catch; (*picaporte*) (door) handle
petaca [pe'taka] *nf* (*de cigarrillos*) cigarette case; (*de pipa*) tobacco pouch; (*Am: maleta*) suitcase
pétalo ['petalo] *nm* petal
petanca [pe'tanka] *nf a game in which metal bowls are thrown at a target bowl*
petardo [pe'tarðo] *nm* firework, firecracker
petición [peti'θjon] *nf* (*pedido*) request, plea; (*memorial*) petition; (*Jur*) plea; **a ~ de** at the request of; ~ **de aumento de salarios** wage demand *o* claim
petirrojo [peti'rroxo] *nm* robin
peto ['peto] *nm* (*corpiño*) bodice; (*Taur*) horse's padding
pétreo, -a ['petreo, a] *adj* stony, rocky
petrificar [petrifi'kar] *vt* to petrify
petrifique *etc* [petri'fike] *vb ver* **petrificar**
PETROVEN [petro'ben] *nm abr* = **Petróleos de Venezuela**
petrodólar [petro'ðolar] *nm* petrodollar
petróleo [pe'troleo] *nm* oil, petroleum
petrolero, -a [petro'lero, a] *adj* petroleum *cpd* ■ *nm* (*Com*) oil man; (*buque*) (oil) tanker
petulancia [petu'lanθja] *nf* (*insolencia*) vanity, opinionated nature
peyorativo, -a [pejora'tiβo, a] *adj* pejorative
pez [peθ] *nm* fish; ~ **de colores** goldfish; ~ **espada** swordfish; **estar como el ~ en el agua** to feel completely at home
pezón [pe'θon] *nm* teat, nipple
pezuña [pe'θuɲa] *nf* hoof
piadoso, -a [pja'ðoso, a] *adj* (*devoto*) pious, devout; (*misericordioso*) kind, merciful
Piamonte [pja'monte] *nm* Piedmont
pianista [pja'nista] *nm/f* pianist
piano ['pjano] *nm* piano; ~ **de cola** grand piano
piar [pjar] *vi* to cheep
piara ['pjara] *nf* (*manada*) herd, drove
PIB *nm abr* (*Esp Com: = Producto Interno Bruto*) GDP
pibe, -a ['piβe, a] *nm/f* (*Am*) boy/girl, kid, child
pica ['pika] *nf* (*Mil*) pike; (*Taur*) goad; **poner una ~ en Flandes** to bring off something difficult
picadero [pika'ðero] *nm* riding school
picadillo [pika'ðiʎo] *nm* mince, minced meat
picado, -a [pi'kaðo, a] *adj* pricked, punctured; (*mar*) choppy; (*diente*) bad; (*tabaco*) cut; (*enfadado*) cross
picador [pika'ðor] *nm* (*Taur*) picador; (*minero*) faceworker
picadora [pika'ðora] *nf* mincer
picadura [pika'ðura] *nf* (*pinchazo*) puncture; (*de abeja*) sting; (*de mosquito*) bite; (*tabaco picado*) cut tobacco
picana [pi'kana] (*Am*) *nf* (*Agr*) cattle prod; (*Pol: para tortura*) electric prod
picante [pi'kante] *adj* (*comida, sabor*) hot; (*comentario*) racy, spicy
picaporte [pika'porte] *nm* (*tirador*) handle; (*pestillo*) latch
picar [pi'kar] *vt* (*agujerear, perforar*) to prick, puncture; (*billete*) to punch, clip; (*abeja*) to sting; (*mosquito, serpiente*) to bite; (*persona*) to nibble (at); (*incitar*) to incite, goad; (*dañar, irritar*) to annoy, bother; (*quemar: lengua*) to burn, sting ■ *vi* (*pez*) to bite, take the bait; (*el sol*) to burn, scorch; (*abeja, Med*) to sting; (*mosquito*) to bite; **picarse** *vr* (*agriarse*) to turn sour, go off; (*mar*) to get choppy; (*ofenderse*) to take offence; **me pican los ojos** my eyes sting; **me pica el brazo** my arm itches
picardía [pikar'ðia] *nf* villainy; (*astucia*) slyness, craftiness; (*una picardía*) dirty trick; (*palabra*) rude/bad word *o* expression
picaresco, -a [pika'resko, a] *adj* (*travieso*) roguish, rascally; (*Lit*) picaresque
pícaro, -a ['pikaro, a] *adj* (*malicioso*) villainous; (*travieso*) mischievous ■ *nm* (*astuto*) sly sort; (*sinvergüenza*) rascal, scoundrel
picazón [pika'θon] *nf* (*comezón*) itch; (*ardor*) sting(ing feeling); (*remordimiento*) pang of conscience
pichón, -ona [pi'tʃon, ona] *nm/f* (*de paloma*) young pigeon; (*apelativo*) darling, dearest
pico ['piko] *nm* (*de ave*) beak; (*punta agudo*) peak, sharp point; (*Tec*) pick, pickaxe; (*Geo*) peak, summit; (*labia*) talkativeness; **no abrir el ~** to keep quiet; ~ **parásito** (*Elec*) spike; **y ~** and a bit; **son las tres y ~** it's just after three; **tiene 50 libros y ~** he has 50-odd books; **me costó un ~** it cost me quite a bit
picor [pi'kor] *nm* itch; (*ardor*) sting(ing feeling)
picota [pi'kota] *nf* pillory; **poner a algn en la ~** (*fig*) to ridicule sb
picotada [piko'taða] *nf*, **picotazo** [piko'taθo] *nm* (*de pájaro*) peck; (*de insecto*) sting, bite
picotear [pikote'ar] *vt* to peck ■ *vi* to nibble, pick
pictórico, -a [pik'toriko, a] *adj* pictorial;

tiene dotes pictóricas she has a talent for painting
picudo, -a [pi'kuðo, a] *adj* pointed, with a point
pidiendo *etc* [pi'ðjendo] *vb ver* **pedir**
pie [pje] (*pl* **pies**) *nm* (*gen, Mat*) foot; (*de cama, página, escalera*) foot, bottom; (*Teat*) cue; (*fig: motivo*) motive, basis; (*: fundamento*) foothold; **pies planos** flat feet; **ir a ~** to go on foot, walk; **estar de ~** to be standing (up); **ponerse de ~** to stand up; **al ~ de la letra** (*citar*) literally, verbatim; (*copiar*) exactly, word for word; **de pies a cabeza** from head to foot; **en ~ de guerra** on a war footing; **sin pies ni cabeza** pointless, absurd; **dar ~ a** to give cause for; **no dar ~ con bola** to be no good at anything; **saber de qué ~ cojea algn** to know sb's weak spots
piedad [pje'ðað] *nf* (*lástima*) pity, compassion; (*clemencia*) mercy; (*devoción*) piety, devotion; **tener ~ de** to take pity on
piedra ['pjeðra] *nf* stone; (*roca*) rock; (*de mechero*) flint; (*Meteorología*) hailstone; **primera ~** foundation stone; **~ de afilar** grindstone; **~ arenisca/caliza** sand-/limestone
piel [pjel] *nf* (*Anat*) skin; (*Zool*) skin, hide; (*de oso*) fur; (*cuero*) leather; (*Bot*) skin, peel ▪ *nm/f*: **~ roja** redskin
pienso *etc* ['pjenso] *vb ver* **pensar** ▪ *nm* (*Agr*) feed
piercing ['pjersiŋ] *nm* piercing
pierda *etc* ['pjerða] *vb ver* **perder**
pierna ['pjerna] *nf* leg; **en piernas** bare-legged
pieza ['pjeθa] *nf* piece; (*esp Am: habitación*) room; (*Mus*) piece, composition; (*Teat*) work, play; **~ de recambio** *o* **repuesto** spare (part), extra (US); **~ de ropa** article of clothing; **quedarse de una ~** to be dumbfounded
pigmento [piɣ'mento] *nm* pigment
pigmeo, -a [piɣ'meo, a] *adj, nm/f* pigmy
pijama [pi'xama] *nm* pyjamas *pl*
pijo, -a ['pixo, a] *nm/f* (*fam*) upper-class twit
pijotada [pixo'taða] *nf* nuisance
pila ['pila] *nf* (*Elec*) battery; (*montón*) heap, pile; (*de fuente*) sink; (*Rel: tb:* **pila bautismal**) font; **nombre de ~** Christian *o* first name; **tengo una ~ de cosas que hacer** (*fam*) I have heaps *o* stacks of things to do
pilar [pi'lar] *nm* pillar; (*de puente*) pier; (*fig*) prop, mainstay
píldora ['pildora] *nf* pill; **la ~ (anticonceptiva)** the pill; **tragarse la ~** to be taken in
pileta [pi'leta] *nf* basin, bowl; (*Am: de cocina*) sink; (*: piscina*) swimming pool
pillaje [pi'ʎaxe] *nm* pillage, plunder
pillar [pi'ʎar] *vt* (*fam: coger*) to catch; (*: agarrar*) to grasp, seize; (*: entender*) to grasp, catch on to; (*suj: coche etc*) to run over; **~ un resfriado** (*fam*) to catch a cold
pillo, -a ['piʎo, a] *adj* villainous; (*astuto*) sly, crafty ▪ *nm/f* rascal, rogue, scoundrel
pilón [pi'lon] *nm* pillar, post; (*Elec*) pylon; (*bebedero*) drinking trough; (*de fuente*) basin
pilotar [pilo'tar] *vt* (*avión*) to pilot; (*barco*) to steer
piloto [pi'loto] *nm* pilot; (*Auto*) rear light, tail light; (*conductor*) driver ▪ *adj inv*: **planta ~** pilot plant; **luz ~** side light
piltrafa [pil'trafa] *nf* (*carne*) poor quality meat; (*fig*) worthless object; (*: individuo*) wretch
pimentón [pimen'ton] *nm* (*polvo*) paprika
pimienta [pi'mjenta] *nf* pepper
pimiento [pi'mjento] *nm* pepper, pimiento
pimpante [pim'pante] *adj* (*encantador*) charming; (*tb:* **tan pimpante**) smug, self-satisfied
PIN *nm abr* (*Esp Com:* = *Producto Interior Neto*) net domestic product
pin (*pl* **pins**) [pin, pins] *nm* badge
pinacoteca [pinako'teka] *nf* art gallery
pinar [pi'nar] *nm* pinewood
pincel [pin'θel] *nm* paintbrush
pincelada [pinθe'laða] *nf* brushstroke; **última ~** (*fig*) finishing touch
pinchadiscos [pintʃa'diskos] *nm/f inv* disc jockey, DJ
pinchar [pin'tʃar] *vt* (*perforar*) to prick, pierce; (*neumático*) to puncture; (*incitar*) to prod ▪ *vi* (*Mus fam*) to be DJ; **pincharse** *vr* (*con droga*) to inject o.s.; (*neumático*) to burst, puncture; **no ~ ni cortar** (*fam*) to cut no ice; **tener un neumático pinchado** to have a puncture *o* a flat tyre
pinchazo [pin'tʃaθo] *nm* (*perforación*) prick; (*de llanta*) puncture, flat (US)
pinche ['pintʃe] *nm* (*de cocina*) kitchen boy, scullion
pinchito [pin'tʃito] *nm* shish kebab
pincho ['pintʃo] *nm* point; (*aguijón*) spike; (*Culin*) savoury (snack); **~ moruno** shish kebab; **~ de tortilla** small slice of omelette
ping-pong ['pimpon] *nm* table tennis
pingüe ['pingwe] *adj* (*cosecha*) bumper *cpd*; (*negocio*) lucrative
pingüino [pin'gwino] *nm* penguin
pinitos [pi'nitos] *nmpl*: **hacer sus primeros ~** to take one's first steps
pino ['pino] *nm* pine (tree); **vivir en el quinto ~** to live at the back of beyond
pinta ['pinta] *nf* spot; (*gota*) spot, drop;

(*aspecto*) appearance, look(s) *pl*; (*medida*) pint; **tener buena ~** to look good, look well; **por la ~** by the look of it

pintado, -a [pin'taðo, a] *adj* spotted; (*de muchos colores*) colourful ■ *nf* piece of political graffiti; **pintados** *nfpl* political graffiti *sg*; **me sienta que ni ~, me viene que ni ~** it suits me a treat

pintar [pin'tar] *vt* to paint ■ *vi* to paint; (*fam*) to count, be important; **pintarse** *vr* to put on make-up; **pintárselas solo para hacer algo** to manage to do sth by o.s.; **no pinta nada** (*fam*) he has no say

pintor, a [pin'tor, a] *nm/f* painter; **~ de brocha gorda** house painter; (*fig*) bad painter

pintoresco, -a [pinto'resko, a] *adj* picturesque

pintura [pin'tura] *nf* painting; **~ a la acuarela** watercolour; **~ al óleo** oil painting; **~ rupestre** cave painting

pinza ['pinθa] *nf* (*Zool*) claw; (*para colgar ropa*) clothes peg, clothespin (US); (*Tec*) pincers *pl*; **pinzas** *nfpl* (*para depilar*) tweezers

piña ['piɲa] *nf* (*fruto del pino*) pine cone; (*fruta*) pineapple; (*fig*) group

piñón [pi'ɲon] *nm* (*Bot*) pine nut; (*Tec*) pinion

PIO *nm abr* (*Esp*: = *Patronato de Igualdad de Oportunidades*) ≈ Equal Opportunities Board

pío, -a ['pio, a] *adj* (*devoto*) pious, devout; (*misericordioso*) merciful ■ *nm*: **no decir ni ~** not to breathe a word

piojo ['pjoxo] *nm* louse

piojoso, -a [pjo'xoso, a] *adj* lousy; (*sucio*) dirty

piolet (*pl* **piolets**) [pjo'le] *nm* ice axe

pionero, -a [pjo'nero, a] *adj* pioneering ■ *nm/f* pioneer

pipa ['pipa] *nf* pipe; (*Bot*) seed, pip

pipí [pi'pi] *nm* (*fam*): **hacer pipí** to have a wee(-wee)

pipiolo [pi'pjolo] *nm* youngster; (*novato*) novice, greenhorn

pique *etc* ['pike] *vb ver* **picar** ■ *nm* (*resentimiento*) pique, resentment; (*rivalidad*) rivalry, competition; **irse a ~** to sink; (*familia*) to be ruined; **tener un ~ con algn** to have a grudge against sb

piqueta [pi'keta] *nf* pick(axe)

piquete [pi'kete] *nm* (*agujerito*) small hole; (*Mil*) squad, party; (*de obreros*) picket; **~ secundario** secondary picket

pirado, -a [pi'raðo, a] *adj* (*fam*) round the bend

piragua [pi'raɣwa] *nf* canoe

piragüismo [pira'ɣwismo] *nm* (*Deporte*) canoeing

pirámide [pi'ramiðe] *nf* pyramid

piraña [pi'raɲa] *nf* piranha

pirarse [pi'rarse] *vr*: **~(las)** (*largarse*) to beat it (*fam*); (*Escol*) to cut class

pirata [pi'rata] *adj*: **edición/disco ~** pirate edition/bootleg record ■ *nm* pirate; (*tb*: **pirata informático**) hacker

pirenaico, -a [pire'naiko, a] *adj* Pyrenean

Pirineo [piri'neo] *nm*, **Pirineos** [piri'neos] *nmpl* Pyrenees *pl*

pirómano, -a [pi'romano, a] *nm/f* (*Psico*) pyromaniac; (*Jur*) arsonist

piropo [pi'ropo] *nm* compliment, (piece of) flattery; **echar piropos a** to make flirtatious remarks to

pirueta [pi'rweta] *nf* pirouette

piruleta [piru'leta] *nf* lollipop

pirulí [piru'li] *nm* lollipop

pis [pis] *nm* (*fam*) pee; **hacer ~** to have a pee

pisada [pi'saða] *nf* (*paso*) footstep; (*huella*) footprint

pisar [pi'sar] *vt* (*caminar sobre*) to walk on, tread on; (*apretar con el pie*) to press; (*fig*) to trample on, walk all over ■ *vi* to tread, step, walk; **~ el acelerador** to step on the accelerator; **~ fuerte** (*fig*) to act determinedly

piscifactoría [pisθifakto'ria] *nf* fish farm

piscina [pis'θina] *nf* swimming pool

Piscis ['pisθis] *nm* (*Astro*) Pisces

piso ['piso] *nm* (*suelo: de edificio*) floor; (*Am*) ground; (*apartamento*) flat, apartment; **primer ~** (*Esp*) first *o* second (US) floor; (*Am*) ground *o* first (US) floor

pisotear [pisote'ar] *vt* to trample (on *o* underfoot); (*fig: humillar*) to trample on

pisotón [piso'ton] *nm* (*con el pie*) stamp

pista ['pista] *nf* track, trail; (*indicio*) clue; (*Inform*) track; **~ de auditoría** (*Com*) audit trail; **~ de aterrizaje** runway; **~ de baile** dance floor; **~ de tenis** tennis court; **~ de hielo** ice rink; **estar sobre la ~ de algn** to be on sb's trail

pisto ['pisto] *nm* (*Culin*) ratatouille; **darse ~** (*fam*) to show off

pistola [pis'tola] *nf* pistol; (*Tec*) spray-gun

pistolero, -a [pisto'lero, a] *nm/f* gunman, gangster ■ *nf* holster

pistón [pis'ton] *nm* (*Tec*) piston; (*Mus*) key

pitar [pi'tar] *vt* (*hacer sonar*) to blow; (*partido*) to referee; (*rechiflar*) to whistle at, boo; (*actor, obra*) to hiss ■ *vi* to whistle; (*Auto*) to sound *o* toot one's horn; (*Am*) to smoke; **salir pitando** to beat it

pitido [pi'tiðo] *nm* whistle; (*sonido agudo*) beep; (*sonido corto*) pip

pitillera [piti'ʎera] *nf* cigarette case

pitillo [pi'tiʎo] *nm* cigarette

pito ['pito] *nm* whistle; (*de coche*) horn; (*cigarrillo*) cigarette; (*fam: de marihuana*) joint; (*fam!*) prick (*!*); **me importa un ~** I don't care two hoots
pitón [pi'ton] *nm* (*Zool*) python
pitonisa [pito'nisa] *nf* fortune-teller
pitorrearse [pitorre'arse] *vr*: **~ de** to scoff at, make fun of
pitorreo [pito'rreo] *nm* joke, laugh; **estar de ~** to be in a joking mood
píxel ['piksel] *nm* (*Inform*) pixel
piyama [pi'jama] *nm* (*Am*) pyjamas *pl*, pajamas (*US*) *pl*
pizarra [pi'θarra] *nf* (*piedra*) slate; (*encerado*) blackboard
pizca ['piθka] *nf* pinch, spot; (*fig*) spot, speck, trace; **ni ~** not a bit
pizza ['pitsa] *nf* pizza
placa ['plaka] *nf* plate; (*Med*) dental plate; (*distintivo*) badge; **~ de matrícula** number plate; **~ madre** (*Inform*) mother board
placaje [pla'kaxe] *nm* tackle
placard [pla'kar] *nm* (*Am*) built-in cupboard, (clothes) closet (*US*)
placenta [pla'θenta] *nf* placenta; (*tras el parto*) afterbirth
placentero, -a [plaθen'tero, a] *adj* pleasant, agreeable
placer [pla'θer] *nm* pleasure; **a ~** at one's pleasure
plácido, -a ['plaθiðo, a] *adj* placid
plafón [pla'fon] *nm* (*Am*) ceiling
plaga ['plaɣa] *nf* pest; (*Med*) plague; (*fig*) swarm
plagar [pla'ɣar] *vt* to infest, plague; (*llenar*) to fill; **plagado de** riddled with; **han plagado la ciudad de carteles** they have plastered the town with posters
plagiar [pla'gjar] *vt* to plagiarize; (*Am*) to kidnap
plagiario, -a [pla'gjario, a] *nm/f* plagiarist; (*Am*) kidnapper
plagio ['plaxjo] *nm* plagiarism; (*Am*) kidnap
plague *etc* ['plaɣe] *vb ver* **plagar**
plan [plan] *nm* (*esquema, proyecto*) plan; (*idea, intento*) idea, intention; (*de curso*) programme; **~ cotizable de jubilación** contributory pension scheme; **~ de estudios** curriculum, syllabus; **~ de incentivos** (*Com*) incentive scheme; **tener ~** (*fam*) to have a date; **tener un ~** (*fam*) to have an affair; **en ~ de cachondeo** for a laugh; **en ~ económico** (*fam*) on the cheap; **vamos en ~ de turismo** we're going as tourists; **si te pones en ese ~ ...** if that's your attitude ...
plana ['plana] *nf ver* **plano**
plancha ['plantʃa] *nf* (*para planchar*) iron; (*rótulo*) plate, sheet; (*Naut*) gangway; (*Culin*) grill; **pescado a la ~** grilled fish
planchado, -a [plan'tʃaðo, a] *adj* (*ropa*) ironed; (*traje*) pressed ■ *nm* ironing
planchar [plan'tʃar] *vt* to iron ■ *vi* to do the ironing
planeador [planea'ðor] *nm* glider
planear [plane'ar] *vt* to plan ■ *vi* to glide
planeta [pla'neta] *nm* planet
planetario, -a [plane'tarjo, a] *adj* planetary ■ *nm* planetarium
planicie [pla'niθje] *nf* plain
planificación [planifika'θjon] *nf* planning; **~ corporativa** (*Com*) corporate planning; **~ familiar** family planning; **diagrama de ~** (*Com*) planner
planilla [pla'niʎa] *nf* (*Am*) form
plano, -a ['plano, a] *adj* flat, level, even; (*liso*) smooth ■ *nm* (*Mat, Tec, Aviat*) plane; (*Foto*) shot; (*Arq*) plan; (*Geo*) map; (*de ciudad*) map, street plan ■ *nf* sheet of paper, page; (*Tec*) trowel; **primer ~** close-up; **caer de ~** to fall flat; **rechazar algo de ~** to turn sth down flat; **le daba el sol de ~** (*fig*) the sun shone directly on it; **en primera plana** on the front page; **plana mayor** staff
planta ['planta] *nf* (*Bot, Tec*) plant; (*Anat*) sole of the foot, foot; **~ baja** ground floor
plantación [planta'θjon] *nf* (*Agr*) plantation; (*acto*) planting
plantar [plan'tar] *vt* (*Bot*) to plant; (*puesto*) to put in; (*levantar*) to erect, set up; **plantarse** *vr* to stand firm; **~ a algn en la calle** to chuck sb out; **dejar plantado a algn** (*fam*) to stand sb up; **plantarse en** to reach, get to
plantear [plante'ar] *vt* (*problema*) to pose; (*dificultad*) to raise; **se lo plantearé** I'll put it to him
plantel [plan'tel] *nm* (*fig*) group, set
plantilla [plan'tiʎa] *nf* (*de zapato*) insole; (*personal*) personnel; **ser de ~** to be on the staff
plantío [plan'tio] *nm* (*acto*) planting; (*lugar*) plot, bed, patch
plantón [plan'ton] *nm* (*Mil*) guard, sentry; (*fam*) long wait; **dar (un) ~ a algn** to stand sb up
plañir [pla'ɲir] *vi* to mourn
plasma ['plasma] *nm* plasma
plasmar [plas'mar] *vt* (*dar forma*) to mould, shape; (*representar*) to represent ■ *vi*: **~ en** to take the form of
plasta ['plasta] *nf* soft mass, lump; (*desastre*) botch, mess
plasticidad [plastiθi'ðað] *nf* (*fig*) expressiveness
plástico, -a ['plastiko, a] *adj* plastic ■ *nf* (art of) sculpture, modelling ■ *nm* plastic

plastificar [plastifi'kar] *vt* (*documento*) to laminate
plastifique *etc* [plasti'fike] *vb ver* **plastificar**
plastilina [plasti'lina] *nf* Plasticine®
plata ['plata] *nf* (*metal*) silver; (*cosas hechas de plata*) silverware; (*Am*) cash, dough (*fam*); **hablar en ~** to speak bluntly *o* frankly
plataforma [plata'forma] *nf* platform; **~ de lanzamiento/perforación** launch(ing) pad/drilling rig
plátano ['platano] *nm* (*fruta*) banana; (*árbol*) plane tree
platea [pla'tea] *nf* (*Teat*) pit
plateado, -a [plate'aðo, a] *adj* silver; (*Tec*) silver-plated
platense [pla'tense] (*fam*) = **ríoplatense**
plática ['platika] *nf* (*Am*) talk, chat; (*Rel*) sermon
platicar [plati'kar] *vi* (*Am*) to talk, chat
platillo [pla'tiʎo] *nm* saucer; (*de limosnas*) collecting bowl; **platillos** *nmpl* cymbals; **~ volador** *o* **volante** flying saucer; **pasar el ~** to pass the hat round
platina [pla'tina] *nf* (*Mus*) tape deck
platino [pla'tino] *nm* platinum; **platinos** *nmpl* (*Auto*) (contact) points
platique *etc* [pla'tike] *vb ver* **platicar**
plato ['plato] *nm* plate, dish; (*parte de comida*) course; (*guiso*) dish; **~ frutero/sopero** fruit/soup dish; **pagar los platos rotos** (*fam*) to carry the can (*fam*)
plató [pla'to] *nm* set
platónico, -a [pla'toniko, a] *adj* platonic
playa ['plaja] *nf* beach; (*costa*) seaside; **~ de estacionamiento** (*Am*) car park
playero, -a [pla'jero, a] *adj* beach *cpd* ■ *nf* (*Am: camiseta*) T-shirt; **playeras** *nfpl* canvas shoes; (*Tenis*) tennis shoes
plaza ['plaθa] *nf* square; (*mercado*) market(place); (*sitio*) room, space; (*en vehículo*) seat, place; (*colocación*) post, job; **~ de abastos** food market; **~ mayor** main square; **~ de toros** bullring; **hacer la ~** to do the daily shopping; **reservar una ~** to reserve a seat; **el hotel tiene 100 plazas** the hotel has 100 beds
plazca *etc* ['plaθka] *vb ver* **placer**
plazo ['plaθo] *nm* (*lapso de tiempo*) time, period, term; (*fecha de vencimiento*) expiry date; (*pago parcial*) instalment; **a corto/largo ~** short-/long-term; **comprar a plazos** to buy on hire purchase, pay for in instalments; **nos dan un ~ de ocho días** they allow us a week
plazoleta [plaθo'leta], **plazuela** [pla'θwela] *nf* small square
pleamar [plea'mar] *nf* high tide
plebe ['pleβe] *nf*: **la ~** the common people *pl*, the masses *pl*; (*pey*) the plebs *pl*
plebeyo, -a [ple'βejo, a] *adj* plebeian; (*pey*) coarse, common
plebiscito [pleβis'θito] *nm* plebiscite
pleca ['pleka] *nf* (*Inform*) backslash
plegable [ple'ɣaβle] *adj* pliable; (*silla*) folding
plegar [ple'ɣar] *vt* (*doblar*) to fold, bend; (*Costura*) to pleat; **plegarse** *vr* to yield, submit
plegaria [ple'ɣarja] *nf* (*oración*) prayer
plegué [ple'ɣe], **pleguemos** *etc* [ple'ɣemos] *vb ver* **plegar**
pleitear [pleite'ar] *vi* (*Jur*) to plead, conduct a lawsuit; (*litigar*) to go to law
pleito ['pleito] *nm* (*Jur*) lawsuit, case; (*fig*) dispute, feud; **pleitos** *nmpl* litigation *sg*; **entablar ~** to bring an action *o* a lawsuit; **poner ~** to sue
plenario, -a [ple'narjo, a] *adj* plenary, full
plenilunio [pleni'lunjo] *nm* full moon
plenitud [pleni'tuð] *nf* plenitude, fullness; (*abundancia*) abundance
pleno, -a ['pleno, a] *adj* full; (*completo*) complete ■ *nm* plenum; **en ~** as a whole; (*por unanimidad*) unanimously; **en ~ día** in broad daylight; **en ~ verano** at the height of summer; **en plena cara** full in the face
pletina *nf* (*Mus*) tape deck
pleuresía [pleure'sia] *nf* pleurisy
plexiglás [pleksi'ɣlas] *nm* acrylic
pliego *etc* ['pljeɣo] *vb ver* **plegar** ■ *nm* (*hoja*) sheet (of paper); (*carta*) sealed letter/document; **~ de condiciones** details *pl*, specifications *pl*
pliegue *etc* ['pljeɣe] *vb ver* **plegar** ■ *nm* fold, crease; (*de vestido*) pleat
plisado [pli'saðo] *nm* pleating
plomero [plo'mero] *nm* (*Am*) plumber
plomizo, -a [plo'miθo, a] *adj* leaden, lead-coloured
plomo ['plomo] *nm* (*metal*) lead; (*Elec*) fuse; **caer a ~** to fall heavily *o* flat
pluma ['pluma] *nf* (*Zool*) feather; **~ estilográfica, ~ fuente** (*Am*) fountain pen
plumazo [plu'maθo] *nm* (*lit, fig*) stroke of the pen
plumero [plu'mero] *nm* (*quitapolvos*) feather duster; **ya te veo el ~** I know what you're up to
plumón [plu'mon] *nm* (*Am*) felt-tip pen
plural [plu'ral] *adj* plural ■ *nm*: **en ~** in the plural
pluralidad [plurali'ðað] *nf* plurality; **una ~ de votos** a majority of votes
pluriempleo [pluriem'pleo] *nm* moonlighting
plus [plus] *nm* bonus

plusmarquista [plusmar'kista] *nm/f* (*Deporte*) record holder
plusvalía [plusβa'lia] *nf* (*mayor valor*) appreciation, added value; (*Com*) goodwill
plutocracia [pluto'kraθja] *nf* plutocracy
PM *nf abr* (*Mil*: = *Policía Militar*) MP
p.m. *abr* (= *post meridiem*) p.m.; (= *por minuto*) per minute
PMA *nm abr* (= *Programa Mundial de Alimentos*) World Food Programme
P.M.A. *nm abr* = **peso máximo autorizado**
pmo. *abr* (= *próximo*) prox.
PN *nf abr* (*Mil*: = *Policía Naval*) Naval Police
PNB *nm abr* (*Esp Com*: = *Producto Nacional Bruto*) GNP
P.N.D. *nm abr* (*Escol*: = *personal no docente*) non-teaching staff
PNN [pe'nene] *nm/f abr* (= *profesor(a) no numerario(-a)*) untenured teacher ■ *nm abr* (*Esp Com*: = *Producto Nacional Neto*) net national product
PNUD *nm abr* (= *Programa de las Naciones Unidas para el Desarrollo*) United Nations Development Programme
PNV *nm abr* (*Esp Pol*) = **Partido Nacional Vasco**
P.° *abr* (= *Paseo*) Av(e).
p.o. *abr* = **por orden**
población [poβla'θjon] *nf* population; (*pueblo, ciudad*) town, city; ~ **activa** working population
poblado, -a [po'βlaðo, a] *adj* inhabited; (*barba*) thick; (*cejas*) bushy ■ *nm* (*aldea*) village; (*pueblo*) (small) town; ~ **de** (*lleno de*) filled with; **densamente** ~ densely populated
poblador, a [poβla'ðor, a] *nm/f* settler, colonist
poblar [po'βlar] *vt* (*colonizar*) to colonize; (*fundar*) to found; (*habitar*) to inhabit; **poblarse** *vr*: **poblarse de** to fill up with; (*irse cubriendo*) to become covered with
pobre ['poβre] *adj* poor ■ *nm/f* poor person; (*mendigo*) beggar; **los pobres** the poor; **¡~!** poor thing!; ~ **diablo** (*fig*) poor wretch *o* devil
pobreza [po'βreθa] *nf* poverty
pocho, -a ['potʃo, a] *adj* (*flor, color*) faded, discoloured; (*persona*) pale; (*fruta*) overripe; (*deprimido*) depressed
pocilga [po'θilɣa] *nf* pigsty
pocillo [po'siʎo] *nm* (*Am*) coffee cup
pócima ['poθima], **poción** [po'θjon] *nf* potion; (*brebaje*) concoction, nasty drink

PALABRA CLAVE

poco, -a ['poko, a] *adj* **1** (*sg*) little, not much; ~ **tiempo** little *o* not much time; **de ~ interés** of little interest, not very interesting; **poca cosa** not much
2 (*pl*) few, not many; **unos pocos** a few, some; **pocos niños comen lo que les conviene** few children eat what they should
■ *adv* **1** little, not much; **cuesta ~** it doesn't cost much; **~ más o menos** more or less
2 (*+ adj*: *negativo, antónimo*): **~ amable/ inteligente** not very nice/intelligent
3: **por ~ me caigo** I almost fell
4 (*tiempo*): **~ después** soon after that; **dentro de ~** shortly; **hace ~** a short time ago, not long ago; **a ~ de haberse casado** shortly after getting married
5: **~ a ~** little by little
6 (*Am*): **¿a ~ no está divino?** isn't it just divine?; **de a ~** gradually
■ *nm* a little, a bit; **un ~ triste/de dinero** a little sad/money

poda ['poða] *nf* (*acto*) pruning; (*temporada*) pruning season
podar [po'ðar] *vt* to prune
podenco [po'ðenko] *nm* hound

PALABRA CLAVE

poder [po'ðer] *vi* **1** (*capacidad*) can, be able to; **no puedo hacerlo** I can't do it, I'm unable to do it
2 (*permiso*) can, may, be allowed to; **¿se puede?** may I (*o* we)?; **puedes irte ahora** you may go now; **no se puede fumar en este hospital** smoking is not allowed in this hospital
3 (*posibilidad*) may, might, could; **puede llegar mañana** he may *o* might arrive tomorrow; **pudiste haberte hecho daño** you might *o* could have hurt yourself; **¡podías habérmelo dicho antes!** you might have told me before!
4: **puede (ser)** perhaps; **puede que lo sepa Tomás** Tomás may *o* might know
5: **¡no puedo más!** I've had enough!; **no pude menos que dejarlo** I couldn't help but leave it; **es tonto a más no ~** he's as stupid as they come
6: **~ con**: **¿puedes con eso?** can you manage that?; **no puedo con este crío** this kid's too much for me
7: **él me puede** (*fam*) he's stronger than me
■ *nm* power; **el ~** the Government; **~ adquisitivo** purchasing power; **detentar** *u* **ocupar** *o* **estar en el ~** to be in power *o* office; **estar** *u* **obrar en ~ de** to be in the hands *o* possession of; **por ~(es)** by proxy

poderío [poðe'rio] *nm* power; (*autoridad*) authority
poderoso, -a [poðe'roso, a] *adj* powerful
podio ['poðjo] *nm* podium
podólogo, -a [po'ðoloɣo, a] *nm/f* chiropodist (*Brit*), podiatrist (*US*)
podré *etc* [po'ðre] *vb ver* **poder**
podrido, -a [po'ðriðo, a] *adj* rotten, bad; (*fig*) rotten, corrupt
podrir [po'ðrir] = **pudrir**
poema [po'ema] *nm* poem
poesía [poe'sia] *nf* poetry
poeta [po'eta] *nm* poet
poético, -a [po'etiko, a] *adj* poetic(al)
poetisa [poe'tisa] *nf* (woman) poet
póker ['poker] *nm* poker
polaco, -a [po'lako, a] *adj* Polish ■ *nm/f* Pole ■ *nm* (*Ling*) Polish
polar [po'lar] *adj* polar
polarice *etc* [pola'riθe] *vb ver* **polarizar**
polaridad [polari'ðað] *nf* polarity
polarizar [polari'θar] *vt* to polarize
polea [po'lea] *nf* pulley
polémica [po'lemika] *nf* polemics *sg*; (*una polémica*) controversy
polemice *etc* [pole'miθe] *vb ver* **polemizar**
polémico, -a [po'lemiko, a] *adj* polemic(al)
polemizar [polemi'θar] *vi* argue
polen ['polen] *nm* pollen
poleo [po'leo] *nm* pennyroyal
poli ['poli] *nm* (*fam*) cop (*fam*) ■ *nf*: **la ~** the cops *pl* (*fam*)
policía [poli'θia] *nm/f* policeman(-woman) ■ *nf* police; *see note*

POLICÍA

There are two branches of the police, both armed: the *policía nacional*, in charge of national security and public order in general, and the *policía municipal*, with duties of regulating traffic and policing the local community. Catalonia and the Basque Country have their own police forces, the *Mossos d'Esquadra* and the *Ertzaintza* respectively.

policíaco, -a [poli'θiako, a] *adj* police *cpd*; **novela policíaca** detective story
polideportivo [poliðepor'tiβo] *nm* sports centre
poliéster [poli'ester] *nm* polyester
polietileno [polieti'leno] *nm* polythene (*Brit*), polyethylene (*US*)
polifacético, -a [polifa'θetiko, a] *adj* (*persona, talento*) many-sided, versatile
poligamia [poli'ɣamja] *nf* polygamy
polígamo, -a [po'liɣamo, a] *adj* polygamous ■ *nm* polygamist
polígono [po'liɣono] *nm* (*Mat*) polygon; (*solar*) building lot; (*zona*) area; (*unidad vecina*) housing estate; **~ industrial** industrial estate
polígrafo [po'liɣrafo] *nm* polygraph
polilla [po'liʎa] *nf* moth
Polinesia [poli'nesja] *nf* Polynesia
polinesio, -a [poli'nesjo, a] *adj, nm/f* Polynesian
polio ['poljo] *nf* polio
Polisario [poli'sarjo] *nm abr* (*Pol*: *tb*: **Frente Polisario**) = **Frente Político de Liberación del Sáhara y Río de Oro**
politécnico [poli'tekniko] *nm* polytechnic
político, -a [po'litiko, a] *adj* political; (*discreto*) tactful; (*pariente*) in-law ■ *nm/f* politician ■ *nf* politics *sg*; (*económica, agraria*) policy; **padre ~** father-in-law; **política exterior/de ingresos y precios** foreign/ prices and incomes policy
póliza ['poliθa] *nf* certificate, voucher; (*impuesto*) tax *o* fiscal stamp; **~ de seguro(s)** insurance policy
polizón [poli'θon] *nm* (*Aviat, Naut*) stowaway
pollera [po'ʎera] *nf* (*criadero*) hencoop; (*Am*) skirt, overskirt
pollería [poʎe'ria] *nf* poulterer's (shop)
pollo ['poʎo] *nm* chicken; (*joven*) young man; (*señorito*) playboy; **~ asado** roast chicken
polo ['polo] *nm* (*Geo, Elec*) pole; (*helado*) ice lolly; (*Deporte*) polo; (*suéter*) polo-neck; **P~ Norte/Sur** North/South Pole; **esto es el ~ opuesto de lo que dijo antes** this is the exact opposite of what he said before
Polonia [po'lonja] *nf* Poland
poltrona [pol'trona] *nf* reclining chair, easy chair
polución [polu'θjon] *nf* pollution; **~ ambiental** environmental pollution
polvera [pol'βera] *nf* powder compact
polvo ['polβo] *nm* dust; (*Química, Culin, Med*) powder; (*fam!*) screw (*!*); **en ~** powdered; **~ de talco** talcum powder; **estar hecho ~** to be worn out *o* exhausted; **hacer algo ~** to smash sth; **hacer ~ a algn** to shatter sb; *ver tb* **polvos**
pólvora ['polβora] *nf* gunpowder; (*fuegos artificiales*) fireworks *pl*; **propagarse como la ~** (*noticia*) to spread like wildfire
polvoriento, -a [polβo'rjento, a] *adj* (*superficie*) dusty; (*sustancia*) powdery
polvorín [polβo'rin] *nm* (*fig*) powder keg
polvorosa [polβo'rosa] *adj* (*fam*): **poner pies en ~** to beat it
polvos ['polβos] *nmpl* powder *sg*

polvoso, -a [pol'βoso, a] *adj* (*Am*) dusty
pomada [po'maða] *nf* pomade
pomelo [po'melo] *nm* grapefruit
pómez ['pomeθ] *nf*: **piedra ~** pumice stone
pomo ['pomo] *nm* handle
pompa ['pompa] *nf* (*burbuja*) bubble; (*bomba*) pump; (*esplendor*) pomp, splendour; **pompas fúnebres** funeral *sg*
pomposo, -a [pom'poso, a] *adj* splendid, magnificent; (*pey*) pompous
pómulo ['pomulo] *nm* cheekbone
ponche ['pontʃe] *nm* punch
poncho ['pontʃo] *nm* (*Am*) poncho, cape
ponderar [ponde'rar] *vt* (*considerar*) to weigh up, consider; (*elogiar*) to praise highly, speak in praise of
pondré *etc* [pon'dre] *vb ver* **poner**
ponencia [po'nenθja] *nf* (*exposición*) (learned) paper, communication; (*informe*) report

PALABRA CLAVE

poner [po'ner] *vt* **1** to put; (*colocar*) to place, set; (*ropa*) to put on; (*problema, la mesa*) to set; (*interés*) to show; (*telegrama*) to send; (*obra de teatro*) to put on; (*película*) to show; **ponlo más alto** turn it up; **¿qué ponen en el Excelsior?** what's on at the Excelsior?; **~ algo a secar** to put sth (out) to dry; **¡no pongas esa cara!** don't look at me like that!
2 (*tienda*) to open; (*instalar: gas etc*) to put in; (*radio, TV*) to switch *o* turn on
3 (*suponer*): **pongamos que ...** let's suppose that ...
4 (*contribuir*): **el gobierno ha puesto otro millón** the government has contributed another million
5 (*Telec*): **póngame con el Sr. López** can you put me through to Mr. López?
6 (*estar escrito*) to say; **¿qué pone aquí?** what does it say here?
7: **~ de, le han puesto de director general** they've appointed him general manager
8 (*+adj*) to make; **me estás poniendo nerviosa** you're making me nervous
9 (*dar nombre*): **al hijo le pusieron Diego** they called their son Diego
■ *vi* (*gallina*) to lay; **ponerse** *vr* **1** (*colocarse*): **se puso a mi lado** he came and stood beside me; **tú ponte en esa silla** you go and sit on that chair
2 (*vestido, cosméticos*) to put on; **¿por qué no te pones el vestido nuevo?** why don't you put on *o* wear your new dress?
3 (*sol*) to set
4 (*+adj*) to get, become; to turn; **ponerse enfermo/gordo/triste** to get ill/fat/sad; **se puso muy serio** he got very serious; **después de lavarla la tela se puso azul** after washing it the material turned blue; **¡no te pongas así!** don't be like that!; **ponerse cómodo** to make o.s. comfortable
5: **ponerse a, se puso a llorar** he started to cry; **tienes que ponerte a estudiar** you must get down to studying
6: **ponerse a bien con algn** to make it up with sb; **ponerse a mal con algn** to get on the wrong side of sb
7 (*Am*): **se me pone que ...** it seems to me that ..., I think that ...

ponga *etc* ['ponga] *vb ver* **poner**
poniente [po'njente] *nm* west
pontevedrés, -esa [ponteβe'ðres, esa] *adj* of *o* from Pontevedra ■ *nm/f* native *o* inhabitant of Pontevedra
pontificado [pontifi'kaðo] *nm* papacy, pontificate
pontífice [pon'tifiθe] *nm* pope, pontiff; **el Sumo P~** His Holiness the Pope
pontón [pon'ton] *nm* pontoon
ponzoña [pon'θoɲa] *nf* poison, venom
ponzoñoso, -a [ponθo'ɲoso, a] *adj* poisonous, venomous
pop [pop] *adj inv, nm* (*Mus*) pop
popa ['popa] *nf* stern; **a ~** astern, abaft; **de ~ a proa** fore and aft
popular [popu'lar] *adj* popular; (*del pueblo*) of the people
popularice *etc* [popula'riθe] *vb ver* **popularizarse**
popularidad [populari'ðað] *nf* popularity
popularizarse [populari'θarse] *vr* to become popular
poquísimo, -a [po'kisimo, a] *adj superlativo de* **poco** very little, very few *pl*; (*casi nada*) hardly any
poquito [po'kito] *nm*: **un ~** a little bit ■ *adv* a little, a bit; **a poquitos** bit by bit

PALABRA CLAVE

por [por] *prep* **1** (*objetivo*) for; **luchar ~ la patria** to fight for one's country; **hazlo ~ mí** do it for my sake
2 (*+infin*): **~ no llegar tarde** so as not to arrive late; **~ citar unos ejemplos** to give a few examples
3 (*causa*) out of, because of; **no es ~ eso** that's not the reason; **~ escasez de fondos** through *o* for lack of funds
4 (*tiempo*): **~ la mañana/noche** in the morning/at night; **se queda ~ una semana** she's staying (for) a week

5 (*lugar*): **pasar ~ Madrid** to pass through Madrid; **ir a Guayaquil ~ Quito** to go to Guayaquil via Quito; **caminar ~ la calle** to walk along the street; **~ allí** over there; **se va ~ ahí** we have to go that way; **¿~ dónde?** which way?; **está ~ el norte** it's somewhere in the north; **~ todo el país** throughout the country
6 (*cambio, precio*): **te doy uno nuevo ~ el que tienes** I'll give you a new one (in return) for the one you've got; **lo vendí ~ 15 dólares** I sold it for 15 dollars
7 (*valor distributivo*): **30 euros ~ hora/cabeza** 30 euros an *o* per hour/a *o* per head; **10 ~ ciento** 10 per cent; **80 (kms) ~ hora** 80 (km) an *o* per hour
8 (*modo, medio*) by; **~ correo/avión** by post/air; **día ~ día** day by day; **~ orden** in order; **entrar ~ la entrada principal** to go in through the main entrance
9 (*agente*) by; **hecho ~ él** done by him; **"dirigido ~"** "directed by"
10: **10 ~ 10 son 100** 10 by 10 is 100
11 (*en lugar de*): **vino él ~ su jefe** he came instead of his boss
12: **~ mí que revienten** as far as I'm concerned they can drop dead
13 (*evidencia*): **~ lo que dicen** judging by *o* from what they say
14: **estar/quedar ~ hacer** to be still *o* remain to be done
15: **~ (muy) difícil que sea** however hard it is *o* may be; **~ más que lo intente** no matter how *o* however hard I try
16: **~ qué** why; **¿~ qué?** why?; **¿~?** (*fam*) why (do you ask)?

porcelana [porθe'lana] *nf* porcelain; (*china*) china
porcentaje [porθen'taxe] *nm* percentage; **~ de actividad** (*Inform*) hit rate
porche ['portʃe] *nm* (*de una plaza*) arcade; (*de casa*) porch
porción [por'θjon] *nf* (*parte*) portion, share; (*cantidad*) quantity, amount
pordiosero, -a [porðjo'sero, a] *nm/f* beggar
porfía [por'fia] *nf* persistence; (*terquedad*) obstinacy
porfiado, -a [por'fjaðo, a] *adj* persistent; obstinate
porfiar [por'fjar] *vi* to persist, insist; (*disputar*) to argue stubbornly
pormenor [porme'nor] *nm* detail, particular
pormenorice *etc* [pormeno'riθe] *vb ver* **pormenorizar**
pormenorizar [pormenori'θar] *vt* to (set out in) detail ■ *vi* to go into detail
porno ['porno] *adj inv* porno ■ *nm* porn
pornografía [pornoɣra'fia] *nf* pornography
poro ['poro] *nm* pore
poroso, -a [po'roso, a] *adj* porous
poroto [po'roto] *nm* (*Am*) kidney bean
porque ['porke] *conj* (*a causa de*) because; (*ya que*) since; **~ sí** because I feel like it
porqué [por'ke] *nm* reason, cause
porquería [porke'ria] *nf* (*suciedad*) filth, muck, dirt; (*acción*) dirty trick; (*objeto*) small thing, trifle; (*fig*) rubbish
porqueriza [porke'riθa] *nf* pigsty
porra ['porra] *nf* (*arma*) stick, club; (*cachiporra*) truncheon; **¡porras!** oh heck!; **¡vete a la ~!** go to heck!
porrazo [po'rraθo] *nm* (*golpe*) blow; (*caída*) bump; **de un ~** in one go
porro ['porro] *nm* joint
porrón [po'rron] *nm glass wine jar with a long spout*
portaaviones [port(a)a'βjones] *nm inv* aircraft carrier
portada [por'taða] *nf* (*Tip*) title page; (*: de revista*) cover
portador, a [porta'ðor, a] *nm/f* carrier, bearer; (*Com*) bearer, payee; (*Med*) carrier; **ser ~ del virus del sida** to be HIV-positive
portaequipajes [portaeki'paxes] *nm inv* boot (*Brit*), trunk (*US*); (*baca*) luggage rack
portafolio [porta'foljo], **portafolios** [porta'foljos] *nm* (*Am*) briefcase; **~(s) de inversiones** (*Com*) investment portfolio
portal [por'tal] *nm* (*entrada*) vestibule, hall; (*pórtico*) porch, doorway; (*puerta de entrada*) main door; (*Deporte*) goal; **portales** *nmpl* arcade *sg*
portaligas [porta'liɣas] *nm inv* (*Am*) suspender belt
portamaletas [portama'letas] *nm inv* roof rack
portamonedas [portamo'neðas] *nm inv* purse
portar [por'tar] *vt* to carry, bear; **portarse** *vr* to behave, conduct o.s.; **portarse mal** to misbehave; **se portó muy bien conmigo** he treated me very well
portátil [por'tatil] *adj* portable
portaviones [porta'βjones] *nm inv* aircraft carrier
portavoz [porta'βoθ] *nm/f* spokesman(-woman)
portazo [por'taθo] *nm*: **dar un ~** to slam the door
porte ['porte] *nm* (*Com*) transport; (*precio*) transport charges *pl*; (*Correos*) postage; **~ debido** (*Com*) carriage forward; **~ pagado** (*Com*) carriage paid, post-paid

portento [por'tento] *nm* marvel, wonder
portentoso, -a [porten'toso, a] *adj* marvellous, extraordinary
porteño, -a [por'teɲo, a] *adj* of *o* from Buenos Aires ■ *nm/f* native *o* inhabitant of Buenos Aires
portería [porte'ria] *nf* (*oficina*) porter's office; (*gol*) goal
portero, -a [por'tero, a] *nm/f* porter; (*conserje*) caretaker; (*Deporte*) goalkeeper
pórtico ['portiko] *nm* (*porche*) portico, porch; (*fig*) gateway; (*arcada*) arcade
portilla [por'tiʎa] *nf*, **portillo** [por'tiʎo] *nm* gate
portón [por'ton] *nm* proton
portorriqueño, -a [portorri'keɲo, a] *adj, nm/f* Puerto Rican
portuario, -a [por'twarjo] *adj* (*del puerto*) port *cpd*, harbour *cpd*; (*del muelle*) dock *cpd*; **trabajador ~** docker
Portugal [portu'ɣal] *nm* Portugal
portugués, -esa [portu'ɣes, esa] *adj, nm/f* Portuguese ■ *nm* (*Ling*) Portuguese
porvenir [porβe'nir] *nm* future
pos [pos]: **en ~ de** *prep* after, in pursuit of
posada [po'saða] *nf* (*refugio*) shelter, lodging; (*mesón*) guest house; **dar ~ a** to give shelter to, take in
posaderas [posa'ðeras] *nfpl* backside *sg*, buttocks
posar [po'sar] *vt* (*en el suelo*) to lay down, put down; (*la mano*) to place, put gently ■ *vi* to sit, pose; **posarse** *vr* to settle; (*pájaro*) to perch; (*avión*) to land, come down
posdata [pos'ðata] *nf* postscript
pose ['pose] *nf* (*Arte, afectación*) pose
poseedor, a [posee'ðor, a] *nm/f* owner, possessor; (*de récord, puesto*) holder
poseer [pose'er] *vt* to have, possess, own; (*ventaja*) to enjoy; (*récord, puesto*) to hold
poseído, -a [pose'iðo, a] *adj* possessed; **estar muy ~ de** to be very vain about
posesión [pose'sjon] *nf* possession; **tomar ~ (de)** to take over
posesionarse [posesjo'narse] *vr*: **~ de** to take possession of, take over
posesivo, -a [pose'siβo, a] *adj* possessive
poseyendo *etc* [pose'jendo] *vb ver* **poseer**
posgrado [pos'ɣraðo] *nm* = **postgrado**
posgraduado, -a [posɣra'ðwaðo, a] *adj, nm/f* = **postgraduado**
posguerra [pos'ɣerra] *nf* = **postguerra**
posibilidad [posiβili'ðað] *nf* possibility; (*oportunidad*) chance
posibilitar [posiβili'tar] *vt* to make possible, permit; (*hacer factible*) to make feasible
posible [po'siβle] *adj* possible; (*factible*) feasible ■ *nm*: **posibles** means; (*bienes*) funds, assets; **de ser ~** if possible; **en** *o* **dentro de lo ~** as far as possible; **lo antes ~** as quickly as possible
posición [posi'θjon] *nf* (*gen*) position; (*rango social*) status
positivo, -a [posi'tiβo, a] *adj* positive ■ *nf* (*Foto*) print
poso ['poso] *nm* sediment
posoperatorio, -a [posopera'torjo, a] *adj, nm* = **postoperatorio**
posponer [pospo'ner] *vt* to put behind *o* below; (*aplazar*) to postpone
posponga *etc* [pos'ponga], **pospuesto** [pos'pwesto], **pospuse** *etc* [pos'puse] *vb ver* **posponer**
posta ['posta] *nf* (*de caballos*) relay, team; **a ~** on purpose, deliberately
postal [pos'tal] *adj* postal ■ *nf* postcard
poste ['poste] *nm* (*de telégrafos*) post, pole; (*columna*) pillar
póster (*pl* **posters**) ['poster 'posters] *nm* poster
postergar [poster'ɣar] *vt* (*esp Am*) to put off, postpone, delay
postergue *etc* [pos'terɣe] *vb ver* **postergar**
posteridad [posteri'ðað] *nf* posterity
posterior [poste'rjor] *adj* back, rear; (*siguiente*) following, subsequent; (*más tarde*) later; **ser ~ a** to be later than
posterioridad [posterjori'ðað] *nf*: **con ~** later, subsequently
postgrado [post'ɣraðo] *nm*: **curso de ~** postgraduate course
postgraduado, -a [postɣra'ðwaðo, a] *adj, nm/f* postgraduate
postguerra [post'ɣerra] *nf* postwar period; **en la ~** after the war
postigo [pos'tiɣo] *nm* (*portillo*) postern; (*contraventana*) shutter
postín [pos'tin] *nm* (*fam*) elegance; **de ~** posh; **darse ~** to show off
postizo, -a [pos'tiθo, a] *adj* false, artificial; (*sonrisa*) false, phoney ■ *nm* hairpiece
postoperatorio, -a [postopera'torjo, a] *adj* postoperative ■ *nm* postoperative period
postor, a [pos'tor, a] *nm/f* bidder; **mejor ~** highest bidder
postrado, -a [pos'traðo, a] *adj* prostrate
postrar [pos'trar] *vt* (*derribar*) to cast down, overthrow; (*humillar*) to humble; (*Med*) to weaken, exhaust; **postrarse** *vr* to prostrate o.s.
postre ['postre] *nm* sweet, dessert ■ *nf*: **a la ~** in the end, when all is said and done; **para ~** (*fam*) to crown it all; **llegar a los postres** (*fig*) to come too late

postrero, -a [pos'trero, a] *adj* (*antes de nmsg* **postrer**) (*último*) last; (*: que viene detrás*) rear
postrimerías [postrime'rias] *nfpl* final stages
postulado [postu'laðo] *nm* postulate
postulante [postu'lante] *nm/f* petitioner; (*Rel*) postulant
póstumo, -a ['postumo, a] *adj* posthumous
postura [pos'tura] *nf* (*del cuerpo*) posture, position; (*fig*) attitude, position
post-venta [pos'βenta] *adj* (*Com*) after-sales
potable [po'taβle] *adj* drinkable
potaje [po'taxe] *nm* thick vegetable soup
pote ['pote] *nm* pot, jar
potencia [po'tenθja] *nf* power; (*capacidad*) capacity; **~ (en caballos)** horsepower; **en ~** potential, in the making; **las grandes potencias** the great powers
potencial [poten'θjal] *adj, nm* potential
potenciar [poten'θjar] *vt* (*promover*) to promote; (*fortalecer*) to boost
potente [po'tente] *adj* powerful
potestad [potes'tað] *nf* authority; **patria ~** paternal authority
potosí [poto'si] *nm* fortune; **cuesta un ~** it costs the earth
potra ['potra] *nf* (*Zool*) filly; **tener ~** to be lucky
potro ['potro] *nm* (*Zool*) colt; (*Deporte*) vaulting horse
pozo ['poθo] *nm* well; (*de río*) deep pool; (*de mina*) shaft; **~ negro** cesspool; **ser un ~ de ciencia** (*fig*) to be deeply learned
PP *abr* (*= por poderes*) pp; (*= porte pagado*) carriage paid ■ *nm abr* = **Partido Popular**
p.p. *abr* = **por poderes**
p.p.m. *abr* (*= palabras por minuto*) wpm
práctica ['praktika] *nf ver* **práctico**
practicable [prakti'kaβle] *adj* practicable; (*camino*) passable, usable
prácticamente ['praktikamente] *adv* practically
practicante [prakti'kante] *nm/f* (*Med: ayudante de doctor*) medical assistant; (*: enfermero*) nurse; (*el que practica algo*) practitioner ■ *adj* practising
practicar [prakti'kar] *vt* to practise; (*deporte*) to go in for, play; (*ejecutar*) to carry out, perform
práctico, -a ['praktiko, a] *adj* (*gen*) practical; (*conveniente*) handy; (*instruído: persona*) skilled, expert ■ *nf* practice; (*método*) method; (*arte, capacidad*) skill; **en la práctica** in practice
practique *etc* [prak'tike] *vb ver* **practicar**
pradera [pra'ðera] *nf* meadow; (*de Canadá*) prairie
prado ['praðo] *nm* (*campo*) meadow, field; (*pastizal*) pasture; (*Am*) lawn
Praga ['praɣa] *nf* Prague
pragmático, -a [praɣ'matiko, a] *adj* pragmatic
preámbulo [pre'ambulo] *nm* preamble, introduction; **decir algo sin preámbulos** to say sth without beating about the bush
precalentamiento [prekalenta'mjento] *nm* (*Deporte*) warm-up
precalentar [prekalen'tar] *vt* to preheat
precaliente *etc* [preka'ljente] *vb ver* **precalentar**
precario, -a [pre'karjo, a] *adj* precarious
precaución [prekau'θjon] *nf* (*medida preventiva*) preventive measure, precaution; (*prudencia*) caution, wariness
precaver [preka'βer] *vt* to guard against; (*impedir*) to forestall; **precaverse** *vr*: **precaverse de** *o* **contra algo** to (be on one's) guard against sth
precavido, -a [preka'βiðo, a] *adj* cautious, wary
precedencia [preθe'ðenθja] *nf* precedence; (*prioridad*) priority; (*superioridad*) greater importance, superiority
precedente [preθe'ðente] *adj* preceding; (*anterior*) former ■ *nm* precedent; **sin ~(s)** unprecedented; **establecer** *o* **sentar un ~** to establish *o* set a precedent
preceder [preθe'ðer] *vt, vi* to precede, go/come before
precepto [pre'θepto] *nm* precept
preceptor [preθep'tor] *nm* (*maestro*) teacher; (*: particular*) tutor
preciado, -a [pre'θjaðo, a] *adj* (*estimado*) esteemed, valuable
preciar [pre'θjar] *vt* to esteem, value; **preciarse** *vr* to boast; **preciarse de** to pride o.s. on
precintar [preθin'tar] *vt* (*local*) to seal off; (*producto*) to seal
precinto [pre'θinto] *nm* (*Com: tb*: **precinto de garantía**) seal
precio ['preθjo] *nm* (*de mercado*) price; (*costo*) cost; (*valor*) value, worth; (*de viaje*) fare; **~ de coste** *o* **de cobertura** cost price; **~ al contado** cash price; **~ al detalle** *o* **al por menor** retail price; **~ al detallista** trade price; **~ de entrega inmediata** spot price; **~ de oferta** offer price; **~ de oportunidad** bargain price; **~ de salida** upset price; **~ tope** top price; **~ unitario** unit price; **no tener ~** (*fig*) to be priceless; **"no importa ~"** "cost no object"
preciosidad [preθjosi'ðað] *nf* (*valor*) (high) value, (great) worth; (*encanto*) charm; (*cosa bonita*) beautiful thing; **es una ~** it's lovely, it's really beautiful

precioso, -a [pre'θjoso, a] *adj* precious; *(de mucho valor)* valuable; *(fam)* lovely, beautiful
precipicio [preθi'piθjo] *nm* cliff, precipice; *(fig)* abyss
precipitación [preθipita'θjon] *nf* *(prisa)* haste; *(lluvia)* rainfall; *(Química)* precipitation
precipitado, -a [preθipi'taðo, a] *adj* hasty, rash; *(salida)* hasty, sudden ■ *nm* *(Química)* precipitate
precipitar [preθipi'tar] *vt* *(arrojar)* to hurl, throw; *(apresurar)* to hasten; *(acelerar)* to speed up, accelerate; *(Química)* to precipitate; **precipitarse** *vr* to throw o.s.; *(apresurarse)* to rush; *(actuar sin pensar)* to act rashly; **precipitarse hacia** to rush towards
precisado, -a [preθi'saðo, a] *adj*: **verse ~ a hacer algo** to be obliged to do sth
precisamente [preθisa'mente] *adv* precisely; *(justo)* precisely, exactly, just; **~ por eso** for that very reason; **~ fue él quien lo dijo** as a matter of fact he said it; **no es eso ~** it's not really that
precisar [preθi'sar] *vt* *(necesitar)* to need, require; *(fijar)* to determine exactly, fix; *(especificar)* to specify; *(señalar)* to pinpoint
precisión [preθi'sjon] *nf* *(exactitud)* precision
preciso, -a [pre'θiso, a] *adj* *(exacto)* precise; *(necesario)* necessary, essential; *(estilo, lenguaje)* concise; **es ~ que lo hagas** you must do it
precocidad [prekoθi'ðað] *nf* precociousness, precocity
preconcebido, -a [prekonθe'βiðo, a] *adj* preconceived
preconice *etc* [preko'niθe] *vb ver* **preconizar**
preconizar [prekoni'θar] *vt* *(aconsejar)* to advise; *(prever)* to foresee
precoz [pre'koθ] *adj* *(persona)* precocious; *(calvicie)* premature
precursor, a [prekur'sor, a] *nm/f* precursor
predecesor, a [preðeθe'sor, a] *nm/f* predecessor
predecir [preðe'θir] *vt* to predict, foretell, forecast
predestinado, -a [preðesti'naðo, a] *adj* predestined
predeterminar [preðetermi'nar] *vt* to predetermine
predicado [preði'kaðo] *nm* predicate
predicador, a [preðika'ðor, a] *nm/f* preacher
predicar [preði'kar] *vt, vi* to preach
predicción [preðik'θjon] *nf* prediction; *(pronóstico)* forecast; **~ del tiempo** weather forecast(ing)
predicho [pre'ðitʃo], **prediga** *etc* [pre'ðiɣa], **predije** *etc* [pre'ðixe] *vb ver* **predecir**
predilecto, -a [preði'lekto, a] *adj* favourite
predique *etc* [pre'ðike] *vb ver* **predicar**
prediré *etc* [preði're] *vb ver* **predecir**
predispondré *etc* [preðispon'dre] *vb ver* **predisponer**
predisponer [preðispo'ner] *vt* to predispose; *(pey)* to prejudice
predisponga *etc* [preðis'ponga] *vb ver* **predisponer**
predisposición [preðisposi'θjon] *nf* predisposition, inclination; prejudice, bias; *(Med)* tendency
predispuesto [preðis'pwesto], **predispuse** *etc* [preðis'puse] *vb ver* **predisponer**
predominante [preðomi'nante] *adj* predominant; *(preponderante)* prevailing; *(interés)* controlling
predominar [preðomi'nar] *vt* to dominate ■ *vi* to predominate; *(prevalecer)* to prevail
predominio [preðo'minjo] *nm* predominance; prevalence
preescolar [preesko'lar] *adj* preschool
preestreno [prees'treno] *nm* preview, press view
prefabricado, -a [prefaβri'kaðo, a] *adj* prefabricated
prefacio [pre'faθjo] *nm* preface
preferencia [prefe'renθja] *nf* preference; **de ~** preferably, for preference; **localidad de ~** reserved seat
preferible [prefe'riβle] *adj* preferable
preferido, a [prefe'riðo, a] *adj, nm/f* favourite, favorite *(US)*
preferir [prefe'rir] *vt* to prefer
prefiera *etc* [pre'fjera] *vb ver* **preferir**
prefijo [pre'fixo] *nm* prefix
prefiriendo *etc* [prefi'rjendo] *vb ver* **preferir**
pregón [pre'ɣon] *nm* proclamation, announcement
pregonar [preɣo'nar] *vt* to proclaim, announce; *(mercancía)* to hawk
pregonero [preɣo'nero] *nm* town crier
pregunta [pre'ɣunta] *nf* question; **~ capciosa** catch question; **hacer una ~** to ask a question; **preguntas frecuentes** FAQs, frequently asked questions
preguntar [preɣun'tar] *vt* to ask; *(cuestionar)* to question ■ *vi* to ask; **preguntarse** *vr* to wonder; **~ por algn** to ask for sb; **~ por la salud de algn** to ask after sb's health
preguntón, -ona [preɣun'ton, ona] *adj* inquisitive
prehistórico, -a [preis'toriko, a] *adj* prehistoric
prejuicio [pre'xwiθjo] *nm* prejudgement; *(preconcepción)* preconception; *(pey)* prejudice, bias
prejuzgar [prexuθ'ɣar] *vt* *(predisponerse)* to prejudge

prejuzgue *etc* [pre'xuθɣe] *vb ver* **prejuzgar**
preliminar [prelimi'nar] *adj, nm* preliminary
preludio [pre'luðjo] *nm* (*Mus, fig*) prelude
premamá [prema'ma] *adj*: **vestido ~** maternity dress
prematrimonial [prematrimo'njal] *adj*: **relaciones prematrimoniales** premarital sex
prematuro, -a [prema'turo, a] *adj* premature
premeditación [premeðita'θjon] *nf* premeditation
premeditado, -a [premeði'taðo, a] *adj* premeditated, deliberate; (*intencionado*) wilful
premeditar [premeði'tar] *vt* to premeditate
premiar [pre'mjar] *vt* to reward; (*en un concurso*) to give a prize to
premio ['premjo] *nm* reward; prize; (*Com*) premium; **~ gordo** first prize
premisa [pre'misa] *nf* premise
premonición [premoni'θjon] *nf* premonition
premura [pre'mura] *nf* (*prisa*) haste, urgency
prenatal [prena'tal] *adj* antenatal, prenatal
prenda ['prenda] *nf* (*de ropa*) garment, article of clothing; (*garantía*) pledge; (*fam*) darling!; **prendas** *nfpl* talents, gifts; **dejar algo en ~** to pawn sth; **no soltar ~** to give nothing away; (*fig*) not to say a word
prendar [pren'dar] *vt* to captivate, enchant; **prendarse de algo** to fall in love with sth
prendedor [prende'ðor] *nm* brooch
prender [pren'der] *vt* (*captar*) to catch, capture; (*detener*) to arrest; (*coser*) to pin, attach; (*sujetar*) to fasten; (*Am*) to switch on ■ *vi* to catch; (*arraigar*) to take root; **prenderse** *vr* (*encenderse*) to catch fire
prendido, -a [pren'diðo, a] *adj* (*Am: luz*) on
prensa ['prensa] *nf* press; **la P~** the press; **tener mala ~** to have *o* get a bad press; **la ~ nacional** the national press
prensar [pren'sar] *vt* to press
preñado, -a [pre'ɲaðo, a] *adj* (*mujer*) pregnant; **~ de** pregnant with, full of
preocupación [preokupa'θjon] *nf* worry, concern; (*ansiedad*) anxiety
preocupado, -a [preoku'paðo, a] *adj* worried, concerned; anxious
preocupar [preoku'par] *vt* to worry; **preocuparse** *vr* to worry; **preocuparse de algo** (*hacerse cargo de algo*) to take care of sth; **preocuparse por algo** to worry about sth
preparación [prepara'θjon] *nf* (*acto*) preparation; (*estado*) preparedness, readiness; (*entrenamiento*) training
preparado, -a [prepa'raðo, a] *adj* (*dispuesto*) prepared; (*Culin*) ready (to serve) ■ *nm* (*Med*) preparation; **¡preparados, listos, ya!** ready, steady, go!
preparar [prepa'rar] *vt* (*disponer*) to prepare, get ready; (*Tec: tratar*) to prepare, process, treat; (*entrenar*) to teach, train; **prepararse** *vr*: **prepararse a** *o* **para hacer algo** to prepare *o* get ready to do sth
preparativo, -a [prepara'tiβo] *adj* preparatory, preliminary ■ *nm*: **preparativos** *nmpl* preparations
preparatoria [prepara'torja] *nf* (*Am*) sixth form college (*Brit*), senior high school (*US*)
preposición [preposi'θjon] *nf* preposition
prepotencia [prepo'tenθja] *nf* abuse of power; (*Pol*) high-handedness; (*soberbia*) arrogance
prepotente [prepo'tente] *adj* (*Pol*) high-handed; (*soberbio*) arrogant
prerrogativa [prerroɣa'tiβa] *nf* prerogative, privilege
presa ['presa] *nf* (*cosa apresada*) catch; (*víctima*) victim; (*de animal*) prey; (*de agua*) dam; **hacer ~ en** to clutch (on to), seize; **ser ~ de** (*fig*) to be a prey to
presagiar [presa'xjar] *vt* to threaten
presagio [pre'saxjo] *nm* omen
presbítero [pres'βitero] *nm* priest
prescindir [presθin'dir] *vi*: **~ de** (*privarse de*) to do without, go without; (*descartar*) to dispense with; **no podemos ~ de él** we can't manage without him
prescribir [preskri'βir] *vt* to prescribe
prescripción [preskrip'θjon] *nf* prescription; **~ facultativa** medical prescription
prescrito [pres'krito] *pp de* **prescribir**
preseleccionar [preselekθjo'nar] *vt* (*Deporte*) to seed
presencia [pre'senθja] *nf* presence; **en ~ de** in the presence of
presencial [presen'θjal] *adj*: **testigo ~** eyewitness
presenciar [presen'θjar] *vt* to be present at; (*asistir a*) to attend; (*ver*) to see, witness
presentación [presenta'θjon] *nf* presentation; (*introducción*) introduction
presentador, a [presenta'ðor, a] *nm/f* compère
presentar [presen'tar] *vt* to present; (*ofrecer*) to offer; (*mostrar*) to show, display; (*renuncia*) to tender; (*moción*) to propose; (*a una persona*) to introduce; **presentarse** *vr* (*llegar inesperadamente*) to appear, turn up; (*ofrecerse: como candidato*) to run, stand; (*aparecer*) to show, appear; (*solicitar empleo*) to apply; **~ al cobro** (*Com*) to present for payment; **presentarse a la policía** to report to the police
presente [pre'sente] *adj* present ■ *nm* present; (*Ling*) present (tense); (*regalo*) gift;

los presentes those present; **hacer ~** to state, declare; **tener ~** to remember, bear in mind; **la carta ~, la ~** this letter
presentimiento [presenti'mjento] *nm* premonition, presentiment
presentir [presen'tir] *vt* to have a premonition of
preservación [preserβa'θjon] *nf* protection, preservation
preservar [preser'βar] *vt* to protect, preserve
preservativo [preserβa'tiβo] *nm* sheath, condom
presidencia [presi'ðenθja] *nf* presidency; (*de comité*) chairmanship; **ocupar la ~** to preside, be in *o* take the chair
presidente [presi'ðente] *nm/f* president; chairman(-woman); (*en parlamento*) speaker; (*Jur*) presiding magistrate
presidiario [presi'ðjarjo] *nm* convict
presidio [pre'siðjo] *nm* prison, penitentiary
presidir [presi'ðir] *vt* (*dirigir*) to preside at, preside over; (*: comité*) to take the chair at; (*dominar*) to dominate, rule ■ *vi* to preside; to take the chair
presienta *etc* [pre'sjenta], **presintiendo** *etc* [presin'tjendo] *vb ver* **presentir**
presión [pre'sjon] *nf* pressure; **~ arterial** *o* **sanguínea** blood pressure; **a ~** under pressure
presionar [presjo'nar] *vt* to press; (*botón*) to push, press; (*fig*) to press, put pressure on ■ *vi*: **~ para** *o* **por** to press for
preso, -a ['preso, a] *adj*: **estar ~ de terror** *o* **pánico** to be panic-stricken ■ *nm/f* prisoner; **tomar** *o* **llevar ~ a algn** to arrest sb, take sb prisoner
prestación [presta'θjon] *nf* (*aportación*) lending; (*Inform*) capability; (*servicio*) service; (*subsidio*) benefit; **prestaciones** *nfpl* (*Auto*) performance features; **~ de juramento** oath-taking; **~ personal** obligatory service; **P~ Social Sustitutoria** community service for conscientious objectors; *ver tb* **mili**
prestado, -a [pres'taðo, a] *adj* on loan; **dar algo ~** to lend sth; **pedir ~** to borrow
prestamista [presta'mista] *nm/f* moneylender
préstamo ['prestamo] *nm* loan; **~ con garantía** loan against collateral; **~ hipotecario** mortgage
prestar [pres'tar] *vt* to lend, loan; (*atención*) to pay; (*ayuda*) to give; (*servicio*) to do, render; (*juramento*) to take, swear; **prestarse** *vr* (*ofrecerse*) to offer *o* volunteer
prestatario, -a [presta'tarjo, a] *nm/f* borrower
presteza [pres'teθa] *nf* speed, promptness
prestidigitador [prestiðixita'ðor] *nm* conjurer
prestigio [pres'tixjo] *nm* prestige; (*reputación*) face; (*renombre*) good name
prestigioso, -a [presti'xjoso, a] *adj* (*honorable*) prestigious; (*famoso, renombrado*) renowned, famous
presto, -a ['presto, a] *adj* (*rápido*) quick, prompt; (*dispuesto*) ready ■ *adv* at once, right away
presumido, -a [presu'miðo, a] *adj* conceited
presumir [presu'mir] *vt* to presume ■ *vi* (*darse aires*) to be conceited; **según cabe ~** as may be presumed, presumably; **~ de listo** to think o.s. very smart
presunción [presun'θjon] *nf* presumption; (*sospecha*) suspicion; (*vanidad*) conceit
presunto, -a [pre'sunto, a] *adj* (*supuesto*) supposed, presumed; (*así llamado*) so-called
presuntuoso, -a [presun'twoso, a] *adj* conceited, presumptuous
presupondré *etc* [presupon'dre] *vb ver* **presuponer**
presuponer [presupo'ner] *vt* to presuppose
presuponga *etc* [presu'ponga] *vb ver* **presuponer**
presupuestar [presupwes'tar] *vi* to budget ■ *vt*: **~ algo** to budget for sth
presupuestario, -a [presupwes'tarjo, a] *adj* (*Finanzas*) budgetary, budget *cpd*
presupuesto [presu'pwesto] *pp de* **presuponer** ■ *nm* (*Finanzas*) budget; (*estimación: de costo*) estimate; **asignación de ~** (*Com*) budget appropriation
presupuse *etc* [presu'puse] *vb ver* **presuponer**
presuroso, -a [presu'roso, a] *adj* (*rápido*) quick, speedy; (*que tiene prisa*) hasty
pretencioso, -a [preten'θjoso, a] *adj* pretentious
pretender [preten'der] *vt* (*intentar*) to try to, seek to; (*reivindicar*) to claim; (*buscar*) to seek, try for; (*cortejar*) to woo, court; **~ que** to expect that; **¿qué pretende usted?** what are you after?
pretendiente [preten'djente] *nm/f* (*candidato*) candidate, applicant; (*amante*) suitor
pretensión [preten'sjon] *nf* (*aspiración*) aspiration; (*reivindicación*) claim; (*orgullo*) pretension
pretérito, -a [pre'terito, a] *adj* (*Ling*) past; (*fig*) past, former
pretextar [preteks'tar] *vt* to plead, use as an excuse
pretexto [pre'teksto] *nm* pretext; (*excusa*) excuse; **so ~ de** under pretext of
pretil [pre'til] *nm* (*valla*) parapet; (*baranda*) handrail

prevalecer [preβale'θer] *vi* to prevail
prevaleciente [preβale'θjente] *adj* prevailing, prevalent
prevalezca *etc* [preβa'leθka] *vb ver* **prevalecer**
prevención [preβen'θjon] *nf (preparación)* preparation; *(estado)* preparedness, readiness; *(medida)* prevention; *(previsión)* foresight, forethought; *(precaución)* precaution
prevendré *etc* [preβen'dre], **prevenga** *etc* [pre'βenga] *vb ver* **prevenir**
prevenido, -a [preβe'niðo, a] *adj* prepared, ready; *(cauteloso)* cautious; **estar ~** *(preparado)* to be ready; **ser ~** *(cuidadoso)* to be cautious; **hombre ~ vale por dos** forewarned is forearmed
prevenir [preβe'nir] *vt (impedir)* to prevent; *(prever)* to foresee, anticipate; *(predisponer)* to prejudice, bias; *(avisar)* to warn; *(preparar)* to prepare, get ready; **prevenirse** *vr* to get ready, prepare; **prevenirse contra** to take precautions against
preventivo, -a [preβen'tiβo, a] *adj* preventive, precautionary
prever [pre'βer] *vt* to foresee; *(anticipar)* to anticipate
previniendo *etc* [preβi'njendo] *vb ver* **prevenir**
previo, -a ['preβjo, a] *adj (anterior)* previous, prior ■ *prep*: **~ acuerdo de los otros** subject to the agreement of the others; **~ pago de los derechos** on payment of the fees
previsible [preβi'siβle] *adj* foreseeable
previsión [preβi'sjon] *nf (perspicacia)* foresight; *(predicción)* forecast; *(prudencia)* caution; **~ de ventas** *(Com)* sales forecast
previsor, a [preβi'sor, a] *adj (precavido)* far-sighted; *(prudente)* thoughtful
previsto [pre'βisto] *pp de* **prever**
P.R.I. ['pri] *nm abr (Am: = Partido Revolucionario Institucional) political party*
prieto, -a ['prjeto, a] *adj (oscuro)* dark; *(Am)* dark(-skinned); *(fig)* mean; *(comprimido)* tight, compressed
prima ['prima] *nf ver* **primo**
primacía [prima'θia] *nf* primacy
primar [pri'mar] *vi (tener primacía)* to occupy first place; **~ sobre** to have priority over
primario, -a [pri'marjo, a] *adj* primary ■ *nf* primary education; *ver tb* **sistema educativo**
primavera [prima'βera] *nf (temporada)* spring; *(período)* springtime
primaveral [primaβe'ral] *adj* spring *cpd*, springlike
primero, -a [pri'mero, a] *adj (antes de nmsg* **primer**) first; *(fig)* prime; *(anterior)* former; *(básico)* fundamental ■ *adv* first; *(más bien)* sooner, rather ■ *nf (Auto)* first gear; *(Ferro)* first class; **de primera** *(fam)* first-class, first-rate; **de buenas a primeras** suddenly; **primera dama** *(Teat)* leading lady
primicia [pri'miθja] *nf (Prensa)* scoop; **primicias** *nfpl (tb fig)* first fruits
primitivo, -a [primi'tiβo, a] *adj* primitive; *(original)* original; *(Com: acción)* ordinary ■ *nf*: **(Lotería) Primitiva** *weekly state-run lottery; ver tb* **lotería**
primo, -a ['primo, a] *adj (Mat)* prime ■ *nm/f* cousin; *(fam)* fool, dupe ■ *nf (Com)* bonus; *(de seguro)* premium; *(a la exportación)* subsidy; **~ hermano** first cousin; **materias primas** raw materials; **hacer el ~** to be taken for a ride
primogénito, -a [primo'xenito, a] *adj* first-born
primor [pri'mor] *nm (cuidado)* care; **es un ~** it's lovely
primordial [primor'ðjal] *adj* basic, fundamental
primoroso, -a [primo'roso, a] *adj* exquisite, fine
princesa [prin'θesa] *nf* princess
principado [prinθi'paðo] *nm* principality
principal [prinθi'pal] *adj* principal, main; *(más destacado)* foremost; *(piso)* first, second *(US)*; *(Inform)* foreground ■ *nm (jefe)* chief, principal
príncipe ['prinθipe] *nm* prince; **~ heredero** crown prince; **P~ de Asturias** *King's son and heir to the Spanish throne*; **~ de gales** *(tela)* check
principiante [prinθi'pjante] *nm/f* beginner; *(novato)* novice
principio [prin'θipjo] *nm (comienzo)* beginning, start; *(origen)* origin; *(base)* rudiment, basic idea; *(moral)* principle; **a principios de** at the beginning of; **desde el ~** from the first; **en un ~** at first
pringar [prin'gar] *vt (Culin: pan)* to dip; *(ensuciar)* to dirty; **pringarse** *vr* to get splashed *o* soiled; **~ a algn en un asunto** *(fam)* to involve sb in a matter
pringoso, -a [prin'goso, a] *adj* greasy; *(pegajoso)* sticky
pringue *etc* ['pringe] *vb ver* **pringar** ■ *nm (grasa)* grease, fat, dripping
prioridad [priori'ðað] *nf* priority; *(Auto)* right of way
prioritario, -a [priori'tarjo, a] *adj (Inform)* foreground
prisa ['prisa] *nf (apresuramiento)* hurry, haste; *(rapidez)* speed; *(urgencia)* (sense of) urgency; **correr ~** to be urgent; **darse ~** to hurry up; **estar de** *o* **tener ~** to be in a hurry
prisión [pri'sjon] *nf (cárcel)* prison; *(período de cárcel)* imprisonment

prisionero, -a [prisjo'nero, a] *nm/f* prisoner
prismáticos [pris'matikos] *nmpl* binoculars
privación [priβa'θjon] *nf* deprivation; (*falta*) want, privation; **privaciones** *nfpl* hardships, privations
privado, -a [pri'βaðo, a] *adj* (*particular*) private; (*Pol: favorito*) favourite (*Brit*), favorite (*US*); **en ~** privately, in private; **"~ y confidencial"** "private and confidential"
privar [pri'βar] *vt* to deprive; **privarse** *vr*: **privarse de** (*abstenerse de*) to deprive o.s. of; (*renunciar a*) to give up
privativo, -a [priβa'tiβo, a] *adj* exclusive
privatizar [priβati'θar] *vt* to privatize
privilegiado, -a [priβile'xjaðo, a] *adj* privileged; (*memoria*) very good ■ *nm/f* (*afortunado*) privileged person
privilegiar [priβile'xjar] *vt* to grant a privilege to; (*favorecer*) to favour
privilegio [priβi'lexjo] *nm* privilege; (*concesión*) concession
pro [pro] *nm o nf* profit, advantage ■ *prep*: **asociación ~ ciegos** association for the blind ■ *pref*: **~ soviético/americano** pro-Soviet/-American; **en ~ de** on behalf of, for; **los pros y los contras** the pros and cons
proa ['proa] *nf* (*Naut*) bow, prow
probabilidad [proβaβili'ðað] *nf* probability, likelihood; (*oportunidad, posibilidad*) chance, prospect
probable [pro'βaβle] *adj* probable, likely; **es ~ que** (*+ subjun*) it is probable *o* likely that; **es ~ que no venga** he probably won't come
probador [proβa'ðor] *nm* (*persona*) taster (*of wine etc*); (*en una tienda*) fitting room
probar [pro'βar] *vt* (*demostrar*) to prove; (*someter a prueba*) to test, try out; (*ropa*) to try on; (*comida*) to taste ■ *vi* to try; **probarse** *vr*: **probarse un traje** to try on a suit
probeta [pro'βeta] *nf* test tube
problema [pro'βlema] *nm* problem
procaz [pro'kaθ] *adj* insolent, impudent
procedencia [proθe'ðenθja] *nf* (*principio*) source, origin; (*lugar de salida*) point of departure
procedente [proθe'ðente] *adj* (*razonable*) reasonable; (*conforme a derecho*) proper, fitting; **~ de** coming from, originating in
proceder [proθe'ðer] *vi* (*avanzar*) to proceed; (*actuar*) to act; (*ser correcto*) to be right (and proper), be fitting ■ *nm* (*comportamiento*) behaviour, conduct; **no procede obrar así** it is not right to act like that; **~ de** to come from, originate in
procedimiento [proθeði'mjento] *nm* procedure; (*proceso*) process; (*método*) means, method; (*trámite*) proceedings *pl*
prócer ['proθer] *nm* (*persona eminente*) worthy; (*líder*) great man, leader; (*esp Am*) national hero
procesado, -a [proθe'saðo, a] *nm/f* accused (person)
procesador [proθesa'ðor] *nm*: **~ de textos** (*Inform*) word processor
procesamiento [proθesa'mjento] *nm* (*Inform*) processing; **~ de datos** data processing; **~ por lotes** batch processing; **~ solapado** multiprogramming; **~ de textos** word processing
procesar [proθe'sar] *vt* to try, put on trial; (*Inform*) to process
procesión [proθe'sjon] *nf* procession; **la ~ va por dentro** he keeps his troubles to himself
proceso [pro'θeso] *nm* process; (*Jur*) trial; (*lapso*) course (of time); (*Inform*): **~ (automático) de datos** (automatic) data processing; **~ no prioritario** background process; **~ por pasadas** batch processing; **~ en tiempo real** real-time programming
proclama [pro'klama] *nf* (*acto*) proclamation; (*cartel*) poster
proclamar [prokla'mar] *vt* to proclaim
proclive [pro'kliβe] *adj*: **~ (a)** inclined *o* prone (to)
procreación [prokrea'θjon] *nf* procreation
procrear [prokre'ar] *vt, vi* to procreate
procurador, a [prokura'ðor, a] *nm/f* attorney, solicitor
procurar [proku'rar] *vt* (*intentar*) to try, endeavour; (*conseguir*) to get, obtain; (*asegurar*) to secure; (*producir*) to produce
prodigar [proði'ɣar] *vt* to lavish; **prodigarse** *vr*: **prodigarse en** to be lavish with
prodigio [pro'ðixjo] *nm* prodigy; (*milagro*) wonder, marvel; **niño ~** child prodigy
prodigioso, -a [proði'xjoso, a] *adj* prodigious, marvellous
pródigo, -a ['proðiɣo, a] *adj* (*rico*) rich, productive; **hijo ~** prodigal son
producción [proðuk'θjon] *nf* production; (*suma de productos*) output; (*producto*) product; **~ en serie** mass production
producir [proðu'θir] *vt* to produce; (*generar*) to cause, bring about; (*impresión*) to give; (*Com: interés*) to bear; **producirse** *vr* (*gen*) to come about, happen; (*hacerse*) to be produced, be made; (*estallar*) to break out; (*accidente*) to take place
productividad [proðuktiβi'ðað] *nf* productivity
productivo, -a [proðuk'tiβo, a] *adj* productive; (*provechoso*) profitable
producto [pro'ðukto] *nm* (*resultado*) product; (*producción*) production; **~ alimenticio**

foodstuff; ~ **(nacional) bruto** gross (national) product; ~ **interno bruto** gross domestic product
productor, a [proðuk'tor, a] *adj* productive, producing ■ *nm/f* producer
produje [pro'ðuxe], **produjera** [proðu'xera], **produzca** *etc* [pro'ðuθka] *vb ver* **producir**
proeza [pro'eθa] *nf* exploit, feat
profanar [profa'nar] *vt* to desecrate, profane
profano, -a [pro'fano, a] *adj* profane ■ *nm/f* (*inexperto*) layman(-woman); **soy ~ en música** I don't know anything about music
profecía [profe'θia] *nf* prophecy
proferir [profe'rir] *vt* (*palabra, sonido*) to utter; (*injuria*) to hurl, let fly
profesar [profe'sar] *vt* (*declarar*) to profess; (*practicar*) to practise
profesión [profe'sjon] *nf* profession; (*confesión*) avowal; **abogado de ~, de ~ abogado** a lawyer by profession
profesional [profesjo'nal] *adj* professional
profesor, a [profe'sor, a] *nm/f* teacher; (*instructor*) instructor; ~ **de universidad** lecturer; ~ **adjunto** assistant lecturer, associate professor (*US*)
profesorado [profeso'raðo] *nm* (*profesión*) teaching profession; (*cuerpo*) teaching staff, faculty (*US*); (*cargo*) professorship
profeta [pro'feta] *nm/f* prophet
profetice *etc* [profe'tiθe] *vb ver* **profetizar**
profetizar [profeti'θar] *vt, vi* to prophesy
profiera *etc* [pro'fjera], **profiriendo** *etc* [profi'rjendo] *vb ver* **proferir**
profilaxis [profi'laksis] *nf inv* prevention
prófugo, -a ['profuɣo, a] *nm/f* fugitive; (*desertor*) deserter
profundice *etc* [profun'diθe] *vb ver* **profundizar**
profundidad [profundi'ðað] *nf* depth; **tener una ~ de 30 cm** to be 30 cm deep
profundizar [profundi'θar] *vt* (*fig*) to go deeply into, study in depth
profundo, -a [pro'fundo, a] *adj* deep; (*misterio, pensador*) profound; **poco ~** shallow
profusión [profu'sjon] *nf* (*abundancia*) profusion; (*prodigalidad*) wealth
progenie [pro'xenje] *nf* offspring
progenitor [proxeni'tor] *nm* ancestor; **progenitores** *nmpl* (*fam*) parents
programa [pro'ɣrama] *nm* programme; (*Inform*) program; ~ **de estudios** curriculum, syllabus; ~ **verificador de ortografía** (*Inform*) spelling checker
programación [proɣrama'θjon] *nf* (*Inform*) programming; ~ **estructurada** structured programming
programador, a [proɣrama'ðor, a] *nm/f* (computer) programmer; ~ **de aplicaciones** applications programmer
programar [proɣra'mar] *vt* (*Inform*) to programme
progre ['proɣre] *adj* (*fam*) liberal
progresar [proɣre'sar] *vi* to progress, make progress
progresión [proɣres'jon] *nf*: ~ **geométrica/aritmética** geometric/arithmetic progression
progresista [proɣre'sista] *adj, nm/f* progressive
progresivo, -a [proɣre'siβo, a] *adj* progressive; (*gradual*) gradual; (*continuo*) continuous
progreso [pro'ɣreso] *nm* (*tb*: **progresos**) progress; **hacer progresos** to progress, advance
prohibición [proiβi'θjon] *nf* prohibition, ban; **levantar la ~ de** to remove the ban on
prohibir [proi'βir] *vt* to prohibit, ban, forbid; **se prohíbe fumar** no smoking
prohibitivo, -a [proiβi'tiβo, a] *adj* prohibitive
prójimo, -a ['proximo, a] *nm* fellow man ■ *nm/f* (*vecino*) neighbour
prole ['prole] *nf* (*descendencia*) offspring
proletariado [proleta'rjaðo] *nm* proletariat
proletario, -a [prole'tarjo, a] *adj, nm/f* proletarian
proliferación [prolifera'θjon] *nf* proliferation; ~ **de armas nucleares** spread of nuclear arms
proliferar [prolife'rar] *vi* to proliferate
prolífico, -a [pro'lifiko, a] *adj* prolific
prolijo, -a [pro'lixo, a] *adj* long-winded, tedious; (*Am*) neat
prólogo ['proloɣo] *nm* prologue; (*preámbulo*) preface, introduction
prolongación [prolonga'θjon] *nf* extension
prolongado, -a [prolon'gaðo, a] *adj* (*largo*) long; (*alargado*) lengthy
prolongar [prolon'gar] *vt* (*gen*) to extend; (*en el tiempo*) to prolong; (*calle, tubo*) to make longer, extend; **prolongarse** *vr* (*alargarse*) to extend, go on
prolongue *etc* [pro'longe] *vb ver* **prolongar**
prom. *abr* (= *promedio*) av.
promedio [pro'meðjo] *nm* average; (*de distancia*) middle, mid-point
promesa [pro'mesa] *nf* promise ■ *adj*: **jugador ~** promising player; **faltar a una ~** to break a promise
prometer [prome'ter] *vt* to promise ■ *vi* to show promise; **prometerse** *vr* (*dos personas*) to get engaged
prometido, -a [prome'tiðo, a] *adj* promised;

engaged ■ *nm/f* fiancé/fiancée
prominente [promi'nente] *adj* prominent
promiscuidad [promiskwi'ðað] *nf* promiscuity
promiscuo, -a [pro'miskwo, a] *adj* promiscuous
promoción [promo'θjon] *nf* promotion; (*año*) class, year; **~ por correspondencia directa** (*Com*) direct mailshot; **~ de ventas** sales promotion *o* drive
promocionar [promoθjo'nar] *vt* (*Com: dar publicidad*) to promote
promontorio [promon'torjo] *nm* promontory
promotor [promo'tor] *nm* promoter; (*instigador*) instigator
promover [promo'βer] *vt* to promote; (*causar*) to cause; (*juicio*) to bring; (*motín*) to instigate, stir up
promueva *etc* [pro'mweβa] *vb ver* **promover**
promulgar [promul'ɣar] *vt* to promulgate; (*fig*) to proclaim
promulgue *etc* [pro'mulɣe] *vb ver* **promulgar**
pronombre [pro'nombre] *nm* pronoun
pronosticar [pronosti'kar] *vt* to predict, foretell, forecast
pronóstico [pro'nostiko] *nm* prediction, forecast; (*profecía*) omen; (*Med: diagnóstico*) prognosis; **de ~ leve** slight, not serious; **~ del tiempo** weather forecast
pronostique *etc* [pronos'tike] *vb ver* **pronosticar**
prontitud [pronti'tuð] *nf* speed, quickness
pronto, -a ['pronto, a] *adj* (*rápido*) prompt, quick; (*preparado*) ready ■ *adv* quickly, promptly; (*en seguida*) at once, right away; (*dentro de poco*) soon; (*temprano*) early ■ *nm* urge, sudden feeling; **tener prontos de enojo** to be quick-tempered; **al ~** at first; **de ~** suddenly; **¡hasta ~!** see you soon!; **lo más ~ posible** as soon as possible; **por lo ~** meanwhile, for the present; **tan ~ como** as soon as
pronunciación [pronunθja'θjon] *nf* pronunciation
pronunciado, -a [pronun'θjaðo, a] *adj* (*marcado*) pronounced; (*curva etc*) sharp; (*facciones*) marked
pronunciamiento [pronunθja'mjento] *nm* (*rebelión*) insurrection
pronunciar [pronun'θjar] *vt* to pronounce; (*discurso*) to make, deliver; (*Jur: sentencia*) to pass, pronounce; **pronunciarse** *vr* to revolt, rise, rebel; (*declararse*) to declare o.s.; **pronunciarse sobre** to pronounce on
propagación [propaɣa'θjon] *nf* propagation; (*difusión*) spread(ing)
propaganda [propa'ɣanda] *nf* (*política*) propaganda; (*comercial*) advertising; **hacer ~ de** (*Com*) to advertise
propagar [propa'ɣar] *vt* to propagate; (*difundir*) to spread, disseminate; **propagarse** *vr* (*Bio*) to propagate; (*fig*) to spread
propague *etc* [pro'paɣe] *vb ver* **propagar**
propalar [propa'lar] *vt* (*divulgar*) to divulge; (*publicar*) to publish an account of
propano [pro'pano] *nm* propane
propasarse [propa'sarse] *vr* (*excederse*) to go too far; (*sexualmente*) to take liberties
propensión [propen'sjon] *nf* inclination, propensity
propenso, -a [pro'penso, a] *adj*: **~ a** prone *o* inclined to; **ser ~ a hacer algo** to be inclined *o* have a tendency to do sth
propiamente [propja'mente] *adv* properly; (*realmente*) really, exactly; **~ dicho** real, true
propicio, -a [pro'piθjo, a] *adj* favourable, propitious
propiedad [propje'ðað] *nf* property; (*posesión*) possession, ownership; (*conveniencia*) suitability; (*exactitud*) accuracy; **~ particular** private property; **~ pública** (*Com*) public ownership; **ceder algo a algn en ~** to transfer to sb the full rights over sth
propietario, -a [propje'tarjo, a] *nm/f* owner, proprietor
propina [pro'pina] *nf* tip; **dar algo de ~** to give something extra
propinar [propi'nar] *vt* (*golpe*) to strike; (*azotes*) to give
propio, -a ['propjo, a] *adj* own, of one's own; (*característico*) characteristic, typical; (*conveniente*) proper; (*mismo*) selfsame, very; **el ~ ministro** the minister himself; **¿tienes casa propia?** have you a house of your own?; **eso es muy ~ de él** that's just like him; **tiene un olor muy ~** it has a smell of its own
propondré *etc* [propon'dre] *vb ver* **proponer**
proponente [propo'nente] *nm* proposer, mover
proponer [propo'ner] *vt* to propose, put forward; (*candidato*) to propose, nominate; (*problema*) to pose; **proponerse** *vr* to propose, plan, intend
proponga *etc* [pro'ponga] *vb ver* **proponer**
proporción [propor'θjon] *nf* proportion; (*Mat*) ratio; (*razón, porcentaje*) rate; **proporciones** *nfpl* dimensions; (*fig*) size *sg*; **en ~ con** in proportion to
proporcionado, -a [proporθjo'naðo, a] *adj* proportionate; (*regular*) medium, middling; (*justo*) just right; **bien ~** well-proportioned
proporcional [proporθjo'nal] *adj* proportional; **~ a** proportional to

proporcionar [proporθjo'nar] *vt* (*dar*) to give, supply, provide; **esto le proporciona una renta anual de ...** this brings him in a yearly income of ...
proposición [proposi'θjon] *nf* proposition; (*propuesta*) proposal
propósito [pro'posito] *nm* (*intención*) purpose; (*intento*) aim, intention ■ *adv*: **a ~** by the way, incidentally; **a ~ de** about, with regard to
propuesto, -a [pro'pwesto, a] *pp de* **proponer** ■ *nf* proposal
propugnar [propuɣ'nar] *vt* to uphold
propulsar [propul'sar] *vt* to drive, propel; (*fig*) to promote, encourage
propulsión [propul'sjon] *nf* propulsion; **~ a chorro** *o* **por reacción** jet propulsion
propuse *etc* [pro'puse] *vb ver* **proponer**
prorrata [pro'rrata] *nf* (*porción*) share, quota, prorate (*US*) ■ *adv* (*Com*) pro rata
prorratear [prorrate'ar] *vt* (*dividir*) to share out, prorate (*US*)
prórroga ['prorroɣa] *nf* (*gen*) extension; (*Jur*) stay; (*Com*) deferment
prorrogable [prorro'ɣaβle] *adj* which can be extended
prorrogar [prorro'ɣar] *vt* (*período*) to extend; (*decisión*) to defer, postpone
prorrogue *etc* [pro'rroɣe] *vb ver* **prorrogar**
prorrumpir [prorrum'pir] *vi* to burst forth, break out; **~ en gritos** to start shouting; **~ en lágrimas** to burst into tears
prosa ['prosa] *nf* prose
prosaico, -a [pro'saiko, a] *adj* prosaic, dull
proscribir [proskri'βir] *vt* to prohibit, ban; (*desterrar*) to exile, banish; (*partido*) to proscribe
proscripción [proskrip'θjon] *nf* prohibition, ban; banishment; proscription
proscrito, -a [pros'krito, a] *pp de* **proscribir** ■ *adj* (*prohibido*) banned; (*desterrado*) outlawed ■ *nm/f* (*exilado*) exile; (*bandido*) outlaw
prosecución [proseku'θjon] *nf* continuation; (*persecución*) pursuit
proseguir [prose'ɣir] *vt* to continue, carry on, proceed with; (*investigación, estudio*) to pursue ■ *vi* to continue, go on
prosiga *etc* [pro'siɣa], **prosiguiendo** *etc* [prosi'ɣjendo] *vb ver* **proseguir**
prosista [pro'sista] *nm/f* (*escritor*) prose writer
prospección [prospek'θjon] *nf* exploration; (*del petróleo, del oro*) prospecting
prospecto [pros'pekto] *nm* prospectus; (*folleto*) leaflet, sheet of instructions
prosperar [prospe'rar] *vi* to prosper, thrive, flourish
prosperidad [prosperi'ðað] *nf* prosperity; (*éxito*) success
próspero, -a ['prospero, a] *adj* prosperous; (*que tiene éxito*) successful
prostíbulo [pros'tiβulo] *nm* brothel
prostitución [prostitu'θjon] *nf* prostitution
prostituir [prosti'twir] *vt* to prostitute; **prostituirse** *vr* to prostitute o.s., become a prostitute
prostituta [prosti'tuta] *nf* prostitute
prostituyendo *etc* [prostitu'jendo] *vb ver* **prostituir**
protagonice *etc* [protaɣo'niθe] *vb ver* **protagonizar**
protagonista [protaɣo'nista] *nm/f* protagonist; (*Lit: personaje*) main character, hero/heroine
protagonizar [protaɣoni'θar] *vt* to head, take the chief role in
protección [protek'θjon] *nf* protection
proteccionismo [protekθjo'nismo] *nm* (*Com*) protectionism
protector, a [protek'tor, a] *adj* protective, protecting; (*tono*) patronizing ■ *nm/f* protector; (*bienhechor*) patron; (*de la tradición*) guardian
proteger [prote'xer] *vt* to protect; **~ contra grabación** *o* **contra escritura** (*Inform*) to write-protect
protegido, -a [prote'xiðo, a] *nm/f* protégé/protégée
proteína [prote'ina] *nf* protein
proteja *etc* [pro'texa] *vb ver* **proteger**
prótesis ['protesis] *nf* (*Med*) prosthesis
protesta [pro'testa] *nf* protest
protestante [protes'tante] *adj* Protestant
protestar [protes'tar] *vt* to protest, declare; (*fe*) to protest ■ *vi* to protest; (*objetar*) to object; **cheque protestado por falta de fondos** cheque referred to drawer
protocolo [proto'kolo] *nm* protocol; **sin protocolos** (*formalismo*) informal(ly)
protón [pro'ton] *nm* proton
prototipo [proto'tipo] *nm* prototype; (*ideal*) model
protuberancia [protuβe'ranθja] *nf* protuberance
prov. *abr* (= *provincia*) prov.
provecho [pro'βetʃo] *nm* advantage, benefit; (*Finanzas*) profit; **¡buen ~!** bon appétit!; **en ~ de** to the benefit of; **sacar ~ de** to benefit from, profit by
provechoso, -a [proβe'tʃoso, a] *adj* (*ventajoso*) advantageous; (*beneficioso*) beneficial, useful; (*Finanzas: lucrativo*) profitable
proveedor, a [proβee'ðor, a] *nm/f* (*abastecedor*) supplier; (*distribuidor*) dealer; **~ de (acceso a) Internet** Internet Service Provider
proveer [proβe'er] *vt* to provide, supply;

(*preparar*) to provide, get ready; (*vacante*) to fill; (*negocio*) to transact, dispatch ■ *vi*: ~ **a** to provide for; **proveerse** *vr*: **proveerse de** to provide o.s. with
provendré *etc* [proβen'dre], **provenga** *etc* [pro'βenga] *vb ver* **provenir**
provenir [proβe'nir] *vi*: ~ **de** to come from
Provenza [pro'βenθa] *nf* Provence
proverbial [proβer'βjal] *adj* proverbial; (*fig*) notorious
proverbio [pro'βerβjo] *nm* proverb
proveyendo *etc* [proβe'jendo] *vb ver* **proveer**
providencia [proβi'ðenθja] *nf* providence; (*previsión*) foresight; **providencias** *nfpl* measures, steps
provincia [pro'βinθja] *nf* province; (*Esp: Admin*) ≈ county, ≈ region (*Scot*); **un pueblo de ~(s)** a country town; *see note*

PROVINCIA

Spain is divided up into 55 administrative *provincias*, including the islands, and territories in North Africa. Each one has a *capital de provincia*, which generally bears the same name. *Provincias* are grouped by geography, history and culture into *comunidades autónomas*. It should be noted that the term *comarca* normally has a purely geographical function in Spanish, but in Catalonia it designates administrative boundaries.

provinciano, -a [proβin'θjano, a] *adj* provincial; (*del campo*) country *cpd*
proviniendo *etc* [proβi'njendo] *vb ver* **provenir**
provisión [proβi'sjon] *nf* provision; (*abastecimiento*) provision, supply; (*medida*) measure, step
provisional [proβisjo'nal] *adj* provisional
provisorio, -a [proβi'sorjo, a] *adj* (*esp Am*) provisional
provisto, -a [pro'βisto, a] *adj*: ~ **de** provided *o* supplied with; (*que tiene*) having, possessing
provocación [proβoka'θjon] *nf* provocation
provocador, a [proβoka'ðor, a] *adj* provocative, provoking
provocar [proβo'kar] *vt* to provoke; (*alentar*) to tempt, invite; (*causar*) to bring about, lead to; (*promover*) to promote; (*estimular*) to rouse, stir, stimulate; (*protesta, explosión*) to cause, spark off; (*Am*): **¿te provoca un café?** would you like a coffee?
provocativo, -a [proβoka'tiβo, a] *adj* provocative
provoque *etc* [pro'βoke] *vb ver* **provocar**
proxeneta [prokse'neta] *nm/f* go-between; (*de prostitutas*) pimp/procuress
próximamente [proksima'mente] *adv* shortly, soon
proximidad [proksimi'ðað] *nf* closeness, proximity
próximo, -a ['proksimo, a] *adj* near, close; (*vecino*) neighbouring; (*el que viene*) next; **en fecha próxima** at an early date; **el mes ~** next month
proyección [projek'θjon] *nf* projection; (*Cine*) showing; (*diapositiva*) slide, transparency; (*influencia*) influence; **el tiempo de ~ es de 35 minutos** the film runs for 35 minutes
proyectar [projek'tar] *vt* (*objeto*) to hurl, throw; (*luz*) to cast, shed; (*Cine*) to screen, show; (*planear*) to plan
proyectil [projek'til] *nm* projectile, missile; **~ (tele)dirigido** guided missile
proyecto [pro'jekto] *nm* plan; (*idea*) project; (*estimación de costo*) detailed estimate; **tener algo en ~** to be planning sth; **~ de ley** (*Pol*) bill
proyector [projek'tor] *nm* (*Cine*) projector
prudencia [pru'ðenθja] *nf* (*sabiduría*) wisdom, prudence; (*cautela*) care
prudente [pru'ðente] *adj* sensible, wise, prudent; (*cauteloso*) careful
prueba *etc* ['prweβa] *vb ver* **probar** ■ *nf* proof; (*ensayo*) test, trial; (*cantidad*) taste, sample; (*saboreo*) testing, sampling; (*de ropa*) fitting; (*Deporte*) event; **a ~** on trial; (*Com*) on approval; **a ~ de** proof against; **a ~ de agua/fuego** waterproof/fireproof; **~ de capacitación** (*Com*) proficiency test; **~ de fuego** (*fig*) acid test; **~ de vallas** hurdles; **someter a ~** to put to the test; **¿tiene usted ~ de ello?** can you prove it?, do you have proof?
prurito [pru'rito] *nm* itch; (*de bebé*) nappy rash; (*anhelo*) urge
psico... [siko] *pref* psycho...
psicoanálisis [sikoa'nalisis] *nm* psychoanalysis
psicoanalista [sikoana'lista] *nm/f* psychoanalyst
psicología [sikolo'xia] *nf* psychology
psicológico, -a [siko'loxiko, a] *adj* psychological
psicólogo, -a [si'koloγo, a] *nm/f* psychologist
psicópata [si'kopata] *nm/f* psychopath
psicosis [si'kosis] *nf inv* psychosis
psicosomático, -a [sikoso'matiko, a] *adj* psychosomatic
psicoterapia [sikote'rapja] *nf* psychotherapy
psiquiatra [si'kjatra] *nm/f* psychiatrist
psiquiátrico, -a [si'kjatriko, a] *adj* psychiatric ■ *nm* mental hospital
psíquico, -a ['sikiko, a] *adj* psychic(al)

PSOE [pe'soe] *nm abr* = **Partido Socialista Obrero Español**
PSS *nf abr* (= *Prestación Social Sustitutoria*) *community service for conscientious objectors*
Pta. *abr* (*Geo:* = *Punta*) Pt.
pta(s). *abr* (*Historia*) = **peseta(s)**
pts. *abr* (*Historia*) = **pesetas**
púa ['pua] *nf* sharp point; (*para guitarra*) plectrum; **alambre de púas** barbed wire
pub [puβ/paβ/paf] *nm* bar
púber, a ['puβer, a] *adj, nm/f* adolescent
pubertad [puβer'tað] *nf* puberty
publicación [puβlika'θjon] *nf* publication
publicar [puβli'kar] *vt* (*editar*) to publish; (*hacer público*) to publicize; (*divulgar*) to make public, divulge
publicidad [puβliθi'ðað] *nf* publicity; (*Com*) advertising; **dar ~ a** to publicize, give publicity to; **~ gráfica** display advertising; **~ en el punto de venta** point-of-sale advertising
publicitar [puβliθi'tar] *vt* to publicize
publicitario, -a [puβliθi'tarjo, a] *adj* publicity *cpd*; advertising *cpd*
público, -a ['puβliko, a] *adj* public ■ *nm* public; (*Teat etc*) audience; (*Deporte*) spectators *pl*, crowd; (*en restaurantes etc*) clients *pl*; **el gran ~** the general public; **hacer ~** to publish; (*difundir*) to disclose; **~ objetivo** (*Com*) target audience
publique *etc* [pu'βlike] *vb ver* **publicar**
pucherazo [putʃe'raθo] *nm* (*fraude*) electoral fiddle; **dar ~** to rig an election
puchero [pu'tʃero] *nm* (*Culin: olla*) cooking pot; (*: guiso*) stew; **hacer pucheros** to pout
pudibundo, -a [puði'βundo, a] *adj* bashful
púdico, -a ['puðiko, a] *adj* modest; (*pudibundo*) bashful
pudiendo *etc* [pu'ðjendo] *vb ver* **poder**
pudiente [pu'ðjente] *adj* (*opulento*) wealthy; (*poderoso*) powerful
pudín [pu'ðin] *nm* pudding
pudor [pu'ðor] *nm* modesty; (*vergüenza*) (sense of) shame
pudoroso, -a [puðo'roso, a] *adj* (*modesto*) modest; (*casto*) chaste
pudrir [pu'ðrir] *vt* to rot; (*fam*) to upset, annoy; **pudrirse** *vr* to rot, decay; (*fig*) to rot, languish
pueblerino, -a [pweβle'rino, a] *adj* (*lugareño*) small-town *cpd*; (*persona*) rustic, provincial ■ *nm/f* (*aldeano*) country person
pueblo *etc* ['pweβlo] *vb ver* **poblar** ■ *nm* people; (*nación*) nation; (*aldea*) village; (*plebe*) common people; (*población pequeña*) small town, country town
pueda *etc* ['pweða] *vb ver* **poder**
puente ['pwente] *nm* (*gen*) bridge; (*Naut: tb:* **puente de mando**) bridge; (*: cubierta*) deck; **~ aéreo** airlift; **~ colgante** suspension bridge; **~ levadizo** drawbridge; **hacer (el) ~** (*fam*) to take a long weekend
puenting ['pwentin] *nm* bungee jumping
puerco, -a ['pwerko, a] *adj* (*sucio*) dirty, filthy; (*obsceno*) disgusting ■ *nm/f* pig/sow
pueril [pwe'ril] *adj* childish
puerro ['pwerro] *nm* leek
puerta ['pwerta] *nf* door; (*de jardín*) gate; (*portal*) doorway; (*fig*) gateway; (*gol*) goal; (*Inform*) port; **a la ~** at the door; **a ~ cerrada** behind closed doors; **~ corredera/giratoria** sliding/swing *o* revolving door; **~ principal/trasera** *o* **de servicio** front/back door; **~ (de transmisión en) paralelo/serie** (*Inform*) parallel/serial port; **tomar la ~** (*fam*) to leave
puerto ['pwerto] *nm* (*tb Inform*) port; (*de mar*) seaport; (*paso*) pass; (*fig*) haven, refuge; **llegar a ~** (*fig*) to get over a difficulty
Puerto Rico [pwerto'riko] *nm* Puerto Rico
puertorriqueño, -a [pwertorri'keɲo, a] *adj, nm/f* Puerto Rican
pues [pwes] *adv* (*entonces*) then; (*¡entonces!*) well, well then; (*así que*) so ■ *conj* (*porque*) since; **~ ... no sé** well ... I don't know
puesto, -a ['pwesto, a] *pp de* **poner** ■ *adj* dressed ■ *nm* (*lugar, posición*) place; (*trabajo*) post, job; (*Mil*) post; (*Com*) stall; (*quiosco*) kiosk ■ *conj*: **~ que** since, as ■ *nf* (*apuesta*) bet, stake; **~ de mercado** market stall; **~ de policía** police station; **~ de socorro** first aid post; **puesta en escena** staging; **puesta en marcha** starting; **puesta del sol** sunset; **puesta a cero** (*Inform*) reset
pugna ['puɣna] *nf* battle, conflict
pugnar [puɣ'nar] *vi* (*luchar*) to struggle, fight; (*pelear*) to fight
puja ['puxa] *nf* (*esfuerzo*) attempt; (*en una subasta*) bid
pujante [pu'xante] *adj* strong, vigorous
pujar [pu'xar] *vt* (*precio*) to raise, push up ■ *vi* (*en licitación*) to bid, bid up; (*fig: esforzarse*) to struggle, strain
pulcro, -a ['pulkro, a] *adj* neat, tidy
pulga ['pulɣa] *nf* flea; **tener malas pulgas** to be short-tempered
pulgada [pul'ɣaða] *nf* inch
pulgar [pul'ɣar] *nm* thumb
pulgón [pul'ɣon] *nm* plant louse, greenfly
pulir [pu'lir] *vt* to polish; (*alisar*) to smooth; (*fig*) to polish up, touch up
pulla ['puʎa] *nf* cutting remark
pulmón [pul'mon] *nm* lung; **a pleno ~** (*respirar*) deeply; (*gritar*) at the top of one's voice; **~ de acero** iron lung

pulmonía [pulmo'nia] *nf* pneumonia
pulpa ['pulpa] *nf* pulp; (*de fruta*) flesh, soft part
pulpería [pulpe'ria] *nf* (*Am*) small grocery store
púlpito ['pulpito] *nm* pulpit
pulpo ['pulpo] *nm* octopus
pulsación [pulsa'θjon] *nf* beat, pulsation; (*Anat*) throb(bing); (*en máquina de escribir*) tap; (*de pianista, mecanógrafo*) touch; **~ (de una tecla)** (*Inform*) keystroke; **~ doble** (*Inform*) strikeover
pulsador [pulsa'ðor] *nm* button, push button
pulsar [pul'sar] *vt* (*tecla*) to touch, tap; (*Mus*) to play; (*botón*) to press, push ▪ *vi* to pulsate; (*latir*) to beat, throb
pulsera [pul'sera] *nf* bracelet; **reloj de ~** wristwatch
pulso ['pulso] *nm* (*Med*) pulse; **hacer algo a ~** to do sth unaided *o* by one's own efforts
pulular [pulu'lar] *vi* (*estar plagado*): **~ (de)** to swarm (with)
pulverice *etc* [pulβe'riθe] *vb ver* **pulverizar**
pulverizador [pulβeriθa'ðor] *nm* spray, spray gun
pulverizar [pulβeri'θar] *vt* to pulverize; (*líquido*) to spray
puna ['puna] *nf* (*Am Med*) mountain sickness
punce *etc* ['punθe] *vb ver* **punzar**
punción [pun'θjon] *nf* (*Med*) puncture
pundonor [pundo'nor] *nm* (*dignidad*) self-respect
punición [puni'θjon] *nf* punishment
punitivo, -a [puni'tiβo, a] *adj* punitive
punki ['punki] *adj, nm/f* punk
punta ['punta] *nf* point, tip; (*extremidad*) end; (*promontorio*) headland; (*Costura*) corner; (*Tec*) small nail; (*fig*) touch, trace; **horas puntas** peak hours, rush hours; **sacar ~ a** to sharpen; **de ~** on end; **de ~ a ~** from one end to the other; **estar de ~** to be edgy; **ir de ~ en blanco** to be all dressed up to the nines; **tener algo en la ~ de la lengua** to have sth on the tip of one's tongue; **se le pusieron los pelos de ~** her hair stood on end
puntada [pun'taða] *nf* (*Costura*) stitch
puntal [pun'tal] *nm* prop, support
puntapié [punta'pje ʃ] (*pl* **~s**) *nm* kick; **echar a algn a ~s** to kick sb out
punteado, -a [punte'aðo, a] *adj* (*moteado*) dotted; (*diseño*) of dots ▪ *nm* (*Mus*) twang
puntear [punte'ar] *vt* to tick, mark; (*Mus*) to pluck
puntería [punte'ria] *nf* (*de arma*) aim, aiming; (*destreza*) marksmanship
puntero, -a [pun'tero, a] *adj* leading ▪ *nm* (*señal, Inform*) pointer; (*dirigente*) leader
puntiagudo, -a [puntja'ɣuðo, a] *adj* sharp, pointed
puntilla [pun'tiʎa] *nf* (*Tec*) tack, braid; (*Costura*) lace edging; **(andar) de puntillas** (to walk) on tiptoe
puntilloso, -a [punti'ʎoso, a] *adj* (*pundonoroso*) punctilious; (*susceptible*) touchy
punto ['punto] *nm* (*gen*) point; (*señal diminuta*) spot, dot; (*lugar*) spot, place; (*momento*) point, moment; (*en un examen*) mark; (*tema*) item; (*Costura*) stitch; (*Inform: impresora*) pitch; (*: pantalla*) pixel; **a ~** ready; **estar a ~ de** to be on the point of *o* about to; **llegar a ~** to come just at the right moment; **al ~** at once; **en ~** on the dot; **estar en su ~** (*Culin*) to be done to a turn; **hasta cierto ~** to some extent; **hacer ~** to knit; **poner un motor en ~** to tune an engine; **~ de partida/de congelación/de fusión** starting/freezing/melting point; **~ de vista** point of view, viewpoint; **~ muerto** dead centre; (*Auto*) neutral (gear); **puntos a tratar** matters to be discussed, agenda *sg*; **~ final** full stop; **dos puntos** colon; **~ y coma** semicolon; **~ acápite** (*Am*) full stop, new paragraph; **~ de interrogación** question mark; **puntos suspensivos** suspension points; **~ de equilibrio/de pedido** (*Com*) breakeven/reorder point; **~ inicial** *o* **de partida** (*Inform*) home; **~ de referencia/de venta** (*Com*) benchmark point/point-of-sale
puntocom [punto'kom] *nf inv, adj inv* dotcom, dot.com
puntuación [puntwa'θjon] *nf* punctuation; (*puntos: en examen*) mark(s) *pl*; (*: Deporte*) score
puntual [pun'twal] *adj* (*a tiempo*) punctual; (*cálculo*) exact, accurate; (*informe*) reliable
puntualice *etc* [puntwa'liθe] *vb ver* **puntualizar**
puntualidad [puntwali'ðað] *nf* punctuality; exactness, accuracy; reliability
puntualizar [puntwali'θar] *vt* to fix, specify
puntuar [pun'twar] *vt* (*Ling, Tip*) to punctuate; (*examen*) to mark ▪ *vi* (*Deporte*) to score, count
punzada [pun'θaða] *nf* (*puntura*) prick; (*Med*) stitch; (*dolor*) twinge (of pain)
punzante [pun'θante] *adj* (*dolor*) shooting, sharp; (*herramienta*) sharp; (*comentario*) biting
punzar [pun'θar] *vt* to prick, pierce ▪ *vi* to shoot, stab
punzón [pun'θon] *nm* (*Tec*) punch
puñado [pu'ɲaðo] *nm* handful (*tb fig*); **a puñados** by handfuls
puñal [pu'ɲal] *nm* dagger
puñalada [puɲa'laða] *nf* stab
puñeta [pu'ɲeta] *nf*: **¡~!, ¡qué ~(s)!** (*fam!*) hell!; **mandar a algn a hacer puñetas** (*fam*) to tell sb to go to hell
puñetazo [puɲe'taθo] *nm* punch

puño ['puɲo] *nm* (*Anat*) fist; (*cantidad*) fistful, handful; (*Costura*) cuff; (*de herramienta*) handle; **como un ~** (*verdad*) obvious; (*palpable*) tangible, visible; **de ~ y letra del poeta** in the poet's own handwriting
pupila [pu'pila] *nf* (*Anat*) pupil
pupitre [pu'pitre] *nm* desk
puré [pu're ʃ] (*pl* **~s**) *nm* puree; (*sopa*) (thick) soup; **~ de patatas** mashed potatoes; **estar hecho ~** (*fig*) to be knackered
pureza [pu'reθa] *nf* purity
purga ['purɣa] *nf* purge
purgante [pur'ɣante] *adj, nm* purgative
purgar [pur'ɣar] *vt* to purge; (*Pol: depurar*) to purge, liquidate; **purgarse** *vr* (*Med*) to take a purge
purgatorio [purɣa'torjo] *nm* purgatory
purgue *etc* ['purɣe] *vb ver* **purgar**
purificar [purifi'kar] *vt* to purify; (*refinar*) to refine
purifique *etc* [puri'fike] *vb ver* **purificar**
puritano, -a [puri'tano, a] *adj* (*actitud*) puritanical; (*iglesia, tradición*) puritan ■ *nm/f* puritan
puro, -a ['puro, a] *adj* pure; (*depurado*) unadulterated; (*oro*) solid; (*cielo*) clear; (*verdad*) simple, plain ■ *adv*: **de ~ cansado** out of sheer tiredness ■ *nm* cigar; **por pura casualidad** by sheer chance
púrpura ['purpura] *nf* purple
purpúreo, -a [pur'pureo, a] *adj* purple
pus [pus] *nm* pus
puse *etc* ['puse] *vb ver* **poner**
pústula ['pustula] *nf* pimple, sore
puta ['puta] *nf* whore, prostitute
putada [pu'taða] *nf* (*fam!*): **hacer una ~ a algn** to play a dirty trick on sb; **¡qué ~!** what a pain in the arse! (!)
putería [pute'ria] *nf* (*prostitución*) prostitution; (*prostíbulo*) brothel
putrefacción [putrefak'θjon] *nf* rotting, putrefaction
pútrido, -a ['putriðo, a] *adj* rotten
puzzle ['puθle] *nm* puzzle
PVP *abr* (*Esp*: = *Precio Venta al Público*) ≈ RRP
PYME ['pime] *nf abr* (= *Pequeña y Mediana Empresa*) SME
Pza *abr* = **plaza**

Qq

Q, q [ku] *nf* (*letra*) Q, q; **Q de Querido** Q for Queen
q.e.p.d. *abr* (= *que en paz descanse*) R.I.P
qm *abr* = **quintal métrico; quintales métricos**
qts. *abr* = **quilates**

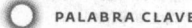

PALABRA CLAVE

que [ke] *conj* **1** (*con oración subordinada: muchas veces no se traduce*) that; **dijo que vendría** he said (that) he would come; **espero que lo encuentres** I hope (that) you find it; **dile que me llame** ask him to call me; *ver tb* **el**
2 (*en oración independiente*): **¡que entre!** send him in; **¡que se mejore tu padre!** I hope your father gets better; **¡que lo haga él!** he can do it!; (*orden*) get him to do it!
3 (*enfático*): **¿me quieres? — ¡que sí!** do you love me? — of course!; **te digo que sí** I'm telling you
4 (*consecutivo: muchas veces no se traduce*) that; **es tan grande que no lo puedo levantar** it's so big (that) I can't lift it
5 (*comparaciones*) than; **yo que tú/él** if I were you/him; *ver tb* **más; menos**
6 (*valor disyuntivo*): **que le guste o no** whether he likes it or not; **que venga o que no venga** whether he comes or not
7 (*porque*): **no puedo, que tengo que quedarme en casa** I can't, I've got to stay in
8: **siguió toca que toca** he kept on playing
■ *pron* **1** (*cosa*) that, which; (*+ prep*) which; **el sombrero que te compraste** the hat (that *o* which) you bought; **la cama en que dormí** the bed (that *o* which) I slept in; **el día (en) que ella nació** the day (when) she was born
2 (*persona: suj*) that, who; (*: objeto*) that, whom; **el amigo que me acompañó al museo** the friend that *o* who went to the museum with me; **la chica que invité** the girl (that *o* whom) I invited

qué [ke] *adj* what?, which? ■ *pron* what?; **¡qué divertido/asco!** how funny/revolting!; **¡qué día más espléndido!** what a glorious day!; **¿qué edad tienes?** how old are you?; **¿de qué me hablas?** what are you saying to me?; **¿qué tal?** how are you?, how are things?; **¿qué hay (de nuevo)?** what's new?; **¿qué más?** anything else?
quebrada [ke'βraða] *nf ver* **quebrado**
quebradero [keβra'ðero] *nm*: **~ de cabeza** headache, worry
quebradizo, -a [keβra'ðiθo, a] *adj* fragile; (*persona*) frail
quebrado, -a [ke'βraðo, a] *adj* (*roto*) broken; (*terreno*) rough, uneven ■ *nm/f* bankrupt ■ *nm* (*Mat*) fraction ■ *nf* ravine; **~ rehabilitado** discharged bankrupt
quebradura [keβra'ðura] *nf* (*fisura*) fissure; (*Med*) rupture
quebrantamiento [keβranta'mjento] *nm* (*acto*) breaking; (*de ley*) violation; (*estado*) exhaustion
quebrantar [keβran'tar] *vt* (*infringir*) to violate, transgress; **quebrantarse** *vr* (*persona*) to fail in health
quebranto [ke'βranto] *nm* damage, harm; (*decaimiento*) exhaustion; (*dolor*) grief, pain
quebrar [ke'βrar] *vt* to break, smash ■ *vi* to go bankrupt; **quebrarse** *vr* to break, get broken; (*Med*) to be ruptured
quechua ['ketʃua] *adj, nm/f* Quechua
queda ['keða] *nf*: **(toque de) ~** curfew
quedar [ke'ðar] *vi* to stay, remain; (*encontrarse*) to be; (*restar*) to remain, be left; **quedarse** *vr* to remain, stay (behind); **~ en** (*acordar*) to agree on/to; (*acabar siendo*) to end up as; **~ por hacer** to be still to be done; **~ ciego/mudo** to be left blind/dumb; **no te queda bien ese vestido** that dress doesn't suit you; **quedamos a las seis** we agreed to meet at six; **eso queda muy lejos** that's a long way (away); **nos quedan 12 kms para llegar al pueblo** there are still 12 kms before

we get to the village; **no queda otra** there's no alternative; **quedarse (con) algo** to keep sth; **quedarse con algn** (*fam*) to swindle sb; **quedarse en nada** to come to nothing *o* nought; **quedarse sin** to run out of

quedo, -a ['keðo, a] *adj* still ■ *adv* softly, gently

quehacer [kea'θer] *nm* task, job; **quehaceres (domésticos)** household chores

queja ['kexa] *nf* complaint

quejarse [ke'xarse] *vr* (*enfermo*) to moan, groan; (*protestar*) to complain; **~ de que ...** to complain (about the fact) that ...

quejica [ke'xika] *adj* grumpy, complaining ■ *nm/f* grumbler, whinger

quejido [ke'xiðo] *nm* moan

quejoso, -a [ke'xoso, a] *adj* complaining

quema ['kema] *nf* fire; (*combustión*) burning

quemado, -a [ke'maðo, a] *adj* burnt; (*irritado*) annoyed

quemadura [kema'ðura] *nf* burn, scald; (*de sol*) sunburn; (*de fusible*) blow-out

quemar [ke'mar] *vt* to burn; (*fig: malgastar*) to burn up, squander; (*Com: precios*) to slash, cut; (*fastidiar*) to annoy, bug ■ *vi* to be burning hot; **quemarse** *vr* (*consumirse*) to burn (up); (*del sol*) to get sunburnt

quemarropa [kema'rropa]: **a ~** *adv* point-blank

quemazón [kema'θon] *nf* burn; (*calor*) intense heat; (*sensación*) itch

quena ['kena] *nf* (*Am*) Indian flute

quepo *etc* ['kepo] *vb ver* **caber**

querella [ke'reʎa] *nf* (*Jur*) charge; (*disputa*) dispute

querellarse [kere'ʎarse] *vr* to file a complaint

querencia [ke'renθja] *nf* (*Zool*) homing instinct; (*fig*) homesickness

PALABRA CLAVE

querer [ke'rer] *vt* **1** (*desear*) to want; **quiero más dinero** I want more money; **quisiera** *o* **querría un té** I'd like a tea; **quiero ayudar/que vayas** I want to help/you to go; **como Vd quiera** as you wish, as you please; **ven cuando quieras** come when you like; **lo hizo sin querer** he didn't mean to do it; **no quiero** I don't want to; **le pedí que me dejara ir pero no quiso** I asked him to let me go but he refused

2 (*preguntas: para pedir u ofrecer algo*): **¿quiere abrir la ventana?** could you open the window?; **¿quieres echarme una mano?** can you give me a hand?; **¿quiere un café?** would you like some coffee?

3 (*amar*) to love; (*tener cariño a*) to be fond of; **quiere mucho a sus hijos** he's very fond of his children

4 (*requerir*): **esta planta quiere más luz** this plant needs more light

5: **querer decir** to mean; **¿qué quieres decir?** what do you mean?

querido, -a [ke'riðo, a] *adj* dear ■ *nm/f* darling; (*amante*) lover; **nuestra querida patria** our beloved country

querosén [kero'sen], **querosene** [kero'sene] *nm* (*Am*) kerosene, paraffin

querré *etc* [ke'rre] *vb ver* **querer**

quesería [kese'ria] *nf* dairy; (*fábrica*) cheese factory

quesero, -a [ke'sero, a] *adj*: **la industria quesera** the cheese industry ■ *nm/f* cheesemaker ■ *nf* cheese dish

queso ['keso] *nm* cheese; **~ rallado** grated cheese; **~ crema** cream cheese; **dárselas con ~ a algn** (*fam*) to take sb in

quetzal [ket'sal] *nm* *monetary unit of Guatemala*

quicio ['kiθjo] *nm* hinge; **estar fuera de ~** to be beside o.s.; **sacar a algn de ~** to drive sb up the wall

quid [kið] *nm* gist, crux; **dar en el ~** to hit the nail on the head

quiebra ['kjeβra] *nf* break, split; (*Com*) bankruptcy; (*Econ*) slump

quiebro *etc* ['kjeβro] *vb ver* **quebrar** ■ *nm* (*del cuerpo*) swerve

quien [kjen] *pron relativo* (*suj*) who; (*complemento*) whom; (*indefinido*): **~ dice eso es tonto** whoever says that is a fool; **hay ~ piensa que** there are those who think that; **no hay ~ lo haga** no-one will do it; **~ más, ~ menos tiene sus problemas** everybody has problems

quién [kjen] *pron interrogativo* who; (*complemento*) whom; **¿~ es?** who is it?, who's there?; (*Telec*) who's calling?

quienquiera [kjen'kjera] (*pl* **quienesquiera**) *pron* whoever

quiera *etc* ['kjera] *vb ver* **querer**

quieto, -a ['kjeto, a] *adj* still; (*carácter*) placid; **¡estáte ~!** keep still!

quietud [kje'tuð] *nf* stillness

quijada [ki'xaða] *nf* jaw, jawbone

quijote [ki'xote] *nm* dreamer; **Don Q~** Don Quixote

quil. *abr* = **quilates**

quilate [ki'late] *nm* carat

quilla ['kiʎa] *nf* keel

quilo ... ['kilo] = **kilo...**

quimera [ki'mera] *nf* (*sueño*) pipe dream

quimérico, -a [ki'meriko, a] *adj* fantastic

químico, -a ['kimiko, a] *adj* chemical ■ *nm/f*

chemist ■ *nf* chemistry
quimioterapia [kimiote'rapia] *nf* chemotherapy
quina ['kina] *nf* quinine
quincallería [kinkaʎe'ria] *nf* ironmonger's (shop), hardware store (*US*)
quince ['kinθe] *num* fifteen; ~ **días** a fortnight
quinceañero, -a [kinθea'ɲero, a] *adj* fifteen-year-old; (*adolescente*) teenage ■ *nm/f* fifteen-year-old; (*adolescente*) teenager
quincena [kin'θena] *nf* fortnight; (*pago*) fortnightly pay
quincenal [kinθe'nal] *adj* fortnightly
quincuagésimo, -a [kinkwa'xesimo, a] *num* fiftieth
quiniela [ki'njela] *nf* football pools *pl*; **quinielas** *nfpl* pools coupon *sg*
quinientos, -as [ki'njentos, as] *num* five hundred
quinina [ki'nina] *nf* quinine
quinqué [kin'ke] *nm* oil lamp
quinquenal [kinke'nal] *adj* five-year *cpd*
quinqui ['kinki] *nm* delinquent
quinta ['kinta] *nf ver* **quinto**
quintaesencia [kintae'senθja] *nf* quintessence
quintal [kin'tal] *nm* (*Castilla: peso*) = *46kg*; ~ **métrico** = *100kg*
quinteto [kin'teto] *nm* quintet
quinto, -a ['kinto, a] *adj* fifth ■ *nm* (*Mil*) conscript, draftee ■ *nf* country house; (*Mil*) call-up, draft
quintuplo, -a [kin'tuplo, a] *adj* quintuple, five-fold
quiosco ['kjosko] *nm* (*de música*) bandstand; (*de periódicos*) news stand (*also selling sweets, cigarettes etc*)
quirófano [ki'rofano] *nm* operating theatre
quiromancia [kiro'manθja] *nf* palmistry
quirúrgico, -a [ki'rurxiko, a] *adj* surgical
quise *etc* ['kise] *vb ver* **querer**
quisque ['kiske] *pron* (*fam*): **cada** *o* **todo** ~ (absolutely) everyone
quisquilloso [kiski'ʎoso, a] *adj* (*susceptible*) touchy; (*meticuloso*) pernickety
quiste ['kiste] *nm* cyst
quitaesmalte [kitaes'malte] *nm* nail polish remover
quitamanchas [kita'mantʃas] *nm inv* stain remover
quitanieves [kita'njeβes] *nm inv* snowplough (*Brit*), snowplow (*US*)
quitar [ki'tar] *vt* to remove, take away; (*ropa*) to take off; (*dolor*) to relieve; (*vida*) to take; (*valor*) to reduce; (*hurtar*) to remove, steal ■ *vi*: **¡quita de ahí!** get away!; **quitarse** *vr* to withdraw; (*mancha*) to come off *o* out; (*ropa*) to take off; **me quita mucho tiempo** it takes up a lot of my time; **el café me quita el sueño** coffee stops me sleeping; **~ de en medio a algn** to get rid of sb; **quitarse algo de encima** to get rid of sth; **quitarse del tabaco** to give up smoking; **se quitó el sombrero** he took off his hat
quitasol [kita'sol] *nm* sunshade (*Brit*), parasol
quite ['kite] *nm* (*en esgrima*) parry; (*evasión*) dodge; **estar al** ~ to be ready to go to sb's aid
Quito ['kito] *n* Quito
quizá [ki'θa]
quizás [ki'θas] *adv* perhaps, maybe
quórum ['kworum] (*pl* **quórums**) ['kworum] *nm* quorum

Rr

R, r ['erre] *nf* (*letra*) R, r; **R de Ramón** R for Robert (*Brit*) *o* Roger (*US*)
R. *abr* (*Rel*) = **real; reverendo; Remite, Remitente; río**
rabadilla [raβa'ðiʎa] *nf* base of the spine
rábano ['raβano] *nm* radish; **me importa un ~** I don't give a damn
rabia ['raβja] *nf* (*Med*) rabies *sg*; (*fig: ira*) fury, rage; **¡qué ~!** isn't it infuriating!; **me da ~** it maddens me; **tener ~ a algn** to have a grudge against sb
rabiar [ra'βjar] *vi* to have rabies; to rage, be furious; **~ por algo** to long for sth
rabieta [ra'βjeta] *nf* tantrum, fit of temper
rabino [ra'βino] *nm* rabbi
rabioso, -a [ra'βjoso, a] *adj* rabid; (*fig*) furious
rabo ['raβo] *nm* tail
racanear [rakane'ar] *vi* (*fam*) to skive
rácano ['rakano] *nm* (*fam*) slacker, skiver
RACE ['raθe] *nm abr* (= *Real Automóvil Club de España*) ≈ RAC
racha ['ratʃa] *nf* gust of wind; (*serie*) string, series; **buena/mala ~** spell of good/bad luck
racial [ra'θjal] *adj* racial, race *cpd*
racimo [ra'θimo] *nm* bunch
raciocinio [raθjo'θinjo] *nm* reason; (*razonamiento*) reasoning
ración [ra'θjon] *nf* portion; **raciones** *nfpl* rations
racional [raθjo'nal] *adj* (*razonable*) reasonable; (*lógico*) rational
racionalice *etc* [raθjona'liθe] *vb ver* **racionalizar**
racionalizar [raθjonali'θar] *vt* to rationalize; (*Com*) to streamline
racionamiento [raθjona'mjento] *nm* (*Com*) rationing
racionar [raθjo'nar] *vt* to ration (out)
racismo [ra'θismo] *nm* racialism, racism
racista [ra'θista] *adj, nm/f* racist
radar [ra'ðar] *nm* radar
radiación [raðja'θjon] *nf* radiation; (*Telec*) broadcasting
radiactividad [raðjaktiβi'ðað] *nf* radioactivity
radiactivo, -a [raðjak'tiβo, a] *adj* radioactive
radiado, -a [ra'ðjaðo, a] *adj* radio *cpd*, broadcast
radiador [raðja'ðor] *nm* radiator
radial [ra'ðjal] *adj* (*Am*) radio *cpd*
radiante [ra'ðjante] *adj* radiant
radiar [ra'ðjar] *vt* to radiate; (*Telec*) to broadcast; (*Med*) to give radiotherapy to
radical [raði'kal] *adj, nm/f* radical ■ *nm* (*Ling*) root; (*Mat*) square-root sign
radicar [raði'kar] *vi* to take root; **~ en** to lie *o* consist in; **radicarse** *vr* to establish o.s., put down (one's) roots
radio ['raðjo] *nf* radio; (*aparato*) radio (set) ■ *nm* (*Mat*) radius; (*Am*) radio; (*Química*) radium; **~ de acción** extent of one's authority, sphere of influence
radioaficionado, -a [raðjoafiθjo'naðo, a] *nm/f* radio ham
radiocasete [raðjoka'sete] *nm* radiocassette (player)
radiodifusión [raðjodifu'sjon] *nf* broadcasting
radioemisora [raðjoemi'sora] *nf* transmitter, radio station
radiofónico, -a [raðjo'foniko, a] *adj* radio *cpd*
radiografía [raðjoɣra'fia] *nf* X-ray
radiólogo, -a [ra'ðjoloɣo, a] *nm/f* radiologist
radionovela [raðjono'βela] *nf* radio series
radiotaxi [raðjo'taksi] *nm* radio taxi
radioterapia [raðjote'rapja] *nf* radiotherapy
radioyente [raðjo'jente] *nm/f* listener
radique *etc* [ra'ðike] *vb ver* **radicar**
RAE ['rae] *nf abr* (= *Real Academia Española*) *ver* **real**
ráfaga ['rafaɣa] *nf* gust; (*de luz*) flash; (*de tiros*) burst
raído, -a [ra'iðo, a] *adj* (*ropa*) threadbare; (*persona*) shabby
raigambre [rai'ɣambre] *nf* (*Bot*) roots *pl*; (*fig*) tradition

raíz [ra'iθ] (*pl* **raíces**) *nf* root; **~ cuadrada** square root; **a ~ de** as a result of; (*después de*) immediately after
raja ['raxa] *nf* (*de melón etc*) slice; (*hendidura*) slit, split; (*grieta*) crack
rajar [ra'xar] *vt* to split; (*fam*) to slash; **rajarse** *vr* to split, crack; **rajarse de** to back out of
rajatabla [raxa'taβla]: **a ~** *adv* (*estrictamente*) strictly, to the letter
RAL *abr* (*Inform*) = **red de área local**
ralea [ra'lea] *nf* (*pey*) kind, sort
ralenti [ra'lenti] *nm* (*TV etc*) slow motion; (*Auto*) neutral; **al ~** in slow motion; (*Auto*) ticking over
rallador [raʎa'ðor] *nm* grater
rallar [ra'ʎar] *vt* to grate
ralo, -a ['ralo, a] *adj* thin, sparse
RAM [ram] *nf abr* (= *random access memory*) RAM
rama ['rama] *nf* bough, branch; **andarse por las ramas** (*fig: fam*) to beat about the bush
ramaje [ra'maje] *nm* branches *pl*, foliage
ramal [ra'mal] *nm* (*de cuerda*) strand; (*Ferro*) branch line; (*Auto*) branch (road)
rambla ['rambla] *nf* (*avenida*) avenue
ramera [ra'mera] *nf* whore, hooker (*US*)
ramificación [ramifika'θjon] *nf* ramification
ramificarse [ramifi'karse] *vr* to branch out
ramifique *etc* [rami'fike] *vb ver* **ramificarse**
ramillete [rami'ʎete] *nm* bouquet; (*fig*) select group
ramo ['ramo] *nm* branch, twig; (*sección*) department, section; (*sector*) field, sector
rampa ['rampa] *nf* ramp
ramplón, -ona [ram'plon, ona] *adj* uncouth, coarse
rana ['rana] *nf* frog; **salto de ~** leapfrog; **cuando las ranas críen pelos** when pigs fly
ranchero [ran'tʃero] *nm* (*Am*) rancher; (*pequeño propietario*) smallholder
rancho ['rantʃo] *nm* (*Mil*) food; (*Am: grande*) ranch; (*: pequeño*) small farm
rancio, -a ['ranθjo, a] *adj* (*comestibles*) stale, rancid; (*vino*) aged, mellow; (*fig*) ancient
rango ['rango] *nm* rank; (*prestigio*) standing
ranura [ra'nura] *nf* groove; (*de teléfono etc*) slot; **~ de expansión** (*Inform*) expansion slot
rap [rap] *nm* (*Mus*) rap
rapacidad [rapaθi'ðað] *nf* rapacity
rapapolvo [rapa'polβo] *nm*: **echar un ~ a algn** to give sb a ticking off
rapar [ra'par] *vt* to shave; (*los cabellos*) to crop
rapaz [ra'paθ] *adj* (*Zool*) predatory ■ *nm* young boy
rapaza [ra'paθa] *nf* young girl
rape ['rape] *nm* quick shave; (*pez*) angler (fish); **al ~** cropped
rapé [ra'pe] *nm* snuff
rapel [ra'pel] *nm* = **rappel**
rapidez [rapi'ðeθ] *nf* speed, rapidity
rápido, -a ['rapiðo, a] *adj* fast, quick ■ *adv* quickly ■ *nm* (*Ferro*) express; **rápidos** *nmpl* rapids
rapiña [ra'piɲa] *nm* robbery; **ave de ~** bird of prey
rappel [ra'pel] *nm* (*Deporte*) abseiling
raptar [rap'tar] *vt* to kidnap
rapto ['rapto] *nm* kidnapping; (*impulso*) sudden impulse; (*éxtasis*) ecstasy, rapture
raqueta [ra'keta] *nf* racquet
raquítico, -a [ra'kitiko, a] *adj* stunted; (*fig*) poor, inadequate
raquitismo [raki'tismo] *nm* rickets *sg*
rareza [ra'reθa] *nf* rarity; (*fig*) eccentricity
raro, -a ['raro, a] *adj* (*poco común*) rare; (*extraño*) odd, strange; (*excepcional*) remarkable; **¡qué ~!** how (very) odd!; **¡(qué) cosa más rara!** how strange!
ras [ras] *nm*: **a ~ de** level with; **a ~ de tierra** at ground level
rasar [ra'sar] *vt* to level
rascacielos [raska'θjelos] *nm inv* skyscraper
rascar [ras'kar] *vt* (*con las uñas etc*) to scratch; (*raspar*) to scrape; **rascarse** *vr* to scratch (o.s.)
rasgar [ras'ɣar] *vt* to tear, rip (up)
rasgo ['rasɣo] *nm* (*con pluma*) stroke; **rasgos** *nmpl* features, characteristics; **a grandes rasgos** in outline, broadly
rasgue *etc* ['rasɣe] *vb ver* **rasgar**
rasguear [rasɣe'ar] *vt* (*Mus*) to strum
rasguñar [rasɣu'ɲar] *vt* to scratch; (*bosquejar*) to sketch
rasguño [ras'ɣuɲo] *nm* scratch
raso, -a ['raso, a] *adj* (*liso*) flat, level; (*a baja altura*) very low ■ *nm* satin; (*campo llano*) flat country; **cielo ~** clear sky; **al ~** in the open
raspado [ras'paðo] *nm* (*Med*) scrape
raspador [raspa'ðor] *nm* scraper
raspadura [raspa'ðura] *nf* (*acto*) scrape, scraping; (*marca*) scratch; **raspaduras** *nfpl* scrapings
raspar [ras'par] *vt* to scrape; (*arañar*) to scratch; (*limar*) to file ■ *vi* (*manos*) to be rough; (*vino*) to be sharp, have a rough taste
rasque *etc* ['raske] *vb ver* **rascar**
rastra ['rastra] *nf*: **a rastras** by dragging; (*fig*) unwillingly
rastreador [rastrea'ðor] *nm* tracker; **~ de minas** minesweeper
rastrear [rastre'ar] *vt* (*seguir*) to track; (*minas*) to sweep
rastrero, -a [ras'trero, a] *adj* (*Bot: Zool*) creeping; (*fig*) despicable, mean
rastrillar [rastri'ʎar] *vt* to rake

rastrillo [ras'triʎo] *nm* rake; (*Am*) safety razor
rastro ['rastro] *nm* (*Agr*) rake; (*pista*) track, trail; (*vestigio*) trace; (*mercado*) flea market; **el R~** *the Madrid flea market*; **perder el ~** to lose the scent; **desaparecer sin ~** to vanish without trace
rastrojo [ras'troxo] *nm* stubble
rasurador [rasura'ðor] *nm*, **rasuradora** (*Am*) [rasura'ðora] ■ *nf* electric shaver *o* razor
rasurarse [rasu'rarse] *vr* to shave
rata ['rata] *nf* rat
ratear [rate'ar] *vt* (*robar*) to steal
ratero, -a [ra'tero, a] *adj* light-fingered ■ *nm/f* pickpocket; (*Am: de casas*) burglar
ratificar [ratifi'kar] *vt* to ratify
ratifique *etc* [rati'fike] *vb ver* **ratificar**
rato ['rato] *nm* while, short time; **a ratos** from time to time; **al poco ~** shortly after, soon afterwards; **ratos libres** *o* **de ocio** leisure *sg*, spare *o* free time *sg*; **hay para ~** there's still a long way to go; **pasar el ~** to kill time; **pasar un buen/mal ~** to have a good/rough time
ratón [ra'ton] *nm* (*tb Inform*) mouse
ratonera [rato'nera] *nf* mousetrap
RAU *nf abr* (= *República Árabe Unida*) UAR
raudal [rau'ðal] *nm* torrent; **a raudales** in abundance; **entrar a raudales** to pour in
raya ['raja] *nf* line; (*marca*) scratch; (*en tela*) stripe; (*Tip*) hyphen; (*de pelo*) parting; (*límite*) boundary; (*pez*) ray; **a rayas** striped; **pasarse de la ~** to overstep the mark; **tener a ~** to keep in check
rayado, -a [ra'jaðo, a] *adj* (*papel*) ruled; (*tela, diseño*) striped
rayar [ra'jar] *vt* to line; to scratch; (*subrayar*) to underline ■ *vi*: **~ en** *o* **con** to border on; **al ~ el alba** at first light; **~ a algn >** (*col*) to do sb's head in (*col*); **está siempre rayándome con esa historia** he's doing my head in with that business (*col*)
rayo ['rajo] *nm* (*del sol*) ray, beam; (*de luz*) shaft; (*en una tormenta*) (flash of) lightning; **~ solar** *o* **de sol** sunbeam; **rayos infrarrojos** infrared rays; **rayos X** X-rays; **como un ~** like a shot; **la noticia cayó como un ~** the news was a bombshell; **pasar como un ~** to flash past
raza ['raθa] *nf* race; (*de animal*) breed; **~ humana** human race; **de pura ~** (*caballo*) thoroughbred; (*perro etc*) pedigree
razón [ra'θon] *nf* reason; (*justicia*) right, justice; (*razonamiento*) reasoning; (*motivo*) reason, motive; (*proporción*) rate; (*Mat*) ratio; **a ~ de 10 cada día** at the rate of 10 a day; **"~: ..."** "inquiries to ..."; **en ~ de** with regard to; **perder la ~** to go out of one's mind; **dar ~ a algn** to agree that sb is right; **dar ~ de** to give an account of, report on; **tener/no tener ~** to be right/wrong; **~ directa/inversa** direct/inverse proportion; **~ de ser** raison d'être
razonable [raθo'naβle] *adj* reasonable; (*justo, moderado*) fair
razonado, -a [raθo'naðo, a] *adj* (*Com: cuenta etc*) itemized
razonamiento [raθona'mjento] *nm* (*juicio*) judgement; (*argumento*) reasoning
razonar [raθo'nar] *vt, vi* to reason, argue
RDA *nf abr* (*Historia:* = *República Democrática Alemana*) *ver* **república**
Rdo. *abr* (*Rel:* = *Reverendo*) Rev
RDSI *nf abr* (= *Red Digital de Servicios Integrados*) ISDN
re [re] *nm* (*Mus*) D
reabierto [rea'βjerto] *pp de* **reabrir**
reabrir [rea'βrir] *vt*, **reabrirse** *vr* to reopen
reacción [reak'θjon] *nf* reaction; **avión a ~** jet plane; **~ en cadena** chain reaction
reaccionar [reakθjo'nar] *vi* to react
reaccionario, -a [reakθjo'narjo, a] *adj* reactionary
reacio, -a [re'aθjo, a] *adj* stubborn; **ser** *o* **estar ~ a** to be opposed to
reactivar [reakti'βar] *vt* to reactivate; **reactivarse** *vr* (*economía*) to be on the upturn
reactor [reak'tor] *nm* reactor; (*avión*) jet plane; **~ nuclear** nuclear reactor
readaptación [reaðapta'θjon] *nf*: **~ profesional** industrial retraining
readmitir [reaðmi'tir] *vt* to readmit
reafirmar [reafir'mar] *vt* to reaffirm
reagrupar [reaɣru'par] *vt* to regroup
reajustar [reaxus'tar] *vt* (*Inform*) to reset
reajuste [rea'xuste] *nm* readjustment; **~ salarial** wage increase; **~ de plantilla** rationalization
real [re'al] *adj* real; (*del rey, fig*) royal; (*espléndido*) grand ■ *nm* (*de feria*) fairground; **la R~ Academia Española** *see note*

REAL

The *Real Academia Española* (*RAE*) is the regulatory body for the Spanish language in Spain and was founded in 1713. It produces dictionaries and grammars bearing its own name, and is considered the authority on the language, although it has been critized for being too conservative. In 1994, along with the Spanish American *academias*, it approved a change to the Spanish alphabet, no longer treating "ch" and "ll" as separate letters. "ñ" continues to be treated separately.

realce *etc* [re'alθe] *vb ver* **realzar** ■ *nm* (*Tec*) embossing; **poner de ~** to emphasize
real-decreto [re'alde'kreto] (*pl* **reales-decretos**) *nm* royal decree
realeza [rea'leθa] *nf* royalty
realice *etc* [rea'liθe] *vb ver* **realizar**
realidad [reali'ðað] *nf* reality; (*verdad*) truth; **~ virtual** virtual reality; **en ~** in fact
realismo [rea'lismo] *nm* realism
realista [rea'lista] *nm/f* realist
realización [realiθa'θjon] *nf* fulfilment, realization; (*Com*) selling up (*Brit*), conversion into money (*US*); **~ de plusvalías** profit-taking
realizador, a [realiθa'ðor, a] *nm/f* (*TV etc*) producer
realizar [reali'θar] *vt* (*objetivo*) to achieve; (*plan*) to carry out; (*viaje*) to make, undertake; (*Com*) to realize; **realizarse** *vr* to come about, come true; **realizarse como persona** to fulfil one's aims in life
realmente [real'mente] *adv* really
realojar [realo'xar] *vt* to rehouse
realquilar [realki'lar] *vt* (*subarrendar*) to sublet; (*alquilar de nuevo*) to relet
realzar [real'θar] *vt* (*Tec*) to raise; (*embellecer*) to enhance; (*acentuar*) to highlight
reanimar [reani'mar] *vt* to revive; (*alentar*) to encourage; **reanimarse** *vr* to revive
reanudar [reanu'ðar] *vt* (*renovar*) to renew; (*historia, viaje*) to resume
reaparición [reapari'θjon] *nf* reappearance; (*vuelta*) return
reapertura [reaper'tura] *nf* reopening
rearme [re'arme] *nm* rearmament
reata [re'ata] *nf* (*Am*) lasso
reavivar [reaβi'βar] *vt* (*persona*) to revive; (*fig*) to rekindle
rebaja [re'βaxa] *nf* reduction, lowering; (*Com*) discount; **"grandes rebajas"** "big reductions", "sale"
rebajar [reβa'xar] *vt* (*bajar*) to lower; (*reducir*) to reduce; (*precio*) to cut; (*disminuir*) to lessen; (*humillar*) to humble; **rebajarse** *vr*: **rebajarse a hacer algo** to stoop to doing sth
rebanada [reβa'naða] *nf* slice
rebañar [reβa'ɲar] *vt* to scrape clean
rebaño [re'βaɲo] *nm* herd; (*de ovejas*) flock
rebasar [reβa'sar] *vt* (*tb*: **rebasar de**) to exceed; (*Auto*) to overtake
rebatir [reβa'tir] *vt* to refute; (*rebajar*) to reduce; (*ataque*) to repel
rebato [re'βato] *nm* alarm; (*ataque*) surprise attack; **llamar** *o* **tocar a ~** (*fig*) to sound the alarm
rebeca [re'βeka] *nf* cardigan
rebelarse [reβe'larse] *vr* to rebel, revolt
rebelde [re'βelde] *adj* rebellious; (*niño*) unruly ■ *nm/f* rebel; **ser ~ a** to be in revolt against, rebel against
rebeldía [reβel'dia] *nf* rebelliousness; (*desobediencia*) disobedience; (*Jur*) default
rebelión [reβe'ljon] *nf* rebellion
rebenque [re'βenke] *nm* (*Am*) whip
reblandecer [reβlande'θer] *vt* to soften
reblandezca *etc* [reβlan'deθka] *vb ver* **reblandecer**
rebobinar [reβoβi'nar] *vt* to rewind
reboce *etc* [re'βoθe] *vb ver* **rebozar**
rebosante [reβo'sante] *adj*: **~ de** (*fig*) brimming *o* overflowing with
rebosar [reβo'sar] *vi* to overflow; (*abundar*) to abound, be plentiful; **~ de salud** to be bursting *o* brimming with health
rebotar [reβo'tar] *vt* to bounce; (*rechazar*) to repel
rebote [re'βote] *nm* rebound; **de ~** on the rebound
rebozado, -a [reβo'θaðo, a] *adj* (*Culin*) fried in batter *o* breadcrumbs *o* flour
rebozar [reβo'θar] *vt* to wrap up; (*Culin*) to fry in batter *etc*
rebozo [reβo'θo] *nm*: **sin ~** openly
rebuscado, -a [reβus'kaðo, a] *adj* affected
rebuscar [reβus'kar] *vi* (*en bolsillo, cajón*) to fish; (*en habitación*) to search high and low
rebuznar [reβuθ'nar] *vi* to bray
recabar [reka'βar] *vt* (*obtener*) to manage to get; **~ fondos** to collect money
recadero [reka'ðero] *nm* messenger
recado [re'kaðo] *nm* message; **dejar/tomar un ~** (*Telec*) to leave/take a message
recaer [reka'er] *vi* to relapse; **~ en** to fall to *o* on; (*criminal etc*) to fall back into, relapse into; (*premio*) to go to
recaída [reka'iða] *nf* relapse
recaiga *etc* [re'kaiɣa] *vb ver* **recaer**
recalcar [rekal'kar] *vt* (*fig*) to stress, emphasize
recalcitrante [rekalθi'trante] *adj* recalcitrant
recalentamiento [rekalenta'mjento] *nm*: **~ global** global warming
recalentar [rekalen'tar] *vt* (*comida*) to warm up, reheat; (*demasiado*) to overheat; **recalentarse** *vr* to overheat, get too hot
recaliente *etc* [reka'ljente] *vb ver* **recalentar**
recalque *etc* [re'kalke] *vb ver* **recalcar**
recámara [re'kamara] *nf* side room; (*Am*) bedroom
recamarera [rekama'rera] *nf* (*Am*) maid
recambio [re'kambjo] *nm* spare; (*de pluma*) refill; **piezas de ~** spares
recapacitar [rekapaθi'tar] *vi* to reflect

recapitular [rekapitu'lar] *vt* to recap
recargable [rekar'ɣaβle] *adj (batería, pila)* rechargeable; *(mechero, pluma)* refillable
recargado, -a [rekar'ɣaðo, a] *adj* overloaded; *(exagerado)* over-elaborate
recargar [rekar'ɣar] *vt* to overload; *(batería)* to recharge; *(mechero, pluma)* to refill; *(tarjeta de móvil)* to top up
recargo [re'karɣo] *nm* surcharge; *(aumento)* increase
recargue *etc* [re'karɣe] *vb ver* **recargar**
recatado, -a [reka'taðo, a] *adj (modesto)* modest, demure; *(prudente)* cautious
recato [re'kato] *nm (modestia)* modesty, demureness; *(cautela)* caution
recauchutado, -a [rekautʃu'taðo, a] *adj* remould *cpd*
recaudación [rekauða'θjon] *nf (acción)* collection; *(cantidad)* takings *pl*; *(en deporte)* gate; *(oficina)* tax office
recaudador, a [rekauða'ðor, a] *nm/f* tax collector
recaudar [rekau'ðar] *vt* to collect
recaudo [re'kauðo] *nm*: **estar a buen ~** to be in safekeeping; **poner algo a buen ~** to put sth in a safe place
recayendo *etc* [reka'jendo] *vb ver* **recaer**
rece *etc* ['reθe] *vb ver* **rezar**
recelar [reθe'lar] *vt*: **~ que** *(sospechar)* to suspect that; *(temer)* to fear that ■ *vi*: **~(se) de** to distrust
recelo [re'θelo] *nm* distrust, suspicion
receloso, -a [reθe'loso, a] *adj* distrustful, suspicious
recepción [reθep'θjon] *nf* reception; *(acto de recibir)* receipt
recepcionista [reθepθjo'nista] *nm/f* receptionist
receptáculo [reθep'takulo] *nm* receptacle
receptivo, -a [reθep'tiβo, a] *adj* receptive
receptor, a [reθep'tor, a] *nm/f* recipient ■ *nm (Telec)* receiver; **descolgar el ~** to pick up the receiver
recesión [reθe'sjon] *nf (Com)* recession
receta [re'θeta] *nf (Culin)* recipe; *(Med)* prescription
recetar [reθe'tar] *vt* to prescribe
rechace *etc* [re'tʃaθe] *vb ver* **rechazar**
rechazar [retʃa'θar] *vt* to repel, drive back; *(idea)* to reject; *(oferta)* to turn down
rechazo [re'tʃaθo] *nm (de fusil)* recoil; *(rebote)* rebound; *(negación)* rebuff
rechifla [re'tʃifla] *nf* hissing, booing; *(fig)* derision
rechinar [retʃi'nar] *vi* to creak; *(dientes)* to grind; *(máquina)* to clank, clatter; *(metal seco)* to grate; *(motor)* to hum
rechistar [retʃis'tar] *vi*: **sin ~** without complaint
rechoncho, -a [re'tʃontʃo, a] *adj (fam)* stocky, thickset (*Brit*), heavy-set (*US*)
rechupete [retʃu'pete]: **de ~** *adj (comida)* delicious
recibidor [reθiβi'ðor] *nm* entrance hall
recibimiento [reθiβi'mjento] *nm* reception, welcome
recibir [reθi'βir] *vt* to receive; *(dar la bienvenida)* to welcome; *(salir al encuentro de)* to go and meet ■ *vi* to entertain; **recibirse** *vr*: **recibirse de** to qualify as
recibo [re'θiβo] *nm* receipt; **acusar ~ de** to acknowledge receipt of
reciclable [reθi'klaβle] *adj* recyclable
reciclaje [reθi'klaxe] *nm* recycling; *(de trabajadores)* retraining; **cursos de ~** refresher courses
reciclar [reθi'klar] *vt* to recycle; *(trabajador)* to retrain
recién [re'θjen] *adv* recently, newly; *(Am)* just, recently; **~ casado** newly-wed; **el ~ llegado** the newcomer; **el ~ nacido** the newborn child; **~ a las seis** only at six o'clock
reciente [re'θjente] *adj* recent; *(fresco)* fresh
recientemente [reθjente'mente] *adv* recently
recinto [re'θinto] *nm* enclosure; *(área)* area, place
recio, -a ['reθjo, a] *adj* strong, tough; *(voz)* loud ■ *adv* hard; loud(ly)
recipiente [reθi'pjente] *nm (objeto)* container, receptacle; *(persona)* recipient
reciprocidad [reθiproθi'ðað] *nf* reciprocity
recíproco, -a [re'θiproco, a] *adj* reciprocal
recital [reθi'tal] *nm (Mus)* recital; *(Lit)* reading
recitar [reθi'tar] *vt* to recite
reclamación [reklama'θjon] *nf* claim, demand; *(queja)* complaint; **~ salarial** pay claim
reclamar [rekla'mar] *vt* to claim, demand ■ *vi*: **~ contra** to complain about; **~ a algn en justicia** to take sb to court
reclamo [re'klamo] *nm (anuncio)* advertisement; *(tentación)* attraction
reclinar [rekli'nar] *vt* to recline, lean; **reclinarse** *vr* to lean back
recluir [reklu'ir] *vt* to intern, confine
reclusión [reklu'sjon] *nf (prisión)* prison; *(refugio)* seclusion; **~ perpetua** life imprisonment
recluso, -a [re'kluso, a] *adj* imprisoned; **población reclusa** prison population ■ *nm/f (solitario)* recluse; *(Jur)* prisoner
recluta [re'kluta] *nm/f* recruit ■ *nf* recruitment

reclutamiento [rekluta'mjento] *nm* recruitment
recluyendo *etc* [reklu'jendo] *vb ver* **recluir**
recobrar [reko'βrar] *vt* (*recuperar*) to recover; (*rescatar*) to get back; (*ciudad*) to recapture; (*tiempo*) to make up (for); **recobrarse** *vr* to recover
recochineo [rekotʃi'neo] *nm* (*fam*) mickey-taking
recodo [re'koðo] *nm* (*de río, camino*) bend
recogedor, a [rekoxe'ðor, a] *nm/f* picker, harvester
recoger [reko'xer] *vt* to collect; (*Agr*) to harvest; (*fruta*) to pick; (*levantar*) to pick up; (*juntar*) to gather; (*pasar a buscar*) to come for, get; (*dar asilo*) to give shelter to; (*faldas*) to gather up; (*mangas*) to roll up; (*pelo*) to put up; **recogerse** *vr* (*retirarse*) to retire; **me recogieron en la estación** they picked me up at the station
recogido, -a [reko'xiðo, a] *adj* (*lugar*) quiet, secluded; (*pequeño*) small ■ *nf* (*Correos*) collection; (*Agr*) harvest; **recogida de datos** (*Inform*) data capture
recogimiento [rekoxi'mjento] *nm* collection; (*Agr*) harvesting
recoja *etc* [re'koxa] *vb ver* **recoger**
recolección [rekolek'θjon] *nf* (*Agr*) harvesting; (*colecta*) collection
recomencé [rekomen'θe], **recomencemos** *etc* [rekomen'θemos] *vb ver* **recomenzar**
recomendable [rekomen'daβle] *adj* recommendable; **poco ~** inadvisable
recomendación [rekomenda'θjon] *nf* (*sugerencia*) suggestion, recommendation; (*referencia*) reference; **carta de ~ para** letter of introduction to
recomendar [rekomen'dar] *vt* to suggest, recommend; (*confiar*) to entrust
recomenzar [rekomen'θar] *vt, vi* to begin again, recommence
recomience *etc* [reko'mjenθe] *vb ver* **recomenzar**
recomiende *etc* [reko'mjende] *vb ver* **recomendar**
recomienzo *etc* [reko'mjenθo] *vb ver* **recomenzar**
recompensa [rekom'pensa] *nf* reward, recompense; (*compensación*): **~ (de una pérdida)** compensation (for a loss); **como** *o* **en ~ por** in return for
recompensar [rekompen'sar] *vt* to reward, recompense
recompondré *etc* [rekompon'dre] *vb ver* **recomponer**
recomponer [rekompo'ner] *vt* to mend; (*Inform: texto*) to reformat
recomponga *etc* [rekom'ponga], **recompuesto** [rekom'pwesto], **recompuse** *etc* [rekom'puse] *vb ver* **recomponer**
reconciliación [rekonθilja'θjon] *nf* reconciliation
reconciliar [rekonθi'ljar] *vt* to reconcile; **reconciliarse** *vr* to become reconciled
recóndito, -a [re'kondito, a] *adj* (*lugar*) hidden, secret
reconfortar [rekonfor'tar] *vt* to comfort
reconocer [rekono'θer] *vt* to recognize; **~ los hechos** to face the facts
reconocido, -a [rekono'θiðo, a] *adj* recognized; (*agradecido*) grateful
reconocimiento [rekonoθi'mjento] *nm* recognition; (*registro*) search; (*inspección*) examination; (*gratitud*) gratitude; (*confesión*) admission; **~ óptico de caracteres** (*Inform*) optical character recognition; **~ de la voz** (*Inform*) speech recognition
reconozca *etc* [reko'noθka] *vb ver* **reconocer**
reconquista [rekon'kista] *nf* reconquest
reconquistar [rekonkis'tar] *vt* (*Mil*) to reconquer; (*fig*) to recover, win back
reconstituyente [rekonstitu'jente] *nm* tonic
reconstruir [rekonstru'ir] *vt* to reconstruct
reconstruyendo *etc* [rekonstru'jendo] *vb ver* **reconstruir**
reconversión [recomber'sjon] *nf* restructuring, reorganization; (*tb:* **reconversión industrial**) rationalization
recopilación [rekopila'θjon] *nf* (*resumen*) summary; (*compilación*) compilation
recopilar [rekopi'lar] *vt* to compile
récord ['rekorð] *adj inv* record; **cifras ~** record figures ■ *nm* (*pl* **records** *o* **récords**) ['rekorð] record; **batir el ~** to break the record
recordar [rekor'ðar] *vt* (*acordarse de*) to remember; (*traer a la memoria*) to recall; (*recordar a otro*) to remind ■ *vi* to remember; **recuérdale que me debe cinco dólares** remind him that he owes me five dollars; **que yo recuerde** as far as I can remember; **creo ~, si mal no recuerdo** if my memory serves me right
recordatorio [rekorða'torjo] *nm* (*de fallecimiento*) in memoriam card; (*de bautizo, comunión*) *commemorative card*
recorrer [reko'rrer] *vt* (*país*) to cross, travel through; (*distancia*) to cover; (*registrar*) to search; (*repasar*) to look over
recorrido [reko'rriðo] *nm* run, journey; **tren de largo ~** main-line *o* inter-city (*Brit*) train
recortado, -a [rekor'taðo, a] *adj* uneven, irregular
recortar [rekor'tar] *vt* (*papel*) to cut out; (*el pelo*) to trim; (*dibujar*) to draw in outline;

recortarse *vr* to stand out, be silhouetted
recorte [re'korte] *nm* (*acción, de prensa*) cutting; (*de telas, chapas*) trimming; ~ **presupuestario** budget cut; ~ **salarial** wage cut
recostado, -a [rekos'taðo, a] *adj* leaning; **estar** ~ to be lying down
recostar [rekos'tar] *vt* to lean; **recostarse** *vr* to lie down
recoveco [reko'βeko] *nm* (*de camino, río etc*) bend; (*en casa*) cubbyhole
recreación [rekrea'θjon] *nf* recreation
recrear [rekre'ar] *vt* (*entretener*) to entertain; (*volver a crear*) to recreate
recreativo, -a [rekrea'tiβo, a] *adj* recreational
recreo [re'kreo] *nm* recreation; (*Escol*) break, playtime
recriminar [rekrimi'nar] *vt* to reproach ■ *vi* to recriminate; **recriminarse** *vr* to reproach each other
recrudecer [rekruðe'θer] *vt, vi*, **recrudecerse** *vr* to worsen
recrudecimiento [rekruðeθi'mjento] *nm* upsurge
recrudezca *etc* [recru'ðeθka] *vb ver* **recrudecer**
recta ['rekta] *nf ver* **recto**
rectangular [rektangu'lar] *adj* rectangular
rectángulo, -a [rek'tangulo, a] *adj* rectangular ■ *nm* rectangle
rectificable [rektifi'kaβle] *adj* rectifiable; **fácilmente** ~ easily rectified
rectificación [rektifika'θjon] *nf* correction
rectificar [rektifi'kar] *vt* to rectify; (*volverse recto*) to straighten ■ *vi* to correct o.s.
rectifique *etc* [rekti'fike] *vb ver* **rectificar**
rectitud [rekti'tuð] *nf* straightness; (*fig*) rectitude
recto, -a ['rekto, a] *adj* straight; (*persona*) honest, upright; (*estricto*) strict; (*juez*) fair; (*juicio*) sound ■ *nm* rectum; (*Atletismo*) straight ■ *nf* straight line; **en el sentido ~ de la palabra** in the proper sense of the word; **recta final** *o* **de llegada** home straight
rector, a [rek'tor, a] *adj* governing ■ *nm/f* head, chief; (*Escol*) rector, president (US)
rectorado [rekto'raðo] *nm* (*cargo*) rectorship, presidency (US); (*oficina*) rector's office
recuadro [re'kwaðro] *nm* box; (*Tip*) inset
recubrir [reku'βir] *vt* to cover
recuento [re'kwento] *nm* inventory; **hacer el ~ de** to count *o* reckon up
recuerdo *etc* [re'kwerðo] *vb ver* **recordar** ■ *nm* souvenir; **recuerdos** *nmpl* memories; **¡~s a tu madre!** give my regards to your mother!; **"R~ de Mallorca"** "a present from Majorca"; **contar los ~s** to reminisce
recueste *etc* [re'kweste] *vb ver* **recostar**
recular [reku'lar] *vi* to back down
recuperable [rekupe'raβle] *adj* recoverable
recuperación [rekupera'θjon] *nf* recovery; ~ **de datos** (*Inform*) data retrieval
recuperar [rekupe'rar] *vt* to recover; (*tiempo*) to make up; (*Inform*) to retrieve; **recuperarse** *vr* to recuperate
recurrir [reku'rrir] *vi* (*Jur*) to appeal; ~ **a** to resort to; (*persona*) to turn to
recurso [re'kurso] *nm* resort; (*medio*) means *pl*, resource; (*Jur*) appeal; **como último ~** as a last resort; **recursos económicos** economic resources; **recursos naturales** natural resources
recusar [reku'sar] *vt* to reject, refuse
red [reð] *nf* net, mesh; (*Ferro: Inform*) network; (*Elec, de agua*) mains, supply system; (*de tiendas*) chain; (*trampa*) trap; **la R~** (*Internet*) the Net; **estar conectado con la ~** to be connected to the mains; ~ **local** (*Inform*) local area network; ~ **de transmisión** (*Inform*) data network
redacción [reðak'θjon] *nf* (*acción*) writing; (*Escol*) essay, composition; (*limpieza de texto*) editing; (*personal*) editorial staff
redactar [reðak'tar] *vt* to draw up, draft; (*periódico, Inform*) to edit
redactor, a [reðak'tor, a] *nm/f* writer; (*en periódico*) editor
redada [re'ðaða] *nf* (*Pesca*) cast, throw; (*fig*) catch; ~ **policial** police raid, round-up
redención [reðen'θjon] *nf* redemption
redentor, a [reðen'tor, a] *adj* redeeming ■ *nm/f* (*Com*) redeemer
redescubierto [reðesku'βjerto] *pp de* **redescubrir**
redescubrir [reðesku'βrir] *vt* to rediscover
redesignar [reðesiɣ'nar] *vt* (*Inform*) to rename
redicho, -a [re'ðitʃo, a] *adj* affected
redil [re'ðil] *nm* sheepfold
redimir [reði'mir] *vt* to redeem; (*rehén*) to ransom
redistribución [reðistriβu'θjon] *nf* (*Com*) redeployment
rédito ['reðito] *nm* interest, yield
redoblar [reðo'βlar] *vt* to redouble ■ *vi* (*tambor*) to play a roll on the drums
redoble [re'ðoβle] *nm* (*Mus*) drumroll, drumbeat; (*de trueno*) roll
redomado, -a [reðo'maðo, a] *adj* (*astuto*) sly, crafty; (*perfecto*) utter
redonda [re'ðonda] *nf ver* **redondo**
redondear [reðonde'ar] *vt* to round, round off; (*cifra*) to round up

redondel [reðon'del] *nm* (*círculo*) circle; (*Taur*) bullring, arena; (*Auto*) roundabout
redondo, -a [re'ðondo, a] *adj* (*circular*) round; (*completo*) complete ■ *nf*: **a la redonda** around, round about; **en muchas millas a la redonda** for many miles around; **rehusar en ~** to give a flat refusal
reducción [reðuk'θjon] *nf* reduction; **~ del activo** (*Com*) divestment; **~ de precios** (*Com*) price-cutting
reducido, -a [reðu'θiðo, a] *adj* reduced; (*limitado*) limited; (*pequeño*) small; **quedar ~ a** to be reduced to
reducir [reðu'θir] *vt* to reduce, limit; (*someter*) to bring under control; **reducirse** *vr* to diminish; (*Mat*): **~ (a)** to reduce (to), convert (into); **~ las millas a kilómetros** to convert miles into kilometres; **reducirse a** (*fig*) to come *o* boil down to
reducto [re'ðukto] *nm* redoubt
reduje *etc* [re'ðuxe] *vb ver* **reducir**
redundancia [reðun'danθja] *nf* redundancy
reduzca *etc* [re'ðuθka] *vb ver* **reducir**
reedición [re(e)ði'θjon] *nf* reissue
reeditar [re(e)ði'tar] *vt* to reissue
reelección [re(e)lek'θjon] *nf* re-election
reelegir [re(e)le'xir] *vt* to re-elect
reembolsable [re(e)mbol'saβle] *adj* (*Com*) redeemable, refundable
reembolsar [re(e)mbol'sar] *vt* (*persona*) to reimburse; (*dinero*) to repay, pay back; (*depósito*) to refund
reembolso [re(e)m'bolso] *nm* reimbursement; refund; **enviar algo contra ~** to send sth cash on delivery; **contra ~ del flete** freight forward; **~ fiscal** tax rebate
reemplace *etc* [re(e)m'plaθe] *vb ver* **reemplazar**
reemplazar [re(e)mpla'θar] *vt* to replace
reemplazo [re(e)m'plaθo] *nm* replacement; **de ~** (*Mil*) reserve
reencuentro [re(e)n'kwentro] *nm* reunion
reengancharse [re(e)ngan'tʃarse] *vr* (*Mil*) to re-enlist
reestreno [re(e)s'treno] *nm* rerun
reestructurar [re(e)struktu'rar] *vt* to restructure
reexportación [re(e)ksporta'θjon] *nf* (*Com*) re-export
reexportar [re(e)kspor'tar] *vt* (*Com*) to re-export
REF *nm abr* (*Esp Econ*) = **Régimen Económico Fiscal**
Ref.ª *abr* (= *referencia*) ref
refacción [refak'θjon] *nf* (*Am*) repair(s); **refacciones** *nfpl* (*piezas de repuesto*) spare parts
referencia [refe'renθja] *nf* reference; **con ~ a** with reference to; **hacer ~ a** to refer *o* allude to; **~ comercial** (*Com*) trade reference
referéndum [refe'rendum] (*pl* **referéndums**) *nm* referendum
referente [refe'rente] *adj*: **~ a** concerning, relating to
referir [refe'rir] *vt* (*contar*) to tell, recount; (*relacionar*) to refer, relate; **referirse** *vr*: **referirse a** to refer to; **~ al lector a un apéndice** to refer the reader to an appendix; **~ a** (*Com*) to convert into; **por lo que se refiere a eso** as for that, as regards that
refiera *etc* [re'fjera] *vb ver* **referir**
refilón [refi'lon]: **de ~** *adv* obliquely; **mirar a algn de ~** to look out of the corner of one's eye at sb
refinado, -a [refi'naðo, a] *adj* refined
refinamiento [refina'mjento] *nm* refinement; **~ por pasos** (*Inform*) stepwise refinement
refinar [refi'nar] *vt* to refine
refinería [refine'ria] *nf* refinery
refiriendo *etc* [refi'rjendo] *vb ver* **referir**
reflector [reflek'tor] *nm* reflector; (*Elec*) spotlight; (*Aviat: Mil*) searchlight
reflejar [refle'xar] *vt* to reflect; **reflejarse** *vr* to be reflected
reflejo, -a [re'flexo, a] *adj* reflected; (*movimiento*) reflex ■ *nm* reflection; (*Anat*) reflex; (*en el pelo*): **reflejos** *nmpl* highlights; **tiene el pelo castaño con reflejos rubios** she has chestnut hair with blond streaks
reflexión [reflek'sjon] *nf* reflection
reflexionar [refleksjo'nar] *vt* to reflect on ■ *vi* to reflect; (*detenerse*) to pause (to think); **¡reflexione!** you think it over!
reflexivo, -a [reflek'siβo, a] *adj* thoughtful; (*Ling*) reflexive
refluir [reflu'ir] *vi* to flow back
reflujo [re'fluxo] *nm* ebb
refluyendo *etc* [reflu'jendo] *vb ver* **refluir**
reforcé [refor'θe], **reforcemos** *etc* [refor'θemos] *vb ver* **reforzar**
reforma [re'forma] *nf* reform; (*Arq etc*) repair; **~ agraria** agrarian reform
reformar [refor'mar] *vt* to reform; (*modificar*) to change, alter; (*texto*) to revise; (*Arq*) to repair; **reformarse** *vr* to mend one's ways
reformatear [reformate'ar] *vt* (*Inform: disco*) to reformat
reformatorio [reforma'torjo] *nm* reformatory; **~ de menores** remand home
reformista [refor'mista] *adj, nm/f* reformist
reforzamiento [reforθa'mjento] *nm* reinforcement
reforzar [refor'θar] *vt* to strengthen; (*Arq*) to reinforce; (*fig*) to encourage

refractario, -a [refrak'tarjo, a] *adj* (*Tec*) heat-resistant; **ser ~ a una reforma** to resist *o* be opposed to a reform
refrán [re'fran] *nm* proverb, saying
refregar [refre'ɣar] *vt* to scrub
refrenar [refre'nar] *vt* to check, restrain
refrendar [refren'dar] *vt* (*firma*) to endorse, countersign; (*ley*) to approve
refrescante [refres'kante] *adj* refreshing, cooling
refrescar [refres'kar] *vt* to refresh ■ *vi* to cool down; **refrescarse** *vr* to get cooler; (*tomar aire fresco*) to go out for a breath of fresh air; (*beber*) to have a drink
refresco [re'fresko] *nm* soft drink, cool drink; **"refrescos"** "refreshments"
refresque *etc* [re'freske] *vb ver* **refrescar**
refriega *etc* [re'frjeɣa] *vb ver* **refregar** ■ *nf* scuffle, brawl
refriegue *etc* [re'frjeɣe] *vb ver* **refregar**
refrigeración [refrixera'θjon] *nf* refrigeration; (*de casa*) air-conditioning
refrigerado, -a [refrixe'raðo, a] *adj* cooled; (*sala*) air-conditioned
refrigerador [refrixera'ðor] *nm*, **refrigeradora** (*Am*) [refrixera'ðora] ■ *nf* refrigerator, icebox (US)
refrigerar [refrixe'rar] *vt* to refrigerate; (*sala*) to air-condition
refrito [re'frito] *nm* (*Culin*): **un ~ de cebolla y tomate** sautéed onions and tomatoes; **un ~** (*fig*) a rehash
refuerce *etc* [re'fwerθe] *vb ver* **reforzar**
refuerzo *etc* [re'fwerθo] *vb ver* **reforzar** ■ *nm* reinforcement; (*Tec*) support
refugiado, -a [refu'xjaðo, a] *nm/f* refugee
refugiarse [refu'xjarse] *vr* to take refuge, shelter
refugio [re'fuxjo] *nm* refuge; (*protección*) shelter; (*Auto*) street *o* traffic island; **~ alpino** *o* **de montaña** mountain hut; **~ subterráneo** (*Mil*) underground shelter
refulgencia [reful'xenθja] *nf* brilliance
refulgir [reful'xir] *vi* to shine, be dazzling
refulja *etc* [re'fulxa] *vb ver* **refulgir**
refundir [refun'dir] *vt* to recast; (*escrito etc*) to adapt, rewrite
refunfuñar [refunfu'ɲar] *vi* to grunt, growl; (*quejarse*) to grumble
refunfuñón, -ona [refunfu'ɲon, ona] (*fam*) *adj* grumpy ■ *nm/f* grouch
refutación [refuta'θjon] *nf* refutation
refutar [refu'tar] *vt* to refute
regadera [reɣa'ðera] *nf* watering can; (*Am*) shower; **estar como una ~** (*fam*) to be as mad as a hatter
regadío [rega'ðio] *nm* irrigated land
regalado, -a [reɣa'laðo, a] *adj* comfortable, luxurious; (*gratis*) free, for nothing; **lo tuvo ~** it was handed to him on a plate
regalar [reɣa'lar] *vt* (*dar*) to give (as a present); (*entregar*) to give away; (*mimar*) to pamper, make a fuss of; **regalarse** *vr* to treat o.s. to
regalía [reɣa'lia] *nf* privilege, prerogative; (*Com*) bonus; (*de autor*) royalty
regaliz [reɣa'liθ] *nm* liquorice
regalo [re'ɣalo] *nm* (*obsequio*) gift, present; (*gusto*) pleasure; (*comodidad*) comfort
regañadientes [reɣaɲa'ðjentes]: **a ~** *adv* reluctantly
regañar [reɣa'ɲar] *vt* to scold ■ *vi* to grumble; (*dos personas*) to fall out, quarrel
regañón, -ona [reɣa'ɲon, ona] *adj* nagging
regar [re'ɣar] *vt* to water, irrigate; (*fig*) to scatter, sprinkle
regata [re'ɣata] *nf* (*Naut*) race
regatear [reɣate'ar] *vt* (*Com*) to bargain over; (*escatimar*) to be mean with ■ *vi* to bargain, haggle; (*Deporte*) to dribble; **no ~ esfuerzo** to spare no effort
regateo [reɣa'teo] *nm* bargaining; (*Deporte*) dribbling; (*con el cuerpo*) swerve, dodge
regazo [re'ɣaθo] *nm* lap
regencia [re'xenθja] *nf* regency
regeneración [rexenera'θjon] *nf* regeneration
regenerar [rexene'rar] *vt* to regenerate
regentar [rexen'tar] *vt* to direct, manage; (*puesto*) to hold in an acting capacity; (*negocio*) to be in charge of
regente, -a [re'xente, a] *adj* (*príncipe*) regent; (*director*) managing ■ *nm* (*Com*) manager; (*Pol*) regent
régimen ['reximen] (*pl* **regímenes**) [re'ximenes] *nm* regime; (*reinado*) rule; (*Med*) diet; (*reglas*) (set of) rules *pl*; (*manera de vivir*) lifestyle; **estar a ~** to be on a diet
regimiento [rexi'mjento] *nm* regiment
regio, -a ['rexjo, a] *adj* royal, regal; (*fig: suntuoso*) splendid; (*Am fam*) great, terrific
región [re'xjon] *nf* region; (*área*) area
regional [rexjo'nal] *adj* regional
regir [re'xir] *vt* to govern, rule; (*dirigir*) to manage, run; (*Econ: Jur: Ling*) to govern ■ *vi* to apply, be in force
registrador [rexistra'ðor] *nm* registrar, recorder
registrar [rexis'trar] *vt* (*buscar*) to search; (*en cajón*) to look through; (*inspeccionar*) to inspect; (*anotar*) to register, record; (*Inform: Mus*) to record; **registrarse** *vr* to register; (*ocurrir*) to happen
registro [re'xistro] *nm* (*acto*) registration;

(*Mus, libro*) register; (*lista*) list, record; (*Inform*) record; (*inspección*) inspection, search; **~ civil** registry office; **~ electoral** voting register; **~ de la propiedad** land registry (office)
regla ['reɣla] *nf* (*ley*) rule, regulation; (*de medir*) ruler, rule; (*Med: período*) period; (*regla científica*) law, principle; **no hay ~ sin excepción** every rule has its exception
reglamentación [reɣlamenta'θjon] *nf* (*acto*) regulation; (*lista*) rules *pl*
reglamentar [reɣlamen'tar] *vt* to regulate
reglamentario, -a [reɣlamen'tarjo, a] *adj* statutory; **en la forma reglamentaria** in the properly established way
reglamento [reɣla'mento] *nm* rules *pl*, regulations *pl*; **~ del tráfico** highway code
reglar [re'ɣlar] *vt* (*acciones*) to regulate; **reglarse** *vr*: **reglarse por** to be guided by
regocijarse [reɣoθi'xarse] *vr*: **~ de** *o* **por** to rejoice at, be glad about
regocijo [reɣo'θixo] *nm* joy, happiness
regodearse [reɣoðe'arse] *vr* to be glad, be delighted; (*pey*): **~ con** *o* **en** to gloat over
regodeo [reɣo'ðeo] *nm* delight; (*pey*) perverse pleasure
regresar [reɣre'sar] *vi* to come/go back, return; **regresarse** *vr* (*Am*) to return
regresivo, -a [reɣre'siβo, a] *adj* backward; (*fig*) regressive
regreso [re'ɣreso] *nm* return; **estar de ~** to be back, be home
regué [re'ɣe], **reguemos** *etc* [re'ɣemos] *vb ver* **regar**
reguero [re'ɣero] *nm* (*de sangre*) trickle; (*de humo*) trail
regulación [reɣula'θjon] *nf* regulation; (*Tec*) adjustment; (*control*) control; **~ de empleo** redundancies *pl*; **~ del tráfico** traffic control
regulador [reɣula'ðor] *nm* (*Tec*) regulator; (*de radio etc*) knob, control
regular [reɣu'lar] *adj* regular; (*normal*) normal, usual; (*común*) ordinary; (*organizado*) regular, orderly; (*mediano*) average; (*fam*) not bad, so-so ■ *adv*: **estar ~** to be so-so *o* alright ■ *vt* (*controlar*) to control, regulate; (*Tec*) to adjust; **por lo ~** as a rule
regularice *etc* [reɣula'riθe] *vb ver* **regularizar**
regularidad [reɣulari'ðað] *nf* regularity; **con ~** regularly
regularizar [reɣulari'θar] *vt* to regularize
regusto [re'ɣusto] *nm* aftertaste
rehabilitación [reaβilita'θjon] *nf* rehabilitation; (*Arq*) restoration
rehabilitar [reaβili'tar] *vt* to rehabilitate; (*Arq*) to restore; (*reintegrar*) to reinstate
rehacer [rea'θer] *vt* (*reparar*) to mend, repair; (*volver a hacer*) to redo, repeat; **rehacerse** *vr* (*Med*) to recover
rehaga *etc* [re'aɣa], **reharé** *etc* [rea're], **rehaz** [re'aθ], **rehecho** [re'etʃo] *vb ver* **rehacer**
rehén [re'en] *nm/f* hostage
rehice *etc* [re'iθe], **rehizo** [re'iθo] *vb ver* **rehacer**
rehogar [reo'ɣar] *vt* to sauté, toss in oil
rehuir [reu'ir] *vt* to avoid, shun
rehusar [reu'sar] *vt, vi* to refuse
rehuyendo *etc* [reu'jendo] *vb ver* **rehuir**
reina ['reina] *nf* queen
reinado [rei'naðo] *nm* reign
reinante [rei'nante] *adj* (*fig*) prevailing
reinar [rei'nar] *vi* to reign; (*fig: prevalecer*) to prevail, be general
reincidir [reinθi'ðir] *vi* to relapse; (*criminal*) to repeat an offence
reincorporarse [reinkorpo'rarse] *vr*: **~ a** to rejoin
reinicializar [reiniθjali'θar] *vt* (*Inform*) to reset
reino ['reino] *nm* kingdom; **el R~ Unido** the United Kingdom
reinserción [reinser'θjon] *nf* rehabilitation
reinsertar [reinser'tar] *vt* to rehabilitate
reintegración [reinteɣra'θjon] *nf* (*Com*) reinstatement
reintegrar [reinte'ɣrar] *vt* (*reconstituir*) to reconstruct; (*persona*) to reinstate; (*dinero*) to refund, pay back; **reintegrarse** *vr*: **reintegrarse a** to return to
reintegro [rein'teɣro] *nm* refund, reimbursement; (*en banco*) withdrawal
reír [re'ir] *vi*, **reírse** *vr* to laugh; **reírse de** to laugh at
reiterado, -a [reite'raðo, a] *adj* repeated
reiterar [reite'rar] *vt* to reiterate; (*repetir*) to repeat
reivindicación [reiβindika'θjon] *nf* (*demanda*) claim, demand; (*justificación*) vindication
reivindicar [reiβindi'kar] *vt* to claim
reivindique *etc* [reiβin'dike] *vb ver* **reivindicar**
reja ['rexa] *nf* (*de ventana*) grille, bars *pl*; (*en la calle*) grating
rejilla [re'xiʎa] *nf* grating, grille; (*muebles*) wickerwork; (*de ventilación*) vent; (*de coche etc*) luggage rack
rejuvenecer [rexuβene'θer] *vt, vi* to rejuvenate
rejuvenezca *etc* [rexuβe'neθka] *vb ver* **rejuvenecer**
relación [rela'θjon] *nf* relation, relationship; (*Mat*) ratio; (*lista*) list; (*narración*) report; **~ costo-efectivo** *o* **costo-rendimiento** (*Com*) cost-effectiveness; **relaciones** *nfpl* (*enchufes*) influential friends, connections; **relaciones carnales** sexual relations; **relaciones**

comerciales business connections; **relaciones empresariales/humanas** industrial/human relations; **relaciones laborales/públicas** labour/public relations; **con ~ a, en ~ con** in relation to; **estar en** *o* **tener buenas relaciones con** to be on good terms with
relacionar [relaθjo'nar] *vt* to relate, connect; **relacionarse** *vr* to be connected *o* linked
relajación [relaxa'θjon] *nf* relaxation
relajado, -a [rela'xaðo, a] *adj* (*disoluto*) loose; (*cómodo*) relaxed; (*Med*) ruptured
relajante [rela'xante] *adj* relaxing; (*Med*) sedative
relajar [rela'xar] *vt*, **relajarse** *vr* to relax
relamerse [rela'merse] *vr* to lick one's lips
relamido, -a [rela'miðo, a] *adj* (*pulcro*) overdressed; (*afectado*) affected
relámpago [re'lampaɣo] *nm* flash of lightning ▪ *adj* lightning *cpd*; **como un ~** as quick as lightning, in a flash; **visita/huelga ~** lightning visit/strike
relampaguear [relampaɣe'ar] *vi* to flash
relanzar [relan'θar] *vt* to relaunch
relatar [rela'tar] *vt* to tell, relate
relatividad [relatiβi'ðað] *nf* relativity
relativo, -a [rela'tiβo, a] *adj* relative; **en lo ~ a** concerning
relato [re'lato] *nm* (*narración*) story, tale
relax [re'las] *nm* rest; **"R~"** (*en anuncio*) "Personal services"
relegar [rele'ɣar] *vt* to relegate; **~ algo al olvido** to banish sth from one's mind
relegue *etc* [re'leɣe] *vb ver* **relegar**
relevante [rele'βante] *adj* eminent, outstanding
relevar [rele'βar] *vt* (*sustituir*) to relieve; **relevarse** *vr* to relay; **~ a algn de un cargo** to relieve sb of his post
relevo [re'leβo] *nm* relief; **carrera de relevos** relay race; **coger** *o* **tomar el ~** to take over, stand in
relieve [re'ljeβe] *nm* (*Arte*: *Tec*) relief; (*fig*) prominence, importance; **bajo ~** bas-relief; **un personaje de ~** an important man; **dar ~ a** to highlight
religión [reli'xjon] *nf* religion
religioso, -a [reli'xjoso, a] *adj* religious ▪ *nm/f* monk/nun
relinchar [relin'tʃar] *vi* to neigh
relincho [re'lintʃo] *nm* neigh; (*acto*) neighing
reliquia [re'likja] *nf* relic; **~ de familia** heirloom
rellano [re'ʎano] *nm* (*Arq*) landing
rellenar [reʎe'nar] *vt* (*llenar*) to fill up; (*Culin*) to stuff; (*Costura*) to pad; (*formulario etc*) to fill in *o* out
relleno, -a [re'ʎeno, a] *adj* full up; (*Culin*) stuffed ▪ *nm* stuffing; (*de tapicería*) padding
reloj [re'lo(x)] *nm* clock; **~ de pie** grandfather clock; **~ (de pulsera)** wristwatch; **~ de sol** sundial; **~ despertador** alarm (clock); **como un ~** like clockwork; **contra (el) ~** against the clock
relojería [reloxe'ria] (*tienda*) watchmaker's (shop); **aparato de ~** clockwork; **bomba de ~** time bomb
relojero, -a [relo'xero, a] *nm/f* clockmaker; watchmaker
reluciente [relu'θjente] *adj* brilliant, shining
relucir [relu'θir] *vi* to shine; (*fig*) to excel; **sacar algo a ~** to show sth off
relumbrante [relum'brante] *adj* dazzling
relumbrar [relum'brar] *vi* to dazzle, shine brilliantly
reluzca *etc* [re'luθka] *vb ver* **relucir**
remachar [rema'tʃar] *vt* to rivet; (*fig*) to hammer home, drive home
remache [re'matʃe] *nm* rivet
remanente [rema'nente] *nm* remainder; (*Com*) balance; (*de producto*) surplus
remangarse [reman'garse] *vr* to roll one's sleeves up
remanso [re'manso] *nm* pool
remar [re'mar] *vi* to row
rematado, -a [rema'taðo, a] *adj* complete, utter; **es un loco ~** he's a raving lunatic
rematar [rema'tar] *vt* to finish off; (*animal*) to put out of its misery; (*Com*) to sell off cheap ▪ *vi* to end, finish off; (*Deporte*) to shoot
remate [re'mate] *nm* end, finish; (*punta*) tip; (*Deporte*) shot; (*Arq*) top; (*Com*) auction sale; **de** *o* **para ~** to crown it all (*Brit*), to top it off
remediable [reme'ðjaβle] *adj*: **fácilmente ~** easily remedied
remediar [reme'ðjar] *vt* (*gen*) to remedy; (*subsanar*) to make good, repair; (*evitar*) to avoid; **sin poder remediarlo** without being able to prevent it
remedio [re'meðjo] *nm* remedy; (*Jur*) recourse, remedy; **poner ~ a** to correct, stop; **no tener más ~** to have no alternative; **¡qué ~!** there's no other way; **como último ~** as a last resort; **sin ~** inevitable; (*Med*) hopeless
remedo [re'meðo] *nm* imitation; (*pey*) parody
remendar [remen'dar] *vt* to repair; (*con parche*) to patch; (*fig*) to correct
remesa [re'mesa] *nf* remittance; (*Com*) shipment
remiendo *etc* [re'mjendo] *vb ver* **remendar** ▪ *nm* mend; (*con parche*) patch; (*cosido*) darn; (*fig*) correction
remilgado, -a [remil'ɣaðo, a] *adj* prim; (*afectado*) affected

remilgo [re'milɣo] *nm* primness; *(afectación)* affectation
reminiscencia [reminis'θenθja] *nf* reminiscence
remirar [remi'rar] *vt (volver a mirar)* to look at again; *(examinar)* to look hard at
remisión [remi'sjon] *nf (acto)* sending, shipment; *(Rel)* forgiveness, remission; **sin ~** hopelessly
remiso, -a [re'miso, a] *adj* remiss
remite [re'mite] *nm (en sobre)* name and address of sender
remitente [remi'tente] *nm/f (Correos)* sender
remitir [remi'tir] *vt* to remit, send ▪ *vi* to slacken
remo ['remo] *nm (de barco)* oar; *(Deporte)* rowing; **cruzar un río a ~** to row across a river
remoce *etc* [re'moθe] *vb ver* **remozar**
remodelación [remodela'θjon] *nf (Pol)*: **~ del gobierno** cabinet reshuffle
remojar [remo'xar] *vt* to steep, soak; *(galleta etc)* to dip, dunk; *(fam)* to celebrate with a drink
remojo [re'moxo] *nm* steeping, soaking; *(por la lluvia)* drenching, soaking; **dejar la ropa en ~** to leave clothes to soak
remojón [remo'xon] *nm* soaking; **darse un ~** *(fam)* to go (in) for a dip
remolacha [remo'latʃa] *nf* beet, beetroot *(Brit)*
remolcador [remolka'ðor] *nm (Naut)* tug; *(Auto)* breakdown lorry
remolcar [remol'kar] *vt* to tow
remolino [remo'lino] *nm* eddy; *(de agua)* whirlpool; *(de viento)* whirlwind; *(de gente)* crowd
remolón, -ona [remo'lon, ona] *adj* lazy ▪ *nm/f* slacker, shirker
remolque *etc* [re'molke] *vb ver* **remolcar** ▪ *nm* tow, towing; *(cuerda)* towrope; **llevar a ~** to tow
remontar [remon'tar] *vt* to mend; *(obstáculo)* to negotiate, get over; **remontarse** *vr* to soar; **remontarse a** *(Com)* to amount to; *(en tiempo)* to go back to, date from; **~ el vuelo** to soar
rémora ['remora] *nf* hindrance
remorder [remor'ðer] *vt* to distress, disturb
remordimiento [remorði'mjento] *nm* remorse
remotamente [remota'mente] *adv* vaguely
remoto, -a [re'moto, a] *adj* remote
remover [remo'βer] *vt* to stir; *(tierra)* to turn over; *(objetos)* to move round
remozar [remo'θar] *vt (Arq)* to refurbish; *(fig)* to brighten *o* polish up
remuerda *etc* [re'mwerða] *vb ver* **remorder**
remueva *etc* [re'mweβa] *vb ver* **remover**
remuneración [remunera'θjon] *nf* remuneration
remunerado, -a [remune'raðo, a] *adj*: **trabajo bien/mal ~** well-/badly-paid job
remunerar [remune'rar] *vt* to remunerate; *(premiar)* to reward
renacer [rena'θer] *vi* to be reborn; *(fig)* to revive
renacimiento [renaθi'mjento] *nm* rebirth; **el R~** the Renaissance
renacuajo [rena'kwaxo] *nm (Zool)* tadpole
renal [re'nal] *adj* renal, kidney *cpd*
Renania [re'nanja] *nf* Rhineland
renazca *etc* [re'naθka] *vb ver* **renacer**
rencilla [ren'θiʎa] *nf* quarrel; **rencillas** *nfpl* bickering *sg*
rencor [ren'kor] *nm* rancour, bitterness; *(resentimiento)* ill feeling, resentment; **guardar ~ a** to have a grudge against
rencoroso, -a [renko'roso, a] *adj* spiteful
rendición [rendi'θjon] *nf* surrender
rendido, -a [ren'diðo, a] *adj (sumiso)* submissive; *(agotado)* worn-out, exhausted; *(enamorado)* devoted
rendija [ren'dixa] *nf (hendidura)* crack; *(abertura)* aperture; *(fig)* rift, split; *(Jur)* loophole
rendimiento [rendi'mjento] *nm (producción)* output; *(Com)* yield, profit(s) *(pl)*; *(Tec: Com)* efficiency; **~ de capital** *(Com)* return on capital
rendir [ren'dir] *vt (vencer)* to defeat; *(producir)* to produce; *(dar beneficio)* to yield; *(agotar)* to exhaust ▪ *vi* to pay; *(Com)* to yield, produce; **rendirse** *vr (someterse)* to surrender; *(ceder)* to yield; *(cansarse)* to wear o.s. out; **~ homenaje** *o* **culto a** to pay homage to; **el negocio no rinde** the business doesn't pay
renegado, -a [rene'ɣaðo, a] *adj, nm/f* renegade
renegar [rene'ɣar] *vt (negar)* to deny vigorously ▪ *vi (blasfemar)* to blaspheme; **~ de** *(renunciar)* to renounce; *(quejarse)* to complain about
renegué [rene'ɣe], **reneguemos** *etc* [rene'ɣemos] *vb ver* **renegar**
RENFE ['renfe] *nf abr (Esp: Ferro)* = **Red Nacional de Ferrocarriles Españoles**
renglón [ren'glon] *nm (línea)* line; *(Com)* item, article; **a ~ seguido** immediately after
rengo, -a ['rengo, a] *adj (Am)* lame
reniego *etc* [re'njeɣo], **reniegue** *etc* [re'njeɣe] *vb ver* **renegar**
reno ['reno] *nm* reindeer
renombrado, -a [renom'braðo, a] *adj* renowned

renombre [re'nombre] *nm* renown
renovable [reno'βaβle] *adj* renewable
renovación [renoβa'θjon] *nf* (*de contrato*) renewal; (*Arq*) renovation
renovar [reno'βar] *vt* to renew; (*Arq*) to renovate; (*sala*) to redecorate
renquear [renke'ar] *vi* to limp; (*fam*) to get along, scrape by
renta ['renta] *nf* (*ingresos*) income; (*beneficio*) profit; (*alquiler*) rent; **~ gravable** *o* **imponible** taxable income; **~ nacional (bruta)** (gross) national income; **~ no salarial** unearned income; **~ sobre el terreno** (*Com*) ground rent; **~ vitalicia** annuity; **política de rentas** incomes policy; **vivir de sus rentas** to live on one's private income
rentabilizar [rentaβili'θar] *vt* to make profitable
rentable [ren'taβle] *adj* profitable; **no ~** unprofitable
rentar [ren'tar] *vt* to produce, yield; (*Am*) to rent
rentista [ren'tista] *nm/f* (*accionista*) shareholder (*Brit*), stockholder (*US*)
renuencia [re'nwenθja] *nf* reluctance
renuente [re'nwente] *adj* reluctant
renueve *etc* [re'nweβe] *vb ver* **renovar**
renuncia [re'nunθja] *nf* resignation
renunciar [renun'θjar] *vt* to renounce, give up ■ *vi* to resign; **~ a hacer algo** to give up doing sth
reñido, -a [re'ɲiðo, a] *adj* (*batalla*) bitter, hard-fought; **estar ~ con algn** to be on bad terms with sb; **está ~ con su familia** he has fallen out with his family
reñir [re'ɲir] *vt* (*regañar*) to scold ■ *vi* (*estar peleado*) to quarrel, fall out; (*combatir*) to fight
reo ['reo] *nm/f* culprit, offender; (*Jur*) accused
reojo [re'oxo]: **de ~** *adv* out of the corner of one's eye
reorganice *etc* [reorɣa'niθe] *vb ver* **reorganizar**
reorganizar [reorɣani'θar] *vt* to reorganize
Rep *abr* = **República**
reparación [repara'θjon] *nf* (*acto*) mending, repairing; (*Tec*) repair; (*fig*) amends, reparation; **"reparaciones en el acto"** "repairs while you wait"
reparar [repa'rar] *vt* to repair; (*fig*) to make amends for; (*suerte*) to retrieve; (*observar*) to observe ■ *vi*: **~ en** (*darse cuenta de*) to notice; (*poner atención en*) to pay attention to; **sin ~ en los gastos** regardless of the cost
reparo [re'paro] *nm* (*advertencia*) observation; (*duda*) doubt; (*dificultad*) difficulty; (*escrúpulo*) scruple, qualm; **poner reparos (a)** to raise objections (to); (*criticar*) to criticize; **no tuvo ~ en hacerlo** he did not hesitate to do it
repartición [reparti'θjon] *nf* distribution; (*división*) division
repartidor, a [reparti'ðor, a] *nm/f* distributor; **~ de leche** milkman
repartir [repar'tir] *vt* to distribute, share out; (*Com: Correos*) to deliver; (*Mil*) to partition; (*libros*) to give out; (*comida*) to serve out; (*Naipes*) to deal
reparto [re'parto] *nm* distribution; (*Com: Correos*) delivery; (*Teat: Cine*) cast; (*Am: urbanización*) housing estate (*Brit*), real estate development (*US*); **"~ a domicilio"** "home delivery service"
repasar [repa'sar] *vt* (*Escol*) to revise; (*Mecánica*) to check, overhaul; (*Costura*) to mend
repaso [re'paso] *nm* revision; (*Mecánica*) overhaul, checkup; (*Costura*) mending; **~ general** servicing, general overhaul; **curso de ~** refresher course
repatriar [repa'trjar] *vt* to repatriate; **repatriarse** *vr* to return home
repelente [repe'lente] *adj* repellent, repulsive
repeler [repe'ler] *vt* to repel; (*idea, oferta*) to reject
repensar [repen'sar] *vt* to reconsider
repente [re'pente] *nm* sudden movement; (*fig*) impulse; **de ~** suddenly; **~ de ira** fit of anger
repentice *etc* [repen'tiθe] *vb ver* **repentizar**
repentino, -a [repen'tino, a] *adj* sudden; (*imprevisto*) unexpected
repentizar [repenti'θar] *vi* (*Mus*) to sight-read
repercusión [reperku'sjon] *nf* repercussion; **de amplia** *o* **ancha ~** far-reaching
repercutir [reperku'tir] *vi* (*objeto*) to rebound; (*sonido*) to echo; **~ en** (*fig*) to have repercussions *o* effects on
repertorio [reper'torjo] *nm* list; (*Teat*) repertoire
repesca [re'peska] *nf* (*Escol fam*) resit
repetición [repeti'θjon] *nf* repetition
repetido, -a [repe'tiðo, a] *adj* repeated; **repetidas veces** repeatedly
repetir [repe'tir] *vt* to repeat; (*plato*) to have a second helping of; (*Teat*) to give as an encore, sing *etc* again ■ *vi* to repeat; (*sabor*) to come back; **repetirse** *vr* to repeat o.s.; (*suceso*) to recur
repetitivo, -a [repeti'tiβo, a] *adj* repetitive, repetitious
repicar [repi'kar] *vi* (*campanas*) to ring (out)
repiense *etc* [re'pjense] *vb ver* **repensar**

repipi [re'pipi] *adj* la-di-da ■ *nf*: **es una ~** she's a little madam
repique *etc* [re'pike] *vb ver* **repicar** ■ *nm* pealing, ringing
repiqueteo [repike'teo] *nm* pealing; (*de tambor*) drumming
repisa [re'pisa] *nf* ledge, shelf; **~ de chimenea** mantelpiece; **~ de ventana** windowsill
repitiendo *etc* [repi'tjendo] *vb ver* **repetir**
replantear [replante'ar] *vt* (*cuestión pública*) to readdress; (*problema personal*) to reconsider; (*en reunión*) to raise again; **replantearse** *vr*: **replantearse algo** to reconsider sth
replegarse [reple'ɣarse] *vr* to fall back, retreat
replegué [reple'ɣe], **repleguemos** *etc* [reple'ɣemos] *vb ver* **replegarse**
repleto, -a [re'pleto, a] *adj* replete, full up; **~ de** filled *o* crammed with
réplica ['replika] *nf* answer; (*Arte*) replica; **derecho de ~** right of *o* to reply
replicar [repli'kar] *vi* to answer; (*objetar*) to argue, answer back
repliego *etc* [re'pljeɣo] *vb ver* **replegarse**
repliegue *etc* [re'pljeɣe] *vb ver* **replegarse** ■ *nm* (*Mil*) withdrawal
replique *etc* [re'plike] *vb ver* **replicar**
repoblación [repoβla'θjon] *nf* repopulation; (*de río*) restocking; **~ forestal** reafforestation
repoblar [repo'βlar] *vt* to repopulate; to restock
repollo [re'poʎo] *nm* cabbage
repondré *etc* [repon'dre] *vb ver* **reponer**
reponer [repo'ner] *vt* to replace, put back; (*máquina*) to re-set; (*Teat*) to revive; **reponerse** *vr* to recover; **~ que** to reply that
reponga *etc* [re'ponga] *vb ver* **reponer**
reportaje [repor'taxe] *nm* report, article; **~ gráfico** illustrated report
reportar [repor'tar] *vt* (*traer*) to bring, carry; (*conseguir*) to obtain; (*fig*) to check; **reportarse** *vr* (*contenerse*) to control o.s.; (*calmarse*) to calm down; **la cosa no le reportó sino disgustos** the affair brought him nothing but trouble
reportero, -a [repor'tero, a] *nm/f* reporter; **~ gráfico/a** news photographer
reposacabezas [reposaka'βeθas] *nm inv* headrest
reposado, -a [repo'saðo, a] *adj* (*descansado*) restful; (*tranquilo*) calm
reposar [repo'sar] *vi* to rest, repose; (*muerto*) to lie, rest
reposición [reposi'θjon] *nf* replacement; (*Cine*) second showing; (*Teat*) revival
reposo [re'poso] *nm* rest
repostar [repos'tar] *vt* to replenish; (*Auto*) to fill up (with petrol *o* gasoline)
repostería [reposte'ria] *nf* (*arte*) confectionery, pastry-making; (*tienda*) confectioner's (shop)
repostero, -a [repos'tero, a] *nm/f* confectioner
reprender [repren'der] *vt* to reprimand; (*niño*) to scold
reprensión [repren'sjon] *nf* rebuke, reprimand; (*de niño*) telling-off, scolding
represa [re'presa] *nf* dam; (*lago artificial*) lake, pool
represalia [repre'salja] *nf* reprisal; **tomar represalias** to take reprisals, retaliate
representación [representa'θjon] *nf* representation; (*Teat*) performance; **en ~ de** representing; **por ~** by proxy
representante [represen'tante] *nm/f* (*Pol: Com*) representative; (*Teat*) performer
representar [represen'tar] *vt* to represent; (*significar*) to mean; (*Teat*) to perform; (*edad*) to look; **representarse** *vr* to imagine; **tal acto ~ía la guerra** such an act would mean war
representativo, -a [representa'tiβo, a] *adj* representative
represión [repre'sjon] *nf* repression
represivo, -a [repre'siβo, a] *adj* repressive
reprimenda [repri'menda] *nf* reprimand, rebuke
reprimir [repri'mir] *vt* to repress; **reprimirse** *vr*: **reprimirse de hacer algo** to stop o.s. from doing sth
reprobación [reproβa'θjon] *nf* reproval; (*culpa*) blame
reprobar [repro'βar] *vt* to censure, reprove
réprobo, -a ['reproβo, a] *nm/f* reprobate
reprochar [repro'tʃar] *vt* to reproach; (*censurar*) to condemn, censure
reproche [re'protʃe] *nm* reproach
reproducción [reproðuk'θjon] *nf* reproduction
reproducir [reproðu'θir] *vt* to reproduce; **reproducirse** *vr* to breed; (*situación*) to recur
reproductor, a [reproðuk'tor, a] *adj* reproductive ■ *nm*: **~ de discos compactos** CD player; **~ MP3/MP4** MP3/MP4 player
reproduje [repro'ðuxe], **reprodujera** *etc* [reproðu'xera], **reproduzca** *etc* [repro'duθka] *vb ver* **reproducir**
repruebe *etc* [re'prweβe] *vb ver* **reprobar**
reptar [rep'tar] *vi* to creep, crawl
reptil [rep'til] *nm* reptile
república [re'puβlika] *nf* republic; **R~ Dominicana** Dominican Republic; **R~ Democrática Alemana (RDA)** German

Democratic Republic; **R~ Federal Alemana (RFA)** Federal Republic of Germany; **R~ Árabe Unida** United Arab Republic
republicano, -a [repuβli'kano, a] *adj, nm/f* republican
repudiar [repu'ðjar] *vt* to repudiate; (*fe*) to renounce
repudio [re'puðjo] *nm* repudiation
repueble *etc* [re'pweβle] *vb ver* **repoblar**
repuesto [re'pwesto] *pp de* **reponer** ■ *nm* (*pieza de recambio*) spare (part); (*abastecimiento*) supply; **rueda de ~** spare wheel; **y llevamos otro de ~** and we have another as a spare *o* in reserve
repugnancia [repuɣ'nanθja] *nf* repugnance
repugnante [repuɣ'nante] *adj* repugnant, repulsive
repugnar [repuɣ'nar] *vt* to disgust ■ *vi*, **repugnarse** *vr* (*contradecirse*) to contradict each other
repujar [repu'xar] *vt* to emboss
repulsa [re'pulsa] *nf* rebuff
repulsión [repul'sjon] *nf* repulsion, aversion
repulsivo, -a [repul'siβo, a] *adj* repulsive
repuse *etc* [re'puse] *vb ver* **reponer**
reputación [reputa'θjon] *nf* reputation
reputar [repu'tar] *vt* to consider, deem
requemado, -a [reke'maðo, a] *adj* (*quemado*) scorched; (*bronceado*) tanned
requemar [reke'mar] *vt* (*quemar*) to scorch; (*secar*) to parch; (*Culin*) to overdo, burn; (*la lengua*) to burn, sting
requerimiento [rekeri'mjento] *nm* request; (*demanda*) demand; (*Jur*) summons
requerir [reke'rir] *vt* (*pedir*) to ask, request; (*exigir*) to require; (*ordenar*) to call for; (*llamar*) to send for, summon
requesón [reke'son] *nm* cottage cheese
requete ... [rekete] *pref* extremely
requiebro [re'kjeβro] *nm* (*piropo*) compliment, flirtatious remark
réquiem ['rekjem] *nm* requiem
requiera *etc* [re'kjera], **requiriendo** *etc* [reki'rjendo] *vb ver* **requerir**
requisa [re'kisa] *nf* (*inspección*) survey, inspection; (*Mil*) requisition
requisar [reki'sar] *vt* (*Mil*) to requisition; (*confiscar*) to seize, confiscate
requisito [reki'sito] *nm* requirement, requisite; **~ previo** prerequisite; **tener los requisitos para un cargo** to have the essential qualifications for a post
res [res] *nf* beast, animal
resabio [re'saβjo] *nm* (*maña*) vice, bad habit; (*dejo*) (unpleasant) aftertaste
resaca [re'saka] *nf* (*en el mar*) undertow, undercurrent; (*fig*) backlash; (*fam*) hangover
resaltar [resal'tar] *vi* to project, stick out; (*fig*) to stand out
resarcir [resar'θir] *vt* to compensate; (*pagar*) to repay; **resarcirse** *vr* to make up for; **~ a algn de una pérdida** to compensate sb for a loss; **~ a algn de una cantidad** to repay sb a sum
resarza *etc* [re'sarθa] *vb ver* **resarcir**
resbalada [resβa'laða] *nf* (*Am*) slip
resbaladizo, -a [resβala'ðiθo, a] *adj* slippery
resbalar [resβa'lar] *vi*, **resbalarse** *vr* to slip, slide; (*fig*) to slip (up); **le resbalaban las lágrimas por las mejillas** tears were trickling down his cheeks
resbalón [resβa'lon] *nm* (*acción*) slip; (*deslizamiento*) slide; (*fig*) slip
rescatar [reska'tar] *vt* (*salvar*) to save, rescue; (*objeto*) to get back, recover; (*cautivos*) to ransom
rescate [res'kate] *nm* rescue; (*de objeto*) recovery; **pagar un ~** to pay a ransom
rescindir [resθin'dir] *vt* (*contrato*) to annul, rescind
rescisión [resθi'sjon] *nf* cancellation
rescoldo [res'koldo] *nm* embers *pl*
resecar [rese'kar] *vt* to dry off, dry thoroughly; (*Med*) to cut out, remove; **resecarse** *vr* to dry up
reseco, -a [re'seko, a] *adj* very dry; (*fig*) skinny
resentido, -a [resen'tiðo, a] *adj* resentful; **es un ~** he's bitter
resentimiento [resenti'mjento] *nm* resentment, bitterness
resentirse [resen'tirse] *vr* (*debilitarse: persona*) to suffer; **~ con** to resent; **~ de** (*sufrir las consecuencias de*) to feel the effects of
reseña [re'seɲa] *nf* (*cuenta*) account; (*informe*) report; (*Lit*) review
reseñar [rese'ɲar] *vt* to describe; (*Lit*) to review
reseque *etc* [re'seke] *vb ver* **resecar**
reserva [re'serβa] *nf* reserve; (*reservación*) reservation; **a ~ de que ...** unless ...; **con toda ~** in strictest confidence; **de ~** spare; **tener algo de ~** to have sth in reserve; **~ de indios** Indian reservation; (*Com*): **~ para amortización** depreciation allowance; **~ de caja *o* en efectivo** cash reserves; **reservas del Estado** government stock; **reservas en oro** gold reserves
reservado, -a [reser'βaðo, a] *adj* reserved; (*retraído*) cold, distant ■ *nm* private room; (*Ferro*) reserved compartment
reservar [reser'βar] *vt* (*guardar*) to keep; (*Ferro: Teat etc*) to reserve, book; **reservarse** *vr* to save o.s.; (*callar*) to keep to o.s.; **~ con exceso** to overbook

resfriado [res'friaðo] *nm* cold
resfriarse [res'friarse] *vr* to cool off; (*Med*) to catch (a) cold
resfrío [resf'rio] *nm* (*esp Am*) cold
resguardar [resɣwar'ðar] *vt* to protect, shield; **resguardarse** *vr*: **resguardarse de** to guard against
resguardo [res'ɣwarðo] *nm* defence; (*vale*) voucher; (*recibo*) receipt, slip
residencia [resi'ðenθja] *nf* residence; (*Univ*) hall of residence; **~ para ancianos** *o* **jubilados** rest home
residencial [resiðen'θjal] *adj* residential ■ *nf* (*urbanización*) housing estate (*Brit*), real estate development (*US*)
residente [resi'ðente] *adj, nm/f* resident
residir [resi'ðir] *vi* to reside, live; **~ en** to reside *o* lie in; (*consistir en*) to consist of
residual [resi'ðwal] *adj* residual; **aguas residuales** sewage
residuo [re'siðwo] *nm* residue; **residuos atmosféricos** *o* **radiactivos** fallout *sg*
resienta *etc* [re'sjenta] *vb ver* **resentirse**
resignación [resiɣna'θjon] *nf* resignation
resignarse [resiɣ'narse] *vr*: **~ a** *o* **con** to resign o.s. to, be resigned to
resina [re'sina] *nf* resin
resintiendo *etc* [resin'tjendo] *vb ver* **resentirse**
resistencia [resis'tenθja] *nf* (*dureza*) endurance, strength; (*oposición, Elec*) resistance; **la R~** (*Mil*) the Resistance
resistente [resis'tente] *adj* strong, hardy; (*Tec*) resistant; **~ al calor** heat-resistant
resistir [resis'tir] *vt* (*soportar*) to bear; (*oponerse a*) to resist, oppose; (*aguantar*) to put up with ■ *vi* to resist; (*aguantar*) to last, endure; **resistirse** *vr*: **resistirse a** to refuse to, resist; **no puedo ~ este frío** I can't bear *o* stand this cold; **me resisto a creerlo** I refuse to believe it; **se le resiste la química** chemistry escapes her
resol [re'sol] *nm* glare of the sun
resollar [reso'ʎar] *vi* to breathe noisily, wheeze
resolución [resolu'θjon] *nf* resolution; (*decisión*) decision; (*moción*) motion; **~ judicial** legal ruling; **tomar una ~** to take a decision
resoluto, -a [reso'luto, a] *adj* resolute
resolver [resol'βer] *vt* to resolve; (*solucionar*) to solve, resolve; (*decidir*) to decide, settle; **resolverse** *vr* to make up one's mind
resonancia [reso'nanθja] *nf* (*del sonido*) resonance; (*repercusión*) repercussion; (*fig*) wide effect, impact
resonante [reso'nante] *adj* resonant, resounding; (*fig*) tremendous
resonar [reso'nar] *vi* to ring, echo
resoplar [reso'plar] *vi* to snort; (*por cansancio*) to puff
resoplido [reso'pliðo] *nm* heavy breathing
resorte [re'sorte] *nm* spring; (*fig*) lever
respaldar [respal'dar] *vt* to back (up), support; (*Inform*) to back up; **respaldarse** *vr* to lean back; **respaldarse con** *o* **en** (*fig*) to take one's stand on
respaldo [res'paldo] *nm* (*de sillón*) back; (*fig*) support, backing
respectivo, -a [respek'tiβo, a] *adj* respective; **en lo ~ a** with regard to
respecto [res'pekto] *nm*: **al ~** on this matter; **con ~ a, ~ de** with regard to, in relation to
respetable [respe'taβle] *adj* respectable
respetar [respe'tar] *vt* to respect
respeto [res'peto] *nm* respect; (*acatamiento*) deference; **respetos** *nmpl* respects; **por ~ a** out of consideration for; **presentar sus respetos a** to pay one's respects to
respetuoso, -a [respe'twoso, a] *adj* respectful
respingo [res'pingo] *nm* start, jump
respiración [respira'θjon] *nf* breathing; (*Med*) respiration; (*ventilación*) ventilation
respirar [respi'rar] *vt, vi* to breathe; **no dejar ~ a algn** to keep on at sb; **estuvo escuchándole sin ~** he listened to him in complete silence
respiratorio, -a [respira'torjo, a] *adj* respiratory
respiro [res'piro] *nm* breathing; (*fig: descanso*) respite, rest; (*Com*) period of grace
resplandecer [resplande'θer] *vi* to shine
resplandeciente [resplande'θjente] *adj* resplendent, shining
resplandezca *etc* [resplan'deθka] *vb ver* **resplandecer**
resplandor [resplan'dor] *nm* brilliance, brightness; (*del fuego*) blaze
responder [respon'der] *vt* to answer ■ *vi* to answer; (*fig*) to respond; (*pey*) to answer back; (*corresponder*) to correspond; **~ a** (*situación etc*) to respond to; **~ a una pregunta** to answer a question; **~ a una descripción** to fit a description; **~ de** *o* **por** to answer for
respondón, -ona [respon'don, ona] *adj* cheeky
responsabilice *etc* [responsaβi'liθe] *vb ver* **responsabilizarse**
responsabilidad [responsaβili'ðað] *nf* responsibility; **bajo mi ~** on my authority; **~ ilimitada** (*Com*) unlimited liability
responsabilizarse [responsaβili'θarse] *vr* to make o.s. responsible, take charge

responsable [respon'sable] *adj* responsible; **la persona ~** the person in charge; **hacerse ~ de algo** to assume responsibility for sth
respuesta [res'pwesta] *nf* answer, reply; (*reacción*) response
resquebrajar [reskeβra'xar] *vt*, **resquebrajarse** *vr* to crack, split
resquemor [reske'mor] *nm* resentment
resquicio [res'kiθjo] *nm* chink; (*hendidura*) crack
resta ['resta] *nf* (*Mat*) remainder
restablecer [restaβle'θer] *vt* to re-establish, restore; **restablecerse** *vr* to recover
restablecimiento [restaβleθi'mjento] *nm* re-establishment; (*restauración*) restoration; (*Med*) recovery
restablezca *etc* [resta'βleθka] *vb ver* **restablecer**
restallar [resta'ʎar] *vi* to crack
restante [res'tante] *adj* remaining; **lo ~** the remainder; **los restantes** the rest, those left (over)
restar [res'tar] *vt* (*Mat*) to subtract; (*descontar*) to deduct; (*fig*) to take away ■ *vi* to remain, be left
restauración [restaura'θjon] *nf* restoration
restaurador, a [restaura'ðor, a] *nm/f* (*persona*) restorer
restaurante [restau'rante] *nm* restaurant
restaurar [restau'rar] *vt* to restore
restitución [restitu'θjon] *nf* return, restitution
restituir [restitu'ir] *vt* (*devolver*) to return, give back; (*rehabilitar*) to restore
restituyendo *etc* [restitu'jendo] *vb ver* **restituir**
resto ['resto] *nm* (*residuo*) rest, remainder; (*apuesta*) stake; **restos** *nmpl* remains; (*Culin*) leftovers, scraps; **restos mortales** mortal remains
restregar [restre'ɣar] *vt* to scrub, rub
restregué [restre'ɣe], **restreguemos** *etc* [restre'ɣemos] *vb ver* **restregar**
restricción [restrik'θjon] *nf* restriction; **sin ~ de** without restrictions on *o* as to; **hablar sin restricciones** to talk freely
restrictivo, -a [restrik'tiβo, a] *adj* restrictive
restriego *etc* [res'trjeɣo], **restriegue** *etc* [res'trjeɣe] *vb ver* **restregar**
restringir [restrin'xir] *vt* to restrict, limit
restrinja *etc* [res'trinxa] *vb ver* **restringir**
resucitar [resuθi'tar] *vt, vi* to resuscitate, revive
resuello *etc* [re'sweʎo] *vb ver* **resollar** ■ *nm* (*aliento*) breath
resuelto, -a [re'swelto, a] *pp de* **resolver** ■ *adj* resolute, determined; **estar ~ a algo** to be set on sth; **estar ~ a hacer algo** to be determined to do sth
resuelva *etc* [re'swelβa] *vb ver* **resolver**
resuene *etc* [re'swene] *vb ver* **resonar**
resulta [re'sulta] *nf* result; **de resultas de** as a result of
resultado [resul'taðo] *nm* result; (*conclusión*) outcome; **resultados** *nmpl* (*Inform*) output *sg*; **dar ~** to produce results
resultante [resul'tante] *adj* resulting, resultant
resultar [resul'tar] *vi* (*ser*) to be; (*llegar a ser*) to turn out to be; (*salir bien*) to turn out well; (*seguir*) to ensue; **~ a** (*Com*) to amount to; **~ de** to stem from; **~ en** to result in, produce; **resulta que ...** (*en consecuencia*) it follows that ...; (*parece que*) it seems that ...; **el conductor resultó muerto** the driver was killed; **no resultó** it didn't work *o* come off; **me resulta difícil hacerlo** it's difficult for me to do it
resumen [re'sumen] *nm* summary, résumé; **en ~** in short
resumir [resu'mir] *vt* to sum up; (*condensar*) to summarize; (*cortar*) to abridge, cut down; **resumirse** *vr*: **la situación se resume en pocas palabras** the situation can be summed up in a few words
resurgir [resur'xir] *vi* (*reaparecer*) to reappear
resurrección [resurrek'θjon] *nf* resurrection
retablo [re'taβlo] *nm* altarpiece
retaguardia [reta'ɣwarðja] *nf* rearguard
retahíla [reta'ila] *nf* series, string; (*de injurias*) volley, stream
retal [re'tal] *nm* remnant
retar [re'tar] *vt* (*gen*) to challenge; (*desafiar*) to defy, dare
retardar [retar'ðar] *vt* (*demorar*) to delay; (*hacer más lento*) to slow down; (*retener*) to hold back
retardo [re'tarðo] *nm* delay
retazo [re'taθo] *nm* snippet (*Brit*), fragment
RETD *nf abr* (*Esp Telec*) = **Red Especial de Transmisión de Datos**
rete ... ['rete] *pref* very, extremely
retén [re'ten] *nm* (*Am*) roadblock, checkpoint
retención [reten'θjon] *nf* retention; (*de pago*) deduction; **~ de llamadas** (*Telec*) hold facility
retendré *etc* [reten'dre] *vb ver* **retener**
retener [rete'ner] *vt* (*guardar*) to retain, keep; (*intereses*) to withhold
retenga *etc* [re'tenga] *vb ver* **retener**
reticencia [reti'θenθja] *nf* (*insinuación*) insinuation, (malevolent) suggestion; (*verdad a medias*) half-truth
reticente [reti'θente] *adj* (*insinuador*)

insinuating; (*engañoso*) deceptive
retiene *etc* [re'tjene] *vb ver* **retener**
retina [re'tina] *nf* retina
retintín [retin'tin] *nm* jangle, jingle; **decir algo con ~** to say sth sarcastically
retirado, -a [reti'raðo, a] *adj* (*lugar*) remote; (*vida*) quiet; (*jubilado*) retired ▪ *nf* (*Mil*) retreat; (*de dinero*) withdrawal; (*de embajador*) recall; **batirse en retirada** to retreat
retirar [reti'rar] *vt* to withdraw; (*la mano*) to draw back; (*quitar*) to remove; (*dinero*) to take out, withdraw; (*jubilar*) to retire, pension off; **retirarse** *vr* to retreat, withdraw; (*jubilarse*) to retire; (*acostarse*) to retire, go to bed
retiro [re'tiro] *nm* retreat; (*jubilación, tb Deporte*) retirement; (*pago*) pension; (*lugar*) quiet place
reto ['reto] *nm* dare, challenge
retocar [reto'kar] *vt* to touch up, retouch
retoce *etc* [re'toθe] *vb ver* **retozar**
retoño [re'toɲo] *nm* sprout, shoot; (*fig*) offspring, child
retoque *etc* [re'toke] *vb ver* **retocar** ▪ *nm* retouching
retorcer [retor'θer] *vt* to twist; (*argumento*) to turn, twist; (*manos, lavado*) to wring; **retorcerse** *vr* to become twisted; (*persona*) to writhe; **retorcerse de dolor** to writhe in *o* squirm with pain
retorcido, -a [retor'θiðo, a] *adj* (*tb fig*) twisted
retorcimiento [retorθi'mjento] *nm* twist, twisting; (*fig*) deviousness
retórico, -a [re'toriko, a] *adj* rhetorical; (*pey*) affected, windy ▪ *nf* rhetoric; (*pey*) affectedness
retornable [retor'naβle] *adj* returnable
retornar [retor'nar] *vt* to return, give back ▪ *vi* to return, go/come back
retorno [re'torno] *nm* return; **~ del carro** (*Inform: Tip*) carriage return
retortero [retor'tero] *nm*: **andar al ~** to bustle about, have heaps of things to do; **andar al ~ por algn** to be madly in love with sb
retortijón [retorti'xon] *nm* twist, twisting; **~ de tripas** stomach cramp
retorzamos *etc* [retor'θamos] *vb ver* **retorcer**
retozar [reto'θar] *vi* (*juguetear*) to frolic, romp; (*saltar*) to gambol
retozón, -ona [reto'θon, ona] *adj* playful
retracción [retrak'θjon] *nf* retraction
retractarse [retrak'tarse] *vr* to retract; **me retracto** I take that back
retraerse [retra'erse] *vr* to retreat, withdraw
retraído, -a [retra'iðo, a] *adj* shy, retiring
retraiga *etc* [re'traiɣa] *vb ver* **retraerse**
retraimiento [retrai'mjento] *nm* retirement; (*timidez*) shyness
retraje *etc* [re'traxe], **retrajera** *etc* [retra'xera] *vb ver* **retraerse**
retransmisión [retransmi'sjon] *nf* repeat (broadcast)
retransmitir [retransmi'tir] *vt* (*mensaje*) to relay; (*TV etc*) to repeat, retransmit; (*: en vivo*) to broadcast live
retrasado, -a [retra'saðo, a] *adj* late; (*Med*) mentally retarded; (*país etc*) backward, underdeveloped; **estar ~** (*reloj*) to be slow; (*persona, industria*) to be *o* lag behind
retrasar [retra'sar] *vt* (*demorar*) to postpone, put off; (*retardar*) to slow down ▪ *vi*, **retrasarse** *vr* (*atrasarse*) to be late; (*reloj*) to be slow; (*producción*) to fall (away); (*quedarse atrás*) to lag behind
retraso [re'traso] *nm* (*demora*) delay; (*lentitud*) slowness; (*tardanza*) lateness; (*atraso*) backwardness; **retrasos** *nmpl* (*Com*) arrears; (*deudas*) deficit *sg*, debts; **llegar con ~** to arrive late; **llegar con 25 minutos de ~** to be 25 minutes late; **llevo un ~ de seis semanas** I'm six weeks behind (with my work *etc*); **~ mental** mental deficiency
retratar [retra'tar] *vt* (*Arte*) to paint the portrait of; (*fotografiar*) to photograph; (*fig*) to depict, describe; **retratarse** *vr* to have one's portrait painted; to have one's photograph taken
retratista [retra'tista] *nm/f* (*Arte*) (portrait) painter; (*Foto*) photographer
retrato [re'trato] *nm* portrait; (*Foto*) photograph; (*descripción*) portrayal, depiction; (*fig*) likeness; **ser el vivo ~ de** to be the spitting image of
retrato-robot [re'tratoro'βo(t)] (*pl* **retratos-robot**) *nm* identikit picture
retrayendo *etc* [retra'jendo] *vb ver* **retraerse**
retreta [re'treta] *nf* retreat
retrete [re'trete] *nm* toilet
retribución [retriβu'θjon] *nf* (*recompensa*) reward; (*pago*) pay, payment
retribuir [retriβu'ir] *vt* (*recompensar*) to reward; (*pagar*) to pay
retribuyendo *etc* [retriβu'jendo] *vb ver* **retribuir**
retro ... [retro] *pref* retro...
retroactivo, -a [retroak'tiβo, a] *adj* retroactive, retrospective; **dar efecto ~ a un pago** to backdate a payment
retroalimentación [retroalimenta'θjon] *nf* (*Inform*) feedback
retroceder [retroθe'ðer] *vi* (*echarse atrás*) to move back(wards); (*fig*) to back down; **no ~** to stand firm; **la policía hizo ~ a la multitud** the police forced the crowd back
retroceso [retro'θeso] *nm* backward

movement; (*Med*) relapse; (*Com*) recession, depression; (*fig*) backing down
retrógrado, -a [re'troɣraðo, a] *adj* retrograde, retrogressive; (*Pol*) reactionary
retropropulsión [retropropul'sjon] *nf* jet propulsion
retrospectivo, -a [retrospek'tiβo, a] *adj* retrospective; **mirada retrospectiva** backward glance
retrovisor [retroβi'sor] *nm* rear-view mirror
retuerce *etc* [re'twerθe], **retuerza** *etc* [re'twerθa] *vb ver* **retorcer**
retumbante [retum'bante] *adj* resounding
retumbar [retum'bar] *vi* to echo, resound; (*continuamente*) to reverberate
retuve *etc* [re'tuβe] *vb ver* **retener**
reuma ['reuma] *nm* rheumatism
reumático, -a [reu'matiko, a] *adj* rheumatic
reumatismo [reuma'tismo] *nm* rheumatism
reunificar [reunifi'kar] *vt* to reunify
reunifique *etc* [reuni'fike] *vb ver* **reunificar**
reunión [reu'njon] *nf* (*asamblea*) meeting; (*fiesta*) party; **~ en la cumbre** summit meeting; **~ de ventas** (*Com*) sales meeting
reunir [reu'nir] *vt* (*juntar*) to reunite, join (together); (*recoger*) to gather (together); (*personas*) to bring *o* get together; (*cualidades*) to combine; **reunirse** *vr* (*personas: en asamblea*) to meet, gather; **reunió a sus amigos para discutirlo** he got his friends together to talk it over
reválida [re'βaliða] *nf* (*Escol*) final examination
revalidar [reβali'ðar] *vt* (*ratificar*) to confirm, ratify
revalorar [reβalo'rar] *vt* to revalue, reassess
revalorización [reβaloriθa'θjon], **revaloración** [reβalora'θjon] *nf* revaluation; (*Econ*) reassessment
revancha [re'βantʃa] *nf* revenge; (*Deporte*) return match; (*Boxeo*) return fight
revelación [reβela'θjon] *nf* revelation
revelado [reβe'laðo] *nm* developing
revelador, a [reβela'ðor, a] *adj* revealing
revelar [reβe'lar] *vt* to reveal; (*secreto*) to disclose; (*mostrar*) to show; (*Foto*) to develop
revendedor, a [reβende'ðor, a] *nm/f* retailer; (*pey*) ticket tout
revendré *etc* [reβen'dre], **revenga** *etc* [re'βenga] *vb ver* **revenirse**
revenirse [reβe'nirse] *vr* to shrink; (*comida*) to go bad *o* off; (*vino*) to sour; (*Culin*) to get tough
reventa [re'βenta] *nf* resale; (*especulación*) speculation; (*de entradas*) touting
reventar [reβen'tar] *vt* to burst, explode; (*molestar*) to annoy, rile ■ *vi*, **reventarse** *vr* (*estallar*) to burst, explode; **me revienta tener que ponérmelo** I hate having to wear it; **~ de** (*fig*) to be bursting with; **~ por** to be bursting to
reventón [reβen'ton] *nm* (*Auto*) blow-out (*Brit*), flat (*US*)
reverberación [reβerβera'θjon] *nf* reverberation
reverberar [reβerβe'rar] *vi* (*luz*) to play, be reflected; (*superficie*) to shimmer; (*nieve*) to glare; (*sonido*) to reverberate
reverbero [reβer'βero] *nm* play; shimmer, shine; glare; reverberation
reverencia [reβe'renθja] *nf* reverence; (*inclinación*) bow
reverenciar [reβeren'θjar] *vt* to revere
reverendo, -a [reβe'rendo, a] *adj* reverend; (*fam*) big, awful; **un ~ imbécil** an awful idiot
reverente [reβe'rente] *adj* reverent
reversible [reβer'siβle] *adj* reversible
reverso [re'βerso] *nm* back, other side; (*de moneda*) reverse
revertir [reβer'tir] *vi* to revert; **~ en beneficio de** to be to the advantage of; **~ en perjuicio de** to be to the detriment of
revés [re'βes] *nm* back, wrong side; (*fig*) reverse, setback; (*Deporte*) backhand; **al ~** the wrong way round; (*de arriba abajo*) upside down; (*ropa*) inside out; **y al ~** and vice versa; **volver algo del ~** to turn sth round; (*ropa*) to turn sth inside out; **los reveses de la fortuna** the blows of fate
revestir [reβes'tir] *vt* (*poner*) to put on; (*cubrir*) to cover, coat; (*cualidad*) to have, possess; **revestirse** *vr* (*Rel*) to put on one's vestments; (*ponerse*) to put on; **~ con** *o* **de** to arm o.s. with; **el acto revestía gran solemnidad** the ceremony had great dignity
reviejo, -a [re'βjexo, a] *adj* very old, ancient
reviene *etc* [re'βjene] *vb ver* **revenirse**
reviente *etc* [re'βjente] *vb ver* **reventar**
revierta *etc* [re'βjerta] *vb ver* **revertir**
reviniendo *etc* [reβi'njendo] *vb ver* **revenirse**
revirtiendo *etc* [reβir'tjendo] *vb ver* **revertir**
revisar [reβi'sar] *vt* (*examinar*) to check; (*texto etc*) to revise; (*Jur*) to review
revisión [reβi'sjon] *nf* revision; **~ aduanera** customs inspection; **~ de cuentas** audit
revisor, a [reβi'sor, a] *nm/f* inspector; (*Ferro*) ticket collector; **~ de cuentas** auditor
revista *etc* [re'βista] *vb ver* **revestir** ■ *nf* magazine, review; (*Teat*) revue; (*inspección*) inspection; **~ literaria** literary review; **~ de libros** book reviews (page); **pasar ~ a** to review, inspect
revivir [reβi'βir] *vt* (*recordar*) to revive memories of ■ *vi* to revive
revocación [reβoka'θjon] *nf* repeal

revocar [reβo'kar] *vt* *(decisión)* to revoke; *(Arq)* to plaster
revolcar [reβol'kar] *vt* to knock down, send flying; **revolcarse** *vr* to roll about
revolcón [reβol'kon] *nm* tumble
revolotear [reβolote'ar] *vi* to flutter
revoloteo [reβolo'teo] *nm* fluttering
revolqué [reβol'ke], **revolquemos** *etc* [reβol'kemos] *vb ver* **revolcar**
revoltijo [reβol'tixo] *nm* mess, jumble
revoltoso, -a [reβol'toso, a] *adj* *(travieso)* naughty, unruly
revolución [reβolu'θjon] *nf* revolution
revolucionar [reβoluθjo'nar] *vt* to revolutionize
revolucionario, -a [reβoluθjo'narjo, a] *adj, nm/f* revolutionary
revolver [reβol'βer] *vt* *(desordenar)* to disturb, mess up; *(agitar)* to shake; *(líquido)* to stir; *(mover)* to move about; *(Pol)* to stir up ■ *vi*: ~ **en** to go through, rummage (about) in; **revolverse** *vr* *(en cama)* to toss and turn; *(Meteorología)* to break, turn stormy; **revolverse contra** to turn on *o* against; **han revuelto toda la casa** they've turned the whole house upside down
revólver [re'βolβer] *nm* revolver
revoque *etc* [re'βoke] *vb ver* **revocar**
revuelco *etc* [re'βwelko] *vb ver* **revolcar**
revuelo [re'βwelo] *nm* fluttering; *(fig)* commotion; **armar** *o* **levantar un gran ~** to cause a great stir
revuelque *etc* [re'βwelke] *vb ver* **revolcar**
revuelto, -a [re'βwelto, a] *pp de* **revolver** ■ *adj* *(mezclado)* mixed-up, in disorder; *(mar)* rough; *(tiempo)* unsettled ■ *nf* *(motín)* revolt; *(agitación)* commotion; **todo estaba ~** everything was in disorder *o* was topsy-turvy
revuelva *etc* [re'βwelβa] *vb ver* **revolver**
revulsivo [reβul'siβo] *nm*: **servir de ~** to have a salutary effect
rey [rei] *nm* king; **los Reyes** the King and Queen; *ver tb* **Baraja Española**; *see note*

REY

The night before the 6th of January (the Epiphany), which is a holiday in Spain, children go to bed expecting *los Reyes Magos*, the Three Wise Men who visited the baby Jesus, to bring them presents. Twelfth night processions, known as *cabalgatas*, take place that evening, when 3 people dressed as *los Reyes Magos* arrive in the town by land or sea to the delight of the children.

reyerta [re'jerta] *nf* quarrel, brawl
rezagado, -a [reθa'ɣaðo, a] *adj*: **quedar ~** to be left behind; *(estar retrasado)* to be late, be behind ■ *nm/f* straggler
rezagar [reθa'ɣar] *vt* *(dejar atrás)* to leave behind; *(retrasar)* to delay, postpone; **rezagarse** *vr* *(atrasarse)* to fall behind
rezague *etc* [re'θaɣe] *vb ver* **rezagar**
rezar [re'θar] *vi* to pray; ~ **con** *(fam)* to concern, have to do with
rezo ['reθo] *nm* prayer
rezongar [reθon'gar] *vi* to grumble; *(murmurar)* to mutter; *(refunfuñar)* to growl
rezongue *etc* [re'θonge] *vb ver* **rezongar**
rezumar [reθu'mar] *vt* to ooze ■ *vi* to leak; **rezumarse** *vr* to leak out
RFA *nf abr* (= *República Federal Alemana*) *ver* **república**
RI *abr* = **regimiento de infantería**
ría ['ria] *nf* estuary
riachuelo [rja'tʃwelo] *nm* stream
riada [ri'aða] *nf* flood
ribera [ri'βera] *nf* *(de río)* bank; (: *área*) riverside
ribete [ri'βete] *nm* *(de vestido)* border; *(fig)* addition
ribetear [riβete'ar] *vt* to edge, border
rice *etc* ['riθe] *vb ver* **rizar**
ricino [ri'θino] *nm*: **aceite de ~** castor oil
rico, -a ['riko, a] *adj* *(adinerado)* rich, wealthy; *(lujoso)* luxurious; *(comida)* delicious; *(niño)* lovely, cute ■ *nm/f* rich person; **nuevo ~** nouveau riche
rictus ['riktus] *nm* *(mueca)* sneer, grin; **~ de amargura** bitter smile
ridiculez [riðiku'leθ] *nf* absurdity
ridiculice *etc* [riðiku'liθe] *vb ver* **ridiculizar**
ridiculizar [riðikuli'θar] *vt* to ridicule
ridículo, -a [ri'ðikulo, a] *adj* ridiculous; **hacer el ~** to make a fool of o.s.; **poner a algn en ~** to make a fool of sb; **ponerse en ~** to make a fool of o.s.
riego *etc* ['rjeɣo] *vb ver* **regar** ■ *nm* *(aspersión)* watering; *(irrigación)* irrigation
riegue *etc* ['rjeɣe] *vb ver* **regar**
riel [rjel] *nm* rail
rienda ['rjenda] *nf* rein; *(fig)* restraint, moderating influence; **dar ~ suelta a** to give free rein to; **llevar las riendas** to be in charge
riendo ['rjendo] *vb ver* **reír**
riesgo ['rjesɣo] *nm* risk; **seguro a** *o* **contra todo ~** comprehensive insurance; **~ para la salud** health hazard; **correr el ~ de** to run the risk of
Rif [rif] *nm* Rif(f)
rifa ['rifa] *nf* *(lotería)* raffle

rifar [ri'far] *vt* to raffle
rifeño, -a [ri'feɲo, a] *adj* of the Rif(f), Rif(f)ian ■ *nm/f* Rif(f)ian, Rif(f)
rifle ['rifle] *nm* rifle
rigidez [rixi'ðeθ] *nf* rigidity, stiffness; *(fig)* strictness
rígido, -a ['rixiðo, a] *adj* rigid, stiff; *(moralmente)* strict, inflexible; *(cara)* wooden, expressionless
rigiendo *etc* [ri'xjendo] *vb ver* **regir**
rigor [ri'ɣor] *nm* strictness, rigour; *(dureza)* toughness; *(inclemencia)* harshness; *(meticulosidad)* accuracy; **el ~ del verano** the hottest part of the summer; **con todo ~ científico** with scientific precision; **de ~** de rigueur, essential; **después de los saludos de ~** after the inevitable greetings
riguroso, -a [riɣu'roso, a] *adj* rigorous; *(Meteorología)* harsh; *(severo)* severe
rija *etc* ['rixa] *vb ver* **regir** ■ *nf* quarrel
rima ['rima] *nf* rhyme; **rimas** *nfpl* verse *sg*; **~ imperfecta** assonance; **~ rimando** *(fam)* merrily
rimar [ri'mar] *vi* to rhyme
rimbombante [rimbom'bante] *adj* *(fig)* pompous
rímel, rímmel ['rimel] *nm* mascara
rimero [ri'mero] *nm* stack, pile
Rin [rin] *nm* Rhine
rincón [rin'kon] *nm* corner *(inside)*
rindiendo *etc* [rin'djendo] *vb ver* **rendir**
ring [riŋ] *nm* *(Boxeo)* ring
rinoceronte [rinoθe'ronte] *nm* rhinoceros
riña ['riɲa] *nf* *(disputa)* argument; *(pelea)* brawl
riñendo *etc* [ri'ɲendo] *vb ver* **reñir**
riñón [ri'ɲon] *nm* kidney; **me costó un ~** *(fam)* it cost me an arm and a leg; **tener riñones** to have guts
río *etc* ['rio] *vb ver* **reír** ■ *nm* river; *(fig)* torrent, stream; **~ abajo/arriba** downstream/ upstream; **cuando el ~ suena, agua lleva** there's no smoke without fire
rió [ri'o] *vb ver* **reír**
Río de Janeiro ['rioðexa'neiro] *nm* Rio de Janeiro
Río de la Plata ['rioðela'plata] *nm* Rio de la Plata, River Plate
Rioja [ri'oxa] *nf*: **La ~** La Rioja ■ *nm*: **rioja** rioja wine
riojano, -a [rjo'xano, a] *adj, nm/f* Riojan
rioplatense [riopla'tense] *adj* of *o* from the River Plate region ■ *nm/f* native *o* inhabitant of the River Plate region
riqueza [ri'keθa] *nf* wealth, riches *pl*; *(cualidad)* richness
risa ['risa] *nf* laughter; *(una risa)* laugh; **¡qué ~!** what a laugh!; **caerse** *o* **morirse de ~** to split one's sides laughing, die laughing; **tomar algo a ~** to laugh sth off
risco ['risko] *nm* crag, cliff
risible [ri'siβle] *adj* ludicrous, laughable
risotada [riso'taða] *nf* guffaw, loud laugh
ristra ['ristra] *nf* string
ristre ['ristre] *nm*: **en ~** at the ready
risueño, -a [ri'sweɲo, a] *adj* *(sonriente)* smiling; *(contento)* cheerful
ritmo ['ritmo] *nm* rhythm; **a ~ lento** slowly; **trabajar a ~ lento** to go slow
rito ['rito] *nm* rite
ritual [ri'twal] *adj, nm* ritual
rival [ri'βal] *adj, nm/f* rival
rivalice *etc* [riβa'liθe] *vb ver* **rivalizar**
rivalidad [riβali'ðað] *nf* rivalry, competition
rivalizar [riβali'θar] *vi*: **~ con** to rival, compete with
rizado, -a [ri'θaðo, a] *adj* *(pelo)* curly; *(superficie)* ridged; *(terreno)* undulating; *(mar)* choppy ■ *nm* curls *pl*
rizar [ri'θar] *vt* to curl; **rizarse** *vr* *(el pelo)* to curl; *(agua)* to ripple; *(el mar)* to become choppy
rizo ['riθo] *nm* curl; *(en agua)* ripple
Rma. *abr (= Reverendísima) courtesy title*
Rmo. *abr (= Reverendísimo)* Rt. Rev.
RNE *nf abr* = **Radio Nacional de España**
R. O. *abr (= Real Orden)* royal order
robar [ro'βar] *vt* to rob; *(objeto)* to steal; *(casa etc)* to break into; *(Naipes)* to draw; *(atención)* to steal, capture; *(paciencia)* to exhaust
roble ['roβle] *nm* oak
robledal [roβle'ðal], **robledo** [ro'βleðo] *nm* oakwood
robo ['roβo] *nm* robbery, theft; *(objeto robado)* stolen article *o* goods *pl*; **¡esto es un ~!** this is daylight robbery!
robot [ro'βo(t)] *(pl* **robots***)* *adj, nm* robot ■ *nm* *(tb:* **robot de cocina***)* food processor
robótica [ro'βotika] *nf* robotics *sg*
robustecer [roβuste'θer] *vt* to strengthen
robustezca *etc* [roβus'teθka] *vb ver* **robustecer**
robusto, -a [ro'βusto, a] *adj* robust, strong
ROC *abr (Inform: = reconocimiento óptico de caracteres)* OCR
roca ['roka] *nf* rock; **la R~** the Rock (of Gibraltar)
roce *etc* ['roθe] *vb ver* **rozar** ■ *nm* rub, rubbing; *(caricia)* brush; *(Tec)* friction; *(en la piel)* graze; **tener ~ con** to have a brush with
rociar [ro'θjar] *vt* to sprinkle, spray
rocín [ro'θin] *nm* nag, hack
rocío [ro'θio] *nm* dew
rock [rok] *adj inv, nm* *(Mus)* rock *(cpd)*

rockero, -a [ro'kero, a] *adj* rock *cpd* ■ *nm/f* rocker
rocoso, -a [ro'koso, a] *adj* rocky
rodado, -a [ro'ðaðo, a] *adj* (*con ruedas*) wheeled ■ *nf* rut
rodaja [ro'ðaxa] *nf* (*raja*) slice
rodaje [ro'ðaxe] *nm* (*Cine*) shooting, filming; (*Auto*): **en ~** running in
rodamiento [roða'mjento] *nm* (*Auto*) tread
Ródano ['roðano] *nm* Rhône
rodar [ro'ðar] *vt* (*vehículo*) to wheel (along); (*escalera*) to roll down; (*viajar por*) to travel (over) ■ *vi* to roll; (*coche*) to go, run; (*Cine*) to shoot, film; (*persona*) to move about (from place to place), drift; **echarlo todo a ~** (*fig*) to mess it all up
Rodas ['roðas] *nf* Rhodes
rodear [roðe'ar] *vt* to surround ■ *vi* to go round; **rodearse** *vr*: **rodearse de amigos** to surround o.s. with friends
rodeo [ro'ðeo] *nm* (*ruta indirecta*) long way round, roundabout way; (*desvío*) detour; (*evasión*) evasion; (*Am*) rodeo; **dejarse de rodeos** to talk straight; **hablar sin rodeos** to come to the point, speak plainly
rodilla [ro'ðiʎa] *nf* knee; **de rodillas** kneeling
rodillo [ro'ðiʎo] *nm* roller; (*Culin*) rolling-pin; (*en máquina de escribir, impresora*) platen
rododendro [roðo'ðendro] *nm* rhododendron
roedor, a [roe'ðor, a] *adj* gnawing ■ *nm* rodent
roer [ro'er] *vt* (*masticar*) to gnaw; (*corroer, fig*) to corrode
rogar [ro'ɣar] *vt* (*pedir*) to beg, ask for ■ *vi* (*suplicar*) to beg, plead; **rogarse** *vr*: **se ruega no fumar** please do not smoke; **~ que** (*+ subjun*) to ask to ...; **ruegue a este señor que nos deje en paz** please ask this gentleman to leave us alone; **no se hace de ~** he doesn't have to be asked twice
rogué [ro'ɣe], **roguemos** *etc* [ro'ɣemos] *vb ver* **rogar**
rojizo, -a [ro'xiθo, a] *adj* reddish
rojo, -a ['roxo, a] *adj* red ■ *nm* red (colour); (*Pol*) red; **ponerse ~** to turn red, blush; **al ~ vivo** red-hot
rol [rol] *nm* list, roll; (*esp Am: papel*) role
rollizo, -a [ro'ʎiθo, a] *adj* (*objeto*) cylindrical; (*persona*) plump
rollo, -a ['roʎo, a] *adj* (*fam*) boring, tedious ■ *nm* roll; (*de cuerda*) coil; (*de madera*) log; (*fam*) bore; (*discurso*) boring speech; **¡qué ~!** what a carry-on!; **la conferencia fue un ~** the lecture was a big drag
ROM [rom] *nf abr* (= *memoria de sólo lectura*) ROM
Roma ['roma] *nf* Rome; **por todas partes se va a ~** all roads lead to Rome
romance [ro'manθe] *nm* (*Ling*) Romance language; (*Lit*) ballad; **hablar en ~** to speak plainly
románico, -a [ro'maniko, a] *adj, nm* Romanesque
romano, -a [ro'mano, a] *adj* Roman, of Rome ■ *nm/f* Roman
romanticismo [romanti'θismo] *nm* romanticism
romántico, -a [ro'mantiko, a] *adj* romantic
rombo ['rombo] *nm* (*Geom*) rhombus; (*diseño*) diamond; (*Tip*) lozenge
romería [rome'ria] *nf* (*Rel*) pilgrimage; (*excursión*) trip, outing; *see note*

ROMERÍA

Originally a pilgrimage to a shrine or church to express devotion to Our Lady or a local Saint, the *romería* has also become a rural *fiesta* which accompanies the pilgrimage. People come from all over to attend, bringing their own food and drink, and spend the day in celebration.

romero, -a [ro'mero, a] *nm/f* pilgrim ■ *nm* rosemary
romo, -a ['romo, a] *adj* blunt; (*fig*) dull
rompecabezas [rompeka'βeθas] *nm inv* riddle, puzzle; (*juego*) jigsaw (puzzle)
rompehielos [rompe'jelos] *nm inv* icebreaker
rompeolas [rompe'olas] *nm inv* breakwater
romper [rom'per] *vt* to break; (*hacer pedazos*) to smash; (*papel, tela etc*) to tear, rip; (*relaciones*) to break off ■ *vi* (*olas*) to break; (*sol, diente*) to break through; **~ un contrato** to break a contract; **~ a** to start (suddenly) to; **~ a llorar** to burst into tears; **~ con algn** to fall out with sb; **ha roto con su novio** she has broken up with her fiancé
rompimiento [rompi'mjento] *nm* (*acto*) breaking; (*fig*) break; (*quiebra*) crack; **~ de relaciones** breaking off of relations
ron [ron] *nm* rum
roncar [ron'kar] *vi* (*al dormir*) to snore; (*animal*) to roar
roncha ['rontʃa] *nf* (*cardenal*) bruise; (*hinchazón*) swelling
ronco, -a ['ronko, a] *adj* (*afónico*) hoarse; (*áspero*) raucous
ronda ['ronda] *nf* (*de bebidas etc*) round; (*patrulla*) patrol; (*de naipes*) hand, game; **ir de ~** to do one's round
rondar [ron'dar] *vt* to patrol; (*a una persona*) to hang round; (*molestar*) to harass; (*a una chica*) to court ■ *vi* to patrol; (*fig*) to prowl round;

(*Mus*) to go serenading
rondeño, -a [ron'deɲo, a] *adj* of *o* from Ronda ■ *nm/f* native *o* inhabitant of Ronda
ronque *etc* ['ronke] *vb ver* **roncar**
ronquido [ron'kiðo] *nm* snore, snoring
ronronear [ronrone'ar] *vi* to purr
ronroneo [ronro'neo] *nm* purr
roña ['roɲa] *nf* (*en veterinaria*) mange; (*mugre*) dirt, grime; (*óxido*) rust
roñica [ro'ɲika] *nm/f* (*fam*) skinflint
roñoso, -a [ro'ɲoso, a] *adj* (*mugriento*) filthy; (*tacaño*) mean
ropa ['ropa] *nf* clothes *pl*, clothing; **~ blanca** linen; **~ de cama** bed linen; **~ interior** underwear; **~ lavada** *o* **para lavar** washing; **~ planchada** ironing; **~ sucia** dirty clothes *pl*, washing; **~ usada** secondhand clothes
ropaje [ro'paxe] *nm* gown, robes *pl*
ropero [ro'pero] *nm* linen cupboard; (*guardarropa*) wardrobe
rosa ['rosa] *adj inv* pink ■ *nf* rose; (*Anat*) red birthmark; **~ de los vientos** the compass; **estar como una ~** to feel as fresh as a daisy; **(color) de ~** pink
rosado, -a [ro'saðo, a] *adj* pink ■ *nm* rosé
rosal [ro'sal] *nm* rosebush
rosaleda [rosa'leða] *nf* rose bed *o* garden
rosario [ro'sarjo] *nm* (*Rel*) rosary; (*fig: serie*) string; **rezar el ~** to say the rosary
rosbif [ros'βif] *nm* roast beef
rosca ['roska] *nf* (*de tornillo*) thread; (*de humo*) coil, spiral; (*pan, postre*) ring-shaped roll/ pastry; **hacer la ~ a algn** (*fam*) to suck up to sb; **pasarse de ~** (*fig*) to go too far
Rosellón [rose'ʎon] *nm* Roussillon
rosetón [rose'ton] *nm* rosette; (*Arq*) rose window
rosquilla [ros'kiʎa] *nf* *small ring-shaped cake*; (*de humo*) ring
rosticería [rostise'ria] *nf* (*Am*) *roast chicken shop*
rostro ['rostro] *nm* (*cara*) face; (*fig*) cheek
rotación [rota'θjon] *nf* rotation; **~ de cultivos** crop rotation
rotativo, -a [rota'tiβo, a] *adj* rotary ■ *nm* newspaper
roto, -a ['roto, a] *pp de* **romper** ■ *adj* broken; (*en pedazos*) smashed; (*tela, papel*) torn; (*vida*) shattered ■ *nm* (*en vestido*) hole, tear
rótula ['rotula] *nf* kneecap; (*Tec*) ball-and-socket joint
rotulador [rotula'ðor] *nm* felt-tip pen
rotular [rotu'lar] *vt* (*carta, documento*) to head, entitle; (*objeto*) to label
rótulo ['rotulo] *nm* (*título*) heading, title; (*etiqueta*) label; (*letrero*) sign
rotundo, -a [ro'tundo, a] *adj* round; (*enfático*) emphatic
rotura [ro'tura] *nf* (*rompimiento*) breaking; (*Med*) fracture
roturar [rotu'rar] *vt* to plough
roulote [ru'lote] *nf* caravan (*Brit*), trailer (*US*)
rozado, -a [ro'θaðo, a] *adj* worn
rozadura [roθa'ðura] *nf* abrasion, graze
rozar [ro'θar] *vt* (*frotar*) to rub; (*ensuciar*) to dirty; (*Med*) to graze; (*tocar ligeramente*) to shave, skim; (*fig*) to touch *o* border on; **rozarse** *vr* to rub (together); **~ con** (*fam*) to rub shoulders with
Rte. *abr* = **remite, remitente**
RTVE *nf abr* (*TV*) = **Radiotelevisión Española**
Ruán [ru'an] *nm* Rouen
rubéola [ru'βeola] *nf* German measles, rubella
rubí [ru'βi] *nm* ruby; (*de reloj*) jewel
rubio, -a ['ruβjo, a] *adj* fair-haired, blond(e) ■ *nm/f* blond/blonde; **tabaco ~** Virginia tobacco; **(cerveza) rubia** lager
rubor [ru'βor] *nm* (*sonrojo*) blush; (*timidez*) bashfulness
ruborice *etc* [ruβo'riθe] *vb ver* **ruborizarse**
ruborizarse [ruβori'θarse] *vr* to blush
ruboroso, -a [ruβo'roso, a] *adj* blushing
rúbrica ['ruβrika] *nf* (*título*) title, heading; (*de la firma*) flourish; **bajo la ~ de** under the heading of
rubricar [ruβri'kar] *vt* (*firmar*) to sign with a flourish; (*concluir*) to sign and seal
rubrique *etc* [ru'βrike] *vb ver* **rubricar**
rudeza [ru'ðeθa] *nf* (*tosquedad*) coarseness; (*sencillez*) simplicity
rudimentario, -a [ruðimen'tarjo, a] *adj* rudimentary, basic
rudo, -a ['ruðo, a] *adj* (*sin pulir*) unpolished; (*grosero*) coarse; (*violento*) violent; (*sencillo*) simple
rueda ['rweða] *nf* wheel; (*círculo*) ring, circle; (*rodaja*) slice, round; (*en impresora etc*) sprocket; **~ delantera/trasera/de repuesto** front/ back/spare wheel; **~ impresora** (*Inform*) print wheel; **~ de prensa** press conference
ruedo *etc* ['rweðo] *vb ver* **rodar** ■ *nm* (*contorno*) edge, border; (*de vestido*) hem; (*círculo*) circle; (*Taur*) arena, bullring; (*esterilla*) (round) mat
ruego *etc* ['rweɣo] *vb ver* **rogar** ■ *nm* request; **a ~ de** at the request of; **"~s y preguntas"** "question and answer session"
ruegue *etc* ['rweɣe] *vb ver* **rogar**
rufián [ru'fjan] *nm* scoundrel
rugby ['ruɣβi] *nm* rugby
rugido [ru'xiðo] *nm* roar
rugir [ru'xir] *vi* to roar; (*toro*) to bellow; (*estómago*) to rumble
rugoso, -a [ru'ɣoso, a] *adj* (*arrugado*) wrinkled; (*áspero*) rough; (*desigual*) ridged

ruibarbo [rwi'βarβo] *nm* rhubarb
ruido ['rwiðo] *nm* noise; *(sonido)* sound; *(alboroto)* racket, row; *(escándalo)* commotion, rumpus; **~ de fondo** background noise; **hacer** *o* **meter ~** to cause a stir
ruidoso, -a [rwi'ðoso, a] *adj* noisy, loud; *(fig)* sensational
ruin [rwin] *adj* contemptible, mean
ruina ['rwina] *nf* ruin; *(hundimiento)* collapse; *(de persona)* ruin, downfall; **estar hecho una ~** to be a wreck; **la empresa le llevó a la ~** the venture ruined him (financially)
ruindad [rwin'dað] *nf* lowness, meanness; *(acto)* low *o* mean act
ruinoso, -a [rwi'noso, a] *adj* ruinous; *(destartalado)* dilapidated, tumbledown; *(Com)* disastrous
ruiseñor [rwise'ɲor] *nm* nightingale
ruja *etc* ['ruxa] *vb ver* **rugir**
ruleta [ru'leta] *nf* roulette
rulo ['rulo] *nm* *(para el pelo)* curler
rulot [ru'lot], **rulote** [ru'lote] *nf* caravan *(Brit)*, trailer *(US)*
Rumania [ru'manja] *nf* Rumania
rumano, -a [ru'mano, a] *adj, nm/f* Rumanian
rumba ['rumba] *nf* rumba
rumbo ['rumbo] *nm* *(ruta)* route, direction; *(ángulo de dirección)* course, bearing; *(fig)* course of events; **con ~ a** in the direction of; **ir con ~ a** to be heading for; *(Naut)* to be bound for
rumboso, -a [rum'boso, a] *adj* *(generoso)* generous
rumiante [ru'mjante] *nm* ruminant
rumiar [ru'mjar] *vt* to chew; *(fig)* to chew over ■ *vi* to chew the cud
rumor [ru'mor] *nm* *(ruido sordo)* low sound; *(murmuración)* murmur, buzz
rumorearse [rumore'arse] *vr*: **se rumorea que** it is rumoured that
rumoroso, -a [rumo'roso, a] *adj* full of sounds; *(arroyo)* murmuring
runrún [run'run] *nm* *(de voces)* murmur, sound of voices; *(fig)* rumour; *(de una máquina)* whirr
rupestre [ru'pestre] *adj* rock *cpd*; **pintura ~** cave painting
ruptura [rup'tura] *nf* *(gen)* rupture; *(disputa)* split; *(de contrato)* breach; *(de relaciones)* breaking-off
rural [ru'ral] *adj* rural
Rusia ['rusja] *nf* Russia
ruso, -a ['ruso, a] *adj, nm/f* Russian ■ *nm* *(Ling)* Russian
rústico, -a ['rustiko, a] *adj* rustic; *(ordinario)* coarse, uncouth ■ *nm/f* yokel ■ *nf*: **libro en rústica** paperback (book)
ruta ['ruta] *nf* route
rutina [ru'tina] *nf* routine; **~ diaria** daily routine; **por ~** as a matter of course
rutinario, -a [ruti'narjo, a] *adj* routine

Ss

S, s ['ese] *nf* (*letra*) S, s; **S de Sábado** S for Sugar
S *abr* (= *san, santo, a*) St.; (= *sur*) S
s. *abr* (*tb*: **S.**: = *siglo*) c.; (= *siguiente*) foll.
s/ *abr* (*Com*) = **su; sus**
S.Sª *abr* (= *Sierra*) Mts
S.A. *abr* (= *Sociedad Anónima*) Ltd., Inc. (US); (= *Su Alteza*) H.H.
sáb. *abr* (= *sábado*) Sat.
sábado ['saβaðo] *nm* Saturday; (*de los judíos*) Sabbath; **del ~ en ocho días** a week on Saturday; **un ~ sí y otro no, cada dos sábados** every other Saturday; **S~ Santo** Holy Saturday; *ver tb* **Semana Santa**
sabana [sa'βana] *nf* savannah
sábana ['saβana] *nf* sheet; **se le pegan las sábanas** he can't get up in the morning
sabandija [saβan'dixa] *nf* (*bicho*) bug; (*fig*) louse
sabañón [saβa'ɲon] *nm* chilblain
sabático, -a [sa'βatiko, a] *adj* (*Rel: Univ*) sabbatical
sabelotodo [saβelo'toðo] *nm/f inv* know-all
saber [sa'βer] *vt* to know; (*llegar a conocer*) to find out, learn; (*tener capacidad de*) to know how to ■ *vi*: **~ a** to taste of, taste like ■ *nm* knowledge, learning; **saberse** *vr*: **se sabe que ...** it is known that ...; **no se sabe** nobody knows; **a ~** namely; **¿sabes conducir/nadar?** can you drive/swim?; **¿sabes francés?** do you *o* can you speak French?; **~ de memoria** to know by heart; **lo sé** I know; **hacer ~** to inform, let know; **que yo sepa** as far as I know; **vete** *o* **anda a ~** your guess is as good as mine, who knows!; **¿sabe?** (*fam*) you know (what I mean)?; **le sabe mal que otro la saque a bailar** it upsets him that anybody else should ask her to dance
sabido, -a [sa'βiðo, a] *adj* (*consabido*) well-known; **como es ~** as we all know
sabiduría [saβiðu'ria] *nf* (*conocimientos*) wisdom; (*instrucción*) learning; **~ popular** folklore
sabiendas [sa'βjendas]: **a ~** *adv* knowingly; **a ~ de que ...** knowing full well that ...
sabihondo, -a [sa'βjondo, a] *adj, nm/f* know-all, know-it-all (US)
sabio, -a ['saβjo, a] *adj* (*docto*) learned; (*prudente*) wise, sensible
sablazo [sa'βlaθo] *nm* (*herida*) sword wound; (*fam*) sponging; **dar un ~ a algn** to tap sb for money
sable [sa'βle] *nm* sabre
sabor [sa'βor] *nm* taste, flavour; (*fig*) flavour; **sin ~** flavourless
saborear [saβore'ar] *vt* to taste, savour; (*fig*) to relish
sabotaje [saβo'taxe] *nm* sabotage
saboteador, a [saβotea'ðor, a] *nm/f* saboteur
sabotear [saβote'ar] *vt* to sabotage
Saboya [sa'βoja] *nf* Savoy
sabré *etc* [sa'βre] *vb ver* **saber**
sabroso, -a [sa'βroso, a] *adj* tasty; (*fig fam*) racy, salty
saca ['saka] *nf* big sack; **~ de correo(s)** mailbag; (*Com*) withdrawal
sacacorchos [saka'kortʃos] *nm inv* corkscrew
sacapuntas [saka'puntas] *nm inv* pencil sharpener
sacar [sa'kar] *vt* to take out; (*fig: extraer*) to get (out); (*quitar*) to remove, get out; (*hacer salir*) to bring out; (*fondos: de cuenta*) to draw out, withdraw; (*obtener: legado etc*) to get; (*demostrar*) to show; (*conclusión*) to draw; (*novela etc*) to publish, bring out; (*ropa*) to take off; (*obra*) to make; (*premio*) to receive; (*entradas*) to get; (*Tenis*) to serve; (*Fútbol*) to put into play; **~ adelante** (*niño*) to bring up; **~ a algn a bailar** to dance with sb; **~ a algn de sí** to infuriate sb; **~ una foto** to take a photo; **~ la lengua** to stick out one's tongue; **~ buenas/malas notas** to get good/bad marks
sacarina [saka'rina] *nf* saccharin(e)
sacerdote [saθer'ðote] *nm* priest
saciar [sa'θjar] *vt* (*hartar*) to satiate; (*fig*) to satisfy; **saciarse** *vr* (*fig*) to be satisfied

saciedad [saθje'ðað] *nf* satiety; **hasta la ~** (*comer*) one's fill; (*repetir*) ad nauseam
saco ['sako] *nm* bag; (*grande*) sack; (*contenido*) bagful; (*Am: chaqueta*) jacket; **~ de dormir** sleeping bag
sacramento [sakra'mento] *nm* sacrament
sacrificar [sakrifi'kar] *vt* to sacrifice; (*animal*) to slaughter; (*perro etc*) to put to sleep; **sacrificarse** *vr* to sacrifice o.s.
sacrificio [sakri'fiθjo] *nm* sacrifice
sacrifique *etc* [sakri'fike] *vb ver* **sacrificar**
sacrilegio [sakri'lexjo] *nm* sacrilege
sacrílego, -a [sa'krileɣo, a] *adj* sacrilegious
sacristán [sakris'tan] *nm* verger
sacristía [sakris'tia] *nf* sacristy
sacro, -a ['sakro, a] *adj* sacred
sacudida [saku'ðiða] *nf* (*agitación*) shake, shaking; (*sacudimiento*) jolt, bump; (*fig*) violent change; (*Pol etc*) upheaval; **~ eléctrica** electric shock
sacudir [saku'ðir] *vt* to shake; (*golpear*) to hit; (*ala*) to flap; (*alfombra*) to beat; **~ a algn** (*fam*) to belt sb
S.A. de C.V. *abr* (*Am: = Sociedad Anónima de Capital Variable*) ≈ PLC (*Brit*), ≈ Corps (*US*), ≈ Inc. (*US*)
sádico, -a ['saðiko, a] *adj* sadistic ■ *nm/f* sadist
sadismo [sa'ðismo] *nm* sadism
sadomasoquismo [saðomaso'kismo] *nm* sadomasochism, S & M
sadomasoquista [saðomaso'kista] *adj* sadomasochistic ■ *nm/f* sadomasochist
saeta [sa'eta] *nf* (*flecha*) arrow; (*Mus*) *sacred song in flamenco style*
safari [sa'fari] *nm* safari
sagacidad [saɣaθi'ðað] *nf* shrewdness, cleverness
sagaz [sa'ɣaθ] *adj* shrewd, clever
Sagitario [saxi'tarjo] *nm* (*Astro*) Sagittarius
sagrado, -a [sa'ɣraðo, a] *adj* sacred, holy
Sáhara ['saara] *nm*: **el ~** the Sahara (desert)
saharaui [saxa'rawi] *adj* Saharan ■ *nm/f* native *o* inhabitant of the Sahara
sajón, -ona [sa'xon, 'xona] *adj, nm/f* Saxon
Sajonia [sa'xonja] *nf* Saxony
sal [sal] *vb ver* **salir** ■ *nf* salt; (*gracia*) wit; (*encanto*) charm; **sales de baño** bath salts; **~ gorda** *o* **de cocina** kitchen *o* cooking salt
sala ['sala] *nf* (*cuarto grande*) large room; (*tb*: **sala de estar**) living room; (*Teat*) house, auditorium; (*de hospital*) ward; **~ de apelación** court; **~ de conferencias** lecture hall; **~ de espera** waiting room; **~ de embarque** departure lounge; **~ de estar** living room; **~ de fiestas** function room; **~ de juntas** (*Com*) boardroom; **~ VIP** (*en aeropuerto, discoteca*) VIP lounge
salado, -a [sa'laðo, a] *adj* salty; (*fig*) witty, amusing; **agua salada** salt water
salar [sa'lar] *vt* to salt, add salt to
salarial [sala'rjal] *adj* (*aumento, revisión*) wage *cpd*, salary *cpd*, pay *cpd*
salario [sa'larjo] *nm* wage, pay
salchicha [sal'tʃitʃa] *nf* (pork) sausage
salchichón [saltʃi'tʃon] *nm* (salami-type) sausage
saldar [sal'dar] *vt* to pay; (*vender*) to sell off; (*fig*) to settle, resolve
saldo ['saldo] *nm* (*pago*) settlement; (*de una cuenta*) balance; (*lo restante*) remnant(s) (*pl*), remainder; (*liquidación*) sale; (*Com*): **~ anterior** balance brought forward; **~ acreedor/deudor** *o* **pasivo** credit/debit balance; **~ final** final balance
saldré *etc* [sal'dre] *vb ver* **salir**
salero [sa'lero] *nm* salt cellar; (*ingenio*) wit; (*encanto*) charm
salga *etc* ['salɣa] *vb ver* **salir**
salida [sa'liða] *nf* (*puerta etc*) exit, way out; (*acto*) leaving, going out; (*de tren, Aviat*) departure; (*Com: Tec*) output, production; (*fig*) way out; (*resultado*) outcome; (*Com: oportunidad*) opening; (*Geo, válvula*) outlet; (*de gas*) escape; (*ocurrencia*) joke; **calle sin ~** cul-de-sac; **a la ~ del teatro** after the theatre; **dar la ~** (*Deporte*) to give the starting signal; **~ de incendios** fire escape; **~ impresa** (*Inform*) hard copy; **no hay ~** there's no way out of it; **no tenemos otra ~** we have no option; **tener salidas** to be witty
salido, -a [sa'liðo, a] *adj* (*fam*) randy
saliente [sa'ljente] *adj* (*Arq*) projecting; (*sol*) rising; (*fig*) outstanding
salina [sa'lina] *nf* salt mine; **salinas** *nfpl* saltworks *sg*

PALABRA CLAVE

salir [sa'lir] *vi* **1** (*persona*) to come *o* go out; (*tren, avión*) to leave; **Juan ha salido** Juan has gone out; **salió de la cocina** he came out of the kitchen; **salimos de Madrid a las ocho** we left Madrid at eight (o'clock); **salió corriendo (del cuarto)** he ran out (of the room); **salir de un apuro** to get out of a jam
2 (*pelo*) to grow; (*diente*) to come through; (*disco, libro*) to come out; (*planta, número de lotería*) to come up; **salir a la superficie** to come to the surface; **anoche salió en la tele** she appeared *o* was on TV last night; **salió en todos los periódicos** it was in all the papers; **le salió un trabajo** he got a job
3 (*resultar*): **la muchacha nos salió muy**

trabajadora the girl turned out to be a very hard worker; **la comida te ha salido exquisita** the food was delicious; **sale muy caro** it's very expensive; **la entrevista que hice me salió bien/mal** the interview I did turned out *o* went well/badly; **nos salió a 5.000 ptas cada uno** it worked out at 5,000 pesetas each; **no salen las cuentas** it doesn't work out *o* add up; **salir ganando** to come out on top; **salir perdiendo** to lose out
4 (*Deporte*) to start; (*Naipes*) to lead
5: **salir con algn** to go out with sb
6: **salir adelante**: **no sé como haré para salir adelante** I don't know how I'll get by
salirse *vr* **1** (*líquido*) to spill; (*animal*) to escape
2 (*desviarse*): **salirse de la carretera** to leave *o* go off the road; **salirse de lo normal** to be unusual; **salirse del tema** to get off the point
3: **salirse con la suya** to get one's own way

saliva [sa'liβa] *nf* saliva
salivadera [saliβa'ðera] *nf* (*Am*) spittoon
salmantino, -a [salman'tino, a] *adj* of *o* from Salamanca ■ *nm/f* native *o* inhabitant of Salamanca
salmo ['salmo] *nm* psalm
salmón [sal'mon] *nm* salmon
salmonete [salmo'nete] *nm* red mullet
salmuera [sal'mwera] *nf* pickle, brine
salón [sa'lon] *nm* (*de casa*) living-room, lounge; (*muebles*) lounge suite; **~ de belleza** beauty parlour; **~ de baile** dance hall; **~ de sesiones** assembly hall
salpicadero [salpika'ðero] *nm* (*Auto*) dashboard
salpicar [salpi'kar] *vt* (*de barro, pintura*) to splash; (*rociar*) to sprinkle, spatter; (*esparcir*) to scatter
salpicón [salpi'kon] *nm* (*acto*) splashing; (*Culin*) meat *o* fish salad
salpimentar [salpimen'tar] *vt* (*Culin*) to season
salpique *etc* [sal'pike] *vb ver* **salpicar**
salsa ['salsa] *nf* sauce; (*con carne asada*) gravy; (*fig*) spice; **~ mayonesa** mayonnaise; **estar en su ~** (*fam*) to be in one's element
saltamontes [salta'montes] *nm inv* grasshopper
saltar [sal'tar] *vt* to jump (over), leap (over); (*dejar de lado*) to skip, miss out ■ *vi* to jump, leap; (*pelota*) to bounce; (*al aire*) to fly up; (*quebrarse*) to break; (*al agua*) to dive; (*fig*) to explode, blow up; (*botón*) to come off; (*corcho*) to pop out; **saltarse** *vr* (*omitir*) to skip, miss; **salta a la vista** it's obvious; **saltarse todas las reglas** to break all the rules
salteado, -a [salte'aðo, a] *adj* (*Culin*) sauté(ed)
salteador [saltea'ðor] *nm* (*tb*: **salteador de caminos**) highwayman
saltear [salte'ar] *vt* (*robar*) to rob (in a holdup); (*asaltar*) to assault, attack; (*Culin*) to sauté
saltimbanqui [saltim'banki] *nm/f* acrobat
salto ['salto] *nm* jump, leap; (*al agua*) dive; **a saltos** by jumping; **~ de agua** waterfall; **~ de altura** high jump; **~ de cama** negligee; **~ mortal** somersault; (*Inform*): **~ de línea** line feed; **~ de línea automático** wordwrap; **~ de página** formfeed
saltón, -ona [sal'ton, ona] *adj* (*ojos*) bulging, popping; (*dientes*) protruding
salubre [sa'luβre] *adj* healthy, salubrious
salud [sa'luð] *nf* health; **estar bien/mal de ~** to be in good/poor health; **¡(a su) ~!** cheers!, good health!; **beber a la ~ de** to drink (to) the health of
saludable [salu'ðaβle] *adj* (*de buena salud*) healthy; (*provechoso*) good, beneficial
saludar [salu'ðar] *vt* to greet; (*Mil*) to salute; **ir a ~ a algn** to drop in to see sb; **salude de mi parte a X** give my regards to X; **le saluda atentamente** (*en carta*) yours faithfully
saludo [sa'luðo] *nm* greeting; **saludos** (*en carta*) best wishes, regards; **un ~ afectuoso** *o* **cordial** yours sincerely
salva ['salβa] *nf* (*Mil*) salvo; **una ~ de aplausos** thunderous applause
salvación [salβa'θjon] *nf* salvation; (*rescate*) rescue
salvado [sal'βaðo] *nm* bran
salvador [salβa'ðor] *nm* rescuer, saviour; **el S~** the Saviour; **El S~** El Salvador; **San S~** San Salvador
salvadoreño, -a [salβaðo'reɲo, a] *adj, nm/f* Salvadoran, Salvadorian
salvaguardar [salβaɣwar'ðar] *vt* to safeguard; (*Inform*) to back up, make a backup copy of
salvajada [salβa'xaða] *nf* savage deed, atrocity
salvaje [sal'βaxe] *adj* wild; (*tribu*) savage
salvajismo [salβa'xismo] *nm* savagery
salvamento [salβa'mento] *nm* (*acción*) rescue; (*de naufragio*) salvage; **~ y socorrismo** life-saving
salvapantallas [salβapan'taʎas] *nm inv* screensaver
salvar [sal'βar] *vt* (*rescatar*) to save, rescue; (*resolver*) to overcome, resolve; (*cubrir distancias*) to cover, travel; (*hacer excepción*) to except, exclude; (*un barco*) to salvage; **salvarse** *vr* to save o.s., escape; **¡sálvese el que pueda!** every man for himself!

salvavidas [salβa'βiðas] *adj inv*: **bote/chaleco/cinturón** ~ lifeboat/lifejacket/lifebelt
salvedad [salβe'ðað] *nf* reservation, qualification; **con la ~ de que ...** with the proviso that ...
salvia ['salβja] *nf* sage
salvo, -a ['salβo, a] *adj* safe ■ *prep* except (for), save; **~ error u omisión** (*Com*) errors and omissions excepted; **a ~** out of danger; **~ que** unless
salvoconducto [salβokon'dukto] *nm* safe-conduct
samba ['samba] *nf* samba
san [san] *n* (*apócope de* **santo**) saint; **~ Juan** St. John; *ver tb* **Juan**
sanar [sa'nar] *vt* (*herida*) to heal; (*persona*) to cure ■ *vi* (*persona*) to get well, recover; (*herida*) to heal
sanatorio [sana'torjo] *nm* sanatorium
sanción [san'θjon] *nf* sanction
sancionar [sanθjo'nar] *vt* to sanction
sancocho [san'kotʃo] *nm* (*Am*) stew
sandalia [san'dalja] *nf* sandal
sándalo ['sandalo] *nm* sandal(wood)
sandez [san'deθ] *nf* (*cualidad*) foolishness; (*acción*) stupid thing; **decir sandeces** to talk nonsense
sandía [san'dia] *nf* watermelon
sandinista [sanði'nista] *adj, nm/f* Sandinist(a)
sandwich ['sandwitʃ] (*pl* **sandwichs** *o* **sandwiches**) *nm* sandwich
saneamiento [sanea'mjento] *nm* sanitation
sanear [sane'ar] *vt* to drain; (*indemnizar*) to compensate; (*Econ*) to reorganize
sanfermines [sanfer'mines] *nmpl see note*

SANFERMINES

The *Sanfermines* are a week of *fiestas* in Pamplona, the capital of Navarre, made famous by Ernest Hemingway. From the 7th of July, the feast of San Fermín, crowds of mainly young people take to the streets drinking, singing and dancing. Early in the morning bulls are released along the narrow streets leading to the bullring, and people risk serious injury by running out in front of them, a custom which is also typical of many Spanish villages.

sangrar [san'grar] *vt, vi* to bleed; (*texto*) to indent
sangre ['sangre] *nf* blood; **~ fría** sangfroid; **a ~ fría** in cold blood
sangría [san'gria] *nf* (*Med*) bleeding; (*Culin*) sangria, *sweetened drink of red wine with fruit*, ≈ fruit cup
sangriento, -a [san'grjento, a] *adj* bloody
sanguijuela [sangi'xwela] *nf* (*Zool, fig*) leech
sanguinario, -a [sangi'narjo, a] *adj* bloodthirsty
sanguíneo, -a [san'gineo, a] *adj* blood *cpd*
sanidad [sani'ðað] *nf* sanitation; (*calidad de sano*) health, healthiness; **~ pública** public health (department)
sanitario, -a [sani'tarjo, a] *adj* sanitary; (*de la salud*) health *cpd* ■ *nm*: **sanitarios** *nmpl* toilets (*Brit*), restroom *sg* (*US*)
San Marino [sanma'rino] *nm*: **(La República de)** ~ San Marino
sano, -a ['sano, a] *adj* healthy; (*sin daños*) sound; (*comida*) wholesome; (*entero*) whole, intact; **~ y salvo** safe and sound
santanderino, -a [santande'rino, a] *adj* of *o* from Santander ■ *nm/f* native *o* inhabitant of Santander
Santiago [san'tjaγo] *nm*: **~ (de Chile)** Santiago
santiamén [santja'men] *nm*: **en un ~** in no time at all
santidad [santi'ðað] *nf* holiness, sanctity
santificar [santifi'kar] *vt* to sanctify
santifique *etc* [santi'fike] *vb ver* **santificar**
santiguarse [santi'γwarse] *vr* to make the sign of the cross
santigüe *etc* [san'tiγwe] *vb ver* **santiguarse**
santo, -a ['santo, a] *adj* holy; (*fig*) wonderful, miraculous ■ *nm/f* saint ■ *nm* saint's day; **hacer su santa voluntad** to do as one jolly well pleases; **¿a ~ de qué ...?** why on earth ...?; **se le fue el ~ al cielo** he forgot what he was about to say; **~ y seña** password; *see note*

SANTO

As well as celebrating their birthday Spaniards have traditionally celebrated *el santo*, their Saint's day, when the Saint they were called after at birth, eg San Pedro or la Virgen de los Dolores, is honoured in the Christian calendar. This is a custom which is gradually dying out.

santuario [san'twarjo] *nm* sanctuary, shrine
saña ['saɲa] *nf* rage, fury
sapo ['sapo] *nm* toad
saque *etc* ['sake] *vb ver* **sacar** ■ *nm* (*Tenis*) service, serve; (*Fútbol*) throw-in; **~ inicial** kick-off; **~ de esquina** corner (kick); **tener buen ~** to eat heartily
saquear [sake'ar] *vt* (*Mil*) to sack; (*robar*) to loot, plunder; (*fig*) to ransack

saqueo [sa'keo] *nm* sacking; looting, plundering; ransacking
S.A.R. *abr* (*= Su Alteza Real*) HRH
sarampión [saram'pjon] *nm* measles *sg*
sarape [sa'rape] *nm* (*Am*) blanket
sarcasmo [sar'kasmo] *nm* sarcasm
sarcástico, -a [sar'kastiko, a] *adj* sarcastic
sarcófago [sar'kofaɣo] *nm* sarcophagus
sardina [sar'ðina] *nf* sardine
sardo, -a ['sarðo, a] *adj, nm/f* Sardinian
sardónico, -a [sar'ðoniko, a] *adj* sardonic; (*irónico*) ironical, sarcastic
sargento [sar'xento] *nm* sergeant
sarmiento [sar'mjento] *nm* vine shoot
sarna ['sarna] *nf* itch; (*Med*) scabies
sarpullido [sarpu'ʎiðo] *nm* (*Med*) rash
sarro ['sarro] *nm* deposit; (*en dientes*) tartar
sarta ['sarta] *nf* (*fig*): **una ~ de mentiras** a pack of lies
sartén [sar'ten] *nf* frying pan; **tener la ~ por el mango** to rule the roost
sastre ['sastre] *nm* tailor
sastrería [sastre'ria] *nf* (*arte*) tailoring; (*tienda*) tailor's (shop)
Satanás [sata'nas] *nm* Satan
satélite [sa'telite] *nm* satellite
satinado, -a [sati'naðo, a] *adj* glossy ■ *nm* gloss, shine
sátira ['satira] *nf* satire
satírico, -a [sa'tiriko, a] *adj* satiric(al)
sátiro ['satiro] *nm* (*Mitología*) satyr; (*fig*) sex maniac
satisfacción [satisfak'θjon] *nf* satisfaction
satisfacer [satisfa'θer] *vt* to satisfy; (*gastos*) to meet; (*deuda*) to pay; (*Com: letra de cambio*) to honour (*Brit*), honor (*US*); (*pérdida*) to make good; **satisfacerse** *vr* to satisfy o.s., be satisfied; (*vengarse*) to take revenge
satisfaga *etc* [satis'faɣa], **satisfaré** *etc* [satisfa're] *vb ver* **satisfacer**
satisfecho, -a [satis'fetʃo, a] *pp de* **satisfacer** ■ *adj* satisfied; (*contento*) content(ed), happy; (*tb*: **satisfecho de sí mismo**) self-satisfied, smug
satisfice *etc* [satis'fiθe] *vb ver* **satisfacer**
saturación [satura'θjon] *nf* saturation; **llegar a la ~** to reach saturation point
saturar [satu'rar] *vt* to saturate; **saturarse** *vr* (*mercado, aeropuerto*) to reach saturation point; **¡estoy saturado de tanta televisión!** I can't take any more television!
sauce ['sauθe] *nm* willow; **~ llorón** weeping willow
saúco [sa'uko] *nm* (*Bot*) elder
saudí [sau'ði] *adj, nm/f* Saudi
sauna ['sauna] *nf* sauna
savia ['saβja] *nf* sap
saxo ['sakso] *nm* sax
saxofón [sakso'fon] *nm* saxophone
saya ['saja] *nf* (*falda*) skirt; (*enagua*) petticoat
sayo ['sajo] *nm* smock
sazón [sa'θon] *nf* (*de fruta*) ripeness; **a la ~** then, at that time
sazonado, -a [saθo'naðo, a] *adj* (*fruta*) ripe; (*Culin*) flavoured, seasoned
sazonar [saθo'nar] *vt* to ripen; (*Culin*) to flavour, season
s/c *abr* (*Com: = su casa*) your firm; (*: = su cuenta*) your account
Sdo. *abr* (*Com: = Saldo*) bal
SE *abr* (*= sudeste*) SE

PALABRA CLAVE

se [se] *pron* **1** (*reflexivo: sg: m*) himself; (*: f*) herself; (*: pl*) themselves; (*: cosa*) itself; (*: de Vd*) yourself; (*: de Vds*) yourselves; (*indefinido*) oneself; **se mira en el espejo** he looks at himself in the mirror; **¡siéntese!** sit down!; **se durmió** he fell asleep; **se está preparando** she's getting (herself) ready; (*para usos léxicos del pron ver el vb en cuestión, p.ej.* **arrepentirse**)
2 (*como complemento indirecto*) to him; to her; to them; to it; to you; **se lo dije ayer** (*a Vd*) I told you yesterday; **se compró un sombrero** he bought himself a hat; **se rompió la pierna** he broke his leg; **cortarse el pelo** to get one's hair cut; (*uno mismo*) to cut one's hair; **se comió un pastel** he ate a cake
3 (*uso recíproco*) each other, one another; **se miraron (el uno al otro)** they looked at each other *o* one another
4 (*en oraciones pasivas*): **se han vendido muchos libros** a lot of books have been sold; **"se vende coche"** "car for sale"
5 (*impers*): **se dice que** people say that, it is said that; **allí se come muy bien** the food there is very good, you can eat very well there

sé [se] *vb ver* **saber; ser**
sea *etc* ['sea] *vb ver* **ser**
SEAT ['seat] *nf abr* = **Sociedad Española de Automóviles de Turismo**
sebo ['seβo] *nm* fat, grease
Sec. *abr* (*= Secretario*) Sec
seca ['seka] *nf ver* **seco**
secado [se'kaðo] *nm* drying; **~ a mano** blow-dry
secador [seka'ðor] *nm*: **~ para el pelo** hairdryer
secadora [seka'ðora] *nf* tumble dryer; **~ centrífuga** spin-dryer

secano [se'kano] *nm* (*Agr*: *tb*: **tierra de secano**) dry land *o* region; **cultivo de ~** dry farming
secante [se'kante] *adj* (*viento*) drying ■ *nm* blotting paper
secar [se'kar] *vt* to dry; (*superficie*) to wipe dry; (*frente, suelo*) to mop; (*líquido*) to mop up; (*tinta*) to blot; **secarse** *vr* to dry (off); (*río, planta*) to dry up
sección [sek'θjon] *nf* section; (*Com*) department; **~ deportiva** (*en periódico*) sports page(s)
seco, -a ['seko, a] *adj* dry; (*fruta*) dried; (*persona*: *magro*) thin, skinny; (*carácter*) cold; (*antipático*) disagreeable; (*respuesta*) sharp, curt ■ *nf* dry season; **habrá pan a secas** there will be just bread; **decir algo a secas** to say sth curtly; **parar en ~** to stop dead
secreción [sekre'θjon] *nf* secretion
secretaría [sekreta'ria] *nf* secretariat; (*oficina*) secretary's office
secretariado [sekreta'rjaðo] *nm* (*oficina*) secretariat; (*cargo*) secretaryship; (*curso*) secretarial course
secretario, -a [sekre'tarjo, a] *nm/f* secretary; **~ adjunto** (*Com*) assistant secretary
secreto, -a [se'kreto, a] *adj* secret; (*información*) confidential; (*persona*) secretive ■ *nm* secret; (*calidad*) secrecy
secta ['sekta] *nf* sect
sectario, -a [sek'tarjo, a] *adj* sectarian
sector [sek'tor] *nm* sector (*tb Inform*); (*de opinión*) section; (*fig*: *campo*) area, field; **~ privado/público** (*Com*: *Econ*) private/public sector
secuela [se'kwela] *nf* consequence
secuencia [se'kwenθja] *nf* sequence
secuestrar [sekwes'trar] *vt* to kidnap; (*avión*) to hijack; (*bienes*) to seize, confiscate
secuestro [se'kwestro] *nm* kidnapping; hijack; seizure, confiscation
secular [seku'lar] *adj* secular
secundar [sekun'dar] *vt* to second, support
secundario, -a [sekun'darjo, a] *adj* secondary; (*carretera*) side *cpd*; (*Inform*) background *cpd* ■ *nf* secondary education; *ver tb* **sistema educativo**
sed [seð] *nf* thirst; (*fig*) thirst, craving; **tener ~** to be thirsty
seda ['seða] *nf* silk; **~ dental** dental floss
sedal [se'ðal] *nm* fishing line
sedante [se'ðante] *nm* sedative
sede ['seðe] *nf* (*de gobierno*) seat; (*de compañía*) headquarters *pl*, head office; **Santa S~** Holy See
sedentario, -a [seðen'tarjo, a] *adj* sedentary
SEDIC [se'ðik] *nf abr* = **Sociedad Española de Documentación e Información Científica**
sedición [seði'θjon] *nf* sedition
sediento, -a [se'ðjento, a] *adj* thirsty
sedimentar [seðimen'tar] *vt* to deposit; **sedimentarse** *vr* to settle
sedimento [seði'mento] *nm* sediment
sedoso, -a [se'ðoso, a] *adj* silky, silken
seducción [seðuk'θjon] *nf* seduction
seducir [seðu'θir] *vt* to seduce; (*sobornar*) to bribe; (*cautivar*) to charm, fascinate; (*atraer*) to attract
seductor, a [seðuk'tor, a] *adj* seductive; charming, fascinating; attractive; (*engañoso*) deceptive, misleading ■ *nm/f* seducer
seduje *etc* [se'ðuxe], **seduzca** *etc* [se'ðuθka] *vb ver* **seducir**
sefardí [sefar'ði], **sefardita** [sefar'ðita] *adj* Sephardi(c) ■ *nm/f* Sephardi
segador, a [seɣa'ðor, a] *nm/f* (*persona*) harvester ■ *nf* (*Tec*) mower, reaper
segadora-trilladora [seɣa'ðoratriʎa'ðora] *nf* combine harvester
segar [se'ɣar] *vt* (*mies*) to reap, cut; (*hierba*) to mow, cut; (*esperanzas*) to ruin
seglar [se'ɣlar] *adj* secular, lay
segoviano, -a [seɣo'βjano, a] *adj* of *o* from Segovia ■ *nm/f* native *o* inhabitant of Segovia
segregación [seɣreɣa'θjon] *nf* segregation; **~ racial** racial segregation
segregar [seɣre'ɣar] *vt* to segregate, separate
segregue *etc* [se'ɣreɣe] *vb ver* **segregar**
segué [se'ɣe], **seguemos** *etc* [se'ɣemos] *vb ver* **segar**
seguidamente [seɣiða'mente] *adv* (*sin parar*) without a break; (*inmediatamente después*) immediately after
seguido, -a [se'ɣiðo, a] *adj* (*continuo*) continuous, unbroken; (*recto*) straight ■ *adv* (*directo*) straight (on); (*después*) after; (*Am*: *a menudo*) often ■ *nf*: **en seguida** at once, right away; **cinco días seguidos** five days running, five days in a row; **en seguida termino** I've nearly finished, I shan't be long now
seguimiento [seɣi'mjento] *nm* chase, pursuit; (*continuación*) continuation
seguir [se'ɣir] *vt* to follow; (*venir después*) to follow on, come after; (*proseguir*) to continue; (*perseguir*) to chase, pursue; (*indicio*) to follow up; (*mujer*) to court ■ *vi* (*gen*) to follow; (*continuar*) to continue, carry *o* go on; **seguirse** *vr* to follow; **a ~** to be continued; **sigo sin comprender** I still don't understand; **sigue lloviendo** it's still raining; **sigue** (*en carta*) P.T.O.; (*en libro, TV*)

continued; **"hágase ~"** "please forward"; **¡siga!** (*Am: pase*) come in!
según [se'ɣun] *prep* according to ■ *adv*: **~ (y conforme)** it all depends ■ *conj* as; **~ esté el tiempo** depending on the weather; **~ me consta** as far as I know; **está ~ lo dejaste** it is just as you left it
segundo, -a [se'ɣundo, a] *adj* second; (*en discurso*) secondly ■ *nm* (*gen, medida de tiempo*) second; (*piso*) second floor ■ *nf* (*sentido*) second meaning; **~ (de a bordo)** (*Naut*) first mate; **segunda (clase)** (*Ferro*) second class; **segunda (marcha)** (*Auto*) second (gear); **de segunda mano** second hand
seguramente [seɣura'mente] *adv* surely; (*con certeza*) for sure, with certainty; (*probablemente*) probably; **¿lo va a comprar?** — **~** is he going to buy it? — I should think so
seguridad [seɣuri'ðað] *nf* safety; (*del estado, de casa etc*) security; (*certidumbre*) certainty; (*confianza*) confidence; (*estabilidad*) stability; **~ social** social security; **~ contra incendios** fire precautions *pl*; **~ en sí mismo** (self-) confidence
seguro, -a [se'ɣuro, a] *adj* (*cierto*) sure, certain; (*fiel*) trustworthy; (*libre de peligro*) safe; (*bien defendido, firme*) secure; (*datos etc*) reliable; (*fecha*) firm ■ *adv* for sure, certainly ■ *nm* (*dispositivo*) safety device; (*de cerradura*) tumbler; (*de arma*) safety catch; (*Com*) insurance; **~ contra accidentes/incendios** fire/accident insurance; **~ contra terceros/ a todo riesgo** third party/comprehensive insurance; **~ dotal con beneficios** with-profits endowment assurance; **S~ de Enfermedad** ≈ National Insurance; **~ marítimo** marine insurance; **~ mixto** endowment assurance; **~ temporal** term insurance; **~ de vida** life insurance
seis [seis] *num* six; **~ mil** six thousand; **tiene ~ años** she is six (years old); **unos ~** about six; **hoy es el ~** today is the sixth
seiscientos, -as [seis'θjentos, as] *num* six hundred
seísmo [se'ismo] *nm* tremor, earthquake
SELA *sigla m* = **Sistema Económico Latinoamericano**
selección [selek'θjon] *nf* selection; **~ múltiple** multiple choice; **~ nacional** (*Deporte*) national team
seleccionador, a [selekθjona'ðor, a] *nm/f* (*Deporte*) selector
seleccionar [selekθjo'nar] *vt* to pick, choose, select
selectividad [selektiβi'ðað] *nf* (*Univ*) entrance examination; *see note*

SELECTIVIDAD

School leavers wishing to go on to University sit the dreaded *selectividad* in June, with resits in September. When student numbers are too high for a particular course only the best students get their choice. Some of the others then wait a year to sit the exam again rather than do a course they don't want.

selecto, -a [se'lekto, a] *adj* select, choice; (*escogido*) selected
sellado, -a [se'ʎaðo, a] *adj* (*documento oficial*) sealed; (*pasaporte*) stamped
sellar [se'ʎar] *vt* (*documento oficial*) to seal; (*pasaporte, visado*) to stamp; (*marcar*) to brand; (*pacto, labios*) to seal
sello ['seʎo] *nm* stamp; (*precinto*) seal; (*fig: tb:* **sello distintivo**) hallmark; **~ fiscal** revenue stamp; **sellos de prima** (*Com*) trading stamps
selva ['selβa] *nf* (*bosque*) forest, woods *pl*; (*jungla*) jungle; **la S~ Negra** the Black Forest
S.Em. *abr* = **Su Eminencia**
semáforo [se'maforo] *nm* (*Auto*) traffic lights *pl*; (*Ferro*) signal
semana [se'mana] *nf* week; **~ inglesa** five-day (working) week; **~ laboral** working week; **S~ Santa** Holy Week; *see note;* **entre ~** during the week

SEMANA SANTA

Semana Santa is a holiday in Spain. All regions take *Viernes Santo*, Good Friday, *Sábado Santo*, Holy Saturday, and *Domingo de Resurrección*, Easter Sunday. Other holidays at this time vary according to each region. There are spectacular *procesiones* all over the country, with members of *cofradías* (brotherhoods) dressing in hooded robes and parading their *pasos* (religious floats or sculptures) through the streets. Seville has the most renowned celebrations, on account of the religious fervour shown by the locals.

semanal [sema'nal] *adj* weekly
semanario [sema'narjo] *nm* weekly (magazine)
semántica [se'mantika] *nf* semantics *sg*
semblante [sem'blante] *nm* face; (*fig*) look
sembrar [sem'brar] *vt* to sow; (*objetos*) to sprinkle, scatter about; (*noticias etc*) to spread
semejante [seme'xante] *adj* (*parecido*) similar; (*tal*) such; **semejantes** alike,

similar ■ *nm* fellow man, fellow creature; **son muy semejantes** they are very much alike; **nunca hizo cosa ~** he never did such a thing
semejanza [seme'xanθa] *nf* similarity, resemblance; **a ~ de** like, as
semejar [seme'xar] *vi* to seem like, resemble; **semejarse** *vr* to look alike, be similar
semen ['semen] *nm* semen
semental [semen'tal] *nm* (*macho*) stud
sementera [semen'tera] *nf* (*acto*) sowing; (*temporada*) seedtime; (*tierra*) sown land
semestral [semes'tral] *adj* half-yearly, bi-annual
semestre [se'mestre] *nm* period of six months; (*Univ*) semester; (*Com*) half-yearly payment
semicírculo [semi'θirkulo] *nm* semicircle
semiconductor [semikonduk'tor] *nm* semiconductor
semiconsciente [semikons'θjente] *adj* semiconscious
semidesnatado, -a [semiðesna'taðo, a] *adj* semi-skimmed
semifinal [semifi'nal] *nf* semifinal
semiinconsciente [semi(i)nkons'θjente] *adj* semiconscious
semilla [se'miʎa] *nf* seed
semillero [semi'ʎero] *nm* (*Agr etc*) seedbed; (*fig*) hotbed
seminario [semi'narjo] *nm* (*Rel*) seminary; (*Escol*) seminar
semiseco [semi'seko] *nm* medium-dry
semita [se'mita] *adj* Semitic ■ *nm/f* Semite
sémola ['semola] *nf* semolina
sempiterno, -a [sempi'terno, a] *adj* everlasting
Sena ['sena] *nm*: **el ~** the (river) Seine
senado [se'naðo] *nm* senate; *ver tb* **Las Cortes (españolas)**
senador, a [sena'ðor, a] *nm/f* senator
sencillez [senθi'ʎeθ] *nf* simplicity; (*de persona*) naturalness
sencillo, -a [sen'θiʎo, a] *adj* simple; (*carácter*) natural, unaffected; (*billete*) single ■ *nm* (*disco*) single; (*Am*) small change
senda ['senda] *nf*, **sendero** [sen'dero] *nm* path, track; **Sendero Luminoso** the Shining Path (guerrilla movement)
senderismo [sende'rismo] *nm* trekking
sendos, -as ['sendos, as] *adj pl*: **les dio ~ golpes** he hit both of them
senil [se'nil] *adj* senile
seno ['seno] *nm* (*Anat*) bosom, bust; (*fig*) bosom; **senos** *nmpl* breasts; **~ materno** womb
sensación [sensa'θjon] *nf* sensation; (*sentido*) sense; (*sentimiento*) feeling; **causar** *o* **hacer ~** to cause a sensation
sensacional [sensaθjo'nal] *adj* sensational
sensatez [sensa'teθ] *nf* common sense
sensato, -a [sen'sato, a] *adj* sensible
sensibilidad [sensiβili'ðað] *nf* sensitivity; (*para el arte*) feel
sensibilizar [sensiβili'θar] *vt*: **~ a la población/opinión pública** to raise public awareness
sensible [sen'sible] *adj* sensitive; (*apreciable*) perceptible, appreciable; (*pérdida*) considerable
sensiblero, -a [sensi'βlero, a] *adj* sentimental, slushy
sensitivo, -a [sensi'tiβo, a], **sensorial** [senso'rjal] *adj* sense *cpd*
sensor [sen'sor] *nm*: **~ de fin de papel** paper out sensor
sensual [sen'swal] *adj* sensual
sentado, -a [sen'taðo, a] *adj* (*establecido*) settled; (*carácter*) sensible ■ *nf* sitting; (*Pol*) sit-in, sit-down protest; **dar por ~** to take for granted, assume; **dejar algo ~** to establish sth firmly; **estar ~** to sit, be sitting (down); **de una sentada** at one sitting
sentar [sen'tar] *vt* to sit, seat; (*fig*) to establish ■ *vi* (*vestido*) to suit; (*alimento*): **~ bien/mal a** to agree/disagree with; **sentarse** *vr* (*persona*) to sit, sit down; (*el tiempo*) to settle (down); (*los depósitos*) to settle; **¡siéntese!** (do) sit down, take a seat
sentencia [sen'tenθja] *nf* (*máxima*) maxim, saying; (*Jur*) sentence; **~ de muerte** death sentence
sentenciar [senten'θjar] *vt* to sentence
sentido, -a [sen'tiðo, a] *adj* (*pérdida*) regrettable; (*carácter*) sensitive ■ *nm* sense; (*sentimiento*) feeling; (*significado*) sense, meaning; (*dirección*) direction; **mi más ~ pésame** my deepest sympathy; **~ del humor** sense of humour; **~ común** common sense; **en el buen ~ de la palabra** in the best sense of the word; **sin ~** meaningless; **tener ~** to make sense; **~ único** one-way (street)
sentimental [sentimen'tal] *adj* sentimental; **vida ~** love life
sentimiento [senti'mjento] *nm* (*emoción*) feeling, emotion; (*sentido*) sense; (*pesar*) regret, sorrow
sentir [sen'tir] *vt* to feel; (*percibir*) to perceive, sense; (*esp Am: oír*) to hear; (*lamentar*) to regret, be sorry for; (*música etc*) to have a feeling for ■ *vi* to feel; (*lamentarse*) to feel sorry ■ *nm* opinion, judgement; **sentirse** *vr* to feel; **lo siento** I'm sorry; **sentirse mejor/mal** to feel better/ill; **sentirse como en su**

casa to feel at home
seña ['seɲa] *nf* sign; (*Mil*) password; **señas** *nfpl* address *sg*; **señas personales** personal description *sg*; **por más señas** moreover; **dar señas de** to show signs of
señal [se'ɲal] *nf* sign; (*síntoma*) symptom; (*indicio*) indication; (*Ferro: Telec*) signal; (*marca*) mark; (*Com*) deposit; (*Inform*) marker, mark; **en ~ de** as a token of, as a sign of; **dar señales de** to show signs of; **~ de auxilio/de peligro** distress/danger signal; **~ de llamada** ringing tone; **~ para marcar** dialling tone
señalado, -a [seɲa'laðo, a] *adj* (*persona*) distinguished; (*pey*) notorious
señalar [seɲa'lar] *vt* to mark; (*indicar*) to point out, indicate; (*significar*) to denote; (*referirse a*) to allude to; (*fijar*) to fix, settle; (*pey*) to criticize
señalice *etc* [seɲa'liθe] *vb ver* **señalizar**
señalización [seɲaliθa'θjon] *nf* signposting; signals *pl*
señalizar [seɲali'θar] *vt* (*Auto*) to put up road signs on; (*Ferro*) to put signals on; (*Auto: ruta*): **está bien señalizada** it's well signposted
señas ['seɲas] *nfpl ver* **seña**
señor, a [se'ɲor, a] *adj* (*fam*) lordly ■ *nm* (*hombre*) man; (*caballero*) gentleman; (*dueño*) owner, master; (*trato: antes de nombre propio*) Mr; (*: hablando directamente*) sir ■ *nf* (*dama*) lady; (*trato: antes de nombre propio*) Mrs; (*: hablando directamente*) madam; (*esposa*) wife; **los señores González** Mr and Mrs González; **S~ Don Jacinto Benavente** (*en sobre*) Mr J. Benavente, J. Benavente Esq.; **S~ Director ...** (*de periódico*) Dear Sir ...; **~ juez** my lord, your worship (*US*); **~ Presidente** Mr Chairman *o* President; **Muy ~ mío** Dear Sir; **Muy señores nuestros** Dear Sirs; **Nuestro S~** (*Rel*) Our Lord; **¿está la señora?** is the lady of the house in?; **la señora de Smith** Mrs Smith; **Nuestra Señora** (*Rel*) Our Lady
señoría [seɲo'ria] *nf* rule; **su** *o* **vuestra S~** your *o* his/her lordship/ladyship
señorío [seɲo'rio] *nm* manor; (*fig*) rule
señorita [seɲo'rita] *nf* (*gen*) Miss; (*mujer joven*) young lady; (*maestra*) schoolteacher
señorito [seɲo'rito] *nm* young gentleman; (*lenguaje de criados*) master; (*pey*) toff
señuelo [se'ɲwelo] *nm* decoy
Sep. *abr* (= *septiembre*) Sept
sepa *etc* ['sepa] *vb ver* **saber**
separable [sepa'raβle] *adj* separable; (*Tec*) detachable
separación [separa'θjon] *nf* separation; (*división*) division; (*distancia*) gap, distance; **~ de bienes** division of property
separado, -a [sepa'raðo, a] *adj* separate; (*Tec*) detached; **vive ~ de su mujer** he is separated from his wife; **por ~** separately
separador [separa'ðor] *nm* (*Inform*) delimiter
separadora [separa'ðora] *nf*: **~ de hojas** burster
separar [sepa'rar] *vt* to separate; (*silla (de la mesa)*) to move away; (*Tec: pieza*) to detach; (*persona: de un cargo*) to remove, dismiss; (*dividir*) to divide; **separarse** *vr* (*parte*) to come away; (*partes*) to come apart; (*persona*) to leave, go away; (*matrimonio*) to separate
separata [sepa'rata] *nf* offprint
separatismo [separa'tismo] *nm* (*Pol*) separatism
sepelio [se'peljo] *nm* burial, interment
sepia ['sepja] *nf* cuttlefish
Sept. *abr* (= *septiembre*) Sept
septentrional [septentrjo'nal] *adj* north *cpd*, northern
septiembre [sep'tjembre] *nm* September; *ver tb* **julio**
séptimo, -a ['septimo, a] *adj, nm* seventh
septuagésimo, -a [septwa'xesimo, a] *adj* seventieth
sepulcral [sepul'kral] *adj* sepulchral; (*fig*) gloomy, dismal
sepulcro [se'pulkro] *nm* tomb, grave, sepulchre
sepultar [sepul'tar] *vt* to bury; (*en accidente*) to trap; **quedaban sepultados en la caverna** they were trapped in the cave
sepultura [sepul'tura] *nf* (*acto*) burial; (*tumba*) grave, tomb; **dar ~ a** to bury; **recibir ~** to be buried
sepulturero, -a [sepultu'rero, a] *nm/f* gravedigger
seque *etc* ['seke] *vb ver* **secar**
sequedad [seke'ðað] *nf* dryness; (*fig*) brusqueness, curtness
sequía [se'kia] *nf* drought
séquito ['sekito] *nm* (*de rey etc*) retinue; (*Pol*) followers *pl*
SER *nf abr* (*Radio: = Sociedad Española de Radiodifusión*) *Spanish radio network*

PALABRA CLAVE

ser [ser] *vi* **1** (*descripción, identidad*) to be; **es médica/muy alta** she's a doctor/very tall; **la familia es de Cuzco** his (*o her etc*) family is from Cuzco; **ser de madera** to be made of wood; **soy Ana** I'm Ana
2 (*propiedad*): **es de Joaquín** it's Joaquín's, it belongs to Joaquín
3 (*horas, fechas, números*): **es la una** it's one o'clock; **son las seis y media** it's half-past

six; **es el 1 de junio** it's the first of June; **somos/son seis** there are six of us/them; **2 y 2 son 4** 2 and 2 are *o* make 4
4 (*suceso*): **¿qué ha sido eso?** what was that?; **la fiesta es en mi casa** the party's at my house; **¿qué será de mí?** what will become of me?; **"érase una vez ..."** "once upon a time ..."
5 (*en oraciones pasivas*): **ha sido descubierto ya** it's already been discovered
6: **es de esperar que ...** it is to be hoped *o* I *etc* hope that ...
7 (*locuciones con sub*): **o sea** that is to say; **sea él sea su hermana** either him or his sister; **tengo que irme, no sea que mis hijos estén esperándome** I have to go in case my children are waiting for me
8: **a** *o* **de no ser por él ...** but for him ...
9: **a no ser que**: **a no ser que tenga uno ya** unless he's got one already
■ *nm* being; **ser humano** human being; **ser vivo** living creature

Serbia ['serβja] *nf* Serbia
serbio, -a ['serβjo, a] *adj* Serbian ■ *nm/f* Serb
serenarse [sere'narse] *vr* to calm down; (*mar*) to grow calm; (*tiempo*) to clear up
serenidad [sereni'ðað] *nf* calmness
sereno, -a [se'reno, a] *adj* (*persona*) calm, unruffled; (*tiempo*) fine, settled; (*ambiente*) calm, peaceful ■ *nm* night watchman
serial [se'rjal] *nm* serial
serie ['serje] *nf* series; (*cadena*) sequence, succession; (*TV etc*) serial; (*de inyecciones*) course; **fuera de ~** out of order; (*fig*) special, out of the ordinary; **fabricación en ~** mass production; (*Inform*): **interface/impresora en ~** serial interface/printer
seriedad [serje'ðað] *nf* seriousness; (*formalidad*) reliability; (*de crisis*) gravity, seriousness
serigrafía [seriɣra'fia] *nf* silk screen printing
serio, -a ['serjo, a] *adj* serious; reliable, dependable; grave, serious; **poco ~** (*actitud*) undignified; (*carácter*) unreliable; **en ~** seriously
sermón [ser'mon] *nm* (*Rel*) sermon
sermonear [sermone'ar] *vt* (*fam*) to lecture ■ *vi* to sermonize
seropositivo, -a [seroposi'tiβo, a] *adj* HIV-positive
serpentear [serpente'ar] *vi* to wriggle; (*camino, río*) to wind, snake
serpentina [serpen'tina] *nf* streamer
serpiente [ser'pjente] *nf* snake; **~ boa** boa constrictor; **~ de cascabel** rattlesnake
serranía [serra'nia] *nf* mountainous area
serrano, -a [se'rrano, a] *adj* highland *cpd*, hill *cpd* ■ *nm/f* highlander
serrar [se'rrar] *vt* to saw
serrín [se'rrin] *nm* sawdust
serrucho [se'rrutʃo] *nm* handsaw
Servia ['serβja] *nf* Serbia
servicial [serβi'θjal] *adj* helpful, obliging
servicio [ser'βiθjo] *nm* service; (*Culin etc*) set; **servicios** *nmpl* toilet(s) (*pl*); **estar de ~** to be on duty; **~ aduanero** *o* **de aduana** customs service; **~ a domicilio** home delivery service; **~ incluido** (*en hotel etc*) service charge included; **~ militar** military service; **~ público** (*Com*) public utility
servidor, a [serβi'ðor, a] *nm/f* servant ■ *nm* (*Inform*) server; **su seguro ~ (s.s.s.)** yours faithfully; **un ~** (*el que habla o escribe*) your humble servant
servidumbre [serβi'ðumbre] *nf* (*sujeción*) servitude; (*criados*) servants *pl*, staff
servil [ser'βil] *adj* servile
servilleta [serβi'ʎeta] *nf* serviette, napkin
servilletero [serβiʎe'tero] *nm* napkin ring
servir [ser'βir] *vt* to serve; (*comida*) to serve out *o* up; (*Tenis etc*) to serve ■ *vi* to serve; (*camarero*) to serve, wait; (*tener utilidad*) to be of use, be useful; **servirse** *vr* to serve *o* help o.s.; **¿en qué puedo servirle?** how can I help you?; **~ vino a algn** to pour out wine for sb; **~ de guía** to act *o* serve as a guide; **no sirve para nada** it's no use at all; **servirse de algo** to make use of sth, use sth; **sírvase pasar** please come in
sesenta [se'senta] *num* sixty
sesentón, -ona [sesen'ton, ona] *adj, nm/f* sixty-year-old
sesgado, -a [ses'ɣaðo, a] *adj* slanted, slanting
sesgo ['sesɣo] *nm* slant; (*fig*) slant, twist
sesión [se'sjon] *nf* (*Pol*) session, sitting; (*Cine*) showing; (*Teat*) performance; **abrir/levantar la ~** to open/close *o* adjourn the meeting; **la segunda ~** the second house
seso ['seso] *nm* brain; (*fig*) intelligence; **sesos** *nmpl* (*Culin*) brains; **devanarse los sesos** to rack one's brains
sesudo, -a [se'suðo, a] *adj* sensible, wise
set (*pl* **sets**) [set, sets] *nm* (*Tenis*) set
Set. *abr* (= *setiembre*) Sept.
seta ['seta] *nf* mushroom; **~ venenosa** toadstool
setecientos, -as [sete'θjentos, as] *num* seven hundred
setenta [se'tenta] *num* seventy
setiembre [se'tjembre] *nm* = **septiembre**; *ver tb* **julio**
seto ['seto] *nm* fence; **~ vivo** hedge

seudo… [seuðo] *pref* pseudo…
seudónimo [seu'ðonimo] *nm* pseudonym
Seúl [se'ul] *nm* Seoul
s.e.u.o. *abr* (= *salvo error u omisión*) E & O E
severidad [seβeri'ðað] *nf* severity
severo, -a [se'βero, a] *adj* severe; (*disciplina*) strict; (*frío*) bitter
Sevilla [se'βiʎa] *nf* Seville
sevillano, -a [seβi'ʎano, a] *adj* of *o* from Seville ■ *nm/f* native *o* inhabitant of Seville
S.Exc. *abr* = **Su Excelencia**
sexagenario, -a [seksaxe'narjo, a] *adj* sixty-year-old ■ *nm/f* person in his/her sixties
sexagésimo, -a [seksa'xesimo, a] *num* sixtieth
sexo ['sekso] *nm* sex; **el ~ femenino/ masculino** the female/male sex
sexto, -a ['seksto, a] *num* sixth; **Juan S~** John the Sixth
sexual [sek'swal] *adj* sexual; **vida ~** sex life
sexualidad [sekswali'ðað] *nf* sexuality
s.f. *abr* (= *sin fecha*) no date
s/f *abr* (*Com*: = *su favor*) your favour
sgte(s). *abr* (= *siguiente*) foll
si [si] *conj* if; (*en pregunta indirecta*) if, whether ■ *nm* (*Mus*) B; **si … si …** whether … or …; **me pregunto si …** I wonder if *o* whether …; **si no** if not, otherwise; **¡si fuera verdad!** if only it were true!; **por si viene** in case he comes
sí [si] *adv* yes ■ *nm* consent ■ *pron* (*uso impersonal*) oneself; (*sg*: *m*) himself; (: *f*) herself; (: *de cosa*) itself; (: *de usted*) yourself; (*pl*) themselves; (: *de ustedes*) yourselves; (: *recíproco*) each other; **él no quiere pero yo sí** he doesn't want to but I do; **ella sí vendrá** she will certainly come, she is sure to come; **claro que sí** of course; **creo que sí** I think so; **porque sí** because that's the way it is; (*porque lo digo yo*) because I say so; **¡sí que lo es!** I'll say it is!; **¡eso sí que no!** never!; **se ríe de sí misma** she laughs at herself; **cambiaron una mirada entre sí** they gave each other a look; **de por sí** in itself
siamés, -esa [sja'mes, esa] *adj, nm/f* Siamese
sibarita [siβa'rita] *adj* sybaritic ■ *nm/f* sybarite
sicario [si'karjo] *nm* hired killer
Sicilia [si'θilja] *nf* Sicily
siciliano, -a [siθi'ljano, a] *adj, nm/f* Sicilian ■ *nm* (*Ling*) Sicilian
SIDA ['siða] *nm abr* (= *síndrome de inmunodeficiencia adquirida*) AIDS
siderurgia [siðe'rurxja] *nf* iron and steel industry
siderúrgico, -a [siðe'rurxico, a] *adj* iron and steel *cpd*
sidra ['siðra] *nf* cider
siega *etc* ['sjeɣa] *vb ver* **segar** ■ *nf* (*el cosechar*) reaping; (*el segar*) mowing; (*época*) harvest (time)
siegue *etc* ['sjeɣe] *vb ver* **segar**
siembra *etc* ['sjembra] *vb ver* **sembrar** ■ *nf* sowing
siempre ['sjempre] *adv* always; (*todo el tiempo*) all the time; (*Am*: *así y todo*) still ■ *conj*: **~ que …** (+ *indic*) whenever …; (+ *subjun*) provided that …; **es lo de ~** it's the same old story; **como ~** as usual; **para ~** forever; **~ me voy mañana** (*Am*) I'm still leaving tomorrow
sien [sjen] *nf* (*Anat*) temple
siento *etc* ['sjento] *vb ver* **sentar; sentir**
sierra *etc* ['sjerra] *vb ver* **serrar** ■ *nf* (*Tec*) saw; (*Geo*) mountain range; **S~ Leona** Sierra Leone
siervo, -a ['sjerβo, a] *nm/f* slave
siesta ['sjesta] *nf* siesta, nap; **dormir la** *o* **echarse una** *o* **tomar una ~** to have an afternoon nap *o* a doze
siete ['sjete] *num* seven ■ *excl* (*Am fam*): **¡la gran ~!** wow!, hell!; **hijo de la gran ~** (*fam!*) bastard (*!*), son of a bitch (*US !*)
sífilis ['sifilis] *nf* syphilis
sifón [si'fon] *nm* syphon; **whisky con ~** whisky and soda
siga *etc* ['siɣa] *vb ver* **seguir**
sigilo [si'xilo] *nm* secrecy; (*discreción*) discretion
sigla ['siɣla] *nf* initial, abbreviation
siglo ['siɣlo] *nm* century; (*fig*) age; **S~ de las Luces** Age of Enlightenment; **S~ de Oro** Golden Age
significación [siɣnifika'θjon] *nf* significance
significado [siɣnifi'kaðo] *nm* significance; (*de palabra etc*) meaning
significar [siɣnifi'kar] *vt* to mean, signify; (*notificar*) to make known, express
significativo, -a [siɣnifika'tiβo, a] *adj* significant
signifique *etc* [siɣni'fike] *vb ver* **significar**
signo ['siɣno] *nm* sign; **~ de admiración** *o* **exclamación** exclamation mark; **~ igual** equals sign; **~ de interrogación** question mark; **~ de más/de menos** plus/minus sign; **signos de puntuación** punctuation marks
siguiendo *etc* [si'ɣjendo] *vb ver* **seguir**
siguiente [si'ɣjente] *adj* following; (*próximo*) next
silbar [sil'βar] *vt, vi* to whistle; (*silbato*) to blow; (*Teat etc*) to hiss
silbato [sil'βato] *nm* (*instrumento*) whistle
silbido [sil'βiðo] *nm* whistle, whistling; (*abucheo*) hiss
silenciador [silenθja'ðor] *nm* silencer

silenciar [silen'θjar] *vt* (*persona*) to silence; (*escándalo*) to hush up
silencio [si'lenθjo] *nm* silence, quiet; **en el ~ más absoluto** in dead silence; **guardar ~** to keep silent
silencioso, -a [silen'θjoso, a] *adj* silent, quiet
sílfide ['silfiðe] *nf* sylph
silicio [si'liθjo] *nm* silicon
silla ['siʎa] *nf* (*asiento*) chair; (*tb*: **silla de montar**) saddle; **~ de ruedas** wheelchair
sillería [siʎe'ria] *nf* (*asientos*) chairs *pl*, set of chairs; (*Rel*) choir stalls *pl*; (*taller*) chairmaker's workshop
sillín [si'ʎin] *nm* saddle, seat
sillón [si'ʎon] *nm* armchair, easy chair
silueta [si'lweta] *nf* silhouette; (*de edificio*) outline; (*figura*) figure
silvestre [sil'βestre] *adj* (*Bot*) wild; (*fig*) rustic, rural
sima ['sima] *nf* abyss, chasm
simbolice *etc* [simbo'liθe] *vb ver* **simbolizar**
simbólico, -a [sim'boliko, a] *adj* symbolic(al)
simbolizar [simboli'θar] *vt* to symbolize
símbolo ['simbolo] *nm* symbol; **~ gráfico** (*Inform*) icon
simetría [sime'tria] *nf* symmetry
simétrico, -a [si'metriko, a] *adj* symmetrical
simiente [si'mjente] *nf* seed
similar [simi'lar] *adj* similar
similitud [simili'tuð] *nf* similarity, resemblance
simio ['simjo] *nm* ape
simpatía [simpa'tia] *nf* liking; (*afecto*) affection; (*amabilidad*) kindness; (*de ambiente*) friendliness; (*de persona, lugar*) charm, attractiveness; (*solidaridad*) mutual support, solidarity; **tener ~ a** to like; **la famosa ~ andaluza** that well-known Andalusian charm
simpatice *etc* [simpa'tiθe] *vb ver* **simpatizar**
simpático, -a [sim'patiko, a] *adj* nice, pleasant; (*bondadoso*) kind; **no le hemos caído muy simpáticos** she didn't much take to us
simpatiquísimo, -a [simpati'kisimo, a] *adj superlativo de* **simpático** ever so nice; ever so kind
simpatizante [simpati'θante] *nm/f* sympathizer
simpatizar [simpati'θar] *vi*: **~ con** to get on well with
simple ['simple] *adj* simple; (*elemental*) simple, easy; (*mero*) mere; (*puro*) pure, sheer ■ *nm/f* simpleton; **un ~ soldado** an ordinary soldier
simpleza [sim'pleθa] *nf* simpleness; (*necedad*) silly thing
simplicidad [simpliθi'ðað] *nf* simplicity
simplificar [simplifi'kar] *vt* to simplify
simplifique *etc* [simpli'fike] *vb ver* **simplificar**
simplón, -ona [sim'plon, ona] *adj* simple, gullible ■ *nm/f* simple soul
simposio [sim'posjo] *nm* symposium
simulacro [simu'lakro] *nm* (*apariencia*) semblance; (*fingimiento*) sham
simular [simu'lar] *vt* to simulate; (*fingir*) to feign, sham
simultanear [simultane'ar] *vt*: **~ dos cosas** to do two things simultaneously
simultáneo, -a [simul'taneo, a] *adj* simultaneous
sin [sin] *prep* without; (*a no ser por*) but for ■ *conj*: **~ que** (*+subjun*) without; **~ decir nada** without a word; **~ verlo yo** without my seeing it; **platos ~ lavar** unwashed *o* dirty dishes; **la ropa está ~ lavar** the clothes are unwashed; **~ que lo sepa él** without his knowing; **~ embargo** however
sinagoga [sina'ɣoɣa] *nf* synagogue
Sinaí [sina'i] *nm*: **El Sinaí** Sinai, the Sinai Peninsula; **el Monte Sinaí** Mount Sinai
sinceridad [sinθeri'ðað] *nf* sincerity
sincero, -a [sin'θero, a] *adj* sincere; (*persona*) genuine; (*opinión*) frank; (*felicitaciones*) heartfelt
síncope ['sinkope] *nm* (*desmayo*) blackout; **~ cardíaco** (*Med*) heart failure
sincronice *etc* [sinkro'niθe] *vb ver* **sincronizar**
sincronizar [sinkroni'θar] *vt* to synchronize
sindical [sindi'kal] *adj* union *cpd*, trade-union *cpd*
sindicalista [sindika'lista] *adj* trade-union *cpd* ■ *nm/f* trade unionist
sindicar [sindi'kar] *vt* (*obreros*) to organize, unionize; **sindicarse** *vr* (*obrero*) to join a union
sindicato [sindi'kato] *nm* (*de trabajadores*) trade(s) *o* labor (*US*) union; (*de negociantes*) syndicate
sindique *etc* [sin'dike] *vb ver* **sindicar**
síndrome ['sindrome] *nm* syndrome; **~ de abstinencia** withdrawal symptoms
sine qua non [sine'kwanon] *adj*: **condición ~** sine qua non
sinfín [sin'fin] *nm*: **un ~ de** a great many, no end of
sinfonía [sinfo'nia] *nf* symphony
sinfónico, -a [sin'foniko, a] *adj* (*música*) symphonic; **orquesta sinfónica** symphony orchestra
Singapur [singa'pur] *nm* Singapore
singular [singu'lar] *adj* singular; (*fig*) outstanding, exceptional; (*pey*) peculiar, odd ■ *nm* (*Ling*) singular; **en ~** in the singular

singularice *etc* [singula'riθe] *vb ver* **singularizar**
singularidad [singulari'ðað] *nf* singularity, peculiarity
singularizar [singulari'θar] *vt* to single out; **singularizarse** *vr* to distinguish o.s., stand out
siniestro, -a [si'njestro, a] *adj* left; (*fig*) sinister ■ *nm* (*accidente*) accident; (*desastre*) natural disaster
sinnúmero [sin'numero] *nm* = **sinfín**
sino ['sino] *nm* fate, destiny ■ *conj* (*pero*) but; (*salvo*) except, save; **no son 8 ~ 9** there are not 8 but 9; **todos ~ él** all except him
sinónimo, -a [si'nonimo, a] *adj* synonymous ■ *nm* synonym
sinrazón [sinra'θon] *nf* wrong, injustice
sinsabor [sinsa'βor] *nm* (*molestia*) trouble; (*dolor*) sorrow; (*preocupación*) uneasiness
sintaxis [sin'taksis] *nf* syntax
síntesis ['sintesis] *nf inv* synthesis
sintetice *etc* [sinte'tiθe] *vb ver* **sintetizar**
sintético, -a [sin'tetiko, a] *adj* synthetic
sintetizador [sintetiθa'ðor] *nm* synthesizer
sintetizar [sinteti'θar] *vt* to synthesize
sintiendo *etc* [sin'tjendo] *vb ver* **sentir**
síntoma ['sintoma] *nm* symptom
sintomático, -a [sinto'matiko, a] *adj* symptomatic
sintonía [sinto'nia] *nf* (*Radio*) tuning; (*melodía*) signature tune
sintonice *etc* [sinto'niθe] *vb ver* **sintonizar**
sintonizador [sintoniθa'ðor] *nm* (*Radio*) tuner
sintonizar [sintoni'θar] *vt* (*Radio*) to tune (in) to, pick up
sinuoso, -a [si'nwoso, a] *adj* (*camino*) winding; (*rumbo*) devious
sinvergüenza [simber'ɣwenθa] *nm/f* rogue, scoundrel
sionismo [sjo'nismo] *nm* Zionism
siquiera [si'kjera] *conj* even if, even though ■ *adv* (*esp Am*) at least; **ni ~** not even; **~ bebe algo** at least drink something
sirena [si'rena] *nf* siren, mermaid; (*bocina*) siren, hooter
Siria ['sirja] *nf* Syria
sirio, -a ['sirjo, a] *adj, nm/f* Syrian
sirviendo *etc* [sir'βjendo] *vb ver* **servir**
sirviente, -a [sir'βjente, a] *nm/f* servant
sisa ['sisa] *nf* petty theft; (*Costura*) dart; (*sobaquera*) armhole
sisar [si'sar] *vt* (*robar*) to thieve; (*Costura*) to take in
sisear [sise'ar] *vt, vi* to hiss
sísmico, -a ['sismiko, a] *adj*: **movimiento ~** earthquake
sismógrafo [sis'moɣrafo] *nm* seismograph
sistema [sis'tema] *nm* system; (*método*) method; **~ impositivo** *o* **tributario** taxation, tax system; **~ pedagógico** educational system; **~ de alerta inmediata** early-warning system; **~ binario** (*Inform*) binary system; **~ experto** expert system; **~ de facturación** (*Com*) invoicing system; **~ de fondo fijo** (*Com*) imprest system; **~ de lógica compartida** (*Inform*) shared logic system; **~ métrico** metric system; **~ operativo (en disco)** (*Inform*) (disk-based) operating system; *see note*

SISTEMA EDUCATIVO

The reform of the Spanish *sistema educativo* (education system) begun in the early 90s has replaced the courses EGB, BUP and COU with the following: *Primaria* a compulsory 6 years; *Secundaria* a compulsory 4 years; *Bachillerato* an optional 2 year secondary school course, essential for those wishing to go on to higher education.

sistemático, -a [siste'matiko, a] *adj* systematic
sitiar [si'tjar] *vt* to besiege, lay siege to
sitio ['sitjo] *nm* (*lugar*) place; (*espacio*) room, space; (*Mil*) siege; **~ web** website; **¿hay ~?** is there any room?; **hay ~ de sobra** there's plenty of room
situación [sitwa'θjon] *nf* situation, position; (*estatus*) position, standing
situado, -a [si'twaðo, a] *adj* situated, placed; **estar ~** (*Com*) to be financially secure
situar [si'twar] *vt* to place, put; (*edificio*) to locate, situate
S.L. *abr* (*Com*: = *Sociedad Limitada*) Ltd
slip [es'lip] (*pl* **slips**) *nm* pants *pl*, briefs *pl*
slot [es'lot] (*pl* **slots**) *nm*: **~ de expansión** expansion slot
S.M. *abr* (= *Su Majestad*) HM
SME *nm abr* (= *Sistema Monetario Europeo*) EMS; **(mecanismo de cambios del) ~** ERM
smoking [(e)'smokin] (*pl* **smokings**) *nm* dinner jacket (*Brit*), tuxedo (*US*)
SMS *nm* (*mensaje*) text (message), SMS (message)
s/n *abr* (= *sin número*) no number
snob [es'nob] = **esnob**
SO *abr* (= *suroeste*) SW
so [so] *excl* whoa!; **¡so burro!** you idiot! ■ *prep* under
s/o *abr* (*Com*: = *su orden*) your order
sobaco [so'βako] *nm* armpit

sobado, -a [so'βaðo, a] *adj* *(ropa)* worn; *(arrugado)* crumpled; *(libro)* well-thumbed; *(Culin: bizcocho)* short
sobar [so'βar] *vt* *(tela)* to finger; *(ropa)* to rumple, mess up; *(músculos)* to rub, massage
soberanía [soβera'nia] *nf* sovereignty
soberano, -a [soβe'rano, a] *adj* sovereign; *(fig)* supreme ▪ *nm/f* sovereign; **los soberanos** the king and queen
soberbio, -a [so'βerβjo, a] *adj* *(orgulloso)* proud; *(altivo)* haughty, arrogant; *(fig)* magnificent, superb ▪ *nf* pride; haughtiness, arrogance; magnificence
sobornar [soβor'nar] *vt* to bribe
soborno [so'βorno] *nm* *(un soborno)* bribe; *(el soborno)* bribery
sobra ['soβra] *nf* excess, surplus; **sobras** *nfpl* left-overs, scraps; **de ~** surplus, extra; **lo sé de ~** I'm only too aware of it; **tengo de ~** I've more than enough
sobradamente [soβraða'mente] *adv* amply; *(saber)* only too well
sobrado, -a [so'βraðo, a] *adj* *(más que suficiente)* more than enough; *(superfluo)* excessive ▪ *adv* too, exceedingly; **sobradas veces** repeatedly
sobrante [so'βrante] *adj* remaining, extra ▪ *nm* surplus, remainder
sobrar [so'βrar] *vt* to exceed, surpass ▪ *vi* *(tener de más)* to be more than enough; *(quedar)* to remain, be left (over)
sobrasada [soβra'saða] *nf* ≈ sausage spread
sobre ['soβre] *prep* *(gen)* on; *(encima)* on (top of); *(por encima de, arriba de)* over, above; *(más que)* more than; *(además)* in addition to, besides; *(alrededor de)* about; *(porcentaje)* in, out of; *(tema)* about, on ▪ *nm* envelope; **~ todo** above all; **3 ~ 100** 3 in a 100, 3 out of every 100; **un libro ~ Tirso** a book about Tirso; **~ de ventanilla** window envelope
sobrecama [soβre'kama] *nf* bedspread
sobrecapitalice *etc* [soβrekapita'liθe] *vb ver* **sobrecapitalizar**
sobrecapitalizar [soβrekapitali'θar] *vi* to overcapitalize
sobrecargar [soβrekar'ɣar] *vt* *(camión)* to overload; *(Com)* to surcharge
sobrecargue *etc* [soβre'karɣe] *vb ver* **sobrecargar**
sobrecoger [soβreko'xer] *vt* *(sobresaltar)* to startle; *(asustar)* to scare; **sobrecogerse** *vr* *(sobresaltarse)* to be startled; *(asustarse)* to get scared; *(quedar impresionado)*: **sobrecogerse (de)** to be overawed (by)
sobrecoja *etc* [soβre'koxa] *vb ver* **sobrecoger**
sobredosis [soβre'ðosis] *nf inv* overdose
sobreentender [soβreenten'der] *vt* to understand; *(adivinar)* to deduce, infer; **sobreentenderse** *vr*: **se sobreentiende que ...** it is implied that ...
sobreescribir [soβreeskri'βir] *vt* *(Inform)* to overwrite
sobreestimar [soβreesti'mar] *vt* to overestimate
sobregiro [soβre'xiro] *nm* *(Com)* overdraft
sobrehumano, -a [soβreu'mano, a] *adj* superhuman
sobreimprimir [soβreimpri'mir] *vt* *(Com)* to merge
sobrellevar [soβreʎe'βar] *vt* *(fig)* to bear, endure
sobremesa [soβre'mesa] *nf* *(después de comer)* sitting on after a meal; *(Inform)* desktop; **conversación de ~** table talk
sobremodo [soβre'moðo] *adv* very much, enormously
sobrenatural [soβrenatu'ral] *adj* supernatural
sobrenombre [soβre'nombre] *nm* nickname
sobrentender [soβrenten'der] *vt* = **sobreentender**
sobrepasar [soβrepa'sar] *vt* to exceed, surpass
sobrepondré *etc* [soβrepon'dre] *vb ver* **sobreponer**
sobreponer [soβrepo'ner] *vt* *(poner encima)* to put on top; *(añadir)* to add; **sobreponerse** *vr*: **sobreponerse a** to overcome
sobreponga *etc* [soβre'ponga] *vb ver* **sobreponer**
sobreprima [soβre'prima] *nf* *(Com)* loading
sobreproducción [soβreproðuk'θjon] *nf* overproduction
sobrepuesto [soβre'pwesto], **sobrepuse** *etc* [soβre'puse] *vb ver* **sobreponer**
sobresaldré *etc* [soβresal'dre], **sobresalga** *etc* [soβre'salɣa] *vb ver* **sobresalir**
sobresaliente [soβresa'ljente] *adj* projecting; *(fig)* outstanding, excellent; *(Univ etc)* first class ▪ *nm* *(Univ etc)* first class (mark), distinction
sobresalir [soβresa'lir] *vi* to project, jut out; *(fig)* to stand out, excel
sobresaltar [soβresal'tar] *vt* *(asustar)* to scare, frighten; *(sobrecoger)* to startle
sobresalto [soβre'salto] *nm* *(movimiento)* start; *(susto)* scare; *(turbación)* sudden shock
sobreseer [soβrese'er] *vt*: **~ una causa** *(Jur)* to stop a case
sobrestadía [soβresta'ðia] *nf* *(Com)* demurrage
sobrestimar [soβresti'mar] *vt* = **sobreestimar**
sobretensión [soβreten'sjon] *nf* *(Elec)*: **~ transitoria** surge

sobretiempo [soβre'tjempo] *nm* (*Am*) overtime
sobretodo [soβre'toðo] *nm* overcoat
sobrevendré *etc* [soβreβen'dre], **sobrevenga** *etc* [soβre'βenga] *vb ver* **sobrevenir**
sobrevenir [soβreβe'nir] *vi* (*ocurrir*) to happen (unexpectedly); (*resultar*) to follow, ensue
sobreviene *etc* [soβre'βjene], **sobrevine** *etc* [soβre'βine] *vb ver* **sobrevenir**
sobreviviente [soβreβi'βjente] *adj* surviving ■ *nm/f* survivor
sobrevivir [soβreβi'βir] *vi* to survive; (*persona*) to outlive; (*objeto etc*) to outlast
sobrevolar [soβreβo'lar] *vt* to fly over
sobrevuele *etc* [soβre'βwele] *vb ver* **sobrevolar**
sobriedad [soβrje'ðað] *nf* sobriety, soberness; (*moderación*) moderation, restraint
sobrino, -a [so'βrino, a] *nm/f* nephew/niece
sobrio, -a ['soβrjo, a] *adj* (*moderado*) moderate, restrained
socarrón, -ona [soka'rron, ona] *adj* (*sarcástico*) sarcastic, ironic(al)
socavar [soka'βar] *vt* to undermine; (*excavar*) to dig underneath *o* below
socavón [soka'βon] *nm* (*en mina*) gallery; (*hueco*) hollow; (*en la calle*) hole
sociable [so'θjaβle] *adj* (*persona*) sociable, friendly; (*animal*) social
social [so'θjal] *adj* social; (*Com*) company *cpd*
socialdemócrata [soθjalde'mokrata] *adj* social-democratic ■ *nm/f* social democrat
socialice *etc* [soθja'liθe] *vb ver* **socializar**
socialista [soθja'lista] *adj, nm/f* socialist
socializar [soθjali'θar] *vt* to socialize
sociedad [soθje'ðað] *nf* society; (*Com*) company; **~ de ahorro y préstamo** savings and loan society; **~ anónima (S.A.)** limited company (Ltd) (*Brit*), incorporated company (Inc) (*US*); **~ de beneficiencia** friendly society (*Brit*), benefit association (*US*); **~ de cartera** investment trust; **~ comanditaria** (*Com*) co-ownership; **~ conjunta** (*Com*) joint venture; **~ inmobiliaria** building society (*Brit*), savings and loan (society) (*US*); **~ de responsabilidad limitada** (*Com*) private limited company
socio, -a ['soθjo, a] *nm/f* (*miembro*) member; (*Com*) partner; **~ activo** active partner; **~ capitalista** *o* **comanditario** sleeping *o* silent (*US*) partner
socioeconómico, -a [soθjoeko'nomiko, a] *adj* socio-economic
sociología [soθjolo'xia] *nf* sociology
sociólogo, -a [so'θjoloɣo, a] *nm/f* sociologist
socorrer [soko'rrer] *vt* to help
socorrido, -a [soko'rriðo, a] *adj* (*tienda*) well-stocked; (*útil*) handy; (*persona*) helpful
socorrismo [soko'rrismo] *nm* life-saving
socorrista [soko'rrista] *nm/f* first aider; (*en piscina, playa*) lifeguard
socorro [so'korro] *nm* (*ayuda*) help, aid; (*Mil*) relief; **¡~!** help!
soda ['soða] *nf* (*sosa*) soda; (*bebida*) soda (water)
sódico, -a ['soðiko, a] *adj* sodium *cpd*
soez [so'eθ] *adj* dirty, obscene
sofá [so'fa] *nm* sofa, settee
sofá-cama [so'fakama] *nm* studio couch, sofa bed
Sofia ['sofja] *nf* Sofia
sofisticación [sofistika'θjon] *nf* sophistication
sofisticado, -a [sofisti'kaðo, a] *adj* sophisticated
sofocado, -a [sofo'kaðo, a] *adj*: **estar ~** (*fig*) to be out of breath; (*ahogarse*) to feel stifled
sofocar [sofo'kar] *vt* to suffocate; (*apagar*) to smother, put out; **sofocarse** *vr* to suffocate; (*fig*) to blush, feel embarrassed
sofoco [so'foko] *nm* suffocation; (*azoro*) embarrassment
sofocón [sofo'kon] *nm*: **llevarse** *o* **pasar un ~** to have a sudden shock
sofreír [sofre'ir] *vt* to fry lightly
sofría *etc* [so'fria], **sofriendo** *etc* [so'frjendo], **sofrito** [so'frito] *vb ver* **sofreír**
soft ['sof], **software** ['sofwer] *nm* (*Inform*) software
soga ['soɣa] *nf* rope
sois [sois] *vb ver* **ser**
soja ['soxa] *nf* soya
sojuzgar [soxuθ'ɣar] *vt* to subdue, rule despotically
sojuzgue *etc* [so'xuθɣe] *vb ver* **sojuzgar**
sol [sol] *nm* sun; (*luz*) sunshine, sunlight; (*Mus*) G; **~ naciente/poniente** rising/setting sun; **tomar el ~** to sunbathe; **hace ~** it is sunny
solace *etc* [so'laθe] *vb ver* **solazar**
solamente [sola'mente] *adv* only, just
solapa [so'lapa] *nf* (*de chaqueta*) lapel; (*de libro*) jacket
solapado, -a [sola'paðo, a] *adj* sly, underhand
solar [so'lar] *adj* solar, sun *cpd* ■ *nm* (*terreno*) plot (of ground); (*local*) undeveloped site
solaz [so'laθ] *nm* recreation, relaxation
solazar [sola'θar] *vt* (*divertir*) to amuse; **solazarse** *vr* to enjoy o.s., relax
soldada [sol'daða] *nf* pay
soldado [sol'daðo] *nm* soldier; **~ raso** private
soldador [solda'ðor] *nm* soldering iron; (*persona*) welder
soldar [sol'dar] *vt* to solder, weld; (*unir*) to join, unite

soleado, -a [sole'aðo, a] *adj* sunny
soledad [sole'ðað] *nf* solitude; (*estado infeliz*) loneliness
solemne [so'lemne] *adj* solemn; (*tontería*) utter; (*error*) complete
solemnidad [solemni'ðað] *nf* solemnity
soler [so'ler] *vi* to be in the habit of, be accustomed to; **suele salir a las ocho** she usually goes out at 8 o'clock; **solíamos ir todos los años** we used to go every year
solera [so'lera] *nf* (*tradición*) tradition; **vino de ~** vintage wine
solfeo [sol'feo] *nm* singing of scales; **ir a clases de ~** to take singing lessons
solicitar [soliθi'tar] *vt* (*permiso*) to ask for, seek; (*puesto*) to apply for; (*votos*) to canvass for; (*atención*) to attract; (*persona*) to pursue, chase after
solícito, -a [so'liθito, a] *adj* (*diligente*) diligent; (*cuidadoso*) careful
solicitud [soliθi'tuð] *nf* (*calidad*) great care; (*petición*) request; (*a un puesto*) application
solidaridad [soliðari'ðað] *nf* solidarity; **por ~ con** (*Pol etc*) out of *o* in solidarity with
solidario, -a [soli'ðarjo, a] *adj* (*participación*) joint, common; (*compromiso*) mutually binding; **hacerse ~ de** to declare one's solidarity with
solidarizarse [soliðari'θarse] *vr*: **~ con algn** to support sb, sympathize with sb
solidez [soli'ðeθ] *nf* solidity
sólido, -a ['soliðo, a] *adj* solid; (*Tec*) solidly made; (*bien construido*) well built
soliloquio [soli'lokjo] *nm* soliloquy
solista [so'lista] *nm/f* soloist
solitario, -a [soli'tarjo, a] *adj* (*persona*) lonely, solitary; (*lugar*) lonely, desolate ■ *nm/f* (*reclusa*) recluse; (*en la sociedad*) loner ■ *nm* solitaire ■ *nf* tapeworm
soliviantar [soliβjan'tar] *vt* to stir up, rouse (to revolt); (*enojar*) to anger; (*sacar de quicio*) to exasperate
solloce *etc* [so'ʎoθe] *vb ver* **sollozar**
sollozar [soʎo'θar] *vi* to sob
sollozo [so'ʎoθo] *nm* sob
solo, -a ['solo, a] *adj* (*único*) single, sole; (*sin compañía*) alone; (*Mus*) solo; (*solitario*) lonely; **hay una sola dificultad** there is just one difficulty; **a solas** alone, by o.s.
sólo ['solo] *adv* only, just; (*exclusivamente*) solely; **tan ~** only just
solomillo [solo'miʎo] *nm* sirloin
solsticio [sols'tiθjo] *nm* solstice
soltar [sol'tar] *vt* (*dejar ir*) to let go of; (*desprender*) to unfasten, loosen; (*librar*) to release, set free; (*amarras*) to cast off; (*Auto: freno etc*) to release; (*suspiro*) to heave; (*risa etc*) to let out; **soltarse** *vr* (*desanudarse*) to come undone; (*desprenderse*) to come off; (*adquirir destreza*) to become expert; (*en idioma*) to become fluent
soltero, -a [sol'tero, a] *adj* single, unmarried ■ *nm* bachelor ■ *nf* single woman, spinster
solterón [solte'ron] *nm* confirmed bachelor
solterona [solte'rona] *nf* spinster, maiden lady; (*pey*) old maid
soltura [sol'tura] *nf* looseness, slackness; (*de los miembros*) agility, ease of movement; (*en el hablar*) fluency, ease
soluble [so'luβle] *adj* (*Química*) soluble; (*problema*) solvable; **~ en agua** soluble in water
solución [solu'θjon] *nf* solution; **~ de continuidad** break in continuity
solucionar [soluθjo'nar] *vt* (*problema*) to solve; (*asunto*) to settle, resolve
solvencia [sol'βenθja] *nf* (*Com: estado*) solvency; (*: acción*) settlement, payment
solventar [solβen'tar] *vt* (*pagar*) to settle, pay; (*resolver*) to resolve
solvente [sol'βente] *adj* solvent, free of debt
Somalia [so'malja] *nf* Somalia
sombra ['sombra] *nf* shadow; (*como protección*) shade; **sombras** *nfpl* darkness *sg*, shadows; **sin ~ de duda** without a shadow of doubt; **tener buena/mala ~** (*suerte*) to be lucky/unlucky; (*carácter*) to be likeable/disagreeable
sombrero [som'brero] *nm* hat; **~ hongo** bowler (hat), derby (*US*); **~ de copa** *o* **de pelo** (*Am*) top hat
sombrilla [som'briʎa] *nf* parasol, sunshade
sombrío, -a [som'brio, a] *adj* (*oscuro*) shady; (*fig*) sombre, sad; (*persona*) gloomy
somero, -a [so'mero, a] *adj* superficial
someter [some'ter] *vt* (*país*) to conquer; (*persona*) to subject to one's will; (*informe*) to present, submit; **someterse** *vr* to give in, yield, submit; **someterse a** to submit to; **someterse a una operación** to undergo an operation
sometimiento [someti'mjento] *nm* (*estado*) submission; (*acción*) presentation
somier [so'mjer] (*pl* **somiers**) *nm* spring mattress
somnífero [som'nifero] *nm* sleeping pill *o* tablet
somnolencia [somno'lenθja] *nf* sleepiness, drowsiness
somos ['somos] *vb ver* **ser**
son [son] *vb ver* **ser** ■ *nm* sound; **en ~ de broma** as a joke
sonado, -a [so'naðo, a] *adj* (*comentado*) talked-of; (*famoso*) famous; (*Com: pey*) hyped(-up)

sonajero [sona'xero] *nm* (baby's) rattle
sonambulismo [sonambu'lismo] *nm* sleepwalking
sonámbulo, -a [so'nambulo, a] *nm/f* sleepwalker
sonar [so'nar] *vt* (*campana*) to ring; (*trompeta, sirena*) to blow ■ *vi* to sound; (*hacer ruido*) to make a noise; (*Ling*) to be sounded, be pronounced; (*ser conocido*) to sound familiar; (*campana*) to ring; (*reloj*) to strike, chime; **sonarse** *vr*: **sonarse (la nariz)** to blow one's nose; **es un nombre que suena** it's a name that's in the news; **me suena ese nombre** that name rings a bell
sonda ['sonda] *nf* (*Naut*) sounding; (*Tec*) bore, drill; (*Med*) probe
sondear [sonde'ar] *vt* to sound; to bore (into), drill; to probe, sound; (*fig*) to sound out
sondeo [son'deo] *nm* sounding; boring, drilling; (*encuesta*) poll, enquiry; **~ de la opinión pública** public opinion poll
sónico, -a ['soniko, a] *adj* sonic, sound *cpd*
sonido [so'niðo] *nm* sound
sonoro, -a [so'noro, a] *adj* sonorous; (*resonante*) loud, resonant; (*Ling*) voiced; **efectos sonoros** sound effects
sonreír [sonre'ir] *vi*, **sonreírse** *vr* to smile
sonría *etc* [son'ria], **sonriendo** *etc* [son'rjendo] *vb ver* **sonreír**
sonriente [son'rjente] *adj* smiling
sonrisa [son'risa] *nf* smile
sonrojar [sonro'xar] *vt*: **~ a algn** to make sb blush; **sonrojarse** *vr*: **sonrojarse (de)** to blush (at)
sonrojo [son'roxo] *nm* blush
sonsacar [sonsa'kar] *vt* to wheedle, coax; **~ a algn** to pump sb for information
sonsaque *etc* [son'sake] *vb ver* **sonsacar**
sonsonete [sonso'nete] *nm* (*golpecitos*) tap(ping); (*voz monótona*) monotonous delivery, singsong (voice)
soñador, a [soɲa'ðor, a] *nm/f* dreamer
soñar [so'ɲar] *vt, vi* to dream; **~ con** to dream about *o* of; **soñé contigo anoche** I dreamed about you last night
soñoliento, -a [soɲo'ljento, a] *adj* sleepy, drowsy
sopa ['sopa] *nf* soup; **~ de fideos** noodle soup
sopero, -a [so'pero, a] *adj* (*plato, cuchara*) soup *cpd* ■ *nm* soup plate ■ *nf* soup tureen
sopesar [sope'sar] *vt* to try the weight of; (*fig*) to weigh up
sopetón [sope'ton] *nm*: **de ~** suddenly, unexpectedly
soplar [so'plar] *vt* (*polvo*) to blow away, blow off; (*inflar*) to blow up; (*vela*) to blow out; (*ayudar a recordar*) to prompt; (*birlar*) to nick; (*delatar*) to split on ■ *vi* to blow; (*delatar*) to squeal; (*beber*) to booze, bend the elbow
soplete [so'plete] *nm* blowlamp; **~ soldador** welding torch
soplo ['soplo] *nm* blow, puff; (*de viento*) puff, gust
soplón, -ona [so'plon, ona] *nm/f* (*fam: chismoso*) telltale; (*: de policía*) informer, grass
soponcio [so'ponθjo] *nm* dizzy spell
sopor [so'por] *nm* drowsiness
soporífero, -a [sopo'rifero, a] *adj* sleep-inducing; (*fig*) soporific ■ *nm* sleeping pill
soportable [sopor'taβle] *adj* bearable
soportal [sopor'tal] *nm* porch; **soportales** *nmpl* arcade *sg*
soportar [sopor'tar] *vt* to bear, carry; (*fig*) to bear, put up with
soporte [so'porte] *nm* support; (*fig*) pillar, support; (*Inform*) medium; **~ de entrada/salida** input/output medium
soprano [so'prano] *nf* soprano
sor [sor] *nf*: **S~ María** Sister Mary
sorber [sor'βer] *vt* (*chupar*) to sip; (*inhalar*) to sniff, inhale; (*absorber*) to soak up, absorb
sorbete [sor'βete] *nm* sherbet
sorbo ['sorβo] *nm* (*trago*) gulp, swallow; (*chupada*) sip; **beber a sorbos** to sip
sordera [sor'ðera] *nf* deafness
sórdido, -a ['sorðiðo, a] *adj* dirty, squalid
sordo, -a ['sorðo, a] *adj* (*persona*) deaf; (*ruido*) dull; (*Ling*) voiceless ■ *nm/f* deaf person; **quedarse ~** to go deaf
sordomudo, -a [sorðo'muðo, a] *adj* deaf and dumb ■ *nm/f* deaf-mute
soriano, -a [so'rjano, a] *adj* of *o* from Soria ■ *nm/f* native *o* inhabitant of Soria
sorna ['sorna] *nf* (*malicia*) slyness; (*tono burlón*) sarcastic tone
soroche [so'rotʃe] *nm* (*Am Med*) mountain sickness
sorprendente [sorpren'dente] *adj* surprising
sorprender [sorpren'der] *vt* to surprise; (*asombrar*) to amaze; (*sobresaltar*) to startle; (*coger desprevenido*) to catch unawares; **sorprenderse** *vr*: **sorprenderse (de)** to be surprised *o* amazed (at)
sorpresa [sor'presa] *nf* surprise
sorpresivo, -a [sorpre'siβo, a] *adj* (*Am*) surprising; (*imprevisto*) sudden
sortear [sorte'ar] *vt* to draw lots for; (*rifar*) to raffle; (*dificultad*) to dodge, avoid
sorteo [sor'teo] *nm* (*en lotería*) draw; (*rifa*) raffle
sortija [sor'tixa] *nf* ring; (*rizo*) ringlet, curl
sortilegio [sorti'lexjo] *nm* (*hechicería*) sorcery; (*hechizo*) spell
SOS *sigla m* SOS

sosegado, -a [sose'ɣaðo, a] *adj* quiet, calm
sosegar [sose'ɣar] *vt* to quieten, calm; (*el ánimo*) to reassure ▪ *vi* to rest
sosegué [sose'ɣe], **soseguemos** *etc* [sose'ɣemos] *vb ver* **sosegar**
sosiego *etc* [so'sjeɣo] *vb ver* **sosegar** ▪ *nm* quiet(ness), calm(ness)
sosiegue *etc* [so'sjeɣe] *vb ver* **sosegar**
soslayar [sosla'jar] *vt* (*preguntas*) to get round
soslayo [sos'lajo]: **de ~** *adv* obliquely, sideways; **mirar de ~** to look out of the corner of one's eye (at)
soso, -a ['soso, a] *adj* (*Culin*) tasteless; (*fig*) dull, uninteresting
sospecha [sos'petʃa] *nf* suspicion
sospechar [sospe'tʃar] *vt* to suspect ▪ *vi*: **~ de** to be suspicious of
sospechoso, -a [sospe'tʃoso, a] *adj* suspicious; (*testimonio, opinión*) suspect ▪ *nm/f* suspect
sostén [sos'ten] *nm* (*apoyo*) support; (*sujetador*) bra; (*alimentación*) sustenance, food
sostendré *etc* [sosten'dre] *vb ver* **sostener**
sostener [soste'ner] *vt* to support; (*mantener*) to keep up, maintain; (*alimentar*) to sustain, keep going; **sostenerse** *vr* to support o.s.; (*seguir*) to continue, remain
sostenga *etc* [sos'tenga] *vb ver* **sostener**
sostenido, -a [soste'niðo, a] *adj* continuous, sustained; (*prolongado*) prolonged; (*Mus*) sharp ▪ *nm* (*Mus*) sharp
sostuve *etc* [sos'tuβe] *vb ver* **sostener**
sota ['sota] *nf* (*Naipes*) ≈ jack; *ver tb* **baraja española**
sotana [so'tana] *nf* (*Rel*) cassock
sótano ['sotano] *nm* basement
sotavento [sota'βento] *nm* (*Naut*) lee, leeward
soterrar [sote'rrar] *vt* to bury; (*esconder*) to hide away
sotierre *etc* [so'tjerre] *vb ver* **soterrar**
soviético, -a [so'βjetiko, a] *adj, nm/f* Soviet; **los soviéticos** the Soviets, the Russians
soy [soi] *vb ver* **ser**
soya ['soja] *nf* (*Am*) soya (bean)
SP *abr* (*Auto*) = **servicio público**
SPM *nm abr* (= *síndrome premenstrual*) PMS
spooling [es'pulin] *nm* (*Inform*) spooling
sport [es'por(t)] *nm* sport
spot [es'pot] (*pl* **~**) *nm* (*publicitario*) ad
squash [es'kwas] *nm* (*Deporte*) squash
Sr. *abr* (= *Señor*) Mr
Sra. *abr* (= *Señora*) Mrs
S.R.C. *abr* (= *se ruega contestación*) R.S.V.P.
Sres., Srs. *abr* (= *Señores*) Messrs
Sri Lanka [sri'lanka] *nm* Sri Lanka
Srta. *abr* = **Señorita**
SS *abr* (= *Santos, Santas*) SS
S.S. *abr* (*Rel*: = *Su Santidad*) H.H.; = **Seguridad Social**
ss. *abr* (= *siguientes*) foll
SSE *abr* (= *sursudeste*) SSE
SS.MM. *abr* (= *Sus Majestades*) Their Royal Highnesses
SSO *abr* (= *sursudoeste*) SSW
Sta. *abr* (= *Santa*) St; (= *Señorita*) Miss
stand (*pl* **stands**) [es'tan, es'tan(s)] *nm* (*Com*) stand
stárter [es'tarter] *nm* (*Auto*) self-starter, starting motor
statu quo [es'tatu'kuo], **status quo** [es'tatus'kuo] *nm* status quo
status ['status, es'tatus] *nm inv* status
Sto. *abr* (= *Santo*) St
stop (*pl* **stops**) [es'top, es'top(s)] *nm* (*Auto*) stop sign
su [su] *pron* (*de él*) his; (*de ella*) her; (*de una cosa*) its; (*de ellos, ellas*) their; (*de usted, ustedes*) your
suave ['swaβe] *adj* gentle; (*superficie*) smooth; (*trabajo*) easy; (*música, voz*) soft, sweet; (*clima, sabor*) mild
suavice *etc* [swa'βiθe] *vb ver* **suavizar**
suavidad [swaβi'ðað] *nf* gentleness; (*de superficie*) smoothness; (*de música*) softness, sweetness
suavizante [swaβi'θante] *nm* conditioner
suavizar [swaβi'θar] *vt* to soften; (*quitar la aspereza*) to smooth (out); (*pendiente*) to ease; (*colores*) to tone down; (*carácter*) to mellow; (*dureza*) to temper
subalimentado, -a [suβalimen'taðo, a] *adj* undernourished
subalterno, -a [suβal'terno, a] *adj* (*importancia*) secondary; (*personal*) minor, auxiliary ▪ *nm* subordinate
subarrendar [suβarren'dar] *vt* (*Com*) to lease back
subarriendo [suβa'rrjendo] *nm* (*Com*) leaseback
subasta [su'βasta] *nf* auction; **poner en** *o* **sacar a pública ~** to put up for public auction; **~ a la rebaja** Dutch auction
subastador, a [suβasta'ðor, a] *nm/f* auctioneer
subastar [suβas'tar] *vt* to auction (off)
subcampeón, -ona [suβkampe'on, ona] *nm/f* runner-up
subconsciente [suβkons'θjente] *adj* subconscious
subcontratar [suβkontra'tar] *vt* (*Com*) to subcontract
subcontrato [suβkon'trato] *nm* (*Com*) subcontract

subdesarrollado, -a [suβðesarro'ʎaðo, a] *adj* underdeveloped
subdesarrollo [suβðesa'rroʎo] *nm* underdevelopment
subdirector, a [suβðirek'tor, a] *nm/f* assistant *o* deputy manager
subdirectorio [suβðirek'torjo] *nm* (*Inform*) subdirectory
súbdito, -a ['suβðito, a] *nm/f* subject
subdividir [suβðiβi'ðir] *vt* to subdivide
subempleo [suβem'pleo] *nm* underemployment
subestimar [suβesti'mar] *vt* to underestimate, underrate
subido, -a [su'βiðo, a] *adj* (*color*) bright, strong; (*precio*) high ■ *nf* (*de montaña etc*) ascent, climb; (*de precio*) rise, increase; (*pendiente*) slope, hill
subíndice [su'βindiθe] *nm* (*Inform: Tip*) subscript
subir [su'βir] *vt* (*objeto*) to raise, lift up; (*cuesta, calle*) to go up; (*colina, montaña*) to climb; (*precio*) to raise, put up; (*empleado etc*) to promote ■ *vi* to go/come up; (*a un coche*) to get in; (*a un autobús, tren*) to get on; (*precio*) to rise, go up; (*en el empleo*) to be promoted; (*río, marea*) to rise; **subirse** *vr* to get up, climb; **subirse a un coche** to get in(to) a car
súbito, -a ['suβito, a] *adj* (*repentino*) sudden; (*imprevisto*) unexpected
subjetivo, -a [suβxe'tiβo, a] *adj* subjective
subjuntivo [suβxun'tiβo] *nm* subjunctive (mood)
sublevación [suβleβa'θjon] *nf* revolt, rising
sublevar [suβle'βar] *vt* to rouse to revolt; **sublevarse** *vr* to revolt, rise
sublimar [suβli'mar] *vt* (*persona*) to exalt; (*deseos etc*) to sublimate
sublime [su'βlime] *adj* sublime
subliminal [suβlimi'nal] *adj* subliminal
submarinista [suβmari'nista] *nm/f* underwater explorer
submarino, -a [suβma'rino, a] *adj* underwater ■ *nm* submarine
subnormal [suβnor'mal] *adj* subnormal ■ *nm/f* subnormal person
suboficial [suβofi'θjal] *nm* non-commissioned officer
subordinado, -a [suβorði'naðo, a] *adj, nm/f* subordinate
subproducto [suβpro'ðukto] *nm* by-product
subrayado [suβra'jaðo] *nm* underlining
subrayar [suβra'jar] *vt* to underline; (*recalcar*) to underline, emphasize
subrepticio, -a [suβrep'tiθjo, a] *adj* surreptitious
subrutina [suβru'tina] *nf* (*Inform*) subroutine
subsanar [suβsa'nar] *vt* (*reparar*) to make good; (*perdonar*) to excuse; (*sobreponerse a*) to overcome
subscribir [suβskri'βir] *vt* = **suscribir**
subscrito [suβs'krito] *pp de* **subscribir**
subsecretario, -a [suβsekre'tarjo, a] *nm/f* undersecretary, assistant secretary
subsidiariedad [suβsiðjarie'ðað] *nf* (*Pol*) subsidiarity
subsidiario, -a [suβsi'ðjarjo, a] *adj* subsidiary
subsidio [suβ'siðjo] *nm* (*ayuda*) aid, financial help; (*subvención*) subsidy, grant; (*de enfermedad, paro etc*) benefit, allowance
subsistencia [suβsis'tenθja] *nf* subsistence
subsistir [suβsis'tir] *vi* to subsist; (*vivir*) to live; (*sobrevivir*) to survive, endure
subsuelo [suβ'swelo] *nm* subsoil
subte *nm abr* (*CSur*) = **subterráneo**
subterfugio [suβter'fuxjo] *nm* subterfuge
subterráneo, -a [suβte'rraneo, a] *adj* underground, subterranean ■ *nm* underpass, underground passage; (*Am*) underground railway, subway (*US*)
subtítulo [suβ'titulo] *nm* subtitle, subheading
suburbano, -a [suβur'βano, a] *adj* suburban
suburbio [su'βurβjo] *nm* (*barrio*) slum quarter; (*afueras*) suburbs *pl*
subvención [suββen'θjon] *nf* subsidy, subvention, grant; **~ estatal** state subsidy *o* support; **~ para la inversión** (*Com*) investment grant
subvencionar [suββenθjo'nar] *vt* to subsidize
subversión [suββer'sjon] *nf* subversion
subversivo, -a [suββer'siβo, a] *adj* subversive
subyacente [suβja'θente] *adj* underlying
subyugar [suβju'ɣar] *vt* (*país*) to subjugate, subdue; (*enemigo*) to overpower; (*voluntad*) to dominate
subyugue *etc* [sub'juɣe] *vb ver* **subyugar**
succión [suk'θjon] *nf* suction
succionar [sukθjo'nar] *vt* (*sorber*) to suck; (*Tec*) to absorb, soak up
sucedáneo, -a [suθe'ðaneo, a] *adj* substitute ■ *nm* substitute (food)
suceder [suθe'ðer] *vi* to happen; **~ a** (*seguir*) to succeed, follow; **lo que sucede es que ...** the fact is that ...; **~ al trono** to succeed to the throne
sucesión [suθe'sjon] *nf* succession; (*serie*) sequence, series; (*hijos*) issue, offspring
sucesivamente [suθesiβa'mente] *adv*: **y así ~** and so on
sucesivo, -a [suθe'siβo, a] *adj* successive,

following; **en lo ~** in future, from now on
suceso [su'θeso] *nm (hecho)* event, happening; *(incidente)* incident
sucesor, a [suθe'sor, a] *nm/f* successor; *(heredero)* heir/heiress
suciedad [suθje'ðað] *nf (estado)* dirtiness; *(mugre)* dirt, filth
sucinto, -a [su'θinto, a] *adj (conciso)* succinct, concise
sucio, -a ['suθjo, a] *adj* dirty; *(mugriento)* grimy; *(manchado)* grubby; *(borroso)* smudged; *(conciencia)* bad; *(conducta)* vile; *(táctica)* dirty, unfair
Sucre ['sukre] *n* Sucre
sucre ['sukre] *nm Ecuadorean monetary unit*
suculento, -a [suku'lento, a] *adj (sabroso)* tasty; *(jugoso)* succulent
sucumbir [sukum'bir] *vi* to succumb
sucursal [sukur'sal] *nf* branch (office); *(filial)* subsidiary
Sudáfrica [su'ðafrika] *nf* South Africa
sudafricano, -a [suðafri'kano, a] *adj, nm/f* South African
Sudamérica [suða'merika] *nf* South America
sudamericano, -a [suðameri'kano, a] *adj, nm/f* South American
sudanés, -esa [suða'nes, esa] *adj, nm/f* Sudanese
sudar [su'ðar] *vt, vi* to sweat; *(Bot)* to ooze, give out *o* off
sudeste [su'ðeste] *adj* south-east(ern); *(rumbo, viento)* south-easterly ■ *nm* south-east; *(viento)* south-east wind
sudoeste [suðo'este] *adj* south-west(ern); *(rumbo, viento)* south-westerly ■ *nm* south-west; *(viento)* south-west wind
sudor [su'ðor] *nm* sweat
sudoroso, a [suðo'roso, a] *adj* sweaty, sweating
Suecia ['sweθja] *nf* Sweden
sueco, -a ['sweko, a] *adj* Swedish ■ *nm/f* Swede ■ *nm (Ling)* Swedish; **hacerse el ~** to pretend not to hear *o* understand
suegro, -a ['sweɣro, a] *nm/f* father-/mother-in-law; **los suegros** one's in-laws
suela ['swela] *nf (de zapato, tb pescado)* sole
sueldo *etc* ['sweldo] *vb ver* **soldar** ■ *nm* pay, wage(s) *(pl)*
suelo *etc* ['swelo] *vb ver* **soler** ■ *nm (tierra)* ground; *(de casa)* floor
suelto, -a *etc* ['swelto, a] *vb ver* **soltar** ■ *adj* loose; *(libre)* free; *(separado)* detached; *(ágil)* quick, agile; *(fue corre)* fluent, flowing ■ *nm* (loose) change, small change; **está muy ~ en inglés** he is very good at *o* fluent in English
suene *etc* ['swene] *vb ver* **sonar**
sueño *etc* ['sweɲo] *vb ver* **soñar** ■ *nm* sleep; *(somnolencia)* sleepiness, drowsiness; *(lo soñado, fig)* dream; **~ pesado** *o* **profundo** deep *o* heavy sleep; **tener ~** to be sleepy
suero ['swero] *nm (Med)* serum; *(de leche)* whey
suerte ['swerte] *nf (fortuna)* luck; *(azar)* chance; *(destino)* fate, destiny; *(condición)* lot; *(género)* sort, kind; **lo echaron a suertes** they drew lots *o* tossed up for it; **tener ~** to be lucky; **de otra ~** otherwise, if not; **de ~ que** so that, in such a way that
suéter ['sweter] *(pl* **suéters***) nm* sweater
suficiencia [sufi'θjenθja] *nf (cabida)* sufficiency; *(idoneidad)* suitability; *(aptitud)* adequacy
suficiente [sufi'θjente] *adj* enough, sufficient
sufijo [su'fixo] *nm* suffix
sufragar [sufra'ɣar] *vt (ayudar)* to help; *(gastos)* to meet; *(proyecto)* to pay for
sufragio [su'fraxjo] *nm (voto)* vote; *(derecho de voto)* suffrage
sufrague *etc* [su'fraɣe] *vb ver* **sufragar**
sufrido, -a [su'friðo, a] *adj (de carácter fuerte)* tough; *(paciente)* long-suffering; *(tela)* hard-wearing; *(color)* that does not show the dirt; *(marido)* complaisant
sufrimiento [sufri'mjento] *nm* suffering
sufrir [su'frir] *vt (padecer)* to suffer; *(soportar)* to bear, stand, put up with; *(apoyar)* to hold up, support ■ *vi* to suffer
sugerencia [suxe'renθja] *nf* suggestion
sugerir [suxe'rir] *vt* to suggest; *(sutilmente)* to hint; *(idea: incitar)* to prompt
sugestión [suxes'tjon] *nf* suggestion; *(sutil)* hint; *(poder)* hypnotic power
sugestionar [suxestjo'nar] *vt* to influence
sugestivo, -a [suxes'tiβo, a] *adj* stimulating; *(atractivo)* attractive; *(fascinante)* fascinating
sugiera *etc* [su'xjera], **sugiriendo** *etc* [suxi'rjendo] *vb ver* **sugerir**
suicida [sui'θiða] *adj* suicidal ■ *nm/f* suicidal person; *(muerto)* suicide, person who has committed suicide
suicidarse [suiθi'ðarse] *vr* to commit suicide, kill o.s.
suicidio [sui'θiðjo] *nm* suicide
Suiza ['swiθa] *nf* Switzerland
suizo, -a ['swiθo, a] *adj, nm/f* Swiss ■ *nm* sugared bun
sujeción [suxe'θjon] *nf* subjection
sujetador [suxeta'ðor] *nm* fastener, clip; *(prenda femenina)* bra, brassiere
sujetapapeles [suxetapa'peles] *nm inv* paper clip
sujetar [suxe'tar] *vt (fijar)* to fasten; *(detener)* to hold down; *(fig)* to subject, subjugate;

(pelo etc) to keep *o* hold in place; *(papeles)* to fasten together; **sujetarse** *vr* to subject o.s.
sujeto, -a [su'xeto, a] *adj* fastened, secure ■ *nm* subject; *(individuo)* individual; *(fam: tipo)* fellow, character, type, guy (US); **~ a** subject to
sulfurar [sulfu'rar] *vt (Tec)* to sulphurate; *(sacar de quicio)* to annoy; **sulfurarse** *vr (enojarse)* to get riled, see red, blow up
sulfuro [sul'furo] *nm* sulphide
suma ['suma] *nf (cantidad)* total, sum; *(de dinero)* sum; *(acto)* adding (up), addition; **en ~** in short; **~ y sigue** *(Com)* carry forward
sumador [suma'ðor] *nm (Inform)* adder
sumamente [suma'mente] *adv* extremely, exceedingly
sumar [su'mar] *vt* to add (up); *(reunir)* to collect, gather ■ *vi* to add up
sumario, -a [su'marjo, a] *adj* brief, concise ■ *nm* summary
sumergir [sumer'xir] *vt* to submerge; *(hundir)* to sink; *(bañar)* to immerse, dip; **sumergirse** *vr (hundirse)* to sink beneath the surface
sumerja *etc* [su'merxa] *vb ver* **sumergir**
sumidero [sumi'ðero] *nm* drain, sewer; *(Tec)* sump
suministrador, a [suministra'ðor, a] *nm/f* supplier
suministrar [suminis'trar] *vt* to supply, provide
suministro [sumi'nistro] *nm* supply; *(acto)* supplying, providing
sumir [su'mir] *vt* to sink, submerge; *(fig)* to plunge; **sumirse** *vr (objeto)* to sink; **sumirse en el estudio** to become absorbed in one's studies
sumisión [sumi'sjon] *nf (acto)* submission; *(calidad)* submissiveness, docility
sumiso, -a [su'miso, a] *adj* submissive, docile
súmmum ['sumum] *nm inv (fig)* height
sumo, -a ['sumo, a] *adj* great, extreme; *(mayor)* highest, supreme ■ *nm* sumo (wrestling); **a lo ~** at most
suntuoso, -a [sun'twoso, a] *adj* sumptuous, magnificent; *(lujoso)* lavish
sup. *abr (= superior)* sup
supe *etc* ['supe] *vb ver* **saber**
supeditar [supeði'tar] *vt* to subordinate; *(sojuzgar)* to subdue; *(oprimir)* to oppress; **supeditarse** *vr*: **supeditarse a** to subject o.s. to
super... [super] *pref* super..., over...
súper ['super] *adj (fam)* super, great
superable [supe'raβle] *adj (dificultad)* surmountable; *(tarea)* that can be performed
superación [supera'θjon] *nf (tb:* **superación personal**) self-improvement
superar [supe'rar] *vt (sobreponerse a)* to overcome; *(rebasar)* to surpass, do better than; *(pasar)* to go beyond; *(marca, récord)* to break; *(etapa: dejar atrás)* to get past; **superarse** *vr* to excel o.s.
superávit [supe'raβit] *(pl* **superávits**) *nm* surplus
superchería [supertʃe'ria] *nf* fraud, trick, swindle
superficial [superfi'θjal] *adj* superficial; *(medida)* surface *cpd*
superficie [super'fiθje] *nf* surface; *(área)* area; **grandes superficies** *(Com)* superstores
superfluo, -a [su'perflwo, a] *adj* superfluous
superíndice [supe'rindiθe] *nm (Inform: Tip)* superscript
superintendente [superinten'dente] *nm/f* supervisor, superintendent
superior [supe'rjor] *adj (piso, clase)* upper; *(temperatura, número, nivel)* higher; *(mejor: calidad, producto)* superior, better ■ *nm/f* superior
superiora [supe'rjora] *nf (Rel)* mother superior
superioridad [superjori'ðað] *nf* superiority
superlativo, -a [superla'tiβo, a] *adj, nm* superlative
supermercado [supermer'kaðo] *nm* supermarket
superpoblación [superpoβla'θjon] *nf* overpopulation; *(congestionamiento)* overcrowding
superponer [superpo'ner] *vt (Inform)* to overstrike
superposición [superposi'θjon] *nf (en impresora)* overstrike
superpotencia [superpo'tenθja] *nf* superpower, great power
superproducción [superproðuk'θjon] *nf* overproduction
supersónico, -a [super'soniko, a] *adj* supersonic
superstición [supersti'θjon] *nf* superstition
supersticioso, -a [supersti'θjoso, a] *adj* superstitious
supervisar [superβi'sar] *vt* to supervise; *(Com)* to superintend
supervisor, a [superβi'sor, a] *nm/f* supervisor
supervivencia [superβi'βenθja] *nf* survival
superviviente [superβi'βjente] *adj* surviving ■ *nm/f* survivor
suplantar [suplan'tar] *vt (persona)* to supplant; *(hacerse pasar por otro)* to take the place of
suplementario, -a [suplemen'tarjo, a] *adj* supplementary

suplemento [suple'mento] *nm* supplement
suplencia [su'plenθja] *nf* substitution, replacement; (*etapa*) period during which one deputizes *etc*
suplente [su'plente] *adj* substitute; (*disponible*) reserve ■ *nm/f* substitute
supletorio, -a [suple'torjo, a] *adj* supplementary; (*adicional*) extra ■ *nm* supplement; **mesa supletoria** spare table
súplica ['suplika] *nf* request; (*Rel*) supplication; (*Jur: instancia*) petition; **súplicas** *nfpl* entreaties
suplicar [supli'kar] *vt* (*cosa*) to beg (for), plead for; (*persona*) to beg, plead with; (*Jur*) to appeal to, petition
suplicio [su'pliθjo] *nm* torture; (*tormento*) torment; (*emoción*) anguish; (*experiencia penosa*) ordeal
suplique *etc* [su'plike] *vb ver* **suplicar**
suplir [su'plir] *vt* (*compensar*) to make good, make up for; (*reemplazar*) to replace, substitute ■ *vi*: **~ a** to take the place of, substitute for
supo *etc* ['supo] *vb ver* **saber**
supondré *etc* [supon'dre] *vb ver* **suponer**
suponer [supo'ner] *vt* to suppose; (*significar*) to mean; (*acarrear*) to involve ■ *vi* to count, have authority; **era de ~ que ...** it was to be expected that ...
suponga *etc* [su'ponga] *vb ver* **suponer**
suposición [suposi'θjon] *nf* supposition
supositorio [suposi'torjo] *nm* suppository
supremacía [suprema'θia] *nf* supremacy
supremo, -a [su'premo, a] *adj* supreme
supresión [supre'sjon] *nf* suppression; (*de derecho*) abolition; (*de dificultad*) removal; (*de palabra etc*) deletion; (*de restricción*) cancellation, lifting
suprimir [supri'mir] *vt* to suppress; (*derecho, costumbre*) to abolish; (*dificultad*) to remove; (*palabra etc, Inform*) to delete; (*restricción*) to cancel, lift
supuestamente [supwesta'mente] *adv* supposedly
supuesto, -a [su'pwesto, a] *pp de* **suponer** ■ *adj* (*hipotético*) supposed; (*falso*) false ■ *nm* assumption, hypothesis ■ *conj*: **~ que** since; **dar por ~ algo** to take sth for granted; **por ~** of course
supurar [supu'rar] *vi* to fester, suppurate
supuse *etc* [su'puse] *vb ver* **suponer**
sur [sur] *adj* southern; (*rumbo*) southerly ■ *nm* south; (*viento*) south wind
Suráfrica *etc* [su'rafrika] = **Sudáfrica** *etc*
Suramérica *etc* [sura'merika] = **Sudamérica** *etc*
surcar [sur'kar] *vt* to plough; (*superficie*) to cut, score
surco ['surko] *nm* (*en metal, disco*) groove; (*Agr*) furrow
surcoreano, -a [surkore'ano, a] *adj, nm/f* South Korean
sureño, -a [su'reɲo, a] *adj* southern ■ *nm/f* southerner
sureste [su'reste] = **sudeste**
surf [surf] *nm* surfing
surgir [sur'xir] *vi* to arise, emerge; (*dificultad*) to come up, crop up
surja *etc* ['surxa] *vb ver* **surgir**
suroeste [suro'este] = **sudoeste**
surque *etc* ['surke] *vb ver* **surcar**
surrealismo [surrea'lismo] *nm* surrealism
surrealista [surrea'lista] *adj, nm/f* surrealist
surtido, -a [sur'tiðo, a] *adj* mixed, assorted ■ *nm* (*selección*) selection, assortment; (*abastecimiento*) supply, stock
surtidor [surti'ðor] *nm* (*chorro*) jet, spout; (*fuente*) fountain; **~ de gasolina** petrol (*Brit*) *o* gas (US) pump
surtir [sur'tir] *vt* to supply, provide; (*efecto*) to have, produce ■ *vi* to spout, spurt; **surtirse** *vr*: **surtirse de** to provide o.s. with
susceptible [susθep'tiβle] *adj* susceptible; (*sensible*) sensitive; **~ de** capable of
suscitar [susθi'tar] *vt* to cause, provoke; (*discusión*) to start; (*duda, problema*) to raise; (*interés, sospechas*) to arouse
suscribir [suskri'βir] *vt* (*firmar*) to sign; (*respaldar*) to subscribe to, endorse; (*Com: acciones*) to take out an option on; **suscribirse** *vr* to subscribe; **~ a algn a una revista** to take out a subscription to a journal for sb
suscripción [suskrip'θjon] *nf* subscription
suscrito, -a [sus'krito, a] *pp de* **suscribir** ■ *adj*: **~ en exceso** oversubscribed
sushi ['suʃi] *nm* sushi
susodicho, -a [suso'ditʃo, a] *adj* above-mentioned
suspender [suspen'der] *vt* (*objeto*) to hang (up), suspend; (*trabajo*) to stop, suspend; (*Escol*) to fail
suspense [sus'pense] *nm* suspense
suspensión [suspen'sjon] *nf* suspension; (*fig*) stoppage, suspension; (*Jur*) stay; **~ de fuego** *o* **de hostilidades** ceasefire, cessation of hostilities; **~ de pagos** suspension of payments
suspensivo, -a [suspen'siβo, a] *adj*: **puntos suspensivos** dots, suspension points
suspenso, -a [sus'penso, a] *adj* hanging, suspended; (*Escol*) failed ■ *nm* (*Escol*) fail(ure); **quedar** *o* **estar en ~** to be pending
suspicacia [suspi'kaθja] *nf* suspicion, mistrust
suspicaz [suspi'kaθ] *adj* suspicious, distrustful

suspirar [suspi'rar] *vi* to sigh
suspiro [sus'piro] *nm* sigh
sustancia [sus'tanθja] *nf* substance; **~ gris** (*Anat*) grey matter; **sin ~** lacking in substance, shallow
sustancial [sustan'θjal] *adj* substantial
sustancioso, -a [sustan'θjoso, a] *adj* substantial; (*discurso*) solid
sustantivo, -a [sustan'tiβo, a] *adj* substantive; (*Ling*) substantival, noun *cpd* ■ *nm* noun, substantive
sustentar [susten'tar] *vt* (*alimentar*) to sustain, nourish; (*objeto*) to hold up, support; (*idea, teoría*) to maintain, uphold; (*fig*) to sustain, keep going
sustento [sus'tento] *nm* support; (*alimento*) sustenance, food
sustituir [sustitu'ir] *vt* to substitute, replace
sustituto, -a [susti'tuto, a] *nm/f* substitute, replacement
sustituyendo *etc* [sustitu'jendo] *vb ver* **sustituir**
susto ['susto] *nm* fright, scare; **dar un ~ a algn** to give sb a fright; **darse** *o* **pegarse un ~** (*fam*) to get a fright
sustraer [sustra'er] *vt* to remove, take away; (*Mat*) to subtract
sustraiga *etc* [sus'traiɣa], **sustraje** *etc* [sus'traxe] *vb ver* **sustraer**
sustrato [sus'trato] *nm* substratum
sustrayendo *etc* [sustra'jendo] *vb ver* **sustraer**
susurrar [susu'rrar] *vi* to whisper
susurro [su'surro] *nm* whisper
sutil [su'til] *adj* (*aroma*) subtle; (*tenue*) thin; (*hilo, hebra*) fine; (*olor*) delicate; (*brisa*) gentle; (*diferencia*) fine, subtle; (*inteligencia*) sharp, keen
sutileza [suti'leθa] *nf* subtlety; (*delgadez*) thinness; (*delicadeza*) delicacy; (*agudeza*) keenness
sutura [su'tura] *nf* suture
suturar [sutu'rar] *vt* to suture; (*juntar con puntos*) to stitch
suyo, -a ['sujo, a] *adj* (*con artículo o después del verbo* **ser**: *de él*) his; (: *de ella*) hers; (: *de ellos, ellas*) theirs; (: *de usted, ustedes*) yours; (*después de un nombre*: *de él*) of his; (: *de ella*) of hers; (: *de ellos, ellas*) of theirs; (: *de usted, ustedes*) of yours; **lo ~** (what is) his; (*su parte*) his share, what he deserves; **los suyos** (*su familia*) one's family *o* relations; (*sus partidarios*) one's own people *o* supporters; **~ afectísimo** (*en carta*) yours faithfully *o* sincerely; **de ~** in itself; **eso es muy ~** that's just like him; **hacer de las suyas** to get up to one's old tricks; **ir a la suya, ir a lo ~** to go one's own way; **salirse con la suya** to get one's way

Tt

T, t [te] *nf* (*letra*) T, t; **T de Tarragona** T for Tommy
t *abr* = **tonelada**
T. *abr* (= *Telefón, Telégrafo*) tel.; (*Com*) = **Tarifa**; **Tasa**
t. *abr* (= *tomo(s)*) vol(s)
TA *abr* = **traducción automática**
Tabacalera [taβaka'lera] *nf Spanish state tobacco monopoly*
tabaco [ta'βako] *nm* tobacco; (*fam*) cigarettes *pl*
tábano ['taβano] *nm* horsefly
tabaquería [tabake'ria] *nf* tobacconist's (*Brit*), cigar store (*US*)
tabarra [ta'βarra] *nf* (*fam*) nuisance; **dar la ~** to be a pain in the neck
taberna [ta'βerna] *nf* bar
tabernero, -a [taβer'nero, a] *nm/f* (*encargado*) publican; (*camarero*) barman/barmaid
tabique [ta'βike] *nm* (*pared*) thin wall; (*para dividir*) partition
tabla ['taβla] *nf* (*de madera*) plank; (*estante*) shelf; (*de anuncios*) board; (*lista, catálogo*) list; (*de vestido*) pleat; (*Arte*) panel; **tablas** *nfpl* (*Taur: Teat*) boards; **hacer tablas** to draw; **~ de consulta** (*Inform*) lookup table
tablado [ta'βlaðo] *nm* (*plataforma*) platform; (*suelo*) plank floor; (*Teat*) stage
tablao [ta'βlao] *nm* (*tb*: **tablao flamenco**) flamenco show
tablero [ta'βlero] *nm* (*de madera*) plank, board; (*pizarra*) blackboard; (*de ajedrez, damas*) board; (*Auto*) dashboard; **~ de gráficos** (*Inform*) graph pad
tableta [ta'βleta] *nf* (*Med*) tablet; (*de chocolate*) bar
tablilla [ta'βliʎa] *nf* small board; (*Med*) splint
tablón [ta'βlon] *nm* (*de suelo*) plank; (*de techo*) beam; (*de anuncios*) notice board
tabú [ta'βu] *nm* taboo
tabulación [taβula'θjon] *nf* (*Inform*) tab(bing)
tabulador [taβula'ðor] *nm* (*Inform: Tip*) tab
tabuladora [taβula'ðora] *nf*: **~ eléctrica** electric accounting machine
tabular [taβu'lar] *vt* to tabulate; (*Inform*) to tab
taburete [taβu'rete] *nm* stool
tacaño, -a [ta'kaɲo, a] *adj* (*avaro*) mean; (*astuto*) crafty
tacha ['tatʃa] *nf* (*defecto*) flaw, defect; (*Tec*) stud; **poner ~ a** to find fault with; **sin ~** flawless
tachar [ta'tʃar] *vt* (*borrar*) to cross out; (*corregir*) to correct; (*criticar*) to criticize; **~ de** to accuse of
tacho ['tatʃo] *nm* (*Am*) bucket, pail
tachón [ta'tʃon] *nm* erasure; (*tachadura*) crossing-out; (*Tec*) ornamental stud; (*Costura*) trimming
tachuela [ta'tʃwela] *nf* (*clavo*) tack
tácito, -a ['taθito, a] *adj* tacit; (*acuerdo*) unspoken; (*Ling*) understood; (*ley*) unwritten
taciturno, -a [taθi'turno, a] *adj* (*callado*) silent; (*malhumorado*) sullen
taco ['tako] *nm* (*Billar*) cue; (*libro de billetes*) book; (*manojo de billetes*) wad; (*Am*) heel; (*tarugo*) peg; (*fam: bocado*) snack; (*: palabrota*) swear word; (*: trago de vino*) swig; (*México*) filled tortilla; **armarse** *o* **hacerse un ~** to get into a mess
tacógrafo [ta'koɣrafo] *nm* (*Com*) tachograph
tacón [ta'kon] *nm* heel; **de ~ alto** high-heeled
taconear [takone'ar] *vi* (*dar golpecitos*) to tap with one's heels; (*Mil etc*) to click one's heels
taconeo [tako'neo] *nm* (heel) tapping *o* clicking
táctico, -a ['taktiko, a] *adj* tactical ■ *nf* tactics *pl*
tacto ['takto] *nm* touch; (*acción*) touching; (*fig*) tact
TAE *nf abr* (= *tasa anual equivalente*) APR
tafetán [tafe'tan] *nm* taffeta; **tafetanes** *nmpl* (*fam*) frills; **~ adhesivo** *o* **inglés** sticking plaster
tafilete [tafi'lete] *nm* morocco leather
tahona [ta'ona] *nf* (*panadería*) bakery; (*molino*) flourmill

tahur [ta'ur] *nm* gambler; *(pey)* cheat
tailandés, -esa [tailan'des, esa] *adj, nm/f* Thai ▪ *nm (Ling)* Thai
Tailandia [tai'landja] *nf* Thailand
taimado, -a [tai'maðo, a] *adj (astuto)* sly; *(resentido)* sullen
taita ['taita] *nm* dad, daddy
tajada [ta'xaða] *nf* slice; *(fam)* rake-off; **sacar ~** to get one's share
tajante [ta'xante] *adj* sharp; *(negativa)* emphatic; **es una persona ~** he's an emphatic person
tajar [ta'xar] *vt* to cut, slice
Tajo ['taxo] *nm* Tagus
tajo ['taxo] *nm (corte)* cut; *(filo)* cutting edge; *(Geo)* cleft
tal [tal] *adj* such; **un ~ García** a man called García; **~ vez** perhaps ▪ *pron (persona)* someone, such a one; *(cosa)* something, such a thing; **~ como** such as; **~ para cual** tit for tat; *(dos iguales)* two of a kind; **hablábamos de que si ~ si cual** we were talking about this, that and the other ▪ *adv*: **~ como** *(igual)* just as; **~ cual** *(como es)* just as it is; **~ el padre, cual el hijo** like father, like son; **¿qué ~?** how are things?; **¿qué ~ te gusta?** how do you like it? ▪ *conj*: **con ~ (de) que** provided that
tala ['tala] *nf (de árboles)* tree felling
taladradora [talaðra'ðora] *nf* drill; **~ neumática** pneumatic drill
taladrar [tala'ðrar] *vt* to drill; *(fig: ruido)* to pierce
taladro [ta'laðro] *nm (gen)* drill; *(hoyo)* drill hole; **~ neumático** pneumatic drill
talante [ta'lante] *nm (humor)* mood; *(voluntad)* will, willingness
talar [ta'lar] *vt* to fell, cut down; *(fig)* to devastate
talco ['talko] *nm (polvos)* talcum powder; *(Mineralogía)* talc
talega [ta'leɣa] *nf* sack
talego [ta'leɣo] *nm* sack; **tener ~** *(fam)* to have money
talento [ta'lento] *nm* talent; *(capacidad)* ability; *(don)* gift
Talgo ['talgo] *nm abr (Ferro: = tren articulado ligero Goicoechea-Oriol) high-speed train*
talidomida [taliðo'miða] *nm* thalidomide
talismán [talis'man] *nm* talisman
talla ['taʎa] *nf (estatura, fig, Med)* height, stature; *(de ropa)* size, fitting; *(palo)* measuring rod; *(Arte: de madera)* carving; *(de piedra)* sculpture
tallado, -a [ta'ʎaðo, a] *adj* carved ▪ *nm (de madera)* carving; *(de piedra)* sculpture
tallar [ta'ʎar] *vt (trabajar)* to work, carve; *(grabar)* to engrave; *(medir)* to measure; *(repartir)* to deal ▪ *vi* to deal
tallarín [taʎa'rin] *nm* noodle
talle ['taʎe] *nm (Anat)* waist; *(medida)* size; *(física)* build; *(: de mujer)* figure; *(fig)* appearance; **de ~ esbelto** with a slim figure
taller [ta'ʎer] *nm (Tec)* workshop; *(fábrica)* factory; *(Auto)* garage; *(de artista)* studio
tallo ['taʎo] *nm (de planta)* stem; *(de hierba)* blade; *(brote)* shoot; *(col)* cabbage; *(Culin)* candied peel
talmente [tal'mente] *adv (de esta forma)* in such a way; *(hasta tal punto)* to such an extent; *(exactamente)* exactly
talón [ta'lon] *nm (gen)* heel; *(Com)* counterfoil; *(Tec)* rim; **~ de Aquiles** Achilles heel
talonario [talo'narjo] *nm (de cheques)* cheque book; *(de billetes)* book of tickets; *(de recibos)* receipt book
tamaño, -a [ta'maɲo, a] *adj (tan grande)* such a big; *(tan pequeño)* such a small ▪ *nm* size; **de ~ natural** full-size; **¿de qué ~ es?** what size is it?
tamarindo [tama'rindo] *nm* tamarind
tambaleante [tambale'ante] *adj (persona)* staggering; *(mueble)* wobbly; *(vehículo)* swaying
tambalearse [tambale'arse] *vr (persona)* to stagger; *(mueble)* to wobble; *(vehículo)* to sway
también [tam'bjen] *adv (igualmente)* also, too, as well; *(además)* besides; **estoy cansado — yo ~** I'm tired — so am I *o* me too
tambor [tam'bor] *nm* drum; *(Anat)* eardrum; **~ del freno** brake drum; **~ magnético** *(Inform)* magnetic drum
tamboril [tambo'ril] *nm* small drum
tamborilear [tamborile'ar] *vi (Mus)* to drum; *(con los dedos)* to drum with one's fingers
tamborilero [tambori'lero] *nm* drummer
Támesis ['tamesis] *nm* Thames
tamice *etc* [ta'miθe] *vb ver* **tamizar**
tamiz [ta'miθ] *nm* sieve
tamizar [tami'θar] *vt* to sieve
tampoco [tam'poko] *adv* nor, neither; **yo ~ lo compré** I didn't buy it either
tampón [tam'pon] *nm* plug; *(Med)* tampon
tan [tan] *adv* so; **~ es así que** so much so that; **¡qué cosa ~ rara!** how strange!; **no es una idea ~ buena** it is not such a good idea
tanatorio [tana'torjo] *nm (privado)* funeral home *o* parlour; *(público)* mortuary
tanda ['tanda] *nf (gen)* series; *(de inyecciones)* course; *(juego)* set; *(turno)* shift; *(grupo)* gang
tándem ['tandem] *nm* tandem; *(Pol)* duo
tanga ['tanga] *nm (bikini)* tanga; *(ropa interior)* tanga briefs

tangente [tan'xente] *nf* tangent; **salirse por la ~** to go off at a tangent
Tánger ['tanxer] *n* Tangier
tangerino, -a [tanxe'rino, a] *adj* of *o* from Tangier ■ *nm/f* native *o* inhabitant of Tangier
tangible [tan'xiβle] *adj* tangible
tango ['tango] *nm* tango
tanino [ta'nino] *nm* tannin
tanque ['tanke] *nm* (*gen*) tank; (*Auto: Naut*) tanker
tanqueta [tan'keta] *nf* (*Mil*) small tank, armoured vehicle
tantear [tante'ar] *vt* (*calcular*) to reckon (up); (*medir*) to take the measure of; (*probar*) to test, try out; (*tomar la medida: persona*) to take the measurements of; (*considerar*) to weigh up ■ *vi* (*Deporte*) to score
tanteo [tan'teo] *nm* (*cálculo aproximado*) (rough) calculation; (*prueba*) test, trial; (*Deporte*) scoring; (*adivinanzas*) guesswork; **al ~** by trial and error
tantísimo, -a [tan'tisimo, a] *adj* so much; **tantísimos** so many
tanto, -a ['tanto, a] *adj* (*cantidad*) so much, as much; **tantos** so many, as many; **20 y tantos** 20-odd ■ *adv* (*cantidad*) so much, as much; (*tiempo*) so long, as long; **~ tú como yo** both you and I; **~ como eso** it's not as bad as that; **~ más ... cuanto que** it's all the more ... because; **~ mejor/peor** so much the better/the worse; **~ si viene como si va** whether he comes or whether he goes; **~ es así que** so much so that; **por ~, por lo ~** therefore; **me he vuelto ronco de** *o* **con ~ hablar** I have become hoarse with so much talking ■ *conj*: **con ~ que** provided (that); **en ~ que** while; **hasta ~ (que)** until such time as ■ *nm* (*suma*) certain amount; (*proporción*) so much; (*punto*) point; (*gol*) goal; **~ alzado** agreed price; **~ por ciento** percentage; **al ~** up to date; **estar al ~ de los acontecimientos** to be fully abreast of events; **un ~ perezoso** somewhat lazy; **al ~ de que** because of the fact that ■ *pron*: **cado uno paga ~** each one pays so much; **uno de tantos** one of many; **a tantos de agosto** on such and such a day in August; **entre ~** meanwhile
tañer [ta'ɲer] *vt* (*Mus*) to play; (*campana*) to ring
T/año *abr* = **toneladas por año**
TAO *nf abr* (= *traducción asistida por ordenador*) MAT
tapa ['tapa] *nf* (*de caja, olla*) lid; (*de botella*) top; (*de libro*) cover; (*de comida*) snack
tapacubos [tapa'kuβos] *nm inv* hub cap
tapadera [tapa'ðera] *nf* lid, cover
tapado [ta'paðo] *nm* (*Am: abrigo*) coat
tapar [ta'par] *vt* (*cubrir*) to cover; (*envolver*) to wrap *o* cover up; (*la vista*) to obstruct; (*persona, falta*) to conceal; (*Am*) to fill; **taparse** *vr* to wrap o.s. up
tapete [ta'pete] *nm* table cover; **estar sobre el ~** (*fig*) to be under discussion
tapia ['tapja] *nf* (garden) wall
tapiar [ta'pjar] *vt* to wall in
tapice *etc* [ta'piθe] *vb ver* **tapizar**
tapicería [tapiθe'ria] *nf* tapestry; (*para muebles*) upholstery; (*tienda*) upholsterer's (shop)
tapicero, -a [tapi'θero, a] *nm/f* (*de muebles*) upholsterer
tapiz [ta'piθ] *nm* (*alfombra*) carpet; (*tela tejida*) tapestry
tapizar [tapi'θar] *vt* (*pared*) to wallpaper; (*suelo*) to carpet; (*muebles*) to upholster
tapón [ta'pon] *nm* (*corcho*) stopper; (*Tec*) plug; (*Med*) tampon; **~ de rosca** *o* **de tuerca** screw-top
taponar [tapo'nar] *vt* (*botella*) to cork; (*tubería*) to block
taponazo [tapo'naθo] *nm* (*de tapón*) pop
tapujo [ta'puxo] *nm* (*embozo*) muffler; (*engaño*) deceit; **sin tapujos** honestly
taquigrafía [takiɣra'fia] *nf* shorthand
taquígrafo, -a [ta'kiɣrafo, a] *nm/f* shorthand writer
taquilla [ta'kiʎa] *nf* (*de estación etc*) booking office; (*de teatro*) box office; (*suma recogida*) takings *pl*; (*archivador*) filing cabinet
taquillero, -a [taki'ʎero, a] *adj*: **función taquillera** box office success ■ *nm/f* ticket clerk
taquimecanografía [takimekanoɣra'fia] *nf* shorthand and typing
taquímetro [ta'kimetro] *nm* speedometer; (*de control*) tachymeter
tara ['tara] *nf* (*defecto*) defect; (*Com*) tare
tarado, -a [ta'raðo, a] *adj* (*Com*) defective, imperfect; (*idiota*) stupid; (*loco*) crazy, nuts ■ *nm/f* idiot, cretin
tarántula [ta'rantula] *nf* tarantula
tararear [tarare'ar] *vi* to hum
tardanza [tar'ðanθa] *nf* (*demora*) delay; (*lentitud*) slowness
tardar [tar'ðar] *vi* (*tomar tiempo*) to take a long time; (*llegar tarde*) to be late; (*demorar*) to delay; **¿tarda mucho el tren?** does the train take long?; **a más ~** at the (very) latest; **~ en hacer algo** to be slow *o* take a long time to do sth; **no tardes en venir** come soon, come before long
tarde ['tarðe] *adv* (*hora*) late; (*fuera de tiempo*)

too late ■ *nf* (*de día*) afternoon; (*de noche*) evening; **~ o temprano** sooner or later; **de ~ en ~** from time to time; **¡buenas tardes!** (*de día*) good afternoon!; (*de noche*) good evening!; **a** *o* **por la ~** in the afternoon; in the evening
tardío, -a [tar'ðio, a] *adj* (*retrasado*) late; (*lento*) slow (to arrive)
tardo, -a ['tarðo, a] *adj* (*lento*) slow; (*torpe*) dull; **~ de oído** hard of hearing
tarea [ta'rea] *nf* task; **tareas** *nfpl* (*Escol*) homework *sg*; **~ de ocasión** chore
tarifa [ta'rifa] *nf* (*lista de precios*) price list; (*Com*) tariff; **~ básica** basic rate; **~ completa** all-in cost; **~ a destajo** piece rate; **~ doble** double time
tarima [ta'rima] *nf* (*plataforma*) platform
tarjeta [tar'xeta] *nf* card; **~ postal/de crédito/de Navidad** postcard/credit card/ Christmas card; **~ de circuitos** (*Inform*) circuit board; **~ cliente** loyalty card; **~ comercial** (*Com*) calling card; **~ dinero** cash card; **~ gráficos** (*Inform*) graphics card; **~ monedero** electronic purse *o* wallet; **~ prepago** top-up card; **~ SIM** SIM card
tarot [ta'rot] *nm* tarot
tarraconense [tarrako'nense] *adj* of *o* from Tarragona ■ *nm/f* native *o* inhabitant of Tarragona
tarro ['tarro] *nm* jar, pot
tarta ['tarta] *nf* (*pastel*) cake; (*torta*) tart
tartajear [tartaxe'ar] *vi* to stammer
tartamudear [tartamuðe'ar] *vi* to stutter, stammer
tartamudo, -a [tarta'muðo, a] *adj* stuttering, stammering ■ *nm/f* stutterer, stammerer
tartárico, -a [tar'tariko, a] *adj*: **ácido ~** tartaric acid
tártaro ['tartaro] *adj, nm* Tartar ■ *nm* (*Química*) tartar
tarugo, -a [ta'ruɣo, a] *adj* stupid ■ *nm* (*de madera*) lump
tarumba [ta'rumba] *adj* (*confuso*) confused
tasa ['tasa] *nf* (*precio*) (fixed) price, rate; (*valoración*) valuation; (*medida, norma*) measure, standard; **~ básica** (*Com*) basic rate; **~ de cambio** exchange rate; **de ~ cero** (*Com*) zero-rated; **~ de crecimiento** growth rate; **~ de interés/de nacimiento** rate of interest/birth rate; **~ de rendimiento** (*Com*) rate of return; **tasas universitarias** university fees
tasación [tasa'θjon] *nf* assessment, valuation; (*fig*) appraisal
tasador, a [tasa'ðor, a] *nm/f* valuer; (*Com: de impuestos*) assessor
tasar [ta'sar] *vt* (*arreglar el precio*) to fix a price for; (*valorar*) to value, assess; (*limitar*) to limit
tasca ['taska] *nf* (*fam*) pub
tata ['tata] *nm* (*fam*) dad(dy) ■ *nf* (*niñera*) nanny, maid
tatarabuelo, -a [tatara'βwelo, a] *nm/f* great-great-grandfather/mother; **los tatarabuelos** one's great-great-grandparents
tatuaje [ta'twaxe] *nm* (*dibujo*) tattoo; (*acto*) tattooing
tatuar [ta'twar] *vt* to tattoo
taumaturgo [tauma'turɣo] *nm* miracle-worker
taurino, -a [tau'rino, a] *adj* bullfighting *cpd*
Tauro ['tauro] *nm* Taurus
tauromaquia [tauro'makja] *nf* (art of) bullfighting
tautología [tautolo'xia] *nf* tautology
taxativo, -a [taksa'tiβo, a] *adj* (*restringido*) limited; (*sentido*) specific
taxi ['taksi] *nm* taxi
taxidermia [taksi'ðermja] *nf* taxidermy
taxímetro [tak'simetro] *nm* taximeter
taxista [tak'sista] *nm/f* taxi driver
Tayikistán [tajikis'tan] *nm* Tajikistan
taza ['taθa] *nf* cup; (*de retrete*) bowl; **~ para café** coffee cup
tazón [ta'θon] *nm* mug, large cup; (*escudilla*) basin
TCI *nf abr* (= *tarjeta de circuito impreso*) PCB
te [te] *pron* (*complemento de objeto*) you; (*complemento indirecto*) (to) you; (*reflexivo*) (to) yourself; **¿te duele mucho el brazo?** does your arm hurt a lot?; **te equivocas** you're wrong; **¡cálmate!** calm yourself!
té [te] (*pl* **tés**) *nm* tea; (*reunión*) tea party
tea ['tea] *nf* (*antorcha*) torch
teatral [tea'tral] *adj* theatre *cpd*; (*fig*) theatrical
teatro [te'atro] *nm* theatre; (*Lit*) plays *pl*, drama; **el ~** (*carrera*) the theatre, acting; **~ de aficionados/de variedades** amateur/variety theatre, vaudeville theater (*US*); **hacer ~** (*fig*) to make a fuss
tebeo [te'βeo] *nm* children's comic
techado [te'tʃaðo] *nm* (*techo*) roof; **bajo ~** under cover
techo ['tetʃo] *nm* (*externo*) roof; (*interno*) ceiling
techumbre [te'tʃumbre] *nf* roof
tecla ['tekla] *nf* (*Inform: Mus: Tip*) key; (*Inform*): **~ de anulación/de borrar** cancel/delete key; **~ de control/de edición** control/edit key; **~ con flecha** arrow key; **~ programable** user-defined key; **~ de retorno/de tabulación** return/tab key; **~ del cursor** cursor key; **teclas de control direccional del cursor** cursor control keys

teclado [te'klaðo] *nm* keyboard (*tb Inform*); **~ numérico** (*Inform*) numeric keypad
teclear [tekle'ar] *vi* to strum; (*fam*) to drum ■ *vt* (*Inform*) to key (in), type in, keyboard
tecleo [te'kleo] *nm* (*Mus: sonido*) strumming; (*: forma de tocar*) fingering; (*fam*) drumming
tecnicismo [tekni'θismo] *nm* (*carácter técnico*) technical nature; (*Ling*) technical term
técnico, -a ['tekniko, a] *adj* technical ■ *nm* technician; (*experto*) expert ■ *nf* (*procedimientos*) technique; (*arte, oficio*) craft
tecnicolor [tekniko'lor] *nm* Technicolor®
tecnócrata [tek'nokrata] *nm/f* technocrat
tecnología [teknolo'xia] *nf* technology; **~ de estado sólido** (*Inform*) solid-state technology; **~ de la información** information technology
tecnológico, -a [tekno'loxiko, a] *adj* technological
tecnólogo, -a [tek'noloɣo, a] *nm/f* technologist
tedio ['teðjo] *nm* (*aburrimiento*) boredom; (*apatía*) apathy; (*fastidio*) depression
tedioso, -a [te'ðjoso, a] *adj* boring; (*cansado*) wearisome, tedious
Teherán [tee'ran] *nm* Teheran
teja ['texa] *nf* (*azulejo*) tile; (*Bot*) lime (tree)
tejado [te'xaðo] *nm* (tiled) roof
tejano, -a [te'xano, a] *adj, nm/f* Texan ■ *nmpl*: **tejanos** (*vaqueros*) jeans
Tejas ['texas] *nm* Texas
tejemaneje [texema'nexe] *nm* (*actividad*) bustle; (*lío*) fuss, to-do; (*intriga*) intrigue
tejer [te'xer] *vt* to weave; (*tela de araña*) to spin; (*Am*) to knit; (*fig*) to fabricate ■ *vi*: **~ y destejer** to chop and change
tejido [te'xiðo] *nm* fabric; (*estofa, tela*) (knitted) material; (*Anat*) tissue; (*textura*) texture
tejo ['texo] *nm* (*Bot*) yew (tree)
tel. *abr* (= *teléfono*) tel.
tela ['tela] *nf* (*material*) material; (*de fruta, en líquido*) skin; (*del ojo*) film; **hay ~ para rato** there's lots to talk about; **poner en ~ de juicio** to (call in) question; **~ de araña** cobweb, spider's web
telar [te'lar] *nm* (*máquina*) loom; (*de teatro*) gridiron; **telares** *nmpl* textile mill *sg*
telaraña [tela'ɾaɲa] *nf* cobweb, spider's web
tele... [tele] *pref* tele...
tele ['tele] *nf* (*fam*) TV
telecargar [telekar'ɣar] *vt* (*Inform*) to download
telecomunicación [telekomunika'θjon] *nf* telecommunication
teleconferencia [telekonfe'renθja] *nf* (*reunión*) teleconference; (*sistema*) teleconferencing
telecontrol [telekon'trol] *nm* remote control
telecopiadora [telekopja'ðora] *nf*: **~ facsímil** fax copier
telediario [tele'ðjarjo] *nm* television news
teledifusión [teleðifu'sjon] *nf* (television) broadcast
teledirigido, -a [teleðiri'xiðo, a] *adj* remote-controlled
teléf. *abr* (= *teléfono*) tel.
teleférico [tele'feriko] *nm* (*tren*) cable-railway; (*de esquí*) ski-lift
telefilm [tele'film], **telefilme** [tele'filme] *nm* TV film
telefonazo [telefo'naθo] *nm* (*fam*) telephone call; **te daré un ~** I'll give you a ring
telefonear [telefone'ar] *vi* to telephone
telefónicamente [tele'fonikamente] *adv* by (tele)phone
telefónico, -a [tele'foniko, a] *adj* telephone *cpd* ■ *nf*: **Telefónica** (*Esp*) *Spanish national telephone company*, ≈ British Telecom
telefonista [telefo'nista] *nm/f* telephonist
teléfono [te'lefono] *nm* (tele)phone; **~ móvil** mobile phone; **está hablando por ~** he's on the phone
telefoto [tele'foto] *nf* telephoto
telegrafía [teleɣra'fia] *nf* telegraphy
telégrafo [te'leɣrafo] *nm* telegraph; (*fam: persona*) telegraph boy
telegrama [tele'ɣrama] *nm* telegram
teleimpresor [teleimpre'sor] *nm* teleprinter
telemática [tele'matika] *nf* telematics *sg*
telémetro [te'lemetro] *nm* rangefinder
telenovela [teleno'βela] *nf* soap (opera)
teleobjetivo [teleobxe'tiβo] *nm* telephoto lens
telepatía [telepa'tia] *nf* telepathy
telepático, -a [tele'patiko, a] *adj* telepathic
teleproceso [telepro'θeso] *nm* teleprocessing
telescópico, -a [tele'skopiko, a] *adj* telescopic
telescopio [tele'skopjo] *nm* telescope
telesilla [tele'siʎa] *nm* chairlift
telespectador, a [telespekta'ðor, a] *nm/f* viewer
telesquí [teles'ki] *nm* ski-lift
teletex [tele'teks], **teletexto** [tele'teksto] *nm* teletext
teletipista [teleti'pista] *nm/f* teletypist
teletipo [tele'tipo] *nm* teletype(writer)
teletrabajo [teletra'βaxo] *nm* teleworking
televentas [tele'βentas] *nfpl* telesales
televidente [teleβi'ðente] *nm/f* viewer
televisar [teleβi'sar] *vt* to televise
televisión [teleβi'sjon] *nf* television; **~ en color/por satélite** colour/satellite television; **~ digital** digital television

televisivo, -a [teleβi'siβo, a] *adj* television *cpd*
televisor [teleβi'sor] *nm* television set
télex ['teleks] *nm* telex; **máquina ~** telex (machine); **enviar por ~** to telex
telón [te'lon] *nm* curtain; **~ de boca/ seguridad** front/safety curtain; **~ de acero** (*Pol*) iron curtain; **~ de fondo** backcloth, background
telonero, -a [telo'nero, a] *nm/f* support act; **los teloneros** (*Mus*) the support band
tema ['tema] *nm* (*asunto*) subject, topic; (*Mus*) theme; **temas de actualidad** current affairs ■ *nf* (*obsesión*) obsession; (*manía*) ill-will; **tener ~ a algn** to have a grudge against sb
temario [te'marjo] *nm* (*Escol*) set of topics; (*de una conferencia*) agenda
temático, -a [te'matiko, a] *adj* thematic ■ *nf* subject matter
tembladera [tembla'ðera] *nf* shaking; (*Am*) quagmire
temblar [tem'blar] *vi* to shake, tremble; (*de frío*) to shiver
tembleque [tem'bleke] *adj* shaking ■ *nm* shaking
temblón, -ona [tem'blon, ona] *adj* shaking
temblor [tem'blor] *nm* trembling; (*de tierra*) earthquake
tembloroso, -a [temblo'roso, a] *adj* trembling
temer [te'mer] *vt* to fear ■ *vi* to be afraid; **temo que Juan llegue tarde** I am afraid Juan may be late
temerario, -a [teme'rarjo, a] *adj* (*imprudente*) rash; (*descuidado*) reckless; (*arbitrario*) hasty
temeridad [temeri'ðað] *nf* (*imprudencia*) rashness; (*audacia*) boldness
temeroso, -a [teme'roso, a] *adj* (*miedoso*) fearful; (*que inspira temor*) frightful
temible [te'miβle] *adj* fearsome
temor [te'mor] *nm* (*miedo*) fear; (*duda*) suspicion
témpano ['tempano] *nm* (*Mus*) kettledrum; **~ de hielo** ice floe
temperamento [tempera'mento] *nm* temperament; **tener ~** to be temperamental
temperar [tempe'rar] *vt* to temper, moderate
temperatura [tempera'tura] *nf* temperature
tempestad [tempes'tað] *nf* storm; **~ en un vaso de agua** (*fig*) storm in a teacup
tempestuoso, -a [tempes'twoso, a] *adj* stormy
templado, -a [tem'plaðo, a] *adj* (*moderado*) moderate; (*: en el comer*) frugal; (*: en el beber*) abstemious; (*agua*) lukewarm; (*clima*) mild; (*Mus*) in tune, well-tuned
templanza [tem'planθa] *nf* moderation; (*en el beber*) abstemiousness; (*del clima*) mildness
templar [tem'plar] *vt* (*moderar*) to moderate; (*furia*) to restrain; (*calor*) to reduce; (*solución*) to dilute; (*afinar*) to tune (up); (*acero*) to temper ■ *vi* to moderate; **templarse** *vr* to be restrained
temple ['temple] *nm* (*humor*) mood; (*coraje*) courage; (*ajuste*) tempering; (*afinación*) tuning; (*pintura*) tempera
templo ['templo] *nm* (*iglesia*) church; (*pagano etc*) temple; **~ metodista** Methodist chapel
temporada [tempo'raða] *nf* time, period; (*estación, social, Deporte*) season; **en plena ~** at the height of the season
temporal [tempo'ral] *adj* (*no permanente*) temporary; (*Rel*) temporal ■ *nm* storm
temporario, -a [tempo'rarjo, a] *adj* (*Am*) temporary
tempranero, -a [tempra'nero, a] *adj* (*Bot*) early; (*persona*) early-rising
temprano, -a [tem'prano, a] *adj* early ■ *adv* early; (*demasiado pronto*) too soon, too early; **lo más ~ posible** as soon as possible
ten [ten] *vb ver* **tener**
tenacidad [tenaθi'ðað] *nf* (*gen*) tenacity; (*dureza*) toughness; (*terquedad*) stubbornness
tenacillas [tena'θiʎas] *nfpl* (*gen*) tongs; (*para el pelo*) curling tongs; (*Med*) forceps
tenaz [te'naθ] *adj* (*material*) tough; (*persona*) tenacious; (*pegajoso*) sticky; (*terco*) stubborn
tenaza [te'naθa] *nf*, **tenazas** [te'naθas] *nfpl* (*Med*) forceps; (*Tec*) pliers; (*Zool*) pincers
tendal [ten'dal] *nm* awning
tendedero [tende'ðero] *nm* (*para ropa*) drying-place; (*cuerda*) clothes line
tendencia [ten'denθja] *nf* tendency; (*proceso*) trend; **~ imperante** prevailing tendency; **~ del mercado** run of the market; **tener ~ a** to tend *o* have a tendency to
tendenciosidad [tendenθjosi'ðað] *nf* tendentiousness
tendencioso, -a [tenden'θjoso, a] *adj* tendentious
tender [ten'der] *vt* (*extender*) to spread out; (*ropa*) to hang out; (*vía férrea, cable*) to lay; (*cuerda*) to stretch; (*trampa*) to set ■ *vi* to tend; **tenderse** *vr* to lie down; (*fig: dejarse llevar*) to let o.s. go; (*: dejar ir*) to let things go; **~ la cama/la mesa** (*Am*) to make the bed/lay the table
ténder ['tender] *nm* (*Ferro*) tender
tenderete [tende'rete] *nm* (*puesto*) stall; (*carretilla*) barrow; (*exposición*) display of goods
tendero, -a [ten'dero, a] *nm/f* shopkeeper
tendido, -a [ten'diðo, a] *adj* (*acostado*) lying down, flat; (*colgado*) hanging ■ *nm* (*ropa*) washing; (*Taur*) front rows *pl* of seats; (*colocación*) laying; (*Arq: enyesado*) coat of

plaster; **a galope ~** flat out
tendón [ten'don] *nm* tendon
tendré *etc* [ten'dre] *vb ver* **tener**
tenducho [ten'dutʃo] *nm* small dirty shop
tenebroso, -a [tene'βroso, a] *adj* (*oscuro*) dark; (*fig*) gloomy; (*siniestro*) sinister
tenedor [tene'ðor] *nm* (*Culin*) fork; (*poseedor*) holder; **~ de libros** book-keeper; **~ de acciones** shareholder; **~ de póliza** policyholder
teneduría [teneðu'ria] *nf* keeping; **~ de libros** book-keeping
tenencia [te'nenθja] *nf* (*de casa*) tenancy; (*de oficio*) tenure; (*de propiedad*) possession; **~ asegurada** security of tenure; **~ ilícita de armas** illegal possession of weapons

PALABRA CLAVE

tener [te'ner] *vt* **1** (*poseer, gen*) to have; (*en la mano*) to hold; **¿tienes un boli?** have you got a pen?; **va a tener un niño** she's going to have a baby; **tiene los ojos azules** he's got blue eyes; **¡ten (*o* tenga)!**, **¡aquí tienes (*o* tiene)!** here you are!
2 (*edad, medidas*) to be; **tiene siete años** she's seven (years old); **tiene 15 cm de largo** it's 15 cm long
3 (*sentimientos, sensaciones*): **tener sed/hambre/frío/calor** to be thirsty/hungry/cold/hot; **tener celos** to be jealous; **tener cuidado** to be careful; **tener razón** to be right; **tener suerte** to be lucky
4 (*considerar*): **lo tengo por brillante** I consider him to be brilliant; **tener en mucho a algn** to think very highly of sb
5 (*+ pp: + adj: + gerundio*): **tengo terminada ya la mitad del trabajo** I've done half the work already; **tenía el sombrero puesto** he had his hat on; **tenía pensado llamarte** I had been thinking of phoning you; **nos tiene hartos** we're fed up with him; **me ha tenido tres horas esperando** he kept me waiting three hours
6: **tener que hacer algo** to have to do sth; **tengo que acabar este trabajo hoy** I have to finish this job today
7: **¿qué tienes, estás enfermo?** what's the matter with you, are you ill?
8 (*locuciones*): **¿conque ésas tenemos?** so it's like that, then?; **no las tengo todas conmigo** I'm a bit unsure (about it); **lo tiene difícil** he'll have a hard job
tenerse *vr* **1**: **tenerse en pie** to stand up
2: **tenerse por** to think o.s.; **se tiene por un gran cantante** he thinks himself a great singer

tenga *etc* ['tenga] *vb ver* **tener**
tenia ['tenja] *nf* tapeworm
teniente [te'njente] *nm* lieutenant; **~ coronel** lieutenant colonel
tenis ['tenis] *nm* tennis; **~ de mesa** table tennis
tenista [te'nista] *nm/f* tennis player
tenor [te'nor] *nm* (*tono*) tone; (*sentido*) meaning; (*Mus*) tenor; **a ~ de** on the lines of
tenorio [te'norjo] *nm* (*fam*) ladykiller, Don Juan
tensar [ten'sar] *vt* to tauten; (*arco*) to draw
tensión [ten'sjon] *nf* tension; (*Tec*) stress; (*Med*): **~ arterial** blood pressure; **~ nerviosa** nervous strain; **tener la ~ alta** to have high blood pressure
tenso, -a ['tenso, a] *adj* tense; (*relaciones*) strained
tentación [tenta'θjon] *nf* temptation
tentáculo [ten'takulo] *nm* tentacle
tentador, a [tenta'ðor, a] *adj* tempting ▪ *nm/f* tempter/temptress
tentar [ten'tar] *vt* (*tocar*) to touch, feel; (*seducir*) to tempt; (*atraer*) to attract; (*probar*) to try (out); (*Med*) to probe; **~ hacer algo** to try to do sth
tentativa [tenta'tiβa] *nf* attempt; **~ de asesinato** attempted murder
tentempié [tentem'pje] *nm* (*fam*) snack
tenue ['tenwe] *adj* (*delgado*) thin, slender; (*alambre*) fine; (*insustancial*) tenuous; (*sonido*) faint; (*neblina*) light; (*lazo, vínculo*) slight
teñir [te'ɲir] *vt* to dye; (*fig*) to tinge; **teñirse el pelo** to dye one's hair
teología [teolo'xia] *nf* theology
teólogo, -a [te'oloɣo, a] *nm/f* theologist, theologian
teorema [teo'rema] *nm* theorem
teoría [teo'ria] *nf* theory; **en ~** in theory
teóricamente [te'orikamente] *adv* theoretically
teorice *etc* [teo'riθe] *vb ver* **teorizar**
teórico, -a [te'oriko, a] *adj* theoretic(al) ▪ *nm/f* theoretician, theorist
teorizar [teori'θar] *vi* to theorize
tequila [te'kila] *nm o f* tequila
TER [ter] *nm abr* (*Ferro*) = **tren español rápido**
terapeuta [tera'peuta] *nm/f* therapist
terapéutico, -a [tera'peutiko, a] *adj* therapeutic(al) ▪ *nf* therapeutics *sg*
terapia [te'rapja] *nf* therapy; **~ laboral** occupational therapy
tercer [ter'θer] *adj ver* **tercero**
tercermundista [terθermun'dista] *adj* Third World *cpd*
tercero, -a [ter'θero, a] *adj* third (*antes de nmsg* **tercer**) ▪ *nm* (*árbitro*) mediator; (*Jur*) third party

terceto [ter'θeto] *nm* trio
terciado, -a [ter'θjaðo, a] *adj* slanting; **azúcar ~** brown sugar
terciar [ter'θjar] *vt* (*Mat*) to divide into three; (*inclinarse*) to slope; (*llevar*) to wear across one's chest ■ *vi* (*participar*) to take part; (*hacer de árbitro*) to mediate; **terciarse** *vr* to arise
terciario, -a [ter'θjarjo, a] *adj* tertiary
tercio ['terθjo] *nm* third
terciopelo [terθjo'pelo] *nm* velvet
terco, -a ['terko, a] *adj* obstinate, stubborn; (*material*) tough
tergal® [ter'ɣal] *nm* Terylene®
tergiversación [terxiβersa'θjon] *nf* (*deformación*) distortion; (*evasivas*) prevarication
tergiversar [terxiβer'sar] *vt* to distort ■ *vi* to prevaricate
termal [ter'mal] *adj* thermal
termas ['termas] *nfpl* hot springs
térmico, -a ['termiko, a] *adj* thermic, thermal, heat *cpd*
terminación [termina'θjon] *nf* (*final*) end; (*conclusión*) conclusion, ending
terminal [termi'nal] *adj* terminal ■ *nm* (*Elec: Inform*) terminal; **~ conversacional** interactive terminal; **~ de pantalla** visual display unit ■ *nf* (*Aviat: Ferro*) terminal
terminante [termi'nante] *adj* (*final*) final, definitive; (*tajante*) categorical
terminar [termi'nar] *vt* (*completar*) to complete, finish; (*concluir*) to end ■ *vi* (*llegar a su fin*) to end; (*parar*) to stop; (*acabar*) to finish; **terminarse** *vr* to come to an end; **~ por hacer algo** to end up (by) doing sth
término ['termino] *nm* end, conclusion; (*parada*) terminus; (*límite*) boundary; (*en discusión*) point; (*Ling: Com*) term; **~ medio** average; (*fig*) middle way; **en otros términos** in other words; **en último ~** (*a fin de cuentas*) in the last analysis; (*como último recurso*) as a last resort; **en términos de** in terms of; **según los términos del contrato** according to the terms of the contract
terminología [terminolo'xia] *nf* terminology
termita [ter'mita] *nf* termite
termo ['termo] *nm* Thermos® (flask)
termodinámico, -a [termoði'namiko, a] *adj* thermodynamic ■ *nf* thermodynamics *sg*
termoimpresora [termoimpre'sora] *nf* thermal printer
termómetro [ter'mometro] *nm* thermometer
termonuclear [termonukle'ar] *adj* thermonuclear
termostato [termos'tato] *nm* thermostat
ternero, -a [ter'nero, a] *nm/f* (*animal*) calf ■ *nf* (*carne*) veal
terneza [ter'neθa] *nf* tenderness
ternilla [ter'niʎa] *nf* gristle; (*cartílago*) cartilage
terno ['terno] *nm* (*traje*) three-piece suit; (*conjunto*) set of three
ternura [ter'nura] *nf* (*trato*) tenderness; (*palabra*) endearment; (*cariño*) fondness
terquedad [terke'ðað] *nf* obstinacy; (*dureza*) harshness
terrado [te'rraðo] *nm* terrace
Terranova [terra'noβa] *nf* Newfoundland
terraplén [terra'plen] *nm* (*Agr*) terrace; (*Ferro*) embankment; (*Mil*) rampart; (*cuesta*) slope
terráqueo, -a [te'rrakeo, a] *adj*: **globo ~** globe
terrateniente [terrate'njente] *nm* landowner
terraza [te'rraθa] *nf* (*balcón*) balcony; (*techo*) flat roof; (*Agr*) terrace
terremoto [terre'moto] *nm* earthquake
terrenal [terre'nal] *adj* earthly
terreno, -a [te'rreno, a] *adj* (*de la tierra*) earthly, worldly ■ *nm* (*tierra*) land; (*parcela*) plot; (*suelo*) soil; (*fig*) field; **un ~** a piece of land; **sobre el ~** on the spot; **ceder/perder ~** to give/lose ground; **preparar el ~ (a)** (*fig*) to pave the way (for)
terrestre [te'rrestre] *adj* terrestrial; (*ruta*) land *cpd*
terrible [te'rriβle] *adj* (*espantoso*) terrible; (*aterrador*) dreadful; (*tremendo*) awful
territorial [territo'rjal] *adj* territorial
territorio [terri'torjo] *nm* territory; **~ bajo mandato** mandated territory
terrón [te'rron] *nm* (*de azúcar*) lump; (*de tierra*) clod, lump; **terrones** *nmpl* land *sg*
terror [te'rror] *nm* terror
terrorífico, -a [terro'rifiko, a] *adj* terrifying
terrorismo [terro'rismo] *nm* terrorism
terrorista [terro'rista] *adj, nm/f* terrorist
terroso, -a [te'rroso, a] *adj* earthy
terruño [te'rruɲo] *nm* (*pedazo*) clod; (*parcela*) plot; (*fig*) native soil; **apego al ~** attachment to one's native soil
terso, -a ['terso, a] *adj* (*liso*) smooth; (*pulido*) polished; (*fig: estilo*) flowing
tersura [ter'sura] *nf* smoothness; (*brillo*) shine
tertulia [ter'tulja] *nf* (*reunión informal*) social gathering; (*grupo*) group, circle; (*sala*) clubroom; **~ literaria** literary circle
tesina [te'sina] *nf* dissertation
tesis ['tesis] *nf inv* thesis
tesón [te'son] *nm* (*firmeza*) firmness; (*tenacidad*) tenacity
tesorería [tesore'ria] *nf* treasurership

tesorero, -a [teso'rero, a] *nm/f* treasurer
tesoro [te'soro] *nm* treasure; **T~ público** (*Pol*) Exchequer
test (*pl* **tests**) [tes(t), tes(t)] *nm* test
testaferro [testa'ferro] *nm* figurehead
testamentaría [testamenta'ria] *nf* execution of a will
testamentario, -a [testamen'tarjo, a] *adj* testamentary ■ *nm/f* executor/executrix
testamento [testa'mento] *nm* will
testar [tes'tar] *vi* to make a will
testarada [testa'raða] *nf*, **testarazo** [testa'raθo] *nm*: **darse una ~ o un testarazo** (*fam*) to bump one's head
testarudo, -a [testa'ruðo, a] *adj* stubborn
testículo [tes'tikulo] *nm* testicle
testificar [testifi'kar] *vt* to testify; (*fig*) to attest ■ *vi* to give evidence
testifique *etc* [testi'fike] *vb ver* **testificar**
testigo [tes'tiɣo] *nm/f* witness; **~ de cargo/descargo** witness for the prosecution/defence; **~ ocular** eye witness; **poner a algn por ~** to cite sb as a witness
testimonial [testimo'njal] *adj* (*prueba*) testimonial; (*gesto*) token
testimoniar [testimo'njar] *vt* to testify to; (*fig*) to show
testimonio [testi'monjo] *nm* testimony; **en ~ de** as a token *o* mark of; **falso ~** perjured evidence, false witness
teta ['teta] *nf* (*de biberón*) teat; (*Anat*) nipple; (*fam*) breast; (*fam!*) tit (*!*)
tétanos ['tetanos] *nm* tetanus
tetera [te'tera] *nf* teapot; **~ eléctrica** (electric) kettle
tetilla [te'tiʎa] *nf* (*Anat*) nipple; (*de biberón*) teat
tétrico, -a ['tetriko, a] *adj* gloomy, dismal
textil [teks'til] *adj* textile
texto ['teksto] *nm* text
textual [teks'twal] *adj* textual; **palabras textuales** exact words
textura [teks'tura] *nf* (*de tejido*) texture; (*de mineral*) structure
tez [teθ] *nf* (*cutis*) complexion; (*color*) colouring
tfno. *abr* (= *teléfono*) tel.
ti [ti] *pron* you; (*reflexivo*) yourself
tía ['tia] *nf* (*pariente*) aunt; (*fam: mujer*) girl
Tibet [ti'βet] *nm*: **El ~** Tibet
tibetano, -a [tiβe'tano, a] *adj, nm/f* Tibetan ■ *nm* (*Ling*) Tibetan
tibia ['tiβja] *nf* tibia
tibieza [ti'βjeθa] *nf* (*temperatura*) tepidness; (*fig*) coolness
tibio, -a ['tiβjo, a] *adj* lukewarm, tepid
tiburón [tiβu'ron] *nm* shark
tic [tik] *nm* (*ruido*) click; (*de reloj*) tick; **~ nervioso** (*Med*) nervous tic
tico, -a ['tiko, a] *adj, nm/f* (*Am fam*) Costa Rican
tictac [tik'tak] *nm* (*de reloj*) tick tock
tiemble *etc* ['tjemble] *vb ver* **temblar**
tiempo ['tjempo] *nm* (*gen*) time; (*época, período*) age, period; (*Meteorología*) weather; (*Ling*) tense; (*edad*) age; (*de juego*) half; **a ~** in time; **a un o al mismo ~** at the same time; **al poco ~** very soon (after); **andando el ~** in due course; **cada cierto ~** every so often; **con ~** in time; **con el ~** eventually; **de ~ en ~** from time to time; **en mis tiempos** in my time; **en los buenos tiempos** in the good old days; **hace buen/mal ~** the weather is fine/bad; **estar a ~** to be in time; **hace ~** some time ago; **hacer ~** to while away the time; **¿qué ~ tiene?** how old is he?; **motor de 2 tiempos** two-stroke engine; **~ compartido** (*Inform*) time sharing; **~ de ejecución** (*Inform*) run time; **~ inactivo** (*Com*) downtime; **~ libre** spare time; **~ de paro** (*Com*) idle time; **a ~ partido** (*trabajar*) part-time; **~ preferencial** (*Com*) prime time; **en ~ real** (*Inform*) real time
tienda *etc* ['tjenda] *vb ver* **tender** ■ *nf* shop; (*más grande*) store; (*Naut*) awning; **~ de campaña** tent; **~ de comestibles** grocer's shop (*esp Brit*), grocery (*US*)
tiene *etc* ['tjene] *vb ver* **tener**
tienta ['tjenta] *nf* (*Med*) probe; (*fig*) tact; **andar a tientas** to grope one's way along
tiento *etc* ['tjento] *vb ver* **tentar** ■ *nm* (*tacto*) touch; (*precaución*) wariness; (*pulso*) steady hand; (*Zool*) feeler, tentacle
tierno, -a ['tjerno, a] *adj* (*blando, dulce*) tender; (*fresco*) fresh
tierra ['tjerra] *nf* earth; (*suelo*) soil; (*mundo*) world; (*país*) country, land; (*Elec*) earth, ground (*US*); **~ adentro** inland; **~ natal** native land; **echar ~ a un asunto** to hush an affair up; **no es de estas tierras** he's not from these parts; **la T~ Santa** the Holy Land
tieso, -a ['tjeso, a] *adj* (*rígido*) rigid; (*duro*) stiff; (*fig: testarudo*) stubborn; (*fam: orgulloso*) conceited ■ *adv* strongly
tiesto ['tjesto] *nm* flowerpot; (*pedazo*) piece of pottery
tifoidea [tifoi'ðea] *nf* typhoid
tifón [ti'fon] *nm* (*huracán*) typhoon; (*de mar*) tidal wave
tifus ['tifus] *nm* typhus; **~ icteroides** yellow fever
tigre ['tiɣre] *nm* tiger; (*Am*) jaguar
TIJ *sigla m* (= *Tribunal Internacional de Justicia*) ICJ
tijera [ti'xera] *nf* (*una tijera*) (pair of) scissors *pl*; (*Zool*) claw; (*persona*) gossip; **de ~** folding;

tijeras *nfpl* scissors; (*para plantas*) shears; **unas tijeras** a pair of scissors
tijeretear [tixerete'ar] *vt* to snip ■ *vi* (*fig*) to meddle
tila ['tila] *nf* (*Bot*) lime tree; (*Culin*) lime flower tea
tildar [til'dar] *vt*: ~ **de** to brand as
tilde ['tilde] *nf* (*defecto*) defect; (*trivialidad*) triviality; (*Tip*) tilde
tilín [ti'lin] *nm* tinkle
tilo ['tilo] *nm* lime tree
timador, a [tima'ðor, a] *nm/f* swindler
timar [ti'mar] *vt* (*robar*) to steal; (*estafar*) to swindle; (*persona*) to con; **timarse** *vr* (*fam*): **timarse con algn** to make eyes at sb
timbal [tim'bal] *nm* small drum
timbrar [tim'brar] *vt* to stamp; (*sellar*) to seal; (*carta*) to postmark
timbrazo [tim'braθo] *nm* ring; **dar un ~** to ring the bell
timbre ['timbre] *nm* (*sello*) stamp; (*campanilla*) bell; (*tono*) timbre; (*Com*) stamp duty
timidez [timi'ðeθ] *nf* shyness
tímido, -a ['timiðo, a] *adj* shy, timid
timo ['timo] *nm* swindle; **dar un ~ a algn** to swindle sb
timón [ti'mon] *nm* helm, rudder; (*Am*) steering wheel; **coger el ~** (*fig*) to take charge
timonel [timo'nel] *nm* helmsman
timorato, -a [timo'rato, a] *adj* God-fearing; (*mojigato*) sanctimonious
tímpano ['timpano] *nm* (*Anat*) eardrum; (*Mus*) small drum
tina ['tina] *nf* tub; (*Am: baño*) bath(tub)
tinaja [ti'naxa] *nf* large earthen jar
tinerfeño, -a [tiner'feɲo, a] *adj* of *o* from Tenerife ■ *nm/f* native *o* inhabitant of Tenerife
tinglado [tin'glaðo] *nm* (*cobertizo*) shed; (*fig: truco*) trick; (*intriga*) intrigue; **armar un ~** to lay a plot
tinieblas [ti'njeβlas] *nfpl* darkness *sg*; (*sombras*) shadows; **estamos en ~ sobre sus proyectos** (*fig*) we are in the dark about his plans
tino ['tino] *nm* (*habilidad*) skill; (*Mil*) marksmanship; (*juicio*) insight; (*moderación*) moderation; **sin ~** immoderately; **coger el ~** to get the feel *o* hang of it
tinta ['tinta] *nf* ink; (*Tec*) dye; (*Arte*) colour; **~ china** Indian ink; **tintas** *nfpl* (*fig*) shades; **medias tintas** (*fig*) half measures; **saber algo de buena ~** to have sth on good authority
tinte ['tinte] *nm* (*acto*) dyeing; (*fig*) tinge; (*barniz*) veneer
tintero [tin'tero] *nm* inkwell; **se le quedó en el ~** he clean forgot about it
tintinear [tintine'ar] *vt* to tinkle
tinto, -a ['tinto, a] *adj* (*teñido*) dyed; (*manchado*) stained ■ *nm* red wine
tintorera [tinto'rera] *nf* shark
tintorería [tintore'ria] *nf* dry cleaner's
tintorero [tinto'rero] *nm* dry cleaner('s)
tintura [tin'tura] *nf* (*acto*) dyeing; (*Química*) dye; (*farmacéutico*) tincture
tiña *etc* ['tiɲa] *vb ver* **teñir** ■ *nf* (*Med*) ringworm
tío ['tio] *nm* (*pariente*) uncle; (*fam: hombre*) bloke, guy (*US*)
tiovivo [tio'βiβo] *nm* roundabout
típico, -a ['tipiko, a] *adj* typical; (*pintoresco*) picturesque
tiple ['tiple] *nm* soprano (voice) ■ *nf* soprano
tipo ['tipo] *nm* (*clase*) type, kind; (*norma*) norm; (*patrón*) pattern; (*fam: hombre*) fellow, bloke, guy (*US*); (*Anat*) build; (*: de mujer*) figure; (*Imprenta*) type; **~ bancario/de descuento** bank/discount rate; **~ de interés** interest rate; **~ de interés vigente** (*Com*) standard rate; **~ de cambio** exchange rate; **~ base** (*Com*) base rate; **~ a término** (*Com*) forward rate; **dos tipos sospechosos** two suspicious characters; **~ de letra** (*Inform: Tip*) typeface; **~ de datos** (*Inform*) data type
tipografía [tipoɣra'fia] *nf* (*tipo*) printing; (*lugar*) printing press
tipográfico, -a [tipo'ɣrafiko, a] *adj* printing
tipógrafo, -a [ti'poɣrafo, a] *nm/f* printer
tíque, tíquet ['tike] (*pl* **~(t)s**) ['tikes] *nm* ticket; (*en tienda*) cash slip
tiquismiquis [tikis'mikis] *nm* fussy person ■ *nmpl* (*querellas*) squabbling *sg*; (*escrúpulos*) silly scruples
tira ['tira] *nf* strip; (*fig*) abundance ■ *nm*: **~ y afloja** give and take; (*cautela*) caution; **la ~ de ...** (*fam*) lots of ...
tirabuzón [tiraβu'θon] *nm* corkscrew; (*rizo*) curl
tiradero [tira'ðero] *nm* (*Am*) rubbish dump
tirado, -a [ti'raðo, a] *adj* (*barato*) dirt-cheap; (*fam: fácil*) very easy ■ *nf* (*acto*) cast, throw; (*distancia*) distance; (*serie*) series; (*Tip*) printing, edition; **de una tirada** at one go; **está ~** (*fam*) it's a cinch
TIR *sigla mpl* = **Transportes internacionales por carretera**
tirador, a [tira'ðor, a] *nm/f* (*persona*) shooter ■ *nm* (*mango*) handle; (*Elec*) flex; **~ certero** sniper
tiralíneas [tira'lineas] *nm inv* ruling-pen
tiranía [tira'nia] *nf* tyranny
tiránico, -a [ti'raniko, a] *adj* tyrannical

tiranizar [tirani'θar] *vt (pueblo, empleado)* to tyrannize
tirano, -a [ti'rano, a] *adj* tyrannical ■ *nm/f* tyrant
tirante [ti'rante] *adj (cuerda)* tight, taut; *(relaciones)* strained ■ *nm (Arq)* brace; *(Tec)* stay; *(correa)* shoulder strap; **tirantes** *nmpl* braces, suspenders (US)
tirantez [tiran'teθ] *nf* tightness; *(fig)* tension
tirar [ti'rar] *vt* to throw; *(volcar)* to upset; *(derribar)* to knock down *o* over; *(tiro)* to fire; *(cohete)* to launch; *(bomba)* to drop; *(edificio)* to pull down; *(desechar)* to throw out *o* away; *(disipar)* to squander; *(imprimir)* to print; *(dar: golpe)* to deal ■ *vi (disparar)* to shoot; *(dar un tirón)* to pull; *(fig)* to draw; *(interesar)* to appeal; *(fam: andar)* to go; *(tender a)* to tend to; *(Deporte)* to shoot; **tirarse** *vr* to throw o.s.; *(fig)* to demean o.s.; *(fam!)* to screw *(!)*; **~ abajo** to bring down, destroy; **tira más a su padre** he takes more after his father; **~ de algo** to pull *o* tug (on) sth; **ir tirando** to manage; **~ a la derecha** to turn *o* go right; **a todo ~** at the most
tirita [ti'rita] *nf* (sticking) plaster, bandaid (US)
tiritar [tiri'tar] *vi* to shiver
tiritona [tiri'tona] *nf* shivering (fit)
tiro ['tiro] *nm (lanzamiento)* throw; *(disparo)* shot; *(tiroteo)* shooting; *(Deporte)* shot; *(Tenis: Golf)* drive; *(alcance)* range; *(de escalera)* flight (of stairs); *(golpe)* blow; *(engaño)* hoax; **~ al blanco** target practice; **caballo de ~** cart-horse; **andar de tiros largos** to be all dressed up; **al ~** *(Am)* at once; **de a ~** *(Am fam)* completely; **se pegó un ~** he shot himself; **le salió el ~ por la culata** it backfired on him
tiroides [ti'roiðes] *nm inv* thyroid
Tirol [ti'rol] *nm*: **El ~** the Tyrol
tirolés, -esa [tiro'les, esa] *adj, nm/f* Tyrolean
tirón [ti'ron] *nm (sacudida)* pull, tug; **de un ~** in one go; **dar un ~ a** to pull at, tug at
tirotear [tirote'ar] *vt* to shoot at; **tirotearse** *vr* to exchange shots
tiroteo [tiro'teo] *nm* exchange of shots, shooting; *(escaramuza)* skirmish
tirria ['tirrja] *nf*: **tener una ~ a algn** to have a grudge against sb
tísico, -a ['tisiko, a] *adj, nm/f* consumptive
tisis ['tisis] *nf* consumption, tuberculosis
tít. *abr* = **título**
titánico, -a [ti'taniko, a] *adj* titanic
títere ['titere] *nm* puppet; **no dejar ~ con cabeza** to turn everything upside-down
titilar [titi'lar] *vi (luz, estrella)* to twinkle; *(párpado)* to flutter
titiritero, -a [titiri'tero, a] *nm/f (acróbata)* acrobat; *(malabarista)* juggler
titubeante [tituβe'ante] *adj (inestable)* shaky, tottering; *(farfullante)* stammering; *(dudoso)* hesitant
titubear [tituβe'ar] *vi* to stagger; *(tartamudear)* to stammer; *(vacilar)* to hesitate
titubeo [titu'βeo] *nm* staggering; stammering; hesitation
titulado, -a [titu'laðo, a] *adj (libro)* entitled; *(persona)* titled
titular [titu'lar] *adj* titular ■ *nm/f (de oficina)* occupant; *(de pasaporte)* holder ■ *nm* headline ■ *vt* to title; **titularse** *vr* to be entitled
título ['titulo] *nm (gen)* title; *(de diario)* headline; *(certificado)* professional qualification; *(universitario)* university degree; *(Com)* bond; *(fig)* right; **títulos** *nmpl* qualifications; **a ~ de** by way of; *(en calidad de)* in the capacity of; **a ~ de curiosidad** as a matter of interest; **~ de propiedad** title deed; **títulos convertibles de interés fijo** *(Com)* convertible loan stock *sg*
tiza ['tiθa] *nf* chalk; **una ~** a piece of chalk
tizna ['tiθna] *nf* grime
tiznar [tiθ'nar] *vt* to blacken; *(manchar)* to smudge, stain; *(fig)* to tarnish
tizón [ti'θon], **tizo** ['tiθo] *nm* brand; *(fig)* stain
TLC *nm abr (= Tratado de Libre Comercio)* NAFTA
Tm. *abr* = **tonelada(s) métrica(s)**
TNT *sigla m (= trinitrotolueno)* TNT
toalla [to'aʎa] *nf* towel
tobillo [to'βiʎo] *nm* ankle
tobogán [toβo'ɣan] *nm* toboggan; *(montaña rusa)* switchback; *(resbaladilla)* chute, slide
toca ['toka] *nf* headdress
tocadiscos [toka'ðiskos] *nm inv* record player
tocado, -a [to'kaðo, a] *adj (fruta etc)* rotten ■ *nm* headdress; **estar ~ de la cabeza** *(fam)* to be weak in the head
tocador [toka'ðor] *nm (mueble)* dressing table; *(cuarto)* boudoir; *(neceser)* toilet case; *(fam)* ladies' room
tocante [to'kante]: **~ a** *prep* with regard to; **en lo ~ a** as for, so far as concerns
tocar [to'kar] *vt* to touch; *(sentir)* to feel; *(con la mano)* to handle; *(Mus)* to play; *(campana)* to ring; *(tambor)* to beat; *(trompeta)* to blow; *(topar con)* to run into, strike; *(referirse a)* to allude to; *(estar emparentado con)* to be related to ■ *vi (a la puerta)* to knock (on *o* at the door); *(ser el turno)* to fall to, be the turn of; *(ser hora)* to be due; *(atañer)* to concern; **tocarse** *vr (cubrirse la cabeza)* to cover one's head; *(tener contacto)* to touch (each other); **tocarle a**

algn to fall to sb's lot; ~ **en** (*Naut*) to call at; **por lo que a mí me toca** as far as I am concerned; **esto toca en la locura** this verges on madness
tocateja [toka'texa] (*fam*): **a ~** *adv* in readies
tocayo, -a [to'kajo, a] *nm/f* namesake
tocino [to'θino] *nm* (bacon) fat; ~ **de panceta** bacon
todavía [toða'βia] *adv* (*aun*) even; (*aún*) still, yet; ~ **más** yet *o* still more; ~ **no** not yet; ~ **en 1970** as late as 1970; **está lloviendo ~** it's still raining
toditito, -a [toði'tito, a], **todito a** [to'ðito, a] *adj* (*Am fam*) (absolutely) all

PALABRA CLAVE

todo, -a ['toðo, a] *adj* **1** (*sg*) all; **toda la carne** all the meat; **toda la noche** all night, the whole night; **todo el libro** the whole book; **toda una botella** a whole bottle; **todo lo contrario** quite the opposite; **está toda sucia** she's all dirty; **a toda velocidad** at full speed; **por todo el país** throughout the whole country; **es todo un hombre** he's every inch a man; **soy todo oídos** I'm all ears
2 (*pl*) all; every; **todos los libros** all the books; **todas las noches** every night; **todos los que quieran salir** all those who want to leave; **todos vosotros** all of you
■ *pron* **1** everything, all; **todos** everyone, everybody; **lo sabemos todo** we know everything; **todos querían más tiempo** everybody *o* everyone wanted more time; **nos marchamos todos** all of us left; **corriendo y todo, no llegaron a tiempo** even though they ran, they still didn't arrive in time
2 (*con preposición*): **a pesar de todo** even so, in spite of everything; **con todo él me sigue gustando** even so I still like him; **le llamaron de todo** they called him all the names under the sun; **no me agrada del todo** I don't entirely like it
■ *adv* all; **vaya todo seguido** keep straight on *o* ahead
■ *nm*: **como un todo** as a whole; **arriba del todo** at the very top; **todo a cien** ≈ pound store (*Brit*), ≈ dollar store (*US*)

todopoderoso, -a [toðopoðe'roso, a] *adj* all powerful; (*Rel*) almighty
todoterreno [toðote'rreno] *nm* (*tb*: **vehículo todoterreno**) four-by-four
toga ['toɣa] *nf* toga; (*Escol*) gown
Tokio ['tokjo] *n* Tokyo
toldo ['toldo] *nm* (*para el sol*) sunshade; (*en tienda*) marquee; (*fig*) pride
tole ['tole] *nm* (*fam*) commotion
toledano, -a [tole'ðano, a] *adj* of *o* from Toledo ■ *nm/f* native *o* inhabitant of Toledo
tolerable [tole'raβle] *adj* tolerable
tolerancia [tole'ranθja] *nf* tolerance
tolerante [tole'rante] *adj* tolerant; (*fig*) open-minded
tolerar [tole'rar] *vt* to tolerate; (*resistir*) to endure
Tolón [to'lon] *nm* Toulon
toma ['toma] *nf* (*gen*) taking; (*Med*) dose; (*Elec*: *tb*: **toma de corriente**) socket; (*Mec*) inlet; ~ **de posesión** (*por presidente*) taking up office; ~ **de tierra** (*Aviat*) landing
tomadura [toma'ðura] *nf*: ~ **de pelo** hoax
tomar [to'mar] *vt* (*gen, Cine*: *Foto*: *TV*) to take; (*actitud*) to adopt; (*aspecto*) to take on; (*notas*) to take down; (*beber*) to drink ■ *vi* to take; (*Am*) to drink; **tomarse** *vr* to take; **tomarse por** to consider o.s. to be; **¡toma!** here you are!; ~ **asiento** to sit down; ~ **a algn por loco** to think sb mad; ~ **a bien/a mal** to take well/badly; ~ **en serio** to take seriously; ~ **el pelo a algn** to pull sb's leg; **tomarla con algn** to pick a quarrel with sb; ~ **por escrito** to write down; **toma y daca** give and take
tomate [to'mate] *nm* tomato
tomatera [toma'tera] *nf* tomato plant
tomavistas [toma'βistas] *nm inv* movie camera
tomillo [to'miʎo] *nm* thyme
tomo ['tomo] *nm* (*libro*) volume; (*fig*) importance
ton [ton] *abr* = **tonelada** ■ *nm*: **sin ~ ni son** without rhyme or reason
tonada [to'naða] *nf* tune
tonalidad [tonali'ðað] *nf* tone
tonel [to'nel] *nm* barrel
tonelada [tone'laða] *nf* ton; **~(s) métrica(s)** metric ton(s)
tonelaje [tone'laxe] *nm* tonnage
tonelero [tone'lero] *nm* cooper
tongo ['tongo] *nm* (*Deporte*) fix
tónico, -a ['toniko, a] *adj* tonic ■ *nm* (*Med*) tonic ■ *nf* (*Mus*) tonic; (*fig*) keynote
tonificador, a [tonifika'ðor, a], **tonificante** [tonifi'kante] *adj* invigorating, stimulating
tonificar [tonifi'kar] *vt* to tone up
tonifique *etc* [toni'fike] *vb ver* **tonificar**
tonillo [to'niʎo] *nm* monotonous voice
tono ['tono] *nm* (*Mus*) tone; (*altura*) pitch; (*color*) shade; **fuera de ~** inappropriate; ~ **de marcar** (*Telec*) dialling tone; **darse ~** to put on airs
tontear [tonte'ar] *vi* (*fam*) to fool about; (*enamorados*) to flirt

tontería [tonte'ria] *nf* (*estupidez*) foolishness; (*una tontería*) silly thing; **tonterías** *nfpl* rubbish *sg*, nonsense *sg*
tonto, -a ['tonto, a] *adj* stupid; (*ridículo*) silly ■ *nm/f* fool; (*payaso*) clown; **a tontas y a locas** anyhow; **hacer(se) el ~** to act the fool
topacio [to'paθjo] *nm* topaz
topar [to'par] *vt* (*tropezar*) to bump into; (*encontrar*) to find, come across; (*cabra etc*) to butt ■ *vi*: **~ contra** *o* **en** to run into; **~ con** to run up against; **el problema topa en eso** that's where the problem lies
tope ['tope] *adj* maximum ■ *nm* (*fin*) end; (*límite*) limit; (*Ferro*) buffer; (*Auto*) bumper; **al ~** end to end; **fecha ~** closing date; **precio ~** top price; **sueldo ~** maximum salary; **~ de tabulación** tab stop
tópico, -a ['topiko, a] *adj* topical; (*Med*) local ■ *nm* platitude, cliché; **de uso ~** for external application
topo ['topo] *nm* (*Zool*) mole; (*fig*) blunderer
topografía [topoɣra'fia] *nf* topography
topógrafo, -a [to'poɣrafo, a] *nm/f* topographer; (*agrimensor*) surveyor
toponimia [topo'nimja] *nf* place names *pl*; (*estudio*) study of place names
toque *etc* ['toke] *vb ver* **tocar** ■ *nm* touch; (*Mus*) beat; (*de campana*) ring, chime; (*Mil*) bugle call; (*fig*) crux; **dar un ~ a** to test; **dar el último ~ a** to put the final touch to; **~ de queda** curfew
toquetear [tokete'ar] *vt* to handle; (*fam!*) to touch up
toquilla [to'kiʎa] *nf* (*chal*) shawl
tórax ['toraks] *nm inv* thorax
torbellino [torbe'ʎino] *nm* whirlwind; (*fig*) whirl
torcedura [torθe'ðura] *nf* twist; (*Med*) sprain
torcer [tor'θer] *vt* to twist; (*la esquina*) to turn; (*Med*) to sprain; (*cuerda*) to plait; (*ropa, manos*) to wring; (*persona*) to corrupt; (*sentido*) to distort ■ *vi* (*cambiar de dirección*) to turn; **torcerse** *vr* to twist; (*doblar*) to bend; (*desviarse*) to go astray; (*fracasar*) to go wrong; **~ el gesto** to scowl; **torcerse un pie** to twist one's foot; **el coche torció a la derecha** the car turned right
torcido, -a [tor'θiðo, a] *adj* twisted; (*fig*) crooked ■ *nm* curl
tordo, -a ['torðo, a] *adj* dappled ■ *nm* thrush
torear [tore'ar] *vt* (*fig: evadir*) to dodge; (*toro*) to fight ■ *vi* to fight bulls
toreo [to'reo] *nm* bullfighting
torero, -a [to'rero, a] *nm/f* bullfighter
toril [to'ril] *nm* bullpen
tormenta [tor'menta] *nf* storm; (*fig: confusión*) turmoil
tormento [tor'mento] *nm* torture; (*fig*) anguish
tormentoso, -a [tormen'toso, a] *adj* stormy
tornar [tor'nar] *vt* (*devolver*) to return, give back; (*transformar*) to transform ■ *vi* to go back; **tornarse** *vr* (*ponerse*) to become; (*volver*) to return
tornasol [torna'sol] *nm* (*Bot*) sunflower; **papel de ~** litmus paper
tornasolado, -a [tornaso'laðo, a] *adj* (*brillante*) iridescent; (*reluciente*) shimmering
torneo [tor'neo] *nm* tournament
tornero, -a [tor'nero, a] *nm/f* machinist
tornillo [tor'niʎo] *nm* screw; **apretar los tornillos a algn** to apply pressure on sb; **le falta un ~** (*fam*) he's got a screw loose
torniquete [torni'kete] *nm* (*puerta*) turnstile; (*Med*) tourniquet
torno ['torno] *nm* (*Tec: grúa*) winch; (*: de carpintero*) lathe; (*tambor*) drum; **~ de banco** vice, vise (*US*); **en ~ (a)** round, about
toro ['toro] *nm* bull; (*fam*) he-man; **los toros** bullfighting *sg*
toronja [to'ronxa] *nf* grapefruit
torpe ['torpe] *adj* (*poco hábil*) clumsy, awkward; (*movimiento*) sluggish; (*necio*) dim; (*lento*) slow; (*indecente*) crude; (*no honrado*) dishonest
torpedo [tor'peðo] *nm* torpedo
torpemente [torpe'mente] *adv* (*sin destreza*) clumsily; (*lentamente*) slowly
torpeza [tor'peθa] *nf* (*falta de agilidad*) clumsiness; (*lentitud*) slowness; (*rigidez*) stiffness; (*error*) mistake; (*crudeza*) obscenity
torre ['torre] *nf* tower; (*de petróleo*) derrick; (*de electricidad*) pylon; (*Ajedrez*) rook; (*Aviat: Mil: Naut*) turret
torrefacto, -a [torre'fakto, a] *adj*: **café ~** high roast coffee
torrencial [torren'θjal] *adj* torrential
torrente [to'rrente] *nm* torrent
tórrido, -a ['torriðo, a] *adj* torrid
torrija [to'rrixa] *nf* fried bread; **torrijas** French toast *sg*
torsión [tor'sjon] *nf* twisting
torso ['torso] *nm* torso
torta ['torta] *nf* cake; (*fam*) slap; **~ de huevos** (*Am*) omelette; **no entendió ni ~** he didn't understand a word of it
tortazo [tor'taθo] *nm* (*bofetada*) slap; (*de coche*) crash
tortícolis [tor'tikolis] *nm inv* stiff neck
tortilla [tor'tiʎa] *nf* omelette; (*Am*) maize pancake; **~ francesa/española** plain/potato omelette; **cambiar** *o* **volver la ~ a algn** to turn the tables on sb
tortillera [torti'ʎera] *nf* (*fam!*) lesbian

tórtola ['tortola] *nf* turtledove
tortuga [tor'tuɣa] *nf* tortoise; **~ marina** turtle
tortuoso, -a [tor'twoso, a] *adj* winding
tortura [tor'tura] *nf* torture
torturar [tortu'rar] *vt* to torture
torvo, -a ['torβo, a] *adj* grim, fierce
torzamos *etc* [tor'θamos] *vb ver* **torcer**
tos [tos] *nf inv* cough; **~ ferina** whooping cough
Toscana [tos'kana] *nf*: **La ~** Tuscany
tosco, -a ['tosko, a] *adj* coarse
toser [to'ser] *vi* to cough; **no hay quien le tosa** he's in a class by himself
tostado, -a [tos'taðo, a] *adj* toasted; (*por el sol*) dark brown; (*piel*) tanned ■ *nf* tan; (*pan*) piece of toast; **tostadas** *nfpl* toast *sg*
tostador [tosta'ðor] *nm* toaster
tostar [tos'tar] *vt* to toast; (*café*) to roast; (*al sol*) to tan; **tostarse** *vr* to get brown
tostón [tos'ton] *nm*: **ser un ~** to be a drag
total [to'tal] *adj* total ■ *adv* in short; (*al fin y al cabo*) when all is said and done ■ *nm* total; **en ~** in all; **~ que** to cut a long story short; **~ de comprobación** (*Inform*) hash total; **~ debe/haber** (*Com*) debit/assets total
totalidad [totali'ðað] *nf* whole
totalitario, -a [totali'tarjo, a] *adj* totalitarian
totalmente [to'talmente] *adv* totally
tóxico, -a ['toksiko, a] *adj* toxic ■ *nm* poison
toxicómano, -a [toksi'komano, a] *adj* addicted to drugs ■ *nm/f* drug addict
toxina [to'ksina] *nf* toxin
tozudo, -a [to'θuðo, a] *adj* obstinate
traba ['traβa] *nf* bond, tie; (*cadena*) fetter; **poner trabas a** to restrain
trabajador, a [traβaxa'ðor, a] *nm/f* worker ■ *adj* hard-working
trabajar [traβa'xar] *vt* to work; (*arar*) to till; (*empeñarse en*) to work at; (*empujar: persona*) to push; (*convencer*) to persuade ■ *vi* to work; (*esforzarse*) to strive; **¡a ~!** let's get to work!; **~ por hacer algo** to strive to do sth
trabajo [tra'βaxo] *nm* work; (*tarea*) task; (*Pol*) labour; (*fig*) effort; **tomarse el ~ de** to take the trouble to; **~ por turno/a destajo** shift work/piecework; **~ en proceso** (*Com*) work-in-progress
trabajoso, -a [traβa'xoso, a] *adj* hard; (*Med*) pale
trabalenguas [traβa'lengwas] *nm inv* tongue twister
trabar [tra'βar] *vt* (*juntar*) to join, unite; (*atar*) to tie down, fetter; (*agarrar*) to seize; (*amistad*) to strike up; **trabarse** *vr* to become entangled; (*reñir*) to squabble; **se le traba la lengua** he gets tongue-tied
trabazón [traβa'θon] *nf* (*Tec*) joining, assembly; (*fig*) bond, link
trabucar [traβu'kar] *vt* (*confundir*) to confuse, mix up; (*palabras*) to misplace
trabuque *etc* [tra'βuke] *vb ver* **trabucar**
tracción [trak'θjon] *nf* traction; **~ delantera/trasera** front-wheel/rear-wheel drive
trace *etc* ['traθe] *vb ver* **trazar**
tractor [trak'tor] *nm* tractor
trad. *abr* (*= traducido*) trans
tradición [traði'θjon] *nf* tradition
tradicional [traðiθjo'nal] *adj* traditional
traducción [traðuk'θjon] *nf* translation; **~ asistida por ordenador** computer-assisted translation
traducible [traðu'θiβle] *adj* translatable
traducir [traðu'θir] *vt* to translate; **traducirse** *vr*: **traducirse en** (*fig*) to entail, result in
traductor, a [traðuk'tor, a] *nm/f* translator
traduzca *etc* [tra'ðuθka] *vb ver* **traducir**
traer [tra'er] *vt* to bring; (*llevar*) to carry; (*ropa*) to wear; (*incluir*) to carry; (*fig*) to cause; **traerse** *vr*: **traerse algo** to be up to sth; **traerse bien/mal** to dress well/badly; **traérselas** to be annoying; **~ consigo** to involve, entail; **es un problema que se las trae** it's a difficult problem
traficante [trafi'kante] *nm/f* trader, dealer
traficar [trafi'kar] *vi* to trade; **~ con** (*pey*) to deal illegally in
tráfico ['trafiko] *nm* (*Com*) trade; (*Auto*) traffic
trafique *etc* [tra'fike] *vb ver* **traficar**
tragaderas [traɣa'ðeras] *nfpl* (*garganta*) throat *sg*, gullet *sg*; (*credulidad*) gullibility *sg*
tragaluz [traɣa'luθ] *nm* skylight
tragamonedas [traɣamo'neðas] *nm inv*, **tragaperras** [traɣa'perras] *nm inv* slot machine
tragar [tra'ɣar] *vt* to swallow; (*devorar*) to devour, bolt down; **tragarse** *vr* to swallow; (*tierra*) to absorb, soak up; **no le puedo ~** (*persona*) I can't stand him
tragedia [tra'xeðja] *nf* tragedy
trágico, -a ['traxiko, a] *adj* tragic
trago ['traɣo] *nm* (*de líquido*) drink; (*comido de golpe*) gulp; (*fam: de bebida*) swig; (*desgracia*) blow; **~ amargo** (*fig*) hard time
trague *etc* ['traɣe] *vb ver* **tragar**
traición [trai'θjon] *nf* treachery; (*Jur*) treason; (*una traición*) act of treachery
traicionar [traiθjo'nar] *vt* to betray
traicionero, -a [traiθjo'nero, a] = **traidor, a**
traída [tra'iða] *nf* carrying; **~ de aguas** water supply
traidor, a [trai'ðor, a] *adj* treacherous ■ *nm/f* traitor

traiga *etc* ['traiɣa] *vb ver* **traer**
trailer (*pl* **trailers**) ['trailer, 'trailer(s)] *nm* trailer
traje *etc* ['traxe] *vb ver* **traer** ■ *nm* (*gen*) dress; (*de hombre*) suit; (*traje típico*) costume; (*fig*) garb; **~ de baño** swimsuit; **~ de luces** bullfighter's costume; **~ hecho a la medida** made-to-measure suit
trajera *etc* [tra'xera] *vb ver* **traer**
trajín [tra'xin] *nm* haulage; (*fam*: *movimiento*) bustle; **trajines** *nmpl* goings-on
trajinar [traxi'nar] *vt* (*llevar*) to carry, transport ■ *vi* (*moverse*) to bustle about; (*viajar*) to travel around
trama ['trama] *nf* (*fig*) link; (: *intriga*) plot; (*de tejido*) weft
tramar [tra'mar] *vt* to plot; (*Tec*) to weave; **tramarse** *vr* (*fig*): **algo se está tramando** there's something going on
tramitar [trami'tar] *vt* (*asunto*) to transact; (*negociar*) to negotiate; (*manejar*) to handle
trámite ['tramite] *nm* (*paso*) step; (*Jur*) transaction; **trámites** *nmpl* (*burocracia*) paperwork *sg*, procedures; (*Jur*) proceedings
tramo ['tramo] *nm* (*de tierra*) plot; (*de escalera*) flight; (*de vía*) section
tramoya [tra'moja] *nf* (*Teat*) piece of stage machinery; (*fig*) trick
tramoyista [tramo'jista] *nm/f* scene shifter; (*fig*) trickster
trampa ['trampa] *nf* trap; (*en el suelo*) trapdoor; (*prestidigitación*) conjuring trick; (*engaño*) trick; (*fam*) fiddle; **caer en la ~** to fall into the trap; **hacer trampas** (*trampear*) to cheat
trampear [trampe'ar] *vt, vi* to cheat
trampilla [tram'piʎa] *nf* trap, hatchway
trampolín [trampo'lin] *nm* trampoline; (*de piscina etc*) diving board
tramposo, -a [tram'poso, a] *adj* crooked, cheating ■ *nm/f* crook, cheat
tranca ['tranka] *nf* (*palo*) stick; (*viga*) beam; (*de puerta, ventana*) bar; (*borrachera*) binge; **a trancas y barrancas** with great difficulty
trancar [tran'kar] *vt* to bar ■ *vi* to stride along
trancazo [tran'kaθo] *nm* (*golpe*) blow
trance ['tranθe] *nm* (*momento difícil*) difficult moment; (*situación crítica*) critical situation; (*estado de hipnosis*) trance; **estar en ~ de muerte** to be at death's door
tranco ['tranko] *nm* stride
tranque *etc* ['tranke] *vb ver* **trancar**
tranquilamente [tran'kilamente] *adv* (*sin preocupaciones*: *leer, trabajar*) peacefully; (*sin enfadarse*: *hablar, discutir*) calmly
tranquilice *etc* [tranki'liθe] *vb ver* **tranquilizar**
tranquilidad [trankili'ðað] *nf* (*calma*) calmness, stillness; (*paz*) peacefulness
tranquilizador, a [trankiliθa'ðor, a] *adj* (*música*) soothing; (*hecho*) reassuring
tranquilizante [trankili'θante] *nm* tranquillizer
tranquilizar [trankili'θar] *vt* (*calmar*) to calm (down); (*asegurar*) to reassure
tranquilo, -a [tran'kilo, a] *adj* (*calmado*) calm; (*apacible*) peaceful; (*mar*) calm; (*mente*) untroubled
Trans. *abr* (*Com*) = **transferencia**
transacción [transak'θjon] *nf* transaction
transar [tran'sar] *vi* (*Am*) = **transigir**
transatlántico, -a [transat'lantiko, a] *adj* transatlantic ■ *nm* (ocean) liner
transbordador [transβorða'ðor] *nm* ferry
transbordar [transβor'ðar] *vt* to transfer; **transbordarse** *vr* to change
transbordo [trans'βorðo] *nm* transfer; **hacer ~** to change (trains)
transcender [transθen'der] *vt* = **trascender**
transcribir [transkri'βir] *vt* to transcribe
transcurrir [transku'rrir] *vi* (*tiempo*) to pass; (*hecho*) to turn out
transcurso [trans'kurso] *nm* passing, lapse; **en el ~ de ocho días** in the course of a week
transeúnte [transe'unte] *adj* transient ■ *nm/f* passer-by
transexual [transe'kswal] *adj, nm/f* transsexual
transferencia [transfe'renθja] *nf* transference; (*Com*) transfer; **~ bancaria** banker's order; **~ de crédito** (*Com*) credit transfer; **~ electrónica de fondos** (*Com*) electronic funds transfer
transferir [transfe'rir] *vt* to transfer; (*aplazar*) to postpone
transfiera *etc* [trans'fjera] *vb ver* **transferir**
transfigurar [transfiɣu'rar] *vt* to transfigure
transfiriendo *etc* [transfi'rjendo] *vb ver* **transferir**
transformación [transforma'θjon] *nf* transformation
transformador [transforma'ðor] *nm* transformer
transformar [transfor'mar] *vt* to transform; (*convertir*) to convert
tránsfuga ['transfuɣa] *nm/f* (*Mil*) deserter; (*Pol*) turncoat
transfusión [transfu'sjon] *nf* (*tb*: **transfusión de sangre**) (blood) transfusion
transgénico, -a [trans'xeniko, a] *adj* genetically modified
transgredir [transɣre'dir] *vt* to transgress
transgresión [transɣre'sjon] *nf* transgression

transición [transi'θjon] *nf* transition; **período de ~** transitional period
transido, -a [tran'siðo, a] *adj* overcome; **~ de angustia** beset with anxiety; **~ de dolor** racked with pain
transigir [transi'xir] *vi* to compromise; (*ceder*) to make concessions
transija *etc* [tran'sixa] *vb ver* **transigir**
Transilvania [transil'βanja] *nf* Transylvania
transistor [transis'tor] *nm* transistor
transitable [transi'taβle] *adj* (*camino*) passable
transitar [transi'tar] *vi* to go (from place to place)
transitivo, -a [transi'tiβo, a] *adj* transitive
tránsito ['transito] *nm* transit; (*Auto*) traffic; (*parada*) stop; **horas de máximo ~** rush hours; **"se prohíbe el ~"** "no thoroughfare"
transitorio, -a [transi'torjo, a] *adj* transitory
transmisión [transmi'sjon] *nf* (*Radio*: *TV*) transmission, broadcast(ing); (*transferencia*) transfer; **~ en circuito** hookup; **~ en directo/exterior** live/outside broadcast; **~ de datos (en paralelo/en serie)** (*Inform*) (parallel/serial) data transfer *o* transmission; **plena/media ~ bidireccional** (*Inform*) full/half duplex
transmitir [transmi'tir] *vt* to transmit; (*Radio*: *TV*) to broadcast; (*enfermedad*) to give, pass on
transparencia [transpa'renθja] *nf* transparency; (*claridad*) clearness, clarity; (*foto*) slide
transparentar [transparen'tar] *vt* to reveal ■ *vi* to be transparent
transparente [transpa'rente] *adj* transparent; (*aire*) clear; (*ligero*) diaphanous ■ *nm* curtain
transpirar [transpi'rar] *vi* to perspire; (*fig*) to transpire
transpondré *etc* [transpon'dre] *vb ver* **transponer**
transponer [transpo'ner] *vt* to transpose; (*cambiar de sitio*) to move about ■ *vi* (*desaparecer*) to disappear; (*ir más allá*) to go beyond; **transponerse** *vr* to change places; (*ocultarse*) to hide; (*sol*) to go down
transponga *etc* [trans'ponga] *vb ver* **transponer**
transportador [transporta'ðor] *nm* (*Mecánica*): **~ de correa** belt conveyor
transportar [transpor'tar] *vt* to transport; (*llevar*) to carry
transporte [trans'porte] *nm* transport; (*Com*) haulage; **Ministerio de Transportes** Ministry of Transport
transpuesto [trans'pwesto], **transpuse** *etc* [trans'puse] *vb ver* **transponer**
transversal [transβer'sal] *adj* transverse, cross ■ *nf* (*tb*: **calle transversal**) cross street
transversalmente [transβersal'mente] *adv* obliquely
tranvía [tram'bia] *nm* tram, streetcar (US)
trapecio [tra'peθjo] *nm* trapeze
trapecista [trape'θista] *nm/f* trapeze artist
trapero, -a [tra'pero, a] *nm/f* ragman
trapicheos [trapi'tʃeos] *nmpl* (*fam*) schemes, fiddles
trapisonda [trapi'sonda] *nf* (*jaleo*) row; (*estafa*) swindle
trapo ['trapo] *nm* (*tela*) rag; (*de cocina*) cloth; **trapos** *nmpl* (*fam*: *de mujer*) clothes, dresses; **a todo ~** under full sail; **soltar el ~** (*llorar*) to burst into tears
tráquea ['trakea] *nf* trachea, windpipe
traqueteo [trake'teo] *nm* (*crujido*) crack; (*golpeteo*) rattling
tras [tras] *prep* (*detrás*) behind; (*después*) after; **~ de** besides; **día ~ día** day after day; **uno ~ otro** one after the other
trascendencia [trasθen'denθja] *nf* (*importancia*) importance; (*en filosofía*) transcendence
trascendental [trasθenden'tal] *adj* important; transcendental
trascender [trasθen'der] *vi* (*oler*) to smell; (*noticias*) to come out, leak out; (*sucesos, sentimientos*) to spread, have a wide effect; **~ a** (*afectar*) to reach, have an effect on; (*oler a*) to smack of; **en su novela todo trasciende a romanticismo** everything in his novel smacks of romanticism
trascienda *etc* [tras'θjenda] *vb ver* **trascender**
trasegar [trase'ɣar] *vt* (*mover*) to move about; (*vino*) to decant
trasegué [trase'ɣe], **traseguemos** *etc* [trase'ɣemos] *vb ver* **trasegar**
trasero, -a [tra'sero, a] *adj* back, rear ■ *nm* (*Anat*) bottom; **traseros** *nmpl* ancestors
trasfondo [tras'fondo] *nm* background
trasgo ['trasɣo] *nm* (*duende*) goblin
trasgredir [trasɣre'ðir] *vt* to contravene
trashumante [trasu'mante] *adj* migrating
trasiego *etc* [tra'sjeɣo] *vb ver* **trasegar** ■ *nm* (*cambiar de sitio*) move, switch; (*de vino*) decanting; (*trastorno*) upset
trasiegue *etc* [tra'sjeɣe] *vb ver* **trasegar**
trasladar [trasla'ðar] *vt* to move; (*persona*) to transfer; (*postergar*) to postpone; (*copiar*) to copy; (*interpretar*) to interpret; **trasladarse** *vr* (*irse*) to go; (*mudarse*) to move; **trasladarse a otro puesto** to move to a new job
traslado [tras'laðo] *nm* move; (*mudanza*) move, removal; (*de persona*) transfer; (*copia*)

copy; ~ **de bloque** (*Inform*) block move, cut-and-paste
traslucir [traslu'θir] *vt* to show; **traslucirse** *vr* to be translucent; (*fig*) to be revealed
trasluz [tras'luθ] *nm* reflected light; **al ~** against *o* up to the light
trasluzca *etc* [tras'luθka] *vb ver* **traslucir**
trasmano [tras'mano]: **a ~** *adv* (*fuera de alcance*) out of reach; (*apartado*) out of the way
trasnochado, -a [trasno'tʃaðo, a] *adj* dated
trasnochador, a [trasnotʃa'ðor, a] *adj* given to staying up late ■ *nm/f* (*fig*) night bird
trasnochar [trasno'tʃar] *vi* (*acostarse tarde*) to stay up late; (*no dormir*) to have a sleepless night; (*pasar la noche*) to stay the night
traspasar [traspa'sar] *vt* (*bala*) to pierce, go through; (*propiedad*) to sell, transfer; (*calle*) to cross over; (*límites*) to go beyond; (*ley*) to break; **"traspaso negocio"** "business for sale"
traspaso [tras'paso] *nm* transfer; (*fig*) anguish
traspié [tras'pje] (*pl* **~s**) *nm* (*caída*) stumble; (*tropezón*) trip; (*fig*) blunder
trasplantar [trasplan'tar] *vt* to transplant
trasplante [tras'plante] *nm* transplant
traspuesto, -a [tras'pwesto, a] *adj*: **quedarse** ~ to doze off
trastada [tras'taða] *nf* (*fam*) prank
trastazo [tras'taθo] *nm* (*fam*) bump; **darse un ~** (*persona*) to bump o.s.; (*en coche*) to have a bump
traste ['traste] *nm* (*Mus*) fret; **dar al ~ con algo** to ruin sth; **ir al ~** to fall through
trastero [tras'tero] *nm* lumber room
trastienda [tras'tjenda] *nf* backshop; **obtener algo por la ~** to get sth by underhand means
trasto ['trasto] *nm* (*mueble*) piece of furniture; (*tarro viejo*) old pot; (*pey: cosa*) piece of junk; (*: persona*) dead loss; **trastos** *nmpl* (*Teat*) scenery *sg*; **tirar los trastos a la cabeza** to have a blazing row
trastocar [trasto'kar] *vt* (*papeles*) to mix up
trastornado, -a [trastor'naðo, a] *adj* (*loco*) mad; (*agitado*) crazy
trastornar [trastor'nar] *vt* to overturn, upset; (*fig: ideas*) to confuse; (*: nervios*) to shatter; (*: persona*) to drive crazy; **trastornarse** *vr* (*plan*) to fall through
trastorno [tras'torno] *nm* (*acto*) overturning; (*confusión*) confusion; (*Pol*) disturbance, upheaval; (*Med*) upset; ~ **estomacal** stomach upset; ~ **mental** mental disorder, breakdown
trasunto [tra'sunto] *nm* copy
trasvase [tras'βase] *nm* (*de río*) diversion
tratable [tra'taβle] *adj* friendly
tratado [tra'taðo] *nm* (*Pol*) treaty; (*Com*) agreement; (*Lit*) treatise
tratamiento [trata'mjento] *nm* treatment; (*Tec*) processing; (*de problema*) handling; ~ **de datos** (*Inform*) data processing; ~ **de gráficos** (*Inform*) graphics; ~ **de márgenes** margin settings; ~ **de textos** (*Inform*) word processing; ~ **por lotes** (*Inform*) batch processing; ~ **de tú** familiar address
tratante [tra'tante] *nm/f* dealer, merchandizer
tratar [tra'tar] *vt* (*ocuparse de*) to treat; (*manejar, Tec*) to handle; (*Inform*) to process; (*Med*) to treat; (*dirigirse a: persona*) to address ■ *vi*: ~ **de** (*hablar sobre*) to deal with, be about; (*intentar*) to try to; ~ **con** (*Com*) to trade in; (*negociar con*) to negotiate with; (*tener tratos con*) to have dealings with; **tratarse** *vr* to treat each other; **se trata de la nueva piscina** it's about the new pool; **¿de qué se trata?** what's it about?
trato ['trato] *nm* dealings *pl*; (*relaciones*) relationship; (*comportamiento*) manner; (*Com: Jur*) agreement, contract; (*título*) (form of) address; **de ~ agradable** pleasant; **de fácil ~** easy to get on with; ~ **equitativo** fair deal; **¡~ hecho!** it's a deal!; **malos tratos** ill-treatment *sg*
trauma ['trauma] *nm* trauma
traumático, -a [trau'matiko, a] *adj* traumatic
través [tra'βes] *nm* (*contratiempo*) reverse; **al ~** across, crossways; **a ~ de** across; (*sobre*) over; (*por*) through; **de ~** across; (*de lado*) sideways
travesaño [traβe'saɲo] *nm* (*Arq*) crossbeam; (*Deporte*) crossbar
travesía [traβe'sia] *nf* (*calle*) cross-street; (*Naut*) crossing
travesti [tra'βesti] *nm/f* transvestite
travesura [traβe'sura] *nf* (*broma*) prank; (*ingenio*) wit
travieso, -a [tra'βjeso, a] *adj* (*niño*) naughty; (*adulto*) restless; (*ingenioso*) witty ■ *nf* crossing; (*Arq*) crossbeam; (*Ferro*) sleeper
trayecto [tra'jekto] *nm* (*ruta*) road, way; (*viaje*) journey; (*tramo*) stretch; (*curso*) course; **final del ~** end of the line
trayectoria [trajek'torja] *nf* trajectory; (*desarrollo*) development, path; **la ~ actual del partido** the party's present line
trayendo *etc* [tra'jendo] *vb ver* **traer**
traza ['traθa] *nf* (*Arq*) plan, design; (*aspecto*) looks *pl*; (*señal*) sign; (*engaño*) trick; (*habilidad*) skill; (*Inform*) trace
trazado, -a [tra'θaðo, a] *adj*: **bien ~** shapely, well-formed ■ *nm* (*Arq*) plan, design; (*fig*)

outline; *(de carretera etc)* line, route
trazador [traθa'ðor] *nm* plotter; **~ plano** flatbed plotter
trazar [tra'θar] *vt (Arq)* to plan; *(Arte)* to sketch; *(fig)* to trace; *(itinerario: hacer)* to plot; *(plan)* to follow
trazo ['traθo] *nm (línea)* line; *(bosquejo)* sketch; **trazos** *nmpl (de cara)* lines, features
TRB *abr* = **toneladas de registro bruto**
trébol ['treβol] *nm (Bot)* clover; **tréboles** *nmpl (Naipes)* clubs
trece ['treθe] *num* thirteen; **estar en sus ~** to stand firm
trecho ['tretʃo] *nm (distancia)* distance; *(de tiempo)* while; *(fam)* piece; **de ~ en ~** at intervals
tregua ['treɣwa] *nf (Mil)* truce; *(fig)* lull; **sin ~** without respite
treinta ['treinta] *num* thirty
treintena [trein'tena] *nf* (about) thirty
tremendo, -a [tre'mendo, a] *adj (terrible)* terrible; *(imponente: cosa)* imposing; *(fam: fabuloso)* tremendous; *(divertido)* entertaining
trémulo, -a ['tremulo, a] *adj* quivering; *(luz)* flickering
tren [tren] *nm (Ferro)* train; **~ de aterrizaje** undercarriage; **~ directo/expreso/(de) mercancías/de pasajeros/suplementario** through/fast/goods *o* freight/passenger/ relief train; **~ de vida** way of life
trenca ['trenka] *nf* duffel coat
trence *etc* ['trenθe] *vb ver* **trenzar**
trenza ['trenθa] *nf (de pelo)* plait
trenzar [tren'θar] *vt (el pelo)* to plait ■ *vi (en baile)* to weave in and out; **trenzarse** *vr (Am)* to become involved
trepa ['trepa] *nf (subida)* climb; *(ardid)* trick
trepador, a [trepa'ðor(a)] *nm/f (fam)*: **ser un(a) ~(a)** to be on the make ■ *nf (Bot)* climber
trepar [tre'par] *vt, vi* to climb; *(Tec)* to drill
trepidación [trepiða'θjon] *nf* shaking, vibration
trepidar [trepi'ðar] *vi* to shake, vibrate
tres [tres] *num* three; *(fecha)* third; **las ~** three o'clock
trescientos, -as [tres'θjentos, as] *num* three hundred
tresillo [tre'siʎo] *nm* three-piece suite; *(Mus)* triplet
treta ['treta] *nf (Com etc)* gimmick; *(fig)* trick
tri ... [tri] *pref* tri..., three-...
tríada ['triaða] *nf* triad
triangular [trjangu'lar] *adj* triangular
triángulo [tri'angulo] *nm* triangle
tribal [tri'βal] *adj* tribal
tribu ['triβu] *nf* tribe
tribuna [tri'βuna] *nf (plataforma)* platform; *(Deporte)* stand; *(fig)* public speaking; **~ de la prensa** press box; **~ del acusado** *(Jur)* dock; **~ del jurado** jury box
tribunal [triβu'nal] *nm (en juicio)* court; *(comisión, fig)* tribunal; *(Escol: examinadores)* board of examiners; **T~ Supremo** High Court, Supreme Court *(US)*; **T~ de Justicia de las Comunidades Europeas** European Court of Justice; **~ popular** jury
tributar [triβu'tar] *vt* to pay; *(las gracias)* to give; *(cariño)* to show
tributario, -a [triβu'tarjo, a] *adj (Geo: Pol)* tributary *cpd*; *(Econ)* tax *cpd*, taxation *cpd* ■ *nm (Geo)* tributary ■ *nm/f (Com)* taxpayer; **sistema ~** tax system
tributo [tri'βuto] *nm (Com)* tax
triciclo [tri'θiklo] *nm* tricycle
tricornio [tri'kornjo] *nm* three-cornered hat
tricota [tri'kota] *nf (Am)* knitted sweater
tricotar [triko'tar] *vi* to knit
tridimensional [triðimensjo'nal] *adj* three-dimensional
trienal [trje'nal] *adj* three-year
trifulca [tri'fulka] *nf (fam)* row, shindy
trigal [tri'ɣal] *nm* wheat field
trigésimo, -a [tri'xesimo, a] *num* thirtieth
trigo ['triɣo] *nm* wheat; **trigos** *nmpl* wheat field(s) *(pl)*
trigueño, -a [tri'ɣeɲo, a] *adj (pelo)* corn-coloured; *(piel)* olive-skinned
trillado, -a [tri'ʎaðo, a] *adj* threshed; *(fig)* trite, hackneyed
trilladora [triʎa'ðora] *nf* threshing machine
trillar [tri'ʎar] *vt (Agr)* to thresh; *(fig)* to frequent
trillizos, -as [tri'ʎiθos, as] *nmpl/nfpl* triplets
trilogía [trilo'xia] *nf* trilogy
trimestral [trimes'tral] *adj* quarterly; *(Escol)* termly
trimestre [tri'mestre] *nm (Escol)* term; *(Com)* quarter, financial period; *(: pago)* quarterly payment
trinar [tri'nar] *vi (Mus)* to trill; *(ave)* to sing, warble; **está que trina** he's hopping mad
trincar [trin'kar] *vt (atar)* to tie up; *(Naut)* to lash; *(agarrar)* to pinion
trinchante [trin'tʃante] *nm (para cortar carne)* carving knife; *(tenedor)* meat fork
trinchar [trin'tʃar] *vt* to carve
trinchera [trin'tʃera] *nf (fosa)* trench; *(para vía)* cutting; *(impermeable)* trench-coat
trineo [tri'neo] *nm* sledge
trinidad [trini'ðað] *nf* trio; *(Rel)*: **la T~** the Trinity
trino ['trino] *nm* trill
trinque *etc* ['trinke] *vb ver* **trincar**

trinquete [trin'kete] *nm* (*Tec*) pawl; (*Naut*) foremast
trío ['trio] *nm* trio
tripa ['tripa] *nf* (*Anat*) intestine; (*fig: fam*) belly; **tripas** *nfpl* (*Anat*) insides; (*Culin*) tripe *sg*; **tener mucha ~** to be fat; **me duelen las tripas** I have a stomach ache
tripartito, -a [tripar'tito, a] *adj* tripartite
triple ['triple] *adj* triple; (*tres veces*) threefold
triplicado, -a [tripli'kaðo, a] *adj*: **por ~** in triplicate
triplicar [tripli'kar] *vt* to treble
triplo ['triplo] *adj* = **triple**
trípode ['tripoðe] *nm* tripod
Trípoli ['tripoli] *nm* Tripoli
tríptico ['triptiko] *nm* (*Arte*) triptych; (*documento*) three-part document
tripulación [tripula'θjon] *nf* crew
tripulante [tripu'lante] *nm/f* crewman/woman
tripular [tripu'lar] *vt* (*barco*) to man; (*Auto*) to drive
triquiñuela [triki'ɲwela] *nf* trick
tris [tris] *nm* crack; **en un ~** in an instant; **estar en un ~ de hacer algo** to be within an inch of doing sth
triste ['triste] *adj* (*afligido*) sad; (*sombrío*) melancholy, gloomy; (*desolado*) desolate; (*lamentable*) sorry, miserable; (*viejo*) old; (*único*) single; **no queda sino un ~ penique** there's just one miserable penny left
tristeza [tris'teθa] *nf* (*aflicción*) sadness; (*melancolía*) melancholy; (*de lugar*) desolation; (*pena*) misery
tristón, -ona [tris'ton, ona] *adj* sad, downhearted
trituradora [tritura'ðora] *nf* shredder
triturar [tritu'rar] *vt* (*moler*) to grind; (*mascar*) to chew; (*documentos*) to shred
triunfador, a [triunfa'ðor, a] *adj* triumphant; (*ganador*) winning ▪ *nm/f* winner
triunfal [triun'fal] *adj* triumphant; (*arco*) triumphal
triunfante [triun'fante] *adj* triumphant; (*ganador*) winning
triunfar [triun'far] *vi* (*tener éxito*) to triumph; (*ganar*) to win; (*Naipes*) to be trumps; **triunfan corazones** hearts are trumps; **~ en la vida** to succeed in life
triunfo [tri'unfo] *nm* triumph; (*Naipes*) trump
trivial [tri'βjal] *adj* trivial
trivialice *etc* [triβja'liθe] *vb ver* **trivializar**
trivializar [triβjali'θar] *vt* to minimize, play down
triza ['triθa] *nf* bit, piece; **hacer algo trizas** to smash sth to bits; (*papel*) to tear sth to shreds
trocar [tro'kar] *vt* (*Com*) to exchange; (*dinero, de lugar*) to change; (*palabras*) to exchange; (*confundir*) to confuse; **trocarse** *vr* (*confundirse*) to get mixed up; (*transformarse*): **trocarse (en)** to change (into)
trocear [troθe'ar] *vt* to cut up
trocha ['trotʃa] *nf* (*sendero*) by-path; (*atajo*) short cut
troche ['trotʃe]: **a ~ y moche** *adv* helter-skelter, pell-mell
trofeo [tro'feo] *nm* (*premio*) trophy
trola ['trola] *nf* (*fam*) fib
tromba ['tromba] *nf* whirlwind; **~ de agua** cloudburst
trombón [trom'bon] *nm* trombone
trombosis [trom'bosis] *nf inv* thrombosis
trompa ['trompa] *nf* (*Mus*) horn; (*de elefante*) trunk; (*trompo*) humming top; (*hocico*) snout; (*Anat*) tube, duct ▪ *nm* (*Mus*) horn player; **~ de Falopio** Fallopian tube; **cogerse una ~** (*fam*) to get tight
trompada [trom'paða] *nf*, **trompazo** [trom'paθo] *nm* (*choque*) bump, bang; (*puñetazo*) punch
trompeta [trom'peta] *nf* trumpet; (*clarín*) bugle ▪ *nm* trumpeter
trompetilla [trompe'tiʎa] *nf* ear trumpet
trompicón [trompi'kon]: **a trompicones** *adv* in fits and starts
trompo ['trompo] *nm* spinning top
trompón [trom'pon] *nm* bump
tronado, -a [tro'naðo, a] *adj* broken-down
tronar [tro'nar] *vt* (*Am*) to shoot, execute ▪ *vi* to thunder; (*fig*) to rage; (*fam*) to go broke
tronchar [tron'tʃar] *vt* (*árbol*) to chop down; (*fig: vida*) to cut short; (*esperanza*) to shatter; (*persona*) to tire out; **troncharse** *vr* to fall down; **troncharse de risa** to split one's sides with laughter
tronco ['tronko] *nm* (*de árbol, Anat*) trunk; (*de planta*) stem; **estar hecho un ~** to be sound asleep
tronera [tro'nera] *nf* (*Mil*) loophole; (*Arq*) small window
trono ['trono] *nm* throne
tropa ['tropa] *nf* (*Mil*) troop; (*soldados*) soldiers *pl*; (*soldados rasos*) ranks *pl*; (*gentío*) mob
tropecé [trope'θe], **tropecemos** *etc* [trope'θemos] *vb ver* **tropezar**
tropel [tro'pel] *nm* (*muchedumbre*) crowd; (*prisa*) rush; (*montón*) throng; **acudir** *etc* **en ~** to come *etc* in a mad rush
tropelía [trope'lia] *nm* outrage
tropezar [trope'θar] *vi* to trip, stumble; (*fig*) to slip up; **tropezarse** *vr* (*dos personas*) to run

into each other; **~ con** *(encontrar)* to run into; *(topar con)* to bump into
tropezón [trope'θon] *nm* trip; *(fig)* blunder; *(traspié)*: **dar un ~** to trip
tropical [tropi'kal] *adj* tropical
trópico ['tropiko] *nm* tropic
tropiece *etc* [tro'pjeθe] *vb ver* **tropezar**
tropiezo *etc* [tro'pjeθo] *vb ver* **tropezar** ■ *nm* *(error)* slip, blunder; *(desgracia)* misfortune; *(revés)* setback; *(obstáculo)* snag; *(discusión)* quarrel
troqué [tro'ke], **troquemos** *etc* [tro'kemos] *vb ver* **trocar**
trotamundos [trota'mundos] *nm inv* globetrotter
trotar [tro'tar] *vi* to trot; *(viajar)* to travel about
trote ['trote] *nm* trot; *(fam)* travelling; **de mucho ~** hard-wearing
Troya ['troja] *nf* Troy; **aquí fue ~** now there's nothing but ruins
trozo ['troθo] *nm* bit, piece; *(Lit: Mus)* passage; **a trozos** in bits
trucha ['trutʃa] *nf* *(pez)* trout; *(Tec)* crane
truco ['truko] *nm* *(habilidad)* knack; *(engaño)* trick; *(Cine)* trick effect *o* photography; **trucos** *nmpl* billiards *sg*; **~ publicitario** advertising gimmick
trueco *etc* ['trweko] *vb ver* **trocar**
trueno *etc* ['trweno] *vb ver* **tronar** ■ *nm* *(gen)* thunder; *(estampido)* boom; *(de arma)* bang
trueque *etc* ['trweke] *vb ver* **trocar** ■ *nm* exchange; *(Com)* barter
trufa ['trufa] *nf* *(Bot)* truffle; *(fig: fam)* fib
truhán, -ana [tru'an, ana] *nm/f* rogue
truncado, -a [trun'kaðo, a] *adj* truncated
truncar [trun'kar] *vt* *(cortar)* to truncate; *(la vida etc)* to cut short; *(el desarrollo)* to stunt
trunque *etc* ['trunke] *vb ver* **truncar**
Tte. *abr* (= *Teniente*) Lt.
tu [tu] *adj* your
tú [tu] *pron* you
tubérculo [tu'βerkulo] *nm* *(Bot)* tuber
tuberculosis [tuβerku'losis] *nf inv* tuberculosis
tubería [tuβe'ria] *nf* pipes *pl*, piping; *(conducto)* pipeline
tubo ['tuβo] *nm* tube, pipe; **~ de desagüe** drainpipe; **~ de ensayo** test-tube; **~ de escape** exhaust (pipe); **~ digestivo** alimentary canal
tuerca ['twerka] *nf* *(Tec)* nut
tuerce *etc* ['twerθe] *vb ver* **torcer**
tuerto, -a ['twerto, a] *adj* *(torcido)* twisted; *(ciego)* blind in one eye ■ *nm/f* one-eyed person ■ *nm* *(ofensa)* wrong; **a tuertas** upside-down
tuerza *etc* ['twerθa] *vb ver* **torcer**
tueste *etc* ['tweste] *vb ver* **tostar**
tuétano ['twetano] *nm* *(Anat: médula)* marrow; *(Bot)* pith; **hasta los tuétanos** through and through, utterly
tufo ['tufo] *nm* vapour; *(fig: pey)* stench
tugurio [tu'ɣurjo] *nm* slum
tul [tul] *nm* tulle
tulipán [tuli'pan] *nm* tulip
tullido, -a [tu'ʎiðo, a] *adj* crippled; *(cansado)* exhausted
tumba ['tumba] *nf* *(sepultura)* tomb; *(sacudida)* shake; *(voltereta)* somersault; **ser (como) una ~** to keep one's mouth shut
tumbar [tum'bar] *vt* to knock down; *(doblar)* to knock over; *(fam: suj: olor)* to overpower ■ *vi* to fall down; **tumbarse** *vr* *(echarse)* to lie down; *(extenderse)* to stretch out
tumbo ['tumbo] *nm* *(caída)* fall; *(de vehículo)* jolt; *(momento crítico)* critical moment
tumbona [tum'bona] *nf* lounger
tumor [tu'mor] *nm* tumour
tumulto [tu'multo] *nm* turmoil; *(Pol: motín)* riot
tuna ['tuna] *nf* *(Mus)* student music group; *ver tb* **tuno**; *see note*

TUNA

A *tuna* is made up of university students, or quite often former students, who dress up in costumes from the *Edad de Oro*, the Spanish Golden Age. These musical troupes go through the town playing their guitars, lutes and tambourines and serenade the young ladies in the halls of residence, or make impromptu appearances at weddings or parties singing traditional Spanish songs for a few pesetas.

tunante [tu'nante] *adj* rascally ■ *nm* rogue, villain; **¡~!** you villain!
tunda ['tunda] *nf* *(de tela)* shearing; *(de golpes)* beating
tundir [tun'dir] *vt* *(tela)* to shear; *(hierba)* to mow; *(fig)* to exhaust; *(fam: golpear)* to beat
tunecino, -a [tune'θino, a] *adj, nm/f* Tunisian
túnel ['tunel] *nm* tunnel
Túnez ['tuneθ] *nm* Tunis
túnica ['tunika] *nf* tunic; *(vestido largo)* long dress; *(Anat: Bot)* tunic
Tunicia [tu'niθja] *nf* Tunisia
tuno, -a ['tuno, a] *nm/f* *(fam)* rogue ■ *nm* *(Mus)* *member of a "tuna"*
tuntún [tun'tun]: **al ~** *adv* thoughtlessly
tupamaro, -a [tupa'maro, a] *adj, nm/f* *(Am)* urban guerrilla

tupé [tu'pe] *nm* quiff
tupí [tu'pi], **tupí-guaraní** [tupigwara'ni] *adj, nm/f* Tupi-Guarani
tupido, -a [tu'piðo, a] *adj* (*denso*) dense; (*fig: torpe*) dim; (*tela*) close-woven
turba ['turβa] *nf* (*combustible*) turf; (*muchedumbre*) crowd
turbación [turβa'θjon] *nf* (*molestia*) disturbance; (*preocupación*) worry
turbado, -a [tur'βaðo, a] *adj* (*molesto*) disturbed; (*preocupado*) worried
turbante [tur'βante] *nm* turban
turbar [tur'βar] *vt* (*molestar*) to disturb; (*incomodar*) to upset; **turbarse** *vr* to be disturbed
turbina [tur'βina] *nf* turbine
turbio, -a ['turβjo, a] *adj* (*agua etc*) cloudy; (*vista*) dim, blurred; (*tema*) unclear, confused; (*negocio*) shady ■ *adv* indistinctly
turbión [tur'βjon] *nf* downpour; (*fig*) shower, hail
turbo ['turβo] *adj inv* turbo(-charged) ■ *nm* (*tb coche*) turbo
turbulencia [turβu'lenθja] *nf* turbulence; (*fig*) restlessness
turbulento, -a [turβu'lento, a] *adj* turbulent; (*fig: intranquilo*) restless; (*: ruidoso*) noisy
turco, -a ['turko, a] *adj* Turkish ■ *nm/f* Turk ■ *nm* (*Ling*) Turkish
Turena [tu'rena] *nf* Touraine
turgente [tur'xente], **túrgido, a** ['turxiðo, a] *adj* (*tirante*) turgid, swollen
Turín [tu'rin] *nm* Turin
turismo [tu'rismo] *nm* tourism; (*coche*) saloon car; **hacer ~** to go travelling (abroad)
turista [tu'rista] *nm/f* tourist; (*vacacionista*) holidaymaker (*Brit*), vacationer (*US*)
turístico, -a [tu'ristiko, a] *adj* tourist *cpd*
Turkmenistán [turkmeni'stan] *nm* Turkmenistan
turnar [tur'nar] *vi*, **turnarse** *vr* to take (it in) turns
turno ['turno] *nm* (*oportunidad, orden de prioridad*) opportunity; (*Deporte etc*) turn; **es su ~** it's his turn (next); **~ de día/de noche** (*Industria*) day/night shift
turolense [turo'lense] *adj* of *o* from Teruel ■ *nm/f* native *o* inhabitant of Teruel
turquesa [tur'kesa] *nf* turquoise
Turquía [tur'kia] *nf* Turkey
turrón [tu'rron] *nm* (*dulce*) nougat; (*fam*) sinecure, cushy job *o* number
tute ['tute] *nm* (*Naipes*) *card game*; **darse un ~** to break one's back
tutear [tute'ar] *vt* to address as familiar "tú"; **tutearse** *vr* to be on familiar terms
tutela [tu'tela] *nf* (*legal*) guardianship; (*instrucción*) guidance; **estar bajo la ~ de** (*fig*) to be under the protection of
tutelar [tute'lar] *adj* tutelary ■ *vt* to protect
tutor, a [tu'tor, a] *nm/f* (*legal*) guardian; (*Escol*) tutor; **~ de curso** form master/mistress
tuve *etc* ['tuβe] *vb ver* **tener**
tuyo, -a ['tujo, a] *adj* yours, of yours ■ *pron* yours; **los tuyos** (*fam*) your relations, your family
TVE *nf abr* = **Televisión Española**

Uu

U, u [u] *nf* (*letra*) U, u; **viraje en U** U-turn; **U de Ulises** U for Uncle
u [u] *conj* or
u. *abr* = **unidad**
UAR [war] *nfpl abr* (*Esp*) = **Unidades Antiterroristas Rurales**
ubérrimo, -a [u'βerrimo, a] *adj* very rich, fertile
ubicación [uβika'θjon] *nf* (*esp Am*) place, position, location
ubicado, -a [uβi'kaðo, a] *adj* (*esp Am*) situated
ubicar [uβi'kar] *vt* (*esp Am*) to place, situate; (*: fig*) to install in a post; (*: encontrar*) to find; **ubicarse** *vr* to be situated, be located
ubicuo, -a [u'βikwo, a] *adj* ubiquitous
ubique *etc* [u'βike] *vb ver* **ubicar**
ubre ['uβre] *nf* udder
UCI ['uθi] *sigla f* (= *Unidad de Cuidados Intensivos*) ICU
Ucrania [u'kranja] *nf* Ukraine
ucraniano, -a [ukra'njano, a] *adj, nm/f* Ukrainian ■ *nm* (*Ling*) Ukrainian
ucranio [u'kranjo] *nm* (*Ling*) Ukrainian
Ud(s) *abr* = **usted(es)**; *ver* **usted**
UDV *sigla f* = **Unidad de Despliegue Visual**
UE *nf abr* (= *Unión Europea*) EU
UEFA [w'efa] *nf abr* (= *Unión de Asociaciones de Fútbol Europeo*) UEFA
UEO *nf abr* (= *Unión Europea Occidental*) WEU
UEP *nf abr* = **Unión Europea de Pagos**
UER *sigla f* = **Unión Europea de Radiodifusión**
uf [uf] *excl* (*cansancio*) phew!; (*repugnancia*) ugh!
ufanarse [ufa'narse] *vr* to boast; **~ de** to pride o.s. on
ufano, -a [u'fano, a] *adj* (*arrogante*) arrogant; (*presumido*) conceited
UGT *nf abr ver* **Unión General de Trabajadores**
UIT *sigla f* = **Unión Internacional de Telecomunicaciones**
ujier [u'xjer] *nm* usher; (*portero*) doorkeeper
úlcera ['ulθera] *nf* ulcer
ulcerar [ulθe'rar] *vt* to make sore; **ulcerarse** *vr* to ulcerate
ulterior [ulte'rjor] *adj* (*más allá*) farther, further; (*subsecuente, siguiente*) subsequent
ulteriormente [ulterjor'mente] *adv* later, subsequently
últimamente ['ultimamente] *adv* (*recientemente*) lately, recently; (*finalmente*) finally; (*como último recurso*) as a last resort
ultimar [ulti'mar] *vt* to finish; (*finalizar*) to finalize; (*Am: rematar*) to finish off, murder
ultimátum [ulti'matum] *nm* (*pl* **ultimátums**) ultimatum
último, -a ['ultimo, a] *adj* last; (*más reciente*) latest, most recent; (*más bajo*) bottom; (*más alto*) top; (*fig*) final, extreme; **en las últimas** on one's last legs; **por último** finally
ultra ['ultra] *adj* ultra ■ *nm/f* extreme right-winger
ultracongelar [ultrakonxe'lar] *vt* to deep-freeze
ultraderecha [ultraðe'retʃa] *nf* extreme right (wing)
ultrajar [ultra'xar] *vt* (*escandalizar*) to outrage; (*insultar*) to insult, abuse
ultraje [ul'traxe] *nm* outrage; insult
ultraligero [ultrali'xero] *nm* microlight (*Brit*), microlite (*US*)
ultramar [ultra'mar] *nm*: **de** *o* **en ~** abroad, overseas; **los países de ~** the overseas countries
ultramarino, -a [ultrama'rino, a] *adj* overseas, foreign ■ *nmpl*: **ultramarinos** groceries; **tienda de ultramarinos** grocer's (shop)
ultranza [ul'tranθa]: **a ~** *adv* to the death; (*a toda costa*) at all costs; (*completo*) outright; (*Pol etc*) out-and-out, extreme; **un nacionalista a ~** a rabid nationalist
ultrarrojo, -a [ultra'rroxo, a] *adj* = **infrarrojo, a**
ultrasónico, -a [ultra'soniko, a] *adj* ultrasonic
ultratumba [ultra'tumba] *nf*: **la vida de ~** the next life; **una voz de ~** a ghostly voice

ultravioleta [ultraβjo'leta] *adj inv* ultraviolet
ulular [ulu'lar] *vi* to howl; (*búho*) to hoot
umbilical [umbili'kal] *adj*: **cordón ~** umbilical cord
umbral [um'bral] *nm* (*gen*) threshold; **~ de rentabilidad** (*Com*) break-even point
umbrío, -a [um'brio, a] *adj* shady
UME *nf abr* (= *Unión Monetaria y Económica*) EMU

PALABRA CLAVE

un, una [un, 'una] *artículo indefinido* a; (*antes de vocal*) an; **una mujer/naranja** a woman/an orange
■ *adj* **1**: **unos** (*o* **unas**): **hay unos regalos para ti** there are some presents for you; **hay unas cervezas en la nevera** there are some beers in the fridge
2 (*enfático*): **¡hace un frío!** it's so cold!; **¡tiene una casa!** he's got some house!

U.N.A.M. ['unam] *nf abr* = **Universidad Nacional Autónoma de México**
unánime [u'nanime] *adj* unanimous
unanimidad [unanimi'ðað] *nf* unanimity; **por ~** unanimously
unción [un'θjon] *nf* anointing
uncir [un'θir] *vt* to yoke
undécimo, -a [un'deθimo, a] *adj, nm/f* eleventh
UNED [u'ned] *nf abr* (*Esp Univ*: = *Universidad Nacional de Enseñanza a Distancia*) ≈ Open University (*Brit*)
UNEF [u'nef] *sigla f* = **Fuerzas de Urgencia de las Naciones Unidas**
UNESCO, Unesco [u'nesko] *sigla f* (= *United Nations Educational, Scientific and Cultural Organization*) UNESCO
ungir [un'xir] *vt* to rub with ointment; (*Rel*) to anoint
ungüento [un'gwento] *nm* ointment; (*fig*) salve, balm
únicamente ['unikamente] *adv* solely; (*solamente*) only
UNICEF, Unicef [uni'θef] *sigla m* (= *United Nations International Children's Emergency Fund*) ≈ UNICEF
unicidad [uniθi'ðað] *nf* uniqueness
único, -a ['uniko, a] *adj* only; (*solo*) sole, single; (*sin par*) unique; **hijo único** only child
unidad [uni'ðað] *nf* unity; (*Tec*) unit; **~ móvil** (*TV*) mobile unit; (*Inform*): **~ central** system unit, central processing unit; **~ de control** control unit; **~ de disco** disk drive; **~ de entrada/salida** input/output device; **~ de información** data item; **~ periférica** peripheral device; **~ de presentación visual** *o* **de visualización** visual display unit; **~ procesadora central** central processing unit
unido, -a [u'niðo, a] *adj* joined, linked; (*fig*) united
unifamiliar [unifamil'jar] *adj*: **vivienda ~** single-family home
unificar [unifi'kar] *vt* to unite, unify
unifique *etc* [uni'fike] *vb ver* **unificar**
uniformado, -a [unifor'maðo, a] *adj* uniformed, in uniform
uniformar [unifor'mar] *vt* to make uniform; (*Tec*) to standardize
uniforme [uni'forme] *adj* uniform, equal; (*superficie*) even ■ *nm* uniform
uniformidad [uniformi'ðað] *nf* uniformity; (*llaneza*) levelness, evenness
unilateral [unilate'ral] *adj* unilateral
unión [u'njon] *nf* (*gen*) union; (*acto*) uniting, joining; (*calidad*) unity; (*Tec*) joint; (*fig*) closeness, togetherness; **en ~ con** (together) with, accompanied by; **~ aduanera** customs union; **U~ General de Trabajadores (UGT)** (*Esp*) *Socialist Union Confederation*; **U~ Europea** European Union; **la U~ Soviética** the Soviet Union; **punto de ~** (*Tec*) junction
unir [u'nir] *vt* (*juntar*) to join, unite; (*atar*) to tie, fasten; (*combinar*) to combine ■ *vi* (*ingredientes*) to mix well; **unirse** *vr* to join together, unite; (*empresas*) to merge; **les une una fuerte simpatía** they are bound by (a) strong affection; **unirse en matrimonio** to marry
unisex [uni'seks] *adj inv* unisex
unísono [u'nisono] *nm*: **al ~** in unison
unitario, -a [uni'tarjo, a] *adj* unitary; (*Rel*) Unitarian ■ *nm/f* (*Rel*) Unitarian
universal [uniβer'sal] *adj* universal; (*mundial*) world *cpd*; **historia ~** world history
universidad [uniβersi'ðað] *nf* university; **~ laboral** polytechnic, poly
universitario, -a [uniβersi'tarjo, a] *adj* university *cpd* ■ *nm/f* (*profesor*) lecturer; (*estudiante*) (university) student
universo [uni'βerso] *nm* universe
unja *etc* ['unxa] *vb ver* **ungir**

PALABRA CLAVE

uno, -a ['uno, a] *adj* one; **es todo uno** it's all one and the same; **unos pocos** a few; **unos cien** about a hundred
■ *pron* **1** one; **quiero uno solo** I only want one; **uno de ellos** one of them; **una de dos** either one or the other; **no doy una hoy** I can't do anything right today
2 (*alguien*) somebody, someone; **conozco a**

uno que se te parece I know somebody *o* someone who looks like you; **unos querían quedarse** some (people) wanted to stay
3 (*impersonal*) one; **uno mismo** oneself; **uno nunca sabe qué hacer** one never knows what to do
4: **unos ... otros ...** some ... others; **una y otra son muy agradables** they're both very nice; **(los) uno(s) a (los) otro(s)** each other, one another
■ *nf* one; **es la una** it's one o'clock
■ *num* (number) one; **el día uno** the first

untar [un'tar] *vt* (*gen*) to rub; (*engrasar*) to grease, oil; (*Med*) to rub (with ointment); (*fig*) to bribe; **untarse** *vr* (*fig*) to be crooked; **~ el pan con mantequilla** to spread butter on one's bread
unto ['unto] *nm* animal fat; (*Med*) ointment
unza *etc* ['unθa] *vb ver* **uncir**
uña ['uɲa] *nf* (*Anat*) nail; (*del pie*) toenail; (*garra*) claw; (*casco*) hoof; (*arrancaclavos*) claw; **ser ~ y carne** to be as thick as thieves; **enseñar** *o* **mostrar** *o* **sacar las uñas** to show one's claws
UOE *nf abr* (*Esp Mil*) = **Unidad de Operaciones Especiales**
UPA *nf abr* = **Unión Panamericana**
UPC *nf abr* (= *unidad procesadora central*) CPU
uperizado, -a [uperi'θaðo, a] *adj*: **leche uperizada** UHT milk
Urales [u'rales] *nmpl* (*tb*: **Montes Urales**) Urals
uralita® [ura'lita] *nf* corrugated asbestos cement
uranio [u'ranjo] *nm* uranium
urbanidad [urβani'ðað] *nf* courtesy, politeness
urbanismo [urβa'nismo] *nm* town planning
urbanista [urβa'nista] *nm/f* town planner
urbanización [urβaniθa'θjon] *nf* (*colonia, barrio*) estate, housing scheme
urbanizar [urβani'θar] *vt* to develop
urbano, -a [ur'βano, a] *adj* (*de ciudad*) urban, town *cpd*; (*cortés*) courteous, polite
urbe ['urβe] *nf* large city, metropolis
urdimbre [ur'ðimbre] *nf* (*de tejido*) warp; (*intriga*) intrigue
urdir [ur'ðir] *vt* to warp; (*fig*) to plot, contrive
urgencia [ur'xenθja] *nf* urgency; (*prisa*) haste, rush; **salida de ~** emergency exit; **servicios de ~** emergency services
urgente [ur'xente] *adj* urgent; (*insistente*) insistent; **carta ~** registered (*Brit*) *o* special delivery (*US*) letter
urgir [ur'xir] *vi* to be urgent; **me urge** I'm in a hurry for it; **me urge terminarlo** I must finish it as soon as I can
urinario, -a [uri'narjo, a] *adj* urinary ■ *nm* urinal, public lavatory, comfort station (*US*)
urja *etc* ['urxa] *vb ver* **urgir**
urna ['urna] *nf* urn; (*Pol*) ballot box; **acudir a las urnas** (*fig*: *persona*) to (go and) vote; (: *gobierno*) to go to the country
urología [urolo'xia] *nf* urology
urólogo, -a [u'roloɣo, a] *nm/f* urologist
urraca [u'rraka] *nf* magpie
URSS *nf abr* (*Historia*: = *Unión de Repúblicas Socialistas Soviéticas*) USSR
Uruguay [uru'ɣwai] *nm*: **El ~** Uruguay
uruguayo, -a [uru'ɣwajo, a] *adj, nm/f* Uruguayan
usado, -a [u'saðo, a] *adj* (*gen*) used; (*ropa etc*) worn; **muy ~** worn out
usanza [u'sanθa] *nf* custom, usage
usar [u'sar] *vt* to use; (*ropa*) to wear; (*tener costumbre*) to be in the habit of ■ *vi*: **~ de** to make use of; **usarse** *vr* to be used; (*ropa*) to be worn *o* in fashion
USO ['uso] *nf abr* (*Esp*: = *Unión Sindical Obrera*) *workers' union*
uso ['uso] *nm* use; (*Mecánica etc*) wear; (*costumbre*) usage, custom; (*moda*) fashion; **al ~** in keeping with custom; **al ~ de** in the style of; **de ~ externo** (*Med*) for external application; **estar en el ~ de la palabra** to be speaking, have the floor; **~ y desgaste** (*Com*) wear and tear
usted [us'teð] *pron* (*sg formal*: *abr* **Ud** *o* **Vd**) you *sg*; **ustedes** (*pl formal*: *abr* **Uds** *o* **Vds**) you *pl*; (*Am*: *formal y fam*) you *pl*
usual [u'swal] *adj* usual
usuario, -a [usw'arjo, a] *nm/f* user; **~ final** (*Com*) end user
usufructo [usu'frukto] *nm* use; **~ vitalicio (de)** life interest (in)
usura [u'sura] *nf* usury
usurero, -a [usu'rero, a] *nm/f* usurer
usurpar [usur'par] *vt* to usurp
utensilio [uten'siljo] *nm* tool; (*Culin*) utensil
útero ['utero] *nm* uterus, womb
útil ['util] *adj* useful; (*servible*) usable, serviceable ■ *nm* tool; **día útil** working day, weekday; **es muy útil tenerlo aquí cerca** it's very handy having it here close by
utilice *etc* [uti'liθe] *vb ver* **utilizar**
utilidad [utili'ðað] *nf* usefulness, utility; (*Com*) profit; **utilidades líquidas** net profit *sg*
utilitario [utili'tarjo] *nm* (*Inform*) utility
utilizar [utili'θar] *vt* to use, utilize; (*explotar*) to harness
utopía [uto'pia] *nf* Utopia
utópico, -a [u'topiko, a] *adj* Utopian
UVA *sigla mpl* (= *ultravioleta*) UV, UVA

uva ['uβa] *nf* grape; **~ pasa** raisin; **~ de Corinto** currant; **estar de mala ~** to be in a bad mood; *see note*

UVA

In Spain *Las uvas* play a big part on New Years' Eve (*Nochevieja*), when on the stroke of midnight people from every part of Spain, at home, in restaurants or in the plaza mayor eat a grape for each stroke of the clock of the Puerta del Sol in Madrid. It is said to bring luck for the following year.

uve ['uβe] *nf name of the letter V*; **en forma de ~** V-shaped; **~ doble** *name of the letter W*

UVI ['uβi] *nf abr* (*Esp Med*: = *unidad de vigilancia intensiva*) ICU

Vv

V, v (*Esp*) ['uβe] (*Am*) [be'korta, betʃika] *nf* (*letra*) V, v; **V de Valencia** V for Victor
V. *abr* = **usted**; (= *visto*) approved, passed
v. *abr* (= *voltio*) v; (= *ver, véase*) v.; (*Lit*: = *verso*) v
va [ba] *vb ver* **ir**
V.A. *abr* = **Vuestra Alteza**
vaca ['baka] *nf* (*animal*) cow; (*carne*) beef; (*cuero*) cowhide; **vacas flacas/gordas** (*fig*) bad/good times
vacaciones [baka'θjones] *nfpl* holiday(s); **estar/irse** *o* **marcharse de ~** to be/go (away) on holiday
vacante [ba'kante] *adj* vacant, empty ■ *nf* vacancy
vaciado, -a [ba'θjaðo, a] *adj* (*hecho en molde*) cast in a mould; (*hueco*) hollow ■ *nm* cast, mould(ing)
vaciar [ba'θjar] *vt* to empty (out); (*ahuecar*) to hollow out; (*moldear*) to cast; (*Inform*) to dump ■ *vi* (*río*): **~ en** to flow into; **vaciarse** *vr* to empty; (*fig*) to blab, spill the beans
vaciedad [baθje'ðað] *nf* emptiness
vacilación [baθila'θjon] *nf* hesitation
vacilante [baθi'lante] *adj* unsteady; (*habla*) faltering; (*luz*) flickering; (*fig*) hesitant
vacilar [baθi'lar] *vi* to be unsteady; to falter; to flicker; to hesitate, waver; (*persona*) to stagger, stumble; (*memoria*) to fail; (*esp Am*: *divertirse*) to have a great time
vacilón [baθi'lon] *nm* (*esp Am*): **estar** *o* **ir de ~** to have a great time
vacío, -a [ba'θio, a] *adj* empty; (*puesto*) vacant; (*desocupado*) idle; (*vano*) vain; (*charla etc*) light, superficial ■ *nm* emptiness; (*Física*) vacuum; (*un vacío*) (empty) space; **hacer el ~ a algn** to send sb to Coventry
vacuna [ba'kuna] *nf* vaccine
vacunar [baku'nar] *vt* to vaccinate; **vacunarse** *vr* to get vaccinated
vacuno, -a [ba'kuno, a] *adj* bovine
vacuo, -a ['bakwo, a] *adj* empty
vadear [baðe'ar] *vt* (*río*) to ford; (*problema*) to overcome; (*persona*) to sound out
vado ['baðo] *nm* ford; (*solución*) solution; (*descanso*) respite
vagabundo, -a [baɣa'βundo, a] *adj* wandering; (*pey*) vagrant ■ *nm/f* (*errante*) wanderer; (*vago*) tramp, bum (US)
vagamente [baɣa'mente] *adv* vaguely
vagancia [ba'ɣanθja] *nf* vagrancy
vagar [ba'ɣar] *vi* to wander; (*pasear*) to saunter up and down; (*no hacer nada*) to idle ■ *nm* leisure
vagido [ba'xiðo] *nm* wail
vagina [ba'xina] *nf* vagina
vago, -a ['baɣo, a] *adj* vague; (*perezoso*) lazy; (*ambulante*) wandering ■ *nm/f* (*vagabundo*) tramp, bum (US); (*perezoso*) lazybones *sg*, idler
vagón [ba'ɣon] *nm* (*de pasajeros*) carriage; (*de mercancías*) wagon; **~ cama/restaurante** sleeping/dining car
vague *etc* ['baɣe] *vb ver* **vagar**
vaguear [baɣe'ar] *vi* to laze around
vaguedad [baɣe'ðað] *nf* vagueness
vahído [ba'iðo] *nm* dizzy spell
vaho ['bao] *nm* (*vapor*) vapour, steam; (*olor*) smell; (*respiración*) breath; **vahos** *nmpl* (*Med*) inhalation *sg*
vaina ['baina] *nf* sheath ■ *nm* (*Am*) nuisance
vainilla [bai'niʎa] *nf* vanilla
vainita [bai'nita] *nf* (*Am*) green *o* French bean
vais [bais] *vb ver* **ir**
vaivén [bai'βen] *nm* to-and-fro movement; (*de tránsito*) coming and going; **vaivenes** *nmpl* (*fig*) ups and downs
vajilla [ba'xiʎa] *nf* crockery, dishes *pl*; (*una vajilla*) service; **~ de porcelana** chinaware
val [bal], **valdré** *etc* [bal'dre] *vb ver* **valer**
vale ['bale] *nm* voucher; (*recibo*) receipt; (*pagaré*) I.O.U.; **~ de regalo** gift voucher *o* token
valedero, -a [bale'ðero, a] *adj* valid
valenciano, -a [balen'θjano, a] *adj, nm/f* Valencian ■ *nm* (*Ling*) Valencian
valentía [balen'tia] *nf* courage, bravery; (*pey*) boastfulness; (*acción*) heroic deed

valentísimo, -a [balen'tisimo, a] *adj superlativo de* **valiente** very brave, courageous

valentón, -ona [balen'ton, ona] *adj* blustering

valer [ba'ler] *vt* to be worth; (*Mat*) to equal; (*costar*) to cost; (*amparar*) to aid, protect ■ *vi* (*ser útil*) to be useful; (*ser válido*) to be valid; **valerse** *vr* to defend o.s. ■ *nm* worth, value; **~ la pena** to be worthwhile; **¿vale?** O.K.?; **¡vale!** (*¡basta!*) that'll do!; **¡eso no vale!** that doesn't count!; **no vale nada** it's no good; (*mercancía*) it's worthless; (*argumento*) it's no use; **no vale para nada** he's no good at all; **más vale tarde que nunca** better late than never; **más vale que nos vayamos** we'd better go; **valerse de** to make use of, take advantage of; **valerse por sí mismo** to help *o* manage by o.s.

valga *etc* ['balɣa] *vb ver* **valer**

valía [ba'lia] *nf* worth; **de gran ~** (*objeto*) very valuable

validar [bali'ðar] *vt* to validate; (*Pol*) to ratify

validez [bali'ðeθ] *nf* validity; **dar ~ a** to validate

válido, -a ['baliðo, a] *adj* valid

valiente [ba'ljente] *adj* brave, valiant; (*audaz*) bold; (*pey*) boastful; (*con ironía*) fine, wonderful ■ *nm/f* brave man/woman

valija [ba'lixa] *nf* case; (*Am*) suitcase; (*mochila*) satchel; (*Correos*) mailbag; **~ diplomática** diplomatic bag

valioso, -a [ba'ljoso, a] *adj* valuable; (*rico*) wealthy

valla ['baʎa] *nf* fence; (*Deporte*) hurdle; (*fig*) barrier; **~ publicitaria** billboard

vallar [ba'ʎar] *vt* to fence in

valle ['baʎe] *nm* valley, vale

vallisoletano, -a [baʎisole'tano, a] *adj* of *o* from Valladolid ■ *nm/f* native *o* inhabitant of Valladolid

valor [ba'lor] *nm* value, worth; (*precio*) price; (*valentía*) valour, courage; (*importancia*) importance; (*cara*) nerve, cheek (*fam*); **sin ~** worthless; **~ adquisitivo** *o* **de compra** purchasing power; **dar ~ a** to attach importance to; **quitar ~ a** to minimize the importance of; (*Com*): **~ según balance** book value; **~ comercial** *o* **de mercado** market value; **~ contable/desglosado** asset/break-up value; **~ de escasez** scarcity value; **~ intrínseco** intrinsic value; **~ a la par** par value; **~ neto** net worth; **~ de rescate/de sustitución** surrender/replacement value; *ver tb* **valores**

valoración [balora'θjon] *nf* valuation

valorar [balo'rar] *vt* to value; (*tasar*) to price; (*fig*) to assess

valores [ba'lores] *nmpl* (*Com*) securities; **~ en cartera** *o* **habidos** investments

vals [bals] *nm* waltz

válvula ['balβula] *nf* valve

vamos ['bamos] *vb ver* **ir**

vampiro, -iresa [bam'piro, i'resa] *nm/f* vampire ■ *nf* (*Cine*) vamp, femme fatale

van [ban] *vb ver* **ir**

vanagloriarse [banaɣlo'rjarse] *vr* to boast

vandalismo [banda'lismo] *nm* vandalism

vándalo, -a ['bandalo, a] *nm/f* vandal

vanguardia [ban'gwardja] *nf* vanguard; **de ~** (*Arte*) avant-garde; **estar en** *o* **ir a la ~ de** (*fig*) to be in the forefront of

vanguardista [bangwar'ðista] *adj* avant-garde

vanidad [bani'ðað] *nf* vanity; (*inutilidad*) futility; (*irrealidad*) unreality

vanidoso, -a [bani'ðoso, a] *adj* vain, conceited

vano, -a ['bano, a] *adj* (*irreal*) unreal; (*irracional*) unreasonable; (*inútil*) vain, useless; (*persona*) vain, conceited; (*frívolo*) frivolous

vapor [ba'por] *nm* vapour; (*vaho*) steam; (*de gas*) fumes *pl*; (*neblina*) mist; **vapores** *nmpl* (*Med*) hysterics; **al ~** (*Culin*) steamed

vaporice *etc* [bapo'riθe] *vb ver* **vaporizar**

vaporizador [baporiθa'ðor] *nm* (*de perfume etc*) spray

vaporizar [bapori'θar] *vt* to vaporize; (*perfume*) to spray

vaporoso, -a [bapo'roso, a] *adj* vaporous; (*vahoso*) steamy; (*tela*) light, airy

vapulear [bapule'ar] *vt* to thrash; (*fig*) to slate

vaquería [bake'ria] *nf* dairy

vaquero, -a [ba'kero, a] *adj* cattle *cpd* ■ *nm* cowboy; **vaqueros** *nmpl* jeans

vaquilla [ba'kiʎa] *nf* heifer

vara ['bara] *nf* stick, pole; (*Tec*) rod; **~ mágica** magic wand

varado, -a [ba'raðo, a] *adj* (*Naut*) stranded; **estar ~** to be aground

varar [ba'rar] *vt* to beach ■ *vi*, **vararse** *vr* to be beached

varear [bare'ar] *vt* to hit, beat; (*frutas*) to knock down (with poles)

variable [ba'rjaβle] *adj, nf* variable (*tb Inform*)

variación [barja'θjon] *nf* variation; **sin ~** unchanged

variado, -a [ba'rjaðo, a] *adj* varied; (*dulces, galletas*) assorted; **entremeses variados** a selection of starters

variante [ba'rjante] *adj* variant ■ *nf* (*alternativa*) alternative; (*Auto*) bypass

variar [ba'rjar] *vt* (*cambiar*) to change; (*poner variedad*) to vary; (*modificar*) to modify;

(*cambiar de posición*) to switch around ■ *vi* to vary; ~ **de** to differ from; ~ **de opinión** to change one's mind; **para** ~ just for a change
varicela [bari'θela] *nf* chicken pox
varices [ba'riθes] *nfpl* varicose veins
variedad [barje'ðað] *nf* variety
varilla [ba'riʎa] *nf* stick; (*Bot*) twig; (*Tec*) rod; (*de rueda*) spoke; ~ **mágica** magic wand
vario, -a ['barjo, a] *adj* (*variado*) varied; (*multicolor*) motley; (*cambiable*) changeable; **varios** various, several
variopinto, -a [barjo'pinto, a] *adj* diverse; **un público** ~ a mixed audience
varita [ba'rita] *nf*: ~ **mágica** magic wand
varón [ba'ron] *nm* male, man
varonil [baro'nil] *adj* manly
Varsovia [bar'soβja] *nf* Warsaw
vas [bas] *vb ver* **ir**
vasco, -a ['basko, a], **vascongado a** [baskon'gaðo, a] *adj, nm/f* Basque ■ *nm* (*Ling*) Basque ■ *nfpl*: **las Vascongadas** the Basque Country *sg o* Provinces
vascuence [bas'kwenθe] *nm* (*Ling*) Basque
vasectomía [basekto'mia] *nf* vasectomy
vaselina [base'lina] *nf* Vaseline®
vasija [ba'sixa] *nf* (earthenware) vessel
vaso ['baso] *nm* glass, tumbler; (*Anat*) vessel; (*cantidad*) glass(ful); ~ **de vino** glass of wine; ~ **para vino** wineglass
vástago ['bastaɣo] *nm* (*Bot*) shoot; (*Tec*) rod; (*fig*) offspring
vasto, -a ['basto, a] *adj* vast, huge
váter ['bater] *nm* lavatory, W.C.
Vaticano [bati'kano] *nm*: **el** ~ the Vatican; **la Ciudad del** ~ the Vatican City
vaticinar [batiθi'nar] *vt* to prophesy, predict
vaticinio [bati'θinjo] *nm* prophecy
vatio ['batjo] *nm* (*Elec*) watt
vaya *etc* ['baja] *vb ver* **ir**
Vda. *abr* (= *viuda*) = **viudo**
Vd *abr* = **usted**
Vds *abr* = **ustedes**
ve [be] *vb ver* **ir; ver**
vea *etc* ['bea] *vb ver* **ver**
vecinal [beθi'nal] *adj* (*camino, impuesto etc*) local
vecindad [beθin'dað] *nf*, **vecindario** [beθin'darjo] *nm* neighbourhood; (*habitantes*) residents *pl*
vecino, -a [be'θino, a] *adj* neighbouring ■ *nm/f* neighbour; (*residente*) resident; **somos vecinos** we live next door to one another
vector [bek'tor] *nm* vector
veda ['beða] *nf* prohibition; (*temporada*) close season
vedado [be'ðaðo] *nm* preserve
vedar [be'ðar] *vt* (*prohibir*) to ban, prohibit; (*idea, plan*) to veto; (*impedir*) to stop, prevent
vedette [be'ðet] *nf* (*Teat: Cine*) star(let)
vega ['beɣa] *nf* fertile plain *o* valley
vegetación [bexeta'θjon] *nf* vegetation
vegetal [bexe'tal] *adj, nm* vegetable
vegetar [bexe'tar] *vi* to vegetate
vegetariano, -a [bexeta'rjano, a] *adj, nm/f* vegetarian
vegetativo, -a [bexeta'tiβo, a] *adj* vegetative
vehemencia [bee'menθja] *nf* (*insistencia*) vehemence; (*pasión*) passion; (*fervor*) fervour; (*violencia*) violence
vehemente [bee'mente] *adj* vehement; passionate; fervent; violent
vehículo [be'ikulo] *nm* vehicle; (*Med*) carrier; ~ **de servicio público** public service vehicle; ~ **espacial** spacecraft
veinte ['beinte] *num* twenty; (*orden, fecha*) twentieth; **el siglo** ~ the twentieth century
veintena [bein'tena] *nf*: **una** ~ (about) twenty, a score
vejación [bexa'θjon] *nf* vexation; (*humillación*) humiliation
vejamen [be'xamen] *nm* satire
vejar [be'xar] *vt* (*irritar*) to annoy, vex; (*humillar*) to humiliate
vejatorio, -a [bexa'torjo, a] *adj* humiliating, degrading
vejez [be'xeθ] *nf* old age
vejiga [be'xiɣa] *nf* (*Anat*) bladder
vela ['bela] *nf* (*de cera*) candle; (*Naut*) sail; (*insomnio*) sleeplessness; (*vigilia*) vigil; (*Mil*) sentry duty; (*fam*) snot; **a toda** ~ (*Naut*) under full sail; **estar a dos velas** (*fam*) to be skint; **pasar la noche en** ~ to have a sleepless night
velado, -a [be'laðo, a] *adj* veiled; (*sonido*) muffled; (*Foto*) blurred ■ *nf* soirée
velador [bela'ðor] *nm* watchman; (*candelero*) candlestick; (*Am*) bedside table
velar [be'lar] *vt* (*vigilar*) to keep watch over; (*cubrir*) to veil ■ *vi* to stay awake; ~ **por** to watch over, look after
velatorio [bela'torjo] *nm* (funeral) wake
veleidad [belei'ðað] *nf* (*ligereza*) fickleness; (*capricho*) whim
velero [be'lero] *nm* (*Naut*) sailing ship; (*Aviat*) glider
veleta [be'leta] *nm/f* fickle person ■ *nf* weather vane
veliz [be'lis] *nm* (*Am*) suitcase
vello ['beʎo] *nm* down, fuzz
vellón [be'ʎon] *nm* fleece
velloso, -a [be'ʎoso, a] *adj* fuzzy
velludo, -a [be'ʎuðo, a] *adj* shaggy ■ *nm* plush, velvet

velo ['belo] *nm* veil; **~ de paladar** *(Anat)* soft palate
velocidad [beloθi'ðað] *nf* speed; *(Tec)* rate, pace, velocity; *(Mecánica: Auto)* gear; **¿a qué ~?** how fast?; **de alta ~** high-speed; **cobrar ~** to pick up *o* gather speed; **meter la segunda ~** to change into second gear; **~ máxima de impresión** *(Inform)* maximum print speed
velocímetro [belo'θimetro] *nm* speedometer
velódromo [be'loðromo] *nm* cycle track
veloz [be'loθ] *adj* fast, swift
ven [ben] *vb ver* **venir**
vena ['bena] *nf* vein; *(fig)* vein, disposition; *(Geo)* seam, vein
venablo [be'naβlo] *nm* javelin
venado [be'naðo] *nm* deer; *(Culin)* venison
venal [be'nal] *adj (Anat)* venous; *(pey)* venal
venalidad [benali'ðað] *nf* venality
vencedor, a [benθe'ðor, a] *adj* victorious ■ *nm/f* victor, winner
vencer [ben'θer] *vt (dominar)* to defeat, beat; *(derrotar)* to vanquish; *(superar, controlar)* to overcome, master ■ *vi (triunfar)* to win (through), triumph; *(pago)* to fall due; *(plazo)* to expire; **dejarse ~** to yield, give in
vencido, -a [ben'θiðo, a] *adj (derrotado)* defeated, beaten; *(Com)* payable, due ■ *adv*: **pagar ~** to pay in arrears; **le pagan por meses vencidos** he is paid at the end of the month; **darse por ~** to give up
vencimiento [benθi'mjento] *nm* collapse; *(Com: de plazo)* expiration; **a su ~** when it falls due
venda ['benda] *nf* bandage
vendaje [ben'daxe] *nm* bandage, dressing
vendar [ben'dar] *vt* to bandage; **~ los ojos** to blindfold
vendaval [benda'βal] *nm (viento)* gale; *(huracán)* hurricane
vendedor, a [bende'ðor, a] *nm/f* seller; **~ ambulante** hawker, pedlar (Brit), peddler (US)
vender [ben'der] *vt* to sell; *(comerciar)* to market; *(traicionar)* to sell out, betray; **venderse** *vr* to be sold; **~ al contado/al por mayor/al por menor/a plazos** to sell for cash/wholesale/retail/on credit; **"se vende"** "for sale"; **"véndese coche"** "car for sale"; **~ al descubierto** to sell short
vendimia [ben'dimja] *nf* grape harvest; **la ~ de 1973** the 1973 vintage
vendimiar [bendi'mjar] *vi* to pick grapes
vendré *etc* [ben'dre] *vb ver* **venir**
Venecia [be'neθja] *nf* Venice
veneciano, -a [bene'θjano, a] *adj, nm/f* Venetian
veneno [be'neno] *nm* poison, venom
venenoso, -a [bene'noso, a] *adj* poisonous
venerable [bene'raβle] *adj* venerable
veneración [benera'θjon] *nf* veneration
venerar [bene'rar] *vt (reconocer)* to venerate; *(adorar)* to worship
venéreo, -a [be'nereo, a] *adj* venereal
venezolano, -a [beneθo'lano, a] *adj, nm/f* Venezuelan
Venezuela [bene'θwela] *nf* Venezuela
venga *etc* ['benga] *vb ver* **venir**
vengador, a [benga'ðor, a] *adj* avenging ■ *nm/f* avenger
venganza [ben'ganθa] *nf* vengeance, revenge
vengar [ben'gar] *vt* to avenge; **vengarse** *vr* to take revenge
vengativo, -a [benga'tiβo, a] *adj (persona)* vindictive
vengue *etc* ['benge] *vb ver* **vengar**
venia ['benja] *nf (perdón)* pardon; *(permiso)* consent; **con su ~** by your leave
venial [be'njal] *adj* venial
venida [be'niða] *nf (llegada)* arrival; *(regreso)* return; *(fig)* rashness
venidero, -a [beni'ðero, a] *adj* coming, future; **en lo ~** in (the) future
venir [be'nir] *vi* to come; *(llegar)* to arrive; *(ocurrir)* to happen; **venirse** *vr*: **venirse abajo** to collapse; **~ a menos** *(persona)* to lose status; *(empresa)* to go downhill; **~ bien** to be suitable, come just right; *(ropa, gusto)* to suit; **~ mal** to be unsuitable *o* inconvenient, come awkwardly; **el año que viene** next year; **¡ven acá!** come (over) here!; **¡venga!** *(fam)* come on!
venta ['benta] *nf (Com)* sale; *(posada)* inn; **~ a plazos** hire purchase; **~ al contado/al por mayor/al por menor** *o* **al detalle** cash sale/wholesale/retail; **~ a domicilio** door-to-door selling; **~ y arrendamiento al vendedor** sale and lease back; **~ de liquidación** clearance sale; **estar de** *o* **en ~** to be (up) for sale *o* on the market; **ventas brutas** gross sales; **ventas a término** forward sales
ventaja [ben'taxa] *nf* advantage; **llevar la ~** *(en carrera)* to be leading *o* ahead
ventajoso, -a [benta'xoso, a] *adj* advantageous
ventana [ben'tana] *nf* window; **~ de guillotina/galería** sash/bay window; **~ de la nariz** nostril
ventanilla [venta'niʎa] *nf (de taquilla, tb Inform)* window
ventearse [bente'arse] *vr (romperse)* to crack; *(Anat)* to break wind
ventilación [bentila'θjon] *nf* ventilation; *(corriente)* draught; *(fig)* airing

ventilador [bentila'ðor] *nm* ventilator; (*eléctrico*) fan
ventilar [benti'lar] *vt* to ventilate; (*poner a secar*) to put out to dry; (*fig*) to air, discuss
ventisca [ben'tiska] *nf* blizzard
ventisquero [bentis'kero] *nm* snowdrift
ventolera [bento'lera] *nf* (*ráfaga*) gust of wind; (*idea*) whim, wild idea; **le dio la ~ de comprarlo** he had a sudden notion to buy it
ventosear [bentose'ar] *vi* to break wind
ventosidad [bentosi'ðað] *nf* flatulence
ventoso, -a [ben'toso, a] *adj* windy ▪ *nf* (*Zool*) sucker; (*instrumento*) suction pad
ventrículo [ben'trikulo] *nm* ventricle
ventrílocuo, -a [ben'trilokwo, a] *nm/f* ventriloquist
ventriloquia [bentri'lokja] *nf* ventriloquism
ventura [ben'tura] *nf* (*felicidad*) happiness; (*buena suerte*) luck; (*destino*) fortune; **a la (buena) ~** at random
venturoso, -a [bentu'roso, a] *adj* happy; (*afortunado*) lucky, fortunate
venza *etc* ['benθa] *vb ver* **vencer**
ver [ber] *vt, vi* to see; (*mirar*) to look at, watch; (*investigar*) to look into; (*entender*) to see, understand; **verse** *vr* (*encontrarse*) to meet; (*dejarse ver*) to be seen; (*hallarse: en un apuro*) to find o.s., be ▪ *nm* looks *pl*, appearance; **a ~** let's see; **a ~ si ...** I wonder if ...; **por lo que veo** apparently; **dejarse ~** to become apparent; **no tener nada que ~ con** to have nothing to do with; **a mi modo de ~** as I see it; **merece verse** it's worth seeing; **no lo veo** I can't see it; **¡nos vemos!** see you (later)!; **¡habráse visto!** did you ever! (*fam*); **¡viera(n)** *o* **hubiera(n) visto qué casa!** (*Am fam*) if only you'd seen the house!, what a house!; **ya se ve que ...** it is obvious that ...; **si te vi no me acuerdo** they *etc* just don't want to know
vera ['bera] *nf* edge, verge; (*de río*) bank; **a la ~ de** near, next to
veracidad [beraθi'ðað] *nf* truthfulness
veraneante [berane'ante] *nm/f* holidaymaker, (summer) vacationer (*US*)
veranear [berane'ar] *vi* to spend the summer
veraneo [bera'neo] *nm*: **estar de ~** to be away on (one's summer) holiday; **lugar de ~** holiday resort
veraniego, -a [bera'njeɣo, a] *adj* summer *cpd*
verano [be'rano] *nm* summer
veras ['beras] *nfpl* truth *sg*; **de ~** really, truly; **esto va de ~** this is serious
veraz [be'raθ] *adj* truthful
verbal [ber'βal] *adj* verbal; (*mensaje etc*) oral
verbena [ber'βena] *nf* street party
verbigracia [berβi'ɣraθja] *adv* for example
verbo ['berβo] *nm* verb
verborrea [berβo'rrea] *nf* verbosity, verbal diarrhoea
verboso, -a [ber'βoso, a] *adj* verbose
verdad [ber'ðað] *nf* (*lo verídico*) truth; (*fiabilidad*) reliability ▪ *adv* really; **¿~?, ¿no es ~?** isn't it?, aren't you?, don't you? *etc*; **de ~** *adj* real, proper; **a decir ~, no quiero** to tell (you) the truth, I don't want to; **la pura ~** the plain truth
verdaderamente [berðaðera'mente] *adv* really, indeed, truly
verdadero, -a [berða'ðero, a] *adj* (*veraz*) true, truthful; (*fiable*) reliable; (*fig*) real
verde ['berðe] *adj* green; (*fruta etc*) green, unripe; (*chiste etc*) blue, smutty, dirty ▪ *nm* green; **viejo ~** dirty old man; **poner ~ a algn** to give sb a dressing-down
verdear [berðe'ar], **verdecer** [berðe'θer] *vi* to turn green
verdezca *etc* [ber'ðeθka] *vb ver* **verdecer**
verdor [ber'ðor] *nm* (*lo verde*) greenness; (*Bot*) verdure; (*fig*) youthful vigour
verdugo [ber'ðuɣo] *nm* executioner; (*Bot*) shoot; (*cardenal*) weal
verdulero, -a [berðu'lero, a] *nm/f* greengrocer
verdura [ber'ðura] *nf* greenness; **verduras** *nfpl* (*Culin*) greens
vereda [be'reða] *nf* path; (*Am*) pavement, sidewalk (*US*); **meter a algn en ~** to bring sb into line
veredicto [bere'ðikto] *nm* verdict
vergel [ber'xel] *nm* lush garden
vergonzoso, -a [berɣon'θoso, a] *adj* shameful; (*tímido*) timid, bashful
vergüenza [ber'ɣwenθa] *nf* shame, sense of shame; (*timidez*) bashfulness; (*pudor*) modesty; **tener ~** to be ashamed; **me da ~ decírselo** I feel too shy *o* it embarrasses me to tell him; **¡qué ~!** (*de situación*) what a disgrace!; (*a persona*) shame on you!
vericueto [beri'kweto] *nm* rough track
verídico, -a [be'riðiko, a] *adj* true, truthful
verificar [berifi'kar] *vt* to check; (*corroborar*) to verify (*tb Inform*); (*testamento*) to prove; (*llevar a cabo*) to carry out; **verificarse** *vr* to occur, happen; (*mitin etc*) to be held; (*profecía etc*) to come *o* prove true
verifique *etc* [beri'fike] *vb ver* **verificar**
verja ['berxa] *nf* iron gate; (*cerca*) railing(s) (*pl*); (*rejado*) grating
vermut [ber'mu] (*pl* **vermuts**) *nm* vermouth ▪ *nf* (*esp Am*) matinée
verosímil [bero'simil] *adj* likely, probable; (*relato*) credible

verosimilitud [berosimili'tuð] *nf* likeliness, probability
verruga [be'rruɣa] *nf* wart
versado, -a [ber'saðo, a] *adj*: **~ en** versed in
Versalles [ber'saʎes] *nm* Versailles
versar [ber'sar] *vi* to go round, turn; **~ sobre** to deal with, be about
versátil [ber'satil] *adj* versatile
versículo [ber'sikulo] *nm* (*Rel*) verse
versión [ber'sjon] *nf* version; (*traducción*) translation
verso ['berso] *nm* verse; **un ~** a line of poetry; **~ libre/suelto** free/blank verse
vértebra ['berteβra] *nf* vertebra
vertebrado, -a [berte'βraðo, a] *adj, nm/f* vertebrate
vertebral [berte'βral] *adj* vertebral; **columna ~** spine
vertedero [berte'ðero] *nm* rubbish dump, tip
verter [ber'ter] *vt* (*vaciar*) to empty, pour (out); (*tirar*) to dump ■ *vi* to flow
vertical [berti'kal] *adj* vertical; (*postura, piano etc*) upright ■ *nf* vertical
vértice ['bertiθe] *nm* vertex, apex
vertiente [ber'tjente] *nf* slope
vertiginoso, -a [bertixi'noso, a] *adj* giddy, dizzy
vértigo ['bertiɣo] *nm* vertigo; (*mareo*) dizziness; (*actividad*) intense activity; **de ~** (*fam: velocidad*) giddy; (*: ruido*) tremendous; (*: talento*) fantastic
vesícula [be'sikula] *nf* blister; **~ biliar** gall bladder
vespa® ['bespa] *nf* (motor) scooter
vespertino, -a [besper'tino, a] *adj* evening *cpd*
vespino® [bes'pino] *nm o f* ≈ moped
vestíbulo [bes'tiβulo] *nm* hall; (*de teatro*) foyer
vestido [bes'tiðo] *nm* (*ropa*) clothes *pl*, clothing; (*de mujer*) dress, frock
vestigio [bes'tixjo] *nm* (*trazo*) trace; (*señal*) sign; **vestigios** *nmpl* remains
vestimenta [besti'menta] *nf* clothing
vestir [bes'tir] *vt* (*poner: ropa*) to put on; (*llevar: ropa*) to wear; (*cubrir*) to clothe, cover; (*pagar: la ropa*) to clothe, pay for the clothing of; (*sastre*) to make clothes for ■ *vi* (*ponerse: ropa*) to dress; (*verse bien*) to look good; **vestirse** *vr* to get dressed, dress o.s.; **traje de ~** (*formal*) formal suit; **estar vestido de** to be dressed *o* clad in; (*como disfraz*) to be dressed as
vestuario [bes'twarjo] *nm* clothes *pl*, wardrobe; (*Teat: para actores*) dressing room; (*: para público*) cloakroom; (*Deporte*) changing room
Vesubio [be'suβjo] *nm* Vesuvius
veta ['beta] *nf* (*vena*) vein, seam; (*raya*) streak; (*de madera*) grain
vetar [be'tar] *vt* to veto
veterano, -a [bete'rano, a] *adj, nm/f* veteran
veterinario, -a [beteri'narjo, a] *nm/f* vet(erinary surgeon) ■ *nf* veterinary science
veto ['beto] *nm* veto
vetusto, -a [be'tusto, a] *adj* ancient
vez [beθ] *nf* time; (*turno*) turn; **a la ~ que** at the same time as; **a su ~** in its turn; **cada ~ más/menos** more and more/less and less; **una ~** once; **dos veces** twice; **de una ~** in one go; **de una ~ para siempre** once and for all; **en ~ de** instead of; **a veces** sometimes; **otra ~** again; **una y otra ~** repeatedly; **muchas veces** (*con frecuencia*) often; **pocas veces** seldom; **de ~ en cuando** from time to time; **7 veces 9** 7 times 9; **hacer las veces de** to stand in for; **tal ~** perhaps; **¿lo viste alguna ~?** did you ever see it?; **¿cuántas veces?** how often?; **érase una ~** once upon a time (there was)
v. g., v. gr. *abr* (= *verbigracia*) viz
VHF *sigla f* (= *Very High Frequency*) VHF
vía ['bia] *nf* (*calle*) road; (*ruta*) track, route; (*Ferro*) line; (*fig*) way; (*Anat*) passage, tube ■ *prep* via, by way of; **por ~ bucal** orally; **por ~ judicial** by legal means; **por ~ oficial** through official channels; **por ~ de** by way of; **en vías de** in the process of; **un país en vías de desarrollo** a developing country; **~ aérea** airway; **V~ Láctea** Milky Way; **~ pública** public highway *o* thoroughfare; **~ única** one-way street; **el tren está en la ~ 8** the train is (standing) at platform 8
viable ['bjaβle] *adj* (*Com*) viable; (*plan etc*) feasible
viaducto [bja'ðukto] *nm* viaduct
viajante [bja'xante] *nm* commercial traveller, traveling salesman (US)
viajar [bja'xar] *vi* to travel, journey
viaje ['bjaxe] *nm* journey; (*gira*) tour; (*Naut*) voyage; (*Com: carga*) load; **los viajes** travel *sg*; **estar de ~** to be on a journey; **~ de ida y vuelta** round trip; **~ de novios** honeymoon
viajero, -a [bja'xero, a] *adj* travelling (*Brit*), traveling (*US*); (*Zool*) migratory ■ *nm/f* (*quien viaja*) traveller; (*pasajero*) passenger
vial [bjal] *adj* road *cpd*, traffic *cpd*
vianda ['bjanda] *nf* (*tb:* **viandas**) food
viáticos ['bjatikos] *nmpl* (*Com*) travelling (*Brit*) *o* traveling (*US*) expenses
víbora ['biβora] *nf* viper
vibración [biβra'θjon] *nf* vibration
vibrador [biβra'ðor] *nm* vibrator
vibrante [bi'βrante] *adj* vibrant, vibrating
vibrar [bi'βrar] *vt* to vibrate ■ *vi* to vibrate;

(*pulsar*) to throb, beat, pulsate
vicario [bi'karjo] *nm* curate
vicecónsul [biθe'konsul] *nm* vice-consul
vicegerente [biθexe'rente] *nm/f* assistant manager
vicepresidente [biθepresi'ðente] *nm/f* vice president; (*de comité etc*) vice-chairman
viceversa [biθe'βersa] *adv* vice versa
viciado, -a [bi'θjaðo, a] *adj* (*corrompido*) corrupt; (*contaminado*) foul, contaminated
viciar [bi'θjar] *vt* (*pervertir*) to pervert; (*adulterar*) to adulterate; (*falsificar*) to falsify; (*Jur*) to nullify; (*estropear*) to spoil; (*sentido*) to twist; **viciarse** *vr* to become corrupted; (*aire, agua*) to be(come) polluted
vicio ['biθjo] *nm* (*libertinaje*) vice; (*mala costumbre*) bad habit; (*mimo*) spoiling; (*alabeo*) warp, warping; **de** *o* **por ~** out of sheer habit
vicioso, -a [bi'θjoso, a] *adj* (*muy malo*) vicious; (*corrompido*) depraved; (*mimado*) spoiled ■ *nm/f* depraved person; (*adicto*) addict
vicisitud [biθisi'tuð] *nf* vicissitude
víctima ['biktima] *nf* victim; (*de accidente etc*) casualty
victimario [bikti'marjo] *nm* (*Am*) killer, murderer
victoria [bik'torja] *nf* victory
victorioso, -a [bikto'rjoso, a] *adj* victorious
vicuña [bi'kuɲa] *nf* vicuna
vid [bið] *nf* vine
vida ['biða] *nf* life; (*duración*) lifetime; (*modo de vivir*) way of life; **¡~!, ¡~ mía!** (*saludo cariñoso*) my love!; **de por ~** for life; **de ~ airada** *o* **libre** loose-living; **en la/mi ~** never; **estar con ~** to be still alive; **ganarse la ~** to earn one's living; **¡esto es ~!** this is the life!; **le va la ~ en esto** his life depends on it
vidente [bi'ðente] *nm/f* (*adivino*) clairvoyant; (*no ciego*) sighted person
vídeo ['biðeo] *nm* video; (*aparato*) video (recorder); **cinta de ~** videotape; **película de ~** videofilm; **grabar en ~** to record, (video)tape; **~ compuesto/inverso** (*Inform*) composite/reverse video
videocámara [biðeo'kamara] *nf* video camera; (*pequeña*) camcorder
videocassette [biðeoka'set] *nm* video cassette
videoclip [biðeo'klip] *nm* (music) video
videoclub [biðeo'klub] *nm* video club; (*tienda*) video shop
videodatos [biðeo'ðatos] *nmpl* (*Com*) viewdata
videojuego [biðeo'xweɣo] *nm* video game
videotex [biðeo'teks], **videotexto** [biðeo'tekso] *nm* Videotex®
vidriero, -a [bi'ðrjero, a] *nm/f* glazier ■ *nf* (*ventana*) stained-glass window; (*Am: de tienda*) shop window; (*puerta*) glass door
vidrio ['biðrjo] *nm* glass; (*Am*) window; **~ cilindrado/inastillable** plate/splinter-proof glass
vidrioso, -a [bi'ðrjoso, a] *adj* glassy; (*frágil*) fragile, brittle; (*resbaladizo*) slippery
viejo, -a ['bjexo, a] *adj* old ■ *nm/f* old man/woman; **mi ~/vieja** (*fam*) my old man/woman; **hacerse** *o* **ponerse ~** to grow *o* get old
Viena ['bjena] *nf* Vienna
viene *etc* ['bjene] *vb ver* **venir**
vienés, -esa [bje'nes, esa] *adj, nm/f* Viennese
viento ['bjento] *nm* wind; **contra ~ y marea** at all costs; **ir ~ en popa** to go splendidly; (*negocio*) to prosper
vientre ['bjentre] *nm* belly; (*matriz*) womb; **vientres** *nmpl* bowels; **hacer de ~** to have a movement of the bowels
vier. *abr* (= *viernes*) Fri.
viernes ['bjernes] *nm inv* Friday; **V~ Santo** Good Friday; *ver tb* **Semana Santa; sábado**
vierta *etc* ['bjerta] *vb ver* **verter**
Vietnam [bjet'nam] *nm*: **el ~** Vietnam
vietnamita [bjetna'mita] *adj, nm/f* Vietnamese
viga ['biɣa] *nf* beam, rafter; (*de metal*) girder
vigencia [bi'xenθja] *nf* validity; (*de contrato etc*) term, life; **estar/entrar en ~** to be in/come into effect *o* force
vigente [bi'xente] *adj* valid, in force; (*imperante*) prevailing
vigésimo, -a [bi'xesimo, a] *num* twentieth
vigía [bi'xia] *nm* look-out ■ *nf* (*atalaya*) watchtower; (*acción*) watching
vigilancia [bixi'lanθja] *nf* vigilance
vigilante [bixi'lante] *adj* vigilant ■ *nm* caretaker; (*en cárcel*) warder; (*en almacén*) shopwalker (*Brit*), floor-walker (*US*); **~ jurado** security guard (*licensed to carry a gun*); **~ nocturno** night watchman
vigilar [bixi'lar] *vt* to watch over; (*cuidar*) to look after, keep an eye on ■ *vi* to be vigilant; (*hacer guardia*) to keep watch
vigilia [vi'xilja] *nf* wakefulness; (*Rel*) fast; **comer de ~** to fast
vigor [bi'ɣor] *nm* vigour, vitality; **en ~** in force; **entrar/poner en ~** to take/put into effect
vigoroso, -a [biɣo'roso, a] *adj* vigorous
VIH *nm abr* (= *virus de inmunodeficiencia humana*) HIV
vil [bil] *adj* vile, low
vileza [bi'leθa] *nf* vileness; (*acto*) base deed
vilipendiar [bilipen'djar] *vt* to vilify, revile
villa ['biʎa] *nf* (*pueblo*) small town;

(*municipalidad*) municipality; **la V~** (*Esp*) Madrid; **~ miseria** shanty town
villancico [biʎan'θiko] *nm* (Christmas) carol
villorrio [bi'ʎorrjo] *nm* one-horse town, dump; (*Am: barrio pobre*) shanty town
vilo ['bilo]: **en ~** *adv* in the air, suspended; (*fig*) on tenterhooks, in suspense; **estar** *o* **quedar en ~** to be left in suspense
vinagre [bi'naɣre] *nm* vinegar
vinagrera [bina'ɣrera] *nf* vinegar bottle; **vinagreras** *nfpl* cruet stand *sg*
vinagreta [bina'ɣreta] *nf* French dressing
vinatería [binate'ria] *nf* wine shop
vinatero, -a [bina'tero, a] *adj* wine *cpd* ▪ *nm* wine merchant
vinculación [binkula'θjon] *nf* (*lazo*) link, bond; (*acción*) linking
vincular [binku'lar] *vt* to link, bind
vínculo ['binkulo] *nm* link, bond
vindicar [bindi'kar] *vt* to vindicate; (*vengar*) to avenge; (*Jur*) to claim
vinícola [bi'nikola] *adj* (*industria*) wine *cpd*; (*región*) wine-growing *cpd*
vinicultura [binikul'tura] *nf* wine growing
vino *etc* ['bino] *vb ver* **venir** ▪ *nm* wine; **~ de solera/seco/tinto** vintage/dry/red wine; **~ de Jerez** sherry; **~ de Oporto** port (wine)
viña ['biɲa] *nf*, **viñedo** [bi'ɲeðo] *nm* vineyard
viñeta [bi'ɲeta] *nf* (*en historieta*) cartoon
viola ['bjola] *nf* viola
violación [bjola'θjon] *nf* violation; (*Jur*) offence, infringement; (*estupro*): **~ (sexual)** rape; **~ de contrato** (*Com*) breach of contract
violar [bjo'lar] *vt* to violate; (*Jur*) to infringe; (*cometer estupro*) to rape
violencia [bjo'lenθja] *nf* (*fuerza*) violence, force; (*embarazo*) embarrassment; (*acto injusto*) unjust act
violentar [bjolen'tar] *vt* to force; (*casa*) to break into; (*agredir*) to assault; (*violar*) to violate
violento, -a [bjo'lento, a] *adj* violent; (*furioso*) furious; (*situación*) embarrassing; (*acto*) forced, unnatural; (*difícil*) awkward; **me es muy ~** it goes against the grain with me
violeta [bjo'leta] *nf* violet
violín [bjo'lin] *nm* violin
violón [bjo'lon] *nm* double bass
violoncelo [bjolon'θelo] *nm* cello
V.I.P. ['bip] *sigla m* (= *Very Important Person*) VIP
virador [bira'ðor] *nm* (*para fotocopiadora*) toner
viraje [bi'raxe] *nm* turn; (*de vehículo*) swerve; (*de carretera*) bend; (*fig*) change of direction
virar [bi'rar] *vi* to turn; to swerve; to change direction
virgen ['birxen] *adj* virgin; (*cinta*) blank ▪ *nm/f* virgin; **la Santísima V~** (*Rel*) the Blessed Virgin
virginidad [birxini'ðað] *nf* virginity
Virgo ['birɣo] *nm* Virgo
viril [bi'ril] *adj* virile
virilidad [birili'ðað] *nf* virility
virrey [bi'rrei] *nm* viceroy
virtual [bir'twal] *adj* (*real*) virtual; (*en potencia*) potential
virtud [bir'tuð] *nf* virtue; **en ~ de** by virtue of
virtuoso, -a [bir'twoso, a] *adj* virtuous ▪ *nm/f* virtuoso
viruela [bi'rwela] *nf* smallpox; **viruelas** *nfpl* pockmarks; **viruelas locas** chickenpox *sg*
virulento, -a [biru'lento, a] *adj* virulent
virus ['birus] *nm inv* virus
viruta [bi'ruta] *nf* wood *o* metal shaving
vis [bis] *nf*: **~ cómica** sense of humour
visa ['bisa] *nf* (*Am*), **visado** [bi'saðo] *nm* visa; **~ de permanencia** residence permit
visar [bi'sar] *vt* (*pasaporte*) to visa; (*documento*) to endorse
víscera ['bisθera] *nf* internal organ; **vísceras** *nfpl* entrails
visceral [bisθe'ral] *adj* (*odio*) deep-rooted; **reacción ~** gut reaction
viscoso, -a [bis'koso, a] *adj* viscous
visera [bi'sera] *nf* visor
visibilidad [bisiβili'ðað] *nf* visibility
visible [bi'siβle] *adj* visible; (*fig*) obvious; **exportaciones/importaciones visibles** (*Com*) visible exports/imports
visillo [bi'siʎo] *nm* lace curtain
visión [bi'sjon] *nf* (*Anat*) vision, (eye)sight; (*fantasía*) vision, fantasy; (*panorama*) view; **ver visiones** to see *o* be seeing things
visionario, -a [bisjo'narjo, a] *adj* (*que prevé*) visionary; (*alucinado*) deluded ▪ *nm/f* visionary; (*chalado*) lunatic
visita [bi'sita] *nf* call, visit; (*persona*) visitor; **horas/tarjeta de ~** visiting hours/card; **~ de cortesía/de cumplido/de despedida** courtesy/formal/farewell visit; **hacer una ~** to pay a visit; **ir de ~** to go visiting
visitar [bisi'tar] *vt* to visit, call on; (*inspeccionar*) to inspect
vislumbrar [bislum'brar] *vt* to glimpse, catch a glimpse of
vislumbre [bis'lumbre] *nf* glimpse; (*centelleo*) gleam; (*idea vaga*) glimmer
viso ['biso] *nm* (*de metal*) glint, gleam; (*de tela*) sheen; (*aspecto*) appearance; **hay un ~ de verdad en esto** there is an element of truth in this
visón [bi'son] *nm* mink
visor [bi'sor] *nm* (*Foto*) viewfinder
víspera ['bispera] *nf* eve, day before; **la ~** *o* **en**

vísperas de on the eve of
vista ['bista] *nf* sight, vision; (*capacidad de ver*) (eye)sight; (*mirada*) look(s) (*pl*); (*Foto etc*) view; (*Jur*) hearing ■ *nm* customs officer; **a primera ~** at first glance; **~ general** overview; **fijar** *o* **clavar la ~ en** to stare at; **hacer la ~ gorda** to turn a blind eye; **volver la ~** to look back; **está a la ~ que** it's obvious that; **a la ~** (*Com*) at sight; **en ~ de** in view of; **en ~ de que** in view of the fact that; **¡hasta la ~!** so long!, see you!; **con vistas a** with a view to; *ver tb* **visto, a**
vistazo [bis'taθo] *nm* glance; **dar** *o* **echar un ~ a** to glance at
visto, -a *etc* ['bisto, a] *vb ver* **vestir** ■ *pp de* **ver** ■ *adj* seen; (*considerado*) considered ■ *nm*: **~ bueno** approval; **"~ bueno"** "approved"; **por lo ~** evidently; **dar el ~ bueno a algo** to give sth the go-ahead; **está ~ que** it's clear that; **está bien/mal ~** it's acceptable/ unacceptable; **está muy ~** it is very common; **estaba ~** it had to be; **~ que** *conj* since, considering that
vistoso, -a [bis'toso, a] *adj* colourful; (*alegre*) gay; (*pey*) gaudy
visual [bi'swal] *adj* visual
visualice *etc* [biswa'liθe] *vb ver* **visualizar**
visualizador [biswaliθa'ðor] *nm* (*Inform*) display screen, VDU
visualizar [biswali'θar] *vt* (*imaginarse*) to visualize; (*Inform*) to display
vital [bi'tal] *adj* life *cpd*, living *cpd*; (*fig*) vital; (*persona*) lively, vivacious
vitalicio, -a [bita'liθjo, a] *adj* for life
vitalidad [bitali'ðað] *nf* vitality
vitamina [bita'mina] *nf* vitamin
vitaminado, -a [bitami'naðo, a] *adj* with added vitamins
vitamínico, -a [bita'miniko, a] *adj* vitamin *cpd*; **complejos vitamínicos** vitamin compounds
viticultor, a [bitikul'tor, a] *nm/f* vine grower
viticultura [bitikul'tura] *nf* vine growing
vitorear [bitore'ar] *vt* to cheer, acclaim
vítores ['bitores] *nmpl* cheers
vitoriano, -a [bito'rjano, a] *adj* of *o* from Vitoria ■ *nm/f* native *o* inhabitant of Vitoria
vítreo, -a ['bitreo, a] *adj* vitreous
vitrina [bi'trina] *nf* glass case; (*en casa*) display cabinet; (*Am*) shop window
vituperar [bitupe'rar] *vt* to condemn
vituperio [bitu'perjo] *nm* (*condena*) condemnation; (*censura*) censure; (*insulto*) insult
viudez [bju'ðeθ] *nf* widowhood
viudo, -a ['bjuðo, a] *adj* widowed ■ *nm* widower ■ *nf* widow
viva ['biβa] *excl* hurrah! ■ *nm* cheer; **¡~ el rey!** long live the King!
vivacidad [biβaθi'ðað] *nf* (*vigor*) vigour; (*vida*) vivacity
vivamente [biβa'mente] *adv* in lively fashion; (*describir*) vividly; (*protestar*) sharply; (*emocionarse*) acutely
vivaracho, -a [biβa'ratʃo, a] *adj* jaunty, lively; (*ojos*) bright, twinkling
vivaz [bi'βaθ] *adj* (*que dura*) enduring; (*vigoroso*) vigorous; (*vivo*) lively
vivencia [bi'βenθja] *nf* experience
víveres ['biβeres] *nmpl* provisions
vivero [bi'βero] *nm* (*Horticultura*) nursery; (*para peces*) fishpond; (: *Com*) fish farm
viveza [bi'βeθa] *nf* liveliness; (*agudeza*) sharpness
vividor, a [biβi'ðor, a] *adj* (*pey*) opportunistic ■ *nm* (*aprovechado*) hustler
vivienda [bi'βjenda] *nf* (*alojamiento*) housing; (*morada*) dwelling; **viviendas protegidas** *o* **sociales** council housing *sg* (*Brit*), public housing *sg* (*US*)
viviente [bi'βjente] *adj* living
vivificar [biβifi'kar] *vt* to give life to
vivifique *etc* [biβi'fike] *vb ver* **vivificar**
vivir [bi'βir] *vt* (*experimentar*) to live *o* go through ■ *vi* (*gen, Com*): **~ (de)** to live (by, off, on) ■ *nm* life, living; **¡viva!** hurray!; **¡viva el rey!** long live the king!
vivo, -a ['biβo, a] *adj* living, live, alive; (*fig*) vivid; (*movimiento*) quick; (*color*) bright; (*protesta etc*) strong; (*astuto*) smart, clever; **en ~** (*TV etc*) live; **llegar a lo ~** to cut to the quick
vizcaíno, -a [biθka'ino, a] *adj, nm/f* Biscayan
Vizcaya [biθ'kaja] *nf* Biscay; **el Golfo de ~** the Bay of Biscay
V.M. *abr* = **Vuestra Majestad**
V.O. *abr* = **versión original**
V.ºB.º *abr* = **visto bueno**
vocablo [bo'kaβlo] *nm* (*palabra*) word; (*término*) term
vocabulario [bokaβu'larjo] *nm* vocabulary, word list
vocación [boka'θjon] *nf* vocation
vocacional [bokasjo'nal] *nf* (*Am*) ≈ technical college
vocal [bo'kal] *adj* vocal ■ *nm/f* member (of a committee *etc*) ■ *nm* non-executive director ■ *nf* vowel
vocalice *etc* [boka'liθe] *vb ver* **vocalizar**
vocalizar [bokali'θar] *vt* to vocalize
voceador [bosea'ðor] *nm* (*Am*): **~ de periódicos** newspaper vendor *o* seller
vocear [boθe'ar] *vt* (*para vender*) to cry; (*aclamar*) to acclaim; (*fig*) to proclaim ■ *vi* to yell

vocerío [boθe'rio] *nm* shouting; (*escándalo*) hullabaloo
vocero, -a [bo'sero, a] *nm/f* (*Am*) spokesman/woman
vociferar [boθife'rar] *vt* to shout; (*jactarse*) to proclaim boastfully ■ *vi* to yell
vocinglero, -a [boθin'glero, a] *adj* vociferous; (*gárrulo*) garrulous; (*fig*) blatant
vodevil [boðe'βil] *nm* music hall, variety, vaudeville (*US*)
vodka ['boðka] *nm* vodka
vodú [bo'ðu] *nm* voodoo
vol *abr* = **volumen**
volado, -a [bo'laðo, a] *adj*: **estar ~** (*fam: inquieto*) to be worried; (*: loco*) to be crazy
volador, a [bola'ðor, a] *adj* flying
voladura [bola'ðura] *nf* blowing up, demolition; (*Minería*) blasting
volandas [bo'landas]: **en ~** *adv* in *o* through the air; (*fig*) swiftly
volante [bo'lante] *adj* flying ■ *nm* (*de máquina, coche*) steering wheel; (*de reloj*) balance; (*nota*) note; **ir al ~** to be at the wheel, be driving
volar [bo'lar] *vt* (*demoler*) to blow up, demolish ■ *vi* to fly; (*fig: correr*) to rush, hurry; (*fam: desaparecer*) to disappear; **voy volando** I must dash; **¡cómo vuela el tiempo!** how time flies!
volátil [bo'latil] *adj* volatile; (*fig*) changeable
volcán [bol'kan] *nm* volcano
volcánico, -a [bol'kaniko, a] *adj* volcanic
volcar [bol'kar] *vt* to upset, overturn; (*tumbar, derribar*) to knock over; (*vaciar*) to empty out ■ *vi* to overturn; **volcarse** *vr* to tip over; (*barco*) to capsize
voleibol [bolei'βol] *nm* volleyball
voleo [bo'leo] *nm* volley; **a(l) ~** haphazardly; **de un ~** quickly
Volga ['bolɣa] *nm* Volga
volición [boli'θjon] *nf* volition
volqué [bol'ke], **volquemos** *etc* [bol'kemos] *vb ver* **volcar**
volquete [bol'kete] *nm* dumper, dump truck (*US*)
voltaje [bol'taxe] *nm* voltage
voltear [bolte'ar] *vt* to turn over; (*volcar*) to knock over; (*doblar*) to peal ■ *vi* to roll over; **voltearse** *vr* (*Am*) to turn round; **~ a hacer algo** (*Am*) to do sth again
voltereta [bolte'reta] *nf* somersault; **~ sobre las manos** handspring; **~ lateral** cartwheel
voltio ['boltjo] *nm* volt
voluble [bo'luβle] *adj* fickle
volumen [bo'lumen] *nm* volume; **~ monetario** money supply; **~ de negocios** turnover; **bajar el ~** to turn down the volume; **poner la radio a todo ~** to turn the radio up full
voluminoso, -a [bolumi'noso, a] *adj* voluminous; (*enorme*) massive
voluntad [bolun'tað] *nf* will, willpower; (*deseo*) desire, wish; (*afecto*) fondness; **a ~** at will; (*cantidad*) as much as one likes; **buena ~** goodwill; **mala ~** ill will, malice; **por causas ajenas a mi ~** for reasons beyond my control
voluntario, -a [bolun'tarjo, a] *adj* voluntary ■ *nm/f* volunteer
voluntarioso, -a [bolunta'rjoso, a] *adj* headstrong
voluptuoso, -a [bolup'twoso, a] *adj* voluptuous
volver [bol'βer] *vt* to turn; (*boca abajo*) to turn (over); (*voltear*) to turn round, turn upside down; (*poner del revés*) to turn inside out; (*devolver*) to return; (*transformar*) to change, transform; (*manga*) to roll up ■ *vi* to return, go/come back; **volverse** *vr* to turn round; (*llegar a ser*) to become; **~ la espalda** to turn one's back; **~ bien por mal** to return good for evil; **~ a hacer** to do again; **~ en sí** to come to *o* round, regain consciousness; **~ la vista atrás** to look back; **~ loco a algn** to drive sb mad; **volverse loco** to go mad
vomitar [bomi'tar] *vt, vi* to vomit
vómito ['bomito] *nm* (*acto*) vomiting; (*resultado*) vomit
voracidad [boraθi'ðað] *nf* voracity
vorágine [bo'raxine] *nf* whirlpool; (*fig*) maelstrom
voraz [bo'raθ] *adj* voracious; (*fig*) fierce
vórtice ['bortiθe] *nm* whirlpool; (*de aire*) whirlwind
VOS *abr* = **versión original subtitulada**
vos [bos] *pron* (*Am*) you
voseo [bo'seo] *nm* (*Am*) addressing a person as "vos", *familiar usage*
Vosgos ['bosɣos] *nmpl* Vosges
vosotros, -as [bo'sotros, as] *pron* you *pl*; (*reflexivo*) yourselves; **entre ~** among yourselves
votación [bota'θjon] *nf* (*acto*) voting; (*voto*) vote; **~ a mano alzada** show of hands; **someter algo a ~** to put sth to the vote
votar [bo'tar] *vt* (*Pol: partido etc*) to vote for; (*proyecto: aprobar*) to pass; (*Rel*) to vow ■ *vi* to vote
voto ['boto] *nm* vote; (*promesa*) vow; (*maldición*) oath, curse; **votos** *nmpl* (good) wishes; **~ de bloque/de grupo** block/card vote; **~ de censura/de (des)confianza/de gracias** vote of censure/(no) confidence/thanks; **dar su ~** to cast one's vote
voy [boi] *vb ver* **ir**

voz [boθ] *nf* voice; (*grito*) shout; (*chisme*) rumour; (*Ling: palabra*) word; (*: forma*) voice; **dar voces** to shout, yell; **llamar a algn a voces** to shout to sb; **llevar la ~ cantante** (*fig*) to be the boss; **tener la ~ tomada** to be hoarse; **tener ~ y voto** to have the right to speak; **a media ~** in a low voice; **a ~ en cuello** *o* **en grito** at the top of one's voice; **de viva ~** verbally; **en ~ alta** aloud; **~ de mando** command

vozarrón [boθa'rron] *nm* booming voice

vra., vro. *abr* = **vuestra**; **vuestro**

Vto. *abr* (*Com*) = **vencimiento**

vudú [bu'ðu] *nm* voodoo

vuelco *etc* ['bwelko] *vb ver* **volcar** ■ *nm* spill, overturning; (*fig*) collapse; **mi corazón dio un ~** my heart missed a beat

vuelo *etc* ['bwelo] *vb ver* **volar** ■ *nm* flight; (*encaje*) lace, frill; (*de falda etc*) loose part; (*fig*) importance; **de altos ~s** (*fig: plan*) grandiose; (*: persona*) ambitious; **alzar el ~** to take flight; (*fig*) to dash off; **coger al ~** to catch in flight; **~ de bajo coste** low-cost flight; **~ en picado** dive; **~ libre** hang-gliding; **~ regular** scheduled flight; **falda de mucho ~** full *o* wide skirt

vuelque *etc* ['bwelke] *vb ver* **volcar**

vuelta ['bwelta] *nf* turn; (*curva*) bend, curve; (*regreso*) return; (*revolución*) revolution; (*paseo*) stroll; (*circuito*) lap; (*de papel, tela*) reverse; (*de pantalón*) turn-up (*Brit*), cuff (*US*); (*cambio*) change; **~ a empezar** back to square one; **~ al mundo** world trip; **V~ de Francia** Tour de France; **~ cerrada** hairpin bend; **a la ~** (*Esp*) on one's return; **a la ~ de la esquina, a la ~** (*Am*) round the corner; **a ~ de correo** by return of post; **dar vueltas** to turn, revolve; **dar vueltas a una idea** to turn over an idea (in one's mind); **dar una ~** to go for a walk; **dar media ~** (*Auto*) to do a U-turn; (*fam*) to beat it; **estar de ~** (*fam*) to be back; **poner a algn de ~ y media** to heap abuse on sb; **no tiene ~ de hoja** there's no alternative

vueltita [bwel'tita] *nf* (*esp Am fam*) (little) walk; (*: en coche*) (little) drive

vuelto ['bwelto] *pp de* **volver** ■ *nm* (*Am: moneda*) change

vuelva *etc* ['bwelβa] *vb ver* **volver**

vuestro, -a ['bwestro, a] *adj* your; (*después de n*) of yours ■ *pron*: **el ~/la vuestra/los vuestros/las vuestras** yours; **lo ~** (what is) yours; **un amigo ~** a friend of yours; **una idea vuestra** an idea of yours

vulgar [bul'ɣar] *adj* (*ordinario*) vulgar; (*común*) common

vulgarice *etc* [bulɣa'riθe] *vb ver* **vulgarizar**

vulgaridad [bulɣari'ðað] *nf* commonness; (*acto*) vulgarity; (*expresión*) coarse expression; **vulgaridades** *nfpl* banalities

vulgarismo [bulɣa'rismo] *nm* popular form of a word

vulgarizar [bulɣari'θar] *vt* to popularize

vulgo ['bulɣo] *nm* common people

vulnerable [bulne'raβle] *adj* vulnerable

vulnerar [bulne'rar] *vt* to harm, damage; (*derechos*) to interfere with; (*Jur: Com*) to violate

vulva ['bulβa] *nf* vulva

Ww

W *abr* (= *vatio(s)*) w
W, w ['uβe'doβle] (*Am*) ['doβleβe] *nf* (*letra*) W, w; **W de Washington** W for William
walkie-talkie [walki'talki] *nm* walkie-talkie
walkman® ['wal(k)man] *nm* Walkman®
WAP [wap] *adj, nm* WAP; **teléfono ~** WAP phone
wáter ['bater] *nm* lavatory
waterpolo [water'polo] *nm* waterpolo
web [web] *nm o nf* (*página*) website; (*red*) (World Wide) Web
web site ['websait] *nm* website
webcam ['webkam] *nf* webcam
web master ['webmaster] *nm/f* webmaster
whisky ['wiski] *nm* whisky
Winchester ['wintʃester] *nm* (*Inform*): **disco ~** Winchester disk
windsurf ['winsurf] *nm* windsurfing
WWW *nm o nf abr* (*Inform*: = *World Wide Web*) WWW

Xx

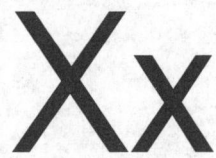

X, x ['ekis] *nf* (*letra*) X, x; **X de Xiquena** X for Xmas
xenofobia [seno'foβja] *nf* xenophobia
xenófobo, -a [se'nofoβo, a] *adj* xenophobic ▪ *nm/f* xenophobe
xerografía [seroɣra'fia] *nf* xerography
xilófono [si'lofono] *nm* xylophone
Xunta ['shunta] *nf* (*tb*: **Xunta de Galicia**) *regional government of Galicia*

Yy

Y, y [i'ɣrjeɣa] *nf* (*letra*) Y, y; **Y de Yegua** Y for Yellow (*Brit*) *o* Yoke (*US*)
y [i] *conj* and; (*Am fam: pues*) well; **¿y eso?** why?, how so?; **¿y los demás?** what about the others?; **y bueno ...** (*Am*) well ...
ya [ja] *adv* (*gen*) already; (*ahora*) now; (*en seguida*) at once; (*pronto*) soon ■ *excl* all right!; (*por supuesto*) of course! ■ *conj* (*ahora que*) now that; **ya no** not any more, no longer; **ya lo sé** I know; **ya dice que sí, ya dice que no** first he says yes, then he says no; **¡ya, ya!** yes, yes!; (*con impaciencia*) all right!, O.K.!; **¡ya voy!** (*enfático: no se suele traducir*) coming!; **ya que** since
yacer [ja'θer] *vi* to lie
yacimiento [jaθi'mjento] *nm* bed, deposit; **~ petrolífero** oilfield
Yakarta [ja'karta] *nf* Jakarta
yanqui ['janki] *adj* Yankee ■ *nm/f* Yank, Yankee
yate ['jate] *nm* yacht
yazca *etc* ['jaθka] *vb ver* **yacer**
yedra ['jeðra] *nf* ivy
yegua ['jeɣwa] *nf* mare
yema ['jema] *nf* (*del huevo*) yoke; (*Bot*) leaf bud; (*fig*) best part; **~ del dedo** fingertip
Yemen ['jemen] *nm*: **el ~ del Norte** Yemen; **el ~ del Sur** Southern Yemen
yemení [jeme'ni] *adj, nm/f* Yemeni
yendo ['jendo] *vb ver* **ir**
yerba ['jerβa] *nf* = **hierba**
yerbatero, -a [jerβa'tero, a] *adj* (*Am*) maté ■ *nm/f* (*Am*) herbal healer
yerga *etc* ['jerɣa], **yergue** *etc* ['jerɣe] *vb ver* **erguir**
yermo, -a ['jermo, a] *adj* barren; (*de gente*) uninhabited ■ *nm* waste land
yerno ['jerno] *nm* son-in-law
yerre *etc* ['jerre] *vb ver* **errar**
yerto, -a ['jerto, a] *adj* stiff
yesca ['jeska] *nf* tinder
yeso ['jeso] *nm* (*Geo*) gypsum; (*Arq*) plaster
yo [jo] *pron personal* I; **soy yo** it's me, it is I; **yo que tú/usted** if I were you
yodo ['joðo] *nm* iodine
yoga ['joɣa] *nm* yoga
yogur [jo'ɣur], **yogurt** [jo'ɣurt] *nm* yogurt
yogurtera [joɣur'tera] *nf* yogurt maker
yuca ['juka] *nf* yucca
yudo ['juðo] *nm* judo
yugo ['juɣo] *nm* yoke
Yugoslavia [juɣos'laβja] *nf* Yugoslavia
yugoslavo, -a [juɣos'laβo, a] *adj* Yugoslavian ■ *nm/f* Yugoslav
yugular [juɣu'lar] *adj* jugular
yunque ['junke] *nm* anvil
yunta ['junta] *nf* yoke
yuntero [jun'tero] *nm* ploughman
yute ['jute] *nm* jute
yuxtapondré *etc* [jukstapond're] *vb ver* **yuxtaponer**
yuxtaponer [jukstapo'ner] *vt* to juxtapose
yuxtaponga *etc* [juksta'ponga] *vb ver* **yuxtaponer**
yuxtaposición [jukstaposi'θjon] *nf* juxtaposition
yuxtapuesto [juksta'pwesto], **yuxtapuse** *etc* [juksta'puse] *vb ver* **yuxtaponer**

Zz

Z, z ['θeta] (*esp Am*) ['seta] *nf* (*letra*) Z, z; **Z de Zaragoza** Z for Zebra
zafar [θa'far] *vt* (*soltar*) to untie; (*superficie*) to clear; **zafarse** *vr* (*escaparse*) to escape; (*ocultarse*) to hide o.s. away; (*Tec*) to slip off; **zafarse de** (*persona*) to get away from
zafio, -a ['θafjo, a] *adj* coarse
zafiro [θa'firo] *nm* sapphire
zaga ['θaɣa] *nf* rear; **a la ~** behind, in the rear
zagal [θa'ɣal] *nm* boy, lad
zagala [θa'ɣala] *nf* girl, lass
zaguán [θa'ɣwan] *nm* hallway
zaherir [θae'rir] *vt* (*criticar*) to criticize; (*fig: herir*) to wound
zahiera *etc*, **zahiriendo** *etc* [θa'jera, θai'rjendo] *vb ver* **zaherir**
zahorí [θao'ri] *nm* clairvoyant
zaino, -a ['θaino, a] *adj* (*color de caballo*) chestnut; (*pérfido*) treacherous; (*animal*) vicious
zalamería [θalame'ria] *nf* flattery
zalamero, -a [θala'mero, a] *adj* flattering; (*relamido*) suave
zamarra [θa'marra] *nf* (*piel*) sheepskin; (*chaqueta*) sheepskin jacket
Zambeze [θam'beθe] *nm* Zambezi
zambo, -a ['θambo, a] *adj* knock-kneed ■ *nm/f* (*Am*) half-breed (*of Negro and Indian parentage*); (*mulato*) mulatto ■ *nf* samba
zambullida [θambu'ʎiða] *nf* dive, plunge
zambullirse [θambu'ʎirse] *vr* to dive; (*ocultarse*) to hide o.s.
zamorano, -a [θamo'rano, a] *adj* of *o* from Zamora ■ *nm/f* native *o* inhabitant of Zamora
zampar [θam'par] *vt* (*esconder*) to hide *o* put away (hurriedly); (*comer*) to gobble; (*arrojar*) to hurl ■ *vi* to eat voraciously; **zamparse** *vr* (*chocar*) to bump; (*fig*) to gatecrash
zanahoria [θana'orja] *nf* carrot
zancada [θan'kaða] *nf* stride
zancadilla [θanka'ðiʎa] *nf* trip; (*fig*) stratagem; **echar la ~ a algn** to trip sb up
zancajo [θan'kaxo] *nm* (*Anat*) heel; (*fig*) dwarf
zanco ['θanko] *nm* stilt
zancudo, -a [θan'kuðo, a] *adj* long-legged ■ *nm* (*Am*) mosquito
zángano ['θangano] *nm* drone; (*holgazán*) idler, slacker
zanja ['θanxa] *nf* (*fosa*) ditch; (*tumba*) grave
zanjar [θan'xar] *vt* (*fosa*) to ditch, trench; (*problema*) to surmount; (*conflicto*) to resolve
zapapico [θapa'piko] *nm* pick, pickaxe
zapata [θa'pata] *nf* half-boot; (*Mecánica*) shoe
zapateado [θapate'aðo] *nm* (flamenco) tap dance
zapatear [θapate'ar] *vt* (*tocar*) to tap with one's foot; (*patear*) to kick; (*fam*) to ill-treat ■ *vi* to tap with one's feet
zapatería [θapate'ria] *nf* (*oficio*) shoemaking; (*tienda*) shoe-shop; (*fábrica*) shoe factory
zapatero, -a [θapa'tero, a] *nm/f* shoemaker; **~ remendón** cobbler
zapatilla [θapa'tiʎa] *nf* slipper; (*Tec*) washer; (*de deporte*) training shoe
zapato [θa'pato] *nm* shoe
zapear [θape'ar] *vi* to flick through the channels
zapping ['θapin] *nm* channel-hopping; **hacer ~** to channel-hop
zar [θar] *nm* tsar, czar
zarabanda [θara'βanda] *nf* saraband; (*fig*) whirl
Zaragoza [θara'ɣoθa] *nf* Saragossa
zaragozano, -a [θaraɣo'θano, a] *adj* of *o* from Saragossa ■ *nm/f* native *o* inhabitant of Saragossa
zaranda [θa'randa] *nf* sieve
zarandear [θarande'ar] *vt* to sieve; (*fam*) to shake vigorously
zarpa ['θarpa] *nf* (*garra*) claw, paw; **echar la ~ a** to claw at; (*fam*) to grab
zarpar [θar'par] *vi* to weigh anchor
zarpazo [θar'paθo] *nm*: **dar un ~** to claw
zarza ['θarθa] *nf* (*Bot*) bramble
zarzal [θar'θal] *nm* (*matorral*) bramble patch

zarzamora [θarθa'mora] *nf* blackberry
zarzuela [θar'θwela] *nf* Spanish light opera; **la Z~** *home of the Spanish Royal Family*
zigzag [θiɣ'θaɣ] *adj* zigzag
zigzaguear [θiɣθaɣe'ar] *vi* to zigzag
zinc [θink] *nm* zinc
zíper ['siper] *nm* (*Am*) zip, zipper (*US*)
zócalo ['θokalo] *nm* (*Arq*) plinth, base; (*de pared*) skirting board
zoco ['θoko] *nm* (Arab) market, souk
zodíaco [θo'ðiako] *nm* zodiac; **signo del ~** star sign
zona ['θona] *nf* zone; **~ cero** Ground Zero; **~ euro** Eurozone; **los países de la ~ euro** the Eurozone countries; **~ fronteriza** border area; **~ del dólar** (*Com*) dollar area; **~ de fomento** *o* **de desarrollo** development area
zonzo, -a ['sonso, a] *adj* (*Am*) silly
zoología [θoolo'xia] *nf* zoology
zoológico, -a [θoo'loxiko, a] *adj* zoological ▪ *nm* (*tb*: **parque zoológico**) zoo
zoólogo, -a [θo'oloɣo, a] *nm/f* zoologist
zoom [θum] *nm* zoom lens
zopenco, -a [θo'penko, a] (*fam*) *adj* dull, stupid ▪ *nm/f* clot, nitwit
zopilote [sopi'lote] *nm* (*Am*) buzzard
zoquete [θo'kete] *nm* (*de madera*) block; (*de pan*) crust; (*fam*) blockhead
zorro, -a ['θorro, a] *adj* crafty ▪ *nm/f* fox/vixen ▪ *nf* (*fam*) whore, tart, hooker (*US*)
zote ['θote] (*fam*) *adj* dim, stupid ▪ *nm/f* dimwit
zozobra [θo'θoβra] *nf* (*fig*) anxiety
zozobrar [θoθo'βrar] *vi* (*hundirse*) to capsize; (*fig*) to fail
zueco ['θweko] *nm* clog
zulo ['θulo] *nm* (*de armas*) cache
zumbar [θum'bar] *vt* (*burlar*) to tease; (*golpear*) to hit ▪ *vi* to buzz; (*fam*) to be very close; **zumbarse** *vr*: **zumbarse de** to tease; **me zumban los oídos** I have a buzzing *o* ringing in my ears
zumbido [θum'biðo] *nm* buzzing; (*fam*) punch; **~ de oídos** buzzing *o* ringing in the ears
zumo ['θumo] *nm* juice; (*ganancia*) profit; **~ de naranja** (fresh) orange juice
zurcir [θur'θir] *vt* (*coser*) to darn; (*fig*) to put together; **¡que las zurzan!** to blazes with them!
zurdo, -a ['θurðo, a] *adj* (*mano*) left; (*persona*) left-handed
zurrar [θu'rrar] *vt* (*Tec*) to dress; (*fam: pegar duro*) to wallop; (*: aplastar*) to flatten; (*: criticar*) to criticize harshly
zurriagazo [θurrja'ɣaθo] *nm* lash, stroke; (*desgracia*) stroke of bad luck
zurrón [θu'rron] *nm* pouch
zurza *etc* ['θurθa] *vb ver* **zurcir**
zutano, -a [θu'tano, a] *nm/f* so-and-so

Aa

A, a [eɪ] *n* (*letter*) A, a; (*Scol: mark*) ≈ sobresaliente; (*Mus*): **A** la *m*; **A for Andrew,** (*US*) **A for Able** A de Antonio; **A road** *n* (*Brit Aut*) ≈ carretera nacional

KEYWORD

a [ə] *indef art* (*before vowel and silent h* **an**) **1** un(a); **a book** un libro; **an apple** una manzana; **she's a nurse** (ella) es enfermera; **I haven't got a car** no tengo coche
2 (*instead of the number "one"*) un(a); **a year ago** hace un año; **a hundred/thousand pounds** cien/mil libras
3 (*in expressing ratios, prices etc*): **three a day/week** tres al día/a la semana; **10 km an hour** 10 km por hora; **£5 a person** £5 por persona; **30p a kilo** 30p el kilo; **three times a month** tres veces al mes

a. *abbr* = **acre**
A2 *n* (*Brit Scol*) *segunda parte de los "A levels" (módulos 4–6)*
AA *n abbr* (*Brit: = Automobile Association*) ≈ RACE *m* (*SP*); = **Alcoholics Anonymous** A.A.; (*US: = Associate in/of Arts*) *título universitario*; = **anti-aircraft**
AAA *n abbr* (*= American Automobile Association*) ≈ RACE *m* (*SP*) ['θri:'eɪz] (*Brit: = Amateur Athletics Association*) *asociación de atletismo amateur*
A & R *n abbr* (*Mus: = artists and repertoire*) *nuevos artistas y canciones*; **~ man** *descubridor de jóvenes talentos*
AAUP *n abbr* (*= American Association of University Professors*) *asociación de profesores universitarios*
AB *abbr* (*Brit*) = **able-bodied seaman**; (*Canada*) = **Alberta**
aback [ə'bæk] *adv*: **to be taken ~** quedar(se) desconcertado
abandon [ə'bændən] *vt* abandonar; (*renounce*) renunciar a ■ *n* abandono; (*wild behaviour*): **with ~** con desenfreno; **to ~ ship** abandonar el barco
abandoned [ə'bændənd] *adj* (*child, house etc*) abandonado; (*unrestrained: manner*) desinhibido
abase [ə'beɪs] *vt*: **to ~ o.s. (so far as to do ...)** rebajarse (hasta el punto de hacer ...)
abashed [ə'bæʃt] *adj* avergonzado
abate [ə'beɪt] *vi* moderarse; (*lessen*) disminuir; (*calm down*) calmarse
abatement [ə'beɪtmənt] *n* (*of pollution, noise*) disminución *f*
abattoir ['æbətwɑːʳ] *n* (*Brit*) matadero
abbey ['æbɪ] *n* abadía
abbot ['æbət] *n* abad *m*
abbreviate [ə'bri:vɪeɪt] *vt* abreviar
abbreviation [əbri:vɪ'eɪʃən] *n* (*short form*) abreviatura; (*act*) abreviación *f*
ABC *n abbr* (*= American Broadcasting Company*) *cadena de televisión*
abdicate ['æbdɪkeɪt] *vt, vi* abdicar
abdication [æbdɪ'keɪʃən] *n* abdicación *f*
abdomen ['æbdəmən] *n* abdomen *m*
abdominal [æb'dɔmɪnl] *adj* abdominal
abduct [æb'dʌkt] *vt* raptar, secuestrar
abduction [æb'dʌkʃən] *n* rapto, secuestro
abductor [æb'dʌktəʳ] *n* raptor(a) *m(f)*, secuestrador(a) *m(f)*
Aberdonian [æbə'dəunɪən] *adj* de Aberdeen ■ *n* nativo(-a) *or* habitante *m/f* de Aberdeen
aberration [æbə'reɪʃən] *n* aberración *f*; **in a moment of mental ~** en un momento de enajenación mental
abet [ə'bɛt] *vt see* **aid**
abeyance [ə'beɪəns] *n*: **in ~** (*law*) en desuso; (*matter*) en suspenso
abhor [əb'hɔːʳ] *vt* aborrecer, abominar (de)
abhorrent [əb'hɔrənt] *adj* aborrecible, detestable
abide [ə'baɪd] *vt*: **I can't ~ it/him** no lo/le puedo ver *or* aguantar; **to ~ by** *vt fus* atenerse a
abiding [ə'baɪdɪŋ] *adj* (*memory etc*) perdurable
ability [ə'bɪlɪtɪ] *n* habilidad *f*, capacidad *f*;

(*talent*) talento; **to the best of my ~** lo mejor que pueda *etc*
abject ['æbdʒɛkt] *adj* (*poverty*) sórdido; (*apology*) rastrero; (*coward*) vil
ablaze [ə'bleɪz] *adj* en llamas, ardiendo
able ['eɪbl] *adj* capaz; (*skilled*) hábil; **to be ~ to do sth** poder hacer algo
able-bodied ['eɪbl'bɔdɪd] *adj* sano; **~ seaman** marinero de primera
ably ['eɪblɪ] *adv* hábilmente
ABM *n abbr* = **anti-ballistic missile**
abnormal [æb'nɔːməl] *adj* anormal
abnormality [æbnɔː'mælɪtɪ] *n* (*condition*) anormalidad *f*; (*instance*) anomalía
aboard [ə'bɔːd] *adv* a bordo ▪ *prep* a bordo de; **~ the train** en el tren
abode [ə'bəud] *n* (*old*) morada; (*Law*) domicilio; **of no fixed ~** sin domicilio fijo
abolish [ə'bɔlɪʃ] *vt* suprimir, abolir
abolition [æbəu'lɪʃən] *n* supresión *f*, abolición *f*
abominable [ə'bɔmɪnəbl] *adj* abominable
aborigine [æbə'rɪdʒɪnɪ] *n* aborigen *m/f*
abort [ə'bɔːt] *vt* abortar; (*Comput*) interrumpir ▪ *vi* (*Comput*) interrumpir el programa
abortion [ə'bɔːʃən] *n* aborto (provocado); **to have an ~** abortar
abortionist [ə'bɔːʃənɪst] *n* persona que practica abortos
abortive [ə'bɔːtɪv] *adj* fracasado
abound [ə'baund] *vi*: **to ~ (in** *or* **with)** abundar (de *or* en)

KEYWORD

about [ə'baut] *adv* **1** (*approximately*) más o menos, aproximadamente; **about a hundred/thousand** *etc* unos (unas) *or* como cien/mil *etc*; **it takes about 10 hours** se tarda unas *or* más o menos 10 horas; **at about two o'clock** sobre las dos; **I've just about finished** casi he terminado
2 (*referring to place*) por todas partes; **to leave things lying about** dejar las cosas (tiradas) por ahí; **to run about** correr por todas partes; **to walk about** pasearse, ir y venir; **is Paul about?** ¿está por aquí Paul?; **it's the other way about** es al revés
3: **to be about to do sth** estar a punto de hacer algo; **I'm not about to do all that for nothing** no pienso hacer todo eso para nada
▪ *prep* **1** (*relating to*) de, sobre, acerca de; **a book about London** un libro sobre *or* acerca de Londres; **what is it about?** (*book, film*) ¿de qué se trata?; **we talked about it** hablamos de eso *or* ello; **what** *or* **how about doing this?** ¿qué tal si hacemos esto?
2 (*referring to place*) por; **to walk about the town** caminar por la ciudad

about face, about turn *n* (*Mil*) media vuelta; (*fig*) cambio radical
above [ə'bʌv] *adv* encima, por encima, arriba ▪ *prep* encima de; **mentioned ~** susodicho; **~ all** sobre todo; **he's not ~ a bit of blackmail** es capaz hasta de hacer chantaje
above board *adj* legítimo
above-mentioned [əbʌv'mɛnʃnd] *adj* susodicho
abrasion [ə'breɪʒən] *n* (*on skin*) abrasión *f*
abrasive [ə'breɪzɪv] *adj* abrasivo
abreast [ə'brɛst] *adv* uno al lado de otro; **to keep ~ of** mantenerse al corriente de
abridge [ə'brɪdʒ] *vt* abreviar
abroad [ə'brɔːd] *adv* (*be*) en el extranjero; (*go*) al extranjero; **there is a rumour ~ that ...** corre el rumor de que ...
abrupt [ə'brʌpt] *adj* (*sudden: departure*) repentino; (*manner*) brusco
abruptly [ə'brʌptlɪ] *adv* (*leave*) repentinamente; (*speak*) bruscamente
abscess ['æbsɪs] *n* absceso
abscond [əb'skɔnd] *vi* fugarse
absence ['æbsəns] *n* ausencia; **in the ~ of** (*person*) en ausencia de; (*thing*) a falta de
absent ['æbsənt] *adj* ausente; **~ without leave (AWOL)** ausente sin permiso
absentee [æbsən'tiː] *n* ausente *m/f*
absenteeism [æbsən'tiːɪzəm] *n* absentismo
absent-minded [æbsənt'maɪndɪd] *adj* distraído
absolute ['æbsəluːt] *adj* absoluto; **~ monopoly** monopolio total
absolutely [æbsə'luːtlɪ] *adv* totalmente; **oh yes, ~!** ¡claro *or* por supuesto que sí!
absolution [æbsə'luːʃən] *n* (*Rel*) absolución *f*
absolve [əb'zɔlv] *vt*: **to ~ sb (from)** absolver a algn (de)
absorb [əb'zɔːb] *vt* absorber; **to be absorbed in a book** estar enfrascado en un libro
absorbent [əb'zɔːbənt] *adj* absorbente
absorbent cotton *n* (*US*) algodón *m* hidrófilo
absorbing [əb'zɔːbɪŋ] *adj* absorbente; (*book etc*) interesantísimo
absorption [əb'zɔːpʃən] *n* absorción *f*
abstain [əb'steɪn] *vi*: **to ~ (from)** abstenerse (de)
abstemious [əb'stiːmɪəs] *adj* abstemio
abstention [əb'stɛnʃən] *n* abstención *f*
abstinence ['æbstɪnəns] *n* abstinencia
abstract ['æbstrækt] *adj* abstracto
abstruse [æb'struːs] *adj* abstruso, oscuro
absurd [əb'səːd] *adj* absurdo

absurdity [əb'sə:dɪtɪ] *n* absurdo
ABTA ['æbtə] *n abbr* = **Association of British Travel Agents**
abundance [ə'bʌndəns] *n* abundancia
abundant [ə'bʌndənt] *adj* abundante
abuse [ə'bju:s] *n* (*insults*) insultos *mpl*, improperios *mpl*; (*misuse*) abuso ■ *vt* [ə'bju:z] (*ill-treat*) maltratar; (*take advantage of*) abusar de; **open to ~** sujeto al abuso
abusive [ə'bju:sɪv] *adj* ofensivo
abysmal [ə'bɪzməl] *adj* pésimo; (*ignorance*) supino
abyss [ə'bɪs] *n* abismo
AC *abbr* (= *alternating current*) corriente *f* alterna ■ *n abbr* (*US*) = **athletic club**
a/c *abbr* (*Banking etc*: = *account, account current*) c/c
academic [ækə'dɛmɪk] *adj* académico, universitario; (*pej*: *issue*) puramente teórico ■ *n* estudioso(-a); (*lecturer*) profesor(a) *m(f)* universitario(-a)
academic year *n* (*Univ*) año académico
academy [ə'kædəmɪ] *n* (*learned body*) academia; (*school*) instituto, colegio
academy of music *n* conservatorio
ACAS ['eɪkæs] *n abbr* (*Brit*: = *Advisory, Conciliation and Arbitration Service*) ≈ Instituto de Mediación, Arbitraje y Conciliación
accede [æk'si:d] *vi*: **to ~ to** acceder a
accelerate [æk'sɛləreɪt] *vt* acelerar ■ *vi* acelerarse
acceleration [æksɛlə'reɪʃən] *n* aceleración *f*
accelerator [æk'sɛləreɪtə^r] *n* (*Brit*) acelerador *m*
accent ['æksɛnt] *n* acento
accentuate [æk'sɛntjueɪt] *vt* (*syllable*) acentuar; (*need, difference etc*) recalcar, subrayar
accept [ək'sɛpt] *vt* aceptar; (*approve*) aprobar; (*concede*) admitir
acceptable [ək'sɛptəbl] *adj* aceptable, admisible
acceptance [ək'sɛptəns] *n* aceptación *f*; aprobación *f*; **to meet with general ~** recibir la aprobación general
access ['æksɛs] *n* acceso ■ *vt* (*Comput*) acceder a; **the burglars gained ~ through a window** los ladrones lograron entrar por una ventana; **to have ~ to** tener acceso a
accessible [æk'sɛsəbl] *adj* accesible
accession [æk'sɛʃən] *n* (*of monarch*) subida, ascenso; (*addition*) adquisición *f*
accessory [æk'sɛsərɪ] *n* accesorio; **toilet accessories** artículos *mpl* de tocador
access road *n* carretera de acceso; (*to motorway*) carril *m* de acceso
access time *n* (*Comput*) tiempo de acceso
accident ['æksɪdənt] *n* accidente *m*; (*chance*) casualidad *f*; **by ~** (*unintentionally*) sin querer; (*by coincidence*) por casualidad; **accidents at work** accidentes *mpl* de trabajo; **to meet with** *or* **to have an ~** tener *or* sufrir un accidente
accidental [æksɪ'dɛntl] *adj* accidental, fortuito
accidentally [æksɪ'dɛntəlɪ] *adv* sin querer; por casualidad
accident insurance *n* seguro contra accidentes
accident-prone ['æksɪdənt'prəun] *adj* propenso a los accidentes
acclaim [ə'kleɪm] *vt* aclamar, aplaudir ■ *n* aclamación *f*, aplausos *mpl*
acclamation [æklə'meɪʃən] *n* (*approval*) aclamación *f*; (*applause*) aplausos *mpl*; **by ~** por aclamación
acclimatize [ə'klaɪmətaɪz], **acclimate** (*US*) [ə'klaɪmət] *vt*: **to become acclimatized** aclimatarse
accolade ['ækəuleɪd] *n* (*prize*) premio; (*praise*) alabanzas *fpl*, homenaje *m*
accommodate [ə'kɔmədeɪt] *vt* alojar, hospedar; (*oblige, help*) complacer; **this car accommodates four people comfortably** en este coche caben cuatro personas cómodamente
accommodating [ə'kɔmədeɪtɪŋ] *adj* servicial, complaciente
accommodation *n*, **accommodations** (*US*) ■ *npl* [əkɔmə'deɪʃən(z)] alojamiento; **"~ to let"** "se alquilan habitaciones"; **seating ~** asientos *mpl*
accompaniment [ə'kʌmpənɪmənt] *n* acompañamiento
accompanist [ə'kʌmpənɪst] *n* (*Mus*) acompañante *m/f*
accompany [ə'kʌmpənɪ] *vt* acompañar
accomplice [ə'kʌmplɪs] *n* cómplice *m/f*
accomplish [ə'kʌmplɪʃ] *vt* (*finish*) acabar; (*aim*) realizar; (*task*) llevar a cabo
accomplished [ə'kʌmplɪʃt] *adj* experto, hábil
accomplishment [ə'kʌmplɪʃmənt] *n* (*ending*) conclusión *f*; (*bringing about*) realización *f*; (*skill*) talento
accord [ə'kɔ:d] *n* acuerdo ■ *vt* conceder; **of his own ~** espontáneamente; **with one ~** de *or* por común acuerdo
accordance [ə'kɔ:dəns] *n*: **in ~ with** de acuerdo con
according [ə'kɔ:dɪŋ]: **~ to** *prep* según; (*in accordance with*) conforme a; **it went ~ to plan** salió según lo previsto
accordingly [ə'kɔ:dɪŋlɪ] *adv* (*thus*) por consiguiente

accordion [ə'kɔ:dɪən] *n* acordeón *m*
accordionist [ə'kɔ:dɪənɪst] *n* acordeonista *m/f*
accost [ə'kɔst] *vt* abordar, dirigirse a
account [ə'kaunt] *n* (*Comm*) cuenta, factura; (*report*) informe *m*; **accounts** *npl* (*Comm*) cuentas *fpl*; **"~ payee only"** "únicamente en cuenta del beneficiario"; **your ~ is still outstanding** su cuenta está todavía pendiente; **of little ~** de poca importancia; **on ~** a crédito; **to buy sth on ~** comprar algo a crédito; **on no ~** bajo ningún concepto; **on ~ of** a causa de, por motivo de; **to take into ~, take ~ of** tener en cuenta; **to keep an ~ of** llevar la cuenta de; **to bring sb to ~ for sth/for having done sth** pedirle cuentas a algn por algo/por haber hecho algo
▸ **account for** *vt fus* (*explain*) explicar; **all the children were accounted for** no faltaba ningún niño
accountability [əkauntə'bɪlɪtɪ] *n* responsabilidad *f*
accountable [ə'kauntəbl] *adj*: **~ (for)** responsable (de)
accountancy [ə'kauntənsɪ] *n* contabilidad *f*
accountant [ə'kauntənt] *n* contable *m/f*, contador(a) *m(f)* (*LAm*)
accounting [ə'kauntɪŋ] *n* contabilidad *f*
accounting period *n* período contable, ejercicio financiero
account number *n* (*at bank etc*) número de cuenta
account payable *n* cuenta por pagar
account receivable *n* cuenta por cobrar
accoutrements [ə'ku:trəmənts] *npl* equipo, pertrechos *mpl*
accredited [ə'krɛdɪtɪd] *adj* (*agent etc*) autorizado, acreditado
accretion [ə'kri:ʃən] *n* acumulación *f*
accrue [ə'kru:] *vi* (*mount up*) aumentar, incrementarse; (*interest*) acumularse; **to ~ to** corresponder a; **accrued charges** gastos *mpl* vencidos; **accrued interest** interés *m* acumulado
accumulate [ə'kju:mjuleɪt] *vt* acumular ▪ *vi* acumularse
accumulation [əkju:mju'leɪʃən] *n* acumulación *f*
accuracy ['ækjurəsɪ] *n* exactitud *f*, precisión *f*
accurate ['ækjurɪt] *adj* (*number*) exacto; (*answer*) acertado; (*shot*) certero
accurately ['ækjurɪtlɪ] *adv* (*count, shoot, answer*) con precisión
accursed [ə'kə:st] *adj* maldito
accusation [ækju'zeɪʃən] *n* acusación *f*
accusative [ə'kju:zətɪv] *n* acusativo
accuse [ə'kju:z] *vt* acusar; (*blame*) echar la culpa a
accused [ə'kju:zd] *n* acusado(-a)
accuser [ə'kju:zə[r]] *n* acusador(a) *m(f)*
accustom [ə'kʌstəm] *vt* acostumbrar; **to ~ o.s. to sth** acostumbrarse a algo
accustomed [ə'kʌstəmd] *adj*: **~ to** acostumbrado a
AC/DC *abbr* (= *alternating current/direct current*) CA/CC
ACE [eɪs] *n abbr* = **American Council on Education**
ace [eɪs] *n* as *m*
acerbic [ə'sə:bɪk] *adj* acerbo; (*fig*) mordaz
acetate ['æsɪteɪt] *n* acetato
ache [eɪk] *n* dolor *m* ▪ *vi* doler; (*yearn*): **to ~ to do sth** ansiar hacer algo; **I've got stomach ~** *or* (*US*) **a stomach ~** tengo dolor de estómago, me duele el estómago; **my head aches** me duele la cabeza
achieve [ə'tʃi:v] *vt* (*reach*) alcanzar; (*realize*) realizar; (*victory, success*) lograr, conseguir
achievement [ə'tʃi:vmənt] *n* (*completion*) realización *f*; (*success*) éxito
Achilles heel [ə'kɪli:z-] *n* talón *m* de Aquiles
acid ['æsɪd] *adj* ácido; (*bitter*) agrio ▪ *n* ácido
acidity [ə'sɪdɪtɪ] *n* acidez *f*; (*Med*) acedía
acid rain *n* lluvia ácida
acid test *n* (*fig*) prueba de fuego
acknowledge [ək'nɔlɪdʒ] *vt* (*letter: also:* **acknowledge receipt of**) acusar recibo de; (*fact*) reconocer
acknowledgement [ək'nɔlɪdʒmənt] *n* acuse *m* de recibo; reconocimiento; **acknowledgements** (*in book*) agradecimientos *mpl*
ACLU *n abbr* (= *American Civil Liberties Union*) *unión americana por libertades civiles*
acme ['ækmɪ] *n* súmmum *m*
acne ['æknɪ] *n* acné *m*
acorn ['eɪkɔ:n] *n* bellota
acoustic [ə'ku:stɪk] *adj* acústico
acoustics [ə'ku:stɪks] *n, npl* acústica *sg*
acquaint [ə'kweɪnt] *vt*: **to ~ sb with sth** (*inform*) poner a algn al corriente de algo; **to be acquainted with** (*person*) conocer; (*fact*) estar al corriente de
acquaintance [ə'kweɪntəns] *n* conocimiento; (*person*) conocido(-a); **to make sb's ~** conocer a algn
acquiesce [ækwɪ'ɛs] *vi* (*agree*): **to ~ (in)** consentir (en), conformarse (con)
acquire [ə'kwaɪə[r]] *vt* adquirir
acquired [ə'kwaɪəd] *adj* adquirido; **it's an ~ taste** es algo a lo que uno se aficiona poco a poco
acquisition [ækwɪ'zɪʃən] *n* adquisición *f*
acquisitive [ə'kwɪzɪtɪv] *adj* codicioso

acquit [ə'kwɪt] *vt* absolver, exculpar; **to ~ o.s. well** defenderse bien
acquittal [ə'kwɪtl] *n* absolución *f*, exculpación *f*
acre ['eɪkə^r] *n* acre *m*
acreage ['eɪkərɪdʒ] *n* extensión *f*
acrid ['ækrɪd] *adj* (*smell*) acre; (*fig*) mordaz, sarcástico
acrimonious [ækrɪ'məunɪəs] *adj* (*remark*) mordaz; (*argument*) reñido
acrobat ['ækrəbæt] *n* acróbata *m/f*
acrobatic [ækrə'bætɪk] *adj* acrobático
acrobatics [ækrə'bætɪks] *npl* acrobacias *fpl*
acronym ['ækrənɪm] *n* siglas *fpl*
across [ə'krɔs] *prep* (*on the other side of*) al otro lado de; (*crosswise*) a través de ■ *adv* de un lado a otro, de una parte a otra a través, al través; **to run/swim ~** atravesar corriendo/nadando; **~ from** enfrente de; **the lake is 12 km ~** el lago tiene 12 km de ancho; **to get sth ~ to sb** (*fig*) hacer comprender algo a algn
acrylic [ə'krɪlɪk] *adj* acrílico
ACT *n abbr* (*= American College Test*) *prueba de aptitud estándar que por lo general hacen los estudiantes que quieren entrar a la universidad por primera vez*
act [ækt] *n* acto, acción *f*; (*Theat*) acto; (*in music-hall etc*) número; (*Law*) decreto, ley *f* ■ *vi* (*behave*) comportarse; (*Theat*) actuar; (*pretend*) fingir; (*take action*) tomar medidas ■ *vt* (*part*) hacer, representar; **~ of God** fuerza mayor; **it's only an ~** es cuento; **to catch sb in the ~** coger a algn in fraganti *or* con las manos en la masa; **to ~ Hamlet** hacer el papel de Hamlet; **to ~ as** actuar *or* hacer de; **acting in my capacity as chairman, I ...** en mi calidad de presidente, yo ...; **it acts as a deterrent** sirve para disuadir; **he's only acting** está fingiendo nada más
▸ **act on** *vt*: **to ~ on sth** actuar *or* obrar sobre algo
▸ **act out** *vt* (*event*) representar; (*fantasies*) realizar
acting ['æktɪŋ] *adj* suplente ■ *n*: **to do some ~** hacer algo de teatro; **he is the ~ manager** es el gerente en funciones
action ['ækʃən] *n* acción *f*, acto; (*Mil*) acción *f*; (*Law*) proceso, demanda; **to put a plan into ~** poner un plan en acción *or* en marcha; **killed in ~** (*Mil*) muerto en acto de servicio *or* en combate; **out of ~** (*person*) fuera de combate; (*thing*) averiado, descompuesto; **to take ~** tomar medidas; **to bring an ~ against sb** entablar *or* presentar demanda contra algn
action replay *n* (*TV*) repetición *f*
activate ['æktɪveɪt] *vt* activar
active ['æktɪv] *adj* activo, enérgico; (*volcano*) en actividad; **to play an ~ part in** colaborar activamente en
active duty *n* (*US Mil*) servicio activo
actively ['æktɪvlɪ] *adv* (*participate*) activamente; (*discourage, dislike*) enérgicamente
active partner *n* (*Comm*) socio activo
activist ['æktɪvɪst] *n* activista *m/f*
activity [æk'tɪvɪtɪ] *n* actividad *f*
actor ['æktə^r] *n* actor *m*
actress ['aektrɪs] *n* actriz *f*
actual ['æktjuəl] *adj* verdadero, real
actually ['æktjuəlɪ] *adv* realmente, en realidad
actuary ['æktjuərɪ] *n* (*Comm*) actuario(-a) (de seguros)
actuate ['æktjueɪt] *vt* mover, impulsar
acumen ['ækjumən] *n* perspicacia; **business ~** talento para los negocios
acupuncture ['ækjupʌŋktʃə^r] *n* acupuntura
acute [ə'kju:t] *adj* agudo
acutely [ə'kju:tlɪ] *adv* profundamente, extremadamente
AD *adv abbr* (*= Anno Domini*) A.C. ■ *n abbr* (*US Mil*) = **active duty**
ad [æd] *n abbr* = **advertisement**
adage ['ædɪdʒ] *n* refrán *m*, adagio
Adam ['ædəm] *n* Adán; **~'s apple** *n* nuez *f* (de la garganta)
adamant ['ædəmənt] *adj* firme, inflexible
adapt [ə'dæpt] *vt* adaptar; (*reconcile*) acomodar ■ *vi*: **to ~ (to)** adaptarse (a), ajustarse (a)
adaptability [ədæptə'bɪlɪtɪ] *n* (*of person, device etc*) adaptabilidad *f*
adaptable [ə'dæptəbl] *adj* (*device*) adaptable; (*person*) acomodadizo, que se adapta
adaptation [ædæp'teɪʃən] *n* adaptación *f*
adapter, adaptor [ə'dæptə^r] *n* (*Elec*) adaptador *m*
ADC *n abbr* (*Mil: = aide-de-camp*: *US: = Aid to Dependent Children*) *ayuda para niños dependientes*
add [æd] *vt* añadir, agregar (*esp LAm*); (*figures: also*: **add up**) sumar ■ *vi*: **to ~ to** (*increase*) aumentar, acrecentar
▸ **add on** *vt* añadir
▸ **add up** *vt* (*figures*) sumar ■ *vi* (*fig*): **it doesn't ~ up** no tiene sentido; **it doesn't ~ up to much** es poca cosa, no tiene gran *or* mucha importancia
addendum [ə'dɛndəm] *n* ad(d)enda *m or f*
adder ['ædə^r] *n* víbora
addict ['ædɪkt] *n* (*to drugs etc*) adicto(-a); (*enthusiast*) aficionado(-a), entusiasta *m/f*; **heroin ~** heroinómano(-a)
addicted [ə'dɪktɪd] *adj*: **to be ~ to** ser adicto a;

ser aficionado a
addiction [ə'dɪkʃən] *n* (*dependence*) hábito morboso; (*enthusiasm*) afición *f*
addictive [ə'dɪktɪv] *adj* que causa adicción
adding machine ['ædɪŋ-] *n* calculadora
Addis Ababa ['ædɪs'æbəbə] *n* Addis Abeba *m*
addition [ə'dɪʃən] *n* (*adding up*) adición *f*; (*thing added*) añadidura, añadido; **in ~** además, por añadidura; **in ~ to** además de
additional [ə'dɪʃənl] *adj* adicional
additive ['ædɪtɪv] *n* aditivo
addled ['ædld] *adj* (*Brit: rotten*) podrido; (*: fig*) confuso
address [ə'drɛs] *n* dirección *f*, señas *fpl*; (*speech*) discurso; (*Comput*) dirección *f* ■ *vt* (*letter*) dirigir; (*speak to*) dirigirse a, dirigir la palabra a; **form of ~** tratamiento; **absolute/relative ~** (*Comput*) dirección *f* absoluta/relativa; **to ~ o.s. to sth** (*issue, problem*) abordar
address book *n* agenda (de direcciones)
addressee [ædrɛ'si:] *n* destinatario(-a)
Aden ['eɪdn] *n* Adén *m*
adenoids ['ædɪnɔɪdz] *npl* vegetaciones *fpl* (adenoideas)
adept ['ædɛpt] *adj*: **~ at** experto *or* ducho en
adequacy ['ædɪkwəsɪ] *n* idoneidad *f*
adequate ['ædɪkwɪt] *adj* (*satisfactory*) adecuado; (*enough*) suficiente; **to feel ~ to a task** sentirse con fuerzas para una tarea
adequately ['ædɪkwɪtlɪ] *adv* adecuadamente
adhere [əd'hɪəʳ] *vi*: **to ~ to** adherirse a; (*fig: abide by*) observar
adherent [əd'hɪərənt] *n* partidario(-a)
adhesion [əd'hi:ʒən] *n* adherencia
adhesive [əd'hi:zɪv] *adj, n* adhesivo
adhesive tape *n* (*Brit*) cinta adhesiva; (*US Med*) esparadrapo
ad hoc [æd'hɔk] *adj* (*decision*) ad hoc; (*committee*) formado con fines específicos ■ *adv* ad hoc
adieu [ə'dju:] *excl* ¡vaya con Dios!
ad inf ['æd'ɪnf] *adv* hasta el infinito
adjacent [ə'dʒeɪsənt] *adj*: **~ to** contiguo a, inmediato a
adjective ['ædʒɛktɪv] *n* adjetivo
adjoin [ə'dʒɔɪn] *vt* estar contiguo a; (*land*) lindar con
adjoining [ə'dʒɔɪnɪŋ] *adj* contiguo, vecino
adjourn [ə'dʒə:n] *vt* aplazar; (*session*) suspender, levantar; (*US: end*) terminar ■ *vi* suspenderse; **the meeting has been adjourned till next week** se ha levantado la sesión hasta la semana que viene; **they adjourned to the pub** (*col*) se trasladaron al bar
adjournment [ə'dʒə:nmənt] *n* (*period*) suspensión *f*; (*postponement*) aplazamiento
Adjt. *abbr* (*Mil*) = **adjutant**
adjudicate [ə'dʒu:dɪkeɪt] *vi* sentenciar ■ *vt* (*contest*) hacer de árbitro en, juzgar; (*claim*) decidir
adjudication [ədʒu:dɪ'keɪʃən] *n* fallo
adjudicator [ə'dʒu:dɪkeɪtəʳ] *n* juez *m*, árbitro
adjust [ə'dʒʌst] *vt* (*change*) modificar; (*arrange*) arreglar; (*machine*) ajustar ■ *vi*: **to ~ (to)** adaptarse (a)
adjustable [ə'dʒʌstəbl] *adj* ajustable
adjuster [ə'dʒʌstəʳ] *n see* **loss adjuster**
adjustment [ə'dʒʌstmənt] *n* modificación *f*; arreglo; (*of prices, wages*) ajuste *m*
adjutant ['ædʒətənt] *n* ayudante *m*
ad-lib [æd'lɪb] *vt, vi* improvisar ■ *adv*: **ad lib** a voluntad, a discreción
adman ['ædmæn] *n* (*col*) publicista *m*
admin ['ædmin] *n abbr* (*col*) = **administration**
administer [əd'mɪnɪstəʳ] *vt* proporcionar; (*justice*) administrar
administration [ædmɪnɪ'streɪʃən] *n* administración *f*; (*government*) gobierno; **the A~** (*US*) la Administración
administrative [əd'mɪnɪstrətɪv] *adj* administrativo
administrator [əd'mɪnɪstreɪtəʳ] *n* administrador(a) *m(f)*
admirable ['ædmərəbl] *adj* admirable
admiral ['ædmərəl] *n* almirante *m*
Admiralty ['ædmərəltɪ] *n* (*Brit*) Ministerio de Marina, Almirantazgo
admiration [ædmə'reɪʃən] *n* admiración *f*
admire [əd'maɪəʳ] *vt* admirar
admirer [əd'maɪərəʳ] *n* admirador(a) *m(f)*; (*suitor*) pretendiente *m*
admiring [əd'maɪərɪŋ] *adj* (*expression*) de admiración
admissible [əd'mɪsəbl] *adj* admisible
admission [əd'mɪʃən] *n* (*to exhibition, nightclub*) entrada; (*enrolment*) ingreso; (*confession*) confesión *f*; **"~ free"** "entrada gratis *or* libre"; **by his own ~** él mismo reconoce que
admit [əd'mɪt] *vt* dejar entrar, dar entrada a; (*permit*) admitir; (*acknowledge*) reconocer; **"this ticket admits two"** "entrada para dos personas"; **children not admitted** se prohíbe la entrada a (los) menores de edad; **I must ~ that ...** debo reconocer que ...
▸ **admit of** *vt fus* admitir, permitir
▸ **admit to** *vt fus* confesarse culpable de
admittance [əd'mɪtəns] *n* entrada; **"no ~"** "se prohíbe la entrada", "prohibida la entrada"
admittedly [əd'mɪtədlɪ] *adv* de acuerdo que
admonish [əd'mɔnɪʃ] *vt* amonestar; (*advise*) aconsejar

ad nauseam [æd'nɔːsɪæm] *adv* hasta la saciedad
ado [ə'duː] *n*: **without (any) more ~** sin más (ni más)
adolescence [ædəu'lɛsns] *n* adolescencia
adolescent [ædəu'lɛsnt] *adj, n* adolescente *m/f*
adopt [ə'dɔpt] *vt* adoptar
adopted [ə'dɔptɪd] *adj* adoptivo
adoption [ə'dɔpʃən] *n* adopción *f*
adoptive [ə'dɔptɪv] *adj* adoptivo
adorable [ə'dɔːrəbl] *adj* adorable
adoration [ædə'reɪʃən] *n* adoración *f*
adore [ə'dɔːʳ] *vt* adorar
adoring [ə'dɔːrɪŋ] *adj*: **to his ~ public** a un público que le adora *or* le adoraba *etc*
adorn [ə'dɔːn] *vt* adornar
adornment [ə'dɔːnmənt] *n* adorno
ADP *n abbr* = **automatic data processing**
adrenalin [ə'drɛnəlɪn] *n* adrenalina
Adriatic [eɪdrɪ'ætɪk] *n*: **the ~ (Sea)** el (Mar) Adriático
adrift [ə'drɪft] *adv* a la deriva; **to come ~** (*boat*) ir a la deriva, soltarse; (*wire, rope etc*) soltarse
adroit [ə'drɔɪt] *adj* diestro, hábil
ADSL *n abbr* (= *asymmetrical digital subscriber line*) ADSL *m*
ADT *abbr* (*US*: = *Atlantic Daylight Time*) *hora de verano de Nueva York*
adulation [ædju'leɪʃən] *n* adulación *f*
adult ['ædʌlt] *n* adulto(-a) ■ *adj*: **~ education** educación *f* para adultos
adulterate [ə'dʌltəreɪt] *vt* adulterar
adulterer [ə'dʌltərəʳ] *n* adúltero
adulteress [ə'dʌltrɪs] *n* adúltera
adultery [ə'dʌltərɪ] *n* adulterio
adulthood ['ædʌlthud] *n* edad *f* adulta
advance [əd'vɑːns] *n* adelanto, progreso; (*money*) anticipo; (*Mil*) avance *m* ■ *vt* avanzar, adelantar; (*money*) anticipar ■ *vi* avanzar, adelantarse; **in ~** por adelantado; (*book*) con antelación; **to make advances to sb** (*gen*) ponerse en contacto con algn; (*amorously*) insinuarse a algn
advanced *adj* avanzado; (*Scol: studies*) adelantado; **~ in years** entrado en años
Advanced Higher *n* (*Scottish Scol*) *titulación que sigue al "Higher"*, ≈ Bachillerato
advancement [əd'vɑːnsmənt] *n* progreso; (*in rank*) ascenso
advance notice *n* previo aviso
advance payment *n* (*part sum*) anticipo
advantage [əd'vɑːntɪdʒ] *n* (*also Tennis*) ventaja; **to take ~ of** aprovecharse de; **it's to our ~** es ventajoso para nosotros
advantageous [ædvən'teɪdʒəs] *adj* ventajoso, provechoso
advent ['ædvənt] *n* advenimiento; **A~** Adviento
adventure [əd'vɛntʃəʳ] *n* aventura
adventure playground *n* parque *m* infantil
adventurous [əd'vɛntʃərəs] *adj* aventurero; (*bold*) arriesgado
adverb ['ædvəːb] *n* adverbio
adversary ['ædvəsərɪ] *n* adversario, contrario
adverse ['ædvəːs] *adj* adverso, contrario; **~ to** adverso a
adversity [əd'vəːsɪtɪ] *n* infortunio
advert ['ædvəːt] *n abbr* (*Brit*) = **advertisement**
advertise ['ædvətaɪz] *vi* hacer propaganda; (*in newspaper etc*) poner un anuncio, anunciarse; **to ~ for** (*staff*) buscar por medio de anuncios ■ *vt* anunciar
advertisement [əd'vəːtɪsmənt] *n* anuncio
advertiser ['ædvətaɪzəʳ] *n* anunciante *m/f*
advertising ['ædvətaɪzɪŋ] *n* publicidad *f*, propaganda; anuncios *mpl*
advertising agency *n* agencia de publicidad
advertising campaign *n* campaña de publicidad
advice [əd'vaɪs] *n* consejo, consejos *mpl*; (*notification*) aviso; **a piece of ~** un consejo; **to take legal ~** consultar a un abogado; **to ask (sb) for ~** pedir consejo (a algn)
advice note *n* (*Brit*) nota de aviso
advisable [əd'vaɪzəbl] *adj* aconsejable, conveniente
advise [əd'vaɪz] *vt* aconsejar; **to ~ sb of sth** (*inform*) informar a algn de algo; **to ~ sb against sth/doing sth** desaconsejar algo a algn/aconsejar a algn que no haga algo; **you will be well/ill advised to go** deberías/no deberías ir
advisedly [əd'vaɪzɪdlɪ] *adv* deliberadamente
adviser [əd'vaɪzəʳ] *n* consejero(-a); (*business adviser*) asesor(a) *m(f)*
advisory [əd'vaɪzərɪ] *adj* consultivo; **in an ~ capacity** como asesor
advocate ['ædvəkeɪt] *vt* (*argue for*) abogar por; (*give support to*) ser partidario de ■ *n* ['ædvəkɪt] abogado(-a)
advt. *abbr* = **advertisement**
AEA *n abbr* (*Brit*: = *Atomic Energy Authority*) *consejo de energía nuclear*; (*Brit Scol*: = *Advanced Extension Award*) *titulación opcional para los alumnos mejor preparados de los "A levels"*
AEC *n abbr* (*US*: = *Atomic Energy Commission*) AEC *f*
Aegean [iː'dʒiːən] *n*: **the ~ (Sea)** el (Mar) Egeo
aegis ['iːdʒɪs] *n*: **under the ~ of** bajo la tutela de
aeon ['iːən] *n* eón *m*
aerial ['ɛərɪəl] *n* antena ■ *adj* aéreo
aerie ['ɛərɪ] *n* (*US*) aguilera

aero- ['ɛərəu] *pref* aero-
aerobatics [ɛərəu'bætɪks] *npl* acrobacia aérea
aerobics [ɛə'rəubɪks] *nsg* aerobic *m*, aerobismo (*LAm*)
aerodrome ['ɛərədrəum] *n* (*Brit*) aeródromo
aerodynamic [ɛərəudaɪ'næmɪk] *adj* aerodinámico
aeronautics [ɛərəu'nɔ:tɪks] *nsg* aeronáutica
aeroplane ['ɛərəpleɪn] *n* (*Brit*) avión *m*
aerosol ['ɛərəsɔl] *n* aerosol *m*
aerospace industry ['ɛərəuspeɪs-] *n* industria aeroespacial
aesthetic [i:s'θɛtɪk] *adj* estético
aesthetics [i:s'θɛtɪks] *npl* estética
afar [ə'fɑ:ʳ] *adv* lejos; **from ~** desde lejos
AFB *n abbr* (*US*) = **Air Force Base**
AFDC *n abbr* (*US: = Aid to Families with Dependent Children) ayuda a familias con hijos menores*
affable ['æfəbl] *adj* afable
affair [ə'fɛəʳ] *n* asunto; (*also:* **love affair**) aventura *f* amorosa; **affairs** (*business*) asuntos *mpl*; **the Watergate ~** el asunto (de) Watergate
affect [ə'fɛkt] *vt* afectar, influir en; (*move*) conmover
affectation [æfɛk'teɪʃən] *n* afectación *f*
affected [ə'fɛktɪd] *adj* afectado
affection [ə'fɛkʃən] *n* afecto, cariño
affectionate [ə'fɛkʃənɪt] *adj* afectuoso, cariñoso
affectionately [ə'fɛkʃənɪtlɪ] *adv* afectuosamente
affidavit [æfɪ'deɪvɪt] *n* (*Law*) declaración *f* jurada
affiliated [ə'fɪlɪeɪtɪd] *adj* afiliado; **~ company** empresa *or* compañía filial *or* subsidiaria
affinity [ə'fɪnɪtɪ] *n* afinidad *f*
affirm [ə'fə:m] *vt* afirmar
affirmation [æfə'meɪʃən] *n* afirmación *f*
affirmative [ə'fə:mətɪv] *adj* afirmativo
affix [ə'fɪks] *vt* (*signature*) estampar; (*stamp*) pegar
afflict [ə'flɪkt] *vt* afligir
affliction [ə'flɪkʃən] *n* enfermedad *f*, aflicción *f*
affluence ['æfluəns] *n* opulencia, riqueza
affluent ['aefluənt] *adj* adinerado, acaudalado; **the ~ society** la sociedad opulenta
afford [ə'fɔ:d] *vt* poder permitirse; (*provide*) proporcionar; **can we ~ a car?** ¿podemos permitirnos el gasto de comprar un coche?
affordable [ə'fɔ:dəbl] *adj* asequible
affray [ə'freɪ] *n* refriega, reyerta
affront [ə'frʌnt] *n* afrenta, ofensa
affronted [ə'frʌntɪd] *adj* ofendido
Afghan ['æfgæn] *adj, n* afgano(-a) *m(f)*
Afghanistan [æf'gænɪstæn] *n* Afganistán *m*
afield [ə'fi:ld] *adv*: **far ~** muy lejos
AFL-CIO *n abbr* (*US: = American Federation of Labor and Congress of Industrial Organizations) confederación sindicalista*
afloat [ə'fləut] *adv* (*floating*) a flote; (*at sea*) en el mar
afoot [ə'fut] *adv*: **there is something ~** algo se está tramando
aforesaid [ə'fɔ:sɛd] *adj* susodicho; (*Comm*) mencionado anteriormente
afraid [ə'freɪd] *adj*: **to be ~ of** (*person*) tener miedo a; (*thing*) tener miedo de; **to be ~ to** tener miedo de, temer; **I am ~ that** me temo que; **I'm ~ so** ¡me temo que sí!, ¡lo siento, pero es así!; **I'm ~ not** me temo que no
afresh [ə'frɛʃ] *adv* de nuevo, otra vez
Africa ['æfrɪkə] *n* África
African ['æfrɪkən] *adj, n* africano(-a) *m(f)*
Afrikaans [æfrɪ'kɑ:ns] *n* africaans *m*
Afrikaner [æfrɪ'kɑ:nəʳ] *n* africánder *m/f*
Afro-American ['æfrəuə'mɛrɪkən] *adj, n* afroamericano(-a) *m(f)*
AFT *n abbr* (*= American Federation of Teachers*) *sindicato de profesores*
aft [ɑ:ft] *adv* (*be*) en popa; (*go*) a popa
after ['ɑ:ftəʳ] *prep* (*time*) después de; (*place, order*) detrás de, tras ■ *adv* después ■ *conj* después (de) que; **what/who are you ~?** ¿qué/a quién buscas?; **the police are ~ him** la policía le está buscando; **~ having done/he left** después de haber hecho/después de que se marchó; **~ dinner** después de cenar *or* comer; **the day ~ tomorrow** pasado mañana; **to ask ~ sb** preguntar por algn; **~ all** después de todo, al fin y al cabo; **~ you!** ¡Vd primero!; **quarter ~ two** (*US*) las dos y cuarto
afterbirth ['ɑ:ftəbə:θ] *n* placenta
aftercare ['ɑ:ftəkɛəʳ] *n* (*Med*) asistencia postoperatoria
after-effects ['ɑ:ftərɪfɛkts] *npl* secuelas *fpl*, efectos *mpl*
afterlife ['ɑ:ftəlaɪf] *n* vida después de la muerte
aftermath ['ɑ:ftəmɑ:θ] *n* consecuencias *fpl*, resultados *mpl*
afternoon [ɑ:ftə'nu:n] *n* tarde *f*; **good ~!** ¡buenas tardes!
afters ['ɑ:ftəz] *n* (*col: dessert*) postre *m*
after-sales service [ɑ:ftə'seɪlz-] *n* (*Brit Comm: for car, washing machine etc*) servicio de asistencia pos-venta
after-shave ['ɑ:ftəʃeɪv], **after-shave lotion** *n* loción *f* para después del afeitado, aftershave *m*

aftershock ['ɑ:ftəʃɔk] *n* (*of earthquake*) pequeño temblor *m* posterior
aftersun ['ɑ:ftəsʌn], **aftersun lotion** *n* after-sun *m inv*
aftertaste ['ɑ:ftəteɪst] *n* regusto
afterthought ['ɑ:ftəθɔ:t] *n* ocurrencia (tardía)
afterwards ['ɑ:ftəwədz] *adv* después, más tarde
again [ə'gɛn] *adv* otra vez, de nuevo; **to do sth ~** volver a hacer algo; **~ and ~** una y otra vez; **now and ~** de vez en cuando
against [ə'gɛnst] *prep* (*opposed*) en contra de; (*close to*) contra, junto a; **I was leaning ~ the desk** estaba apoyado en el escritorio; **(as) ~** frente a
age [eɪdʒ] *n* edad *f*; (*old age*) vejez *f*; (*period*) época ■ *vi* envejecer(se) ■ *vt* envejecer; **what ~ is he?** ¿qué edad *or* cuántos años tiene?; **he is 20 years of ~** tiene 20 años; **under ~** menor de edad; **to come of ~** llegar a la mayoría de edad; **it's been ages since I saw you** hace siglos que no te veo
aged [eɪdʒd] *adj*: **~ 10** de 10 años de edad ■ *npl* ['eɪdʒɪd]: **the ~** los ancianos
age group *n*: **to be in the same ~** tener la misma edad; **the 40 to 50 ~** las personas de 40 a 50 años
ageing ['eɪdʒɪŋ] *adj* que envejece; (*pej*) en declive ■ *n* envejecimiento
ageless ['eɪdʒlɪs] *adj* (*eternal*) eterno; (*ever young*) siempre joven
age limit *n* límite *m* de edad, edad *f* tope
agency ['eɪdʒənsɪ] *n* agencia; **through** *or* **by the ~ of** por medio de
agenda [ə'dʒɛndə] *n* orden *m* del día; **on the ~** (*Comm*) en el orden del día
agent ['eɪdʒənt] *n* (*gen*) agente *m/f*; (*representative*) representante *m/f* delegado(-a)
aggravate ['ægrəveɪt] *vt* agravar; (*annoy*) irritar, exasperar
aggravating ['ægrəveɪtɪŋ] *adj* irritante, molesto
aggravation [ægrə'veɪʃən] *n* agravamiento
aggregate ['ægrɪgeɪt] *n* conjunto
aggression [ə'grɛʃən] *n* agresión *f*
aggressive [ə'grɛsɪv] *adj* agresivo; (*vigorous*) enérgico
aggressiveness [ə'grɛsɪvnɪs] *n* agresividad *f*
aggressor [ə'grɛsə^r] *n* agresor(a) *m(f)*
aggrieved [ə'gri:vd] *adj* ofendido, agraviado
aggro ['ægrəu] *n* (*col: physical violence*) bronca; (*bad feeling*) mal rollo; (*hassle*) rollo, movida
aghast [ə'gɑ:st] *adj* horrorizado
agile ['ædʒaɪl] *adj* ágil
agility [ə'dʒɪlɪtɪ] *n* agilidad *f*
agitate ['ædʒɪteɪt] *vt* (*shake*) agitar; (*trouble*) inquietar; **to ~ for** hacer campaña en pro de *or* en favor de
agitated ['ædʒɪteɪtɪd] *adj* agitado
agitator ['ædʒɪteɪtə^r] *n* agitador(a) *m(f)*
AGM *n abbr* = **annual general meeting**
agnostic [æg'nɔstɪk] *adj, n* agnóstico(-a) *m(f)*
ago [ə'gəu] *adv*: **two days ~** hace dos días; **not long ~** hace poco; **how long ~?** ¿hace cuánto tiempo?; **as long ~ as 1980** ya en 1980
agog [ə'gɔg] *adj* (*anxious*) ansioso; (*excited*): **(all) ~ (for)** (todo) emocionado (por)
agonize ['ægənaɪz] *vi*: **to ~ (over)** atormentarse (por)
agonized ['ægənaɪzd] *adj* angustioso
agonizing ['ægənaɪzɪŋ] *adj* (*pain*) atroz; (*suspense*) angustioso
agony ['ægənɪ] *n* (*pain*) dolor *m* atroz; (*distress*) angustia; **to be in ~** retorcerse de dolor
agony aunt *n* (*Brit col*) consejera sentimental
agony column *n* consultorio sentimental
agree [ə'gri:] *vt* (*price*) acordar, quedar en ■ *vi* (*statements etc*) coincidir, concordar; **to ~ (with)** (*person*) estar de acuerdo (con), ponerse de acuerdo (con); **to ~ to do** aceptar hacer; **to ~ to sth** consentir en algo; **to ~ that** (*admit*) estar de acuerdo en que; **it was agreed that ...** se acordó que ...; **garlic doesn't ~ with me** el ajo no me sienta bien
agreeable [ə'gri:əbl] *adj* agradable; (*person*) simpático; (*willing*) de acuerdo, conforme
agreeably [ə'gri:əblɪ] *adv* agradablemente
agreed [ə'gri:d] *adj* (*time, place*) convenido
agreement [ə'gri:mənt] *n* acuerdo; (*Comm*) contrato; **in ~** de acuerdo, conforme; **by mutual ~** de común acuerdo
agricultural [ægrɪ'kʌltʃərəl] *adj* agrícola
agriculture ['ægrɪkʌltʃə^r] *n* agricultura
aground [ə'graund] *adv*: **to run ~** encallar, embarrancar
ahead [ə'hɛd] *adv* delante; **~ of** delante de; (*fig: schedule etc*) antes de; **~ of time** antes de la hora; **to be ~ of sb** (*fig*) llevar ventaja *or* la delantera a algn; **go right** *or* **straight ~** siga adelante; **they were (right) ~ of us** iban (justo) delante de nosotros
ahoy [ə'hɔɪ] *excl* ¡oiga!
AI *n abbr* (= *Amnesty International*) (*Comput*) = **artificial intelligence**
AIB *n abbr* (*Brit*: = *Accident Investigation Bureau*) *oficina de investigación de accidentes*
AID *n abbr* (= *artificial insemination by donor*) inseminación artificial por donante; (*US*: = *Agency for International Development*) Agencia Internacional para el Desarrollo
aid [eɪd] *n* ayuda, auxilio ■ *vt* ayudar, auxiliar; **in ~ of** a beneficio de; **with the ~ of** con la ayuda de; **to ~ and abet** (*Law*) ser cómplice

aide [eɪd] *n* (*Pol*) ayudante *m/f*
AIDS [eɪdz] *n abbr* (= *acquired immune (or immuno-) deficiency syndrome*) SIDA *m*, sida *m*
AIH *n abbr* (= *artificial insemination by husband*) *inseminación artificial por esposo*
ailing ['eɪlɪŋ] *adj* (*person, economy*) enfermizo
ailment ['eɪlmənt] *n* enfermedad *f*, achaque *m*
aim [eɪm] *vt* (*gun*) apuntar; (*missile, remark*) dirigir; (*blow*) asestar ■ *vi* (*also*: **take aim**) apuntar ■ *n* puntería; (*objective*) propósito, meta; **to ~ at** (*objective*) aspirar a, pretender; **to ~ to do** tener como objetivo hacer, aspirar a hacer
aimless ['eɪmlɪs] *adj* sin propósito, sin objeto
aimlessly ['eɪmlɪslɪ] *adv* sin rumbo fijo
ain't [eɪnt] (*col*) = **am not; aren't; isn't**
air [ɛəʳ] *n* aire *m*; (*appearance*) aspecto ■ *vt* (*room*) ventilar; (*clothes, bed, grievances, ideas*) airear; (*views*) hacer público ■ *cpd* aéreo; **to throw sth into the ~** (*ball etc*) lanzar algo al aire; **by ~** (*travel*) en avión; **to be on the ~** (*Radio, TV: programme*) estarse emitiendo; (*: station*) estar emitiendo
airbag ['ɛəbæg] *n* airbag *m inv*
air base *n* (*Mil*) base *f* aérea
air bed *n* (*Brit*) colchoneta inflable *or* neumática
airborne ['ɛəbɔːn] *adj* (*in the air*) en el aire; (*Mil*) aerotransportado; **as soon as the plane was ~** tan pronto como el avión estuvo en el aire
air cargo *n* carga aérea
air-conditioned ['ɛəkən'dɪʃənd] *adj* climatizado
air conditioning [-kən'dɪʃənɪŋ] *n* aire *m* acondicionado
air-cooled ['ɛəkuːld] *adj* refrigerado por aire
aircraft ['ɛəkrɑːft] *n pl inv* avión *m*
aircraft carrier *n* porta(a)viones *m inv*
air cushion *n* cojín *m* de aire; (*Aviat*) colchón *m* de aire
airdrome ['ɛədrəum] *n* (*US*) aeródromo
airfield ['ɛəfiːld] *n* campo de aviación
Air Force *n* fuerzas aéreas *fpl*, aviación *f*
air freight *n* flete *m* por avión
air freshener *n* ambientador *m*
air gun *n* escopeta de aire comprimido
air hostess (*Brit*) *n* azafata, aeromoza (*LAm*)
airily ['ɛərɪlɪ] *adv* muy a la ligera
airing ['ɛərɪŋ] *n*: **to give an ~ to** (*linen*) airear; (*room*) ventilar; (*fig: ideas etc*) airear, someter a discusión
air letter *n* (*Brit*) carta aérea
airlift ['ɛəlɪft] *n* puente *m* aéreo
airline ['ɛəlaɪn] *n* línea aérea
airliner ['ɛəlaɪnəʳ] *n* avión *m* de pasajeros
airlock ['ɛəlɔk] *n* (*in pipe*) esclusa de aire
airmail ['ɛəmeɪl] *n*: **by ~** por avión
air mattress *n* colchón *m* inflable *or* neumático
airplane ['ɛəpleɪn] *n* (*US*) avión *m*
air pocket *n* bolsa de aire
airport ['ɛəpɔːt] *n* aeropuerto
air rage *n conducta agresiva de pasajeros a bordo de un avión*
air raid *n* ataque *m* aéreo
air rifle *n* escopeta de aire comprimido
airsick ['ɛəsɪk] *adj*: **to be ~** marearse (en avión)
airspeed ['ɛəspiːd] *n* velocidad *f* de vuelo
airstrip ['ɛəstrɪp] *n* pista de aterrizaje
air terminal *n* terminal *f*
airtight ['ɛətaɪt] *adj* hermético
air time *n* (*Radio, TV*) tiempo en antena
air traffic control *n* control *m* de tráfico aéreo
air traffic controller *n* controlador(a) *m(f)* aéreo(-a)
airway ['ɛəweɪ] *n* (*Aviat*) vía aérea; (*Anat*) vía respiratoria
airy ['ɛərɪ] *adj* (*room*) bien ventilado; (*manners*) despreocupado
aisle [aɪl] *n* (*of church*) nave *f* lateral; (*of theatre, plane*) pasillo
ajar [ə'dʒɑːʳ] *adj* entreabierto
AK *abbr* (*US*) = **Alaska**
aka *abbr* (= *also known as*) alias
akin [ə'kɪn] *adj*: **~ to** semejante a
AL *abbr* (*US*) = **Alabama**
ALA *n abbr* = **American Library Association**
Ala. *abbr* (*US*) = **Alabama**
alabaster ['æləbɑːstəʳ] *n* alabastro
à la carte [ælæ'kɑːt] *adv* a la carta
alacrity [ə'lækrɪtɪ] *n*: **with ~** con la mayor prontitud
alarm [ə'lɑːm] *n* alarma; (*anxiety*) inquietud *f* ■ *vt* asustar, alarmar
alarm clock *n* despertador *m*
alarmed [ə'lɑːmd] *adj* (*person*) alarmado, asustado; (*house, car etc*) con alarma
alarming [ə'lɑːmɪŋ] *adj* alarmante
alarmingly [ə'lɑːmɪŋlɪ] *adv* de forma alarmante; **~ quickly** a una velocidad alarmante
alarmist [ə'lɑːmɪst] *n* alarmista *m/f*
alas [ə'læs] *adv* desgraciadamente ■ *excl* ¡ay!
Alas. *abbr* (*US*) = **Alaska**
Alaska [ə'læskə] *n* Alaska
Albania [æl'beɪnɪə] *n* Albania
Albanian [æl'beɪnɪən] *adj* albanés(-esa) ■ *n* albanés(-esa) *m(f)*; (*Ling*) albanés *m*
albatross ['ælbətrɔs] *n* albatros *m*
albeit [ɔːl'biːɪt] *conj* (*although*) aunque

album ['ælbəm] *n* álbum *m*; (*L.P.*) elepé *m*
albumen ['ælbjumɪn] *n* albúmina
alchemy ['ælkɪmɪ] *n* alquimia
alcohol ['ælkəhɔl] *n* alcohol *m*
alcohol-free *adj* sin alcohol
alcoholic [ælkə'hɔlɪk] *adj, n* alcohólico(-a) *m(f)*
alcoholism ['ælkəhɔlɪzəm] *n* alcoholismo
alcove ['ælkəuv] *n* nicho, hueco
Ald. *abbr* = **alderman**
alderman ['ɔ:ldəmən] *n* concejal *m*
ale [eɪl] *n* cerveza
alert [ə'lə:t] *adj* alerta *inv*; (*sharp*) despierto, despabilado ■ *n* alerta *m*, alarma ■ *vt* poner sobre aviso; **to ~ sb (to sth)** poner sobre aviso *or* alertar a algn (de algo); **to ~ sb to the dangers of sth** poner sobre aviso *or* alertar a algn de los peligros de algo; **to be on the ~** estar alerta *or* sobre aviso
alertness [ə'lə:tnɪs] *n* vigilancia
Aleutian Islands [ə'lu:ʃən-] *npl* Islas *fpl* Aleutianas
A level *n abbr* (*Brit Scol*: = *Advanced level*) ≈ Bachillerato
Alexandria [ælɪg'zɑ:ndrɪə] *n* Alejandría
alfresco [æl'frɛskəu] *adj, adv* al aire libre
algebra ['ældʒɪbrə] *n* álgebra
Algeria [æl'dʒɪərɪə] *n* Argelia
Algerian [æl'dʒɪərɪən] *adj, n* argelino(-a) *m(f)*
Algiers [æl'dʒɪəz] *n* Argel *m*
algorithm ['ælgərɪðəm] *n* algoritmo
alias ['eɪlɪəs] *adv* alias, conocido por ■ *n* alias *m*
alibi ['ælɪbaɪ] *n* coartada
alien ['eɪlɪən] *n* (*foreigner*) extranjero(-a) ■ *adj*: **~ to** ajeno a
alienate ['eɪlɪəneɪt] *vt* enajenar, alejar
alienation [eɪlɪə'neɪʃən] *n* alejamiento *m*
alight [ə'laɪt] *adj* ardiendo ■ *vi* apearse, bajar
align [ə'laɪn] *vt* alinear
alignment [ə'laɪnmənt] *n* alineación *f*; **the desks are out of ~** los pupitres no están bien alineados
alike [ə'laɪk] *adj* semejantes, iguales ■ *adv* igualmente, del mismo modo; **to look ~** parecerse
alimony ['ælɪmənɪ] *n* (*Law*) pensión *f* alimenticia
alive [ə'laɪv] *adj* (*gen*) vivo; (*lively*) activo
alkali ['ælkəlaɪ] *n* álcali *m*

KEYWORD

all [ɔ:l] *adj* todo(-a) *sg*, todos(-as) *pl*; **all day** todo el día; **all night** toda la noche; **all men** todos los hombres; **all five came** vinieron los cinco; **all the books** todos los libros; **all the time/his life** todo el tiempo/toda su vida; **for all their efforts** a pesar de todos sus esfuerzos
■ *pron* **1** todo; **I ate it all, I ate all of it** me lo comí todo; **all of them** todos (ellos); **all of us went** fuimos todos; **all the boys went** fueron todos los chicos; **is that all?** ¿eso es todo?, ¿algo más?; (*in shop*) ¿algo más?, ¿alguna cosa más?
2 (*in phrases*): **above all** sobre todo; por encima de todo; **after all** después de todo; **at all**: **anything at all** lo que sea; **not at all** (*in answer to question*) en absoluto; (*in answer to thanks*) ¡de nada!, ¡no hay de qué!; **I'm not at all tired** no estoy nada cansado(-a); **anything at all will do** cualquier cosa viene bien; **all in all** a fin de cuentas
■ *adv*: **all alone** completamente solo(-a); **to be/feel all in** estar rendido; **it's not as hard as all that** no es tan difícil como lo pintas; **all the more/the better** tanto más/mejor; **all but** casi; **the score is two all** están empatados a dos

all-around ['ɔ:lə'raund] *adj* (*US*) = **all-round**
allay [ə'leɪ] *vt* (*fears*) aquietar; (*pain*) aliviar
all clear *n* (*after attack etc*) fin *m* de la alerta; (*fig*) luz *f* verde
allegation [ælɪ'geɪʃən] *n* alegato
allege [ə'lɛdʒ] *vt* pretender; **he is alleged to have said ...** se afirma que él dijo ...
alleged [ə'lɛdʒd] *adj* supuesto, presunto
allegedly [ə'lɛdʒɪdlɪ] *adv* supuestamente, según se afirma
allegiance [ə'li:dʒəns] *n* lealtad *f*
allegory ['ælɪgərɪ] *n* alegoría
all-embracing ['ɔ:ləm'breɪsɪŋ] *adj* universal
allergic [ə'lə:dʒɪk] *adj*: **~ to** alérgico a
allergy ['ælədʒɪ] *n* alergia
alleviate [ə'li:vɪeɪt] *vt* aliviar
alleviation [əli:vɪ'eɪʃən] *n* alivio
alley ['ælɪ] *n* (*street*) callejuela; (*in garden*) paseo
alleyway ['ælɪweɪ] *n* callejón *m*
alliance [ə'laɪəns] *n* alianza
allied ['ælaɪd] *adj* aliado; (*related*) relacionado
alligator ['ælɪgeɪtə^r] *n* caimán *m*
all-important ['ɔ:lɪm'pɔ:tənt] *adj* de suma importancia
all-in ['ɔ:lɪn] *adj* (*Brit*: *also adv*: *charge*) todo incluido
all-in wrestling *n* lucha libre
alliteration [əlɪtə'reɪʃən] *n* aliteración *f*
all-night ['ɔ:l'naɪt] *adj* (*café*) abierto toda la noche; (*party*) que dura toda la noche
allocate ['æləkeɪt] *vt* (*share out*) repartir; (*devote*) asignar

allocation [ælə'keɪʃən] *n* (*of money*) ración *f*, cuota; (*distribution*) reparto
allot [ə'lɔt] *vt* asignar; **in the allotted time** en el tiempo asignado
allotment [ə'lɔtmənt] *n* porción *f*; (*garden*) parcela
all-out ['ɔːlaut] *adj* (*effort etc*) supremo ■ *adv*: **all out** con todas las fuerzas, a fondo
allow [ə'lau] *vt* (*permit*) permitir, dejar; (*a claim*) admitir; (*sum to spend, time estimated*) dar, conceder; (*concede*): **to ~ that** reconocer que; **to ~ sb to do** permitir a algn hacer; **smoking is not allowed** prohibido *or* se prohíbe fumar; **he is allowed to ...** se le permite ...; **we must ~ three days for the journey** debemos dejar tres días para el viaje
▸ **allow for** *vt fus* tener en cuenta
allowance [ə'lauəns] *n* concesión *f*; (*payment*) subvención *f*, pensión *f*; (*discount*) descuento, rebaja; **to make allowances for** (*person*) disculpar a; (*thing*: *take into account*) tener en cuenta
alloy ['ælɔɪ] *n* aleación *f*
all right *adv* (*feel, work*) bien; (*as answer*) ¡de acuerdo!, ¡está bien!
all-round ['ɔːl'raund] *adj* completo; (*view*) amplio
all-rounder ['ɔːl'raundəʳ] *n*: **to be a good ~** ser una persona que hace de todo
allspice ['ɔːlspaɪs] *n* pimienta inglesa *or* de Jamaica
all-time ['ɔːl'taɪm] *adj* (*record*) de todos los tiempos
allude [ə'luːd] *vi*: **to ~ to** aludir a
alluring [ə'ljuərɪŋ] *adj* seductor(a), atractivo
allusion [ə'luːʒən] *n* referencia, alusión *f*
ally *n* ['ælaɪ] aliado(-a) ■ *vt* [ə'laɪ]: **to ~ o.s. with** aliarse con
almanac ['ɔːlmənæk] *n* almanaque *m*
almighty [ɔːl'maɪtɪ] *adj* todopoderoso
almond ['ɑːmənd] *n* (*fruit*) almendra; (*tree*) almendro
almost ['ɔːlməust] *adv* casi; **he ~ fell** casi *or* por poco se cae
alms [ɑːmz] *npl* limosna *sg*
aloft [ə'lɔft] *adv* arriba
alone [ə'ləun] *adj* solo ■ *adv* sólo, solamente; **to leave sb ~** dejar a algn en paz; **to leave sth ~** no tocar algo; **let ~ ...** y mucho menos, y no digamos ...
along [ə'lɔŋ] *prep* a lo largo de, por ■ *adv*: **is he coming ~ with us?** ¿viene con nosotros?; **he was limping ~** iba cojeando; **~ with** junto con; **all ~** (*all the time*) desde el principio
alongside [ə'lɔŋ'saɪd] *prep* al lado de ■ *adv* (*Naut*) de costado; **we brought our boat ~** atracamos nuestro barco
aloof [ə'luːf] *adj* distante ■ *adv*: **to stand ~** mantenerse a distancia
aloud [ə'laud] *adv* en voz alta
alphabet ['ælfəbɛt] *n* alfabeto
alphabetical [ælfə'bɛtɪkəl] *adj* alfabético; **in ~ order** por orden alfabético
alphanumeric [ælfənjuː'mɛrɪk] *adj* alfanumérico
alpine ['ælpaɪn] *adj* alpino, alpestre
Alps [ælps] *npl*: **the ~** los Alpes
already [ɔːl'rɛdɪ] *adv* ya
alright ['ɔːl'raɪt] *adv* (*Brit*) = **all right**
Alsatian [æl'seɪʃən] *n* (*dog*) pastor *m* alemán
also ['ɔːlsəu] *adv* también, además
Alta. *abbr* (*Canada*) = **Alberta**
altar ['ɔltəʳ] *n* altar *m*
alter ['ɔltəʳ] *vt* cambiar, modificar ■ *vi* cambiarse, modificarse
alteration [ɔltə'reɪʃən] *n* cambio, modificación *f*; **alterations** *npl* (*Arch*) reformas *fpl*; (*Sewing*) arreglos *mpl*; **timetable subject to ~** el horario puede cambiar
altercation [ɔltə'keɪʃən] *n* altercado
alternate [ɔl'təːnɪt] *adj* alterno ■ *vi* ['ɔltəneɪt]: **to ~ (with)** alternar (con); **on ~ days** en días alternos
alternately [ɔl'təːnɪtlɪ] *adv* alternativamente, por turno
alternating ['ɔltəneɪtɪŋ] *adj* (*current*) alterno
alternative [ɔl'təːnətɪv] *adj* alternativo ■ *n* alternativa
alternatively [ɔl'təːnətɪvlɪ] *adv*: **~ one could ...** por otra parte se podría ...
alternative medicine *n* medicina alternativa
alternator ['ɔltəneɪtəʳ] *n* (*Aut*) alternador *m*
although [ɔːl'ðəu] *conj* aunque, si bien
altitude ['æltɪtjuːd] *n* altitud *f*, altura
altitude sickness *n* mal *m* de altura, soroche *m* (*LAm*)
alto ['æltəu] *n* (*female*) contralto *f*; (*male*) alto
altogether [ɔːltə'gɛðəʳ] *adv* completamente, del todo; (*on the whole, in all*) en total, en conjunto; **how much is that ~?** ¿cuánto es todo *or* en total?
altruism ['æltruɪzəm] *n* altruismo
altruistic [æltru'ɪstɪk] *adj* altruista
aluminium [ælju'mɪnɪəm], **aluminum** (*US*) [ə'luːmɪnəm] *n* aluminio
always ['ɔːlweɪz] *adv* siempre
Alzheimer's ['æltshaɪməz] *n* (*also*: **Alzheimer's disease**) enfermedad *f* de Alzheimer
AM *abbr* (= *amplitude modulation*) A.M. *f* ■ *n abbr* (*Pol*: *in Wales*) = **Assembly Member**
am [æm] *vb see* **be**

a.m. *adv abbr* (*= ante meridiem*) de la mañana
AMA *n abbr* = **American Medical Association**
amalgam [ə'mælgəm] *n* amalgama
amalgamate [ə'mælgəmeɪt] *vi* amalgamarse ■ *vt* amalgamar
amalgamation [əmælgə'meɪʃən] *n* (*Comm*) fusión *f*
amass [ə'mæs] *vt* amontonar, acumular
amateur ['æmətəʳ] *n* aficionado(-a), amateur *m/f*; ~ **dramatics** dramas *mpl* presentados por aficionados, representación *f* de aficionados
amateurish ['æmətərɪʃ] *adj* (*pej*) torpe, inexperto
amaze [ə'meɪz] *vt* asombrar, pasmar; **to be amazed (at)** asombrarse (de)
amazement [ə'meɪzmənt] *n* asombro, sorpresa; **to my ~** para mi sorpresa
amazing [ə'meɪzɪŋ] *adj* extraordinario, asombroso; (*bargain, offer*) increíble
amazingly [ə'meɪzɪŋlɪ] *adv* extraordinariamente
Amazon ['æməzən] *n* (*Geo*) Amazonas *m*; (*Mythology*) amazona ■ *cpd*: **the ~ basin/jungle** la cuenca/selva del Amazonas
Amazonian [æmə'zəunɪən] *adj* amazónico
ambassador [æm'bæsədəʳ] *n* embajador(a) *m(f)*
amber ['æmbəʳ] *n* ámbar *m*; **at ~** (*Brit Aut*) en amarillo
ambidextrous [æmbɪ'dɛkstrəs] *adj* ambidextro
ambience ['æmbɪəns] *n* ambiente *m*
ambiguity [æmbɪ'gjuɪtɪ] *n* ambigüedad *f*; (*of meaning*) doble sentido
ambiguous [æm'bɪgjuəs] *adj* ambiguo
ambition [æm'bɪʃən] *n* ambición *f*; **to achieve one's ~** realizar su ambición
ambitious [æm'bɪʃəs] *adj* ambicioso; (*plan*) grandioso
ambivalent [æm'bɪvələnt] *adj* ambivalente; (*pej*) equívoco
amble ['æmbl] *vi* (*gen: also:* **amble along**) deambular, andar sin prisa
ambulance ['æmbjuləns] *n* ambulancia
ambulanceman/woman ['æmbjulənsmən/wumən] *n* ambulanciero(-a)
ambush ['æmbuʃ] *n* emboscada ■ *vt* tender una emboscada a; (*fig*) coger (*SP*) *or* agarrar (*LAm*) por sorpresa
ameba [ə'mi:bə] *n* (*US*) = **amoeba**
ameliorate [ə'mi:lɪəreɪt] *vt* mejorar
amelioration [əmi:lɪə'reɪʃən] *n* mejora
amen [ɑ:'mɛn] *excl* amén
amenable [ə'mi:nəbl] *adj*: ~ **to** (*advice etc*) sensible a
amend [ə'mɛnd] *vt* (*law, text*) enmendar; **to make amends** (*apologize*) enmendarlo, dar cumplida satisfacción
amendment [ə'mɛndmənt] *n* enmienda
amenities [ə'mi:nɪtɪz] *npl* comodidades *fpl*
amenity [ə'mi:nɪtɪ] *n* servicio
America [ə'mɛrɪkə] *n* América (del Norte)
American [ə'mɛrɪkən] *adj, n* (norte)americano(-a) *m(f)*, estadounidense *m/f*
Americanism [ə'mɛrɪkənɪzəm] *n* americanismo
americanize [ə'mɛrɪkənaɪz] *vt* americanizar
Amerindian [æmər'ɪndɪən] *adj, n* amerindio(-a)
amethyst ['æmɪθɪst] *n* amatista
Amex ['æmɛks] *n abbr* = **American Stock Exchange**
amiable ['eɪmɪəbl] *adj* (*kind*) amable, simpático
amicable ['æmɪkəbl] *adj* amistoso, amigable
amicably ['æmɪkəblɪ] *adv* amigablemente, amistosamente; **to part ~** separarse amistosamente
amid [ə'mɪd], **amidst** [ə'mɪdst] *prep* entre, en medio de
amiss [ə'mɪs] *adv*: **to take sth ~** tomar algo a mal; **there's something ~** pasa algo
ammo ['æməu] *n abbr* (*col*) = **ammunition**
ammonia [ə'məunɪə] *n* amoníaco
ammunition [æmju'nɪʃən] *n* municiones *fpl*; (*fig*) argumentos *mpl*
ammunition dump *n* depósito de municiones
amnesia [æm'ni:zɪə] *n* amnesia
amnesty ['æmnɪstɪ] *n* amnistía; **to grant an ~ to** amnistiar (a); **A~ International** Amnistía Internacional
amoeba, ameba (*US*) [ə'mi:bə] *n* amiba
amok [ə'mɔk] *adv*: **to run ~** enloquecerse, desbocarse
among [ə'mʌŋ], **amongst** [ə'mʌŋst] *prep* entre, en medio de
amoral [æ'mɔrəl] *adj* amoral
amorous ['æmərəs] *adj* cariñoso
amorphous [ə'mɔ:fəs] *adj* amorfo
amortization [əmɔ:taɪ'zeɪʃən] *n* amortización *f*
amount [ə'maunt] *n* (*gen*) cantidad *f*; (*of bill etc*) suma, importe *m* ■ *vi*: **to ~ to** (*total*) sumar; (*be same as*) equivaler a, significar; **this amounts to a refusal** esto equivale a una negativa; **the total ~** (*of money*) la suma total
amp [æmp], **ampère** ['æmpɛəʳ] *n* amperio; **a 13 ~ plug** un enchufe de 13 amperios
ampersand ['æmpəsænd] *n* signo &, "y" comercial

amphetamine [æm'fɛtəmi:n] *n* anfetamina
amphibian [æm'fɪbɪən] *n* anfibio
amphibious [æm'fɪbɪəs] *adj* anfibio
amphitheatre, amphitheater (*US*) ['æmfɪθɪətəʳ] *n* anfiteatro
ample ['æmpl] *adj* (*spacious*) amplio; (*abundant*) abundante; **to have ~ time** tener tiempo de sobra
amplifier ['æmplɪfaɪəʳ] *n* amplificador *m*
amplify ['æmplɪfaɪ] *vt* amplificar, aumentar; (*explain*) explicar
amply ['æmplɪ] *adv* ampliamente
ampoule, ampule (*US*) ['æmpu:l] *n* (*Med*) ampolla
amputate ['æmpjuteɪt] *vt* amputar
amputee [æmpju'ti:] *n* persona que ha sufrido una amputación
Amsterdam ['æmstədæm] *n* Amsterdam *m*
amt *abbr* = **amount**
amuck [ə'mʌk] *adv* = **amok**
amuse [ə'mju:z] *vt* divertir; (*distract*) distraer, entretener; **to ~ o.s. with sth/by doing sth** distraerse con algo/haciendo algo; **he was amused at the joke** le divirtió el chiste
amusement [ə'mju:zmənt] *n* diversión *f*; (*pastime*) pasatiempo; (*laughter*) risa; **much to my ~** con gran regocijo mío
amusement arcade *n* salón *m* de juegos
amusement park *n* parque *m* de atracciones
amusing [ə'mju:zɪŋ] *adj* divertido
an [æn, ən, n] *indef art see* **a**
ANA *n abbr* = **American Newspaper Association; American Nurses Association**
anachronism [ə'nækrənɪzəm] *n* anacronismo
anaemia [ə'ni:mɪə] *n* anemia
anaemic [ə'ni:mɪk] *adj* anémico; (*fig*) flojo
anaesthetic [ænɪs'θɛtɪk] *n* anestesia; **local/general ~** anestesia local/general
anaesthetist [æ'ni:sθɪtɪst] *n* anestesista *m/f*
anagram ['ænəgræm] *n* anagrama *m*
anal ['eɪnl] *adj* anal
analgesic [ænæl'dʒi:sɪk] *adj, n* analgésico
analogous [ə'næləgəs] *adj*: **~ to** *or* **with** análogo a
analogue, analog ['ænəlɔg] *adj* (*watch*) analógico
analogy [ə'nælədʒɪ] *n* analogía; **to draw an ~ between** señalar la analogía entre
analyse ['ænəlaɪz] *vt* (*Brit*) analizar
analysis (*pl* **analyses**) [ə'næləsɪs, -si:z] *n* análisis *m inv*
analyst ['ænəlɪst] *n* (*political analyst*) analista *m/f*; (*psychoanalyst*) psicoanalista *m/f*
analytic [ænə'lɪtɪk], **analytical** [ænə'lɪtɪkəl] *adj* analítico
analyze ['ænəlaɪz] *vt* (*US*) = **analyse**
anarchic [æ'nɑ:kɪk] *adj* anárquico
anarchist ['ænəkɪst] *adj, n* anarquista *m/f*
anarchy ['ænəkɪ] *n* anarquía, desorden *m*
anathema [ə'næθɪmə] *n*: **that is ~ to him** eso es pecado para él
anatomical [ænə'tɔmɪkəl] *adj* anatómico
anatomy [ə'nætəmɪ] *n* anatomía
ANC *n abbr* = **African National Congress**
ancestor ['ænsɪstəʳ] *n* antepasado
ancestral [æn'sɛstrəl] *adj* ancestral
ancestry ['ænsɪstrɪ] *n* ascendencia, abolengo
anchor ['æŋkəʳ] *n* ancla, áncora ▪ *vi* (*also*: **to drop anchor**) anclar, echar el ancla ▪ *vt* (*fig*) sujetar, afianzar; **to weigh ~** levar anclas
anchorage ['æŋkərɪdʒ] *n* ancladero
anchor man, anchor woman *n* (*Radio, TV*) presentador(a) *m(f)*
anchovy ['æntʃəvɪ] *n* anchoa
ancient ['eɪnʃənt] *adj* antiguo; **~ monument** monumento histórico
ancillary [æn'sɪlərɪ] *adj* (*worker, staff*) auxiliar
and [ænd] *conj* y; (*before i, hi*) e; **~ so on** etcétera; **try ~ come** procure *or* intente venir; **better ~ better** cada vez mejor
Andalusia [ændə'lu:zɪə] *n* Andalucía
Andean ['ændɪən] *adj* andino(-a); **~ high plateau** altiplanicie *f*, altiplano (*LAm*)
Andes ['ændi:z] *npl*: **the ~** los Andes
anecdote ['ænɪkdəut] *n* anécdota
anemia [ə'ni:mɪə] *n* (*US*) = **anaemia**
anemic [ə'ni:mɪk] *adj* (*US*) = **anaemic**
anemone [ə'nɛmənɪ] *n* (*Bot*) anémone *f*; **sea ~** anémona
anesthetic [ænɪs'θɛtɪk] *adj, n* (*US*) = **anaesthetic**
anesthetist [æ'ni:sθɪtɪst] *n* (*US*) = **anaesthetist**
anew [ə'nju:] *adv* de nuevo, otra vez
angel ['eɪndʒəl] *n* ángel *m*
angel dust *n* polvo de ángel
angelic [æn'dʒɛlɪk] *adj* angélico
anger ['æŋgəʳ] *n* ira, cólera, enojo (*LAm*) ▪ *vt* enojar, enfurecer
angina [æn'dʒaɪnə] *n* angina (del pecho)
angle ['æŋgl] *n* ángulo; **from their ~** desde su punto de vista
angler ['æŋgləʳ] *n* pescador(a) *m(f)* (de caña)
Anglican ['æŋglɪkən] *adj, n* anglicano(-a)
anglicize ['æŋglɪsaɪz] *vt* anglicanizar
angling ['æŋglɪŋ] *n* pesca con caña
Anglo- [æŋgləu] *pref* anglo...
Angola [æŋ'gəulə] *n* Angola
Angolan [æŋ'gəulən] *adj, n* angoleño(-a) *m(f)*
angrily ['æŋgrɪlɪ] *adv* enojado, enfadado
angry ['æŋgrɪ] *adj* enfadado, enojado (*esp LAm*); **to be ~ with sb/at sth** estar enfadado con algn/por algo; **to get ~** enfadarse,

enojarse (*esp LAm*)
anguish ['æŋgwɪʃ] *n* (*physical*) tormentos *mpl*; (*mental*) angustia
anguished ['æŋgwɪʃt] *adj* angustioso
angular ['æŋgjuləʳ] *adj* (*shape*) angular; (*features*) anguloso
animal ['ænɪməl] *adj, n* animal *m*
animal rights [-raɪts] *npl* derechos *mpl* de los animales
animate *vt* ['ænɪmeɪt] (*enliven*) animar; (*encourage*) estimular, alentar ■ *adj* ['ænɪmɪt] vivo, animado
animated ['ænɪmeɪtɪd] *adj* vivo, animado
animation [ænɪ'meɪʃən] *n* animación *f*
animosity [ænɪ'mɔsɪtɪ] *n* animosidad *f*, rencor *m*
aniseed ['ænɪsi:d] *n* anís *m*
Ankara ['æŋkərə] *n* Ankara
ankle ['æŋkl] *n* tobillo *m*
ankle sock *n* calcetín *m*
annex *n* ['ænɛks] (*Brit*: *also*: **annexe**: *building*) edificio anexo ■ *vt* [æ'nɛks] (*territory*) anexar
annihilate [ə'naɪəleɪt] *vt* aniquilar
annihilation [ənaɪə'leɪʃən] *n* aniquilación *f*
anniversary [ænɪ'və:sərɪ] *n* aniversario
annotate ['ænəuteɪt] *vt* anotar
announce [ə'nauns] *vt* (*gen*) anunciar; (*inform*) comunicar; **he announced that he wasn't going** declaró que no iba
announcement [ə'naunsmənt] *n* (*gen*) anuncio; (*declaration*) declaración *f*; **I'd like to make an ~** quisiera anunciar algo
announcer [ə'naunsəʳ] *n* (*Radio, TV*) locutor(a) *m(f)*
annoy [ə'nɔɪ] *vt* molestar, fastidiar, fregar (*LAm*), embromar (*LAm*); **to be annoyed (at sth/with sb)** estar enfadado *or* molesto (por algo/con algn); **don't get annoyed!** ¡no se enfade!
annoyance [ə'nɔɪəns] *n* enojo; (*thing*) molestia
annoying [ə'nɔɪɪŋ] *adj* molesto, fastidioso, fregado (*LAm*), embromado (*LAm*); (*person*) pesado
annual ['ænjuəl] *adj* anual ■ *n* (*Bot*) anual *m*; (*book*) anuario
annual general meeting *n* junta general anual
annually ['ænjuəlɪ] *adv* anualmente, cada año
annual report *n* informe *m or* memoria anual
annuity [ə'nju:ɪtɪ] *n* renta *or* pensión *f* vitalicia
annul [ə'nʌl] *vt* anular; (*law*) revocar
annulment [ə'nʌlmənt] *n* anulación *f*
annum ['ænəm] *n see* **per annum**
Annunciation [ənʌnsɪ'eɪʃən] *n* Anunciación *f*
anode ['ænəud] *n* ánodo
anoint [ə'nɔɪnt] *vt* untar
anomalous [ə'nɔmələs] *adj* anómalo
anomaly [ə'nɔməlɪ] *n* anomalía
anon. [ə'nɔn] *abbr* = **anonymous**
anonymity [ænə'nɪmɪtɪ] *n* anonimato
anonymous [ə'nɔnɪməs] *adj* anónimo; **to remain ~** quedar en el anonimato
anorak ['ænəræk] *n* anorak *m*
anorexia [ænə'rɛksɪə] *n* (*Med*) anorexia
anorexic [ænə'rɛksɪk] *adj, n* anoréxico(-a) *m(f)*
another [ə'nʌðəʳ] *adj*: **~ book** otro libro; **~ beer?** ¿(quieres) otra cerveza?; **in ~ five years** en cinco años más ■ *pron* otro; *see also* **one**
ANSI *n abbr* (= *American National Standards Institution*) *oficina de normalización de* EEUU
answer ['ɑ:nsəʳ] *n* respuesta, contestación *f*; (*to problem*) solución *f* ■ *vi* contestar, responder ■ *vt* (*reply to*) contestar a, responder a; (*problem*) resolver; **to ~ the phone** contestar el teléfono; **in ~ to your letter** contestando *or* en contestación a su carta; **to ~ the bell** *or* **the door** abrir la puerta
▸ **answer back** *vi* replicar, ser respondón(-ona)
▸ **answer for** *vt fus* responder de *or* por
▸ **answer to** *vt fus* (*description*) corresponder a
answerable ['ɑ:nsərəbl] *adj*: **~ to sb for sth** responsable ante algn de algo
answering machine ['ɑ:nsərɪŋ-] *n* contestador *m* automático
ant [ænt] *n* hormiga
ANTA *n abbr* = **American National Theater and Academy**
antagonism [æn'tægənɪzəm] *n* antagonismo *m*
antagonist [æn'tægənɪst] *n* antagonista *m/f*, adversario(-a)
antagonistic [æntægə'nɪstɪk] *adj* antagónico; (*opposed*) contrario, opuesto
antagonize [æn'tægənaɪz] *vt* provocar la enemistad de
Antarctic [ænt'ɑ:ktɪk] *adj* antártico ■ *n*: **the ~** el Antártico
Antarctica [æn'tɑ:ktɪkə] *n* Antártida
Antarctic Circle *n* Círculo Polar Antártico
Antarctic Ocean *n* Océano Antártico
ante ['æntɪ] *n*: **to up the ~** subir la apuesta
ante... ['æntɪ] *pref* ante...
anteater ['ænti:təʳ] *n* oso hormiguero
antecedent [æntɪ'si:dənt] *n* antecedente *m*
antechamber ['æntɪtʃeɪmbəʳ] *n* antecámara

antelope ['æntɪləup] *n* antílope *m*
antenatal [æntɪ'neɪtl] *adj* prenatal
antenatal clinic *n* clínica prenatal
antenna [æn'tɛnə] (*pl* **antennae** [-ni:]) *n* antena
anteroom ['æntɪrum] *n* antesala
anthem ['ænθəm] *n*: **national ~** himno nacional
anthology [æn'θɔlədʒɪ] *n* antología
anthropologist [ænθrə'pɔlədʒɪst] *n* antropólogo(-a)
anthropology [ænθrə'pɔlədʒɪ] *n* antropología
anti... [æntɪ] *pref* anti...
anti-aircraft ['æntɪ'ɛəkrɑ:ft] *adj* antiaéreo
antiballistic [æntɪbə'lɪstɪk] *adj* antibalístico
antibiotic [æntɪbaɪ'ɔtɪk] *adj, n* antibiótico
antibody ['æntɪbɔdɪ] *n* anticuerpo
anticipate [æn'tɪsɪpeɪt] *vt* (*foresee*) prever; (*expect*) esperar, contar con; (*forestall*) anticiparse a, adelantarse a; **this is worse than I anticipated** esto es peor de lo que esperaba; **as anticipated** según se esperaba
anticipation [æntɪsɪ'peɪʃən] *n* previsión *f*; esperanza; anticipación *f*
anticlimax [æntɪ'klaɪmæks] *n* decepción *f*
anticlockwise [æntɪ'klɔkwaɪz] *adv* en dirección contraria a la de las agujas del reloj
antics ['æntɪks] *npl* payasadas *fpl*
anticyclone [æntɪ'saɪkləun] *n* anticiclón *m*
antidepressant [ˌæntɪdɪ'presnt] *n* antidepresivo
antidote ['æntɪdəut] *n* antídoto
antifreeze ['æntɪfri:z] *n* anticongelante *m*
anti-globalization ['æntɪgləubəlaɪ'zeɪʃən] *n* antiglobalización *f*; **~ protesters** manifestantes *m/fpl* antiglobalización
antihistamine [æntɪ'hɪstəmi:n] *n* antihistamínico
Antilles [æn'tɪli:z] *npl*: **the ~** las Antillas
antipathy [æn'tɪpəθɪ] *n* (*between people*) antipatía; (*to person, thing*) aversión *f*
antiperspirant ['æntɪpə:spɪrənt] *n* antitranspirante *m*
Antipodean [æntɪpə'di:ən] *adj* antípoda
Antipodes [æn'tɪpədi:z] *npl*: **the ~** las Antípodas
antiquarian [æntɪ'kwɛərɪən] *n* anticuario(-a)
antiquated ['æntɪkweɪtɪd] *adj* anticuado
antique [æn'ti:k] *n* antigüedad *f* ■ *adj* antiguo
antique dealer *n* anticuario(-a)
antique shop *n* tienda de antigüedades
antiquity [æn'tɪkwɪtɪ] *n* antigüedad *f*
anti-Semitic ['æntɪsɪ'mɪtɪk] *adj* antisemita
anti-Semitism [æntɪ'sɛmɪtɪzəm] *n* antisemitismo
antiseptic [æntɪ'sɛptɪk] *adj, n* antiséptico
antisocial [æntɪ'səuʃəl] *adj* antisocial
antitank [æntɪ'tæŋk] *adj* antitanque
antithesis (*pl* **antitheses**) [æn'tɪθɪsɪs, -si:z] *n* antítesis *f inv*
antitrust [æntɪ'trʌst] *adj*: **~ legislation** legislación *f* antimonopolio
antivirus [æntɪ'vaɪərəs] *adj* antivirus; **~ software** antivirus *m*
antlers ['æntləz] *npl* cornamenta
anus ['eɪnəs] *n* ano
anvil ['ænvɪl] *n* yunque *m*
anxiety [æŋ'zaɪətɪ] *n* (*worry*) inquietud *f*; (*eagerness*) ansia, anhelo
anxious ['æŋkʃəs] *adj* (*worried*) inquieto; (*keen*) deseoso; **I'm very ~ about you** me tienes muy preocupado
anxiously ['æŋkʃəslɪ] *adv* con inquietud, de manera angustiada

KEYWORD

any ['ɛnɪ] *adj* **1** (*in questions etc*) algún/alguna; **have you any butter/children?** ¿tienes mantequilla/hijos?; **if there are any tickets left** si quedan billetes, si queda algún billete
2 (*with negative*): **I haven't any money/books** no tengo dinero/libros
3 (*no matter which*) cualquier; **any excuse will do** valdrá *or* servirá cualquier excusa; **choose any book you like** escoge el libro que quieras; **any teacher you ask will tell you** cualquier profesor al que preguntes te lo dirá
4 (*in phrases*): **in any case** de todas formas, en cualquier caso; **any day now** cualquier día (de estos); **at any moment** en cualquier momento, de un momento a otro; **at any rate** en todo caso; **any time**: **come (at) any time** ven cuando quieras; **he might come (at) any time** podría llegar de un momento a otro
■ *pron* **1** (*in questions etc*): **have you got any?** ¿tienes alguno/a?; **can any of you sing?** ¿sabe cantar alguno de vosotros/ustedes?
2 (*with negative*): **I haven't any (of them)** no tengo ninguno
3 (*no matter which one(s)*): **take any of those books (you like)** toma el libro que quieras de ésos
■ *adv* **1** (*in questions etc*): **do you want any more soup/sandwiches?** ¿quieres más sopa/bocadillos?; **are you feeling any better?** ¿te sientes algo mejor?
2 (*with negative*): **I can't hear him any more** ya no le oigo; **don't wait any longer** no esperes más

anybody ['ɛnıbɔdı] *pron* cualquiera, cualquier persona; (*in interrogative sentences*) alguien; (*in negative sentences*): **I don't see ~** no veo a nadie
anyhow ['ɛnıhau] *adv* de todos modos, de todas maneras; (*carelessly*) de cualquier manera; (*haphazardly*) de cualquier modo; **I shall go ~** iré de todas maneras
anyone ['ɛnıwʌn] = **anybody**
anyplace ['ɛnıpleıs] *adv* (*US*) = **anywhere**
anything ['ɛnıθıŋ] *pron* cualquier cosa; (*in interrogative sentences*) algo; (*in negative sentences*) nada; (*everything*) todo; **~ else?** ¿algo más?; **it can cost ~ between £15 and £20** puede costar entre 15 y 20 libras
anytime ['ɛnıtaım] *adv* (*at any moment*) en cualquier momento, de un momento a otro; (*whenever*) no importa cuándo, cuando quiera
anyway ['ɛnıweı] *adv* de todas maneras; de cualquier modo
anywhere ['ɛnıwɛəʳ] *adv* dondequiera; (*interrogative*) en algún sitio; (*negative sense*) en ningún sitio; (*everywhere*) en *or* por todas partes; **I don't see him ~** no le veo en ningún sitio; **~ in the world** en cualquier parte del mundo
Anzac ['ænzæk] *n abbr* = **Australia-New Zealand Army Corps**
apace [ə'peıs] *adv* aprisa
apart [ə'pɑ:t] *adv* aparte, separadamente; **10 miles ~** separados por 10 millas; **to take ~** desmontar; **~ from** *prep* aparte de
apartheid [ə'pɑ:teıt] *n* apartheid *m*
apartment [ə'pɑ:tmənt] *n* (*US*) piso, departamento (*LAm*), apartamento; (*room*) cuarto
apartment block *or* **building** *n* (*US*) bloque *m* de pisos
apathetic [æpə'θɛtık] *adj* apático, indiferente
apathy ['æpəθı] *n* apatía, indiferencia
APB *n abbr* (*US: = all points bulletin: police expression*) *expresión usada por la policía que significa "descubrir y aprehender al sospechoso"*
ape [eıp] *n* mono ■ *vt* imitar, remedar
Apennines ['æpənaınz] *npl*: **the ~** los Apeninos *mpl*
aperitif [ə'pɛrıti:f] *n* aperitivo
aperture ['æpətʃjuəʳ] *n* rendija, resquicio; (*Phot*) abertura
APEX ['eıpɛks] *n abbr* (*Aviat: = advance purchase excursion*) APEX *m*
apex ['eıpɛks] *n* ápice *m*; (*fig*) cumbre *f*
aphid ['eıfıd] *n* pulgón *m*
aphorism ['æfərızəm] *n* aforismo
aphrodisiac [æfrəu'dızıæk] *adj, n* afrodisíaco
API *n abbr* = **American Press Institute**
apiece [ə'pi:s] *adv* cada uno
aplomb [ə'plɔm] *n* aplomo, confianza
APO *n abbr* (*US: = Army Post Office*) *servicio postal del ejército*
Apocalypse [ə'pɔkəlıps] *n* Apocalipsis *m*
apocryphal [ə'pɔkrıfəl] *adj* apócrifo
apolitical [eıpə'lıtıkl] *adj* apolítico
apologetic [əpɔlə'dʒɛtık] *adj* (*look, remark*) de disculpa
apologetically [əpɔlə'dʒɛtıkəlı] *adv* con aire de disculpa, excusándose, disculpándose
apologize [ə'pɔlədʒaız] *vi*: **to ~ (for sth to sb)** disculparse (con algn por algo)
apology [ə'pɔlədʒı] *n* disculpa, excusa; **please accept my apologies** le ruego me disculpe
apoplectic [æpə'plɛktık] *adj* (*Med*) apoplético; (*col*): **~ with rage** furioso
apoplexy ['æpəplɛksı] *n* apoplejía
apostle [ə'pɔsl] *n* apóstol *m/f*
apostrophe [ə'pɔstrəfı] *n* apóstrofo *m*
appal [ə'pɔ:l] *vt* horrorizar, espantar
Appalachian Mountains [æpə'leıʃən-] *npl*: **the ~** los (Montes) Apalaches
appalling [ə'pɔ:lıŋ] *adj* espantoso; (*awful*) pésimo; **she's an ~ cook** es una cocinera malísima
apparatus [æpə'reıtəs] *n* aparato; (*in gymnasium*) aparatos *mpl*
apparel [ə'pærl] *n* (*US*) indumentaria
apparent [ə'pærənt] *adj* aparente; (*obvious*) manifiesto, evidente; **it is ~ that** está claro que
apparently [ə'pærəntlı] *adv* por lo visto, al parecer, dizque (*LAm*)
apparition [æpə'rıʃən] *n* aparición *f*
appeal [ə'pi:l] *vi* (*Law*) apelar ■ *n* (*Law*) apelación *f*; (*request*) llamamiento, llamado (*LAm*); (*plea*) súplica; (*charm*) atractivo, encanto; **to ~ for** solicitar; **to ~ to** (*person*) rogar a, suplicar a; (*thing*) atraer, interesar; **to ~ to sb for mercy** rogarle misericordia a algn; **it doesn't ~ to me** no me atrae, no me llama la atención; **right of ~** derecho de apelación
appealing [ə'pi:lıŋ] *adj* (*nice*) atractivo; (*touching*) conmovedor(a), emocionante
appear [ə'pıəʳ] *vi* aparecer, presentarse; (*Law*) comparecer; (*publication*) salir (a luz), publicarse; (*seem*) parecer; **it would ~ that** parecería que
appearance [ə'pıərəns] *n* aparición *f*; (*look, aspect*) apariencia, aspecto; **to keep up appearances** salvar las apariencias; **to all appearances** al parecer
appease [ə'pi:z] *vt* (*pacify*) apaciguar; (*satisfy*) satisfacer

appeasement [ə'pi:zmənt] *n* (*Pol*) apaciguamiento
append [ə'pɛnd] *vt* (*Comput*) añadir (al final)
appendage [ə'pɛndɪdʒ] *n* añadidura
appendicitis [əpɛndɪ'saɪtɪs] *n* apendicitis *f*
appendix (*pl* **appendices**) [ə'pɛndɪks, -dɪsi:z] *n* apéndice *m*; **to have one's ~ out** operarse de apendicitis
appetite ['æpɪtaɪt] *n* apetito; (*fig*) deseo, anhelo; **that walk has given me an ~** ese paseo me ha abierto el apetito
appetizer ['æpɪtaɪzəʳ] *n* (*drink*) aperitivo; (*food*) tapas *fpl* (*SP*)
appetizing ['æpɪtaɪzɪŋ] *adj* apetitoso
applaud [ə'plɔ:d] *vt, vi* aplaudir
applause [ə'plɔ:z] *n* aplausos *mpl*
apple ['æpl] *n* manzana
apple tree *n* manzano
appliance [ə'plaɪəns] *n* aparato; **electrical appliances** electrodomésticos *mpl*
applicable [ə'plɪkəbl] *adj* aplicable, pertinente; **the law is ~ from January** la ley es aplicable *or* se pone en vigor a partir de enero; **to be ~ to** referirse a
applicant ['æplɪkənt] *n* candidato(-a); solicitante *m/f*
application [æplɪ'keɪʃən] *n* aplicación *f*; (*for a job, a grant etc*) solicitud *f*
application form *n* solicitud *f*
application program *n* (*Comput*) (programa *m* de) aplicación *f*
applications package *n* (*Comput*) paquete *m* de programas de aplicación
applied [ə'plaɪd] *adj* (*science, art*) aplicado
apply [ə'plaɪ] *vt*: **to ~ (to)** aplicar (a); (*fig*) emplear (para) ■ *vi*: **to ~ to** (*ask*) dirigirse a; (*be suitable for*) ser aplicable a; (*be relevant to*) tener que ver con; **to ~ for** (*permit, grant, job*) solicitar; **to ~ the brakes** echar el freno; **to ~ o.s. to** aplicarse a, dedicarse a
appoint [ə'pɔɪnt] *vt* (*to post*) nombrar; (*date, place*) fijar, señalar
appointee [əpɔɪn'ti:] *n* persona nombrada
appointment [ə'pɔɪntmənt] *n* (*engagement*) cita; (*date*) compromiso; (*act*) nombramiento; (*post*) puesto; **to make an ~ (with)** (*doctor*) pedir hora (con); (*friend*) citarse (con); **"appointments"** "ofertas de trabajo"; **by ~** mediante cita
apportion [ə'pɔ:ʃən] *vt* repartir
appraisal [ə'preɪzl] *n* evaluación *f*
appraise [ə'preɪz] *vt* (*value*) tasar, valorar; (*situation etc*) evaluar
appreciable [ə'pri:ʃəbl] *adj* sensible
appreciably [ə'pri:ʃəblɪ] *adv* sensiblemente, de manera apreciable
appreciate [ə'pri:ʃɪeɪt] *vt* (*like*) apreciar, tener en mucho; (*be grateful for*) agradecer; (*be aware of*) comprender ■ *vi* (*Comm*) aumentar en valor; **I appreciated your help** agradecí tu ayuda
appreciation [əpri:ʃɪ'eɪʃən] *n* aprecio; reconocimiento, agradecimiento; aumento en valor
appreciative [ə'pri:ʃɪətɪv] *adj* agradecido
apprehend [æprɪ'hɛnd] *vt* percibir; (*arrest*) detener
apprehension [æprɪ'hɛnʃən] *n* (*fear*) aprensión *f*
apprehensive [æprɪ'hɛnsɪv] *adj* aprensivo
apprentice [ə'prɛntɪs] *n* aprendiz(a) *m(f)* ■ *vt*: **to be apprenticed to** estar de aprendiz con
apprenticeship [ə'prɛntɪsʃɪp] *n* aprendizaje *m*; **to serve one's ~** hacer el aprendizaje
appro. ['æprəu] *abbr* (*Brit Comm: col*) *see* **approval**
approach [ə'prəutʃ] *vi* acercarse ■ *vt* acercarse a; (*be approximate*) aproximarse a; (*ask, apply to*) dirigirse a; (*problem*) abordar ■ *n* acercamiento; aproximación *f*; (*access*) acceso; (*proposal*) proposición *f*; (*to problem etc*) enfoque *m*; **to ~ sb about sth** hablar con algn sobre algo
approachable [ə'prəutʃəbl] *adj* (*person*) abordable; (*place*) accesible
approach road *n* vía de acceso
approbation [æprə'beɪʃən] *n* aprobación *f*
appropriate [ə'prəuprɪɪt] *adj* apropiado, conveniente ■ *vt* [-rɪeɪt] (*take*) apropiarse de; (*allot*): **to ~ sth for** destinar algo a; **~ for** *or* **to** apropiado para; **it would not be ~ for me to comment** no estaría bien *or* sería pertinente que yo diera mi opinión
appropriation [əprəuprɪ'eɪʃən] *n* asignación *f*
approval [ə'pru:vəl] *n* aprobación *f*, visto bueno; **on ~** (*Comm*) a prueba; **to meet with sb's ~** obtener la aprobación de algn
approve [ə'pru:v] *vt* aprobar
▸ **approve of** *vt fus* aprobar
approved school *n* (*Brit*) correccional *m*
approx. *abbr* (= *approximately*) aprox
approximate [ə'prɔksɪmɪt] *adj* aproximado
approximately [ə'prɔksɪmɪtlɪ] *adv* aproximadamente, más o menos
approximation [əprɔksɪ'meɪʃən] *n* aproximación *f*
Apr. *abbr* (= *April*) abr
apr *n abbr* (= *annual percentage rate*) tasa de interés anual
apricot ['eɪprɪkɔt] *n* albaricoque *m* (*SP*), damasco (*LAm*)
April ['eɪprəl] *n* abril *m*; *see also* **July**

April Fools' Day *n* ≈ día *m* de los (Santos) Inocentes; *ver nota*

> **APRIL FOOLS' DAY**
>
> El 1 de abril es *April Fools' Day* en la tradición anglosajona. Tal día se les gastan bromas a los más desprevenidos, quienes reciben la denominación de "April Fool" (= inocente), y tanto la prensa escrita como la televisión difunden alguna historia falsa con la que sumarse al espíritu del día.

apron ['eɪprən] *n* delantal *m*; (*Aviat*) pista
apse [æps] *n* (*Arch*) ábside *m*
APT *n abbr* (*Brit*) = **advanced passenger train**
Apt. *abbr* = **apartment**
apt [æpt] *adj* (*to the point*) acertado, oportuno; (*appropriate*) apropiado; **~ to do** (*likely*) propenso a hacer
aptitude ['æptɪtju:d] *n* aptitud *f*, capacidad *f*
aptitude test *n* prueba de aptitud
aptly ['æptlɪ] *adj* acertadamente
aqualung ['ækwəlʌŋ] *n* escafandra autónoma
aquarium [ə'kwɛərɪəm] *n* acuario
Aquarius [ə'kwɛərɪəs] *n* Acuario
aquatic [ə'kwætɪk] *adj* acuático
aqueduct ['ækwɪdʌkt] *n* acueducto
AR *abbr* (*US*) = **Arkansas**
ARA *n abbr* (*Brit*) = **Associate of the Royal Academy**
Arab ['ærəb] *adj*, *n* árabe *m/f*
Arabia [ə'reɪbɪə] *n* Arabia
Arabian [ə'reɪbɪən] *adj* árabe, arábigo
Arabian Desert *n* Desierto de Arabia
Arabian Sea *n* Mar *m* de Omán
Arabic ['ærəbɪk] *adj* (*language, manuscripts*) árabe, arábigo ■ *n* árabe *m*; **~ numerals** numeración *f* arábiga
arable ['ærəbl] *adj* cultivable
Aragon ['ærəgən] *n* Aragón *m*
ARAM *n abbr* (*Brit*) = **Associate of the Royal Academy of Music**
arbiter ['ɑ:bɪtəʳ] *n* árbitro
arbitrary ['ɑ:bɪtrərɪ] *adj* arbitrario
arbitrate ['ɑ:bɪtreɪt] *vi* arbitrar
arbitration [ɑ:bɪ'treɪʃən] *n* arbitraje *m*; **the dispute went to ~** el conflicto laboral fue sometido al arbitraje
arbitrator ['ɑ:bɪtreɪtəʳ] *n* árbitro
ARC *n abbr* = **American Red Cross**
arc [ɑ:k] *n* arco
arcade [ɑ:'keɪd] *n* (*Arch*) arcada; (*round a square*) soportales *mpl*; (*shopping arcade*) galería comercial
arch [ɑ:tʃ] *n* arco; (*vault*) bóveda; (*of foot*) empeine *m* ■ *vt* arquear
archaeological [ɑ:kɪə'lɔdʒɪkl] *adj* arqueológico
archaeologist [ɑ:kɪ'ɔlədʒɪst] *n* arqueólogo(-a)
archaeology [ɑ:kɪ'ɔlədʒɪ] *n* arqueología
archaic [ɑ:'keɪɪk] *adj* arcaico
archangel ['ɑ:keɪndʒəl] *n* arcángel *m*
archbishop [ɑ:tʃ'bɪʃəp] *n* arzobispo
arched [ɑ:tʃt] *adj* abovedado
archenemy ['ɑ:tʃ'ɛnəmɪ] *n* enemigo jurado
archeology *etc* [ɑ:kɪ'ɔlədʒɪ] (*US*) *see* **archaeology** *etc*
archer ['ɑ:tʃəʳ] *n* arquero(-a)
archery ['ɑ:tʃərɪ] *n* tiro al arco
archetypal ['ɑ:kɪtaɪpəl] *adj* arquetípico
archetype ['ɑ:kɪtaɪp] *n* arquetipo
archipelago [ɑ:kɪ'pɛlɪgəu] *n* archipiélago
architect ['ɑ:kɪtɛkt] *n* arquitecto(-a)
architectural [ɑ:kɪ'tɛktʃərəl] *adj* arquitectónico
architecture ['ɑ:kɪtɛktʃəʳ] *n* arquitectura
archive ['ɑ:kaɪv] *n* (*often pl: also Comput*) archivo
archive file *n* (*Comput*) fichero archivado
archives ['ɑ:kaɪvz] *npl* archivo *sg*
archivist ['ɑ:kɪvɪst] *n* archivero(-a)
archway ['ɑ:tʃweɪ] *n* arco, arcada
ARCM *n abbr* (*Brit*) = **Associate of the Royal College of Music**
Arctic ['ɑ:ktɪk] *adj* ártico ■ *n*: **the ~** el Ártico
Arctic Circle *n* Círculo Polar Ártico
Arctic Ocean *n* Océano (Glacial) Ártico
ARD *n abbr* (*US Med*) = **acute respiratory disease**
ardent ['ɑ:dənt] *adj* (*desire*) ardiente; (*supporter, lover*) apasionado
ardour, ardor (*US*) ['ɑ:dəʳ] *n* ardor *m*, pasión *f*
arduous ['ɑ:djuəs] *adj* (*gen*) arduo; (*journey*) penoso
are [ɑ:ʳ] *vb see* **be**
area ['ɛərɪə] *n* área; (*Math etc*) superficie *f*, extensión *f*; (*zone*) región *f*, zona; **the London ~** la zona de Londres
area code *n* (*US Tel*) prefijo
arena [ə'ri:nə] *n* arena; (*of circus*) pista; (*for bullfight*) plaza, ruedo
aren't [ɑ:nt] = **are not**
Argentina [ɑ:dʒən'ti:nə] *n* Argentina
Argentinian [ɑ:dʒən'tɪnɪən] *adj*, *n* argentino(-a) *m(f)*
arguable ['ɑ:gjuəbl] *adj*: **it is ~ whether ...** es dudoso que + *subjun*
arguably ['ɑ:gjuəblɪ] *adv*: **it is ~ ...** es discutiblemente ...
argue ['ɑ:gju:] *vt* (*debate: case, matter*)

mantener, argüir ■ *vi* (*quarrel*) discutir; (*reason*) razonar, argumentar; **to ~ that** sostener que; **to ~ about sth (with sb)** pelearse (con algn) por algo
argument ['ɑ:gjumənt] *n* (*reasons*) argumento; (*quarrel*) discusión *f*; (*debate*) debate *m*; **~ for/against** argumento en pro/contra de
argumentative [ɑ:gju'mɛntətɪv] *adj* discutidor(a)
aria ['ɑ:rɪə] *n* (*Mus*) aria
ARIBA *n abbr* (*Brit*) = **Associate of the Royal Institute of British Architects**
arid ['ærɪd] *adj* árido
aridity [ə'rɪdɪtɪ] *n* aridez *f*
Aries ['ɛərɪz] *n* Aries *m*
arise [ə'raɪz] (*pt* **arose**, *pp* **arisen** [ə'rɪzn]) *vi* (*rise up*) levantarse, alzarse; (*emerge*) surgir, presentarse; **to ~ from** derivar de; **should the need ~** si fuera necesario
aristocracy [ærɪs'tɔkrəsɪ] *n* aristocracia
aristocrat ['ærɪstəkræt] *n* aristócrata *m/f*
aristocratic [ərɪstə'krætɪk] *adj* aristocrático
arithmetic [ə'rɪθmətɪk] *n* aritmética
arithmetical [ærɪθ'mɛtɪkl] *adj* aritmético
Ariz. *abbr* (*US*) = **Arizona**
Ark [ɑ:k] *n*: **Noah's ~** el Arca *f* de Noé
Ark. *abbr* (*US*) = **Arkansas**
arm [ɑ:m] *n* (*Anat*) brazo ■ *vt* armar; **~ in ~** cogidos del brazo; *see also* **arms**
armaments ['ɑ:məmənts] *npl* (*weapons*) armamentos *mpl*
armchair ['ɑ:mtʃɛə^r] *n* sillón *m*, butaca
armed [ɑ:md] *adj* armado; **the ~ forces** las fuerzas armadas
armed robbery *n* robo a mano armada
Armenia [ɑ:'mi:nɪə] *n* Armenia
Armenian [ɑ:'mi:nɪən] *adj* armenio ■ *n* armenio(-a); (*Ling*) armenio
armful ['ɑ:mful] *n* brazada
armistice ['ɑ:mɪstɪs] *n* armisticio
armour, armor (*US*) ['ɑ:mə^r] *n* armadura
armoured car, armored car (*US*) *n* coche *m* *or* carro (*LAm*) blindado
armoury, armory (*US*) ['ɑ:mərɪ] *n* arsenal *m*
armpit ['ɑ:mpɪt] *n* sobaco, axila
armrest ['ɑ:mrɛst] *n* reposabrazos *m inv*, brazo
arms [ɑ:mz] *npl* (*weapons*) armas *fpl*; (*Heraldry*) escudo *sg*
arms control *n* control *m* de armamentos
arms race *n* carrera de armamentos
army ['ɑ:mɪ] *n* ejército
aroma [ə'rəumə] *n* aroma *m*, fragancia
aromatherapy [ərəumə'θɛrəpɪ] *n* aromaterapia
aromatic [ærə'mætɪk] *adj* aromático, fragante
arose [ə'rəuz] *pt of* **arise**
around [ə'raund] *adv* alrededor; (*in the area*) a la redonda ■ *prep* alrededor de
arousal [ə'rauzəl] *n* (*sexual*) excitación *f*; (*of feelings, interest*) despertar *m*
arouse [ə'rauz] *vt* despertar
arrange [ə'reɪndʒ] *vt* arreglar, ordenar; (*programme*) organizar; (*appointment*) concertar ■ *vi*: **we have arranged for a taxi to pick you up** hemos organizado todo para que le recoja un taxi; **to ~ to do sth** quedar en hacer algo; **it was arranged that …** se quedó en que …
arrangement [ə'reɪndʒmənt] *n* arreglo; (*agreement*) acuerdo; **arrangements** *npl* (*plans*) planes *mpl*, medidas *fpl*; (*preparations*) preparativos *mpl*; **to come to an ~ (with sb)** llegar a un acuerdo (con algn); **by ~** a convenir; **I'll make arrangements for you to be met** haré los preparativos para que le estén esperando
arrant ['ærənt] *adj*: **~ nonsense** una verdadera tontería
array [ə'reɪ] *n* (*Comput*) matriz *f*; **~ of** (*things*) serie *f* *or* colección *f* de; (*people*) conjunto de
arrears [ə'rɪəz] *npl* atrasos *mpl*; **in ~** (*Comm*) en mora; **to be in ~ with one's rent** estar retrasado en el pago del alquiler
arrest [ə'rɛst] *vt* detener; (*sb's attention*) llamar ■ *n* detención *f*; **under ~** detenido
arresting [ə'rɛstɪŋ] *adj* (*fig*) llamativo
arrival [ə'raɪvəl] *n* llegada, arribo (*LAm*); **new ~** recién llegado(-a)
arrive [ə'raɪv] *vi* llegar, arribar (*LAm*)
arrogance ['ærəgəns] *n* arrogancia, prepotencia (*LAm*)
arrogant ['ærəgənt] *adj* arrogante, prepotente (*LAm*)
arrow ['ærəu] *n* flecha
arse [ɑ:s] *n* (*Brit col!*) culo, trasero
arsenal ['ɑ:sɪnl] *n* arsenal *m*
arsenic ['ɑ:snɪk] *n* arsénico
arson ['ɑ:sn] *n* incendio provocado
art [ɑ:t] *n* arte *m*; (*skill*) destreza; (*technique*) técnica; **Arts** *npl* (*Scol*) Letras *fpl*; **work of ~** obra de arte
art and design *n* (*Brit Scol*) arte *m* y diseño, dibujo
artefact ['ɑ:tɪfækt] *n* artefacto
arterial [ɑ:'tɪərɪəl] *adj* (*Anat*) arterial; (*road etc*) principal
artery ['ɑ:tərɪ] *n* (*Med*: *road etc*) arteria
artful ['ɑ:tful] *adj* (*cunning*: *person, trick*) mañoso
art gallery *n* pinacoteca, museo de pintura; (*Comm*) galería de arte

arthritis [ɑ:'θraɪtɪs] *n* artritis *f*
artichoke ['ɑ:tɪtʃəuk] *n* alcachofa; **Jerusalem ~** aguaturma
article ['ɑ:tɪkl] *n* artículo, objeto, cosa; (*in newspaper*) artículo; (*Brit Law: training*); **articles** *npl* contrato *sg* de aprendizaje; **articles of clothing** prendas *fpl* de vestir
articles of association *npl* (*Comm*) estatutos *mpl* sociales, escritura social
articulate *adj* [ɑ:'tɪkjulɪt] (*speech*) claro; (*person*) que se expresa bien ■ *vi* [ɑ:'tɪkjuleɪt] articular
articulated lorry *n* (*Brit*) trailer *m*
artifice ['ɑ:tɪfɪs] *n* artificio, truco
artificial [ɑ:tɪ'fɪʃəl] *adj* artificial; (*teeth etc*) postizo
artificial insemination *n* inseminación *f* artificial
artificial intelligence *n* inteligencia artificial
artificial respiration *n* respiración *f* artificial
artillery [ɑ:'tɪlərɪ] *n* artillería
artisan ['ɑ:tɪzæn] *n* artesano(-a)
artist ['ɑ:tɪst] *n* artista *m/f*; (*Mus*) intérprete *m/f*
artistic [ɑ:'tɪstɪk] *adj* artístico
artistry ['ɑ:tɪstrɪ] *n* arte *m*, habilidad *f* (artística)
artless ['ɑ:tlɪs] *adj* (*innocent*) natural, sencillo; (*clumsy*) torpe
art school *n* escuela de bellas artes
artwork ['ɑ:twə:k] *n* material *m* gráfico
arty ['ɑ:tɪ] *adj* artistoide
ARV *n abbr* (*= American Revised Version*) *traducción americana de la Biblia*
AS *n abbr* (*US Scol*) = **Associate in Science**

KEYWORD

as [æz] *conj* **1** (*referring to time: while*) mientras; (*: when*) cuando; **she wept as she told her story** lloraba mientras contaba lo que le ocurrió; **as the years go by** a medida que pasan los años, con el paso de los años; **he came in as I was leaving** entró cuando me marchaba; **as from tomorrow** a partir de *or* desde mañana
2 (*in comparisons*): **as big as** tan grande como; **twice as big as** el doble de grande que; **as much money/many books as** tanto dinero/tantos libros como; **as soon as** en cuanto, no bien (*LAm*)
3 (*since, because*) como, ya que; **as I don't speak German I can't understand him** como no hablo alemán no le entiendo, no le entiendo ya que no hablo alemán
4 (*although*): **much as I like them, ...** aunque me gustan, ...
5 (*referring to manner, way*): **do as you wish** haz lo que quieras; **as she said** como dijo; **he gave it to me as a present** me lo dio de regalo; **it's on the left as you go in** según se entra, a la izquierda
6 (*concerning*): **as for** *or* **to that** por *or* en lo que respecta a eso
7: **as if** *or* **though** como si; **he looked as if he was ill** parecía como si estuviera enfermo, tenía aspecto de enfermo; *see also* **long**; **such**; **well**
■ *prep* (*in the capacity of*): **he works as a barman** trabaja de barman; **as chairman of the company, he ...** como presidente de la compañía, ...

ASA *n abbr* (*= American Standards Association*) *instituto de normalización*; (*Brit: = Advertising Standards Association*) *departamento de control de la publicidad*; (*= Amateur Swimming Association*) *federación amateur de natación*
a.s.a.p. *abbr* (*= as soon as possible*) cuanto antes, lo más pronto posible
asbestos [æz'bɛstəs] *n* asbesto, amianto
ascend [ə'sɛnd] *vt* subir, ascender
ascendancy [ə'sɛndənsɪ] *n* ascendiente *m*, dominio
ascendant [ə'sɛndənt] *n*: **to be in the ~** estar en auge, ir ganando predominio
Ascension [ə'sɛnʃən] *n*: **the ~** la Ascensión
Ascension Island *n* Isla Ascensión
ascent [ə'sɛnt] *n* subida; (*slope*) cuesta, pendiente *f*; (*of plane*) ascenso
ascertain [æsə'teɪn] *vt* averiguar
ascetic [ə'sɛtɪk] *adj* ascético
asceticism [ə'sɛtɪsɪzəm] *n* ascetismo
ASCII ['æski:] *n abbr* (*= American Standard Code for Information Interchange*) ASCII
ascribe [ə'skraɪb] *vt*: **to ~ sth to** atribuir algo a
ASCU *n abbr* (*US*) = **Association of State Colleges and Universities**
ASE *n abbr* = **American Stock Exchange**
ASH [æʃ] *n abbr* (*Brit: = Action on Smoking and Health*) *organización anti-tabaco*
ash [æʃ] *n* ceniza; (*tree*) fresno
ashamed [ə'ʃeɪmd] *adj* avergonzado; **to be ~ of** avergonzarse de
ashcan ['æʃkæn] *n* (*US*) cubo *or* bote *m* (*LAm*) de la basura
ashen ['æʃn] *adj* pálido
ashore [ə'ʃɔ:ʳ] *adv* en tierra
ashtray ['æʃtreɪ] *n* cenicero
Ash Wednesday *n* miércoles *m* de ceniza
Asia ['eɪʃə] *n* Asia

Asian ['eɪʃən], **Asiatic** [eɪsɪ'ætɪk] *adj, n* asiático(-a) *m(f)*
aside [ə'saɪd] *adv* a un lado ■ *n* aparte *m*; **~ from** *prep* (*as well as*) aparte *or* además de
ask [ɑːsk] *vt* (*question*) preguntar; (*demand*) pedir; (*invite*) invitar ■ *vi*: **to ~ about sth** preguntar acerca de algo; **to ~ sb sth/to do sth** preguntar algo a algn/pedir a algn que haga algo; **to ~ sb about sth** preguntar algo a algn; **to ~ (sb) a question** hacer una pregunta (a algn); **to ~ sb the time** preguntar la hora a algn; **to ~ sb out to dinner** invitar a cenar a algn
▸ **ask after** *vt fus* preguntar por
▸ **ask for** *vt fus* pedir; **it's just asking for trouble** *or* **for it** es buscarse problemas
askance [ə'skɑːns] *adv*: **to look ~ at sb** mirar con recelo a algn
askew [ə'skjuː] *adv* sesgado, ladeado
asking price *n* (*Comm*) precio inicial
asleep [ə'sliːp] *adj* dormido; **to fall ~** dormirse, quedarse dormido
ASLEF ['æzlɛf] *n abbr* (*Brit: = Associated Society of Locomotive Engineers and Firemen*) *sindicato de ferroviarios*
AS level *n abbr* (*Brit Scol: = Advanced Subsidiary level*) *título intermedio entre los "GCSEs" y los "A levels"*
asp [æsp] *n* áspid *m*
asparagus [əs'pærəgəs] *n* espárragos *mpl*
ASPCA *n abbr* = **American Society for the Prevention of Cruelty to Animals**
aspect ['æspɛkt] *n* aspecto, apariencia; (*direction in which a building etc faces*) orientación *f*
aspersions [əs'pəːʃənz] *npl*: **to cast ~ on** difamar a, calumniar a
asphalt ['æsfælt] *n* asfalto
asphyxiate [æs'fɪksɪeɪt] *vt* asfixiar
asphyxiation [aesfɪksɪ'eɪʃən] *n* asfixia
aspirate ['æspəreɪt] *vt* aspirar ■ *adj* ['æspərɪt] aspirado
aspirations [æspə'reɪʃənz] *npl* aspiraciones *fpl*; (*ambition*) ambición *f*
aspire [əs'paɪə^r] *vi*: **to ~ to** aspirar a, ambicionar
aspirin ['æsprɪn] *n* aspirina
aspiring [əs'paɪərɪŋ] *adj*: **an ~ actor** un aspirante a actor
ass [æs] *n* asno, burro; (*col*) imbécil *m/f*; (*US col!*) culo, trasero
assailant [ə'seɪlənt] *n* agresor(a) *m(f)*
assassin [ə'sæsɪn] *n* asesino(-a)
assassinate [ə'sæsɪneɪt] *vt* asesinar
assassination [əsæsɪ'neɪʃən] *n* asesinato
assault [ə'sɔːlt] *n* (*gen: attack*) asalto, agresión *f* ■ *vt* asaltar, agredir; (*sexually*) violar
assemble [ə'sɛmbl] *vt* reunir, juntar; (*Tech*) montar ■ *vi* reunirse, juntarse
assembly [ə'sɛmblɪ] *n* (*meeting*) reunión *f*, asamblea; (*construction*) montaje *m*
assembly language *n* (*Comput*) lenguaje *m* ensamblador
assembly line *n* cadena de montaje
Assembly Member *n* (*in Wales*) miembro *m/f* de la Asamblea Nacional (de Gales)
assent [ə'sɛnt] *n* asentimiento, aprobación *f* ■ *vi* consentir, asentir; **to ~ (to sth)** consentir (en algo)
assert [ə'səːt] *vt* afirmar; (*insist on*) hacer valer; **to ~ o.s.** imponerse
assertion [ə'səːʃən] *n* afirmación *f*
assertive [ə'səːtɪv] *adj* enérgico, agresivo, perentorio
assess [ə'sɛs] *vt* valorar, calcular; (*tax, damages*) fijar; (*property etc: for tax*) gravar
assessment [ə'sɛsmənt] *n* valoración *f*; gravamen *m*; (*judgment*): **~ (of)** juicio (sobre)
assessor [ə'sɛsə^r] *n* asesor(a) *m(f)*; (*of tax*) tasador(a) *m(f)*
asset ['æsɛt] *n* posesión *f*; (*quality*) ventaja; **assets** *npl* (*funds*) activo *sg*, fondos *mpl*
asset-stripping ['æsɛt'strɪpɪŋ] *n* (*Comm*) acaparamiento de activos
assiduous [ə'sɪdjuəs] *adj* asiduo
assign [ə'saɪn] *vt* (*date*) fijar; (*task*) asignar; (*resources*) destinar; (*property*) traspasar
assignment [ə'saɪnmənt] *n* asignación *f*; (*task*) tarea
assimilate [ə'sɪmɪleɪt] *vt* asimilar
assimilation [əsɪmɪ'leɪʃən] *n* asimilación *f*
assist [ə'sɪst] *vt* ayudar
assistance [ə'sɪstəns] *n* ayuda, auxilio
assistant [ə'sɪstənt] *n* ayudante *m/f*; (*Brit: also*: **shop assistant**) dependiente(-a) *m(f)*
assistant manager *n* subdirector(a) *m(f)*
assizes [ə'saɪzɪz] *npl* sesión *f* de un tribunal
associate [*adj, n* ə'səuʃɪɪt, *vt, vi* ə'səuʃɪeɪt] *adj* asociado ■ *n* socio(-a), colega *m/f*; (*in crime*) cómplice *m/f*; (*member*) miembro(-a) ■ *vt* asociar; (*ideas*) relacionar ■ *vi*: **to ~ with sb** tratar con algn; **~ director** subdirector(a) *m(f)*; **associated company** compañía afiliada
association [əsəusɪ'eɪʃən] *n* asociación *f*; (*Comm*) sociedad *f*; **in ~ with** en asociación con
association football *n* (*Brit*) fútbol *m*
assorted [ə'sɔːtɪd] *adj* surtido, variado; **in ~ sizes** en distintos tamaños
assortment [ə'sɔːtmənt] *n* surtido
Asst. *abbr* = **Assistant**
assuage [ə'sweɪdʒ] *vt* mitigar
assume [ə'sjuːm] *vt* (*suppose*) suponer;

(*responsibilities etc*) asumir; (*attitude, name*) adoptar, tomar
assumed name *n* nombre *m* falso
assumption [ə'sʌmpʃən] *n* (*supposition*) suposición *f*, presunción *f*; (*act*) asunción *f*; **on the ~ that** suponiendo que
assurance [ə'ʃuərəns] *n* garantía, promesa; (*confidence*) confianza, aplomo; (*Brit: insurance*) seguro; **I can give you no assurances** no puedo hacerle ninguna promesa
assure [ə'ʃuəʳ] *vt* asegurar
assured [ə'ʃuəd] *adj* seguro
assuredly [ə'ʃuərɪdlɪ] *adv* indudablemente
AST *abbr* (= *Atlantic Standard Time*) *hora oficial del este del Canadá*
asterisk ['æstərɪsk] *n* asterisco
astern [ə'stəːn] *adv* a popa
asteroid ['æstərɔɪd] *n* asteroide *m*
asthma ['æsmə] *n* asma
asthmatic [æs'mætɪk] *adj, n* asmático(-a) *m(f)*
astigmatism [ə'stɪgmətɪzəm] *n* astigmatismo
astir [ə'stəːʳ] *adv* en acción
astonish [ə'stɔnɪʃ] *vt* asombrar, pasmar
astonishing [ə'stɔnɪʃɪŋ] *adj* asombroso, pasmoso; **I find it ~ that ...** me asombra *or* pasma que ...
astonishingly [ə'stɔnɪʃɪŋlɪ] *adv* increíblemente, asombrosamente
astonishment [ə'stɔnɪʃmənt] *n* asombro, sorpresa; **to my ~** con gran sorpresa mía
astound [ə'staund] *vt* asombrar, pasmar
astounding [ə'staundɪŋ] *adj* asombroso
astray [ə'streɪ] *adv*: **to go ~** extraviarse; **to lead ~** llevar por mal camino; **to go ~ in one's calculations** equivocarse en sus cálculos
astride [ə'straɪd] *prep* a caballo *or* horcajadas sobre
astringent [əs'trɪndʒənt] *adj, n* astringente *m*
astrologer [əs'trɔlədʒəʳ] *n* astrólogo(-a)
astrology [əs'trɔlədʒɪ] *n* astrología
astronaut ['æstrənɔːt] *n* astronauta *m/f*
astronomer [əs'trɔnəməʳ] *n* astrónomo(-a)
astronomical [æstrə'nɔmɪkəl] *adj* astronómico
astronomy [aes'trɔnəmɪ] *n* astronomía
astrophysics ['æstrəu'fɪzɪks] *n* astrofísica
astute [əs'tjuːt] *adj* astuto
asunder [ə'sʌndəʳ] *adv*: **to tear ~** hacer pedazos
ASV *n abbr* (= *American Standard Version*) *traducción de la Biblia*
asylum [ə'saɪləm] *n* (*refuge*) asilo; (*hospital*) manicomio; **to seek political ~** pedir asilo político
asymmetric [eɪsɪ'mɛtrɪk], **asymmetrical** [eɪsɪ'mɛtrɪkl] *adj* asimétrico

KEYWORD

at [æt] *prep* **1** (*referring to position*) en; (*direction*) a; **at the top** en lo alto; **at home/school** en casa/la escuela; **to look at sth/sb** mirar algo/a algn
2 (*referring to time*): **at four o'clock** a las cuatro; **at night** por la noche; **at Christmas** en Navidad; **at times** a veces
3 (*referring to rates, speed etc*): **at £1 a kilo** a una libra el kilo; **two at a time** de dos en dos; **at 50 km/h** a 50 km/h
4 (*referring to manner*): **at a stroke** de un golpe; **at peace** en paz
5 (*referring to activity*): **to be at work** estar trabajando; (*in office*) estar en el trabajo; **to play at cowboys** jugar a los vaqueros; **to be good at sth** ser bueno en algo
6 (*referring to cause*): **shocked/surprised/annoyed at sth** asombrado/sorprendido/fastidiado por algo; **I went at his suggestion** fui a instancias suyas
■ *n* (*symbol @*) arroba

ate [ɛt, eɪt] *pt of* **eat**
atheism ['eɪθɪɪzəm] *n* ateísmo
atheist ['eɪθɪɪst] *n* ateo(-a)
Athenian [ə'θiːnɪən] *adj, n* ateniense *m/f*
Athens ['æθɪnz] *n* Atenas *f*
athlete ['æθliːt] *n* atleta *m/f*
athletic [æθ'lɛtɪk] *adj* atlético
athletics [æθ'lɛtɪks] *n* atletismo
Atlantic [ət'læntɪk] *adj* atlántico ■ *n*: **the ~ (Ocean)** el (Océano) Atlántico
atlas ['ætləs] *n* atlas *m inv*
Atlas Mountains *npl*: **the ~** el Atlas
A.T.M. *n abbr* (= *Automated Telling Machine*) *cajero automático*
atmosphere ['ætməsfɪəʳ] *n* (*air*) atmósfera; (*fig*) ambiente *m*
atom ['ætəm] *n* átomo
atom bomb *n* bomba atómica
atomic [ə'tɔmɪk] *adj* atómico
atomic bomb *n* bomba atómica
atomic power *n* energía atómica
atomizer ['ætəmaɪzəʳ] *n* atomizador *m*
atone [ə'təun] *vi*: **to ~ for** expiar
atonement [ə'təunmənt] *n* expiación *f*
A to Z® *n* guía alfabética; (*map*) callejero
ATP *n abbr* (= *Association of Tennis Professionals*) *sindicato de jugadores de tenis profesionales*
atrocious [ə'trəuʃəs] *adj* atroz; (*fig*) horrible, infame
atrocity [ə'trɔsɪtɪ] *n* atrocidad *f*

atrophy ['ætrəfɪ] *n* atrofia ■ *vi* atrofiarse
attach [ə'tætʃ] *vt* sujetar; (*stick*) pegar; (*document, letter*) adjuntar; **to be attached to sb/sth** (*like*) tener cariño a algn/algo; **the attached letter** la carta adjunta
attaché [ə'tæʃeɪ] *n* agregado(-a)
attaché case *n* (*Brit*) maletín *m*
attachment [ə'tætʃmənt] *n* (*tool*) accesorio; (*Comput*) archivo *o* documento adjunto; (*love*): **~ (to)** apego (a), cariño (a)
attack [ə'tæk] *vt* (*Mil*) atacar; (*criminal*) agredir, asaltar; (*task etc*) emprender ■ *n* ataque *m*, asalto; (*on sb's life*) atentado; **heart ~** infarto (de miocardio)
attacker [ə'tækə^r] *n* agresor(a) *m(f)*, asaltante *m/f*
attain [ə'teɪn] *vt* (*also*: **attain to**) alcanzar; (*achieve*) lograr, conseguir
attainments [ə'teɪnmənts] *npl* (*skill*) talento *sg*
attempt [ə'tɛmpt] *n* tentativa, intento; (*attack*) atentado ■ *vt* intentar, tratar de; **he made no ~ to help** ni siquiera intentó ayudar
attempted [ə'tɛmptɪd] *adj*: **~ murder/burglary/suicide** tentativa *or* intento de asesinato/robo/suicidio
attend [ə'tɛnd] *vt* asistir a; (*patient*) atender
▸ **attend to** *vt fus* (*needs, affairs etc*) ocuparse de; (*speech etc*) prestar atención a; (*customer*) atender a
attendance [ə'tɛndəns] *n* asistencia, presencia; (*people present*) concurrencia
attendant [ə'tɛndənt] *n* sirviente(-a) *m(f)*, mozo(-a); (*Theat*) acomodador(a) *m(f)* ■ *adj* concomitante
attention [ə'tɛnʃən] *n* atención *f* ■ *excl* (*Mil*) ¡firme(s)!; **for the ~ of ...** (*Admin*) a la atención de ...; **it has come to my ~ that ...** me he enterado de que ...
attentive [ə'tɛntɪv] *adj* atento; (*polite*) cortés
attenuate [ə'tɛnjueɪt] *vt* atenuar
attest [ə'tɛst] *vi*: **to ~ to** dar fe de
attic ['ætɪk] *n* desván *m*, altillo (*LAm*), entretecho (*LAm*)
attitude ['ætɪtju:d] *n* (*gen*) actitud *f*; (*disposition*) disposición *f*
attorney [ə'tə:nɪ] *n* (*US: lawyer*) abogado(-a); (*having proxy*) apoderado
Attorney General *n* (*Brit*) ≈ Presidente *m* del Consejo del Poder Judicial (*SP*); (*US*) ≈ ministro de justicia
attract [ə'trækt] *vt* atraer; (*attention*) llamar
attraction [ə'trækʃən] *n* (*gen*) encanto, atractivo; (*Physics*) atracción *f*; (*towards sth*) atracción *f*
attractive [ə'træktɪv] *adj* atractivo
attribute ['ætrɪbju:t] *n* atributo ■ *vt* [ə'trɪbju:t]: **to ~ sth to** atribuir algo a; (*accuse*) achacar algo a
attrition [ə'trɪʃən] *n*: **war of ~** guerra de agotamiento *or* desgaste
Atty. Gen. *abbr* = **Attorney General**
ATV *n abbr* (= *all terrain vehicle*) vehículo todo terreno
atypical [eɪ'tɪpɪkl] *adj* atípico
AU *n abbr* (= *African Union*) UA *f* (= *Unión Africana*)
aubergine ['əubəʒi:n] *n* (*Brit*) berenjena
auburn ['ɔ:bən] *adj* color castaño rojizo
auction ['ɔ:kʃən] *n* (*also*: **sale by auction**) subasta ■ *vt* subastar
auctioneer [ɔ:kʃə'nɪə^r] *n* subastador(a) *m(f)*
auction room *n* sala de subastas
audacious [ɔ:'deɪʃəs] *adj* (*bold*) audaz, osado; (*impudent*) atrevido, descarado
audacity [ɔ:'dæsɪtɪ] *n* audacia, atrevimiento; (*pej*) descaro
audible ['ɔ:dɪbl] *adj* audible, que se puede oír
audience ['ɔ:dɪəns] *n* auditorio; (*gathering*) público; (*interview*) audiencia
audio-typist ['ɔ:dɪəu'taɪpɪst] *n* mecanógrafo(-a) de dictáfono
audiovisual [ɔ:dɪəu'vɪzjuəl] *adj* audiovisual
audiovisual aid *n* ayuda *or* medio audiovisual
audit ['ɔ:dɪt] *vt* revisar, intervenir
audition [ɔ:'dɪʃən] *n* audición *f* ■ *vi*: **to ~ for the part of** hacer una audición para el papel de
auditor ['ɔ:dɪtə^r] *n* interventor(a) *m(f)*, censor(a) *m(f)* de cuentas
auditorium [ɔ:dɪ'tɔ:rɪəm] *n* auditorio
Aug. *abbr* (= *August*) ag
augment [ɔ:g'mɛnt] *vt, vi* aumentar
augur ['ɔ:gə^r] *vi*: **it augurs well** es de buen agüero
August ['ɔ:gəst] *n* agosto; *see also* **July**
august [ɔ:'gʌst] *adj* augusto
aunt [ɑ:nt] *n* tía
auntie, aunty ['ɑ:ntɪ] *n diminutive of* **aunt**
au pair ['əu'pɛə^r] *n* (*also*: **au pair girl**) chica *f* au pair
aura ['ɔ:rə] *n* aura; (*atmosphere*) ambiente *m*
auspices ['ɔ:spɪsɪz] *npl*: **under the ~ of** bajo los auspicios de
auspicious [ɔ:s'pɪʃəs] *adj* propicio, de buen augurio
austere [ɔs'tɪə^r] *adj* austero; (*manner*) adusto
austerity [ɔ'stɛrɪtɪ] *n* austeridad *f*
Australasia [ɔ:strə'leɪzɪə] *n* Australasia
Australia [ɔs'treɪlɪə] *n* Australia
Australian [ɔs'treɪlɪən] *adj, n* australiano(-a) *m(f)*
Austria ['ɔstrɪə] *n* Austria

Austrian ['ɔstrɪən] *adj, n* austríaco(-a) *m(f)*
AUT *n abbr (Brit: = Association of University Teachers) sindicato de profesores de universidad*
authentic [ɔː'θɛntɪk] *adj* auténtico
authenticate [ɔː'θɛntɪkeɪt] *vt* autentificar
authenticity [ɔːθɛn'tɪsɪtɪ] *n* autenticidad *f*
author ['ɔːθəʳ] *n* autor(a) *m(f)*
authoritarian [ɔːθɔrɪ'tɛərɪən] *adj* autoritario
authoritative [ɔː'θɔrɪtətɪv] *adj* autorizado; (*manner*) autoritario
authority [ɔː'θɔrɪtɪ] *n* autoridad *f*; **the authorities** *npl* las autoridades; **to have ~ to do sth** tener autoridad para hacer algo
authorization [ɔːθəraɪ'zeɪʃən] *n* autorización *f*
authorize ['ɔːθəraɪz] *vt* autorizar
authorized capital *n* (*Comm*) capital *m* autorizado *or* social
autistic [ɔː'tɪstɪk] *adj* autista
auto ['ɔːtəu] *n* (*US*) coche *m*, carro (*LAm*), auto (*LAm*), automóvil *m*
autobiographical [ɔːtəbaɪə'græfɪkəl] *adj* autobiográfico
autobiography [ɔːtəbaɪ'ɔgrəfɪ] *n* autobiografía
autocratic [ɔːtə'krætɪk] *adj* autocrático
Autocue® ['ɔːtəukjuː] *n* autocue *m*, teleapuntador *m*
autograph ['ɔːtəgrɑːf] *n* autógrafo ■ *vt* firmar; (*photo etc*) dedicar
autoimmune [ɔːtəuɪ'mjuːn] *adj* autoinmune
automat ['ɔːtəmæt] *n* (*US*) restaurante *m* de autoservicio
automate ['ɔːtəmeɪt] *vt* automatizar
automated ['ɔːtəmeɪtɪd] *adj* automatizado
automatic [ɔːtə'mætɪk] *adj* automático ■ *n* (*gun*) pistola automática; (*washing machine*) lavadora
automatically [ɔːtə'mætɪklɪ] *adv* automáticamente
automatic data processing *n* proceso automático de datos
automation [ɔːtə'meɪʃən] *n* automatización *f*
automaton (*pl* **automata**) [ɔː'tɔmətən, -tə] *n* autómata
automobile ['ɔːtəməbiːl] *n* (*US*) coche *m*, carro (*LAm*), auto (*LAm*), automóvil *m*
autonomous [ɔː'tɔnəməs] *adj* autónomo
autonomy [ɔː'tɔnəmɪ] *n* autonomía
autopsy ['ɔːtɔpsɪ] *n* autopsia
autumn ['ɔːtəm] *n* otoño
auxiliary [ɔːg'zɪlɪərɪ] *adj* auxiliar
AV *n abbr (= Authorized Version) traducción inglesa de la Biblia* ■ *abbr* = **audiovisual**
Av. *abbr* (= *avenue*) Av., Avda
avail [ə'veɪl] *vt*: **to ~ o.s. of** aprovechar(se) de, valerse de ■ *n*: **to no ~** en vano, sin resultado
availability [əveɪlə'bɪlɪtɪ] *n* disponibilidad *f*
available [ə'veɪləbl] *adj* disponible; (*obtainable*) asequible; **to make sth ~ to sb** poner algo a la disposición de algn; **is the manager ~?** ¿está libre el gerente?
avalanche ['ævəlɑːnʃ] *n* alud *m*, avalancha
avant-garde ['ævɑ̃ŋ'gɑːd] *adj* de vanguardia
avarice ['ævərɪs] *n* avaricia
avaricious [ævə'rɪʃəs] *adj* avaricioso
avdp. *abbr* = **avoirdupois**
Ave. *abbr* (= *avenue*) Av., Avda
avenge [ə'vɛndʒ] *vt* vengar
avenue ['ævənjuː] *n* avenida; (*fig*) camino, vía
average ['ævərɪdʒ] *n* promedio, media ■ *adj* (*mean*) medio; (*ordinary*) regular, corriente ■ *vt* calcular el promedio de; **on ~** por término medio
▸ **average out** *vi*: **to ~ out at** salir a un promedio de
averse [ə'vəːs] *adj*: **to be ~ to sth/doing** sentir aversión *or* antipatía por algo/por hacer
aversion [ə'vəːʃən] *n* aversión *f*, repugnancia
avert [ə'vəːt] *vt* prevenir; (*blow*) desviar; (*one's eyes*) apartar
aviary ['eɪvɪərɪ] *n* pajarera
aviation [eɪvɪ'eɪʃən] *n* aviación *f*
aviator ['eɪvɪeɪtəʳ] *n* aviador(a) *m(f)*
avid ['ævɪd] *adj* ávido, ansioso
avidly ['ævɪdlɪ] *adv* ávidamente, con avidez
avocado [ævə'kɑːdəu] *n* (*Brit: also*: **avocado pear**) aguacate *m*, palta (*LAm*)
avoid [ə'vɔɪd] *vt* evitar, eludir
avoidable [ə'vɔɪdəbl] *adj* evitable, eludible
avoidance [ə'vɔɪdəns] *n* evasión *f*
avow [ə'vau] *vt* prometer
avowal [ə'vauəl] *n* promesa, voto
avowed [ə'vaud] *adj* declarado
AVP *n abbr* (*US*) = **assistant vice-president**
avuncular [ə'vʌŋkjuləʳ] *adj* paternal
AWACS ['eɪwæks] *n abbr* (= *airborne warning and control system*) AWACS *m*
await [ə'weɪt] *vt* esperar, aguardar; **long awaited** largamente esperado
awake [ə'weɪk] (*pt* **awoke**, *pp* **awoken** *or* **awaked**) *adj* despierto ■ *vt* despertar ■ *vi* despertarse; **to be ~** estar despierto
awakening [ə'weɪknɪŋ] *n* despertar *m*
award [ə'wɔːd] *n* (*prize*) premio; (*medal*) condecoración *f*; (*Law*) fallo, sentencia; (*act*) concesión *f* ■ *vt* (*prize*) otorgar, conceder; (*Law: damages*) adjudicar
aware [ə'wɛəʳ] *adj* consciente; (*awake*) despierto; (*informed*) enterado; **to become ~ of** darse cuenta de, enterarse de; **I am fully ~ that** sé muy bien que
awareness [ə'wɛənɪs] *n* conciencia, conocimiento
awash [ə'wɔʃ] *adj* inundado

away [ə'weɪ] *adv* (*gen*) fuera; (*far away*) lejos; **two kilometres ~** a dos kilómetros (de distancia); **two hours ~ by car** a dos horas en coche; **the holiday was two weeks ~** faltaban dos semanas para las vacaciones; **~ from** lejos de, fuera de; **he's ~ for a week** estará ausente una semana; **he's ~ in Barcelona** está en Barcelona; **to take ~** llevar(se); **to work/pedal ~** seguir trabajando/pedaleando; **to fade ~** desvanecerse; (*sound*) apagarse
away game *n* (*Sport*) partido de fuera
awe [ɔː] *n* respeto, temor *m* reverencial
awe-inspiring ['ɔːɪnspaɪərɪŋ], **awesome** ['ɔːsəm] *adj* imponente, pasmoso
awestruck ['ɔːstrʌk] *adj* pasmado
awful ['ɔːfəl] *adj* terrible; **an ~ lot of** (*people, cars, dogs*) la mar de, muchísimos
awfully ['ɔːfəlɪ] *adv* (*very*) terriblemente
awhile [ə'waɪl] *adv* (durante) un rato, algún tiempo
awkward ['ɔːkwəd] *adj* (*clumsy*) desmañado, torpe; (*shape, situation*) incómodo; (*difficult: question*) difícil; (*problem*) complicado
awkwardness ['ɔːkwədnɪs] *n* (*clumsiness*) torpeza; (*of situation*) incomodidad *f*
awl [ɔːl] *n* lezna, subilla
awning ['ɔːnɪŋ] *n* (*of shop*) toldo; (*of window etc*) marquesina
awoke [ə'wəuk], **awoken** [ə'wəukən] *pt, pp of* **awake**
AWOL ['eɪwɔl] *abbr* (*Mil etc*) *see* **absent without leave**
awry [ə'raɪ] *adv*: **to be ~** estar descolocado *or* atravesado; **to go ~** salir mal, fracasar
axe, ax (*US*) [æks] *n* hacha ■ *vt* (*employee*) despedir; (*project etc*) cortar; (*jobs*) reducir; **to have an ~ to grind** (*fig*) tener un interés creado *or* algún fin interesado
axes ['æksiːz] *npl of* **axis**
axiom ['æksɪəm] *n* axioma *m*
axiomatic [æksɪə'mætɪk] *adj* axiomático
axis (*pl* **axes**) ['æksɪs, -siːz] *n* eje *m*
axle ['æksl] *n* eje *m*, árbol *m*
ay, aye [aɪ] *excl* (*yes*) sí; **the ayes** los que votan a favor
AYH *n abbr* = **American Youth Hostels**
AZ *abbr* (*US*) = **Arizona**
azalea [ə'zeɪlɪə] *n* azalea
Azerbaijan [æzəbaɪ'dʒɑːn] *n* Azerbaiyán *m*
Azerbaijani [æzəbaɪ'dʒɑːnɪ], **Azeri** [ə'zɛərɪ] *adj, n* azerbaiyano(-a), azerí *m/f*
Azores [ə'zɔːz] *npl*: **the ~** las (Islas) Azores
AZT *n abbr* (= *azidothymidine*) AZT *m*
Aztec ['æztɛk] *adj, n* azteca *m/f*
azure ['eɪʒə^r] *adj* celeste

Bb

B, b [bi:] *n* (*letter*) B, b *f*; (*Scol: mark*) N; (*Mus*) si *m*; **B for Benjamin,** (*US*) **B for Baker** B de Barcelona; **B road** (*Brit Aut*) ≈ carretera secundaria
b. *abbr* = **born**
BA *n abbr* = **British Academy**; (*Scol*) = **Bachelor of Arts**; *see also* **Bachelor's Degree**
babble ['bæbl] *vi* farfullar
babe [beɪb] *n* criatura
baboon [bə'bu:n] *n* mandril *m*
baby ['beɪbɪ] *n* bebé *m/f*
baby carriage *n* (*US*) cochecito
babyish ['beɪbɪɪʃ] *adj* infantil
baby-minder ['beɪbɪ'maɪndə^{r}] *n* niñera *f* (cualificada)
baby-sit ['beɪbɪsɪt] *vi* hacer de canguro
baby-sitter ['beɪbɪsɪtə^{r}] *n* canguro *m/f*
bachelor ['bætʃələ^{r}] *n* soltero; **B~ of Arts/ Science (BA/BSc)** licenciado(-a) en Filosofía y Letras/Ciencias
bachelor's degree *n* licenciatura; *ver nota*

BACHELOR'S DEGREE

Se denomina *Bachelor's Degree* a la titulación que se recibe al finalizar el primer ciclo universitario, normalmente después de un período de estudio de tres o cuatro años. Las titulaciones más frecuentes son las de Letras, "BA (Bachelor of Arts)", Ciencias, "BSc (Bachelor of Science)", Educación, "BEd (Bachelor of Education)" y Derecho, "LLB (Bachelor of Laws)".

back [bæk] *n* (*of person*) espalda; (*of animal*) lomo; (*of hand, page*) dorso; (*as opposed to front*) parte *f* de atrás; (*of room*) fondo; (*of chair*) respaldo; (*Football*) defensa *m*; **to have one's ~ to the wall** (*fig*) estar entre la espada y la pared; **to break the ~ of a job** hacer lo más difícil de un trabajo; **~ to front** al revés; **at the ~ of my mind was the thought that ...** en el fondo tenía la idea de que ... ■ *vt* (*candidate: also:* **back up**) respaldar, apoyar; (*horse: at races*) apostar a; (*car*) dar marcha atrás a *or* con ■ *vi* (*car etc*) dar marcha atrás ■ *adj* (*in compounds*) de atrás; **~ seats/wheels** (*Aut*) asientos *mpl* traseros, ruedas *fpl* traseras; **~ garden/room** jardín *m*/ habitación *f* de atrás; **~ payments** pagos *mpl* con efecto retroactivo; **~ rent** renta atrasada; **to take a ~ seat** (*fig*) pasar a segundo plano ■ *adv* (*not forward*) (hacia) atrás; **he's ~** (*returned*) ha vuelto; **he ran ~** volvió corriendo; **throw the ball ~** (*restitution*) devuelve la pelota; **can I have it ~?** ¿me lo devuelve?; **he called ~** (*again*) volvió a llamar; **~ and forth** de acá para allá; **as far ~ as the 13th century** ya en el siglo XIII; **when will you be ~?** ¿cuándo volverá?
▸ **back down** *vi* echarse atrás
▸ **back on to** *vt fus*: **the house backs on to the golf course** por atrás la casa da al campo de golf
▸ **back out** *vi* (*of promise*) volverse atrás
▸ **back up** *vt* (*support: person*) apoyar, respaldar; (*: theory*) defender; (*car*) dar marcha atrás a; (*Comput*) hacer una copia de reserva de
backache ['bækeɪk] *n* dolor *m* de espalda
backbencher ['bæk'bɛntʃə^{r}] *n* (*Brit*) *diputado sin cargo oficial en el gobierno o la oposición*
back benches *npl* (*Brit*) *ver nota*

BACK BENCHES

Reciben el nombre genérico de the *back benches* los escaños más alejados del pasillo central en la Cámara de los Comunes del Parlamento británico, que son ocupados por los "backbenchers", los miembros de la cámara que no tienen cargo en el gobierno o en la oposición.

backbiting ['bækbaɪtɪŋ] *n* murmuración *f*

backbone ['bækbəun] *n* columna vertebral; **the ~ of the organization** el pilar de la organización
backchat ['bæktʃæt] *n* réplicas *fpl*
backcloth ['bækklɔθ] *n* telón *m* de fondo
backcomb ['bækkəum] *vt* cardar
backdate [bæk'deɪt] *vt* (*letter*) poner fecha atrasada a; **backdated pay rise** aumento de sueldo con efecto retroactivo
backdrop ['bækdrɔp] *n* = **backcloth**
backer ['bækəʳ] *n* partidario(-a); (*Comm*) promotor(a) *m(f)*
backfire [bæk'faɪəʳ] *vi* (*Aut*) petardear; (*plans*) fallar, salir mal
backgammon ['bækgæmən] *n* backgammon *m*
background ['bækgraund] *n* fondo; (*of events*) antecedentes *mpl*; (*basic knowledge*) bases *fpl*; (*experience*) conocimientos *mpl*, educación *f* ■ *cpd* (*noise, music*) de fondo; (*Comput*) secundario; **~ reading** lectura de preparación; **family ~** origen *m*, antecedentes *mpl* familiares
backhand ['bækhænd] *n* (*Tennis: also:* **backhand stroke**) revés *m*
backhanded ['bæk'hændɪd] *adj* (*fig*) ambiguo, equívoco
backhander ['bæk'hændəʳ] *n* (*Brit: bribe*) soborno
backing ['bækɪŋ] *n* (*fig*) apoyo, respaldo; (*Comm*) respaldo financiero; (*Mus*) acompañamiento
backlash ['bæklæʃ] *n* reacción *f* (en contra)
backlog ['bæklɔg] *n*: **~ of work** trabajo atrasado
back number *n* (*of magazine etc*) número atrasado
backpack ['bækpæk] *n* mochila
backpacker ['bækpækəʳ] *n* mochilero(-a)
back pay *n* atrasos *mpl*
backpedal ['bækpɛdl] *vi* (*fig*) volverse/echarse atrás
backseat driver ['bæksi:t-] *n* *pasajero que se empeña en aconsejar al conductor*
backside ['bæksaɪd] *n* (*col*) trasero
backslash ['bækslæʃ] *n* pleca, barra inversa
backslide ['bækslaɪd] *vi* reincidir, recaer
backspace ['bækspeɪs] *vi* (*in typing*) retroceder
backstage [bæk'steɪdʒ] *adv* entre bastidores
back-street ['bækstri:t] *adj* de barrio; **~ abortionist** persona que practica abortos clandestinos
backstroke ['bækstrəuk] *n* espalda
backtrack ['bæktræk] *vi* (*fig*) = **backpedal**
backup ['bækʌp] *adj* (*train, plane*) suplementario; (*Comput: disk, file*) de reserva ■ *n* (*support*) apoyo; (*also:* **backup file**) copia de reserva; (*US: congestion*) embotellamiento, retención *f*
back-up lights *npl* (*US*) luces *fpl* de marcha atrás
backward ['bækwəd] *adj* (*movement*) hacia atrás; (*person, country*) atrasado; (*shy*) tímido
backwardness ['bækwədnɪs] *n* atraso
backwards ['bækwədz] *adv* (*move, go*) hacia atrás; (*read a list*) al revés; (*fall*) de espaldas; **to know sth ~** *or* (*US*) **~ and forwards** (*col*) saberse algo al dedillo
backwater ['bækwɔ:təʳ] *n* (*fig*) lugar *m* atrasado *or* apartado
backyard [bæk'jɑ:d] *n* patio trasero
bacon ['beɪkən] *n* tocino, bacon *m*, beicon *m*
bacteria [bæk'tɪərɪə] *npl* bacterias *fpl*
bacteriology [bæktɪərɪ'ɔlədʒɪ] *n* bacteriología
bad [bæd] *adj* malo; (*serious*) grave; (*meat, food*) podrido, pasado; **to go ~** pasarse; **to have a ~ time of it** pasarlo mal; **I feel ~ about it** (*guilty*) me siento culpable; **~ debt** (*Comm*) cuenta incobrable; **in ~ faith** de mala fe
baddie, baddy ['bædɪ] *n* (*col: Cine etc*) malo(-a)
bade [bæd] [beɪd] *pt of* **bid**
badge [bædʒ] *n* insignia; (*metal badge*) chapa; (*of policeman*) placa; (*stick-on*) pegatina
badger ['bædʒəʳ] *n* tejón *m*
badly ['bædlɪ] *adv* (*work, dress etc*) mal; **~ wounded** gravemente herido; **he needs it ~** le hace mucha falta; **to be ~ off (for money)** andar mal de dinero; **things are going ~** las cosas van muy mal
bad-mannered ['bæd'mænəd] *adj* mal educado
badminton ['bædmɪntən] *n* bádminton *m*
bad-tempered ['bæd'tɛmpəd] *adj* de mal genio *or* carácter; (*temporary*) de mal humor
baffle ['bæfl] *vt* desconcertar, confundir
baffling ['bæflɪŋ] *adj* incomprensible
bag [bæg] *n* bolsa; (*handbag*) bolso; (*satchel*) mochila; (*case*) maleta; (*of hunter*) caza ■ *vt* (*col: take*) coger (*SP*), agarrar (*LAm*), pescar; **bags of** (*col: lots of*) un montón de; **to pack one's bags** hacer las maletas
bagful ['bægful] *n* saco (lleno)
baggage ['bægɪdʒ] *n* equipaje *m*
baggage claim *n* recogida de equipajes
baggy ['bægɪ] *adj* (*trousers*) ancho, holgado
Baghdad [bæg'dæd] *n* Bagdad *m*
bag lady *n* (*col*) *mujer sin hogar cargada de bolsas*
bagpipes ['bægpaɪps] *npl* gaita *sg*
bag-snatcher ['bægsnætʃəʳ] *n* (*Brit*) ladrón(-ona) *m(f)* de bolsos
bag-snatching ['bægsnætʃɪŋ] *n* (*Brit*) tirón *m* (de bolsos)

Bahamas [bə'hɑːməz] *npl*: **the ~** las (Islas) Bahama
Bahrain [bɑː'reɪn] *n* Bahrein *m*
bail [beɪl] *n* fianza ■ *vt* (*prisoner: also*: **grant bail to**) poner en libertad bajo fianza; (*boat: also*: **bail out**) achicar; **on ~** (*prisoner*) bajo fianza; **to be released on ~** ser puesto en libertad bajo fianza; **to ~ sb out** pagar la fianza de algn; *see also* **bale**
bailiff ['beɪlɪf] *n* alguacil *m*
bait [beɪt] *n* cebo ■ *vt* poner el cebo en
bake [beɪk] *vt* cocer (al horno) ■ *vi* (*cook*) cocerse; (*be hot*) hacer un calor terrible
baked beans *npl* judías *fpl* en salsa de tomate
baker ['beɪkə^r] *n* panadero(-a)
baker's dozen *n* docena del fraile
bakery ['beɪkərɪ] *n* (*for bread*) panadería; (*for cakes*) pastelería
baking ['beɪkɪŋ] *n* (*act*) cocción *f*; (*batch*) hornada
baking powder *n* levadura (en polvo)
baking tin *n* molde *m* (para horno)
balaclava [bælə'klɑːvə] *n* (*also*: **balaclava helmet**) pasamontañas *m inv*
balance ['bæləns] *n* equilibrio; (*Comm: sum*) balance *m*; (*remainder*) resto; (*scales*) balanza ■ *vt* equilibrar; (*budget*) nivelar; (*account*) saldar; (*compensate*) compensar; **~ of trade/payments** balanza de comercio/pagos; **~ carried forward** balance *m* pasado a cuenta nueva; **~ brought forward** saldo de hoja anterior; **to ~ the books** hacer el balance
balanced ['bælənst] *adj* (*personality, diet*) equilibrado
balance sheet *n* balance *m*
balcony ['bælkənɪ] *n* (*open*) balcón *m*; (*closed*) galería
bald [bɔːld] *adj* calvo; (*tyre*) liso
baldness ['bɔːldnɪs] *n* calvicie *f*
bale [beɪl] *n* (*Agr*) paca, fardo
▸ **bale out** *vi* (*of a plane*) lanzarse en paracaídas ■ *vt* (*Naut*) achicar; **to ~ sb out of a difficulty** sacar a algn de un apuro
Balearic Islands [bælɪ'ærɪk-] *npl*: **the ~** las (Islas) Baleares
baleful ['beɪlful] *adj* (*look*) triste; (*sinister*) funesto, siniestro
balk [bɔːk] *vi*: **to ~ (at)** resistirse (a); (*horse*) plantarse (ante)
Balkan ['bɔːlkən] *adj* balcánico ■ *n*: **the Balkans** los Balcanes
ball [bɔːl] *n* (*sphere*) bola; (*football*) balón *m*; (*for tennis, golf etc*) pelota; (*dance*) baile *m*; **to be on the ~** (*fig: competent*) ser un enterado; (*: alert*) estar al tanto; **to play ~ (with sb)** jugar a la pelota (con algn); (*fig*) cooperar; **to start the ~ rolling** (*fig*) empezar; **the ~ is in your court** (*fig*) le toca a usted
ballad ['bæləd] *n* balada, romance *m*
ballast ['bæləst] *n* lastre *m*
ball bearing *n* cojinete *m* de bolas
ballcock ['bɔːlkɔk] *n* llave *f* de bola *or* de flotador
ballerina [bælə'riːnə] *n* bailarina
ballet ['bæleɪ] *n* ballet *m*
ballet dancer *n* bailarín(-ina) *m(f)* (de ballet)
ballistic [bə'lɪstɪk] *adj* balístico; **intercontinental ~ missile** misil *m* balístico intercontinental
ballistics [bə'lɪstɪks] *n* balística
balloon [bə'luːn] *n* globo; (*in comic strip*) bocadillo ■ *vi* dispararse
balloonist [bə'luːnɪst] *n* aeróstata *m/f*
ballot ['bælət] *n* votación *f*
ballot box *n* urna (electoral)
ballot paper *n* papeleta
ballpark ['bɔːlpɑːk] *n* (*US*) estadio de béisbol
ball-point pen ['bɔːlpɔɪnt-] *n* bolígrafo
ballroom ['bɔːlrum] *n* salón *m* de baile
balm [bɑːm] *n* (*also fig*) bálsamo
balmy ['bɑːmɪ] *adj* (*breeze, air*) suave; (*col*) = **barmy**
BALPA ['bælpə] *n abbr* (= *British Airline Pilots' Association*) *sindicato de pilotos de líneas aéreas*
balsa ['bɔːlsə], **balsa wood** *n* (madera de) balsa
Baltic ['bɔːltɪk] *adj* báltico ■ *n*: **the ~ (Sea)** el (Mar) Báltico
balustrade ['bæləstreɪd] *n* barandilla
bamboo [bæm'buː] *n* bambú *m*
bamboozle [bæm'buːzl] *vt* (*col*) embaucar, engatusar
ban [bæn] *n* prohibición *f* ■ *vt* prohibir; (*exclude*) excluir; **he was banned from driving** le retiraron el carnet de conducir
banal [bə'nɑːl] *adj* banal, vulgar
banana [bə'nɑːnə] *n* plátano, banana (*LAm*)
band [bænd] *n* (*group*) banda; (*gang*) pandilla; (*strip*) faja, tira; (*at a dance*) orquesta; (*Mil*) banda; (*rock band*) grupo
▸ **band together** *vi* juntarse, asociarse
bandage ['bændɪdʒ] *n* venda, vendaje *m* ■ *vt* vendar
Band-Aid® ['bændeɪd] *n* (*US*) tirita, curita (*LAm*)
B & B *n abbr* = **bed and breakfast**
bandit ['bændɪt] *n* bandido; **one-armed ~** máquina tragaperras
bandstand ['bændstænd] *n* quiosco de música
bandwagon ['bændwægən] *n*: **to jump on the ~** (*fig*) subirse al carro
bandy ['bændɪ] *vt* (*jokes, insults*) intercambiar
bandy-legged ['bændɪ'lɛgd] *adj* patizambo

bane [beɪn] *n*: **it** *(or* **he** *etc)* **is the ~ of my life** me amarga la vida
bang [bæŋ] *n* estallido; *(of door)* portazo; *(blow)* golpe *m* ■ *vt* golpear ■ *vi* estallar ■ *adv*: **to be ~ on time** *(col)* llegar en punto; **to ~ the door** dar un portazo; **to ~ into sth** chocar con algo, golpearse contra algo; *see also* **bangs**
banger ['bæŋəʳ] *n* *(Brit: car: also:* **old banger***)* armatoste *m*, cacharro; *(Brit col: sausage)* salchicha; *(firework)* petardo
Bangkok [bæŋ'kɔk] *n* Bangkok *m*
Bangladesh [bæŋglə'dɛʃ] *n* Bangladesh *f*
bangle ['bæŋgl] *n* brazalete *m*, ajorca
bangs [bæŋz] *npl* *(US)* flequillo *sg*
banish ['bænɪʃ] *vt* desterrar
banister ['bænɪstəʳ] *n*, **banisters** ['bænɪstəz] ■ *npl* barandilla *f*, pasamanos *m inv*
banjo *(pl* **banjoes** *or* **banjos***)* ['bændʒəu] *n* banjo
bank [bæŋk] *n* *(Comm)* banco; *(of river, lake)* ribera, orilla; *(of earth)* terraplén *m* ■ *vi* *(Aviat)* ladearse; *(Comm)*: **to ~ with** tener la cuenta en
▸ **bank on** *vt fus* contar con
bank account *n* cuenta bancaria
bank balance *n* saldo
bank card *n* = **banker's card**
bank charges *npl* comisión *fsg*
bank draft *n* letra de cambio
banker ['bæŋkəʳ] *n* banquero; **~'s card** *(Brit)* tarjeta bancaria; **~'s order** orden *f* bancaria
bank giro *n* giro bancario
bank holiday *n* *(Brit)* día *m* festivo *or* de fiesta; *ver nota*

BANK HOLIDAY

El término *bank holiday* se aplica en el Reino Unido a todo día festivo oficial en el que cierran bancos y comercios. Los más destacados coinciden con Navidad, Semana Santa, finales de mayo y finales de agosto. Al contrario que en los países de tradición católica, no se celebran las festividades dedicadas a los santos.

banking ['bæŋkɪŋ] *n* banca
bank loan *n* préstamo bancario
bank manager *n* director(a) *m(f)* (de sucursal) de banco
banknote ['bæŋknəut] *n* billete *m* de banco
bank rate *n* tipo de interés bancario
bankrupt ['bæŋkrʌpt] *n* quebrado(-a) ■ *adj* quebrado, insolvente; **to go ~** quebrar, hacer bancarrota; **to be ~** estar en quiebra
bankruptcy ['bæŋkrʌptsɪ] *n* quiebra, bancarrota
bank statement *n* extracto de cuenta
banned substance ['bænd -] *n* *(Sport)* sustancia prohibida
banner ['bænəʳ] *n* bandera; *(in demonstration)* pancarta
banns [bænz] *npl* amonestaciones *fpl*
banquet ['bæŋkwɪt] *n* banquete *m*
banter ['bæntəʳ] *n* guasa, bromas *fpl*
baptism ['bæptɪzəm] *n* bautismo; *(act)* bautizo
baptize [bæp'taɪz] *vt* bautizar
bar [bɑːʳ] *n* barra; *(on door)* tranca; *(of window, cage)* reja; *(of soap)* pastilla; *(fig: hindrance)* obstáculo; *(prohibition)* prohibición *f*; *(pub)* bar *m*, cantina *(esp LAm)*; *(counter: in pub)* barra, mostrador *m*; *(Mus)* barra ■ *vt* *(road)* obstruir; *(window, door)* atrancar; *(person)* excluir; *(activity)* prohibir; **behind bars** entre rejas; **the B~** *(Law: profession)* la abogacía; *(: people)* el cuerpo de abogados; **~ none** sin excepción
Barbados [bɑː'beɪdɔs] *n* Barbados *m*
barbarian [bɑː'bɛərɪən] *n* bárbaro(-a)
barbaric [bɑː'bærɪk] *adj* bárbaro
barbarity [bɑː'bærɪtɪ] *n* barbaridad *f*
barbarous ['bɑːbərəs] *adj* bárbaro
barbecue ['bɑːbɪkjuː] *n* barbacoa, asado *(LAm)*
barbed wire ['bɑːbd-] *n* alambre *m* de espino
barber ['bɑːbəʳ] *n* peluquero, barbero
barbiturate [bɑː'bɪtjurɪt] *n* barbitúrico
Barcelona [bɑːsɪ'ləunə] *n* Barcelona
bar chart *n* gráfico de barras
bar code *n* código de barras
bare [bɛəʳ] *adj* desnudo; *(head)* descubierto ■ *vt* desnudar; **to ~ one's teeth** enseñar los dientes
bareback ['bɛəbæk] *adv* a pelo
barefaced ['bɛəfeɪst] *adj* descarado
barefoot ['bɛəfut] *adj, adv* descalzo
bareheaded [bɛə'hɛdɪd] *adj* descubierto, sin sombrero
barely ['bɛəlɪ] *adv* apenas
bareness ['bɛənɪs] *n* desnudez *f*
Barents Sea ['bærənts-] *n*: **the ~** el Mar de Barents
bargain ['bɑːgɪn] *n* pacto; *(transaction)* negocio; *(good buy)* ganga ■ *vi* negociar; *(haggle)* regatear; **into the ~** además, por añadidura
▸ **bargain for** *vt fus* *(col)*: **he got more than he bargained for** le resultó peor de lo que esperaba
bargaining ['bɑːgənɪŋ] *n* negociación *f*, regateo; **~ table** mesa de negociaciones
bargaining position *n*: **to be in a strong/weak ~** estar/no estar en una posición de fuerza para negociar

barge [bɑ:dʒ] *n* barcaza
▸ **barge in** *vi* irrumpir; (*in conversation*) entrometerse
▸ **barge into** *vt fus* dar contra
baritone ['bærɪtəun] *n* barítono
barium meal ['bɛərɪəm-] *n* (*Med*) sulfato de bario
bark [bɑ:k] *n* (*of tree*) corteza; (*of dog*) ladrido ■ *vi* ladrar
barley ['bɑ:lɪ] *n* cebada
barley sugar *n* azúcar *m* cande
barmaid ['bɑ:meɪd] *n* camarera
barman ['bɑ:mən] *n* camarero, barman *m*
barmy ['bɑ:mɪ] *adj* (*col*) chiflado, chalado
barn [bɑ:n] *n* granero; (*for animals*) cuadra
barnacle ['bɑ:nəkl] *n* percebe *m*
barn owl *n* lechuza
barometer [bə'rɔmɪtə^r] *n* barómetro
baron ['bærən] *n* barón *m*; (*fig*) magnate *m*; **the press barons** los magnates de la prensa
baroness ['bærənɪs] *n* baronesa
baroque [bə'rɔk] *adj* barroco
barrack ['bærək] *vt* (*Brit*) abuchear
barracking ['bærəkɪŋ] *n*: **to give sb a ~** (*Brit*) abuchear a algn
barracks ['bærəks] *npl* cuartel *msg*
barrage ['bærɑ:ʒ] *n* (*Mil*) cortina de fuego; (*dam*) presa; (*fig: of criticism etc*) lluvia, aluvión *m*; **a ~ of questions** una lluvia de preguntas
barrel ['bærəl] *n* barril *m*; (*of wine*) tonel *m*, cuba; (*of gun*) cañón *m*
barren ['bærən] *adj* estéril
barricade [bærɪ'keɪd] *n* barricada ■ *vt* cerrar con barricadas
barrier ['bærɪə^r] *n* barrera; (*crash barrier*) barrera
barrier cream *n* crema protectora
barring ['bɑ:rɪŋ] *prep* excepto, salvo
barrister ['bærɪstə^r] *n* (*Brit*) abogado(-a); *ver nota*

BARRISTER

En el sistema legal inglés *barrister* es el abogado que se ocupa de defender los casos de sus clientes en los tribunales superiores. El equivalente escocés es "advocate". Normalmente actúan según instrucciones de un "solicitor", abogado de despacho que no toma parte activa en los juicios de dichos tribunales. El título de *barrister* lo otorga el órgano colegiado correspondiente, "the Inns of Court".

barrow ['bærəu] *n* (*cart*) carretilla
barstool ['bɑ:stu:l] *n* taburete *m* (de bar)
Bart. *abbr* (*Brit*) = **baronet**
bartender ['bɑ:tɛndə^r] *n* (*US*) camarero, barman *m*
barter ['bɑ:tə^r] *vt*: **to ~ sth for sth** trocar algo por algo
base [beɪs] *n* base *f* ■ *vt*: **to ~ sth on** basar *or* fundar algo en ■ *adj* bajo, infame; **to ~ at** (*troops*) estacionar en; **I'm based in London** (*work*) trabajo en Londres
baseball ['beɪsbɔ:l] *n* béisbol *m*
base camp *n* campamento base
Basel ['bɑ:zəl] *n* Basilea
baseless ['beɪslɪs] *adj* infundado
baseline ['beɪslaɪn] *n* (*Tennis*) línea de fondo
basement ['beɪsmənt] *n* sótano
base rate *n* tipo base
bases ['beɪsi:z] *npl of* **basis** ['beɪsɪz] ■ *npl of* **base**
bash [bæʃ] *n*: **I'll have a ~ (at it)** lo intentaré ■ *vt* (*col*) golpear
▸ **bash up** *vt* (*col: car*) destrozar; (*: person*) aporrear, vapulear
bashful ['bæʃful] *adj* tímido, vergonzoso
bashing ['bæʃɪŋ] *n* (*col*) paliza; **to go Paki-/queer-~** ir a dar una paliza a los paquistaníes/a los maricas
BASIC ['beɪsɪk] *n* (*Comput*) BASIC *m*
basic ['beɪsɪk] *adj* (*salary etc*) básico; (*elementary: principles*) fundamental
basically ['beɪsɪklɪ] *adv* fundamentalmente, en el fondo
basic rate *n* (*of tax*) base *f* mínima imponible
basil ['bæzl] *n* albahaca
basin ['beɪsn] *n* (*vessel*) cuenco, tazón *m*; (*Geo*) cuenca; (*also:* **washbasin**) palangana, jofaina; (*in bathroom*) lavabo
basis ['beɪsɪs] (*pl* **-ses**) [-si:z] *n* base *f*; **on the ~ of what you've said** en base a lo que has dicho
bask [bɑ:sk] *vi*: **to ~ in the sun** tomar el sol
basket ['bɑ:skɪt] *n* cesta, cesto
basketball ['bɑ:skɪtbɔ:l] *n* baloncesto
basketball player *n* jugador(a) *m(f)* de baloncesto
basketwork ['bɑ:skɪtwə:k] *n* cestería
Basle [bɑ:l] *n* Basilea
basmati rice [bəz'mætɪ-] *n* arroz *m* basmati
Basque [bæsk] *adj, n* vasco(-a) *m(f)*
Basque Country *n* Euskadi *m*, País *m* Vasco
bass [beɪs] *n* (*Mus*) bajo
bass clef *n* clave *f* de fa
bassoon [bə'su:n] *n* fagot *m*
bastard ['bɑ:stəd] *n* bastardo(-a); (*col!*) cabrón *m*, hijo de puta (*!*)
baste [beɪst] *vt* (*Culin*) rociar (con su salsa)
bastion ['bæstɪən] *n* bastión *m*, baluarte *m*
bat [bæt] *n* (*Zool*) murciélago; (*for ball games*) palo; (*for cricket, baseball*) bate *m*; (*Brit: for*

table tennis) pala; **he didn't ~ an eyelid** ni pestañeó, ni se inmutó
batch [bætʃ] *n* lote *m*, remesa; (*of bread*) hornada
bated ['beɪtɪd] *adj*: **with ~ breath** sin respirar
bath [bɑːθ, *pl* bɑːðz] *n* (*act*) baño; (*bathtub*) bañera, tina (*esp LAm*) ▪ *vt* bañar; **to have a ~** bañarse, darse un baño; *see also* **baths**
bathchair ['bɑːθtʃɛəʳ] *n* silla de ruedas
bathe [beɪð] *vi* bañarse; (*US*) darse un baño, bañarse ▪ *vt* (*wound etc*) lavar; (*US*) bañar, dar un baño a
bather ['beɪðəʳ] *n* bañista *m/f*
bathing ['beɪðɪŋ] *n* baño
bathing cap *n* gorro de baño
bathing costume, bathing suit (*US*) *n* bañador *m*, traje *m* de baño
bathing trunks *npl* bañador *msg*
bathmat ['bɑːθmæt] *n* alfombrilla de baño
bathrobe ['bɑːθrəub] *n* albornoz *m*
bathroom ['bɑːθrum] *n* (cuarto de) baño
baths [bɑːðz] *npl* piscina *sg*
bath towel *n* toalla de baño
bathtub ['bɑːθtʌb] *n* bañera
batman ['bætmən] *n* (*Brit*) ordenanza *m*
baton ['bætən] *n* (*Mus*) batuta
battalion [bə'tæliən] *n* batallón *m*
batten ['bætn] *n* (*Carpentry*) listón *m*; (*Naut*) junquillo, sable *m*
▸ **batten down** *vt* (*Naut*): **to ~ down the hatches** atrancar las escotillas
batter ['bætəʳ] *vt* maltratar; (*wind, rain*) azotar ▪ *n* batido
battered ['bætəd] *adj* (*hat, pan*) estropeado
battery ['bætərɪ] *n* batería; (*of torch*) pila
battery charger *n* cargador *m* de baterías
battery farming *n* cría intensiva
battle ['bætl] *n* batalla; (*fig*) lucha ▪ *vi* luchar; **that's half the ~** (*col*) ya hay medio camino andado; **to fight a losing ~** (*fig*) luchar por una causa perdida
battlefield ['bætlfiːld] *n* campo *m* de batalla
battlements ['bætlmənts] *npl* almenas *fpl*
battleship ['bætlʃɪp] *n* acorazado
batty ['bætɪ] *adj* (*col: person*) chiflado; (*: idea*) de chiflado
bauble ['bɔːbl] *n* chuchería
baud rate *n* (*Comput*) velocidad *f* (de transmisión) en baudios
bauxite ['bɔːksaɪt] *n* bauxita
Bavaria [bə'vɛərɪə] *n* Baviera
Bavarian [bə'vɛərɪən] *adj, n* bávaro(-a) *m(f)*
bawdy ['bɔːdɪ] *adj* indecente; (*joke*) verde
bawl [bɔːl] *vi* chillar, gritar
bay [beɪ] *n* (*Geo*) bahía; (*for parking*) parking *m*, estacionamiento; (*loading bay*) patio de carga; (*Bot*) laurel *m* ▪ *vi* aullar; **to hold sb at ~** mantener a alguien a raya
bay leaf *n* (hoja de) laurel *m*
bayonet ['beɪənɪt] *n* bayoneta
bay window *n* ventana salediza
bazaar [bə'zɑːʳ] *n* bazar *m*
bazooka [bə'zuːkə] *n* bazuca
BB *n abbr* (*Brit: = Boys' Brigade*) *organización juvenil para chicos*
BBB *n abbr* (*US: = Better Business Bureau*) *organismo para la defensa del consumidor*
BBC *n abbr* (*= British Broadcasting Corporation*) BBC *f*; *ver nota*

BBC

La BBC es el organismo público británico de radio y televisión, autónomo en cuanto a su política de programas pero regulado por un estatuto ("BBC charter") que ha de aprobar el Parlamento. Además de cadenas nacionales de televisión y de radio, transmite también un servicio informativo mundial ("BBC World Service"). A no tener publicidad, se financia a través de operaciones comerciales paralelas y del cobro de una licencia anual obligatoria ("TV licence") para los que tienen aparato de televisión.

BBE *n abbr* (*US*) = **Benevolent and Protective Order of Elks**
BC *adv abbr* (*= before Christ*) a. de J.C. ▪ *abbr* (*Canada*) = **British Columbia**
BCG *n abbr* (*= Bacillus Calmette-Guérin*) *vacuna de la tuberculosis*
BD *n abbr* (*= Bachelor of Divinity*) *Licenciado/a en Teología*
B/D *abbr* = **bank draft**
BDS *n abbr* (*= Bachelor of Dental Surgery*) *título universitario*

KEYWORD

be [biː] (*pt* **was, were**, *pp* **been**) *aux vb* **1** (*with present participle: forming continuous tenses*): **what are you doing?** ¿qué estás haciendo?, ¿qué haces?; **they're coming tomorrow** vienen mañana; **I've been waiting for you for hours** llevo horas esperándote
2 (*with pp: forming passives*) ser (*but often replaced by active or reflexive constructions*); **to be murdered** ser asesinado; **the box had been opened** habían abierto la caja; **the thief was nowhere to be seen** no se veía al ladrón por ninguna parte

3 (*in tag questions*): **it was fun, wasn't it?** fue divertido, ¿no? *or* ¿verdad?; **he's good-looking, isn't he?** es guapo, ¿no te parece?; **she's back again, is she?** entonces, ¿ha vuelto?
4 (*+to +infin*): **the house is to be sold** (*necessity*) hay que vender la casa; (*future*) van a vender la casa; **he's not to open it** no tiene que abrirlo; **he was to have come yesterday** debía de haber venido ayer; **am I to understand that ...?** ¿debo entender que ...?
■ *vb +complement* **1** (*with n or num complement*) ser; **he's a doctor** es médico; **2 and 2 are 4** 2 y 2 son 4
2 (*with adj complement: expressing permanent or inherent quality*) ser; (*: expressing state seen as temporary or reversible*) estar; **I'm English** soy inglés(-esa); **she's tall/pretty** es alta/bonita; **he's young** es joven; **be careful/good/quiet** ten cuidado/pórtate bien/cállate; **I'm tired** estoy cansado(-a); **I'm warm** tengo calor; **it's dirty** está sucio(-a)
3 (*of health*) estar; **how are you?** ¿cómo estás?; **he's very ill** está muy enfermo; **I'm better now** ya estoy mejor
4 (*of age*) tener; **how old are you?** ¿cuántos años tienes?; **I'm sixteen (years old)** tengo dieciséis años
5 (*cost*) costar; ser; **how much was the meal?** ¿cuánto fue *or* costó la comida?; **that'll be £5.75, please** son £5.75, por favor; **this shirt is £17** esta camisa cuesta £17
■ *vi* **1** (*exist, occur etc*) existir, haber; **the best singer that ever was** el mejor cantante que existió jamás; **is there a God?** ¿hay un Dios?, ¿existe Dios?; **be that as it may** sea como sea; **so be it** así sea
2 (*referring to place*) estar; **I won't be here tomorrow** no estaré aquí mañana
3 (*referring to movement*): **where have you been?** ¿dónde has estado?
■ *impers vb* **1** (*referring to time*): **it's 5 o'clock** son las 5; **it's the 28th of April** estamos a 28 de abril
2 (*referring to distance*): **it's 10 km to the village** el pueblo está a 10 km
3 (*referring to the weather*): **it's too hot/cold** hace demasiado calor/frío; **it's windy today** hace viento hoy
4 (*emphatic*): **it's me** soy yo; **it was Maria who paid the bill** fue María la que pagó la cuenta

B/E *abbr* = **bill of exchange**
beach [biːtʃ] *n* playa ■ *vt* varar
beach buggy [-bʌgɪ] *n* buggy *m*
beachcomber ['biːtʃkəuməʳ] *n* raquero(-a)
beachwear ['biːtʃwɛəʳ] *n* ropa de playa
beacon ['biːkən] *n* (*lighthouse*) faro; (*marker*) guía; (*radio beacon*) radiofaro
bead [biːd] *n* cuenta, abalorio; (*of dew, sweat*) gota; **beads** *npl* (*necklace*) collar *m*
beady ['biːdɪ] *adj* (*eyes*) pequeño y brillante
beagle ['biːgl] *n* sabueso pequeño, beagle *m*
beak [biːk] *n* pico
beaker ['biːkəʳ] *n* vaso
beam [biːm] *n* (*Arch*) viga; (*of light*) rayo, haz *m* de luz; (*Radio*) rayo ■ *vi* brillar; (*smile*) sonreír; **to drive on full** *or* **main ~** conducir con las luces largas
beaming ['biːmɪŋ] *adj* (*sun, smile*) radiante
bean [biːn] *n* judía, fríjol/frijol *m* (*esp LAm*); **runner/broad ~** habichuela/haba; **coffee ~** grano de café
beanpole ['biːnpəul] *n* (*col*) espárrago
beansprouts ['biːnsprauts] *npl* brotes *mpl* de soja
bear [bɛəʳ] (*pt* **bore**, *pp* **borne**) *n* oso; (*Stock Exchange*) bajista *m* ■ *vt* (*weight etc*) llevar; (*cost*) pagar; (*responsibility*) tener; (*traces, signs*) mostrar; (*produce: fruit*) dar; (*Comm: interest*) devengar; (*endure*) soportar, aguantar; (*stand up to*) resistir a; (*children*) tener, dar a luz ■ *vi*: **to ~ right/left** torcer a la derecha/izquierda; **I can't ~ him** no le puedo ver, no lo soporto; **to bring pressure to ~ on sb** ejercer presión sobre algn
▸ **bear on** *vt fus* tener que ver con, referirse a
▸ **bear out** *vt fus* (*suspicions*) corroborar, confirmar; (*person*) confirmar lo dicho por
▸ **bear up** *vi* (*cheer up*) animarse; **he bore up well under the strain** resistió bien la presión
▸ **bear with** *vt fus* (*sb's moods, temper*) tener paciencia con
bearable ['bɛərəbl] *adj* soportable, aguantable
beard [bɪəd] *n* barba
bearded ['bɪədɪd] *adj* con barba
bearer ['bɛərəʳ] *n* (*of news, cheque*) portador(a) *m(f)*; (*of passport*) titular *m/f*
bearing ['bɛərɪŋ] *n* porte *m*; (*connection*) relación *f*; **(ball) bearings** *npl* cojinetes *mpl* a bolas; **to take a ~** marcarse; **to find one's bearings** orientarse
bearskin ['bɛəskɪn] *n* (*Mil*) gorro militar (*de piel de oso*)
beast [biːst] *n* bestia; (*col*) bruto, salvaje *m*
beastly ['biːstlɪ] *adj* bestial; (*awful*) horrible
beat [biːt] (*pt* **~**, *pp* **beaten**) *n* (*of heart*) latido; (*Mus*) ritmo, compás *m*; (*of policeman*) ronda ■ *vt* (*hit*) golpear; (*eggs*) batir; (*defeat*) vencer, derrotar; (*better*) sobrepasar; (*drum*) tocar;

(*rhythm*) marcar ■ *vi* (*heart*) latir; **off the beaten track** aislado; **to ~ about the bush** andarse con rodeos; **to ~ it** largarse; **that beats everything!** (*col*) ¡eso es el colmo!; **to ~ on a door** dar golpes en una puerta
▸ **beat down** *vt* (*door*) derribar a golpes; (*price*) conseguir rebajar, regatear; (*seller*) hacer rebajar el precio ■ *vi* (*rain*) llover a cántaros; (*sun*) caer de plomo
▸ **beat off** *vt* rechazar
▸ **beat up** *vt* (*col: person*) dar una paliza a
beater ['bi:tə^r] *n* (*for eggs, cream*) batidora
beating ['bi:tɪŋ] *n* paliza, golpiza (*LAm*); **to take a ~** recibir una paliza
beat-up ['bi:t'ʌp] *adj* (*col*) destartalado
beautiful ['bju:tɪful] *adj* hermoso, bello, lindo (*esp LAm*)
beautifully ['bju:tɪfəlɪ] *adv* de maravilla
beautify ['bju:tɪfaɪ] *vt* embellecer
beauty ['bju:tɪ] *n* belleza, hermosura; (*concept, person*) belleza; **the ~ of it is that ...** lo mejor de esto es que ...
beauty contest *n* concurso de belleza
beauty queen *n* reina de la belleza
beauty salon *n* salón *m* de belleza
beauty sleep *n*: **to get one's ~** *no perder horas de sueño*
beauty spot *n* lunar *m* postizo; (*Brit: Tourism*) lugar *m* pintoresco
beaver ['bi:və^r] *n* castor *m*
becalmed [bɪ'kɑ:md] *adj* encalmado
became [bɪ'keɪm] *pt of* **become**
because [bɪ'kɔz] *conj* porque; **~ of** *prep* debido a, a causa de
beck [bɛk] *n*: **to be at the ~ and call of** estar a disposición de
beckon ['bɛkən] *vt* (*also:* **beckon to**) llamar con señas
become [bɪ'kʌm] (*irreg: like* **come**) *vi* (*+ noun*) hacerse, llegar a ser; (*+ adj*) ponerse, volverse ■ *vt* (*suit*) favorecer, sentar bien a; **to ~ fat** engordar; **to ~ angry** enfadarse; **it became known that ...** se descubrió que ...
becoming [bɪ'kʌmɪŋ] *adj* (*behaviour*) decoroso; (*clothes*) favorecedor(a)
becquerel [bɛkə'rɛl] *n* becquerelio
BECTU ['bɛktu:] *n abbr* (*Brit*) = **Broadcasting Entertainment Cinematographic and Theatre Union**
BEd *n abbr* (*= Bachelor of Education*) *título universitario; see also* **Bachelor's Degree**
bed [bɛd] *n* cama; (*of flowers*) macizo; (*of sea, lake*) fondo; (*of coal, clay*) capa; **to go to ~** acostarse
▸ **bed down** *vi* acostarse
bed and breakfast *n* ≈ pensión *f*; *ver nota*

BED AND BREAKFAST

Se llama *Bed and Breakfast* a la casa de hospedaje particular, o granja si es en el campo, que ofrece cama y desayuno a tarifas inferiores a las de un hotel. El servicio se suele anunciar con carteles colocados en las ventanas del establecimiento, en el jardín o en la carretera y en ellos aparece a menudo únicamente el símbolo "B & B".

bedbug ['bɛdbʌg] *n* chinche *f*
bedclothes ['bɛdkləuðz] *npl* ropa de cama
bedding ['bɛdɪŋ] *n* ropa de cama
bedeck [bɪ'dɛk] *vt* engalanar, adornar
bedevil [bɪ'dɛvl] *vt* (*dog*) acosar; (*trouble*) fastidiar
bedfellow ['bɛdfɛləu] *n*: **they are strange bedfellows** (*fig*) hacen una pareja rara
bedlam ['bɛdləm] *n* confusión *f*
bedpan ['bɛdpæn] *n* cuña
bedraggled [bɪ'drægld] *adj* desastrado
bedridden ['bɛdrɪdn] *adj* postrado (en cama)
bedrock ['bɛdrɔk] *n* (*Geo*) roca firme; (*fig*) pilar *m*
bedroom ['bɛdrum] *n* dormitorio, alcoba
Beds *abbr* (*Brit*) = **Bedfordshire**
bed settee *n* sofá-cama *m*
bedside ['bɛdsaɪd] *n*: **at sb's ~** a la cabecera de alguien
bedside lamp *n* lámpara de noche
bedsit ['bɛdsɪt], **bedsitter** ['bɛdsɪtə^r] *n* (*Brit*) estudio
bedspread ['bɛdsprɛd] *n* cubrecama *m*, colcha
bedtime ['bɛdtaɪm] *n* hora de acostarse; **it's ~** es hora de acostarse *or* de irse a la cama
bee [bi:] *n* abeja; **to have a ~ in one's bonnet (about sth)** tener una idea fija (de algo)
beech [bi:tʃ] *n* haya
beef [bi:f] *n* carne *f* de vaca; **roast ~** rosbif *m*
▸ **beef up** *vt* (*col*) reforzar
beefburger ['bi:fbə:gə^r] *n* hamburguesa
beefeater ['bi:fi:tə^r] *n alabardero de la Torre de Londres*
beehive ['bi:haɪv] *n* colmena
bee-keeping ['bi:ki:pɪŋ] *n* apicultura
beeline ['bi:laɪn] *n*: **to make a ~ for** ir derecho a
been [bi:n] *pp of* **be**
beep [bi:p] *n* pitido ■ *vi* pitar
beeper ['bi:pə^r] *n* (*of doctor etc*) busca *m inv*
beer [bɪə^r] *n* cerveza
beer belly *n* (*col*) barriga (*de bebedor de cerveza*)
beer can *n* bote *m or* lata de cerveza
beet [bi:t] *n* (*US*) remolacha

beetle ['bi:tl] *n* escarabajo
beetroot ['bi:tru:t] *n* (*Brit*) remolacha
befall [bɪ'fɔ:l] *vi, vt* (*irreg: like* **fall**) acontecer (a)
befit [bɪ'fɪt] *vt* convenir a, corresponder a
before [bɪ'fɔ:ʳ] *prep* (*of time*) antes de; (*of space*) delante de ■ *conj* antes (de) que ■ *adv* (*time*) antes; (*space*) delante, adelante; **~ going** antes de marcharse; **~ she goes** antes de que se vaya; **the week ~** la semana anterior; **I've never seen it ~** no lo he visto nunca
beforehand [bɪ'fɔ:hænd] *adv* de antemano, con anticipación
befriend [bɪ'frɛnd] *vt* ofrecer amistad a
befuddled [bɪ'fʌdld] *adj* aturdido, atontado
beg [bɛg] *vi* pedir limosna, mendigar ■ *vt* pedir, rogar; (*entreat*) suplicar; **I ~ your pardon** (*apologising*) perdóneme; (*not hearing*) ¿perdón?
began [bɪ'gæn] *pt of* **begin**
beggar ['bɛgəʳ] *n* mendigo(-a)
begin (*pt* **began**, *pp* **begun**) [bɪ'gɪn, -gæn, -gʌn] *vt, vi* empezar, comenzar; **to ~ doing** *or* **to do sth** empezar a hacer algo; **I can't ~ to thank you** no encuentro palabras para agradecerle; **to ~ with, I'd like to know ...** en primer lugar, quisiera saber ...; **beginning from Monday** a partir del lunes
beginner [bɪ'gɪnəʳ] *n* principiante *m/f*
beginning [bɪ'gɪnɪŋ] *n* principio, comienzo; **right from the ~** desde el principio
begrudge [bɪ'grʌdʒ] *vt*: **to ~ sb sth** tenerle envidia a alguien por algo
beguile [bɪ'gaɪl] *vt* (*enchant*) seducir
beguiling [bɪ'gaɪlɪŋ] *adj* seductor(a), atractivo
begun [bɪ'gʌn] *pp of* **begin**
behalf [bɪ'hɑ:f] *n*: **on ~ of,** (*US*) **in ~ of** en nombre de; (*for benefit of*) por
behave [bɪ'heɪv] *vi* (*person*) portarse, comportarse; (*thing*) funcionar; (*well: also*: **behave o.s.**) portarse bien
behaviour, behavior (*US*) [bɪ'heɪvjəʳ] *n* comportamiento, conducta
behead [bɪ'hɛd] *vt* decapitar
beheld [bɪ'hɛld] *pt, pp of* **behold**
behind [bɪ'haɪnd] *prep* detrás de ■ *adv* detrás, por detrás, atrás ■ *n* trasero; **to be ~ (schedule)** ir retrasado; **~ the scenes** (*fig*) entre bastidores; **we're ~ them in technology** (*fig*) nos dejan atrás en tecnología; **to leave sth ~** olvidar *or* dejarse algo; **to be ~ with sth** estar atrasado en algo; **to be ~ with payments (on sth)** estar atrasado en el pago (de algo)
behold [bɪ'həuld] (*irreg: like* **hold**) *vt* contemplar
beige [beɪʒ] *adj* (color) beige
being ['bi:ɪŋ] *n* ser *m*; **to come into ~** nacer, aparecer
Beirut [beɪ'ru:t] *n* Beirut *m*
Belarus [bɛlə'rus] *n* Bielorrusia
Belarussian [bɛlə'rʌʃən] *adj, n* bielorruso(-a) ■ *n* (*Ling*) bielorruso
belated [bɪ'leɪtɪd] *adj* atrasado, tardío
belch [bɛltʃ] *vi* eructar ■ *vt* (*also*: **belch out**: *smoke etc*) vomitar, arrojar
beleaguered [bɪ'li:gəd] *adj* asediado
Belfast ['bɛlfɑ:st] *n* Belfast *m*
belfry ['bɛlfrɪ] *n* campanario
Belgian ['bɛldʒən] *adj, n* belga *m/f*
Belgium ['bɛldʒəm] *n* Bélgica
Belgrade [bel'greɪd] *n* Belgrado
belie [bɪ'laɪ] *vt* (*give false impression of*) desmentir, contradecir
belief [bɪ'li:f] *n* (*opinion*) opinión *f*; (*trust, faith*) fe *f*; (*acceptance as true*) creencia; **it's beyond ~** es increíble; **in the ~ that** creyendo que
believable [bɪ'li:vəbl] *adj* creíble
believe [bɪ'li:v] *vt, vi* creer; **to ~ (that)** creer (que); **to ~ in** (*God, ghosts*) creer en; (*method*) ser partidario de; **he is believed to be abroad** se cree que está en el extranjero; **I don't ~ in corporal punishment** no soy partidario del castigo corporal
believer [bɪ'li:vəʳ] *n* (*in idea, activity*) partidario(-a); (*Rel*) creyente *m/f*, fiel *m/f*
belittle [bɪ'lɪtl] *vt* despreciar
Belize [bɛ'li:z] *n* Belice *f*
bell [bɛl] *n* campana; (*small*) campanilla; (*on door*) timbre *m*; (*animal's*) cencerro; (*on toy etc*) cascabel *m*; **that rings a ~** (*fig*) eso me suena
bellboy ['bɛlbɔɪ] *n*, **bellhop** (*US*) ['bɛlhɔp] ■ *n* botones *m inv*
belligerent [bɪ'lɪdʒərənt] *adj* (*at war*) beligerante; (*fig*) agresivo
bellow ['bɛləu] *vi* bramar; (*person*) rugir ■ *vt* (*orders*) gritar
bellows ['bɛləuz] *npl* fuelle *msg*
bell push *n* pulsador *m* de timbre
belly ['bɛlɪ] *n* barriga, panza
bellyache ['bɛlɪeɪk] *n* dolor *m* de barriga *or* de tripa ■ *vi* (*col*) gruñir
bellyful ['bɛlɪful] *n*: **to have had a ~ of ...** (*col*) estar más que harto de ...
belong [bɪ'lɔŋ] *vi*: **to ~ to** pertenecer a; (*club etc*) ser socio de; **this book belongs here** este libro va aquí
belongings [bɪ'lɔŋɪŋz] *npl*: **personal ~** pertenencias *fpl*
Belorussia [bɛləu'rʌʃə] *n* Bielorrusia
Belorussian [bɛləu'rʌʃən] *adj, n* = **Belarussian**
beloved [bɪ'lʌvɪd] *adj, n* querido(-a) *m(f)*, amado(-a) *m(f)*

below [bɪ'ləu] *prep* bajo, debajo de ■ *adv* abajo, (por) debajo; **see ~** véase más abajo
belt [bɛlt] *n* cinturón *m*; *(Tech)* correa, cinta ■ *vt (thrash)* golpear con correa; **industrial ~** cinturón industrial
▸ **belt out** *vt (song)* cantar a voz en grito *or* a grito pelado
▸ **belt up** *vi (Aut)* ponerse el cinturón de seguridad; *(fig, col)* cerrar el pico
beltway ['bɛltweɪ] *n (US Aut)* carretera de circunvalación
bemoan [bɪ'məun] *vt* lamentar
bemused [bɪ'mju:zd] *adj* perplejo
bench [bɛntʃ] *n* banco; **the B~** *(Law)* el tribunal; *(people)* la judicatura
bench mark *n* punto de referencia
bend [bɛnd] *vb (pt, pp* **bent**) ■ *vt* doblar; *(body, head)* inclinar ■ *vi* inclinarse; *(road)* curvarse ■ *n (Brit: in road, river)* recodo; *(in pipe)* codo; *see also* **bends**
▸ **bend down** *vi* inclinarse, doblarse
▸ **bend over** *vi* inclinarse
bends [bɛndz] *npl (Med) apoplejía por cambios bruscos de presión*
beneath [bɪ'ni:θ] *prep* bajo, debajo de; *(unworthy of)* indigno de ■ *adv* abajo, (por) debajo
benefactor ['bɛnɪfæktəʳ] *n* bienhechor *m*
benefactress ['bɛnɪfæktrɪs] *n* bienhechora
beneficial [bɛnɪ'fɪʃəl] *adj*: **~ to** beneficioso para
beneficiary [bɛnɪ'fɪʃərɪ] *n (Law)* beneficiario(-a)
benefit ['bɛnɪfɪt] *n* beneficio, provecho; *(allowance of money)* subsidio ■ *vt* beneficiar ■ *vi*: **he'll ~ from it** le sacará provecho; **unemployment ~** subsidio de desempleo
Benelux ['bɛnɪlʌks] *n* Benelux *m*
benevolence [bɪ'nɛvələns] *n* benevolencia
benevolent [bɪ'nɛvələnt] *adj* benévolo
BEng *n abbr (= Bachelor of Engineering) título universitario*
benign [bɪ'naɪn] *adj (person)* benigno; *(Med)* benigno; *(smile)* afable
bent [bɛnt] *pt, pp of* **bend** ■ *n* inclinación *f* ■ *adj (wire, pipe)* doblado, torcido; **to be ~ on** estar empeñado en
bequeath [bɪ'kwi:ð] *vt* legar
bequest [bɪ'kwɛst] *n* legado
bereaved [bɪ'ri:vd] *adj* afligido ■ *n*: **the ~** los afligidos *mpl*
bereavement [bɪ'ri:vmənt] *n* aflicción *f*
beret ['bɛreɪ] *n* boina
Bering Sea ['bɛərɪŋ-] *n*: **the ~** el Mar de Bering
berk [bə:k] *n (Brit col)* capullo(-a) *(!)*
Berks *abbr (Brit)* = **Berkshire**
Berlin [bə:'lɪn] *n* Berlín *m*; **East/West ~** Berlín del Este/Oeste
berm [bə:m] *n (US Aut)* arcén *m*
Bermuda [bə:'mju:də] *n* las (Islas) Bermudas
Bermuda shorts *npl* bermudas *mpl or fpl*
Bern [bə:n] *n* Berna
berry ['bɛrɪ] *n* baya
berserk [bə'sə:k] *adj*: **to go ~** perder los estribos
berth [bə:θ] *n (bed)* litera; *(cabin)* camarote *m*; *(for ship)* amarradero ■ *vi* atracar, amarrar; **to give sb a wide ~** *(fig)* evitar encontrarse con algn
beseech *(pt, pp* **besought**) [bɪ'si:tʃ, -'sɔ:t] *vt* suplicar
beset *(pt, pp* **~**) [bɪ'sɛt] *vt (person)* acosar ■ *adj*: **a policy ~ with dangers** una política rodeada de peligros
besetting [bɪ'sɛtɪŋ] *adj*: **his ~ sin** su principal falta
beside [bɪ'saɪd] *prep* junto a, al lado de; *(compared with)* comparado con; **to be ~ o.s. with anger** estar fuera de sí; **that's ~ the point** eso no tiene nada que ver con el asunto
besides [bɪ'saɪdz] *adv* además ■ *prep (as well as)* además de; *(except)* excepto
besiege [bɪ'si:dʒ] *vt (town)* sitiar; *(fig)* asediar
besmirch [bɪ'smə:tʃ] *vt (fig)* manchar, mancillar
besotted [bɪ'sɔtɪd] *adj*: **~ with** chiflado por
bespoke [bɪ'spəuk] *adj (garment)* hecho a la medida; **~ tailor** sastre *m* que confecciona a la medida
best [bɛst] *adj* (el/la) mejor ■ *adv* (lo) mejor; **the ~ part of** *(most)* la mayor parte de; **at ~** en el mejor de los casos; **to make the ~ of sth** sacar el mejor partido de algo; **to do one's ~** hacer todo lo posible; **to the ~ of my knowledge** que yo sepa; **to the ~ of my ability** como mejor puedo; **the ~ thing to do is ...** lo mejor (que se puede hacer) es ...; **he's not exactly patient at the ~ of times** no es que tenga mucha paciencia precisamente
bestial ['bɛstɪəl] *adj* bestial
best man *n* padrino de boda
bestow [bɪ'stəu] *vt* otorgar; *(honour, praise)* dispensar; **to ~ sth on sb** conceder *or* dar algo a algn
bestseller ['bɛst'sɛləʳ] *n* éxito de ventas, best-seller *m*
bet [bɛt] *n* apuesta ■ *vt, vi (pt, pp* **bet** *or* **betted**); **to ~ (on)** apostar (a); **it's a safe ~** *(fig)* es cosa segura
Bethlehem ['bɛθlɪhɛm] *n* Belén *m*
betray [bɪ'treɪ] *vt* traicionar; *(inform on)* delatar

betrayal [bɪ'treɪəl] *n* traición *f*
better ['bɛtəʳ] *adj* mejor ■ *adv* mejor ■ *vt* mejorar; (*record etc*) superar ■ *n*: **to get the ~ of sb** quedar por encima de algn; **you had ~ do it** más vale que lo hagas; **he thought ~ of it** cambió de parecer; **to get ~** mejorar(se); (*Med*) reponerse; **that's ~!** ¡eso es!; **I had ~ go** tengo que irme; **a change for the ~** una mejora; **~ off** *adj* más acomodado
betting ['bɛtɪŋ] *n* juego, apuestas *fpl*
betting shop *n* (*Brit*) casa de apuestas
between [bɪ'twi:n] *prep* entre ■ *adv* (*also*: **in between**: *time*) mientras tanto; (*: place*) en medio; **the road ~ here and London** la carretera de aquí a Londres; **we only had 5 ~ us** teníamos sólo 5 entre todos
bevel ['bɛvəl] *n* (*also*: **bevel edge**) bisel *m*, chaflán *m*
beverage ['bɛvərɪdʒ] *n* bebida
bevy ['bɛvɪ] *n*: **a ~ of** una bandada de
bewail [bɪ'weɪl] *vt* lamentar
beware [bɪ'wɛəʳ] *vi*: **to ~ (of)** tener cuidado (con) ■ *excl* ¡cuidado!
bewildered [bɪ'wɪldəd] *adj* aturdido, perplejo
bewildering [bɪ'wɪldərɪŋ] *adj* desconcertante
bewitching [bɪ'wɪtʃɪŋ] *adj* hechicero, encantador(a)
beyond [bɪ'jɔnd] *prep* más allá de; (*exceeding*) además de, fuera de; (*above*) superior a ■ *adv* más allá, más lejos; **~ doubt** fuera de toda duda; **~ repair** irreparable
b/f *abbr* (*= brought forward*) saldo previo
BFPO *n abbr* (*= British Forces Post Office*) *servicio postal del ejército*
bhp *n abbr* (*Aut*: *= brake horsepower*) potencia al freno
bi ... [baɪ] *pref* bi ...
biannual [baɪ'ænjuəl] *adj* semestral
bias ['baɪəs] *n* (*prejudice*) prejuicio; (*preference*) predisposición *f*
biased, biassed ['baɪəst] *adj* parcial; **to be bias(s)ed against** tener perjuicios contra
biathlon [baɪ'æθlən] *n* biatlón *m*
bib [bɪb] *n* babero
Bible ['baɪbl] *n* Biblia
biblical ['bɪblɪkəl] *adj* bíblico
bibliography [bɪblɪ'ɔgrəfɪ] *n* bibliografía
bicarbonate of soda [baɪ'kɑ:bənɪt-] *n* bicarbonato de soda
bicentenary [baɪsɛn'ti:nərɪ], **bicentennial** (*US*) [baɪsɛn'tɛnɪəl] *n* bicentenario
biceps ['baɪsɛps] *n* bíceps *m*
bicker ['bɪkəʳ] *vi* reñir
bickering ['bɪkərɪŋ] *n* riñas *fpl*, altercados *mpl*
bicycle ['baɪsɪkl] *n* bicicleta
bicycle path *n* camino para ciclistas
bicycle pump *n* bomba de bicicleta
bid [bɪd] *n* (*at auction*) oferta, puja, postura; (*attempt*) tentativa, conato ■ *vi* (*pt, pp* **bid**) hacer una oferta ■ *vt* (*pt* **bade**) [bæd] (*pp* **bidden**) ['bɪdn] mandar, ordenar; **to ~ sb good day** dar a algn los buenos días
bidder ['bɪdəʳ] *n*: **the highest ~** el mejor postor
bidding ['bɪdɪŋ] *n* (*at auction*) ofertas *fpl*, puja; (*order*) orden *f*, mandato
bide [baɪd] *vt*: **to ~ one's time** esperar el momento adecuado
bidet ['bi:deɪ] *n* bidet *m*
bidirectional ['baɪdɪ'rɛkʃənl] *adj* bidireccional
biennial [baɪ'ɛnɪəl] *adj, n* bienal *f*
bier [bɪəʳ] *n* féretro
bifocals [baɪ'fəuklz] *npl* gafas *fpl or* anteojos *mpl* (*LAm*) bifocales
big [bɪg] *adj* grande; **~ business** gran negocio; **to do things in a ~ way** hacer las cosas en grande
bigamy ['bɪgəmɪ] *n* bigamia
big dipper [-'dɪpəʳ] *n* montaña rusa
big end *n* (*Aut*) cabeza de biela
biggish ['bɪgɪʃ] *adj* más bien grande; (*man*) más bien alto
bigheaded ['bɪg'hɛdɪd] *adj* engreído
bigot ['bɪgət] *n* fanático(-a), intolerante *m/f*
bigoted ['bɪgətɪd] *adj* fanático, intolerante
bigotry ['bɪgətrɪ] *n* fanatismo, intolerancia
big toe *n* dedo gordo (del pie)
big top *n* (*circus*) circo; (*main tent*) carpa principal
big wheel *n* (*at fair*) noria
bigwig ['bɪgwɪg] *n* (*col*) pez *m* gordo
bike [baɪk] *n* bici *f*
bike lane *n* carril *m* de bicicleta, carril *m* bici
bikini [bɪ'ki:nɪ] *n* bikini *m*
bilateral [baɪ'lætərl] *adj* (*agreement*) bilateral
bile [baɪl] *n* bilis *f*
bilge [bɪldʒ] *n* (*water*) agua de sentina
bilingual [baɪ'lɪŋgwəl] *adj* bilingüe
bilious ['bɪlɪəs] *adj* bilioso (*also fig*)
bill [bɪl] *n* (*gen*) cuenta; (*invoice*) factura; (*Pol*) proyecto de ley; (*US*: *banknote*) billete *m*; (*of bird*) pico; (*notice*) cartel *m*; (*Theat*) programa *m* ■ *vt* extender *or* pasar la factura a; **may I have the ~ please?** ¿puede traerme la cuenta, por favor?; **~ of exchange** letra de cambio; **~ of lading** conocimiento de embarque; **~ of sale** escritura de venta; **"post no bills"** "prohibido fijar carteles"
billboard ['bɪlbɔ:d] *n* valla publicitaria
billet ['bɪlɪt] *n* alojamiento ■ *vt*: **to ~ sb (on sb)** alojar a algn (con algn)
billfold ['bɪlfəuld] *n* (*US*) cartera
billiards ['bɪljədz] *n* billar *m*

billion ['bɪljən] *n* (*Brit*) billón *m*; (*US*) mil millones *mpl*
billow ['bɪləu] *n* (*of smoke*) nube *f*; (*of sail*) ondulación *f* ■ *vi* (*smoke*) salir en nubes; (*sail*) ondear, ondular
billy ['bɪlɪ] *n* (*US*) porra
billy goat *n* macho cabrío
bimbo ['bɪmbəu] *n* (*col*) tía buena sin seso
bin [bɪn] *n* (*gen*) cubo *or* bote *m* (*LAm*) de la basura; **litterbin** *n* (*Brit*) papelera
binary ['baɪnərɪ] *adj* (*Math*) binario; **~ code** código binario
bind (*pt, pp* **bound**) [baɪnd, baund] *vt* atar, liar; (*wound*) vendar; (*book*) encuadernar; (*oblige*) obligar
▸ **bind over** *vt* (*Law*) obligar por vía legal
▸ **bind up** *vt* (*wound*) vendar; **to be bound up in** (*work, research etc*) estar absorto en; **to be bound up with** (*person*) estar estrechamente ligado a
binder ['baɪndə^r] *n* (*file*) archivador *m*
binding ['baɪndɪŋ] *adj* (*contract*) vinculante
binge [bɪndʒ] *n* borrachera, juerga; **to go on a ~** ir de juerga
bingo ['bɪŋgəu] *n* bingo *m*
bin-liner ['bɪnlaɪnə^r] *n* bolsa de la basura
binoculars [bɪ'nɔkjuləz] *npl* prismáticos *mpl*, gemelos *mpl*
bio [baɪə'] *adj* (*fam*) biológico
biochemistry [baɪə'kɛmɪstrɪ] *n* bioquímica
biodegradable ['baɪəudɪ'greɪdəbl] *adj* biodegradable
biodiversity ['baɪəudaɪ'vəːsɪtɪ] *n* biodiversidad *f*
biographer [baɪ'ɔgrəfə^r] *n* biógrafo(-a)
biographical [baɪə'græfɪkəl] *adj* biográfico
biography [baɪ'ɔgrəfɪ] *n* biografía
biological [baɪə'lɔdʒɪkəl] *adj* biológico; (*products, foodstuffs etc*) orgánico(-a)
biological clock *n* reloj *m* biológico
biologist [baɪ'ɔlədʒɪst] *n* biólogo(-a)
biology [baɪ'ɔlədʒɪ] *n* biología
biophysics ['baɪəu'fɪzɪks] *nsg* biofísica
biopic ['baɪəupɪk] *n* filme *m* biográfico
biopsy ['baɪɔpsɪ] *n* biopsia
biosphere ['baɪəsfɪə^r] *n* biosfera
biotechnology ['baɪəutɛk'nɔlədʒɪ] *n* biotecnología
bioterrorism ['baɪəu'tɛrərɪzəm] *n* bioterrorismo
biped ['baɪpɛd] *n* bípedo
birch [bəːtʃ] *n* abedul *m*; (*cane*) vara
bird [bəːd] *n* ave *f*, pájaro; (*Brit col: girl*) chica
birdcage ['bəːdkeɪdʒ] *n* jaula
bird flu *n* gripe aviar
bird of prey *n* ave *f* de presa
bird's-eye view ['bəːdzaɪ-] *n* vista de pájaro
bird watcher *n* ornitólogo(-a)
Biro® ['baɪrəu] *n* bolígrafo
birth [bəːθ] *n* nacimiento; (*Med*) parto; **to give ~ to** parir, dar a luz a; (*fig*) dar origen a
birth certificate *n* partida de nacimiento
birth control *n* control *m* de natalidad; (*methods*) métodos *mpl* anticonceptivos
birthday ['bəːθdeɪ] *n* cumpleaños *m inv*
birthday card *n* tarjeta de cumpleaños
birthplace ['bəːθpleɪs] *n* lugar *m* de nacimiento
birth rate *n* (tasa de) natalidad *f*
Biscay ['bɪskeɪ] *n*: **the Bay of ~** el Mar Cantábrico, el golfo de Vizcaya
biscuit ['bɪskɪt] *n* (*Brit*) galleta
bisect [baɪ'sɛkt] *vt* (*also Math*) bisecar
bisexual ['baɪ'sɛksjuəl] *adj, n* bisexual *m/f*
bishop ['bɪʃəp] *n* obispo; (*Chess*) alfil *m*
bistro ['biːstrəu] *n* café-bar *m*
bit [bɪt] *pt of* **bite** ■ *n* trozo, pedazo, pedacito; (*Comput*) bit *m*; (*for horse*) freno, bocado; **a ~ of** un poco de; **a ~ mad** algo loco; **~ by ~** poco a poco; **to come to bits** (*break*) hacerse pedazos; **to do one's ~** aportar su granito de arena; **bring all your bits and pieces** trae todas tus cosas
bitch [bɪtʃ] *n* (*dog*) perra; (*col!*) zorra (*!*)
bite [baɪt] *vt, vi* (*pt* **bit**) [bɪt] (*pp* **bitten**) ['bɪtn] morder; (*insect etc*) picar ■ *n* (*wound: of dog, snake etc*) mordedura; (*of insect*) picadura; (*mouthful*) bocado; **to ~ one's nails** morderse las uñas; **let's have a ~ (to eat)** comamos algo
biting ['baɪtɪŋ] *adj* (*wind*) que traspasa los huesos; (*criticism*) mordaz
bit part *n* (*Theat*) papel *m* sin importancia, papelito
bitten ['bɪtn] *pp of* **bite**
bitter ['bɪtə^r] *adj* amargo; (*wind, criticism*) cortante, penetrante; (*icy: weather*) glacial; (*battle*) encarnizado ■ *n* (*Brit: beer*) *cerveza típica británica a base de lúpulos*
bitterly ['bɪtəlɪ] *adv* (*disappoint, complain, weep*) desconsoladamente; (*oppose, criticise*) implacablemente; (*jealous*) agriamente; **it's ~ cold** hace un frío glacial
bitterness ['bɪtənɪs] *n* amargura; (*anger*) rencor *m*
bitty ['bɪtɪ] *adj* deshilvanado
bitumen ['bɪtjumɪn] *n* betún *m*
bivouac ['bɪvuæk] *n* vivac *m*, vivaque *m*
bizarre [bɪ'zɑː^r] *adj* raro, estrafalario
bk *abbr* = **bank; book**
BL *n abbr* (= *Bachelor of Law(s), Bachelor of Letters*) *título universitario*; (*US: = Bachelor of Literature*) *título universitario*
B/L *abbr* = **bill of lading**

blab [blæb] *vi* cantar ■ *vt* (*also*: **blab out**) soltar, contar
black [blæk] *adj* (*colour*) negro; (*dark*) oscuro ■ *n* (*colour*) color *m* negro; (*person*): **B~** negro(-a) ■ *vt* (*shoes*) lustrar; (*Brit Industry*) boicotear; **to give sb a ~ eye** ponerle a algn el ojo morado; **~ coffee** café *m* solo; **there it is in ~ and white** (*fig*) ahí está bien claro; **to be in the ~** (*in credit*) tener saldo positivo; **~ and blue** *adj* amoratado
▸ **black out** *vi* (*faint*) desmayarse
black belt *n* (*Sport*) cinturón *m* negro; (*US*: *area*) zona negra
blackberry ['blækbərɪ] *n* zarzamora
blackbird ['blækbə:d] *n* mirlo
blackboard ['blækbɔ:d] *n* pizarra
black box *n* (*Aviat*) caja negra
Black Country *n* (*Brit*): **the ~** *región industrial del centro de Inglaterra*
blackcurrant ['blæk'kʌrənt] *n* grosella negra
black economy *n* economía sumergida
blacken ['blækən] *vt* ennegrecer; (*fig*) denigrar
Black Forest *n*: **the ~** la Selva Negra
blackguard ['blægɑ:d] *n* canalla *m*, pillo
black hole *n* (*Astro*) agujero negro
black ice *n* hielo invisible en la carretera
blackjack ['blækdʒæk] *n* (*US*) veintiuna
blackleg ['blæklɛg] *n* (*Brit*) esquirol *m/f*
blacklist ['blæklɪst] *n* lista negra ■ *vt* poner en la lista negra
blackmail ['blækmeɪl] *n* chantaje *m* ■ *vt* chantajear
blackmailer ['blækmeɪlə^r] *n* chantajista *m/f*
black market *n* mercado negro, estraperlo
blackness ['blæknɪs] *n* negrura
blackout ['blækaut] *n* (*TV, Elec*) apagón *m*; (*fainting*) desmayo, pérdida de conocimiento
Black Sea *n*: **the ~** el Mar Negro
black sheep *n* oveja negra
blacksmith ['blæksmɪθ] *n* herrero
black spot *n* (*Aut*) punto negro
bladder ['blædə^r] *n* vejiga
blade [bleɪd] *n* hoja; (*cutting edge*) filo; **a ~ of grass** una brizna de hierba
Blairite ['blɛərait] *n, adj* blairista *m/f*
blame [bleɪm] *n* culpa ■ *vt*: **to ~ sb for sth** echar a algn la culpa de algo; **to be to ~ (for)** tener la culpa (de); **I'm not to ~** yo no tengo la culpa; **and I don't ~ him** y lo comprendo perfectamente
blameless ['bleɪmlɪs] *adj* (*person*) inocente
blanch [blɑ:ntʃ] *vi* (*person*) palidecer; (*Culin*) escaldar
bland [blænd] *adj* suave; (*taste*) soso
blank [blæŋk] *adj* en blanco; (*shot*) de fogueo; (*look*) sin expresión ■ *n* blanco, espacio en blanco; cartucho de fogueo; **to draw a ~** (*fig*) no conseguir nada
blank cheque, blank check (*US*) *n* cheque *m* en blanco
blanket ['blæŋkɪt] *n* manta, frazada (*LAm*), cobija (*LAm*) ■ *adj* (*statement, agreement*) comprensivo, general; **to give ~ cover** (*insurance policy*) dar póliza a todo riesgo
blankly ['blæŋklɪ] *adv*: **she looked at me ~** me miró sin comprender
blare [blɛə^r] *vi* (*brass band, horns, radio*) resonar
blasé ['blɑ:zeɪ] *adj* de vuelta de todo
blaspheme [blæs'fi:m] *vi* blasfemar
blasphemous ['blæsfɪməs] *adj* blasfemo
blasphemy ['blæsfɪmɪ] *n* blasfemia
blast [blɑ:st] *n* (*of wind*) ráfaga, soplo; (*of whistle*) toque *m*; (*of explosive*) carga explosiva; (*force*) choque *m* ■ *vt* (*blow up*) volar; (*blow open*) abrir con carga explosiva ■ *excl* (*Brit col*) ¡maldito sea!; **(at) full ~** (*also fig*) a toda marcha
▸ **blast off** *vi* (*spacecraft etc*) despegar
blast furnace *n* alto horno
blast-off ['blɑ:stɔf] *n* (*Space*) lanzamiento
blatant ['bleɪtənt] *adj* descarado
blatantly ['bleɪtəntlɪ] *adv*: **it's ~ obvious** está clarísimo
blather ['blæðə^r] *vi* decir tonterías
blaze [bleɪz] *n* (*fire*) fuego; (*flames*) llamarada; (*glow*: *of fire, sun etc*) resplandor *m*; (*fig*) arranque *m* ■ *vi* (*fire*) arder con llamaradas; (*fig*) brillar ■ *vt*: **to ~ a trail** (*fig*) abrir (un) camino; **in a ~ of publicity** bajo los focos de la publicidad
blazer ['bleɪzə^r] *n chaqueta de uniforme de colegial o de socio de club*
bleach [bli:tʃ] *n* (*also*: **household bleach**) lejía ■ *vt* (*linen*) blanquear
bleached [bli:tʃt] *adj* (*hair*) de colorado; (*clothes*) blanqueado
bleachers ['bli:tʃəz] *npl* (*US Sport*) gradas *fpl*
bleak [bli:k] *adj* (*countryside*) desierto; (*landscape*) desolado, desierto; (*weather*) desapacible; (*smile*) triste; (*prospect, future*) poco prometedor(a)
bleary-eyed ['blɪərɪ'aɪd] *adj*: **to be ~** tener ojos de cansado
bleat [bli:t] *vi* balar
bleed (*pt, pp* **bled**) [bli:d, blɛd] *vt* sangrar; (*brakes, radiator*) desaguar ■ *vi* sangrar
bleeding ['bli:dɪŋ] *adj* sangrante
bleep [bli:p] *n* pitido ■ *vi* pitar ■ *vt* llamar por el busca
bleeper ['bli:pə^r] *n* (*of doctor etc*) busca *m*
blemish ['blɛmɪʃ] *n* mancha, tacha
blench [blɛntʃ] *vi* (*shrink back*) acobardarse; (*grow pale*) palidecer

blend [blɛnd] *n* mezcla ■ *vt* mezclar ■ *vi* (*colours etc*) combinarse, mezclarse
blender ['blɛndə^r] *n* (*Culin*) batidora
bless (*pt, pp* **blessed** *or* **blest**) [blɛs, blɛst] *vt* bendecir
blessed ['blɛsɪd] *adj* (*Rel: holy*) santo, bendito; (*: happy*) dichoso; **every ~ day** cada santo día
blessing ['blɛsɪŋ] *n* bendición *f*; (*advantage*) beneficio, ventaja; **to count one's blessings** agradecer lo que se tiene; **it was a ~ in disguise** no hay mal que por bien no venga
blew [blu:] *pt of* **blow**
blight [blaɪt] *vt* (*hopes etc*) frustrar, arruinar
blimey ['blaɪmɪ] *excl* (*Brit col*) ¡caray!
blind [blaɪnd] *adj* ciego ■ *n* (*for window*) persiana ■ *vt* cegar; (*dazzle*) deslumbrar
blind alley *n* callejón *m* sin salida
blind corner *n* (*Brit*) esquina *or* curva sin visibilidad
blind date *n* cita a ciegas
blinders ['blaɪndəz] *npl* (*US*) anteojeras *fpl*
blindfold ['blaɪndfəuld] *n* venda ■ *adj, adv* con los ojos vendados ■ *vt* vendar los ojos a
blinding ['blaɪndɪŋ] *adj* (*flash, light*) cegador; (*pain*) intenso
blindingly ['blaɪndɪŋlɪ] *adv*: **it's ~ obvious** salta a la vista
blindly ['blaɪndlɪ] *adv* a ciegas, ciegamente
blindness ['blaɪndnɪs] *n* ceguera
blind spot *n* (*Aut*) ángulo muerto; **to have a ~ about sth** estar ciego para algo
blink [blɪŋk] *vi* parpadear, pestañear; (*light*) oscilar; **to be on the ~** (*col*) estar estropeado
blinkers ['blɪŋkəz] *npl* (*esp Brit*) anteojeras *fpl*
blinking ['blɪŋkɪŋ] *adj* (*col*): **this ~ ...** este condenado ...
blip [blɪp] *n* señal *f* luminosa; (*on graph*) pequeña desviación *f*; (*fig*) pequeña anomalía
bliss [blɪs] *n* felicidad *f*
blissful ['blɪsful] *adj* dichoso; **in ~ ignorance** feliz en la ignorancia
blissfully ['blɪsfulɪ] *adv* (*sigh, smile*) con felicidad; **~ happy** sumamente feliz
blister ['blɪstə^r] *n* (*on skin, paint*) ampolla ■ *vi* ampollarse
blistering ['blɪstərɪŋ] *adj* (*heat*) abrasador(a)
BLit, BLitt *n abbr* (*= Bachelor of Literature*) *título universitario*
blithely ['blaɪðlɪ] *adv* alegremente, despreocupadamente
blithering ['blɪðərɪŋ] *adj* (*col*): **this ~ idiot** este tonto perdido
blitz [blɪts] *n* bombardeo aéreo; **to have a ~ on sth** (*fig*) emprenderla con algo
blizzard ['blɪzəd] *n* ventisca
BLM *n abbr* (*US*) = **Bureau of Land Management**
bloated ['bləutɪd] *adj* hinchado
blob [blɔb] *n* (*drop*) gota; (*stain, spot*) mancha
bloc [blɔk] *n* (*Pol*) bloque *m*
block [blɔk] *n* bloque *m* (*also Comput*); (*in pipes*) obstáculo; (*of buildings*) manzana ■ *vt* (*gen*) obstruir, cerrar; (*progress*) estorbar; (*Comput*) agrupar; **~ of flats** (*Brit*) bloque *m* de pisos; **mental ~** amnesia temporal; **~ and tackle** (*Tech*) aparejo de polea; **3 blocks from here** a 3 manzanas *or* cuadras (*LAm*) de aquí
▸ **block up** *vt* tapar, obstruir; (*pipe*) atascar
blockade [blɔ'keɪd] *n* bloqueo ■ *vt* bloquear
blockage ['blɔkɪdʒ] *n* estorbo, obstrucción *f*
block booking *n* reserva en grupo
blockbuster ['blɔkbʌstə^r] *n* (*book*) best-seller *m*; (*film*) éxito de público
block capitals *npl* mayúsculas *fpl*
block letters *npl* letras *fpl* de molde
block release *n* (*Brit*) exención *f* por estudios
block vote *n* (*Brit*) voto por delegación
blog [blɔg] *n* (*Comput*) blog *m* ■ *vi* bloguear
blogger ['blɔgə^r] *n* (*col: person*) blogger *mf*
bloke [bləuk] *n* (*Brit col*) tipo, tío
blond, blonde [blɔnd] *adj, n* rubio(-a) *m(f)*
blood [blʌd] *n* sangre *f*; **new ~** (*fig*) gente *f* nueva
blood bank *n* banco de sangre
blood count *n* recuento de glóbulos rojos y blancos
blood donor *n* donante *m/f* de sangre
blood group *n* grupo sanguíneo
bloodhound ['blʌdhaund] *n* sabueso
bloodless ['blʌdlɪs] *adj* (*pale*) exangüe; (*revolt etc*) sin derramamiento de sangre, incruento
bloodletting ['blʌdlɛtɪŋ] *n* (*Med*) sangría; (*fig*) sangría, carnicería
blood poisoning *n* septicemia de la sangre
blood pressure *n* tensión *f* sanguínea; **to have high/low ~** tener la tensión alta/baja
bloodshed ['blʌdʃɛd] *n* baño de sangre
bloodshot ['blʌdʃɔt] *adj* inyectado en sangre
bloodstained ['blʌdsteɪnd] *adj* manchado de sangre
bloodstream ['blʌdstri:m] *n* corriente *f* sanguínea
blood test *n* análisis *m* de sangre
bloodthirsty ['blʌdθə:stɪ] *adj* sanguinario
blood transfusion *n* transfusión *f* de sangre
blood type *n* grupo sanguíneo
blood vessel *n* vaso sanguíneo
bloody ['blʌdɪ] *adj* sangriento; (*Brit col!*): **this ~ ...** este condenado *or* puñetero *or* fregado (*LAm*) ... (*!*) ■ *adv* (*Brit col!*): **~ strong/good** terriblemente fuerte/bueno

bloody-minded ['blʌdɪ'maɪndɪd] *adj* (*Brit col*) con malas pulgas
bloom [blu:m] *n* floración *f*; **in ~** en flor ■ *vi* florecer
blooming ['blu:mɪŋ] *adj* (*col*): **this ~ ...** este condenado ...
blossom ['blɔsəm] *n* flor *f* ■ *vi* florecer; (*fig*) desarrollarse; **to ~ into** (*fig*) convertirse en
blot [blɔt] *n* borrón *m* ■ *vt* (*dry*) secar; (*stain*) manchar; **to ~ out** *vt* (*view*) tapar; (*memories*) borrar; **to be a ~ on the landscape** estropear el paisaje; **to ~ one's copy book** (*fig*) manchar su reputación
blotchy ['blɔtʃɪ] *adj* (*complexion*) lleno de manchas
blotter ['blɔtəʳ] *n* secante *m*
blotting paper ['blɔtɪŋ-] *n* papel *m* secante
blotto ['blɔtəu] *adj* (*col*) mamado
blouse [blauz] *n* blusa
blow [bləu] (*pt* **blew**, *pp* **blown**) *n* golpe *m* ■ *vi* soplar; (*fuse*) fundirse ■ *vt* (*glass*) soplar; (*fuse*) quemar; (*instrument*) tocar; **to come to blows** llegar a golpes; **to ~ one's nose** sonarse
▸ **blow away** *vt* llevarse, arrancar
▸ **blow down** *vt* derribar
▸ **blow off** *vt* arrebatar
▸ **blow out** *vt* apagar ■ *vi* apagarse; (*tyre*) reventar
▸ **blow over** *vi* amainar
▸ **blow up** *vi* estallar ■ *vt* volar; (*tyre*) inflar; (*Phot*) ampliar
blow-dry ['bləudraɪ] *n* secado con secador de mano ■ *vt* secar con secador de mano
blowlamp ['bləulæmp] *n* (*Brit*) soplete *m*, lámpara de soldar
blown [bləun] *pp of* **blow**
blow-out ['bləuaut] *n* (*of tyre*) pinchazo; (*col: big meal*) banquete *m*, festín *m*
blowtorch ['bləutɔ:tʃ] *n* = **blowlamp**
blow-up ['bləuʌp] *n* (*Phot*) ampliación *f*
BLS *n abbr* (*US*) = **Bureau of Labor Statistics**
blubber ['blʌbəʳ] *n* grasa de ballena ■ *vi* (*pej*) lloriquear
bludgeon ['blʌdʒən] *vt*: **to ~ sb into doing sth** coaccionar a algn a hacer algo
blue [blu:] *adj* azul; **~ film** película porno; **~ joke** chiste verde; **once in a ~ moon** de higos a brevas; **to come out of the ~** (*fig*) ser completamente inesperado; *see also* **blues**
blue baby *n* niño azul *or* cianótico
bluebell ['blu:bɛl] *n* campanilla, campánula azul
blue-blooded [blu:'blʌdɪd] *adj* de sangre azul
bluebottle ['blu:bɔtl] *n* moscarda, mosca azul
blue cheese *n* queso azul
blue-chip ['blu:tʃɪp] *n*: **~ investment** inversión *f* asegurada
blue-collar worker ['blu:kɔləʳ-] *n* obrero(-a)
blue jeans *npl* tejanos *mpl*, vaqueros *mpl*
blueprint ['blu:prɪnt] *n* proyecto; **~ (for)** (*fig*) anteproyecto (de)
blues [blu:z] *npl*: **the ~** (*Mus*) el blues; **to have the ~** estar triste
Bluetooth® ['blu:tu:θ] *n* Bluetooth® *f*; **~ technology®** tecnología Bluetooth®
bluff [blʌf] *vi* tirarse un farol, farolear ■ *n* bluff *m*, farol *m*; (*Geo*) precipicio, despeñadero; **to call sb's ~** coger a algn en un renuncio
bluish ['blu:ɪʃ] *adj* azulado
blunder ['blʌndəʳ] *n* patinazo, metedura de pata ■ *vi* cometer un error, meter la pata; **to ~ into sb/sth** tropezar con algn/algo
blunt [blʌnt] *adj* (*knife*) desafilado; (*person*) franco, directo ■ *vt* embotar, desafilar; **this pencil is ~** este lápiz está despuntado; **~ instrument** (*Law*) instrumento contundente
bluntly ['blʌntlɪ] *adv* (*speak*) francamente, de modo terminante
bluntness ['blʌntnɪs] *n* (*of person*) franqueza, brusquedad *f*
blur [blə:ʳ] *n* aspecto borroso ■ *vt* (*vision*) enturbiar; (*memory*) empañar
blurb [blə:b] *n* propaganda
blurred [blə:d] *adj* borroso
blurt [blə:t]: **to ~ out** *vt* (*say*) descolgarse con, dejar escapar
blush [blʌʃ] *vi* ruborizarse, ponerse colorado ■ *n* rubor *m*
blusher ['blʌʃəʳ] *n* colorete *m*
bluster ['blʌstəʳ] *n* fanfarronada, bravata ■ *vi* fanfarronear, echar bravatas
blustering ['blʌstərɪŋ] *adj* (*person*) fanfarrón(-ona)
blustery ['blʌstərɪ] *adj* (*weather*) tempestuoso, tormentoso
Blvd *abbr* = **boulevard**
BM *n abbr* (= *British Museum*: *Univ*: = *Bachelor of Medicine*) *título universitario*
BMA *n abbr* = **British Medical Association**
BMJ *n abbr* = **British Medical Journal**
BMus *n abbr* (= *Bachelor of Music*) *título universitario*
BMX *n abbr* (= *bicycle motocross*) BMX *f*; **~ bike** bici(cleta) *f* BMX
bn *abbr* = **billion**
BO *n abbr* (*col*: = *body odour*) olor *m* a sudor; (*US*) = **box office**
boa ['bəuə] *n* boa
boar [bɔ:ʳ] *n* verraco, cerdo
board [bɔ:d] *n* tabla, tablero; (*on wall*) tablón

m; (*for chess etc*) tablero; (*committee*) junta, consejo; (*in firm*) mesa *or* junta directiva; (*Naut, Aviat*): **on ~** a bordo ■ *vt* (*ship*) embarcarse en; (*train*) subir a; **full ~** (*Brit*) pensión *f* completa; **half ~** (*Brit*) media pensión; **~ and lodging** alojamiento y comida; **to go by the ~** (*fig*) irse por la borda; **above ~** (*fig*) sin tapujos; **across the ~** (*fig: adv*) en todos los niveles; (*: adj*) general
▸ **board up** *vt* (*door*) tapar, cegar
boarder ['bɔːdəʳ] *n* huésped(a) *m(f)*; (*Scol*) interno(-a)
board game *n* juego de tablero
boarding card ['bɔːdɪŋ-] *n* (*Brit: Aviat, Naut*) tarjeta de embarque
boarding house ['bɔːdɪŋ-] *n* casa de huéspedes
boarding party ['bɔːdɪŋ-] *n* brigada de inspección
boarding pass ['bɔːdɪŋ-] *n* (*US*) = **boarding card**
boarding school ['bɔːdɪŋ-] *n* internado
board meeting *n* reunión *f* de la junta directiva
board room *n* sala de juntas
boardwalk ['bɔːdwɔːk] *n* (*US*) paseo entablado
boast [bəust] *vi*: **to ~ (about** *or* **of)** alardear (de) ■ *vt* ostentar ■ *n* alarde *m*, baladronada
boastful ['bəustfəl] *adj* presumido, jactancioso
boastfulness ['bəustfulnɪs] *n* fanfarronería, jactancia
boat [bəut] *n* barco, buque *m*; (*small*) barca, bote *m*; **to go by ~** ir en barco
boater ['bəutəʳ] *n* (*hat*) canotié *m*
boating ['bəutɪŋ] *n* canotaje *m*
boatman ['bəutmən] *n* barquero
boat people *npl refugiados que huyen en barca*
boatswain ['bəusn] *n* contramaestre *m*
bob [bɔb] *vi* (*boat, cork on water: also:* **bob up and down**) menearse, balancearse ■ *n* (*Brit col*) = **shilling**
▸ **bob up** *vi* (re)aparecer de repente
bobbin ['bɔbɪn] *n* (*of sewing machine*) carrete *m*, bobina
bobby ['bɔbɪ] *n* (*Brit col*) poli *m/f*
bobsleigh ['bɔbsleɪ] *n* bob *m*, trineo de competición *f*
bode [bəud] *vi*: **to ~ well/ill (for)** ser de buen/mal agüero (para)
bodice ['bɔdɪs] *n* corpiño
-bodied ['bɔdɪd] *adj suff* de cuerpo ...
bodily ['bɔdɪlɪ] *adj* (*comfort, needs*) corporal; (*pain*) corpóreo ■ *adv* (*in person*) en persona; (*carry*) corporalmente; (*lift*) en peso
body ['bɔdɪ] *n* cuerpo; (*corpse*) cadáver *m*; (*of car*) caja, carrocería; (*also:* **body stocking**) body *m*; (*fig: organization*) organización *f*; (*: public body*) organismo; (*: quantity*) masa; (*: of speech, document*) parte *f* principal; **ruling ~** directiva; **in a ~** todos juntos, en masa
body blow *n* (*fig*) palo
body-building ['bɔdɪ'bɪldɪŋ] *n* culturismo
bodyguard ['bɔdɪgɑːd] *n* guardaespaldas *m inv*
body language *n* lenguaje *m* gestual
body search *n* cacheo; **to carry out a ~ on sb** registrar a algn; **to submit to** *or* **undergo a ~** ser registrado
bodywork ['bɔdɪwəːk] *n* carrocería
boffin ['bɔfɪn] *n* (*Brit*) científico(-a)
bog [bɔg] *n* pantano, ciénaga ■ *vt*: **to get bogged down** (*fig*) empantanarse, atascarse
boggle ['bɔgl] *vi*: **the mind boggles!** ¡no puedo creerlo!
Bogotá [bəugə'tɑː] *n* Bogotá
bogus ['bəugəs] *adj* falso, fraudulento; (*person*) fingido
Bohemia [bə'hiːmɪə] *n* Bohemia
Bohemian [bə'hiːmɪən] *adj, n* bohemio(-a) *m(f)*
boil [bɔɪl] *vt* cocer; (*eggs*) pasar por agua ■ *vi* hervir ■ *n* (*Med*) furúnculo, divieso; **to bring to the ~** calentar hasta que hierva; **to come to the** (*Brit*) *or* **a** (*US*) **~** comenzar a hervir; **boiled egg** huevo pasado por agua; **boiled potatoes** patatas *fpl or* papas *fpl* (*LAm*) cocidas
▸ **boil down** *vi* (*fig*): **to ~ down to** reducirse a
▸ **boil over** *vi* (*liquid*) rebosar; (*anger, resentment*) llegar al colmo
boiler ['bɔɪləʳ] *n* caldera
boiler suit *n* (*Brit*) mono, overol *m* (*LAm*)
boiling ['bɔɪlɪŋ] *adj*: **I'm ~ (hot)** (*col*) estoy asado
boiling point *n* punto de ebullición *f*
boil-in-the-bag [bɔɪlɪnðə'bæg] *adj*: **~ meals** platos que se cuecen en su misma bolsa
boisterous ['bɔɪstərəs] *adj* (*noisy*) bullicioso; (*excitable*) exuberante; (*crowd*) tumultuoso
bold [bəuld] *adj* (*brave*) valiente, audaz; (*pej*) descarado; (*outline*) grueso; (*colour*) vivo; **~ type** (*Typ*) negrita
boldly ['bəuldlɪ] *adv* audazmente
boldness ['bəuldnɪs] *n* valor *m*, audacia; (*cheek*) descaro
Bolivia [bə'lɪvɪə] *n* Bolivia
Bolivian [bə'lɪvɪən] *adj, n* boliviano(-a) *m(f)*
bollard ['bɔləd] *n* (*Brit Aut*) poste *m*
bolshy ['bɔlʃɪ] *adj* (*Brit col*) protestón(-ona); **to be in a ~ mood** tener el día protestón
bolster ['bəulstəʳ] *n* travesero, cabezal *m*

▸ **bolster up** *vt* reforzar; (*fig*) alentar
bolt [bəult] *n* (*lock*) cerrojo; (*with nut*) perno, tornillo ■ *adv*: ~ **upright** rígido, erguido ■ *vt* (*door*) echar el cerrojo a; (*food*) engullir ■ *vi* fugarse; (*horse*) desbocarse
bomb [bɔm] *n* bomba ■ *vt* bombardear
bombard [bɔm'bɑ:d] *vt* bombardear; (*fig*) asediar
bombardment [bɔm'bɑ:dmənt] *n* bombardeo
bombastic [bɔm'bæstɪk] *adj* rimbombante; (*person*) pomposo
bomb disposal *n* desactivación *f* de explosivos
bomb disposal expert *n* artificiero(-a)
bomber ['bɔmə^r] *n* (*Aviat*) bombardero; (*terrorist*) persona que pone bombas
bombing ['bɔmɪŋ] *n* bombardeo
bomb scare *n* amenaza de bomba
bombshell ['bɔmʃɛl] *n* obús *m*, granada; (*fig*) bomba
bomb site *n* lugar *m* donde estalló una bomba
bona fide ['bəunə'faɪdɪ] *adj* genuino, auténtico
bonanza [bə'nænzə] *n* bonanza
bond [bɔnd] *n* (*binding promise*) fianza; (*Finance*) bono; (*link*) vínculo, lazo; **in ~** (*Comm*) en depósito bajo fianza
bondage ['bɔndɪdʒ] *n* esclavitud *f*
bonded goods ['bɔndɪd-] *npl* mercancías *fpl* en depósito de aduanas
bonded warehouse ['bɔndɪd-] *n* depósito de aduanas
bone [bəun] *n* hueso; (*of fish*) espina ■ *vt* deshuesar; quitar las espinas a; **~ of contention** manzana de la discordia
bone china *n* porcelana fina
bone-dry ['bəun'draɪ] *adj* completamente seco
bone idle *adj* gandul
bone marrow *n* médula; **~ transplant** transplante *m* de médula
boner ['bəunə^r] *n* (*US col*) plancha, patochada
bonfire ['bɔnfaɪə^r] *n* hoguera, fogata
bonk [bɔŋk] *vt, vi* (*humorous, col*) chingar (*!*)
bonkers ['bɔŋkəz] *adj* (*Brit col*) majareta
Bonn [bɔn] *n* Bonn *m*
bonnet ['bɔnɪt] *n* gorra; (*Brit: of car*) capó *m*
bonny ['bɔnɪ] *adj* (*esp Scottish*) bonito, hermoso, lindo
bonus ['bəunəs] *n* (*at Christmas etc*) paga extraordinaria; (*merit award*) sobrepaga, prima
bony ['bəunɪ] *adj* (*arm, face*) huesudo; (*Med: tissue*) huesudo; (*meat*) lleno de huesos; (*fish*) lleno de espinas; (*thin: person*) flaco, delgado
boo [bu:] *vt* abuchear
boob [bu:b] *n* (*col: mistake*) disparate *m*, sandez *f*; (*: breast*) teta
booby prize ['bu:bɪ-] *n* premio de consolación (*al último*)
booby trap ['bu:bɪ-] *n* (*Mil etc*) trampa explosiva
book [buk] *n* libro; (*notebook*) libreta; (*of stamps etc*) librillo; **books** (*Comm*) cuentas *fpl*, contabilidad *f* ■ *vt* (*ticket, seat, room*) reservar; (*driver*) fichar; (*Football*) amonestar; **to keep the books** llevar las cuentas *or* los libros; **by the ~** según las reglas; **to throw the ~ at sb** echar un rapapolvo a algn
▸ **book in** *vi* (*at hotel*) registrarse
▸ **book up** *vt*: **all seats are booked up** todas las plazas están reservadas; **the hotel is booked up** el hotel está lleno
bookable ['bukəbl] *adj*: **seats are ~** los asientos se pueden reservar (de antemano)
bookcase ['bukkeɪs] *n* librería, estante *m* para libros
booking office ['bukɪŋ-] *n* (*Brit: Rail*) despacho de billetes *or* boletos (*LAm*); (*: Theat*) taquilla, boletería (*LAm*)
book-keeping ['buk'ki:pɪŋ] *n* contabilidad *f*
booklet ['buklɪt] *n* folleto
bookmaker ['bukmeɪkə^r] *n* corredor *m* de apuestas
bookmark ['bukmɑ:k] (*Comput*) favorito *m*
bookseller ['buksɛlə^r] *n* librero(-a)
bookshelf ['bukʃɛlf] *n* estante *m*
bookshop ['bukʃɔp] *n* librería
bookstall ['bukstɔ:l] *n* quiosco de libros
book store *n* = **bookshop**
book token *n* vale *m* para libros
book value *n* (*Comm*) valor *m* contable
bookworm ['bukwə:m] *n* (*fig*) ratón *m* de biblioteca
boom [bu:m] *n* (*noise*) trueno, estampido; (*in prices etc*) alza rápida; (*Econ*) boom *m*, auge *m* ■ *vi* (*cannon*) hacer gran estruendo, retumbar; (*Econ*) estar en alza
boomerang ['bu:məræŋ] *n* bumerang *m* (*also fig*) ■ *vi*: **to ~ on sb** (*fig*) ser contraproducente para algn
boom town *n* ciudad *f* de crecimiento rápido
boon [bu:n] *n* favor *m*, beneficio
boorish ['buərɪʃ] *adj* grosero
boost [bu:st] *n* estímulo, empuje *m* ■ *vt* estimular, empujar; (*increase: sales, production*) aumentar; **to give a ~ to** (*morale*) levantar; **it gave a ~ to his confidence** le dio confianza en sí mismo
booster ['bu:stə^r] *n* (*Med*) reinyección *f*; (*TV*) repetidor *m*; (*Elec*) elevador *m* de tensión; (*also*: **booster rocket**) cohete *m*

boot [buːt] *n* bota; (*ankle boot*) botín *m*, borceguí *m*; (*Brit: of car*) maleta, maletero, baúl *m* (*LAm*) ■ *vt* dar un puntapié a; (*Comput*) arrancar; **to ~** (*in addition*) además, por añadidura; **to give sb the ~** (*col*) despedir a algn, poner a algn en la calle

booth [buːð] *n* (*at fair*) barraca; (*telephone booth, voting booth*) cabina

bootleg [ˈbuːtlɛg] *adj* de contrabando; **~ record** disco pirata

booty [ˈbuːtɪ] *n* botín *m*

booze [buːz] (*col*) *n* bebida ■ *vi* emborracharse

boozer [ˈbuːzəʳ] *n* (*col: person*) bebedor(a) *m(f)*; (*: Brit: pub*) bar *m*

border [ˈbɔːdəʳ] *n* borde *m*, margen *m*; (*of a country*) frontera ■ *adj* fronterizo; **the Borders** *región fronteriza entre Escocia e Inglaterra*
▸ **border on** *vt fus* lindar con; (*fig*) rayar en

borderline [ˈbɔːdəlaɪn] *n* (*fig*) frontera

bore [bɔːʳ] *pt of* **bear** ■ *vt* (*hole*) taladrar; (*person*) aburrir ■ *n* (*person*) pelmazo, pesado; (*of gun*) calibre *m*

bored [bɔːd] *adj* aburrido; **he's ~ to tears** *or* **to death** *or* **stiff** está aburrido como una ostra, está muerto de aburrimiento

boredom [ˈbɔːdəm] *n* aburrimiento

boring [ˈbɔːrɪŋ] *adj* aburrido, pesado

born [bɔːn] *adj*: **to be ~** nacer; **I was ~ in 1960** nací en 1960

born-again [bɔːnəˈgɛn] *adj*: **~ Christian** evangelista *m/f*

borne [bɔːn] *pp of* **bear**

Borneo [ˈbɔːnɪəu] *n* Borneo

borough [ˈbʌrə] *n* municipio

borrow [ˈbɔrəu] *vt*: **to ~ sth (from sb)** tomar algo prestado (a alguien); **may I ~ your car?** ¿me prestas tu coche?

borrower [ˈbɔrəuəʳ] *n* prestatario(-a)

borrowing [ˈbɔrəuɪŋ] *n* préstamos *mpl*

borstal [ˈbɔːstl] *n* (*Brit*) reformatorio (de menores)

Bosnia [ˈbɔznɪə] *n* Bosnia

Bosnia-Herzegovina, Bosnia-Hercegovina [ˈbɔːsnɪəhɛrzəˈgəuviːnə] *n* Bosnia-Herzegovina

Bosnian [ˈbɔznɪən] *adj, n* bosnio(-a)

bosom [ˈbuzəm] *n* pecho; (*fig*) seno

bosom friend *n* amigo(-a) íntimo(-a) *or* del alma

boss [bɔs] *n* jefe(-a) *m(f)*; (*employer*) patrón(-ona) *m(f)*; (*political etc*) cacique *m* ■ *vt* (*also*: **boss about** *or* **around**) mangonear; **stop bossing everyone about!** ¡deja de dar órdenes *or* de mangonear a todos!

bossy [ˈbɔsɪ] *adj* mandón(-ona)

bosun [ˈbəusn] *n* contramaestre *m*

botanical [bəˈtænɪkl] *adj* botánico

botanist [ˈbɔtənɪst] *n* botanista *m/f*

botany [ˈbɔtənɪ] *n* botánica

botch [bɔtʃ] *vt* (*also*: **botch up**) arruinar, estropear

both [bəuθ] *adj, pron* ambos(-as), los/las dos; **~ of us went, we ~ went** fuimos los dos, ambos fuimos ■ *adv*: **~ A and B** tanto A como B

bother [ˈbɔðəʳ] *vt* (*worry*) preocupar; (*disturb*) molestar, fastidiar, fregar (*LAm*), embromar (*LAm*) ■ *vi* (*gen*): **~ o.s.** molestarse ■ *n*: **what a ~!** ¡qué lata! ■ *excl* ¡maldita sea!, ¡caramba!; **I'm sorry to ~ you** perdona que te moleste; **to ~ doing** tomarse la molestia de hacer; **please don't ~** no te molestes

Botswana [bɔtˈswɑːnə] *n* Botswana

bottle [ˈbɔtl] *n* botella; (*small*) frasco; (*baby's*) biberón *m* ■ *vt* embotellar; **~ of wine/milk** botella de vino/de leche; **wine/milk ~** botella de vino/de leche
▸ **bottle up** *vt* (*fig*) contener, reprimir

bottle bank *n* contenedor *m* de vidrio, iglú *m*

bottleneck [ˈbɔtlnɛk] *n* embotellamiento

bottle-opener [ˈbɔtləupnəʳ] *n* abrebotellas *m inv*

bottom [ˈbɔtəm] *n* (*of box, sea*) fondo; (*buttocks*) trasero, culo; (*of page, mountain, tree*) pie *m*; (*of list*) final *m* ■ *adj* (*lowest*) más bajo; (*last*) último; **to get to the ~ of sth** (*fig*) llegar al fondo de algo

bottomless [ˈbɔtəmlɪs] *adj* sin fondo, insondable

bottom line *n*: **the ~** lo fundamental; **the ~ is he has to go** el caso es que tenemos que despedirle

botulism [ˈbɔtjulɪzəm] *n* botulismo

bough [bau] *n* rama

bought [bɔːt] *pt, pp of* **buy**

bouillon cube [ˈbuːjɔn-] *n* (*US*) cubito de caldo

boulder [ˈbəuldəʳ] *n* canto rodado

bounce [bauns] *vi* (*ball*) (re)botar; (*cheque*) ser rechazado ■ *vt* hacer (re)botar ■ *n* (*rebound*) (re)bote *m*; **he's got plenty of ~** (*fig*) tiene mucha energía

bouncer [ˈbaunsəʳ] *n* (*col*) forzudo, gorila *m*

bouncy castle® [ˈbaunsɪ-] *n* castillo inflable

bound [baund] *pt, pp of* **bind** ■ *n* (*leap*) salto; (*gen pl: limit*) límite *m* ■ *vi* (*leap*) saltar ■ *adj*: **~ by** rodeado de; **to be ~ to do sth** (*obliged*) tener el deber de hacer algo; **he's ~ to come** es seguro que vendrá; **"out of bounds to the public"** "prohibido el paso"; **~ for** con destino a

boundary [ˈbaundrɪ] *n* límite *m*, lindero

boundless [ˈbaundlɪs] *adj* ilimitado

bountiful [ˈbauntɪful] *adj* (*person*) liberal,

generoso; (*God*) bondadoso; (*supply*) abundante
bounty ['baunti] *n* (*generosity*) generosidad *f*; (*reward*) prima
bounty hunter *n* cazarrecompensas *m inv*
bouquet ['bukeɪ] *n* (*of flowers*) ramo, ramillete *m*; (*of wine*) aroma *m*
bourbon ['buəbən] *n* (*US: also:* **bourbon whiskey**) whisky *m* americano, bourbon *m*
bourgeois ['bueʒwɑː] *adj, n* burgués(-esa) *m(f)*
bout [baut] *n* (*of malaria etc*) ataque *m*; (*Boxing etc*) combate *m*, encuentro
boutique [buː'tiːk] *n* boutique *f*, tienda de ropa
bow [bəu] *n* (*knot*) lazo; (*weapon*) arco; (*Mus*) arco [bau] (*of the head*) reverencia; (*Naut: also:* **bows**) proa ■ *vi* [bau] inclinarse, hacer una reverencia; (*yield*): **to ~ to** *or* **before** ceder ante, someterse a; **to ~ to the inevitable** resignarse a lo inevitable
bowels ['bauəlz] *npl* intestinos *mpl*, vientre *m*
bowl [bəul] *n* tazón *m*, cuenco; (*for washing*) palangana, jofaina; (*ball*) bola; (*US: stadium*) estadio ■ *vi* (*Cricket*) arrojar la pelota; *see also* **bowls**
bow-legged ['bəu'lɛgɪd] *adj* estevado
bowler ['bəuləʳ] *n* (*Cricket*) lanzador *m* (de la pelota); (*Brit: also:* **bowler hat**) hongo, bombín *m*
bowling ['bəulɪŋ] *n* (*game*) bolos *mpl*, bochas *fpl*
bowling alley *n* bolera
bowling green *n* pista para bochas
bowls [bəulz] *n* juego de los bolos, bochas *fpl*
bow tie ['bəu-] *n* corbata de lazo, pajarita
box [bɔks] *n* (*also:* **cardboard box**) caja, cajón *m*; (*for jewels*) estuche *m*; (*for money*) cofre *m*; (*crate*) cofre *m*, arca; (*Theat*) palco ■ *vt* encajonar ■ *vi* (*Sport*) boxear
boxer ['bɔksəʳ] *n* (*person*) boxeador *m*; (*dog*) bóxer *m*
box file *n* fichero
boxing ['bɔksɪŋ] *n* (*Sport*) boxeo, box *m* (*LAm*)
Boxing Day *n* (*Brit*) día *m* de San Esteban; *ver nota*

Boxing Day

El día después de Navidad es *Boxing Day*, fiesta en todo el Reino Unido, aunque si el 26 de diciembre cae en domingo el día de descanso se traslada al lunes. En dicho día solía ser tradición entregar "Christmas boxes" (aguinaldos) a empleados, proveedores a domicilio, carteros etc.

boxing gloves *npl* guantes *mpl* de boxeo
boxing ring *n* ring *m*, cuadrilátero
box number *n* (*for advertisements*) apartado
box office *n* taquilla, boletería (*LAm*)
boxroom ['bɔksrum] *n* trastero
boy [bɔɪ] *n* (*young*) niño; (*older*) muchacho
boycott ['bɔɪkɔt] *n* boicot *m* ■ *vt* boicotear
boyfriend ['bɔɪfrɛnd] *n* novio
boyish ['bɔɪɪʃ] *adj* de muchacho, inmaduro
boy scout *n* boy scout *m*
bp *abbr* = **bishop**
Br. *abbr* (*Rel*) = **brother**
bra [brɑː] *n* sostén *m*, sujetador *m*, corpiño (*LAm*)
brace [breɪs] *n* refuerzo, abrazadera; (*Brit: on teeth*) corrector *m*; (*tool*) berbiquí *m* ■ *vt* asegurar, reforzar; **to ~ o.s. (for)** (*fig*) prepararse (para); *see also* **braces**
bracelet ['breɪslɪt] *n* pulsera, brazalete *m*, pulso (*LAm*)
braces ['breɪsɪz] *npl* (*Brit*) tirantes *mpl*, suspensores *mpl* (*LAm*); (*US: on teeth*) corrector *m*
bracing ['breɪsɪŋ] *adj* vigorizante, tónico
bracken ['brækən] *n* helecho
bracket ['brækɪt] *n* (*Tech*) soporte *m*, puntal *m*; (*group*) clase *f*, categoría; (*also:* **brace bracket**) soporte *m*, abrazadera; (*also:* **round bracket**) paréntesis *m inv*; (*gen*): **square ~** corchete *m* ■ *vt* (*fig: also:* **bracket together**) agrupar; **income ~** nivel *m* económico; **in brackets** entre paréntesis
brackish ['brækɪʃ] *adj* (*water*) salobre
brag [bræg] *vi* jactarse
braid [breɪd] *n* (*trimming*) galón *m*; (*of hair*) trenza
Braille [breɪl] *n* Braille *m*
brain [breɪn] *n* cerebro; **brains** *npl* sesos *mpl*; **she's got brains** es muy lista
brainchild ['breɪntʃaɪld] *n* invención *f*
braindead ['breɪndɛd] *adj* (*Med*) clínicamente muerto; (*col*) subnormal, tarado
brainless ['breɪnlɪs] *adj* estúpido, insensato
brainstorm ['breɪnstɔːm] *n* (*fig*) ataque *m* de locura, frenesí *m*; (*US: brainwave*) idea luminosa *or* genial, inspiración *f*
brainstorming ['breɪnstɔːmɪŋ] *n discusión intensa para solucionar problemas*
brainwash ['breɪnwɔʃ] *vt* lavar el cerebro a
brainwave ['breɪnweɪv] *n* idea luminosa *or* genial, inspiración *f*
brainy ['breɪnɪ] *adj* muy listo *or* inteligente
braise [breɪz] *vt* cocer a fuego lento
brake [breɪk] *n* (*on vehicle*) freno ■ *vt, vi* frenar
brake drum *n* tambor *m* de freno
brake fluid *n* líquido de frenos
brake light *n* luz *f* de frenado

brake pedal *n* pedal *m* de freno
bramble ['bræmbl] *n* (*fruit*) zarza
bran [bræn] *n* salvado
branch [brɑːntʃ] *n* rama; (*fig*) ramo; (*Comm*) sucursal *f* ■ *vi* ramificarse; (*fig*) extenderse
▸ **branch out** *vi* ramificarse
branch line *n* (*Rail*) ramal *m*, línea secundaria
branch manager *n* director(a) *m(f)* de sucursal
brand [brænd] *n* marca; (*iron*) hierro de marcar ■ *vt* (*cattle*) marcar con hierro candente
brandish ['brændɪʃ] *vt* blandir
brand name *n* marca
brand-new ['brænd'njuː] *adj* flamante, completamente nuevo
brandy ['brændɪ] *n* coñac *m*, brandy *m*
brash [bræʃ] *adj* (*rough*) tosco; (*cheeky*) descarado
Brasilia [brə'zɪlɪə] *n* Brasilia
brass [brɑːs] *n* latón *m*; **the ~** (*Mus*) los cobres
brass band *n* banda de metal
brassière ['bræsɪəʳ] *n* sostén *m*, sujetador *m*, corpiño (*LAm*)
brass tacks *npl*: **to get down to ~** ir al grano
brat [bræt] *n* (*pej*) mocoso(-a)
bravado [brə'vɑːdəu] *n* fanfarronería
brave [breɪv] *adj* valiente, valeroso ■ *n* guerrero indio ■ *vt* (*challenge*) desafiar; (*resist*) aguantar
bravely ['breɪvlɪ] *adv* valientemente, con valor
bravery ['breɪvərɪ] *n* valor *m*, valentía
bravo [brɑː'vəu] *excl* ¡bravo!, ¡olé!
brawl [brɔːl] *n* pendencia, reyerta ■ *vi* pelearse
brawn [brɔːn] *n* fuerza muscular; (*meat*) carne *f* en gelatina
brawny ['brɔːnɪ] *adj* fornido, musculoso
bray [breɪ] *n* rebuzno ■ *vi* rebuznar
brazen ['breɪzn] *adj* descarado, cínico ■ *vt*: **to ~ it out** echarle cara al asunto
brazier ['breɪzɪəʳ] *n* brasero
Brazil [brə'zɪl] *n* (el) Brasil
Brazilian [brə'zɪlɪən] *adj, n* brasileño(-a) *m(f)*
breach [briːtʃ] *vt* abrir brecha en ■ *n* (*gap*) brecha; (*estrangement*) ruptura; (*breaking*): **~ of confidence** abuso de confianza; **~ of contract** infracción *f* de contrato; **~ of the peace** perturbación *f* del orden público; **in ~ of** por incumplimiento *or* infracción de
bread [brɛd] *n* pan *m*; (*col: money*) pasta, lana (*LAm*); **~ and butter** *n* pan con mantequilla; (*fig*) pan (de cada día) ■ *adj* común y corriente; **to earn one's daily ~** ganarse el pan; **to know which side one's ~ is buttered (on)** saber dónde aprieta el zapato
breadbin ['brɛdbɪn] *n* panera
breadboard ['brɛdbɔːd] *n* (*Comput*) circuito experimental
breadbox ['brɛdbɔks] *n* (*US*) panera
breadcrumbs ['brɛdkrʌmz] *npl* migajas *fpl*; (*Culin*) pan *msg* rallado
breadline ['brɛdlaɪn] *n*: **on the ~** en la miseria
breadth [brɛtθ] *n* anchura; (*fig*) amplitud *f*
breadwinner ['brɛdwɪnəʳ] *n* sostén *m* de la familia
break [breɪk] *vb* (*pt* **broke**, *pp* **broken**) ■ *vt* (*gen*) romper; (*promise*) no cumplir; (*fall*) amortiguar; (*journey*) interrumpir; (*law*) violar, infringir; (*record*) batir; (*news*) comunicar ■ *vi* romperse, quebrarse; (*storm*) estallar; (*weather*) cambiar ■ *n* (*gap*) abertura; (*crack*) grieta; (*fracture*) fractura; (*in relations*) ruptura; (*rest*) descanso; (*time*) intervalo; (*: at school*) (período de) recreo; (*holiday*) vacaciones *fpl*; (*chance*) oportunidad *f*; (*escape*) evasión *f*, fuga; **to ~ with sb** (*fig*) romper con algn; **to ~ even** *vi* cubrir los gastos; **to ~ free** *or* **loose** *vi* escaparse; **lucky ~** (*col*) chiripa, racha de buena suerte; **to have** *or* **take a ~** (*few minutes*) descansar; **without a ~** sin descanso *or* descansar
▸ **break down** *vt* (*door etc*) echar abajo, derribar; (*resistance*) vencer, acabar con; (*figures, data*) analizar, descomponer; (*undermine*) acabar con ■ *vi* estropearse; (*Med*) sufrir un colapso; (*Aut*) averiarse, descomponerse (*LAm*); (*person*) romper a llorar
▸ **break in** *vt* (*horse etc*) domar ■ *vi* (*burglar*) forzar una entrada
▸ **break into** *vt fus* (*house*) forzar
▸ **break off** *vi* (*speaker*) pararse, detenerse; (*branch*) partir ■ *vt* (*talks*) suspender; (*engagement*) romper
▸ **break open** *vt* (*door etc*) abrir por la fuerza, forzar
▸ **break out** *vi* estallar; **to ~ out in spots** salir a algn granos
▸ **break through** *vi*: **the sun broke through** asomó el sol ■ *vt fus* (*defences, barrier, crowd*) abrirse paso por
▸ **break up** *vi* (*partnership*) disolverse; (*friends*) romper ■ *vt* (*rocks, ice etc*) partir; (*crowd*) disolver
breakable ['breɪkəbl] *adj* quebradizo ■ *n*: **breakables** cosas *fpl* frágiles
breakage ['breɪkɪdʒ] *n* rotura; **to pay for breakages** pagar por los objetos rotos
breakaway ['breɪkəweɪ] *adj* (*group etc*) disidente
break-dancing ['breɪkdɑːnsɪŋ] *n* break *m*

breakdown ['breɪkdaun] *n* (*Aut*) avería; (*in communications*) interrupción *f*; (*Med*: *also*: **nervous breakdown**) colapso, crisis *f* nerviosa; (*of figures*) desglose *m*
breakdown van *n* (*Brit*) (camión *m*) grúa
breaker ['breɪkə^r] *n* rompiente *m*, ola grande
breakeven ['breɪk'i:vn] *cpd*: ~ **chart** gráfico del punto de equilibrio; ~ **point** punto de break-even *or* de equilibrio
breakfast ['brɛkfəst] *n* desayuno
breakfast cereal *n* cereales *mpl* para el desayuno
break-in ['breɪkɪn] *n* robo con allanamiento de morada
breaking and entering ['breɪkɪŋənd'ɛntərɪŋ] *n* (*Law*) violación *f* de domicilio, allanamiento de morada
breaking point ['breɪkɪŋ-] *n* punto de ruptura
breakthrough ['breɪkθru:] *n* ruptura; (*fig*) avance *m*, adelanto
break-up ['breɪkʌp] *n* (*of partnership, marriage*) disolución *f*
break-up value *n* (*Comm*) valor *m* de liquidación
breakwater ['breɪkwɔ:tə^r] *n* rompeolas *m inv*
breast [brɛst] *n* (*of woman*) pecho, seno; (*chest*) pecho; (*of bird*) pechuga
breast-feed ['brɛstfi:d] *vt, vi* (*irreg*: *like* **feed**) amamantar, dar el pecho
breaststroke ['brɛststrəuk] *n* braza de pecho
breath [brɛθ] *n* aliento, respiración *f*; **out of ~** sin aliento, sofocado; **to go out for a ~ of air** salir a tomar el fresco
Breathalyser® ['brɛθəlaɪzə^r] *n* (*Brit*) alcoholímetro *m*; ~ **test** *n* prueba de alcoholemia
breathe [bri:ð] *vt, vi* respirar; (*noisily*) resollar; **I won't ~ a word about it** no diré ni una palabra de ello
▸ **breathe in** *vt, vi* aspirar
▸ **breathe out** *vt, vi* espirar
breather ['bri:ðə^r] *n* respiro, descanso
breathing ['bri:ðɪŋ] *n* respiración *f*
breathing space *n* (*fig*) respiro, pausa
breathless ['brɛθlɪs] *adj* sin aliento, jadeante; (*with excitement*) pasmado
breathtaking ['brɛθteɪkɪŋ] *adj* imponente, pasmoso
breath test *n* prueba de la alcoholemia
-bred [brɛd] *suff*: **to be well/ill~** estar bien/mal criado
breed [bri:d] *vb* (*pt, pp* **bred**) [brɛd] ■ *vt* criar; (*fig*: *hate, suspicion*) crear, engendrar ■ *vi* reproducirse, procrear ■ *n* raza, casta
breeder ['bri:də^r] *n* (*person*) criador(a) *m(f)*; (*Physics*: *also*: **breeder reactor**) reactor *m*
breeding ['bri:dɪŋ] *n* (*of person*) educación *f*
breeze [bri:z] *n* brisa
breezeblock ['bri:zblɔk] *n* (*Brit*) bovedilla
breezy ['bri:zɪ] *adj* de mucho viento, ventoso; (*person*) despreocupado
Breton ['brɛtən] *adj* bretón(-ona) ■ *n* bretón(-ona) *m(f)*; (*Ling*) bretón *m*
brevity ['brɛvɪtɪ] *n* brevedad *f*
brew [bru:] *vt* (*tea*) hacer; (*beer*) elaborar; (*plot*) tramar ■ *vi* hacerse; elaborarse; tramarse; (*storm*) amenazar
brewer ['bru:ə^r] *n* cervecero, fabricante *m* de cerveza
brewery ['bru:ərɪ] *n* fábrica de cerveza
briar ['braɪə^r] *n* (*thorny bush*) zarza; (*wild rose*) escaramujo, rosa silvestre
bribe [braɪb] *n* soborno ■ *vt* sobornar, cohechar; **to ~ sb to do sth** sobornar a algn para que haga algo
bribery ['braɪbərɪ] *n* soborno, cohecho
bric-a-brac ['brɪkəbræk] *n inv* baratijas *fpl*
brick [brɪk] *n* ladrillo
bricklayer ['brɪkleɪə^r] *n* albañil *m*
brickwork ['brɪkwə:k] *n* enladrillado
brickworks ['brɪkwə:ks] *n* ladrillar *m*
bridal ['braɪdl] *adj* nupcial
bride [braɪd] *n* novia
bridegroom ['braɪdgru:m] *n* novio
bridesmaid ['braɪdzmeɪd] *n* dama de honor
bridge [brɪdʒ] *n* puente *m*; (*Naut*) puente *m* de mando; (*of nose*) caballete *m*; (*Cards*) bridge *m* ■ *vt* (*river*) tender un puente sobre
bridgehead ['brɪdʒhɛd] *n* cabeza de puente
bridging loan ['brɪdʒɪŋ-] *n* crédito provisional
bridle ['braɪdl] *n* brida, freno ■ *vt* poner la brida a; (*fig*) reprimir, refrenar ■ *vi* (*in anger etc*) picarse
bridle path *n* camino de herradura
brief [bri:f] *adj* breve, corto ■ *n* (*Law*) escrito ■ *vt* (*inform*) informar; (*instruct*) dar instrucciones a; **in ~ ...** en resumen ...; **to ~ sb (about sth)** informar a algn (sobre algo)
briefcase ['bri:fkeɪs] *n* cartera, portafolio(s) *m inv* (*LAm*)
briefing ['bri:fɪŋ] *n* (*Press*) informe *m*
briefly *adv* (*smile, glance*) brevemente; (*explain, say*) brevemente, en pocas palabras
briefs [bri:fs] *npl* (*for men*) calzoncillos *mpl*; (*for women*) bragas *fpl*
Brig. *abbr* = **brigadier**
brigade [brɪ'geɪd] *n* (*Mil*) brigada
brigadier [brɪgə'dɪə^r] *n* general *m* de brigada
bright [braɪt] *adj* claro; (*room*) luminoso; (*day*) de sol; (*person*: *clever*) listo, inteligente; (: *lively*) alegre, animado; (*colour*) vivo; **to look on the ~ side** mirar el lado bueno

brighten ['braɪtn] (*also:* **brighten up**) *vt* (*room*) hacer más alegre ■ *vi* (*weather*) despejarse; (*person*) animarse, alegrarse
brill [brɪl] *adj* (*Brit col*) guay
brilliance ['brɪljəns] *n* brillo, brillantez *f*; (*fig: of person*) inteligencia
brilliant ['brɪljənt] *adj* (*light, idea, person, success*) brillante; (*clever*) genial
brilliantly ['brɪljəntlɪ] *adv* brillantemente
brim [brɪm] *n* borde *m*; (*of hat*) ala
brimful ['brɪm'ful] *adj* lleno hasta el borde; (*fig*) rebosante
brine [braɪn] *n* (*Culin*) salmuera
bring (*pt, pp* **brought**) [brɪŋ, brɔːt] *vt* (*thing*) traer; (*person*) conducir; **to ~ sth to an end** terminar con algo; **I can't ~ myself to sack him** no soy capaz de echarle
▸ **bring about** *vt* ocasionar, producir
▸ **bring back** *vt* volver a traer; (*return*) devolver
▸ **bring down** *vt* bajar; (*price*) rebajar
▸ **bring forward** *vt* adelantar; (*Bookkeeping*) sumar y seguir
▸ **bring in** *vt* (*harvest*) recoger; (*person*) hacer entrar *or* pasar; (*object*) traer; (*Pol: bill, law*) presentar; (*Law: verdict*) pronunciar; (*produce: income*) producir, rendir
▸ **bring off** *vt* (*task, plan*) lograr, conseguir; (*deal*) cerrar
▸ **bring out** *vt* (*object*) sacar; (*new product*) sacar; (*book*) publicar
▸ **bring round** *vt* (*unconscious person*) hacer volver en sí; (*convince*) convencer
▸ **bring up** *vt* (*person*) educar, criar; (*carry up*) subir; (*question*) sacar a colación; (*food: vomit*) devolver, vomitar
brink [brɪŋk] *n* borde *m*; **on the ~ of doing sth** a punto de hacer algo; **she was on the ~ of tears** estaba al borde de las lágrimas
brisk [brɪsk] *adj* (*walk*) enérgico, vigoroso; (*speedy*) rápido; (*wind*) fresco; (*trade*) activo, animado; (*abrupt*) brusco; **business is ~** el negocio va bien *or* a paso activo
brisket ['brɪskɪt] *n* falda de vaca
bristle ['brɪsl] *n* cerda ■ *vi* erizarse
bristly ['brɪslɪ] *adj* (*beard, hair*) erizado; **to have a ~ chin** tener la barba crecida
Brit [brɪt] *n abbr* (*col:* = *British person*) británico(-a)
Britain ['brɪtən] *n* (*also:* **Great Britain**) Gran Bretaña
British ['brɪtɪʃ] *adj* británico; **the British** *npl* los británicos; **the British Isles** *npl* las Islas Británicas
British Rail *n* ≈ RENFE *f* (*SP*)
British Summer Time *n hora de verano británica*
Briton ['brɪtən] *n* británico(-a)
brittle ['brɪtl] *adj* quebradizo, frágil
Bro. *abbr* (*Rel*) = **brother**
broach [brəutʃ] *vt* (*subject*) abordar
broad [brɔːd] *adj* ancho, amplio; (*accent*) cerrado ■ *n* (*US col*) tía; **in ~ daylight** en pleno día; **the ~ outlines** las líneas generales
broadband ['brɔːdbænd] *n* banda ancha
broad bean *n* haba
broadcast ['brɔːdkaːst] (*pt, pp* **~**) *n* emisión *f* ■ *vt* (*Radio*) emitir; (*TV*) transmitir ■ *vi* emitir; transmitir
broadcaster ['brɔːdkaːstə^r] *n* locutor(a) *m(f)*
broadcasting ['brɔːdkaːstɪŋ] *n* radiodifusión *f*, difusión *f*
broadcasting station *n* emisora
broaden ['brɔːdn] *vt* ensanchar ■ *vi* ensancharse
broadly ['brɔːdlɪ] *adv* en general
broad-minded ['brɔːd'maɪndɪd] *adj* tolerante, liberal
broadsheet ['brɔːdʃiːt] *n* (*Brit*) periódico de gran formato (*no sensacionalista*); *see also* **quality press**
brocade [brə'keɪd] *n* brocado
broccoli ['brɔkəlɪ] *n* brécol *m*, bróculi *m*
brochure ['brəuʃjuə^r] *n* folleto
brogue [brəug] *n* (*accent*) acento regional; (*shoe*) (*tipo de*) *zapato de cuero grueso*
broil [brɔɪl] *vt* (*US*) asar a la parrilla
broiler ['brɔɪlə^r] *n* (*fowl*) pollo (para asar)
broke [brəuk] *pt of* **break** ■ *adj* (*col*) pelado, sin una perra; **to go ~** quebrar
broken ['brəukən] *pp of* **break** ■ *adj* (*stick*) roto; (*fig: marriage*) deshecho; (*: promise, vow*) violado; **~ leg** pierna rota; **in ~ English** en un inglés chapurreado
broken-down ['brəukn'daun] *adj* (*car*) averiado; (*machine*) estropeado; (*house*) destartalado
broken-hearted ['brəukn'haːtɪd] *adj* con el corazón destrozado
broker ['brəukə^r] *n* corredor(a) *m(f)* de bolsa
brokerage ['brəukərɪdʒ] *n* corretaje *m*
brolly ['brɔlɪ] *n* (*Brit col*) paraguas *m inv*
bronchitis [brɔŋ'kaɪtɪs] *n* bronquitis *f*
bronze [brɔnz] *n* bronce *m*
bronzed [brɔnzd] *adj* bronceado
brooch [brəutʃ] *n* broche *m*
brood [bruːd] *n* camada, cría; (*children*) progenie *f* ■ *vi* (*hen*) empollar; **to ~ over** dar vueltas a, rumiar
broody ['bruːdɪ] *adj* (*fig*) triste, melancólico
brook [bruk] *n* arroyo
broom [brum] *n* escoba; (*Bot*) retama
broomstick ['brumstɪk] *n* palo de escoba
Bros. *abbr* (*Comm:* = *Brothers*) Hnos

broth [brɔθ] *n* caldo
brothel ['brɔθl] *n* burdel *m*
brother ['brʌðə^r] *n* hermano
brotherhood ['brʌðəhud] *n* hermandad *f*
brother-in-law ['brʌðərɪn'lɔː] *n* cuñado
brotherly ['brʌðəlɪ] *adj* fraternal
brought [brɔːt] *pt, pp of* **bring**
brow [brau] *n* (*forehead*) frente *f*; (*of hill*) cumbre *f*
browbeat ['braubiːt] *vt* (*irreg: like* **beat**) intimidar
brown [braun] *adj* marrón; (*hair*) castaño; (*tanned*) moreno ■ *n* (*colour*) marrón *m* ■ *vt* (*tan*) poner moreno; (*Culin*) dorar; **to go ~** (*person*) ponerse moreno; (*leaves*) dorarse
brown bread *n* pan *m* moreno
brownie ['braunɪ] *n* niña exploradora
brown paper *n* papel *m* de estraza
brown rice *n* arroz *m* integral
brown sugar *n* azúcar *m* moreno
browse [brauz] *vi* (*animal*) pacer; (*among books*) hojear libros; **to ~ through a book** hojear un libro
browser ['braʊzə^r] *n* (*Comput*) navegador *m*
bruise [bruːz] *n* (*on person*) cardenal *m*, hematoma *m* ■ *vt* (*leg etc*) magullar; (*fig: feelings*) herir
Brum [brʌm] *n abbr*, **Brummagem** ['brʌmədʒəm] *n* (*col*) = **Birmingham**
Brummie ['brʌmɪ] *n* (*col*) habitante *m/f* de Birmingham
brunch [brʌntʃ] *n desayuno-almuerzo*
brunette [bruː'nɛt] *n* morena, morocha (*LAm*)
brunt [brʌnt] *n*: **to bear the ~ of** llevar el peso de
brush [brʌʃ] *n* cepillo, escobilla (*LAm*); (*large*) escoba; (*for painting, shaving etc*) brocha; (*artist's*) pincel *m*; (*Bot*) maleza ■ *vt* cepillar; (*gen*): **~ past, ~ against** rozar al pasar; **to have a ~ with the police** tener un roce con la policía
▸ **brush aside** *vt* rechazar, no hacer caso a
▸ **brush up** *vt* (*knowledge*) repasar, refrescar
brushed [brʌʃt] *adj* (*nylon, denim etc*) afelpado; (*Tech: steel, chrome etc*) cepillado
brushwood ['brʌʃwud] *n* (*bushes*) maleza; (*sticks*) leña
brusque [bruːsk] *adj* (*person, manner*) brusco; (*tone*) áspero
Brussels ['brʌslz] *n* Bruselas
Brussels sprout *n* col *f* de Bruselas
brutal ['bruːtl] *adj* brutal
brutality [bruː'tælɪtɪ] *n* brutalidad *f*
brutalize ['bruːtəlaɪz] *vt* (*harden*) embrutecer; (*ill-treat*) tratar brutalmente a
brute [bruːt] *n* bruto; (*person*) bestia ■ *adj*: **by ~ force** por la fuerza bruta
brutish ['bruːtɪʃ] *adj* brutal
BS *n abbr* (*US: = Bachelor of Science*) *título universitario*
bs *abbr* = **bill of sale**
BSA *n abbr* (*US*) = **Boy Scouts of America**
BSc *abbr* = **Bachelor of Science**; *see also* **Bachelor's Degree**
BSE *n abbr* (*= bovine spongiform encephalopathy*) encefalopatía espongiforme bovina
BSI *n abbr* (*= British Standards Institution*) *institución británica de normalización*
BST *n abbr* (*= British Summer Time*) *hora de verano británica*
Bt. *abbr* (*Brit*) = **baronet**
btu *n abbr* (*= British thermal unit*) *= 1054.2 julios*
BTW *abbr* (*= by the way*) por cierto
bubble ['bʌbl] *n* burbuja; (*in paint*) ampolla ■ *vi* burbujear, borbotar
bubble bath *n* espuma para el baño
bubble gum *n* chicle *m*
bubblejet printer ['bʌbldʒɛt-] *n* impresora de injección por burbujas
bubbly ['bʌblɪ] *adj* (*person*) vivaracho; (*liquid*) con burbujas ■ *n* (*col*) champán *m*
Bucharest [buːkə'rɛst] *n* Bucarest *m*
buck [bʌk] *n* macho; (*US col*) dólar *m* ■ *vi* corcovear; **to pass the ~ (to sb)** echar (a algn) el muerto
▸ **buck up** *vi* (*cheer up*) animarse, cobrar ánimo ■ *vt*: **to ~ one's ideas up** poner más empeño
bucket ['bʌkɪt] *n* cubo, balde *m* (*esp LAm*) ■ *vi*: **the rain is bucketing (down)** (*col*) está lloviendo a cántaros
Buckingham Palace ['bʌkɪŋəm-] *n* el Palacio de Buckingham; *ver nota*

BUCKINGHAM PALACE

Buckingham Palace es la residencia oficial del monarca británico en Londres. Data de 1703 y fue en principio el palacio del Duque de Buckingham, para pasar a manos de Jorge III en 1762. Fue reconstruido el siglo pasado y reformado después a principios de este siglo. Hoy en día parte del palacio está abierto al público.

buckle ['bʌkl] *n* hebilla ■ *vt* abrochar con hebilla ■ *vi* torcerse, combarse
▸ **buckle down** *vi* poner empeño
Bucks [bʌks] *abbr* (*Brit*) = **Buckinghamshire**
bud [bʌd] *n* brote *m*, yema; (*of flower*) capullo ■ *vi* brotar, echar brotes
Budapest [bjuːdə'pɛst] *n* Budapest *m*

Buddhism ['budɪzm] *n* Budismo
Buddhist ['budɪst] *adj, n* budista *m/f*
budding ['bʌdɪŋ] *adj* en ciernes, en embrión
buddy ['bʌdɪ] *n* (*US*) compañero, compinche *m*
budge [bʌdʒ] *vt* mover; (*fig*) hacer ceder ■ *vi* moverse
budgerigar ['bʌdʒərɪgɑːʳ] *n* periquito
budget ['bʌdʒɪt] *n* presupuesto ■ *vi*: **to ~ for sth** presupuestar algo; **I'm on a tight ~** no puedo gastar mucho; **she works out her ~ every month** planea su presupuesto todos los meses
budgie ['bʌdʒɪ] *n* = **budgerigar**
Buenos Aires ['bweɪnɔs'aɪrɪz] *n* Buenos Aires *m* ■ *adj* bonaerense, porteño (*LAm*)
buff [bʌf] *adj* (*colour*) color *m* de ante ■ *n* (*enthusiast*) entusiasta *m/f*
buffalo ['bʌfələu] (*pl* **~** *or* **buffaloes**) *n* (*Brit*) búfalo; (*US: bison*) bisonte *m*
buffer ['bʌfəʳ] *n* amortiguador *m*; (*Comput*) memoria intermedia, buffer *m*
buffering ['bʌfərɪŋ] *n* (*Comput*) almacenamiento en memoria intermedia
buffer zone *n* zona (que sirve de) colchón
buffet ['bufeɪ] *n* (*Brit: bar*) bar *m*, cafetería; (*food*) buffet *m* ■ *vt* ['bʌfɪt] (*strike*) abofetear; (*wind etc*) golpear
buffet car *n* (*Brit Rail*) coche-restaurante *m*
buffet lunch *n* buffet *m* (almuerzo)
buffoon [bə'fuːn] *n* bufón *m*
bug [bʌg] *n* (*insect*) chinche *m*; (*: gen*) bicho, sabandija; (*germ*) microbio, bacilo; (*spy device*) micrófono oculto; (*Comput*) fallo, error *m* ■ *vt* (*annoy*) fastidiar; (*room*) poner un micrófono oculto en; (*phone*) pinchar; **I've got the travel ~** (*fig*) me encanta viajar; **it really bugs me** me fastidia *or* molesta mucho
bugbear ['bʌgbɛəʳ] *n* pesadilla
bugle ['bjuːgl] *n* corneta, clarín *m*
build [bɪld] *n* (*of person*) talle *m*, tipo ■ *vt* (*pt, pp* **built**) [bɪlt] construir, edificar
▸ **build on** *vt fus* (*fig*) basar en
▸ **build up** *vt* (*Med*) fortalecer; (*stocks*) acumular; (*establish: business*) fomentar, desarrollar; (*: reputation*) crear(se); (*increase: production*) aumentar; **don't ~ your hopes up too soon** no te hagas demasiadas ilusiones
builder ['bɪldəʳ] *n* constructor(a) *m(f)*; (*contractor*) contratista *m/f*
building ['bɪldɪŋ] *n* (*act*) construcción *f*; (*habitation, offices*) edificio
building contractor *n* contratista *m/f* de obras
building industry *n* construcción *f*
building site *n* solar *m* (*SP*), obra (*LAm*)
building society *n* (*Brit*) sociedad *f* de préstamo inmobiliario; *ver nota*

BUILDING SOCIETY

En el Reino Unido existe un tipo de entidad financiera llamada *building society* de la que sus clientes son también propietarios y cuyos servicios son similares a los de los bancos, aunque se centran fundamentalmente en créditos hipotecarios y cuentas de ahorro. Son la entidad más utilizada por el público en general a la hora de pedir créditos para la compra de la vivienda.

building trade *n* = **building industry**
build-up ['bɪldʌp] *n* (*publicity*): **to give sb/sth a good ~** hacer mucha propaganda de algn/algo
built [bɪlt] *pt, pp of* **build**
built-in ['bɪlt'ɪn] *adj* (*cupboard*) empotrado; (*device*) interior, incorporado; **~ obsolescence** caducidad *f* programada
built-up ['bɪltʌp] *adj* (*area*) urbanizado
bulb [bʌlb] *n* (*Bot*) bulbo; (*Elec*) bombilla, bombillo (*LAm*), foco (*LAm*)
bulbous ['bʌlbəs] *adj* bulboso
Bulgaria [bʌl'gɛərɪə] *n* Bulgaria
Bulgarian [bʌl'gɛərɪən] *adj* búlgaro ■ *n* búlgaro(-a); (*Ling*) búlgaro
bulge [bʌldʒ] *n* bombeo, pandeo; (*in birth rate, sales*) alza, aumento ■ *vi* bombearse, pandearse; (*pocket etc*) hacer bulto
bulimia [bə'lɪmɪə] *n* bulimia
bulk [bʌlk] *n* (*mass*) bulto, volumen *m*; (*major part*) grueso; **in ~** (*Comm*) a granel; **the ~ of** la mayor parte de; **to buy in ~** comprar en grandes cantidades
bulk buying *n* compra a granel
bulk carrier *n* (buque *m*) granelero
bulkhead ['bʌlkhɛd] *n* mamparo
bulky ['bʌlkɪ] *adj* voluminoso, abultado
bull [bul] *n* toro; (*Stock Exchange*) alcista *m/f* de bolsa; (*Rel*) bula
bulldog ['buldɔg] *n* dogo
bulldoze ['buldəuz] *vt* mover con excavadora; **I was bulldozed into doing it** (*fig col*) me obligaron a hacerlo
bulldozer ['buldəuzəʳ] *n* buldozer *m*, excavadora
bullet ['bulɪt] *n* bala; **~ wound** balazo
bulletin ['bulɪtɪn] *n* comunicado, parte *m*; (*journal*) boletín *m*
bulletin board *n* (*US*) tablón *m* de anuncios; (*Comput*) tablero de noticias
bulletproof ['bulɪtpruːf] *adj* a prueba de balas; **~ vest** chaleco antibalas
bullfight ['bulfaɪt] *n* corrida de toros
bullfighter ['bulfaɪtəʳ] *n* torero

bullfighting ['bulfaitiŋ] *n* los toros *mpl*, el toreo; *(art of bullfighting)* tauromaquia
bullion ['buljən] *n* oro *or* plata en barras
bullock ['bulək] *n* novillo
bullring ['bulriŋ] *n* plaza de toros
bull's-eye ['bulzai] *n* blanco, diana
bullshit ['bulʃit] *(col!)* *excl* chorradas ■ *n* chorradas *fpl* ■ *vi* decir chorradas ■ *vt*: **to ~ sb** quedarse con algn
bully ['buli] *n* valentón *m*, matón *m* ■ *vt* intimidar, tiranizar
bum [bʌm] *n* *(Brit: col: backside)* culo; *(: tramp)* vagabundo; *(col: esp US: idler)* holgazán(-ana) *m(f)*, flojo(-a)
bumble ['bʌmbl] *vi* *(walk unsteadily)* andar de forma vacilante; *(fig)* farfullar, trastabillar
bumblebee ['bʌmblbi:] *n* abejorro
bumbling ['bʌmbliŋ] *n* divagación *f*
bumf [bʌmf] *n* *(col: forms etc)* papeleo
bump [bʌmp] *n* *(blow)* tope *m*, choque *m*; *(jolt)* sacudida; *(noise)* choque *m*, topetón *m*; *(on road etc)* bache *m*; *(on head)* chichón *m* ■ *vt* *(strike)* chocar contra, topetar ■ *vi* dar sacudidas
▸ **bump into** *vt fus* chocar contra, tropezar con; *(person)* topar con; *(col: meet)* tropezar con, toparse con
bumper ['bʌmpər] *n* *(Brit)* parachoques *m inv* ■ *adj*: **~ crop/harvest** cosecha abundante
bumper cars *npl* *(US)* autos *or* coches *mpl* de choque
bumph [bʌmf] *n* = **bumf**
bumptious ['bʌmpʃəs] *adj* engreído, presuntuoso
bumpy ['bʌmpi] *adj* *(road)* lleno de baches; *(journey, flight)* agitado
bun [bʌn] *n* *(Brit: cake)* pastel *m*; *(US: bread)* bollo; *(of hair)* moño
bunch [bʌntʃ] *n* *(of flowers)* ramo; *(of keys)* manojo; *(of bananas)* piña; *(of people)* grupo; *(pej)* pandilla
bundle ['bʌndl] *n* *(gen)* bulto, fardo; *(of sticks)* haz *m*; *(of papers)* legajo ■ *vt* *(also:* **bundle up***)* atar, envolver; **to ~ sth/sb into** meter algo/a algn precipitadamente en
bun fight *n* *(Brit col: tea party)* merienda; *(: function)* fiesta oficial
bung [bʌŋ] *n* tapón *m*, bitoque *m* ■ *vt* *(throw: also:* **bung into***)* arrojar; *(also:* **bung up***: pipe, hole)* tapar; **my nose is bunged up** *(col)* tengo la nariz atascada *or* taponada
bungalow ['bʌŋgələu] *n* bungalow *m*, chalé *m*
bungee jumping ['bʌndʒi:'dʒʌmpiŋ] *n* puenting *m*, banyi *m*
bungle ['bʌŋgl] *vt* chapucear
bunion ['bʌnjən] *n* juanete *m*
bunk [bʌŋk] *n* litera; **~ beds** *npl* literas *fpl*
bunker ['bʌŋkər] *n* *(coal store)* carbonera; *(Mil)* refugio; *(Golf)* bunker *m*
bunk off *vi*: **to ~ school** *(Brit col)* pirarse las clases; **I'll ~ at 3 this afternoon** me voy a pirar a las 3 esta tarde
bunny ['bʌni] *n* *(also:* **bunny rabbit***)* conejito
Bunsen burner ['bʌnsn-] *n* mechero Bunsen
bunting ['bʌntiŋ] *n* empavesada, banderas *fpl*
buoy [bɔi] *n* boya
▸ **buoy up** *vt* mantener a flote; *(fig)* animar
buoyancy ['bɔiənsi] *n* *(of ship)* flotabilidad *f*
buoyant ['bɔiənt] *adj* *(carefree)* boyante, optimista; *(Comm: market, prices etc)* sostenido
BUPA ['bu:pə] *n abbr* *(= British United Provident Association) seguro médico privado*
burden ['bə:dn] *n* carga ■ *vt* cargar; **to be a ~ to sb** ser una carga para algn
bureau *(pl* **bureaux***)* ['bjuərəu, -z] *n* *(Brit: writing desk)* escritorio, buró *m*; *(US: chest of drawers)* cómoda; *(office)* oficina, agencia
bureaucracy [bjuə'rɔkrəsi] *n* burocracia
bureaucrat ['bjuərəkræt] *n* burócrata *m/f*
bureaucratic [bjuərə'krætik] *adj* burocrático
burgeon ['bə:dʒən] *vi* *(develop rapidly)* crecer, incrementarse; *(trade etc)* florecer
burger ['bə:gər] *n* hamburguesa
burglar ['bə:glər] *n* ladrón(-ona) *m(f)*
burglar alarm *n* alarma *f* contra robo
burglarize ['bə:gləraiz] *vt* *(US)* robar (con allanamiento)
burglary ['bə:gləri] *n* robo con allanamiento *or* fractura, robo de una casa
burgle ['bə:gl] *vt* robar (con allanamiento)
Burgundy ['bə:gəndi] *n* Borgoña
burial ['beriəl] *n* entierro
burial ground *n* cementerio
burlap ['bə:læp] *n* arpillera
burlesque [bə:'lesk] *n* parodia
burly ['bə:li] *adj* fornido, membrudo
Burma ['bə:mə] *n* Birmania; *see also* **Myanmar**
Burmese [bə:'mi:z] *adj* birmano ■ *n* *(pl inv)* birmano(-a); *(Ling)* birmano
burn [bə:n] *vb* *(pt, pp* **burned** *or* **burnt***)* ■ *vt* quemar; *(house)* incendiar ■ *vi* quemarse, arder; incendiarse; *(sting)* escocer ■ *n* *(Med)* quemadura; **the cigarette burnt a hole in her dress** se ha quemado el vestido con el cigarrillo; **I've burnt myself!** ¡me he quemado!
▸ **burn down** *vt* incendiar
▸ **burn out** *vt* *(writer etc)*: **to ~ o.s. out** agotarse
burner ['bə:nər] *n* *(gas)* quemador *m*
burning ['bə:niŋ] *adj* ardiente; *(building, forest)* en llamas

Burns' Night [bə:nz-] *n ver nota*

Burns' Night

Cada veinticinco de enero los escoceses celebran la llamada *Burns' Night* (noche de Burns), en honor al poeta escocés Robert Burns (1759-1796). Es tradición hacer una cena en la que, al son de la música de la gaita escocesa, se sirve "haggis", plato tradicional de asadura de cordero cocida en el estómago del animal, acompañado de nabos y puré de patatas. Durante la misma se recitan poemas del autor y varios discursos conmemorativos de carácter festivo.

burnt [bə:nt] *pt, pp of* **burn**
burp [bə:p] (*col*) *n* eructo ■ *vi* eructar
burqa ['bə:kə] *n* burka *m*, burqa *m*
burrow ['bʌrəu] *n* madriguera ■ *vt* hacer una madriguera
bursar ['bə:səʳ] *n* tesorero; (*Brit: student*) becario(-a)
bursary ['bə:sərɪ] *n* (*Brit*) beca
burst [bə:st] *vb* (*pt, pp* **burst**) ■ *vt* (*balloon, pipe*) reventar; (*banks etc*) romper ■ *vi* reventarse; romperse; (*tyre*) pincharse; (*bomb*) ■ *n* (*explosion*) estallido; (*also*: **burst pipe**) reventón *m*; **the river has ~ its banks** el río se ha desbordado; **to ~ into flames** estallar en llamas; **to ~ out laughing** soltar la carcajada; **to ~ into tears** deshacerse en lágrimas; **to be bursting with** reventar de; **a ~ of energy** una explosión de energía; **a ~ of applause** una salva de aplausos; **a ~ of speed** una escapada; **to ~ open** *vi* abrirse de golpe
▸ **burst into** *vt fus* (*room etc*) irrumpir en
bury ['bɛrɪ] *vt* enterrar; (*body*) enterrar, sepultar; **to ~ the hatchet** enterrar el hacha (de guerra), echar pelillos a la mar
bus [bʌs] *n* autobús *m*, camión *m* (*LAm*)
bus boy *n* (*US*) ayudante *m/f* de camarero
bush [buʃ] *n* arbusto; (*scrub land*) monte *m* bajo; **to beat about the ~** andar(se) con rodeos
bushed [buʃt] *adj* (*col*) molido
bushel ['buʃl] *n* (*measure: Brit*) *= 36,36 litros*; (*US*) *= 35,24 litros*
bush fire *n* incendio en el monte
bushy ['buʃɪ] *adj* (*beard, eyebrows*) poblado; (*hair*) espeso; (*fur*) tupido
busily ['bɪzɪlɪ] *adv* afanosamente
business ['bɪznɪs] *n* (*matter, affair*) asunto; (*trading*) comercio, negocios *mpl*; (*firm*) empresa, casa; (*occupation*) oficio; **to be away on ~** estar en viaje de negocios; **it's my ~ to ...** me toca *or* corresponde ...; **it's none of my ~** no es asunto mío; **he means ~** habla en serio; **he's in the insurance ~** se dedica a los seguros; **I'm here on ~** estoy aquí por mi trabajo; **to do ~ with sb** hacer negocios con algn
business address *n* dirección *f* comercial
business card *n* tarjeta de visita
businesslike ['bɪznɪslaɪk] *adj* (*company*) serio; (*person*) eficiente
businessman ['bɪznɪsmən] *n* hombre *m* de negocios
business trip *n* viaje *m* de negocios
businesswoman ['bɪznɪswumən] *n* mujer *f* de negocios
busker ['bʌskəʳ] *n* (*Brit*) músico(-a) ambulante
bus route *n* recorrido del autobús
bus station *n* estación *f or* terminal *f* de autobuses
bus-stop ['bʌsstɔp] *n* parada de autobús, paradero (*LAm*)
bust [bʌst] *n* (*Anat*) pecho ■ *adj* (*col: broken*) roto, estropeado ■ *vt* (*col: Police: arrest*) detener; **to go ~** quebrar
bustle ['bʌsl] *n* bullicio, movimiento ■ *vi* menearse, apresurarse
bustling ['bʌslɪŋ] *adj* (*town*) animado, bullicioso
bust-up ['bʌstʌp] *n* (*col*) riña
busty ['bʌstɪ] *adj* (*col*) pechugona, con buena delantera
busy ['bɪzɪ] *adj* ocupado, atareado; (*shop, street*) concurrido, animado ■ *vt*: **to ~ o.s. with** ocuparse en; **he's a ~ man** (*normally*) es un hombre muy ocupado; (*temporarily*) está muy ocupado; **the line's ~** (*esp US*) está comunicando
busybody ['bɪzɪbɔdɪ] *n* entrometido(-a)
busy signal *n* (*US Tel*) señal *f* de comunicando

KEYWORD

but [bʌt] *conj* **1** pero; **he's not very bright, but he's hard-working** no es muy inteligente, pero es trabajador
2 (*in direct contradiction*) sino; **he's not English but French** no es inglés sino francés; **he didn't sing but he shouted** no cantó sino que gritó
3 (*showing disagreement, surprise etc*): **but that's far too expensive!** ¡pero eso es carísimo!; **but it does work!** ¡(pero) sí que funciona!
■ *prep* (*apart from, except*) menos, salvo; **we've had nothing but trouble** no hemos tenido más que problemas; **no-one but him can**

do it nadie más que él puede hacerlo; **the last but one** el penúltimo; **who but a lunatic would do such a thing?** ¡sólo un loco haría una cosa así!; **but for you/your help** si no fuera por ti/tu ayuda; **anything but that** cualquier cosa menos eso
■ *adv* (*just, only*): **she's but a child** no es más que una niña; **had I but known** si lo hubiera sabido; **I can but try** al menos lo puedo intentar; **it's all but finished** está casi acabado

butane ['bju:teɪn] *n* (*also*: **butane gas**) (gas *m*) butano
butch [butʃ] *adj* (*pej*: *woman*) machirula, marimacho; (*col*: *man*) muy macho
butcher ['butʃəʳ] *n* carnicero(-a) ■ *vt* hacer una carnicería con; (*cattle etc for meat*) matar; **~'s (shop)** carnicería
butler ['bʌtləʳ] *n* mayordomo
butt [bʌt] *n* (*cask*) tonel *m*; (*for rain*) tina; (*thick end*) cabo, extremo; (*of gun*) culata; (*of cigarette*) colilla; (*Brit fig*: *target*) blanco ■ *vt* dar cabezadas contra, topetar
▸ **butt in** *vi* (*interrupt*) interrumpir
butter ['bʌtəʳ] *n* mantequilla, manteca (*LAm*) ■ *vt* untar con mantequilla
butter bean *n* judía blanca
buttercup ['bʌtəkʌp] *n* ranúnculo
butterfingers ['bʌtəfɪŋgəz] *n* (*col*) torpe *m/f*
butterfly ['bʌtəflaɪ] *n* mariposa; (*Swimming*: *also*: **butterfly stroke**) (braza de) mariposa
buttocks ['bʌtəks] *npl* nalgas *fpl*
button ['bʌtn] *n* botón *m* ■ *vt* (*also*: **button up**) abotonar, abrochar ■ *vi* abrocharse
buttonhole ['bʌtnhəul] *n* ojal *m*; (*flower*) flor *f* que se lleva en el ojal ■ *vt* obligar a escuchar
buttress ['bʌtrɪs] *n* contrafuerte *m*; (*fig*) apoyo, sostén *m*
buxom ['bʌksəm] *adj* (*woman*) frescachona, rolliza
buy [baɪ] *vb* (*pt, pp* **bought**) ■ *vt* comprar ■ *n* compra; **to ~ sb sth/sth from sb** comprarle algo a algn; **to ~ sb a drink** invitar a algn a una copa; **a good/bad ~** una buena/mala compra
▸ **buy back** *vt* volver a comprar
▸ **buy in** *vt* proveerse *or* abastecerse de
▸ **buy into** *vt fus* comprar acciones en
▸ **buy off** *vt* (*col*: *bribe*) sobornar
▸ **buy out** *vt* (*partner*) comprar la parte de
buyer ['baɪəʳ] *n* comprador(a) *m(f)*; **~'s market** mercado favorable al comprador
buy-out ['baɪaut] *n* (*Comm*) adquisición *f* de (la totalidad de) las acciones
buzz [bʌz] *n* zumbido; (*col*: *phone call*) llamada (telefónica) ■ *vt* (*call on intercom*) llamar; (*with buzzer*) hacer sonar; (*Aviat*: *plane, building*) pasar rozando ■ *vi* zumbar; **my head is buzzing** me zumba la cabeza
▸ **buzz off** *vi* (*Brit col*) largarse
buzzard ['bʌzəd] *n* (*Brit*) águila ratonera; (*US*) buitre *m*, gallinazo (*LAm*)
buzzer ['bʌzəʳ] *n* timbre *m*
buzz word *n* palabra que está de moda

KEYWORD

by [baɪ] *prep* **1** (*referring to cause, agent*) por; de; **abandoned by his mother** abandonado por su madre; **surrounded by enemies** rodeado de enemigos; **a painting by Picasso** un cuadro de Picasso
2 (*referring to method, manner, means*): **by bus/car/train** en autobús/coche/tren; **to pay by cheque** pagar con cheque(s); **by moonlight/candlelight** a la luz de la luna/una vela; **by saving hard, he ...** ahorrando, ...
3 (*via, through*) por; **we came by Dover** vinimos por Dover
4 (*close to, past*): **the house by the river** la casa junto al río; **she rushed by me** pasó a mi lado como una exhalación; **I go by the post office every day** paso por delante de Correos todos los días
5 (*time*: *not later than*) para; (: *during*): **by daylight** de día; **by 4 o'clock** para las cuatro; **by this time tomorrow** mañana a estas horas; **by the time I got here it was too late** cuando llegué ya era demasiado tarde
6 (*amount*): **by the metre/kilo** por metro/kilo; **paid by the hour** pagado por hora
7 (*in measurements, sums*): **to divide/multiply by 3** dividir/multiplicar por 3; **a room 3 metres by 4** una habitación de 3 metros por 4; **it's broader by a metre** es un metro más ancho; **the bus missed me by inches** no me pilló el autobús por un pelo
8 (*according to*) según, de acuerdo con; **it's 3 o'clock by my watch** según mi reloj, son las tres; **it's all right by me** por mí, está bien
9: **(all) by oneself** *etc* todo solo; **he did it (all) by himself** lo hizo él solo; **he was standing (all) by himself in a corner** estaba de pie solo en un rincón
10: **by the way** a propósito, por cierto; **this wasn't my idea, by the way** pues, no fue idea mía
■ *adv* **1** *see* **go**; **pass** *etc*
2: **by and by** finalmente; **they'll come back by and by** acabarán volviendo; **by and large** en líneas generales, en general

bye ['baɪ], **bye-bye** ['baɪ'baɪ] *excl* adiós, hasta luego, chao (*esp LAm*)

bye-law ['baɪlɔː] *n see* **by-law**
by-election ['baɪɪlɛkʃən] *n* (*Brit*) elección *f* parcial; *ver nota*

BY-ELECTION

Se celebra una *by-election* en el Reino Unido y otros países de la "Commonwealth" cuando es necesario reemplazar a un parlamentario ("Member of Parliament") cesado o fallecido durante una legislatura. Dichas elecciones tienen lugar únicamente en el área electoral representada por el citado parlamentario, su "constituency".

Byelorussia [bjɛləu'rʌʃə] *n* Bielorrusia
Byelorussian [bjɛləu'rʌʃən] *adj, n* = **Belorussian**
bygone ['baɪgɔn] *adj* pasado, del pasado ■ *n*: **let bygones be bygones** lo pasado, pasado está
by-law ['baɪlɔː] *n* ordenanza municipal
bypass ['baɪpɑːs] *n* carretera de, circunvalación; (*Med*) (operación *f* de) bypass *m* ■ *vt* evitar
by-product ['baɪprɔdʌkt] *n* subproducto, derivado
bystander ['baɪstændə^r] *n* espectador(a) *m(f)*
byte [baɪt] *n* (*Comput*) byte *m*, octeto
byway ['baɪweɪ] *n* camino poco frecuentado
byword ['baɪwəːd] *n*: **to be a ~ for** ser sinónimo de
by-your-leave ['baɪjɔː'liːv] *n*: **without so much as a ~** sin decir nada, sin dar ningún tipo de explicación

Cc

C, c [siː] *n* (*letter*) C, c *f*; (*Mus*): **C** do *m*; **C for Charlie** C de Carmen
C *abbr* (= *Celsius, centigrade*) C
c *abbr* (= *century*) S.; (= *circa*) hacia; (*US etc*) = **cent**; **cents**
CA *n abbr* = **Central America**; (*Brit*) = **chartered accountant**; (*US*) = **California**
ca. *abbr* (= *circa*) c
c/a *abbr* = **capital account**; **credit account**; **current account**
CAA *n abbr* (*Brit*: = *Civil Aviation Authority*) *organismo de control y desarrollo de la aviación civil*; = **Civil Aeronautics Authority**
CAB *n abbr* (*Brit*: = *Citizens' Advice Bureau*) ≈ Servicio de Información Ciudadana
cab [kæb] *n* taxi *m*; (*of truck*) cabina
cabaret ['kæbəreɪ] *n* cabaret *m*
cabbage ['kæbɪdʒ] *n* col *f*, berza
cabbie, cabby ['kæbɪ] *n* (*col*) taxista *m/f*
cab driver *n* taxista *m/f*
cabin ['kæbɪn] *n* cabaña; (*on ship*) camarote *m*
cabin cruiser *n* yate *m* de motor
cabinet ['kæbɪnɪt] *n* (*Pol*) consejo de ministros; (*furniture*) armario; (*also*: **display cabinet**) vitrina
cabinet-maker ['kæbɪnɪt'meɪkəʳ] *n* ebanista *m*
cabinet minister *n* ministro(-a) (del gabinete)
cable ['keɪbl] *n* cable *m* ■ *vt* cablegrafiar
cable-car ['keɪblkɑːʳ] *n* teleférico
cablegram ['keɪblgræm] *n* cablegrama *m*
cable television *n* televisión *f* por cable
cache [kæʃ] *n* (*of drugs*) alijo; (*of arms*) zulo
cackle ['kækl] *vi* cacarear
cactus (*pl* **cacti**) ['kæktəs, -taɪ] *n* cacto
CAD ['kæd] *n* (= *computer-aided design*) DAO *m*
caddie, caddy ['kædɪ] *n* (*Golf*) cadi *m*
cadence ['keɪdəns] *n* ritmo; (*Mus*) cadencia
cadet [kə'dɛt] *n* (*Mil*) cadete *m*; **police ~** cadete *m* de policía
cadge [kædʒ] *vt* gorronear
cadger ['kædʒəʳ] *n* gorrón(-ona) *m(f)*
cadre ['kædrɪ] *n* cuadro
Caesarean, Cesarean (*US*) [siː'zɛərɪən] *adj*: **~ (section)** cesárea
CAF *abbr* (*Brit*: = *cost and freight*) C y F
café ['kæfeɪ] *n* café *m*
cafeteria [kæfɪ'tɪərɪə] *n* cafetería (*con autoservicio para comer*)
caffeine ['kæfiːn] *n* cafeína
cage [keɪdʒ] *n* jaula ■ *vt* enjaular
cagey ['keɪdʒɪ] *adj* (*col*) cauteloso, reservado
cagoule [kə'guːl] *n* canguro
cahoots [kə'huːts] *n*: **to be in ~ (with sb)** estar conchabado (con algn)
Cairo ['kaɪərəu] *n* El Cairo
cajole [kə'dʒəul] *vt* engatusar
cake [keɪk] *n* pastel *m*; (*of soap*) pastilla; **he wants to have his ~ and eat it** (*fig*) quiere estar en misa y repicando; **it's a piece of ~** (*col*) es pan comido
caked [keɪkt] *adj*: **~ with** cubierto de
cake shop *n* pastelería
Cal. *abbr* (*US*) = **California**
calamine ['kæləmaɪn] *n* calamina
calamitous [kə'læmɪtəs] *adj* calamitoso
calamity [kə'læmɪtɪ] *n* calamidad *f*
calcium ['kælsɪəm] *n* calcio
calculate ['kælkjuleɪt] *vt* (*estimate*: *chances, effect*) calcular
▸ **calculate on** *vt fus*: **to ~ on sth/on doing sth** contar con algo/con hacer algo
calculated ['kælkjuleɪtɪd] *adj*: **we took a ~ risk** calculamos el riesgo
calculating ['kælkjuleɪtɪŋ] *adj* (*scheming*) calculador(a)
calculation [kælkju'leɪʃən] *n* cálculo, cómputo
calculator ['kælkjuleɪtəʳ] *n* calculadora
calculus ['kælkjuləs] *n* cálculo
calendar ['kæləndəʳ] *n* calendario; **~ month/year** *n* mes *m*/año civil
calf (*pl* **calves**) [kɑːf, kɑːvz] *n* (*of cow*) ternero, becerro; (*of other animals*) cría; (*also*: **calfskin**) piel *f* de becerro; (*Anat*) pantorrilla, canilla (*LAm*)

caliber ['kælɪbər] *n* (*US*) = **calibre**
calibrate ['kælɪbreɪt] *vt* (*gun etc*) calibrar; (*scale of measuring instrument*) graduar
calibre, caliber (*US*) ['kælɪbər] *n* calibre *m*
calico ['kælɪkəu] *n* calicó *m*
Calif. *abbr* (*US*) = **California**
California [kælɪ'fɔːnɪə] *n* California
calipers ['kælɪpəz] *npl* (*US*) = **callipers**
call [kɔːl] *vt* (*gen*) llamar; (*Tel*) llamar; (*announce: flight*) anunciar; (*meeting, strike*) convocar ■ *vi* (*shout*) llamar; (*telephone*) llamar (por teléfono), telefonear; (*visit: also*: **call in, call round**) hacer una visita ■ *n* (*shout*) llamada, llamado (*LAm*); (*Tel*) llamada, llamado (*LAm*); (*of bird*) canto; (*appeal*) llamamiento, llamado (*LAm*); (*summons: for flight etc*) llamada; (*fig: lure*) llamada; **to be called** (*person, object*) llamarse; **to ~ sb names** poner verde a algn; **let's ~ it a day** (*col*) ¡dejémoslo!, ¡ya está bien!; **who is calling?** ¿de parte de quién?; **London calling** (*Radio*) aquí Londres; **on ~** (*nurse, doctor etc*) de guardia; **please give me a ~ at seven** despiérteme *or* llámeme a las siete, por favor; **long-distance ~** conferencia (interurbana); **to make a ~** llamar por teléfono; **port of ~** puerto de escala; **to pay a ~ on sb** pasarse a ver a algn; **there's not much ~ for these items** estos artículos no tienen mucha demanda
▸ **call at** *vt fus* (*ship*) hacer escala en, tocar en; (*train*) parar en
▸ **call back** *vi* (*return*) volver; (*Tel*) volver a llamar
▸ **call for** *vt fus* (*demand*) pedir, exigir; (*fetch*) venir por
▸ **call in** *vt* (*doctor, expert, police*) llamar
▸ **call off** *vt* suspender; **the strike was called off** se desconvocó la huelga
▸ **call on** *vt fus* (*visit*) ir a ver; (*turn to*) acudir a
▸ **call out** *vi* gritar, dar voces ■ *vt* (*doctor*) llamar; (*police, troops*) hacer intervenir
▸ **call up** *vt* (*Mil*) llamar a filas
Callanetics® [kælə'nɛtɪks] *nsg gimnasia de repetición de pequeños ejercicios musculares*
callbox ['kɔːlbɔks] *n* (*Brit*) cabina telefónica
call centre *n* (*Brit*) centro de llamadas
caller ['kɔːlər] *n* visita *f*; (*Tel*) usuario(-a); **hold the line, ~!** ¡no cuelgue!
call girl *n* prostituta
call-in ['kɔːlɪn] *n* (*US*) *programa de línea abierta al público*
calling ['kɔːlɪŋ] *n* vocación *f*; (*profession*) profesión *f*
calling card *n* tarjeta de visita
callipers, calipers (*US*) ['kælɪpəz] *npl* (*Med*) aparato ortopédico; (*Math*) calibrador *m*
callous ['kæləs] *adj* insensible, cruel
callousness ['kæləsnɪs] *n* insensibilidad, crueldad *f*
callow ['kæləu] *adj* inexperto, novato
calm [kɑːm] *adj* tranquilo; (*sea*) tranquilo, en calma ■ *n* calma, tranquilidad *f* ■ *vt* calmar, tranquilizar
▸ **calm down** *vi* calmarse, tranquilizarse ■ *vt* calmar, tranquilizar
calmly ['kɑːmlɪ] *adv* tranquilamente, con calma
calmness ['kɑːmnɪs] *n* calma
Calor gas® ['kælər-] *n* butano, camping gas® *m inv*
calorie ['kælərɪ] *n* caloría; **low-~ product** producto bajo en calorías
calve [kɑːv] *vi* parir
calves [kɑːvz] *npl of* **calf**
CAM *n abbr* (= *computer-aided manufacturing*) producción *f* asistida por ordenador
camber ['kæmbər] *n* (*of road*) combadura
Cambodia [kæm'bəudjə] *n* Camboya
Cambodian [kæm'bəudjən] *adj, n* camboyano(-a) *m(f)*
Cambs *abbr* (*Brit*) = **Cambridgeshire**
camcorder ['kæmkɔːdər] *n* videocámara
came [keɪm] *pt of* **come**
camel ['kæməl] *n* camello
cameo ['kæmɪəu] *n* camafeo
camera ['kæmərə] *n* cámara *or* máquina fotográfica; (*Cine, TV*) cámara; (*movie camera*) cámara, tomavistas *m inv*; **in ~** a puerta cerrada
cameraman ['kæmərəmən] *n* cámara *m*
camera phone *n* teléfono *m* con cámara
Cameroon, Cameroun [kæme'ruːn] *n* Camerún *m*
camomile tea ['kæməmaɪl-] *n* manzanilla
camouflage ['kæməflɑːʒ] *n* camuflaje *m* ■ *vt* camuflar
camp [kæmp] *n* campo, campamento ■ *vi* acampar ■ *adj* afectado, afeminado; **to go camping** ir de *or* hacer camping
campaign [kæm'peɪn] *n* (*Mil, Pol etc*) campaña ■ *vi*: **to ~ (for/against)** hacer campaña (a favor de/en contra de)
campaigner [kæm'peɪnər] *n*: **~ for** defensor(a) *m(f)* de; **~ against** persona que hace campaña contra
campbed ['kæmpbɛd] *n* (*Brit*) cama plegable
camper ['kæmpər] *n* campista *m/f*; (*vehicle*) caravana
camping ['kæmpɪŋ] *n* camping *m*
campsite ['kæmpsaɪt] *n* camping *m*
campus ['kæmpəs] *n* campus *m*
camshaft ['kæmʃɑːft] *n* árbol *m* de levas
can [kæn] (*aux vb see keyword*) *n* (*of oil, water*)

bidón *m*; (*tin*) lata, bote *m* ■ *vt* enlatar; (*preserve*) conservar en lata; **a ~ of beer** una lata *or* un bote de cerveza; **to carry the ~** (*col*) pagar el pato

KEYWORD

can (*negative* **cannot, can't,** *conditional and pt* **could**) *aux vb* **1** (*be able to*) poder; **you can do it if you try** puedes hacerlo si lo intentas; **I can't see you** no te veo; **can you hear me?** (*not translated*) ¿me oyes?
2 (*know how to*) saber; **I can swim/play tennis/drive** sé nadar/jugar al tenis/conducir; **can you speak French?** ¿hablas *or* sabes hablar francés?
3 (*may*) poder; **can I use your phone?** ¿me dejas *or* puedo usar tu teléfono?; **could I have a word with you?** ¿podría hablar contigo un momento?
4 (*expressing disbelief, puzzlement etc*): **it can't be true!** ¡no puede ser (verdad)!; **what CAN he want?** ¿qué querrá?
5 (*expressing possibility, suggestion etc*): **he could be in the library** podría estar en la biblioteca; **she could have been delayed** puede que se haya retrasado

Canada ['kænədə] *n* Canadá *m*
Canadian [kə'neɪdɪən] *adj, n* canadiense *m/f*
canal [kə'næl] *n* canal *m*
canary [kə'nɛərɪ] *n* canario
Canary Islands, Canaries [kə'nɛərɪz] *npl* las (Islas) Canarias
Canberra ['kænbərə] *n* Camberra
cancel ['kænsəl] *vt* cancelar; (*train*) suprimir; (*appointment, cheque*) anular; (*cross out*) tachar
▸ **cancel out** *vt* (*Math*) anular; (*fig*) contrarrestar; **they ~ each other out** se anulan mutuamente
cancellation [kænsə'leɪʃən] *n* cancelación *f*; supresión *f*
cancer ['kænsəʳ] *n* cáncer *m*; **C~** (*Astro*) Cáncer *m*
cancerous ['kænsərəs] *adj* canceroso
cancer patient *n* enfermo(-a) *m(f)* de cáncer
cancer research *n* investigación *f* del cáncer
C and F *abbr* (= *cost and freight*) C y F
candid ['kændɪd] *adj* franco, abierto
candidacy ['kændɪdəsɪ] *n* candidatura
candidate ['kændɪdeɪt] *n* candidato(-a)
candidature ['kændɪdətʃəʳ] *n* (*Brit*) = **candidacy**
candidly ['kændɪdlɪ] *adv* francamente, con franqueza
candle ['kændl] *n* vela; (*in church*) cirio
candle holder *n see* **candlestick**
candlelight ['kændllaɪt] *n*: **by ~** a la luz de una vela
candlestick ['kændlstɪk] *n* (*also*: **candle holder**: *single*) candelero; (: *low*) palmatoria; (*bigger, ornate*) candelabro
candour, candor (*US*) ['kændəʳ] *n* franqueza
C & W *n abbr* = **country and western (music)**
candy ['kændɪ] *n* azúcar *m* cande; (*US*) caramelo ■ *vt* (*fruit*) escarchar
candy-floss ['kændɪflɔs] *n* (*Brit*) algodón *m* (azucarado)
cane [keɪn] *n* (*Bot*) caña; (*for baskets, chairs etc*) mimbre *m*; (*stick*) vara, palmeta; (*for walking*) bastón *m* ■ *vt* (*Brit Scol*) castigar (con palmeta); **~ liquor** caña
canine ['kænaɪn] *adj* canino
canister ['kænɪstəʳ] *n* bote *m*
cannabis ['kænəbɪs] *n* canabis *m*
canned [kænd] *adj* en lata, de lata; (*col*: *music*) grabado; (: *drunk*) mamado
cannibal ['kænɪbəl] *n* caníbal *m/f*, antropófago(-a)
cannibalism ['kænɪbəlɪzəm] *n* canibalismo
cannon (*pl* **~** *or* **cannons**) ['kænən] *n* cañón *m*
cannonball ['kænənbɔːl] *n* bala (de cañón)
cannon fodder *n* carne *f* de cañón
cannot ['kænɔt] = **can not**
canny ['kænɪ] *adj* avispado
canoe [kə'nuː] *n* canoa; (*Sport*) piragua
canoeing [kə'nuːɪŋ] *n* (*Sport*) piragüismo
canoeist [kə'nuːɪst] *n* piragüista *m/f*
canon ['kænən] *n* (*clergyman*) canónigo; (*standard*) canon *m*
canonize ['kænənaɪz] *vt* canonizar
can opener *n* abrelatas *m inv*
canopy ['kænəpɪ] *n* dosel *m*, toldo
can't [kænt] = **can not**
Cantab. *abbr* (*Brit*: = *cantabrigiensis*) *of Cambridge*
cantankerous [kæn'tæŋkərəs] *adj* arisco, malhumorado
canteen [kæn'tiːn] *n* (*eating place*) comedor *m*; (*Brit*: *of cutlery*) juego
canter ['kæntəʳ] *n* medio galope ■ *vi* ir a medio galope
cantilever ['kæntɪliːvəʳ] *n* viga voladiza
canvas ['kænvəs] *n* (*material*) lona; (*painting*) lienzo; (*Naut*) velamen *m*; **under ~** (*camping*) en tienda de campaña
canvass ['kænvəs] *vt* (*Pol*: *district*) hacer campaña (puerta a puerta) en; (: *person*) hacer campaña (puerta a puerta) a favor de; (*Comm*: *district*) sondear el mercado en; (: *citizens, opinions*) sondear
canvasser ['kænvəsəʳ] *n* (*Pol*) representante *m/f* electoral; (*Comm*) corredor(a) *m(f)*
canyon ['kænjən] *n* cañón *m*
CAP *n abbr* (= *Common Agricultural Policy*) PAC *f*

cap [kæp] *n* (*hat*) gorra; (*for swimming*) gorro; (*of pen*) capuchón *m*; (*of bottle*) tapón *m*; (*: metal*) chapa; (*contraceptive*) diafragma *m* ■ *vt* (*outdo*) superar; (*Brit Sport*) seleccionar (para el equipo nacional); **and to ~ it all, he ...** y para colmo, él ...
capability [keɪpəˈbɪlɪtɪ] *n* capacidad *f*
capable [ˈkeɪpəbl] *adj* capaz
capacious [kəˈpeɪʃəs] *adj* amplio
capacity [kəˈpæsɪtɪ] *n* capacidad *f*; (*position*) calidad *f*; **filled to ~** lleno a reventar; **this work is beyond my ~** este trabajo es superior a mí; **in an advisory ~** como asesor
cape [keɪp] *n* capa; (*Geo*) cabo
Cape of Good Hope *n* Cabo de Buena Esperanza
caper [ˈkeɪpəʳ] *n* (*Culin: also:* **capers**) alcaparra; (*prank*) travesura
Cape Town *n* Ciudad *f* del Cabo
capital [ˈkæpɪtl] *n* (*also:* **capital city**) capital *f*; (*money*) capital *m*; (*also:* **capital letter**) mayúscula
capital account *n* cuenta de capital
capital allowance *n* desgravación *f* sobre bienes del capital
capital assets *n* activo fijo
capital expenditure *n* inversión *f* de capital
capital gains tax *n* impuesto sobre la plusvalía
capital goods *npl* bienes *mpl* de capital
capital-intensive [kæpɪtlɪnˈtɛnsɪv] *adj* de utilización intensiva de capital
capital investment *n* inversión *f* de capital
capitalism [ˈkæpɪtəlɪzəm] *n* capitalismo
capitalist [ˈkæpɪtəlɪst] *adj, n* capitalista *m/f*
capitalize [ˈkæpɪtəlaɪz] *vt* (*Comm: provide with capital*) capitalizar
▸ **capitalize on** *vt fus* (*fig*) sacar provecho de, aprovechar
capital punishment *n* pena de muerte
capital transfer tax *n* impuesto sobre plusvalía de cesión
Capitol [ˈkæpɪtl] *n*: **the ~** el Capitolio

CAPITOL

El Capitolio (*Capitol*) es el edificio en el que se reúne el Congreso de los Estados Unidos ("Congress"), situado en la ciudad de Washington. Por extensión, también se suele llamar así al edificio en el que tienen lugar las sesiones parlamentarias de la cámara de representantes de muchos de los estados.

capitulate [kəˈpɪtjuleɪt] *vi* capitular, rendirse
capitulation [kəpɪtjuˈleɪʃən] *n* capitulación *f*, rendición *f*
capricious [kəˈprɪʃəs] *adj* caprichoso
Capricorn [ˈkæprɪkɔːn] *n* Capricornio
caps [kæps] *abbr* (= *capital letters*) may
capsize [kæpˈsaɪz] *vt* volcar, hacer zozobrar ■ *vi* volcarse, zozobrar
capstan [ˈkæpstən] *n* cabrestante *m*
capsule [ˈkæpsjuːl] *n* cápsula
Capt. *abbr* = **Captain**
captain [ˈkæptɪn] *n* capitán *m* ■ *vt* capitanear, ser el capitán de
caption [ˈkæpʃən] *n* (*heading*) título; (*to picture*) leyenda, pie *m*
captivate [ˈkæptɪveɪt] *vt* cautivar, encantar
captive [ˈkæptɪv] *adj, n* cautivo(-a) *m(f)*
captivity [kæpˈtɪvɪtɪ] *n* cautiverio
captor [ˈkæptəʳ] *n* captor(a) *m(f)*
capture [ˈkæptʃəʳ] *vt* capturar; (*place*) tomar; (*attention*) captar, llamar ■ *n* captura; toma; (*Comput: also:* **data capture**) formulación *f* de datos
car [kɑːʳ] *n* coche *m*, carro (*LAm*), automóvil *m*, auto (*LAm*); (*US Rail*) vagón *m*; **by ~** en coche
Caracas [kəˈrækəs] *n* Caracas *m*
carafe [kəˈræf] *n* garrafa
caramel [ˈkærəməl] *n* caramelo
carat [ˈkærət] *n* quilate *m*; **18-~ gold** oro de 18 quilates
caravan [ˈkærəvæn] *n* (*Brit*) caravana, remolque *m*; (*of camels*) caravana
caravan site *n* (*Brit*) camping *m* para caravanas
caraway [ˈkærəweɪ] *n*: **~ seed** carvi *m*
carbohydrates [kɑːbəuˈhaɪdreɪts] *npl* (*foods*) hidratos *mpl* de carbono
carbolic [kɑːˈbɔlɪk] *adj*: **~ acid** ácido carbólico, fenol *m*
car bomb *n* coche-bomba *m*
carbon [ˈkɑːbən] *n* carbono
carbonated [ˈkɑːbəneɪtɪd] *adj* (*drink*) con gas
carbon copy *n* copia al carbón
carbon dioxide *n* dióxido de carbono, anhídrido carbónico
carbon footprint *n* impacto ecológico
carbon monoxide *n* monóxido de carbono
carbon paper *n* papel *m* carbón
carbon ribbon *n* cinta de carbón
car boot sale *n* mercadillo (*de objetos usados expuestos en el maletero del coche*)
carburettor, carburetor (*US*) [kɑːbjuˈrɛtəʳ] *n* carburador *m*
carcass [ˈkɑːkəs] *n* (*of animal*) res *f* muerta; (*dead body*) cadáver *m*
carcinogenic [kɑːsɪnəˈdʒɛnɪk] *adj* cancerígeno
card [kɑːd] *n* (*thin cardboard*) cartulina; (*playing*

card) carta, naipe *m*; (*visiting card, greetings card etc*) tarjeta; (*index card*) ficha; **membership ~** carnet *m*; **to play cards** jugar a las cartas *or* los naipes
cardamom ['kɑːdəməm] *n* cardamomo
cardboard ['kɑːdbɔːd] *n* cartón *m*, cartulina
cardboard box *n* caja de cartón
cardboard city *n* zona de marginados sin hogar (*que se refugian entre cartones*)
card-carrying member ['kɑːdkærɪɪŋ-] *n* miembro con carnet
card game *n* juego de naipes *or* cartas
cardiac ['kɑːdɪæk] *adj* cardíaco
cardigan ['kɑːdɪgən] *n* chaqueta (de punto), rebeca
cardinal ['kɑːdɪnl] *adj* cardinal ■ *n* cardenal *m*
cardinal number *n* número cardinal
card index *n* fichero
cardphone ['kɑːdfəun] *n cabina que funciona con tarjetas telefónicas*
cardsharp ['kɑːdʃɑːp] *n* fullero(-a)
card vote *n* voto por delegación
CARE [kɛəʳ] *n abbr* (= *Cooperative for American Relief Everywhere*) *sociedad benéfica*
care [kɛəʳ] *n* cuidado; (*worry*) preocupación *f*; (*charge*) cargo, custodia ■ *vi*: **to ~ about** preocuparse por; **~ of (c/o)** en casa de, al cuidado de; (*on letter*) para (entregar a); **in sb's ~** a cargo de algn; **the child has been taken into ~** pusieron al niño bajo custodia del gobierno; **"with ~"** "¡frágil!"; **to take ~ to** cuidarse de, tener cuidado de; **to take ~ of** *vt* cuidar; (*details, arrangements*) encargarse de; **I don't ~** no me importa; **I couldn't ~ less** me trae sin cuidado
▸ **care for** *vt fus* cuidar; (*like*) querer
careen [kə'riːn] *vi* (*ship*) inclinarse, escorar ■ *vt* carenar
career [kə'rɪəʳ] *n* carrera (profesional); (*occupation*) profesión *f* ■ *vi* (*also*: **career along**) correr a toda velocidad
career girl *n* mujer *f* dedicada a su profesión
careers officer *n* consejero(-a) de orientación profesional
carefree ['kɛəfriː] *adj* despreocupado
careful ['kɛəful] *adj* cuidadoso; (*cautious*) cauteloso; **(be) ~!** ¡ten cuidado!; **he's very ~ with his money** mira mucho el dinero; (*pej*) es muy tacaño
carefully ['kɛəfəlɪ] *adv* con cuidado, cuidadosamente
careless ['kɛəlɪs] *adj* descuidado; (*heedless*) poco atento
carelessly ['kɛəlɪslɪ] *adv* sin cuidado, a la ligera
carelessness ['kɛəlɪsnɪs] *n* descuido, falta de atención
carer ['kɛərəʳ] *n persona que cuida de enfermos, ancianos o disminuidos*
caress [kə'rɛs] *n* caricia ■ *vt* acariciar
caretaker ['kɛəteɪkəʳ] *n* portero(-a), conserje *m/f*
caretaker government *n* gobierno provisional
car-ferry ['kɑːfɛrɪ] *n* transbordador *m* para coches
cargo (*pl* **cargoes**) ['kɑːgəu] *n* cargamento, carga
cargo boat *n* buque *m* de carga, carguero
cargo plane *n* avión *m* de carga
car hire *n* alquiler *m* de coches
Caribbean [kærɪ'biːən] *adj* caribe, caribeño; **the ~ (Sea)** el (Mar) Caribe
caricature ['kærɪkətjuəʳ] *n* caricatura
caring ['kɛərɪŋ] *adj* humanitario
carnage ['kɑːnɪdʒ] *n* matanza, carnicería
carnal ['kɑːnl] *adj* carnal
carnation [kɑː'neɪʃən] *n* clavel *m*
carnival ['kɑːnɪvəl] *n* carnaval *m*; (*US*) parque *m* de atracciones
carnivore ['kɑːnɪvɔːʳ] *n* carnívoro(-a)
carnivorous [kɑː'nɪvrəs] *adj* carnívoro
carol ['kærəl] *n*: **(Christmas) ~** villancico
carouse [kə'rauz] *vi* estar de juerga
carousel [kærə'sɛl] *n* (*US*) tiovivo, caballitos *mpl*
carp [kɑːp] *n* (*fish*) carpa
▸ **carp at** *or* **about** *vt fus* sacar faltas de
car park *n* (*Brit*) aparcamiento, parking *m*, playa de estacionamiento (*LAm*)
carpenter ['kɑːpɪntəʳ] *n* carpintero
carpentry ['kɑːpɪntrɪ] *n* carpintería
carpet ['kɑːpɪt] *n* alfombra ■ *vt* alfombrar; **fitted ~** moqueta
carpet bombing *n* bombardeo de arrasamiento
carpet slippers *npl* zapatillas *fpl*
carpet sweeper [-'swiːpəʳ] *n* cepillo mecánico
car phone *n* teléfono de coche
carping ['kɑːpɪŋ] *adj* (*critical*) criticón(-ona)
carriage ['kærɪdʒ] *n* coche *m*; (*Brit Rail*) vagón *m*; (*for goods*) transporte *m*; (*of typewriter*) carro; (*bearing*) porte *m*; **~ forward** porte *m* debido; **~ free** franco de porte; **~ paid** porte pagado; **~ inwards/outwards** gastos *mpl* de transporte a cargo del comprador/vendedor
carriage return *n* (*on typewriter etc*) tecla de regreso
carriageway ['kærɪdʒweɪ] *n* (*Brit*: *part of road*) calzada; **dual ~** autovía

carrier ['kærɪəʳ] *n* transportista *m/f*; (*company*) empresa de transportes; (*Med*) portador(a) *m(f)*
carrier bag *n* (*Brit*) bolsa de papel *or* plástico
carrier pigeon *n* paloma mensajera
carrion ['kærɪən] *n* carroña
carrot ['kærət] *n* zanahoria
carry ['kærɪ] *vt* (*person*) llevar; (*transport*) transportar; (*a motion, bill*) aprobar; (*involve: responsibilities etc*) entrañar, conllevar; (*Comm: stock*) tener en existencia; (*interest*) llevar; (*Math: figure*) llevarse ■ *vi* (*sound*) oírse; **to get carried away** (*fig*) entusiasmarse; **this loan carries 10% interest** este empréstito devenga un interés del 10 por ciento
▸ **carry forward** *vt* (*Math, Comm*) pasar a la página/columna siguiente
▸ **carry on** *vi* (*continue*) seguir (adelante), continuar; (*fam: complain*) montar el número ■ *vt* seguir, continuar
▸ **carry out** *vt* (*orders*) cumplir; (*investigation*) llevar a cabo, realizar
carrycot ['kærɪkɔt] *n* (*Brit*) cuna portátil, capazo
carry-on ['kærɪ'ɔn] *n* (*col*) follón *m*
cart [kɑːt] *n* carro, carreta ■ *vt* cargar con
carte blanche ['kɑːt'blɔnʃ] *n*: **to give sb ~** dar carta blanca a algn
cartel [kɑː'tɛl] *n* (*Comm*) cartel *m*
cartilage ['kɑːtɪlɪdʒ] *n* cartílago
cartographer [kɑː'tɔgrəfəʳ] *n* cartógrafo(-a)
carton ['kɑːtən] *n* caja (de cartón); (*of cigarettes*) cartón *m*
cartoon [kɑː'tuːn] *n* (*Press*) chiste *m*; (*comic strip*) historieta, tira cómica; (*film*) dibujos *mpl* animados
cartoonist [kɑː'tuːnɪst] *n* humorista *m/f* gráfico
cartridge ['kɑːtrɪdʒ] *n* cartucho
cartwheel ['kɑːtwiːl] *n*: **to turn a ~** dar una voltereta lateral
carve [kɑːv] *vt* (*meat*) trinchar; (*wood*) tallar; (*stone*) cincelar, esculpir; (*on tree*) grabar
▸ **carve up** *vt* dividir, repartir; (*meat*) trinchar
carving ['kɑːvɪŋ] *n* (*in wood etc*) escultura, talla
carving knife *n* trinchante *m*
car wash *n* túnel *m* de lavado
Casablanca [kæsə'blæŋkə] *n* Casablanca
cascade [kæs'keɪd] *n* salto de agua, cascada; (*fig*) chorro ■ *vi* caer a chorros
case [keɪs] *n* (*container*) caja; (*Med*) caso; (*for jewels etc*) estuche *m*; (*Law*) causa, proceso; (*Brit: also:* **suitcase**) maleta; **lower/upper ~** (*Typ*) caja baja/alta; **in ~ of** en caso de; **in any ~** en todo caso; **just in ~** por si acaso; **to have a good ~** tener buenas razones; **there's a strong ~ for reform** hay razones sólidas para exigir una reforma
case history *n* (*Med*) historial *m* médico, historia clínica
case study *n* estudio de casos prácticos
cash [kæʃ] *n* (dinero) efectivo; (*col: money*) dinero ■ *vt* cobrar, hacer efectivo; **to pay (in) ~** pagar al contado; **~ on delivery (COD)** entrega contra reembolso; **~ with order** paga al hacer el pedido; **to be short of ~** estar pelado, estar sin blanca
▸ **cash in** *vt* (*insurance policy etc*) cobrar ■ *vi*: **to ~ in on sth** sacar partido *or* aprovecharse de algo
cash account *n* cuenta de caja
cash and carry *n* cash and carry *m*, autoservicio mayorista
cashbook ['kæʃbuk] *n* libro de caja
cash box *n* hucha
cash card *n* tarjeta *f* de(l) cajero (automático)
cash desk *n* (*Brit*) caja
cash discount *n* descuento por pago al contado
cash dispenser *n* cajero automático
cashew [kæ'ʃuː] *n* (*also:* **cashew nut**) anacardo
cash flow *n* flujo de fondos, cash-flow *m*, movimiento de efectivo
cashier [kæ'ʃɪəʳ] *n* cajero(-a) ■ *vt* (*Mil*) destituir, expulsar
cashmere ['kæʃmɪəʳ] *n* cachemir *m*, cachemira
cash payment *n* pago al contado
cash price *n* precio al contado
cash register *n* caja
cash reserves *npl* reserva en efectivo
cash sale *n* venta al contado
casing ['keɪsɪŋ] *n* revestimiento
casino [kə'siːnəu] *n* casino
cask [kɑːsk] *n* tonel *m*, barril *m*
casket ['kɑːskɪt] *n* cofre *m*, estuche *m*; (*US: coffin*) ataúd *m*
Caspian Sea ['kæspɪən-] *n*: **the ~** el Mar Caspio
cassava [kə'sɑːvə] *n* mandioca
casserole ['kæsərəul] *n* (*food, pot*) cazuela
cassette [kæ'sɛt] *n* cas(s)et(t)e *m or f*
cassette deck *n* platina
cassette player, cassette recorder *n* cas(s)et(t)e *m*
cassock ['kæsək] *n* sotana
cast [kɑːst] *vb* (*pt, pp* **cast**) ■ *vt* (*throw*) echar, arrojar, lanzar; (*skin*) mudar, perder; (*metal*) fundir; (*Theat*): **to ~ sb as Othello** dar a algn el papel de Otelo ■ *n* (*Theat*) reparto; (*mould*) forma, molde *m*; (*also:* **plaster cast**) vaciado;

to ~ loose soltar; **to ~ one's vote** votar
▸ **cast aside** *vt* (*reject*) descartar, desechar
▸ **cast away** *vt* desechar
▸ **cast down** *vt* derribar
▸ **cast off** *vi* (*Naut*) soltar amarras; (*Knitting*) cerrar los puntos ■ *vt* (*Knitting*) cerrar; **to ~ sb off** abandonar a algn, desentenderse de algn
▸ **cast on** *vt* (*Knitting*) montar
castanets [kæstəˈnɛts] *npl* castañuelas *fpl*
castaway [ˈkɑːstəwəɪ] *n* náufrago(-a)
caste [kɑːst] *n* casta
caster sugar [ˈkɑːstəʳ-] *n* (*Brit*) azúcar *m* en polvo
Castile [kæsˈtiːl] *n* Castilla
Castilian [kæsˈtɪlɪən] *adj, n* castellano(-a) ■ *n* (*Ling*) castellano
casting vote [ˈkɑːstɪŋ-] *n* (*Brit*) voto decisivo
cast iron *n* hierro fundido *or* colado ■ *adj* (*fig*: *alibi*) irrebatible; (*will*) férreo
castle [ˈkɑːsl] *n* castillo; (*Chess*) torre *f*
castor [ˈkɑːstəʳ] *n* (*wheel*) ruedecilla
castor oil *n* aceite *m* de ricino
castrate [kæsˈtreɪt] *vt* castrar
casual [ˈkæʒjul] *adj* (*by chance*) fortuito; (*irregular*: *work etc*) eventual, temporero; (*unconcerned*) despreocupado; (*informal*: *clothes*) de sport
casually [ˈkæzjulɪ] *adv* por casualidad; de manera despreocupada
casualty [ˈkæʒjultɪ] *n* víctima, herido; (*dead*) muerto; (*Mil*) baja; **heavy casualties** numerosas bajas *fpl*
casualty ward *n* urgencias *fpl*
cat [kæt] *n* gato
catacombs [ˈkætəkuːmz] *npl* catacumbas *fpl*
Catalan [ˈkætəlæn] *adj, n* catalán(-ana) *m(f)*
catalogue, catalog (*US*) [ˈkætəlɔg] *n* catálogo ■ *vt* catalogar
Catalonia [kætəˈləunɪə] *n* Cataluña
catalyst [ˈkætəlɪst] *n* catalizador *m*
catalytic converter [kætəˈlɪtɪkkənˈvəːtəʳ] *n* catalizador *m*
catapult [ˈkætəpʌlt] *n* tirachinas *m inv*
cataract [ˈkætərækt] *n* (*Med*) cataratas *fpl*
catarrh [kəˈtɑːʳ] *n* catarro
catastrophe [kəˈtæstrəfɪ] *n* catástrofe *f*
catastrophic [kætəˈstrɔfɪk] *adj* catastrófico
catcall [ˈkætkɔːl] *n* (*at meeting etc*) rechifla, silbido
catch [kætʃ] *vb* (*pt, pp* **caught**) ■ *vt* coger (*SP*), agarrar (*LAm*); (*arrest*) atrapar, coger (*SP*); (*grasp*) asir; (*breath*) recobrar; (*person*: *by surprise*) pillar; (*attract*: *attention*) captar; (*Med*) pillar, coger; (*also*: **catch up**) alcanzar ■ *vi* (*fire*) encenderse; (*in branches etc*) engancharse ■ *n* (*fish etc*) captura; (*act of catching*) cogida; (*trick*) trampa; (*of lock*) pestillo, cerradura; **to ~ fire** prenderse; (*house*) incendiarse; **to ~ sight of** divisar
▸ **catch on** *vi* (*understand*) caer en la cuenta; (*grow popular*) tener éxito, cuajar
▸ **catch out** *vt* (*fig*: *with trick question*) hundir
▸ **catch up** *vi* (*fig*) ponerse al día
catching [ˈkætʃɪŋ] *adj* (*Med*) contagioso
catchment area [ˈkætʃmənt-] *n* (*Brit*) zona de captación
catch phrase *n* frase *f* de moda
catch-22 [ˈkætʃtwɛntɪˈtuː] *n*: **it's a ~ situation** es un callejón sin salida, es un círculo vicioso
catchy [ˈkætʃɪ] *adj* (*tune*) pegadizo
catechism [ˈkætɪkɪzəm] *n* (*Rel*) catecismo
categoric [kætɪˈgɔrɪk], **categorical** [kætɪˈgɔrɪkəl] *adj* categórico, terminante
categorically [kætɪˈgɔrɪkəlɪ] *adv* categóricamente, terminantemente
categorize [ˈkætɪgəraɪz] *vt* clasificar
category [ˈkætɪgərɪ] *n* categoría
cater [ˈkeɪtəʳ] *vi*: **to ~ for** (*Brit*) abastecer a; (*needs*) atender a; (*consumers*) proveer a
caterer [ˈkeɪtərəʳ] *n* abastecedor(a) *m(f)*, proveedor(a) *m(f)*
catering [ˈkeɪtərɪŋ] *n* (*trade*) hostelería
caterpillar [ˈkætəpɪləʳ] *n* oruga
caterpillar track *n* rodado de oruga
cat flap *n* gatera
cathedral [kəˈθiːdrəl] *n* catedral *f*
cathode-ray tube [ˈkæθəudreɪˈtjuːb] *n* tubo de rayos catódicos
catholic [ˈkæθəlɪk] *adj* católico; **C~** *adj, n* (*Rel*) católico(-a) *m(f)*
CAT scanner [kæt-] (*Med*) *n abbr* (*= computerized axial tomography scanner*) escáner *m* TAC
cat's-eye [ˈkætsaɪ] *n* (*Brit Aut*) catafaro
catsup [ˈkætsəp] *n* (*US*) ketchup, catsup *m*
cattle [ˈkætl] *npl* ganado *sg*
catty [ˈkætɪ] *adj* malicioso
catwalk [ˈkætwɔːk] *n* pasarela
Caucasian [kɔːˈkeɪzɪən] *adj, n* caucásico(-a) *m(f)*
Caucasus [ˈkɔːkəsəs] *n* Cáucaso
caucus [ˈkɔːkəs] *n* (*Pol*: *local committee*) comité *m* local; (: *US*: *to elect candidates*) comité *m* electoral; (: *group*) camarilla política
caught [kɔːt] *pt, pp of* **catch**
cauliflower [ˈkɔlɪflauəʳ] *n* coliflor *f*
cause [kɔːz] *n* causa; (*reason*) motivo, razón *f* ■ *vt* causar; (*provoke*) provocar; **to ~ sb to do sth** hacer que algn haga algo
causeway [ˈkɔːzweɪ] *n* (*road*) carretera elevada; (*embankment*) terraplén *m*
caustic [ˈkɔːstɪk] *adj* cáustico; (*fig*) mordaz

cauterize ['kɔːtəraɪz] *vt* cauterizar
caution ['kɔːʃən] *n* cautela, prudencia; (*warning*) advertencia, amonestación *f* ■ *vt* amonestar
cautious ['kɔːʃəs] *adj* cauteloso, prudente, precavido
cautiously ['kɔːʃəslɪ] *adv* con cautela
cautiousness ['kɔːʃəsnɪs] *n* cautela
cavalcade [kævəl'keɪd] *n* cabalgata
cavalier [kævə'lɪəʳ] *n* (*knight*) caballero ■ *adj* (*pej: offhand: person, attitude*) arrogante, desdeñoso
cavalry ['kævəlrɪ] *n* caballería
cave [keɪv] *n* cueva, caverna ■ *vi*: **to go caving** ir en una expedición espeleológica ▸ **cave in** *vi* (*roof etc*) derrumbarse, hundirse
caveman ['keɪvmæn] *n* cavernícola *m*
cavern ['kævən] *n* caverna
cavernous ['kævənəs] *adj* (*cheeks, eyes*) hundido
caviar, caviare ['kævɪɑːʳ] *n* caviar *m*
cavity ['kævɪtɪ] *n* hueco, cavidad *f*
cavity wall insulation *n* aislamiento térmico
cavort [kə'vɔːt] *vi* hacer cabrioladas
cayenne [keɪ'ɛn] *n*: ~ **pepper** pimentón *m* picante
CB *n abbr* (= *Citizens' Band (Radio)*) *frecuencias de radio usadas para la comunicación privada*; (Brit: = *Companion of (the Order of) the Bath*) *título de nobleza*
CBC *n abbr* (= *Canadian Broadcasting Corporation*) *cadena de radio y televisión*
CBE *n abbr* (Brit: = *Companion of (the Order of) the British Empire*) *título de nobleza*
CBI *n abbr* (= *Confederation of British Industry*) ≈ C.E.O.E. *f* (*SP*)
CBS *n abbr* (US: = *Columbia Broadcasting System*) *cadena de radio y televisión*
CC *abbr* (Brit) = **county council**
cc *abbr* (= *cubic centimetres*) cc, cm^3; (*on letter etc*) = **carbon copy**
CCA *n abbr* (US: = *Circuit Court of Appeals*) *tribunal de apelación itinerante*
CCTV *n abbr* = **closed-circuit television**
CCU *n abbr* (*esp US*: = *coronary care unit*) unidad *f* de cuidados cardiológicos
CD *n abbr* (= *compact disc*) CD *m*; (*Mil*: = *Civil Defence (Corps)*: Brit: = *Civil Defense*: US) ■ *abbr* (Brit: = *Corps Diplomatique*) CD
CD burner *n* tostadora/grabadora *f* de CDs
CD player *n* reproductor *m* de compact disc
CDC *n abbr* (US) = **center for disease control**
Cdr. *abbr* = **commander**
CD-ROM ['siː'diː'rɔm] *n abbr* (= *compact disc read-only memory*) CD-ROM *m*
CDT *n abbr* (US: = *Central Daylight Time*) *hora de verano del centro*; (Brit: *Scol*: = *Craft, Design and Technology*) *artesanía, diseño y tecnología*
CDW *n abbr* = **collision damage waiver**
CD writer *n* tostadora/grabadora *f* de CDs
cease [siːs] *vt* cesar
ceasefire ['siːsfaɪəʳ] *n* alto *m* el fuego
ceaseless ['siːslɪs] *adj* incesante
ceaselessly ['siːslɪslɪ] *adv* sin cesar
CED *n abbr* (US) = **Committee for Economic Development**
cedar ['siːdəʳ] *n* cedro
cede [siːd] *vt* ceder
CEEB *n abbr* (US: = *College Entrance Examination Board*) *tribunal para las pruebas de acceso a la universidad*
ceilidh ['keɪlɪ] *n baile con música y danzas tradicionales escocesas o irlandesas*
ceiling ['siːlɪŋ] *n* techo; (*fig: upper limit*) límite *m*, tope *m*
celebrate ['sɛlɪbreɪt] *vt* celebrar; (*have a party*) festejar ■ *vi*: **let's ~!** ¡vamos a celebrarlo!
celebrated ['sɛlɪbreɪtɪd] *adj* célebre
celebration [sɛlɪ'breɪʃən] *n* celebración *f*, festejo
celebrity [sɪ'lɛbrɪtɪ] *n* celebridad *f*
celeriac [sə'lɛrɪæk] *n* apio-nabo
celery ['sɛlərɪ] *n* apio
celestial [sɪ'lɛstɪəl] *adj* (*of the sky*) celeste; (*divine*) celestial
celibacy ['sɛlɪbəsɪ] *n* celibato
cell [sɛl] *n* celda; (*Biol*) célula; (*Elec*) elemento
cellar ['sɛləʳ] *n* sótano; (*for wine*) bodega
cellist ['tʃɛlɪst] *n* violoncelista *m/f*
cello ['tʃɛləu] *n* violoncelo
cellophane ['sɛləfeɪn] *n* celofán *m*
cellphone ['sɛlfəun] *n* teléfono celular
cellular ['sɛljuləʳ] *adj* celular
celluloid ['sɛljulɔɪd] *n* celuloide *m*
cellulose ['sɛljuləus] *n* celulosa
Celsius ['sɛlsɪəs] *adj* centígrado
Celt [kɛlt, sɛlt] *n* celta *m/f*
Celtic ['kɛltɪk, 'sɛltɪk] *adj* celta, céltico ■ *n* (*Ling*) celta *m*
cement [sə'mɛnt] *n* cemento ■ *vt* cementar; (*fig*) cimentar
cement mixer *n* hormigonera
cemetery ['sɛmɪtrɪ] *n* cementerio
cenotaph ['sɛnətɑːf] *n* cenotafio
censor ['sɛnsəʳ] *n* censor(a) *m(f)* ■ *vt* (*cut*) censurar
censorship ['sɛnsəʃɪp] *n* censura
censure ['sɛnʃəʳ] *vt* censurar
census ['sɛnsəs] *n* censo
cent [sɛnt] *n* (US: *unit of dollar*) centavo; (*unit of euro*) céntimo; *see also* **per**
centenary [sɛn'tiːnərɪ], **centennial** [sɛn'tɛnɪəl] (US) *n* centenario

center ['sɛntəʳ] *n* (US) = **centre**
centigrade ['sɛntɪgreɪd] *adj* centígrado
centilitre, centiliter (US) ['sɛntɪli:təʳ] *n* centilitro
centimetre, centimeter (US) ['sɛntɪmi:təʳ] *n* centímetro
centipede ['sɛntɪpi:d] *n* ciempiés *m inv*
central ['sɛntrəl] *adj* central; (*house etc*) céntrico
Central African Republic *n* República Centroafricana
Central America *n* Centroamérica
Central American *adj, n* centroamericano(-a) *m(f)*
central heating *n* calefacción *f* central
centralize ['sɛntrəlaɪz] *vt* centralizar
central processing unit *n* (*Comput*) unidad *f* procesadora central, unidad *f* central de proceso
central reservation *n* (*Brit Aut*) mediana
centre, center (US) ['sɛntəʳ] *n* centro ■ *vt* centrar; **to ~ (on)** (*concentrate*) concentrar (en)
centrefold, centerfold (US) ['sɛntəfəuld] *n* página central plegable
centre-forward ['sɛntə'fɔ:wəd] *n* (*Sport*) delantero centro
centre-half ['sɛntə'hɑ:f] *n* (*Sport*) medio centro
centrepiece, centerpiece (US) ['sɛntəpi:s] *n* punto central
centre spread *n* (*Brit*) páginas *fpl* centrales
centre-stage *n*: **to take ~** pasar a primer plano
centrifuge ['sɛntrɪfju:dʒ] *n* centrifugadora
century ['sɛntjurɪ] *n* siglo; **20th ~** siglo veinte; **in the twentieth ~** en el siglo veinte
CEO *n abbr* = **chief executive officer**
ceramic [sɪ'ræmɪk] *adj* de cerámica
ceramics [sɪ'ræmɪks] *n* cerámica
cereal ['si:rɪəl] *n* cereal *m*
cerebral ['sɛrɪbrəl] *adj* cerebral
ceremonial [sɛrɪ'məunɪəl] *n* ceremonial
ceremony ['sɛrɪmənɪ] *n* ceremonia; **to stand on ~** hacer ceremonias, andarse con cumplidos
cert [sə:t] *n* (*Brit col*): **it's a dead ~** ¡es cosa segura!
certain ['sə:tən] *adj* seguro; (*correct*) cierto; (*particular*) cierto; **for ~** a ciencia cierta
certainly ['sə:tənlɪ] *adv* desde luego, por supuesto
certainty ['sə:təntɪ] *n* certeza, certidumbre *f*, seguridad *f*
certificate [sə'tɪfɪkɪt] *n* certificado
certified ['sə:tɪfaɪd] *adj*: **~ mail** (US) correo certificado
certified public accountant *n* (US) contable *m/f* diplomado(-a)
certify ['sə:tɪfaɪ] *vt* certificar
cervical ['sə:vɪkl] *adj*: **~ cancer** cáncer *m* cervical; **~ smear** citología
cervix ['sə:vɪks] *n* cerviz *f*, cuello del útero
Cesarean [sɪ'zɛərɪən] *adj, n* (US) = **Caesarean**
cessation [sə'seɪʃən] *n* cese *m*, suspensión *f*
cesspit ['sɛspɪt] *n* pozo negro
CET *n abbr* (= *Central European Time*) *hora de Europa central*
Ceylon [sɪ'lɔn] *n* Ceilán *m*
cf. *abbr* (= *compare*) cfr
c/f *abbr* (*Comm*) = **carried forward**
CFC *n abbr* (= *chlorofluorocarbon*) CFC *m*
CG *n abbr* (US) = **coastguard**
cg *abbr* (= *centigram*) cg
CH *n abbr* (*Brit*: = *Companion of Honour*) *título de nobleza*
ch. *abbr* (= *chapter*) cap
Chad [tʃæd] *n* Chad *m*
chafe [tʃeɪf] *vt* (*rub*) rozar; (*irritate*) irritar; **to ~ (against)** (*fig*) irritarse *or* enojarse (con)
chaffinch ['tʃæfɪntʃ] *n* pinzón *m* (vulgar)
chagrin ['ʃægrɪn] *n* (*annoyance*) disgusto; (*disappointment*) desazón *f*
chain [tʃeɪn] *n* cadena ■ *vt* (*also*: **chain up**) encadenar
chain reaction *n* reacción *f* en cadena
chain-smoke ['tʃeɪnsməuk] *vi* fumar un cigarrillo tras otro
chain store *n* tienda de una cadena, ≈ grandes almacenes *mpl*
chair [tʃɛəʳ] *n* silla; (*armchair*) sillón *m*; (*of university*) cátedra ■ *vt* (*meeting*) presidir; **the ~** (*US: electric chair*) la silla eléctrica; **please take a ~** siéntese *or* tome asiento, por favor
chairlift ['tʃɛəlɪft] *n* telesilla *m*
chairman ['tʃɛəmən] *n* presidente *m*
chairperson ['tʃɛəpə:sn] *n* presidente(-a) *m(f)*
chairwoman ['tʃɛəwumən] *n* presidenta
chalet ['ʃæleɪ] *n* chalet *m* (de madera)
chalice ['tʃælɪs] *n* cáliz *m*
chalk [tʃɔ:k] *n* (*Geo*) creta; (*for writing*) tiza, gis *m* (*LAm*)
▸ **chalk up** *vt* apuntar; (*fig: success, victory*) apuntarse
challenge ['tʃælɪndʒ] *n* desafío, reto ■ *vt* desafiar, retar; (*statement, right*) poner en duda; **to ~ sb to do sth** retar a algn a que haga algo
challenger ['tʃælɪndʒəʳ] *n* (*Sport*) contrincante *m/f*
challenging ['tʃælɪndʒɪŋ] *adj* que supone un reto; (*tone*) de desafío
chamber ['tʃeɪmbəʳ] *n* cámara, sala
chambermaid ['tʃeɪmbəmeɪd] *n* camarera

chamber music *n* música de cámara
chamber of commerce *n* cámara de comercio
chamberpot ['tʃeɪmbəpɔt] *n* orinal *m*
chameleon [kə'mi:lɪən] *n* camaleón *m*
chamois ['ʃæmwɑ:] *n* gamuza
champagne [ʃæm'peɪn] *n* champaña *m*, champán *m*
champers ['ʃæmpəz] *nsg* (*col*) champán *m*
champion ['tʃæmpɪən] *n* campeón(-ona) *m(f)*; (*of cause*) defensor(a) *m(f)*, paladín *m/f* ■ *vt* defender, apoyar
championship ['tʃæmpɪənʃɪp] *n* campeonato
chance [tʃɑ:ns] *n* (*coincidence*) casualidad *f*; (*luck*) suerte *f*; (*fate*) azar *m*; (*opportunity*) ocasión *f*, oportunidad *f*, chance *m or f* (*LAm*); (*likelihood*) posibilidad *f*; (*risk*) riesgo ■ *vt* arriesgar, probar ■ *adj* fortuito, casual; **to ~ it** arriesgarse, intentarlo; **to take a ~** arriesgarse; **by ~** por casualidad; **it's the ~ of a lifetime** es la oportunidad de su vida; **the chances are that ...** lo más probable es que ...; **to ~ to do sth** (*happen*) hacer algo por casualidad
▸ **chance (up)on** *vt fus* tropezar(se) con
chancel ['tʃɑ:nsəl] *n* coro y presbiterio
chancellor ['tʃɑ:nsələʳ] *n* canciller *m*; **C~ of the Exchequer** (*Brit*) Ministro de Economía y Hacienda; *see also* **Downing Street**
chancy ['tʃɑ:nsɪ] *adj* (*col*) arriesgado
chandelier [ʃændə'lɪəʳ] *n* araña (de luces)
change [tʃeɪndʒ] *vt* cambiar; (*clothes, house*) cambiarse de, mudarse de; (*transform*) transformar ■ *vi* cambiar(se); (*change trains*) hacer transbordo; (*be transformed*): **to ~ into** transformarse en ■ *n* cambio; (*alteration*) modificación *f*, transformación *f*; (*coins*) suelto; (*money returned*) vuelta, vuelto (*LAm*); **to ~ one's mind** cambiar de opinión *or* idea; **to ~ gear** (*Aut*) cambiar de marcha; **she changed into an old skirt** se puso una falda vieja; **for a ~** para variar; **can you give me ~ for £1?** ¿tiene cambio de una libra?; **keep the ~** quédese con la vuelta
changeable ['tʃeɪndʒəbl] *adj* (*weather*) cambiable; (*person*) variable
changeless ['tʃeɪndʒlɪs] *adj* inmutable
change machine *n* máquina de cambio
changeover ['tʃeɪndʒəuvəʳ] *n* (*to new system*) cambio
changing ['tʃeɪndʒɪŋ] *adj* cambiante
changing room *n* (*Brit*) vestuario
channel ['tʃænl] *n* (*TV*) canal *m*; (*of river*) cauce *m*; (*of sea*) estrecho; (*groove: fig: medium*) conducto, medio ■ *vt* (*river etc*) encauzar; **to ~ into** (*fig: interest, energies*) encauzar a, dirigir a; **the (English) C~** el Canal (de la Mancha); **the C~ Islands** las Islas Anglonormandas; **channels of communication** canales *mpl* de comunicación; **green/red ~** (*Customs*) pasillo verde/rojo
Channel Tunnel *n*: **the ~** el túnel del Canal de la Mancha, el Eurotúnel
chant [tʃɑ:nt] *n* canto; (*of crowd*) gritos *mpl* ■ *vt* cantar; **the demonstrators chanted their disapproval** los manifestantes corearon su desaprobación
chaos ['keɪɔs] *n* caos *m*
chaos theory *n* teoría del caos
chaotic [keɪ'ɔtɪk] *adj* caótico
chap [tʃæp] *n* (*Brit col: man*) tío, tipo; **old ~** amigo (mío)
chapel ['tʃæpəl] *n* capilla
chaperone ['ʃæpərəun] *n* carabina
chaplain ['tʃæplɪn] *n* capellán *m*
chapped [tʃæpt] *adj* agrietado
chapter ['tʃæptəʳ] *n* capítulo
char [tʃɑ:ʳ] *vt* (*burn*) carbonizar, chamuscar ■ *n* (*Brit*) = **charlady**
character ['kærɪktəʳ] *n* carácter *m*, naturaleza, índole *f*; (*in novel, film*) personaje *m*; (*role*) papel *m*; (*individuality*) carácter *m*; (*Comput*) carácter *m*; **a person of good ~** una persona de buena reputación
character code *n* código de caracteres
characteristic [kærɪktə'rɪstɪk] *adj* característico ■ *n* característica
characterize ['kærɪktəraɪz] *vt* caracterizar
charade [ʃə'rɑ:d] *n* farsa, comedia; **charades** (*game*) charadas *fpl*
charcoal ['tʃɑ:kəul] *n* carbón *m* vegetal; (*Art*) carboncillo
charge [tʃɑ:dʒ] *n* carga; (*Law*) cargo, acusación *f*; (*cost*) precio, coste *m*; (*responsibility*) cargo; (*task*) encargo ■ *vt* (*Law*): **to ~ (with)** acusar (de); (*gun, battery*) cargar; (*Mil: enemy*) cargar; (*price*) pedir; (*customer*) cobrar; (*person: with task*) encargar ■ *vi* precipitarse; (*make pay*) cobrar; **charges** *npl*: **bank charges** comisiones *fpl* bancarias; **extra ~** recargo, suplemento; **free of ~** gratis; **to reverse the charges** (*Brit Tel*) llamar a cobro revertido; **to take ~ of** hacerse cargo de, encargarse de; **to be in ~ of** estar encargado de; **how much do you ~?** ¿cuánto cobra usted?; **to ~ an expense (up) to sb's account** cargar algo a cuenta de algn; **~ it to my account** póngalo *or* cárguelo a mi cuenta
charge account *n* (*US*) cuenta abierta *or* a crédito
charge card *n* tarjeta de cuenta
chargé d'affaires [ʃɑ:ʒeɪdæ'fɛəʳ] *n* encargado de negocios

chargehand ['tʃɑ:dʒhænd] *n* capataz *m*
charger ['tʃɑ:dʒəʳ] *n* (*also*: **battery charger**) cargador *m* (de baterías)
chariot ['tʃærɪət] *n* carro
charisma [kæ'rɪzmə] *n* carisma *m*
charitable ['tʃærɪtəbl] *adj* caritativo
charity ['tʃærɪtɪ] *n* (*gen*) caridad *f*; (*organization*) organización *f* benéfica
charlady ['tʃɑ:leɪdɪ] *n* (*Brit*) mujer *f* de la limpieza
charlatan ['ʃɑ:lətən] *n* charlatán *m*
charm [tʃɑ:m] *n* encanto, atractivo; (*spell*) hechizo; (*object*) amuleto ■ *vt* encantar; hechizar
charm bracelet *n* pulsera amuleto
charming ['tʃɑ:mɪŋ] *adj* encantador(a); (*person*) simpático
chart [tʃɑ:t] *n* (*table*) cuadro; (*graph*) gráfica; (*map*) carta de navegación; (*weather chart*) mapa *m* meteorológico ■ *vt* (*course*) trazar; (*sales, progress*) hacer una gráfica de; **to be in the charts** (*record, pop group*) estar en la lista de éxitos
charter ['tʃɑ:təʳ] *vt* (*bus*) alquilar; (*plane, ship*) fletar ■ *n* (*document*) estatuto, carta; **on ~** en alquiler, alquilado
chartered accountant *n* (*Brit*) contable *m/f* diplomado(-a)
charter flight *n* vuelo chárter
charwoman ['tʃɑ:wumən] *n* = **charlady**
chase [tʃeɪs] *vt* (*pursue*) perseguir; (*hunt*) cazar ■ *n* persecución *f*; caza; **to ~ after** correr tras
▸ **chase up** *vt* (*information*) tratar de conseguir; **to ~ sb up about sth** recordar algo a algn
chasm ['kæzəm] *n* abismo
chassis ['ʃæsɪ] *n* chasis *m*
chaste [tʃeɪst] *adj* casto
chastened ['tʃeɪsənd] *adj* escarmentado
chastening ['tʃeɪsnɪŋ] *adj* aleccionador(a)
chastity ['tʃæstɪtɪ] *n* castidad *f*
chat [tʃæt] *vi* (*also*: **have a chat**) charlar; (*Internet*) chatear ■ *n* charla; (*Internet*) chat *m*
▸ **chat up** *vt* (*col: girl*) ligar con, enrollarse con
chatline ['tʃætlaɪn] *n* línea (telefónica) múltiple, party line *f*
chat room *n* (*internet*) chat *m*, canal *m* de charla
chat show *n* (*Brit*) programa *m* de entrevistas
chattel ['tʃætl] *n* bien *m* mueble
chatter ['tʃætəʳ] *vi* (*person*) charlar; (*teeth*) castañetear ■ *n* (*of birds*) parloteo; (*of people*) charla, cháchara
chatterbox ['tʃætəbɔks] *n* parlanchín(-ina) *m(f)*
chattering classes ['tʃætərɪŋ'klɑ:sɪz] *npl*: **the ~** (*col, pej*) los intelectualillos
chatty ['tʃætɪ] *adj* (*style*) informal; (*person*) hablador(a)
chauffeur ['ʃəufəʳ] *n* chófer *m*
chauvinist ['ʃəuvɪnɪst] *n* (*also*: **male chauvinist**) machista *m*; (*nationalist*) chovinista *m/f*, patriotero(-a) *m(f)*
ChE *abbr* = **chemical engineer**
cheap [tʃi:p] *adj* barato; (*joke*) de mal gusto, chabacano; (*poor quality*) malo; (*reduced: ticket*) económico; (*: fare*) barato ■ *adv* barato
cheapen ['tʃi:pn] *vt* rebajar el precio de, abaratar
cheaply ['tʃi:plɪ] *adv* barato, a bajo precio
cheat [tʃi:t] *vi* hacer trampa; (*in exam*) copiar ■ *vt* estafar, timar ■ *n* trampa; estafa; (*person*) tramposo(-a); **he's been cheating on his wife** ha estado engañando a su esposa
cheating ['tʃi:tɪŋ] *n* trampa
Chechnia ['tʃɛtʃni:ə] *n* Chechenia
check [tʃɛk] *vt* comprobar; (*count*) contar; (*halt*) frenar; (*restrain*) refrenar, restringir ■ *vi*: **to ~ with sb** consultar con algn; (*official etc*) informarse por ■ *n* (*inspection*) control *m*, inspección *f*; (*curb*) freno; (*bill*) nota, cuenta; (*US*) = **cheque**; (*pattern: gen pl*) cuadro ■ *adj* (*also*: **checked**: *pattern, cloth*) a cuadros; **to keep a ~ on sth/sb** controlar algo/a algn
▸ **check in** *vi* (*in hotel*) registrarse; (*at airport*) facturar ■ *vt* (*luggage*) facturar
▸ **check out** *vi* (*of hotel*) desocupar la habitación ■ *vt* (*investigate: story*) comprobar; (*: person*) informarse sobre
▸ **check up** *vi*: **to ~ up on sth** comprobar algo; **to ~ up on sb** investigar a algn
checkbook ['tʃɛkbuk] *n* (*US*) = **chequebook**
checkered ['tʃɛkəd] *adj* (*US*) = **chequered**
checkers ['tʃɛkəz] *n* (*US*) damas *fpl*
check-in ['tʃɛkɪn] *n* (*also*: **check-in desk**: *at airport*) mostrador *m* de facturación
checking account ['tʃɛkɪŋ-] *n* (*US*) cuenta corriente
checklist ['tʃɛklɪst] *n* lista
checkmate ['tʃɛkmeɪt] *n* jaque *m* mate
checkout ['tʃɛkaut] *n* (*in supermarket*) caja
checkpoint ['tʃɛkpɔɪnt] *n* (punto de) control *m*, retén *m* (*LAm*)
checkroom ['tʃɛkrum] *n* (*US*) consigna
checkup ['tʃɛkʌp] *n* (*Med*) reconocimiento general; (*of machine*) revisión *f*
cheek [tʃi:k] *n* mejilla; (*impudence*) descaro
cheekbone ['tʃi:kbəun] *n* pómulo
cheeky ['tʃi:kɪ] *adj* fresco, descarado
cheep [tʃi:p] *n* (*of bird*) pío ■ *vi* piar
cheer [tʃɪəʳ] *vt* vitorear, ovacionar; (*gladden*) alegrar, animar ■ *vi* dar vivas ■ *n* viva *m*; **cheers** *npl* vítores *mpl*; **cheers!** ¡salud!

▸**cheer on** *vt* (*person etc*) animar con aplausos *or* gritos
▸**cheer up** *vi* animarse ■ *vt* alegrar, animar
cheerful ['tʃɪəful] *adj* alegre
cheerfulness ['tʃɪəfulnɪs] *n* alegría
cheering ['tʃɪərɪŋ] *n* ovaciones *fpl*, vítores *mpl*
cheerio [tʃɪərɪ'əu] *excl* (*Brit*) ¡hasta luego!
cheerleader ['tʃɪəli:də^r] *n* animador(a) *m(f)*
cheerless ['tʃɪəlɪs] *adj* triste, sombrío
cheese [tʃi:z] *n* queso
cheeseboard ['tʃi:zbɔ:d] *n* tabla de quesos
cheeseburger ['tʃi:zbə:gə^r] *n* hamburguesa con queso
cheesecake ['tʃi:zkeɪk] *n* pastel *m* de queso
cheetah ['tʃi:tə] *n* guepardo
chef [ʃɛf] *n* jefe(-a) *m(f)* de cocina
chemical ['kɛmɪkəl] *adj* químico ■ *n* producto químico
chemist ['kɛmɪst] *n* (*Brit: pharmacist*) farmacéutico(-a); (*scientist*) químico(-a); **~'s (shop)** *n* (*Brit*) farmacia
chemistry ['kɛmɪstrɪ] *n* química
chemotherapy [ki:məu'θɛrəpɪ] *n* quimioterapia
cheque, check (*US*) [tʃɛk] *n* cheque *m*; **to pay by ~** pagar con cheque
chequebook, checkbook (*US*) ['tʃɛkbuk] *n* talonario (de cheques), chequera (*LAm*)
cheque card *n* (*Brit*) tarjeta de identificación bancaria
chequered, checkered (*US*) ['tʃɛkəd] *adj* (*fig*) accidentado; (*pattern*) de cuadros
cherish ['tʃɛrɪʃ] *vt* (*love*) querer, apreciar; (*protect*) cuidar; (*hope etc*) abrigar
cheroot [ʃə'ru:t] *n* puro (*cortado en los dos extremos*)
cherry ['tʃɛrɪ] *n* cereza
Ches *abbr* (*Brit*) = **Cheshire**
chess [tʃɛs] *n* ajedrez *m*
chessboard ['tʃɛsbɔ:d] *n* tablero (de ajedrez)
chessman ['tʃɛsmən] *n* pieza (de ajedrez)
chest [tʃɛst] *n* (*Anat*) pecho; (*box*) cofre *m*; **to get sth off one's ~** (*col*) desahogarse; **~ of drawers** *n* cómoda
chest measurement *n* talla (*de chaqueta etc*)
chestnut ['tʃɛsnʌt] *n* castaña; (*also*: **chestnut tree**) castaño; (*colour*) castaño ■ *adj* (*color*) castaño *inv*
chesty ['tʃɛstɪ] *adj* (*cough*) de bronquios, de pecho
chew [tʃu:] *vt* mascar, masticar
chewing gum ['tʃu:ɪŋ-] *n* chicle *m*
chic [ʃi:k] *adj* elegante
chicanery [ʃɪ'keɪnərɪ] *n* embustes *mpl*, sofismas *mpl*
Chicano [tʃɪ'kɑ:nəu] *adj, n* chicano(-a)
chick [tʃɪk] *n* pollito, polluelo; (*US col*) chica
chicken ['tʃɪkɪn] *n* gallina, pollo; (*food*) pollo; (*col: coward*) gallina *m/f*
▸**chicken out** *vi* (*col*) rajarse; **to ~ out of doing sth** rajarse y no hacer algo
chickenpox ['tʃɪkɪnpɔks] *n* varicela
chickpea ['tʃɪkpi:] *n* garbanzo
chicory ['tʃɪkərɪ] *n* (*for coffee*) achicoria; (*salad*) escarola
chide [tʃaɪd] *vt*: **to ~ sb for sth** reprender a algn por algo
chief [tʃi:f] *n* jefe(-a) *m(f)* ■ *adj* principal, esp máximo (*LAm*); **C~ of Staff** (*esp Mil*) Jefe *m* del Estado mayor
chief executive, chief executive officer (*US*) *n* director *m* general
chiefly ['tʃi:flɪ] *adv* principalmente
chieftain ['tʃi:ftən] *n* jefe *m*, cacique *m*
chiffon ['ʃɪfɔn] *n* gasa
chilblain ['tʃɪlbleɪn] *n* sabañón *m*
child (*pl* **children**) [tʃaɪld, 'tʃɪldrən] *n* niño(-a); (*offspring*) hijo(-a)
child benefit *n* (*Brit*) *subsidio por cada hijo pequeño*
childbirth ['tʃaɪldbə:θ] *n* parto
childhood ['tʃaɪldhud] *n* niñez *f*, infancia
childish ['tʃaɪldɪʃ] *adj* pueril, infantil
childless ['tʃaɪldlɪs] *adj* sin hijos
childlike ['tʃaɪldlaɪk] *adj* de niño, infantil
child minder *n* (*Brit*) niñera, madre *f* de día
child prodigy *n* niño(-a) prodigio *inv*
children's home *n* centro de acogida para niños
child's play *n* (*fig*): **this is ~** esto es coser y cantar
Chile ['tʃɪlɪ] *n* Chile *m*
Chilean ['tʃɪlɪən] *adj, n* chileno(-a) *m(f)*
chill [tʃɪl] *n* frío; (*Med*) resfriado ■ *adj* frío ■ *vt* enfriar; (*Culin*) refrigerar
▸**chill out** *vi* (*esp US col*) tranquilizarse
chilli, chili ['tʃɪlɪ] *n* (*Brit*) chile *m*, ají *m* (*LAm*)
chilling ['tʃɪlɪŋ] *adj* escalofriante
chilly ['tʃɪlɪ] *adj* frío
chime [tʃaɪm] *n* repique *m*, campanada ■ *vi* repicar, sonar
chimney ['tʃɪmnɪ] *n* chimenea
chimney sweep *n* deshollinador *m*
chimpanzee [tʃɪmpæn'zi:] *n* chimpancé *m*
chin [tʃɪn] *n* mentón *m*, barbilla
China ['tʃaɪnə] *n* China
china ['tʃaɪnə] *n* porcelana; (*crockery*) loza
Chinese [tʃaɪ'ni:z] *adj* chino ■ *n* (*pl inv*) chino(-a); (*Ling*) chino
chink [tʃɪŋk] *n* (*opening*) rendija, hendedura; (*noise*) tintineo
chintz [tʃɪnts] *n* cretona
chinwag ['tʃɪnwæg] *n* (*Brit col*): **to have a ~** echar una parrafada

chip [tʃɪp] *n (gen pl: Culin: Brit)* patata *or (LAm)* papa frita; *(: US: also:* **potato chip**) patata *or (LAm)* papa frita; *(of wood)* astilla; *(stone)* lasca; *(in gambling)* ficha; *(Comput)* chip *m* ■ *vt (cup, plate)* desconchar; **when the chips are down** *(fig)* a la hora de la verdad
▸ **chip in** *vi (col: interrupt)* interrumpir, meterse; *(: contribute)* contribuir
chipboard ['tʃɪpbɔ:d] *n* madera aglomerada
chipmunk ['tʃɪpmʌŋk] *n* ardilla listada
chip shop *n ver nota*

CHIP SHOP

Se denomina *chip shop* o "fish-and-chip shop" a un tipo de tienda popular de comida rápida en la que se despachan platos tradicionales británicos, principalmente filetes de pescado rebozado frito y patatas fritas.

chiropodist [kɪ'rɔpədɪst] *n (Brit)* podólogo(-a)
chiropody [kɪ'rɔpədɪ] *n* podología
chirp [tʃə:p] *vi* gorjear; *(cricket)* cantar ■ *n (of cricket)* canto
chirpy ['tʃə:pɪ] *adj* alegre, animado
chisel ['tʃɪzl] *n (for wood)* escoplo; *(for stone)* cincel *m*
chit [tʃɪt] *n* nota
chitchat ['tʃɪttʃæt] *n* chismes *mpl*, habladurías *fpl*
chivalrous ['ʃɪvəlrəs] *adj* caballeroso
chivalry ['ʃɪvəlrɪ] *n* caballerosidad *f*
chives [tʃaɪvz] *npl* cebollinos *mpl*
chloride ['klɔ:raɪd] *n* cloruro
chlorinate ['klɔ:rɪneɪt] *vt* clorar
chlorine ['klɔ:ri:n] *n* cloro
chock-a-block ['tʃɔkə'blɔk], **chock-full** [tʃɔk'ful] *adj* atestado
chocolate ['tʃɔklɪt] *n* chocolate *m*
choice [tʃɔɪs] *n* elección *f*; *(preference)* preferencia ■ *adj* escogido; **I did it by** *or* **from ~** lo hice de buena gana; **a wide ~** un gran surtido, una gran variedad
choir ['kwaɪəʳ] *n* coro
choirboy ['kwaɪəbɔɪ] *n* niño de coro
choke [tʃəuk] *vi* ahogarse; *(on food)* atragantarse ■ *vt* ahogar; *(block)* atascar ■ *n (Aut)* estárter *m*
choker ['tʃəukəʳ] *n (necklace)* gargantilla
cholera ['kɔlərə] *n* cólera *m*
cholesterol [kɔ'lɛstərəl] *n* colesterol *m*
choose [tʃu:z] *(pt* **chose**) [tʃəʊz] *(pp* **chosen**) [tʃəuzn] *vt* escoger, elegir; *(team)* seleccionar; **to ~ between** elegir *or* escoger entre; **to ~ from** escoger entre
choosy ['tʃu:zɪ] *adj* remilgado
chop [tʃɔp] *vt (wood)* cortar, talar; *(Culin: also:* **chop up**) picar ■ *n* tajo, golpe *m* cortante; *(Culin)* chuleta; **chops** *npl (jaws)* boca *sg*; **to get the ~** *(col: project)* ser suprimido; *(: person: be sacked)* ser despedido
chopper ['tʃɔpəʳ] *n (helicopter)* helicóptero
choppy ['tʃɔpɪ] *adj (sea)* picado, agitado
chopsticks ['tʃɔpstɪks] *npl* palillos *mpl*
choral ['kɔ:rəl] *adj* coral
chord [kɔ:d] *n (Mus)* acorde *m*
chore [tʃɔ:ʳ] *n* faena, tarea; *(routine task)* trabajo rutinario
choreographer [kɔrɪ'ɔgrəfəʳ] *n* coreógrafo(-a)
choreography [kɔrɪ'ɔgrəfɪ] *n* coreografía
chorister ['kɔrɪstəʳ] *n* corista *m/f*; (US) director(a) *m(f)* de un coro
chortle ['tʃɔ:tl] *vi* reírse satisfecho
chorus ['kɔ:rəs] *n* coro; *(repeated part of song)* estribillo
chose [tʃəuz] *pt of* **choose**
chosen ['tʃəuzn] *pp of* **choose**
chow [tʃau] *n (dog)* perro chino
chowder ['tʃaudəʳ] *n (esp US)* sopa de pescado
Christ [kraɪst] *n* Cristo
christen ['krɪsn] *vt* bautizar
christening ['krɪsnɪŋ] *n* bautizo
Christian ['krɪstɪən] *adj, n* cristiano(-a) *m(f)*
Christianity [krɪstɪ'ænɪtɪ] *n* cristianismo
Christian name *n* nombre *m* de pila
Christmas ['krɪsməs] *n* Navidad *f*; **Merry ~!** ¡Felices Navidades!, ¡Felices Pascuas!
Christmas card *n* crismas *m inv*, tarjeta de Navidad
Christmas Day *n* día *m* de Navidad
Christmas Eve *n* Nochebuena
Christmas Island *n* Isla Christmas
Christmas tree *n* árbol *m* de Navidad
chrome [krəum] *n* = **chromium plating**
chromium ['krəumɪəm] *n* cromo; *(also:* **chromium plating**) cromado
chromosome ['krəuməsəum] *n* cromosoma *m*
chronic ['krɔnɪk] *adj* crónico; *(fig: liar, smoker)* empedernido
chronicle ['krɔnɪkl] *n* crónica
chronological [krɔnə'lɔdʒɪkəl] *adj* cronológico
chrysalis ['krɪsəlɪs] *n (Bio)* crisálida
chrysanthemum [krɪ'sænθəməm] *n* crisantemo
chubby ['tʃʌbɪ] *adj* rechoncho
chuck [tʃʌk] *vt* tirar; **to ~ (up** *or* **in)** *vt (Brit)* dejar, mandar a paseo
chuckle ['tʃʌkl] *vi* reírse entre dientes
chuffed [tʃʌft] *adj (col)*: **to be ~ (about sth)** estar encantado (con algo)

chug [tʃʌg] *vi* (*also*: **chug along**: *train*) ir despacio; (: *fig*) ir tirando
chum [tʃʌm] *n* amiguete(-a) *m(f)*, coleguilla *m/f*
chump [tʃʌmp] *n* (*col*) tonto(-a), estúpido(-a)
chunk [tʃʌŋk] *n* pedazo, trozo
chunky ['tʃʌŋkɪ] *adj* (*furniture etc*) achaparrado; (*person*) fornido; (*knitwear*) de lana gorda, grueso
Chunnel [tʃʌnl] *n* = **Channel Tunnel**
church [tʃə:tʃ] *n* iglesia; **the C~ of England** la Iglesia Anglicana
churchyard ['tʃə:tʃɑ:d] *n* cementerio, camposanto
churlish ['tʃə:lɪʃ] *adj* grosero; (*mean*) arisco
churn [tʃə:n] *n* (*for butter*) mantequera; (*for milk*) lechera
▸ **churn out** *vt* producir en serie
chute [ʃu:t] *n* (*also*: **rubbish chute**) vertedero; (*Brit*: *children's slide*) tobogán *m*
chutney ['tʃʌtnɪ] *n* *salsa picante de frutas y especias*
CIA *n abbr* (*US*: = *Central Intelligence Agency*) CIA *f*, Agencia Central de Inteligencia
cicada [sɪ'kɑ:də] *n* cigarra
CID *n abbr* (*Brit*: = *Criminal Investigation Department*) ≈ B.I.C. *f* (*SP*)
cider ['saɪdə^r] *n* sidra
CIF *abbr* (= *cost, insurance, and freight*) c.s.f.
cigar [sɪ'gɑ:^r] *n* puro
cigarette [sɪgə'rɛt] *n* cigarrillo, pitillo
cigarette case *n* pitillera
cigarette end *n* colilla
cigarette holder *n* boquilla
C-in-C *abbr* (= *commander-in-chief*) comandante *mf* general
cinch [sɪntʃ] *n*: **it's a ~** está tirado
Cinderella [sɪndə'rɛlə] *n* Cenicienta
cinders ['sɪndəz] *npl* cenizas *fpl*
cine-camera ['sɪnɪ'kæmərə] *n* (*Brit*) cámara cinematográfica
cine-film ['sɪnɪfɪlm] *n* (*Brit*) película de cine
cinema ['sɪnəmə] *n* cine *m*
cinnamon ['sɪnəmən] *n* canela
cipher ['saɪfə^r] *n* clave *f*; (*fig*) cero; **in ~** en clave
circle ['sə:kl] *n* círculo; (*in theatre*) anfiteatro ■ *vi* dar vueltas ■ *vt* (*surround*) rodear, cercar; (*move round*) dar la vuelta a
circuit ['sə:kɪt] *n* circuito; (*track*) pista; (*lap*) vuelta
circuit board *n* tarjeta de circuitos
circuitous [sə:'kjuɪtəs] *adj* indirecto
circular ['sə:kjulə^r] *adj* circular ■ *n* circular *f*; (*as advertisement*) panfleto
circulate ['sə:kjuleɪt] *vi* circular; (*person*: *socially*) alternar, circular ■ *vt* poner en circulación
circulation [sə:kju'leɪʃən] *n* circulación *f*; (*of newspaper etc*) tirada
circumcise ['sə:kəmsaɪz] *vt* circuncidar
circumference [sə'kʌmfərəns] *n* circunferencia
circumscribe ['sə:kəmskraɪb] *vt* circunscribir
circumspect ['sə:kəmspɛkt] *adj* circunspecto, prudente
circumstances ['sə:kəmstənsɪz] *npl* circunstancias *fpl*; (*financial condition*) situación *f* económica; **in the ~** en *or* dadas las circunstancias; **under no ~** de ninguna manera, bajo ningún concepto
circumstantial [sə:kəm'stænʃəl] *adj* detallado; **~ evidence** prueba indiciaria
circumvent ['sə:kəmvɛnt] *vt* (*rule etc*) burlar
circus ['sə:kəs] *n* circo; (*also*: **Circus**: *in place names*) Plaza
cirrhosis [sɪ'rəusɪs] *n* (*also*: **cirrhosis of the liver**) cirrosis *f inv*
CIS *n abbr* (= *Commonwealth of Independent States*) CEI *f*
cissy ['sɪsɪ] *n* = **sissy**
cistern ['sɪstən] *n* tanque *m*, depósito; (*in toilet*) cisterna
citation [saɪ'teɪʃən] *n* cita; (*Law*) citación *f*; (*Mil*) mención *f*
cite [saɪt] *vt* citar
citizen ['sɪtɪzn] *n* (*Pol*) ciudadano(-a); (*of city*) habitante *m/f*
Citizens' Advice Bureau *n* (*Brit*) *organización voluntaria británica que aconseja especialmente en temas legales o financieros*
citizenship ['sɪtɪznʃɪp] *n* ciudadanía; (*Brit Scol*) civismo
citric ['sɪtrɪk] *adj*: **~ acid** ácido cítrico
citrus fruits ['sɪtrəs-] *npl* cítricos *mpl*
city ['sɪtɪ] *n* ciudad *f*; **the C~** *centro financiero de Londres*
city centre *n* centro de la ciudad
City Hall *n* (*US*) ayuntamiento
City Technology College *n* (*Brit*) ≈ Centro de formación profesional
civic ['sɪvɪk] *adj* cívico; (*authorities*) municipal
civic centre *n* (*Brit*) centro de administración municipal
civil ['sɪvɪl] *adj* civil; (*polite*) atento, cortés; (*well-bred*) educado
civil defence *n* protección *f* civil
civil engineer *n* ingeniero(-a) de caminos
civil engineering *n* ingeniería de caminos
civilian [sɪ'vɪlɪən] *adj* civil; (*clothes*) de paisano ■ *n* civil *m/f*
civilization [sɪvɪlaɪ'zeɪʃən] *n* civilización *f*
civilized ['sɪvɪlaɪzd] *adj* civilizado

civil law *n* derecho civil
civil liberties *npl* libertades *fpl* civiles
civil rights *npl* derechos *mpl* civiles
civil servant *n* funcionario(-a) (del Estado)
Civil Service *n* administración *f* pública
civil war *n* guerra civil
civvies ['sɪvɪz] *npl*: **in ~** (*col*) de paisano
CJD *n abbr* (= *Creutzfeld-Jakob disease*) *enfermedad de Creutzfeldt-Jakob*
cl *abbr* (= *centilitre*) cl
clad [klæd] *adj*: **~ (in)** vestido (de)
claim [kleɪm] *vt* exigir, reclamar; (*rights etc*) reivindicar; (*assert*) pretender ■ *vi* (*for insurance*) reclamar ■ *n* (*for expenses*) reclamación *f*; (*Law*) demanda; (*pretension*) pretensión *f*; **to put in a ~ for sth** presentar una demanda por algo
claimant ['kleɪmənt] *n* (*Admin, Law*) demandante *m/f*
claim form *n* solicitud *f*
clairvoyant [klɛə'vɔɪənt] *n* clarividente *m/f*
clam [klæm] *n* almeja
▸ **clam up** *vi* (*col*) cerrar el pico
clamber ['klæmbəʳ] *vi* trepar
clammy ['klæmɪ] *adj* (*cold*) frío y húmedo; (*sticky*) pegajoso
clamour, clamor (*US*) ['klæməʳ] *n* (*noise*) clamor *m*; (*protest*) protesta ■ *vi*: **to ~ for sth** clamar por algo, pedir algo a voces
clamp [klæmp] *n* abrazadera; (*laboratory clamp*) grapa; (*wheel clamp*) cepo ■ *vt* afianzar (con abrazadera)
▸ **clamp down on** *vt fus* (*government, police*) poner coto a
clampdown ['klæmpdaun] *n* restricción *f*; **there has been a ~ on terrorism** se ha puesto coto al terrorismo
clan [klæn] *n* clan *m*
clandestine [klæn'dɛstɪn] *adj* clandestino
clang [klæŋ] *n* estruendo ■ *vi* sonar con estruendo
clanger [klæŋəʳ] *n*: **to drop a ~** (*Brit col*) meter la pata
clansman ['klænzmən] *n* miembro del clan
clap [klæp] *vi* aplaudir ■ *vt* (*hands*) batir ■ *n* (*of hands*) palmada; **to ~ one's hands** dar palmadas, batir las palmas; **a ~ of thunder** un trueno
clapping ['klæpɪŋ] *n* aplausos *mpl*
claptrap ['klæptræp] *n* (*col*) gilipolleces *fpl*
claret ['klærət] *n* burdeos *m inv*
clarification [klærɪfɪ'keɪʃən] *n* aclaración *f*
clarify ['klærɪfaɪ] *vt* aclarar
clarinet [klærɪ'nɛt] *n* clarinete *m*
clarity ['klærɪtɪ] *n* claridad *f*
clash [klæʃ] *n* estruendo; (*fig*) choque *m* ■ *vi* enfrentarse; (*personalities, interests*) oponerse, chocar; (*colours*) desentonar; (*dates, events*) coincidir
clasp [klɑːsp] *n* broche *m*; (*on jewels*) cierre *m* ■ *vt* abrochar; (*hand*) apretar; (*embrace*) abrazar
class [klɑːs] *n* (*gen*) clase *f*; (*group, category*) clase *f*, categoría ■ *cpd* de clase ■ *vt* clasificar
class-conscious ['klɑːs'kɔnʃəs] *adj* clasista, con conciencia de clase
classic ['klæsɪk] *adj* clásico ■ *n* (*work*) obra clásica, clásico; **classics** *npl* (*Univ*) clásicas *fpl*
classical ['klæsɪkəl] *adj* clásico; **~ music** música clásica
classification [klæsɪfɪ'keɪʃən] *n* clasificación *f*
classified ['klæsɪfaɪd] *adj* (*information*) reservado
classified advertisement *n* anuncio por palabras
classify ['klæsɪfaɪ] *vt* clasificar
classless ['klɑːslɪs] *adj*: **~ society** sociedad *f* sin clases
classmate ['klɑːsmeɪt] *n* compañero(-a) de clase
classroom ['klɑːsrum] *n* aula
classy ['klɑːsɪ] *adj* (*col*) elegante, con estilo
clatter ['klætəʳ] *n* ruido, estruendo; (*of hooves*) trápala ■ *vi* hacer ruido *or* estruendo
clause [klɔːz] *n* cláusula; (*Ling*) oración *f*
claustrophobia [klɔːstrə'fəubɪə] *n* claustrofobia
claustrophobic [klɔːstrə'fəubɪk] *adj* claustrofóbico; **I feel ~** me entra claustrofobia
claw [klɔː] *n* (*of cat*) uña; (*of bird of prey*) garra; (*of lobster*) pinza; (*Tech*) garfio ■ *vi*: **to ~ at** arañar; (*tear*) desgarrar
clay [kleɪ] *n* arcilla
clean [kliːn] *adj* limpio; (*copy*) en limpio; (*lines*) bien definido ■ *vt* limpiar ■ *adv*: **he ~ forgot** lo olvidó por completo; **to come ~** (*col: admit guilt*) confesarlo todo; **to have a ~ driving licence** tener el carnet de conducir sin sanciones; **to ~ one's teeth** lavarse los dientes
▸ **clean off** *vt* limpiar
▸ **clean out** *vt* limpiar (a fondo)
▸ **clean up** *vt* limpiar, asear ■ *vi* (*fig: make profit*): **to ~ up on** sacar provecho de
clean-cut ['kliːn'kʌt] *adj* bien definido; (*outline*) nítido; (*person*) de buen parecer
cleaner ['kliːnəʳ] *n* encargado(-a) *m(f)* de la limpieza; (*also:* **dry cleaner**) tintorero(-a)
cleaning ['kliːnɪŋ] *n* limpieza
cleaning lady *n* señora de la limpieza, asistenta

cleanliness ['klɛnlɪnɪs] *n* limpieza
cleanse [klɛnz] *vt* limpiar
cleanser ['klɛnzəʳ] *n* detergente *m*; (*cosmetic*) loción *f or* crema limpiadora
clean-shaven ['kli:n'ʃeɪvn] *adj* bien afeitado
cleansing department ['klɛnzɪŋ-] *n* (*Brit*) servicio municipal de limpieza
clean sweep *n*: **to make a ~** (*Sport*) arrasar, barrer
clear [klɪəʳ] *adj* claro; (*road, way*) libre; (*profit*) neto; (*majority*) absoluto ■ *vt* (*space*) despejar, limpiar; (*Law: suspect*) absolver; (*obstacle*) salvar, saltar por encima de; (*debt*) liquidar; (*cheque*) aceptar; (*site, woodland*) desmontar ■ *vi* (*fog etc*) despejarse ■ *n*: **to be in the ~** (*out of debt*) estar libre de deudas; (*out of suspicion*) estar fuera de toda sospecha; (*out of danger*) estar fuera de peligro ■ *adv*: **~ of** a distancia de; **to make o.s. ~** explicarse claramente; **to make it ~ to sb that ...** hacer entender a algn que ...; **I have a ~ day tomorrow** mañana tengo el día libre; **to keep ~ of sth/sb** evitar algo/a algn; **to ~ a profit of ...** sacar una ganancia de ...; **to ~ the table** recoger *or* quitar la mesa
▸ **clear off** *vi* (*col: leave*) marcharse, mandarse mudar (*LAm*)
▸ **clear up** *vt* limpiar; (*mystery*) aclarar, resolver
clearance ['klɪərəns] *n* (*removal*) despeje *m*; (*permission*) acreditación *f*
clear-cut ['klɪə'kʌt] *adj* bien definido, claro
clearing ['klɪərɪŋ] *n* (*in wood*) claro
clearing bank *n* (*Brit*) banco central
clearing house *n* (*Comm*) cámara de compensación
clearly ['klɪəlɪ] *adv* claramente
clearway ['klɪəweɪ] *n* (*Brit*) *carretera en la que no se puede estacionar*
cleaver ['kli:və] *n* cuchilla (de carnicero)
clef [klɛf] *n* (*Mus*) clave *f*
cleft [klɛft] *n* (*in rock*) grieta, hendedura
clemency ['klɛmənsɪ] *n* clemencia
clench [klɛntʃ] *vt* apretar, cerrar
clergy ['klə:dʒɪ] *n* clero
clergyman ['klə:dʒɪmən] *n* clérigo
clerical ['klɛrɪkəl] *adj* de oficina; (*Rel*) clerical; (*error*) de copia
clerk [klɑ:k] (*US*) [klə:k] *n* oficinista *m/f*; (*US*) dependiente(-a) *m(f)*, vendedor(a) *m(f)*; **C~ of the Court** secretario(-a) de juzgado
clever ['klɛvəʳ] *adj* (*mentally*) inteligente, listo; (*skilful*) hábil; (*device, arrangement*) ingenioso
cleverly ['klɛvəlɪ] *adv* ingeniosamente
clew [klu:] *n* (*US*) = **clue**
cliché ['kli:ʃeɪ] *n* cliché *m*, frase *f* hecha
click [klɪk] *vt* (*tongue*) chasquear ■ *vi* (*Comput*) hacer clic; **to ~ one's heels** taconear
clickable ['klɪkəbl] *adj* (*Comput*) cliqueable
client ['klaɪənt] *n* cliente *m/f*
clientele [kli:ɑ̃:n'tɛl] *n* clientela
cliff [klɪf] *n* acantilado
cliffhanger ['klɪfhæŋəʳ] *n*: **it was a ~** estuvimos *etc* en ascuas hasta el final
climactic [klaɪ'mæktɪk] *adj* culminante
climate ['klaɪmɪt] *n* clima *m*; (*fig*) clima *m*, ambiente *m*
climax ['klaɪmæks] *n* punto culminante; (*of play etc*) clímax *m*; (*sexual climax*) orgasmo
climb [klaɪm] *vi* subir, trepar; (*plane*) elevarse, remontar el vuelo ■ *vt* (*stairs*) subir; (*tree*) trepar a; (*mountain*) escalar ■ *n* subida, ascenso; **to ~ over a wall** saltar una tapia
▸ **climb down** *vi* (*fig*) volverse atrás
climbdown ['klaɪmdaun] *n* vuelta atrás
climber ['klaɪməʳ] *n* escalador(a) *m(f)*
climbing ['klaɪmɪŋ] *n* escalada
clinch [klɪntʃ] *vt* (*deal*) cerrar; (*argument*) rematar
clincher ['klɪntʃəʳ] *n* (*col*): **that was the ~ for me** eso me hizo decidir
cling [klɪŋ] (*pt, pp* **clung**) [klʌŋ] *vi*: **to ~ (to)** agarrarse (a); (*clothes*) pegarse (a)
clingfilm ['klɪŋfɪlm] *n* plástico adherente
clinic ['klɪnɪk] *n* clínica
clinical ['klɪnɪkl] *adj* clínico; (*fig*) frío, impasible
clink [klɪŋk] *vi* tintinear
clip [klɪp] *n* (*for hair*) horquilla; (*also*: **paper clip**) sujetapapeles *m inv*, clip *m*; (*clamp*) grapa ■ *vt* (*cut*) cortar; (*hedge*) podar; (*also*: **clip together**) unir
clippers ['klɪpəz] *npl* (*for gardening*) tijeras *fpl* de podar; (*for hair*) maquinilla *sg*; (*for nails*) cortauñas *m inv*
clipping ['klɪpɪŋ] *n* (*from newspaper*) recorte *m*
clique [kli:k] *n* camarilla
cloak [kləuk] *n* capa, manto ■ *vt* (*fig*) encubrir, disimular
cloakroom ['kləukrum] *n* guardarropa *m*; (*Brit: WC*) lavabo, aseos *mpl*, baño (*esp LAm*)
clobber ['klɔbəʳ] *n* (*col*) bártulos *mpl*, trastos *mpl* ■ *vt* dar una paliza a
clock [klɔk] *n* reloj *m*; (*in taxi*) taxímetro; **to work against the ~** trabajar contra reloj; **around the ~** las veinticuatro horas; **to sleep round the ~** dormir un día entero; **30,000 on the ~** (*Aut*) treinta mil millas en el cuentakilómetros
▸ **clock in, clock on** *vi* fichar, picar
▸ **clock off, clock out** *vi* fichar *or* picar la salida
▸ **clock up** *vt* hacer

clockwise ['klɔkwaɪz] *adv* en el sentido de las agujas del reloj
clockwork ['klɔkwəːk] *n* aparato de relojería ■ *adj* (*toy, train*) de cuerda
clog [klɔg] *n* zueco, chanclo ■ *vt* atascar ■ *vi* atascarse
cloister ['klɔɪstəʳ] *n* claustro
clone [kləun] *n* clon *m*
close [*adj, adv* kləus, *vb, n* kləuz] *adj* cercano, próximo; (*near*): **~ (to)** cerca (de); (*print, weave*) tupido, compacto; (*friend*) íntimo; (*connection*) estrecho; (*examination*) detallado, minucioso; (*weather*) bochornoso; (*atmosphere*) sofocante; (*room*) mal ventilado ■ *adv* cerca; **~ by, ~ at hand** *adj, adv* muy cerca; **~ to** *prep* cerca de; **to have a ~ shave** (*fig*) escaparse por un pelo; **how ~ is Edinburgh to Glasgow?** ¿qué distancia hay de Edimburgo a Glasgow?; **at ~ quarters** de cerca ■ *vt* cerrar; (*end*) concluir, terminar ■ *vi* (*shop etc*) cerrar; (*end*) concluir(se), terminar(se) ■ *n* (*end*) fin *m*, final *m*, conclusión *f*; **to bring sth to a ~** terminar algo
▸ **close down** *vi* cerrar definitivamente
▸ **close in** *vi* (*hunters*) acercarse rodeando, rodear; (*evening, night*) caer; (*fog*) cerrarse; **to ~ in on sb** rodear *or* cercar a algn; **the days are closing in** los días son cada vez más cortos
▸ **close off** *vt* (*area*) cerrar al tráfico *or* al público
closed [kləuzd] *adj* (*shop etc*) cerrado
closed-circuit ['kləuzd'səːkɪt] *adj*: **~ television** televisión *f* por circuito cerrado
closed shop *n empresa en la que todo el personal está afiliado a un sindicato*
close-knit ['kləus'nɪt] *adj* (*fig*) muy unido
closely ['kləuslɪ] *adv* (*study*) con detalle; (*listen*) con atención; (*watch*) de cerca; **we are ~ related** somos parientes cercanos; **a ~ guarded secret** un secreto rigurosamente guardado
close season [kləuz-] *n* (*Football*) temporada de descanso; (*Hunting*) veda
closet ['klɔzɪt] *n* (*cupboard*) armario, placar(d) *m* (*LAm*)
close-up ['kləusʌp] *n* primer plano
closing ['kləuzɪŋ] *adj* (*stages, remarks*) último, final; **~ price** (*Stock Exchange*) cotización *f* de cierre
closing time *n* hora de cierre
closure ['kləuʒəʳ] *n* cierre *m*
clot [klɔt] *n* (*gen: also:* **blood clot**) embolia; (*col: idiot*) imbécil *m/f* ■ *vi* (*blood*) coagularse
cloth [klɔθ] *n* (*material*) tela, paño; (*table cloth*) mantel *m*; (*rag*) trapo
clothe [kləuð] *vt* vestir; (*fig*) revestir
clothes [kləuðz] *npl* ropa *sg*; **to put one's ~ on** vestirse, ponerse la ropa; **to take one's ~ off** desvestirse, desnudarse
clothes brush *n* cepillo (para la ropa)
clothes line *n* cuerda (para tender la ropa)
clothes peg, clothes pin (US) *n* pinza
clothing ['kləuðɪŋ] *n* = **clothes**
clotted cream ['klɔtɪd-] *n nata muy espesa*
cloud [klaud] *n* nube *f*; (*storm cloud*) nubarrón *m* ■ *vt* (*liquid*) enturbiar; **every ~ has a silver lining** no hay mal que por bien no venga; **to ~ the issue** empañar el problema
▸ **cloud over** *vi* (*also fig*) nublarse
cloudburst ['klaudbəːst] *n* chaparrón *m*
cloud-cuckoo-land ['klaud'kukuː'lænd] *n* Babia
cloudy ['klaudɪ] *adj* nublado; (*liquid*) turbio
clout [klaut] *n* (*fig*) influencia, peso ■ *vt* dar un tortazo a
clove [kləuv] *n* clavo; **~ of garlic** diente *m* de ajo
clover ['kləuvəʳ] *n* trébol *m*
clown [klaun] *n* payaso ■ *vi* (*also:* **clown about, clown around**) hacer el payaso
cloying ['klɔɪɪŋ] *adj* (*taste*) empalagoso
club [klʌb] *n* (*society*) club *m*; (*weapon*) porra, cachiporra; (*also:* **golf club**) palo ■ *vt* aporrear ■ *vi*: **to ~ together** (*join forces*) unir fuerzas; **clubs** *npl* (*Cards*) tréboles *mpl*
club car *n* (*US Rail*) coche *m* salón
club class *n* (*Aviat*) clase *f* preferente
clubhouse ['klʌbhaus] *n local social, sobre todo en clubs deportivos*
club soda *n* (US) soda
cluck [klʌk] *vi* cloquear
clue [kluː] *n* pista; (*in crosswords*) indicación *f*; **I haven't a ~** no tengo ni idea
clued up, clued in (US) [kluːd-] *adj* (*col*) al tanto, al corriente
clueless ['kluːlɪs] *adj* (*col*) desorientado
clump [klʌmp] *n* (*of trees*) grupo
clumsy ['klʌmzɪ] *adj* (*person*) torpe; (*tool*) difícil de manejar
clung [klʌŋ] *pt, pp of* **cling**
cluster ['klʌstəʳ] *n* grupo; (*Bot*) racimo ■ *vi* agruparse, apiñarse
clutch [klʌtʃ] *n* (*Aut*) embrague *m*; (*pedal*) (pedal *m* de) embrague *m*; **to fall into sb's clutches** caer en las garras de algn ■ *vt* agarrar
clutter ['klʌtəʳ] *vt* (*also:* **clutter up**) atestar, llenar desordenadamente ■ *n* desorden *m*, confusión *f*
CM *abbr* (US) = **North Mariana Islands**
cm *abbr* (= *centimetre*) cm
CNAA *n abbr* (*Brit:* = *Council for National Academic Awards*) *organismo no universitario que otorga diplomas*

CND *n abbr* (*Brit*: = *Campaign for Nuclear Disarmament*) *plataforma pro desarme nuclear*
CO *n abbr* = **commanding officer**; (*Brit*) = **Commonwealth Office** ■ *abbr* (*US*) = **Colorado**
Co. *abbr* = **county**; **company**
c/o *abbr* (= *care of*) c/a, a/c
coach [kəutʃ] *n* (*bus*) autocar *m* (*SP*), autobús *m*; (*horse-drawn*) coche *m*; (*ceremonial*) carroza; (*of train*) vagón *m*, coche *m*; (*Sport*) entrenador(a) *m(f)*, instructor(a) *m(f)* ■ *vt* (*Sport*) entrenar; (*student*) preparar, enseñar
coach trip *n* excursión *f* en autocar
coagulate [kəu'ægjuleɪt] *vi* coagularse
coal [kəul] *n* carbón *m*
coal face *n* frente *m* de carbón
coalfield ['kəulfi:ld] *n* yacimiento de carbón
coalition [kəuə'lɪʃən] *n* coalición *f*
coal man *n* carbonero
coalmine ['kəulmaɪn] *n* mina de carbón
coalminer ['kəulmaɪnəʳ] *n* minero (de carbón)
coalmining ['keulmaɪnɪŋ] *n* minería (de carbón)
coarse [kɔ:s] *adj* basto, burdo; (*vulgar*) grosero, ordinario
coast [kəust] *n* costa, litoral *m* ■ *vi* (*Aut*) ir en punto muerto
coastal ['kəustl] *adj* costero
coaster ['kəustəʳ] *n* buque *m* costero, barco de cabotaje
coastguard ['kəustgɑ:d] *n* guardacostas *m inv*
coastline ['kəustlaɪn] *n* litoral *m*
coat [kəut] *n* (*jacket*) chaqueta, saco (*LAm*); (*overcoat*) abrigo; (*of animal*) pelo, lana; (*of paint*) mano *f*, capa ■ *vt* cubrir, revestir
coat hanger *n* percha, gancha (*LAm*)
coating ['kəutɪŋ] *n* capa, baño
coat of arms *n* escudo de armas
co-author ['kəu'ɔ:θəʳ] *n* coautor(a) *m(f)*
coax [kəuks] *vt* engatusar
cob [kɔb] *n see* **corn**
cobbler ['kɔbləʳ] *n* zapatero (remendón)
cobbles ['kɔblz], **cobblestones** ['kɔblstəunz] *npl* adoquines *mpl*
COBOL ['kəubɔl] *n* COBOL *m*
cobra ['kəubrə] *n* cobra
cobweb ['kɔbwɛb] *n* telaraña
cocaine [kə'keɪn] *n* cocaína
cock [kɔk] *n* (*rooster*) gallo; (*male bird*) macho ■ *vt* (*gun*) amartillar
cock-a-hoop [kɔkə'hu:p] *adj*: **to be ~** estar más contento que unas pascuas
cockatoo [kɔkə'tu:] *n* cacatúa
cockerel ['kɔkərl] *n* gallito, gallo joven
cock-eyed ['kɔkaɪd] *adj* bizco; (*fig: crooked*) torcido; (*: idea*) disparatado
cockle ['kɔkl] *n* berberecho
cockney ['kɔknɪ] *n habitante de ciertos barrios de Londres*
cockpit ['kɔkpɪt] *n* (*in aircraft*) cabina
cockroach ['kɔkrəutʃ] *n* cucaracha
cocktail ['kɔkteɪl] *n* combinado, cóctel *m*; **prawn ~** cóctel *m* de gambas
cocktail cabinet *n* mueble-bar *m*
cocktail party *n* cóctel *m*
cocktail shaker [-ʃeɪkəʳ] *n* coctelera
cocky ['kɔkɪ] *adj* farruco, flamenco
cocoa ['kəukəu] *n* cacao; (*drink*) chocolate *m*
coconut ['kəukənʌt] *n* coco
cocoon [kə'ku:n] *n* capullo
cod [kɔd] *n* bacalao
COD *abbr* = **cash on delivery**; (*US*) = **collect on delivery**
code [kəud] *n* código; (*cipher*) clave *f*; (*Tel*) prefijo; **~ of behaviour** código de conducta; **~ of practice** código profesional
codeine ['kəudi:n] *n* codeína
codger [kɔdʒəʳ] *n* (*Brit col*): **an old ~** un abuelo
codicil ['kɔdɪsɪl] *n* codicilo
codify ['kəudɪfaɪ] *vt* codificar
cod-liver oil ['kɔdlɪvəʳ-] *n* aceite *m* de hígado de bacalao
co-driver ['kəu'draɪvəʳ] *n* (*in race*) copiloto *m/f*; (*of lorry*) segundo conductor *m*
co-ed ['kəuɛd] *adj abbr* = **coeducational** ■ *n abbr* (*US*: = *female student*) *alumna de una universidad mixta*; (*Brit: school*) colegio mixto
coeducational [kəuɛdju'keɪʃənl] *adj* mixto
coerce [kəu'ə:s] *vt* forzar, coaccionar
coercion [kəu'ə:ʃən] *n* coacción *f*
coexistence ['kəuɪg'zɪstəns] *n* coexistencia
C. of C. *n abbr* = **chamber of commerce**
C of E *abbr* = **Church of England**
coffee ['kɔfɪ] *n* café *m*; **white ~**, (*US*) **~ with cream** café con leche
coffee bar *n* (*Brit*) cafetería
coffee bean *n* grano de café
coffee break *n* descanso (para tomar café)
coffee cup *n* taza de café, pocillo (*LAm*)
coffeepot ['kɔfɪpɔt] *n* cafetera
coffee table *n* mesita baja
coffin ['kɔfɪn] *n* ataúd *m*
C of I *abbr* = **Church of Ireland**
C of S *abbr* = **Church of Scotland**
cog [kɔg] *n* diente *m*
cogent ['kəudʒənt] *adj* lógico, convincente
cognac ['kɔnjæk] *n* coñac *m*
cogwheel ['kɔgwi:l] *n* rueda dentada
cohabit [kəu'hæbɪt] *vi* (*formal*): **to ~ (with sb)** cohabitar (con algn)
coherent [kəu'hɪərənt] *adj* coherente
cohesion [kəu'hi:ʒen] *n* cohesión *f*
cohesive [kəu'hi:sɪv] *adj* (*fig*) cohesivo, unido

COI *n abbr* (*Brit*: = *Central Office of Information*) *servicio de información gubernamental*
coil [kɔɪl] *n* rollo; (*of rope*) vuelta; (*of smoke*) espiral *f*; (*Aut, Elec*) bobina, carrete *m*; (*contraceptive*) DIU *m* ■ *vt* enrollar
coin [kɔɪn] *n* moneda ■ *vt* acuñar; (*word*) inventar, acuñar
coinage ['kɔɪnɪdʒ] *n* moneda
coin-box ['kɔɪnbɔks] *n* (*Brit*) caja recaudadora
coincide [kəuɪn'saɪd] *vi* coincidir
coincidence [kəu'ɪnsɪdəns] *n* casualidad *f*, coincidencia
coin-operated ['kɔɪn'ɔpəreɪtɪd] *adj* (*machine*) que funciona con monedas
Coke® [kəuk] *n* Coca Cola® *f*
coke [kəuk] *n* (*coal*) coque *m*
Col. *abbr* (= *colonel*) col; (US) = **Colorado**
COLA *n abbr* (*US*: = *cost-of-living adjustment*) *reajuste salarial de acuerdo con el coste de la vida*
colander ['kɔləndə^r] *n* escurridor *m*
cold [kəuld] *adj* frío ■ *n* frío; (*Med*) resfriado; **it's ~** hace frío; **to be ~** tener frío; **to catch a ~** coger un catarro, resfriarse, acatarrarse; **in ~ blood** a sangre fría; **the room's getting ~** está empezando a hacer frío en la habitación; **to give sb the ~ shoulder** tratar a algn con frialdad
cold-blooded ['kəuld'blʌdɪd] *adj* (*Zool*) de sangre fría
cold cream *n* crema
coldly ['kəuldlɪ] *adj* fríamente
cold sore *n* calentura, herpes *m* labial
cold sweat *n*: **to be in a ~ (about sth)** tener sudores fríos (por algo)
cold turkey *n* (*col*) mono
Cold War *n*: **the ~** la guerra fría
coleslaw ['kəulslɔ:] *n* ensalada de col con zanahoria
colic ['kɔlɪk] *n* cólico
colicky ['kɔlɪkɪ] *adj*: **to be ~** tener un cólico
collaborate [kə'læbəreɪt] *vi* colaborar
collaboration [kəlæbə'reɪʃən] *n* colaboración *f*; (*Pol*) colaboracionismo
collaborator [kə'læbəreɪtə^r] *n* colaborador(a) *m(f)*; (*Pol*) colaboracionista *m/f*
collage [kɔ'lɑ:ʒ] *n* collage *m*
collagen ['kɔlədʒən] *n* colágeno
collapse [kə'læps] *vi* (*gen*) hundirse, derrumbarse; (*Med*) sufrir un colapso ■ *n* (*gen*) hundimiento; (*Med*) colapso; (*of government*) caída; (*of plans, scheme*) fracaso; (*of business*) ruina
collapsible [kə'læpsəbl] *adj* plegable
collar ['kɔlə^r] *n* (*of coat, shirt*) cuello; (*for dog*) collar *m*; (*Tech*) collar *m* ■ *vt* (*col: person*) agarrar; (*: object*) birlar
collarbone ['kɔləbəun] *n* clavícula
collate [kɔ'leɪt] *vt* cotejar
collateral [kɔ'lætərəl] *n* (*Comm*) garantía subsidiaria
collation [kə'leɪʃən] *n* colación *f*
colleague ['kɔli:g] *n* colega *m/f*, compañero(-a) *m(f)*
collect [kə'lɛkt] *vt* reunir; (*as a hobby*) coleccionar; (*Brit: call and pick up*) recoger; (*wages*) cobrar; (*debts*) recaudar; (*donations, subscriptions*) colectar ■ *vi* (*crowd*) reunirse ■ *adv*: **to call ~** (*US Tel*) llamar a cobro revertido; **to ~ one's thoughts** reponerse, recobrar el dominio de sí mismo; **~ on delivery (COD)** (*US*) entrega contra reembolso
collection [kə'lɛkʃən] *n* colección *f*; (*of fares, wages*) cobro; (*of post*) recogida
collective [kə'lɛktɪv] *adj* colectivo
collective bargaining *n* negociación *f* del convenio colectivo
collector [kə'lɛktə^r] *n* coleccionista *m/f*; (*of taxes etc*) recaudador(a) *m(f)*; **~'s item** *or* **piece** pieza de coleccionista
college ['kɔlɪdʒ] *n* colegio; (*of technology, agriculture etc*) escuela
collide [kə'laɪd] *vi* chocar
collie ['kɔlɪ] *n* (*dog*) collie *m*, perro pastor escocés
colliery ['kɔlɪərɪ] *n* (*Brit*) mina de carbón
collision [kə'lɪʒən] *n* choque *m*, colisión *f*; **to be on a ~ course** (*also fig*) ir rumbo al desastre
colloquial [kə'ləukwɪəl] *adj* coloquial
collusion [kə'lu:ʒən] *n* confabulación *f*, connivencia; **in ~ with** en connivencia con
Colo. *abbr* (*US*) = **Colorado**
cologne [kə'ləun] *n* (*also*: **eau de cologne**) (agua de) colonia
Colombia [kə'lɔmbɪə] *n* Colombia
Colombian [kə'lɔmbɪən] *adj, n* colombiano(-a) *m(f)*
colon ['kəulən] *n* (*sign*) dos puntos; (*Med*) colon *m*
colonel ['kə:nl] *n* coronel *m*
colonial [kə'ləunɪəl] *adj* colonial
colonize ['kɔlənaɪz] *vt* colonizar
colonnade [kɔlə'neɪd] *n* columnata
colony ['kɔlənɪ] *n* colonia
color ['kʌlə^r] (*US*) = **colour**
Colorado beetle [kɔlə'rɑ:dəu-] *n* escarabajo de la patata
colossal [kə'lɔsl] *adj* colosal
colour, color (*US*) ['kʌlə^r] *n* color *m* ■ *vt* colorear, pintar; (*dye*) teñir ■ *vi* (*blush*) sonrojarse; **colours** *npl* (*of party, club*) colores *mpl*
colour bar, color bar (*US*) *n* segregación *f* racial

colour-blind, color-blind (*US*) ['kʌləblaɪnd] *adj* daltónico
coloured, colored (*US*) ['kʌləd] *adj* de color; (*photo*) en color; (*of race*) de color
colour film, color film (*US*) *n* película en color
colourful, colorful (*US*) ['kʌləful] *adj* lleno de color; (*person*) pintoresco
colouring, coloring (*US*) ['kʌlərɪŋ] *n* colorido, color; (*substance*) colorante *m*
colourless, colorless (*US*) ['kʌləlɪs] *adj* incoloro, sin color
colour scheme, color scheme (*US*) *n* combinación *f* de colores
colour supplement *n* (*Brit Press*) suplemento semanal *or* dominical
colour television, color television (*US*) *n* televisión *f* en color
colt [kəult] *n* potro
column ['kɔləm] *n* columna; (*fashion column, sports column etc*) sección *f*, columna; **the editorial ~** el editorial
columnist ['kɔləmnɪst] *n* columnista *m/f*
coma ['kəumə] *n* coma *m*
comb [kəum] *n* peine *m*; (*ornamental*) peineta ▪ *vt* (*hair*) peinar; (*area*) registrar a fondo, peinar
combat ['kɔmbæt] *n* combate *m* ▪ *vt* combatir
combination [kɔmbɪ'neɪʃən] *n* (*gen*) combinación *f*
combination lock *n* cerradura de combinación
combine [kəm'baɪn] *vt* combinar; (*qualities*) reunir ▪ *vi* combinarse ▪ *n* ['kɔmbaɪn] (*Econ*) cartel *m*; (*also*: **combine harvester**) cosechadora; **a combined effort** un esfuerzo conjunto
combine harvester *n* cosechadora
combo ['kɔmbəu] *n* (*jazz etc*) conjunto
combustion [kəm'bʌstʃən] *n* combustión *f*

KEYWORD

come [kʌm] (*pt* **came**, *pp* **come**) *vi* **1** (*movement towards*) venir; **to come running** venir corriendo; **come with me** ven conmigo
2 (*arrive*) llegar; **he's come here to work** ha venido aquí para trabajar; **to come home** volver a casa; **we've just come from Seville** acabamos de llegar de Sevilla; **coming!** ¡voy!
3 (*reach*): **to come to** llegar a; **the bill came to £40** la cuenta ascendía a cuarenta libras
4 (*occur*): **an idea came to me** se me ocurrió una idea; **if it comes to it** llegado el caso
5 (*be, become*): **to come loose/undone** *etc* aflojarse/desabrocharse, desatarse *etc*; **I've come to like him** por fin ha llegado a gustarme
▸ **come about** *vi* suceder, ocurrir
▸ **come across** *vt fus* (*person*) encontrarse con; (*thing*) encontrar
▪ *vi*: **to come across well/badly** causar buena/mala impresión
▸ **come away** *vi* (*leave*) marcharse; (*become detached*) desprenderse
▸ **come back** *vi* (*return*) volver; (*reply*): **can I come back to you on that one?** volvamos sobre ese punto
▸ **come by** *vt fus* (*acquire*) conseguir
▸ **come down** *vi* (*price*) bajar; (*building*) derrumbarse; (*be demolished*) ser derribado
▸ **come forward** *vi* presentarse
▸ **come from** *vt fus* (*place, source*) ser de
▸ **come in** *vi* (*visitor*) entrar; (*train, report*) llegar; (*fashion*) ponerse de moda; (*on deal etc*) entrar
▸ **come in for** *vt fus* (*criticism etc*) recibir
▸ **come into** *vt fus* (*money*) heredar; (*be involved*) tener que ver con; **to come into fashion** ponerse de moda
▸ **come off** *vi* (*button*) soltarse, desprenderse; (*attempt*) salir bien
▸ **come on** *vi* (*pupil, work, project*) marchar; (*lights*) encenderse; (*electricity*) volver; **come on!** ¡vamos!
▸ **come out** *vi* (*fact*) salir a la luz; (*book, sun*) salir; (*stain*) quitarse; **to come out (on strike)** declararse en huelga; **to come out for/against** declararse a favor/en contra de
▸ **come over** *vt fus*: **I don't know what's come over him!** ¡no sé lo que le pasa!
▸ **come round** *vi* (*after faint, operation*) volver en sí
▸ **come through** *vi* (*survive*) sobrevivir; (*telephone call*): **the call came through** recibimos la llamada
▸ **come to** *vi* (*wake*) volver en sí; (*total*) sumar; **how much does it come to?** ¿cuánto es en total?, ¿a cuánto asciende?
▸ **come under** *vt fus* (*heading*) entrar dentro de; (*influence*) estar bajo
▸ **come up** *vi* (*sun*) salir; (*problem*) surgir; (*event*) aproximarse; (*in conversation*) mencionarse
▸ **come up against** *vt fus* (*resistance etc*) tropezar con
▸ **come up to** *vt fus* llegar hasta; **the film didn't come up to our expectations** la película no fue tan buena como esperábamos
▸ **come up with** *vt fus* (*idea*) sugerir; (*money*) conseguir
▸ **come upon** *vt fus* (*find*) dar con

comeback ['kʌmbæk] *n* (*reaction*) reacción *f*; (*response*) réplica; **to make a ~** (*Theat*) volver a las tablas
comedian [kə'miːdɪən] *n* humorista *m*
comedienne [kəmiːdɪ'ɛn] *n* humorista
comedown ['kʌmdaun] *n* revés *m*
comedy ['kɔmɪdɪ] *n* comedia
comet ['kɔmɪt] *n* cometa *m*
comeuppance [kʌm'ʌpəns] *n*: **to get one's ~** llevar su merecido
comfort ['kʌmfət] *n* comodidad *f*, confort *m*; (*well-being*) bienestar *m*; (*solace*) consuelo; (*relief*) alivio ■ *vt* consolar; *see also* **comforts**
comfortable ['kʌmfətəbl] *adj* cómodo; (*income*) adecuado; (*majority*) suficiente; **I don't feel very ~ about it** la cosa me tiene algo preocupado
comfortably ['kʌmfətəblɪ] *adv* (*sit*) cómodamente; (*live*) holgadamente
comforter ['kʌmfətə^r] *n* (*US: pacifier*) chupete *m*; (*: bed cover*) colcha
comforts ['kʌmfəts] *npl* comodidades *fpl*
comfort station *n* (*US*) servicios *mpl*
comic ['kɔmɪk] *adj* (*also:* **comical**) cómico, gracioso ■ *n* (*magazine*) tebeo; (*for adults*) cómic *m*
comic strip *n* tira cómica
coming ['kʌmɪŋ] *n* venida, llegada ■ *adj* que viene; (*next*) próximo; (*future*) venidero; **~(s) and going(s)** *n(pl)* ir y venir *m*, ajetreo; **in the ~ weeks** en las próximas semanas
Comintern ['kɔmɪntəːn] *n* Comintern *m*
comma ['kɔmə] *n* coma
command [kə'mɑːnd] *n* orden *f*, mandato; (*Mil: authority*) mando; (*mastery*) dominio; (*Comput*) orden *f*, comando ■ *vt* (*troops*) mandar; (*give orders to*) mandar, ordenar; (*be able to get*) disponer de; (*deserve*) merecer; **to have at one's ~** (*money, resources etc*) disponer de; **to have/take ~ of** estar al/asumir el mando de
command economy *n* economía dirigida
commandeer [kɔmən'dɪə^r] *vt* requisar
commander [kə'mɑːndə^r] *n* (*Mil*) comandante *m/f*, jefe(-a) *m(f)*
commanding [kə'mɑːndɪŋ] *adj* (*appearance*) imponente; (*voice, tone*) imperativo; (*lead*) abrumador(-a); (*position*) dominante
commanding officer *n* comandante *m*
commandment [kə'mɑːndmənt] *n* (*Rel*) mandamiento
command module *n* módulo de mando
commando [kə'mɑːndəu] *n* comando
commemorate [kə'mɛməreɪt] *vt* conmemorar
commemoration [kəmɛmə'reɪʃən] *n* conmemoración *f*
commemorative [kə'mɛmərətɪv] *adj* conmemorativo
commence [kə'mɛns] *vt, vi* comenzar
commend [kə'mɛnd] *vt* (*praise*) elogiar, alabar; (*recommend*) recomendar; (*entrust*) encomendar
commendable [kə'mɛndəbl] *adj* encomiable
commendation [kɔmɛn'deɪʃən] *n* (*for bravery etc*) elogio, encomio
commensurate [kə'mɛnʃərɪt] *adj*: **~ with** en proporción a
comment ['kɔmɛnt] *n* comentario ■ *vt*: **to ~ that** comentar *or* observar que ■ *vi*: **to ~ (on)** comentar, hacer comentarios (sobre); **"no ~"** "no tengo nada que decir", "sin comentarios"
commentary ['kɔməntərɪ] *n* comentario
commentator ['kɔmənteɪtə^r] *n* comentarista *m/f*
commerce ['kɔməːs] *n* comercio
commercial [kə'məːʃəl] *adj* comercial ■ *n* (*TV*) anuncio
commercial bank *n* banco comercial
commercial break *n* intermedio para publicidad
commercialism [kə'məːʃəlɪzəm] *n* comercialismo
commercial television *n* televisión *f* comercial
commercial vehicle *n* vehículo comercial
commiserate [kə'mɪzəreɪt] *vi*: **to ~ with** compadecerse de, condolerse de
commission [kə'mɪʃən] *n* (*committee, fee, order for work of art etc*) comisión *f*; (*act*) perpetración *f* ■ *vt* (*Mil*) nombrar; (*work of art*) encargar; **out of ~** (*machine*) fuera de servicio; **~ of inquiry** comisión *f* investigadora; **I get 10% ~** me dan el diez por ciento de comisión; **to ~ sb to do sth** encargar a algn que haga algo; **to ~ sth from sb** (*painting etc*) encargar algo a algn
commissionaire [kəmɪʃə'nɛə^r] *n* (*Brit*) portero, conserje *m*
commissioner [kə'mɪʃənə^r] *n* comisario; (*Police*) comisario *m* de policía
commit [kə'mɪt] *vt* (*act*) cometer; (*to sb's care*) entregar; **to ~ o.s. (to do)** comprometerse (a hacer); **to ~ suicide** suicidarse; **to ~ sb for trial** remitir a algn al tribunal
commitment [kə'mɪtmənt] *n* compromiso
committed [kə'mɪtɪd] *adj* (*writer, politician etc*) comprometido
committee [kə'mɪtɪ] *n* comité *m*; **to be on a ~** ser miembro(-a) de un comité
committee meeting *n* reunión *f* del comité
commodious [kə'məudɪəs] *adj* grande, espacioso

commodity [kə'mɔdɪtɪ] *n* mercancía
commodity exchange *n* bolsa de productos *or* de mercancías
commodity market *n* mercado de productos básicos
commodore ['kɔmədɔːʳ] *n* comodoro
common ['kɔmən] *adj* (*gen*) común; (*pej*) ordinario ▪ *n* campo común; **in ~** en común; **in ~ use** de uso corriente
common cold *n*: **the ~** el resfriado
common denominator *n* común denominador *m*
commoner ['kɔmənəʳ] *n* plebeyo(-a)
common land *n* campo comunal, ejido
common law *n* ley *f* consuetudinaria
common-law ['kɔmənlɔː] *adj*: **~ wife** esposa de hecho
commonly ['kɔmənlɪ] *adv* comúnmente
Common Market *n* Mercado Común
commonplace ['kɔmənpleɪs] *adj* corriente
commonroom ['kɔmənrum] *n* sala de reunión
Commons ['kɔmənz] *npl* (*Brit Pol*): **the ~** (la Cámara de) los Comunes
common sense *n* sentido común
Commonwealth ['kɔmənwɛlθ] *n*: **the ~** la Comunidad (Británica) de Naciones, la Commonwealth; *ver nota*

COMMONWEALTH

La *Commonwealth* es la asociación de estados soberanos independientes y territorios asociados que formaban parte del antiguo Imperio Británico. Éste pasó a llamarse así después de la Segunda Guerra Mundial, aunque ya desde 1931 se le conocía como "British Commonwealth of Nations". Todos los estados miembros reconocen al monarca británico como "Head of the Commonwealth".

commotion [kə'məuʃən] *n* tumulto, confusión *f*
communal ['kɔmjuːnl] *adj* comunal; (*kitchen*) común
commune ['kɔmjuːn] *n* (*group*) comuna ▪ *vi* [kə'mjuːn]: **to ~ with** comunicarse con
communicate [kə'mjuːnɪkeɪt] *vt* comunicar ▪ *vi*: **to ~ (with)** comunicarse (con)
communication [kəmjuːnɪ'keɪʃən] *n* comunicación *f*
communication cord *n* (*Brit*) timbre *m* de alarma
communications network *n* red *f* de comunicaciones
communications satellite *n* satélite *m* de comunicaciones
communicative [kə'mjuːnɪkətɪv] *adj* comunicativo
communion [kə'mjuːnɪən] *n* (*also*: **Holy Communion**) comunión *f*
communiqué [kə'mjuːnɪkeɪ] *n* comunicado, parte *m*
communism ['kɔmjunɪzəm] *n* comunismo
communist ['kɔmjunɪst] *adj, n* comunista *m/f*
community [kə'mjuːnɪtɪ] *n* comunidad *f*; (*large group*) colectividad *f*; (*local*) vecindario
community centre *n* centro social
community chest *n* (*US*) fondo social
community health centre *n* centro médico, casa de salud
community spirit *n* civismo
commutation ticket [kɔmju'teɪʃən-] *n* (*US*) billete *m* de abono
commute [kə'mjuːt] *vi viajar a diario de casa al trabajo* ▪ *vt* conmutar
commuter [kə'mjuːtəʳ] *n persona que viaja a diario de casa al trabajo*
compact [kəm'pækt] *adj* compacto; (*style*) conciso; (*dense*) apretado ▪ *n* ['kɔmpækt] (*pact*) pacto; (*also*: **powder compact**) polvera
compact disc *n* compact disc *m*, disco compacto
compact disc player *n* lector *m or* reproductor *m* de discos compactos
companion [kəm'pænɪən] *n* compañero(-a)
companionship [kəm'pænjənʃɪp] *n* compañerismo
companionway [kəm'pænjənweɪ] *n* (*Naut*) escalerilla
company ['kʌmpənɪ] *n* (*gen*) compañía; (*Comm*) empresa, compañía; **to keep sb ~** acompañar a algn; **Smith and C~** Smith y Compañía
company car *n* coche *m* de la empresa
company director *n* director(a) *m(f)* de empresa
company secretary *n* (*Brit*) administrador(a) *m(f)* de empresa
comparable ['kɔmpərəbl] *adj* comparable
comparative [kəm'pærətɪv] *adj* (*freedom, luxury, cost*) relativo; (*study, linguistics*) comparado
comparatively [kəm'pærətɪvlɪ] *adv* (*relatively*) relativamente
compare [kəm'pɛəʳ] *vt* comparar ▪ *vi*: **to ~ (with)** poder compararse (con); **compared with** *or* **to** comparado con *or* a; **how do the prices ~?** ¿cómo son los precios en comparación?
comparison [kəm'pærɪsn] *n* comparación *f*; **in ~ (with)** en comparación (con)

compartment [kəm'pɑ:tmənt] *n* compartim(i)ento; (*Rail*) departamento, compartimento
compass ['kʌmpəs] *n* brújula; **compasses** *npl* compás *m*; **within the ~ of** al alcance de
compassion [kəm'pæʃən] *n* compasión *f*
compassionate [kəm'pæʃənɪt] *adj* compasivo; **on ~ grounds** por compasión
compassionate leave *n* permiso por asuntos familiares
compatibility [kəmpætɪ'bɪlɪtɪ] *n* compatibilidad *f*
compatible [kəm'pætɪbl] *adj* compatible
compel [kəm'pɛl] *vt* obligar
compelling [kəm'pɛlɪŋ] *adj* (*fig: argument*) convincente
compendium [kəm'pɛndɪəm] *n* compendio
compensate ['kɔmpənseɪt] *vt* compensar ■ *vi*: **to ~ for** compensar
compensation [kɔmpən'seɪʃən] *n* (*for loss*) indemnización *f*
compère ['kɔmpɛəʳ] *n* presentador(a) *m(f)*
compete [kəm'pi:t] *vi* (*take part*) competir; (*vie with*) competir, hacer la competencia
competence ['kɔmpɪtəns] *n* capacidad *f*, aptitud *f*
competent ['kɔmpɪtənt] *adj* competente, capaz
competing [kəm'pi:tɪŋ] *adj* (*rival*) competidor(-a); (*ideas*) contrapuesto
competition [kɔmpɪ'tɪʃən] *n* (*contest*) concurso; (*Sport*) competición *f*; (*Econ: rivalry*) competencia; **in ~ with** en competencia con
competitive [kəm'pɛtɪtɪv] *adj* (*Econ, Sport*) competitivo; (*spirit*) competidor(a), de competencia; (*selection*) por concurso
competitor [kəm'pɛtɪtəʳ] *n* (*rival*) competidor(a) *m(f)*; (*participant*) concursante *m/f*
compile [kəm'paɪl] *vt* recopilar
complacency [kəm'pleɪsnsɪ] *n* autosatisfacción *f*
complacent [kəm'pleɪsənt] *adj* autocomplaciente
complain [kəm'pleɪn] *vi* (*gen*) quejarse; (*Comm*) reclamar
complaint [kəm'pleɪnt] *n* (*gen*) queja; (*Comm*) reclamación *f*; (*Law*) demanda, querella; (*Med*) enfermedad *f*
complement ['kɔmplɪmənt] *n* complemento; (*esp ship's crew*) dotación *f* ■ *vt* ['kɔmplɪmɛnt] (*enhance*) complementar
complementary [kɔmplɪ'mɛntərɪ] *adj* complementario
complete [kəm'pli:t] *adj* (*full*) completo; (*finished*) acabado ■ *vt* (*fulfil*) completar; (*finish*) acabar; (*a form*) rellenar; **it's a ~ disaster** es un desastre total
completely [kəm'pli:tlɪ] *adv* completamente
completion [kəm'pli:ʃən] *n* (*gen*) conclusión *f*, terminación *f*; **to be nearing ~** estar a punto de terminarse; **on ~ of contract** cuando se realice el contrato
complex ['kɔmplɛks] *adj* complejo ■ *n* (*gen*) complejo
complexion [kəm'plɛkʃən] *n* (*of face*) tez *f*, cutis *m*; (*fig*) aspecto
complexity [kəm'plɛksɪtɪ] *n* complejidad *f*
compliance [kəm'plaɪəns] *n* (*submission*) sumisión *f*; (*agreement*) conformidad *f*; **in ~ with** de acuerdo con
compliant [kəm'plaɪənt] *adj* sumiso; conforme
complicate ['kɔmplɪkeɪt] *vt* complicar
complicated ['kɔmplɪkeɪtɪd] *adj* complicado
complication [kɔmplɪ'keɪʃən] *n* complicación *f*
complicity [kəm'plɪsɪtɪ] *n* complicidad *f*
compliment ['kɔmplɪmənt] *n* (*formal*) cumplido; (*flirtation*) piropo ■ *vt* felicitar; **compliments** *npl* saludos *mpl*; **to pay sb a ~** (*formal*) hacer cumplidos a algn; (*flirt*) piropear, echar piropos a algn; **to ~ sb (on sth/on doing sth)** felicitar a algn (por algo/ por haber hecho algo)
complimentary [kɔmplɪ'mɛntərɪ] *adj* elogioso; (*copy*) de regalo; **~ ticket** invitación *f*
compliments slip *n* saluda *m*
comply [kəm'plaɪ] *vi*: **to ~ with** acatar
component [kəm'pəunənt] *adj* componente ■ *n* (*Tech*) pieza, componente *m*
compose [kəm'pəuz] *vt* componer; **to be composed of** componerse de, constar de; **to ~ o.s.** tranquilizarse
composed [kəm'pəuzd] *adj* sosegado
composer [kəm'pəuzəʳ] *n* (*Mus*) compositor(a) *m(f)*
composite ['kɔmpəzɪt] *adj* compuesto; **~ motion** (*Comm*) moción *f* compuesta
composition [kɔmpə'zɪʃən] *n* composición *f*
compositor [kəm'pɔzɪtəʳ] *n* (*Typ*) cajista *m/f*
compos mentis ['kɔmpəs'mɛntɪs] *adj*: **to be ~** estar en su sano juicio
compost ['kɔmpɔst] *n* abono
compost heap *n* *montón de basura orgánica para abono*
composure [kəm'pəuʒəʳ] *n* serenidad *f*, calma
compound ['kɔmpaund] *n* (*Chem*) compuesto; (*Ling*) término compuesto; (*enclosure*) recinto ■ *adj* (*gen*) compuesto; (*fracture*) complicado ■ *vt* [kəm'paund] (*fig: problem, difficulty*) agravar
comprehend [kɔmprɪ'hɛnd] *vt* comprender

comprehension [kɔmprɪ'hɛnʃən] *n* comprensión *f*
comprehensive [kɔmprɪ'hɛnsɪv] *adj* (*broad*) extenso; (*general*) de conjunto; **~ (school)** *n* *centro estatal de enseñanza secundaria*, ≈ Instituto Nacional de Bachillerato (*SP*); *ver nota*

COMPREHENSIVE SCHOOL

En los años 60 se creó un nuevo tipo de centro educativo de enseñanza secundaria (aproximadamente de los once años en adelante) denominado *comprehensive school*, abierto a todos los alumnos independientemente de sus capacidades, con el que se intentó poner fin a la división tradicional entre centros de enseñanzas teóricas para acceder a la educación superior ("grammar schools") y otros de enseñanzas básicamente profesionales ("secondary modern schools").

comprehensive insurance policy *n* seguro a todo riesgo
compress [kəm'prɛs] *vt* comprimir; (*Inform*) comprimir ■ *n* ['kɔmprɛs] (*Med*) compresa
compression [kəm'prɛʃən] *n* compresión *f*
comprise [kəm'praɪz] *vt* (*also*: **be comprised of**) comprender, constar de
compromise ['kɔmprəmaɪz] *n* solución *f* intermedia; (*agreement*) arreglo ■ *vt* comprometer ■ *vi* transigir, transar (*LAm*) ■ *cpd* (*decision, solution*) de término medio
compulsion [kəm'pʌlʃən] *n* obligación *f*; **under ~** a la fuerza, por obligación
compulsive [kəm'pʌlsɪv] *adj* compulsivo
compulsory [kəm'pʌlsərɪ] *adj* obligatorio
compulsory purchase *n* expropiación *f*
compunction [kəm'pʌŋkʃən] *n* escrúpulo; **to have no ~ about doing sth** no tener escrúpulos en hacer algo
computer [kəm'pju:tə^r] *n* ordenador *m*, computador *m*, computadora
computer game *n* juego de ordenador
computerize [kəm'pju:təraɪz] *vt* (*data*) computerizar; (*system*) informatizar
computer language *n* lenguaje *m* de ordenador *or* computadora
computer literate *adj*: **to be ~** tener conocimientos de informática a nivel de usuario
computer peripheral *n* periférico
computer program *n* programa *m* informático *or* de ordenador
computer programmer *n* programador(a) *m(f)*
computer programming *n* programación *f*
computer science *n* informática
computing [kəm'pju:tɪŋ] *n* (*activity*) informática
comrade ['kɔmrɪd] *n* compañero(-a)
comradeship ['kɔmrɪdʃɪp] *n* camaradería, compañerismo
comsat® ['kɔmsæt] *n abbr* = **communications satellite**
con [kɔn] *vt* timar, estafar ■ *n* timo, estafa; **to ~ sb into doing sth** (*col*) engañar a algn para que haga algo
concave ['kɔn'keɪv] *adj* cóncavo
conceal [kən'si:l] *vt* ocultar; (*thoughts etc*) disimular
concede [kən'si:d] *vt* reconocer; (*game*) darse por vencido en; (*territory*) ceder ■ *vi* darse por vencido
conceit [kən'si:t] *n* orgullo, presunción *f*
conceited [kən'si:tɪd] *adj* orgulloso
conceivable [kən'si:vəbl] *adj* concebible; **it is ~ that ...** es posible que ...
conceivably [kən'si:vəblɪ] *adv*: **he may ~ be right** es posible que tenga razón
conceive [kən'si:v] *vt, vi* concebir; **to ~ of sth/of doing sth** imaginar algo/imaginarse haciendo algo
concentrate ['kɔnsəntreɪt] *vi* concentrarse ■ *vt* concentrar
concentration [kɔnsən'treɪʃən] *n* concentración *f*
concentration camp *n* campo de concentración
concentric [kən'sɛntrɪk] *adj* concéntrico
concept ['kɔnsɛpt] *n* concepto
conception [kən'sɛpʃən] *n* (*idea*) concepto, idea; (*Biol*) concepción *f*
concern [kən'sə:n] *n* (*matter*) asunto; (*Comm*) empresa; (*anxiety*) preocupación *f* ■ *vt* tener que ver con; (*affect*) atañer, concernir; **to be concerned (about)** interesarse (por), preocuparse (por); **to be concerned with** tratar de; **"to whom it may ~"** "a quien corresponda"; **the department concerned** (*under discussion*) el departamento en cuestión; (*relevant*) el departamento competente; **as far as I am concerned** en cuanto a mí, por lo que a mí se refiere
concerning [kən'sə:nɪŋ] *prep* sobre, acerca de
concert ['kɔnsət] *n* concierto
concerted [kən'sə:təd] *adj* (*efforts etc*) concertado
concert hall *n* sala de conciertos
concertina [kɔnsə'ti:nə] *n* concertina
concerto [kən'tʃə:təu] *n* concierto
concession [kən'sɛʃən] *n* concesión *f*; (*price concession*) descuento; **tax ~** privilegio fiscal

concessionaire [kənsɛʃə'nɛəʳ] *n* concesionario(-a)
concessionary [kən'sɛʃənərɪ] *adj* (*ticket, fare*) con descuento, a precio reducido
conciliation [kənsɪlɪ'eɪʃən] *n* conciliación *f*
conciliatory [kən'sɪlɪətrɪ] *adj* conciliador(a)
concise [kən'saɪs] *adj* conciso
conclave ['kɔnkleɪv] *n* cónclave *m*
conclude [kən'klu:d] *vt* (*finish*) concluir; (*treaty etc*) firmar; (*agreement*) llegar a; (*decide*): **to ~ that ...** llegar a la conclusión de que ... ▪ *vi* (*events*) concluir, terminar
concluding [kən'klu:dɪŋ] *adj* (*remarks etc*) final
conclusion [kən'klu:ʒən] *n* conclusión *f*; **to come to the ~ that** llegar a la conclusión de que
conclusive [kən'klu:sɪv] *adj* decisivo, concluyente
conclusively [kən'klu:sɪvlɪ] *adv* concluyentemente
concoct [kən'kɔkt] *vt* (*food, drink*) preparar; (*story*) inventar; (*plot*) tramar
concoction [kən'kɔkʃən] *n* (*food*) mezcla; (*drink*) brebaje *m*
concord ['kɔŋkɔ:d] *n* (*harmony*) concordia; (*treaty*) acuerdo
concourse ['kɔŋkɔ:s] *n* (*hall*) vestíbulo
concrete ['kɔnkri:t] *n* hormigón *m* ▪ *adj* concreto
concrete mixer *n* hormigonera
concur [kən'kə:ʳ] *vi* estar de acuerdo
concurrently [kən'kʌrntlɪ] *adv* al mismo tiempo
concussion [kən'kʌʃən] *n* conmoción *f* cerebral
condemn [kən'dɛm] *vt* condenar
condemnation [kɔndɛm'neɪʃən] *n* (*gen*) condena; (*blame*) censura
condensation [kɔndɛn'seɪʃən] *n* condensación *f*
condense [kən'dɛns] *vi* condensarse ▪ *vt* condensar; (*text*) abreviar
condensed milk *n* leche *f* condensada
condescend [kɔndɪ'sɛnd] *vi* condescender; **to ~ to sb** tratar a algn con condescendencia; **to ~ to do sth** dignarse hacer algo
condescending [kɔndɪ'sɛndɪŋ] *adj* superior
condition [kən'dɪʃən] *n* condición *f*; (*of health*) estado; (*disease*) enfermedad *f* ▪ *vt* condicionar; **on ~ that** a condición (de) que; **weather conditions** condiciones atmosféricas; **in good/poor ~** en buenas/malas condiciones, en buen/mal estado; **conditions of sale** condiciones de venta
conditional [kən'dɪʃənl] *adj* condicional
conditioned reflex [kən'dɪʃənd-] *n* reflejo condicionado
conditioner [kən'dɪʃənəʳ] *n* (*for hair*) suavizante *m*, acondicionador *m*
condo ['kɔndəu] *n abbr* (*US col*) = **condominium**
condolences [kən'dəulənsɪz] *npl* pésame *msg*
condom ['kɔndəm] *n* condón *m*
condominium [kɔndə'mɪnɪəm] *n* (*US: building*) bloque *m* de pisos *or* apartamentos (*propiedad de quienes lo habitan*), condominio (*LAm*); (*: apartment*) piso *or* apartamento (en propiedad), condominio (*LAm*)
condone [kən'dəun] *vt* condonar
conducive [kən'dju:sɪv] *adj*: **~ to** conducente a
conduct ['kɔndʌkt] *n* conducta, comportamiento ▪ *vt* [kən'dʌkt] (*lead*) conducir; (*manage*) llevar, dirigir; (*Mus*) dirigir ▪ *vi* (*Mus*) llevar la batuta; **to ~ o.s.** comportarse
conducted tour *n* (*Brit*) visita con guía
conductor [kən'dʌktəʳ] *n* (*of orchestra*) director(a) *m(f)*; (*US: on train*) revisor(a) *m(f)*; (*on bus*) cobrador *m*; (*Elec*) conductor *m*
cone [kəun] *n* cono; (*pine cone*) piña; (*for ice cream*) cucurucho
confectioner [kən'fɛkʃənəʳ] *n* (*of cakes*) pastelero(-a); (*of sweets*) confitero(-a); **~'s (shop)** *n* pastelería; confitería
confectionery [kən'fɛkʃənrɪ] *n* pasteles *mpl*; dulces *mpl*
confederate [kən'fɛdrɪt] *adj* confederado ▪ *n* (*pej*) cómplice *m/f*; (*US History*) confederado(-a)
confederation [kənfɛdə'reɪʃən] *n* confederación *f*
confer [kən'fə:ʳ] *vt*: **~ (on)** otorgar (a) ▪ *vi* conferenciar; **to ~ (with sb about sth)** consultar (con algn sobre algo)
conference ['kɔnfərns] *n* (*meeting*) reunión *f*; (*convention*) congreso; **to be in ~** estar en una reunión
conference room *n* sala de conferencias
confess [kən'fɛs] *vt* confesar ▪ *vi* confesar; (*Rel*) confesarse
confession [kən'fɛʃən] *n* confesión *f*
confessional [kən'fɛʃənl] *n* confesionario
confessor [kən'fɛsəʳ] *n* confesor *m*
confetti [kən'fɛtɪ] *n* confeti *m*
confide [kən'faɪd] *vi*: **to ~ in** confiar en
confidence ['kɔnfɪdns] *n* (*gen: also:* **self-confidence**) confianza; (*secret*) confidencia; **in ~** (*speak, write*) en confianza; **to have (every) ~ that** estar seguro *or* confiado de que; **motion of no ~** moción *f* de censura; **to tell sb sth in strict ~** decir algo a algn de manera confidencial

confidence trick *n* timo
confident ['kɔnfɪdənt] *adj* seguro de sí mismo
confidential [kɔnfɪ'dɛnʃəl] *adj* confidencial; (*secretary*) de confianza
confidentiality [kɔnfɪdɛnʃɪ'ælɪtɪ] *n* confidencialidad *f*
configuration [kənfɪgju'reɪʃən] *n* (*Comput*) configuración *f*
confine [kən'faɪn] *vt* (*limit*) limitar; (*shut up*) encerrar; **to ~ o.s. to doing sth** limitarse a hacer algo
confined [kən'faɪnd] *adj* (*space*) reducido
confinement [kən'faɪnmənt] *n* (*prison*) reclusión *f*; (*Med*) parto; **in solitary ~** incomunicado
confines ['kɔnfaɪnz] *npl* confines *mpl*
confirm [kən'fə:m] *vt* confirmar
confirmation [kɔnfə'meɪʃən] *n* confirmación *f*
confirmed [kən'fə:md] *adj* empedernido
confiscate ['kɔnfɪskeɪt] *vt* confiscar
confiscation [kɔnfɪs'keɪʃən] *n* incautación *f*
conflagration [kɔnflə'greɪʃən] *n* conflagración *f*
conflict ['kɔnflɪkt] *n* conflicto ■ *vi* [kən'flɪkt] (*opinions*) estar reñido; (*reports, evidence*) contradecirse
conflicting [kən'flɪktɪŋ] *adj* (*reports, evidence, opinions*) contradictorio
conform [kən'fɔ:m] *vi*: **to ~ to** (*laws*) someterse a; (*usages, mores*) amoldarse a; (*standards*) ajustarse a
conformist [kən'fɔ:mɪst] *n* conformista *m/f*
confound [kən'faund] *vt* confundir; (*amaze*) pasmar
confounded [kən'faundɪd] *adj* condenado
confront [kən'frʌnt] *vt* (*problems*) hacer frente a; (*enemy, danger*) enfrentarse con
confrontation [kɔnfrən'teɪʃən] *n* enfrentamiento, confrontación *f*
confrontational [kɔnfrən'teɪʃənəl] *adj* conflictivo
confuse [kən'fju:z] *vt* (*perplex*) desconcertar; (*mix up*) confundir
confused [kən'fju:zd] *adj* confuso; (*person*) desconcertado; **to get ~** desconcertarse; (*muddled up*) hacerse un lío
confusing [kən'fju:zɪŋ] *adj* confuso
confusion [kən'fju:ʒən] *n* confusión *f*
congeal [kən'dʒi:l] *vi* coagularse
congenial [kən'dʒi:nɪəl] *adj* agradable
congenital [kən'dʒɛnɪtl] *adj* congénito
congested [kən'dʒɛstɪd] *adj* (*gen*) atestado; (*telephone lines*) saturado
congestion [kən'dʒɛstʃən] *n* congestión *f*
congestion charge *n*, **congestion charges** ■ *npl* tasa por congestión
conglomerate [kən'glɔmərət] *n* (*Comm, Geo*) conglomerado
conglomeration [kənglɔmə'reɪʃən] *n* conglomeración *f*
Congo ['kɔŋgəu] *n* (*state*) Congo
congratulate [kən'grætjuleɪt] *vt* felicitar
congratulations [kəngrætju'leɪʃənz] *npl*: **~ (on)** felicitaciones *fpl* (por); **~!** ¡enhorabuena!, ¡felicidades!
congregate ['kɔŋgrɪgeɪt] *vi* congregarse
congregation [kɔŋgrɪ'geɪʃən] *n* (*in church*) fieles *mpl*
congress ['kɔŋgrɛs] *n* congreso; (*US Pol*): **C~** el Congreso (de los Estados Unidos); *ver nota*

CONGRESS

En el Congreso de los Estados Unidos (*Congress*) se elaboran y aprueban las leyes federales. Consta de dos cámaras: la Cámara de Representantes ("House of Representatives"), cuyos 435 miembros son elegidos cada dos años por voto popular directo y en número proporcional a los habitantes de cada estado, y el Senado ("Senate"), con 100 senadores ("senators"), 2 por estado, de los que un tercio se elige cada dos años y el resto cada seis.

congressman ['kɔŋgrɛsmən] *n* (*US*) diputado, miembro del Congreso
congresswoman ['kɔŋgrɛswumən] *n* (*US*) diputada, miembro *f* del Congreso
conical ['kɔnɪkl] *adj* cónico
conifer ['kɔnɪfə^r] *n* conífera
coniferous [kə'nɪfərəs] *adj* (*forest*) conífero
conjecture [kən'dʒɛktʃə^r] *n* conjetura
conjugal ['kɔndʒugl] *adj* conyugal
conjugate ['kɔndʒugeɪt] *vt* conjugar
conjunction [kən'dʒʌŋkʃən] *n* conjunción *f*; **in ~ with** junto con
conjunctivitis [kəndʒʌŋktɪ'vaɪtɪs] *n* conjuntivitis *f*
conjure ['kʌndʒə^r] *vi* hacer juegos de manos
▸ **conjure up** *vt* (*ghost, spirit*) hacer aparecer; (*memories*) evocar
conjurer ['kʌndʒərə^r] *n* ilusionista *m/f*
conjuring trick ['kʌndʒərɪŋ-] *n* juego de manos
conker ['kɔŋkə^r] *n* (*Brit*) castaño de Indias
conk out [kɔŋk-] *vi* (*col*) estropearse, fastidiarse, descomponerse (*LAm*)
con man *n* timador *m*
Conn. *abbr* (*US*) = **Connecticut**
connect [kə'nɛkt] *vt* juntar, unir; (*Elec*) conectar; (*pipes*) empalmar; (*fig*) relacionar,

asociar ■ *vi*: **to ~ with** (*train*) enlazar con; **to be connected with** (*associated*) estar relacionado con; (*related*) estar emparentado con; **I am trying to ~ you** (*Tel*) estoy intentando ponerle al habla
connection [kə'nɛkʃən] *n* juntura, unión *f*; (*Elec*) conexión *f*; (*Tech*) empalme *m*; (*Rail*) enlace *m*; (*Tel*) comunicación *f*; (*fig*) relación *f*; **what is the ~ between them?** ¿qué relación hay entre ellos?; **in ~ with** con respecto a, en relación a; **she has many business connections** tiene muchos contactos profesionales; **to miss/make a ~** perder/coger el enlace
connive [kə'naɪv] *vi*: **to ~ at** hacer la vista gorda a
connoisseur [kɔnɪ'səːʳ] *n* experto(-a), entendido(-a)
connotation [kɔnə'teɪʃən] *n* connotación *f*
conquer ['kɔŋkəʳ] *vt* (*territory*) conquistar; (*enemy, feelings*) vencer
conqueror ['kɔŋkərəʳ] *n* conquistador(a) *m(f)*
conquest ['kɔŋkwɛst] *n* conquista
cons [kɔnz] *npl see* **convenience**; **pro**
conscience ['kɔnʃəns] *n* conciencia; **in all ~** en conciencia
conscientious [kɔnʃɪ'ɛnʃəs] *adj* concienzudo; (*objection*) de conciencia
conscientious objector *n* objetor *m* de conciencia
conscious ['kɔnʃəs] *adj* consciente; (*deliberate: insult, error*) premeditado, intencionado; **to become ~ of sth/that** darse cuenta de algo/de que
consciousness ['kɔnʃəsnɪs] *n* conciencia; (*Med*) conocimiento
conscript ['kɔnskrɪpt] *n* recluta *m/f*
conscription [kən'skrɪpʃən] *n* servicio militar (obligatorio)
consecrate ['kɔnsɪkreɪt] *vt* consagrar
consecutive [kən'sɛkjutɪv] *adj* consecutivo; **on 3 ~ occasions** en 3 ocasiones consecutivas
consensus [kən'sɛnsəs] *n* consenso; **the ~ of opinion** el consenso general
consent [kən'sɛnt] *n* consentimiento ■ *vi*: **to ~ to** consentir en; **by common ~** de común acuerdo
consenting adults [kən'sɛntɪŋ-] *npl* adultos con capacidad de consentir
consequence ['kɔnsɪkwəns] *n* consecuencia; **in ~** por consiguiente
consequently ['kɔnsɪkwəntlɪ] *adv* por consiguiente
conservation [kɔnsə'veɪʃən] *n* conservación *f*; (*of nature*) conservación, protección *f*
conservationist [kɔnsə'veɪʃnɪst] *n* conservacionista *m/f*
conservative [kən'səːvətɪv] *adj* conservador(a); (*cautious*) moderado; **C~** *adj, n* (*Brit Pol*) conservador(a) *m(f)*; **the C~ Party** el partido conservador (británico)
conservatory [kən'səːvətrɪ] *n* (*greenhouse*) invernadero
conserve [kən'səːv] *vt* conservar ■ *n* conserva
consider [kən'sɪdəʳ] *vt* considerar; (*take into account*) tomar en cuenta; (*study*) estudiar, examinar; **to ~ doing sth** pensar en (la posibilidad de) hacer algo; **all things considered** pensándolo bien; **~ yourself lucky** ¡date por satisfecho!
considerable [kən'sɪdərəbl] *adj* considerable
considerably [kən'sɪdərəblɪ] *adv* bastante, considerablemente
considerate [kən'sɪdərɪt] *adj* considerado
consideration [kənsɪdə'reɪʃən] *n* consideración *f*; (*reward*) retribución *f*; **to be under ~** estar estudiándose; **my first ~ is my family** mi primera consideración es mi familia
considered [kən'sɪdəd] *adj*: **it's my ~ opinion that ...** después de haber reflexionado mucho, pienso que ...
considering [kən'sɪdərɪŋ] *prep*: **~ (that)** teniendo en cuenta (que)
consign [kən'saɪn] *vt* consignar
consignee [kɔnsaɪ'niː] *n* consignatario(-a)
consignment [kən'saɪnmənt] *n* envío
consignment note *n* (*Comm*) talón *m* de expedición
consignor [kən'saɪnəʳ] *n* remitente *m/f*
consist [kən'sɪst] *vi*: **to ~ of** consistir en
consistency [kən'sɪstənsɪ] *n* (*of person etc*) consecuencia, coherencia; (*thickness*) consistencia
consistent [kən'sɪstənt] *adj* (*person, argument*) consecuente, coherente; (*results*) constante
consolation [kɔnsə'leɪʃən] *n* consuelo
console [kən'səul] *vt* consolar ■ *n* ['kɔnsəul] (*control panel*) consola
consolidate [kən'sɔlɪdeɪt] *vt* consolidar
consols ['kɔnsɔlz] *npl* (*Brit Stock Exchange*) valores *mpl* consolidados
consommé [kən'sɔmeɪ] *n* consomé *m*, caldo
consonant ['kɔnsənənt] *n* consonante *f*
consort ['kɔnsɔːt] *n* consorte *m/f* ■ *vi* [kən'sɔːt]: **to ~ with sb** (*often pej*) asociarse con algn; **prince ~** príncipe *m* consorte
consortium [kən'sɔːtɪəm] *n* consorcio
conspicuous [kən'spɪkjuəs] *adj* (*visible*) visible; (*garish etc*) llamativo; (*outstanding*) notable; **to make o.s. ~** llamar la atención
conspiracy [kən'spɪrəsɪ] *n* conjura, complot *m*

conspiratorial [kənspɪrə'tɔːrɪəl] *adj* de conspirador
conspire [kən'spaɪəʳ] *vi* conspirar
constable ['kʌnstəbl] *n* (*Brit*) agente *m/f* (de policía); **chief ~** ≈ jefe *m/f* de policía
constabulary [kən'stæbjulərɪ] *n* ≈ policía
constancy ['kɔnstənsɪ] *n* constancia; fidelidad *f*
constant ['kɔnstənt] *adj* (*gen*) constante; (*loyal*) leal, fiel
constantly ['kɔnstəntlɪ] *adv* constantemente
constellation [kɔnstə'leɪʃən] *n* constelación *f*
consternation [kɔnstə'neɪʃən] *n* consternación *f*
constipated ['kɔnstɪpeɪtəd] *adj* estreñido
constipation [kɔnstɪ'peɪʃən] *n* estreñimiento
constituency [kən'stɪtjuənsɪ] *n* (*Pol*) distrito electoral; (*people*) electorado; *ver nota*

CONSTITUENCY

Constituency es la denominación que recibe un distrito o circunscripción electoral y el grupo de electores registrados en ella en el sistema electoral británico. Cada circunscripción elige a un diputado ("Member of Parliament"), el cual se halla disponible semanalmente para las consultas y peticiones de sus electores durante ciertas horas a la semana, tiempo al que se llama "surgery".

constituency party *n* partido local
constituent [kən'stɪtjuənt] *n* (*Pol*) elector(a) *m(f)*; (*part*) componente *m*
constitute ['kɔnstɪtjuːt] *vt* constituir
constitution [kɔnstɪ'tjuːʃən] *n* constitución *f*
constitutional [kɔnstɪ'tjuːʃənl] *adj* constitucional; **~ monarchy** monarquía constitucional
constrain [kən'streɪn] *vt* obligar
constrained [kən'streɪnd] *adj*: **to feel ~ to ...** sentirse obligado a ...
constraint [kən'streɪnt] *n* (*force*) fuerza; (*limit*) restricción *f*; (*restraint*) reserva; (*embarrassment*) cohibición *f*
constrict [kən'strɪkt] *vt* oprimir
constriction [kən'strɪkʃən] *n* constricción *f*, opresión *f*
construct [kən'strʌkt] *vt* construir
construction [kən'strʌkʃən] *n* construcción *f*; (*fig: interpretation*) interpretación *f*; **under ~** en construcción
construction industry *n* industria de la construcción
constructive [kən'strʌktɪv] *adj* constructivo
construe [kən'struː] *vt* interpretar
consul ['kɔnsl] *n* cónsul *m/f*
consulate ['kɔnsjulɪt] *n* consulado
consult [kən'sʌlt] *vt, vi* consultar; **to ~ sb (about sth)** consultar a algn (sobre algo)
consultancy [kən'sʌltənsɪ] *n* (*Comm*) consultoría; (*Med*) puesto de especialista
consultant [kən'sʌltənt] *n* (*Brit Med*) especialista *m/f*; (*other specialist*) asesor(a) *m(f)*, consultor(a) *m(f)*
consultation [kɔnsəl'teɪʃən] *n* consulta; **in ~ with** en consulta con
consultative [kən'sʌltətɪv] *adj* consultivo
consulting room *n* (*Brit*) consulta, consultorio
consume [kən'sjuːm] *vt* (*eat*) comerse; (*drink*) beberse; (*fire etc*) consumir; (*Comm*) consumir
consumer [kən'sjuːməʳ] *n* (*of electricity, gas etc*) consumidor(a) *m(f)*
consumer association *n* asociación *f* de consumidores
consumer credit *n* crédito al consumidor
consumer durables *npl* bienes *mpl* de consumo duraderos
consumer goods *npl* bienes *mpl* de consumo
consumerism [kən'sjuːmərɪzəm] *n* consumismo
consumer society *n* sociedad *f* de consumo
consumer watchdog *n* organización *f* protectora del consumidor
consummate ['kɔnsʌmeɪt] *vt* consumar
consumption [kən'sʌmpʃən] *n* consumo; (*Med*) tisis *f*; **not fit for human ~** no apto para el consumo humano
cont. *abbr* (= *continued*) sigue
contact ['kɔntækt] *n* contacto; (*person: pej*) enchufe *m* ■ *vt* ponerse en contacto con; **~ lenses** *npl* lentes *fpl* de contacto; **to be in ~ with sb/sth** estar en contacto con algn/algo; **business contacts** relaciones *fpl* comerciales
contagious [kən'teɪdʒəs] *adj* contagioso
contain [kən'teɪn] *vt* contener; **to ~ o.s.** contenerse
container [kən'teɪnəʳ] *n* recipiente *m*; (*for shipping etc*) contenedor *m*
containerize [kən'teɪnəraɪz] *vt* transportar en contenedores
container ship *n* buque *m* contenedor, portacontenedores *m inv*
contaminate [kən'tæmɪneɪt] *vt* contaminar
contamination [kəntæmɪ'neɪʃən] *n* contaminación *f*
cont'd *abbr* (= *continued*) sigue
contemplate ['kɔntəmpleɪt] *vt* (*gen*) contemplar; (*reflect upon*) considerar; (*intend*) pensar

contemplation [kɔntəm'pleɪʃən] *n* contemplación *f*
contemporary [kən'tɛmpərərɪ] *adj, n* (*of the same age*) contemporáneo(-a) *m(f)*
contempt [kən'tɛmpt] *n* desprecio; **~ of court** (*Law*) desacato (a los tribunales *or* a la justicia)
contemptible [kən'tɛmptɪbl] *adj* despreciable, desdeñable
contemptuous [kən'tɛmptjuəs] *adj* desdeñoso
contend [kən'tɛnd] *vt* (*argue*) afirmar ■ *vi* (*struggle*) luchar; **he has a lot to ~ with** tiene que hacer frente a muchos problemas
contender [kən'tɛndə^r] *n* (*Sport*) contendiente *m/f*
content [kən'tɛnt] *adj* (*happy*) contento; (*satisfied*) satisfecho ■ *vt* contentar; satisfacer ■ *n* ['kɔntɛnt] contenido; **contents** *npl* contenido *msg*; **(table of) contents** índice *m* de materias; (*in magazine*) sumario; **to be ~ with** conformarse con; **to ~ o.s. with sth/with doing sth** conformarse con algo/con hacer algo
contented [kən'tɛntɪd] *adj* contento; satisfecho
contentedly [kən'tɛntɪdlɪ] *adv* con aire satisfecho
contention [kən'tɛnʃən] *n* discusión *f*; (*belief*) argumento; **bone of ~** manzana de la discordia
contentious [kən'tɛnʃəs] *adj* discutible
contentment [kən'tɛntmənt] *n* satisfacción *f*
contest ['kɔntɛst] *n* contienda; (*competition*) concurso ■ *vt* [kən'tɛst] (*dispute*) impugnar; (*Law*) disputar, litigar; (*Pol: election, seat*) presentarse como candidato(-a) a
contestant [kən'tɛstənt] *n* concursante *m/f*; (*in fight*) contendiente *m/f*
context ['kɔntɛkst] *n* contexto; **in/out of ~** en/fuera de contexto
continent ['kɔntɪnənt] *n* continente *m*; **the C~** (*Brit*) el continente europeo, Europa; **on the C~** en el continente europeo, en Europa
continental [kɔntɪ'nɛntl] *adj* continental; (*Brit: European*) europeo
continental breakfast *n* desayuno estilo europeo
continental quilt *n* (*Brit*) edredón *m*
contingency [kən'tɪndʒənsɪ] *n* contingencia
contingent [kən'tɪndʒənt] *n* (*group*) representación *f*
continual [kən'tɪnjuəl] *adj* continuo
continually [kən'tɪnjuəlɪ] *adv* continuamente
continuation [kəntɪnju'eɪʃən] *n* prolongación *f*; (*after interruption*) reanudación *f*; (*of story, episode*) continuación *f*
continue [kən'tɪnju:] *vi, vt* seguir, continuar; **continued on page 10** sigue en la página 10
continuing education [kən'tɪnjuɪŋ-] *n* educación *f* continua de adultos
continuity [kɔntɪ'njuɪtɪ] *n* (*also Cine*) continuidad *f*
continuity girl *n* (*Cine*) secretaria de continuidad
continuous [kən'tɪnjuəs] *adj* continuo; **~ performance** (*Cine*) sesión *f* continua
continuously [kən'tɪnjuəslɪ] *adv* continuamente
contort [kən'tɔ:t] *vt* retorcer
contortion [kən'tɔ:ʃən] *n* (*movement*) contorsión *f*
contortionist [kən'tɔ:ʃənɪst] *n* contorsionista *m/f*
contour ['kɔntuə^r] *n* contorno; (*also:* **contour line**) curva de nivel
contraband ['kɔntrəbænd] *n* contrabando ■ *adj* de contrabando
contraception [kɔntrə'sɛpʃən] *n* contracepción *f*
contraceptive [kɔntrə'sɛptɪv] *adj, n* anticonceptivo
contract [*n* 'kɔntrækt, *vb* kən'trækt] *n* contrato ■ *cpd* ['kɔntrækt] (*price, date*) contratado, de contrato; (*work*) bajo contrato ■ *vi* (*Comm*): **to ~ to do sth** comprometerse por contrato a hacer algo; (*become smaller*) contraerse, encogerse ■ *vt* contraer; **to be under ~ to do sth** estar bajo contrato para hacer algo; **~ of employment** *or* **of service** contrato de trabajo
▸ **contract in** *vi* tomar parte
▸ **contract out** *vi*: **to ~ out (of)** optar por no tomar parte (en); **to ~ out of a pension scheme** dejar de cotizar en un plan de jubilación
contraction [kən'trækʃən] *n* contracción *f*
contractor [kən'træktə^r] *n* contratista *m/f*
contractual [kən'træktjuəl] *adj* contractual
contradict [kɔntrə'dɪkt] *vt* (*declare to be wrong*) desmentir; (*be contrary to*) contradecir
contradiction [kɔntrə'dɪkʃən] *n* contradicción *f*; **to be in ~ with** contradecir
contradictory [kɔntrə'dɪktərɪ] *adj* (*statements*) contradictorio; **to be ~ to** contradecir
contralto [kən'træltəu] *n* contralto *f*
contraption [kən'træpʃən] *n* (*pej*) artilugio *m*
contrary ['kɔntrərɪ] *adj* (*opposite, different*) contrario [kən'trɛərɪ] (*perverse*) terco ■ *n*: **on the ~** al contrario; **unless you hear to the ~** a no ser que le digan lo contrario; **~ to what we thought** al contrario de lo que pensábamos

contrast ['kɔntrɑːst] *n* contraste *m* ■ *vt* [kən'trɑːst] contrastar; **in ~ to** *or* **with** a diferencia de
contrasting [kən'trɑːstɪŋ] *adj* (*opinion*) opuesto; (*colour*) que hace contraste
contravene [kɔntrə'viːn] *vt* contravenir
contravention [kɔntrə'vɛnʃən] *n*: **~ (of)** contravención *f* (de)
contribute [kən'trɪbjuːt] *vi* contribuir ■ *vt*: **to ~ to** (*gen*) contribuir a; (*newspaper*) colaborar en; (*discussion*) intervenir en
contribution [kɔntrɪ'bjuːʃən] *n* (*money*) contribución *f*; (*to debate*) intervención *f*; (*to journal*) colaboración *f*
contributor [kən'trɪbjutəʳ] *n* (*to newspaper*) colaborador(a) *m(f)*
contributory [kən'trɪbjutərɪ] *adj* (*cause*) contribuyente; **it was a ~ factor in ...** fue un factor que contribuyó en ...
contributory pension scheme *n* plan *m* cotizable de jubilación
contrivance [kən'traɪvəns] *n* (*machine, device*) aparato, dispositivo
contrive [kən'traɪv] *vt* (*invent*) idear ■ *vi*: **to ~ to do** lograr hacer; (*try*) procurar hacer
control [kən'trəul] *vt* controlar; (*traffic etc*) dirigir; (*machinery*) manejar; (*temper*) dominar; (*disease, fire*) dominar, controlar ■ *n* (*command*) control *m*; (*of car*) conducción *f*; (*check*) freno; **controls** *npl* mandos *mpl*; **to ~ o.s.** controlarse, dominarse; **everything is under ~** todo está bajo control; **to be in ~ of** estar al mando de; **the car went out of ~** el coche se descontroló
control group *n* (*Med, Psych etc*) grupo de control
control key *n* (*Comput*) tecla de control
controlled economy *n* economía dirigida
controller [kən'trəuləʳ] *n* controlador(a) *m(f)*
controlling interest [kən'trəulɪŋ-] *n* participación *f* mayoritaria
control panel *n* (*on aircraft, ship, TV etc*) tablero de instrumentos
control point *n* (puesto de) control *m*
control room *n* (*Naut, Mil*) sala de mandos; (*Radio, TV*) sala de control
control tower *n* (*Aviat*) torre *f* de control
control unit *n* (*Comput*) unidad *f* de control
controversial [kɔntrə'vəːʃl] *adj* polémico
controversy ['kɔntrəvəːsɪ] *n* polémica
conurbation [kɔnəː'beɪʃən] *n* conurbación *f*
convalesce [kɔnvə'lɛs] *vi* convalecer
convalescence [kɔnvə'lɛsns] *n* convalecencia
convalescent [kɔnvə'lɛsnt] *adj, n* convaleciente *m/f*
convector [kən'vɛktəʳ] *n* calentador *m* de convección
convene [kən'viːn] *vt* (*meeting*) convocar ■ *vi* reunirse
convenience [kən'viːnɪəns] *n* (*comfort*) comodidad *f*; (*advantage*) ventaja; **at your earliest ~** (*Comm*) tan pronto como le sea posible; **all modern conveniences,** (*Brit*) **all mod cons** todo confort
convenience foods *npl* platos *mpl* preparados
convenient [kən'viːnɪənt] *adj* (*useful*) útil; (*place*) conveniente; (*time*) oportuno; **if it is ~ for you** si le viene bien
conveniently [kən'viːnɪəntlɪ] *adv* (*happen*) oportunamente; (*situated*) convenientemente
convent ['kɔnvənt] *n* convento
convention [kən'vɛnʃən] *n* convención *f*; (*meeting*) asamblea
conventional [kən'vɛnʃənl] *adj* convencional
convent school *n* colegio de monjas
converge [kən'vəːdʒ] *vi* converger
conversant [kən'vəːsnt] *adj*: **to be ~ with** estar familiarizado con
conversation [kɔnvə'seɪʃən] *n* conversación *f*
conversational [kɔnvə'seɪʃənl] *adj* (*familiar*) familiar; (*talkative*) locuaz; **~ mode** (*Comput*) modo de conversación
converse ['kɔnvəːs] *n* inversa ■ *vi* [kən'vəːs] conversar; **to ~ (with sb about sth)** conversar *or* platicar (*LAm*) (con algn de algo)
conversely [kɔn'vəːslɪ] *adv* a la inversa
conversion [kən'vəːʃən] *n* conversión *f*; (*house conversion*) reforma, remodelación *f*
conversion table *n* tabla de equivalencias
convert [kən'vəːt] *vt* (*Rel, Comm*) convertir; (*alter*) transformar ■ *n* ['kɔnvəːt] converso(-a)
convertible [kən'vəːtəbl] *adj* convertible ■ *n* descapotable *m*; **~ loan stock** obligaciones *fpl* convertibles
convex ['kɔn'vɛks] *adj* convexo
convey [kən'veɪ] *vt* transportar; (*thanks*) comunicar; (*idea*) expresar
conveyance [kən'veɪəns] *n* (*of goods*) transporte *m*; (*vehicle*) vehículo, medio de transporte
conveyancing [kən'veɪənsɪŋ] *n* (*Law*) preparación *f* de escrituras de traspaso
conveyor belt [kən'veɪəʳ-] *n* cinta transportadora
convict [kən'vɪkt] *vt* (*gen*) condenar; (*find guilty*) declarar culpable a ■ *n* ['kɔnvɪkt] presidiario(-a)
conviction [kən'vɪkʃən] *n* condena; (*belief*) creencia, convicción *f*
convince [kən'vɪns] *vt* convencer; **to ~ sb (of sth/that)** convencer a algn (de algo/de que)

convinced [kən'vɪnst] *adj*: **~ of/that** convencido de/de que
convincing [kən'vɪnsɪŋ] *adj* convincente
convincingly [kən'vɪnsɪŋlɪ] *adv* de modo convincente, convincentemente
convivial [kən'vɪvɪəl] *adj* (*person*) sociable; (*atmosphere*) alegre
convoluted ['kɔnvəlu:tɪd] *adj* (*argument etc*) enrevesado; (*shape*) enrollado, enroscado
convoy ['kɔnvɔɪ] *n* convoy *m*
convulse [kən'vʌls] *vt* convulsionar; **to be convulsed with laughter** dislocarse de risa
convulsion [kən'vʌlʃən] *n* convulsión *f*
coo [ku:] *vi* arrullar
cook [kuk] *vt* cocinar; (*stew etc*) guisar; (*meal*) preparar ■ *vi* hacerse; (*person*) cocinar ■ *n* cocinero(-a)
▸ **cook up** *vt* (*col: excuse, story*) inventar
cookbook ['kukbuk] *n* libro de cocina
cooker ['kukəʳ] *n* cocina
cookery ['kukərɪ] *n* cocina
cookery book *n* (*Brit*) = **cookbook**
cookie ['kukɪ] *n* (*US*) galleta
cooking ['kukɪŋ] *n* cocina ■ *cpd* (*apples*) para cocinar; (*utensils, salt, foil*) de cocina
cooking chocolate *n* chocolate *m* fondant *or* de hacer
cookout ['kukaut] *n* (*US*) comida al aire libre
cool [ku:l] *adj* fresco; (*not hot*) tibio; (*not afraid*) tranquilo; (*unfriendly*) frío ■ *vt* enfriar ■ *vi* enfriarse; **it is ~** (*weather*) hace fresco; **to keep sth ~** *or* **in a ~ place** conservar algo fresco *or* en un sitio fresco
▸ **cool down** *vi* enfriarse; (*fig: person, situation*) calmarse
coolant ['ku:lənt] *n* refrigerante *m*
cool box, cooler (*US*) ['ku:ləʳ] *n* nevera portátil
cooling ['ku:lɪŋ] *adj* refrescante
cooling-off period [ku:lɪŋ'ɔf-] *n* (*Industry*) plazo de negociaciones
cooling tower *n* torre *f* de refrigeración
coolly ['ku:lɪ] *adv* (*calmly*) con tranquilidad; (*audaciously*) descaradamente; (*unenthusiastically*) fríamente, con frialdad
coolness ['ku:lnɪs] *n* frescura; tranquilidad *f*; (*hostility*) frialdad *f*; (*indifference*) falta de entusiasmo
coop [ku:p] *n* gallinero ■ *vt*: **to ~ up** (*fig*) encerrar
co-op ['kəuɔp] *n abbr* (= *cooperative (society)*) cooperativa
cooperate [kəu'ɔpəreɪt] *vi* cooperar, colaborar; **will he ~?** ¿querrá cooperar?
cooperation [kəuɔpə'reɪʃən] *n* cooperación *f*, colaboración *f*
cooperative [kəu'ɔpərətɪv] *adj* cooperativo; (*person*) dispuesto a colaborar ■ *n* cooperativa
co-opt [kəu'ɔpt] *vt*: **to ~ sb into sth** nombrar a algn para algo
coordinate [kəu'ɔ:dɪneɪt] *vt* coordinar ■ *n* [kəu'ɔ:dɪnət] (*Math*) coordenada; **coordinates** *npl* (*clothes*) coordinados *mpl*
coordination [kəuɔ:dɪ'neɪʃən] *n* coordinación *f*
coot [ku:t] *n* focha *f* (común)
co-ownership [kəu'əunəʃɪp] *n* copropiedad *f*
cop [kɔp] *n* (*col*) poli *m*
cope [kəup] *vi*: **to ~ with** poder con; (*problem*) hacer frente a
Copenhagen [kəupən'heɪgən] *n* Copenhague *m*
copier ['kɔpɪəʳ] *n* (*photocopier*) (foto)copiadora
co-pilot ['kəu'paɪlət] *n* copiloto *m/f*
copious ['kəupɪəs] *adj* copioso, abundante
copper ['kɔpəʳ] *n* (*metal*) cobre *m*; (*col: policeman*) poli *m*; **coppers** *npl* perras *fpl*; (*small change*) calderilla
coppice ['kɔpɪs], **copse** [kɔps] *n* bosquecillo
copulate ['kɔpjuleɪt] *vi* copular
copulation [kɔpju'leɪʃən] *n* cópula
copy ['kɔpɪ] *n* copia; (*of book*) ejemplar *m*; (*of magazine*) número; (*material: for printing*) original *m* ■ *vt* copiar (*also Comput*); (*imitate*) copiar, imitar; **to make good ~** (*fig*) ser una noticia de interés; **rough ~** borrador *m*; **fair ~** copia en limpio
▸ **copy out** *vt* copiar
copycat ['kɔpɪkæt] *n* (*pej*) imitador(a) *m(f)*
copyright ['kɔpɪraɪt] *n* derechos *mpl* de autor
copy typist *n* mecanógrafo(-a)
coral ['kɔrəl] *n* coral *m*
coral reef *n* arrecife *m* (de coral)
Coral Sea *n*: **the ~** el Mar del Coral
cord [kɔ:d] *n* cuerda; (*Elec*) cable *m*; (*fabric*) pana; **cords** *npl* (*trousers*) pantalones *mpl* de pana
cordial ['kɔ:dɪəl] *adj* cordial ■ *n* cordial *m*
cordless ['kɔ:dlɪs] *adj* sin hilos; **~ telephone** teléfono inalámbrico
cordon ['kɔ:dn] *n* cordón *m*
▸ **cordon off** *vt* acordonar
Cordova ['kɔ:dəvə] *n* Córdoba
corduroy ['kɔ:dərɔɪ] *n* pana
CORE [kɔ:ʳ] *n abbr* (*US*) = **Congress of Racial Equality**
core [kɔ:ʳ] *n* (*of earth, nuclear reactor*) centro, núcleo; (*of fruit*) corazón *m*; (*of problem etc*) esencia, meollo ■ *vt* quitar el corazón de
Corfu [kɔ:'fu] *n* Corfú *m*
coriander [kɔrɪ'ændəʳ] *n* culantro, cilantro
cork [kɔ:k] *n* corcho; (*tree*) alcornoque *m*
corkage ['kɔ:kɪdʒ] *n precio que se cobra en un restaurante por una botella de vino traída de fuera*

corked [kɔːkt] *adj* (*wine*) con sabor a corcho
corkscrew [ˈkɔːkskruː] *n* sacacorchos *m inv*
cormorant [ˈkɔːmərnt] *n* cormorán *m*
Corn *abbr* (*Brit*) = **Cornwall**
corn [kɔːn] *n* (*Brit: wheat*) trigo; (*US: maize*) maíz *m*, choclo (*LAm*); (*on foot*) callo; **~ on the cob** (*Culin*) maíz en la mazorca
cornea [ˈkɔːnɪə] *n* córnea
corned beef [ˈkɔːnd-] *n* carne *f* de vaca acecinada
corner [ˈkɔːnə^r] *n* (*outside*) esquina; (*inside*) rincón *m*; (*in road*) curva; (*Football*) córner *m*, saque *m* de esquina ■ *vt* (*trap*) arrinconar; (*Comm*) acaparar ■ *vi* (*in car*) tomar las curvas; **to cut corners** atajar
corner flag *n* (*Football*) banderola de esquina
corner kick *n* (*Football*) córner *m*, saque *m* de esquina
cornerstone [ˈkɔːnəstəun] *n* piedra angular
cornet [ˈkɔːnɪt] *n* (*Mus*) corneta; (*Brit: of ice cream*) cucurucho
cornflakes [ˈkɔːnfleɪks] *npl* copos *mpl* de maíz, cornflakes *mpl*
cornflour [ˈkɔːnflauə^r] *n* (*Brit*) harina de maíz
cornice [ˈkɔːnɪs] *n* cornisa
Cornish [ˈkɔːnɪʃ] *adj* de Cornualles
corn oil *n* aceite *m* de maíz
cornstarch [ˈkɔːnstɑːtʃ] *n* (*US*) = **cornflour**
cornucopia [kɔːnjuˈkəupɪə] *n* cornucopia
Cornwall [ˈkɔːnwəl] *n* Cornualles *m*
corny [ˈkɔːnɪ] *adj* (*col*) gastado
corollary [kəˈrɔlərɪ] *n* corolario
coronary [ˈkɔrənərɪ] *n*: **~ (thrombosis)** infarto
coronation [kɔrəˈneɪʃən] *n* coronación *f*
coroner [ˈkɔrənə^r] *n* juez *m/f* de instrucción
coronet [ˈkɔrənɪt] *n* corona
Corp. *abbr* = **corporation**
corporal [ˈkɔːpərl] *n* cabo ■ *adj*: **~ punishment** castigo corporal
corporate [ˈkɔːpərɪt] *adj* corporativo
corporate hospitality *n obsequios a los clientes por cortesía de la empresa*
corporate identity, corporate image *n* (*of organization*) identidad *f* corporativa
corporation [kɔːpəˈreɪʃən] *n* (*of town*) ayuntamiento; (*Comm*) corporación *f*
corps [kɔː^r] (*pl* **~**) [kɔːz] *n* cuerpo; **press ~** gabinete *m* de prensa
corpse [kɔːps] *n* cadáver *m*
corpulent [ˈkɔːpjulənt] *adj* corpulento(-a)
Corpus Christi [ˈkɔːpəsˈkrɪstɪ] *n* Corpus *m* (Christi)
corpuscle [ˈkɔːpʌsl] *n* corpúsculo
corral [kəˈrɑːl] *n* corral *m*
correct [kəˈrɛkt] *adj* correcto; (*accurate*) exacto ■ *vt* corregir; **you are ~** tiene razón
correction [kəˈrɛkʃən] *n* rectificación *f*; (*erasure*) tachadura
correlate [ˈkɔrɪleɪt] *vi*: **to ~ with** tener correlación con
correlation [kɔrɪˈleɪʃən] *n* correlación *f*
correspond [kɔrɪsˈpɔnd] *vi* (*write*) escribirse; (*be equal to*) corresponder
correspondence [kɔrɪsˈpɔndəns] *n* correspondencia
correspondence course *n* curso por correspondencia
correspondent [kɔrɪsˈpɔndənt] *n* corresponsal *m/f*
corresponding [kɔrɪsˈpɔndɪŋ] *adj* correspondiente
corridor [ˈkɔrɪdɔː^r] *n* pasillo
corroborate [kəˈrɔbəreɪt] *vt* corroborar
corroboration [kərɔbəˈreɪʃən] *n* corroboración *f*, confirmación *f*
corrode [kəˈrəud] *vt* corroer ■ *vi* corroerse
corrosion [kəˈrəuʒən] *n* corrosión *f*
corrosive [kəˈrəusɪv] *adj* corrosivo
corrugated [ˈkɔrəgeɪtɪd] *adj* ondulado
corrugated cardboard *n* cartón *m* ondulado
corrugated iron *n* chapa ondulada
corrupt [kəˈrʌpt] *adj* corrompido; (*person*) corrupto ■ *vt* corromper; (*bribe*) sobornar; (*Comput: data*) degradar; **~ practices** (*dishonesty, bribery*) corrupción *f*
corruption [kəˈrʌpʃən] *n* corrupción *f*; (*Comput: of data*) alteración *f*
corset [ˈkɔːsɪt] *n* faja; (*old-style*) corsé *m*
Corsica [ˈkɔːsɪkə] *n* Córcega
Corsican [ˈkɔːsɪkən] *adj, n* corso(-a) *m(f)*
cortège [kɔːˈteɪʒ] *n* cortejo, comitiva
cortisone [ˈkɔːtɪzəun] *n* cortisona
cosh [kɔʃ] *n* (*Brit*) cachiporra
cosignatory [ˈkəuˈsɪgnətərɪ] *n* cosignatario(-a)
cosine [ˈkəusaɪn] *n* coseno
cosiness [ˈkəuzɪnɪs] *n* comodidad *f*; (*atmosphere*) lo acogedor
cos lettuce [kɔs-] *n* lechuga romana
cosmetic [kɔzˈmɛtɪk] *n* cosmético ■ *adj* (*also fig*) cosmético; (*surgery*) estético
cosmic [ˈkɔzmɪk] *adj* cósmico
cosmonaut [ˈkɔzmənɔːt] *n* cosmonauta *m/f*
cosmopolitan [kɔzməˈpɔlɪtn] *adj* cosmopolita
cosmos [ˈkɔzmɔs] *n* cosmos *m*
cosset [ˈkɔsɪt] *vt* mimar
cost [kɔst] (*pt, pp* **~**) *n* (*gen*) coste *m*, costo; (*price*) precio; **costs** *npl* (*Law*) costas *fpl* ■ *vi* costar, valer ■ *vt* preparar el presupuesto de; **how much does it ~?** ¿cuánto cuesta?, ¿cuánto vale?; **what will it ~ to have it**

repaired? ¿cuánto costará repararlo?; **the ~ of living** el coste *or* costo de la vida; **at all costs** cueste lo que cueste
cost accountant *n* contable *m* de costos
co-star ['kəustɑːʳ] *n* coprotagonista *m/f*
Costa Rica ['kɔstə'riːkə] *n* Costa Rica
Costa Rican ['kɔstə'riːkən] *adj, n* costarriqueño(-a) *m(f)*, costarricense *m/f*
cost centre *n* centro (de determinación) de coste
cost control *n* control *m* de costes
cost-effective [kɔstɪ'fɛktɪv] *adj (Comm)* rentable
cost-effectiveness ['kɔstɪ'fɛktɪvnɪs] *n* relación *f* coste-rendimiento
costing ['kɔstɪŋ] *n* cálculo del coste
costly ['kɔstlɪ] *adj (expensive)* costoso
cost-of-living [kɔstəv'lɪvɪŋ] *adj*: **~ allowance** *n* plus *m* de carestía de vida; **~ index** *n* índice *m* del coste de vida
cost price *n (Brit)* precio de coste
costume ['kɔstjuːm] *n* traje *m*; *(Brit: also:* **swimming costume**) traje de baño
costume jewellery *n* bisutería
cosy, cozy *(US)* ['kəuzɪ] *adj* cómodo, a gusto; *(room, atmosphere)* acogedor(a)
cot [kɔt] *n (Brit: child's)* cuna; *(US: folding bed)* cama plegable
cot death *n* muerte *f* en la cuna
Cotswolds ['kɔtswəuldz] *npl región de colinas del suroeste inglés*
cottage ['kɔtɪdʒ] *n* casita de campo
cottage cheese *n* requesón *m*
cottage industry *n* industria artesanal
cottage pie *n pastel de carne cubierta de puré de patatas*
cotton ['kɔtn] *n* algodón *m*; *(thread)* hilo
▸ **cotton on** *vi (col)*: **to ~ on (to sth)** caer en la cuenta (de algo)
cotton candy *n (US)* algodón *m* (azucarado)
cotton wool *n (Brit)* algodón *m* (hidrófilo)
couch [kautʃ] *n* sofá *m*; *(in doctor's surgery)* camilla
couchette [kuː'ʃɛt] *n* litera
couch potato *n (col) persona comodona que no se mueve en todo el día*
cough [kɔf] *vi* toser ■ *n* tos *f*
▸ **cough up** *vt* escupir
cough drop *n* pastilla para la tos
cough mixture *n* jarabe *m* para la tos
could [kud] *pt of* **can**
couldn't ['kudnt] = **could not**
council ['kaunsl] *n* consejo; **city** *or* **town ~** ayuntamiento; **C~ of Europe** Consejo de Europa
council estate *n (Brit)* barriada de viviendas sociales de alquiler
council house *n (Brit)* vivienda social de alquiler
councillor ['kaunsləʳ] *n* concejal *m/f*
council tax *n (Brit)* contribución *f* municipal *(dependiente del valor de la vivienda)*
counsel ['kaunsl] *n (advice)* consejo; *(lawyer)* abogado(-a) ■ *vt* aconsejar; **~ for the defence/the prosecution** abogado(-a) defensor(a)/fiscal; **to ~ sth/sb to do sth** aconsejar algo/a algn que haga algo
counsellor, counselor *(US)* ['kaunsləʳ] *n* consejero(-a); *(US Law)* abogado(-a)
count [kaunt] *vt (gen)* contar; *(include)* incluir ■ *vi* contar ■ *n* cuenta; *(of votes)* escrutinio; *(nobleman)* conde *m*; *(sum)* total *m*, suma; **to ~ the cost of** calcular el coste de; **not counting the children** niños aparte; **10 counting him** diez incluyéndolo a él, diez con él; **~ yourself lucky** date por satisfecho; **that doesn't ~!** ¡eso no vale!; **to ~ (up) to 10** contar hasta diez; **it counts for very little** cuenta poco; **to keep ~ of sth** llevar la cuenta de algo
▸ **count on** *vt fus* contar con; **to ~ on doing sth** contar con hacer algo
▸ **count up** *vt* contar
countdown ['kauntdaun] *n* cuenta atrás
countenance ['kauntɪnəns] *n* semblante *m*, rostro ■ *vt (tolerate)* aprobar, consentir
counter ['kauntəʳ] *n (in shop)* mostrador *m*; *(position: in post office, bank)* ventanilla; *(in games)* ficha; *(Tech)* contador *m* ■ *vt* contrarrestar; *(blow)* parar; *(attack)* contestar a ■ *adv*: **~ to** contrario a; **to buy under the ~** *(fig)* comprar de estraperlo *or* bajo mano; **to ~ sth with sth/by doing sth** contestar algo con algo/haciendo algo
counteract ['kauntər'ækt] *vt* contrarrestar
counterattack ['kauntərə'tæk] *n* contraataque *m* ■ *vi* contraatacar
counterbalance ['kauntə'bæləns] *n* contrapeso
counter-clockwise ['kauntə'klɔkwaɪz] *adv* en sentido contrario al de las agujas del reloj
counter-espionage ['kauntər'ɛspɪənɑːʒ] *n* contraespionaje *m*
counterfeit ['kauntəfɪt] *n* falsificación *f* ■ *vt* falsificar ■ *adj* falso, falsificado
counterfoil ['kauntəfɔɪl] *n (Brit)* matriz *f*, talón *m*
counterintelligence ['kauntərɪn'tɛlɪdʒəns] *n* contraespionaje *m*
countermand ['kauntəmɑːnd] *vt* revocar
counter-measure ['kauntəmɛʒəʳ] *n* contramedida
counteroffensive ['kauntərə'fɛnsɪv] *n* contraofensiva

counterpane ['kauntəpeɪn] *n* colcha
counterpart ['kauntəpɑːt] *n* (*of person*) homólogo(-a)
counter-productive [kauntəprə'dʌktɪv] *adj* contraproducente
counterproposal ['kauntəprə'pəuzl] *n* contrapropuesta
countersign ['kauntəsaɪn] *vt* ratificar, refrendar
countess ['kauntɪs] *n* condesa
countless ['kauntlɪs] *adj* innumerable
countrified ['kʌntrɪfaɪd] *adj* rústico
country ['kʌntrɪ] *n* país *m*; (*native land*) patria; (*as opposed to town*) campo; (*region*) región *f*, tierra; **in the ~** en el campo; **mountainous ~** región *f* montañosa
country and western, country and western music *n* música country
country dancing *n* (*Brit*) baile *m* regional
country house *n* casa de campo
countryman ['kʌntrɪmən] *n* (*national*) compatriota *m*; (*rural*) hombre *m* del campo
countryside ['kʌntrɪsaɪd] *n* campo
countrywide ['kʌntrɪ'waɪd] *adj* nacional ■ *adv* por todo el país
county ['kauntɪ] *n* condado; *see also* **district council**
county council *n* (*Brit*) ≈ diputación *f* provincial
county town *n* cabeza de partido
coup [kuː] (*pl* **coups**) [kuːz] *n* golpe *m*; (*triumph*) éxito; (*also*: **coup d'état**) golpe de estado
coupé ['kuːpeɪ] *n* cupé *m*
couple ['kʌpl] *n* (*of things*) par *m*; (*of people*) pareja; (*married couple*) matrimonio ■ *vt* (*ideas, names*) unir, juntar; (*machinery*) acoplar; **a ~ of** un par de
couplet ['kʌplɪt] *n* pareado
coupling ['kʌplɪŋ] *n* (*Rail*) enganche *m*
coupon ['kuːpɔn] *n* cupón *m*; (*pools coupon*) boleto (de quiniela)
courage ['kʌrɪdʒ] *n* valor *m*, valentía
courageous [kə'reɪdʒəs] *adj* valiente
courgette [kuə'ʒɛt] *n* (*Brit*) calabacín *m*
courier ['kurɪə^r] *n* mensajero(-a); (*diplomatic*) correo; (*for tourists*) guía *m/f* (de turismo)
course [kɔːs] *n* (*direction*) dirección *f*; (*of river*) curso; (*Scol*) curso; (*of ship*) rumbo; (*fig*) proceder *m*; (*Golf*) campo; (*part of meal*) plato; **of ~** *adv* desde luego, naturalmente; **of ~!** ¡claro!, ¡cómo no! (*LAm*); **(no) of ~ not!** ¡claro que no!, ¡por supuesto que no!; **in due ~** a su debido tiempo; **in the ~ of the next few days** durante los próximos días; **we have no other ~ but to ...** no tenemos más remedio que ...; **there are 2 courses open to us** se nos ofrecen dos posibilidades; **the best ~ would be to ...** lo mejor sería ...; **~ of treatment** (*Med*) tratamiento
court [kɔːt] *n* (*royal*) corte *f*; (*Law*) tribunal *m*, juzgado; (*Tennis*) pista, cancha (*LAm*) ■ *vt* (*woman*) cortejar; (*fig: favour, popularity*) solicitar, buscar; (*: death, disaster, danger etc*) buscar; **to take to ~** demandar; **~ of appeal** tribunal *m* de apelación
courteous ['kəːtɪəs] *adj* cortés
courtesan [kɔːtɪ'zæn] *n* cortesana
courtesy ['kəːtəsɪ] *n* cortesía; **by ~ of** (por) cortesía de
courtesy light *n* (*Aut*) luz *f* interior
court-house ['kɔːthaus] *n* (*US*) palacio de justicia
courtier ['kɔːtɪə^r] *n* cortesano
court martial (*pl* **courts martial**) ['kɔːt'mɑːʃəl] *n* consejo de guerra ■ *vt* someter a consejo de guerra
courtroom ['kɔːtrum] *n* sala de justicia
court shoe *n* *zapato de mujer de estilo clásico*
courtyard ['kɔːtjɑːd] *n* patio
cousin ['kʌzn] *n* primo(-a); **first ~** primo(-a) carnal
cove [kəuv] *n* cala, ensenada
covenant ['kʌvənənt] *n* convenio ■ *vt*: **to ~ £20 per year to a charity** concertar el pago de veinte libras anuales a una sociedad benéfica
Coventry ['kɔvəntrɪ] *n*: **to send sb to ~** (*fig*) hacer el vacío a algn
cover ['kʌvə^r] *vt* cubrir; (*with lid*) tapar; (*chairs etc*) revestir; (*distance*) cubrir, recorrer; (*include*) abarcar; (*protect*) abrigar; (*journalist*) investigar; (*issues*) tratar ■ *n* cubierta; (*lid*) tapa; (*for chair etc*) funda; (*for bed*) cobertor *m*; (*envelope*) sobre *m*; (*of magazine*) portada; (*shelter*) abrigo; (*insurance*) cobertura; **to take ~** (*shelter*) protegerse, resguardarse; **under ~** (*indoors*) bajo techo; **under ~ of darkness** al amparo de la oscuridad; **under separate ~** (*Comm*) por separado; **£10 will ~ everything** con diez libras cubriremos todos los gastos
▸ **cover up** *vt* (*child, object*) cubrir completamente, tapar; (*fig: hide: truth, facts*) ocultar; **to ~ up for sb** (*fig*) encubrir a algn
coverage ['kʌvərɪdʒ] *n* alcance *m*; (*in media*) reportaje *m*; (*Insurance*) cobertura
coveralls ['kʌvərɔːlz] *npl* (*US*) mono *sg*
cover charge *n* precio del cubierto
covering ['kʌvərɪŋ] *n* cubierta, envoltura
covering letter, cover letter (*US*) *n* carta de explicación
cover note *n* (*Insurance*) póliza provisional
cover price *n* precio de cubierta

covert ['kəuvət] *adj (secret)* secreto, encubierto; *(dissembled)* furtivo
cover-up ['kʌvərʌp] *n* encubrimiento
covet ['kʌvɪt] *vt* codiciar
covetous ['kʌvɪtəs] *adj* codicioso
cow [kau] *n* vaca ■ *vt* intimidar
coward ['kauəd] *n* cobarde *m/f*
cowardice ['kauədɪs] *n* cobardía
cowardly ['kauədlɪ] *adj* cobarde
cowboy ['kaubɔɪ] *n* vaquero
cower ['kauə^r] *vi* encogerse (de miedo)
co-worker ['kəuwəːkə^r] *n* colaborador(a) *m(f)*
cowshed ['kauʃɛd] *n* establo
cowslip ['kauslɪp] *n (Bot)* primavera, prímula
cox ['kɔks], **coxswain** ['kɔksn] *n* timonel *m*
coy [kɔɪ] *adj* tímido
coyote [kɔɪ'əutɪ] *n* coyote *m*
cozy ['kəuzɪ] *adj (US)* = **cosy**
CP *n abbr (= Communist Party)* PC *m*
cp. *abbr (= compare)* cfr.
CPA *n abbr (US)* = **certified public accountant**
CPI *n abbr (= Consumer Price Index)* IPC *m*
Cpl. *abbr (Mil)* = **corporal**
c.p.s. *abbr (= characters per second)* c.p.s.
CPSA *n abbr (Brit: = Civil and Public Services Association) sindicato de funcionarios*
CPU *n abbr* = **central processing unit**
cr. *abbr* = **credit**; **creditor**
crab [kræb] *n* cangrejo
crab apple *n* manzana silvestre
crack [kræk] *n* grieta; *(noise)* crujido; *(: of whip)* chasquido; *(joke)* chiste *m*; *(col: drug)* crack *m*; *(attempt)*: **to have a ~ at sth** intentar algo ■ *vt* agrietar, romper; *(nut)* cascar; *(safe)* forzar; *(whip etc)* chasquear; *(knuckles)* crujir; *(joke)* contar; *(case: solve)* resolver; *(code)* descifrar ■ *adj (athlete)* de primera clase; **to ~ jokes** *(col)* bromear
▸ **crack down on** *vt fus* reprimir fuertemente, adoptar medidas severas contra
▸ **crack up** *vi* sufrir una crisis nerviosa
crackdown ['krækdaun] *n*: **~ (on)** *(on crime)* campaña (contra); *(on spending)* reducción *f* (en)
cracker ['krækə^r] *n (biscuit)* galleta salada, crácker *m*; *(Christmas cracker)* sorpresa (navideña)
crackle ['krækl] *vi* crepitar
crackling ['kræklɪŋ] *n (on radio, telephone)* interferencia; *(of fire)* chisporroteo, crepitación *f*; *(of leaves etc)* crujido; *(of pork)* chicharrón *m*
crackpot ['krækpɔt] *(col) n* pirado(-a) ■ *adj* de pirado
cradle ['kreɪdl] *n* cuna ■ *vt (child)* mecer, acunar; *(object)* abrazar
craft [krɑːft] *n (skill)* arte *m*; *(trade)* oficio; *(cunning)* astucia; *(boat)* embarcación *f*
craftsman ['krɑːftsmən] *n* artesano
craftsmanship ['krɑːftsmənʃɪp] *n* artesanía
crafty ['krɑːftɪ] *adj* astuto
crag [kræg] *n* peñasco
craggy ['krægɪ] *adj* escarpado
cram [kræm] *vt (fill)*: **to ~ sth with** llenar algo (a reventar) de; *(put)*: **to ~ sth into** meter algo a la fuerza en ■ *vi (for exams)* empollar
crammed [kræmd] *adj* atestado
cramp [kræmp] *n (Med)* calambre *m*; *(Tech)* grapa ■ *vt (limit)* poner trabas a
cramped [kræmpt] *adj* apretado; *(room)* minúsculo
crampon ['kræmpən] *n* crampón *m*
cranberry ['krænbərɪ] *n* arándano
crane [kreɪn] *n (Tech)* grúa; *(bird)* grulla ■ *vt, vi*: **to ~ forward, to ~ one's neck** estirar el cuello
cranium ['kreɪnɪəm] *n* cráneo
crank [kræŋk] *n* manivela; *(person)* chiflado(-a)
crankshaft ['kræŋkʃɑːft] *n* cigüeñal *m*
cranky ['kræŋkɪ] *adj (eccentric)* maniático; *(bad-tempered)* de mal genio
cranny ['krænɪ] *n see* **nook**
crap [kræp] *n (col!)* mierda *(!)*
crappy ['kræpɪ] *adj (col)* chungo
craps [kræps] *n (US)* dados *mpl*
crash [kræʃ] *n (noise)* estrépito; *(of cars, plane)* accidente *m*; *(of business)* quiebra; *(Stock Exchange)* crac *m* ■ *vt (plane)* estrellar ■ *vi (plane)* estrellarse; *(two cars)* chocar; *(fall noisily)* caer con estrépito; **he crashed the car into a wall** estrelló el coche contra una pared *or* tapia
crash barrier *n (Aut)* barrera de protección
crash course *n* curso acelerado
crash helmet *n* casco (protector)
crash landing *n* aterrizaje *m* forzoso
crass [kræs] *adj* grosero, maleducado
crate [kreɪt] *n* caja, cajón *m* de embalaje; *(col)* armatoste *m*
crater ['kreɪtə^r] *n* cráter *m*
cravat, cravate [krə'væt] *n* pañuelo
crave [kreɪv] *vt, vi*: **to ~ (for)** ansiar, anhelar
craving ['kreɪvɪŋ] *n (for food, cigarettes etc)* ansias *fpl*; *(during pregnancy)* antojo
crawl [krɔːl] *vi (drag o.s.)* arrastrarse; *(child)* andar a gatas, gatear; *(vehicle)* avanzar (lentamente); *(col)*: **to ~ to sb** dar coba a algn, hacerle la pelota a algn ■ *n (Swimming)* crol *m*
crawler lane [krɔːlə-] *n (Brit Aut)* carril *m* para tráfico lento

crayfish ['kreɪfɪʃ] *n pl inv* (*freshwater*) cangrejo (de río); (*saltwater*) cigala
crayon ['kreɪən] *n* lápiz *m* de color
craze [kreɪz] *n* manía; (*fashion*) moda
crazed [kreɪzd] *adj* (*look, person*) loco, demente; (*pottery, glaze*) agrietado, cuarteado
crazy ['kreɪzɪ] *adj* (*person*) loco; (*idea*) disparatado; **to go ~** volverse loco; **to be ~ about sb/sth** (*col*) estar loco por algn/algo
crazy paving *n pavimento de baldosas irregulares*
creak [kri:k] *vi* crujir; (*hinge etc*) chirriar, rechinar
cream [kri:m] *n* (*of milk*) nata, crema; (*lotion*) crema; (*fig*) flor *f* y nata ■ *adj* (*colour*) color *m* crema; **whipped ~** nata batida
▸ **cream off** *vt* (*fig: best talents, part of profits*) separar lo mejor de
cream cake *n* pastel *m* de nata
cream cheese *n* queso fresco cremoso
creamery ['kri:mərɪ] *n* (*shop*) quesería; (*factory*) central *f* lechera
creamy ['kri:mɪ] *adj* cremoso
crease [kri:s] *n* (*fold*) pliegue *m*; (*in trousers*) raya; (*wrinkle*) arruga ■ *vt* (*fold*) doblar, plegar; (*wrinkle*) arrugar ■ *vi* (*wrinkle up*) arrugarse
crease-resistant ['kri:srɪzɪstənt] *adj* inarrugable
create [kri:'eɪt] *vt* (*also Comput*) crear; (*impression*) dar; (*fuss, noise*) hacer
creation [kri:'eɪʃən] *n* creación *f*
creative [kri:'eɪtɪv] *adj* creativo
creativity [kri:eɪ'tɪvɪtɪ] *n* creatividad *f*
creator [kri:'eɪtə^r] *n* creador(a) *m(f)*
creature ['kri:tʃə^r] *n* (*living thing*) criatura; (*animal*) animal *m*; (*insect*) bicho
creature comforts *npl* comodidades *fpl* materiales
crèche, creche [krɛʃ] *n* (*Brit*) guardería (infantil)
credence ['kri:dəns] *n*: **to lend** *or* **give ~ to** creer en, dar crédito a
credentials [krɪ'dɛnʃlz] *npl* credenciales *fpl*; (*letters of reference*) referencias *fpl*
credibility [krɛdɪ'bɪlɪtɪ] *n* credibilidad *f*
credible ['krɛdɪbl] *adj* creíble; (*witness, source*) fidedigno
credit ['krɛdɪt] *n* (*gen*) crédito; (*merit*) honor *m*, mérito ■ *vt* (*Comm*) abonar; (*believe*) creer, dar crédito a ■ *adj* crediticio; **to be in ~** (*person, bank account*) tener saldo a favor; **on ~** a crédito; (*col*) al fiado; **he's a ~ to his family** hace honor a su familia; **to ~ sb with** (*fig*) reconocer a algn el mérito de; *see also* **credits**
creditable ['krɛdɪtəbl] *adj* estimable, digno de elogio
credit account *n* cuenta de crédito
credit agency *n* agencia de informes comerciales
credit balance *n* saldo acreedor
credit card *n* tarjeta de crédito
credit control *n* control *m* de créditos
credit facilities *npl* facilidades *fpl* de crédito
credit limit *n* límite *m* de crédito
credit note *n* nota de crédito
creditor ['krɛdɪtə^r] *n* acreedor(a) *m(f)*
credits ['krɛdɪts] *npl* (*Cine*) títulos *mpl or* rótulos *mpl* de crédito, créditos *mpl*
credit transfer *n* transferencia de crédito
creditworthy ['krɛdɪtwə:ðɪ] *adj* solvente
credulity [krɪ'dju:lɪtɪ] *n* credulidad *f*
creed [kri:d] *n* credo
creek [kri:k] *n* cala, ensenada; (*US*) riachuelo
creel [kri:l] *n* nasa
creep [kri:p] (*pt, pp* **crept**) [krɛpt] *vi* (*animal*) deslizarse; (*plant*) trepar; **to ~ up on sb** acercarse sigilosamente a algn; (*fig: old age etc*) acercarse ■ *n* (*col*): **he's a ~** ¡qué lameculos es!; **it gives me the creeps** me da escalofríos
creeper ['kri:pə^r] *n* enredadera
creepers ['kri:pəz] *npl* (*US: for baby*) pelele *msg*
creepy ['kri:pɪ] *adj* (*frightening*) horripilante
creepy-crawly ['kri:pɪ'krɔ:lɪ] *n* (*col*) bicho
cremate [krɪ'meɪt] *vt* incinerar
cremation [krɪ'meɪʃən] *n* incineración *f*, cremación *f*
crematorium [krɛmə'tɔ:rɪəm] (*pl* **crematoria**) [krɛmə'tɔ:rɪə] *n* crematorio
creosote ['krɪəsəut] *n* creosota
crêpe [kreɪp] *n* (*fabric*) crespón *m*; (*also*: **crêpe rubber**) crep(é) *m*
crêpe bandage *n* (*Brit*) venda elástica
crêpe paper *n* papel *m* crep(é)
crêpe sole *n* (*on shoes*) suela de crep(é)
crept [krɛpt] *pt, pp of* **creep**
crescent ['krɛsnt] *n* media luna; (*street*) calle *f* (*en forma de semicírculo*)
cress [krɛs] *n* berro
crest [krɛst] *n* (*of bird*) cresta; (*of hill*) cima, cumbre *f*; (*of helmet*) cimera; (*of coat of arms*) blasón *m*
crestfallen ['krɛstfɔ:lən] *adj* alicaído
Crete [kri:t] *n* Creta
cretin ['krɛtɪn] *n* cretino(-a)
crevasse [krɪ'væs] *n* grieta
crevice ['krɛvɪs] *n* grieta, hendedura
crew [kru:] *n* (*of ship etc*) tripulación *f*; (*Cine etc*) equipo; (*gang*) pandilla, banda; (*Mil*) dotación *f*
crew-cut ['kru:kʌt] *n* corte *m* al rape
crew-neck ['kru:nɛk] *n* cuello de caja
crib [krɪb] *n* pesebre *m* ■ *vt* (*col*) plagiar; (*Scol*) copiar

crick [krɪk] *n*: **~ in the neck** tortícolis *f inv*
cricket ['krɪkɪt] *n* (*insect*) grillo; (*game*) críquet *m*
cricketer ['krɪkɪtəʳ] *n* jugador(a) *m(f)* de críquet
crime [kraɪm] *n* crimen *m*; (*less serious*) delito
crime wave *n* ola de crímenes *or* delitos
criminal ['krɪmɪnl] *n* criminal *m/f*, delincuente *m/f* ■ *adj* criminal; (*law*) penal
Criminal Investigation Department *n* ≈ Brigada de Investigación Criminal *f* (*SP*)
crimp [krɪmp] *vt* (*hair*) rizar
crimson ['krɪmzn] *adj* carmesí
cringe [krɪndʒ] *vi* encogerse
crinkle ['krɪŋkl] *vt* arrugar
crinkly ['krɪŋklɪ] *adj* (*hair*) rizado, crespo
cripple ['krɪpl] *n* lisiado(-a), cojo(-a) ■ *vt* lisiar, mutilar; (*ship, plane*) inutilizar; (*production, exports*) paralizar; **crippled with arthritis** paralizado por la artritis
crippling ['krɪplɪŋ] *adj* (*injury etc*) debilitador(a); (*prices, taxes*) devastador(a)
crisis ['kraɪsɪs] (*pl* **crises**) ['kraɪsi:z] *n* crisis *f*
crisp [krɪsp] *adj* fresco; (*toast, snow*) crujiente; (*manner*) seco
crisps [krɪsps] *npl* (*Brit*) patatas *fpl* fritas
crisscross ['krɪskrɔs] *adj* entrelazado, entrecruzado ■ *vt* entrecruzar(se)
criterion [kraɪ'tɪərɪən] (*pl* **criteria**) [kraɪ'tɪərɪə] *n* criterio
critic ['krɪtɪk] *n* crítico(-a)
critical ['krɪtɪkl] *adj* (*gen*) crítico; (*illness*) grave; **to be ~ of sb/sth** criticar a algn/algo
critically ['krɪtɪklɪ] *adv* (*speak etc*) en tono crítico; (*ill*) gravemente
criticism ['krɪtɪsɪzm] *n* crítica
criticize ['krɪtɪsaɪz] *vt* criticar
critique [krɪ'ti:k] *n* crítica
croak [krəuk] *vi* (*frog*) croar; (*raven*) graznar ■ *n* (*of raven*) graznido
Croat ['krəuæt] *adj, n* = **Croatian**
Croatia [krəu'eɪʃə] *n* Croacia
Croatian [krəu'eɪʃən] *adj, n* croata *m/f* ■ *n* (*Ling*) croata *m*
crochet ['krəuʃeɪ] *n* ganchillo
crock [krɔk] *n* cántaro; (*col: person: also:* **old crock**) carcamal *m/f*, vejestorio; (*: car etc*) cacharro
crockery ['krɔkərɪ] *n* (*plates, cups etc*) loza, vajilla
crocodile ['krɔkədaɪl] *n* cocodrilo
crocus ['krəukəs] *n* azafrán *m*
croft [krɔft] *n* granja pequeña
crofter ['krɔftəʳ] *n* pequeño granjero
croissant ['krwas] *n* croissant *m*, medialuna (*esp LAm*)
crone [krəun] *n* arpía, bruja
crony ['krəunɪ] *n* compinche *m/f*
crook [kruk] *n* (*fam*) ladrón(-ona) *m(f)*; (*of shepherd*) cayado; (*of arm*) pliegue *m*
crooked ['krukɪd] *adj* torcido; (*path*) tortuoso; (*fam*) sucio
crop [krɔp] *n* (*produce*) cultivo; (*amount produced*) cosecha; (*riding crop*) látigo de montar; (*of bird*) buche *m* ■ *vt* cortar, recortar; (*animals: grass*) pacer
▸ **crop up** *vi* surgir, presentarse
crop spraying [-'spreɪɪŋ] *n* fumigación *f* de los cultivos
croquet ['krəukeɪ] *n* croquet *m*
croquette [krə'kɛt] *n* croqueta (*de patata*)
cross [krɔs] *n* cruz *f* ■ *vt* (*street etc*) cruzar, atravesar; (*thwart: person*) contrariar, ir contra ■ *vi*: **the boat crosses from Santander to Plymouth** el barco hace la travesía de Santander a Plymouth ■ *adj* de mal humor, enojado; **it's a ~ between geography and sociology** es una mezcla de geografía y sociología; **to ~ o.s.** santiguarse; **they've got their lines crossed** (*fig*) hay un malentendido entre ellos; **to be/get ~ with sb (about sth)** estar enfadado/enfadarse con algn (por algo)
▸ **cross out** *vt* tachar
▸ **cross over** *vi* cruzar
crossbar ['krɔsbɑ:ʳ] *n* travesaño; (*of bicycle*) barra
crossbow ['krɔsbəu] *n* ballesta
cross-Channel ferry ['krɔs'tʃænl-] *n* transbordador *m* que cruza el Canal de la Mancha
cross-check ['krɔstʃɛk] *n* verificación *f* ■ *vt* verificar
cross-country ['krɔs'kʌntrɪ], **cross-country race** *n* carrera a campo traviesa, cross *m*
cross-dressing [krɔs'drɛsɪŋ] *n* travestismo
cross-examination ['krɔsɪgzæmɪ'neɪʃən] *n* interrogatorio
cross-examine ['krɔsɪg'zæmɪn] *vt* interrogar
cross-eyed ['krɔsaɪd] *adj* bizco
crossfire ['krɔsfaɪəʳ] *n* fuego cruzado
crossing ['krɔsɪŋ] *n* (*on road*) cruce *m*; (*Rail*) paso a nivel; (*sea passage*) travesía; (*also:* **pedestrian crossing**) paso de peatones
crossing guard *n* (*US*) *persona encargada de ayudar a los niños a cruzar la calle*
crossing point *n* paso; (*at border*) paso fronterizo
cross purposes *npl*: **to be at ~ with sb** tener un malentendido con algn
cross-question ['krɔs'kwɛstʃən] *vt* interrogar
cross-reference ['krɔs'rɛfrəns] *n* remisión *f*
crossroads ['krɔsrəudz] *nsg* cruce *m*; (*fig*) encrucijada

cross section *n* corte *m* transversal; (*of population*) muestra (representativa)
crosswalk ['krɔswɔːk] *n* (*US*) paso de peatones
crosswind ['krɔswɪnd] *n* viento de costado
crossword ['krɔswəːd] *n* crucigrama *m*
crotch [krɔtʃ] *n* (*of garment*) entrepierna
crotchet ['krɔtʃɪt] *n* (*Brit Mus*) negra
crotchety ['krɔtʃɪtɪ] *adj* (*person*) arisco
crouch [krautʃ] *vi* agacharse
croup [kruːp] *n* (*Med*) crup *m*
croupier ['kruːpɪə] *n* crupier *m/f*
crouton ['kruːtɔn] *n* cubito de pan frito
crow [krəu] *n* (*bird*) cuervo; (*of cock*) canto, cacareo ■ *vi* (*cock*) cantar; (*fig*) jactarse
crowbar ['krəubɑːʳ] *n* palanca
crowd [kraud] *n* muchedumbre *f*; (*Sport*) público; (*common herd*) vulgo ■ *vt* (*gather*) amontonar; (*fill*) llenar ■ *vi* (*gather*) reunirse; (*pile up*) amontonarse; **crowds of people** gran cantidad de gente
crowded ['kraudɪd] *adj* (*full*) atestado; (*well-attended*) concurrido
crowd scene *n* (*Cine, Theat*) escena con muchos comparsas
crown [kraun] *n* corona; (*of head*) coronilla; (*of hat*) copa; (*of hill*) cumbre *f* ■ *vt* (*also tooth*) coronar; **and to ~ it all ...** (*fig*) y para colmo *or* remate ...
crown court *n* (*Law*) tribunal *m* superior; *ver nota*

CROWN COURT

En el sistema legal inglés los delitos graves como asesinato, violación o atraco son juzgados por un jurado en un tribunal superior llamado *crown court* con sede en noventa ciudades. Los jueces de paz ("Justice of the Peace") juzgan delitos menores e infracciones de la ley en juzgados llamados "Magistrates' Courts". Es el juez de paz quien decide remitir los casos pertinentes a la *crown court*, que en caso de recursos se remite al tribunal de apelación, "Court of Appeal".

crowning ['kraunɪŋ] *adj* (*achievement, glory*) máximo
crown jewels *npl* joyas *fpl* reales
crown prince *n* príncipe *m* heredero
crow's feet ['krəuzfiːt] *npl* patas *fpl* de gallo
crucial ['kruːʃl] *adj* crucial, decisivo; **his approval is ~ to the success of the project** su aprobación es crucial para el éxito del proyecto
crucifix ['kruːsɪfɪks] *n* crucifijo
crucifixion [kruːsɪ'fɪkʃən] *n* crucifixión *f*
crucify ['kruːsɪfaɪ] *vt* crucificar; (*fig*) martirizar
crude [kruːd] *adj* (*materials*) bruto; (*fig: basic*) tosco; (*: vulgar*) ordinario ■ *n* (*also:* **crude oil**) (petróleo) crudo
crude oil *n* petróleo crudo
cruel ['kruəl] *adj* cruel
cruelty ['kruəltɪ] *n* crueldad *f*
cruet ['kruːɪt] *n* vinagreras *fpl*
cruise [kruːz] *n* crucero ■ *vi* (*ship*) navegar; (*holidaymakers*) hacer un crucero; (*car*) ir a velocidad constante
cruise missile *n* misil *m* de crucero
cruiser ['kruːzəʳ] *n* crucero
cruising speed ['kruːzɪŋ-] *n* velocidad *f* de crucero
crumb [krʌm] *n* miga, migaja
crumble ['krʌmbl] *vt* desmenuzar ■ *vi* (*gen*) desmenuzarse; (*building*) desmoronarse
crumbly ['krʌmblɪ] *adj* desmenuzable
crummy ['krʌmɪ] *adj* (*col: poor quality*) pésimo, cutre (*SP*); (*: unwell*) fatal
crumpet ['krʌmpɪt] *n* ≈ bollo para tostar
crumple ['krʌmpl] *vt* (*paper*) estrujar; (*material*) arrugar
crunch [krʌntʃ] *vt* (*with teeth*) ronzar; (*underfoot*) hacer crujir ■ *n* (*fig*) hora de la verdad
crunchy ['krʌntʃɪ] *adj* crujiente
crusade [kruː'seɪd] *n* cruzada ■ *vi*: **to ~ for/against** (*fig*) hacer una campaña en pro de/en contra de
crusader [kruː'seɪdəʳ] *n* (*fig*) paladín *m/f*
crush [krʌʃ] *n* (*crowd*) aglomeración *f* ■ *vt* (*gen*) aplastar; (*paper*) estrujar; (*cloth*) arrugar; (*grind, break up: garlic, ice*) picar; (*fruit*) exprimir; (*grapes*) exprimir, prensar; **to have a ~ on sb** estar enamorado de algn
crush barrier *n* barrera de seguridad
crushing ['krʌʃɪŋ] *adj* aplastante; (*burden*) agobiante
crust [krʌst] *n* corteza
crustacean [krʌs'teɪʃən] *n* crustáceo
crusty ['krʌstɪ] *adj* (*bread*) crujiente; (*person*) de mal carácter; (*remark*) brusco
crutch [krʌtʃ] *n* (*Med*) muleta; (*support*) apoyo
crux [krʌks] *n*: **the ~** lo esencial, el quid
cry [kraɪ] *vi* llorar; (*shout: also:* **cry out**) gritar ■ *n* grito; (*of animal*) aullido; (*weep*): **she had a good ~** lloró a lágrima viva; **what are you crying about?** ¿por qué lloras?; **to ~ for help** pedir socorro a voces; **it's a far ~ from ...** (*fig*) dista mucho de ...
▸ **cry off** *vi* retirarse
crypt [krɪpt] *n* cripta
cryptic ['krɪptɪk] *adj* enigmático

crystal ['krɪstl] *n* cristal *m*
crystal-clear ['krɪstl'klɪəʳ] *adj* claro como el agua; (*fig*) cristalino
crystallize ['krɪstəlaɪz] *vt* (*fig*) cristalizar ■ *vi* cristalizarse; **crystallized fruits** frutas *fpl* escarchadas
CSA *n abbr* (= *Confederate States of America, Child Support Agency*) *organismo que supervisa el pago de la pensión a hijos de padres separados*
CSC *n abbr* (= *Civil Service Commission*) *comisión para la contratación de funcionarios*
CS gas *n* (*Brit*) gas *m* lacrimógeno
CST *n abbr* (*US*: = *Central Standard Time*) *huso horario*
CT, Ct. *abbr* (*US*) = **Connecticut**
ct *abbr* = **cent**; **court**; **carat**
CTC *n abbr* (*Brit*: = *city technology college*) ≈ centro de formación profesional
cu. *abbr* = **cubic**
cub [kʌb] *n* cachorro; (*also*: **cub scout**) niño explorador
Cuba ['kju:bə] *n* Cuba
Cuban ['kju:bən] *adj, n* cubano(-a) *m(f)*
cubbyhole ['kʌbɪhəul] *n* cuchitril *m*
cube [kju:b] *n* cubo; (*of sugar*) terrón *m* ■ *vt* (*Math*) elevar al cubo
cube root *n* raíz *f* cúbica
cubic ['kju:bɪk] *adj* cúbico; **~ capacity** (*Aut*) capacidad *f* cúbica
cubicle ['kju:bɪkl] *n* (*at pool*) caseta; (*for bed*) cubículo
cubism ['kju:bɪzəm] *n* cubismo
cuckoo ['kuku:] *n* cuco
cuckoo clock *n* reloj *m* de cuco
cucumber ['kju:kʌmbəʳ] *n* pepino
cuddle ['kʌdl] *vt* abrazar ■ *vi* abrazarse
cuddly ['kʌdlɪ] *adj* mimoso; (*toy*) de peluche
cudgel ['kʌdʒəl] *vt*: **to ~ one's brains** devanarse los sesos
cue [kju:] *n* (*snooker cue*) taco; (*Theat etc*) entrada
cuff [kʌf] *n* (*Brit*: *of shirt, coat etc*) puño; (*US*: *of trousers*) vuelta; (*blow*) bofetada ■ *vt* bofetear; **off the ~** *adv* improvisado
cufflinks ['kʌflɪŋks] *npl* gemelos *mpl*
cu. ft. *abbr* = **cubic feet**
cu. in. *abbr* = **cubic inches**
cuisine [kwɪ'zi:n] *n* cocina
cul-de-sac ['kʌldəsæk] *n* callejón *m* sin salida
culinary ['kʌlɪnərɪ] *adj* culinario
cull [kʌl] *vt* (*select*) entresacar; (*kill selectively*: *animals*) matar selectivamente ■ *n* matanza selectiva; **seal ~** matanza selectiva de focas
culminate ['kʌlmɪneɪt] *vi*: **to ~ in** culminar en
culmination [kʌlmɪ'neɪʃən] *n* culminación *f*, colmo
culottes [ku:'lɔts] *npl* falda *f* pantalón
culpable ['kʌlpəbl] *adj* culpable
culprit ['kʌlprɪt] *n* culpable *m/f*
cult [kʌlt] *n* culto; **a ~ figure** un ídolo
cultivate ['kʌltɪveɪt] *vt* (*also fig*) cultivar
cultivated ['kʌltɪveɪtɪd] *adj* culto
cultivation [kʌltɪ'veɪʃən] *n* cultivo; (*fig*) cultura
cultural ['kʌltʃərəl] *adj* cultural
culture ['kʌltʃəʳ] *n* (*also fig*) cultura
cultured ['kʌltʃəd] *adj* culto
cumbersome ['kʌmbəsəm] *adj* voluminoso
cumin ['kʌmɪn] *n* (*spice*) comino
cummerbund ['kʌməbʌnd] *n* faja, fajín *m*
cumulative ['kju:mjulətɪv] *adj* cumulativo
cunning ['kʌnɪŋ] *n* astucia ■ *adj* astuto; (*clever*: *device, idea*) ingenioso
cunt [kʌnt] *n* (*col!*) coño (*!*); (*insult*) mamonazo(-a) (*!*)
cup [kʌp] *n* taza; (*prize, event*) copa; **a ~ of tea** una taza de té
cupboard ['kʌbəd] *n* armario, placar(d) *m* (*LAm*)
cup final *n* (*Football*) final *f* de copa
cupful ['kʌpful] *n* taza
Cupid ['kju:pɪd] *n* Cupido
cupola ['kju:pələ] *n* cúpula
cuppa ['kʌpa] *n* (*Brit col*) (taza de) té *m*
cup-tie ['kʌptaɪ] *n* (*Brit*) partido de copa
cur [kə:ʳ] *n* perro de mala raza; (*person*) canalla *m*
curable ['kjuərəbl] *adj* curable
curate ['kjuərɪt] *n* coadjutor *m*
curator [kjuə'reɪtəʳ] *n* director(a) *m(f)*
curb [kə:b] *vt* refrenar; (*powers, spending*) limitar ■ *n* freno; (*US*: *kerb*) bordillo
curd cheese [kə:d-] *n* requesón *m*
curdle ['kə:dl] *vi* cuajarse
curds [kə:dz] *npl* requesón *msg*
cure [kjuəʳ] *vt* curar ■ *n* cura, curación *f*; **to be cured of sth** curarse de algo; **to take a ~** tomar un remedio
cure-all ['kjuərɔ:l] *n* (*also fig*) panacea
curfew ['kə:fju:] *n* toque *m* de queda
curio ['kjuərɪəu] *n* curiosidad *f*
curiosity [kjuərɪ'ɔsɪtɪ] *n* curiosidad *f*
curious ['kjuərɪəs] *adj* curioso; **I'm ~ about him** me intriga
curiously ['kjuərɪəslɪ] *adv* curiosamente; **~ enough, ...** aunque parezca extraño ...
curl [kə:l] *n* rizo; (*of smoke etc*) espiral *f*, voluta ■ *vt* (*hair*) rizar; (*paper*) arrollar; (*lip*) fruncir ■ *vi* rizarse; arrollarse
▸ **curl up** *vi* arrollarse; (*person*) hacerse un ovillo; (*fam*) morirse de risa
curler ['kə:ləʳ] *n* bigudí *m*
curlew ['kə:lu:] *n* zarapito

curling tongs, curling irons *(US)* ['kə:lɪŋ-] *npl* tenacillas *fpl*
curly ['kə:lɪ] *adj* rizado
currant ['kʌrnt] *n* pasa; *(black, red)* grosella
currency ['kʌrnsɪ] *n* moneda; **to gain ~** *(fig)* difundirse
current ['kʌrnt] *n* corriente *f* ■ *adj* actual; **direct/alternating ~** corriente directa/alterna; **the ~ issue of a magazine** el último número de una revista; **in ~ use** de uso corriente
current account *n (Brit)* cuenta corriente
current affairs *npl* (noticias *fpl* de) actualidad *f*
current assets *npl (Comm)* activo disponible
current liabilities *npl (Comm)* pasivo circulante
currently ['kʌrntlɪ] *adv* actualmente
curriculum *(pl* **curriculums** *or* **curricula**) [kə'rɪkjuləm, -lə] *n* plan *m* de estudios
curriculum vitae [-'vi:taɪ] *n* currículum *m* (vitae)
curry ['kʌrɪ] *n* curry *m* ■ *vt*: **to ~ favour with** buscar el favor de
curry powder *n* curry *m* en polvo
curse [kə:s] *vi* echar pestes ■ *vt* maldecir ■ *n* maldición *f*; *(swearword)* palabrota
cursor ['kə:sə^r] *n (Comput)* cursor *m*
cursory ['kə:sərɪ] *adj* rápido, superficial
curt [kə:t] *adj* seco
curtail [kə:'teɪl] *vt (cut short)* acortar; *(restrict)* restringir
curtain ['kə:tn] *n* cortina; *(Theat)* telón *m*; **to draw the curtains** *(together)* cerrar las cortinas; *(apart)* abrir las cortinas
curtain call *n (Theat)* llamada a escena
curtain ring *n* anilla
curtsey, curtsy ['kə:tsɪ] *n* reverencia ■ *vi* hacer una reverencia
curve [kə:v] *n* curva ■ *vt, vi* torcer
curved [kə:vd] *adj* curvo
cushion ['kuʃən] *n* cojín *m*; *(Snooker)* banda ■ *vt (seat)* acolchar; *(shock)* amortiguar
cushy ['kuʃɪ] *adj (col)*: **a ~ job** un chollo; **to have a ~ time** tener la vida arreglada
custard ['kʌstəd] *n (for pouring)* natillas *fpl*
custard powder *n* polvos *mpl* para natillas
custodial sentence [kʌs'təudɪəl-] *n* pena de prisión
custodian [kʌs'təudɪən] *n* guardián(-ana) *m(f)*; *(of museum etc)* conservador(a) *m(f)*
custody ['kʌstədɪ] *n* custodia; **to take sb into ~** detener a algn; **in the ~ of** al cuidado *or* cargo de
custom ['kʌstəm] *n* costumbre *f*; *(Comm)* clientela; *see also* **customs**
customary ['kʌstəmərɪ] *adj* acostumbrado; **it is ~ to do ...** es la costumbre hacer ...
custom-built ['kʌstəm'bɪlt] *adj* = **custom-made**
customer ['kʌstəmə^r] *n* cliente *m/f*; **he's an awkward ~** *(col)* es un tipo difícil
customer profile *n* perfil *m* del cliente
customized ['kʌstəmaɪzd] *adj (car etc)* hecho a encargo
custom-made ['kʌstəm'meɪd] *adj* hecho a la medida
customs ['kʌstəmz] *npl* aduana *sg*; **to go through (the) ~** pasar la aduana
Customs and Excise *n (Brit)* Aduanas *fpl* y Arbitrios
customs officer *n* aduanero(-a), funcionario(-a) de aduanas
cut [kʌt] *vb (pt, pp* **cut**) ■ *vt* cortar; *(price)* rebajar; *(record)* grabar; *(reduce)* reducir; *(col: avoid: class, lecture)* fumarse, faltar a ■ *vi* cortar; *(intersect)* cruzarse ■ *n* corte *m*; *(in skin)* corte, cortadura; *(with sword)* tajo; *(of knife)* cuchillada; *(in salary etc)* recorte *m*; *(slice of meat)* tajada; **to ~ one's finger** cortarse un dedo; **to get one's hair ~** cortarse el pelo; **to ~ and paste** *(Comput)* cortar y pegar; **to ~ sb dead** negarle el saludo *or* cortarle *(LAm)* a algn; **it cuts both ways** *(fig)* tiene doble filo; **to ~ a tooth** echar un diente; **power ~** *(Brit)* apagón *m*
▸ **cut back** *vt (plants)* podar; *(production, expenditure)* reducir
▸ **cut down** *vt (tree)* cortar, derribar; *(consumption, expenses)* reducir; **to ~ sb down to size** *(fig)* bajarle los humos a algn
▸ **cut in** *vi*: **to ~ in (on)** *(interrupt: conversation)* interrumpir, intervenir (en); *(Aut)* cerrar el paso (a)
▸ **cut off** *vt* cortar; *(fig)* aislar; *(troops)* cercar; **we've been ~ off** *(Tel)* nos han cortado la comunicación
▸ **cut out** *vt (shape)* recortar; *(delete)* suprimir
▸ **cut up** *vt* cortar (en pedazos); *(chop: food)* trinchar, cortar
cut-and-dried ['kʌtən'draɪd] *adj (also:* **cut-and-dry**) arreglado de antemano, seguro
cutback ['kʌtbæk] *n* reducción *f*
cute [kju:t] *adj* lindo, mono; *(shrewd)* listo
cuticle ['kju:tɪkl] *n* cutícula
cutlery ['kʌtlərɪ] *n* cubiertos *mpl*
cutlet ['kʌtlɪt] *n* chuleta
cutoff ['kʌtɔf] *n (also:* **cutoff point**) límite *m*
cutout ['kʌtaut] *n (cardboard cutout)* recortable *m*
cut-price ['kʌt'praɪs], **cut-rate** *(US)* ['kʌt'reɪt] *adj* a precio reducido
cutthroat ['kʌtθrəut] *n* asesino(-a) ■ *adj* feroz; **~ competition** competencia encarnizada *or* despiadada

cutting ['kʌtɪŋ] *adj* (*gen*) cortante; (*remark*) mordaz ■ *n* (*Brit: from newspaper*) recorte *m*; (*: Rail*) desmonte *m*; (*Cine*) montaje *m*
cutting edge *n* (*of knife*) filo; (*fig*) vanguardia; **a country on** *or* **at the ~ of space technology** un país puntero en tecnología del espacio
CV *n abbr* = **curriculum vitae**
cwo *abbr* (*Comm*) = **cash with order**
cwt. *abbr* = **hundredweight(s)**
cyanide ['saɪənaɪd] *n* cianuro
cybercafé ['saɪbəˌkæfeɪ] *n* cibercafé *m*
cybernetics [saɪbə'nɛtɪks] *nsg* cibernética
cyberspace ['saɪbəspeɪs] *n* ciberespacio
cyberterrorism ['saɪbətɛrərɪzəm] *n* ciberterrorismo *m*
cyclamen ['sɪkləmən] *n* ciclamen *m*
cycle ['saɪkl] *n* ciclo; (*bicycle*) bicicleta ■ *vi* ir en bicicleta
cycle lane *n* carril *m* de bicicleta, carril *m* bici
cycle race *n* carrera ciclista
cycle rack *n* soporte *m* para bicicletas
cycling ['saɪklɪŋ] *n* ciclismo
cycling holiday *n* vacaciones *fpl* en bicicleta
cyclist ['saɪklɪst] *n* ciclista *m/f*
cyclone ['saɪkləun] *n* ciclón *m*
cygnet ['sɪgnɪt] *n* pollo de cisne
cylinder ['sɪlɪndəʳ] *n* cilindro
cylinder block *n* bloque *m* de cilindros
cylinder head *n* culata de cilindro
cylinder-head gasket *n* junta de culata
cymbals ['sɪmblz] *npl* platillos *mpl*, címbalos *mpl*
cynic ['sɪnɪk] *n* cínico(-a)
cynical ['sɪnɪkl] *adj* cínico
cynicism ['sɪnɪsɪzəm] *n* cinismo
cypress ['saɪprɪs] *n* ciprés *m*
Cypriot ['sɪprɪət] *adj, n* chipriota *m/f*
Cyprus ['saɪprəs] *n* Chipre *f*
cyst [sɪst] *n* quiste *m*
cystitis [sɪs'taɪtɪs] *n* cistitis *f*
CZ *n abbr* (*US: = Canal Zone*) *zona del Canal de Panamá*
czar [zɑːʳ] *n* zar *m*
czarina [zɑː'riːnə] *n* zarina
Czech [tʃɛk] *adj* checo ■ *n* checo(-a); (*Ling*) checo; **the ~ Republic** la República Checa
Czechoslovak [tʃɛkə'sləuvæk] *adj, n* = **Czechoslovakian**
Czechoslovakia [tʃɛkəslə'vækɪə] *n* Checoslovaquia
Czechoslovakian [tʃɛkəslə'vækɪən] *adj, n* checoslovaco(-a) *m(f)*

Dd

D, d [diː] *n* (*letter*) D, d; (*Mus*): **D** re *m*; **D for David,** (*US*) **D for Dog** D de Dolores
D *abbr* (*US Pol*) = **democrat; democratic**
d *abbr* (*Brit: old*) = **penny**
d. *abbr* = **died**
DA *n abbr* (*US*) = **district attorney**
dab [dæb] *vt*: **to ~ ointment onto a wound** aplicar pomada sobre una herida; **to ~ with paint** dar unos toques de pintura ■ *n* (*light stroke*) toque *m*; (*small amount*) pizca
dabble ['dæbl] *vi*: **to ~ in** hacer por afición
Dacca ['dækə] *n* Dacca
dachshund ['dækshund] *n* perro tejonero
Dacron® ['deɪkrɔn] *n* (*US*) terylene *m*
dad [dæd], **daddy** ['dædɪ] *n* papá *m*
daddy-long-legs [dædɪ'lɔŋlɛgz] *n* típula
daffodil ['dæfədɪl] *n* narciso
daft [dɑːft] *adj* chiflado
dagger ['dægə^r] *n* puñal *m*, daga; **to look daggers at sb** fulminar a algn con la mirada
dahlia ['deɪljə] *n* dalia
daily ['deɪlɪ] *adj* diario, cotidiano ■ *n* (*paper*) diario; (*domestic help*) asistenta ■ *adv* todos los días, cada día; **twice ~** dos veces al día
dainty ['deɪntɪ] *adj* delicado; (*tasteful*) elegante
dairy ['dɛərɪ] *n* (*shop*) lechería; (*on farm*) vaquería ■ *adj* (*cow etc*) lechero
dairy cow *n* vaca lechera
dairy farm *n* vaquería
dairy produce *n* productos *mpl* lácteos
dais ['deɪɪs] *n* estrado
daisy ['deɪzɪ] *n* margarita
daisy-wheel printer *n* impresora de margarita
dale [deɪl] *n* valle *m*
dally ['dælɪ] *vi* entretenerse
dalmatian [dæl'meɪʃən] *n* (*dog*) (perro) dálmata *m*
dam [dæm] *n* presa; (*reservoir*) embalse ■ *vt* embalsar
damage ['dæmɪdʒ] *n* daño; (*fig*) perjuicio; (*to machine*) avería ■ *vt* dañar; perjudicar; averiar; **~ to property** daños materiales
damages ['dæmɪdʒɪz] *npl* (*Law*) daños y perjuicios; **to pay £5000 in ~** pagar £5000 por daños y perjuicios
damaging ['dæmɪdʒɪŋ] *adj*: **~ (to)** perjudicial (a)
Damascus [də'mɑːskəs] *n* Damasco
dame [deɪm] *n* (*title*) dama; (*US col*) tía; (*Theat*) vieja; *see also* **pantomime**
damn [dæm] *vt* condenar; (*curse*) maldecir ■ *n* (*col*): **I don't give a ~** me importa un pito ■ *adj* (*col: also:* **damned**) maldito, fregado (*LAm*); **~ (it)!** ¡maldito sea!
damnable ['dæmnəbl] *adj* (*col: behaviour*) detestable; (*weather*) horrible
damnation [dæm'neɪʃən] *n* (*Rel*) condenación *f* ■ *excl* (*col*) ¡maldición!, ¡maldito sea!
damning ['dæmɪŋ] *adj* (*evidence*) irrecusable
damp [dæmp] *adj* húmedo, mojado ■ *n* humedad *f* ■ *vt* (*also:* **dampen**: *cloth, rag*) mojar; (*enthusiasm*) enfriar
dampcourse ['dæmpkɔːs] *n* aislante *m* hidrófugo
damper ['dæmpə^r] *n* (*Mus*) sordina; (*of fire*) regulador *m* de tiro; **to put a ~ on things** ser un jarro de agua fría
dampness ['dæmpnɪs] *n* humedad *f*
damson ['dæmzən] *n* ciruela damascena
dance [dɑːns] *n* baile *m* ■ *vi* bailar; **to ~ about** saltar
dance hall *n* salón *m* de baile
dancer ['dɑːnsə^r] *n* bailador(a) *m(f)*; (*professional*) bailarín(-ina) *m(f)*
dancing ['dɑːnsɪŋ] *n* baile *m*
D and C *n abbr* (*Med:* = *dilation and curettage*) raspado
dandelion ['dændɪlaɪən] *n* diente *m* de león
dandruff ['dændrəf] *n* caspa
D and T *n abbr* (*Brit Scol*) = **design and technology**
dandy ['dændɪ] *n* dandi *m* ■ *adj* (*US col*) estupendo

Dane [deɪn] *n* danés(-esa) *m(f)*
danger ['deɪndʒəʳ] *n* peligro; (*risk*) riesgo; **~!** (*on sign*) ¡peligro!; **to be in ~ of** correr riesgo de; **out of ~** fuera de peligro
danger list *n* (*Med*): **to be on the ~** estar grave
dangerous ['deɪndʒərəs] *adj* peligroso
dangerously ['deɪndʒərəslɪ] *adv* peligrosamente; **~ ill** gravemente enfermo
danger zone *n* área *or* zona de peligro
dangle ['dæŋgl] *vt* colgar ■ *vi* pender, estar colgado
Danish ['deɪnɪʃ] *adj* danés(-esa) ■ *n* (*Ling*) danés *m*
Danish pastry *n* pastel *m* de almendra
dank [dæŋk] *adj* húmedo y malsano
dapper ['dæpəʳ] *adj* pulcro, apuesto
Dardanelles [dɑːdə'nɛlz] *npl* Dardanelos *mpl*
dare [dɛəʳ] *vt*: **to ~ sb to do** desafiar a algn a hacer ■ *vi*: **to ~ (to) do sth** atreverse a hacer algo; **I ~ say** (*I suppose*) puede ser, a lo mejor; **I ~ say he'll turn up** puede ser que *or* quizás venga; **I daren't tell him** no me atrevo a decírselo
daredevil ['dɛədɛvl] *n* temerario(-a), atrevido(-a)
Dar-es-Salaam ['dɑːrɛssə'lɑːm] *n* Dar es Salaam *m*
daring ['dɛərɪŋ] *adj* (*person*) osado; (*plan, escape*) atrevido ■ *n* atrevimiento, osadía
dark [dɑːk] *adj* oscuro; (*hair, complexion*) moreno; (*fig: cheerless*) triste, sombrío ■ *n* (*gen*) oscuridad *f*; (*night*) tinieblas *fpl*; **~ chocolate** chocolate *m* amargo; **it is/is getting ~** es de noche/está oscureciendo; **in the ~ about** (*fig*) ignorante de; **after ~** después del anochecer
darken ['dɑːkn] *vt* oscurecer; (*colour*) hacer más oscuro ■ *vi* oscurecerse; (*cloud over*) nublarse
dark glasses *npl* gafas *fpl* oscuras
dark horse *n* (*fig*) incógnita
darkly ['dɑːklɪ] *adv* (*gloomily*) tristemente; (*sinisterly*) siniestramente
darkness ['dɑːknɪs] *n* (*in room*) oscuridad *f*; (*night*) tinieblas *fpl*
darkroom ['dɑːkrum] *n* cuarto oscuro
darling ['dɑːlɪŋ] *adj, n* querido(-a) *m(f)*
darn [dɑːn] *vt* zurcir
dart [dɑːt] *n* dardo; (*in sewing*) pinza ■ *vi* precipitarse; **to ~ away/along** salir/marchar disparado
dartboard ['dɑːtbɔːd] *n* diana
darts [dɑːts] *n* dardos *mpl*
dash [dæʃ] *n* (*small quantity: of liquid*) gota, chorrito; (*of solid*) pizca; (*sign*) guión *m*; (*: long*) raya ■ *vt* (*break*) romper, estrellar; (*hopes*) defraudar ■ *vi* precipitarse, ir de prisa; **a ~ of soda** un poco *or* chorrito de sifón *or* soda
▸ **dash away, dash off** *vi* marcharse apresuradamente
dashboard ['dæʃbɔːd] *n* (*Aut*) salpicadero
dashing ['dæʃɪŋ] *adj* gallardo
dastardly ['dæstədlɪ] *adj* ruin, vil
DAT *n abbr* (*= digital audio tape*) cas(s)et(t)e *m or f* digital
data ['deɪtə] *npl* datos *mpl*
database ['deɪtəbeɪs] *n* base *f* de datos
data capture *n* recogida de datos
data link *n* enlace *m* de datos
data processing *n* proceso *or* procesamiento de datos
data transmission *n* transmisión *f* de datos
date [deɪt] *n* (*day*) fecha; (*with friend*) cita; (*fruit*) dátil *m* ■ *vt* fechar; (*col: girl etc*) salir con; **what's the ~ today?** ¿qué fecha es hoy?; **~ of birth** fecha de nacimiento; **closing ~** fecha tope; **to ~** *adv* hasta la fecha; **out of ~** pasado de moda; **up to ~** moderno; puesto al día; **to bring up to ~** (*correspondence, information*) poner al día; (*method*) actualizar; **to bring sb up to ~** poner a algn al corriente; **letter dated 5th July** *or* (US) **July 5th** carta fechada el 5 de julio
dated ['deɪtɪd]] *adj* anticuado
date rape *n violación ocurrida durante una cita con un conocido*
date stamp *n* matasellos *m inv*; (*on fresh foods*) sello de fecha
dative ['deɪtɪv] *n* dativo
daub [dɔːb] *vt* embadurnar
daughter ['dɔːtəʳ] *n* hija
daughter-in-law ['dɔːtərɪnlɔː] *n* nuera, hija política
daunting ['dɔːntɪŋ] *adj* desalentador(-a)
davenport ['dævnpɔːt] *n* escritorio; (*US: sofa*) sofá *m*
dawdle ['dɔːdl] *vi* (*waste time*) perder el tiempo; (*go slowly*) andar muy despacio; **to ~ over one's work** trabajar muy despacio
dawn [dɔːn] *n* alba, amanecer *m* ■ *vi* amanecer; (*fig*): **it dawned on him that ...** cayó en la cuenta de que ...; **at ~** al amanecer; **from ~ to dusk** de sol a sol
dawn chorus *n* canto de los pájaros al amanecer
day [deɪ] *n* día *m*; (*working day*) jornada; **the ~ before** el día anterior; **the ~ after tomorrow** pasado mañana; **the ~ before yesterday** anteayer, antes de ayer; **the ~ after, the following ~** el día siguiente; **by ~** de día; **~ by ~** día a día; **(on) the ~ that ...** el día que ...; **to work an eight-hour ~** trabajar ocho horas diarias *or* al día; **he works eight hours a ~** trabaja ocho horas al día; **paid**

by the ~ pagado por día; **these days, in the present ~** hoy en día
daybook ['deɪbuk] *n* (*Brit*) diario *or* libro de entradas y salidas
daybreak ['deɪbreɪk] *n* amanecer *m*
day-care centre ['deɪkɛə-] *n* centro de día; (*for children*) guardería infantil
daydream ['deɪdri:m] *n* ensueño ■ *vi* soñar despierto
daylight ['deɪlaɪt] *n* luz *f* (del día)
daylight robbery *n*: **it's ~!** (*fig, col*) ¡es un robo descarado!
Daylight Saving Time *n* (*US*) hora de verano
day-release course [deɪrɪ'li:s-] *n* curso de formación de un día a la semana
day return, day return ticket *n* (*Brit*) billete *m* de ida y vuelta (en un día)
day shift *n* turno de día
daytime ['deɪtaɪm] *n* día *m*
day-to-day ['deɪtə'deɪ] *adj* cotidiano, diario; (*expenses*) diario; **on a ~ basis** día por día
day trip *n* excursión *f* (de un día)
day tripper *n* excursionista *m/f*
daze [deɪz] *vt* (*stun*) aturdir ■ *n*: **in a ~** aturdido
dazed [deɪzd] *adj* aturdido
dazzle ['dæzl] *vt* deslumbrar
dazzling ['dæzlɪŋ] *adj* (*light, smile*) deslumbrante; (*colour*) fuerte
dB *abbr* = **decibel**
DBS *n abbr* (= *direct broadcasting by satellite*) transmisión vía satélite
DC *abbr* (*Elec*) = **direct current**; (*US*) = **District of Columbia**
DCC® *n abbr* (= *digital compact cassette*) cas(s)et(t)e *m* digital compacto
DD *n abbr* (= *Doctor of Divinity*) *título universitario* ■ *abbr* = **direct debit**
dd. *abbr* (*Comm*) = **delivered**
D-day ['di:deɪ] *n* (*fig*) día *m* clave
DDS *n abbr* (*US*: = *Doctor of Dental Science, Doctor of Dental Surgery*) *títulos universitarios*
DDT *n abbr* (= *dichlorodiphenyl trichloroethane*) DDT *m*
DE *abbr* (*US*) = **Delaware**
DEA *n abbr* (*US*: = *Drug Enforcement Administration*) *brigada especial dedicada a la lucha contra el tráfico de estupefacientes*
deacon ['di:kən] *n* diácono
dead [dɛd] *adj* muerto; (*limb*) dormido; (*battery*) agotado ■ *adv* totalmente; (*exactly*) justo; **he was ~ on arrival** ingresó cadáver; **to shoot sb ~** matar a algn a tiros; **~ tired** muerto (de cansancio); **to stop ~** parar en seco; **the line has gone ~** (*Tel*) se ha cortado la línea; **the ~** *npl* los muertos
dead beat *adj*: **to be ~** (*col*) estar hecho polvo
deaden ['dɛdn] *vt* (*blow, sound*) amortiguar; (*pain*) calmar, aliviar
dead end *n* callejón *m* sin salida
dead-end ['dɛdɛnd] *adj*: **a ~ job** un trabajo sin porvenir
dead heat *n* (*Sport*) empate *m*
deadline ['dɛdlaɪn] *n* fecha tope; **to work to a ~** trabajar con una fecha tope
deadlock ['dɛdlɔk] *n* punto muerto
dead loss *n* (*col*): **to be a ~** (*person*) ser un inútil; (*thing*) ser una birria
deadly ['dɛdlɪ] *adj* mortal, fatal; **~ dull** aburridísimo
deadly nightshade [-'naɪtʃeɪd] *n* belladona
deadpan ['dɛdpæn] *adj* sin expresión
Dead Sea *n*: **the ~** el Mar Muerto
dead season *n* (*Tourism*) temporada baja
deaf [dɛf] *adj* sordo; **to turn a ~ ear to sth** hacer oídos sordos a algo
deaf-aid ['dɛfeɪd] *n* audífono
deaf-and-dumb ['dɛfən'dʌm] *adj* (*person*) sordomudo; (*alphabet*) para sordomudos
deafen ['dɛfn] *vt* ensordecer
deafening ['dɛfnɪŋ] *adj* ensordecedor(-a)
deaf-mute ['dɛfmju:t] *n* sordomudo(-a)
deafness ['dɛfnɪs] *n* sordera
deal [di:l] *n* (*agreement*) pacto, convenio; (*business*) negocio, transacción *f*; (*Cards*) reparto ■ *vt* (*pt, pp* **dealt**) (*gen*) dar; **a great ~ (of)** bastante, mucho; **it's a ~!** (*col*) ¡trato hecho!, ¡de acuerdo!; **to do a ~ with sb** hacer un trato con algn; **he got a bad/fair ~ from them** le trataron mal/bien
▸ **deal in** *vt fus* tratar en, comerciar en
▸ **deal with** *vt fus* (*people*) tratar con; (*problem*) ocuparse de; (*subject*) tratar de
dealer ['di:ləʳ] *n* comerciante *m/f*; (*Cards*) mano *f*
dealership ['di:ləʃɪp] *n* concesionario
dealings ['di:lɪŋz] *npl* (*Comm*) transacciones *fpl*; (*relations*) relaciones *fpl*
dealt [dɛlt] *pt, pp of* **deal**
dean [di:n] *n* (*Rel*) deán *m*; (*Scol*) decano(-a)
dear [dɪəʳ] *adj* querido; (*expensive*) caro ■ *n*: **my ~** querido(-a); **~ me!** ¡Dios mío!; **D~ Sir/Madam** (*in letter*) Muy señor mío, Estimado señor/Estimada señora, De mi/nuestra (mayor) consideración (*esp LAm*); **D~ Mr/Mrs X** Estimado(-a) señor(a) X
dearly ['dɪəlɪ] *adv* (*love*) mucho; (*pay*) caro
dearth [də:θ] *n* (*of food, resources, money*) escasez *f*
death [dɛθ] *n* muerte *f*
deathbed ['dɛθbɛd] *n* lecho de muerte
death certificate *n* partida de defunción
death duties *npl* (*Brit*) derechos *mpl* de sucesión

deathly ['dɛθlɪ] *adj* mortal; (*silence*) profundo
death penalty *n* pena de muerte
death rate *n* tasa de mortalidad
death row *n*: **to be on ~** (*US*) estar condenado a muerte
death sentence *n* condena a muerte
death squad *n* escuadrón *m* de la muerte
deathtrap ['dɛθtræp] *n* lugar *m* (*or* vehículo *etc*) muy peligroso
deb [dɛb] *n abbr* (*col*) = **debutante**
debacle [deɪ'bɑːkl] *n* desastre *m*, catástrofe *f*
debar [dɪ'bɑːʳ] *vt*: **to ~ sb from doing** prohibir a algn hacer
debase [dɪ'beɪs] *vt* degradar
debatable [dɪ'beɪtəbl] *adj* discutible; **it is ~ whether ...** es discutible si ...
debate [dɪ'beɪt] *n* debate *m* ■ *vt* discutir
debauched [dɪ'bɔːtʃt] *adj* vicioso
debauchery [dɪ'bɔːtʃərɪ] *n* libertinaje *m*
debenture [dɪ'bɛntʃəʳ] *n* (*Comm*) bono, obligación *f*
debenture capital *n* capital *m* hipotecario
debilitate [dɪ'bɪlɪteɪt] *vt* debilitar
debilitating [dɪ'bɪlɪteɪtɪŋ] *adj* (*illness etc*) debilitante
debit ['dɛbɪt] *n* debe *m* ■ *vt*: **to ~ a sum to sb** *or* **to sb's account** cargar una suma en cuenta a algn
debit balance *n* saldo deudor *or* pasivo
debit note *n* nota de débito *or* cargo
debonair [dɛbə'nɛəʳ] *adj* jovial, cortés(-esa)
debrief [diː'briːf] *vt* hacer dar parte
debriefing [diː'briːfɪŋ] *n* relación *f* (de un informe)
debris ['dɛbriː] *n* escombros *mpl*
debt [dɛt] *n* deuda; **to be in ~** tener deudas; **debts of £5000** deudas de cinco mil libras; **bad ~** deuda incobrable
debt collector *n* cobrador(a) *m(f)* de deudas
debtor ['dɛtəʳ] *n* deudor(a) *m(f)*
debug ['diː'bʌg] *vt* (*Comput*) depurar
debunk [diː'bʌŋk] *vt* (*col: theory*) desprestigiar, desacreditar; (*claim*) desacreditar; (*person, institution*) desenmascarar
début ['deɪbjuː] *n* presentación *f*
debutante ['dɛbjutænt] *n* debutante *f*
Dec. *abbr* (= *December*) dic
decade ['dɛkeɪd] *n* década, decenio
decadence ['dɛkədəns] *n* decadencia
decadent ['dɛkədənt] *adj* decadente
de-caff ['diːkæf] *n* (*col*) descafeinado
decaffeinated [dɪ'kæfɪneɪtɪd] *adj* descafeinado
decamp [dɪ'kæmp] *vi* (*col*) escaparse, largarse, rajarse (*LAm*)
decant [dɪ'kænt]] *vt* decantar
decanter [dɪ'kæntəʳ] *n* jarra, decantador *m*
decathlon [dɪ'kæθlən] *n* decatlón *m*
decay [dɪ'keɪ] *n* (*fig*) decadencia; (*of building*) desmoronamiento; (*of tooth*) caries *f inv* ■ *vi* (*rot*) pudrirse; (*fig*) decaer
decease [dɪ'siːs] *n* fallecimiento ■ *vi* fallecer
deceased [dɪ'siːst] *adj* difunto
deceit [dɪ'siːt] *n* engaño
deceitful [dɪ'siːtful] *adj* engañoso
deceive [dɪ'siːv] *vt* engañar
decelerate [diː'sɛləreɪt] *vt* moderar la marcha de ■ *vi* decelerar
December [dɪ'sɛmbəʳ] *n* diciembre *m*; *see also* **July**
decency ['diːsənsɪ] *n* decencia
decent ['diːsənt] *adj* (*proper*) decente; (*person*) amable, bueno
decently ['diːsəntlɪ] *adv* (*respectably*) decentemente; (*kindly*) amablemente
decentralization [diːsɛntrəlaɪ'zeɪʃən] *n* descentralización *f*
decentralize [diː'sɛntrəlaɪz] *vt* descentralizar
deception [dɪ'sɛpʃən] *n* engaño
deceptive [dɪ'sɛptɪv] *adj* engañoso
decibel ['dɛsɪbɛl] *n* decibel(io) *m*
decide [dɪ'saɪd] *vt* (*person*) decidir; (*question, argument*) resolver ■ *vi*: **to ~ to do/that** decidir hacer/que; **to ~ on sth** tomar una decisión sobre algo; **to ~ against doing sth** decidir en contra de hacer algo
decided [dɪ'saɪdɪd] *adj* (*resolute*) decidido; (*clear, definite*) indudable
decidedly [dɪ'saɪdɪdlɪ] *adv* decididamente
deciding [dɪ'saɪdɪŋ] *adj* decisivo
deciduous [dɪ'sɪdjuəs] *adj* de hoja caduca
decimal ['dɛsɪməl] *adj* decimal ■ *n* decimal *f*; **to three ~ places** con tres cifras decimales
decimalize ['dɛsɪməlaɪz] *vt* convertir al, sistema decimal
decimal point *n* coma decimal
decimal system *n* sistema *m* métrico decimal
decimate ['dɛsɪmeɪt] *vt* diezmar
decipher [dɪ'saɪfəʳ] *vt* descifrar
decision [dɪ'sɪʒən] *n* decisión *f*; **to make a ~** tomar una decisión
decisive [dɪ'saɪsɪv] *adj* (*influence*) decisivo; (*manner, person*) decidido; (*reply*) tajante
deck [dɛk] *n* (*Naut*) cubierta; (*of bus*) piso; (*of cards*) baraja; **cassette ~** platina; **to go up on ~** subir a (la) cubierta; **below ~** en la bodega
deckchair ['dɛktʃɛəʳ]] *n* tumbona
deckhand ['dɛkhænd] *n* marinero de cubierta
declaration [dɛklə'reɪʃən] *n* declaración *f*
declare [dɪ'klɛəʳ] *vt* (*gen*) declarar

declassify [di:'klæsɪfaɪ] *vt* permitir que salga a la luz

decline [dɪ'klaɪn] *n* decaimiento, decadencia; (*lessening*) disminución *f* ■ *vt* rehusar ■ *vi* decaer; disminuir; **~ in living standards** disminución *f* del nivel de vida; **to ~ to do sth** rehusar hacer algo

declutch ['di:'klʌtʃ] *vi* desembragar

decode [di:'kəud] *vt* descifrar

decoder [di:'kəudəʳ] *n* (*Comput, TV*) de(s)codificador *m*

decompose [di:kəm'pəuz] *vi* descomponerse

decomposition [di:kɔmpə'zɪʃən] *n* descomposición *f*

decompression [di:kəm'prɛʃən] *n* descompresión *f*

decompression chamber *n* cámara de descompresión

decongestant [di:kən'dʒɛstənt] *n* descongestionante *m*

decontaminate [di:kən'tæmɪneɪt] *vt* descontaminar

decontrol [di:kən'trəul] *vt* (*trade*) quitar controles a; (*prices*) descongelar

décor ['deɪkɔ:ʳ] *n* decoración *f*; (*Theat*) decorado

decorate ['dɛkəreɪt] *vt* (*paint*) pintar; (*paper*) empapelar; (*adorn*): **to ~ (with)** adornar (de), decorar (de)

decoration [dɛkə'reɪʃən] *n* adorno; (*act*) decoración *f*; (*medal*) condecoración *f*

decorative ['dɛkərətɪv] *adj* decorativo

decorator ['dɛkəreɪtəʳ] *n* (*workman*) pintor *m* decorador

decorum [dɪ'kɔ:rəm] *n* decoro

decoy ['di:kɔɪ] *n* señuelo; **police ~** trampa *or* señuelo policial

decrease [*n* 'di:kri:s] *n* disminución *f* ■ *vt* [dɪ'kri:s] disminuir, reducir ■ *vi* reducirse; **to be on the ~** ir disminuyendo

decreasing [dɪ'kri:sɪŋ] *adj* decreciente

decree [dɪ'kri:] *n* decreto ■ *vt*: **to ~ (that)** decretar (que); **~ absolute/nisi** sentencia absoluta/provisional de divorcio

decrepit [dɪ'krɛpɪt] *adj* (*person*) decrépito; (*building*) ruinoso

decry [dɪ'kraɪ] *vt* criticar, censurar

dedicate ['dɛdɪkeɪt] *vt* dedicar

dedicated ['dɛdɪkeɪtɪd] *adj* dedicado; (*Comput*) especializado; **~ word processor** procesador *m* de textos especializado *or* dedicado

dedication [dɛdɪ'keɪʃən] *n* (*devotion*) dedicación *f*; (*in book*) dedicatoria

deduce [dɪ'dju:s] *vt* deducir

deduct [dɪ'dʌkt] *vt* restar; (*from wage etc*) descontar, deducir

deduction [dɪ'dʌkʃən] *n* (*amount deducted*) descuento; (*conclusion*) deducción *f*, conclusión *f*

deed [di:d] *n* hecho, acto; (*feat*) hazaña; (*Law*) escritura; **~ of covenant** escritura de contrato

deem [di:m] *vt* (*formal*) juzgar, considerar; **to ~ it wise to do** considerar prudente hacer

deep [di:p] *adj* profundo; (*voice*) bajo; (*breath*) profundo, a pleno pulmón ■ *adv*: **the spectators stood 20 ~** los espectadores se formaron de 20 en fondo; **to be four metres ~** tener cuatro metros de profundidad

deepen ['di:pn] *vt* ahondar, profundizar ■ *vi* (*darkness*) intensificarse

deep-freeze ['di:p'fri:z] *n* arcón *m* congelador

deep-fry ['di:p'fraɪ] *vt* freír en aceite abundante

deeply ['di:plɪ] *adv* (*breathe*) profundamente, a pleno pulmón; (*interested, moved, grateful*) profundamente, hondamente; **to regret sth ~** sentir algo profundamente

deep-rooted ['di:p'ru:tɪd] *adj* (*prejudice, habit*) profundamente arraigado; (*affection*) profundo

deep-sea ['di:p'si:] *adj*: **~ diver** buzo; **~ diving** buceo de altura

deep-seated ['di:p'si:tɪd] *adj* (*beliefs*) (profundamente) arraigado

deep-set ['di:psɛt] *adj* (*eyes*) hundido

deep-vein thrombosis *n* (*Med*) trombosis *f* venosa profunda

deer (*pl* **~**) [dɪəʳ] *n* ciervo

deerstalker ['dɪəstɔ:kəʳ] *n* (*hat*) gorro de cazador

deface [dɪ'feɪs] *vt* desfigurar, mutilar

defamation [dɛfə'meɪʃən] *n* difamación *f*

defamatory [dɪ'fæmətrɪ] *adj* difamatorio

default [dɪ'fɔ:lt] *vi* faltar al pago; (*Sport*) no presentarse, no comparecer ■ *n* (*Comput*) defecto; **by ~** (*Law*) en rebeldía; (*Sport*) por incomparecencia; **to ~ on a debt** dejar de pagar una deuda

defaulter [dɪ'fɔ:ltəʳ] *n* (*in debt*) moroso(-a)

default option *n* (*Comput*) opción *f* por defecto

defeat [dɪ'fi:t] *n* derrota ■ *vt* derrotar, vencer; (*fig: efforts*) frustrar

defeatism [dɪ'fi:tɪzəm] *n* derrotismo

defeatist [dɪ'fi:tɪst] *adj, n* derrotista *m/f*

defecate ['dɛfəkeɪt] *vi* defecar

defect ['di:fɛkt] *n* defecto ■ *vi* [dɪ'fɛkt]: **to ~ to the enemy** pasarse al enemigo; **physical ~** defecto físico; **mental ~** deficiencia mental

defective [dɪ'fɛktɪv] *adj* (*gen*) defectuoso; (*person*) anormal

defector [dɪ'fɛktə] *n* tránsfuga *m/f*
defence, (*US*) **defense** [dɪ'fɛns] *n* defensa; **the Ministry of D~** el Ministerio de Defensa; **witness for the ~** testigo de descargo
defenceless [dɪ'fɛnslɪs] *adj* indefenso
defence spending *n* gasto militar
defend [dɪ'fɛnd] *vt* defender; (*decision, action*) defender; (*opinion*) mantener
defendant [dɪ'fɛndənt] *n* acusado(-a); (*in civil case*) demandado(-a)
defender [dɪ'fɛndə^r] *n* defensor(a) *m(f)*
defending champion [dɪ'fɛndɪŋ-] *n* (*Sport*) defensor(-a) *m(f)* del título
defending counsel *n* (*Law*) abogado defensor
defense [dɪ'fɛns] *n* (*US*) = **defence**
defensive [dɪ'fɛnsɪv] *adj* defensivo ■ *n* defensiva; **on the ~** a la defensiva
defer [dɪ'fəː^r] *vt* (*postpone*) aplazar; **to ~ to** diferir a; (*submit*): **to ~ to sb/sb's opinion** someterse a algn/a la opinión de algn
deference ['dɛfərəns] *n* deferencia, respeto; **out of** *or* **in ~ to** por respeto a
deferential [dɛfə'rɛnʃəl] *adj* respetuoso
deferred [dɪ'fəːd] *adj*: **~ creditor** acreedor *m* diferido
defiance [dɪ'faɪəns] *n* desafío; **in ~ of** en contra de
defiant [dɪ'faɪənt] *adj* (*insolent*) insolente; (*challenging*) retador(a)
defiantly [dɪ'faɪəntlɪ] *adv* con aire de desafío
deficiency [dɪ'fɪʃənsɪ] *n* (*lack*) falta; (*Comm*) déficit *m*; (*defect*) defecto
deficient [dɪ'fɪʃənt] *adj* (*lacking*) insuficiente; (*incomplete*) incompleto; (*defective*) defectuoso; (*mentally*) anormal; **~ in** deficiente en
deficit ['dɛfɪsɪt] *n* déficit *m*
defile [dɪ'faɪl] *vt* manchar; (*violate*) violar
define [dɪ'faɪn] *vt* (*Comput*) definir
definite ['dɛfɪnɪt] *adj* (*fixed*) determinado; (*clear, obvious*) claro; **he was ~ about it** no dejó lugar a dudas (sobre ello)
definitely ['dɛfɪnɪtlɪ] *adv*: **he's ~ mad** no cabe duda de que está loco
definition [dɛfɪ'nɪʃən] *n* definición *f*
definitive [dɪ'fɪnɪtɪv] *adj* definitivo
deflate [diː'fleɪt] *vt* (*gen*) desinflar; (*pompous person*) quitar *or* rebajar los humos a; (*Econ*) deflacionar
deflation [diː'fleɪʃən] *n* (*Econ*) deflación *f*
deflationary [diː'fleɪʃənrɪ] *adj* (*Econ*) deflacionario
deflect [dɪ'flɛkt] *vt* desviar
defog [diː'fɔg] *vt* desempañar
defogger [diː'fɔgə^r] *n* (*US Aut*) dispositivo antivaho
deform [dɪ'fɔːm] *vt* deformar
deformed [dɪ'fɔːmd] *adj* deformado
deformity [dɪ'fɔːmɪtɪ] *n* deformación *f*
Defra *n abbr* (*Brit*) = **Department for Environment, Food and Rural Affairs**
defraud [dɪ'frɔːd] *vt* estafar; **to ~ sb of sth** estafar algo a algn
defray [dɪ'freɪ] *vt*: **to ~ sb's expenses** reembolsar a algn los gastos
defrost [diː'frɔst] *vt* (*frozen food, fridge*) descongelar
defroster [diː'frɔstə^r] *n* (*US*) eliminador *m* de vaho
deft [dɛft] *adj* diestro, hábil
defunct [dɪ'fʌŋkt] *adj* difunto; (*organization etc*) ya desaparecido
defuse [diː'fjuːz] *vt* desarmar; (*situation*) calmar, apaciguar
defy [dɪ'faɪ] *vt* (*resist*) oponerse a; (*challenge*) desafiar; (*order*) contravenir
degenerate [dɪ'dʒɛnəreɪt] *vi* degenerar ■ *adj* [dɪ'dʒɛnərɪt] degenerado
degradation [dɛgrə'deɪʃən] *n* degradación *f*
degrade [dɪ'greɪd] *vt* degradar
degrading [dɪ'greɪdɪŋ] *adj* degradante
degree [dɪ'griː] *n* grado; (*Scol*) título; **10 degrees below freezing** 10 grados bajo cero; **to have a ~ in maths** ser licenciado(-a) en matemáticas; **by degrees** (*gradually*) poco a poco, por etapas; **to some ~, to a certain ~** hasta cierto punto; **a considerable ~ of risk** un gran índice de riesgo
dehydrated [diːhaɪ'dreɪtɪd] *adj* deshidratado; (*milk*) en polvo
dehydration [diːhaɪ'dreɪʃən] *n* deshidratación *f*
de-ice [diː'aɪs] *vt* (*windscreen*) deshelar
de-icer [diː'aɪsə^r] *n* descongelador *m*
deign [deɪn] *vi*: **to ~ to do** dignarse hacer
deity ['diːɪtɪ] *n* deidad *f*, divinidad *f*
déjà vu [deɪʒɑː'vuː] *n*: **I had a sense of ~** sentía como si ya lo hubiera vivido
dejected [dɪ'dʒɛktɪd] *adj* abatido, desanimado
dejection [dɪ'dʒɛkʃən] *n* abatimiento
Del. *abbr* (*US*) = **Delaware**
delay [dɪ'leɪ] *vt* demorar, aplazar; (*person*) entretener; (*train*) retrasar; (*payment*) aplazar ■ *vi* tardar ■ *n* demora, retraso; **without ~** en seguida, sin tardar
delayed-action [dɪleɪd'ækʃən] *adj* (*bomb etc*) de acción retardada
delectable [dɪ'lɛktəbl] *adj* (*person*) encantador(-a); (*food*) delicioso
delegate ['dɛlɪgɪt] *n* delegado(-a) ■ *vt* ['dɛlɪgeɪt] delegar; **to ~ sth to sb/sb to do sth** delegar algo en algn/en algn para hacer algo

delegation [dɛlɪˈgeɪʃən] *n* (*of work etc*) delegación *f*
delete [dɪˈliːt] *vt* suprimir, tachar; (*Comput*) suprimir, borrar
Delhi [ˈdɛlɪ] *n* Delhi *m*
deli [ˈdɛlɪ] *n* = **delicatessen**
deliberate [dɪˈlɪbərɪt] *adj* (*intentional*) intencionado; (*slow*) pausado, lento ■ *vi* [dɪˈlɪbəreɪt] deliberar
deliberately [dɪˈlɪbərɪtlɪ] *adv* (*on purpose*) a propósito; (*slowly*) pausadamente
deliberation [dɪlɪbəˈreɪʃən] *n* (*consideration*) reflexión *f*; (*discussion*) deliberación *f*, discusión *f*
delicacy [ˈdɛlɪkəsɪ] *n* delicadeza; (*choice food*) manjar *m*
delicate [ˈdɛlɪkɪt] *adj* (*gen*) delicado; (*fragile*) frágil
delicately [ˈdɛlɪkɪtlɪ] *adv* con delicadeza, delicadamente; (*act, express*) con discreción
delicatessen [dɛlɪkəˈtɛsn] *n tienda especializada en comida exótica*
delicious [dɪˈlɪʃəs] *adj* delicioso, rico
delight [dɪˈlaɪt] *n* (*feeling*) placer *m*, deleite *m*; (*object*) encanto, delicia ■ *vt* encantar, deleitar; **to take ~ in** deleitarse en
delighted [dɪˈlaɪtɪd] *adj*: **~ (at** *or* **with/to do)** encantado (con/de hacer); **to be ~ that** estar encantado de que; **I'd be ~** con mucho *or* todo gusto
delightful [dɪˈlaɪtful] *adj* encantador(a), delicioso
delimit [diːˈlɪmɪt] *vt* delimitar
delineate [dɪˈlɪnɪeɪt] *vt* delinear
delinquency [dɪˈlɪŋkwənsɪ] *n* delincuencia
delinquent [dɪˈlɪŋkwənt] *adj, n* delincuente *m/f*
delirious [dɪˈlɪrɪəs] *adj* (*Med: fig*) delirante; **to be ~** delirar, desvariar
delirium [dɪˈlɪrɪəm] *n* delirio
deliver [dɪˈlɪvəʳ] *vt* (*distribute*) repartir; (*hand over*) entregar; (*message*) comunicar; (*speech*) pronunciar; (*blow*) lanzar, dar; (*Med*) asistir al parto de
deliverance [dɪˈlɪvrəns] *n* liberación *f*
delivery [dɪˈlɪvərɪ] *n* reparto; entrega; (*of speaker*) modo de expresarse; (*Med*) parto, alumbramiento; **to take ~ of** recibir
delivery note *n* nota de entrega
delivery van *n* furgoneta de reparto
delta [ˈdɛltə] *n* delta *m*
delude [dɪˈluːd] *vt* engañar
deluge [ˈdɛljuːdʒ] *n* diluvio ■ *vt* (*fig*): **to ~ (with)** inundar (de)
delusion [dɪˈluːʒən] *n* ilusión *f*, engaño
de luxe [dəˈlʌks] *adj* de lujo
delve [dɛlv] *vi*: **to ~ into** hurgar en
Dem. *abbr* (*US Pol*) = **Democrat**; **Democratic**
demand [dɪˈmɑːnd] *vt* (*gen*) exigir; (*rights*) reclamar; (*need*) requerir ■ *n* (*gen*) exigencia; (*claim*) reclamación *f*; (*Econ*) demanda; **to ~ sth (from** *or* **of sb)** exigir algo (a algn); **to be in ~** ser muy solicitado; **on ~** a solicitud
demanding [dɪˈmɑːndɪŋ] *adj* (*boss*) exigente; (*work*) absorbente
demarcation [diːmɑːˈkeɪʃən] *n* demarcación *f*
demarcation dispute *n* conflicto de definición *or* demarcación del trabajo
demean [dɪˈmiːn] *vt*: **to ~ o.s.** rebajarse
demeanour, demeanor (*US*) [dɪˈmiːnəʳ] *n* porte *m*, conducta, comportamiento
demented [dɪˈmɛntɪd] *adj* demente
demi- [ˈdɛmɪ] *pref* semi..., medio...
demilitarize [diːˈmɪlɪtəraɪz] *vt* desmilitarizar; **demilitarized zone** zona desmilitarizada
demise [dɪˈmaɪz] *n* (*death*) fallecimiento
demist [diːˈmɪst] *vt* (*Aut*) eliminar el vaho de
demister [diːˈmɪstəʳ] *n* (*Aut*) eliminador *m* de vaho
demo [ˈdɛməu] *n abbr* (*col*: = *demonstration*) manifestación *f*
demobilization [diːˈməubɪlaɪˈzeɪʃən] *n* desmovilización *f*
democracy [dɪˈmɔkrəsɪ] *n* democracia
democrat [ˈdɛməkræt] *n* demócrata *m/f*
democratic [dɛməˈkrætɪk] *adj* democrático; **the D~ Party** el partido demócrata (estadounidense)
demography [dɪˈmɔgrəfɪ] *n* demografía
demolish [dɪˈmɔlɪʃ] *vt* derribar, demoler
demolition [dɛməˈlɪʃən] *n* derribo, demolición *f*
demon [ˈdiːmən] *n* (*evil spirit*) demonio ■ *cpd* temible
demonstrate [ˈdɛmənstreɪt] *vt* demostrar ■ *vi* manifestarse; **to ~ (for/against)** manifestarse (a favor de/en contra de)
demonstration [dɛmənˈstreɪʃən] *n* (*Pol*) manifestación *f*; (*proof*) prueba, demostración *f*; **to hold a ~** (*Pol*) hacer una manifestación
demonstrative [dɪˈmɔnstrətɪv] *adj* (*person*) expresivo; (*Ling*) demostrativo
demonstrator [ˈdɛmənstreɪtəʳ] *n* (*Pol*) manifestante *m/f*
demoralize [dɪˈmɔrəlaɪz] *vt* desmoralizar
demote [dɪˈməut] *vt* degradar
demotion [dɪˈməuʃən] *n* degradación *f*; (*Comm*) descenso
demur [dɪˈməːʳ] *vi*: **to ~ (at)** hacer objeciones (a), vacilar (ante) ■ *n*: **without ~** sin objeción

demure [dɪ'mjuəʳ] *adj* recatado
demurrage [dɪ'mʌrɪdʒ] *n* sobrestadía
den [dɛn] *n* (*of animal*) guarida; (*study*) estudio
denationalization [di:næʃnəlaɪ'zeɪʃən] *n* desnacionalización *f*
denationalize [di:'næʃnəlaɪz] *vt* desnacionalizar
denatured alcohol [di:'neɪtʃəd-] *n* (*US*) alcohol *m* desnaturalizado
denial [dɪ'naɪəl] *n* (*refusal*) negativa; (*of report etc*) denegación *f*
denier ['dɛnɪəʳ] *n* denier *m*
denim ['dɛnɪm] *n* tela vaquera; *see also* **denims**
denim jacket *n* chaqueta vaquera, saco vaquero (*LAm*)
denims ['dɛnɪms] *npl* vaqueros *mpl*
denizen ['dɛnɪzn] *n* (*inhabitant*) habitante *m/f*; (*foreigner*) residente *m/f* extranjero(-a)
Denmark ['dɛnmɑ:k] *n* Dinamarca
denomination [dɪnɔmɪ'neɪʃən] *n* valor *m*; (*Rel*) confesión *f*
denominator [dɪ'nɔmɪneɪtəʳ] *n* denominador *m*
denote [dɪ'nəut] *vt* indicar, significar
denounce [dɪ'nauns] *vt* denunciar
dense [dɛns] *adj* (*thick*) espeso; (*foliage etc*) tupido; (*stupid*) torpe
densely [dɛnslɪ] *adv*: **~ populated** con una alta densidad de población
density ['dɛnsɪtɪ] *n* densidad *f*; **single/double-~ disk** *n* disco de densidad sencilla/de doble densidad
dent [dɛnt] *n* abolladura ■ *vt* (*also*: **make a dent in**) abollar
dental ['dɛntl] *adj* dental
dental floss [-flɔs] *n* seda dental
dental surgeon *n* odontólogo(-a)
dentifrice ['dɛntɪfrɪs] *n* dentífrico
dentist ['dɛntɪst] *n* dentista *m/f*; **~'s surgery** (*Brit*) consultorio dental
dentistry ['dɛntɪstrɪ] *n* odontología
dentures ['dɛntʃəz] *npl* dentadura *sg* (postiza)
denude [dɪ'nju:d] *vt*: **to ~ of** despojar de
denunciation [dɪnʌnsɪ'eɪʃən] *n* denuncia, denunciación *f*
deny [dɪ'naɪ] *vt* negar; (*charge*) rechazar; (*report*) desmentir; **to ~ o.s.** privarse (de); **he denies having said it** niega haberlo dicho
deodorant [di:'əudərənt] *n* desodorante *m*
depart [dɪ'pɑ:t] *vi* irse, marcharse; (*train*) salir; **to ~ from** (*fig: differ from*) apartarse de
departed [dɪ'pɑ:tɪd] *adj* (*bygone: days, glory*) pasado; (*dead*) difunto ■ *n*: **the (dear) ~** el/la/los/las difunto/a/os/as
department [dɪ'pɑ:tmənt] *n* (*Comm*) sección *f*; (*Scol*) departamento; (*Pol*) ministerio; **that's not my ~** (*fig*) no tiene que ver conmigo; **D~ of State** (*US*) Ministerio de Asuntos Exteriores
departmental [di:pɑ:t'mɛntl] *adj* (*dispute*) departamental; (*meeting*) departamental, de departamento; **~ manager** jefe(-a) *m(f)* de sección *or* de departamento *or* de servicio
department store *n* grandes almacenes *mpl*
departure [dɪ'pɑ:tʃəʳ] *n* partida, ida; (*of train*) salida; **a new ~** un nuevo rumbo
departure lounge *n* (*at airport*) sala de embarque
depend [dɪ'pɛnd] *vi*: **to ~ (up)on** (*be dependent upon*) depender de; (*rely on*) contar con; **it depends** depende, según; **depending on the result** según el resultado
dependable [dɪ'pɛndəbl] *adj* (*person*) formal, serio
dependant [dɪ'pɛndənt] *n* dependiente *m/f*
dependence [dɪ'pɛndəns] *n* dependencia
dependent [dɪ'pɛndənt] *adj*: **to be ~ (on)** depender (de) ■ *n* = **dependant**
depict [dɪ'pɪkt] *vt* (*in picture*) pintar; (*describe*) representar
depilatory [dɪ'pɪlətrɪ] *n* (*also*: **depilatory cream**) depilatorio
depleted [dɪ'pli:tɪd] *adj* reducido
deplorable [dɪ'plɔ:rəbl] *adj* deplorable
deplore [dɪ'plɔ:ʳ] *vt* deplorar
deploy [dɪ'plɔɪ] *vt* desplegar
depopulate [di:'pɔpjuleɪt] *vt* despoblar
depopulation ['di:pɔpju'leɪʃən] *n* despoblación *f*
deport [dɪ'pɔ:t] *vt* deportar
deportation [di:pɔ:'teɪʃən] *n* deportación *f*
deportation order *n* orden *f* de expulsión *or* deportación
deportee [di:pɔ:'ti:] *n* deportado(-a)
deportment [dɪ'pɔ:tmənt] *n* comportamiento
depose [dɪ'pəuz] *vt* deponer
deposit [dɪ'pɔzɪt] *n* depósito; (*Chem*) sedimento; (*of ore, oil*) yacimiento ■ *vt* (*gen*) depositar; **to put down a ~ of £50** dejar un depósito de 50 libras
deposit account *n* (*Brit*) cuenta de ahorros
depositor [dɪ'pɔzɪtəʳ] *n* depositante *m/f*, cuentacorrentista *m/f*
depository [dɪ'pɔzɪtərɪ] *n* almacén *m* depositario
depot ['dɛpəu] *n* (*storehouse*) depósito; (*for vehicles*) parque *m*
deprave [dɪ'preɪv] *vt* depravar
depraved [dɪ'preɪvd] *adj* depravado, vicioso
depravity [dɪ'prævɪtɪ] *n* depravación *f*, vicio
deprecate ['dɛprɪkeɪt] *vt* desaprobar, lamentar

deprecating ['dɛprɪkeɪtɪŋ] *adj* (*disapproving*) de desaprobación; (*apologetic*): **a ~ smile** una sonrisa de disculpa
depreciate [dɪ'pri:ʃɪeɪt] *vi* depreciarse, perder valor
depreciation [dɪpri:ʃɪ'eɪʃən] *n* depreciación *f*
depress [dɪ'prɛs] *vt* deprimir; (*press down*) apretar
depressant [dɪ'prɛsnt] *n* (*Med*) calmante *m*, sedante *m*
depressed [dɪ'prɛst] *adj* deprimido; (*Comm: market, economy*) deprimido; (*area*) deprimido (económicamente); **to get ~** deprimirse
depressing [dɪ'prɛsɪŋ] *adj* deprimente
depression [dɪ'prɛʃən] *n* depresión *f*; **the economy is in a state of ~** la economía está deprimida
deprivation [dɛprɪ'veɪʃən] *n* privación *f*; (*loss*) pérdida
deprive [dɪ'praɪv] *vt*: **to ~ sb of** privar a algn de
deprived [dɪ'praɪvd] *adj* necesitado
dept. *abbr* (= *department*) dto
depth [dɛpθ] *n* profundidad *f*; **at a ~ of three metres** a tres metros de profundidad; **to be out of one's ~** (*swimmer*) perder pie; (*fig*) estar perdido; **to study sth in ~** estudiar algo a fondo; **in the depths of** en lo más hondo de
depth charge *n* carga de profundidad
deputation [dɛpju'teɪʃən] *n* delegación *f*
deputize ['dɛpjutaɪz] *vi*: **to ~ for sb** sustituir a algn
deputy ['dɛpjutɪ] *adj*: **~ head** subdirector(-a) *m(f)* ■ *n* sustituto(-a), suplente *m/f*; (*Pol*) diputado(-a); (*agent*) representante *m/f*
deputy leader *n* vicepresidente(-a) *m(f)*
derail [dɪ'reɪl] *vt*: **to be derailed** descarrilarse
derailment [dɪ'reɪlmənt] *n* descarrilamiento
deranged [dɪ'reɪndʒd] *adj* trastornado
derby ['də:bɪ] *n* (*US*) hongo
deregulate [di:'rɛgjuleɪt] *vt* desreglamentar
deregulation [di:rɛgju'leɪʃən] *n* desreglamentación *f*
derelict ['dɛrɪlɪkt] *adj* abandonado
deride [dɪ'raɪd] *vt* ridiculizar, mofarse de
derision [dɪ'rɪʒən] *n* irrisión *f*, mofas *fpl*
derisive [dɪ'raɪsɪv] *adj* burlón(-ona)
derisory [dɪ'raɪzərɪ] *adj* (*sum*) irrisorio; (*laughter, person*) burlón(-ona), irónico
derivation [dɛrɪ'veɪʃən] *n* derivación *f*
derivative [dɪ'rɪvətɪv] *n* derivado ■ *adj* (*work*) poco original
derive [dɪ'raɪv] *vt* derivar ■ *vi*: **to ~ from** derivarse de
derived [dɪ'raɪvd] *adj* derivado
dermatitis [də:mə'taɪtɪs] *n* dermatitis *f*
dermatology [də:mə'tɔlədʒɪ] *n* dermatología
derogatory [dɪ'rɔgətərɪ] *adj* despectivo
derrick ['dɛrɪk] *n* torre *f* de perforación
derv [də:v] *n* (*Brit*) gasoil *m*
descend [dɪ'sɛnd] *vt, vi* descender, bajar; **to ~ from** descender de; **in descending order of importance** de mayor a menor importancia
▸ **descend on** *vt fus* (*enemy, angry person*) caer sobre; (*misfortune*) sobrevenir; (*gloom, silence*) invadir; **visitors descended on us** las visitas nos invadieron
descendant [dɪ'sɛndənt] *n* descendiente *m/f*
descent [dɪ'sɛnt] *n* descenso; (*Geo*) pendiente *f*, declive *m*; (*origin*) descendencia
describe [dɪs'kraɪb] *vt* describir
description [dɪs'krɪpʃən] *n* descripción *f*; (*sort*) clase *f*, género; **of every ~** de toda clase
descriptive [dɪs'krɪptɪv] *adj* descriptivo
desecrate ['dɛsɪkreɪt] *vt* profanar
desegregation [di:sɛgrɪ'geɪʃən] *n* desegregación *f*
desert [*n* 'dɛzət, *vb* dɪ'zə:t] *n* desierto ■ *vt* abandonar, desamparar ■ *vi* (*Mil*) desertar; *see also* **deserts**
deserter [dɪ'zə:təʳ] *n* desertor(-a) *m(f)*
desertion [dɪ'zə:ʃən] *n* deserción *f*
desert island *n* isla desierta
deserts [dɪ'zə:ts] *npl*: **to get one's just ~** llevarse su merecido
deserve [dɪ'zə:v] *vt* merecer, ser digno de, ameritar (*LAm*)
deservedly [dɪ'zə:vɪdlɪ] *adv* con razón
deserving [dɪ'zə:vɪŋ] *adj* (*person*) digno; (*action, cause*) meritorio
desiccated ['dɛsɪkeɪtɪd] *adj* desecado
design [dɪ'zaɪn] *n* (*sketch*) bosquejo; (*of dress, car*) diseño; (*pattern*) dibujo ■ *vt* (*gen*) diseñar; **industrial ~** diseño industrial; **to have designs on sb** tener la(s) mira(s) puesta(s) en algn; **to be designed for sb/sth** estar hecho para algn/algo
design and technology *n* (*Brit Scol*) diseño y tecnología
designate ['dɛzɪgneɪt] *vt* (*appoint*) nombrar; (*destine*) designar ■ *adj* ['dɛzɪgnɪt] designado
designation [dɛzɪg'neɪʃən] *n* (*appointment*) nombramiento; (*name*) denominación *f*
designer [dɪ'zaɪnəʳ] *n* diseñador(-a) *m(f)*; (*fashion designer*) modisto(-a)
designer baby *n* bebé *m* de diseño
desirability [dɪzaɪərə'bɪlɪtɪ] *n* ventaja, atractivo
desirable [dɪ'zaɪərəbl] *adj* (*proper*) deseable; (*attractive*) atractivo; **it is ~ that** es conveniente que
desire [dɪ'zaɪəʳ] *n* deseo ■ *vt* desear; **to ~ sth/to do sth/that** desear algo/hacer algo/que

desirous [dɪ'zaɪərəs] *adj* deseoso
desist [dɪ'zɪst] *vi*: **to ~ (from)** desistir (de)
desk [dɛsk] *n* (*in office*) escritorio; (*for pupil*) pupitre *m*; (*in hotel, at airport*) recepción *f*; (*Brit: in shop, restaurant*) caja
desktop computer ['dɛsktɔp-] *n* ordenador *m* de sobremesa
desktop publishing ['dɛsktɔp-] *n* autoedición *f*
desolate ['dɛsəlɪt] *adj* (*place*) desierto; (*person*) afligido
desolation [dɛsə'leɪʃən] *n* (*of place*) desolación *f*; (*of person*) aflicción *f*
despair [dɪs'pɛə^r] *n* desesperación *f* ■ *vi*: **to ~ of** desesperar de; **in** ~ desesperado
despatch [dɪs'pætʃ] *n*, *vt* = **dispatch**
desperate ['dɛspərɪt] *adj* desesperado; (*fugitive*) peligroso; (*measures*) extremo; **we are getting** ~ estamos al borde de desesperación
desperately ['dɛspərɪtlɪ] *adv* desesperadamente; (*very*) terriblemente, gravemente; ~ **ill** gravemente enfermo
desperation [dɛspə'reɪʃən] *n* desesperación *f*; **in** ~ desesperado
despicable [dɪs'pɪkəbl] *adj* vil, despreciable
despise [dɪs'paɪz] *vt* despreciar
despite [dɪs'paɪt] *prep* a pesar de, pese a
despondent [dɪs'pɔndənt] *adj* deprimido, abatido
despot ['dɛspɔt] *n* déspota *m/f*
dessert [dɪ'zə:t] *n* postre *m*
dessertspoon [dɪ'zə:tspu:n] *n* cuchara (de postre)
destabilize [di:'steɪbɪlaɪz] *vt* desestabilizar
destination [dɛstɪ'neɪʃən] *n* destino
destine ['dɛstɪn] *vt* destinar
destined ['dɛstɪnd] *adj*: ~ **for London** con destino a Londres
destiny ['dɛstɪnɪ] *n* destino
destitute ['dɛstɪtju:t] *adj* desamparado, indigente
destitution [dɛstɪ'tju:ʃən] *n* indigencia, miseria
destroy [dɪs'trɔɪ] *vt* destruir; (*finish*) acabar con
destroyer [dɪs'trɔɪə^r] *n* (*Naut*) destructor *m*
destruction [dɪs'trʌkʃən] *n* destrucción *f*; (*fig*) ruina
destructive [dɪs'trʌktɪv] *adj* destructivo, destructor(a)
desultory ['dɛsəltərɪ] *adj* (*reading*) poco metódico; (*conversation*) inconexo; (*contact*) intermitente
detach [dɪ'tætʃ] *vt* separar; (*unstick*) despegar
detachable [dɪ'tætʃəbl] *adj* separable; (*Tech*) desmontable
detached [dɪ'tætʃt] *adj* (*attitude*) objetivo, imparcial
detached house *n* chalé *m*, chalet *m*
detachment [dɪ'tætʃmənt] *n* separación *f*; (*Mil*) destacamento; (*fig*) objetividad *f*, imparcialidad *f*
detail ['di:teɪl] *n* detalle *m*; (*Mil*) destacamento ■ *vt* detallar; (*Mil*) destacar; **in** ~ detalladamente; **to go into ~(s)** entrar en detalles
detailed ['di:teɪld] *adj* detallado
detain [dɪ'teɪn] *vt* retener; (*in captivity*) detener
detainee [di:teɪ'ni:] *n* detenido(-a)
detect [dɪ'tɛkt] *vt* (*discover*) descubrir; (*Med, Police*) identificar; (*Mil, Radar, Tech*) detectar; (*notice*) percibir
detection [dɪ'tɛkʃən] *n* descubrimiento; identificación *f*; **crime** ~ investigación *f*; **to escape** ~ (*criminal*) escaparse sin ser descubierto; (*mistake*) pasar inadvertido
detective [dɪ'tɛktɪv] *n* detective *m*
detective story *n* novela policíaca
detector [dɪ'tɛktə^r] *n* detector *m*
détente [deɪ'tɑ:nt] *n* distensión *f*, detente *f*
detention [dɪ'tɛnʃən] *n* detención *f*, arresto
deter [dɪ'tə:^r] *vt* (*dissuade*) disuadir; (*prevent*) impedir; **to ~ sb from doing sth** disuadir a algn de que haga algo
detergent [dɪ'tə:dʒənt] *n* detergente *m*
deteriorate [dɪ'tɪərɪəreɪt] *vi* deteriorarse
deterioration [dɪtɪərɪə'reɪʃən] *n* deterioro
determination [dɪtə:mɪ'neɪʃən] *n* resolución *f*
determine [dɪ'tə:mɪn] *vt* determinar; **to ~ to do sth** decidir hacer algo
determined [dɪ'tə:mɪnd] *adj*: **to be ~ to do sth** estar decidido *or* resuelto a hacer algo; **a ~ effort** un esfuerzo enérgico
deterrence [dɪ'tɛrns] *n* disuasión *f*
deterrent [dɪ'tɛrənt] *n* fuerza de disuasión; **to act as a** ~ servir para prevenir
detest [dɪ'tɛst] *vt* aborrecer
detestable [dɪ'tɛstəbl] *adj* aborrecible
dethrone [di:'θrəun] *vt* destronar
detonate ['dɛtəneɪt] *vi* estallar ■ *vt* hacer detonar
detonator ['dɛtəneɪtə^r] *n* detonador *m*, fulminante *m*
detour ['di:tuə^r] *n* (*gen: US Aut: diversion*) desvío ■ *vt* (*US: traffic*) desviar; **to make a** ~ dar un rodeo
detract [dɪ'trækt] *vt*: **to ~ from** quitar mérito a, restar valor a
detractor [dɪ'træktə^r] *n* detractor(-a) *m(f)*
detriment ['dɛtrɪmənt] *n*: **to the ~ of** en perjuicio de; **without ~ to** sin detrimento de, sin perjuicio para

detrimental [dɛtrɪ'mɛntl] *adj* perjudicial
deuce [dju:s] *n* (*Tennis*) cuarenta iguales
devaluation [dɪvælju'eɪʃən] *n* devaluación *f*
devalue [dɪ'vælju:] *vt* devaluar
devastate ['dɛvəsteɪt] *vt* devastar; **he was devastated by the news** las noticias le dejaron desolado
devastating ['dɛvəsteɪtɪŋ] *adj* devastador(-a); (*fig*) arrollador(-a)
devastation [dɛvəs'teɪʃən] *n* devastación *f*, ruina
develop [dɪ'vɛləp] *vt* desarrollar; (*Phot*) revelar; (*disease*) contraer; (*habit*) adquirir ■ *vi* desarrollarse; (*advance*) progresar; **this land is to be developed** se va a construir en este terreno; **to ~ a taste for sth** tomar gusto a algo; **to ~ into** transformarse *or* convertirse en
developer [dɪ'vɛləpə^r] *n* (*property developer*) promotor(-a) *m(f)*
developing country *n* país *m* en (vías de) desarrollo
development [dɪ'vɛləpmənt] *n* desarrollo; (*advance*) progreso; (*of affair, case*) desenvolvimiento; (*of land*) urbanización *f*
development area *n* zona de fomento *or* desarrollo
deviant ['di:vɪənt] *adj* anómalo, pervertido
deviate ['di:vɪeɪt] *vi*: **to ~ (from)** desviarse (de)
deviation [di:vɪ'eɪʃən] *n* desviación *f*
device [dɪ'vaɪs] *n* (*scheme*) estratagema, recurso; (*apparatus*) aparato, mecanismo; (*explosive device*) artefacto explosivo
devil ['dɛvl] *n* diablo, demonio
devilish ['dɛvlɪʃ] *adj* diabólico
devil-may-care ['dɛvlmeɪ'kɛə^r] *adj* despreocupado
devil's advocate *n*: **to play (the) ~** hacer de abogado del diablo
devious ['di:vɪəs] *adj* intricado, enrevesado; (*person*) taimado
devise [dɪ'vaɪz] *vt* idear, inventar
devoid [dɪ'vɔɪd] *adj*: **~ of** desprovisto de
devolution [di:və'lu:ʃən] *n* (*Pol*) descentralización *f*
devolve [dɪ'vɔlv] *vi*: **to ~ (up) on** recaer sobre
devote [dɪ'vəut] *vt*: **to ~ sth to** dedicar algo a
devoted [dɪ'vəutɪd] *adj* (*loyal*) leal, fiel; **the book is ~ to politics** el libro trata de política
devotee [dɛvəu'ti:] *n* devoto(-a)
devotion [dɪ'vəuʃən] *n* dedicación *f*; (*Rel*) devoción *f*
devour [dɪ'vauə^r] *vt* devorar
devout [dɪ'vaut] *adj* devoto
dew [dju:] *n* rocío
dexterity [dɛks'tɛrɪtɪ] *n* destreza
dexterous, dextrous ['dɛkstrəs] *adj* (*skilful*) diestro, hábil; (*movement*) ágil
DfEE *n abbr* (*Brit*) = **Department for Education and Employment**
dg *abbr* (= *decigram*) dg
diabetes [daɪə'bi:ti:z] *n* diabetes *f*
diabetic [daɪə'bɛtɪk] *n* diabético(-a) ■ *adj* diabético; (*chocolate, jam*) para diabéticos
diabolical [daɪə'bɔlɪkəl] *adj* diabólico; (*col: dreadful*) horrendo, horroroso
diagnose ['daɪəgnəuz] *vt* diagnosticar
diagnosis (*pl* **diagnoses**) [daɪəg'nəusɪs, -si:z] *n* diagnóstico
diagonal [daɪ'ægənl] *adj* diagonal ■ *n* diagonal *f*
diagram ['daɪəgræm] *n* diagrama *m*, esquema *m*
dial ['daɪəl] *n* esfera; (*of radio*) dial *m*; (*tuner*) sintonizador *m*; (*of phone*) disco ■ *vt* (*number*) marcar, discar (*LAm*); **to ~ a wrong number** equivocarse de número; **can I ~ London direct?** ¿puedo marcar un número de Londres directamente?
dial. *abbr* = **dialect**
dial code *n* (*US*) prefijo
dialect ['daɪəlɛkt] *n* dialecto
dialling code ['daɪəlɪŋ-] *n* (*Brit*) prefijo
dialling tone *n* (*Brit*) señal *f or* tono de marcar
dialogue, (*US*) **dialog** ['daɪəlɔg] *n* diálogo
dial tone *n* (*US*) señal *f or* tono de marcar
dialysis [daɪ'ælɪsɪs] *n* diálisis *f*
diameter [daɪ'æmɪtə^r] *n* diámetro
diametrically [daɪə'mɛtrɪklɪ] *adv*: **~ opposed (to)** diametralmente opuesto (a)
diamond ['daɪəmənd] *n* diamante *m*; **diamonds** *npl* (*Cards*) diamantes *mpl*
diamond ring *n* anillo *or* sortija de diamantes
diaper ['daɪəpə^r] *n* (*US*) pañal *m*
diaphragm ['daɪəfræm] *n* diafragma *m*
diarrhoea, diarrhea (*US*) [daɪə'ri:ə] *n* diarrea
diary ['daɪərɪ] *n* (*daily account*) diario; (*book*) agenda; **to keep a ~** escribir un diario
diatribe ['daɪətraɪb] *n*: **~ (against)** diatriba (contra)
dice [daɪs] *n pl inv* dados *mpl* ■ *vt* (*Culin*) cortar en cuadritos
dicey ['daɪsɪ] *adj* (*col*): **it's a bit ~** (*risky*) es un poco arriesgado; (*doubtful*) es un poco dudoso
dichotomy [daɪ'kɔtəmɪ] *n* dicotomía
dickhead ['dɪkhɛd] *n* (*Brit col!*) gilipollas *m inv*
Dictaphone® ['dɪktəfəun] *n* dictáfono®
dictate [dɪk'teɪt] *vt* dictar ■ *n* ['dɪkteɪt] dictado
▸ **dictate to** *vt fus* (*person*) dar órdenes a;

I won't be dictated to no recibo órdenes de nadie
dictation [dɪk'teɪʃən] *n* (*to secretary etc*) dictado; **at ~ speed** para tomar al dictado
dictator [dɪk'teɪtəʳ] *n* dictador *m*
dictatorship [dɪk'teɪtəʃɪp] *n* dictadura
diction ['dɪkʃən] *n* dicción *f*
dictionary ['dɪkʃənrɪ] *n* diccionario
did [dɪd] *pt of* **do**
didactic [daɪ'dæktɪk] *adj* didáctico
diddle ['dɪdl] *vt* estafar, timar
didn't ['dɪdənt] = **did not**
die [daɪ] *vi* morir; **to ~ (of** *or* **from)** morirse (de); **to be dying** morirse, estar muriéndose; **to be dying for sth/to do sth** morirse por algo/de ganas de hacer algo
▸ **die away** *vi* (*sound, light*) desvanecerse
▸ **die down** *vi* (*gen*) apagarse; (*wind*) amainar
▸ **die out** *vi* desaparecer, extinguirse
diehard ['daɪhɑːd] *n* intransigente *m/f*
diesel ['diːzl] *n* diesel *m*
diesel engine *n* motor *m* diesel
diesel fuel, diesel oil *n* gas-oil *m*
diet ['daɪət] *n* dieta; (*restricted food*) régimen *m* ■ *vi* (*also*: **be on a diet**) estar a dieta, hacer régimen; **to live on a ~ of** alimentarse de
dietician [daɪə'tɪʃən] *n* dietista *mf*
differ ['dɪfəʳ] *vi* (*be different*) ser distinto, diferenciarse; (*disagree*) discrepar
difference ['dɪfrəns] *n* diferencia; (*quarrel*) desacuerdo; **it makes no ~ to me** me da igual *or* lo mismo; **to settle one's differences** arreglarse
different ['dɪfrənt] *adj* diferente, distinto
differential [dɪfə'rɛnʃəl] *n* diferencial *f*
differentiate [dɪfə'rɛnʃɪeɪt] *vt* distinguir ■ *vi* diferenciarse; **to ~ between** distinguir entre
differently ['dɪfrəntlɪ] *adv* de otro modo, en forma distinta
difficult ['dɪfɪkəlt] *adj* difícil; **~ to understand** difícil de entender
difficulty ['dɪfɪkəltɪ] *n* dificultad *f*; **to have difficulties with** (*police, landlord etc*) tener problemas con; **to be in ~** estar en apuros
diffidence ['dɪfɪdəns] *n* timidez *f*, falta de confianza en sí mismo
diffident ['dɪfɪdənt] *adj* tímido
diffuse [dɪ'fjuːs] *adj* difuso ■ *vt* [dɪ'fjuːz] difundir
dig [dɪg] *vt* (*pt, pp* **dug**) [dʌg] (*hole*) cavar; (*ground*) remover; (*coal*) extraer; (*nails etc*) clavar ■ *n* (*prod*) empujón *m*; (*archaeological*) excavación *f*; (*remark*) indirecta; **to ~ into** (*savings*) consumir; **to ~ into one's pockets for sth** hurgar en el bolsillo buscando algo; **to ~ one's nails into** clavar las uñas en; *see also* **digs**
▸ **dig in** *vi* (*also*: **dig o.s. in**: *Mil*) atrincherarse; (*col*: *eat*) hincar los dientes ■ *vt* (*compost*) añadir al suelo; (*knife, claw*) clavar; **to ~ in one's heels** (*fig*) mantenerse en sus trece
▸ **dig out** *vt* (*hole*) excavar; (*survivors, car from snow*) sacar
▸ **dig up** *vt* desenterrar; (*plant*) desarraigar
digest [daɪ'dʒɛst] *vt* (*food*) digerir; (*facts*) asimilar ■ *n* ['daɪdʒɛst] resumen *m*
digestible [daɪ'dʒɛstəbl] *adj* digerible
digestion [dɪ'dʒɛstʃən] *n* digestión *f*
digestive [daɪ'dʒɛstɪv] *adj* (*juices, system*) digestivo
digit ['dɪdʒɪt] *n* (*number*) dígito; (*finger*) dedo
digital ['dɪdʒɪtl] *adj* digital
digital camera *n* cámara digital
digital compact cassette *n* cas(s)et(t)e *m or f* digital compacto
digital TV *n* televisión *f* digital
dignified ['dɪgnɪfaɪd] *adj* grave, solemne; (*action*) decoroso
dignify ['dɪgnɪfaɪ] *vt* dignificar
dignitary ['dɪgnɪtərɪ] *n* dignatario(-a)
dignity ['dɪgnɪtɪ] *n* dignidad *f*
digress [daɪ'grɛs] *vi*: **to ~ from** apartarse de
digression [daɪ'grɛʃən] *n* digresión *f*
digs [dɪgz] *npl* (*Brit*: *col*) pensión *f*, alojamiento
dike [daɪk] *n* = **dyke**
dilapidated [dɪ'læpɪdeɪtɪd] *adj* desmoronado, ruinoso
dilate [daɪ'leɪt] *vt* dilatar ■ *vi* dilatarse
dilatory ['dɪlətərɪ] *adj* (*person*) lento; (*action*) dilatorio
dilemma [daɪ'lɛmə] *n* dilema *m*; **to be in a ~** estar en un dilema
dilettante [dɪlɪ'tæntɪ] *n* diletante *m/f*
diligence ['dɪlɪdʒəns] *n* diligencia
diligent ['dɪlɪdʒənt] *adj* diligente
dill [dɪl] *n* eneldo
dilly-dally ['dɪlɪ'dælɪ] *vi* (*hesitate*) vacilar; (*dawdle*) entretenerse
dilute [daɪ'luːt] *vt* diluir
dim [dɪm] *adj* (*light*) débil; (*sight*) turbio; (*outline*) borroso; (*stupid*) lerdo; (*room*) oscuro ■ *vt* (*light*) bajar; **to take a ~ view of sth** tener una pobre opinión de algo
dime [daɪm] *n* (*US*) *moneda de diez centavos*
dimension [dɪ'mɛnʃən] *n* dimensión *f*
-dimensional [dɪ'mɛnʃənl] *adj suff*: **two~** de dos dimensiones
dimensions [dɪ'mɛnʃənz] *npl* dimensiones *fpl*
diminish [dɪ'mɪnɪʃ] *vt, vi* disminuir
diminished [dɪ'mɪnɪʃt] *adj*: **~ responsibility** (*Law*) responsabilidad *f* disminuida
diminutive [dɪ'mɪnjutɪv] *adj* diminuto ■ *n* (*Ling*) diminutivo

dimly ['dɪmlɪ] *adv* débilmente; (*not clearly*) vagamente
dimmer ['dɪməʳ] *n* (*also*: **dimmer switch**) regulador *m* (de intensidad); (*US Aut*) interruptor *m*
dimple ['dɪmpl] *n* hoyuelo
dimwitted ['dɪm'wɪtɪd] *adj* (*col*) lerdo, de pocas luces
din [dɪn] *n* estruendo, estrépito ■ *vt*: **to ~ sth into sb** (*col*) meter algo en la cabeza a algn
dine [daɪn] *vi* cenar
diner ['daɪnəʳ] *n* (*person: in restaurant*) comensal *m/f*; (*Brit Rail*) = **dining car**; (*US*) restaurante económico
dinghy ['dɪŋgɪ] *n* bote *m*; (*also*: **rubber dinghy**) lancha (neumática)
dingy ['dɪndʒɪ] *adj* (*room*) sombrío; (*dirty*) sucio; (*dull*) deslucido
dining car ['daɪnɪŋ-] *n* (*Brit*) coche-restaurante *m*
dining room ['daɪnɪŋ-] *n* comedor *m*
dinner ['dɪnəʳ] *n* (*evening meal*) cena, comida (*LAm*); (*lunch*) comida; (*public*) cena, banquete *m*; **~'s ready!** ¡la cena está servida!
dinner jacket *n* smoking *m*
dinner party *n* cena
dinner time *n* hora de cenar *or* comer
dinosaur ['daɪnəsɔːʳ] *n* dinosaurio
dint [dɪnt] *n*: **by ~ of (doing) sth** a fuerza de (hacer) algo
diocese ['daɪəsɪs] *n* diócesis *f*
dioxide [daɪ'ɔksaɪd] *n* bióxido; **carbon ~** bióxido de carbono
Dip. *abbr* (*Brit*) = **diploma**
dip [dɪp] *n* (*slope*) pendiente *f*; (*in sea*) chapuzón *m* ■ *vt* (*in water*) mojar; (*ladle etc*) meter; (*Brit Aut*): **to ~ one's lights** poner la luz de cruce ■ *vi* inclinarse hacia abajo
diphtheria [dɪf'θɪərɪə] *n* difteria
diphthong ['dɪfθɔŋ] *n* diptongo
diploma [dɪ'pləumə] *n* diploma *m*
diplomacy [dɪ'pləuməsɪ] *n* diplomacia
diplomat ['dɪpləmæt] *n* diplomático(-a) *m(f)*
diplomatic [dɪplə'mætɪk] *adj* diplomático; **to break off ~ relations** romper las relaciones diplomáticas
diplomatic corps *n* cuerpo diplomático
diplomatic immunity *n* inmunidad *f* diplomática
dipstick ['dɪpstɪk] *n* (*Aut*) varilla de nivel (del aceite)
dipswitch ['dɪpswɪtʃ] *n* (*Brit Aut*) interruptor *m*
dire [daɪəʳ] *adj* calamitoso
direct [daɪ'rɛkt] *adj* (*gen*) directo; (*manner, person*) franco ■ *vt* dirigir; **can you ~ me to ...?** ¿puede indicarme dónde está ...?; **to ~ sb to do sth** mandar a algn hacer algo
direct cost *n* costo directo
direct current *n* corriente *f* continua
direct debit *n* domiciliación *f* bancaria de recibos; **to pay by ~** domiciliar el pago
direct dialling *n* servicio automático de llamadas
direction [dɪ'rɛkʃən] *n* dirección *f*; **sense of ~** sentido de la orientación; **directions** *npl* (*advice*) órdenes *fpl*, instrucciones *fpl*; (*to a place*) señas *fpl*; **in the ~ of** hacia, en dirección a; **directions for use** modo de empleo; **to ask for directions** preguntar el camino
directional [dɪ'rɛkʃənl] *adj* direccional
directive [daɪ'rɛktɪv] *n* orden *f*, instrucción *f*; **a government ~** una orden del gobierno
direct labour *n* mano *f* de obra directa
directly [dɪ'rɛktlɪ] *adv* (*in straight line*) directamente; (*at once*) en seguida
direct mail *n* correspondencia personalizada
direct mailshot *n* (*Brit*) promoción *f* por correspondencia personalizada
directness [dɪ'rɛktnɪs] *n* (*of person, speech*) franqueza
director [dɪ'rɛktəʳ] *n* director(a) *m(f)*; **managing ~** director(a) *m(f)* gerente
Director of Public Prosecutions *n* ≈ fiscal *m/f* general del Estado
directory [dɪ'rɛktərɪ] *n* (*Tel*) guía (telefónica); (*street directory*) callejero; (*trade directory*) directorio de comercio; (*Comput*) directorio
directory enquiries, (*US*) **directory assistance** *n* (*service*) (servicio *m* de) información
dirt [dəːt] *n* suciedad *f*
dirt-cheap ['dəːt'tʃiːp] *adj* baratísimo
dirt road *n* (*US*) camino sin firme
dirty ['dəːtɪ] *adj* sucio; (*joke*) verde, colorado (*LAm*) ■ *vt* ensuciar; (*stain*) manchar
dirty trick *n* mala jugada, truco sucio
disability [dɪsə'bɪlɪtɪ] *n* incapacidad *f*
disability allowance *n* pensión *f* de invalidez
disable [dɪs'eɪbl] *vt* (*illness, accident*) dejar incapacitado *or* inválido; (*tank, gun*) inutilizar; (*Law: disqualify*) incapacitar
disabled [dɪs'eɪbld] *adj* minusválido
disabuse [dɪsə'bjuːz] *vt* desengañar
disadvantage [dɪsəd'vɑːntɪdʒ] *n* desventaja, inconveniente *m*
disadvantaged [dɪsəd'vɑːntɪdʒd] *adj* (*person*) desventajado
disadvantageous [dɪsædvən'teɪdʒəs] *adj* desventajoso
disaffected [dɪsə'fɛktɪd] *adj* descontento; **to be ~ (to *or* towards)** estar descontento (de)

disaffection [dɪsəˈfɛkʃən] *n* desafecto, descontento
disagree [dɪsəˈgriː] *vi* (*differ*) discrepar; **to ~ (with)** no estar de acuerdo (con); **I ~ with you** no estoy de acuerdo contigo
disagreeable [dɪsəˈgrɪəbl] *adj* desagradable
disagreement [dɪsəˈgriːmənt] *n* (*gen*) desacuerdo; (*quarrel*) riña; **to have a ~ with sb** estar en desacuerdo con algn
disallow [ˈdɪsəˈlau] *vt* (*goal*) anular; (*claim*) rechazar
disappear [dɪsəˈpɪəʳ] *vi* desaparecer
disappearance [dɪsəˈpɪərəns] *n* desaparición *f*
disappoint [dɪsəˈpɔɪnt] *vt* decepcionar; (*hopes*) defraudar
disappointed [dɪsəˈpɔɪntɪd] *adj* decepcionado
disappointing [dɪsəˈpɔɪntɪŋ] *adj* decepcionante
disappointment [dɪsəˈpɔɪntmənt] *n* decepción *f*
disapproval [dɪsəˈpruːvəl] *n* desaprobación *f*
disapprove [dɪsəˈpruːv] *vi*: **to ~ of** desaprobar
disapproving [dɪsəˈpruːvɪŋ] *adj* de desaprobación, desaprobador(a)
disarm [dɪsˈɑːm] *vt* desarmar
disarmament [dɪsˈɑːməmənt] *n* desarme *m*
disarmament talks *npl* conversaciones *fpl* de *or* sobre desarme
disarming [dɪsˈɑːmɪŋ] *adj* (*smile*) que desarma, encantador(a)
disarray [dɪsəˈreɪ] *n*: **in ~** (*troops*) desorganizado; (*thoughts*) confuso; (*hair, clothes*) desarreglado; **to throw into ~** provocar el caos
disaster [dɪˈzɑːstəʳ] *n* desastre *m*
disaster area *n* zona catastrófica
disastrous [dɪˈzɑːstrəs] *adj* desastroso
disband [dɪsˈbænd] *vt* disolver ■ *vi* desbandarse
disbelief [dɪsbəˈliːf] *n* incredulidad *f*; **in ~** con incredulidad
disbelieve [ˈdɪsbəˈliːv] *vt* (*person, story*) poner en duda, no creer
disc [dɪsk] *n* disco; (*Comput*) = **disk**
disc. *abbr* (*Comm*) = **discount**
discard [dɪsˈkɑːd] *vt* tirar; (*fig*) descartar
discern [dɪˈsəːn] *vt* percibir, discernir; (*understand*) comprender
discernible [dɪˈsəːnəbl] *adj* perceptible
discerning [dɪˈsəːnɪŋ] *adj* perspicaz
discharge [dɪsˈtʃɑːdʒ] *vt* (*task, duty*) cumplir; (*ship etc*) descargar; (*patient*) dar de alta; (*employee*) despedir; (*soldier*) licenciar; (*defendant*) poner en libertad; (*settle: debt*) saldar ■ *n* [ˈdɪstʃɑːdʒ] (*Elec*) descarga; (*vaginal discharge*) emisión *f* vaginal; (*dismissal*) despedida; (*of duty*) desempeño; (*of debt*) pago, descargo; (*of gas, chemicals*) escape *m*; **discharged bankrupt** quebrado/a rehabilitado/a
disciple [dɪˈsaɪpl] *n* discípulo(-a)
disciplinary [ˈdɪsɪplɪnərɪ] *adj*: **to take ~ action against sb** disciplinar a algn
discipline [ˈdɪsɪplɪn] *n* disciplina ■ *vt* disciplinar; **to ~ o.s. to do sth** obligarse a hacer algo
disc jockey, DJ *n* pinchadiscos *m/f inv*
disclaim [dɪsˈkleɪm] *vt* negar tener
disclaimer [dɪsˈkleɪməʳ] *n* rectificación *f*; **to issue a ~** hacer una rectificación
disclose [dɪsˈkləuz] *vt* revelar
disclosure [dɪsˈkləuʒəʳ] *n* revelación *f*
Discman® [ˈdɪskmən] *n* Discman® *m*
disco [ˈdɪskəu] *n abbr* = **discothèque**
discolouration, discoloration (*US*) [dɪskʌləˈreɪʃən] *n* descoloramiento, decoloración *f*
discoloured, discolored (*US*) [dɪsˈkʌləd] *adj* descolorido
discomfort [dɪsˈkʌmfət] *n* incomodidad *f*; (*unease*) inquietud *f*; (*physical*) malestar *m*
disconcert [dɪskənˈsəːt] *vt* desconcertar
disconnect [dɪskəˈnɛkt] *vt* (*gen*) separar; (*Elec etc*) desconectar; (*supply*) cortar (el suministro) a
disconsolate [dɪsˈkɔnsəlɪt] *adj* desconsolado
discontent [dɪskənˈtɛnt] *n* descontento
discontented [dɪskənˈtɛntɪd] *adj* descontento
discontinue [dɪskənˈtɪnjuː] *vt* interrumpir; (*payments*) suspender
discord [ˈdɪskɔːd] *n* discordia; (*Mus*) disonancia
discordant [dɪsˈkɔːdənt] *adj* disonante
discothèque [ˈdɪskəutɛk] *n* discoteca
discount [ˈdɪskaunt] *n* descuento ■ *vt* [dɪsˈkaunt] descontar; (*report etc*) descartar; **at a ~** con descuento; **~ for cash** descuento por pago en efectivo; **to give sb a ~ on sth** hacer un descuento a algn en algo
discount house *n* (*Finance*) banco de descuento; (*Comm*: *also*: **discount store**) ≈ tienda de saldos
discount rate *n* (*Comm*) tipo de descuento
discount store *n* ≈ tienda de saldos
discourage [dɪsˈkʌrɪdʒ] *vt* desalentar; (*oppose*) oponerse a; (*dissuade, deter*) desanimar, disuadir
discouragement [dɪsˈkʌrɪdʒmənt] *n* (*dissuasion*) disuasión *f*; (*depression*) desánimo, desaliento; **to act as a ~ to** servir para disuadir

discouraging [dɪs'kʌrɪdʒɪŋ] *adj* desalentador(a)
discourteous [dɪs'kə:tɪəs] *adj* descortés
discover [dɪs'kʌvəʳ] *vt* descubrir
discovery [dɪs'kʌvərɪ] *n* descubrimiento
discredit [dɪs'krɛdɪt] *vt* desacreditar
discreet [dɪ'skri:t] *adj* (*tactful*) discreto; (*careful*) circunspecto, prudente
discreetly [dɪ'skri:tlɪ] *adv* discretamente
discrepancy [dɪ'skrɛpənsɪ] *n* (*difference*) diferencia; (*disagreement*) discrepancia
discretion [dɪ'skrɛʃən] *n* (*tact*) discreción *f*; (*care*) prudencia, circunspección *f*; **use your own ~** haz lo que creas oportuno
discretionary [dɪ'skrɛʃənrɪ] *adj* (*powers*) discrecional
discriminate [dɪ'skrɪmɪneɪt] *vi*: **to ~ between** distinguir entre; **to ~ against** discriminar contra
discriminating [dɪ'skrɪmɪneɪtɪŋ] *adj* entendido
discrimination [dɪskrɪmɪ'neɪʃən] *n* (*discernment*) perspicacia; (*bias*) discriminación *f*; **racial/sexual ~** discriminación racial/sexual
discus ['dɪskəs] *n* disco
discuss [dɪ'skʌs] *vt* (*gen*) discutir; (*a theme*) tratar
discussion [dɪ'skʌʃən] *n* discusión *f*; **under ~** en discusión
disdain [dɪs'deɪn] *n* desdén *m* ■ *vt* desdeñar
disease [dɪ'zi:z] *n* enfermedad *f*
diseased [dɪ'zi:zd] *adj* enfermo
disembark [dɪsɪm'bɑ:k] *vt, vi* desembarcar
disembarkation [dɪsɛmbɑ:'keɪʃən] *n* desembarque *m*
disenchanted [dɪsɪn'tʃɑ:ntɪd] *adj*: **~ (with)** desilusionado (con)
disenfranchise ['dɪsɪn'fræntʃaɪz] *vt* privar del derecho al voto; (*Comm*) privar de franquicias
disengage [dɪsɪn'geɪdʒ] *vt* soltar; **to ~ the clutch** (*Aut*) desembragar
disentangle [dɪsɪn'tæŋgl] *vt* desenredar
disfavour, disfavor (*US*) [dɪs'feɪvəʳ] *n* desaprobación *f*
disfigure [dɪs'fɪgəʳ] *vt* desfigurar
disgorge [dɪs'gɔ:dʒ] *vt* verter
disgrace [dɪs'greɪs] *n* ignominia; (*downfall*) caída; (*shame*) vergüenza, escándalo ■ *vt* deshonrar
disgraceful [dɪs'greɪsful] *adj* vergonzoso; (*behaviour*) escandaloso
disgruntled [dɪs'grʌntld] *adj* disgustado, descontento
disguise [dɪs'gaɪz] *n* disfraz *m* ■ *vt* disfrazar; (*voice*) disimular; (*feelings etc*) ocultar; **in ~** disfrazado; **to ~ o.s. as** disfrazarse de; **there's no disguising the fact that ...** no puede ocultarse el hecho de que ...
disgust [dɪs'gʌst] *n* repugnancia ■ *vt* repugnar, dar asco a
disgusting [dɪs'gʌstɪŋ] *adj* repugnante, asqueroso
dish [dɪʃ] *n* (*gen*) plato; **to do** *or* **wash the dishes** fregar los platos
▸ **dish out** *vt* (*money, exam papers*) repartir; (*food*) servir; (*advice*) dar
▸ **dish up** *vt* servir
dishcloth ['dɪʃklɔθ] *n* paño de cocina, bayeta
dishearten [dɪs'hɑ:tn] *vt* desalentar
dishevelled, disheveled (*US*) [dɪ'ʃɛvəld] *adj* (*hair*) despeinado; (*clothes, appearance*) desarreglado
dishonest [dɪs'ɔnɪst] *adj* (*person*) poco honrado, tramposo; (*means*) fraudulento
dishonesty [dɪs'ɔnɪstɪ] *n* falta de honradez
dishonour, dishonor (*US*) [dɪs'ɔnəʳ] *n* deshonra
dishonourable, dishonorable (*US*) [dɪs'ɔnərəbl] *adj* deshonroso
dish soap *n* (*US*) lavavajillas *m inv*
dishtowel ['dɪʃtauəl] *n* (*US*) trapo de fregar
dishwasher ['dɪʃwɔʃəʳ] *n* lavaplatos *m inv*; (*person*) friegaplatos *m/f inv*
dishy ['dɪʃɪ] *adj* (*Brit col*) buenón(-ona)
disillusion [dɪsɪ'lu:ʒən] *vt* desilusionar; **to become disillusioned (with)** quedar desilusionado (con)
disillusionment [dɪsɪ'lu:ʒənmənt] *n* desilusión *f*
disincentive [dɪsɪn'sɛntɪv] *n* freno; **to act as a ~ (to)** actuar de freno (a); **to be a ~ to** ser un freno a
disinclined ['dɪsɪn'klaɪnd] *adj*: **to be ~ to do sth** estar poco dispuesto a hacer algo
disinfect [dɪsɪn'fɛkt] *vt* desinfectar
disinfectant [dɪsɪn'fɛktənt] *n* desinfectante *m*
disinflation [dɪsɪn'fleɪʃən] *n* desinflación *f*
disinformation [dɪsɪnfə'meɪʃən] *n* desinformación *f*
disingenuous [dɪsɪn'dʒɛnjuəs] *adj* poco sincero, falso
disinherit [dɪsɪn'hɛrɪt] *vt* desheredar
disintegrate [dɪs'ɪntɪgreɪt] *vi* disgregarse, desintegrarse
disinterested [dɪs'ɪntrəstɪd] *adj* desinteresado
disjointed [dɪs'dʒɔɪntɪd] *adj* inconexo
disk [dɪsk] *n* (*Comput*) disco, disquete *m*; **single-/double-sided ~** disco de una cara/dos caras
disk drive *n* unidad *f* (de disco)

diskette [dɪs'kɛt] *n* diskette *m*, disquete *m*, disco flexible
disk operating system *n* sistema *m* operativo de discos
dislike [dɪs'laɪk] *n* antipatía, aversión *f* ■ *vt* tener antipatía a; **to take a ~ to sb/sth** cogerle *or* (*LAm*) agarrarle antipatía a algn/algo; **I ~ the idea** no me gusta la idea
dislocate ['dɪsləkeɪt] *vt* dislocar; **he dislocated his shoulder** se dislocó el hombro
dislodge [dɪs'lɔdʒ] *vt* sacar; (*enemy*) desalojar
disloyal [dɪs'lɔɪəl] *adj* desleal
dismal ['dɪzml] *adj* (*dark*) sombrío; (*depressing*) triste; (*very bad*) fatal
dismantle [dɪs'mæntl] *vt* desmontar, desarmar
dismay [dɪs'meɪ] *n* consternación *f* ■ *vt* consternar; **much to my ~** para gran consternación mía
dismiss [dɪs'mɪs] *vt* (*worker*) despedir; (*official*) destituir; (*idea*) rechazar; (*Law*) rechazar; (*possibility*) descartar ■ *vi* (*Mil*) romper filas
dismissal [dɪs'mɪsl] *n* despedida; destitución *f*
dismount [dɪs'maunt] *vi* apearse; (*rider*) desmontar
disobedience [dɪsə'bi:dɪəns] *n* desobediencia
disobedient [dɪsə'bi:dɪənt] *adj* desobediente
disobey [dɪsə'beɪ] *vt* desobedecer; (*rule*) infringir
disorder [dɪs'ɔ:dəʳ] *n* desorden *m*; (*rioting*) disturbio; (*Med*) trastorno; (*disease*) enfermedad *f*; **civil ~** desorden *m* civil
disorderly [dɪs'ɔ:dəlɪ] *adj* (*untidy*) desordenado; (*meeting*) alborotado; **~ conduct** (*Law*) conducta escandalosa
disorganized [dɪs'ɔ:gənaɪzd] *adj* desorganizado
disorientated [dɪs'ɔ:rɪɛnteɪtəd] *adj* desorientado
disown [dɪs'əun] *vt* renegar de
disparaging [dɪs'pærɪdʒɪŋ] *adj* despreciativo; **to be ~ about sth/sb** menospreciar algo/a algn
disparate ['dɪspərɪt] *adj* dispar
disparity [dɪs'pærɪtɪ] *n* disparidad *f*
dispassionate [dɪs'pæʃənɪt] *adj* (*unbiased*) imparcial; (*unemotional*) desapasionado
dispatch [dɪs'pætʃ] *vt* enviar; (*kill*) despachar; (*deal with: business*) despachar ■ *n* (*sending*) envío; (*speed*) prontitud *f*; (*Press*) informe *m*; (*Mil*) parte *m*
dispatch department *n* (*Comm*) departamento de envíos
dispatch rider *n* (*Mil*) correo
dispel [dɪs'pɛl] *vt* disipar, dispersar
dispensary [dɪs'pɛnsərɪ] *n* dispensario
dispensation [dɪspɛn'seɪʃən] *n* (*Rel*) dispensa
dispense [dɪs'pɛns] *vt* dispensar, repartir; (*medicine*) preparar
▸ **dispense with** *vt fus* (*make unnecessary*) prescindir de
dispenser [dɪs'pɛnsəʳ] *n* (*container*) distribuidor *m* automático
dispensing chemist [dɪs'pɛnsɪŋ-] *n* (*Brit*) farmacia
dispersal [dɪs'pə:sl] *n* dispersión *f*
disperse [dɪs'pə:s] *vt* dispersar ■ *vi* dispersarse
dispirited [dɪ'spɪrɪtɪd] *adj* desanimado, desalentado
displace [dɪs'pleɪs] *vt* (*person*) desplazar; (*replace*) reemplazar
displaced person *n* (*Pol*) desplazado(-a)
displacement [dɪs'pleɪsmənt] *n* cambio de sitio
display [dɪs'pleɪ] *n* (*exhibition*) exposición *f*; (*Comput*) visualización *f*; (*Mil*) desfile *m*; (*of feeling*) manifestación *f*; (*pej*) aparato, pompa ■ *vt* exponer; manifestar; (*ostentatiously*) lucir; **on ~** (*exhibits*) expuesto, exhibido; (*goods*) en el escaparate
display advertising *n* publicidad *f* gráfica
displease [dɪs'pli:z] *vt* (*offend*) ofender; (*annoy*) fastidiar; **displeased with** disgustado con
displeasure [dɪs'plɛʒəʳ] *n* disgusto
disposable [dɪs'pəuzəbl] *adj* (*not reusable*) desechable; **~ personal income** ingresos *mpl* personales disponibles
disposable nappy *n* pañal *m* desechable
disposal [dɪs'pəuzl] *n* (*sale*) venta; (*of house*) traspaso; (*by giving away*) donación *f*; (*arrangement*) colocación *f*; (*of rubbish*) destrucción *f*; **at one's ~** a la disposición de algn; **to put sth at sb's ~** poner algo a disposición de algn
disposed [dɪs'pəuzd] *adj*: **~ to do** dispuesto a hacer
dispose of [dɪs'pəuz] *vt fus* (*time, money*) disponer de; (*unwanted goods*) deshacerse de; (*Comm: sell*) traspasar, vender; (*throw away*) tirar
disposition [dɪspə'zɪʃən] *n* disposición *f*; (*temperament*) carácter *m*
dispossess ['dɪspə'zɛs] *vt*: **to ~ sb (of)** desposeer a algn (de)
disproportion [dɪsprə'pɔ:ʃən] *n* desproporción *f*
disproportionate [dɪsprə'pɔ:ʃənət] *adj* desproporcionado
disprove [dɪs'pru:v] *vt* refutar

dispute [dɪs'pjuːt] *n* disputa; (*verbal*) discusión *f*; (*also*: **industrial dispute**) conflicto (laboral) ■ *vt* (*argue*) disputar; (*question*) cuestionar; **to be in** *or* **under ~** (*matter*) discutirse; (*territory*) estar en disputa; (*Jur*) estar en litigio
disqualification [dɪskwɔlɪfɪ'keɪʃən] *n* inhabilitación *f*; (*Sport*) descalificación *f*; (*from driving*) descalificación *f*
disqualify [dɪs'kwɔlɪfaɪ] *vt* (*Sport*) desclasificar; **to ~ sb for sth/from doing sth** incapacitar a algn para algo/para hacer algo
disquiet [dɪs'kwaɪət] *n* preocupación *f*, inquietud *f*
disquieting [dɪs'kwaɪətɪŋ] *adj* inquietante
disregard [dɪsrɪ'gɑːd] *vt* desatender; (*ignore*) no hacer caso de ■ *n* (*indifference*: *to feelings, danger, money*): **~ (for)** indiferencia (a); **~ (of)** (*non-observance*: *of law, rules*) violación *f* (de)
disrepair [dɪsrɪ'pɛəʳ] *n*: **to fall into ~** (*building*) desmoronarse; (*street*) deteriorarse
disreputable [dɪs'rɛpjutəbl] *adj* (*person, area*) de mala fama; (*behaviour*) vergonzoso
disrepute ['dɪsrɪ'pjuːt] *n* descrédito, ignominia; **to bring into ~** desacreditar
disrespectful [dɪsrɪ'spɛktful] *adj* irrespetuoso
disrupt [dɪs'rʌpt] *vt* (*meeting, public transport, conversation*) interrumpir; (*plans*) desbaratar, alternar, trastornar
disruption [dɪs'rʌpʃən] *n* trastorno; desbaratamiento; interrupción *f*
disruptive [dɪs'rʌptɪv] *adj* (*influence*) disruptivo; (*strike action*) perjudicial
dissatisfaction [dɪssætɪs'fækʃən] *n* disgusto, descontento
dissatisfied [dɪs'sætɪsfaɪd] *adj* insatisfecho
dissect [dɪ'sɛkt] *vt* (*also fig*) disecar
disseminate [dɪ'sɛmɪneɪt] *vt* divulgar, difundir
dissent [dɪ'sɛnt] *n* disensión *f*
dissenter [dɪ'sɛntəʳ] *n* (*Rel, Pol etc*) disidente *m/f*
dissertation [dɪsə'teɪʃən] *n* (*Univ*) tesina; *see also* **master's degree**
disservice [dɪs'səːvɪs] *n*: **to do sb a ~** perjudicar a algn
dissident ['dɪsɪdnt] *adj, n* disidente *m/f*
dissimilar [dɪ'sɪmɪləʳ] *adj* distinto
dissipate ['dɪsɪpeɪt] *vt* disipar; (*waste*) desperdiciar
dissipated ['dɪsɪpeɪtɪd] *adj* disoluto
dissipation [dɪsɪ'peɪʃən] *n* disipación *f* (*moral*), libertinaje *m*, vicio; (*waste*) derroche *m*
dissociate [dɪ'səuʃɪeɪt] *vt* disociar; **to ~ o.s. from** disociarse de
dissolute ['dɪsəluːt] *adj* disoluto
dissolution [dɪsə'luːʃən] *n* disolución *f*
dissolve [dɪ'zɔlv] *vt* disolver ■ *vi* disolverse
dissuade [dɪ'sweɪd] *vt*: **to ~ sb (from)** disuadir a algn (de)
distaff ['dɪstæf] *n*: **~ side** rama femenina
distance ['dɪstns] *n* distancia; **in the ~** a lo lejos; **what ~ is it to London?** ¿qué distancia hay de aquí a Londres?; **it's within walking ~** se puede ir andando
distant ['dɪstnt] *adj* lejano; (*manner*) reservado, frío
distaste [dɪs'teɪst] *n* repugnancia
distasteful [dɪs'teɪstful] *adj* repugnante, desagradable
Dist. Atty. *abbr* (*US*) = **district attorney**
distemper [dɪs'tɛmpəʳ] *n* (*of dogs*) moquillo
distend [dɪ'stɛnd] *vt* dilatar, hinchar ■ *vi* dilatarse, hincharse
distended [dɪ'stɛndɪd] *adj* (*stomach*) hinchado
distil, distill (*US*) [dɪs'tɪl] *vt* destilar
distillery [dɪs'tɪlərɪ] *n* destilería
distinct [dɪs'tɪŋkt] *adj* (*different*) distinto; (*clear*) claro; (*unmistakeable*) inequívoco; **as ~ from** a diferencia de
distinction [dɪs'tɪŋkʃən] *n* distinción *f*; (*in exam*) sobresaliente *m*; **a writer of ~** un escritor destacado; **to draw a ~ between** hacer una distinción entre
distinctive [dɪs'tɪŋktɪv] *adj* distintivo
distinctly [dɪs'tɪŋktlɪ] *adv* claramente
distinguish [dɪs'tɪŋgwɪʃ] *vt* distinguir ■ *vi*: **to ~ (between)** distinguir (entre)
distinguished [dɪs'tɪŋgwɪʃt] *adj* (*eminent*) distinguido; (*career*) eminente; (*refined*) distinguido, de categoría
distinguishing [dɪs'tɪŋgwɪʃɪŋ] *adj* (*feature*) distintivo
distort [dɪs'tɔːt] *vt* torcer, retorcer; (*account, news*) desvirtuar, deformar
distortion [dɪs'tɔːʃən] *n* deformación *f*; (*of sound*) distorsión *f*; (*of truth etc*) tergiversación *f*; (*of facts*) falseamiento
distract [dɪs'trækt] *vt* distraer
distracted [dɪs'træktɪd] *adj* distraído
distracting [dɪs'træktɪŋ] *adj* que distrae la atención, molesto
distraction [dɪs'trækʃən] *n* distracción *f*; (*confusion*) aturdimiento; (*amusement*) diversión *f*; **to drive sb to ~** (*distress, anxiety*) volver loco a algn
distraught [dɪs'trɔːt] *adj* turbado, enloquecido
distress [dɪs'trɛs] *n* (*anguish*) angustia; (*want*) miseria; (*pain*) dolor *m*; (*danger*) peligro ■ *vt*

afligir; *(pain)* doler; **in ~** *(ship etc)* en peligro
distressing [dɪs'trɛsɪŋ] *adj* angustioso; doloroso
distress signal *n* señal *f* de socorro
distribute [dɪs'trɪbju:t] *vt (gen)* distribuir; *(share out)* repartir
distribution [dɪstrɪ'bju:ʃən] *n* distribución *f*
distribution cost *n* gastos *mpl* de distribución
distributor [dɪs'trɪbjutəʳ] *n (Aut)* distribuidor *m*; *(Comm)* distribuidora
district ['dɪstrɪkt] *n (of country)* zona, región *f*; *(of town)* barrio; *(Admin)* distrito
district attorney *n (US)* fiscal *m/f*
district council *n* ≈ municipio; *ver nota*

DISTRICT COUNCIL

En Inglaterra y Gales, con la excepción de Londres, la administración local corre a cargo del *district council*, responsable de los servicios municipales como vivienda, urbanismo, recolección de basuras, salud medioambiental etc. La mayoría de sus miembros son elegidos a nivel local cada cuatro años. Hay un total de 369 "districts" (distritos), repartidos en 53 "counties" (condados), que se financian a través de los impuestos municipales y partidas presupuestarias del Estado. Éste controla sus gastos a través de una comisión independiente.

district manager *n* representante *m/f* regional
district nurse *n (Brit) enfermera que atiende a pacientes a domicilio*
distrust [dɪs'trʌst] *n* desconfianza ■ *vt* desconfiar de
distrustful [dɪs'trʌstful] *adj* desconfiado
disturb [dɪs'tə:b] *vt (person: bother, interrupt)* molestar; *(meeting)* interrumpir; *(disorganize)* desordenar; **sorry to ~ you** perdone la molestia
disturbance [dɪs'tə:bəns] *n (political etc)* disturbio; *(violence)* alboroto; *(of mind)* trastorno; **to cause a ~** causar alboroto; **~ of the peace** alteración *f* del orden público
disturbed [dɪs'tə:bd] *adj (worried, upset)* preocupado, angustiado; **to be emotionally/mentally ~** tener problemas emocionales/ser un trastornado mental
disturbing [dɪs'tə:bɪŋ] *adj* inquietante, perturbador(a)
disuse [dɪs'ju:s] *n*: **to fall into ~** caer en desuso
disused [dɪs'ju:zd] *adj* abandonado
ditch [dɪtʃ] *n* zanja; *(irrigation ditch)* acequia ■ *vt (col)* deshacerse de
dither ['dɪðəʳ] *vi* vacilar
ditto ['dɪtəu] *adv* ídem, lo mismo
divan [dɪ'væn] *n* diván *m*
divan bed *n* cama turca
dive [daɪv] *n (from board)* salto; *(underwater)* buceo; *(of submarine)* inmersión *f*; *(Aviat)* picada ■ *vi* saltar; bucear; sumergirse; picar
diver ['daɪvəʳ] *n (Sport)* saltador(a) *m(f)*; *(underwater)* buzo
diverge [daɪ'və:dʒ] *vi* divergir
divergent [daɪ'və:dʒənt] *adj* divergente
diverse [daɪ'və:s] *adj* diversos(-as), varios(-as)
diversification [daɪvə:sɪfɪ'keɪʃən] *n* diversificación *f*
diversify [daɪ'və:sɪfaɪ] *vt* diversificar
diversion [daɪ'və:ʃən] *n (Brit Aut)* desviación *f*; *(distraction)* diversión *f*; *(Mil)* diversión *f*
diversionary tactics [daɪ'və:ʃənrɪ-] *npl* tácticas *fpl* de diversión
diversity [daɪ'və:sɪtɪ] *n* diversidad *f*
divert [daɪ'və:t] *vt (Brit: train, plane, traffic)* desviar; *(amuse)* divertir
divest [daɪ'vɛst] *vt*: **to ~ sb of sth** despojar a algn de algo
divide [dɪ'vaɪd] *vt* dividir; *(separate)* separar ■ *vi* dividirse; *(road)* bifurcarse; **to ~ (between, among)** repartir *or* dividir (entre); **40 divided by 5** 40 dividido por 5
▸ **divide out** *vt*: **to ~ out (between, among)** *(sweets, tasks etc)* repartir (entre)
divided [dɪ'vaɪdɪd] *adj (country, couple)* dividido, separado; *(opinions)* en desacuerdo
divided highway *n (US)* carretera de doble calzada
dividend ['dɪvɪdɛnd] *n* dividendo; *(fig)* beneficio
dividend cover *n* cobertura de dividendo
dividers [dɪ'vaɪdəz] *npl* compás *msg* de puntas
divine [dɪ'vaɪn] *adj* divino ■ *vt (future)* vaticinar; *(truth)* alumbrar; *(water, metal)* descubrir, detectar
diving ['daɪvɪŋ] *n (Sport)* salto; *(underwater)* buceo
diving board *n* trampolín *m*
diving suit *n* escafandra
divinity [dɪ'vɪnɪtɪ] *n* divinidad *f*; *(Scol)* teología
divisible [dɪ'vɪzɪbl] *adj* divisible
division [dɪ'vɪʒən] *n (also Brit Football)* división *f*; *(sharing out)* repartimiento; *(Brit Pol)* votación *f*; **~ of labour** división *f* del trabajo
divisive [dɪ'vaɪsɪv] *adj* divisivo
divorce [dɪ'vɔ:s] *n* divorcio ■ *vt* divorciarse de
divorced [dɪ'vɔ:st] *adj* divorciado

divorcee [dɪvɔːˈsiː] *n* divorciado(-a)
divot [ˈdɪvət] *n* (*Golf*) chuleta
divulge [daɪˈvʌldʒ] *vt* divulgar, revelar
D.I.Y. *adj, n abbr* (*Brit*) = **do-it-yourself**
dizziness [ˈdɪzɪnɪs] *n* vértigo
dizzy [ˈdɪzɪ] *adj* (*person*) mareado; (*height*) vertiginoso; **to feel ~** marearse; **I feel ~** estoy mareado
DJ *n abbr see* **disc jockey**
dj *n abbr* = **dinner jacket**
Djakarta [dʒəˈkɑːtə] *n* Yakarta
DJIA *n abbr* (*US Stock Exchange*) = **Dow-Jones Industrial Average**
dl *abbr* (= *decilitre(s)*) dl
DLit, DLitt *abbr* (= *Doctor of Literature, Doctor of Letters*) *título universitario*
dm *abbr* (= *decimetre(s)*) dm
DMus *abbr* (= *Doctor of Music*) *título universitario*
DMZ *n abbr* (= *demilitarized zone*) zona desmilitarizada
DNA *n abbr* (= *deoxyribonucleic acid*) ADN *m*
DNA test *n* prueba *f* del ADN

KEYWORD

do [duː] (*pt* **did**, *pp* **done**) *n* **1** (*col: party etc*): **we're having a little do on Saturday** damos una fiestecita el sábado; **it was rather a grand do** fue un acontecimiento a lo grande
2: **the dos and don'ts** lo que se debe y no se debe hacer
■ *aux vb* **1** (*in negative constructions: not translated*): **I don't understand** no entiendo
2 (*to form questions: not translated*): **do you speak English?** ¿habla (usted) inglés?; **didn't you know?** ¿no lo sabías?; **what do you think?** ¿qué opinas?
3 (*for emphasis, in polite expressions*): **people do make mistakes sometimes** a veces sí se cometen errores; **she does seem rather late** a mí también me parece que se ha retrasado; **do sit down/help yourself** siéntate/sírvete por favor; **do take care!** ¡ten cuidado! ¿eh?; **I DO wish I could ...** ojalá (que) pudiera ...; **but I DO like it** pero, sí (que) me gusta
4 (*used to avoid repeating vb*): **she sings better than I do** canta mejor que yo; **do you agree? — yes, I do/no, I don't** ¿estás de acuerdo? — sí (lo estoy)/no (lo estoy); **she lives in Glasgow — so do I** vive en Glasgow — yo también; **he didn't like it and neither did we** no le gustó y a nosotros tampoco; **who made this mess? — I did** ¿quién hizo esta chapuza? — yo; **he asked me to help him and I did** me pidió que le ayudara y lo hice
5 (*in question tags*): **you like him, don't you?** te gusta, ¿verdad? *or* ¿no?; **I don't know him, do I?** creo que no le conozco; **he laughed, didn't he?** se rió ¿no?
■ *vt* **1** (*gen*): **what are you doing tonight?** ¿qué haces esta noche?; **what can I do for you?** (*in shop*) ¿en qué puedo servirle?; **what does he do for a living?** ¿a qué se dedica?; **I'll do all I can** haré todo lo que pueda; **what have you done with my slippers?** ¿qué has hecho con mis zapatillas?; **to do the washing-up/cooking** fregar los platos/cocinar; **to do one's teeth/hair/nails** lavarse los dientes/arreglarse el pelo/arreglarse las uñas
2 (*Aut etc*): **the car was doing 100** el coche iba a 100; **we've done 200 km already** ya hemos hecho 200 km; **he can do 100 in that car** puede ir a 100 en ese coche
3 (*visit: city, museum*) visitar, recorrer
4 (*cook*): **a steak – well done please** un filete bien hecho, por favor
■ *vi* **1** (*act, behave*) hacer; **do as I do** haz como yo
2 (*get on, fare*): **he's doing well/badly at school** va bien/mal en la escuela; **the firm is doing well** la empresa anda *or* va bien; **how do you do?** mucho gusto; (*less formal*) ¿qué tal?
3 (*suit*): **will it do?** ¿sirve?, ¿está *or* va bien?; **it doesn't do to upset her** cuidado en ofenderla
4 (*be sufficient*) bastar; **will £10 do?** ¿será bastante con £10?; **that'll do** así está bien; **that'll do!** (*in annoyance*) ¡ya está bien!, ¡basta ya!; **to make do (with)** arreglárselas (con)
▸ **do away with** *vt fus* (*kill*) eliminar; (*eradicate: disease*) eliminar; (*abolish: law etc*) abolir; (*withdraw*) retirar
▸ **do out of** *vt fus*: **to do sb out of sth** pisar algo a algn
▸ **do up** *vt* (*laces*) atar; (*zip, dress, shirt*) abrochar; (*renovate: room, house*) renovar
▸ **do with** *vt fus* (*need*): **I could do with a drink/some help** no me vendría mal un trago/un poco de ayuda; (*be connected with*) tener que ver con; **what has it got to do with you?** ¿qué tiene que ver contigo?
▸ **do without** *vi*: **if you're late for dinner then you'll do without** si llegas tarde tendrás que quedarte sin cenar
■ *vt fus* pasar sin; **I can do without a car** puedo pasar sin coche

do. *abbr* = **ditto**
DOA *abbr* = **dead on arrival**
d.o.b. *abbr* = **date of birth**

doc [dɔk] *n* (*col*) médico(-a)
docile ['dəusaɪl] *adj* dócil
dock [dɔk] *n* (*Naut: wharf*) dársena, muelle *m*; (*Law*) banquillo (de los acusados); **docks** *npl* muelles *mpl*, puerto *sg* ■ *vi* (*enter dock*) atracar (en el muelle) ■ *vt* (*pay etc*) descontar
dock dues *npl* derechos *mpl* de muelle
docker ['dɔkəʳ] *n* trabajador *m* portuario, estibador *m*
docket ['dɔkɪt] *n* (*on parcel etc*) etiqueta
dockyard ['dɔkjɑːd] *n* astillero
doctor ['dɔktəʳ] *n* médico; (*Ph.D. etc*) doctor(a) *m(f)* ■ *vt* (*fig*) arreglar, falsificar; (*drink etc*) adulterar
doctorate ['dɔktərɪt] *n* doctorado; *ver nota*

DOCTORATE

El grado más alto que conceden las universidades es el doctorado (*doctorate*), tras un período de estudio e investigación original no inferior a tres años que culmina con la presentación de una tesis ("thesis") en la que se exponen los resultados. El título más frecuente es el de "PhD" ("Doctor of Philosophy"), que se obtiene en Letras, Ciencias e Ingeniería, aunque también existen otros doctorados específicos en Música, Derecho etc.

Doctor of Philosophy *n* Doctor *m* (en Filosofía y Letras)
doctrinaire [dɔktrɪ'nɛəʳ] *adj* doctrinario
doctrine ['dɔktrɪn] *n* doctrina
docudrama [dɔkju'drɑːmə] *n* (*TV*) docudrama *m*
document ['dɔkjumənt] *n* documento ■ *vt* documentar
documentary [dɔkju'mɛntərɪ] *adj* documental ■ *n* documental *m*
documentation [dɔkjumɛn'teɪʃən] *n* documentación *f*
DOD *n abbr* (*US: = Department of Defense*) Ministerio de Defensa
doddering ['dɔdərɪŋ] *adj*, **doddery** ['dɔdərɪ] ■ *adj* vacilante
doddle ['dɔdl] *n*: **it's a ~** (*Brit col*) es pan comido
Dodecanese [dəudɪkə'niːz], **Dodecanese Islands** *npl* Dodecaneso *sg*
dodge [dɔdʒ] *n* (*of body*) regate *m*; (*fig*) truco ■ *vt* (*gen*) evadir; (*blow*) esquivar ■ *vi* escabullirse; (*Sport*) hacer una finta; **to ~ out of the way** echarse a un lado; **to ~ through the traffic** esquivar el tráfico
dodgems ['dɔdʒəmz] *npl* (*Brit*) autos *or* coches *mpl* de choque
dodgy ['dɔdʒɪ] *adj* (*col: uncertain*) dudoso; (*shady*) sospechoso; (*risky*) arriesgado
DOE *n abbr* (*Brit*) = **Department of the Environment**; (*US*) = **Department of Energy**
doe [dəu] *n* (*deer*) cierva, gama; (*rabbit*) coneja
does [dʌz] *vb see* **do**
doesn't ['dʌznt] = **does not**
dog [dɔg] *n* perro ■ *vt* seguir (de cerca); (*fig: memory etc*) perseguir; **to go to the dogs** (*person*) echarse a perder; (*nation etc*) ir a la ruina
dog biscuit *n* galleta de perro
dog collar *n* collar *m* de perro; (*fig*) alzacuello(s) *msg*
dog-eared ['dɔgɪəd] *adj* sobado; (*page*) con la esquina doblada
dogfish ['dɔgfɪʃ] *n* cazón *m*, perro marino
dog food *n* comida para perros
dogged ['dɔgɪd] *adj* tenaz, obstinado
doggy ['dɔgɪ] *n* (*col*) perrito
doggy bag *n* *bolsa para llevarse las sobras de la comida*
dogma ['dɔgmə] *n* dogma *m*
dogmatic [dɔg'mætɪk] *adj* dogmático
do-gooder [duː'gudəʳ] *n* (*col pej*): **to be a ~** ser una persona bien intencionada *or* un filantropista
dogsbody ['dɔgzbɔdɪ] *n* (*Brit*) burro de carga
doily ['dɔɪlɪ] *n* pañito de adorno
doing ['duɪŋ] *n*: **this is your ~** esto es obra tuya
doings ['duɪŋz] *npl* (*events*) sucesos *mpl*; (*acts*) hechos *mpl*
do-it-yourself [duːɪtjɔː'sɛlf] *n* bricolaje *m*
doldrums ['dɔldrəmz] *npl*: **to be in the ~** (*person*) estar abatido; (*business*) estar estancado
dole [dəul] *n* (*Brit: payment*) subsidio de paro; **on the ~** parado
▸ **dole out** *vt* repartir
doleful ['dəulful] *adj* triste, lúgubre
doll [dɔl] *n* muñeca
▸ **doll up** *vt*: **to ~ o.s. up** ataviarse
dollar ['dɔləʳ] *n* dólar *m*
dollop ['dɔləp] *n* buena cucharada
dolphin ['dɔlfɪn] *n* delfín *m*
domain [də'meɪn] *n* (*fig*) campo, competencia; (*land*) dominios *mpl*
dome [dəum] *n* (*Arch*) cúpula; (*shape*) bóveda
domestic [də'mɛstɪk] *adj* (*animal, duty*) doméstico; (*flight, news, policy*) nacional
domesticated [də'mɛstɪkeɪtɪd] *adj* domesticado; (*person: home-loving*) casero, hogareño
domesticity [dəumɛs'tɪsɪtɪ] *n* vida casera
domestic servant *n* sirviente(-a) *m(f)*
domicile ['dɔmɪsaɪl] *n* domicilio

dominant ['dɔmɪnənt] *adj* dominante
dominate ['dɔmɪneɪt] *vt* dominar
domination [dɔmɪ'neɪʃən] *n* dominación *f*
domineering [dɔmɪ'nɪərɪŋ] *adj* dominante
Dominican Republic [də'mɪnɪkən-] *n* República Dominicana
dominion [də'mɪnɪən] *n* dominio
domino (*pl* **dominoes**) ['dɔmɪnəu] *n* ficha de dominó
dominoes ['dɔmɪnəuz] *n* (*game*) dominó
don [dɔn] *n* (*Brit*) profesor(a) *m(f)* de universidad
donate [də'neɪt] *vt* donar
donation [də'neɪʃən] *n* donativo
done [dʌn] *pp of* **do**
donkey ['dɔŋkɪ] *n* burro
donkey-work ['dɔŋkɪwəːk] *n* (*Brit col*) trabajo pesado
donor ['dəunəʳ] *n* donante *m/f*
donor card *n* carnet *m* de donante de órganos
don't [dəunt] = **do not**
donut ['dəunʌt] *n* (*US*) = **doughnut**
doodle ['duːdl] *n* garabato ■ *vi* pintar dibujitos *or* garabatos
doom [duːm] *n* (*fate*) suerte *f*; (*death*) muerte *f* ■ *vt*: **to be doomed to failure** estar condenado al fracaso
doomsday ['duːmzdeɪ] *n* día *m* del juicio final
door [dɔːʳ] *n* puerta; (*of car*) portezuela; (*entry*) entrada; **from ~ to ~** de puerta en puerta
doorbell ['dɔːbɛl] *n* timbre *m*
door handle *n* tirador *m*; (*of car*) manija
door knocker *n* aldaba
doorman ['dɔːmən] *n* (*in hotel*) portero
doormat ['dɔːmæt] *n* felpudo, estera
doorstep ['dɔːstɛp] *n* peldaño; **on your ~** en la puerta de casa; (*fig*) al lado de casa
door-to-door ['dɔːtə'dɔːʳ] *adj*: **~ selling** venta a domicilio
doorway ['dɔːweɪ] *n* entrada, puerta; **in the ~** en la puerta
dope [dəup] *n* (*col: person*) imbécil *m/f*; (*: information*) información *f*, informes *mpl* ■ *vt* (*horse etc*) drogar
dopey ['dəupɪ] *adj* atontado
dormant ['dɔːmənt] *adj* inactivo; (*latent*) latente
dormer ['dɔːməʳ] *n* (*also:* **dormer window**) buhardilla
dormitory ['dɔːmɪtrɪ] *n* (*Brit*) dormitorio; (*US: hall of residence*) residencia, colegio mayor
dormouse (*pl* **dormice**) ['dɔːmaus, -maɪs] *n* lirón *m*
Dors *abbr* (*Brit*) = **Dorset**
DOS [dɔs] *n abbr* = **disk operating system**
dosage ['dəusɪdʒ] *n* (*on medicine bottle*) dosis *f inv*, dosificación *f*
dose [dəus] *n* (*of medicine*) dosis *f inv*; **a ~ of flu** un ataque de gripe ■ *vt*: **to ~ o.s. with** automedicarse con
dosser ['dɔsəʳ] *n* (*Brit col*) mendigo(-a); (*lazy person*) vago(-a)
doss house ['dɔs-] *n* (*Brit*) pensión *f* de mala muerte
dossier ['dɔsɪeɪ] *n*: **~ (on)** expediente *m* (sobre)
DOT *n abbr* (*US:* = *Department of Transportation*) *ministerio de transporte*
dot [dɔt] *n* punto; **dotted with** salpicado de; **on the ~** en punto
dotcom ['dɔtkɔm] *n* puntocom *f*
dot command *n* (*Comput*) instrucción *f* (precedida) de punto
dote [dəut]: **to ~ on** *vt fus* adorar, idolatrar
dot-matrix printer [dɔt'meɪtrɪks-] *n* impresora matricial *or* de matriz
dotted line ['dɔtɪd-] *n* línea de puntos; **to sign on the ~** firmar
dotty ['dɔtɪ] *adj* (*col*) disparatado, chiflado
double ['dʌbl] *adj* doble ■ *adv* (*twice*): **to cost ~** costar el doble ■ *n* (*gen*) doble *m* ■ *vt* doblar; (*efforts*) redoblar ■ *vi* doblarse; (*have two uses etc*): **to ~ as** hacer las veces de; **~ five two six (5526)** (*Telec*) cinco cinco dos seis; **spelt with a ~ "s"** escrito con dos "eses"; **on the ~,** (*Brit*) **at the ~** corriendo
▸ **double back** *vi* (*person*) volver sobre sus pasos
▸ **double up** *vi* (*bend over*) doblarse; (*share bedroom*) compartir
double bass *n* contrabajo
double bed *n* cama matrimonial
double-breasted ['dʌbl'brɛstɪd] *adj* cruzado
double-check ['dʌbltʃɛk] *vt* volver a revisar ■ *vi*: **I'll ~** voy a revisarlo otra vez
double-click ['dʌblˌklɪk] (*Comput*) *vi* hacer doble clic
double cream *n* nata enriquecida
doublecross ['dʌbl'krɔs] *vt* (*trick*) engañar; (*betray*) traicionar
doubledecker ['dʌbl'dɛkəʳ] *n* autobús *m* de dos pisos
double glazing *n* (*Brit*) doble acristalamiento
double indemnity *n* doble indemnización *f*
double-page ['dʌblpeɪdʒ] *adj*: **~ spread** doble página
double room *n* cuarto para dos
doubles ['dʌblz] *n* (*Tennis*) juego de dobles
double time *n* tarifa doble
double whammy [-'wæmɪ] *n* (*col*) palo doble
doubly ['dʌblɪ] *adv* doblemente
doubt [daut] *n* duda ■ *vt* dudar; (*suspect*)

dudar de; **to ~ that** dudar que; **there is no ~ that** no cabe duda de que; **without (a) ~** sin duda (alguna); **beyond ~** fuera de duda; **I ~ it very much** lo dudo mucho
doubtful ['dautful] *adj* dudoso; (*arousing suspicion: person*) sospechoso; **to be ~ about sth** tener dudas sobre algo; **I'm a bit ~** no estoy convencido
doubtless ['dautlıs] *adv* sin duda
dough [dəu] *n* masa, pasta; (*col: money*) pasta, lana (*LAm*)
doughnut ['dəunʌt] *n* buñuelo
douse [daus] *vt* (*drench: with water*) mojar; (*extinguish: flames*) apagar
dove [dʌv] *n* paloma
Dover ['dəuvəʳ] *n* Dover
dovetail ['dʌvteıl] *vi* (*fig*) encajar
dowager ['dauıdʒəʳ] *n*: **~ duchess** duquesa viuda
dowdy ['daudı] *adj* desaliñado; (*inelegant*) poco elegante
Dow-Jones average ['daudʒəunz-] *n* (*US*) índice *m* Dow-Jones
Dow-Jones Index *n* (*US*) índice *m* Dow-Jones
down [daun] *n* (*fluff*) pelusa; (*feathers*) plumón *m*, flojel *m*; (*hill*) loma ■ *adv* (*also*: **downwards**) abajo, hacia abajo; (*on the ground*) por/en tierra ■ *prep* abajo ■ *vt* (*col: drink*) beberse, tragar(se); **~ with X!** ¡abajo X!; **~ there** allí abajo; **~ here** aquí abajo; **I'll be ~ in a minute** ahora bajo; **England is two goals ~** Inglaterra está perdiendo por dos tantos; **I've been ~ with flu** he estado con gripe; **the price of meat is ~** ha bajado el precio de la carne; **I've got it ~ in my diary** lo he apuntado en mi agenda; **to pay £2 ~** dejar £2 de depósito; **he went ~ the hill** fue cuesta abajo; **~ under** (*in Australia etc*) en Australia/Nueva Zelanda; **to ~ tools** (*fig*) declararse en huelga
down-and-out ['daunəndaut] *n* (*tramp*) vagabundo(-a)
down-at-heel ['daunət'hi:l] *adj* venido a menos; (*appearance*) desaliñado
downbeat ['daunbi:t] *n* (*Mus*) compás *m* ■ *adj* (*gloomy*) pesimista
downcast ['daunkɑ:st] *adj* abatido
downer ['daunəʳ] *n* (*col: drug*) tranquilizante; **to be on a ~** estar pasando un mal bache
downfall ['daunfɔ:l] *n* caída, ruina
downgrade [daun'greıd] *vt* (*job*) degradar; (*hotel*) bajar de categoría
downhearted [daun'hɑ:tıd] *adj* desanimado
downhill [daun'hıl] *adv*: **to go ~** ir cuesta abajo; (*business*) estar en declive
Downing Street ['daunıŋ-] *n* (*Brit*) Downing Street *f*; *ver nota*

DOWNING STREET

Downing Street es la calle de Londres en la que tienen su residencia oficial tanto el Primer Ministro ("Prime Minister") como el Ministro de Economía ("Chancellor of the Exchequer"). El primero vive en el nº10 y el segundo en el nº11. Es una calle cerrada al público que se encuentra en el barrio de Westminster, en el centro de Londres. *Downing Street* se usa también en lenguaje periodístico para referirse al jefe del gobierno británico.

download ['daunləud] *vt* (*Comput*) transferir, telecargar
down-market ['daun'mɑ:kıt] *adj* de escasa calidad
down payment *n* entrada, pago al contado
downplay ['daunpleı] *vt* (*US*) quitar importancia a
downpour ['daunpɔ:ʳ] *n* aguacero
downright ['daunraıt] *adj* (*nonsense, lie*) manifiesto; (*refusal*) terminante
downsize [daun'saız] *vt* reducir la plantilla de
Down's syndrome [daunz-] *n* síndrome *m* de Down
downstairs [daun'stɛəz] *adv* (*below*) (en el piso de) abajo; (*motion*) escaleras abajo; **to come (***or* **go) ~** bajar la escalera
downstream [daun'stri:m] *adv* aguas *or* río abajo
downtime ['dauntaım] *n* (*Comm*) tiempo inactivo
down-to-earth [dauntu'ə:θ] *adj* práctico
downtown [daun'taun] *adv* en el centro de la ciudad
downtrodden ['dauntrɔdn] *adj* oprimido
downward ['daunwəd] *adv* hacia abajo; **face ~** (*person*) boca abajo; (*object*) cara abajo ■ *adj*: **a ~ trend** una tendencia descendente
downwards ['daunwədz] *adv* hacia abajo; **face ~** (*person*) boca abajo; (*object*) cara abajo
dowry ['daurı] *n* dote *f*
doz. *abbr* = **dozen**
doze [dəuz] *vi* dormitar
▸ **doze off** *vi* echar una cabezada
dozen ['dʌzn] *n* docena; **a ~ books** una docena de libros; **dozens of** cantidad de; **dozens of times** cantidad de veces; **80p a ~** 80 peniques la docena
DPh, DPhil *n abbr* (= *Doctor of Philosophy*) *título universitario*
DPP *n abbr* (*Brit*) = **Director of Public Prosecutions**

DPT *n abbr* (*Med*: = *diphtheria, pertussis, tetanus*) vacuna trivalente
DPW *n abbr* (*US*: = *Department of Public Works*) *ministerio de obras públicas*
Dr, Dr. *abbr* (= *doctor*) Dr
Dr. *abbr* (= *in street names*) = **Drive**
dr *abbr* (*Comm*) = **debtor**
drab [dræb] *adj* gris, monótono
draft [drɑ:ft] *n* (*first copy: of document, report*) borrador *m*; (*Comm*) giro; (*US: call-up*) quinta ■ *vt* (*write roughly*) hacer un borrador de; *see also* **draught**
draftsman *etc* ['drɑ:ftsmən] (*US*) = **draughtsman** *etc*
drag [dræg] *vt* arrastrar; (*river*) dragar, rastrear ■ *vi* arrastrarse por el suelo ■ *n* (*Aviat: resistance*) resistencia aerodinámica; (*col*) lata; (*women's clothing*): **in ~** travestido; **to ~ and drop** (*Comput*) arrastrar y soltar
▸ **drag away** *vt*: **to ~ away (from)** separar a rastras (de)
▸ **drag on** *vi* ser interminable
dragnet ['drægnɛt] *n* (*Naut*) rastra; (*fig*) emboscada
dragon ['drægən] *n* dragón *m*
dragonfly ['drægənflaɪ] *n* libélula
dragoon [drə'gu:n] *n* (*cavalryman*) dragón *m* ■ *vt*: **to ~ sb into doing sth** forzar a algn a hacer algo
drain [dreɪn] *n* desaguadero; (*in street*) sumidero; (*drain cover*) rejilla del sumidero ■ *vt* (*land, marshes*) desecar; (*Med*) drenar; (*reservoir*) desecar; (*fig*) agotar ■ *vi* escurrirse; **to be a ~ on** consumir, agotar; **to feel drained (of energy)** (*fig*) sentirse agotado
drainage ['dreɪnɪdʒ] *n* (*act*) desagüe *m*; (*Med, Agr*) drenaje *m*; (*sewage*) alcantarillado
draining board ['dreɪnɪŋ-], **drainboard** (*US*) ['dreɪnbɔ:d] *n* escurridero, escurridor *m*
drainpipe ['dreɪnpaɪp] *n* tubo de desagüe
drake [dreɪk] *n* pato (macho)
dram [dræm] *n* (*drink*) traguito, copita
drama ['drɑ:mə] *n* (*art*) teatro; (*play*) drama *m*
dramatic [drə'mætɪk] *adj* dramático
dramatist ['dræmətɪst] *n* dramaturgo(-a)
dramatize ['dræmətaɪz] *vt* (*events etc*) dramatizar; (*adapt: novel: for TV, cinema*) adaptar
drank [dræŋk] *pt of* **drink**
drape [dreɪp] *vt* cubrir
draper ['dreɪpər] *n* (*Brit*) pañero, mercero
drapes [dreɪps] *npl* (*US*) cortinas *fpl*
drastic ['dræstɪk] *adj* (*measure, reduction*) severo; (*change*) radical
draught, draft (*US*) [drɑ:ft] *n* (*of air*) corriente *f* de aire; (*drink*) trago; (*Naut*) calado; **on ~** (*beer*) de barril
draught beer *n* cerveza de barril
draughtboard ['drɑ:ftbɔ:d] (*Brit*) *n* tablero de damas
draughts [drɑ:fts] *n* (*Brit*) juego de damas
draughtsman, draftsman (*US*) ['drɑ:ftsmən] *n* proyectista *m*, delineante *m*
draughtsmanship, draftsmanship (*US*) ['drɑ:ftsmənʃɪp] *n* (*drawing*) dibujo lineal; (*skill*) habilidad *f* para el dibujo
draw [drɔ:] *vb* (*pt* **drew**, *pp* **drawn**) ■ *vt* (*pull*) tirar; (*take out*) sacar; (*attract*) atraer; (*picture*) dibujar; (*money*) retirar; (*formulate: conclusion*): **to ~ (from)** sacar (de); (*comparison, distinction*): **to ~ (between)** hacer (entre) ■ *vi* (*Sport*) empatar ■ *n* (*Sport*) empate *m*; (*lottery*) sorteo; (*attraction*) atracción *f*; **to ~ near** *vi* acercarse
▸ **draw back** *vi*: **to ~ back (from)** echarse atrás (de)
▸ **draw in** *vi* (*car*) aparcar; (*train*) entrar en la estación
▸ **draw on** *vt* (*resources*) utilizar, servirse de; (*imagination, person*) recurrir a
▸ **draw out** *vi* (*lengthen*) alargarse
▸ **draw up** *vi* (*stop*) pararse ■ *vt* (*document*) redactar; (*plan*) trazar
drawback ['drɔ:bæk] *n* inconveniente *m*, desventaja
drawbridge ['drɔ:brɪdʒ] *n* puente *m* levadizo
drawee [drɔ:'i:] *n* girado, librado
drawer [drɔ:r] *n* cajón *m*; (*of cheque*) librador(a) *m(f)*
drawing ['drɔ:ɪŋ] *n* dibujo
drawing board *n* tablero (de dibujante)
drawing pin *n* (*Brit*) chincheta *m*
drawing room *n* salón *m*
drawl [drɔ:l] *n* habla lenta y cansina
drawn [drɔ:n] *pp of* **draw** ■ *adj* (*haggard: with tiredness*) ojeroso; (*: with pain*) macilento
drawstring ['drɔ:strɪŋ] *n* cordón *m*
dread [drɛd] *n* pavor *m*, terror *m* ■ *vt* temer, tener miedo *or* pavor a
dreadful ['drɛdful] *adj* espantoso; **I feel ~!** (*ill*) ¡me siento fatal *or* malísimo!; (*ashamed*) ¡qué vergüenza!
dream [dri:m] *n* sueño ■ *vt, vi* (*pt, pp* **dreamed** *or* **dreamt**) [drɛmt] soñar; **to have a ~ about sb/sth** soñar con algn/algo; **sweet dreams!** ¡que sueñes con los angelitos!
▸ **dream up** *vt* (*reason, excuse*) inventar; (*plan, idea*) idear
dreamer ['dri:mər] *n* soñador(a) *m(f)*
dream world *n* mundo imaginario *or* de ensueño
dreamy ['dri:mɪ] *adj* (*person*) soñador(a), distraído; (*music*) de sueño
dreary ['drɪərɪ] *adj* monótono, aburrido

dredge [drɛdʒ] *vt* dragar
▸ **dredge up** *vt* sacar con draga; (*fig: unpleasant facts*) pescar, sacar a luz
dredger ['drɛdʒəʳ] *n* (*ship, machine*) draga; (*Culin*) tamiz *m*
dregs [drɛgz] *npl* heces *fpl*
drench [drɛntʃ] *vt* empapar; **drenched to the skin** calado hasta los huesos
dress [drɛs] *n* vestido; (*clothing*) ropa ▪ *vt* vestir; (*wound*) vendar; (*Culin*) aliñar; (*shop window*) decorar, arreglar ▪ *vi* vestirse; **to ~ o.s., get dressed** vestirse; **she dresses very well** se viste muy bien
▸ **dress up** *vi* vestirse de etiqueta; (*in fancy dress*) disfrazarse
dress circle *n* (*Brit*) principal *m*
dress designer *n* modisto(-a)
dresser ['drɛsəʳ] *n* (*furniture*) aparador *m*; (*: US*) tocador *m*; (*Theat*) camarero(-a)
dressing ['drɛsɪŋ] *n* (*Med*) vendaje *m*; (*Culin*) aliño
dressing gown *n* (*Brit*) bata
dressing room *n* (*Theat*) camarín *m*; (*Sport*) vestidor *m*
dressing table *n* tocador *m*
dressmaker ['drɛsmeɪkəʳ] *n* modista, costurera
dressmaking ['drɛsmeɪkɪŋ] *n* costura
dress rehearsal *n* ensayo general
dress shirt *n* camisa de frac
dressy ['drɛsɪ] *adj* (*col*) elegante
drew [dru:] *pt of* **draw**
dribble ['drɪbl] *vi* gotear, caer gota a gota; (*baby*) babear ▪ *vt* (*ball*) driblar, regatear
dried [draɪd] *adj* (*gen*) seco; (*fruit*) paso; (*milk*) en polvo
drier ['draɪəʳ] *n* = **dryer**
drift [drɪft] *n* (*of current etc*) velocidad *f*; (*of sand*) montón *m*; (*of snow*) ventisquero; (*meaning*) significado ▪ *vi* (*boat*) ir a la deriva; (*sand, snow*) amontonarse; **to catch sb's ~** cogerle el hilo a algn; **to let things ~** dejar las cosas como están; **to ~ apart** (*friends*) seguir su camino; (*lovers*) disgustarse, romper
drifter ['drɪftəʳ] *n* vagabundo(-a)
driftwood ['drɪftwud] *n* madera flotante
drill [drɪl] *n* taladro; (*bit*) broca; (*of dentist*) fresa; (*for mining etc*) perforadora, barrena; (*Mil*) instrucción *f* ▪ *vt* perforar, taladrar; (*soldiers*) ejercitar; (*pupils: in grammar*) hacer ejercicios con ▪ *vi* (*for oil*) perforar
drilling ['drɪlɪŋ] *n* (*for oil*) perforación *f*
drilling rig *n* (*on land*) torre *f* de perforación; (*at sea*) plataforma de perforación
drily ['draɪlɪ] *adv* secamente
drink [drɪŋk] *n* bebida ▪ *vt, vi* (*pt* **drank**, *pp* **drunk**) beber, tomar (*LAm*); **to have a ~** tomar algo; tomar una copa *or* un trago; **a ~ of water** un trago de agua; **to invite sb for drinks** invitar a algn a tomar unas copas; **there's food and ~ in the kitchen** hay de comer y de beber en la cocina; **would you like something to ~?** ¿quieres beber *or* tomar algo?
▸ **drink in** *vt* (*person: fresh air*) respirar; (*: story, sight*) beberse
drinkable ['drɪŋkəbl] *adj* (*not poisonous*) potable; (*palatable*) aguantable
drink-driving [drɪŋk'draɪvɪŋ] *n*: **to be charged with ~** ser acusado de conducir borracho *or* en estado de embriaguez
drinker ['drɪŋkəʳ] *n* bebedor(a) *m(f)*
drinking ['drɪŋkɪŋ] *n* (*drunkenness*) beber *m*
drinking fountain *n* fuente *f* de agua potable
drinking water *n* agua potable
drip [drɪp] *n* (*act*) goteo; (*one drip*) gota; (*Med*) gota a gota *m*; (*sound: of water etc*) goteo; (*col: spineless person*) soso(-a) ▪ *vi* gotear, caer gota a gota
drip-dry ['drɪp'draɪ] *adj* (*shirt*) de lava y pon
dripping ['drɪpɪŋ] *n* (*animal fat*) pringue *m* ▪ *adj*: **~ wet** calado
drive [draɪv] (*pt* **drove**, *pp* **driven**) *n* paseo (en coche); (*journey*) viaje *m* (en coche); (*also*: **driveway**) entrada; (*street*) calle; (*energy*) energía, vigor *m*; (*Psych*) impulso; (*Sport*) ataque *m*; (*Comput: also*: **disk drive**) unidad *f* (de disco) ▪ *vt* (*car*) conducir, manejar (*LAm*); (*nail*) clavar; (*push*) empujar; (*Tech: motor*) impulsar ▪ *vi* (*Aut: at controls*) conducir, manejar (*LAm*); (*: travel*) pasearse en coche; **to go for a ~** dar una vuelta en coche; **it's three hours' ~ from London** es un viaje de tres horas en coche desde Londres; **left-/right-hand ~** conducción *f* a la izquierda/derecha; **front-/rear-wheel ~** tracción *f* delantera/trasera; **sales ~** promoción *f* de ventas; **to ~ sb mad** volverle loco a algn; **to ~ sb to (do) sth** empujar a algn a (hacer) algo; **he drives a taxi** es taxista; **he drives a Mercedes** tiene un Mercedes; **can you ~?** ¿sabes conducir *or* (*LAm*) manejar?; **to ~ at 50 km an hour** ir a 50km por hora
▸ **drive at** *vt fus* (*fig: intend, mean*) querer decir, insinuar
▸ **drive on** *vi* no parar, seguir adelante ▪ *vt* (*incite, encourage*) empujar
drive-by ['draɪvbaɪ] *n*: **~ shooting** tiroteo desde el coche
drive-in ['draɪvɪn] *adj* (*esp US*): **~ cinema** autocine *m*
drivel ['drɪvl] *n* (*col*) tonterías *fpl*
driven ['drɪvn] *pp of* **drive**

driver ['draɪvə^r] *n* conductor(a) *m(f)*, chofer *m* (*LAm*); (*of taxi*) taxista *m/f*
driver's license *n* (*US*) carnet *m or* permiso de conducir
driveway ['draɪvweɪ] *n* camino de entrada
driving ['draɪvɪŋ] *n* conducir *m*, manejar *m* (*LAm*) ■ *adj* (*force*) impulsor(a)
driving instructor *n* instructor(a) *m(f)* de autoescuela
driving lesson *n* clase *f* de conducir
driving licence *n* (*Brit*) carnet *m or* permiso de conducir
driving school *n* autoescuela
driving test *n* examen *m* de conducir
drizzle ['drɪzl] *n* llovizna, garúa (*LAm*) ■ *vi* lloviznar
droll [drəul] *adj* gracioso
dromedary ['drɔmɪdərɪ] *n* dromedario
drone [drəun] *vi* (*bee, aircraft, engine*) zumbar; (*also*: **drone on**) murmurar sin interrupción ■ *n* zumbido; (*male bee*) zángano
drool [dru:l] *vi* babear; **to ~ over sb/sth** caérsele la baba por algn/algo
droop [dru:p] *vi* (*fig*) decaer, desanimarse
drop [drɔp] *n* (*of water*) gota; (*fall: in price*) bajada; (*: in salary*) disminución *f* ■ *vt* (*allow to fall*) dejar caer; (*voice, eyes, price*) bajar; (*set down from car*) dejar ■ *vi* (*price, temperature*) bajar; (*wind*) calmarse, amainar; (*numbers, attendance*) disminuir; **drops** *npl* (*Med*) gotas *fpl*; **cough drops** pastillas *fpl* para la tos; **a ~ of 10%** una bajada del 10 por ciento; **to ~ anchor** echar el ancla; **to ~ sb a line** mandar unas líneas a algn
▸ **drop in** *vi* (*col: visit*): **to ~ in (on)** pasar por casa (de)
▸ **drop off** *vi* (*sleep*) dormirse ■ *vt* (*passenger*) bajar, dejar
▸ **drop out** *vi* (*withdraw*) retirarse
droplet ['drɔplɪt] *n* gotita
dropout ['drɔpaut] *n* (*from society*) marginado(-a); (*from university*) estudiante *m/f* que ha abandonado los estudios
dropper ['drɔpə^r] *n* (*Med*) cuentagotas *m inv*
droppings ['drɔpɪŋz] *npl* excremento *sg*
dross [drɔs] *n* (*fig*) escoria
drought [draut] *n* sequía
drove [drəuv] *pt of* **drive**
drown [draun] *vt* (*also*: **drown out**: *sound*) ahogar ■ *vi* ahogarse
drowse [drauz] *vi* estar medio dormido
drowsy ['drauzɪ] *adj* soñoliento; **to be ~** tener sueño
drudge [drʌdʒ] *n* esclavo del trabajo
drudgery ['drʌdʒərɪ] *n* trabajo pesado *or* monótono
drug [drʌg] *n* (*Med*) medicamento, droga; (*narcotic*) droga ■ *vt* drogar; **to be on drugs** drogarse; **he's on drugs** se droga
drug addict *n* drogadicto(-a)
druggist ['drʌgɪst] *n* (*US*) farmacéutico(-a)
drug peddler *n* traficante *m/f* de drogas
drugstore ['drʌgstɔ:^r] *n* (*US*) tienda (*de comestibles, periódicos y medicamentos*)
drug trafficker *n* narcotraficante *m/f*
drum [drʌm] *n* tambor *m*; (*large*) bombo; (*for oil, petrol*) bidón *m* ■ *vi* tocar el tambor; (*with fingers*) tamborilear ■ *vt*: **to ~ one's fingers on the table** tamborilear con los dedos sobre la mesa; **drums** *npl* batería *sg*
▸ **drum up** *vt* (*enthusiasm, support*) movilizar, fomentar
drummer ['drʌmə^r] *n* (*in military band*) tambor *m/f*; (*in jazz/pop group*) batería *m/f*
drumstick ['drʌmstɪk] *n* (*Mus*) palillo, baqueta; (*chicken leg*) muslo (de pollo)
drunk [drʌŋk] *pp of* **drink** ■ *adj* borracho ■ *n* (*also*: **drunkard**) borracho(-a); **to get ~** emborracharse
drunken ['drʌŋkən] *adj* borracho
drunkenness ['drʌŋkənnɪs] *n* embriaguez *f*
dry [draɪ] *adj* seco; (*day*) sin lluvia; (*climate*) árido, seco; (*humour*) agudo; (*uninteresting: lecture*) aburrido, pesado ■ *vt* secar; (*tears*) enjugarse ■ *vi* secarse; **on ~ land** en tierra firme; **to ~ one's hands/hair/eyes** secarse las manos/el pelo/las lágrimas
▸ **dry up** *vi* (*supply, imagination etc*) agotarse; (*in speech*) atascarse
dry-clean ['draɪ'kli:n] *vt* limpiar *or* lavar en seco; **"~ only"** (*on label*) "limpieza *or* lavado en seco"
dry-cleaner's ['draɪ'kli:nəz] *n* tintorería
dry-cleaning ['draɪ'kli:nɪŋ] *n* lavado en seco
dry dock *n* (*Naut*) dique *m* seco
dryer ['draɪə^r] *n* (*for hair*) secador *m*; (*for clothes*) secadora
dry goods *npl* (*Comm*) mercería *sg*
dry goods store *n* (*US*) mercería
dry ice *n* nieve *f* carbónica, hielo seco
dryness ['draɪnɪs] *n* sequedad *f*
dry rot *n* putrefacción *f*
dry run *n* (*fig*) ensayo
dry ski slope *n* pista artificial de esquí
DSc *n abbr* (= *Doctor of Science*) *título universitario*
DSS *n abbr* (*Brit*) = **Department of Social Security**; *see* **social security**
DST *n abbr* (*US*: = *Daylight Saving Time*) *hora de verano*
DT *n abbr* (*Comput*) = **data transmission**
DTI *n abbr* (*Brit*) = **Department of Trade and Industry**
DTP *n abbr* = **desktop publishing**; (*Med*) = **diphtheria, tetanus, pertussis**

DT's *n abbr* (*col*: = *delirium tremens*) delirium *m* tremens
dual ['djuəl] *adj* doble
dual carriageway *n* (*Brit*) ≈ autovía
dual-control ['djuəlkən'trəul] *adj* de doble mando
dual nationality *n* doble nacionalidad *f*
dual-purpose ['djuəl'pə:pəs] *adj* de doble uso
dubbed [dʌbd] *adj* (*Cine*) doblado
dubious ['dju:bɪəs] *adj* indeciso; (*reputation, company*) dudoso; (*character*) sospechoso; **I'm very ~ about it** tengo mis dudas sobre ello
Dublin ['dʌblɪn] *n* Dublín
Dubliner ['dʌblɪnə^r] *n* dublinés(-esa) *m(f)*
duchess ['dʌtʃɪs] *n* duquesa
duck [dʌk] *n* pato ▪ *vi* agacharse ▪ *vt* (*plunge in water*) zambullir
duckling ['dʌklɪŋ] *n* patito
duct [dʌkt] *n* conducto, canal *m*
dud [dʌd] *n* (*shell*) obús *m* que no estalla; (*object, tool*): **it's a ~** es una filfa ▪ *adj*: **~ cheque** (*Brit*) cheque *m* sin fondos
due [dju:] *adj* (*proper*) debido; (*fitting*) conveniente, oportuno ▪ *adv*: **~ north** derecho al norte; **dues** *npl* (*for club, union*) cuota *sg*; (*in harbour*) derechos *mpl*; **in ~ course** a su debido tiempo; **~ to** debido a; **to be ~ to** deberse a; **the train is ~ to arrive at 8.00** el tren tiene (prevista) la llegada a las ocho; **the rent's ~ on the 30th** hay que pagar el alquiler el día 30; **I am ~ six days' leave** me deben seis días de vacaciones; **she is ~ back tomorrow** ella debe volver mañana
due date *n* fecha de vencimiento
duel ['djuəl] *n* duelo
duet [dju:'ɛt] *n* dúo
duff [dʌf] *adj* sin valor
duffel bag ['dʌfl-] *n* macuto
duffel coat ['dʌfl-] *n* trenca
dug [dʌg] *pt, pp of* **dig**
dugout ['dʌgaut] *n* (*canoe*) piragua (*hecha de un solo tronco*); (*Sport*) banquillo; (*Mil*) refugio subterráneo
duke [dju:k] *n* duque *m*
dull [dʌl] *adj* (*light*) apagado; (*stupid*) torpe; (*boring*) pesado; (*sound, pain*) sordo; (*weather, day*) gris ▪ *vt* (*pain, grief*) aliviar; (*mind, senses*) entorpecer
duly ['dju:lɪ] *adv* debidamente; (*on time*) a su debido tiempo
dumb [dʌm] *adj* mudo; (*stupid*) estúpido; **to be struck ~** (*fig*) quedar boquiabierto
dumbbell ['dʌmbɛl] *n* (*Sport*) pesa
dumbfounded [dʌm'faundɪd] *adj* pasmado
dummy ['dʌmɪ] *n* (*tailor's model*) maniquí *m*; (*Brit: for baby*) chupete *m* ▪ *adj* falso, postizo; **~ run** ensayo
dump [dʌmp] *n* (*heap*) montón *m* de basura; (*place*) basurero, vertedero; (*col*) tugurio; (*Mil*) depósito; (*Comput*) copia vaciada ▪ *vt* (*put down*) dejar; (*get rid of*) deshacerse de; (*Comput*) tirar (a la papelera); (*Comm: goods*) inundar el mercado de; **to be (down) in the dumps** (*col*) tener murria, estar deprimido
dumping ['dʌmpɪŋ] *n* (*Econ*) dumping *m*; (*of rubbish*): **"no ~"** "prohibido verter basura"
dumpling ['dʌmplɪŋ] *n* *bola de masa hervida*
dumpy ['dʌmpɪ] *adj* regordete(-a)
dunce [dʌns] *n* zopenco
dune [dju:n] *n* duna
dung [dʌŋ] *n* estiércol *m*
dungarees [dʌŋgə'ri:z] *npl* mono *sg*, overol *msg* (*LAm*)
dungeon ['dʌndʒən] *n* calabozo
dunk [dʌŋk] *vt* mojar
duo ['dju:əu] *n* (*Mus*) dúo
duodenal [dju:ə'di:nl] *adj* (*ulcer*) de duodeno
duodenum [dju:ə'di:nəm] *n* duodeno
dupe [dju:p] *n* (*victim*) víctima ▪ *vt* engañar
duplex ['dju:plɛks] *n* (*US: also:* **duplex apartment**) dúplex *m*
duplicate ['dju:plɪkət] *n* duplicado; (*copy of letter etc*) copia ▪ *adj* (*copy*) duplicado ▪ *vt* ['dju:plɪkeɪt] duplicar; (*on machine*) multicopiar; **in ~** por duplicado
duplicate key *n* duplicado de una llave
duplicating machine ['dju:plɪkeɪtɪŋ-], **duplicator** ['dju:plɪkeɪtə^r] *n* multicopista *m*
duplicity [dju:'plɪsɪtɪ] *n* doblez *f*, duplicidad *f*
Dur. *abbr* (*Brit*) = **Durham**
durability [djuərə'bɪlɪtɪ] *n* durabilidad *f*
durable ['djuərəbl] *adj* duradero
duration [djuə'reɪʃən] *n* duración *f*
duress [djuə'rɛs] *n*: **under ~** por coacción
Durex® ['djuərɛks] *n* (*Brit*) preservativo
during ['djuərɪŋ] *prep* durante
dusk [dʌsk] *n* crepúsculo, anochecer *m*
dusky ['dʌskɪ] *adj* oscuro; (*complexion*) moreno
dust [dʌst] *n* polvo ▪ *vt* (*furniture*) desempolvar; (*cake etc*): **to ~ with** espolvorear de
▸**dust off** *vt* (*also fig*) desempolvar, quitar el polvo de
dustbin ['dʌstbɪn] *n* (*Brit*) cubo de la basura, balde *m* (*LAm*)
dustbin liner *n* bolsa de basura
duster ['dʌstə^r] *n* paño, trapo; (*feather duster*) plumero
dust jacket *n* sobrecubierta
dustman ['dʌstmən] *n* (*Brit*) basurero
dustpan ['dʌstpæn] *n* cogedor *m*
dust storm *n* vendaval *m* de polvo
dusty ['dʌstɪ] *adj* polvoriento

Dutch [dʌtʃ] *adj* holandés(-esa) ■ *n* (*Ling*) holandés *m* ■ *adv*: **to go ~** pagar a escote; **the Dutch** *npl* los holandeses
Dutch auction *n* subasta a la rebaja
Dutchman ['dʌtʃmən], **Dutchwoman** ['dʌtʃwumən] *n* holandés(-esa) *m(f)*
dutiful ['dju:tɪful] *adj* (*child*) obediente; (*husband*) sumiso; (*employee*) cumplido
duty ['dju:tɪ] *n* deber *m*; (*tax*) derechos *mpl* de aduana; (*Med: in hospital*) servicio, guardia; **on ~** de servicio; (*at night etc*) de guardia; **off ~** libre (de servicio); **to make it one's ~ to do sth** encargarse de hacer algo sin falta; **to pay ~ on sth** pagar los derechos sobre algo
duty-free [dju:tɪ'fri:] *adj* libre de derechos de aduana; **~ shop** tienda libre de impuestos
duty officer *n* (*Mil etc*) oficial *m/f* de guardia
duvet ['du:veɪ] *n* (*Brit*) edredón *m* (nórdico)
DV *abbr* (= *Deo volente*) Dios mediante
DVD *n abbr* (= *digital versatile or video disc*) DVD *m*
DVLA *n abbr* (*Brit*: = *Driver and Vehicle Licensing Agency*) *organismo encargado de la expedición de permisos de conducir y matriculación de vehículos*
DVM *n abbr* (*US*: = *Doctor of Veterinary Medicine*) *título universitario*
DVT *n abbr* = **deep-vein thrombosis**
dwarf [dwɔ:f] (*pl* **dwarves**) [dwɔ:vz] *n* enano ■ *vt* empequeñecer
dwell [dwɛl] (*pt, pp* **dwelt**) [dwɛlt] *vi* morar
▸ **dwell on** *vt fus* explayarse en
dweller ['dwɛlə^r] *n* habitante *m*; **city ~** habitante *m* de la ciudad
dwelling ['dwɛlɪŋ] *n* vivienda
dwelt [dwɛlt] *pt, pp of* **dwell**
dwindle ['dwɪndl] *vi* menguar, disminuir
dwindling ['dwɪndlɪŋ] *adj* (*strength, interest*) menguante; (*resources, supplies*) en disminución
dye [daɪ] *n* tinte *m* ■ *vt* teñir; **hair ~** tinte *m* para el pelo
dying ['daɪɪŋ] *adj* moribundo, agonizante; (*moments*) final; (*words*) último
dyke [daɪk] *n* (*Brit*) dique *m*; (*channel*) arroyo, acequia; (*causeway*) calzada
dynamic [daɪ'næmɪk] *adj* dinámico
dynamics [daɪ'næmɪks] *n or npl* dinámica *sg*
dynamite ['daɪnəmaɪt] *n* dinamita ■ *vt* dinamitar
dynamo ['daɪnəməu] *n* dinamo *f*, dinamo *m* (*LAm*)
dynasty ['dɪnəstɪ] *n* dinastía
dysentery ['dɪsɪntrɪ] *n* disentería
dyslexia [dɪs'lɛksɪə] *n* dislexia
dyslexic [dɪs'lɛksɪk] *adj, n* disléxico(-a) *m(f)*
dyspepsia [dɪs'pɛpsɪə] *n* dispepsia
dystrophy ['dɪstrəfɪ] *n* distrofia; **muscular ~** distrofia muscular

Ee

E, e [iː] *n* (*letter*) E, e *f*; (*Mus*) mi *m*; **E for Edward,** (*US*) **E for Easy** E de Enrique
E *abbr* (= *east*) E ■ *n abbr* (= *Ecstasy*) éxtasis *m*
E111 *n abbr* (= *form E111*) impreso E111
ea. *abbr* = **each**
E.A. *abbr* (*US*: = *educational age*) *nivel escolar*
each [iːtʃ] *adj* cada *inv* ■ *pron* cada uno; (*also*: **each other**) el uno al otro; **they hate ~ other** se odian (entre ellos *or* mutuamente); **~ day** cada día; **they have two books ~** tienen dos libros cada uno; **they cost £5 ~** cuestan cinco libras cada uno; **~ of us** cada uno de nosotros
eager [ˈiːgəʳ] *adj* (*gen*) impaciente; (*hopeful*) ilusionado; (*keen*) entusiasmado; (*pupil*) apasionado; **to be ~ to do sth** estar deseoso de hacer algo; **to be ~ for** ansiar, anhelar
eagerly [ˈiːgəlɪ] *adv* con impaciencia; con ilusión; con entusiasmo
eagerness [ˈiːgənɪs] *n* impaciencia; ilusión *f*; entusiasmo
eagle [ˈiːgl] *n* águila
E & OE *abbr* = **errors and omissions excepted**
ear [ɪəʳ] *n* oreja; (*sense of hearing*) oído; (*of corn*) espiga; **up to the ears in debt** abrumado de deudas
earache [ˈɪəreɪk] *n* dolor *m* de oídos
eardrum [ˈɪədrʌm] *n* tímpano
earful [ˈɪəful] *n*: **to give sb an ~** (*col*) echar una bronca a algn
earl [əːl] *n* conde *m*
early [ˈəːlɪ] *adv* (*gen*) temprano; (*ahead of time*) con tiempo, con anticipación ■ *adj* (*gen*) temprano; (*reply*) pronto; (*man*) primitivo; (*first*: *Christians, settlers*) primero; **to have an ~ night** acostarse temprano; **in the ~** *or* **~ in the spring/19th century** a principios de primavera/del siglo diecinueve; **you're ~!** ¡has llegado temprano *or* pronto!; **~ in the morning/afternoon** a primeras horas de la mañana/tarde; **she's in her ~ forties** tiene poco más de cuarenta años; **at your earliest convenience** (*Comm*) con la mayor brevedad posible; **I can't come any earlier** no puedo llegar antes
early retirement *n* jubilación *f* anticipada
early warning system *n* sistema *m* de alerta inmediata
earmark [ˈɪəmɑːk] *vt*: **to ~ for** reservar para, destinar a
earn [əːn] *vt* (*gen*) ganar; (*interest*) devengar; (*praise*) ganarse; **to ~ one's living** ganarse la vida
earned income *n* renta del trabajo
earnest [ˈəːnɪst] *adj* serio, formal ■ *n* (*also*: **earnest money**) anticipo, señal *f*; **in ~** *adv* en serio
earnings [ˈəːnɪŋz] *npl* (*personal*) ingresos *mpl*; (*of company etc*) ganancias *fpl*
earphones [ˈɪəfəunz] *npl* auriculares *mpl*
earplugs [ˈɪəplʌgz] *npl* tapones *mpl* para los oídos
earring [ˈɪərɪŋ] *n* pendiente *m*, arete *m* (*LAm*)
earshot [ˈɪəʃɔt] *n*: **out of/within ~** fuera del/al alcance del oído
earth [əːθ] *n* (*gen*) tierra; (*Brit Elec*) toma de tierra ■ *vt* (*Brit Elec*) conectar a tierra
earthenware [ˈəːθnwɛəʳ] *n* loza (de barro)
earthly [ˈəːθlɪ] *adj* terrenal, mundano; **~ paradise** paraíso terrenal; **there is no ~ reason to think ...** no existe razón para pensar ...
earthquake [ˈəːθkweɪk] *n* terremoto
earth-shattering [ˈəːθʃætərɪŋ] *adj* trascendental
earthworm [ˈəːθwəːm] *n* lombriz *f*
earthy [ˈəːθɪ] *adj* (*fig*: *uncomplicated*) sencillo; (*coarse*) grosero
earwig [ˈɪəwɪg] *n* tijereta
ease [iːz] *n* facilidad *f*; (*comfort*) comodidad *f* ■ *vt* (*task*) facilitar; (*pain*) aliviar; (*loosen*) soltar; (*relieve*: *pressure, tension*) aflojar; (*weight*) aligerar; (*help pass*): **to ~ sth in/out** meter/sacar algo con cuidado ■ *vi* (*situation*) relajarse; **with ~** con facilidad; **to feel at ~/ill at ~** sentirse a gusto/a disgusto; **at ~!** (*Mil*) ¡descansen!

▸ **ease off, ease up** *vi* (*work, business*) aflojar; (*person*) relajarse
easel ['i:zl] *n* caballete *m*
easily ['i:zɪlɪ] *adv* fácilmente
easiness ['i:zɪnɪs] *n* facilidad *f*; (*of manners*) soltura
east [i:st] *n* este *m*, oriente *m* ■ *adj* del este, oriental ■ *adv* al este, hacia el este; **the E~** el Oriente; (*Pol*) el Este
Easter ['i:stəʳ] *n* Pascua (de Resurrección)
Easter egg *n* huevo de Pascua
Easter holidays *npl* Semana Santa *sg*
Easter Island *n* Isla de Pascua
easterly ['i:stəlɪ] *adj* (*to the east*) al este; (*from the east*) del este
Easter Monday *n* lunes *m* de Pascua
eastern ['i:stən] *adj* del este, oriental; **E~ Europe** Europa del Este; **the E~ bloc** (*Pol*) los países del Este
Easter Sunday *n* Domingo de Resurrección
East Germany *n* (*formerly*) Alemania Oriental *or* del Este
eastward ['i:stwəd], **eastwards** ['i:stwədz] *adv* hacia el este
easy ['i:zɪ] *adj* fácil; (*life*) holgado, cómodo; (*relaxed*) natural ■ *adv*: **to take it** *or* **things ~** (*not worry*) no preocuparse; (*go slowly*) tomarlo con calma; (*rest*) descansar; **payment on ~ terms** (*Comm*) facilidades de pago; **I'm ~** (*col*) me da igual, no me importa; **easier said than done** del dicho al hecho hay buen trecho
easy chair *n* butaca
easy-going ['i:zɪ'gəuɪŋ] *adj* acomodadizo
easy touch [i:zɪ'tʌtʃ] *n*: **he's an ~** (*col*) es fácil de convencer
eat (*pt* **ate**, *pp* **eaten**) [i:t, eɪt, 'i:tn] *vt* comer
▸ **eat away** *vt* (*sea*) desgastar; (*acid*) corroer
▸ **eat into, eat away at** *vt fus* corroer
▸ **eat out** *vi* comer fuera
▸ **eat up** *vt* (*meal etc*) comerse; **it eats up electricity** devora la electricidad
eatable ['i:təbl] *adj* comestible
eau de Cologne [əudəkə'ləun] *n* (agua de) colonia
eaves [i:vz] *npl* alero *sg*
eavesdrop ['i:vzdrɔp] *vi*: **to ~ (on sb)** escuchar a escondidas *or* con disimulo (a algn)
ebb [ɛb] *n* reflujo ■ *vi* bajar; (*fig*: *also*: **ebb away**) decaer; **~ and flow** el flujo y reflujo; **to be at a low ~** (*fig*: *person*) estar de capa caída
ebb tide *n* marea menguante
ebony ['ɛbənɪ] *n* ébano
e-book ['i:buk] *n* libro electrónico
ebullient [ɪ'bʌlɪənt] *adj* entusiasta, animado
e-business [i:bɪznɪs] *n* (*commerce*) comercio electrónico; (*company*) negocio electrónico
ECB *n abbr* (= *European Central Bank*) BCE *m*
eccentric [ɪk'sɛntrɪk] *adj, n* excéntrico(-a)
ecclesiastical [ɪkli:zɪ'æstɪkəl] *adj* eclesiástico
ECG *n abbr* (= *electrocardiogram*) E.C.G. *m*
echo (*pl* **echoes**) ['ɛkəu] *n* eco *m* ■ *vt* (*sound*) repetir ■ *vi* resonar, hacer eco
ECLA *n abbr* (= *Economic Commission for Latin America*) CEPAL *f*
éclair ['eɪklɛəʳ] *n* petisú *m*
eclipse [ɪ'klɪps] *n* eclipse *m* ■ *vt* eclipsar
ECM *n abbr* (*US*: = *European Common Market*) MCE *m*
eco- ['i:kəu] *pref* eco-
eco-friendly ['i:kəufrɛndlɪ] *adj* ecológico
ecological [i:kə'lɔdʒɪkl] *adj* ecológico
ecologist [ɪ'kɔlədʒɪst] *n* ecologista *m/f*; (*scientist*) ecólogo(-a) *m(f)*
ecology [ɪ'kɔlədʒɪ] *n* ecología
e-commerce ['i:,kɔmə:s] *n* comercio electrónico
economic [i:kə'nɔmɪk] *adj* (*profitable*: *price*) económico; (*business etc*) rentable
economical [i:kə'nɔmɪkl] *adj* económico
economically [i:kə'nɔmɪklɪ] *adv* económicamente
economics [i:kə'nɔmɪks] *n* economía ■ *npl* (*financial aspects*) finanzas *fpl*
economic warfare *n* guerra económica
economist [ɪ'kɔnəmɪst] *n* economista *m/f*
economize [ɪ'kɔnəmaɪz] *vi* economizar, ahorrar
economy [ɪ'kɔnəmɪ] *n* economía; **economies of scale** economías *fpl* de escala
economy class *n* (*Aviat etc*) clase *f* turista
economy class syndrome *n* síndrome *m* de la clase turista
economy size *n* tamaño familiar
ecosystem ['i:kəusɪstəm] *n* ecosistema *m*
eco-tourism [i:kəu'tuərɪzm] *n* turismo verde *or* ecológico
ECSC *n abbr* (= *European Coal and Steel Community*) CECA *f*
ecstasy ['ɛkstəsɪ] *n* éxtasis *m inv*
ecstatic [ɛks'tætɪk] *adj* extático, extasiado
ECT *n abbr* = **electroconvulsive therapy**
Ecuador ['ɛkwədɔ:ʳ] *n* Ecuador *m*
Ecuadoran [ɛkwə'dɔ:rən], **Ecuadorian** [ɛkwə'dɔ:rɪən] *adj, n* ecuatoriano(-a) *m(f)*
ecumenical [i:kju'mɛnɪkl] *adj* ecuménico
eczema ['ɛksɪmə] *n* eczema *m*
eddy ['ɛdɪ] *n* remolino
edge [ɛdʒ] *n* (*of knife etc*) filo; (*of object*) borde *m*; (*of lake etc*) orilla ■ *vt* (*Sewing*) ribetear ■ *vi*: **to ~ past** pasar con dificultad; **on ~** (*fig*) = **edgy**; **to ~ away from** alejarse poco a poco de; **to ~ forward** avanzar poco a poco; **to ~ up** subir lentamente

edgeways ['ɛdʒweɪz] *adv*: **he couldn't get a word in** ~ no pudo meter baza
edging ['ɛdʒɪŋ] *n (Sewing)* ribete *m*; *(of path)* borde *m*
edgy ['ɛdʒɪ] *adj* nervioso, inquieto
edible ['ɛdɪbl] *adj* comestible
edict ['i:dɪkt] *n* edicto
edifice ['ɛdɪfɪs] *n* edificio
edifying ['ɛdɪfaɪɪŋ] *adj* edificante
Edinburgh ['ɛdɪnbərə] *n* Edimburgo
edit ['ɛdɪt] *vt (be editor of)* dirigir; *(re-write)* redactar; *(cut)* cortar; *(Comput)* editar
edition [ɪ'dɪʃən] *n (gen)* edición *f*; *(number printed)* tirada
editor ['ɛdɪtə^r] *n (of newspaper)* director(a) *m(f)*; *(of book)* redactor(a) *m(f)*; *(also:* **film editor**) montador(a) *m(f)*
editorial [ɛdɪ'tɔ:rɪəl] *adj* editorial ■ *n* editorial *m*; **~ staff** redacción *f*
EDP *n abbr (= electronic data processing)* PED *m*
EDT *n abbr (US: = Eastern Daylight Time) hora de verano de Nueva York*
educate ['ɛdjukeɪt] *vt (gen)* educar; *(instruct)* instruir
educated guess ['ɛdjukeɪtɪd-] *n* hipótesis *f* sólida
education [ɛdju'keɪʃən] *n* educación *f*; *(schooling)* enseñanza; *(Scol: subject etc)* pedagogía; **primary/secondary ~** enseñanza primaria/secundaria
educational [ɛdju'keɪʃənl] *adj (policy etc)* de educación, educativo; *(teaching)* docente; *(instructive)* educativo; **~ technology** tecnología educacional
Edwardian [ɛd'wɔ:dɪən] *adj* eduardiano
EE *abbr* = **electrical engineer**
EEG *n abbr* = **electroencephalogram**
eel [i:l] *n* anguila
EENT *n abbr (US Med)* = **eye, ear, nose and throat**
EEOC *n abbr (US: = Equal Employment Opportunity Commission) comisión que investiga discriminación racial o sexual en el empleo*
eerie ['ɪərɪ] *adj (sound, experience)* espeluznante
EET *n abbr (= Eastern European Time) hora de Europa oriental*
efface [ɪ'feɪs] *vt* borrar
effect [ɪ'fɛkt] *n* efecto ■ *vt* efectuar, llevar a cabo; **effects** *npl (property)* efectos *mpl*; **to take ~** *(law)* entrar en vigor *or* vigencia; *(drug)* surtir efecto; **in ~** en realidad; **to have an ~ on sb/sth** hacerle efecto a algn/afectar algo; **to put into ~** *(plan)* llevar a la práctica; **his letter is to the ~ that ...** su carta viene a decir que ...
effective [ɪ'fɛktɪv] *adj (gen)* eficaz; *(striking: display, outfit)* impresionante; *(real)* efectivo; **to become ~** *(law)* entrar en vigor; **~ date** fecha de vigencia
effectively [ɪ'fɛktɪvlɪ] *adv (efficiently)* eficazmente; *(strikingly)* de manera impresionante; *(in reality)* en efecto
effectiveness [ɪ'fɛktɪvnɪs] *n* eficacia
effeminate [ɪ'fɛmɪnɪt] *adj* afeminado
effervescent [ɛfə'vɛsnt] *adj* efervescente
efficacy ['ɛfɪkəsɪ] *n* eficacia
efficiency [ɪ'fɪʃənsɪ] *n (gen)* eficiencia; *(of machine)* rendimiento
efficient [ɪ'fɪʃənt] *adj* eficiente; *(remedy, product, system)* eficaz; *(machine, car)* de buen rendimiento
effigy ['ɛfɪdʒɪ] *n* efigie *f*
effluent ['ɛfluənt] *n* vertidos *mpl*
effort ['ɛfət] *n* esfuerzo; **to make an ~ to do sth** hacer un esfuerzo *or* esforzarse para hacer algo
effortless ['ɛfətlɪs] *adj* sin ningún esfuerzo
effrontery [ɪ'frʌntərɪ] *n* descaro
effusive [ɪ'fju:sɪv] *adj* efusivo
EFL *n abbr (Scol)* = **English as a foreign language**
EFTA ['ɛftə] *n abbr (= European Free Trade Association)* EFTA *f*
e.g. *adv abbr (= exempli gratia)* p.ej.
egg [ɛg] *n* huevo; **hard-boiled/soft-boiled/poached ~** huevo duro *or (LAm)* a la copa *or (LAm)* tibio /pasado por agua/escalfado; **scrambled eggs** huevos revueltos
▸ **egg on** *vt* incitar
eggcup ['ɛgkʌp] *n* huevera
eggnog [ɛg'nɔg] *n* ponche *m* de huevo
eggplant ['ɛgplɑ:nt] *n (esp US)* berenjena
eggshell ['ɛgʃɛl] *n* cáscara de huevo
egg-timer ['ɛgtaɪmə^r] *n* reloj *m* de arena *(para cocer huevos)*
egg white *n* clara de huevo
egg yolk *n* yema de huevo
ego ['i:gəu] *n* ego
egotism ['ɛgəutɪzəm] *n* egoísmo
egotist ['ɛgəutɪst] *n* egoísta *m/f*
ego trip *n*: **to be on an ~** creerse el centro del mundo
Egypt ['i:dʒɪpt] *n* Egipto
Egyptian [ɪ'dʒɪpʃən] *adj, n* egipcio(-a) *m(f)*
eiderdown ['aɪdədaun] *n* edredón *m*
eight [eɪt] *num* ocho
eighteen [eɪ'ti:n] *num* dieciocho
eighth [eɪtθ] *adj* octavo
eighty ['eɪtɪ] *num* ochenta
Eire ['ɛərə] *n* Eire *m*
EIS *n abbr (= Educational Institute of Scotland) sindicato de profesores escoceses*

either ['aɪðəʳ] *adj* cualquiera de los dos ...; (*both, each*) cada ■ *pron*: **~ (of them)** cualquiera (de los dos) ■ *adv* tampoco ■ *conj*: **~ yes or no** o sí o no; **on ~ side** en ambos lados; **I don't like ~** no me gusta ninguno de los dos; **no, I don't ~** no, yo tampoco
eject [ɪ'dʒɛkt] *vt* echar; (*tenant*) desahuciar ■ *vi* eyectarse
ejector seat [ɪ'dʒɛktə-] *n* asiento proyectable
eke out [iːk-] *vt fus* (*money*) hacer que llegue
EKG *n abbr* (*US*) *see* **electrocardiogram**
el [ɛl] *n abbr* (*US col*) = **elevated railroad**
elaborate [*adj* ɪ'læbərɪt, *vb* ɪ'læbəreɪt] *adj* (*design, pattern*) complicado ■ *vt* elaborar ■ *vi* explicarse con muchos detalles
elaborately [ɪ'læbərɪtlɪ] *adv* de manera complicada; (*decorated*) profusamente
elaboration [ɪlæbə'reɪʃən] *n* elaboración *f*
elapse [ɪ'læps] *vi* transcurrir
elastic [ɪ'læstɪk] *adj, n* elástico
elastic band *n* (*Brit*) gomita
elated [ɪ'leɪtɪd] *adj*: **to be ~** estar eufórico
elation [ɪ'leɪʃən] *n* euforia
elbow ['ɛlbəu] *n* codo ■ *vt*: **to ~ one's way through the crowd** abrirse paso a codazos por la muchedumbre
elbow grease *n* (*col*): **to use some** *or* **a bit of ~** menearse
elder ['ɛldəʳ] *adj* mayor ■ *n* (*tree*) saúco; (*person*) mayor; (*of tribe*) anciano
elderly ['ɛldəlɪ] *adj* de edad, mayor ■ *npl*: **the ~** la gente mayor, los ancianos
elder statesman *n* estadista *m* veterano; (*fig*) figura respetada
eldest ['ɛldɪst] *adj, n* el/la mayor
elect [ɪ'lɛkt] *vt* elegir; (*choose*): **to ~ to do** optar por hacer ■ *adj*: **the president ~** el presidente electo
election [ɪ'lɛkʃən] *n* elección *f*; **to hold an ~** convocar elecciones
election campaign *n* campaña electoral
electioneering [ɪlɛkʃə'nɪərɪŋ] *n* campaña electoral
elector [ɪ'lɛktəʳ] *n* elector(a) *m(f)*
electoral [ɪ'lɛktərəl] *adj* electoral
electoral college *n* colegio electoral
electoral roll *n* censo electoral
electorate [ɪ'lɛktərɪt] *n* electorado
electric [ɪ'lɛktrɪk] *adj* eléctrico
electrical [ɪ'lɛktrɪkl] *adj* eléctrico
electrical engineer *n* ingeniero(-a) electricista
electrical failure *n* fallo eléctrico
electric blanket *n* manta eléctrica
electric chair *n* silla eléctrica
electric cooker *n* cocina eléctrica
electric current *n* corriente *f* eléctrica
electric fire *n* estufa eléctrica
electrician [ɪlɛk'trɪʃən] *n* electricista *m/f*
electricity [ɪlɛk'trɪsɪtɪ] *n* electricidad *f*; **to switch on/off the ~** conectar/desconectar la electricidad
electricity board *n* (*Brit*) compañía eléctrica (estatal)
electric light *n* luz *f* eléctrica
electric shock *n* electrochoque *m*
electrification [ɪlɛktrɪfɪ'keɪʃən] *n* electrificación *f*
electrify [ɪ'lɛktrɪfaɪ] *vt* (*Rail*) electrificar; (*fig: audience*) electrizar
electro... [ɪ'lɛktrəu] *pref* electro...
electrocardiogram [ɪ'lɛktrə'kɑːdɪəgræm] *n* electrocardiograma *m*
electrocardiograph [ɪ'lɛktrəu'kɑːdɪəgræf] *n* electrocardiógrafo
electro-convulsive therapy [ɪ'lɛktrə-kən'vʌlsɪv-] *n* electroterapia
electrocute [ɪ'lɛktrəukjuːt] *vt* electrocutar
electrode [ɪ'lɛktrəud] *n* electrodo
electroencephalogram [ɪ'lɛktrəuɛn'sɛfələ-græm] *n* electroencefalograma *m*
electrolysis [ɪlɛk'trɔlɪsɪs] *n* electrólisis *f inv*
electromagnetic [ɪ'lɛktrəmæg'nɛtɪk] *adj* electromagnético
electron [ɪ'lɛktrɔn] *n* electrón *m*
electronic [ɪlɛk'trɔnɪk] *adj* electrónico
electronic data processing *n* tratamiento *or* proceso electrónico de datos
electronic mail *n* correo electrónico
electronics [ɪlɛk'trɔnɪks] *n* electrónica
electron microscope *n* microscopio electrónico
electroplated [ɪ'lɛktrə'pleɪtɪd] *adj* galvanizado
electrotherapy [ɪ'lɛktrə'θɛrəpɪ] *n* electroterapia
elegance ['ɛlɪgəns] *n* elegancia
elegant ['ɛlɪgənt] *adj* elegante
elegy ['ɛlɪdʒɪ] *n* elegía
element ['ɛlɪmənt] *n* (*gen*) elemento; (*of heater, kettle etc*) resistencia
elementary [ɛlɪ'mɛntərɪ] *adj* elemental; (*primitive*) rudimentario; (*school, education*) primario
elementary school *n* (*US*) escuela de enseñanza primaria; *ver nota*

ELEMENTARY SCHOOL

En Estados Unidos y Canadá se llama *elementary school* al centro estatal en el que los niños reciben los primeros seis u ocho años de su educación, también llamado "grade school" o "grammar school".

elephant ['ɛlɪfənt] *n* elefante *m*
elevate ['ɛlɪveɪt] *vt* (*gen*) elevar; (*in rank*) ascender
elevated railroad *n* (*US*) *ferrocarril urbano elevado*
elevation [ɛlɪ'veɪʃən] *n* elevación *f*; (*rank*) ascenso; (*height*) altitud *f*
elevator ['ɛlɪveɪtə^r] *n* (*US*) ascensor *m*, elevador *m* (*LAm*)
eleven [ɪ'lɛvn] *num* once
elevenses [ɪ'lɛvnzɪz] *npl* (*Brit*) ≈ café *m* de media mañana
eleventh [ɪ'lɛvnθ] *adj* undécimo; **at the ~ hour** (*fig*) a última hora
elf (*pl* **elves**) [ɛlf, ɛlvz] *n* duende *m*
elicit [ɪ'lɪsɪt] *vt*: **to ~ sth (from sb)** obtener algo (de algn)
eligible ['ɛlɪdʒəbl] *adj* cotizado; **to be ~ for a pension** tener derecho a una pensión
eliminate [ɪ'lɪmɪneɪt] *vt* eliminar; (*score out*) suprimir; (*a suspect, possibility*) descartar
elimination [ɪlɪmɪ'neɪʃən] *n* eliminación *f*; supresión *f*; **by process of ~** por eliminación
elite [eɪ'li:t] *n* élite *f*
elitist [eɪ'li:tɪst] *adj* (*pej*) elitista
elixir [ɪ'lɪksɪə^r] *n* elixir *m*
Elizabethan [ɪlɪzə'bi:θən] *adj* isabelino
elm [ɛlm] *n* olmo
elocution [ɛlə'kju:ʃən] *n* elocución *f*
elongated ['i:lɔŋgeɪtɪd] *adj* alargado
elope [ɪ'ləup] *vi* fugarse
elopement [ɪ'ləupmənt] *n* fuga
eloquence ['ɛləkwəns] *n* elocuencia
eloquent ['ɛləkwənt] *adj* elocuente
else [ɛls] *adv*: **or ~** si no; **something ~** otra cosa *or* algo más; **somewhere ~** en otra parte; **everywhere ~** en los demás sitios; **everyone ~** todos los demás; **nothing ~** nada más; **is there anything ~ I can do?** ¿puedo hacer algo más?; **where ~?** ¿dónde más?, ¿en qué otra parte?; **there was little ~ to do** apenas quedaba otra cosa que hacer; **nobody ~** nadie más
elsewhere [ɛls'wɛə^r] *adv* (*be*) en otra parte; (*go*) a otra parte
ELT *n abbr* (*Scol*) = **English Language Teaching**
elucidate [ɪ'lu:sɪdeɪt] *vt* esclarecer, elucidar
elude [ɪ'lu:d] *vt* eludir; (*blow, pursuer*) esquivar
elusive [ɪ'lu:sɪv] *adj* escurridizo; (*answer*) difícil de encontrar; **he is very ~** no es fácil encontrarlo
elves [ɛlvz] *npl of* **elf**
emaciated [ɪ'meɪsɪeɪtɪd] *adj* escuálido
e-mail ['i:meɪl] *n abbr* (= *electronic mail*) email *m*, correo electrónico ■ *vt*: **to ~ sb** mandar un email *or* un correo electrónico a algn; **to ~ sb sth** mandar algo a algn por Internet, mandar algo a algn en un email *or* un correo electrónico
e-mail account *n* cuenta de correo
e-mail address *n* dirección *f* electrónica, email *m*
emanate ['ɛməneɪt] *vi* emanar, provenir
emancipate [ɪ'mænsɪpeɪt] *vt* emancipar
emancipated [ɪ'mænsɪpeɪtɪd] *adj* liberado
emancipation [ɪmænsɪ'peɪʃən] *n* emancipación *f*, liberación *f*
emasculate [ɪ'mæskjuleɪt] *vt* castrar; (*fig*) debilitar
embalm [ɪm'bɑ:m] *vt* embalsamar
embankment [ɪm'bæŋkmənt] *n* (*of railway*) terraplén *m*; (*riverside*) dique *m*
embargo (*pl* **embargoes**) [ɪm'bɑ:gəu] *n* prohibición *f*; (*Comm, Naut*) embargo; **to put an ~ on sth** poner un embargo en algo
embark [ɪm'bɑ:k] *vi* embarcarse ■ *vt* embarcar; **to ~ on** (*journey*) comenzar, iniciar; (*fig*) emprender
embarkation [ɛmbɑ:'keɪʃən] *n* (*of people*) embarco; (*of goods*) embarque *m*
embarrass [ɪm'bærəs] *vt* avergonzar, dar vergüenza a; (*financially etc*) poner en un aprieto
embarrassed [ɪm'baerəst] *adj* azorado, violento; **to be ~** sentirse azorado *or* violento
embarrassing [ɪm'bærəsɪŋ] *adj* (*situation*) violento; (*question*) embarazoso
embarrassment [ɪm'bærəsmənt] *n* vergüenza, azoramiento; (*financial*) apuros *mpl*
embassy ['ɛmbəsɪ] *n* embajada
embed [ɪm'bɛd] *vt* (*jewel*) empotrar; (*teeth etc*) clavar
embellish [ɪm'bɛlɪʃ] *vt* embellecer; (*fig: story, truth*) adornar
embers ['ɛmbəz] *npl* rescoldo *sg*, ascuas
embezzle [ɪm'bɛzl] *vt* desfalcar, malversar
embezzlement [ɪm'bɛzlmənt] *n* desfalco, malversación *f*
embezzler [ɪm'bɛzlə^r] *n* malversador(a) *m(f)*
embitter [ɪm'bɪtə^r] *vt* (*person*) amargar; (*relationship*) envenenar
embittered [ɪm'bɪtəd] *adj* resentido, amargado
emblem ['ɛmbləm] *n* emblema *m*
embody [ɪm'bɔdɪ] *vt* (*spirit*) encarnar; (*ideas*) expresar
embolden [ɪm'bəuldən] *vt* envalentonar
embolism ['ɛmbəlɪzəm] *n* embolia
emboss [ɪm'bɔs] *vt* estampar en relieve; (*metal, leather*) repujar
embossed [ɪm'bɔst] *adj* realzado; **~ with ...** con ... en relieve
embrace [ɪm'breɪs] *vt* abrazar, dar un abrazo a; (*include*) abarcar; (*adopt: idea*) adherirse a ■ *vi* abrazarse ■ *n* abrazo

embroider [ɪmˈbrɔɪdə^r] *vt* bordar; (*fig: story*) adornar, embellecer
embroidery [ɪmˈbrɔɪdərɪ] *n* bordado
embroil [ɪmˈbrɔɪl] *vt*: **to become embroiled (in sth)** enredarse (en algo)
embryo [ˈɛmbrɪəu] *n* (*also fig*) embrión *m*
emcee [ɛmˈsiː] *n abbr* (*US: = master of ceremonies*) presentador(a) *m(f)*
emend [ɪˈmɛnd] *vt* (*text*) enmendar
emerald [ˈɛmərəld] *n* esmeralda
emerge [ɪˈməːdʒ] *vi* (*gen*) salir; (*arise*) surgir; **it emerges that** resulta que
emergence [ɪˈməːdʒəns] *n* (*of nation*) surgimiento
emergency [ɪˈməːdʒənsɪ] *n* (*event*) emergencia; (*crisis*) crisis *f inv*; **in an ~** en caso de urgencia; **(to declare a) state of ~** (declarar) estado de emergencia *or* de excepción
emergency cord *n* (*US*) timbre *m* de alarma
emergency exit *n* salida de emergencia
emergency landing *n* aterrizaje *m* forzoso
emergency lane *n* (*US*) arcén *m*
emergency meeting *n* reunión *f* extraordinaria
emergency service *n* servicio de urgencia
emergency stop *n* (*Aut*) parada en seco
emergent [ɪˈməːdʒənt] *adj* (*nation*) recientemente independizado
emery board [ˈɛmərɪ-] *n* lima de uñas
emetic [ɪˈmɛtɪk] *n* vomitivo, emético
emigrant [ˈɛmɪgrənt] *n* emigrante *m/f*
emigrate [ˈɛmɪgreɪt] *vi* emigrar
emigration [ɛmɪˈgreɪʃən] *n* emigración *f*
émigré [ˈɛmɪgreɪ] *n* emigrado(-a)
eminence [ˈɛmɪnəns] *n* eminencia; **to gain** *or* **win ~** ganarse fama
eminent [ˈɛmɪnənt] *adj* eminente
eminently [ˈɛmɪnəntlɪ] *adv* eminentemente
emirate [ˈɛmɪrɪt] *n* emirato
emission [ɪˈmɪʃən] *n* emisión *f*
emit [ɪˈmɪt] *vt* emitir; (*smell, smoke*) despedir
emolument [ɪˈmɔljumənt] *n* (*often pl: formal*) honorario, emolumento
emotion [ɪˈməuʃən] *n* emoción *f*
emotional [ɪˈməuʃənl] *adj* (*person*) sentimental; (*scene*) conmovedor(a), emocionante
emotionally [ɪˈməuʃnəlɪ] *adv* (*behave, speak*) con emoción; (*be involved*) sentimentalmente
emotive [ɪˈməutɪv] *adj* emotivo
empathy [ˈɛmpəθɪ] *n* empatía; **to feel ~ with sb** sentirse identificado con algn
emperor [ˈɛmpərə^r] *n* emperador *m*
emphasis (*pl* **emphases**) [ˈɛmfəsɪs, -siːz] *n* énfasis *m inv*; **to lay** *or* **place ~ on sth** (*fig*) hacer hincapié en algo; **the ~ is on sport** se da mayor importancia al deporte
emphasize [ˈɛmfəsaɪz] *vt* (*word, point*) subrayar, recalcar; (*feature*) hacer resaltar
emphatic [ɛmˈfætɪk] *adj* (*condemnation*) enérgico; (*denial*) rotundo
emphatically [ɛmˈfætɪklɪ] *adv* con énfasis
emphysema [ɛmfɪˈsiːmə] *n* (*Med*) enfisema *m*
empire [ˈɛmpaɪə^r] *n* imperio
empirical [ɛmˈpɪrɪkl] *adj* empírico
employ [ɪmˈplɔɪ] *vt* (*give job to*) emplear; (*make use of: thing, method*) emplear, usar; **he's employed in a bank** está empleado en un banco
employee [ɪmplɔɪˈiː] *n* empleado(-a)
employer [ɪmˈplɔɪə^r] *n* patrón(-ona) *m(f)*; (*businessman*) empresario(-a)
employment [ɪmˈplɔɪmənt] *n* empleo; **full ~** pleno empleo; **without ~** sin empleo; **to find ~** encontrar trabajo; **place of ~** lugar *m* de trabajo
employment agency *n* agencia de colocaciones *or* empleo
employment exchange *n* bolsa de trabajo
empower [ɪmˈpauə^r] *vt*: **to ~ sb to do sth** autorizar a algn para hacer algo
empress [ˈɛmprɪs] *n* emperatriz *f*
emptiness [ˈɛmptɪnɪs] *n* vacío
empty [ˈɛmptɪ] *adj* vacío; (*street, area*) desierto; (*threat*) vano ■ *n* (*bottle*) envase *m* ■ *vt* vaciar; (*place*) dejar vacío ■ *vi* vaciarse; (*house*) quedar(se) vacío *or* desocupado; (*place*) quedar(se) desierto; **to ~ into** (*river*) desembocar en
empty-handed [ˈɛmptɪˈhændɪd] *adj* con las manos vacías
empty-headed [ˈɛmptɪˈhɛdɪd] *adj* casquivano
EMS *n abbr* (= *European Monetary System*) SME *m*
EMT *n abbr* (*US*) = **emergency medical technician**
EMU *n abbr* (= *European Monetary Union, Economic and Monetary Union*) UME *f*
emulate [ˈɛmjuleɪt] *vt* emular
emulsion [ɪˈmʌlʃən] *n* emulsión *f*
enable [ɪˈneɪbl] *vt*: **to ~ sb to do sth** (*allow*) permitir a algn hacer algo; (*prepare*) capacitar a algn para hacer algo
enact [ɪnˈækt] *vt* (*law*) promulgar; (*play, scene, role*) representar
enamel [ɪˈnæməl] *n* esmalte *m*
enamel paint *n* esmalte *m*
enamoured [ɪˈnæməd] *adj*: **to be ~ of** (*person*) estar enamorado de; (*activity etc*) tener gran afición a; (*idea*) aferrarse a
enc. *abbr* (*on letters etc: = enclosed, enclosure*) adj
encampment [ɪnˈkæmpmənt] *n* campamento

encase [ɪn'keɪs] *vt*: **to ~ in** (*contain*) encajar; (*cover*) cubrir
encased [ɪn'keɪst] *adj*: **~ in** (*covered*) revestido de
enchant [ɪn'tʃɑ:nt] *vt* encantar
enchanting [ɪn'tʃɑ:ntɪŋ] *adj* encantador(a)
encircle [ɪn'sə:kl] *vt* (*gen*) rodear; (*waist*) ceñir
encl. *abbr* (= *enclosed*) adj
enclave ['ɛnkleɪv] *n* enclave *m*
enclose [ɪn'kləuz] *vt* (*land*) cercar; (*with letter etc*) adjuntar; (*in receptacle*): **to ~ (with)** encerrar (con); **please find enclosed** le mandamos adjunto
enclosure [ɪn'kləuʒə^r] *n* cercado, recinto; (*Comm*) carta adjunta
encoder [ɪn'kəudə^r] *n* (*Comput*) codificador *m*
encompass [ɪn'kʌmpəs] *vt* abarcar
encore [ɔŋ'kɔ:^{r}] *excl* ¡otra!, ¡bis! ■ *n* bis *m*
encounter [ɪn'kauntə^r] *n* encuentro ■ *vt* encontrar, encontrarse con; (*difficulty*) tropezar con
encourage [ɪn'kʌrɪdʒ] *vt* alentar, animar; (*growth*) estimular; **to ~ sb (to do sth)** animar a algn (a hacer algo)
encouragement [ɪn'kʌrɪdʒmənt] *n* estímulo; (*of industry*) fomento
encouraging [ɪn'kʌrɪdʒɪŋ] *adj* alentador(a)
encroach [ɪn'krəutʃ] *vi*: **to ~ (up)on** (*gen*) invadir; (*time*) adueñarse de
encrust [ɪn'krʌst] *vt* incrustar
encrusted [ɪn'krʌstəd] *adj*: **~ with** recubierto de
encumber [ɪn'kʌmbə^r] *vt*: **to be encumbered with** (*carry*) estar cargado de; (*debts*) estar gravado de
encyclopaedia, encyclopedia [ɛnsaɪkləu'pi:dɪə] *n* enciclopedia
end [ɛnd] *n* fin *m*; (*of table*) extremo; (*of line, rope etc*) cabo; (*of pointed object*) punta; (*of town*) barrio; (*of street*) final *m*; (*Sport*) lado ■ *vt* terminar, acabar; (*also*: **bring to an end, put an end to**) acabar con ■ *vi* terminar, acabar; **to ~ (with)** terminar (con); **in the ~** al final; **to be at an ~** llegar a su fin; **at the ~ of the day** (*fig*) al fin y al cabo, a fin de cuentas; **to this ~, with this ~ in view** con este propósito; **from ~ to ~** de punta a punta; **on ~** (*object*) de punta, de cabeza; **to stand on ~** (*hair*) erizarse, ponerse de punta; **for hours on ~** hora tras hora
▸ **end up** *vi*: **to ~ up in** terminar en; (*place*) ir a parar a
endanger [ɪn'deɪndʒə^r] *vt* poner en peligro; **an endangered species** (*of animal*) una especie en peligro de extinción
endear [ɪn'dɪə^r] *vt*: **to ~ o.s. to sb** ganarse la simpatía de algn
endearing [ɪn'dɪərɪŋ] *adj* entrañable
endearment [ɪn'dɪərmənt] *n* cariño, palabra cariñosa; **to whisper endearments** decir unas palabras cariñosas al oído; **term of ~** nombre *m* cariñoso
endeavour, endeavor (*US*) [ɪn'dɛvə^r] *n* esfuerzo; (*attempt*) tentativa ■ *vi*: **to ~ to do** esforzarse por hacer; (*try*) procurar hacer
endemic [ɛn'dɛmɪk] *adj* (*poverty, disease*) endémico
ending ['ɛndɪŋ] *n* fin *m*, final *m*; (*of book*) desenlace *m*; (*Ling*) terminación *f*
endive ['ɛndaɪv] *n* (*curly*) escarola; (*smooth, flat*) endibia
endless ['ɛndlɪs] *adj* interminable, inacabable; (*possibilities*) infinito
endorse [ɪn'dɔ:s] *vt* (*cheque*) endosar; (*approve*) aprobar
endorsee [ɪndɔ:'si:] *n* endorsatario(-a)
endorsement [ɪn'dɔ:smənt] *n* (*approval*) aprobación *f*; (*signature*) endoso; (*Brit*: *on driving licence*) nota de sanción
endorser [ɪn'dɔ:sə^r] *n* avalista *m/f*
endow [ɪn'dau] *vt* (*provide with money*) dotar; (*found*) fundar; **to be endowed with** (*fig*) estar dotado de
endowment [ɪn'daumənt] *adj* (*amount*) donación *f*
endowment mortgage *n* hipoteca dotal
endowment policy *n* póliza dotal
end product *n* (*Industry*) producto final; (*fig*) resultado
end result *n* resultado
endurable [ɪn'djuərəbl] *adj* soportable, tolerable
endurance [ɪn'djuərəns] *n* resistencia
endurance test *n* prueba de resistencia
endure [ɪn'djuə^r] *vt* (*bear*) aguantar, soportar; (*resist*) resistir ■ *vi* (*last*) perdurar; (*resist*) resistir
enduring [ɪn'djuərɪŋ] *adj* duradero
end user *n* (*Comput*) usuario final
enema ['ɛnɪmə] *n* (*Med*) enema *m*
enemy ['ɛnəmɪ] *adj, n* enemigo(-a) *m(f)*; **to make an ~ of sb** enemistarse con algn
energetic [ɛnə'dʒɛtɪk] *adj* enérgico
energy ['ɛnədʒɪ] *n* energía
energy crisis *n* crisis *f* energética
energy-saving ['ɛnədʒɪseɪvɪŋ] *adj* (*policy*) para ahorrar energía; (*device*) que ahorra energía ■ *n* ahorro de energía
enervating ['ɛnəveɪtɪŋ] *adj* deprimente
enforce [ɪn'fɔ:s] *vt* (*law*) hacer cumplir
enforced [ɪn'fɔ:st] *adj* forzoso, forzado
enfranchise [ɪn'fræntʃaɪz] *vt* (*give vote to*) conceder el derecho de voto a; (*set free*) emancipar

engage [ɪn'geɪdʒ] *vt (attention)* captar; *(in conversation)* abordar; *(worker, lawyer)* contratar ■ *vi (Tech)* engranar; **to ~ in** dedicarse a, ocuparse en; **to ~ sb in conversation** entablar conversación con algn; **to ~ the clutch** embragar
engaged [ɪn'geɪdʒd] *adj (Brit: busy, in use)* ocupado; *(betrothed)* prometido; **to get ~** prometerse; **he is ~ in research** se dedica a la investigación
engaged tone *n (Brit Tel)* señal *f* de comunicando
engagement [ɪn'geɪdʒmənt] *n (appointment)* compromiso, cita; *(battle)* combate *m*; *(to marry)* compromiso; *(period)* noviazgo; **I have a previous ~** ya tengo un compromiso
engagement ring *n* anillo de pedida
engaging [ɪn'geɪdʒɪŋ] *adj* atractivo, simpático
engender [ɪn'dʒɛndə^r] *vt* engendrar
engine ['ɛndʒɪn] *n (Aut)* motor *m*; *(Rail)* locomotora
engine driver *n (Brit: of train)* maquinista *m/f*
engineer [ɛndʒɪ'nɪə^r] *n* ingeniero(-a); *(Brit: for repairs)* técnico(-a); *(US Rail)* maquinista *m/f*; **civil/mechanical ~** ingeniero(-a) de caminos, canales y puertos/industrial
engineering [ɛndʒɪ'nɪərɪŋ] *n* ingeniería ■ *cpd (works, factory)* de componentes mecánicos
engine failure, engine trouble *n* avería del motor
England ['ɪŋglənd] *n* Inglaterra
English ['ɪŋglɪʃ] *adj* inglés(-esa) ■ *n (Ling)* el inglés; **the English** *npl* los ingleses
English Channel *n*: **the ~** el Canal de la Mancha
Englishman ['ɪŋglɪʃmən], **Englishwoman** ['ɪŋglɪʃwumən] *n* inglés(-esa) *m(f)*
English-speaker ['ɪŋglɪʃspiːkə^r] *n* persona de habla inglesa
English-speaking ['ɪŋglɪʃspiːkɪŋ] *adj* de habla inglesa
engraving [ɪn'greɪvɪŋ] *n* grabado
engrossed [ɪn'grəust] *adj*: **~ in** absorto en
engulf [ɪn'gʌlf] *vt* sumergir, hundir; *(fire)* devorar
enhance [ɪn'hɑːns] *vt (gen)* aumentar; *(beauty)* realzar; *(position, reputation)* mejorar
enigma [ɪ'nɪgmə] *n* enigma *m*
enigmatic [ɛnɪg'mætɪk] *adj* enigmático
enjoy [ɪn'dʒɔɪ] *vt (have: health, fortune)* disfrutar de, gozar de; *(food)* comer con gusto; **I ~ doing ...** me gusta hacer ...; **to ~ o.s.** divertirse, pasarlo bien
enjoyable [ɪn'dʒɔɪəbl] *adj (pleasant)* agradable; *(amusing)* divertido
enjoyment [ɪn'dʒɔɪmənt] *n (use)* disfrute *m*; *(joy)* placer *m*
enlarge [ɪn'lɑːdʒ] *vt* aumentar; *(broaden)* extender; *(Phot)* ampliar ■ *vi*: **to ~ on** *(subject)* tratar con más detalles
enlarged [ɪn'lɑːdʒd] *adj (edition)* aumentado; *(Med: organ, gland)* dilatado
enlargement [ɪn'lɑːdʒmənt] *n (Phot)* ampliación *f*
enlighten [ɪn'laɪtn] *vt* informar, instruir
enlightened [ɪn'laɪtnd] *adj* iluminado; *(tolerant)* comprensivo
enlightening [ɪn'laɪtnɪŋ] *adj* informativo, instructivo
Enlightenment [ɪn'laɪtnmənt] *n (History)*: **the ~** la Ilustración, el Siglo de las Luces
enlist [ɪn'lɪst] *vt* alistar; *(support)* conseguir ■ *vi* alistarse; **enlisted man** *(US Mil)* soldado raso
enliven [ɪn'laɪvn] *vt (people)* animar; *(events)* avivar, animar
enmity ['ɛnmɪtɪ] *n* enemistad *f*
ennoble [ɪ'nəubl] *vt* ennoblecer
enormity [ɪ'nɔːmɪtɪ] *n* enormidad *f*
enormous [ɪ'nɔːməs] *adj* enorme
enough [ɪ'nʌf] *adj*: **~ time/books** bastante tiempo/bastantes libros ■ *n*: **have you got ~?** ¿tiene usted bastante? ■ *adv*: **big ~** bastante grande; **he has not worked ~** no ha trabajado bastante; **(that's) ~!** ¡basta ya!, ¡ya está bien!; **that's ~, thanks** con eso basta, gracias; **will five be ~?** ¿bastará con cinco?; **I've had ~** estoy harto; **he was kind ~ to lend me the money** tuvo la bondad *or* amabilidad de prestarme el dinero; **... which, funnily ~ ...** ... lo que, por extraño que parezca ...
enquire [ɪn'kwaɪə^r] *vt, vi* = **inquire**
enrage [ɪn'reɪdʒ] *vt* enfurecer
enrich [ɪn'rɪtʃ] *vt* enriquecer
enrol, enroll *(US)* [ɪn'rəul] *vt (member)* inscribir; *(Scol)* matricular ■ *vi* inscribirse; *(Scol)* matricularse
enrolment, enrollment *(US)* [ɪn'rəulmənt] *n* inscripción *f*; matriculación *f*
en route [ɔn'ruːt] *adv* durante el viaje; **~ for/from/to** camino de/de/a
ensconce [ɪn'skɔns] *vt*: **to ~ o.s.** instalarse cómodamente, acomodarse
ensemble [ɔn'sɔmbl] *n (Mus)* conjunto
enshrine [ɪn'ʃraɪn] *vt* recoger
ensign ['ɛnsaɪn] *n (flag)* bandera; *(Naut)* alférez *m*
enslave [ɪn'sleɪv] *vt* esclavizar
ensue [ɪn'sjuː] *vi* seguirse; *(result)* resultar
ensuing [ɪn'sjuːɪŋ] *adj* subsiguiente
ensure [ɪn'ʃuə^r] *vt* asegurar

ENT *n abbr* (*Med*: = *ear, nose and throat*) otorrinolaringología
entail [ɪn'teɪl] *vt* (*imply*) suponer; (*result in*) acarrear
entangle [ɪn'tæŋgl] *vt* (*thread etc*) enredar, enmarañar; **to become entangled in sth** (*fig*) enredarse en algo
entanglement [ɪn'tæŋglmənt] *n* enredo
enter ['ɛntə^r] *vt* (*room, profession*) entrar en; (*club*) hacerse socio de; (*army*) alistarse en; (*sb for a competition*) inscribir; (*write down*) anotar, apuntar; (*Comput*) introducir ■ *vi* entrar; **to ~ for** *vt fus* presentarse a; **to ~ into** *vt fus* (*relations*) establecer; (*plans*) formar parte de; (*debate*) tomar parte en; (*negotiations*) entablar; (*agreement*) llegar a, firmar; **to ~ (up)on** *vt fus* (*career*) emprender
enteritis [ɛntə'raɪtɪs] *n* enteritis *f*
enterprise ['ɛntəpraɪz] *n* empresa; (*spirit*) iniciativa; **free ~** la libre empresa; **private ~** la iniciativa privada
enterprising ['ɛntəpraɪzɪŋ] *adj* emprendedor(a)
entertain [ɛntə'teɪn] *vt* (*amuse*) divertir; (*receive: guest*) recibir (en casa); (*idea*) abrigar
entertainer [ɛntə'teɪnə^r] *n* artista *m/f*
entertaining [ɛntə'teɪnɪŋ] *adj* divertido, entretenido ■ *n*: **to do a lot of ~** dar muchas fiestas, tener muchos invitados
entertainment [ɛntə'teɪnmənt] *n* (*amusement*) diversión *f*; (*show*) espectáculo; (*party*) fiesta
entertainment allowance *n* (*Comm*) gastos *mpl* de representación
enthral [ɪn'θrɔːl] *vt* embelesar, cautivar
enthralled [ɪn'θrɔːld] *adj* cautivado
enthralling [ɪn'θrɔːlɪŋ] *adj* cautivador(a)
enthuse [ɪn'θuːz] *vi*: **to ~ about** *or* **over** entusiasmarse por
enthusiasm [ɪn'θuːzɪæzəm] *n* entusiasmo
enthusiast [ɪn'θuːzɪæst] *n* entusiasta *m/f*
enthusiastic [ɪnθuːzɪ'æstɪk] *adj* entusiasta; **to be ~ about sb/sth** estar entusiasmado con algn/algo
entice [ɪn'taɪs] *vt* tentar; (*seduce*) seducir
entire [ɪn'taɪə^r] *adj* entero, todo
entirely [ɪn'taɪəlɪ] *adv* totalmente
entirety [ɪn'taɪərətɪ] *n*: **in its ~** en su totalidad
entitle [ɪn'taɪtl] *vt*: **to ~ sb to sth** dar a algn derecho a algo
entitled [ɪn'taɪtld] *adj* (*book*) titulado; **to be ~ to sth/to do sth** tener derecho a algo/a hacer algo
entity ['ɛntɪtɪ] *n* entidad *f*
entourage [ɔntu'rɑːʒ] *n* séquito
entrails ['ɛntreɪlz] *npl* entrañas *fpl*; (*US: offal*) asadura *sg*, menudos *mpl*
entrance ['ɛntrəns] *n* entrada ■ *vt* [ɪn'trɑːns] encantar, hechizar; **to gain ~ to** (*university etc*) ingresar en
entrance examination *n* (*to school*) examen *m* de ingreso
entrance fee *n* entrada
entrance ramp *n* (*US Aut*) rampa de acceso
entrancing [ɪn'trɑːnsɪŋ] *adj* encantador(a)
entrant ['ɛntrənt] *n* (*in race, competition*) participante *m/f*; (*in exam*) candidato(-a)
entreat [ɛn'triːt] *vt* rogar, suplicar
entrenched [ɛn'trɛntʃd] *adj*: **~ interests** intereses *mpl* creados
entrepreneur [ɔntrəprə'nəː^r] *n* empresario(-a), capitalista *m/f*
entrepreneurial [ɔntrəprə'nəːrɪəl] *adj* empresarial
entrust [ɪn'trʌst] *vt*: **to ~ sth to sb** confiar algo a algn
entry ['ɛntrɪ] *n* entrada; (*permission to enter*) acceso; (*in register, diary, ship's log*) apunte *m*; (*in account book, ledger, list*) partida; **no ~** prohibido el paso; (*Aut*) dirección prohibida; **single/double ~ book-keeping** contabilidad *f* simple/por partida doble
entry form *n* boletín *m* de inscripción
entry phone *n* (*Brit*) portero automático
E-number ['iːnʌmbə^r] *n* número E
enumerate [ɪ'njuːməreɪt] *vt* enumerar
enunciate [ɪ'nʌnsɪeɪt] *vt* pronunciar; (*principle etc*) enunciar
envelop [ɪn'vɛləp] *vt* envolver
envelope ['ɛnvələup] *n* sobre *m*
enviable ['ɛnvɪəbl] *adj* envidiable
envious ['ɛnvɪəs] *adj* envidioso; (*look*) de envidia
environment [ɪn'vaɪərnmənt] *n* medio ambiente; (*surroundings*) entorno; **Department of the E~** ministerio del medio ambiente
environmental [ɪnvaɪərn'mɛntl] *adj* (medio) ambiental; **~ studies** (*in school etc*) ecología *sg*
environmentalist [ɪnvaɪərn'mɛntlɪst] *n* ecologista *m/f*
environmentally [ɪnvaɪərn'mɛntlɪ] *adv*: **~ sound/friendly** ecológico
envisage [ɪn'vɪzɪdʒ] *vt* (*foresee*) prever; (*imagine*) concebir
envision [ɪn'vɪʒən] *vt* imaginar
envoy ['ɛnvɔɪ] *n* enviado(-a)
envy ['ɛnvɪ] *n* envidia ■ *vt* tener envidia a; **to ~ sb sth** envidiar algo a algn
enzyme ['ɛnzaɪm] *n* enzima *m or f*
EPA *n abbr* (*US*: = *Environmental Protection Agency*) *Agencia del Medio Ambiente*
ephemeral [ɪ'fɛmərl] *adj* efímero
epic ['ɛpɪk] *n* epopeya ■ *adj* épico

epicentre, (*US*) **epicenter** ['ɛpɪsɛntəʳ] *n* epicentro
epidemic [ɛpɪ'dɛmɪk] *n* epidemia
epigram ['ɛpɪgræm] *n* epigrama *m*
epilepsy ['ɛpɪlɛpsɪ] *n* epilepsia
epileptic [ɛpɪ'lɛptɪk] *adj, n* epiléptico(-a) *m(f)*
epilogue ['ɛpɪlɔg] *n* epílogo
episcopal [ɪ'pɪskəpl] *adj* episcopal
episode ['ɛpɪsəud] *n* episodio
epistle [ɪ'pɪsl] *n* epístola
epitaph ['ɛpɪtɑːf] *n* epitafio
epithet ['ɛpɪθɛt] *n* epíteto
epitome [ɪ'pɪtəmɪ] *n* arquetipo
epitomize [ɪ'pɪtəmaɪz] *vt* representar
epoch ['iːpɔk] *n* época
eponymous [ɪ'pɔnɪməs] *adj* epónimo
equable ['ɛkwəbl] *adj* (*climate*) estable; (*character*) ecuánime
equal ['iːkwl] *adj* (*gen*) igual; (*treatment*) equitativo ■ *n* igual *m/f* ■ *vt* ser igual a; (*fig*) igualar; **to be ~ to** (*task*) estar a la altura de; **the E~ Opportunities Commission** (*Brit*) *comisión para la igualdad de la mujer en el trabajo*
equality [iː'kwɔlɪtɪ] *n* igualdad *f*
equalize ['iːkwəlaɪz] *vt, vi* igualar; (*Sport*) empatar
equalizer ['iːkwəlaɪzəʳ] *n* igualada
equally ['iːkwəlɪ] *adv* igualmente; (*share etc*) a partes iguales; **they are ~ clever** son tan listos uno como otro
equals sign *n* signo igual
equanimity [ɛkwə'nɪmɪtɪ] *n* ecuanimidad *f*
equate [ɪ'kweɪt] *vt*: **to ~ sth with** equiparar algo con
equation [ɪ'kweɪʒən] *n* (*Math*) ecuación *f*
equator [ɪ'kweɪtəʳ] *n* ecuador *m*
equatorial [ɛkwə'tɔːrɪəl] *adj* ecuatorial
Equatorial Guinea *n* Guinea Ecuatorial
equestrian [ɪ'kwɛstrɪən] *adj* ecuestre ■ *n* jinete *m/f*
equilibrium [iːkwɪ'lɪbrɪəm] *n* equilibrio
equinox ['iːkwɪnɔks] *n* equinoccio
equip [ɪ'kwɪp] *vt* (*gen*) equipar; (*person*) proveer; **equipped with** (*machinery etc*) provisto de; **to be well equipped** estar bien equipado; **he is well equipped for the job** está bien preparado para este puesto
equipment [ɪ'kwɪpmənt] *n* equipo
equitable ['ɛkwɪtəbl] *adj* equitativo
equities ['ɛkwɪtɪz] *npl* (*Brit Comm*) acciones *fpl* ordinarias
equity ['ɛkwɪtɪ] *n* (*fairness*) equidad *f*; (*Econ: of debtor*) valor *m* líquido
equity capital *n* capital *m* propio, patrimonio neto
equivalent [ɪ'kwɪvəlnt] *adj, n* equivalente *m*; **to be ~ to** equivaler a
equivocal [ɪ'kwɪvəkl] *adj* equívoco
equivocate [ɪ'kwɪvəkeɪt] *vi* andarse con ambigüedades
equivocation [ɪkwɪvə'keɪʃən] *n* ambigüedad *f*
ER *abbr* (*Brit: = Elizabeth Regina*) *la reina Isabel*
er [əː] *interj* (*col: in hesitation*) esto, este (*LAm*)
ERA *n abbr* (*US Pol: = Equal Rights Amendment*) *enmienda sobre la igualdad de derechos de la mujer*
era ['ɪərə] *n* era, época
eradicate [ɪ'rædɪkeɪt] *vt* erradicar, extirpar
erase [ɪ'reɪz] *vt* (*Comput*) borrar
eraser [ɪ'reɪzəʳ] *n* goma de borrar
erect [ɪ'rɛkt] *adj* erguido ■ *vt* erigir, levantar; (*assemble*) montar
erection [ɪ'rɛkʃən] *n* (*of building*) construcción *f*; (*of machinery*) montaje *m*; (*structure*) edificio; (*Med*) erección *f*
ergonomics [əːgə'nɔmɪks] *n* ergonomía
ERISA *n abbr* (*US: = Employee Retirement Income Security Act*) *ley que regula las pensiones de jubilados*
Eritrea [ɛrɪ'treɪə] *n* Eritrea
ERM *n abbr* (*= Exchange Rate Mechanism*) (mecanismo de cambios del) SME *m*
ermine ['əːmɪn] *n* armiño
ERNIE ['əːnɪ] *n abbr* (*Brit: = Electronic Random Number Indicator Equipment*) *ordenador que elige al azar los números ganadores de los bonos del Estado*
erode [ɪ'rəud] *vt* (*Geo*) erosionar; (*metal*) corroer, desgastar
erogenous zone [ɪ'rɔdʒənəs-] *n* zona erógena
erosion [ɪ'rəuʒən] *n* erosión *f*; desgaste *m*
erotic [ɪ'rɔtɪk] *adj* erótico
eroticism [ɪ'rɔtɪsɪzm] *n* erotismo
err [əːʳ] *vi* errar; (*Rel*) pecar
errand ['ɛrnd] *n* recado, mandado; **to run errands** hacer recados; **~ of mercy** misión *f* de caridad
errand boy *n* recadero
erratic [ɪ'rætɪk] *adj* variable; (*results etc*) desigual, poco uniforme
erroneous [ɪ'rəunɪəs] *adj* erróneo
error ['ɛrəʳ] *n* error *m*, equivocación *f*; **typing/spelling ~** error de mecanografía/ortografía; **in ~** por equivocación; **errors and omissions excepted** salvo error u omisión
error message *n* (*Comput*) mensaje *m* de error
erstwhile ['əːstwaɪl] *adj* antiguo, previo
erudite ['ɛrudaɪt] *adj* erudito
erudition [ɛru'dɪʃən] *n* erudición *f*
erupt [ɪ'rʌpt] *vi* entrar en erupción; (*Med*) hacer erupción; (*fig*) estallar
eruption [ɪ'rʌpʃən] *n* erupción *f*; (*fig: of anger, violence*) explosión *f*, estallido
ESA *n abbr* (*= European Space Agency*) Agencia Espacial Europea

escalate ['ɛskəleɪt] *vi* extenderse, intensificarse; (*costs*) aumentar vertiginosamente
escalation clause [ɛskə'leɪʃən-] *n* cláusula de reajuste de los precios
escalator ['ɛskəleɪtə^{r}] *n* escalera mecánica
escapade [ɛskə'peɪd] *n* aventura
escape [ɪ'skeɪp] *n* (*gen*) fuga; (*Tech*) escape *m*; (*from duties*) escapatoria; (*from chase*) evasión *f* ■ *vi* (*gen*) escaparse; (*flee*) huir, evadirse ■ *vt* evitar, eludir; (*consequences*) escapar a; **to ~ from** (*place*) escaparse de; (*person*) huir de; (*clutches*) librarse de; **to ~ to** (*another place, freedom, safety*) huir a; **to ~ notice** pasar desapercibido
escape artist *n* artista *m/f* de la evasión
escape clause *n* (*fig: in agreement*) cláusula de excepción
escapee [ɪskeɪ'pi:] *n* fugado(-a)
escape hatch *n* (*in submarine, space rocket*) escotilla de salvamento
escape key *n* (*Comput*) tecla de escape
escape route *n* (*from fire*) vía de escape
escapism [ɪ'skeɪpɪzəm] *n* escapismo, evasión *f*
escapist [ɪ'skeɪpɪst] *adj* escapista, de evasión ■ *n* escapista *m/f*
escapologist [ɛskə'pɔlədʒɪst] *n* (*Brit*) = **escape artist**
escarpment [ɪ'skɑ:pmənt] *n* escarpa
eschew [ɪs'tʃu:] *vt* evitar, abstenerse de
escort ['ɛskɔ:t] *n* acompañante *m/f*; (*Mil*) escolta; (*Naut*) convoy *m* ■ *vt* [ɪ'skɔ:t] acompañar; (*Mil, Naut*) escoltar
escort agency *n* agencia de acompañantes
Eskimo ['ɛskɪməu] *adj* esquimal ■ *n* esquimal *m/f*; (*Ling*) esquimal *m*
ESL *n abbr* (*Scol*) = **English as a Second Language**
esophagus [i:'sɔfəgəs] *n* (*US*) = **oesophagus**
esoteric [ɛsəu'tɛrɪk] *adj* esotérico
ESP *n abbr* = **extrasensory perception**; (*Scol: = English for Specific (or Special) Purposes*) *inglés especializado*
esp. *abbr* = **especially**
especially [ɪ'spɛʃlɪ] *adv* (*gen*) especialmente; (*above all*) sobre todo; (*particularly*) en especial
espionage ['ɛspɪənɑ:ʒ] *n* espionaje *m*
esplanade [ɛsplə'neɪd] *n* (*by sea*) paseo marítimo
espouse [ɪ'spauz] *vt* adherirse a
Esq. *abbr* (*= Esquire*) D.
Esquire [ɪ'skwaɪə^{r}] *n*: **J. Brown, ~** Sr. D. J. Brown
essay ['ɛseɪ] *n* (*Scol*) redacción *f*; (*: longer*) trabajo
essayist ['ɛseɪɪst] *n* ensayista *m/f*
essence ['ɛsns] *n* esencia; **in ~** esencialmente; **speed is of the ~** es esencial hacerlo con la mayor prontitud
essential [ɪ'sɛnʃl] *adj* (*necessary*) imprescindible; (*basic*) esencial ■ *n* (*often pl*) lo esencial; **it is ~ that** es imprescindible que
essentially [ɪ'sɛnʃlɪ] *adv* esencialmente
EST *n abbr* (*US: = Eastern Standard Time*) *hora de invierno de Nueva York*
est. *abbr* (*= established*) fundado; (*= estimated*) aprox.
establish [ɪ'stæblɪʃ] *vt* establecer; (*prove: fact*) comprobar, demostrar; (*identity*) verificar; (*relations*) entablar
established [ɪ'stæblɪʃt] *adj* (*business*) de buena reputación; (*staff*) de plantilla
establishment [ɪ'stæblɪʃmənt] *n* establecimiento; (*also:* **the Establishment**) la clase dirigente; **a teaching ~** un centro de enseñanza
estate [ɪ'steɪt] *n* (*land*) finca, hacienda; (*property*) propiedad *f*; (*inheritance*) herencia; (*Pol*) estado; **housing ~** (*Brit*) urbanización *f*; **industrial ~** polígono industrial
estate agency *n* (*Brit*) agencia inmobiliaria
estate agent *n* (*Brit*) agente *m/f* inmobiliario(-a)
estate agent's *n* agencia inmobiliaria
estate car *n* (*Brit*) ranchera
esteem [ɪ'sti:m] *n*: **to hold sb in high ~** estimar en mucho a algn ■ *vt* estimar
esthetic [i:s'θɛtɪk] *adj* (*US*) = **aesthetic**
estimate ['ɛstɪmət] *n* estimación *f*; (*assessment*) tasa, cálculo; (*Comm*) presupuesto ■ *vt* ['ɛstɪmeɪt] estimar; tasar, calcular; **to give sb an ~ of** presentar a algn un presupuesto de; **at a rough ~** haciendo un cálculo aproximado; **to ~ for** (*Comm*) hacer un presupuesto de, presupuestar
estimation [ɛstɪ'meɪʃən] *n* opinión *f*, juicio; (*esteem*) aprecio; **in my ~** a mi juicio
Estonia [ɛ'stəunɪə] *n* Estonia
Estonian [ɛ'stəunɪən] *adj* estonio ■ *n* estonio(-a); (*Ling*) estonio
estranged [ɪ'streɪndʒd] *adj* separado
estrangement [ɪ'streɪndʒmənt] *n* alejamiento, distanciamiento
estrogen ['i:strəudʒən] *n* (*US*) = **oestrogen**
estuary ['ɛstjuərɪ] *n* estuario, ría
ET *n abbr* (*Brit: = Employment Training*) *plan estatal de formación para los desempleados* ■ *abbr* (*US*) = **Eastern Time**
ETA *n abbr* = **estimated time of arrival**
e-tailing ['i:teɪlɪŋ] *n* venta en línea, venta vía *or* por Internet
et al. *abbr* (*= et alii: and others*) et al.

etc *abbr* (= *et cetera*) etc
etch [ɛtʃ] *vt* grabar al aguafuerte
etching ['ɛtʃɪŋ] *n* aguafuerte *m or f*
ETD *n abbr* = **estimated time of departure**
eternal [ɪ'tə:nl] *adj* eterno
eternity [ɪ'tə:nɪtɪ] *n* eternidad *f*
ether ['i:θəʳ] *n* éter *m*
ethereal [ɪ'θɪərɪəl] *adj* etéreo
ethical ['ɛθɪkl] *adj* ético; (*honest*) honrado
ethics ['ɛθɪks] *n* ética ■ *npl* moralidad *f*
Ethiopia [i:θɪ'əupɪə] *n* Etiopía
Ethiopian [i:θɪ'əupɪən] *adj, n* etíope *m/f*
ethnic ['ɛθnɪk] *adj* étnico
ethnic cleansing [-klɛnzɪŋ] *n* limpieza étnica
ethos ['i:θɔs] *n* (*of culture, group*) sistema *m* de valores
e-ticket ['i:tɪkɪt] *n* billete electrónico, boleto electrónico (*LAm*)
etiquette ['ɛtɪkɛt] *n* etiqueta
ETV *n abbr* (*US*: = *Educational Television*) *televisión escolar*
etymology [ɛtɪ'mɔlədʒɪ] *n* etimología
EU *n abbr* (= *European Union*) UE *f*
eucalyptus [ju:kə'lɪptəs] *n* eucalipto
Eucharist ['ju:kərɪst] *n* Eucaristía
eulogy ['ju:lədʒɪ] *n* elogio, encomio
eunuch ['ju:nək] *n* eunuco
euphemism ['ju:fəmɪzm] *n* eufemismo
euphemistic [ju:fə'mɪstɪk] *adj* eufemístico
euphoria [ju:'fɔ:rɪə] *n* euforia
Eurasia [juə'reɪʃə] *n* Eurasia
Eurasian [juə'reɪʃən] *adj, n* eurasiático(-a) *m(f)*
Euratom [juə'rætəm] *n abbr* (= *European Atomic Energy Commission*) Euratom *m*
Euro- *pref* euro-
euro ['jʊərəʊ] *n* (*currency*) euro
Eurocheque ['juərəutʃɛk] *n* Eurocheque *m*
Eurocrat ['juərəukræt] *n* eurócrata *m/f*
Eurodollar ['juərəudɔləʳ] *n* eurodólar *m*
Euroland ['jʊərəʊlænd] *n* Eurolandia
Europe ['juərəp] *n* Europa
European [juərə'pi:ən] *adj, n* europeo(-a) *m(f)*
European Court of Justice *n* Tribunal *m* de Justicia de las Comunidades Europeas
Euro-sceptic [juərəu'skɛptɪk] *n* euroescéptico(-a)
Eurozone ['juərəuzəun] *n* eurozona, zona euro
euthanasia [ju:θə'neɪzɪə] *n* eutanasia
evacuate [ɪ'vækjueɪt] *vt* evacuar; (*place*) desocupar
evacuation [ɪvækju'eɪʃən] *n* evacuación *f*
evacuee [ɪvækju'i:] *n* evacuado(-a)
evade [ɪ'veɪd] *vt* evadir, eludir
evaluate [ɪ'væljueɪt] *vt* evaluar; (*value*) tasar; (*evidence*) interpretar
evangelical [i:væn'dʒɛlɪkəl] *adj* evangélico
evangelist [ɪ'vændʒəlɪst] *n* evangelista *m*; (*preacher*) evangelizador(a) *m(f)*
evaporate [ɪ'væpəreɪt] *vi* evaporarse; (*fig*) desvanecerse ■ *vt* evaporar
evaporation [ɪvæpə'reɪʃən] *n* evaporación *f*
evasion [ɪ'veɪʒən] *n* evasión *f*
evasive [ɪ'veɪsɪv] *adj* evasivo
eve [i:v] *n*: **on the ~ of** en vísperas de
even ['i:vn] *adj* (*level*) llano; (*smooth*) liso; (*speed, temperature*) uniforme; (*number*) par; (*Sport*) igual(es) ■ *adv* hasta, incluso; **~ if**, **~ though** aunque + *subjun*, así + *subjun* (*LAm*); **~ more** aun más; **~ so** aun así; **not ~** ni siquiera; **~ he was there** hasta él estaba allí; **~ on Sundays** incluso los domingos; **~ faster** aún más rápido; **to break ~** cubrir los gastos; **to get ~ with sb** ajustar cuentas con algn; **to ~ out** *vi* nivelarse
even-handed [i:vn'hændɪd] *adj* imparcial
evening ['i:vnɪŋ] *n* tarde *f*; (*dusk*) atardecer *m*; (*night*) noche *f*; **in the ~** por la tarde; **this ~** esta tarde *or* noche; **tomorrow/yesterday ~** mañana/ayer por la tarde *or* noche
evening class *n* clase *f* nocturna
evening dress *n* (*man's*) traje *m* de etiqueta; (*woman's*) traje *m* de noche
evenly ['i:vnlɪ] *adv* (*distribute, space, spread*) de modo uniforme; (*divide*) equitativamente
evensong ['i:vnsɔŋ] *n* vísperas *fpl*
event [ɪ'vɛnt] *n* suceso, acontecimiento; (*Sport*) prueba; **in the ~ of** en caso de; **in the ~** en realidad; **in the course of events** en el curso de los acontecimientos; **at all events**, **in any ~** en cualquier caso
eventful [ɪ'vɛntful] *adj* azaroso; (*game*) lleno de emoción; (*journey*) lleno de incidentes
eventing [ɪ'vɛntɪŋ] *n* (*Horseriding*) competición *f*
eventual [ɪ'vɛntʃuəl] *adj* final
eventuality [ɪvɛntʃu'ælɪtɪ] *n* eventualidad *f*
eventually [ɪ'vɛntʃuəlɪ] *adv* (*finally*) por fin; (*in time*) con el tiempo
ever ['ɛvəʳ] *adv* nunca, jamás; (*at all times*) siempre; **for ~** (para) siempre; **the best ~** lo nunca visto; **did you ~ meet him?** ¿llegaste a conocerle?; **have you ~ been there?** ¿has estado allí alguna vez?; **have you ~ seen it?** ¿lo has visto alguna vez?; **better than ~** mejor que nunca; **thank you ~ so much** muchísimas gracias; **yours ~** (*in letters*) un abrazo de; **~ since** *adv* desde entonces ■ *conj* después de que
Everest ['ɛvərɪst] *n* (*also*: **Mount Everest**) el Everest *m*
evergreen ['ɛvəgri:n] *n* árbol *m* de hoja perenne
everlasting [ɛvə'lɑ:stɪŋ] *adj* eterno, perpetuo

KEYWORD

every ['ɛvrɪ] *adj* **1** (*each*) cada; **every one of them** (*persons*) todos ellos(-as); (*objects*) cada uno de ellos(-as); **every shop in the town was closed** todas las tiendas de la ciudad estaban cerradas
2 (*all possible*) todo(-a); **I gave you every assistance** te di toda la ayuda posible; **I have every confidence in him** tiene toda mi confianza; **we wish you every success** te deseamos toda suerte de éxitos
3 (*showing recurrence*) todo(-a); **every day/ week** todos los días/todas las semanas; **every other car had been broken into** habían forzado uno de cada dos coches; **she visits me every other/third day** me visita cada dos/tres días; **every now and then** de vez en cuando

everybody ['ɛvrɪbɔdɪ] *pron* todos *pron pl*, todo el mundo; **~ knows about it** todo el mundo lo sabe; **~ else** todos los demás
everyday ['ɛvrɪdeɪ] *adj* (*daily: use, occurrence, experience*) diario, cotidiano; (*usual: expression*) corriente; (*common*) vulgar; (*routine*) rutinario
everyone ['ɛvrɪwʌn] = **everybody**
everything ['ɛvrɪθɪŋ] *pron* todo; **~ is ready** todo está dispuesto; **he did ~ possible** hizo todo lo posible
everywhere ['ɛvrɪwɛəʳ] *adv* (*be*) en todas partes; (*go*) a *or* por todas partes; **~ you go you meet ...** en todas partes encontrarás ...
evict [ɪ'vɪkt] *vt* desahuciar
eviction [ɪ'vɪkʃən] *n* desahucio
eviction notice *n* orden *f* de desahucio *or* desalojo (*LAm*)
evidence ['ɛvɪdəns] *n* (*proof*) prueba; (*of witness*) testimonio; (*facts*) datos *mpl*, hechos *mpl*; **to give ~** prestar declaración, dar testimonio
evident ['ɛvɪdənt] *adj* evidente, manifiesto
evidently ['ɛvɪdəntlɪ] *adv* (*obviously*) obviamente, evidentemente; (*apparently*) por lo visto
evil ['i:vl] *adj* malo; (*influence*) funesto; (*smell*) horrible ■ *n* mal *m*
evildoer ['i:vldu:əʳ] *n* malhechor(a) *m(f)*
evince [ɪ'vɪns] *vt* mostrar, dar señales de
evocative [ɪ'vɔkətɪv] *adj* sugestivo, evocador(a)
evoke [ɪ'vəuk] *vt* evocar; (*admiration*) provocar
evolution [i:və'lu:ʃən] *n* evolución *f*, desarrollo
evolve [ɪ'vɔlv] *vt* desarrollar ■ *vi* evolucionar, desarrollarse
ewe [ju:] *n* oveja
ex- [ɛks] *pref* (*former: husband, president etc*) ex-; (*out of*): **the price ~works** precio de fábrica
exacerbate [ɛk'sæsəbeɪt] *vt* exacerbar
exact [ɪg'zækt] *adj* exacto ■ *vt*: **to ~ sth (from)** exigir algo (de)
exacting [ɪg'zæktɪŋ] *adj* exigente; (*conditions*) arduo
exactitude [ɪg'zæktɪtju:d] *n* exactitud *f*
exactly [ɪg'zæktlɪ] *adv* exactamente; (*time*) en punto; **~!** ¡exacto!
exactness [ɪg'zæktnɪs] *n* exactitud *f*
exaggerate [ɪg'zædʒəreɪt] *vt*, *vi* exagerar
exaggerated [ɪg'zædʒəreɪtɪd] *adj* exagerado
exaggeration [ɪgzædʒə'reɪʃən] *n* exageración *f*
exalt [ɪg'zɔ:lt] *vt* (*praise*) ensalzar; (*elevate*) elevar
exalted [ɪg'zɔ:ltɪd] *adj* (*position*) elevado; (*elated*) enardecido
exam [ɪg'zæm] *n abbr* (*Scol*) = **examination**
examination [ɪgzæmɪ'neɪʃən] *n* (*gen*) examen *m*; (*Law*) interrogación *f*; (*inquiry*) investigación *f*; **to take** *or* **sit an ~** hacer un examen; **the matter is under ~** se está examinando el asunto
examine [ɪg'zæmɪn] *vt* (*gen*) examinar; (*inspect: machine, premises*) inspeccionar; (*Scol, Law: person*) interrogar; (*at customs: luggage, passport*) registrar; (*Med*) hacer un reconocimiento médico de, examinar
examiner [ɪg'zæmɪnəʳ] *n* examinador(a) *m(f)*
example [ɪg'zɑ:mpl] *n* ejemplo; **for ~** por ejemplo; **to set a good/bad ~** dar buen/mal ejemplo
exasperate [ɪg'zɑ:spəreɪt] *vt* exasperar, irritar; **exasperated by** *or* **at** *or* **with** exasperado por *or* con
exasperating [ɪg'zɑ:spəreɪtɪŋ] *adj* irritante
exasperation [ɪgzɑ:spə'reɪʃən] *n* exasperación *f*, irritación *f*
excavate ['ɛkskəveɪt] *vt* excavar
excavation [ɛkskə'veɪʃən] *n* excavación *f*
excavator ['ɛkskəveɪtəʳ] *n* excavadora
exceed [ɪk'si:d] *vt* exceder; (*number*) pasar de; (*speed limit*) sobrepasar; (*limits*) rebasar; (*powers*) excederse en; (*hopes*) superar
exceedingly [ɪk'si:dɪŋlɪ] *adv* sumamente, sobremanera
excel [ɪk'sɛl] *vi* sobresalir; **to ~ o.s.** lucirse
excellence ['ɛksələns] *n* excelencia
Excellency ['ɛksələnsɪ] *n*: **His ~** Su Excelencia
excellent ['ɛksələnt] *adj* excelente
except [ɪk'sɛpt] *prep* (*also*: **except for, excepting**) excepto, salvo ■ *vt* exceptuar, excluir; **~ if/when** excepto si/cuando; **~ that** salvo que

exception [ɪk'sɛpʃən] *n* excepción *f*; **to take ~ to** ofenderse por; **with the ~ of** a excepción de; **to make an ~** hacer una excepción
exceptional [ɪk'sɛpʃənl] *adj* excepcional
excerpt ['ɛksə:pt] *n* extracto
excess [ɪk'sɛs] *n* exceso; **in ~ of** superior a; *see also* **excesses**
excess baggage *n* exceso de equipaje
excesses *npl* excesos *mpl*
excess fare *n* suplemento
excessive [ɪk'sɛsɪv] *adj* excesivo
excess supply *n* exceso de oferta
excess weight *n* exceso de peso
exchange [ɪks'tʃeɪndʒ] *n* cambio; (*of prisoners*) canje *m*; (*of ideas*) intercambio; (*also*: **telephone exchange**) central *f* (telefónica) ■ *vt* intercambiar; **to ~ (for)** cambiar (por); **in ~ for** a cambio de; **foreign ~** (*Comm*) divisas *fpl*
exchange control *n* control *m* de divisas
exchange rate *n* tipo de cambio
exchequer [ɪks'tʃɛkə^r] *n*: **the ~** (*Brit*) Hacienda
excisable [ɛk'saɪzəbl] *adj* sujeto al pago de impuestos sobre el consumo
excise ['ɛksaɪz] *n* impuestos sobre el consumo interior
excitable [ɪk'saɪtəbl] *adj* excitable
excite [ɪk'saɪt] *vt* (*stimulate*) entusiasmar; (*anger*) suscitar, provocar; (*move*) emocionar; **to get excited** emocionarse
excitement [ɪk'saɪtmənt] *n* emoción *f*
exciting [ɪk'saɪtɪŋ] *adj* emocionante
excl. *abbr* = **excluding; exclusive (of)**
exclaim [ɪk'skleɪm] *vi* exclamar
exclamation [ɛksklə'meɪʃən] *n* exclamación *f*
exclamation mark *n* signo de admiración
exclude [ɪk'sklu:d] *vt* excluir; (*except*) exceptuar
excluding [ɪks'klu:dɪŋ] *prep*: **~ VAT** IVA no incluido
exclusion [ɪk'sklu:ʒən] *n* exclusión *f*; **to the ~ of** con exclusión de
exclusion clause *n* cláusula de exclusión
exclusion zone *n* zona de exclusión
exclusive [ɪk'sklu:sɪv] *adj* exclusivo; (*club, district*) selecto; **~ of tax** excluyendo impuestos; **~ of postage/service** franqueo/ servicio no incluido; **from 1st to 13th March ~** del 1 al 13 de marzo exclusive
exclusively [ɪk'sklu:sɪvlɪ] *adv* únicamente
excommunicate [ɛkskə'mju:nɪkeɪt] *vt* excomulgar
excrement ['ɛkskrəmənt] *n* excremento
excrete [ɪk'skri:t] *vi* excretar
excruciating [ɪk'skru:ʃɪeɪtɪŋ] *adj* (*pain*) agudísimo, atroz
excursion [ɪk'skə:ʃən] *n* excursión *f*
excursion ticket *n* billete *m* (especial) de excursión
excusable [ɪk'skju:səbl] *adj* perdonable
excuse *n* [ɪk'skju:s] disculpa, excusa; (*evasion*) pretexto ■ *vt* [ɪk'skju:z] disculpar, perdonar; (*justify*) justificar; **to make excuses for sb** presentar disculpas por algn; **to ~ sb from doing sth** dispensar a algn de hacer algo; **to ~ o.s. (for (doing) sth)** pedir disculpas a algn (por (hacer) algo); **~ me!** ¡perdone!; (*attracting attention*) ¡oiga (, por favor)!; **if you will ~ me** con su permiso
ex-directory ['ɛksdɪ'rɛktərɪ] *adj* (*Brit*): **~ (phone) number** número que no figura en la guía (telefónica)
execrable ['ɛksɪkrəbl] *adj* execrable, abominable; (*manners*) detestable
execute ['ɛksɪkju:t] *vt* (*plan*) realizar; (*order*) cumplir; (*person*) ajusticiar, ejecutar
execution [ɛksɪ'kju:ʃən] *n* realización *f*; cumplimiento; ejecución *f*
executioner [ɛksɪ'kju:ʃənə^r] *n* verdugo
executive [ɪg'zɛkjutɪv] *n* (*Comm*) ejecutivo(-a); (*Pol*) poder *m* ejecutivo ■ *adj* ejecutivo; (*car, plane, position*) de ejecutivo; (*offices, suite*) de la dirección; (*secretary*) de dirección
executive director *n* director(a) *m(f)* ejecutivo(-a)
executor [ɪg'zɛkjutə^r] *n* albacea *m*, testamentario
exemplary [ɪg'zɛmplərɪ] *adj* ejemplar
exemplify [ɪg'zɛmplɪfaɪ] *vt* ejemplificar
exempt [ɪg'zɛmpt] *adj*: **~ from** exento de ■ *vt*: **to ~ sb from** eximir a algn de
exemption [ɪg'zɛmpʃən] *n* exención *f*; (*immunity*) inmunidad *f*
exercise ['ɛksəsaɪz] *n* ejercicio ■ *vt* ejercer; (*patience etc*) proceder con; (*dog*) sacar de paseo ■ *vi* hacer ejercicio
exercise bike *n* bicicleta estática
exercise book *n* cuaderno de ejercicios
exert [ɪg'zə:t] *vt* ejercer; (*strength, force*) emplear; **to ~ o.s.** esforzarse
exertion [ɪg'zə:ʃən] *n* esfuerzo
exfoliant [ɛks'fəulɪənt] *n* exfoliante *m*
ex gratia ['ɛks'greɪʃə] *adj*: **~ payment** pago a título voluntario
exhale [ɛks'heɪl] *vt* despedir, exhalar ■ *vi* espirar
exhaust [ɪg'zɔ:st] *n* (*pipe*) (tubo de) escape *m*; (*fumes*) gases *mpl* de escape ■ *vt* agotar; **to ~ o.s.** agotarse
exhausted [ɪg'zɔ:stɪd] *adj* agotado

exhausting [ɪɡ'zɔːstɪŋ] *adj*: **an ~ journey/day** un viaje/día agotador
exhaustion [ɪɡ'zɔːstʃən] *n* agotamiento; **nervous ~** agotamiento nervioso
exhaustive [ɪɡ'zɔːstɪv] *adj* exhaustivo
exhibit [ɪɡ'zɪbɪt] *n* (*Art*) obra expuesta; (*Law*) objeto expuesto ■ *vt* (*show*: *emotions*) manifestar; (: *courage, skill*) demostrar; (*paintings*) exponer
exhibition [ɛksɪ'bɪʃən] *n* exposición *f*
exhibitionist [ɛksɪ'bɪʃənɪst] *n* exhibicionista *m/f*
exhibitor [ɪɡ'zɪbɪtəʳ] *n* expositor(a) *m(f)*
exhilarating [ɪɡ'zɪləreɪtɪŋ] *adj* estimulante, tónico
exhilaration [ɪɡzɪlə'reɪʃən] *n* júbilo
exhort [ɪɡ'zɔːt] *vt* exhortar
exile ['ɛksaɪl] *n* exilio; (*person*) exiliado(-a) ■ *vt* desterrar, exiliar
exist [ɪɡ'zɪst] *vi* existir
existence [ɪɡ'zɪstəns] *n* existencia
existentialism [ɛɡzɪs'tɛnʃəlɪzəm] *n* existencialismo
existing [ɪɡ'zɪstɪŋ] *adj* existente, actual
exit ['ɛksɪt] *n* salida ■ *vi* (*Theat*) hacer mutis; (*Comput*) salir (del sistema)
exit poll *n encuesta a la salida de los colegios electorales*
exit ramp *n* (*US Aut*) vía de acceso
exit visa *n* visado de salida
exodus ['ɛksədəs] *n* éxodo
ex officio ['ɛksə'fɪʃɪəu] *adj* de pleno derecho ■ *adv* ex oficio
exonerate [ɪɡ'zɔnəreɪt] *vt*: **to ~ from** exculpar de
exorbitant [ɪɡ'zɔːbɪtənt] *adj* (*price, demands*) exorbitante, excesivo
exorcize ['ɛksɔːsaɪz] *vt* exorcizar
exotic [ɪɡ'zɔtɪk] *adj* exótico
expand [ɪk'spænd] *vt* ampliar, extender; (*number*) aumentar ■ *vi* (*trade etc*) ampliarse, expandirse; (*gas, metal*) dilatarse; **to ~ on** (*notes, story etc*) ampliar
expanse [ɪk'spæns] *n* extensión *f*
expansion [ɪk'spænʃən] *n* ampliación *f*; aumento; (*of trade*) expansión *f*
expansionism [ɪk'spænʃənɪzəm] *n* expansionismo
expansionist [ɪk'spænʃənɪst] *adj* expansionista
expatriate [ɛks'pætrɪət] *n* expatriado(-a)
expect [ɪk'spɛkt] *vt* (*gen*) esperar; (*count on*) contar con; (*suppose*) suponer ■ *vi*: **to be expecting** estar encinta; **to ~ to do sth** esperar hacer algo; **as expected** como era de esperar; **I ~ so** supongo que sí
expectancy [ɪk'spɛktənsɪ] *n* (*anticipation*) expectación *f*; **life ~** esperanza de vida
expectantly [ɪk'spɛktəntlɪ] *adv* (*look, listen*) con expectación
expectant mother [ɪk'spɛktənt-] *n* futura madre *f*
expectation [ɛkspɛk'teɪʃən] *n* esperanza, expectativa; **in ~ of** esperando; **against** *or* **contrary to all ~(s)** en contra de todas las previsiones; **to come** *or* **live up to sb's expectations** resultar tan bueno como se esperaba; **to fall short of sb's expectations** no cumplir las esperanzas de algn, decepcionar a algn
expedience [ɪk'spiːdɪəns], **expediency** [ɪk'spiːdɪənsɪ] *n* conveniencia
expedient [ɪk'spiːdɪənt] *adj* conveniente, oportuno ■ *n* recurso, expediente *m*
expedite ['ɛkspɪdaɪt] *vt* (*speed up*) acelerar; (: *progress*) facilitar
expedition [ɛkspə'dɪʃən] *n* expedición *f*
expeditionary force [ɛkspə'dɪʃnrɪ-] *n* cuerpo expedicionario
expel [ɪk'spɛl] *vt* expulsar
expend [ɪk'spɛnd] *vt* gastar; (*use up*) consumir
expendable [ɪk'spɛndəbl] *adj* prescindible
expenditure [ɪk'spɛndɪtʃəʳ] *n* gastos *mpl*, desembolso; (*of time, effort*) gasto
expense [ɪk'spɛns] *n* gasto, gastos *mpl*; (*high cost*) coste *m*; **expenses** *npl* (*Comm*) gastos *mpl*; **at the ~ of** a costa de; **to meet the ~ of** hacer frente a los gastos de
expense account *n* cuenta de gastos (de representación)
expensive [ɪk'spɛnsɪv] *adj* caro, costoso
experience [ɪk'spɪərɪəns] *n* experiencia ■ *vt* experimentar; (*suffer*) sufrir; **to learn by ~** aprender con la experiencia
experienced [ɪk'spɪərɪənst] *adj* experimentado
experiment [ɪk'spɛrɪmənt] *n* experimento ■ *vi* hacer experimentos, experimentar; **to perform** *or* **carry out an ~** realizar un experimento; **as an ~** como experimento; **to ~ with a new vaccine** experimentar con una vacuna nueva
experimental [ɪkspɛrɪ'mɛntl] *adj* experimental; **the process is still at the ~ stage** el proceso está todavía en prueba
expert ['ɛkspəːt] *adj* experto, perito ■ *n* experto(-a), perito(-a); (*specialist*) especialista *m/f*; **~ witness** (*Law*) testigo pericial; **~ in** *or* **at doing sth** experto *or* perito en hacer algo; **an ~ on sth** un experto en algo
expertise [ɛkspəː'tiːz] *n* pericia
expiration [ɛkspɪ'reɪʃən] *n* (*gen*) expiración *f*, vencimiento

expire [ɪk'spaɪəʳ] *vi* (*gen*) caducar, vencerse
expiry [ɪk'spaɪərɪ] *n* caducidad *f*, vencimiento
explain [ɪk'spleɪn] *vt* explicar; (*mystery*) aclarar
▸ **explain away** *vt* justificar
explanation [ɛksplə'neɪʃən] *n* explicación *f*; aclaración *f*; **to find an ~ for sth** encontrarle una explicación a algo
explanatory [ɪk'splænətrɪ] *adj* explicativo; aclaratorio
expletive [ɪk'spli:tɪv] *n* imprecación *f*
explicable [ɪk'splɪkəbl] *adj* explicable
explicit [ɪk'splɪsɪt] *adj* explícito
explicitly [ɪk'splɪsɪtlɪ] *adv* explícitamente
explode [ɪk'spləud] *vi* estallar, explotar; (*with anger*) reventar ■ *vt* hacer explotar; (*fig: theory, myth*) demoler
exploit ['ɛksplɔɪt] *n* hazaña ■ *vt* [ɪk'splɔɪt] explotar
exploitation [ɛksplɔɪ'teɪʃən] *n* explotación *f*
exploration [ɛksplə'reɪʃən] *n* exploración *f*
exploratory [ɪk'splɔrətrɪ] *adj* (*fig: talks*) exploratorio, preliminar
explore [ɪk'splɔ:ʳ] *vt* explorar; (*fig*) examinar, sondear
explorer [ɪk'splɔ:rəʳ] *n* explorador(a) *m(f)*
explosion [ɪk'spləuʒən] *n* explosión *f*
explosive [ɪk'spləusɪv] *adj, n* explosivo
exponent [ɪk'spəunənt] *n* partidario(-a); (*of skill, activity*) exponente *m/f*
export *vt* [ɛk'spɔ:t] exportar ■ *n* ['ɛkspɔ:t] exportación *f* ■ *cpd* de exportación
exportation [ɛkspɔ:'teɪʃən] *n* exportación *f*
export drive *n* campaña de exportación
exporter [ɛk'spɔ:təʳ] *n* exportador(a) *m(f)*
export licence *n* licencia de exportación
export manager *n* gerente *m/f* de exportación
export trade *n* comercio exterior
expose [ɪk'spəuz] *vt* exponer; (*unmask*) desenmascarar
exposé [ɪk'spəuzeɪ] *n* revelación *f*
exposed [ɪk'spəuzd] *adj* expuesto; (*land, house*) desprotegido; (*Elec: wire*) al aire; (*pipe, beam*) al descubierto
exposition [ɛkspə'zɪʃən] *n* exposición *f*
exposure [ɪk'spəuʒəʳ] *n* exposición *f*; (*Phot: speed*) (tiempo *m* de) exposición *f*; (*: shot*) fotografía; **to die from ~** (*Med*) morir de frío
exposure meter *n* fotómetro
expound [ɪk'spaund] *vt* exponer; (*theory, text*) comentar; (*one's views*) explicar
express [ɪk'sprɛs] *adj* (*definite*) expreso, explícito; (*Brit: letter etc*) urgente ■ *n* (*train*) rápido ■ *adv* (*send*) por correo extraordinario ■ *vt* expresar; (*squeeze*) exprimir; **to send sth ~** enviar algo por correo urgente; **to ~ o.s.** expresarse
expression [ɪk'sprɛʃən] *n* expresión *f*
expressionism [ɪk'sprɛʃənɪzm] *n* expresionismo
expressive [ɪk'sprɛsɪv] *adj* expresivo
expressly [ɪk'sprɛslɪ] *adv* expresamente
expressway [ɪk'sprɛsweɪ] *n* (*US: urban motorway*) autopista
expropriate [ɛks'prəuprɪeɪt] *vt* expropiar
expulsion [ɪk'spʌlʃən] *n* expulsión *f*
expurgate ['ɛkspəgeɪt] *vt* expurgar
exquisite [ɛk'skwɪzɪt] *adj* exquisito
exquisitely [ɛk'skwɪzɪtlɪ] *adv* exquisitamente
ex-serviceman ['ɛks'sə:vɪsmən] *n* ex-combatiente *m*
ext. *abbr* (*Tel*) = **extension**
extemporize [ɪk'stɛmpəraɪz] *vi* improvisar
extend [ɪk'stɛnd] *vt* (*visit, street*) prolongar; (*building*) ampliar; (*thanks, friendship etc*) extender; (*Comm: credit*) conceder; (*deadline*) prorrogar ■ *vi* (*land*) extenderse; **the contract extends to/for ...** el contrato se prolonga hasta/por ...
extension [ɪk'stɛnʃən] *n* extensión *f*; (*building*) ampliación *f*; (*Tel: line*) extensión *f*; (*: telephone*) supletorio *m*; (*of deadline*) prórroga; **~ 3718** extensión 3718
extension cable *n* (*Elec*) alargador *m*
extensive [ɪk'stɛnsɪv] *adj* (*gen*) extenso; (*damage*) importante; (*knowledge*) amplio
extensively [ɪk'stɛnsɪvlɪ] *adv* (*altered, damaged etc*) extensamente; **he's travelled ~** ha viajado por muchos países
extent [ɪk'stɛnt] *n* (*breadth*) extensión *f*; (*scope: of knowledge, activities*) alcance *m*; (*degree: of damage, loss*) grado; **to some ~** hasta cierto punto; **to a certain ~** hasta cierto punto; **to a large ~** en gran parte; **to the ~ of ...** hasta el punto de ...; **to such an ~ that ...** hasta tal punto que ...; **to what ~?** ¿hasta qué punto?; **debts to the ~ of £5000** deudas por la cantidad de £5000
extenuating [ɪk'stɛnjueɪtɪŋ] *adj*: **~ circumstances** circunstancias *fpl* atenuantes
exterior [ɛk'stɪərɪəʳ] *adj* exterior, externo ■ *n* exterior *m*
exterminate [ɪk'stə:mɪneɪt] *vt* exterminar
extermination [ɪkstə:mɪ'neɪʃən] *n* exterminio
external [ɛk'stə:nl] *adj* externo, exterior ■ *n*: **the externals** la apariencia exterior; **~ affairs** asuntos *mpl* exteriores; **for ~ use only** (*Med*) para uso tópico
externally [ɛk'stə:nəlɪ] *adv* por fuera

extinct [ɪk'stɪŋkt] *adj* (*volcano*) extinguido, apagado; (*race*) extinguido
extinction [ɪk'stɪŋkʃən] *n* extinción *f*
extinguish [ɪk'stɪŋgwɪʃ] *vt* extinguir, apagar
extinguisher [ɪk'stɪŋgwɪʃəʳ] *n* extintor *m*
extol, extoll (US) [ɪk'stəul] *vt* (*merits, virtues*) ensalzar, alabar; (*person*) alabar, elogiar
extort [ɪk'stɔ:t] *vt* sacar a la fuerza; (*confession*) arrancar
extortion [ɪk'stɔ:ʃən] *n* extorsión *f*
extortionate [ɪk'stɔ:ʃnət] *adj* excesivo, exorbitante
extra ['ɛkstrə] *adj* adicional ■ *adv* (*in addition*) más ■ *n* (*addition*) extra *m*, suplemento; (*Theat*) extra *m/f*, comparsa *m/f*; (*newspaper*) edición *f* extraordinaria; **wine will cost ~** el vino se paga aparte; **~ large sizes** tallas extragrandes; *see also* **extras**
extra... ['ɛkstrə] *pref* extra...
extract *vt* [ɪk'strækt] sacar; (*tooth*) extraer; (*confession*) arrancar ■ *n* ['ɛkstrækt] fragmento; (*Culin*) extracto
extraction [ɪk'strækʃən] *n* extracción *f* (*origin*), origen *m*
extractor fan [ɪk'stræktə-] *n* extractor *m* de humos
extracurricular [ɛkstrəkə'rɪkjuləʳ] *adj* (*Scol*) extraescolar
extradite ['ɛkstrədaɪt] *vt* extraditar
extradition [ɛkstrə'dɪʃən] *n* extradición *f*
extramarital [ɛkstrə'mærɪtl] *adj* extramatrimonial
extramural [ɛkstrə'mjuərl] *adj* extra-académico
extraneous [ɪk'streɪnɪəs] *adj* extraño, ajeno
extraordinary [ɪk'strɔ:dnrɪ] *adj* extraordinario; (*odd*) raro; **the ~ thing is that ...** lo más extraordinario es que ...
extraordinary general meeting *n* junta general extraordinaria
extrapolation [ɪkstræpə'leɪʃən] *n* extrapolación *f*
extras *npl* (*additional expense*) extras *mpl*
extrasensory perception ['ɛkstrə'sɛnsərɪ-] *n* percepción *f* extrasensorial
extra time *n* (*Football*) prórroga
extravagance [ɪk'strævəgəns] *n* (*excessive spending*) derroche *m*; (*thing bought*) extravagancia
extravagant [ɪk'strævəgənt] *adj* (*wasteful*) derrochador(a); (*taste, gift*) excesivamente caro; (*price*) exorbitante; (*praise*) excesivo
extreme [ɪk'stri:m] *adj* extremo; (*poverty etc*) extremado; (*case*) excepcional ■ *n* extremo; **the ~ left/right** (*Pol*) la extrema izquierda/derecha; **extremes of temperature** temperaturas extremas
extremely [ɪk'stri:mlɪ] *adv* sumamente, extremadamente
extremist [ɪk'stri:mɪst] *adj, n* extremista *m/f*
extremity [ɪk'strɛmətɪ] *n* extremidad *f*, punta; (*need*) apuro, necesidad *f*; **extremities** *npl* (*hands and feet*) extremidades *fpl*
extricate ['ɛkstrɪkeɪt] *vt*: **to ~ o.s. from** librarse de
extrovert ['ɛkstrəvə:t] *n* extrovertido(-a)
exuberance [ɪg'zju:bərns] *n* exuberancia
exuberant [ɪg'zju:bərnt] *adj* (*person*) eufórico; (*style*) exuberante
exude [ɪg'zju:d] *vt* rezumar
exult [ɪg'zʌlt] *vi* regocijarse
exultant [ɪg'zʌltənt] *adj* (*person*) regocijado, jubiloso; (*shout, expression, smile*) de júbilo
exultation [ɛgzʌl'teɪʃən] *n* regocijo, júbilo
eye [aɪ] *n* ojo ■ *vt* mirar; **to keep an ~ on** vigilar; **as far as the ~ can see** hasta donde alcanza la vista; **with an ~ to doing sth** con vistas *or* miras a hacer algo; **to have an ~ for sth** tener mucha vista *or* buen ojo para algo; **there's more to this than meets the ~** esto tiene su miga
eyeball ['aɪbɔ:l] *n* globo ocular
eyebath ['aɪbɑ:θ] *n* baño ocular, lavaojos *m inv*
eyebrow ['aɪbrau] *n* ceja
eyebrow pencil *n* lápiz *m* de cejas
eye-catching ['aɪkætʃɪŋ] *adj* llamativo
eye cup *n* (US) = **eyebath**
eyedrops ['aɪdrɔps] *npl* gotas *fpl* para los ojos
eyeful ['aɪful] *n* (*col*): **to get an ~ of sth** ver bien algo
eyelash ['aɪlæʃ] *n* pestaña
eyelet ['aɪlɪt] *n* ojete *m*
eye-level ['aɪlɛvl] *adj* a la altura de los ojos
eyelid ['aɪlɪd] *n* párpado
eyeliner ['aɪlaɪnəʳ] *n* lápiz *m* de ojos
eye-opener ['aɪəupnəʳ] *n* revelación *f*, gran sorpresa
eyeshadow ['aɪʃædəu] *n* sombra de ojos
eyesight ['aɪsaɪt] *n* vista
eyesore ['aɪsɔ:ʳ] *n* monstruosidad *f*
eyestrain ['aɪstreɪn] *n*: **to get ~** cansar la vista *or* los ojos
eyetooth (*pl* **eyeteeth**) ['aɪtu:θ, -ti:θ] *n* colmillo; **to give one's eyeteeth for sth/to do sth** (*col, fig*) dar un ojo de la cara por algo/por hacer algo
eyewash ['aɪwɔʃ] *n* (*fig*) disparates *mpl*, tonterías *fpl*
eye witness *n* testigo *m/f* ocular
eyrie ['ɪərɪ] *n* aguilera

Ff

F, f [ɛf] *n* (*letter*) F, f *f*; (*Mus*) fa *m*; **F for Frederick,** (*US*) **F for Fox** F de Francia

F. *abbr* = **Fahrenheit**

FA *n abbr* (*Brit: = Football Association*) ≈ AFE *f* (*SP*)

FAA *n abbr* (*US*) = **Federal Aviation Administration**

fable ['feɪbl] *n* fábula

fabric ['fæbrɪk] *n* tejido, tela

fabricate ['fæbrɪkeɪt] *vt* fabricar; (*fig*) inventar

fabrication [fæbrɪ'keɪʃən] *n* fabricación *f*; (*fig*) invención *f*

fabric ribbon *n* (*for typewriter*) cinta de tela

fabulous ['fæbjuləs] *adj* fabuloso

façade [fə'sɑːd] *n* fachada

face [feɪs] *n* (*Anat*) cara, rostro; (*of clock*) esfera, cara; (*side*) cara; (*surface*) superficie *f* ■ *vt* mirar a; (*fig*) enfrentarse a; **~ down** (*person, card*) boca abajo; **to lose ~** desprestigiarse; **to save ~** salvar las apariencias; **to make** *or* **pull a ~** hacer muecas; **in the ~ of** (*difficulties etc*) en vista de, ante; **on the ~ of it** a primera vista; **~ to ~** cara a cara; **to ~ the fact that ...** reconocer que ...
▸ **face up to** *vt fus* hacer frente a, enfrentarse a

face cloth *n* (*Brit*) toallita

face cream *n* crema (de belleza)

faceless ['feɪslɪs] *adj* (*fig*) anónimo

face lift *n* lifting *m*, estirado facial

face powder *n* polvos *mpl* para la cara

face-saving ['feɪsseɪvɪŋ] *adj* para salvar las apariencias

facet ['fæsɪt] *n* faceta

facetious [fə'siːʃəs] *adj* chistoso

facetiously [fə'siːʃəslɪ] *adv* chistosamente

face value *n* (*of stamp*) valor *m* nominal; **to take sth at ~** (*fig*) tomar algo en sentido literal, aceptar las apariencias de algo

facial ['feɪʃəl] *adj* de la cara ■ *n* (*also*: **beauty facial**) tratamiento facial, limpieza

facile ['fæsaɪl] *adj* superficial

facilitate [fə'sɪlɪteɪt] *vt* facilitar

facility [fə'sɪlɪtɪ] *n* facilidad *f*; **facilities** *npl* instalaciones *fpl*; **credit ~** facilidades de crédito

facing ['feɪsɪŋ] *prep* frente a ■ *adj* de enfrente

facsimile [fæk'sɪmɪlɪ] *n* facsímil(e) *m*

fact [fækt] *n* hecho; **in ~** en realidad; **to know for a ~ that ...** saber a ciencia cierta que ...

fact-finding ['fæktfaɪndɪŋ] *adj*: **a ~ tour/mission** un viaje/una misión de reconocimiento

faction ['fækʃən] *n* facción *f*

factional ['fækʃənl] *adj* (*fighting*) entre distintas facciones

factor ['fæktəʳ] *n* factor *m*; (*Comm: person*) agente *m/f* comisionado(-a) ■ *vi* (*Comm*) comprar deudas; **safety ~** factor de seguridad

factory ['fæktərɪ] *n* fábrica

factory farming *n* cría industrial

factory floor *n* (*workers*) trabajadores *mpl*, mano *f* de obra directa; (*area*) talleres *mpl*

factory ship *n* buque *m* factoría

factual ['fæktjuəl] *adj* basado en los hechos

faculty ['fækəltɪ] *n* facultad *f*; (*US: teaching staff*) personal *m* docente

fad [fæd] *n* novedad *f*, moda

fade [feɪd] *vi* descolorarse, desteñirse; (*sound, hope*) desvanecerse; (*light*) apagarse; (*flower*) marchitarse
▸ **fade away** *vi* (*sound*) apagarse
▸ **fade in** *vt* (*TV, Cine*) fundir; (*Radio: sound*) mezclar ■ *vi* (*TV, Cine*) fundirse; (*Radio*) oírse por encima
▸ **fade out** *vt* (*TV, Cine*) fundir; (*Radio*) apagar, disminuir el volumen de ■ *vi* (*TV, Cine*) desvanecerse; (*Radio*) apagarse, dejarse de oír

faded ['feɪdɪd] *adj* (*clothes, colour*) descolorido; (*flower*) marchito

faeces, feces (*US*) ['fiːsiːz] *npl* excremento *sg*, heces *fpl*

fag [fæg] *n* (*Brit col: cigarette*) pitillo (*SP*), cigarro; (*US col: homosexual*) maricón *m*
fag end *n* (*Brit col*) colilla
fagged [fægd] *adj* (*Brit col: exhausted*) rendido, agotado
Fahrenheit ['fɑːrənhaɪt] *n* Fahrenheit *m*
fail [feɪl] *vt* suspender; (*memory etc*) fallar a ■ *vi* suspender; (*be unsuccessful*) fracasar; (*strength, brakes, engine*) fallar; **to ~ to do sth** (*neglect*) dejar de hacer algo; (*be unable*) no poder hacer algo; **without ~** sin falta; **words ~ me!** ¡no sé qué decir!
failing ['feɪlɪŋ] *n* falta, defecto ■ *prep* a falta de; **~ that** de no ser posible eso
failsafe ['feɪlseɪf] *adj* (*device etc*) de seguridad
failure ['feɪljə^r] *n* fracaso; (*person*) fracasado(-a); (*mechanical etc*) fallo; (*in exam*) suspenso; (*of crops*) pérdida, destrucción *f*; **it was a complete ~** fue un fracaso total
faint [feɪnt] *adj* débil; (*smell, breeze, trace*) leve; (*recollection*) vago; (*mark*) apenas visible ■ *n* desmayo ■ *vi* desmayarse; **to feel ~** estar mareado, marearse
faintest ['feɪntɪst] *adj*: **I haven't the ~ idea** no tengo la más remota idea
faint-hearted ['feɪnt'hɑːtɪd] *adj* apocado
faintly ['feɪntlɪ] *adv* débilmente; (*vaguely*) vagamente
faintness ['feɪntnɪs] *n* debilidad *f*; vaguedad *f*
fair [fɛə^r] *adj* justo; (*hair, person*) rubio; (*weather*) bueno; (*good enough*) suficiente; (*sizeable*) considerable ■ *adv*: **to play ~** jugar limpio ■ *n* feria; (*Brit: funfair*) parque *m* de atracciones; **it's not ~!** ¡no es justo!, ¡no hay derecho!; **~ copy** copia en limpio; **~ play** juego limpio; **a ~ amount of** bastante; **~ wear and tear** desgaste *m* natural; **trade ~** feria de muestras
fair game *n*: **to be ~** ser blanco legítimo
fairground ['fɛəgraund] *n* recinto ferial
fair-haired [fɛə'hɛəd] *adj* (*person*) rubio
fairly ['fɛəlɪ] *adv* (*justly*) con justicia; (*equally*) equitativamente; (*quite*) bastante; **I'm ~ sure** estoy bastante seguro
fairness ['fɛənɪs] *n* justicia; (*impartiality*) imparcialidad *f*; **in all ~** a decir verdad
fair trade *n* comercio justo
fairy ['fɛərɪ] *n* hada
fairy godmother *n* hada madrina
fairyland ['fɛərɪlænd] *n* el país de ensueño
fairy lights *npl* bombillas *fpl* de colores
fairy tale *n* cuento de hadas
faith [feɪθ] *n* fe *f*; (*trust*) confianza; (*sect*) religión *f*; **to have ~ in sb/sth** confiar en algn/algo
faithful ['feɪθful] *adj* fiel
faithfully ['feɪθfulɪ] *adv* fielmente; **yours ~** (*Brit: in letters*) le saluda atentamente
faith healer *n* curador(a) *m(f)* por fe
fake [feɪk] *n* (*painting etc*) falsificación *f*; (*person*) impostor(a) *m(f)* ■ *adj* falso ■ *vt* fingir; (*painting etc*) falsificar
falcon ['fɔːlkən] *n* halcón *m*
Falkland Islands ['fɔːlklənd-] *npl* Islas *fpl* Malvinas
fall [fɔːl] *n* caída; (*US*) otoño; (*decrease*) disminución *f* ■ *vi* (*pt* **fell**, *pp* **fallen**) ['fɔːlən] caer; (*accidentally*) caerse; (*price*) bajar; **falls** *npl* (*waterfall*) cataratas *fpl*, salto *sg* de agua; **a ~ of earth** un desprendimiento de tierra; **a ~ of snow** una nevada; **to ~ flat** *vi* (*on one's face*) caerse de bruces; (*joke, story*) no hacer gracia; **to ~ short of sb's expectations** decepcionar a algn; **to ~ in love (with sb/sth)** enamorarse (de algn/algo)
▸ **fall apart** *vi* deshacerse
▸ **fall back** *vi* retroceder
▸ **fall back on** *vt fus* (*remedy etc*) recurrir a; **to have sth to ~ back on** tener algo a que recurrir
▸ **fall behind** *vi* quedarse atrás; (*fig: with payments*) retrasarse
▸ **fall down** *vi* (*person*) caerse; (*building*) derrumbarse
▸ **fall for** *vt fus* (*trick*) tragar; (*person*) enamorarse de
▸ **fall in** *vi* (*roof*) hundirse; (*Mil*) alinearse
▸ **fall in with** *vt fus*: **to ~ in with sb's plans** acomodarse con los planes de algn
▸ **fall off** *vi* caerse; (*diminish*) disminuir
▸ **fall out** *vi* (*friends etc*) reñir; (*Mil*) romper filas
▸ **fall over** *vi* caer(se)
▸ **fall through** *vi* (*plan, project*) fracasar
fallacy ['fæləsɪ] *n* error *m*
fallback position ['fɔːlbæk-] *n* posición *f* de repliegue
fallen ['fɔːlən] *pp of* **fall**
fallible ['fæləbl] *adj* falible
falling ['fɔːlɪŋ] *adj*: **~ market** mercado en baja
falling-off ['fɔːlɪŋ'ɔf] *n* (*reduction*) disminución *f*
Fallopian tube [fə'ləupɪən-] *n* (*Anat*) trompa de Falopio
fallout ['fɔːlaut] *n* lluvia radioactiva
fallout shelter *n* refugio antinuclear
fallow ['fæləu] *adj* (*land, field*) en barbecho
false [fɔːls] *adj* (*gen*) falso; (*teeth etc*) postizo; (*disloyal*) desleal, traidor(a); **under ~ pretences** con engaños
false alarm *n* falsa alarma
falsehood ['fɔːlshud] *n* falsedad *f*
falsely ['fɔːlslɪ] *adv* falsamente

false teeth *npl* (*Brit*) dentadura *sg* postiza
falsify ['fɔːlsɪfaɪ] *vt* falsificar
falter ['fɔːltəʳ] *vi* vacilar
fame [feɪm] *n* fama
familiar [fə'mɪlɪəʳ] *adj* familiar; (*well-known*) conocido; (*tone*) de confianza; **to be ~ with** (*subject*) estar enterado de; **to make o.s. ~ with** familiarizarse con; **to be on ~ terms with sb** tener confianza con algn
familiarity [fəmɪlɪ'ærɪtɪ] *n* familiaridad *f*
familiarize [fə'mɪlɪəraɪz] *vt*: **to ~ o.s. with** familiarizarse con
family ['fæmɪlɪ] *n* familia
family allowance *n subsidio que se recibe por cada hijo*
family business *n* negocio familiar
family credit *n* (*Brit*) ≈ ayuda familiar
family doctor *n* médico(-a) de cabecera
family life *n* vida doméstica *or* familiar
family man *n* (*home-loving*) hombre *m* casero; (*having family*) padre *m* de familia
family planning *n* planificación *f* familiar
family planning clinic *n* clínica de planificación familiar
family tree *n* árbol *m* genealógico
famine ['fæmɪn] *n* hambre *f*, hambruna
famished ['fæmɪʃt] *adj* hambriento; **I'm ~!** (*col*) ¡estoy muerto de hambre!, ¡tengo un hambre canina!
famous ['feɪməs] *adj* famoso, célebre
famously ['feɪməslɪ] *adv* (*get on*) estupendamente
fan [fæn] *n* abanico; (*Elec*) ventilador *m*; (*person*) aficionado(-a); (*Sport*) hincha *m/f*; (*of pop star*) fan *m/f* ■ *vt* abanicar; (*fire, quarrel*) atizar
▸ **fan out** *vi* desplegarse
fanatic [fə'nætɪk] *n* fanático(-a)
fanatical [fə'nætɪkəl] *adj* fanático
fan belt *n* correa de ventilador
fancied ['fænsɪd] *adj* imaginario
fanciful ['fænsɪful] *adj* (*gen*) fantástico; (*imaginary*) fantasioso; (*design*) rebuscado
fan club *n* club *m* de fans
fancy ['fænsɪ] *n* (*whim*) capricho, antojo; (*imagination*) imaginación *f* ■ *adj* (*luxury*) de lujo; (*price*) exorbitado ■ *vt* (*feel like, want*) tener ganas de; (*imagine*) imaginarse, figurarse; **to take a ~ to sb** tomar cariño a algn; **when the ~ takes him** cuando se le antoja; **it took** *or* **caught my ~** me cayó en gracia; **to ~ that ...** imaginarse que ...; **he fancies her** le gusta (ella) mucho
fancy dress *n* disfraz *m*
fancy-dress ball ['fænsɪdrɛs-] *n* baile *m* de disfraces
fancy goods *n* artículos *mpl* de fantasía
fanfare ['fænfɛəʳ] *n* fanfarria (de trompeta)
fanfold paper ['fænfəuld-] *n* papel *m* plegado en abanico *or* en acordeón
fang [fæŋ] *n* colmillo
fan heater *n* calefactor *m* de aire
fanlight ['fænlaɪt] *n* (montante *m* en) abanico
fanny ['fænɪ] *n* (*Brit col!*) chocho (*!*); (*US col*) pompis *m*, culo (*!*)
fantasize ['fæntəsaɪz] *vi* fantasear, hacerse ilusiones
fantastic [fæn'tæstɪk] *adj* fantástico
fantasy ['fæntəzɪ] *n* fantasía
fanzine ['fænziːn] *n* fanzine *m*
FAO *n abbr* (= *Food and Agriculture Organization*) OAA *f*, FAO *f*
FAQ *abbr* (= *free alongside quay*) franco sobre muelle
FAQs *npl abbr* (= *frequently asked questions*) preguntas *fpl* frecuentes
far [fɑːʳ] *adj* (*distant*) lejano ■ *adv* lejos; **the ~ left/right** (*Pol*) la extrema izquierda/derecha; **~ away**, **~ off** (a lo) lejos; **~ better** mucho mejor; **~ from** lejos de; **by ~** con mucho; **it's by ~ the best** es con mucho el mejor; **go as ~ as the farm** vaya hasta la granja; **is it ~ to London?** ¿estamos lejos de Londres?, ¿Londres queda lejos?; **it's not ~ (from here)** no está lejos (de aquí); **as ~ as I know** que yo sepa; **how ~ have you got with your work?** ¿hasta dónde has llegado en tu trabajo?
faraway ['fɑːrəweɪ] *adj* remoto; (*look*) ausente, perdido
farce [fɑːs] *n* farsa
farcical ['fɑːsɪkəl] *adj* absurdo
fare [fɛəʳ] *n* (*on trains, buses*) precio (del billete); (*in taxi: cost*) tarifa; (*: passenger*) pasajero; (*food*) comida; **half/full ~** medio billete *m*/billete *m* completo
Far East *n*: **the ~** el Extremo *or* Lejano Oriente
farewell [fɛə'wɛl] *excl, n* adiós *m*
far-fetched [fɑː'fɛtʃt] *adj* inverosímil
farm [fɑːm] *n* granja, finca, estancia (*LAm*), chacra (*LAm*), rancho (*LAm*) ■ *vt* cultivar
▸ **farm out** *vt* (*work*): **to ~ out (to sb)** mandar hacer fuera (a algn)
farmer ['fɑːməʳ] *n* granjero(-a), estanciero(-a) (*LAm*)
farmhand ['fɑːmhænd] *n* peón *m*
farmhouse ['fɑːmhaus] *n* granja, casa de hacienda (*LAm*)
farming ['fɑːmɪŋ] *n* (*gen*) agricultura; (*tilling*) cultivo; **sheep ~** cría de ovejas
farm labourer *n* = **farmhand**
farmland ['fɑːmlænd] *n* tierra de cultivo
farm produce *n* productos *mpl* agrícolas

farm worker *n* = **farmhand**
farmyard ['fɑːmjɑːd] *n* corral *m*
Faroe Islands ['fɛərəu-], **Faroes** ['fɛərəuz] *npl*: **the ~** las Islas Feroe
far-reaching [fɑː'riːtʃɪŋ] *adj* (*reform, effect*) de gran alcance
far-sighted [fɑː'saɪtɪd] *adj* previsor(a)
fart [fɑːt] (*col!*) *n* pedo (*!*) ■ *vi* tirarse un pedo (*!*)
farther ['fɑːðəʳ] *adv* más lejos, más allá ■ *adj* más lejano
farthest ['fɑːðɪst] *superlative of* **far**
FAS *abbr* (*Brit*: = *free alongside ship*) franco al costado del buque
fascinate ['fæsɪneɪt] *vt* fascinar
fascinating ['fæsɪneɪtɪŋ] *adj* fascinante
fascination [fæsɪ'neɪʃən] *n* fascinación *f*
fascism ['fæʃɪzəm] *n* fascismo
fascist ['fæʃɪst] *adj, n* fascista *m/f*
fashion ['fæʃən] *n* moda; (*manner*) manera ■ *vt* formar; **in ~** a la moda; **out of ~** pasado de moda; **in the Greek ~** a la griega, al estilo griego; **after a ~** (*finish, manage etc*) en cierto modo
fashionable ['fæʃnəbl] *adj* de moda; (*writer*) de moda, popular; **it is ~ to do ...** está de moda hacer ...
fashion designer *n* diseñador(a) *m(f)* de modas, modisto(-a)
fashion show *n* desfile *m* de modelos
fast [fɑːst] *adj* (*also Phot*: *film*) rápido; (*dye, colour*) sólido; (*clock*): **to be ~** estar adelantado ■ *adv* rápidamente, de prisa; (*stuck, held*) firmemente ■ *n* ayuno ■ *vi* ayunar; **~ asleep** profundamente dormido; **in the ~ lane** (*Aut*) en el carril de adelantamiento; **my watch is five minutes ~** mi reloj está adelantado cinco minutos; **as ~ as I** *etc* **can** lo más rápido posible; **to make a boat ~** amarrar una barca
fasten ['fɑːsn] *vt* asegurar, sujetar; (*coat, belt*) abrochar ■ *vi* cerrarse
▸ **fasten (up)on** *vt fus* (*idea*) aferrarse a
fastener ['fɑːsnəʳ] *n* cierre *m*; (*of door etc*) cerrojo; (*Brit*: *also*: **zip fastener**) cremallera
fastening ['fɑːsnɪŋ] *n* = **fastener**
fast food *n* comida rápida, platos *mpl* preparados
fastidious [fæs'tɪdɪəs] *adj* (*fussy*) delicado; (*demanding*) exigente
fat [fæt] *adj* gordo; (*meat*) con mucha grasa; (*greasy*) grasiento ■ *n* grasa; (*on person*) carnes *fpl*; (*lard*) manteca; **to live off the ~ of the land** vivir a cuerpo de rey
fatal ['feɪtl] *adj* (*mistake*) fatal; (*injury*) mortal; (*consequence*) funesto
fatalism ['feɪtəlɪzəm] *n* fatalismo
fatality [fə'tælɪtɪ] *n* (*road death etc*) víctima *f* mortal
fatally ['feɪtəlɪ] *adv*: **~ injured** herido de muerte
fate [feɪt] *n* destino, sino
fated ['feɪtɪd] *adj* predestinado
fateful ['feɪtful] *adj* fatídico
fat-free ['fætfriː] *adj* sin grasa
father ['fɑːðəʳ] *n* padre *m*
Father Christmas *n* Papá *m* Noel
fatherhood ['fɑːðəhud] *n* paternidad *f*
father-in-law ['fɑːðərɪnlɔː] *n* suegro
fatherland ['fɑːðəlænd] *n* patria
fatherly ['fɑːðəlɪ] *adj* paternal
fathom ['fæðəm] *n* braza ■ *vt* (*unravel*) desentrañar; (*understand*) explicarse
fatigue [fə'tiːg] *n* fatiga, cansancio; **metal ~** fatiga del metal
fatness ['fætnɪs] *n* gordura
fatten ['fætn] *vt, vi* engordar; **chocolate is fattening** el chocolate engorda
fatty ['fætɪ] *adj* (*food*) graso ■ *n* (*fam*) gordito(-a), gordinflón(-ona) *m(f)*
fatuous ['fætjuəs] *adj* fatuo, necio
faucet ['fɔːsɪt] *n* (*US*) grifo, llave *f*, canilla (*LAm*)
fault [fɔːlt] *n* (*blame*) culpa; (*defect*: *in character*) defecto; (*in manufacture*) desperfecto; (*Geo*) falla ■ *vt* criticar; **it's my ~** es culpa mía; **to find ~ with** criticar, poner peros a; **at ~** culpable
faultless ['fɔːltlɪs] *adj* (*action*) intachable; (*person*) sin defectos
faulty ['fɔːltɪ] *adj* defectuoso
fauna ['fɔːnə] *n* fauna
faux pas ['fəu'pɑː] *n* desacierto
favour, favor (*US*) ['feɪvəʳ] *n* favor *m*; (*approval*) aprobación *f* ■ *vt* (*proposition*) estar a favor de, aprobar; (*person etc*) preferir; (*assist*) favorecer; **to ask a ~ of** pedir un favor a; **to do sb a ~** hacer un favor a algn; **to find ~ with sb** (*person*) caerle bien a algn; (*: suggestion*) tener buena acogida por parte de algn; **in ~ of** a favor de; **to be in ~ of sth/of doing sth** ser partidario *or* estar a favor de algo/de hacer algo
favourable, favorable (*US*) ['feɪvərəbl] *adj* favorable
favourably, favorably (*US*) ['feɪvərəblɪ] *adv* favorablemente
favourite, favorite (*US*) ['feɪvərɪt] *adj, n* favorito(-a) *m(f)*, preferido(-a) *m(f)*
favouritism, favoritism (*US*) ['feɪvərɪtɪzəm] *n* favoritismo
fawn [fɔːn] *n* cervato ■ *adj* (*also*: **fawn-coloured**) de color cervato, leonado ■ *vi*: **to ~ (up)on** adular

fax [fæks] *n* fax *m* ■ *vt* mandar *or* enviar por fax
FBI *n abbr* (*US*: = *Federal Bureau of Investigation*) FBI *m*
FCC *n abbr* (*US*) = **Federal Communications Commission**
FCO *n abbr* (*Brit*: = *Foreign and Commonwealth Office*) ≈ Min. de AA. EE
FD *n abbr* (*US*) = **fire department**
FDA *n abbr* (*US*: = *Food and Drug Administration*) *oficina que se ocupa del control de los productos alimenticios y farmacéuticos*
FE *n abbr* = **further education**
fear [fɪəʳ] *n* miedo, temor *m* ■ *vt* temer; **for ~ of** por temor a; **~ of heights** vértigo; **to ~ for/that** temer por/que
fearful [ˈfɪəful] *adj* temeroso; (*awful*) espantoso; **to be ~ of** (*frightened*) tener miedo de
fearfully [ˈfɪəfulɪ] *adv* (*timidly*) con miedo; (*col: very*) terriblemente
fearless [ˈfɪəlɪs] *adj* (*gen*) sin miedo *or* temor; (*bold*) audaz
fearlessly [ˈfɪəlɪslɪ] *adv* temerariamente
fearlessness [ˈfɪəlɪsnɪs] *n* temeridad *f*
fearsome [ˈfɪəsəm] *adj* (*opponent*) temible; (*sight*) espantoso
feasibility [fiːzəˈbɪlɪtɪ] *n* factibilidad *f*, viabilidad *f*
feasibility study *n* estudio de viabilidad
feasible [ˈfiːzəbl] *adj* factible, viable
feast [fiːst] *n* banquete *m*; (*Rel*: *also*: **feast day**) fiesta ■ *vi* banquetear
feat [fiːt] *n* hazaña
feather [ˈfɛðəʳ] *n* pluma ■ *vt*: **to ~ one's nest** (*fig*) hacer su agosto, sacar tajada ■ *cpd* (*mattress, bed, pillow*) de plumas
feather-weight [ˈfɛðəweɪt] *n* (*Boxing*) peso pluma
feature [ˈfiːtʃəʳ] *n* (*gen*) característica; (*Anat*) rasgo; (*article*) reportaje *m* ■ *vt* (*film*) presentar ■ *vi* figurar; **features** *npl* (*of face*) facciones *fpl*; **a (special) ~ on sth/sb** un reportaje (especial) sobre algo/algn; **it featured prominently in ...** tuvo un papel destacado en ...
feature film *n* largometraje *m*
Feb. *abbr* (= *February*) feb
February [ˈfɛbruərɪ] *n* febrero; *see also* **July**
feces [ˈfiːsiːz] *npl* (*US*) = **faeces**
feckless [ˈfɛklɪs] *adj* irresponsable, irreflexivo
Fed [fɛd] *abbr* (*US*) = **federal; federation**
Fed. [fɛd] *n abbr* (*US col*) = **Federal Reserve Board**
fed [fɛd] *pt, pp of* **feed**
federal [ˈfɛdərəl] *adj* federal
Federal Republic of Germany *n* República Federal de Alemania
federation [fɛdəˈreɪʃən] *n* federación *f*
fed-up [fɛdˈʌp] *adj*: **to be ~ (with)** estar harto (de)
fee [fiː] *n* (*professional*) honorarios *mpl*; (*for examination*) derechos *mpl*; (*of school*) matrícula; (*also*: **membership fee**) cuota; (*also*: **entrance fee**) entrada; **for a small ~** por poco dinero
feeble [ˈfiːbl] *adj* débil
feeble-minded [fiːblˈmaɪndɪd] *adj* imbécil
feed [fiːd] *n* (*gen*) comida; (*of animal*) pienso; (*on printer*) dispositivo de alimentación ■ *vt* (*pp, pt* **fed**) (*gen*) alimentar; (*Brit*: *breastfeed*) dar el pecho a; (*animal, baby*) dar de comer a ■ *vi* (*baby, animal*) comer
▸ **feed back** *vt* (*results*) pasar
▸ **feed in** *vt* (*Comput*) introducir
▸ **feed into** *vt* (*data, information*) suministrar a; **to ~ sth into a machine** introducir algo en una máquina
▸ **feed on** *vt fus* alimentarse de
feedback [ˈfiːdbæk] *n* (*from person*) reacción *f*; (*Tech*) realimentación *f*, feedback *m*
feeder [ˈfiːdəʳ] *n* (*bib*) babero
feeding bottle [ˈfiːdɪŋ-] *n* (*Brit*) biberón *m*
feel [fiːl] *n* (*sensation*) sensación *f*; (*sense of touch*) tacto ■ *vt* (*pt, pp* **felt**) tocar; (*cold, pain etc*) sentir; (*think, believe*) creer; **to get the ~ of sth** (*fig*) acostumbrarse a algo; **to ~ hungry/cold** tener hambre/frío; **to ~ lonely/better** sentirse solo/mejor; **I don't ~ well** no me siento bien; **it feels soft** es suave al tacto; **it feels colder out here** se siente más frío aquí fuera; **to ~ like** (*want*) tener ganas de; **I'm still feeling my way** (*fig*) todavía me estoy orientando; **I ~ that you ought to do it** creo que debes hacerlo; **to ~ about** *or* **around** *vi* tantear
feeler [ˈfiːləʳ] *n* (*of insect*) antena; **to put out feelers** (*fig*) tantear el terreno
feeling [ˈfiːlɪŋ] *n* (*physical*) sensación *f*; (*foreboding*) presentimiento; (*impression*) impresión *f*; (*emotion*) sentimiento; **what are your feelings about the matter?** ¿qué opinas tú del asunto?; **to hurt sb's feelings** herir los sentimientos de algn; **feelings ran high about it** causó mucha controversia; **I got the ~ that ...** me dio la impresión de que ...; **there was a general ~ that ...** la opinión general fue que ...
fee-paying school [ˈfiːpeɪɪŋ-] *n* colegio de pago
feet [fiːt] *npl of* **foot**
feign [feɪn] *vt* fingir
feigned [feɪnd] *adj* fingido

feline ['fi:laɪn] *adj* felino
fell [fɛl] *pt of* **fall** ■ *vt* (*tree*) talar ■ *adj*: **with one ~ blow** con un golpe feroz; **at one ~ swoop** de un solo golpe ■ *n* (*Brit: mountain*) montaña; (*moorland*): **the fells** los páramos
fellow ['fɛləu] *n* tipo, tío (*SP*); (*of learned society*) socio(-a); (*Univ*) *miembro de la junta de gobierno de un colegio* ■ *cpd*: ~ **students** compañeros(-as) *m(f)pl* de curso, de curso, condiscípulos(-as) *m(f)pl*
fellow citizen *n* conciudadano(-a)
fellow countryman *n* compatriota *m*
fellow feeling *n* compañerismo
fellow men *npl* semejantes *mpl*
fellowship ['fɛləuʃɪp] *n* compañerismo; (*grant*) beca
fellow traveller *n* compañero(-a) de viaje; (*Pol: with communists*) simpatizante *m/f*
fellow worker *n* colega *m/f*
felon ['fɛlən] *n* criminal *m/f*
felony ['fɛlənɪ] *n* crimen *m*, delito mayor
felt [fɛlt] *pt, pp of* **feel** ■ *n* fieltro
felt-tip pen ['fɛlttɪp-] *n* rotulador *m*
female ['fi:meɪl] *n* (*woman*) mujer *f*; (*Zool*) hembra ■ *adj* femenino
feminine ['fɛmɪnɪn] *adj* femenino
femininity [fɛmɪ'nɪnɪtɪ] *n* feminidad *f*
feminism ['fɛmɪnɪzəm] *n* feminismo
feminist ['fɛmɪnɪst] *n* feminista *m/f*
fence [fɛns] *n* valla, cerca; (*Racing*) valla ■ *vt* (*also*: **fence in**) cercar ■ *vi* hacer esgrima; **to sit on the ~** (*fig*) nadar entre dos aguas
▸ **fence in** *vt* cercar
▸ **fence off** *vt* separar con cerca
fencing ['fɛnsɪŋ] *n* esgrima
fend [fɛnd] *vi*: **to ~ for o.s.** valerse por sí mismo
▸ **fend off** *vt* (*attack, attacker*) rechazar, repeler; (*blow*) desviar; (*awkward question*) esquivar
fender ['fɛndə^r] *n* pantalla; (*US Aut*) parachoques *m inv*; (*Rail*) trompa
fennel ['fɛnl] *n* hinojo
Fens [fɛnz] *npl* (*Brit*): **the ~** *las tierras bajas de Norfolk (antiguamente zona de marismas)*
ferment *vi* [fə'mɛnt] fermentar ■ *n* ['fə:mɛnt] (*fig*) agitación *f*
fermentation [fə:mɛn'teɪʃən] *n* fermentación *f*
fern [fə:n] *n* helecho
ferocious [fə'rəuʃəs] *adj* feroz
ferociously [fə'rəuʃəslɪ] *adv* ferozmente, con ferocidad
ferocity [fə'rɔsɪtɪ] *n* ferocidad *f*
ferret ['fɛrɪt] *n* hurón *m*
▸ **ferret about, ferret around** *vi* rebuscar
▸ **ferret out** *vt* (*secret, truth*) desentrañar

ferry ['fɛrɪ] *n* (*small*) barca de pasaje, balsa; (*large: also*: **ferryboat**) transbordador *m*, ferry *m* ■ *vt* transportar; **to ~ sth/sb across** *or* **over** transportar algo/a algn a la otra orilla; **to ~ sb to and fro** llevar a algn de un lado para otro
ferryman ['fɛrɪmən] *n* barquero
fertile ['fə:taɪl] *adj* fértil; (*Biol*) fecundo
fertility [fə'tɪlɪtɪ] *n* fertilidad *f*; fecundidad *f*
fertility drug *n* medicamento contra la infertilidad
fertilization [fə:tɪlaɪ'zeɪʃən] *n* fertilización *f*; (*Biol*) fecundación *f*
fertilize ['fə:tɪlaɪz] *vt* fertilizar; (*Biol*) fecundar; (*Agr*) abonar
fertilizer ['fə:tɪlaɪzə^r] *n* abono, fertilizante *m*
fervent ['fə:vənt] *adj* ferviente
fervour, fervor (US) ['fə:və^r] *n* fervor *m*, ardor *m*
fester ['fɛstə^r] *vi* supurar
festival ['fɛstɪvəl] *n* (*Rel*) fiesta; (*Art, Mus*) festival *m*
festive ['fɛstɪv] *adj* festivo; **the ~ season** (*Brit: Christmas*) las Navidades
festivities [fɛs'tɪvɪtɪz] *npl* festejos *mpl*
festoon [fɛs'tu:n] *vt*: **to ~ with** festonear *or* engalanar de
fetch [fɛtʃ] *vt* ir a buscar; (*Brit: sell for*) venderse por; **how much did it ~?** ¿por cuánto se vendió?
▸ **fetch up** *vi* ir a parar
fetching ['fɛtʃɪŋ] *adj* atractivo
fête [feɪt] *n* fiesta
fetid ['fɛtɪd] *adj* fétido
fetish ['fɛtɪʃ] *n* fetiche *m*
fetter ['fɛtə^r] *vt* (*person*) encadenar, poner grillos a; (*horse*) trabar; (*fig*) poner trabas a
fetters ['fɛtəz] *npl* grillos *mpl*
fettle ['fɛtl] *n*: **in fine ~** en buenas condiciones
fetus ['fi:təs] *n* (US) = **foetus**
feud [fju:d] *n* (*hostility*) enemistad *f*; (*quarrel*) disputa; **a family ~** una pelea familiar
feudal ['fju:dl] *adj* feudal
feudalism ['fju:dəlɪzəm] *n* feudalismo
fever ['fi:və^r] *n* fiebre *f*; **he has a ~** tiene fiebre
feverish ['fi:vərɪʃ] *adj* febril
feverishly ['fi:vərɪʃlɪ] *adv* febrilmente
few [fju:] *adj* (*not many*) pocos; (*some*) algunos, unos ■ *pron* algunos; **a ~** *adj* unos pocos; few people, poca gente; **a good ~, quite a ~** bastantes; **in** *or* **over the next ~ days** en los próximos días; **every ~ weeks** cada dos o tres semanas; **a ~ more days** unos días más
fewer ['fju:ə^r] *adj* menos
fewest ['fju:ɪst] *adj* los/las menos

FFA *n abbr* = **Future Farmers of America**
FH *abbr* (*Brit*) = **fire hydrant**
FHA *n abbr* (*US*: = *Federal Housing Administration*) *oficina federal de la vivienda*
fiancé [fɪ'ɑ̃:ŋseɪ] *n* novio, prometido
fiancée [fɪ'ɑ̃:ŋseɪ] *n* novia, prometida
fiasco [fɪ'æskəu] *n* fiasco
fib [fɪb] *n* mentirijilla ■ *vi* decir mentirijillas
fibre, fiber (*US*) ['faɪbə^r] *n* fibra
fibreboard, fiberboard (*US*) ['faɪbəbɔ:d] *n* fibra vulcanizada
fibreglass, fiberglass (*US*) ['faɪbəglɑ:s] *n* fibra de vidrio
fibrositis [faɪbrə'saɪtɪs] *n* fibrositis *f inv*
FICA *n abbr* (*US*) = **Federal Insurance Contributions Act**
fickle ['fɪkl] *adj* inconstante
fiction ['fɪkʃən] *n* (*gen*) ficción *f*
fictional ['fɪkʃənl] *adj* novelesco
fictionalize ['fɪkʃənəlaɪz] *vt* novelar
fictitious [fɪk'tɪʃəs] *adj* ficticio
fiddle ['fɪdl] *n* (*Mus*) violín *m*; (*cheating*) trampa ■ *vt* (*Brit*: *accounts*) falsificar; **tax ~** evasión *f* fiscal; **to work a ~** hacer trampa
▸ **fiddle with** *vt fus* juguetear con
fiddler ['fɪdlə^r] *n* violinista *m/f*
fiddly ['fɪdlɪ] *adj* (*task*) delicado, mañoso; (*object*) enrevesado
fidelity [fɪ'dɛlɪtɪ] *n* fidelidad *f*
fidget ['fɪdʒɪt] *vi* moverse (nerviosamente)
fidgety ['fɪdʒɪtɪ] *adj* nervioso
fiduciary [fɪ'du:ʃɪərɪ] *n* fiduciario(-a)
field [fi:ld] *n* (*gen*) campo; (*Comput*) campo; (*fig*) campo, esfera; (*Sport*) campo, cancha (*LAm*); (*competitors*) competidores *mpl* ■ *cpd*: **to have a ~ day** (*fig*) ponerse las botas; **to lead the ~** (*Sport, Comm*) llevar la delantera; **to give sth a year's trial in the ~** (*fig*) sacar algo al mercado a prueba por un año; **my particular ~** mi especialidad
field glasses *npl* gemelos *mpl*
field hospital *n* hospital *m* de campaña
field marshal *n* mariscal *m*
fieldwork ['fi:ldwə:k] *n* (*Archaeology, Geo*) trabajo de campo
fiend [fi:nd] *n* demonio
fiendish ['fi:ndɪʃ] *adj* diabólico
fierce [fɪəs] *adj* feroz; (*wind, attack*) violento; (*heat*) intenso; (*fighting, enemy*) encarnizado
fiercely ['fɪəslɪ] *adv* con ferocidad; violentamente; intensamente; encarnizadamente
fierceness ['fɪəsnɪs] *n* ferocidad *f*; violencia; intensidad *f*; encarnizamiento
fiery ['faɪərɪ] *adj* (*burning*) ardiente; (*temperament*) apasionado

FIFA ['fi:fə] *n abbr* (= *Fédération Internationale de Football Association*) FIFA *f*
fifteen [fɪf'ti:n] *num* quince
fifth [fɪfθ] *adj* quinto
fiftieth ['fɪftɪɪθ] *adj* quincuagésimo
fifty ['fɪftɪ] *num* cincuenta; **the fifties** los años cincuenta; **to be in one's fifties** andar por los cincuenta
fifty-fifty ['fɪftɪ'fɪftɪ] *adv*: **to go ~ with sb** ir a medias con algn ■ *adj*: **we have a ~ chance of success** tenemos un cincuenta por ciento de posibilidades de tener éxito
fig [fɪg] *n* higo
fight [faɪt] (*pt, pp* **fought**) *n* (*gen*) pelea; (*Mil*) combate *m*; (*struggle*) lucha ■ *vt* luchar contra; (*cancer, alcoholism*) combatir; (*Law*): **to ~ a case** defenderse ■ *vi* pelear, luchar; (*quarrel*): **to ~ (with sb)** pelear (con algn); (*fig*): **to ~ (for/against)** luchar (por/contra)
▸ **fight back** *vi* defenderse; (*after illness*) recuperarse ■ *vt* (*tears*) contener
▸ **fight down** *vt* (*anger, anxiety, urge*) reprimir
▸ **fight off** *vt* (*attack, attacker*) rechazar; (*disease, sleep, urge*) luchar contra
▸ **fight out** *vt*: **to ~ it out** decidirlo en una pelea
fighter ['faɪtə^r] *n* combatiente *m/f*; (*fig*) luchador(a) *m(f)*; (*plane*) caza *m*
fighter-bomber ['faɪtəbɔmə^r] *n* cazabombardero
fighter pilot *n* piloto de caza
fighting ['faɪtɪŋ] *n* (*gen*) el luchar; (*battle*) combate *m*; (*in streets*) disturbios *mpl*
figment ['fɪgmənt] *n*: **a ~ of the imagination** un producto de la imaginación
figurative ['fɪgjurətɪv] *adj* (*meaning*) figurado; (*Art*) figurativo
figure ['fɪgə^r] *n* (*Drawing, Geom*) figura, dibujo; (*number, cipher*) cifra; (*person, outline*) figura; (*body shape*) línea; (: *attractive*) tipo ■ *vt* (*esp US*: *think, calculate*) calcular, imaginarse ■ *vi* (*appear*) figurar; (*esp US*: *make sense*) ser lógico; **~ of speech** (*Ling*) figura retórica; **public ~** personaje *m*
▸ **figure on** *vt fus* (*US*) contar con
▸ **figure out** *vt* (*understand*) comprender
figurehead ['fɪgəhɛd] *n* (*fig*) figura decorativa
figure skating *n* patinaje *m* artístico
Fiji ['fi:dʒi:], **Fiji Islands** *npl* (Islas *fpl*) Fiji
filament ['fɪləmənt] *n* (*Elec*) filamento
filch [fɪltʃ] *vt* (*col*: *steal*) birlar
file [faɪl] *n* (*tool*) lima; (*for nails*) lima de uñas; (*dossier*) expediente *m*; (*folder*) carpeta; (*in cabinet*) archivo; (*Comput*) fichero; (*row*) fila ■ *vt* limar; (*papers*) clasificar; (*Law*: *claim*) presentar; (*store*) archivar; **to open/close a ~** (*Comput*) abrir/cerrar un fichero; **to ~ in/out**

vi entrar/salir en fila; **to ~ a suit against sb** entablar pleito contra algn; **to ~ past** desfilar ante
file name *n* (*Comput*) nombre *m* de fichero
filibuster ['fɪlɪbʌstəʳ] (*esp US Pol*) *n* obstruccionista *m/f*, filibustero(-a) ■ *vi* usar maniobras obstruccionistas
filing ['faɪlɪŋ] *n*: **to do the ~** llevar los archivos
filing cabinet *n* fichero, archivo
filing clerk *n* oficinista *m/f*
fill [fɪl] *vt* llenar; (*tooth*) empastar; (*vacancy*) cubrir ■ *n*: **to eat one's ~** comer hasta hartarse; **we've already filled that vacancy** ya hemos cubierto esa vacante; **filled with admiration (for)** lleno de admiración (por)
▸ **fill in** *vt* rellenar; (*details, report*) completar; **to ~ sb in on sth** (*col*) poner a algn al corriente *or* al día sobre algo
▸ **fill out** *vt* (*form, receipt*) rellenar
▸ **fill up** *vt* llenar (hasta el borde) ■ *vi* (*Aut*) echar gasolina
fillet ['fɪlɪt] *n* filete *m*
fillet steak *n* filete *m* de ternera
filling ['fɪlɪŋ] *n* (*Culin*) relleno; (*for tooth*) empaste *m*
filling station *n* estación *f* de servicio
fillip ['fɪlɪp] *n* estímulo
filly ['fɪlɪ] *n* potra
film [fɪlm] *n* película ■ *vt* (*scene*) filmar ■ *vi* rodar
film script *n* guión *m*
film star *n* estrella de cine
filmstrip ['fɪlmstrɪp] *n* tira de diapositivas
film studio *n* estudio de cine
Filofax® ['faɪləufæks] *n* agenda (profesional)
filter ['fɪltəʳ] *n* filtro ■ *vt* filtrar
▸ **filter in, filter through** *vi* filtrarse
filter coffee *n* café *m* (molido) para filtrar
filter lane *n* (*Brit*) carril *m* de selección
filter-tipped ['fɪltətɪpt] *adj* con filtro
filth [fɪlθ] *n* suciedad *f*
filthy ['fɪlθɪ] *adj* sucio; (*language*) obsceno
fin [fɪn] *n* (*gen*) aleta
final ['faɪnl] *adj* (*last*) final, último; (*definitive*) definitivo ■ *n* (*Sport*) final *f*; **finals** *npl* (*Scol*) exámenes *mpl* finales
final demand *n* (*on invoice etc*) último aviso
final dividend *n* dividendo final
finale [fɪ'nɑːlɪ] *n* final *m*
finalist ['faɪnəlɪst] *n* (*Sport*) finalista *m/f*
finality [faɪ'nælɪtɪ] *n* finalidad *f*; **with an air of ~** en tono resuelto, de modo terminante
finalize ['faɪnəlaɪz] *vt* ultimar
finally ['faɪnəlɪ] *adv* (*lastly*) por último, finalmente; (*eventually*) por fin; (*irrevocably*) de modo definitivo; (*once and for all*) definitivamente
finance [faɪ'næns] *n* (*money, funds*) fondos *mpl*; **finances** *npl* finanzas *fpl* ■ *cpd* (*page, section, company*) financiero ■ *vt* financiar
financial [faɪ'nænʃəl] *adj* financiero
financially [faɪ'nænʃəlɪ] *adv* económicamente
financial management *n* gestión *f* financiera
financial statement *n* estado financiero
financial year *n* ejercicio (financiero)
financier [faɪ'nænsɪəʳ] *n* financiero(-a)
find [faɪnd] *vt* (*pt, pp* **found**) [faund] (*gen*) encontrar, hallar; (*come upon*) descubrir ■ *n* hallazgo; descubrimiento; **to ~ sb guilty** (*Law*) declarar culpable a algn; **I ~ it easy** me resulta fácil
▸ **find out** *vt* averiguar; (*truth, secret*) descubrir ■ *vi*: **to ~ out about** enterarse de
findings ['faɪndɪŋz] *npl* (*Law*) veredicto *sg*, fallo *sg*; (*of report*) recomendaciones *fpl*
fine [faɪn] *adj* (*delicate*) fino; (*beautiful*) hermoso ■ *adv* (*well*) bien ■ *n* (*Law*) multa ■ *vt* (*Law*) multar; **the weather is ~** hace buen tiempo; **he's ~** está muy bien; **you're doing ~** lo estás haciendo muy bien; **to cut it ~** (*of time, money*) calcular muy justo; **to get a ~ for (doing) sth** recibir una multa por (hacer) algo
fine arts *npl* bellas artes *fpl*
finely ['faɪnlɪ] *adv* (*splendidly*) con elegancia; (*chop*) en trozos pequeños, fino; (*adjust*) con precisión
fineness ['faɪnnɪs] *n* (*of cloth*) finura
fine print *n*: **the ~** la letra pequeña *or* menuda
finery ['faɪnərɪ] *n* galas *fpl*
finesse [fɪ'nɛs] *n* sutileza
fine-tooth comb ['faɪntuːθ-] *n*: **to go through sth with a ~** revisar algo a fondo
finger ['fɪŋgəʳ] *n* dedo ■ *vt* (*touch*) manosear; (*Mus*) puntear; **little/index ~** (dedo) meñique *m*/índice *m*
fingernail ['fɪŋgəneɪl] *n* uña
fingerprint ['fɪŋgəprɪnt] *n* huella dactilar
fingertip ['fɪŋgətɪp] *n* yema del dedo; **to have sth at one's fingertips** saberse algo al dedillo
finicky ['fɪnɪkɪ] *adj* (*fussy*) delicado
finish ['fɪnɪʃ] *n* (*end*) fin *m*; (*Sport*) meta; (*polish etc*) acabado ■ *vt, vi* acabar, terminar; **to ~ doing sth** acabar de hacer algo; **to ~ first/second/third** (*Sport*) llegar el primero/ segundo/tercero; **I've finished with the paper** he terminado con el periódico; **she's finished with him** ha roto *or* acabado con él
▸ **finish off** *vt* acabar, terminar; (*kill*) rematar
▸ **finish up** *vt* acabar, terminar ■ *vi* ir a parar, terminar

finished ['fɪnɪʃt] *adj* (*product*) acabado; (*performance*) pulido; (*col: tired*) rendido, hecho polvo
finishing ['fɪnɪʃɪŋ] *adj*: **~ touches** toque *m* final
finishing line *n* línea de llegada *or* meta
finishing school *n colegio para la educación social de señoritas*
finite ['faɪnaɪt] *adj* finito
Finland ['fɪnlənd] *n* Finlandia
Finn [fɪn] *n* finlandés(-esa) *m(f)*
Finnish ['fɪnɪʃ] *adj* finlandés(-esa) ■ *n* (*Ling*) finlandés *m*
fiord [fjɔ:d] *n* fiordo
fir [fəːʳ] *n* abeto
fire ['faɪəʳ] *n* fuego; (*accidental, damaging*) incendio ■ *vt* (*gun*) disparar; (*set fire to*) incendiar; (*excite*) exaltar; (*interest*) despertar; (*dismiss*) despedir ■ *vi* encenderse; (*Aut: engine*) encender; **electric/gas ~** estufa eléctrica/de gas; **on ~** ardiendo, en llamas; **to be on ~** estar ardiendo; **to catch ~** prenderse fuego; **to set ~ to sth, set sth on ~** prender fuego a algo; **insured against ~** asegurado contra incendios; **to be/come under ~** estar/caer bajo el fuego enemigo
fire alarm *n* alarma de incendios
firearm ['faɪərɑ:m] *n* arma de fuego
fire brigade, fire department (*US*) *n* (cuerpo de) bomberos *mpl*
fire door *n* puerta contra incendios
fire drill *n* (ejercicio de) simulacro de incendio
fire engine *n* coche *m* de bomberos
fire escape *n* escalera de incendios
fire extinguisher *n* extintor *m*
fireguard ['faɪəgɑ:d] *n* pantalla (guardallama)
fire hazard *n* = **fire risk**
fire hydrant *n* boca de incendios
fire insurance *n* seguro contra incendios
fireman ['faɪəmən] *n* bombero
fireplace ['faɪəpleɪs] *n* chimenea
fireplug ['faɪəplʌg] *n* (*US*) boca de incendios
fire practice *n* = **fire drill**
fireproof ['faɪəpru:f] *adj* a prueba de fuego; (*material*) incombustible
fire regulations *npl* reglamentos *mpl* contra incendios
fire risk *n* peligro de incendio
firescreen ['faɪəskri:n] *n* pantalla refractaria
fireside ['faɪəsaɪd] *n*: **by the ~** al lado de la chimenea
fire station *n* parque *m* de bomberos
firewall ['faɪəwɔ:l] *n* (*Internet*) firewall *m*
firewood ['faɪəwud] *n* leña
fireworks ['faɪəwə:ks] *npl* fuegos *mpl* artificiales
firing ['faɪərɪŋ] *n* (*Mil*) disparos *mpl*, tiroteo
firing line *n* línea de fuego; **to be in the ~** (*fig: liable to be criticised*) estar en la línea de fuego
firing squad *n* pelotón *m* de ejecución
firm [fə:m] *adj* firme; (*offer, decision*) en firme ■ *n* empresa; **to be a ~ believer in sth** ser un partidario convencido de algo; **to stand ~** *or* **take a ~ stand on sth** (*fig*) mantenerse firme ante algo
firmly ['fə:mlɪ] *adv* firmemente
firmness ['fə:mnɪs] *n* firmeza
first [fə:st] *adj* primero ■ *adv* (*before others*) primero; (*when listing reasons etc*) en primer lugar, primeramente ■ *n* (*person: in race*) primero(-a); (*Aut: also:* **first gear**) primera; **at ~** al principio; **~ of all** ante todo; **the ~ of January** el uno *or* primero de enero; **in the ~ instance** en primer lugar; **I'll do it ~ thing tomorrow** lo haré mañana a primera hora; **for the ~ time** por primera vez; **head ~** de cabeza; **from the (very) ~** desde el principio
first aid *n* primeros auxilios *mpl*
first aid kit *n* botiquín *m*
first aid post, first aid station (*US*) *n* puesto de auxilio
first-class ['fə:stklɑ:s] *adj* de primera clase; **~ ticket** (*Rail etc*) billete *m or* (*LAm*) boleto de primera clase; **~ mail** correo de primera clase
first-hand [fə:st'hænd] *adj* de primera mano
first lady *n* (*esp US*) primera dama
firstly ['fə:stlɪ] *adv* en primer lugar
first name *n* nombre *m* de pila
first night *n* estreno
first-rate [fə:st'reɪt] *adj* de primera (clase)
first-time buyer [fə:sttaɪm-] *n persona que compra su primera vivienda*
fir tree *n* abeto
fiscal ['fɪskəl] *adj* fiscal; **~ year** año fiscal, ejercicio
fish [fɪʃ] *n pl inv* pez *m*; (*food*) pescado ■ *vt* pescar en ■ *vi* pescar; **to go fishing** ir de pesca
▸ **fish out** *vt* (*from water, box etc*) sacar
fish-and-chip shop *n* = **chip shop**
fishbone ['fɪʃbəun] *n* espina
fisherman ['fɪʃəmən] *n* pescador *m*
fishery ['fɪʃərɪ] *n* pesquería
fish factory *n* fábrica de elaboración de pescado
fish farm *n* piscifactoría
fish fingers *npl* (*Brit*) palitos *mpl* de pescado (empanado)
fishing boat ['fɪʃɪŋ-] *n* barca de pesca
fishing industry *n* industria pesquera

fishing line *n* sedal *m*
fishing net *n* red *f* de pesca
fishing rod *n* caña (de pescar)
fishing tackle *n* aparejo (de pescar)
fish market *n* mercado de pescado
fishmonger ['fɪʃmʌŋgəʳ] *n* (*Brit*) pescadero(-a)
fishmonger's, fishmonger's shop *n* (*Brit*) pescadería
fishseller ['fɪʃsɛləʳ] *n* (*US*) = **fishmonger**
fish slice *n* paleta para pescado
fish sticks *npl* (*US*) = **fish fingers**
fishstore ['fɪʃstɔːʳ] *n* (*US*) = **fishmonger's**
fishy ['fɪʃɪ] *adj* (*fig*) sospechoso
fission ['fɪʃən] *n* fisión *f*; **atomic/nuclear ~** fisión *f* atómica/nuclear
fissure ['fɪʃəʳ] *n* fisura
fist [fɪst] *n* puño
fistfight ['fɪstfaɪt] *n* lucha a puñetazos
fit [fɪt] *adj* (*Med, Sport*) en (buena) forma; (*proper*) adecuado, apropiado ■ *vt* (*clothes*) quedar bien a; (*try on: clothes*) probar; (*match: facts*) cuadrar *or* corresponder *or* coincidir con; (*: description*) estar de acuerdo con; (*accommodate*) ajustar, adaptar ■ *vi* (*clothes*) quedar bien; (*in space, gap*) caber; (*facts*) coincidir ■ *n* (*Med*) ataque *m*; (*outburst*) arranque *m*; **~ to** apto para; **~ for** apropiado para; **do as you think** *or* **see ~** haz lo que te parezca mejor; **to keep ~** mantenerse en forma; **to be ~ for work** (*after illness*) estar en condiciones para trabajar; **~ of coughing** acceso de tos; **~ of anger/enthusiasm** arranque de cólera/entusiasmo; **to have** *or* **suffer a ~** tener un ataque *or* acceso; **this dress is a good ~** este vestido me queda bien; **by fits and starts** a rachas
▸ **fit in** *vi* encajar ■ *vt* (*object*) acomodar; (*fig: appointment, visitor*) encontrar un hueco para; **to ~ in with sb's plans** acomodarse a los planes de algn
▸ **fit out** *vt*, (*Brit*) **fit up** equipar
fitful ['fɪtful] *adj* espasmódico, intermitente
fitfully ['fɪtfəlɪ] *adv* irregularmente; **to sleep ~** dormir a rachas
fitment ['fɪtmənt] *n* mueble *m*
fitness ['fɪtnɪs] *n* (*Med*) forma física; (*of remark*) conveniencia
fitted carpet ['fɪtɪd-] *n* moqueta
fitted cupboards ['fɪtɪd-] *npl* armarios *mpl* empotrados
fitted kitchen ['fɪtɪd-] *n* cocina amueblada
fitter ['fɪtəʳ] *n* ajustador(a) *m(f)*
fitting ['fɪtɪŋ] *adj* apropiado ■ *n* (*of dress*) prueba; *see also* **fittings**
fitting room *n* (*in shop*) probador *m*
fittings ['fɪtɪŋz] *npl* instalaciones *fpl*
five [faɪv] *num* cinco; **she is ~ (years old)** tiene cinco años (de edad); **it costs ~ pounds** cuesta cinco libras; **it's ~ (o'clock)** son las cinco
five-day week ['faɪvdeɪ] *n* semana inglesa
fiver ['faɪvəʳ] *n* (*col: Brit*) billete *m* de cinco libras; (*: US*) billete *m* de cinco dólares
fix [fɪks] *vt* (*secure*) fijar, asegurar; (*mend*) arreglar; (*make ready: meal, drink*) preparar ■ *n*: **to be in a ~** estar en un aprieto; **to ~ sth in one's mind** fijar algo en la memoria; **the fight was a ~** (*col*) la pelea estaba amañada
▸ **fix on** *vt* (*decide on*) fijar
▸ **fix up** *vt* (*arrange: date, meeting*) arreglar; **to ~ sb up with sth** conseguirle algo a algn
fixation [fɪk'seɪʃən] *n* (*Psych*) fijación *f*
fixative ['fiksətɪv] *n* fijador *m*
fixed [fɪkst] *adj* (*prices etc*) fijo; **how are you ~ for money?** (*col*) ¿qué tal andas de dinero?
fixed assets *npl* activo *sg* fijo
fixed charge *n* gasto fijo
fixture ['fɪkstʃəʳ] *n* (*Sport*) encuentro; **fixtures** *npl* instalaciones *fpl* fijas
fizz [fɪz] *vi* burbujear
fizzle out ['fɪzl-] *vi* apagarse; (*enthusiasm, interest*) decaer; (*plan*) quedar en agua de borrajas
fizzy ['fɪzɪ] *adj* (*drink*) gaseoso
fjord [fjɔːd] *n* = **fiord**
FL, Fla. *abbr* (*US*) = **Florida**
flabbergasted ['flæbəgɑːstɪd] *adj* pasmado
flabby ['flæbɪ] *adj* flojo (de carnes); (*skin*) fofo
flag [flæg] *n* bandera; (*stone*) losa ■ *vi* decaer; **~ of convenience** pabellón *m* de conveniencia
▸ **flag down** *vt*: **to ~ sb down** hacer señas a algn para que se pare
flagpole ['flægpəul] *n* asta de bandera
flagrant ['fleɪgrənt] *adj* flagrante
flagship ['flægʃɪp] *n* buque *m* insignia *or* almirante
flagstone ['flægstəun] *n* losa
flag stop *n* (*US*) parada discrecional
flair [flɛəʳ] *n* aptitud *f* especial
flak [flæk] *n* (*Mil*) fuego antiaéreo; (*col: criticism*) lluvia de críticas
flake [fleɪk] *n* (*of rust, paint*) desconchón *m*; (*of snow*) copo; (*of soap powder*) escama ■ *vi* (*also:* **flake off**: *paint*) desconcharse; (*skin*) descamarse
flaky ['fleɪkɪ] *adj* (*paintwork*) desconchado; (*skin*) escamoso
flaky pastry *n* (*Culin*) hojaldre *m*
flamboyant [flæm'bɔɪənt] *adj* (*dress*) vistoso; (*person*) extravagante
flame [fleɪm] *n* llama; **to burst into flames** incendiarse; **old ~** (*col*) antiguo amor *m/f*
flamingo [flə'mɪŋgəu] *n* flamenco

flammable ['flæməbl] *adj* inflamable
flan [flæn] *n* (*Brit*) tarta
flank [flæŋk] *n* flanco; (*of person*) costado ■ *vt* flanquear
flannel ['flænl] *n* (*Brit*: *also*: **face flannel**) toallita; (*fabric*) franela; **flannels** *npl* pantalones *mpl* de franela
flannelette [flænə'lɛt] *n* franela de algodón
flap [flæp] *n* (*of pocket, envelope*) solapa; (*of table*) hoja (plegadiza); (*wing movement*) aletazo; (*Aviat*) flap *m* ■ *vt* (*wings*) batir ■ *vi* (*sail, flag*) ondear
flapjack ['flæpdʒæk] *n* (*US*: *pancake*) torta, panqueque *m* (*LAm*)
flare [flɛəʳ] *n* llamarada; (*Mil*) bengala; (*in skirt etc*) vuelo
▸ **flare up** *vi* encenderse; (*fig*: *person*) encolerizarse; (: *revolt*) estallar
flash [flæʃ] *n* relámpago; (*also*: **news flash**) noticias *fpl* de última hora; (*Phot*) flash *m*; (*US*: *torch*) linterna ■ *vt* (*light, headlights*) lanzar destellos con; (*torch*) encender ■ *vi* destellar; **in a ~** en un santiamén; **~ of inspiration** ráfaga de inspiración; **to ~ sth about** (*fig, col*: *flaunt*) ostentar algo, presumir con algo; **he flashed by** *or* **past** pasó como un rayo
flashback ['flæʃbæk] *n* flashback *m*, escena retrospectiva
flashbulb ['flæʃbʌlb] *n* bombilla de flash
flash card *n* (*Scol*) tarjeta
flasher ['flæʃəʳ] *n* exhibicionista *m*
flashlight ['flæʃlaɪt] *n* (*US*: *torch*) linterna
flashpoint ['flæʃpɔɪnt] *n* punto de inflamación; (*fig*) punto de explosión
flashy ['flæʃɪ] *adj* (*pej*) ostentoso
flask [flɑːsk] *n* petaca; (*also*: **vacuum flask**) termo
flat [flæt] *adj* llano; (*smooth*) liso; (*tyre*) desinflado; (*battery*) descargado; (*beer*) sin gas; (*Mus*: *instrument*) desafinado ■ *n* (*Brit*: *apartment*) piso (*SP*), departamento (*LAm*), apartamento; (*Aut*) pinchazo; (*Mus*) bemol *m*; **(to work) ~ out** (trabajar) a tope; **~ rate of pay** sueldo fijo
flatfooted [flæt'futɪd] *adj* de pies planos
flatly ['flætlɪ] *adv* rotundamente, de plano
flatmate ['flætmeɪt] *n* compañero(-a) de piso
flatness ['flætnɪs] *n* (*of land*) llanura, lo llano
flat pack *n*: **it comes in a ~** viene en un paquete plano para su automontaje
flat-pack *adj*: **~ furniture** muebles *mpl* automontables (*embalados en paquetes planos*)
flat-screen ['flætskriːn] *adj* de pantalla plana
flatten ['flætn] *vt* (*also*: **flatten out**) allanar; (*smooth out*) alisar; (*house, city*) arrasar
flatter ['flætəʳ] *vt* adular, halagar; (*show to advantage*) favorecer
flatterer ['flætərəʳ] *n* adulador(a) *m(f)*
flattering ['flætərɪŋ] *adj* halagador(a); (*clothes etc*) que favorece, favorecedor(a)
flattery ['flætərɪ] *n* adulación *f*
flatulence ['flætjuləns] *n* flatulencia
flaunt [flɔːnt] *vt* ostentar, lucir
flavour, flavor (*US*) ['fleɪvəʳ] *n* sabor *m*, gusto ■ *vt* sazonar, condimentar; **strawberry flavoured** con sabor a fresa
flavouring, flavoring (*US*) ['fleɪvərɪŋ] *n* (*in product*) aromatizante *m*
flaw [flɔː] *n* defecto
flawless ['flɔːlɪs] *adj* intachable
flax [flæks] *n* lino
flaxen ['flæksən] *adj* muy rubio
flea [fliː] *n* pulga
flea market *n* rastro, mercadillo
fleck [flɛk] *n* mota ■ *vt* (*with blood, mud etc*) salpicar; **brown flecked with white** marrón con motas blancas
fledgeling, fledgling ['flɛdʒlɪŋ] *n* (*fig*) novato(-a), principiante *m/f*
flee [fliː] (*pt, pp* **fled**) [flɛd] *vt* huir de, abandonar ■ *vi* huir
fleece [fliːs] *n* (*of sheep*) vellón *m*; (*wool*) lana; (*top*) forro polar ■ *vt* (*col*) desplumar
fleecy ['fliːsɪ] *adj* (*blanket*) lanoso, lanudo; (*cloud*) aborregado
fleet [fliːt] *n* flota; (*of cars, lorries etc*) parque *m*
fleeting ['fliːtɪŋ] *adj* fugaz
Flemish ['flɛmɪʃ] *adj* flamenco ■ *n* (*Ling*) flamenco; **the ~** los flamencos
flesh [flɛʃ] *n* carne *f*; (*of fruit*) pulpa; **of ~ and blood** de carne y hueso
flesh wound *n* herida superficial
flew [fluː] *pt of* **fly**
flex [flɛks] *n* cable *m* ■ *vt* (*muscles*) tensar
flexibility [flɛksɪ'bɪlɪtɪ] *n* flexibilidad *f*
flexible ['flɛksəbl] *adj* flexible; **~ working hours** horario *sg* flexible
flexitime ['flɛksɪtaɪm] *n* horario flexible
flick [flɪk] *n* golpecito; (*with finger*) capirotazo; (*Brit*: *col*: *film*) película ■ *vt* dar un golpecito a
▸ **flick off** *vt* quitar con el dedo
▸ **flick through** *vt fus* hojear
flicker ['flɪkəʳ] *vi* (*light*) parpadear; (*flame*) vacilar ■ *n* parpadeo
flick knife *n* navaja de muelle
flier ['flaɪəʳ] *n* aviador(a) *m(f)*
flies [flaɪz] *npl of* **fly**
flight [flaɪt] *n* vuelo; (*escape*) huida, fuga; (*also*: **flight of steps**) tramo (de escaleras); **to take ~** huir, darse a la fuga; **to put to ~** ahuyentar; **how long does the ~ take?** ¿cuánto dura el vuelo?

flight attendant *n* (US) auxiliar *m/f* de vuelo
flight deck *n* (*Aviat*) cabina de mandos
flight path *n* trayectoria de vuelo
flight recorder *n* registrador *m* de vuelo
flighty ['flaɪtɪ] *adj* caprichoso
flimsy ['flɪmzɪ] *adj* (*thin*) muy ligero; (*excuse*) flojo
flinch [flɪntʃ] *vi* encogerse
fling [flɪŋ] *vt* (*pt, pp* **flung**) [flʌŋ] arrojar ■ *n* (*love affair*) aventura amorosa
flint [flɪnt] *n* pedernal *m*; (*in lighter*) piedra
flip [flɪp] *vt*: **to ~ a coin** echar a cara o cruz
▸ **flip over** *vt* dar la vuelta a
▸ **flip through** *vt fus* (*book*) hojear; (*records*) ver de pasada
flippancy ['flɪpənsɪ] *n* ligereza
flippant ['flɪpənt] *adj* poco serio
flipper ['flɪpəʳ] *n* aleta
flip side *n* (*of record*) cara B
flirt [flə:t] *vi* coquetear, flirtear ■ *n* coqueta *f*
flirtation [flə:'teɪʃən] *n* coqueteo, flirteo
flit [flɪt] *vi* revolotear
float [fləut] *n* flotador *m*; (*in procession*) carroza; (*sum of money*) (dinero suelto para) cambio ■ *vi* (*Comm: currency*) flotar ■ *vt* (*gen*) hacer flotar; (*company*) lanzar; **to ~ an idea** plantear una idea
floating ['fləutɪŋ] *adj*: ~ **vote** voto indeciso; ~ **voter** votante *m/f* indeciso(-a)
flock [flɔk] *n* (*of sheep*) rebaño; (*of birds*) bandada; (*of people*) multitud *f*
floe [fləu] *n*: **ice ~** témpano de hielo
flog [flɔg] *vt* azotar; (*col*) vender
flood [flʌd] *n* inundación *f*; (*of words, tears etc*) torrente *m* ■ *vt* (*Aut: carburettor*) inundar; (*also*: **to flood the market**: *Comm*) inundar el mercado
flooding ['flʌdɪŋ] *n* inundación *f*
floodlight ['flʌdlaɪt] *n* foco ■ *vt* (*irreg: like* **light**) iluminar con focos
floodlit ['flʌdlɪt] *pt, pp of* **floodlight** ■ *adj* iluminado
flood tide *n* pleamar *f*
floodwater ['flʌdwɔ:təʳ] *n* aguas *fpl* (*de la inundación*)
floor [flɔ:ʳ] *n* suelo, piso (*LAm*); (*storey*) piso; (*of sea, valley*) fondo; (*dance floor*) pista ■ *vt* (*fig: baffle*) dejar anonadado; **ground ~,** (US) **first ~** planta baja; **first ~,** (US) **second ~** primer piso; **top ~** último piso; **to have the ~** (*speaker*) tener la palabra
floorboard ['flɔ:bɔ:d] *n* tabla
flooring ['flɔ:rɪŋ] *n* suelo; (*material*) solería
floor lamp *n* (US) lámpara de pie
floor show *n* cabaret *m*
floorwalker ['flɔ:wɔ:kəʳ] *n* (*US Comm*) supervisor(a) *m(f)*
flop [flɔp] *n* fracaso ■ *vi* (*fail*) fracasar
flora ['flɔ:rə] *n* flora
floral ['flɔ:rl] *adj* floral; (*dress, wallpaper*) de flores
Florence ['flɔrəns] *n* Florencia
Florentine ['flɔrəntaɪn] *adj, n* florentino(-a) *m(f)*
florid ['flɔrɪd] *adj* (*style*) florido
florist ['flɔrɪst] *n* florista *m/f*; **~'s (shop)** *n* floristería
flotation [fləu'teɪʃən] *n* (*of shares*) emisión *f*; (*of company*) lanzamiento
flounce [flauns] *n* volante *m*
▸ **flounce in** *vi* entrar con gesto exagerado
▸ **flounce out** *vi* salir con gesto airado
flounder ['flaundəʳ] *vi* tropezar ■ *n* (*Zool*) platija
flour ['flauəʳ] *n* harina
flourish ['flʌrɪʃ] *vi* florecer ■ *n* ademán *m*, movimiento (ostentoso)
flourishing ['flʌrɪʃɪŋ] *adj* floreciente
flout [flaut] *vt* burlarse de; (*order*) no hacer caso de, hacer caso omiso de
flow [fləu] *n* (*movement*) flujo; (*direction*) curso; (*Elec*) corriente *f* ■ *vi* correr, fluir
flow chart *n* organigrama *m*
flow diagram *n* organigrama *m*
flower ['flauəʳ] *n* flor *f* ■ *vi* florecer; **in ~** en flor
flower bed *n* macizo
flowerpot ['flauəpɔt] *n* tiesto
flowery ['flauərɪ] *adj* florido; (*perfume, pattern*) de flores
flowing ['fləuɪŋ] *adj* (*hair, clothes*) suelto; (*style*) fluido
flown [fləun] *pp of* **fly**
flu [flu:] *n* gripe *f*
fluctuate ['flʌktjueɪt] *vi* fluctuar
fluctuation [flʌktju'eɪʃən] *n* fluctuación *f*
flue [flu:] *n* cañón *m*
fluency ['flu:ənsɪ] *n* fluidez *f*, soltura
fluent ['flu:ənt] *adj* (*speech*) elocuente; **he speaks ~ French, he's ~ in French** domina el francés
fluently ['flu:əntlɪ] *adv* con soltura
fluff [flʌf] *n* pelusa
fluffy ['flʌfɪ] *adj* lanoso
fluid ['flu:ɪd] *adj, n* fluido, líquido; (*in diet*) líquido
fluke [flu:k] *n* (*col*) chiripa
flummox ['flʌməks] *vt* desconcertar
flung [flʌŋ] *pt, pp of* **fling**
flunky ['flʌŋkɪ] *n* lacayo
fluorescent [fluə'rɛsnt] *adj* fluorescente
fluoride ['fluəraɪd] *n* fluoruro
fluoride toothpaste *n* pasta de dientes con flúor

flurry ['flʌrɪ] *n* (*of snow*) ventisca; (*haste*) agitación *f*; **~ of activity** frenesí *m* de actividad
flush [flʌʃ] *n* (*on face*) rubor *m*; (*fig: of youth, beauty*) resplandor *m* ■ *vt* limpiar con agua; (*also:* **flush out**: *game, birds*) levantar; (*fig: criminal*) poner al descubierto ■ *vi* ruborizarse ■ *adj*: **~ with** a ras de; **to ~ the toilet** tirar de la cadena (del wáter); **hot flushes** (*Med*) sofocos *mpl*
flushed [flʌʃt] *adj* ruborizado
fluster ['flʌstəʳ] *n* aturdimiento ■ *vt* aturdir
flustered ['flʌstəd] *adj* aturdido
flute [flu:t] *n* flauta travesera
flutter ['flʌtəʳ] *n* (*of wings*) revoloteo, aleteo; (*col: bet*) apuesta ■ *vi* revolotear; **to be in a ~** estar nervioso
flux [flʌks] *n* flujo; **in a state of ~** cambiando continuamente
fly [flaɪ] (*pt* **flew**, *pp* **flown**) *n* (*insect*) mosca; (*on trousers: also:* **flies**) bragueta ■ *vt* (*plane*) pilotar; (*cargo*) transportar (en avión); (*distance*) recorrer (en avión) ■ *vi* volar; (*passenger*) ir en avión; (*escape*) evadirse; (*flag*) ondear
▸ **fly away** *vi* (*bird, insect*) irse volando
▸ **fly in** *vi* (*person*) llegar en avión; (*plane*) aterrizar; **he flew in from Bilbao** llegó en avión desde Bilbao
▸ **fly off** *vi* irse volando
▸ **fly out** *vi* irse en avión
fly-fishing ['flaɪfɪʃɪŋ] *n* pesca con mosca
flying ['flaɪɪŋ] *n* (*activity*) (el) volar ■ *adj*: **~ visit** visita relámpago; **with ~ colours** con lucimiento
flying buttress *n* arbotante *m*
flying picket *n* piquete *m* volante
flying saucer *n* platillo volante
flying squad *n* (*Police*) brigada móvil
flying start *n*: **to get off to a ~** empezar con buen pie
flyleaf (*pl* **flyleaves**) ['flaɪli:f, -li:vz] *n* (hoja de) guarda
flyover ['flaɪəuvəʳ] *n* (*Brit: bridge*) paso elevado *or* (*LAm*) a desnivel
flypast ['flaɪpɑ:st] *n* desfile *m* aéreo
flysheet ['flaɪʃi:t] *n* (*for tent*) doble techo
flyswatter ['flaɪswɔtəʳ] *n* matamoscas *m inv*
flyweight ['flaɪweɪt] *adj* de peso mosca ■ *n* peso mosca
flywheel ['flaɪwi:l] *n* volante *m* (de motor)
FM *abbr* (*Radio: = frequency modulation*) FM; (*Brit Mil*) = **field marshal**
FMB *n abbr* (*US*) = **Federal Maritime Board**
FMCS *n abbr* (*US: = Federal Mediation and Conciliation Services*) *organismo de conciliación en conflictos laborales*
FO *n abbr* (*Brit: = Foreign Office*) ≈ Min. de AA. EE
foal [fəul] *n* potro
foam [fəum] *n* espuma ■ *vi* hacer espuma
foam rubber *n* goma espuma
FOB *abbr* (*= free on board*) f.a.b.
fob [fɔb] *n* (*also:* **watch fob**) leontina ■ *vt*: **to ~ sb off with sth** deshacerse de algn con algo
foc *abbr* (*Brit: = free of charge*) gratis
focal ['fəukəl] *adj* focal; **~ point** punto focal; (*fig*) centro de atención
focus ['fəukəs ʃ] (*pl* **focuses**) *n* foco ■ *vt* (*field glasses etc*) enfocar ■ *vi*: **to ~ (on)** enfocar (a); (*issue etc*) centrarse en; **in/out of ~** enfocado/desenfocado
fodder ['fɔdəʳ] *n* pienso
FOE *n abbr* (*= Friends of the Earth*) Amigos *mpl* de la Tierra; (*US: = Fraternal Order of Eagles*) *organización benéfica*
foe [fəu] *n* enemigo
foetus, fetus (*US*) ['fi:təs] *n* feto
fog [fɔg] *n* niebla
fogbound ['fɔgbaund] *adj* inmovilizado por la niebla
foggy ['fɔgɪ] *adj*: **it's ~** hay niebla
fog lamp, fog light (*US*) *n* (*Aut*) faro antiniebla
foible ['fɔɪbl] *n* manía
foil [fɔɪl] *vt* frustrar ■ *n* hoja; (*also:* **kitchen foil**) papel *m* (de) aluminio; (*Fencing*) florete *m*
foist [fɔɪst] *vt*: **to ~ sth on sb** endilgarle algo a algn
fold [fəuld] *n* (*bend, crease*) pliegue *m*; (*Agr*) redil *m* ■ *vt* doblar; (*map etc*) plegar; **to ~ one's arms** cruzarse de brazos
▸ **fold up** *vi* plegarse, doblarse; (*business*) quebrar
folder ['fəuldəʳ] *n* (*for papers*) carpeta; (*binder*) carpeta de anillas; (*brochure*) folleto
folding ['fəuldɪŋ] *adj* (*chair, bed*) plegable
foliage ['fəulɪɪdʒ] *n* follaje *m*
folio ['fəulɪəu] *n* folio
folk [fəuk] *npl* gente *f* ■ *adj* popular, folklórico; **folks** *npl* familia, parientes *mpl*
folklore ['fəuklɔ:ʳ] *n* folklore *m*
folk music *n* música folk
folk singer *n* cantante *m/f* de música folk
folk song *n* canción *f* popular *or* folk
follow ['fɔləu] *vt* seguir ■ *vi* seguir; (*result*) resultar; **he followed suit** hizo lo mismo; **to ~ sb's advice** seguir el consejo de algn; **I don't quite ~ you** no te comprendo muy bien; **to ~ in sb's footsteps** seguir los pasos de algn; **it doesn't ~ that ...** no se deduce que ....
▸ **follow on** *vi* seguir; (*continue*): **to ~ on from** ser la consecuencia lógica de

▸ **follow out** *vt* (*implement: idea, plan*) realizar, llevar a cabo
▸ **follow through** *vt* llevar hasta el fin ■ *vi* (*Sport*) dar el remate
▸ **follow up** *vt* (*letter, offer*) responder a; (*case*) investigar
follower ['fɔləuəʳ] *n* seguidor(a) *m(f)*; (*Pol*) partidario(-a)
following ['fɔləuɪŋ] *adj* siguiente ■ *n* seguidores *mpl*
follow-up ['fɔləuʌp] *n* continuación *f*
follow-up letter *n* carta recordatoria
folly ['fɔlɪ] *n* locura
fond [fɔnd] *adj* (*loving*) cariñoso; **to be ~ of sb** tener cariño a algn; **she's ~ of swimming** tiene afición a la natación, le gusta nadar
fondle ['fɔndl] *vt* acariciar
fondly ['fɔndlɪ] *adv* (*lovingly*) con cariño; **he ~ believed that ...** creía ingenuamente que ...
fondness ['fɔndnɪs] *n* (*for things*) afición *f*; (*for people*) cariño
font [fɔnt] *n* pila bautismal
food [fu:d] *n* comida
food chain *n* cadena alimenticia
food mixer *n* batidora
food poisoning *n* intoxicación *f* alimentaria
food processor *n* robot *m* de cocina
food stamp *n* (*US*) vale *m* para comida
foodstuffs ['fu:dstʌfs] *npl* comestibles *mpl*
fool [fu:l] *n* tonto(-a); (*Culin*) mousse *m* de frutas ■ *vt* engañar; **to make a ~ of o.s.** ponerse en ridículo; **you can't ~ me** a mí no me engañas; *see also* **April Fool's Day**
▸ **fool about, fool around** *vi* hacer el tonto
foolhardy ['fu:lhɑ:dɪ] *adj* temerario
foolish ['fu:lɪʃ] *adj* tonto; (*careless*) imprudente
foolishly ['fu:lɪʃlɪ] *adv* tontamente, neciamente
foolproof ['fu:lpru:f] *adj* (*plan etc*) infalible
foolscap ['fu:lskæp] *n* ≈ papel *m* tamaño folio
foot [fut ʃ] (*pl* **feet**) *n* (*Anat*) pie *m*; (*of page, stairs, mountain*) pie *m*; (*measure*) pie (= *304 mm*); (*of animal, table*) pata ■ *vt* (*bill*) pagar; **on ~** a pie; **to find one's feet** acostumbrarse; **to put one's ~ down** (*say no*) plantarse; (*Aut*) pisar el acelerador
footage ['futɪdʒ] *n* (*Cine*) imágenes *fpl*
foot-and-mouth [futənd'mauθ-], **foot-and-mouth disease** *n* fiebre *f* aftosa
football ['futbɔ:l] *n* balón *m*; (*game: Brit*) fútbol *m*; (*US*) fútbol *m* americano
footballer ['futbɔ:ləʳ] *n* (*Brit*) = **football player**
football match *n* partido de fútbol
football player *n* futbolista *m/f*, jugador(a) *m(f)* de fútbol
footbrake ['futbreɪk] *n* freno de pie
footbridge ['futbrɪdʒ] *n* pasarela, puente *m* para peatones
foothills ['futhɪlz] *npl* estribaciones *fpl*
foothold ['futhəuld] *n* pie *m* firme
footing ['futɪŋ] *n* (*fig*) nivel *m*; **to lose one's ~** perder el equilibrio; **on an equal ~** en pie de igualdad
footlights ['futlaɪts] *npl* candilejas *fpl*
footman ['futmən] *n* lacayo
footnote ['futnəut] *n* nota (de pie de página)
footpath ['futpɑ:θ] *n* sendero
footprint ['futprɪnt] *n* huella, pisada
footrest ['futrɛst] *n* apoyapiés *m inv*
footsie ['futsɪ] *n*: **to play ~ with sb** (*col*) juguetear con los pies de algn
footsore ['futsɔ:ʳ] *adj* con los pies doloridos
footstep ['futstɛp] *n* paso
footwear ['futwɛəʳ] *n* calzado
FOR *abbr* (= *free on rail*) franco (puesto sobre) vagón

KEYWORD

for [fɔ:] *prep* **1** (*indicating destination, intention*) para; **the train for London** el tren para Londres; (*in announcements*) el tren con destino a Londres; **he left for Rome** marchó para Roma; **he went for the paper** fue por el periódico; **is this for me?** ¿es esto para mí?; **it's time for lunch** es la hora de comer
2 (*indicating purpose*) para; **what('s it) for?** ¿para qué (es)?; **what's this button for?** ¿para qué sirve este botón?; **to pray for peace** rezar por la paz
3 (*on behalf of, representing*): **the MP for Hove** el diputado por Hove; **he works for the government/a local firm** trabaja para el gobierno/en una empresa local; **I'll ask him for you** se lo pediré por ti; **G for George** G de Gerona
4 (*because of*) por esta razón; **for fear of being criticized** por temor a ser criticado
5 (*with regard to*) para; **it's cold for July** hace frío para julio; **he has a gift for languages** tiene don de lenguas
6 (*in exchange for*) por; **I sold it for £5** lo vendí por £5; **to pay 50 pence for a ticket** pagar 50 peniques por un billete
7 (*in favour of*): **are you for or against us?** ¿estás con nosotros o contra nosotros?; **I'm all for it** estoy totalmente a favor; **vote for X** vote (a) X
8 (*referring to distance*): **there are roadworks for 5 km** hay obras en 5 km; **we walked for miles** caminamos kilómetros y kilómetros
9 (*referring to time*): **he was away for two**

years estuvo fuera (durante) dos años; **it hasn't rained for three weeks** no ha llovido durante *or* en tres semanas; **I have known her for years** la conozco desde hace años; **can you do it for tomorrow?** ¿lo podrás hacer para mañana?
10 (*with infinitive clauses*): **it is not for me to decide** la decisión no es cosa mía; **it would be best for you to leave** sería mejor que te fueras; **there is still time for you to do it** todavía te queda tiempo para hacerlo; **for this to be possible ...** para que esto sea posible ...
11 (*in spite of*) a pesar de; **for all his complaints** a pesar de sus quejas
■ *conj* (*since, as: rather formal*) puesto que

forage [ˈfɔrɪdʒ] *n* forraje *m*
foray [ˈfɔreɪ] *n* incursión *f*
forbid (*pt* **forbad(e)**, *pp* **forbidden**) [fəˈbɪd, -ˈbæd, -ˈbɪdn] *vt* prohibir; **to ~ sb to do sth** prohibir a algn hacer algo
forbidding [fəˈbɪdɪŋ] *adj* (*landscape*) inhóspito; (*severe*) severo
force [fɔːs] *n* fuerza ■ *vt* obligar, forzar; **to ~ o.s. to do** hacer un esfuerzo por hacer; **the Forces** *npl* (*Brit*) las Fuerzas Armadas; **sales ~** (*Comm*) personal *m* de ventas; **a ~ 5 wind** un viento fuerza 5; **to join forces** unir fuerzas; **in ~** (*law etc*) en vigor; **to ~ sb to do sth** obligar a algn a hacer algo
▸ **force back** *vt* (*crowd, enemy*) hacer retroceder; (*tears*) reprimir
▸ **force down** *vt* (*food*) tragar con esfuerzo
forced [fɔːst] *adj* (*smile*) forzado; (*landing*) forzoso
force-feed [ˈfɔːsfiːd] *vt* (*animal, prisoner*) alimentar a la fuerza
forceful [ˈfɔːsful] *adj* enérgico
forcemeat [ˈfɔːsmiːt] *n* (*Culin*) relleno
forceps [ˈfɔːsɛps] *npl* fórceps *m inv*
forcible [ˈfɔːsəbl] *adj* (*violent*) a la fuerza; (*telling*) convincente
forcibly [ˈfɔːsəblɪ] *adv* a la fuerza
ford [fɔːd] *n* vado ■ *vt* vadear
fore [fɔːʳ] *n*: **to bring to the ~** sacar a la luz pública; **to come to the ~** empezar a destacar
forearm [ˈfɔːrɑːm] *n* antebrazo
forebear [ˈfɔːbɛəʳ] *n* antepasado
foreboding [fɔːˈbəudɪŋ] *n* presentimiento
forecast [ˈfɔːkɑːst] *n* pronóstico ■ *vt* (*irreg: like* **cast**) pronosticar; **weather ~** previsión *f* meteorológica
foreclose [fɔːˈkləuz] *vt* (*Law: also:* **foreclose on**) extinguir el derecho de redimir
foreclosure [fɔːˈkləuʒəʳ] *n* apertura de un juicio hipotecario
forecourt [ˈfɔːkɔːt] *n* (*of garage*) área de entrada
forefathers [ˈfɔːfɑːðəz] *npl* antepasados *mpl*
forefinger [ˈfɔːfɪŋgəʳ] *n* (dedo) índice *m*
forefront [ˈfɔːfrʌnt] *n*: **in the ~ of** en la vanguardia de
forego (*pt* **forewent**, *pp* **foregone**) [fɔːˈgəu, -ˈwɛnt, -ˈgɔn] *vt* = **forgo**
foregoing [ˈfɔːgəuɪŋ] *adj* anterior, precedente
foregone [ˈfɔːgɔn] *pp of* **forego** ■ *adj*: **it's a ~ conclusion** es una conclusión inevitable
foreground [ˈfɔːgraund] *n* primer plano *m* (*also Comput*)
forehand [ˈfɔːhænd] *n* (*Tennis*) derechazo directo
forehead [ˈfɔrɪd] *n* frente *f*
foreign [ˈfɔrɪn] *adj* extranjero; (*trade*) exterior
foreign currency *n* divisas *fpl*
foreigner [ˈfɔrɪnəʳ] *n* extranjero(-a)
foreign exchange *n* (*system*) cambio de divisas; (*money*) divisas *fpl*, moneda extranjera
foreign investment *n* inversión *f* en el extranjero; (*money, stock*) inversiones *fpl* extranjeras
Foreign Minister *n* Ministro(-a) de Asuntos Exteriores, Canciller *m* (*LAm*)
Foreign Office *n* Ministerio de Asuntos Exteriores
Foreign Secretary *n* (*Brit*) Ministro(-a) de Asuntos Exteriores, Canciller *m* (*LAm*)
foreleg [ˈfɔːlɛg] *n* pata delantera
foreman [ˈfɔːmən] *n* capataz *m*; (*Law: of jury*) presidente *m/f*
foremost [ˈfɔːməust] *adj* principal ■ *adv*: **first and ~** ante todo, antes que nada
forename [ˈfɔːneɪm] *n* nombre *m* (de pila)
forensic [fəˈrɛnsɪk] *adj* forense; **~ scientist** forense *m/f*
foreplay [ˈfɔːpleɪ] *n* preámbulos *mpl* (*de estimulación sexual*)
forerunner [ˈfɔːrʌnəʳ] *n* precursor(a) *m(f)*
foresee (*pt* **foresaw**, *pp* **foreseen**) [fɔːˈsiː, -ˈsɔː, -ˈsiːn] *vt* prever
foreseeable [fɔːˈsiːəbl] *adj* previsible
foreshadow [fɔːˈʃædəu] *vt* prefigurar, anunciar
foreshore [ˈfɔːʃɔːʳ] *n* playa
foreshorten [fɔːˈʃɔːtn] *vt* (*figure, scene*) escorzar
foresight [ˈfɔːsaɪt] *n* previsión *f*
foreskin [ˈfɔːskɪn] *n* (*Anat*) prepucio
forest [ˈfɔrɪst] *n* bosque *m*
forestall [fɔːˈstɔːl] *vt* anticiparse a
forestry [ˈfɔrɪstrɪ] *n* silvicultura
foretaste [ˈfɔːteɪst] *n* anticipo

foretell (*pt, pp* **foretold**) [fɔːˈtɛl, -ˈtəuld] *vt* predecir, pronosticar
forethought [ˈfɔːθɔːt] *n* previsión *f*
forever [fəˈrɛvəʳ] *adv* siempre; (*for good*) para siempre
forewarn [fɔːˈwɔːn] *vt* avisar, advertir
forewent [fɔːˈwɛnt] *pt of* **forego**
foreword [ˈfɔːwəːd] *n* prefacio
forfeit [ˈfɔːfɪt] *n* (*in game*) prenda ■ *vt* perder (derecho a)
forgave [fəˈgeɪv] *pt of* **forgive**
forge [fɔːdʒ] *n* fragua; (*smithy*) herrería ■ *vt* (*signature: Brit: money*) falsificar; (*metal*) forjar
▸ **forge ahead** *vi* avanzar mucho
forger [ˈfɔːdʒəʳ] *n* falsificador(a) *m(f)*
forgery [ˈfɔːdʒərɪ] *n* falsificación *f*
forget (*pt* **forgot**, *pp* **forgotten**) [fəˈgɛt, -ˈgɔt, -ˈgɔtn] *vt* olvidar, olvidarse de ■ *vi* olvidarse
forgetful [fəˈgɛtful] *adj* olvidadizo
forget-me-not [fəˈgɛtmɪnɔt] *n* nomeolvides *f inv*
forgive (*pt* **forgave**, *pp* **forgiven**) [fəˈgɪv, -ˈgeɪv, -ˈgɪvn] *vt* perdonar; **to ~ sb for sth/for doing sth** perdonar algo a algn/a algn por haber hecho algo
forgiveness [fəˈgɪvnɪs] *n* perdón *m*
forgiving [fəˈgɪvɪŋ] *adj* compasivo
forgo (*pt* **forwent**, *pp* **forgone**) [fɔːˈgəu, -ˈwɛnt, -ˈgɔn] *vt* (*give up*) renunciar a; (*go without*) privarse de
forgot [fəˈgɔt] *pt of* **forget**
forgotten [fəˈgɔtn] *pp of* **forget**
fork [fɔːk] *n* (*for eating*) tenedor *m*; (*for gardening*) horca; (*of roads*) bifurcación *f*; (*in tree*) horcadura ■ *vi* (*road*) bifurcarse
▸ **fork out** *vt* (*col: pay*) soltar
forked [fɔːkt] *adj* (*lightning*) en zigzag
fork-lift truck [ˈfɔːklɪft-] *n* máquina elevadora
forlorn [fəˈlɔːn] *adj* (*person*) triste, melancólico; (*deserted: cottage*) abandonado; (*desperate: attempt*) desesperado
form [fɔːm] *n* forma; (*Brit Scol*) curso; (*document*) formulario, planilla (*LAm*) ■ *vt* formar; **in the ~ of** en forma de; **in top ~** en plena forma; **to be in good ~** (*Sport: fig*) estar en plena forma; **to ~ part of sth** formar parte de algo; **to ~ a circle/a queue** hacer una curva/una cola
formal [ˈfɔːməl] *adj* (*offer, receipt*) por escrito; (*person etc*) correcto; (*occasion, dinner*) ceremonioso; **~ dress** traje *m* de vestir; (*evening dress*) traje *m* de etiqueta
formalities [fɔːˈmælɪtɪz] *npl* formalidades *fpl*
formality [fɔːˈmælɪtɪ] *n* ceremonia
formalize [ˈfɔːməlaɪz] *vt* formalizar
formally [ˈfɔːməlɪ] *adv* oficialmente
format [ˈfɔːmæt] *n* formato ■ *vt* (*Comput*) formatear
formation [fɔːˈmeɪʃən] *n* formación *f*
formative [ˈfɔːmətɪv] *adj* (*years*) de formación
former [ˈfɔːməʳ] *adj* anterior; (*earlier*) antiguo; (*ex*) ex; **the ~ ... the latter ...** aquél ... éste ...; **the ~ president** el antiguo *or* ex presidente; **the ~ Yugoslavia/Soviet Union** la antigua *or* ex Yugoslavia/Unión Soviética
formerly [ˈfɔːməlɪ] *adv* antiguamente
form feed *n* (*on printer*) salto de página
Formica® [fɔːˈmaɪkə] *n* formica®
formidable [ˈfɔːmɪdəbl] *adj* formidable
formula [ˈfɔːmjulə] *n* fórmula; **F~ One** (*Aut*) Fórmula Uno
formulate [ˈfɔːmjuleɪt] *vt* formular
fornicate [ˈfɔːnɪkeɪt] *vi* fornicar
forsake (*pt* **forsook**, *pp* **forsaken**) [fəˈseɪk, -ˈsuk, -ˈseɪkən] *vt* (*gen*) abandonar; (*plan*) renunciar a
fort [fɔːt] *n* fuerte *m*; **to hold the ~** (*fig*) quedarse a cargo
forte [ˈfɔːtɪ] *n* fuerte *m*
forth [fɔːθ] *adv*: **back and ~** de acá para allá; **and so ~** y así sucesivamente
forthcoming [fɔːθˈkʌmɪŋ] *adj* próximo, venidero; (*character*) comunicativo
forthright [ˈfɔːθraɪt] *adj* franco
forthwith [ˈfɔːθˈwɪθ] *adv* en el acto, acto seguido
fortification [fɔːtɪfɪˈkeɪʃən] *n* fortificación *f*
fortified wine [ˈfɔːtɪfaɪd-] *n* vino encabezado
fortify [ˈfɔːtɪfaɪ] *vt* fortalecer
fortitude [ˈfɔːtɪtjuːd] *n* fortaleza
fortnight [ˈfɔːtnaɪt] *n* (*Brit*) quincena; **it's a ~ since ...** hace quince días que ...
fortnightly [ˈfɔːtnaɪtlɪ] *adj* quincenal ■ *adv* quincenalmente
FORTRAN [ˈfɔːtræn] *n* FORTRAN *m*
fortress [ˈfɔːtrɪs] *n* fortaleza
fortuitous [fɔːˈtjuːɪtəs] *adj* fortuito
fortunate [ˈfɔːtʃənɪt] *adj*: **it is ~ that ...** (es una) suerte que ...
fortunately [ˈfɔːtʃənɪtlɪ] *adv* afortunadamente
fortune [ˈfɔːtʃən] *n* suerte *f*; (*wealth*) fortuna; **to make a ~** hacer un dineral
fortune-teller [ˈfɔːtʃəntɛləʳ] *n* adivino(-a)
forty [ˈfɔːtɪ] *num* cuarenta
forum [ˈfɔːrəm] *n* (*also fig*) foro
forward [ˈfɔːwəd] *adj* (*position*) avanzado; (*movement*) hacia delante; (*front*) delantero; (*not shy*) atrevido ■ *n* (*Sport*) delantero ■ *vt* (*letter*) remitir; (*career*) promocionar; **to move ~** avanzar; **"please ~"** "remítase al destinatario"

forward contract *n* contrato a término
forward exchange *n* cambio a término
forward planning *n* planificación *f* por anticipado
forward rate *n* tipo a término
forwards ['fɔːwədz] *adv* (hacia) adelante
forward sales *npl* ventas *fpl* a término
forwent [fɔː'wɛnt] *pt of* **forgo**
fossil ['fɔsl] *n* fósil *m*
fossil fuel *n* combustible *m* fósil
foster ['fɔstəʳ] *vt* (*child*) acoger en familia; (*idea*) fomentar
foster brother *n* hermano de leche
foster child *n* hijo(-a) adoptivo(-a)
foster mother *n* madre *f* adoptiva
fought [fɔːt] *pt, pp of* **fight**
foul [faul] *adj* (*gen*) sucio, puerco; (*weather, smell etc*) asqueroso ■ *n* (*Football*) falta ■ *vt* (*dirty*) ensuciar; (*block*) atascar; (*entangle: anchor, propeller*) atascar, enredarse en; (*football player*) cometer una falta contra
foul play *n* (*Sport*) mala jugada; (*Law*) muerte *f* violenta
found [faund] *pt, pp of* **find** ■ *vt* (*establish*) fundar
foundation [faun'deɪʃən] *n* (*act*) fundación *f*; (*basis*) base *f*; (*also*: **foundation cream**) base *f* de maquillaje
foundations [faun'deɪʃənz] *npl* (*of building*) cimientos *mpl*; **to lay the ~** poner los cimientos
foundation stone *n*: **to lay the ~** poner la primera piedra
founder ['faundəʳ] *n* fundador(a) *m(f)* ■ *vi* irse a pique
founding ['faundɪŋ] *adj*: **~ fathers** (*esp US*) fundadores *mpl*, próceres *mpl*; **~ member** miembro fundador
foundry ['faundrɪ] *n* fundición *f*
fountain ['fauntɪn] *n* fuente *f*
fountain pen *n* (pluma) estilográfica, plumafuente *f* (*LAm*)
four [fɔːʳ] *num* cuatro; **on all fours** a gatas
four-footed [fɔː'futɪd] *adj* cuadrúpedo
four-letter word ['fɔːlɛtə-] *n* taco
four-poster ['fɔː'pəustəʳ] *n* (*also*: **four-poster bed**) cama de columnas
foursome ['fɔːsəm] *n* grupo de cuatro personas
fourteen ['fɔː'tiːn] *num* catorce
fourteenth [fɔː'tiːnθ] *adj* decimocuarto
fourth [fɔːθ] *adj* cuarto ■ *n* (*Aut*: *also*: **fourth gear**) cuarta (velocidad)
four-wheel drive ['fɔːwiːl-] *n* tracción *f* a las cuatro ruedas
fowl [faul] *n* ave *f* (de corral)
fox [fɔks] *n* zorro ■ *vt* confundir
fox fur *n* piel *f* de zorro
foxglove ['fɔksglʌv] *n* (*Bot*) dedalera
fox-hunting ['fɔkshʌntɪŋ] *n* caza de zorros
foxtrot ['fɔkstrɔt] *n* fox(trot) *m*
foyer ['fɔɪeɪ] *n* vestíbulo
FPA *n abbr* (*Brit*: = *Family Planning Association*) *asociación de planificación familiar*
Fr. *abbr* (*Rel*: = *father*) P.; (= *friar*) Fr.
fracas ['frækɑː] *n* gresca, refriega
fraction ['frækʃən] *n* fracción *f*
fractionally ['frækʃnəlɪ] *adv* ligeramente
fractious ['frækʃəs] *adj* (*person, mood*) irascible
fracture ['fræktʃəʳ] *n* fractura ■ *vt* fracturar
fragile ['frædʒaɪl] *adj* frágil
fragment ['frægmənt] *n* fragmento
fragmentary [fræg'mɛntərɪ] *adj* fragmentario
fragrance ['freɪgrəns] *n* fragancia
fragrant ['freɪgrənt] *adj* fragante, oloroso
frail [freɪl] *adj* (*fragile*) frágil, quebradizo; (*weak*) delicado
frame [freɪm] *n* (*Tech*) armazón *f*; (*of picture, door etc*) marco; (*of spectacles*: *also*: **frames**) montura ■ *vt* encuadrar; (*picture*) enmarcar; (*reply*) formular; **to ~ sb** (*col*) inculpar por engaños a algn
frame of mind *n* estado de ánimo
framework ['freɪmwəːk] *n* marco
France [frɑːns] *n* Francia
franchise ['fræntʃaɪz] *n* (*Pol*) derecho al voto, sufragio; (*Comm*) licencia, concesión *f*
franchisee [fræntʃaɪ'ziː] *n* concesionario(-a)
franchiser ['fræntʃaɪzəʳ] *n* compañía concesionaria
frank [fræŋk] *adj* franco ■ *vt* (*Brit*: *letter*) franquear
frankfurter ['fræŋkfəːtəʳ] *n* salchicha de Frankfurt
frankincense ['fræŋkɪnsens] *n* incienso
franking machine ['fræŋkɪŋ-] *n* máquina de franqueo
frankly ['fræŋklɪ] *adv* francamente
frankness ['fræŋknɪs] *n* franqueza
frantic ['fræntɪk] *adj* (*desperate*: *need, desire*) desesperado; (*: search*) frenético; (*: person*) desquiciado
fraternal [frə'təːnl] *adj* fraterno
fraternity [frə'təːnɪtɪ] *n* (*club*) fraternidad *f*; (*US*) club *m* de estudiantes; (*guild*) gremio
fraternization [frætənaɪ'zeɪʃən] *n* fraternización *f*
fraternize ['frætənaɪz] *vi* confraternizar
fraud [frɔːd] *n* fraude *m*; (*person*) impostor(a) *m(f)*
fraudulent ['frɔːdjulənt] *adj* fraudulento
fraught [frɔːt] *adj* (*tense*) tenso; **~ with** cargado de

fray [freɪ] *n* combate *m*, lucha, refriega ■ *vi* deshilacharse; **tempers were frayed** el ambiente se ponía tenso
FRB *n abbr* (*US*) = **Federal Reserve Board**
FRCM *n abbr* (*Brit*) = **Fellow of the Royal College of Music**
FRCO *n abbr* (*Brit*) = **Fellow of the Royal College of Organists**
FRCP *n abbr* (*Brit*) = **Fellow of the Royal College of Physicians**
FRCS *n abbr* (*Brit*) = **Fellow of the Royal College of Surgeons**
freak [fri:k] *n* (*person*) fenómeno; (*event*) suceso anormal; (*col: enthusiast*) adicto(-a) ■ *adj* (*storm, conditions*) anormal; **health ~** (*col*) maniático(-a) en cuestión de salud ▸ **freak out** *vi* (*col: on drugs*) flipar
freakish ['fri:kɪʃ] *adj* (*result*) inesperado; (*appearance*) estrambótico; (*weather*) cambiadizo
freckle ['frɛkl] *n* peca
freckled ['frɛkld] *adj* pecoso, lleno de pecas
free [fri:] *adj* (*person: at liberty*) libre; (*not fixed*) suelto; (*gratis*) gratuito; (*unoccupied*) desocupado; (*liberal*) generoso ■ *vt* (*prisoner etc*) poner en libertad; (*jammed object*) soltar; **to give sb a ~ hand** dar carta blanca a algn; **~ and easy** despreocupado; **is this seat ~?** ¿está libre este asiento?; **~ of tax** libre de impuestos; **admission ~** entrada libre; **~ (of charge), for ~** *adv* gratis
freebie ['fri:bɪ] *n* (*col*): **it's a ~** es gratis
freedom ['fri:dəm] *n* libertad *f*; **~ of association** libertad de asociación
freedom fighter *n* luchador(a) *m(f)* por la libertad
free enterprise *n* libre empresa
Freefone® ['fri:fəun] *n* (*Brit*) número gratuito
free-for-all ['fri:fərɔ:l] *n* riña general
free gift *n* regalo
freehold ['fri:həuld] *n* propiedad *f* absoluta
free kick *n* tiro libre
freelance ['fri:lɑ:ns] *adj, adv* por cuenta propia; **to do ~ work** trabajar por su cuenta
freely ['fri:lɪ] *adv* libremente; (*liberally*) generosamente
free-market economy ['fri:'mɑ:kɪt-] *n* economía de libre mercado
freemason ['fri:meɪsn] *n* francmasón *m*
freemasonry ['fri:meɪsnrɪ] *n* (franc)masonería
freepost ['fri:pəust] *n* porte *m* pagado
free-range ['fri:'reɪndʒ] *adj* (*hen, egg*) de granja
free sample *n* muestra gratuita
freesia ['fri:ʒə] *n* fresia
free speech *n* libertad *f* de expresión
free trade *n* libre comercio
freeway ['fri:weɪ] *n* (*US*) autopista
freewheel [fri:'wi:l] *vi* ir en punto muerto
freewheeling [fri:'wi:lɪŋ] *adj* libre, espontáneo; (*careless*) irresponsable
free will *n* libre albedrío; **of one's own ~** por su propia voluntad
freeze [fri:z] (*pt* **froze**, *pp* **frozen**) *vi* helarse, congelarse ■ *vt* helar; (*prices, food, salaries*) congelar ■ *n* helada; congelación *f* ▸ **freeze over** *vi* (*lake, river*) helarse, congelarse; (*window, windscreen*) cubrirse de escarcha ▸ **freeze up** *vi* helarse, congelarse
freeze-dried ['fri:zdraɪd] *adj* liofilizado
freezer ['fri:zəʳ] *n* congelador *m*, congeladora
freezing ['fri:zɪŋ] *adj* helado
freezing point *n* punto de congelación; **3 degrees below ~** tres grados bajo cero
freight [freɪt] *n* (*goods*) carga; (*money charged*) flete *m*
freight car *n* vagón *m* de mercancías
freighter ['freɪtəʳ] *n* buque *m* de carga; (*Aviat*) avión *m* de transporte de mercancías
freight forward *n* contra reembolso del flete, flete por pagar
freight forwarder [-'fɔ:wədəʳ] *n* agente *m* expedidor
freight inward *n* flete sobre compras
freight train *n* (*US*) tren *m* de mercancías
French [frɛntʃ] *adj* francés(-esa) ■ *n* (*Ling*) francés *m*; **the French** *npl* los franceses
French bean *n* judía verde
French bread *n* pan *m* francés
French Canadian *adj, n* francocanadiense *m/f*
French dressing *n* (*Culin*) vinagreta
French fried potatoes, French fries (*US*) *npl* patatas *fpl or* (*LAm*) papas *fpl* fritas
French Guiana [-gaɪ'ænə] *n* la Guayana Francesa
French loaf *n* barra de pan
Frenchman ['frɛntʃmən] *n* francés *m*
French Riviera *n*: **the ~** la Riviera, la Costa Azul
French stick *n* barra de pan
French window *n* puertaventana
Frenchwoman ['frɛntʃwumən] *n* francesa
frenetic [frə'nɛtɪk] *adj* frenético
frenzy ['frɛnzɪ] *n* frenesí *m*
frequency ['fri:kwənsɪ] *n* frecuencia
frequency modulation *n* frecuencia modulada
frequent *adj* ['fri:kwənt] frecuente ■ *vt* [frɪ'kwɛnt] frecuentar
frequently ['fri:kwəntlɪ] *adv* frecuentemente, a menudo

fresco ['frɛskəu] *n* fresco
fresh [frɛʃ] *adj* (*gen*) fresco; (*new*) nuevo; (*water*) dulce; **to make a ~ start** empezar de nuevo
freshen ['frɛʃən] *vi* (*wind*) arreciar; (*air*) refrescar
▸**freshen up** *vi* (*person*) refrescarse
freshener ['frɛʃnəʳ] *n*: **air ~** ambientador *m*; **skin ~** tónico
fresher ['frɛʃəʳ] *n* (*Brit Scol: col*) estudiante *m/f* de primer año
freshly ['frɛʃlɪ] *adv*: **~ painted/arrived** recién pintado/llegado
freshman ['frɛʃmən] *n* (*US Scol*) = **fresher**
freshness ['frɛʃnɪs] *n* frescura
freshwater ['frɛʃwɔːtəʳ] *adj* (*fish*) de agua dulce
fret [frɛt] *vi* inquietarse
fretful ['frɛtful] *adj* (*child*) quejumbroso
Freudian ['frɔɪdɪən] *adj* freudiano; **~ slip** lapsus *m* (freudiano)
FRG *n abbr* (= *Federal Republic of Germany*) RFA *f*
Fri. *abbr* (= *Friday*) vier
friar ['fraɪəʳ] *n* fraile *m*; (*before name*) fray
friction ['frɪkʃən] *n* fricción *f*
friction feed *n* (*on printer*) avance *m* por fricción
Friday ['fraɪdɪ] *n* viernes *m inv*; *see also* **Tuesday**
fridge [frɪdʒ] *n* (*Brit*) nevera, frigo, refrigeradora (*LAm*), heladera (*LAm*)
fridge-freezer ['frɪdʒ'friːzəʳ] *n* frigorífico-congelador *m*, combi *m*
fried [fraɪd] *pt, pp of* **fry** ■ *adj*: **~ egg** huevo frito, huevo estrellado
friend [frɛnd] *n* amigo(-a)
friendliness ['frɛndlɪnɪs] *n* simpatía
friendly ['frɛndlɪ] *adj* simpático
friendly fire *n* fuego amigo, disparos *mpl* del propio bando
friendly society *n* mutualidad *f*, montepío
friendship ['frɛndʃɪp] *n* amistad *f*
frieze [friːz] *n* friso
frigate ['frɪgɪt] *n* fragata
fright [fraɪt] *n* susto; **to take ~** asustarse
frighten ['fraɪtn] *vt* asustar
▸**frighten away, frighten off** *vt* (*birds, children etc*) espantar, ahuyentar
frightened ['fraɪtnd] *adj* asustado
frightening ['fraɪtnɪŋ] *adj*: **it's ~** da miedo
frightful ['fraɪtful] *adj* espantoso, horrible
frightfully ['fraɪtfulɪ] *adv* terriblemente; **I'm ~ sorry** lo siento muchísimo
frigid ['frɪdʒɪd] *adj* (*Med*) frígido
frigidity [frɪ'dʒɪdɪtɪ] *n* (*Med*) frigidez *f*
frill [frɪl] *n* volante *m*; **without frills** (*fig*) sin adornos
frilly ['frɪlɪ] *adj* con volantes
fringe [frɪndʒ] *n* (*Brit: of hair*) flequillo; (*edge: of forest etc*) borde *m*, margen *m*
fringe benefits *npl* ventajas *fpl* complementarias
fringe theatre *n* teatro experimental
Frisbee® ['frɪzbɪ] *n* frisbee® *m*
frisk [frɪsk] *vt* cachear, registrar
frisky ['frɪskɪ] *adj* juguetón(-ona)
fritter ['frɪtəʳ] *n* buñuelo
▸**fritter away** *vt* desperdiciar
frivolity [frɪ'vɔlɪtɪ] *n* frivolidad *f*
frivolous ['frɪvələs] *adj* frívolo
frizzy ['frɪzɪ] *adj* crespo
fro [frəu] *see* **to**
frock [frɔk] *n* vestido
frog [frɔg] *n* rana; **to have a ~ in one's throat** tener carraspera
frogman ['frɔgmən] *n* hombre-rana *m*
frogmarch ['frɔgmɑːtʃ] *vt*: **to ~ sb in/out** meter/sacar a algn a rastras
frolic ['frɔlɪk] *vi* juguetear

KEYWORD

from [frɔm] *prep* **1** (*indicating starting place*) de, desde; **where do you come from?, where are you from?** ¿de dónde eres?; **where has he come from?** ¿de dónde ha venido?; **from London to Glasgow** de Londres a Glasgow; **to escape from sth/sb** escaparse de algo/algn
2 (*indicating origin etc*) de; **a letter/telephone call from my sister** una carta/llamada de mi hermana; **tell him from me that ...** dígale de mi parte que ...
3 (*indicating time*): **from one o'clock to** *or* **until** *or* **till nine** de la una a las nueve, desde la una hasta las nueve; **from January (on)** a partir de enero; **(as) from Friday** a partir del viernes
4 (*indicating distance*) de; **the hotel is 1 km from the beach** el hotel está a 1 km de la playa
5 (*indicating price, number etc*) de; **prices range from £10 to £50** los precios van desde £10 a *or* hasta £50; **the interest rate was increased from 9% to 10%** el tipo de interés fue incrementado de un 9% a un 10%
6 (*indicating difference*) de; **he can't tell red from green** no sabe distinguir el rojo del verde; **to be different from sb/sth** ser diferente a algn/algo
7 (*because of, on the basis of*): **from what he says** por lo que dice; **weak from hunger** debilitado por el hambre

frond [frɔnd] *n* fronda
front [frʌnt] *n* *(foremost part)* parte *f* delantera; *(of house)* fachada; *(promenade: also:* **sea front***)* paseo marítimo; *(Mil, Pol, Meteorology)* frente *m*; *(fig: appearances)* apariencia ■ *adj* *(wheel, leg)* delantero; *(row, line)* primero ■ *vi*: **to ~ onto sth** dar a algo; **in ~ (of)** delante (de)
frontage ['frʌntɪdʒ] *n* *(of building)* fachada
frontal ['frʌntl] *adj* frontal
front bench *n* *(Brit: Pol)* *ver nota*

FRONT BENCH

El término genérico *front bench* se usa para referirse a los escaños situados en primera fila a ambos lados del Presidente ("Speaker") de la Cámara de los Comunes ("House of Commons") del Parlamento británico. Dichos escaños son ocupados por los miembros del gobierno a un lado y los del gobierno en la oposición ("shadow cabinet") al otro. Por esta razón a todos ellos se les denomina "frontbenchers".

frontbencher ['frʌnt'bɛntʃəʳ] *n* *(Brit)* *see* **front bench**
front desk *n* *(US)* recepción *f*
front door *n* puerta principal
frontier ['frʌntɪəʳ] *n* frontera
frontispiece ['frʌntɪspi:s] *n* frontispicio
front page *n* primera plana
front room *n* *(Brit)* salón *m*, sala
front runner *n* favorito(-a)
front-wheel drive ['frʌntwi:l-] *n* tracción *f* delantera
frost [frɔst] *n* *(gen)* helada; *(also:* **hoarfrost***)* escarcha ■ *vt* *(US Culin)* escarchar
frostbite ['frɔstbaɪt] *n* congelación *f*
frosted ['frɔstɪd] *adj* *(glass)* esmerilado; *(esp US: cake)* glaseado
frosting ['frɔstɪŋ] *n* *(esp US: icing)* glaseado
frosty ['frɔstɪ] *adj* *(surface)* cubierto de escarcha; *(welcome etc)* glacial
froth [frɔθ] *n* espuma
frothy ['frɔθɪ] *adj* espumoso
frown [fraun] *vi* fruncir el ceño ■ *n*: **with a ~** frunciendo el entrecejo
▸ **frown on** *vt fus* desaprobar
froze [frəuz] *pt of* **freeze**
frozen ['frəuzn] *pp of* **freeze** ■ *adj* *(food)* congelado; *(Comm)*: **~ assets** activos *mpl* congelados *or* bloqueados
FRS *n abbr* *(Brit: = Fellow of the Royal Society) miembro de la principal asociación de investigación científica*; *(US: = Federal Reserve System) banco central de los EE. UU.*
frugal ['fru:gəl] *adj* *(person)* frugal
fruit [fru:t] *n pl inv* fruta
fruiterer ['fru:tərəʳ] *n* frutero(-a); **~'s (shop)** frutería
fruit fly *n* mosca de la fruta
fruitful ['fru:tful] *adj* provechoso
fruition [fru:'ɪʃən] *n*: **to come to ~** realizarse
fruit juice *n* jugo *or* *(SP)* zumo de fruta
fruitless ['fru:tlɪs] *adj* *(fig)* infructuoso, inútil
fruit machine *n* *(Brit)* máquina tragaperras
fruit salad *n* macedonia *or* *(LAm)* ensalada de frutas
frump [frʌmp] *n* espantajo, adefesio
frustrate [frʌs'treɪt] *vt* frustrar
frustrated [frʌs'treɪtɪd] *adj* frustrado
frustrating [frʌs'treɪtɪŋ] *adj* *(job, day)* frustrante
frustration [frʌs'treɪʃən] *n* frustración *f*
fry *(pt, pp* **fried***)* [fraɪ, -d] *vt* freír ■ *n*: **small ~** gente *f* menuda
frying pan ['fraɪɪŋ-] *n* sartén *f*, sartén *m* *(LAm)*
FT *n abbr* *(Brit: = Financial Times) periódico financiero*; *(= the FT index) el índice de valores del Financial Times*
ft. *abbr* = **foot; feet**
FTC *n abbr* *(US)* = **Federal Trade Commission**
FTSE 100 Index *n abbr* *(= Financial Times Stock Exchange 100 Index) índice bursátil del Financial Times*
fuchsia ['fju:ʃə] *n* fucsia
fuck [fʌk] *(col!)* *vt* joder *(SP)* *(!)*, coger *(LAm)* *(!)* ■ *vi* joder *(SP)* *(!)*, coger *(LAm)* *(!)*; **~ off!** ¡vete a tomar por culo! *(!)*
fuddled ['fʌdld] *adj* *(muddled)* confuso, aturdido; *(col: tipsy)* borracho
fuddy-duddy ['fʌdɪdʌdɪ] *(pej)* *n* carcamal *m*, carroza *m/f* ■ *adj* chapado a la antigua
fudge [fʌdʒ] *n* *(Culin) caramelo blando* ■ *vt* *(issue, problem)* rehuir, esquivar
fuel [fjuəl] *n* *(for heating)* combustible *m*; *(coal)* carbón *m*; *(wood)* leña; *(for engine)* carburante *m* ■ *vt* *(furnace etc)* alimentar; *(aircraft, ship etc)* aprovisionar de combustible
fuel oil *n* fuel oil *m*
fuel pump *n* *(Aut)* surtidor *m* de gasolina
fuel tank *n* depósito de combustible
fug [fʌg] *n* aire *m* viciado
fugitive ['fju:dʒɪtɪv] *n* *(from prison)* fugitivo(-a)
fulfil, fulfill *(US)* [ful'fɪl] *vt* *(function)* desempeñar; *(condition)* cumplir; *(wish, desire)* realizar
fulfilled [ful'fɪld] *adj* *(person)* realizado
fulfilment, fulfillment *(US)* [ful'fɪlmənt] *n* realización *f*; *(of promise)* cumplimiento
full [ful] *adj* lleno; *(fig)* pleno; *(complete)* completo; *(information)* detallado; *(price)* íntegro, sin descuento ■ *adv*: **~ well** perfectamente; **we're ~ up for July** estamos completos para julio; **I'm ~ (up)** estoy lleno;

~ **employment** pleno empleo; ~ **name** nombre *m* completo; **a ~ two hours** dos horas enteras; **at ~ speed** a toda velocidad; **in ~** (*reproduce, quote*) íntegramente; **to write sth in ~** escribir algo por extenso; **to pay in ~** pagar la deuda entera
fullback ['fulbæk] *n* (*Football*) defensa *m*; (*Rugby*) zaguero
full-blooded ['ful'blʌdɪd] *adj* (*vigorous: attack*) vigoroso; (*pure*) puro
full-cream ['ful'kri:m] *adj*: ~ **milk** leche *f* entera
full driving licence *n* (*Brit Aut*) carnet *m* de conducir (*definitivo*); *see also* **L-plates**
full-fledged ['fulflɛdʒd] *adj* (*US*) = **fully-fledged**
full-grown ['ful'grəun] *adj* maduro
full-length ['ful'lɛŋθ] *adj* (*portrait*) de cuerpo entero; (*film*) de largometraje
full moon *n* luna llena, plenilunio
fullness ['fulnɪs] *n* plenitud *f*, amplitud *f*
full-scale ['fulskeɪl] *adj* (*attack, war, search, retreat*) en gran escala; (*plan, model*) de tamaño natural
full stop *n* punto
full-time ['fultaɪm] *adj* (*work*) de tiempo completo ■ *adv*: **to work ~** trabajar a tiempo completo
fully ['fulɪ] *adv* completamente; (*at least*) al menos
fully-fledged ['fulɪ'flɛdʒd], (*US*) **full-fledged** *adj* (*teacher, barrister*) diplomado; (*bird*) con todas sus plumas, capaz de volar; (*fig*) de pleno derecho
fully-paid ['fulɪpeɪd] *adj*: ~ **share** acción *f* liberada
fulsome ['fulsəm] *adj* (*pej: praise, gratitude*) excesivo, exagerado; (*manner*) obsequioso
fumble with ['fʌmbl-] *vt fus* manosear
fume [fju:m] *vi* humear, echar humo
fumes [fju:mz] *npl* humo *sg*, gases *mpl*
fumigate ['fju:mɪgeɪt] *vt* fumigar
fun [fʌn] *n* (*amusement*) diversión *f*; (*joy*) alegría; **to have ~** divertirse; **for ~** por gusto; **to make ~ of** reírse de
function ['fʌŋkʃən] *n* función *f* ■ *vi* funcionar; **to ~ as** hacer (las veces) de, fungir de (*LAm*)
functional ['fʌŋkʃənl] *adj* funcional
function key *n* (*Comput*) tecla de función
fund [fʌnd] *n* fondo; (*reserve*) reserva; **funds** *npl* fondos *mpl*
fundamental [fʌndə'mɛntl] *adj* fundamental ■ *n*; **fundamentals** *npl* fundamentos *mpl*
fundamentalism [fʌndə'mɛntəlɪzəm] *n* fundamentalismo, integrismo
fundamentalist [fʌndə'mɛntəlɪst] *n* fundamentalista *m/f*, integrista *m/f*
fundamentally [fʌndə'mɛntəlɪ] *adv* fundamentalmente
funding ['fʌndɪŋ] *n* financiación *f*
fund-raising ['fʌndreɪzɪŋ] *n* recaudación *f* de fondos
funeral ['fju:nərəl] *n* (*burial*) entierro; (*ceremony*) funerales *mpl*
funeral director *n* director(a) *m(f)* de pompas fúnebres
funeral parlour *n* (*Brit*) funeraria
funeral service *n* misa de cuerpo presente
funereal [fju:'nɪərɪəl] *adj* fúnebre
funfair ['fʌnfɛəʳ] *n* (*Brit*) parque *m* de atracciones; (*travelling*) feria
fungus (*pl* **fungi**) ['fʌŋgəs, -gaɪ] *n* hongo
funicular [fju:'nɪkjuləʳ] *n* (*also*: **funicular railway**) funicular *m*
funky ['fʌŋkɪ] *adj* (*music*) funky; (*col: good*) guay
funnel ['fʌnl] *n* embudo; (*of ship*) chimenea
funnily ['fʌnɪlɪ] *adv* de modo divertido, graciosamente; (*oddly*) de una manera rara; **~ enough** aunque parezca extraño
funny ['fʌnɪ] *adj* gracioso, divertido; (*strange*) curioso, raro
funny bone *n* hueso de la alegría
fun run *n* maratón *m* popular
fur [fə:ʳ] *n* piel *f*; (*Brit: on tongue etc*) sarro
fur coat *n* abrigo de pieles
furious ['fjuərɪəs] *adj* furioso; (*effort, argument*) violento; **to be ~ with sb** estar furioso con algn
furiously ['fjuərɪəslɪ] *adv* con furia
furl [fə:l] *vt* (*sail*) recoger
furlong ['fə:lɔŋ] *n* *octava parte de una milla*
furlough ['fə:ləu] *n* (*US Mil*) permiso
furnace ['fə:nɪs] *n* horno
furnish ['fə:nɪʃ] *vt* amueblar; (*supply*) proporcionar; (*information*) facilitar
furnished ['fə:nɪʃt] *adj*: ~ **flat** *or* (*US*) **apartment** piso amueblado
furnishings ['fə:nɪʃɪŋz] *npl* mobiliario *sg*
furniture ['fə:nɪtʃəʳ] *n* muebles *mpl*; **piece of ~** mueble *m*
furniture polish *n* cera para muebles
furore [fjuə'rɔ:rɪ] *n* (*protests*) escándalo
furrier ['fʌrɪəʳ] *n* peletero(-a)
furrow ['fʌrəu] *n* surco ■ *vt* (*forehead*) arrugar
furry ['fə:rɪ] *adj* peludo; (*toy*) de peluche
further ['fə:ðəʳ] *adj* (*new*) nuevo; (*place*) más lejano ■ *adv* más lejos; (*more*) más; (*moreover*) además ■ *vt* hacer avanzar; **how much ~ is it?** ¿a qué distancia queda?; **~ to your letter of ...** (*Comm*) con referencia a su carta de ...; **to ~ one's interests** fomentar sus intereses
further education *n* educación *f* postescolar

furthermore [fəːðəˈmɔːʳ] *adv* además
furthermost [ˈfəːðəməust] *adj* más lejano
furthest [ˈfəːðɪst] *superlative of* **far**
furtive [ˈfəːtɪv] *adj* furtivo
furtively [ˈfəːtɪvlɪ] *adv* furtivamente, a escondidas
fury [ˈfjuərɪ] *n* furia
fuse, (*US*) **fuze** [fjuːz] *n* fusible *m*; (*for bomb etc*) mecha ▪ *vt* (*metal*) fundir; (*fig*) fusionar ▪ *vi* fundirse; fusionarse; (*Brit Elec*): **to ~ the lights** fundir los plomos; **a ~ has blown** se ha fundido un fusible
fuse box *n* caja de fusibles
fuselage [ˈfjuːzəlɑːʒ] *n* fuselaje *m*
fuse wire *n* hilo fusible
fusillade [fjuːzɪˈleɪd] *n* descarga cerrada; (*fig*) lluvia
fusion [ˈfjuːʒən] *n* fusión *f*
fuss [fʌs] *n* (*noise*) bulla; (*dispute*) lío, jaleo; (*complaining*) protesta ▪ *vi* preocuparse (por pequeñeces) ▪ *vt* (*person*) molestar; **to make a ~** armar jaleo
▸ **fuss over** *vt fus* (*person*) contemplar, mimar
fusspot [ˈfʌspɔt] *n* (*col*) quisquilloso(-a)
fussy [ˈfʌsɪ] *adj* (*person*) quisquilloso; **I'm not ~** (*col*) me da igual
fusty [ˈfʌstɪ] *adj* (*pej*) rancio; **to smell ~** oler a cerrado
futile [ˈfjuːtaɪl] *adj* vano
futility [fjuːˈtɪlɪtɪ] *n* inutilidad *f*
futon [ˈfuːtɔn] *n* futón *m*
future [ˈfjuːtʃəʳ] *adj* (*gen*) futuro; (*coming*) venidero ▪ *n* futuro, porvenir; **in ~** de ahora en adelante
futures [ˈfjuːtʃəz] *npl* (*Comm*) operaciones *fpl* a término, futuros *mpl*
futuristic [fjuːtʃəˈrɪstɪk] *adj* futurista
fuze [fjuːz] (*US*) = **fuse**
fuzzy [ˈfʌzɪ] *adj* (*Phot*) borroso; (*hair*) muy rizado
fwd. *abbr* = **forward**
fwy *abbr* (*US*) = **freeway**
FY *abbr* = **fiscal year**
FYI *abbr* = **for your information**

Gg

G, g [dʒiː] *n* (*letter*) G, g *f*; **G** (*Mus*) sol *m*; **G for George** G de Gerona
G *n abbr* (*Brit Scol*: *mark*: = *good*) N; (*US Cine*: = *general audience*) todos los públicos
g. *abbr* (= *gram(s), gravity*) g
G8 *n abbr* (*Pol*: = *Group of Eight*) G8 *m*
GA *abbr* (*US Post*) = **Georgia**
gab [gæb] *n*: **to have the gift of the ~** (*col*) tener mucha labia
gabble ['gæbl] *vi* hablar atropelladamente; (*gossip*) cotorrear
gaberdine [gæbə'diːn] *n* gabardina
gable ['geɪbl] *n* aguilón *m*
Gabon [gə'bɔn] *n* Gabón *m*
gad about [gæd-] *vi* (*col*) moverse mucho
gadget ['gædʒɪt] *n* aparato
gadgetry ['gædʒɪtrɪ] *n* chismes *mpl*
Gaelic ['geɪlɪk] *adj, n* (*Ling*) gaélico
gaffe [gæf] *n* plancha, patinazo, metedura de pata
gaffer ['gæfəʳ] *n* (*Brit col*) jefe *m*; ((*old*) *man*) vejete *m*
gag [gæg] *n* (*on mouth*) mordaza; (*joke*) chiste *m* ■ *vt* (*prisoner etc*) amordazar ■ *vi* (*choke*) tener arcadas
gaga ['gɑːgɑː] *adj*: **to go ~** (*senile*) chochear; (*ecstatic*) caérsele a algn la baba
gage [geɪdʒ] *n, vt* (*US*) = **gauge**
gaiety ['geɪɪtɪ] *n* alegría
gaily ['geɪlɪ] *adv* alegremente
gain [geɪn] *n* ganancia ■ *vt* ganar ■ *vi* (*watch*) adelantarse; **to ~ by sth** ganar con algo; **to ~ ground** ganar terreno; **to ~ 3 lbs (in weight)** engordar 3 libras
▸ **gain (up)on** *vt fus* alcanzar
gainful ['geɪnful] *adj* (*employment*) remunerado
gainfully ['geɪnfulɪ] *adv*: **to be ~ employed** tener un trabajo remunerado
gait [geɪt] *n* forma de andar, andares *mpl*
gala ['gɑːlə] *n* gala; **swimming ~** certamen *m* de natación
Galapagos Islands [gə'læpəgəs-] *npl*: **the ~** las Islas Galápagos
galaxy ['gæləksɪ] *n* galaxia
gale [geɪl] *n* (*wind*) vendaval *m*; **~ force 10** vendaval de fuerza 10
gall [gɔːl] *n* (*Anat*) bilis *f*, hiel *f*; (*fig*: *impudence*) descaro, caradura ■ *vt* molestar
gal., gall. *abbr* = **gallon; gallons**
gallant ['gælənt] *adj* valeroso; (*towards ladies*) galante
gallantry ['gæləntrɪ] *n* valentía; (*courtesy*) galantería
gall bladder *n* vesícula biliar
galleon ['gælɪən] *n* galeón *m*
gallery ['gælərɪ] *n* (*Theat*) galería; (*for spectators*) tribuna; (*also*: **art gallery**: *state-owned*) pinacoteca *or* museo de arte; (: *private*) galería de arte
galley ['gælɪ] *n* (*ship's kitchen*) cocina; (*ship*) galera
galley proof *n* (*Typ*) prueba de galera, galerada
Gallic ['gælɪk] *adj* galo
gallon ['gæln] *n* galón *m* (= *8 pints; BRIT = 4,546 litros; US = 3,785 litros*)
gallop ['gæləp] *n* galope *m* ■ *vi* galopar; **galloping inflation** inflación *f* galopante
gallows ['gæləuz] *n* horca
gallstone ['gɔːlstəun] *n* cálculo biliar
Gallup poll ['gæləp-] *n* sondeo de opinión
galore [gə'lɔːʳ] *adv* en cantidad, en abundancia
galvanize ['gælvənaɪz] *vt* (*metal*) galvanizar; (*fig*): **to ~ sb into action** mover *or* impulsar a algn a actuar
Gambia ['gæmbɪə] *n* Gambia
gambit ['gæmbɪt] *n* (*fig*): **opening ~** táctica inicial
gamble ['gæmbl] *n* (*risk*) jugada arriesgada; (*bet*) apuesta ■ *vt*: **to ~ on** apostar a; (*fig*) confiar en que ■ *vi* jugar; (*Comm*) especular; **to ~ on the Stock Exchange** jugar a la bolsa
gambler ['gæmbləʳ] *n* jugador(a) *m(f)*
gambling ['gæmblɪŋ] *n* juego

gambol ['gæmbl] *vi* brincar, juguetear
game [geɪm] *n* (*gen*) juego; (*match*) partido; (*of cards*) partida; (*Hunting*) caza ■ *adj* valiente; (*ready*): **to be ~ for anything** estar dispuesto a todo; **games** (*Scol*) deportes *mpl*; **big ~** caza mayor
game bird *n* ave *f* de caza
gamekeeper ['geɪmki:pəʳ] *n* guardabosque *m/f*
gamely ['geɪmlɪ] *adv* con decisión
game reserve *n* coto de caza
games console [geɪmz-] *n* consola de juegos
game show *n* programa *m* concurso *inv*, concurso
gamesmanship ['geɪmzmənʃɪp] *n* (uso de) artimañas *fpl* para ganar
gammon ['gæmən] *n* (*bacon*) tocino ahumado; (*ham*) jamón *m* ahumado
gamut ['gæmət] *n* (*Mus*) gama; **to run the (whole) ~ of emotions** (*fig*) recorrer toda la gama de emociones
gander ['gændəʳ] *n* ganso
gang [gæŋ] *n* pandilla; (*of criminals etc*) banda; (*of kids*) pandilla; (*of colleagues*) peña; (*of workmen*) brigada ■ *vi*: **to ~ up on sb** conchabarse contra algn
Ganges ['gændʒi:z] *n*: **the ~** el Ganges
gangland ['gæŋglænd] *adj*: **~ bosses** cabecillas mafiosos; **~ killings** asesinatos entre bandas
gangling ['gæŋglɪŋ] *adj* larguirucho
gangly ['gæŋglɪ] *adj* desgarbado
gangplank ['gæŋplæŋk] *n* pasarela, plancha
gangrene ['gæŋgri:n] *n* gangrena
gangster ['gæŋstəʳ] *n* gángster *m*
gang warfare *n* guerra entre bandas
gangway ['gæŋweɪ] *n* (*Brit: in theatre, bus etc*) pasillo; (*on ship*) pasarela
gantry ['gæntrɪ] *n* (*for crane, railway signal*) pórtico; (*for rocket*) torre *f* de lanzamiento
GAO *n abbr* (*US: = General Accounting Office*) *tribunal de cuentas*
gaol [dʒeɪl] *n, vt* (*Brit*): **jail**
gap [gæp] *n* hueco; (*in trees, traffic*) claro; (*in market, records*) laguna; (*in time*) intervalo
gape [geɪp] *vi* mirar boquiabierto
gaping ['geɪpɪŋ] *adj* (*hole*) muy abierto
gap year *n* año sabático
garage ['gærɑ:ʒ] *n* garaje *m*
garb [gɑ:b] *n* atuendo
garbage ['gɑ:bɪdʒ] *n* (*US*) basura; (*nonsense*) bobadas *fpl*; (*fig: film, book etc*) basura
garbage can *n* (*US*) cubo *or* balde *m* (*LAm*) *or* bote *m* (*LAm*) de la basura
garbage collector *n* (*US*) basurero(-a)
garbage disposal unit *n* triturador *m* (de basura)
garbage man *n* basurero
garbage truck *n* (*US*) camión *m* de la basura
garbled ['gɑ:bld] *adj* (*account, explanation*) confuso
garden ['gɑ:dn] *n* jardín *m*; **gardens** *npl* (*public*) parque *m*, jardines *mpl*; (*private*) huertos *mpl*
garden centre *n* centro de jardinería
garden city *n* (*Brit*) ciudad *f* jardín
gardener ['gɑ:dnəʳ] *n* jardinero(-a)
gardening ['gɑ:dnɪŋ] *n* jardinería
garden party *n* recepción *f* al aire libre
gargle ['gɑ:gl] *vi* hacer gárgaras, gargarear (*LAm*)
gargoyle ['gɑ:gɔɪl] *n* gárgola
garish ['gɛərɪʃ] *adj* chillón(-ona)
garland ['gɑ:lənd] *n* guirnalda
garlic ['gɑ:lɪk] *n* ajo
garment ['gɑ:mənt] *n* prenda (de vestir)
garner ['gɑ:nəʳ] *vt* hacer acopio de
garnish ['gɑ:nɪʃ] *vt* adornar; (*Culin*) aderezar
garret ['gærɪt] *n* desván *m*, buhardilla
garrison ['gærɪsn] *n* guarnición *f* ■ *vt* guarnecer
garrulous ['gærjuləs] *adj* charlatán(-ana)
garter ['gɑ:təʳ] *n* (*US*) liga
garter belt *n* (*US*) liguero, portaligas *m inv*
gas [gæs] *n* gas *m*; (*US: gasoline*) gasolina ■ *vt* asfixiar con gas; **Calor ~®** (gas *m*) butano
gas chamber *n* cámara de gas
Gascony ['gæskənɪ] *n* Gascuña
gas cooker *n* (*Brit*) cocina de gas
gas cylinder *n* bombona de gas
gaseous ['gæsɪəs] *adj* gaseoso
gas fire *n* estufa de gas
gas-fired ['gæsfaɪəd] *adj* de gas
gash [gæʃ] *n* brecha, raja; (*from knife*) cuchillada ■ *vt* rajar; (*with knife*) acuchillar
gasket ['gæskɪt] *n* (*Aut*) junta
gas mask *n* careta antigás
gas meter *n* contador *m* de gas
gasoline ['gæsəli:n] *n* (*US*) gasolina
gasp [gɑ:sp] *n* grito sofocado ■ *vi* (*pant*) jadear
▸ **gasp out** *vt* (*say*) decir jadeando
gas pedal *n* (*esp US*) acelerador *m*
gas ring *n* hornillo de gas
gas station *n* (*US*) gasolinera
gas stove *n* cocina de gas
gassy ['gæsɪ] *adj* con mucho gas
gas tank *n* (*US Aut*) depósito (de gasolina)
gas tap *n* llave *f* del gas
gastric ['gæstrɪk] *adj* gástrico
gastric ulcer *n* úlcera gástrica
gastroenteritis ['gæstrəuɛntə'raɪtɪs] *n* gastroenteritis *f*
gasworks ['gæswə:ks] *nsg or npl* fábrica de gas

gate [geɪt] *n (also at airport)* puerta; *(Rail: at level crossing)* barrera; *(metal)* verja
gâteau (*pl* **gâteaux**) ['gætəu, z] *n* tarta
gatecrash ['geɪtkræʃ] *vt* colarse en
gatecrasher ['geɪtkræʃə'] *n* intruso(-a)
gatehouse ['geɪthaus] *n* casa del guarda
gateway ['geɪtweɪ] *n* puerta
gather ['gæðə'] *vt (flowers, fruit)* coger *(SP)*, recoger *(LAm)*; *(assemble)* reunir; *(pick up)* recoger; *(Sewing)* fruncir; *(understand)* sacar en consecuencia ■ *vi (assemble)* reunirse; *(dust)* acumularse; *(clouds)* cerrarse; **to ~ speed** ganar velocidad; **to ~ (from/that)** deducir (por/que); **as far as I can ~** por lo que tengo entendido
gathering ['gæðərɪŋ] *n* reunión *f*, asamblea
GATT [gæt] *n abbr (= General Agreement on Tariffs and Trade)* GATT *m*
gauche [gəuʃ] *adj* torpe
gaudy ['gɔ:dɪ] *adj* chillón(-ona)
gauge, gage *(US)* [geɪdʒ] *n* calibre *m*; *(Rail)* ancho de vía, entrevía; *(instrument)* indicador *m* ■ *vt* medir; *(fig: sb's capabilities, character)* juzgar, calibrar; **petrol ~** indicador *m* (del nivel) de gasolina; **to ~ the right moment** elegir el momento (oportuno)
gaunt [gɔ:nt] *adj* descarnado; *(fig)* adusto
gauntlet ['gɔ:ntlɪt] *n (fig)*: **to run the ~ of sth** exponerse a algo; **to throw down the ~** arrojar el guante
gauze [gɔ:z] *n* gasa
gave [geɪv] *pt of* **give**
gawk [gɔ:k] *vi* mirar pasmado
gawky ['gɔ:kɪ] *adj* desgarbado
gay [geɪ] *adj (colour, person)* alegre; *(homosexual)* gay
gaze [geɪz] *n* mirada fija ■ *vi*: **to ~ at sth** mirar algo fijamente
gazelle [gə'zɛl] *n* gacela
gazette [gə'zɛt] *n (newspaper)* gaceta; *(official publication)* boletín *m* oficial
gazetteer [gæzə'tɪə'] *n* índice geográfico
gazump [gə'zʌmp] *vti (Brit) echarse atrás en la venta ya acordada de una casa por haber una oferta más alta*
GB *abbr (= Great Britain)* GB
GBH *n abbr (Brit Law: col)* = **grievous bodily harm**
GC *n abbr (Brit: = George Cross) distinción honorífica*
GCE *n abbr (Brit: = General Certificate of Education)* ≈ certificado de bachillerato
GCHQ *n abbr (Brit: = Government Communications Headquarters) centro de intercepción de las telecomunicaciones internacionales*
GCSE *n abbr (Brit: = General Certificate of Secondary Education) certificado del último ciclo de la enseñanza secundaria obligatoria*

Gdns. *abbr (= gardens)* jdns
GDP *n abbr (= gross domestic product)* PIB *m*
GDR *n abbr (= German Democratic Republic)* RDA *f*
gear [gɪə'] *n* equipo; *(Tech)* engranaje *m*; *(Aut)* velocidad *f*, marcha ■ *vt (fig: adapt)*: **to ~ sth to** adaptar *or* ajustar algo a; **top** *or (US)* **high/low ~** cuarta/primera; **in ~** con la marcha metida; **our service is geared to meet the needs of the disabled** nuestro servicio va enfocado a responder a las necesidades de los minusválidos
▸ **gear up** *vi* prepararse
gear box *n* caja de cambios
gear lever, gear shift *(US) n* palanca de cambio
gear wheel *n* rueda dentada
GED *n abbr (US Scol)* = **general educational development**
geese [gi:s] *npl of* **goose**
geezer ['gi:zə'] *n (Brit col)* tipo, maromo *(SP)*
Geiger counter ['gaɪgə-] *n* contador *m* Geiger
gel [dʒɛl] *n* gel *m*
gelatin, gelatine ['dʒɛləti:n] *n* gelatina
gelignite ['dʒɛlɪgnaɪt] *n* gelignita
gem [dʒɛm] *n* gema, piedra preciosa; *(fig)* joya
Gemini ['dʒɛmɪnaɪ] *n* Géminis *m*
gen [dʒɛn] *n (Brit col)*: **to give sb the ~ on sth** poner a algn al tanto de algo
Gen. *abbr (Mil: = General)* Gen., Gral
gen. *abbr (= general)* grl.; = **generally**
gender ['dʒɛndə'] *n* género
gene [dʒi:n] *n* gen(e) *m*
genealogy [dʒi:nɪ'ælədʒɪ] *n* genealogía
general ['dʒɛnərl] *n* general *m* ■ *adj* general; **in ~** en general; **~ audit** auditoría general; **the ~ public** el gran público
general anaesthetic, general anesthetic *(US) n* anestesia general
general delivery *n (US)* lista de correos
general election *n* elecciones *fpl* generales
generalization [dʒɛnrəlaɪ'zeɪʃən] *n* generalización *f*
generalize ['dʒɛnrəlaɪz] *vi* generalizar
generally ['dʒɛnrəlɪ] *adv* generalmente, en general
general manager *n* director(a) *m(f)* general
general practitioner *n* médico(-a) de medicina general
general strike *n* huelga general
generate ['dʒɛnəreɪt] *vt* generar
generation [dʒɛnə'reɪʃən] *n (of electricity etc)* generación *f*
generator ['dʒɛnəreɪtə'] *n* generador *m*
generic [dʒɪ'nɛrɪk] *adj* genérico
generosity [dʒɛnə'rɔsɪtɪ] *n* generosidad *f*
generous ['dʒɛnərəs] *adj* generoso; *(copious)* abundante

generously ['dʒɛnərəslɪ] *adv* generosamente; abundantemente
genesis ['dʒɛnɪsɪs] *n* génesis *f*
genetic [dʒɪ'nɛtɪk] *adj* genético
genetically modified organism [dʒɪ'nɛtɪkəlɪ] *n* organismo genéticamente modificado, organismo transgénico
genetic engineering *n* ingeniería genética
genetic fingerprinting [-'fɪŋgəprɪntɪŋ] *n* identificación *f* genética
genetics [dʒɪ'nɛtɪks] *n* genética
Geneva [dʒɪ'ni:və] *n* Ginebra
genial ['dʒi:nɪəl] *adj* afable
genitals ['dʒɛnɪtlz] *npl* (órganos *mpl*) genitales *mpl*
genitive ['dʒɛnɪtɪv] *n* genitivo
genius ['dʒi:nɪəs] *n* genio
Genoa ['dʒɛnəuə] *n* Génova
genocide ['dʒɛnəusaɪd] *n* genocidio
gent [dʒɛnt] *n abbr* (*Brit col*) = **gentleman**
genteel [dʒɛn'ti:l] *adj* fino, distinguido
gentle ['dʒɛntl] *adj* (*sweet*) dulce; (*touch etc*) ligero, suave
gentleman ['dʒɛntlmən] *n* señor *m*; (*well-bred man*) caballero; **~'s agreement** acuerdo entre caballeros
gentlemanly ['dʒɛntlmənlɪ] *adj* caballeroso
gentleness ['dʒɛntlnɪs] *n* dulzura; (*of touch*) suavidad *f*
gently ['dʒɛntlɪ] *adv* suavemente
gentrification [dʒɛntrɪfɪ'keɪʃən] *n* aburguesamiento
gentry ['dʒɛntrɪ] *npl* pequeña nobleza *sg*
gents [dʒɛnts] *n* servicios *mpl* (de caballeros)
genuine ['dʒɛnjuɪn] *adj* auténtico; (*person*) sincero
genuinely ['dʒɛnjuɪnlɪ] *adv* sinceramente
geographer [dʒɪ'ɔgrəfə^r] *n* geógrafo(-a)
geographic [dʒɪə'græfɪk], **geographical** [dʒɪə'græfɪkl] *adj* geográfico
geography [dʒɪ'ɔgrəfɪ] *n* geografía
geological [dʒɪə'lɔdʒɪkl] *adj* geológico
geologist [dʒɪ'ɔlədʒɪst] *n* geólogo(-a)
geology [dʒɪ'ɔlədʒɪ] *n* geología
geometric [dʒɪə'mɛtrɪk], **geometrical** [dʒɪə'mɛtrɪkl] *adj* geométrico
geometry [dʒɪ'ɔmətrɪ] *n* geometría
Geordie ['dʒɔ:dɪ] *n* habitante *m/f* de Tyneside
Georgia ['dʒɔ:dʒə] *n* Georgia
Georgian ['dʒɔ:dʒən] *adj* georgiano
■ *n* georgiano(-a); (*Ling*) georgiano
geranium [dʒɪ'reɪnjəm] *n* geranio
gerbil ['dʒerbl] *n* gerbo
geriatric [dʒɛrɪ'ætrɪk] *adj, n* geriátrico(-a) *m(f)*
germ [dʒə:m] *n* (*microbe*) microbio, bacteria; (*seed*) germen *m*
German ['dʒə:mən] *adj* alemán(-ana)
■ *n* alemán(-ana) *m(f)*; (*Ling*) alemán *m*
German Democratic Republic *n* República Democrática Alemana
germane [dʒə:'meɪn] *adj*: **~ (to)** pertinente (a)
German measles *n* rubeola, rubéola
German Shepherd *n* (*dog*) pastor *m* alemán
Germany ['dʒə:mənɪ] *n* Alemania; **East/West ~** Alemania Oriental *or* Democrática/Occidental *or* Federal
germination [dʒə:mɪ'neɪʃən] *n* germinación *f*
germ warfare *n* guerra bacteriológica
gesticulate [dʒɛs'tɪkjuleɪt] *vi* gesticular
gesticulation [dʒɛstɪkju'leɪʃən] *n* gesticulación *f*
gesture ['dʒɛstjə^r] *n* gesto; **as a ~ of friendship** en señal de amistad

KEYWORD

get [gɛt] (*pt, pp* **got**) (*US*) (*pp* **gotten**) *vi*
1 (*become, be*) ponerse, volverse; **to get old/tired** envejecer/cansarse; **to get drunk** emborracharse; **to get dirty** ensuciarse; **to get ready/washed** prepararse/lavarse; **to get married** casarse; **when do I get paid?** ¿cuándo me pagan *or* se me paga?; **it's getting late** se está haciendo tarde
2 (*go*): **to get to/from** llegar a/de; **to get home** llegar a casa; **he got under the fence** pasó por debajo de la barrera
3 (*begin*) empezar a; **to get to know sb** (llegar a) conocer a algn; **I'm getting to like him** me está empezando a gustar; **let's get going** *or* **started** ¡vamos (a empezar)!
4 (*modal aux vb*): **you've got to do it** tienes que hacerlo
■ *vt* **1**: **to get sth done** (*finish*) hacer algo; (*have done*) mandar hacer algo; **to get one's hair cut** cortarse el pelo; **to get the car going** *or* **to go** arrancar el coche; **to get sb to do sth** conseguir *or* hacer que algn haga algo; **to get sth/sb ready** preparar algo/a algn
2 (*obtain: money, permission, results*) conseguir; (*find: job, flat*) encontrar; (*fetch: person, doctor*) buscar; (*object*) ir a buscar, traer; **to get sth for sb** conseguir algo para algn; **get me Mr Jones, please** (*Tel*) póngame *or* (*LAm*) comuníqueme con el Sr. Jones, por favor; **can I get you a drink?** ¿quieres algo de beber?
3 (*receive: present, letter*) recibir; (*acquire: reputation*) alcanzar; (*: prize*) ganar; **what did you get for your birthday?** ¿qué te regalaron por tu cumpleaños?; **how much did you get for the painting?** ¿cuánto sacaste por el cuadro?

4 (*catch*) coger (*SP*), agarrar (*LAm*); (*hit: target etc*) dar en; **to get sb by the arm/throat** coger *or* agarrar a algn por el brazo/cuello; **get him!** ¡cógelo! (*SP*), ¡atrápalo! (*LAm*); **the bullet got him in the leg** la bala le dio en la pierna
5 (*take, move*) llevar; **to get sth to sb** hacer llegar algo a algn; **do you think we'll get it through the door?** ¿crees que lo podremos meter por la puerta?
6 (*catch, take: plane, bus etc*) coger (*SP*), tomar (*LAm*); **where do I get the train for Birmingham?** ¿dónde se coge *or* se toma el tren para Birmingham?
7 (*understand*) entender; (*hear*) oír; **I've got it!** ¡ya lo tengo!, ¡eureka!; **I don't get your meaning** no te entiendo; **I'm sorry, I didn't get your name** lo siento, no me he enterado de tu nombre
8 (*have, possess*): **to have got** tener
9 (*col: annoy*) molestar; (*: thrill*) chiflar
▸ **get about** *vi* salir mucho; (*news*) divulgarse
▸ **get across** *vt* (*message, meaning*) lograr comunicar
▪ *vi*: **to get across to sb** hacer que algn comprenda
▸ **get along** *vi* (*agree*) llevarse bien; (*depart*) marcharse; (*manage*) = **get by**
▸ **get at** *vt fus* (*attack*) meterse con; (*reach*) alcanzar; (*the truth*) descubrir; **what are you getting at?** ¿qué insinúas?
▸ **get away** *vi* marcharse; (*escape*) escaparse
▸ **get away with** *vt fus* hacer impunemente
▸ **get back** *vi* (*return*) volver
▪ *vt* recobrar
▸ **get back at** *vt fus* (*col*): **to get back at sb (for sth)** vengarse de algn (por algo)
▸ **get by** *vi* (*pass*) (lograr) pasar; (*manage*) arreglárselas; **I can get by in Dutch** me defiendo en holandés
▸ **get down** *vi* bajar(se)
▪ *vt fus* bajar
▪ *vt* bajar; (*depress*) deprimir
▸ **get down to** *vt fus* (*work*) ponerse a
▸ **get in** *vi* entrar; (*train*) llegar; (*arrive home*) volver a casa, regresar; (*political party*) salir
▪ *vt* (*bring in: harvest*) recoger; (*: coal, shopping, supplies*) comprar, traer; (*insert*) meter
▸ **get into** *vt fus* entrar en; (*vehicle*) subir a; **to get into a rage** enfadarse
▸ **get off** *vi* (*from train etc*) bajar(se); (*depart: person, car*) marcharse
▪ *vt* (*remove*) quitar; (*send off*) mandar; (*have as leave: day, time*) tener libre
▪ *vt fus* (*train, bus*) bajar(se) de; **to get off to a good start** (*fig*) empezar muy bien *or* con buen pie
▸ **get on** *vi* (*at exam etc*): **how are you getting on?** ¿cómo te va?; (*agree*): **to get on (with)** llevarse bien (con)
▪ *vt fus* subir(se) a
▸ **get on to** *vt fus* (*deal with*) ocuparse de; (*col: contact on phone etc*) hablar con
▸ **get out** *vi* salir; (*of vehicle*) bajar(se); (*news*) saberse
▪ *vt* sacar
▸ **get out of** *vt fus* salir de; (*duty etc*) escaparse de; (*gain from: pleasure, benefit*) sacar de
▸ **get over** *vt fus* (*illness*) recobrarse de
▸ **get round** *vt fus* rodear; (*fig: person*) engatusar a
▪ *vi*: **to get round to doing sth** encontrar tiempo para hacer algo
▸ **get through** *vt fus* (*finish*) acabar
▪ *vi* (*Tel*) (lograr) comunicar
▸ **get through to** *vt fus* (*Tel*) comunicar con
▸ **get together** *vi* reunirse
▪ *vt* reunir, juntar
▸ **get up** *vi* (*rise*) levantarse
▪ *vt fus* subir; **to get up enthusiasm for sth** cobrar entusiasmo por algo
▸ **get up to** *vt fus* (*reach*) llegar a; (*prank*) hacer

getaway ['gɛtəweɪ] *n* fuga
getaway car *n*: **the thieves' ~** el coche en que huyeron los ladrones
get-together ['gɛttəgɛðəʳ] *n* reunión *f*; (*party*) fiesta
get-up ['gɛtʌp] *n* (*Brit col: outfit*) atavío, atuendo
get-well card [gɛt'wɛl-] *n* *tarjeta en la que se desea a un enfermo que se mejore*
geyser ['gi:zəʳ] *n* (*water heater*) calentador *m* de agua; (*Geo*) géiser *m*
Ghana ['gɑ:nə] *n* Ghana
Ghanaian [gɑ:'neɪən] *adj, n* ghanés(-esa) *m(f)*
ghastly ['gɑ:stlɪ] *adj* horrible; (*pale*) pálido
gherkin ['gə:kɪn] *n* pepinillo
ghetto ['gɛtəu] *n* gueto
ghetto blaster [-'blɑ:stəʳ] *n* radiocas(s)et(t)e *m* portátil (*de gran tamaño*)
ghost [gəust] *n* fantasma *m* ▪ *vt* (*book*) escribir por otro
ghostly ['gəustlɪ] *adj* fantasmal
ghost story *n* cuento de fantasmas
ghostwriter ['gəustraɪtəʳ] *n* negro(-a)
ghoul [gu:l] *n* espíritu *m* necrófago
GHQ *n abbr* (*Mil: = general headquarters*) cuartel *m* general
GI *n abbr* (*US col: = government issue*) *soldado del ejército norteamericano*
giant ['dʒaɪənt] *n* gigante *m/f* ▪ *adj* gigantesco, gigante; **~ (size) packet** paquete *m* (de tamaño) gigante *or* familiar

giant killer *n* (*Sport*) matagigantes *m inv*
gibber ['dʒɪbəʳ] *vi* farfullar
gibberish ['dʒɪbərɪʃ] *n* galimatías *m*
gibe [dʒaɪb] *n* pulla
giblets ['dʒɪblɪts] *npl* menudillos *mpl*
Gibraltar [dʒɪ'brɔːltəʳ] *n* Gibraltar *m*
giddiness ['gɪdɪnɪs] *n* mareo
giddy ['gɪdɪ] *adj* (*dizzy*) mareado; (*height, speed*) vertiginoso; **it makes me ~** me marea; **I feel ~** me siento mareado
gift [gɪft] *n* (*gen*) regalo; (*Comm*: *also*: **free gift**) obsequio; (*ability*) don *m*; **to have a ~ for sth** tener dotes para algo
gifted ['gɪftɪd] *adj* dotado
gift token, gift voucher *n* vale-regalo *m*
gig [gɪg] *n* (*col*: *concert*) actuación *f*
gigabyte ['dʒɪgəbaɪt] *n* gigabyte *m*
gigantic [dʒaɪ'gæntɪk] *adj* gigantesco
giggle ['gɪgl] *vi* reírse tontamente ▪ *n* risilla
GIGO ['gaɪgəu] *abbr* (*Comput*: *col*) = **garbage in, garbage out**
gill [dʒɪl] *n* (*measure*) *0.25 pints* (*BRIT = 0,148 litros; US = 0,118 litros.*)
gills [gɪlz] *npl* (*of fish*) branquias *fpl*, agallas *fpl*
gilt [gɪlt] *adj, n* dorado
gilt-edged ['gɪltɛdʒd] *adj* (*Comm*: *stocks, securities*) de máxima garantía
gimlet ['gɪmlɪt] *n* barrena de mano
gimmick ['gɪmɪk] *n* reclamo; **sales ~** reclamo promocional
gimmicky ['gɪmɪkɪ] *adj* de reclamo
gin [dʒɪn] *n* (*liquor*) ginebra
ginger ['dʒɪndʒəʳ] *n* jengibre *m*
ginger ale *n* ginger ale *m*
ginger beer *n* refresco *m* de jengibre
gingerbread ['dʒɪndʒəbrɛd] *n* pan *m* de jengibre
ginger-haired [dʒɪndʒə'hɛəd] *adj* pelirrojo
gingerly ['dʒɪndʒəlɪ] *adv* con pies de plomo
ginseng ['dʒɪnsɛŋ] *n* ginseng *m*
gipsy ['dʒɪpsɪ] *n* gitano(-a)
giraffe [dʒɪ'rɑːf] *n* jirafa
girder ['gəːdəʳ] *n* viga
girdle ['gəːdl] *n* (*corset*) faja ▪ *vt* ceñir
girl [gəːl] *n* (*small*) niña; (*young woman*) chica, joven *f*, muchacha; **an English ~** una (chica) inglesa
girlfriend ['gəːlfrɛnd] *n* (*of girl*) amiga; (*of boy*) novia
Girl Guide *n* exploradora
girlish ['gəːlɪʃ] *adj* de niña
Girl Scout *n* (*US*) = **Girl Guide**
giro ['dʒaɪrəu] *n* (*Brit*: *bank giro*) giro bancario; (*post office giro*) giro postal
girth [gəːθ] *n* circunferencia; (*of saddle*) cincha
gist [dʒɪst] *n* lo esencial
give [gɪv] (*pt* **gave**, *pp* **given**) [geɪv, 'gɪvn] *vt* dar; (*deliver*) entregar; (*as gift*) regalar ▪ *vi* (*break*) romperse; (*stretch*: *fabric*) dar de sí; **to ~ sb sth, ~ sth to sb** dar algo a algn; **how much did you ~ for it?** ¿cuánto pagaste por él?; **12 o'clock, ~ or take a few minutes** más o menos las doce; **~ them my regards** dales recuerdos de mi parte; **I can ~ you 10 minutes** le puedo conceder 10 minutos; **to ~ way** (*Brit Aut*) ceder el paso; **to ~ way to despair** ceder a la desesperación
▸ **give away** *vt* (*give free*) regalar; (*betray*) traicionar; (*disclose*) revelar
▸ **give back** *vt* devolver
▸ **give in** *vi* ceder ▪ *vt* entregar
▸ **give off** *vt* despedir
▸ **give out** *vt* distribuir ▪ *vi* (*be exhausted*: *supplies*) agotarse; (*fail*: *engine*) averiarse; (*strength*) fallar
▸ **give up** *vi* rendirse, darse por vencido ▪ *vt* renunciar a; **to ~ up smoking** dejar de fumar; **to ~ o.s. up** entregarse
give-and-take ['gɪvənd'teɪk] *n* (*col*) toma y daca *m*
giveaway ['gɪvəweɪ] *n* (*col*): **her expression was a ~** su expresión la delataba; **the exam was a ~!** ¡el examen estaba tirado! ▪ *cpd*: **~ prices** precios *mpl* de regalo
given ['gɪvn] *pp of* **give** ▪ *adj* (*fixed*: *time, amount*) determinado ▪ *conj*: **~ (that) ...** dado (que) ...; **~ the circumstances ...** dadas las circunstancias ...
glacial ['gleɪsɪəl] *adj* glacial
glacier ['glæsɪəʳ] *n* glaciar *m*
glad [glæd] *adj* contento; **to be ~ about sth/that** alegrarse de algo/de que; **I was ~ of his help** agradecí su ayuda
gladden ['glædn] *vt* alegrar
glade [gleɪd] *n* claro
gladiator ['glædɪeɪtəʳ] *n* gladiador *m*
gladioli [glædɪ'əulaɪ] *npl* gladiolos *mpl*
gladly ['glædlɪ] *adv* con mucho gusto
glamorous ['glæmərəs] *adj* con encanto, atractivo
glamour ['glæməʳ] *n* encanto, atractivo
glance [glɑːns] *n* ojeada, mirada ▪ *vi*: **to ~ at** echar una ojeada a
▸ **glance off** *vt fus* (*bullet*) rebotar en
glancing ['glɑːnsɪŋ] *adj* (*blow*) oblicuo
gland [glænd] *n* glándula
glandular ['glændjuləʳ] *adj*: **~ fever** mononucleosis *f* infecciosa
glare [glɛəʳ] *n* deslumbramiento, brillo ▪ *vi* deslumbrar; **to ~ at** mirar con odio
glaring ['glɛərɪŋ] *adj* (*mistake*) manifiesto
glass [glɑːs] *n* vidrio, cristal *m*; (*for drinking*) vaso; (*with stem*) copa; (*also*: **looking glass**) espejo

glass-blowing ['glɑːsbləuɪŋ] *n* soplado de vidrio
glass ceiling *n* (*fig*) techo *or* barrera invisible (*que impide ascender profesionalmente a las mujeres o miembros de minorías étnicas*)
glasses ['glɑːsəs] *npl* gafas *fpl*, anteojos *mpl* (*LAm*)
glass fibre, (*US*) **glass fiber** *n* fibra de vidrio
glasshouse ['glɑːshaus] *n* invernadero
glassware ['glɑːswɛəʳ] *n* cristalería
glassy ['glɑːsɪ] *adj* (*eyes*) vidrioso
Glaswegian [glæs'wiːdʒən] *adj* de Glasgow ■ *n* nativo(-a) *or* habitante *m(f)* de Glasgow
glaze [gleɪz] *vt* (*window*) acristalar; (*pottery*) vidriar; (*Culin*) glasear ■ *n* barniz *m*; (*Culin*) glaseado
glazed [gleɪzd] *adj* (*eye*) vidrioso; (*pottery*) vidriado
glazier ['gleɪzɪəʳ] *n* vidriero(-a)
gleam [gliːm] *n* destello ■ *vi* relucir; **a ~ of hope** un rayo de esperanza
gleaming ['gliːmɪŋ] *adj* reluciente
glean [gliːn] *vt* (*gather: information*) recoger
glee [gliː] *n* alegría, regocijo
gleeful ['gliːful] *adj* alegre
glen [glɛn] *n* cañada
glib [glɪb] *adj* (*person*) de mucha labia; (*comment*) fácil
glibly ['glɪblɪ] *adv* (*explain*) con mucha labia
glide [glaɪd] *vi* deslizarse; (*Aviat: bird*) planear
glider ['glaɪdəʳ] *n* (*Aviat*) planeador *m*
gliding ['glaɪdɪŋ] *n* (*Aviat*) vuelo sin motor
glimmer ['glɪməʳ] *n* luz *f* tenue
glimpse [glɪmps] *n* vislumbre *m* ■ *vt* vislumbrar, entrever; **to catch a ~ of** vislumbrar
glint [glɪnt] *n* destello; (*in the eye*) chispa ■ *vi* centellear
glisten ['glɪsn] *vi* relucir, brillar
glitter ['glɪtəʳ] *vi* relucir, brillar ■ *n* brillo
glittering ['glɪtərɪŋ] *adj* reluciente, brillante
glitz [glɪts] *n* (*col*) vistosidad *f*
gloat [gləut] *vi*: **to ~ over** regodearse con
global ['gləubl] *adj* (*world-wide*) mundial; (*comprehensive*) global
globalization ['gləubəlaɪzeɪʃən] *n* globalización *f*, mundialización *f*
global warming [-'wɔːmɪŋ] *n* (re)calentamiento global *or* de la tierra
globe [gləub] *n* globo, esfera; (*model*) bola del mundo; globo terráqueo
globetrotter ['gləubtrɔtəʳ] *n* trotamundos *m inv*
globule ['glɔbjuːl] *n* glóbulo
gloom [gluːm] *n* penumbra; (*sadness*) desaliento, melancolía
gloomily ['gluːmɪlɪ] *adv* tristemente; de modo pesimista
gloomy ['gluːmɪ] *adj* (*dark*) oscuro; (*sad*) triste; (*pessimistic*) pesimista; **to feel ~** sentirse pesimista
glorification [glɔːrɪfɪ'keɪʃən] *n* glorificación *f*
glorify ['glɔːrɪfaɪ] *vt* glorificar
glorious ['glɔːrɪəs] *adj* glorioso; (*weather, sunshine*) espléndido
glory ['glɔːrɪ] *n* gloria
Glos *abbr* (*Brit*) = **Gloucestershire**
gloss [glɔs] *n* (*shine*) brillo; (*also:* **gloss paint**) (pintura) esmalte *m*
▸ **gloss over** *vt fus* restar importancia a; (*omit*) pasar por alto
glossary ['glɔsərɪ] *n* glosario
glossy ['glɔsɪ] *adj* (*hair*) brillante; (*photograph*) con brillo; (*magazine*) de papel satinado *or* cuché
glove [glʌv] *n* guante *m*
glove compartment *n* (*Aut*) guantera
glow [gləu] *vi* (*shine*) brillar ■ *n* brillo
glower ['glauəʳ] *vi*: **to ~ at** mirar con ceño
glowing ['gləuɪŋ] *adj* (*fire*) vivo; (*complexion*) encendido; (*fig: report, description*) entusiasta
glow-worm ['gləuwəːm] *n* luciérnaga
glucose ['gluːkəus] *n* glucosa
glue [gluː] *n* pegamento, cemento (*LAm*) ■ *vt* pegar
glue-sniffing ['gluːsnɪfɪŋ] *n* inhalación *f* de pegamento *or* (*LAm*) cemento
glum [glʌm] *adj* (*mood*) abatido; (*person, tone*) melancólico
glut [glʌt] *n* superabundancia
glutinous ['gluːtɪnəs] *adj* glutinoso, pegajoso
glutton ['glʌtn] *n* glotón(-ona) *m(f)*; **~ for punishment** masoquista *m/f*
gluttony ['glʌtənɪ] *n* gula, glotonería
glycerin, glycerine ['glɪsəriːn] *n* glicerina
GM *adj abbr* (= *genetically-modified*) transgénico
gm *abbr* (= *gram*) g
GMAT *n abbr* (*US:* = *Graduate Management Admissions Test*) *examen de admisión al segundo ciclo de la enseñanza superior*
GMB *n abbr* (*Brit*) = **General, Municipal, and Boilermakers (Union)**
GMo *n abbr* (= *genetically modified organism*) organismo transgénico, OGM *m*
GMT *abbr* (= *Greenwich Mean Time*) GMT
gnarled [nɑːld] *adj* nudoso
gnash [næʃ] *vt*: **to ~ one's teeth** hacer rechinar los dientes
gnat [næt] *n* mosquito
gnaw [nɔː] *vt* roer
gnome [nəum] *n* gnomo
GNP *n abbr* (= *gross national product*) PNB *m*
GNVQ *n abbr* (*Brit:* = *general national vocational qualification*) *título general de formación profesional*

go [gəu] *vb* (*pt* **went**, *pp* **gone**) ■ *vi* ir; (*travel*) viajar; (*depart*) irse, marcharse; (*work*) funcionar, marchar; (*be sold*) venderse; (*time*) pasar; (*become*) ponerse; (*break etc*) estropearse, romperse; (*fit, suit*): **to go with** hacer juego con ■ *n* (*pl* **goes**); **to have a go (at)** probar suerte (con); **to be on the go** no parar; **whose go is it?** ¿a quién le toca?; **to go by car/on foot** ir en coche/a pie; **he's going to do it** va a hacerlo; **to go for a walk** ir a dar un paseo; **to go dancing** ir a bailar; **to go looking for sth/sb** ir a buscar algo/a algn; **to make sth go, get sth going** poner algo en marcha; **my voice has gone** he perdido la voz; **the cake is all gone** se acabó la tarta; **the money will go towards our holiday** el dinero es para (ayuda de) nuestras vacaciones; **how did it go?** ¿qué tal salió *or* resultó?, ¿cómo ha ido?; **the meeting went well** la reunión salió bien; **to go and see sb** ir a ver a algn; **to go to sleep** dormirse; **I'll take whatever is going** acepto lo que haya; **... to go** (*US: food*) ... para llevar; **to go round the back** pasar por detrás

▸ **go about** *vi* (*rumour*) propagarse; (*also:* **go round**: *wander about*) andar (de un sitio para otro) ■ *vt fus*: **how do I go about this?** ¿cómo me las arreglo para hacer esto?; **to go about one's business** ocuparse de sus asuntos

▸ **go after** *vt fus* (*pursue*) perseguir; (*job, record etc*) andar tras

▸ **go against** *vt fus* (*be unfavourable to: results*) ir en contra de; (*be contrary to: principles*) ser contrario a

▸ **go ahead** *vi* seguir adelante

▸ **go along** *vi* ir; **as you go along** sobre la marcha ■ *vt fus* bordear

▸ **go along with** *vt fus* (*accompany*) acompañar; (*agree with: idea*) estar de acuerdo con

▸ **go around** *vi* = **go round**

▸ **go away** *vi* irse, marcharse

▸ **go back** *vi* volver

▸ **go back on** *vt fus* (*promise*) faltar a

▸ **go by** *vi* (*years, time*) pasar ■ *vt fus* guiarse por

▸ **go down** *vi* bajar; (*ship*) hundirse; (*sun*) ponerse ■ *vt fus* bajar por; **that should go down well with him** eso le va a gustar; **he's gone down with flu** ha cogido la gripe

▸ **go for** *vt fus* (*fetch*) ir por; (*like*) gustar; (*attack*) atacar

▸ **go in** *vi* entrar

▸ **go in for** *vt fus* (*competition*) presentarse a

▸ **go into** *vt fus* entrar en; (*investigate*) investigar; (*embark on*) dedicarse a

▸ **go off** *vi* irse, marcharse; (*food*) pasarse; (*lights etc*) apagarse; (*explode*) estallar; (*event*) realizarse ■ *vt fus* perder el interés por; **the party went off well** la fiesta salió bien

▸ **go on** *vi* (*continue*) seguir, continuar; (*lights*) encenderse; (*happen*) pasar, ocurrir; (*be guided by: evidence etc*) partir de; **to go on doing sth** seguir haciendo algo; **what's going on here?** ¿qué pasa aquí?

▸ **go on at** *vt fus* (*nag*) soltarle el rollo a

▸ **go out** *vi* salir; (*fire, light*) apagarse; (*ebb: tide*) bajar, menguar; **to go out with sb** salir con algn

▸ **go over** *vi* (*ship*) zozobrar ■ *vt fus* (*check*) revisar; **to go over sth in one's mind** repasar algo mentalmente

▸ **go round** *vi* (*circulate: news, rumour*) correr; (*suffice*) alcanzar, bastar; (*revolve*) girar, dar vueltas; (*visit*): **to go round (to sb's)** pasar a ver (a algn); **to go round (by)** (*make a detour*) dar la vuelta (por)

▸ **go through** *vt fus* (*town etc*) atravesar; (*search through*) revisar; (*perform: ceremony*) realizar; (*examine: list, book*) repasar

▸ **go through with** *vt fus* (*plan, crime*) llevar a cabo; **I couldn't go through with it** no pude llevarlo a cabo

▸ **go together** *vi* entenderse

▸ **go under** *vi* (*sink: ship, person*) hundirse; (*fig: business, firm*) quebrar

▸ **go up** *vi* subir; **to go up in flames** estallar en llamas

▸ **go without** *vt fus* pasarse sin

goad [gəud] *vt* aguijonear

go-ahead ['gəuəhɛd] *adj* emprendedor(a) ■ *n* luz *f* verde; **to give sth/sb the ~** dar luz verde a algo/algn

goal [gəul] *n* meta, arco (*LAm*); (*score*) gol *m*

goal difference *n* diferencia por goles

goalie ['gəulı] *n* (*col*) = **goalkeeper**

goalkeeper ['gəulki:pə^r] *n* portero, guardameta *m/f*, arquero (*LAm*)

goal post *n* poste *m* (de la portería)

goat [gəut] *n* cabra *f*

gobble ['gɔbl] *vt* (*also:* **gobble down, gobble up**) engullir

go-between ['gəubıtwi:n] *n* intermediario(-a)

Gobi Desert ['gəubı-] *n* Desierto de Gobi

goblet ['gɔblıt] *n* copa

goblin ['gɔblın] *n* duende *m*

go-cart ['gəukɑ:t] *n* = **go-kart**

god [gɔd] *n* dios *m*; **G~** Dios *m*

god-awful [gɔd'ɔ:fəl] *adj* (*col*) de puta pena

godchild ['gɔdtʃaıld] *n* ahijado(-a)

goddamn ['gɔddæm] *adj* (*col: also:* **goddamned**) maldito, puñetero ■ *excl*: **~!** ¡cagüen diez!

goddess ['gɔdɪs] *n* diosa
godfather ['gɔdfɑːðə^r] *n* padrino
god-fearing ['gɔdfɪərɪŋ] *adj* temeroso de Dios
god-forsaken ['gɔdfəseɪkən] *adj* dejado de la mano de Dios
godmother ['gɔdmʌðə^r] *n* madrina
godparents ['gɔdpɛərənts] *npl*: **the ~** los padrinos
godsend ['gɔdsɛnd] *n*: **to be a ~** venir como llovido del cielo
godson ['gɔdsʌn] *n* ahijado
goes [gəuz] *vb see* **go**
gofer ['gəufə^r] *n* (*col*) chico(-a) para todo
go-getter ['gəugɛtə^r] *n* ambicioso(-a)
goggle ['gɔgl] *vi*: **to ~ (at)** mirar con ojos desorbitados
goggles ['gɔglz] *npl* (*Aut*) gafas *fpl*, anteojos *mpl* (*LAm*); (*diver's*) gafas *fpl* submarinas
going ['gəuɪŋ] *n* (*conditions*) cosas *fpl* ■ *adj*: **the ~ rate** la tarifa corriente *or* en vigor; **it was slow ~** las cosas iban lentas
going-over [gəuɪŋ'əuvə^r] *n* revisión *f*; (*col: beating*) paliza
goings-on ['gəuɪŋz'ɔn] *npl* (*col*) tejemanejes *mpl*
go-kart ['gəukɑːt] *n* kart *m*
gold [gəuld] *n* oro ■ *adj* (*reserves*) de oro
golden ['gəuldn] *adj* (*made of gold*) de oro; (*golden in colour*) dorado
Golden Age *n* Siglo de Oro
golden handshake *n cuantiosa gratificación por los servicios prestados*
golden rule *n* regla de oro
goldfish ['gəuldfɪʃ] *n* pez *m* de colores
gold leaf *n* pan *m* de oro
gold medal *n* (*Sport*) medalla de oro
goldmine ['gəuldmaɪn] *n* mina de oro
gold-plated ['gəuld'pleɪtɪd] *adj* chapado en oro
goldsmith ['gəuldsmɪθ] *n* orfebre *m/f*
gold standard *n* patrón *m* oro
golf [gɔlf] *n* golf *m*
golf ball *n* (*for game*) pelota de golf; (*on typewriter*) esfera impresora
golf club *n* club *m* de golf; (*stick*) palo (de golf)
golf course *n* campo de golf
golfer ['gɔlfə^r] *n* jugador(a) *m(f)* de golf, golfista *m/f*
golfing ['gɔlfɪŋ] *n*: **to go ~** jugar al golf
gondola ['gɔndələ] *n* góndola
gondolier [gɔndə'lɪə^r] *n* gondolero
gone [gɔn] *pp of* **go**
goner ['gɔnə^r] *n* (*col*): **to be a ~** estar en las últimas
gong [gɔŋ] *n* gong *m*
gonorrhea [gɔnə'rɪə] *n* gonorrea
good [gud] *adj* bueno; (*before m sing n*) buen; (*well-behaved*) educado ■ *n* bien *m*; **~!** ¡qué bien!; **he's ~ at it** se le da bien; **to be ~ for** servir para; **it's ~ for you** te hace bien; **would you be ~ enough to ...?** ¿podría hacerme el favor de ...?, ¿sería tan amable de ...?; **that's very ~ of you** es usted muy amable; **to feel ~** sentirse bien; **it's ~ to see you** me alegro de verte; **a ~ deal (of)** mucho; **a ~ many** muchos; **to make ~** reparar; **it's no ~ complaining** no sirve de nada quejarse; **is this any ~?** (*will it do?*) ¿sirve esto?; (*what's it like?*) ¿qué tal es esto?; **it's a ~ thing you were there** menos mal que estabas allí; **for ~** (*for ever*) para siempre, definitivamente; **~ morning/afternoon** ¡buenos días/buenas tardes!; **~ evening!** ¡buenas noches!; **~ night!** ¡buenas noches!; **he's up to no ~** está tramando algo; **for the common ~** para el bien común; *see also* **goods**
goodbye [gud'baɪ] *excl* ¡adiós!; **to say ~ (to)** (*person*) despedirse (de)
good faith *n* buena fe *f*
good-for-nothing ['gudfənʌθɪŋ] *n* inútil *m/f*
Good Friday *n* Viernes *m* Santo
good-humoured ['gud'hjuːməd] *adj* (*person*) afable, de buen humor; (*remark, joke*) bien intencionado
good-looking ['gud'lukɪŋ] *adj* guapo
good-natured ['gud'neɪtʃəd] *adj* (*person*) de buen carácter; (*discussion*) cordial
goodness ['gudnɪs] *n* (*of person*) bondad *f*; **for ~ sake!** ¡por Dios!; **~ gracious!** ¡madre mía!
goods [gudz] *npl* bienes *mpl*; (*Comm etc*) géneros *mpl*, mercancías *fpl*, artículos *mpl*; **all his ~ and chattels** todos sus bienes
goods train *n* (*Brit*) tren *m* de mercancías
goodwill [gud'wɪl] *n* buena voluntad *f*; (*Comm*) fondo de comercio; (*customer connections*) clientela
goody-goody ['gudɪgudɪ] *n* (*pej*) santurrón(-ona) *m(f)*
gooey ['guːɪ] *adj* (*Brit col*) pegajoso; (*cake, behaviour*) empalagoso
google® ['gugl] *vi, vt* googlear
goose, geese [guːs, giːs] *n* ganso, oca
gooseberry ['guzbərɪ] *n* grosella espinosa *or* silvestre
gooseflesh ['guːsflɛʃ] *n*, **goosepimples** ['guːspɪmplz] *npl* carne *f* de gallina
goose step *n* (*Mil*) paso de la oca
GOP *n abbr* (*US Pol: col: = Grand Old Party*) *Partido Republicano*
gopher ['gəufə^r] *n* = **gofer**
gore [gɔː^r] *vt* dar una cornada a, cornear ■ *n* sangre *f*
gorge [gɔːdʒ] *n* garganta ■ *vr*: **to ~ o.s. (on)** atracarse (de)

gorgeous ['gɔːdʒəs] *adj* precioso; (*weather*) estupendo; (*person*) guapísimo
gorilla [gə'rɪlə] *n* gorila *m*
gormless ['gɔːmlɪs] *adj* (*col*) ceporro, zoquete
gorse [gɔːs] *n* tojo
gory ['gɔːrɪ] *adj* sangriento
go-slow ['gəu'sləu] *n* (*Brit*) huelga de celo
gospel ['gɔspl] *n* evangelio
gossamer ['gɔsəməʳ] *n* gasa
gossip ['gɔsɪp] *n* cotilleo; (*person*) cotilla *m/f* ■ *vi* cotillear, comadrear (*LAm*); **a piece of ~** un cotilleo
gossip column *n* ecos *mpl* de sociedad
got [gɔt] *pt, pp of* **get**
Gothic ['gɔθɪk] *adj* gótico
gotten ['gɔtn] (*US*) *pp of* **get**
gouge [gaudʒ] *vt* (*also*: **gouge out**: *hole etc*) excavar; (: *initials*) grabar; **to ~ sb's eyes out** sacar los ojos a algn
goulash ['guːlæʃ] *n* g(o)ulash *m*
gourd [guəd] *n* calabaza
gourmet ['guəmeɪ] *n* gastrónomo(-a) *m(f)*
gout [gaut] *n* gota
govern ['gʌvən] *vt* (*gen*) gobernar; (*event, conduct*) regir
governess ['gʌvənɪs] *n* institutriz *f*
governing ['gʌvənɪŋ] *adj* (*Pol*) de gobierno, gubernamental; **~ body** organismo de gobierno
government ['gʌvnmənt] *n* gobierno; **local ~** administración *f* municipal
governmental [gʌvn'mɛntl] *adj* gubernamental
government stock *n* papel *m* del Estado
governor ['gʌvənəʳ] *n* gobernador(a) *m(f)*; (*of jail*) director(a) *m(f)*
Govt *abbr* (= *Government*) gobno
gown [gaun] *n* vestido; (*of teacher*: *Brit*: *of judge*) toga
GP *n abbr* (*Med*) = **general practitioner**
GPMU *n abbr* (*Brit*: = *Graphical, Paper and Media Union*) *sindicato de trabajadores del sector editorial*
GPO *n abbr* (*Brit*: *old*: = *General Post Office*) (*US*) = **Government Printing Office**
GPS *n abbr* (= *global positioning system*) GPS *m*
gr. *abbr* (*Comm*: = *gross*) bto
grab [græb] *vt* coger (*SP*) *or* agarrar; **to ~ at** intentar agarrar
grace [greɪs] *n* (*Rel*) gracia; (*gracefulness*) elegancia, gracia; (*graciousness*) cortesía, gracia ■ *vt* (*favour*) honrar; (*adorn*) adornar; **5 days' ~** un plazo de 5 días; **to say ~** bendecir la mesa; **his sense of humour is his saving ~** lo que le salva es su sentido del humor
graceful ['greɪsful] *adj* elegante
gracious ['greɪʃəs] *adj* amable ■ *excl*: **good ~!** ¡Dios mío!
grade [greɪd] *n* (*quality*) clase *f*, calidad *f*; (*in hierarchy*) grado; (*US Scol*) curso; (: *gradient*) pendiente *f*, cuesta ■ *vt* clasificar; **to make the ~** (*fig*) dar el nivel; *see also* **high school**
grade crossing *n* (*US*) paso a nivel
grade school *n* (*US*) escuela primaria; *see also* **elementary school**
gradient ['greɪdɪənt] *n* pendiente *f*
gradual ['grædjuəl] *adj* gradual
gradually ['grædjuəlɪ] *adv* gradualmente
graduate *n* ['grædjuɪt] licenciado(-a), graduado(-a), egresado(-a) (*LAm*); (*US Scol*) bachiller *m/f* ■ *vi* ['grædjueɪt] licenciarse, graduarse, recibirse (*LAm*); (*US*) obtener el título de bachillerato
graduated pension ['grædjueɪtɪd-] *n* pensión *f* escalonada
graduation [grædju'eɪʃən] *n* graduación *f*; (*US Scol*) entrega de los títulos de bachillerato
graffiti [grə'fiːtɪ] *npl* pintadas *fpl*
graft [grɑːft] *n* (*Agr, Med*) injerto; (*bribery*) corrupción *f* ■ *vt* injertar; **hard ~** (*col*) trabajo duro
grain [greɪn] *n* (*single particle*) grano; (*no pl*: *cereals*) cereales *mpl*; (*US*: *corn*) trigo; (*in wood*) veta
gram [græm] *n* (*US*) gramo
grammar ['græməʳ] *n* gramática
grammar school *n* (*Brit*) ≈ instituto (de segunda enseñanza); (*US*) escuela primaria; *see also* **comprehensive school**
grammatical [grə'mætɪkl] *adj* gramatical
gramme [græm] *n* = **gram**
gramophone ['græməfəun] *n* (*Brit*) gramófono
granary ['grænərɪ] *n* granero
grand [grænd] *adj* grandioso ■ *n* (*US*: *col*) mil dólares *mpl*
grandchildren ['græntʃɪldrən] *npl* nietos *mpl*
granddad ['grændæd] *n* yayo, abuelito
granddaughter ['grændɔːtəʳ] *n* nieta
grandeur ['grændjəʳ] *n* grandiosidad *f*
grandfather ['grænfɑːðəʳ] *n* abuelo
grandiose ['grændɪəuz] *adj* grandioso; (*pej*) pomposo
grand jury *n* (*US*) jurado de acusación
grandma ['grænmɑː] *n* yaya, abuelita
grandmother ['grænmʌðəʳ] *n* abuela
grandpa ['grænpɑː] *n* = **granddad**
grandparents ['grændpɛərənts] *npl* abuelos *mpl*
grand piano *n* piano de cola
Grand Prix ['grɑ̃ː'priː] *n* (*Aut*) gran premio, Grand Prix *m*
grandson ['grænsʌn] *n* nieto
grandstand ['grændstænd] *n* (*Sport*) tribuna
grand total *n* suma total, total *m*

granite ['grænɪt] *n* granito
granny ['grænɪ] *n* abuelita, yaya
grant [grɑːnt] *vt* (*concede*) conceder; (*admit*): **to ~ (that)** reconocer (que) ■ *n* (*Scol*) beca; **to take sth for granted** dar algo por sentado
granulated sugar ['grænjuleɪtɪd-] *n* (*Brit*) azúcar *m* granulado
granule ['grænjuːl] *n* gránulo
grape [greɪp] *n* uva; **sour grapes** (*fig*) envidia *sg*; **a bunch of grapes** un racimo de uvas
grapefruit ['greɪpfruːt] *n* pomelo, toronja
grape juice *n* jugo *or* (*SP*) zumo de uva
grapevine ['greɪpvaɪn] *n* vid *f*, parra; **I heard it on the ~** (*fig*) me enteré, me lo contaron
graph [grɑːf] *n* gráfica
graphic ['græfɪk] *adj* gráfico
graphic designer *n* diseñador(a) *m(f)* gráfico(-a)
graphic equalizer *n* ecualizador *m* gráfico
graphics ['græfɪks] *n* (*art, process*) artes *fpl* gráficas ■ *npl* (*drawings: Comput*) gráficos *mpl*
graphite ['græfaɪt] *n* grafito
graph paper *n* papel *m* cuadriculado
grapple ['græpl] *vi* (*also*: **to grapple with a problem**) enfrentarse a un problema
grappling iron ['græplɪŋ-] *n* (*Naut*) rezón *m*
grasp [grɑːsp] *vt* agarrar, asir; (*understand*) comprender ■ *n* (*grip*) asimiento; (*reach*) alcance *m*; (*understanding*) comprensión *f*; **to have a good ~ of** (*subject*) dominar
▸ **grasp at** *vt fus* (*rope etc*) tratar de agarrar; (*fig: opportunity*) aprovechar
grasping ['grɑːspɪŋ] *adj* avaro
grass [grɑːs] *n* hierba; (*lawn*) césped *m*; (*pasture*) pasto; (*col: informer*) soplón(-ona) *m(f)*
grasshopper ['grɑːshɔpəʳ] *n* saltamontes *m inv*
grassland ['grɑːslænd] *n* pradera, pampa (*LAm*)
grass roots *adj* de base ■ *npl* (*Pol*) bases *fpl*
grass snake *n* culebra
grassy ['grɑːsɪ] *adj* cubierto de hierba
grate [greɪt] *n* parrilla ■ *vi* chirriar, rechinar ■ *vt* (*Culin*) rallar
grateful ['greɪtful] *adj* agradecido
gratefully ['greɪtfəlɪ] *adv* con agradecimiento
grater ['greɪtəʳ] *n* rallador *m*
gratification [grætɪfɪ'keɪʃən] *n* satisfacción *f*
gratify ['grætɪfaɪ] *vt* complacer; (*whim*) satisfacer
gratifying ['grætɪfaɪɪŋ] *adj* gratificante
grating ['greɪtɪŋ] *n* (*iron bars*) rejilla ■ *adj* (*noise*) chirriante
gratitude ['grætɪtjuːd] *n* agradecimiento
gratuitous [grə'tjuːɪtəs] *adj* gratuito
gratuity [grə'tjuːɪtɪ] *n* gratificación *f*
grave [greɪv] *n* tumba ■ *adj* serio, grave
gravedigger ['greɪvdɪgəʳ] *n* sepulturero(-a)
gravel ['grævl] *n* grava
gravely ['greɪvlɪ] *adv* seriamente; **~ ill** muy grave
gravestone ['greɪvstəun] *n* lápida
graveyard ['greɪvjɑːd] *n* cementerio, camposanto
gravitate ['grævɪteɪt] *vi* gravitar
gravitation [grævɪ'teɪʃən] *n* gravitación *f*
gravity ['grævɪtɪ] *n* gravedad *f*; (*seriousness*) seriedad *f*
gravy ['greɪvɪ] *n* salsa de carne
gravy boat *n* salsera
gravy train *n* (*esp US: col*): **to get on the ~** coger un chollo
gray [greɪ] *adj* (*US*) = **grey**
graze [greɪz] *vi* pacer ■ *vt* (*touch lightly, scrape*) rozar ■ *n* (*Med*) rozadura
grazing ['greɪzɪŋ] *n* (*for livestock*) pastoreo
grease [griːs] *n* (*fat*) grasa; (*lubricant*) lubricante *m* ■ *vt* engrasar; **to ~ the skids** (*US: fig*) engrasar el mecanismo
grease gun *n* pistola engrasadora
greasepaint ['griːspeɪnt] *n* maquillaje *m*
greaseproof ['griːspruːf] *adj* a prueba de grasa; (*Brit: paper*) de grasa
greasy ['griːsɪ] *adj* (*hands, clothes*) grasiento; (*road, surface*) resbaladizo
great [greɪt] *adj* grande; (*before n sing*) gran; (*col*) estupendo, macanudo (*LAm*), regio (*LAm*); (*pain, heat*) intenso; **we had a ~ time** nos lo pasamos muy bien; **they're ~ friends** son íntimos *or* muy amigos; **the ~ thing is that ...** lo bueno es que ...; **it was ~!** ¡fue estupendo!
Great Barrier Reef *n* Gran Barrera de Coral
Great Britain *n* Gran Bretaña
greater ['greɪtəʳ] *adj* mayor; **G~ London** el área metropolitana de Londres
greatest ['greɪtɪst] *adj* (el/la) mayor
great-grandchild (*pl* **-children**) [greɪt'grændtʃaɪld, 'tʃɪldrən] *n* bisnieto(-a)
great-grandfather [greɪt'grændfɑːðəʳ] *n* bisabuelo
great-grandmother [greɪt'grændmʌðəʳ] *n* bisabuela
Great Lakes *npl*: **the ~** los Grandes Lagos
greatly ['greɪtlɪ] *adv* sumamente, muy
greatness ['greɪtnɪs] *n* grandeza
Greece [griːs] *n* Grecia
greed [griːd] *n* (*also*: **greediness**) codicia; (*for food*) gula
greedily ['griːdɪlɪ] *adv* con avidez
greedy ['griːdɪ] *adj* codicioso; (*for food*) glotón(-ona)

Greek [gri:k] *adj* griego ■ *n* griego(-a); (*Ling*) griego; **ancient/modern ~** griego antiguo/moderno
green [gri:n] *adj* verde; (*inexperienced*) novato ■ *n* verde *m*; (*stretch of grass*) césped *m*; (*of golf course*) campo, "green" *m*; **the G~ party** (*Pol*) el partido verde; **greens** *npl* verduras *fpl*; **to have ~ fingers** (*fig*) tener buena mano para las plantas
green belt *n* cinturón *m* verde
green card *n* (*Aut*) carta verde
greenery ['gri:nərɪ] *n* vegetación *f*
greenfly ['gri:nflaɪ] *n* pulgón *m*
greengage ['gri:ngeɪdʒ] *n* (ciruela) claudia
greengrocer ['gri:ngrəusəʳ] *n* (*Brit*) frutero(-a), verdulero(-a)
greenhouse ['gri:nhaus] *n* invernadero
greenhouse effect *n*: **the ~** el efecto invernadero
greenhouse gas *n* gas *m* que produce el efecto invernadero
greenish ['gri:nɪʃ] *adj* verdoso
Greenland ['gri:nlənd] *n* Groenlandia
Greenlander ['gri:nləndəʳ] *n* groenlandés(-esa) *m(f)*
green light *n* luz *f* verde
green pepper *n* pimiento verde
greet [gri:t] *vt* saludar; (*news*) recibir
greeting ['gri:tɪŋ] *n* (*gen*) saludo; (*welcome*) bienvenida; **greetings** saludos *mpl*; **season's greetings** Felices Pascuas
greeting card, greetings card *n* tarjeta de felicitación
gregarious [grə'gɛərɪəs] *adj* gregario
grenade [grə'neɪd] *n* (*also*: **hand grenade**) granada
grew [gru:] *pt of* **grow**
grey [greɪ] *adj* gris; **to go ~** salirle canas
grey-haired [greɪ'hɛəd] *adj* canoso
greyhound ['greɪhaund] *n* galgo
grid [grɪd] *n* rejilla; (*Elec*) red *f*
griddle ['grɪdl] *n* (*esp US*) plancha
gridiron ['grɪdaɪən] *n* (*Culin*) parrilla
gridlock ['grɪdlɔk] *n* (*esp US*) retención *f*
grief [gri:f] *n* dolor *m*, pena; **to come to ~** (*plan*) fracasar, ir al traste; (*person*) acabar mal, desgraciarse
grievance ['gri:vəns] *n* (*cause for complaint*) motivo de queja, agravio
grieve [gri:v] *vi* afligirse, acongojarse ■ *vt* afligir, apenar; **to ~ for** llorar por; **to ~ for sb** (*dead person*) llorar la pérdida de algn
grievous ['gri:vəs] *adj* grave; (*loss*) cruel; **~ bodily harm** (*Law*) daños *mpl* corporales graves
grill [grɪl] *n* (*on cooker*) parrilla ■ *vt* (*Brit*) asar a la parrilla; (*question*) interrogar; **grilled meat** carne *f* (asada) a la parrilla *or* plancha
grille [grɪl] *n* rejilla
grim [grɪm] *adj* (*place*) lúgubre; (*person*) adusto
grimace [grɪ'meɪs] *n* mueca ■ *vi* hacer muecas
grime [graɪm] *n* mugre *f*
grimly ['grɪmlɪ] *adv* (*say*) sombríamente
grimy ['graɪmɪ] *adj* mugriento
grin [grɪn] *n* sonrisa abierta ■ *vi*: **to ~ (at)** sonreír abiertamente (a)
grind [graɪnd] (*pt, pp* **ground**) *vt* (*coffee, pepper etc*) moler; (*US: meat*) picar; (*make sharp*) afilar; (*polish: gem, lens*) esmerilar ■ *vi* (*car gears*) rechinar ■ *n*: **the daily ~** (*col*) la rutina diaria; **to ~ one's teeth** hacer rechinar los dientes; **to ~ to a halt** (*vehicle*) pararse con gran estruendo de frenos; (*fig: talks, scheme*) interrumpirse; (*work, production*) paralizarse
grinder ['graɪndəʳ] *n* (*machine: for coffee*) molinillo
grindstone ['graɪndstəun] *n*: **to keep one's nose to the ~** trabajar sin descanso
grip [grɪp] *n* (*hold*) asimiento; (*of hands*) apretón *m*; (*handle*) asidero; (*of racquet etc*) mango; (*understanding*) comprensión *f* ■ *vt* agarrar; **to get to grips with** enfrentarse con; **to lose one's ~** (*fig*) perder el control; **he lost his ~ of the situation** la situación se le fue de las manos
gripe [graɪp] *n* (*col: complaint*) queja ■ *vi* (*col: complain*): **to ~ (about)** quejarse (de); **gripes** *npl* retortijones *mpl*
gripping ['grɪpɪŋ] *adj* absorbente
grisly ['grɪzlɪ] *adj* horripilante, horrible
gristle ['grɪsl] *n* cartílago
grit [grɪt] *n* gravilla; (*courage*) valor *m* ■ *vt* (*road*) poner gravilla en; **I've got a piece of ~ in my eye** tengo una arenilla en el ojo; **to ~ one's teeth** apretar los dientes
grits [grɪts] *npl* (*US*) maíz *msg* a medio moler
grizzle ['grɪzl] *vi* (*cry*) lloriquear
grizzly ['grɪzlɪ] *n* (*also*: **grizzly bear**) oso pardo
groan [grəun] *n* gemido, quejido ■ *vi* gemir, quejarse
grocer ['grəusəʳ] *n* tendero (de ultramarinos); **~'s (shop)** *n* tienda de ultramarinos *or* (*LAm*) de abarrotes
groceries ['grəusərɪz] *npl* comestibles *mpl*
grocery ['grəusərɪ] *n* (*shop*) tienda de ultramarinos
grog [grɔg] *n* (*Brit*) grog *m*
groggy ['grɔgɪ] *adj* atontado
groin [grɔɪn] *n* ingle *f*
groom [gru:m] *n* mozo(-a) de cuadra; (*also*: **bridegroom**) novio ■ *vt* (*horse*) almohazar; **well-groomed** acicalado
groove [gru:v] *n* ranura; (*of record*) surco

grope [grəup] *vi* ir a tientas; **to ~ for** buscar a tientas
gross [grəus] *adj* grueso; (*Comm*) bruto ■ *vt* (*Comm*) recaudar en bruto
gross domestic product *n* producto interior bruto
gross income *n* ingresos *mpl* brutos
grossly ['grəuslɪ] *adv* (*greatly*) enormemente
gross national product *n* producto nacional bruto
gross profit *n* beneficios *mpl* brutos
gross sales *npl* ventas *fpl* brutas
grotesque [grə'tɛsk] *adj* grotesco
grotto ['grɔtəu] *n* gruta
grotty ['grɔtɪ] *adj* asqueroso
grouch [grautʃ] *vi* (*col*) refunfuñar ■ *n* (*col: person*) refunfuñón(-ona) *m(f)*
ground [graund] *pt, pp of* **grind** ■ *n* suelo, tierra; (*Sport*) campo, terreno; (*reason: gen pl*) motivo, razón *f*; (*US: also:* **ground wire**) tierra ■ *vt* (*plane*) mantener en tierra; (*US Elec*) conectar con tierra ■ *vi* (*ship*) varar, encallar ■ *adj* (*coffee etc*) molido; **grounds** *npl* (*of coffee etc*) poso *sg*; (*gardens etc*) jardines *mpl*, parque *m*; **on the ~** en el suelo; **common ~** terreno común; **to gain/lose ~** ganar/perder terreno; **to the ~** al suelo; **below ~** bajo tierra; **he covered a lot of ~ in his lecture** abarcó mucho en la clase
ground cloth *n* (*US*) = **groundsheet**
ground control *n* control *m* desde tierra
ground floor *n* (*Brit*) planta baja
grounding ['graundɪŋ] *n* (*in education*) conocimientos *mpl* básicos
groundkeeper ['graundki:pəʳ] *n*: **groundsman**
groundless ['graundlɪs] *adj* infundado, sin fundamento
groundnut ['graundnʌt] *n* cacahuete *m*
ground rent *n* alquiler *m* del terreno
ground rules *npl* normas básicas
groundsheet ['graundʃi:t] (*Brit*) *n* tela impermeable
groundsman ['graundzmən], **groundskeeper** (*US*) ['graundzki:pəʳ] *n* (*Sport*) encargado de pista de deportes
ground staff *n* personal *m* de tierra
ground swell *n* mar *m or f* de fondo; (*fig*) ola
ground-to-air ['grauntə'ɛə] *adj* tierra-aire
ground-to-ground ['grauntə'graund] *adj* tierra-tierra
groundwork ['graundwə:k] *n* trabajo preliminar
Ground Zero *n* zona cero
group [gru:p] *n* grupo; (*Mus: pop group*) conjunto, grupo; (*vb: also:* **group together**) ■ *vt* agrupar ■ *vi* agruparse
groupie ['gru:pɪ] *n* groupie *f*
group therapy *n* terapia de grupo
grouse [graus] *n* (*pl inv: bird*) urogallo ■ *vi* (*complain*) quejarse
grove [grəuv] *n* arboleda
grovel ['grɔvl] *vi* (*fig*) arrastrarse
grow (*pt* **grew**, *pp* **grown**) [grəu, gru:, grəun] *vi* crecer; (*increase*) aumentar; (*expand*) desarrollarse; (*become*) volverse ■ *vt* cultivar; (*hair, beard*) dejar crecer; **to ~ rich/weak** enriquecerse/debilitarse; **to ~ tired of waiting** cansarse de esperar
▸ **grow apart** *vi* (*fig*) alejarse uno del otro
▸ **grow away from** *vt fus* (*fig*) alejarse de
▸ **grow on** *vt fus*: **that painting is growing on me** ese cuadro me gusta cada vez más
▸ **grow out of** *vt fus* (*clothes*): **I've grown out of this shirt** esta camisa se me ha quedado pequeña; (*habit*) perder
▸ **grow up** *vi* crecer, hacerse hombre/mujer
grower ['grəuəʳ] *n* (*Agr*) cultivador(a) *m(f)*, productor(a) *m(f)*
growing ['grəuɪŋ] *adj* creciente; **~ pains** (*also fig*) problemas *mpl* de crecimiento
growl [graul] *vi* gruñir
grown [grəun] *pp of* **grow**
grown-up [grəun'ʌp] *n* adulto(-a), mayor *m/f*
growth [grəuθ] *n* crecimiento, desarrollo; (*what has grown*) brote *m*; (*Med*) tumor *m*
growth rate *n* tasa de crecimiento
grub [grʌb] *n* gusano; (*col: food*) comida
grubby ['grʌbɪ] *adj* sucio, mugriento, mugroso (*LAm*)
grudge [grʌdʒ] *n* rencor ■ *vt*: **to ~ sb sth** dar algo a algn de mala gana; **to bear sb a ~** guardar rencor a algn; **he grudges (giving) the money** da el dinero de mala gana
grudgingly ['grʌdʒɪŋlɪ] *adv* de mala gana
gruelling, grueling (*US*) ['gruəlɪŋ] *adj* agotador
gruesome ['gru:səm] *adj* horrible
gruff [grʌf] *adj* (*voice*) ronco; (*manner*) brusco
grumble ['grʌmbl] *vi* refunfuñar, quejarse
grumpy ['grʌmpɪ] *adj* gruñón(-ona)
grunge [grʌndʒ] *n* (*Mus: fashion*) grunge *m*
grunt [grʌnt] *vi* gruñir ■ *n* gruñido
G-string ['dʒi:strɪŋ] *n* tanga *m*
GSUSA *n abbr* = **Girl Scouts of the United States of America**
GT *abbr* (*Aut: = gran turismo*) GT
GU *abbr* (*US Post*) = **Guam**
guarantee [gærən'ti:] *n* garantía ■ *vt* garantizar; **he can't ~ (that) he'll come** no está seguro de poder venir
guarantor [gærən'tɔ:ʳ] *n* garante *m/f*, fiador(a) *m(f)*
guard [gɑ:d] *n* guardia; (*person*) guarda

m/f; (*Brit Rail*) jefe *m* de tren; (*safety device*: *on machine*) cubierta de protección; (*protection*) protección *f*; (*fireguard*) pantalla; (*mudguard*) guardabarros *m inv* ■ *vt* guardar; **to ~ (against** *or* **from)** proteger (de); **to be on one's ~** (*fig*) estar en guardia
▸ **guard against** *vi*: **to ~ against doing sth** guardarse de hacer algo
guard dog *n* perro guardián
guarded ['gɑːdɪd] *adj* (*fig*) cauteloso
guardian ['gɑːdɪən] *n* guardián(-ana) *m(f)*; (*of minor*) tutor(a) *m(f)*
guardrail ['gɑːdreɪl] *n* pretil *m*
guard's van *n* (*Brit Rail*) furgón *m* del jefe de tren
Guatemala [gwɑːtə'mɑːlə] *n* Guatemala
Guatemalan [gwɑːtə'mɑːlən] *adj*, *n* guatemalteco(-a) *m(f)*
Guernsey ['gəːnzɪ] *n* Guernsey *m*
guerrilla [gə'rɪlə] *n* guerrillero(-a)
guerrilla warfare *n* guerra de guerrillas
guess [gɛs] *vi*, *vt* (*gen*) adivinar; (*suppose*) suponer ■ *n* suposición *f*, conjetura; **I ~ you're right** (*esp US*) supongo que tienes razón; **to keep sb guessing** mantener a algn a la expectativa; **to take** *or* **have a ~** tratar de adivinar; **my ~ is that ...** yo creo que ...
guesstimate ['gɛstɪmɪt] *n* cálculo aproximado
guesswork ['gɛswəːk] *n* conjeturas *fpl*; **I got the answer by ~** acerté a ojo de buen cubero
guest [gɛst] *n* invitado(-a); (*in hotel*) huésped(a) *m(f)*; **be my ~** (*col*) estás en tu casa
guest-house ['gɛsthaus] *n* casa de huéspedes, pensión *f*
guest room *n* cuarto de huéspedes
guff [gʌf] *n* (*col*) bobadas *fpl*
guffaw [gʌ'fɔː] *n* carcajada ■ *vi* reírse a carcajadas
guidance ['gaɪdəns] *n* (*gen*) dirección *f*; (*advice*) consejos *mpl*; **marriage/vocational ~** orientación *f* matrimonial/profesional
guide [gaɪd] *n* (*person*) guía *m/f*; (*book*) guía *f*; (*fig*) guía *f*; (*also*: **girl guide**) exploradora ■ *vt* guiar; **to be guided by sb/sth** dejarse guiar por algn/algo
guidebook ['gaɪdbuk] *n* guía
guided missile ['gaɪdɪd-] *n* misil *m* teledirigido
guide dog *n* perro guía
guidelines ['gaɪdlaɪnz] *npl* (*fig*) directrices *fpl*
guild [gɪld] *n* gremio
guildhall ['gɪldhɔːl] *n* (*Brit*: *town hall*) ayuntamiento
guile [gaɪl] *n* astucia
guileless ['gaɪllɪs] *adj* cándido
guillotine ['gɪlətiːn] *n* guillotina
guilt [gɪlt] *n* culpabilidad *f*
guilty ['gɪltɪ] *adj* culpable; **to feel ~ (about)** sentirse culpable (de); **to plead ~/not ~** declararse culpable/inocente
Guinea ['gɪnɪ] *n*: **Republic of ~** República de Guinea
guinea ['gɪnɪ] *n* (*Brit*: *old*) guinea (*21 chelines*: *en la actualidad ya no se usa esta moneda*)
guinea pig *n* cobaya; (*fig*) conejillo de Indias
guise [gaɪz] *n*: **in** *or* **under the ~ of** bajo la apariencia de
guitar [gɪ'tɑːʳ] *n* guitarra
guitarist [gɪ'tɑːrɪst] *n* guitarrista *m/f*
gulch [gʌltʃ] *n* (*US*) barranco
gulf [gʌlf] *n* golfo; (*abyss*) abismo; **the G~** el Golfo (Pérsico)
Gulf States *npl*: **the ~** los países del Golfo
Gulf Stream *n*: **the ~** la Corriente del Golfo
gull [gʌl] *n* gaviota
gullet ['gʌlɪt] *n* esófago
gullibility [gʌlɪ'bɪlɪtɪ] *n* credulidad *f*
gullible ['gʌlɪbl] *adj* crédulo
gully ['gʌlɪ] *n* barranco
gulp [gʌlp] *vi* tragar saliva ■ *vt* (*also*: **gulp down**) tragarse ■ *n* (*of liquid*) trago; (*of food*) bocado; **in** *or* **at one ~** de un trago
gum [gʌm] *n* (*Anat*) encía; (*glue*) goma, cemento (*LAm*); (*sweet*) gominola; (*also*: **chewing-gum**) chicle *m* ■ *vt* pegar con goma
▸ **gum up** *vt*: **to ~ up the works** (*col*) entorpecerlo todo
gumboots ['gʌmbuːts] *npl* (*Brit*) botas *fpl* de goma
gumption ['gʌmpʃən] *n* (*col*) iniciativa
gum tree *n* árbol *m* gomero
gun [gʌn] *n* (*small*) pistola; (*shotgun*) escopeta; (*rifle*) fusil *m*; (*cannon*) cañón *m* ■ *vt* (*also*: **gun down**) abatir a tiros; **to stick to one's guns** (*fig*) mantenerse firme *or* en sus trece
gunboat ['gʌnbəut] *n* cañonero
gun dog *n* perro de caza
gunfire ['gʌnfaɪəʳ] *n* disparos *mpl*
gung-ho [gʌŋ'həu] *adj* (*col*) patriotero
gunk [gʌŋk] *n* (*col*) masa viscosa
gunman ['gʌnmən] *n* pistolero
gunner ['gʌnəʳ] *n* artillero
gunpoint ['gʌnpɔɪnt] *n*: **at ~** a mano armada
gunpowder ['gʌnpaudəʳ] *n* pólvora
gunrunner ['gʌnrʌnəʳ] *n* traficante *m/f* de armas
gunrunning ['gʌnrʌnɪŋ] *n* tráfico de armas
gunshot ['gʌnʃɔt] *n* disparo
gunsmith ['gʌnsmɪθ] *n* armero

gurgle ['gəːgl] *vi* gorgotear
guru ['guːruː] *n* guru *m*
gush [gʌʃ] *vi* chorrear; (*fig*) deshacerse en efusiones
gushing ['gʌʃɪŋ] *adj* efusivo
gusset ['gʌsɪt] *n* (*in tights, pants*) escudete *m*
gust [gʌst] *n* (*of wind*) ráfaga
gusto ['gʌstəu] *n* entusiasmo
gusty ['gʌstɪ] *adj* racheado
gut [gʌt] *n* intestino; (*Mus etc*) cuerda de tripa ■ *vt* (*poultry, fish*) destripar; (*building*): **the blaze gutted the entire building** el fuego destruyó el edificio entero
gut reaction *n* reacción *f* instintiva
guts [gʌts] *npl* (*courage*) agallas *fpl*, valor *m*; (*col: innards: of people, animals*) tripas *fpl*; **to hate sb's ~** odiar a algn (a muerte)
gutsy ['gʌtsɪ] *adj*: **to be ~** (*col*) tener agallas
gutted ['gʌtɪd] *adj* (*col: disappointed*): **I was ~** me quedé hecho polvo
gutter ['gʌtəʳ] *n* (*of roof*) canalón *m*; (*in street*) cuneta; **the ~** (*fig*) el arroyo
gutter press *n* (*col*): **the ~** la prensa sensacionalista *or* amarilla; *see also* **tabloid press**
guttural ['gʌtərl] *adj* gutural
guy [gaɪ] *n* (*also*: **guyrope**) viento, cuerda; (*col: man*) tío (*SP*), tipo
Guyana [gaɪ'ænə] *n* Guayana
Guy Fawkes' Night [gaɪ'fɔːks-] *n*

GUY FAWKES' NIGHT

La noche del cinco de noviembre, *Guy Fawkes' Night*, se celebra el fracaso de la conspiración de la pólvora ("Gunpowder Plot"), el intento fallido de volar el parlamento de Jaime I en 1605. Esa noche se lanzan fuegos artificiales y se queman en muchas hogueras muñecos de trapo que representan a "Guy Fawkes", uno de los cabecillas. Días antes los niños tienen por costumbre pedir a los viandantes "a penny for the guy", dinero para comprar los cohetes.

guzzle ['gʌzl] *vi* tragar ■ *vt* engullir
gym [dʒɪm] *n* (*also*: **gymnasium**) gimnasio; (*also*: **gymnastics**) gimnasia
gymkhana [dʒɪm'kɑːnə] *n* gincana
gymnast ['dʒɪmnæst] *n* gimnasta *m/f*
gymnastics [dʒɪm'næstɪks] *n* gimnasia
gym shoes *npl* zapatillas *fpl* de gimnasia
gym slip *n* (*Brit*) pichi *m*
gynaecologist, (*US*) **gynecologist** [gaɪnɪ'kɔlədʒɪst] *n* ginecólogo(-a)
gynaecology, (*US*) **gynecology** [gaɪnə'kɔlədʒɪ] *n* ginecología
gypsy ['dʒɪpsɪ] *n* = **gipsy**
gyrate [dʒaɪ'reɪt] *vi* girar
gyroscope ['dʒaɪrəskəup] *n* giroscopio

Hh

H, h [eɪtʃ] *n* (*letter*) H, h *f*; **H for Harry,** (*US*) **H for How** H de Historia
habeas corpus ['heɪbɪəs'kɔːpəs] *n* (*Law*) hábeas corpus *m*
haberdashery ['hæbə'dæʃərɪ] *n* (*Brit*) mercería; (*US: men's clothing*) prendas *fpl* de caballero
habit ['hæbɪt] *n* hábito, costumbre *f*; **to get out of/into the ~ of doing sth** perder la costumbre de/acostumbrarse a hacer algo
habitable ['hæbɪtəbl] *adj* habitable
habitat ['hæbɪtæt] *n* hábitat *m*
habitation [hæbɪ'teɪʃən] *n* habitación *f*
habitual [hə'bɪtjuəl] *adj* acostumbrado, habitual; (*drinker, liar*) empedernido
habitually [hə'bɪtjuəlɪ] *adv* por costumbre
hack [hæk] *vt* (*cut*) cortar; (*slice*) tajar ■ *n* corte *m*; (*axe blow*) hachazo; (*pej: writer*) escritor(a) *m(f)* a sueldo; (*old horse*) jamelgo
hacker ['hækəʳ] *n* (*Comput*) pirata *m* informático
hackles ['hæklz] *npl*: **to make sb's ~ rise** (*fig*) poner furioso a algn
hackney cab ['hæknɪ-] *n* coche *m* de alquiler
hackneyed ['hæknɪd] *adj* trillado, gastado
hacksaw ['hæksɔː] *n* sierra para metales
had [hæd] *pt, pp of* **have**
haddock (*pl* **~** *or* **haddocks**) ['hædək] *n especie de merluza*
hadn't ['hædnt] = **had not**
haematology, hematology (*US*) ['hiːmə'tɔlədʒɪ] *n* hematología
haemoglobin, hemoglobin (*US*) ['hiːmə'gləubɪn] *n* hemoglobina
haemophilia, hemophilia (*US*) ['hiːmə'fɪlɪə] *n* hemofilia
haemorrhage, hemorrhage (*US*) ['hɛmərɪdʒ] *n* hemorragia
haemorrhoids, hemorrhoids (*US*) ['hɛmərɔɪdz] *npl* hemorroides *fpl*, almorranas *fpl*
hag [hæg] *n* (*ugly*) vieja fea, tarasca; (*nasty*) bruja; (*witch*) hechicera
haggard ['hægəd] *adj* ojeroso
haggis ['hægɪs] *n* (*Scottish*) *asadura de cordero cocida*; *see also* **Burns' Night**
haggle ['hægl] *vi* (*argue*) discutir; (*bargain*) regatear
haggling ['hæglɪŋ] *n* regateo
Hague [heɪg] *n*: **The ~** La Haya
hail [heɪl] *n* (*weather*) granizo ■ *vt* saludar; (*call*) llamar a ■ *vi* granizar; **to ~ (as)** aclamar (como), celebrar (como); **he hails from Scotland** es natural de Escocia
hailstone ['heɪlstəun] *n* (piedra de) granizo
hailstorm ['heɪlstɔːm] *n* granizada
hair [hɛəʳ] *n* (*gen*) pelo, cabellos *mpl*; (*one hair*) pelo, cabello; (*head of hair*) pelo, cabellera; (*on legs etc*) vello; **to do one's ~** arreglarse el pelo; **grey ~** canas *fpl*
hairbrush ['hɛəbrʌʃ] *n* cepillo (para el pelo)
haircut ['hɛəkʌt] *n* corte *m* de pelo
hairdo ['hɛəduː] *n* peinado
hairdresser ['hɛədrɛsəʳ] *n* peluquero(-a); **~'s** peluquería
hair-dryer ['hɛədraɪəʳ] *n* secador *m* (de pelo)
-haired [hɛəd] *adj suff*: **fair/long~** (de pelo) rubio *or* (*LAm*) güero/de pelo largo
hairgrip ['hɛəgrɪp] *n* horquilla
hairline ['hɛəlaɪn] *n* nacimiento del pelo
hairline fracture *n* fractura muy fina
hairnet ['hɛənɛt] *n* redecilla
hair oil *n* brillantina
hairpiece ['hɛəpiːs] *n* trenza postiza
hairpin ['hɛəpɪn] *n* horquilla
hairpin bend, (*US*) **hairpin curve** *n* curva muy cerrada
hair-raising ['hɛəreɪzɪŋ] *adj* espeluznante
hair remover *n* depilatorio
hair's breadth *n*: **by a ~** por un pelo
hair spray *n* laca
hairstyle ['hɛəstaɪl] *n* peinado
hairy ['hɛərɪ] *adj* peludo, velludo
Haiti ['heɪtɪ] *n* Haití *m*
hake [heɪk] *n* merluza
halcyon ['hælsɪən] *adj* feliz
hale [heɪl] *adj*: **~ and hearty** sano y fuerte

half [hɑːf] *n* (*pl* **halves**) [hɑːvz] mitad *f*; (*Sport: of match*) tiempo, parte *f*; (*: of ground*) campo ■ *adj* medio ■ *adv* medio, a medias; **~-an-hour** media hora; **two and a ~** dos y media; **~ a dozen** media docena; **~ a pound** media libra, ≈ 250 gr.; **to cut sth in ~** cortar algo por la mitad; **to go halves (with sb)** ir a medias (con algn); **halfempty/closed** medio vacío/entreabierto; **~ asleep** medio dormido; **~ past 3** las 3 y media
half-back ['hɑːfbæk] *n* (*Sport*) medio
half-baked ['hɑːf'beɪkt] *adj* (*col: idea, scheme*) mal concebido *or* pensado
half-breed ['hɑːfbriːd] *n* = **half-caste**
half-brother ['hɑːfbrʌðə^r] *n* hermanastro
half-caste ['hɑːfkɑːst] *n* mestizo(-a)
half-hearted ['hɑːf'hɑːtɪd] *adj* indiferente, poco entusiasta
half-hour [hɑːf'auə^r] *n* media hora
half-mast ['hɑːf'mɑːst] *n*: **at ~** (*flag*) a media asta
halfpenny ['heɪpnɪ] *n* medio penique *m*
half-price ['hɑːf'praɪs] *adj* a mitad de precio
half term *n* (*Brit Scol*) *vacaciones de mediados del trimestre*
half-time [hɑːf'taɪm] *n* descanso
halfway ['hɑːf'weɪ] *adv* a medio camino; **to meet sb ~** (*fig*) llegar a un acuerdo con algn
halfway house *n centro de readaptación de antiguos presos*; (*fig*) solución *f* intermedia
half-wit ['hɑːfwɪt] *n* (*col*) zoquete *m*
half-yearly [hɑːf'jɪəlɪ] *adv* semestralmente ■ *adj* semestral
halibut ['hælɪbət] *n* (*pl inv*) halibut *m*
halitosis [hælɪ'təusɪs] *n* halitosis *f*
hall [hɔːl] *n* (*for concerts*) sala; (*entrance way*) entrada, vestíbulo
hallmark ['hɔːlmɑːk] *n* (*mark*) rasgo distintivo; (*seal*) sello
hallo [hə'ləu] *excl* = **hello**
hall of residence *n* (*Brit*) colegio mayor, residencia universitaria
Hallowe'en [hæləu'iːn] *n* víspera de Todos los Santos; *ver nota*

HALLOWE'EN

La tradición anglosajona dice que en la noche del 31 de octubre, *Hallowe'en*, víspera de Todos los Santos, es fácil ver a brujas y fantasmas. Es una ocasión festiva en la que los niños se disfrazan y van de puerta en puerta llevando un farol hecho con una calabaza en forma de cabeza humana. Cuando se les abre la puerta gritan "trick or treat" para indicar que gastarán una broma a quien no les dé un pequeño regalo (como golosinas o dinero).

hallucination [həluːsɪ'neɪʃən] *n* alucinación *f*
hallucinogenic [həluːsɪnəu'dʒɛnɪk] *adj* alucinógeno
hallway ['hɔːlweɪ] *n* vestíbulo
halo ['heɪləu] *n* (*of saint*) aureola
halt [hɔːlt] *n* (*stop*) alto, parada; (*Rail*) apeadero ■ *vt* parar ■ *vi* pararse; (*process*) interrumpirse; **to call a ~ (to sth)** (*fig*) poner fin (a algo)
halter ['hɔːltə^r] *n* (*for horse*) cabestro
halterneck ['hɔːltənɛk] *adj* de espalda escotada
halve [hɑːv] *vt* partir por la mitad
halves [hɑːvz] *pl of* **half**
ham [hæm] *n* jamón *m* (cocido); (*col: also:* **radio ham**) radioaficionado(-a) *m(f)*; (*: also:* **ham actor**) comicastro
hamburger ['hæmbəːgə^r] *n* hamburguesa
ham-fisted ['hæm'fɪstɪd] *adj* torpe, desmañado
hamlet ['hæmlɪt] *n* aldea
hammer ['hæmə^r] *n* martillo ■ *vt* (*nail*) clavar; **to ~ a point home to sb** remacharle un punto a algn
▸ **hammer out** *vt* (*metal*) forjar a martillo; (*fig: solution, agreement*) elaborar (trabajosamente)
hammock ['hæmək] *n* hamaca
hamper ['hæmpə^r] *vt* estorbar ■ *n* cesto
hamster ['hæmstə^r] *n* hámster *m*
hand [hænd] *n* mano *f*; (*of clock*) aguja, manecilla; (*writing*) letra; (*worker*) obrero; (*measurement: of horse*) palmo ■ *vt* (*give*) dar, pasar; (*deliver*) entregar; **to give sb a ~** echar una mano a algn, ayudar a algn; **to force sb's ~** forzarle la mano a algn; **at ~** a mano; **in ~** entre manos; **we have the matter in ~** tenemos el asunto entre manos; **to have in one's ~** (*knife, victory*) tener en la mano; **to have a free ~** tener carta blanca; **on ~** (*person, services*) a mano, al alcance; **to ~** (*information etc*) a mano; **on the one ~ ..., on the other ~ ...** por una parte ... por otra (parte) ...
▸ **hand down** *vt* pasar, bajar; (*tradition*) transmitir; (*heirloom*) dejar en herencia; (*US: sentence, verdict*) imponer
▸ **hand in** *vt* entregar
▸ **hand out** *vt* (*leaflets, advice*) repartir, distribuir
▸ **hand over** *vt* (*deliver*) entregar; (*surrender*) ceder
▸ **hand round** *vt* (*Brit: information, papers*) pasar (de mano en mano); (*: chocolates etc*) ofrecer
handbag ['hændbæg] *n* bolso, cartera (*LAm*)

hand baggage *n* = **hand luggage**
handball ['hændbɔ:l] *n* balonmano
handbasin ['hændbeɪsn] *n* lavabo
handbook ['hændbuk] *n* manual *m*
handbrake ['hændbreɪk] *n* freno de mano
hand cream *n* crema para las manos
handcuffs ['hændkʌfs] *npl* esposas *fpl*
handful ['hændful] *n* puñado
hand-held ['hænd'hɛld] *adj* de mano
handicap ['hændɪkæp] *n* desventaja; (*Sport*) hándicap *m* ■ *vt* estorbar
handicapped ['hændɪkæpt] *adj*: **to be mentally ~** ser deficiente *m/f* mental; **to be physically ~** ser minusválido(-a)
handicraft ['hændɪkrɑ:ft] *n* artesanía
handiwork ['hændɪwə:k] *n* manualidad(es) *f(pl)*; (*fig*) obra; **this looks like his ~** (*pej*) es obra de él, parece
handkerchief ['hæŋkətʃɪf] *n* pañuelo
handle ['hændl] *n* (*of door etc*) pomo; (*of cup etc*) asa; (*of knife etc*) mango; (*for winding*) manivela ■ *vt* (*touch*) tocar; (*deal with*) encargarse de; (*treat: people*) manejar; **"~ with care"** "(manéjese) con cuidado"; **to fly off the ~** perder los estribos
handlebar ['hændlbɑ:ʳ] *n*, **handlebars** ['hændlbɑ:z] *npl* manillar *msg*
handling ['hændlɪŋ] *n* (*Aut*) conducción *f*; **his ~ of the matter** su forma de llevar el asunto
handling charges *npl* gastos *mpl* de tramitación
hand luggage *n* equipaje *m* de mano
handmade ['hændmeɪd] *adj* hecho a mano
handout ['hændaut] *n* (*distribution*) repartición *f*; (*charity*) limosna; (*leaflet*) folleto, octavilla; (*press handout*) nota
hand-picked ['hænd'pɪkt] *adj* (*produce*) escogido a mano; (*staff etc*) seleccionado cuidadosamente
handrail ['hændreɪl] *n* (*on staircase etc*) pasamanos *m inv*, barandilla
handset ['hændsɛt] *n* (*Tel*) auricular *m*
handsfree ['hændzfri:] *adj* (*Tel: telephone, kit*) manos libres
handshake ['hændʃeɪk] *n* apretón *m* de manos; (*Comput*) coloquio
handsome ['hænsəm] *adj* guapo
hands-on ['hændz'ɔn] *adj* práctico; **she has a very ~ approach** le gusta tomar parte activa; **~ experience** (*Comput*) experiencia práctica
handstand ['hændstænd] *n* voltereta, salto mortal
hand-to-mouth ['hændtə'mauθ] *adj* (*existence*) precario
handwriting ['hændraɪtɪŋ] *n* letra
handwritten ['hændrɪtn] *adj* escrito a mano, manuscrito
handy ['hændɪ] *adj* (*close at hand*) a mano; (*useful: machine, tool etc*) práctico; (*skilful*) hábil, diestro; **to come in ~** venir bien
handyman ['hændɪmæn] *n* manitas *m inv*
hang (*pt, pp* **hung**) [hæŋ, hʌŋ] *vt* colgar; (*head*) bajar; (*criminal*) (*pt, pp* **hanged**) ahorcar; **to get the ~ of sth** (*col*) coger el tranquillo a algo
▸ **hang about** *vi* haraganear
▸ **hang back** *vi* (*hesitate*): **to ~ back (from doing)** vacilar (en hacer)
▸ **hang on** *vi* (*wait*) esperar ■ *vt fus* (*depend on: decision etc*) depender de; **to ~ on to** (*keep*) guardar, quedarse con
▸ **hang out** *vt* (*washing*) tender, colgar ■ *vi* (*col: live*) vivir; (*: often be found*) moverse; **to ~ out of sth** colgar fuera de algo
▸ **hang together** *vi* (*cohere: argument etc*) sostenerse
▸ **hang up** *vt* (*coat*) colgar ■ *vi* (*Tel*) colgar; **to ~ up on sb** colgarle a algn
hangar ['hæŋəʳ] *n* hangar *m*
hangdog ['hæŋdɔg] *adj* (*guilty: look, expression*) avergonzado
hanger ['hæŋəʳ] *n* percha
hanger-on [hæŋər'ɔn] *n* parásito
hang-glider ['hæŋglaɪdəʳ] *n* ala delta
hang-gliding ['hæŋglaɪdɪŋ] *n* vuelo con ala delta
hanging ['hæŋɪŋ] *n* (*execution*) ejecución *f* (en la horca)
hangman ['hæŋmən] *n* verdugo
hangover ['hæŋəuvəʳ] *n* (*after drinking*) resaca
hang-up ['hæŋʌp] *n* complejo
hanker ['hæŋkəʳ] *vi*: **to ~ after** (*miss*) echar de menos; (*long for*) añorar
hankie, hanky ['hæŋkɪ] *n abbr* = **handkerchief**
Hansard ['hænsɑ:d] *n actas oficiales de las sesiones del parlamento británico*
Hants *abbr* (*Brit*) = **Hampshire**
haphazard [hæp'hæzəd] *adj* fortuito
hapless ['hæplɪs] *adj* desventurado
happen ['hæpən] *vi* suceder, ocurrir; (*take place*) tener lugar, realizarse; **as it happens** da la casualidad de que; **what's happening?** ¿qué pasa?
▸ **happen (up)on** *vt fus* tropezar *or* dar con
happening ['hæpnɪŋ] *n* suceso, acontecimiento
happily ['hæpɪlɪ] *adv* (*luckily*) afortunadamente; (*cheerfully*) alegremente
happiness ['hæpɪnɪs] *n* (*contentment*) felicidad *f*; (*joy*) alegría
happy ['hæpɪ] *adj* feliz; (*cheerful*) alegre; **to be ~ (with)** estar contento (con); **yes, I'd be ~ to** sí, con mucho gusto; **H~ Christmas!** ¡Feliz

Navidad!; **H~ New Year!** ¡Feliz Año Nuevo!; **~ birthday!** ¡felicidades!, ¡feliz cumpleaños!
happy-go-lucky ['hæpɪgəu'lʌkɪ] *adj* despreocupado
happy hour *n horas en las que la bebida es más barata en un bar*
harangue [hə'ræŋ] *vt* arengar
harass ['hærəs] *vt* acosar, hostigar
harassed ['hærəst] *adj* agobiado, presionado
harassment ['hærəsmənt] *n* persecución *f*, acoso; (*worry*) preocupación *f*
harbour, harbor (*US*) ['hɑːbəʳ] *n* puerto ■ *vt* (*hope etc*) abrigar; (*hide*) dar abrigo a; (*retain: grudge etc*) guardar
harbour dues, harbor dues (*US*) *npl* derechos *mpl* portuarios
hard [hɑːd] *adj* duro; (*difficult*) difícil; (*person*) severo ■ *adv* (*work*) mucho, duro; (*think*) profundamente; **to look ~ at sb/sth** clavar los ojos en algn/algo; **to try ~** esforzarse; **no ~ feelings!** ¡sin rencor(es)!; **to be ~ of hearing** ser duro de oído; **to be ~ done by** ser tratado injustamente; **to be ~ on sb** ser muy duro con algn; **I find it ~ to believe that ...** me cuesta trabajo creer que ...
hard-and-fast ['hɑːdən'fɑːst] *adj* rígido, definitivo
hardback ['hɑːdbæk] *n* libro de tapas duras
hard cash *n* dinero en efectivo
hard copy *n* (*Comput*) copia impresa
hard-core ['hɑːd'kɔːʳ] *adj* (*pornography*) duro; (*supporters*) incondicional
hard court *n* (*Tennis*) pista *or* cancha (de tenis) de cemento
hard disk *n* (*Comput*) disco duro
harden ['hɑːdn] *vt* endurecer; (*steel*) templar; (*fig*) curtir; (*: determination*) fortalecer ■ *vi* (*substance*) endurecerse
hardened ['hɑːdnd] *adj* (*criminal*) habitual; **to be ~ to sth** estar acostumbrado a algo
hard-headed ['hɑːd'hɛdɪd] *adj* poco sentimental, realista
hard-hearted ['hɑːd'hɑːtɪd] *adj* insensible
hard-hitting ['hɑːd'hɪtɪŋ] *adj* (*speech, article*) contundente
hard labour *n* trabajos *mpl* forzados
hardliner [hɑːd'laɪnəʳ] *n* partidario(-a) de la línea dura
hard-luck story ['hɑːdlʌk-] *n* dramón *m*
hardly ['hɑːdlɪ] *adv* (*scarcely*) apenas; **that can ~ be true** eso difícilmente puede ser cierto; **~ ever** casi nunca; **I can ~ believe it** apenas me lo puedo creer
hardness ['hɑːdnɪs] *n* dureza
hard-nosed ['hɑːd'nəuzd] *adj* duro, sin contemplaciones
hard-pressed ['hɑːd'prɛst] *adj* en apuros
hard sell *n* publicidad *f* agresiva; **~ techniques** técnicas *fpl* agresivas de venta
hardship ['hɑːdʃɪp] *n* (*troubles*) penas *fpl*; (*financial*) apuro
hard shoulder *n* (*Aut*) arcén *m*
hard-up [hɑːd'ʌp] *adj* (*col*) sin un duro (*SP*), sin plata (*LAm*)
hardware ['hɑːdwɛəʳ] *n* ferretería; (*Comput*) hardware *m*
hardware shop *n* ferretería
hard-wearing [hɑːd'wɛərɪŋ] *adj* resistente, duradero; (*shoes*) resistente
hard-won ['hɑːd'wʌn] *adj* ganado con esfuerzo
hard-working [hɑːd'wəːkɪŋ] *adj* trabajador(a)
hardy ['hɑːdɪ] *adj* fuerte; (*plant*) resistente
hare [hɛəʳ] *n* liebre *f*
hare-brained ['hɛəbreɪnd] *adj* atolondrado
harelip ['hɛəlɪp] *n* labio leporino
harem [hɑː'riːm] *n* harén *m*
haricot ['hærɪkəu], **haricot bean** *n* alubia
hark back [hɑːk-] *vi*: **to ~ to** (*former days, earlier occasion*) recordar
harm [hɑːm] *n* daño, mal *m* ■ *vt* (*person*) hacer daño a; (*health, interests*) perjudicar; (*thing*) dañar; **out of ~'s way** a salvo; **there's no ~ in trying** no se pierde nada con intentar
harmful ['hɑːmful] *adj* (*gen*) dañino; (*reputation*) perjudicial
harmless ['hɑːmlɪs] *adj* (*person*) inofensivo; (*drug*) inocuo
harmonica [hɑː'mɔnɪkə] *n* armónica
harmonious [hɑː'məunɪəs] *adj* armonioso
harmonize ['hɑːmənaɪz] *vt, vi* armonizar
harmony ['hɑːmənɪ] *n* armonía
harness ['hɑːnɪs] *n* arreos *mpl* ■ *vt* (*horse*) enjaezar; (*resources*) aprovechar
harp [hɑːp] *n* arpa ■ *vi*: **to ~ on (about)** machacar (con)
harpoon [hɑː'puːn] *n* arpón *m*
harrow ['hærəu] *n* grada ■ *vt* gradar
harrowing ['hærəuɪŋ] *adj* angustioso
harry ['hærɪ] *vt* (*Mil*) acosar; (*person*) hostigar
harsh [hɑːʃ] *adj* (*cruel*) duro, cruel; (*severe*) severo; (*words*) hosco; (*colour*) chillón(-ona); (*contrast*) violento
harshly ['hɑːʃlɪ] *adv* (*say*) con aspereza; (*treat*) con mucha dureza
harshness ['hɑːʃnɪs] *n* dureza
harvest ['hɑːvɪst] *n* cosecha; (*of grapes*) vendimia ■ *vt, vi* cosechar
harvester ['hɑːvɪstəʳ] *n* (*machine*) cosechadora; (*person*) segador(a) *m(f)*; **combine ~** segadora trilladora
has [hæz] *vb see* **have**

has-been ['hæzbi:n] *n* (*col: person*) persona acabada; (*: thing*) vieja gloria
hash [hæʃ] *n* (*Culin*) picadillo; (*fig: mess*) lío
hashish ['hæʃɪʃ] *n* hachís *m*
hasn't ['hæznt] = **has not**
hassle ['hæsl] *n* (*col*) lío, rollo ■ *vt* incordiar
haste [heɪst] *n* prisa
hasten ['heɪsn] *vt* acelerar ■ *vi* darse prisa; **I ~ to add that ...** me apresuro a añadir que ...
hastily ['heɪstɪlɪ] *adv* de prisa
hasty ['heɪstɪ] *adj* apresurado
hat [hæt] *n* sombrero
hatbox ['hætbɔks] *n* sombrerera
hatch [hætʃ] *n* (*Naut: also:* **hatchway**) escotilla ■ *vi* salir del cascarón ■ *vt* incubar; (*fig: scheme, plot*) idear, tramar
hatchback ['hætʃbæk] *n* (*Aut*) tres *or* cinco puertas *m*
hatchet ['hætʃɪt] *n* hacha
hatchet job *n* (*col*) varapalo
hatchet man *n* (*col*) ejecutor de faenas desagradables por cuenta de otro
hate [heɪt] *vt* odiar, aborrecer ■ *n* odio; **I ~ to trouble you, but ...** siento *or* lamento molestarle, pero ...
hateful ['heɪtful] *adj* odioso
hatred ['heɪtrɪd] *n* odio
hat trick *n*: **to score a ~** (*Brit Sport*) marcar tres tantos (*or* triunfos) seguidos
haughtily ['hɔ:tɪlɪ] *adv* con arrogancia
haughty ['hɔ:tɪ] *adj* altanero, arrogante
haul [hɔ:l] *vt* tirar, jalar (*LAm*); (*by lorry*) transportar ■ *n* (*of fish*) redada; (*of stolen goods etc*) botín *m*
haulage ['hɔ:lɪdʒ] *n* (*Brit*) transporte *m*; (*costs*) gastos *mpl* de transporte
haulage contractor *n* (*firm*) empresa de transportes; (*person*) transportista *m/f*
haulier ['hɔ:lɪə^r], **hauler** (*US*) ['hɔ:lə^r] *n* transportista *m/f*
haunch [hɔ:ntʃ] *n* anca; (*of meat*) pierna
haunt [hɔ:nt] *vt* (*ghost*) aparecer en; (*frequent*) frecuentar; (*obsess*) obsesionar ■ *n* guarida
haunted ['hɔ:ntɪd] *adj* (*castle etc*) embrujado; (*look*) de angustia
haunting ['hɔ:ntɪŋ] *adj* (*sight, music*) evocativo
Havana [hə'vɑ:nə] *n* La Habana

KEYWORD

have [haev] (*pt, pp* **had**) *aux vb* **1** (*gen*) haber; **to have arrived/eaten** haber llegado/comido; **having finished** *or* **when he had finished, he left** cuando hubo acabado, se fue
2 (*in tag questions*): **you've done it, haven't you?** lo has hecho, ¿verdad? *or* ¿no?
3 (*in short answers and questions*): **I haven't** no; **so I have** pues, es verdad; **we haven't paid — yes we have!** no hemos pagado — ¡sí que hemos pagado!; **I've been there before, have you?** he estado allí antes, ¿y tú?
■ *modal aux vb* (*be obliged*): **to have (got) to do sth** tener que hacer algo; **you haven't to tell her** no hay que *or* no debes decírselo
■ *vt* **1** (*possess*) tener; **he has (got) blue eyes/dark hair** tiene los ojos azules/el pelo negro
2 (*referring to meals etc*): **to have breakfast/lunch/dinner** desayunar/comer/cenar; **to have a drink/a cigarette** tomar algo/fumar un cigarrillo
3 (*receive*) recibir; (*obtain*) obtener; **may I have your address?** ¿puedes darme tu dirección?; **you can have it for £5** te lo puedes quedar por £5; **I must have it by tomorrow** lo necesito para mañana; **to have a baby** tener un niño *or* bebé
4 (*maintain, allow*): **I won't have it!** ¡no lo permitiré!; **I won't have this nonsense!** ¡no permitiré estas tonterías!; **we can't have that** no podemos permitir eso
5: **to have sth done** hacer *or* mandar hacer algo; **to have one's hair cut** cortarse el pelo; **to have sb do sth** hacer que algn haga algo
6 (*experience, suffer*): **to have a cold/flu** tener un resfriado/la gripe; **she had her bag stolen/her arm broken** le robaron el bolso/se rompió un brazo; **to have an operation** operarse
7 (*+ noun*): **to have a swim/walk/bath/rest** nadar/dar un paseo/darse un baño/descansar; **let's have a look** vamos a ver; **to have a meeting/party** celebrar una reunión/una fiesta; **let me have a try** déjame intentarlo
▸ **have in** *vt*: **to have it in for sb** (*col*) tenerla tomada con algn
▸ **have on** *vt*: **have you anything on tomorrow?** ¿vas a hacer algo mañana?; **I don't have any money on me** no llevo dinero (encima); **to have sb on** (*Brit col*) tomarle el pelo a algn
▸ **have out** *vt*: **to have it out with sb** (*settle a problem etc*) dejar las cosas en claro con algn

haven ['heɪvn] *n* puerto; (*fig*) refugio
haven't ['hævnt] = **have not**
haversack ['hævəsæk] *n* macuto
haves [hævz] *npl*: **the ~ and the have-nots** los ricos y los pobres
havoc ['hævək] *n* estragos *mpl*; **to play ~ with sth** hacer estragos en algo
Hawaii [hə'waii:] *n* (Islas *fpl*) Hawai *m*
Hawaiian [hə'waɪjən] *adj, n* hawaiano(-a) *m(f)*

hawk [hɔːk] *n* halcón *m* ■ *vt* (*goods for sale*) pregonar
hawkish ['hɔːkɪʃ] *adj* beligerante
hawthorn ['hɔːθɔːn] *n* espino
hay [heɪ] *n* heno
hay fever *n* fiebre *f* del heno
haystack ['heɪstæk] *n* almiar *m*
haywire ['heɪwaɪəʳ] *adj* (*col*): **to go ~** (*person*) volverse loco; (*plan*) irse al garete
hazard ['hæzəd] *n* riesgo; (*danger*) peligro ■ *vt* (*remark*) aventurar; (*one's life*) arriesgar; **to be a health ~** ser un peligro para la salud; **to ~ a guess** aventurar una respuesta *or* hipótesis
hazardous ['hæzədəs] *adj* (*dangerous*) peligroso; (*risky*) arriesgado
hazard warning lights *npl* (*Aut*) señales *fpl* de emergencia
haze [heɪz] *n* neblina
hazel ['heɪzl] *n* (*tree*) avellano ■ *adj* (*eyes*) color *m* de avellano
hazelnut ['heɪzlnʌt] *n* avellana
hazy ['heɪzɪ] *adj* brumoso; (*idea*) vago
H-bomb ['eɪtʃbɔm] *n* bomba H
h & c *abbr* (*Brit*) = **hot and cold (water)**
HE *abbr* = **high explosive**; (*Rel, Diplomacy*: = His (*or Her*) *Excellency*) S. Excª
he [hiː] *pron* él; **he who ...** aquél que ..., quien ...
head [hɛd] *n* cabeza; (*leader*) jefe(-a) *m(f)* ■ *vt* (*list*) encabezar; (*group*) capitanear; **heads (or tails)** cara (o cruz); **~ first** de cabeza; **~ over heels** patas arriba; **~ over heels in love** perdidamente enamorado; **on your ~ be it!** ¡allá tú!; **they went over my ~ to the manager** fueron directamente al gerente sin hacerme caso; **it was above** *or* **over their heads** no alcanzaron a entenderlo; **to come to a ~** (*fig: situation etc*) llegar a un punto crítico; **to have a ~ for business** tener talento para los negocios; **to have no ~ for heights** no resistir las alturas; **to lose/keep one's ~** perder la cabeza/mantener la calma; **to sit at the ~ of the table** sentarse a la cabecera de la mesa; **to ~ the ball** cabecear (el balón)
▸ **head for** *vt fus* dirigirse a
▸ **head off** *vt* (*threat, danger*) evitar
headache ['hɛdeɪk] *n* dolor *m* de cabeza; **to have a ~** tener dolor de cabeza
headband ['hɛdbænd] *n* cinta (para la cabeza), vincha (*LAm*)
headboard ['hɛdbɔːd] *n* cabecera
headdress ['hɛddrɛs] *n* (*of bride, Indian*) tocado
headed notepaper ['hɛdɪd-] *n* papel *m* con membrete
header ['hɛdəʳ] *n* (*Brit col: Football*) cabezazo; (*: fall*) caída de cabeza
headfirst [hɛd'fəːst] *adv* de cabeza
headhunt ['hɛdhʌnt] *vt*: **to be headhunted** ser seleccionado por un cazatalentos
headhunter ['hɛdhʌntəʳ] *n* (*fig*) cazaejecutivos *m inv*
heading ['hɛdɪŋ] *n* título
headlamp ['hɛdlæmp] *n* (*Brit*) = **headlight**
headland ['hɛdlənd] *n* promontorio
headlight ['hɛdlaɪt] *n* faro
headline ['hɛdlaɪn] *n* titular *m*
headlong ['hɛdlɔŋ] *adv* (*fall*) de cabeza; (*rush*) precipitadamente
headmaster/mistress [hɛd'mɑːstəʳ/mɪstrɪs] *n* director(a) *m(f)* (de escuela)
head office *n* oficina central, central *f*
head-on [hɛd'ɔn] *adj* (*collision*) de frente
headphones ['hɛdfəunz] *npl* auriculares *mpl*
headquarters ['hɛdkwɔːtəz] *npl* sede *f* central; (*Mil*) cuartel *m* general
head-rest ['hɛdrɛst] *n* reposa-cabezas *m inv*
headroom ['hɛdrum] *n* (*in car*) altura interior; (*under bridge*) (límite *m* de) altura
headscarf ['hɛdskɑːf] *n* pañuelo
headset ['hɛdsɛt] *n* cascos *mpl*
headstone ['hɛdstəun] *n* lápida
headstrong ['hɛdstrɔŋ] *adj* testarudo
head waiter *n* maître *m*
headway ['hɛdweɪ] *n*: **to make ~** (*fig*) hacer progresos
headwind ['hɛdwɪnd] *n* viento contrario
heady ['hɛdɪ] *adj* (*experience, period*) apasionante; (*wine*) fuerte
heal [hiːl] *vt* curar ■ *vi* cicatrizar
health [hɛlθ] *n* salud *f*
health care *n* asistencia sanitaria
health centre *n* ambulatorio, centro médico
health food *n*, **health foods** *npl* alimentos *mpl* orgánicos
health hazard *n* riesgo para la salud
Health Service *n* (*Brit*) servicio de salud pública, ≈ Insalud *m* (*SP*)
healthy ['hɛlθɪ] *adj* (*gen*) sano; (*economy, bank balance*) saludable
heap [hiːp] *n* montón *m* ■ *vt* amontonar; (*plate*) colmar; **heaps (of)** (*col: lots*) montones (de); **to ~ favours/praise/gifts** *etc* **on sb** colmar a algn de favores/elogios/regalos *etc*
hear (*pt, pp* **heard**) [hɪəʳ, həːd] *vt* oír; (*perceive*) sentir; (*listen to*) escuchar; (*lecture*) asistir a; (*Law: case*) ver ■ *vi* oír; **to ~ about** oír hablar de; **to ~ from sb** tener noticias de algn; **I've never heard of that book** nunca he oído hablar de ese libro
▸ **hear out** *vt*: **to ~ sb out** dejar que algn termine de hablar
hearing ['hɪərɪŋ] *n* (*sense*) oído; (*Law*) vista; **to give sb a ~** dar a algn la oportunidad de

hablar, escuchar a algn
hearing aid *n* audífono
hearsay ['hɪəseɪ] *n* rumores *mpl*, habladurías *fpl*
hearse [hə:s] *n* coche *m* fúnebre
heart [hɑ:t] *n* corazón *m*; **hearts** *npl* (*Cards*) corazones *mpl*; **at ~** en el fondo; **by ~** (*learn, know*) de memoria; **to have a weak ~** tener el corazón débil; **to set one's ~ on sth/on doing sth** anhelar algo/hacer algo; **I did not have the ~ to tell her** no tuve valor para decírselo; **to take ~** cobrar ánimos; **the ~ of the matter** lo esencial *or* el meollo del asunto
heartache ['hɑ:teɪk] *n* angustia
heart attack *n* infarto (de miocardio)
heartbeat ['hɑ:tbi:t] *n* latido (del corazón)
heartbreak ['hɑ:tbreɪk] *n* angustia, congoja
heartbreaking ['hɑ:tbreɪkɪŋ] *adj* desgarrador(a)
heartbroken ['hɑ:tbrəukən] *adj*: **she was ~ about it** le partió el corazón
heartburn ['hɑ:tbə:n] *n* acedía
-hearted ['hɑ:tɪd] *adj suff*: **a kind~ person** una persona bondadosa
heartening ['hɑ:tnɪŋ] *adj* alentador(a)
heart failure *n* (*Med*) paro cardíaco
heartfelt ['hɑ:tfɛlt] *adj* (*cordial*) cordial; (*deeply felt*) sincero
hearth [hɑ:θ] *n* (*gen*) hogar *m*; (*fireplace*) chimenea
heartily ['hɑ:tɪlɪ] *adv* sinceramente, cordialmente; (*laugh*) a carcajadas; (*eat*) con buen apetito; **to be ~ sick of** estar completamente harto de
heartland ['hɑ:tlænd] *n* zona interior *or* central; (*fig*) corazón *m*
heartless ['hɑ:tlɪs] *adj* despiadado
heartstrings ['hɑ:tstrɪŋz] *npl*: **to tug (at) sb's ~** tocar la fibra sensible de algn
heart-throb ['hɑ:tθrɔb] *n* ídolo
heart-to-heart ['hɑ:ttə'hɑ:t] *n* (*also*: **heart-to-heart talk**) conversación *f* íntima
heart transplant *n* transplante *m* de corazón
hearty ['hɑ:tɪ] *adj* cordial
heat [hi:t] *n* (*gen*) calor *m*; (*Sport*: *also*: **qualifying heat**) prueba eliminatoria; (*Zool*): **in** *or* **on ~** en celo ■ *vt* calentar
▸ **heat up** *vi* (*gen*) calentarse
heated ['hi:tɪd] *adj* caliente; (*fig*) acalorado
heater ['hi:tə^r] *n* calentador *m*
heath [hi:θ] *n* (*Brit*) brezal *m*
heathen ['hi:ðn] *adj*, *n* pagano(-a) *m(f)*
heather ['hɛðə^r] *n* brezo
heating ['hi:tɪŋ] *n* calefacción *f*
heat-resistant ['hi:trɪzɪstənt] *adj* refractario
heat-seeking ['hi:tsi:kɪŋ] *adj* guiado por infrarrojos, termoguiado
heatstroke ['hi:tstrəuk] *n* insolación *f*
heatwave ['hi:tweɪv] *n* ola de calor
heave [hi:v] *vt* (*pull*) tirar; (*push*) empujar con esfuerzo; (*lift*) levantar (con esfuerzo) ■ *vi* (*water*) subir y bajar ■ *n* tirón *m*; empujón *m*; (*effort*) esfuerzo; (*throw*) echada; **to ~ a sigh** dar *or* echar un suspiro, suspirar
▸ **heave to** *vi* (*Naut*) ponerse al pairo
heaven ['hɛvn] *n* cielo; (*Rel*) paraíso; **thank ~!** ¡gracias a Dios!; **for ~'s sake!** (*pleading*) ¡por el amor de Dios!, ¡por lo que más quiera!; (*protesting*) ¡por Dios!
heavenly ['hɛvnlɪ] *adj* celestial; (*Rel*) divino
heavenly body *n* cuerpo celeste
heavily ['hɛvɪlɪ] *adv* pesadamente; (*drink, smoke*) en exceso; (*sleep, sigh*) profundamente
heavy ['hɛvɪ] *adj* pesado; (*work*) duro; (*sea, rain, meal*) fuerte; (*drinker, smoker*) empedernido; (*eater*) comilón(-ona)
heavy-duty ['hɛvɪ'dju:tɪ] *adj* resistente
heavy goods vehicle *n* (*Brit*) vehículo pesado
heavy-handed ['hɛvɪ'hændɪd] *adj* (*clumsy, tactless*) torpe
heavy industry *n* industria pesada
heavy metal *n* (*Mus*) heavy *m* (metal)
heavy-set [hevɪ'sɛt] *adj* (*esp US*) corpulento, fornido
heavy user *n* consumidor *m* intensivo
heavyweight ['hɛvɪweɪt] *n* (*Sport*) peso pesado
Hebrew ['hi:bru:] *adj*, *n* (*Ling*) hebreo
Hebrides ['hɛbrɪdi:z] *npl*: **the ~** las Hébridas
heck [hɛk] *n* (*col*): **why the ~ ...?** ¿por qué porras ...?; **a ~ of a lot of** cantidad de
heckle ['hɛkl] *vt* interrumpir
heckler ['hɛklə^r] *n* *el/la que interrumpe a un orador*
hectare ['hɛktɑ:^r] *n* (*Brit*) hectárea
hectic ['hɛktɪk] *adj* agitado; (*busy*) ocupado
hector ['hɛktə^r] *vt* intimidar con bravatas
he'd [hi:d] = **he would**; **he had**
hedge [hɛdʒ] *n* seto ■ *vt* cercar (con un seto) ■ *vi* contestar con evasivas; **as a ~ against inflation** como protección contra la inflación; **to ~ one's bets** (*fig*) cubrirse
hedgehog ['hɛdʒhɔg] *n* erizo
hedgerow ['hɛdʒrəu] *n* seto vivo
hedonism ['hi:dənɪzəm] *n* hedonismo
heed [hi:d] *vt* (*also*: **take heed of**: *pay attention*) hacer caso de; (*bear in mind*) tener en cuenta; **to pay (no) ~ to, take (no) ~ of** (no) hacer caso a, (no) tener en cuenta
heedless ['hi:dlɪs] *adj* desatento
heel [hi:l] *n* talón *m* ■ *vt* (*shoe*) poner tacón a; **to take to one's heels** (*col*) poner pies en polvorosa; **to bring to ~** meter en cintura; *see also* **dig**
hefty ['hɛftɪ] *adj* (*person*) fornido; (*piece*) grande; (*price*) alto

heifer ['hɛfəʳ] *n* novilla, ternera
height [haɪt] *n* (*of person*) talla *f*; (*of building*) altura; (*high ground*) cerro; (*altitude*) altitud *f*; **what ~ are you?** ¿cuánto mides?; **of average ~** de estatura mediana; **to be afraid of heights** tener miedo a las alturas; **it's the ~ of fashion** es el último grito en moda
heighten ['haɪtn] *vt* elevar; (*fig*) aumentar
heinous ['heɪnəs] *adj* atroz, nefasto
heir [ɛəʳ] *n* heredero
heir apparent *n* presunto heredero
heiress ['ɛərɛs] *n* heredera
heirloom ['ɛəlu:m] *n* reliquia de familia
heist [haɪst] *n* (*col: hold-up*) atraco a mano armada
held [hɛld] *pt, pp of* **hold**
helicopter ['hɛlɪkɔptəʳ] *n* helicóptero
heliport ['hɛlɪpɔ:t] *n* (*Aviat*) helipuerto
helium ['hi:lɪəm] *n* helio
hell [hɛl] *n* infierno; **oh ~!** (*col*) ¡demonios!, ¡caramba!
he'll [hi:l] = **he will; he shall**
hellbent [hɛl'bɛnt] *adj* (*col*): **he was ~ on going** se le metió entre ceja y ceja ir
hellish ['hɛlɪʃ] *adj* infernal; (*col*) horrible
hello [hə'ləu] *excl* ¡hola!; (*surprise*) ¡caramba!; (*Tel*) ¡dígame! (*esp SP*), ¡aló! (*LAm*)
helm [hɛlm] *n* (*Naut*) timón *m*
helmet ['hɛlmɪt] *n* casco
helmsman ['hɛlmzmən] *n* timonel *m*
help [hɛlp] *n* ayuda; (*charwoman*) criada, asistenta ■ *vt* ayudar; **~!** ¡socorro!; **with the ~ of** con la ayuda de; **can I ~ you?** (*in shop*) ¿qué desea?; **to be of ~ to sb** servir a algn; **to ~ sb (to) do sth** echarle una mano *or* ayudar a algn a hacer algo; **~ yourself** sírvete; **he can't ~ it** no lo puede evitar
helper ['hɛlpəʳ] *n* ayudante *m/f*
helpful ['hɛlpful] *adj* útil; (*person*) servicial
helping ['hɛlpɪŋ] *n* ración *f*
helping hand *n*: **to give sb a ~** echar una mano a algn
helpless ['hɛlplɪs] *adj* (*incapable*) incapaz; (*defenceless*) indefenso
helpline ['hɛlplaɪn] *n* teléfono de asistencia al público
Helsinki ['hɛlsɪŋkɪ] *n* Helsinki *m*
helter-skelter ['hɛltə'skɛltəʳ] *n* (*in funfair*) tobogán *m*
hem [hɛm] *n* dobladillo ■ *vt* poner *or* coser el dobladillo a
▸ **hem in** *vt* cercar; **to feel hemmed in** (*fig*) sentirse acosado
he-man ['hi:mæn] *n* macho
hematology [hi:mə'tɔlədʒɪ] *n* (*US*) = **haematology**
hemisphere ['hɛmɪsfɪəʳ] *n* hemisferio
hemline ['hɛmlaɪn] *n* bajo (del vestido)
hemlock ['hɛmlɔk] *n* cicuta
hemoglobin [hi:mə'gləubɪn] *n* (*US*) = **haemoglobin**
hemophilia [hi:mə'fɪlɪə] *n* (*US*) = **haemophilia**
hemorrhage ['hɛmərɪdʒ] *n* (*US*) = **haemorrhage**
hemorrhoids ['hɛmərɔɪdz] *npl* (*US*) = **haemorrhoids**
hemp [hɛmp] *n* cáñamo
hen [hɛn] *n* gallina; (*female bird*) hembra
hence [hɛns] *adv* (*therefore*) por lo tanto; **two years ~** de aquí a dos años
henceforth [hɛns'fɔ:θ] *adv* de hoy en adelante
henchman ['hɛntʃmən] *n* (*pej*) secuaz *m*
henna ['hɛnə] *n* alheña
hen night *n* (*col*) despedida de soltera
hen party *n* (*col*) reunión *f* de mujeres
henpecked ['hɛnpɛkt] *adj*: **to be ~** ser un calzonazos
hepatitis [hɛpə'taɪtɪs] *n* hepatitis *f inv*
her [hə:ʳ] *pron* (*direct*) la; (*indirect*) le; (*stressed, after prep*) ella ■ *adj* su; *see also* **me; my**
herald ['hɛrəld] *n* (*forerunner*) precursor(a) *m(f)* ■ *vt* anunciar
heraldic [hɛ'rældɪk] *adj* heráldico
heraldry ['hɛrəldrɪ] *n* heráldica
herb [hə:b] *n* hierba
herbaceous [hə:'beɪʃəs] *adj* herbáceo
herbal ['hə:bl] *adj* de hierbas
herbicide ['hə:bɪsaɪd] *n* herbicida *m*
herd [hə:d] *n* rebaño; (*of wild animals, swine*) piara ■ *vt* (*drive, gather: animals*) llevar en manada; (*: people*) reunir
▸ **herd together** *vt* agrupar, reunir ■ *vi* apiñarse, agruparse
here [hɪəʳ] *adv* aquí; **~!** (*present*) ¡presente!; **~ is/are** aquí está/están; **~ she is** aquí está; **come ~!** ¡ven aquí *or* acá!; **~ and there** aquí y allá
hereabouts ['hɪərə'bauts] *adv* por aquí (cerca)
hereafter [hɪər'ɑ:ftəʳ] *adv* en el futuro ■ *n*: **the ~** el más allá
hereby [hɪə'baɪ] *adv* (*in letter*) por la presente
hereditary [hɪ'rɛdɪtrɪ] *adj* hereditario
heredity [hɪ'rɛdɪtɪ] *n* herencia
heresy ['hɛrəsɪ] *n* herejía
heretic ['hɛrətɪk] *n* hereje *m/f*
heretical [hɪ'rɛtɪkəl] *adj* herético
herewith [hɪə'wɪð] *adv*: **I send you ~ ...** le mando adjunto ...
heritage ['hɛrɪtɪdʒ] *n* (*gen*) herencia; (*fig*) patrimonio; **our national ~** nuestro patrimonio nacional

hermetically [hə:ˈmɛtɪkəlɪ] *adv*: **~ sealed** herméticamente cerrado
hermit [ˈhə:mɪt] *n* ermitaño(-a)
hernia [ˈhə:nɪə] *n* hernia
hero (*pl* **heroes**) [ˈhɪərəu] *n* héroe *m*; (*in book, film*) protagonista *m*
heroic [hɪˈrəuɪk] *adj* heroico
heroin [ˈhɛrəuɪn] *n* heroína
heroin addict *n* heroinómano(-a), adicto(-a) a la heroína
heroine [ˈhɛrəuɪn] *n* heroína; (*in book, film*) protagonista
heroism [ˈhɛrəuɪzm] *n* heroísmo
heron [ˈhɛrən] *n* garza
hero worship *n* veneración *f*
herring [ˈhɛrɪŋ] *n* arenque *m*
hers [hə:z] *pron* (el) suyo/(la) suya *etc*; **a friend of ~** un amigo suyo; **this is ~** esto es suyo *or* de ella; *see also* **mine**
herself [hə:ˈsɛlf] *pron* (*reflexive*) se; (*emphatic*) ella misma; (*after prep*) sí (misma); *see also* **oneself**
Herts *abbr* (*Brit*) = **Hertfordshire**
he's [hi:z] = **he is; he has**
hesitant [ˈhɛzɪtənt] *adj* indeciso; **to be ~ about doing sth** no decidirse a hacer algo
hesitate [ˈhɛzɪteɪt] *vi* dudar, vacilar; **don't ~ to ask (me)** no dudes en pedírmelo
hesitation [hɛzɪˈteɪʃən] *n* indecisión *f*; **I have no ~ in saying (that)...** no tengo el menor reparo en afirmar que ...
hessian [ˈhɛsɪən] *n* arpillera
heterogeneous [ˈhɛtərəˈdʒi:nɪəs] *adj* heterogéneo
heterosexual [hɛtərəuˈsɛksjuəl] *adj, n* heterosexual *m/f*
het up [hɛtˈʌp] *adj* (*col*) agitado, nervioso
HEW *n abbr* (*US:* = *Department of Health, Education, and Welfare*) *ministerio de sanidad, educación y bienestar público*
hew [hju:] *vt* cortar
hex [hɛks] (*US*) *n* maleficio, mal *m* de ojo ■ *vt* embrujar
hexagon [ˈhɛksəgən] *n* hexágono
hexagonal [hɛkˈsægənl] *adj* hexagonal
hey [heɪ] *excl* ¡oye!, ¡oiga!
heyday [ˈheɪdeɪ] *n*: **the ~ of** el apogeo de
HF *n abbr* = **high frequency**
HGV *n abbr* = **heavy goods vehicle**
HI *abbr* (*US*) = **Hawaii**
hi [haɪ] *excl* ¡hola!
hiatus [haɪˈeɪtəs] *n* vacío, interrupción *f*; (*Ling*) hiato
hibernate [ˈhaɪbəneɪt] *vi* invernar
hibernation [haɪbəˈneɪʃən] *n* hibernación *f*
hiccough, hiccup [ˈhɪkʌp] *vi* hipar; **hiccoughs** *npl* hipo *sg*
hick [hɪk] *n* (*US col*) paleto(-a)
hid [hɪd] *pt of* **hide**
hidden [ˈhɪdn] *pp of* **hide** ■ *adj*: **there are no ~ extras** no hay suplementos ocultos; **~ agenda** plan *m* encubierto
hide [haɪd] (*pt* **hid**, *pp* **hidden**) *n* (*skin*) piel *f* ■ *vt* esconder, ocultar; (*feelings, truth*) encubrir, ocultar ■ *vi*: **to ~ (from sb)** esconderse *or* ocultarse (de algn)
hide-and-seek [ˈhaɪdənˈsi:k] *n* escondite *m*
hideaway [ˈhaɪdəweɪ] *n* escondite *m*
hideous [ˈhɪdɪəs] *adj* horrible
hideously [ˈhɪdɪəslɪ] *adv* horriblemente
hide-out [ˈhaɪdaut] *n* escondite *m*, refugio
hiding [ˈhaɪdɪŋ] *n* (*beating*) paliza; **to be in ~** (*concealed*) estar escondido
hiding place *n* escondrijo
hierarchy [ˈhaɪərɑ:kɪ] *n* jerarquía
hieroglyphic [haɪərəˈglɪfɪk] *adj* jeroglífico ■ *n*: **hieroglyphics** jeroglíficos *mpl*
hi-fi [ˈhaɪfaɪ] *abbr* (= *high fidelity*) *n* estéreo, hifi *m* ■ *adj* de alta fidelidad
higgledy-piggledy [ˈhɪgldɪˈpɪgldɪ] *adv* en desorden, de cualquier modo
high [haɪ] *adj* alto; (*speed, number*) grande, alto; (*price*) elevado; (*wind*) fuerte; (*voice*) agudo; (*col: on drugs*) colocado; (*: on drink*) borracho; (*Culin: meat, game*) pasado; (*: spoilt*) estropeado ■ *adv* alto, a gran altura ■ *n*: **exports have reached a new ~** las exportaciones han alcanzado niveles inusitados; **it is 20 m ~** tiene 20 m de altura; **~ in the air** en las alturas; **to pay a ~ price for sth** pagar algo muy caro
highball [ˈhaɪbɔ:l] *n* (*US: drink*) whisky *m* soda, highball *m* (*LAm*), jaibol *m* (*LAm*)
highboy [ˈhaɪbɔɪ] *n* (*US*) cómoda alta
highbrow [ˈhaɪbrau] *adj* culto
highchair [ˈhaɪtʃɛəʳ] *n* silla alta (para niños)
high-class [ˈhaɪˈklɑ:s] *adj* (*neighbourhood*) de alta sociedad; (*hotel*) de lujo; (*person*) distinguido, de categoría; (*food*) de alta categoría
High Court *n* (*Law*) tribunal *m* supremo; *ver nota*

HIGH COURT

En el sistema legal de Inglaterra y Gales *High Court* es la forma abreviada de "High Court of Justice", tribunal superior que junto con el de apelación ("Court of Appeal") forma el Tribunal Supremo ("Supreme Court of Judicature"). En el sistema legal escocés es la forma abreviada de "High Court of Justiciary", tribunal con jurado que juzga los delitos más serios, que pueden dar lugar a una pena de gran severidad.

higher ['haɪəʳ] *adj* (*form of life, study etc*) superior ■ *adv* más alto ■ *n* (*Scottish Scol*): **H~** *cada una de las asignaturas que se estudian entre los 16 y los 17 años generalmente, así como el certificado de haberlas probado*
higher education *n* educación *f or* enseñanza superior
high explosive *n* explosivo de gran potencia
highfalutin [haɪfə'lu:tɪn] *adj* (*col*) de altos vuelos, encopetado
high finance *n* altas finanzas *fpl*
high-flier, high-flyer [haɪ'flaɪəʳ] *n* ambicioso(-a)
high-handed [haɪ'hændɪd] *adj* despótico
high-heeled [haɪ'hi:ld] *adj* de tacón alto
highjack ['haɪdʒæk] = **hijack**
high jump *n* (*Sport*) salto de altura
highlands ['haɪləndz] *npl* tierras *fpl* altas; **the H~** (*in Scotland*) las Tierras Altas de Escocia
high-level ['haɪlɛvl] *adj* (*talks etc*) de alto nivel
highlight ['haɪlaɪt] *n* (*fig: of event*) punto culminante ■ *vt* subrayar
highly ['haɪlɪ] *adv* sumamente; **~ paid** muy bien pagado; **to speak ~ of** hablar muy bien de; **~ strung** muy excitable
High Mass *n* misa mayor
highness ['haɪnɪs] *n* altura; **Her** *or* **His H~** Su Alteza
high-pitched [haɪ'pɪtʃt] *adj* agudo
high point *n*: **the ~** el punto culminante
high-powered ['haɪ'pauəd] *adj* (*engine*) de gran potencia; (*fig: person*) importante
high-pressure ['haɪprɛʃəʳ] *adj* de alta presión; (*fig: salesman etc*) enérgico
high-rise ['haɪraɪz] *n* (*also*: **high-rise block, high-rise building**) torre *f* de pisos
high school *n* centro de enseñanza secundaria, ≈ Instituto Nacional de Bachillerato (*SP*), liceo (*LAm*); *ver nota*

HIGH SCHOOL

El término *high school* se aplica en Estados Unidos a dos tipos de centros de educación secundaria: "Junior High Schools", en los que se imparten normalmente del 7° al 9° curso (llamado "grade") y "Senior High Schools", que abarcan los cursos 10°, 11° y 12° y en ocasiones el 9°. Aquí pueden estudiarse asignaturas tanto de contenido académico como profesional. En Gran Bretaña también se llaman *high school* algunos centros de enseñanza secundaria.

high season *n* (*Brit*) temporada alta
high-speed ['haɪspi:d] *adj* de alta velocidad
high-spirited [haɪ'spɪrɪtɪd] *adj* animado
high spirits *npl* ánimos *mpl*
high street *n* (*Brit*) calle *f* mayor
high tide *n* marea alta
highway ['haɪweɪ] *n* carretera; (*US*) autopista
Highway Code *n* (*Brit*) código de la circulación
highwayman ['haɪweɪmən] *n* salteador *m* de caminos
hijack ['haɪdʒæk] *vt* secuestrar ■ *n* (*also*: **hijacking**) secuestro
hijacker ['haɪdʒækəʳ] *n* secuestrador(a) *m(f)*
hike [haɪk] *vi* (*go walking*) ir de excursión (a pie); (*tramp*) caminar ■ *n* caminata; (*col: in prices etc*) aumento
▸ **hike up** *vt* (*raise*) aumentar
hiker ['haɪkəʳ] *n* excursionista *m/f*
hilarious [hɪ'lɛərɪəs] *adj* divertidísimo
hilarity [hɪ'lærɪtɪ] *n* (*laughter*) risas *fpl*, carcajadas *fpl*
hill [hɪl] *n* colina; (*high*) montaña; (*slope*) cuesta
hillbilly ['hɪlbɪlɪ] *n* (*US*) rústico(-a) montañés(-esa); (*pej*) palurdo(-a)
hillock ['hɪlək] *n* montecillo, altozano
hillside ['hɪlsaɪd] *n* ladera
hilltop ['hɪltɔp] *n* cumbre *f*
hilly ['hɪlɪ] *adj* montañoso; (*uneven*) accidentado
hilt [hɪlt] *n* (*of sword*) empuñadura; **to the ~** (*fig: support*) incondicionalmente; **to be in debt up to the ~** estar hasta el cuello de deudas
him [hɪm] *pron* (*direct*) le, lo; (*indirect*) le; (*stressed, after prep*) él; *see also* **me**
Himalayas [hɪmə'leɪəz] *npl*: **the ~** el Himalaya
himself [hɪm'sɛlf] *pron* (*reflexive*) se; (*emphatic*) él mismo; (*after prep*) sí (mismo); *see also* **oneself**
hind [haɪnd] *adj* posterior ■ *n* cierva
hinder ['hɪndəʳ] *vt* estorbar, impedir
hindquarters ['haɪndkwɔ:təz] *npl* (*Zool*) cuartos *mpl* traseros
hindrance ['hɪndrəns] *n* estorbo, obstáculo
hindsight ['haɪndsaɪt] *n* percepción *f* tardía *or* retrospectiva; **with the benefit of ~** con la perspectiva del tiempo transcurrido
Hindu ['hɪndu:] *n* hindú *m/f*
hinge [hɪndʒ] *n* bisagra, gozne *m* ■ *vi* (*fig*): **to ~ on** depender de
hint [hɪnt] *n* indirecta; (*advice*) consejo ■ *vt*: **to ~ that** insinuar que ■ *vi*: **to ~ at** aludir a; **to drop a ~** soltar *or* tirar una indirecta; **give me a ~** dame una pista
hip [hɪp] *n* cadera; (*Bot*) escaramujo

hip flask *n* petaca
hip-hop ['hɪphɔp] *n* hip hop *m*
hippie ['hɪpɪ] *n* hippie *m/f*, jipi *m/f*
hip pocket *n* bolsillo de atrás
hippopotamus (*pl* **hippopotamuses** *or* **hippopotami**) *n* [hɪpə'pɔtəməs, -'pɔtəmaɪ] hipopótamo
hippy ['hɪpɪ] *n* = **hippie**
hire ['haɪəʳ] *vt* (*Brit: car, equipment*) alquilar; (*worker*) contratar ■ *n* alquiler *m*; **for ~** se alquila; (*taxi*) libre; **on ~** de alquiler
▸ **hire out** *vt* alquilar, arrendar
hire car, hired car *n* (*Brit*) coche *m* de alquiler
hire purchase *n* (*Brit*) compra a plazos; **to buy sth on ~** comprar algo a plazos
his [hɪz] *pron* (el) suyo/(la) suya *etc* ■ *adj* su; **this is ~** esto es suyo *or* de él; *see also* **my; mine**
Hispanic [hɪs'pænɪk] *adj* hispánico
hiss [hɪs] *vi* sisear; (*in protest*) silbar ■ *n* siseo; silbido
histogram ['hɪstəgræm] *n* histograma *m*
historian [hɪ'stɔːrɪən] *n* historiador(a) *m(f)*
historic [hɪ'stɔrɪk], **historical** [hɪ'stɔrɪkl] *adj* histórico
history ['hɪstərɪ] *n* historia; **there's a long ~ of that illness in his family** esa enfermedad corre en su familia
histrionics [hɪstrɪ'ɔnɪks] *npl* histrionismo
hit [hɪt] *vt* (*pt, pp* **hit**) (*strike*) golpear, pegar; (*reach: target*) alcanzar; (*collide with: car*) chocar contra; (*fig: affect*) afectar ■ *n* golpe *m*; (*success*) éxito; **to ~ the headlines** salir en primera plana; **to ~ the road** (*col*) largarse; **to ~ it off with sb** llevarse bien con algn
▸ **hit back** *vi* defenderse; (*fig*) devolver golpe por golpe
▸ **hit out at** *vt fus* asestar un golpe a; (*fig*) atacar
▸ **hit (up)on** *vt fus* (*answer*) dar con; (*solution*) hallar, encontrar
hit and miss *adj*: **it's very ~, it's a ~ affair** es cuestión de suerte
hit-and-run driver ['hɪtən'rʌn-] *n conductor que tras atropellar a algn se da a la fuga*
hitch [hɪtʃ] *vt* (*fasten*) atar, amarrar; (*also:* **hitch up**) arremangarse ■ *n* (*difficulty*) problema, pega; **to ~ a lift** hacer autostop; **technical ~** problema *m* técnico
▸ **hitch up** *vt* (*horse, cart*) enganchar, uncir
hitch-hike ['hɪtʃhaɪk] *vi* hacer autostop
hitch-hiker ['hɪtʃhaɪkəʳ] *n* autostopista *m/f*
hi-tech [haɪ'tɛk] *adj* de alta tecnología
hitherto ['hɪðə'tuː] *adv* hasta ahora, hasta aquí
hit list *n* lista negra
hitman ['hɪtmæn] *n* asesino a sueldo
hit or miss ['hɪtə'mɪs] *adj* = **hit and miss**
hit parade *n*: **the ~** los cuarenta principales
HIV *n abbr* (= *human immunodeficiency virus*) VIH *m*; **~-negative** no portador(a) del virus del sida, no seropositivo; **~-positive** portador(a) del virus del sida, seropositivo
hive [haɪv] *n* colmena; **the shop was a ~ of activity** (*fig*) la tienda era una colmena humana
▸ **hive off** *vt* (*col: separate*) separar; (*: privatize*) privatizar
hl *abbr* (= *hectolitre*) hl
HM *abbr* (= *His (or Her) Majesty*) S.M.
HMG *abbr* (*Brit*) = **His** (*or* **Her**) **Majesty's Government**
HMI *n abbr* (*Brit Scol*) = **His** (*or* **Her**) **Majesty's Inspector**
HMO *n abbr* (*US: = Health Maintenance Organization*) *seguro médico global*
HMS *abbr* = **His** (*or* **Her**) **Majesty's Ship**
HMSO *n abbr* (*Brit: = His (or Her) Majesty's Stationery Office*) *distribuidor oficial de las publicaciones del gobierno del Reino Unido*
HNC *n abbr* (*Brit: = Higher National Certificate*) *título académico*
HND *n abbr* (*Brit: = Higher National Diploma*) *título académico*
hoard [hɔːd] *n* (*treasure*) tesoro; (*stockpile*) provisión *f* ■ *vt* acumular
hoarding ['hɔːdɪŋ] *n* (*for posters*) valla publicitaria
hoarfrost ['hɔːfrɔst] *n* escarcha
hoarse [hɔːs] *adj* ronco
hoax [həuks] *n* engaño
hob [hɔb] *n* quemador *m*
hobble ['hɔbl] *vi* cojear
hobby ['hɔbɪ] *n* pasatiempo, afición *f*
hobby-horse ['hɔbɪhɔːs] *n* (*fig*) tema preferido
hobnob ['hɔbnɔb] *vi*: **to ~ (with)** alternar (con)
hobo ['həubəu] *n* (*US*) vagabundo
hock [hɔk] *n* corvejón *m*; (*col*): **to be in ~** (*person*) estar empeñado *or* endeudado; (*object*) estar empeñado
hockey ['hɔkɪ] *n* hockey *m*
hocus-pocus [həukəs'pəukəs] *n* (*trickery*) engañifa; (*words: of magician*) abracadabra *m*
hod [hɔd] *n* capacho
hodge-podge ['hɔdʒpɔdʒ] *n* (*US*) = **hotchpotch**
hoe [həu] *n* azadón *m* ■ *vt* azadonar
hog [hɔg] *n* cerdo, puerco ■ *vt* (*fig*) acaparar; **to go the whole ~** echar el todo por el todo
Hogmanay [hɔgmə'neɪ] *n* (*Scottish*) Nochevieja
hoist [hɔɪst] *n* (*crane*) grúa ■ *vt* levantar, alzar
hoity-toity [hɔɪtɪ'tɔɪtɪ] *adj* (*col*): **to be ~** darse humos

hold [həuld] (*pt, pp* **held**) *vt* tener; (*contain*) contener; (*keep back*) retener; (*believe*) sostener; (*take hold of*) coger (*SP*), agarrar (*LAm*); (*bear: weight*) soportar; (*meeting*) celebrar ■ *vi* (*withstand: pressure*) resistir; (*be valid*) ser válido; (*stick*) pegarse ■ *n* (*grasp*) asimiento; (*fig*) dominio; (*Wrestling*) presa; (*Naut*) bodega; **~ the line!** (*Tel*) ¡no cuelgue!; **to ~ one's own** (*fig*) defenderse; **to ~ office** (*Pol*) ocupar un cargo; **to ~ firm** *or* **fast** mantenerse firme; **he holds the view that ...** opina *or* es su opinión que ...; **to ~ sb responsible for sth** culpar *or* echarle la culpa a algn de algo; **where can I get ~ of ...?** ¿dónde puedo encontrar (a) ...?; **to catch** *or* **get (a) ~ of** agarrarse *or* asirse de
▸ **hold back** *vt* retener; (*secret*) ocultar; **to ~ sb back from doing sth** impedir a algn hacer algo, impedir que algn haga algo
▸ **hold down** *vt* (*person*) sujetar; (*job*) mantener
▸ **hold forth** *vi* perorar
▸ **hold off** *vt* (*enemy*) rechazar ■ *vi*: **if the rain holds off** si no llueve
▸ **hold on** *vi* agarrarse bien; (*wait*) esperar
▸ **hold on to** *vt fus* agarrarse a; (*keep*) guardar
▸ **hold out** *vt* ofrecer ■ *vi* (*resist*) resistir; **to ~ out (against)** resistir (a), sobrevivir
▸ **hold over** *vt* (*meeting etc*) aplazar
▸ **hold up** *vt* (*raise*) levantar; (*support*) apoyar; (*delay*) retrasar; (*: traffic*) demorar; (*rob: bank*) asaltar, atracar

holdall [ˈhəuldɔːl] *n* (*Brit*) bolsa

holder [ˈhəuldəʳ] *n* (*of ticket, record*) poseedor(a) *m(f)*; (*of passport, post, office, title etc*) titular *m/f*

holding [ˈhəuldɪŋ] *n* (*share*) participación *f*

holding company *n* holding *m*

holdup [ˈhəuldʌp] *n* (*robbery*) atraco; (*delay*) retraso; (*Brit: in traffic*) embotellamiento

hole [həul] *n* agujero ■ *vt* agujerear; **~ in the heart** (*Med*) boquete *m* en el corazón; **to pick holes in** (*fig*) encontrar defectos en; **the ship was holed** se abrió una vía de agua en el barco
▸ **hole up** *vi* esconderse

holiday [ˈhɔlədɪ] *n* vacaciones *fpl*; (*day off*) (día *m* de) fiesta, día *m* festivo *or* feriado (*LAm*); **on ~** de vacaciones; **to be on ~** estar de vacaciones

holiday camp *n* colonia *or* centro vacacional; (*for children*) colonia veraniega infantil

holiday job *n* (*Brit*) trabajo para las vacaciones

holidaymaker [ˈhɔlədɪmeɪkəʳ] *n* (*Brit*) turista *m/f*

holiday pay *n* paga de las vacaciones

holiday resort *n* centro turístico

holiday season *n* temporada de vacaciones

holiness [ˈhəulɪnɪs] *n* santidad *f*

holistic [həuˈlɪstɪk] *adj* holístico

Holland [ˈhɔlənd] *n* Holanda

holler [ˈhɔləʳ] *vi* (*col*) gritar, vocear

hollow [ˈhɔləu] *adj* hueco; (*fig*) vacío; (*eyes*) hundido; (*sound*) sordo ■ *n* (*gen*) hueco; (*in ground*) hoyo ■ *vt*: **to ~ out** ahuecar

holly [ˈhɔlɪ] *n* acebo

hollyhock [ˈhɔlɪhɔk] *n* malva loca

holocaust [ˈhɔləkɔːst] *n* holocausto

hologram [ˈhɔləgræm] *n* holograma *m*

holster [ˈhəulstəʳ] *n* pistolera

holy [ˈhəulɪ] *adj* (*gen*) santo, sagrado; (*water*) bendito; **the H~ Father** el Santo Padre

Holy Communion *n* Sagrada Comunión *f*

Holy Ghost, Holy Spirit *n* Espíritu *m* Santo

homage [ˈhɔmɪdʒ] *n* homenaje *m*; **to pay ~ to** rendir homenaje a

home [həum] *n* casa; (*country*) patria; (*institution*) asilo; (*Comput*) punto inicial *or* de partida ■ *adj* (*domestic*) casero, de casa; (*Econ, Pol*) nacional; (*Sport: team*) de casa; (*: match, win*) en casa ■ *adv* (*direction*) a casa; **at ~** en casa; **to go/come ~** ir/volver a casa; **make yourself at ~** ¡estás en tu casa!; **it's near my ~** está cerca de mi casa
▸ **home in on** *vt fus* (*missile*) dirigirse hacia

home address *n* domicilio

home-brew [həumˈbru] *n* cerveza *etc* casera

homecoming [ˈhəumkʌmɪŋ] *n* regreso (al hogar)

home computer *n* ordenador *m* doméstico

Home Counties *npl* *condados que rodean Londres*

home economics *n* economía doméstica

home ground *n*: **to be on ~** estar en su *etc* terreno

home-grown [ˈhəumgrəun] *adj* de cosecha propia

home help *n* (*Brit*) trabajador(a) *m(f)* del servicio de atención domiciliaria

homeland [ˈhəumlænd] *n* tierra natal

homeless [ˈhəumlɪs] *adj* sin hogar, sin casa ■ *npl*: **the ~** las personas sin hogar

home loan *n* préstamo para la vivienda

homely [ˈhəumlɪ] *adj* (*domestic*) casero; (*simple*) sencillo

home-made [həumˈmeɪd] *adj* hecho en casa

Home Office *n* (*Brit*) Ministerio del Interior

homeopathy *etc* [həumɪˈɔpəθɪ] (*US*) = **homoeopathy** *etc*

home page *n* (*Comput*) página de inicio

home rule *n* autonomía

Home Secretary *n* (*Brit*) Ministro del Interior

homesick ['həumsɪk] *adj*: **to be ~** tener morriña *or* nostalgia
homestead ['həumstɛd] *n* hacienda
home town *n* ciudad *f* natal
home truth *n*: **to tell sb a few home truths** decir cuatro verdades a algn
homeward ['həumwəd] *adj* (*journey*) de vuelta ■ *adv* hacia casa
homewards ['həumwədz] *adv* hacia casa
homework ['həumwəːk] *n* deberes *mpl*
homicidal [hɔmɪ'saɪdl] *adj* homicida
homicide ['hɔmɪsaɪd] *n* (*US*) homicidio
homily ['hɔmɪlɪ] *n* homilía
homing ['həumɪŋ] *adj* (*device, missile*) buscador(a); **~ pigeon** paloma mensajera
homoeopath, homeopath (*US*) ['həumɪəupæθ] *n* homeópata *m/f*
homoeopathic, homeopathic (*US*) [həumɪəu'pæθɪk] *adj* homeopático
homoeopathy, homeopathy (*US*) [həumɪ'ɔpəθɪ] *n* homeopatía
homogeneous [hɔmə'dʒiːnɪəs] *adj* homogéneo
homogenize [hə'mɔdʒənaɪz] *vt* homogeneizar
homosexual [hɔməu'sɛksjuəl] *adj, n* homosexual *m/f*
Hon *abbr* (= *honourable, honorary*) *en títulos*
Honduras [hɔn'djuərəs] *n* Honduras *fpl*
hone [həun] *vt* (*sharpen*) afilar; (*fig*) perfeccionar
honest ['ɔnɪst] *adj* honrado; (*sincere*) franco, sincero; **to be quite ~ with you ...** para serte franco ...
honestly ['ɔnɪstlɪ] *adv* honradamente; francamente, de verdad
honesty ['ɔnɪstɪ] *n* honradez *f*
honey ['hʌnɪ] *n* miel *f*; (*US col*) cariño; (*: to strangers*) guapo, linda
honeycomb ['hʌnɪkəum] *n* panal *m*; (*fig*) laberinto
honeymoon ['hʌnɪmuːn] *n* luna de miel
honeysuckle ['hʌnɪsʌkl] *n* madreselva
Hong Kong ['hɔŋ'kɔŋ] *n* Hong-Kong *m*
honk [hɔŋk] *vi* (*Aut*) tocar la bocina
Honolulu [hɔnə'luːluː] *n* Honolulú *m*
honorary ['ɔnərərɪ] *adj* no remunerado; (*duty, title*) honorario
honour, honor (*US*) ['ɔnəʳ] *vt* honrar ■ *n* honor *m*, honra; **in ~ of** en honor de; **it's a great ~** es un gran honor
honourable, honorable (*US*) ['ɔnərəbl] *adj* honrado, honorable
honour-bound, honor-bound (*US*) ['ɔnə'baund] *adj* moralmente obligado
honours degree *n* (*Univ*) *licenciatura superior*; *ver nota*

HONOURS DEGREE

Tras un período de estudios de tres años normalmente (cuatro en Escocia), los universitarios obtienen una licenciatura llamada *honours degree*. La calificación global que se recibe, en una escala de mayor a menor es la siguiente: "first class" (I), "upper-second class" (II:1), "lower-second class" (II:2) y "third class" (III). El licenciado puede añadir las letras "Hons" al título obtenido tras su nombre y apellidos, por ejemplo "BA Hons" *see also* **ordinary degree**

honours list *n* (*Brit*) *lista de distinciones honoríficas que entrega la reina*; *ver nota*

HONOURS LIST

A la lista con los títulos honoríficos y condecoraciones que el monarca británico otorga en Año Nuevo y en el día de su cumpleaños se la conoce con el nombre de *honours list*. Las personas que reciben dichas distinciones suelen ser miembros destacados de la vida pública (ámbito empresarial, ejército, deportes, espectáculos), aunque últimamente también se reconoce con ellas el trabajo abnegado y anónimo de la gente de la calle.

Hons. [ɔnz] *abbr* (*Univ*) = **hono(u)rs degree**
hood [hud] *n* capucha; (*Brit Aut*) capota; (*US Aut*) capó *m*; (*US col*) matón *m*
hooded ['hudɪd] *adj* (*robber*) encapuchado
hoodie ['hudɪ] *n* (*pullover*) sudadera *f* con capucha; (*young person*) capuchero(-a) *m(f)*
hoodlum ['huːdləm] *n* matón *m*
hoodwink ['hudwɪŋk] *vt* (*Brit*) timar, engañar
hoof (*pl* **hoofs** *or* **hooves**) [huːf, huːvz] *n* pezuña
hook [huk] *n* gancho; (*on dress*) corchete *m*, broche *m*; (*for fishing*) anzuelo ■ *vt* enganchar; **hooks and eyes** corchetes *mpl*, macho y hembra *m*; **by ~ or by crook** por las buenas o por las malas, cueste lo que cueste; **to be hooked on** (*col*) estar enganchado a
▸ **hook up** *vt* (*Radio, TV*) transmitir en cadena
hooligan ['huːlɪgən] *n* gamberro
hooliganism ['huːlɪgənɪzəm] *n* gamberrismo
hoop [huːp] *n* aro
hoot [huːt] *vi* (*Brit Aut*) tocar la bocina; (*siren*) sonar; (*owl*) ulular ■ *n* bocinazo, toque *m* de sirena; **to ~ with laughter** morirse de risa

hooter ['huːtəʳ] *n* (*Brit Aut*) bocina; (*of ship, factory*) sirena
hoover® ['huːvəʳ] (*Brit*) *n* aspiradora ■ *vt* pasar la aspiradora por
hooves [huːvz] *pl of* **hoof**
hop [hɔp] *vi* saltar, brincar; (*on one foot*) saltar con un pie ■ *n* salto, brinco; *see also* **hops**
hope [həup] *vt, vi* esperar ■ *n* esperanza; **I ~ so/not** espero que sí/no
hopeful ['həupful] *adj* (*person*) optimista; (*situation*) prometedor(a); **I'm ~ that she'll manage to come** confío en que podrá venir
hopefully ['həupfulɪ] *adv* con optimismo, con esperanza
hopeless ['həuplɪs] *adj* desesperado
hopelessly ['həuplɪslɪ] *adv* (*live etc*) sin esperanzas; **I'm ~ confused/lost** estoy totalmente despistado/perdido
hopper ['hɔpəʳ] *n* (*chute*) tolva
hops [hɔps] *npl* lúpulo *sg*
horde [hɔːd] *n* horda
horizon [hə'raɪzn] *n* horizonte *m*
horizontal [hɔrɪ'zɔntl] *adj* horizontal
hormone ['hɔːməun] *n* hormona
hormone replacement therapy *n* terapia hormonal sustitutiva
horn [hɔːn] *n* cuerno, cacho (*LAm*); (*Mus: also:* **French horn**) trompa; (*Aut*) bocina, claxon *m*
horned [hɔːnd] *adj* con cuernos
hornet ['hɔːnɪt] *n* avispón *m*
horny ['hɔːnɪ] *adj* (*material*) córneo; (*hands*) calloso; (*US col*) cachondo
horoscope ['hɔrəskəup] *n* horóscopo
horrendous [hɔ'rɛndəs] *adj* horrendo
horrible ['hɔrɪbl] *adj* horrible
horribly ['hɔrɪblɪ] *adv* horriblemente
horrid ['hɔrɪd] *adj* horrible, horroroso
horridly ['hɔrɪdlɪ] *adv* (*behave*) tremendamente mal
horrific [hɔ'rɪfɪk] *adj* (*accident*) horroroso; (*film*) horripilante
horrify ['hɔrɪfaɪ] *vt* horrorizar
horrifying ['hɔrɪfaɪɪŋ] *adj* horroroso
horror ['hɔrəʳ] *n* horror *m*
horror film *n* película de terror *or* miedo
horror-struck ['hɔrəstrʌk], **horror-stricken** ['hɔrəstrɪkn] *adj* horrorizado
hors d'œuvre [ɔː'dəːvrə] *n* entremeses *mpl*
horse [hɔːs] *n* caballo
horseback ['hɔːsbæk] *n*: **on ~** a caballo
horsebox ['hɔːsbɔks] *n* remolque *m* para transportar caballos
horse chestnut *n* (*tree*) castaño de Indias
horsedrawn ['hɔːsdrɔːn] *adj* de tracción animal
horsefly ['hɔːsflaɪ] *n* tábano
horseman ['hɔːsmən] *n* jinete *m*
horsemanship ['hɔːsmənʃɪp] *n* equitación *f*, manejo del caballo
horseplay ['hɔːspleɪ] *n* pelea amistosa
horsepower ['hɔːspauəʳ] *n* caballo (de fuerza), potencia en caballos
horse-racing ['hɔːsreɪsɪŋ] *n* carreras *fpl* de caballos
horseradish ['hɔːsrædɪʃ] *n* rábano picante
horseshoe ['hɔːsʃuː] *n* herradura
horse show *n* concurso hípico
horse-trader ['hɔːstreɪdəʳ] *n* chalán(-ana) *m(f)*
horse trials *npl* = **horse show**
horsewhip ['hɔːswɪp] *vt* azotar
horsewoman ['hɔːswumən] *n* amazona
horsey ['hɔːsɪ] *adj* (*col: person*) aficionado a los caballos
horticulture ['hɔːtɪkʌltʃəʳ] *n* horticultura
hose [həuz] *n* (*also:* **hosepipe**) manguera
▸ **hose down** *vt* limpiar con manguera
hosiery ['həuzɪərɪ] *n* calcetería
hospice ['hɔspɪs] *n* hospicio
hospitable ['hɔspɪtəbl] *adj* hospitalario
hospital ['hɔspɪtl] *n* hospital *m*
hospitality [hɔspɪ'tælɪtɪ] *n* hospitalidad *f*
hospitalize ['hɔspɪtəlaɪz] *vt* hospitalizar
host [həust] *n* anfitrión *m*; (*TV, Radio*) presentador(a) *m(f)*; (*of inn etc*) mesonero; (*Rel*) hostia; (*large number*): **a ~ of** multitud de
hostage ['hɔstɪdʒ] *n* rehén *m*
hostel ['hɔstl] *n* hostal *m*; (*for students, nurses etc*) residencia; (*also:* **youth hostel**) albergue *m* juvenil; (*for homeless people*) hospicio
hostelling ['hɔstlɪŋ] *n*: **to go (youth) ~** hospedarse en albergues
hostess ['həustɪs] *n* anfitriona; (*Brit: air hostess*) azafata; (*in night-club*) señorita de compañía
hostile ['hɔstaɪl] *adj* hostil
hostility [hɔ'stɪlɪtɪ] *n* hostilidad *f*
hot [hɔt] *adj* caliente; (*weather*) caluroso, de calor; (*as opposed to only warm*) muy caliente; (*spicy*) picante; (*fig*) ardiente, acalorado; **to be ~** (*person*) tener calor; (*object*) estar caliente; (*weather*) hacer calor
▸ **hot up** *vi* (*col: situation*) ponerse difícil *or* apurado; (*: party*) animarse ■ *vt* (*col: pace*) apretar; (*: engine*) aumentar la potencia de
hot air *n* (*col*) palabras *fpl* huecas
hot-air balloon [hɔt'ɛə-] *n* (*Aviat*) globo aerostático *or* de aire caliente
hotbed ['hɔtbɛd] *n* (*fig*) semillero
hot-blooded [hɔt'blʌdɪd] *adj* impetuoso
hotchpotch ['hɔtʃpɔtʃ] *n* mezcolanza, baturrillo
hot dog *n* perrito caliente
hotel [həu'tɛl] *n* hotel *m*

hotelier [həu'tɛlɪəʳ] *n* hotelero
hotel industry *n* industria hotelera
hotel room *n* habitación *f* de hotel
hot flush *n* (*Brit*) sofoco
hotfoot ['hɔtfut] *adv* a toda prisa
hothead ['hɔthɛd] *n* (*fig*) exaltado(-a)
hotheaded [hɔt'hɛdɪd] *adj* exaltado
hothouse ['hɔthaus] *n* invernadero
hot line *n* (*Pol*) teléfono rojo, línea directa
hotly ['hɔtlɪ] *adv* con pasión, apasionadamente
hotplate ['hɔtpleɪt] *n* (*on cooker*) hornillo
hotpot ['hɔtpɔt] *n* (*Brit Culin*) estofado
hot potato *n* (*Brit col*) asunto espinoso; **to drop sth/sb like a ~** no querer saber ya nada de algo/algn
hot seat *n* primera fila
hot spot *n* (*trouble spot*) punto caliente; (*night club etc*) lugar *m* popular
hot spring *n* terma, fuente *f* de aguas termales
hot-tempered ['hɔt'tɛmpəd] *adj* de mal genio *or* carácter
hot-water bottle [hɔt'wɔːtə-] *n* bolsa de agua caliente
hot-wire ['hɔtwaɪəʳ] *vt* (*col: car*) hacer el puente en
hound [haund] *vt* acosar ■ *n* perro de caza
hour ['auəʳ] *n* hora; **at 30 miles an ~** a 30 millas por hora; **lunch ~** la hora del almuerzo *or* de comer; **to pay sb by the ~** pagar a algn por horas
hourly ['auəlɪ] *adj* (de) cada hora; (*rate*) por hora ■ *adv* cada hora
house *n* [haus] (*pl* **houses** ['hauzɪz]) casa; (*Pol*) cámara; (*Theat*) sala ■ *vt* [hauz] (*person*) alojar; **at/to my ~** en/a mi casa; **the H~ (of Commons/Lords)** (*Brit*) la Cámara de los Comunes/Lores; **the H~ (of Representatives)** (*US*) la Cámara de Representantes; **it's on the ~** (*fig*) la casa invita
house arrest *n* arresto domiciliario
houseboat ['hausbəut] *n* casa flotante
housebound ['hausbaund] *adj* confinado en casa
housebreaking ['hausbreɪkɪŋ] *n* allanamiento de morada
house-broken ['hausbrəukən] *adj* (*US*) = **house-trained**
housecoat ['hauskəut] *n* bata
household ['haushəuld] *n* familia
householder ['haushəuldəʳ] *n* propietario(-a); (*head of house*) cabeza de familia
househunting ['haushʌntɪŋ] *n*: **to go ~** ir en busca de vivienda
housekeeper ['hauskiːpəʳ] *n* ama de llaves
housekeeping ['hauskiːpɪŋ] *n* (*work*) trabajos *mpl* domésticos; (*Comput*) gestión *f* interna; (*also*: **housekeeping money**) dinero para gastos domésticos
houseman ['hausmən] *n* (*Brit Med*) médico residente
house-owner ['hausəunəʳ] *n* propietario(a) de una vivienda
house plant *n* planta de interior
house-proud ['hauspraud] *adj* preocupado por el embellecimiento de la casa
house-to-house ['haustə'haus] *adj* (*collection*) de casa en casa; (*search*) casa por casa
house-train ['haustreɪn] *vt* (*pet*) enseñar (*a hacer sus necesidades en el sitio apropiado*)
house-trained ['haustreɪnd] *adj* (*Brit: animal*) enseñado
house-warming ['hauswɔːmɪŋ] *n* (*also*: **house-warming party**) fiesta de estreno de una casa
housewife ['hauswaɪf] *n* ama de casa
housework ['hauswəːk] *n* faenas *fpl* (de la casa)
housing ['hauzɪŋ] *n* (*act*) alojamiento; (*houses*) viviendas *fpl* ■ *cpd* (*problem, shortage*) de (la) vivienda
housing association *n* asociación *f* de la vivienda
housing benefit *n* (*Brit*) subsidio por alojamiento
housing conditions *npl* condiciones *fpl* de habitabilidad
housing development, (*Brit*) **housing estate** *n* urbanización *f*
hovel ['hɔvl] *n* casucha
hover ['hɔvəʳ] *vi* flotar (en el aire); (*helicopter*) cernerse; **to ~ on the brink of disaster** estar al borde mismo del desastre
hovercraft ['hɔvəkrɑːft] *n* aerodeslizador *m*, hovercraft *m*
hoverport ['hɔvəpɔːt] *n* puerto de aerodeslizadores
how [hau] *adv* cómo; **~ are you?** ¿cómo está usted?, ¿cómo estás?; **~ do you do?** encantado, mucho gusto; **~ far is it to ...?** ¿qué distancia hay de aquí a ...?; **~ long have you been here?** ¿cuánto (tiempo) hace que estás aquí?, ¿cuánto (tiempo) llevas aquí?; **~ lovely!** ¡qué bonito!; **~ many/much?** ¿cuántos/cuánto?; **~ old are you?** ¿cuántos años tienes?; **~ is school?** ¿qué tal la escuela?; **~ about a drink?** ¿te gustaría algo de beber?, ¿qué te parece una copa?
however [hau'ɛvəʳ] *adv* de cualquier manera; (*+ adjective*) por muy ... que; (*in questions*) cómo ■ *conj* sin embargo, no obstante

howitzer ['haʊɪtsəʳ] *n* (*Mil*) obús *m*
howl [haul] *n* aullido ■ *vi* aullar
howler ['hauləʳ] *n* plancha, falta garrafal
howling ['haulɪŋ] *adj* (*wind*) huracanado
HP *n abbr* (*Brit*) = **hire purchase**
hp *abbr* (*Aut*) = **horsepower**
HQ *n abbr* = **headquarters**
HR *n abbr* (*US*) = **House of Representatives**; **human resources**
hr, hrs *abbr* (= *hour(s)*) h
HRH *abbr* (= *His (or Her) Royal Highness*) S.A.R.
HRT *n abbr* = **hormone replacement therapy**
HS *abbr* (*US*) = **high school**
HST *abbr* (*US*: = *Hawaiian Standard Time*) *hora de Hawai*
HT *abbr* = **high tension**
HTML *n abbr* (*Comput*: = *hypertext markup language*) HTML *m*
hub [hʌb] *n* (*of wheel*) cubo; (*fig*) centro
hubbub ['hʌbʌb] *n* barahúnda, barullo
hubcap ['hʌbkæp] *n* tapacubos *m inv*
HUD *n abbr* (*US*: = *Department of Housing and Urban Development*) *ministerio de la vivienda y urbanismo*
huddle ['hʌdl] *vi*: **to ~ together** amontonarse
hue [hju:] *n* color *m*, matiz *m*; **~ and cry** *n* protesta
huff [hʌf] *n*: **in a ~** enojado
huffy ['hʌfɪ] *adj* (*col*) mosqueado
hug [hʌg] *vt* abrazar ■ *n* abrazo
huge [hju:dʒ] *adj* enorme
hulk [hʌlk] *n* (*ship*) barco viejo; (*person, building etc*) mole *f*
hulking ['hʌlkɪŋ] *adj* pesado
hull [hʌl] *n* (*of ship*) casco
hullabaloo ['hʌləbə'lu:] *n* (*col*: *noise*) algarabía, jaleo
hullo [hə'ləu] *excl* = **hello**
hum [hʌm] *vt* tararear, canturrear ■ *vi* tararear, canturrear; (*insect*) zumbar ■ *n* (*Elec*) zumbido; (*of traffic, machines*) zumbido, ronroneo; (*of voices etc*) murmullo
human ['hju:mən] *adj* humano ■ *n* (*also*: **human being**) ser *m* humano
humane [hju:'meɪn] *adj* humano, humanitario
humanism ['hju:mənɪzəm] *n* humanismo
humanitarian [hju:mænɪ'tɛərɪən] *adj* humanitario
humanity [hju:'mænɪtɪ] *n* humanidad *f*
humanly ['hju:mənlɪ] *adv* humanamente
humanoid ['hju:mənɔɪd] *adj, n* humanoide *m/f*
human relations *npl* relaciones *fpl* humanas
human rights *npl* derechos *mpl* humanos
humble ['hʌmbl] *adj* humilde ■ *vt* humillar
humbly ['hʌmblɪ] *adv* humildemente
humbug ['hʌmbʌg] *n* patrañas *fpl*; (*Brit*: *sweet*) caramelo de menta
humdrum ['hʌmdrʌm] *adj* (*boring*) monótono, aburrido; (*routine*) rutinario
humid ['hju:mɪd] *adj* húmedo
humidifier [hju:'mɪdɪfaɪəʳ] *n* humectador *m*
humidity [hju'mɪdɪtɪ] *n* humedad *f*
humiliate [hju:'mɪlɪeɪt] *vt* humillar
humiliation [hju:mɪlɪ'eɪʃən] *n* humillación *f*
humility [hju:'mɪlɪtɪ] *n* humildad *f*
humorist ['hju:mərɪst] *n* humorista *m/f*
humorous ['hju:mərəs] *adj* gracioso, divertido
humour, humor (*US*) ['hju:məʳ] *n* humorismo, sentido del humor; (*mood*) humor *m* ■ *vt* (*person*) complacer; **sense of ~** sentido del humor; **to be in a good/bad ~** estar de buen/mal humor
humourless, humorless (*US*) ['hju:məlɪs] *adj* serio
hump [hʌmp] *n* (*in ground*) montículo; (*camel's*) giba
humus ['hju:məs] *n* (*Bio*) humus *m*
hunch [hʌntʃ] *n* (*premonition*) presentimiento; **I have a ~ that** tengo la corazonada *or* el presentimiento de que
hunchback ['hʌntʃbæk] *n* jorobado(-a)
hunched [hʌntʃt] *adj* jorobado
hundred ['hʌndrəd] *num* ciento; (*before n*) cien; **about a ~ people** unas cien personas, alrededor de cien personas; **hundreds of** centenares de; **hundreds of people** centenares de personas; **I'm a ~ per cent sure** estoy completamente seguro
hundredweight ['hʌndrədweɪt] *n* (*Brit*) = *50.8 kg; 112 lb;* (*US*) = *45.3 kg; 100 lb*
hung [hʌŋ] *pt, pp of* **hang**
Hungarian [hʌŋ'gɛərɪən] *adj* húngaro ■ *n* húngaro(-a) *m(f)*; (*Ling*) húngaro
Hungary ['hʌŋgərɪ] *n* Hungría
hunger ['hʌŋgəʳ] *n* hambre *f* ■ *vi*: **to ~ for** (*fig*) tener hambre de, anhelar
hunger strike *n* huelga de hambre
hungover [hʌŋ'əuvəʳ] *adj* (*col*): **to be ~** tener resaca
hungrily ['hʌŋgrəlɪ] *adv* ávidamente, con ganas
hungry ['hʌŋgrɪ] *adj* hambriento; **to be ~** tener hambre; **~ for** (*fig*) sediento de
hunk [hʌŋk] *n* (*of bread etc*) trozo, pedazo
hunt [hʌnt] *vt* (*seek*) buscar; (*Sport*) cazar ■ *vi* cazar ■ *n* caza, cacería
▸ **hunt down** *vt* acorralar, seguir la pista a
hunter ['hʌntəʳ] *n* cazador(a) *m(f)*; (*horse*) caballo de caza
hunting ['hʌntɪŋ] *n* caza
hurdle ['hə:dl] *n* (*Sport*) valla; (*fig*) obstáculo

hurl [hə:l] *vt* lanzar, arrojar
hurling ['hə:lɪŋ] *n* (*Sport*) *juego irlandés semejante al hockey*
hurly-burly ['hə:lɪ'bə:lɪ] *n* jaleo, follón *m*
hurrah [hu'rɑ:], **hurray** [hu'reɪ] *n* ¡viva!, ¡hurra!
hurricane ['hʌrɪkən] *n* huracán *m*
hurried ['hʌrɪd] *adj* (*fast*) apresurado; (*rushed*) hecho de prisa
hurriedly ['hʌrɪdlɪ] *adv* con prisa, apresuradamente
hurry ['hʌrɪ] *n* prisa ■ *vb* (*also:* **hurry up**) ■ *vi* apresurarse, darse prisa, apurarse (*LAm*) ■ *vt* (*person*) dar prisa a; (*work*) apresurar, hacer de prisa; **to be in a ~** tener prisa, tener apuro (*LAm*), estar apurado (*LAm*); **to ~ back/home** darse prisa en volver/volver a casa
▸ **hurry along** *vi* pasar de prisa
▸ **hurry away, hurry off** *vi* irse corriendo
▸ **hurry on** *vi*: **to ~ on to say** apresurarse a decir
▸ **hurry up** *vi* darse prisa, apurarse (*LAm*)
hurt [hə:t] (*pl* **hurt**) *vt* hacer daño a; (*business, interests etc*) perjudicar ■ *vi* doler ■ *adj* lastimado; **I ~ my arm** me lastimé el brazo; **where does it ~?** ¿dónde te duele?
hurtful ['hə:tful] *adj* (*remark etc*) hiriente, dañino
hurtle ['hə:tl] *vi*: **to ~ past** pasar como un rayo
husband ['hʌzbənd] *n* marido
hush [hʌʃ] *n* silencio ■ *vt* hacer callar; (*cover up*) encubrir; **~!** ¡chitón!, ¡cállate!
▸ **hush up** *vt* (*fact*) encubrir, callar
hushed [hʌʃt] *adj* (*voice*) bajo
hush-hush [hʌʃ'hʌʃ] *adj* (*col*) muy secreto
husk [hʌsk] *n* (*of wheat*) cáscara
husky ['hʌskɪ] *adj* ronco; (*burly*) fornido ■ *n* perro esquimal
hustings ['hʌstɪŋz] *npl* (*Pol*) mítin *msg* preelectoral
hustle ['hʌsl] *vt* (*push*) empujar; (*hurry*) dar prisa a ■ *n* bullicio, actividad *f* febril; **~ and bustle** ajetreo
hut [hʌt] *n* cabaña; (*shed*) cobertizo
hutch [hʌtʃ] *n* conejera
hyacinth ['haɪəsɪnθ] *n* jacinto
hybrid ['haɪbrɪd] *adj, n* híbrido
hydrant ['haɪdrənt] *n* (*also:* **fire hydrant**) boca de incendios
hydraulic [haɪ'drɔ:lɪk] *adj* hidráulico
hydraulics [haɪ'drɔ:lɪks] *n* hidráulica
hydrochloric ['haɪdrəu'klɔrɪk] *adj*: **~ acid** ácido clorhídrico
hydroelectric [haɪdrəuɪ'lɛktrɪk] *adj* hidroeléctrico
hydrofoil ['haɪdrəfɔɪl] *n* aerodeslizador *m*
hydrogen ['haɪdrədʒən] *n* hidrógeno
hydrogen bomb *n* bomba de hidrógeno
hydrophobia [haɪdrə'fəubɪə] *n* hidrofobia
hydroplane ['haɪdrəpleɪn] *n* hidroavión *m*, hidroavioneta
hyena [haɪ'i:nə] *n* hiena
hygiene ['haɪdʒi:n] *n* higiene *f*
hygienic [haɪ'dʒi:nɪk] *adj* higiénico
hymn [hɪm] *n* himno
hype [haɪp] *n* (*col*) bombo
hyperactive [haɪpər'æktɪv] *adj* hiperactivo
hypermarket ['haɪpəmɑ:kɪt] *n* hipermercado
hypertension ['haɪpə'tɛnʃən] *n* hipertensión *f*
hypertext ['haɪpə'tɛkst] *n* (*Comput*) hipertexto *m*
hyphen ['haɪfn] *n* guión *m*
hypnosis [hɪp'nəusɪs] *n* hipnosis *f*
hypnotic [hɪp'nɔtɪk] *adj* hipnótico
hypnotism ['hɪpnətɪzəm] *n* hipnotismo
hypnotist ['hɪpnətɪst] *n* hipnotista *m/f*
hypnotize ['hɪpnətaɪz] *vt* hipnotizar
hypoallergenic ['haɪpəuælə'dʒɛnɪk] *adj* hipoalérgeno
hypochondriac [haɪpəu'kɔndrɪæk] *n* hipocondríaco(-a)
hypocrisy [hɪ'pɔkrɪsɪ] *n* hipocresía
hypocrite ['hɪpəkrɪt] *n* hipócrita *m/f*
hypocritical [hɪpə'krɪtɪkl] *adj* hipócrita
hypodermic [haɪpə'də:mɪk] *adj* hipodérmico ■ *n* (*syringe*) aguja hipodérmica
hypotenuse [haɪ'pɔtɪnju:z] *n* hipotenusa
hypothermia [haɪpəu'θə:mɪə] *n* hipotermia
hypothesis, hypotheses [haɪ'pɔθɪsɪs, -si:z] *n* hipótesis *f inv*
hypothetical [haɪpə'θɛtɪkl] *adj* hipotético
hysterectomy [hɪstə'rɛktəmɪ] *n* histerectomía
hysteria [hɪ'stɪərɪə] *n* histeria
hysterical [hɪ'stɛrɪkl] *adj* histérico
hysterics [hɪ'stɛrɪks] *npl* histeria *sg*, histerismo *sg*; **to have ~** ponerse histérico
Hz *abbr* (= *Hertz*) Hz

I i

I, i [aɪ] *n* (*letter*) I, i *f*; **I for Isaac,** (*US*) **I for Item** I de Inés, I de Israel
I [aɪ] *pron* yo ▪ *abbr* = **island; isle**
IA, Ia. *abbr* (*US*) = **Iowa**
IAEA *n abbr* = **International Atomic Energy Agency**
ib., ibid. *abbr* (= *ibidem: from the same source*) ibídem
IBA *n abbr* (*Brit:* = *Independent Broadcasting Authority*) *see* **ITV**
Iberian [aɪ'bɪərɪən] *adj* ibero, ibérico
Iberian Peninsula *n*: **the** ~ la Península Ibérica
IBEW *n abbr* (*US:* = *International Brotherhood of Electrical Workers*) *sindicato internacional de electricistas*
i/c *abbr* (*Brit*) = **in charge**
ICBM *n abbr* (= *intercontinental ballistic missile*) misil *m* balístico intercontinental
ICC *n abbr* (= *International Chamber of Commerce*) CCI *f*; (*US*) = **Interstate Commerce Commission**
ice [aɪs] *n* hielo ▪ *vt* (*cake*) alcorzar ▪ *vi* (*also:* **ice over, ice up**) helarse; **to keep sth on** ~ (*fig: plan, project*) tener algo en reserva
ice age *n* período glaciar
ice axe *n* piqueta (de alpinista)
iceberg ['aɪsbə:g] *n* iceberg *m*; **the tip of the** ~ la punta del iceberg
icebox ['aɪsbɔks] *n* (*Brit*) congelador *m*; (*US*) nevera, refrigeradora (*LAm*)
icebreaker ['aɪsbreɪkə^r] *n* rompehielos *m inv*
ice bucket *n* cubo para el hielo
icecap ['aɪskæp] *n* casquete *m* polar
ice-cold [aɪs'kəuld] *adj* helado
ice cream *n* helado
ice-cream soda *n* soda mezclada con helado
ice cube *n* cubito de hielo
iced [aɪst] *adj* (*drink*) con hielo; (*cake*) escarchado
ice hockey *n* hockey *m* sobre hielo
Iceland ['aɪslənd] *n* Islandia
Icelander ['aɪsləndə^r] *n* islandés(-esa) *m(f)*
Icelandic [aɪs'lændɪk] *adj* islandés(-esa) ▪ *n* (*Ling*) islandés *m*
ice lolly *n* (*Brit*) polo
ice pick *n* piolet *m*
ice rink *n* pista de hielo
ice-skate ['aɪsskeɪt] *n* patín *m* de hielo ▪ *vi* patinar sobre hielo
ice-skating ['aɪsskeɪtɪŋ] *n* patinaje *m* sobre hielo
icicle ['aɪsɪkl] *n* carámbano
icing ['aɪsɪŋ] *n* (*Culin*) alcorza; (*Aviat etc*) formación *f* de hielo
icing sugar *n* (*Brit*) azúcar *m* glas(eado)
ICJ *n abbr* = **International Court of Justice**
icon ['aɪkɔn] *n* (*gen*) icono; (*Comput*) icono
ICR *n abbr* (*US*) = **Institute for Cancer Research**
ICT *n abbr* (= *Information and Communication(s) Technology*) TIC *f*, tecnología de la información; (*Brit Scol*) informática
ICU *n abbr* (= *intensive care unit*) UVI *f*
icy ['aɪsɪ] *adj* (*road*) helado; (*fig*) glacial
ID *abbr* (*US: Post*) = **Idaho**
I'd [aɪd] = **I would; I had**
Ida. *abbr* (*US: Post*) = **Idaho**
ID card *n* (*identity card*) DNI *m*
IDD *n abbr* (*Brit Tel:* = *international direct dialling*) *servicio automático internacional*
idea [aɪ'dɪə] *n* idea; **good ~!** ¡buena idea!; **to have an ~ that ...** tener la impresión de que ...; **I haven't the least** ~ no tengo ni (la más remota) idea
ideal [aɪ'dɪəl] *n* ideal *m* ▪ *adj* ideal
idealism [aɪ'dɪəlɪzəm] *n* idealismo
idealist [aɪ'dɪəlɪst] *n* idealista *m/f*
ideally [aɪ'dɪəlɪ] *adv* perfectamente; **~, the book should have ...** idealmente, el libro debería tener ...
identical [aɪ'dɛntɪkl] *adj* idéntico
identification [aɪdɛntɪfɪ'keɪʃən] *n* identificación *f*; **means of** ~ documentos *mpl* personales

identify [aɪ'dɛntɪfaɪ] *vt* identificar ▪ *vi*: **to ~ with** identificarse con
Identikit® [aɪ'dɛntɪkɪt] *n*: **~ (picture)** retrato-robot *m*
identity [aɪ'dɛntɪtɪ] *n* identidad *f*
identity card *n* carnet *m* de identidad, cédula (de identidad) (*LAm*)
identity papers *npl* documentos *mpl* (de identidad), documentación *fsg*
identity parade *n* identificación *f* de acusados
ideological [aɪdɪə'lɔdʒɪkəl] *adj* ideológico
ideology [aɪdɪ'ɔlədʒɪ] *n* ideología
idiocy ['ɪdɪəsɪ] *n* idiotez *f*; (*stupid act*) estupidez *f*
idiom ['ɪdɪəm] *n* modismo; (*style of speaking*) lenguaje *m*
idiomatic [ɪdɪə'mætɪk] *adj* idiomático
idiosyncrasy [ɪdɪəu'sɪŋkrəsɪ] *n* idiosincrasia
idiot ['ɪdɪət] *n* (*gen*) idiota *m/f*; (*fool*) tonto(-a)
idiotic [ɪdɪ'ɔtɪk] *adj* idiota; tonto
idle ['aɪdl] *adj* (*lazy*) holgazán(-ana); (*unemployed*) parado, desocupado; (*talk*) frívolo ▪ *vi* (*machine*) funcionar *or* marchar en vacío; **~ capacity** (*Comm*) capacidad *f* sin utilizar; **~ money** (*Comm*) capital *m* improductivo; **~ time** (*Comm*) tiempo de paro
▸ **idle away** *vt*: **to ~ away one's time** malgastar *or* desperdiciar el tiempo
idleness ['aɪdlnɪs] *n* holgazanería; paro, desocupación *f*
idler ['aɪdləʳ] *n* holgazán(-ana) *m(f)*, vago(-a)
idol ['aɪdl] *n* ídolo
idolize ['aɪdəlaɪz] *vt* idolatrar
idyllic [ɪ'dɪlɪk] *adj* idílico
i.e. *abbr* (*= id est: that is*) es decir
if [ɪf] *conj* si ▪ *n*: **there are a lot of ifs and buts** hay muchas dudas sin resolver; **(even) if** aunque, si bien; **I'd be pleased if you could do it** yo estaría contento si pudieras hacerlo; **if necessary** si resultase necesario; **if only** si solamente; **as if** como si
iffy ['ɪfɪ] *adj* (*col*) dudoso
igloo ['ɪglu:] *n* iglú *m*
ignite [ɪg'naɪt] *vt* (*set fire to*) encender ▪ *vi* encenderse
ignition [ɪg'nɪʃən] *n* (*Aut*) encendido; **to switch on/off the ~** arrancar/apagar el motor
ignition key *n* (*Aut*) llave *f* de contacto
ignoble [ɪg'nəubl] *adj* innoble, vil
ignominious [ɪgnə'mɪnɪəs] *adj* ignominioso, vergonzoso
ignoramus [ɪgnə'reɪməs] *n* ignorante *m/f*, inculto(-a)
ignorance ['ɪgnərəns] *n* ignorancia; **to keep sb in ~ of sth** ocultarle algo a algn
ignorant ['ɪgnərənt] *adj* ignorante; **to be ~ of** (*subject*) desconocer; (*events*) ignorar
ignore [ɪg'nɔ:ʳ] *vt* (*person*) no hacer caso de; (*fact*) pasar por alto
ikon ['aɪkɔn] *n* = **icon**
IL *abbr* (*US: Post*) = **Illinois**
ILA *n abbr* (*US: = International Longshoremen's Association*) *sindicato internacional de trabajadores portuarios*
ill [ɪl] *adj* enfermo, malo ▪ *n* mal *m*; (*fig*) infortunio ▪ *adv* mal; **to take** *or* **be taken ~** caer *or* ponerse enfermo; **to feel ~ (with)** encontrarse mal (de); **to speak/think ~ of sb** hablar/pensar mal de algn; *see also* **ills**
Ill. *abbr* (*US: Post*) = **Illinois**
I'll [aɪl] = **I will; I shall**
ill-advised [ɪləd'vaɪzd] *adj* poco recomendable; **he was ~ to go** se equivocaba al ir
ill-at-ease [ɪlət'i:z] *adj* incómodo
ill-considered [ɪlkən'sɪdəd] *adj* (*plan*) poco pensado
ill-disposed [ɪldɪs'pəuzd] *adj*: **to be ~ towards sb/sth** estar maldispuesto hacia algn/algo
illegal [ɪ'li:gl] *adj* ilegal
illegible [ɪ'lɛdʒɪbl] *adj* ilegible
illegitimate [ɪlɪ'dʒɪtɪmət] *adj* ilegítimo
ill-fated [ɪl'feɪtɪd] *adj* malogrado
ill-favoured, ill-favored (*US*) [ɪl'feɪvəd] *adj* poco agraciado
ill feeling *n* rencor *m*
ill-gotten ['ɪlgɔtn] *adj* (*gains etc*) mal adquirido
ill health *n* mala salud *f*; **to be in ~** estar mal de salud
illicit [ɪ'lɪsɪt] *adj* ilícito
ill-informed [ɪlɪn'fɔ:md] *adj* (*judgement*) erróneo; (*person*) mal informado
illiterate [ɪ'lɪtərət] *adj* analfabeto
ill-mannered [ɪl'mænəd] *adj* mal educado
illness ['ɪlnɪs] *n* enfermedad *f*
illogical [ɪ'lɔdʒɪkl] *adj* ilógico
ills [ɪlz] *npl* males *mpl*
ill-suited [ɪl'su:tɪd] *adj* (*couple*) incompatible; **he is ~ to the job** no es la persona indicada para el trabajo
ill-timed [ɪl'taɪmd] *adj* inoportuno
ill-treat [ɪl'tri:t] *vt* maltratar
ill-treatment [ɪl'tri:tmənt] *n* malos tratos *mpl*
illuminate [ɪ'lu:mɪneɪt] *vt* (*room, street*) iluminar, alumbrar; (*subject*) aclarar; **illuminated sign** letrero luminoso
illuminating [ɪ'lu:mɪneɪtɪŋ] *adj* revelador(a)
illumination [ɪlu:mɪ'neɪʃən] *n* alumbrado; **illuminations** *npl* luminarias *fpl*, luces *fpl*

illusion [ɪ'luːʒən] *n* ilusión *f*; **to be under the ~ that ...** estar convencido de que ...
illusive [ɪ'luːsɪv], **illusory** [ɪ'luːsərɪ] *adj* ilusorio
illustrate ['ɪləstreɪt] *vt* ilustrar
illustration [ɪlə'streɪʃən] *n* (*example*) ejemplo, ilustración *f*; (*in book*) lámina, ilustración *f*
illustrator ['ɪləstreɪtəʳ] *n* ilustrador(a) *m(f)*
illustrious [ɪ'lʌstrɪəs] *adj* ilustre
ill will *n* rencor *m*
ILO *n abbr* (= *International Labour Organization*) OIT *f*
I'm [aɪm] = **I am**
image ['ɪmɪdʒ] *n* imagen *f*
imagery ['ɪmɪdʒərɪ] *n* imágenes *fpl*
imaginable [ɪ'mædʒɪnəbl] *adj* imaginable
imaginary [ɪ'mædʒɪnərɪ] *adj* imaginario
imagination [ɪmædʒɪ'neɪʃən] *n* imaginación *f*; (*inventiveness*) inventiva; (*illusion*) fantasía
imaginative [ɪ'mædʒɪnətɪv] *adj* imaginativo
imagine [ɪ'mædʒɪn] *vt* imaginarse; (*suppose*) suponer
imbalance [ɪm'bæləns] *n* desequilibrio
imbecile ['ɪmbəsiːl] *n* imbécil *m/f*
imbue [ɪm'bjuː] *vt*: **to ~ sth with** imbuir algo de
IMF *n abbr* (= *International Monetary Fund*) FMI *m*
imitate ['ɪmɪteɪt] *vt* imitar
imitation [ɪmɪ'teɪʃən] *n* imitación *f*; (*copy*) copia; (*pej*) remedo
imitator ['ɪmɪteɪtəʳ] *n* imitador(a) *m(f)*
immaculate [ɪ'mækjulət] *adj* limpísimo, inmaculado; (*Rel*) inmaculado
immaterial [ɪmə'tɪərɪəl] *adj* incorpóreo; **it is ~ whether ...** no importa si ...
immature [ɪmə'tjuəʳ] *adj* (*person*) inmaduro; (*of one's youth*) joven
immaturity [ɪmə'tjuərɪtɪ] *n* inmadurez *f*
immeasurable [ɪ'mɛʒrəbl] *adj* inconmensurable
immediacy [ɪ'miːdɪəsɪ] *n* urgencia, proximidad *f*
immediate [ɪ'miːdɪət] *adj* inmediato; (*pressing*) urgente, apremiante; **in the ~ future** en un futuro próximo
immediately [ɪ'miːdɪətlɪ] *adv* (*at once*) en seguida; **~ next to** justo al lado de
immense [ɪ'mɛns] *adj* inmenso, enorme
immensely [ɪ'mɛnslɪ] *adv* enormemente
immensity [ɪ'mɛnsɪtɪ] *n* (*of size, difference*) inmensidad *f*; (*of problem*) enormidad *f*
immerse [ɪ'məːs] *vt* (*submerge*) sumergir; **to be immersed in** (*fig*) estar absorto en
immersion heater [ɪ'məːʃən-] *n* (*Brit*) calentador *m* de inmersión
immigrant ['ɪmɪgrənt] *n* inmigrante *m/f*
immigrate ['ɪmɪgreɪt] *vi* inmigrar
immigration [ɪmɪ'greɪʃən] *n* inmigración *f*
immigration authorities *npl* servicio *sg* de inmigración
immigration laws *npl* leyes *fpl* de inmigración
imminent ['ɪmɪnənt] *adj* inminente
immobile [ɪ'məubaɪl] *adj* inmóvil
immobilize [ɪ'məubɪlaɪz] *vt* inmovilizar
immoderate [ɪ'mɔdərɪt] *adj* (*person*) desmesurado; (*opinion, reaction, demand*) excesivo
immodest [ɪ'mɔdɪst] *adj* (*indecent*) desvergonzado, impúdico; (*boasting*) jactancioso
immoral [ɪ'mɔrl] *adj* inmoral
immorality [ɪmɔ'rælɪtɪ] *n* inmoralidad *f*
immortal [ɪ'mɔːtl] *adj* inmortal
immortality [ɪmɔː'tælɪtɪ] *n* inmortalidad *f*
immortalize [ɪ'mɔːtlaɪz] *vt* inmortalizar
immovable [ɪ'muːvəbl] *adj* (*object*) imposible de mover; (*person*) inconmovible
immune [ɪ'mjuːn] *adj*: **~ (to)** inmune (a)
immune system *n* sistema *m* inmunitario
immunity [ɪ'mjuːnɪtɪ] *n* (*Med, of diplomat*) inmunidad *f*; (*Comm*) exención *f*
immunization [ɪmjunaɪ'zeɪʃən] *n* inmunización *f*
immunize ['ɪmjunaɪz] *vt* inmunizar
imp [ɪmp] *n* (*small devil, child*) diablillo
impact ['ɪmpækt] *n* (*gen*) impacto
impair [ɪm'pɛəʳ] *vt* perjudicar
-impaired [ɪm'pɛəd] *suff*: **visually-impaired** con defectos de visión
impale [ɪm'peɪl] *vt* (*with sword*) atravesar
impart [ɪm'pɑːt] *vt* comunicar; (*make known*) participar; (*bestow*) otorgar
impartial [ɪm'pɑːʃl] *adj* imparcial
impartiality [ɪmpɑːʃɪ'ælɪtɪ] *n* imparcialidad *f*
impassable [ɪm'pɑːsəbl] *adj* (*barrier*) infranqueable; (*road*) intransitable
impasse [ɪm'pɑːs] *n* callejón *m* sin salida; **to reach an ~** llegar a un punto muerto
impassioned [ɪm'pæʃənd] *adj* apasionado, exaltado
impassive [ɪm'pæsɪv] *adj* impasible
impatience [ɪm'peɪʃəns] *n* impaciencia
impatient [ɪm'peɪʃənt] *adj* impaciente; **to get** *or* **grow ~** impacientarse
impatiently [ɪm'peɪʃəntlɪ] *adv* con impaciencia
impeachment [ɪm'piːtʃmənt] *n* denuncia, acusación *f*
impeccable [ɪm'pɛkəbl] *adj* impecable
impecunious [ɪmpɪ'kjuːnɪəs] *adj* sin dinero
impede [ɪm'piːd] *vt* estorbar, dificultar
impediment [ɪm'pɛdɪmənt] *n* obstáculo, estorbo; (*also*: **speech impediment**) defecto (del habla)

impel [ɪm'pɛl] *vt (force)*: **to ~ sb (to do sth)** obligar a algn (a hacer algo)
impending [ɪm'pɛndɪŋ] *adj* inminente
impenetrable [ɪm'pɛnɪtrəbl] *adj (jungle, fortress)* impenetrable; *(unfathomable)* insondable
imperative [ɪm'pɛrətɪv] *adj (tone)* imperioso; *(necessary)* imprescindible ■ *n (Ling)* imperativo
imperceptible [ɪmpə'sɛptɪbl] *adj* imperceptible
imperfect [ɪm'pə:fɪkt] *adj* imperfecto; *(goods etc)* defectuoso
imperfection [ɪmpə:'fɛkʃən] *n (blemish)* desperfecto; *(fault, flaw)* defecto
imperial [ɪm'pɪərɪəl] *adj* imperial
imperialism [ɪm'pɪərɪəlɪzəm] *n* imperialismo
imperil [ɪm'pɛrɪl] *vt* poner en peligro
imperious [ɪm'pɪərɪəs] *adj* señorial, apremiante
impersonal [ɪm'pə:sənl] *adj* impersonal
impersonate [ɪm'pə:səneɪt] *vt* hacerse pasar por
impersonation [ɪmpə:sə'neɪʃən] *n* imitación *f*
impersonator [ɪm'pə:səneɪtə^r] *n (Theat etc)* imitador(a) *m(f)*
impertinence [ɪm'pə:tɪnəns] *n* impertinencia, insolencia
impertinent [ɪm'pə:tɪnənt] *adj* impertinente, insolente
imperturbable [ɪmpə'tə:bəbl] *adj* imperturbable, impasible
impervious [ɪm'pə:vɪəs] *adj* impermeable; *(fig)*: **~ to** insensible a
impetuous [ɪm'pɛtjuəs] *adj* impetuoso
impetus ['ɪmpətəs] *n* ímpetu *m*; *(fig)* impulso
impinge [ɪm'pɪndʒ]: **to ~ on** *vt fus (affect)* afectar a
impish ['ɪmpɪʃ] *adj* travieso
implacable [ɪm'plækəbl] *adj* implacable
implant [ɪm'plɑ:nt] *vt (Med)* injertar, implantar; *(fig: idea, principle)* inculcar
implausible [ɪm'plɔ:zɪbl] *adj* implausible
implement *n* ['ɪmplɪmənt] instrumento, herramienta ■ *vt* ['ɪmplɪmɛnt] hacer efectivo; *(carry out)* realizar
implicate ['ɪmplɪkeɪt] *vt (compromise)* comprometer; *(involve)* enredar; **to ~ sb in sth** comprometer a algn en algo
implication [ɪmplɪ'keɪʃən] *n* consecuencia; **by ~** indirectamente
implicit [ɪm'plɪsɪt] *adj (gen)* implícito; *(complete)* absoluto
implicitly [ɪm'plɪsɪtlɪ] *adv* implícitamente
implore [ɪm'plɔ:^{r}] *vt (person)* suplicar
imploring [ɪm'plɔ:rɪŋ] *adj* de súplica
imply [ɪm'plaɪ] *vt (involve)* implicar, suponer; *(hint)* insinuar
impolite [ɪmpə'laɪt] *adj* mal educado
impolitic [ɪm'pɔlɪtɪk] *adj* poco diplomático
imponderable [ɪm'pɔndərəbl] *adj* imponderable
import *vt* [ɪm'pɔ:t] importar ■ *n* ['ɪmpɔ:t] *(Comm)* importación *f*; *(meaning)* significado, sentido ■ *cpd (duty, licence etc)* de importación
importance [ɪm'pɔ:təns] *n* importancia; **to be of great/little ~** tener mucha/poca, importancia
important [ɪm'pɔ:tənt] *adj* importante; **it's not ~** no importa, no tiene importancia; **it is ~ that** es importante que
importantly [ɪm'pɔ:təntlɪ] *adv (pej)* dándose importancia; **but, more ~ ...** pero, lo que es aún más importante ...
import duty *n* derechos *mpl* de importación
imported [ɪm'pɔ:tɪd] *adj* importado
importer [ɪm'pɔ:tə^r] *n* importador(a) *m(f)*
import licence, import license (US) *n* licencia de importación
impose [ɪm'pəuz] *vt* imponer ■ *vi*: **to ~ on sb** abusar de algn
imposing [ɪm'pəuzɪŋ] *adj* imponente, impresionante
imposition [ɪmpə'zɪʃn] *n (of tax etc)* imposición *f*; **to be an ~** *(on person)* molestar
impossibility [ɪmpɔsə'bɪlɪtɪ] *n* imposibilidad *f*
impossible [ɪm'pɔsɪbl] *adj* imposible; *(person)* insoportable; **it is ~ for me to leave now** me es imposible salir ahora
impossibly [ɪm'pɔsɪblɪ] *adv* imposiblemente
impostor [ɪm'pɔstə^r] *n* impostor(a) *m(f)*
impotence ['ɪmpətəns] *n* impotencia
impotent ['ɪmpətənt] *adj* impotente
impound [ɪm'paund] *vt* embargar
impoverished [ɪm'pɔvərɪʃt] *adj* necesitado; *(land)* agotado
impracticable [ɪm'præktɪkəbl] *adj* no factible, irrealizable
impractical [ɪm'præktɪkl] *adj (person)* poco práctico
imprecise [ɪmprɪ'saɪs] *adj* impreciso
impregnable [ɪm'prɛgnəbl] *adj* invulnerable; *(castle)* inexpugnable
impregnate ['ɪmprɛgneɪt] *vt (gen)* impregnar; *(soak)* empapar; *(fertilize)* fecundar
impresario [ɪmprɪ'sɑ:rɪəu] *n* empresario(-a)
impress [ɪm'prɛs] *vt* impresionar; *(mark)* estampar ■ *vi* causar buena impresión; **to ~ sth on sb** convencer a algn de la importancia de algo

impression [ɪm'prɛʃən] *n* impresión *f*; (*footprint etc*) huella; (*print run*) edición *f*; **to be under the ~ that** tener la idea de que; **to make a good/bad ~ on sb** causar buena/mala impresión a algn
impressionable [ɪm'prɛʃnəbl] *adj* impresionable
impressionist [ɪm'prɛʃənɪst] *n* impresionista *m/f*
impressive [ɪm'prɛsɪv] *adj* impresionante
imprint ['ɪmprɪnt] *n* (*Publishing*) pie *m* de imprenta; (*fig*) sello
imprison [ɪm'prɪzn] *vt* encarcelar
imprisonment [ɪm'prɪznmənt] *n* encarcelamiento; (*term of imprisonment*) cárcel *f*; **life ~** cadena perpetua
improbable [ɪm'prɔbəbl] *adj* improbable, inverosímil
impromptu [ɪm'prɔmptju:] *adj* improvisado ■ *adv* de improviso
improper [ɪm'prɔpəʳ] *adj* (*incorrect*) impropio; (*unseemly*) indecoroso; (*indecent*) indecente
impropriety [ɪmprə'praɪətɪ] *n* falta de decoro; (*indecency*) indecencia; (*of language*) impropiedad *f*
improve [ɪm'pru:v] *vt* mejorar; (*foreign language*) perfeccionar ■ *vi* mejorar
▸ **improve (up)on** *vt fus* (*offer*) mejorar
improvement [ɪm'pru:vmənt] *n* mejora; perfeccionamiento; **to make improvements to** mejorar
improvise ['ɪmprəvaɪz] *vt, vi* improvisar
imprudence [ɪm'pru:dns] *n* imprudencia
imprudent [ɪm'pru:dnt] *adj* imprudente
impudent ['ɪmpjudnt] *adj* descarado, insolente
impugn [ɪm'pju:n] *vt* impugnar
impulse ['ɪmpʌls] *n* impulso; **to act on ~** actuar sin reflexionar, dejarse llevar por el impulso
impulse buying *n* compra impulsiva
impulsive [ɪm'pʌlsɪv] *adj* irreflexivo, impulsivo
impunity [ɪm'pju:nɪtɪ] *n*: **with ~** impunemente
impure [ɪm'pjuəʳ] *adj* (*adulterated*) adulterado; (*morally*) impuro
impurity [ɪm'pjuərɪtɪ] *n* impureza
IN *abbr* (*US: Post*) = **Indiana**

KEYWORD

in [ɪn] *prep* **1** (*indicating place, position, with place names*) en; **in the house/garden** en (la) casa/el jardín; **in here/there** aquí/ahí *or* allí dentro; **in London/England** en Londres/Inglaterra; **in town** en el centro (de la ciudad)

2 (*indicating time*) en; **in spring** en (la) primavera; **in 1988/May** en 1988/mayo; **in the afternoon** por la tarde; **at four o'clock in the afternoon** a las cuarto de la tarde; **I did it in three hours/days** lo hice en tres horas/días; **I'll see you in two weeks** *or* **in two weeks' time** te veré dentro de dos semanas; **once in a hundred years** una vez cada cien años

3 (*indicating manner etc*) en; **in a loud/soft voice** en voz alta/baja; **in pencil/ink** a lápiz/bolígrafo; **the boy in the blue shirt** el chico de la camisa azul; **in writing** por escrito; **to pay in dollars** pagar en dólares

4 (*indicating circumstances*): **in the sun/shade** al sol/a la sombra; **in the rain** bajo la lluvia; **a change in policy** un cambio de política; **a rise in prices** un aumento de precios

5 (*indicating mood, state*): **in tears** llorando; **in anger/despair** enfadado/desesperado; **to live in luxury** vivir lujosamente

6 (*with ratios, numbers*): **1 in 10 households, 1 household in 10** una de cada 10 familias; **20 pence in the pound** 20 peniques por libra; **they lined up in twos** se alinearon de dos en dos; **in hundreds** a *or* por centenares

7 (*referring to people, works*) en; entre; **the disease is common in children** la enfermedad es común entre los niños; **in (the works of) Dickens** en (las obras de) Dickens

8 (*indicating profession etc*): **to be in teaching** dedicarse a la enseñanza

9 (*after superlative*) de; **the best pupil in the class** el/la mejor alumno(-a) de la clase

10 (*with present participle*): **in saying this** al decir esto

■ *adv*: **to be in** (*person: at home*) estar en casa; (*: at work*) estar; (*train, ship, plane*) haber llegado; (*in fashion*) estar de moda; **she'll be in later today** llegará más tarde hoy; **to ask sb in** hacer pasar a algn; **to run/limp** *etc* **in** entrar corriendo/cojeando *etc*; **in that** *conj* ya que

■ *npl*: **the ins and outs** (*of proposal, situation etc*) los detalles

in., ins *abbr* = **inch; inches**
inability [ɪnə'bɪlɪtɪ] *n* incapacidad *f*; **~ to pay** insolvencia en el pago
inaccessible [ɪnək'sɛsɪbl] *adj* inaccesible
inaccuracy [ɪn'ækjurəsɪ] *n* inexactitud *f*
inaccurate [ɪn'ækjurət] *adj* inexacto, incorrecto
inaction [ɪn'ækʃən] *n* inacción *f*
inactive [ɪn'æktɪv] *adj* inactivo
inactivity [ɪnæk'tɪvɪtɪ] *n* inactividad *f*

inadequacy [ɪn'ædɪkwəsɪ] *n* insuficiencia; incapacidad *f*
inadequate [ɪn'ædɪkwət] *adj* (*insufficient*) insuficiente; (*unsuitable*) inadecuado; (*person*) incapaz
inadmissible [ɪnəd'mɪsəbl] *adj* improcedente, inadmisible
inadvertent [ɪnəd'vəːtənt] *adj* descuidado, involuntario
inadvertently [ɪnəd'vəːtntlɪ] *adv* por descuido
inadvisable [ɪnəd'vaɪzəbl] *adj* poco aconsejable
inane [ɪ'neɪn] *adj* necio, fatuo
inanimate [ɪn'ænɪmət] *adj* inanimado
inapplicable [ɪn'æplɪkəbl] *adj* inaplicable
inappropriate [ɪnə'prəuprɪət] *adj* inadecuado
inapt [ɪn'æpt] *adj* impropio
inaptitude [ɪn'æptɪtjuːd] *n* incapacidad *f*
inarticulate [ɪnɑː'tɪkjulət] *adj* (*person*) incapaz de expresarse; (*speech*) mal pronunciado
inartistic [ɪnɑː'tɪstɪk] *adj* antiestético
inasmuch as [ɪnəz'mʌtʃ-] *adv* en la medida en que
inattention [ɪnə'tɛnʃən] *n* desatención *f*
inattentive [ɪnə'tɛntɪv] *adj* distraído
inaudible [ɪn'ɔːdɪbl] *adj* inaudible
inaugural [ɪ'nɔːgjurəl] *adj* inaugural; (*speech*) de apertura
inaugurate [ɪ'nɔːgjureɪt] *vt* inaugurar; (*president, official*) investir
inauguration [ɪnɔːgju'reɪʃən] *n* inauguración *f*; (*of official*) investidura; (*of event*) ceremonia de apertura
inauspicious [ɪnɔːs'pɪʃəs] *adj* poco propicio, inoportuno
in-between [ɪnbɪ'twiːn] *adj* intermedio
inborn [ɪn'bɔːn] *adj* (*feeling*) innato
inbred [ɪn'brɛd] *adj* innato; (*family*) consanguíneo
inbreeding [ɪn'briːdɪŋ] *n* endogamia
Inc. *abbr* = **incorporated**
Inca ['ɪŋkə] *adj* (*also*: **Incan**) inca, de los incas ■ *n* inca *m/f*
incalculable [ɪn'kælkjuləbl] *adj* incalculable
incapability [ɪnkeɪpə'bɪlɪtɪ] *n* incapacidad *f*
incapable [ɪn'keɪpəbl] *adj*: **~ (of doing sth)** incapaz (de hacer algo)
incapacitate [ɪnkə'pæsɪteɪt] *vt*: **to ~ sb** incapacitar a algn
incapacitated [ɪnkə'pæsɪteɪtɪd] *adj* incapacitado
incapacity [ɪnkə'pæsɪtɪ] *n* (*inability*) incapacidad *f*
incarcerate [ɪn'kɑːsəreɪt] *vt* encarcelar
incarnate *adj* [ɪn'kɑːnɪt] en persona ■ *vt* ['ɪnkɑːneɪt] encarnar
incarnation [ɪnkɑː'neɪʃən] *n* encarnación *f*
incendiary [ɪn'sɛndɪərɪ] *adj* incendiario ■ *n* (*bomb*) bomba incendiaria
incense *n* ['ɪnsɛns] incienso ■ *vt* [ɪn'sɛns] (*anger*) indignar, encolerizar
incentive [ɪn'sɛntɪv] *n* incentivo, estímulo
incentive bonus *n* prima
incentive scheme *n* plan *m* de incentivos
inception [ɪn'sɛpʃən] *n* comienzo, principio
incessant [ɪn'sɛsnt] *adj* incesante, continuo
incessantly [ɪn'sɛsəntlɪ] *adv* constantemente
incest ['ɪnsɛst] *n* incesto
inch [ɪntʃ] *n* pulgada; **to be within an ~ of** estar a dos dedos de; **he didn't give an ~** no hizo la más mínima concesión; **a few inches** unas pulgadas
▸ **inch forward** *vi* avanzar palmo a palmo
incidence ['ɪnsɪdns] *n* (*of crime, disease*) incidencia
incident ['ɪnsɪdnt] *n* incidente *m*; (*in book*) episodio
incidental [ɪnsɪ'dɛntl] *adj* circunstancial, accesorio; (*unplanned*) fortuito; **~ to** relacionado con; **~ expenses** (gastos *mpl*) imprevistos *mpl*
incidentally [ɪnsɪ'dɛntəlɪ] *adv* (*by the way*) por cierto
incidental music *n* música de fondo
incident room *n* (*Police*) centro de coordinación
incinerate [ɪn'sɪnəreɪt] *vt* incinerar, quemar
incinerator [ɪn'sɪnəreɪtə[r]] *n* incinerador *m*, incineradora
incipient [ɪn'sɪpɪənt] *adj* incipiente
incision [ɪn'sɪʒən] *n* incisión *f*
incisive [ɪn'saɪsɪv] *adj* (*mind*) penetrante; (*remark etc*) incisivo
incisor [ɪn'saɪzə[r]] *n* incisivo
incite [ɪn'saɪt] *vt* provocar, incitar
incl. *abbr* = **including**; **inclusive (of)**
inclement [ɪn'klɛmənt] *adj* inclemente
inclination [ɪnklɪ'neɪʃən] *n* (*tendency*) tendencia, inclinación *f*
incline [*n* 'ɪnklaɪn, *vb* ɪn'klaɪn] *n* pendiente *f*, cuesta ■ *vt* (*slope*) inclinar; (*head*) poner de lado ■ *vi* inclinarse; **to be inclined to** (*tend*) ser propenso a; (*be willing*) estar dispuesto a
include [ɪn'kluːd] *vt* incluir, comprender; (*in letter*) adjuntar; **the tip is/is not included** la propina está/no está incluida
including [ɪn'kluːdɪŋ] *prep* incluso, inclusive; **~ tip** propina incluida
inclusion [ɪn'kluːʒən] *n* inclusión *f*
inclusive [ɪn'kluːsɪv] *adj* inclusivo ■ *adv*

inclusive; **~ of tax** incluidos los impuestos; **$50, ~ of all surcharges** 50 dólares, incluidos todos los recargos
incognito [ɪnkɔg'ni:təu] *adv* de incógnito
incoherent [ɪnkəu'hɪərənt] *adj* incoherente
income ['ɪnkʌm] *n* (*personal*) ingresos *mpl*; (*from property etc*) renta; (*profit*) rédito; **gross/net ~** ingresos *mpl* brutos/netos; **~ and expenditure account** cuenta de gastos e ingresos
income bracket *n* categoría económica
income support *n* (*Brit*) ≈ ayuda familiar
income tax *n* impuesto sobre la renta
income tax inspector *n* inspector(a) *m(f)* de Hacienda
income tax return *n* declaración *f* de ingresos
incoming ['ɪnkʌmɪŋ] *adj* (*passengers, flight*) de llegada; (*government*) entrante; (*tenant*) nuevo
incommunicado ['ɪnkəmjunɪ'kɑ:dəu] *adj*: **to hold sb ~** mantener incomunicado a algn
incomparable [ɪn'kɔmpərəbl] *adj* incomparable, sin par
incompatible [ɪnkəm'pætɪbl] *adj* incompatible
incompetence [ɪn'kɔmpɪtəns] *n* incompetencia
incompetent [ɪn'kɔmpɪtənt] *adj* incompetente
incomplete [ɪnkəm'pli:t] *adj* incompleto; (*unfinished*) sin terminar
incomprehensible [ɪnkɔmprɪ'hɛnsɪbl] *adj* incomprensible
inconceivable [ɪnkən'si:vəbl] *adj* inconcebible
inconclusive [ɪnkən'klu:sɪv] *adj* sin resultado (definitivo); (*argument*) poco convincente
incongruity [ɪnkɔŋ'gru:ɪtɪ] *n* incongruencia
incongruous [ɪn'kɔŋgruəs] *adj* discordante
inconsequential [ɪnkɔnsɪ'kwɛnʃl] *adj* intranscendente
inconsiderable [ɪnkən'sɪdərəbl] *adj* insignificante
inconsiderate [ɪnkən'sɪdərət] *adj* desconsiderado; **how ~ of him!** ¡qué falta de consideración (de su parte)!
inconsistency [ɪnkən'sɪstənsɪ] *n* inconsecuencia; (*of actions etc*) falta de lógica; (*of work*) carácter *m* desigual, inconsistencia; (*of statement etc*) contradicción *f*
inconsistent [ɪnkən'sɪstnt] *adj* inconsecuente; **~ with** que no concuerda con
inconsolable [ɪnkən'səuləbl] *adj* inconsolable
inconspicuous [ɪnkən'spɪkjuəs] *adj* (*discreet*) discreto; (*person*) que llama poco la atención
inconstancy [ɪn'kɔnstənsɪ] *n* inconstancia
inconstant [ɪn'kɔnstənt] *adj* inconstante
incontinence [ɪn'kɔntɪnəns] *n* incontinencia
incontinent [ɪn'kɔntɪnənt] *adj* incontinente
incontrovertible [ɪnkɔntrə'və:təbl] *adj* incontrovertible
inconvenience [ɪnkən'vi:njəns] *n* (*gen*) inconvenientes *mpl*; (*trouble*) molestia ■ *vt* incomodar; **to put sb to great ~** causar mucha molestia a algn; **don't ~ yourself** no se moleste
inconvenient [ɪnkən'vi:njənt] *adj* incómodo, poco práctico; (*time, place*) inoportuno; **that time is very ~ for me** esa hora me es muy inconveniente
incorporate [ɪn'kɔ:pəreɪt] *vt* incorporar; (*contain*) comprender; (*add*) agregar
incorporated [ɪn'kɔ:pəreɪtɪd] *adj*: **~ company** (US) ≈ Sociedad *f* Anónima (S.A.)
incorrect [ɪnkə'rɛkt] *adj* incorrecto
incorrigible [ɪn'kɔrɪdʒəbl] *adj* incorregible
incorruptible [ɪnkə'rʌptɪbl] *adj* incorruptible
increase [*n* 'ɪnkri:s, *vb* ɪn'kri:s] *n* aumento ■ *vi* aumentar; (*grow*) crecer; (*price*) subir ■ *vt* aumentar; **an ~ of 5%** un aumento de 5%; **to be on the ~** ir en aumento
increasing [ɪn'kri:sɪŋ] *adj* (*number*) creciente, que va en aumento
increasingly [ɪn'kri:sɪŋlɪ] *adv* cada vez más
incredible [ɪn'krɛdɪbl] *adj* increíble
incredibly [ɪn'krɛdɪblɪ] *adv* increíblemente
incredulity [ɪnkrɪ'dju:lɪtɪ] *n* incredulidad *f*
incredulous [ɪn'krɛdjuləs] *adj* incrédulo
increment ['ɪnkrɪmənt] *n* aumento, incremento
incriminate [ɪn'krɪmɪneɪt] *vt* incriminar
incriminating [ɪn'krɪmɪneɪtɪŋ] *adj* incriminatorio
incrust [ɪn'krʌst] *vt* = **encrust**
incubate ['ɪnkjubeɪt] *vt* (*egg*) incubar, empollar ■ *vi* (*egg, disease*) incubar
incubation [ɪnkju'beɪʃən] *n* incubación *f*
incubation period *n* período de incubación
incubator ['ɪnkjubeɪtə^r] *n* incubadora
inculcate ['ɪnkʌlkeɪt] *vt*: **to ~ sth in sb** inculcar algo en algn
incumbent [ɪn'kʌmbənt] *n* ocupante *m/f* ■ *adj*: **it is ~ on him to ...** le incumbe ...
incur [ɪn'kə:^r] *vt* (*expenses*) incurrir en; (*loss*) sufrir
incurable [ɪn'kjuərəbl] *adj* incurable
incursion [ɪn'kə:ʃən] *n* incursión *f*
Ind. *abbr* (US) = **Indiana**
indebted [ɪn'dɛtɪd] *adj*: **to be ~ to sb** estar agradecido a algn
indecency [ɪn'di:snsɪ] *n* indecencia

indecent [ɪn'di:snt] *adj* indecente
indecent assault *n* (*Brit*) atentado contra el pudor
indecent exposure *n* exhibicionismo
indecipherable [ɪndɪ'saɪfərəbl] *adj* indescifrable
indecision [ɪndɪ'sɪʒən] *n* indecisión *f*
indecisive [ɪndɪ'saɪsɪv] *adj* indeciso; (*discussion*) no resuelto, inconcluyente
indeed [ɪn'di:d] *adv* efectivamente, en realidad; **yes ~!** ¡claro que sí!
indefatigable [ɪndɪ'fætɪgəbl] *adj* incansable, infatigable
indefensible [ɪndɪ'fɛnsəbl] *adj* (*conduct*) injustificable
indefinable [ɪndɪ'faɪnəbl] *adj* indefinible
indefinite [ɪn'dɛfɪnɪt] *adj* indefinido; (*uncertain*) incierto
indefinitely [ɪn'dɛfɪnɪtlɪ] *adv* (*wait*) indefinidamente
indelible [ɪn'dɛlɪbl] *adj* imborrable
indelicate [ɪn'dɛlɪkɪt] *adj* (*tactless*) indiscreto, inoportuno; (*not polite*) poco delicado
indemnify [ɪn'dɛmnɪfaɪ] *vt* indemnizar, resarcir
indemnity [ɪn'dɛmnɪtɪ] *n* (*insurance*) indemnidad *f*; (*compensation*) indemnización *f*
indent [ɪn'dɛnt] *vt* (*text*) sangrar
indentation [ɪndɛn'teɪʃən] *n* mella; (*Typ*) sangría
indenture [ɪn'dɛntʃə^r] *n* escritura, instrumento
independence [ɪndɪ'pɛndns] *n* independencia
Independence Day *n* Día *m* de la Independencia

INDEPENDENCE DAY

El cuatro de julio es la fiesta nacional de los Estados Unidos, *Independence Day*, en conmemoración de la Declaración de Independencia escrita por Thomas Jefferson y adoptada en 1776. En ella se proclamaba la ruptura total con Gran Bretaña de las trece colonias americanas que fueron el origen de los Estados Unidos de América.

independent [ɪndɪ'pɛndənt] *adj* independiente; **to become ~** independizarse
in-depth ['ɪndɛpθ] *adj* en profundidad, a fondo
indescribable [ɪndɪ'skraɪbəbl] *adj* indescriptible
indestructible [ɪndɪs'trʌktəbl] *adj* indestructible
indeterminate [ɪndɪ'tə:mɪnɪt] *adj* indeterminado
index ['ɪndɛks] *n* (*pl* **indexes**) (*in book*) índice *m*; (*in library etc*) catálogo; (*pl* **indices**) ['ɪndɪsi:z] (*ratio, sign*) exponente *m*
index card *n* ficha
index finger *n* índice *m*
index-linked ['ɪndɛks'lɪŋkt], (*US*) **indexed** ['ɪndɛkst] *adj* indexado
India ['ɪndɪə] *n* la India
Indian ['ɪndɪən] *adj, n* indio(-a) *m(f)*; (*also*: **American Indian**) indio(-a) *m(f)* de América, amerindio(-a) *m(f)*; (*pej*): **Red ~** piel roja *m/f*
Indian Ocean *n*: **the ~** el Océano Índico, el Mar de las Indias
Indian summer *n* (*fig*) veranillo de San Martín
india rubber *n* caucho
indicate ['ɪndɪkeɪt] *vt* indicar ■ *vi* (*Brit Aut*): **to ~ left/right** indicar a la izquierda/a la derecha
indication [ɪndɪ'keɪʃən] *n* indicio, señal *f*
indicative [ɪn'dɪkətɪv] *adj*: **to be ~ of sth** indicar algo ■ *n* (*Ling*) indicativo
indicator ['ɪndɪkeɪtə^r] *n* (*gen*) indicador *m*; (*Aut*) intermitente *m*, direccional *m* (*LAm*)
indices ['ɪndɪsi:z] *npl of* **index**
indict [ɪn'daɪt] *vt* acusar
indictable [ɪn'daɪtəbl] *adj*: **~ offence** delito procesable
indictment [ɪn'daɪtmənt] *n* acusación *f*
indifference [ɪn'dɪfrəns] *n* indiferencia
indifferent [ɪn'dɪfrənt] *adj* indiferente; (*poor*) regular
indigenous [ɪn'dɪdʒɪnəs] *adj* indígena
indigestible [ɪndɪ'dʒɛstɪbl] *adj* indigesto
indigestion [ɪndɪ'dʒɛstʃən] *n* indigestión *f*
indignant [ɪn'dɪgnənt] *adj*: **to be ~ about sth** indignarse por algo
indignation [ɪndɪg'neɪʃən] *n* indignación *f*
indignity [ɪn'dɪgnɪtɪ] *n* indignidad *f*
indigo ['ɪndɪgəu] *adj* (*colour*) (de color) añil ■ *n* añil *m*
indirect [ɪndɪ'rɛkt] *adj* indirecto
indirectly [ɪndɪ'rɛktlɪ] *adv* indirectamente
indiscernible [ɪndɪ'sə:nəbl] *adj* imperceptible
indiscreet [ɪndɪ'skri:t] *adj* indiscreto, imprudente
indiscretion [ɪndɪ'skrɛʃən] *n* indiscreción *f*, imprudencia
indiscriminate [ɪndɪ'skrɪmɪnət] *adj* indiscriminado
indispensable [ɪndɪ'spɛnsəbl] *adj* indispensable, imprescindible
indisposed [ɪndɪ'spəuzd] *adj* (*unwell*) indispuesto

indisposition [ɪndɪspə'zɪʃən] *n* indisposición *f*
indisputable [ɪndɪ'spju:təbl] *adj* incontestable
indistinct [ɪndɪ'stɪŋkt] *adj* indistinto
indistinguishable [ɪndɪ'stɪŋgwɪʃəbl] *adj* indistinguible
individual [ɪndɪ'vɪdjuəl] *n* individuo ■ *adj* individual; (*personal*) personal; (*for/of one only*) particular
individualist [ɪndɪ'vɪdjuəlɪst] *n* individualista *m/f*
individuality [ɪndɪvɪdju'ælɪtɪ] *n* individualidad *f*
individually [ɪndɪ'vɪdjuəlɪ] *adv* individualmente; particularmente
indivisible [ɪndɪ'vɪzəbl] *adj* indivisible
Indo-China ['ɪndəu'tʃaɪnə] *n* Indochina
indoctrinate [ɪn'dɔktrɪneɪt] *vt* adoctrinar
indoctrination [ɪndɔktrɪ'neɪʃən] *n* adoctrinamiento
indolence ['ɪndələns] *n* indolencia
indolent ['ɪndələnt] *adj* indolente, perezoso
Indonesia [ɪndə'ni:zɪə] *n* Indonesia
Indonesian [ɪndə'ni:zɪən] *adj* indonesio ■ *n* indonesio(-a); (*Ling*) indonesio
indoor ['ɪndɔ:ʳ] *adj* (*swimming pool*) cubierto; (*plant*) de interior; (*sport*) bajo cubierta
indoors [ɪn'dɔ:z] *adv* dentro; (*at home*) en casa
indubitable [ɪn'dju:bɪtəbl] *adj* indudable
indubitably [ɪn'dju:bɪtəblɪ] *adv* indudablemente
induce [ɪn'dju:s] *vt* inducir, persuadir; (*bring about*) producir; **to ~ sb to do sth** persuadir a algn a que haga algo
inducement [ɪn'dju:smənt] *n* (*incentive*) incentivo, aliciente *m*
induct [ɪn'dʌkt] *vt* iniciar; (*in job, rank, position*) instalar
induction [ɪn'dʌkʃən] *n* (*Med: of birth*) inducción *f*
induction course *n* (*Brit*) cursillo introductorio *or* de iniciación
indulge [ɪn'dʌldʒ] *vt* (*whim*) satisfacer; (*person*) complacer; (*child*) mimar ■ *vi*: **to ~ in** darse el gusto de
indulgence [ɪn'dʌldʒəns] *n* vicio
indulgent [ɪn'dʌldʒənt] *adj* indulgente
industrial [ɪn'dʌstrɪəl] *adj* industrial
industrial action *n* huelga
industrial estate *n* (*Brit*) polígono *or* (*LAm*) zona industrial
industrial goods *npl* bienes *mpl* de producción
industrialist [ɪn'dʌstrɪəlɪst] *n* industrial *m/f*
industrialize [ɪn'dʌstrɪəlaɪz] *vt* industrializar
industrial park *n* (*US*) = **industrial estate**
industrial relations *npl* relaciones *fpl* empresariales
industrial tribunal *n* magistratura de trabajo, tribunal *m* laboral
industrial unrest *n* (*Brit*) agitación *f* obrera
industrious [ɪn'dʌstrɪəs] *adj* (*gen*) trabajador(a); (*student*) aplicado
industry ['ɪndəstrɪ] *n* industria; (*diligence*) aplicación *f*
inebriated [ɪ'ni:brɪeɪtɪd] *adj* borracho
inedible [ɪn'ɛdɪbl] *adj* incomible; (*plant etc*) no comestible
ineffective [ɪnɪ'fɛktɪv], **ineffectual** [ɪnɪ'fɛktʃuəl] *adj* ineficaz, inútil
inefficiency [ɪnɪ'fɪʃənsɪ] *n* ineficacia
inefficient [ɪnɪ'fɪʃənt] *adj* ineficaz, ineficiente
inelegant [ɪn'ɛlɪgənt] *adj* poco elegante
ineligible [ɪn'ɛlɪdʒɪbl] *adj* inelegible
inept [ɪ'nɛpt] *adj* incompetente, incapaz
ineptitude [ɪ'nɛptɪtju:d] *n* incapacidad *f*, ineptitud *f*
inequality [ɪnɪ'kwɔlɪtɪ] *n* desigualdad *f*
inequitable [ɪn'ɛkwɪtəbl] *adj* injusto
ineradicable [ɪnɪ'rædɪkəbl] *adj* inextirpable
inert [ɪ'nə:t] *adj* inerte, inactivo; (*immobile*) inmóvil
inertia [ɪ'nə:ʃə] *n* inercia; (*laziness*) pereza
inertia-reel seat-belt [ɪ'nə:ʃə'ri:l-] *n* cinturón *m* de seguridad retráctil
inescapable [ɪnɪ'skeɪpəbl] *adj* ineludible, inevitable
inessential [ɪnɪ'sɛnʃl] *adj* no esencial
inestimable [ɪn'ɛstɪməbl] *adj* inestimable
inevitability [ɪnɛvɪtə'bɪlɪtɪ] *n* inevitabilidad *f*
inevitable [ɪn'ɛvɪtəbl] *adj* inevitable; (*necessary*) forzoso
inevitably [ɪn'ɛvɪtəblɪ] *adv* inevitablemente; **as ~ happens ...** como siempre pasa ...
inexact [ɪnɪg'zaekt] *adj* inexacto
inexcusable [ɪnɪks'kju:zəbl] *adj* imperdonable
inexhaustible [ɪnɪg'zɔ:stɪbl] *adj* inagotable
inexorable [ɪn'ɛksərəbl] *adj* inexorable, implacable
inexpensive [ɪnɪk'spɛnsɪv] *adj* económico
inexperience [ɪnɪk'spɪərɪəns] *n* falta de experiencia
inexperienced [ɪnɪk'spɪərɪənst] *adj* inexperto; **to be ~ in sth** no tener experiencia en algo
inexplicable [ɪnɪk'splɪkəbl] *adj* inexplicable
inexpressible [ɪnɪk'sprɛsəbl] *adj* inexpresable
inextricable [ɪnɪks'trɪkəbl] *adj* inseparable
inextricably [ɪnɪks'trɪkəblɪ] *adv* indisolublemente

infallibility [ɪnfælə'bɪlɪtɪ] *n* infalibilidad *f*
infallible [ɪn'fælɪbl] *adj* infalible
infamous ['ɪnfəməs] *adj* infame
infamy ['ɪnfəmɪ] *n* infamia
infancy ['ɪnfənsɪ] *n* infancia
infant ['ɪnfənt] *n* niño(-a)
infantile ['ɪnfəntaɪl] *adj* infantil; (*pej*) aniñado
infant mortality *n* mortalidad *f* infantil
infantry ['ɪnfəntrɪ] *n* infantería
infantryman ['ɪnfəntrɪmən] *n* soldado de infantería
infant school *n* (*Brit*) escuela de párvulos; *see also* **primary school**
infatuated [ɪn'fætjueɪtɪd] *adj*: **~ with** (*in love*) loco por; **to become ~ (with sb)** enamoriscarse (de algn), encapricharse (con algn)
infatuation [ɪnfætju'eɪʃən] *n* enamoramiento
infect [ɪn'fɛkt] *vt* (*wound*) infectar; (*person*) contagiar; (*fig: pej*) corromper; **infected with** (*illness*) contagiado de; **to become infected** (*wound*) infectarse
infection [ɪn'fɛkʃən] *n* infección *f*; (*fig*) contagio
infectious [ɪn'fɛkʃəs] *adj* contagioso; (*fig*) infeccioso
infer [ɪn'fəːʳ] *vt* deducir, inferir; **to ~ (from)** inferir (de), deducir (de)
inference ['ɪnfərəns] *n* deducción *f*, inferencia
inferior [ɪn'fɪərɪəʳ] *adj, n* inferior *m/f*; **to feel ~** sentirse inferior
inferiority [ɪnfɪərɪ'ɔrətɪ] *n* inferioridad *f*
inferiority complex *n* complejo de inferioridad
infernal [ɪn'fəːnl] *adj* infernal
inferno [ɪn'fəːnəu] *n* infierno; (*fig*) hoguera
infertile [ɪn'fəːtaɪl] *adj* estéril; (*person*) infecundo
infertility [ɪnfəː'tɪlɪtɪ] *n* esterilidad *f*; infecundidad *f*
infest [ɪn'fɛst] *vt* infestar
infested [ɪn'fɛstɪd] *adj*: **~ (with)** plagado (de)
infidel ['ɪnfɪdəl] *n* infiel *m/f*
infidelity [ɪnfɪ'dɛlɪtɪ] *n* infidelidad *f*
in-fighting ['ɪnfaɪtɪŋ] *n* (*fig*) lucha(s) *f(pl)* interna(s)
infiltrate ['ɪnfɪltreɪt] *vt* (*troops etc*) infiltrarse en ■ *vi* infiltrarse
infinite ['ɪnfɪnɪt] *adj* infinito; **an ~ amount of money/time** un sinfín de dinero/tiempo
infinitely ['ɪnfɪnɪtlɪ] *adv* infinitamente
infinitesimal [ɪnfɪnɪ'tɛsɪməl] *adj* infinitésimo
infinitive [ɪn'fɪnɪtɪv] *n* infinitivo
infinity [ɪn'fɪnɪtɪ] *n* (*Math*) infinito; **an ~** infinidad *f*
infirm [ɪn'fəːm] *adj* enfermizo, débil
infirmary [ɪn'fəːmərɪ] *n* hospital *m*
infirmity [ɪn'fəːmɪtɪ] *n* debilidad *f*; (*illness*) enfermedad *f*, achaque *m*
inflame [ɪn'fleɪm] *vt* inflamar
inflamed [ɪn'fleɪmd] *adj*: **to become ~** inflamarse
inflammable [ɪn'flæməbl] *adj* (*Brit*) inflamable; (*situation etc*) explosivo
inflammation [ɪnflə'meɪʃən] *n* inflamación *f*
inflammatory [ɪn'flæmətərɪ] *adj* (*speech*) incendiario
inflatable [ɪn'fleɪtəbl] *adj* inflable
inflate [ɪn'fleɪt] *vt* (*tyre*) inflar; (*fig*) hinchar
inflated [ɪn'fleɪtɪd] *adj* (*tyre etc*) inflado; (*price, self-esteem etc*) exagerado
inflation [ɪn'fleɪʃən] *n* (*Econ*) inflación *f*
inflationary [ɪn'fleɪʃnərɪ] *adj* inflacionario
inflationary spiral *n* espiral *f* inflacionista
inflexible [ɪn'flɛksɪbl] *adj* inflexible
inflict [ɪn'flɪkt] *vt*: **to ~ on** infligir en; (*tax etc*) imponer a
in-flight ['ɪnflaɪt] *adj* durante el vuelo
inflow ['ɪnfləu] *n* afluencia
influence ['ɪnfluəns] *n* influencia ■ *vt* influir en, influenciar; **under the ~ of alcohol** en estado de embriaguez
influential [ɪnflu'ɛnʃl] *adj* influyente
influenza [ɪnflu'ɛnzə] *n* gripe *f*
influx ['ɪnflʌks] *n* afluencia
inform [ɪn'fɔːm] *vt*: **to ~ sb of sth** informar a algn sobre *or* de algo; (*warn*) avisar a algn de algo; (*communicate*) comunicar algo a algn ■ *vi*: **to ~ on sb** delatar a algn
informal [ɪn'fɔːml] *adj* (*manner, tone*) desenfadado; (*dress, occasion*) informal
informality [ɪnfɔː'mælɪtɪ] *n* falta de ceremonia; (*intimacy*) intimidad *f*; (*familiarity*) familiaridad *f*; (*ease*) afabilidad *f*
informally [ɪn'fɔːməlɪ] *adv* sin ceremonia; (*invite*) informalmente
informant [ɪn'fɔːmənt] *n* informante *m/f*
informatics [ɪnfɔː'mætɪks] *n* informática
information [ɪnfə'meɪʃən] *n* información *f*; (*news*) noticias *fpl*; (*knowledge*) conocimientos *mpl*; (*Law*) delación *f*; **a piece of ~** un dato; **for your ~** para su información
information and communication technology, information and communications technology *n* (*gen*) tecnología de la información y de las comunicaciones; (*Brit Scol*) informática
information bureau *n* oficina de información
information processing *n* procesamiento de datos

information retrieval *n* recuperación *f* de información
information science *n* gestión *f* de la información
information technology *n* informática
informative [ɪn'fɔ:mətɪv] *adj* informativo
informed [ɪn'fɔ:md] *adj* (*observer*) informado, al corriente; **an ~ guess** una opinión bien fundamentada
informer [ɪn'fɔ:məʳ] *n* delator(a) *m(f)*; (*also*: **police informer**) soplón(-ona) *m(f)*
infra dig ['ɪnfrə'dɪg] *adj abbr* (*col*: = *infra dignitatem*: = *beneath one's dignity*) denigrante
infra-red [ɪnfrə'rɛd] *adj* infrarrojo
infrastructure ['ɪnfrəstrʌktʃəʳ] *n* infraestructura
infrequent [ɪn'fri:kwənt] *adj* infrecuente
infringe [ɪn'frɪndʒ] *vt* infringir, violar ■ *vi*: **to ~ on** invadir
infringement [ɪn'frɪndʒmənt] *n* infracción *f*; (*of rights*) usurpación *f*; (*Sport*) falta
infuriate [ɪn'fjuərɪeɪt] *vt*: **to become infuriated** ponerse furioso
infuriating [ɪn'fjuərɪeɪtɪŋ] *adj*: **I find it ~** me saca de quicio
infuse [ɪn'fju:z] *vt* (*with courage, enthusiasm*): **to ~ sb with sth** infundir algo a algn
infusion [ɪn'fju:ʒən] *n* (*tea etc*) infusión *f*
ingenious [ɪn'dʒi:njəs] *adj* ingenioso
ingenuity [ɪndʒɪ'nju:ɪtɪ] *n* ingeniosidad *f*
ingenuous [ɪn'dʒɛnjuəs] *adj* ingenuo
ingot ['ɪŋgət] *n* lingote *m*, barra
ingrained [ɪn'greɪnd] *adj* arraigado
ingratiate [ɪn'greɪʃɪeɪt] *vt*: **to ~ o.s. with** congraciarse con
ingratiating [ɪn'greɪʃɪeɪtɪŋ] *adj* (*smile, speech*) insinuante; (*person*) zalamero, congraciador(a)
ingratitude [ɪn'grætɪtju:d] *n* ingratitud *f*
ingredient [ɪn'gri:dɪənt] *n* ingrediente *m*
ingrowing ['ɪngrəuɪŋ] *adj*: **~ (toe)nail** uña encarnada
inhabit [ɪn'hæbɪt] *vt* vivir en; (*occupy*) ocupar
inhabitable [ɪn'hæbɪtəbl] *adj* habitable
inhabitant [ɪn'hæbɪtənt] *n* habitante *m/f*
inhale [ɪn'heɪl] *vt* inhalar ■ *vi* (*in smoking*) tragar
inhaler [ɪn'heɪləʳ] *n* inhalador *m*
inherent [ɪn'hɪərənt] *adj*: **~ in** *or* **to** inherente a
inherently [ɪn'hɪərəntlɪ] *adv* intrínsecamente
inherit [ɪn'hɛrɪt] *vt* heredar
inheritance [ɪn'hɛrɪtəns] *n* herencia; (*fig*) patrimonio
inhibit [ɪn'hɪbɪt] *vt* inhibir, impedir; **to ~ sb from doing sth** impedir a algn hacer algo
inhibited [ɪn'hɪbɪtɪd] *adj* (*person*) cohibido
inhibition [ɪnhɪ'bɪʃən] *n* cohibición *f*
inhospitable [ɪnhɔs'pɪtəbl] *adj* (*person*) inhospitalario; (*place*) inhóspito
in-house ['ɪnhaus] *adj* dentro de la empresa
inhuman [ɪn'hju:mən] *adj* inhumano
inhumane [ɪnhju:'meɪn] *adj* inhumano
inimitable [ɪ'nɪmɪtəbl] *adj* inimitable
iniquity [ɪ'nɪkwɪtɪ] *n* iniquidad *f*; (*injustice*) injusticia
initial [ɪ'nɪʃl] *adj* inicial; (*first*) primero ■ *n* inicial *f* ■ *vt* firmar con las iniciales; **initials** *npl* iniciales *fpl*; (*abbreviation*) siglas *fpl*
initialize [ɪ'nɪʃəlaɪz] *vt* (*Comput*) inicializar
initially [ɪ'nɪʃəlɪ] *adv* en un principio
initiate [ɪ'nɪʃɪeɪt] *vt* (*start*) iniciar; **to ~ sb into a secret** iniciar a algn en un secreto; **to ~ proceedings against sb** (*Law*) poner una demanda contra algn
initiation [ɪnɪʃɪ'eɪʃən] *n* (*into secret etc*) iniciación *f*; (*beginning*) comienzo
initiative [ɪ'nɪʃətɪv] *n* iniciativa; **to take the ~** tomar la iniciativa
inject [ɪn'dʒɛkt] *vt* inyectar; (*money, enthusiasm*) aportar
injection [ɪn'dʒɛkʃən] *n* inyección *f*; **to have an ~** ponerse una inyección
injudicious [ɪndʒu'dɪʃəs] *adj* imprudente, indiscreto
injunction [ɪn'dʒʌŋkʃən] *n* entredicho, interdicto
injure ['ɪndʒəʳ] *vt* herir; (*hurt*) lastimar; (*fig: reputation etc*) perjudicar; (*feelings*) herir; **to ~ o.s.** hacerse daño, lastimarse
injured ['ɪndʒəd] *adj* (*also fig*) herido; **~ party** (*Law*) parte *f* perjudicada
injurious [ɪn'dʒuərɪəs] *adj*: **~ (to)** perjudicial (para)
injury ['ɪndʒərɪ] *n* herida, lesión *f*; (*wrong*) perjuicio, daño; **to escape without ~** salir ileso
injury time *n* (*Sport*) descuento
injustice [ɪn'dʒʌstɪs] *n* injusticia; **you do me an ~** usted es injusto conmigo
ink [ɪŋk] *n* tinta
ink-jet printer ['ɪŋkdʒɛt-] *n* impresora de chorro de tinta
inkling ['ɪŋklɪŋ] *n* sospecha; (*idea*) idea
inkpad ['ɪŋkpæd] *n* almohadilla
inlaid ['ɪnleɪd] *adj* (*wood*) taraceado; (*tiles*) entarimado
inland *adj* ['ɪnlənd] interior; (*town*) del interior ■ *adv* [ɪn'lænd] tierra adentro
Inland Revenue *n* (*Brit*) ≈ Hacienda
in-laws ['ɪnlɔ:z] *npl* suegros *mpl*
inlet ['ɪnlɛt] *n* (*Geo*) ensenada, cala; (*Tech*) admisión *f*, entrada

inmate ['ɪnmeɪt] *n* (*in prison*) preso(-a), presidiario(-a); (*in asylum*) internado(-a)
inmost ['ɪnməust] *adj* más íntimo, más secreto
inn [ɪn] *n* posada, mesón *m*; **the Inns of Court** *see* **barrister**
innards ['ɪnədz] *npl* (*col*) tripas *fpl*
innate [ɪ'neɪt] *adj* innato
inner ['ɪnəʳ] *adj* interior, interno
inner city *n barrios deprimidos del centro de una ciudad*
innermost ['ɪnəməust] *adj* más íntimo, más secreto
inner tube *n* (*of tyre*) cámara, llanta (*LAm*)
innings ['ɪnɪŋz] *n* (*Cricket*) entrada, turno
innocence ['ɪnəsns] *n* inocencia
innocent ['ɪnəsnt] *adj* inocente
innocuous [ɪ'nɔkjuəs] *adj* inocuo
innovation [ɪnəu'veɪʃən] *n* novedad *f*
innuendo (*pl* **innuendoes**) [ɪnju'ɛndəu, -əuz] *n* indirecta
innumerable [ɪ'nju:mrəbl] *adj* innumerable
inoculate [ɪ'nɔkjuleɪt] *vt*: **to ~ sb with sth/against sth** inocular *or* vacunar a algn con algo/contra algo
inoculation [ɪnɔkju'leɪʃən] *n* inoculación *f*
inoffensive [ɪnə'fɛnsɪv] *adj* inofensivo
inopportune [ɪn'ɔpətju:n] *adj* inoportuno
inordinate [ɪ'nɔ:dɪnət] *adj* excesivo, desmesurado
inordinately [ɪ'nɔ:dɪnətlɪ] *adv* excesivamente, desmesuradamente
inorganic [ɪnɔ:'gaenɪk] *adj* inorgánico
in-patient ['ɪnpeɪʃənt] *n* (paciente *m/f*) interno(-a)
input ['ɪnput] *n* (*Elec*) entrada; (*Comput*) entrada de datos ■ *vt* (*Comput*) introducir, entrar
inquest ['ɪnkwɛst] *n* (*coroner's*) investigación *f* post-mortem
inquire [ɪn'kwaɪəʳ] *vi* preguntar ■ *vt*: **to ~ when/where/whether** preguntar cuándo/dónde/si; **to ~ about** (*person*) preguntar por; (*fact*) informarse de
▸ **inquire into** *vt fus*: **to ~ into sth** investigar *or* indagar algo
inquiring [ɪn'kwaɪərɪŋ] *adj* (*mind*) inquieto; (*look*) interrogante
inquiry [ɪn'kwaɪərɪ] *n* pregunta; (*Law*) investigación *f*, pesquisa; (*commission*) comisión *f* investigadora; **to hold an ~ into sth** emprender una investigación sobre algo
inquiry desk *n* mesa de información
inquiry office *n* (*Brit*) oficina de información
inquisition [ɪnkwɪ'zɪʃən] *n* inquisición *f*
inquisitive [ɪn'kwɪzɪtɪv] *adj* (*mind*) inquisitivo; (*person*) fisgón(-ona)
inroad ['ɪnrəud] *n* incursión *f*; (*fig*) invasión *f*; **to make inroads into** (*time*) ocupar parte de; (*savings, supplies*) agotar parte de
insane [ɪn'seɪn] *adj* loco; (*Med*) demente
insanitary [ɪn'sænɪtərɪ] *adj* insalubre
insanity [ɪn'sænɪtɪ] *n* demencia, locura
insatiable [ɪn'seɪʃəbl] *adj* insaciable
inscribe [ɪn'skraɪb] *vt* inscribir; (*book etc*): **to ~ (to sb)** dedicar (a algn)
inscription [ɪn'skrɪpʃən] *n* (*gen*) inscripción *f*; (*in book*) dedicatoria
inscrutable [ɪn'skru:təbl] *adj* inescrutable, insondable
inseam measurement ['ɪnsi:m-] *n* (*US*) = **inside leg measurement**
insect ['ɪnsɛkt] *n* insecto
insect bite *n* picadura
insecticide [ɪn'sɛktɪsaɪd] *n* insecticida *m*
insect repellent *n* loción *f* contra los insectos
insecure [ɪnsɪ'kjuəʳ] *adj* inseguro
insecurity [ɪnsɪ'kjuərɪtɪ] *n* inseguridad *f*
insemination [ɪnsɛmɪ'neɪʃn] *n*: **artificial ~** inseminación *f* artificial
insensible [ɪn'sɛnsɪbl] *adj* inconsciente; (*unconscious*) sin conocimiento
insensitive [ɪn'sɛnsɪtɪv] *adj* insensible
insensitivity [ɪnsɛnsɪ'tɪvɪtɪ] *n* insensibilidad *f*
inseparable [ɪn'sɛprəbl] *adj* inseparable; **they were ~ friends** los unía una estrecha amistad
insert *vt* [ɪn'sə:t] (*into sth*) introducir; (*Comput*) insertar ■ *n* ['ɪnsə:t] encarte *m*
insertion [ɪn'sə:ʃən] *n* inserción *f*
in-service [ɪn'sə:vɪs] *adj* (*training, course*) en el trabajo, a cargo de la empresa
inshore [ɪn'ʃɔ:ʳ] *adj*: **~ fishing** pesca *f* costera ■ *adv* (*fish*) a lo largo de la costa; (*move*) hacia la orilla
inside ['ɪn'saɪd] *n* interior *m*; (*lining*) forro; (*of road: Brit*) izquierdo; (*: in US, Europe etc*) derecho ■ *adj* interior, interno ■ *adv* (*within*) (por) dentro, adentro (*esp LAm*); (*with movement*) hacia dentro; (*col: in prison*) en chirona ■ *prep* dentro de; (*of time*): **~ 10 minutes** en menos de 10 minutos; **insides** *npl* (*col*) tripas *fpl*; **~ out** *adv* (*turn*) al revés; (*know*) a fondo
inside forward *n* (*Sport*) interior *m*
inside information *n* información *f* confidencial
inside lane *n* (*Aut: Brit*) carril *m* izquierdo; (*: in US, Europe etc*) carril *m* derecho
inside leg measurement *n* medida de pernera
insider [ɪn'saɪdəʳ] *n* enterado(-a)
insider dealing, insider trading *n* (*Stock Exchange*) abuso de información privilegiada

inside story *n* historia íntima
insidious [ɪn'sɪdɪəs] *adj* insidioso
insight ['ɪnsaɪt] *n* perspicacia, percepción *f*; **to gain** *or* **get an ~ into sth** comprender algo mejor
insignia [ɪn'sɪgnɪə] *npl* insignias *fpl*
insignificant [ɪnsɪg'nɪfɪknt] *adj* insignificante
insincere [ɪnsɪn'sɪəʳ] *adj* poco sincero
insincerity [ɪnsɪn'sɛrɪtɪ] *n* falta de sinceridad, doblez *f*
insinuate [ɪn'sɪnjueɪt] *vt* insinuar
insinuation [ɪnsɪnju'eɪʃən] *n* insinuación *f*
insipid [ɪn'sɪpɪd] *adj* soso, insulso
insist [ɪn'sɪst] *vi* insistir; **to ~ on doing** empeñarse en hacer; **to ~ that** insistir en que; (*claim*) exigir que
insistence [ɪn'sɪstəns] *n* insistencia; (*stubbornness*) empeño
insistent [ɪn'sɪstənt] *adj* insistente; empeñado
insofar as [ɪnsəu'fɑ:-] *conj* en la medida en que, en tanto que
insole ['ɪnsəul] *n* plantilla
insolence ['ɪnsələns] *n* insolencia, descaro
insolent ['ɪnsələnt] *adj* insolente, descarado
insoluble [ɪn'sɔljubl] *adj* insoluble
insolvency [ɪn'sɔlvənsɪ] *n* insolvencia
insolvent [ɪn'sɔlvənt] *adj* insolvente
insomnia [ɪn'sɔmnɪə] *n* insomnio
insomniac [ɪn'sɔmnɪæk] *n* insomne *m/f*
inspect [ɪn'spɛkt] *vt* inspeccionar, examinar; (*troops*) pasar revista a
inspection [ɪn'spɛkʃən] *n* inspección *f*, examen *m*
inspector [ɪn'spɛktəʳ] *n* inspector(a) *m(f)*; (*Brit: on buses, trains*) revisor(a) *m(f)*
inspiration [ɪnspə'reɪʃən] *n* inspiración *f*
inspire [ɪn'spaɪəʳ] *vt* inspirar; **to ~ sb (to do sth)** alentar a algn (a hacer algo)
inspired [ɪn'spaɪəd] *adj* (*writer, book etc*) inspirado, genial, iluminado; **in an ~ moment** en un momento de inspiración
inspiring [ɪn'spaɪərɪŋ] *adj* inspirador(a)
inst. [ɪnst] *abbr* (*Brit Comm: = instant, of the present month*) cte
instability [ɪnstə'bɪlɪtɪ] *n* inestabilidad *f*
install [ɪn'stɔ:l] *vt* instalar
installation [ɪnstə'leɪʃən] *n* instalación *f*
installment plan *n* (*US*) compra a plazos
instalment, (*US*) **installment** [ɪn'stɔ:lmənt] *n* plazo; (*of story*) entrega; (*of TV serial etc*) capítulo; **in instalments** (*pay, receive*) a plazos; **to pay in instalments** pagar a plazos *or* por abonos
instance ['ɪnstəns] *n* ejemplo, caso; **for ~** por ejemplo; **in the first ~** en primer lugar; **in that ~** en ese caso
instant ['ɪnstənt] *n* instante *m*, momento ■ *adj* inmediato; (*coffee*) instantáneo
instantaneous [ɪnstən'teɪnɪəs] *adj* instantáneo
instantly ['ɪnstəntlɪ] *adv* en seguida, al instante
instant replay *n* (*US TV*) repetición *f* de la jugada
instead [ɪn'stɛd] *adv* en cambio; **~ of** en lugar de, en vez de
instep ['ɪnstɛp] *n* empeine *m*
instigate ['ɪnstɪgeɪt] *vt* (*rebellion, strike, crime*) instigar; (*new ideas etc*) fomentar
instigation [ɪnstɪ'geɪʃən] *n* instigación *f*; **at sb's ~** a instigación de algn
instil [ɪn'stɪl] *vt*: **to ~ into** inculcar a
instinct ['ɪnstɪŋkt] *n* instinto
instinctive [ɪn'stɪŋktɪv] *adj* instintivo
instinctively [ɪn'stɪŋktɪvlɪ] *adv* por instinto
institute ['ɪnstɪtju:t] *n* instituto; (*professional body*) colegio ■ *vt* (*begin*) iniciar, empezar; (*proceedings*) entablar
institution [ɪnstɪ'tju:ʃən] *n* institución *f*; (*beginning*) iniciación *f*; (*Med: home*) asilo; (*asylum*) manicomio; (*custom*) costumbre *f* arraigada
institutional [ɪnstɪ'tju:ʃənl] *adj* institucional
instruct [ɪn'strʌkt] *vt*: **to ~ sb in sth** instruir a algn en *or* sobre algo; **to ~ sb to do sth** dar instrucciones a algn de *or* mandar a algn hacer algo
instruction [ɪn'strʌkʃən] *n* (*teaching*) instrucción *f*; **instructions** *npl* órdenes *fpl*; **instructions (for use)** modo *sg* de empleo
instruction book *n* manual *m*
instructive [ɪn'strʌktɪv] *adj* instructivo
instructor [ɪn'strʌktəʳ] *n* instructor(a) *m(f)*
instrument ['ɪnstrəmənt] *n* instrumento
instrumental [ɪnstrə'mɛntl] *adj* (*Mus*) instrumental; **to be ~ in** ser el artífice de; **to be ~ in sth/in doing sth** ser responsable de algo/de hacer algo
instrumentalist [ɪnstrə'mɛntəlɪst] *n* instrumentista *m/f*
instrument panel *n* tablero (de instrumentos)
insubordinate [ɪnsə'bɔ:dənɪt] *adj* insubordinado
insubordination [ɪnsəbɔ:də'neɪʃən] *n* insubordinación *f*
insufferable [ɪn'sʌfrəbl] *adj* insoportable
insufficient [ɪnsə'fɪʃənt] *adj* insuficiente
insufficiently [ɪnsə'fɪʃəntlɪ] *adv* insuficientemente
insular ['ɪnsjuləʳ] *adj* insular; (*outlook*) estrecho de miras

insularity [ɪnsju'lærɪtɪ] *n* insularidad *f*
insulate ['ɪnsjuleɪt] *vt* aislar
insulating tape ['ɪnsjuleɪtɪŋ-] *n* cinta aislante
insulation [ɪnsju'leɪʃən] *n* aislamiento
insulator ['ɪnsjuleɪtəʳ] *n* aislante *m*
insulin ['ɪnsjulɪn] *n* insulina
insult *n* ['ɪnsʌlt] insulto; (*offence*) ofensa ▪ *vt* [ɪn'sʌlt] insultar; ofender
insulting [ɪn'sʌltɪŋ] *adj* insultante; ofensivo
insuperable [ɪn'sju:prəbl] *adj* insuperable
insurance [ɪn'ʃuərəns] *n* seguro; **fire/life ~** seguro de incendios/vida; **to take out ~ (against)** hacerse un seguro (contra)
insurance agent *n* agente *m/f* de seguros
insurance broker *n* corredor(a) *m(f)* *or* agente *m/f* de seguros
insurance policy *n* póliza (de seguros)
insurance premium *n* prima de seguros
insure [ɪn'ʃuəʳ] *vt* asegurar; **to ~ sb** *or* **sb's life** hacer un seguro de vida a algn; **to ~ (against)** asegurar (contra); **to be insured for £5000** tener un seguro de 5000 libras
insured [ɪn'ʃuəd] *n*: **the ~** el/la asegurado(-a)
insurer [ɪn'ʃuərəʳ] *n* asegurador(a)
insurgent [ɪn'sə:dʒənt] *adj, n* insurgente *m/f*, insurrecto(-a) *m(f)*
insurmountable [ɪnsə'mauntəbl] *adj* insuperable
insurrection [ɪnsə'rɛkʃən] *n* insurrección *f*
intact [ɪn'tækt] *adj* íntegro; (*untouched*) intacto
intake ['ɪnteɪk] *n* (*Tech*) entrada, toma; (*: pipe*) tubo de admisión; (*of food*) ingestión *f*; (*Brit Scol*): **an ~ of 200 a year** 200 matriculados al año
intangible [ɪn'tændʒɪbl] *adj* intangible
integer ['ɪntɪdʒəʳ] *n* (número) entero
integral ['ɪntɪgrəl] *adj* (*whole*) íntegro; (*part*) integrante
integrate ['ɪntɪgreɪt] *vt* integrar ▪ *vi* integrarse
integrated circuit ['ɪntɪgreɪtɪd-] *n* (*Comput*) circuito integrado
integration [ɪntɪ'greɪʃən] *n* integración *f*; **racial ~** integración de razas
integrity [ɪn'tɛgrɪtɪ] *n* honradez *f*, rectitud *f*; (*Comput*) integridad *f*
intellect ['ɪntəlɛkt] *n* intelecto
intellectual [ɪntə'lɛktjuəl] *adj, n* intelectual *m/f*
intelligence [ɪn'tɛlɪdʒəns] *n* inteligencia
intelligence quotient *n* coeficiente *m* intelectual
Intelligence Service *n* Servicio de Inteligencia
intelligence test *n* prueba de inteligencia
intelligent [ɪn'tɛlɪdʒənt] *adj* inteligente
intelligently [ɪn'tɛlɪdʒəntlɪ] *adv* inteligentemente
intelligentsia [ɪntɛlɪ'dʒɛntsɪə] *n* intelectualidad *f*
intelligible [ɪn'tɛlɪdʒɪbl] *adj* inteligible, comprensible
intemperate [ɪn'tɛmpərət] *adj* inmoderado
intend [ɪn'tɛnd] *vt* (*gift etc*): **to ~ sth for** destinar algo a; **to ~ to do sth** tener intención de *or* pensar hacer algo
intended [ɪn'tɛndɪd] *adj* (*effect*) deseado
intense [ɪn'tɛns] *adj* intenso; **to be ~** (*person*) tomárselo todo muy en serio
intensely [ɪn'tɛnslɪ] *adv* intensamente; (*very*) sumamente
intensify [ɪn'tɛnsɪfaɪ] *vt* intensificar; (*increase*) aumentar
intensity [ɪn'tɛnsɪtɪ] *n* (*gen*) intensidad *f*
intensive [ɪn'tɛnsɪv] *adj* intensivo
intensive care *n*: **to be in ~** estar bajo cuidados intensivos; **~ unit** *n* unidad *f* de vigilancia intensiva
intensively [ɪn'tɛnsɪvlɪ] *adv* intensivamente
intent [ɪn'tɛnt] *n* propósito ▪ *adj* (*absorbed*) absorto; (*attentive*) atento; **to all intents and purposes** a efectos prácticos; **to be ~ on doing sth** estar resuelto *or* decidido a hacer algo
intention [ɪn'tɛnʃən] *n* intención *f*, propósito
intentional [ɪn'tɛnʃənl] *adj* deliberado
intentionally [ɪn'tɛnʃnəlɪ] *adv* a propósito
intently [ɪn'tɛntlɪ] *adv* atentamente, fijamente
inter [ɪn'tə:ʳ] *vt* enterrar, sepultar
inter- ['ɪntəʳ] *pref* inter-
interact [ɪntər'ækt] *vi* (*substances*) influirse mutuamente; (*people*) relacionarse
interaction [ɪntər'ækʃən] *n* interacción *f*, acción *f* recíproca
interactive [ɪntər'æktɪv] *adj* (*Comput*) interactivo
intercede [ɪntə'si:d] *vi* (*also*: **to intercede (with)**) interceder (con); **to ~ with sb/on behalf of sb** interceder con algn/en nombre de algn
intercept [ɪntə'sɛpt] *vt* interceptar; (*stop*) detener
interception [ɪntə'sɛpʃən] *n* interceptación *f*; detención *f*
interchange *n* ['ɪntətʃeɪndʒ] intercambio; (*on motorway*) intersección *f* ▪ *vt* [ɪntə'tʃeɪndʒ] intercambiar
interchangeable [ɪntə'tʃeɪndʒəbl] *adj* intercambiable
intercity [ɪntə'sɪtɪ] *adj*: **~ (train)** (tren *m*) intercity *m*

intercom ['ɪntəkɔm] *n* interfono
interconnect [ɪntəkə'nɛkt] *vi* (*rooms*) comunicar(se)
intercontinental ['ɪntəkɔntɪ'nɛntl] *adj* intercontinental
intercourse ['ɪntəkɔ:s] *n* (*also*: **sexual intercourse**) relaciones *fpl* sexuales, contacto sexual; (*social*) trato
interdependence [ɪntədɪ'pɛndəns] *n* interdependencia
interdependent [ɪntədɪ'pɛndənt] *adj* interdependiente
interest ['ɪntrɪst] *n* (*Comm*) interés *m* ■ *vt* interesar; **compound/simple ~** interés compuesto/simple; **business interests** negocios *mpl*; **British interests in the Middle East** los intereses británicos en el Medio Oriente
interested ['ɪntrɪstɪd] *adj* interesado; **to be ~ in** interesarse por
interest-free ['ɪntrɪst'fri:] *adj* libre de interés
interesting ['ɪntrɪstɪŋ] *adj* interesante
interest rate *n* tipo de interés
interface ['ɪntəfeɪs] *n* (*Comput*) junción *f*, interface *m*
interfere [ɪntə'fɪə^r] *vi*: **to ~ in** (*quarrel, other people's business*) entrometerse en; **to ~ with** (*hinder*) estorbar; (*damage*) estropear; (*Radio*) interferir con
interference [ɪntə'fɪərəns] *n* (*gen*) intromisión *f*; (*Radio, TV*) interferencia
interfering [ɪntə'fɪərɪŋ] *adj* entrometido
interim ['ɪntərɪm] *adj*: **~ dividend** dividendo parcial ■ *n*: **in the ~** en el ínterin
interior [ɪn'tɪərɪə^r] *n* interior *m* ■ *adj* interior
interior decorator, interior designer *n* interiorista *m/f*, diseñador(a) *m(f)* de interiores
interjection [ɪntə'dʒɛkʃən] *n* interrupción *f*
interlock [ɪntə'lɔk] *vi* entrelazarse; (*wheels etc*) endentarse
interloper ['ɪntələupə^r] *n* intruso(-a)
interlude ['ɪntəlu:d] *n* intervalo; (*rest*) descanso; (*Theat*) intermedio
intermarriage [ɪntə'mærɪdʒ] *n* endogamia
intermarry [ɪntə'mærɪ] *vi* casarse (entre parientes)
intermediary [ɪntə'mi:dɪərɪ] *n* intermediario(-a)
intermediate [ɪntə'mi:dɪət] *adj* intermedio
interminable [ɪn'tə:mɪnəbl] *adj* inacabable
intermission [ɪntə'mɪʃən] *n* (*Theat*) descanso
intermittent [ɪntə'mɪtnt] *adj* intermitente
intermittently [ɪntə'mɪtntlɪ] *adv* intermitentemente
intern *vt* [ɪn'tə:n] internar; (*enclose*) encerrar ■ *n* ['ɪntə:n] (*US*) médico(-a) *m(f)* interno(-a)
internal [ɪn'tə:nl] *adj* interno, interior; **~ injuries** heridas *fpl or* lesiones *fpl* internas
internally [ɪn'tə:nəlɪ] *adv* interiormente; **"not to be taken ~"** "uso externo"
Internal Revenue Service *n* (*US*) ≈ Hacienda
international [ɪntə'næʃənl] *adj* internacional; **~ (game)** partido internacional; **~ (player)** jugador(a) *m(f)* internacional
International Atomic Energy Agency *n* Organismo Internacional de Energía Atómica
International Chamber of Commerce *n* Cámara de Comercio Internacional
International Court of Justice *n* Corte *f* Internacional de Justicia
international date line *n* línea de cambio de fecha
internationally [ɪntə'næʃnəlɪ] *adv* internacionalmente
International Monetary Fund *n* Fondo Monetario Internacional
internecine [ɪntə'ni:saɪn] *adj* de aniquilación mutua
internee [ɪntə:'ni:] *n* interno(-a), recluso(-a)
Internet ['ɪntənɛt] *n*: **the ~** (el *or* la) Internet
Internet café *n* cibercafé *m*
Internet Service Provider *n* proveedor *m* de (acceso a) Internet
Internet user *n* internauta *m/f*
internment [ɪn'tə:nmənt] *n* internamiento
interplanetary [ɪntə'plænɪtərɪ] *adj* interplanetario
interplay ['ɪntəpleɪ] *n* interacción *f*
Interpol ['ɪntəpɔl] *n* Interpol *f*
interpret [ɪn'tə:prɪt] *vt* interpretar; (*translate*) traducir; (*understand*) entender ■ *vi* hacer de intérprete
interpretation [ɪntə:prɪ'teɪʃən] *n* interpretación *f*; traducción *f*
interpreter [ɪn'tə:prɪtə^r] *n* intérprete *m/f*
interrelated [ɪntərɪ'leɪtɪd] *adj* interrelacionado
interrogate [ɪn'tɛrəugeɪt] *vt* interrogar
interrogation [ɪntɛrəu'geɪʃən] *n* interrogatorio
interrogative [ɪntə'rɔgətɪv] *adj* interrogativo
interrupt [ɪntə'rʌpt] *vt, vi* interrumpir
interruption [ɪntə'rʌpʃən] *n* interrupción *f*
intersect [ɪntə'sɛkt] *vt* cruzar ■ *vi* (*roads*) cruzarse
intersection [ɪntə'sɛkʃən] *n* intersección *f*; (*of roads*) cruce *m*
intersperse [ɪntə'spə:s] *vt*: **to ~ with** salpicar de
intertwine [ɪntə'twaɪn] *vt* entrelazar ■ *vi* entrelazarse

interval ['ɪntəvl] *n* intervalo; (*Brit Theat, Sport*) descanso; **at intervals** a ratos, de vez en cuando; **sunny intervals** (*Meteorology*) claros *mpl*
intervene [ɪntə'vi:n] *vi* intervenir; (*take part*) participar; (*occur*) sobrevenir
intervening [ɪntə'vi:nɪŋ] *adj* intermedio
intervention [ɪntə'vɛnʃən] *n* intervención *f*
interview ['ɪntəvju:] *n* (*Radio, TV etc*) entrevista ▪ *vt* entrevistar a
interviewee [ɪntəvju:'i:] *n* entrevistado(-a)
interviewer ['ɪntəvju:əʳ] *n* entrevistador(a) *m(f)*
intestate [ɪn'tɛsteɪt] *adj* intestado
intestinal [ɪn'tɛstɪnl] *adj* intestinal
intestine [ɪn'tɛstɪn] *n*: **large/small ~** intestino grueso/delgado
intimacy ['ɪntɪməsɪ] *n* intimidad *f*; (*relations*) relaciones *fpl* íntimas
intimate *adj* ['ɪntɪmət] íntimo; (*friendship*) estrecho; (*knowledge*) profundo ▪ *vt* ['ɪntɪmeɪt] (*announce*) dar a entender
intimately ['ɪntɪmətlɪ] *adv* íntimamente
intimidate [ɪn'tɪmɪdeɪt] *vt* intimidar, amedrentar
intimidation [ɪntɪmɪ'deɪʃən] *n* intimidación *f*
into ['ɪntu:] *prep* (*gen*) en; (*towards*) a; (*inside*) hacia el interior de; **~ three pieces/French** en tres pedazos/al francés; **to change pounds ~ euros** cambiar libras por euros
intolerable [ɪn'tɔlərəbl] *adj* intolerable, insoportable
intolerance [ɪn'tɔlərəns] *n* intolerancia
intolerant [ɪn'tɔlərənt] *adj*: **~ (of)** intolerante (con)
intonation [ɪntəu'neɪʃən] *n* entonación *f*
intoxicate [ɪn'tɔksɪkeɪt] *vt* embriagar
intoxicated [ɪn'tɔksɪkeɪtɪd] *adj* embriagado
intoxication [ɪntɔksɪ'keɪʃən] *n* embriaguez *f*
intractable [ɪn'træktəbl] *adj* (*person*) intratable; (*problem*) irresoluble; (*illness*) incurable
intranet ['ɪntrənɛt] *n* intranet *f*
intransigence [ɪn'trænsɪdʒəns] *n* intransigencia
intransigent [ɪn'trænsɪdʒənt] *adj* intransigente
intransitive [ɪn'trænsɪtɪv] *adj* intransitivo
intravenous [ɪntrə'vi:nəs] *adj* intravenoso
in-tray ['ɪntreɪ] *n* bandeja de entrada
intrepid [ɪn'trɛpɪd] *adj* intrépido
intricacy ['ɪntrɪkəsɪ] *n* complejidad *f*
intricate ['ɪntrɪkət] *adj* intrincado; (*plot, problem*) complejo
intrigue [ɪn'tri:g] *n* intriga ▪ *vt* fascinar ▪ *vi* andar en intrigas
intriguing [ɪn'tri:gɪŋ] *adj* fascinante
intrinsic [ɪn'trɪnsɪk] *adj* intrínseco
introduce [ɪntrə'dju:s] *vt* introducir, meter; **to ~ sb (to sb)** presentar algn (a algn); **to ~ sb to** (*pastime, technique*) introducir a algn a; **may I ~ ...?** permítame presentarle a ...
introduction [ɪntrə'dʌkʃən] *n* introducción *f*; (*of person*) presentación *f*; **a letter of ~** una carta de recomendación
introductory [ɪntrə'dʌktərɪ] *adj* introductorio; **an ~ offer** una oferta introductoria; **~ remarks** comentarios *mpl* preliminares
introspection [ɪntrəu'spɛkʃən] *n* introspección *f*
introspective [ɪntrəu'spɛktɪv] *adj* introspectivo
introvert ['ɪntrəuvə:t] *adj, n* introvertido(-a) *m(f)*
intrude [ɪn'tru:d] *vi* (*person*) entrometerse; **to ~ on** estorbar
intruder [ɪn'tru:dəʳ] *n* intruso(-a)
intrusion [ɪn'tru:ʒən] *n* invasión *f*
intrusive [ɪn'tru:sɪv] *adj* intruso
intuition [ɪntju:'ɪʃən] *n* intuición *f*
intuitive [ɪn'tju:ɪtɪv] *adj* intuitivo
intuitively [ɪn'tju:ɪtɪvlɪ] *adv* por intuición, intuitivamente
inundate ['ɪnʌndeɪt] *vt*: **to ~ with** inundar de
inure [ɪn'juəʳ] *vt*: **to ~ (to)** acostumbrar *or* habituar (a)
invade [ɪn'veɪd] *vt* invadir
invader [ɪn'veɪdəʳ] *n* invasor(a) *m(f)*
invalid *n* ['ɪnvəlɪd] minusválido(-a) ▪ *adj* [ɪn'vælɪd] (*not valid*) inválido, nulo
invalidate [ɪn'vælɪdeɪt] *vt* invalidar, anular
invalid chair *n* silla de ruedas
invaluable [ɪn'væljuəbl] *adj* inestimable
invariable [ɪn'vɛərɪəbl] *adj* invariable
invariably [ɪn'vɛərɪəblɪ] *adv* sin excepción, siempre; **she is ~ late** siempre llega tarde
invasion [ɪn'veɪʒən] *n* invasión *f*
invective [ɪn'vɛktɪv] *n* invectiva
inveigle [ɪn'vi:gl] *vt*: **to ~ sb into (doing) sth** embaucar *or* engatusar a algn para (que haga) algo
invent [ɪn'vɛnt] *vt* inventar
invention [ɪn'vɛnʃən] *n* invento; (*inventiveness*) inventiva; (*lie*) invención *f*
inventive [ɪn'vɛntɪv] *adj* inventivo
inventiveness [ɪn'vɛntɪvnɪs] *n* ingenio, inventiva
inventor [ɪn'vɛntəʳ] *n* inventor(a) *m(f)*
inventory ['ɪnvəntrɪ] *n* inventario
inventory control *n* control *m* de existencias
inverse [ɪn'və:s] *adj, n* inverso; **in ~ proportion (to)** en proporción inversa (a)

inversely [ɪn'vəːslɪ] *adv* a la inversa
invert [ɪn'vəːt] *vt* invertir
invertebrate [ɪn'vəːtɪbrət] *n* invertebrado
inverted commas [ɪn'vəːtɪd-] *npl* (*Brit*) comillas *fpl*
invest [ɪn'vɛst] *vt* invertir; (*fig: time, effort*) dedicar ■ *vi* invertir; **to ~ sb with sth** conferir algo a algn
investigate [ɪn'vɛstɪgeɪt] *vt* investigar; (*study*) estudiar, examinar
investigation [ɪnvɛstɪ'geɪʃən] *n* investigación *f*, pesquisa; examen *m*
investigative journalism [ɪn'vɛstɪgətɪv-] *n* periodismo de investigación
investigator [ɪn'vɛstɪgeɪtəʳ] *n* investigador(a) *m(f)*; **private ~** investigador(a) *m(f)* privado(-a)
investiture [ɪn'vɛstɪtʃəʳ] *n* investidura
investment [ɪn'vɛstmənt] *n* inversión *f*
investment grant *n* subvención *f* para la inversión
investment income *n* ingresos *mpl* procedentes de inversiones
investment portfolio *n* cartera de inversiones
investment trust *n* compañía inversionista, sociedad *f* de cartera
investor [ɪn'vɛstəʳ] *n* inversor(a) *m(f)*
inveterate [ɪn'vɛtərət] *adj* empedernido
invidious [ɪn'vɪdɪəs] *adj* odioso
invigilate [ɪn'vɪdʒɪleɪt] *vt, vi* (*in exam*) vigilar
invigilator [ɪn'vɪdʒɪleɪtəʳ] *n* celador(a) *m(f)*
invigorating [ɪn'vɪgəreɪtɪŋ] *adj* vigorizante
invincible [ɪn'vɪnsɪbl] *adj* invencible
inviolate [ɪn'vaɪələt] *adj* inviolado
invisible [ɪn'vɪzɪbl] *adj* invisible
invisible assets *npl* activo invisible
invisible ink *n* tinta simpática
invisible mending *n* puntada invisible
invitation [ɪnvɪ'teɪʃən] *n* invitación *f*; **at sb's ~** a invitación de algn; **by ~ only** solamente por invitación
invite [ɪn'vaɪt] *vt* invitar; (*opinions etc*) solicitar, pedir; (*trouble*) buscarse; **to ~ sb (to do)** invitar a algn (a hacer); **to ~ sb to dinner** invitar a algn a cenar
▸ **invite out** *vt* invitar a salir
▸ **invite over** *vt* invitar a casa
inviting [ɪn'vaɪtɪŋ] *adj* atractivo; (*look*) provocativo; (*food*) apetitoso
invoice ['ɪnvɔɪs] *n* factura ■ *vt* facturar; **to ~ sb for goods** facturar a algn las mercancías
invoicing ['ɪnvɔɪsɪŋ] *n* facturación *f*
invoke [ɪn'vəuk] *vt* invocar; (*aid*) pedir; (*law*) recurrir a
involuntary [ɪn'vɔləntrɪ] *adj* involuntario
involve [ɪn'vɔlv] *vt* (*entail*) suponer, implicar; **to ~ sb (in)** involucrar a algn (en)
involved [ɪn'vɔlvd] *adj* complicado; **to be/become ~ in sth** estar involucrado/involucrarse en algo
involvement [ɪn'vɔlvmənt] *n* (*gen*) enredo; (*obligation*) compromiso; (*difficulty*) apuro
invulnerable [ɪn'vʌlnərəbl] *adj* invulnerable
inward ['ɪnwəd] *adj* (*movement*) interior, interno; (*thought, feeling*) íntimo ■ *adv* hacia dentro
inwardly ['ɪnwədlɪ] *adv* (*feel, think etc*) para sí, para dentro
inwards ['ɪnwədz] *adv* hacia dentro
I/O *abbr* (*Comput:* = *input/output*) E/S; **~ error** error *m* de E/S
IOC *n abbr* (= *International Olympic Committee*) COI *m*
iodine ['aɪəudiːn] *n* yodo
IOM *abbr* (*Brit*) = **Isle of Man**
ion ['aɪən] *n* ion *m*
Ionian Sea [aɪ'əunɪən-] *n*: **the ~** el Mar Jónico
ioniser ['aɪənaɪzəʳ] *n* ionizador *m*
iota [aɪ'əutə] *n* (*fig*) jota, ápice *m*
IOU *n abbr* (= *I owe you*) pagaré *m*
IOW *abbr* (*Brit*) = **Isle of Wight**
IPA *n abbr* (= *International Phonetic Alphabet*) AFI *m*
IQ *n abbr* (= *intelligence quotient*) C.I. *m*
IRA *n abbr* (= *Irish Republican Army*) IRA *m*; (*US*) = **individual retirement account**
Iran [ɪ'rɑːn] *n* Irán *m*
Iranian [ɪ'reɪnɪən] *adj* iraní ■ *n* iraní *m/f*; (*Ling*) iraní *m*
Iraq [ɪ'rɑːk] *n* Irak *m*
Iraqi [ɪ'rɑːkɪ] *adj, n* irakí *m/f*
irascible [ɪ'ræsɪbl] *adj* irascible
irate [aɪ'reɪt] *adj* enojado, airado
Ireland ['aɪələnd] *n* Irlanda; **Republic of ~** República de Irlanda
iris (*pl* **irises**) ['aɪrɪs, -ɪz] *n* (*Anat*) iris *m*; (*Bot*) lirio
Irish ['aɪrɪʃ] *adj* irlandés(-esa) ■ *n* (*Ling*) irlandés *m*; **the ~** *npl* los irlandeses
Irishman ['aɪrɪʃmən] *n* irlandés *m*
Irish Sea *n*: **the ~** el Mar de Irlanda
Irishwoman ['aɪrɪʃwumən] *n* irlandesa
irk [əːk] *vt* fastidiar
irksome ['əːksəm] *adj* fastidioso
IRN *n abbr* (= *Independent Radio News*) *servicio de noticias en las cadenas de radio privadas*
IRO *n abbr* (*US*) = **International Refugee Organization**
iron ['aɪən] *n* hierro; (*for clothes*) plancha ■ *adj* de hierro ■ *vt* (*clothes*) planchar; **irons** *npl* (*chains*) grilletes *mpl*
▸ **iron out** *vt* (*crease*) quitar; (*fig*) allanar, resolver

Iron Curtain *n*: **the ~** el Telón de Acero
iron foundry *n* fundición *f*, fundidora
ironic [aɪ'rɔnɪk], **ironical** [aɪ'rɔnɪkl] *adj* irónico
ironically [aɪ'rɔnɪklɪ] *adv* irónicamente
ironing ['aɪənɪŋ] *n* (*act*) planchado; (*ironed clothes*) ropa planchada; (*clothes to be ironed*) ropa por planchar
ironing board *n* tabla de planchar
iron lung *n* (*Med*) pulmón *m* de acero
ironmonger ['aɪənmʌŋgəʳ] *n* (*Brit*) ferretero(-a); **~'s (shop)** ferretería
iron ore *n* mineral *m* de hierro
ironworks ['aɪənwə:ks] *n* fundición *f*
irony ['aɪrənɪ] *n* ironía; **the ~ of it is that ...** lo irónico del caso es que ...
irrational [ɪ'ræʃənl] *adj* irracional
irreconcilable [ɪrɛkən'saɪləbl] *adj* inconciliable; (*enemies*) irreconciliable
irredeemable [ɪrɪ'di:məbl] *adj* irredimible
irrefutable [ɪrɪ'fju:təbl] *adj* irrefutable
irregular [ɪ'rɛgjuləʳ] *adj* irregular; (*surface*) desigual
irregularity [ɪrɛgju'lærɪtɪ] *n* irregularidad *f*; desigualdad *f*
irrelevance [ɪ'rɛləvəns] *n* irrelevancia
irrelevant [ɪ'rɛləvənt] *adj* irrelevante; **to be ~** estar fuera de lugar, no venir al caso
irreligious [ɪrɪ'lɪdʒəs] *adj* irreligioso
irreparable [ɪ'rɛprəbl] *adj* irreparable
irreplaceable [ɪrɪ'pleɪsəbl] *adj* irremplazable
irrepressible [ɪrɪ'prɛsəbl] *adj* incontenible
irreproachable [ɪrɪ'prəutʃəbl] *adj* irreprochable
irresistible [ɪrɪ'zɪstɪbl] *adj* irresistible
irresolute [ɪ'rɛzəlu:t] *adj* indeciso
irrespective [ɪrɪ'spɛktɪv]: **~ of** *prep* sin tener en cuenta, no importa
irresponsibility [ɪrɪspɔnsɪ'bɪlɪtɪ] *n* irresponsabilidad *f*
irresponsible [ɪrɪ'spɔnsɪbl] *adj* (*act*) irresponsable; (*person*) poco serio
irretrievable [ɪrɪ'tri:vəbl] *adj* (*object*) irrecuperable; (*loss, damage*) irremediable, irreparable
irretrievably [ɪrɪ'tri:vəblɪ] *adv* irremisiblemente
irreverence [ɪ'rɛvərns] *n* irreverencia
irreverent [ɪ'rɛvərnt] *adj* irreverente, irrespetuoso
irrevocable [ɪ'rɛvəkəbl] *adj* irrevocable
irrigate ['ɪrɪgeɪt] *vt* regar
irrigation [ɪrɪ'geɪʃən] *n* riego
irritability [ɪrɪtə'bɪlɪtɪ] *n* irritabilidad *f*
irritable ['ɪrɪtəbl] *adj* (*person: temperament*) irritable; (*: mood*) de mal humor
irritant ['ɪrɪtənt] *n* agente *m* irritante
irritate ['ɪrɪteɪt] *vt* fastidiar; (*Med*) picar
irritating ['ɪrɪteɪtɪŋ] *adj* fastidioso
irritation [ɪrɪ'teɪʃən] *n* fastidio; picazón *f*, picor *m*
IRS *n abbr* (*US*) = **Internal Revenue Service**
is [ɪz] *vb see* **be**
ISA ['aɪsə] *n abbr* (*Brit: = individual savings account*) *plan de ahorro personal para pequeños inversores con fiscalidad cero*
ISBN *n abbr* (*= International Standard Book Number*) ISBN *m*
ISDN *n abbr* (*= Integrated Services Digital Network*) RDSI *f*
Islam ['ɪzlɑ:m] *n* Islam *m*
island ['aɪlənd] *n* isla; (*also:* **traffic island**) isleta
islander ['aɪləndəʳ] *n* isleño(-a)
isle [aɪl] *n* isla
isn't ['ɪznt] = **is not**
isobar ['aɪsəubɑ:ʳ] *n* isobara
isolate ['aɪsəleɪt] *vt* aislar
isolated ['aɪsəleɪtɪd] *adj* aislado
isolation [aɪsə'leɪʃən] *n* aislamiento
isolationism [aɪsə'leɪʃənɪzəm] *n* aislacionismo
isolation ward *n* pabellón *m* de aislamiento
isotope ['aɪsəutəup] *n* isótopo
ISP *n abbr* = **Internet service provider**
Israel ['ɪzreɪl] *n* Israel *m*
Israeli [ɪz'reɪlɪ] *adj, n* israelí *m/f*
issue ['ɪsju:] *n* cuestión *f*, asunto; (*outcome*) resultado; (*of banknotes etc*) emisión *f*; (*of newspaper etc*) número; (*offspring*) sucesión *f*, descendencia ■ *vt* (*rations, equipment*) distribuir, repartir; (*orders*) dar; (*certificate, passport*) expedir; (*decree*) promulgar; (*magazine*) publicar; (*cheque*) extender; (*banknotes, stamp*) emitir ■ *vi*: **to ~ (from)** derivar (de), brotar (de); **at ~** en cuestión; **to take ~ with sb (over)** disentir con algn (en); **to avoid the ~** andarse con rodeos; **to confuse** *or* **obscure the ~** confundir las cosas; **to make an ~ of sth** dar a algo más importancia de lo necesario; **to ~ sth to sb, ~ sb with sth** entregar algo a algn
Istanbul [ɪstæn'bu:l] *n* Estambul *m*
isthmus ['ɪsməs] *n* istmo
IT *n abbr* = **information technology**

KEYWORD

it [ɪt] *pron* **1** (*specific: subject: not generally translated*) él/ella; (*: direct object*) lo/la; (*: indirect object*) le; (*after prep*) él/ella; (*abstract concept*)

ello; **it's on the table** está en la mesa; **I can't find it** no lo (*or* la) encuentro; **give it to me** dámelo (*or* dámela); **I spoke to him about it** le hablé del asunto; **what did you learn from it?** ¿qué aprendiste de él (*or* ella)?; **did you go to it?** (*party, concert etc*) ¿fuiste?
2 (*impersonal*): **it's raining** llueve, está lloviendo; **it's 6 o'clock/the 10th of August** son las 6/es el 10 de agosto; **how far is it? — it's 10 miles/2 hours on the train** ¿a qué distancia está? — a 10 millas/ 2 horas en tren; **who is it? — it's me** ¿quién es? — soy yo

ITA *n abbr* (*Brit*: = *initial teaching alphabet*) *alfabeto parcialmente fonético, ayuda para enseñar a leer*
Italian [ɪ'tæljən] *adj* italiano ■ *n* italiano(-a); (*Ling*) italiano
italic [ɪ'tælɪk] *adj* cursivo; **italics** *npl* cursiva *sg*
Italy ['ɪtəlɪ] *n* Italia
ITC *n abbr* (*Brit*) = **Independent Television Commission**
itch [ɪtʃ] *n* picazón *f*; (*fig*) prurito ■ *vi* (*person*) sentir *or* tener comezón; (*part of body*) picar; **to be itching to do sth** rabiar por *or* morirse de ganas de hacer algo
itching ['ɪtʃɪŋ] *n* picazón *f*, comezón *f*
itchy ['ɪtʃɪ] *adj*: **to be ~** picar
it'd ['ɪtd] = **it would; it had**
item ['aɪtəm] *n* artículo; (*on agenda*) asunto (a tratar); (*in programme*) número; (*also*: **news item**) noticia; **items of clothing** prendas *fpl* de vestir
itemize ['aɪtəmaɪz] *vt* detallar
itemized bill ['aɪtəmaɪzd-] *n* recibo detallado
itinerant [ɪ'tɪnərənt] *adj* ambulante
itinerary [aɪ'tɪnərərɪ] *n* itinerario
it'll ['ɪtl] = **it will; it shall**
ITN *n abbr* (*Brit*) = **Independent Television News**
its [ɪts] *adj* su
it's [ɪts] = **it is; it has**
itself [ɪt'sɛlf] *pron* (*reflexive*) sí mismo(-a); (*emphatic*) él/ella mismo(-a)
ITV *n abbr* (*Brit*: = *Independent Television*) *ver nota*

ITV

En el Reino Unido la *ITV* ("Independent Television") es una cadena de emisoras comerciales regionales con licencia exclusiva para emitir en su región. Suelen producir sus propios programas, se financian con publicidad y están bajo el control del organismo oficial independiente "Independent Broadcasting Authority" ("IBA"). El servicio de noticias nacionales e internacionales, "ITN" ("Independent Television News"), funciona como una compañía productora para toda la cadena.

IUD *n abbr* (= *intra-uterine device*) DIU *m*
I've [aɪv] = **I have**
ivory ['aɪvərɪ] *n* marfil *m*
Ivory Coast *n*: **the ~** la Costa de Marfil
ivory tower *n* (*fig*) torre *f* de marfil
ivy ['aɪvɪ] *n* hiedra
Ivy League *n* (*US*) *ver nota*

IVY LEAGUE

Las ocho universidades más prestigiosas del nordeste de los Estados Unidos reciben el nombre colectivo de *Ivy League*, por sus muros cubiertos de hiedra. Son: Brown, Columbia, Cornell, Dartmouth College, Harvard, Princeton, la universidad de Pennsylvania y Yale. También se llaman así las competiciones deportivas que celebran entre ellas.

Jj

J, j [dʒeɪ] *n* (*letter*) J, j *f*; **J for Jack,** (*US*) **J for Jig** J de José
JA *n abbr* = **judge advocate**
J/A *abbr* = **joint account**
jab [dʒæb] *vt* (*elbow*) dar un codazo a; (*punch*) dar un golpe rápido a ■ *vi*: **to ~ at** intentar golpear a; **to ~ sth into sth** clavar algo en algo ■ *n* codazo; golpe *m* (rápido); (*Med: col*) pinchazo
jabber ['dʒæbəʳ] *vt, vi* farfullar
jack [dʒæk] *n* (*Aut*) gato; (*Bowls*) boliche *m*; (*Cards*) sota
▸**jack in** *vt* (*col*) dejar
▸**jack up** *vt* (*Aut*) levantar con el gato
jackal ['dʒækl] *n* (*Zool*) chacal *m*
jackass ['dʒækæs] *n* (*also fig*) asno, burro
jackdaw ['dʒækdɔː] *n* grajo(-a), chova
jacket ['dʒækɪt] *n* chaqueta, americana, saco (*LAm*); (*of boiler etc*) camisa; (*of book*) sobrecubierta
jacket potato *n* patata asada (con piel)
jack-in-the-box ['dʒækɪnðəbɔks] *n* caja sorpresa, caja de resorte
jack-knife ['dʒæknaɪf] *vi* colear
jack-of-all-trades ['dʒækəv'ɔːltreɪdz] *n* aprendiz *m* de todo
jack plug *n* (*Elec*) enchufe *m* de clavija
jackpot ['dʒækpɔt] *n* premio gordo
Jacuzzi® [dʒə'kuːzɪ] *n* jacuzzi® *m*
jade [dʒeɪd] *n* (*stone*) jade *m*
jaded ['dʒeɪdɪd] *adj* (*tired*) cansado; (*fed up*) hastiado
jagged ['dʒægɪd] *adj* dentado
jaguar ['dʒægjuəʳ] *n* jaguar *m*
jail [dʒeɪl] *n* cárcel *f* ■ *vt* encarcelar
jailbird ['dʒeɪlbəːd] *n* preso(-a) reincidente
jailbreak ['dʒeɪlbreɪk] *n* fuga *or* evasión *f* (de la cárcel)
jailer ['dʒeɪləʳ] *n* carcelero(-a)
jalopy [dʒə'lɔpɪ] *n* (*col*) cacharro, armatoste *m*
jam [dʒæm] *n* mermelada; (*also*: **traffic jam**) atasco, embotellamiento; (*difficulty*) apuro ■ *vt* (*passage etc*) obstruir; (*mechanism, drawer etc*) atascar; (*Radio*) interferir ■ *vi* atascarse, trabarse; **to get sb out of a ~** sacar a algn del paso *or* de un apuro; **to ~ sth into sth** meter algo a la fuerza en algo; **the telephone lines are jammed** las líneas están saturadas
Jamaica [dʒə'meɪkə] *n* Jamaica
Jamaican [dʒə'meɪkən] *adj, n* jamaicano(-a) *m(f)*
jamb [dʒæm] *n* jamba
jamboree [dʒæmbə'riː] *n* congreso de niños exploradores
jam-packed [dʒæm'pækt] *adj*: **~ (with)** atestado (de)
jam session *n* concierto improvisado de jazz/rock *etc*
Jan *abbr* (= *January*) ene
jangle ['dʒæŋgl] *vi* sonar (de manera) discordante
janitor ['dʒænɪtəʳ] *n* (*caretaker*) portero, conserje *m*
January ['dʒænjuərɪ] *n* enero; *see also* **July**
Japan [dʒə'pæn] *n* (el) Japón
Japanese [dʒæpə'niːz] *adj* japonés(-esa) ■ *n* (*pl inv*) japonés(-esa) *m(f)*; (*Ling*) japonés *m*
jar [dʒɑːʳ] *n* (*glass: large*) jarra; (*: small*) tarro ■ *vi* (*sound*) chirriar; (*colours*) desentonar
jargon ['dʒɑːgən] *n* jerga
jarring ['dʒɑːrɪŋ] *adj* (*sound*) discordante, desafinado; (*colour*) chocante
Jas. *abbr* = **James**
jasmine, jasmin ['dʒæzmɪn] *n* jazmín *m*
jaundice ['dʒɔːndɪs] *n* ictericia
jaundiced ['dʒɔːndɪst] *adj* (*fig: embittered*) amargado; (*: disillusioned*) desilusionado
jaunt [dʒɔːnt] *n* excursión *f*
jaunty ['dʒɔːntɪ] *adj* alegre; (*relaxed*) desenvuelto
Java ['dʒɑːvə] *n* Java
javelin ['dʒævlɪn] *n* jabalina
jaw [dʒɔː] *n* mandíbula; **jaws** *npl* (*Tech: of vice etc*) mordaza *sg*
jawbone ['dʒɔːbəun] *n* mandíbula, quijada
jay [dʒeɪ] *n* (*Zool*) arrendajo
jaywalker ['dʒeɪwɔːkəʳ] *n* peatón(-ona) *m(f)* imprudente

jazz [dʒæz] *n* jazz *m*
▸**jazz up** *vt* (*liven up*) animar
jazz band *n* orquesta de jazz
jazzy ['dʒæzɪ] *adj* de colores llamativos
JCB® *n abbr* excavadora
JCS *n abbr* (*US*) = **Joint Chiefs of Staff**
JD *n abbr* (*US: = Doctor of Laws*) *título universitario*; (*= Justice Department*) Ministerio de Justicia
jealous ['dʒɛləs] *adj* (*gen*) celoso; (*envious*) envidioso; **to be ~** tener celos
jealously ['dʒɛləslɪ] *adv* (*enviously*) envidiosamente; (*watchfully*) celosamente
jealousy ['dʒɛləsɪ] *n* celos *mpl*; envidia
jeans [dʒi:nz] *npl* (pantalones *mpl*) vaqueros *mpl or* tejanos *mpl*, bluejean *m inv* (*LAm*)
Jeep® [dʒi:p] *n* jeep *m*
jeer [dʒɪə^r] *vi*: **to ~ (at)** (*boo*) abuchear; (*mock*) mofarse (de)
jeering ['dʒɪərɪŋ] *adj* (*crowd*) insolente, ofensivo ▪ *n* protestas *fpl*; (*mockery*) burlas *fpl*
jelly ['dʒɛlɪ] *n* gelatina, jalea
jellyfish ['dʒɛlɪfɪʃ] *n* medusa
jemmy ['dʒɛmɪ] *n* palanqueta
jeopardize ['dʒɛpədaɪz] *vt* arriesgar, poner en peligro
jeopardy ['dʒɛpədɪ] *n*: **to be in ~** estar en peligro
jerk [dʒə:k] *n* (*jolt*) sacudida; (*wrench*) tirón *m*; (*US col*) imbécil *m/f*, pendejo(-a) (*LAm*) ▪ *vt* dar una sacudida a; tirar bruscamente de ▪ *vi* (*vehicle*) dar una sacudida
jerkin ['dʒə:kɪn] *n* chaleco
jerky ['dʒə:kɪ] *adj* espasmódico
jerry-built ['dʒɛrɪbɪlt] *adj* mal construido
jerry can ['dʒɛrɪ-] *n* bidón *m*
Jersey ['dʒə:zɪ] *n* Jersey *m*
jersey ['dʒə:zɪ] *n* jersey *m*; (*fabric*) tejido de punto
Jerusalem [dʒə'ru:sləm] *n* Jerusalén *m*
jest [dʒɛst] *n* broma
jester ['dʒɛstə^r] *n* bufón *m*
Jesus ['dʒi:zəs] *n* Jesús *m*; **~ Christ** Jesucristo
jet [dʒɛt] *n* (*of gas, liquid*) chorro; (*Aviat*) avión *m* a reacción
jet-black ['dʒɛt'blæk] *adj* negro como el azabache
jet engine *n* motor *m* a reacción
jet lag *n* desorientación *f* por desfase horario
jetsam ['dʒɛtsəm] *n* echazón *f*
jet-setter ['dʒɛtsɛtə^r] *n* personaje *m* de la jet
jettison ['dʒɛtɪsn] *vt* desechar
jetty ['dʒɛtɪ] *n* muelle *m*, embarcadero
Jew [dʒu:] *n* judío
jewel ['dʒu:əl] *n* joya; (*in watch*) rubí *m*
jeweller, jeweler (*US*) ['dʒu:ələ^r] *n* joyero(-a); **~'s (shop)** joyería
jewellery, jewelry (*US*) ['dʒu:əlrɪ] *n* joyas *fpl*, alhajas *fpl*
Jewess ['dʒu:ɪs] *n* judía
Jewish ['dʒu:ɪʃ] *adj* judío
JFK *n abbr* (*US*) = **John Fitzgerald Kennedy International Airport**
jib [dʒɪb] *vi* (*horse*) plantarse; **to ~ at doing sth** resistirse a hacer algo
jibe [dʒaɪb] *n* mofa
jiffy ['dʒɪfɪ] *n* (*col*): **in a ~** en un santiamén
jig [dʒɪg] *n* (*dance, tune*) giga
jigsaw ['dʒɪgsɔ:] *n* (*also*: **jigsaw puzzle**) rompecabezas *m inv*; (*tool*) sierra de vaivén
jilt [dʒɪlt] *vt* dejar plantado a
jingle ['dʒɪŋgl] *n* (*advert*) musiquilla ▪ *vi* tintinear
jingoism ['dʒɪŋgəuɪzəm] *n* patriotería, jingoísmo
jinx [dʒɪŋks] *n*: **there's a ~ on it** está gafado
jitters ['dʒɪtəz] *npl* (*col*): **to get the ~** ponerse nervioso
jittery ['dʒɪtərɪ] *adj* (*col*) agitado
jiujitsu [dʒu:'dʒɪtsu:] *n* jiujitsu *m*
job [dʒɔb] *n* trabajo; (*task*) tarea; (*duty*) deber *m*; (*post*) empleo; (*col: difficulty*) dificultad *f*; **it's a good ~ that ...** menos mal que ...; **just the ~!** ¡justo lo que necesito!; **a part-time/ full-time ~** un trabajo a tiempo parcial/ tiempo completo; **that's not my ~** eso no me incumbe *or* toca a mí; **he's only doing his ~** está cumpliendo nada más
job centre *n* (*Brit*) oficina de empleo
job creation scheme *n* plan *m* de creación de puestos de trabajo
job description *n* descripción *f* del puesto de trabajo
jobless ['dʒɔblɪs] *adj* sin trabajo ▪ *n*: **the ~** los parados
job lot *n* lote *m* de mercancías, saldo
job satisfaction *n* satisfacción *f* en el trabajo
job security *n* garantía de trabajo
job specification *n* especificación *f* del trabajo, profesiograma *m*
Jock *n* (*col: Scotsman*) escocés *m*
jockey ['dʒɔkɪ] *n* jockey *m/f* ▪ *vi*: **to ~ for position** maniobrar para sacar delantera
jockey box *n* (*US Aut*) guantera
jockstrap ['dʒɔkstræp] *n* suspensorio
jocular ['dʒɔkjulə^r] *adj* (*humorous*) gracioso; (*merry*) alegre
jodhpurs ['dʒɔdpə:z] *npl* pantalón *msg* de montar
jog [dʒɔg] *vt* empujar (ligeramente) ▪ *vi* (*run*) hacer footing; **to ~ along** (*fig*) ir tirando; **to ~ sb's memory** refrescar la memoria a algn
jogger ['dʒɔgə^r] *n* corredor(a) *m(f)*
jogging ['dʒɔgɪŋ] *n* footing *m*

john [dʒɔn] *n* (*US col*) wáter *m*
join [dʒɔɪn] *vt* (*things*) unir, juntar; (*become member of: club*) hacerse socio de; (*Pol: party*) afiliarse a; (*meet: people*) reunirse con; (*fig*) unirse a ■ *vi* (*roads*) empalmar; (*rivers*) confluir ■ *n* juntura; **will you ~ us for dinner?** ¿quieres cenar con nosotros?; **I'll ~ you later** me reuniré contigo luego; **to ~ forces (with)** aliarse (con)
▸**join in** *vi* tomar parte, participar ■ *vt fus* tomar parte *or* participar en
▸**join up** *vi* unirse; (*Mil*) alistarse
joiner ['dʒɔɪnəʳ] *n* carpintero(-a)
joinery ['dʒɔɪnərɪ] *n* carpintería
joint [dʒɔɪnt] *n* (*Tech*) juntura, unión *f*; (*Anat*) articulación *f*; (*Brit Culin*) pieza de carne (para asar); (*col: place*) garito ■ *adj* (*common*) común; (*combined*) conjunto; (*responsibility*) compartido; (*committee*) mixto
joint account *n* (*with bank etc*) cuenta común
jointly ['dʒɔɪntlɪ] *adv* (*gen*) en común; (*together*) conjuntamente
joint owners *npl* copropietarios *mpl*
joint ownership *n* copropiedad *f*, propiedad *f* común
joint-stock bank ['dʒɔɪntstɔk-] *n* banco por acciones
joint-stock company ['dʒɔɪntstɔk-] *n* sociedad *f* anónima
joint venture *n* empresa conjunta
joist [dʒɔɪst] *n* viga
joke [dʒəuk] *n* chiste *m*; (*also*: **practical joke**) broma ■ *vi* bromear; **to play a ~ on** gastar una broma a
joker ['dʒəukəʳ] *n* chistoso(-a), bromista *m/f*; (*Cards*) comodín *m*
joking ['dʒəukɪŋ] *n* bromas *fpl*
jokingly ['dʒəukɪŋlɪ] *adv* en broma
jollity ['dʒɔlɪtɪ] *n* alegría
jolly ['dʒɔlɪ] *adj* (*merry*) alegre; (*enjoyable*) divertido ■ *adv* (*col*) muy, la mar de ■ *vt*: **to ~ sb along** animar *or* darle ánimos a algn; **~ good!** ¡estupendo!
jolt [dʒəult] *n* (*shake*) sacudida; (*blow*) golpe *m*; (*shock*) susto ■ *vt* sacudir
Jordan ['dʒɔ:dən] *n* (*country*) Jordania; (*river*) Jordán *m*
joss stick [dʒɔs-] *n* barrita de incienso, pebete *m*
jostle ['dʒɔsl] *vt* dar empujones *or* empellones a
jot [dʒɔt] *n*: **not one ~** ni pizca, ni un ápice
▸**jot down** *vt* apuntar
jotter ['dʒɔtəʳ] *n* (*Brit*) bloc *m*
journal ['dʒə:nl] *n* (*paper*) periódico; (*magazine*) revista; (*diary*) diario
journalese [dʒə:nə'li:z] *n* (*pej*) lenguaje *m* periodístico
journalism ['dʒə:nəlɪzəm] *n* periodismo
journalist ['dʒə:nəlɪst] *n* periodista *m/f*
journey ['dʒə:nɪ] *n* viaje *m*; (*distance covered*) trayecto ■ *vi* viajar; **return ~** viaje de regreso; **a five-hour ~** un viaje de cinco horas
jovial ['dʒəuvɪəl] *adj* risueño, alegre
jowl [dʒaul] *n* quijada
joy [dʒɔɪ] *n* alegría
joyful ['dʒɔɪful] *adj* alegre
joyfully ['dʒɔɪfulɪ] *adv* alegremente
joyous ['dʒɔɪəs] *adj* alegre
joyride ['dʒɔɪraɪd] *n*: **to go for a ~** darse una vuelta en un coche robado
joyrider ['dʒɔɪraɪdəʳ] *n persona que se da una vuelta en un coche robado*
joystick ['dʒɔɪstɪk] *n* (*Aviat*) palanca de mando; (*Comput*) palanca de control
JP *n abbr see* **Justice of the Peace**
Jr *abbr* = **junior**
JTPA *n abbr* (*US: = Job Training Partnership Act*) *programa gubernamental de formación profesional*
jubilant ['dʒu:bɪlnt] *adj* jubiloso
jubilation [dʒu:bɪ'leɪʃən] *n* júbilo
jubilee ['dʒu:bɪli:] *n* aniversario; **silver ~** vigésimo quinto aniversario
judge [dʒʌdʒ] *n* juez *m/f* ■ *vt* juzgar; (*competition*) actuar de *or* ser juez en; (*estimate*) considerar; (*: weight, size etc*) calcular ■ *vi*: **judging** *or* **to ~ by his expression** a juzgar por su expresión; **as far as I can ~** por lo que puedo entender, a mi entender; **I judged it necessary to inform him** consideré necesario informarle
judge advocate *n* (*Mil*) auditor *m* de guerra
judgment, judgement ['dʒʌdʒmənt] *n* juicio; (*punishment*) sentencia, fallo; **to pass judg(e)ment (on)** (*Law*) pronunciar *or* dictar sentencia (sobre); (*fig*) emitir un juicio crítico *or* dictaminar (sobre); **in my judg(e)ment** a mi juicio
judicial [dʒu:'dɪʃl] *adj* judicial
judiciary [dʒu:'dɪʃɪərɪ] *n* poder *m* judicial, magistratura
judicious [dʒu:'dɪʃəs] *adj* juicioso
judo ['dʒu:dəu] *n* judo
jug [dʒʌg] *n* jarro
jugged hare [dʒʌgd-] *n* (*Brit*) estofado de liebre
juggernaut ['dʒʌgənɔ:t] *n* (*Brit: huge truck*) camión *m* de carga pesada
juggle ['dʒʌgl] *vi* hacer juegos malabares
juggler ['dʒʌgləʳ] *n* malabarista *m/f*
Jugoslav *etc* ['ju:gəuslɑ:v] = **Yugoslav** *etc*
jugular ['dʒʌgjuləʳ] *adj*: **~ vein** (vena) yugular *f*

juice [dʒu:s] *n* jugo, zumo (*SP*); (*of meat*) jugo; (*col: petrol*): **we've run out of ~** se nos acabó la gasolina
juiciness ['dʒu:sɪnɪs] *n* jugosidad *f*
juicy ['dʒu:sɪ] *adj* jugoso
juijitsu, jujitsu [dʒu:'dʒɪtsu:] *n* jujitsu *m*
jukebox ['dʒu:kbɔks] *n* máquina de discos
Jul. *abbr* (= *July*) jul
July [dʒu:'laɪ] *n* julio; **the first of ~** el uno *or* primero de julio; **during ~** en el mes de julio; **in ~ of next year** en julio del año que viene
jumble ['dʒʌmbl] *n* revoltijo ■ *vt* (*also*: **jumble together, jumble up**: *mix up*) revolver; (: *disarrange*) mezclar
jumble sale *n* (*Brit*) mercadillo; *ver nota*

JUMBLE SALE

En cada *jumble sale* pueden comprarse todo tipo de objetos baratos de segunda mano, especialmente ropa, juguetes, libros, vajillas y muebles. Suelen organizarse en los locales de un colegio, iglesia, ayuntamiento o similar, con fines benéficos, bien en ayuda de una organización benéfica conocida o para solucionar problemas más concretos de la comunidad.

jumbo ['dʒʌmbəu], **jumbo jet** *n* jumbo
jump [dʒʌmp] *vi* saltar, dar saltos; (*start*) sobresaltarse; (*increase*) aumentar ■ *vt* saltar ■ *n* salto; (*fence*) obstáculo; (*increase*) aumento; **to ~ the queue** (*Brit*) colarse
▸**jump about** *vi* dar saltos, brincar
▸**jump at** *vt fus* (*fig*) apresurarse a aprovechar; **he jumped at the offer** se apresuró a aceptar la oferta
▸**jump down** *vi* bajar de un salto, saltar a tierra
▸**jump up** *vi* levantarse de un salto
jumped-up ['dʒʌmptʌp] *adj* (*pej*) engreído
jumper ['dʒʌmpə^r^] *n* (*Brit: pullover*) jersey *m*, suéter *m*; (*US: pinafore dress*) pichi *m*; (*Sport*) saltador(a) *m(f)*
jump leads, (*US*) **jumper cables** *npl* cables *mpl* puente de batería
jump-start ['djʌmpstɑ:t] *vt* (*car*) arrancar con ayuda de otra batería *or* empujando; (*fig: economy*) reactivar
jump suit *n* mono
jumpy ['dʒʌmpɪ] *adj* nervioso
Jun. *abbr* = **junior**; (= *June*) jun
junction ['dʒʌŋkʃən] *n* (*Brit: of roads*) cruce *m*; (*Rail*) empalme *m*
juncture ['dʒʌŋktʃə^r^] *n*: **at this ~** en este momento, en esta coyuntura
June [dʒu:n] *n* junio; *see also* **July**
jungle ['dʒʌŋgl] *n* selva, jungla
junior ['dʒu:nɪə^r^] *adj* (*in age*) menor, más joven; (*competition*) juvenil; (*position*) subalterno ■ *n* menor *m/f*, joven *m/f*; **he's ~ to me** es menor que yo
junior executive *n* ejecutivo/a subalterno/a
junior high school *n* (*US*) *centro de educación secundaria*; *see also* **high school**
junior school *n* (*Brit*) escuela primaria; *see also* **primary school**
junk [dʒʌŋk] *n* (*cheap goods*) baratijas *fpl*; (*lumber*) trastos *mpl* viejos; (*rubbish*) basura; (*ship*) junco ■ *vt* (*esp US*) deshacerse de
junk bond *n* (*Comm*) obligación *f* basura *inv*
junk dealer *n* vendedor(a) *m(f)* de objetos usados
junket ['dʒʌŋkɪt] *n* (*Culin*) *dulce de leche cuajada*; (*Brit col*): **to go on a ~, go junketing** viajar a costa ajena *or* del erario público
junk food *n* comida basura *or* de plástico
junkie ['dʒʌŋkɪ] *n* (*col*) yonqui *m/f*, heroinómano(-a)
junk mail *n* propaganda (buzoneada), correo *m* basura *inv*
junk room *n* trastero
junk shop *n* tienda de objetos usados
junta ['dʒʌntə] *n* junta militar
Jupiter ['dʒu:pɪtə^r^] *n* (*Mythology, Astro*) Júpiter *m*
jurisdiction [dʒuərɪs'dɪkʃən] *n* jurisdicción *f*; **it falls** *or* **comes within/outside our ~** es/no es de nuestra competencia
jurisprudence [dʒuərɪs'pru:dəns] *n* jurisprudencia
juror ['dʒuərə^r^] *n* jurado
jury ['dʒuərɪ] *n* jurado
jury box *n* tribuna del jurado
juryman ['dʒuərɪmən] *n* miembro del jurado
just [dʒʌst] *adj* justo ■ *adv* (*exactly*) exactamente; (*only*) sólo, solamente, no más (*LAm*); **he's ~ done it/left** acaba de hacerlo/irse; **I've ~ seen him** acabo de verle; **~ right** perfecto; **~ two o'clock** las dos en punto; **she's ~ as clever as you** es tan lista como tú; **~ as well that ...** menos mal que ...; **it's ~ as well you didn't go** menos mal que no fuiste; **it's ~ as good (as)** es igual (que), es tan bueno (como); **~ as he was leaving** en el momento en que se marchaba; **we were ~ going** ya nos íbamos; **I was ~ about to phone** estaba a punto de llamar; **~ before/enough** justo antes/lo suficiente; **~ here** aquí mismo; **he ~ missed** falló por poco; **~ listen to this** escucha esto un momento; **~ ask someone the way** simplemente

preguntale a alguien por dónde se va; **not ~ now** ahora no
justice ['dʒʌstɪs] *n* justicia; **this photo doesn't do you ~** esta foto no te favorece
Justice of the Peace *n* juez *m/f* de paz; *see also* **Crown Court**
justifiable [dʒʌstɪ'faɪəbl] *adj* justificable, justificado
justifiably [dʒʌstɪ'faɪəblɪ] *adv* justificadamente, con razón
justification [dʒʌstɪfɪ'keɪʃən] *n* justificación *f*
justify ['dʒʌstɪfaɪ] *vt* justificar; (*text*) alinear, justificar; **to be justified in doing sth** tener motivo para *or* razón al hacer algo
justly ['dʒʌstlɪ] *adv* (*gen*) justamente; (*with reason*) con razón
justness ['dʒʌstnɪs] *n* justicia
jut [dʒʌt] *vi* (*also*: **jut out**) sobresalir
jute [dʒu:t] *n* yute *m*
juvenile ['dʒu:vənaɪl] *adj* juvenil; (*court*) de menores ■ *n* joven *m/f*, menor *m/f* de edad
juvenile delinquency *n* delincuencia juvenil
juvenile delinquent *n* delincuente *m/f* juvenil
juxtapose ['dʒʌkstəpəuz] *vt* yuxtaponer
juxtaposition ['dʒʌkstəpə'zɪʃən] *n* yuxtaposición *f*

Kk

K, k [keɪ] *n* (*letter*) K, k *f*; **K for King** K de Kilo

K *n abbr* (*= one thousand*) mille ■ *abbr* (*Brit: = Knight*) *titolo*; (*= kilobyte*) K

kaftan ['kæftæn] *n* caftán *m*

Kalahari Desert [kælə'hɑːrɪ-] *n* desierto de Kalahari

kale [keɪl] *n* col *f* rizada

kaleidoscope [kə'laɪdəskəup] *n* calidoscopio

kamikaze [kæmɪ'kɑːzɪ] *adj* kamikaze

Kampala [kæm'pɑːlə] *n* Kampala

Kampuchea [kæmpu'tʃɪə] *n* Kampuchea

kangaroo [kæŋgə'ruː] *n* canguro

Kans. *abbr* (*US*) = **Kansas**

kaput [kə'put] *adj* (*col*) roto, estropeado

karaoke [kɑːrə'əukɪ] *n* karaoke

karate [kə'rɑːtɪ] *n* karate *m*

Kashmir [kæʃ'mɪə^r] *n* Cachemira

kayak ['kaɪæk] *n* kayak *m*

Kazakhstan [kɑːzɑːk'stæn] *n* Kazajstán *m*

KC *n abbr* (*Brit Law: = King's Counsel*) *título concedido a determinados abogados*

kebab [kə'bæb] *n* pincho moruno, brocheta

keel [kiːl] *n* quilla; **on an even ~** (*fig*) en equilibrio
▸ **keel over** *vi* (*Naut*) zozobrar, volcarse; (*person*) desplomarse

keen [kiːn] *adj* (*interest, desire*) grande, vivo; (*eye, intelligence*) agudo; (*competition*) intenso; (*edge*) afilado; (*Brit: eager*) entusiasta; **to be ~ to do** *or* **on doing sth** tener muchas ganas de hacer algo; **to be ~ on sth/sb** interesarse por algo/algn; **I'm not ~ on going** no tengo ganas de ir

keenly ['kiːnlɪ] *adv* (*enthusiastically*) con entusiasmo; (*acutely*) vivamente; (*intensely*) intensamente

keenness ['kiːnnɪs] *n* (*eagerness*) entusiasmo, interés *m*

keep [kiːp] (*pt, pp* **kept**) *vt* (*retain, preserve*) guardar; (*hold back*) quedarse con; (*shop*) ser propietario de; (*feed: family etc*) mantener; (*promise*) cumplir; (*chickens, bees etc*) criar ■ *vi* (*food*) conservarse; (*remain*) seguir, continuar ■ *n* (*of castle*) torreón *m*; (*food etc*) comida, sustento; **to ~ doing sth** seguir haciendo algo; **to ~ sb from doing sth** impedir a algn hacer algo; **to ~ sth from happening** impedir que algo ocurra; **to ~ sb happy** tener a algn contento; **to ~ sb waiting** hacer esperar a algn; **to ~ a place tidy** mantener un lugar limpio; **to ~ sth to o.s.** no decirle algo a nadie; **to ~ time** (*clock*) mantener la hora exacta; **~ the change** quédese con la vuelta; **to ~ an appointment** acudir a una cita; **to ~ a record** *or* **note of sth** tomar nota de *or* apuntar algo; *see also* **keeps**
▸ **keep away** *vt*: **to ~ sth/sb away from sb** mantener algo/a algn apartado de algn ■ *vi*: **to ~ away (from)** mantenerse apartado (de)
▸ **keep back** *vt* (*crowd, tears*) contener; (*money*) quedarse con; (*conceal: information*): **to ~ sth back from sb** ocultar algo a algn ■ *vi* hacerse a un lado
▸ **keep down** *vt* (*control: prices, spending*) controlar; (*retain: food*) retener ■ *vi* seguir agachado, no levantar la cabeza
▸ **keep in** *vt* (*invalid, child*) impedir que salga, no dejar salir; (*Scol*) castigar (a quedarse en el colegio) ■ *vi* (*col*): **to ~ in with sb** mantener la relación con algn
▸ **keep off** *vt* (*dog, person*) mantener a distancia ■ *vi* evitar; **~ your hands off!** ¡no toques!; **"~ off the grass"** "prohibido pisar el césped"
▸ **keep on** *vi* seguir, continuar
▸ **keep out** *vi* (*stay out*) permanecer fuera; **"~ out"** "prohibida la entrada"
▸ **keep up** *vt* mantener, conservar ■ *vi* no rezagarse; (*fig: in comprehension*) seguir (el hilo); **to ~ up with** (*pace*) ir al paso de; (*level*) mantenerse a la altura de; **to ~ up with sb** seguir el ritmo a algn; (*fig*) seguir a algn

keeper ['kiːpə^r] *n* guarda *m/f*

keep-fit [kiːp'fɪt] *n* gimnasia (de mantenimiento)

keeping ['kiːpɪŋ] *n* (*care*) cuidado; **in ~ with** de acuerdo con

keeps [ki:ps] *n*: **for ~** (*col*) para siempre
keepsake ['ki:pseɪk] *n* recuerdo
keg [kɛg] *n* barrilete *m*, barril *m*
Ken. *abbr* (*US*) = **Kentucky**
kennel ['kɛnl] *n* perrera; **kennels** *npl* perrera
Kenya ['kɛnjə] *n* Kenia
Kenyan ['kɛnjən] *adj, n* keniata *m/f*, keniano(-a) *m(f)*
kept [kɛpt] *pt, pp of* **keep**
kerb [kə:b] *n* (*Brit*) bordillo
kerb crawler [-krɔ:ləʳ] *n conductor en busca de prostitutas desde su coche*
kernel ['kə:nl] *n* (*nut*) fruta; (*fig*) meollo
kerosene ['kɛrəsi:n] *n* keroseno
kestrel ['kɛstrəl] *n* cernícalo
ketchup ['kɛtʃəp] *n* salsa de tomate, ketchup *m*
kettle ['kɛtl] *n* hervidor *m*
kettle drum *n* (*Mus*) timbal *m*
key [ki:] *n* (*gen*) llave *f*; (*Mus*) tono; (*of piano, typewriter*) tecla; (*on map*) clave *f* ■ *cpd* (*vital: position, industry etc*) clave ■ *vt* (*also*: **key in**) teclear
keyboard ['ki:bɔ:d] *n* teclado ■ *vt* (*text*) teclear
keyboarder ['ki:bɔ:dəʳ] *n* teclista *m/f*
keyed up [ki:d-] *adj* (*person*) nervioso; **to be (all) ~** estar nervioso *or* emocionado
keyhole ['ki:həul] *n* ojo (de la cerradura)
keyhole surgery *n* cirugía cerrada *or* no invasiva
key man *n* hombre *m* clave
keynote ['ki:nəut] *n* (*Mus*) tónica; (*fig*) idea fundamental
keynote speech *n* discurso de apertura
keypad ['ki:pæd] *n* teclado numérico
keyring ['ki:rɪŋ] *n* llavero
keystone ['ki:stəun] *n* piedra clave
keystroke ['ki:strəuk] *n* pulsación *f* (de una tecla)
kg *abbr* (= *kilogram*) kg
KGB *n abbr* KGB *m*
khaki ['kɑ:kɪ] *n* caqui
kibbutz, kibbutzim [kɪ'buts, -ɪm] *n* kibutz *m*
kick [kɪk] *vt* (*person*) dar una patada a; (*ball*) dar un puntapié a ■ *vi* (*horse*) dar coces ■ *n* patada; puntapié *m*, tiro; (*of rifle*) culetazo; (*col: thrill*): **he does it for kicks** lo hace por pura diversión
▸ **kick around** *vt* (*idea*) dar vueltas a; (*person*) tratar a patadas a
▸ **kick off** *vi* (*Sport*) hacer el saque inicial
kick-start ['kɪkstɑ:t] *n* (*also*: **kick-starter**) (pedal *m* de) arranque *m*
kid [kɪd] *n* (*col: child*) niño(-a), chiquillo(-a); (*animal*) cabrito; (*leather*) cabritilla ■ *vi* (*col*) bromear
kid gloves *npl*: **to treat sb with ~** andarse con pies de plomo con algn
kidnap ['kɪdnæp] *vt* secuestrar
kidnapper ['kɪdnæpəʳ] *n* secuestrador(a) *m(f)*
kidnapping ['kɪdnæpɪŋ] *n* secuestro
kidney ['kɪdnɪ] *n* riñón *m*
kidney bean *n* judía, alubia
kidney machine *n* riñón *m* artificial
kill [kɪl] *vt* matar; (*murder*) asesinar; (*fig: rumour, conversation*) acabar con ■ *n* matanza; **to ~ time** matar el tiempo
▸ **kill off** *vt* exterminar, terminar con; (*fig*) echar por tierra
killer ['kɪləʳ] *n* asesino(-a)
killer app [- 'æp] *n abbr* (*col*: = *killer application*) aplicación *f* rompedora, aplicación *f* excelente rendimiento
killer instinct *n*: **to have the ~** ir a por todas
killing ['kɪlɪŋ] *n* (*one*) asesinato; (*several*) matanza; (*Comm*): **to make a ~** tener un gran éxito financiero
killjoy ['kɪldʒɔɪ] *n* (*Brit*) aguafiestas *m/f inv*
kiln [kɪln] *n* horno
kilo ['ki:ləu] *n abbr* (= *kilogram(me)*) kilo
kilobyte ['kɪləubaɪt] *n* (*Comput*) kilobyte *m*
kilogram, kilogramme ['kɪləugræm] *n* kilogramo
kilometre, (*US*) **kilometer** ['kɪləmi:təʳ] *n* kilómetro
kilowatt ['kɪləuwɔt] *n* kilovatio
kilt [kɪlt] *n* falda escocesa
kilter ['kɪltəʳ] *n*: **out of ~** desbaratado
kimono [kɪ'məunəu] *n* quimono
kin [kɪn] *n* parientes *mpl*
kind [kaɪnd] *adj* (*treatment*) bueno, cariñoso; (*person, act, word*) amable, atento ■ *n* clase *f*, especie *f*; (*species*) género; **in ~** (*Comm*) en especie; **a ~ of** una especie de; **to be two of a ~** ser tal para cual; **would you be ~ enough to ...?, would you be so ~ as to ...?** ¿me hace el favor de ...?; **it's very ~ of you (to do)** le agradezco mucho (el que haya hecho)
kindergarten ['kɪndəgɑ:tn] *n* jardín *m* de infancia
kind-hearted [kaɪnd'hɑ:tɪd] *adj* bondadoso, de buen corazón
kindle ['kɪndl] *vt* encender
kindliness ['kaɪndlɪnəs] *n* bondad *f*, amabilidad *f*
kindling ['kɪndlɪŋ] *n* leña (menuda)
kindly ['kaɪndlɪ] *adj* bondadoso; (*gentle*) cariñoso ■ *adv* bondadosamente, amablemente; **will you ~ ...** sería usted tan amable de ...
kindness ['kaɪndnɪs] *n* bondad *f*, amabilidad *f*
kindred ['kɪndrɪd] *n* familia, parientes *mpl* ■ *adj*: **~ spirits** almas *fpl* gemelas

kinetic [kɪ'nɛtɪk] *adj* cinético
king [kɪŋ] *n* rey *m*
kingdom ['kɪŋdəm] *n* reino
kingfisher ['kɪŋfɪʃəʳ] *n* martín *m* pescador
kingpin ['kɪŋpɪn] *n* (*Tech*) perno real *or* pinzote; (*fig*) persona clave
king-size ['kɪŋsaɪz], **king-sized** ['kɪŋsaɪzd] *adj* de tamaño gigante; (*cigarette*) extra largo
kink [kɪŋk] *n* (*in rope etc*) enroscadura; (*in hair*) rizo; (*fig: emotional, psychological*) manía
kinky ['kɪŋkɪ] *adj* (*pej*) perverso
kinship ['kɪnʃɪp] *n* parentesco; (*fig*) afinidad *f*
kinsman ['kɪnzmən] *n* pariente *m*
kinswoman ['kɪnzwumən] *n* parienta
kiosk ['ki:ɔsk] *n* quiosco; (*Brit Tel*) cabina; **newspaper ~** quiosco, kiosco
kipper ['kɪpəʳ] *n* arenque *m* ahumado
Kirghizia [kəː'gɪzɪə] *n* Kirguizistán *m*
kiss [kɪs] *n* beso ■ *vt* besar; **~ of life** (*artificial respiration*) respiración *f* artificial; **to ~ sb goodbye** dar un beso de despedida a algn; **to ~ (each other)** besarse
kissogram ['kɪsəgræm] *n* *servicio de felicitaciones mediante el que se envía a una persona vestida de manera sugerente para besar a algn*
kit [kɪt] *n* equipo; (*set of tools etc*) (caja de) herramientas *fpl*; (*assembly kit*) juego de armar; **tool ~** juego *or* estuche *m* de herramientas
▸ **kit out** *vt* equipar
kitbag ['kɪtbæg] *n* (*Mil*) macuto
kitchen ['kɪtʃɪn] *n* cocina
kitchen garden *n* huerto
kitchen sink *n* fregadero
kitchen unit *n* módulo de cocina
kitchenware ['kɪtʃɪnwɛəʳ] *n* batería de cocina
kite [kaɪt] *n* (*toy*) cometa
kith [kɪθ] *n*: **~ and kin** parientes *mpl* y allegados
kitten ['kɪtn] *n* gatito(-a)
kitty ['kɪtɪ] *n* (*pool of money*) fondo común; (*Cards*) bote *m*
kiwi ['ki:wi:] *n* (*col: New Zealander*) neozelandés(-esa) *m(f)*; (*also*: **kiwi fruit**) kiwi *m*
KKK *n abbr* (*US*) = **Ku Klux Klan**
kleptomaniac [klɛptəu'meɪnɪæk] *n* cleptómano(-a)
km *abbr* (= *kilometre*) km
km/h *abbr* (= *kilometres per hour*) km/h
knack [næk] *n*: **to have the ~ of doing sth** tener facilidad para hacer algo
knackered ['nækəd] *adj* (*col*) hecho polvo
knapsack ['næpsæk] *n* mochila
knead [ni:d] *vt* amasar
knee [ni:] *n* rodilla
kneecap ['ni:kæp] *vt* destrozar a tiros la rótula de ■ *n* rótula
knee-deep ['ni:'di:p] *adj*: **the water was ~** el agua llegaba hasta la rodilla
kneel [ni:l] (*pt, pp* **knelt** [nɛlt]) *vi* (*also*: **kneel down**) arrodillarse
kneepad ['ni:pæd] *n* rodillera
knell [nɛl] *n* toque *m* de difuntos
knelt [nɛlt] *pt, pp of* **kneel**
knew [nju:] *pt of* **know**
knickers ['nɪkəz] *npl* (*Brit*) bragas *fpl*, calzones *mpl* (*LAm*)
knick-knack ['nɪknæk] *n* chuchería, baratija
knife [naɪf] (*pl* **knives**) *n* cuchillo ■ *vt* acuchillar; **~, fork and spoon** cubiertos *mpl*
knife edge *n*: **to be on a ~** estar en la cuerda floja
knight [naɪt] *n* caballero; (*Chess*) caballo
knighthood ['naɪthud] *n* (*title*): **to get a ~** recibir el título de *Sir*
knit [nɪt] *vt* tejer, tricotar; (*brows*) fruncir; (*fig*): **to ~ together** unir, juntar ■ *vi* hacer punto, tejer, tricotar; (*bones*) soldarse
knitted ['nɪtɪd] *adj* de punto
knitting ['nɪtɪŋ] *n* labor *f* de punto
knitting machine *n* máquina de tricotar
knitting needle, knit pin (*US*) *n* aguja de hacer punto *or* tejer
knitting pattern *n* patrón *m* para tricotar
knitwear ['nɪtwɛəʳ] *n* prendas *fpl* de punto
knives [naɪvz] *pl of* **knife**
knob [nɔb] *n* (*of door*) pomo; (*of stick*) puño; (*lump*) bulto; (*fig*): **a ~ of butter** (*Brit*) un pedazo de mantequilla
knobbly ['nɔblɪ], **knobby** (*US*) ['nɔbɪ] *adj* (*wood, surface*) nudoso; (*knee*) huesudo
knock [nɔk] *vt* (*strike*) golpear; (*bump into*) chocar contra; (*fig: col*) criticar ■ *vi* (*at door etc*): **to ~ at/on** llamar a ■ *n* golpe *m*; (*on door*) llamada; **he knocked at the door** llamó a la puerta
▸ **knock down** *vt* (*pedestrian*) atropellar; (*price*) rebajar
▸ **knock off** *vi* (*col: finish*) salir del trabajo ■ *vt* (*col: steal*) birlar; (*strike off*) quitar; (*fig: from price, record*): **to ~ off £10** rebajar en £10
▸ **knock out** *vt* dejar sin sentido; (*Boxing*) poner fuera de combate, dejar K.O.; (*stop*) estropear, dejar fuera de servicio
▸ **knock over** *vt* (*object*) derribar, tirar; (*pedestrian*) atropellar
knockdown ['nɔkdaun] *adj* (*price*) de saldo
knocker ['nɔkəʳ] *n* (*on door*) aldaba
knocking ['nɔkɪŋ] *n* golpes *mpl*, golpeteo
knock-kneed [nɔk'ni:d] *adj* patizambo
knockout ['nɔkaut] *n* (*Boxing*) K.O. *m*, knockout *m*
knock-up ['nɔkʌp] *n* (*Tennis*) peloteo

knot [nɔt] *n* *(gen)* nudo ■ *vt* anudar; **to tie a ~** hacer un nudo
knotted ['nɔtɪd] *adj* anudado
knotty ['nɔtɪ] *adj* *(fig)* complicado
know [nəu] *(pt* **knew**, *pp* **known**) [nju:, nəun] *vt* *(gen)* saber; *(person, author, place)* conocer ■ *vi*: **as far as I ~ ...** que yo sepa ...; **yes, I ~** sí, ya lo sé; **I don't ~** no lo sé; **to ~ how to do** saber hacer; **to ~ how to swim** saber nadar; **to ~ about** *or* **of sb/sth** saber de algn/algo; **to get to ~ sth** enterarse de algo; **I ~ nothing about it** no sé nada de eso; **I don't ~ him** no lo *or* le conozco; **to ~ right from wrong** saber distinguir el bien del mal
know-all ['nəuɔ:l] *n* *(Brit pej)* sabelotodo *m/f inv*, sabihondo(-a)
know-how ['nəuhau] *n* conocimientos *mpl*
knowing ['nəuɪŋ] *adj* *(look etc)* de complicidad
knowingly ['nəuɪŋlɪ] *adv* *(purposely)* a sabiendas; *(smile, look)* con complicidad
know-it-all ['nəuɪtɔ:l] *n* (US) = **know-all**
knowledge ['nɔlɪdʒ] *n* *(gen)* conocimiento; *(learning)* saber *m*, conocimientos *mpl*; **to have no ~ of** no saber nada de; **with my ~** con mis conocimientos, sabiéndolo; **to (the best of) my ~** a mi entender, que yo sepa; **not to my ~** que yo sepa, no; **it is common ~ that ...** es del dominio público que ...; **it has come to my ~ that ...** me he enterado de que ...; **to have a working ~ of Spanish** defenderse con el español
knowledgeable ['nɔlɪdʒəbl] *adj* entendido, erudito
known [nəun] *pp of* **know** ■ *adj* *(thief, facts)* conocido; *(expert)* reconocido
knuckle ['nʌkl] *n* nudillo
▸ **knuckle down** *vi* *(col)* ponerse a trabajar en serio
▸ **knuckle under** *vi* someterse
knuckleduster ['nʌkldʌstəʳ] *n* puño de hierro
KO *abbr* (= *knock out*) K.O. *m* ■ *vt* *(knock out)* dejar K.O.
koala [kəu'ɑ:lə] *n* *(also:* **koala bear**) koala *m*
kook [ku:k] *n* *(US col)* chiflado(-a) *m(f)*, majareta *m/f*
Koran [kɔ'rɑ:n] *n* Corán *m*
Korea [kə'rɪə] *n* Corea; **North/South ~** Corea del Norte/Sur
Korean [kə'rɪən] *adj, n* coreano(-a) *m(f)*
kosher ['kəuʃəʳ] *adj* autorizado por la ley judía
Kosovan ['kɒsəvən], **Kosovar** ['kɒsəvɑ:ʳ] *adj* kosovar
Kosovo ['kɒsəvəu] *n* Kosovo *m*
kowtow ['kau'tau] *vi*: **to ~ to sb** humillarse ante algn
KS *abbr* (US) = **Kansas**
Kt *abbr* (Brit: = *Knight*) *caballero de una orden*
Kuala Lumpur ['kwɑ:lə'lumpuəʳ] *n* Kuala Lumpur *m*
kudos ['kju:dɔs] *n* gloria, prestigio
Kurd [kə:d] *n* kurdo(-a)
Kuwait [ku'weɪt] *n* Kuwait *m*
Kuwaiti [ku'weɪtɪ] *adj, n* Kuwaití *m/f*
kW *abbr* (= *kilowatt*) Kv
KY, Ky. *abbr* (US) = **Kentucky**

Ll

L, l [ɛl] *n* (*letter*) L, l *f*; **L for Lucy,** (*US*) **L for Love** L de Lorenzo
L *abbr* (*on maps etc*) = **lake**; **large**; (= *left*) izq.; (*Brit Aut*: = *learner*) L
l *abbr* = **litre**
LA *n abbr* (*US*: = *Los Angeles*) ■ *abbr* (*US*) = **Louisiana**
La. *abbr* (*US*) = **Louisiana**
lab [læb] *n abbr* = **laboratory**
Lab. *abbr* (*Canada*) = **Labrador**
label ['leɪbl] *n* etiqueta; (*brand*: *of record*) sello (discográfico) ■ *vt* poner una etiqueta a, etiquetar
labor ['leɪbəʳ] (*US*) = **labour**
laboratory [lə'bɔrətərɪ] *n* laboratorio
Labor Day *n* (*US*) día *m* de los trabajadores (*primer lunes de septiembre*)
laborious [lə'bɔːrɪəs] *adj* penoso
laboriously [lə'bɔːrɪəslɪ] *adv* penosamente
labor union *n* (*US*) sindicato
labor unrest *n* (*US*) conflictividad *f* laboral
Labour ['leɪbəʳ] *n* (*Brit Pol*: *also*: **the Labour Party**) el partido laborista, los laboristas
labour, labor (*US*) ['leɪbəʳ] *n* (*task*) trabajo; (*also*: **labour force**) mano *f* de obra; (*workers*) trabajadores *mpl*; (*Med*) (dolores *mpl* de) parto ■ *vi*: **to ~ (at)** trabajar (en) ■ *vt* insistir en; **hard ~** trabajos *mpl* forzados; **to be in ~** estar de parto
labour cost, labor cost (*US*) *n* costo de la mano de obra
labour dispute, labor dispute (*US*) *n* conflicto laboral
laboured, labored (*US*) ['leɪbəd] *adj* (*breathing*) fatigoso; (*style*) forzado, pesado
labourer, laborer (*US*) ['leɪbərəʳ] *n* peón *m*; (*on farm*) peón *m*, obrero; (*day labourer*) jornalero
labour force, labor force (*US*) *n* mano *f* de obra
labour-intensive, labor-intensive (*US*) [leɪbərɪn'tɛnsɪv] *adj* que necesita mucha mano de obra
labour relations, labor relations (*US*) *npl* relaciones *fpl* laborales
labour-saving, labor-saving (*US*) ['leɪbəseɪvɪŋ] *adj* que ahorra trabajo
laburnum [lə'bəːnəm] *n* codeso
labyrinth ['læbɪrɪnθ] *n* laberinto
lace [leɪs] *n* encaje *m*; (*of shoe etc*) cordón *m* ■ *vt* (*shoes*: *also*: **lace up**) atarse; (*drink*: *fortify with spirits*) echar licor a
lacemaking ['leɪsmeɪkɪŋ] *n* obra de encaje
lacerate ['læsəreɪt] *vt* lacerar
laceration [læsə'reɪʃən] *n* laceración *f*
lace-up ['leɪsʌp] *adj* (*shoes etc*) con cordones
lack [læk] *n* (*absence*) falta, carencia; (*scarcity*) escasez *f* ■ *vt* faltarle a algn, carecer de; **through** *or* **for ~ of** por falta de; **to be lacking** faltar, no haber
lackadaisical [lækə'deɪzɪkl] *adj* (*careless*) descuidado; (*indifferent*) indiferente
lackey ['lækɪ] *n* (*also fig*) lacayo
lacklustre, lackluster (*US*) ['læklʌstəʳ] *adj* (*surface*) deslustrado, deslucido; (*style*) inexpresivo; (*eyes*) apagado
laconic [lə'kɔnɪk] *adj* lacónico
lacquer ['lækəʳ] *n* laca; **hair ~** laca para el pelo
lacrosse [lə'krɔs] *n* lacrosse *f*
lacy ['leɪsɪ] *adj* (*like lace*) parecido al encaje
lad [læd] *n* muchacho, chico; (*in stable etc*) mozo
ladder ['lædəʳ] *n* escalera (de mano); (*Brit*: *in tights*) carrera ■ *vt* (*Brit*: *tights*) hacer una carrera en
laden ['leɪdn] *adj*: **~ (with)** cargado (de); **fully ~** (*truck, ship*) cargado hasta el tope
ladle ['leɪdl] *n* cucharón *m*
lady ['leɪdɪ] *n* señora; (*distinguished, noble*) dama; **young ~** señorita; **the ladies' (room)** los servicios de señoras
ladybird ['leɪdɪbəːd], **ladybug** (*US*) ['leɪdɪbʌg] *n* mariquita
lady doctor *n* médica, doctora
lady-in-waiting ['leɪdɪɪn'weɪtɪŋ] *n* dama de honor

ladykiller ['leɪdɪkɪlə^r] *n* robacorazones *m inv*
ladylike ['leɪdɪlaɪk] *adj* fino
Ladyship ['leɪdɪʃɪp] *n*: **your ~** su Señoría
LAFTA *n abbr* (= *Latin American Free Trade Association*) ALALC *f*
lag [læg] *vi* (*also*: **lag behind**) retrasarse, quedarse atrás ■ *vt* (*pipes*) revestir
lager ['lɑːgə^r] *n* cerveza (rubia)
lager lout *n* (*Brit col*) gamberro borracho
lagging ['lægɪŋ] *n* revestimiento
lagoon [lə'guːn] *n* laguna
Lagos ['leɪgɔs] *n* Lagos *m*
laid [leɪd] *pt, pp of* **lay**
laid-back [leɪd'bæk] *adj* (*col*) tranquilo, relajado
laid up *adj*: **to be ~** (*person*) tener que guardar cama
lain [leɪn] *pp of* **lie**
lair [lɛə^r] *n* guarida
laissez-faire [lɛseɪ'fɛə^r] *n* laissez-faire *m*
laity ['leɪtɪ] *n* laicado
lake [leɪk] *n* lago
Lake District *n* (*Brit*): **the ~** la Región de los Lagos
lamb [læm] *n* cordero; (*meat*) carne *f* de cordero
lamb chop *n* chuleta de cordero
lambswool ['læmzwul] *n* lana de cordero
lame [leɪm] *adj* cojo, rengo (*LAm*); (*weak*) débil, poco convincente; **~ duck** (*fig: person*) inútil *m/f*; (*: firm*) empresa en quiebra
lamely ['leɪmlɪ] *adv* (*fig*) sin convicción
lament [lə'mɛnt] *n* lamento ■ *vt* lamentarse de
lamentable ['læməntəbl] *adj* lamentable
lamentation [læmən'teɪʃən] *n* lamento
laminated ['læmɪneɪtɪd] *adj* laminado
lamp [læmp] *n* lámpara
lamplight ['læmplaɪt] *n*: **by ~** a la luz de la lámpara
lampoon [læm'puːn] *vt* satirizar
lamppost ['læmppəust] *n* (*Brit*) farola
lampshade ['læmpʃeɪd] *n* pantalla
lance [lɑːns] *n* lanza ■ *vt* (*Med*) abrir con lanceta
lance corporal *n* (*Brit*) soldado de primera clase
lancet ['lɑːnsɪt] *n* (*Med*) lanceta
Lancs [læŋks] *abbr* (*Brit*) = **Lancashire**
land [lænd] *n* tierra; (*country*) país *m*; (*piece of land*) terreno; (*estate*) tierras *fpl*, finca; (*Agr*) campo ■ *vi* (*from ship*) desembarcar; (*Aviat*) aterrizar; (*fig: fall*) caer ■ *vt* (*obtain*) conseguir; (*passengers, goods*) desembarcar; **to go/travel by ~** ir/viajar por tierra; **to own ~** ser dueño de tierras; **to ~ on one's feet** caer de pie; (*fig: to be lucky*) salir bien parado
▸ **land up** *vi*: **to ~ up in/at** ir a parar a/en
landed ['lændɪd] *adj*: **~ gentry** terratenientes *mpl*
landfill site ['lændfɪl-] *n* vertedero
landing ['lændɪŋ] *n* desembarco; aterrizaje *m*; (*of staircase*) rellano
landing card *n* tarjeta de desembarque
landing craft *n* lancha de desembarco
landing gear *n* (*Aviat*) tren *m* de aterrizaje
landing stage *n* (*Brit*) desembarcadero
landing strip *n* pista de aterrizaje
landlady ['lændleɪdɪ] *n* (*of boarding house*) patrona; (*owner*) dueña
landlocked ['lændlɔkt] *adj* cercado de tierra
landlord ['lændlɔːd] *n* propietario; (*of pub etc*) patrón *m*
landlubber ['lændlʌbə^r] *n* marinero de agua dulce
landmark ['lændmɑːk] *n* lugar *m* conocido; **to be a ~** (*fig*) hacer época
landowner ['lændəunə^r] *n* terrateniente *m/f*
landscape ['lænskeɪp] *n* paisaje *m*
landscape architecture *n* arquitectura paisajista
landscaped ['lænskeɪpt] *adj* reformado artísticamente
landscape gardener *n* diseñador(-a) *m(f)* de paisajes
landscape gardening *n* jardinería paisajista
landscape painting *n* (*Art*) paisaje *m*
landslide ['lændslaɪd] *n* (*Geo*) corrimiento de tierras; (*fig: Pol*) victoria arrolladora
lane [leɪn] *n* (*in country*) camino; (*in town*) callejón *m*; (*Aut*) carril *m*; (*in race*) calle *f*; (*for air or sea traffic*) ruta; **shipping ~** ruta marina
language ['læŋgwɪdʒ] *n* lenguaje *m*; (*national tongue*) idioma *m*, lengua; **bad ~** palabrotas *fpl*
language laboratory *n* laboratorio de idiomas
language studies *npl* estudios *mpl* filológicos
languid ['læŋgwɪd] *adj* lánguido
languish ['læŋgwɪʃ] *vi* languidecer
languor ['læŋgə^r] *n* languidez *f*
languorous ['læŋgərəs] *adj* lánguido
lank [læŋk] *adj* (*hair*) lacio
lanky ['læŋkɪ] *adj* larguirucho
lanolin, lanoline ['lænəlɪn] *n* lanolina
lantern ['læntn] *n* linterna, farol *m*
lanyard ['lænjed] *n* acollador *m*
Laos [laus] *n* Laos *m*
lap [læp] *n* (*of track*) vuelta; (*of body*): **to sit on sb's ~** sentarse en las rodillas de algn ■ *vt* (*also*: **lap up**) beber a lengüetadas *or* con la lengua ■ *vi* (*waves*) chapotear
▸ **lap up** *vt* beber a lengüetadas *or* con la lengua; (*fig: compliments, attention*) disfrutar; (*: lies etc*) tragarse

La Paz [læ'pæz] *n* La Paz
lapdog ['læpdɔg] *n* perro faldero
lapel [lə'pɛl] *n* solapa
Lapland ['læplænd] *n* Laponia
Laplander ['læplændəʳ] *n* lapón(-ona) *m(f)*
lapse [læps] *n* (*fault*) error *m*, fallo; (*moral*) desliz *m* ■ *vi* (*expire*) caducar; (*morally*) cometer un desliz; (*time*) pasar, transcurrir; **to ~ into bad habits** volver a las andadas; **~ of time** lapso, período; **a ~ of memory** un lapsus de memoria
laptop ['læptɔp] *n* (*also*: **laptop computer**) (ordenador *m*) portátil *m*
larceny ['lɑːsənɪ] *n* latrocinio
lard [lɑːd] *n* manteca (de cerdo)
larder ['lɑːdəʳ] *n* despensa
large [lɑːdʒ] *adj* grande ■ *adv*: **by and ~** en general, en términos generales; **at ~** (*free*) en libertad; (*generally*) en general; **to make ~(r)** hacer mayor *or* más extenso; **a ~ number of people** una gran cantidad de personas; **on a ~ scale** a gran escala
largely ['lɑːdʒlɪ] *adv* en gran parte
large-scale ['lɑːdʒ'skeɪl] *adj* (*map, drawing*) a gran escala; (*reforms, business activities*) importante
largesse [lɑː'ʒɛs] *n* generosidad *f*
lark [lɑːk] *n* (*bird*) alondra; (*joke*) broma
▸ **lark about** *vi* bromear, hacer el tonto
larva (*pl* **larvae**) ['lɑːvə, -iː] *n* larva
laryngitis [lærɪn'dʒaɪtɪs] *n* laringitis *f*
larynx ['lærɪŋks] *n* laringe *f*
lasagne [lə'zænjə] *n* lasaña
lascivious [lə'sɪvɪəs] *adj* lascivo
laser ['leɪzəʳ] *n* láser *m*
laser beam *n* rayo láser
laser printer *n* impresora láser
lash [læʃ] *n* latigazo; (*punishment*) azote *m*; (*also*: **eyelash**) pestaña ■ *vt* azotar; (*tie*) atar
▸ **lash down** *vt* sujetar con cuerdas ■ *vi* (*rain*) caer a trombas
▸ **lash out** *vi* (*col*: *spend*) gastar a la loca; **to ~ out at** *or* **against sb** (*fig*) lanzar invectivas contra algn
lashing ['læʃɪŋ] *n* (*beating*) azotaina, flagelación *f*; **lashings of** (*col*) montones *mpl* de
lass [læs] *n* chica
lassitude ['læsɪtjuːd] *n* lasitud *f*
lasso [læ'suː] *n* lazo ■ *vt* coger con lazo
last [lɑːst] *adj* (*gen*) último; (*final*) último, final ■ *adv* por último ■ *vi* (*endure*) durar; (*continue*) continuar, seguir; **~ night** anoche; **~ week** la semana pasada; **at ~** por fin; **~ but one** penúltimo; **~ time** la última vez; **it lasts (for) two hours** dura dos horas
last-ditch ['lɑːst'dɪtʃ] *adj* (*attempt*) de último recurso, último, desesperado
lasting ['lɑːstɪŋ] *adj* duradero
lastly ['lɑːstlɪ] *adv* por último, finalmente
last-minute ['lɑːstmɪnɪt] *adj* de última hora
latch [lætʃ] *n* picaporte *m*, pestillo
▸ **latch on to** *vt fus* (*cling to*: *person*) pegarse a; (: *idea*) agarrarse de
latchkey ['lætʃkiː] *n* llavín *m*
latchkey child *n* niño cuyos padres trabajan
late [leɪt] *adj* (*not on time*) tarde, atrasado; (*towards end of period, life*) tardío; (*hour*) avanzado; (*deceased*) fallecido ■ *adv* tarde; (*behind time, schedule*) con retraso; **to be (10 minutes) ~** llegar con (10 minutos de) retraso; **to be ~ with** estar atrasado con; **~ delivery** entrega tardía; **~ in life** a una edad avanzada; **of ~** últimamente; **in ~ May** hacia fines de mayo; **the ~ Mr X** el difunto Sr. X; **to work ~** trabajar hasta tarde
latecomer ['leɪtkʌməʳ] *n* recién llegado(-a)
lately ['leɪtlɪ] *adv* últimamente
lateness ['leɪtnɪs] *n* (*of person*) demora; (*of event*) tardanza
latent ['leɪtnt] *adj* latente; **~ defect** defecto latente
later ['leɪtəʳ] *adj* (*date etc*) posterior; (*version etc*) más reciente ■ *adv* más tarde, después; **~ on today** hoy más tarde
lateral ['lætərl] *adj* lateral
latest ['leɪtɪst] *adj* último; **at the ~** a más tardar
latex ['leɪtɛks] *n* látex *m*
lathe [leɪð] *n* torno
lather ['lɑːðəʳ] *n* espuma (de jabón) ■ *vt* enjabonar
Latin ['lætɪn] *n* latín *m* ■ *adj* latino
Latin America *n* América Latina, Latinoamérica
Latin American *adj, n* latinoamericano(-a) *m(f)*
Latino [læ'tiːnəu] *adj, n* latino(-a) *m(f)*
latitude ['lætɪtjuːd] *n* latitud *f*; (*fig*: *freedom*) libertad *f*
latrine [lə'triːn] *n* letrina
latter ['lætəʳ] *adj* último; (*of two*) segundo ■ *n*: **the ~** el último, éste
latter-day ['lætədeɪ] *adj* moderno
latterly ['lætəlɪ] *adv* últimamente
lattice ['lætɪs] *n* enrejado
lattice window *n* ventana enrejada *or* de celosía
lattice work *n* enrejado
Latvia ['lætvɪə] *n* Letonia
Latvian ['lætvɪən] *adj* letón(-ona) ■ *n* letón(-ona) *m(f)*; (*Ling*) letón *m*
laudable ['lɔːdəbl] *adj* loable
laugh [lɑːf] *n* risa; (*loud*) carcajada ■ *vi* reírse, reír; reírse a carcajadas

▸ **laugh at** *vt fus* reírse de
▸ **laugh off** *vt* tomar a risa
laughable ['lɑːfəbl] *adj* ridículo
laughing ['lɑːfɪŋ] *adj* risueño ■ *n*: **it's no ~ matter** no es cosa de risa
laughing gas *n* gas *m* hilarante
laughing stock *n*: **to be the ~ of the town** ser el hazmerreír de la ciudad
laughter ['lɑːftəʳ] *n* risa
launch [lɔːntʃ] *n* (*boat*) lancha; *see also* **launching** ■ *vt* (*ship*) botar; (*rocket, plan*) lanzar
▸ **launch forth** *vi*: **to ~ forth (into)** lanzarse a *or* en, emprender
▸ **launch out** *vi* = **launch forth**
launching ['lɔːntʃɪŋ] *n* (*of rocket etc*) lanzamiento; (*inauguration*) estreno
launching pad, launch pad *n* plataforma de lanzamiento
launder ['lɔːndəʳ] *vt* lavar
Launderette® [lɔːn'drɛt], **Laundromat®** (*US*) ['lɔːndrəmæt] *n* lavandería (automática)
laundry ['lɔːndrɪ] *n* lavandería; (*clothes*) ropa sucia; **to do the ~** hacer la colada
laureate ['lɔːrɪət] *adj see* **poet**
laurel ['lɔrl] *n* laurel *m*; **to rest on one's laurels** dormirse en *or* sobre los laureles
lava ['lɑːvə] *n* lava
lavatory ['lævətərɪ] *n* wáter *m*; **lavatories** *npl* servicios *mpl*, aseos *mpl*, sanitarios *mpl* (*LAm*)
lavatory paper *n* papel *m* higiénico
lavender ['lævəndəʳ] *n* lavanda
lavish ['lævɪʃ] *adj* abundante; (*giving freely*): **~ with** pródigo en ■ *vt*: **to ~ sth on sb** colmar a algn de algo
lavishly ['lævɪʃlɪ] *adv* (*give, spend*) generosamente; (*furnished*) lujosamente
law [lɔː] *n* ley *f*; (*study*) derecho; (*of game*) regla; **against the ~** contra la ley; **to study ~** estudiar derecho; **to go to ~** recurrir a la justicia
law-abiding ['lɔːəbaɪdɪŋ] *adj* respetuoso con la ley
law and order *n* orden *m* público
lawbreaker ['lɔːbreɪkəʳ] *n* infractor(a) *m(f)* de la ley
law court *n* tribunal *m* (de justicia)
lawful ['lɔːful] *adj* legítimo, lícito
lawfully ['lɔːfulɪ] *adv* legalmente
lawless ['lɔːlɪs] *adj* (*act*) ilegal; (*person*) rebelde; (*country*) ingobernable
Law Lord *n* (*Brit*) *miembro de la Cámara de los Lores y del más alto tribunal de apelación*
lawmaker ['lɔːmeɪkəʳ] *n* legislador(a) *m(f)*
lawn [lɔːn] *n* césped *m*
lawnmower ['lɔːnməuəʳ] *n* cortacésped *m*
lawn tennis *n* tenis *m* sobre hierba
law school *n* (*US*) facultad *f* de derecho
law student *n* estudiante *m/f* de derecho
lawsuit ['lɔːsuːt] *n* pleito; **to bring a ~ against** entablar un pleito contra
lawyer ['lɔːjəʳ] *n* abogado(-a); (*for sales, wills etc*) notario(-a)
lax [læks] *adj* (*discipline*) relajado; (*person*) negligente
laxative ['læksətɪv] *n* laxante *m*
laxity ['læksɪtɪ] *n* flojedad *f*; (*moral*) relajamiento; (*negligence*) negligencia
lay [leɪ] *pt of* **lie** ■ *adj* laico; (*not expert*) lego ■ *vt* (*pt, pp* **laid** [leɪd]) (*place*) colocar; (*eggs, table*) poner; (*trap*) tender; **to ~ the facts/ one's proposals before sb** presentar los hechos/sus propuestas a algn
▸ **lay aside, lay by** *vt* dejar a un lado
▸ **lay down** *vt* (*pen etc*) dejar; (*arms*) rendir; (*policy*) trazar; **to ~ down the law** imponer las normas
▸ **lay in** *vt* abastecerse de
▸ **lay into** *vt fus* (*col: attack, scold*) arremeter contra
▸ **lay off** *vt* (*workers*) despedir
▸ **lay on** *vt* (*water, gas*) instalar; (*meal, facilities*) proveer
▸ **lay out** *vt* (*plan*) trazar; (*display*) exponer; (*spend*) gastar
▸ **lay up** *vt* (*store*) guardar; (*ship*) desarmar; (*illness*) obligar a guardar cama
layabout ['leɪəbaut] *n* vago(-a)
lay-by ['leɪbaɪ] *n* (*Brit Aut*) apartadero
lay days *npl* días *mpl* de inactividad
layer ['leɪəʳ] *n* capa
layette [leɪ'ɛt] *n* ajuar *m* (de niño)
layman ['leɪmən] *n* lego
lay-off ['leɪɔf] *n* despido, paro forzoso
layout ['leɪaut] *n* (*design*) plan *m*, trazado; (*disposition*) disposición *f*; (*Press*) composición *f*
laze [leɪz] *vi* no hacer nada; (*pej*) holgazanear
lazily ['leɪzɪlɪ] *adv* perezosamente
laziness ['leɪzɪnɪs] *n* pereza
lazy ['leɪzɪ] *adj* perezoso, vago, flojo (*LAm*)
LB *abbr* (*Canada*) = **Labrador**
lb. *abbr* = **pound** (*weight*)
lbw *abbr* (*Cricket*) = **leg before wicket**
LC *n abbr* (*US*) = **Library of Congress**
lc *abbr* (*Typ*: = *lower case*) min
L/C *abbr* = **letter of credit**
LCD *n abbr see* **liquid crystal display**
Ld *abbr* (*Brit*: = *Lord*) *título de nobleza*
LDS *n abbr* (= *Licentiate in Dental Surgery*) *diploma universitario*; (= *Latter-day Saints*) Iglesia de Jesucristo de los Santos del último día

LEA *n abbr* (*Brit*: = *local education authority*) *organismo local encargado de la enseñanza*
lead [li:d] (*pt, pp* **led** [lɛd]) *n* (*front position*) delantera; (*distance, time ahead*) ventaja; (*clue*) pista; (*Elec*) cable *m*; (*for dog*) correa; (*Theat*) papel *m* principal; (*metal*) plomo; (*in pencil*) mina ■ *vt* conducir; (*life*) llevar; (*be leader of*) dirigir; (*Sport*) ir en cabeza de; (*orchestra*: *Brit*) ser el primer violín en; (: *US*) dirigir ■ *vi* ir primero; **to be in the ~** (*Sport*) llevar la delantera; (*fig*) ir a la cabeza; **to take the ~** (*Sport*) tomar la delantera; (*fig*) tomar la iniciativa; **to ~ sb to believe that ...** hacer creer a algn que ...; **to ~ sb to do sth** llevar a algn a hacer algo
▸ **lead astray** *vt* llevar por mal camino
▸ **lead away** *vt* llevar
▸ **lead back** *vt* hacer volver
▸ **lead off** *vt* llevar ■ *vi* (*in game*) abrir
▸ **lead on** *vt* (*tease*) engañar; **to ~ sb on to** (*induce*) incitar a algn a
▸ **lead to** *vt fus* producir, provocar
▸ **lead up to** *vt fus* conducir a
leaded ['lɛdɪd] *adj*: **~ windows** ventanas *fpl* emplomadas
leaden ['lɛdn] *adj* (*sky, sea*) plomizo; (*heavy*: *footsteps*) pesado
leader ['li:dəʳ] *n* jefe(-a) *m(f)*, líder *m*; (*of union etc*) dirigente *m/f*; (*guide*) guía *m/f*; (*of newspaper*) editorial *m*; **they are leaders in their field** (*fig*) llevan la delantera en su especialidad
leadership ['li:dəʃɪp] *n* dirección *f*; **qualities of ~** iniciativa *sg*; **under the ~ of ...** bajo la dirección de ..., al mando de ...
lead-free ['lɛdfri:] *adj* sin plomo
leading ['li:dɪŋ] *adj* (*main*) principal; (*outstanding*) destacado; (*first*) primero; (*front*) delantero; **a ~ question** una pregunta tendenciosa
leading lady *n* (*Theat*) primera actriz *f*
leading light *n* (*fig*: *person*) figura principal
leading man *n* (*Theat*) primer actor *m*
leading role *n* papel *m* principal
lead pencil *n* lápiz *m*
lead poisoning *n* envenenamiento plúmbico
lead time *n* (*Comm*) plazo de entrega
lead-up ['li:dʌp] *n*: **in the ~ to the election** cuando falta *etc* poco para las elecciones
lead weight *n* peso de plomo
leaf (*pl* **leaves**) [li:f, li:vz] *n* hoja; **to turn over a new ~** (*fig*) volver la hoja, hacer borrón y cuenta nueva; **to take a ~ out of sb's book** (*fig*) seguir el ejemplo de algn
▸ **leaf through** *vt fus* (*book*) hojear
leaflet ['li:flɪt] *n* folleto
leafy ['li:fɪ] *adj* frondoso
league [li:g] *n* sociedad *f*; (*Football*) liga; **to be in ~ with** estar confabulado con
league table *n* clasificación *f*
leak [li:k] *n* (*of liquid, gas*) escape *m*, fuga; (*in pipe*) agujero; (*in roof*) gotera; (*fig*: *of information, in security*) filtración *f* ■ *vi* (*ship*) hacer agua; (*shoes*) tener un agujero; (*pipe*) tener un escape; (*roof*) tener goteras; (*also*: **leak out**: *liquid, gas*) escaparse, salirse; (*fig*: *news*) trascender, divulgarse ■ *vt* (*gen*) dejar escapar; (*fig*: *information*) filtrar
leakage ['li:kɪdʒ] *n* (*of water, gas etc*) escape *m*, fuga
leaky ['li:kɪ] *adj* (*roof*) con goteras; (*bucket, shoe*) con agujeros; (*pipe*) con un escape; (*boat*) que hace agua
lean [li:n] (*pt, pp* **leaned** *or* **leant**) *adj* (*thin*) flaco; (*meat*) magro ■ *vt*: **to ~ sth on sth** apoyar algo en algo ■ *vi* (*slope*) inclinarse; (*rest*): **to ~ against** apoyarse contra; **to ~ on** apoyarse en
▸ **lean back** *vi* inclinarse hacia atrás
▸ **lean forward** *vi* inclinarse hacia adelante
▸ **lean out** *vi*: **to ~ out (of)** asomarse (a)
▸ **lean over** *vi* inclinarse
leaning ['li:nɪŋ] *adj* inclinado ■ *n*: **~ (towards)** inclinación *f* (hacia); **the L~ Tower of Pisa** la Torre Inclinada de Pisa
leant [lɛnt] *pt, pp of* **lean**
lean-to ['li:ntu:] *n* (*roof*) tejado de una sola agua; (*building*) cobertizo
leap [li:p] *n* salto ■ *vi* (*pt, pp* **leaped** *or* **leapt**) [lɛpt] saltar; **to ~ at an offer** apresurarse a aceptar una oferta
▸ **leap up** *vi* (*person*) saltar
leapfrog ['li:pfrɔg] *n* pídola ■ *vi*: **to ~ over sb/sth** saltar por encima de algn/algo
leapt [lɛpt] *pt, pp of* **leap**
leap year *n* año bisiesto
learn (*pt, pp* **learned** *or* **learnt**) [lə:n, -t] *vt* (*gen*) aprender; (*come to know of*) enterarse de ■ *vi* aprender; **to ~ how to do sth** aprender a hacer algo; **to ~ that ...** enterarse *or* informarse de que ...; **to ~ about sth** (*Scol*) aprender algo; (*hear*) enterarse *or* informarse de algo; **we were sorry to ~ that ...** nos dio tristeza saber que ...
learned ['lə:nɪd] *adj* erudito
learner ['lə:nəʳ] *n* principiante *m/f*; (*Brit*: *also*: **learner driver**) conductor(a) *m(f)* en prácticas; *see also* **L-plates**
learning ['lə:nɪŋ] *n* saber *m*, conocimientos *mpl*
learnt [lə:nt] *pp of* **learn**
lease [li:s] *n* arriendo ■ *vt* arrendar; **on ~** en arriendo
▸ **lease back** *vt* subarrendar

leaseback ['li:sbæk] *n* subarriendo
leasehold ['li:shəuld] *n* (*contract*) derechos *mpl* de arrendamiento ■ *adj* arrendado
leash [li:ʃ] *n* correa
least [li:st] *adj* (*slightest*) menor, más pequeño; (*smallest amount of*) mínimo ■ *adv* menos ■ *n*: **the ~** lo menos; **the ~ expensive car** el coche menos caro; **at ~** por lo menos, al menos; **not in the ~** en absoluto
leather ['lɛðə^r] *n* cuero ■ *cpd*: **~ goods** artículos *mpl* de cuero *or* piel
leathery ['lɛðərɪ] *adj* (*skin*) curtido
leave [li:v] (*pt, pp* **left**) *vt* dejar; (*go away from*) abandonar ■ *vi* irse; (*train*) salir ■ *n* permiso; **to ~ school** dejar la escuela *or* el colegio; **~ it to me!** ¡yo me encargo!; **he's already left for the airport** ya se ha marchado al aeropuerto; **to be left** quedar, sobrar; **there's some milk left over** sobra *or* queda algo de leche; **on ~** de permiso; **to take one's ~ of** despedirse de
▸ **leave behind** *vt* (*on purpose*) dejar (atrás); (*accidentally*) olvidar
▸ **leave off** *vt* (*lid*) no poner; (*switch*) no encender; (*col: stop*): **to ~ off doing sth** dejar de hacer algo
▸ **leave on** *vt* (*lid*) dejar puesto; (*light, fire, cooker*) dejar encendido
▸ **leave out** *vt* omitir
▸ **leave over** *vt* (*postpone*) dejar, aplazar
leave of absence *n* excedencia
leaves [li:vz] *pl of* **leaf**
leavetaking ['li:vteɪkɪŋ] *n* despedida
Lebanon ['lɛbənən] *n*: **the ~** el Líbano
lecherous ['lɛtʃərəs] *adj* lascivo
lectern ['lɛktə:n] *n* atril *m*
lecture ['lɛktʃə^r] *n* conferencia; (*Scol*) clase *f* ■ *vi* dar clase(s) ■ *vt* (*scold*) sermonear; (*reprove*) echar una reprimenda a; **to give a ~ on** dar una conferencia sobre
lecture hall *n* sala de conferencias; (*Univ*) aula
lecturer ['lɛktʃərə^r] *n* conferenciante *m/f*; (*Brit: at university*) profesor(a) *m(f)*
lecture theatre *n* = **lecture hall**
LED *n abbr* (*Elec: = light-emitting diode*) LED *m*
led [lɛd] *pt, pp of* **lead**
ledge [lɛdʒ] *n* (*of window, on wall*) repisa, reborde *m*; (*of mountain*) saliente *m*
ledger ['lɛdʒə^r] *n* libro mayor
lee [li:] *n* sotavento; **in the ~ of** al abrigo de
leech [li:tʃ] *n* sanguijuela
leek [li:k] *n* puerro
leer [lɪə^r] *vi*: **to ~ at sb** mirar de manera lasciva a algn
leeway ['li:weɪ] *n* (*fig*): **to have some ~** tener cierta libertad de acción
left [lɛft] *pt, pp of* **leave** ■ *adj* izquierdo ■ *n* izquierda ■ *adv* a la izquierda; **on** *or* **to the ~** a la izquierda; **the L~** (*Pol*) la izquierda
left-click ['lɛftklɪk] *vi* clicar con el botón izquierdo del ratón ■ *vt*: **to ~ an icon** clicar en un icono con el botón izquierdo del ratón
left-hand drive ['lɛfthænd-] *n* conducción *f* por la izquierda
left-handed [lɛft'hændɪd] *adj* zurdo; **~ scissors** tijeras *fpl* zurdas *or* para zurdos
left-hand side ['lɛfthænd-] *n* izquierda
leftie ['lɛftɪ] *n* = **lefty**
leftist ['lɛftɪst] *adj* (*Pol*) izquierdista
left-luggage [lɛft'lʌgɪdʒ], **left-luggage office** *n* (*Brit*) consigna
left-overs ['lɛftəuvəz] *npl* sobras *fpl*
left-wing [lɛft'wɪŋ] *adj* (*Pol*) de izquierda(s), izquierdista
left-winger ['lɛft'wɪŋə^r] *n* (*Pol*) izquierdista *m/f*
lefty ['lɛftɪ] *n* (*col: Pol*) rojillo(-a)
leg [lɛg] *n* pierna; (*of animal, chair*) pata; (*Culin: of meat*) pierna; (*of journey*) etapa; **1st/2nd ~** (*Sport*) partido de ida/de vuelta; **to pull sb's ~** tomar el pelo a algn; **to stretch one's legs** dar una vuelta
legacy ['lɛgəsɪ] *n* herencia; (*fig*) herencia, legado
legal ['li:gl] *adj* (*permitted by law*) lícito; (*of law*) legal; (*inquiry etc*) jurídico; **to take ~ action** *or* **proceedings against sb** entablar *or* levantar un pleito contra algn
legal adviser *n* asesor(a) *m(f)* jurídico(-a)
legal holiday *n* (*US*) fiesta oficial
legality [lɪ'gælɪtɪ] *n* legalidad *f*
legalize ['li:gəlaɪz] *vt* legalizar
legally ['li:gəlɪ] *adv* legalmente; **~ binding** con fuerza legal
legal tender *n* moneda de curso legal
legend ['lɛdʒənd] *n* leyenda
legendary ['lɛdʒəndərɪ] *adj* legendario
-legged ['lɛgɪd] *suff*: **two~** (*table etc*) de dos patas
leggings ['lɛgɪŋz] *npl* mallas *fpl*, leggins *mpl*
leggy ['lɛgɪ] *adj* de piernas largas
legibility [lɛdʒɪ'bɪlɪtɪ] *n* legibilidad *f*
legible ['lɛdʒəbl] *adj* legible
legibly ['lɛdʒəblɪ] *adv* legiblemente
legion ['li:dʒən] *n* legión *f*
legionnaire [li:dʒə'nɛə^r] *n* legionario
legionnaire's disease *n* enfermedad *f* del legionario
legislation [lɛdʒɪs'leɪʃən] *n* legislación *f*; **a piece of ~** (*bill*) un proyecto de ley; (*act*) una ley
legislative ['lɛdʒɪslətɪv] *adj* legislativo
legislator ['lɛdʒɪsleɪtə^r] *n* legislador(a) *m(f)*

legislature ['lɛdʒɪslətʃəʳ] *n* cuerpo legislativo
legitimacy [lɪ'dʒɪtɪməsɪ] *n* legitimidad *f*
legitimate [lɪ'dʒɪtɪmət] *adj* legítimo
legitimize [lɪ'dʒɪtɪmaɪz] *vt* legitimar
legless ['lɛglɪs] *adj* (*Brit col*) mamado
leg-room ['lɛgru:m] *n* espacio para las piernas
Leics *abbr* (*Brit*) = **Leicestershire**
leisure ['lɛʒəʳ] *n* ocio, tiempo libre; **at ~** con tranquilidad
leisure centre *n* centro recreativo
leisurely ['lɛʒəlɪ] *adj* sin prisa; lento
leisure suit *n* conjunto tipo chandal
lemon ['lɛmən] *n* limón *m*
lemonade [lɛmə'neɪd] *n* (*fruit juice*) limonada; (*fizzy*) gaseosa
lemon cheese, lemon curd *n* queso de limón
lemon juice *n* zumo de limón
lemon tea *n* té *m* con limón
lend [lɛnd] (*pt, pp* **lent** [lɛnt]) *vt*: **to ~ sth to sb** prestar algo a algn
lender ['lɛndəʳ] *n* prestamista *m/f*
lending library ['lɛndɪŋ-] *n* biblioteca de préstamo
length [lɛŋθ] *n* (*size*) largo, longitud *f*; (*section: of road, pipe*) tramo; (*: of rope etc*) largo; **at ~** (*at last*) por fin, finalmente; (*lengthily*) largamente; **it is two metres in ~** tiene dos metros de largo; **what ~ is it?** ¿cuánto tiene de largo?; **to fall full ~** caer de bruces; **to go to any ~(s) to do sth** ser capaz de hacer cualquier cosa para hacer algo
lengthen ['lɛŋθn] *vt* alargar ■ *vi* alargarse
lengthways ['lɛŋθweɪz] *adv* a lo largo
lengthy ['lɛŋθɪ] *adj* largo, extenso; (*meeting*) prolongado
lenient ['li:nɪənt] *adj* indulgente
lens [lɛnz] *n* (*of spectacles*) lente *f*; (*of camera*) objetivo
Lent [lɛnt] *n* Cuaresma
lent [lɛnt] *pt, pp of* **lend**
lentil ['lɛntl] *n* lenteja
Leo ['li:əu] *n* Leo
leopard ['lɛpəd] *n* leopardo
leotard ['li:ətɑ:d] *n* leotardo
leper ['lɛpəʳ] *n* leproso(-a)
leper colony *n* colonia de leprosos
leprosy ['lɛprəsɪ] *n* lepra
lesbian ['lɛzbɪən] *adj* lesbiano ■ *n* lesbiana
lesion ['li:ʒən] *n* (*Med*) lesión *f*
Lesotho [lɪ'su:tu:] *n* Lesotho
less [lɛs] *adj* (*in size, degree etc*) menor; (*in quantity*) menos ■ *pron, adv* menos; **~ than half** menos de la mitad; **~ than £1/a kilo/3 metres** menos de una libra/un kilo/3 metros; **~ than ever** menos que nunca; **~ 5%** menos el cinco por ciento; **~ and ~** cada vez menos; **the ~ he works ...** cuanto menos trabaja ...
lessee [lɛ'si:] *n* inquilino(-a), arrendatario(-a)
lessen ['lɛsn] *vi* disminuir, reducirse ■ *vt* disminuir, reducir
lesser ['lɛsəʳ] *adj* menor; **to a ~ extent** *or* **degree** en menor grado
lesson ['lɛsn] *n* clase *f*; **a maths ~** una clase de matemáticas; **to give lessons in** dar clases de; **it taught him a ~** (*fig*) le sirvió de lección
lessor ['lɛsɔ:ʳ, lɛ'sɔ:ʳ] *n* arrendador(a) *m(f)*
lest [lɛst] *conj*: **~ it happen** para que no pase
let (*pt, pp* **let**) [lɛt] *vt* (*allow*) dejar, permitir; (*Brit: lease*) alquilar; **to ~ sb do sth** dejar que algn haga algo; **to ~ sb have sth** dar algo a algn; **to ~ sb know sth** comunicar algo a algn; **~'s go** ¡vamos!; **~ him come** que venga; **"to ~"** "se alquila"
▸ **let down** *vt* (*lower*) bajar; (*dress*) alargar; (*tyre*) desinflar; (*hair*) soltar; (*disappoint*) defraudar
▸ **let go** *vi* soltar; (*fig*) dejarse ir ■ *vt* soltar
▸ **let in** *vt* dejar entrar; (*visitor etc*) hacer pasar; **what have you ~ yourself in for?** ¿en qué te has metido?
▸ **let off** *vt* dejar escapar; (*firework etc*) disparar; (*bomb*) accionar; (*passenger*) dejar, bajar; **to ~ off steam** (*fig, col*) desahogarse, desfogarse
▸ **let on** *vi*: **to ~ on that ...** revelar que ...
▸ **let out** *vt* dejar salir; (*dress*) ensanchar; (*rent out*) alquilar
▸ **let up** *vi* disminuir; (*rain etc*) amainar
let-down ['lɛtdaun] *n* (*disappointment*) decepción *f*
lethal ['li:θl] *adj* (*weapon*) mortífero; (*poison, wound*) mortal
lethargic [lɛ'θɑ:dʒɪk] *adj* aletargado
lethargy ['lɛθədʒɪ] *n* letargo
letter ['lɛtəʳ] *n* (*of alphabet*) letra; (*correspondence*) carta; **letters** *npl* (*literature, learning*) letras *fpl*; **small/capital ~** minúscula/mayúscula; **covering ~** carta adjunta
letter bomb *n* carta-bomba
letterbox ['lɛtəbɔks] *n* (*Brit*) buzón *m*
letterhead ['lɛtəhɛd] *n* membrete *m*, encabezamiento
lettering ['lɛtərɪŋ] *n* letras *fpl*
letter of credit *n* carta de crédito; **documentary ~** carta de crédito documentaria; **irrevocable ~** carta de crédito irrevocable
letter-opener ['lɛtərəupnəʳ] *n* abrecartas *m inv*

letterpress ['lɛtəprɛs] *n* (*method*) prensa de copiar; (*printed page*) impresión *f* tipográfica
letter quality *n* calidad *f* de correspondencia
letters patent *npl* letra *sg* de patente
lettuce ['lɛtɪs] *n* lechuga
let-up ['lɛtʌp] *n* descanso, tregua
leukaemia, (US) **leukemia** [lu:'ki:mɪə] *n* leucemia
level ['lɛvl] *adj* (*flat*) llano; (*flattened*) nivelado; (*uniform*) igual ■ *adv* a nivel ■ *n* nivel *m* ■ *vt* nivelar, allanar; (*gun*) apuntar; (*accusation*): **to ~ (against)** levantar (contra) ■ *vi* (*col*): **to ~ with sb** ser franco con algn; **to be ~ with** estar a nivel de; **a ~ spoonful** (*Culin*) una cucharada rasa; **to draw ~ with** (*team*) igualar; (*runner, car*) alcanzar a; **O levels** *npl* (*Brit: formerly*) ≈ bachillerato *sg* elemental, octavo *sg* de Básica; **on the ~** (*fig: honest*) en serio; **talks at ministerial ~** charlas *fpl* a nivel ministerial
▸ **level off** *or* **out** *vi* (*prices etc*) estabilizarse; (*ground*) nivelarse; (*aircraft*) ponerse en una trayectoria horizontal
level crossing *n* (*Brit*) paso a nivel
level-headed [lɛvl'hɛdɪd] *adj* sensato
levelling, leveling (US) ['lɛvlɪŋ] *adj* (*process, effect*) de nivelación ■ *n* igualación *f*, allanamiento
level playing field *n* situación *f* de igualdad; **to compete on a ~** competir en igualdad de condiciones
lever ['li:vəʳ] *n* palanca ■ *vt*: **to ~ up** levantar con palanca
leverage ['li:vərɪdʒ] *n* (*fig: influence*) influencia
levity ['lɛvɪtɪ] *n* frivolidad *f*, informalidad *f*
levy ['lɛvɪ] *n* impuesto ■ *vt* exigir, recaudar
lewd [lu:d] *adj* lascivo, obsceno, colorado (*LAm*)
lexicographer [lɛksɪ'kɔgrəfəʳ] *n* lexicógrafo(-a) *m(f)*
lexicography [lɛksɪ'kɔgrəfɪ] *n* lexicografía
LGV *n abbr* (= *Large Goods Vehicle*) vehículo pesado
LI *abbr* (US) = **Long Island**
liabilities [laɪə'bɪlətɪz] *npl* obligaciones *fpl*; pasivo *sg*
liability [laɪə'bɪlətɪ] *n* responsabilidad *f*; (*handicap*) desventaja
liable ['laɪəbl] *adj* (*subject*): **~ to** sujeto a; (*responsible*): **~ for** responsable de; (*likely*): **~ to do** propenso a hacer; **to be ~ to a fine** exponerse a una multa
liaise [li:'eɪz] *vi*: **to ~ (with)** colaborar (con); **to ~ with sb** mantener informado a algn
liaison [li:'eɪzɔn] *n* (*coordination*) enlace *m*; (*affair*) relación *f*
liar ['laɪəʳ] *n* mentiroso(-a)
libel ['laɪbl] *n* calumnia ■ *vt* calumniar
libellous ['ləɪbləs] *adj* difamatorio, calumnioso
liberal ['lɪbərl] *adj* (*gen*) liberal; (*generous*): **~ with** generoso con ■ *n*: **L~** (*Pol*) liberal *m/f*
Liberal Democrat *n* (*Brit*) demócrata *m/f* liberal
liberality [lɪbə'rælɪtɪ] *n* (*generosity*) liberalidad *f*, generosidad *f*
liberalize ['lɪbərəlaɪz] *vt* liberalizar
liberally ['lɪbərəlɪ] *adv* liberalmente
liberal-minded ['lɪbərl'maɪndɪd] *adj* de miras anchas, liberal
liberate ['lɪbəreɪt] *vt* liberar
liberation [lɪbə'reɪʃən] *n* liberación *f*
liberation theology *n* teología de la liberación
Liberia [laɪ'bɪərɪə] *n* Liberia
Liberian [laɪ'bɪərɪən] *adj, n* liberiano(-a) *m(f)*
liberty ['lɪbətɪ] *n* libertad *f*; **to be at ~ to do** estar libre para hacer; **to take the ~ of doing sth** tomarse la libertad de hacer algo
libido [lɪ'bi:dəu] *n* libido
Libra ['li:brə] *n* Libra
librarian [laɪ'brɛərɪən] *n* bibliotecario(-a)
library ['laɪbrərɪ] *n* biblioteca
library book *n* libro de la biblioteca
libretto [lɪ'brɛtəu] *n* libreto
Libya ['lɪbɪə] *n* Libia
Libyan ['lɪbɪən] *adj, n* libio(-a) *m(f)*
lice [laɪs] *pl of* **louse**
licence, license (US) ['laɪsns] *n* licencia; (*permit*) permiso; (*also*: **driving licence,** (US) **driver's license**) carnet *m* de conducir; (*excessive freedom*) libertad *f*; **import ~** licencia *or* permiso de importación; **produced under ~** elaborado bajo licencia
licence number *n* (número de) matrícula
licence plate *n* (placa de) matrícula
license ['laɪsns] (US) = **licence**; *vt* autorizar, dar permiso a; (*car*) sacar la matrícula de *or* (*LAm*) la patente de
licensed ['laɪsnst] *adj* (*for alcohol*) autorizado para vender bebidas alcohólicas
licensed trade *n* comercio *or* negocio autorizado
licensee [laɪsən'si:] *n* (*in a pub*) concesionario(-a), dueño(-a) de un bar
licentious [laɪ'sɛnʃəs] *adj* licencioso
lichen ['laɪkən] *n* liquen *m*
lick [lɪk] *vt* lamer; (*col: defeat*) dar una paliza a ■ *n* lamedura; **a ~ of paint** una mano de pintura
licorice ['lɪkərɪs] *n* = **liquorice**

lid [lɪd] *n* (*of box, case*) tapa; (*of pan*) cobertera; **to take the ~ off sth** (*fig*) exponer algo a la luz pública
lido ['laɪdəu] *n* (*Brit*) piscina, alberca (*LAm*)
lie [laɪ] *n* mentira ■ *vi* mentir; (*pt* **lay**, *pp* **lain**) [leɪ, leɪn] (*rest*) estar echado, estar acostado; (*of object: be situated*) estar, encontrarse; **to tell lies** mentir; **to ~ low** (*fig*) mantenerse a escondidas
▸ **lie about, lie around** *vi* (*things*) estar tirado; (*Brit: people*) estar acostado *or* tumbado
▸ **lie back** *vi* recostarse
▸ **lie down** *vi* echarse, tumbarse
▸ **lie up** *vi* (*hide*) esconderse
Liechtenstein ['lɪktənstaɪn] *n* Liechtenstein *m*
lie detector *n* detector *m* de mentiras
lie-down ['laɪdaun] *n* (*Brit*): **to have a ~** echarse (una siesta)
lie-in ['laɪɪn] *n* (*Brit*): **to have a ~** quedarse en la cama
lieu [lu:]: **in ~ of** *prep* en lugar de
Lieut. *abbr* = **lieutenant**
lieutenant [lɛf'tɛnənt, (*US*) lu:'tɛnənt] *n* (*Mil*) teniente *m*
lieutenant colonel *n* teniente *m* coronel
life (*pl* **lives**) [laɪf, laɪvz] *n* vida; (*of licence etc*) vigencia; **to be sent to prison for ~** ser condenado a cadena perpetua; **country/city ~** la vida en el campo/en la ciudad; **true to ~** fiel a la realidad; **to paint from ~** pintar del natural; **to put** *or* **breathe new ~ into** (*person*) reanimar; (*project, area etc*) infundir nueva vida a
life assurance *n* (*Brit*) seguro de vida
lifebelt ['laɪfbɛlt] *n* (*Brit*) cinturón *m* salvavidas
lifeblood ['laɪfblʌd] *n* (*fig*) alma, nervio
lifeboat ['laɪfbəut] *n* lancha de socorro
life-buoy ['laɪfbɔɪ] *n* boya *or* guindola salvavidas
life coach *n* *profesional encargado de mejorar la situación laboral y personal de sus clientes*
life expectancy *n* esperanza de vida
lifeguard ['laɪfgɑ:d] *n* vigilante *m/f*
life imprisonment *n* cadena perpetua
life insurance *n* = **life assurance**
life jacket *n* chaleco salvavidas
lifeless ['laɪflɪs] *adj* sin vida; (*dull*) soso
lifelike ['laɪflaɪk] *adj* natural
lifeline ['laɪflaɪn] *n* (*fig*) cordón *m* umbilical
lifelong ['laɪflɔŋ] *adj* de toda la vida
life preserver *n* (*US*) = **lifebelt**
lifer ['laɪfə^r] *n* (*col*) condenado(-a) *m(f)* a cadena perpetua
life-saver ['laɪfseɪvə^r] *n* socorrista *m/f*
life sentence *n* cadena perpetua
life-sized ['laɪfsaɪzd] *adj* de tamaño natural
life span *n* vida
lifestyle ['laɪfstaɪl] *n* estilo de vida
life support system *n* (*Med*) sistema *m* de respiración asistida
lifetime ['laɪftaɪm] *n*: **in his ~** durante su vida; **once in a ~** una vez en la vida; **the chance of a ~** una oportunidad única
lift [lɪft] *vt* levantar; (*copy*) plagiar ■ *vi* (*fog*) disiparse ■ *n* (*Brit: elevator*) ascensor *m*, elevador *m* (*LAm*); **to give sb a ~** (*Brit*) llevar a algn en coche
▸ **lift off** *vt* levantar, quitar ■ *vi* (*rocket, helicopter*) despegar
▸ **lift out** *vt* sacar; (*troops, evacuees etc*) evacuar
▸ **lift up** *vt* levantar
lift-off ['lɪftɔf] *n* despegue *m*
ligament ['lɪgəmənt] *n* ligamento
light [laɪt] *n* luz *f*; (*flame*) lumbre *f*; (*lamp*) luz *f*, lámpara; (*daylight*) luz *f* del día; (*headlight*) faro; (*rear light*) luz *f* trasera; (*for cigarette etc*): **have you got a ~?** ¿tienes fuego? ■ *vt* (*pt, pp* **lighted**, *pt, pp* **lit** [lɪt]) (*candle, cigarette, fire*) encender; (*room*) alumbrar ■ *adj* (*colour*) claro ligero, liviano (*LAm*); (*room*) alumbrado ■ *adv* (*travel*) con poco equipaje; **to turn the ~ on/off** encender/apagar la luz; **in the ~ of** a la luz de; **to come to ~** salir a la luz; **to cast** *or* **shed** *or* **throw ~ on** arrojar luz sobre; **to make ~ of sth** (*fig*) no dar importancia a algo
▸ **light up** *vi* (*smoke*) encender un cigarrillo; (*face*) iluminarse ■ *vt* (*illuminate*) iluminar, alumbrar
light bulb *n* bombilla, bombillo (*LAm*), foco (*LAm*)
lighten ['laɪtn] *vi* (*grow light*) clarear ■ *vt* (*give light to*) iluminar; (*make lighter*) aclarar; (*make less heavy*) aligerar
lighter ['laɪtə^r] *n* (*also*: **cigarette lighter**) encendedor *m* (*LAm*), mechero
light-fingered [laɪt'fɪŋgəd] *adj* de manos largas
light-headed [laɪt'hɛdɪd] *adj* (*dizzy*) mareado; (*excited*) exaltado; (*by nature*) atolondrado
light-hearted [laɪt'hɑ:tɪd] *adj* alegre
lighthouse ['laɪthaus] *n* faro
lighting ['laɪtɪŋ] *n* (*act*) iluminación *f*; (*system*) alumbrado
lighting-up time [laɪtɪŋ'ʌp-] *n* (*Brit*) hora de encendido del alumbrado
lightly ['laɪtlɪ] *adv* ligeramente; (*not seriously*) con poca seriedad; **to get off ~** ser castigado con poca severidad
light meter *n* (*Phot*) fotómetro
lightness ['laɪtnɪs] *n* claridad *f*; (*in weight*) ligereza

lightning ['laɪtnɪŋ] *n* relámpago, rayo
lightning conductor, lightning rod (*US*) *n* pararrayos *m inv*
lightning strike *n* huelga relámpago
lightweight ['laɪtweɪt] *adj* (*suit*) ligero ■ *n* (*Boxing*) peso ligero
light year *n* año luz
like [laɪk] *vt* (*person*) querer a; (*thing*): **I ~ swimming/apples** me gusta nadar/me gustan las manzanas ■ *prep* como ■ *adj* parecido, semejante ■ *n*: **did you ever see the ~ (of it)?** ¿has visto cosa igual?; **his likes and dislikes** sus gustos y aversiones; **the likes of him** personas como él; **I would ~, I'd ~** me gustaría; (*for purchase*) quisiera; **would you ~ a coffee?** ¿te apetece un café?; **to be** *or* **look ~ sb/sth** parecerse a algn/algo; **that's just ~ him** es muy de él, es típico de él; **do it ~ this** hazlo así; **it is nothing ~ ...** no tiene parecido alguno con ...; **what's he ~?** ¿cómo es (él)?; **what's the weather ~?** ¿qué tiempo hace?; **something ~ that** algo así *or* por el estilo; **I feel ~ a drink** me apetece algo de beber; **if you ~** si quieres
likeable ['laɪkəbl] *adj* simpático, agradable
likelihood ['laɪklɪhud] *n* probabilidad *f*; **in all ~** según todas las probabilidades
likely ['laɪklɪ] *adj* probable, capaz (*LAm*); **he's ~ to leave** es probable *or* (*LAm*) capaz que se vaya; **not ~!** ¡ni hablar!
like-minded [laɪk'maɪndɪd] *adj* de la misma opinión
liken ['laɪkən] *vt*: **to ~ to** comparar con
likeness ['laɪknɪs] *n* (*similarity*) semejanza, parecido
likewise ['laɪkwaɪz] *adv* igualmente
liking ['laɪkɪŋ] *n*: **~ (for)** (*person*) cariño (a); (*thing*) afición (a); **to take a ~ to sb** tomar cariño a algn; **to be to sb's ~** ser del gusto de algn
lilac ['laɪlək] *n* lila ■ *adj* (*colour*) de color lila
Lilo® ['laɪləu] *n* colchoneta inflable
lilt [lɪlt] *n* deje *m*
lilting ['lɪltɪŋ] *adj* melodioso
lily ['lɪlɪ] *n* lirio, azucena
lily of the valley *n* lirio de los valles
Lima ['li:mə] *n* Lima
limb [lɪm] *n* miembro; (*of tree*) rama; **to be out on a ~** (*fig*) estar aislado
limber up ['lɪmbə^r-] *vi* (*fig*) entrenarse; (*Sport*) hacer (ejercicios de) precalentamiento
limbo ['lɪmbəu] *n*: **to be in ~** (*fig*) quedar a la expectativa
lime [laɪm] *n* (*tree*) limero; (*fruit*) lima; (*Geo*) cal *f*
lime juice *n* zumo (*SP*) *or* jugo de lima
limelight ['laɪmlaɪt] *n*: **to be in the ~** (*fig*) ser el centro de atención
limerick ['lɪmərɪk] *n* quintilla humorística
limestone ['laɪmstəun] *n* piedra caliza
limit ['lɪmɪt] *n* límite *m* ■ *vt* limitar; **weight/speed ~** peso máximo/velocidad *f* máxima; **within limits** entre límites
limitation [lɪmɪ'teɪʃən] *n* limitación *f*
limited ['lɪmɪtɪd] *adj* limitado; **to be ~ to** limitarse a; **~ edition** edición limitada
limited company, limited liability company *n* (*Brit*) sociedad *f* anónima
limitless ['lɪmɪtlɪs] *adj* sin límites
limousine ['lɪməzi:n] *n* limusina
limp [lɪmp] *n*: **to have a ~** tener cojera ■ *vi* cojear, renguear (*LAm*) ■ *adj* flojo
limpet ['lɪmpɪt] *n* lapa
limpid ['lɪmpɪd] *adj* (*poetic*) límpido, cristalino
limply ['lɪmplɪ] *adv* desmayadamente; **to say ~** decir débilmente
linchpin ['lɪntʃpɪn] *n* pezonera; (*fig*) eje *m*
Lincs [lɪŋks] *abbr* (*Brit*) = **Lincolnshire**
line [laɪn] *n* (*Comm*) línea; (*straight line*) raya; (*rope*) cuerda; (*for fishing*) sedal *m*; (*wire*) hilo; (*row, series*) fila, hilera; (*of writing*) renglón *m*; (*on face*) arruga; (*speciality*) rama ■ *vt* (*Sewing*): **to ~ (with)** forrar (de); **to ~ the streets** ocupar las aceras; **in ~ with** de acuerdo con; **she's in ~ for promotion** (*fig*) tiene muchas posibilidades de que la asciendan; **to bring sth into ~ with sth** poner algo de acuerdo con algo; **~ of research/business** campo de investigación/comercio; **to take the ~ that ...** ser de la opinión que ...; **hold the ~ please** (*Tel*) no cuelgue usted, por favor; **to draw the ~ at doing sth** negarse a hacer algo; no permitir que se haga algo; **on the right lines** por buen camino; **a new ~ in cosmetics** una nueva línea en cosméticos; *see also* **lines**
▸ **line up** *vi* hacer cola ■ *vt* alinear, poner en fila; **to have sth lined up** tener algo arreglado
linear ['lɪnɪə^r] *adj* lineal
lined [laɪnd] *adj* (*face*) arrugado; (*paper*) rayado; (*clothes*) forrado
line editing *n* (*Comput*) corrección *f* por líneas
line feed *n* (*Comput*) avance *m* de línea
lineman ['laɪnmən] *n* (*US*) técnico de las líneas; (*Football*) delantero
linen ['lɪnɪn] *n* ropa blanca; (*cloth*) lino
line printer *n* impresora de línea
liner ['laɪnə^r] *n* vapor *m* de línea transatlántico; **dustbin ~** bolsa de la basura
lines [laɪnz] *npl* (*Rail*) vía *sg*, raíles *mpl*
linesman ['laɪnzmən] *n* (*Sport*) juez *m* de línea
line-up ['laɪnʌp] *n* alineación *f*
linger ['lɪŋgə^r] *vi* retrasarse, tardar en marcharse; (*smell, tradition*) persistir

lingerie ['lænʒəri:] *n* ropa interior *or* íntima (de mujer)
lingering ['lɪŋgərɪŋ] *adj* persistente; (*death*) lento
lingo (*pl* **lingoes**) ['lɪŋgəu, -gəuz] *n* (*pej*) jerga
linguist ['lɪŋgwɪst] *n* lingüista *m/f*
linguistic [lɪŋ'gwɪstɪk] *adj* lingüístico
linguistics [lɪŋ'gwɪstɪks] *n* lingüística
liniment ['lɪnɪmənt] *n* linimento
lining ['laɪnɪŋ] *n* forro; (*Tech*) revestimiento; (*of brake*) guarnición *f*
link [lɪŋk] *n* (*of chain*) eslabón *m*; (*connection*) conexión *f*; (*bond*) vínculo, lazo; (*Internet*) enlace *m* ■ *vt* vincular, unir; **rail ~** línea de ferrocarril, servicio de trenes
▶ **link up** *vt* acoplar ■ *vi* unirse
links [lɪŋks] *npl* (*Golf*) campo *sg* de golf
link-up ['lɪŋkʌp] *n* (*gen*) unión *f*; (*meeting*) encuentro, reunión *f*; (*of roads*) empalme *m*; (*of spaceships*) acoplamiento; (*Radio, TV*) enlace *m*
lino ['laɪnəu], (*Brit*) **linoleum** [lɪ'nəulɪəm] *n* linóleo
linseed oil ['lɪnsi:d-] *n* aceite *m* de linaza
lint [lɪnt] *n* gasa
lintel ['lɪntl] *n* dintel *m*
lion ['laɪən] *n* león *m*
lioness ['laɪənɪs] *n* leona
lip [lɪp] *n* labio; (*of jug*) pico; (*of cup etc*) borde *m*
liposuction ['lɪpəusʌkʃən] *n* liposucción *f*
lipread ['lɪpri:d] *vi* leer los labios
lip salve *n* crema protectora para labios
lip service *n*: **to pay ~ to sth** alabar algo pero sin hacer nada
lipstick ['lɪpstɪk] *n* lápiz *m or* barra de labios, carmín *m*
liquefy ['lɪkwɪfaɪ] *vt* licuar ■ *vi* licuarse
liqueur [lɪ'kjuəʳ] *n* licor *m*
liquid ['lɪkwɪd] *adj, n* líquido
liquidate ['lɪkwɪdeɪt] *vt* liquidar
liquidation [lɪkwɪ'deɪʃən] *n* liquidación *f*; **to go into ~** entrar en liquidación
liquid crystal display *n* pantalla de cristal líquido
liquidity [lɪ'kwɪdɪtɪ] *n* (*Comm*) liquidez *f*
liquidize ['lɪkwɪdaɪz] *vt* (*Culin*) licuar
liquidizer ['lɪkwɪdaɪzəʳ] *n* (*Culin*) licuadora
liquor ['lɪkəʳ] *n* licor *m*, bebidas *fpl* alcohólicas
liquorice ['lɪkərɪs] *n* regaliz *m*
liquor store *n* (*US*) bodega, *tienda de vinos y bebidas alcohólicas*
Lisbon ['lɪzbən] *n* Lisboa
lisp [lɪsp] *n* ceceo
lissom ['lɪsəm] *adj* ágil
list [lɪst] *n* lista; (*of ship*) inclinación *f* ■ *vt* (*write down*) hacer una lista de; (*enumerate*) catalogar; (*Comput*) hacer un listado de ■ *vi* (*ship*) inclinarse; **shopping ~** lista de las compras; *see also* **lists**
listed building ['lɪstɪd-] *n* (*Arch*) edificio de interés histórico-artístico
listed company ['lɪstɪd-] *n* compañía cotizable
listen ['lɪsn] *vi* escuchar, oír; (*pay attention*) atender
listener ['lɪsnəʳ] *n* oyente *m/f*
listeria [lɪs'tɪərɪə] *n* listeria
listing ['lɪstɪŋ] *n* (*Comput*) listado
listless ['lɪstlɪs] *adj* apático, indiferente
listlessly ['lɪstlɪslɪ] *adv* con indiferencia
listlessness ['lɪstlɪsnɪs] *n* indiferencia, apatía
list price *n* precio de catálogo
lists [lɪsts] *npl* (*History*) liza *sg*; **to enter the ~ (against sb/sth)** salir a la palestra (contra algn/algo)
lit [lɪt] *pt, pp of* **light**
litany ['lɪtənɪ] *n* letanía
liter ['li:təʳ] *n* (*US*) = **litre**
literacy ['lɪtərəsɪ] *n* capacidad *f* de leer y escribir
literacy campaign *n* campaña de alfabetización
literal ['lɪtərl] *adj* literal
literally ['lɪtrəlɪ] *adv* literalmente
literary ['lɪtərərɪ] *adj* literario
literate ['lɪtərət] *adj* que sabe leer y escribir; (*fig*) culto
literature ['lɪtərɪtʃəʳ] *n* literatura; (*brochures etc*) folletos *mpl*
lithe [laɪð] *adj* ágil
lithography [lɪ'θɔgrəfɪ] *n* litografía
Lithuania [lɪθju'eɪnɪə] *n* Lituania
Lithuanian [lɪθju'eɪnɪən] *adj* lituano ■ *n* lituano(-a); (*Ling*) lituano
litigate ['lɪtɪgeɪt] *vi* litigar
litigation [lɪtɪ'geɪʃən] *n* litigio
litmus paper ['lɪtməs-] *n* papel *m* de tornasol
litre, liter (*US*) ['li:təʳ] *n* litro
litter ['lɪtəʳ] *n* (*rubbish*) basura; (*paper*) papeles *mpl* (tirados); (*young animals*) camada, cría
litter bin *n* (*Brit*) papelera
littered ['lɪtəd] *adj*: **~ with** lleno de
litter lout, litterbug (*US*) ['lɪtəbʌg] *n persona que tira papeles usados en la vía pública*
little ['lɪtl] *adj* (*small*) pequeño, chico (*LAm*); (*not much*) poco; (*often translated by suffix, eg*): **~ house** casita ■ *adv* poco; **a ~** un poco (de); **~ by ~** poco a poco; **~ finger** (dedo) meñique *m*; **for a ~ while** (durante) un rato; **with ~ difficulty** sin problema *or* dificultad; **as ~ as possible** lo menos posible
little-known ['lɪtl'nəun] *adj* poco conocido
liturgy ['lɪtədʒɪ] *n* liturgia

live [*vb* lɪv, *adj* laɪv] *vi* vivir ■ *vt* (*a life*) llevar; (*experience*) vivir ■ *adj* (*animal*) vivo; (*wire*) conectado; (*broadcast*) en directo; (*issue*) de actualidad; (*unexploded*) sin explotar; **to ~ in London** vivir en Londres; **to ~ together** vivir juntos
▸ **live down** *vt* hacer olvidar
▸ **live off** *vt fus* (*land, fish etc*) vivir de; (*pej: parents etc*) vivir a costa de
▸ **live on** *vt fus* (*food*) vivir de, alimentarse de; **to ~ on £50 a week** vivir con 50 libras semanales *or* a la semana
▸ **live out** *vi* (*student*) ser externo ■ *vt*: **to ~ out one's days** *or* **life** pasar el resto de la vida
▸ **live up** *vt*: **to ~ it up** (*col*) tirarse la gran vida
▸ **live up to** *vt fus* (*fulfil*) cumplir con; (*justify*) justificar

live-in ['lɪvɪn] *adj*: **~ partner** pareja, compañero(-a) sentimental; **~ maid** asistenta interna
livelihood ['laɪvlɪhud] *n* sustento
liveliness ['laɪvlɪnɪs] *n* viveza
lively ['laɪvlɪ] *adj* (*gen*) vivo; (*talk*) animado; (*pace*) rápido; (*party, tune*) alegre
liven up ['laɪvn-] *vt* (*discussion, evening*) animar
liver ['lɪvə^r] *n* hígado
liverish ['lɪvərɪʃ] *adj*: **to feel ~** sentirse *or* encontrarse mal, no estar muy católico
Liverpudlian [lɪvə'pʌdlɪən] *adj* de Liverpool ■ *n* nativo(-a) *or* habitante *m(f)* de Liverpool
livery ['lɪvərɪ] *n* librea
lives [laɪvz] *npl of* **life**
livestock ['laɪvstɔk] *n* ganado
live wire [laɪv-] *n* (*fig, col*): **he's a real ~!** ¡tiene una marcha!
livid ['lɪvɪd] *adj* lívido; (*furious*) furioso
living ['lɪvɪŋ] *adj* (*alive*) vivo ■ *n*: **to earn** *or* **make a ~** ganarse la vida; **cost of ~** coste *m* de la vida; **in ~ memory** que se recuerde *or* recuerda
living conditions *npl* condiciones *fpl* de vida
living expenses *npl* gastos *mpl* de mantenimiento
living room *n* sala (de estar), living *m* (*LAm*)
living standards *npl* nivel *msg* de vida
living wage *n* sueldo suficiente para vivir
lizard ['lɪzəd] *n* lagartija
llama ['lɑːmə] *n* llama
LLB *n abbr* (*= Bachelor of Laws*) Ldo.(-a.) en Dcho.; *see also* **Bachelor's Degree**
LLD *n abbr* (*= Doctor of Laws*) Dr(a). en Dcho.
LMT *n abbr* (*US: = Local Mean Time*) *hora local*
load [ləud] *n* (*gen*) carga; (*weight*) peso ■ *vt* (*Comput*) cargar; (*also*: **load up**): **to ~ (with)** cargar (con *or* de); **a ~ of, loads of** (*fig*) (gran) cantidad de, montones de
loaded ['ləudɪd] *adj* (*dice*) cargado; (*question*) intencionado; (*col: rich*) forrado (de dinero)
loading ['ləudɪŋ] *n* (*Comm*) sobreprima
loading bay *n* área de carga y descarga
loaf (*pl* **loaves**) [ləuf, ləuvz] *n* (barra de) pan *m* ■ *vi* (*also*: **loaf about, loaf around**) holgazanear
loam [ləum] *n* marga
loan [ləun] *n* préstamo; (*Comm*) empréstito ■ *vt* prestar; **on ~** (*book, painting*) prestado; **to raise a ~** (*money*) procurar un empréstito
loan account *n* cuenta de crédito
loan capital *n* empréstito
loan shark *n* (*col: pej*) prestamista *m/f* sin escrúpulos
loath [ləuθ] *adj*: **to be ~ to do sth** ser reacio a hacer algo
loathe [ləuð] *vt* aborrecer; (*person*) odiar
loathing ['ləuðɪŋ] *n* aversión *f*; odio
loathsome ['ləuðsəm] *adj* asqueroso, repugnante; (*person*) odioso
loaves [ləuvz] *pl of* **loaf**
lob [lɔb] *vt* (*ball*) volear por alto
lobby ['lɔbɪ] *n* vestíbulo, sala de espera; (*Pol: pressure group*) grupo de presión ■ *vt* presionar
lobbyist ['lɔbɪɪst] *n* cabildero(-a)
lobe [ləub] *n* lóbulo
lobster ['lɔbstə^r] *n* langosta
lobster pot *n* nasa, langostera
local ['ləukl] *adj* local ■ *n* (*pub*) bar *m*; **the locals** *npl* los vecinos, los del lugar
local anaesthetic *n* (*Med*) anestesia local
local authority *n* municipio, ayuntamiento (*SP*)
local call *n* (*Tel*) llamada local
local government *n* gobierno municipal
locality [ləu'kælɪtɪ] *n* localidad *f*
localize ['ləukəlaɪz] *vt* localizar
locally ['ləukəlɪ] *adv* en la vecindad
locate [ləu'keɪt] *vt* (*find*) localizar; (*situate*) situar, ubicar (*LAm*)
location [ləu'keɪʃən] *n* situación *f*; **on ~** (*Cine*) en exteriores, fuera del estudio
loch [lɔx] *n* lago
lock [lɔk] *n* (*of door, box*) cerradura, chapa (*LAm*); (*of canal*) esclusa; (*of hair*) mechón *m* ■ *vt* (*with key*) cerrar con llave; (*immobilize*) inmovilizar ■ *vi* (*door etc*) cerrarse con llave; (*wheels*) trabarse; **~, stock and barrel** (*fig*) por completo *or* entero; **on full ~** (*Aut*) con el volante girado al máximo
▸ **lock away** *vt* (*valuables*) guardar bajo llave; (*criminal*) encerrar
▸ **lock out** *vt*: **the workers were locked out** los trabajadores tuvieron que enfrentarse con un cierre patronal

▶ **lock up** *vi* echar la llave
locker ['lɔkəʳ] *n* casillero
locker-room ['lɔkərum] *n* (*US Sport*) vestuario
locket ['lɔkɪt] *n* medallón *m*
lockout ['lɔkaut] *n* (*Industry*) paro *or* cierre *m* patronal, lockout *m*
locksmith ['lɔksmɪθ] *n* cerrajero(-a)
lock-up ['lɔkʌp] *n* (*prison*) cárcel *f*; (*cell*) jaula; (*also*: **lock-up garage**) jaula, cochera
locomotive [ləukə'məutɪv] *n* locomotora
locum ['ləukəm] *n* (*Med*) (médico(-a)) suplente *m(f)*
locust ['ləukəst] *n* langosta
lodge [lɔdʒ] *n* casa del guarda; (*porter's*) portería; (*Freemasonry*) logia ■ *vi* (*person*): **to ~ (with)** alojarse (en casa de) ■ *vt* (*complaint*) presentar
lodger ['lɔdʒəʳ] *n* huésped(a) *m(f)*
lodging house ['lɔdʒɪŋ-] *n* pensión *f*, casa de huéspedes
lodgings ['lɔdʒɪŋz] *npl* alojamiento *sg*; (*house*) casa *sg* de huéspedes
loft [lɔft] *n* desván *m*
lofty ['lɔftɪ] *adj* alto; (*haughty*) altivo, arrogante; (*sentiments, aims*) elevado, noble
log [lɔg] *n* (*of wood*) leño, tronco; (*book*) = **logbook** ■ *n abbr* (= *logarithm*) log ■ *vt* anotar, registrar
▶ **log in, log on** *vi* (*Comput*) iniciar la (*or* una) sesión
▶ **log off, log out** *vi* (*Comput*) finalizar la sesión
logarithm ['lɔgərɪðəm] *n* logaritmo
logbook ['lɔgbuk] *n* (*Naut*) diario de a bordo; (*Aviat*) libro de vuelo; (*of car*) documentación *f* (del coche)
log cabin *n* cabaña de troncos
log fire *n* fuego de leña
logger ['lɔgəʳ] *n* leñador(a) *m(f)*
loggerheads ['lɔgəhɛdz] *npl*: **at ~ (with)** de pique (con)
logic ['lɔdʒɪk] *n* lógica
logical ['lɔdʒɪkl] *adj* lógico
logically ['lɔdʒɪkəlɪ] *adv* lógicamente
login ['lɔgɪn] *n* login *m*
logistics [lɔ'dʒɪstɪks] *n* logística
log jam *n*: **to break the ~** poner fin al estancamiento
logo ['ləugəu] *n* logotipo
loin [lɔɪn] *n* (*Culin*) lomo, solomillo; **loins** *npl* lomos *mpl*
loin cloth *n* taparrabos *m inv*
loiter ['lɔɪtəʳ] *vi* vagar; (*pej*) merodear
loll [lɔl] *vi* (*also*: **loll about**) repantigarse
lollipop ['lɔlɪpɔp] *n* pirulí *m*; (*iced*) polo
lollipop lady *n* (*Brit*) *ver nota*
lollipop man *n* (*Brit*) *ver nota*

LOLLIPOP LADY, LOLLIPOP MAN

Se llama *lollipop man* o *lollipop lady* a la persona encargada de parar el tráfico en las carreteras cercanas a los colegios británicos para que los niños las crucen sin peligro. Suelen ser personas ya jubiladas, vestidas con un abrigo de color luminoso y llevando una señal de stop en un poste portátil, la cual recuerda por su forma a un chupachups, de ahí su nombre.

lollop ['lɔləp] *vi* (*Brit*) moverse desgarbadamente
lolly ['lɔlɪ] *n* (*col*: *ice cream*) polo; (: *lollipop*) piruleta; (: *money*) guita
London ['lʌndən] *n* Londres *m*
Londoner ['lʌndənəʳ] *n* londinense *m/f*
lone [ləun] *adj* solitario
loneliness ['ləunlɪnɪs] *n* soledad *f*, aislamiento
lonely ['ləunlɪ] *adj* solitario, solo
lonely hearts *adj*: **~ ad** anuncio de la sección de contactos; **~ column** sección *f* de contactos
lone parent family *n* familia monoparental
loner ['ləunəʳ] *n* solitario(-a)
lonesome ['ləunsəm] *adj* (*esp US*) = **lonely**
long [lɔŋ] *adj* largo ■ *adv* mucho tiempo, largamente ■ *vi*: **to ~ for sth** anhelar algo ■ *n*: **the ~ and the short of it is that ...** (*fig*) en resumidas cuentas ...; **in the ~ run** a la larga; **so** *or* **as ~ as** mientras, con tal de que; **don't be ~!** ¡no tardes!, ¡vuelve pronto!; **how ~ is the street?** ¿cuánto tiene la calle de largo?; **how ~ is the lesson?** ¿cuánto dura la clase?; **six metres ~** que mide seis metros, de seis metros de largo; **six months ~** que dura seis meses, de seis meses de duración; **all night ~** toda la noche; **~ ago** hace mucho (tiempo); **he no longer comes** ya no viene; **~ before** mucho antes; **before ~** (+ *future*) dentro de poco; (+ *past*) poco tiempo después; **at ~ last** al fin, por fin; **I shan't be ~** termino pronto
long-distance [lɔŋ'dɪstəns] *adj* (*race*) de larga distancia; (*call*) interurbano
longevity [lɔn'dʒɛvɪtɪ] *n* longevidad *f*
long-haired ['lɔŋ'hɛəd] *adj* de pelo largo
longhand ['lɔŋhænd] *n* escritura (corriente)
longing ['lɔŋɪŋ] *n* anhelo, ansia; (*nostalgia*) nostalgia ■ *adj* anhelante
longingly ['lɔŋɪŋlɪ] *adv* con ansia
longitude ['lɔŋgɪtju:d] *n* longitud *f*
long jump *n* salto de longitud
long-lost ['lɔŋlɔst] *adj* desaparecido hace mucho tiempo

long-playing record ['lɔŋpleɪɪŋ-] *n* elepé *m*, disco de larga duración
long-range ['lɔŋ'reɪndʒ] *adj* de gran alcance; (*weather forecast*) a largo plazo
longshoreman ['lɔŋʃɔ:mən] *n* (*US*) estibador *m*
long-sighted ['lɔŋ'saɪtɪd] *adj* (*Brit*) présbita
long-standing ['lɔŋ'stændɪŋ] *adj* de mucho tiempo
long-suffering [lɔŋ'sʌfərɪŋ] *adj* sufrido
long-term ['lɔŋtə:m] *adj* a largo plazo
long wave *n* onda larga
long-winded [lɔŋ'wɪndɪd] *adj* prolijo
loo [lu:] *n* (*Brit: col*) wáter *m*
loofah ['lu:fə] *n* esponja de lufa
look [luk] *vi* mirar; (*seem*) parecer; (*building etc*): **to ~ south/on to the sea** dar al sur/al mar ■ *n* mirada; (*glance*) vistazo; (*appearance*) aire *m*, aspecto; **looks** *npl* físico *sg*, belleza *sg*; **to ~ ahead** mirar hacia delante; **it looks about four metres long** yo calculo que tiene unos cuarto metros de largo; **it looks all right to me** a mí me parece que está bien; **to have a ~ at sth** echar un vistazo a algo; **to have a ~ for sth** buscar algo
▸ **look after** *vt fus* cuidar
▸ **look around** *vi* echar una mirada alrededor
▸ **look at** *vt fus* mirar; (*consider*) considerar
▸ **look back** *vi* mirar hacia atrás; **to ~ back at sb/sth** mirar hacia atrás algo/a algn; **to ~ back on** (*event, period*) recordar
▸ **look down on** *vt fus* (*fig*) despreciar, mirar con desprecio
▸ **look for** *vt fus* buscar
▸ **look forward to** *vt fus* esperar con ilusión; (*in letters*): **we ~ forward to hearing from you** quedamos a la espera de su respuesta *or* contestación; **I'm not looking forward to it** no tengo ganas de eso, no me hace ilusión
▸ **look in** *vi*: **to ~ in on sb** (*visit*) pasar por casa de algn
▸ **look into** *vt fus* investigar
▸ **look on** *vi* mirar (como espectador)
▸ **look out** *vi* (*beware*): **to ~ out (for)** tener cuidado (de)
▸ **look out for** *vt fus* (*seek*) buscar; (*await*) esperar
▸ **look over** *vt* (*essay*) revisar; (*town, building*) inspeccionar, registrar; (*person*) examinar
▸ **look round** *vi* (*turn*) volver la cabeza; **to ~ round for sth** buscar algo
▸ **look through** *vt fus* (*papers, book*) hojear; (*briefly*) echar un vistazo a; (*telescope*) mirar por
▸ **look to** *vt fus* ocuparse de; (*rely on*) contar con
▸ **look up** *vi* mirar hacia arriba; (*improve*) mejorar ■ *vt* (*word*) buscar; (*friend*) visitar
▸ **look up to** *vt fus* admirar
look-out ['lukaut] *n* (*tower etc*) puesto de observación; (*person*) vigía *m/f*; **to be on the ~ for sth** estar al acecho de algo
look-up table ['lukʌp-] *n* (*Comput*) tabla de consulta
loom [lu:m] *n* telar *m* ■ *vi* (*threaten*) amenazar
loony ['lu:nɪ] *adj, n* (*col*) loco(-a) *m(f)*
loop [lu:p] *n* lazo; (*bend*) vuelta, recodo; (*Comput*) bucle *m*
loophole ['lu:phəul] *n* laguna
loose [lu:s] *adj* (*gen*) suelto; (*not tight*) flojo; (*wobbly etc*) movedizo; (*clothes*) ancho; (*morals, discipline*) relajado ■ *vt* (*free*) soltar; (*slacken*) aflojar; (*also*: **loose off**: *arrow*) disparar, soltar; **~ connection** (*Elec*) hilo desempalmado; **to be at a ~ end** *or* (*US*) **at ~ ends** no saber qué hacer; **to tie up ~ ends** (*fig*) no dejar ningún cabo suelto, atar cabos
loose change *n* cambio
loose chippings [-'tʃɪpɪŋz] *npl* (*on road*) gravilla *sg* suelta
loose-fitting ['lu:sfɪtɪŋ] *adj* suelto
loose-leaf ['lu:sli:f] *adj*: **~ binder** *or* **folder** carpeta de anillas
loose-limbed ['lu:slɪmd] *adj* ágil, suelto
loosely ['lu:slɪ] *adv* libremente, aproximadamente
loosely-knit [-nɪt] *adj* de estructura abierta
loosen ['lu:sn] *vt* (*free*) soltar; (*untie*) desatar; (*slacken*) aflojar
▸ **loosen up** *vi* (*before game*) hacer (ejercicios de) precalentamiento; (*col: relax*) soltarse, relajarse
looseness ['lu:snɪs] *n* soltura; flojedad *f*
loot [lu:t] *n* botín *m* ■ *vt* saquear
looter ['lu:tə^r] *n* saqueador(a) *m(f)*
looting ['lu:tɪŋ] *n* pillaje *m*
lop [lɔp]: **to ~ off** *vt* cortar; (*branches*) podar
lop-sided ['lɔp'saɪdɪd] *adj* desequilibrado
lord [lɔ:d] *n* señor *m*; **L~ Smith** Lord Smith; **the L~** el Señor; **the (House of) Lords** (*Brit*) la Cámara de los Lores
lordly ['lɔ:dlɪ] *adj* señorial
Lordship ['lɔ:dʃɪp] *n*: **your ~** su Señoría
lore [lɔ:^{r}] *n* saber *m* popular, tradiciones *fpl*
lorry ['lɔrɪ] *n* (*Brit*) camión *m*
lorry driver *n* camionero(-a)
lorry load *n* carga
lose (*pt, pp* **lost**) [lu:z, lɔst] *vt* perder ■ *vi* perder, ser vencido; **to ~ (time)** (*clock*) atrasarse; **to ~ no time (in doing sth)** no tardar (en hacer algo); **to get lost** (*object*) extraviarse; (*person*) perderse
▸ **lose out** *vi* salir perdiendo

loser ['lu:zə^r] *n* perdedor(a) *m(f)*; **to be a bad ~** no saber perder
losing ['lu:zɪŋ] *adj* (*team etc*) vencido, perdedor(a)
loss [lɔs] *n* pérdida; **heavy losses** (*Mil*) grandes pérdidas *fpl*; **to be at a ~** no saber qué hacer; **to be a dead ~** ser completamente inútil; **to cut one's losses** reducir las pérdidas; **to sell sth at a ~** vender algo perdiendo dinero
loss adjuster *n* (*Insurance*) perito(-a) *m(f)* *or* tasador(-a) *m/f* de pérdidas
loss leader *n* (*Comm*) artículo de promoción
lost [lɔst] *pt, pp of* **lose** ■ *adj* perdido; **~ in thought** absorto, ensimismado
lost and found *n* (*US*) = **lost property; lost property office** *or* **department**
lost cause *n* causa perdida
lost property *n* (*Brit*) objetos *mpl* perdidos
lost property office *or* **department** *n* (*Brit*) departamento de objetos perdidos
lot [lɔt] *n* (*at auction*) lote *m*; (*destiny*) suerte *f*; **the ~** el todo, todos *mpl*, todas *fpl*; **a ~** mucho, bastante; **a ~ of, lots of** muchos(-as), mucho(-a) *adj sg*; **I read a ~** leo bastante; **to draw lots (for sth)** echar suertes (para decidir algo)
lotion ['ləuʃən] *n* loción *f*
lottery ['lɔtərɪ] *n* lotería
loud [laud] *adj* (*voice, sound*) fuerte; (*laugh, shout*) estrepitoso; (*gaudy*) chillón(-ona) ■ *adv* (*speak etc*) fuerte; **out ~** en voz alta
loudhailer [laud'heɪlə^r] *n* (*Brit*) megáfono
loudly ['laudlɪ] *adv* (*noisily*) fuerte; (*aloud*) en alta voz
loudness ['laudnɪs] *n* (*of sound etc*) fuerza
loudspeaker [laud'spi:kə^r] *n* altavoz *m*
lounge [laundʒ] *n* salón *m*, sala de estar; (*of hotel*) salón *m*; (*of airport*) sala de embarque ■ *vi* (*also*: **lounge about, lounge around**) holgazanear, no hacer nada; *see also* **pub**
lounge bar *n* salón *m*
lounge suit *n* (*Brit*) traje *m* de calle
louse (*pl* **lice**) [laus, laɪs] *n* piojo
▸ **louse up** *vt* (*col*) echar a perder
lousy ['lauzɪ] *adj* (*fig*) vil, asqueroso
lout [laut] *n* gamberro(-a)
louvre, louver (*US*) ['lu:və^r] *adj*: **~ door** puerta de rejilla; **~ window** ventana de libro
lovable ['lʌvəbl] *adj* amable, simpático
love [lʌv] *n* amor *m* ■ *vt* amar, querer; **to send one's ~ to sb** dar sus recuerdos a algn; **~ from Anne** (*in letter*) con cariño de Anne; **I ~ to read** me encanta leer; **to be in ~ with** estar enamorado de; **to make ~** hacer el amor; **for the ~ of** por amor a; **"15 ~"** (*Tennis*) "15 a cero"; **I ~ paella** me encanta la paella; **I'd ~ to come** me gustaría muchísimo venir
love affair *n* aventura sentimental *or* amorosa
love child *n* hijo(-a) natural
loved ones ['lʌvdwʌnz] *npl* seres *mpl* queridos
love-hate relationship ['lʌvheɪt-] *n* relación *f* de amor y odio
love letter *n* carta de amor
love life *n* vida sentimental
lovely ['lʌvlɪ] *adj* (*delightful*) precioso, encantador(a), lindo (*esp LAm*); (*beautiful*) hermoso, lindo (*esp LAm*); **we had a ~ time** lo pasamos estupendo
lovemaking ['lʌvmeɪkɪŋ] *n* relaciones *fpl* sexuales
lover ['lʌvə^r] *n* amante *m/f*; (*amateur*): **a ~ of** un(a) aficionado(-a) *or* un(a) amante de
lovesick ['lʌvsɪk] *adj* enfermo de amor, amartelado
lovesong ['lʌvsɔŋ] *n* canción *f* de amor
loving ['lʌvɪŋ] *adj* amoroso, cariñoso
lovingly ['lʌvɪŋlɪ] *adv* amorosamente, cariñosamente
low [ləu] *adj, adv* bajo ■ *n* (*Meteorology*) área de baja presión ■ *vi* (*cow*) mugir; **to feel ~** sentirse deprimido; **to turn (down) ~** bajar; **to reach a new** *or* **an all-time ~** llegar a su punto más bajo
low-alcohol [ləu'ælkəhɔl] *adj* bajo en alcohol
lowbrow ['ləubrau] *adj* (*person*) de poca cultura
low-calorie ['ləu'kælərɪ] *adj* bajo en calorías
low-cut ['ləukʌt] *adj* (*dress*) escotado
low-down ['ləudaun] *n* (*col*): **he gave me the ~ on it** me puso al corriente ■ *adj* (*mean*) vil, bajo
lower ['ləuə^r] *vt* bajar; (*reduce: price*) reducir, rebajar; (*: resistance*) debilitar; **to ~ o.s. to** (*fig*) rebajarse a ■ *vi* ['lauə^r]: **to ~ (at sb)** fulminar (a algn) con la mirada
lower case *n* (*Typ*) minúscula
Lower House *n* (*Pol*): **the ~** la Cámara baja
lowering ['lauərɪŋ] *adj* (*sky*) amenazador(a)
low-fat ['ləu'fæt] *adj* (*milk, yoghurt*) desnatado; (*diet*) bajo en calorías
low-key ['ləu'ki:] *adj* de mínima intensidad; (*operation*) de poco perfil
lowland ['ləulənd] *n* tierra baja
low-level ['ləulɛvl] *adj* de bajo nivel; (*flying*) a poca altura
low-loader ['ləuləudə^r] *n* camión *m* de caja a bajo nivel
lowly ['ləulɪ] *adj* humilde
low-lying [ləu'laɪɪŋ] *adj* bajo
low-rise ['ləuraɪz] *adj* bajo
low-tech ['ləutɛk] *adj* de baja tecnología, tradicional

loyal ['lɔɪəl] *adj* leal
loyalist ['lɔɪəlɪst] *n* legitimista *m/f*
loyally ['lɔɪəlɪ] *adv* lealmente
loyalty ['lɔɪəltɪ] *n* lealtad *f*
loyalty card *n* (*Brit*) tarjeta cliente
lozenge ['lɔzɪndʒ] *n* (*Med*) pastilla
LP *n abbr* (= *long-playing record*) elepé *m*
LPG *n abbr* (= *liquefied petroleum gas*) GLP *m* (= *Gas Licuado de Petróleo*)
L-plates ['ɛlpleɪts] *npl* (*Brit*) (placas *fpl* de) la L; *ver nota*

L-PLATES

En el Reino Unido las personas que están aprendiendo a conducir han de llevar indicativos blancos con una L en rojo llamados normalmente *L-plates* (de "learner") en la parte delantera y trasera de los automóviles que conducen. No tienen que ir a clases teóricas, sino que desde el principio se les entrega un carnet de conducir provisional ("provisional driving licence") para que realicen sus prácticas, que han de estar supervisadas por un conductor con carnet definitivo ("full driving licence"). Tampoco se les permite hacer prácticas en autopistas aunque vayan acompañados.

LPN *n abbr* (*US*: = *Licensed Practical Nurse*) enfermero(-a) practicante
LRAM *n abbr* (*Brit*) = **Licentiate of the Royal Academy of Music**
LSAT *n abbr* (*US*) = **Law School Admissions Test**
LSD *n abbr* (= *lysergic acid diethylamide*) LSD *m*; (*Brit*: = *pounds, shillings and pence*) *sistema monetario usado en Gran Bretaña hasta 1971*
LSE *n abbr* = **London School of Economics**
LT *abbr* (*Elec*) = **low tension**
Lt. *abbr* (= *lieutenant*) Tte.
Ltd *abbr* (*Comm*) = **limited**
lubricant ['lu:brɪkənt] *n* lubricante *m*
lubricate ['lu:brɪkeɪt] *vt* lubricar, engrasar
lubrication [lu:brɪ'keɪʃən] *n* lubricación *f*
lucid ['lu:sɪd] *adj* lúcido
lucidity [lu:'sɪdɪtɪ] *n* lucidez *f*
lucidly ['lu:sɪdlɪ] *adv* lúcidamente
luck [lʌk] *n* suerte *f*; **good/bad ~** buena/mala suerte; **good ~!** ¡(que tengas) suerte!; **to be in ~** estar de suerte; **to be out of ~** tener mala suerte
luckily ['lʌkɪlɪ] *adv* afortunadamente
luckless ['lʌklɪs] *adj* desafortunado
lucky ['lʌkɪ] *adj* afortunado
lucrative ['lu:krətɪv] *adj* lucrativo
ludicrous ['lu:dɪkrəs] *adj* absurdo
ludo ['lu:dəu] *n* parchís *m*
lug [lʌg] *vt* (*drag*) arrastrar
luggage ['lʌgɪdʒ] *n* equipaje *m*
luggage rack *n* (*in train*) rejilla, redecilla; (*on car*) baca, portaequipajes *m inv*
luggage van *n* furgón *m or* vagón *m* de equipaje
lugubrious [lu'gu:brɪəs] *adj* lúgubre
lukewarm ['lu:kwɔ:m] *adj* tibio, templado
lull [lʌl] *n* tregua ■ *vt* (*child*) acunar; (*person, fear*) calmar
lullaby ['lʌləbaɪ] *n* nana
lumbago [lʌm'beɪgəu] *n* lumbago
lumber ['lʌmbə^r] *n* (*junk*) trastos *mpl* viejos; (*wood*) maderos *mpl* ■ *vt* (*Brit col*): **to ~ sb with sth/sb** hacer que algn cargue con algo/algn ■ *vi* (*also*: **lumber about, lumber along**) moverse pesadamente
lumberjack ['lʌmbədʒæk] *n* maderero
lumber room *n* (*Brit*) cuarto trastero
lumber yard *n* (*US*) almacén *m* de madera
luminous ['lu:mɪnəs] *adj* luminoso
lump [lʌmp] *n* terrón *m*; (*fragment*) trozo; (*in sauce*) grumo; (*in throat*) nudo; (*swelling*) bulto ■ *vt* (*also*: **lump together**) juntar; (*persons*) poner juntos
lump sum *n* suma global
lumpy ['lʌmpɪ] *adj* (*sauce*) lleno de grumos
lunacy ['lu:nəsɪ] *n* locura
lunar ['lu:nə^r] *adj* lunar
lunatic ['lu:nətɪk] *adj, n* loco(-a) *m(f)*
lunatic asylum *n* manicomio
lunch [lʌntʃ] *n* almuerzo, comida ■ *vi* almorzar; **to invite sb to** *or* **for ~** invitar a algn a almorzar
lunch break, lunch hour *n* hora del almuerzo
luncheon ['lʌntʃən] *n* almuerzo
luncheon meat *n tipo de fiambre*
luncheon voucher *n* vale *m* de comida
lunchtime ['lʌntʃtaɪm] *n* hora del almuerzo *or* de comer
lung [lʌŋ] *n* pulmón *m*
lung cancer *n* cáncer *m* del pulmón
lunge [lʌndʒ] *vi* (*also*: **lunge forward**) abalanzarse; **to ~ at** arremeter contra
lupin ['lu:pɪn] *n* altramuz *m*
lurch [lə:tʃ] *vi* dar sacudidas ■ *n* sacudida; **to leave sb in the ~** dejar a algn plantado
lure [luə^r] *n* (*bait*) cebo; (*decoy*) señuelo ■ *vt* convencer con engaños
lurid ['luərɪd] *adj* (*colour*) chillón(-ona); (*account*) sensacional; (*detail*) horripilante
lurk [lə:k] *vi* (*hide*) esconderse; (*wait*) estar al acecho
luscious ['lʌʃəs] *adj* delicioso

lush [lʌʃ] *adj* exuberante
lust [lʌst] *n* lujuria; (*greed*) codicia
▸ **lust after** *vt fus* codiciar
lustful ['lʌstful] *adj* lascivo, lujurioso
lustre, luster (*US*) ['lʌstəʳ] *n* lustre *m*, brillo
lustrous ['lʌstrəs] *adj* brillante
lusty ['lʌstɪ] *adj* robusto, fuerte
lute [lu:t] *n* laúd *m*
Luxembourg ['lʌksəmbə:g] *n* Luxemburgo
luxuriant [lʌg'zjuərɪənt] *adj* exuberante
luxurious [lʌg'zjuərɪəs] *adj* lujoso
luxury ['lʌkʃərɪ] *n* lujo ■ *cpd* de lujo
luxury tax *n* impuesto de lujo
LV *n abbr* (*Brit*) = **luncheon voucher**
LW *abbr* (*Radio*) = **long wave**
Lycra® ['laɪkrə] *n* licra®
lying ['laɪɪŋ] *n* mentiras *fpl* ■ *adj* (*statement, story*) falso; (*person*) mentiroso
lynch [lɪntʃ] *vt* linchar
lynx [lɪŋks] *n* lince *m*
Lyons ['laɪənz] *n* Lyón *m*
lyre ['laɪəʳ] *n* lira
lyric ['lɪrɪk] *adj* lírico; **lyrics** *npl* (*of song*) letra *sg*
lyrical ['lɪrɪkl] *adj* lírico

Mm

M, m [ɛm] *n* (*letter*) M, m *f*; **M for Mary,** (*US*) **M for Mike** M de Madrid
M *n abbr* (*Brit:* = *motorway*): **the M8** ≈ la A8; = **million; millions** ■ *abbr* (= *medium*) M
m *abbr* (= *metre*) m.; = **mile; miles**
MA *n abbr* (*Scol*) *see* **Master of Arts**; (*US*) = **Military Academy** ■ *abbr* (*US*) = **Massachusetts**
mac [mæk] *n* (*Brit*) impermeable *m*
macabre [mə'kɑːbrə] *adj* macabro
macaroni [mækə'rəunɪ] *n* macarrones *mpl*
macaroon [mækə'ruːn] *n* macarrac *m*, mostachón *m*
mace [meɪs] *n* (*weapon, ceremonial*) maza; (*spice*) macis *f*
Macedonia [mæsɪ'dəunɪə] *n* Macedonia
Macedonian [mæsɪ'dəunɪən] *adj* macedonio ■ *n* macedonio(-a); (*Ling*) macedonio
machinations [mæʃɪ'neɪʃənz] *npl* intrigas *fpl*, maquinaciones *fpl*
machine [mə'ʃiːn] *n* máquina ■ *vt* (*dress etc*) coser a máquina; (*Tech*) trabajar a máquina
machine code *n* (*Comput*) código máquina
machine gun *n* ametralladora
machine language *n* (*Comput*) lenguaje *m* máquina
machine readable *adj* (*Comput*) legible por máquina
machinery [mə'ʃiːnərɪ] *n* maquinaria; (*fig*) mecanismo
machine shop *n* taller *m* de máquinas
machine tool *n* máquina herramienta
machine translation *n* traducción *f* automática
machine washable *adj* lavable a máquina
machinist [mə'ʃiːnɪst] *n* operario(-a) *m(f)* (de máquina)
macho ['mætʃəu] *adj* macho
mackerel ['mækrl] *n pl inv* caballa
mackintosh ['mækɪntɔʃ] *n* (*Brit*) impermeable *m*
macro ... ['mækrəu] *pref* macro...
macro-economics ['mækrəuiːkə'nɔmɪks] *n* macroeconomía
mad [mæd] *adj* loco; (*idea*) disparatado; (*angry*) furioso, enojado (*LAm*); **~ (at** *or* **with sb)** furioso (con algn); **to be ~ (keen) about** *or* **on sth** estar loco por algo; **to go ~** volverse loco, enloquecer(se)
madam ['mædəm] *n* señora; **can I help you, ~?** ¿le puedo ayudar, señora?; **M~ Chairman** señora presidenta
madcap ['mædkæp] *adj* (*col*) alocado, disparatado
mad cow disease *n* encefalopatía espongiforme bovina
madden ['mædn] *vt* volver loco
maddening ['mædnɪŋ] *adj* enloquecedor(a)
made [meɪd] *pt, pp of* **make**
Madeira [mə'dɪərə] *n* (*Geo*) Madeira; (*wine*) madeira *m*
made-to-measure ['meɪdtəmɛʒə^r] *adj* (*Brit*) hecho a la medida
made-up ['meɪdʌp] *adj* (*story*) ficticio
madhouse ['mædhaus] *n* (*also fig*) manicomio
madly ['mædlɪ] *adv* locamente
madman ['mædmən] *n* loco
madness ['mædnɪs] *n* locura
Madonna [mə'dɔnə] *n* Virgen *f*
Madrid [mə'drɪd] *n* Madrid *m*
madrigal ['mædrɪgəl] *n* madrigal *m*
Mafia ['mæfɪə] *n* Mafia
mag [mæg] *n abbr* (*Brit col*) = **magazine**
magazine [mægə'ziːn] *n* revista; (*Mil: store*) almacén *m*; (*of firearm*) recámara
maggot ['mægət] *n* gusano
magic ['mædʒɪk] *n* magia ■ *adj* mágico
magical ['mædʒɪkəl] *adj* mágico
magician [mə'dʒɪʃən] *n* mago(-a)
magistrate ['mædʒɪstreɪt] *n* juez *m/f* (municipal); **Magistrates' Court** (*Brit*) *see* **crown court**
magnanimity [mægnə'nɪmɪtɪ] *n* magnanimidad *f*

magnanimous [mæg'nænɪməs] *adj* magnánimo
magnate ['mægneɪt] *n* magnate *m/f*
magnesium [mæg'ni:zɪəm] *n* magnesio
magnet ['mægnɪt] *n* imán *m*
magnetic [mæg'nɛtɪk] *adj* magnético
magnetic disk *n* (*Comput*) disco magnético
magnetic tape *n* cinta magnética
magnetism ['mægnɪtɪzəm] *n* magnetismo
magnification [mægnɪfɪ'keɪʃən] *n* aumento
magnificence [mæg'nɪfɪsns] *n* magnificencia
magnificent [mæg'nɪfɪsnt] *adj* magnífico
magnificently [mæg'nɪfɪsntlɪ] *adv* magníficamente
magnify ['mægnɪfaɪ] *vt* aumentar; (*fig*) exagerar
magnifying glass ['mægnɪfaɪɪŋ-] *n* lupa
magnitude ['mægnɪtju:d] *n* magnitud *f*
magnolia [mæg'nəulɪə] *n* magnolia
magpie ['mægpaɪ] *n* urraca
maharajah [mɑ:hə'rɑ:dʒə] *n* maharajá *m*
mahogany [mə'hɔgənɪ] *n* caoba ■ *cpd* de caoba
maid [meɪd] *n* criada; **old ~** (*pej*) solterona
maiden ['meɪdn] *n* doncella ■ *adj* (*aunt etc*) solterona; (*speech, voyage*) inaugural
maiden name *n* apellido de soltera
mail [meɪl] *n* correo; (*letters*) cartas *fpl* ■ *vt* (*post*) echar al correo; (*send*) mandar por correo; **by ~** por correo
mailbox ['meɪlbɔks] *n* (*US: for letters etc: Comput*) buzón *m*
mailing list ['meɪlɪŋ-] *n* lista de direcciones
mailman ['meɪlmæn] *n* (*US*) cartero
mail-order ['meɪlɔ:dəʳ] *n* pedido postal; (*business*) venta por correo ■ *adj*: **~ firm** *or* **house** casa de venta por correo
mailshot ['meɪlʃɔt] *n* mailing *m inv*
mailtrain ['meɪltreɪn] *n* tren *m* correo
mail van, mail truck (*US*) *n* (*Aut*) camioneta de correos *or* de reparto
maim [meɪm] *vt* mutilar, lisiar
main [meɪn] *adj* principal, mayor ■ *n* (*pipe*) cañería principal *or* maestra; (*US*) red *f* eléctrica; **the mains** (*Brit Elec*) la red eléctrica; **in the ~** en general
main course *n* (*Culin*) plato principal
mainframe ['meɪnfreɪm] *n* (*also*: **mainframe computer**) ordenador *m or* computadora central
mainland ['meɪnlənd] *n* continente *m*
main line *n* línea principal
mainly ['meɪnlɪ] *adv* principalmente, en su mayoría
main road *n* carretera principal
mainstay ['meɪnsteɪ] *n* (*fig*) pilar *m*
mainstream ['meɪnstri:m] *n* (*fig*) corriente *f* principal
main street *n* calle *f* mayor
maintain [meɪn'teɪn] *vt* mantener; (*affirm*) sostener; **to ~ that ...** mantener *or* sostener que ...
maintenance ['meɪntənəns] *n* mantenimiento; (*alimony*) pensión *f* alimenticia
maintenance contract *n* contrato de mantenimiento
maintenance order *n* (*Law*) obligación *f* de pagar una pensión alimenticia al cónyuge
maisonette [meɪzə'nɛt] *n* dúplex *m*
maize [meɪz] *n* (*Brit*) maíz *m*, choclo (*LAm*)
Maj. *abbr* (*Mil*) = **major**
majestic [mə'dʒɛstɪk] *adj* majestuoso
majesty ['mædʒɪstɪ] *n* majestad *f*
major ['meɪdʒəʳ] *n* (*Mil*) comandante *m* ■ *adj* principal; (*Mus*) mayor ■ *vi* (*US Univ*): **to ~ in** especializarse en; **a ~ operation** una operación *or* intervención de gran importancia
Majorca [mə'jɔ:kə] *n* Mallorca
major general *n* (*Mil*) general *m* de división
majority [mə'dʒɔrɪtɪ] *n* mayoría ■ *cpd* (*verdict*) mayoritario
majority holding *n* (*Comm*): **to have a ~** tener un interés mayoritario
make [meɪk] *vt* (*pt, pp* **made** [meɪd]) hacer; (*manufacture*) hacer, fabricar; (*cause to be*): **to ~ sb sad** poner triste *or* entristecer a algn; (*force*): **to ~ sb do sth** obligar a algn a hacer algo; (*equal*): **2 and 2 ~ 4** 2 y 2 son 4 ■ *n* marca; **to ~ a fool of sb** poner a algn en ridículo; **to ~ a profit/loss** obtener ganancias/sufrir pérdidas; **to ~ a profit of £500** sacar una ganancia de 500 libras; **to ~ it** (*arrive*) llegar; (*achieve sth*) tener éxito; **what time do you ~ it?** ¿qué hora tienes?; **to ~ do with** contentarse con
▸**make for** *vt fus* (*place*) dirigirse a
▸**make off** *vi* largarse
▸**make out** *vt* (*decipher*) descifrar; (*understand*) entender; (*see*) distinguir; (*write: cheque*) extender; **to ~ out (that)** (*claim, imply*) dar a entender (que); **to ~ out a case for sth** dar buenas razones en favor de algo
▸**make over** *vt* (*assign*): **to ~ over (to)** ceder *or* traspasar (a)
▸**make up** *vt* (*invent*) inventar; (*parcel*) hacer ■ *vi* reconciliarse; (*with cosmetics*) maquillarse; **to be made up of** estar compuesto de
▸**make up for** *vt fus* compensar
make-believe ['meɪkbɪli:v] *n* ficción *f*, fantasía

maker ['meɪkəʳ] *n* fabricante *m/f*
makeshift ['meɪkʃɪft] *adj* improvisado
make-up ['meɪkʌp] *n* maquillaje *m*
make-up bag *n* bolsita del maquillaje *or* de los cosméticos
make-up remover *n* desmaquillador *m*
making ['meɪkɪŋ] *n* (*fig*): **in the ~** en vías de formación; **to have the makings of** (*person*) tener madera de
maladjusted [mælə'dʒʌstɪd] *adj* inadaptado
maladroit [maelə'drɔɪt] *adj* torpe
malaise [mæ'leɪz] *n* malestar *m*
malaria [mə'lɛərɪə] *n* malaria
Malawi [mə'lɑːwɪ] *n* Malawi *m*
Malay [mə'leɪ] *adj* malayo ■ *n* malayo(-a); (*Ling*) malayo
Malaya [mə'leɪə] *n* Malaya, Malaca
Malayan [mə'leɪən] *adj, n* = **Malay**
Malaysia [mə'leɪzɪə] *n* Malaisia, Malaysia
Malaysian [mə'leɪzɪən] *adj, n* malaisio(-a) *m(f)*, malaysio(-a) *m(f)*
Maldive Islands ['mɔːldaɪv-], **Maldives** ['mɔːldaɪvz] *npl*: **the ~** las Maldivas
male [meɪl] *n* (*Biol, Elec*) macho ■ *adj* (*sex, attitude*) masculino; (*child etc*) varón
male chauvinist, male chauvinist pig *n* machista *m*
male nurse *n* enfermero
malevolence [mə'lɛvələns] *n* malevolencia
malevolent [mə'lɛvələnt] *adj* malévolo
malfunction [mæl'fʌŋkʃən] *n* mal funcionamiento
malice ['mælɪs] *n* (*ill will*) malicia; (*rancour*) rencor *m*
malicious [mə'lɪʃəs] *adj* malicioso; rencoroso
maliciously [mə'lɪʃəslɪ] *adv* con malevolencia, con malicia; rencorosamente
malign [mə'laɪn] *vt* difamar, calumniar ■ *adj* maligno
malignant [mə'lɪgnənt] *adj* (*Med*) maligno
malinger [mə'lɪŋgəʳ] *vi* fingirse enfermo
malingerer [mə'lɪŋgərəʳ] *n* enfermo(-a) fingido(-a)
mall [mɔːl] *n* (*US: also:* **shopping mall**) centro comercial
malleable ['mælɪəbl] *adj* maleable
mallet ['mælɪt] *n* mazo
malnutrition [mælnjuː'trɪʃən] *n* desnutrición *f*
malpractice [mæl'præktɪs] *n* negligencia profesional
malt [mɔːlt] *n* malta
Malta ['mɔːltə] *n* Malta
Maltese [mɔːl'tiːz] *adj* maltés(-esa) ■ *n* (*pl inv*) maltés(-esa) *m(f)*; (*Ling*) maltés *m*
maltreat [mæl'triːt] *vt* maltratar
mammal ['mæml] *n* mamífero
mammoth ['mæməθ] *n* mamut *m* ■ *adj* gigantesco
man (*pl* **men**) [mæn, mɛn] *n* hombre *m*; (*Chess*) pieza ■ *vt* (*Naut*) tripular; (*Mil*) defender; **an old ~** un viejo; **~ and wife** marido y mujer
Man. *abbr* (*Canada*) = **Manitoba**
manacle ['mænəkl] *n* esposa, manilla; **manacles** *npl* grillos *mpl*
manage ['mænɪdʒ] *vi* arreglárselas ■ *vt* (*be in charge of*) dirigir; (*person etc*) manejar; **to ~ to do sth** conseguir hacer algo; **to ~ without sth/sb** poder prescindir de algo/algn
manageable ['mænɪdʒəbl] *adj* manejable
management ['mænɪdʒmənt] *n* dirección *f*, administración *f*; **"under new ~"** "bajo nueva dirección"
management accounting *n* contabilidad *f* de gestión
management buyout *n* adquisición *f* por parte de la dirección
management consultant *n* consultor(a) *m(f)* en dirección de empresas
manager ['mænɪdʒəʳ] *n* director(a) *m(f)*; (*Sport*) entrenador(a) *m(f)*; **sales ~** jefe(-a) *m(f)* de ventas
manageress ['mænɪdʒərɛs] *n* directora; (*Sport*) entrenadora
managerial [mænə'dʒɪerɪəl] *adj* directivo
managing director ['mænɪdʒɪŋ-] *n* director(a) *m(f)* general
Mancunian [mæŋ'kjuːnɪən] *adj* de Manchester ■ *n* nativo(-a) *or* habitante *m(f)* de Manchester
mandarin ['mændərɪn] *n* (*also:* **mandarin orange**) mandarina; (*person*) mandarín *m*
mandate ['mændeɪt] *n* mandato
mandatory ['mændətərɪ] *adj* obligatorio
mandolin, mandoline ['mændəlɪn] *n* mandolina
mane [meɪn] *n* (*of horse*) crin *f*; (*of lion*) melena
maneuver [mə'nuːvəʳ] (*US*) = **manoeuvre**
manful ['mænful] *adj* resuelto
manfully ['mænfəlɪ] *adv* resueltamente
mangetout [mɔnʒ'tuː] *n* tirabeque *m*
mangle ['mæŋgl] *vt* mutilar, destrozar ■ *n* escurridor *m*
mango (*pl* **mangoes**) ['mæŋgəu] *n* mango
mangrove ['mæŋgrəuv] *n* mangle *m*
mangy ['meɪndʒɪ] *adj* roñoso; (*Med*) sarnoso
manhandle ['mænhændl] *vt* maltratar; (*move by hand: goods*) manipular
manhole ['mænhəul] *n* boca de acceso
manhood ['mænhud] *n* edad *f* viril; (*manliness*) virilidad *f*
man-hour ['mæn'auəʳ] *n* hora-hombre *f*
manhunt ['mænhʌnt] *n* caza de hombre

mania ['meɪnɪə] *n* manía
maniac ['meɪnɪæk] *n* maníaco(-a); (*fig*) maniático
manic ['mænɪk] *adj* (*behaviour, activity*) frenético
manic-depressive ['mænɪkdɪ'prɛsɪv] *adj, n* maniacodepresivo(-a) *m(f)*
manicure ['mænɪkjuəʳ] *n* manicura
manicure set *n* estuche *m* de manicura
manifest ['mænɪfɛst] *vt* manifestar, mostrar ■ *adj* manifiesto ■ *n* manifiesto
manifestation [mænɪfɛs'teɪʃən] *n* manifestación *f*
manifestly ['mænɪfɛstlɪ] *adv* evidentemente
manifesto [mænɪ'fɛstəu] *n* manifiesto
manifold ['mænɪfəuld] *adj* múltiples ■ *n* (*Aut etc*): **exhaust ~** colector *m* de escape
Manila [mə'nɪlə] *n* Manila
manila, manilla [mə'nɪlə] *n* (*paper, envelope*) manila
manipulate [mə'nɪpjuleɪt] *vt* manipular
manipulation [mənɪpju'leɪʃən] *n* manipulación *f*, manejo
mankind [mæn'kaɪnd] *n* humanidad *f*, género humano
manliness ['mænlɪnɪs] *n* virilidad *f*, hombría
manly ['mænlɪ] *adj* varonil
man-made ['mæn'meɪd] *adj* artificial
manna ['mænə] *n* maná *m*
mannequin ['maenɪkɪn] *n* (*dummy*) maniquí *m*; (*fashion model*) maniquí *m/f*
manner ['mænəʳ] *n* manera, modo; (*behaviour*) conducta, manera de ser; (*type*) clase *f*; **manners** *npl* modales *mpl*, educación *fsg*; **(good) manners** (buena) educación *fsg*, (buenos) modales *mpl*; **bad manners** falta *sg* de educación, pocos modales *mpl*; **all ~ of** toda clase *or* suerte de
mannerism ['mænərɪzəm] *n* gesto típico
mannerly ['mænəlɪ] *adj* bien educado, formal
manoeuvrable, maneuvrable (*US*) [mə'nu:vrəbl] *adj* (*car etc*) manejable
manoeuvre, maneuver (*US*) [mə'nu:vəʳ] *vt, vi* maniobrar ■ *n* maniobra; **to ~ sb into doing sth** manipular a algn para que haga algo
manor ['mænəʳ] *n* (*also*: **manor house**) casa solariega
manpower ['mænpauəʳ] *n* mano *f* de obra
Manpower Services Commission *n* (*Brit*) *comisión para el aprovechamiento de los recursos humanos*
manservant ['mænsə:vənt] *n* criado
mansion ['mænʃən] *n* mansión *f*
manslaughter ['mænslɔ:təʳ] *n* homicidio involuntario
mantelpiece ['mæntlpi:s] *n* repisa de la chimenea
mantle ['mæntl] *n* manto
man-to-man ['mæntə'mæn] *adj* de hombre a hombre
manual ['mænjuəl] *adj* manual ■ *n* manual *m*; **~ worker** obrero(-a), trabajador(a) *m(f)* manual
manufacture [mænju'fæktʃəʳ] *vt* fabricar ■ *n* fabricación *f*
manufactured goods [mænju'fæktʃəd-] *npl* manufacturas *fpl*, bienes *mpl* manufacturados
manufacturer [mænju'fæktʃərəʳ] *n* fabricante *m/f*
manufacturing industries [mænju'fæktʃərɪŋ-] *npl* industrias *fpl* manufactureras
manure [mə'njuəʳ] *n* estiércol *m*, abono
manuscript ['mænjuskrɪpt] *n* manuscrito
Manx [mæŋks] *adj* de la Isla de Man
many ['mɛnɪ] *adj* muchos(-as) ■ *pron* muchos(-as); **a great ~** muchísimos, un buen número de; **~ a time** muchas veces; **too ~ difficulties** demasiadas dificultades; **twice as ~** el doble; **how ~?** ¿cuántos?
Maori ['maurɪ] *adj, n* maorí *m/f*
map [mæp] *n* mapa *m* ■ *vt* trazar el mapa de
▸ **map out** *vt* (*fig: career, holiday, essay*) proyectar, planear
maple ['meɪpl] *n* arce *m*, maple *m* (*LAm*)
mar [mɑ:ʳ] *vt* estropear
Mar *abbr* (= *March*) mar
marathon ['mærəθən] *n* maratón *m* ■ *adj*: **a ~ session** una sesión maratoniana
marathon runner *n* corredor(a) *m(f)* de maratones
marauder [mə'rɔ:dəʳ] *n* merodeador(a) *m(f)*
marble ['mɑ:bl] *n* mármol *m*; (*toy*) canica
March [mɑ:tʃ] *n* marzo; *see also* **July**
march [mɑ:tʃ] *vi* (*Mil*) marchar; (*fig*) caminar con resolución ■ *n* marcha; (*demonstration*) manifestación *f*
marcher ['mɑ:tʃəʳ] *n* manifestante *m/f*
marching ['mɑ:tʃɪŋ] *n*: **to give sb his ~ orders** (*fig*) mandar a paseo a algn; (*employee*) poner de patitas en la calle a algn
march-past ['mɑ:tʃpɑ:st] *n* desfile *m*
mare [mɛəʳ] *n* yegua
margarine [mɑ:dʒə'ri:n] *n* margarina
marg(e) [mɑ:dʒ] *n abbr* (*col*) = **margarine**
margin ['mɑ:dʒɪn] *n* margen *m*
marginal ['mɑ:dʒɪnl] *adj* marginal
marginally ['mɑ:dʒɪnəlɪ] *adv* ligeramente
marginal seat *n* (*Pol*) circunscripción *f* políticamente no definida
marigold ['mærɪgəuld] *n* caléndula

marijuana [mærɪ'wɑːnə] *n* marihuana
marina [mə'riːnə] *n* marina
marinade [mærɪ'neɪd] *n* adobo
marinate ['mærɪneɪt] *vt* adobar
marine [mə'riːn] *adj* marino ■ *n* soldado de infantería de marina
marine insurance *n* seguro marítimo
mariner ['mærɪnə^r] *n* marinero, marino
marionette [mærɪə'nɛt] *n* marioneta, títere *m*
marital ['mærɪtl] *adj* matrimonial; **~ status** estado civil
maritime ['mærɪtaɪm] *adj* marítimo
marjoram ['mɑːdʒərəm] *n* mejorana
mark [mɑːk] *n* marca, señal *f*; (*imprint*) huella; (*stain*) mancha; (*Brit Scol*) nota; (*currency*) marco ■ *vt* (*Sport: player*) marcar; (*stain*) manchar; (*Brit Scol*) calificar, corregir; **punctuation marks** signos *mpl* de puntuación; **to be quick off the ~** (*fig*) ser listo; **up to the ~** (*in efficiency*) a la altura de las circunstancias; **to ~ time** marcar el paso
▸ **mark down** *vt* (*reduce: prices, goods*) rebajar
▸ **mark off** *vt* (*tick*) indicar, señalar
▸ **mark out** *vt* trazar
▸ **mark up** *vt* (*price*) aumentar
marked [mɑːkt] *adj* marcado, acusado
markedly ['mɑːkɪdlɪ] *adv* marcadamente, apreciablemente
marker ['mɑːkə^r] *n* (*sign*) marcador *m*; (*bookmark*) registro
market ['mɑːkɪt] *n* mercado ■ *vt* (*Comm*) comercializar; (*promote*) publicitar; **open ~** mercado libre; **to be on the ~** estar en venta; **to play the ~** jugar a la bolsa
marketable ['mɑːkɪtəbl] *adj* comerciable
market analysis *n* análisis *m* del mercado
market day *n* día *m* de mercado
market demand *n* demanda de mercado
market economy *n* economía de mercado
market forces *npl* tendencias *fpl* del mercado
market garden *n* (*Brit*) huerto
marketing ['mɑːkɪtɪŋ] *n* marketing *m*, mercadotecnia
marketing manager *n* director *m* de marketing
market leader *n* líder *m* de ventas
marketplace ['mɑːkɪtpleɪs] *n* mercado
market price *n* precio de mercado
market research *n* (*Comm*) estudios *mpl* de mercado
market value *n* valor *m* en el mercado
marking ['mɑːkɪŋ] *n* (*on animal*) pinta; (*on road*) señal *f*
marking ink *n* tinta indeleble *or* de marcar
marksman ['mɑːksmən] *n* tirador *m*
marksmanship ['mɑːksmənʃɪp] *n* puntería
mark-up ['mɑːkʌp] *n* (*Comm: margin*) margen *m* de beneficio; (*: increase*) aumento
marmalade ['mɑːməleɪd] *n* mermelada de naranja
maroon [mə'ruːn] *vt*: **to be marooned** (*shipwrecked*) naufragar; (*fig*) quedar abandonado ■ *adj* granate *inv*
marquee [mɑː'kiː] *n* carpa, entoldado
marquess, marquis ['mɑːkwɪs] *n* marqués *m*
Marrakech, Marrakesh [mærə'kɛʃ] *n* Marrakech *m*
marriage ['mærɪdʒ] *n* (*state*) matrimonio; (*wedding*) boda; (*act*) casamiento
marriage bureau *n* agencia matrimonial
marriage certificate *n* partida de casamiento
marriage guidance, marriage counseling (*US*) *n* orientación *f* matrimonial
marriage of convenience *n* matrimonio de conveniencia
married ['mærɪd] *adj* casado; (*life, love*) conyugal
marrow ['mærəu] *n* médula; (*vegetable*) calabacín *m*
marry ['mærɪ] *vt* casarse con; (*father, priest etc*) casar ■ *vi* (*also*: **get married**) casarse
Mars [mɑːz] *n* Marte *m*
Marseilles [mɑː'seɪ] *n* Marsella
marsh [mɑːʃ] *n* pantano; (*salt marsh*) marisma
marshal ['mɑːʃl] *n* (*Mil*) mariscal *m*; (*at sports meeting, demonstration etc*) oficial *m*; (*US: of police, fire department*) jefe(-a) *m(f)* ■ *vt* (*facts*) ordenar; (*soldiers*) formar
marshalling yard ['mɑːʃəlɪŋ-] *n* (*Rail*) estación *f* clasificadora
marshmallow ['mɑːʃmæləu] *n* (*Bot*) malvavisco; (*sweet*) esponja, dulce *m* de merengue blando
marshy ['mɑːʃɪ] *adj* pantanoso
marsupial [mɑː'suːpɪəl] *adj, n* marsupial *m*
martial ['mɑːʃl] *adj* marcial
martial arts *npl* artes *fpl* marciales
martial law *n* ley *f* marcial
martin ['mɑːtɪn] *n* (*also*: **house martin**) avión *m*
martyr ['mɑːtə^r] *n* mártir *m/f* ■ *vt* martirizar
martyrdom ['mɑːtədəm] *n* martirio
marvel ['mɑːvl] *n* maravilla, prodigio ■ *vi*: **to ~ (at)** maravillarse (de)
marvellous, (US) **marvelous** ['mɑːvləs] *adj* maravilloso
marvellously, (US) **marvelously** ['mɑːvləslɪ] *adv* maravillosamente
Marxism ['mɑːksɪzəm] *n* marxismo
Marxist ['mɑːksɪst] *adj, n* marxista *m/f*
marzipan ['mɑːzɪpæn] *n* mazapán *m*
mascara [mæs'kɑːrə] *n* rimel *m*
mascot ['mæskət] *n* mascota

masculine ['mæskjulɪn] *adj* masculino
masculinity [mæskju'lɪnɪtɪ] *n* masculinidad *f*
MASH [mæʃ] *n abbr (US Mil)* = **mobile army surgical hospital**
mash [mæʃ] *n (mix)* mezcla; *(Culin)* puré *m*; *(pulp)* amasijo
mashed potatoes [mæʃt-] *npl* puré *m* de patatas *or (LAm)* papas
mask [mɑ:sk] *n (Elec)* máscara ■ *vt* enmascarar
masochism ['mæsəkɪzəm] *n* masoquismo
masochist ['mæsəukɪst] *n* masoquista *m/f*
mason ['meɪsn] *n (also:* **stonemason***)* albañil *m*; *(also:* **freemason***)* masón *m*
masonic [mə'sɔnɪk] *adj* masónico
masonry ['meɪsnrɪ] *n* masonería; *(building)* mampostería
masquerade [mæskə'reɪd] *n* baile *m* de máscaras; *(fig)* mascarada ■ *vi*: **to ~ as** disfrazarse de, hacerse pasar por
mass [mæs] *n (people)* muchedumbre *f*; *(Physics)* masa; *(Rel)* misa; *(great quantity)* montón *m* ■ *vi* reunirse; *(Mil)* concentrarse; **the masses** las masas; **to go to ~** ir a *or* oír misa
Mass. *abbr (US)* = **Massachusetts**
massacre ['mæsəkə^r] *n* masacre *f* ■ *vt* masacrar
massage ['mæsɑ:ʒ] *n* masaje *m* ■ *vt* dar masajes *or* un masaje a
masseur [mæ'sə:^r] *n* masajista *m*
masseuse [mæ'sə:z] *n* masajista *f*
massive ['mæsɪv] *adj* enorme; *(support, intervention)* masivo
mass media *npl* medios *mpl* de comunicación de masas
mass meeting *n (of everyone concerned)* reunión *f* en masa; *(huge)* mitin *m*
mass-produce ['mæsprə'dju:s] *vt* fabricar en serie
mass-production ['mæsprə'dʌkʃən] *n* fabricación *f or* producción *f* en serie
mast [mɑ:st] *n (Naut)* mástil *m*; *(Radio etc)* torre *f*, antena
mastectomy [mæs'tɛktəmɪ] *n* mastectomía
master ['mɑ:stə^r] *n (of servant, animal)* amo; *(fig: of situation)* dueño; *(Art, Mus)* maestro; *(in secondary school)* profesor *m*; *(title for boys)*: **M~ X** Señorito X ■ *vt* dominar
master disk *n (Comput)* disco maestro
masterful ['mɑ:stəful] *adj* magistral, dominante
master key *n* llave *f* maestra
masterly ['mɑ:stəlɪ] *adj* magistral
mastermind ['mɑ:stəmaɪnd] *n* inteligencia superior ■ *vt* dirigir, planear
Master of Arts *n* licenciatura superior en Letras; *see also* **master's degree**
Master of Ceremonies *n* encargado de protocolo
Master of Science *n* licenciatura superior en Ciencias; *see also* **master's degree**
masterpiece ['mɑ:stəpi:s] *n* obra maestra
master plan *n* plan *m* rector
master's degree *n* máster *m*

MASTER'S DEGREE

Los estudios de postgrado británicos que llevan a la obtención de un *master's degree* consisten generalmente en una combinación de curso(s) académico(s) y tesina ("dissertation") sobre un tema original, o bien únicamente la redacción de una tesina. El primer caso es el más frecuente para los títulos de "MA" ("Master of Arts") y "MSc" ("Master of Science"), mientras que los de "MLitt" ("Master of Letters") o "MPhil" ("Master of Philosophy") se obtienen normalmente mediante tesina. En algunas universidades, como las escocesas, el título de *master's degree* no es de postgrado, sino que corresponde a la licenciatura.

master stroke *n* golpe *m* maestro
mastery ['mɑ:stərɪ] *n* maestría
mastiff ['mæstɪf] *n* mastín *m*
masturbate ['mæstəbeɪt] *vi* masturbarse
masturbation [mæstə'beɪʃən] *n* masturbación *f*
mat [mæt] *n* alfombrilla; *(also:* **doormat***)* felpudo ■ *adj* = **matt**
MAT *n abbr (= machine-assisted translation)* TAO
match [mætʃ] *n* cerilla, fósforo; *(game)* partido; *(fig)* igual *m/f* ■ *vt* emparejar; *(go well with)* hacer juego con; *(equal)* igualar ■ *vi* hacer juego; **to be a good ~** hacer buena pareja
matchbox ['mætʃbɔks] *n* caja de cerillas
matching ['mætʃɪŋ] *adj* que hace juego
matchless ['mætʃlɪs] *adj* sin par, incomparable
matchmaker ['mætʃmeɪkə^r] *n* casamentero
mate [meɪt] *n (workmate)* compañero(-a), colega *m/f*; *(col: friend)* amigo(-a), compadre *m/f (LAm)*; *(animal)* macho/hembra; *(in merchant navy)* primer oficial *m* ■ *vi* acoplarse, parearse ■ *vt* acoplar, parear
maté ['mɑ:teɪ] *n* mate *m* (cocido), yerba mate
material [mə'tɪərɪəl] *n (substance)* materia; *(equipment)* material *m*; *(cloth)* tela, tejido ■ *adj* material; *(important)* esencial;

materials *npl* materiales *mpl*; (*equipment etc*) artículos *mpl*
materialistic [mətɪərɪə'lɪstɪk] *adj* materialista
materialize [mə'tɪərɪəlaɪz] *vi* materializarse
materially [mə'tɪərɪəlɪ] *adv* materialmente
maternal [mə'tə:nl] *adj* maternal; **~ grandmother** abuela materna
maternity [mə'tə:nɪtɪ] *n* maternidad *f*
maternity benefit *n* subsidio por maternidad
maternity dress *n* vestido premamá
maternity hospital *n* hospital *m* de maternidad
maternity leave *n* baja por maternidad
math [mæθ] *n abbr* (*US*: = *mathematics*) matemáticas *fpl*
mathematical [mæθə'mætɪkl] *adj* matemático
mathematically [mæθɪ'mætɪklɪ] *adv* matemáticamente
mathematician [mæθəmə'tɪʃən] *n* matemático
mathematics [mæθə'mætɪks] *n* matemáticas *fpl*
maths [mæθs] *n abbr* (*Brit*: = *mathematics*) matemáticas *fpl*
matinée ['mætɪneɪ] *n* función *f* de la tarde, vermú(t) *m* (*LAm*)
mating ['meɪtɪŋ] *n* aparejamiento
mating call *n* llamada del macho
mating season *n* época de celo
matins ['mætɪnz] *n* maitines *mpl*
matriarchal [meɪtrɪ'ɑ:kl] *adj* matriarcal
matrices ['meɪtrɪsi:z] *pl of* **matrix**
matriculation [mətrɪkju'leɪʃən] *n* matriculación *f*, matrícula
matrimonial [mætrɪ'məunɪəl] *adj* matrimonial
matrimony ['mætrɪmənɪ] *n* matrimonio
matrix (*pl* **matrices**) ['meɪtrɪks, 'meɪtrɪsi:z] *n* matriz *f*
matron ['meɪtrən] *n* (*in hospital*) enfermera jefe; (*in school*) ama de llaves
matronly ['meɪtrənlɪ] *adj* de matrona; (*fig*: *figure*) corpulento
matt [mæt] *adj* mate
matted ['mætɪd] *adj* enmarañado
matter ['mætəʳ] *n* cuestión *f*, asunto; (*Physics*) sustancia, materia; (*content*) contenido; (*Med*: *pus*) pus *m* ■ *vi* importar; **it doesn't ~** no importa; **what's the ~?** ¿qué pasa?; **no ~ what** pase lo que pase; **as a ~ of course** por rutina; **as a ~ of fact** en realidad; **printed ~** impresos *mpl*; **reading ~** material *m* de lectura, lecturas *fpl*
matter-of-fact ['mætərəv'fækt] *adj* (*style*) prosaico; (*person*) práctico; (*voice*) neutro
mattress ['mætrɪs] *n* colchón *m*
mature [mə'tjuəʳ] *adj* maduro ■ *vi* madurar
mature student *n estudiante de más de 21 años*
maturity [mə'tjuərɪtɪ] *n* madurez *f*
maudlin ['mɔ:dlɪn] *adj* llorón(-ona)
maul [mɔ:l] *vt* magullar
Mauritania [mɔ:rɪ'teɪnɪə] *n* Mauritania
Mauritius [mə'rɪʃəs] *n* Mauricio
mausoleum [mɔ:sə'lɪəm] *n* mausoleo
mauve [məuv] *adj* de color malva
maverick ['mævrɪk] *n* (*fig*) inconformista *m/f*, persona independiente
mawkish ['mɔ:kɪʃ] *adj* sensiblero, empalagoso
max *abbr* = **maximum**
maxim ['mæksɪm] *n* máxima
maxima ['mæksɪmə] *pl of* **maximum**
maximize ['mæksɪmaɪz] *vt* (*profits etc*) llevar al máximo; (*chances*) maximizar
maximum ['mæksɪməm] *adj* máximo ■ *n* (*pl* **maxima**) ['mæksɪmə] máximo
May [meɪ] *n* mayo; *see also* **July**
may [meɪ] *vi* (*conditional* **might**) (*indicating possibility*): **he ~ come** puede que venga; (*be allowed to*): **~ I smoke?** ¿puedo fumar?; (*wishes*): **~ God bless you!** ¡que Dios le bendiga!; **~ I sit here?** ¿me puedo sentar aquí?
maybe ['meɪbi:] *adv* quizá(s); **~ not** quizá(s) no
May Day *n* el primero de Mayo
mayday ['meɪdeɪ] *n* señal *f* de socorro
mayhem ['meɪhɛm] *n* caos *m* total
mayonnaise [meɪə'neɪz] *n* mayonesa
mayor [mɛəʳ] *n* alcalde *m*
mayoress ['mɛərɛs] *n* alcaldesa
maypole ['meɪpəul] *n* mayo
maze [meɪz] *n* laberinto
MB *abbr* (*Comput*) = **megabyte**; (*Canada*) = **Manitoba**
MBA *n abbr* (= *Master of Business Administration*) *título universitario*
MBBS, MBChB *n abbr* (*Brit*: = *Bachelor of Medicine and Surgery*) *título universitario*
MBE *n abbr* (*Brit*: = *Member of the Order of the British Empire*) *título ceremonial*
MBO *n abbr see* **management buyout**
MC *n abbr* (= *master of ceremonies*) e.p.; (*US*: = *Member of Congress*) *diputado del Congreso de los Estados Unidos*
MCAT *n abbr* (*US*: = *Medical College Admissions Test*) *examen de ingreso en los estudios superiores de Medicina*
MD *n abbr* (= *Doctor of Medicine*) *título universitario*; (*Comm*) = **managing director**; (= *MiniDisc®*) MiniDisc® *m*, minidisc *m* ■ *abbr* (*US*) = **Maryland**

Md. *abbr* (*US*) = **Maryland**
MD player *n* MiniDisc® *m*, minidisc *m*
MDT *n abbr* (*US*: = *Mountain Daylight Time*) *hora de verano de las Montañas Rocosas*
ME *abbr* (*US Post*: = *Maine*) ■ *n abbr* (*US Med*: = *medical examiner*); (*Med*: = *myalgic encephalomyelitis*) encefalomielitis *f* miálgica
me [mi:] *pron* (*direct*) me; (*stressed, after pronoun*) mí; **can you hear me?** ¿me oyes?; **he heard ME!** me oyó a mí; **it's me** soy yo; **give them to me** dámelos; **with/without me** conmigo/sin mí; **it's for me** es para mí
meadow ['mɛdəu] *n* prado, pradera
meagre, (*US*) **meager** ['mi:gəʳ] *adj* escaso, pobre
meal [mi:l] *n* comida; (*flour*) harina; **to go out for a ~** salir a comer
meals on wheels *nsg* (*Brit*) *servicio de alimentación a domicilio para necesitados y tercera edad*
mealtime ['mi:ltaɪm] *n* hora de comer
mealy-mouthed ['mi:lɪmauðd] *adj*: **to be ~** no decir nunca las cosas claras
mean [mi:n] *adj* (*with money*) tacaño; (*unkind*) mezquino, malo; (*average*) medio; (*US*: *vicious*: *animal*) resabiado; (: *person*) malicioso ■ *vt* (*pt, pp* **meant** [mɛnt]) (*signify*) querer decir, significar; (*intend*): **to ~ to do sth** tener la intención de *or* pensar hacer algo ■ *n* medio, término medio; **do you ~ it?** ¿lo dices en serio?; **what do you ~?** ¿qué quiere decir?; **to be meant for sb/sth** ser para algn/algo; *see also* **means**
meander [mɪ'ændəʳ] *vi* (*river*) serpentear; (*person*) vagar
meaning ['mi:nɪŋ] *n* significado, sentido
meaningful ['mi:nɪŋful] *adj* significativo
meaningless ['mi:nɪŋlɪs] *adj* sin sentido
meanness ['mi:nnɪs] *n* (*with money*) tacañería; (*unkindness*) maldad *f*, mezquindad *f*
means [mi:nz] *npl* medio *sg*, manera *sg*; (*resource*) recursos *mpl*, medios *mpl*; **by ~ of** mediante, por medio de; **by all ~!** ¡naturalmente!, ¡claro que sí!
means test *n* control *m* de los recursos económicos
meant [mɛnt] *pt, pp of* **mean**
meantime ['mi:ntaɪm], **meanwhile** ['mi:nwaɪl] *adv* (*also*: **in the meantime**) mientras tanto
measles ['mi:zlz] *n* sarampión *m*
measly ['mi:zlɪ] *adj* (*col*) miserable
measurable ['mɛʒərəbl] *adj* mensurable, que se puede medir
measure ['mɛʒəʳ] *vt* medir; (*for clothes etc*) tomar las medidas a ■ *vi* medir ■ *n* medida; (*ruler*) cinta métrica, metro; **a litre ~** una medida de un litro; **some ~ of success** cierto éxito; **to take measures to do sth** tomar medidas para hacer algo
▸ **measure up** *vi*: **to ~ up (to)** estar a la altura (de)
measured ['mɛʒəd] *adj* moderado; (*tone*) mesurado
measurement ['mɛʒəmənt] *n* (*measure*) medida; (*act*) medición *f*; **to take sb's measurements** tomar las medidas a algn
meat [mi:t] *n* carne *f*; **cold meats** fiambres *mpl*; **crab ~** carne *f* de cangrejo
meatball ['mi:tbɔ:l] *n* albóndiga
meat pie *n* pastel *m* de carne
meaty ['mi:tɪ] *adj* (*person*) fuerte, corpulento; (*role*) sustancioso; **a ~ meal** una comida con bastante carne
Mecca ['mɛkə] *n* (*city*) la Meca; (*fig*) meca
mechanic [mɪ'kænɪk] *n* mecánico(-a)
mechanical [mɪ'kænɪkl] *adj* mecánico
mechanical engineering *n* (*science*) ingeniería mecánica; (*industry*) construcción *f* mecánica
mechanics [mə'kænɪks] *n* mecánica ■ *npl* mecanismo *sg*
mechanism ['mɛkənɪzəm] *n* mecanismo
mechanization [mɛkənaɪ'zeɪʃən] *n* mecanización *f*
mechanize ['mɛkənaɪz] *vt* mecanizar; (*factory etc*) automatizar
MEd *n abbr* (= *Master of Education*) *título universitario*
medal ['mɛdl] *n* medalla
medallion [mɪ'dælɪən] *n* medallón *m*
medallist, (*US*) **medalist** ['mɛdlɪst] *n* (*Sport*) medallista *m/f*
meddle ['mɛdl] *vi*: **to ~ in** entrometerse en; **to ~ with sth** manosear algo
meddlesome ['mɛdlsəm], **meddling** ['mɛdlɪŋ] *adj* (*interfering*) entrometido; (*touching things*) curioso
media ['mi:dɪə] *npl* medios *mpl* de comunicación
media circus *n excesivo despliegue informativo*
mediaeval [mɛdɪ'i:vl] *adj* = **medieval**
median ['mi:dɪən] *n* (*US*: *also*: **median strip**) mediana
media research *n* estudio de los medios de publicidad
mediate ['mi:dɪeɪt] *vi* mediar
mediation [mi:dɪ'eɪʃən] *n* mediación *f*
mediator ['mi:dɪeɪtəʳ] *n* mediador(a) *m(f)*
Medicaid ['mɛdɪkeɪd] *n* (*US*) *programa de ayuda médica*
medical ['mɛdɪkl] *adj* médico ■ *n* (*also*: **medical examination**) reconocimiento médico

medical certificate *n* certificado *m* médico
Medicare ['mɛdɪkɛəʳ] *n* (*US*) *seguro médico del Estado*
medicated ['mɛdɪkeɪtɪd] *adj* medicinal
medication [mɛdɪ'keɪʃən] *n* (*drugs etc*) medicación *f*
medicinal [mɛ'dɪsɪnl] *adj* medicinal
medicine ['mɛdsɪn] *n* medicina; (*drug*) medicamento
medicine chest *n* botiquín *m*
medicine man *n* hechicero
medieval, mediaeval [mɛdɪ'i:vl] *adj* medieval
mediocre [mi:dɪ'əukəʳ] *adj* mediocre
mediocrity [mi:dɪ'ɔkrɪtɪ] *n* mediocridad *f*
meditate ['mɛdɪteɪt] *vi* meditar
meditation [mɛdɪ'teɪʃən] *n* meditación *f*
Mediterranean [mɛdɪtə'reɪnɪən] *adj* mediterráneo; **the ~ (Sea)** el (Mar *m*) Mediterráneo
medium ['mi:dɪəm] *adj* mediano; (*level, height*) medio ■ *n* (*pl* **media**) (*means*) medio (*pl* **mediums**) (*person*) médium *m/f*; **happy ~** punto justo
medium-dry ['mi:dɪəm'draɪ] *adj* semiseco
medium-sized ['mi:dɪəm'saɪzd] *adj* de tamaño mediano; (*clothes*) de (la) talla mediana
medium wave *n* onda media
medley ['mɛdlɪ] *n* mezcla; (*Mus*) popurrí *m*
meek [mi:k] *adj* manso, sumiso
meekly ['mi:klɪ] *adv* mansamente, dócilmente
meet [mi:t] (*pt, pp* **met**) *vt* encontrar; (*accidentally*) encontrarse con; (*by arrangement*) reunirse con; (*for the first time*) conocer; (*go and fetch*) ir a buscar; (*opponent*) enfrentarse con; (*obligations*) cumplir; (*bill, expenses*) pagar, costear ■ *vi* encontrarse; (*in session*) reunirse; (*join: objects*) unirse; (*get to know*) conocerse ■ *n* (*Brit Hunting*) cacería; (*US Sport*) encuentro; **pleased to ~ you!** ¡encantado (de conocerle)!, ¡mucho gusto!
▸ **meet up** *vi*: **to ~ up with sb** reunirse con algn
▸ **meet with** *vt fus* reunirse con; (*difficulty*) tropezar con
meeting ['mi:tɪŋ] *n* (*also Sport: rally*) encuentro; (*arranged*) cita, compromiso (*LAm*); (*formal session, business meeting*) reunión *f*; (*Pol*) mitin *m*; **to call a ~** convocar una reunión
meeting place *n* lugar *m* de reunión *or* encuentro
megabyte ['mɛgə'baɪt] *n* (*Comput*) megabyte *m*, megaocteto
megalomaniac [mɛgələu'meɪnɪæk] *adj, n* megalómano(-a) *m(f)*
megaphone ['mɛgəfəun] *n* megáfono
megawatt ['mɛgəwɔt] *n* megavatio
melancholy ['mɛlənkəlɪ] *n* melancolía ■ *adj* melancólico
melee ['mɛleɪ] *n* refriega
mellow ['mɛləu] *adj* (*wine*) añejo; (*sound, colour*) suave; (*fruit*) maduro ■ *vi* (*person*) madurar
melodious [mɪ'ləudɪəs] *adj* melodioso
melodrama ['mɛləudrɑ:mə] *n* melodrama *m*
melodramatic [mɛləudrə'mætɪk] *adj* melodramático
melody ['mɛlədɪ] *n* melodía
melon ['mɛlən] *n* melón *m*
melt [mɛlt] *vi* (*metal*) fundirse; (*snow*) derretirse; (*fig*) ablandarse ■ *vt* (*also:* **melt down**) fundir; **melted butter** mantequilla derretida
▸ **melt away** *vi* desvanecerse
meltdown ['mɛltdaun] *n* (*in nuclear reactor*) fusión *f* (de un reactor nuclear)
melting point ['mɛltɪŋ-] *n* punto de fusión
melting pot ['mɛltɪŋ-] *n* (*fig*) crisol *m*; **to be in the ~** estar sobre el tapete
member ['mɛmbəʳ] *n* (*of political party*) miembro; (*of club*) socio(-a); **M~ of Parliament (MP)** (*Brit*) diputado(-a); **M~ of the European Parliament (MEP)** (*Brit*) eurodiputado(-a); **M~ of the House of Representatives (MHR)** (*US*) diputado(-a) del Congreso de los Estados Unidos; **M~ of the Scottish Parliament (MSP)** (*Brit*) diputado(-a) *m(f)* del Parlamento escocés
membership ['mɛmbəʃɪp] *n* (*members*) miembros *mpl*; socios *mpl*; (*numbers*) número de miembros *or* socios; **to seek ~ of** pedir el ingreso a
membership card *n* carnet *m* de socio
membrane ['mɛmbreɪn] *n* membrana
memento [mə'mɛntəu] *n* recuerdo
memo ['mɛməu] *n abbr* (= *memorandum*) nota (de servicio)
memoirs ['mɛmwɑ:z] *npl* memorias *fpl*
memo pad *n* bloc *m* de notas
memorable ['mɛmərəbl] *adj* memorable
memorandum (**memoranda**) [mɛmə'rændəm, -də] *n* nota (de servicio); (*Pol*) memorándum *m*
memorial [mɪ'mɔ:rɪəl] *n* monumento conmemorativo ■ *adj* conmemorativo
Memorial Day *n* (*US*) *día de conmemoración de los caídos en la guerra*
memorize ['mɛməraɪz] *vt* aprender de memoria
memory ['mɛmərɪ] *n* memoria; (*recollection*) recuerdo; (*Comput*) memoria; **to have a**

good/bad ~ tener buena/mala memoria; **loss of ~** pérdida de memoria
men [mɛn] *pl of* **man**
menace ['mɛnəs] *n* amenaza; (*col: nuisance*) lata ■ *vt* amenazar; **a public ~** un peligro público
menacing ['mɛnɪsɪŋ] *adj* amenazador(-a)
menacingly ['mɛnɪsɪŋlɪ] *adv* amenazadoramente
menagerie [mɪ'nædʒərɪ] *n* casa de fieras
mend [mɛnd] *vt* reparar, arreglar; (*darn*) zurcir ■ *vi* reponerse ■ *n* (*gen*) remiendo; (*darn*) zurcido; **to be on the ~** ir mejorando
mending ['mɛndɪŋ] *n* arreglo, reparación *f*; (*clothes*) ropa por remendar
menial ['mi:nɪəl] *adj* (*pej*) bajo, servil
meningitis [mɛnɪn'dʒaɪtɪs] *n* meningitis *f*
menopause ['mɛnəupɔ:z] *n* menopausia
men's room *n* (*US*): **the ~** el servicio de caballeros
menstrual ['mɛnstruəl] *adj* menstrual
menstruate ['mɛnstrueɪt] *vi* menstruar
menstruation [mɛnstru'eɪʃən] *n* menstruación *f*
menswear ['mɛnzwɛəʳ] *n* confección *f* de caballero
mental ['mɛntl] *adj* mental; **~ illness** enfermedad *f* mental
mental hospital *n* (hospital *m*) psiquiátrico
mentality [mɛn'tælɪtɪ] *n* mentalidad *f*
mentally ['mɛntlɪ] *adv*: **to be ~ handicapped** ser un disminuido mental
menthol ['mɛnθɔl] *n* mentol *m*
mention ['mɛnʃən] *n* mención *f* ■ *vt* mencionar; (*speak of*) hablar de; **don't ~ it!** ¡de nada!; **I need hardly ~ that ...** huelga decir que ...; **not to ~, without mentioning** sin contar
mentor ['mɛntɔ:ʳ] *n* mentor *m*
menu ['mɛnju:] *n* (*set menu*) menú *m*; (*printed*) carta; (*Comput*) menú *m*
menu-driven ['mɛnju:drɪvn] *adj* (*Comput*) guiado por menú
MEP *n abbr* = **Member of the European Parliament**
mercantile ['mə:kəntaɪl] *adj* mercantil
mercenary ['mə:sɪnərɪ] *adj, n* mercenario(-a)
merchandise ['mə:tʃəndaɪz] *n* mercancías *fpl*
merchandiser ['mə:tʃəndaɪzəʳ] *n* comerciante *m/f*, tratante *m*
merchant ['mə:tʃənt] *n* comerciante *m/f*
merchant bank *n* (*Brit*) banco comercial
merchantman ['mə:tʃəntmən] *n* buque *m* mercante
merchant navy, (*US*) **merchant marine** *n* marina mercante
merciful ['mə:sɪful] *adj* compasivo
mercifully ['mə:sɪfulɪ] *adv* con compasión; (*fortunately*) afortunadamente
merciless ['mə:sɪlɪs] *adj* despiadado
mercilessly ['mə:sɪlɪslɪ] *adv* despiadadamente, sin piedad
mercurial [mə:'kjuərɪəl] *adj* veleidoso, voluble
mercury ['mə:kjurɪ] *n* mercurio
mercy ['mə:sɪ] *n* compasión *f*; (*Rel*) misericordia; **at the ~ of** a la merced de
mercy killing *n* eutanasia
mere [mɪəʳ] *adj* simple, mero
merely ['mɪəlɪ] *adv* simplemente, sólo
merge [mə:dʒ] *vt* (*join*) unir; (*mix*) mezclar; (*fuse*) fundir; (*Comput: files, text*) intercalar ■ *vi* unirse; (*Comm*) fusionarse
merger ['mə:dʒəʳ] *n* (*Comm*) fusión *f*
meridian [mə'rɪdɪən] *n* meridiano
meringue [mə'ræŋ] *n* merengue *m*
merit ['mɛrɪt] *n* mérito ■ *vt* merecer
meritocracy [mɛrɪ'tɔkrəsɪ] *n* meritocracia
mermaid ['mə:meɪd] *n* sirena
merrily ['mɛrɪlɪ] *adv* alegremente
merriment ['mɛrɪmənt] *n* alegría
merry ['mɛrɪ] *adj* alegre; **M~ Christmas!** ¡Felices Pascuas!
merry-go-round ['mɛrɪgəuraund] *n* tiovivo
mesh [mɛʃ] *n* malla; (*Tech*) engranaje *m* ■ *vi* (*gears*) engranar; **wire ~** tela metálica
mesmerize ['mɛzməraɪz] *vt* hipnotizar
mess [mɛs] *n* confusión *f*; (*of objects*) revoltijo; (*tangle*) lío; (*Mil*) comedor *m*; **to be (in) a ~** (*room*) estar revuelto; **to be/get o.s. in a ~** estar/meterse en un lío
▸ **mess about, mess around** *vi* (*col*) perder el tiempo; (*pass the time*) pasar el rato
▸ **mess about** *or* **around with** *vt fus* (*col: play with*) divertirse con; (*: handle*) manosear
▸ **mess up** *vt* (*disarrange*) desordenar; (*spoil*) estropear; (*dirty*) ensuciar
message ['mɛsɪdʒ] *n* recado, mensaje *m*; **to get the ~** (*fig, col*) enterarse
message switching *n* (*Comput*) conmutación *f* de mensajes
messenger ['mɛsɪndʒəʳ] *n* mensajero(-a)
Messiah [mɪ'saɪə] *n* Mesías *m*
Messrs, Messrs. *abbr* (*on letters:* = *Messieurs*) Sres
messy ['mɛsɪ] *adj* (*dirty*) sucio; (*untidy*) desordenado; (*confused: situation etc*) confuso
Met [mɛt] *n abbr* (*US*) = **Metropolitan Opera**
met [mɛt] *pt, pp of* **meet** ■ *adj abbr* = **meteorological**
metabolism [mɛ'tæbəlɪzəm] *n* metabolismo
metal ['mɛtl] *n* metal *m*
metallic [mɛ'tælɪk] *adj* metálico
metallurgy [mɛ'tælədʒɪ] *n* metalurgia

metalwork ['mɛtlwəːk] *n* (*craft*) metalistería
metamorphosis (*pl* **metamorphoses**) [mɛtə'mɔːfəsɪs, -siːz] *n* metamorfosis *f inv*
metaphor ['mɛtəfəʳ] *n* metáfora
metaphorical [mɛtə'fɔrɪkl] *adj* metafórico
metaphysics [mɛtə'fɪzɪks] *n* metafísica
mete [miːt]: **to ~ out** *vt fus* (*punishment*) imponer
meteor ['miːtɪəʳ] *n* meteoro
meteoric [miːtɪ'ɔrɪk] *adj* (*fig*) meteórico
meteorite ['miːtɪəraɪt] *n* meteorito
meteorological [miːtɪərə'lɔdʒɪkl] *adj* meteorológico
meteorology [miːtɪə'rɔlədʒɪ] *n* meteorología
meter ['miːtəʳ] *n* (*instrument*) contador *m*; (*US: unit*) = **metre** ■ *vt* (*US Post*) franquear; **parking ~** parquímetro
methane ['miːθeɪn] *n* metano
method ['mɛθəd] *n* método; **~ of payment** método de pago
methodical [mɪ'θɔdɪkl] *adj* metódico
Methodist ['mɛθədɪst] *adj, n* metodista *m/f*
methodology [mɛθə'dɔlədʒɪ] *n* metodología
meths [mɛθs] *n* (*Brit*) = **methylated spirit**
methylated spirit ['mɛθɪleɪtɪd-] *n* (*Brit*) alcohol *m* metilado *or* desnaturalizado
meticulous [mɛ'tɪkjuləs] *adj* meticuloso
metre, meter (*US*) ['miːtəʳ] *n* metro
metric ['mɛtrɪk] *adj* métrico; **to go ~** pasar al sistema métrico
metrication [mɛtrɪ'keɪʃən] *n* conversión *f* al sistema métrico
metric system *n* sistema *m* métrico
metric ton *n* tonelada métrica
metronome ['mɛtrənəum] *n* metrónomo
metropolis [mɪ'trɔpəlɪs] *n* metrópoli(s) *f*
metropolitan [mɛtrə'pɔlɪtən] *adj* metropolitano
Metropolitan Police *n* (*Brit*): **the ~** la policía londinense
mettle ['mɛtl] *n* valor *m*, ánimo
mew [mjuː] *vi* (*cat*) maullar
mews [mjuːz] (*Brit*) *n*: **~ cottage** *casa acondicionada en antiguos establos o cocheras*; **~ flat** *piso en antiguos establos o cocheras*
Mexican ['mɛksɪkən] *adj, n* mejicano(-a) *m(f)*, mexicano(-a) *m(f)* (*LAm*)
Mexico ['mɛksɪkəu] *n* Méjico, México (*LAm*)
Mexico City *n* Ciudad *f* de Méjico *or* (*LAm*) México
mezzanine ['mɛtsəniːn] *n* entresuelo
MFA *n abbr* (*US:* = *Master of Fine Arts*) *título universitario*
mfr *abbr* (= *manufacturer*) fab; = **manufacture**
mg *abbr* (= *milligram*) mg
Mgr *abbr* (= *Monseigneur, Monsignor*) Mons; (*Comm*) = **manager**
mgr *abbr* = **manager**
MHR *n abbr* (*US*) *see* **Member of the House of Representatives**
MHz *abbr* (= *megahertz*) MHz
MI *abbr* (*US*) = **Michigan**
MI5 *n abbr* (*Brit:* = *Military Intelligence, section five*) *servicio de contraespionaje del gobierno británico*
MI6 *n abbr* (*Brit:* = *Military Intelligence, section six*) *servicio de inteligencia del gobierno británico*
MIA *abbr* (*Mil:* = *missing in action*) desaparecido
miaow [miː'au] *vi* maullar
mice [maɪs] *pl of* **mouse**
Mich. *abbr* (*US*) = **Michigan**
mickey ['mɪkɪ] *n*: **to take the ~ out of sb** tomar el pelo a algn
micro ['maɪkrəu] *n* = **microcomputer**
micro... [maɪkrəu] *pref* micro...
microbe ['maɪkrəub] *n* microbio
microbiology [maɪkrəubaɪ'ɔlədʒɪ] *n* microbiología
microchip ['maɪkrəutʃɪp] *n* microchip *m*, microplaqueta
microcomputer ['maɪkrəukəm'pjuːtəʳ] *n* microordenador *m*, microcomputador *m* (*LAm*)
microcosm ['maɪkrəukɔzəm] *n* microcosmo
microeconomics ['maɪkrəuiːkə'nɔmɪks] *n* microeconomía
microfiche ['maɪkrəufiːʃ] *n* microficha
microfilm ['maɪkrəufɪlm] *n* microfilm *m*
microlight ['maɪkrəulaɪt] *n* ultraligero
micrometer [maɪ'krɔmɪtəʳ] *n* micrómetro
microphone ['maɪkrəfəun] *n* micrófono
microprocessor ['maɪkrəu'prəusɛsəʳ] *n* microprocesador *m*
microscope ['maɪkrəskəup] *n* microscopio; **under the ~** al microscopio
microscopic [maɪkrə'skɔpɪk] *adj* microscópico
microwave ['maɪkrəuweɪv] *n* (*also:* **microwave oven**) horno microondas
mid [mɪd] *adj*: **in ~ May** a mediados de mayo; **in ~ afternoon** a media tarde; **in ~ air** en el aire; **he's in his ~ thirties** tiene unos treinta y cinco años
midday [mɪd'deɪ] *n* mediodía *m*
middle ['mɪdl] *n* medio, centro; (*waist*) cintura ■ *adj* de en medio; **in the ~ of the night** en plena noche; **I'm in the ~ of reading it** lo estoy leyendo ahora mismo
middle-aged [mɪdl'eɪdʒd] *adj* de mediana edad
Middle Ages *npl*: **the ~** la Edad *sg* Media
middle class *n*: **the ~(es)** la clase media ■ *adj*: **middle-class** de clase media
Middle East *n* Oriente *m* Medio
middleman ['mɪdlmæn] *n* intermediario

middle management *n* dirección *f* de nivel medio
middle name *n* segundo nombre *m*
middle-of-the-road ['mɪdləvðə'rəud] *adj* moderado
middleweight ['mɪdlweɪt] *n* (*Boxing*) peso medio
middling ['mɪdlɪŋ] *adj* mediano
Middx *abbr* (*Brit*) = **Middlesex**
midge [mɪdʒ] *n* mosquito
midget ['mɪdʒɪt] *n* enano(-a)
midi system *n* cadena midi
Midlands ['mɪdləndz] *npl región central de Inglaterra*
midnight ['mɪdnaɪt] *n* medianoche *f*; **at ~** a medianoche
midriff ['mɪdrɪf] *n* diafragma *m*
midst [mɪdst] *n*: **in the ~ of** entre, en medio de
midsummer [mɪd'sʌməʳ] *n*: **a ~ day** un día de pleno verano
Midsummer's Day *n* Día *m* de San Juan
midway [mɪd'weɪ] *adj, adv*: **~ (between)** a mitad de camino *or* a medio camino (entre)
midweek [mɪd'wi:k] *adv* entre semana
midwife (*pl* **midwives**) ['mɪdwaɪf, -waɪvz] *n* comadrona
midwifery ['mɪdwɪfərɪ] *n* tocología
midwinter [mɪd'wɪntəʳ] *n*: **in ~** en pleno invierno
miffed [mɪft] *adj* (*col*) mosqueado
might [maɪt] *vb see* **may** ▪ *n* fuerza, poder *m*; **he ~ be there** puede que esté allí, a lo mejor está allí; **I ~ as well go** más vale que vaya; **you ~ like to try** podría intentar
mightily ['maɪtɪlɪ] *adv* fuertemente, poderosamente; **I was ~ surprised** me sorprendí enormemente
mightn't ['maɪtnt] = **might not**
mighty ['maɪtɪ] *adj* fuerte, poderoso
migraine ['mi:greɪn] *n* jaqueca
migrant ['maɪgrənt] *adj* migratorio ▪ *n* (*bird*) ave *f* migratoria; (*worker*) emigrante *m/f*
migrate [maɪ'greɪt] *vi* emigrar
migration [maɪ'greɪʃən] *n* emigración *f*
mike [maɪk] *n abbr* (= *microphone*) micro
Milan [mɪ'læn] *n* Milán *m*
mild [maɪld] *adj* (*person*) apacible; (*climate*) templado; (*slight*) ligero; (*taste*) suave; (*illness*) leve
mildew ['mɪldju:] *n* moho
mildly ['maɪldlɪ] *adv* ligeramente; suavemente; **to put it ~** por no decir algo peor
mildness ['maɪldnɪs] *n* suavidad *f*; (*of illness*) levedad *f*
mile [maɪl] *n* milla; **to do 20 miles per gallon** hacer 20 millas por galón
mileage ['maɪlɪdʒ] *n* número de millas; (*Aut*) kilometraje *m*
mileage allowance *n* ≈ asignación *f* por kilometraje
mileometer [maɪ'lɔmɪtəʳ] *n* (*Brit*) = **milometer**
milestone ['maɪlstəun] *n* mojón *m*; (*fig*) hito
milieu ['mi:ljə:] *n* (medio) ambiente *m*, entorno
militant ['mɪlɪtnt] *adj, n* militante *m/f*
militarism ['mɪlɪtərɪzəm] *n* militarismo
militaristic [mɪlɪtə'rɪstɪk] *adj* militarista
military ['mɪlɪtərɪ] *adj* militar
military service *n* servicio militar
militate ['mɪlɪteɪt] *vi*: **to ~ against** militar en contra de
militia [mɪ'lɪʃə] *n* milicia
milk [mɪlk] *n* leche *f* ▪ *vt* (*cow*) ordeñar; (*fig*) chupar
milk chocolate *n* chocolate *m* con leche
milk float *n* (*Brit*) furgoneta de la leche
milking ['mɪlkɪŋ] *n* ordeño
milkman ['mɪlkmən] *n* lechero, repartidor *m* de la leche
milk shake *n* batido, malteada (*LAm*)
milk tooth *n* diente *m* de leche
milk truck *n* (*US*) = **milk float**
milky ['mɪlkɪ] *adj* lechoso
Milky Way *n* Vía Láctea
mill [mɪl] *n* (*windmill etc*) molino; (*coffee mill*) molinillo; (*factory*) fábrica; (*spinning mill*) hilandería ▪ *vt* moler ▪ *vi* (*also*: **mill about**) arremolinarse
milled [mɪld] (*grain*) molido; (*coin, edge*) acordonado
millennium (*pl* **millenniums** *or* **millennia**) [mɪ'lɛnɪəm, 'lɛnɪə] *n* milenio, milenario
millennium bug *n* (*Comput*): **the ~** el (problema del) efecto 2000
miller ['mɪləʳ] *n* molinero
millet ['mɪlɪt] *n* mijo
milli... ['mɪlɪ] *pref* mili...
milligram, milligramme ['mɪlɪgraem] *n* miligramo
millilitre, (*US*) **milliliter** ['mɪlɪli:təʳ] *n* mililitro
millimetre, (*US*) **millimeter** ['mɪlɪmi:təʳ] *n* milímetro
milliner ['mɪlɪnəʳ] *n* sombrerero(-a)
millinery ['mɪlɪnərɪ] *n* sombrerería
million ['mɪljən] *n* millón *m*; **a ~ times** un millón de veces
millionaire [mɪljə'nɛəʳ] *n* millonario(-a)
millipede ['mɪlɪpi:d] *n* milpiés *m inv*
millstone ['mɪlstəun] *n* piedra de molino
millwheel ['mɪlwi:l] *n* rueda de molino

milometer [maɪˈlɔmɪtəʳ] *n* (*Brit*) cuentakilómetros *m inv*
mime [maɪm] *n* mímica; (*actor*) mimo(-a) ■ *vt* remedar ■ *vi* actuar de mimo
mimic [ˈmɪmɪk] *n* imitador(a) *m(f)* ■ *adj* mímico ■ *vt* remedar, imitar
mimicry [ˈmɪmɪkrɪ] *n* imitación *f*
Min *abbr* (*Brit Pol: = Ministry*) Min
min. *abbr* (*= minute(s)*) m.; *=* **minimum**
minaret [mɪnəˈrɛt] *n* alminar *m*, minarete *m*
mince [mɪns] *vt* picar ■ *vi* (*in walking*) andar con pasos menudos ■ *n* (*Brit Culin*) carne *f* picada, picadillo
mincemeat [ˈmɪnsmiːt] *n conserva de fruta picada*
mince pie *n pastelillo relleno de fruta picada*
mincer [ˈmɪnsəʳ] *n* picadora de carne
mincing [ˈmɪnsɪŋ] *adj* afectado
mind [maɪnd] *n* (*gen*) mente *f*; (*contrasted with matter*) espíritu *m* ■ *vt* (*attend to, look after*) ocuparse de, cuidar; (*be careful of*) tener cuidado con; (*object to*): **I don't ~ the noise** no me molesta el ruido; **it is on my ~** me preocupa; **to my ~** a mi parecer *or* juicio; **to change one's ~** cambiar de idea *or* de parecer; **to bring** *or* **call sth to ~** recordar algo; **to have sth/sb in ~** tener algo/a algn en mente; **to be out of one's ~** haber perdido el juicio; **to bear sth in ~** tomar *or* tener algo en cuenta; **to make up one's ~** decidirse; **it went right out of my ~** se me fue por completo (de la cabeza); **to be in two minds about sth** estar indeciso *or* dudar ante algo; **I don't ~** me es igual; **~ you, ...** te advierto que ...; **never ~!** ¡es igual!, ¡no importa!; (*don't worry*) ¡no te preocupes!; **'~ the step'** 'cuidado con el escalón'
mind-boggling [ˈmaɪndbɔglɪŋ] *adj* (*col*) alucinante, increíble
-minded [-maɪndɪd] *adj*: **fair~** imparcial; **an industrially~ nation** una nación orientada a la industria
minder [ˈmaɪndəʳ] *n* guardaespaldas *m inv*
mindful [ˈmaɪndful] *adj*: **~ of** consciente de
mindless [ˈmaɪndlɪs] *adj* (*violence, crime*) sin sentido; (*work*) de autómata
mine [maɪn] *pron* (el) mío/(la) mía *etc*; **a friend of ~** un(a) amigo(-a) mío/mía ■ *adj*: **this book is ~** este libro es mío ■ *n* mina ■ *vt* (*coal*) extraer; (*ship, beach*) minar
mine detector *n* detector *m* de minas
minefield [ˈmaɪnfiːld] *n* campo de minas
miner [ˈmaɪnəʳ] *n* minero(-a)
mineral [ˈmɪnərəl] *adj* mineral ■ *n* mineral *m*; **minerals** *npl* (*Brit: soft drinks*) refrescos *mpl* con gas
mineral water *n* agua mineral
minesweeper [ˈmaɪnswiːpəʳ] *n* dragaminas *m inv*
mingle [ˈmɪŋgl] *vi*: **to ~ with** mezclarse con
mingy [ˈmɪndʒɪ] *adj* (*col*) tacaño
mini ... [mɪnɪ] *pref* mini..., micro...
miniature [ˈmɪnətʃəʳ] *adj* (en) miniatura ■ *n* miniatura
minibus [ˈmɪnɪbʌs] *n* microbús *m*
minicab [ˈmɪnɪkæb] *n* taxi *m* (*que sólo puede pedirse por teléfono*)
minicomputer [ˈmɪnɪkəmˈpjuːtəʳ] *n* miniordenador *m*, minicomputador *m* (*LAm*)
MiniDisc® [ˈmɪnɪdɪsk] *n* MiniDisc® *m*
minim [ˈmɪnɪm] *n* (*Brit Mus*) blanca
minimal [ˈmɪnɪml] *adj* mínimo
minimalist [ˈmɪnɪməlɪst] *adj, n* minimalista *m/f*
minimize [ˈmɪnɪmaɪz] *vt* minimizar
minimum [ˈmɪnɪməm] *n* (*pl* **minima**) [ˈmɪnɪmə] mínimo ■ *adj* mínimo; **to reduce to a ~** reducir algo al mínimo; **~ wage** salario mínimo
minimum lending rate *n* tipo de interés mínimo
mining [ˈmaɪnɪŋ] *n* minería ■ *adj* minero
minion [ˈmɪnjən] *n* secuaz *m*
mini-series [ˈmɪnɪsɪəriːz] *n* serie *f* de pocos capítulos, miniserie *f*
miniskirt [ˈmɪnɪskəːt] *n* minifalda
minister [ˈmɪnɪstəʳ] *n* (*Brit Pol*) ministro(-a); (*Rel*) pastor *m* ■ *vi*: **to ~ to** atender a
ministerial [mɪnɪsˈtɪərɪəl] *adj* (*Brit Pol*) ministerial
ministry [ˈmɪnɪstrɪ] *n* (*Brit Pol*) ministerio; (*Rel*) sacerdocio; **M~ of Defence** Ministerio de Defensa
mink [mɪŋk] *n* visón *m*
mink coat *n* abrigo de visón
Minn. *abbr* (*US*) = **Minnesota**
minnow [ˈmɪnəu] *n* pececillo (de agua dulce)
minor [ˈmaɪnəʳ] *adj* (*unimportant*) secundario; (*Mus*) menor ■ *n* (*Law*) menor *m/f* de edad
Minorca [mɪˈnɔːkə] *n* Menorca
minority [maɪˈnɔrɪtɪ] *n* minoría; **to be in a ~** estar en *or* ser minoría
minority interest *n* participación *f* minoritaria
minster [ˈmɪnstəʳ] *n* catedral *f*
minstrel [ˈmɪnstrəl] *n* juglar *m*
mint [mɪnt] *n* (*plant*) menta, hierbabuena; (*sweet*) caramelo de menta ■ *vt* (*coins*) acuñar; **the (Royal) M~,** (*US*) **the (US) M~** la Casa de la Moneda; **in ~ condition** en perfecto estado
mint sauce *n* salsa de menta
minuet [mɪnjuˈɛt] *n* minué *m*
minus [ˈmaɪnəs] *n* (*also:* **minus sign**) signo menos ■ *prep* menos

minuscule ['mɪnəskju:l] *adj* minúsculo
minute *n* ['mɪnɪt] minuto; (*fig*) momento; **minutes** *npl* (*of meeting*) actas *fpl* ■ *adj* [maɪ'nju:t] diminuto; (*search*) minucioso; **it is 5 minutes past 3** son las 3 y 5 (minutos); **at the last ~** a última hora; **wait a ~!** ¡espera un momento!; **up to the ~** de última hora; **in ~ detail** con todo detalle
minute book *n* libro de actas
minute hand *n* minutero
minutely [maɪ'nju:tlɪ] *adv* (*by a small amount*) por muy poco; (*in detail*) detalladamente, minuciosamente
minutiae [mɪ'nju:ʃii:] *npl* minucias *fpl*
miracle ['mɪrəkl] *n* milagro
miracle play *n* auto, milagro
miraculous [mɪ'rækjuləs] *adj* milagroso
miraculously [mɪ'rækjuləslɪ] *adv* milagrosamente
mirage ['mɪrɑ:ʒ] *n* espejismo
mire [maɪə[r]] *n* fango, lodo
mirror ['mɪrə[r]] *n* espejo; (*in car*) retrovisor *m* ■ *vt* reflejar
mirror image *n* reflejo inverso
mirth [mə:θ] *n* alegría; (*laughter*) risa, risas *fpl*
misadventure [mɪsəd'ventʃə[r]] *n* desventura; **death by ~** muerte *f* accidental
misanthropist [mɪ'zænθrəpɪst] *n* misántropo(-a)
misapply [mɪsə'plaɪ] *vt* emplear mal
misapprehension ['mɪsæprɪ'hɛnʃən] *n* equivocación *f*
misappropriate [mɪsə'prəuprɪeɪt] *vt* (*funds*) malversar
misappropriation ['mɪsəprəuprɪ'eɪʃən] *n* malversación *f*, desfalco
misbehave [mɪsbɪ'heɪv] *vi* portarse mal
misbehaviour, misbehavior (*US*) [mɪsbɪ'heɪvjə[r]] *n* mala conducta
misc. *abbr* = **miscellaneous**
miscalculate [mɪs'kælkjuleɪt] *vt* calcular mal
miscalculation [mɪskælkju'leɪʃən] *n* error *m* (de cálculo)
miscarriage ['mɪskærɪdʒ] *n* (*Med*) aborto (no provocado); **~ of justice** error *m* judicial
miscarry [mɪs'kærɪ] *vi* (*Med*) abortar (de forma natural); (*fail: plans*) fracasar, malograrse
miscellaneous [mɪsɪ'leɪnɪəs] *adj* varios(-as), diversos(-as); **~ expenses** gastos diversos
miscellany [mɪ'sɛlənɪ] *n* miscelánea
mischance [mɪs'tʃɑ:ns] *n* desgracia, mala suerte *f*; **by (some) ~** por (alguna) desgracia
mischief ['mɪstʃɪf] *n* (*naughtiness*) travesura; (*harm*) mal *m*, daño; (*maliciousness*) malicia
mischievous ['mɪstʃɪvəs] *adj* travieso; dañino; (*playful*) malicioso
mischievously ['mɪstʃɪvəslɪ] *adv* por travesura; maliciosamente
misconception ['mɪskən'sɛpʃən] *n* concepto erróneo; equivocación *f*
misconduct [mɪs'kɔndʌkt] *n* mala conducta; **professional ~** falta profesional
misconstrue [mɪskən'stru:] *vt* interpretar mal
miscount [mɪs'kaunt] *vt, vi* contar mal
misdeed [mɪs'di:d] *n* (*old*) fechoría, delito
misdemeanour, misdemeanor (*US*) [mɪsdɪ'mi:nə[r]] *n* delito, ofensa
misdirect [mɪsdɪ'rɛkt] *vt* (*person*) informar mal; (*letter*) poner señas incorrectas en
miser ['maɪzə[r]] *n* avaro(-a)
miserable ['mɪzərəbl] *adj* (*unhappy*) triste, desgraciado; (*wretched*) miserable; **to feel ~** sentirse triste
miserably ['mɪzərəblɪ] *adv* (*smile, answer*) tristemente; (*fail*) rotundamente; **to pay ~** pagar una miseria
miserly ['maɪzəlɪ] *adj* avariento, tacaño
misery ['mɪzərɪ] *n* (*unhappiness*) tristeza; (*wretchedness*) miseria, desdicha
misfire [mɪs'faɪə[r]] *vi* fallar
misfit ['mɪsfɪt] *n* (*person*) inadaptado(-a)
misfortune [mɪs'fɔ:tʃən] *n* desgracia
misgiving [mɪs'gɪvɪŋ] *n*, **misgivings** [mɪs'gɪvɪŋz] *npl* (*mistrust*) recelo; (*apprehension*) presentimiento; **to have misgivings about sth** tener dudas sobre algo
misguided [mɪs'gaɪdɪd] *adj* equivocado
mishandle [mɪs'hændl] *vt* (*treat roughly*) maltratar; (*mismanage*) manejar mal
mishap ['mɪshæp] *n* desgracia, contratiempo
mishear [mɪs'hɪə[r]] *vt, vi* (*irreg: like* **hear**) oír mal
mishmash ['mɪʃmæʃ] *n* (*col*) revoltijo
misinform [mɪsɪn'fɔ:m] *vt* informar mal
misinterpret [mɪsɪn'tə:prɪt] *vt* interpretar mal
misinterpretation ['mɪsɪntə:prɪ'teɪʃən] *n* mala interpretación *f*
misjudge [mɪs'dʒʌdʒ] *vt* juzgar mal
mislay [mɪs'leɪ] *vt* (*irreg: like* **lay**) extraviar, perder
mislead [mɪs'li:d] *vt* (*irreg: like* **lead**) llevar a conclusiones erróneas; (*deliberately*) engañar
misleading [mɪs'li:dɪŋ] *adj* engañoso
misled [mɪs'lɛd] *pt, pp of* **mislead**
mismanage [mɪs'mænɪdʒ] *vt* administrar mal
mismanagement [mɪs'mænɪdʒmənt] *n* mala administración *f*
misnomer [mɪs'nəumə[r]] *n* término inapropiado *or* equivocado

misogynist [mɪ'sɔdʒɪnɪst] *n* misógino
misplace [mɪs'pleɪs] *vt* (*lose*) extraviar; **misplaced** (*trust etc*) inmerecido
misprint ['mɪsprɪnt] *n* errata, error *m* de imprenta
mispronounce [mɪsprə'nauns] *vt* pronunciar mal
misquote ['mɪs'kwəut] *vt* citar incorrectamente
misread [mɪs'ri:d] *vt* (*irreg*: *like* **read**) leer mal
misrepresent [mɪsrɛprɪ'zɛnt] *vt* falsificar
misrepresentation [mɪsrɛprɪzɛn'teɪʃən] *n* (*Law*) falsa declaración *f*
Miss [mɪs] *n* Señorita; **Dear ~ Smith** Estimada Señorita Smith
miss [mɪs] *vt* (*train etc*) perder; (*shot*) errar, fallar; (*appointment, class*) faltar a; (*escape, avoid*) evitar; (*notice loss of*: *money etc*) notar la falta de, echar en falta; (*regret the absence of*): **I ~ him** le echo de menos ■ *vi* fallar ■ *n* (*shot*) tiro fallido; **the bus just missed the wall** faltó poco para que el autobús se estrella contra el muro; **you're missing the point** no has entendido la idea
▸ **miss out** *vt* (*Brit*) omitir
▸ **miss out on** *vt fus* (*fun, party, opportunity*) perderse
Miss. *abbr* (*US*) = **Mississippi**
missal ['mɪsl] *n* misal *m*
misshapen [mɪs'ʃeɪpən] *adj* deforme
missile ['mɪsaɪl] *n* (*Aviat*) misil *m*; (*object thrown*) proyectil *m*
missile base *n* base *f* de misiles
missile launcher *n* lanzamisiles *m inv*
missing ['mɪsɪŋ] *adj* (*pupil*) ausente, que falta; (*thing*) perdido; (*Mil*) desaparecido; **to be ~** faltar; **~ person** desaparecido(-a)
mission ['mɪʃən] *n* misión *f*; **on a ~ for sb** en una misión para algn
missionary ['mɪʃənrɪ] *n* misionero(-a)
misspell [mɪs'spɛl] *vt* (*irreg*: *like* **spell**) escribir mal
misspent ['mɪs'spɛnt] *adj*: **his ~ youth** su juventud disipada
mist [mɪst] *n* (*light*) neblina; (*heavy*) niebla; (*at sea*) bruma ■ *vi* (*also*: **mist over, mist up**: *weather*) nublarse; (*Brit*: *windows*) empañarse
mistake [mɪs'teɪk] *n* error *m* ■ *vt* (*irreg*: *like* **take**) entender mal; **by ~** por equivocación; **to make a ~** (*about sb/sth*) equivocarse; (*in writing, calculating etc*) cometer un error; **to ~ A for B** confundir A con B
mistaken [mɪs'teɪkən] *pp of* **mistake** ■ *adj* (*idea etc*) equivocado; **to be ~** equivocarse, engañarse; **~ identity** identificación *f* errónea
mistakenly [mɪs'teɪkənlɪ] *adv* erróneamente
mister ['mɪstəʳ] *n* (*col*) señor *m*; *see* **Mr**
mistletoe ['mɪsltəu] *n* muérdago
mistook [mɪs'tuk] *pt of* **mistake**
mistranslation [mɪstræns'leɪʃən] *n* mala traducción *f*
mistreat [mɪs'tri:t] *vt* maltratar, tratar mal
mistress ['mɪstrɪs] *n* (*lover*) amante *f*; (*of house*) señora (de la casa); (*Brit*: *in primary school*) maestra; (*in secondary school*) profesora; *see also* **Mrs**
mistrust [mɪs'trʌst] *vt* desconfiar de ■ *n*: **~ (of)** desconfianza (de)
mistrustful [mɪs'trʌstful] *adj*: **~ (of)** desconfiado (de), receloso (de)
misty ['mɪstɪ] *adj* nebuloso, brumoso; (*day*) de niebla; (*glasses*) empañado
misty-eyed ['mɪstɪ'aɪd] *adj* sentimental
misunderstand [mɪsʌndə'stænd] *vt, vi* (*irreg*: *like* **understand**) entender mal
misunderstanding [mɪsʌndə'stændɪŋ] *n* malentendido
misunderstood [mɪsʌndə'stud] *pt, pp of* **misunderstand** ■ *adj* (*person*) incomprendido
misuse *n* [mɪs'ju:s] mal uso; (*of power*) abuso ■ *vt* [mɪs'ju:z] abusar de; (*funds*) malversar
MIT *n abbr* (*US*) = **Massachusetts Institute of Technology**
mite [maɪt] *n* (*small quantity*) pizca; **poor ~!** ¡pobrecito!
mitigate ['mɪtɪgeɪt] *vt* mitigar; **mitigating circumstances** circunstancias *fpl* atenuantes
mitigation [mɪtɪ'geɪʃən] *n* mitigación *f*, alivio
mitre, (*US*) **miter** ['maɪtəʳ] *n* mitra
mitt ['mɪt], **mitten** ['mɪtn] *n* manopla
mix [mɪks] *vt* (*gen*) mezclar; (*combine*) unir ■ *vi* mezclarse; (*people*) llevarse bien ■ *n* mezcla; **to ~ sth with sth** mezclar algo con algo; **to ~ business with pleasure** combinar los negocios con el placer; **cake ~** preparado para pastel
▸ **mix in** *vt* (*eggs etc*) añadir
▸ **mix up** *vt* mezclar; (*confuse*) confundir; **to be mixed up in sth** estar metido en algo
mixed [mɪkst] *adj* (*assorted*) variado, surtido; (*school, marriage etc*) mixto
mixed-ability ['mɪkstə'bɪlɪtɪ] *adj* (*class etc*) de alumnos de distintas capacidades
mixed blessing *n*: **it's a ~** tiene su lado bueno y su lado malo
mixed doubles *n* (*Sport*) mixtos *mpl*
mixed economy *n* economía mixta
mixed grill *n* (*Brit*) parrillada mixta
mixed-up [mɪkst'ʌp] *adj* (*confused*) confuso, revuelto

mixer ['mɪksəʳ] *n (for food)* batidora; *(person)*: **he's a good ~** tiene don de gentes
mixer tap *n* (grifo) monomando
mixture ['mɪkstʃəʳ] *n* mezcla
mix-up ['mɪksʌp] *n* confusión *f*
Mk *abbr* (*Brit Tech*: = *mark*) Mk
mkt *abbr* = **market**
MLA *n abbr* (*Brit Pol: Northern Ireland*: = *Member of the Legislative Assembly*) miembro de la asamblea legislativa
MLitt *n abbr* (= *Master of Literature, Master of Letters*) *título universitario de postgrado*; *see also* **master's degree**
MLR *n abbr* (*Brit*) = **minimum lending rate**
mm *abbr* (= *millimetre*) mm
MMR vaccine *n* (*against measles, mumps, rubella*) vacuna triple vírica
MMS *n abbr* (= *multimedia messaging service*) MMS *m*
MN *abbr* (*Brit*) = **Merchant Navy**; (*US*) = **Minnesota**
MO *n abbr* (*Med*) = **medical officer**; (*US col*) = **modus operandi** ■ *abbr* (*US*) = **Missouri**
Mo. *abbr* (*US*) = **Missouri**
m.o. *abbr* (= *money order*) g/
moan [məun] *n* gemido ■ *vi* gemir; (*col: complain*): **to ~ (about)** quejarse (de)
moaning ['məunɪŋ] *n* gemidos *mpl*; quejas *fpl*
moat [məut] *n* foso
mob [mɔb] *n* multitud *f*; (*pej*): **the ~** el populacho ■ *vt* acosar
mobile ['məubaɪl] *adj* móvil ■ *n* móvil *m*
mobile home *n* caravana
mobile phone *n* teléfono móvil
mobility [məu'bɪlɪtɪ] *n* movilidad *f*; **~ of labour** *or* (*US*) **labor** movilidad *f* de la mano de obra
mobilize ['məubɪlaɪz] *vt* movilizar
moccasin ['mɔkəsɪn] *n* mocasín *m*
mock [mɔk] *vt* (*make ridiculous*) ridiculizar; (*laugh at*) burlarse de ■ *adj* fingido
mockery ['mɔkərɪ] *n* burla; **to make a ~ of** desprestigiar
mocking ['mɔkɪŋ] *adj* (*tone*) burlón(-ona)
mockingbird ['mɔkɪŋbə:d] *n* sinsonte *m* (*LAm*), zenzontle *m* (*LAm*)
mock-up ['mɔkʌp] *n* maqueta
MOD *n abbr* (*Brit*) = **Ministry of Defence**; *see* **defence**
mod cons ['mɔd'kɔnz] *npl abbr* (= *modern conveniences*) *see* **convenience**
mode [məud] *n* modo; (*of transport*) medio; (*Comput*) modo, modalidad *f*
model ['mɔdl] *n* (*gen*) modelo; (*Arch*) maqueta; (*person: for fashion, art*) modelo *m/f* ■ *adj* modelo *inv* ■ *vt* modelar ■ *vi* ser modelo; **~ railway** ferrocarril *m* de juguete; **to ~ clothes** pasar modelos, ser modelo; **to ~ on** crear a imitación de
modelling, (*US*) **modeling** ['mɔdlɪŋ] *n* (*modelmaking*) modelado
modem ['məudəm] *n* módem *m*
moderate [*adj, n* 'mɔdərət, *vb* 'mɔdəreɪt] *adj, n* moderado(-a) *m(f)* ■ *vi* moderarse, calmarse ■ *vt* moderar
moderately ['mɔdərətlɪ] *adv* (*act*) con moderación; (*expensive, difficult*) medianamente; (*pleased, happy*) bastante
moderation [mɔdə'reɪʃən] *n* moderación *f*; **in ~** con moderación
moderator ['mɔdəreɪtəʳ] *n* (*mediator*) moderador(a) *m(f)*
modern ['mɔdən] *adj* moderno; **~ languages** lenguas *fpl* modernas
modernity [mə'də:nɪtɪ] *n* modernidad *f*
modernization [mɔdənaɪ'zeɪʃən] *n* modernización *f*
modernize ['mɔdənaɪz] *vt* modernizar
modest ['mɔdɪst] *adj* modesto
modestly ['mɔdɪstlɪ] *adv* modestamente
modesty ['mɔdɪstɪ] *n* modestia
modicum ['mɔdɪkəm] *n*: **a ~ of** un mínimo de
modification [mɔdɪfɪ'keɪʃən] *n* modificación *f*; **to make modifications** hacer cambios *or* modificaciones
modify ['mɔdɪfaɪ] *vt* modificar
modish ['məudɪʃ] *adj* de moda
Mods [mɔdz] *n abbr* (*Brit*: = (*Honour*) *Moderations*) *examen de licenciatura de la universidad de Oxford*
modular ['mɔdjuləʳ] *adj* (*filing, unit*) modular
modulate ['mɔdjuleɪt] *vt* modular
modulation [mɔdju'leɪʃən] *n* modulación *f*
module ['mɔdju:l] *n* módulo
modus operandi ['məudəsɔpə'rændi:] *n* manera de actuar
Mogadishu [mɔgə'dɪʃu:] *n* Mogadiscio
mogul ['məugəl] *n* (*fig*) magnate *m*
MOH *n abbr* (*Brit*) = **Medical Officer of Health**
mohair ['məuhɛəʳ] *n* mohair *m*
Mohammed [mə'hæmɛd] *n* Mahoma *m*
moist [mɔɪst] *adj* húmedo
moisten ['mɔɪsn] *vt* humedecer
moisture ['mɔɪstʃəʳ] *n* humedad *f*
moisturize ['mɔɪstʃəraɪz] *vt* (*skin*) hidratar
moisturizer ['mɔɪstʃəraɪzəʳ] *n* crema hidratante
molar ['məuləʳ] *n* muela
molasses [məu'læsɪz] *n* melaza
mold [məuld] *n, vt* (*US*) = **mould**
Moldavia [mɔl'deɪvɪə], **Moldova** [mɔl'dəuvə] *n* Moldavia, Moldova
Moldavian [mɔl'deɪvɪən], **Moldovan** [mɔl'dəuvən] *adj, n* moldavo(-a) *m(f)*

mole [məul] *n* (*animal*) topo; (*spot*) lunar *m*
molecular [mə'lɛkjuləʳ] *adj* molecular
molecule ['mɔlɪkju:l] *n* molécula
molest [məu'lɛst] *vt* importunar; (*sexually*) abordar con propósitos deshonestos
moll [mɔl] *n* (*slang*) amiga
mollusc, mollusk (US) ['mɔləsk] *n* molusco
mollycoddle ['mɔlɪkɔdl] *vt* mimar
Molotov cocktail ['mɔlətɔf-] *n* cóctel *m* Molotov
molt [məult] *vi* (US) = **moult**
molten ['məultən] *adj* fundido; (*lava*) líquido
mom [mɔm] *n* (US) = **mum**
moment ['məumənt] *n* momento; **at** *or* **for the ~** de momento, por el momento, por ahora; **in a ~** dentro de un momento
momentarily ['məuməntrɪlɪ] *adv* momentáneamente; (US: *very soon*) de un momento a otro
momentary ['məuməntərɪ] *adj* momentáneo
momentous [məu'mɛntəs] *adj* trascendental, importante
momentum [məu'mɛntəm] *n* momento; (*fig*) ímpetu *m*; **to gather ~** cobrar velocidad; (*fig*) cobrar fuerza
mommy ['mɔmɪ] *n* (US) = **mummy**
Mon *abbr* (= *Monday*) lun
Monaco ['mɔnəkəu] *n* Mónaco
monarch ['mɔnək] *n* monarca *m/f*
monarchist ['mɔnəkɪst] *n* monárquico(-a)
monarchy ['mɔnəkɪ] *n* monarquía
monastery ['mɔnəstərɪ] *n* monasterio
monastic [mə'næstɪk] *adj* monástico
Monday ['mʌndɪ] *n* lunes *m inv*; *see also* **Tuesday**
Monegasque [mɔnɪ'gæsk] *adj, n* monegasco(-a) *m(f)*
monetarist ['mʌnɪtərɪst] *n* monetarista *m/f*
monetary ['mʌnɪtərɪ] *adj* monetario
monetary policy *n* política monetaria
money ['mʌnɪ] *n* dinero, plata (*LAm*); **to make ~** ganar dinero; **I've got no ~ left** no me queda dinero
moneyed ['mʌnɪd] *adj* adinerado
moneylender ['mʌnɪlɛndəʳ] *n* prestamista *m/f*
moneymaker ['mʌnɪmeɪkəʳ] *n* (*Brit col: business*) filón *m*
moneymaking ['mʌnɪmeɪkɪŋ] *adj* rentable
money market *n* mercado monetario
money order *n* giro
money-spinner ['mʌnɪspɪnəʳ] *n* (*col: person, idea, business*) filón *m*
money supply *n* oferta monetaria, medio circulante, volumen *m* monetario
Mongol ['mɔŋgəl] *n* mongol(a) *m(f)*; (*Ling*) mongol *m*
mongol ['mɔŋgəl] *adj, n* (*Med*) mongólico
Mongolia [mɔŋ'gəulɪə] *n* Mongolia
Mongolian [mɔŋ'gəulɪən] *adj* mongol(a) ■ *n* mongol(a) *m(f)*; (*Ling*) mongol *m*
mongoose ['mɔŋgu:s] *n* mangosta
mongrel ['mʌŋgrəl] *n* (*dog*) perro cruzado
monitor ['mɔnɪtəʳ] *n* monitor *m* ■ *vt* controlar; (*foreign station*) escuchar
monk [mʌŋk] *n* monje *m*
monkey ['mʌŋkɪ] *n* mono
monkey business *n*, **monkey tricks** ■ *npl* tejemanejes *mpl*
monkey nut *n* (*Brit*) cacahuete *m*, maní *m* (*LAm*)
monkey wrench *n* llave *f* inglesa
mono ['mɔnəu] *adj* (*broadcast etc*) mono *inv*
mono... [mɔnəu] *pref* mono ...
monochrome ['mɔnəukrəum] *adj* monocromo
monocle ['mɔnəkl] *n* monóculo
monogamous [mə'nɔgəməs] *adj* monógamo
monogram ['mɔnəgræm] *n* monograma *m*
monolith ['mɔnəlɪθ] *n* monolito
monolithic [mɔnə'lɪθɪk] *adj* monolítico
monologue ['mɔnəlɔg] *n* monólogo
monoplane ['mɔnəpleɪn] *n* monoplano
monopolist [mə'nɔpəlɪst] *n* monopolista *m/f*
monopolize [mə'nɔpəlaɪz] *vt* monopolizar
monopoly [mə'nɔpəlɪ] *n* monopolio; **Monopolies and Mergers Commission** (*Brit*) *comisión reguladora de monopolios y fusiones*
monorail ['mɔnəureɪl] *n* monocarril *m*, monorraíl *m*
monosodium glutamate [mɔnə'səudɪəm 'glu:təmeɪt] *n* glutamato monosódico
monosyllabic [mɔnɔsɪ'læbɪk] *adj* monosílabo
monosyllable ['mɔnəsɪləbl] *n* monosílabo
monotone ['mɔnətəun] *n* voz *f* (*or* tono) monocorde
monotonous [mə'nɔtənəs] *adj* monótono
monotony [mə'nɔtənɪ] *n* monotonía
monoxide [mə'nɔksaɪd] *n*: **carbon ~** monóxido de carbono
monseigneur [mɔnsɛn'jə:ʳ], **monsignor** [mɔn'si:njəʳ] *n* monseñor *m*
monsoon [mɔn'su:n] *n* monzón *m*
monster ['mɔnstəʳ] *n* monstruo
monstrosity [mɔns'trɔsɪtɪ] *n* monstruosidad *f*
monstrous ['mɔnstrəs] *adj* (*huge*) enorme; (*atrocious*) monstruoso
Mont. *abbr* (US) = **Montana**
montage [mɔn'tɑ:ʒ] *n* montaje *m*
Mont Blanc [mɔ̃'blɑ̃] *n* Mont Blanc *m*
month [mʌnθ] *n* mes *m*; **300 dollars a ~** 300 dólares al mes; **every ~** cada mes

monthly ['mʌnθlɪ] *adj* mensual ■ *adv* mensualmente ■ *n* (*magazine*) revista, mensual; **twice ~** dos veces al mes; **~ instalment** mensualidad *f*
monument ['mɔnjumənt] *n* monumento
monumental [mɔnju'mɛntl] *adj* monumental
moo [muː] *vi* mugir
mood [muːd] *n* humor *m*; **to be in a good/bad ~** estar de buen/mal humor
moodily ['muːdɪlɪ] *adv* malhumoradamente
moodiness ['muːdɪnɪs] *n* humor *m* cambiante; (*bad mood*) mal humor *m*
moody ['muːdɪ] *adj* (*variable*) de humor variable; (*sullen*) malhumorado
moon [muːn] *n* luna
moonbeam ['muːnbiːm] *n* rayo de luna
moon landing *n* alunizaje *m*
moonless ['muːnlɪs] *adj* sin luna
moonlight ['muːnlaɪt] *n* luz *f* de la luna ■ *vi* hacer pluriempleo
moonlighting ['muːnlaɪtɪŋ] *n* pluriempleo
moonlit ['muːnlɪt] *adj*: **a ~ night** una noche de luna
moonshot ['muːnʃɔt] *n* lanzamiento de una astronave a la luna
moonstruck ['muːnstrʌk] *adj* chiflado
moony ['muːnɪ] *adj*: **to have ~ eyes** estar soñando despierto, estar pensando en las musarañas
Moor [muəʳ] *n* moro(-a)
moor [muəʳ] *n* páramo ■ *vt* (*ship*) amarrar ■ *vi* echar las amarras
moorings ['muərɪŋz] *npl* (*chains*) amarras *fpl*; (*place*) amarradero *sg*
Moorish ['muərɪʃ] *adj* moro; (*architecture*) árabe
moorland ['muələnd] *n* páramo, brezal *m*
moose [muːs] *n pl inv* alce *m*
moot [muːt] *vt* proponer para la discusión, sugerir ■ *adj*: **~ point** punto discutible
mop [mɔp] *n* fregona; (*of hair*) greñas *fpl* ■ *vt* fregar
▸ **mop up** *vt* limpiar
mope [məup] *vi* estar deprimido
▸ **mope about, mope around** *vi* andar abatido
moped ['məupɛd] *n* ciclomotor *m*
moquette [mɔ'kɛt] *n* moqueta
MOR *adj abbr* (*Mus*: = *middle-of-the-road*) para el gran público
moral ['mɔrl] *adj* moral ■ *n* moraleja; **morals** *npl* moralidad *f*, moral *f*
morale [mɔ'rɑːl] *n* moral *f*
morality [mə'rælɪtɪ] *n* moralidad *f*
moralize ['mɔrəlaɪz] *vi*: **to ~ (about)** moralizar (sobre)
morally ['mɔrəlɪ] *adv* moralmente
moral victory *n* victoria moral
morass [mə'ræs] *n* pantano
moratorium [mɔrə'tɔːrɪəm] *n* moratoria
morbid ['mɔːbɪd] *adj* (*interest*) morboso; (*Med*) mórbido

KEYWORD

more [mɔːʳ] *adj* **1** (*greater in number etc*) más; **more people/work than before** más gente/trabajo que antes
2 (*additional*) más; **do you want (some) more tea?** ¿quieres más té?; **is there any more wine?** ¿queda vino?; **it'll take a few more weeks** tardará unas semanas más; **it's 2 kms more to the house** faltan 2 kms para la casa; **more time/letters than we expected** más tiempo del que/más cartas de las que esperábamos; **I have no more money, I don't have any more money** (ya) no tengo más dinero
■ *pron* (*greater amount, additional amount*) más; **more than 10** más de 10; **it cost more than the other one/than we expected** costó más que el otro/más de lo que esperábamos; **is there any more?** ¿hay más?; **I want more** quiero más; **and what's more ...** y además ...; **many/much more** muchos(-as)/mucho(-a) más
■ *adv* más; **more dangerous/easily (than)** más peligroso/fácilmente (que); **more and more expensive** cada vez más caro; **more or less** más o menos; **more than ever** más que nunca; **she doesn't live here any more** ya no vive aquí

moreover [mɔː'rəuvəʳ] *adv* además, por otra parte
morgue [mɔːg] *n* depósito de cadáveres
MORI ['mɔːrɪ] *n abbr* (*Brit*) = **Market and Opinion Research Institute**
moribund ['mɔrɪbʌnd] *adj* moribundo
Mormon ['mɔːmən] *n* mormón(-ona) *m(f)*
morning ['mɔːnɪŋ] *n* (*gen*) mañana; (*early morning*) madrugada; **in the ~** por la mañana; **7 o'clock in the ~** las 7 de la mañana; **this ~** esta mañana
morning-after pill ['mɔːnɪŋ'ɑːftə-] *n* píldora del día después
morning sickness *n* (*Med*) náuseas *fpl* del embarazo
Moroccan [mə'rɔkən] *adj, n* marroquí *m/f*
Morocco [mə'rɔkəu] *n* Marruecos *m*
moron ['mɔːrɔn] *n* imbécil *m/f*
morose [mə'rəus] *adj* hosco, malhumorado
morphine ['mɔːfiːn] *n* morfina

morris dancing ['mɔrɪs-] *n (Brit) baile tradicional inglés en el que se llevan cascabeles en la ropa*
Morse [mɔːs] *n* (*also*: **Morse code**) (alfabeto) morse *m*
morsel ['mɔːsl] *n* (*of food*) bocado
mortal ['mɔːtl] *adj, n* mortal *m*
mortality [mɔː'tælɪtɪ] *n* mortalidad *f*
mortality rate *n* tasa de mortalidad
mortally ['mɔːtəlɪ] *adv* mortalmente
mortar ['mɔːtə^r] *n* argamasa; (*implement*) mortero
mortgage ['mɔːgɪdʒ] *n* hipoteca ■ *vt* hipotecar; **to take out a ~** sacar una hipoteca
mortgage company *n* (*US*) ≈ banco hipotecario
mortgagee [mɔːgə'dʒiː] *n* acreedor(a) *m(f)* hipotecario(-a)
mortgager ['mɔːgədʒə^r] *n* deudor(a) *m(f)* hipotecario(-a)
mortice ['mɔːtɪs] = **mortise**
mortician [mɔː'tɪʃən] *n* (*US*) director(a) *m(f)* de pompas fúnebres
mortification ['mɔːtɪfɪ'keɪʃən] *n* mortificación *f*, humillación *f*
mortified ['mɔːtɪfaɪd] *adj*: **I was ~** me dio muchísima vergüenza
mortise ['mɔːtɪs], **mortise lock** *n* cerradura de muesca
mortuary ['mɔːtjuərɪ] *n* depósito de cadáveres
mosaic [məu'zeɪɪk] *n* mosaico
Moscow ['mɔskəu] *n* Moscú *m*
Moslem ['mɔzləm] *adj, n* = **Muslim**
mosque [mɔsk] *n* mezquita
mosquito (*pl* **mosquitoes**) [mɔs'kiːtəu] *n* mosquito
moss [mɔs] *n* musgo
mossy ['mɔsɪ] *adj* musgoso, cubierto de musgo
most [məust] *adj* la mayor parte de, la mayoría de ■ *pron* la mayor parte, la mayoría ■ *adv* el más; (*very*) muy; **the ~** (*also: + adjective*) el más; **~ of them** la mayor parte de ellos; **I saw the ~** yo fui el que más vi; **at the (very) ~** a lo sumo, todo lo más; **to make the ~ of** aprovechar (al máximo); **a ~ interesting book** un libro interesantísimo
mostly ['məustlɪ] *adv* en su mayor parte, principalmente
MOT *n abbr* (*Brit*: = *Ministry of Transport*): **the ~ (test)** ≈ la ITV
motel [məu'tɛl] *n* motel *m*
moth [mɔθ] *n* mariposa nocturna; (*clothes moth*) polilla
mothball ['mɔθbɔːl] *n* bola de naftalina
moth-eaten ['mɔθiːtn] *adj* apolillado
mother ['mʌðə^r] *n* madre *f* ■ *adj* materno ■ *vt* (*care for*) cuidar (como una madre)
mother board *n* (*Comput*) placa madre
motherhood ['mʌðəhud] *n* maternidad *f*
mother-in-law ['mʌðərɪnlɔː] *n* suegra
motherly ['mʌðəlɪ] *adj* maternal
mother-of-pearl ['mʌðərəv'pəːl] *n* nácar *m*
mother's help *n* niñera
mother-to-be ['mʌðətə'biː] *n* futura madre
mother tongue *n* lengua materna
mothproof ['mɔθpruːf] *adj* a prueba de polillas
motif [məu'tiːf] *n* motivo; (*theme*) tema *m*
motion ['məuʃən] *n* movimiento; (*gesture*) ademán *m*, señal *f*; (*at meeting*) moción *f*; (*Brit*: *also*: **bowel motion**) evacuación *f* intestinal ■ *vt, vi*: **to ~ (to) sb to do sth** hacer señas a algn para que haga algo; **to be in ~** (*vehicle*) estar en movimiento; **to set in ~** poner en marcha; **to go through the motions of doing sth** (*fig*) hacer algo mecánicamente *or* sin convicción
motionless ['məuʃənlɪs] *adj* inmóvil
motion picture *n* película
motivate ['məutɪveɪt] *vt* motivar
motivated ['məutɪveɪtɪd] *adj* motivado
motivation [məutɪ'veɪʃən] *n* motivación *f*
motivational research [məutɪ'veɪʃənl-] *n* estudios *mpl* de motivación
motive ['məutɪv] *n* motivo; **from the best motives** con las mejores intenciones
motley ['mɔtlɪ] *adj* variopinto
motor ['məutə^r] *n* motor *m*; (*Brit: col: vehicle*) coche *m*, carro (*LAm*), automóvil *m*, auto *m* (*LAm*) ■ *adj* motor/motora, motriz
motorbike ['məutəbaɪk] *n* moto *f*
motorboat ['məutəbəut] *n* lancha motora
motorcade ['məutəkeɪd] *n* desfile *m* de automóviles
motorcar ['məutəkɑː^r] *n* (*Brit*) coche *m*, carro (*LAm*), automóvil *m*, auto *m* (*LAm*)
motorcoach ['məutəkəutʃ] *n* autocar *m*, autobús *m*, camión *m* (*LAm*)
motorcycle ['məutəsaɪkl] *n* motocicleta
motorcycle racing *n* motociclismo
motorcyclist ['məutəsaɪklɪst] *n* motociclista *m/f*
motoring ['məutərɪŋ] *n* (*Brit*) automovilismo ■ *adj* (*accident, offence*) de tráfico *or* tránsito
motorist ['məutərɪst] *n* conductor(a) *m(f)*, automovilista *m/f*
motorize ['məutəraɪz] *vt* motorizar
motor oil *n* aceite *m* para motores
motor racing *n* (*Brit*) carreras *fpl* de coches, automovilismo

motor scooter *n* vespa®
motor vehicle *n* automóvil *m*
motorway ['məutəweɪ] *n* (*Brit*) autopista
mottled ['mɔtld] *adj* moteado
motto (*pl* **mottoes**) ['mɔtəu] *n* lema *m*; (*watchword*) consigna
mould, mold (*US*) [məuld] *n* molde *m*; (*mildew*) moho ■ *vt* moldear; (*fig*) formar
moulder, molder (*US*) ['məuldə^r] *vi* (*decay*) decaer
moulding, molding (*US*) ['məuldɪŋ] *n* (*Arch*) moldura
mouldy, moldy (*US*) ['məuldɪ] *adj* enmohecido
moult, molt (*US*) [məult] *vi* mudar la piel; (*bird*) mudar las plumas
mound [maund] *n* montón *m*, montículo
mount [maunt] *n* monte *m*; (*horse*) montura; (*for jewel etc*) engarce *m*; (*for picture*) marco ■ *vt* montar en, subir a; (*stairs*) subir; (*exhibition*) montar; (*attack*) lanzar; (*stamp*) pegar, fijar; (*picture*) enmarcar ■ *vi* (*also*: **mount up**) subirse, montarse
mountain ['mauntɪn] *n* montaña ■ *cpd* de montaña; **to make a ~ out of a molehill** hacer una montaña de un grano de arena
mountain bike *n* bicicleta de montaña
mountaineer [mauntɪ'nɪə^r] *n* montañero(-a), alpinista *m/f*, andinista *m/f* (*LAm*)
mountaineering [mauntɪ'nɪərɪŋ] *n* montañismo, alpinismo, andinismo (*LAm*)
mountainous ['mauntɪnəs] *adj* montañoso
mountain range *n* sierra
mountain rescue team *n* equipo de rescate de montaña
mountainside ['mauntɪnsaɪd] *n* ladera de la montaña
mounted ['mauntɪd] *adj* montado
Mount Everest *n* Monte *m* Everest
mourn [mɔ:n] *vt* llorar, lamentar ■ *vi*: **to ~ for** llorar la muerte de, lamentarse por
mourner ['mɔ:nə^r] *n* doliente *m/f*
mournful ['mɔ:nful] *adj* triste, lúgubre
mourning ['mɔ:nɪŋ] *n* luto ■ *cpd* (*dress*) de luto; **in ~** de luto
mouse (*pl* **mice**) [maus, maɪs] *n* (*also Comput*) ratón *m*
mouse mat, mouse pad *n* (*Comput*) alfombrilla, almohadilla
mousetrap ['maustræp] *n* ratonera
mousse [mu:s] *n* (*Culin*) mousse *f*; (*for hair*) espuma (moldeadora)
moustache [məs'tɑ:ʃ], (*US*) **mustache** ['mʌstæʃ] *n* bigote *m*
mousy ['mausɪ] *adj* (*person*) tímido; (*hair*) pardusco
mouth (*pl* **mouths**) [mauθ, -ðz] *n* boca; (*of river*) desembocadura
mouthful ['mauθful] *n* bocado
mouth organ *n* armónica
mouthpiece ['mauθpi:s] *n* (*of musical instrument*) boquilla; (*Tel*) micrófono; (*spokesman*) portavoz *m/f*
mouth-to-mouth ['mauθtə'mauθ] *adj* (*also*: **mouth-to-mouth resuscitation**) boca a boca *m*
mouthwash ['mauθwɔʃ] *n* enjuague *m* bucal
mouth-watering ['mauθwɔ:tərɪŋ] *adj* apetitoso
movable ['mu:vəbl] *adj* movible
move [mu:v] *n* (*movement*) movimiento; (*in game*) jugada; (*: turn to play*) turno; (*change of house*) mudanza ■ *vt* mover; (*emotionally*) conmover; (*Pol: resolution etc*) proponer ■ *vi* (*gen*) moverse; (*traffic*) circular; (*Brit: also*: **move house**) trasladarse, mudarse; **to ~ sb to do sth** mover a algn a hacer algo; **to be moved** estar conmovido; **to get a ~ on** darse prisa
▸ **move about** *or* **around** *vi* moverse; (*travel*) viajar
▸ **move along** *vi* (*stop loitering*) circular; (*along seat etc*) correrse
▸ **move away** *vi* (*leave*) marcharse
▸ **move back** *vi* (*return*) volver
▸ **move down** *vt* (*demote*) degradar
▸ **move forward** *vi* avanzar ■ *vt* adelantar
▸ **move in** *vi* (*to a house*) instalarse
▸ **move off** *vi* ponerse en camino
▸ **move on** *vi* seguir viaje ■ *vt* (*onlookers*) hacer circular
▸ **move out** *vi* (*of house*) mudarse
▸ **move over** *vi* hacerse a un lado, correrse
▸ **move up** *vi* subir; (*employee*) ascender
movement ['mu:vmənt] *n* movimiento; (*Tech*) mecanismo; **~ (of the bowels)** (*Med*) evacuación *f*
mover ['mu:və^r] *n* proponente *m/f*
movie ['mu:vɪ] *n* película; **to go to the movies** ir al cine
movie camera *n* cámara cinematográfica
moviegoer ['mu:vɪgəuə^r] *n* (*US*) aficionado(-a) al cine
moving ['mu:vɪŋ] *adj* (*emotional*) conmovedor(a); (*that moves*) móvil; (*instigating*) motor(a)
mow (*pt* **mowed**, *pp* **mowed** *or* **mown**) [məu, -n] *vt* (*grass*) cortar; (*corn*) segar; (*also*: **mow down**: *shoot*) acribillar
mower ['məuə^r] *n* (*also*: **lawnmower**) cortacésped *m*
Mozambique [məuzæm'bi:k] *n* Mozambique *m*

MP *n abbr* (= *Military Police*) PM; (*Brit*) = **Member of Parliament**; (*Canada*) = **Mounted Police**
mpg *n abbr* (= *miles per gallon*) *30 mpg = 9.4 l. per 100 km*
mph *abbr* (= *miles per hour*) *60 mph = 96 km/h*
MPhil *n abbr* (= *Master of Philosophy*) *título universitario de postgrado*; *see also* **master's degree**
MPS *n abbr* (*Brit*) = **Member of the Pharmaceutical Society**
MP3 ['ɛmpi:'θri:] *n* MP3 *m*
MP3 player *n* reproductor *m* MP3
Mr, Mr. ['mɪstəʳ] *n*: **Mr Smith** (el) Sr. Smith
MRC *n abbr* (*Brit*: = *Medical Research Council*) *departamento estatal que controla la investigación médica*
MRCP *n abbr* (*Brit*) = **Member of the Royal College of Physicians**
MRCS *n abbr* (*Brit*) = **Member of the Royal College of Surgeons**
MRCVS *n abbr* (*Brit*) = **Member of the Royal College of Veterinary Surgeons**
Mrs, Mrs. ['mɪsɪz] *n*: **~ Smith** (la) Sra. de Smith
MS *n abbr* (= *manuscript*) MS; = **multiple sclerosis**; (*US*: = *Master of Science*) *título universitario* ■ *abbr* (*US*) = **Mississippi**
Ms, Ms. [mɪz] *n* (*Miss or Mrs*) *abreviatura con la que se evita hacer expreso el estado civil de una mujer*
MSA *n abbr* (*US*: = *Master of Science in Agriculture*) *título universitario*
MSc *abbr see* **Master of Science**
MSG *n abbr* = **monosodium glutamate**
MSP *n abbr* (*Brit*) = **Member of the Scottish Parliament**
MST *abbr* (*US*: = *Mountain Standard Time*) *hora de invierno de las Montañas Rocosas*
MSW *n abbr* (*US*: = *Master of Social Work*) *título universitario*
MT *abbr* (*US*: = *Montana*) ■ *n abbr* = **machine translation**
Mt *abbr* (*Geo*: = *mount*) m
mth *abbr* (= *month*) m
MTV *n abbr* = **music television**
much [mʌtʃ] *adj* mucho ■ *adv, n, pron* mucho; (*before pp*) muy; **how ~ is it?** ¿cuánto es?, ¿cuánto cuesta?; **too ~** demasiado; **so ~** tanto; **it's not ~** no es mucho; **as ~ as** tanto como; **however ~ he tries** por mucho que se esfuerce; **I like it very/so ~** me gusta mucho/tanto; **thank you very ~** muchas gracias, muy agradecido
muck [mʌk] *n* (*dirt*) suciedad *f*; (*fig*) porquería
▸ **muck about** *or* **around** *vi* (*col*) perder el tiempo; (*enjoy o.s.*) entretenerse; (*tinker*) manosear
▸ **muck in** *vi* (*col*) arrimar el hombro
▸ **muck out** *vt* (*stable*) limpiar
▸ **muck up** *vt* (*col*: *dirty*) ensuciar; (: *spoil*) echar a perder; (: *ruin*) estropear
muckraking ['mʌkreɪkɪŋ] (*fig col*) *n* amarillismo ■ *adj* especializado en escándalos
mucky ['mʌkɪ] *adj* (*dirty*) sucio
mucus ['mju:kəs] *n* mucosidad *f*, moco
mud [mʌd] *n* barro, lodo
muddle ['mʌdl] *n* desorden *m*, confusión *f*; (*mix-up*) embrollo, lío ■ *vt* (*also*: **muddle up**) embrollar, confundir
▸ **muddle along, muddle on** *vi* arreglárselas de alguna manera
▸ **muddle through** *vi* salir del paso
muddle-headed [mʌdl'hɛdɪd] *adj* (*person*) despistado, confuso
muddy ['mʌdɪ] *adj* fangoso, cubierto de lodo
mudguard ['mʌdgɑ:d] *n* guardabarros *m inv*
mudpack ['mʌdpæk] *n* mascarilla
mud-slinging ['mʌdslɪŋɪŋ] *n* injurias *fpl*, difamación *f*
muesli ['mju:zlɪ] *n* muesli *m*
muff [mʌf] *n* manguito ■ *vt* (*chance*) desperdiciar; (*lines*) estropear; (*shot, catch etc*) fallar; **to ~ it** fracasar
muffin ['mʌfɪn] *n* bollo
muffle ['mʌfl] *vt* (*sound*) amortiguar; (*against cold*) abrigar
muffled ['mʌfld] *adj* sordo, apagado
muffler ['mʌfləʳ] *n* (*scarf*) bufanda; (*US Aut*) silenciador *m*; (*on motorbike*) silenciador *m*, mofle *m*
mufti ['mʌftɪ] *n*: **in ~** (vestido) de paisano
mug [mʌg] *n* (*cup*) taza alta; (*for beer*) jarra; (*col*: *face*) jeta; (: *fool*) bobo ■ *vt* (*assault*) atracar; **it's a ~'s game** es cosa de bobos
▸ **mug up** *vt* (*col*: *also*: **mug up on**) empollar
mugger ['mʌgəʳ] *n* atracador(a) *m(f)*
mugging ['mʌgɪŋ] *n* atraco callejero
muggins ['mʌgɪnz] *nsg* (*col*) tonto(-a) el bote
muggy ['mʌgɪ] *adj* bochornoso
mug shot *n* (*col*) foto *f* (para la ficha policial)
mulatto (*pl* **mulattoes**) [mju:'lætəu] *n* mulato(-a)
mulberry ['mulbrɪ] *n* (*fruit*) mora; (*tree*) morera, moral *m*
mule [mju:l] *n* mula
mull [mʌl]: **to ~ over** *vt* meditar sobre
mulled [mʌld] *adj*: **~ wine** vino caliente (*con especias*)
mullioned ['mʌlɪənd] *adj* (*window*) dividido por parteluces
multi... [mʌltɪ] *pref* multi...
multi-access ['mʌltɪ'æksɛs] *adj* (*Comput*) multiacceso, de acceso múltiple

multicoloured, (*US*) **multicolored** ['mʌltɪkʌləd] *adj* multicolor
multifarious [mʌltɪ'fɛərɪəs] *adj* múltiple, vario
multilateral [mʌltɪ'lætərl] *adj* (*Pol*) multilateral
multi-level [mʌltɪ'lɛvl] *adj* (*US*) = **multi-storey**
multimillionaire [mʌltɪmɪljə'nɛəʳ] *n* multimillonario(-a)
multinational [mʌltɪ'næʃənl] *n* multinacional *f* ■ *adj* multinacional
multiple ['mʌltɪpl] *adj* múltiple ■ *n* múltiplo; (*Brit: also:* **multiple store**) (cadena de) grandes almacenes *mpl*
multiple choice *n* examen *m* de tipo test
multiple crash *n* colisión *f* en cadena
multiple sclerosis [-sklɪ'rəusɪs] *n* esclerosis *f* múltiple
multiplex ['mʌltɪplɛks] *n* (*also:* **multiplex cinema**) multicines *m inv*
multiplication [mʌltɪplɪ'keɪʃən] *n* multiplicación *f*
multiplication table *n* tabla de multiplicar
multiplicity [mʌltɪ'plɪsɪtɪ] *n* multiplicidad *f*
multiply ['mʌltɪplaɪ] *vt* multiplicar ■ *vi* multiplicarse
multiracial [mʌltɪ'reɪʃl] *adj* multirracial
multistorey [mʌltɪ'stɔːrɪ] *adj* (*Brit: building, car park*) de muchos pisos
multi-tasking ['mʌltɪtɑːskɪŋ] *n* (*Comput*) ejecución *f* de tareas múltiples, multitarea
multitude ['mʌltɪtjuːd] *n* multitud *f*
mum [mʌm] *n* (*Brit*) mamá ■ *adj*: **to keep ~ (about sth)** no decir ni mu (de algo)
mumble ['mʌmbl] *vt* decir entre dientes ■ *vi* hablar entre dientes, musitar
mumbo jumbo ['mʌmbəu-] *n* (*col*) galimatías *m inv*
mummify ['mʌmɪfaɪ] *vt* momificar
mummy ['mʌmɪ] *n* (*Brit: mother*) mamá; (*embalmed*) momia
mumps [mʌmps] *n* paperas *fpl*
munch [mʌntʃ] *vt, vi* mascar
mundane [mʌn'deɪn] *adj* mundano
municipal [mjuː'nɪsɪpl] *adj* municipal
municipality [mjuːnɪsɪ'pælɪtɪ] *n* municipio
munificence [muː'nɪfɪsns] *n* munificencia
munitions [mjuː'nɪʃənz] *npl* municiones *fpl*
mural ['mjuərl] *n* (pintura) mural *m*
murder ['məːdəʳ] *n* asesinato; (*in law*) homicidio ■ *vt* asesinar, matar; **to commit ~** cometer un asesinato *or* homicidio
murderer ['məːdərəʳ] *n* asesino
murderess ['məːdərɪs] *n* asesina
murderous ['məːdərəs] *adj* homicida
murk [məːk] *n* oscuridad *f*, tinieblas *fpl*
murky ['məːkɪ] *adj* (*water, past*) turbio; (*room*) sombrío
murmur ['məːməʳ] *n* murmullo ■ *vt, vi* murmurar; **heart ~** soplo cardíaco
MusB, MusBac *n abbr* (= *Bachelor of Music*) *título universitario*
muscle ['mʌsl] *n* músculo
▸ **muscle in** *vi* entrometerse
muscular ['mʌskjuləʳ] *adj* muscular; (*person*) musculoso
muscular dystrophy *n* distrofia muscular
MusD, MusDoc *n abbr* (= *Doctor of Music*) *título universitario*
muse [mjuːz] *vi* meditar ■ *n* musa
museum [mjuː'zɪəm] *n* museo
mush [mʌʃ] *n* gachas *fpl*
mushroom ['mʌʃrum] *n* (*gen*) seta, hongo; (*small*) champiñón *m* ■ *vi* (*fig*) crecer de la noche a la mañana
mushy ['mʌʃɪ] *adj* (*vegetables*) casi hecho puré; (*story*) sentimentaloide
music ['mjuːzɪk] *n* música
musical ['mjuːzɪkl] *adj* melodioso; (*person*) musical ■ *n* (*show*) (comedia) musical *m*
musical box *n* = **music box**
musical chairs *n* juego de las sillas; (*fig*): **to play ~** cambiar de puesto continuamente
musical instrument *n* instrumento musical
musically ['mjuːzɪklɪ] *adv* melodiosamente, armoniosamente
music box *n* caja de música
music centre *n* equipo de música
music hall *n* teatro de variedades
musician [mjuː'zɪʃən] *n* músico(-a)
music stand *n* atril *m*
musk [mʌsk] *n* (perfume *m* de) almizcle *m*
musket ['mʌskɪt] *n* mosquete *m*
musk rat *n* ratón *m* almizclero
musk rose *n* (*Bot*) rosa almizcleña
Muslim ['mʌzlɪm] *adj, n* musulmán(-ana) *m(f)*
muslin ['mʌzlɪn] *n* muselina
musquash ['mʌskwɔʃ] *n* (*fur*) piel *f* del ratón almizclero
muss [mʌs] *vt* (*col: hair*) despeinar; (*: dress*) arrugar
mussel ['mʌsl] *n* mejillón *m*
must [mʌst] *aux vb* (*obligation*): **I ~ do it** debo hacerlo, tengo que hacerlo; (*probability*): **he ~ be there by now** ya debe (de) estar allí ■ *n*: **it's a ~** es imprescindible
mustache ['mʌstæʃ] *n* (*US*) = **moustache**
mustard ['mʌstəd] *n* mostaza
mustard gas *n* gas *m* mostaza
muster ['mʌstəʳ] *vt* juntar, reunir; (*also:* **muster up**) reunir; (*: courage*) armarse de
mustiness ['mʌstɪnɪs] *n* olor *m* a cerrado
mustn't ['mʌsnt] = **must not**

musty ['mʌstɪ] *adj* mohoso, que huele a humedad
mutant ['mju:tənt] *adj, n* mutante *m*
mutate [mju:'teɪt] *vi* sufrir mutación, transformarse
mutation [mju:'teɪʃən] *n* mutación *f*
mute [mju:t] *adj, n* mudo(-a) *m(f)*
muted ['mju:tɪd] *adj* (*noise*) sordo; (*criticism*) callado
mutilate ['mju:tɪleɪt] *vt* mutilar
mutilation [mju:tɪ'leɪʃən] *n* mutilación *f*
mutinous ['mju:tɪnəs] *adj* (*troops*) amotinado; (*attitude*) rebelde
mutiny ['mju:tɪnɪ] *n* motín *m* ■ *vi* amotinarse
mutter ['mʌtəʳ] *vt, vi* murmurar
mutton ['mʌtn] *n* (carne *f* de) cordero
mutual ['mju:tʃuəl] *adj* mutuo; (*friend*) común
mutually ['mju:tʃuəlɪ] *adv* mutuamente
Muzak® ['mju:zæk] *n* hilo musical
muzzle ['mʌzl] *n* hocico; (*protective device*) bozal *m*; (*of gun*) boca ■ *vt* amordazar; (*dog*) poner un bozal a
MV *abbr* = **motor vessel**
MVP *n abbr* (*US Sport*) = **most valuable player**
MW *abbr* (*Radio*: = *medium wave*) onda media
my [maɪ] *adj* mi(s); **my house/brother/sisters** mi casa/hermano/mis hermanas; **I've washed my hair/cut my finger** me he lavado el pelo/cortado un dedo; **is this my pen or yours?** ¿este bolígrafo es mío o tuyo?
Myanmar ['maɪænmɑ:ʳ] *n* Myanmar
myopic [maɪ'ɔpɪk] *adj* miope
myriad ['mɪrɪəd] *n* (*of people, things*) miríada
myrrh [mə:ʳ] *n* mirra
myself [maɪ'sɛlf] *pron* (*reflexive*) me; (*emphatic*) yo mismo; (*after prep*) mí (mismo); *see also* **oneself**
mysterious [mɪs'tɪərɪəs] *adj* misterioso
mysteriously [mɪs'tɪərɪəslɪ] *adv* misteriosamente
mystery ['mɪstərɪ] *n* misterio
mystery play *n* auto, misterio
mystic ['mɪstɪk] *adj, n* místico(-a) *m(f)*
mystical ['mɪstɪkl] *adj* místico
mysticism ['mɪstɪsɪzəm] *n* misticismo
mystification [mɪstɪfɪ'keɪʃən] *n* perplejidad *f*; desconcierto
mystify ['mɪstɪfaɪ] *vt* (*perplex*) dejar perplejo; (*disconcert*) desconcertar
mystique [mɪs'ti:k] *n* misterio
myth [mɪθ] *n* mito
mythical ['mɪθɪkl] *adj* mítico
mythological [mɪθə'lɔdʒɪkl] *adj* mitológico
mythology [mɪ'θɔlədʒɪ] *n* mitología

Nn

N, n [ɛn] *n* (*letter*) N, n *f*; **N for Nellie,** (*US*) **N for Nan** N de Navarra
N *abbr* (= *North*) N
NA *n abbr* (*US*: = *Narcotics Anonymous*) *organización de ayuda a los drogadictos*; (*US*) = **National Academy**
n/a *abbr* (= *not applicable*) no interesa; (*Comm etc*) = **no account**
NAACP *n abbr* (*US*) = **National Association for the Advancement of Colored People**
NAAFI ['næfɪ] *n abbr* (*Brit*: = *Navy, Army & Air Force Institutes*) *servicio de cantinas etc para las fuerzas armadas*
nab [næb] *vt* (*col*: *grab*) coger (*SP*), agarrar (*LAm*); (: *catch out*) pillar
NACU *n abbr* (*US*) = **National Association of Colleges and Universities**
nadir ['neɪdɪəʳ] *n* (*Astro*) nadir *m*; (*fig*) punto más bajo
NAFTA ['næftə] *n abbr* (= *North Atlantic Free Trade Agreement*) TLC *m*
nag [næg] *n* (*pej*: *horse*) rocín *m* ■ *vt* (*scold*) regañar; (*annoy*) fastidiar
nagging ['nægɪŋ] *adj* (*doubt*) persistente; (*pain*) continuo ■ *n* quejas *fpl*
nail [neɪl] *n* (*human*) uña; (*metal*) clavo ■ *vt* clavar; (*fig*: *catch*) coger (*SP*), pillar; **to pay cash on the ~** pagar a tocateja; **to ~ sb down to a date/price** hacer que algn se comprometa a una fecha/un precio
nailbrush ['neɪlbrʌʃ] *n* cepillo para las uñas
nailfile ['neɪlfaɪl] *n* lima para las uñas
nail polish *n* esmalte *m or* laca para las uñas
nail polish remover *n* quitaesmalte *m*
nail scissors *npl* tijeras *fpl* para las uñas
nail varnish *n* (*Brit*) = **nail polish**
Nairobi [naɪ'rəubɪ] *n* Nairobi *m*
naïve [naɪ'i:v] *adj* ingenuo
naïvely [naɪ'i:vlɪ] *adv* ingenuamente
naïveté [nɑ:'i:vteɪ], **naivety** [naɪ'i:vɪtɪ] *n* ingenuidad *f*, candidez *f*
naked ['neɪkɪd] *adj* (*nude*) desnudo; (*flame*) expuesto al aire; **with the ~ eye** a simple vista
NAM *n abbr* (*US*) = **National Association of Manufacturers**
name [neɪm] *n* (*gen*) nombre *m*; (*surname*) apellido; (*reputation*) fama, renombre *m* ■ *vt* (*child*) poner nombre a; (*appoint*) nombrar; **by ~** de nombre; **in the ~ of** en nombre de; **what's your ~?** ¿cómo se llama usted?; **my ~ is Peter** me llamo Pedro; **to give one's ~ and address** dar sus señas; **to take sb's ~ and address** apuntar las señas de algn; **to make a ~ for o.s.** hacerse famoso; **to get (o.s.) a bad ~** forjarse una mala reputación
name-drop ['neɪmdrɔp] *vi*: **he's always name-dropping** siempre está presumiendo de la gente que conoce
nameless ['neɪmlɪs] *adj* anónimo, sin nombre
namely ['neɪmlɪ] *adv* a saber
nameplate ['neɪmpleɪt] *n* (*on door etc*) placa
namesake ['neɪmseɪk] *n* tocayo(-a)
nan bread [nɑ:n-] *n pan indio sin apenas levadura*
nanny ['nænɪ] *n* niñera
nap [næp] *n* (*sleep*) sueñecito, siesta; **they were caught napping** les pilló desprevenidos
NAPA *n abbr* (*US*: = *National Association of Performing Artists*) *sindicato de trabajadores del espectáculo*
napalm ['neɪpɑ:m] *n* napalm *m*
nape [neɪp] *n*: **~ of the neck** nuca, cogote *m*
napkin ['næpkɪn] *n* (*also*: **table napkin**) servilleta
Naples ['neɪplz] *n* Nápoles
nappy ['næpɪ] *n* (*Brit*) pañal *m*
nappy liner *n* gasa
nappy rash *n* prurito
narcissism [nɑ:'sɪsɪzəm] *n* narcisismo
narcissus (*pl* **narcissi**) [nɑ:'sɪsəs, -saɪ] *n* narciso
narcotic [nɑ:'kɔtɪk] *adj*, *n* narcótico
narrate [nə'reɪt] *vt* narrar, contar
narration [nə'reɪʃən] *n* narración *f*, relato
narrative ['nærətɪv] *n* narrativa ■ *adj* narrativo

narrator [nə'reɪtəʳ] *n* narrador(a) *m(f)*
narrow ['nærəu] *adj* estrecho; (*resources, means*) escaso ■ *vi* estrecharse; (*diminish*) reducirse; **to have a ~ escape** escaparse por los pelos; **to ~ sth down** reducir algo
narrow gauge *adj* (*Rail*) de vía estrecha
narrowly ['nærəlɪ] *adv* (*miss*) por poco
narrow-minded [nærəu'maɪndɪd] *adj* de miras estrechas
narrow-mindedness ['nærəu'maɪndɪdnɪs] *n* estrechez *f* de miras
NAS *n abbr* (*US*) = **National Academy of Sciences**
NASA *n abbr* (*US: = National Aeronautics and Space Administration*) NASA *f*
nasal ['neɪzl] *adj* nasal
Nassau ['næsɔ:] *n* (*in Bahamas*) Nassau *m*
nastily ['nɑ:stɪlɪ] *adv* (*unpleasantly*) de mala manera; (*spitefully*) con rencor
nastiness ['nɑ:stɪnɪs] *n* (*malice*) malevolencia; (*rudeness*) grosería; (*of person, remark*) maldad *f*; (*spitefulness*) rencor *m*
nasturtium [nəs'tə:ʃəm] *n* capuchina
nasty ['nɑ:stɪ] *adj* (*remark*) feo; (*person*) antipático; (*revolting: taste, smell*) asqueroso; (*wound, disease etc*) peligroso, grave; **to turn ~** (*situation*) ponerse feo; (*weather*) empeorar; (*person*) ponerse negro
NAS/UWT *n abbr* (*Brit: = National Association of Schoolmasters/Union of Women Teachers*) *sindicato de profesores*
nation ['neɪʃən] *n* nación *f*
national ['næʃənl] *adj* nacional ■ *n* súbdito(-a)
national anthem *n* himno nacional
National Curriculum *n* (*Brit*) plan *m* general de estudios (*en Inglaterra y Gales*)
national debt *n* deuda pública
national dress *n* traje *m* típico del país
National Guard *n* (*US*) Guardia Nacional
National Health Service *n* (*Brit*) servicio nacional de sanidad, ≈ INSALUD *m* (*SP*)
National Insurance *n* (*Brit*) seguro social nacional, ≈ Seguridad *f* Social
nationalism ['næʃnəlɪzəm] *n* nacionalismo
nationalist ['næʃnəlɪst] *adj, n* nacionalista *m/f*
nationality [næʃə'nælɪtɪ] *n* nacionalidad *f*
nationalization [næʃnəlaɪ'zeɪʃən] *n* nacionalización *f*
nationalize ['næʃnəlaɪz] *vt* nacionalizar; **nationalized industry** industria nacionalizada
nationally ['næʃnəlɪ] *adv* (*nationwide*) a escala nacional; (*as a nation*) como nación
national press *n* prensa nacional
national service *n* (*Mil*) servicio militar
National Trust *n* (*Brit*) *organización encargada de preservar el patrimonio histórico británico*
nationwide ['neɪʃənwaɪd] *adj* a escala nacional
native ['neɪtɪv] *n* (*local inhabitant*) natural *m/f*; (*in colonies*) indígena *m/f*, nativo(-a) ■ *adj* (*indigenous*) indígena; (*country*) natal; (*innate*) natural, innato; **a ~ of Russia** un(a) natural de Rusia; **~ language** lengua materna; **a ~ speaker of French** un hablante nativo de francés
Native American *adj, n* americano(-a) indígena *m(f)*, amerindio(-a) *m(f)*
Nativity [nə'tɪvɪtɪ] *n*: **the ~** Navidad *f*
nativity play *n* auto del nacimiento
NATO ['neɪtəu] *n abbr* (*= North Atlantic Treaty Organization*) OTAN *f*
natter ['nætəʳ] *vi* (*Brit*) charlar ■ *n*: **to have a ~** charlar
natural ['nætʃrəl] *adj* natural; **death from ~ causes** (*Law*) muerte *f* por causas naturales
natural childbirth *n* parto natural
natural gas *n* gas *m* natural
natural history *n* historia natural
naturalist ['nætʃrəlɪst] *n* naturalista *m/f*
naturalization [nætʃrəlaɪ'zeɪʃən] *n* naturalización *f*
naturalize ['nætʃrəlaɪz] *vt*: **to become naturalized** (*person*) naturalizarse; (*plant*) aclimatarse
naturally ['nætʃrəlɪ] *adv* (*speak etc*) naturalmente; (*of course*) desde luego, por supuesto, ¡cómo no! (*LAm*); (*instinctively*) por naturaleza
naturalness ['nætʃrəlnɪs] *n* naturalidad *f*
natural resources *npl* recursos *mpl* naturales
natural selection *n* selección *f* natural
natural wastage *n* (*Industry*) desgaste *m* natural
nature ['neɪtʃəʳ] *n* naturaleza; (*group, sort*) género, clase *f*; (*character*) modo de ser, carácter *m*; **by ~** por naturaleza; **documents of a confidential ~** documentos *mpl* de tipo confidencial
-natured ['neɪtʃəd] *suff*: **ill~** malhumorado
nature reserve *n* reserva natural
nature trail *n* camino forestal educativo
naturist ['neɪtʃərɪst] *n* naturista *m/f*
naught [nɔ:t] = **nought**
naughtily ['nɔ:tɪlɪ] *adv* (*behave*) mal; (*say*) con malicia
naughtiness ['nɔ:tɪnɪs] *n* travesuras *fpl*
naughty ['nɔ:tɪ] *adj* (*child*) travieso; (*story, film*) picante, escabroso, colorado (*LAm*)
nausea ['nɔ:sɪə] *n* náusea
nauseate ['nɔ:sɪeɪt] *vt* dar náuseas a; (*fig*) dar asco a

nauseating ['nɔːsɪeɪtɪŋ] *adj* nauseabundo; (*fig*) asqueroso, repugnante
nauseous ['nɔːsɪəs] *adj* nauseabundo; **to feel** ~ sentir náuseas
nautical ['nɔːtɪkl] *adj* náutico, marítimo; ~ **mile** milla marina
naval ['neɪvl] *adj* naval, de marina
naval officer *n* oficial *m/f* de marina
nave [neɪv] *n* nave *f*
navel ['neɪvl] *n* ombligo
navigable ['nævɪgəbl] *adj* navegable
navigate ['nævɪgeɪt] *vt* (*ship*) gobernar; (*river etc*) navegar por ■ *vi* navegar; (*Aut*) hacer de copiloto
navigation [nævɪ'geɪʃən] *n* (*action*) navegación *f*; (*science*) náutica
navigator ['nævɪgeɪtə^r] *n* navegante *m/f*
navvy ['nævɪ] *n* (*Brit*) peón *m* caminero
navy ['neɪvɪ] *n* marina de guerra; (*ships*) armada, flota ■ *adj* azul marino
navy-blue ['neɪvɪ'bluː] *adj* azul marino
Nazareth ['næzərɪθ] *n* Nazaret *m*
Nazi ['nɑːtsɪ] *adj, n* nazi *m/f*
NB *abbr* (= *nota bene*) nótese; (*Canada*) = **New Brunswick**
NBA *n abbr* (*US*) = **National Basketball Association; National Boxing Association**
NBC *n abbr* (*US*: = *National Broadcasting Company*) *cadena de televisión*
NBS *n abbr* (*US*: = *National Bureau of Standards*) ≈ Oficina Nacional de Normalización
NC *abbr* (*Comm etc*: = *no charge*: *US*) = **North Carolina**
NCC *n abbr* (*Brit*: = *Nature Conservancy Council*) ≈ ICONA *m*; (*US*) = **National Council of Churches**
NCCL *n abbr* (*Brit*: = *National Council for Civil Liberties*) *asociación para la defensa de las libertades públicas*
NCO *n abbr* = **non-commissioned officer**
ND, N. Dak. *abbr* (*US*) = **North Dakota**
NE *abbr* (*US*) = **Nebraska; New England**
NEA *n abbr* (*US*) = **National Education Association**
Neapolitan [nɪə'pɔlɪtən] *adj, n* napolitano(-a) *m(f)*
neap tide [niːp-] *n* marea muerta
near [nɪə^r] *adj* (*place, relation*) cercano; (*time*) próximo ■ *adv* cerca ■ *prep* (*also*: **near to**: *space*) cerca de, junto a; (: *time*) cerca de ■ *vt* acercarse a, aproximarse a; ~ **here/there** cerca de aquí/de allí; **£25,000 or nearest offer** 25,000 libras o precio a discutir; **in the ~ future** en fecha próxima; **the building is nearing completion** el edificio está casi terminado
nearby [nɪə'baɪ] *adj* cercano, próximo ■ *adv* cerca
nearly ['nɪəlɪ] *adv* casi, por poco; **I ~ fell** por poco me caigo; **not** ~ ni mucho menos, ni con mucho
near miss *n* (*shot*) tiro casi en el blanco; (*Aviat*) *accidente evitado por muy poco*
nearness ['nɪənɪs] *n* cercanía, proximidad *f*
nearside ['nɪəsaɪd] *n* (*Aut*: *right-hand drive*) lado izquierdo; (: *left-hand drive*) lado derecho
near-sighted [nɪə'saɪtɪd] *adj* miope, corto de vista
neat [niːt] *adj* (*place*) ordenado, bien cuidado; (*person*) pulcro; (*plan*) ingenioso; (*spirits*) solo
neatly ['niːtlɪ] *adv* (*tidily*) con esmero; (*skilfully*) ingeniosamente
neatness ['niːtnɪs] *n* (*tidiness*) orden *m*; (*skilfulness*) destreza, habilidad *f*
Nebr. *abbr* (*US*) = **Nebraska**
nebulous ['nɛbjuləs] *adj* (*fig*) vago, confuso
necessarily ['nɛsɪsrɪlɪ] *adv* necesariamente; **not** ~ no necesariamente
necessary ['nɛsɪsrɪ] *adj* necesario, preciso; **he did all that was** ~ hizo todo lo necesario; **if** ~ si es necesario
necessitate [nɪ'sɛsɪteɪt] *vt* necesitar, precisar
necessity [nɪ'sɛsɪtɪ] *n* necesidad *f*; **necessities** *npl* artículos *mpl* de primera necesidad; **in case of** ~ en caso de urgencia
neck [nɛk] *n* (*Anat*) cuello; (*of animal*) pescuezo ■ *vi* besuquearse; **~ and ~** parejos; **to stick one's ~ out** (*col*) arriesgarse
necklace ['nɛklɪs] *n* collar *m*
neckline ['nɛklaɪn] *n* escote *m*
necktie ['nɛktaɪ] *n* (*US*) corbata
nectar ['nɛktə^r] *n* néctar *m*
nectarine ['nɛktərɪn] *n* nectarina
née [neɪ] *adj*: ~ **Scott** de soltera Scott
need [niːd] *n* (*lack*) escasez *f*, falta; (*necessity*) necesidad *f* ■ *vt* (*require*) necesitar; **in case of** ~ en caso de necesidad; **there's no ~ for** ... no hace(n) falta ...; **to be in ~ of, have ~ of** necesitar; **10 will meet my immediate needs** 10 satisfacerán mis necesidades más apremiantes; **the needs of industry** las necesidades de la industria; **I ~ it** lo necesito; **a signature is needed** se requiere una firma; **I ~ to do it** tengo que hacerlo; **you don't ~ to go** no hace falta que vayas
needle ['niːdl] *n* aguja ■ *vt* (*fig*: *col*) picar, fastidiar
needless ['niːdlɪs] *adj* innecesario, inútil; **~ to say** huelga decir que
needlessly ['niːdlɪslɪ] *adv* innecesariamente, inútilmente
needlework ['niːdlwəːk] *n* (*activity*) costura, labor *f* de aguja

needn't ['ni:dnt] = **need not**
needy ['ni:dɪ] *adj* necesitado
negation [nɪ'geɪʃən] *n* negación *f*
negative ['nɛgətɪv] *n* (*Phot*) negativo; (*answer*) negativa; (*Ling*) negación *f* ■ *adj* negativo
negative cash flow *n* flujo negativo de efectivo
negative equity *n* *situación en la que el valor de la vivienda es menor que el de la hipoteca que pesa sobre ella*
neglect [nɪ'glɛkt] *vt* (*one's duty*) faltar a, no cumplir con; (*child*) descuidar, desatender ■ *n* (*state*) abandono; (*personal*) dejadez *f*; (*of duty*) incumplimiento; **to ~ to do sth** olvidarse de hacer algo
neglected [nɪ'glɛktɪd] *adj* abandonado
neglectful [nɪ'glɛktful] *adj* negligente; **to be ~ of sth/sb** desatender algo/a algn
negligee ['nɛglɪʒeɪ] *n* (*nightdress*) salto de cama
negligence ['nɛglɪdʒəns] *n* negligencia
negligent ['nɛglɪdʒənt] *adj* negligente; (*casual*) descuidado
negligently ['nɛglɪdʒəntlɪ] *adv* negligentemente; (*casually*) con descuido
negligible ['nɛglɪdʒɪbl] *adj* insignificante, despreciable
negotiable [nɪ'gəuʃɪəbl] *adj* negociable; **not ~** (*cheque*) no trasferible
negotiate [nɪ'gəuʃɪeɪt] *vt* (*treaty, loan*) negociar; (*obstacle*) franquear; (*bend in road*) tomar ■ *vi*: **to ~ (with)** negociar (con); **to ~ with sb for sth** tratar *or* negociar con algn por algo
negotiating table [nɪ'gəuʃɪeɪtɪŋ-] *n* mesa de negociaciones
negotiation [nɪgəuʃɪ'eɪʃən] *n* negociación *f*, gestión *f*; **to enter into negotiations with sb** entrar en negociaciones con algn
negotiator [nɪ'gəuʃɪeɪtə^r] *n* negociador(a) *m(f)*
Negress ['ni:grɪs] *n* negra
Negro ['ni:grəu] *adj, n* negro
neigh [neɪ] *n* relincho ■ *vi* relinchar
neighbour, neighbor (*US*) ['neɪbə^r] *n* vecino(-a)
neighbourhood, neighborhood (*US*) ['neɪbəhud] *n* (*place*) vecindad *f*, barrio; (*people*) vecindario
neighbourhood watch *n* (*Brit: also:* **neighbourhood watch scheme**) *vigilancia del barrio por los propios vecinos*
neighbouring, neighboring (*US*) ['neɪbərɪŋ] *adj* vecino
neighbourly, neighborly (*US*) ['neɪbəlɪ] *adj* amigable, sociable
neither ['naɪðə^r] *adj* ni ■ *conj*: **I didn't move and ~ did John** no me he movido, ni Juan tampoco ■ *pron* ninguno; **~ is true** ninguno(-a) de los/las dos es cierto(-a) ■ *adv*: **~ good nor bad** ni bueno ni malo
neo... [ni:əu] *pref* neo...
neolithic [ni:əu'lɪθɪk] *adj* neolítico
neologism [nɪ'ɔlədʒɪzəm] *n* neologismo
neon ['ni:ɔn] *n* neón *m*
neon light *n* lámpara de neón
Nepal [nɪ'pɔ:l] *n* Nepal *m*
nephew ['nɛvju:] *n* sobrino
nepotism ['nɛpətɪzəm] *n* nepotismo
nerd [nə:d] *n* (*col*) primo(-a)
nerve [nə:v] *n* (*Anat*) nervio; (*courage*) valor *m*; (*impudence*) descaro, frescura; **a fit of nerves** un ataque de nervios; **to lose one's ~** (*self-confidence*) perder el valor
nerve centre *n* (*Anat*) centro nervioso; (*fig*) punto neurálgico
nerve gas *n* gas *m* nervioso
nerve-racking ['nə:vrækɪŋ] *adj* angustioso
nervous ['nə:vəs] *adj* (*anxious*) nervioso; (*Anat*) nervioso; (*timid*) tímido, miedoso
nervous breakdown *n* crisis *f* nerviosa
nervously ['nə:vəslɪ] *adv* nerviosamente; tímidamente
nervousness ['nə:vəsnɪs] *n* nerviosismo; timidez *f*
nervous wreck *n* (*col*): **to be a ~** estar de los nervios
nervy ['nə:vɪ] *adj*: **to be ~** estar nervioso
nest [nɛst] *n* (*of bird*) nido ■ *vi* anidar
nest egg *n* (*fig*) ahorros *mpl*
nestle ['nɛsl] *vi*: **to ~ down** acurrucarse
nestling ['nɛstlɪŋ] *n* pajarito
Net ['nɛt] *n* (*Comput*) Internet *m or f*
net [nɛt] *n* (*gen*) red *f*; (*fabric*) tul *m* ■ *adj* (*Comm*) neto, líquido; (*weight, price, salary*) neto ■ *vt* coger (*SP*) *or* agarrar (*LAm*) con red; (*money: person*) cobrar; (*: deal, sale*) conseguir; (*Sport*) marcar; **~ of tax** neto; **he earns £10,000 ~ per year** gana 10,000 libras netas por año; **the N~** (*Internet*) la Red
netball ['nɛtbɔ:l] *n* básquet *m*
net curtain *n* visillo
Netherlands ['nɛðələndz] *npl*: **the ~** los Países Bajos
net income *n* renta neta
net loss *n* pérdida neta
net profit *n* beneficio neto
nett [nɛt] *adj* = **net**
netting ['nɛtɪŋ] *n* red *f*, redes *fpl*
nettle ['nɛtl] *n* ortiga
network ['nɛtwə:k] *n* red *f* ■ *vt* (*Radio, TV*) difundir por la red de emisores; **local area ~** red local; **there's no ~ coverage here** (*Tel*) aquí no hay cobertura

neuralgia [njuəˈrældʒə] *n* neuralgia
neurological [njuərəˈlɔdʒɪkl] *adj* neurológico
neurosis (*pl* **-ses**) [njuəˈrəusɪs, -si:z] *n* neurosis *f inv*
neurotic [njuəˈrɔtɪk] *adj, n* neurótico(-a) *m(f)*
neuter [ˈnju:təʳ] *adj* (*Ling*) neutro ■ *vt* castrar, capar
neutral [ˈnju:trəl] *adj* (*person*) neutral; (*colour etc*) neutro; (*Elec*) neutro ■ *n* (*Aut*) punto muerto
neutrality [nju:ˈtrælɪtɪ] *n* neutralidad *f*
neutralize [ˈnju:trəlaɪz] *vt* neutralizar
neutron [ˈnju:trɔn] *n* neutrón *m*
neutron bomb *n* bomba de neutrones
Nev. *abbr* (*US*) = **Nevada**
never [ˈnɛvəʳ] *adv* nunca, jamás; **I ~ went** no fui nunca; **~ in my life** jamás en la vida; *see also* **mind**
never-ending [nɛvərˈɛndɪŋ] *adj* interminable, sin fin
nevertheless [nɛvəðəˈlɛs] *adv* sin embargo, no obstante
new [nju:] *adj* nuevo; (*recent*) reciente; **as good as ~** como nuevo
New Age *n* Nueva era
newborn [ˈnju:bɔ:n] *adj* recién nacido
newcomer [ˈnju:kʌməʳ] *n* recién venido *or* llegado
new-fangled [ˈnju:fæŋgld] *adj* (*pej*) modernísimo
new-found [ˈnju:faund] *adj* (*friend*) nuevo; (*enthusiasm*) recién adquirido
New Guinea *n* Nueva Guinea
newly [ˈnju:lɪ] *adv* recién
newly-weds [ˈnju:lɪwɛdz] *npl* recién casados
new moon *n* luna nueva
newness [ˈnju:nɪs] *n* novedad *f*; (*fig*) inexperiencia
news [nju:z] *n* noticias *fpl*; **a piece of ~** una noticia; **the ~** (*Radio, TV*) las noticias *fpl*, el telediario; **good/bad ~** buenas/malas noticias *fpl*; **financial ~** noticias *fpl* financieras
news agency *n* agencia de noticias
newsagent [ˈnju:zeɪdʒənt] *n* (*Brit*) vendedor(a) *m(f)* de periódicos
news bulletin *n* (*Radio, TV*) noticiario
newscaster [ˈnju:zkɑ:stəʳ] *n* presentador(a) *m(f)*, locutor(a) *m(f)*
news dealer *n* (*US*) = **newsagent**
news flash *n* noticia de última hora
newsletter [ˈnju:zlɛtəʳ] *n* hoja informativa, boletín *m*
newspaper [ˈnju:zpeɪpəʳ] *n* periódico, diario; **daily ~** diario; **weekly ~** periódico semanal
newsprint [ˈnju:zprɪnt] *n* papel *m* de periódico
newsreader [ˈnju:zri:dəʳ] *n* = **newscaster**
newsreel [ˈnju:zri:l] *n* noticiario
newsroom [ˈnju:zru:m] *n* (*Press, Radio, TV*) sala de redacción
news stand *n* quiosco *or* puesto de periódicos
newsworthy [ˈnju:zwə:ðɪ] *adj*: **to be ~** ser de interés periodístico
newt [nju:t] *n* tritón *m*
new town *n* (*Brit*) ciudad *f* nueva (*construida con subsidios estatales*)
New Year *n* Año Nuevo; **Happy ~!** ¡Feliz Año Nuevo!; **to wish sb a happy ~** desear a algn un feliz año nuevo
New Year's Day *n* Día *m* de Año Nuevo
New Year's Eve *n* Nochevieja
New York [-ˈjɔ:k] *n* Nueva York
New Zealand [-ˈzi:lənd] *n* Nueva Zelanda (*SP*), Nueva Zelandia (*LAm*) ■ *adj* neozelandés(-esa)
New Zealander [-ˈzi:ləndəʳ] *n* neozelandés(-esa) *m(f)*
next [nɛkst] *adj* (*house, room*) vecino, de al lado; (*meeting*) próximo; (*page*) siguiente ■ *adv* después; **the ~ day** el día siguiente; **~ time** la próxima vez; **~ year** el año próximo *or* que viene; **~ month** el mes que viene *or* entrante; **the week after ~** no la semana que viene sino la otra; **"turn to the ~ page"** "vuelva a la página siguiente"; **you're ~** le toca; **~ to** *prep* junto a, al lado de; **~ to nothing** casi nada
next door *adv* en la casa de al lado ■ *adj* vecino, de al lado
next-of-kin [ˈnɛkstəvˈkɪn] *n* pariente(s) *m(pl)* más cercano(s)
NF *n abbr* (*Brit Pol: = National Front*) *partido político de la extrema derecha* ■ *abbr* (*Canada*) = **Newfoundland**
NFL *n abbr* (*US*) = **National Football League**
Nfld. *abbr* (*Canada*) = **Newfoundland**
NG *abbr* (*US*) = **National Guard**
NGO *n abbr* (*= non-governmental organization*) ONG *f*
NH *abbr* (*US*) = **New Hampshire**
NHL *n abbr* (*US*) = **National Hockey League**
NHS *n abbr* (*Brit*) = **National Health Service**
NI *abbr* = **Northern Ireland**; (*Brit*) = **National Insurance**
nib [nɪb] *n* plumilla
nibble [ˈnɪbl] *vt* mordisquear
Nicaragua [nɪkəˈrægjuə] *n* Nicaragua
Nicaraguan [nɪkəˈrægjuən] *adj, n* nicaragüense *m/f*, nicaragüeño(-a) *m(f)*
Nice [ni:s] *n* Niza
nice [naɪs] *adj* (*likeable*) simpático, majo; (*kind*) amable; (*pleasant*) agradable; (*attractive*) bonito, mono; (*distinction*) fino; (*taste, smell, meal*) rico

nice-looking ['naɪslukɪŋ] *adj* guapo
nicely ['naɪslɪ] *adv* amablemente; (*of health etc*) bien; **that will do** ~ perfecto
niceties ['naɪsɪtɪz] *npl* detalles *mpl*
niche [niːʃ] *n* (*Arch*) nicho, hornacina
nick [nɪk] *n* (*wound*) rasguño; (*cut, indentation*) mella, muesca ■ *vt* (*cut*) cortar; (*col*) birlar, mangar; (*: arrest*) pillar; **in the ~ of time** justo a tiempo; **in good** ~ en buen estado; **to ~ o.s.** cortarse
nickel ['nɪkl] *n* níquel *m*; (*US*) *moneda de 5 centavos*
nickname ['nɪkneɪm] *n* apodo, mote *m* ■ *vt* apodar
Nicosia [nɪkə'siːə] *n* Nicosia
nicotine ['nɪkətiːn] *n* nicotina
nicotine patch *n* parche *m* de nicotina
niece [niːs] *n* sobrina
nifty ['nɪftɪ] *adj* (*col: car, jacket*) elegante, chulo; (*: gadget, tool*) ingenioso
Niger ['naɪdʒəʳ] *n* (*country, river*) Níger *m*
Nigeria [naɪ'dʒɪərɪə] *n* Nigeria
Nigerian [naɪ'dʒɪərɪən] *adj, n* nigeriano(-a) *m(f)*
niggardly ['nɪgədlɪ] *adj* (*person*) avaro, tacaño, avariento; (*allowance, amount*) miserable
nigger ['nɪgəʳ] *n* (*col!: highly offensive*) negro(-a)
niggle ['nɪgl] *vt* preocupar ■ *vi* (*complain*) quejarse; (*fuss*) preocuparse por minucias
niggling ['nɪglɪŋ] *adj* (*detail: trifling*) nimio, insignificante; (*annoying*) molesto; (*doubt, pain*) constante
night [naɪt] *n* (*gen*) noche *f*; (*evening*) tarde *f*; **last** ~ anoche; **the ~ before last** anteanoche, antes de ayer por la noche; **at** ~, **by** ~ de noche, por la noche; **in the ~, during the** ~ durante la noche, por la noche
night-bird ['naɪtbəːd] *n* (*fig*) trasnochador(a) *m(f)*, madrugador(a) *m(f)* (*LAm*)
nightcap ['naɪtkæp] *n* (*drink*) *bebida que se toma antes de acostarse*
night club *n* club nocturno, discoteca
nightdress ['naɪtdrɛs] *n* (*Brit*) camisón *m*
nightfall ['naɪtfɔːl] *n* anochecer *m*
nightgown ['naɪtgaun], **nightie** ['naɪtɪ] (*Brit*) *n* = **nightdress**
nightingale ['naɪtɪŋgeɪl] *n* ruiseñor *m*
night life *n* vida nocturna
nightly ['naɪtlɪ] *adj* de todas las noches ■ *adv* todas las noches, cada noche
nightmare ['naɪtmɛəʳ] *n* pesadilla
night porter *n* guardián *m* nocturno
night safe *n* caja fuerte
night school *n* clase(s) *f(pl)* nocturna(s)
nightshade ['naɪtʃeɪd] *n*: **deadly ~** (*Bot*) belladona
night shift *n* turno nocturno *or* de noche
night-time ['naɪttaɪm] *n* noche *f*
night watchman *n* vigilante *m* nocturno, sereno
nihilism ['naɪɪlɪzəm] *n* nihilismo
nil [nɪl] *n* (*Brit Sport*) cero, nada
Nile [naɪl] *n*: **the** ~ el Nilo
nimble ['nɪmbl] *adj* (*agile*) ágil, ligero; (*skilful*) diestro
nimbly ['nɪmblɪ] *adv* ágilmente; con destreza
nine [naɪn] *num* nueve
9-11, Nine-Eleven [naɪnɪ'lɛvn] *n* 11-S *m*
nineteen ['naɪn'tiːn] *num* diecinueve
nineteenth [naɪn'tiːnθ] *adj* decimonoveno, decimonono
ninety ['naɪntɪ] *num* noventa
ninth [naɪnθ] *adj* noveno
nip [nɪp] *vt* (*pinch*) pellizcar; (*bite*) morder ■ *vi* (*Brit col*): **to ~ out/down/up** salir/bajar/subir un momento ■ *n* (*drink*) trago
nipple ['nɪpl] *n* (*Anat*) pezón *m*; (*of bottle*) tetilla; (*Tech*) boquilla, manguito
nippy ['nɪpɪ] *adj* (*Brit: person*) rápido; (*taste*) picante; **it's a very ~ car** es un coche muy potente para el tamaño que tiene
nit [nɪt] *n* (*of louse*) liendre *f*; (*col: idiot*) imbécil *m/f*
nit-pick ['nɪtpɪk] *vi* (*col*) sacar punta a todo
nitrogen ['naɪtrədʒən] *n* nitrógeno
nitroglycerin, nitroglycerine ['naɪtrəu'glɪsəriːn] *n* nitroglicerina
nitty-gritty ['nɪtɪ'grɪtɪ] *n* (*col*): **to get down to the** ~ ir al grano
nitwit ['nɪtwɪt] *n* cretino(-a)
NJ *abbr* (*US*) = **New Jersey**
NLF *n abbr* (= *National Liberation Front*) FLN *m*
NLRB *n abbr* (*US: = National Labor Relations Board*) *organismo de protección al trabajador*
NM, N. Mex. *abbr* (*US*) = **New Mexico**

KEYWORD

no [nəu] (*pl* **noes**) *adv* (*opposite of "yes"*) no; **are you coming? — no (I'm not)** ¿vienes? — no; **would you like some more? — no thank you** ¿quieres más? — no gracias
■ *adj* (*not any*): **I have no money/time/books** no tengo dinero/tiempo/libros; **no other man would have done it** ningún otro lo hubiera hecho; **"no entry"** "prohibido el paso"; **"no smoking"** "prohibido fumar"
■ *n* no *m*

no. *abbr* (= *number*) nº, núm
nobble ['nɔbl] *vt* (*Brit col: bribe*) sobornar; (*: catch*) pescar; (*: Racing*) drogar
Nobel prize [nəu'bɛl-] *n* premio Nobel
nobility [nəu'bɪlɪtɪ] *n* nobleza

noble ['nəubl] *adj* *(person)* noble; *(title)* de nobleza
nobleman ['nəublmən] *n* noble *m*
nobly ['nəublı] *adv* *(selflessly)* noblemente
nobody ['nəubədı] *pron* nadie
no-claims bonus ['nəukleımz-] *n* bonificación *f* por carencia de reclamaciones
nocturnal [nɔk'tə:nl] *adj* nocturno
nod [nɔd] *vi* saludar con la cabeza; *(in agreement)* asentir con la cabeza ■ *vt*: **to ~ one's head** inclinar la cabeza ■ *n* inclinación *f* de cabeza; **they nodded their agreement** asintieron con la cabeza
▸ **nod off** *vi* cabecear
no-fly zone [nəu'flaı-] *n* zona de exclusión aérea
noise [nɔız] *n* ruido; *(din)* escándalo, estrépito
noisily ['nɔızılı] *adv* ruidosamente, estrepitosamente
noisy ['nɔızı] *adj* *(gen)* ruidoso; *(child)* escandaloso
nomad ['nəumæd] *n* nómada *m/f*
nomadic [nəu'mædık] *adj* nómada
no man's land *n* tierra de nadie
nominal ['nɔmınl] *adj* nominal
nominate ['nɔmıneıt] *vt* *(propose)* proponer; *(appoint)* nombrar
nomination [nɔmı'neıʃən] *n* propuesta; nombramiento
nominee [nɔmı'ni:] *n* candidato(-a)
non... [nɔn] *pref* no, des..., in...
nonalcoholic [nɔnælkə'hɔlık] *adj* sin alcohol
nonaligned [nɔnə'laınd] *adj* no alineado
nonarrival [nɔnə'raıvl] *n* falta de llegada
nonce word [nɔns-] *n* hápax *m*
nonchalant ['nɔnʃələnt] *adj* indiferente
noncommissioned [nɔnkə'mıʃənd] *adj*: **~ officer** suboficial *m/f*
noncommittal ['nɔnkə'mıtl] *adj* *(reserved)* reservado; *(uncommitted)* evasivo
nonconformist [nɔnkən'fɔ:mıst] *adj* inconformista ■ *n* inconformista *m/f*; *(Brit Rel)* no conformista *m/f*
noncontributory [nɔnkən'trıbjutərı] *adj*: **~ pension scheme** *or* (*US*) **plan** fondo de pensiones no contributivo
noncooperation ['nɔnkəuɔpə'reıʃən] *n* no cooperación *f*
nondescript ['nɔndıskrıpt] *adj* anodino, soso
none [nʌn] *pron* ninguno(-a) ■ *adv* de ninguna manera; **~ of you** ninguno de vosotros; **I've ~ left** no me queda ninguno(-a); **he's ~ the worse for it** no le ha perjudicado; **I have ~** no tengo ninguno; **~ at all** *(not one)* ni uno
nonentity [nɔ'nɛntıtı] *n* cero a la izquierda, nulidad *f*
nonessential [nɔnı'sɛnʃl] *adj* no esencial ■ *n*: **nonessentials** cosas *fpl* secundarias *or* sin importancia
nonetheless [nʌnðə'lɛs] *adv* sin embargo, no obstante, aún así
non-EU [nɔni:'ju:] *adj* *(citizen, passport)* no comunitario; *(imports)* de fuera de la Unión Europea
non-event [nɔnı'vɛnt] *n* acontecimiento sin importancia; **it was a ~** no pasó absolutamente nada
nonexecutive [nɔnıg'zɛkjutıv] *adj*: **~ director** director *m* no ejecutivo
nonexistent [nɔnıg'zıstənt] *adj* inexistente
nonfiction [nɔn'fıkʃən] *n* no ficción *f*
nonintervention [nɔnıntə'vɛnʃən] *n* no intervención *f*
no-no ['nəunəu] *n* *(col)*: **it's a ~** de eso ni hablar
non obst. *abbr* (*= non obstante: notwithstanding*) no obstante
no-nonsense [nəu'nɔnsəns] *adj* sensato
nonpayment [nɔn'peımənt] *n* falta de pago
nonplussed [nɔn'plʌst] *adj* perplejo
non-profit-making [nɔn'prɔfıtmeıkıŋ] *adj* no lucrativo
nonsense ['nɔnsəns] *n* tonterías *fpl*, disparates *fpl*; **~!** ¡qué tonterías!; **it is ~ to say that ...** es absurdo decir que ...
nonsensical [nɔn'sɛnsıkl] *adj* disparatado, absurdo
nonshrink [nɔn'ʃrıŋk] *adj* que no encoge
nonskid [nɔn'skıd] *adj* antideslizante
nonsmoker ['nɔn'sməukə^r] *n* no fumador(a) *m(f)*
nonstarter [nɔn'stɑ:tə^r] *n*: **it's a ~** no tiene futuro
nonstick ['nɔn'stık] *adj* *(pan, surface)* antiadherente
nonstop ['nɔn'stɔp] *adj* continuo; *(Rail)* directo ■ *adv* sin parar
nontaxable [nɔn'tæksəbl] *adj*: **~ income** renta no imponible
non-U ['nɔnju:] *adj abbr* (*Brit col: = non-upper class*) *que no pertenece a la clase alta*
nonvolatile [nɔn'vɔlətaıl] *adj*: **~ memory** *(Comput)* memoria permanente
nonvoting [nɔn'vəutıŋ] *adj*: **~ shares** acciones *fpl* sin derecho a voto
nonwhite ['nɔn'waıt] *adj* de color ■ *n* *(person)* persona de color
noodles ['nu:dlz] *npl* tallarines *mpl*
nook [nuk] *n* rincón *m*; **nooks and crannies** escondrijos *mpl*
noon [nu:n] *n* mediodía *m*
no-one ['nəuwʌn] *pron* = **nobody**
noose [nu:s] *n* lazo corredizo

nor [nɔː^r] *conj* = **neither** ■ *adv see* **neither**
Norf *abbr (Brit)* = **Norfolk**
norm [nɔːm] *n* norma
normal ['nɔːml] *adj* normal; **to return to ~** volver a la normalidad
normality [nɔː'mælɪtɪ] *n* normalidad *f*
normally ['nɔːməlɪ] *adv* normalmente
Normandy ['nɔːməndɪ] *n* Normandía
north [nɔːθ] *n* norte *m* ■ *adj* del norte ■ *adv* al *or* hacia el norte
North Africa *n* África del Norte
North African *adj, n* norteafricano(-a) *m(f)*
North America *n* América del Norte
North American *adj, n* norteamericano(-a) *m(f)*
Northants [nɔː'θænts] *abbr (Brit)* = **Northamptonshire**
northbound ['nɔːθbaund] *adj (traffic)* que se dirige al norte; *(carriageway)* de dirección norte
Northd *abbr (Brit)* = **Northumberland**
north-east [nɔːθ'iːst] *n* nor(d)este *m*
northerly ['nɔːðəlɪ] *adj (point, direction)* hacia el norte, septentrional; *(wind)* del norte
northern ['nɔːðən] *adj* norteño, del norte
Northern Ireland *n* Irlanda del Norte
North Korea *n* Corea del Norte
North Pole *n*: **the ~** el Polo Norte
North Sea *n*: **the ~** el Mar del Norte
North Sea oil *n* petróleo del Mar del Norte
northward ['nɔːθwəd], **northwards** ['nɔːθwədz] *adv* hacia el norte
north-west [nɔːθ'wɛst] *n* noroeste *m*
Norway ['nɔːweɪ] *n* Noruega
Norwegian [nɔː'wiːdʒən] *adj* noruego ■ *n* noruego(-a); *(Ling)* noruego
nos. *abbr (= numbers)* núms.
nose [nəuz] *n (Anat)* nariz *f*; *(Zool)* hocico; *(sense of smell)* olfato ■ *vi (also:* **nose one's way***)* avanzar con cautela; **to pay through the ~ (for sth)** *(col)* pagar un dineral (por algo)
▸ **nose about, nose around** *vi* curiosear
nosebleed ['nəuzbliːd] *n* hemorragia, nasal
nose-dive ['nəuzdaɪv] *n* picado vertical
nose drops *npl* gotas *fpl* para la nariz
nosey ['nəuzɪ] *adj* curioso, fisgón(-ona)
nostalgia [nɔs'tældʒɪə] *n* nostalgia
nostalgic [nɔs'tældʒɪk] *adj* nostálgico
nostril ['nɔstrɪl] *n* ventana *or* orificio de la nariz
nosy ['nəuzɪ] *adj* = **nosey**
not [nɔt] *adv* no; **~ at all** no ... en absoluto; **~ that ...** no es que ...; **it's too late, isn't it?** es demasiado tarde, ¿verdad?; **~ yet** todavía no; **~ now** ahora no; **why ~?** ¿por qué no?; **I hope ~** espero que no; **~ at all** no ... nada; *(after thanks)* de nada
notable ['nəutəbl] *adj* notable
notably ['nəutəblɪ] *adv* especialmente; *(in particular)* sobre todo
notary ['nəutərɪ] *n (also:* **notary public***)* notario(-a)
notation [nəu'teɪʃən] *n* notación *f*
notch [nɔtʃ] *n* muesca, corte *m*
▸ **notch up** *vt (score, victory)* apuntarse
note [nəut] *n (Mus, record, letter)* nota; *(banknote)* billete *m*; *(tone)* tono ■ *vt (observe)* notar, observar; *(write down)* apuntar, anotar; **delivery ~** nota de entrega; **to compare notes** *(fig)* cambiar impresiones; **of ~** conocido, destacado; **to take ~** prestar atención a; **just a quick ~ to let you know that ...** sólo unas líneas para informarte que ...
notebook ['nəutbuk] *n* libreta, cuaderno; *(for shorthand)* libreta
notecase ['nəutkeɪs] *n (Brit)* cartera, billetero
noted ['nəutɪd] *adj* célebre, conocido
notepad ['nəutpæd] *n* bloc *m*
notepaper ['nəutpeɪpə] *n* papel *m* para cartas
noteworthy ['nəutwəːðɪ] *adj* notable, digno de atención
nothing ['nʌθɪŋ] *n* nada; *(zero)* cero; **he does ~** no hace nada; **~ new** nada nuevo; **for ~** *(free)* gratis; *(in vain)* en balde; **~ at all** nada en absoluto
notice ['nəutɪs] *n (announcement)* anuncio; *(dismissal)* despido; *(resignation)* dimisión *f*; *(review: of play etc)* reseña ■ *vt (observe)* notar, observar; **to take ~ of** hacer caso de, prestar atención a; **at short ~** con poca antelación; **without ~** sin previo aviso; **advance ~** previo aviso; **until further ~** hasta nuevo aviso; **to give sb ~ of sth** avisar a algn de algo; **to give ~, hand in one's ~** dimitir, renunciar; **it has come to my ~ that ...** he llegado a saber que ...; **to escape** *or* **avoid ~** pasar inadvertido
noticeable ['nəutɪsəbl] *adj* evidente, obvio
notice board *n (Brit)* tablón *m* de anuncios
notification [nəutɪfɪ'keɪʃən] *n* aviso; *(announcement)* anuncio
notify ['nəutɪfaɪ] *vt*: **to ~ sb (of sth)** comunicar (algo) a algn
notion ['nəuʃən] *n* noción *f*, concepto; *(opinion)* opinión *f*
notions ['nəuʃənz] *npl (US)* mercería
notoriety [nəutə'raɪətɪ] *n* notoriedad *f*, mala fama
notorious [nəu'tɔːrɪəs] *adj* notorio, tristemente célebre
notoriously [nəu'tɔːrɪəslɪ] *adv* notoriamente
Notts [nɔts] *abbr (Brit)* = **Nottinghamshire**
notwithstanding [nɔtwɪθ'stændɪŋ] *adv* no obstante, sin embargo; **~ this** a pesar de esto

nougat ['nu:gɑ:] *n* turrón *m*
nought [nɔ:t] *n* cero
noun [naun] *n* nombre *m*, sustantivo
nourish ['nʌrɪʃ] *vt* nutrir, alimentar; (*fig*) fomentar, nutrir
nourishing ['nʌrɪʃɪŋ] *adj* nutritivo, rico
nourishment ['nʌrɪʃmənt] *n* alimento, sustento
Nov. *abbr* (= *November*) nov
novel ['nɔvl] *n* novela ■ *adj* (*new*) nuevo, original; (*unexpected*) insólito
novelist ['nɔvəlɪst] *n* novelista *m/f*
novelty ['nɔvəltɪ] *n* novedad *f*
November [nəu'vɛmbəʳ] *n* noviembre *m*; *see also* **July**
novice ['nɔvɪs] *n* principiante *m/f*, novato(-a); (*Rel*) novicio(-a)
NOW [nau] *n abbr* (*US*) = **National Organization for Women**
now [nau] *adv* (*at the present time*) ahora; (*these days*) actualmente, hoy día ■ *conj*: ~ **(that)** ya que, ahora que; **right** ~ ahora mismo; **by** ~ ya; **just** ~: **I'll do it just now** ahora mismo lo hago; **~ and then, ~ and again** de vez en cuando; **from ~ on** de ahora en adelante; **between ~ and Monday** entre hoy y el lunes; **in 3 days from** ~ de hoy en 3 días; **that's all for** ~ eso es todo por ahora
nowadays ['nauədeɪz] *adv* hoy (en) día, actualmente
nowhere ['nəuwɛəʳ] *adv* (*direction*) a ninguna parte; (*location*) en ninguna parte; **~ else** en *or* a ninguna otra parte
no-win situation [nəu'wɪn-] *n*: **I'm in a ~** haga lo que haga, llevo las de perder
noxious ['nɔkʃəs] *adj* nocivo
nozzle ['nɔzl] *n* boquilla
NP *n abbr* = **notary public**
NS *abbr* (*Canada*) = **Nova Scotia**
NSC *n abbr* (*US*) = **National Security Council**
NSF *n abbr* (*US*) = **National Science Foundation**
NSPCC *n abbr* (*Brit*) = **National Society for the Prevention of Cruelty to Children**
NSW *abbr* (*Australia*) = **New South Wales**
NT *n abbr* (= *New Testament*) ■ *abbr* (*Canada*) = **Northwest Territories**
nth [ɛnθ] *adj*: **for the ~ time** (*col*) por enésima vez
nuance ['nju:ɑ:ns] *n* matiz *m*
nubile ['nju:baɪl] *adj* núbil
nuclear ['nju:klɪəʳ] *adj* nuclear
nuclear disarmament *n* desarme *m* nuclear
nuclear family *n* familia nuclear
nuclear-free zone ['nju:klɪə'fri:-] *n* zona desnuclearizada
nucleus (*pl* **nuclei**) ['nju:klɪəs, 'nju:klɪaɪ] *n* núcleo
NUCPS *n abbr* (*Brit*: = *National Union of Civil and Public Servants*) *sindicato de funcionarios*
nude [nju:d] *adj, n* desnudo(-a) *m(f)*; **in the** ~ desnudo
nudge [nʌdʒ] *vt* dar un codazo a
nudist ['nju:dɪst] *n* nudista *m/f*
nudist colony *n* colonia de desnudistas
nudity ['nju:dɪtɪ] *n* desnudez *f*
nugget ['nʌgɪt] *n* pepita
nuisance ['nju:sns] *n* molestia, fastidio; (*person*) pesado, latoso; **what a ~!** ¡qué lata!
NUJ *n abbr* (*Brit*: = *National Union of Journalists*) *sindicato de periodistas*
nuke [nju:k] (*col*) *n* bomba atómica ■ *vt* atacar con arma nuclear
null [nʌl] *adj*: **~ and void** nulo y sin efecto
nullify ['nʌlɪfaɪ] *vt* anular, invalidar
NUM *n abbr* (*Brit*: = *National Union of Mineworkers*) *sindicato de mineros*
numb [nʌm] *adj* entumecido; (*fig*) insensible ■ *vt* quitar la sensación a, entumecer, entorpecer; **to be ~ with cold** estar entumecido de frío; **~ with fear/grief** paralizado de miedo/dolor
number ['nʌmbəʳ] *n* número; (*numeral*) número, cifra ■ *vt* (*pages etc*) numerar, poner número a; (*amount to*) sumar, ascender a; **reference** ~ número de referencia; **telephone** ~ número de teléfono; **wrong** ~ (*Tel*) número equivocado; **opposite** ~ (*person*) homólogo(-a); **to be numbered among** figurar entre; **a ~ of** varios, algunos; **they were ten in** ~ eran diez
number plate *n* (*Brit*) matrícula, placa
Number Ten *n* (*Brit*: *10 Downing Street*) *residencia del primer ministro*
numbness ['nʌmnɪs] *n* insensibilidad *f*, parálisis *f inv*; (*due to cold*) entumecimiento
numbskull ['nʌmskʌl] *n* (*col*) papanatas *m/f inv*
numeral ['nju:mərəl] *n* número, cifra
numerate ['nju:mərɪt] *adj* competente en aritmética
numerical [nju:'mɛrɪkl] *adj* numérico
numerous ['nju:mərəs] *adj* numeroso, muchos
nun [nʌn] *n* monja, religiosa
nunnery ['nʌnərɪ] *n* convento de monjas
nuptial ['nʌpʃəl] *adj* nupcial
nurse [nə:s] *n* enfermero(-a); (*nanny*) niñera ■ *vt* (*patient*) cuidar, atender; (*baby*: *Brit*) mecer; (: *US*) criar, amamantar; **male ~** enfermero
nursery ['nə:sərɪ] *n* (*institution*) guardería infantil; (*room*) cuarto de los niños; (*for plants*) criadero, semillero
nursery rhyme *n* canción *f* infantil
nursery school *n* escuela de preescolar

nursery slope *n* (*Brit Ski*) cuesta para principiantes
nursing ['nə:sɪŋ] *n* (*profession*) profesión *f* de enfermera; (*care*) asistencia, cuidado ■ *adj* (*mother*) lactante
nursing home *n* clínica de reposo
nurture ['nə:tʃəʳ] *vt* (*child, plant*) alimentar, nutrir
NUS *n abbr* (*Brit: = National Union of Students*) *sindicato de estudiantes*
NUT *n abbr* (*Brit: = National Union of Teachers*) *sindicato de profesores*
nut [nʌt] *n* (*Tech*) tuerca; (*Bot*) nuez *f* ■ *adj* (*chocolate etc*) con nueces; **nuts** (*Culin*) frutos secos
nutcrackers ['nʌtkrækəz] *npl* cascanueces *m inv*
nutmeg ['nʌtmɛg] *n* nuez *f* moscada
nutrient ['nju:trɪənt] *adj* nutritivo ■ *n* elemento nutritivo
nutrition [nju:'trɪʃən] *n* nutrición *f*, alimentación *f*
nutritionist [nju:'trɪʃənɪst] *n* dietista *m/f*
nutritious [nju:'trɪʃəs] *adj* nutritivo
nuts [nʌts] *adj* (*col*) chiflado
nutshell ['nʌtʃɛl] *n* cáscara de nuez; **in a ~** en resumidas cuentas
nutty ['nʌtɪ] *adj* (*flavour*) a frutos secos; (*col: foolish*) chalado
nuzzle ['nʌzl] *vi*: **to ~ up to** arrimarse a
NV *abbr* (US) = **Nevada**
NVQ *n abbr* (*Brit: = national vocational qualification*) *título de formación profesional*
NWT *abbr* (*Canada*) = **Northwest Territories**
NY *abbr* (US) = **New York**
NYC *abbr* (US) = **New York City**
nylon ['naɪlɔn] *n* nylon *m*, nilón *m* ■ *adj* de nylon *or* nilón
nymph [nɪmf] *n* ninfa
nymphomaniac ['nɪmfəu'meɪnɪæk] *adj, n* ninfómana
NYSE *n abbr* (US) = **New York Stock Exchange**

Oo

O, o [əu] *n* (*letter*) O, o *f*; **O for Oliver,** (*US*) **O for Oboe** O de Oviedo
oaf [əuf] *n* zoquete *m/f*
oak [əuk] *n* roble *m* ▪ *adj* de roble
O & M *n abbr* = **organization and method**
OAP *n abbr* (*Brit*) = **old-age pensioner**
oar [ɔːʳ] *n* remo; **to put** *or* **shove one's ~ in** (*fig col*) entrometerse
oarsman ['ɔːzmən] *n* remero
OAS *n abbr* (= *Organization of American States*) OEA *f*
oasis (*pl* **oases**) [əu'eɪsɪs, əu'eɪsiːz] *n* oasis *m inv*
oath [əuθ] *n* juramento; (*swear word*) palabrota; **on** (*Brit*) *or* **under ~** bajo juramento
oatmeal ['əutmiːl] *n* harina de avena
oats [əuts] *n* avena
OAU *n abbr* (= *Organization of African Unity*) OUA *f*
obdurate ['ɔbdjurɪt] *adj* (*stubborn*) terco, obstinado; (*sinner*) empedernido; (*unyielding*) inflexible, firme
OBE *n abbr* (*Brit*: = *Order of the British Empire*) *título ceremonial*
obedience [ə'biːdɪəns] *n* obediencia; **in ~ to** de acuerdo con
obedient [ə'biːdɪənt] *adj* obediente
obelisk ['ɔbɪlɪsk] *n* obelisco
obese [əu'biːs] *adj* obeso
obesity [əu'biːsɪtɪ] *n* obesidad *f*
obey [ə'beɪ] *vt* obedecer; (*instructions*) cumplir
obituary [ə'bɪtjuərɪ] *n* necrología
object ['ɔbdʒɪkt] *n* (*gen*) objeto; (*purpose*) objeto, propósito; (*Ling*) objeto, complemento ▪ *vi* [əb'dʒɛkt]: **to ~ to** (*attitude*) protestar contra; (*proposal*) oponerse a; **expense is no ~** no importan los gastos; **I ~!** ¡protesto!; **to ~ that** objetar que
objection [əb'dʒɛkʃən] *n* objeción *f*; **I have no ~ to ...** no tengo inconveniente en, que ...
objectionable [əb'dʒɛkʃənəbl] *adj* (*gen*) desagradable; (*conduct*) censurable
objective [əb'dʒɛktɪv] *adj, n* objetivo
objectively [əb'dʒɛktɪvlɪ] *adv* objetivamente
objectivity [ɔbdʒɪk'tɪvɪtɪ] *n* objetividad *f*
object lesson *n* (*fig*) (buen) ejemplo
objector [əb'dʒɛktəʳ] *n* objetor(a) *m(f)*
obligation [ɔblɪ'geɪʃən] *n* obligación *f*; (*debt*) deber *m*; **"without ~"** "sin compromiso"; **to be under an ~ to sb/to do sth** estar comprometido con algn/a hacer algo
obligatory [ə'blɪgətərɪ] *adj* obligatorio
oblige [ə'blaɪdʒ] *vt* (*do a favour for*) complacer, hacer un favor a; **to ~ sb to do sth** obligar a algn a hacer algo; **to be obliged to sb for sth** estarle agradecido a algn por algo; **anything to ~!** todo sea por complacerte
obliging [ə'blaɪdʒɪŋ] *adj* servicial, atento
oblique [ə'bliːk] *adj* oblicuo; (*allusion*) indirecto ▪ *n* (*Typ*) barra
obliterate [ə'blɪtəreɪt] *vt* arrasar; (*memory*) borrar
oblivion [ə'blɪvɪən] *n* olvido
oblivious [ə'blɪvɪəs] *adj*: **~ of** inconsciente de
oblong ['ɔblɔŋ] *adj* rectangular ▪ *n* rectángulo
obnoxious [əb'nɔkʃəs] *adj* odioso, detestable; (*smell*) nauseabundo
o.b.o. *abbr* (*US*: = *or best offer*: *in classified ads*) abierto ofertas
oboe ['əubəu] *n* oboe *m*
obscene [əb'siːn] *adj* obsceno
obscenity [əb'sɛnɪtɪ] *n* obscenidad *f*
obscure [əb'skjuəʳ] *adj* oscuro ▪ *vt* oscurecer; (*hide*: *sun*) ocultar
obscurity [əb'skjuərɪtɪ] *n* oscuridad *f*; (*obscure point*) punto oscuro; **to rise from ~** salir de la nada
obsequious [əb'siːkwɪəs] *adj* servil
observable [əb'zəːvəbl] *adj* observable, perceptible
observance [əb'zəːvns] *n* observancia, cumplimiento; (*ritual*) práctica; **religious observances** prácticas *fpl* religiosas
observant [əb'zəːvnt] *adj* observador(a)
observation [ɔbzə'veɪʃən] *n* (*Med*) observación *f*; (*by police etc*) vigilancia

observation post *n* (*Mil*) puesto de observación
observatory [əb'zə:vətrɪ] *n* observatorio
observe [əb'zə:v] *vt* (*gen*) observar; (*rule*) cumplir
observer [əb'zə:vəʳ] *n* observador(a) *m(f)*
obsess [əb'sɛs] *vt* obsesionar; **to be obsessed by** *or* **with sb/sth** estar obsesionado con algn/algo
obsession [əb'sɛʃən] *n* obsesión *f*
obsessive [əb'sɛsɪv] *adj* obsesivo
obsolescence [ɔbsə'lɛsns] *n* obsolescencia
obsolescent [ɔbsə'lɛsnt] *adj* que está cayendo en desuso
obsolete ['ɔbsəli:t] *adj* obsoleto
obstacle ['ɔbstəkl] *n* obstáculo; (*nuisance*) estorbo
obstacle race *n* carrera de obstáculos
obstetrician [ɔbstə'trɪʃən] *n* obstetra *m/f*
obstetrics [ɔb'stɛtrɪks] *n* obstetricia
obstinacy ['ɔbstɪnəsɪ] *n* terquedad *f*, obstinación *f*; tenacidad *f*
obstinate ['ɔbstɪnɪt] *adj* terco, obstinado; (*determined*) tenaz
obstinately ['ɔbstɪnɪtlɪ] *adv* tercamente, obstinadamente
obstreperous [əb'strɛpərəs] *adj* ruidoso; (*unruly*) revoltoso
obstruct [əb'strʌkt] *vt* (*block*) obstruir; (*hinder*) estorbar, obstaculizar
obstruction [əb'strʌkʃən] *n* obstrucción *f*; estorbo, obstáculo
obstructive [əb'strʌktɪv] *adj* obstruccionista; **stop being ~!** ¡deja de poner peros!
obtain [əb'teɪn] *vt* (*get*) obtener; (*achieve*) conseguir; **to ~ sth (for o.s.)** conseguir *or* adquirir algo
obtainable [əb'teɪnəbl] *adj* asequible
obtrusive [əb'tru:sɪv] *adj* (*person*) importuno; (*: interfering*) entrometido; (*building etc*) demasiado visible
obtuse [əb'tju:s] *adj* obtuso
obverse ['ɔbvə:s] *n* (*of medal*) anverso; (*fig*) complemento
obviate ['ɔbvɪeɪt] *vt* obviar, evitar
obvious ['ɔbvɪəs] *adj* (*clear*) obvio, evidente; (*unsubtle*) poco sutil; **it's ~ that ...** está claro que ..., es evidente que ...
obviously ['ɔbvɪəslɪ] *adv* obviamente, evidentemente; **~ not!** ¡por supuesto que no!; **he was ~ not drunk** era evidente que no estaba borracho; **he was not ~ drunk** no se le notaba que estaba borracho
OCAS *n abbr* (= *Organization of Central American States*) ODECA *f*
occasion [ə'keɪʒən] *n* oportunidad *f*, ocasión *f*; (*event*) acontecimiento ■ *vt* ocasionar, causar; **on that ~** esa vez, en aquella ocasión; **to rise to the ~** ponerse a la altura de las circunstancias
occasional [ə'keɪʒənl] *adj* poco frecuente, ocasional
occasionally [ə'keɪʒənlɪ] *adv* de vez en cuando; **very ~** muy de tarde en tarde, en muy contadas ocasiones
occasional table *n* mesita
occult [ɔ'kʌlt] *adj* (*gen*) oculto
occupancy ['ɔkjupənsɪ] *n* ocupación *f*
occupant ['ɔkjupənt] *n* (*of house*) inquilino(-a); (*of boat, car*) ocupante *m/f*
occupation [ɔkju'peɪʃən] *n* (*of house*) tenencia; (*job*) trabajo; (*calling*) oficio
occupational accident [ɔkju'peɪʃənl-] *n* accidente *m* laboral
occupational guidance *n* orientación *f* profesional
occupational hazard *n* gajes *mpl* del oficio
occupational pension scheme *n* plan *m* profesional de jubilación
occupational therapy *n* terapia ocupacional
occupier ['ɔkjupaɪəʳ] *n* inquilino(-a)
occupy ['ɔkjupaɪ] *vt* (*seat, post, time*) ocupar; (*house*) habitar; **to ~ o.s. with** *or* **by doing** (*as job*) dedicarse a hacer; (*to pass time*) entretenerse haciendo; **to be occupied with sth/in doing sth** estar ocupado con algo/haciendo algo
occur [ə'kə:ʳ] *vi* ocurrir, suceder; **to ~ to sb** ocurrírsele a algn
occurrence [ə'kʌrəns] *n* suceso
ocean ['əuʃən] *n* océano; **oceans of** (*col*) la mar de
ocean bed *n* fondo del océano
ocean-going ['əuʃəngəuɪŋ] *adj* de alta mar
Oceania [əuʃɪ'ɑ:nɪə] *n* Oceanía
ocean liner *n* buque *m* transoceánico
ochre, (*US*) **ocher** ['əukəʳ] *n* ocre *m*
o'clock [ə'klɔk] *adv*: **it is five ~** son las cinco
OCR *n abbr* = **optical character recognition/reader**
Oct. *abbr* (= *October*) oct
octagonal [ɔk'tægənl] *adj* octagonal
octane ['ɔkteɪn] *n* octano; **high ~ petrol** *or* (*US*) **gas** gasolina de alto octanaje
octave ['ɔktɪv] *n* octava
October [ɔk'təubəʳ] *n* octubre *m*; *see also* **July**
octogenarian ['ɔktəudʒɪ'nɛərɪən] *n* octogenario(-a)
octopus ['ɔktəpəs] *n* pulpo
oculist ['ɔkjulɪst] *n* oculista *m/f*
odd [ɔd] *adj* (*strange*) extraño, raro; (*number*) impar; (*left over*) sobrante, suelto; **60-~** 60 y pico; **at ~ times** de vez en cuando; **to be**

the ~ one out estar de más; **if you have the ~ minute** si tienes unos minutos libres; *see also* **odds**
oddball ['ɔdbɔ:l] *n* (*col*) bicho raro
oddity ['ɔdɪtɪ] *n* rareza; (*person*) excéntrico(-a)
odd-job man [ɔd'dʒɔb-] *n* hombre *m* que hace chapuzas
odd jobs *npl* chapuzas *fpl*
oddly ['ɔdlɪ] *adv* extrañamente
oddments ['ɔdmənts] *npl* (*Brit Comm*) restos *mpl*
odds [ɔdz] *npl* (*in betting*) puntos *mpl* de ventaja; **it makes no ~** da lo mismo; **at ~** reñidos(-as); **to succeed against all the ~** tener éxito contra todo pronóstico; **~ and ends** cachivaches *mpl*
odds-on [ɔdz'ɔn] *adj* (*col*): **the ~ favourite** el máximo favorito; **it's ~ he'll come** seguro que viene
ode [əud] *n* oda
odious ['əudɪəs] *adj* odioso
odometer [ɔ'dɔmɪtəʳ] *n* (*US*) cuentakilómetros *m inv*
odour, odor (*US*) ['əudəʳ] *n* olor *m*; (*perfume*) perfume *m*
odourless, odorless (*US*) ['əudəlɪs] *adj* sin olor
OECD *n abbr* (= *Organization for Economic Cooperation and Development*) OCDE *f*
oesophagus, esophagus (*US*) [i:'sɔfəgəs] *n* esófago
oestrogen, estrogen (*US*) ['i:strədʒən] *n* estrógeno

KEYWORD

of [ɔv, əv] *prep* **1** (*gen*) de; **a friend of ours** un amigo nuestro; **a boy of 10** un chico de 10 años; **that was kind of you** eso fue muy amable de tu parte
2 (*expressing quantity, amount, dates etc*) de; **a kilo of flour** un kilo de harina; **there were three of them** había tres; **three of us went** tres de nosotros fuimos; **the 5th of July** el 5 de julio; **a quarter of four** (*US*) las cuarto menos cuarto
3 (*from, out of*) de; **made of wood** (hecho) de madera

Ofcom ['ɔfkɔm] *n abbr* (*Brit*) = **Office of Communications**
off [ɔf] *adj, adv* (*engine, light*) apagado; (*tap*) cerrado; (*Brit: food: bad*) pasado, malo; (*: milk*) cortado; (*cancelled*) suspendido; (*removed*): **the lid was ~** no estaba puesta la tapadera ■ *prep* de; **to be ~** (*leave*) irse, marcharse; **to be ~ sick** estar enfermo *or* de baja; **a day ~** un día libre; **to have an ~ day** tener un mal día; **he had his coat ~** se había quitado el abrigo; **10% ~** (*Comm*) (con el) 10% de descuento; **it's a long way ~** está muy lejos; **5 km ~ (the road)** a 5 km (de la carretera); **~ the coast** frente a la costa; **I'm ~ meat** (*no longer eat/like it*) paso de la carne; **on the ~ chance** por si acaso; **~ and on, on and ~** de vez en cuando; **I must be ~** tengo que irme; **to be well/badly ~** andar bien/mal de dinero; **I'm afraid the chicken is ~** desgraciadamente ya no queda pollo; **that's a bit ~, isn't it?** (*fig, col*) ¡eso no se hace!
offal ['ɔfl] *n* (*Brit Culin*) menudillos *mpl*, asaduras *fpl*
off-centre, (*US*) **off-center** [ɔf'sɛntəʳ] *adj* descentrado, ladeado
off-colour ['ɔf'kʌləʳ] *adj* (*Brit: ill*) indispuesto; **to feel ~** sentirse *or* estar mal
offence, offense (*US*) [ə'fɛns] *n* (*crime*) delito; (*insult*) ofensa; **to take ~ at** ofenderse por; **to commit an ~** cometer un delito
offend [ə'fɛnd] *vt* (*person*) ofender ■ *vi*: **to ~ against** (*law, rule*) infringir
offender [ə'fɛndəʳ] *n* delincuente *m/f*; (*against regulations*) infractor(a) *m(f)*
offending [ə'fɛndɪŋ] *adj* culpable; (*object*) molesto; (*word*) problemático
offense [ə'fɛns] *n* (*US*) = **offence**
offensive [ə'fɛnsɪv] *adj* ofensivo; (*smell etc*) repugnante ■ *n* (*Mil*) ofensiva
offer ['ɔfəʳ] *n* (*gen*) oferta, ofrecimiento; (*proposal*) propuesta ■ *vt* ofrecer; **"on ~"** (*Comm*) "en oferta"; **to make an ~ for sth** hacer una oferta por algo; **to ~ sth to sb, ~ sb sth** ofrecer algo a algn; **to ~ to do sth** ofrecerse a hacer algo
offering ['ɔfərɪŋ] *n* (*Rel*) ofrenda
offer price *n* precio de oferta
offertory ['ɔfətrɪ] *n* (*Rel*) ofertorio
offhand [ɔf'hænd] *adj* informal; (*brusque*) desconsiderado ■ *adv* de improviso, sin pensarlo; **I can't tell you ~** no te lo puedo decir así de improviso *or* (*LAm*) así nomás
office ['ɔfɪs] *n* (*place*) oficina; (*room*) despacho; (*position*) cargo, oficio; **doctor's ~** (*US*) consultorio; **to take ~** entrar en funciones; **through his good offices** gracias a sus buenos oficios; **O~ of Fair Trading** (*Brit*) *oficina que regula normas comerciales*
office automation *n* ofimática, buromática
office bearer *n* (*of club etc*) titular *m/f* (de una cartera)
office block, office building (*US*) *n* bloque *m* de oficinas
office boy *n* ordenanza *m*
office hours *npl* horas *fpl* de oficina; (*US Med*) horas *fpl* de consulta

office manager *n* jefe(-a) *m(f)* de oficina
officer ['ɔfɪsəʳ] *n* (*Mil etc*) oficial *m/f*; (*of organization*) director(a) *m(f)*; (*also*: **police officer**) agente *m/f* de policía
office work *n* trabajo de oficina
office worker *n* oficinista *m/f*
official [ə'fɪʃl] *adj* (*authorized*) oficial, autorizado; (*strike*) oficial ■ *n* funcionario(-a)
officialdom [ə'fɪʃldəm] *n* burocracia
officially [ə'fɪʃəlɪ] *adv* oficialmente
official receiver *n* síndico
officiate [ə'fɪʃɪeɪt] *vi* (*Rel*) oficiar; **to ~ as Mayor** ejercer las funciones de alcalde; **to ~ at a marriage** celebrar una boda
officious [ə'fɪʃəs] *adj* oficioso
offing ['ɔfɪŋ] *n*: **in the ~** (*fig*) en perspectiva
off-key [ɔf'ki:] *adj* desafinado ■ *adv* desafinadamente
off-licence ['ɔflaɪsns] *n* (*Brit*: *shop*) *tienda de bebidas alcohólicas; ver nota*

OFF-LICENCE

En el Reino Unido una *off-licence* es una tienda especializada en la venta de bebidas alcohólicas para el consumo fuera del establecimiento. De ahí su nombre, pues se necesita un permiso especial para tal venta, que está estrictamente regulada. Suelen vender además bebidas sin alcohol, tabaco, chocolate, patatas fritas etc y a menudo son parte de grandes cadenas nacionales.

off-limits [ɔf'lɪmɪts] *adj* (*US Mil*) prohibido al personal militar
off line *adj, adv* (*Comput*) fuera de línea; (*switched off*) desconectado
off-load ['ɔfləud] *vt* descargar, desembarcar
off-peak ['ɔf'pi:k] *adj* (*holiday*) de temporada baja; (*electricity*) de banda económica
off-putting ['ɔfputɪŋ] *adj* (*Brit*: *person*) poco amable, difícil; (*behaviour*) chocante
off-season ['ɔf'si:zn] *adj, adv* fuera de temporada
offset ['ɔfsɛt] *vt* (*irreg*: *like* **set**) (*counteract*) contrarrestar, compensar ■ *n* (*also*: **offset printing**) offset *m*
offshoot ['ɔfʃu:t] *n* (*Bot*) vástago; (*fig*) ramificación *f*
offshore [ɔf'ʃɔ:ʳ] *adj* (*breeze, island*) costero; (*fishing*) de bajura; **~ oilfield** campo petrolífero submarino
offside ['ɔf'saɪd] *n* (*Aut*: *with right-hand drive*) lado derecho; (: *with left-hand drive*) lado izquierdo ■ *adj* (*Sport*) fuera de juego; (*Aut*) del lado derecho; del lado izquierdo
offspring ['ɔfsprɪŋ] *n* descendencia
offstage [ɔf'steɪdʒ] *adv* entre bastidores
off-the-cuff [ɔfðə'kʌf] *adj* espontáneo
off-the-job [ɔfðə'dʒɔb] *adj*: **~ training** formación *f* fuera del trabajo
off-the-peg [ɔfðə'pɛg], (*US*) **off-the-rack** [ɔfðə'ræk] *adv* confeccionado
off-the-record ['ɔfðə'rɛkɔ:d] *adj* extraoficial, confidencial ■ *adv* extraoficialmente, confidencialmente
off-white ['ɔfwaɪt] *adj* blanco grisáceo
Ofgas ['ɔfgæs] *n abbr* (*Brit*: = *Office of Gas Supply*) *organismo que controla a las empresas del gas en Gran Bretaña*
Ofgem ['ɔfdʒɛm] *n abbr* (*Brit*) = **Office of Gas and Electricity Markets**
Oftel ['ɔftɛl] *n abbr* (*Brit*: = *Office of Telecommunications*) *organismo que controla las telecomunicaciones británicas*
often ['ɔfn] *adv* a menudo, con frecuencia, seguido (*LAm*); **how ~ do you go?** ¿cada cuánto vas?
Ofwat ['ɔfwɔt] *n abbr* (*Brit*: = *Office of Water Services*) *organismo que controla a las empresas suministradoras del agua en Inglaterra y Gales*
ogle ['əugl] *vt* comerse con los ojos a
ogre ['əugəʳ] *n* ogro
OH *abbr* (*US*) = **Ohio**
oh [əu] *excl* ¡ah!
OHMS *abbr* (*Brit*) = **On His** (*or* **Her**) **Majesty's Service**
oil [ɔɪl] *n* aceite *m*; (*petroleum*) petróleo ■ *vt* (*machine*) engrasar; **fried in ~** frito en aceite
oilcan ['ɔɪlkæn] *n* lata de aceite
oilfield ['ɔɪlfi:ld] *n* campo petrolífero
oil filter *n* (*Aut*) filtro de aceite
oil-fired ['ɔɪlfaɪəd] *adj* de fuel-oil
oil gauge *n* indicador *m* del aceite
oil industry *n* industria petrolífera
oil level *n* nivel *m* del aceite
oil painting *n* pintura al óleo
oil refinery *n* refinería de petróleo
oil rig *n* torre *f* de perforación
oilskins ['ɔɪlskɪnz] *npl* impermeable *msg*, chubasquero *sg*
oil tanker *n* petrolero
oil well *n* pozo (de petróleo)
oily ['ɔɪlɪ] *adj* aceitoso; (*food*) grasiento
ointment ['ɔɪntmənt] *n* ungüento
OK *abbr* (*US*) = **Oklahoma**
O.K., okay ['əu'keɪ] *excl* O.K., ¡está bien!, ¡vale! ■ *adj* bien ■ *n*: **to give sth one's O.K.** dar el visto bueno a *or* aprobar algo ■ *vt* dar el visto bueno a; **it's O.K. with** *or* **by me** estoy de acuerdo, me parece bien; **are you O.K. for money?** ¿andas *or* vas bien de dinero?

Okla. *abbr* (*US*) = **Oklahoma**
old [əuld] *adj* viejo; (*former*) antiguo; **how ~ are you?** ¿cuántos años tienes?, ¿qué edad tienes?; **he's 10 years ~** tiene 10 años; **older brother** hermano mayor; **any ~ thing will do** sirve cualquier cosa
old age *n* vejez *f*
old-age pension ['əuldeɪdʒ-] *n* (*Brit*) jubilación *f*, pensión *f*
old-age pensioner ['əuldeɪdʒ-] *n* (*Brit*) jubilado(-a)
olden ['əuldən] *adj* antiguo
old-fashioned ['əuld'fæʃənd] *adj* anticuado, pasado de moda
old maid *n* solterona
old-style ['əuldstaɪl] *adj* tradicional, chapado a la antigua
old-time ['əuld'taɪm] *adj* antiguo, de antaño
old-timer [əuld'taɪməʳ] *n* veterano(-a); (*old person*) anciano(-a)
old wives' tale *n* cuento de viejas, patraña
olive ['ɔlɪv] *n* (*fruit*) aceituna; (*tree*) olivo ■ *adj* (*also*: **olive-green**) verde oliva *inv*
olive branch *n* (*fig*): **to offer an ~ to sb** ofrecer hacer las paces con algn
olive oil *n* aceite *m* de oliva
Olympic [əu'lɪmpɪk] *adj* olímpico; **the ~ Games, the Olympics** *npl* las Olimpíadas
OM *n abbr* (*Brit*: = *Order of Merit*) *título ceremonial*
Oman [əu'mɑːn] *n* Omán *m*
OMB *n abbr* (*US*: = *Office of Management and Budget*) *servicio que asesora al presidente en materia presupuestaria*
omelette, omelet ['ɔmlɪt] *n* tortilla, tortilla de huevo (*LAm*)
omen ['əumən] *n* presagio
ominous ['ɔmɪnəs] *adj* de mal agüero, amenazador(a)
omission [əu'mɪʃən] *n* omisión *f*; (*error*) descuido
omit [əu'mɪt] *vt* omitir; (*by mistake*) olvidar, descuidar; **to ~ to do sth** olvidarse *or* dejar de hacer algo
omnivorous [ɔm'nɪvərəs] *adj* omnívoro
ON *abbr* (*Canada*) = **Ontario**

KEYWORD

on [ɔn] *prep* **1** (*indicating position*) en; sobre; **on the wall** en la pared; **it's on the table** está sobre *or* en la mesa; **on the left** a la izquierda; **I haven't got any money on me** no llevo dinero encima
2 (*indicating means, method, condition etc*): **on foot** a pie; **on the train/plane** (*go*) en tren/avión; (*be*) en el tren/el avión; **on the radio/television** por *or* en la radio/televisión; **on the telephone** al teléfono; **to be on drugs** drogarse; (*Med*) estar a tratamiento; **to be on holiday/business** estar de vacaciones/en viaje de negocios; **we're on irregular verbs** estamos con los verbos irregulares
3 (*referring to time*): **on Friday** el viernes; **on Fridays** los viernes; **on June 20th** el 20 de junio; **a week on Friday** del viernes en una semana; **on arrival** al llegar; **on seeing this** al ver esto
4 (*about, concerning*) sobre, acerca de; **a book on physics** un libro de *or* sobre física
5 (*at the expense of*): **this round's on me** esta ronda la pago yo, invito yo a esta ronda; (*earning*): **he's on sixteen thousand pounds a year** gana dieciséis mil libras al año
■ *adv* **1** (*referring to dress*): **to have one's coat on** tener *or* llevar el abrigo puesto; **she put her gloves on** se puso los guantes
2 (*referring to covering*): **"screw the lid on tightly"** "cerrar bien la tapa"
3 (*further, continuously*): **to walk/run** *etc* **on** seguir caminando/corriendo *etc*; **from that day on** desde aquel día; **it was well on in the evening** estaba ya entrada la tarde
4 (*in phrases*): **I'm on to sth** creo haber encontrado algo; **my father's always on at me to get a job** (*col*) mi padre siempre me está dando la lata para que me ponga a trabajar
■ *adj* **1** (*functioning, in operation*: *machine, radio, TV, light*) encendido(-a) (*SP*), prendido(-a) (*LAm*); (: *tap*) abierto(-a); (: *brakes*) echado(-a), puesto(-a); **is the meeting still on?** (*in progress*) ¿todavía continúa la reunión?; (*not cancelled*) ¿va a haber reunión al fin?; **there's a good film on at the cinema** ponen una buena película en el cine
2: **that's not on!** (*col*: *not possible*) ¡eso ni hablar!; (: *not acceptable*) ¡eso no se hace!

ONC *n abbr* (*Brit*: = *Ordinary National Certificate*) *título escolar*
once [wʌns] *adv* una vez; (*formerly*) antiguamente ■ *conj* una vez que; **~ he had left/it was done** una vez que se había marchado/se hizo; **at ~** en seguida, inmediatamente; (*simultaneously*) a la vez; **~ a week** una vez a la semana; **~ more** otra vez; **~ and for all** de una vez por todas; **~ upon a time** érase una vez; **I knew him ~** le conocía hace tiempo
oncoming ['ɔnkʌmɪŋ] *adj* (*traffic*) que viene de frente
OND *n abbr* (*Brit*: = *Ordinary National Diploma*) *título escolar*

KEYWORD

one [wʌn] *num* un/una; **one hundred and fifty** ciento cincuenta; **one by one** uno a uno; **it's one (o'clock)** es la una
■ *adj* 1 (*sole*) único; **the one book which** el único libro que; **the one man who** el único que
2 (*same*) mismo(-a); **they came in the one car** vinieron en un solo coche
■ *pron* 1: **this one** éste/ésta; **that one** ése/ésa; (*more remote*) aquél/aquélla; **I've already got (a red) one** ya tengo uno(-a) (rojo(-a)); **one by one** uno(-a) por uno(-a); **to be one up on sb** llevar ventaja a algn; **to be at one (with sb)** estar completamente de acuerdo (con algn)
2: **one another** (*US*) nos; (*you*) os (*SP*); (*you: polite: them*) se; **do you two ever see one another?** ¿os veis alguna vez? (*SP*), ¿se ven alguna vez?; **the two boys didn't dare look at one another** los dos chicos no se atrevieron a mirarse (el uno al otro); **they all kissed one another** se besaron unos a otros
3 (*impers*): **one never knows** nunca se sabe; **to cut one's finger** cortarse el dedo; **one needs to eat** hay que comer

one-armed bandit ['wʌnɑːmd-] *n* máquina tragaperras
one-day excursion ['wʌndeɪ-] *n* (*US*) billete *m* de ida y vuelta en un día
One-hundred share index ['wʌnhʌndrəd-] *n* índice *m* bursátil (*del Financial Times*)
one-man ['wʌn'mæn] *adj* (*business*) individual
one-man band *n* hombre-orquesta *m*
one-off [wʌn'ɔf] *n* (*Brit col: object*) artículo único; (*: event*) caso especial
one-parent family ['wʌnpɛərənt-] *n* familia monoparental
one-piece ['wʌnpiːs] *adj* (*bathing suit*) de una pieza
onerous ['ɔnərəs] *adj* (*task, duty*) pesado; (*responsibility*) oneroso
oneself [wʌn'sɛlf] *pron* uno mismo; (*after prep, also emphatic*) sí (mismo(-a)); **to do sth by ~** hacer algo solo *or* por sí solo
one-shot [wʌn'ʃɔt] *n* (*US*) = **one-off**
one-sided [wʌn'saɪdɪd] *adj* (*argument*) parcial; (*decision, view*) unilateral; (*game, contest*) desigual
one-time ['wʌntaɪm] *adj* antiguo, ex-
one-to-one ['wʌntəwʌn] *adj* (*relationship*) individualizado
one-upmanship [wʌn'ʌpmənʃɪp] *n*: **the art of ~** el arte de quedar siempre por encima
one-way ['wʌnweɪ] *adj* (*street, traffic*) de dirección única; (*ticket*) sencillo
ongoing ['ɔngəuɪŋ] *adj* continuo
onion ['ʌnjən] *n* cebolla
online *adj, adv* (*Comput*) en línea; (*switched on*) conectado
onlooker ['ɔnlukə^r] *n* espectador(a) *m(f)*
only ['əunlɪ] *adv* solamente, sólo, nomás (*LAm*) ■ *adj* único, solo ■ *conj* solamente que, pero; **an ~ child** un hijo único; **not ~ ... but also ...** no sólo ... sino también ...; **I'd be ~ too pleased to help** encantado de ayudarles; **I saw her ~ yesterday** le vi ayer mismo; **I would come, ~ I'm very busy** iría, sólo que estoy muy atareado
ono *abbr* (= *or nearest offer: in classified ads*) abierto ofertas
onset ['ɔnsɛt] *n* comienzo
onshore ['ɔnʃɔː^r] *adj* (*wind*) que sopla del mar hacia la tierra
onslaught ['ɔnslɔːt] *n* ataque *m*, embestida
Ont. *abbr* (*Canada*) = **Ontario**
on-the-job ['ɔnðə'dʒɔb] *adj*: **~ training** formación *f* en el trabajo *or* sobre la práctica
onto ['ɔntu] *prep* = **on to**
onus ['əunəs] *n* responsabilidad *f*; **the ~ is upon him to prove it** le incumbe a él demostrarlo
onward ['ɔnwəd], **onwards** ['ɔnwədz] *adv* (*move*) (hacia) adelante
onyx ['ɔnɪks] *n* ónice *m*, onyx *m*
oops [ups] *excl* (*also*: **oops-a-daisy!**) ¡huy!
ooze [uːz] *vi* rezumar
opal ['əupl] *n* ópalo
opaque [əu'peɪk] *adj* opaco
OPEC ['əupɛk] *n abbr* (= *Organization of Petroleum-Exporting Countries*) OPEP *f*
open ['əupn] *adj* abierto; (*car*) descubierto; (*road, view*) despejado; (*meeting*) público; (*admiration*) manifiesto ■ *vt* abrir ■ *vi* (*flower, eyes, door, debate*) abrirse; (*book etc: commence*) comenzar; **in the ~ (air)** al aire libre; **~ verdict** veredicto inconcluso; **~ ticket** billete *m* sin fecha; **~ ground** (*among trees*) claro; (*waste ground*) solar *m*; **to have an ~ mind (on sth)** estar sin decidirse aún (sobre algo); **to ~ a bank account** abrir una cuenta en el banco
▸ **open on to** *vt fus* (*room, door*) dar a
▸ **open out** *vt* abrir ■ *vi* (*person*) abrirse
▸ **open up** *vt* abrir; (*blocked road*) despejar ■ *vi* abrirse
open-and-shut ['əupənən'ʃʌt] *adj*: **~ case** caso claro *or* evidente
open day *n* (*Brit*) jornada de puertas abiertas *or* acceso público

open-ended [əupn'ɛndɪd] *adj (fig)* indefinido, sin definir
opener ['əupnəʳ] *n (also:* **can opener, tin opener**) abrelatas *m inv*
open-heart surgery [əupn'hɑːt-] *n* cirugía a corazón abierto
opening ['əupnɪŋ] *n* abertura; *(beginning)* comienzo; *(opportunity)* oportunidad *f*; *(job)* puesto vacante, vacante *f*
opening night *n* estreno
open learning *n enseñanza flexible a tiempo parcial*
openly ['əupnlɪ] *adv* abiertamente
open-minded [əupn'maɪndɪd] *adj* de amplias miras, sin prejuicios
open-necked ['əupnnɛkt] *adj* sin corbata
openness ['əupnnɪs] *n (frankness)* franqueza
open-plan ['əupn'plæn] *adj* sin tabiques, de plan abierto
open prison *n* centro penitenciario de régimen abierto
open return *n* vuelta con fecha abierta
open shop *n empresa que contrata a mano de obra no afiliada a ningún sindicato*
Open University *n (Brit)* ≈ Universidad *f* Nacional de Enseñanza a Distancia, UNED *f*; *ver nota*

Open University

La *Open University*, fundada en 1969, está especializada en impartir cursos a distancia y a tiempo parcial con sus propios materiales de apoyo diseñados para tal fin, entre ellos programas de radio y televisión emitidos por la "BBC". Los trabajos se envían por correo y se complementan con la asistencia obligatoria a cursos de verano. Para obtener la licenciatura es necesario estudiar un mínimo de módulos y alcanzar un determinado número de créditos.

opera ['ɔpərə] *n* ópera
opera glasses *npl* gemelos *mpl*
opera house *n* teatro de la ópera
opera singer *n* cantante *m/f* de ópera
operate ['ɔpəreɪt] *vt (machine)* hacer funcionar; *(company)* dirigir ■ *vi* funcionar; *(drug)* hacer efecto; **to ~ on sb** *(Med)* operar a algn
operatic [ɔpə'rætɪk] *adj* de ópera
operating costs ['ɔpəreɪtɪŋ-] *npl* gastos *mpl* operacionales
operating profit *n* beneficio de explotación
operating room *n (US)* quirófano, sala de operaciones
operating table *n* mesa de operaciones
operating theatre *n* quirófano, sala de operaciones
operation [ɔpə'reɪʃən] *n (gen)* operación *f*; *(of machine)* funcionamiento; **to be in ~** estar funcionando *or* en funcionamiento; **to have an ~** *(Med)* ser operado; **to have an ~ for** operarse de; **the company's operations during the year** las actividades de la compañía durante el año
operational [ɔpə'reɪʃənl] *adj* operacional, en buen estado; *(Comm)* en condiciones de servicio; *(ready for use or action)* en condiciones de funcionar; **when the service is fully ~** cuando el servicio esté en pleno funcionamiento
operative ['ɔpərətɪv] *adj (measure)* en vigor; **the ~ word** la palabra clave
operator ['ɔpəreɪtəʳ] *n (of machine)* operario(-a); *(Tel)* operador(a) *m(f)*, telefonista *m/f*
operetta [ɔpə'rɛtə] *n* opereta
ophthalmic [ɔf'θælmɪk] *adj* oftálmico
ophthalmologist [ɔfθæl'mɔlədʒɪst] *n* oftalmólogo(-a)
opinion [ə'pɪnjən] *n (gen)* opinión *f*; **in my ~** en mi opinión, a mi juicio; **to seek a second ~** pedir una segunda opinión
opinionated [ə'pɪnjəneɪtɪd] *adj* testarudo
opinion poll *n* encuesta, sondeo
opium ['əupɪəm] *n* opio
opponent [ə'pəunənt] *n* adversario(-a), contrincante *m/f*
opportune ['ɔpətjuːn] *adj* oportuno
opportunism [ɔpə'tjuːnɪzm] *n* oportunismo
opportunist [ɔpə'tjuːnɪst] *n* oportunista *m/f*
opportunity [ɔpə'tjuːnɪtɪ] *n* oportunidad *f*, chance *m or f (LAm)*; **to take the ~ to do** *or* **of doing** aprovechar la ocasión para hacer
oppose [ə'pəuz] *vt* oponerse a; **to be opposed to sth** oponerse a algo; **as opposed to** en vez de; *(unlike)* a diferencia de
opposing [ə'pəuzɪŋ] *adj (side)* opuesto, contrario
opposite ['ɔpəzɪt] *adj* opuesto, contrario; *(house etc)* de enfrente ■ *adv* en frente ■ *prep* en frente de, frente a ■ *n* lo contrario; **the ~ sex** el otro sexo, el sexo opuesto
opposite number *n (Brit)* homólogo(-a)
opposition [ɔpə'zɪʃən] *n* oposición *f*
oppress [ə'prɛs] *vt* oprimir
oppression [ə'prɛʃən] *n* opresión *f*
oppressive [ə'prɛsɪv] *adj* opresivo
opprobrium [ə'prəubrɪəm] *n (formal)* oprobio
opt [ɔpt] *vi*: **to ~ for** optar por; **to ~ to do** optar por hacer; **to ~ out** *(of NHS etc)* salirse

optical ['ɔptɪkl] *adj* óptico
optical character reader *n* lector *m* óptico de caracteres
optical character recognition *n* reconocimiento *m* óptico de caracteres
optical fibre *n* fibra óptica
optician [ɔp'tɪʃən] *n* óptico *m/f*
optics ['ɔptɪks] *n* óptica
optimism ['ɔptɪmɪzəm] *n* optimismo
optimist ['ɔptɪmɪst] *n* optimista *m/f*
optimistic [ɔptɪ'mɪstɪk] *adj* optimista
optimum ['ɔptɪməm] *adj* óptimo
option ['ɔpʃən] *n* opción *f*; **to keep one's options open** (*fig*) mantener las opciones abiertas; **I have no ~** no tengo más *or* otro remedio
optional ['ɔpʃənl] *adj* opcional; (*course*) optativo; **~ extras** opciones *fpl* extras
opulence ['ɔpjuləns] *n* opulencia
opulent ['ɔpjulənt] *adj* opulento
OR *abbr* (*US*) = **Oregon**
or [ɔːʳ] *conj* o; (*before o, ho*) u; (*with negative*): **he hasn't seen or heard anything** no ha visto ni oído nada; **or else** si no; **let me go or I'll scream!** ¡suélteme, o me pongo a gritar!
oracle ['ɔrəkl] *n* oráculo
oral ['ɔːrəl] *adj* oral ■ *n* examen *m* oral
orange ['ɔrɪndʒ] *n* (*fruit*) naranja ■ *adj* (de color) naranja
orangeade [ɔrɪndʒ'eɪd] *n* naranjada, refresco de naranja
orange squash *n* zumo (*SP*) *or* jugo de naranja
orang-outang, orang-utan [ɔ'ræŋuː'tæn] *n* orangután *m*
oration [ɔː'reɪʃən] *n* discurso solemne; **funeral ~** oración *f* fúnebre
orator ['ɔrətəʳ] *n* orador(a) *m(f)*
oratorio [ɔrə'tɔːrɪəu] *n* oratorio
orbit ['ɔːbɪt] *n* órbita ■ *vt, vi* orbitar; **to be in/go into ~ (round)** estar en/entrar en órbita (alrededor de)
orbital ['ɔːbɪtl] *n* (*also*: **orbital motorway**) autopista de circunvalación
orchard ['ɔːtʃəd] *n* huerto; **apple ~** manzanar *m*, manzanal *m*
orchestra ['ɔːkɪstrə] *n* orquesta; (*US: seating*) platea
orchestral [ɔː'kɛstrəl] *adj* de orquesta
orchestrate ['ɔːkɪstreɪt] *vt* orquestar
orchid ['ɔːkɪd] *n* orquídea
ordain [ɔː'deɪn] *vt* (*Rel*) ordenar
ordeal [ɔː'diːl] *n* experiencia terrible
order ['ɔːdəʳ] *n* orden *m*; (*command*) orden *f*; (*type, kind*) clase *f*; (*state*) estado; (*Comm*) pedido, encargo ■ *vt* (*also*: **put in order**) ordenar, poner en orden; (*Comm*) encargar, pedir; (*command*) mandar, ordenar; **in ~** (*gen*) en orden; (*of document*) en regla; **in (working) ~** en funcionamiento; **a machine in working ~** una máquina en funcionamiento; **to be out of ~** (*machine, toilets*) estar estropeado *or* (*LAm*) descompuesto; **in ~ to do** para hacer; **in ~ that** para que + *subjun*; **on ~** (*Comm*) pedido; **to be on ~** estar pedido; **we are under orders to do it** tenemos orden de hacerlo; **a point of ~** una cuestión de procedimiento; **to place an ~ for sth with sb** hacer un pedido de algo a algn; **made to ~** hecho a la medida; **his income is of the ~ of £24,000 per year** sus ingresos son del orden de 24 mil libras al año; **to the ~ of** (*Banking*) a la orden de; **to ~ sb to do sth** mandar a algn hacer algo
order book *n* cartera de pedidos
order form *n* hoja de pedido
orderly ['ɔːdəlɪ] *n* (*Mil*) ordenanza *m*; (*Med*) auxiliar *m/f* (de hospital) ■ *adj* ordenado
orderly officer *n* (*Mil*) oficial *m* del día
order number *n* número de pedido
ordinal ['ɔːdɪnl] *adj* ordinal
ordinarily ['ɔːdnrɪlɪ] *adv* por lo común
ordinary ['ɔːdnrɪ] *adj* corriente, normal; (*pej*) común y corriente; **out of the ~** fuera de lo común, extraordinario
ordinary degree *n* (*Brit*) diploma *m*; *ver nota*

ORDINARY DEGREE

Después de tres años de estudios, algunos universitarios obtienen la titulación de *ordinary degree*. Esto ocurre en el caso poco frecuente de que no aprueben los exámenes que conducen al título de "honours degree" pero sus examinadores consideren que a lo largo de la carrera han logrado unos resultados mínimos satisfactorios. También es una opción que tienen los estudiantes de las universidades escocesas no interesados en estudiar en la universidad más de tres años.

ordinary seaman *n* (*Brit*) marinero
ordinary shares *npl* acciones *fpl* ordinarias
ordination [ɔːdɪ'neɪʃən] *n* ordenación *f*
ordnance ['ɔːdnəns] *n* (*Mil: unit*) artillería
ordnance factory *n* fábrica de artillería
Ordnance Survey *n* (*Brit*) *servicio oficial de topografía y cartografía*
ore [ɔːʳ] *n* mineral *m*
Ore., Oreg. *abbr* (*US*) = **Oregon**
organ ['ɔːgən] *n* órgano

organic [ɔːˈgænɪk] *adj* orgánico; (*vegetables, produce*) biológico
organism [ˈɔːgənɪzəm] *n* organismo
organist [ˈɔːgənɪst] *n* organista *m/f*
organization [ɔːgənaɪˈzeɪʃən] *n* organización *f*
organization chart *n* organigrama *m*
organize [ˈɔːgənaɪz] *vt* organizar; **to get organized** organizarse
organized crime *n* crimen organizado
organizer [ˈɔːgənaɪzəʳ] *n* organizador(-a) *m(f)*
orgasm [ˈɔːgæzəm] *n* orgasmo
orgy [ˈɔːdʒɪ] *n* orgía
Orient [ˈɔːrɪənt] *n* Oriente *m*
oriental [ɔːrɪˈɛntl] *adj* oriental
orientate [ˈɔːrɪənteɪt] *vt* orientar
origin [ˈɔrɪdʒɪn] *n* origen *m*; (*point of departure*) procedencia
original [əˈrɪdʒɪnl] *adj* original; (*first*) primero; (*earlier*) primitivo ■ *n* original *m*
originality [ərɪdʒɪˈnælɪtɪ] *n* originalidad *f*
originally [əˈrɪdʒɪnəlɪ] *adv* (*at first*) al principio; (*with originality*) con originalidad
originate [əˈrɪdʒɪneɪt] *vi*: **to ~ from, to ~ in** surgir de, tener su origen en
originator [əˈrɪdʒɪneɪtəʳ] *n* inventor(a) *m(f)*, autor(a) *m(f)*
Orkneys [ˈɔːknɪz] *npl*: **the ~** (*also*: **the Orkney Islands**) las Orcadas
ornament [ˈɔːnəmənt] *n* adorno
ornamental [ɔːnəˈmɛntl] *adj* decorativo, de adorno
ornamentation [ɔːnəmɛnˈteɪʃən] *n* ornamentación *f*
ornate [ɔːˈneɪt] *adj* recargado
ornithologist [ɔːnɪˈθɔlədʒɪst] *n* ornitólogo(-a)
ornithology [ɔːnɪˈθɔlədʒɪ] *n* ornitología
orphan [ˈɔːfn] *n* huérfano(-a) ■ *vt*: **to be orphaned** quedar huérfano(-a)
orphanage [ˈɔːfənɪdʒ] *n* orfanato
orthodox [ˈɔːθədɔks] *adj* ortodoxo
orthodoxy [ˈɔːθədɔksɪ] *n* ortodoxia
orthopaedic, orthopedic (US) [ɔːθəˈpiːdɪk] *adj* ortopédico
orthopaedics, orthopedics (US) [ɔːθəˈpiːdɪks] *n* ortopedia
OS *abbr* (*Brit*: = *Ordnance Survey*) *servicio oficial de topografía y cartografía*; (: *Dress*) = **outsize**
O.S. *abbr* = **out of stock**
Oscar [ˈɔskəʳ] *n* óscar *m*
oscillate [ˈɔsɪleɪt] *vi* oscilar; (*person*) vacilar
oscillation [ɔsɪˈleɪʃən] *n* oscilación *f*; (*of prices*) fluctuación *f*
OSHA *n abbr* (*US*: = *Occupational Safety and Health Administration*) *oficina de la higiene y la seguridad en el trabajo*
Oslo [ˈɔzləu] *n* Oslo
ostensible [ɔsˈtɛnsɪbl] *adj* aparente
ostensibly [ɔsˈtɛnsɪblɪ] *adv* aparentemente
ostentatious [ɔstɛnˈteɪʃəs] *adj* pretencioso, aparatoso; (*person*) ostentativo
osteopath [ˈɔstɪəpæθ] *n* osteópata *m/f*
ostracize [ˈɔstrəsaɪz] *vt* hacer el vacío a
ostrich [ˈɔstrɪtʃ] *n* avestruz *m*
OT *n abbr* (= *Old Testament*) A.T. *m*
OTB *n abbr* (*US*: = *off-track betting*) *apuestas hechas fuera del hipódromo*
OTE *abbr* (= *on-target earnings*) *beneficios según objetivos*
other [ˈʌðəʳ] *adj* otro ■ *pron*: **the ~** (*one*) el/la otro(-a); **others** (*other people*) otros; **~ than** (*apart from*) aparte de; **the ~ day** el otro día; **some ~ people have still to arrive** quedan por llegar otros; **some actor or ~** un actor cualquiera; **somebody or ~** alguien, alguno; **it was no ~ than the bishop** no era otro que el obispo
otherwise [ˈʌðəwaɪz] *adv, conj* de otra manera; (*if not*) si no; **an ~ good piece of work** un trabajo que, quitando eso, es bueno
OTT *abbr* (*col*) = **over the top**; *see* **top**
otter [ˈɔtəʳ] *n* nutria
OU *n abbr* (*Brit*) = **Open University**
ouch [autʃ] *excl* ¡ay!
ought (*pt* **ought**) [ɔːt] *aux vb*: **I ~ to do it** debería hacerlo; **this ~ to have been corrected** esto debiera de haberse corregido; **he ~ to win** (*probability*) debiera ganar; **you ~ to go and see it** vale la pena ir a verlo
ounce [auns] *n* onza (*28.35g: 16 in a pound*)
our [ˈauəʳ] *adj* nuestro; *see also* **my**
ours [ˈauəz] *pron* (el) nuestro/(la) nuestra *etc*; *see also* **mine**
ourselves [auəˈsɛlvz] *pron pl* (*reflexive, after prep*) nosotros; (*emphatic*) nosotros mismos; **we did it (all) by ~** lo hicimos nosotros solos; *see also* **oneself**
oust [aust] *vt* desalojar
out [aut] *adv* fuera, afuera; (*not at home*) fuera (de casa); (*light, fire*) apagado; (*on strike*) en huelga ■ *vt*: **to ~ sb** revelar públicamente la homosexualidad de algn; **~ there** allí (fuera); **he's ~** (*absent*) no está, ha salido; **to be ~ in one's calculations** equivocarse (en sus cálculos); **to run ~** salir corriendo; **~ loud** en alta voz; **~ of** *prep* (*outside*) fuera de; (*because of*: *anger etc*) por; **to look ~ of the window** mirar por la ventana; **to drink ~ of a cup** beber de una taza; **made ~ of wood** de madera; **~ of petrol** sin gasolina; **"~ of order"** "no funciona"; **it's ~ of stock** (*Comm*) está agotado; **to be ~ and about again** estar repuesto y levantado; **the journey ~** el viaje de ida; **the boat was 10**

km ~ el barco estaba a 10 kilómetros de la costa; **before the week was** ~ antes del fin de la semana; **he's ~ for all he can get** busca sus propios fines, anda detrás de lo suyo
out-and-out [ˈautəndaut] *adj (liar, thief etc)* redomado, empedernido
outback [ˈautbæk] *n* interior *m*
outbid [autˈbɪd] *vt* pujar más alto que, sobrepujar
outboard [ˈautbɔːd] *adj*: **~ motor** (motor *m*) fuera borda *m*
outbound [ˈautbaund] *adj*: **~ from/for** con salida de/hacia
outbreak [ˈautbreɪk] *n (of war)* comienzo; *(of disease)* epidemia; *(of violence etc)* ola
outbuilding [ˈautbɪldɪŋ] *n* dependencia; *(shed)* cobertizo
outburst [ˈautbəːst] *n* explosión *f*, arranque *m*
outcast [ˈautkɑːst] *n* paria *m/f*
outclass [autˈklɑːs] *vt* aventajar, superar
outcome [ˈautkʌm] *n* resultado
outcrop [ˈautkrɔp] *n (of rock)* afloramiento
outcry [ˈautkraɪ] *n* protestas *fpl*
outdated [autˈdeɪtɪd] *adj* anticuado
outdistance [autˈdɪstəns] *vt* dejar atrás
outdo [autˈduː] *vt (irreg: like* **do**) superar
outdoor [autˈdɔːʳ] *adj* al aire libre
outdoors [autˈdɔːz] *adv* al aire libre
outer [ˈautəʳ] *adj* exterior, externo
outer space *n* espacio exterior
outfit [ˈautfɪt] *n* equipo; *(clothes)* traje *m*; *(col: organization)* grupo, organización *f*
outfitter's [ˈautfɪtəz] *n (Brit)* sastrería
outgoing [ˈautgəuɪŋ] *adj (president, tenant)* saliente; *(means of transport)* que sale; *(character)* extrovertido
outgoings [ˈautgəuɪŋz] *npl (Brit)* gastos *mpl*
outgrow [autˈgrəu] *vt (irreg: like* **grow**) **he has outgrown his clothes** su ropa le queda pequeña ya
outhouse [ˈauthaus] *n* dependencia
outing [ˈautɪŋ] *n* excursión *f*, paseo
outlandish [autˈlændɪʃ] *adj* estrafalario
outlast [autˈlɑːst] *vt* durar más tiempo que, sobrevivir a
outlaw [ˈautlɔː] *n* proscrito(-a) ■ *vt (person)* declarar fuera de la ley; *(practice)* declarar ilegal
outlay [ˈautleɪ] *n* inversión *f*
outlet [ˈautlɛt] *n* salida; *(of pipe)* desagüe *m*; *(US Elec)* toma de corriente; *(for emotion)* desahogo; *(also:* **retail outlet**) punto de venta
outline [ˈautlaɪn] *n (shape)* contorno, perfil *m*; **in ~** *(fig)* a grandes rasgos
outlive [autˈlɪv] *vt* sobrevivir a
outlook [ˈautluk] *n* perspectiva; *(opinion)* punto de vista
outlying [ˈautlaɪɪŋ] *adj* remoto, aislado
outmanoeuvre, *(US)* **outmaneuver** [autməˈnuːvəʳ] *vt (Mil: fig)* superar en la estrategia
outmoded [autˈməudɪd] *adj* anticuado, pasado de moda
outnumber [autˈnʌmbəʳ] *vt* exceder *or* superar en número
out of bounds [autəvˈbaundz] *adj*: **it's ~** está prohibido el paso
out-of-court [autəvˈkɔːt] *adj, adv* sin ir a juicio
out-of-date [autəvˈdeɪt] *adj (passport)* caducado, vencido; *(theory, idea)* anticuado; *(clothes, customs)* pasado de moda
out-of-doors [autəvˈdɔːz] *adv* al aire libre
out-of-the-way [autəvðəˈweɪ] *adj (remote)* apartado; *(unusual)* poco común *or* corriente
out-of-touch [autəvˈtʌtʃ] *adj*: **to be ~** estar desconectado
outpatient [ˈautpeɪʃənt] *n* paciente *m/f* externo(-a)
outpost [ˈautpəust] *n* puesto avanzado
outpouring [ˈautpɔːrɪŋ] *n (fig)* efusión *f*
output [ˈautput] *n* (volumen *m* de) producción *f*, rendimiento; *(Comput)* salida ■ *vt (Comput: to power)* imprimir
outrage [ˈautreɪdʒ] *n (scandal)* escándalo; *(atrocity)* atrocidad *f* ■ *vt* ultrajar
outrageous [autˈreɪdʒəs] *adj (clothes)* extravagante; *(behaviour)* escandaloso
outright [autˈraɪt] *adv (win)* de manera absoluta; *(be killed)* en el acto; *(ask)* abiertamente; *(completely)* completamente ■ *adj* [ˈautraɪt] completo; *(winner)* absoluto; *(refusal)* rotundo
outrun [autˈrʌn] *vt (irreg: like* **run**) correr más que, dejar atrás
outset [ˈautsɛt] *n* principio
outshine [autˈʃaɪn] *vt (irreg: like* **shine**) *(fig)* eclipsar, brillar más que
outside [autˈsaɪd] *n* exterior *m* ■ *adj* exterior, externo ■ *adv* fuera, afuera *(LAm)* ■ *prep* fuera de; *(beyond)* más allá de; **at the ~** *(fig)* a lo sumo; **an ~ chance** una posibilidad remota; **~ left/right** *(esp Football)* extremo izquierdo/derecho
outside broadcast *n (Radio, TV)* emisión *f* exterior
outside contractor *n* contratista *m/f* independiente
outside lane *n (Aut)* carril *m* de adelantamiento
outside line *n (Tel)* línea (exterior)
outsider [autˈsaɪdəʳ] *n (stranger)* forastero(-a)
outsize [ˈautsaɪz] *adj (clothes)* de talla grande
outskirts [ˈautskəːts] *npl* alrededores *mpl*, afueras *fpl*

outsmart [aut'smɑːt] *vt* ser más listo que
outspoken [aut'spəukən] *adj* muy franco
outspread [aut'sprɛd] *adj* extendido; (*wings*) desplegado
outstanding [aut'stændɪŋ] *adj* excepcional, destacado; (*unfinished*) pendiente
outstay [aut'steɪ] *vt*: **to ~ one's welcome** quedarse más de la cuenta
outstretched [aut'strɛtʃt] *adj* (*arm*) extendido
outstrip [aut'strɪp] *vt* (*competitors, demand: also fig*) dejar atrás, aventajar
out-tray ['auttreɪ] *n* bandeja de salida
outvote [aut'vəut] *vt*: **it was outvoted (by ...)** fue rechazado en el voto (por ...)
outward ['autwəd] *adj* (*sign, appearances*) externo; (*journey*) de ida
outwardly ['autwədlɪ] *adv* por fuera
outweigh [aut'weɪ] *vt* pesar más que
outwit [aut'wɪt] *vt* ser más listo que
outworn [aut'wɔːn] *adj* (*expression*) cansado
oval ['əuvl] *adj* ovalado ■ *n* óvalo
ovarian [əu'vɛərɪən] *adj* ovárico; (*cancer*) de ovario
ovary ['əuvərɪ] *n* ovario
ovation [əu'veɪʃən] *n* ovación *f*
oven ['ʌvn] *n* horno
ovenproof ['ʌvnpruːf] *adj* refractario, resistente al horno
oven-ready ['ʌvnrɛdɪ] *adj* listo para el horno
ovenware ['ʌvnwɛə^r] *n* artículos *mpl* para el horno
over ['əuvə^r] *adv* encima, por encima ■ *adj* (*finished*) terminado; (*surplus*) de sobra; (*excessively*) demasiado ■ *prep* (por) encima de; (*above*) sobre; (*on the other side of*) al otro lado de; (*more than*) más de; (*during*) durante; (*about, concerning*): **they fell out ~ money** riñeron por una cuestión de dinero; **~ here** (por) aquí; **~ there** (por) allí *or* allá; **all ~** (*everywhere*) por todas partes; **~ and ~ (again)** una y otra vez; **~ and above** además de; **to ask sb ~** invitar a algn a casa; **to bend ~** inclinarse; **now ~ to our Paris correspondent** damos la palabra a nuestro corresponsal de París; **the world ~** en todo el mundo, en el mundo entero; **she's not ~ intelligent** no es muy lista que digamos
over... [əuvə^r] *pref* sobre..., super...
overact [əuvər'ækt] *vi* (*Theat*) exagerar el papel
overall ['əuvərɔːl] *adj* (*length*) total; (*study*) de conjunto ■ *adv* [əuvər'ɔːl] en conjunto ■ *n* (*Brit*) guardapolvo; **overalls** *npl* mono *sg*, overol *msg* (*LAm*)
overall majority *n* mayoría absoluta
overanxious [əuvər'æŋkʃəs] *adj* demasiado preocupado *or* ansioso
overawe [əuvər'ɔː] *vt* intimidar
overbalance [əuvə'bæləns] *vi* perder el equilibrio
overbearing [əuvə'bɛərɪŋ] *adj* autoritario, imperioso
overboard ['əuvəbɔːd] *adv* (*Naut*) por la borda; **to go ~ for sth** (*fig*) enloquecer por algo
overbook [əuvə'buk] *vt* sobrereservar, reservar con exceso
overcapitalize [əuvə'kæpɪtəlaɪz] *vi* sobrecapitalizar
overcast ['əuvəkɑːst] *adj* encapotado
overcharge [əuvə'tʃɑːdʒ] *vt*: **to ~ sb** cobrar un precio excesivo a algn
overcoat ['əuvəkəut] *n* abrigo
overcome [əuvə'kʌm] *vt* (*irreg: like* **come**) (*gen*) vencer; (*difficulty*) superar; **she was quite ~ by the occasion** la ocasión le conmovió mucho
overconfident [əuvə'kɔnfɪdənt] *adj* demasiado confiado
overcrowded [əuvə'kraudɪd] *adj* atestado de gente; (*city, country*) superpoblado
overcrowding [əuvə'kraudɪŋ] *n* (*in town, country*) superpoblación *f*; (*in bus etc*) hacinamiento, apiñamiento
overdo [əuvə'duː] *vt* (*irreg: like* **do**) exagerar; (*overcook*) cocer demasiado; **to ~ it, ~ things** (*work too hard*) trabajar demasiado
overdose ['əuvədəus] *n* sobredosis *f inv*
overdraft ['əuvədrɑːft] *n* saldo deudor
overdrawn [əuvə'drɔːn] *adj* (*account*) en descubierto
overdrive ['əuvədraɪv] *n* (*Aut*) sobremarcha, superdirecta
overdue [əuvə'djuː] *adj* retrasado; (*recognition*) tardío; (*bill*) vencido y no pagado; **that change was long ~** ese cambio tenía que haberse hecho hace tiempo
overemphasis [əuvər'ɛmfəsɪs] *n*: **to put an ~ on** poner énfasis excesivo en
overenthusiastic ['əuvərənθuːzɪ'æstɪk] *adj* demasiado entusiasta
overestimate [əuvər'ɛstɪmeɪt] *vt* sobreestimar
overexcited [əuvərɪk'saɪtɪd] *adj* sobreexcitado
overexertion [əuvərɪg'zəːʃən] *n* agotamiento, fatiga
overexpose [əuvərɪk'spəuz] *vt* (*Phot*) sobreexponer
overflow [əuvə'fləu] *vi* desbordarse ■ *n* ['əuvəfləu] (*excess*) exceso; (*of river*) desbordamiento; (*also:* **overflow pipe**) (cañería de) desagüe *m*
overfly [əuvə'flaɪ] *vt* (*irreg: like* **fly**) sobrevolar

overgenerous [əuvə'dʒɛnərəs] *adj* demasiado generoso
overgrown [əuvə'grəun] *adj* (*garden*) cubierto de hierba; **he's just an ~ schoolboy** es un niño en grande
overhang [əuvə'hæŋ] *vt* (*irreg: like* **hang**) sobresalir por encima de ■ *vi* sobresalir
overhaul *vt* [əuvə'hɔ:l] revisar, repasar ■ *n* ['əuvəhɔ:l] revisión *f*
overhead *adv* [əuvə'hɛd] por arriba *or* encima ■ *adj* ['əuvəhɛd] (*cable*) aéreo; (*railway*) elevado, aéreo ■ *n* ['əuvəhɛd] (*US*) = **overheads**
overheads ['əuvəhɛdz] *npl* (*Brit*) gastos *mpl* generales
overhear [əuvə'hɪə^r] *vt* (*irreg: like* **hear**) oír por casualidad
overheat [əuvə'hi:t] *vi* (*engine*) recalentarse
overjoyed [əuvə'dʒɔɪd] *adj* encantado, lleno de alegría
overkill ['əuvəkɪl] *n* (*Mil*) capacidad *f* excesiva de destrucción; (*fig*) exceso
overland ['əuvəlænd] *adj, adv* por tierra
overlap *vi* [əuvə'læp] superponerse ■ *n* ['əuvəlæp] superposición *f*
overleaf [əuvə'li:f] *adv* al dorso
overload [əuvə'ləud] *vt* sobrecargar
overlook [əuvə'luk] *vt* (*have view of*) dar a, tener vistas a; (*miss*) pasar por alto; (*forgive*) hacer la vista gorda a
overlord ['əuvəlɔ:d] *n* señor *m*
overmanning [əuvə'mænɪŋ] *n* exceso de mano de obra; (*in organization*) exceso de personal
overnight [əuvə'naɪt] *adv* durante la noche; (*fig*) de la noche a la mañana ■ *adj* de noche; **to stay ~** pasar la noche
overnight bag *n* fin *m* de semana, neceser *m* de viaje
overnight stay *n* estancia de una noche
overpass ['əuvəpɑ:s] *n* (*US*) paso elevado *or* a desnivel
overpay [əuvə'peɪ] *vt*: **to ~ sb by £50** pagar 50 libras de más a algn
overplay [əuvə'pleɪ] *vt* exagerar; **to ~ one's hand** desmedirse
overpower [əuvə'pauə^r] *vt* dominar; (*fig*) embargar
overpowering [əuvə'pauərɪŋ] *adj* (*heat*) agobiante; (*smell*) penetrante
overproduction [əuvəprə'dʌkʃən] *n* superproducción *f*
overrate [əuvə'reɪt] *vt* sobrevalorar
overreach [əuvə'ri:tʃ] *vt*: **to ~ o.s.** ir demasiado lejos, pasarse
override [əuvə'raɪd] *vt* (*irreg: like* **ride**) (*order, objection*) no hacer caso de
overriding [əuvə'raɪdɪŋ] *adj* predominante
overrule [əuvə'ru:l] *vt* (*decision*) anular; (*claim*) denegar
overrun [əuvə'rʌn] *vt* (*irreg: like* **run**) (*Mil: country*) invadir; (*time limit*) rebasar, exceder ■ *vi* rebasar el límite previsto; **the town is ~ with tourists** el pueblo está inundado de turistas
overseas [əuvə'si:z] *adv* en ultramar; (*abroad*) en el extranjero ■ *adj* (*trade*) exterior; (*visitor*) extranjero
oversee [əuvə'si:] *vt* supervisar
overseer ['əuvəsɪə^r] *n* (*in factory*) supervisor(a) *m(f)*; (*foreman*) capataz *m*
overshadow [əuvə'ʃædəu] *vt* (*fig*) eclipsar
overshoot [əuvə'ʃu:t] *vt* (*irreg: like* **shoot**) excederse
oversight ['əuvəsaɪt] *n* descuido; **due to an ~** a causa de un descuido *or* una equivocación
oversimplify [əuvə'sɪmplɪfaɪ] *vt* simplificar demasiado
oversleep [əuvə'sli:p] *vi* (*irreg: like* **sleep**) dormir más de la cuenta, no despertarse a tiempo
overspend [əuvə'spɛnd] *vi* gastar más de la cuenta; **we have overspent by five dollars** hemos excedido el presupuesto en cinco dólares
overspill ['əuvəspɪl] *n* exceso de población
overstaffed [əuvə'stɑ:ft] *adj*: **to be ~** tener exceso de plantilla
overstate [əuvə'steɪt] *vt* exagerar
overstatement ['əuvəsteɪtmənt] *n* exageración *f*
overstay [əuvə'steɪ] *vt*: **to ~ one's time** *or* **welcome** quedarse más de lo conveniente
overstep [əuvə'stɛp] *vt*: **to ~ the mark** *or* **the limits** pasarse de la raya
overstock [əuvə'stɔk] *vt* abarrotar
overstretched [əuvə'strɛtʃt] *adj* utilizado por encima de su capacidad
overstrike *n* ['əuvəstraɪk] (*on printer*) superposición *f* ■ *vt* (*irreg: like* **strike**) [əuvə'straɪk] superponer
oversubscribed [əuvəsəb'skraɪbd] *adj* suscrito en exceso
overt [əu'və:t] *adj* abierto
overtake [əuvə'teɪk] *vt* (*irreg: like* **take**) sobrepasar; (*Brit Aut*) adelantar
overtax [əuvə'tæks] *vt* (*Econ*) exigir contribuciones *fpl* excesivas *or* impuestos *mpl* excesivos a; (*fig: strength*) poner a prueba; (*patience*) agotar, abusar de; **to ~ o.s.** fatigarse demasiado
overthrow [əuvə'θrəu] *vt* (*irreg: like* **throw**) (*government*) derrocar
overtime ['əuvətaɪm] *n* horas *fpl*

extraordinarias; **to do** *or* **work ~** hacer *or* trabajar horas extraordinarias *or* extras
overtime ban *n* prohibición *f* de (hacer) horas extraordinarias
overtone ['əuvətəun] *n* (*fig*) tono
overture ['əuvətʃuəʳ] *n* (*Mus*) obertura; (*fig*) propuesta
overturn [əuvə'tə:n] *vt, vi* volcar
overview ['əuvəvju:] *n* visión *f* de conjunto
overweight [əuvə'weɪt] *adj* demasiado gordo *or* pesado
overwhelm [əuvə'wɛlm] *vt* aplastar
overwhelming [əuvə'wɛlmɪŋ] *adj* (*victory, defeat*) arrollador(a); (*desire*) irresistible; **one's ~ impression is of heat** lo que más impresiona es el calor
overwhelmingly [əuvə'wɛlmɪŋlɪ] *adv* abrumadoramente
overwork [əuvə'wə:k] *n* trabajo excesivo ■ *vt* hacer trabajar demasiado ■ *vi* trabajar demasiado
overwrite [əuvə'raɪt] *vt* (*irreg: like* **write**) (*Comput*) sobreescribir
overwrought [əuvə'rɔ:t] *adj* sobreexcitado
ovulation [ɔvju'leɪʃən] *n* ovulación *f*
owe [əu] *vt* deber; **to ~ sb sth, ~ sth to sb** deber algo a algn
owing to ['əuɪŋtu:] *prep* debido a, por causa de
owl [aul] *n* (*also:* **long-eared owl**) búho; (*also:* **barn owl**) lechuza
own [əun] *vt* tener, poseer ■ *vi:* **to ~ to sth/ to having done sth** confesar *or* reconocer algo/haber hecho algo ■ *adj* propio; **a room of my ~** mi propia habitación; **to get one's ~ back** tomarse la revancha; **on one's ~** solo, a solas; **can I have it for my (very) ~?** ¿puedo quedarme con él?; **to come into one's ~** llegar a realizarse
▸ **own up** *vi* confesar
own brand *n* (*Comm*) marca propia
owner ['əunəʳ] *n* dueño(-a)
owner-occupier ['əunər'ɔkjupaɪəʳ] *n* ocupante propietario(-a) *m(f)*
ownership ['əunəʃɪp] *n* posesión *f*; **it's under new ~** está bajo nueva dirección
own goal *n* (*Sport*) autogol *m*; **to score an ~** marcar un gol en propia puerta, marcar un autogol
ox (*pl* **oxen**) [ɔks, 'ɔksn] *n* buey *m*
Oxbridge ['ɔksbrɪdʒ] *n universidades de Oxford y Cambridge; ver nota*

OXBRIDGE

El término *Oxbridge* es una fusión de Ox(ford) y (Cam)bridge, las dos universidades británicas más antiguas y con mayor prestigio académico y social. Muchos miembros destacados de la clase dirigente del país son antiguos alumnos de una de las dos. El mismo término suele aplicarse a todo lo que ambas representan en cuestión de prestigio y privilegios sociales.

Oxfam ['ɔksfæm] *n abbr* (*Brit:* = *Oxford Committee for Famine Relief*) OXFAM
oxide ['ɔksaɪd] *n* óxido
Oxon. ['ɔksn] *abbr* (*Brit*) = **Oxoniensis; of Oxford**
oxtail ['ɔksteɪl] *n:* **~ soup** sopa de rabo de buey
oxyacetylene ['ɔksɪə'sɛtɪli:n] *adj* oxiacetilénico; **~ burner, ~ torch** soplete *m* oxiacetilénico
oxygen ['ɔksɪdʒən] *n* oxígeno
oxygen mask *n* máscara de oxígeno
oxygen tent *n* tienda de oxígeno
oyster ['ɔɪstəʳ] *n* ostra
oz. *abbr* = **ounce; ounces**
ozone ['əuzəun] *n* ozono
ozone layer *n* capa de ozono

Pp

P, p [piː] *n* (*letter*) P, p *f*; **P for Peter** P de París
P *abbr* = **president; prince**
p *abbr* (= *page*) pág.; (*Brit*) = **penny; pence**
PA *n abbr see* **personal assistant; public address system** ■ *abbr* (*US*) = **Pennsylvania**
pa [pɑː] *n* (*col*) papá *m*
p.a. *abbr* = **per annum**
PAC *n abbr* (*US*) = **political action committee**
pace [peɪs] *n* paso; (*rhythm*) ritmo ■ *vi*: **to ~ up and down** pasearse de un lado a otro; **to keep ~ with** llevar el mismo paso que; (*events*) mantenerse a la altura de *or* al corriente de; **to set the ~** (*running*) marcar el paso; (*fig*) marcar la pauta; **to put sb through his paces** (*fig*) poner a algn a prueba
pacemaker ['peɪsmeɪkəʳ] *n* (*Med*) marcapasos *m inv*
pacific [pə'sɪfɪk] *adj* pacífico ■ *n*: **the P~ (Ocean)** el (Océano) Pacífico
pacification [pæsɪfɪ'keɪʃən] *n* pacificación *f*
pacifier ['pæsɪfaɪəʳ] *n* (*US: dummy*) chupete *m*
pacifism ['pæsɪfɪzəm] *n* pacifismo
pacifist ['pæsɪfɪst] *n* pacifista *m/f*
pacify ['pæsɪfaɪ] *vt* (*soothe*) apaciguar; (*country*) pacificar
pack [pæk] *n* (*packet*) paquete *m*; (*Comm*) embalaje *m*; (*of hounds*) jauría; (*of wolves*) manada; (*of thieves etc*) banda; (*of cards*) baraja; (*bundle*) fardo; (*US: of cigarettes*) paquete *m*, cajetilla ■ *vt* (*wrap*) empaquetar; (*fill*) llenar; (*in suitcase etc*) meter, poner; (*cram*) llenar, atestar; (*fig: meeting etc*) llenar de partidarios; (*Comput*) comprimir; **to ~ (one's bags)** hacer las maletas; **to ~ sb off** despachar a algn; **the place was packed** el local estaba (lleno) hasta los topes; **to send sb packing** (*col*) echar a algn con cajas destempladas
▸ **pack in** *vi* (*break down: watch, car*) estropearse ■ *vt* (*col*) dejar; **~ it in!** ¡para!, ¡basta ya!
▸ **pack up** *vi* (*col: machine*) estropearse; (*person*) irse ■ *vt* (*belongings, clothes*) recoger; (*goods, presents*) empaquetar, envolver
package ['pækɪdʒ] *n* paquete *m*; (*bulky*) bulto; (*Comput*) paquete *m* (*de software*); (*also:* **package deal**) acuerdo global ■ *vt* (*Comm: goods*) envasar, embalar
package holiday *n* viaje *m* organizado (con todo incluido)
package tour *n* viaje *m* organizado
packaging ['pækɪdʒɪŋ] *n* envase *m*
packed lunch [pækt-] *n* almuerzo frío
packer ['pækəʳ] *n* (*person*) empacador(a) *m(f)*
packet ['pækɪt] *n* paquete *m*
packet switching [-'swɪtʃɪŋ] *n* (*Comput*) conmutación *f* por paquetes
packhorse ['pækhɔːs] *n* caballo de carga
pack ice *n* banco de hielo
packing ['pækɪŋ] *n* embalaje *m*
packing case *n* cajón *m* de embalaje
pact [pækt] *n* pacto
pad [pæd] *n* (*of paper*) bloc *m*; (*cushion*) cojinete *m*; (*launching pad*) plataforma (de lanzamiento); (*col: flat*) casa ■ *vt* rellenar
padded cell ['pædɪd-] *n* celda acolchada
padding ['pædɪŋ] *n* relleno; (*fig*) paja
paddle ['pædl] *n* (*oar*) canalete *m*, pala; (*US: for table tennis*) pala ■ *vt* remar ■ *vi* (*with feet*) chapotear
paddle steamer *n* vapor *m* de ruedas
paddling pool ['pædlɪŋ-] *n* (*Brit*) piscina para niños
paddock ['pædək] *n* (*field*) potrero
paddy field ['pædɪ-] *n* arrozal *m*
padlock ['pædlɔk] *n* candado ■ *vt* cerrar con candado
padre ['pɑːdrɪ] *n* capellán *m*
paediatrician, (*US*) **pediatrician** [piːdɪə'trɪʃən] *n* pediatra *m/f*
paediatrics, (*US*) **pediatrics** [piːdɪ'ætrɪks] *n* pediatría
paedophile, (*US*) **pedophile** ['piːdəufaɪl] *adj* de pedófilos ■ *n* pedófilo(-a)
pagan ['peɪgən] *adj, n* pagano(-a) *m(f)*
page [peɪdʒ] *n* página; (*also:* **page boy**) paje *m* ■ *vt* (*in hotel etc*) llamar por altavoz a

pageant ['pædʒənt] *n* *(procession)* desfile *m*; *(show)* espectáculo
pageantry ['pædʒəntrɪ] *n* pompa
page break *n* límite *m* de la página
pager ['peɪdʒəʳ] *n* busca *m*
paginate ['pædʒɪneɪt] *vt* paginar
pagination [pædʒɪ'neɪʃən] *n* paginación *f*
pagoda [pə'gəudə] *n* pagoda
paid [peɪd] *pt, pp of* **pay** ■ *adj* *(work)* remunerado; *(official)* asalariado; **to put ~ to** *(Brit)* acabar con
paid-up ['peɪdʌp], **paid-in** *(US)* ['peɪdɪn] *adj* *(member)* con sus cuotas pagadas *or* al día; *(share)* liberado; **~ capital** capital *m* desembolsado
pail [peɪl] *n* cubo, balde *m*
pain [peɪn] *n* dolor *m*; **to be in ~** sufrir; **on ~ of death** so *or* bajo pena de muerte; *see also* **pains**
pained [peɪnd] *adj* *(expression)* afligido
painful ['peɪnful] *adj* doloroso; *(difficult)* penoso; *(disagreeable)* desagradable
painfully ['peɪnfəlɪ] *adv* *(fig: very)* terriblemente
painkiller ['peɪnkɪləʳ] *n* analgésico
painless ['peɪnlɪs] *adj* sin dolor; *(method)* fácil
pains [peɪnz] *npl* *(efforts)* esfuerzos *mpl*; **to take ~ to do sth** tomarse trabajo en hacer algo
painstaking ['peɪnzteɪkɪŋ] *adj* *(person)* concienzudo, esmerado
paint [peɪnt] *n* pintura ■ *vt* pintar; **a tin of ~** un bote de pintura; **to ~ the door blue** pintar la puerta de azul
paintbox ['peɪntbɔks] *n* caja de pinturas
paintbrush ['peɪntbrʌʃ] *n* *(artist's)* pincel *m*; *(decorator's)* brocha
painter ['peɪntəʳ] *n* pintor(a) *m(f)*
painting ['peɪntɪŋ] *n* pintura
paintwork ['peɪntwə:k] *n* pintura
pair [pεəʳ] *n* *(of shoes, gloves etc)* par *m*; *(of people)* pareja; **a ~ of scissors** unas tijeras; **a ~ of trousers** unos pantalones, un pantalón
▸ **pair off** *vi*: **to ~ off (with sb)** hacer pareja (con algn)
pajamas [pɪ'dʒɑ:məz] *npl* *(US)* pijama *msg*, piyama *msg* *(LAm)*
Pakistan [pɑ:kɪ'stɑ:n] *n* Paquistán *m*
Pakistani [pɑ:kɪ'stɑ:nɪ] *adj, n* paquistaní *m/f*
PAL [pæl] *n abbr* *(TV)* = **phase alternation line**
pal [pæl] *n* *(col)* amiguete(-a) *m(f)*, colega *m/f*
palace ['pæləs] *n* palacio
palatable ['pælɪtəbl] *adj* sabroso; *(acceptable)* aceptable
palate ['pælɪt] *n* paladar *m*
palatial [pə'leɪʃəl] *adj* *(surroundings, residence)* suntuoso, espléndido
palaver [pə'lɑ:vəʳ] *n* *(fuss)* lío
pale [peɪl] *adj* *(gen)* pálido; *(colour)* claro ■ *n*: **to be beyond the ~** pasarse de la raya ■ *vi* palidecer; **to grow** *or* **turn ~** palidecer; **to ~ into insignificance (beside)** no poderse comparar (con)
paleness ['peɪlnɪs] *n* palidez *f*
Palestine ['pælɪstaɪn] *n* Palestina
Palestinian [pælɪs'tɪnɪən] *adj, n* palestino(-a) *m(f)*
palette ['pælɪt] *n* paleta
paling ['peɪlɪŋ] *n* *(stake)* estaca; *(fence)* valla
palisade [pælɪ'seɪd] *n* palizada
pall [pɔ:l] *n* *(of smoke)* cortina ■ *vi* cansar
pallbearer ['pɔ:lbεərəʳ] *n* portador *m* del féretro
pallet ['pælɪt] *n* *(for goods)* pallet *m*
palletization [pælɪtaɪ'zeɪʃən] *n* paletización *f*
palliative ['pælɪətɪv] *n* paliativo
pallid ['pælɪd] *adj* pálido
pallor ['pæləʳ] *n* palidez *f*
pally ['pælɪ] *adj* *(col)*: **to be very ~ with sb** ser muy amiguete de algn
palm [pɑ:m] *n* *(Anat)* palma; *(also:* **palm tree***)* palmera, palma ■ *vt*: **to ~ sth off on sb** *(Brit col)* endosarle algo a algn
palmist ['pɑ:mɪst] *n* quiromántico(-a), palmista *m/f*
Palm Sunday *n* Domingo de Ramos
palpable ['pælpəbl] *adj* palpable
palpably ['pælpəblɪ] *adv* obviamente
palpitation [pælpɪ'teɪʃən] *n* palpitación *f*; **to have palpitations** tener palpitaciones
paltry ['pɔ:ltrɪ] *adj* *(amount etc)* miserable; *(insignificant: person)* insignificante
pamper ['pæmpəʳ] *vt* mimar
pamphlet ['pæmflət] *n* folleto; *(political: handed out in street)* panfleto
pan [pæn] *n* *(also:* **saucepan***)* cacerola, cazuela, olla; *(also:* **frying pan***)* sartén *m*; *(of lavatory)* taza ■ *vi* *(Cine)* tomar panorámicas; **to ~ for gold** cribar oro
pan- [pæn] *pref* pan-
panacea [pænə'sɪə] *n* panacea
panache [pə'næʃ] *n* gracia, garbo
Panama ['pænəmɑ:] *n* Panamá *m*
Panama Canal *n* el Canal de Panamá
pancake ['pænkeɪk] *n* crepe *f*, panqueque *m* *(LAm)*
Pancake Day *n* martes *m* de carnaval
pancake roll *n* rollito de primavera
pancreas ['pæŋkrɪəs] *n* páncreas *m*
panda ['pændə] *n* panda *m*
panda car *n* *(Brit)* coche *m* de la policía
pandemonium [pændɪ'məunɪəm] *n* *(noise)*: **there was ~** se armó un tremendo jaleo; *(mess)* caos *m*
pander ['pændəʳ] *vi*: **to ~ to** complacer a

p & h *abbr* (*US*: = *postage and handling*) gastos de envío
P & L *abbr* = **profit and loss**
p & p *abbr* (*Brit*: = *postage and packing*) gastos de envío
pane [peɪn] *n* cristal *m*
panel ['pænl] *n* (*of wood*) panel *m*; (*of cloth*) paño; (*Radio, TV*) panel *m* de invitados
panel game *n* (*TV*) programa *m* concurso para equipos
panelling, (*US*) **paneling** ['pænəlɪŋ] *n* paneles *mpl*
panellist, panelist (*US*) ['pænəlɪst] *n* miembro del jurado
pang [pæŋ] *n*: **pangs of conscience** remordimientos *mpl*; **pangs of hunger** dolores *mpl* del hambre
panhandler ['pænhændləʳ] *n* (*US col*) mendigo(-a)
panic ['pænɪk] *n* pánico ■ *vi* dejarse llevar por el pánico
panic buying [-baɪɪŋ] *n compras masivas por miedo a futura escasez*
panicky ['pænɪkɪ] *adj* (*person*) asustadizo
panic-stricken ['pænɪkstrɪkən] *adj* preso del pánico
pannier ['pænɪəʳ] *n* (*on bicycle*) cartera; (*on mule etc*) alforja
panorama [pænə'rɑːmə] *n* panorama *m*
panoramic [pænə'ræmɪk] *adj* panorámico
pansy ['pænzɪ] *n* (*Bot*) pensamiento; (*col: pej*) maricón *m*
pant [pænt] *vi* jadear
panther ['pænθəʳ] *n* pantera
panties ['pæntɪz] *npl* bragas *fpl*
pantihose ['pæntɪhəuz] *n* (*US*) medias *fpl*, panties *mpl*
panto ['pæntəu] *n* (*Brit col*) = **pantomime**
pantomime ['pæntəmaɪm] *n* (*Brit*) representación *f* musical navideña; *ver nota*

PANTOMIME

En época navideña los teatros británicos ponen en escena representaciones llamadas *pantomimes*, versiones libres de cuentos tradicionales como Aladino o El gato con botas. En ella nunca faltan personajes como la dama ("dame"), papel que siempre interpreta un actor; el protagonista joven ("principal boy"), normalmente interpretado por una actriz, y el malvado ("villain"). Es un espectáculo familiar dirigido a los niños pero con grandes dosis de humor para adultos en el que se alienta la participación del público.

pantry ['pæntrɪ] *n* despensa
pants [pænts] *npl* (*Brit: underwear: woman's*) bragas *fpl*; (*: man's*) calzoncillos *mpl*; (*US: trousers*) pantalones *mpl*
pantsuit ['pæntsjuːt] *n* (*US*) traje *m* de chaqueta y pantalón
papal ['peɪpəl] *adj* papal
paparazzi [pæpə'rætsɪ] *npl* paparazzi *mpl*
paper ['peɪpəʳ] *n* papel *m*; (*also*: **newspaper**) periódico, diario; (*study, article*) artículo; (*exam*) examen *m* ■ *adj* de papel ■ *vt* empapelar; **(identity) papers** *npl* papeles *mpl*, documentos *mpl*; **a piece of ~** un papel; **to put sth down on ~** poner algo por escrito
paper advance *n* (*on printer*) avance *m* de papel
paperback ['peɪpəbæk] *n* libro de bolsillo
paper bag *n* bolsa de papel
paperboy ['peɪpəbɔɪ] *n* (*selling*) vendedor *m* de periódicos; (*delivering*) repartidor *m* de periódicos
paper clip *n* clip *m*
paper hankie *n* pañuelo de papel
paper money *n* papel *m* moneda
paper profit *n* beneficio no realizado
paper shop *n* (*Brit*) tienda de periódicos
paperweight ['peɪpəweɪt] *n* pisapapeles *m inv*
paperwork ['peɪpəwəːk] *n* trabajo administrativo; (*pej*) papeleo
papier-mâché ['pæpɪeɪ'mæʃeɪ] *n* cartón *m* piedra
paprika ['pæprɪkə] *n* pimentón *m*
Pap test ['pæp-] *n* (*Med*) frotis *m* (cervical)
papyrus [pə'paɪərəs] *n* papiro
par [pɑːʳ] *n* par *f*; (*Golf*) par *m* ■ *adj* a la par; **to be on a ~ with** estar a la par con; **at ~** a la par; **to be above/below ~** estar sobre/bajo par; **to feel under ~** sentirse en baja forma
parable ['pærəbl] *n* parábola
parachute ['pærəʃuːt] *n* paracaídas *m inv* ■ *vi* lanzarse en paracaídas
parachutist ['pærəʃuːtɪst] *n* paracaidista *m/f*
parade [pə'reɪd] *n* desfile *m* ■ *vt* (*gen*) recorrer, desfilar por; (*show off*) hacer alarde de ■ *vi* desfilar; (*Mil*) pasar revista; **a fashion ~** un desfile de modelos
parade ground *n* plaza de armas
paradise ['pærədaɪs] *n* paraíso
paradox ['pærədɔks] *n* paradoja
paradoxical [pærə'dɔksɪkl] *adj* paradójico
paradoxically [pærə'dɔksɪklɪ] *adv* paradójicamente
paraffin ['pærəfɪn] *n* (*Brit*): **~ (oil)** parafina
paraffin heater *n* estufa de parafina
paraffin lamp *n* quinqué *m*
paragon ['pærəgən] *n* modelo
paragraph ['pærəgrɑːf] *n* párrafo, acápite *m*

(*LAm*); **new ~** punto y aparte, punto acápite (*LAm*)
Paraguay ['pærəgwaɪ] *n* Paraguay *m*
Paraguayan [pærə'gwaɪən] *adj, n* paraguayo(-a) *m(f)*, paraguayano(-a) *m(f)*
parallel ['pærəlɛl] *adj*: **~ (with/to)** en paralelo (con/a); (*fig*) semejante (a) ■ *n* (*line*) paralela; (*fig*) paralelo; (*Geo*) paralelo
paralysis [pə'rælɪsɪs] *n* parálisis *f inv*
paralytic [pærə'lɪtɪk] *adj* paralítico
paralyze ['pærəlaɪz] *vt* paralizar
paramedic [pærə'mɛdɪk] *n* auxiliar *m/f* sanitario(-a)
parameter [pə'ræmɪtə^r] *n* parámetro
paramilitary [pærə'mɪlɪtərɪ] *adj* (*organization, operations*) paramilitar
paramount ['pærəmaunt] *adj*: **of ~ importance** de suma importancia
paranoia [pærə'nɔɪə] *n* paranoia
paranoid ['pærənɔɪd] *adj* (*person, feeling*) paranoico
paranormal [pærə'nɔːml] *adj* paranormal
parapet ['pærəpɪt] *n* parapeto
paraphernalia [pærəfə'neɪlɪə] *n* parafernalia
paraphrase ['pærəfreɪz] *vt* parafrasear
paraplegic [pærə'pliːdʒɪk] *n* parapléjico(-a)
parapsychology [pærəsaɪ'kɔlədʒɪ] *n* parasicología
parasite ['pærəsaɪt] *n* parásito(-a)
parasol ['pærəsɔl] *n* sombrilla, quitasol *m*
paratrooper ['pærətruːpə^r] *n* paracaidista *m/f*
parcel ['pɑːsl] *n* paquete *m* ■ *vt* (*also*: **parcel up**) empaquetar, embalar; **to be part and ~ of** ser parte integrante de
▸ **parcel out** *vt* parcelar, repartir
parcel bomb *n* paquete *m* bomba
parcel post *n* servicio de paquetes postales
parch [pɑːtʃ] *vt* secar, resecar
parched [pɑːtʃt] *adj* (*person*) muerto de sed
parchment ['pɑːtʃmənt] *n* pergamino
pardon ['pɑːdn] *n* perdón *m*; (*Law*) indulto ■ *vt* perdonar; indultar; **~ me!, I beg your ~!** ¡perdone usted!; **(I beg your) ~?**, (*US*) **~ me?** ¿cómo (dice)?
pare [pɛə^r] *vt* (*nails*) cortar; (*fruit etc*) pelar
parent ['pɛərənt] *n*: **parents** *npl* padres *mpl*
parentage ['pɛərəntɪdʒ] *n* familia, linaje *m*; **of unknown ~** de padres desconocidos
parental [pə'rɛntl] *adj* paternal/maternal
parent company *n* casa matriz
parenthesis (*pl* **parentheses**) [pə'rɛnθɪsɪs, -θɪsiːz] *n* paréntesis *m inv*; **in parentheses** entre paréntesis
parenthood ['pɛərənthud] *n* el ser padres
parent ship *n* buque *m* nodriza
Paris ['pærɪs] *n* París *m*
parish ['pærɪʃ] *n* parroquia
parish council *n* consejo parroquial
parishioner [pə'rɪʃənə^r] *n* feligrés(-esa) *m(f)*
Parisian [pə'rɪzɪən] *adj, n* parisino(-a) *m(f)*, parisiense *m/f*
parity ['pærɪtɪ] *n* paridad *f*, igualdad *f*
park [pɑːk] *n* parque *m*, jardín *m* público ■ *vt* aparcar, estacionar ■ *vi* aparcar, estacionar
parka ['pɑːkə] *n* parka
parking ['pɑːkɪŋ] *n* aparcamiento, estacionamiento; **"no ~"** "prohibido aparcar *or* estacionarse"
parking lights *npl* luces *fpl* de estacionamiento
parking lot *n* (*US*) parking *m*, aparcamiento, playa *f* de estacionamiento (*LAm*)
parking meter *n* parquímetro
parking offence, (*US*) **parking violation** *n* ofensa por aparcamiento indebido
parking place *n* sitio para aparcar, aparcamiento
parking ticket *n* multa de aparcamiento
Parkinson's *n* (*also*: **Parkinson's disease**) (enfermedad *f* de) Parkinson *m*
parkway ['pɑːkweɪ] *n* (*US*) alameda
parlance ['pɑːləns] *n* lenguaje *m*; **in common/modern ~** en lenguaje corriente/moderno
parliament ['pɑːləmənt] *n* parlamento; (*Spanish*) las Cortes *fpl*; *ver nota*

PARLIAMENT

El Parlamento británico (*Parliament*) tiene como sede el palacio de Westminster, también llamado "Houses of Parliament". Consta de dos cámaras: la Cámara de los Comunes ("House of Commons") está formada por 650 diputados ("Members of Parliament") que acceden a ella tras ser elegidos por sufragio universal en su respectiva área o circunscripción electoral ("constituency"). Se reúne 175 días al año y sus sesiones son presididas y moderadas por el Presidente de la Cámara ("Speaker"). La cámara alta es la Cámara de los Lores ("House of Lords") y sus miembros son nombrados por el monarca o bien han heredado su escaño. Su poder es limitado, aunque actúa como tribunal supremo de apelación, excepto en Escocia.

parliamentary [pɑːlə'mɛntərɪ] *adj* parlamentario
parlour, parlor (*US*) ['pɑːlə^r] *n* salón *m*, living *m* (*LAm*)

parlous ['pɑːləs] *adj* peligroso, alarmante
Parmesan [pɑːmɪ'zæn] *n* (*also*: **Parmesan cheese**) queso parmesano
parochial [pə'rəukɪəl] *adj* parroquial; (*pej*) de miras estrechas
parody ['pærədɪ] *n* parodia ■ *vt* parodiar
parole [pə'rəul] *n*: **on ~** en libertad condicional
paroxysm ['pærəksɪzəm] *n* (*Med*) paroxismo, ataque *m*; (*of anger, laughter, coughing*) ataque *m*; (*of grief*) crisis *f*
parquet ['pɑːkeɪ] *n*: **~ floor(ing)** parquet *m*
parrot ['pærət] *n* loro, papagayo
parrot fashion *adv* como un loro
parry ['pærɪ] *vt* parar
parsimonious [pɑːsɪ'məunɪəs] *adj* tacaño
parsley ['pɑːslɪ] *n* perejil *m*
parsnip ['pɑːsnɪp] *n* chirivía
parson ['pɑːsn] *n* cura *m*
part [pɑːt] *n* (*gen*) parte *f*; (*Mus*) parte *f*; (*bit*) trozo; (*of machine*) pieza; (*Theat etc*) papel *m*; (*of serial*) entrega; (*US: in hair*) raya ■ *adv* = **partly** ■ *vt* separar; (*break*) partir ■ *vi* (*people*) separarse; (*roads*) bifurcarse; (*crowd*) apartarse; (*break*) romperse; **to take ~ in** participar *or* tomar parte en; **to take sb's ~** tomar partido por algn; **for my ~** por mi parte; **for the most ~** en su mayor parte; (*people*) en su mayoría; **for the better ~ of the day** durante la mayor parte del día; **~ of speech** (*Ling*) categoría gramatical, parte *f* de la oración; **to take sth in good/bad ~** aceptar algo bien/tomarse algo a mal
▸ **part with** *vt fus* ceder, entregar; (*money*) pagar; (*get rid of*) deshacerse de
partake [pɑː'teɪk] *vi* (*irreg: like* **take**) (*formal*): **to ~ of sth** (*food*) comer algo; (*drink*) tomar *or* beber algo
part exchange *n* (*Brit*): **in ~** como parte del pago
partial ['pɑːʃl] *adj* parcial; **to be ~ to** (*like*) ser aficionado a
partially ['pɑːʃəlɪ] *adv* en parte, parcialmente
participant [pɑː'tɪsɪpənt] *n* (*in competition*) concursante *m/f*
participate [pɑː'tɪsɪpeɪt] *vi*: **to ~ in** participar en
participation [pɑːtɪsɪ'peɪʃən] *n* participación *f*
participle ['pɑːtɪsɪpl] *n* participio
particle ['pɑːtɪkl] *n* partícula; (*of dust*) mota; (*fig*) pizca
particular [pə'tɪkjuləʳ] *adj* (*special*) particular; (*concrete*) concreto; (*given*) determinado; (*detailed*) detallado, minucioso; (*fussy*) quisquilloso, exigente; **particulars** *npl* (*information*) datos *mpl*, detalles *mpl*; (*details*) pormenores *mpl*; **in ~** en particular; **to be very ~ about** ser muy exigente en cuanto a; **I'm not ~** me es *or* da igual
particularly [pə'tɪkjuləlɪ] *adv* especialmente, en particular
parting ['pɑːtɪŋ] *n* (*act of*) separación *f*; (*farewell*) despedida; (*Brit: in hair*) raya ■ *adj* de despedida; **~ shot** (*fig*) golpe *m* final
partisan [pɑːtɪ'zæn] *adj* partidista ■ *n* partidario(-a); (*fighter*) partisano(-a)
partition [pɑː'tɪʃən] *n* (*Pol*) división *f*; (*wall*) tabique *m* ■ *vt* dividir; dividir con tabique
partly ['pɑːtlɪ] *adv* en parte
partner ['pɑːtnəʳ] *n* (*Comm*) socio(-a); (*Sport*) pareja; (*at dance*) pareja; (*spouse*) cónyuge *m/f*; (*friend etc*) compañero(-a) ■ *vt* acompañar
partnership ['pɑːtnəʃɪp] *n* (*gen*) asociación *f*; (*Comm*) sociedad *f*; **to go into ~ (with), form a ~ (with)** asociarse (con)
part payment *n* pago parcial
partridge ['pɑːtrɪdʒ] *n* perdiz *f*
part-time ['pɑːt'taɪm] *adj, adv* a tiempo parcial
part-timer [pɑːt'taɪməʳ] *n* trabajador(a) *m(f)* a tiempo parcial
party ['pɑːtɪ] *n* (*Pol*) partido; (*celebration*) fiesta; (*group*) grupo; (*Law*) parte *f*, interesado ■ *adj* (*Pol*) de partido; (*dress etc*) de fiesta, de gala; **to have** *or* **give** *or* **throw a ~** organizar una fiesta; **dinner ~** cena; **to be a ~ to a crime** ser cómplice *m/f* de un crimen
party line *n* (*Pol*) línea política del partido; (*Tel*) línea compartida
party piece *n*: **to do one's ~** hacer su numerito (de fiesta)
party political broadcast *n* ≈ espacio electoral
pass [pɑːs] *vt* (*time, object*) pasar; (*place*) pasar por; (*exam, law*) aprobar; (*overtake, surpass*) rebasar; (*approve*) aprobar ■ *vi* pasar; (*Scol*) aprobar ■ *n* (*permit*) permiso, pase *m*; (*membership card*) carnet *m*; (*in mountains*) puerto; (*Sport*) pase *m*; (*Scol: also*: **pass mark**) aprobado; **to ~ sth through sth** pasar algo por algo; **to ~ the time of day with sb** pasar el rato con algn; **things have come to a pretty ~!** ¡hasta dónde hemos llegado!; **to make a ~ at sb** (*col*) insinuársele a algn
▸ **pass away** *vi* fallecer
▸ **pass by** *vi* pasar ■ *vt* (*ignore*) pasar por alto
▸ **pass down** *vt* (*customs, inheritance*) pasar, transmitir
▸ **pass for** *vt fus* pasar por; **she could ~ for 25** se podría creer que sólo tiene 25 años
▸ **pass on** *vi* (*die*) fallecer, morir ■ *vt* (*hand on*): **to ~ on (to)** transmitir (a); (*cold, illness*) pegar (a); (*benefits*) dar (a); (*price rises*) pasar (a)

▸ **pass out** *vi* desmayarse; (*Mil*) graduarse
▸ **pass over** *vi* (*die*) fallecer ■ *vt* omitir, pasar por alto
▸ **pass up** *vt* (*opportunity*) dejar pasar, no aprovechar
passable ['pɑːsəbl] *adj* (*road*) transitable; (*tolerable*) pasable
passably ['pɑːsəblɪ] *adv* pasablemente
passage ['pæsɪdʒ] *n* pasillo; (*act of passing*) tránsito; (*fare, in book*) pasaje *m*; (*by boat*) travesía
passageway ['pæsɪdʒweɪ] *n* (*in house*) pasillo, corredor *m*; (*between buildings etc*) pasaje *m*, pasadizo
passenger ['pæsɪndʒəʳ] *n* pasajero(-a), viajero(-a)
passer-by [pɑːsə'baɪ] *n* transeúnte *m/f*
passing ['pɑːsɪŋ] *adj* (*fleeting*) pasajero; **in ~** de paso
passing place *n* (*Aut*) apartadero
passion ['pæʃən] *n* pasión *f*
passionate ['pæʃənɪt] *adj* apasionado
passionately ['pæʃənɪtlɪ] *adv* apasionadamente, con pasión
passion fruit *n* fruta de la pasión, granadilla
passion play *n* drama *m* de la Pasión
passive ['pæsɪv] *adj* (*also Ling*) pasivo
passive smoking *n efectos del tabaco en fumadores pasivos*
passkey ['pɑːskiː] *n* llave *f* maestra
Passover ['pɑːsəuvəʳ] *n* Pascua (de los judíos)
passport ['pɑːspɔːt] *n* pasaporte *m*
passport control *n* control *m* de pasaporte
password ['pɑːswəːd] *n* (*also Comput*) contraseña
past [pɑːst] *prep* (*further than*) más allá de; (*later than*) después de ■ *adj* pasado; (*president etc*) antiguo ■ *n* (*time*) pasado; (*of person*) antecedentes *mpl*; **quarter/half ~ four** las cuatro y cuarto/media; **he's ~ forty** tiene más de cuarenta años; **I'm ~ caring** ya no me importa; **to be ~ it** (*col: person*) estar acabado; **for the ~ few/three days** durante los últimos días/últimos tres días; **to run ~** pasar corriendo por; **in the ~** en el pasado, antes
pasta ['pæstə] *n* pasta
paste [peɪst] *n* (*gen*) pasta; (*glue*) engrudo ■ *vt* (*stick*) pegar; (*glue*) engomar; **tomato ~** tomate concentrado
pastel ['pæstl] *adj* pastel; (*painting*) al pastel
pasteurized ['pæstəraɪzd] *adj* pasteurizado
pastille ['pæstl] *n* pastilla
pastime ['pɑːstaɪm] *n* pasatiempo
past master *n*: **to be a ~ at** ser un maestro en
pastor ['pɑːstəʳ] *n* pastor *m*
pastoral ['pɑːstərl] *adj* pastoral
pastry ['peɪstrɪ] *n* (*dough*) pasta; (*cake*) pastel *m*
pasture ['pɑːstʃəʳ] *n* (*grass*) pasto
pasty *n* ['pæstɪ] empanada ■ *adj* ['peɪstɪ] pastoso; (*complexion*) pálido
pat [pæt] *vt* dar una palmadita a; (*dog etc*) acariciar ■ *n* (*of butter*) porción *f* ■ *adj*: **he knows it (off) ~** se lo sabe de memoria *or* al dedillo; **to give sb/o.s. a ~ on the back** (*fig*) felicitar a algn/felicitarse
patch [pætʃ] *n* (*of material*) parche *m*; (*mended part*) remiendo; (*of land*) terreno; (*Comput*) ajuste *m* ■ *vt* (*clothes*) remendar; **(to go through) a bad ~** (pasar por) una mala racha
▸ **patch up** *vt* (*mend temporarily*) reparar; **to ~ up a quarrel** hacer las paces
patchwork ['pætʃwəːk] *n* labor *f* de retales
patchy ['pætʃɪ] *adj* desigual
pate [peɪt] *n*: **bald ~** calva
pâté ['pæteɪ] *n* paté *m*
patent ['peɪtnt] *n* patente *f* ■ *vt* patentar ■ *adj* patente, evidente
patent leather *n* charol *m*
patently ['peɪtntlɪ] *adv* evidentemente
patent medicine *n* específico
patent office *n* oficina de patentes y marcas
patent rights *npl* derechos *mpl* de patente
paternal [pə'təːnl] *adj* paternal; (*relation*) paterno
paternalistic [pətəːnə'lɪstɪk] *adj* paternalista
paternity [pə'təːnɪtɪ] *n* paternidad *f*
paternity suit *n* (*Law*) caso de paternidad
path [pɑːθ] *n* camino, sendero; (*trail, track*) pista; (*of missile*) trayectoria
pathetic [pə'θɛtɪk] *adj* (*pitiful*) penoso, patético; (*very bad*) malísimo; (*moving*) conmovedor(a)
pathetically [pə'θɛtɪklɪ] *adv* penosamente, patéticamente; (*very badly*) malísimamente mal, de pena
pathological [pæθə'lɔdʒɪkəl] *adj* patológico
pathologist [pə'θɔlədʒɪst] *n* patólogo(-a)
pathology [pə'θɔlədʒɪ] *n* patología
pathos ['peɪθɔs] *n* patetismo
pathway ['pɑːθweɪ] *n* sendero, vereda
patience ['peɪʃns] *n* paciencia; (*Brit Cards*) solitario; **to lose one's ~** perder la paciencia
patient ['peɪʃnt] *n* paciente *m/f* ■ *adj* paciente, sufrido; **to be ~ with sb** tener paciencia con algn
patiently ['peɪʃəntlɪ] *adv* pacientemente, con paciencia
patio ['pætɪəu] *n* patio
patriot ['peɪtrɪət] *n* patriota *m/f*
patriotic [pætrɪ'ɔtɪk] *adj* patriótico
patriotism ['pætrɪətɪzəm] *n* patriotismo
patrol [pə'trəul] *n* patrulla ■ *vt* patrullar por; **to be on ~** patrullar, estar de patrulla

patrol boat *n* patrullero, patrullera
patrol car *n* coche *m* patrulla
patrolman [pə'trəulmən] *n* (*US*) policía *m*
patron ['peɪtrən] *n* (*in shop*) cliente *m/f*; (*of charity*) patrocinador(a) *m(f)*; **~ of the arts** mecenas *m*
patronage ['pætrənɪdʒ] *n* patrocinio, protección *f*
patronize ['pætrənaɪz] *vt* (*shop*) ser cliente de; (*look down on*) tratar con condescendencia a
patronizing ['pætrənaɪzɪŋ] *adj* condescendiente
patron saint *n* santo(-a) patrón(-ona)
patter ['pætəʳ] *n* golpeteo; (*sales talk*) labia ■ *vi* (*rain*) tamborilear
pattern ['pætən] *n* (*Sewing*) patrón *m*; (*design*) dibujo; (*behaviour, events*) esquema *m*; **~ of events** curso de los hechos; **behaviour patterns** modelos *mpl* de comportamiento
patterned ['pætənd] *adj* (*material*) estampado
paucity ['pɔːsɪtɪ] *n* escasez *f*
paunch [pɔːntʃ] *n* panza, barriga
pauper ['pɔːpəʳ] *n* pobre *m/f*
pause [pɔːz] *n* pausa; (*interval*) intervalo ■ *vi* hacer una pausa; **to ~ for breath** detenerse para tomar aliento
pave [peɪv] *vt* pavimentar; **to ~ the way for** preparar el terreno para
pavement ['peɪvmənt] *n* (*Brit*) acera, vereda (*LAm*), andén *m* (*LAm*), banqueta (*LAm*); (*US*) calzada, pavimento
pavilion [pə'vɪlɪən] *n* pabellón *m*; (*Sport*) vestuarios *mpl*
paving ['peɪvɪŋ] *n* pavimento
paving stone *n* losa
paw [pɔː] *n* pata; (*claw*) garra ■ *vt* (*animal*) tocar con la pata; (*pej: touch*) tocar, manosear
pawn [pɔːn] *n* (*Chess*) peón *m*; (*fig*) instrumento ■ *vt* empeñar
pawnbroker ['pɔːnbrəukəʳ] *n* prestamista *m/f*
pawnshop ['pɔːnʃɔp] *n* casa de empeños
pay [peɪ] (*pt, pp* **paid**) *n* paga; (*wage etc*) sueldo, salario ■ *vt* pagar; (*visit*) hacer; (*respect*) ofrecer ■ *vi* pagar; (*be profitable*) rendir, compensar, ser rentable; **to be in sb's ~** estar al servicio de algn; **to ~ attention (to)** prestar atención (a); **I paid £5 for that record** pagué 5 libras por ese disco; **how much did you ~ for it?** ¿cuánto pagaste por él?; **to ~ one's way** (*contribute one's share*) pagar su parte; (*remain solvent: company*) ser solvente; **to ~ dividends** (*Comm*) pagar dividendos; (*fig*) compensar; **it won't ~ you to do that** no te merece la pena hacer eso; **to put paid to** (*plan, person*) acabar con
▸ **pay back** *vt* (*money*) devolver, reembolsar; (*person*) pagar
▸ **pay for** *vt fus* pagar
▸ **pay in** *vt* ingresar
▸ **pay off** *vt* liquidar; (*person*) pagar; (*debts*) liquidar, saldar; (*creditor*) cancelar, redimir; (*workers*) despedir; (*mortgage*) cancelar, redimir ■ *vi* (*scheme, decision*) dar resultado; **to ~ sth off in instalments** pagar algo a plazos
▸ **pay out** *vt* (*rope*) ir dando; (*money*) gastar, desembolsar
▸ **pay up** *vt* pagar
payable ['peɪəbl] *adj* pagadero; **to make a cheque ~ to sb** extender un cheque a favor de algn
pay-as-you-go [peɪəzjə'gəu] *adj* (*mobile phone*) (de) prepago
pay award *n* aumento de sueldo
pay day *n* día *m* de paga
PAYE *n abbr* (*Brit:* = *pay as you earn*) *sistema de retención fiscal en la fuente de ingresos*
payee [peɪ'iː] *n* portador(a) *m(f)*
pay envelope *n* (*US*) = **pay packet**
paying ['peɪɪŋ] *adj*: **~ guest** huésped(a) *m(f)* que la paga
payload ['peɪləud] *n* carga útil
payment ['peɪmənt] *n* pago; **advance ~** (*part sum*) anticipo, adelanto; (*total sum*) saldo; **monthly ~** mensualidad *f*; **deferred ~, ~ by instalments** pago a plazos *or* diferido; **on ~ of £5** mediante pago de *or* pagando £5; **in ~ for** en pago de
pay packet *n* (*Brit*) sobre *m* (de la paga)
pay-phone ['peɪfəun] *n* teléfono público
payroll ['peɪrəul] *n* nómina; **to be on a firm's ~** estar en la nómina de una compañía
pay slip *n* hoja del sueldo
pay station *n* (*US*) teléfono público
PBS *n abbr* (*US:* = *Public Broadcasting Service*) *agrupación de ayuda a la realización de emisiones para la TV pública*
PBX *abbr* (*Tel*) = **private branch exchange**
PC *n abbr* (= *personal computer*) PC *m*, OP *m*; (*Brit*) = **police constable** ■ *abbr* (*Brit*) = **Privy Councillor** ■ *adj abbr* = **politically correct**
pc *abbr* = **per cent; postcard**
p/c *abbr* = **petty cash**
PCB *n abbr* (= *printed circuit board*) TCI *f*
pcm *abbr* = **per calendar month**
PD *n abbr* (*US*) = **police department**
pd *abbr* = **paid**
PDA *n abbr* (= *personal digital assistant*) agenda electrónica
PDSA *n abbr* (*Brit*) = **People's Dispensary for Sick Animals**
PDT *n abbr* (*US:* = *Pacific Daylight Time*) *hora de verano del Pacífico*

PE *n abbr* (= *physical education*) ed. física ■ *abbr* (*Canada*) = **Prince Edward Island**
pea [pi:] *n* guisante *m*, chícharo (*LAm*), arveja (*LAm*)
peace [pi:s] *n* paz *f*; (*calm*) paz *f*, tranquilidad *f*; **to be at ~ with sb/sth** estar en paz con algn/algo; **to keep the ~** (*policeman*) mantener el orden; (*citizen*) guardar el orden
peaceable ['pi:səbl] *adj* pacífico
peaceably [pɪ:səblɪ] *adv* pacíficamente
peaceful ['pi:sful] *adj* (*gentle*) pacífico; (*calm*) tranquilo, sosegado
peacekeeping ['pi:ski:pɪŋ] *adj* de pacificación ■ *n* pacificación *f*
peacekeeping force *n* fuerza de pacificación
peace offering *n* (*fig*) prenda de paz
peacetime ['pi:staɪm] *n*: **in ~** en tiempo de paz
peach [pi:tʃ] *n* melocotón *m*, durazno (*LAm*)
peacock ['pi:kɔk] *n* pavo real
peak [pi:k] *n* (*of mountain: top*) cumbre *f*, cima; (*: point*) pico; (*of cap*) visera; (*fig*) cumbre *f*
peak-hour ['pi:kauəʳ] *adj* (*traffic etc*) de horas punta
peak hours *npl*, **peak period** ■ *n* horas *fpl* punta
peak rate *n* tarifa máxima
peaky ['pi:kɪ] *adj* (*Brit col*) pálido, paliducho; **I'm feeling a bit ~** estoy malucho, no me encuentro bien
peal [pi:l] *n* (*of bells*) repique *m*; **~ of laughter** carcajada
peanut ['pi:nʌt] *n* cacahuete *m*, maní *m* (*LAm*)
peanut butter *n* mantequilla de cacahuete
pear [pɛəʳ] *n* pera
pearl [pə:l] *n* perla
peasant ['pɛznt] *n* campesino(-a)
peat [pi:t] *n* turba
pebble ['pɛbl] *n* guijarro
peck [pɛk] *vt* (*also*: **peck at**) picotear; (*food*) comer sin ganas ■ *n* picotazo; (*kiss*) besito
pecking order ['pɛkɪŋ-] *n* orden *m* de jerarquía
peckish ['pɛkɪʃ] *adj* (*Brit col*): **I feel ~** tengo ganas de picar algo
peculiar [pɪ'kju:lɪəʳ] *adj* (*odd*) extraño, raro; (*typical*) propio, característico; (*particular: importance, qualities*) particular; **~ to** propio de
peculiarity [pɪkju:lɪ'ærɪtɪ] *n* peculiaridad *f*, característica
peculiarly [pɪ'kju:lɪəlɪ] *adv* extrañamente; particularmente
pedal ['pɛdl] *n* pedal *m* ■ *vi* pedalear
pedal bin *n* cubo de la basura con pedal
pedant ['pɛdənt] *n* pedante *m/f*
pedantic [pɪ'dæntɪk] *adj* pedante
pedantry ['pɛdəntrɪ] *n* pedantería
peddle ['pɛdl] *vt* (*goods*) ir vendiendo *or* vender de puerta en puerta; (*drugs*) traficar con; (*gossip*) divulgar
peddler ['pɛdləʳ] *n* vendedor(a) *m(f)* ambulante
pedestal ['pɛdəstl] *n* pedestal *m*
pedestrian [pɪ'dɛstrɪən] *n* peatón *m* ■ *adj* pedestre
pedestrian crossing *n* (*Brit*) paso de peatones
pedestrian precinct *n* zona reservada para peatones
pediatrics [pi:dɪ'ætrɪks] *n* (*US*) = **paediatrics**
pedigree ['pɛdɪgri:] *n* genealogía; (*of animal*) pedigrí *m* ■ *cpd* (*animal*) de raza, de casta
pedlar ['pɛdləʳ] *n* (*Brit*) = **peddler**
pee [pi:] *vi* (*col*) mear
peek [pi:k] *vi* mirar a hurtadillas; (*Comput*) inspeccionar
peel [pi:l] *n* piel *f*; (*of orange, lemon*) cáscara; (*: removed*) peladuras *fpl* ■ *vt* pelar ■ *vi* (*paint etc*) desconcharse; (*wallpaper*) despegarse, desprenderse
▸ **peel back** *vt* pelar
peeler ['pi:ləʳ] *n*: **potato ~** mondador *m or* pelador *m* de patatas, pelapatatas *m inv*
peep [pi:p] *n* (*Brit: look*) mirada furtiva; (*sound*) pío ■ *vi* (*Brit*) piar
▸ **peep out** *vi* asomar la cabeza
peephole ['pi:phəul] *n* mirilla
peer [pɪəʳ] *vi*: **to ~ at** escudriñar ■ *n* (*noble*) par *m*; (*equal*) igual *m*
peerage ['pɪərɪdʒ] *n* nobleza
peerless ['pɪəlɪs] *adj* sin par, incomparable, sin igual
peeved [pi:vd] *adj* enojado
peevish ['pi:vɪʃ] *adj* malhumorado
peevishness ['pɪ:vɪʃnɪs] *n* mal humor *m*
peg [pɛg] *n* clavija; (*for coat etc*) gancho, colgador *m*; (*Brit: also*: **clothes peg**) pinza; (*also*: **tent peg**) estaca ■ *vt* (*clothes*) tender; (*groundsheet*) fijar con estacas; (*fig: wages, prices*) fijar
pejorative [pɪ'dʒɔrətɪv] *adj* peyorativo
Pekin [pi:'kɪn], **Peking** [pi:'kɪŋ] *n* Pekín *m*
pekinese [pi:kɪ'ni:z] *n* pequinés(-esa) *m(f)*
pelican ['pɛlɪkən] *n* pelícano
pelican crossing *n* (*Brit Aut*) paso de peatones señalizado
pellet ['pɛlɪt] *n* bolita; (*bullet*) perdigón *m*
pell-mell ['pɛl'mɛl] *adv* en tropel
pelmet ['pɛlmɪt] *n* galería
pelt [pɛlt] *vt*: **to ~ sb with sth** arrojarle algo a algn ■ *vi* (*rain: also*: **pelt down**) llover a cántaros ■ *n* pellejo
pelvis ['pɛlvɪs] *n* pelvis *f*
pen [pɛn] *n* (*also*: **ballpoint pen**) bolígrafo;

(*also*: **fountain pen**) pluma; (*for sheep*) redil *m*; (*US col*: *prison*) cárcel *f*, chirona; **to put ~ to paper** tomar la pluma
penal ['pi:nl] *adj* penal; **~ servitude** trabajos *mpl* forzados
penalize ['pi:nəlaɪz] *vt* (*punish*) castigar; (*Sport*) sancionar, penalizar
penalty ['pɛnltɪ] *n* (*gen*) pena; (*fine*) multa; (*Sport*) sanción *f*; (*also*: **penalty kick**: *Football*) penalty *m*
penalty area *n* (*Brit Sport*) área de castigo
penalty clause *n* cláusula de penalización
penalty shoot-out [-'ʃu:taut] *n* (*Football*) tanda de penaltis
penance ['pɛnəns] *n* penitencia
pence [pɛns] *pl of* **penny**
penchant ['pɑ̃:ʃɑ̃:ŋ] *n* predilección *f*, inclinación *f*
pencil ['pɛnsl] *n* lápiz *m*, lapicero (*LAm*) ■ *vt* (*also*: **pencil in**) escribir con lápiz
pencil case *n* estuche *m*
pencil sharpener *n* sacapuntas *m inv*
pendant ['pɛndnt] *n* pendiente *m*
pending ['pɛndɪŋ] *prep* antes de ■ *adj* pendiente; **~ the arrival of ...** hasta que llegue ..., hasta llegar ...
pendulum ['pɛndjuləm] *n* péndulo
penetrate ['pɛnɪtreɪt] *vt* penetrar
penetrating ['pɛnɪtreɪtɪŋ] *adj* penetrante
penetration [pɛnɪ'treɪʃən] *n* penetración *f*
penfriend ['pɛnfrɛnd] *n* (*Brit*) amigo(-a) por correspondencia
penguin ['pɛŋgwɪn] *n* pingüino
penicillin [pɛnɪ'sɪlɪn] *n* penicilina
peninsula [pə'nɪnsjulə] *n* península
penis ['pi:nɪs] *n* pene *m*
penitence ['pɛnɪtns] *n* penitencia
penitent ['pɛnɪtnt] *adj* arrepentido; (*Rel*) penitente
penitentiary [pɛnɪ'tɛnʃərɪ] *n* (*US*) cárcel *f*, presidio
penknife ['pɛnnaɪf] *n* navaja
Penn., Penna. *abbr* (*US*) = **Pennsylvania**
pen name *n* seudónimo
pennant ['pɛnənt] *n* banderola; banderín *m*
penniless ['pɛnɪlɪs] *adj* sin dinero
Pennines ['pɛnaɪnz] *npl* (Montes *mpl*) Peninos *mpl*
penny (*pl* **pennies** *or* (*BRIT*) **pence**) ['pɛnɪ, 'pɛnɪz, pɛns] *n* (*Brit*) penique *m*; (*US*) centavo
penpal ['pɛnpæl] *n* amigo(-a) por correspondencia
penpusher ['pɛnpuʃəʳ] *n* (*pej*) chupatintas *m/f inv*
pension ['pɛnʃən] *n* (*allowance, state payment*) pensión *f*; (*old-age*) jubilación *f*
▸ **pension off** *vt* jubilar
pensioner ['pɛnʃənəʳ] *n* (*Brit*) jubilado(-a)
pension fund *n* fondo de pensiones
pensive ['pɛnsɪv] *adj* pensativo; (*withdrawn*) preocupado
pentagon ['pɛntəgən] *n* pentágono; **the P~** (*US Pol*) el Pentágono

PENTAGON

Se conoce como el Pentágono (*the Pentagon*) al edificio de planta pentagonal que acoge las dependencias del Ministerio de Defensa estadounidense ("Department of Defense") en Arlington, Virginia. En lenguaje periodístico se aplica también a la dirección militar del país.

Pentecost ['pɛntɪkɔst] *n* Pentecostés *m*
penthouse ['pɛnthaus] *n* ático (de lujo)
pent-up ['pɛntʌp] *adj* (*feelings*) reprimido
penultimate [pɛ'nʌltɪmət] *adj* penúltimo
penury ['pɛnjurɪ] *n* miseria, pobreza
people ['pi:pl] *npl* gente *f*; (*citizens*) pueblo *sg*, ciudadanos *mpl* ■ *n* (*nation, race*) pueblo, nación *f* ■ *vt* poblar; **several ~ came** vinieron varias personas; **~ say that ...** dice la gente que ...; **old/young ~** los ancianos/jóvenes; **~ at large** la gente en general; **a man of the ~** un hombre del pueblo
PEP [pɛp] *n abbr* (*= personal equity plan*) *plan personal de inversión con desgravación fiscal*
pep [pɛp] *n* (*col*) energía
▸ **pep up** *vt* animar
pepper ['pɛpəʳ] *n* (*spice*) pimienta; (*vegetable*) pimiento, ají *m* (*LAm*), chile *m* (*LAm*) ■ *vt* (*fig*) salpicar
peppermint ['pɛpəmɪnt] *n* menta; (*sweet*) pastilla de menta
pepperoni [pɛpə'rəunɪ] *n* ≈ salchichón *m* picante
pepperpot ['pɛpəpɔt] *n* pimentero
peptalk ['pɛptɔ:k] *n* (*col*): **to give sb a ~** darle a algn una inyección de ánimo
per [pə:ʳ] *prep* por; **~ day/person** por día/persona; **as ~ your instructions** de acuerdo con sus instrucciones
per annum *adv* al año
per capita *adj, adv* per cápita
perceive [pə'si:v] *vt* percibir; (*realize*) darse cuenta de
per cent, (*US*) **percent** [pə'sɛnt] *n* por ciento; **a 20 ~ discount** un descuento del 20 por ciento
percentage [pə'sɛntɪdʒ] *n* porcentaje *m*; **to get a ~ on all sales** percibir un tanto por ciento sobre todas las ventas; **on a ~ basis** a porcentaje

percentage point *n* punto (porcentual)
perceptible [pə'sɛptəbl] *adj* perceptible; (*notable*) sensible
perception [pə'sɛpʃən] *n* percepción *f*; (*insight*) perspicacia
perceptive [pə'sɛptɪv] *adj* perspicaz
perch [pəːtʃ] *n* (*fish*) perca; (*for bird*) percha ■ *vi* posarse
percolate ['pəːkəleɪt] *vt* (*coffee*) filtrar ■ *vi* (*coffee*) filtrarse; (*fig*) filtrarse
percolator ['pəːkəleɪtəʳ] *n* cafetera de filtro
percussion [pə'kʌʃən] *n* percusión *f*
percussionist [pə'kʌʃənɪst] *n* percusionista *m/f*
peremptory [pə'rɛmptərɪ] *adj* perentorio
perennial [pə'rɛnɪəl] *adj* perenne
perfect *adj* ['pəːfɪkt] perfecto ■ *n* (*also*: **perfect tense**) perfecto ■ *vt* [pə'fɛkt] perfeccionar; **he's a ~ stranger to me** no le conozco de nada, me es completamente desconocido
perfection [pə'fɛkʃən] *n* perfección *f*
perfectionist [pə'fɛkʃənɪst] *n* perfeccionista *m/f*
perfectly ['pəːfɪktlɪ] *adv* perfectamente; **I'm ~ happy with the situation** estoy muy contento con la situación; **you know ~ well** lo sabes muy bien *or* perfectamente
perforate ['pəːfəreɪt] *vt* perforar
perforated ulcer *n* úlcera perforada
perforation [pəːfə'reɪʃən] *n* perforación *f*
perform [pə'fɔːm] *vt* (*carry out*) realizar, llevar a cabo; (*Theat*) representar; (*piece of music*) interpretar ■ *vi* (*Theat*) actuar; (*Tech*) funcionar
performance [pə'fɔːməns] *n* (*of task*) realización *f*; (*of a play*) representación *f*; (*of player etc*) actuación *f*; (*of engine*) rendimiento; (*of car*) prestaciones *fpl*; (*of function*) desempeño; **the team put up a good ~** el equipo se defendió bien
performer [pə'fɔːməʳ] *n* (*actor*) actor *m*, actriz *f*; (*Mus*) intérprete *m/f*
performing [pə'fɔːmɪŋ] *adj* (*animal*) amaestrado
performing arts *npl*: **the ~** las artes teatrales
perfume ['pəːfjuːm] *n* perfume *m*
perfunctory [pə'fʌŋktərɪ] *adj* superficial
perhaps [pə'hæps] *adv* quizá(s), tal vez; **~ so/not** puede que sí/no
peril ['pɛrɪl] *n* peligro, riesgo
perilous ['pɛrɪləs] *adj* peligroso
perilously ['pɛrɪləslɪ] *adv*: **they came ~ close to being caught** por poco les cogen *or* agarran
perimeter [pə'rɪmɪtəʳ] *n* perímetro
period ['pɪərɪəd] *n* período, periodo; (*History*) época; (*Scol*) clase *f*; (*full stop*) punto; (*Med*) regla, periodo; (*US Sport*) tiempo ■ *adj* (*costume, furniture*) de época; **for a ~ of three weeks** durante (un período de) tres semanas; **the holiday ~** el período de vacaciones
periodic [pɪərɪ'ɔdɪk] *adj* periódico
periodical [pɪərɪ'ɔdɪkl] *adj* periódico ■ *n* revista, publicación *f* periódica
periodically [pɪərɪ'ɔdɪklɪ] *adv* de vez en cuando, cada cierto tiempo
period pains *npl* dolores *mpl* de la regla *or* de la menstruación
peripatetic [pɛrɪpə'tɛtɪk] *adj* (*salesman*) ambulante; (*teacher*) con trabajo en varios colegios
peripheral [pə'rɪfərəl] *adj* periférico ■ *n* (*Comput*) periférico, unidad *f* periférica
periphery [pə'rɪfərɪ] *n* periferia
periscope ['pɛrɪskəup] *n* periscopio
perish ['pɛrɪʃ] *vi* perecer; (*decay*) echarse a perder
perishable ['pɛrɪʃəbl] *adj* perecedero
perishables ['pɛrɪʃəblz] *npl* productos *mpl* perecederos
peritonitis [pɛrɪtə'naɪtɪs] *n* peritonitis *f*
perjure ['pəːdʒəʳ] *vt*: **to ~ o.s.** perjurar
perjury ['pəːdʒərɪ] *n* (*Law*) perjurio
perk [pəːk] *n* beneficio, extra *m*
▸ **perk up** *vi* (*cheer up*) animarse
perky ['pəːkɪ] *adj* alegre, animado
perm [pəːm] *n* permanente *f* ■ *vt*: **to have one's hair permed** hacerse una permanente
permanence ['pəːmənəns] *n* permanencia
permanent ['pəːmənənt] *adj* permanente; (*job, position*) fijo; (*dye, ink*) indeleble; **~ address** domicilio permanente; **I'm not ~ here** no estoy fijo aquí
permanently ['pəːmənəntlɪ] *adv* (*lastingly*) para siempre, de modo definitivo; (*all the time*) permanentemente
permeate ['pəːmɪeɪt] *vi* penetrar, trascender ■ *vt* penetrar, trascender a
permissible [pə'mɪsɪbl] *adj* permisible, lícito
permission [pə'mɪʃən] *n* permiso; **to give sb ~ to do sth** autorizar a algn para que haga algo; **with your ~** con su permiso
permissive [pə'mɪsɪv] *adj* permisivo
permit *n* ['pəːmɪt] permiso, licencia; (*entrance pass*) pase *m* ■ *vt* [pə'mɪt] permitir; (*accept*) tolerar ■ *vi* [pə'mɪt]: **weather permitting** si el tiempo lo permite; **fishing ~** permiso de pesca; **building/export ~** licencia *or* permiso de construcción/exportación
permutation [pəːmju'teɪʃən] *n* permutación *f*
pernicious [pəː'nɪʃəs] *adj* nocivo; (*Med*) pernicioso

pernickety [pəˈnɪkɪtɪ] *adj* (*col: person*) quisquilloso; (*: task*) delicado
perpendicular [pəːpənˈdɪkjuləʳ] *adj* perpendicular
perpetrate [ˈpəːpɪtreɪt] *vt* cometer
perpetual [pəˈpɛtjuəl] *adj* perpetuo
perpetually [pəˈpɛtjuəlɪ] *adv* (*eternally*) perpetuamente; (*continuously*) constantemente, continuamente
perpetuate [pəˈpɛtjueɪt] *vt* perpetuar
perpetuity [pəːpɪˈtjuːɪtɪ] *n*: **in ~** a perpetuidad
perplex [pəˈplɛks] *vt* dejar perplejo
perplexed [pəˈplɛkst] *adj* perplejo, confuso
perplexing [pəˈplɛksɪŋ] *adj* que causa perplejidad
perplexity [pəˈplɛksɪtɪ] *n* perplejidad *f*, confusión *f*
perquisites [ˈpəːkwɪzɪts] *npl* (*also*: **perks**) beneficios *mpl*
persecute [ˈpəːsɪkjuːt] *vt* (*pursue*) perseguir; (*harass*) acosar
persecution [pəːsɪˈkjuːʃən] *n* persecución *f*
perseverance [pəːsɪˈvɪərəns] *n* perseverancia
persevere [pəːsɪˈvɪəʳ] *vi* perseverar
Persia [ˈpəːʃə] *n* Persia
Persian [ˈpəːʃən] *adj, n* persa *m/f* ■ *n* (*Ling*) persa *m*; **the ~ Gulf** el Golfo Pérsico
Persian cat *n* gato persa
persist [pəˈsɪst] *vi* persistir; **to ~ in doing sth** empeñarse en hacer algo
persistence [pəˈsɪstəns] *n* empeño
persistent [pəˈsɪstənt] *adj* (*lateness, rain*) persistente; (*determined*) porfiado; (*continuing*) constante; **~ offender** (*Law*) multirreincidente *m/f*
persistently [pəˈsɪstəntlɪ] *adv* persistentemente; (*continually*) constantemente
persnickety [pəˈsnɪkətɪ] *adj* (*US col*) = **pernickety**
person [ˈpəːsn] *n* persona; **in ~** en persona; **on** *or* **about one's ~** encima; **a ~ to ~ call** una llamada (de) persona a persona
personable [ˈpəːsnəbl] *adj* atractivo
personal [ˈpəːsnl] *adj* personal, individual; (*visit*) en persona; (*Brit Tel*) (de) persona a persona
personal allowance *n* desgravación *f* personal
personal assistant *n* ayudante *m/f* personal
personal belongings *npl* efectos *mpl* personales
personal column *n* anuncios *mpl* personales
personal computer *n* ordenador *m* personal
personal effects *npl* efectos *mpl* personales
personal identification number *n* número personal de identificación
personality [pəːsəˈnælɪtɪ] *n* personalidad *f*
personally [ˈpəːsnəlɪ] *adv* personalmente
personal organizer *n* agenda (profesional); (*electronic*) organizador *m* personal
personal property *n* bienes *mpl* muebles
personal, social and health education *n* (*Brit Scol*) *formación social y sanitaria para la vida adulta*
personal stereo *n* walkman® *m*
personification [pəːsɔnɪfɪˈkeɪʃən] *n* personificación *f*
personify [pəːˈsɔnɪfaɪ] *vt* encarnar, personificar
personnel [pəːsəˈnɛl] *n* personal *m*
personnel department *n* departamento de personal
personnel management *n* gestión *f* de personal
personnel manager *n* jefe *m* de personal
perspective [pəˈspɛktɪv] *n* perspectiva; **to get sth into ~** ver algo en perspectiva *or* como es
Perspex® [ˈpəːspɛks] *n* (*Brit*) vidrio acrílico, plexiglás® *m*
perspiration [pəːspɪˈreɪʃən] *n* transpiración *f*, sudor *m*
perspire [pəˈspaɪəʳ] *vi* transpirar, sudar
persuade [pəˈsweɪd] *vt*: **to ~ sb to do sth** persuadir a algn para que haga algo; **to ~ sb of sth/that** persuadir *or* convencer a algn de algo/de que; **I am persuaded that ...** estoy convencido de que ...
persuasion [pəˈsweɪʒən] *n* persuasión *f*; (*persuasiveness*) persuasiva; (*creed*) creencia
persuasive [pəˈsweɪsɪv] *adj* persuasivo
persuasively [pəˈsweɪsɪvlɪ] *adv* de modo persuasivo
pert [pəːt] *adj* impertinente, fresco, atrevido
pertaining [pəːˈteɪnɪŋ]: **~ to** *prep* relacionado con
pertinent [ˈpəːtɪnənt] *adj* pertinente, a propósito
perturb [pəˈtəːb] *vt* perturbar
perturbing [pəˈtəːbɪŋ] *adj* inquietante, perturbador(a)
Peru [pəˈruː] *n* el Perú
perusal [pəˈruːzəl] *n* (*quick*) lectura somera; (*careful*) examen *m*
peruse [pəˈruːz] *vt* (*examine*) leer con detención, examinar; (*glance at*) mirar por encima
Peruvian [pəˈruːvɪən] *adj, n* peruano(-a) *m(f)*
pervade [pəˈveɪd] *vt* impregnar; (*influence, ideas*) extenderse por
pervasive [pəˈveɪsɪv] *adj* (*smell*) penetrante;

(*influence*) muy extendido; (*gloom, feelings, ideas*) reinante
perverse [pə'və:s] *adj* perverso; (*stubborn*) terco; (*wayward*) travieso
perversely [pə'və:slɪ] *adv* perversamente; tercamente; traviesamente
perverseness [pə'və:snɪs] *n* perversidad *f*; terquedad *f*; travesura
perversion [pə'və:ʃən] *n* perversión *f*
pervert *n* ['pə:və:t] pervertido(-a) ■ *vt* [pə'və:t] pervertir
pessary ['pɛsərɪ] *n* pesario
pessimism ['pɛsɪmɪzəm] *n* pesimismo
pessimist ['pɛsɪmɪst] *n* pesimista *m/f*
pessimistic [pɛsɪ'mɪstɪk] *adj* pesimista
pest [pɛst] *n* (*insect*) insecto nocivo; (*fig*) lata, molestia; **pests** *npl* plaga
pest control *n* control *m* de plagas
pester ['pɛstə^r] *vt* molestar, acosar
pesticide ['pɛstɪsaɪd] *n* pesticida *m*
pestilence ['pɛstɪləns] *n* pestilencia
pestle ['pɛsl] *n* mano *f* de mortero *or* de almirez
pet [pɛt] *n* animal *m* doméstico; (*favourite*) favorito(-a) ■ *vt* acariciar ■ *vi* (*col*) besuquearse ■ *cpd*: **my ~ aversion** mi manía
petal ['pɛtl] *n* pétalo
peter ['pi:tə^r]: **to ~ out** *vi* agotarse, acabarse
petite [pə'ti:t] *adj* menuda, chiquita
petition [pə'tɪʃən] *n* petición *f* ■ *vt* presentar una petición a ■ *vi*: **to ~ for divorce** pedir el divorcio
pet name *n* nombre *m* cariñoso, apodo
petrified ['pɛtrɪfaɪd] *adj* (*fig*) pasmado, horrorizado
petrochemical [pɛtrə'kɛmɪkl] *adj* petroquímico
petrodollars ['pɛtrəudɔləz] *npl* petrodólares *mpl*
petrol ['pɛtrəl] (*Brit*) *n* gasolina; (*for lighter*) bencina; **two/four-star ~** gasolina normal/súper
petrol bomb *n* cóctel *m* Molotov
petrol can *n* bidón *m* de gasolina
petrol engine *n* (*Brit*) motor *m* de gasolina
petroleum [pə'trəulɪəm] *n* petróleo
petroleum jelly *n* vaselina
petrol pump *n* (*Brit: in car*) bomba de gasolina; (*in garage*) surtidor *m* de gasolina
petrol station *n* (*Brit*) gasolinera
petrol tank *n* (*Brit*) depósito (de gasolina)
petticoat ['pɛtɪkəut] *n* combinación *f*, enagua(s) *f(pl)* (*LAm*)
pettifogging ['pɛtɪfɔgɪŋ] *adj* quisquilloso
pettiness ['pɛtɪnɪs] *n* mezquindad *f*
petty ['pɛtɪ] *adj* (*mean*) mezquino; (*unimportant*) insignificante
petty cash *n* dinero para gastos menores
petty cash book *n* libro de caja auxiliar
petty officer *n* contramaestre *m*
petulant ['pɛtjulənt] *adj* malhumorado
pew [pju:] *n* banco
pewter ['pju:tə^r] *n* peltre *m*
Pfc *abbr* (*US Mil*) = **private first class**
PG *n abbr* (*Cine*) = **parental guidance**
PG 13 *abbr* (*US: Cine: = Parental Guidance 13*) no apto para menores de 13 años
PGA *n abbr* = **Professional Golfers' Association**
PH *n abbr* (*US Mil: = Purple Heart*) *decoración otorgada a los heridos de guerra*
pH *n abbr* (= *pH value*) pH
PHA *n abbr* (*US*) = **Public Housing Administration**
phallic ['fælɪk] *adj* fálico
phantom ['fæntəm] *n* fantasma *m*
Pharaoh ['fɛərəu] *n* faraón *m*
pharmaceutical [fɑ:mə'sju:tɪkl] *adj* farmaceútico
pharmacist ['fɑ:məsɪst] *n* farmacéutico(-a)
pharmacy ['fɑ:məsɪ] *n* (*US*) farmacia
phase [feɪz] *n* fase *f* ■ *vt*: **to ~ sth in/out** introducir/retirar algo por etapas; **phased withdrawal** retirada progresiva
PhD *abbr* = **Doctor of Philosophy**
pheasant ['fɛznt] *n* faisán *m*
phenomenal [fɪ'nɔmɪnl] *adj* fenomenal, extraordinario
phenomenally [fɪ'nɔmɪnlɪ] *adv* extraordinariamente
phenomenon (*pl* **phenomena**) [fə'nɔmɪnən, -nə] *n* fenómeno
phial ['faɪəl] *n* ampolla
philanderer [fɪ'lændərə^r] *n* donjuán *m*, don Juan *m*
philanthropic [fɪlən'θrɔpɪk] *adj* filantrópico
philanthropist [fɪ'lænθrəpɪst] *n* filántropo(-a)
philatelist [fɪ'lætəlɪst] *n* filatelista *m/f*
philately [fɪ'lætəlɪ] *n* filatelia
Philippines ['fɪlɪpi:nz] *npl*: **the ~** (las Islas) Filipinas
philosopher [fɪ'lɔsəfə^r] *n* filósofo(-a)
philosophical [fɪlə'sɔfɪkl] *adj* filosófico
philosophy [fɪ'lɔsəfɪ] *n* filosofía
phishing ['fɪʃɪŋ] *n* phishing *m*, *método de estafa a través de Internet*
phlegm [flɛm] *n* flema
phlegmatic [flɛg'mætɪk] *adj* flemático
phobia ['fəubjə] *n* fobia
phone [fəun] *n* teléfono ■ *vt* telefonear, llamar por teléfono; **to be on the ~** tener teléfono; (*be calling*) estar hablando por teléfono

▸ **phone back** *vt, vi* volver a llamar
▸ **phone up** *vt, vi* llamar por teléfono
phone book *n* guía telefónica
phone box, phone booth *n* cabina telefónica
phone call *n* llamada (telefónica)
phonecard ['fəunka:d] *n* tarjeta telefónica
phone-in ['fəunɪn] *n* (*Brit Radio, TV*) *programa de radio o televisión con las líneas abiertas al público*
phone tapping [-tæpɪŋ] *n* escuchas telefónicas
phonetics [fə'nɛtɪks] *n* fonética
phoney ['fəunɪ] *adj* = **phony**
phonograph ['fəunəgræf] *n* (*US*) fonógrafo, tocadiscos *m inv*
phonology [fəu'nɔlədʒɪ] *n* fonología
phony ['fəunɪ] *adj* falso ■ *n* (*person*) farsante *m/f*
phosphate ['fɔsfeɪt] *n* fosfato
phosphorus ['fɔsfərəs] *n* fósforo
photo ['fəutəu] *n* foto *f*
photo... ['fəutəu] *pref* foto...
photocall ['fəutəukɔ:l] *n* sesión *f* fotográfica para la prensa
photocopier ['fəutəukɔpɪə^r] *n* fotocopiadora
photocopy ['fəutəukɔpɪ] *n* fotocopia ■ *vt* fotocopiar
photoelectric [fəutəuɪ'lɛktrɪk] *adj*: **~ cell** célula fotoeléctrica
photo finish *n* resultado comprobado por fotocontrol
Photofit® ['fəutəufɪt] *n* (*also*: **Photofit picture**) retrato robot
photogenic [fəutəu'dʒɛnɪk] *adj* fotogénico
photograph ['fəutəgræf] *n* fotografía ■ *vt* fotografiar; **to take a ~ of sb** sacar una foto de algn
photographer [fə'tɔgrəfə^r] *n* fotógrafo
photographic [fəutə'græfɪk] *adj* fotográfico
photography [fə'tɔgrəfɪ] *n* fotografía
photo opportunity *n oportunidad de salir en la foto*
Photostat® ['fəutəustæt] *n* fotóstato
photosynthesis [fəutəu'sɪnθəsɪs] *n* fotosíntesis *f*
phrase [freɪz] *n* frase *f* ■ *vt* (*letter*) expresar, redactar
phrase book *n* libro de frases
physical ['fɪzɪkl] *adj* físico; **~ examination** reconocimiento médico; **~ exercises** ejercicios *mpl* físicos
physical education *n* educación *f* física
physically ['fɪsɪklɪ] *adv* físicamente
physical training *n* gimnasia
physician [fɪ'zɪʃən] *n* médico(-a)
physicist ['fɪzɪsɪst] *n* físico(-a)
physics ['fɪzɪks] *n* física
physiological [fɪzɪə'lɔdʒɪkl] *adj* fisiológico
physiology [fɪzɪ'ɔlədʒɪ] *n* fisiología
physiotherapy [fɪzɪəu'θɛrəpɪ] *n* fisioterapia
physique [fɪ'zi:k] *n* físico
pianist ['pɪənɪst] *n* pianista *m/f*
piano [pɪ'ænəu] *n* piano
piano accordion *n* (*Brit*) acordeón-piano *m*
piccolo ['pɪkələu] *n* (*Mus*) flautín *m*
pick [pɪk] *n* (*tool*: *also*: **pick-axe**) pico, piqueta ■ *vt* (*select*) elegir, escoger; (*gather*) coger (*SP*), recoger (*LAm*); (*lock*) abrir con ganzúa; (*scab, spot*) rascar ■ *vi*: **to ~ and choose** ser muy exigente; **take your ~** escoja lo que quiera; **the ~ of** lo mejor de; **to ~ one's nose/teeth** hurgarse las narices/escarbarse los dientes; **to ~ pockets** ratear, ser carterista; **to ~ one's way through** andar a tientas, abrirse camino; **to ~ a fight/quarrel with sb** buscar pelea/camorra con algn; **to ~ sb's brains** aprovecharse de los conocimientos de algn
▸ **pick at** *vt fus*: **to ~ at one's food** comer con poco apetito
▸ **pick off** *vt* (*kill*) matar de un tiro
▸ **pick on** *vt fus* (*person*) meterse con
▸ **pick out** *vt* escoger; (*distinguish*) identificar
▸ **pick up** *vi* (*improve*: *sales*) ir mejor; (*: patient*) reponerse; (*: Finance*) recobrarse ■ *vt* (*from floor*) recoger; (*buy*) comprar; (*find*) encontrar; (*learn*) aprender; (*Radio, TV, Tel*) captar; **to ~ up speed** acelerarse; **to ~ o.s. up** levantarse; **to ~ up where one left off** volver a empezar algo donde lo había dejado
pickaxe, pickax (*US*) ['pɪkæks] *n* pico, zapapico
picket ['pɪkɪt] *n* (*in strike*) piquete *m* ■ *vt* hacer un piquete en, piquetear; **to be on ~ duty** estar de piquete
picketing ['pɪkɪtɪŋ] *n* organización *f* de piquetes
picket line *n* piquete *m*
pickings ['pɪkɪŋz] *npl* (*pilferings*): **there are good ~ to be had here** se pueden sacar buenas ganancias de aquí
pickle ['pɪkl] *n* (*also*: **pickles**: *as condiment*) escabeche *m*; (*fig*: *mess*) apuro ■ *vt* conservar en escabeche; (*in vinegar*) conservar en vinagre; **in a ~** en un lío, en apuros
pick-me-up ['pɪkmɪʌp] *n* reconstituyente *m*
pickpocket ['pɪkpɔkɪt] *n* carterista *m/f*
pickup ['pɪkʌp] *n* (*also*: **pickup truck, pickup van**) furgoneta
picnic ['pɪknɪk] *n* picnic *m*, merienda ■ *vi* merendar en el campo
pictorial [pɪk'tɔ:rɪəl] *adj* pictórico; (*magazine etc*) ilustrado
picture ['pɪktʃə^r] *n* cuadro; (*painting*) pintura; (*photograph*) fotografía; (*film*) película; (*TV*)

imagen *f* ■ *vt* pintar; **the pictures** (*Brit*) el cine; **we get a good ~ here** captamos bien la imagen aquí; **to take a ~ of sb/sth** hacer *or* sacar una foto a algn/de algo; **the garden is a ~ in June** el jardín es una preciosidad en junio; **the overall ~** la impresión general; **to put sb in the ~** poner a algn al corriente *or* al tanto
picture book *n* libro de dibujos
picture message *n* mensaje *m* con foto
picture messaging *n* (envío de) mensajes *mpl* con imágenes
picturesque [pɪktʃəˈrɛsk] *adj* pintoresco
piddling [ˈpɪdlɪŋ] *adj* insignificante
pidgin [ˈpɪdʒɪn] *adj*: **~ English** *lengua franca basada en el inglés*
pie [paɪ] *n* (*of meat etc: large*) pastel *m*; (*: small*) empanada; (*sweet*) tarta
piebald [ˈpaɪbɔːld] *adj* pío
piece [piːs] *n* pedazo, trozo; (*of cake*) trozo; (*Draughts etc*) ficha; (*Chess*) pieza; (*part of a set*) pieza; (*item*): **a ~ of furniture/advice** un mueble/un consejo ■ *vt*: **to ~ together** juntar; (*Tech*) armar; **to take to pieces** desmontar; **a ~ of news** una noticia; **a 10p ~** una moneda de 10 peniques; **a six-~ band** un conjunto de seis (músicos); **in one ~** (*object*) de una sola pieza; **~ by ~** pieza por *or* a pieza; **to say one's ~** decir su parecer
piecemeal [ˈpiːsmiːl] *adv* poco a poco
piece rate *n* tarifa a destajo
piecework [ˈpiːswəːk] *n* trabajo a destajo
pie chart *n* gráfico de sectores *or* de tarta
pier [pɪəʳ] *n* muelle *m*, embarcadero
pierce [pɪəs] *vt* penetrar en, perforar; **to have one's ears pierced** hacerse los agujeros de las orejas
piercing [ˈpɪəsɪŋ] *adj* (*cry*) penetrante ■ *n* (*body art*) piercing *m*
piety [ˈpaɪətɪ] *n* piedad *f*
pig [pɪg] *n* cerdo, puerco, chancho (*LAm*); (*person: greedy*) tragón(-ona) *m(f)*, comilón(-ona) *m(f)*; (*nasty*) cerdo(-a)
pigeon [ˈpɪdʒən] *n* paloma; (*as food*) pichón *m*
pigeonhole [ˈpɪdʒənhəul] *n* casilla
piggy bank [ˈpɪgɪbæŋk] *n* hucha (*en forma de cerdito*)
pigheaded [ˈpɪgˈhɛdɪd] *adj* terco, testarudo
piglet [ˈpɪglɪt] *n* cerdito, cochinillo
pigment [ˈpɪgmənt] *n* pigmento
pigmentation [pɪgmənˈteɪʃən] *n* pigmentación *f*
pigmy [ˈpɪgmɪ] *n* = **pygmy**
pigskin [ˈpɪgskɪn] *n* piel *f* de cerdo
pigsty [ˈpɪgstaɪ] *n* pocilga
pigtail [ˈpɪgteɪl] *n* (*girl's*) trenza; (*Chinese*) coleta; (*Taur*) coleta
pike [paɪk] *n* (*spear*) pica; (*fish*) lucio
pilchard [ˈpɪltʃəd] *n* sardina
pile [paɪl] *n* (*heap*) montón *m*; (*of carpet*) pelo; (*vb: also*: **pile up**) ■ *vt* amontonar; (*fig*) acumular ■ *vi* amontonarse; **in a ~** en un montón; **to ~ into** (*car*) meterse en
▸ **pile on** *vt*: **to ~ it on** (*col*) exagerar
piles [paɪlz] *npl* (*Med*) almorranas *fpl*, hemorroides *mpl*
pile-up [ˈpaɪlʌp] *n* (*Aut*) accidente *m* múltiple
pilfer [ˈpɪlfəʳ] *vt, vi* ratear, robar, sisar
pilfering [ˈpɪlfərɪŋ] *n* ratería
pilgrim [ˈpɪlgrɪm] *n* peregrino(-a); **the P~ Fathers** *or* **Pilgrims** *los primeros colonos norteamericanos*; *see also* **Thanksgiving**
pilgrimage [ˈpɪlgrɪmɪdʒ] *n* peregrinación *f*, romería
pill [pɪl] *n* píldora; **the ~** la píldora; **to be on the ~** tomar la píldora (anticonceptiva)
pillage [ˈpɪlɪdʒ] *vt* pillar, saquear
pillar [ˈpɪləʳ] *n* pilar *m*, columna
pillar box *n* (*Brit*) buzón *m*
pillion [ˈpɪljən] *n* (*of motorcycle*) asiento trasero; **to ride ~** ir en el asiento trasero
pillion passenger *n* pasajero que va detrás
pillory [ˈpɪlərɪ] *vt* poner en ridículo
pillow [ˈpɪləu] *n* almohada
pillowcase [ˈpɪləukeɪs], **pillowslip** [ˈpɪləuslɪp] *n* funda (de almohada)
pilot [ˈpaɪlət] *n* piloto *inv* ■ *adj* (*scheme etc*) piloto ■ *vt* pilotar; (*fig*) guiar, conducir
pilot light *n* piloto
pimento [pɪˈmɛntəu] *n* pimiento morrón
pimp [pɪmp] *n* chulo, cafiche *m* (*LAm*)
pimple [ˈpɪmpl] *n* grano
pimply [ˈpɪmplɪ] *adj* lleno de granos
PIN *n abbr* (*= personal identification number*) NPI *m*
pin [pɪn] *n* alfiler *m*; (*Elec: of plug*) clavija; (*Tech*) perno; (*: wooden*) clavija; (*drawing pin*) chincheta; (*in grenade*) percutor *m* ■ *vt* prender con (alfiler); sujetar con perno; **pins and needles** hormigueo *sg*; **to ~ sth on sb** (*fig*) cargar a algn con la culpa de algo
▸ **pin down** *vt* (*fig*): **there's something strange here, but I can't quite ~ it down** aquí hay algo raro pero no puedo precisar qué es; **to ~ sb down** hacer que algn concrete
pinafore [ˈpɪnəfɔːʳ] *n* delantal *m*
pinafore dress *n* (*Brit*) pichi *m*
pinball [ˈpɪnbɔːl] *n* (*also*: **pinball machine**) millón *m*, fliper *m*
pincers [ˈpɪnsəz] *npl* pinzas *fpl*, tenazas *fpl*
pinch [pɪntʃ] *n* pellizco; (*of salt etc*) pizca ■ *vt* pellizcar; (*col: steal*) birlar ■ *vi* (*shoe*) apretar; **at a ~** en caso de apuro; **to feel the ~** (*fig*) pasar apuros *or* estrecheces
pinched [pɪntʃt] *adj* (*drawn*) cansado; **~ with**

cold transido de frío; **~ for money/space** mal *or* falto de dinero/espacio *or* sitio
pincushion ['pɪnkuʃən] *n* acerico
pine [paɪn] *n* (*also*: **pine tree**) pino ■ *vi*: **to ~ for** suspirar por
▸ **pine away** *vi* morirse de pena
pineapple ['paɪnæpl] *n* piña, ananá(s) *m* (*LAm*)
pine cone *n* piña
pine needle *n* aguja de pino
Ping-Pong® ['pɪŋpɔŋ] *n* pingpong *m*
pink [pɪŋk] *adj* (de color) rosa ■ *n* (*colour*) rosa; (*Bot*) clavel *m*
pinking shears ['pɪŋkɪŋ-] *npl* tijeras *fpl* dentadas
pin money *n* dinero para gastos extra
pinnacle ['pɪnəkl] *n* cumbre *f*
pinpoint ['pɪnpɔɪnt] *vt* precisar
pinstripe ['pɪnstraɪp] *adj*: **~ suit** traje *m* a rayas
pint [paɪnt] *n* (*Brit*) pinta (= *0,57 l*); (*US*) pinta (= *0,47 l*); (*Brit col*: *of beer*) pinta de cerveza, ≈ jarra (*SP*)
pin-up ['pɪnʌp] *n* (*picture*) *fotografía de mujer u hombre medio desnudos*; **~ (girl)** ≈ chica de calendario
pioneer [paɪə'nɪəʳ] *n* pionero(-a) ■ *vt* promover
pious ['paɪəs] *adj* piadoso, devoto
pip [pɪp] *n* (*seed*) pepita; **the pips** (*Brit Tel*) la señal
pipe [paɪp] *n* tubería, cañería; (*for smoking*) pipa, cachimba (*LAm*), cachimbo (*LAm*) ■ *vt* conducir en cañerías; **(bag)pipes** *npl* gaita *sg*
▸ **pipe down** *vi* (*col*) callarse
pipe cleaner *n* limpiapipas *m inv*
piped music [paɪpt-] *n* música ambiental
pipe dream *n* sueño imposible
pipeline ['paɪplaɪn] *n* tubería, cañería; (*for oil*) oleoducto; (*for natural gas*) gaseoducto; **it is in the ~** (*fig*) está en trámite
piper ['paɪpəʳ] *n* (*gen*) flautista *m/f*; (*with bagpipes*) gaitero(-a)
pipe tobacco *n* tabaco de pipa
piping ['paɪpɪŋ] *adv*: **to be ~ hot** estar calentito
piquant ['pi:kənt] *adj* picante
pique [pi:k] *n* pique *m*, resentimiento
pirate ['paɪərət] *n* pirata *m/f* ■ *vt* (*record, video, book*) hacer una copia pirata de
pirated ['paɪərətɪd] *adj* (*book, record etc*) pirata *inv*
pirate radio *n* (*Brit*) emisora pirata
pirouette [pɪru'ɛt] *n* pirueta ■ *vi* piruetear
Pisces ['paɪsi:z] *n* Piscis *m*
piss [pɪs] *vi* (*col*) mear
pissed [pɪst] *adj* (*col*: *drunk*) mamado
pistol ['pɪstl] *n* pistola
piston ['pɪstən] *n* pistón *m*, émbolo
pit [pɪt] *n* hoyo; (*also*: **coal pit**) mina; (*in garage*) foso de inspección; (*also*: **orchestra pit**) foso de la orquesta; (*quarry*) cantera ■ *vt* (*chickenpox*) picar; (*rust*) comer; **to ~ A against B** oponer A a B; **pits** *npl* (*Aut*) box *msg*; **pitted with** (*chickenpox*) picado de
pitapat ['pɪtə'pæt] *adv*: **to go ~** (*heart*) latir rápidamente; (*rain*) golpetear
pitch [pɪtʃ] *n* (*throw*) lanzamiento; (*Mus*) tono; (*Brit Sport*) campo, terreno; (*tar*) brea; (*in market etc*) puesto; (*fig*: *degree*) nivel *m*, grado ■ *vt* (*throw*) arrojar, lanzar ■ *vi* (*fall*) caer(se); (*Naut*) cabecear; **I can't keep working at this ~** no puedo seguir trabajando a este ritmo; **at its (highest) ~** en su punto máximo; **his anger reached such a ~ that ...** su ira *or* cólera llegó a tal extremo que ...; **to ~ a tent** montar una tienda (de campaña); **to ~ one's aspirations too high** tener ambiciones desmesuradas
pitch-black ['pɪtʃ'blæk] *adj* negro como boca de lobo
pitched battle [pɪtʃt-] *n* batalla campal
pitcher ['pɪtʃəʳ] *n* cántaro, jarro
pitchfork ['pɪtʃfɔ:k] *n* horca
piteous ['pɪtɪəs] *adj* lastimoso
pitfall ['pɪtfɔ:l] *n* riesgo
pith [pɪθ] *n* (*of orange*) piel *f* blanca; (*fig*) meollo
pithead ['pɪthɛd] *n* (*Brit*) bocamina
pithy ['pɪθɪ] *adj* jugoso
pitiful ['pɪtɪful] *adj* (*touching*) lastimoso, conmovedor(a); (*contemptible*) lamentable
pitifully ['pɪtɪfəlɪ] *adv*: **it's ~ obvious** es tan evidente que da pena
pitiless ['pɪtɪlɪs] *adj* despiadado, implacable
pitilessly ['pɪtɪlɪslɪ] *adv* despiadadamente, implacablemente
pittance ['pɪtns] *n* miseria
pity ['pɪtɪ] *n* (*compassion*) compasión *f*, piedad *f*; (*shame*) lástima ■ *vt* compadecer(se de); **to have** *or* **take ~ on sb** compadecerse de algn; **what a ~!** ¡qué pena!; **it is a ~ that you can't come** ¡qué pena que no puedas venir!
pitying ['pɪtɪɪŋ] *adj* compasivo, de lástima
pivot ['pɪvət] *n* eje *m* ■ *vi*: **to ~ on** girar sobre; (*fig*) depender de
pixel ['pɪksl] *n* (*Comput*) pixel *m*, punto
pixie ['pɪksɪ] *n* duendecillo
pizza ['pi:tsə] *n* pizza
placard ['plækɑ:d] *n* (*in march etc*) pancarta
placate [plə'keɪt] *vt* apaciguar
place [pleɪs] *n* lugar *m*, sitio; (*rank*) rango; (*seat*) plaza, asiento; (*post*) puesto; (*in street names*) plaza; (*home*): **at/to his ~** en/a su

casa ▪ *vt* (*object*) poner, colocar; (*identify*) reconocer; (*find a post for*) dar un puesto a, colocar; (*goods*) vender; **to take ~** tener lugar; **to be placed** (*in race, exam*) colocarse; **out of ~** (*not suitable*) fuera de lugar; **in the first ~** (*first of all*) en primer lugar; **to change places with sb** cambiarse de sitio con algn; **from ~ to ~** de un sitio a *or* para otro; **all over the ~** por todas partes; **he's going places** (*fig, col*) llegará lejos; **I feel rather out of ~ here** me encuentro algo desplazado; **to put sb in his ~** (*fig*) poner a algn en su lugar; **it is not my ~ to do it** no me incumbe a mí hacerlo; **to ~ an order with sb (for)** hacer un pedido a algn (de); **we are better placed than a month ago** estamos en mejor posición que hace un mes

placebo [plə'si:bəu] *n* placebo

place mat *n* (*wooden etc*) salvamanteles *m inv*; (*in linen etc*) mantel *m* individual

placement ['pleɪsmənt] *n* colocación *f*

place name *n* topónimo

placid ['plæsɪd] *adj* apacible, plácido

placidity [plæ'sɪdɪtɪ] *n* placidez *f*

plagiarism ['pleɪdʒjərɪzm] *n* plagio

plagiarist ['pleɪdʒjərɪst] *n* plagiario(-a)

plagiarize ['pleɪdʒjəraɪz] *vt* plagiar

plague [pleɪg] *n* plaga; (*Med*) peste *f* ▪ *vt* (*fig*) acosar, atormentar; **to ~ sb with questions** acribillar a algn a preguntas

plaice [pleɪs] *n pl inv* platija

plaid [plæd] *n* (*material*) tela de cuadros

plain [pleɪn] *adj* (*clear*) claro, evidente; (*simple*) sencillo; (*frank*) franco, abierto; (*not handsome*) poco atractivo; (*pure*) natural, puro ▪ *adv* claramente ▪ *n* llano, llanura; **in ~ clothes** (*police*) vestido de paisano; **to make sth ~ to sb** dejar algo en claro a algn

plain chocolate *n* chocolate *m* oscuro *or* amargo

plainly ['pleɪnlɪ] *adv* claramente, evidentemente; (*frankly*) francamente

plainness ['pleɪnnɪs] *n* (*clarity*) claridad *f*; (*simplicity*) sencillez *f*; (*of face*) falta de atractivo

plain speaking *n*: **there has been some ~** se ha hablado claro

plaintiff ['pleɪntɪf] *n* demandante *m/f*

plaintive ['pleɪntɪv] *adj* (*cry, voice*) lastimero, quejumbroso; (*look*) que da lástima

plait [plæt] *n* trenza ▪ *vt* trenzar

plan [plæn] *n* (*drawing*) plano; (*scheme*) plan *m*, proyecto ▪ *vt* (*think*) pensar; (*prepare*) proyectar, planear; (*intend*) pensar, tener la intención de ▪ *vi* hacer proyectos; **have you any plans for today?** ¿piensas hacer algo hoy?; **to ~ to do** pensar hacer; **how long do you ~ to stay?** ¿cuánto tiempo piensas quedarte?; **to ~ (for)** planear, proyectar
▸ **plan out** *vt* planear detalladamente

plane [pleɪn] *n* (*Aviat*) avión *m*; (*tree*) plátano; (*tool*) cepillo; (*Math*) plano

planet ['plænɪt] *n* planeta *m*

planetarium [plænɪ'tɛərɪəm] *n* planetario

planetary ['plænɪtərɪ] *adj* planetario

plank [plæŋk] *n* tabla

plankton ['plæŋktən] *n* plancton *m*

planned economy [plænd-] *n* economía planificada

planner ['plænəʳ] *n* planificador(-a) *m(f)*; (*chart*) diagrama *m* de planificación; **town ~** urbanista *m/f*

planning ['plænɪŋ] *n* (*Pol, Econ*) planificación *f*; **family ~** planificación familiar

planning committee *n* (*in local government*) comité *m* de planificación

planning permission *n* licencia de obras

plant [plɑ:nt] *n* planta; (*machinery*) maquinaria; (*factory*) fábrica ▪ *vt* plantar; (*field*) sembrar; (*bomb*) colocar

plantain ['plænteɪn] *n* llantén *m*

plantation [plæn'teɪʃən] *n* plantación *f*; (*estate*) hacienda

planter ['plɑ:ntəʳ] *n* hacendado

plant pot *n* maceta, tiesto

plaque [plæk] *n* placa

plasma ['plæzmə] *n* plasma *m*

plaster ['plɑ:stəʳ] *n* (*for walls*) yeso; (*also*: **plaster of Paris**) yeso mate; (*Med: for broken leg etc*) escayola; (*Brit: also*: **sticking plaster**) tirita, esparadrapo ▪ *vt* enyesar; (*cover*): **to ~ with** llenar *or* cubrir de; **to be plastered with mud** estar cubierto de barro

plasterboard ['plɑ:stəbɔ:d] *n* cartón *m* yeso

plaster cast *n* (*Med*) escayola; (*model, statue*) vaciado de yeso

plastered ['plɑ:stəd] *adj* (*col*) borracho

plasterer ['plɑ:stərəʳ] *n* yesero

plastic ['plæstɪk] *n* plástico ▪ *adj* de plástico

plastic bag *n* bolsa de plástico

plastic bullet *n* bala de goma

plastic explosive *n* goma 2®

plasticine® ['plæstɪsi:n] *n* (*Brit*) plastilina®

plastic surgery *n* cirugía plástica

plastinate ['plæstɪneɪt] *vt* plastinar

plate [pleɪt] *n* (*dish*) plato; (*metal, in book*) lámina; (*Phot*) placa; (*on door*) placa; (*Aut: also*: **number plate**) matrícula

plateau (*pl* **plateaus** *or* **plateaux**) ['plætəu, -z] *n* meseta, altiplanicie *f*

plateful ['pleɪtful] *n* plato

plate glass *n* vidrio *or* cristal *m* cilindrado

platen ['plætən] *n* (*on typewriter, printer*) rodillo

plate rack *n* escurreplatos *m inv*

platform ['plætfɔ:m] *n* (*Rail*) andén *m*; (*stage*) plataforma; (*at meeting*) tribuna; (*Pol*) programa *m* (electoral); **the train leaves from ~ seven** el tren sale del andén número siete
platform ticket *n* (*Brit*) billete *m* de andén
platinum ['plætɪnəm] *n* platino
platitude ['plætɪtju:d] *n* tópico, lugar *m* común
platonic [plə'tɔnɪk] *adj* platónico
platoon [plə'tu:n] *n* pelotón *m*
platter ['plætəʳ] *n* fuente *f*
plaudits ['plɔ:dɪts] *npl* aplausos *mpl*
plausibility [plɔ:zɪ'bɪlɪtɪ] *n* verosimilitud *f*, credibilidad *f*
plausible ['plɔ:zɪbl] *adj* verosímil; (*person*) convincente
play [pleɪ] *n* (*gen*) juego; (*Theat*) obra ■ *vt* (*game*) jugar; (*instrument*) tocar; (*Theat*) representar; (*: part*) hacer el papel de; (*fig*) desempeñar ■ *vi* jugar; (*frolic*) juguetear; **to ~ safe** ir a lo seguro; **to bring** *or* **call into ~** poner en juego; **to ~ a trick on sb** gastar una broma a algn; **they're playing at soldiers** están jugando a (los) soldados; **to ~ for time** (*fig*) tratar de ganar tiempo; **to ~ into sb's hands** (*fig*) hacerle el juego a algn; **a smile played on his lips** una sonrisa le bailaba en los labios
▸ **play about, play around** *vi* (*person*) hacer el tonto; **to ~ about** *or* **around with** (*fiddle with*) juguetear con; (*idea*) darle vueltas a
▸ **play along** *vi*: **to ~ along with** seguirle el juego a ■ *vt*: **to ~ sb along** (*fig*) jugar con algn
▸ **play back** *vt* poner
▸ **play down** *vt* quitar importancia a
▸ **play on** *vt fus* (*sb's feelings, credulity*) aprovecharse de; **to ~ on sb's nerves** atacarle los nervios a algn
▸ **play up** *vi* (*cause trouble*) dar guerra
playact ['pleɪækt] *vi* (*fig*) hacer comedia *or* teatro
play-acting ['pleɪæktɪŋ] *n* teatro
playboy ['pleɪbɔɪ] *n* playboy *m*
player ['pleɪəʳ] *n* jugador(a) *m(f)*; (*Theat*) actor *m*, actriz *f*; (*Mus*) músico(-a) *m(f)*
playful ['pleɪful] *adj* juguetón(-ona)
playground ['pleɪgraund] *n* (*in school*) patio de recreo
playgroup ['pleɪgru:p] *n* jardín *m* de infancia
playing card ['pleɪɪŋ-] *n* naipe *m*, carta
playing field *n* campo de deportes
playmaker ['pleɪmeɪkəʳ] *n* (*Sport*) *jugador encargado de facilitar buenas jugadas a sus compañeros*
playmate ['pleɪmeɪt] *n* compañero(-a) de juego
play-off ['pleɪɔf] *n* (*Sport*) (partido de) desempate *m*
playpen ['pleɪpɛn] *n* corral *m*
playroom ['pleɪru:m] *n* cuarto de juego
playschool ['pleɪsku:l] *n* = **playgroup**
plaything ['pleɪθɪŋ] *n* juguete *m*
playtime ['pleɪtaɪm] *n* (*Scol*) (hora de) recreo
playwright ['pleɪraɪt] *n* dramaturgo(-a)
plc *abbr* (*Brit: = public limited company*) S.A.
plea [pli:] *n* (*request*) súplica, petición *f*; (*excuse*) pretexto, disculpa; (*Law*) alegato, defensa
plea bargaining *n* (*Law*) *acuerdo entre fiscal y defensor para agilizar los trámites judiciales*
plead [pli:d] *vt* (*Law*): **to ~ sb's case** defender a alguien; (*give as excuse*) poner como pretexto ■ *vi* (*Law*) declararse; (*beg*): **to ~ with sb** suplicar *or* rogar a algn; **to ~ guilty/not guilty** (*defendant*) declararse culpable/inocente; **to ~ for sth** (*beg for*) suplicar algo
pleasant ['plɛznt] *adj* agradable
pleasantly ['plɛzntlɪ] *adv* agradablemente
pleasantries ['plɛzntrɪz] *npl* (*polite remarks*) cortesías *fpl*; **to exchange ~** conversar amablemente
please [pli:z] *vt* (*give pleasure to*) dar gusto a, agradar ■ *vi* (*think fit*): **do as you ~** haz lo que quieras *or* lo que te dé la gana; **to ~ o.s.** hacer lo que le parezca; **~!** ¡por favor!; **~ yourself!** ¡haz lo que quieras!, ¡como quieras!; **~ don't cry!** ¡no llores! te lo ruego
pleased [pli:zd] *adj* (*happy*) alegre, contento; (*satisfied*): **~ (with)** satisfecho (de); **~ to meet you** (*col*) ¡encantado!, ¡tanto *or* mucho gusto!; **to be ~ (about sth)** alegrarse (de algo); **we are ~ to inform you that ...** tenemos el gusto de comunicarle que ...
pleasing ['pli:zɪŋ] *adj* agradable, grato
pleasurable ['plɛʒərəbl] *adj* agradable, grato
pleasurably ['plɛʒərəblɪ] *adv* agradablemente, gratamente
pleasure ['plɛʒəʳ] *n* placer *m*, gusto; (*will*) voluntad *f* ■ *cpd* de recreo; **"it's a ~"** "el gusto es mío"; **it's a ~ to see him** da gusto verle; **I have much ~ in informing you that ...** tengo el gran placer de comunicarles que ...; **with ~** con mucho *or* todo gusto; **is this trip for business or ~?** ¿este viaje es de negocios o de placer?
pleasure cruise *n* crucero de placer
pleasure ground *n* parque *m* de atracciones
pleasure-seeking ['plɛʒəsi:kɪŋ] *adj* hedonista
pleat [pli:t] *n* pliegue *m*
pleb [plɛb] *n*: **the plebs** la gente baja, la plebe

plebeian [plɪ'bi:ən] *n* plebeyo(-a) ■ *adj* plebeyo; (*pej*) ordinario
plebiscite ['plɛbɪsɪt] *n* plebiscito
plectrum ['plɛktrəm] *n* plectro
pledge [plɛdʒ] *n* (*object*) prenda; (*promise*) promesa, voto ■ *vt* (*pawn*) empeñar; (*promise*) prometer; **to ~ support for sb** prometer su apoyo a algn; **to ~ sb to secrecy** hacer jurar a algn que guardará el secreto
plenary ['pli:nərɪ] *adj*: **in ~ session** en sesión plenaria
plentiful ['plɛntɪful] *adj* copioso, abundante
plenty ['plɛntɪ] *n* abundancia; **~ of** mucho(s)(-a(s)); **we've got ~ of time to get there** tenemos tiempo de sobra para llegar
plethora ['plɛθərə] *n* plétora
pleurisy ['pluərɪsɪ] *n* pleuresía
pliability [plaɪə'bɪlɪtɪ] *n* flexibilidad *f*
pliable ['plaɪəbl] *adj* flexible
pliers ['plaɪəz] *npl* alicates *mpl*, tenazas *fpl*
plight [plaɪt] *n* condición *f or* situación *f* difícil
plimsolls ['plɪmsəlz] *npl* (*Brit*) zapatillas *fpl* de tenis
plinth [plɪnθ] *n* plinto
PLO *n abbr* (*= Palestine Liberation Organization*) OLP *f*
plod [plɔd] *vi* caminar con paso pesado; (*fig*) trabajar laboriosamente
plodder ['plɔdə^r] *n trabajador(a) diligente pero lento/a*
plodding ['plɔdɪŋ] *adj* (*student*) empollón(-ona); (*worker*) más aplicado que brillante
plonk [plɔŋk] (*col*) *n* (*Brit: wine*) vino peleón ■ *vt*: **to ~ sth down** dejar caer algo
plot [plɔt] *n* (*scheme*) complot *m*, conjura; (*of story, play*) argumento; (*of land*) terreno, parcela ■ *vt* (*mark out*) trazar; (*conspire*) tramar, urdir ■ *vi* conspirar; **a vegetable ~** un cuadro de hortalizas
plotter ['plɔtə^r] *n* (*instrument*) trazador *m* (de gráficos)
plotting ['plɔtɪŋ] *n* conspiración *f*, intrigas *fpl*
plough, plow (US) [plau] *n* arado ■ *vt* (*earth*) arar
▸ **plough back** *vt* (*Comm*) reinvertir
▸ **plough through** *vt fus* (*crowd*) abrirse paso a la fuerza por
ploughing ['plauɪŋ] *n* labranza
ploughman ['plaumən] *n*: **~'s lunch** pan *m* con queso y cebolla
plow [plau] (US) = **plough**
ploy [plɔɪ] *n* truco, estratagema
pluck [plʌk] *vt* (*fruit*) coger (*SP*), recoger (*LAm*); (*musical instrument*) puntear; (*bird*) desplumar ■ *n* valor *m*, ánimo; **to ~ up courage** hacer de tripas corazón; **to ~ one's eyebrows** depilarse las cejas
plucky ['plʌkɪ] *adj* valiente
plug [plʌg] *n* tapón *m*; (*Elec*) enchufe *m*, clavija; (*Aut: also:* **spark(ing) plug**) bujía ■ *vt* (*hole*) tapar; (*col: advertise*) dar publicidad a; **to give sb/sth a ~** dar publicidad a algn/algo; **to ~ a lead into a socket** enchufar un hilo en una toma
▸ **plug in** *vt, vi* (*Elec*) enchufar
plughole ['plʌghəul] *n* desagüe *m*
plum [plʌm] *n* (*fruit*) ciruela; (*also:* **plum job**) chollo
plumage ['plu:mɪdʒ] *n* plumaje *m*
plumb [plʌm] *adj* vertical ■ *n* plomo ■ *adv* (*exactly*) exactamente, en punto ■ *vt* sondar; (*fig*) sondear
▸ **plumb in** *vt* (*washing machine*) conectar
plumber ['plʌmə^r] *n* fontanero(-a), plomero(-a) (*LAm*)
plumbing ['plʌmɪŋ] *n* (*trade*) fontanería, plomería (*LAm*); (*piping*) cañerías
plume [plu:m] *n* (*gen*) pluma; (*on helmet*) penacho
plummet ['plʌmɪt] *vi*: **to ~ (down)** caer a plomo
plump [plʌmp] *adj* rechoncho, rollizo ■ *vt*: **to ~ sth (down) on** dejar caer algo en
▸ **plump for** *vt fus* (*col: choose*) optar por
▸ **plump up** *vt* ahuecar
plumpness ['plʌmpnɪs] *n* gordura
plunder ['plʌndə^r] *n* pillaje *m*; (*loot*) botín *m* ■ *vt* saquear, pillar
plunge [plʌndʒ] *n* zambullida ■ *vt* sumergir, hundir ■ *vi* (*fall*) caer; (*dive*) saltar; (*person*) arrojarse; (*sink*) hundirse; **to take the ~** lanzarse; **to ~ a room into darkness** sumir una habitación en la oscuridad
plunger ['plʌndʒə^r] *n* émbolo; (*for drain*) desatascador *m*
plunging ['plʌndʒɪŋ] *adj* (*neckline*) escotado
pluperfect [plu:'pə:fɪkt] *n* pluscuamperfecto
plural ['pluərl] *n* plural *m*
plus [plʌs] *n* (*also:* **plus sign**) signo más; (*fig*) punto a favor ■ *adj*: **a ~ factor** (*fig*) un factor *m* a favor ■ *prep* más, y, además de; **ten/twenty ~** más de diez/veinte
plush [plʌʃ] *adj* de felpa
plutonium [plu:'təunɪəm] *n* plutonio
ply [plaɪ] *vt* (*a trade*) ejercer ■ *vi* (*ship*) ir y venir; (*for hire*) ofrecerse (para alquilar); **three ~** (*wool*) de tres cabos; **to ~ sb with drink** no dejar de ofrecer copas a algn
plywood ['plaɪwud] *n* madera contrachapada
PM *n abbr* (*Brit*) *see* **Prime Minister**
p.m. *adv abbr* (*= post meridiem*) de la tarde *or* noche

PMS *n abbr* (= *premenstrual syndrome*) SPM *m*
PMT *n abbr* (= *premenstrual tension*) SPM *m*
pneumatic [nju:ˈmætɪk] *adj* neumático
pneumatic drill *n* taladradora neumática
pneumonia [nju:ˈməunɪə] *n* pulmonía, neumonía
PO *n abbr* (= *Post Office*) Correos *mpl*; (*Naut*) = **petty officer**
po *abbr* = **postal order**
POA *n abbr* (*Brit*) = **Prison Officers' Association**
poach [pəutʃ] *vt* (*cook*) escalfar; (*steal*) cazar/pescar en vedado ■ *vi* cazar/pescar en vedado
poached [pəutʃt] *adj* (*egg*) escalfado
poacher [ˈpəutʃəʳ] *n* cazador(a) *m(f)* furtivo(-a)
poaching [ˈpəutʃɪŋ] *n* caza/pesca furtiva
PO Box *n abbr see* **Post Office Box**
pocket [ˈpɔkɪt] *n* bolsillo; (*of air,: Geo*) bolsa; (*fig*) bolsa; (*Billiards*) tronera ■ *vt* meter en el bolsillo; (*steal*) embolsarse; (*Billiards*) entronerar; **breast ~** bolsillo de pecho; **~ of resistance** foco de resistencia; **~ of warm air** bolsa de aire caliente; **to be out of ~** salir perdiendo; **to be £5 in/out of ~** salir ganando/perdiendo 5 libras
pocketbook [ˈpɔkɪtbuk] *n* (*US: wallet*) cartera; (*: handbag*) bolso
pocketful [ˈpɔkɪtful] *n* bolsillo lleno
pocket knife *n* navaja
pocket money *n* asignación *f*
pockmarked [ˈpɔkma:kt] *adj* (*face*) picado de viruelas
pod [pɔd] *n* vaina
podcast [ˈpɔdka:st] *n* podcast *m* ■ *vi* podcastear
podcasting [ˈpɔdka:stɪŋ] *n* podcasting *m*
podgy [ˈpɔdʒɪ] *adj* gordinflón(-ona)
podiatrist [pɔˈdi:ətrɪst] *n* (*US*) podólogo(-a)
podiatry [pɔˈdi:ətrɪ] *n* (*US*) podología
podium [ˈpəudɪəm] *n* podio
POE *n abbr* = **port of embarkation; port of entry**
poem [ˈpəuɪm] *n* poema *m*
poet [ˈpəuɪt] *n* poeta *m/f*
poetic [pəuˈɛtɪk] *adj* poético
poet laureate [-ˈlɔ:rɪɪt] *n* poeta *m* laureado; *ver nota*

POET LAUREATE

El poeta de la corte, denominado *Poet Laureate*, ocupa como tal un puesto vitalicio al servicio de la Casa Real británica. Era tradición que escribiera poemas conmemorativos para ocasiones oficiales, aunque hoy día esto es poco frecuente. El primer poeta así distinguido fue Ben Jonson, en 1616.

poetry [ˈpəuɪtrɪ] *n* poesía
poignant [ˈpɔɪnjənt] *adj* conmovedor(a)
poignantly [ˈpɔɪnjəntlɪ] *adv* de modo conmovedor
point [pɔɪnt] *n* punto; (*tip*) punta; (*purpose*) fin *m*, propósito; (*Brit Elec: also:* **power point**) toma de corriente, enchufe *m*; (*use*) utilidad *f*; (*significant part*) lo esencial; (*place*) punto, lugar *m*; (*also:* **decimal point**): **2 ~ 3 (2.3)** dos coma tres (2,3) ■ *vt* (*gun etc*): **to ~ sth at sb** apuntar con algo a algn ■ *vi* señalar con el dedo; **points** *npl* (*Aut*) contactos *mpl*; (*Rail*) agujas *fpl*; **to be on the ~ of doing sth** estar a punto de hacer algo; **to make a ~ of doing sth** poner empeño en hacer algo; **to get the ~** comprender; **to come to the ~** ir al meollo; **there's no ~ (in doing)** no tiene sentido (hacer); **~ of departure** (*also fig*) punto de partida; **~ of order** cuestión *f* de procedimiento; **~ of sale** (*Comm*) punto de venta; **~-of-sale advertising** publicidad *f* en el punto de venta; **the train stops at Carlisle and all points south** el tren para en Carlisle, y en todas las estaciones al sur; **when it comes to the ~** a la hora de la verdad; **in ~ of fact** en realidad; **that's the whole ~!** ¡de eso se trata!; **to be beside the ~** no venir al caso; **you've got a ~ there!** ¡tienes razón!
▸ **point out** *vt* señalar
▸ **point to** *vt fus* indicar con el dedo; (*fig*) indicar, señalar
point-blank [ˈpɔɪntˈblæŋk] *adv* (*also:* **at point-blank range**) a quemarropa
point duty *n* (*Brit*) control *m* de circulación
pointed [ˈpɔɪntɪd] *adj* (*shape*) puntiagudo, afilado; (*remark*) intencionado
pointedly [ˈpɔɪntɪdlɪ] *adv* intencionadamente
pointer [ˈpɔɪntəʳ] *n* (*stick*) puntero; (*needle*) aguja, indicador *m*; (*clue*) indicación *f*, pista; (*advice*) consejo
pointless [ˈpɔɪntlɪs] *adj* sin sentido
pointlessly [ˈpɔɪntlɪslɪ] *adv* inútilmente, sin motivo
point of view *n* punto de vista
poise [pɔɪz] *n* (*of head, body*) porte *m*; (*calmness*) aplomo
poised [pɔɪzd] *adj* (*in temperament*) sereno
poison [ˈpɔɪzn] *n* veneno ■ *vt* envenenar
poisoning [ˈpɔɪznɪŋ] *n* envenenamiento
poisonous [ˈpɔɪznəs] *adj* venenoso; (*fumes etc*) tóxico; (*fig: ideas, literature*) pernicioso; (*: rumours, individual*) nefasto

poke [pəuk] *vt* (*fire*) hurgar, atizar; (*jab with finger, stick etc*) dar; (*Comput*) almacenar; (*put*): **to ~ sth in(to)** introducir algo en ■ *n* (*jab*) empujoncito; (*with elbow*) codazo; **to ~ one's head out of the window** asomar la cabeza por la ventana; **to ~ fun at sb** ridiculizar a algn; **to give the fire a ~** atizar el fuego
▸ **poke about** *vi* fisgonear
poker ['pəukə^r] *n* atizador *m*; (*Cards*) póker *m*
poker-faced ['pəukə'feɪst] *adj* de cara impasible
poky ['pəukɪ] *adj* estrecho
Poland ['pəulənd] *n* Polonia
polar ['pəulə^r] *adj* polar
polar bear *n* oso polar
polarization [pəulərаɪ'zeɪʃən] *n* polarización *f*
polarize ['pəuləraɪz] *vt* polarizar
Pole [pəul] *n* polaco(-a)
pole [pəul] *n* palo; (*Geo*) polo; (*Tel*) poste *m*; (*flagpole*) asta; (*tent pole*) mástil *m*
poleaxe ['pəulæks] *vt* (*fig*) desnucar
pole bean *n* (*US*) judía trepadora
polecat ['pəulkæt] *n* (*Brit*) turón *m*; (*US*) mofeta
Pol. Econ. ['pɔlɪkɔn] *n abbr* = **political economy**
polemic [pɔ'lɛmɪk] *n* polémica
polemicist [pɔ'lɛmɪsɪst] *n* polemista *m/f*
pole star *n* estrella polar
pole vault *n* salto con pértiga
police [pə'li:s] *n* policía ■ *vt* (*streets, city, frontier*) vigilar
police car *n* coche-patrulla *m*
police constable *n* (*Brit*) guardia *m*, policía *m*
police department *n* (*US*) policía
police force *n* cuerpo de policía
policeman [pə'li:smən] *n* guardia *m*, policía *m*, agente *m* (*LAm*)
police officer *n* guardia *m*, policía *m*
police record *n*: **to have a ~** tener antecedentes penales
police state *n* estado policial
police station *n* comisaría
policewoman [pə'li:swumən] *n* mujer *f* policía
policy ['pɔlɪsɪ] *n* política; (*also*: **insurance policy**) póliza; (*of newspaper, company*) política; **it is our ~ to do that** tenemos por norma hacer eso; **to take out a ~** sacar una póliza, hacerse un seguro
policy holder *n* asegurado(-a)
policy-making ['pɔlɪsɪmeɪkɪŋ] *n* elaboración *f* de directrices generales
policy-making body *n* organismo encargado de elaborar las directrices generales
polio ['pəulɪəu] *n* polio *f*
Polish ['pəulɪʃ] *adj* polaco ■ *n* (*Ling*) polaco
polish ['pɔlɪʃ] *n* (*for shoes*) betún *m*; (*for floor*) cera (de lustrar); (*for nails*) esmalte *m*; (*shine*) brillo, lustre *m*; (*fig: refinement*) refinamiento ■ *vt* (*shoes*) limpiar; (*make shiny*) pulir, sacar brillo a; (*fig: improve*) perfeccionar, refinar
▸ **polish off** *vt* (*work*) terminar; (*food*) despachar
▸ **polish up** *vt* (*shoes, furniture etc*) limpiar, sacar brillo a; (*fig: language*) perfeccionar
polished ['pɔlɪʃt] *adj* (*fig: person*) refinado
polite [pə'laɪt] *adj* cortés, atento; (*formal*) correcto; **it's not ~ to do that** es de mala educación hacer eso
politely [pə'laɪtlɪ] *adv* cortésmente
politeness [pə'laɪtnɪs] *n* cortesía
politic ['pɔlɪtɪk] *adj* prudente
political [pə'lɪtɪkl] *adj* político
political asylum *n* asilo político
politically [pə'lɪtɪkəlɪ] *adv* políticamente
politically correct *adj* políticamente correcto
politician [pɔlɪ'tɪʃən] *n* político(-a)
politics ['pɔlɪtɪks] *n* política
polka ['pɔlkə] *n* polca
polka dot *n* lunar *m*
poll [pəul] *n* (*votes*) votación *f*, votos *mpl*; (*also*: **opinion poll**) sondeo, encuesta ■ *vt* (*votes*) obtener; (*in opinion poll*) encuestar; **to go to the polls** (*voters*) votar; (*government*) acudir a las urnas
pollen ['pɔlən] *n* polen *m*
pollen count *n* índice *m* de polen
pollination [pɔlɪ'neɪʃən] *n* polinización *f*
polling ['pəulɪŋ] *n* (*Brit Pol*) votación *f*; (*Tel*) interrogación *f*
polling booth *n* cabina de votar
polling day *n* día *m* de elecciones
polling station *n* centro electoral
pollster ['pəulstə^r] *n* (*person*) encuestador(a) *m(f)*; (*organization*) empresa de encuestas *or* sondeos
poll tax *n* (*Brit*) contribución *f* municipal (*no progresiva*)
pollutant [pə'lu:tənt] *n* (agente *m*) contaminante *m*
pollute [pə'lu:t] *vt* contaminar
pollution [pə'lu:ʃən] *n* contaminación *f*, polución *f*
polo ['pəuləu] *n* (*sport*) polo
polo-neck ['pəuləunɛk] *adj* de cuello vuelto ■ *n* (*sweater*) suéter *m* de cuello vuelto
poly ['pɔlɪ] *n abbr* (*Brit*) = **polytechnic**
poly... [pɔlɪ] *pref* poli...
poly bag *n* (*Brit col*) bolsa de plástico
polyester [pɔlɪ'ɛstə^r] *n* poliéster *m*
polyethylene [pɔlɪ'ɛθɪli:n] *n* (*US*) polietileno

polygamy [pəˈlɪgəmɪ] *n* poligamia
polygraph [ˈpɔlɪgrɑːf] *n* polígrafo
Polynesia [pɔlɪˈniːzɪə] *n* Polinesia
Polynesian [pɔlɪˈniːzɪən] *adj, n* polinesio(-a) *m(f)*
polyp [ˈpɔlɪp] *n* (*Med*) pólipo
polystyrene [pɔlɪˈstaɪriːn] *n* poliestireno
polytechnic [pɔlɪˈtɛknɪk] *n* escuela politécnica
polythene [ˈpɔlɪθiːn] *n* (*Brit*) polietileno
polythene bag *n* bolsa de plástico
polyurethane [pɔlɪˈjuərɪθeɪn] *n* poliuretano
pomegranate [ˈpɔmɪgrænɪt] *n* granada
pommel [ˈpɔml] *n* pomo ■ *vt* = **pummel**
pomp [pɔmp] *n* pompa
pompom [ˈpɔmpɔm] *n* borla
pompous [ˈpɔmpəs] *adj* pomposo; (*person*) presumido
pond [pɔnd] *n* (*natural*) charca; (*artificial*) estanque *m*
ponder [ˈpɔndəʳ] *vt* meditar
ponderous [ˈpɔndərəs] *adj* pesado
pong [pɔŋ] *n* (*Brit col*) peste *f* ■ *vi* (*Brit col*) apestar
pontiff [ˈpɔntɪf] *n* pontífice *m*
pontificate [pɔnˈtɪfɪkeɪt] *vi* (*fig*): **to ~ (about)** pontificar (sobre)
pontoon [pɔnˈtuːn] *n* pontón *m*; (*Brit: card game*) veintiuna
pony [ˈpəunɪ] *n* poney *m*, potro
ponytail [ˈpəunɪteɪl] *n* coleta, cola de caballo
pony trekking *n* (*Brit*) excursión *f* a caballo
poodle [ˈpuːdl] *n* caniche *m*
pool [puːl] *n* (*natural*) charca; (*pond*) estanque *m*; (*also*: **swimming pool**) piscina, alberca (*LAm*); (*billiards*) billar *m* americano; (*Comm: consortium*) consorcio; (*: US: monopoly trust*) trust *m* ■ *vt* juntar; **typing ~** servicio de mecanografía; **(football) pools** *npl* quinielas *fpl*
poor [puəʳ] *adj* pobre; (*bad*) malo ■ *npl*: **the ~** los pobres
poorly [ˈpuəlɪ] *adj* mal, enfermo
pop [pɔp] *n* ¡pum!; (*sound*) ruido seco; (*Mus*) (música) pop *m*; (*US col: father*) papá *m*; (*col: drink*) gaseosa ■ *vt* (*burst*) hacer reventar ■ *vi* reventar; (*cork*) saltar; **she popped her head out (of the window)** sacó de repente la cabeza (por la ventana)
▸ **pop in** *vi* entrar un momento
▸ **pop out** *vi* salir un momento
▸ **pop up** *vi* aparecer inesperadamente
pop concert *n* concierto pop
popcorn [ˈpɔpkɔːn] *n* palomitas *fpl* (de maíz)
pope [pəup] *n* papa *m*
poplar [ˈpɔpləʳ] *n* álamo
poplin [ˈpɔplɪn] *n* popelina
popper [ˈpɔpəʳ] *n* corchete *m*, botón *m* automático
poppy [ˈpɔpɪ] *n* amapola; *see also* **Remembrance Sunday**
poppycock [ˈpɔpɪkɔk] *n* (*col*) tonterías *fpl*
Popsicle® [ˈpɔpsɪkl] *n* (*US*) polo
populace [ˈpɔpjuləs] *n* pueblo
popular [ˈpɔpjuləʳ] *adj* popular; **a ~ song** una canción popular; **to be ~ (with)** (*person*) caer bien (a); (*decision*) ser popular (entre)
popularity [pɔpjuˈlærɪtɪ] *n* popularidad *f*
popularize [ˈpɔpjuləraɪz] *vt* popularizar; (*disseminate*) vulgarizar
populate [ˈpɔpjuleɪt] *vt* poblar
population [pɔpjuˈleɪʃən] *n* población *f*
population explosion *n* explosión *f* demográfica
populous [ˈpɔpjuləs] *adj* populoso
pop-up menu [ˈpɔpʌp-] *n* (*Comput*) menú *m* emergente
porcelain [ˈpɔːslɪn] *n* porcelana
porch [pɔːtʃ] *n* pórtico, entrada
porcupine [ˈpɔːkjupaɪn] *n* puerco *m* espín
pore [pɔːʳ] *n* poro ■ *vi*: **to ~ over** enfrascarse en
pork [pɔːk] *n* (carne *f* de) cerdo *or* chancho (*LAm*)
pork chop *n* chuleta de cerdo
porn [pɔːn] *adj* (*col*) porno *inv* ■ *n* porno
pornographic [pɔːnəˈgræfɪk] *adj* pornográfico
pornography [pɔːˈnɔgrəfɪ] *n* pornografía
porous [ˈpɔːrəs] *adj* poroso
porpoise [ˈpɔːpəs] *n* marsopa
porridge [ˈpɔrɪdʒ] *n* gachas *fpl* de avena
port [pɔːt] *n* (*harbour*) puerto; (*Naut: left side*) babor *m*; (*wine*) oporto; (*Comput*) puerta, puerto, port *m*; **~ of call** puerto de escala
portable [ˈpɔːtəbl] *adj* portátil
portal [ˈpɔːtl] *n* puerta (grande), portalón *m*
port authorities *npl* autoridades *fpl* portuarias
portcullis [pɔːtˈkʌlɪs] *n* rastrillo
portend [pɔːˈtɛnd] *vt* presagiar, anunciar
portent [ˈpɔːtɛnt] *n* presagio, augurio
porter [ˈpɔːtəʳ] *n* (*for luggage*) maletero; (*doorkeeper*) portero(-a), conserje *m/f*; (*US Rail*) mozo de los coches-cama
portfolio [pɔːtˈfəulɪəu] *n* (*case, of artist*) cartera, carpeta; (*Pol, Finance*) cartera
porthole [ˈpɔːthəul] *n* portilla
portico [ˈpɔːtɪkəu] *n* pórtico
portion [ˈpɔːʃən] *n* porción *f*; (*helping*) ración *f*
portly [ˈpɔːtlɪ] *adj* corpulento
portrait [ˈpɔːtreɪt] *n* retrato
portray [pɔːˈtreɪ] *vt* retratar; (*in writing*) representar

portrayal [pɔː'treɪəl] *n* representación *f*
Portugal ['pɔːtjugl] *n* Portugal *m*
Portuguese [pɔːtju'giːz] *adj* portugués(-esa) ■ *n pl inv* portugués(-esa) *m(f)*; (*Ling*) portugués *m*
Portuguese man-of-war [-mænəu'wɔːʳ] *n* (*jellyfish*) *especie de medusa*
pose [pəuz] *n* postura, actitud *f*; (*pej*) afectación *f*, pose *f* ■ *vi* posar; (*pretend*): **to ~ as** hacerse pasar por ■ *vt* (*question*) plantear; **to strike a ~** tomar *or* adoptar una pose *or* actitud
poser ['pəuzəʳ] *n* problema *m*/pregunta difícil; (*person*) = **poseur**
poseur [pəu'zəːʳ] *n* presumido(-a), persona afectada
posh [pɔʃ] *adj* (*col*) elegante, de lujo ■ *adv* (*col*): **to talk ~** hablar con acento afectado
position [pə'zɪʃən] *n* posición *f*; (*job*) puesto ■ *vt* colocar; **to be in a ~ to do sth** estar en condiciones de hacer algo
positive ['pɔzɪtɪv] *adj* positivo; (*certain*) seguro; (*definite*) definitivo; **we look forward to a ~ reply** (*Comm*) esperamos que pueda darnos una respuesta en firme; **he's a ~ nuisance** es un auténtico pelmazo; **~ cash flow** (*Comm*) flujo positivo de efectivo
positively ['pɔzɪtɪvlɪ] *adv* (*affirmatively, enthusiastically*) de forma positiva; (*col: really*) absolutamente
posse ['pɔsɪ] *n* (*US*) pelotón *m*
possess [pə'zɛs] *vt* poseer; **like one possessed** como un poseído; **whatever can have possessed you?** ¿cómo se te ocurrió?
possessed [pə'zɛst] *adj* poseso, poseído
possession [pə'zɛʃən] *n* posesión *f*; **to take ~ of sth** tomar posesión de algo
possessive [pə'zɛsɪv] *adj* posesivo
possessiveness [pə'zɛsɪvnɪs] *n* posesividad *f*
possessor [pə'zɛsəʳ] *n* poseedor(a) *m(f)*, dueño(-a)
possibility [pɔsɪ'bɪlɪtɪ] *n* posibilidad *f*; **he's a ~ for the part** es uno de los posibles para el papel
possible ['pɔsɪbl] *adj* posible; **as big as ~** lo más grande posible; **it is ~ to do it** es posible hacerlo; **as far as ~** en la medida de lo posible; **a ~ candidate** un(a) posible candidato(-a)
possibly ['pɔsɪblɪ] *adv* (*perhaps*) posiblemente, tal vez; **I cannot ~ come** me es imposible venir; **could you ~ ...?** ¿podrías ...?
post [pəust] *n* (*Brit: letters, delivery*) correo; (*job, situation*) puesto; (*trading post*) factoría; (*pole*) poste *m* ■ *vt* (*Brit: send by post*) mandar por correo; (*: put in mailbox*) echar al correo; (*Mil*) apostar; (*bills*) fijar, pegar; (*Brit: appoint*): **to ~ to** destinar a; **by ~** por correo; **by return of ~** a vuelta de correo; **to keep sb posted** tener a algn al corriente
post ... [pəust] *pref* post..., pos...; **post 1950** pos(t) 1950
postage ['pəustɪdʒ] *n* porte *m*, franqueo
postage stamp *n* sello (de correo)
postal ['pəustl] *adj* postal, de correos
postal order *n* giro postal
postbag ['pəustbæg] *n* (*Brit*) correspondencia, cartas *fpl*
postbox ['pəustbɔks] *n* (*Brit*) buzón *m*
postcard ['pəustkɑːd] *n* (tarjeta) postal *f*
postcode ['pəustkəud] *n* (*Brit*) código postal
postdate [pəust'deɪt] *vt* (*cheque*) poner fecha adelantada a
poster ['pəustəʳ] *n* cartel *m*, afiche *m* (*LAm*)
poste restante [pəust'rɛstɔ̃nt] *n* (*Brit*) lista de correos
posterior [pɔs'tɪərɪəʳ] *n* (*col*) trasero
posterity [pɔs'tɛrɪtɪ] *n* posteridad *f*
poster paint *n* pintura al agua
post-free [pəust'friː] *adj* (con) porte pagado
postgraduate ['pəust'grædjuɪt] *n* posgraduado(-a)
posthumous ['pɔstjuməs] *adj* póstumo
posthumously ['pɔstjuməslɪ] *adv* póstumamente, con carácter póstumo
posting ['pəustɪŋ] *n* destino
postman ['pəustmən] *n* cartero
postmark ['pəustmɑːk] *n* matasellos *m inv*
postmaster ['pəustmɑːstəʳ] *n* administrador *m* de correos
Postmaster General *n* director *m* general de correos
postmistress ['pəustmɪstrɪs] *n* administradora de correos
post-mortem [pəust'mɔːtəm] *n* autopsia
postnatal ['pəust'neɪtl] *adj* postnatal, postparto
post office *n* (*building*) (oficina de) correos *m*; (*organization*): **the Post Office** Administración *f* General de Correos
Post Office Box *n* apartado postal, casilla de correos (*LAm*)
post-paid ['pəust'peɪd] *adj* porte pagado
postpone [pəs'pəun] *vt* aplazar, postergar (*LAm*)
postponement [pəs'pəunmənt] *n* aplazamiento
postscript ['pəustskrɪpt] *n* posdata
postulate ['pɔstjuleɪt] *vt* postular
posture ['pɔstʃəʳ] *n* postura, actitud *f*
postwar [pəust'wɔːʳ] *adj* de la posguerra
posy ['pəuzɪ] *n* ramillete *m* (de flores)
pot [pɔt] *n* (*for cooking*) olla; (*for flowers*) maceta; (*for jam*) tarro, pote *m* (*LAm*); (*piece of*

pottery) cacharro; (*col: marijuana*) costo ■ *vt* (*plant*) poner en tiesto; (*conserve*) conservar (en tarros); **pots of** (*col*) montones de; **to go to ~** (*col: work, performance*) irse al traste
potash ['pɔtæʃ] *n* potasa
potassium [pə'tæsɪəm] *n* potasio
potato (*pl* **potatoes**) [pə'teɪtəu] *n* patata, papa (*LAm*)
potato crisps, potato chips (*US*) *npl* patatas *fpl or* papas *fpl* (*LAm*)
potato peeler *n* pelapatatas *m inv*
potbellied ['pɔtbɛlɪd] *adj* (*from overeating*) barrigón(-ona); (*from malnutrition*) con el vientre hinchado
potency ['pəutnsɪ] *n* potencia
potent ['pəutnt] *adj* potente, poderoso; (*drink*) fuerte
potentate ['pəutnteɪt] *n* potentado
potential [pə'tɛnʃl] *adj* potencial, posible ■ *n* potencial *m*; **to have ~** prometer
potentially [pə'tɛnʃəlɪ] *adv* en potencia
pothole ['pɔthəul] *n* (*in road*) bache *m*; (*Brit: underground*) gruta
potholer ['pɔthəuləʳ] *n* (*Brit*) espeleólogo(-a)
potholing ['pɔthəulɪŋ] *n* (*Brit*): **to go ~** dedicarse a la espeleología
potion ['pəuʃən] *n* poción *f*, pócima
potluck [pɔt'lʌk] *n*: **to take ~** conformarse con lo que haya
pot roast *n* carne *f* asada
potshot ['pɔtʃɔt] *n*: **to take a ~ at sth** tirar a algo sin apuntar
potted ['pɔtɪd] *adj* (*food*) en conserva; (*plant*) en tiesto *or* maceta; (*fig: shortened*) resumido
potter ['pɔtəʳ] *n* alfarero(-a) ■ *vi*: **to ~ around, ~ about** entretenerse haciendo cosillas; **to ~ round the house** estar en casa haciendo cosillas; **~'s wheel** torno de alfarero
pottery ['pɔtərɪ] *n* cerámica, alfarería; **a piece of ~** un objeto de cerámica
potty ['pɔtɪ] *adj* (*col: mad*) chiflado ■ *n* orinal *m* de niño
potty-trained ['pɔtɪtreɪnd] *adj* que ya no necesita pañales
pouch [pautʃ] *n* (*Zool*) bolsa; (*for tobacco*) petaca
pouf, pouffe [pu:f] *n* (*stool*) pouf *m*
poultry ['pəultrɪ] *n* aves *fpl* de corral; (*dead*) pollos *mpl*
poultry farm *n* granja avícola
poultry farmer *n* avicultor(-a) *m(f)*
pounce [pauns] *vi*: **to ~ on** precipitarse sobre ■ *n* salto, ataque *m*
pound [paund] *n* libra; (*for dogs*) perrera; (*for cars*) depósito ■ *vt* (*beat*) golpear; (*crush*) machacar ■ *vi* (*beat*) dar golpes; **half a ~** media libra; **a one ~ note** un billete de una libra
pounding ['paundɪŋ] *n*: **to take a ~** (*team*) recibir una paliza
pound sterling *n* libra esterlina
pour [pɔ:ʳ] *vt* echar; (*tea*) servir ■ *vi* correr, fluir; (*rain*) llover a cántaros
▸ **pour away, pour off** *vt* vaciar, verter
▸ **pour in** *vi* (*people*) entrar en tropel; **to come pouring in** (*water*) entrar a raudales; (*letters*) llegar a montones; (*cars, people*) llegar en tropel
▸ **pour out** *vi* (*people*) salir en tropel ■ *vt* (*drink*) echar, servir
pouring ['pɔ:rɪŋ] *adj*: **~ rain** lluvia torrencial
pout [paut] *vi* hacer pucheros
poverty ['pɔvətɪ] *n* pobreza, miseria; (*fig*) falta, escasez *f*
poverty line *n*: **below the ~** por debajo del umbral de pobreza
poverty-stricken ['pɔvətɪstrɪkn] *adj* necesitado
poverty trap *n* trampa de la pobreza
POW *n abbr* = **prisoner of war**
powder ['paudəʳ] *n* polvo; (*also*: **face powder**) polvos *mpl*; (*also*: **gun powder**) pólvora ■ *vt* empolvar; **to ~ one's face** ponerse polvos; **to ~ one's nose** empolvarse la nariz, ponerse polvos; (*euphemism*) ir al baño
powder compact *n* polvera
powdered milk ['paudəd-] *n* leche *f* en polvo
powder keg *n* (*fig*) polvorín *m*
powder puff *n* borla (para empolvarse)
powder room *n* aseos *mpl*
powdery ['paudərɪ] *adj* polvoriento
power ['pauəʳ] *n* poder *m*; (*strength*) fuerza; (*nation*) potencia; (*drive*) empuje *m*; (*Tech*) potencia; (*Elec*) energía ■ *vt* impulsar; **to be in ~** (*Pol*) estar en el poder; **to do all in one's ~ to help sb** hacer todo lo posible por ayudar a algn; **the world powers** las potencias mundiales
powerboat ['pauəbəut] *n* lancha a motor
power cut *n* (*Brit*) apagón *m*
powered ['pauəd] *adj*: **~ by** impulsado por; **nuclear-~ submarine** submarino nuclear
power failure *n* = **power cut**
powerful ['pauəful] *adj* poderoso; (*engine*) potente; (*strong*) fuerte; (*play, speech*) conmovedor(a)
powerhouse ['pauəhaus] *n* (*fig: person*) fuerza motriz; **a ~ of ideas** una cantera de ideas
powerless ['pauəlɪs] *adj* impotente, ineficaz
power line *n* línea de conducción eléctrica
power of attorney *n* poder *m*, procuración *f*
power point *n* (*Brit*) enchufe *m*
power station *n* central *f* eléctrica

power steering *n (Aut)* dirección *f* asistida
powwow ['pauwau] *n* conferencia ■ *vi* conferenciar
pp *abbr (= per procurationem: by proxy)* p.p.; = **pages**
PPE *n abbr (Brit Scol)* = **philosophy, politics, and economics**
PPS *n abbr (= post postscriptum) posdata adicional; (Brit: = Parliamentary Private Secretary) ayudante de un ministro*
PQ *abbr (Canada)* = **Province of Quebec**
PR *n abbr see* **proportional representation**; *(= public relations)* relaciones *fpl* públicas ■ *abbr (US)* = **Puerto Rico**
Pr. *abbr (= prince)* P
practicability [præktɪkə'bɪlɪtɪ] *n* factibilidad *f*
practicable ['præktɪkəbl] *adj (scheme)* factible
practical ['præktɪkl] *adj* práctico
practicality [præktɪ'kælɪtɪ] *n (of situation etc)* aspecto práctico
practical joke *n* broma pesada
practically ['præktɪklɪ] *adv (almost)* casi, prácticamente
practice ['præktɪs] *n (habit)* costumbre *f*; *(exercise)* práctica; *(training)* adiestramiento; *(Med)* clientela ■ *vt, vi (US)* = **practise**; **in ~** *(in reality)* en la práctica; **out of ~** desentrenado; **to put sth into ~** poner algo en práctica; **it's common ~** es bastante corriente; **target ~** práctica de tiro; **he has a small ~** *(doctor)* tiene pocos pacientes; **to set up in ~ as** establecerse como
practise, practice *(US)* ['præktɪs] *vt (carry out)* practicar; *(profession)* ejercer; *(train at)* practicar ■ *vi* ejercer; *(train)* practicar
practised, *(US)* **practiced** ['præktɪst] *adj (person)* experto; *(performance)* bien ensayado; *(liar)* consumado; **with a ~ eye** con ojo experto
practising, practicing *(US)* ['præktɪsɪŋ] *adj (Christian etc)* practicante; *(lawyer)* que ejerce; *(homosexual)* activo
practitioner [præk'tɪʃənəʳ] *n* practicante *m/f*; *(Med)* médico(-a)
pragmatic [præg'mætɪk] *adj* pragmático
pragmatism ['prægmətɪzəm] *n* pragmatismo
pragmatist ['prægmətɪst] *n* pragmatista *m/f*
Prague [prɑ:g] *n* Praga
prairie ['prɛərɪ] *n (US)* pampa
praise [preɪz] *n* alabanza(s) *f(pl)*, elogio(s) *m(pl)*
praiseworthy ['preɪswə:ðɪ] *adj* loable
pram [præm] *n (Brit)* cochecito de niño
prance [prɑ:ns] *vi (horse)* hacer cabriolas
prank [præŋk] *n* travesura
prat [præt] *n (Brit col)* imbécil *m/f*
prattle ['prætl] *vi* parlotear; *(child)* balbucear
prawn [prɔ:n] *n* gamba
pray [preɪ] *vi* rezar; **to ~ for forgiveness** pedir perdón
prayer [prɛəʳ] *n* oración *f*, rezo; *(entreaty)* ruego, súplica
prayer book *n* devocionario, misal *m*
pre- ['pri:] *pref* pre..., ante-; **~1970** pre 1970
preach [pri:tʃ] *vi* predicar
preacher ['pri:tʃəʳ] *n* predicador(a) *m(f)*; *(US: minister)* pastor(a) *m(f)*
preamble [prɪ'æmbl] *n* preámbulo
prearrange [pri:ə'reɪndʒ] *vt* organizar *or* acordar de antemano
prearrangement [pri:ə'reɪndʒmənt] *n*: **by ~** por previo acuerdo
precarious [prɪ'kɛərɪəs] *adj* precario
precariously [prɪ'kɛərɪəslɪ] *adv* precariamente
precaution [prɪ'kɔ:ʃən] *n* precaución *f*
precautionary [prɪ'kɔ:ʃənrɪ] *adj (measure)* de precaución
precede [prɪ'si:d] *vt, vi* preceder
precedence ['prɛsɪdəns] *n* precedencia; *(priority)* preferencia
precedent ['prɛsɪdənt] *n* precedente *m*; **to establish** *or* **set a ~** sentar un precedente
preceding [prɪ'si:dɪŋ] *adj* precedente
precept ['pri:sɛpt] *n* precepto
precinct ['pri:sɪŋkt] *n* recinto; *(US: district)* distrito, barrio; **precincts** *npl* recinto; **pedestrian ~** *(Brit)* zona peatonal; **shopping ~** *(Brit)* centro comercial
precious ['prɛʃəs] *adj* precioso; *(treasured)* querido; *(stylized)* afectado ■ *adv (col)*: **~ little/few** muy poco/pocos; **your ~ dog** *(ironic)* tu querido perro
precipice ['prɛsɪpɪs] *n* precipicio
precipitate *adj* [prɪ'sɪpɪtɪt] *(hasty)* precipitado ■ *vt* [prɪ'sɪpɪteɪt] precipitar
precipitation [prɪsɪpɪ'teɪʃən] *n* precipitación *f*
precipitous [prɪ'sɪpɪtəs] *adj (steep)* escarpado; *(hasty)* precipitado
précis ['preɪsi:] *n* resumen *m*
precise [prɪ'saɪs] *adj* preciso, exacto; *(person)* escrupuloso
precisely [prɪ'saɪslɪ] *adv* exactamente, precisamente
precision [prɪ'sɪʒən] *n* precisión *f*
preclude [prɪ'klu:d] *vt* excluir
precocious [prɪ'kəuʃəs] *adj* precoz
preconceived [pri:kən'si:vd] *adj (idea)* preconcebido
preconception [pri:kən'sɛpʃən] *n (idea)* idea preconcebida

precondition [pri:kən'dɪʃən] *n* condición *f* previa
precursor [pri:'kə:sə[r]] *n* precursor(a) *m(f)*
predate ['pri:'deɪt] *vt* (*precede*) preceder
predator ['prɛdətə[r]] *n* depredador *m*
predatory ['prɛdətərɪ] *adj* depredador(a)
predecessor ['pri:dɪsɛsə[r]] *n* antecesor(a) *m(f)*
predestination [pri:dɛstɪ'neɪʃən] *n* predestinación *f*
predestine [pri:'dɛstɪn] *vt* predestinar
predetermine [pri:dɪ'tə:mɪn] *vt* predeterminar
predicament [prɪ'dɪkəmənt] *n* apuro
predicate ['prɛdɪkɪt] *n* predicado
predict [prɪ'dɪkt] *vt* predecir, pronosticar
predictable [prɪ'dɪktəbl] *adj* previsible
predictably [prɪ'dɪktəblɪ] *adv* (*behave, react*) de forma previsible; **~ she didn't arrive** como era de prever, no llegó
prediction [prɪ'dɪkʃən] *n* pronóstico, predicción *f*
predispose ['pri:dɪs'pəuz] *vt* predisponer
predominance [prɪ'dɔmɪnəns] *n* predominio
predominant [prɪ'dɔmɪnənt] *adj* predominante
predominantly [prɪ'dɔmɪnəntlɪ] *adv* en su mayoría
predominate [prɪ'dɔmɪneɪt] *vi* predominar
pre-eminent [pri:'ɛmɪnənt] *adj* preeminente
pre-empt [pri:'ɛmt] *vt* (*Brit*) adelantarse a
pre-emptive [pri:'ɛmtɪv] *adj*: **~ strike** ataque *m* preventivo
preen [pri:n] *vt*: **to ~ itself** (*bird*) limpiarse las plumas; **to ~ o.s.** pavonearse
prefab ['pri:fæb] *n* casa prefabricada
prefabricated [pri:'fæbrɪkeɪtɪd] *adj* prefabricado
preface ['prɛfəs] *n* prefacio
prefect ['pri:fɛkt] *n* (*Brit: in school*) monitor(a) *m(f)*
prefer [prɪ'fə:[r]] *vt* preferir; (*Law: charges, complaint*) presentar; (*: action*) entablar; **to ~ coffee to tea** preferir el café al té
preferable ['prɛfrəbl] *adj* preferible
preferably ['prɛfrəblɪ] *adv* preferentemente, más bien
preference ['prɛfrəns] *n* preferencia; **in ~ to sth** antes que algo
preference shares *npl* acciones *fpl* privilegiadas
preferential [prɛfə'rɛnʃəl] *adj* preferente
prefix ['pri:fɪks] *n* prefijo
pregnancy ['prɛgnənsɪ] *n* embarazo
pregnancy test *n* prueba del embarazo
pregnant ['prɛgnənt] *adj* embarazada; **3 months ~** embarazada de tres meses; **~ with meaning** cargado de significado
prehistoric ['pri:hɪs'tɔrɪk] *adj* prehistórico
prehistory [pri:'hɪstərɪ] *n* prehistoria
prejudge [pri:'dʒʌdʒ] *vt* prejuzgar
prejudice ['prɛdʒudɪs] *n* (*bias*) prejuicio; (*harm*) perjuicio ■ *vt* (*bias*) predisponer; (*harm*) perjudicar; **to ~ sb in favour of/against** (*bias*) predisponer a algn a favor de/en contra de
prejudiced ['prɛdʒudɪst] *adj* (*person*) predispuesto; (*view*) parcial, interesado; **to be ~ against sb/sth** estar predispuesto en contra de algn/algo
prelate ['prɛlət] *n* prelado
preliminaries [prɪ'lɪmɪnərɪz] *npl* preliminares *mpl*, preparativos *mpl*
preliminary [prɪ'lɪmɪnərɪ] *adj* preliminar
prelude ['prɛlju:d] *n* preludio
premarital ['pri:'mærɪtl] *adj* prematrimonial, premarital
premature ['prɛmətʃuə[r]] *adj* (*arrival etc*) prematuro; **you are being a little ~** te has adelantado
prematurely [prɛmə'tʃuəlɪ] *adv* prematuramente, antes de tiempo
premeditate [pri:'mɛdɪteɪt] *vt* premeditar
premeditated [pri:'mɛdɪteɪtɪd] *adj* premeditado
premeditation [pri:mɛdɪ'teɪʃən] *n* premeditación *f*
premenstrual [pri:'mɛnstruəl] *adj* premenstrual
premenstrual tension *n* (*Med*) tensión *f* premenstrual
premier ['prɛmɪə[r]] *adj* primero, principal ■ *n* (*Pol*) primer(a) ministro(-a)
première ['prɛmɪɛə[r]] *n* estreno
premise ['prɛmɪs] *n* premisa
premises ['prɛmɪsɪs] *npl* local *msg*; **on the ~** en el lugar mismo; **business ~** locales *mpl* comerciales
premium ['pri:mɪəm] *n* prima; **to be at a ~** estar muy solicitado; **to sell at a ~** (*shares*) vender caro
premium bond *n* (*Brit*) *bono del estado que participa en una lotería nacional*; *ver nota*

PREMIUM BOND

Se conoce como *Premium Bonds* o *Premium Savings Bonds* a los bonos emitidos por el Ministerio de Economía británico (*Treasury*) en los que se pueden invertir los ahorros. No producen intereses, pero dan acceso a un sorteo mensual de premios en metálico.

premium deal *n* (*Comm*) oferta extraordinaria
premium gasoline *n* (*US*) (gasolina) súper *m*
premonition [prɛmə'nɪʃən] *n* presentimiento
preoccupation [pri:ɔkju'peɪʃən] *n* preocupación *f*
preoccupied [pri:'ɔkjupaɪd] *adj* (*worried*) preocupado; (*absorbed*) ensimismado
prep [prɛp] *adj abbr*: **~ school** = **preparatory school** ■ *n abbr* (*Scol*: = *preparation*) deberes *mpl*
prepaid [pri:'peɪd] *adj* porte pagado; **~ envelope** sobre *m* de porte pagado
preparation [prɛpə'reɪʃən] *n* preparación *f*; **preparations** *npl* preparativos *mpl*; **in ~ for sth** en preparación para algo
preparatory [prɪ'pærətərɪ] *adj* preparatorio, preliminar; **~ to sth/to doing sth** como preparación para algo/para hacer algo
preparatory school *n* (*Brit*) *colegio privado de enseñanza primaria*; (*US*) *colegio privado de enseñanza secundaria*; *see also* **public school**
prepare [prɪ'pɛə^r] *vt* preparar, disponer ■ *vi*: **to ~ for** prepararse *or* disponerse para; (*make preparations*) hacer preparativos para
prepared [prɪ'pɛəd] *adj* (*willing*): **to be ~ to help sb** estar dispuesto a ayudar a algn
preponderance [prɪ'pɔndərns] *n* preponderancia, predominio
preposition [prɛpə'zɪʃən] *n* preposición *f*
prepossessing [pri:pə'zɛsɪŋ] *adj* agradable, atractivo
preposterous [prɪ'pɔstərəs] *adj* absurdo, ridículo
prerecorded ['pri:rɪ'kɔ:dɪd] *adj*: **~ broadcast** programa *m* grabado de antemano; **~ cassette** cassette *f* pregrabada
prerequisite [pri:'rɛkwɪzɪt] *n* requisito previo
prerogative [prɪ'rɔgətɪv] *n* prerrogativa
Presbyterian [prɛzbɪ'tɪərɪən] *adj, n* presbiteriano(-a) *m(f)*
presbytery ['prɛzbɪtərɪ] *n* casa parroquial
preschool ['pri:'sku:l] *adj* (*child, age*) preescolar
prescribe [prɪ'skraɪb] *vt* prescribir; (*Med*) recetar; **prescribed books** (*Brit Scol*) libros *mpl* del curso
prescription [prɪ'skrɪpʃən] *n* (*Med*) receta; **to make up** *or* (*US*) **fill a ~** preparar una receta; **only available on ~** se vende solamente con receta (médica)
prescription charges *npl* (*Brit*) precio *sg* de las recetas
prescriptive [prɪ'skrɪptɪv] *adj* normativo
presence ['prɛzns] *n* presencia; (*attendance*) asistencia
presence of mind *n* aplomo
present *adj* ['prɛznt] (*in attendance*) presente; (*current*) actual ■ *n* (*gift*) regalo; (*actuality*) actualidad *f*, presente *m* ■ *vt* [prɪ'zɛnt] (*introduce*) presentar; (*expound*) exponer; (*give*) presentar, dar, ofrecer; (*Theat*) representar; **to be ~ at** asistir a, estar presente en; **those ~** los presentes; **to give sb a ~, make sb a ~ of sth** regalar algo a algn; **at ~** actualmente; **to ~ o.s. for an interview** presentarse a una entrevista; **may I ~ Miss Clark** permítame presentarle *or* le presento a la Srta Clark
presentable [prɪ'zɛntəbl] *adj*: **to make o.s. ~** arreglarse
presentation [prɛzn'teɪʃən] *n* presentación *f*; (*gift*) obsequio; (*of case*) exposición *f*; (*Theat*) representación *f*; **on ~ of the voucher** al presentar el vale
present-day ['prɛzntdeɪ] *adj* actual
presenter [prɪ'zɛntə^r] *n* (*Radio, TV*) locutor(a) *m(f)*
presently ['prɛzntlɪ] *adv* (*soon*) dentro de poco; (*US*: *now*) ahora
present participle *n* participio (de) presente
present tense *n* (tiempo) presente *m*
preservation [prɛzə'veɪʃən] *n* conservación *f*
preservative [prɪ'zə:vətɪv] *n* conservante *m*
preserve [prɪ'zə:v] *vt* (*keep safe*) preservar, proteger; (*maintain*) mantener; (*food*) conservar; (*in salt*) salar ■ *n* (*for game*) coto, vedado; (*often pl*: *jam*) confitura
preshrunk [pri:'ʃrʌŋk] *adj* inencogible
preside [prɪ'zaɪd] *vi* presidir
presidency ['prɛzɪdənsɪ] *n* presidencia
president ['prɛzɪdənt] *n* presidente *m/f*; (*US*: *of company*) director(a) *m(f)*
presidential [prɛzɪ'dɛnʃl] *adj* presidencial
press [prɛs] *n* (*tool, machine, newspapers*) prensa; (*printer's*) imprenta; (*of hand*) apretón *m* ■ *vt* (*push*) empujar; (*squeeze*) apretar; (*grapes*) pisar; (*clothes*: *iron*) planchar; (*pressure*) presionar; (*doorbell*) apretar, pulsar, tocar; (*insist*): **to ~ sth on sb** insistir en que algn acepte algo ■ *vi* (*squeeze*) apretar; (*pressurize*) ejercer presión; **to go to ~** (*newspaper*) entrar en prensa; **to be in the ~** (*being printed*) estar en prensa; (*in the newspapers*) aparecer en la prensa; **we are pressed for time** tenemos poco tiempo; **to ~ sb to do** *or* **into doing sth** (*urge, entreat*) presionar a algn para que haga algo; **to ~ sb for an answer** insistir a algn para que conteste; **to ~ charges against sb** (*Law*) demandar a algn
▸ **press ahead** *vi* seguir adelante
▸ **press on** *vi* avanzar; (*hurry*) apretar el paso
press agency *n* agencia de prensa
press clipping *n* = **press cutting**

press conference *n* rueda de prensa
press cutting *n* recorte *m* (de periódico)
pressing ['prɛsɪŋ] *adj* apremiante
pressman ['prɛsmæn] *n* periodista *m*
press officer *n* jefe(-a) *m(f)* de prensa
press release *n* comunicado de prensa
press stud *n* (*Brit*) botón *m* de presión
press-up ['prɛsʌp] *n* (*Brit*) flexión *f*
pressure ['prɛʃəʳ] *n* presión *f*; (*urgency*) apremio, urgencia; (*influence*) influencia; **high/low ~** alta/baja presión; **to put ~ on sb** presionar a algn, hacer presión sobre algn
pressure cooker *n* olla a presión
pressure gauge *n* manómetro
pressure group *n* grupo de presión
pressurize ['prɛʃəraɪz] *vt* presurizar; **to ~ sb (into doing sth)** presionar a algn (para que haga algo)
pressurized ['prɛʃəraɪzd] *adj* (*container*) a presión
Prestel® ['prɛstɛl] *n* videotex *m*
prestige [prɛs'tiːʒ] *n* prestigio
prestigious [prɛs'tɪdʒəs] *adj* prestigioso
presumably [prɪ'zjuːməblɪ] *adv* es de suponer que, cabe presumir que; **~ he did it** es de suponer que lo hizo él
presume [prɪ'zjuːm] *vt* suponer, presumir; **to ~ to do** (*dare*) atreverse a hacer
presumption [prɪ'zʌmpʃən] *n* suposición *f*; (*pretension*) presunción *f*
presumptuous [prɪ'zʌmptjuəs] *adj* presumido
presuppose [priːsə'pəuz] *vt* presuponer
presupposition [priːsʌpə'zɪʃən] *n* presuposición *f*
pre-tax [priː'tæks] *adj* anterior al impuesto
pretence, pretense (*US*) [prɪ'tɛns] *n* (*claim*) pretensión *f*; (*pretext*) pretexto; (*make-believe*) fingimiento; **on** *or* **under the ~ of doing sth** bajo *or* con el pretexto de hacer algo; **she is devoid of all ~** no es pretenciosa
pretend [prɪ'tɛnd] *vt* (*feign*) fingir ■ *vi* (*feign*) fingir; (*claim*): **to ~ to sth** pretender a algo
pretense [prɪ'tɛns] *n* (*US*) = **pretence**
pretension [pri'tɛnʃən] *n* (*claim*) pretensión *f*; **to have no pretensions to sth/to being sth** no engañarse en cuanto a algo/a ser algo
pretentious [prɪ'tɛnʃəs] *adj* pretencioso
pretext ['priːtɛkst] *n* pretexto; **on** *or* **under the ~ of doing sth** con el pretexto de hacer algo
prettily ['prɪtɪlɪ] *adv* encantadoramente, con gracia
pretty ['prɪtɪ] *adj* (*gen*) bonito, lindo (*LAm*) ■ *adv* bastante
prevail [prɪ'veɪl] *vi* (*gain mastery*) prevalecer; (*be current*) predominar; (*persuade*): **to ~ (up)on sb to do sth** persuadir a algn para que haga algo
prevailing [prɪ'veɪlɪŋ] *adj* (*dominant*) predominante
prevalent ['prɛvələnt] *adj* (*dominant*) dominante; (*widespread*) extendido; (*fashionable*) de moda
prevarication [prɪværɪ'keɪʃən] *n* evasivas *fpl*
prevent [prɪ'vɛnt] *vt*: **to ~ (sb) from doing sth** impedir (a algn) hacer algo
preventable [prɪ'vɛntəbl] *adj* evitable
preventative [prɪ'vɛntətɪv] *adj* preventivo
prevention [prɪ'vɛnʃən] *n* prevención *f*
preventive [prɪ'vɛntɪv] *adj* preventivo
preview ['priːvjuː] *n* (*of film*) preestreno
previous ['priːvɪəs] *adj* previo, anterior; **he has no ~ experience in that field** no tiene experiencia previa en ese campo; **I have a ~ engagement** tengo un compromiso anterior
previously ['priːvɪəslɪ] *adv* antes
prewar [priː'wɔːʳ] *adj* antes de la guerra
prey [preɪ] *n* presa ■ *vi*: **to ~ on** vivir a costa de; (*feed on*) alimentarse de; **it was preying on his mind** le obsesionaba
price [praɪs] *n* precio; (*Betting*: *odds*) puntos *mpl* de ventaja ■ *vt* (*goods*) fijar el precio de; **to go up** *or* **rise in ~** subir de precio; **what is the ~ of ...?** ¿qué precio tiene ...?; **to put a ~ on sth** poner precio a algo; **what ~ his promises now?** ¿para qué sirven ahora sus promesas?; **he regained his freedom, but at a ~** recobró su libertad, pero le había costado caro; **to be priced out of the market** (*article*) no encontrar comprador por ese precio; (*nation*) no ser competitivo
price control *n* control *m* de precios
price-cutting ['praɪskʌtɪŋ] *n* reducción *f* de precios
priceless ['praɪslɪs] *adj* que no tiene precio; (*col*: *amusing*) divertidísimo
price list *n* tarifa
price range *n* gama de precios; **it's within my ~** está al alcance de mi bolsillo
price tag *n* etiqueta
price war *n* guerra de precios
pricey ['praɪsɪ] *adj* (*Brit col*) caro
prick [prɪk] *n* pinchazo; (*with pin*) alfilerazo; (*sting*) picadura ■ *vt* pinchar; picar; **to ~ up one's ears** aguzar el oído
prickle ['prɪkl] *n* (*sensation*) picor *m*; (*Bot*) espina; (*Zool*) púa
prickly ['prɪklɪ] *adj* espinoso; (*fig*: *person*) enojadizo
prickly heat *n* sarpullido causado por exceso de calor
prickly pear *n* higo chumbo

pride [praɪd] *n* orgullo; *(pej)* soberbia ■ *vt*: **to ~ o.s. on** enorgullecerse de; **to take (a) ~ in** enorgullecerse de; **her ~ and joy** su orgullo; **to have ~ of place** tener prioridad
priest [pri:st] *n* sacerdote *m*
priestess ['pri:stɪs] *n* sacerdotisa
priesthood ['pri:sthud] *n (practice)* sacerdocio; *(priests)* clero
prig [prɪg] *n* gazmoño(-a)
prim [prɪm] *adj (demure)* remilgado; *(prudish)* gazmoño
primacy ['praɪməsɪ] *n* primacía
prima donna ['pri:mə'dɔnə] *n* primadonna, diva
prima facie ['praɪmə'feɪʃɪ] *adj*: **to have a ~ case** *(Law)* tener razón a primera vista
primal ['praɪməl] *adj* original; *(important)* principal
primarily ['praɪmərɪlɪ] *adv (above all)* ante todo, primordialmente
primary ['praɪmərɪ] *adj* primario; *(first in importance)* principal ■ *n (US: also:* **primary election**) (elección *f*) primaria; *ver nota*

PRIMARY

Las elecciones primarias *(primaries)* sirven para preseleccionar a los candidatos de los partidos Demócrata ("Democratic") y Republicano ("Republican") durante la campaña que precede a las elecciones a presidente de los Estados Unidos. Se inician en New Hampshire y tienen lugar en 35 estados de febrero a junio. El número de votos obtenidos por cada candidato determina el número de delegados que votarán en el congreso general ("National Convention") de julio y agosto, cuando se decide el candidato definitivo de cada partido.

primary colour, (US) **primary color** *n* color *m* primario
primary education *n* enseñanza primaria
primary school *n (Brit)* escuela primaria; *ver nota*

PRIMARY SCHOOL

En el Reino Unido la escuela a la que van los niños entre cinco y once años se llama *primary school*, a menudo dividida en "infant school" (entre cinco y siete años de edad) y "junior school" (entre siete y once).

primate *n* ['praɪmɪt] *(Rel)* primado; ['praɪmeɪt] *(Zool)* primate *m*
prime [praɪm] *adj* primero, principal; *(basic)* fundamental; *(excellent)* selecto, de primera clase ■ *n*: **in the ~ of life** en la flor de la vida ■ *vt (gun, pump)* cebar; *(fig)* preparar
Prime Minister *n* primer(a) ministro(-a); *see also* **Downing Street**
primer ['praɪmə^r] *n (book)* texto elemental; *(paint)* capa preparatoria
prime time *n (Radio, TV)* horas *fpl* de mayor audiencia
primeval [praɪ'mi:vəl] *adj* primitivo
primitive ['prɪmɪtɪv] *adj* primitivo; *(crude)* rudimentario; *(uncivilized)* inculto
primly ['prɪmlɪ] *adv* remilgadamente; con gazmoñería
primrose ['prɪmrəuz] *n* primavera, prímula
primus® ['praɪməs], **primus stove** *n (Brit)* hornillo de camping
prince [prɪns] *n* príncipe *m*
prince charming *n* príncipe *m* azul
princess [prɪn'sɛs] *n* princesa
principal ['prɪnsɪpl] *adj* principal ■ *n* director(a) *m(f)*; *(in play)* protagonista principal *m/f*; *(Comm)* capital *m*, principal *m*; *see also* **pantomime**
principality [prɪnsɪ'pælɪtɪ] *n* principado
principle ['prɪnsɪpl] *n* principio; **in ~** en principio; **on ~** por principio
print [prɪnt] *n (impression)* marca, impresión *f*; huella; *(letters)* letra de molde; *(fabric)* estampado; *(Art)* grabado; *(Phot)* impresión *f* ■ *vt (gen)* imprimir; *(on mind)* grabar; *(write in capitals)* escribir en letras de molde; **out of ~** agotado
▸ **print out** *vt (Comput)* imprimir
printed circuit ['prɪntɪd-] *n* circuito impreso
printed circuit board *n* tarjeta de circuito impreso
printed matter *n* impresos *mpl*
printer ['prɪntə^r] *n (person)* impresor(a) *m(f)*; *(machine)* impresora
printhead ['prɪnthɛd] *n* cabeza impresora
printing ['prɪntɪŋ] *n (art)* imprenta; *(act)* impresión *f*; *(quantity)* tirada
printing press *n* prensa
printout ['prɪntaut] *n (Comput)* printout *m*
print wheel *n* rueda impresora
prior ['praɪə^r] *adj* anterior, previo ■ *n* prior *m*; **~ to doing** antes de *or* hasta hacer; **without ~ notice** sin previo aviso; **to have a ~ claim to sth** tener prioridad en algo
prioress [praɪə'rɛs] *n* priora
priority [praɪ'ɔrɪtɪ] *n* prioridad *f*; **to have** *or* **take ~ over sth** tener prioridad sobre algo
priory ['praɪərɪ] *n* priorato

prise, prize (*US*) [praɪz] *vt*: **to ~ open** abrir con palanca
prism ['prɪzəm] *n* prisma *m*
prison ['prɪzn] *n* cárcel *f*, prisión *f* ■ *cpd* carcelario
prison camp *n* campamento para prisioneros
prisoner ['prɪznəʳ] *n* (*in prison*) preso(-a); (*under arrest*) detenido(-a); (*in dock*) acusado(-a); **the ~ at the bar** el/la acusado(-a); **to take sb ~** hacer *or* tomar prisionero a algn
prisoner of war *n* prisionero(-a) *or* preso(-a) de guerra
prissy ['prɪsɪ] *adj* remilgado
pristine ['prɪsti:n] *adj* pristino
privacy ['prɪvəsɪ] *n* (*seclusion*) soledad *f*; (*intimacy*) intimidad *f*; **in the strictest ~** con el mayor secreto
private ['praɪvɪt] *adj* (*personal*) particular; (*confidential*) secreto, confidencial; (*intimate*) privado, íntimo; (*sitting etc*) a puerta cerrada ■ *n* soldado raso; **"~"** (*on envelope*) "confidencial"; (*on door*) "privado"; **in ~** en privado; **in (his) ~ life** en su vida privada; **to be in ~ practice** tener consulta particular
private enterprise *n* la empresa privada
private eye *n* detective *m/f* privado(-a)
private hearing *n* (*Law*) vista a puerta cerrada
private limited company *n* (*Brit*) sociedad *f* de responsabilidad limitada
privately ['praɪvɪtlɪ] *adv* en privado; (*in o.s.*) en secreto
private parts *npl* partes *fpl* pudendas
private property *n* propiedad *f* privada
private school *n* colegio privado
privation [praɪ'veɪʃən] *n* (*state*) privación *f*; (*hardship*) privaciones *fpl*, estrecheces *fpl*
privatize ['praɪvɪtaɪz] *vt* privatizar
privet ['prɪvɪt] *n* alheña
privilege ['prɪvɪlɪdʒ] *n* privilegio; (*prerogative*) prerrogativa
privileged ['prɪvɪlɪdʒd] *adj* privilegiado; **to be ~ to do sth** gozar del privilegio de hacer algo
privy ['prɪvɪ] *adj*: **to be ~ to** estar enterado de
Privy Council *n* consejo privado (de la Corona); *ver nota*

PRIVY COUNCIL

El consejo de asesores de la Corona conocido como *Privy Council* tuvo su origen en la época de los normandos, y fue adquiriendo mayor importancia hasta ser substituido en 1688 por el actual Consejo de Ministros ("Cabinet"). Hoy día sigue existiendo con un carácter fundamentalmente honorífico y los ministros del gobierno y otras personalidades políticas, eclesiásticas y jurídicas adquieren el rango de "privy councillors" de manera automática.

prize [praɪz] *n* premio ■ *adj* (*first class*) de primera clase ■ *vt* apreciar, estimar; (*US*) = **prise**
prize fighter *n* boxeador *m* profesional
prize fighting *n* boxeo *m* profesional
prize-giving ['praɪzgɪvɪŋ] *n* distribución *f* de premios
prize money *n* (*Sport*) bolsa
prizewinner ['praɪzwɪnəʳ] *n* premiado(-a)
prizewinning ['praɪzwɪnɪŋ] *adj* (*novel, essay*) premiado
PRO *n abbr* = **public relations officer**
pro [prəu] *n* (*Sport*) profesional *m/f*; **the pros and cons** los pros y los contras
pro- [prəu] *pref* (*in favour of*) pro, en pro de; **~Soviet** pro-soviético
proactive [prəu'æktɪv] *adj*: **to be ~** impulsar la actividad
probability [prɔbə'bɪlɪtɪ] *n* probabilidad *f*; **in all ~** lo más probable
probable ['prɔbəbl] *adj* probable; **it is ~/hardly ~ that** es probable/poco probable que
probably ['prɔbəblɪ] *adv* probablemente
probate ['prəubeɪt] *n* (*Law*) legalización *f* de un testamento
probation [prə'beɪʃən] *n*: **on ~** (*employee*) a prueba; (*Law*) en libertad condicional
probationary [prə'beɪʃənrɪ] *adj*: **~ period** período de prueba
probationer [prə'beɪʃənəʳ] *n* (*Law*) persona en libertad condicional; (*nurse*) ≈ ATS *m/f* (*SP*) *or* enfermero(-a) en prácticas
probation officer *n persona a cargo de los presos en libertad condicional*
probe [prəub] *n* (*Med, Space*) sonda; (*enquiry*) investigación *f* ■ *vt* sondar; (*investigate*) investigar
probity ['prəubɪtɪ] *n* probidad *f*
problem ['prɔbləm] *n* problema *m*; **what's the ~?** ¿cuál es el problema?, ¿qué pasa?; **no ~!** ¡por supuesto!; **to have problems with the car** tener problemas con el coche
problematic [prɔblə'mætɪk], **problematical** [prɔblə'mætɪkl] *adj* problemático
problem-solving [prɔbləm'sɔlvɪŋ] *n* resolución *f* de problemas; **~ skills** técnicas de resolución de problemas
procedural [prəu'si:dʒərəl] *adj* de procedimiento; (*Law*) procesal
procedure [prə'si:dʒəʳ] *n* procedimiento; (*bureaucratic*) trámites *mpl*; **cashing a cheque**

is a simple ~ cobrar un cheque es un trámite sencillo
proceed [prə'si:d] *vi* proceder; (*continue*): **to ~ (with)** continuar (con); **to ~ against sb** (*Law*) proceder contra algn; **I am not sure how to ~** no sé cómo proceder; *see also* **proceeds**
proceedings [prə'si:dɪŋz] *npl* acto *sg*, actos *mpl*; (*Law*) proceso *sg*; (*meeting*) función *fsg*; (*records*) actas *fpl*
proceeds ['prəusi:dz] *npl* ganancias *fpl*, ingresos *mpl*
process ['prəusɛs] *n* proceso; (*method*) método, sistema *m*; (*proceeding*) procedimiento ▪ *vt* tratar, elaborar ▪ *vi* [prə'sɛs] (*Brit: formal: go in procession*) desfilar; **in ~** en curso; **we are in the ~ of moving to ...** estamos en vías de mudarnos a ...
processed cheese ['prəusɛst-], (*US*) **process cheese** *n* queso fundido
processing ['prəusɛsɪŋ] *n* elaboración *f*
procession [prə'sɛʃən] *n* desfile *m*; **funeral ~** cortejo fúnebre
pro-choice [prəu'tʃɔɪs] *adj* en favor del derecho de elegir de la madre
proclaim [prə'kleɪm] *vt* proclamar; (*announce*) anunciar
proclamation [prɔklə'meɪʃən] *n* proclamación *f*; (*written*) proclama
proclivity [prə'klɪvɪtɪ] *n* propensión *f*, inclinación *f*
procrastinate [prəu'kræstɪneɪt] *vi* demorarse
procrastination [prəukræstɪ'neɪʃən] *n* dilación *f*
procreation [prəukrɪ'eɪʃən] *n* procreación *f*
Procurator Fiscal ['prɔkjureɪtə-] *n* (*Scottish*) fiscal *m/f*
procure [prə'kjuəʳ] *vt* conseguir, obtener
procurement [prə'kjuəmənt] *n* obtención *f*
prod [prɔd] *vt* (*push*) empujar; (*with elbow*) dar un codazo a ▪ *n* empujoncito; codazo
prodigal ['prɔdɪgl] *adj* pródigo
prodigious [prə'dɪdʒəs] *adj* prodigioso
prodigy ['prɔdɪdʒɪ] *n* prodigio
produce *n* ['prɔdju:s] (*Agr*) productos *mpl* agrícolas ▪ *vt* [prə'dju:s] producir; (*yield*) rendir; (*bring*) sacar; (*show*) presentar, mostrar; (*proof of identity*) enseñar, presentar; (*Theat*) presentar, poner en escena; (*offspring*) dar a luz
produce dealer *n* (*US*) verdulero(-a)
producer [prə'dju:səʳ] *n* (*Theat*) director(a) *m(f)*; (*Agr, Cine*) productor(a) *m(f)*
product ['prɔdʌkt] *n* producto
production [prə'dʌkʃən] *n* (*act*) producción *f*; (*Theat*) representación *f*, montaje *m*; **to put into ~** lanzar a la producción
production agreement *n* (*US*) acuerdo de productividad
production line *n* línea de producción
production manager *n* jefe/jefa *m/f* de producción
productive [prə'dʌktɪv] *adj* productivo
productivity [prɔdʌk'tɪvɪtɪ] *n* productividad *f*
productivity agreement *n* (*Brit*) acuerdo de productividad
productivity bonus *n* bono de productividad
Prof. [prɔf] *abbr* (= *professor*) Prof
profane [prə'feɪn] *adj* profano
profess [prə'fɛs] *vt* profesar; **I do not ~ to be an expert** no pretendo ser experto
professed [prə'fɛst] *adj* (*self-declared*) declarado
profession [prə'fɛʃən] *n* profesión *f*
professional [prə'fɛʃnl] *n* profesional *m/f* ▪ *adj* profesional; (*by profession*) de profesión; **to take ~ advice** buscar un consejo profesional
professionalism [prə'fɛʃnəlɪzm] *n* profesionalismo
professionally [prə'fɛʃnəlɪ] *adv*: **I only know him ~** sólo le conozco por nuestra relación de trabajo
professor [prə'fɛsəʳ] *n* (*Brit*) catedrático(-a) *m(f)*; (*US: teacher*) profesor(a) *m(f)*
professorship [prə'fɛsəʃɪp] *n* cátedra
proffer ['prɔfəʳ] *vt* ofrecer
proficiency [prə'fɪʃənsɪ] *n* capacidad *f*, habilidad *f*
proficiency test *n* prueba de capacitación
proficient [prə'fɪʃənt] *adj* experto, hábil
profile ['prəufaɪl] *n* perfil *m*; **to keep a high/low ~** tratar de llamar la atención/pasar inadvertido
profit ['prɔfɪt] *n* (*Comm*) ganancia; (*fig*) provecho ▪ *vi*: **to ~ by** *or* **from** aprovechar *or* sacar provecho de; **~ and loss account** cuenta de ganancias y pérdidas; **with profits endowment assurance** seguro dotal con beneficios; **to sell sth at a ~** vender algo con ganancia
profitability [prɔfɪtə'bɪlɪtɪ] *n* rentabilidad *f*
profitable ['prɔfɪtəbl] *adj* (*Econ*) rentable; (*beneficial*) provechoso, útil
profitably ['prɔfɪtəblɪ] *adv* rentablemente; provechosamente
profit centre, (*US*) **profit center** *n* centro de beneficios
profiteering [prɔfɪ'tɪərɪŋ] *n* (*pej*) explotación *f*
profit-making ['prɔfɪtmeɪkɪŋ] *adj* rentable
profit margin *n* margen *m* de ganancia

profit-sharing ['prɔfɪtʃɛərɪŋ] *n* participación *f* de empleados en los beneficios
profits tax *n* impuesto sobre los beneficios
profligate ['prɔflɪgɪt] *adj* (*dissolute: behaviour, act*) disoluto; (*: person*) libertino; (*extravagant*): **he's very ~ with his money** es muy derrochador
pro forma ['prəu'fɔːmə] *adj*: **~ invoice** factura pro-forma
profound [prə'faund] *adj* profundo
profoundly [prə'faundlɪ] *adv* profundamente
profusely [prə'fjuːslɪ] *adv* profusamente
profusion [prə'fjuːʒən] *n* profusión *f*, abundancia
progeny ['prɔdʒɪnɪ] *n* progenie *f*
programme, program (US) ['prəugræm] *n* programa *m* ■ *vt* programar
programmer, program (US) ['prəugræməʳ] *n* programador(a) *m(f)*
programming, program (US) ['prəugræmɪŋ] *n* programación *f*
programming language, programing language (US) *n* lenguaje *m* de programación
progress *n* ['prəugrɛs] progreso; (*development*) desarrollo ■ *vi* [prə'grɛs] progresar, avanzar; desarrollarse; **in ~** (*meeting, work etc*) en curso; **as the match progressed** a medida que avanzaba el partido
progression [prə'grɛʃən] *n* progresión *f*
progressive [prə'grɛsɪv] *adj* progresivo; (*person*) progresista
progressively [prə'grɛsɪvlɪ] *adv* progresivamente, poco a poco
progress report *n* (*Med*) informe *m* sobre el estado del paciente; (*Admin*) informe *m* sobre la marcha del trabajo
prohibit [prə'hɪbɪt] *vt* prohibir; **to ~ sb from doing sth** prohibir a algn hacer algo; **"smoking prohibited"** "prohibido fumar"
prohibition [prəuɪ'bɪʃən] *n* (*US*) prohibicionismo
prohibitive [prə'hɪbɪtɪv] *adj* (*price etc*) prohibitivo
project [*n* 'prɔdʒɛkt, *vb* prə'dʒɛkt] *n* proyecto; (*Scol, Univ: research*) trabajo, proyecto ■ *vt* proyectar ■ *vi* (*stick out*) salir, sobresalir
projectile [prə'dʒɛktaɪl] *n* proyectil *m*
projection [prə'dʒɛkʃən] *n* proyección *f*; (*overhang*) saliente *m*
projectionist [prə'dʒɛkʃənɪst] *n* (*Cine*) operador(a) *m(f)* de cine
projection room *n* (*Cine*) cabina de proyección
projector [prə'dʒɛktəʳ] *n* proyector *m*
proletarian [prəulɪ'tɛərɪən] *adj* proletario
proletariat [prəulɪ'tɛərɪət] *n* proletariado
pro-life [prəu'laɪf] *adj* pro-vida
proliferate [prə'lɪfəreɪt] *vi* proliferar, multiplicarse
proliferation [prəlɪfə'reɪʃən] *n* proliferación *f*
prolific [prə'lɪfɪk] *adj* prolífico
prologue, (US) **prolog** ['prəulɔg] *n* prólogo
prolong [prə'lɔŋ] *vt* prolongar, extender
prom [prɔm] *n abbr* (*Brit*) = **promenade**; **promenade concert**; (*US: ball*) baile *m* de gala; *ver nota*

PROM

Los conciertos de música clásica más conocidos en Inglaterra son los llamados *Proms* (o *promenade concerts*), que tienen lugar en el "Royal Albert Hall" de Londres, aunque también se llama así a cualquier concierto de esas características. Su nombre se debe al hecho de que en un principio el público paseaba durante las actuaciones; en la actualidad parte de la gente que acude a ellos permanece de pie. En Estados Unidos se llama *prom* a un baile de gala en un colegio o universidad.

promenade [prɔmə'nɑːd] *n* (*by sea*) paseo marítimo ■ *vi* (*stroll*) pasearse
promenade concert *n* concierto (*en que parte del público permanece de pie*)
promenade deck *n* cubierta de paseo
prominence ['prɔmɪnəns] *n* (*fig*) importancia
prominent ['prɔmɪnənt] *adj* (*standing out*) saliente; (*important*) eminente, importante; **he is ~ in the field of ...** destaca en el campo de ...
prominently ['prɔmɪnəntlɪ] *adv* (*display, set*) muy a la vista; **he figured ~ in the case** desempeñó un papel destacado en el juicio
promiscuity [prɔmɪs'kjuːɪtɪ] *n* promiscuidad *f*
promiscuous [prə'mɪskjuəs] *adj* (*sexually*) promiscuo
promise ['prɔmɪs] *n* promesa ■ *vt, vi* prometer; **to make sb a ~** prometer algo a algn; **a young man of ~** un joven con futuro; **to ~ (sb) to do sth** prometer (a algn) hacer algo; **to ~ well** ser muy prometedor
promising ['prɔmɪsɪŋ] *adj* prometedor(a)
promissory note ['prɔmɪsərɪ-] *n* pagaré *m*
promontory ['prɔməntrɪ] *n* promontorio
promote [prə'məut] *vt* promover; (*new product*) dar publicidad a, lanzar; (*Mil*) ascender; **the team was promoted to the second division** (*Brit Football*) el equipo ascendió a la segunda división

promoter [prəˈməutəʳ] *n* (*of sporting event*) promotor(a) *m(f)*; (*of company, business*) patrocinador(a) *m(f)*
promotion [prəˈməuʃən] *n* (*gen*) promoción *f*; (*Mil*) ascenso
prompt [prɔmpt] *adj* pronto ■ *adv*: **at six o'clock ~** a las seis en punto ■ *n* (*Comput*) aviso, guía ■ *vt* (*urge*) mover, incitar; (*Theat*) apuntar; **to ~ sb to do sth** instar a algn a hacer algo; **to be ~ to do sth** no tardar en hacer algo; **they're very ~** (*punctual*) son muy puntuales
prompter [ˈprɔmptəʳ] *n* (*Theat*) apuntador(a) *m(f)*
promptly [ˈprɔmptlɪ] *adv* (*punctually*) puntualmente; (*rapidly*) rápidamente
promptness [ˈprɔmptnɪs] *n* puntualidad *f*; rapidez *f*
promulgate [ˈprɔməlgeɪt] *vt* promulgar
prone [prəun] *adj* (*lying*) postrado; **~ to** propenso a
prong [prɔŋ] *n* diente *m*, punta
pronoun [ˈprəunaun] *n* pronombre *m*
pronounce [prəˈnauns] *vt* pronunciar; (*declare*) declarar ■ *vi*: **to ~ (up)on** pronunciarse sobre; **they pronounced him unfit to plead** le declararon incapaz de defenderse
pronounced [prəˈnaunst] *adj* (*marked*) marcado
pronouncement [prəˈnaunsmənt] *n* declaración *f*
pronunciation [prənʌnsɪˈeɪʃən] *n* pronunciación *f*
proof [pru:f] *n* prueba; **70° ~** graduación *f* del 70 por 100 ■ *adj*: **~ against** a prueba de ■ *vt* (*tent, anorak*) impermeabilizar
proofreader [ˈpru:fri:dəʳ] *n* corrector(a) *m(f)* de pruebas
prop [prɔp] *n* apoyo; (*fig*) sostén *m* ■ *vt* (*also*: **prop up**) apoyar; (*lean*): **to ~ sth against** apoyar algo contra
Prop. *abbr* (*Comm*) = **proprietor**
propaganda [prɔpəˈgændə] *n* propaganda
propagate [ˈprɔpəgeɪt] *vt* propagar
propagation [prɔpəˈgeɪʃən] *n* propagación *f*
propel [prəˈpɛl] *vt* impulsar, propulsar
propeller [prəˈpɛləʳ] *n* hélice *f*
propelling pencil [prəˈpɛlɪŋ-] *n* (*Brit*) lapicero
propensity [prəˈpɛnsɪtɪ] *n* propensión *f*
proper [ˈprɔpəʳ] *adj* (*suited, right*) propio; (*exact*) justo; (*apt*) apropiado, conveniente; (*timely*) oportuno; (*seemly*) correcto, decente; (*authentic*) verdadero; (*col: real*) auténtico; **to go through the ~ channels** (*Admin*) ir por la vía oficial
properly [ˈprɔpəlɪ] *adv* (*adequately*) correctamente; (*decently*) decentemente
proper noun *n* nombre *m* propio
properties [ˈprɔpətɪz] *npl* (*Theat*) accesorios *mpl*, atrezzo *msg*
property [ˈprɔpətɪ] *n* propiedad *f*; (*estate*) finca; **lost ~** objetos *mpl* perdidos; **personal ~** bienes *mpl* muebles
property developer *n* promotor(a) *m(f)* de construcciones
property owner *n* dueño(-a) de propiedades
property tax *n* impuesto sobre la propiedad
prophecy [ˈprɔfɪsɪ] *n* profecía
prophesy [ˈprɔfɪsaɪ] *vt* profetizar; (*fig*) predecir
prophet [ˈprɔfɪt] *n* profeta *m/f*
prophetic [prəˈfɛtɪk] *adj* profético
proportion [prəˈpɔ:ʃən] *n* proporción *f*; (*share*) parte *f*; **to be in/out of ~ to** *or* **with sth** estar en/no guardar proporción con algo; **to see sth in ~** (*fig*) ver algo en su justa medida
proportional [prəˈpɔ:ʃənl] *adj* proporcional
proportionally [prəpɔ:ʃnəlɪ] *adv* proporcionalmente, en proporción
proportional representation *n* (*Pol*) representación *f* proporcional
proportional spacing *n* (*on printer*) espaciado proporcional
proportionate [prəˈpɔ:ʃənɪt] *adj* proporcionado
proportionately [prəˈpɔ:ʃnɪtlɪ] *adv* proporcionadamente, en proporción
proportioned [prəˈpɔ:ʃənd] *adj* proporcionado
proposal [prəˈpəuzl] *n* propuesta; (*offer of marriage*) oferta de matrimonio; (*plan*) proyecto; (*suggestion*) sugerencia
propose [prəˈpəuz] *vt* proponer; (*have in mind*): **to ~ sth/to do** *or* **doing sth** proponer algo/proponerse hacer algo ■ *vi* declararse
proposer [prəˈpəuzəʳ] *n* (*of motion*) proponente *m/f*
proposition [prɔpəˈzɪʃən] *n* propuesta, proposición *f*; **to make sb a ~** proponer algo a algn
propound [prəˈpaund] *vt* (*theory*) exponer
proprietary [prəˈpraɪətərɪ] *adj* (*Comm*): **~ article** artículo de marca; **~ brand** marca comercial
proprietor [prəˈpraɪətəʳ] *n* propietario(-a), dueño(-a)
propriety [prəˈpraɪətɪ] *n* decoro
propulsion [prəˈpʌlʃən] *n* propulsión *f*
pro rata [prəuˈrɑ:tə] *adv* a prorrata
prosaic [prəuˈzeɪɪk] *adj* prosaico
Pros. Atty. *abbr* (*US*) = **prosecuting attorney**
proscribe [prəˈskraɪb] *vt* proscribir

prose [prəuz] *n* prosa; (*Scol*) traducción *f* inversa
prosecute ['prɔsɪkju:t] *vt* (*Law*) procesar; **"trespassers will be prosecuted"** (*Law*) "se procesará a los intrusos"
prosecution [prɔsɪ'kju:ʃən] *n* proceso, causa; (*accusing side*) acusación *f*
prosecutor ['prɔsɪkju:tə^r] *n* acusador(a) *m(f)*; (*also*: **public prosecutor**) fiscal *m/f*
prospect [*n* 'prɔspɛkt, *vb* prə'spɛkt] *n* (*chance*) posibilidad *f*; (*outlook*) perspectiva; (*hope*) esperanza ■ *vt* explorar ■ *vi* buscar; **prospects** *npl* (*for work etc*) perspectivas *fpl*; **to be faced with the ~ of** tener que enfrentarse a la posibilidad de que ...; **we were faced with the ~ of leaving early** se nos planteó la posibilidad de marcharnos pronto; **there is every ~ of an early victory** hay buenas perspectivas de una pronta victoria
prospecting [prə'spɛktɪŋ] *n* prospección *f*
prospective [prə'spɛktɪv] *adj* (*possible*) probable, eventual; (*certain*) futuro; (*buyer*) presunto; (*legislation, son-in-law*) futuro
prospector [prə'spɛktə^r] *n* explorador(a) *m(f)*; **gold ~** buscador *m* de oro
prospectus [prə'spɛktəs] *n* prospecto
prosper ['prɔspə^r] *vi* prosperar
prosperity [prɔ'spɛrɪtɪ] *n* prosperidad *f*
prosperous ['prɔspərəs] *adj* próspero
prostate ['prɔsteɪt] *n* (*also*: **prostate gland**) próstata
prostitute ['prɔstɪtju:t] *n* prostituta; **male ~** prostituto
prostitution [prɔstɪ'tju:ʃən] *n* prostitución *f*
prostrate ['prɔstreɪt] *adj* postrado; (*fig*) abatido ■ *vt*: **to ~ o.s.** postrarse
protagonist [prə'tægənɪst] *n* protagonista *m/f*
protect [prə'tɛkt] *vt* proteger
protection [prə'tɛkʃən] *n* protección *f*; **to be under sb's ~** estar amparado por algn
protectionism [prə'tɛkʃənɪzəm] *n* proteccionismo
protection racket *n* chantaje *m*
protective [prə'tɛktɪv] *adj* protector(a); **~ custody** (*Law*) detención *f* preventiva
protector [prə'tɛktə^r] *n* protector(a) *m(f)*
protégé ['prəutɛʒeɪ] *n* protegido(-a)
protein ['prəuti:n] *n* proteína
pro tem [prəu'tɛm] *adv abbr* (= *pro tempore*: *for the time being*) provisionalmente
protest [*n* 'prəutɛst, *vb* prə'tɛst] *n* protesta ■ *vi* protestar ■ *vt* (*affirm*) afirmar, declarar; **to do sth under ~** hacer algo bajo protesta; **to ~ against/about** protestar en contra de/por
Protestant ['prɔtɪstənt] *adj, n* protestante *m/f*
protester, protestor [prə'tɛstə^r] *n* (*in demonstration*) manifestante *m/f*
protest march *n* manifestación *f or* marcha (de protesta)
protocol ['prəutəkɔl] *n* protocolo
prototype ['prəutətaɪp] *n* prototipo
protracted [prə'træktɪd] *adj* prolongado
protractor [prə'træktə^r] *n* (*Geom*) transportador *m*
protrude [prə'tru:d] *vi* salir, sobresalir
protuberance [prə'tju:bərəns] *n* protuberancia
proud [praud] *adj* orgulloso; (*pej*) soberbio, altanero ■ *adv*: **to do sb ~** tratar a algn a cuerpo de rey; **to do o.s. ~** no privarse de nada; **to be ~ to do sth** estar orgulloso de hacer algo
proudly ['praudlɪ] *adv* orgullosamente, con orgullo; (*pej*) con soberbia, con altanería
prove [pru:v] *vt* probar; (*verify*) comprobar; (*show*) demostrar ■ *vi*: **to ~ correct** resultar correcto; **to ~ o.s.** ponerse a prueba; **he was proved right in the end** al final se vio que tenía razón
proverb ['prɔvə:b] *n* refrán *m*
proverbial [prə'və:bɪəl] *adj* proverbial
proverbially [prə'və:bɪəlɪ] *adv* proverbialmente
provide [prə'vaɪd] *vt* proporcionar, dar; **to ~ sb with sth** proveer a algn de algo; **to be provided with** ser provisto de
▸ **provide for** *vt fus* (*person*) mantener a; (*problem etc*) tener en cuenta
provided [prə'vaɪdɪd] *conj*: **~ (that)** con tal de que, a condición de que
Providence ['prɔvɪdəns] *n* Divina Providencia
providing [prə'vaɪdɪŋ] *conj* a condición de que, con tal de que
province ['prɔvɪns] *n* provincia; (*fig*) esfera
provincial [prə'vɪnʃəl] *adj* provincial; (*pej*) provinciano
provision [prə'vɪʒən] *n* provisión *f*; (*supply*) suministro, abastecimiento; **provisions** *npl* provisiones *fpl*, víveres *mpl*; **to make ~ for** (*one's family, future*) atender las necesidades de
provisional [prə'vɪʒənl] *adj* provisional, provisorio (*LAm*); (*temporary*) interino ■ *n*: **P~** (*Ireland Pol*) Provisional *m* (*miembro de la tendencia activista del IRA*)
provisional driving licence *n* (*Brit Aut*) carnet *m* de conducir provisional; *see also* **L-plates**
proviso [prə'vaɪzəu] *n* condición *f*, estipulación *f*; **with the ~ that** a condición de que
Provo ['prɔvəu] *n abbr* (*col*) = **Provisional**

provocation [prɔvəˈkeɪʃən] *n* provocación *f*
provocative [prəˈvɔkətɪv] *adj* provocativo
provoke [prəˈvəuk] *vt* (*arouse*) provocar, incitar; (*cause*) causar, producir; (*anger*) enojar; **to ~ sb to sth/to do** *or* **into doing sth** provocar a algn a algo/a hacer algo
provoking [prəˈvəukɪŋ] *adj* provocador(a)
provost [ˈprɔvəst] *n* (*Brit: of university*) rector(a) *m(f)*; (*Scottish*) alcalde(-esa) *m(f)*
prow [prau] *n* proa
prowess [ˈprauɪs] *n* (*skill*) destreza, habilidad *f*; (*courage*) valor *m*; **his ~ as a footballer** (*skill*) su habilidad como futbolista
prowl [praul] *vi* (*also*: **prowl about, prowl around**) merodear ▪ *n*: **on the ~** de merodeo, merodeando
prowler [ˈpraulə^r] *n* merodeador(a) *m(f)*
proximity [prɔkˈsɪmɪtɪ] *n* proximidad *f*
proxy [ˈprɔksɪ] *n* poder *m*; (*person*) apoderado(-a); **by ~** por poderes
PRP *n abbr* (= *performance related pay*) *retribución en función del rendimiento en el trabajo*
prude [pru:d] *n* gazmoño(-a), mojigato(-a)
prudence [ˈpru:dns] *n* prudencia
prudent [ˈpru:dnt] *adj* prudente
prudently [ˈpru:dntlɪ] *adv* prudentemente, con prudencia
prudish [ˈpru:dɪʃ] *adj* gazmoño
prudishness [pru:dɪʃnɪs] *n* gazmoñería
prune [pru:n] *n* ciruela pasa ▪ *vt* podar
pry [praɪ] *vi*: **to ~ into** entrometerse en
PS *abbr* (= *postscript*) P.D.
psalm [sɑ:m] *n* salmo
PSAT *n abbr* (*US*) = **Preliminary Scholastic Aptitude Test**
PSBR *n abbr* (*Brit:* = *public sector borrowing requirement*) *necesidades de endeudamiento del sector público*
pseud [sju:d] *n* (*Brit col: intellectually*) farsante *m/f*; (*: socially*) pretencioso(-a)
pseudo... [sju:dəu] *pref* seudo...
pseudonym [ˈsju:dənɪm] *n* seudónimo
PSHE *n abbr* (*Brit Scol:* = *personal, social, and health education*) *formación social y sanitaria para la vida adulta*
PST *n abbr* (*US:* = *Pacific Standard Time*) *hora de invierno del Pacífico*
PSV *n abbr* (*Brit*) *see* **public service vehicle**
psyche [ˈsaɪkɪ] *n* psique *f*
psychiatric [saɪkɪˈætrɪk] *adj* psiquiátrico
psychiatrist [saɪˈkaɪətrɪst] *n* psiquiatra *m/f*
psychiatry [saɪˈkaɪətrɪ] *n* psiquiatría
psychic [ˈsaɪkɪk] *adj* (*also*: **psychical**) psíquico
psycho [ˈsaɪkəu] *n* (*col*) psicópata *m/f*, pirado(-a)
psychoanalyse, psychoanalyze [saɪkəuˈænəlaɪz] *vt* psicoanalizar
psychoanalysis (*pl* **psychoanalyses**) [saɪkəuəˈnælɪsɪs, -si:z] *n* psicoanálisis *m inv*
psychoanalyst [saɪkəuˈænəlɪst] *n* psicoanalista *m/f*
psychological [saɪkəˈlɔdʒɪkl] *adj* psicológico
psychologically [saɪkəˈlɔdʒɪklɪ] *adv* psicológicamente
psychologist [saɪˈkɔlədʒɪst] *n* psicólogo(-a)
psychology [saɪˈkɔlədʒɪ] *n* psicología
psychopath [ˈsaɪkəupæθ] *n* psicópata *m/f*
psychosis (*pl* **psychoses**) [saɪˈkəusɪs, -si:z] *n* psicosis *f inv*
psychosomatic [ˈsaɪkəusəˈmætɪk] *adj* psicosomático
psychotherapy [saɪkəuˈθɛrəpɪ] *n* psicoterapia
psychotic [saɪˈkɔtɪk] *adj, n* psicótico(-a)
PT *n abbr* (*Brit:* = *physical training*) Ed. Fís.
pt *abbr* = **pint; pints; point; points**
Pt. *abbr* (*Geo: in place names:* = *Point*) Pta
PTA *n abbr* (*Brit:* = *Parent-Teacher Association*) ≈ Asociación *f* de Padres de Alumnos
Pte. *abbr* (*Brit Mil*) = **private**
PTO *abbr* (= *please turn over*) sigue
PTV *n abbr* (*US*) = **pay television; public television**
pub [pʌb] *n abbr* (= *public house*) pub *m*, bar *m*; *ver nota*

PUB

En un *pub* (o *public house*) se pueden consumir fundamentalmente bebidas alcohólicas, aunque en la actualidad también se sirven platos ligeros durante el almuerzo. Es, además, un lugar de encuentro donde se juega a los dardos o al billar, entre otras actividades. La estricta regulación sobre la venta de alcohol controla las horas de apertura, aunque éstas son más flexibles desde hace unos años. No se puede servir alcohol a los menores de 18 años.

pub crawl *n* (*col*): **to go on a ~** ir a recorrer bares
puberty [ˈpju:bətɪ] *n* pubertad *f*
pubic [ˈpju:bɪk] *adj* púbico
public [ˈpʌblɪk] *adj, n* público; **in ~** en público; **to make sth ~** revelar *or* hacer público algo; **to be ~ knowledge** ser del dominio público; **to go ~** (*Comm*) proceder a la venta pública de acciones
public address system *n* megafonía, sistema *m* de altavoces
publican [ˈpʌblɪkən] *n* dueño(-a) *or* encargado(-a) de un bar

publication [pʌblɪ'keɪʃən] *n* publicación *f*
public company *n* sociedad *f* anónima
public convenience *n* (*Brit*) aseos *mpl* públicos, sanitarios *mpl* (*LAm*)
public holiday *n* día *m* de fiesta, (día) feriado (*LAm*)
public house *n* (*Brit*) bar *m*, pub *m*
publicity [pʌb'lɪsɪtɪ] *n* publicidad *f*
publicize ['pʌblɪsaɪz] *vt* publicitar; (*advertise*) hacer propaganda para
public limited company *n* sociedad *f* anónima (S.A.)
publicly ['pʌblɪklɪ] *adv* públicamente, en público
public opinion *n* opinión *f* pública
public ownership *n* propiedad *f* pública; **to be taken into ~** ser nacionalizado
Public Prosecutor *n* Fiscal *m/f* del Estado
public relations *n* relaciones *fpl* públicas
public relations officer *n* encargado(-a) de relaciones públicas
public school *n* (*Brit*) colegio privado; (*US*) instituto; *ver nota*

PUBLIC SCHOOL

En Inglaterra el término *public school* se usa para referirse a un colegio privado de pago, generalmente de alto prestigio social y en régimen de internado. Algunos de los más conocidos son Eton o Harrow. Muchos de sus alumnos estudian previamente hasta los 13 años en un centro privado de pago llamado "prep(aratory) school" y al terminar el bachiller pasan a estudiar en las universidades de Oxford y Cambridge. En otros lugares como Estados Unidos el mismo término se refiere a una escuela pública de enseñanza gratuita administrada por el Estado.

public sector *n* sector *m* público
public service vehicle *n* vehículo de servicio público
public-spirited [pʌblɪk'spɪrɪtɪd] *adj* cívico
public transport, public transportation (*US*) *n* transporte *m* público
public utility *n* servicio público
public works *npl* obras *fpl* públicas
publish ['pʌblɪʃ] *vt* publicar
publisher ['pʌblɪʃəʳ] *n* (*person*) editor(a) *m(f)*; (*firm*) editorial *f*
publishing ['pʌblɪʃɪŋ] *n* (*industry*) industria del libro
publishing company *n* (casa) editorial *f*
puce [pju:s] *adj* de color pardo rojizo
puck [pʌk] *n* (*ice hockey*) puck *m*
pucker ['pʌkəʳ] *vt* (*pleat*) arrugar; (*brow etc*) fruncir
pudding ['pudɪŋ] *n* pudín *m*; (*Brit: sweet*) postre *m*; **black ~** morcilla; **rice ~** arroz *m* con leche
puddle ['pʌdl] *n* charco
puerile ['pjuəraɪl] *adj* pueril
Puerto Rican ['pwə:təu'ri:kən] *adj, n* puertorriqueño(-a) *m(f)*
Puerto Rico [-'ri:kəu] *n* Puerto Rico
puff [pʌf] *n* soplo; (*of smoke*) bocanada; (*of breathing, engine*) resoplido; (*also:* **powder puff**) borla ■ *vt*: **to ~ one's pipe** dar chupadas a la pipa; (*also:* **puff out**: *sails, cheeks*) hinchar, inflar ■ *vi* (*gen*) soplar; (*pant*) jadear; **to ~ out smoke** echar humo
puffed [pʌft] *adj* (*col: out of breath*) sin aliento
puffin ['pʌfɪn] *n* frailecillo
puff pastry, puff paste (*US*) *n* hojaldre *m*
puffy ['pʌfɪ] *adj* hinchado
pull [pul] *n* (*tug*): **to give sth a ~** dar un tirón a algo; (*fig: advantage*) ventaja; (*: influence*) influencia ■ *vt* tirar de, jalar (*LAm*); (*haul*) tirar, jalar (*LAm*), arrastrar; (*strain*): **to ~ a muscle** sufrir un tirón ■ *vi* tirar, jalar (*LAm*); **to ~ to pieces** hacer pedazos; **to ~ one's punches** andarse con bromas; **to ~ one's weight** hacer su parte; **to ~ o.s. together** tranquilizarse; **to ~ sb's leg** tomar el pelo a algn; **to ~ strings (for sb)** enchufar (a algn)
▸ **pull about** *vt* (*handle roughly: object*) manosear; (*: person*) maltratar
▸ **pull apart** *vt* (*take apart*) desmontar
▸ **pull down** *vt* (*house*) derribar
▸ **pull in** *vi* (*Aut: at the kerb*) parar (junto a la acera); (*Rail*) llegar
▸ **pull off** *vt* (*deal etc*) cerrar
▸ **pull out** *vi* irse, marcharse; (*Aut: from kerb*) salir ■ *vt* sacar, arrancar
▸ **pull over** *vi* (*Aut*) hacerse a un lado
▸ **pull round, pull through** *vi* salvarse; (*Med*) recobrar la salud
▸ **pull up** *vi* (*stop*) parar ■ *vt* (*uproot*) arrancar, desarraigar; (*stop*) parar
pulley ['pulɪ] *n* polea
pull-out ['pulaut] *n* suplemento ■ *cpd* (*pages, magazine*) separable
pullover ['puləuvəʳ] *n* jersey *m*, suéter *m*
pulp [pʌlp] *n* (*of fruit*) pulpa; (*for paper*) pasta; (*pej: also:* **pulp magazines** *etc*) prensa amarilla; **to reduce sth to ~** hacer algo papilla
pulpit ['pulpɪt] *n* púlpito
pulsate [pʌl'seɪt] *vi* pulsar, latir
pulse [pʌls] *n* (*Anat*) pulso; (*of music, engine*) pulsación *f*; (*Bot*) legumbre *f*; **to feel** *or* **take sb's ~** tomar el pulso a algn

pulverize ['pʌlvəraɪz] *vt* pulverizar; (*fig*) hacer polvo
puma ['pju:mə] *n* puma *m*
pumice ['pʌmɪs], **pumice stone** *n* piedra pómez
pummel ['pʌml] *vt* aporrear
pump [pʌmp] *n* bomba; (*shoe*) zapatilla de tenis ■ *vt* sacar con una bomba; (*fig: col*) (son)sacar; **to ~ sb for information** (son)sacarle información a algn
▸ **pump up** *vt* inflar
pumpkin ['pʌmpkɪn] *n* calabaza
pun [pʌn] *n* juego de palabras
punch [pʌntʃ] *n* (*blow*) golpe *m*, puñetazo; (*tool*) punzón *m*; (*for paper*) perforadora; (*for tickets*) taladro; (*drink*) ponche *m* ■ *vt* (*hit*): **to ~ sb/sth** dar un puñetazo *or* golpear a algn/algo; (*make a hole in*) punzar; perforar
punch card, punched card [pʌntʃt-] *n* tarjeta perforada
punch-drunk ['pʌntʃdrʌŋk] *adj* (*Brit*) grogui, sonado
punch line *n* (*of joke*) remate *m*
punch-up ['pʌntʃʌp] *n* (*Brit col*) riña
punctual ['pʌŋktjuəl] *adj* puntual
punctuality [pʌŋktju'ælɪtɪ] *n* puntualidad *f*
punctually ['pʌŋktjuəlɪ] *adv*: **it will start ~ at six** empezará a las seis en punto
punctuate ['pʌŋktjueɪt] *vt* puntuar; (*fig*) interrumpir
punctuation [pʌŋktju'eɪʃən] *n* puntuación *f*
punctuation mark *n* signo de puntuación
puncture ['pʌŋktʃər] (*Brit*) *n* pinchazo ■ *vt* pinchar; **to have a ~** tener un pinchazo
pundit ['pʌndɪt] *n* experto(-a)
pungent ['pʌndʒənt] *adj* acre
punish ['pʌnɪʃ] *vt* castigar; **to ~ sb for sth/for doing sth** castigar a algn por algo/por haber hecho algo
punishable ['pʌnɪʃəbl] *adj* punible, castigable
punishing ['pʌnɪʃɪŋ] *adj* (*fig: exhausting*) agotador(a)
punishment ['pʌnɪʃmənt] *n* castigo; (*fig, col*): **to take a lot of ~** (*boxer*) recibir una paliza; (*car*) ser maltratado
punitive ['pju:nɪtɪv] *adj* punitivo
punk [pʌŋk] *n* (*also:* **punk rocker**) punki *m/f*; (*also:* **punk rock**) música punk; (*US col: hoodlum*) matón *m*
punt [pʌnt] *n* (*boat*) batea; (*Ireland*) libra irlandesa ■ *vi* (*bet*) apostar
punter ['pʌntər] *n* (*gambler*) jugador(a) *m(f)*
puny ['pju:nɪ] *adj* enclenque
pup [pʌp] *n* cachorro
pupil ['pju:pl] *n* alumno(-a); (*of eye*) pupila
puppet ['pʌpɪt] *n* títere *m*
puppet government *n* gobierno títere
puppy ['pʌpɪ] *n* cachorro, perrito
purchase ['pə:tʃɪs] *n* compra; (*grip*) agarre *m*, asidero ■ *vt* comprar
purchase order *n* orden *f* de compra
purchase price *n* precio de compra
purchaser ['pə:tʃɪsər] *n* comprador(a) *m(f)*
purchase tax *n* (*Brit*) impuesto sobre la venta
purchasing power ['pə:tʃɪsɪŋ-] *n* poder *m* adquisitivo
pure [pjuər] *adj* puro; **a ~ wool jumper** un jersey de pura lana; **it's laziness, ~ and simple** es pura vagancia
purebred ['pjuəbrɛd] *adj* de pura sangre
purée ['pjuəreɪ] *n* puré *m*
purely ['pjuəlɪ] *adv* puramente
purgatory ['pə:gətərɪ] *n* purgatorio
purge [pə:dʒ] *n* (*Med, Pol*) purga ■ *vt* purgar
purification [pjuərɪfɪ'keɪʃən] *n* purificación *f*, depuración *f*
purify ['pjuərɪfaɪ] *vt* purificar, depurar
purist ['pjuərɪst] *n* purista *m/f*
puritan ['pjuərɪtən] *n* puritano(-a)
puritanical [pjuərɪ'tænɪkl] *adj* puritano
purity ['pjuərɪtɪ] *n* pureza
purl [pə:l] *n* punto del revés
purloin [pə:'lɔɪn] *vt* hurtar, robar
purple ['pə:pl] *adj* morado
purport [pə:'pɔ:t] *vi*: **to ~ to be/do** dar a entender que es/hace
purpose ['pə:pəs] *n* propósito; **on ~** a propósito, adrede; **to no ~** para nada, en vano; **for teaching purposes** con fines pedagógicos; **for the purposes of this meeting** para los fines de esta reunión
purpose-built ['pə:pəs'bɪlt] *adj* (*Brit*) construido especialmente
purposeful ['pə:pəsful] *adj* resuelto, determinado
purposely ['pə:pəslɪ] *adv* a propósito, adrede
purr [pə:r] *n* ronroneo ■ *vi* ronronear
purse [pə:s] *n* monedero; (*US: handbag*) bolso ■ *vt* fruncir
purser ['pə:sər] *n* (*Naut*) comisario(-a)
purse snatcher [-snætʃər] *n* (*US*) *persona que roba por el procedimiento del tirón*
pursue [pə'sju:] *vt* seguir; (*harass*) perseguir; (*profession*) ejercer; (*pleasures*) buscar; (*inquiry, matter*) seguir
pursuer [pə'sju:ər] *n* perseguidor(a) *m(f)*
pursuit [pə'sju:t] *n* (*chase*) caza; (*of pleasure etc*) busca; (*occupation*) actividad *f*; **in (the) ~ of sth** en busca de algo
purveyor [pə'veɪər] *n* proveedor(a) *m(f)*
pus [pʌs] *n* pus *m*
push [puʃ] *n* empujón *m*; (*Mil*) ataque *m*; (*drive*) empuje *m* ■ *vt* empujar; (*button*)

apretar; (*promote*) promover; (*fig: press, advance: views*) fomentar; (*thrust*): **to ~ sth (into)** meter algo a la fuerza (en) ■ *vi* empujar; (*fig*) hacer esfuerzos; **at a ~** (*col*) a duras penas; **she is pushing 50** (*col*) raya en los 50; **to be pushed for time/money** andar justo de tiempo/escaso de dinero; **to ~ a door open/shut** abrir/cerrar una puerta empujándola; **to ~ for** (*better pay, conditions*) reivindicar; **"~"** (*on door*) "empujar"; (*on bell*) "pulse"
▸ **push aside** *vt* apartar con la mano
▸ **push in** *vi* colarse
▸ **push off** *vi* (*col*) largarse
▸ **push on** *vi* (*continue*) seguir adelante
▸ **push through** *vt* (*measure*) despachar
▸ **push up** *vt* (*total, prices*) hacer subir

push-bike ['puʃbaɪk] *n* (*Brit*) bicicleta

push-button ['puʃbʌtn] *adj* con botón de mando

pushchair ['puʃtʃɛəʳ] *n* (*Brit*) silla de niño

pusher ['puʃəʳ] *n* (*also*: **drug pusher**) traficante *m/f* de drogas

pushover ['puʃəuvəʳ] *n* (*col*): **it's a ~** está tirado

push-up ['puʃʌp] *n* (*US*) flexión *f*

pushy ['puʃɪ] *adj* (*pej*) agresivo

puss [pus], **pussy** ['pusɪ], **pussy-cat** ['pusɪkæt] *n* minino

put [put] (*pt, pp* **put**) *vt* (*place*) poner, colocar; (*put into*) meter; (*express, say*) expresar; (*a question*) hacer; (*estimate*) calcular; (*cause to be*): **to ~ sb in a good/bad mood** poner a algn de buen/mal humor; **to ~ a lot of time into sth** dedicar mucho tiempo a algo; **to ~ money on a horse** apostar dinero en un caballo; **to ~ money into a company** invertir dinero en una compañía; **to ~ sb to a lot of trouble** causar mucha molestia a algn; **we ~ the children to bed** acostamos a los niños; **how shall I ~ it?** ¿cómo puedo explicarlo *or* decirlo?; **I ~ it to you that ...** le sugiero que ...; **to stay ~** no moverse
▸ **put about** *vi* (*Naut*) virar ■ *vt* (*rumour*) hacer correr
▸ **put across** *vt* (*ideas etc*) comunicar
▸ **put aside** *vt* (*lay down: book etc*) dejar *or* poner a un lado; (*save*) ahorrar; (*in shop*) guardar
▸ **put away** *vt* (*store*) guardar
▸ **put back** *vt* (*replace*) devolver a su lugar; (*postpone*) posponer; (*set back: watch, clock*) retrasar; **this will ~ us back 10 years** esto nos retrasará 10 años
▸ **put by** *vt* (*money*) guardar
▸ **put down** *vt* (*on ground*) poner en el suelo; (*animal*) sacrificar; (*in writing*) apuntar; (*suppress: revolt etc*) sofocar; (*attribute*) atribuir; **~ me down for £15** apúntame por 15 libras; **~ it down on my account** (*Comm*) póngalo en mi cuenta
▸ **put forward** *vt* (*ideas*) presentar, proponer; (*date*) adelantar
▸ **put in** *vt* (*application, complaint*) presentar
▸ **put in for** *vt fus* (*job*) solicitar; (*promotion*) pedir
▸ **put off** *vt* (*postpone*) aplazar; (*discourage*) desanimar, quitar las ganas a
▸ **put on** *vt* (*clothes, lipstick etc*) ponerse; (*light etc*) encender; (*play etc*) presentar; (*brake*) echar; (*assume: accent, manner*) afectar, fingir; (*airs*) adoptar, darse; (*concert, exhibition etc*) montar; (*extra bus, train etc*) poner; (*col: kid, have on: esp US*) tomar el pelo a; (*inform, indicate*): **to ~ sb on to sb/sth** informar a algn de algn/algo; **to ~ on weight** engordar
▸ **put out** *vt* (*fire, light*) apagar; (*one's hand*) alargar; (*news, rumour*) hacer circular; (*tongue etc*) sacar; (*person: inconvenience*) molestar, fastidiar; (*dislocate: shoulder, vertebra, knee*) dislocar(se); (*vi: Naut*): **to ~ out to sea** hacerse a la mar; **to ~ out from Plymouth** salir de Plymouth
▸ **put through** *vt* (*call*) poner; **~ me through to Mr Low** póngame *or* comuníqueme (*LAm*) con el Señor Low
▸ **put together** *vt* unir, reunir; (*assemble: furniture*) armar, montar; (*meal*) preparar
▸ **put up** *vt* (*raise*) levantar, alzar; (*hang*) colgar; (*build*) construir; (*increase*) aumentar; (*accommodate*) alojar; (*incite*): **to ~ sb up to doing sth** instar *or* incitar a algn a hacer algo; **to ~ sth up for sale** poner algo a la venta
▸ **put upon** *vt fus*: **to be ~ upon** (*imposed upon*) dejarse explotar
▸ **put up with** *vt fus* aguantar

putrid ['pju:trɪd] *adj* podrido

putsch [putʃ] *n* golpe *m* de estado

putt [pʌt] *vt* hacer un putt ■ *n* putt *m*

putter ['pʌtəʳ] *n* putter *m*

putting green ['pʌtɪŋ-] *n* green *m*, minigolf *m*

putty ['pʌtɪ] *n* masilla

put-up ['putʌp] *adj*: **~ job** (*Brit*) estafa

puzzle ['pʌzl] *n* (*riddle*) acertijo; (*jigsaw*) rompecabezas *m inv*; (*also*: **crossword puzzle**) crucigrama *m*; (*mystery*) misterio ■ *vt* dejar perplejo, confundir ■ *vi*: **to ~ about** quebrar la cabeza por; **to ~ over** (*sb's actions*) quebrarse la cabeza por; (*mystery, problem*) devanarse los sesos sobre; **to be puzzled about sth** no llegar a entender algo

puzzling ['pʌzlɪŋ] *adj* (*question*) misterioso, extraño; (*attitude, instructions*) extraño

PVC *n abbr* (*= polyvinyl chloride*) P.V.C. *m*
Pvt. *abbr* (*US Mil*) = **private**
PW *n abbr* (*US*) = **prisoner of war**
pw *abbr* (*= per week*) por semana
PX *n abbr* (*US Mil*: *= post exchange*) *economato militar*
pygmy ['pɪgmɪ] *n* pigmeo(-a)
pyjamas, pajamas (*US*) [pɪ'dʒɑːməz] *npl* pijama *m*, piyama *m* (*LAm*); **a pair of** ~ un pijama
pylon ['paɪlən] *n* torre *f* de conducción eléctrica
pyramid ['pɪrəmɪd] *n* pirámide *f*
Pyrenean [pɪrə'niːən] *adj* pirenaico
Pyrenees [pɪrə'niːz] *npl*: **the** ~ los Pirineos
Pyrex® ['paɪreks] *n* pírex *m* ■ *cpd*: ~ **casserole** cazuela de pírex
python ['paɪθən] *n* pitón *m*

Qq

Q, q [kju:] *n (letter)* Q, q *f*; **Q for Queen** Q de Quebec
Qatar [kæ'tɑ:] *n* Qatar *m*
QC *n abbr (Brit: = Queen's Counsel) título concedido a determinados abogados*
QCA *n abbr (Brit: = Qualifications and Curriculum Authority) organismo que se encarga del currículum educativo en Inglaterra*
QED *abbr (= quod erat demonstrandum)* Q.E.D.
QM *n abbr see* **quartermaster**
q.t. *n abbr (col: = quiet)*: **on the q.t.** a hurtadillas
qty *abbr (= quantity)* cantidad
quack [kwæk] *n (of duck)* graznido; *(pej: doctor)* curandero(-a), matasanos *m inv* ■ *vi* graznar
quad [kwɔd] *abbr* = **quadrangle**; **quadruple**; **quadruplet**
quadrangle ['kwɔdræŋgl] *n (Brit: courtyard: abbr: quad)* patio
quadruple [kwɔ'dru:pl] *vt, vi* cuadruplicar
quadruplet [kwɔ'dru:plɪt] *n* cuatrillizo
quagmire ['kwægmaɪə^r] *n* lodazal *m*, cenegal *m*
quail [kweɪl] *n (bird)* codorniz *f* ■ *vi* amedrentarse
quaint [kweɪnt] *adj* extraño; *(picturesque)* pintoresco
quaintly ['kweɪntlɪ] *adv* extrañamente; pintorescamente
quaintness ['kweɪntnɪs] *n* lo pintoresco, tipismo
quake [kweɪk] *vi* temblar ■ *n abbr* = **earthquake**
Quaker ['kweɪkə^r] *n* cuáquero(-a)
qualification [kwɔlɪfɪ'keɪʃən] *n (reservation)* reserva; *(modification)* modificación *f*; *(act)* calificación *f*; *(paper qualification)* título; **what are your qualifications?** ¿qué títulos tienes?
qualified ['kwɔlɪfaɪd] *adj (trained)* cualificado; *(fit)* capacitado; *(limited)* limitado; *(professionally)* titulado; **~ for/to do sth** capacitado para/para hacer algo; **he's not ~ for the job** no está capacitado para ese trabajo; **it was a ~ success** fue un éxito relativo
qualify ['kwɔlɪfaɪ] *vt (Ling)* calificar a; *(capacitate)* capacitar; *(modify)* matizar; *(limit)* moderar ■ *vi (Sport)* clasificarse; **to ~ (as)** calificarse (de), graduarse (en), recibirse (de) *(LAm)*; **to ~ (for)** reunir los requisitos (para); **to ~ as an engineer** sacar el título de ingeniero
qualifying ['kwɔlɪfaɪɪŋ] *adj (exam, round)* eliminatorio
qualitative ['kwɔlɪtətɪv] *adj* cualitativo
quality ['kwɔlɪtɪ] *n* calidad *f*; *(moral)* cualidad *f*; **of good/poor ~** de buena *or* alta/poca calidad
quality control *n* control *m* de calidad
quality of life *n* calidad *f* de vida
quality press *n* prensa seria; *ver nota*

> **QUALITY PRESS**
>
> La expresión *quality press* se refiere los periódicos que dan un tratamiento serio de las noticias, ofreciendo información detallada sobre un amplio espectro de temas y análisis en profundidad de la actualidad. Por su tamaño, considerablemente mayor que el de los periódicos sensacionalistas, se les llama también "broadsheets".

qualm [kwɑ:m] *n* escrúpulo; **to have qualms about sth** sentir escrúpulos por algo
quandary ['kwɔndrɪ] *n*: **to be in a ~** verse en un dilema
quango ['kwæŋgəu] *n abbr (Brit: = quasi-autonomous non-governmental organization) organismo semiautónomo de subvención estatal*
quantifiable [kwɔntɪ'faɪəbl] *adj* cuantificable
quantitative ['kwɔntɪtətɪv] *adj* cuantitativo
quantity ['kwɔntɪtɪ] *n* cantidad *f*; **in ~** en grandes cantidades
quantity surveyor *n* aparejador(a) *m(f)*

quantum leap ['kwɔntəm-] *n (fig)* avance *m* espectacular
quarantine ['kwɔrnti:n] *n* cuarentena
quark [kwɑ:k] *n* cuark *m*
quarrel ['kwɔrl] *n* riña, pelea ■ *vi* reñir, pelearse; **to have a ~ with sb** reñir *or* pelearse con algn; **I can't ~ with that** no le veo pegas
quarrelsome ['kwɔrəlsəm] *adj* pendenciero
quarry ['kwɔrɪ] *n (for stone)* cantera; *(animal)* presa
quart [kwɔ:t] *n cuarto de galón = 1.136 l*
quarter ['kwɔ:tə^r] *n* cuarto, cuarta parte *f*; *(of year)* trimestre *m*; *(district)* barrio; *(US, Canada: 25 cents)* cuarto de dólar ■ *vt* dividir en cuartos; *(Mil: lodge)* alojar; **quarters** *npl (barracks)* cuartel *m*; *(living quarters)* alojamiento *sg*; **a ~ of an hour** un cuarto de hora; **to pay by the ~** pagar trimestralmente *or* cada tres meses; **it's a ~ to** *or (US)* **of three** son las tres menos cuarto; **it's a ~ past** *or (US)* **after three** son las tres y cuarto; **from all quarters** de todas partes; **at close quarters** de cerca
quarterback ['kwɔ:təbæk] *n (US: football)* mariscal *m* de campo
quarter-deck ['kwɔ:tədɛk] *n (Naut)* alcázar *m*
quarter final *n* cuarto de final
quarterly ['kwɔ:təlɪ] *adj* trimestral ■ *adv* cada 3 meses, trimestralmente
quartermaster ['kwɔ:təmɑ:stə^r] *n (Mil)* comisario, intendente *m* militar
quartet, quartette [kwɔ:'tɛt] *n* cuarteto
quarto ['kwɔ:təu] *n* tamaño holandés ■ *adj* de tamaño holandés
quartz [kwɔ:ts] *n* cuarzo
quash [kwɔʃ] *vt (verdict)* anular, invalidar
quasi- ['kweɪzaɪ] *pref* cuasi
quaver ['kweɪvə^r] *n (Brit Mus)* corchea ■ *vi* temblar
quay [ki:] *n (also:* **quayside***)* muelle *m*
Que. *abbr (Canada)* = **Quebec**
queasiness ['kwi:zɪnɪs] *n* malestar *m*, náuseas *fpl*
queasy ['kwi:zɪ] *adj*: **to feel ~** tener náuseas
Quebec [kwɪ'bɛk] *n* Quebec *m*
queen [kwi:n] *n* reina; *(Cards etc)* dama
queen mother *n* reina madre
Queen's Speech *n ver nota*

QUEEN'S SPEECH

Se llama *Queen's Speech* (o "King's Speech") al discurso que pronuncia el monarca durante la sesión de apertura del Parlamento británico, en el que se expresan las líneas generales de la política del gobierno para la nueva legislatura. El Primer Ministro se encarga de redactarlo con la ayuda del Consejo de Ministros y es leído en la Cámara de los Lores ("House of Lords") ante los miembros de ambas cámaras.

queer [kwɪə^r] *adj (odd)* raro, extraño ■ *n (pej: col)* marica *m*
quell [kwɛl] *vt* calmar; *(put down)* sofocar
quench [kwɛntʃ] *vt (flames)* apagar; **to ~ one's thirst** apagar la sed
querulous ['kwɛruləs] *adj (person, voice)* quejumbroso
query ['kwɪərɪ] *n (question)* pregunta; *(doubt)* duda ■ *vt* preguntar; *(disagree with, dispute)* no estar conforme con, dudar de
quest [kwɛst] *n* busca, búsqueda
question ['kwɛstʃən] *n* pregunta; *(matter)* asunto, cuestión *f* ■ *vt (doubt)* dudar de; *(interrogate)* interrogar, hacer preguntas a; **to ask sb a ~, put a ~ to sb** hacerle una pregunta a algn; **the ~ is ...** el asunto es ...; **to bring** *or* **call sth into ~** poner algo en (tela de) duda; **beyond ~** fuera de toda duda; **it's out of the ~** imposible, ni hablar
questionable ['kwɛstʃənəbl] *adj* discutible; *(doubtful)* dudoso
questioner ['kwɛstʃənə^r] *n* interrogador(a) *m(f)*
questioning ['kwɛstʃənɪŋ] *adj* inquisitivo ■ *n* preguntas *fpl*; *(by police etc)* interrogatorio
question mark *n* punto de interrogación
questionnaire [kwɛstʃə'nɛə^r] *n* cuestionario
queue [kju:] *(Brit) n* cola ■ *vi* hacer cola; **to jump the ~** colarse
quibble ['kwɪbl] *vi* andarse con sutilezas
quick [kwɪk] *adj* rápido; *(temper)* vivo; *(agile)* ágil; *(mind)* listo; *(eye)* agudo; *(ear)* fino ■ *n*: **cut to the ~** *(fig)* herido en lo más vivo; **be ~!** ¡date prisa!; **to be ~ to act** obrar con prontitud; **she was ~ to see that** se dio cuenta de eso en seguida
quicken ['kwɪkən] *vt* apresurar ■ *vi* apresurarse, darse prisa
quick-fire ['kwɪkfaɪə^r] *adj (questions etc)* rápido, (hecho) a quemarropa
quick fix *n (pej)* parche *m*
quickly ['kwɪklɪ] *adv* rápidamente, de prisa; **we must act ~** tenemos que actuar cuanto antes
quickness ['kwɪknɪs] *n* rapidez *f*; *(of temper)* viveza; *(agility)* agilidad *f*; *(of mind, eye etc)* agudeza
quicksand ['kwɪksænd] *n* arenas *fpl* movedizas
quickstep ['kwɪkstɛp] *n baile de ritmo rápido*

quick-tempered [kwɪk'tɛmpəd] *adj* de genio vivo
quick-witted [kwɪk'wɪtɪd] *adj* listo, despabilado
quid [kwɪd] *n pl inv* (*Brit: col*) libra
quid pro quo ['kwɪdprəu'kwəu] *n* quid pro quo *m*, compensación *f*
quiet ['kwaɪət] *adj* (*not busy: day*) tranquilo; (*silent*) callado; (*reserved*) reservado; (*discreet*) discreto; (*not noisy: engine*) silencioso ■ *n* tranquilidad *f* ■ *vt, vi* (*US*) = **quieten**; **keep ~!** ¡cállate!, ¡silencio!; **business is ~ at this time of year** hay poco movimiento en esta época
quieten ['kwaɪətn] (*also*: **quieten down**) *vi* (*grow calm*) calmarse; (*grow silent*) callarse ■ *vt* calmar; hacer callar
quietly ['kwaɪətlɪ] *adv* tranquilamente; (*silently*) silenciosamente
quietness ['kwaɪətnɪs] *n* (*silence*) silencio; (*calm*) tranquilidad *f*
quill [kwɪl] *n* (*of porcupine*) púa; (*pen*) pluma
quilt [kwɪlt] *n* (*Brit*) edredón *m*
quin [kwɪn] *n abbr* = **quintuplet**
quince [kwɪns] *n* membrillo
quinine [kwɪ'ni:n] *n* quinina
quintet, quintette [kwɪn'tɛt] *n* quinteto
quintuplet [kwɪn'tju:plɪt] *n* quintillizo
quip [kwɪp] *n* ocurrencia ■ *vi* decir con ironía
quire ['kwaɪəʳ] *n* mano *f* de papel
quirk [kwə:k] *n* peculiaridad *f*; **by some ~ of fate** por algún capricho del destino
quit (*pt, pp* **~** *or* **quitted**) [kwɪt] *vt* dejar, abandonar; (*premises*) desocupar; (*Comput*) abandonar ■ *vi* (*give up*) renunciar; (*go away*) irse; (*resign*) dimitir; **~ stalling!** (*US col*) ¡déjate de evasivas!
quite [kwaɪt] *adv* (*rather*) bastante; (*entirely*) completamente; **~ a few of them** un buen número de ellos; **~ (so)!** ¡así es!, ¡exactamente!; **~ new** bastante nuevo; **that's not ~ right** eso no está del todo bien; **not ~ as many as last time** no tantos como la última vez; **she's ~ pretty** es bastante guapa
Quito ['ki:təu] *n* Quito
quits [kwɪts] *adj*: **~ (with)** en paz (con); **let's call it ~** quedamos en paz
quiver ['kwɪvəʳ] *vi* estremecerse ■ *n* (*for arrows*) carcaj *m*
quiz [kwɪz] *n* (*game*) concurso; (: *TV, Radio*) programa-concurso; (*questioning*) interrogatorio ■ *vt* interrogar
quizzical ['kwɪzɪkl] *adj* burlón(-ona)
quoits [kwɔɪts] *npl* juego de aros
quorum ['kwɔ:rəm] *n* quórum *m*
quota ['kwəutə] *n* cuota
quotation [kwəu'teɪʃən] *n* cita; (*estimate*) presupuesto
quotation marks *npl* comillas *fpl*
quote [kwəut] *n* cita ■ *vt* (*sentence*) citar; (*Comm: sum, figure*) cotizar ■ *vi*: **to ~ from** citar de; **quotes** *npl* (*inverted commas*) comillas *fpl*; **in quotes** entre comillas; **the figure quoted for the repairs** el presupuesto dado para las reparaciones; **~ ... unquote** (*in dictation*) comillas iniciales ... finales
quotient ['kwəuʃənt] *n* cociente *m*
qv *n abbr* (= *quod vide: which see*) q.v.
qwerty keyboard ['kwə:tɪ-] *n* teclado QWERTY

Rr

R, r [ɑːʳ] *n* (*letter*) R, r *f*; **R for Robert,** (*US*) **R for Roger** R de Ramón
R *abbr* (= *right*) dcha.; (= *river*) R.; (= *Réaumur (scale)*) R; (*US Cine*: = *restricted*) *sólo mayores*; (*US Pol*: = *republican*; *Brit*: = *Rex, Regina*) R
RA *abbr* = **rear admiral** ■ *n abbr* (*Brit*) = **Royal Academy; Royal Academician**
RAAF *n abbr* = **Royal Australian Air Force**
Rabat [rəˈbɑːt] *n* Rabat *m*
rabbi [ˈræbaɪ] *n* rabino
rabbit [ˈræbɪt] *n* conejo ■ *vi*: **to ~ (on)** (*Brit col*) hablar sin ton ni son
rabbit hutch *n* conejera
rabble [ˈræbl] *n* (*pej*) chusma, populacho
rabies [ˈreɪbiːz] *n* rabia
RAC *n abbr* (*Brit*: = *Royal Automobile Club*) ≈ RACE *m* (*SP*)
raccoon [rəˈkuːn] *n* mapache *m*
race [reɪs] *n* carrera; (*species*) raza ■ *vt* (*horse*) hacer correr; (*person*) competir contra; (*engine*) acelerar ■ *vi* (*compete*) competir; (*run*) correr; (*pulse*) latir a ritmo acelerado; **the arms ~** la carrera armamentista; **the human ~** el género humano; **he raced across the road** cruzó corriendo la carretera; **to ~ in/out** entrar/salir corriendo
race car *n* (*US*) = **racing car**
race car driver *n* (*US*) = **racing driver**
racecourse [ˈreɪskɔːs] *n* hipódromo
racehorse [ˈreɪshɔːs] *n* caballo de carreras
race meeting *n* concurso hípico
race relations *npl* relaciones *fpl* raciales
racetrack [ˈreɪstræk] *n* hipódromo; (*for cars*) circuito de carreras
racial [ˈreɪʃl] *adj* racial
racial discrimination *n* discriminación *f* racial
racial integration *n* integración *f* racial
racialism [ˈreɪʃəlɪzəm] *n* racismo
racialist [ˈreɪʃəlɪst] *adj, n* racista *m/f*
racing [ˈreɪsɪŋ] *n* carreras *fpl*
racing car *n* (*Brit*) coche *m* de carreras
racing driver *n* (*Brit*) corredor(a) *m(f)* de coches
racism [ˈreɪsɪzəm] *n* racismo
racist [ˈreɪsɪst] *adj, n* racista *m/f*
rack [ræk] *n* (*also*: **luggage rack**) rejilla (portaequipajes); (*shelf*) estante *m*; (*also*: **roof rack**) baca; (*also*: **clothes rack**) perchero ■ *vt* (*cause pain to*) atormentar; **to go to ~ and ruin** venirse abajo; **to ~ one's brains** devanarse los sesos
▸ **rack up** *vt* conseguir, ganar
racket [ˈrækɪt] *n* (*for tennis*) raqueta; (*noise*) ruido, estrépito; (*swindle*) estafa, timo
racketeer [rækɪˈtɪəʳ] *n* (*esp US*) estafador(a) *m(f)*
racoon [rəˈkuːn] *n* = **raccoon**
racquet [ˈrækɪt] *n* raqueta
racy [ˈreɪsɪ] *adj* picante, subido
RADA [ˈrɑːdə] *n abbr* (*Brit*) = **Royal Academy of Dramatic Art**
radar [ˈreɪdɑːʳ] *n* radar *m*
radar trap *n* trampa radar
radial [ˈreɪdɪəl] *adj* (*tyre*: *also*: **radial-ply**) radial
radiance [ˈreɪdɪəns] *n* brillantez *f*, resplandor *m*
radiant [ˈreɪdɪənt] *adj* brillante, resplandeciente
radiate [ˈreɪdɪeɪt] *vt* (*heat*) radiar, irradiar ■ *vi* (*lines*) extenderse
radiation [reɪdɪˈeɪʃən] *n* radiación *f*
radiation sickness *n* enfermedad *f* de radiación
radiator [ˈreɪdɪeɪtəʳ] *n* (*Aut*) radiador *m*
radiator cap *n* tapón *m* de radiador
radiator grill *n* (*Aut*) rejilla del radiador
radical [ˈrædɪkl] *adj* radical
radically [ˈrædɪkəlɪ] *adv* radicalmente
radii [ˈreɪdɪaɪ] *npl of* **radius**
radio [ˈreɪdɪəu] *n* radio *f or m* (*LAm*) ■ *vi*: **to ~ to sb** mandar un mensaje por radio a algn ■ *vt* (*information*) radiar, transmitir por radio; (*one's position*) indicar por radio; (*person*) llamar por radio; **on the ~** en *or* por la radio
radioactive [reɪdɪəuˈæktɪv] *adj* radi(o)activo
radioactivity [reɪdɪəuækˈtɪvɪtɪ] *n* radi(o)actividad *f*

radio announcer *n* locutor(a) *m(f)* de radio
radio-controlled [reɪdɪəukən'trəuld] *adj* teledirigido
radiographer [reɪdɪ'ɔgrəfəʳ] *n* radiógrafo(-a)
radiography [reɪdɪ'ɔgrəfɪ] *n* radiografía
radiology [reɪdɪ'ɔlədʒɪ] *n* radiología
radio station *n* emisora
radio taxi *n* radio taxi *m*
radiotelephone [reɪdɪəu'tɛlɪfəun] *n* radioteléfono
radiotelescope [reɪdɪəu'tɛlɪskəup] *n* radiotelescopio
radiotherapist [reɪdɪəu'θɛrəpɪst] *n* radioterapeuta *m/f*
radiotherapy ['reɪdɪəuθɛrəpɪ] *n* radioterapia
radish ['rædɪʃ] *n* rábano
radium ['reɪdɪəm] *n* radio
radius (*pl* **radii**) ['reɪdɪəs, -ɪaɪ] *n* radio; **within a ~ of 50 miles** en un radio de 50 millas
RAF *n abbr* (*Brit*) *see* **Royal Air Force**
raffia ['ræfɪə] *n* rafia
raffle ['ræfl] *n* rifa, sorteo ■ *vt* (*object*) rifar
raft [rɑ:ft] *n* (*craft*) balsa; (*also*: **life raft**) balsa salvavidas
rafter ['rɑ:ftəʳ] *n* viga
rag [ræg] *n* (*piece of cloth*) trapo; (*torn cloth*) harapo; (*pej*: *newspaper*) periodicucho; (*for charity*) *actividades estudiantiles benéficas* ■ *vt* (*Brit*) tomar el pelo a; **rags** *npl* harapos *mpl*; **in rags** en harapos, hecho jirones
rag-and-bone man [rægən'bəunmæn] *n* (*Brit*) trapero
rag doll *n* muñeca de trapo
rage [reɪdʒ] *n* (*fury*) rabia, furor *m* ■ *vi* (*person*) rabiar, estar furioso; (*storm*) bramar; **to fly into a ~** montar en cólera; **it's all the ~** es lo último
ragged ['rægɪd] *adj* (*edge*) desigual, mellado; (*cuff*) roto; (*appearance*) andrajoso, harapiento; **~ left/right** (*text*) margen *m* izquierdo/derecho irregular
raging ['reɪdʒɪŋ] *adj* furioso; **in a ~ temper** de un humor de mil demonios
rag trade *n*: **the ~** (*col*) el ramo de la confección
rag week *n ver nota*

RAG WEEK

En la universidad los estudiantes suelen organizar cada año lo que llaman *rag week*. Consiste en una serie de actos festivos y de participación general como teatro en la calle, marchas patrocinadas etc, para hacer colectas con fines benéficos. En ocasiones hacen también una revista ("rag mag"), que consiste básicamente en chistes más bien picantes para vender a los transeúntes, e incluso un baile de gala ("rag ball").

raid [reɪd] *n* (*Mil*) incursión *f*; (*criminal*) asalto; (*by police*) redada, allanamiento (*LAm*) ■ *vt* invadir, atacar; asaltar
raider ['reɪdəʳ] *n* invasor(a) *m(f)*
rail [reɪl] *n* (*on stair*) barandilla, pasamanos *m inv*; (*on bridge*) pretil *m*; (*of balcony, ship*) barandilla; (*for train*) riel *m*, carril *m*; **rails** *npl* vía *sg*; **by ~** por ferrocarril, en tren
railcard ['reɪlkɑ:d] *n* (*Brit*) *tarjeta para obtener descuentos en el tren*; **Young Person's ~** ≈ Tarjeta joven (*SP*)
railing ['reɪlɪŋ] *n*, **railings** ['reɪlɪŋz] *npl* verja *sg*
railway ['reɪlweɪ], (*US*) **railroad** ['reɪlrəud] *n* ferrocarril *m*, vía férrea
railway engine *n* (máquina) locomotora
railway line *n* (*Brit*) línea (de ferrocarril)
railwayman ['reɪlweɪmən] *n* (*Brit*) ferroviario
railway station *n* (*Brit*) estación *f* de ferrocarril
rain [reɪn] *n* lluvia ■ *vi* llover; **in the ~** bajo la lluvia; **it's raining** llueve, está lloviendo; **it's raining cats and dogs** está lloviendo a cántaros *or* a mares
rainbow ['reɪnbəu] *n* arco iris
raincoat ['reɪnkəut] *n* impermeable *m*
raindrop ['reɪndrɔp] *n* gota de lluvia
rainfall ['reɪnfɔ:l] *n* lluvia
rainforest ['reɪnfɔrɪst] *n* selva tropical
rainproof ['reɪnpru:f] *adj* impermeable, a prueba de lluvia
rainstorm ['reɪnstɔ:m] *n* temporal *m* (de lluvia)
rainwater ['reɪnwɔ:təʳ] *n* agua de lluvia
rainy ['reɪnɪ] *adj* lluvioso
raise [reɪz] *n* aumento ■ *vt* (*lift*) levantar; (*build*) erigir, edificar; (*increase*) aumentar; (*doubts*) suscitar; (*a question*) plantear; (*cattle, family*) criar; (*crop*) cultivar; (*army*) reclutar; (*funds*) reunir; (*loan*) obtener; (*end*: *embargo*) levantar; **to ~ one's voice** alzar la voz; **to ~ one's glass to sb/sth** brindar por algn/algo; **to ~ a laugh/a smile** provocar risa/una sonrisa; **to ~ sb's hopes** dar esperanzas a algn
raisin ['reɪzn] *n* pasa de Corinto
rake [reɪk] *n* (*tool*) rastrillo; (*person*) libertino ■ *vt* (*garden*) rastrillar; (*fire*) hurgar; (*with machine gun*) barrer
▸ **rake in, rake together** *vt* sacar
rake-off ['reɪkɔf] *n* (*col*) comisión *f*, tajada
rakish ['reɪkɪʃ] *adj* (*dissolute*) libertino; **at a ~ angle** (*hat*) echado a un lado, de lado

rally ['rælɪ] *n* reunión *f*; (*Pol*) mitin *m*; (*Aut*) rallye *m*; (*Tennis*) peloteo ■ *vt* reunir ■ *vi* reunirse; (*sick person*) recuperarse; (*Stock Exchange*) recuperarse
▸ **rally round** *vt fus* (*fig*) dar apoyo a
rallying point ['rælɪɪŋ-] *n* (*Pol, Mil*) punto de reunión
RAM [ræm] *n abbr* (*Comput: = random access memory*) RAM *f*
ram [ræm] *n* carnero; (*Tech*) pisón *m* ■ *vt* (*crash into*) dar contra, chocar con; (*tread down*) apisonar
Ramadan ['ræmədæn] *n* Ramadán *m*
ramble ['ræmbl] *n* caminata, excursión *f* en el campo ■ *vi* (*pej: also:* **ramble on**) divagar
rambler ['ræmblə^r] *n* excursionista *m/f*; (*Bot*) trepadora
rambling ['ræmblɪŋ] *adj* (*speech*) inconexo; (*Bot*) trepador(a); (*house*) laberíntico
rambunctious [ræm'bʌŋkʃəs] *adj* (*US*) = **rumbustious**
RAMC *n abbr* (*Brit*) = **Royal Army Medical Corps**
ramification [ræmɪfɪ'keɪʃən] *n* ramificación *f*
ramp [ræmp] *n* rampa; **on/off ~** *n* (*US Aut*) vía de acceso/salida; **"~"** (*Aut*) "rampa"
rampage [ræm'peɪdʒ] *n*: **to be on the ~** desmandarse
rampant ['ræmpənt] *adj* (*disease etc*): **to be ~** estar muy extendido
rampart ['ræmpɑːt] *n* terraplén *m*; (*wall*) muralla
ram raid *vt* atracar (*rompiendo el escaparate con un coche*)
ramshackle ['ræmʃækl] *adj* destartalado
RAN *n abbr* = **Royal Australian Navy**
ran [ræn] *pt of* **run**
R & B *n abbr* = **rhythm and blues**
ranch [rɑːntʃ] *n* (*US*) hacienda, estancia
rancher ['rɑːntʃə^r] *n* ganadero
rancid ['rænsɪd] *adj* rancio
rancour, rancor (*US*) ['ræŋkə^r] *n* rencor *m*
R & D *n abbr* (*= research and development*) I + D
random ['rændəm] *adj* fortuito, sin orden; (*Comput, Math*) aleatorio ■ *n*: **at ~** al azar
random access *n* (*Comput*) acceso aleatorio
R & R *n abbr* (*also US Mil*) = **rest and recreation**
randy ['rændɪ] *adj* (*Brit col*) cachondo, caliente
rang [ræŋ] *pt of* **ring**
range [reɪndʒ] *n* (*of mountains*) cadena de montañas, cordillera; (*of missile*) alcance *m*; (*of voice*) registro; (*series*) serie *f*; (*of products*) surtido; (*Mil: also:* **shooting range**) campo de tiro; (*also:* **kitchen range**) fogón *m* ■ *vt* (*place*) colocar; (*arrange*) arreglar ■ *vi*: **to ~ over** (*wander*) recorrer; (*extend*) extenderse por; **within (firing) ~** a tiro; **do you have anything else in this price ~?** ¿tiene algo más de esta gama de precios?; **intermediate-/short-~ missile** proyectil *m* de medio/corto alcance; **to ~ from ... to ...** oscilar entre ... y ...; **ranged left/right** (*text*) alineado a la izquierda/derecha
ranger [reɪndʒə^r] *n* guardabosques *m inv*
Rangoon [ræŋ'guːn] *n* Rangún *m*
rangy ['reɪndʒɪ] *adj* alto y delgado
rank [ræŋk] *n* (*row*) fila; (*Mil*) rango; (*status*) categoría; (*Brit: also:* **taxi rank**) parada ■ *vi*: **to ~ among** figurar entre ■ *adj* (*stinking*) fétido, rancio; (*hypocrisy, injustice etc*) manifiesto; **the ~ and file** (*fig*) las bases; **to close ranks** (*Mil*) cerrar filas; (*fig*) hacer un frente común; **~ outsider** participante *m/f* sin probabilidades de vencer; **I ~ him sixth** yo le pongo en sexto lugar
rankle ['ræŋkl] *vi* (*insult*) doler
ransack ['rænsæk] *vt* (*search*) registrar; (*plunder*) saquear
ransom ['rænsəm] *n* rescate *m*; **to hold sb to ~** (*fig*) poner a algn entre la espada y la pared
rant [rænt] *vi* despotricar
ranting ['ræntɪŋ] *n* desvaríos *mpl*
rap [ræp] *vt* golpear, dar un golpecito en
rape [reɪp] *n* violación *f*; (*Bot*) colza ■ *vt* violar
rape oil, rapeseed oil ['reɪpsiːd-] *n* aceite *m* de colza
rapid ['ræpɪd] *adj* rápido
rapidity [rə'pɪdɪtɪ] *n* rapidez *f*
rapidly ['ræpɪdlɪ] *adv* rápidamente
rapids ['ræpɪdz] *npl* (*Geo*) rápidos *mpl*
rapier ['reɪpɪə^r] *n* estoque *m*
rapist ['reɪpɪst] *n* violador *m*
rapport [ræ'pɔː^r] *n* entendimiento
rapprochement [ræ'prɔʃmɑ̃ːŋ] *n* acercamiento
rapt [ræpt] *adj* (*attention*) profundo; **to be ~ in contemplation** estar ensimismado
rapture ['ræptʃə^r] *n* éxtasis *m*
rapturous ['ræptʃərəs] *adj* extático; (*applause*) entusiasta; **a ~ (party)** *macrofiesta con música máquina*; **~ music** música máquina
rare [rɛə^r] *adj* raro, poco común; (*Culin: steak*) poco hecho; **it is ~ to find that ...** es raro descubrir que ...
rarefied ['rɛərɪfaɪd] *adj* (*air, atmosphere*) enrarecido
rarely ['rɛəlɪ] *adv* rara vez, pocas veces
raring ['rɛərɪŋ] *adj*: **to be ~ to go** (*col*) tener muchas ganas de empezar
rarity ['rɛərɪtɪ] *n* rareza
rascal ['rɑːskl] *n* pillo(-a), pícaro(-a)

rash [ræʃ] *adj* imprudente, precipitado ▪ *n* (*Med*) salpullido, erupción *f* (cutánea); **to come out in a ~** salir salpullidos
rasher ['ræʃəʳ] *n* loncha
rashly ['ræʃlɪ] *adv* imprudentemente, precipitadamente
rashness ['ræʃnɪs] *n* imprudencia, precipitación *f*
rasp [rɑːsp] *n* (*tool*) escofina ▪ *vt* (*speak*: *also*: **rasp out**) decir con voz áspera
raspberry ['rɑːzbərɪ] *n* frambuesa
rasping ['rɑːspɪŋ] *adj*: **a ~ noise** un ruido áspero
Rastafarian [ræstə'fɛərɪən] *adj, n* rastafari *m/f*
rat [ræt] *n* rata
ratchet ['rætʃɪt] *n* (*Tech*) trinquete *m*
rate [reɪt] *n* (*ratio*) razón *f*; (*percentage*) tanto por ciento; (*price*) precio; (: *of hotel*) tarifa; (*of interest*) tipo; (*speed*) velocidad *f* ▪ *vt* (*value*) tasar; (*estimate*) estimar; **to ~ as** ser considerado como; **rates** *npl* (*Brit*) impuesto *sg* municipal; (*fees*) tarifa *sg*; **failure ~** porcentaje *m* de fallos; **pulse ~** pulsaciones *fpl* por minuto; **~ of pay** tipos *mpl* de sueldo; **at a ~ of 60 kph** a una velocidad de 60 kph; **~ of growth** ritmo de crecimiento; **~ of return** (*Comm*) tasa de rendimiento; **bank ~** tipo *or* tasa de interés bancario; **at any ~** en todo caso; **to ~ sb/sth highly** tener a algn/algo en alta estima; **the house is rated at £84 per annum** (*Brit*) la casa está tasada en 84 libras al año
rateable value ['reɪtəbl-] *n* (*Brit*) valor *m* impuesto
rate-capping ['reɪtkæpɪŋ] *n* (*Brit*) fijación *f* de las contribuciones
ratepayer ['reɪtpeɪəʳ] *n* (*Brit*) contribuyente *m/f*
rather ['rɑːðəʳ] *adv* antes, más bien; (*somewhat*) algo, un poco; (*quite*) bastante; **it's ~ expensive** es algo caro; (*too much*) es demasiado caro; **there's ~ a lot** hay bastante; **I would** *or* **I'd ~ go** preferiría ir; **I'd ~ not** prefiero que no; **I ~ think he won't come** me inclino a creer que no vendrá; **or ~** (*more accurately*) o mejor dicho
ratification [rætɪfɪ'keɪʃən] *n* ratificación *f*
ratify ['rætɪfaɪ] *vt* ratificar
rating ['reɪtɪŋ] *n* (*valuation*) tasación *f*; (*standing*) posición *f*; (*Brit Naut*: *sailor*) marinero; **ratings** *npl* (*Radio, TV*) clasificación *f*
ratio ['reɪʃɪəu] *n* razón *f*; **in the ~ of 100 to 1** a razón de *or* en la proporción de 100 a 1
ration ['ræʃən] *n* ración *f*; **rations** *npl* víveres *mpl* ▪ *vt* racionar
rational ['ræʃənl] *adj* racional; (*solution, reasoning*) lógico, razonable; (*person*) cuerdo, sensato
rationale [ræʃə'nɑːl] *n* razón *f* fundamental
rationalism ['ræʃnəlɪzəm] *n* racionalismo
rationalization [ræʃnəlaɪ'zeɪʃən] *n* racionalización *f*
rationalize ['ræʃnəlaɪz] *vt* (*reorganize*: *industry*) racionalizar
rationally ['ræʃnəlɪ] *adv* racionalmente; (*logically*) lógicamente
rationing ['ræʃnɪŋ] *n* racionamiento
ratpack ['rætpæk] *n* (*Brit col*) *periodistas que persiguen a los famosos*
rat race *n* *lucha incesante por la supervivencia*
rattan [ræ'tæn] *n* rota, caña de Indias
rattle ['rætl] *n* golpeteo; (*of train etc*) traqueteo; (*object*: *of baby*) sonaja, sonajero; (: *of sports fan*) matraca ▪ *vi* sonar, golpear; traquetear; (*small objects*) castañetear ▪ *vt* hacer sonar agitando; (*col*: *disconcert*) poner nervioso a
rattlesnake ['rætlsneɪk] *n* serpiente *f* de cascabel
ratty ['rætɪ] *adj* (*col*) furioso; **to get ~** mosquearse
raucous ['rɔːkəs] *adj* estridente, ronco
raucously ['rɔːkəslɪ] *adv* de modo estridente, roncamente
raunchy ['rɔːntʃɪ] *adj* (*col*) lascivo
ravage ['rævɪdʒ] *vt* hacer estragos en, destrozar; **ravages** *npl* estragos *mpl*
rave [reɪv] *vi* (*in anger*) encolerizarse; (*with enthusiasm*) entusiasmarse; (*Med*) delirar, desvariar ▪ *cpd*: **~ review** reseña entusiasta; **a ~ (party)** *macrofiesta con música máquina*; **~ music** música máquina
raven ['reɪvən] *n* cuervo
ravenous ['rævənəs] *adj*: **to be ~** tener un hambre canina
ravine [rə'viːn] *n* barranco
raving ['reɪvɪŋ] *adj*: **~ lunatic** loco de atar
ravings ['reɪvɪŋz] *npl* desvaríos *mpl*
ravioli [rævɪ'əulɪ] *n* ravioles *mpl*, ravioli *mpl*
ravish ['rævɪʃ] *vt* (*charm*) encantar, embelesar; (*rape*) violar
ravishing ['rævɪʃɪŋ] *adj* encantador(a)
raw [rɔː] *adj* (*uncooked*) crudo; (*not processed*) bruto; (*sore*) vivo; (*inexperienced*) novato, inexperto
Rawalpindi [rɔːl'pɪndɪ] *n* Rawalpindi *m*
raw data *n* (*Comput*) datos *mpl* en bruto
raw deal *n* (*col*: *bad deal*) mala pasada *or* jugada; (: *harsh treatment*) injusticia
raw material *n* materia prima
ray [reɪ] *n* rayo; **~ of hope** (rayo de) esperanza
rayon ['reɪɔn] *n* rayón *m*

raze [reɪz] *vt* (*also*: **raze to the ground**) arrasar, asolar
razor ['reɪzəʳ] *n* (*open*) navaja; (*safety razor*) máquina de afeitar
razor blade *n* hoja de afeitar
razzle ['ræzl], **razzle-dazzle** ['ræzl'dæzl] *n* (*Brit col*): **to be/go on the ~(-dazzle)** estar/irse de juerga
razzmatazz ['ræzmə'tæz] *n* (*col*) animación *f*, bullicio
RC *abbr* = **Roman Catholic**
RCAF *n abbr* = **Royal Canadian Air Force**
RCMP *n abbr* = **Royal Canadian Mounted Police**
RCN *n abbr* = **Royal Canadian Navy**
RD *abbr* (*US Post*) = **rural delivery**
Rd *abbr* = **road**
RDC *n abbr* (*Brit*) = **rural district council**
RE *n abbr* (*Brit*: = *religious education*) (*Brit Mil*) = **Royal Engineers**
re [ri:] *prep* con referencia a
re... [ri:] *pref* re...
reach [ri:tʃ] *n* alcance *m*; (*Boxing*) envergadura; (*of river etc*) extensión *f* entre dos recodos ■ *vt* alcanzar, llegar a; (*achieve*) lograr ■ *vi* extenderse; (*stretch out hand: also*: **reach down, reach over**: *also*: **reach across** *etc*) tender la mano; **within ~** al alcance (de la mano); **out of ~** fuera del alcance; **to ~ out for sth** alargar *or* tender la mano para tomar algo; **can I ~ you at your hotel?** ¿puedo localizarte en tu hotel?; **to ~ sb by phone** comunicarse con algn por teléfono
react [ri:'ækt] *vi* reaccionar
reaction [ri:'ækʃən] *n* reacción *f*
reactionary [ri:'ækʃənrɪ] *adj, n* reaccionario(-a) *m(f)*
reactor [ri:'æktəʳ] *n* reactor *m*
read (*pt, pp* ~) [ri:d, rɛd] *vi* leer ■ *vt* leer; (*understand*) entender; (*study*) estudiar; **to take sth as ~** (*fig*) dar algo por sentado; **do you ~ me?** (*Tel*) ¿me escucha?; **to ~ between the lines** leer entre líneas
▸ **read out** *vt* leer en alta voz
▸ **read over** *vt* repasar
▸ **read through** *vt* (*quickly*) leer rápidamente, echar un vistazo a; (*thoroughly*) leer con cuidado *or* detenidamente
▸ **read up** *vt*, **read up on** *vt fus* documentarse sobre
readable ['ri:dəbl] *adj* (*writing*) legible; (*book*) que merece la pena leer
reader ['ri:dəʳ] *n* lector(a) *m(f)*; (*book*) libro de lecturas; (*Brit: at university*) profesor(a) *m(f)*
readership ['ri:dəʃɪp] *n* (*of paper etc*) número de lectores
readily ['rɛdɪlɪ] *adv* (*willingly*) de buena gana; (*easily*) fácilmente; (*quickly*) en seguida
readiness ['rɛdɪnɪs] *n* buena voluntad; (*preparedness*) preparación *f*; **in ~** (*prepared*) listo, preparado
reading ['ri:dɪŋ] *n* lectura; (*understanding*) comprensión *f*; (*on instrument*) indicación *f*
reading lamp *n* lámpara portátil
reading matter *n* lectura
reading room *n* sala de lectura
readjust [ri:ə'dʒʌst] *vt* reajustar ■ *vi* (*person*): **to ~ to** reajustarse a
readjustment [ri:ə'dʒʌstmənt] *n* reajuste *m*
ready ['rɛdɪ] *adj* listo, preparado; (*willing*) dispuesto; (*available*) disponible ■ *n*: **at the ~** (*Mil*) listo para tirar; **~ for use** listo para usar; **to be ~ to do sth** estar listo para hacer algo; **to get ~** *vi* prepararse ■ *vt* preparar
ready cash *n* efectivo
ready-made ['rɛdɪ'meɪd] *adj* confeccionado
ready money *n* dinero contante
ready reckoner *n* tabla de cálculos hechos
ready-to-wear ['rɛdɪtə'wɛəʳ] *adj* confeccionado
reaffirm [ri:ə'fə:m] *vt* reafirmar
reagent [ri:'eɪdʒənt] *n* reactivo
real [rɪəl] *adj* verdadero, auténtico; **in ~ terms** en términos reales; **in ~ life** en la vida real, en la realidad
real ale *n* cerveza elaborada tradicionalmente
real estate *n* bienes *mpl* raíces
real estate agency *n* = **estate agency**
realism ['rɪəlɪzəm] *n* (*also Art*) realismo
realist ['rɪəlɪst] *n* realista *m/f*
realistic [rɪə'lɪstɪk] *adj* realista
realistically [rɪə'lɪstɪklɪ] *adv* de modo realista
reality [ri:'ælɪtɪ] *n* realidad *f*; **in ~** en realidad
reality TV *n* telerrealidad *f*
realization [rɪəlaɪ'zeɪʃən] *n* comprensión *f*; (*of a project*) realización *f*; (*Comm: of assets*) realización *f*
realize ['rɪəlaɪz] *vt* (*understand*) darse cuenta de; (*a project*) realizar; (*Comm: asset*) realizar; **I ~ that ...** comprendo *or* entiendo que ...
really ['rɪəlɪ] *adv* realmente; **~?** ¿de veras?
realm [rɛlm] *n* reino; (*fig*) esfera
real time *n* (*Comput*) tiempo real
Realtor® ['rɪəltɔ:ʳ] *n* (*US*) corredor(a) *m(f)* de bienes raíces
ream [ri:m] *n* resma; **reams** (*fig, col*) montones *mpl*
reap [ri:p] *vt* segar; (*fig*) cosechar, recoger
reaper ['ri:pəʳ] *n* segador(a) *m(f)*
reappear [ri:ə'pɪəʳ] *vi* reaparecer
reappearance [ri:ə'pɪərəns] *n* reaparición *f*
reapply [ri:ə'plaɪ] *vi* volver a presentarse, hacer *or* presentar una nueva solicitud

reappoint [riːəˈpɔɪnt] *vt* volver a nombrar
reappraisal [riːəˈpreɪzl] *n* revaluación *f*
rear [rɪəʳ] *adj* trasero ■ *n* parte *f* trasera ■ *vt* (*cattle, family*) criar ■ *vi* (*also*: **rear up**: *animal*) encabritarse
rear-engined [ˈrɪərˈɛndʒɪnd] *adj* (*Aut*) con motor trasero
rearguard [ˈrɪəgɑːd] *n* retaguardia
rearm [riːˈɑːm] *vt* rearmar ■ *vi* rearmarse
rearmament [riːˈɑːməmənt] *n* rearme *m*
rearrange [riːəˈreɪndʒ] *vt* ordenar *or* arreglar de nuevo
rear-view [ˈrɪəvjuː]: **~ mirror** *n* (*Aut*) espejo retrovisor
reason [ˈriːzn] *n* razón *f* ■ *vi*: **to ~ with sb** tratar de que algn entre en razón; **it stands to ~ that** es lógico que; **the ~ for/why** la causa de/la razón por la cual; **she claims with good ~ that she's underpaid** dice con razón que está mal pagada; **all the more ~ why you should not sell it** razón de más para que no lo vendas
reasonable [ˈriːznəbl] *adj* razonable; (*sensible*) sensato
reasonably [ˈriːznəblɪ] *adv* razonablemente; **a ~ accurate report** un informe bastante exacto
reasoned [ˈriːznd] *adj* (*argument*) razonado
reasoning [ˈriːznɪŋ] *n* razonamiento, argumentos *mpl*
reassemble [riːəˈsɛmbl] *vt* volver a reunir; (*machine*) montar de nuevo ■ *vi* volver a reunirse
reassert [riːəˈsəːt] *vt* reafirmar, reiterar
reassurance [riːəˈʃuərəns] *n* consuelo
reassure [riːəˈʃuəʳ] *vt* tranquilizar; **to ~ sb that** tranquilizar a algn asegurándole que
reassuring [riːəˈʃuərɪŋ] *adj* tranquilizador(a)
reawakening [riːəˈweɪknɪŋ] *n* despertar *m*
rebate [ˈriːbeɪt] *n* (*on product*) rebaja; (*on tax etc*) desgravación *f*; (*repayment*) reembolso
rebel [ˈrɛbl] *n* rebelde *m/f* ■ *vi* [rɪˈbɛl] rebelarse, sublevarse
rebellion [rɪˈbɛljən] *n* rebelión *f*, sublevación *f*
rebellious [rɪˈbɛljəs] *adj* rebelde; (*child*) revoltoso
rebirth [riːˈbəːθ] *n* renacimiento
rebound [rɪˈbaund] *vi* (*ball*) rebotar ■ *n* [ˈriːbaund] rebote *m*
rebuff [rɪˈbʌf] *n* desaire *m*, rechazo ■ *vt* rechazar
rebuild [riːˈbɪld] *vt* (*irreg: like* **build**) reconstruir
rebuilding [riːˈbɪldɪŋ] *n* reconstrucción *f*
rebuke [rɪˈbjuːk] *n* reprimenda ■ *vt* reprender
rebut [rɪˈbʌt] *vt* rebatir
recalcitrant [rɪˈkælsɪtrənt] *adj* reacio
recall [rɪˈkɔːl] *vt* (*remember*) recordar; (*ambassador etc*) retirar; (*Comput*) volver a llamar ■ *n* recuerdo
recant [rɪˈkænt] *vi* retractarse
recap [ˈriːkæp] *vt, vi* recapitular
recapitulate [riːkəˈpɪtjuleɪt] *vt, vi* = **recap**
recapture [riːˈkæptʃəʳ] *vt* (*town*) reconquistar; (*atmosphere*) hacer revivir
recd., rec'd *abbr* (= *received*) recibido
recede [rɪˈsiːd] *vi* retroceder
receding [rɪˈsiːdɪŋ] *adj* (*forehead, chin*) hundido; **~ hairline** entradas *fpl*
receipt [rɪˈsiːt] *n* (*document*) recibo; (*act of receiving*) recepción *f*; **receipts** *npl* (*Comm*) ingresos *mpl*; **to acknowledge ~ of** acusar recibo de; **we are in ~ of ...** obra en nuestro poder ...
receivable [rɪˈsiːvəbl] *adj* (*Comm*) a cobrar
receive [rɪˈsiːv] *vt* recibir; (*guest*) acoger; (*wound*) sufrir; **"received with thanks"** "recibí"
Received Pronunciation [rɪˈsiːvd-] *n see* **RP**
receiver [rɪˈsiːvəʳ] *n* (*Tel*) auricular *m*; (*Radio*) receptor *m*; (*of stolen goods*) perista *m/f*; (*Law*) administrador *m* jurídico
receivership [rɪˈsiːvəʃɪp] *n*: **to go into ~** entrar en liquidación
recent [ˈriːsnt] *adj* reciente; **in ~ years** en los últimos años
recently [ˈriːsntlɪ] *adv* recientemente, recién (*LAm*); **~ arrived** recién llegado; **until ~** hasta hace poco
receptacle [rɪˈsɛptɪkl] *n* receptáculo
reception [rɪˈsɛpʃən] *n* (*in building, office etc*) recepción *f*; (*welcome*) acogida
reception centre *n* (*Brit*) centro de recepción
reception desk *n* recepción *f*
receptionist [rɪˈsɛpʃənɪst] *n* recepcionista *m/f*
receptive [rɪˈsɛptɪv] *adj* receptivo
recess [rɪˈsɛs] *n* (*in room*) hueco; (*for bed*) nicho; (*secret place*) escondrijo; (*Pol etc: holiday*) período vacacional; (*US Law: short break*) descanso; (*Scol: esp US*) recreo
recession [rɪˈsɛʃən] *n* recesión *f*, depresión *f*
recharge [riːˈtʃɑːdʒ] *vt* (*battery*) recargar
rechargeable [riːˈtʃɑːdʒəbl] *adj* recargable
recipe [ˈrɛsɪpɪ] *n* receta
recipient [rɪˈsɪpɪənt] *n* recibidor(a) *m(f)*; (*of letter*) destinatario(-a)
reciprocal [rɪˈsɪprəkl] *adj* recíproco
reciprocate [rɪˈsɪprəkeɪt] *vt* devolver, corresponder a ■ *vi* corresponder
recital [rɪˈsaɪtl] *n* (*Mus*) recital *m*
recitation [rɛsɪˈteɪʃən] *n* (*of poetry*) recitado; (*of complaints etc*) enumeración *f*, relación *f*

recite [rɪ'saɪt] *vt* (*poem*) recitar; (*complaints etc*) enumerar
reckless ['rɛkləs] *adj* temerario, imprudente; (*speed*) peligroso
recklessly ['rɛkləslɪ] *adv* imprudentemente; de modo peligroso
recklessness ['rɛkləsnɪs] *n* temeridad *f*, imprudencia
reckon ['rɛkən] *vt* (*count*) contar; (*consider*) considerar ■ *vi*: **to ~ without sb/sth** dejar de contar con algn/algo; **he is somebody to be reckoned with** no se le puede descartar; **I ~ that ...** me parece que ..., creo que ...
▸ **reckon on** *vt fus* contar con
reckoning ['rɛkənɪŋ] *n* (*calculation*) cálculo
reclaim [rɪ'kleɪm] *vt* (*land*) recuperar; (*: from sea*) rescatar; (*demand back*) reclamar
reclamation [rɛklə'meɪʃən] *n* recuperación *f*; rescate *m*
recline [rɪ'klaɪn] *vi* reclinarse
reclining [rɪ'klaɪnɪŋ] *adj* (*seat*) reclinable
recluse [rɪ'klu:s] *n* recluso(-a)
recognition [rɛkəg'nɪʃən] *n* reconocimiento; **transformed beyond ~** irreconocible; **in ~ of** en reconocimiento de
recognizable ['rɛkəgnaɪzəbl] *adj*: **~ (by)** reconocible (por)
recognize ['rɛkəgnaɪz] *vt* reconocer, conocer; **to ~ (by/as)** reconocer (por/como)
recoil [rɪ'kɔɪl] *vi* (*person*): **to ~ from doing sth** retraerse de hacer algo ■ *n* (*of gun*) retroceso
recollect [rɛkə'lɛkt] *vt* recordar, acordarse de
recollection [rɛkə'lɛkʃən] *n* recuerdo; **to the best of my ~** que yo recuerde
recommend [rɛkə'mɛnd] *vt* recomendar; **she has a lot to ~ her** tiene mucho a su favor
recommendation [rɛkəmɛn'deɪʃən] *n* recomendación *f*
recommended retail price *n* (*Brit*) precio (recomendado) de venta al público
recompense ['rɛkəmpɛns] *vt* recompensar ■ *n* recompensa
reconcilable ['rɛkənsaɪləbl] *adj* (re)conciliable
reconcile ['rɛkənsaɪl] *vt* (*two people*) reconciliar; (*two facts*) conciliar; **to ~ o.s. to sth** resignarse *or* conformarse a algo
reconciliation [rɛkənsɪlɪ'eɪʃən] *n* reconciliación *f*
recondite [rɪ'kɔndaɪt] *adj* recóndito
recondition [ri:kən'dɪʃən] *vt* (*machine*) reparar, reponer
reconditioned [ri:kən'dɪʃənd] *adj* renovado, reparado
reconnaissance [rɪ'kɔnɪsns] *n* (*Mil*) reconocimiento
reconnoitre, (*US*) **reconnoiter** [rɛkə'nɔɪtə^r] *vt*, *vi* (*Mil*) reconocer
reconsider [ri:kən'sɪdə^r] *vt* repensar
reconstitute [ri:'kɔnstɪtju:t] *vt* reconstituir
reconstruct [ri:kən'strʌkt] *vt* reconstruir
reconstruction [ri:kən'strʌkʃən] *n* reconstrucción *f*
reconvene [ri:kən'vi:n] *vt* volver a convocar ■ *vi* volver a reunirse
record *n* ['rɛkɔ:d] (*Mus*) disco; (*of meeting etc*) relación *f*; (*register*) registro, partida; (*file*) archivo; (*also*: **police** *or* **criminal record**) antecedentes *mpl* penales; (*written*) expediente *m*; (*Sport*) récord *m*; (*Comput*) registro ■ *vt* [rɪ'kɔ:d] (*set down*) registrar; (*Comput*) registrar; (*relate*) hacer constar; (*Mus: song etc*) grabar; **in ~ time** en un tiempo récord; **public records** archivos *mpl* nacionales; **he is on ~ as saying that ...** hay pruebas de que ha dicho públicamente que ...; **Spain's excellent ~** el excelente historial de España; **off the ~** *adj* no oficial ■ *adv* confidencialmente
record card *n* (*in file*) ficha
recorded delivery letter [rɪ'kɔ:dɪd-] *n* (*Brit Post*) carta de entrega con acuse de recibo
recorded music *n* música grabada
recorder [rɪ'kɔ:də^r] *n* (*Mus*) flauta de pico; (*Tech*) contador *m*
record holder *n* (*Sport*) actual poseedor(a) *m(f)* del récord
recording [rɪ'kɔ:dɪŋ] *n* (*Mus*) grabación *f*
recording studio *n* estudio de grabación
record library *n* discoteca
record player *n* tocadiscos *m inv*
recount *vt* [rɪ'kaunt] contar
re-count ['ri:kaunt] *n* (*Pol: of votes*) segundo escrutinio, recuento ■ *vt* [ri:'kaunt] volver a contar
recoup [rɪ'ku:p] *vt*: **to ~ one's losses** recuperar las pérdidas
recourse [rɪ'kɔ:s] *n* recurso; **to have ~ to** recurrir a
recover [rɪ'kʌvə^r] *vt* recuperar; (*rescue*) rescatar ■ *vi* recuperarse
recovery [rɪ'kʌvərɪ] *n* recuperación *f*; rescate *m*; (*Med*): **to make a ~** restablecerse
recreate [ri:krɪ'eɪt] *vt* recrear
recreation [rɛkrɪ'eɪʃən] *n* recreación *f*; (*amusement*) recreo
recreational [rɛkrɪ'eɪʃənl] *adj* de, recreo
recreational drug *n* droga recreativa
recreational vehicle *n* (*US*) caravana *or* roulotte *f* pequeña
recrimination [rɪkrɪmɪ'neɪʃən] *n* recriminación *f*
recruit [rɪ'kru:t] *n* recluta *m/f* ■ *vt* reclutar; (*staff*) contratar
recruiting office [rɪ'kru:tɪŋ-] *n* caja de reclutas

recruitment [rɪ'kru:tmənt] *n* reclutamiento
rectangle ['rɛktæŋgl] *n* rectángulo
rectangular [rɛk'tæŋgjulə^r] *adj* rectangular
rectify ['rɛktɪfaɪ] *vt* rectificar
rector ['rɛktə^r] *n* (*Rel*) párroco; (*Scol*) rector(a) *m(f)*
rectory ['rɛktərɪ] *n* casa del párroco
rectum ['rɛktəm] *n* (*Anat*) recto
recuperate [rɪ'ku:pəreɪt] *vi* reponerse, restablecerse
recur [rɪ'kə:^r] *vi* repetirse; (*pain, illness*) producirse de nuevo
recurrence [rɪ'kə:rns] *n* repetición *f*
recurrent [rɪ'kə:rnt] *adj* repetido
recyclable [ri:'saɪkləbl] *adj* reciclable
recycle [ri:'saɪkl] *vt* reciclar
recycling [ri:'saɪklɪŋ] *vt* reciclaje *m*
red [rɛd] *n* rojo ■ *adj* rojo; **to be in the ~** (*account*) estar en números rojos; (*business*) tener un saldo negativo; **to give sb the ~ carpet treatment** recibir a algn con todos los honores
red alert *n* alerta roja
red-blooded ['rɛd'blʌdɪd] *adj* (*col*) viril
redbrick university ['rɛdbrɪk-] *n ver nota*

REDBRICK UNIVERSITY

El término *redbrick university* se aplica a las universidades construidas en los grandes centros urbanos industriales como Birmingham, Liverpool o Manchester a finales del siglo XIX o principios del XX. Deben su nombre a que sus edificios son normalmente de ladrillo, a diferencia de las universidades tradicionales de Oxford y Cambridge, cuyos edificios suelen ser de piedra.

Red Cross *n* Cruz *f* Roja
redcurrant ['rɛdkʌrənt] *n* grosella
redden ['rɛdn] *vt* enrojecer ■ *vi* enrojecerse
reddish ['rɛdɪʃ] *adj* (*hair*) rojizo
redecorate [ri:'dɛkəreɪt] *vt* pintar de nuevo; volver a decorar
redecoration [ri:dɛkə'reɪʃən] *n* renovación *f*
redeem [rɪ'di:m] *vt* (*sth in pawn*) desempeñar; (*Rel*) rescatar; (*fig*) rescatar
redeemable [rɪ'di:məbl] *adj* canjeable
redeeming [rɪ'di:mɪŋ] *adj*: **~ feature** punto bueno *or* favorable
redefine [ri:dɪ'faɪn] *vt* redefinir
redemption [rɪ'dɛmpʃən] *n* (*Rel*) redención *f*; **to be past** *or* **beyond ~** no tener remedio
redeploy [ri:dɪ'plɔɪ] *vt* disponer de nuevo
redeployment [ri:dɪ'plɔɪmənt] *n* redistribución *f*
redevelop [ri:dɪ'vɛləp] *vt* reorganizar
redevelopment [ri:dɪ'vɛləpmənt] *n* reorganización *f*
red-handed [rɛd'hændɪd] *adj*: **he was caught ~** le pillaron con las manos en la masa
redhead ['rɛdhɛd] *n* pelirrojo(-a)
red herring *n* (*fig*) pista falsa
red-hot [rɛd'hɔt] *adj* candente
redirect [ri:daɪ'rɛkt] *vt* (*mail*) reexpedir
rediscover [ri:dɪs'kʌvə^r] *vt* redescubrir
rediscovery [ri:dɪs'kʌvərɪ] *n* redescubrimiento
redistribute [ri:dɪs'trɪbju:t] *vt* redistribuir, hacer una nueva distribución de
red-letter day [rɛd'lɛtə-] *n* día *m* señalado, día *m* especial
red light *n*: **to go through** *or* **jump a ~** (*Aut*) saltarse un semáforo
red-light district *n* barrio chino, zona de tolerancia
red meat *n* carne *f* roja
redness ['rɛdnɪs] *n* rojez *f*
redo [ri:'du:] *vt* (*irreg: like* **do**) rehacer
redolent ['rɛdələnt] *adj*: **~ of** (*smell*) con fragancia a; **to be ~ of** (*fig*) evocar
redouble [ri:'dʌbl] *vt*: **to ~ one's efforts** redoblar los esfuerzos
redraft [ri:'drɑ:ft] *vt* volver a redactar
redress [rɪ'drɛs] *n* reparación *f* ■ *vt* reparar, corregir; **to ~ the balance** restablecer el equilibrio
Red Sea *n*: **the ~** el mar Rojo
redskin ['rɛdskɪn] *n* piel roja *m/f*
red tape *n* (*fig*) trámites *mpl*, papeleo (*fam*)
reduce [rɪ'dju:s] *vt* reducir; (*lower*) rebajar; **to ~ sth by/to** reducir algo en/a; **to ~ sb to silence/despair/tears** hacer callar/desesperarse/llorar a algn; **"~ speed now"** (*Aut*) "reduzca la velocidad"
reduced [rɪ'dju:st] *adj* (*decreased*) reducido, rebajado; **at a ~ price** con rebaja *or* descuento; **"greatly ~ prices"** "grandes rebajas"
reduction [rɪ'dʌkʃən] *n* reducción *f*; (*of price*) rebaja; (*discount*) descuento
redundancy [rɪ'dʌndənsɪ] *n* despido; (*unemployment*) desempleo; **voluntary ~** baja voluntaria
redundancy payment *n* indemnización *f* por desempleo
redundant [rɪ'dʌndənt] *adj* (*Brit: worker*) parado, sin trabajo; (*detail, object*) superfluo; **to be made ~** quedar(se) sin trabajo, perder el empleo
reed [ri:d] *n* (*Bot*) junco, caña; (*Mus: of clarinet etc*) lengüeta

re-educate [ri:ˈɛdjukeɪt] *vt* reeducar
reedy [ˈri:dɪ] *adj (voice, instrument)* aflautado
reef [ri:f] *n (at sea)* arrecife *m*
reek [ri:k] *vi*: **to ~ (of)** oler *or* apestar (a)
reel [ri:l] *n* carrete *m*, bobina; *(of film)* rollo ■ *vt (Tech)* devanar; *(also:* **reel in**) sacar ■ *vi (sway)* tambalear(se); **my head is reeling** me da vueltas la cabeza
▶ **reel off** *vt* recitar de memoria
re-election [ri:ɪˈlɛkʃən] *n* reelección *f*
re-engage [ri:ɪnˈgeɪdʒ] *vt* contratar de nuevo
re-enter [ri:ˈɛntəʳ] *vt* reingresar en, volver a entrar en
re-entry [ri:ˈɛntrɪ] *n* reingreso, reentrada
re-examine [ri:ɪgˈzæmɪn] *vt* reexaminar
re-export *vt* [ˈri:ɪksˈpɔ:t] reexportar ■ *n* [ri:ˈɛkspɔ:t] reexportación *f*
ref [rɛf] *n abbr (col)* = **referee**
ref. *abbr (Comm: = with reference to)* Ref
refectory [rɪˈfɛktərɪ] *n* comedor *m*
refer [rɪˈfə:ʳ] *vt (send)* remitir; *(ascribe)* referir a, relacionar con ■ *vi*: **to ~ to** *(allude to)* referirse a, aludir a; *(apply to)* relacionarse con; *(consult)* remitirse a; **he referred me to the manager** me envió al gerente
referee [rɛfəˈri:] *n* árbitro; *(Brit: for job application)* persona que da referencias de otro ■ *vt (match)* arbitrar en
reference [ˈrɛfrəns] *n (mention: in book)* referencia; *(sending)* remisión *f*; *(relevance)* relación *f*; *(for job application: letter)* carta de recomendación; **with ~ to** con referencia a; *(Comm: in letter)* me remito a
reference book *n* libro de consulta
reference library *n* biblioteca de consulta
reference number *n* número de referencia
referendum *(pl* **referenda**) [rɛfəˈrɛndəm, -də] *n* referéndum *m*
referral [rɪˈfə:rəl] *n* remisión *f*
refill *vt* [ri:ˈfɪl] rellenar ■ *n* [ˈri:fɪl] repuesto, recambio
refine [rɪˈfaɪn] *vt (sugar, oil)* refinar
refined [rɪˈfaɪnd] *adj (person, taste)* refinado, culto
refinement [rɪˈfaɪnmənt] *n (of person)* cultura, educación *f*
refinery [rɪˈfaɪnərɪ] *n* refinería
refit *(also Naut) n* [ˈri:fɪt] reparación *f* ■ *vt* [ri:ˈfɪt] reparar
reflate [ri:ˈfleɪt] *vt (economy)* reflacionar
reflation [ri:ˈfleɪʃən] *n* reflación *f*
reflationary [ri:ˈfleɪʃənrɪ] *adj* reflacionario
reflect [rɪˈflɛkt] *vt (light, image)* reflejar ■ *vi (think)* reflexionar, pensar; **it reflects badly/well on him** le perjudica/le hace honor
reflection [rɪˈflɛkʃən] *n (act)* reflexión *f*; *(image)* reflejo; *(discredit)* crítica; **on ~** pensándolo bien
reflector [rɪˈflɛktəʳ] *n (Aut)* catafaros *m inv*; *(telescope)* reflector *m*
reflex [ˈri:flɛks] *adj, n* reflejo
reflexive [rɪˈflɛksɪv] *adj (Ling)* reflexivo
reform [rɪˈfɔ:m] *n* reforma ■ *vt* reformar
reformat [ri:ˈfɔ:mæt] *vt (Comput)* recomponer
Reformation [rɛfəˈmeɪʃən] *n*: **the ~** la Reforma
reformatory [rɪˈfɔ:mətərɪ] *n (US)* reformatorio
reformer [rɪˈfɔ:məʳ] *n* reformador(a) *m(f)*
refrain [rɪˈfreɪn] *vi*: **to ~ from doing** abstenerse de hacer ■ *n (Mus etc)* estribillo
refresh [rɪˈfrɛʃ] *vt* refrescar
refresher course [rɪˈfrɛʃə-] *n (Brit)* curso de repaso
refreshing [rɪˈfrɛʃɪŋ] *adj (drink)* refrescante; *(sleep)* reparador; *(change etc)* estimulante; *(idea, point of view)* estimulante, interesante
refreshments [rɪˈfrɛʃmənts] *npl (drinks)* refrescos *mpl*
refrigeration [rɪfrɪdʒəˈreɪʃən] *n* refrigeración *f*
refrigerator [rɪˈfrɪdʒəreɪtəʳ] *n* frigorífico, refrigeradora *(LAm)*, heladera *(LAm)*
refuel [ri:ˈfjuəl] *vi* repostar (combustible)
refuelling, *(US)* **refueling** [ri:ˈfjuəlɪŋ] *n* reabastecimiento de combustible
refuge [ˈrɛfju:dʒ] *n* refugio, asilo; **to take ~ in** refugiarse en
refugee [rɛfjuˈdʒi:] *n* refugiado(-a)
refugee camp *n* campamento para refugiados
refund *n* [ˈri:fʌnd] reembolso ■ *vt* [rɪˈfʌnd] devolver, reembolsar
refurbish [ri:ˈfə:bɪʃ] *vt* restaurar, renovar
refurnish [ri:ˈfə:nɪʃ] *vt* amueblar de nuevo
refusal [rɪˈfju:zəl] *n* negativa; **first ~** primera opción; **to have first ~ on sth** tener la primera opción a algo
refuse [*n* ˈrɛfju:s, *vb* rɪˈfju:z] *n* basura ■ *vt (reject)* rehusar; *(say no to)* negarse a ■ *vi* negarse; *(horse)* rehusar; **to ~ to do sth** negarse a *or* rehusar hacer algo
refuse bin *n* cubo *or* bote *m (LAm) or* balde *m (LAm)* de la basura
refuse collection *n* recogida de basuras
refuse disposal *n* eliminación *f* de basuras
refusenik [rɪˈfju:znɪk] *n judío/a que tenía prohibido emigrar de la ex Unión Soviética*
refuse tip *n* vertedero
refute [rɪˈfju:t] *vt* refutar, rebatir
regain [rɪˈgeɪn] *vt* recobrar, recuperar
regal [ˈri:gl] *adj* regio, real
regale [rɪˈgeɪl] *vt* agasajar, entretener

regalia [rɪ'geɪlɪə] *n* galas *fpl*
regard [rɪ'gɑːd] *n* (*gaze*) mirada; (*aspect*) respecto; (*esteem*) respeto, consideración *f* ■ *vt* (*consider*) considerar; (*look at*) mirar; **to give one's regards to** saludar de su parte a; **"(kind) regards"** "muy atentamente"; **"with kindest regards"** "con muchos recuerdos"; **regards to María, please give my regards to María** recuerdos a María, dele recuerdos a María de mi parte; **as regards, with ~ to** con respecto a, en cuanto a
regarding [rɪ'gɑːdɪŋ] *prep* con respecto a, en cuanto a
regardless [rɪ'gɑːdlɪs] *adv* a pesar de todo; **~ of** sin reparar en
regatta [rɪ'gætə] *n* regata
regency ['riːdʒənsɪ] *n* regencia
regenerate [rɪ'dʒɛnəreɪt] *vt* regenerar
regent ['riːdʒənt] *n* regente *m/f*
reggae ['rɛgeɪ] *n* reggae *m*
régime [reɪ'ʒiːm] *n* régimen *m*
regiment *n* ['rɛdʒɪmənt] regimiento ■ *vt* ['rɛdʒɪmɛnt] reglamentar
regimental [rɛdʒɪ'mɛntl] *adj* militar
regimentation [rɛdʒɪmɛn'teɪʃən] *n* regimentación *f*
region ['riːdʒən] *n* región *f*; **in the ~ of** (*fig*) alrededor de
regional ['riːdʒənl] *adj* regional
regional development *n* desarrollo, regional
register ['rɛdʒɪstə^r] *n* registro ■ *vt* registrar; (*birth*) declarar; (*letter*) certificar; (*instrument*) marcar, indicar ■ *vi* (*at hotel*) registrarse; (*sign on*) inscribirse; (*make impression*) producir impresión; **to ~ a protest** presentar una queja; **to ~ for a course** matricularse *or* inscribirse en un curso
registered ['rɛdʒɪstəd] *adj* (*design*) registrado; (*Brit: letter*) certificado; (*student*) matriculado; (*voter*) registrado
registered company *n* sociedad *f* legalmente constituida
registered nurse *n* (*US*) enfermero(-a) titulado(-a)
registered office *n* domicilio social
registered trademark *n* marca registrada
registrar ['rɛdʒɪstrɑː^r] *n* secretario(-a) (del registro civil)
registration [rɛdʒɪs'treɪʃən] *n* (*act*) declaración *f*; (*Aut: also*: **registration number**) matrícula
registry ['rɛdʒɪstrɪ] *n* registro
registry office *n* (*Brit*) registro civil; **to get married in a ~** casarse por lo civil
regret [rɪ'grɛt] *n* sentimiento, pesar *m*; (*remorse*) remordimiento ■ *vt* sentir, lamentar; (*repent of*) arrepentirse de; **we ~ to inform you that ...** sentimos informarle que ...
regretful [rɪ'grɛtful] *adj* pesaroso, arrepentido
regretfully [rɪ'grɛtfəlɪ] *adv* con pesar, sentidamente
regrettable [rɪ'grɛtəbl] *adj* lamentable; (*loss*) sensible
regrettably [rɪ'grɛtəblɪ] *adv* desgraciadamente
regroup [riː'gruːp] *vt* reagrupar ■ *vi* reagruparse
regt *abbr* = **regiment**
regular ['rɛgjulə^r] *adj* regular; (*soldier*) profesional; (*col: intensive*) verdadero; (*listener, reader*) asiduo, habitual ■ *n* (*client etc*) cliente(-a) *m(f)* habitual
regularity [rɛgju'lærɪtɪ] *n* regularidad *f*
regularly ['rɛgjuləlɪ] *adv* con regularidad
regulate ['rɛgjuleɪt] *vt* (*gen*) controlar; (*Tech*) regular, ajustar
regulation [rɛgju'leɪʃən] *n* (*rule*) regla, reglamento; (*adjustment*) regulación *f*
rehabilitate [riːə'bɪlɪteɪt] *vt* rehabilitar
rehabilitation ['riːəbɪlɪ'teɪʃən] *n* rehabilitación *f*
rehash [riː'hæʃ] *vt* (*col*) hacer un refrito de
rehearsal [rɪ'həːsəl] *n* ensayo; **dress ~** ensayo general *or* final
rehearse [rɪ'həːs] *vt* ensayar
rehouse [riː'hauz] *vt* dar nueva vivienda a
reign [reɪn] *n* reinado; (*fig*) predominio ■ *vi* reinar; (*fig*) imperar
reigning ['reɪnɪŋ] *adj* (*monarch*) reinante, actual; (*predominant*) imperante
reiki ['reɪkɪ] *n* reiki *m*
reimburse [riːɪm'bəːs] *vt* reembolsar
rein [reɪn] *n* (*for horse*) rienda; **to give sb free ~** dar rienda suelta a algn
reincarnation [riːɪnkɑː'neɪʃən] *n* reencarnación *f*
reindeer ['reɪndɪə^r] *n* (*pl inv*) reno
reinforce [riːɪn'fɔːs] *vt* reforzar
reinforced concrete [riːɪn'fɔːst-] *n* hormigón *m* armado
reinforcement [riːɪn'fɔːsmənt] *n* (*action*) refuerzo; **reinforcements** *npl* (*Mil*) refuerzos *mpl*
reinstate [riːɪn'steɪt] *vt* (*worker*) reintegrar (a su puesto)
reinstatement [riːɪn'steɪtmənt] *n* reintegración *f*
reissue [riː'ɪʃuː] *vt* (*record, book*) reeditar
reiterate [riː'ɪtəreɪt] *vt* reiterar, repetir
reject *n* ['riːdʒɛkt] (*thing*) desecho ■ *vt* [rɪ'dʒɛkt] rechazar; (*proposition, offer etc*) descartar

rejection [rɪ'dʒɛkʃən] *n* rechazo
rejoice [rɪ'dʒɔɪs] *vi*: **to ~ at** *or* **over** regocijarse *or* alegrarse de
rejoinder [rɪ'dʒɔɪndəʳ] *n* (*retort*) réplica
rejuvenate [rɪ'dʒu:vəneɪt] *vt* rejuvenecer
rekindle [ri:'kɪndl] *vt* volver a encender; (*fig*) despertar
relapse [rɪ'læps] *n* (*Med*) recaída; (*into crime*) reincidencia
relate [rɪ'leɪt] *vt* (*tell*) contar, relatar; (*connect*) relacionar ■ *vi* relacionarse; **to ~ to** (*connect*) relacionarse *or* tener que ver con
related [rɪ'leɪtɪd] *adj* afín; (*person*) emparentado; **~ to** con referencia a, relacionado con
relating [rɪ'leɪtɪŋ]: **~ to** *prep* referente a
relation [rɪ'leɪʃən] *n* (*person*) pariente *m/f*; (*link*) relación *f*; **in ~ to** en relación con, en lo que se refiere a; **to bear a ~ to** guardar relación con; **diplomatic relations** relaciones *fpl* diplomáticas
relationship [rɪ'leɪʃənʃɪp] *n* relación *f*; (*personal*) relaciones *fpl*; (*also*: **family relationship**) parentesco
relative ['rɛlətɪv] *n* pariente *m/f*, familiar *m/f* ■ *adj* relativo
relatively ['rɛlətɪvlɪ] *adv* (*fairly, rather*) relativamente
relative pronoun *n* pronombre *m* relativo
relax [rɪ'læks] *vi* descansar; (*quieten down*) relajarse ■ *vt* relajar; (*grip*) aflojar; **~!** (*calm down*) ¡tranquilo!
relaxation [ri:læk'seɪʃən] *n* (*rest*) descanso; (*easing*) relajación *f*, relajamiento *m*; (*amusement*) recreo; (*entertainment*) diversión *f*
relaxed [rɪ'lækst] *adj* relajado; (*tranquil*) tranquilo
relaxing [rɪ'læksɪŋ] *adj* relajante
relay *n* ['ri:leɪ] (*race*) carrera de relevos ■ *vt* [rɪ'leɪ] (*Radio, TV*) retransmitir; (*pass on*) retransmitir
release [rɪ'li:s] *n* (*liberation*) liberación *f*; (*discharge*) puesta en libertad *f*; (*of gas etc*) escape *m*; (*of film etc*) estreno ■ *vt* (*prisoner*) poner en libertad; (*film*) estrenar; (*book*) publicar; (*piece of news*) difundir; (*gas etc*) despedir, arrojar; (*free: from wreckage etc*) liberar; (*Tech: catch, spring etc*) desenganchar; (*let go*) soltar, aflojar
relegate ['rɛləgeɪt] *vt* relegar; (*Sport*): **to be relegated to** bajar a
relent [rɪ'lɛnt] *vi* ceder, ablandarse; (*let up*) descansar
relentless [rɪ'lɛntlɪs] *adj* implacable
relentlessly [rɪ'lɛntlɪslɪ] *adv* implacablemente
relevance ['rɛləvəns] *n* relación *f*
relevant ['rɛləvənt] *adj* (*fact*) pertinente; **~ to** relacionado con
reliability [rɪlaɪə'bɪlɪtɪ] *n* fiabilidad *f*; seguridad *f*; veracidad *f*
reliable [rɪ'laɪəbl] *adj* (*person, firm*) de confianza, de fiar; (*method, machine*) seguro; (*source*) fidedigno
reliably [rɪ'laɪəblɪ] *adv*: **to be ~ informed that ...** saber de fuente fidedigna que ...
reliance [rɪ'laɪəns] *n*: **~ (on)** dependencia (de)
reliant [rɪ'laɪənt] *adj*: **to be ~ on sth/sb** depender de algo/algn
relic ['rɛlɪk] *n* (*Rel*) reliquia; (*of the past*) vestigio
relief [rɪ'li:f] *n* (*from pain, anxiety*) alivio, desahogo; (*help, supplies*) socorro, ayuda; (*Art, Geo*) relieve *m*; **by way of light ~** a modo de diversión
relief road *n* carretera de descongestionamiento
relieve [rɪ'li:v] *vt* (*pain, patient*) aliviar; (*bring help to*) ayudar, socorrer; (*burden*) aligerar; (*take over from: gen*) sustituir a; (: *guard*) relevar; **to ~ sb of sth** quitar algo a algn; **to ~ sb of his command** (*Mil*) relevar a algn de su mando; **to ~ o.s.** hacer sus necesidades; **I am relieved to hear you are better** me alivia saber que estás *or* te encuentras mejor
religion [rɪ'lɪdʒən] *n* religión *f*
religious [rɪ'lɪdʒəs] *adj* religioso
religious education *n* educación *f* religiosa
religiously [rɪ'lɪdʒəslɪ] *adv* religiosamente
relinquish [rɪ'lɪŋkwɪʃ] *vt* abandonar; (*plan, habit*) renunciar a
relish ['rɛlɪʃ] *n* (*Culin*) salsa; (*enjoyment*) entusiasmo; (*flavour*) sabor *m*, gusto ■ *vt* (*food, challenge etc*) saborear; **to ~ doing** gozar haciendo
relive [ri:'lɪv] *vt* vivir de nuevo, volver a vivir
relocate [ri:ləu'keɪt] *vt* trasladar ■ *vi* trasladarse
reluctance [rɪ'lʌktəns] *n* desgana, renuencia
reluctant [rɪ'lʌktənt] *adj* reacio; **to be ~ to do sth** resistirse a hacer algo
reluctantly [rɪ'lʌktəntlɪ] *adv* de mala gana
rely [rɪ'laɪ]: **to ~ on** *vt fus* confiar en, fiarse de; (*be dependent on*) depender de; **you can ~ on my discretion** puedes contar con mi discreción
remain [rɪ'meɪn] *vi* (*survive*) quedar; (*be left*) sobrar; (*continue*) quedar(se), permanecer; **to ~ silent** permanecer callado; **I ~, yours faithfully** (*in letters*) le saluda atentamente
remainder [rɪ'meɪndəʳ] *n* resto
remaining [rɪ'meɪnɪŋ] *adj* sobrante
remains [rɪ'meɪnz] *npl* restos *mpl*

remand [rɪ'mɑːnd] *n*: **on ~** detenido (bajo custodia) ■ *vt*: **to ~ in custody** mantener bajo custodia
remand home *n* (*Brit*) reformatorio
remark [rɪ'mɑːk] *n* comentario ■ *vt* comentar; **to ~ on sth** hacer observaciones sobre algo
remarkable [rɪ'mɑːkəbl] *adj* notable; (*outstanding*) extraordinario
remarkably [rɪ'mɑːkəblɪ] *adv* extraordinariamente
remarry [riː'mærɪ] *vi* casarse por segunda vez, volver a casarse
remedial [rɪ'miːdɪəl] *adj*: **~ education** educación *f* de los niños atrasados
remedy ['rɛmədɪ] *n* remedio ■ *vt* remediar, curar
remember [rɪ'mɛmbəʳ] *vt* recordar, acordarse de; (*bear in mind*) tener presente; **I ~ seeing it, I ~ having seen it** recuerdo haberlo visto; **she remembered doing it** se acordó de hacerlo; **~ me to your wife and children!** ¡déle recuerdos a su familia!
remembrance [rɪ'mɛmbrəns] *n* (*memory, souvenir*) recuerdo; **in ~ of** en conmemoración de
Remembrance Day, Remembrance Sunday *n* (*Brit*) *ver nota*

REMEMBRANCE DAY

En el Reino Unido el domingo más cercano al 11 de noviembre es *Remembrance Day* o *Remembrance Sunday*, aniversario de la firma del armisticio de 1918 que puso fin a la Primera Guerra Mundial. Tal día se recuerda a todos aquellos que murieron en las dos guerras mundiales con dos minutos de silencio a las once de la mañana hora en que se firmó el armisticio durante los actos de conmemoración celebrados en los monumentos a los caídos. Allí se colocan coronas de amapolas, flor que también se suele llevar prendida en el pecho tras pagar un donativo para los inválidos de guerra.

remind [rɪ'maɪnd] *vt*: **to ~ sb to do sth** recordar a algn que haga algo; **to ~ sb of sth** recordar algo a algn; **she reminds me of her mother** me recuerda a su madre; **that reminds me!** ¡a propósito!
reminder [rɪ'maɪndəʳ] *n* notificación *f*; (*memento*) recuerdo
reminisce [rɛmɪ'nɪs] *vi* recordar (viejas historias)
reminiscences [rɛmɪ'nɪsnsɪz] *npl* reminiscencias *fpl*, recuerdos *mpl*
reminiscent [rɛmɪ'nɪsnt] *adj*: **to be ~ of sth** recordar algo
remiss [rɪ'mɪs] *adj* descuidado; **it was ~ of me** fue un descuido de mi parte
remission [rɪ'mɪʃən] *n* remisión *f*; (*of sentence*) reducción *f* de la pena
remit [rɪ'mɪt] *vt* (*send: money*) remitir, enviar
remittance [rɪ'mɪtns] *n* remesa, envío
remnant ['rɛmnənt] *n* resto; (*of cloth*) retal *m*, retazo; **remnants** *npl* (*Comm*) restos de serie
remonstrate ['rɛmənstreɪt] *vi* protestar
remorse [rɪ'mɔːs] *n* remordimientos *mpl*
remorseful [rɪ'mɔːsful] *adj* arrepentido
remorseless [rɪ'mɔːslɪs] *adj* (*fig*) implacable, inexorable
remorselessly [rɪ'mɔːslɪslɪ] *adv* implacablemente, inexorablemente
remote [rɪ'məut] *adj* remoto; (*distant*) lejano; (*person*) distante; **there is a ~ possibility that ...** hay una posibilidad remota de que ...
remote control *n* mando a distancia
remote-controlled [rɪ'məutkən'trəuld] *adj* teledirigido, con mando a distancia
remotely [rɪ'məutlɪ] *adv* remotamente; (*slightly*) levemente
remoteness [rɪ'məutnɪs] *n* alejamiento; distancia
remould ['riːməuld] *n* (*Brit: tyre*) neumático *or* llanta (*LAm*) recauchutado(-a)
removable [rɪ'muːvəbl] *adj* (*detachable*) separable
removal [rɪ'muːvəl] *n* (*taking away*) (el) quitar; (*Brit: from house*) mudanza; (*from office: dismissal*) destitución *f*; (*Med*) extirpación *f*
removal van *n* (*Brit*) camión *m* de mudanzas
remove [rɪ'muːv] *vt* quitar; (*employee*) destituir; (*name: from list*) tachar, borrar; (*doubt*) disipar; (*Tech*) retirar, separar; (*Med*) extirpar; **first cousin once removed** (*parent's cousin*) tío(-a) segundo(-a); (*cousin's child*) sobrino(-a) segundo(-a)
remover [rɪ'muːvəʳ] *n*: **make-up ~** desmaquilladora
remunerate [rɪ'mjuːnəreɪt] *vt* remunerar
remuneration [rɪmjuːnə'reɪʃən] *n* remuneración *f*
Renaissance [rɪ'neɪsɔ̃ns] *n*: **the ~** el Renacimiento
rename [riː'neɪm] *vt* poner nuevo nombre a
render ['rɛndəʳ] *vt* (*thanks*) dar; (*aid*) proporcionar; (*honour*) dar, conceder; (*assistance*) dar, prestar; **to ~ sth** (*+ adj*) volver algo *+ adj*
rendering ['rɛndərɪŋ] *n* (*Mus etc*) interpretación *f*

rendez-vous ['rɔndɪvuː] *n* cita ■ *vi* reunirse, encontrarse; (*spaceship*) efectuar una reunión espacial
rendition [rɛn'dɪʃən] *n* (*Mus*) interpretación *f*
renegade ['rɛnɪgeɪd] *n* renegado(-a)
renew [rɪ'njuː] *vt* renovar; (*resume*) reanudar; (*extend date*) prorrogar; (*negotiations*) volver a
renewable [rɪ'njuːəbl] *adj* renovable; ~ **energy, renewables** energías renovables
renewal [rɪ'njuːəl] *n* renovación *f*; reanudación *f*; prórroga
renounce [rɪ'nauns] *vt* renunciar a; (*right, inheritance*) renunciar
renovate ['rɛnəveɪt] *vt* renovar
renovation [rɛnə'veɪʃən] *n* renovación *f*
renown [rɪ'naun] *n* renombre *m*
renowned [rɪ'naund] *adj* renombrado
rent [rɛnt] *n* alquiler *m*; (*for house*) arriendo, renta ■ *vt* (*also*: **rent out**) alquilar
rental ['rɛntl] *n* (*for television, car*) alquiler *m*
rent boy *n* (*Brit col*) chapero
renunciation [rɪnʌnsɪ'eɪʃən] *n* renuncia
reopen [riː'əupən] *vt* volver a abrir, reabrir
reorder [riː'ɔːdəʳ] *vt* volver a pedir, repetir el pedido de; (*rearrange*) volver a ordenar *or* arreglar
reorganization [riːɔːgənaɪ'zeɪʃən] *n* reorganización *f*
reorganize [riː'ɔːgənaɪz] *vt* reorganizar
Rep *abbr* (*US Pol*) = **representative**; **Republican**
rep [rɛp] *n abbr* (*Comm*) = **representative**; (*Theat*) = **repertory**
repair [rɪ'pɛəʳ] *n* reparación *f*, arreglo; (*patch*) remiendo ■ *vt* reparar, arreglar; **in good/ bad** ~ en buen/mal estado; **under** ~ en obras
repair kit *n* caja de herramientas
repair man *n* mecánico
repair shop *n* taller *m* de reparaciones
repartee [rɛpɑː'tiː] *n* réplicas *fpl* agudas
repast [rɪ'pɑːst] *n* (*formal*) comida
repatriate [riː'pætrɪeɪt] *vt* repatriar
repay [riː'peɪ] *vt* (*irreg: like* **pay**) (*money*) devolver, reembolsar; (*person*) pagar; (*debt*) liquidar; (*sb's efforts*) devolver, corresponder a
repayment [riː'peɪmənt] *n* reembolso, devolución *f*; (*sum of money*) recompensa
repeal [rɪ'piːl] *n* revocación *f* ■ *vt* revocar
repeat [rɪ'piːt] *n* (*Radio, TV*) reposición *f* ■ *vt* repetir ■ *vi* repetirse
repeatedly [rɪ'piːtɪdlɪ] *adv* repetidas veces
repeat order *n* (*Comm*): **to place a ~ for** renovar un pedido de
repel [rɪ'pɛl] *vt* repugnar
repellent [rɪ'pɛlənt] *adj* repugnante ■ *n*: **insect** ~ crema/loción *f* antiinsectos
repent [rɪ'pɛnt] *vi*: **to ~ (of)** arrepentirse (de)
repentance [rɪ'pɛntəns] *n* arrepentimiento
repercussion [riːpə'kʌʃən] *n* (*consequence*) repercusión *f*; **to have repercussions** repercutir
repertoire ['rɛpətwɑːʳ] *n* repertorio
repertory ['rɛpətərɪ] *n* (*also*: **repertory theatre**) teatro de repertorio
repertory company *n* compañía de repertorio
repetition [rɛpɪ'tɪʃən] *n* repetición *f*
repetitious [rɛpɪ'tɪʃəs] *adj* repetidor(a), que se repite
repetitive [rɪ'pɛtɪtɪv] *adj* (*movement, work*) repetitivo, reiterativo; (*speech*) lleno de repeticiones
rephrase [riː'freɪz] *vt* decir *or* formular de otro modo
replace [rɪ'pleɪs] *vt* (*put back*) devolver a su sitio; (*take the place of*) reemplazar, sustituir
replacement [rɪ'pleɪsmənt] *n* reemplazo; (*act*) reposición *f*; (*thing*) recambio; (*person*) suplente *m/f*
replacement cost *n* costo de sustitución
replacement part *n* repuesto
replacement value *n* valor *m* de sustitución
replay ['riːpleɪ] *n* (*Sport*) partido de desempate; (*TV: playback*) repetición *f*
replenish [rɪ'plɛnɪʃ] *vt* (*tank etc*) rellenar; (*stock etc*) reponer; (*with fuel*) repostar
replete [rɪ'pliːt] *adj* repleto, lleno
replica ['rɛplɪkə] *n* réplica, reproducción *f*
reply [rɪ'plaɪ] *n* respuesta, contestación *f* ■ *vi* contestar, responder; **in ~** en respuesta; **there's no ~** (*Tel*) no contestan
reply coupon *n* cupón-respuesta *m*
reply-paid [rɪ'plaɪ'peɪd] *adj*: **~ postcard** tarjeta postal con respuesta pagada
report [rɪ'pɔːt] *n* informe *m*; (*Press etc*) reportaje *m*; (*Brit: also*: **school report**) informe *m* escolar; (*of gun*) detonación *f* ■ *vt* informar sobre; (*Press etc*) hacer un reportaje sobre; (*notify: accident, culprit*) denunciar ■ *vi* (*make a report*) presentar un informe; (*present o.s.*): **to ~ (to sb)** presentarse (ante algn); **annual ~** (*Comm*) informe *m* anual; **to ~ (on)** hacer un informe (sobre); **it is reported from Berlin that …** se informa desde Berlín que …
report card *n* (*US, Scottish*) cartilla escolar
reportedly [rɪ'pɔːtɪdlɪ] *adv* según se dice, según se informa
reporter [rɪ'pɔːtəʳ] *n* (*Press*) periodista *m/f*, reportero(-a); (*Radio, TV*) locutor(a) *m(f)*
repose [rɪ'pəuz] *n*: **in ~** (*face, mouth*) en reposo
repossess [riːpə'zɛs] *vt* recuperar
repossession order [riːpə'zɛʃən-] *n orden de devolución de la vivienda por el impago de la hipoteca*

reprehensible [rɛprɪ'hɛnsɪbl] *adj* reprensible, censurable
represent [rɛprɪ'zɛnt] *vt* representar; (*Comm*) ser agente de
representation [rɛprɪzɛn'teɪʃən] *n* representación *f*; (*petition*) petición *f*; **representations** *npl* (*protest*) quejas *fpl*
representative [rɛprɪ'zɛntətɪv] *n* (*US Pol*) representante *m/f*, diputado(-a); (*Comm*) representante *m/f* ■ *adj*: **~ (of)** representativo (de)
repress [rɪ'prɛs] *vt* reprimir
repression [rɪ'prɛʃən] *n* represión *f*
repressive [rɪ'prɛsɪv] *adj* represivo
reprieve [rɪ'pri:v] *n* (*Law*) indulto; (*fig*) alivio ■ *vt* indultar; (*fig*) salvar
reprimand ['rɛprɪmɑ:nd] *n* reprimenda ■ *vt* reprender
reprint ['ri:prɪnt] *n* reimpresión *f* ■ *vt* [ri:'prɪnt] reimprimir
reprisal [rɪ'praɪzl] *n* represalia; **to take reprisals** tomar represalias
reproach [rɪ'prəutʃ] *n* reproche *m* ■ *vt*: **to ~ sb with sth** reprochar algo a algn; **beyond ~** intachable
reproachful [rɪ'prəutʃful] *adj* de reproche, de acusación
reproduce [ri:prə'dju:s] *vt* reproducir ■ *vi* reproducirse
reproduction [ri:prə'dʌkʃən] *n* reproducción *f*
reproductive [ri:prə'dʌktɪv] *adj* reproductor(a)
reproof [rɪ'pru:f] *n* reproche *m*
reprove [rɪ'pru:v] *vt*: **to ~ sb for sth** reprochar algo a algn
reptile ['rɛptaɪl] *n* reptil *m*
Repub. *abbr* (*US Pol*) = **Republican**
republic [rɪ'pʌblɪk] *n* república
republican [rɪ'pʌblɪkən] *adj, n* republicano(-a) *m(f)*
repudiate [rɪ'pju:dɪeɪt] *vt* (*accusation*) rechazar; (*obligation*) negarse a reconocer
repudiation [rɪpju:dɪ'eɪʃən] *n* incumplimiento
repugnance [rɪ'pʌgnəns] *n* repugnancia
repugnant [rɪ'pʌgnənt] *adj* repugnante
repulse [rɪ'pʌls] *vt* rechazar
repulsion [rɪ'pʌlʃən] *n* repulsión *f*, repugnancia
repulsive [rɪ'pʌlsɪv] *adj* repulsivo
repurchase [ri:'pə:tʃəs] *vt* volver a comprar, readquirir
reputable ['rɛpjutəbl] *adj* (*make etc*) de renombre
reputation [rɛpju'teɪʃən] *n* reputación *f*; **he has a ~ for being awkward** tiene fama de difícil
repute [rɪ'pju:t] *n* reputación *f*, fama
reputed [rɪ'pju:tɪd] *adj* supuesto; **to be ~ to be rich/intelligent** *etc* tener fama de rico/inteligente *etc*
reputedly [rɪ'pju:tɪdlɪ] *adv* según dicen *or* se dice
request [rɪ'kwɛst] *n* solicitud *f*, petición *f* ■ *vt*: **to ~ sth of** *or* **from sb** solicitar algo a algn; **at the ~ of** a petición de; **"you are requested not to smoke"** "se ruega no fumar"
request stop *n* (*Brit*) parada discrecional
requiem ['rɛkwɪəm] *n* réquiem *m*
require [rɪ'kwaɪə^r] *vt* (*need: person*) necesitar, tener necesidad de; (*: thing, situation*) exigir, requerir; (*want*) pedir; (*demand*) insistir en que; **to ~ sb to do sth/sth of sb** exigir que algn haga algo; **what qualifications are required?** ¿qué títulos se requieren?; **required by law** requerido por la ley
requirement [rɪ'kwaɪəmənt] *n* requisito; (*need*) necesidad *f*
requisite ['rɛkwɪzɪt] *n* requisito ■ *adj* necesario, requerido
requisition [rɛkwɪ'zɪʃən] *n* solicitud *f*; (*Mil*) requisa ■ *vt* (*Mil*) requisar
reroute [ri:'ru:t] *vt* desviar
resale ['ri:seɪl] *n* reventa
resale price maintenance *n* mantenimiento del precio de venta
rescind [rɪ'sɪnd] *vt* (*Law*) abrogar; (*contract*) rescindir; (*order etc*) anular
rescue ['rɛskju:] *n* rescate *m* ■ *vt* rescatar; **to come/go to sb's ~** ir en auxilio de uno, socorrer a algn; **to ~ from** librar de
rescue party *n* equipo de salvamento
rescuer ['rɛskjuə^r] *n* salvador(a) *m(f)*
research [rɪ'sə:tʃ] *n* investigaciones *fpl* ■ *vt* investigar; **a piece of ~** un trabajo de investigación; **to ~ (into sth)** investigar (algo)
research and development *n* investigación *f* y desarrollo
researcher [rɪ'sə:tʃə^r] *n* investigador(a) *m(f)*
research work *n* investigación *f*
resell [ri:'sɛl] *vt* revender
resemblance [rɪ'zɛmbləns] *n* parecido; **to bear a strong ~ to** parecerse mucho a
resemble [rɪ'zɛmbl] *vt* parecerse a
resent [rɪ'zɛnt] *vt* resentirse por, ofenderse por; **he resents my being here** le molesta que esté aquí
resentful [rɪ'zɛntful] *adj* resentido
resentment [rɪ'zɛntmənt] *n* resentimiento
reservation [rɛzə'veɪʃən] *n* reserva; (*Brit: also*: **central reservation**) mediana; **with reservations** con reservas

reservation desk *n* (*US: in hotel*) recepción *f*
reserve [rɪ'zəːv] *n* reserva; (*Sport*) suplente *m/f* ■ *vt* (*seats etc*) reservar; **reserves** *npl* (*Mil*) reserva *sg*; **in ~** en reserva
reserve currency *n* divisa de reserva
reserved [rɪ'zəːvd] *adj* reservado
reserve price *n* (*Brit*) precio mínimo
reserve team *n* (*Sport*) equipo de reserva
reservist [rɪ'zəːvɪst] *n* (*Mil*) reservista *m*
reservoir ['rɛzəvwɑːʳ] *n* (*artificial lake*) embalse *m*, represa; (*small*) depósito
reset [riː'sɛt] *vt* (*Comput*) reinicializar
reshape [riː'ʃeɪp] *vt* (*policy*) reformar, rehacer
reshuffle [riː'ʃʌfl] *n*: **Cabinet ~** (*Pol*) remodelación *f* del gabinete
reside [rɪ'zaɪd] *vi* residir
residence ['rɛzɪdəns] *n* residencia; (*formal: home*) domicilio; (*length of stay*) permanencia; **in ~** (*doctor*) residente; **to take up ~** instalarse
residence permit *n* (*Brit*) permiso de residencia
resident ['rɛzɪdənt] *n* vecino(-a); (*in hotel*) huésped(a) *m(f)* ■ *adj* residente; (*population*) permanente
residential [rɛzɪ'dɛnʃəl] *adj* residencial
residue ['rɛzɪdjuː] *n* resto, residuo
resign [rɪ'zaɪn] *vt* (*gen*) renunciar a ■ *vi*: **to ~ (from)** dimitir (de), renunciar (a); **to ~ o.s. to** (*endure*) resignarse a
resignation [rɛzɪg'neɪʃən] *n* dimisión *f*; (*state of mind*) resignación *f*; **to tender one's ~** presentar la dimisión
resigned [rɪ'zaɪnd] *adj* resignado
resilience [rɪ'zɪlɪəns] *n* (*of material*) elasticidad *f*; (*of person*) resistencia
resilient [rɪ'zɪlɪənt] *adj* (*person*) resistente
resin ['rɛzɪn] *n* resina
resist [rɪ'zɪst] *vt* resistirse a; (*temptation, damage*) resistir
resistance [rɪ'zɪstəns] *n* resistencia
resistant [rɪ'zɪstənt] *adj*: **~ (to)** resistente (a)
resolute ['rɛzəluːt] *adj* resuelto
resolutely ['rɛzəluːtlɪ] *adv* resueltamente
resolution [rɛzə'luːʃən] *n* (*gen*) resolución *f*; (*purpose*) propósito; (*Comput*) definición *f*; **to make a ~** tomar una resolución
resolve [rɪ'zɔlv] *n* (*determination*) resolución *f*; (*purpose*) propósito ■ *vt* resolver ■ *vi* resolverse; **to ~ to do** resolver hacer
resolved [rɪ'zɔlvd] *adj* resuelto
resonance ['rɛzənəns] *n* resonancia
resonant ['rɛzənənt] *adj* resonante
resort [rɪ'zɔːt] *n* (*town*) centro turístico; (*recourse*) recurso ■ *vi*: **to ~ to** recurrir a; **in the last ~** como último recurso; **seaside/winter sports ~** playa, estación *f* balnearia/centro de deportes de invierno
resound [rɪ'zaund] *vi*: **to ~ (with)** resonar (con)
resounding [rɪ'zaundɪŋ] *adj* sonoro; (*fig*) clamoroso
resource [rɪ'sɔːs] *n* recurso; **resources** *npl* recursos *mpl*; **natural resources** recursos *mpl* naturales; **to leave sb to his/her own resources** (*fig*) abandonar a algn/a sus propios recursos
resourceful [rɪ'sɔːsful] *adj* ingenioso
resourcefulness [rɪ'sɔːsfulnɪs] *n* inventiva, iniciativa
respect [rɪs'pɛkt] *n* (*consideration*) respeto; (*relation*) respecto; **respects** *npl* recuerdos *mpl*, saludos *mpl* ■ *vt* respetar; **with ~ to** con respecto a; **in this ~** en cuanto a eso; **to have** *or* **show ~ for** tener *or* mostrar respeto a; **out of ~ for** por respeto a; **in some respects** en algunos aspectos; **with due ~ I still think you're wrong** con el respeto debido, sigo creyendo que está equivocado
respectability [rɪspɛktə'bɪlɪtɪ] *n* respetabilidad *f*
respectable [rɪs'pɛktəbl] *adj* respetable; (*quite big: amount etc*) apreciable; (*passable*) tolerable; (*quite good: player, result etc*) bastante bueno
respected [rɪs'pɛktɪd] *adj* respetado, estimado
respectful [rɪs'pɛktful] *adj* respetuoso
respectfully [rɪs'pɛktfulɪ] *adv* respetuosamente; **Yours ~** Le saluda atentamente
respecting [rɪs'pɛktɪŋ] *prep* (con) respecto a, en cuanto a
respective [rɪs'pɛktɪv] *adj* respectivo
respectively [rɪs'pɛktɪvlɪ] *adv* respectivamente
respiration [rɛspɪ'reɪʃən] *n* respiración *f*
respiratory [rɛs'pɪrətərɪ] *adj* respiratorio
respite ['rɛspaɪt] *n* respiro; (*Law*) prórroga
resplendent [rɪs'plɛndənt] *adj* resplandeciente
respond [rɪs'pɔnd] *vi* responder; (*react*) reaccionar
respondent [rɪs'pɔndənt] *n* (*Law*) demandado(-a)
response [rɪs'pɔns] *n* respuesta; (*reaction*) reacción *f*; **in ~ to** como respuesta a
responsibility [rɪspɔnsɪ'bɪlɪtɪ] *n* responsabilidad *f*; **to take ~ for sth/sb** admitir responsabilidad por algo/uno
responsible [rɪs'pɔnsɪbl] *adj* (*liable*): **~ (for)** responsable (de); (*character*) serio, formal; (*job*) de responsabilidad; **to be ~ to sb (for sth)** ser responsable ante algn (de algo)

responsibly [rɪs'pɔnsɪblɪ] *adv* con seriedad
responsive [rɪs'pɔnsɪv] *adj* sensible
rest [rɛst] *n* descanso, reposo; (*Mus*) pausa, silencio; (*support*) apoyo; (*remainder*) resto ■ *vi* descansar; (*be supported*): **to ~ on** apoyarse en ■ *vt* (*lean*): **to ~ sth on/against** apoyar algo en *or* sobre/contra; **the ~ of them** (*people, objects*) los demás; **to set sb's mind at ~** tranquilizar a algn; **to ~ one's eyes** *or* **gaze on** fijar la mirada en; **it rests with him** depende de él; **~ assured that ...** tenga por seguro que ...
restaurant ['rɛstərɔŋ] *n* restaurante *m*
restaurant car *n* (*Brit*) coche-comedor *m*
restaurant owner *n* dueño(-a) *or* propietario(-a) de un restaurante
rest cure *n* cura de reposo
restful ['rɛstful] *adj* descansado, tranquilo
rest home *n* residencia de ancianos
restitution [rɛstɪ'tju:ʃən] *n*: **to make ~ to sb for sth** restituir algo a algn; (*paying*) indemnizar a algn por algo
restive ['rɛstɪv] *adj* inquieto; (*horse*) rebelón(-ona)
restless ['rɛstlɪs] *adj* inquieto; **to get ~** impacientarse
restlessly ['rɛstlɪslɪ] *adv* inquietamente, con inquietud *f*
restlessness ['rɛstlɪsnɪs] *n* inquietud *f*
restock [ri:'stɔk] *vt* reaprovisionar
restoration [rɛstə'reɪʃən] *n* restauración *f*; (*giving back*) devolución *f*, restitución *f*
restorative [rɪ'stɔ:rətɪv] *adj* reconstituyente, fortalecedor(a) ■ *n* reconstituyente *m*
restore [rɪ'stɔ:ʳ] *vt* (*building*) restaurar; (*sth stolen*) devolver, restituir; (*health*) restablecer
restorer [rɪ'stɔ:rəʳ] *n* (*Art etc*) restaurador(a) *m(f)*
restrain [rɪs'treɪn] *vt* (*feeling*) contener, refrenar; (*person*): **to ~ (from doing)** disuadir (de hacer)
restrained [rɪs'treɪnd] *adj* (*style*) reservado
restraint [rɪs'treɪnt] *n* (*restriction*) freno, control *m*; (*of style*) reserva; **wage ~** control *m* de los salarios
restrict [rɪs'trɪkt] *vt* restringir, limitar
restricted [rɪs'trɪktɪd] *adj* restringido, limitado
restriction [rɪs'trɪkʃən] *n* restricción *f*, limitación *f*
restrictive [rɪs'trɪktɪv] *adj* restrictivo
restrictive practices *npl* (*Industry*) prácticas *fpl* restrictivas
rest room *n* (*US*) aseos *mpl*
restructure [ri:'strʌktʃəʳ] *vt* reestructurar
result [rɪ'zʌlt] *n* resultado ■ *vi*: **to ~ in** terminar en, tener por resultado; **as a ~ of** a *or* como consecuencia de; **to ~ (from)** resultar (de)
resultant [rɪ'zʌltənt] *adj* resultante
resume [rɪ'zju:m] *vt* (*work, journey*) reanudar; (*sum up*) resumir ■ *vi* (*meeting*) continuar
résumé ['reɪzju:meɪ] *n* resumen *m*
resumption [rɪ'zʌmpʃən] *n* reanudación *f*
resurgence [rɪ'sə:dʒəns] *n* resurgimiento
resurrection [rɛzə'rɛkʃən] *n* resurrección *f*
resuscitate [rɪ'sʌsɪteɪt] *vt* (*Med*) resucitar
resuscitation [rɪsʌsɪ'teɪʃn] *n* resucitación *f*
retail ['ri:teɪl] *n* venta al por menor ■ *cpd* al por menor ■ *vt* vender al por menor *or* al detalle ■ *vi*: **to ~ at** (*Comm*) tener precio de venta al público de
retailer ['ri:teɪləʳ] *n* minorista *m/f*, detallista *m/f*
retail outlet *n* punto de venta
retail price *n* precio de venta al público, precio al detalle *or* al por menor
retail price index *n* índice *m* de precios al por menor
retain [rɪ'teɪn] *vt* (*keep*) retener, conservar; (*employ*) contratar
retainer [rɪ'teɪnəʳ] *n* (*servant*) criado; (*fee*) anticipo
retaliate [rɪ'tælɪeɪt] *vi*: **to ~ (against)** tomar represalias (contra)
retaliation [rɪtælɪ'eɪʃən] *n* represalias *fpl*; **in ~ for** como represalia por
retaliatory [rɪ'tælɪətərɪ] *adj* de represalia
retarded [rɪ'tɑ:dɪd] *adj* retrasado
retch [rɛtʃ] *vi* darle a algn arcadas
retentive [rɪ'tɛntɪv] *adj* (*memory*) retentivo
rethink [ri:'θɪŋk] *vt* repensar
reticence ['rɛtɪsns] *n* reticencia, reserva
reticent ['rɛtɪsnt] *adj* reticente, reservado
retina ['rɛtɪnə] *n* retina
retinue ['rɛtɪnju:] *n* séquito, comitiva
retire [rɪ'taɪəʳ] *vi* (*give up work*) jubilarse; (*withdraw*) retirarse; (*go to bed*) acostarse
retired [rɪ'taɪəd] *adj* (*person*) jubilado
retirement [rɪ'taɪəmənt] *n* jubilación *f*; **early ~** jubilación *f* anticipada
retiring [rɪ'taɪərɪŋ] *adj* (*departing: chairman*) saliente; (*shy*) retraído
retort [rɪ'tɔ:t] *n* (*reply*) réplica ■ *vi* replicar
retrace [ri:'treɪs] *vt*: **to ~ one's steps** volver sobre sus pasos, desandar lo andado
retract [rɪ'trækt] *vt* (*statement*) retirar; (*claws*) retraer; (*undercarriage, aerial*) replegar ■ *vi* retractarse
retractable [rɪ'træktəbl] *adj* replegable
retrain [ri:'treɪn] *vt* reciclar
retraining [ri:'treɪnɪŋ] *n* reciclaje *m*, readaptación *f* profesional
retread ['ri:trɛd] *n* neumático *or* llanta (*LAm*) recauchutado(-a)

retreat [rɪ'tri:t] *n* (*place*) retiro; (*Mil*) retirada ■ *vi* retirarse; (*flood*) bajar; **to beat a hasty ~** (*fig*) retirarse en desbandada
retrial ['ri:traɪəl] *n* nuevo proceso
retribution [rɛtrɪ'bju:ʃən] *n* desquite *m*
retrieval [rɪ'tri:vəl] *n* recuperación *f*; **information retrieval** recuperación *f* de datos
retrieve [rɪ'tri:v] *vt* recobrar; (*situation, honour*) salvar; (*Comput*) recuperar; (*error*) reparar
retriever [rɪ'tri:vəʳ] *n* perro cobrador
retroactive [rɛtrəu'æktɪv] *adj* retroactivo
retrograde ['rɛtrəgreɪd] *adj* retrógrado
retrospect ['rɛtrəspɛkt] *n*: **in ~** retrospectivamente
retrospective [rɛtrə'spɛktɪv] *adj* retrospectivo; (*law*) retroactivo ■ *n* exposición *f* retrospectiva
return [rɪ'tə:n] *n* (*going or coming back*) vuelta, regreso; (*of sth stolen etc*) devolución *f*; (*recompense*) recompensa; (*Finance: from land, shares*) ganancia, ingresos *mpl*; (*Comm: of merchandise*) devolución *f* ■ *cpd* (*journey*) de regreso; (*Brit: ticket*) de ida y vuelta; (*match*) de vuelta ■ *vi* (*person etc: come or go back*) volver, regresar; (*symptoms etc*) reaparecer ■ *vt* devolver; (*favour, love etc*) corresponder a; (*verdict*) pronunciar; (*Pol: candidate*) elegir; **returns** *npl* (*Comm*) ingresos *mpl*; **tax ~** declaración *f* de la renta; **in ~ (for)** a cambio (de); **by ~ of post** a vuelta de correo; **many happy returns (of the day)!** ¡feliz cumpleaños!
returnable [rɪ'tə:nəbl] *adj*: **~ bottle** envase *m* retornable
returner [rɪ'tə:nəʳ] *n* *mujer que vuelve a trabajar tras un tiempo dedicada a la familia*
returning officer [rɪ'tə:nɪŋ-] *n* (*Brit Pol*) escrutador(a) *m(f)*
return key *n* (*Comput*) tecla de retorno
reunion [ri:'ju:nɪən] *n* reencuentro
reunite [ri:ju:'naɪt] *vt* reunir; (*reconcile*) reconciliar
rev [rɛv] *n abbr* (*Aut: = revolution*) revolución *f* ■ *vt* (*also*: **rev up**) acelerar
Rev., Revd. *abbr* (*= reverend*) R., Rvdo
revaluation [ri:vælju:'eɪʃən] *n* revalorización *f*
revamp [ri:'væmp] *vt* renovar
reveal [rɪ'vi:l] *vt* (*make known*) revelar
revealing [rɪ'vi:lɪŋ] *adj* revelador(a)
reveille [rɪ'vælɪ] *n* (*Mil*) diana
revel ['rɛvl] *vi*: **to ~ in sth/in doing sth** gozar de algo/haciendo algo
revelation [rɛvə'leɪʃən] *n* revelación *f*
reveller, (*US*) **reveler** ['rɛvləʳ] *n* jaranero, juerguista *m/f*
revelry ['rɛvlrɪ] *n* jarana, juerga
revenge [rɪ'vɛndʒ] *n* venganza; (*in sport*) revancha; **to take ~ on** vengarse de; **to get one's ~ (for sth)** vengarse (de algo)
revengeful [rɪ'vɛndʒful] *adj* vengativo
revenue ['rɛvənju:] *n* ingresos *mpl*, rentas *fpl*
revenue account *n* cuenta de ingresos presupuestarios
revenue expenditure *n* gasto corriente
reverberate [rɪ'və:bəreɪt] *vi* (*sound*) resonar, retumbar
reverberation [rɪvə:bə'reɪʃən] *n* resonancia
revere [rɪ'vɪəʳ] *vt* reverenciar, venerar
reverence ['rɛvərəns] *n* reverencia
Reverend ['rɛvərənd] *adj* (*in titles*): **the ~ John Smith** (*Anglican*) el Reverendo John Smith; (*Catholic*) el Padre John Smith; (*Protestant*) el Pastor John Smith
reverent ['rɛvərənt] *adj* reverente
reverie ['rɛvərɪ] *n* ensueño
reversal [rɪ'və:sl] *n* (*of order*) inversión *f*; (*of policy*) cambio de rumbo; (*of decision*) revocación *f*
reverse [rɪ'və:s] *n* (*opposite*) contrario; (*back: of cloth*) revés *m*; (*: of coin*) reverso; (*: of paper*) dorso; (*Aut: also*: **reverse gear**) marcha atrás ■ *adj* (*order*) inverso; (*direction*) contrario ■ *vt* (*decision*) dar marcha atrás a; (*Aut*) dar marcha atrás a; (*position, function*) invertir ■ *vi* (*Brit Aut*) poner en marcha atrás; **in ~ order** en orden inverso; **the ~** lo contrario; **to go into ~** dar marcha atrás
reverse-charge call [rɪ'və:stʃɑ:dʒ-] *n* (*Brit*) llamada a cobro revertido
reverse video *n* vídeo inverso
reversible [rɪ'və:səbl] *adj* (*garment, procedure*) reversible
reversing lights [rɪ'və:sɪŋ-] *npl* (*Brit Aut*) luces *fpl* de marcha atrás
revert [rɪ'və:t] *vi*: **to ~ to** volver *or* revertir a
review [rɪ'vju:] *n* (*magazine*) revista; (*Mil*) revista; (*of book, film*) reseña; (*US: examination*) repaso, examen *m* ■ *vt* repasar, examinar; (*Mil*) pasar revista a; (*book, film*) reseñar; **to come under ~** ser examinado
reviewer [rɪ'vju:əʳ] *n* crítico(-a)
revile [rɪ'vaɪl] *vt* injuriar, vilipendiar
revise [rɪ'vaɪz] *vt* (*manuscript*) corregir; (*opinion*) modificar; (*Brit: study: subject*) repasar; (*look over*) revisar; **revised edition** edición *f* corregida
revision [rɪ'vɪʒən] *n* corrección *f*; modificación *f*; (*of subject*) repaso; (*revised version*) revisión *f*
revisit [ri:'vɪzɪt] *vt* volver a visitar
revitalize [ri:'vaɪtəlaɪz] *vt* revivificar
revival [rɪ'vaɪvəl] *n* (*recovery*) reanimación *f*;

(*Pol*) resurgimiento; (*of interest*) renacimiento; (*Theat*) reestreno; (*of faith*) despertar *m*
revive [rɪ'vaɪv] *vt* resucitar; (*custom*) restablecer; (*hope, courage*) reanimar; (*play*) reestrenar ■ *vi* (*person*) volver en sí; (*from tiredness*) reponerse; (*business*) reactivarse
revoke [rɪ'vəuk] *vt* revocar
revolt [rɪ'vəult] *n* rebelión *f* ■ *vi* rebelarse, sublevarse ■ *vt* dar asco a, repugnar; **to ~ (against sb/sth)** rebelarse (contra algn/algo)
revolting [rɪ'vəultɪŋ] *adj* asqueroso, repugnante
revolution [rɛvə'lu:ʃən] *n* revolución *f*
revolutionary [rɛvə'lu:ʃənrɪ] *adj, n* revolucionario(-a) *m(f)*
revolutionize [rɛvə'lu:ʃənaɪz] *vt* revolucionar
revolve [rɪ'vɔlv] *vi* dar vueltas, girar
revolver [rɪ'vɔlvə^r] *n* revólver *m*
revolving [rɪ'vɔlvɪŋ] *adj* (*chair, door etc*) giratorio
revue [rɪ'vju:] *n* (*Theat*) revista
revulsion [rɪ'vʌlʃən] *n* asco, repugnancia
reward [rɪ'wɔ:d] *n* premio, recompensa ■ *vt*: **to ~ (for)** recompensar *or* premiar (por)
rewarding [rɪ'wɔ:dɪŋ] *adj* (*fig*) gratificante; **financially ~** económicamente provechoso
rewind [ri:'waɪnd] *vt* (*watch*) dar cuerda a; (*wool etc*) devanar
rewire [ri:'waɪə^r] *vt* (*house*) renovar la instalación eléctrica de
reword [ri:'wə:d] *vt* expresar en otras palabras
rewritable [ri:'raɪtəbl] *adj* reescribible
rewrite [ri:'raɪt] *vt* (*irreg: like* **write**) reescribir
Reykjavik ['reɪkjəvi:k] *n* Reykjavik *m*
RFD *abbr* (*US Post*) = **rural free delivery**
RGN *n abbr* (*Brit*) = **Registered General Nurse**
Rh *abbr* (= *rhesus*) Rh *m*
rhapsody ['ræpsədɪ] *n* (*Mus*) rapsodia; (*fig*): **to go into rhapsodies over** extasiarse por
rhesus negative ['ri:səs-] *adj* (*Med*) Rh negativo
rhesus positive *adj* (*Med*) Rh positivo
rhetoric ['rɛtərɪk] *n* retórica
rhetorical [rɪ'tɔrɪkl] *adj* retórico
rheumatic [ru:'mætɪk] *adj* reumático
rheumatism ['ru:mətɪzəm] *n* reumatismo, reúma
rheumatoid arthritis ['ru:mətɔɪd-] *n* reúma *m* articular
Rhine [raɪn] *n*: **the ~** el (río) Rin
rhinestone ['raɪnstəun] *n* diamante *m* de imitación
rhinoceros [raɪ'nɔsərəs] *n* rinoceronte *m*
Rhodes [rəudz] *n* Rodas *f*
rhododendron [rəudə'dɛndrn] *n* rododendro
Rhone [rəun] *n*: **the ~** el (río) Ródano
rhubarb ['ru:bɑ:b] *n* ruibarbo
rhyme [raɪm] *n* rima; (*verse*) poesía ■ *vi*: **to ~ (with)** rimar (con); **without ~ or reason** sin ton ni son
rhythm ['rɪðm] *n* ritmo
rhythmic ['rɪðmɪk], **rhythmical** ['rɪðmɪkl] *adj* rítmico
rhythmically ['rɪðmɪklɪ] *adv* rítmicamente
rhythm method *n* método (de) Ogino
RI *n abbr* (*Brit*: = *religious instruction*) ed. religiosa ■ *abbr* (*US: Post*) = **Rhode Island**
rib [rɪb] *n* (*Anat*) costilla ■ *vt* (*mock*) tomar el pelo a
ribald ['rɪbəld] *adj* escabroso
ribbon ['rɪbən] *n* cinta; **in ribbons** (*torn*) hecho trizas
rice [raɪs] *n* arroz *m*
ricefield ['raɪsfi:ld] *n* arrozal *m*
rice pudding *n* arroz *m* con leche
rich [rɪtʃ] *adj* rico; (*soil*) fértil; (*food*) pesado; (*: sweet*) empalagoso; **the rich** *npl* los ricos; **riches** *npl* riqueza *sg*; **to be ~ in sth** abundar en algo
richly ['rɪtʃlɪ] *adv* ricamente
richness ['rɪtʃnɪs] *n* riqueza; (*of soil*) fertilidad *f*
rickets ['rɪkɪts] *n* raquitismo
rickety ['rɪkɪtɪ] *adj* (*old*) desvencijado; (*shaky*) tambaleante
rickshaw ['rɪkʃɔ:] *n* carro de culí
ricochet ['rɪkəʃeɪ] *n* rebote *m* ■ *vi* rebotar
rid (*pt, pp* **~**) [rɪd] *vt*: **to ~ sb of sth** librar a algn de algo; **to get ~ of** deshacerse *or* desembarazarse de
riddance ['rɪdns] *n*: **good ~!** ¡y adiós muy buenas!
ridden ['rɪdn] *pp of* **ride**
-ridden ['rɪdn] *suff*: **disease~** plagado de enfermedades; **inflation~** minado por la inflación
riddle ['rɪdl] *n* (*conundrum*) acertijo; (*mystery*) enigma *m*, misterio ■ *vt*: **to be riddled with** ser lleno *or* plagado de
ride [raɪd] (*pt* **rode**, *pp* **ridden**) *n* paseo; (*distance covered*) viaje *m*, recorrido ■ *vi* (*on horse: as sport*) montar; (*go somewhere: on horse, bicycle*) dar un paseo, pasearse; (*journey: on bicycle, motorcycle, bus*) viajar ■ *vt* (*a horse*) montar a; (*distance*) viajar; **to ~ a bicycle** andar en bicicleta; **to ~ at anchor** (*Naut*) estar fondeado; **can you ~ a bike?** ¿sabes montar en bici(cleta)?; **to go for a ~** dar un paseo; **to take sb for a ~** (*fig*) tomar el pelo a algn
▸ **ride out** *vt*: **to ~ out the storm** (*fig*) capear el temporal

rider ['raɪdəʳ] *n* (*on horse*) jinete *m*; (*on bicycle*) ciclista *m/f*; (*on motorcycle*) motociclista *m/f*
ridge [rɪdʒ] *n* (*of hill*) cresta; (*of roof*) caballete *m*; (*wrinkle*) arruga
ridicule ['rɪdɪkjuːl] *n* irrisión *f*, burla ▪ *vt* poner en ridículo a, burlarse de; **to hold sth/sb up to ~** poner algo/a algn en ridículo
ridiculous [rɪ'dɪkjuləs] *adj* ridículo
ridiculously [rɪ'dɪkjuləslɪ] *adv* ridículamente, de modo ridículo
riding ['raɪdɪŋ] *n* equitación *f*; **I like ~** me gusta montar a caballo
riding habit *n* traje *m* de montar
riding school *n* escuela de equitación
rife [raɪf] *adj*: **to be ~** ser muy común; **to be ~ with** abundar en
riffraff ['rɪfræf] *n* chusma, gentuza
rifle ['raɪfl] *n* rifle *m*, fusil *m* ▪ *vt* saquear
▸ **rifle through** *vt fus* saquear
rifle range *n* campo de tiro; (*at fair*) tiro al blanco
rift [rɪft] *n* (*fig: between friends*) desavenencia; (*: in party*) escisión *f*
rig [rɪg] *n* (*also*: **oil rig**: *on land*) torre *f* de perforación; (*: at sea*) plataforma petrolera ▪ *vt* (*election etc*) amañar los resultados de
▸ **rig out** *vt* (*Brit*) ataviar
▸ **rig up** *vt* improvisar
rigging ['rɪgɪŋ] *n* (*Naut*) aparejo
right [raɪt] *adj* (*true, correct*) correcto, exacto; (*suitable*) indicado, debido; (*proper*) apropiado, propio; (*just*) justo; (*morally good*) bueno; (*not left*) derecho ▪ *n* (*title, claim*) derecho; (*not left*) derecha ▪ *adv* (*correctly*) bien, correctamente; (*straight*) derecho, directamente; (*not on the left*) a la derecha; (*to the right*) hacia la derecha ▪ *vt* (*put straight*) enderezar ▪ *excl* ¡bueno!, ¡está bien!; **to be ~** (*person*) tener razón; **to get sth ~** acertar en algo; **you did the ~ thing** hiciste bien; **let's get it ~ this time!** ¡a ver si esta vez nos sale bien!; **to put a mistake ~** corregir un error; **the ~ time** la hora exacta; (*fig*) el momento oportuno; **by rights** en justicia; **~ and wrong** el bien y el mal; **film rights** derechos *mpl* de la película; **on the ~** a la derecha; **to be in the ~** tener razón; **~ now** ahora mismo; **~ before/after** inmediatamente antes/después; **~ in the middle** exactamente en el centro; **~ away** en seguida; **to go ~ to the end of sth** llegar hasta el final de algo; **~, who's next?** bueno, ¿quién sigue?; **all ~!** ¡vale!; **I'm/I feel all ~ now** ya estoy bien
right angle *n* ángulo recto
right-click ['raɪtklɪk] *vi* clicar con el botón derecho del ratón ▪ *vt*: **to ~ an icon** clicar en un icono con el botón derecho del ratón
righteous ['raɪtʃəs] *adj* justo, honrado; (*anger*) justificado
righteousness ['raɪtʃəsnɪs] *n* justicia
rightful ['raɪtful] *adj* (*heir*) legítimo
right-hand ['raɪthænd] *adj* (*drive, turn*) por la derecha
right-handed [raɪt'hændɪd] *adj* (*person*) que usa la mano derecha
right-hand man *n* brazo derecho
right-hand side *n* derecha
rightly ['raɪtlɪ] *adv* correctamente, debidamente; (*with reason*) con razón; **if I remember ~** si recuerdo bien
right-minded ['raɪt'maɪndɪd] *adj* (*sensible*) sensato; (*decent*) honrado
right of way *n* (*on path etc*) derecho de paso; (*Aut*) prioridad *f* de paso
right-wing [raɪt'wɪŋ] *adj* (*Pol*) de derechas, derechista
right-winger [raɪt'wɪŋəʳ] *n* (*Pol*) persona de derechas, derechista *m/f*; (*Sport*) extremo derecha
rigid ['rɪdʒɪd] *adj* rígido; (*person, ideas*) inflexible
rigidity [rɪ'dʒɪdɪtɪ] *n* rigidez *f*; inflexibilidad *f*
rigidly ['rɪdʒɪdlɪ] *adv* rígidamente; (*inflexibly*) inflexiblemente
rigmarole ['rɪgmərəul] *n* galimatías *m inv*
rigor mortis ['rɪgə'mɔːtɪs] *n* rigidez *f* cadavérica
rigorous ['rɪgərəs] *adj* riguroso
rigorously ['rɪgərəslɪ] *adv* rigurosamente
rigour, rigor (*US*) ['rɪgəʳ] *n* rigor *m*, severidad *f*
rile [raɪl] *vt* irritar
rim [rɪm] *n* borde *m*; (*of spectacles*) montura, aro; (*of wheel*) llanta
rimless ['rɪmlɪs] *adj* (*spectacles*) sin aros
rimmed [rɪmd] *adj*: **~ with** con un borde de, bordeado de
rind [raɪnd] *n* (*of bacon, cheese*) corteza; (*of lemon etc*) cáscara
ring [rɪŋ] *n* (*pt* **rang**, *pp* **rung**) (*of metal*) aro; (*on finger*) anillo; (*of people*) corro; (*of objects*) círculo; (*gang*) banda; (*for boxing*) cuadrilátero; (*of circus*) pista; (*bull ring*) ruedo, plaza; (*sound of bell*) toque *m*; (*telephone call*) llamada ▪ *vi* (*on telephone*) llamar por teléfono; (*large bell*) repicar; (*also*: **ring out**: *voice, words*) sonar; (*ears*) zumbar ▪ *vt* (*Brit Tel*: *also*: **ring up**) llamar; (*bell etc*) hacer sonar; (*doorbell*) tocar; **that has the ~ of truth about it** eso suena a verdad; **to give sb a ~** (*Brit Tel*) llamar por teléfono a algn, dar un telefonazo a algn; **the name doesn't ~ a bell (with me)** el nombre no me suena; **to ~ sb (up)** llamar a algn

▸ **ring back** *vt, vi* (*Tel*) devolver la llamada
▸ **ring off** *vi* (*Brit Tel*) colgar, cortar la comunicación
ring binder *n* carpeta de anillas
ring finger *n* (dedo) anular *m*
ringing ['rɪŋɪŋ] *n* (*of bell*) toque *m*, tañido; (*of large bell*) repique *m*; (*in ears*) zumbido
ringing tone *n* (*Tel*) tono de llamada
ringleader ['rɪŋli:dər] *n* cabecilla *m/f*
ringlets ['rɪŋlɪts] *npl* tirabuzones *mpl*, bucles *mpl*
ring road *n* (*Brit*) carretera periférica *or* de circunvalación
ringtone ['rɪŋtəun] *n* tono de llamada
rink [rɪŋk] *n* (*also*: **ice rink**) pista de hielo; (*for roller-skating*) pista de patinaje
rinse [rɪns] *n* (*of dishes*) enjuague *m*; (*of clothes*) aclarado; (*of hair*) reflejo ■ *vt* enjuagar; aclarar; dar reflejos a
Rio ['ri:əu], **Rio de Janeiro** ['ri:əudədʒə'nɪərəu] *n* Río de Janeiro
riot ['raɪət] *n* motín *m*, disturbio ■ *vi* amotinarse; **to run ~** desmandarse
rioter ['raɪətər] *n* amotinado(-a)
riot gear *n* uniforme *m* antidisturbios *inv*
riotous ['raɪətəs] *adj* alborotado; (*party*) bullicioso; (*uncontrolled*) desenfrenado
riotously ['raɪətəslɪ] *adv* bulliciosamente
riot police *n* policía antidisturbios
RIP *abbr* (*= requiescat or requiescant in pace: rest in peace*) q.e.p.d.
rip [rɪp] *n* rasgón *m*, desgarrón *m* ■ *vt* rasgar, desgarrar ■ *vi* rasgarse
▸ **rip up** *vt* hacer pedazos
ripcord ['rɪpkɔ:d] *n* cabo de desgarre
ripe [raɪp] *adj* (*fruit*) maduro
ripen ['raɪpən] *vt, vi* madurar
ripeness ['raɪpnɪs] *n* madurez *f*
rip-off ['rɪpɔf] *n* (*col*): **it's a ~!** ¡es una estafa!, ¡es un timo!
riposte [rɪ'pɔst] *n* respuesta aguda, réplica
ripple ['rɪpl] *n* onda, rizo; (*sound*) murmullo ■ *vi* rizarse ■ *vt* rizar
rise [raɪz] *n* (*slope*) cuesta, pendiente *f*; (*hill*) altura; (*increase: in wages: Brit*) aumento; (*: in prices, temperature*) subida, alza; (*fig: to power etc*) ascenso; (*: ascendancy*) auge *m* ■ *vi* (*pt* **rose**, *pp* **risen**) [rəuz, 'rɪzn] (*gen*) elevarse; (*prices*) subir; (*waters*) crecer; (*river*) nacer; (*sun*) salir; (*person: from bed etc*) levantarse; (*also*: **rise up**: *rebel*) sublevarse; (*in rank*) ascender; **~ to power** ascenso al poder; **to give ~ to** dar lugar *or* origen a; **to ~ to the occasion** ponerse a la altura de las circunstancias
rising ['raɪzɪŋ] *adj* (*increasing: number*) creciente; (*: prices*) en aumento *or* alza; (*tide*) creciente; (*sun, moon*) naciente ■ *n* (*uprising*) sublevación *f*
rising damp *n* humedad *f* de paredes
rising star *n* (*fig*) figura en alza
risk [rɪsk] *n* riesgo, peligro ■ *vt* (*gen*) arriesgar; (*dare*) atreverse a; **to take** *or* **run the ~ of doing** correr el riesgo de hacer; **at ~** en peligro; **at one's own ~** bajo su propia responsabilidad; **fire/health/security ~** peligro de incendio/para la salud/para la seguridad
risk capital *n* capital *m* de riesgo
risky ['rɪskɪ] *adj* arriesgado, peligroso
risqué ['ri:skeɪ] *adj* (*joke*) subido de color
rissole ['rɪsəul] *n* croqueta
rite [raɪt] *n* rito; **last rites** últimos sacramentos *mpl*
ritual ['rɪtjuəl] *adj* ritual ■ *n* ritual *m*, rito
rival ['raɪvl] *n* rival *m/f*; (*in business*) competidor(a) *m(f)* ■ *adj* rival, opuesto ■ *vt* competir con
rivalry ['raɪvlrɪ] *n* rivalidad *f*, competencia
river ['rɪvər] *n* río ■ *cpd* (*port, traffic*) de río, del río; **up/down ~** río arriba/abajo
riverbank ['rɪvəbæŋk] *n* orilla (del río)
riverbed ['rɪvəbɛd] *n* lecho, cauce *m*
rivet ['rɪvɪt] *n* roblón *m*, remache *m* ■ *vt* remachar; (*fig*) fascinar
riveting ['rɪvɪtɪŋ] *adj* (*fig*) fascinante
Riviera [rɪvɪ'ɛərə] *n*: **the (French) ~** la Costa Azul, la Riviera (francesa); **the Italian ~** la Riviera italiana
Riyadh [rɪ'jɑ:d] *n* Riyadh *m*
RMT *n abbr* (*= National Union of Rail, Maritime and Transport Workers*) *sindicato de transportes*
RN *n abbr* (*Brit*) = **Royal Navy**; (*US*) = **registered nurse**
RNA *n abbr* (*= ribonucleic acid*) ARN *m*, RNA *m*
RNLI *n abbr* (*Brit: = Royal National Lifeboat Institution*) *organización benéfica que proporciona un servicio de lanchas de socorro*
RNZAF *n abbr* = **Royal New Zealand Air Force**
RNZN *n abbr* = **Royal New Zealand Navy**
road [rəud] *n* (*gen*) camino; (*motorway etc*) carretera; (*in town*) calle *f*; **major/minor ~** carretera general/secundaria; **main ~** carretera; **it takes four hours by ~** se tarda cuarto horas por carretera; **on the ~ to success** camino del éxito
roadblock ['rəudblɔk] *n* barricada, control *m*, retén *m* (*LAm*)
road haulage *n* transporte *m* por carretera
roadhog ['rəudhɔg] *n* loco(-a) del volante
road map *n* mapa *m* de carreteras
road rage *n conducta agresiva de los conductores*
road safety *n* seguridad *f* vial
roadside ['rəudsaɪd] *n* borde *m* (del camino)

■ *cpd* al lado de la carretera; **by the ~** al borde del camino
roadsign ['rəudsaɪn] *n* señal *f* de tráfico
roadsweeper ['rəudswi:pəʳ] *n* (*Brit: person*) barrendero(-a)
road user *n* usuario(-a) de la vía pública
roadway ['rəudweɪ] *n* calzada
roadworks ['rəudwə:ks] *npl* obras *fpl*
roadworthy ['rəudwə:ðɪ] *adj* (*car*) en buen estado para circular
roam [rəum] *vi* vagar ■ *vt* vagar por
roar [rɔ:ʳ] *n* (*of animal*) rugido, bramido; (*of crowd*) clamor *m*, rugido; (*of vehicle, storm*) estruendo; (*of laughter*) carcajada ■ *vi* rugir, bramar; hacer estruendo; **to ~ with laughter** reírse a carcajadas
roaring ['rɔ:rɪŋ] *adj*: **a ~ success** un tremendo éxito; **to do a ~ trade** hacer buen negocio
roast [rəust] *n* carne *f* asada, asado ■ *vt* (*meat*) asar; (*coffee*) tostar
roast beef *n* rosbif *m*
roasting ['rəustɪŋ] *n*: **to give sb a ~** (*col*) echar una buena bronca a algn
rob [rɔb] *vt* robar; **to ~ sb of sth** robar algo a algn; (*fig: deprive*) quitar algo a algn
robber ['rɔbəʳ] *n* ladrón(-ona) *m(f)*
robbery ['rɔbərɪ] *n* robo
robe [rəub] *n* (*for ceremony etc*) toga; (*also*: **bath robe**) bata
robin ['rɔbɪn] *n* petirrojo
robot ['rəubɔt] *n* robot *m*
robotics [rəu'bɔtɪks] *n* robótica
robust [rəu'bʌst] *adj* robusto, fuerte
rock [rɔk] *n* (*gen*) roca; (*boulder*) peña, peñasco; (*Brit: sweet*) ≈ pirulí *m* ■ *vt* (*swing gently*) mecer; (*shake*) sacudir ■ *vi* mecerse, balancearse; sacudirse; **on the rocks** (*drink*) con hielo; **their marriage is on the rocks** su matrimonio se está yendo a pique; **to ~ the boat** (*fig*) crear problemas
rock and roll *n* rock and roll *m*, rocanrol *m*
rock-bottom ['rɔk'bɔtəm] *adj* (*fig*) por los suelos; **to reach** *or* **touch ~** (*price*) estar por los suelos; (*person*) tocar fondo
rock cake *n* (*Brit*) *bollito de pasas con superficie rugosa*
rock climber *n* escalador(a) *m(f)*
rock climbing *n* (*Sport*) escalada
rockery ['rɔkərɪ] *n* cuadro alpino
rocket ['rɔkɪt] *n* cohete *m* ■ *vi* (*prices*) dispararse, ponerse por las nubes
rocket launcher *n* lanzacohetes *m inv*
rock face *n* pared *f* de roca
rocking chair ['rɔkɪŋ-] *n* mecedora
rocking horse *n* caballo de balancín
rocky ['rɔkɪ] *adj* (*gen*) rocoso; (*unsteady: table*) inestable
Rocky Mountains *npl*: **the ~** las Montañas Rocosas
rococo [rə'kəukəu] *adj* rococó *inv* ■ *n* rococó
rod [rɔd] *n* vara, varilla; (*Tech*) barra; (*also*: **fishing rod**) caña
rode [rəud] *pt of* **ride**
rodent ['rəudnt] *n* roedor *m*
rodeo ['rəudɪəu] *n* rodeo
roe [rəu] *n* (*species: also*: **roe deer**) corzo; (*of fish*): **hard/soft ~** hueva/lecha
rogue [rəug] *n* pícaro, pillo
roguish ['rəugɪʃ] *adj* (*child*) travieso; (*smile etc*) pícaro
role [rəul] *n* papel *m*, rol *m*
role-model ['rəulmɔdl] *n* modelo a imitar
role play *n* (*also*: **role playing**) juego de papeles *or* roles
roll [rəul] *n* rollo; (*of bank notes*) fajo; (*also*: **bread roll**) panecillo; (*register*) lista, nómina; (*sound: of drums etc*) redoble *m*; (*movement: of ship*) balanceo ■ *vt* hacer rodar; (*also*: **roll up**: *string*) enrollar; (*: sleeves*) arremangar; (*cigarettes*) liar; (*also*: **roll out**: *pastry*) aplanar ■ *vi* (*gen*) rodar; (*drum*) redoblar; (*in walking*) bambolearse; (*ship*) balancearse; **cheese ~** panecillo de queso
▸ **roll about, roll around** *vi* (*person*) revolcarse
▸ **roll by** *vi* (*time*) pasar
▸ **roll in** *vi* (*mail, cash*) entrar a raudales
▸ **roll over** *vi* dar una vuelta
▸ **roll up** *vi* (*col: arrive*) presentarse, aparecer ■ *vt* (*carpet, cloth, map*) arrollar; (*sleeves*) arremangar; **to ~ o.s. up into a ball** acurrucarse, hacerse un ovillo
roll call *n*: **to take a ~** pasar lista
rolled [rəuld] *adj* (*umbrella*) plegado
roller ['rəuləʳ] *n* rodillo; (*wheel*) rueda
roller blind *n* (*Brit*) persiana (enrollable)
roller coaster *n* montaña rusa
roller skates *npl* patines *mpl* de rueda
rollicking ['rɔlɪkɪŋ] *adj*: **we had a ~ time** nos divertimos una barbaridad
rolling ['rəulɪŋ] *adj* (*landscape*) ondulado
rolling mill *n* taller *m* de laminación
rolling pin *n* rodillo (de cocina)
rolling stock *n* (*Rail*) material *m* rodante
ROM [rɔm] *n abbr* (*Comput*: = *read-only memory*) (memoria) ROM *f*
Roman ['rəumən] *adj, n* romano(-a) *m(f)*
Roman Catholic *adj, n* católico(-a) *m(f)* (romano(-a))
romance [rə'mæns] *n* (*love affair*) amor *m*, idilio; (*charm*) lo romántico; (*novel*) novela de amor
romanesque [rəumə'nɛsk] *adj* románico
Romania [ru:'meɪnɪə] *n* = **Rumania**

Romanian [ru:'meɪnɪən] *adj, n* = **Rumanian**
Roman numeral *n* número romano
romantic [rə'mæntɪk] *adj* romántico
romanticism [rə'mæntɪsɪzəm] *n* romanticismo
Romany ['rəumənɪ] *adj* gitano ■ *n* (*person*) gitano(-a); (*Ling*) lengua gitana, caló (*SP*)
Rome [rəum] *n* Roma
romp [rɔmp] *n* retozo, jugueteo ■ *vi* (*also*: **romp about**) juguetear; **to ~ home** (*horse*) ganar fácilmente
rompers ['rɔmpəz] *npl* pelele *m*
roof [ru:f] *n* (*gen*) techo; (*of house*) tejado ■ *vt* techar, poner techo a; **~ of the mouth** paladar *m*
roofing ['ru:fɪŋ] *n* techumbre *f*
roof rack *n* (*Aut*) baca
rook [ruk] *n* (*bird*) graja; (*Chess*) torre *f*
rookie ['rukɪ] *n* (*col*) novato(-a); (*Mil*) chivo
room [ru:m] *n* (*in house*) cuarto, habitación *f*, pieza (*esp LAm*); (*also*: **bedroom**) dormitorio; (*in school etc*) sala; (*space*) sitio; **rooms** *npl* (*lodging*) alojamiento *sg*; **"rooms to let"**, (*US*) **"rooms for rent"** "se alquilan pisos *or* cuartos"; **single/double ~** habitación individual/doble *or* para dos personas; **is there ~ for this?** ¿cabe esto?; **to make ~ for sb** hacer sitio para algn; **there is ~ for improvement** podría mejorarse
roominess ['ru:mɪnɪs] *n* amplitud *f*, espaciosidad *f*
rooming house ['ru:mɪŋ-] *n* (*US*) pensión *f*
roommate ['ru:mmeɪt] *n* compañero(-a) de cuarto
room service *n* servicio de habitaciones
room temperature *n* temperatura ambiente
roomy ['ru:mɪ] *adj* espacioso
roost [ru:st] *n* percha ■ *vi* pasar la noche
rooster ['ru:stə^r] *n* gallo
root [ru:t] *n* (*Bot, Math*) raíz *f* ■ *vi* (*plant, belief*) arraigar(se); **to take ~** (*plant*) echar raíces; (*idea*) arraigar(se); **the ~ of the problem is that ...** la raíz del problema es que ...
▸ **root about** *vi* (*fig*) rebuscar
▸ **root for** *vt fus* apoyar a
▸ **root out** *vt* desarraigar
root beer *n* (*US*) *refresco sin alcohol de extractos de hierbas*
rooted ['ru:tɪd] *adj* enraizado; (*opinions etc*) arraigado
rope [rəup] *n* cuerda; (*Naut*) cable *m* ■ *vt* (*box*) atar *or* amarrar con (una) cuerda; (*climbers*: *also*: **rope together**) encordarse; **to ~ sb in** (*fig*) persuadir a algn a tomar parte; **to know the ropes** (*fig*) conocer los trucos (del oficio)
rope ladder *n* escala de cuerda
ropey ['rəupɪ] *adj* (*col*) chungo
rosary ['rəuzərɪ] *n* rosario
rose [rəuz] *pt of* **rise** ■ *n* rosa; (*also*: **rosebush**) rosal *m*; (*on watering can*) roseta ■ *adj* color de rosa
rosé ['rəuzeɪ] *n* vino rosado, clarete *m*
rosebed ['rəuzbɛd] *n* rosaleda
rosebud ['rəuzbʌd] *n* capullo de rosa
rosebush ['rəuzbuʃ] *n* rosal *m*
rosemary ['rəuzmərɪ] *n* romero
rosette [rəu'zɛt] *n* rosetón *m*
ROSPA ['rɔspə] *n abbr* (*Brit*) = **Royal Society for the Prevention of Accidents**
roster ['rɔstə^r] *n*: **duty ~** lista de tareas
rostrum ['rɔstrəm] *n* tribuna
rosy ['rəuzɪ] *adj* rosado, sonrosado; **the future looks ~** el futuro parece prometedor
rot [rɔt] *n* (*decay*) putrefacción *f*, podredumbre *f*; (*fig: pej*) tonterías *fpl* ■ *vt* pudrir, corromper ■ *vi* pudrirse, corromperse; **it has rotted** está podrido; **to stop the ~** (*fig*) poner fin a las pérdidas
rota ['rəutə] *n* lista (de tareas)
rotary ['rəutərɪ] *adj* rotativo
rotate [rəu'teɪt] *vt* (*revolve*) hacer girar, dar vueltas a; (*change round: crops*) cultivar en rotación; (*: jobs*) alternar ■ *vi* (*revolve*) girar, dar vueltas
rotating [rəu'teɪtɪŋ] *adj* (*movement*) rotativo
rotation [rəu'teɪʃən] *n* rotación *f*; **in ~** por turno
rote [rəut] *n*: **by ~** de memoria
rotor ['rəutə^r] *n* rotor *m*
rotten ['rɔtn] *adj* (*decayed*) podrido; (*: wood*) carcomido; (*fig*) corrompido; (*col: bad*) pésimo; **to feel ~** (*ill*) sentirse fatal; **~ to the core** completamente podrido
rotund [rəu'tʌnd] *adj* rotundo
rouble, ruble (*US*) ['ru:bl] *n* rublo
rouge [ru:ʒ] *n* colorete *m*
rough [rʌf] *adj* (*skin, surface*) áspero; (*terrain*) accidentado; (*road*) desigual; (*voice*) bronco; (*person, manner: coarse*) tosco, grosero; (*weather*) borrascoso; (*treatment*) brutal; (*sea*) embravecido; (*cloth*) basto; (*plan*) preliminar; (*guess*) aproximado; (*violent*) violento ■ *n* (*Golf*): **in the ~** en las hierbas altas; **to ~ it** vivir sin comodidades; **to sleep ~** (*Brit*) pasar la noche al raso; **the sea is ~ today** el mar está agitado hoy; **to have a ~ time (of it)** pasar una mala racha; **~ estimate** cálculo aproximado
roughage ['rʌfɪdʒ] *n* fibra(s) *f(pl)*, forraje *m*
rough-and-ready ['rʌfən'rɛdɪ] *adj* improvisado, tosco
rough-and-tumble ['rʌfən'tʌmbl] *n* pelea
roughcast ['rʌfkɑ:st] *n* mezcla gruesa

rough copy, rough draft *n* borrador *m*
roughen ['rʌfn] *vt* (*a surface*) poner áspero
roughly ['rʌflɪ] *adv* (*handle*) torpemente; (*make*) toscamente; (*approximately*) aproximadamente; **~ speaking** más o menos
roughness ['rʌfnɪs] *n* aspereza; tosquedad *f*; brutalidad *f*
roughshod ['rʌfʃɔd] *adv*: **to ride ~ over** (*person*) pisotear a; (*objections*) hacer caso omiso de
rough work *n* (*Scol etc*) borrador *m*
roulette [ru:'lɛt] *n* ruleta
Roumania [ru:'meɪnɪə] *n* = **Rumania**
round [raund] *adj* redondo ■ *n* círculo; (*of policeman*) ronda; (*of milkman*) recorrido; (*of doctor*) visitas *fpl*; (*game: in competition, cards*) partida; (*of ammunition*) cartucho; (*Boxing*) asalto; (*of talks*) ronda ■ *vt* (*corner*) doblar ■ *prep* alrededor de ■ *adv*: **all ~** por todos lados; **the long way ~** por el camino menos directo; **all the year ~** durante todo el año; **it's just ~ the corner** (*fig*) está a la vuelta de la esquina; **to ask sb ~** invitar a algn a casa; **I'll be ~ at six o'clock** llegaré a eso de las seis; **she arrived ~ (about) noon** llegó alrededor del mediodía; **~ the clock** *adv* las 24 horas; **to go ~ to sb's (house)** ir a casa de algn; **to go ~ the back** pasar por atrás; **to go ~ a house** visitar una casa; **enough to go ~** bastante (para todos); **in ~ figures** en números redondos; **to go the rounds** (*story*) divulgarse; **a ~ of applause** una salva de aplausos; **a ~ of drinks/sandwiches** una ronda de bebidas/bocadillos; **a ~ of toast** (*Brit*) una tostada; **the daily ~** la rutina cotidiana
▸ **round off** *vt* (*speech etc*) acabar, poner término a
▸ **round up** *vt* (*cattle*) acorralar; (*people*) reunir; (*prices*) redondear
roundabout ['raundəbaut] *n* (*Brit: Aut*) glorieta, rotonda; (*: at fair*) tiovivo ■ *adj* (*route, means*) indirecto
rounded ['raundɪd] *adj* redondeado, redondo
rounders ['raundəz] *n* (*Brit: game*) *juego similar al béisbol*
roundly ['raundlɪ] *adv* (*fig*) rotundamente
round-robin ['raundrɔbɪn] *n* (*Sport: also*: **round-robin tournament**) liguilla
round-shouldered ['raund'ʃəuldəd] *adj* cargado de espaldas
round trip *n* viaje *m* de ida y vuelta
roundup ['raundʌp] *n* rodeo; (*of criminals*) redada; **a ~ of the latest news** un resumen de las últimas noticias
rouse [rauz] *vt* (*wake up*) despertar; (*stir up*) suscitar
rousing ['rauzɪŋ] *adj* (*applause*) caluroso; (*speech*) conmovedor(a)
rout [raut] *n* (*Mil*) derrota; (*flight*) desbandada ■ *vt* derrotar
route [ru:t] *n* ruta, camino; (*of bus*) recorrido; (*of shipping*) rumbo, derrota; **the best ~ to London** el mejor camino *or* la mejor ruta para ir a Londres; **en ~ from ... to** en el viaje de ... a; **en ~ for** rumbo a, con destino en
route map *n* (*Brit: for journey*) mapa *m* de carreteras
routine [ru:'ti:n] *adj* (*work*) rutinario ■ *n* rutina; (*Theat*) número; (*Comput*) rutina; **~ procedure** trámite *m* rutinario
rover ['rəuvəʳ] *n* vagabundo(-a)
roving ['rəuvɪŋ] *adj* (*wandering*) errante; (*salesman*) ambulante; (*reporter*) volante
row [rəu] *n* (*line*) fila, hilera; (*Knitting*) vuelta [rau] (*noise*) escándalo; (*dispute*) bronca, pelea; (*fuss*) jaleo; (*scolding*) reprimenda ■ *vi* (*in boat*) remar; [rau] reñir(se) ■ *vt* (*boat*) conducir remando; **four days in a ~** cuarto días seguidos; **to make a ~** armar un lío; **to have a ~** pelearse, reñir
rowboat ['rəubəut] *n* (*US*) bote *m* de remos
rowdy ['raudɪ] *adj* (*person: noisy*) ruidoso; (*: quarrelsome*) pendenciero; (*occasion*) alborotado ■ *n* pendenciero
rowdyism ['raudɪɪzəm] *n* gamberrismo
row houses *npl* (*US*) casas *fpl* adosadas
rowing ['rəuɪŋ] *n* remo
rowing boat *n* (*Brit*) bote *m or* barco de remos
rowlock ['rɔlək] *n* (*Brit*) chumacera
royal ['rɔɪəl] *adj* real
Royal Academy, Royal Academy of Arts *n* (*Brit*) la Real Academia (de Bellas Artes); *ver nota*

ROYAL ACADEMY (OF ARTS)

La *Royal Academy (of Arts)*, fundada en 1768 durante el reinado de Jorge III, es una institución dedicada al fomento de la pintura, escultura y arquitectura en el Reino Unido. Además de dar cursos de arte, presenta una exposición anual de artistas contemporáneos en su sede de Burlington House, en el centro de Londres. No existe una institución equivalente a la Real Academia de la Lengua.

Royal Air Force *n* Fuerzas Aéreas Británicas *fpl*
royal blue *n* azul *m* marino
royalist ['rɔɪəlɪst] *adj, n* monárquico(-a) *m(f)*
Royal Navy *n* (*Brit*) Marina Británica

royalty ['rɔɪəltɪ] *n* (*royal persons*) (miembros *mpl* de la) familia real; (*payment to author*) derechos *mpl* de autor
RP (*n abbr: Brit: = Received Pronunciation*) *ver nota*

RP

El acento con el que suelen hablar las clases medias y altas de Inglaterra se denomina RP (o *Received Pronunciation*). Es el acento estándar, sin variaciones regionales, que aún usan los locutores en los informativos nacionales de la "BBC". También suele tomarse como norma en la enseñanza del inglés británico como lengua extranjera. Todavía conserva un gran prestigio, aunque la gran mayoría de la población habla con el acento de su región, que puede ser más o menos fuerte según su educación o clase social.

rpm (*abbr: = revolutions per minute*) r.p.m.
RR *abbr* (*US*) = **railroad**
RRP *n abbr* (*Brit: = recommended retail price*) PVP *m*
RSA *n abbr* (*Brit*) = **Royal Society of Arts**; **Royal Scottish Academy**
RSI *n abbr* (*Med: = repetitive strain injury*) *traumatismo producido por un esfuerzo continuado (como el de las mecanógrafas)*
RSPB *n abbr* (*Brit*) = **Royal Society for the Protection of Birds**
RSPCA *n abbr* (*Brit*) = **Royal Society for the Prevention of Cruelty to Animals**
RSVP *abbr* (*= répondez s'il vous plaît*) SRC
RTA *n abbr* (*= road traffic accident*) accidente *m* de carretera
Rt. Hon. *abbr* (*Brit: = Right Honourable*) *tratamiento honorífico de diputado*
Rt. Rev. *abbr* (*= Right Reverend*) Rvdo.
rub [rʌb] *vt* (*gen*) frotar; (*hard*) restregar ■ *n* (*gen*) frotamiento; (*touch*) roce *m*; **to ~ sb up** *or* (*US*) **~ sb the wrong way** sacar de quicio a algn
▸ **rub down** *vt* (*body*) secar frotando; (*horse*) almohazar
▸ **rub in** *vt* (*ointment*) frotar
▸ **rub off** *vt* borrarse ■ *vi* quitarse (frotando); **to ~ off on sb** influir en algn, pegársele a algn
▸ **rub out** *vt* borrar ■ *vi* borrarse
rubber ['rʌbəʳ] *n* caucho, goma; (*Brit: eraser*) goma de borrar
rubber band *n* goma, gomita
rubber bullet *n* bala de goma
rubber plant *n* ficus *m*
rubber ring *n* (*for swimming*) flotador *m*
rubber stamp *n* sello (de caucho) ■ *vt*:
rubber-stamp (*fig*) aprobar maquinalmente
rubbery ['rʌbərɪ] *adj* (como) de goma
rubbish ['rʌbɪʃ] (*Brit*) *n* (*from household*) basura; (*waste*) desperdicios *mpl*; (*fig: pej*) tonterías *fpl*; (*trash*) basura, porquería ■ *vt* (*col*) poner por los suelos; **what you've just said is ~** lo que acabas de decir es una tontería
rubbish bin *n* cubo *or* bote *m* (*LAm*) de la basura
rubbish dump *n* (*in town*) vertedero, basurero
rubbishy ['rʌbɪʃɪ] *adj* de mala calidad, de pacotilla
rubble ['rʌbl] *n* escombros *mpl*
ruby ['ru:bɪ] *n* rubí *m*
RUC *n abbr* (*= Royal Ulster Constabulary*) *fuerza de policía en Irlanda del Norte*
rucksack ['rʌksæk] *n* mochila
ructions ['rʌkʃənz] *npl*: **there will be ~** se va a armar la gorda
ruddy ['rʌdɪ] *adj* (*face*) rubicundo; (*col: damned*) condenado
rude [ru:d] *adj* (*impolite: person*) grosero, maleducado; (*: word, manners*) rudo, grosero; (*indecent*) indecente; **to be ~ to sb** ser grosero con algn
rudeness ['ru:dnɪs] *n* grosería, tosquedad *f*
rudiment ['ru:dɪmənt] *n* rudimento
rudimentary [ru:dɪ'mɛntərɪ] *adj* rudimentario
rue [ru:] *vt* arrepentirse de
rueful ['ru:ful] *adj* arrepentido
ruffian ['rʌfɪən] *n* matón *m*, criminal *m*
ruffle ['rʌfl] *vt* (*hair*) despeinar; (*clothes*) arrugar; (*fig: person*) agitar
rug [rʌg] *n* alfombra; (*Brit: for knees*) manta
rugby ['rʌgbɪ] *n* (*also:* **rugby football**) rugby *m*
rugged ['rʌgɪd] *adj* (*landscape*) accidentado; (*features*) robusto
rugger ['rʌgəʳ] *n* (*Brit col*) rugby *m*
ruin ['ru:ɪn] *n* ruina ■ *vt* arruinar; (*spoil*) estropear; **ruins** *npl* ruinas *fpl*, restos *mpl*; **in ruins** en ruinas
ruinous ['ru:ɪnəs] *adj* ruinoso
rule [ru:l] *n* (*norm*) norma, costumbre *f*; (*regulation, ruler*) regla; (*government*) dominio; (*dominion etc*): **under British ~** bajo el dominio británico ■ *vt* (*country, person*) gobernar; (*decide*) disponer; (*draw lines*) trazar ■ *vi* gobernar; (*Law*) fallar; **to ~ against/in favour of/on** fallar en contra de/a favor de/sobre; **to ~ that ...** (*umpire, judge*) fallar que ...; **it's against the rules** está prohibido; **as a ~** por regla general, generalmente; **by ~ of thumb** por experiencia; **majority ~** (*Pol*) gobierno mayoritario
▸ **rule out** *vt* excluir
ruled [ru:ld] *adj* (*paper*) rayado

ruler ['ruːləʳ] *n* (*sovereign*) soberano; (*for measuring*) regla
ruling ['ruːlɪŋ] *adj* (*party*) gobernante; (*class*) dirigente ■ *n* (*Law*) fallo, decisión *f*
rum [rʌm] *n* ron *m*
Rumania [ruː'meɪnɪə] *n* Rumanía
Rumanian [ruː'meɪnɪən] *adj, n* rumano(-a) *m(f)*
rumble ['rʌmbl] *n* ruido sordo; (*of thunder*) redoble *m* ■ *vi* retumbar, hacer un ruido sordo; (*stomach, pipe*) sonar
rumbustious [rʌm'bʌstʃəs] *adj* (*person*) bullicioso
rummage ['rʌmɪdʒ] *vi* revolverlo todo
rumour, rumor (*US*) ['ruːməʳ] *n* rumor *m* ■ *vt*: **it is rumoured that ...** se rumorea que ...; ~ **has it that ...** corre la voz de que ...
rump [rʌmp] *n* (*of animal*) ancas *fpl*, grupa
rumple ['rʌmpl] *vt* (*clothes*) arrugar; (*hair*) despeinar
rump steak *n* filete *m* de lomo
rumpus ['rʌmpəs] *n* (*col*) lío, jaleo; (*quarrel*) pelea, riña; **to kick up a ~** armar un follón *or* armar bronca
run [rʌn] (*pt* **ran**, *pp* **~**) *n* (*Sport*) carrera; (*outing*) paseo, excursión *f*; (*distance travelled*) trayecto; (*series*) serie *f*; (*Theat*) temporada; (*Ski*) pista; (*in tights, stockings*) carrera ■ *vt* (*operate: business*) dirigir; (*: competition, course*) organizar; (*: hotel, house*) administrar, llevar; (*Comput: program*) ejecutar; (*to pass: hand*) pasar; (*bath*): **to ~ a bath** llenar la bañera ■ *vi* (*gen*) correr; (*work: machine*) funcionar, marchar; (*bus, train: operate*) circular, ir; (*: travel*) ir; (*continue: play*) seguir en cartel; (*: contract*) ser válido; (*flow: river, bath*) fluir; (*colours, washing*) desteñirse; (*in election*) ser candidato; **to go for a ~** ir a correr; **to make a ~ for it** echar(se) a correr, escapar(se), huir; **to have the ~ of sb's house** tener el libre uso de la casa de algn; **a ~ of luck** una racha de suerte; **there was a ~ on** (*meat, tickets*) hubo mucha demanda de; **in the long ~** a la larga; **on the ~** en fuga; **I'll ~ you to the station** te llevaré a la estación en coche; **to ~ a risk** correr un riesgo; **to ~ errands** hacer recados; **it's very cheap to ~** es muy económico; **to be ~ off one's feet** estar ocupadísimo; **to ~ for the bus** correr tras el autobús; **we shall have to ~ for it** tendremos que escapar; **the train runs between Gatwick and Victoria** el tren circula entre Gatwick y Victoria; **the bus runs every 20 minutes** el autobús pasa cada 20 minutos; **to ~ on petrol/on diesel/off batteries** funcionar con gasolina/gasoil/baterías; **my salary won't ~ to a car** mi sueldo no me da para comprarme un coche; **the car ran into the lamppost** el coche chocó contra el farol
▸**run about, run around** *vi* (*children*) correr por todos lados
▸**run across** *vt fus* (*find*) dar *or* topar con
▸**run away** *vi* huir
▸**run down** *vi* (*clock*) pararse ■ *vt* (*reduce: production*) ir reduciendo; (*factory*) restringir la producción de; (*Aut*) atropellar; (*criticize*) criticar; **to be ~ down** (*person: tired*) encontrarse agotado
▸**run in** *vt* (*Brit: car*) rodar
▸**run into** *vt fus* (*meet: person, trouble*) tropezar con; (*collide with*) chocar con; **to ~ into debt** contraer deudas, endeudarse
▸**run off** *vt* (*water*) dejar correr ■ *vi* huir corriendo
▸**run out** *vi* (*person*) salir corriendo; (*liquid*) irse; (*lease*) caducar, vencer; (*money*) acabarse
▸**run out of** *vt fus* quedar sin; **I've ~ out of petrol** se me acabó la gasolina
▸**run over** *vt* (*Aut*) atropellar ■ *vt fus* (*revise*) repasar
▸**run through** *vt fus* (*instructions*) repasar
▸**run up** *vt* (*debt*) incurrir en; **to ~ up against** (*difficulties*) tropezar con
run-around ['rʌnəraund] *n*: **to give sb the ~** traer a algn al retortero
runaway ['rʌnəweɪ] *adj* (*horse*) desbocado; (*truck*) sin frenos; (*person*) fugitivo
rundown ['rʌndaun] *n* (*Brit: of industry etc*) cierre *m* gradual
rung [rʌŋ] *pp of* **ring** ■ *n* (*of ladder*) escalón *m*, peldaño
run-in ['rʌnɪn] *n* (*col*) altercado
runner ['rʌnəʳ] *n* (*in race: person*) corredor(a) *m(f)*; (*: horse*) caballo; (*on sledge*) patín *m*; (*wheel*) ruedecilla
runner bean *n* (*Brit*) judía escarlata
runner-up [rʌnər'ʌp] *n* subcampeón(-ona) *m(f)*
running ['rʌnɪŋ] *n* (*sport*) atletismo; (*race*) carrera ■ *adj* (*costs, water*) corriente; (*commentary*) en directo; **to be in/out of the ~ for sth** tener/no tener posibilidades de ganar algo; **6 days ~** 6 días seguidos
running costs *npl* (*of business*) gastos *mpl* corrientes; (*of car*) gastos *mpl* de mantenimiento
running head *n* (*Typ*) encabezamiento normal
running mate *n* (*US Pol*) candidato(-a) a la vicepresidencia
runny ['rʌnɪ] *adj* derretido
run-off ['rʌnɔf] *n* (*in contest, election*) desempate *m*; (*extra race*) carrera de desempate
run-of-the-mill ['rʌnəvðə'mɪl] *adj* común y corriente

runt [rʌnt] *n* (*also pej*) enano
run-up ['rʌnʌp] *n*: **~ to** (*election etc*) período previo a
runway ['rʌnweɪ] *n* (*Aviat*) pista (de aterrizaje)
rupee [ru:'pi:] *n* rupia
rupture ['rʌptʃəʳ] *n* (*Med*) hernia ■ *vt*: **to ~ o.s.** causarse una hernia
rural ['ruərl] *adj* rural
ruse [ru:z] *n* ardid *m*
rush [rʌʃ] *n* ímpetu *m*; (*hurry*) prisa, apuro (*LAm*); (*Comm*) demanda repentina; (*Bot*) junco; (*current*) corriente *f* fuerte, ráfaga ■ *vt* apresurar; (*work*) hacer de prisa; (*attack: town etc*) asaltar ■ *vi* correr, precipitarse; **gold ~** fiebre *f* del oro; **we've had a ~ of orders** ha habido una gran demanda; **I'm in a ~ (to do)** tengo prisa *or* apuro (*LAm*) (por hacer); **is there any ~ for this?** ¿te corre prisa esto?; **to ~ sth off** hacer algo de prisa y corriendo
▸ **rush through** *vt fus* (*meal*) comer de prisa; (*book*) leer de prisa; (*work*) hacer de prisa; (*town*) atravesar a toda velocidad ■ *vt sep* (*Comm: order*) despachar rápidamente
rush hour *n* horas *fpl* punta
rush job *n* (*urgent*) trabajo urgente
rusk [rʌsk] *n* bizcocho tostado
Russia ['rʌʃə] *n* Rusia
Russian ['rʌʃən] *adj* ruso ■ *n* ruso(-a); (*Ling*) ruso
rust [rʌst] *n* herrumbre *f*, moho ■ *vi* oxidarse
rustic ['rʌstɪk] *adj* rústico
rustle ['rʌsl] *vi* susurrar ■ *vt* (*paper*) hacer crujir; (*US: cattle*) hurtar, robar
rustproof ['rʌstpru:f] *adj* inoxidable
rusty ['rʌstɪ] *adj* oxidado
rut [rʌt] *n* surco; (*Zool*) celo; **to be in a ~** ser esclavo de la rutina
ruthless ['ru:θlɪs] *adj* despiadado
RV *abbr (= revised version) traducción inglesa de la Biblia de 1855* ■ *n abbr* (*US*) = **recreational vehicle**
rye [raɪ] *n* centeno
rye bread *n* pan de centeno

Ss

S, s [ɛs] *n* (*letter*) S, s *f*; **S for Sugar** S de sábado

S *abbr* (= *Saint*) Sto.(-a.); (*US Scol*: *mark*: = *satisfactory*) suficiente; (= *south*) S; (*on clothes*) = **small**

SA *n abbr* = **South Africa; South America**

sabbath ['sæbəθ] *n* domingo; (*Jewish*) sábado

sabbatical [sə'bætɪkl] *adj*: **~ year** año sabático

sabotage ['sæbətɑːʒ] *n* sabotaje *m* ▪ *vt* sabotear

sabre, saber (*US*) ['seɪbəʳ] *n* sable *m*

saccharin, saccharine ['sækərɪn] *n* sacarina

sachet ['sæʃeɪ] *n* sobrecito

sack [sæk] *n* (*bag*) saco, costal *m* ▪ *vt* (*dismiss*) despedir, echar; (*plunder*) saquear; **to get the ~** ser despedido; **to give sb the ~** despedir *or* echar a algn

sackful ['sækful] *n* saco

sacking ['sækɪŋ] *n* (*material*) arpillera

sacrament ['sækrəmənt] *n* sacramento

sacred ['seɪkrɪd] *adj* sagrado, santo

sacred cow *n* (*fig*) vaca sagrada

sacrifice ['sækrɪfaɪs] *n* sacrificio ▪ *vt* sacrificar; **to make sacrifices (for sb)** sacrificarse (por algn)

sacrilege ['sækrɪlɪdʒ] *n* sacrilegio

sacrosanct ['sækrəusæŋkt] *adj* sacrosanto

sad [sæd] *adj* (*unhappy*) triste; (*deplorable*) lamentable

sadden ['sædn] *vt* entristecer

saddle ['sædl] *n* silla (de montar); (*of cycle*) sillín *m* ▪ *vt* (*horse*) ensillar; **to ~ sb with sth** (*col*: *task, bill, name*) cargar a algn con algo; (*responsibility*) gravar a algn con algo; **to be saddled with sth** (*col*) quedar cargado con algo

saddlebag ['sædlbæg] *n* alforja

sadism ['seɪdɪzm] *n* sadismo

sadist ['seɪdɪst] *n* sádico(-a)

sadistic [sə'dɪstɪk] *adj* sádico

sadly ['sædlɪ] *adv* tristemente; (*regrettably*) desgraciadamente; **~ lacking (in)** muy deficiente (en)

sadness ['sædnɪs] *n* tristeza

sado-masochism [seɪdəu'mæsəkɪzɪm] *n* sadomasoquismo

sae *abbr* (*Brit*: = *stamped addressed envelope*) *sobre con las propias señas de uno y con sello*

safari [sə'fɑːrɪ] *n* safari *m*

safari park *n* safari *m*

safe [seɪf] *adj* (*out of danger*) fuera de peligro; (*not dangerous, sure*) seguro; (*unharmed*) ileso; (*trustworthy*) digno de confianza ▪ *n* caja de caudales, caja fuerte; **~ and sound** sano y salvo; **(just) to be on the ~ side** para mayor seguridad; **~ journey!** ¡buen viaje!; **it is ~ to say that ...** se puede decir con confianza que ...

safe bet *n* apuesta segura; **it's a ~ she'll turn up** seguro que viene

safe-breaker ['seɪfbreɪkəʳ] *n* (*Brit*) ladrón(-ona) *m(f)* de cajas fuertes

safe-conduct [seɪf'kɔndʌkt] *n* salvoconducto

safe-cracker ['seɪfkrækəʳ] *n* (*US*) = **safe-breaker**

safe-deposit ['seɪfdɪpɔzɪt] *n* (*vault*) cámara acorazada; (*box*) caja de seguridad *or* de caudales

safeguard ['seɪfgɑːd] *n* protección *f*, garantía ▪ *vt* proteger, defender

safe haven *n* refugio

safekeeping ['seɪf'kiːpɪn] *n* custodia

safely ['seɪflɪ] *adv* seguramente, con seguridad; (*without mishap*) sin peligro; **I can ~ say** puedo decir *or* afirmar con toda seguridad

safeness ['seɪfnɪs] *n* seguridad *f*

safe passage *n* garantías *fpl* para marcharse en libertad

safe sex *n* sexo seguro *or* sin riesgo

safety ['seɪftɪ] *n* seguridad *f* ▪ *cpd* de seguridad; **road ~** seguridad *f* en carretera; **~ first!** ¡precaución!

safety belt *n* cinturón *m* (de seguridad)

safety catch *n* seguro

safety net *n* red *f* (de seguridad)

safety pin *n* imperdible *m*, seguro (*LAm*)
safety valve *n* válvula de seguridad *or* de escape
saffron ['sæfrən] *n* azafrán *m*
sag [sæg] *vi* aflojarse
saga ['sɑːgə] *n* (*History*) saga; (*fig*) epopeya
sage [seɪdʒ] *n* (*herb*) salvia; (*man*) sabio
Sagittarius [sædʒɪ'tɛərɪəs] *n* Sagitario
sago ['seɪgəu] *n* sagú *m*
Sahara [sə'hɑːrə] *n*: **the ~ (Desert)** el Sáhara
Sahel [sæ'hɛl] *n* Sahel *m*
said [sɛd] *pt, pp of* **say**
Saigon [saɪ'gɔn] *n* Saigón *m*
sail [seɪl] *n* (*on boat*) vela ■ *vt* (*boat*) gobernar ■ *vi* (*travel: ship*) navegar; (*passenger*) pasear en barco; (*set off: also:* **to set sail**) zarpar; **to go for a ~** dar un paseo en barco; **they sailed into Copenhagen** arribaron a Copenhague ▸ **sail through** *vt fus* (*exam*) aprobar fácilmente
sailboat ['seɪlbəut] *n* (US) velero, barco de vela
sailing ['seɪlɪŋ] *n* (*Sport*) balandrismo; **to go ~** salir en balandro
sailing ship *n* barco de vela
sailor ['seɪlə^r] *n* marinero, marino
saint [seɪnt] *n* santo; **S~ John** San Juan
saintliness ['seɪntlɪnɪs] *n* santidad *f*
saintly ['seɪntlɪ] *adj* santo
sake [seɪk] *n*: **for the ~ of** por; **for the ~ of argument** digamos, es un decir; **art for art's ~** el arte por el arte
salad ['sæləd] *n* ensalada; **tomato ~** ensalada de tomate
salad bowl *n* ensaladera
salad cream *n* (*Brit*) mayonesa
salad dressing *n* aliño
salad oil *n* aceite *m* para ensalada
salami [sə'lɑːmɪ] *n* salami *m*, salchichón *m*
salaried ['sælərɪd] *adj* asalariado
salary ['sælərɪ] *n* sueldo
salary earner *n* asalariado(-a)
salary scale *n* escala salarial
sale [seɪl] *n* venta; (*at reduced prices*) liquidación *f*, saldo; **"for ~"** "se vende"; **on ~** en venta; **on ~ or return** (*goods*) venta por reposición; **closing-down** *or* (US) **liquidation ~** liquidación *f*; **~ and lease back** venta y arrendamiento al vendedor
saleroom ['seɪlruːm] *n* sala de subastas
sales assistant *n* (*Brit*) dependiente(-a) *m(f)*
sales campaign *n* campaña de venta
sales clerk *n* (US) dependiente(-a) *m(f)*
sales conference *n* conferencia de ventas
sales drive *n* promoción *f* de ventas
sales figures *npl* cifras *fpl* de ventas
sales force *n* personal *m* de ventas
salesman ['seɪlzmən] *n* vendedor *m*; (*in shop*) dependiente *m*; (*representative*) viajante *m*
sales manager *n* gerente *m/f* de ventas
salesmanship ['seɪlzmənʃɪp] *n* arte *m* de vender
sales meeting *n* reunión *f* de ventas
sales tax *n* (US) = **purchase tax**
saleswoman ['seɪlzwumən] *n* vendedora; (*in shop*) dependienta; (*representative*) viajante *f*
salient ['seɪlɪənt] *adj* (*features, points*) sobresaliente
saline ['seɪlaɪn] *adj* salino
saliva [sə'laɪvə] *n* saliva
sallow ['sæləu] *adj* cetrino
sally forth, sally out ['sælɪ-] *vi* salir, ponerse en marcha
salmon ['sæmən] *n* (*pl inv*) salmón *m*
salon ['sælɔn] *n* (*hairdressing salon, beauty salon*) salón *m*
saloon [sə'luːn] *n* (US) bar *m*, taberna; (*Brit Aut*) (coche *m* de) turismo; (*ship's lounge*) cámara, salón *m*
SALT [sɔːlt] *n abbr* (= *Strategic Arms Limitation Talks/Treaty*) tratado SALT
salt [sɔːlt] *n* sal *f* ■ *vt* salar; (*put salt on*) poner sal en; **an old ~** un lobo de mar ▸ **salt away** *vt* (*col: money*) ahorrar
salt cellar *n* salero
salt mine *n* mina de sal
saltwater ['sɔːlt'wɔːtə^r] *adj* (*fish etc*) de agua salada, de mar
salty ['sɔːltɪ] *adj* salado
salubrious [sa'luːbrɪəs] *adj* sano; (*fig: district etc*) atractivo
salutary ['sæljutərɪ] *adj* saludable
salute [sə'luːt] *n* saludo; (*of guns*) salva ■ *vt* saludar
salvage ['sælvɪdʒ] *n* (*saving*) salvamento, recuperación *f*; (*things saved*) objetos *mpl* salvados ■ *vt* salvar
salvage vessel *n* buque *m* de salvamento
salvation [sæl'veɪʃən] *n* salvación *f*
Salvation Army *n* Ejército de Salvación
salve [sælv] *n* (*cream etc*) ungüento, bálsamo
salvo ['sælvəu] *n* (*Mil*) salva
Samaritan [sə'mærɪtən] *n*: **to call the Samaritans** llamar al teléfono de la esperanza
same [seɪm] *adj* mismo ■ *pron*: **the ~** el mismo/la misma; **the ~ book as** el mismo libro que; **on the ~ day** el mismo día; **at the ~ time** (*at the same moment*) al mismo tiempo; (*yet*) sin embargo; **all** *or* **just the ~** sin embargo, aun así; **they're one and the ~** (*person*) son la misma persona; (*thing*) son iguales; **to do the ~ (as sb)** hacer lo mismo (que otro); **and the ~ to you!** ¡igualmente!;

~ **here!** ¡yo también!; **the ~ again** (*in bar etc*) otro igual
sampan ['sæmpæn] *n* sampán *m*
sample ['sɑːmpl] *n* muestra ■ *vt* (*food, wine*) probar; **to take a ~** tomar una muestra; **free ~** muestra gratuita
sanatorium (*pl* **sanatoria**) [sænə'tɔːrɪəm, -rɪə] *n* (*Brit*) sanatorio
sanctify ['sæŋktɪfaɪ] *vt* santificar
sanctimonious [sæŋktɪ'məunɪəs] *adj* santurrón(-ona)
sanction ['sæŋkʃən] *n* sanción *f* ■ *vt* sancionar; **to impose economic sanctions on** *or* **against** imponer sanciones económicas a *or* contra
sanctity ['sæŋktɪtɪ] *n* (*gen*) santidad *f*; (*inviolability*) inviolabilidad *f*
sanctuary ['sæŋktjuərɪ] *n* (*gen*) santuario; (*refuge*) asilo, refugio
sand [sænd] *n* arena; (*beach*) playa ■ *vt* (*also*: **sand down**: *wood etc*) lijar
sandal ['sændl] *n* sandalia
sandalwood ['sændlwud] *n* sándalo
sandbag ['sændbæg] *n* saco de arena
sandblast ['sændblɑːst] *vt* limpiar con chorro de arena
sandbox ['sændbɔks] *n* (*US*) = **sandpit**
sandcastle ['sændkɑːsl] *n* castillo de arena
sand dune *n* duna
sander ['sændəʳ] *n* pulidora
sandpaper ['sændpeɪpəʳ] *n* papel *m* de lija
sandpit ['sændpɪt] *n* (*for children*) cajón *m* de arena
sands [sændz] *npl* playa *sg* de arena
sandstone ['sændstəun] *n* piedra arenisca
sandstorm ['sændstɔːm] *n* tormenta de arena
sandwich ['sændwɪtʃ] *n* bocadillo (*SP*), sandwich *m* (*LAm*) ■ *vt* (*also*: **sandwich in**) intercalar; **to be sandwiched between** estar apretujado entre; **cheese/ham ~** sandwich de queso/jamón
sandwich board *n* cartelón *m*
sandwich course *n* (*Brit*) *programa que intercala períodos de estudio con prácticas profesionales*
sandy ['sændɪ] *adj* arenoso; (*colour*) rojizo
sane [seɪn] *adj* cuerdo, sensato
sang [sæŋ] *pt of* **sing**
sanitarium [sænɪ'tɛərɪəm] *n* (*US*) = **sanatorium**
sanitary ['sænɪtərɪ] *adj* (*system, arrangements*) sanitario; (*clean*) higiénico
sanitary towel, sanitary napkin (*US*) *n* paño higiénico, compresa
sanitation [sænɪ'teɪʃən] *n* (*in house*) servicios *mpl* higiénicos; (*in town*) servicio de desinfección
sanitation department *n* (*US*) departamento de limpieza y recogida de basuras
sanity ['sænɪtɪ] *n* cordura; (*of judgment*) sensatez *f*
sank [sæŋk] *pt of* **sink**
San Marino ['sænmə'riːnəu] *n* San Marino
Santa Claus [sæntə'klɔːz] *n* San Nicolás *m*, Papá Noel *m*
Santiago [sæntɪ'ɑːgəu] *n* (*also*: **Santiago de Chile**) Santiago (de Chile)
sap [sæp] *n* (*of plants*) savia ■ *vt* (*strength*) minar, agotar
sapling ['sæplɪŋ] *n* árbol nuevo *or* joven
sapphire ['sæfaɪəʳ] *n* zafiro
Saragossa [særə'gɔsə] *n* Zaragoza
sarcasm ['sɑːkæzm] *n* sarcasmo
sarcastic [sɑː'kæstɪk] *adj* sarcástico; **to be ~** ser sarcástico
sarcophagus, sarcophagi [sɑː'kɔfəgəs, -gaɪ] *n* sarcófago
sardine [sɑː'diːn] *n* sardina
Sardinia [sɑː'dɪnɪə] *n* Cerdeña
Sardinian [sɑː'dɪnɪən] *adj, n* sardo(-a) *m(f)*
sardonic [sɑː'dɔnɪk] *adj* sardónico
sari ['sɑːrɪ] *n* sari *m*
SARS ['sɑːz] *n abbr* (= *severe acute respiratory syndrome*) neumonía asiática, SARS *m*
SAS *n abbr* (*Brit Mil*: = *Special Air Service*) *cuerpo del ejército británico encargado de misiones clandestinas*
SASE *n abbr* (*US*: = *self-addressed stamped envelope*) *sobre con las propias señas de uno y con sello*
sash [sæʃ] *n* faja
Sask. *abbr* (*Canada*) = **Saskatchewan**
SAT *n abbr* (*US*) = **Scholastic Aptitude Test**
Sat. *abbr* (= *Saturday*) sáb
sat [sæt] *pt, pp of* **sit**
Satan ['seɪtn] *n* Satanás *m*
satanic [sə'tænɪk] *adj* satánico
satchel ['sætʃl] *n* bolsa; (*child's*) cartera, mochila (*LAm*)
sated ['seɪtɪd] *adj* (*appetite, person*) saciado
satellite ['sætəlaɪt] *n* satélite *m*
satellite dish *n* (antena) parabólica
satellite navigation system *n* sistema *m* de navegación por satélite
satellite television *n* televisión *f* por satélite
satiate ['seɪʃɪeɪt] *vt* saciar, hartar
satin ['sætɪn] *n* raso ■ *adj* de raso; **with a ~ finish** satinado
satire ['sætaɪəʳ] *n* sátira
satirical [sə'tɪrɪkl] *adj* satírico
satirist ['sætɪrɪst] *n* (*writer etc*) escritor(a) *m(f)* satírico(-a); (*cartoonist*) caricaturista *m/f*
satirize ['sætɪraɪz] *vt* satirizar
satisfaction [sætɪs'fækʃən] *n* satisfacción *f*; **it gives me great ~** es para mí una gran

satisfacción; **has it been done to your ~?** ¿se ha hecho a su satisfacción?
satisfactorily [sætɪsˈfæktərɪlɪ] *adv* satisfactoriamente, de modo satisfactorio
satisfactory [sætɪsˈfæktərɪ] *adj* satisfactorio
satisfied [ˈsætɪsfaɪd] *adj* satisfecho; **to be ~ (with sth)** estar satisfecho (de algo)
satisfy [ˈsætɪsfaɪ] *vt* satisfacer; (*pay*) liquidar; (*convince*) convencer; **to ~ the requirements** llenar los requisitos; **to ~ sb that** convencer a algn de que; **to ~ o.s. of sth** convencerse de algo
satisfying [ˈsætɪsfaɪɪŋ] *adj* satisfactorio
satsuma [sætˈsuːmə] *n* satsuma
saturate [ˈsætʃəreɪt] *vt*: **to ~ (with)** empapar *or* saturar (de)
saturated fat [sætʃəreɪtɪd-] *n* grasa saturada
saturation [sætʃəˈreɪʃən] *n* saturación *f*
Saturday [ˈsætədɪ] *n* sábado; *see also* **Tuesday**
sauce [sɔːs] *n* salsa; (*sweet*) crema; (*fig: cheek*) frescura
saucepan [ˈsɔːspən] *n* cacerola, olla
saucer [ˈsɔːsəʳ] *n* platillo
saucily [ˈsɔːsɪlɪ] *adv* con frescura, descaradamente
sauciness [ˈsɔːsɪnɪs] *n* frescura, descaro
saucy [ˈsɔːsɪ] *adj* fresco, descarado
Saudi [ˈsaudɪ] *adj, n* saudí *m/f*, saudita *m/f*
Saudi Arabia *n* Arabia Saudí *or* Saudita
Saudi Arabian *adj, n* = **Saudi**
sauna [ˈsɔːnə] *n* sauna
saunter [ˈsɔːntəʳ] *vi* deambular
sausage [ˈsɔsɪdʒ] *n* salchicha; (*salami etc*) salchichón *m*
sausage roll *n* empanadilla
sauté [ˈsəuteɪ] *adj* (*Culin: potatoes*) salteado; (*: onions*) dorado, rehogado ■ *vt* saltear; dorar
savage [ˈsævɪdʒ] *adj* (*cruel, fierce*) feroz, furioso; (*primitive*) salvaje ■ *n* salvaje *m/f* ■ *vt* (*attack*) embestir
savagely [ˈsævɪdʒlɪ] *adv* con ferocidad, furiosamente; de modo salvaje
savagery [ˈsævɪdʒrɪ] *n* ferocidad *f*; salvajismo
save [seɪv] *vt* (*rescue*) salvar, rescatar; (*money, time*) ahorrar; (*put by*) guardar; (*Comput*) salvar (y guardar); (*avoid: trouble*) evitar ■ *vi* (*also*: **save up**) ahorrar ■ *n* (*Sport*) parada ■ *prep* salvo, excepto; **to ~ face** salvar las apariencias; **God ~ the Queen!** ¡Dios guarde a la Reina!, ¡Viva la Reina!; **I saved you a piece of cake** te he guardado un trozo de tarta; **it will ~ me an hour** con ello ganaré una hora
saving [ˈseɪvɪŋ] *n* (*on price etc*) economía ■ *adj*: **the ~ grace of** el único mérito de;
savings *npl* ahorros *mpl*; **to make savings** economizar
savings account *n* cuenta de ahorros
savings bank *n* caja de ahorros
saviour, savior (*US*) [ˈseɪvjəʳ] *n* salvador(a) *m(f)*
savoir-faire [ˈsævwɑːˈfɛəʳ] *n* don *m* de gentes
savour, savor (*US*) [ˈseɪvəʳ] *n* sabor *m*, gusto ■ *vt* saborear
savoury, savory (*US*) [ˈseɪvərɪ] *adj* sabroso; (*dish: not sweet*) salado
savvy [ˈsævɪ] *n* (*col*) conocimiento, experiencia
saw [sɔː] *pt of* **see** ■ *n* (*tool*) sierra ■ *vt* (*pt* **sawed**, *pp* **sawed** *or* **sawn** [sɔːn]) serrar; **to ~ sth up** (a)serrar algo
sawdust [ˈsɔːdʌst] *n* (a)serrín *m*
sawmill [ˈsɔːmɪl] *n* aserradero
sawn [sɔːn] *pp of* **saw**
sawn-off [ˈsɔːnɔf], **sawed-off** (*US*) [ˈsɔːdɔf] *adj*: **~ shotgun** escopeta de cañones recortados
saxophone [ˈsæksəfəun] *n* saxófono
say [seɪ] *n*: **to have one's ~** expresar su opinión; **to have a** *or* **some ~ in sth** tener voz y voto en algo ■ *vt, vi* (*pt, pp* **said** [sɛd]) decir; **to ~ yes/no** decir que sí/no; **my watch says 3 o'clock** mi reloj marca las tres; **that is to ~** es decir; **that goes without saying** ni que decir tiene; **she said (that) I was to give you this** me pidió que te diera esto; **I should ~ it's worth about £100** yo diría que vale unas 100 libras; **~ after me** repite lo que yo diga; **shall we ~ Tuesday?** ¿quedamos, por ejemplo, el martes?; **that doesn't ~ much for him** eso no dice nada a su favor; **when all is said and done** al fin y al cabo, a fin de cuentas; **there is something** *or* **a lot to be said for it** hay algo *or* mucho que decir a su favor
saying [ˈseɪɪŋ] *n* dicho, refrán *m*
say-so [ˈseɪsəu] *n* (*col*) autorización *f*
SBA *n abbr* (*US*) = **Small Business Administration**
SC *n abbr* (*US*) = **Supreme Court** ■ *abbr* (*US*) = **South Carolina**
s/c *abbr* = **self-contained**
scab [skæb] *n* costra; (*pej*) esquirol(a) *m(f)*
scaffold [ˈskæfəld] *n* (*for execution*) cadalso
scaffolding [ˈskæfəldɪŋ] *n* andamio, andamiaje *m*
scald [skɔːld] *n* escaldadura ■ *vt* escaldar
scalding [ˈskɔːldɪŋ] *adj* (*also*: **scalding hot**) hirviendo, que arde
scale [skeɪl] *n* (*gen*) escala; (*Mus*) escala; (*of fish*) escama; (*of salaries, fees etc*) escalafón *m* ■ *vt* (*mountain*) escalar; (*tree*) trepar; **scales**

npl (*small*) balanza *sg*; (*large*) báscula *sg*; **on a large ~** a gran escala; **~ of charges** tarifa, lista de precios; **pay ~** escala salarial; **to draw sth to ~** dibujar algo a escala
▸ **scale down** *vt* reducir
scaled-down [skeɪld'daun] *adj* reducido proporcionalmente
scale model *n* modelo a escala
scallop ['skɔləp] *n* (*Zool*) venera; (*Sewing*) festón *m*
scalp [skælp] *n* cabellera ■ *vt* escalpar
scalpel ['skælpl] *n* bisturí *m*
scam [skæm] *n* (*col*) estafa, timo
scamper ['skæmpəʳ] *vi*: **to ~ away, ~ off** escabullirse
scampi ['skæmpɪ] *npl* gambas *fpl*
scan [skæn] *vt* (*examine*) escudriñar; (*glance at quickly*) dar un vistazo a; (*TV, Radar*) explorar, registrar; (*Comput*) escanear ■ *n* (*Med*) examen *m* ultrasónico
scandal ['skændl] *n* escándalo; (*gossip*) chismes *mpl*
scandalize ['skændəlaɪz] *vt* escandalizar
scandalous ['skændələs] *adj* escandaloso
Scandinavia [skændɪ'neɪvɪə] *n* Escandinavia
Scandinavian [skændɪ'neɪvɪən] *adj, n* escandinavo(-a) *m(f)*
scanner ['skænəʳ] *n* (*Radar, Med, Comput*) escáner *m*
scant [skænt] *adj* escaso
scantily ['skæntɪlɪ] *adv*: **~ clad** *or* **dressed** ligero de ropa
scantiness ['skæntɪnɪs] *n* escasez *f*, insuficiencia
scanty ['skæntɪ] *adj* (*meal*) insuficiente; (*clothes*) ligero
scapegoat ['skeɪpgəut] *n* cabeza de turco, chivo expiatorio
scar [skɑː] *n* cicatriz *f* ■ *vt* marcar con una cicatriz ■ *vi* cicatrizarse
scarce [skɛəs] *adj* escaso
scarcely ['skɛəslɪ] *adv* apenas; **~ anybody** casi nadie; **I can ~ believe it** casi no puedo creerlo
scarceness ['skɛəsnɪs], **scarcity** ['skɛəsɪtɪ] *n* escasez *f*
scarcity value *n* valor *m* de escasez
scare [skɛəʳ] *n* susto, sobresalto; (*panic*) pánico ■ *vt* asustar, espantar; **to ~ sb stiff** dar a algn un susto de muerte; **bomb ~** amenaza de bomba
▸ **scare away, scare off** *vt* espantar, ahuyentar
scarecrow ['skɛəkrəu] *n* espantapájaros *m inv*
scared [skɛəd] *adj*: **to be ~** asustarse, estar asustado
scaremonger ['skɛəmʌŋgəʳ] *n* alarmista *m/f*
scarf (*pl* **scarves**) [skɑːf, skɑːvz] *n* (*long*) bufanda; (*square*) pañuelo
scarlet ['skɑːlɪt] *adj* escarlata
scarlet fever *n* escarlatina
scarper ['skɑːpəʳ] *vi* (*Brit col*) largarse
scarred [skɑːd] *adj* lleno de cicatrices
scarves [skɑːvz] *npl of* **scarf**
scary ['skɛərɪ] *adj* (*col*) de miedo; **it's ~** da miedo
scathing ['skeɪðɪŋ] *adj* mordaz; **to be ~ about sth** criticar algo duramente
scatter ['skætəʳ] *vt* (*spread*) esparcir, desparramar; (*put to flight*) dispersar ■ *vi* desparramarse; dispersarse
scatterbrained ['skætəbreɪnd] *adj* ligero de cascos
scavenge ['skævɪndʒ] *vi*: **to ~ (for)** (*person*) revolver entre la basura (para encontrar); **to ~ for food** (*hyenas etc*) nutrirse de carroña
scavenger ['skævɪndʒəʳ] *n* (*person*) *mendigo/a que rebusca en la basura*; (*Zool: animal*) animal *m* de carroña; (*: bird*) ave *f* de carroña
SCE *n abbr* = **Scottish Certificate of Education**
scenario [sɪ'nɑːrɪəu] *n* (*Theat*) argumento; (*Cine*) guión *m*; (*fig*) escenario
scene [siːn] *n* (*Theat*) escena; (*of crime, accident*) escenario; (*sight, view*) vista, perspectiva; (*fuss*) escándalo; **the political ~ in Spain** el panorama político español; **behind the scenes** (*also fig*) entre bastidores; **to appear** *or* **come on the ~** (*also fig*) aparecer, presentarse; **to make a ~** (*col: fuss*) armar un escándalo
scenery ['siːnərɪ] *n* (*Theat*) decorado; (*landscape*) paisaje *m*
scenic ['siːnɪk] *adj* (*picturesque*) pintoresco
scent [sɛnt] *n* perfume *m*, olor *m*; (*fig: track*) rastro, pista; (*sense of smell*) olfato ■ *vt* perfumar; (*suspect*) presentir; **to put** *or* **throw sb off the ~** (*fig*) despistar a algn
sceptic, skeptic (*US*) ['skɛptɪk] *n* escéptico(-a)
sceptical, skeptical (*US*) ['skɛptɪkl] *adj* escéptico
scepticism, skepticism (*US*) ['skɛptɪsɪzm] *n* escepticismo
sceptre, scepter (*US*) ['sɛptəʳ] *n* cetro
schedule ['ʃɛdjuːl], (*US*) ['skɛdjuːl] *n* (*of trains*) horario; (*of events*) programa *m*; (*list*) lista ■ *vt* (*timetable*) establecer el horario de; (*list*) catalogar; (*visit*) fijar la hora de; **on ~** a la hora, sin retraso; **to be ahead of/behind ~** estar adelantado/retrasado; **we are working to a very tight ~** tenemos un programa de trabajo muy apretado; **everything went according to ~** todo salió según lo previsto;

the meeting is scheduled for seven *or* **to begin at seven** la reunión está fijada para las siete
scheduled ['ʃɛdju:ld], (*US*) ['skɛdju:ld] *adj* (*date, time*) fijado; (*visit, event, bus, train*) programado; (*stop*) previsto; ~ **flight** vuelo regular
schematic [skɪ'mætɪk], *adj* (*diagram etc*) esquemático
scheme [ski:m] *n* (*plan*) plan *m*, proyecto; (*method*) esquema *m*; (*plot*) intriga; (*trick*) ardid *m*; (*arrangement*) disposición *f*; (*pension scheme etc*) sistema *m* ■ *vt* proyectar ■ *vi* (*plan*) hacer proyectos; (*intrigue*) intrigar; **colour** ~ combinación *f* de colores
scheming ['ski:mɪŋ] *adj* intrigante
schism ['skɪzəm] *n* cisma *m*
schizophrenia [skɪtsə'fri:nɪə] *n* esquizofrenia
schizophrenic [skɪtsə'frɛnɪk] *adj* esquizofrénico
scholar ['skɔləʳ] *n* (*pupil*) alumno(-a), estudiante *m/f*; (*learned person*) sabio(-a), erudito(-a)
scholarly ['skɔləlɪ] *adj* erudito
scholarship ['skɔləʃɪp] *n* erudición *f*; (*grant*) beca
school [sku:l] *n* (*gen*) escuela, colegio; (*in university*) facultad *f*; (*of fish*) banco ■ *vt* (*animal*) amaestrar; **to be at** *or* **go to** ~ ir al colegio *or* a la escuela
school age *n* edad *f* escolar
schoolbook ['sku:lbuk] *n* libro de texto
schoolboy ['sku:lbɔɪ] *n* alumno
schoolchild (*pl* **schoolchildren**) ['sku:ltʃaɪld, -tʃɪldrən] *n* alumno(-a)
schooldays ['sku:ldeɪz] *npl* años *mpl* del colegio
schoolgirl ['sku:lgə:l] *n* alumna
schooling ['sku:lɪŋ] *n* enseñanza
school-leaver ['sku:lli:vəʳ] *n* (*Brit*) *joven que ha terminado la educación secundaria*
schoolmaster ['sku:lmɑ:stəʳ] *n* (*primary*) maestro; (*secondary*) profesor *m*
schoolmistress ['sku:lmɪstrɪs] *n* (*primary*) maestra; (*secondary*) profesora
schoolroom ['sku:lrum] *n* clase *f*
schoolteacher ['sku:lti:tʃəʳ] *n* (*primary*) maestro(-a); (*secondary*) profesor(a) *m(f)*
schoolyard ['sku:ljɑ:d] *n* (*US*) patio del colegio
schooner ['sku:nəʳ] *n* (*ship*) goleta
sciatica [saɪ'ætɪkə] *n* ciática
science ['saɪəns] *n* ciencia; **the sciences** las ciencias
science fiction *n* ciencia-ficción *f*
scientific [saɪən'tɪfɪk] *adj* científico
scientist ['saɪəntɪst] *n* científico(-a)
sci-fi ['saɪfaɪ] *n abbr* (*col*) = **science fiction**
Scilly Isles ['sɪlɪ-], **Scillies** ['sɪlɪz] *npl*: **the** ~ las Islas Sorlingas
scintillating ['sɪntɪleɪtɪŋ] *adj* (*wit, conversation, company*) brillante, chispeante, ingenioso
scissors ['sɪzəz] *npl* tijeras *fpl*; **a pair of** ~ unas tijeras
scoff [skɔf] *vt* (*Brit col: eat*) engullir ■ *vi*: **to ~ (at)** (*mock*) mofarse (de)
scold [skəuld] *vt* regañar
scolding ['skəuldɪŋ] *n* riña, reprimenda
scone [skɔn] *n pastel de pan*
scoop [sku:p] *n* cucharón *m*; (*for flour etc*) pala; (*Press*) exclusiva ■ *vt* (*Comm: market*) adelantarse a; (*: profit*) sacar; (*Comm, Press: competitors*) adelantarse a
▸ **scoop out** *vt* excavar
▸ **scoop up** *vt* recoger
scooter ['sku:təʳ] *n* (*motor cycle*) Vespa®; (*toy*) patinete *m*
scope [skəup] *n* (*of plan, undertaking*) ámbito; (*reach*) alcance *m*; (*of person*) competencia; (*opportunity*) libertad *f* (de acción); **there is plenty of ~ for improvement** hay bastante campo para efectuar mejoras
scorch [skɔ:tʃ] *vt* (*clothes*) chamuscar; (*earth, grass*) quemar, secar
scorcher ['skɔ:tʃəʳ] *n* (*col: hot day*) día *m* abrasador
scorching ['skɔ:tʃɪŋ] *adj* abrasador(a)
score [skɔ:ʳ] *n* (*points etc*) puntuación *f*; (*Mus*) partitura; (*reckoning*) cuenta; (*twenty*) veintena ■ *vt* (*goal, point*) ganar; (*mark, cut*) rayar ■ *vi* marcar un tanto; (*Football*) marcar un gol; (*keep score*) llevar el tanteo; **to keep (the)** ~ llevar la cuenta; **to have an old ~ to settle with sb** (*fig*) tener cuentas pendientes con algn; **on that** ~ en lo que se refiere a eso; **scores of people** (*fig*) muchísima gente, cantidad de gente; **to ~ 6 out of 10** obtener una puntuación de 6 sobre 10
▸ **score out** *vt* tachar
scoreboard ['skɔ:bɔ:d] *n* marcador *m*
scoreline ['skɔ:laɪn] *n* (*Sport*) resultado final
scorer ['skɔ:rəʳ] *n* marcador *m*; (*keeping score*) encargado(-a) del marcador
scorn [skɔ:n] *n* desprecio ■ *vt* despreciar
scornful ['skɔ:nful] *adj* desdeñoso, despreciativo
scornfully ['skɔ:nfulɪ] *adv* desdeñosamente, con desprecio
Scorpio ['skɔ:pɪəu] *n* Escorpión *m*
scorpion ['skɔ:pɪən] *n* alacrán *m*, escorpión *m*
Scot [skɔt] *n* escocés(-esa) *m(f)*
Scotch [skɔtʃ] *n* whisky *m* escocés

scotch [skɔtʃ] *vt* (*rumour*) desmentir; (*plan*) frustrar
Scotch tape® *n* (*US*) cinta adhesiva, celo, scotch® *m*
scot-free [skɔt'fri:] *adv*: **to get off ~** (*unpunished*) salir impune; (*unhurt*) salir ileso
Scotland ['skɔtlənd] *n* Escocia
Scots [skɔts] *adj* escocés(-esa)
Scotsman ['skɔtsmən] *n* escocés *m*
Scotswoman ['skɔtswumən] *n* escocesa
Scottish ['skɔtɪʃ] *adj* escocés(-esa); **the ~ National Party** *partido político independista escocés*; **the ~ Parliament** el Parlamento escocés
scoundrel ['skaundrəl] *n* canalla *m/f*, sinvergüenza *m/f*
scour ['skauəʳ] *vt* (*clean*) fregar, estregar; (*search*) recorrer, registrar
scourer ['skauərəʳ] *n* (*pad*) estropajo; (*powder*) limpiador *m*
scourge [skə:dʒ] *n* azote *m*
scout [skaut] *n* explorador *m*
▸**scout around** *vi* reconocer el terreno
scowl [skaul] *vi* fruncir el ceño; **to ~ at sb** mirar con ceño a algn
scrabble ['skræbl] *vi* (*claw*): **to ~ (at)** arañar ■ *n*: **S~**® Scrabble® *m*, Intelect® *m*; **to ~ around for sth** revolver todo buscando algo
scraggy ['skrægɪ] *adj* flaco, delgaducho
scram [skræm] *vi* (*col*) largarse
scramble ['skræmbl] *n* (*climb*) subida (difícil); (*struggle*) pelea ■ *vi*: **to ~ out/through** salir/abrirse paso con dificultad; **to ~ for** pelear por; **to go scrambling** (*Sport*) hacer motocrós
scrambled eggs ['skræmbld-] *npl* huevos *mpl* revueltos
scrap [skræp] *n* (*bit*) pedacito; (*fig*) pizca; (*fight*) riña, bronca; (*also*: **scrap iron**) chatarra, hierro viejo ■ *vt* (*discard*) desechar, descartar ■ *vi* reñir, armar (una) bronca; **scraps** *npl* (*waste*) sobras *fpl*, desperdicios *mpl*; **to sell sth for ~** vender algo como chatarra
scrapbook ['skræpbuk] *n* álbum *m* de recortes
scrap dealer *n* chatarrero(-a)
scrape [skreɪp] *n* (*fig*) lío, apuro ■ *vt* raspar; (*skin etc*) rasguñar; (*also*: **scrape against**) rozar
▸**scrape through** *vi* (*succeed*) salvarse por los pelos; (*exam*) aprobar por los pelos
scraper ['skreɪpəʳ] *n* raspador *m*
scrap heap *n* (*fig*): **on the ~** desperdiciado; **to throw sth on the ~** desechar *or* descartar algo
scrap iron *n* chatarra
scrap merchant *n* (*Brit*) chatarrero(-a)
scrap metal *n* chatarra, desecho de metal
scrap paper *n* pedazos *mpl* de papel
scrappy ['skræpɪ] *adj* (*essay etc*) deshilvanado; (*education*) incompleto
scrap yard *n* depósito de chatarra; (*for cars*) cementerio de coches
scratch [skrætʃ] *n* rasguño; (*from claw*) arañazo ■ *adj*: **~ team** equipo improvisado ■ *vt* (*record*) rayar; (*with claw, nail*) rasguñar, arañar; (*Comput*) borrar ■ *vi* rascarse; **to start from ~** partir de cero; **to be up to ~** cumplir con los requisitos
scratchpad ['skrætʃpæd] *n* (*US*) bloc *m* de notas
scrawl [skrɔ:l] *n* garabatos *mpl* ■ *vi* hacer garabatos
scrawny ['skrɔ:nɪ] *adj* (*person, neck*) flaco
scream [skri:m] *n* chillido ■ *vi* chillar; **it was a ~** (*fig, col*) fue para morirse de risa *or* muy divertido; **he's a ~** (*fig, col*) es muy divertido *or* de lo más gracioso; **to ~ at sb (to do sth)** gritarle a algn (para que haga algo)
scree [skri:] *n* cono de desmoronamiento
screech [skri:tʃ] *vi* chirriar
screen [skri:n] *n* (*Cine, TV*) pantalla; (*movable*) biombo; (*wall*) tabique *m*; (*also*: **windscreen**) parabrisas *m inv* ■ *vt* (*conceal*) tapar; (*from the wind etc*) proteger; (*film*) proyectar; (*fig*: *person*: *for security*) investigar; (*: for illness*) hacer una exploración a
screen editing *n* (*Comput*) corrección *f* en pantalla
screenful ['skri:nful] *n* pantalla
screening ['skri:nɪŋ] *n* (*of film*) proyección *f*; (*for security*) investigación *f*; (*Med*) exploración *f*
screen memory *n* (*Comput*) memoria de la pantalla
screenplay ['skri:npleɪ] *n* guión *m*
screen saver [-seɪvəʳ] *n* (*Comput*) salvapantallas *m inv*
screen test *n* prueba de pantalla
screw [skru:] *n* tornillo; (*propeller*) hélice *f* ■ *vt* atornillar; **to ~ sth to the wall** fijar algo a la pared con tornillos
▸**screw up** *vt* (*paper, material etc*) arrugar; (*col*: *ruin*) fastidiar; **to ~ up one's eyes** arrugar el entrecejo; **to ~ up one's face** torcer *or* arrugar la cara
screwdriver ['skru:draɪvəʳ] *n* destornillador *m*
screwed-up ['skru:d'ʌp] *adj* (*col*): **she's totally ~** está trastornada
screwy ['skru:ɪ] *adj* (*col*) chiflado
scribble ['skrɪbl] *n* garabatos *mpl* ■ *vt* escribir con prisa; **to ~ sth down** garabatear algo

script [skrɪpt] *n* (*Cine etc*) guión *m*; (*writing*) escritura, letra

scripted ['skrɪptɪd] *adj* (*Radio, TV*) escrito

Scripture ['skrɪptʃə^r] *n* Sagrada Escritura

scriptwriter ['skrɪptraɪtə^r] *n* guionista *m/f*

scroll [skrəul] *n* rollo ■ *vt* (*Comput*) desplazar

scrotum ['skrəutəm] *n* escroto

scrounge [skraundʒ] (*col*) *vt*: **to ~ sth off** *or* **from sb** gorronear algo a algn ■ *vi*: **to ~ on sb** vivir a costa de algn

scrounger ['skraundʒə^r] *n* gorrón(-ona) *m(f)*

scrub [skrʌb] *n* (*clean*) fregado; (*land*) maleza ■ *vt* fregar, restregar; (*reject*) cancelar, anular

scrubbing brush ['skrʌbɪŋ-] *n* cepillo de fregar

scruff [skrʌf] *n*: **by the ~ of the neck** por el pescuezo

scruffy ['skrʌfɪ] *adj* desaliñado, desaseado

scrum ['skrʌm], **scrummage** ['skrʌmɪdʒ] *n* (*Rugby*) melée *f*

scruple ['skru:pl] *n* escrúpulo; **to have no scruples about doing sth** no tener reparos en *or* escrúpulos para hacer algo

scrupulous ['skru:pjuləs] *adj* escrupuloso

scrupulously ['skru:pjuləslɪ] *adv* escrupulosamente; **to be ~ fair/honest** ser sumamente justo/honesto

scrutinize ['skru:tɪnaɪz] *vt* escudriñar; (*votes*) escrutar

scrutiny ['skru:tɪnɪ] *n* escrutinio, examen *m*; **under the ~ of sb** bajo la mirada *or* el escrutinio de algn

scuba ['sku:bə] *n* escafandra autónoma

scuba diving *n* submarinismo

scuff [skʌf] *vt* (*shoes, floor*) rayar

scuffle ['skʌfl] *n* refriega

scullery ['skʌlərɪ] *n* trascocina

sculptor ['skʌlptə^r] *n* escultor(a) *m(f)*

sculpture ['skʌlptʃə^r] *n* escultura

scum [skʌm] *n* (*on liquid*) espuma; (*pej: people*) escoria

scupper ['skʌpə^r] *vt* (*Brit: boat*) hundir; (*: fig: plans etc*) acabar con

scurrilous ['skʌrɪləs] *adj* difamatorio, calumnioso

scurry ['skʌrɪ] *vi*: **to ~ off** escabullirse

scurvy ['skə:vɪ] *n* escorbuto

scuttle ['skʌtl] *n* (*also:* **coal scuttle**) cubo, carbonera ■ *vt* (*ship*) barrenar ■ *vi* (*scamper*): **to ~ away, ~ off** escabullirse

scythe [saɪð] *n* guadaña

SD, S. Dak. *abbr* (*US*) = **South Dakota**

SDI *n abbr* (= *Strategic Defense Initiative*) IDE *f*

SDLP *n abbr* (*Brit Pol*) = **Social Democratic and Labour Party**

sea [si:] *n* mar *m/f*; **by ~** (*travel*) en barco; **on the ~** (*boat*) en el mar; (*town*) junto al mar; **to be all at ~** (*fig*) estar despistado; **out to** *or* **at ~** en alta mar; **to go by ~** ir en barco; **heavy** *or* **rough seas** marejada; **by** *or* **beside the ~** (*holiday*) en la playa; (*village*) a orillas del mar; **a ~ of faces** una multitud de caras

sea bed *n* fondo del mar

sea bird *n* ave *f* marina

seaboard ['si:bɔ:d] *n* litoral *m*

sea breeze *n* brisa de mar

seadog ['si:dɔg] *n* lobo de mar

seafarer ['si:fɛərə^r] *n* marinero

seafaring ['si:fɛərɪŋ] *adj* (*community*) marinero; (*life*) de marinero

seafood ['si:fu:d] *n* mariscos *mpl*

sea front *n* (*beach*) playa; (*prom*) paseo marítimo

seagoing ['si:gəuɪŋ] *adj* (*ship*) de alta mar

seagull ['si:gʌl] *n* gaviota

seal [si:l] *n* (*animal*) foca; (*stamp*) sello ■ *vt* (*close*) cerrar; (*: with seal*) sellar; (*decide: sb's fate*) decidir; (*: bargain*) cerrar; **~ of approval** sello de aprobación

▸ **seal off** *vt* obturar

seal cull *n* matanza de crías de foca

sea level *n* nivel *m* del mar

sealing wax ['si:lɪŋ-] *n* lacre *m*

sea lion *n* león *m* marino

sealskin ['si:lskɪn] *n* piel *f* de foca

seam [si:m] *n* costura; (*of metal*) juntura; (*of coal*) veta, filón *m*; **the hall was bursting at the seams** la sala rebosaba de gente

seaman ['si:mən] *n* marinero

seamanship ['si:mənʃɪp] *n* náutica

seamy ['si:mɪ] *adj* sórdido

seance ['seɪɔns] *n* sesión *f* de espiritismo

seaplane ['si:pleɪn] *n* hidroavión *m*

seaport ['si:pɔ:t] *n* puerto de mar

search [sə:tʃ] *n* (*for person, thing*) busca, búsqueda; (*of drawer, pockets*) registro; (*inspection*) reconocimiento ■ *vt* (*look in*) buscar en; (*examine*) examinar; (*person, place*) registrar; (*Comput*) buscar ■ *vi*: **to ~ for** buscar; **in ~ of** en busca de; **"~ and replace"** (*Comput*) "buscar y reemplazar"

▸ **search through** *vt fus* registrar

search engine *n* (*Comput: Internet*) buscador *m*

searcher ['sə:tʃə^r] *n* buscador(a) *m(f)*

searching ['sə:tʃɪŋ] *adj* (*question*) penetrante

searchlight ['sə:tʃlaɪt] *n* reflector *m*

search party *n* equipo de salvamento

search warrant *n* mandamiento judicial

searing ['sɪərɪŋ] *adj* (*heat*) abrasador(a); (*pain*) agudo

seashore ['si:ʃɔ^r] *n* playa, orilla del mar; **on the ~** a la orilla del mar

seasick ['si:sɪk] *adj* mareado; **to be ~** marearse

seaside ['si:saɪd] *n* playa, orilla del mar; **to go to the ~** ir a la playa
seaside resort *n* playa
season ['si:zn] *n* (*of year*) estación f; (*sporting etc*) temporada; (*gen*) época, período ■ *vt* (*food*) sazonar; **to be in/out of ~** estar en sazón/fuera de temporada; **the busy ~** (*for shops, hotels etc*) la temporada alta; **the open ~** (*Hunting*) la temporada de caza *or* de pesca
seasonal ['si:znl] *adj* estacional
seasoned ['si:znd] *adj* (*wood*) curado; (*fig: worker, actor*) experimentado; (*troops*) curtido; **~ campaigner** veterano(-a)
seasoning ['si:znɪŋ] *n* condimento
season ticket *n* abono
seat [si:t] *n* (*in bus, train: place*) asiento; (*chair*) silla; (*Parliament*) escaño; (*buttocks*) trasero; (*centre: of government etc*) sede *f* ■ *vt* sentar; (*have room for*) tener cabida para; **are there any seats left?** ¿quedan plazas?; **to take one's ~** sentarse, tomar asiento; **to be seated** estar sentado, sentarse
seat belt *n* cinturón *m* de seguridad
seating ['si:tɪŋ] *n* asientos *mpl*
seating arrangements *npl* distribución *fsg* de los asientos
seating capacity *n* número de asientos, aforo
SEATO ['si:təu] *n abbr* (= *Southeast Asia Treaty Organization*) OTASE *f*
sea water *n* agua *m* del mar
seaweed ['si:wi:d] *n* alga marina
seaworthy ['si:wə:ðɪ] *adj* en condiciones de navegar
SEC *n abbr* (*US*: = *Securities and Exchange Commission*) *comisión de operaciones bursátiles*
sec. *abbr* = **second; seconds**
secateurs [sɛkə'tə:z] *npl* podadera *sg*
secede [sɪ'si:d] *vi*: **to ~ (from)** separarse (de)
secluded [sɪ'klu:dɪd] *adj* retirado
seclusion [sɪ'klu:ʒən] *n* retiro
second ['sɛkənd] *adj* segundo ■ *adv* (*in race etc*) en segundo lugar ■ *n* (*gen*) segundo; (*Aut*: *also*: **second gear**) segunda; (*Comm*) artículo con algún desperfecto; (*Brit Scol: degree*) título universitario de segunda clase ■ *vt* (*motion*) apoyar [sɪ'kɔnd] (*employee*) trasladar temporalmente; **~ floor** (*Brit*) segundo piso; (*US*) primer piso; **Charles the S~** Carlos Segundo; **to ask for a ~ opinion** (*Med*) pedir una segunda opinión; **just a ~!** ¡un momento!; **to have ~ thoughts** cambiar de opinión; **on ~ thoughts** *or* (*US*) **thought** pensándolo bien; **~ mortgage** segunda hipoteca
secondary ['sɛkəndərɪ] *adj* secundario
secondary education *n* enseñanza secundaria
secondary school *n* escuela secundaria; *ver nota*

SECONDARY SCHOOL

En el Reino Unido se llama *secondary school* a un centro educativo para alumnos de 11 a 18 años, si bien muchos estudiantes acaban a los 16, edad mínima de escolarización obligatoria. La mayor parte de estos centros funcionan como "comprehensive schools", aunque aún existen algunos de tipo selectivo.

second-best [sɛkənd'bɛst] *n* segundo
second-class ['sɛkənd'klɑ:s] *adj* de segunda clase ■ *adv*: **to send sth ~** enviar algo por correo de segunda clase; **to travel ~** viajar en segunda; **~ citizen** ciudadano(-a) de segunda (clase)
second cousin *n* primo(-a) segundo(-a)
seconder ['sɛkəndə^r] *n* el/la que apoya una moción
second-guess ['sɛkənd'gɛs] *vt* (*evaluate*) juzgar (a posteriori); (*anticipate*): **to ~ sth/sb** (intentar) adivinar algo/lo que va a hacer algn
secondhand ['sɛkənd'hænd] *adj* de segunda mano, usado ■ *adv*: **to buy sth ~** comprar algo de segunda mano; **to hear sth ~** oír algo indirectamente
second hand *n* (*on clock*) segundero
second-in-command ['sɛkəndɪnkə'mɑ:nd] *n* (*Mil*) segundo en el mando; (*Admin*) segundo(-a), ayudante *m/f*
secondly ['sɛkəndlɪ] *adv* en segundo lugar
secondment [sɪ'kɔndmənt] *n* (*Brit*) traslado temporal
second-rate ['sɛkənd'reɪt] *adj* de segunda categoría
secrecy ['si:krəsɪ] *n* secreto
secret ['si:krɪt] *adj, n* secreto; **in ~** *adv* en secreto; **to keep sth ~ (from sb)** ocultarle algo (a algn); **to make no ~ of sth** no ocultar algo
secret agent *n* agente *m/f* secreto(-a), espía *m/f*
secretarial [sɛkrɪ'tɛərɪəl] *adj* (*course*) de secretariado; (*staff*) de secretaría; (*work, duties*) de secretaria
secretariat [sɛkrɪ'tɛərɪət] *n* secretaría
secretary ['sɛkrətərɪ] *n* secretario(-a); **S~ of State** (*Brit Pol*) Ministro (con cartera)
secretary-general ['sɛkrətərɪ'dʒɛnərl] *n* secretario(-a) general

secretary pool *n* (*US*) = **typing pool**
secrete [sɪ'kri:t] *vt* (*Med, Anat, Bio*) secretar; (*hide*) ocultar, esconder
secretion [sɪ'kri:ʃən] *n* secreción *f*
secretive ['si:krətɪv] *adj* reservado, sigiloso
secretly ['si:krɪtlɪ] *adv* en secreto
secret police *n* policía secreta
secret service *n* servicio secreto
sect [sɛkt] *n* secta
sectarian [sɛk'tɛərɪən] *adj* sectario
section ['sɛkʃən] *n* sección *f*; (*part*) parte *f*; (*of document*) artículo; (*of opinion*) sector *m*; **business ~** (*Press*) sección *f* de economía
sectional ['sɛkʃənl] *adj* (*regional*) regional, local
sector ['sɛktə^r] *n* sector *m*
secular ['sɛkjulə^r] *adj* secular, seglar
secure [sɪ'kjuə^r] *adj* (*free from anxiety*) seguro; (*firmly fixed*) firme, fijo ■ *vt* (*fix*) asegurar, afianzar; (*get*) conseguir; (*Comm: loan*) garantizar; **to make sth ~** afianzar algo; **to ~ sth for sb** conseguir algo para algn
secured creditor [sɪ'kjuəd-] *n* acreedor(a) *m(f)* con garantía
securely [sɪ'kjuəlɪ] *adv* firmemente; **it is ~ fastened** está bien sujeto
security [sɪ'kjuərɪtɪ] *n* seguridad *f*; (*for loan*) fianza; (*: object*) prenda; **securities** *npl* (*Comm*) valores *mpl*, títulos *mpl*; **~ of tenure** tenencia asegurada; **to increase/tighten ~** aumentar/estrechar las medidas de seguridad; **job ~** seguridad *f* en el empleo
Security Council *n*: **the ~** el Consejo de Seguridad
security forces *npl* fuerzas *fpl* de seguridad
security guard *n* guardia *m/f* de seguridad
security risk *n* riesgo para la seguridad
secy. *abbr* (= *secretary*) Sec.
sedan [sɪ'dæn] *n* (*US Aut*) sedán *m*
sedate [sɪ'deɪt] *adj* tranquilo ■ *vt* administrar sedantes a, sedar
sedation [sɪ'deɪʃən] *n* (*Med*) sedación *f*; **to be under ~** estar bajo sedación
sedative ['sɛdɪtɪv] *n* sedante *m*, calmante *m*
sedentary ['sɛdntrɪ] *adj* sedentario
sediment ['sɛdɪmənt] *n* sedimento
sedimentary [sɛdɪ'mɛntərɪ] *adj* (*Geo*) sedimentario
sedition [sɪ'dɪʃən] *n* sedición *f*
seduce [sɪ'dju:s] *vt* (*gen*) seducir
seduction [sɪ'dʌkʃən] *n* seducción *f*
seductive [sɪ'dʌktɪv] *adj* seductor(-a)
see [si:] (*pt* **saw**, *pp* **seen**) *vt* (*gen*) ver; (*understand*) ver, comprender; (*look at*) mirar ■ *vi* ver ■ *n* sede *f*; **to ~ sb to the door** acompañar a algn a la puerta; **to ~ that** (*ensure*) asegurarse de que; **~ you soon/later/tomorrow!** ¡hasta pronto/luego/mañana!; **as far as I can ~** por lo visto *or* por lo que veo; **there was nobody to be seen** no se veía a nadie; **let me ~** (*show me*) a ver; (*let me think*) vamos a ver; **to go and ~ sb** ir a ver a algn; **~ for yourself** compruébalo tú mismo; **I don't know what she sees in him** no sé qué le encuentra
▸ **see about** *vt fus* atender a, encargarse de
▸ **see off** *vt* despedir
▸ **see through** *vt fus* calar ■ *vt* llevar a cabo
▸ **see to** *vt fus* atender a, encargarse de
seed [si:d] *n* semilla; (*in fruit*) pepita; (*fig*) germen *m*; (*Tennis*) preseleccionado(-a); **to go to ~** (*plant*) granar; (*fig*) descuidarse
seedless ['si:dlɪs] *adj* sin semillas *or* pepitas
seedling ['si:dlɪŋ] *n* planta de semillero
seedy ['si:dɪ] *adj* (*person*) desaseado; (*place*) sórdido
seeing ['si:ɪŋ] *conj*: **~ (that)** visto que, en vista de que
seek (*pt, pp* **sought**) [si:k, sɔ:t] *vt* (*gen*) buscar; (*post*) solicitar; **to ~ advice/help from sb** pedir consejos/solicitar ayuda a algn
▸ **seek out** *vt* (*person*) buscar
seem [si:m] *vi* parecer; **there seems to be ...** parece que hay ...; **it seems (that) ...** parece que ...; **what seems to be the trouble?** ¿qué pasa?; **I did what seemed best** hice lo que parecía mejor
seemingly ['si:mɪŋlɪ] *adv* aparentemente, según parece
seen [si:n] *pp of* **see**
seep [si:p] *vi* filtrarse
seer [sɪə^r] *n* vidente *m/f*, profeta *m/f*
seersucker [sɪə'sʌkə^r] *n* sirsaca
seesaw ['si:sɔ:] *n* balancín *m*, subibaja *m*
seethe [si:ð] *vi* hervir; **to ~ with anger** enfurecerse
see-through ['si:θru:] *adj* transparente
segment ['sɛgmənt] *n* segmento
segregate ['sɛgrɪgeɪt] *vt* segregar
segregation [sɛgrɪ'geɪʃən] *n* segregación *f*
Seine [seɪn] *n* Sena *m*
seismic ['saɪzmɪk] *adj* sísmico
seize [si:z] *vt* (*grasp*) agarrar, asir; (*take possession of*) secuestrar; (*: territory*) apoderarse de; (*opportunity*) aprovecharse de
▸ **seize up** *vi* (*Tech*) agarrotarse
▸ **seize (up)on** *vt fus* valerse de
seizure ['si:ʒə^r] *n* (*Med*) ataque *m*; (*Law*) incautación *f*
seldom ['sɛldəm] *adv* rara vez
select [sɪ'lɛkt] *adj* selecto, escogido; (*hotel, restaurant, clubs*) exclusivo ■ *vt* escoger, elegir; (*Sport*) seleccionar; **a ~ few** una minoría selecta

selection [sɪ'lɛkʃən] *n* selección *f*, elección *f*; (*Comm*) surtido
selection committee *n* comisión *f* de nombramiento
selective [sɪ'lɛktɪv] *adj* selectivo
self [sɛlf] *n* (*pl* **selves**) [sɛlvz] uno mismo ■ *pref* auto...; **the ~** el yo
self-addressed ['sɛlfə'drɛst] *adj*: **~ envelope** sobre *m* con la dirección propia
self-adhesive [sɛlfəd'hiːzɪv] *adj* autoadhesivo, autoadherente
self-appointed [sɛlfə'pɔɪntɪd] *adj* autonombrado
self-assurance [sɛlfə'ʃuərəns] *n* confianza en sí mismo
self-assured [sɛlfə'ʃuəd] *adj* seguro de sí mismo
self-catering [sɛlf'keɪtərɪŋ] *adj* (*Brit*) sin pensión *or* servicio de comida; **~ apartment** apartamento con cocina propia
self-centred, self-centered (*US*) [sɛlf'sɛntəd] *adj* egocéntrico
self-cleaning [sɛlf'kliːnɪŋ] *adj* autolimpiador
self-confessed [sɛlfkən'fɛst] *adj* (*alcoholic etc*) confeso
self-confidence [sɛlf'kɔnfɪdns] *n* confianza en sí mismo
self-confident [sɛlf'kɔnfɪdnt] *adj* seguro de sí (mismo), lleno de confianza en sí mismo
self-conscious [sɛlf'kɔnʃəs] *adj* cohibido
self-contained [sɛlfkən'teɪnd] *adj* (*gen*) independiente; (*Brit: flat*) con entrada particular
self-control [sɛlfkən'trəul] *n* autodominio
self-defeating [sɛlfdɪ'fiːtɪŋ] *adj* contraproducente
self-defence, self-defense (*US*) [sɛlfdɪ'fɛns] *n* defensa propia
self-discipline [sɛlf'dɪsɪplɪn] *n* autodisciplina
self-employed [sɛlfɪm'plɔɪd] *adj* que trabaja por cuenta propia, autónomo
self-esteem [sɛlfɪ'stiːm] *n* amor *m* propio
self-evident [sɛlf'ɛvɪdnt] *adj* patente
self-explanatory [sɛlfɪks'plænətərɪ] *adj* que no necesita explicación
self-financing [sɛlffaɪ'nænsɪŋ] *adj* autofinanziado
self-governing [sɛlf'gʌvənɪŋ] *adj* autónomo
self-help ['sɛlf'hɛlp] *n* autosuficiencia, ayuda propia
self-importance [sɛlfɪm'pɔːtns] *n* presunción *f*, vanidad *f*
self-important [sɛlfɪm'pɔːtnt] *adj* vanidoso
self-indulgent [sɛlfɪn'dʌldʒənt] *adj* indulgente consigo mismo
self-inflicted [sɛlfɪn'flɪktɪd] *adj* infligido a sí mismo
self-interest [sɛlf'ɪntrɪst] *n* egoísmo
selfish ['sɛlfɪʃ] *adj* egoísta
selfishly ['sɛlfɪʃlɪ] *adv* con egoísmo, de modo egoísta
selfishness ['sɛlfɪʃnɪs] *n* egoísmo
selfless ['sɛlflɪs] *adj* desinteresado
selflessly ['sɛlflɪslɪ] *adv* desinteresadamente
self-made man ['sɛlfmeɪd-] *n hombre que ha triunfado por su propio esfuerzo*
self-pity [sɛlf'pɪtɪ] *n* lástima de sí mismo
self-portrait [sɛlf'pɔːtreɪt] *n* autorretrato
self-possessed [sɛlfpə'zɛst] *adj* sereno, dueño de sí mismo
self-preservation ['sɛlfprɛzə'veɪʃən] *n* propia conservación *f*
self-propelled [sɛlfprə'pɛld] *adj* autopropulsado, automotor(-triz)
self-raising [sɛlf'reɪzɪŋ], **self-rising** (*US*) [sɛlf'raɪzɪŋ] *adj*: **~ flour** harina con levadura
self-reliant [sɛlfrɪ'laɪənt] *adj* independiente, autosuficiente
self-respect [sɛlfrɪ'spɛkt] *n* amor *m* propio
self-respecting [sɛlfrɪ'spɛktɪŋ] *adj* que tiene amor propio
self-righteous [sɛlf'raɪtʃəs] *adj* santurrón(-ona)
self-rising [sɛlf'raɪzɪŋ] *adj* (*US*) = **self-raising**
self-sacrifice [sɛlf'sækrɪfaɪs] *n* abnegación *f*
self-same [sɛlfseɪm] *adj* mismo, mismísimo
self-satisfied [sɛlf'sætɪsfaɪd] *adj* satisfecho de sí mismo
self-service [sɛlf'səːvɪs] *adj* de autoservicio
self-styled ['sɛlfstaɪld] *adj* supuesto, sedicente
self-sufficient [sɛlfsə'fɪʃənt] *adj* autosuficiente
self-supporting [sɛlfsə'pɔːtɪŋ] *adj* económicamente independiente
self-tanning [sɛlf'tænɪŋ] *adj* autobronceador
self-taught [sɛlf'tɔːt] *adj* autodidacta
self-test ['sɛlftɛst] *n* (*Comput*) autocomprobación *f*
sell (*pt, pp* **sold**) [sɛl, səuld] *vt* vender ■ *vi* venderse; **to ~ at** *or* **for £10** venderse a 10 libras; **to ~ sb an idea** (*fig*) convencer a algn de una idea
▸ **sell off** *vt* liquidar
▸ **sell out** *vi* transigir, transar (*LAm*); **to ~ out (to sb/sth)** (*Comm*) vender su negocio (a algn/algo) ■ *vt* agotar las existencias de, venderlo todo; **the tickets are all sold out** las entradas están agotadas
▸ **sell up** *vi* (*Comm*) liquidarse
sell-by date ['sɛlbaɪ-] *n* fecha de caducidad

seller ['sɛləʳ] *n* vendedor(a) *m(f)*; **~'s market** mercado de demanda
selling price ['sɛlɪŋ-] *n* precio de venta
Sellotape® ['sɛləuteɪp] *n* (*Brit*) cinta adhesiva, celo, scotch® *m*
sellout ['sɛlaut] *n* traición *f*; **it was a ~** (*Theat etc*) fue un éxito de taquilla
selves [sɛlvz] *npl of* **self**
semantic [sɪ'mæntɪk] *adj* semántico
semaphore ['sɛməfɔːʳ] *n* semáforo
semblance ['sɛmbləns] *n* apariencia
semen ['siːmən] *n* semen *m*
semester [sɪ'mɛstəʳ] *n* (*US*) semestre *m*
semi ['sɛmɪ] *n* = **semidetached house**
semi... [sɛmɪ] *pref* semi..., medio...
semicircle ['sɛmɪsəːkl] *n* semicírculo
semicircular ['sɛmɪ'səːkjuləʳ] *adj* semicircular
semicolon [sɛmɪ'kəulən] *n* punto y coma
semiconductor [sɛmɪkən'dʌktəʳ] *n* semiconductor *m*
semiconscious [sɛmɪ'kɔnʃəs] *adj* semiconsciente
semidetached [sɛmɪdɪ'tætʃt], **semidetached house** *n* casa adosada
semi-final [sɛmɪ'faɪnl] *n* semifinal *f*
seminar ['sɛmɪnɑːʳ] *n* seminario
seminary ['sɛmɪnərɪ] *n* (*Rel*) seminario
semiprecious stone [sɛmɪ'prɛʃəs-] *n* piedra semipreciosa
semiquaver ['sɛmɪkweɪvəʳ] *n* (*Brit*) semicorchea
semiskilled ['sɛmɪskɪld] *adj* (*work, worker*) semicualificado
semi-skimmed *adj* semidesnatado
semitone ['sɛmɪtəun] *n* semitono
semolina [sɛmə'liːnə] *n* sémola
Sen., sen. *abbr* = **senator**; **senior**
senate ['sɛnɪt] *n* senado; *see also* **Congress**
senator ['sɛnɪtəʳ] *n* senador(a) *m(f)*
send (*pt, pp* **sent**) [sɛnd, sɛnt] *vt* mandar, enviar; **to ~ by post** mandar por correo; **to ~ sb for sth** mandar a algn a buscar algo; **to ~ word that ...** avisar *or* mandar aviso de que ...; **she sends (you) her love** te manda *or* envía cariñosos recuerdos; **to ~ sb to sleep/ into fits of laughter** dormir/hacer reír a algn; **to ~ sb flying** echar a algn; **to ~ sth flying** tirar algo
▸ **send away** *vt* (*letter, goods*) despachar
▸ **send away for** *vt fus* pedir
▸ **send back** *vt* devolver
▸ **send for** *vt fus* mandar traer; (*by post*) escribir pidiendo algo
▸ **send in** *vt* (*report, application, resignation*) mandar
▸ **send off** *vt* (*goods*) despachar; (*Brit Sport: player*) expulsar
▸ **send on** *vt* (*letter*) mandar, expedir; (*luggage etc: in advance*) facturar
▸ **send out** *vt* (*invitation*) mandar; (*emit: light, heat*) emitir, difundir; (*signal*) emitir
▸ **send round** *vt* (*letter, document etc*) hacer circular
▸ **send up** *vt* (*person, price*) hacer subir; (*Brit: parody*) parodiar
sender ['sɛndəʳ] *n* remitente *m/f*
send-off ['sɛndɔf] *n*: **a good ~** una buena despedida
send-up ['sɛndʌp] *n* (*col*) parodia, sátira
Senegal [sɛnɪ'gɔːl] *n* Senegal *m*
Senegalese [sɛnɪgə'liːz] *adj, n* senegalés(-esa) *m(f)*
senile ['siːnaɪl] *adj* senil
senility [sɪ'nɪlɪtɪ] *n* senilidad *f*
senior ['siːnɪəʳ] *adj* (*older*) mayor, más viejo; (*: on staff*) más antiguo; (*of higher rank*) superior ■ *n* mayor *m*; **P. Jones ~** P. Jones padre
senior citizen *n* persona de la tercera edad
senior high school *n* (*US*) ≈ instituto de enseñanza media; *see also* **high school**
seniority [siːnɪ'ɔrɪtɪ] *n* antigüedad *f*; (*in rank*) rango superior
sensation [sɛn'seɪʃən] *n* (*physical feeling, impression*) sensación *f*
sensational [sɛn'seɪʃənl] *adj* sensacional
sense [sɛns] *n* (*faculty, meaning*) sentido; (*feeling*) sensación *f*; (*good sense*) sentido común, juicio ■ *vt* sentir, percibir; **~ of humour** sentido del humor; **it makes ~** tiene sentido; **there is no ~ in (doing) that** no tiene sentido (hacer) eso; **to come to one's senses** (*regain consciousness*) volver en sí, recobrar el sentido; **to take leave of one's senses** perder el juicio
senseless ['sɛnslɪs] *adj* estúpido, insensato; (*unconscious*) sin conocimiento
senselessly ['sɛnslɪslɪ] *adv* estúpidamente, insensatamente
sensibility [sɛnsɪ'bɪlɪtɪ] *n* sensibilidad *f*; **sensibilities** *npl* delicadeza *sg*
sensible ['sɛnsɪbl] *adj* sensato; (*reasonable*) razonable, lógico
sensibly ['sɛnsɪblɪ] *adv* sensatamente; razonablemente, de modo lógico
sensitive ['sɛnsɪtɪv] *adj* sensible; (*touchy*) susceptible; **he is very ~ about it** es muy susceptible acerca de eso
sensitivity [sɛnsɪ'tɪvɪtɪ] *n* sensibilidad *f*; susceptibilidad *f*
sensual ['sɛnsjuəl] *adj* sensual
sensuous ['sɛnsjuəs] *adj* sensual
sent [sɛnt] *pt, pp of* **send**

sentence ['sɛntəns] *n* (*Ling*) frase *f*, oración *f*; (*Law*) sentencia, fallo ■ *vt*: **to ~ sb to death/ to five years** condenar a algn a muerte/a cinco años de cárcel; **to pass ~ on sb** (*also fig*) sentenciar *or* condenar a algn
sentiment ['sɛntɪmənt] *n* sentimiento; (*opinion*) opinión *f*
sentimental [sɛntɪ'mɛntl] *adj* sentimental
sentimentality [sɛntɪmɛn'tælɪtɪ] *n* sentimentalismo, sensiblería
sentinel ['sɛntɪnl] *n* centinela *m*
sentry ['sɛntrɪ] *n* centinela *m*
sentry duty *n*: **to be on ~** estar de guardia, hacer guardia
Seoul [səul] *n* Seúl *m*
separable ['sɛpərəbl] *adj* separable
separate [*adj* 'sɛprɪt, *vb* 'sɛpəreɪt] *adj* separado; (*distinct*) distinto ■ *vt* separar; (*part*) dividir ■ *vi* separarse; **~ from** separado *or* distinto de; **under ~ cover** (*Comm*) por separado; **to ~ into** dividir *or* separar en; **he is separated from his wife, but not divorced** está separado de su mujer, pero no (está) divorciado
separately ['sɛprɪtlɪ] *adv* por separado
separates ['sɛprɪts] *npl* (*clothes*) coordinados *mpl*
separation [sɛpə'reɪʃən] *n* separación *f*
sepia ['si:pɪə] *adj* color sepia *inv*
Sept. *abbr* (= *September*) sep
September [sɛp'tɛmbəʳ] *n* se(p)tiembre *m*; *see also* **July**
septic ['sɛptɪk] *adj* séptico; **to go ~** ponerse séptico
septicaemia, septicemia (*US*) [sɛptɪ'si:mɪə] *n* septicemia
septic tank *n* fosa séptica
sequel ['si:kwl] *n* consecuencia, resultado; (*of story*) continuación *f*
sequence ['si:kwəns] *n* sucesión *f*, serie *f*; (*Cine*) secuencia; **in ~** en orden *or* serie
sequential [sɪ'kwɛnʃəl] *adj*: **~ access** (*Comput*) acceso en serie
sequin ['si:kwɪn] *n* lentejuela
Serb [sə:b] *adj*, *n* = **Serbian**
Serbia ['sə:bɪə] *n* Serbia
Serbian ['sə:bɪən] *adj* serbio ■ *n* serbio(-a); (*Ling*) serbio
Serbo-Croat ['sə:bəu'krəuæt] *n* (*Ling*) serbocroata *m*
serenade [sɛrə'neɪd] *n* serenata ■ *vt* dar serenata a
serene [sɪ'ri:n] *adj* sereno, tranquilo
serenely [sɪ'ri:nlɪ] *adv* serenamente, tranquilamente
serenity [sə'rɛnɪtɪ] *n* serenidad *f*, tranquilidad *f*
sergeant ['sɑ:dʒənt] *n* sargento
sergeant major *n* sargento mayor
serial ['sɪərɪəl] *n* novela por entregas; (*TV*) telenovela
serial access *n* (*Comput*) acceso en serie
serial interface *n* (*Comput*) interface *m* en serie
serialize ['sɪərɪəlaɪz] *vt* publicar/televisar por entregas
serial killer *n* asesino(-a) múltiple
serial number *n* número de serie
series ['sɪəri:z] *n* (*pl inv*) serie *f*
serious ['sɪərɪəs] *adj* serio; (*grave*) grave; **are you ~ (about it)?** ¿lo dices en serio?
seriously ['sɪərɪəslɪ] *adv* en serio; (*ill, wounded etc*) gravemente; (*col: extremely*) de verdad; **to take sth/sb ~** tomar algo/a algn en serio; **he's ~ rich** es una pasada de rico
seriousness ['sɪərɪəsnɪs] *n* seriedad *f*; gravedad *f*
sermon ['sə:mən] *n* sermón *m*
serpent ['sə:pənt] *n* serpiente *f*
serrated [sɪ'reɪtɪd] *adj* serrado, dentellado
serum ['sɪərəm] *n* suero
servant ['sə:vənt] *n* (*gen*) servidor(a) *m(f)*; (*also*: **house servant**) criado(-a) *m(f)*
serve [sə:v] *vt* servir; (*customer*) atender; (*train*) tener parada en; (*apprenticeship*) hacer; (*prison term*) cumplir ■ *vi* (*servant, soldier etc*) servir; (*Tennis*) sacar ■ *n* (*Tennis*) saque *m*; **it serves him right** se lo merece, se lo tiene merecido; **to ~ a summons on sb** entregar una citación a algn; **it serves my purpose** me sirve para lo que quiero; **are you being served?** ¿le atienden?; **the power station serves the entire region** la central eléctrica abastece a toda la región; **to ~ as/for/to do** servir de/para/para hacer; **to ~ on a committee/a jury** ser miembro de una comisión/un jurado
▸ **serve out, serve up** *vt* (*food*) servir
service ['sə:vɪs] *n* (*gen*) servicio; (*Rel: Catholic*) misa; (*: other*) oficio (religioso); (*Aut*) mantenimiento; (*of dishes*) juego ■ *vt* (*car, washing machine*) mantener; (*: repair*) reparar; **the Services** las fuerzas armadas; **funeral ~** exequias *fpl*; **to hold a ~** celebrar un oficio religioso; **the essential services** los servicios esenciales; **medical/social services** servicios *mpl* médicos/sociales; **the train ~ to London** los trenes a Londres; **to be of ~ to sb** ser útil a algn
serviceable ['sə:vɪsəbl] *adj* servible, utilizable
service area *n* (*on motorway*) área de servicios
service charge *n* (*Brit*) servicio

service industries *npl* industrias *fpl* del servicio
serviceman ['sə:vɪsmən] *n* militar *m*
service station *n* estación *f* de servicio
servicing ['sə:vɪsɪŋ] *n* (*of car*) revisión *f*; (*of washing machine etc*) servicio de reparaciones
serviette [sə:vɪ'ɛt] *n* (*Brit*) servilleta
servile ['sə:vaɪl] *adj* servil
session ['sɛʃən] *n* (*sitting*) sesión *f*; **to be in ~** estar en sesión
session musician *n* músico *m/f* de estudio
set [sɛt] (*pt, pp* **~**) *n* juego; (*Radio*) aparato; (*TV*) televisor *m*; (*of utensils*) batería; (*of cutlery*) cubierto; (*of books*) colección *f*; (*Tennis*) set *m*; (*group of people*) grupo; (*Cine*) plató *m*; (*Theat*) decorado; (*Hairdressing*) marcado ■ *adj* (*fixed*) fijo; (*ready*) listo; (*resolved*) resuelto, decidido ■ *vt* (*place*) poner, colocar; (*fix*) fijar; (*adjust*) ajustar, arreglar; (*decide*: *rules etc*) establecer, decidir; (*assign*: *task*) asignar; (: *homework*) poner ■ *vi* (*sun*) ponerse; (*jam, jelly*) cuajarse; (*concrete*) fraguar; **a ~ of false teeth** una dentadura postiza; **a ~ of dining-room furniture** muebles *mpl* de comedor; **~ in one's ways** con costumbres arraigadas; **a ~ phrase** una frase hecha; **to be all ~ to do sth** estar listo para hacer algo; **to be ~ on doing sth** estar empeñado en hacer algo; **a novel ~ in Valencia** una novela ambientada en Valencia; **to ~ to music** poner música a; **to ~ on fire** incendiar, prender fuego a; **to ~ free** poner en libertad; **to ~ sth going** poner algo en marcha; **to ~ sail** zarpar, hacerse a la mar
▸ **set about** *vt fus*: **to ~ about doing sth** ponerse a hacer algo
▸ **set aside** *vt* poner aparte, dejar de lado
▸ **set back** *vt* (*progress*): **to ~ back (by)** retrasar (por); **a house ~ back from the road** una casa apartada de la carretera
▸ **set down** *vt* (*bus, train*) dejar; (*record*) poner por escrito
▸ **set in** *vi* (*infection*) declararse; (*complications*) comenzar; **the rain has ~ in for the day** parece que va a llover todo el día
▸ **set off** *vi* partir ■ *vt* (*bomb*) hacer estallar; (*cause to start*) poner en marcha; (*show up well*) hacer resaltar
▸ **set out** *vi*: **to ~ out to do sth** proponerse hacer algo ■ *vt* (*arrange*) disponer; (*state*) exponer; **to ~ out (from)** salir (de)
▸ **set up** *vt* (*organization*) establecer
setback ['sɛtbæk] *n* (*hitch*) revés *m*, contratiempo; (*in health*) recaída
set menu *n* menú *m*
set phrase *n* frase *f* hecha
set square *n* cartabón *m*
settee [sɛ'ti:] *n* sofá *m*
setting ['sɛtɪŋ] *n* (*scenery*) marco; (*of jewel*) engaste *m*, montadura
setting lotion *n* fijador *m* (para el pelo)
settle ['sɛtl] *vt* (*argument, matter*) resolver; (*pay*: *bill, accounts*) pagar, liquidar; (*colonize*: *land*) colonizar; (*Med*: *calm*) calmar, sosegar ■ *vi* (*dust etc*) depositarse; (*weather*) estabilizarse; (*also*: **settle down**) instalarse; (*calm down*) tranquilizarse; **to ~ for sth** convenir en aceptar algo; **to ~ on sth** decidirse por algo; **that's settled then** bueno, está arreglado; **to ~ one's stomach** asentar el estómago
▸ **settle in** *vi* instalarse
▸ **settle up** *vi*: **to ~ up with sb** ajustar cuentas con algn
settlement ['sɛtlmənt] *n* (*payment*) liquidación *f*; (*agreement*) acuerdo, convenio; (*village etc*) poblado; **in ~ of our account** (*Comm*) en pago *or* liquidación de nuestra cuenta
settler ['sɛtlə^r] *n* colono(-a), colonizador(a) *m(f)*
setup ['sɛtʌp] *n* sistema *m*
seven ['sɛvn] *num* siete
seventeen [sɛvn'ti:n] *num* diez y siete, diecisiete
seventh ['sɛvnθ] *adj* séptimo
seventy ['sɛvntɪ] *num* setenta
sever ['sɛvə^r] *vt* cortar; (*relations*) romper
several ['sɛvərl] *adj, pron* varios(-as) *m(f)pl*, algunos(-as) *m(f)pl*; **~ of us** varios de nosotros; **~ times** varias veces
severance ['sɛvərəns] *n* (*of relations*) ruptura
severance pay *n* indemnización *f* por despido
severe [sɪ'vɪə^r] *adj* severo; (*serious*) grave; (*hard*) duro; (*pain*) intenso
severely [sɪ'vɪəlɪ] *adv* severamente; (*wounded, ill*) de gravedad, gravemente
severity [sɪ'vɛrɪtɪ] *n* severidad *f*; gravedad *f*; intensidad *f*
Seville [sə'vɪl] *n* Sevilla
sew (*pt* **sewed**, *pp* **sewn**) [səu, səud, səun] *vt, vi* coser
▸ **sew up** *vt* coser
sewage ['su:ɪdʒ] *n* (*effluence*) aguas *fpl* residuales; (*system*) alcantarillado
sewage works *n* estación *f* depuradora (de aguas residuales)
sewer ['su:ə^r] *n* alcantarilla, cloaca
sewing ['səuɪŋ] *n* costura
sewing machine *n* máquina de coser
sewn [səun] *pp of* **sew**
sex [sɛks] *n* sexo; **the opposite ~** el sexo opuesto; **to have ~ with sb** tener relaciones (sexuales) con algn

sex act *n* acto sexual, coito
sex appeal *n* sex-appeal *m*, gancho
sex education *n* educación *f* sexual
sexism ['sɛksɪzəm] *n* sexismo
sexist ['sɛksɪst] *adj, n* sexista *m/f*
sex life *n* vida sexual
sex object *n* objeto sexual
sextant ['sɛkstənt] *n* sextante *m*
sextet [sɛks'tɛt] *n* sexteto
sexual ['sɛksjuəl] *adj* sexual; **~ assault** atentado contra el pudor; **~ harassment** acoso sexual; **~ intercourse** relaciones *fpl* sexuales
sexually ['sɛksjuəlɪ] *adv* sexualmente
sexy ['sɛksɪ] *adj* sexy
Seychelles [seɪ'ʃɛlz] *npl*: **the ~** las Seychelles
SF *n abbr* = **science fiction**
SG *n abbr* (*US*: = *Surgeon General*) *jefe del servicio federal de sanidad*
Sgt. *abbr* (= *sergeant*) Sgto.
shabbily ['ʃæbɪlɪ] *adv* (*treat*) injustamente; (*dressed*) pobremente
shabbiness ['ʃæbɪnɪs] *n* (*of dress, person*) aspecto desharrapado; (*of building*) mal estado
shabby ['ʃæbɪ] *adj* (*person*) desharrapado; (*clothes*) raído, gastado
shack [ʃæk] *n* choza, chabola
shackle ['ʃækl] *vt* encadenar; (*fig*): **to be shackled by sth** verse obstaculizado por algo
shackles ['ʃæklz] *npl* grillos *mpl*, grilletes *mpl*
shade [ʃeɪd] *n* sombra; (*for lamp*) pantalla; (*for eyes*) visera; (*of colour*) tono *m*, tonalidad *f*; (*US*: *window shade*) persiana ■ *vt* dar sombra a; **shades** *npl* (*US*: *sunglasses*) gafas *fpl* de sol; **in the ~** a la sombra; (*small quantity*): **a ~ of** un poquito de; **a ~ smaller** un poquito más pequeño
shadow ['ʃædəu] *n* sombra ■ *vt* (*follow*) seguir y vigilar; **without** *or* **beyond a ~ of doubt** sin lugar a dudas
shadow cabinet *n* (*Brit Pol*) gobierno en la oposición
shadowy ['ʃædəuɪ] *adj* oscuro; (*dim*) indistinto
shady ['ʃeɪdɪ] *adj* sombreado; (*fig*: *dishonest*) sospechoso; (*deal*) turbio
shaft [ʃɑːft] *n* (*of arrow, spear*) astil *m*; (*Aut, Tech*) eje *m*, árbol *m*; (*of mine*) pozo; (*of lift*) hueco, caja; (*of light*) rayo; **ventilator ~** chimenea de ventilación
shaggy ['ʃægɪ] *adj* peludo
shake [ʃeɪk] (*pt* **shook**, *pp* **shaken**) ['ʃeɪkn] *vt* sacudir; (*building*) hacer temblar; (*perturb*) inquietar, perturbar; (*weaken*) debilitar; (*alarm*) trastornar ■ *vi* estremecerse; (*tremble*) temblar ■ *n* (*movement*) sacudida; **to ~ one's head** (*in refusal*) negar con la cabeza; (*in dismay*) mover *or* menear la cabeza, incrédulo; **to ~ hands with sb** estrechar la mano a algn; **to ~ in one's shoes** (*fig*) temblar de miedo
▸ **shake off** *vt* sacudirse; (*fig*) deshacerse de
▸ **shake up** *vt* agitar
shake-up ['ʃeɪkʌp] *n* reorganización *f*
shakily ['ʃeɪkɪlɪ] *adv* (*reply*) con voz temblorosa *or* trémula; (*walk*) con paso vacilante; (*write*) con mano temblorosa
shaky ['ʃeɪkɪ] *adj* (*unstable*) inestable, poco firme; (*trembling*) tembloroso; (*health*) delicado; (*memory*) defectuoso; (*person*: *from illness*) temblando; (*premise etc*) incierto
shale [ʃeɪl] *n* esquisto
shall [ʃæl] *aux vb*: **I ~ go** iré
shallot [ʃə'lɔt] *n* (*Brit*) cebollita, chalote *m*
shallow ['ʃæləu] *adj* poco profundo; (*fig*) superficial
shallows ['ʃæləuz] *npl* bajío *sg*, bajos *mpl*
sham [ʃæm] *n* fraude *m*, engaño ■ *adj* falso, fingido ■ *vt* fingir, simular
shambles ['ʃæmblz] *n* desorden *m*, confusión *f*; **the economy is (in) a complete ~** la economía está en un estado desastroso
shambolic [ʃæm'bɔlɪk] *adj* (*col*) caótico
shame [ʃeɪm] *n* vergüenza; (*pity*) lástima, pena ■ *vt* avergonzar; **it is a ~ that/to do** es una lástima *or* pena que/hacer; **what a ~!** ¡qué lástima *or* pena!; **to put sth/sb to ~** (*fig*) ridiculizar algo/a algn
shamefaced ['ʃeɪmfeɪst] *adj* avergonzado
shameful ['ʃeɪmful] *adj* vergonzoso
shamefully ['ʃeɪmfulɪ] *adv* vergonzosamente
shameless ['ʃeɪmlɪs] *adj* descarado
shampoo [ʃæm'puː] *n* champú *m* ■ *vt* lavar con champú
shampoo and set *n* lavado y marcado
shamrock ['ʃæmrɔk] *n* trébol *m*
shandy ['ʃændɪ], **shandygaff** (*US*) ['ʃændɪgæf] *n* clara, cerveza con gaseosa
shan't [ʃɑːnt], **shall not**
shanty town ['ʃæntɪ-] *n* barrio de chabolas
SHAPE [ʃeɪp] *n abbr* (= *Supreme Headquarters Allied Powers, Europe*) *cuartel general de las fuerzas aliadas en Europa*
shape [ʃeɪp] *n* forma ■ *vt* formar, dar forma a; (*clay*) modelar; (*stone*) labrar; (*sb's ideas*) formar; (*sb's life*) determinar ■ *vi* (*also*: **shape up**: *events*) desarrollarse; (*person*) formarse; **to take ~** tomar forma; **to get o.s. into ~** ponerse en forma *or* en condiciones; **in the ~ of a heart** en forma de corazón; **I can't bear gardening in any ~ or form** no aguanto la jardinería de ningún modo

-shaped *suff*: **heart~** en forma de corazón
shapeless ['ʃeɪplɪs] *adj* informe, sin forma definida
shapely ['ʃeɪplɪ] *adj* bien formado *or* proporcionado
share [ʃɛəʳ] *n* (*part*) parte *f*, porción *f*; (*contribution*) cuota; (*Comm*) acción *f* ■ *vt* dividir; (*fig: have in common*) compartir; **to have a ~ in the profits** tener una proporción de las ganancias; **he has a 50% ~ in a new business venture** tiene una participación del 50% en un nuevo negocio; **to ~ in** participar en; **to ~ out (among** *or* **between)** repartir (entre)
share capital *n* (*Comm*) capital *m* social en acciones
share certificate *n* certificado *or* título de una acción
shareholder ['ʃɛəhəuldəʳ] *n* (*Brit*) accionista *m/f*
share index *n* (*Comm*) índice *m* de la bolsa
share issue *n* emisión *f* de acciones
share price *n* (*Comm*) cotización *f*
shark [ʃɑːk] *n* tiburón *m*
sharp [ʃɑːp] *adj* (*razor, knife*) afilado; (*point*) puntiagudo; (*outline*) definido; (*pain*) intenso; (*Mus*) desafinado; (*contrast*) marcado; (*voice*) agudo; (*curve, bend*) cerrado; (*person: quick-witted*) avispado; (*: dishonest*) poco escrupuloso ■ *n* (*Mus*) sostenido ■ *adv*: **at two o'clock ~** a las dos en punto; **to be ~ with sb** hablar a algn de forma brusca y tajante; **turn ~ left** tuerce del todo a la izquierda
sharpen ['ʃɑːpn] *vt* afilar; (*pencil*) sacar punta a; (*fig*) agudizar
sharpener ['ʃɑːpnəʳ] *n* (*gen*) afilador *m*; (*also*: **pencil sharpener**) sacapuntas *m inv*
sharp-eyed [ʃɑːp'aɪd] *adj* de vista aguda
sharpish ['ʃɑːpɪʃ] *adv* (*Brit col: quickly*) prontito, bien pronto
sharply ['ʃɑːplɪ] *adv* (*abruptly*) bruscamente; (*clearly*) claramente; (*harshly*) severamente
sharp-tempered [ʃɑːp'tɛmpəd] *adj* de genio arisco
sharp-witted [ʃɑːp'wɪtɪd] *adj* listo, despabilado
shatter ['ʃætəʳ] *vt* hacer añicos *or* pedazos; (*fig: ruin*) destruir, acabar con ■ *vi* hacerse añicos
shattered ['ʃætəd] *adj* (*grief-stricken*) destrozado, deshecho; (*exhausted*) agotado, hecho polvo
shattering ['ʃætərɪŋ] *adj* (*experience*) devastador(a), anonadante
shatterproof ['ʃætəpruːf] *adj* inastillable
shave [ʃeɪv] *vt* afeitar, rasurar ■ *vi* afeitarse ■ *n*: **to have a ~** afeitarse
shaven ['ʃeɪvn] *adj* (*head*) rapado
shaver ['ʃeɪvəʳ] *n* (*also*: **electric shaver**) máquina de afeitar (eléctrica)
shaving ['ʃeɪvɪŋ] *n* (*action*) afeitado; **shavings** *npl* (*of wood etc*) virutas *fpl*
shaving brush *n* brocha (de afeitar)
shaving cream *n* crema (de afeitar)
shaving point *n* enchufe *m* para máquinas de afeitar
shaving soap *n* jabón *m* de afeitar
shawl [ʃɔːl] *n* chal *m*
she [ʃiː] *pron* ella; **there ~ is** allí está; **~-cat** gata, *NB: for ships, countries follow the gender of your translation*
sheaf (*pl* **sheaves**) [ʃiːf, ʃiːvz] *n* (*of corn*) gavilla; (*of arrows*) haz *m*; (*of papers*) fajo
shear [ʃɪəʳ] *vt* (*pt, pp* **sheared** *or* **shorn**) [ʃɔːn] (*sheep*) esquilar, trasquilar
▸ **shear off** *vi* romperse
shears ['ʃɪəz] *npl* (*for hedge*) tijeras *fpl* de jardín
sheath [ʃiːθ] *n* vaina; (*contraceptive*) preservativo
sheath knife *n* cuchillo de monte
sheaves [ʃiːvz] *npl of* **sheaf**
shed [ʃɛd] *n* cobertizo; (*Industry, Rail*) nave *f* ■ *vt* (*pt, pp* **shed**) (*skin*) mudar; (*tears*) derramar; **to ~ light on** (*problem, mystery*) aclarar, arrojar luz sobre
she'd [ʃiːd] = **she had; she would**
sheen [ʃiːn] *n* brillo, lustre *m*
sheep [ʃiːp] *n* (*pl inv*) oveja
sheepdog ['ʃiːpdɔg] *n* perro pastor
sheep farmer *n* ganadero (de ovejas)
sheepish ['ʃiːpɪʃ] *adj* tímido, vergonzoso
sheepskin ['ʃiːpskɪn] *n* piel *f* de carnero
sheepskin jacket *n* zamarra
sheer [ʃɪəʳ] *adj* (*utter*) puro, completo; (*steep*) escarpado; (*material*) diáfano ■ *adv* verticalmente; **by ~ chance** de pura casualidad
sheet [ʃiːt] *n* (*on bed*) sábana; (*of paper*) hoja; (*of glass, metal*) lámina
sheet feed *n* (*on printer*) alimentador *m* de papel
sheet lightning *n* relámpago (difuso)
sheet metal *n* metal *m* en lámina
sheet music *n* hojas *fpl* de partitura
sheik, sheikh [ʃeɪk] *n* jeque *m*
shelf (*pl* **shelves**) [ʃɛlf, ʃɛlvz] *n* estante *m*
shelf life *n* (*Comm*) periodo de conservación antes de la venta
shell [ʃɛl] *n* (*on beach*) concha, caracol (*LAm*); (*of egg, nut etc*) cáscara; (*explosive*) proyectil *m*, obús *m*; (*of building*) armazón *m* ■ *vt* (*peas*) desenvainar; (*Mil*) bombardear

▸ **shell out** *vi* (*col*): **to ~ out (for)** soltar el dinero (para), desembolsar (para)
she'll [ʃi:l] = **she will; she shall**
shellfish ['ʃɛlfɪʃ] *n pl inv* crustáceo; (*pl: as food*) mariscos *mpl*
shellsuit ['ʃɛlsu:t] *n* chándal *m* (de tactel®)
shelter ['ʃɛltəʳ] *n* abrigo, refugio ■ *vt* (*aid*) amparar, proteger; (*give lodging to*) abrigar; (*hide*) esconder ■ *vi* abrigarse, refugiarse; **to take ~ (from)** refugiarse *or* asilarse (de); **bus ~** parada de autobús cubierta
sheltered ['ʃɛltəd] *adj* (*life*) protegido; (*spot*) abrigado
shelve [ʃɛlv] *vt* (*fig*) dar carpetazo a
shelves [ʃɛlvz] *npl of* **shelf**
shelving ['ʃɛlvɪŋ] *n* estantería
shepherd ['ʃɛpəd] *n* pastor *m* ■ *vt* (*guide*) guiar, conducir
shepherdess ['ʃɛpədɪs] *n* pastora
shepherd's pie *n* *pastel de carne y puré de patatas*
sherbert ['ʃə:bət] *n* (*Brit: powder*) polvos *mpl* azucarados; (*US: water ice*) sorbete *m*
sheriff ['ʃɛrɪf] *n* (*US*) sheriff *m*
sherry ['ʃɛrɪ] *n* jerez *m*
she's [ʃi:z] = **she is; she has**
Shetland ['ʃɛtlənd] *n* (*also:* **the Shetlands, the Shetland Isles**) las Islas *fpl* Shetland
Shetland pony *n* pony *m* de Shetland
shield [ʃi:ld] *n* escudo; (*Tech*) blindaje *m* ■ *vt*: **to ~ (from)** proteger (de)
shift [ʃɪft] *n* (*change*) cambio; (*at work*) turno ■ *vt* trasladar; (*remove*) quitar ■ *vi* moverse; (*change place*) cambiar de sitio; **the wind has shifted to the south** el viento ha virado al sur; **a ~ in demand** (*Comm*) un desplazamiento de la demanda
shift key *n* (*on typewriter*) tecla de mayúsculas
shiftless ['ʃɪftlɪs] *adj* (*person*) vago
shift work *n* (*Brit*) trabajo por turnos; **to do ~** trabajar por turnos
shifty ['ʃɪftɪ] *adj* tramposo; (*eyes*) furtivo
Shiite ['ʃi:aɪt] *adj, n* shiíta *m/f*
shilling ['ʃɪlɪŋ] *n* (*Brit*) chelín *m* (*= 12 old pence; 20 in a pound*)
shilly-shally ['ʃɪlɪʃælɪ] *vi* titubear, vacilar
shimmer ['ʃɪməʳ] *n* reflejo trémulo ■ *vi* relucir
shimmering ['ʃɪmərɪŋ] *adj* reluciente; (*haze*) trémulo; (*satin etc*) lustroso
shin [ʃɪn] *n* espinilla ■ *vi*: **to ~ down/up a tree** bajar de/trepar un árbol
shindig ['ʃɪndɪg] *n* (*col*) fiesta, juerga
shine [ʃaɪn] (*pt, pp* **shone**) *n* brillo, lustre *m* ■ *vi* brillar, relucir ■ *vt* (*shoes*) lustrar, sacar brillo a; **to ~ a torch on sth** dirigir una linterna hacia algo
shingle ['ʃɪŋgl] *n* (*on beach*) guijarras *fpl*
shingles ['ʃɪŋglz] *n* (*Med*) herpes *msg*
shining ['ʃaɪnɪŋ] *adj* (*surface, hair*) lustroso; (*light*) brillante
shiny ['ʃaɪnɪ] *adj* brillante, lustroso
ship [ʃɪp] *n* buque *m*, barco ■ *vt* (*goods*) embarcar; (*oars*) desarmar; (*send*) transportar *or* enviar por vía marítima; **~'s manifest** manifiesto del buque; **on board ~** a bordo
shipbuilder ['ʃɪpbɪldəʳ] *n* constructor(a) *m(f)* naval
shipbuilding ['ʃɪpbɪldɪŋ] *n* construcción *f* naval
ship canal *n* canal *m* de navegación
ship chandler [-'tʃɑ:ndləʳ] *n* proveedor *m* de efectos navales
shipment ['ʃɪpmənt] *n* (*act*) embarque *m*; (*goods*) envío
shipowner ['ʃɪpəunəʳ] *n* naviero, armador *m*
shipper ['ʃɪpəʳ] *n* compañía naviera
shipping ['ʃɪpɪŋ] *n* (*act*) embarque *m*; (*traffic*) buques *mpl*
shipping agent *n* agente *m/f* marítimo(-a)
shipping company *n* compañía naviera
shipping lane *n* ruta de navegación
shipping line *n* = **shipping company**
shipshape ['ʃɪpʃeɪp] *adj* en buen orden
shipwreck ['ʃɪprɛk] *n* naufragio ■ *vt*: **to be shipwrecked** naufragar
shipyard ['ʃɪpjɑ:d] *n* astillero
shire ['ʃaɪəʳ] *n* (*Brit*) condado
shirk [ʃə:k] *vt* eludir, esquivar; (*obligations*) faltar a
shirt [ʃə:t] *n* camisa; **in ~ sleeves** en mangas de camisa
shirty ['ʃə:tɪ] *adj* (*Brit col*): **to be ~** estar de malas pulgas
shit [ʃɪt] (*col!*) *n* mierda (*!*); (*nonsense*) chorradas *fpl*; **to be a ~** ser un cabrón (*!*) ■ *excl* ¡mierda! (*!*); **tough ~!** ¡te jodes! (*!*)
shiver ['ʃɪvəʳ] *vi* temblar, estremecerse; (*with cold*) tiritar
shoal [ʃəul] *n* (*of fish*) banco
shock [ʃɔk] *n* (*impact*) choque *m*; (*Elec*) descarga (eléctrica); (*emotional*) conmoción *f*; (*start*) sobresalto, susto; (*Med*) postración *f* nerviosa ■ *vt* dar un susto a; (*offend*) escandalizar; **to get a ~** (*Elec*) sentir una sacudida eléctrica; **to give sb a ~** dar un susto a algn; **to be suffering from ~** padecer una postración nerviosa; **it came as a ~ to hear that ...** me *etc* asombró descubrir que ...
shock absorber [-əbsɔ:bəʳ] *n* amortiguador *m*
shocker ['ʃɔkəʳ] *n* (*col*): **it was a real ~** fue muy fuerte
shocking ['ʃɔkɪŋ] *adj* (*awful: weather, handwriting*) espantoso, horrible; (*improper*) escandaloso; (*result*) inesperado

shock therapy, shock treatment *n* (*Med*) terapia de choque
shock wave *n* onda expansiva *or* de choque
shod [ʃɔd] *pt, pp of* **shoe** ■ *adj* calzado
shoddiness ['ʃɔdɪnɪs] *n* baja calidad *f*
shoddy ['ʃɔdɪ] *adj* de pacotilla
shoe [ʃu:] *n* zapato; (*for horse*) herradura; (*brake shoe*) zapata ■ *vt* (*pt, pp* **shod**) [ʃɔd] (*horse*) herrar
shoebrush ['ʃu:brʌʃ] *n* cepillo para zapatos
shoehorn ['ʃu:hɔ:n] *n* calzador *m*
shoelace ['ʃu:leɪs] *n* cordón *m*
shoemaker ['ʃu:meɪkə^r] *n* zapatero(-a)
shoe polish *n* betún *m*
shoeshop ['ʃu:ʃɔp] *n* zapatería
shoestring ['ʃu:strɪŋ] *n* (*shoelace*) cordón *m*; (*fig*): **on a ~** con muy poco dinero, a lo barato
shone [ʃɔn] *pt, pp of* **shine**
shoo [ʃu:] *excl* ¡fuera!; (*to animals*) ¡zape! ■ *vt* (*also*: **shoo away, shoo off**) ahuyentar
shook [ʃuk] *pt of* **shake**
shoot [ʃu:t] (*pt, pp* **shot**) *n* (*on branch, seedling*) retoño, vástago; (*shooting party*) cacería; (*competition*) concurso de tiro; (*preserve*) coto de caza ■ *vt* disparar; (*kill*) matar a tiros; (*execute*) fusilar; (*Cine: film, scene*) rodar, filmar ■ *vi* (*Football*) chutar; **to ~ (at)** tirar (a); **to ~ past** pasar como un rayo; **to ~ in/out** *vi* entrar corriendo/salir disparado
▸ **shoot down** *vt* (*plane*) derribar
▸ **shoot up** *vi* (*prices*) dispararse
shooting ['ʃu:tɪŋ] *n* (*shots*) tiros *mpl*, tiroteo; (*Hunting*) caza con escopeta; (*act: murder*) asesinato (a tiros); (*Cine*) rodaje *m*
shooting star *n* estrella fugaz
shop [ʃɔp] *n* tienda; (*workshop*) taller *m* ■ *vi* (*also*: **go shopping**) ir de compras; **to talk ~** (*fig*) hablar del trabajo; **repair ~** taller *m* de reparaciones
▸ **shop around** *vi* comparar precios
shopaholic [ʃɔpə'hɔlɪk] *n* (*col*) adicto(-a) a las compras
shop assistant *n* (*Brit*) dependiente(-a) *m(f)*
shop floor *n* (*Brit fig*) taller *m*, fábrica
shopkeeper ['ʃɔpki:pə^r] *n* (*Brit*) tendero(-a)
shoplift ['ʃɔplɪft] *vi* robar en las tiendas
shoplifter ['ʃɔplɪftə^r] *n* ratero(-a)
shoplifting ['ʃɔplɪftɪŋ] *n* ratería, robo (en las tiendas)
shopper ['ʃɔpə^r] *n* comprador(a) *m(f)*
shopping ['ʃɔpɪŋ] *n* (*goods*) compras *fpl*
shopping bag *n* bolsa (de compras)
shopping centre, shopping center (*US*) *n* centro comercial
shopping mall *n* centro comercial
shop-soiled ['ʃɔpsɔɪld] *adj* (*Brit*) usado
shop steward *n* (*Brit Industry*) enlace *m/f* sindical
shop window *n* escaparate *m*, vidriera (*LAm*)
shopworn ['ʃɔpwɔ:n] *adj* (*US*) usado
shore [ʃɔ:^r] *n* (*of sea, lake*) orilla ■ *vt*: **to ~ (up)** reforzar; **on ~** en tierra
shore leave *n* (*Naut*) permiso para bajar a tierra
shorn [ʃɔ:n] *pp of* **shear**
short [ʃɔ:t] *adj* (*not long*) corto; (*in time*) breve, de corta duración; (*person*) bajo; (*curt*) brusco, seco ■ *vi* (*Elec*) ponerse en cortocircuito ■ *n* (*also*: **short film**) cortometraje *m*; **(a pair of) shorts** (unos) pantalones *mpl* cortos; **to be ~ of sth** estar falto de algo; **in ~** en pocas palabras; **a ~ time ago** hace poco (tiempo); **in the ~ term** a corto plazo; **to be in ~ supply** escasear, haber escasez de; **I'm ~ of time** me falta tiempo; **~ of doing ...** a menos que hagamos *etc* ...; **everything ~ of ...** todo menos ...; **it is ~ for** es la forma abreviada de; **to cut ~** (*speech, visit*) interrumpir, terminar inesperadamente; **to fall ~ of** no alcanzar; **to run ~ of sth** acabársele algo; **to stop ~** parar en seco; **to stop ~ of** detenerse antes de
shortage ['ʃɔ:tɪdʒ] *n* escasez *f*, falta
shortbread ['ʃɔ:tbrɛd] *n pasta de mantequilla*
short-change [ʃɔ:t'tʃeɪndʒ] *vt*: **to ~ sb** no dar el cambio completo a algn
short-circuit [ʃɔ:t'sə:kɪt] *n* cortocircuito ■ *vt* poner en cortocircuito ■ *vi* ponerse, en cortocircuito
shortcoming ['ʃɔ:tkʌmɪŋ] *n* defecto, deficiencia
shortcrust pastry ['ʃɔ:tkrʌst-], **short pastry** *n* (*Brit*) pasta quebradiza
shortcut ['ʃɔ:tkʌt] *n* atajo
shorten ['ʃɔ:tn] *vt* acortar; (*visit*) interrumpir
shortfall ['ʃɔ:tfɔ:l] *n* déficit *m*, deficiencia
shorthand ['ʃɔ:thænd] *n* (*Brit*) taquigrafía; **to take sth down in ~** taquigrafiar algo
shorthand notebook *n* cuaderno de taquigrafía
shorthand typist *n* (*Brit*) taquimecanógrafo(-a)
short list *n* (*Brit: for job*) lista de candidatos pre-seleccionados
short-lived ['ʃɔ:t'lɪvd] *adj* efímero
shortly ['ʃɔ:tlɪ] *adv* en breve, dentro de poco
shortness ['ʃɔ:tnɪs] *n* (*of distance*) cortedad *f*; (*of time*) brevedad *f*; (*manner*) brusquedad *f*
short-sighted [ʃɔ:t'saɪtɪd] *adj* (*Brit*) miope, corto de vista; (*fig*) imprudente
short-sightedness [ʃɔ:t'saɪtɪdnɪs] *n* miopía; (*fig*) falta de previsión, imprudencia

short-staffed [ʃɔːtˈstɑːft] *adj* falto de personal
short story *n* cuento
short-tempered [ʃɔːtˈtɛmpəd] *adj* enojadizo
short-term [ˈʃɔːttəːm] *adj* (*effect*) a corto plazo
short time *n*: **to work ~, be on ~** (*Industry*) trabajar con sistema de horario reducido
short-time working [ˈʃɔːttaɪm-] *n* trabajo de horario reducido
short wave *n* (*Radio*) onda corta
shot [ʃɔt] *pt, pp of* **shoot** ■ *n* (*sound*) tiro, disparo; (*person*) tirador(a) *m(f)*; (*try*) tentativa; (*injection*) inyección *f*; (*Phot*) toma, fotografía; (*shotgun pellets*) perdigones *mpl*; **to fire a ~ at sb/sth** tirar *or* disparar contra algn/algo; **to have a ~ at (doing) sth** probar suerte con algo; **like a ~** (*without any delay*) como un rayo; **a big ~** (*col*) un pez gordo; **to get ~ of sth/sb** (*col*) deshacerse de algo/algn, quitarse algo/a algn de encima
shotgun [ˈʃɔtgʌn] *n* escopeta
should [ʃud] *aux vb*: **I ~ go now** debo irme ahora; **he ~ be there now** debe de haber llegado (ya); **I ~ go if I were you** yo en tu lugar me iría; **I ~ like to** me gustaría; **~ he phone ...** si llamara ..., en caso de que llamase ...
shoulder [ˈʃəuldəʳ] *n* hombro; (*Brit: of road*): **hard ~** arcén *m* ■ *vt* (*fig*) cargar con; **to look over one's ~** mirar hacia atrás; **to rub shoulders with sb** (*fig*) codearse con algn; **to give sb the cold ~** (*fig*) dar de lado a algn
shoulder bag *n* bolso de bandolera
shoulder blade *n* omóplato
shoulder strap *n* tirante *m*
shouldn't [ˈʃudnt] = **should not**
shout [ʃaut] *n* grito ■ *vt* gritar ■ *vi* gritar, dar voces
▸ **shout down** *vt* hundir a gritos
shouting [ˈʃautɪŋ] *n* griterío
shouting match *n* (*col*) discusión *f* a voz en grito
shove [ʃʌv] *n* empujón *m* ■ *vt* empujar; (*col: put*): **to ~ sth in** meter algo a empellones; **he shoved me out of the way** me quitó de en medio de un empujón
▸ **shove off** *vi* (*Naut*) alejarse del muelle; (*fig: col*) largarse
shovel [ˈʃʌvl] *n* pala; (*mechanical*) excavadora ■ *vt* mover con pala
show [ʃəu] (*pt* **showed**, *pp* **shown**) *n* (*of emotion*) demostración *f*; (*semblance*) apariencia; (*Comm, Tech: exhibition*) exhibición *f*, exposición *f*; (*Theat*) función *f*, espectáculo; (*organization*) negocio, empresa ■ *vt* mostrar, enseñar; (*courage etc*) mostrar, manifestar; (*exhibit*) exponer; (*film*) proyectar ■ *vi* mostrarse; (*appear*) aparecer; **on ~** (*exhibits etc*) expuesto; **to be on ~** estar expuesto; **it's just for ~** es sólo para impresionar; **to ask for a ~ of hands** pedir una votación a mano alzada; **who's running the ~ here?** ¿quién manda aquí?; **to ~ a profit/loss** (*Comm*) arrojar un saldo positivo/negativo; **I have nothing to ~ for it** no saqué ningún provecho (de ello); **to ~ sb to his seat/to the door** acompañar a algn a su asiento/a la puerta; **as shown in the illustration** como se ve en el grabado; **it just goes to ~ that ...** queda demostrado que ...; **it doesn't ~** no se ve *or* nota
▸ **show in** *vt* (*person*) hacer pasar
▸ **show off** *vi* (*pej*) presumir ■ *vt* (*display*) lucir; (*pej*) hacer alarde de
▸ **show out** *vt*: **to ~ sb out** acompañar a algn a la puerta
▸ **show up** *vi* (*stand out*) destacar; (*col: turn up*) presentarse ■ *vt* descubrir; (*unmask*) desenmascarar
showbiz [ˈʃəubɪz] *n* (*col*) = **show business**
show business *n* el mundo del espectáculo
showcase [ˈʃəukeɪs] *n* vitrina; (*fig*) escaparate *m*
showdown [ˈʃəudaun] *n* crisis *f*, momento decisivo
shower [ˈʃauəʳ] *n* (*rain*) chaparrón *m*, chubasco; (*of stones etc*) lluvia; (*also*: **shower bath**) ducha ■ *vi* llover ■ *vt*: **to ~ sb with sth** colmar a algn de algo; **to have** *or* **take a ~** ducharse
shower cap *n* gorro de baño
shower gel *n* gel de ducha
showerproof [ˈʃauəpruːf] *adj* impermeable
showery [ˈʃauərɪ] *adj* (*weather*) lluvioso
showground [ˈʃəugraund] *n* ferial *m*, real *m* (de la feria)
showing [ˈʃəuɪŋ] *n* (*of film*) proyección *f*
show jumping *n* hípica
showman [ˈʃəumən] *n* (*at fair, circus*) empresario (de espectáculos); (*fig*) actor *m* consumado
showmanship [ˈʃəumənʃɪp] *n* dotes *fpl* teatrales
shown [ʃəun] *pp of* **show**
show-off [ˈʃəuɔf] *n* (*col: person*) fantasmón(-ona) *m(f)*
showpiece [ˈʃəupiːs] *n* (*of exhibition etc*) objeto más valioso, joya; **that hospital is a ~** ese hospital es un modelo del género
showroom [ˈʃəuruːm] *n* sala de muestras
show trial *n* juicio propagandístico
showy [ˈʃəuɪ] *adj* ostentoso
shrank [ʃræŋk] *pt of* **shrink**
shrapnel [ˈʃræpnl] *n* metralla

shred [ʃrɛd] *n* (*gen pl*) triza, jirón *m*; (*fig*: *of truth, evidence*) pizca, chispa ■ *vt* hacer trizas; (*documents*) triturar; (*Culin*) desmenuzar
shredder ['ʃrɛdəʳ] *n* (*vegetable shredder*) picadora; (*document shredder*) trituradora (de papel)
shrewd [ʃru:d] *adj* astuto
shrewdly ['ʃru:dlɪ] *adv* astutamente
shrewdness ['ʃru:dnɪs] *n* astucia
shriek [ʃri:k] *n* chillido ■ *vt, vi* chillar
shrill [ʃrɪl] *adj* agudo, estridente
shrimp [ʃrɪmp] *n* camarón *m*
shrine [ʃraɪn] *n* santuario, sepulcro
shrink (*pt* **shrank**, *pp* **shrunk**) [ʃrɪŋk, ʃræŋk, ʃrʌŋk] *vi* encogerse; (*be reduced*) reducirse ■ *vt* encoger; **to ~ from (doing) sth** no atreverse a hacer algo
▸ **shrink away** *vi* retroceder, retirarse
shrinkage ['ʃrɪŋkɪdʒ] *n* encogimiento; reducción *f*; (*Comm*: *in shops*) pérdidas *fpl*
shrink-wrap ['ʃrɪŋkræp] *vt* empaquetar en envase termoretráctil
shrivel ['ʃrɪvl] (*also*: **shrivel up**) *vt* (*dry*) secar; (*crease*) arrugar ■ *vi* secarse; arrugarse
shroud [ʃraud] *n* sudario ■ *vt*: **shrouded in mystery** envuelto en el misterio
Shrove Tuesday ['ʃrəuv-] *n* martes *m* de carnaval
shrub [ʃrʌb] *n* arbusto
shrubbery ['ʃrʌbərɪ] *n* arbustos *mpl*
shrug [ʃrʌg] *n* encogimiento de hombros ■ *vt, vi*: **to ~ (one's shoulders)** encogerse de hombros
▸ **shrug off** *vt* negar importancia a; (*cold, illness*) deshacerse de
shrunk [ʃrʌŋk] *pp of* **shrink**
shrunken ['ʃrʌŋkn] *adj* encogido
shudder ['ʃʌdəʳ] *n* estremecimiento, escalofrío ■ *vi* estremecerse
shuffle ['ʃʌfl] *vt* (*cards*) barajar; **to ~ (one's feet)** arrastrar los pies
shun [ʃʌn] *vt* rehuir, esquivar
shunt [ʃʌnt] *vt* (*Rail*) maniobrar
shunting yard ['ʃʌntɪŋ-] *n* estación *f* de maniobras
shut (*pt, pp* **~**) [ʃʌt] *vt* cerrar ■ *vi* cerrarse
▸ **shut down** *vt, vi* cerrar; (*machine*) parar
▸ **shut off** *vt* (*stop*: *power, water supply etc*) interrumpir, cortar; (*engine*) parar
▸ **shut out** *vt* (*person*) excluir, dejar fuera; (*noise, cold*) no dejar entrar; (*block*: *view*) tapar; (*memory*) tratar de olvidar
▸ **shut up** *vi* (*col*: *keep quiet*) callarse ■ *vt* (*close*) cerrar; (*silence*) callar
shutdown ['ʃʌtdaun] *n* cierre *m*
shutter ['ʃʌtəʳ] *n* contraventana; (*Phot*) obturador *m*
shuttle ['ʃʌtl] *n* lanzadera; (*also*: **shuttle service**: *Aviat*) puente *m* aéreo ■ *vi* (*vehicle, person*) ir y venir ■ *vt* (*passengers*) transportar, trasladar
shuttlecock ['ʃʌtlkɔk] *n* volante *m*
shuttle diplomacy *n* viajes *mpl* diplomáticos
shy [ʃaɪ] *adj* tímido ■ *vi*: **to ~ away from doing sth** (*fig*) rehusar hacer algo; **to be ~ of doing sth** esquivar hacer algo
shyly ['ʃaɪlɪ] *adv* tímidamente
shyness ['ʃaɪnɪs] *n* timidez *f*
Siam [saɪ'æm] *n* Siam *m*
Siamese [saɪə'mi:z] *adj* siamés(-esa) ■ *n* (*person*) siamés(-esa) *m(f)*; (*Ling*) siamés *m*; **~ cat** gato siamés; **~ twins** gemelos(-as) *m(f)pl* siameses(-as)
Siberia [saɪ'bɪərɪə] *n* Siberia
sibling ['sɪblɪŋ] *n* (*formal*) hermano(-a)
Sicilian [sɪ'sɪlɪən] *adj, n* siciliano(-a) *m(f)*
Sicily ['sɪsɪlɪ] *n* Sicilia
sick [sɪk] *adj* (*ill*) enfermo; (*nauseated*) mareado; (*humour*) morboso; **to be ~** (*Brit*) vomitar; **to feel ~** estar mareado; **to be ~ of** (*fig*) estar harto de; **a ~ person** un(a) enfermo(-a); **to be (off) ~** estar ausente por enfermedad; **to fall** *or* **take ~** ponerse enfermo
sickbag ['sɪkbæg] *n* bolsa para el mareo
sick bay *n* enfermería
sickbed ['sɪkbɛd] *n* lecho de enfermo
sick building syndrome *n* *enfermedad causada por falta de ventilación y luz natural en un edificio*
sicken ['sɪkn] *vt* dar asco a ■ *vi* enfermar; **to be sickening for** (*cold, flu etc*) mostrar síntomas de
sickening ['sɪknɪŋ] *adj* (*fig*) asqueroso
sickle ['sɪkl] *n* hoz *f*
sick leave *n* baja por enfermedad
sickle-cell anaemia ['sɪklsɛl-] *n* anemia de células falciformes, drepanocitosis *f*
sick list *n*: **to be on the ~** estar de baja
sickly ['sɪklɪ] *adj* enfermizo; (*taste*) empalagoso
sickness ['sɪknɪs] *n* enfermedad *f*, mal *m*; (*vomiting*) náuseas *fpl*
sickness benefit *n* subsidio de enfermedad
sick pay *n* *prestación por enfermedad pagada por la empresa*
sickroom ['sɪkru:m] *n* cuarto del enfermo
side [saɪd] *n* (*gen*) lado; (*face, surface*) cara; (*of paper*) cara; (*slice of bread*) rebanada; (*of body*) costado; (*of animal*) ijar *m*, ijada; (*of lake*) orilla; (*part*) lado; (*aspect*) aspecto; (*team*: *Sport*) equipo; (: *Pol etc*) partido; (*of hill*) ladera ■ *adj* (*door, entrance*) lateral ■ *vi*: **to ~ with sb** ponerse de parte de algn; **by the ~ of** al lado de; **~ by ~** juntos(-as); **from all sides**

de todos lados; **to take sides (with)** tomar partido (por); **~ of beef** flanco de vaca; **the right/wrong** ~ el derecho/revés; **from ~ to ~** de un lado a otro
sideboard ['saɪdbɔːd] *n* aparador *m*
sideboards ['saɪdbɔːdz], (*Brit*) **sideburns** ['saɪdbəːnz] *npl* patillas *fpl*
sidecar ['saɪdkɑːʳ] *n* sidecar *m*
side dish *n* entremés *m*
side drum *n* (*Mus*) tamboril *m*
side effect *n* efecto secundario
sidekick ['saɪdkɪk] *n* compinche *m*
sidelight ['saɪdlaɪt] *n* (*Aut*) luz *f* lateral
sideline ['saɪdlaɪn] *n* (*Sport*) línea lateral; (*fig*) empleo suplementario
sidelong ['saɪdlɔŋ] *adj* de soslayo; **to give a ~ glance at sth** mirar algo de reojo
side plate *n* platito
side road *n* (*Brit*) calle *f* lateral
sidesaddle ['saɪdsædl] *adv* a la amazona
side show *n* (*stall*) caseta; (*fig*) atracción *f* secundaria
sidestep ['saɪdstɛp] *vt* (*question*) eludir; (*problem*) esquivar ■ *vi* (*Boxing etc*) dar un quiebro
side street *n* calle *f* lateral
sidetrack ['saɪdtræk] *vt* (*fig*) desviar (de su propósito)
sidewalk ['saɪdwɔːk] *n* (*US*) acera, vereda (*LAm*), andén *m* (*LAm*), banqueta (*LAm*)
sideways ['saɪdweɪz] *adv* de lado
siding ['saɪdɪŋ] *n* (*Rail*) apartadero, vía muerta
sidle ['saɪdl] *vi*: **to ~ up (to)** acercarse furtivamente (a)
SIDS [sɪdz] *n abbr* (*= sudden infant death syndrome*) (síndrome *m* de la) muerte *f* súbita
siege [siːdʒ] *n* cerco, sitio; **to lay ~ to** cercar, sitiar
siege economy *n* economía de sitio *or* de asedio
Sierra Leone [sɪ'ɛrəlɪ'əun] *n* Sierra Leona
siesta [sɪ'ɛstə] *n* siesta
sieve [sɪv] *n* colador *m* ■ *vt* cribar
sift [sɪft] *vt* cribar ■ *vi*: **to ~ through** pasar por una criba; (*information*) analizar cuidadosamente
sigh [saɪ] *n* suspiro ■ *vi* suspirar
sight [saɪt] *n* (*faculty*) vista; (*spectacle*) espectáculo; (*on gun*) mira, alza ■ *vt* ver, divisar; **in ~** a la vista; **out of ~** fuera de (la) vista; **at ~** a la vista; **at first ~** a primera vista; **to lose ~ of sth/sb** perder algo/a algn de vista; **to catch ~ of sth/sb** divisar algo/a algn; **I know her by ~** la conozco de vista; **to set one's sights on (doing) sth** aspirar a *or* ambicionar (hacer) algo
sighted ['saɪtɪd] *adj* vidente, de vista normal; **partially ~** de vista limitada
sightseeing ['saɪtsiːɪŋ] *n* excursionismo, turismo; **to go ~** visitar monumentos
sightseer ['saɪtsiːəʳ] *n* excursionista *m/f*, turista *m/f*
sign [saɪn] *n* (*with hand*) señal *f*, seña; (*trace*) huella, rastro; (*notice*) letrero; (*written*) signo; (*also*: **road sign**) indicador *m*; (*: with instructions*) señal *f* de tráfico ■ *vt* firmar; **as a ~ of** en señal de; **it's a good/bad ~** es buena/mala señal; **plus/minus ~** signo de más/de menos; **to ~ one's name** firmar
▸**sign away** *vt* (*rights etc*) ceder
▸**sign off** *vi* (*Radio, TV*) cerrar el programa
▸**sign on** *vi* (*Mil*) alistarse; (*as unemployed*) apuntarse al paro; (*employee*) firmar un contrato ■ *vt* (*Mil*) alistar; (*employee*) contratar; **to ~ on for a course** matricularse en un curso
▸**sign out** *vi* firmar el registro (al salir)
▸**sign over** *vt*: **to ~ sth over to sb** traspasar algo a algn
▸**sign up** *vi* (*Mil*) alistarse ■ *vt* (*contract*) contratar
signal ['sɪgnl] *n* señal *f* ■ *vi* (*Aut*) señalizar ■ *vt* (*person*) hacer señas a; (*message*) transmitir; **the engaged ~** (*Tel*) la señal de comunicando; **the ~ is very weak** (*TV*) no captamos bien el canal; **to ~ a left/right turn** (*Aut*) indicar que se va a doblar a la izquierda/derecha; **to ~ to sb (to do sth)** hacer señas a algn (para que haga algo)
signal box *n* (*Rail*) garita de señales
signalman ['sɪgnlmən] *n* (*Rail*) guardavía *m*
signatory ['sɪgnətərɪ] *n* firmante *m/f*
signature ['sɪgnətʃəʳ] *n* firma
signature tune *n* sintonía
signet ring ['sɪgnət-] *n* (anillo de) sello
significance [sɪg'nɪfɪkəns] *n* significado; (*importance*) trascendencia; **that is of no ~** eso no tiene importancia
significant [sɪg'nɪfɪkənt] *adj* significativo; trascendente; **it is ~ that ...** es significativo que ...
significantly [sɪg'nɪfɪkəntlɪ] *adv* (*smile*) expresivamente; (*improve, increase*) sensiblemente; **and, ~ ...** y debe notarse que ...
signify ['sɪgnɪfaɪ] *vt* significar
sign language *n* mímica, lenguaje *m* por *or* de señas
signpost ['saɪnpəust] *n* indicador *m*
silage ['saɪlɪdʒ] *n* ensilaje *m*
silence ['saɪlns] *n* silencio ■ *vt* hacer callar; (*guns*) reducir al silencio

silencer ['saɪlnsəʳ] *n* silenciador *m*
silent ['saɪlnt] *adj* (*gen*) silencioso; (*not speaking*) callado; (*film*) mudo; **to keep** *or* **remain ~** guardar silencio
silently ['saɪlntlɪ] *adv* silenciosamente, en silencio
silent partner *n* (*Comm*) socio(-a) comanditario(-a)
silhouette [sɪlu:'ɛt] *n* silueta; **silhouetted against** destacado sobre *or* contra
silicon ['sɪlɪkən] *n* silicio
silicon chip *n* chip *m*, plaqueta de silicio
silicone ['sɪlɪkəun] *n* silicona
silk [sɪlk] *n* seda ■ *cpd* de seda
silky ['sɪlkɪ] *adj* sedoso
sill [sɪl] *n* (*also*: **windowsill**) alféizar *m*; (*Aut*) umbral *m*
silliness ['sɪlɪnɪs] *n* (*of person*) necedad *f*; (*of idea*) lo absurdo
silly ['sɪlɪ] *adj* (*person*) tonto; (*idea*) absurdo; **to do sth ~** hacer una tontería
silo ['saɪləu] *n* silo
silt [sɪlt] *n* sedimento
silver ['sɪlvəʳ] *n* plata; (*money*) moneda suelta ■ *adj* de plata
silver paper, (*Brit*) **silver foil** *n* papel *m* de plata
silver plate *n* vajilla de plata
silver-plated [sɪlvə'pleɪtɪd] *adj* plateado
silversmith ['sɪlvəsmɪθ] *n* platero(-a)
silverware ['sɪlvəwɛəʳ] *n* plata
silver wedding, silver wedding anniversary *n* (*Brit*) bodas *fpl* de plata
silvery ['sɪlvrɪ] *adj* plateado
similar ['sɪmɪləʳ] *adj*: **~ to** parecido *or* semejante a
similarity [sɪmɪ'lærɪtɪ] *n* parecido, semejanza
similarly ['sɪmɪləlɪ] *adv* del mismo modo; (*in a similar way*) de manera parecida; (*equally*) igualmente
simile ['sɪmɪlɪ] *n* símil *m*
simmer ['sɪməʳ] *vi* hervir a fuego lento
▸ **simmer down** *vi* (*fig, col*) calmarse, tranquilizarse
simpering ['sɪmpərɪŋ] *adj* afectado; (*foolish*) bobo
simple ['sɪmpl] *adj* (*easy*) sencillo; (*foolish*) simple; (*Comm*) simple; **the ~ truth** la pura verdad
simple interest *n* (*Comm*) interés *m* simple
simple-minded [sɪmpl'maɪndɪd] *adj* simple, ingenuo
simpleton ['sɪmpltən] *n* inocentón(-ona) *m(f)*
simplicity [sɪm'plɪsɪtɪ] *n* sencillez *f*; (*foolishness*) ingenuidad *f*
simplification [sɪmplɪfɪ'keɪʃən] *n* simplificación *f*
simplify ['sɪmplɪfaɪ] *vt* simplificar
simply ['sɪmplɪ] *adv* (*in a simple way: live, talk*) sencillamente; (*just, merely*) sólo
simulate ['sɪmjuleɪt] *vt* simular
simulation [sɪmju'leɪʃən] *n* simulación *f*
simultaneous [sɪməl'teɪnɪəs] *adj* simultáneo
simultaneously [sɪməl'teɪnɪəslɪ] *adv* simultáneamente, a la vez
sin [sɪn] *n* pecado ■ *vi* pecar
since [sɪns] *adv* desde entonces ■ *prep* desde ■ *conj* (*time*) desde que; (*because*) ya que, puesto que; **~ then** desde entonces; **~ Monday** desde el lunes; **(ever) ~ I arrived** desde que llegué
sincere [sɪn'sɪəʳ] *adj* sincero
sincerely [sɪn'sɪəlɪ] *adv* sinceramente; **yours ~** (*in letters*) le saluda (afectuosamente); **~ yours** (*US: in letters*) le saluda atentamente
sincerity [sɪn'sɛrɪtɪ] *n* sinceridad *f*
sinecure ['saɪnɪkjuəʳ] *n* chollo
sinew ['sɪnju:] *n* tendón *m*
sinful ['sɪnful] *adj* (*thought*) pecaminoso; (*person*) pecador(a)
sing (*pt* **sang**, *pp* **sung**) [sɪŋ, sæŋ, sʌŋ] *vt* cantar ■ *vi* (*gen*) cantar; (*bird*) trinar; (*ears*) zumbar
Singapore [sɪŋə'pɔ:ʳ] *n* Singapur *m*
singe [sɪndʒ] *vt* chamuscar
singer ['sɪŋəʳ] *n* cantante *m/f*
Singhalese [sɪŋə'li:z] *adj* = **Sinhalese**
singing ['sɪŋɪŋ] *n* (*of person, bird*) canto; (*songs*) canciones *fpl*; (*in the ears*) zumbido; (*of kettle*) silbido
single ['sɪŋgl] *adj* único, solo; (*unmarried*) soltero; (*not double*) individual, sencillo ■ *n* (*Brit: also*: **single ticket**) billete *m* sencillo; (*record*) sencillo, single *m*; **singles** *npl* (*Tennis*) individual *msg*; **not a ~ one was left** no quedaba ni uno; **every ~ day** todos los días (sin excepción)
▸ **single out** *vt* (*choose*) escoger; (*point out*) singularizar
single bed *n* cama individual
single-breasted [sɪŋgl'brɛstɪd] *adj* (*jacket, suit*) recto, sin cruzar
single-entry book-keeping ['sɪŋglɛntrɪ-] *n* contabilidad *f* por partida simple
Single European Market *n*: **the ~** el Mercado Único Europeo
single file *n*: **in ~** en fila de uno
single-handed [sɪŋgl'hændɪd] *adv* sin ayuda
single-minded [sɪŋgl'maɪndɪd] *adj* resuelto, firme
single parent *n* (*mother*) madre *f* soltera; (*father*) padre *m* soltero

single-parent family ['sɪŋglpɛərənt-] *n* familia monoparental
single room *n* habitación *f* individual
singles bar *n* (*esp US*) bar *m* para solteros
single-sex school ['sɪŋglsɛks-] *n* escuela no mixta
single-sided [sɪŋgl'saɪdɪd] *adj* (*Comput: disk*) de una cara
single spacing *n* (*Typ*): **in ~** a un espacio
singlet ['sɪŋglɪt] *n* camiseta
singly ['sɪŋglɪ] *adv* uno por uno
singsong ['sɪŋsɔŋ] *adj* (*tone*) cantarín(-ina) ■ *n* (*songs*): **to have a ~** tener un concierto improvisado
singular ['sɪŋgjuləʳ] *adj* singular, extraordinario; (*odd*) extraño; (*Ling*) singular ■ *n* (*Ling*) singular *m*; **in the feminine ~** en femenino singular
singularly ['sɪŋgjuləlɪ] *adv* singularmente, extraordinariamente
Sinhalese [sɪnhə'li:z] *adj* singhalese
sinister ['sɪnɪstəʳ] *adj* siniestro
sink [sɪŋk] (*pt* **sank**, *pp* **sunk**) *n* fregadero ■ *vt* (*ship*) hundir, echar a pique; (*foundations*) excavar; (*piles etc*): **to ~ sth into** hundir algo en ■ *vi* (*gen*) hundirse; **he sank into a chair/the mud** se dejó caer en una silla/se hundió en el barro; **the shares** *or* **share prices have sunk to three dollars** las acciones han bajado a tres dólares
▸ **sink in** *vi* (*fig*) penetrar, calar; **the news took a long time to ~ in** la noticia tardó mucho en hacer mella en él (*or mí etc*)
sinking ['sɪŋkɪŋ] *adj*: **that ~ feeling** la sensación esa de desmoralización
sinking fund *n* fondo de amortización
sink unit *n* fregadero
sinner ['sɪnəʳ] *n* pecador(a) *m(f)*
Sinn Féin [ʃɪn'feɪn] *n partido político republicano de Irlanda del Norte*
sinuous ['sɪnjuəs] *adj* sinuoso
sinus ['saɪnəs] *n* (*Anat*) seno
sip [sɪp] *n* sorbo ■ *vt* sorber, beber a sorbitos
siphon ['saɪfən] *n* sifón *m* ■ *vt* (*also*: **siphon off**: *funds*) desviar
sir [səːʳ] *n* señor *m*; **S~ John Smith** el Señor John Smith; **yes ~** sí, señor; **Dear S~** (*in letter*) Muy señor mío, Estimado Señor; **Dear Sirs** Muy señores nuestros, Estimados Señores
siren ['saɪərn] *n* sirena
sirloin ['səːlɔɪn] *n* solomillo
sirloin steak *n* filete *m* de solomillo
sisal ['saɪsəl] *n* pita, henequén *m* (*LAm*)
sissy ['sɪsɪ] *n* (*col*) marica *m*
sister ['sɪstəʳ] *n* hermana; (*Brit: nurse*) enfermera jefe
sister-in-law ['sɪstərɪnlɔː] *n* cuñada
sister organization *n* organización *f* hermana
sister ship *n* barco gemelo
sit (*pt, pp* **sat**) [sɪt, sæt] *vi* sentarse; (*be sitting*) estar sentado; (*assembly*) reunirse; (*dress etc*) caer, sentar ■ *vt* (*exam*) presentarse a; **that jacket sits well** esa chaqueta sienta bien; **to ~ on a committee** ser miembro de una comisión *or* un comité
▸ **sit about, sit around** *vi* holgazanear
▸ **sit back** *vi* (*in seat*) recostarse
▸ **sit down** *vi* sentarse; **to be sitting down** estar sentado
▸ **sit in on** *vt fus*: **to ~ in on a discussion** asistir a una discusión
▸ **sit up** *vi* incorporarse; (*not go to bed*) no acostarse
sitcom ['sɪtkɔm] *n abbr* (*TV*: = *situation comedy*) telecomedia
sit-down ['sɪtdaun] *adj*: **~ strike** huelga de brazos caídos; **a ~ meal** una comida sentada
site [saɪt] *n* sitio; (*also*: **building site**) solar *m* ■ *vt* situar
sit-in ['sɪtɪn] *n* (*demonstration*) sentada *f*
siting ['saɪtɪŋ] *n* (*location*) situación *f*, emplazamiento
sitter ['sɪtəʳ] *n* (*Art*) modelo *m/f*; (*babysitter*) canguro *m/f*
sitting ['sɪtɪŋ] *n* (*of assembly etc*) sesión *f*; (*in canteen*) turno
sitting member *n* (*Pol*) titular *m/f* de un escaño
sitting room *n* sala de estar
sitting tenant *n inquilino con derechos de estancia en una vivienda*
situate ['sɪtjueɪt] *vt* situar, ubicar (*LAm*)
situated ['sɪtjueɪtɪd] *adj* situado, ubicado (*LAm*)
situation [sɪtju'eɪʃən] *n* situación *f*; **"situations vacant"** (*Brit*) "ofertas de trabajo"
situation comedy *n* (*TV, Radio*) serie *f* cómica, comedia de situación
six [sɪks] *num* seis
six-pack ['sɪkspæk] *n* (*esp US*) paquete *m* de seis cervezas
sixteen [sɪks'tiːn] *num* dieciséis
sixth [sɪksθ] *adj* sexto; **the upper/lower ~** (*Scol*) el séptimo/sexto año
sixty ['sɪkstɪ] *num* sesenta
size [saɪz] *n* (*gen*) tamaño; (*extent*) extensión *f*; (*of clothing*) talla; (*of shoes*) número; **I take ~ 5 shoes** calzo el número cinco; **I take ~ 14** mi talla es la 42; **I'd like the small/large ~** (*of soap powder etc*) quisiera el tamaño pequeño/grande
▸ **size up** *vt* formarse una idea de

sizeable ['saɪzəbl] *adj* importante, considerable
sizzle ['sɪzl] *vi* crepitar
SK *abbr* (*Canada*) = **Saskatchewan**
skate [skeɪt] *n* patín *m*; (*fish: pl inv*) raya ■ *vi* patinar
▸**skate over, skate round** *vt fus* (*problem, issue*) pasar por alto
skateboard ['skeɪtbɔːd] *n* monopatín *m*
skater ['skeɪtə^r] *n* patinador(a) *m(f)*
skating ['skeɪtɪŋ] *n* patinaje *m*; **figure ~** patinaje *m* artístico
skating rink *n* pista de patinaje
skeleton ['skɛlɪtn] *n* esqueleto; (*Tech*) armazón *m*; (*outline*) esquema *m*
skeleton key *n* llave *f* maestra
skeleton staff *n* personal *m* reducido
skeptic *etc* ['skɛptɪk] (*US*) = **sceptic** *etc*
sketch [skɛtʃ] *n* (*drawing*) dibujo; (*outline*) esbozo, bosquejo; (*Theat*) pieza corta ■ *vt* dibujar; esbozar
sketch book *n* bloc *m* de dibujo
sketching ['skɛtʃɪŋ] *n* dibujo
sketch pad *n* bloc *m* de dibujo
sketchy ['skɛtʃɪ] *adj* incompleto
skewer ['skjuːə^r] *n* broqueta
ski [skiː] *n* esquí *m* ■ *vi* esquiar
ski boot *n* bota de esquí
skid [skɪd] *n* patinazo ■ *vi* patinar; **to go into a ~** comenzar a patinar
skid mark *n* señal *f* de patinazo
skier ['skiːə^r] *n* esquiador(a) *m(f)*
skiing ['skiːɪŋ] *n* esquí *m*; **to go ~** practicar el esquí, (ir a) esquiar
ski instructor *n* instructor(a) *m(f)* de esquí
ski jump *n* pista para salto de esquí
skilful, skillful (US) ['skɪlful] *adj* diestro, experto
skilfully, skillfully (US) ['skɪlfulɪ] *adv* hábilmente, con destreza
ski lift *n* telesilla *m*, telesquí *m*
skill [skɪl] *n* destreza, pericia; (*technique*) arte *m*, técnica; **there's a certain ~ to doing it** se necesita cierta habilidad para hacerlo
skilled [skɪld] *adj* hábil, diestro; (*worker*) cualificado
skillet ['skɪlɪt] *n* sartén *f* pequeña
skillful *etc* ['skɪlful] (US) = **skilful** *etc*
skim [skɪm] *vt* (*milk*) desnatar; (*glide over*) rozar, rasar ■ *vi*: **to ~ through** (*book*) hojear
skimmed milk [skɪmd-] *n* leche *f* desnatada *or* descremada
skimp [skɪmp] *vt* (*work*) chapucear; (*cloth etc*) escatimar; **to ~ on** (*material etc*) economizar; (*work*) escatimar
skimpy ['skɪmpɪ] *adj* (*meagre*) escaso; (*skirt*) muy corto
skin [skɪn] *n* (*gen*) piel *f*; (*complexion*) cutis *m*; (*of fruit, vegetable*) piel *f*, cáscara; (*crust: on pudding, paint*) nata ■ *vt* (*fruit etc*) pelar; (*animal*) despellejar; **wet** *or* **soaked to the ~** calado hasta los huesos
skin cancer *n* cáncer *m* de piel
skin-deep ['skɪn'diːp] *adj* superficial
skin diver *n* buceador(a) *m(f)*
skin diving *n* buceo
skinflint ['skɪnflɪnt] *n* tacaño(-a), roñoso(-a)
skinhead ['skɪnhɛd] *n* cabeza *m/f* rapada, skin(head) *m/f*
skinny ['skɪnɪ] *adj* flaco, magro
skintight ['skɪntaɪt] *adj* (*dress etc*) muy ajustado
skip [skɪp] *n* brinco, salto; (*container*) contenedor *m* ■ *vi* brincar; (*with rope*) saltar a la comba ■ *vt* (*pass over*) omitir, saltar
ski pants *npl* pantalones *mpl* de esquí
ski pole *n* bastón *m* de esquiar
skipper ['skɪpə^r] *n* (*Naut, Sport*) capitán *m*
skipping rope ['skɪpɪŋ-] *n* (*Brit*) comba, cuerda (de saltar)
ski resort *n* estación *f* de esquí
skirmish ['skəːmɪʃ] *n* escaramuza
skirt [skəːt] *n* falda, pollera (*LAm*) ■ *vt* (*surround*) ceñir, rodear; (*go round*) ladear
skirting board ['skəːtɪŋ-] *n* (*Brit*) rodapié *m*
ski run *n* pista de esquí
ski suit *n* traje *m* de esquiar
skit [skɪt] *n* sátira, parodia
ski tow *n* arrastre *m* (de esquí)
skittle ['skɪtl] *n* bolo; **skittles** (*game*) boliche *m*
skive [skaɪv] *vi* (*Brit: col*) gandulear
skulk [skʌlk] *vi* esconderse
skull [skʌl] *n* calavera; (*Anat*) cráneo
skullcap ['skʌlkæp] *n* (*worn by Jews*) casquete *m*; (*worn by Pope*) solideo
skunk [skʌŋk] *n* mofeta
sky [skaɪ] *n* cielo; **to praise sb to the skies** poner a algn por las nubes
sky-blue [skaɪ'bluː] *adj* (azul) celeste
skydiving ['skaɪdaɪvɪŋ] *n* paracaidismo acrobático
sky-high ['skaɪ'haɪ] *adj* (*col*) por las nubes ■ *adv* (*throw*) muy alto; **prices have gone ~** (*col*) los precios están por las nubes
skylark ['skaɪlɑːk] *n* (*bird*) alondra
skylight ['skaɪlaɪt] *n* tragaluz *m*, claraboya
skyline ['skaɪlaɪn] *n* (*horizon*) horizonte *m*; (*of city*) perfil *m*
skyscraper ['skaɪskreɪpə^r] *n* rascacielos *m inv*
slab [slæb] *n* (*stone*) bloque *m*; (*of wood*) tabla, plancha; (*flat*) losa; (*of cake*) trozo; (*of meat, cheese*) tajada, trozo
slack [slæk] *adj* (*loose*) flojo; (*slow*) de poca

actividad; (*careless*) descuidado; (*Comm: market*) poco activo; (*: demand*) débil; (*period*) bajo; **business is ~** hay poco movimiento en el negocio
slacken ['slækn] (*also*: **slacken off**) *vi* aflojarse ▪ *vt* aflojar; (*speed*) disminuir
slackness ['slæknɪs] *n* flojedad *f*; negligencia
slacks [slæks] *npl* pantalones *mpl*
slag [slæg] *n* escoria, escombros *mpl*
slag heap *n* escorial *m*, escombrera
slain [sleɪn] *pp of* **slay**
slake [sleɪk] *vt* (*one's thirst*) apagar
slalom ['slɑːləm] *n* eslálom *m*
slam [slæm] *vt* (*door*) cerrar de golpe; (*throw*) arrojar (violentamente); (*criticize*) vapulear, vituperar ▪ *vi* cerrarse de golpe
slammer [slæmər] *n* (*col*): **the ~** la trena, el talego
slander ['slɑːndər] *n* calumnia, difamación *f* ▪ *vt* calumniar, difamar
slanderous ['slɑːndərəs] *adj* calumnioso, difamatorio
slang [slæŋ] *n* argot *m*; (*jargon*) jerga
slanging match ['slæŋɪŋ-] *n* (*Brit col*) bronca gorda
slant [slɑːnt] *n* sesgo, inclinación *f*; (*fig*) punto de vista; **to get a new ~ on sth** obtener un nuevo punto de vista sobre algo
slanted ['slɑːntɪd], **slanting** ['slɑːntɪŋ] *adj* inclinado
slap [slæp] *n* palmada; (*in face*) bofetada ▪ *vt* dar una palmada/bofetada a ▪ *adv* (*directly*) de lleno
slapdash ['slæpdæʃ] *adj* chapucero
slaphead ['slæphɛd] *n* (*Brit col*) colgado(-a)
slapstick ['slæpstɪk] *n*: **~ comedy** comedia de payasadas
slap-up ['slæpʌp] *adj*: **a ~ meal** (*Brit*) un banquetazo, una comilona
slash [slæʃ] *vt* acuchillar; (*fig: prices*) quemar
slat [slæt] *n* (*of wood, plastic*) tablilla, listón *m*
slate [sleɪt] *n* pizarra ▪ *vt* (*Brit: fig: criticize*) vapulear
slaughter ['slɔːtər] *n* (*of animals*) matanza; (*of people*) carnicería ▪ *vt* matar
slaughterhouse ['slɔːtəhaus] *n* matadero
Slav [slɑːv] *adj* eslavo
slave [sleɪv] *n* esclavo(-a) ▪ *vi* (*also*: **slave away**) trabajar como un negro; **to ~ (away) at sth** trabajar como un negro en algo
slave driver *n* (*col, pej*) tirano(-a)
slave labour, slave labor (*US*) *n* trabajo de esclavos
slaver ['slævər] *vi* (*dribble*) babear
slavery ['sleɪvərɪ] *n* esclavitud *f*
slavish ['sleɪvɪʃ] *adj* (*devotion*) de esclavo; (*imitation*) servil
slay (*pt* **slew**, *pp* **slain**) [sleɪ, sluː, sleɪn] *vt* (*literary*) matar
sleazy ['sliːzɪ] *adj* (*fig: place*) sórdido
sledge [slɛdʒ], **sled** (*US*) [slɛd] *n* trineo
sledgehammer ['slɛdʒhæmər] *n* mazo
sleek [sliːk] *adj* (*shiny*) lustroso
sleep [sliːp] (*pt, pp* **slept**) *n* sueño ▪ *vi* dormir ▪ *vt*: **we can ~ 4** podemos alojar a 4, tenemos cabida para 4; **to go to ~** dormirse; **to have a good night's ~** dormir toda la noche; **to put to ~** (*patient*) dormir; (*animal: euphemism: kill*) sacrificar; **to ~ lightly** tener el sueño ligero; **to ~ with sb** (*euphemism*) acostarse con algn
▸ **sleep in** *vi* (*oversleep*) quedarse dormido
sleeper ['sliːpər] *n* (*person*) durmiente *m/f*; (*Brit Rail: on track*) traviesa; (*: train*) coche-cama *m*
sleepiness ['sliːpɪnɪs] *n* somnolencia
sleeping bag ['sliːpɪŋ-] *n* saco de dormir
sleeping car *n* coche-cama *m*
sleeping partner *n* (*Comm*) socio(-a) comanditario(-a)
sleeping pill *n* somnífero
sleeping sickness *n* enfermedad *f* del sueño
sleepless ['sliːplɪs] *adj*: **a ~ night** una noche en blanco
sleeplessness ['sliːplɪsnɪs] *n* insomnio
sleepover ['sliːpəuvər] *n*: **we're having a ~ at Fiona's** pasamos la noche en casa de Fiona
sleepwalk ['sliːpwɔːk] *vi* caminar dormido; (*habitually*) ser sonámbulo
sleepwalker ['sliːpwɔːkər] *n* sonámbulo(-a)
sleepy ['sliːpɪ] *adj* soñoliento; **to be** *or* **feel ~** tener sueño
sleet [sliːt] *n* aguanieve *f*
sleeve [sliːv] *n* manga; (*Tech*) manguito; (*of record*) funda
sleeveless ['sliːvlɪs] *adj* (*garment*) sin mangas
sleigh [sleɪ] *n* trineo
sleight [slaɪt] *n*: **~ of hand** prestidigitación *f*
slender ['slɛndər] *adj* delgado; (*means*) escaso
slept [slɛpt] *pt, pp of* **sleep**
sleuth [sluːθ] *n* (*col*) detective *m/f*
slew [sluː] *vi* (*veer*) torcerse ▪ *pt of* **slay**
slice [slaɪs] *n* (*of meat*) tajada; (*of bread*) rebanada; (*of lemon*) rodaja; (*utensil*) paleta ▪ *vt* cortar, tajar; rebanar; **sliced bread** pan *m* de molde
slick [slɪk] *adj* (*skilful*) hábil, diestro ▪ *n* (*also*: **oil slick**) capa de aceite
slid [slɪd] *pt, pp of* **slide**
slide [slaɪd] (*pt, pp* **slid**) *n* (*in playground*) tobogán *m*; (*Phot*) diapositiva; (*microscope slide*) portaobjetos *m inv*, plaquilla de vidrio; (*Brit: also*: **hair slide**) pasador *m* ▪ *vt* correr, deslizar ▪ *vi* (*slip*) resbalarse; (*glide*)

deslizarse; **to let things ~** (*fig*) dejar que ruede la bola
slide projector *n* (*Phot*) proyector *m* de diapositivas
slide rule *n* regla de cálculo
sliding ['slaɪdɪŋ] *adj* (*door*) corredizo; **~ roof** (*Aut*) techo de corredera
sliding scale *n* escala móvil
slight [slaɪt] *adj* (*slim*) delgado; (*frail*) delicado; (*pain etc*) leve; (*trifling*) insignificante; (*small*) pequeño ■ *n* desaire *m* ■ *vt* (*offend*) ofender, desairar; **a ~ improvement** una ligera mejora; **not in the slightest** en absoluto; **there's not the slightest possibility** no hay la menor *or* más mínima posibilidad
slightly ['slaɪtlɪ] *adv* ligeramente, un poco; **~ built** delgado
slim [slɪm] *adj* delgado, esbelto ■ *vi* adelgazar
slime [slaɪm] *n* limo, cieno
slimming ['slɪmɪŋ] *n* adelgazamiento ■ *adj* (*diet, pills*) adelgazante
slimness ['slɪmnɪs] *n* delgadez *f*
slimy ['slaɪmɪ] *adj* limoso; (*covered with mud*) fangoso; (*also fig: person*) adulón, zalamero
sling [slɪŋ] *n* (*Med*) cabestrillo; (*weapon*) honda ■ *vt* (*pt, pp* **slung**) [slʌŋ] tirar, arrojar; **to have one's arm in a ~** llevar el brazo en cabestrillo
slink (*pt, pp* **slunk**) [slɪŋk, slʌŋk] *vi*: **to ~ away, ~ off** escabullirse
slinky ['slɪŋkɪ] *adj* (*clothing*) pegado al cuerpo, superajustado
slip [slɪp] *n* (*slide*) resbalón *m*; (*mistake*) descuido; (*underskirt*) combinación *f*; (*of paper*) papelito ■ *vt* (*slide*) deslizar ■ *vi* (*slide*) deslizarse; (*stumble*) resbalar(se); (*decline*) decaer; (*move smoothly*): **to ~ into/out of** (*room etc*) colarse en/salirse de; **to let a chance ~ by** dejar escapar la oportunidad; **to ~ sth on/off** ponerse/quitarse algo; **to ~ on a jumper** ponerse un jersey *or* un suéter; **it slipped from her hand** se la cayó de la mano; **to give sb the ~** dar esquinazo a algn; **wages ~** (*Brit*) hoja del sueldo; **a ~ of the tongue** un lapsus
▸ **slip away** *vi* escabullirse
▸ **slip in** *vt* meter ■ *vi* meterse, colarse
▸ **slip out** *vi* (*go out*) salir (un momento)
slip-on ['slɪpɔn] *adj* de quita y pon; (*shoes*) sin cordones
slipped disc [slɪpt-] *n* vértebra dislocada
slipper ['slɪpəʳ] *n* zapatilla, pantufla
slippery ['slɪpərɪ] *adj* resbaladizo
slip road *n* (*Brit*) carretera de acceso
slipshod ['slɪpʃɔd] *adj* descuidado, chapucero
slipstream ['slɪpstri:m] *n* viento de la hélice
slip-up ['slɪpʌp] *n* (*error*) desliz *m*
slipway ['slɪpweɪ] *n* grada, gradas *fpl*
slit [slɪt] *n* raja; (*cut*) corte *m* ■ *vt* (*pt, pp* **slit**) rajar, cortar; **to ~ sb's throat** cortarle el pescuezo a algn
slither ['slɪðəʳ] *vi* deslizarse
sliver ['slɪvəʳ] *n* (*of glass, wood*) astilla; (*of cheese, sausage*) lonja, loncha
slob [slɔb] *n* (*col*) patán(-ana) *m(f)*, palurdo(-a) *m(f)*
slog [slɔg] (*Brit*) *vi* sudar tinta ■ *n*: **it was a ~** costó trabajo (hacerlo)
slogan ['sləugən] *n* eslogan *m*, lema *m*
slop [slɔp] *vi* (*also*: **slop over**) derramarse, desbordarse ■ *vt* derramar, verter
slope [sləup] *n* (*up*) cuesta, pendiente *f*; (*down*) declive *m*; (*side of mountain*) falda, vertiente *f* ■ *vi*: **to ~ down** estar en declive; **to ~ up** subir (en pendiente)
sloping ['sləupɪŋ] *adj* en pendiente; en declive
sloppily ['slɔpɪlɪ] *adv* descuidadamente; con descuido *or* desaliño
sloppiness ['slɔpɪnɪs] *n* descuido; desaliño
sloppy ['slɔpɪ] *adj* (*work*) descuidado; (*appearance*) desaliñado
slosh [slɔʃ] *vi*: **to ~ about** *or* **around** chapotear
sloshed [slɔʃt] *adj* (*col: drunk*): **to get ~** agarrar una trompa
slot [slɔt] *n* ranura; (*fig: in timetable*) hueco; (*Radio, TV*) espacio ■ *vt*: **to ~ into** encajar en
sloth [sləuθ] *n* (*vice*) pereza; (*Zool*) oso perezoso
slot machine *n* (*Brit: vending machine*) máquina expendedora; (*for gambling*) máquina tragaperras
slot meter *n* contador *m*
slouch [slautʃ] *vi*: **to ~ about, ~ around** (*laze*) gandulear
Slovak ['sləuvæk] *adj* eslovaco ■ *n* eslovaco(-a); (*Ling*) eslovaco; **the ~ Republic** Eslovaquia
Slovakia [sləu'vækɪə] *n* Eslovaquia
Slovakian [sləu'vækɪən] *adj, n* = **Slovak**
Slovene [sləu'vi:n] *adj* esloveno ■ *n* esloveno(-a); (*Ling*) esloveno
Slovenia [sləu'vi:nɪə] *n* Eslovenia
Slovenian [sləu'vi:nɪən] *adj, n* = **Slovene**
slovenly ['slʌvənlɪ] *adj* (*dirty*) desaliñado, desaseado; (*careless*) descuidado
slow [sləu] *adj* lento; (*watch*): **to be ~** estar atrasado ■ *adv* lentamente, despacio ■ *vt* (*also*: **slow down, slow up**) retardar; (*engine, machine*) reducir la marcha de ■ *vi* (*also*: **slow down, slow up**) ir más despacio; **"~"** (*road sign*) "disminuir la velocidad"; **at a ~**

speed a una velocidad lenta; **the ~ lane** el carril derecho; **business is ~** *(Comm)* hay poca actividad; **my watch is 20 minutes ~** mi reloj lleva 20 minutos de retraso; **bake for two hours in a ~ oven** cocer *or* asar dos horas en el horno a fuego lento; **to be ~ to act/decide** tardar en obrar/decidir; **to go ~** *(driver)* conducir despacio; *(in industrial dispute)* trabajar a ritmo lento
slow-acting [sləu'æktɪŋ] *adj* de efecto retardado
slowcoach ['sləukəutʃ] *n (Brit col)* tortuga
slowdown ['sləudaun] *n (US)* huelga de celo
slowly ['sləulɪ] *adv* lentamente, despacio; **to drive ~** conducir despacio; **~ but surely** lento pero seguro
slow motion *n*: **in ~** a cámara lenta
slow-moving ['sləu'mu:vɪŋ] *adj* lento
slowpoke ['sləupəuk] *n (US col)* = **slowcoach**
sludge [slʌdʒ] *n* lodo, fango
slug [slʌg] *n* babosa; *(bullet)* posta
sluggish ['slʌgɪʃ] *adj (slow)* lento; *(lazy)* perezoso; *(business, market, sales)* inactivo
sluggishly ['slʌgɪʃlɪ] *adv* lentamente
sluggishness ['slʌgɪʃnɪs] *n* lentitud *f*
sluice [slu:s] *n (gate)* esclusa; *(channel)* canal *m* ■ *vt*: **to ~ down** *or* **out** regar
slum [slʌm] *n (area)* barrios *mpl* bajos; *(house)* casucha
slumber ['slʌmbə^r] *n* sueño
slum clearance, slum clearance programme *n* (programa *m* de) deschabolización *f*
slump [slʌmp] *n (economic)* depresión *f* ■ *vi* hundirse; **the ~ in the price of copper** la baja repentina del precio del cobre; **he was slumped over the wheel** se había desplomado encima del volante
slung [slʌŋ] *pt, pp of* **sling**
slunk [slʌŋk] *pt, pp of* **slink**
slur [slə:^r] *n* calumnia ■ *vt* calumniar, difamar; *(word)* pronunciar mal; **to cast a ~ on sb** manchar la reputación de algn, difamar a algn
slurp [slə:p] *vt, vi* sorber ruidosamente
slurred [slə:d] *adj (pronunciation)* poco claro
slush [slʌʃ] *n* nieve *f* a medio derretir
slush fund *n* fondos *mpl* para sobornar
slushy ['slʌʃɪ] *adj (col: poetry etc)* sentimentaloide
slut [slʌt] *n* marrana
sly [slaɪ] *adj (clever)* astuto; *(nasty)* malicioso
slyly ['slaɪlɪ] *adv* astutamente; taimadamente
slyness ['slaɪnɪs] *n* astucia
SM *n abbr* = **sadomasochism**
smack [smæk] *n (slap)* manotada; *(blow)* golpe *m* ■ *vt* dar una manotada a; golpear con la mano ■ *vi*: **to ~ of** saber a, oler a ■ *adv*: **it fell ~ in the middle** *(col)* cayó justo en medio
smacker ['smækə^r] *n (col: kiss)* besazo; *(: Brit: pound note)* billete *m* de una libra; *(: US: dollar bill)* billete *m* de un dólar
small [smɔ:l] *adj* pequeño, chico *(LAm)*; *(in height)* bajo, chaparro *(LAm)*; *(letter)* en minúscula ■ *n*: **~ of the back** región *f* lumbar; **~ shopkeeper** pequeño(-a) comerciante *m(f)*; **to get** *or* **grow smaller** *(stain, town)* empequeñecer; *(debt, organization, numbers)* reducir, disminuir; **to make smaller** *(amount, income)* reducir; *(garden, object, garment)* achicar
small ads *npl (Brit)* anuncios *mpl* por palabras
small arms *npl* armas *fpl* cortas
small business *n* pequeño negocio; **small businesses** la pequeña empresa
small change *n* suelto, cambio
smallholder ['smɔ:lhəuldə^r] *n (Brit)* granjero(-a), parcelero(-a)
smallholding ['smɔ:lhəuldɪŋ] *n* parcela, minifundio
small hours *npl*: **in the ~** a altas horas de la noche
smallish ['smɔ:lɪʃ] *adj* más bien pequeño
small-minded [smɔ:l'maɪndɪd] *adj* mezquino, de miras estrechas
smallness ['smɔ:lnɪs] *n* pequeñez *f*
smallpox ['smɔ:lpɔks] *n* viruela
small print *n* letra pequeña *or* menuda
small-scale ['smɔ:lskeɪl] *adj (map, model)* a escala reducida; *(business, farming)* en pequeña escala
small talk *n* cháchara
small-time ['smɔ:ltaɪm] *adj (col)* de poca categoría *or* monta; **a ~ thief** un(a) ratero(-a)
small-town ['smɔ:ltəun] *adj* de provincias
smarmy ['smɑ:mɪ] *adj (Brit pej)* pelotillero *(fam)*
smart [smɑ:t] *adj* elegante; *(clever)* listo, inteligente; *(quick)* rápido, vivo; *(weapon)* inteligente ■ *vi* escocer, picar; **the ~ set** la gente de buen tono; **to look ~** estar elegante; **my eyes are smarting** me pican los ojos
smartcard ['smɑ:tkɑ:d] *n* tarjeta inteligente
smarten up ['smɑ:tn-] *vi* arreglarse ■ *vt* arreglar
smartness ['smɑ:tnɪs] *n* elegancia; *(cleverness)* inteligencia
smash [smæʃ] *n (also*: **smash-up***)* choque *m*; *(sound)* estrépito ■ *vt (break)* hacer pedazos; *(car etc)* estrellar; *(Sport: record)* batir ■ *vi* hacerse pedazos; *(against wall etc)* estrellarse

▸ **smash up** *vt* (*car*) hacer pedazos; (*room*) destrozar
smash hit *n* exitazo
smashing ['smæʃɪŋ] *adj* (*col*) cojonudo
smattering ['smætərɪŋ] *n*: **a ~ of Spanish** algo de español
smear [smɪəʳ] *n* mancha; (*Med*) frotis *m inv* (cervical); (*insult*) calumnia ■ *vt* untar; (*fig*) calumniar, difamar; **his hands were smeared with oil/ink** tenía las manos manchadas de aceite/tinta
smear campaign *n* campaña de calumnias
smear test *n* (*Med*) citología, frotis *m inv* (cervical)
smell [smɛl] (*pt, pp* **smelt** *or* **smelled**) *n* olor *m*; (*sense*) olfato ■ *vt, vi* oler; **it smells good/of garlic** huele bien/a ajo
smelly ['smɛlɪ] *adj* maloliente
smelt [smɛlt] *vt* (*ore*) fundir ■ *pt, pp of* **smell**
smile [smaɪl] *n* sonrisa ■ *vi* sonreír
smiley ['smaɪlɪ] *n* (*in e-mail etc*) smiley *m*, emoticón *m*
smiling ['smaɪlɪŋ] *adj* sonriente, risueño
smirk [smə:k] *n* sonrisa falsa *or* afectada
smith [smɪθ] *n* herrero
smitten ['smɪtn] *adj*: **he's really ~ with her** está totalmente loco por ella
smock [smɔk] *n* blusón; (*children's*) babi *m*; (*US: overall*) guardapolvo, bata
smog [smɔg] *n* smog *m*
smoke [sməuk] *n* humo ■ *vi* fumar; (*chimney*) echar humo ■ *vt* (*cigarettes*) fumar; **to go up in ~** quemarse; (*fig*) quedar en agua de borrajas
smoked [sməukt] *adj* (*bacon, glass*) ahumado
smokeless fuel ['sməuklɪs-] *n* combustible *m* sin humo
smokeless zone ['sməuklɪs-] *n* zona libre de humo
smoker ['sməukəʳ] *n* fumador(a) *m(f)*
smoke screen *n* cortina de humo
smoke shop *n* (US) estanco, tabaquería
smoking ['sməukɪŋ] *n*: **"no ~"** "prohibido fumar"; **he's given up ~** ha dejado de fumar
smoking compartment, smoking car (US) *n* departamento de fumadores
smoky ['sməukɪ] *adj* (*room*) lleno de humo
smolder ['sməuldəʳ] *vi* (US) = **smoulder**
smoochy ['smu:tʃɪ] *adj* (*col*) blandengue
smooth [smu:ð] *adj* liso; (*sea*) tranquilo; (*flavour, movement*) suave; (*person: pej*) meloso ■ *vt* alisar; (*also*: **smooth out**: *creases*) alisar; (*difficulties*) allanar
▸ **smooth over** *vt*: **to ~ things over** (*fig*) limar las asperezas
smoothly ['smu:ðlɪ] *adv* (*easily*) fácilmente; **everything went ~** todo fue sobre ruedas
smoothness ['smu:ðnɪs] *n* (*of skin, cloth*) tersura; (*of surface, flavour, movement*) suavidad *f*
smother ['smʌðəʳ] *vt* sofocar; (*repress*) contener
smoulder, smolder (US) ['sməuldəʳ] *vi* arder sin llama
SMS *n abbr* (= *short message service*) SMS *m*
smudge [smʌdʒ] *n* mancha ■ *vt* manchar
smug [smʌg] *adj* engreído
smuggle ['smʌgl] *vt* pasar de contrabando; **to ~ in/out** (*goods etc*) meter/sacar de contrabando
smuggler ['smʌgləʳ] *n* contrabandista *m/f*
smuggling ['smʌglɪŋ] *n* contrabando
smugly ['smʌglɪ] *adv* con suficiencia
smugness ['smʌgnɪs] *n* suficiencia
smut [smʌt] *n* (*grain of soot*) carbonilla, hollín *m*; (*mark*) tizne *m*; (*in conversation etc*) obscenidades *fpl*
smutty ['smʌtɪ] *adj* (*fig*) verde, obsceno
snack [snæk] *n* bocado, tentempié *m*; **to have a ~** tomar un bocado
snack bar *n* cafetería
snag [snæg] *n* problema *m*; **to run into** *or* **hit a ~** encontrar inconvenientes, dar con un obstáculo
snail [sneɪl] *n* caracol *m*
snake [sneɪk] *n* (*gen*) serpiente *f*; (*harmless*) culebra; (*poisonous*) víbora
snap [snæp] *n* (*sound*) chasquido; golpe *m* seco; (*photograph*) foto *f* ■ *adj* (*decision*) instantáneo ■ *vt* (*fingers etc*) castañetear; (*break*) partir, quebrar; (*photograph*) tomar una foto de ■ *vi* (*break*) partirse, quebrarse; (*fig: person*) contestar bruscamente; **to ~ (at sb)** (*person*) hablar con brusquedad (a algn); (*dog*) intentar morder (a algn); **to ~ shut** cerrarse de golpe; **to ~ one's fingers at sth/sb** (*fig*) burlarse de algo/uno; **a cold ~** (*of weather*) una ola de frío
▸ **snap off** *vi* (*break*) partirse
▸ **snap up** *vt* agarrar
snap fastener *n* (US) botón *m* de presión
snappy ['snæpɪ] *adj* (*col: answer*) instantáneo; (*slogan*) conciso; **make it ~!** (*hurry up*) ¡date prisa!
snapshot ['snæpʃɔt] *n* foto *f* (instantánea)
snare [snɛəʳ] *n* trampa ■ *vt* cazar con trampa; (*fig*) engañar
snarl [snɑ:l] *n* gruñido ■ *vi* gruñir; **to get snarled up** (*wool, plans*) enmarañarse, enredarse; (*traffic*) quedar atascado
snatch [snætʃ] *n* (*fig*) robo; **snatches of** trocitos *mpl* de ■ *vt* (*snatch away*) arrebatar; (*grasp*) coger (SP), agarrar; **snatches of conversation** fragmentos *mpl* de

conversación; **to ~ a sandwich** comer un bocadillo a prisa; **to ~ some sleep** buscar tiempo para dormir; **don't ~!** ¡no me lo quites!

▸ **snatch up** *vt* agarrar

snazzy ['snæzɪ] *adj* (*col*) guapo

sneak [sni:k] *vi*: **to ~ in/out** entrar/salir a hurtadillas ■ *vt*: **to ~ a look at sth** mirar algo de reojo ■ *n* (*fam*) soplón(-ona) *m(f)*

sneakers ['sni:kəz] *npl* (*US*) zapatos *mpl* de lona, zapatillas *fpl*

sneaking ['sni:kɪŋ] *adj*: **to have a ~ feeling/suspicion that ...** tener la sensación/sospecha de que ...

sneaky ['sni:kɪ] *adj* furtivo

sneer [snɪəʳ] *n* sonrisa de desprecio ■ *vi* sonreír con desprecio; **to ~ at sth/sb** burlarse *or* mofarse de algo/uno

sneeze [sni:z] *n* estornudo ■ *vi* estornudar

snide [snaɪd] *adj* (*col: sarcastic*) sarcástico

sniff [snɪf] *vi* sorber (por la nariz) ■ *vt* husmear, oler; (*glue, drug*) esnifar

▸ **sniff at** *vt fus*: **it's not to be sniffed at** no es de despreciar

sniffer dog ['snɪfə-] *n* (*for drugs*) perro antidroga; (*for explosives*) perro antiexplosivos

snigger ['snɪgəʳ] *n* risa disimulada ■ *vi* reírse con disimulo

snip [snɪp] *n* (*piece*) recorte *m*; (*bargain*) ganga ■ *vt* tijeretear

sniper ['snaɪpəʳ] *n* francotirador(a) *m(f)*

snippet ['snɪpɪt] *n* retazo

snivelling, sniveling (*US*) ['snɪvlɪŋ] *adj* llorón(-ona)

snob [snɔb] *n* (e)snob *m/f*

snobbery ['snɔbərɪ] *n* (e)snobismo

snobbish ['snɔbɪʃ] *adj* (e)snob

snobbishness ['snɔbɪʃnɪs] *n* (e)snobismo

snog [snɔg] *vi* (*Brit col*) besuquearse, morrear; **to ~ sb** besuquear a algn

snooker ['snu:kəʳ] *n* snooker *m*

snoop [snu:p] *vi*: **to ~ about** fisgonear

snooper ['snu:pəʳ] *n* fisgón(-ona) *m(f)*

snooty ['snu:tɪ] *adj* (e)snob

snooze [snu:z] *n* siesta ■ *vi* echar una siesta

snore [snɔ:ʳ] *vi* roncar ■ *n* ronquido

snoring ['snɔ:rɪŋ] *n* ronquidos *mpl*

snorkel ['snɔ:kl] *n* tubo de respiración

snort [snɔ:t] *n* bufido ■ *vi* bufar ■ *vt* (*col: drugs*) esnifar

snotty ['snɔtɪ] *adj* (*col*) creído

snout [snaut] *n* hocico, morro

snow [snəu] *n* nieve *f* ■ *vi* nevar ■ *vt*: **to be snowed under with work** estar agobiado de trabajo

snowball ['snəubɔ:l] *n* bola de nieve ■ *vi* ir aumentándose

snow-blind ['snəublaɪnd] *adj* cegado por la nieve

snowbound ['snəubaund] *adj* bloqueado por la nieve

snow-capped ['snəukæpt] *adj* (*peak*) cubierto de nieve, nevado

snowdrift ['snəudrɪft] *n* ventisquero

snowdrop ['snəudrɔp] *n* campanilla

snowfall ['snəufɔ:l] *n* nevada

snowflake ['snəufleɪk] *n* copo de nieve

snowline ['snəulaɪn] *n* límite *m* de las nieves perpetuas

snowman ['snəumæn] *n* figura de nieve

snowplough, snowplow (*US*) ['snəuplau] *n* quitanieves *m inv*

snowshoe ['snəuʃu:] *n* raqueta (de nieve)

snowstorm ['snəustɔ:m] *n* tormenta de nieve, nevasca

Snow White *n* Blancanieves *f*

snowy ['snəuɪ] *adj* de (mucha) nieve

SNP *n abbr* (*Brit Pol*) = **Scottish National Party**

snub [snʌb] *vt*: **to ~ sb** desairar a algn ■ *n* desaire *m*, repulsa

snub-nosed [snʌb'nəuzd] *adj* chato

snuff [snʌf] *n* rapé *m* ■ *vt* (*also*: **snuff out**: *candle*) apagar

snuffbox ['snʌfbɔks] *n* caja de rapé

snuff movie *n* (*col*) película porno (*que acaba con un asesinato real*)

snug [snʌg] *adj* (*cosy*) cómodo; (*fitted*) ajustado

snuggle ['snʌgl] *vi*: **to ~ down in bed** hacerse un ovillo *or* acurrucarse en la cama; **to ~ up to sb** acurrucarse junto a algn

snugly ['snʌglɪ] *adv* cómodamente; **it fits ~** (*object in pocket etc*) cabe perfectamente; (*garment*) ajusta perfectamente

SO *abbr* (*Banking*) = **standing order**

KEYWORD

so [səu] *adv* **1** (*thus, likewise*) así, de este modo; **if so** de ser así; **I like swimming — so do I** a mí me gusta nadar — a mí también; **I've got work to do — so has Paul** tengo trabajo que hacer — Paul también; **it's five o'clock — so it is!** son las cinco — ¡pues es verdad!; **I hope/think so** espero/creo que sí; **so far** hasta ahora; (*in past*) hasta este momento; **so to speak** por decirlo así

2 (*in comparisons etc: to such a degree*) tan; **so quickly (that)** tan rápido (que); **so big (that)** tan grande (que); **she's not so clever as her brother** no es tan lista como su hermano; **we were so worried** estábamos preocupadísimos

3: **so much** *adj* tanto(-a)

■ *adv* tanto; **so many** tantos(-as)
4 (*phrases*): **10 or so** unos 10, 10 o así; **so long!** (*col: goodbye*) ¡hasta luego!; **she didn't so much as send me a birthday card** no me mandó ni una tarjeta siquiera por mi cumpleaños; **so (what)?** (*col*) ¿y (qué)?
■ *conj* **1** (*expressing purpose*): **so as to do** para hacer; **so (that)** para que + *subjun*; **we hurried so (that) we wouldn't be late** nos dimos prisa para no llegar tarde
2 (*expressing result*) así que; **so you see, I could have gone** así que ya ves, (yo) podría haber ido; **so that's the reason!** ¡así que es por eso *or* por eso es!

soak [səuk] *vt* (*drench*) empapar; (*put in water*) remojar ■ *vi* remojarse, estar a remojo
▸**soak in** *vi* penetrar
▸**soak up** *vt* absorber
soaking ['səukɪŋ] *adj* (*also*: **soaking wet**) calado *or* empapado (hasta los huesos *or* el tuétano)
so-and-so ['səuənsəu] *n* (*somebody*) fulano(-a) de tal
soap [səup] *n* jabón *m*
soapbox ['saupbɔks] *n* tribuna improvisada
soapflakes ['səupfleɪks] *npl* jabón *msg* en escamas
soap opera *n* (TV) telenovela; (*Radio*) radionovela
soap powder *n* jabón *m* en polvo
soapsuds ['səupsʌdz] *npl* espuma *sg*
soapy ['səupɪ] *adj* jabonoso
soar [sɔːʳ] *vi* (*on wings*) remontarse; (*building etc*) elevarse; (*price*) subir vertiginosamente; (*morale*) elevarse
soaring ['sɔːrɪŋ] *adj* (*flight*) por lo alto; (*prices*) en alza *or* aumento; **~ inflation** inflación *f* altísima *or* en aumento
sob [sɔb] *n* sollozo ■ *vi* sollozar
s.o.b. *n abbr* (*US col!*: = *son of a bitch*) hijo de puta (*!*)
sober ['səubəʳ] *adj* (*moderate*) moderado; (*serious*) serio; (*not drunk*) sobrio; (*colour, style*) discreto
▸**sober up** *vi* pasársele a algn la borrachera
soberly ['səubəlɪ] *adv* sobriamente
sobriety [sə'braɪətɪ] *n* (*not being drunk*) sobriedad *f*; (*seriousness, sedateness*) seriedad *f*, sensatez *f*
sob story *n* (*col, pej*) dramón *m*
Soc. *abbr* (= *society*) S
so-called ['səu'kɔːld] *adj* presunto, supuesto
soccer ['sɔkəʳ] *n* fútbol *m*
soccer pitch *n* campo *or* cancha (*LAm*) de fútbol
soccer player *n* jugador(a) *m(f)* de fútbol
sociability [səuʃə'bɪlɪtɪ] *n* sociabilidad *f*
sociable ['səuʃəbl] *adj* sociable
social ['səuʃl] *adj* social ■ *n* velada, fiesta
social class *n* clase *f* social
social climber *n* arribista *m/f*
social club *n* club *m*
Social Democrat *n* socialdemócrata *m/f*
social insurance *n* (*US*) seguro social
socialism ['səuʃəlɪzəm] *n* socialismo
socialist ['səuʃəlɪst] *adj, n* socialista *m/f*
socialite ['səuʃəlaɪt] *n persona que alterna con la buena sociedad*
socialize ['səuʃəlaɪz] *vi* hacer vida social; **to ~ with** (*colleagues*) salir con
social life *n* vida social
socially ['səuʃəlɪ] *adv* socialmente
social science *n*, **social sciences** ■ *npl* ciencias *fpl* sociales
social security *n* seguridad *f* social
social services *npl* servicios *mpl* sociales
social welfare *n* asistencia social
social work *n* asistencia social
social worker *n* asistente(-a) *m(f)* social
society [sə'saɪətɪ] *n* sociedad *f*; (*club*) asociación *f*; (*also*: **high society**) buena sociedad ■ *cpd* (*party, column*) social, de sociedad
socio-economic ['səusɪəuiːkə'nɔmɪk] *adj* socioeconómico
sociological [səusɪə'lɔdʒɪkəl] *adj* sociológico
sociologist [səusɪ'ɔlədʒɪst] *n* sociólogo(-a)
sociology [səusɪ'ɔlədʒɪ] *n* sociología
sock [sɔk] *n* calcetín *m*, media (*LAm*); **to pull one's socks up** (*fig*) hacer esfuerzos, despabilarse
socket ['sɔkɪt] *n* (*Elec*) enchufe *m*
sod [sɔd] *n* (*of earth*) césped *m*; (*col!*) cabrón(-ona) *m(f)* (*!*) ■ *excl*: **~ off!** (*col!*) ¡vete a la porra!
soda ['səudə] *n* (*Chem*) sosa; (*also*: **soda water**) soda; (*US*: *also*: **soda pop**) gaseosa
sodden ['sɔdn] *adj* empapado
sodium ['səudɪəm] *n* sodio
sodium chloride *n* cloruro sódico *or* de sodio
sofa ['səufə] *n* sofá *m*
Sofia ['səufɪə] *n* Sofía
soft [sɔft] *adj* (*teacher, parent*) blando; (*gentle, not loud*) suave; (*stupid*) bobo; **~ currency** divisa blanda *or* débil
soft-boiled ['sɔftbɔɪld] *adj* (*egg*) pasado por agua
soft copy *n* (*Comput*) copia transitoria
soft drink *n* bebida no alcohólica
soft drugs *npl* drogas *fpl* blandas
soften ['sɔfn] *vt* ablandar; suavizar ■ *vi* ablandarse; suavizarse
softener ['sɔfnəʳ] *n* suavizante *m*

soft fruit *n* bayas *fpl*
soft furnishings *npl* tejidos *mpl* para el hogar
soft-hearted [sɔft'hɑːtɪd] *adj* bondadoso
softly ['sɔftlɪ] *adv* suavemente; (*gently*) delicadamente, con delicadeza
softness ['sɔftnɪs] *n* blandura; suavidad *f*
soft option *n* alternativa fácil
soft sell *n* venta persuasiva
soft target *n* blanco *or* objetivo fácil
soft toy *n* juguete *m* de peluche
software ['sɔftwɛəʳ] *n* (*Comput*) software *m*
soft water *n* agua blanda
soggy ['sɔgɪ] *adj* empapado
soil [sɔɪl] *n* (*earth*) tierra, suelo ■ *vt* ensuciar
soiled [sɔɪld] *adj* sucio, manchado
sojourn ['sɔdʒəːn] *n* (*formal*) estancia
solace ['sɔlɪs] *n* consuelo
solar ['səuləʳ] *adj* solar
solarium (*pl* **solaria**) [sə'lɛərɪəm, -rɪə] *n* solario
solar panel *n* panel *m* solar
solar plexus [-'plɛksəs] *n* (*Anat*) plexo solar
solar power *n* energía solar
solar system *n* sistema *m* solar
sold [səuld] *pt, pp of* **sell**
solder ['səuldəʳ] *vt* soldar ■ *n* soldadura
soldier ['səuldʒəʳ] *n* (*gen*) soldado; (*army man*) militar *m* ■ *vi*: **to ~ on** seguir adelante; **toy ~** soldadito de plomo
sold out *adj* (*Comm*) agotado
sole [səul] *n* (*of foot*) planta; (*of shoe*) suela; (*fish*: *pl inv*) lenguado ■ *adj* único; **the ~ reason** la única razón
solely ['səullɪ] *adv* únicamente, sólo, solamente; **I will hold you ~ responsible** le consideraré el único responsable
solemn ['sɔləm] *adj* solemne
sole trader *n* (*Comm*) comerciante *m/f* exclusivo(-a)
solicit [sə'lɪsɪt] *vt* (*request*) solicitar ■ *vi* (*prostitute*) abordar clientes
solicitor [sə'lɪsɪtəʳ] *n* abogado(-a); *see also* **barrister**
solid ['sɔlɪd] *adj* sólido; (*gold etc*) macizo; (*line*) continuo; (*vote*) unánime ■ *n* sólido; **we waited two ~ hours** esperamos dos horas enteras; **to be on ~ ground** estar en tierra firme; (*fig*) estar seguro
solidarity [sɔlɪ'dærɪtɪ] *n* solidaridad *f*
solid fuel *n* combustible *m* sólido
solidify [sə'lɪdɪfaɪ] *vi* solidificarse
solidity [sə'lɪdɪtɪ] *n* solidez *f*
solidly ['sɔlɪdlɪ] *adv* sólidamente; (*fig*) unánimemente
solid-state ['sɔlɪdsteɪt] *adj* (*Elec*) estado sólido
soliloquy [sə'lɪləkwɪ] *n* soliloquio
solitaire [sɔlɪ'tɛəʳ] *n* (*game, gem*) solitario
solitary ['sɔlɪtərɪ] *adj* solitario, solo; (*isolated*) apartado, aislado; (*only*) único
solitary confinement *n* incomunicación *f*; **to be in ~** estar incomunicado
solitude ['sɔlɪtjuːd] *n* soledad *f*
solo ['səuləu] *n* solo
soloist ['səuləuɪst] *n* solista *m/f*
Solomon Islands ['sɔləmən-] *npl*: **the ~** las Islas Salomón
solstice ['sɔlstɪs] *n* solsticio
soluble ['sɔljubl] *adj* soluble
solution [sə'luːʃən] *n* solución *f*
solve [sɔlv] *vt* resolver, solucionar
solvency ['sɔlvənsɪ] *n* (*Comm*) solvencia
solvent ['sɔlvənt] *adj* (*Comm*) solvente ■ *n* (*Chem*) solvente *m*
solvent abuse *n* uso indebido de disolventes
Som. *abbr* (*Brit*) = **Somerset**
Somali [sə'mɑːlɪ] *adj, n* somalí *m/f*
Somalia [sə'mɑːlɪə] *n* Somalia
Somaliland [sə'mɑːlɪlænd] *n* Somaliland *f*
sombre, somber (*US*) ['sɔmbəʳ] *adj* sombrío

KEYWORD

some [sʌm] *adj* **1** (*a certain amount or number of*): **some tea/water/biscuits** té/agua/(unas) galletas; **have some tea** tómese un té; **there's some milk in the fridge** hay leche en el frigo; **there were some people outside** había algunas personas fuera; **I've got some money, but not much** tengo algo de dinero, pero no mucho
2 (*certain: in contrasts*) algunos(-as); **some people say that ...** hay quien dice que ...; **some films were excellent, but most were mediocre** hubo películas excelentes, pero la mayoría fueron mediocres
3 (*unspecified*): **some woman was asking for you** una mujer estuvo preguntando por ti; **some day** algún día; **some day next week** un día de la semana que viene; **he was asking for some book (or other)** pedía no se qué libro; **in some way or other** de alguna que otra manera
4 (*considerable amount of*) bastante; **some days ago** hace unos cuantos días; **after some time** pasado algún tiempo; **at some length** con mucho detalle
5 (*col: intensive*): **that was some party!** ¡menuda fiesta!
■ *pron* **1** (*a certain number*): **I've got some** (*books etc*) tengo algunos(-as)
2 (*a certain amount*) algo; **I've got some** (*money, milk*) tengo algo; **would you like some?** (*coffee etc*) ¿quiere un poco?; (*books*

etc) ¿quiere alguno?; **could I have some of that cheese?** ¿me puede dar un poco de ese queso?; **I've read some of the book** he leído parte del libro
■ *adv*: **some 10 people** unas 10 personas, una decena de personas

somebody ['sʌmbədɪ] *pron* alguien; **~ or other** alguien
someday ['sʌmdeɪ] *adv* algún día
somehow ['sʌmhau] *adv* de alguna manera; (*for some reason*) por una u otra razón
someone ['sʌmwʌn] *pron* = **somebody**
someplace ['sʌmpleɪs] *adv* (US) = **somewhere**
somersault ['sʌməsɔːlt] *n* (*deliberate*) salto mortal; (*accidental*) vuelco ■ *vi* dar un salto mortal; dar vuelcos
something ['sʌmθɪŋ] *pron* algo ■ *adv*: **he's ~ like me** es un poco como yo; **~ to do** algo que hacer; **it's ~ of a problem** es bastante problemático
sometime ['sʌmtaɪm] *adv* (*in future*) algún día, en algún momento; **~ last month** durante el mes pasado; **I'll finish it ~** lo terminaré un día de éstos
sometimes ['sʌmtaɪmz] *adv* a veces
somewhat ['sʌmwɔt] *adv* algo
somewhere ['sʌmwɛə^r] *adv* (*be*) en alguna parte; (*go*) a alguna parte; **~ else** (*be*) en otra parte; (*go*) a otra parte
son [sʌn] *n* hijo
sonar ['səunɑː^r] *n* sonar *m*
sonata [sə'nɑːtə] *n* sonata
song [sɔŋ] *n* canción *f*
songwriter ['sɔŋraɪtə^r] *n* compositor(a) *m(f)* de canciones
sonic ['sɔnɪk] *adj* (*boom*) sónico
son-in-law ['sʌnɪnlɔː] *n* yerno
sonnet ['sɔnɪt] *n* soneto
sonny ['sʌnɪ] *n* (*col*) hijo
soon [suːn] *adv* pronto, dentro de poco; **~ afterwards** poco después; **very/quite ~** muy/bastante pronto; **how ~ can you be ready?** ¿cuánto tardas en prepararte?; **it's too ~ to tell** es demasiado pronto para saber; **see you ~!** ¡hasta pronto!; *see also* **as**
sooner ['suːnə^r] *adv* (*time*) antes, más temprano; **I would ~ do that** preferiría hacer eso; **~ or later** tarde o temprano; **no ~ said than done** dicho y hecho; **the ~ the better** cuanto antes mejor; **no ~ had we left than ...** apenas nos habíamos marchado cuando ...
soot [sut] *n* hollín *m*
soothe [suːð] *vt* tranquilizar; (*pain*) aliviar
soothing ['suːðɪŋ] *adj* (*ointment etc*) sedante; (*tone, words etc*) calmante, tranquilizante
SOP *n abbr* = **standard operating procedure**
sophisticated [sə'fɪstɪkeɪtɪd] *adj* sofisticado
sophistication [səfɪstɪ'keɪʃən] *n* sofisticación *f*
sophomore ['sɔfəmɔː^r] *n* (US) estudiante *m/f* de segundo año
soporific [sɔpə'rɪfɪk] *adj* soporífero
sopping ['sɔpɪŋ] *adj*: **~ (wet)** empapado
soppy ['sɔpɪ] *adj* (*pej*) bobo, tonto
soprano [sə'prɑːnəu] *n* soprano *f*
sorbet ['sɔːbeɪ] *n* sorbete *m*
sorcerer ['sɔːsərə^r] *n* hechicero
sordid ['sɔːdɪd] *adj* (*place etc*) sórdido; (*motive etc*) mezquino
sore [sɔː^r] *adj* (*painful*) doloroso, que duele; (*offended*) resentido ■ *n* llaga; **~ throat** dolor *m* de garganta; **my eyes are ~, I have ~ eyes** me duelen los ojos; **it's a ~ point** es un asunto delicado *or* espinoso
sorely *adv*: **I am ~ tempted to (do it)** estoy muy tentado a (hacerlo)
soreness ['sɔːnɪs] *n* dolor *m*
sorrel ['sɔrəl] *n* (*Bot*) acedera
sorrow ['sɔrəu] *n* pena, dolor *m*
sorrowful ['sɔrəuful] *adj* afligido, triste
sorrowfully ['sɔrəufulɪ] *adv* tristemente
sorry ['sɔrɪ] *adj* (*regretful*) arrepentido; (*condition, excuse*) lastimoso; (*sight, failure*) triste; **~!** ¡perdón!, ¡perdone!; **I am ~** lo siento; **I feel ~ for him** me da lástima *or* pena; **I'm ~ to hear that ...** siento saber que ...; **to be ~ about sth** lamentar algo
sort [sɔːt] *n* clase *f*, género, tipo; (*make*: *of coffee, car etc*) marca ■ *vt* (*also*: **sort out**: *papers*) clasificar; (: *problems*) arreglar, solucionar; (*Comput*) clasificar; **what ~ do you want?** (*make*) ¿qué marca quieres?; **what ~ of car?** ¿qué tipo de coche?; **I shall do nothing of the ~** no pienso hacer nada parecido; **it's ~ of awkward** (*col*) es bastante difícil
sortie ['sɔːtɪ] *n* salida
sorting office ['sɔːtɪŋ-] *n* oficina de clasificación del correo
SOS *n* SOS *m*
so-so ['səusəu] *adv* regular, así así
soufflé ['suːfleɪ] *n* suflé *m*
sought [sɔːt] *pt, pp of* **seek**
sought-after ['sɔːtɑːftə^r] *adj* solicitado, codiciado
soul [səul] *n* alma *f*; **God rest his ~** Dios le reciba en su seno *or* en su gloria; **I didn't see a ~** no vi a nadie; **the poor ~ had nowhere to sleep** el pobre no tenía dónde dormir
soul-destroying ['səuldɪstrɔɪɪŋ] *adj* (*work*) deprimente

soulful ['səulful] *adj* lleno de sentimiento
soulmate ['səulmeɪt] *n* compañero(-a) del alma
soul-searching ['səulsəːtʃɪŋ] *n*: **after much ~** después de pensarlo mucho, después de darle muchas vueltas
sound [saund] *adj* (*healthy*) sano; (*safe, not damaged*) en buen estado; (*valid: argument, policy, claim*) válido; (*: move*) acertado; (*dependable: person*) de fiar; (*sensible*) sensato, razonable ■ *adv*: **~ asleep** profundamente dormido ■ *n* (*noise*) sonido, ruido; (*Geo*) estrecho ■ *vt* (*alarm*) sonar; (*also*: **sound out**: *opinions*) consultar, sondear ■ *vi* sonar, resonar; (*fig: seem*) parecer; **to ~ like** sonar a; **to be of ~ mind** estar en su sano juicio; **I don't like the ~ of it** no me gusta nada; **it sounds as if ...** parece que ...
▸ **sound off** *vi* (*col*): **to ~ off (about)** (*give one's opinions*) despotricar (contra)
sound barrier *n* barrera del sonido
sound bite *n* cita jugosa
sound effects *npl* efectos *mpl* sonoros
sound engineer *n* ingeniero(-a) del sonido
sounding ['saundɪŋ] *n* (*Naut etc*) sondeo
sounding board *n* caja de resonancia
soundly ['saundlɪ] *adv* (*sleep*) profundamente; (*beat*) completamente
soundproof ['saundpruːf] *adj* insonorizado
sound system *n* equipo de sonido
soundtrack ['saundtræk] *n* (*of film*) banda sonora
sound wave *n* (*Physics*) onda sonora
soup [suːp] *n* (*thick*) sopa; (*thin*) caldo; **in the ~** (*fig*) en apuros
soup kitchen *n* comedor *m* de beneficencia
soup plate *n* plato sopero
soupspoon ['suːpspuːn] *n* cuchara sopera
sour ['sauəʳ] *adj* agrio; (*milk*) cortado; **it's just ~ grapes!** (*fig*) ¡pura envidia!, ¡están verdes!; **to go** *or* **turn ~** (*milk*) cortarse; (*wine*) agriarse; (*fig: relationship*) agriarse; (*: plans*) irse a pique
source [sɔːs] *n* fuente *f*; **I have it from a reliable ~ that ...** sé de fuente fidedigna que ...
source language *n* (*Comput*) lenguaje *m* fuente *or* de origen
south [sauθ] *n* sur *m* ■ *adj* del sur ■ *adv* al sur, hacia el sur; **(to the) ~ of** al sur de; **the S~ of France** el Sur de Francia; **to travel ~** viajar hacia el sur
South Africa *n* Sudáfrica
South African *adj, n* sudafricano(-a) *m(f)*
South America *n* América del Sur, Sudamérica
South American *adj, n* sudamericano(-a) *m(f)*
southbound ['sauθbaund] *adj* (con) rumbo al sur
south-east [sauθ'iːst] *n* sudeste *m* ■ *adj* (*counties etc*) (del) sudeste
Southeast Asia *n* Sudeste *m* asiático
southerly ['sʌðəlɪ] *adj* sur; (*from the south*) del sur
southern ['sʌðən] *adj* del sur, meridional; **the ~ hemisphere** el hemisferio sur
South Korea *n* Corea del Sur
South Pole *n* Polo Sur
South Sea Islands *npl*: **the ~** Oceanía
South Seas *npl*: **the ~** los Mares del Sur
South Vietnam *n* Vietnam *m* del Sur
southward ['sauθwəd], **southwards** ['sauθwədz] *adv* hacia el sur
south-west [sauθ'wɛst] *n* suroeste *m*
souvenir [suːvə'nɪəʳ] *n* recuerdo
sovereign ['sɔvrɪn] *adj, n* soberano(-a) *m(f)*
sovereignty ['sɔvrɪntɪ] *n* soberanía
soviet ['səuvɪət] *adj* soviético
Soviet Union *n*: **the ~** la Unión Soviética
sow [sau] *n* cerda, puerca ■ *vt* [səu] (*pt* **sowed**, *pp* **sown**) [səun] (*gen*) sembrar; (*spread*) esparcir
soya ['sɔɪə], **soy** (*US*) [sɔɪ] *n* soja
soya bean, soy bean (*US*) *n* semilla de soja
soya sauce, soy sauce (*US*) *n* salsa de soja
sozzled ['sɔzld] *adj* (*Brit col*) mamado
spa [spɑː] *n* balneario
space [speɪs] *n* espacio; (*room*) sitio ■ *vt* (*also*: **space out**) espaciar; **to clear a ~ for sth** hacer sitio para algo; **in a confined ~** en un espacio restringido; **in a short ~ of time** en poco *or* un corto espacio de tiempo; **(with)in the ~ of an hour/three generations** en el espacio de una hora/tres generaciones
space bar *n* (*on typewriter*) barra espaciadora
spacecraft ['speɪskrɑːft] *n* nave *f* espacial, astronave *f*
spaceman ['speɪsmæn] *n* astronauta *m*, cosmonauta *m*
spaceship ['speɪsʃɪp] *n* = **spacecraft**
space shuttle *n* transportador *m* espacial
spacesuit ['speɪssuːt] *n* traje *m* espacial
spacewoman ['speɪswumən] *n* astronauta, cosmonauta
spacing ['speɪsɪŋ] *n* espacio
spacious ['speɪʃəs] *adj* amplio
spade [speɪd] *n* (*tool*) pala; **spades** *npl* (*Cards: British*) picas *fpl*; (*Spanish*) espadas *fpl*
spadework ['speɪdwəːk] *n* (*fig*) trabajo preliminar
spaghetti [spə'gɛtɪ] *n* espaguetis *mpl*
Spain [speɪn] *n* España
spam [spæm] *n* (*junk e-mail*) correo basura

span [spæn] *n* (*of bird, plane*) envergadura; (*of hand*) palmo; (*of arch*) luz *f*; (*in time*) lapso ▪ *vt* extenderse sobre, cruzar; (*fig*) abarcar
Spaniard ['spænjəd] *n* español(a) *m(f)*
spaniel ['spænjəl] *n* perro de aguas
Spanish ['spænɪʃ] *adj* español(a) ▪ *n* (*Ling*) español *m*, castellano; **the Spanish** *npl* (*people*) los españoles; ~ **omelette** tortilla española *or* de patata
spank [spæŋk] *vt* zurrar, dar unos azotes a
spanner ['spænəʳ] *n* (*Brit*) llave *f* inglesa
spar [spɑːʳ] *n* palo, verga ▪ *vi* (*Boxing*) entrenarse (en el boxeo)
spare [spɛəʳ] *adj* de reserva; (*surplus*) sobrante, de más ▪ *n* (*part*) pieza de repuesto ▪ *vt* (*do without*) pasarse sin; (*afford to give*) tener de sobra; (*refrain from hurting*) perdonar; (*details etc*) ahorrar; **to ~** (*surplus*) sobrante, de sobra; **there are two going ~** sobran *or* quedan dos; **to ~ no expense** no escatimar gastos; **can you ~ (me) £10?** ¿puedes prestarme *or* darme 10 libras?; **can you ~ the time?** ¿tienes tiempo?; **I've a few minutes to ~** tengo unos minutos libres; **there is no time to ~** no hay tiempo que perder
spare part *n* pieza de repuesto
spare room *n* cuarto de los invitados
spare time *n* ratos *mpl* de ocio, tiempo libre
spare tyre, spare tire (*US*) *n* (*Aut*) neumático *or* llanta (*LAm*) de recambio
spare wheel *n* (*Aut*) rueda de recambio
sparing ['spɛərɪŋ] *adj*: **to be ~ with** ser parco en
sparingly ['spɛərɪŋlɪ] *adv* escasamente
spark [spɑːk] *n* chispa; (*fig*) chispazo
sparking plug ['spɑːk(ɪŋ)-] *n* = **spark plug**
sparkle ['spɑːkl] *n* centelleo, destello ▪ *vi* centellear; (*shine*) relucir, brillar
sparkler ['spɑːkləʳ] *n* bengala
sparkling ['spɑːklɪŋ] *adj* centelleante; (*wine*) espumoso
spark plug *n* bujía
sparring partner ['spɑːrɪŋ-] *n* sparring *m*; (*fig*) contrincante *m/f*
sparrow ['spærəu] *n* gorrión *m*
sparse [spɑːs] *adj* esparcido, escaso
sparsely ['spɑːslɪ] *adv* escasamente; **a ~ furnished room** un cuarto con pocos muebles
spartan ['spɑːtən] *adj* (*fig*) espartano
spasm ['spæzəm] *n* (*Med*) espasmo; (*fig*) arranque *m*, ataque *m*
spasmodic [spæz'mɔdɪk] *adj* espasmódico
spastic ['spæstɪk] *n* espástico(-a)
spat [spæt] *pt, pp of* **spit** ▪ *n* (*US*) riña
spate [speɪt] *n* (*fig*): **~ of** torrente *m* de; **in ~** (*river*) crecido
spatial ['speɪʃl] *adj* espacial
spatter ['spætəʳ] *vt*: **to ~ with** salpicar de
spatula ['spætjulə] *n* espátula
spawn [spɔːn] *vt* (*pej*) engendrar ▪ *vi* desovar, frezar ▪ *n* huevas *fpl*
SPCA *n abbr* (*US*) = **Society for the Prevention of Cruelty to Animals**
SPCC *n abbr* (*US*) = **Society for the Prevention of Cruelty to Children**
speak (*pt* **spoke**, *pp* **spoken**) [spiːk, spəuk, 'spəukn] *vt* (*language*) hablar; (*truth*) decir ▪ *vi* hablar; (*make a speech*) intervenir; **to ~ one's mind** hablar claro *or* con franqueza; **to ~ to sb/of** *or* **about sth** hablar con algn/de *or* sobre algo; **to ~ at a conference/in a debate** hablar en un congreso/un debate; **he has no money to ~ of** no tiene mucho dinero que digamos; **speaking!** ¡al habla!; **~ up!** ¡habla más alto!
▸ **speak for** *vt fus*: **to ~ for sb** hablar por *or* en nombre de algn; **that picture is already spoken for** (*in shop*) ese cuadro está reservado
speaker ['spiːkəʳ] *n* (*in public*) orador(a) *m(f)*; (*also*: **loudspeaker**) altavoz *m*; (*for stereo etc*) bafle *m*; (*Pol*): **the S~** (*Brit*) *el Presidente de la Cámara de los Comunes*; (*US*) *el Presidente del Congreso*; **are you a Welsh ~?** ¿habla Ud galés?
speaking ['spiːkɪŋ] *adj* hablante
-speaking ['spiːkɪŋ] *suff* -hablante; **Spanish-~ people** los hispanohablantes
spear [spɪəʳ] *n* lanza; (*for fishing*) arpón *m* ▪ *vt* alancear; arponear
spearhead ['spɪəhɛd] *vt* (*attack etc*) encabezar ▪ *n* punta de lanza, vanguardia
spearmint ['spɪəmɪnt] *n* menta verde
spec [spɛk] *n* (*col*): **on ~** por si acaso; **to buy on ~** arriesgarse a comprar
special ['spɛʃl] *adj* especial; (*edition etc*) extraordinario; (*delivery*) urgente ▪ *n* (*train*) tren *m* especial; **nothing ~** nada de particular, nada extraordinario
special agent *n* agente *m/f* especial
special correspondent *n* corresponsal *m/f* especial
special delivery *n* (*Post*): **by ~** por entrega urgente
special effects *npl* (*Cine*) efectos *mpl* especiales
specialist ['spɛʃəlɪst] *n* especialista *m/f*; **a heart ~** (*Med*) un(-a) especialista del corazón
speciality [spɛʃɪ'ælɪtɪ], **specialty** (*US*) ['spɛʃəltɪ] *n* especialidad *f*
specialize ['spɛʃəlaɪz] *vi*: **to ~ (in)** especializarse (en)
specially ['spɛʃlɪ] *adv* especialmente

special offer *n* (*Comm*) oferta especial
special train *n* tren *m* especial
specialty ['spɛʃəltɪ] *n* (*US*) = **speciality**
species ['spi:ʃi:z] *n* especie *f*
specific [spə'sɪfɪk] *adj* específico
specifically [spə'sɪfɪklɪ] *adv* (*explicitly: state, warn*) específicamente, expresamente; (*especially: design, intend*) especialmente
specification [spɛsɪfɪ'keɪʃən] *n* especificación *f*; **specifications** *npl* (*plan*) presupuesto *sg*; (*of car, machine*) descripción *f* técnica; (*for building*) plan *msg* detallado
specify ['spɛsɪfaɪ] *vt, vi* especificar, precisar; **unless otherwise specified** salvo indicaciones contrarias
specimen ['spɛsɪmən] *n* ejemplar *m*; (*Med: of urine*) espécimen *m*; (*: of blood*) muestra
specimen copy *n* ejemplar *m* de muestra
specimen signature *n* muestra de firma
speck [spɛk] *n* grano, mota
speckled ['spɛkld] *adj* moteado
specs [spɛks] *npl* (*col*) gafas *fpl* (*SP*), anteojos *mpl*
spectacle ['spɛktəkl] *n* espectáculo
spectacle case *n* estuche *m* *or* funda (de gafas)
spectacles ['spɛktəklz] *npl* (*Brit*) gafas *fpl* (*SP*), anteojos *mpl*
spectacular [spɛk'tækjulə^r] *adj* espectacular; (*success*) impresionante
spectator [spɛk'teɪtə^r] *n* espectador(a) *m(f)*
spectator sport *n* deporte *m* espectáculo
spectra ['spɛktrə] *npl of* **spectrum**
spectre, specter (*US*) ['spɛktə^r] *n* espectro, fantasma *m*
spectrum (*pl* **spectra**) ['spɛktrəm, -trə] *n* espectro
speculate ['spɛkjuleɪt] *vi* especular; (*try to guess*): **to ~ about** especular sobre
speculation [spɛkju'leɪʃən] *n* especulación *f*
speculative ['spɛkjulətɪv] *adj* especulativo
speculator ['spɛkjuleɪtə^r] *n* especulador(a) *m(f)*
sped [spɛd] *pt, pp of* **speed**
speech [spi:tʃ] *n* (*faculty*) habla; (*formal talk*) discurso; (*words*) palabras *fpl*; (*manner of speaking*) forma de hablar; (*language*) idioma *m*, lenguaje *m*
speech day *n* (*Brit Scol*) ≈ día de reparto de premios
speech impediment *n* defecto del habla
speechless ['spi:tʃlɪs] *adj* mudo, estupefacto
speech therapy *n* logopedia
speed [spi:d] *n* (*also Aut, Tech: gear*) velocidad *f*; (*haste*) prisa; (*promptness*) rapidez *f* ■ *vi* (*pt, pp* **sped**) [spɛd] (*Aut: exceed speed limit*) conducir con exceso de velocidad; **at full** *or* **top ~** a máxima velocidad; **at a ~ of 70 km/h** a una velocidad de 70 km por hora; **at ~** a gran velocidad; **a five-~ gearbox** una caja de cambios de cinco velocidades; **shorthand/typing ~** rapidez *f* en taquigrafía/mecanografía; **the years sped by** los años pasaron volando
▸ **speed up** *vi* acelerarse ■ *vt* acelerar
speedboat ['spi:dbəut] *n* lancha motora
speedily ['spi:dɪlɪ] *adv* rápido, rápidamente
speeding ['spi:dɪŋ] *n* (*Aut*) exceso de velocidad
speed limit *n* límite *m* de velocidad, velocidad *f* máxima
speedometer [spɪ'dɔmɪtə^r] *n* velocímetro
speed trap *n* (*Aut*) control *m* de velocidades
speedway ['spi:dweɪ] *n* (*Sport*) pista de carrera
speedy ['spi:dɪ] *adj* (*fast*) veloz, rápido; (*prompt*) pronto
spell [spɛl] *n* (*also:* **magic spell**) encanto, hechizo; (*period of time*) rato, período; (*turn*) turno ■ *vt* (*pt, pp* **spelt** *or* **spelled**) [spɛlt, spɛld] (*also:* **spell out**) deletrear; (*fig*) anunciar, presagiar; **to cast a ~ on sb** hechizar a algn; **he can't ~** no sabe escribir bien, comete faltas de ortografía; **can you ~ it for me?** ¿cómo se deletrea *or* se escribe?; **how do you ~ your name?** ¿cómo se escribe tu nombre?
spellbound ['spɛlbaund] *adj* embelesado, hechizado
spellchecker *n* (*Comput*) corrector *m* (ortográfico)
spelling ['spɛlɪŋ] *n* ortografía
spelling mistake *n* falta de ortografía
spelt [spɛlt] *pt, pp of* **spell**
spend (*pt, pp* **spent**) [spɛnd, spɛnt] *vt* (*money*) gastar; (*time*) pasar; (*life*) dedicar; **to ~ time/money/effort on sth** gastar tiempo/dinero/energías en algo
spending ['spɛndɪŋ] *n*: **government ~** gastos *mpl* del gobierno
spending money *n* dinero para gastos
spending power *n* poder *m* adquisitivo
spendthrift ['spɛndθrɪft] *n* derrochador(a) *m(f)* manirroto(-a)
spent [spɛnt] *pt, pp of* **spend** ■ *adj* (*cartridge, bullets, match*) usado
sperm [spə:m] *n* esperma
sperm bank *n* banco de esperma
sperm whale *n* cachalote *m*
spew [spju:] *vt* vomitar, arrojar
sphere [sfɪə^r] *n* esfera
spherical ['sfɛrɪkl] *adj* esférico
sphinx [sfɪŋks] *n* esfinge *f*
spice [spaɪs] *n* especia ■ *vt* especiar

spiciness ['spaɪsɪnɪs] *n* lo picante
spick-and-span ['spɪkən'spæn] *adj* impecable
spicy ['spaɪsɪ] *adj* picante
spider ['spaɪdəʳ] *n* araña
spider's web *n* telaraña
spiel [ʃpi:l] *n (col)* rollo
spike [spaɪk] *n (point)* punta; *(Zool)* pincho, púa; *(Bot)* espiga; *(Elec)* pico parásito ■ *vt*: **to ~ a quote** cancelar una cita; **spikes** *npl (Sport)* zapatillas *fpl* con clavos
spiky ['spaɪkɪ] *adj (bush, branch)* cubierto de púas; *(animal)* erizado
spill *(pt, pp* **spilt** *or* **spilled***)* [spɪl, spɪlt, spɪld] *vt* derramar, verter; *(blood)* derramar ■ *vi* derramarse; **to ~ the beans** *(col)* descubrir el pastel
▸ **spill out** *vi* derramarse, desparramarse
▸ **spill over** *vi* desbordarse
spillage ['spɪlɪdʒ] *n (event)* derrame *m*; *(substance)* vertidos
spin [spɪn] *(pt, pp* **spun***) n (revolution of wheel)* vuelta, revolución *f*; *(Aviat)* barrena; *(trip in car)* paseo (en coche) ■ *vt (wool etc)* hilar; *(wheel)* girar ■ *vi* girar, dar vueltas; **the car spun out of control** el coche se descontroló y empezó a dar vueltas
▸ **spin out** *vt* alargar, prolongar
spina bifida ['spaɪnə'bɪfɪdə] *n* espina *f* bífida
spinach ['spɪnɪtʃ] *n* espinacas *fpl*
spinal ['spaɪnl] *adj* espinal
spinal column *n* columna vertebral
spinal cord *n* médula espinal
spin class *n (Sport)* clase *f* de spinning
spindly ['spɪndlɪ] *adj (leg)* zanquivano
spin doctor *n (col) informador(a) parcial al servicio de un partido político*
spin-dry ['spɪn'draɪ] *vt* centrifugar
spin-dryer [spɪn'draɪəʳ] *n (Brit)* secadora centrífuga
spine [spaɪn] *n* espinazo, columna vertebral; *(thorn)* espina
spine-chilling ['spaɪntʃɪlɪŋ] *adj* terrorífico
spineless ['spaɪnlɪs] *adj (fig)* débil, flojo
spinet [spɪ'nɛt] *n* espineta
spinning ['spɪnɪŋ] *n (of thread)* hilado; *(art)* hilandería; *(Sport)* spinning *m*
spinning top *n* peonza
spinning wheel *n* rueca, torno de hilar
spin-off ['spɪnɔf] *n* derivado, producto secundario
spinster ['spɪnstəʳ] *n* soltera; *(pej)* solterona
spiral ['spaɪərl] *n* espiral *f* ■ *adj* en espiral ■ *vi (prices)* dispararse; **the inflationary ~** la espiral inflacionista
spiral staircase *n* escalera de caracol
spire ['spaɪəʳ] *n* aguja, chapitel *m*
spirit ['spɪrɪt] *n (soul)* alma *f*; *(ghost)* fantasma *m*; *(attitude)* espíritu *m*; *(courage)* valor *m*, ánimo; **spirits** *npl (drink)* alcohol *msg*, bebidas *fpl* alcohólicas; **in good spirits** alegre, de buen ánimo; **Holy S~** Espíritu *m* Santo; **community ~, public ~** civismo
spirit duplicator *n* copiadora al alcohol
spirited ['spɪrɪtɪd] *adj* enérgico, vigoroso
spirit level *n* nivel *m* de aire
spiritual ['spɪrɪtjuəl] *adj* espiritual ■ *n (also:* **Negro spiritual***)* canción *f* religiosa, espiritual *m*
spiritualism ['spɪrɪtjuəlɪzəm] *n* espiritualismo
spit [spɪt] *n (for roasting)* asador *m*, espetón *m*; *(spittle)* esputo, escupitajo; *(saliva)* saliva ■ *vi (pt, pp* **spat***)* [spæt] escupir; *(sound)* chisporrotear
spite [spaɪt] *n* rencor *m*, ojeriza ■ *vt* fastidiar; **in ~ of** a pesar de, pese a
spiteful ['spaɪtful] *adj* rencoroso, malévolo
spitting ['spɪtɪŋ] *n*: **"~ prohibited"** "se prohíbe escupir" ■ *adj*: **to be the ~ image of sb** ser la viva imagen de algn
spittle ['spɪtl] *n* saliva, baba
splash [splæʃ] *n (sound)* chapoteo; *(of colour)* mancha ■ *vt* salpicar de ■ *vi (also:* **splash about***)* chapotear; **to ~ paint on the floor** manchar el suelo de pintura
splashdown ['splæʃdaun] *n* amaraje *m*, amerizaje *m*
spleen [spli:n] *n (Anat)* bazo
splendid ['splɛndɪd] *adj* espléndido
splendidly ['splɛndɪdlɪ] *adv* espléndidamente; **everything went ~** todo fue a las mil maravillas
splendour, splendor *(US)* ['splɛndəʳ] *n* esplendor *m*; *(fig)* brillo, gloria
splice [splaɪs] *vt* empalmar
splint [splɪnt] *n* tablilla
splinter ['splɪntəʳ] *n* astilla ■ *vi* astillarse, hacer astillas
splinter group *n* grupo disidente, facción *f*
split [splɪt] *(pt, pp* **~***) n* hendedura, raja; *(fig)* división *f*; *(Pol)* escisión *f* ■ *vt* partir, rajar; *(party)* dividir; *(work, profits)* repartir ■ *vi (divide)* dividirse, escindirse; **to ~ the difference** partir la diferencia; **to do the splits** hacer el spagat; **to ~ sth down the middle** *(also fig)* dividir algo en dos
▸ **split up** *vi (couple)* separarse, romper; *(meeting)* acabarse
split-level ['splɪtlɛvl] *adj (house)* dúplex
split peas *npl* guisantes *mpl* secos
split personality *n* doble personalidad *f*
split second *n* fracción *f* de segundo
splitting ['splɪtɪŋ] *adj (headache)* horrible

splutter ['splʌtəʳ] *vi* chisporrotear; (*person*) balbucear
spoil (*pt, pp* **spoilt** *or* **spoiled**) [spɔɪl, spɔɪlt, spɔɪld] *vt* (*damage*) dañar; (*ruin*) estropear, echar a perder; (*child*) mimar, consentir; (*ballot paper*) invalidar ■ *vi*: **to be spoiling for a fight** estar con ganas de lucha, andar con ganas de pelea
spoiled [spɔɪld] *adj* (*US: food: bad*) pasado, malo; (*milk*) cortado
spoils [spɔɪlz] *npl* despojo *sg*, botín *msg*
spoilsport ['spɔɪlspɔ:t] *n* aguafiestas *m inv*
spoilt [spɔɪlt] *pt, pp of* **spoil** ■ *adj* (*child*) mimado, consentido; (*ballot paper*) invalidado
spoke [spəuk] *pt of* **speak** ■ *n* rayo, radio
spoken ['spəukn] *pp of* **speak**
spokesman ['spəuksmən] *n* portavoz *m*, vocero (*LAm*)
spokesperson ['spəukspə:sn] *n* portavoz *m/f*, vocero(-a) (*LAm*)
spokeswoman ['spəukswumən] *n* portavoz *f*, vocera (*LAm*)
sponge [spʌndʒ] *n* esponja; (*Culin: also:* **sponge cake**) bizcocho ■ *vt* (*wash*) lavar con esponja ■ *vi*: **to ~ on** *or* (*US*) **off sb** vivir a costa de algn
sponge bag *n* (*Brit*) neceser *m*
sponge cake *n* bizcocho, pastel *m*
sponger ['spʌndʒəʳ] *n* gorrón(-ona) *m(f)*
spongy ['spʌndʒɪ] *adj* esponjoso
sponsor ['spɔnsəʳ] *n* (*Radio, TV*) patrocinador(a) *m(f)*; (*for membership*) padrino/madrina; (*Comm*) fiador(a) *m(f)*, avalador(a) *m(f)* ■ *vt* patrocinar; apadrinar; (*parliamentary bill*) apoyar, respaldar; (*idea etc*) presentar, promover; **I sponsored him at 3p a mile** (*in fund-raising race*) me apunté para darle 3 peniques la milla
sponsorship ['spɔnsəʃɪp] *n* patrocinio
spontaneity [spɔntə'neɪɪtɪ] *n* espontaneidad *f*
spontaneous [spɔn'teɪnɪəs] *adj* espontáneo
spontaneously [spɔn'teɪnɪəslɪ] *adv* espontáneamente
spooky ['spu:kɪ] *adj* (*col: place, atmosphere*) espeluznante, horripilante
spool [spu:l] *n* carrete *m*; (*of sewing machine*) canilla
spoon [spu:n] *n* cuchara
spoon-feed ['spu:nfi:d] *vt* dar de comer con cuchara a; (*fig*) dárselo todo mascado a
spoonful ['spu:nful] *n* cucharada
sporadic [spə'rædɪk] *adj* esporádico
sport [spɔ:t] *n* deporte *m*; (*person*) buen(a) perdedor(a) *m/f*; (*amusement*) juego, diversión *f*; **indoor/outdoor sports** deportes *mpl* en sala cubierta/al aire libre; **to say sth in ~** decir algo en broma
sport coat *n* (*US*) = **sports jacket**
sporting ['spɔ:tɪŋ] *adj* deportivo; **to give sb a ~ chance** darle a algn su oportunidad
sports car *n* coche *m* sport
sports coat *n* (*US*) = **sports jacket**
sports ground *n* campo de deportes, centro deportivo
sports jacket, sport jacket (*US*) *n* chaqueta deportiva
sportsman ['spɔ:tsmən] *n* deportista *m*
sportsmanship ['spɔ:tsmənʃɪp] *n* deportividad *f*
sports pages *npl* páginas *fpl* deportivas
sportswear ['spɔ:tswɛəʳ] *n* ropa de deporte
sportswoman ['spɔ:tswumən] *n* deportista
sporty ['spɔ:tɪ] *adj* deportivo
spot [spɔt] *n* sitio, lugar *m*; (*dot: on pattern*) punto, mancha; (*pimple*) grano; (*also:* **advertising spot**) spot *m*; (*small amount*): **a ~ of** un poquito de ■ *vt* (*notice*) notar, observar ■ *adj* (*Comm*) inmediatamente efectivo; **on the ~** en el acto, acto seguido; (*in difficulty*) en un aprieto; **to do sth on the ~** hacer algo en el acto; **to put sb on the ~** poner a algn en un apuro
spot check *n* reconocimiento rápido
spotless ['spɔtlɪs] *adj* (*clean*) inmaculado; (*reputation*) intachable
spotlessly ['spɔtlɪslɪ] *adv*: **~ clean** limpísimo
spotlight ['spɔtlaɪt] *n* foco, reflector *m*; (*Aut*) faro auxiliar
spot-on [spɔt'ɔn] *adj* (*Brit col*) exacto
spot price *n* precio de entrega inmediata
spotted ['spɔtɪd] *adj* (*pattern*) de puntos
spotty ['spɔtɪ] *adj* (*face*) con granos
spouse [spauz] *n* cónyuge *m/f*
spout [spaut] *n* (*of jug*) pico; (*pipe*) caño ■ *vi* chorrear
sprain [spreɪn] *n* torcedura, esguince *m* ■ *vt*: **to ~ one's ankle** torcerse el tobillo
sprang [spræŋ] *pt of* **spring**
sprawl [sprɔ:l] *vi* tumbarse ■ *n*: **urban ~** crecimiento urbano descontrolado; **to send sb sprawling** tirar a algn al suelo
sprawling ['sprɔ:lɪŋ] *adj* (*town*) desparramado
spray [spreɪ] *n* rociada; (*of sea*) espuma; (*container*) atomizador *m*; (*of paint*) pistola rociadora; (*of flowers*) ramita ■ *vt* rociar; (*crops*) regar ■ *cpd* (*deodorant*) en atomizador
spread [sprɛd] (*pt, pp* **~**) *n* extensión *f*; (*of idea*) diseminación *f*; (*col: food*) comilona; (*Press, Typ: two pages*) plana ■ *vt* extender; diseminar; (*butter*) untar; (*wings, sails*) desplegar; (*scatter*) esparcir ■ *vi* extenderse; diseminarse; untarse; desplegarse;

esparcirse; **middle-age ~** gordura de la mediana edad; **repayments will be ~ over 18 months** los pagos se harán a lo largo de 18 meses

spread-eagled ['sprɛdi:gld] *adj*: **to be ~** estar despatarrado

spreadsheet ['sprɛdʃi:t] *n* (*Comput*) hoja de cálculo

spree [spri:] *n*: **to go on a ~** ir de juerga *or* farra (*LAm*)

sprightly ['spraɪtlɪ] *adj* vivo, enérgico

spring [sprɪŋ] (*pt* **sprang**, *pp* **sprung**) *n* (*season*) primavera; (*leap*) salto, brinco; (*coiled metal*) resorte *m*; (*of water*) fuente *f*, manantial *m*; (*bounciness*) elasticidad *f* ■ *vi* (*arise*) brotar, nacer; (*leap*) saltar, brincar ■ *vt*: **to ~ a leak** (*pipe etc*) empezar a hacer agua; **he sprang the news on me** de repente me soltó la noticia; **in (the) ~** en (la) primavera; **to walk with a ~ in one's step** andar dando saltos *or* brincos; **to ~ into action** lanzarse a la acción
▸ **spring up** *vi* (*problem*) surgir

springboard ['sprɪŋbɔ:d] *n* trampolín *m*

spring-clean [sprɪŋ'kli:n] *n* (*also*: **spring-cleaning**) limpieza general

spring onion *n* cebolleta

spring roll *n* rollito de primavera

springtime ['sprɪŋtaɪm] *n* primavera

springy ['sprɪŋɪ] *adj* elástico; (*grass*) mullido

sprinkle ['sprɪŋkl] *vt* (*pour*) rociar; **to ~ water on, ~ with water** rociar *or* salpicar de agua

sprinkler ['sprɪŋklər] *n* (*for lawn*) aspersor *m*; (*to put out fire*) aparato de rociadura automática

sprinkling ['sprɪŋklɪŋ] *n* (*of water*) rociada; (*of salt, sugar*) un poco de

sprint [sprɪnt] *n* (e)sprint *m* ■ *vi* (*gen*) correr a toda velocidad; (*Sport*) esprintar; **the 200 metres ~** el (e)sprint de 200 metros

sprinter ['sprɪntər] *n* velocista *m/f*

spritzer ['sprɪtsər] *n* vino blanco con soda

sprocket ['sprɔkɪt] *n* (*on printer etc*) rueda dentada

sprocket feed *n* avance *m* por rueda dentada

sprout [spraut] *vi* brotar, retoñar ■ *n*: **(Brussels) sprouts** *npl* coles *fpl* de Bruselas

spruce [spru:s] *n* (*Bot*) pícea ■ *adj* aseado, pulcro
▸ **spruce up** *vt* (*tidy*) arreglar, acicalar; (*smarten up: room etc*) ordenar; **to ~ o.s. up** arreglarse

sprung [sprʌŋ] *pp of* **spring**

spry [spraɪ] *adj* ágil, activo

SPUC *n abbr* (= *Society for the Protection of Unborn Children*) ≈ Federación *f* Española de Asociaciones Provida

spun [spʌn] *pt, pp of* **spin**

spur [spə:r] *n* espuela; (*fig*) estímulo, aguijón *m* ■ *vt* (*also*: **spur on**) estimular, incitar; **on the ~ of the moment** de improviso

spurious ['spjuərɪəs] *adj* falso

spurn [spə:n] *vt* desdeñar, rechazar

spurt [spə:t] *n* chorro; (*of energy*) arrebato ■ *vi* chorrear; **to put in** *or* **on a ~** (*runner*) acelerar; (*fig: in work etc*) hacer un gran esfuerzo

sputter ['spʌtər] *vi* = **splutter**

spy [spaɪ] *n* espía *m/f* ■ *vi*: **to ~ on** espiar a ■ *vt* (*see*) divisar, lograr ver ■ *cpd* (*film, story*) de espionaje

spying ['spaɪɪŋ] *n* espionaje *m*

Sq. *abbr* (*in address*: = *Square*) Pl.

sq. *abbr* (*Math etc*) = **square**

squabble ['skwɔbl] *n* riña, pelea ■ *vi* reñir, pelear

squad [skwɔd] *n* (*Mil*) pelotón *m*; (*Police*) brigada; (*Sport*) equipo; **flying ~** (*Police*) brigada móvil

squad car *n* (*Police*) coche-patrulla *m*

squaddie ['skwɔdɪ] *n* (*Mil: col*) chivo

squadron ['skwɔdrn] *n* (*Mil*) escuadrón *m*; (*Aviat, Naut*) escuadra

squalid ['skwɔlɪd] *adj* miserable

squall [skwɔ:l] *n* (*storm*) chubasco; (*wind*) ráfaga

squalor ['skwɔlər] *n* miseria

squander ['skwɔndər] *vt* (*money*) derrochar, despilfarrar; (*chances*) desperdiciar

square [skwɛər] *n* cuadro; (*in town*) plaza; (*US: block of houses*) manzana, cuadra (*LAm*) ■ *adj* cuadrado ■ *vt* (*arrange*) arreglar; (*Math*) cuadrar; (*reconcile*): **can you ~ it with your conscience?** ¿cómo se justifica ante sí mismo? ■ *vi* cuadrar, conformarse; **all ~** igual(es); **a ~ meal** una comida decente; **two metres ~** dos metros por dos; **one ~ metre** un metro cuadrado; **to get one's accounts ~** dejar las cuentas claras; **I'll ~ it with him** (*col*) yo lo arreglo con él; **we're back to ~ one** (*fig*) hemos vuelto al punto de partida
▸ **square up** *vi* (*settle*): **to ~ up (with sb)** ajustar cuentas (con algn)

square bracket *n* (*Typ*) corchete *m*

squarely ['skwɛəlɪ] *adv* (*fully*) de lleno; (*honestly, fairly*) honradamente, justamente

square root *n* raíz *f* cuadrada

squash [skwɔʃ] *n* (*vegetable*) calabaza; (*Sport*) squash *m*; (*Brit: drink*): **lemon/orange ~** zumo (*SP*) *or* jugo (*LAm*) de limón/naranja ■ *vt* aplastar

squat [skwɔt] *adj* achaparrado ■ *vi* agacharse, sentarse en cuclillas; (*on property*) ocupar ilegalmente

squatter ['skwɔtər] *n* ocupante *m/f* ilegal, okupa *m/f*

squawk [skwɔ:k] *vi* graznar
squeak [skwi:k] *vi* (*hinge, wheel*) chirriar, rechinar; (*shoe, wood*) crujir ■ *n* (*of hinge, wheel etc*) chirrido, rechinamiento; (*of shoes*) crujir *m*; (*of mouse etc*) chillido
squeaky ['skwi:kɪ] *adj* que cruje; **to be ~ clean** (*fig*) ser superhonrado
squeal [skwi:l] *vi* chillar, dar gritos agudos
squeamish ['skwi:mɪʃ] *adj* delicado, remilgado
squeeze [skwi:z] *n* presión *f*; (*of hand*) apretón *m*; (*Comm: credit squeeze*) restricción *f* ■ *vt* (*lemon etc*) exprimir; (*hand, arm*) apretar; **a ~ of lemon** unas gotas de limón; **to ~ past/under sth** colarse al lado de/por debajo de algo
▸ **squeeze out** *vt* exprimir; (*fig*) excluir
▸ **squeeze through** *vi* abrirse paso con esfuerzos
squelch [skwɛltʃ] *vi* chapotear
squid [skwɪd] *n* calamar *m*
squiggle ['skwɪgl] *n* garabato
squint [skwɪnt] *vi* entrecerrar los ojos ■ *n* (*Med*) estrabismo; **to ~ at sth** mirar algo entornando los ojos
squire ['skwaɪə^r] *n* (*Brit*) terrateniente *m*
squirm [skwə:m] *vi* retorcerse, revolverse
squirrel ['skwɪrəl] *n* ardilla
squirt [skwə:t] *vi* salir a chorros
Sr *abbr* = **senior**; (*Rel*) = **sister**
SRC *n abbr* (*Brit: = Students' Representative Council*) *consejo de estudiantes*
Sri Lanka [srɪ'læŋkə] *n* Sri Lanka *m*
SRO *abbr* (*US*) = **standing room only**
SS *abbr* (*= steamship*) M.V.
SSA *n abbr* (*US: = Social Security Administration*) ≈ Seguro Social
SST *n abbr* (*US*) = **supersonic transport**
ST *abbr* (*US: = Standard Time*) *hora oficial*
St *abbr* (*= saint*) Sto.(-a); (*= street*) c/
stab [stæb] *n* (*with knife etc*) puñalada; (*of pain*) pinchazo; **to have a ~ at (doing) sth** (*col*) probar (a hacer) algo ■ *vt* apuñalar; **to ~ sb to death** matar a algn a puñaladas
stabbing ['stæbɪŋ] *n*: **there's been a ~** han apuñalado a alguien ■ *adj* (*pain*) punzante
stability [stə'bɪlɪtɪ] *n* estabilidad *f*
stabilization [steɪbəlaɪ'zeɪʃən] *n* estabilización *f*
stabilize ['steɪbəlaɪz] *vt* estabilizar ■ *vi* estabilizarse
stabilizer ['steɪbəlaɪzə^r] *n* (*Aviat, Naut*) estabilizador *m*
stable ['steɪbl] *adj* estable ■ *n* cuadra, caballeriza; **riding stables** escuela hípica
staccato [stə'kɑ:təu] *adj, adv* staccato
stack [stæk] *n* montón *m*, pila; (*col*) mar *f* ■ *vt* amontonar, apilar; **there's stacks of time to finish it** hay cantidad de tiempo para acabarlo
stacker ['stækə^r] *n* (*for printer*) apiladora
stadium ['steɪdɪəm] *n* estadio
staff [stɑ:f] *n* (*work force*) personal *m*, plantilla; (*Brit Scol: also*: **teaching staff**) cuerpo docente; (*stick*) bastón *m* ■ *vt* proveer de personal; **to be staffed by Asians/women** tener una plantilla asiática/femenina
staffroom ['stɑ:fru:m] *n* sala de profesores
Staffs *abbr* (*Brit*) = **Staffordshire**
stag [stæg] *n* ciervo, venado; (*Brit Stock Exchange*) especulador *m* con nuevas emisiones
stage [steɪdʒ] *n* escena; (*point*) etapa; (*platform*) plataforma; **the ~** el escenario, el teatro ■ *vt* (*play*) poner en escena, representar; (*organize*) montar, organizar; (*fig: perform: recovery etc*) efectuar; **in stages** por etapas; **in the early/final stages** en las primeras/últimas etapas; **to go through a difficult ~** pasar una fase *or* etapa mala
stagecoach ['steɪdʒkəutʃ] *n* diligencia
stage door *n* entrada de artistas
stagehand ['steɪdʒhænd] *n* tramoyista *m/f*
stage-manage ['steɪdʒmænɪdʒ] *vt* (*fig*) manipular
stage manager *n* director(a) *m(f)* de escena
stagger ['stægə^r] *vi* tambalear ■ *vt* (*amaze*) asombrar; (*hours, holidays*) escalonar
staggering ['stægərɪŋ] *adj* (*amazing*) asombroso, pasmoso
staging post ['steɪdʒɪŋ-] *n* escala
stagnant ['stægnənt] *adj* estancado
stagnate [stæg'neɪt] *vi* estancarse; (*fig: economy, mind*) quedarse estancado
stagnation [stæg'neɪʃən] *n* estancamiento
stag night, stag party *n* despedida de soltero
staid [steɪd] *adj* (*clothes*) serio, formal
stain [steɪn] *n* mancha; (*colouring*) tintura ■ *vt* manchar; (*wood*) teñir
stained glass window [steɪnd-] *n* vidriera de colores
stainless ['steɪnlɪs] *adj* (*steel*) inoxidable
stain remover *n* quitamanchas *m inv*
stair [stɛə^r] *n* (*step*) peldaño, escalón *m*; **stairs** *npl* escaleras *fpl*
staircase ['stɛəkeɪs], **stairway** ['stɛəweɪ] *n* escalera
stairwell ['stɛəwɛl] *n* hueco *or* caja de la escalera
stake [steɪk] *n* estaca, poste *m*; (*Betting*) apuesta ■ *vt* (*bet*) apostar; (*also*: **stake out**: *area*) cercar con estacas; **to be at ~** estar en juego; **to have a ~ in sth** tener interés

en algo; **to ~ a claim to (sth)** presentar reclamación por *or* reclamar (algo)
stake-out ['steɪkaut] *n* vigilancia; **to be on a** ~ estar de vigilancia
stalactite ['stæləktaɪt] *n* estalactita
stalagmite ['stæləgmaɪt] *n* estalagmita
stale [steɪl] *adj* *(bread)* duro; *(food)* pasado
stalemate ['steɪlmeɪt] *n* tablas *fpl*; **to reach ~** *(fig)* estancarse, alcanzar un punto muerto
stalk [stɔ:k] *n* tallo, caña ■ *vt* acechar, cazar al acecho; **to ~ off** irse airado
stall [stɔ:l] *n* *(in market)* puesto; *(in stable)* casilla (de establo) ■ *vt* *(Aut)* parar, calar ■ *vi* *(Aut)* pararse, calarse; *(fig)* buscar evasivas; **stalls** *npl* *(Brit: in cinema, theatre)* butacas *fpl*; **a newspaper ~** un quiosco (de periódicos); **a flower ~** un puesto de flores
stallholder ['stɔ:lhəuldə^r] *n* dueño(-a) de un puesto
stallion ['stælɪən] *n* semental *m*, garañón *m*
stalwart ['stɔ:lwət] *n* partidario(-a) incondicional
stamen ['steɪmən] *n* estambre *m*
stamina ['stæmɪnə] *n* resistencia
stammer ['stæmə^r] *n* tartamudeo, balbuceo ■ *vi* tartamudear, balbucir
stamp [stæmp] *n* sello, estampilla *(LAm)*; *(mark)* marca, huella; *(on document)* timbre *m* ■ *vi* *(also:* **stamp one's foot***)* patear ■ *vt* patear, golpear con el pie; *(letter)* poner sellos en; *(with rubber stamp)* marcar con sello; **stamped addressed envelope (sae)** sobre *m* sellado con las señas propias
▸ **stamp out** *vt* *(fire)* apagar con el pie; *(crime, opposition)* acabar con
stamp album *n* álbum *m* para sellos
stamp collecting *n* filatelia
stamp duty *n* *(Brit)* derecho de timbre
stampede [stæm'pi:d] *n* *(of cattle)* estampida
stamp machine *n* máquina (expendedora) de sellos
stance [stæns] *n* postura
stand [stænd] *(pt, pp* **stood***)* *n* *(attitude)* posición *f*, postura; *(for taxis)* parada; *(also:* **music stand***)* atril *m*; *(Sport)* tribuna; *(at exhibition)* stand *m* ■ *vi* *(be)* estar, encontrarse; *(be on foot)* estar de pie; *(rise)* levantarse; *(remain)* quedar en pie ■ *vt* *(place)* poner, colocar; *(tolerate, withstand)* aguantar, soportar; **to make a ~** resistir; *(fig)* mantener una postura firme; **to take a ~ on an issue** adoptar una actitud hacia una cuestión; **to ~ for parliament** *(Brit)* presentarse (como candidato) a las elecciones; **nothing stands in our way** nada nos lo impide; **to ~ still** quedarse inmóvil; **to let sth ~ as it is** dejar algo como está; **as things ~** tal como están las cosas; **to ~ sb a drink/meal** invitar a algn a una copa/a comer; **the company will have to ~ the loss** la empresa tendrá que hacer frente a las pérdidas; **I can't ~ him** no le aguanto, no le puedo ver; **to ~ guard** *or* **watch** *(Mil)* hacer guardia
▸ **stand aside** *vi* apartarse, mantenerse aparte
▸ **stand by** *vi* *(be ready)* estar listo ■ *vt fus* *(opinion)* mantener
▸ **stand down** *vi* *(withdraw)* ceder el puesto; *(Mil, Law)* retirarse
▸ **stand for** *vt fus* *(signify)* significar; *(tolerate)* aguantar, permitir
▸ **stand in for** *vt fus* suplir a
▸ **stand out** *vi* *(be prominent)* destacarse
▸ **stand up** *vi* *(rise)* levantarse, ponerse de pie
▸ **stand up for** *vt fus* defender
▸ **stand up to** *vt fus* hacer frente a
stand-alone ['stændələun] *adj* *(Comput)* autónomo
standard ['stændəd] *n* patrón *m*, norma; *(flag)* estandarte *m* ■ *adj* *(size etc)* normal, corriente, estándar; **standards** *npl* *(morals)* valores *mpl* morales; **the gold ~** *(Comm)* el patrón oro; **high/low ~** de alto/bajo nivel; **below** *or* **not up to ~** *(work)* de calidad inferior; **to be** *or* **come up to ~** satisfacer los requisitos; **to apply a double ~** aplicar un doble criterio
Standard Grade *n* *(Scottish Scol) certificado del último ciclo de la enseñanza secundaria obligatoria*
standardization [stændədaɪ'zeɪʃən] *n* normalización *f*
standardize ['stændədaɪz] *vt* estandarizar
standard lamp *n* *(Brit)* lámpara de pie
standard model *n* modelo estándar
standard of living *n* nivel *m* de vida
standard practice *n* norma, práctica común
standard rate *n* tasa de imposición
standard time *n* hora oficial
stand-by ['stændbaɪ] *n* *(alert)* alerta, aviso; *(also:* **stand-by ticket***: Theat) entrada reducida de última hora*; *(: Aviat)* billete *m* standby; **to be on ~** estar preparado; *(doctor)* estar listo para acudir; *(Aviat)* estar en la lista de espera
stand-by generator *n* generador *m* de reserva
stand-by passenger *n* *(Aviat)* pasajero(-a) en lista de espera
stand-by ticket *n* *(Aviat)* (billete *m*) standby *m*
stand-in ['stændɪn] *n* suplente *m/f*; *(Cine)* doble *m/f*
standing ['stændɪŋ] *adj* *(upright)* derecho; *(on foot)* de pie, en pie; *(permanent: committee)* permanente; *(: rule)* fijo; *(: army)* permanente, regular; *(grievance)* constante,

viejo ■ *n* reputación *f*; (*duration*): **of six months'** ~ que lleva seis meses; **of many years'** ~ que lleva muchos años; **he was given a ~ ovation** le dieron una calurosa ovación de pie; ~ **joke** motivo constante de broma; **a man of some** ~ un hombre de cierta posición *or* categoría

standing order *n* (*Brit: at bank*) giro bancario; **standing orders** *npl* (*Mil*) reglamento *sg* general

standing room *n* sitio para estar de pie

stand-off ['stændɔf] *n* punto muerto

stand-offish [stænd'ɔfɪʃ] *adj* distante

standpipe ['stændpaɪp] *n* tubo vertical

standpoint ['stændpɔɪnt] *n* punto de vista

standstill ['stændstɪl] *n*: **at a** ~ paralizado, en un punto muerto; **to come to a** ~ pararse, quedar paralizado

stank [stæŋk] *pt of* **stink**

staple ['steɪpl] *n* (*for papers*) grapa; (*product*) producto *or* artículo de primeva necesidad ■ *adj* (*crop, industry, food etc*) básico ■ *vt* grapar

stapler ['steɪpləʳ] *n* grapadora

star [stɑːʳ] *n* estrella; (*celebrity*) estrella, astro ■ *vi*: **to ~ in** ser la estrella de; **four-~ hotel** hotel *m* de cuatro estrellas; **4-~ petrol** gasolina extra

star attraction *n* atracción *f* principal

starboard ['stɑːbəd] *n* estribor *m*

starch [stɑːtʃ] *n* almidón *m*

starchy ['stɑːtʃɪ] *adj* (*food*) feculento

stardom ['stɑːdəm] *n* estrellato

stare [stɛəʳ] *n* mirada fija ■ *vi*: **to ~ at** mirar fijo

starfish ['stɑːfɪʃ] *n* estrella de mar

stark [stɑːk] *adj* (*bleak*) severo, escueto; (*simplicity, colour*) austero; (*reality, truth*) puro; (*poverty*) absoluto ■ *adv*: ~ **naked** en cueros

starkers ['stɑːkəz] *adj* (*Brit col*): **to be** ~ estar en cueros

starlet ['stɑːlɪt] *n* (*Cine*) actriz *f* principiante

starling ['stɑːlɪŋ] *n* estornino

starry ['stɑːrɪ] *adj* estrellado

starry-eyed [stɑːrɪ'aɪd] *adj* (*gullible, innocent*) inocentón(-ona), ingenuo; (*idealistic*) idealista; (*from wonder*) asombrado; (*from love*) enamoradísimo

Stars and Stripes *npl*: **the** ~ las barras y las estrellas, la bandera de EEUU

star sign *n* signo del zodíaco

star-studded ['stɑːstʌdɪd] *adj*: **a ~ cast** un elenco estelar

start [stɑːt] *n* (*beginning*) principio, comienzo; (*departure*) salida; (*sudden movement*) sobresalto; (*advantage*) ventaja ■ *vt* empezar, comenzar; (*cause*) causar; (*found: business, newspaper*) establecer, fundar; (*engine*) poner en marcha ■ *vi* (*begin*) comenzar, empezar; (*with fright*) asustarse, sobresaltarse; (*train etc*) salir; **to give sb a** ~ dar un susto a algn; **at the** ~ al principio; **for a** ~ en primer lugar; **to make an early** ~ ponerse en camino temprano; **the thieves had three hours'** ~ los ladrones llevaban tres horas de ventaja; **to ~ a fire** provocar un incendio; **to ~ doing** *or* **to do sth** empezar a hacer algo; **to ~ (off) with ...** (*firstly*) para empezar; (*at the beginning*) al principio

▸ **start off** *vi* empezar, comenzar; (*leave*) salir, ponerse en camino

▸ **start over** *vi* (*US*) volver a empezar

▸ **start up** *vi* comenzar; (*car*) ponerse en marcha ■ *vt* comenzar; (*car*) poner en marcha

starter ['stɑːtəʳ] *n* (*Aut*) botón *m* de arranque; (*Sport: official*) juez *m/f* de salida; (*: runner*) corredor(a) *m(f)*; (*Brit Culin*) entrada

starting point ['stɑːtɪŋ-] *n* punto de partida

starting price *n* (*Comm*) precio inicial

startle ['stɑːtl] *vt* asustar, sobresaltar

startling ['stɑːtlɪŋ] *adj* alarmante

star turn *n* (*Brit*) atracción *f* principal

starvation [stɑː'veɪʃən] *n* hambre *f*, hambruna (*LAm*); (*Med*) inanición *f*

starvation wages *npl* sueldo *sg* de hambre

starve [stɑːv] *vi* pasar hambre; (*to death*) morir de hambre ■ *vt* hacer pasar hambre; (*fig*) privar; **I'm starving** estoy muerto de hambre

stash [stæʃ] *vt*: **to ~ sth away** (*col*) poner algo a buen recaudo

state [steɪt] *n* estado; (*pomp*): **in** ~ con mucha ceremonia ■ *vt* (*say, declare*) afirmar; (*a case*) presentar, exponer; ~ **of emergency** estado de excepción *or* emergencia; ~ **of mind** estado de ánimo; **to lie in** ~ (*corpse*) estar de cuerpo presente; **to be in a** ~ estar agitado

State Department *n* (*US*) Ministerio de Asuntos Exteriores

state education *n* (*Brit*) enseñanza pública

stateless ['steɪtlɪs] *adj* desnacionalizado

stately ['steɪtlɪ] *adj* majestuoso, imponente

statement ['steɪtmənt] *n* afirmación *f*; (*Law*) declaración *f*; (*Comm*) estado; **official** ~ informe *m* oficial; ~ **of account, bank** ~ estado de cuenta

state-of-the-art ['steɪtəvðɪ'ɑːt] *adj* (*technology etc*) puntero

state-owned ['steɪtəund] *adj* estatal, del estado

States [steɪts] *npl*: **the** ~ los Estados Unidos

state school *n* escuela *or* colegio estatal

statesman ['steɪtsmən] *n* estadista *m*
statesmanship ['steɪtsmənʃɪp] *n* habilidad *f* política, arte *m* de gobernar
static ['stætɪk] *n* (*Radio*) parásitos *mpl* ■ *adj* estático
static electricity *n* electricidad *f* estática
station ['steɪʃən] *n* (*gen*) estación *f*; (*place*) puesto, sitio; (*Radio*) emisora; (*rank*) posición *f* social ■ *vt* colocar, situar; (*Mil*) apostar; **action stations!** ¡a los puestos de combate!; **to be stationed in** (*Mil*) estar estacionado en
stationary ['steɪʃnərɪ] *adj* estacionario, fijo
stationer ['steɪʃənə^r] *n* papelero(-a)
stationer's, stationer's shop *n* (*Brit*) papelería
stationery ['steɪʃənərɪ] *n* (*writing paper*) papel *m* de escribir; (*writing materials*) artículos *mpl* de escritorio
station master *n* (*Rail*) jefe *m* de estación
station wagon *n* (*US*) coche *m* familiar con ranchera
statistic [stə'tɪstɪk] *n* estadística
statistical [stə'tɪstɪkl] *adj* estadístico
statistics [stə'tɪstɪks] *n* (*science*) estadística
statue ['stætju:] *n* estatua
statuette [stætju'ɛt] *n* figurilla
stature ['stætʃə^r] *n* estatura; (*fig*) talla
status ['steɪtəs] *n* condición *f*, estado; (*reputation*) reputación *f*, estatus *m*; **the ~ quo** el statu quo
status line *n* (*Comput*) línea de situación *or* de estado
status symbol *n* símbolo de prestigio
statute ['stætju:t] *n* estatuto, ley *f*
statute book *n* código de leyes
statutory ['stætjutrɪ] *adj* estatutario; **~ meeting** junta ordinaria
staunch [stɔ:ntʃ] *adj* leal, incondicional ■ *vt* (*flow, blood*) restañar
stave [steɪv] *vt*: **to ~ off** (*attack*) rechazar; (*threat*) evitar
stay [steɪ] *n* (*period of time*) estancia; (*Law*): **~ of execution** aplazamiento de una sentencia ■ *vi* (*remain*) quedar(se); (*as guest*) hospedarse; **to ~ put** seguir en el mismo sitio; **to ~ the night/5 days** pasar la noche/estar *or* quedarse 5 días
▸ **stay behind** *vi* quedar atrás
▸ **stay in** *vi* (*at home*) quedarse en casa
▸ **stay on** *vi* quedarse
▸ **stay out** *vi* (*of house*) no volver a casa; (*strikers*) no volver al trabajo
▸ **stay up** *vi* (*at night*) velar, no acostarse
staying power ['steɪɪŋ-] *n* resistencia, aguante *m*
STD *n abbr* (*Brit: = subscriber trunk dialling*) *servicio de conferencias automáticas*; (*= sexually transmitted disease*) ETS *f*
stead [stɛd] *n*: **in sb's ~** en lugar de algn; **to stand sb in good ~** ser muy útil a algn
steadfast ['stɛdfɑ:st] *adj* firme, resuelto
steadily ['stɛdɪlɪ] *adv* (*firmly*) firmemente; (*unceasingly*) sin parar; (*fixedly*) fijamente; (*walk*) normalmente; (*drive*) a velocidad constante
steady ['stɛdɪ] *adj* (*fixed*) firme, fijo; (*regular*) regular; (*boyfriend etc*) formal, fijo; (*person, character*) sensato, juicioso ■ *vt* (*hold*) mantener firme; (*stabilize*) estabilizar; (*nerves*) calmar; **to ~ o.s. on** *or* **against sth** afirmarse en algo
steak [steɪk] *n* (*gen*) filete *m*; (*beef*) bistec *m*
steal (*pt* **stole**, *pp* **stolen**) [sti:l, stəul, 'stəuln] *vt*, *vi* robar
▸ **steal away, steal off** *vi* marcharse furtivamente, escabullirse
stealth [stɛlθ] *n*: **by ~** a escondidas, sigilosamente
stealthy ['stɛlθɪ] *adj* cauteloso, sigiloso
steam [sti:m] *n* vapor *m*; (*mist*) vaho, humo ■ *vt* (*Culin*) cocer al vapor ■ *vi* echar vapor; (*ship*): **to ~ along** avanzar, ir avanzando; **under one's own ~** (*fig*) por sus propios medios *or* propias fuerzas; **to run out of ~** (*fig: person*) quedar(se) agotado, quemarse; **to let off ~** (*fig*) desahogarse
▸ **steam up** *vi* (*window*) empañarse; **to get steamed up about sth** (*fig*) ponerse negro por algo
steam engine *n* máquina de vapor
steamer ['sti:mə^r] *n* (buque *m* de) vapor *m*; (*Culin*) *recipiente para cocinar al vapor*
steam iron *n* plancha de vapor
steamroller ['sti:mrəulə^r] *n* apisonadora
steamship ['sti:mʃɪp] *n* = **steamer**
steamy ['sti:mɪ] *adj* (*room*) lleno de vapor; (*window*) empañado
steel [sti:l] *n* acero ■ *adj* de acero
steel band *n* banda de percusión del Caribe
steel industry *n* industria siderúrgica
steel mill *n* fábrica de acero
steelworks ['sti:lwə:ks] *n* acería, fundición *f* de acero
steely ['sti:lɪ] *adj* (*determination*) inflexible; (*gaze*) duro; (*eyes*) penetrante; **~ grey** gris *m* metálico
steelyard ['sti:ljɑ:d] *n* romana
steep [sti:p] *adj* escarpado, abrupto; (*stair*) empinado; (*price*) exorbitante, excesivo ■ *vt* empapar, remojar
steeple ['sti:pl] *n* aguja, campanario
steeplechase ['sti:pltʃeɪs] *n* carrera de obstáculos

steeplejack ['sti:pldʒæk] *n* reparador(a) *m(f)* de chimeneas *or* de campanarios
steer [stɪəʳ] *vt* (*car*) conducir (*SP*), manejar (*LAm*); (*person*) dirigir, guiar ■ *vi* conducir; **to ~ clear of sb/sth** (*fig*) esquivar a algn/ evadir algo
steering ['stɪərɪŋ] *n* (*Aut*) dirección *f*
steering committee *n* comisión *f* directiva
steering wheel *n* volante *m*
stellar ['stɛləʳ] *adj* estelar
stem [stɛm] *n* (*of plant*) tallo; (*of glass*) pie *m*; (*of pipe*) cañón *m* ■ *vt* detener; (*blood*) restañar
▸ **stem from** *vt fus* ser consecuencia de
stem cell *n* célula madre
stench [stɛntʃ] *n* hedor *m*
stencil ['stɛnsl] *n* (*typed*) cliché *m*, clisé *m*; (*lettering*) plantilla ■ *vt* hacer un cliché de
stenographer [stɛ'nɔgrəfəʳ] *n* (*US*) taquígrafo(-a)
step [stɛp] *n* paso; (*sound*) paso, pisada; (*stair*) peldaño, escalón *m* ■ *vi*: **to ~ forward** dar un paso adelante; **steps** *npl* (*Brit*) = **stepladder**; **~ by ~** paso a paso; (*fig*) poco a poco; **to keep in ~ (with)** llevar el paso de; (*fig*) llevar el paso de, estar de acuerdo con; **to be in/out of ~ with** estar acorde con/estar en disonancia con; **to take steps to solve a problem** tomar medidas para resolver un problema
▸ **step down** *vi* (*fig*) retirarse
▸ **step in** *vi* entrar; (*fig*) intervenir
▸ **step off** *vt fus* bajar de
▸ **step on** *vt fus* pisar
▸ **step over** *vt fus* pasar por encima de
▸ **step up** *vt* (*increase*) aumentar
step aerobics *npl* step *m*
stepbrother ['stɛpbrʌðəʳ] *n* hermanastro
stepdaughter ['stɛpdɔ:təʳ] *n* hijastra
stepfather ['stɛpfɑ:ðəʳ] *n* padrastro
stepladder ['stɛplædəʳ] *n* escalera doble *or* de tijera
stepmother ['stɛpmʌðəʳ] *n* madrastra
stepping stone ['stɛpɪŋ-] *n* pasadera
step Reebok® [-'ri:bɔk] *n* step *m*
stepsister ['stɛpsɪstəʳ] *n* hermanastra
stepson ['stɛpsʌn] *n* hijastro
stereo ['stɛrɪəu] *n* estéreo ■ *adj* (*also*: **stereophonic**) estéreo, estereofónico; **in ~** en estéreo
stereotype ['stɪərɪətaɪp] *n* estereotipo ■ *vt* estereotipar
sterile ['stɛraɪl] *adj* estéril
sterilization [stɛrɪlaɪ'zeɪʃən] *n* esterilización *f*
sterilize ['stɛrɪlaɪz] *vt* esterilizar
sterling ['stə:lɪŋ] *adj* (*silver*) de ley ■ *n* (*Econ*) libras *fpl* esterlinas; **a pound ~** una libra esterlina; **he is of ~ character** tiene un carácter excelente
stern [stə:n] *adj* severo, austero ■ *n* (*Naut*) popa
sternum ['stə:nəm] *n* esternón *m*
steroid ['stɪərɔɪd] *n* esteroide *m*
stethoscope ['stɛθəskəup] *n* estetoscopio
stevedore ['sti:vədɔ:ʳ] *n* estibador *m*
stew [stju:] *n* cocido, estofado, guisado (*LAm*) ■ *vt, vi* estofar, guisar; (*fruit*) cocer; **stewed fruit** compota de fruta
steward ['stju:əd] *n* (*Brit: gen*) camarero; (*shop steward*) enlace *m/f* sindical
stewardess ['stjuədəs] *n* azafata
stewardship ['stjuədʃɪp] *n* tutela
stewing steak ['stju:ɪŋ-], **stew meat** (*US*) *n* carne *f* de vaca
St. Ex. *abbr* = **stock exchange**
stg *abbr* (= *sterling*) ester
stick [stɪk] (*pt, pp* **stuck**) *n* palo; (*as weapon*) porra; (*also*: **walking stick**) bastón *m* ■ *vt* (*glue*) pegar; (*col: put*) meter; (*: tolerate*) aguantar, soportar ■ *vi* pegarse; (*come to a stop*) quedarse parado; (*get jammed: door, lift*) atascarse; **to get hold of the wrong end of the ~** entender al revés; **to ~ to** (*word, principles*) atenerse a, ser fiel a; (*promise*) cumplir; **it stuck in my mind** se me quedó grabado; **to ~ sth into** clavar *or* hincar algo en
▸ **stick around** *vi* (*col*) quedarse
▸ **stick out** *vi* sobresalir ■ *vt*: **to ~ it out** (*col*) aguantar
▸ **stick up** *vi* sobresalir
▸ **stick up for** *vt fus* defender
sticker ['stɪkəʳ] *n* (*label*) etiqueta adhesiva; (*with slogan*) pegatina
sticking plaster ['stɪkɪŋ-] *n* (*Brit*) esparadrapo
sticking point *n* (*fig*) punto de fricción
stick insect *n* insecto palo
stickler ['stɪkləʳ] *n*: **to be a ~ for** insistir mucho en
stick shift *n* (*US Aut*) palanca de cambios
stick-up ['stɪkʌp] *n* asalto, atraco
sticky ['stɪkɪ] *adj* pegajoso; (*label*) adhesivo; (*fig*) difícil
stiff [stɪf] *adj* rígido, tieso; (*hard*) duro; (*difficult*) difícil; (*person*) inflexible; (*price*) exorbitante; **to have a ~ neck/back** tener tortícolis/dolor de espalda; **the door's ~** la puerta está atrancada
stiffen ['stɪfn] *vt* hacer más rígido; (*limb*) entumecer ■ *vi* endurecerse; (*grow stronger*) fortalecerse
stiffness ['stɪfnɪs] *n* rigidez *f*

stifle ['staɪfl] *vt* ahogar, sofocar
stifling ['staɪflɪŋ] *adj* (*heat*) sofocante, bochornoso
stigma *n* (*Bot, Med, Rel*) (*pl* **stigmata**) (*fig*) (*pl* **stigmas**) ['stɪgmə, stɪg'mɑːtə] ■ *n* estigma *m*
stile [staɪl] *n* escalera (*para pasar una cerca*)
stiletto [stɪ'lɛtəu] *n* (*Brit: also:* **stiletto heel**) tacón *m* de aguja
still [stɪl] *adj* inmóvil, quieto; (*orange juice etc*) sin gas ■ *adv* (*up to this time*) todavía; (*even*) aún; (*nonetheless*) sin embargo, aun así ■ *n* (*Cine*) foto *f* fija; **keep ~!** ¡estate quieto!, ¡no te muevas!; **he ~ hasn't arrived** todavía no ha llegado
stillborn ['stɪlbɔːn] *adj* nacido muerto
still life *n* naturaleza muerta
stilt [stɪlt] *n* zanco; (*pile*) pilar *m*, soporte *m*
stilted ['stɪltɪd] *adj* afectado, artificial
stimulant ['stɪmjulənt] *n* estimulante *m*
stimulate ['stɪmjuleɪt] *vt* estimular
stimulating ['stɪmjuleɪtɪŋ] *adj* estimulante
stimulation [stɪmju'leɪʃən] *n* estímulo
stimulus (*pl* **stimuli**) ['stɪmjuləs, -laɪ] *n* estímulo, incentivo
sting [stɪŋ] (*pt, pp* **stung**) *n* (*wound*) picadura; (*pain*) escozor *m*, picazón *m*; (*organ*) aguijón *m*; (*col: confidence trick*) timo ■ *vt* picar ■ *vi* picar, escocer; **my eyes are stinging** me pican *or* escuecen los ojos
stingy ['stɪndʒɪ] *adj* tacaño
stink [stɪŋk] *n* hedor *m*, tufo ■ *vi* (*pt* **stank**, *pp* **stunk**) [stæŋk, stʌŋk] heder, apestar
stinking ['stɪŋkɪŋ] *adj* hediondo, fétido; (*fig: col*) horrible
stint [stɪnt] *n* tarea, destajo; **to do one's ~ (at sth)** hacer su parte (de algo), hacer lo que corresponde (de algo) ■ *vi*: **to ~ on** escatimar
stipend ['staɪpɛnd] *n* salario, remuneración *f*
stipendiary [staɪ'pɛndɪərɪ] *adj*: **~ magistrate** magistrado(-a) estipendiario(-a)
stipulate ['stɪpjuleɪt] *vt* estipular
stipulation [stɪpju'leɪʃən] *n* estipulación *f*
stir [stəːʳ] *n* (*fig: agitation*) conmoción *f* ■ *vt* (*tea etc*) remover; (*fire*) atizar; (*move*) agitar; (*fig: emotions*) conmover ■ *vi* moverse; **to give sth a ~** remover algo; **to cause a ~** causar conmoción *or* sensación
▸ **stir up** *vt* excitar; (*trouble*) fomentar
stir-fry ['stəːfraɪ] *vt* sofreír removiendo ■ *n plato preparado sofriendo y removiendo los ingredientes*
stirrup ['stɪrəp] *n* estribo
stitch [stɪtʃ] *n* (*Sewing*) puntada; (*Knitting*) punto; (*Med*) punto (de sutura); (*pain*) punzada ■ *vt* coser; (*Med*) suturar
stoat [stəut] *n* armiño
stock [stɔk] *n* (*Comm: reserves*) existencias *fpl*, stock *m*; (*: selection*) surtido; (*Agr*) ganado, ganadería; (*Culin*) caldo; (*fig: lineage*) estirpe *f*, cepa; (*Finance*) capital *m*; (*: shares*) acciones *fpl*; (*Rail: rolling stock*) material *m* rodante ■ *adj* (*Comm: goods, size*) normal, de serie; (*fig: reply etc*) clásico, trillado; (*: greeting*) acostumbrado ■ *vt* (*have in stock*) tener existencias de; (*supply*) proveer, abastecer; **in ~** en existencia *or* almacén; **to have sth in ~** tener existencias de algo; **out of ~** agotado; **to take ~ of** (*fig*) considerar, examinar; **stocks** *npl* (*History: punishment*) cepo *sg*; **stocks and shares** acciones y valores; **government ~** papel *m* del Estado
▸ **stock up with** *vt fus* abastecerse de
stockbroker ['stɔkbrəukəʳ] *n* agente *m/f or* corredor(a) *m/f* de bolsa
stock control *n* (*Comm*) control *m* de existencias
stock cube *n* pastilla *or* cubito de caldo
stock exchange *n* bolsa
stockholder ['stɔkhəuldəʳ] *n* (*US*) accionista *m/f*
Stockholm ['stɔkhəum] *n* Estocolmo
stocking ['stɔkɪŋ] *n* media
stock-in-trade ['stɔkɪn'treɪd] *n* (*tools etc*) herramientas *fpl*; (*stock*) existencia de mercancías; (*fig*): **it's his ~** es su especialidad
stockist ['stɔkɪst] *n* (*Brit*) distribuidor(a) *m(f)*
stock market *n* bolsa (de valores)
stock phrase *n* vieja frase *f*
stockpile ['stɔkpaɪl] *n* reserva ■ *vt* acumular, almacenar
stockroom ['stɔkruːm] *n* almacén *m*, depósito
stocktaking ['stɔkteɪkɪŋ] *n* (*Brit Comm*) inventario, balance *m*
stocky ['stɔkɪ] *adj* (*strong*) robusto; (*short*) achaparrado
stodgy ['stɔdʒɪ] *adj* indigesto, pesado
stoical ['stəuɪkəl] *adj* estoico
stoke [stəuk] *vt* atizar
stole [stəul] *pt of* **steal** ■ *n* estola
stolen ['stəuln] *pp of* **steal**
stolid ['stɔlɪd] *adj* (*person*) imperturbable, impasible
stomach ['stʌmək] *n* (*Anat*) estómago; (*belly*) vientre *m* ■ *vt* tragar, aguantar
stomach ache *n* dolor *m* de estómago
stomach pump *n* bomba gástrica
stomach ulcer *n* úlcera de estómago
stomp [stɔmp] *vi*: **to ~ in/out** entrar/salir con pasos ruidosos
stone [stəun] *n* piedra; (*in fruit*) hueso; (*Brit: weight*) *= 6.348 kg; 14 pounds* ■ *adj* de piedra ■ *vt*

apedrear; **within a ~'s throw of the station** a tiro de piedra *or* a dos pasos de la estación
Stone Age *n*: **the ~** la Edad de Piedra
stone-cold ['stəun'kəuld] *adj* helado
stoned [stəund] *adj* (*col*: *drunk*) trompa, borracho, colocado
stone-deaf ['stəun'dɛf] *adj* sordo como una tapia
stonemason ['stəunmeɪsən] *n* albañil *m*
stonewall [stəun'wɔ:l] *vi* alargar la cosa innecesariamente ■ *vt* dar largas a
stonework ['stəunwə:k] *n* (*art*) cantería
stony ['stəunɪ] *adj* pedregoso; (*glance*) glacial
stood [stud] *pt, pp of* **stand**
stooge [stu:dʒ] *n* (*col*) hombre *m* de paja
stool [stu:l] *n* taburete *m*
stoop [stu:p] *vi* (*also*: **have a stoop**) ser cargado de espaldas; (*bend*) inclinarse, encorvarse; **to ~ to (doing) sth** rebajarse a (hacer) algo
stop [stɔp] *n* parada, alto; (*in punctuation*) punto ■ *vt* parar, detener; (*break off*) suspender; (*block*) tapar, cerrar; (*prevent*) impedir; (*also*: **put a stop to**) poner término a ■ *vi* pararse, detenerse; (*end*) acabarse; **to ~ doing sth** dejar de hacer algo; **to ~ sb (from) doing sth** impedir a algn hacer algo; **to ~ dead** pararse en seco; **~ it!** ¡basta ya!, ¡párate!
▸ **stop by** *vi* pasar por
▸ **stop off** *vi* interrumpir el viaje
▸ **stop up** *vt* (*hole*) tapar
stopcock ['stɔpkɔk] *n* llave *f* de paso
stopgap ['stɔpgæp] *n* interino; (*person*) sustituto(-a); (*measure*) medida provisional ■ *cpd* (*situation*) provisional
stoplights ['stɔplaɪts] *npl* (*Aut*) luces *fpl* de detención
stopover ['stɔpəuvə^r^] *n* parada intermedia; (*Aviat*) escala
stoppage ['stɔpɪdʒ] *n* (*strike*) paro; (*temporary stop*) interrupción *f*; (*of pay*) suspensión *f*; (*blockage*) obstrucción *f*
stopper ['stɔpə^r^] *n* tapón *m*
stop press *n* noticias *fpl* de última hora
stopwatch ['stɔpwɔtʃ] *n* cronómetro
storage ['stɔ:rɪdʒ] *n* almacenaje *m*; (*Comput*) almacenamiento
storage capacity *n* espacio de almacenaje
storage heater *n* acumulador *m* de calor
store [stɔ:^r^] *n* (*stock*) provisión *f*; (*depot*) almacén *m*; (*Brit*: *large shop*) almacén *m*; (*US*) tienda; (*reserve*) reserva, repuesto ■ *vt* (*gen*) almacenar; (*Comput*) almacenar; (*keep*) guardar; (*in filing system*) archivar; **stores** *npl* víveres *mpl*; **who knows what is in ~ for us** quién sabe lo que nos espera; **to set great/little ~ by sth** dar mucha/poca importancia a algo, valorar mucho/poco algo
▸ **store up** *vt* acumular
storehouse ['stɔ:haus] *n* almacén *m*, depósito
storekeeper ['stɔ:ki:pə^r^] *n* (*US*) tendero(-a)
storeroom ['stɔ:ru:m] *n* despensa
storey, story (*US*) ['stɔ:rɪ] *n* piso
stork [stɔ:k] *n* cigüeña
storm [stɔ:m] *n* tormenta; (*wind*) vendaval *m*; (*fig*) tempestad *f* ■ *vi* (*fig*) rabiar ■ *vt* tomar por asalto, asaltar; **to take a town by ~** (*Mil*) tomar una ciudad por asalto
storm cloud *n* nubarrón *m*
storm door *n* contrapuerta
stormy ['stɔ:mɪ] *adj* tempestuoso
story ['stɔ:rɪ] *n* historia; (*Press*) artículo; (*joke*) cuento, chiste *m*; (*plot*) argumento; (*lie*) cuento; (*US*) = **storey**
storybook ['stɔ:rɪbuk] *n* libro de cuentos
storyteller ['stɔ:rɪtɛlə^r^] *n* cuentista *m/f*
stout [staut] *adj* (*strong*) sólido; (*fat*) gordo, corpulento ■ *n* cerveza negra
stove [stəuv] *n* (*for cooking*) cocina; (*for heating*) estufa; **gas/electric ~** cocina de gas/eléctrica
stow [stəu] *vt* meter, poner; (*Naut*) estibar
stowaway ['stəuəweɪ] *n* polizón(-ona) *m(f)*
straddle ['strædl] *vt* montar a horcajadas
straggle ['strægl] *vi* (*wander*) vagar en desorden; (*lag behind*) rezagarse
straggler ['stræglə^r^] *n* rezagado(-a)
straggling ['stræglɪŋ], **straggly** ['stræglɪ] *adj* (*hair*) desordenado
straight [streɪt] *adj* (*direct*) recto, derecho; (*plain, uncomplicated*) sencillo; (*frank*) franco, directo; (*in order*) en orden; (*continuous*) continuo; (*Theat*: *part, play*) serio; (*person*: *conventional*) recto, convencional; (: *heterosexual*) heterosexual ■ *adv* derecho, directamente; (*drink*) solo; **to put** *or* **get sth ~** dejar algo en claro; **10 ~ wins** 10 victorias seguidas; **to be (all) ~** (*tidy*) estar en orden; (*clarified*) estar claro; **I went ~ home** (me) fui directamente a casa; **~ away, ~ off** (*at once*) en seguida
straighten ['streɪtn] *vt* (*also*: **straighten out**) enderezar, poner derecho; **to ~ things out** poner las cosas en orden
straight-faced [streɪt'feɪst] *adj* serio ■ *adv* sin mostrar emoción, impávido
straightforward [streɪt'fɔ:wəd] *adj* (*simple*) sencillo; (*honest*) sincero
strain [streɪn] *n* (*gen*) tensión *f*; (*Tech*) esfuerzo; (*Med*) distensión *f*, torcedura; (*breed*) raza; (*lineage*) linaje *m*; (*of virus*) variedad *f* ■ *vt* (*back etc*) distender, torcerse; (*tire*) cansar; (*stretch*) estirar; (*filter*) filtrar;

(*meaning*) tergiversar ■ *vi* esforzarse; **strains** *npl* (*Mus*) son *m*; **she's under a lot of ~** está bajo mucha tensión
strained [streɪnd] *adj* (*muscle*) torcido; (*laugh*) forzado; (*relations*) tenso
strainer ['streɪnəʳ] *n* colador *m*
strait [streɪt] *n* (*Geo*) estrecho; **to be in dire straits** (*fig*) estar en un gran aprieto
straitjacket ['streɪtdʒækɪt] *n* camisa de fuerza
strait-laced [streɪt'leɪst] *adj* mojigato, gazmoño
strand [strænd] *n* (*of thread*) hebra; (*of rope*) ramal *m*; **a ~ of hair** un pelo
stranded ['strændɪd] *adj* (*person*) colgado
strange [streɪndʒ] *adj* (*not known*) desconocido; (*odd*) extraño, raro
stranger ['streɪndʒəʳ] *n* desconocido(-a); (*from another area*) forastero(-a); **I'm a ~ here** no soy de aquí
strangle ['strængl] *vt* estrangular
stranglehold ['strænglhəuld] *n* (*fig*) dominio completo
strangulation [strængju'leɪʃən] *n* estrangulación *f*
strap [stræp] *n* correa; (*of slip, dress*) tirante *m* ■ *vt* atar con correa
straphanging ['stræphænɪŋ] *n* viajar *m* de pie *or* parado (*LAm*)
strapless ['stræplɪs] *adj* (*bra, dress*) sin tirantes
strapped [stræpt] *adj*: **to be ~ for cash** (*col*) andar mal de dinero
strapping ['stræpɪŋ] *adj* robusto, fornido
Strasbourg ['stræzbəːg] *n* Estrasburgo
strata ['strɑːtə] *npl of* **stratum**
stratagem ['strætɪdʒəm] *n* estratagema
strategic [strə'tiːdʒɪk] *adj* estratégico
strategy ['strætɪdʒɪ] *n* estrategia
stratum, strata ['strɑːtəm, 'strɑːtə] *n* estrato
straw [strɔː] *n* paja; (*also:* **drinking straw**) caña, pajita; **that's the last ~!** ¡eso es el colmo!
strawberry ['strɔːbərɪ] *n* fresa, frutilla (*LAm*)
stray [streɪ] *adj* (*animal*) extraviado; (*bullet*) perdido; (*scattered*) disperso ■ *vi* extraviarse, perderse; (*wander: walker*) vagar, ir sin rumbo fijo; (*: speaker*) desvariar
streak [striːk] *n* raya; (*fig: of madness etc*) vena ■ *vt* rayar ■ *vi*: **to ~ past** pasar como un rayo; **to have streaks in one's hair** tener vetas en el pelo; **a winning/losing ~** una racha de buena/mala suerte
streaker ['striːkəʳ] *n* corredor(a) *m(f)* desnudo(-a)
streaky ['striːkɪ] *adj* rayado
stream [striːm] *n* riachuelo, arroyo; (*jet*) chorro; (*flow*) corriente *f*; (*of people*) oleada ■ *vt* (*Scol*) dividir en grupos por habilidad ■ *vi* correr, fluir; **to ~ in/out** (*people*) entrar/salir en tropel; **against the ~** a contracorriente; **on ~** (*new power plant etc*) en funcionamiento
streamer ['striːməʳ] *n* serpentina
stream feed *n* (*on photocopier etc*) alimentación *f* continua
streamline ['striːmlaɪn] *vt* aerodinamizar; (*fig*) racionalizar
streamlined ['striːmlaɪnd] *adj* aerodinámico
street [striːt] *n* calle *f* ■ *adj* callejero; **the back streets** las callejuelas; **to be on the streets** (*homeless*) estar sin vivienda; (*as prostitute*) hacer la calle
streetcar ['striːtkɑː] *n* (*US*) tranvía *m*
street cred [-krɛd] *n* (*col*) *imagen de estar en la onda*
street lamp *n* farol *m*
street lighting *n* alumbrado público
street market *n* mercado callejero
street plan *n* plano callejero
streetwise ['striːtwaɪz] *adj* (*col*) pícaro
strength [strɛŋθ] *n* fuerza; (*of girder, knot etc*) resistencia; (*of chemical solution*) potencia; (*of wine*) graduación *f* de alcohol; **on the ~ of** a base de, en base a; **to be at full/below ~** tener/no tener completo el cupo
strengthen ['strɛŋθən] *vt* fortalecer, reforzar
strenuous ['strɛnjuəs] *adj* (*tough*) arduo; (*energetic*) enérgico; (*opposition*) firme, tenaz; (*efforts*) intensivo
stress [strɛs] *n* (*force, pressure*) presión *f*; (*mental strain*) estrés *m*, tensión *f*; (*accent, emphasis*) énfasis *m*, acento; (*Ling, Poetry*) acento; (*Tech*) tensión *f*, carga ■ *vt* subrayar, recalcar; **to be under ~** estar estresado; **to lay great ~ on sth** hacer hincapié en algo
stressful ['strɛsful] *adj* (*job*) estresante
stretch [strɛtʃ] *n* (*of sand etc*) trecho; (*of road*) tramo; (*of time*) período, tiempo ■ *vi* estirarse; (*extend*): **to ~ to** *or* **as far as** extenderse hasta; (*be enough: money, food*): **to ~ to** alcanzar para, dar de sí para ■ *vt* extender, estirar; (*make demands of*) exigir el máximo esfuerzo a; **to ~ one's legs** estirar las piernas
▸ **stretch out** *vi* tenderse ■ *vt* (*arm etc*) extender; (*spread*) estirar
stretcher ['strɛtʃəʳ] *n* camilla
stretcher-bearer ['strɛtʃəbɛərəʳ] *n* camillero(-a)
stretch marks *npl* estrías *fpl*
strewn [struːn] *adj*: **~ with** cubierto *or* sembrado de

stricken ['strɪkən] *adj* (*person*) herido; (*city, industry etc*) condenado; **~ with** (*arthritis, disease*) afligido por; **grief-~** destrozado por el dolor
strict [strɪkt] *adj* (*order, rule etc*) estricto; (*discipline, ban*) severo; **in ~ confidence** en la más absoluta confianza
strictly ['strɪktlɪ] *adv* estrictamente; (*totally*) terminantemente; **~ confidential** estrictamente confidencial; **~ speaking** en (el) sentido estricto (de la palabra); **~ between ourselves ...** entre nosotros ...
stridden ['strɪdn] *pp of* **stride**
stride [straɪd] *n* zancada, tranco ■ *vi* (*pt* **strode**, *pp* **stridden**) [strəud, 'strɪdn] dar zancadas, andar a trancos; **to take in one's ~** (*fig: changes etc*) tomar con calma
strident ['straɪdnt] *adj* estridente; (*colour*) chillón(-ona)
strife [straɪf] *n* lucha
strike [straɪk] (*pt, pp* **struck**) *n* huelga; (*of oil etc*) descubrimiento; (*attack*) ataque *m*; (*Sport*) golpe *m* ■ *vt* golpear, pegar; (*oil etc*) descubrir; (*obstacle*) topar con; (*produce: coin, medal*) acuñar; (*: agreement, deal*) concertar ■ *vi* declarar la huelga; (*attack: Mil etc*) atacar; (*clock*) dar la hora; **on ~** (*workers*) en huelga; **to call a ~** declarar una huelga; **to go on** *or* **come out on ~** ponerse *or* declararse en huelga; **to ~ a match** encender una cerilla; **to ~ a balance** (*fig*) encontrar un equilibrio; **to ~ a bargain** cerrar un trato; **the clock struck nine o'clock** el reloj dio las nueve
▸ **strike back** *vi* (*Mil*) contraatacar; (*fig*) devolver el golpe
▸ **strike down** *vt* derribar
▸ **strike off** *vt* (*from list*) tachar; (*doctor etc*) suspender
▸ **strike out** *vt* borrar, tachar
▸ **strike up** *vt* (*Mus*) empezar a tocar; (*conversation*) entablar; (*friendship*) trabar
strikebreaker ['straɪkbreɪkə^r] *n* rompehuelgas *m/f inv*
striker ['straɪkə^r] *n* huelgista *m/f*; (*Sport*) delantero
striking ['straɪkɪŋ] *adj* (*colour*) llamativo; (*obvious*) notorio
Strimmer® ['strɪmə^r] *n* cortacéspedes *m inv* (*especial para los bordes*)
string [strɪŋ] *n* (*gen*) cuerda; (*row*) hilera; (*Comput*) cadena ■ *vt* (*pt, pp* **strung**) [strʌŋ]: **to ~ together** ensartar; **to ~ out** extenderse; **the strings** *npl* (*Mus*) los instrumentos de cuerda; **to pull strings** (*fig*) mover palancas; **to get a job by pulling strings** conseguir un trabajo por enchufe; **with no strings attached** (*fig*) sin compromiso
string bean *n* judía verde, habichuela
stringed instrument [strɪŋ(d)-], **string instrument** *n* (*Mus*) instrumento de cuerda
stringent ['strɪndʒənt] *adj* riguroso, severo
string quartet *n* cuarteto de cuerdas
strip [strɪp] *n* tira; (*of land*) franja; (*of metal*) cinta, lámina ■ *vt* desnudar; (*also*: **strip down**: *machine*) desmontar ■ *vi* desnudarse
strip cartoon *n* tira cómica, historieta (*LAm*)
stripe [straɪp] *n* raya; (*Mil*) galón *m*; **white with green stripes** blanco con rayas verdes
striped [straɪpt] *adj* a rayas, rayado
strip lighting *n* alumbrado fluorescente
stripper ['strɪpə^r] *n* artista *m/f* de striptease
strip-search ['strɪpsə:tʃ] *vt*: **to ~ sb** desnudar y registrar a algn
striptease ['strɪpti:z] *n* striptease *m*
strive (*pt* **strove**, *pp* **striven**) [straɪv, strəuv, 'strɪvn] *vi*: **to ~ to do sth** esforzarse *or* luchar por hacer algo
strobe [strəub] *n* (*also*: **strobe light**) luz *f* estroboscópica
strode [strəud] *pt of* **stride**
stroke [strəuk] *n* (*blow*) golpe *m*; (*Med*) apoplejía; (*caress*) caricia; (*of pen*) trazo; (*Swimming: style*) estilo; (*of piston*) carrera ■ *vt* acariciar; **at a ~** de golpe; **a ~ of luck** un golpe de suerte; **two-~ engine** motor *m* de dos tiempos
stroll [strəul] *n* paseo, vuelta ■ *vi* dar un paseo *or* una vuelta; **to go for a ~, have** *or* **take a ~** dar un paseo
stroller ['strəulə^r] *n* (*US: pushchair*) cochecito
strong [strɔŋ] *adj* fuerte; (*bleach, acid*) concentrado ■ *adv*: **to be going ~** (*company*) marchar bien; (*person*) conservarse bien; **they are 50 ~** son 50
strong-arm ['strɔŋɑ:m] *adj* (*tactics, methods*) represivo
strongbox ['strɔŋbɔks] *n* caja fuerte
strong drink *n* bebida cargada *or* fuerte
stronghold ['strɔŋhəuld] *n* fortaleza; (*fig*) baluarte *m*
strong language *n* lenguaje *m* fuerte
strongly ['strɔŋlɪ] *adv* fuertemente, con fuerza; (*believe*) firmemente; **to feel ~ about sth** tener una opinión firme sobre algo
strongman ['strɔŋmæn] *n* forzudo; (*fig*) hombre *m* robusto
strongroom ['strɔŋru:m] *n* cámara acorazada
stroppy ['strɔpɪ] *adj* (*Brit col*) borde; **to get ~** ponerse borde
strove [strəuv] *pt of* **strive**
struck [strʌk] *pt, pp of* **strike**
structural ['strʌktʃərəl] *adj* estructural

structure ['strʌktʃəʳ] *n* estructura; (*building*) construcción *f*
struggle ['strʌgl] *n* lucha ■ *vi* luchar; **to have a ~ to do sth** esforzarse por hacer algo
strum [strʌm] *vt* (*guitar*) rasguear
strung [strʌŋ] *pt, pp of* **string**
strut [strʌt] *n* puntal *m* ■ *vi* pavonearse
strychnine ['strɪkniːn] *n* estricnina
stub [stʌb] *n* (*of ticket etc*) matriz *f*; (*of cigarette*) colilla ■ *vt*: **to ~ one's toe on sth** dar con el dedo del pie contra algo
▸ **stub out** *vt* (*cigarette*) apagar
stubble ['stʌbl] *n* rastrojo; (*on chin*) barba (incipiente)
stubborn ['stʌbən] *adj* terco, testarudo
stucco ['stʌkəu] *n* estuco
stuck [stʌk] *pt, pp of* **stick** ■ *adj* (*jammed*) atascado
stuck-up [stʌk'ʌp] *adj* engreído, presumido
stud [stʌd] *n* (*shirt stud*) corchete *m*; (*of boot*) taco; (*of horses*) caballeriza; (*also*: **stud horse**) caballo semental ■ *vt* (*fig*): **studded with** salpicado de
student ['stjuːdənt] *n* estudiante *m/f* ■ *adj* estudiantil; **a law/medical ~** un(a) estudiante de derecho/medicina
student driver *n* (*US Aut*) aprendiz(a) *m(f)* de conductor
students' union *n* (*Brit: association*) sindicato de estudiantes; (*: building*) centro de estudiantes
studio ['stjuːdɪəu] *n* estudio; (*artist's*) taller *m*
studio flat, studio apartment (*US*) *n* estudio
studious ['stjuːdɪəs] *adj* estudioso; (*studied*) calculado
studiously ['stjuːdɪəslɪ] *adv* (*carefully*) con esmero
study ['stʌdɪ] *n* estudio ■ *vt* estudiar; (*examine*) examinar, investigar ■ *vi* estudiar; **to make a ~ of sth** realizar una investigación de algo; **to ~ for an exam** preparar un examen
stuff [stʌf] *n* materia; (*cloth*) tela; (*substance*) material *m*, sustancia; (*things, belongings*) cosas *fpl* ■ *vt* llenar; (*Culin*) rellenar; (*animal: for exhibition*) disecar; **my nose is stuffed up** tengo la nariz tapada; **stuffed toy** juguete *m or* muñeco de trapo
stuffing ['stʌfɪŋ] *n* relleno
stuffy ['stʌfɪ] *adj* (*room*) mal ventilado; (*person*) de miras estrechas
stumble ['stʌmbl] *vi* tropezar, dar un traspié
▸ **stumble across** *vt fus* (*fig*) tropezar con
stumbling block ['stʌmblɪŋ-] *n* tropiezo, obstáculo
stump [stʌmp] *n* (*of tree*) tocón *m*; (*of limb*) muñón *m* ■ *vt*: **to be stumped** quedarse perplejo; **to be stumped for an answer** quedarse sin saber qué contestar
stun [stʌn] *vt* aturdir
stung [stʌŋ] *pt, pp of* **sting**
stunk [stʌŋk] *pp of* **stink**
stunning ['stʌnɪŋ] *adj* (*fig*) pasmoso
stunt [stʌnt] *n* (*Aviat*) vuelo acrobático; (*also*: **publicity stunt**) truco publicitario
stunted ['stʌntɪd] *adj* enano, achaparrado
stuntman ['stʌntmæn] *n* especialista *m*
stupefaction [stjuːpɪ'fækʃən] *n* estupefacción *f*
stupefy ['stjuːpɪfaɪ] *vt* dejar estupefacto
stupendous [stjuː'pɛndəs] *adj* estupendo, asombroso
stupid ['stjuːpɪd] *adj* estúpido, tonto
stupidity [stjuː'pɪdɪtɪ] *n* estupidez *f*
stupor ['stjuːpəʳ] *n* estupor *m*
sturdy ['stəːdɪ] *adj* robusto, fuerte
stutter ['stʌtəʳ] *n* tartamudeo ■ *vi* tartamudear
sty [staɪ] *n* (*for pigs*) pocilga
stye [staɪ] *n* (*Med*) orzuelo
style [staɪl] *n* estilo; (*fashion*) moda; (*of dress etc*) hechura; (*hair style*) corte *m*; **in the latest ~** en el último modelo
stylish ['staɪlɪʃ] *adj* elegante, a la moda
stylist ['staɪlɪst] *n* (*hair stylist*) peluquero(-a)
stylus (*pl* **styli** *or* **styluses**) ['staɪləs, -laɪ] *n* (*of record player*) aguja
Styrofoam® ['staɪrəfəum] *n* (*US*) poliestireno ■ *adj* (*cup*) de poliestireno
suave [swɑːv] *adj* cortés, fino
sub [sʌb] *n abbr* = **submarine; subscription**
sub... [sʌb] *pref* sub...
subcommittee ['sʌbkəmɪtɪ] *n* subcomisión *f*
subconscious [sʌb'kɔnʃəs] *adj* subconsciente ■ *n* subconsciente *m*
subcontinent [sʌb'kɔntɪnənt] *n*: **the Indian ~** el subcontinente (de la India)
subcontract *n* ['sʌb'kɔntrækt] subcontrato ■ *vt* ['sʌbkən'trækt] subcontratar
subcontractor ['sʌbkən'træktəʳ] *n* subcontratista *m/f*
subdivide [sʌbdɪ'vaɪd] *vt* subdividir
subdue [səb'djuː] *vt* sojuzgar; (*passions*) dominar
subdued [səb'djuːd] *adj* (*light*) tenue; (*person*) sumiso, manso
sub-editor ['sʌb'ɛdɪtəʳ] *n* (*Brit*) redactor(a) *m(f)*
subject *n* ['sʌbdʒɪkt] súbdito; (*Scol*) tema *m*, materia ■ *vt* [səb'dʒɛkt]: **to ~ sb to sth** someter a algn a algo ■ *adj* ['sʌbdʒɪkt]: **to be ~ to** (*law*) estar sujeto a; **~ to confirmation**

in writing sujeto a confirmación por escrito; **to change the ~** cambiar de tema
subjective [səb'dʒɛktɪv] *adj* subjetivo
subject matter *n* materia; (*content*) contenido
sub judice [sʌb'dju:dɪsɪ] *adj* (*Law*) pendiente de resolución
subjugate ['sʌbdʒugeɪt] *vt* subyugar, sojuzgar
subjunctive [səb'dʒʌŋktɪv] *adj, n* subjuntivo
sublet [sʌb'lɛt] *vt, vi* subarrendar, realquilar
sublime [sə'blaɪm] *adj* sublime
subliminal [sʌb'lɪmɪnl] *adj* subliminal
submachine gun ['sʌbmə'ʃi:n-] *n* metralleta
submarine [sʌbmə'ri:n] *n* submarino
submerge [səb'mə:dʒ] *vt* sumergir; (*flood*) inundar ■ *vi* sumergirse
submersion [səb'mə:ʃən] *n* submersión *f*
submission [səb'mɪʃən] *n* sumisión *f*; (*to committee etc*) ponencia
submissive [səb'mɪsɪv] *adj* sumiso
submit [səb'mɪt] *vt* someter; (*proposal, claim*) presentar ■ *vi* someterse; **I ~ that ...** me permito sugerir que ...
subnormal [sʌb'nɔ:məl] *adj* subnormal
subordinate [sə'bɔ:dɪnət] *adj, n* subordinado(-a) *m(f)*
subpoena [səb'pi:nə] (*Law*) *n* citación *f* ■ *vt* citar
subroutine [sʌbru:'ti:n] *n* (*Comput*) subrutina
subscribe [səb'skraɪb] *vi* suscribir; **to ~ to** (*fund*) suscribir, aprobar; (*opinion*) estar de acuerdo con; (*newspaper*) suscribirse a
subscribed capital [səb'skraɪbd-] *n* capital *m* suscrito
subscriber [səb'skraɪbə^r] *n* (*to periodical*) suscriptor(a) *m(f)*; (*to telephone*) abonado(-a)
subscript ['sʌbskrɪpt] *n* (*Typ*) subíndice *m*
subscription [səb'skrɪpʃən] *n* (*to club*) abono; (*to magazine*) suscripción *f*; **to take out a ~ to** suscribirse a
subsequent ['sʌbsɪkwənt] *adj* subsiguiente, posterior; **~ to** posterior a
subsequently ['sʌbsɪkwəntlɪ] *adv* posteriormente, más tarde
subservient [səb'sə:vɪənt] *adj*: **~ (to)** servil (a)
subside [səb'saɪd] *vi* hundirse; (*flood*) bajar; (*wind*) amainar
subsidence [səb'saɪdns] *n* hundimiento; (*in road*) socavón *m*
subsidiarity [səbsɪdɪ'ærɪtɪ] *n* (*Pol*) subsidiariedad *f*
subsidiary [səb'sɪdɪərɪ] *n* sucursal *f*, filial *f* ■ *adj* (*Univ: subject*) secundario
subsidize ['sʌbsɪdaɪz] *vt* subvencionar
subsidy ['sʌbsɪdɪ] *n* subvención *f*
subsist [səb'sɪst] *vi*: **to ~ on sth** subsistir a base de algo, sustentarse con algo
subsistence [səb'sɪstəns] *n* subsistencia
subsistence allowance *n* dietas *fpl*
subsistence level *n* nivel *m* de subsistencia
subsistence wage *n* sueldo de subsistencia
substance ['sʌbstəns] *n* sustancia; (*fig*) esencia; **to lack ~** (*argument*) ser poco convincente; (*accusation*) no tener fundamento; (*film, book*) tener poca profundidad
substance abuse *n* uso indebido de sustancias tóxicas
substandard [sʌb'stændəd] *adj* (*goods*) inferior; (*housing*) deficiente
substantial [səb'stænʃl] *adj* sustancial, sustancioso; (*fig*) importante
substantially [səb'stænʃəlɪ] *adv* sustancialmente; **~ bigger** bastante más grande
substantiate [səb'stænʃɪeɪt] *vt* comprobar
substitute ['sʌbstɪtju:t] *n* (*person*) suplente *m/f*; (*thing*) sustituto ■ *vt*: **to ~ A for B** sustituir B por A, reemplazar A por B
substitution [sʌbstɪ'tju:ʃən] *n* sustitución *f*
subterfuge ['sʌbtəfju:dʒ] *n* subterfugio
subterranean [sʌbtə'reɪnɪən] *adj* subterráneo
subtitle ['sʌbtaɪtl] *n* subtítulo
subtle ['sʌtl] *adj* sutil
subtlety ['sʌtltɪ] *n* sutileza
subtly ['sʌtlɪ] *adv* sutilmente
subtotal [sʌb'təutl] *n* subtotal *m*
subtract [səb'trækt] *vt* restar; sustraer
subtraction [səb'trækʃən] *n* resta; sustracción *f*
suburb ['sʌbə:b] *n* barrio residencial; **the suburbs** las afueras (de la ciudad)
suburban [sə'bə:bən] *adj* suburbano; (*train etc*) de cercanías
suburbia [sə'bə:bɪə] *n* barrios *mpl* residenciales
subversion [səb'və:ʃən] *n* subversión *f*
subversive [səb'və:sɪv] *adj* subversivo
subway ['sʌbweɪ] *n* (*Brit*) paso subterráneo *or* inferior; (*US*) metro
sub-zero [sʌb'zɪərəu] *adj*: **~ temperatures** temperaturas *fpl* por debajo del cero
succeed [sək'si:d] *vi* (*person*) tener éxito; (*plan*) salir bien ■ *vt* suceder a; **to ~ in doing** lograr hacer
succeeding [sək'si:dɪŋ] *adj* (*following*) sucesivo; **~ generations** generaciones *fpl* futuras
success [sək'sɛs] *n* éxito; (*gain*) triunfo
successful [sək'sɛsful] *adj* (*venture*) de éxito, exitoso (*esp LAm*); **to be ~ (in doing)** lograr (hacer)

successfully [sək'sɛsfulɪ] *adv* con éxito
succession [sək'sɛʃən] *n* (*series*) sucesión *f*, serie *f*; (*descendants*) descendencia; **in ~** sucesivamente
successive [sək'sɛsɪv] *adj* sucesivo, consecutivo; **on three ~ days** tres días seguidos
successor [sək'sɛsəʳ] *n* sucesor(a) *m(f)*
succinct [sək'sɪŋkt] *adj* sucinto
succulent ['sʌkjulənt] *adj* suculento ■ *n* (*Bot*); **succulents** *npl* plantas *fpl* carnosas
succumb [sə'kʌm] *vi* sucumbir
such [sʌtʃ] *adj* tal, semejante; (*of that kind*): **~ a book** tal libro; **~ books** tales libros; (*so much*): **~ courage** tanto valor ■ *adv* tan; **~ a long trip** un viaje tan largo; **~ a lot of** tanto; **~ as** (*like*) tal como; **a noise ~ as to** un ruido tal que; **~ books as I have** cuantos libros tengo; **I said no ~ thing** no dije tal cosa; **it's ~ a long time since we saw each other** hace tanto tiempo que no nos vemos; **~ a long time ago** hace tantísimo tiempo; **as ~** *adv* como tal
such-and-such ['sʌtʃənsʌtʃ] *adj* tal o cual
suchlike ['sʌtʃlaɪk] *pron* (*col*): **and ~** y cosas por el estilo
suck [sʌk] *vt* chupar; (*bottle*) sorber; (*breast*) mamar; (*pump, machine*) aspirar
sucker ['sʌkəʳ] *n* (*Bot*) serpollo; (*Zool*) ventosa; (*col*) bobo, primo
sucrose ['su:krəuz] *n* sacarosa
suction ['sʌkʃən] *n* succión *f*
suction pump *n* bomba aspirante *or* de succión
Sudan [su'dæn] *n* Sudán *m*
Sudanese [su:də'ni:z] *adj, n* sudanés(-esa) *m(f)*
sudden ['sʌdn] *adj* (*rapid*) repentino, súbito; (*unexpected*) imprevisto; **all of a ~** de repente
sudden-death [sʌdn'dɛθ] *n* (*also*: **sudden-death play off**) desempate *m* instantáneo, muerte *f* súbita
suddenly ['sʌdnlɪ] *adv* de repente
sudoku [sʊ'dəʊku:] *n* sudoku *m*
suds [sʌdz] *npl* espuma *sg* de jabón
sue [su:] *vt* demandar; **to ~ (for)** demandar (por); **to ~ for divorce** solicitar *or* pedir el divorcio; **to ~ for damages** demandar por daños y perjuicios
suede [sweɪd] *n* ante *m*, gamuza (*LAm*)
suet ['suɪt] *n* sebo
Suez Canal ['su:ɪz-] *n* Canal *m* de Suez
Suff. *abbr* (*Brit*) = **Suffolk**
suffer ['sʌfəʳ] *vt* sufrir, padecer; (*tolerate*) aguantar, soportar; (*undergo: loss, setback*) experimentar ■ *vi* sufrir, padecer; **to ~ from** sufrir, tener; **to ~ from the effects of alcohol/a fall** sufrir los efectos del alcohol/ resentirse de una caída
sufferance ['sʌfərns] *n*: **he was only there on ~** estuvo allí sólo porque se lo toleraron
sufferer ['sʌfərəʳ] *n* víctima *f*; (*Med*): **~ from** enfermo(-a) de
suffering ['sʌfərɪŋ] *n* (*hardship, deprivation*) sufrimiento; (*pain*) dolor *m*
suffice [sə'faɪs] *vi* bastar, ser suficiente
sufficient [sə'fɪʃənt] *adj* suficiente, bastante
sufficiently [sə'fɪʃəntlɪ] *adv* suficientemente, bastante
suffix ['sʌfɪks] *n* sufijo
suffocate ['sʌfəkeɪt] *vi* ahogarse, asfixiarse
suffocation [sʌfə'keɪʃən] *n* sofocación *f*, asfixia
suffrage ['sʌfrɪdʒ] *n* sufragio
suffuse [sə'fju:z] *vt*: **to ~ (with)** (*colour*) bañar (de); **her face was suffused with joy** su cara estaba llena de alegría
sugar ['ʃugəʳ] *n* azúcar *m* ■ *vt* echar azúcar a, azucarar
sugar basin *n* (*Brit*) = **sugar bowl**
sugar beet *n* remolacha
sugar bowl *n* azucarero
sugar cane *n* caña de azúcar
sugar-coated [ʃugə'kəutɪd] *adj* azucarado
sugar lump *n* terrón *m* de azúcar
sugar refinery *n* refinería de azúcar
sugary ['ʃugərɪ] *adj* azucarado
suggest [sə'dʒɛst] *vt* sugerir; (*recommend*) aconsejar; **what do you ~ I do?** ¿qué sugieres que haga?; **this suggests that ...** esto hace pensar que ...
suggestion [sə'dʒɛstʃən] *n* sugerencia; **there's no ~ of ...** no hay indicación *or* evidencia de ...
suggestive [sə'dʒɛstɪv] *adj* sugestivo; (*pej: indecent*) indecente
suicidal ['suɪsaɪdl] *adj* suicida
suicide ['suɪsaɪd] *n* suicidio; (*person*) suicida *m/f*; **to commit ~** suicidarse
suicide attempt, suicide bid *n* intento de suicidio
suicide bomber *n* terrorista *m/f* suicida
suicide bombing *n* atentado *m* suicida
suit [su:t] *n* (*man's*) traje *m*; (*woman's*) traje de chaqueta; (*Law*) pleito; (*Cards*) palo ■ *vt* convenir; (*clothes*) sentar bien a, ir bien a; (*adapt*): **to ~ sth to** adaptar *or* ajustar algo a; **to be suited to sth** (*suitable for*) ser apto para algo; **well suited** (*couple*) hechos el uno para el otro; **to bring a ~ against sb** entablar demanda contra algn; **to follow ~** (*Cards*) seguir el palo; (*fig*) seguir el ejemplo (de algn); **that suits me** me va bien

suitable ['su:təbl] *adj* conveniente; (*apt*) indicado
suitably ['su:təblɪ] *adv* convenientemente; (*appropriately*) en forma debida
suitcase ['su:tkeɪs] *n* maleta, valija (*LAm*)
suite [swi:t] *n* (*of rooms*) suite *f*; (*Mus*) suite *f*; (*furniture*): **bedroom/dining room ~** (juego de) dormitorio/comedor *m*; **a three-piece ~** un tresillo
suitor ['su:tər] *n* pretendiente *m*
sulfate ['sʌlfeɪt] *n* (*US*) = **sulphate**
sulfur ['sʌlfər] *n* (*US*) = **sulphur**
sulk [sʌlk] *vi* estar de mal humor
sulky ['sʌlkɪ] *adj* malhumorado
sullen ['sʌlən] *adj* hosco, malhumorado
sulphate, sulfate (*US*) ['sʌlfeɪt] *n* sulfato; **copper ~** sulfato de cobre
sulphur, sulfur (*US*) ['sʌlfər] *n* azufre *m*
sulphur dioxide *n* dióxido de azufre
sultan ['sʌltən] *n* sultán *m*
sultana [sʌl'tɑ:nə] *n* (*fruit*) pasa de Esmirna
sultry ['sʌltrɪ] *adj* (*weather*) bochornoso; (*seductive*) seductor(a)
sum [sʌm] *n* suma; (*total*) total *m*
▶ **sum up** *vt* resumir; (*evaluate rapidly*) evaluar ■ *vi* hacer un resumen
Sumatra [su'mɑ:trə] *n* Sumatra
summarize ['sʌməraɪz] *vt* resumir
summary ['sʌmərɪ] *n* resumen *m* ■ *adj* (*justice*) sumario
summer ['sʌmər] *n* verano ■ *adj* de verano; **in (the) ~** en (el) verano
summerhouse ['sʌməhaus] *n* (*in garden*) cenador *m*, glorieta
summertime ['sʌmətaɪm] *n* (*season*) verano
summer time *n* (*by clock*) hora de verano
summery ['sʌmərɪ] *adj* veraniego
summing-up [sʌmɪŋ'ʌp] *n* (*Law*) resumen *m*
summit ['sʌmɪt] *n* cima, cumbre *f*; (*also*: **summit conference**) (conferencia) cumbre *f*
summit conference *n* conferencia cumbre *f*
summon ['sʌmən] *vt* (*person*) llamar; (*meeting*) convocar; **to ~ a witness** citar a un testigo
▶ **summon up** *vt* (*courage*) armarse de
summons ['sʌmənz] *n* llamamiento, llamada ■ *vt* citar, emplazar; **to serve a ~ on sb** citar a algn ante el juicio
sumo ['su:məu] *n* (*also*: **sumo wrestling**) sumo
sump [sʌmp] *n* (*Brit Aut*) cárter *m*
sumptuous ['sʌmptjuəs] *adj* suntuoso
sun [sʌn] *n* sol *m*; **they have everything under the ~** no les falta nada, tienen de todo
Sun. *abbr* (= *Sunday*) dom
sunbathe ['sʌnbeɪð] *vi* tomar el sol
sunbeam ['sʌnbi:m] *n* rayo de sol
sunbed ['sʌnbɛd] *n* cama solar
sunburn ['sʌnbə:n] *n* (*painful*) quemadura del sol; (*tan*) bronceado
sunburnt ['sʌnbə:nt], **sunburned** ['sʌnbə:nd] *adj* (*tanned*) bronceado; (*painfully*) quemado por el sol
sundae ['sʌndeɪ] *n* *helado con frutas y nueces*
Sunday ['sʌndɪ] *n* domingo; *see also* **Tuesday**
Sunday paper *n* (periódico) dominical *m*
Sunday school *n* catequesis *f*
sundial ['sʌndaɪəl] *n* reloj *m* de sol
sundown ['sʌndaun] *n* anochecer *m*, puesta de sol
sundries ['sʌndrɪz] *npl* géneros *mpl* diversos
sundry ['sʌndrɪ] *adj* varios, diversos; **all and ~** todos sin excepción
sunflower ['sʌnflauər] *n* girasol *m*
sung [sʌŋ] *pp of* **sing**
sunglasses ['sʌnglɑ:sɪz] *npl* gafas *fpl* de sol
sunk [sʌŋk] *pp of* **sink**
sunken ['sʌŋkn] *adj* (*bath*) hundido
sunlamp ['sʌnlæmp] *n* lámpara solar ultravioleta
sunlight ['sʌnlaɪt] *n* luz *f* del sol
sunlit ['sʌnlɪt] *adj* iluminado por el sol
sunny ['sʌnɪ] *adj* soleado; (*day*) de sol; (*fig*) alegre; **it is ~** hace sol
sunrise ['sʌnraɪz] *n* salida del sol
sun roof *n* (*Aut*) techo corredizo *or* solar; (*on building*) azotea, terraza
sunscreen ['sʌnskri:n] *n* protector *m* solar
sunset ['sʌnsɛt] *n* puesta del sol
sunshade ['sʌnʃeɪd] *n* (*over table*) sombrilla
sunshine ['sʌnʃaɪn] *n* sol *m*
sunstroke ['sʌnstrəuk] *n* insolación *f*
suntan ['sʌntæn] *n* bronceado
suntanned ['sʌntænd] *adj* bronceado
suntan oil *n* aceite *m* bronceador
super ['su:pər] *adj* (*col*) bárbaro
superannuation [su:pərænju'eɪʃən] *n* jubilación *f*, pensión *f*
superb [su:'pə:b] *adj* magnífico, espléndido
Super Bowl *n* (*US Sport*) *super copa de fútbol americano*
supercilious [su:pə'sɪlɪəs] *adj* (*disdainful*) desdeñoso; (*haughty*) altanero
superconductor [su:pəkən'dʌktər] *n* superconductor *m*
superficial [su:pə'fɪʃəl] *adj* superficial
superfluous [su'pə:fluəs] *adj* superfluo, de sobra
superglue ['su:pəglu:] *n* cola de contacto, supercola
superhighway ['su:pəhaɪweɪ] *n* (*US*) superautopista; **the information ~** la superautopista de la información
superhuman [su:pə'hju:mən] *adj* sobrehumano

superimpose ['su:pərɪm'pəuz] *vt* sobreponer
superintend [su:pərɪn'tɛnd] *vt* supervisar
superintendent [su:pərɪn'tɛndənt] *n* director(a) *m(f)*; (*also*: **police superintendent**) subjefe(-a) *m(f)*
superior [su'pɪərɪə^r] *adj* superior; (*smug: person*) altivo, desdeñoso; (*: smile, air*) de suficiencia; (*: remark*) desdeñoso ■ *n* superior *m*; **Mother S~** (*Rel*) madre *f* superiora
superiority [supɪərɪ'ɔrɪtɪ] *n* superioridad *f*; desdén *m*
superlative [su'pə:lətɪv] *adj, n* superlativo
superman ['su:pəmæn] *n* superhombre *m*
supermarket ['su:pəmɑ:kɪt] *n* supermercado
supermodel ['su:pəmɔdl] *n* top model *f*, supermodelo *f*
supernatural [su:pə'nætʃərəl] *adj* sobrenatural
supernova [su:pə'nəuvə] *n* supernova
superpower ['su:pəpauə^r] *n* (*Pol*) superpotencia
supersede [su:pə'si:d] *vt* suplantar
supersonic ['su:pə'sɔnɪk] *adj* supersónico
superstar ['su:pəstɑ:^r] *n* superestrella ■ *adj* de superestrella
superstition [su:pə'stɪʃən] *n* superstición *f*
superstitious [su:pə'stɪʃəs] *adj* supersticioso
superstore ['su:pəstɔ:^r] *n* (*Brit*) hipermercado
supertanker ['su:pətæŋkə^r] *n* superpetrolero
supertax ['su:pətæks] *n* sobretasa, sobreimpuesto
supervise ['su:pəvaɪz] *vt* supervisar
supervision [su:pə'vɪʒən] *n* supervisión *f*
supervisor ['su:pəvaɪzə^r] *n* supervisor(a) *m(f)*
supervisory ['su:pəvaɪzərɪ] *adj* de supervisión
supper ['sʌpə^r] *n* cena; **to have ~** cenar
supplant [sə'plɑ:nt] *vt* suplantar, reemplazar
supple ['sʌpl] *adj* flexible
supplement *n* ['sʌplɪmənt] suplemento ■ *vt* [sʌplɪ'mɛnt] suplir
supplementary [sʌplɪ'mɛntərɪ] *adj* suplementario
supplementary benefit *n* (*Brit*) subsidio adicional de la seguridad social
supplier [sə'plaɪə^r] *n* suministrador(a) *m(f)*; (*Comm*) distribuidor(a) *m(f)*
supply [sə'plaɪ] *vt* (*provide*) suministrar; (*information*) facilitar; (*fill: need, want*) suplir, satisfacer; (*equip*): **to ~ (with)** proveer (de) ■ *n* provisión *f*; (*of gas, water etc*) suministro ■ *adj* (*Brit: teacher etc*) suplente; **supplies** *npl* (*food*) víveres *mpl*; (*Mil*) pertrechos *mpl*; **office supplies** materiales *mpl* para oficina; **to be in short ~** escasear, haber escasez de; **the electricity/water/gas ~** el suministro de electricidad/agua/gas; **~ and demand** la oferta y la demanda
support [sə'pɔ:t] *n* (*moral, financial etc*) apoyo; (*Tech*) soporte *m* ■ *vt* apoyar; (*financially*) mantener; (*uphold*) sostener; (*Sport: team*) seguir, ser hincha de; **they stopped work in ~ (of)** pararon de trabajar en apoyo (de); **to ~ o.s.** (*financially*) ganarse la vida
support buying [-'baɪɪŋ] *n* compra proteccionista
supporter [sə'pɔ:tə^r] *n* (*Pol etc*) partidario(-a); (*Sport*) aficionado(-a); (*Football*) hincha *m/f*
supporting [sə'pɔ:tɪŋ] *adj* (*wall*) de apoyo; **~ role** papel *m* secundario; **~ actor/actress** actor/actriz *m/f* secundario(-a)
supportive [sə'pɔ:tɪv] *adj* de apoyo; **I have a ~ family/wife** mi familia/mujer me apoya
suppose [sə'pəuz] *vt, vi* suponer; (*imagine*) imaginarse; **to be supposed to do sth** deber hacer algo; **I don't ~ she'll come** no creo que venga; **he's supposed to be an expert** se le supone un experto
supposedly [sə'pəuzɪdlɪ] *adv* según cabe suponer
supposing [sə'pəuzɪŋ] *conj* en caso de que; **always ~ (that) he comes** suponiendo que venga
supposition [sʌpə'zɪʃən] *n* suposición *f*
suppository [sə'pɔzɪtrɪ] *n* supositorio
suppress [sə'prɛs] *vt* suprimir; (*yawn*) ahogar
suppression [sə'prɛʃən] *n* represión *f*
supremacy [su'prɛməsɪ] *n* supremacía
supreme [su'pri:m] *adj* supremo
Supreme Court *n* (*US*) Tribunal *m* Supremo, Corte *f* Suprema
supremo [su'pri:məu] *n* autoridad *f* máxima
Supt. *abbr* (*Police*) = **superintendent**
surcharge ['sə:tʃɑ:dʒ] *n* sobretasa, recargo
sure [ʃuə^r] *adj* seguro; (*definite, convinced*) cierto; (*aim*) certero ■ *adv*: **that ~ is pretty, that's ~ pretty** (*US*) ¡qué bonito es!; **to be ~ of sth** estar seguro de algo; **to be ~ of o.s.** estar seguro de sí mismo; **to make ~ of sth/that** asegurarse de algo/asegurar que; **I'm not ~ how/why/when** no estoy seguro de cómo/por qué/cuándo; **~!** (*of course*) ¡claro!, ¡por supuesto!; **~ enough** efectivamente
sure-fire ['ʃuəfaɪə^r] *adj* (*col*) infalible
sure-footed [ʃuə'futɪd] *adj* de pie firme
surely ['ʃuəlɪ] *adv* (*certainly*) seguramente; **~ you don't mean that!** ¡no lo dices en serio!
surety ['ʃuərətɪ] *n* fianza; (*person*) fiador(a) *m(f)*; **to go** *or* **stand ~ for sb** ser fiador de algn, salir garante por algn
surf [sə:f] *n* olas *fpl* ■ *vi* hacer surf ■ *vt* (*Internet*): **to ~ the Net** navegar por Internet

surface ['sə:fɪs] *n* superficie *f* ■ *vt* (*road*) revestir ■ *vi* salir a la superficie ■ *cpd* (*Mil, Naut*) de (la) superficie; **on the ~ it seems that ...** (*fig*) a primera vista parece que ...
surface area *n* área de la superficie
surface mail *n* vía terrestre
surface-to-air ['sə:fɪstə'ɛəʳ] *adj* (*Mil*) tierra-aire
surface-to-surface ['sə:fɪstə'sə:fɪs] *adj* (*Mil*) tierra-tierra
surfboard ['sə:fbɔ:d] *n* plancha (de surf)
surfeit ['sə:fɪt] *n*: **a ~ of** un exceso de
surfer ['sə:fəʳ] *n* súrfer *m/f*
surfing ['sə:fɪŋ] *n* surf *m*
surge [sə:dʒ] *n* oleada, oleaje *m*; (*Elec*) sobretensión *f* transitoria ■ *vi* avanzar a tropel; **to ~ forward** avanzar rápidamente
surgeon ['sə:dʒən] *n* cirujano(-a)
surgery ['sə:dʒərɪ] *n* cirugía; (*Brit: room*) consultorio; (*: Pol*) *horas en las que los electores pueden reunirse personalmente con su diputado*; **to undergo ~** operarse; *see also* **constituency**
surgery hours *npl* (*Brit*) horas *fpl* de consulta
surgical ['sə:dʒɪkl] *adj* quirúrgico
surgical spirit *n* (*Brit*) alcohol *m*
surly ['sə:lɪ] *adj* hosco, malhumorado
surmount [sə:'maunt] *vt* superar, vencer
surname ['sə:neɪm] *n* apellido
surpass [sə:'pɑ:s] *vt* superar, exceder
surplus ['sə:pləs] *n* excedente *m*; (*Comm*) superávit *m* ■ *adj* (*Comm*) excedente, sobrante; **to have a ~ of sth** tener un excedente de algo; **it is ~ to our requirements** nos sobra; **~ stock** saldos *mpl*
surprise [sə'praɪz] *n* sorpresa ■ *vt* sorprender; **to take by ~** (*person*) coger desprevenido *or* por sorpresa a, sorprender a; (*Mil: town, fort*) atacar por sorpresa
surprising [sə'praɪzɪŋ] *adj* sorprendente
surprisingly [sə'praɪzɪŋlɪ] *adv* (*easy, helpful*) de modo sorprendente; **(somewhat) ~, he agreed** para sorpresa de todos, aceptó
surrealism [sə'rɪəlɪzəm] *n* surrealismo
surrender [sə'rɛndəʳ] *n* rendición *f*, entrega ■ *vi* rendirse, entregarse ■ *vt* renunciar
surrender value *n* valor *m* de rescate
surreptitious [sʌrəp'tɪʃəs] *adj* subrepticio
surrogate ['sʌrəgɪt] *n* (*Brit*) sustituto(-a)
surrogate mother *n* madre *f* de alquiler
surround [sə'raund] *vt* rodear, circundar; (*Mil etc*) cercar
surrounding [sə'raundɪŋ] *adj* circundante
surroundings [sə'raundɪŋz] *npl* alrededores *mpl*, cercanías *fpl*
surtax ['sə:tæks] *n* sobretasa, sobreimpuesto
surveillance [sə:'veɪləns] *n* vigilancia
survey *n* ['sə:veɪ] inspección *f* reconocimiento; (*inquiry*) encuesta; (*comprehensive view: of situation etc*) vista de conjunto ■ *vt* [sə:'veɪ] examinar, inspeccionar; (*Surveying: building*) inspeccionar; (*: land*) hacer un reconocimiento de, reconocer; (*look at*) mirar, contemplar; (*make inquiries about*) hacer una encuesta de; **to carry out a ~ of** inspeccionar, examinar
surveyor [sə'veɪəʳ] *n* (*Brit: of building*) perito *m/f*; (*of land*) agrimensor(a) *m(f)*
survival [sə'vaɪvl] *n* supervivencia
survival course *n* curso de supervivencia
survival kit *n* equipo de emergencia
survive [sə'vaɪv] *vi* sobrevivir; (*custom etc*) perdurar ■ *vt* sobrevivir a
survivor [sə'vaɪvəʳ] *n* superviviente *m/f*
susceptibility [səsɛptə'bɪlɪtɪ] *n* (*to illness*) propensión *f*
susceptible [sə'sɛptəbl] *adj* (*easily influenced*) influenciable; (*to disease, illness*): **~ to** propenso a
sushi [su:ʃɪ] *n* sushi *m*
suspect *adj, n* ['sʌspɛkt] sospechoso(-a) *m(f)* ■ *vt* [səs'pɛkt] sospechar
suspected [səs'pɛktɪd] *adj* presunto; **to have a ~ fracture** tener una posible fractura
suspend [səs'pɛnd] *vt* suspender
suspended animation [səs'pɛndəd-] *n*: **in a state of ~** en (estado de) hibernación
suspended sentence *n* (*Law*) libertad *f* condicional
suspender belt [səs'pɛndəʳ-] *n* (*Brit*) liguero, portaligas *m inv* (*LAm*)
suspenders [səs'pɛndəz] *npl* (*Brit*) ligas *fpl*; (*US*) tirantes *mpl*
suspense [səs'pɛns] *n* incertidumbre *f*, duda; (*in film etc*) suspense *m*
suspension [səs'pɛnʃən] *n* (*gen*) suspensión *f*; (*of driving licence*) privación *f*
suspension bridge *n* puente *m* colgante
suspension file *n* archivador *m* colgante
suspicion [səs'pɪʃən] *n* sospecha; (*distrust*) recelo; (*trace*) traza; **to be under ~** estar bajo sospecha; **arrested on ~ of murder** detenido bajo sospecha de asesinato
suspicious [səs'pɪʃəs] *adj* (*suspecting*) receloso; (*causing suspicion*) sospechoso; **to be ~ of** *or* **about sb/sth** tener sospechas de algn/algo
suss out [sʌs-] *vt* (*Brit col*) calar
sustain [səs'teɪn] *vt* sostener, apoyar; (*suffer*) sufrir, padecer
sustainable [səs'teɪnəbl] *adj* sostenible; **~ development** desarrollo sostenible
sustained [səs'teɪnd] *adj* (*effort*) sostenido
sustenance ['sʌstɪnəns] *n* sustento
suture ['su:tʃəʳ] *n* sutura

SUV ['ɛs'juː'viː] *n abbr (= sports utility vehicle)* todoterreno *m inv*
SVQ *n abbr (= Scottish Vocational Qualification) titulación de formación profesional en Escocia*
SW *abbr* = **short wave**
swab [swɔb] *n (Med)* algodón *m*, frotis *m inv* ■ *vt (Naut: also:* **swab down**) limpiar, fregar
swagger ['swægəʳ] *vi* pavonearse
swallow ['swɔləu] *n (bird)* golondrina; *(of food)* bocado; *(of drink)* trago ■ *vt* tragar
▸ **swallow up** *vt (savings etc)* consumir
swam [swæm] *pt of* **swim**
swamp [swɔmp] *n* pantano, ciénaga ■ *vt* abrumar, agobiar
swampy ['swɔmpɪ] *adj* pantanoso
swan [swɔn] *n* cisne *m*
swank [swæŋk] *(col) n (vanity, boastfulness)* fanfarronada ■ *vi* fanfarronear, presumir
swan song *n (fig)* canto del cisne
swap [swɔp] *n* canje *m*, trueque *m* ■ *vt:* **to ~ (for)** canjear (por)
SWAPO ['swɑːpəu] *n abbr (= South-West Africa People's Organization)* SWAPO *f*
swarm [swɔːm] *n (of bees)* enjambre *m*; *(fig)* multitud *f* ■ *vi (fig)* hormiguear, pulular
swarthy ['swɔːðɪ] *adj* moreno
swashbuckling ['swɔʃbʌklɪŋ] *adj (person)* aventurero; *(film)* de capa y espada
swastika ['swɔstɪkə] *n* esvástika, cruz *f* gamada
swat [swɔt] *vt* aplastar ■ *n (also:* **fly swat**) matamoscas *m inv*
SWAT [swɔt] *n abbr (US: = Special Weapons and Tactics) unidad especial de la policía*
swathe [sweɪð] *vt:* **to ~ in** *(blankets)* envolver en; *(bandages)* vendar en
sway [sweɪ] *vi* mecerse, balancearse ■ *vt (influence)* mover, influir en ■ *n (rule, power):* **~ (over)** dominio (sobre); **to hold ~ over sb** dominar a algn, mantener el dominio sobre algn
Swaziland ['swɑːzɪlænd] *n* Swazilandia
swear *(pt* **swore**, *pp* **sworn**) [swɛəʳ, swɔːʳ, swɔːn] *vi* jurar; *(with swearwords)* decir tacos ■ *vt:* **to ~ an oath** prestar juramento, jurar; **to ~ to sth** declarar algo bajo juramento
▸ **swear in** *vt* tomar juramento (a)
swearword ['swɛəwəːd] *n* taco, palabrota
sweat [swɛt] *n* sudor *m* ■ *vi* sudar
sweatband ['swɛtbænd] *n (Sport: on head)* banda; *(: on wrist)* muñequera
sweater ['swɛtəʳ] *n* suéter *m*
sweatshirt ['swɛtʃəːt] *n* sudadera
sweatshop ['swɛtʃɔp] *n* fábrica donde se explota al obrero
sweaty ['swɛtɪ] *adj* sudoroso
Swede [swiːd] *n* sueco(-a)
swede [swiːd] *n (Brit)* nabo
Sweden ['swiːdn] *n* Suecia
Swedish ['swiːdɪʃ] *adj, n (Ling)* sueco
sweep [swiːp] *(pt, pp* **swept**) *n (act)* barrida; *(of arm)* manotazo *m*; *(curve)* curva, alcance *m*; *(also:* **chimney sweep**) deshollinador(a) *m(f)* ■ *vt* barrer; *(disease, fashion)* recorrer ■ *vi* barrer
▸ **sweep away** *vt* barrer; *(rub out)* borrar
▸ **sweep past** *vi* pasar rápidamente; *(brush by)* rozar
▸ **sweep up** *vi* barrer
sweeper ['swiːpəʳ] *n (person)* barrendero(-a); *(machine)* barredora; *(Football)* líbero, libre *m*
sweeping ['swiːpɪŋ] *adj (gesture)* dramático; *(generalized)* generalizado; *(changes, reforms)* radical
sweepstake ['swiːpsteɪk] *n* lotería
sweet [swiːt] *n (candy)* dulce *m*, caramelo; *(Brit: pudding)* postre *m* ■ *adj* dulce; *(sugary)* azucarado; *(charming: person)* encantador(a); *(: smile, character)* dulce, amable, agradable ■ *adv:* **to smell/taste ~** oler/saber dulce
sweet and sour *adj* agridulce
sweetcorn ['swiːtkɔːn] *n* maíz *m* (dulce)
sweeten ['swiːtn] *vt (person)* endulzar; *(add sugar to)* poner azúcar a
sweetener ['swiːtnəʳ] *n (Culin)* edulcorante *m*
sweetheart ['swiːthɑːt] *n* amor *m*, novio(-a); *(in speech)* amor, cariño
sweetness ['swiːtnɪs] *n (gen)* dulzura
sweet pea *n* guisante *m* de olor
sweet potato *n* batata, camote *m (LAm)*
sweetshop ['swiːtʃɔp] *n (Brit)* confitería, bombonería
swell [swɛl] *(pt* **swelled**, *pp* **swollen** *or* **swelled**) *n (of sea)* marejada, oleaje *m* ■ *adj (US: col: excellent)* estupendo, fenomenal ■ *vt* hinchar, inflar ■ *vi* hincharse, inflarse
swelling ['swɛlɪŋ] *n (Med)* hinchazón *f*
sweltering ['swɛltərɪŋ] *adj* sofocante, de mucho calor
swept [swɛpt] *pt, pp of* **sweep**
swerve [swəːv] *n* regate *m*; *(in car)* desvío brusco ■ *vi* desviarse bruscamente
swift [swɪft] *n (bird)* vencejo ■ *adj* rápido, veloz
swiftly ['swɪftlɪ] *adv* rápidamente
swiftness ['swɪftnɪs] *n* rapidez *f*, velocidad *f*
swig [swɪg] *n (col: drink)* trago
swill [swɪl] *n* bazofia ■ *vt (also:* **swill out, swill down**) lavar, limpiar con agua
swim [swɪm] *(pt* **swam**, *pp* **swum**) *n:* **to go for a ~** ir a nadar *or* a bañarse ■ *vi* nadar; *(head, room)* dar vueltas ■ *vt* pasar a nado; **to go swimming** ir a nadar; **to ~ a length** nadar *or* hacer un largo

swimmer ['swɪmə^r] *n* nadador(a) *m(f)*
swimming ['swɪmɪŋ] *n* natación *f*
swimming cap *n* gorro de baño
swimming costume *n* bañador *m*, traje *m* de baño
swimmingly ['swɪmɪŋlɪ] *adv*: **to go ~** (*wonderfully*) ir como una seda *or* sobre ruedas
swimming pool *n* piscina, alberca (*LAm*)
swimming trunks *npl* bañador *msg*
swimsuit ['swɪmsu:t] *n* = **swimming costume**
swindle ['swɪndl] *n* estafa ■ *vt* estafar
swine [swaɪn] *n pl inv* cerdo, puerco; (*col!*) canalla *m* (*!*)
swing [swɪŋ] (*pt, pp* **swung**) *n* (*in playground*) columpio; (*movement*) balanceo, vaivén *m*; (*change of direction*) viraje *m*; (*rhythm*) ritmo; (*Pol: in votes etc*): **there has been a ~ towards/away from Labour** ha habido un viraje en favor/en contra del Partido Laborista ■ *vt* balancear; (*on a swing*) columpiar; (*also*: **swing round**) voltear, girar ■ *vi* balancearse, columpiarse; (*also*: **swing round**) dar media vuelta; **a ~ to the left** un movimiento hacia la izquierda; **to be in full ~** estar en plena marcha; **to get into the ~ of things** meterse en situación; **the road swings south** la carretera gira hacia el sur
swing bridge *n* puente *m* giratorio
swing door, swinging door (*US*) ['swɪŋɪŋ-] *n* puerta giratoria
swingeing ['swɪndʒɪŋ] *adj* (*Brit*) abrumador(a)
swipe [swaɪp] *n* golpe *m* fuerte ■ *vt* (*hit*) golpear fuerte; (*col: steal*) guindar; (*credit card etc*) pasar
swirl [swə:l] *vi* arremolinarse
swish [swɪʃ] *n* (*sound: of whip*) chasquido; (*: of skirts*) frufrú *m*; (*: of grass*) crujido ■ *adj* (*col: smart*) elegante ■ *vi* chasquear
Swiss [swɪs] *adj, n* (*pl inv*) suizo(-a) *m(f)*
switch [swɪtʃ] *n* (*for light, radio etc*) interruptor *m*; (*change*) cambio ■ *vt* (*change*) cambiar de; (*invert: also*: **switch round, switch over**) intercambiar
▸ **switch off** *vt* apagar; (*engine*) parar
▸ **switch on** *vt* (*Aut: ignition*) encender, prender (*LAm*); (*engine, machine*) arrancar; (*water supply*) conectar
switchboard ['swɪtʃbɔ:d] *n* (*Tel*) centralita (de teléfonos), conmutador *m* (*LAm*)
Switzerland ['swɪtsələnd] *n* Suiza
swivel ['swɪvl] *vi* (*also*: **swivel round**) girar
swollen ['swəulən] *pp of* **swell**
swoon [swu:n] *vi* desmayarse
swoop [swu:p] *n* (*by police etc*) redada; (*of bird etc*) descenso en picado, calada ■ *vi* (*also*: **swoop down**) caer en picado
swop [swɔp] = **swap**
sword [sɔ:d] *n* espada
swordfish ['sɔ:dfɪʃ] *n* pez *m* espada
swore [swɔ:^r] *pt of* **swear**
sworn [swɔ:n] *pp of* **swear**
swot [swɔt] (*Brit*) *vt, vi* empollar ■ *n* empollón(-ona) *m(f)*
swum [swʌm] *pp of* **swim**
swung [swʌŋ] *pt, pp of* **swing**
sycamore ['sɪkəmɔ:^r] *n* sicomoro
sycophant ['sɪkəfænt] *n* adulador(a) *m(f)* pelotillero(-a)
Sydney ['sɪdnɪ] *n* Sidney *m*
syllable ['sɪləbl] *n* sílaba
syllabus ['sɪləbəs] *n* programa *m* de estudios; **on the ~** en el programa de estudios
symbol ['sɪmbl] *n* símbolo
symbolic [sɪm'bɔlɪk], **symbolical** [sɪm'bɔlɪkl] *adj* simbólico; **to be ~(al) of sth** simbolizar algo
symbolism ['sɪmbəlɪzəm] *n* simbolismo
symbolize ['sɪmbəlaɪz] *vt* simbolizar
symmetrical [sɪ'mɛtrɪkl] *adj* simétrico
symmetry ['sɪmɪtrɪ] *n* simetría
sympathetic [sɪmpə'θɛtɪk] *adj* compasivo; (*understanding*) comprensivo; **to be ~ to a cause** (*well-disposed*) apoyar una causa; **to be ~ towards** (*person*) ser comprensivo con
sympathize ['sɪmpəθaɪz] *vi*: **to ~ with sb** compadecerse de algn; (*understand*) comprender a algn
sympathizer ['sɪmpəθaɪzə^r] *n* (*Pol*) simpatizante *m/f*
sympathy ['sɪmpəθɪ] *n* (*pity*) compasión *f*; (*understanding*) comprensión *f*; **a letter of ~** un pésame; **with our deepest ~** nuestro más sentido pésame
symphony ['sɪmfənɪ] *n* sinfonía
symposium [sɪm'pəuzɪəm] *n* simposio
symptom ['sɪmptəm] *n* síntoma *m*, indicio
symptomatic [sɪmptə'mætɪk] *adj*: **~ (of)** sintomático (de)
synagogue ['sɪnəgɔg] *n* sinagoga
sync [sɪŋk] *n* (*col*): **to be in/out of ~ (with)** ir/no ir al mismo ritmo (que); (*fig: people*) conectar/no conectar con
synchromesh ['sɪŋkrəumɛʃ] *n* cambio sincronizado de velocidades
synchronize ['sɪŋkrənaɪz] *vt* sincronizar ■ *vi*: **to ~ with** sincronizarse con
synchronized swimming ['sɪŋkrənaɪzd-] *n* natación *f* sincronizada
syncopated ['sɪŋkəpeɪtɪd] *adj* sincopado
syndicate ['sɪndɪkɪt] *n* (*gen*) sindicato; (*Press*) agencia (de noticias)
syndrome ['sɪndrəum] *n* síndrome *m*
synonym ['sɪnənɪm] *n* sinónimo

synonymous [sɪ'nɔnɪməs] *adj*: ~ **(with)** sinónimo (con)
synopsis, synopses [sɪ'nɔpsɪs, -siːz] *n* sinopsis *f inv*
syntax ['sɪntæks] *n* sintaxis *f*
syntax error *n* (*Comput*) error *m* sintáctico
synthesis, syntheses ['sɪnθəsɪs, -siːz] *n* síntesis *f inv*
synthesizer ['sɪnθəsaɪzə^r] *n* sintetizador *m*
synthetic [sɪn'θɛtɪk] *adj* sintético ■ *n* sintético
syphilis ['sɪfɪlɪs] *n* sífilis *f*
syphon ['saɪfən] = **siphon**
Syria ['sɪrɪə] *n* Siria
Syrian ['sɪrɪən] *adj, n* sirio(-a) *m(f)*
syringe [sɪ'rɪndʒ] *n* jeringa
syrup ['sɪrəp] *n* jarabe *m*, almíbar *m*
system ['sɪstəm] *n* sistema *m*; (*Anat*) organismo; **it was quite a shock to his ~** fue un golpe para él
systematic [sɪstə'mætɪk] *adj* sistemático; metódico
system disk *n* (*Comput*) disco del sistema
systems analyst *n* analista *m/f* de sistemas

Tt

T, t [ti:] *n* (*letter*) T, t *f*; **T for Tommy** T de Tarragona
TA *n abbr* (*Brit*) = **Territorial Army**
ta [tɑ:] *excl* (*Brit: col*) ¡gracias!
tab [tæb] *n abbr* = **tabulator** ■ *n* lengüeta; (*label*) etiqueta; **to keep tabs on** (*fig*) vigilar
tabby ['tæbɪ] *n* (*also:* **tabby cat**) gato atigrado
tabernacle ['tæbənækl] *n* tabernáculo
table ['teɪbl] *n* mesa; (*chart: of statistics etc*) cuadro, tabla ■ *vt* (*Brit: motion etc*) presentar; **to lay** *or* **set the ~** poner la mesa; **to clear the ~** quitar *or* levantar la mesa; **league ~** (*Football, Rugby*) clasificación *f* del campeonato; **~ of contents** índice *m* de materias
tablecloth ['teɪblklɔθ] *n* mantel *m*
table d'hôte [tɑ:bl'dəut] *n* menú *m*
table lamp *n* lámpara de mesa
tablemat ['teɪblmæt] *n* salvamanteles *m inv*, posaplatos *m inv*
tablespoon ['teɪblspu:n] *n* cuchara grande; (*also:* **tablespoonful**: *as measurement*) cucharada
tablet ['tæblɪt] *n* (*Med*) pastilla, comprimido; (*for writing*) bloc *m*; (*of stone*) lápida; **~ of soap** pastilla de jabón
table talk *n* conversación *f* de sobremesa
table tennis *n* ping-pong *m*, tenis *m* de mesa
table wine *n* vino de mesa
tabloid ['tæblɔɪd] *n* (*newspaper*) periódico popular sensacionalista
tabloid press *n ver nota*

TABLOID PRESS

El término genérico *tabloid press* o "tabloids" se usa para referirse a los periódicos populares británicos, por su tamaño reducido. A diferencia de la llamada quality press, estos periódicos se caracterizan por su lenguaje sencillo, presentación llamativa y contenido a menudo sensacionalista, con gran énfasis en noticias sobre escándalos financieros y sexuales de los famosos, por lo que también reciben el nombre peyorativo de "gutter press".

taboo [tə'bu:] *adj, n* tabú *m*
tabulate ['tæbjuleɪt] *vt* disponer en tablas
tabulator ['tæbjuleɪtə^r] *n* tabulador *m*
tachograph ['tækəgrɑ:f] *n* tacógrafo
tachometer [tæ'kɔmɪtə^r] *n* taquímetro
tacit ['tæsɪt] *adj* tácito
tacitly ['tæsɪtlɪ] *adv* tácitamente
taciturn ['tæsɪtə:n] *adj* taciturno
tack [tæk] *n* (*nail*) tachuela; (*stitch*) hilván *m*; (*Naut*) bordada ■ *vt* (*nail*) clavar con tachuelas; (*stitch*) hilvanar ■ *vi* virar; **to ~ sth on to (the end of) sth** (*of letter, book*) añadir algo a(l final de) algo
tackle ['tækl] *n* (*gear*) equipo; (*fishing tackle, for lifting*) aparejo; (*Football*) entrada, tackle *m*; (*Rugby*) placaje *m* ■ *vt* (*difficulty*) enfrentarse a, abordar; (*grapple with*) agarrar; (*Football*) entrar a; (*Rugby*) placar
tacky ['tækɪ] *adj* pegajoso; (*fam*) hortera *inv*
tact [tækt] *n* tacto, discreción *f*
tactful ['tæktful] *adj* discreto, diplomático; **to be ~** tener tacto, actuar discretamente
tactfully ['tæktfulɪ] *adv* diplomáticamente, con tacto
tactical ['tæktɪkl] *adj* táctico
tactical voting *n* voto útil
tactician [tæk'tɪʃən] *n* táctico(-a)
tactics ['tæktɪks] *n, npl* táctica *sg*
tactless ['tæktlɪs] *adj* indiscreto
tactlessly ['tæktlɪslɪ] *adv* indiscretamente, sin tacto
tadpole ['tædpəul] *n* renacuajo
taffy ['tæfɪ] *n* (*US*) melcocha
tag [tæg] *n* (*label*) etiqueta; **price/name ~** etiqueta del precio/con el nombre
▸**tag along** *vi*: **to ~ along with sb** engancharse a algn
tag question *n* pregunta coletilla

Tahiti [tɑːˈhiːtɪ] *n* Tahití *m*
tail [teɪl] *n* cola; (*Zool*) rabo; (*of shirt, coat*) faldón *m* ■ *vt* (*follow*) vigilar a; **heads or tails** cara o cruz; **to turn ~** volver la espalda
▸ **tail away, tail off** *vi* (*in size, quality etc*) ir disminuyendo
tailback [ˈteɪlbæk] *n* (*Brit Aut*) cola
tail coat *n* frac *m*
tail end *n* cola, parte *f* final
tailgate [ˈteɪlgeɪt] *n* (*Aut*) puerta trasera
tail light *n* (*Aut*) luz *f* trasera
tailor [ˈteɪləʳ] *n* sastre *m* ■ *vt*: **to ~ sth (to)** confeccionar algo a medida (para); **~'s (shop)** sastrería
tailoring [ˈteɪlərɪŋ] *n* (*cut*) corte *m*; (*craft*) sastrería
tailor-made [ˈteɪləˈmeɪd] *adj* (*also fig*) hecho a (la) medida
tailwind [ˈteɪlwɪnd] *n* viento de cola
taint [teɪnt] *vt* (*meat, food*) contaminar; (*fig: reputation*) manchar, tachar (*LAm*)
tainted [ˈteɪntɪd] *adj* (*water, air*) contaminado; (*fig*) manchado
Taiwan [taɪˈwɑːn] *n* Taiwán *m*
Tajikistan [tɑːdʒɪkɪˈstɑːn] *n* Tayikistán *m*
take [teɪk] (*pt* **took**, *pp* **taken**) *vt* tomar; (*grab*) coger (*SP*), agarrar (*LAm*); (*gain: prize*) ganar; (*require: effort, courage*) exigir; (*support weight of*) aguantar; (*hold: passengers etc*) tener cabida para; (*accompany, bring, carry*) llevar; (*exam*) presentarse a; (*conduct: meeting*) presidir ■ *vi* (*fire*) prender; (*dye*) coger (*SP*), agarrar, tomar ■ *n* (*Cine*) toma; **to ~ sth from** (*drawer etc*) sacar algo de; (*person*) coger algo a (*SP*); **to ~ sb's hand** tomar de la mano a algn; **to ~ notes** tomar apuntes; **to be taken ill** ponerse enfermo; **~ the first on the left** toma la primera a la izquierda; **I only took Russian for one year** sólo estudié ruso un año; **I took him for a doctor** le tenía por médico; **it won't ~ long** durará poco; **it will ~ at least five litres** tiene cabida por lo menos para cinco litros; **to be taken with sb/sth** (*attracted*) tomarle cariño a algn/ tomarle gusto a algo; **I ~ it that ...** supongo que ...
▸ **take after** *vt fus* parecerse a
▸ **take apart** *vt* desmontar
▸ **take away** *vt* (*remove*) quitar; (*carry off*) llevar ■ *vi*: **to ~ away from** quitar mérito a
▸ **take back** *vt* (*return*) devolver; (*one's words*) retractar
▸ **take down** *vt* (*building*) derribar; (*dismantle: scaffolding*) desmantelar; (*message etc*) apuntar, tomar nota de
▸ **take in** *vt* (*Brit: deceive*) engañar; (*understand*) entender; (*include*) abarcar; (*lodger*) acoger, recibir; (*orphan, stray dog*) recoger; (*Sewing*) achicar
▸ **take off** *vi* (*Aviat*) despegar, decolar (*LAm*) ■ *vt* (*remove*) quitar; (*imitate*) imitar, remedar
▸ **take on** *vt* (*work*) emprender; (*employee*) contratar; (*opponent*) desafiar
▸ **take out** *vt* sacar; (*remove*) quitar; **don't ~ it out on me!** ¡no te desquites conmigo!
▸ **take over** *vt* (*business*) tomar posesión de ■ *vi*: **to ~ over from sb** reemplazar a algn
▸ **take to** *vt fus* (*person*) coger cariño a (*SP*), encariñarse con (*LAm*); (*activity*) aficionarse a; **to ~ to doing sth** aficionarse a (hacer) algo
▸ **take up** *vt* (*a dress*) acortar; (*occupy: time, space*) ocupar; (*engage in: hobby etc*) dedicarse a; (*absorb: liquids*) absorber; (*accept: offer, challenge*) aceptar ■ *vi*: **to ~ up with sb** hacerse amigo de algn
▸ **take upon** *vt*: **to ~ it upon o.s. to do sth** encargarse de hacer algo
takeaway [ˈteɪkəweɪ] *adj* (*Brit: food*) para llevar
take-home pay [ˈteɪkhəum-] *n* salario neto
taken [ˈteɪkən] *pp of* **take**
takeoff [ˈteɪkɔf] *n* (*Aviat*) despegue *m*, decolaje *m* (*LAm*)
takeover [ˈteɪkəuvəʳ] *n* (*Comm*) absorción *f*
takeover bid *n* oferta pública de adquisición
takings [ˈteɪkɪŋz] *npl* (*Comm*) ingresos *mpl*
talc [tælk] *n* (*also:* **talcum powder**) talco
tale [teɪl] *n* (*story*) cuento; (*account*) relación *f*; **to tell tales** (*fig*) contar chismes
talent [ˈtælnt] *n* talento
talented [ˈtæləntɪd] *adj* talentoso, de talento
talisman [ˈtælɪzmən] *n* talismán *m*
talk [tɔːk] *n* charla; (*gossip*) habladurías *fpl*, chismes *mpl*; (*conversation*) conversación *f* ■ *vi* (*speak*) hablar; (*chatter*) charlar; **talks** *npl* (*Pol etc*) conversaciones *fpl*; **to give a ~** dar una charla *or* conferencia; **to ~ about** hablar de; **to ~ sb into doing sth** convencer a algn para que haga algo; **to ~ sb out of doing sth** disuadir a algn de que haga algo; **to ~ shop** hablar del trabajo; **talking of films, have you seen ...?** hablando de películas, ¿has visto ...?
▸ **talk over** *vt* discutir
talkative [ˈtɔːkətɪv] *adj* hablador(a)
talker [ˈtɔːkəʳ] *n* hablador(a) *m(f)*
talking point [ˈtɔːkɪŋ-] *n* tema *m* de conversación
talking-to [ˈtɔːkɪŋtuː] *n*: **to give sb a good ~** echar una buena bronca a algn
talk show *n* programa *m* magazine
tall [tɔːl] *adj* alto; (*tree*) grande; **to be 6 feet ~** ≈ medir 1 metro 80, tener 1 metro 80 de alto; **how ~ are you?** ¿cuánto mides?

tallboy ['tɔ:lbɔɪ] *n* (*Brit*) cómoda alta
tallness ['tɔ:lnɪs] *n* altura
tall story *n* cuento chino
tally ['tælɪ] *n* cuenta ■ *vi*: **to ~ (with)** concordar (con), cuadrar (con); **to keep a ~ of sth** llevar la cuenta de algo
talon ['tælən] *n* garra
tambourine [tæmbə'ri:n] *n* pandereta
tame [teɪm] *adj* (*mild*) manso; (*tamed*) domesticado; (*fig: story, style, person*) soso, anodino
tameness ['teɪmnɪs] *n* mansedumbre *f*
Tamil ['tæmɪl] *adj* tamil ■ *n* tamil *m/f*; (*Ling*) tamil *m*
tamper ['tæmpə^r] *vi*: **to ~ with** (*lock etc*) intentar forzar; (*papers*) falsificar
tampon ['tæmpən] *n* tampón *m*
tan [tæn] *n* (*also*: **suntan**) bronceado ■ *vt* broncear ■ *vi* ponerse moreno ■ *adj* (*colour*) marrón; **to get a ~** broncearse, ponerse moreno
tandem ['tændəm] *n* tándem *m*
tandoori [tæn'duərɪ] *adj, n* tandoori *m* (*asado a la manera hindú, en horno de barro*)
tang [tæŋ] *n* sabor *m* fuerte
tangent ['tændʒənt] *n* (*Math*) tangente *f*; **to go off at a ~** (*fig*) salirse por la tangente
tangerine [tændʒə'ri:n] *n* mandarina
tangible ['tændʒəbl] *adj* tangible; **~ assets** bienes *mpl* tangibles
Tangier [tæn'dʒɪə^r] *n* Tánger *m*
tangle ['tæŋgl] *n* enredo; **to get in(to) a ~** enredarse
tango ['tæŋgəu] *n* tango
tank [tæŋk] *n* (*also*: **water tank**) depósito, tanque *m*; (*for fish*) acuario; (*Mil*) tanque *m*
tankard ['tæŋkəd] *n* bock *m*
tanker ['tæŋkə^r] *n* (*ship*) petrolero; (*truck*) camión *m* cisterna
tankful ['tæŋkful] *n*: **to get a ~ of petrol** llenar el depósito de gasolina
tanned [tænd] *adj* (*skin*) moreno, bronceado
tannin ['tænɪn] *n* tanino
tanning ['tænɪŋ] *n* (*of leather*) curtido
tannoy® ['tænɔɪ] *n*: **over the ~** por el altavoz
tantalizing ['tæntəlaɪzɪŋ] *adj* tentador(a)
tantamount ['tæntəmaunt] *adj*: **~ to** equivalente a
tantrum ['tæntrəm] *n* rabieta; **to throw a ~** coger una rabieta
Tanzania [tænzə'nɪə] *n* Tanzania
Tanzanian [tænzə'nɪən] *adj, n* tanzano(-a) *m(f)*
tap [tæp] *n* (*Brit: on sink etc*) grifo, canilla (*LAm*); (*gentle blow*) golpecito; (*gas tap*) llave *f* ■ *vt* (*table etc*) tamborilear; (*shoulder etc*) dar palmaditas en; (*resources*) utilizar, explotar; (*telephone conversation*) intervenir, pinchar; **on ~** (*fig: resources*) a mano; **beer on ~** cerveza de barril
tap-dancing ['tæpdɑ:nsɪŋ] *n* claqué *m*
tape [teɪp] *n* cinta; (*also*: **magnetic tape**) cinta magnética; (*sticky tape*) cinta adhesiva ■ *vt* (*record*) grabar (en cinta); **on ~** (*song etc*) grabado (en cinta)
tape deck *n* pletina
tape measure *n* cinta métrica, metro
taper ['teɪpə^r] *n* cirio ■ *vi* afilarse
tape-record ['teɪprɪkɔ:d] *vt* grabar (en cinta)
tape recorder *n* grabadora
tape recording *n* grabación *f*
tapered ['teɪpəd], **tapering** ['teɪpərɪŋ] *adj* terminado en punta
tapestry ['tæpɪstrɪ] *n* (*object*) tapiz *m*; (*art*) tapicería
tape-worm ['teɪpwə:m] *n* solitaria, tenia
tapioca [tæpɪ'əukə] *n* tapioca
tappet ['tæpɪt] *n* excéntrica
tar [tɑ:^r] *n* alquitrán *m*, brea; **low/middle ~ cigarettes** cigarrillos con contenido bajo/medio de alquitrán
tarantula [tə'ræntjulə] *n* tarántula
tardy ['tɑ:dɪ] *adj* (*late*) tardío; (*slow*) lento
tare [tɛə^r] *n* (*Comm*) tara
target ['tɑ:gɪt] *n* (*gen*) blanco; **to be on ~** (*project*) seguir el curso previsto
target audience *n público al que va destinado un programa etc*
target market *n* (*Comm*) *mercado al que va destinado un producto etc*
target practice *n* tiro al blanco
tariff ['tærɪf] *n* tarifa
tariff barrier *n* (*Comm*) barrera arancelaria
tarmac ['tɑ:mæk] *n* (*Brit: on road*) alquitranado; (*Aviat*) pista (de aterrizaje)
tarn [tɑ:n] *n* lago pequeño de montaña
tarnish ['tɑ:nɪʃ] *vt* deslustrar
tarot ['tærəu] *n* tarot *m*
tarpaulin [tɑ:'pɔ:lɪn] *n* alquitranado
tarragon ['tærəgən] *n* estragón *m*
tarry ['tærɪ] *vi* entretenerse, quedarse atrás
tart [tɑ:t] *n* (*Culin*) tarta; (*Brit col: pej: woman*) fulana ■ *adj* (*flavour*) agrio, ácido
▸ **tart up** *vt* (*room, building*) dar tono a
tartan ['tɑ:tn] *n* tartán *m* ■ *adj* de tartán
tartar ['tɑ:tə^r] *n* (*on teeth*) sarro
tartar sauce *n* salsa tártara
tartly ['tɑ:tlɪ] *adv* (*answer*) ásperamente
task [tɑ:sk] *n* tarea; **to take to ~** reprender
task force *n* (*Mil, Police*) grupo de operaciones
taskmaster ['tɑ:skmɑ:stə^r] *n*: **he's a hard ~** es muy exigente
tassel ['tæsl] *n* borla
taste [teɪst] *n* sabor *m*, gusto; (*also*: **aftertaste**) dejo; (*sip*) sorbo; (*fig: glimpse, idea*)

muestra, idea ■ *vt* probar ■ *vi*: **to ~ of** *or* **like** (*fish etc*) saber a; **you can ~ the garlic (in it)** se nota el sabor a ajo; **can I have a ~ of this wine?** ¿puedo probar este vino?; **to have a ~ for sth** ser aficionado a algo; **in good/bad ~** de buen/mal gusto; **to be in bad** *or* **poor ~** ser de mal gusto
taste bud *n* papila gustativa *or* del gusto
tasteful ['teɪstful] *adj* de buen gusto
tastefully ['teɪstfulɪ] *adv* elegantemente, con buen gusto
tasteless ['teɪstlɪs] *adj* (*food*) soso; (*remark*) de mal gusto
tastelessly ['teɪstlɪslɪ] *adv* con mal gusto
tastily ['teɪstɪlɪ] *adv* sabrosamente
tastiness ['teɪstɪnɪs] *n* (buen) sabor *m*, lo sabroso
tasty ['teɪstɪ] *adj* sabroso, rico
ta-ta ['tæ'tɑː] *interj* (*Brit col*) hasta luego, adiós
tatters ['tætəz] *npl*: **in ~** (*also*: **tattered**) hecho jirones
tattoo [tə'tuː] *n* tatuaje *m*; (*spectacle*) espectáculo militar ■ *vt* tatuar
tatty ['tætɪ] *adj* (*Brit col*) cochambroso
taught [tɔːt] *pt, pp of* **teach**
taunt [tɔːnt] *n* pulla ■ *vt* lanzar pullas a
Taurus ['tɔːrəs] *n* Tauro
taut [tɔːt] *adj* tirante, tenso
tavern ['tævən] *n* (*old*) posada, fonda
tawdry ['tɔːdrɪ] *adj* de mal gusto
tawny ['tɔːnɪ] *adj* leonado
tax [tæks] *n* impuesto ■ *vt* gravar (con un impuesto); (*fig: test*) poner a prueba; (*: patience*) agotar; **before/after ~** impuestos excluidos/incluidos; **free of ~** libre de impuestos
taxable ['tæksəbl] *adj* (*income*) imponible, sujeto a impuestos
tax allowance *n* desgravación *f* fiscal
taxation [tæk'seɪʃən] *n* impuestos *mpl*; **system of ~** sistema *m* tributario
tax avoidance *n* evasión *f* de impuestos
tax collector *n* recaudador(a) *m(f)*
tax disc *n* (*Brit Aut*) pegatina del impuesto de circulación
tax evasion *n* evasión *f* fiscal
tax exemption *n* exención *f* de impuestos
tax-free ['tæksfriː] *adj* libre de impuestos
tax haven *n* paraíso fiscal
taxi ['tæksɪ] *n* taxi *m* ■ *vi* (*Aviat*) rodar por la pista
taxidermist ['tæksɪdəːmɪst] *n* taxidermista *m/f*
taxi driver *n* taxista *m/f*
tax inspector *n* inspector(a) *m(f)* de Hacienda
taxi rank, (*Brit*) **taxi stand** *n* parada de taxis
tax payer *n* contribuyente *m/f*
tax rebate *n* devolución *f* de impuestos, reembolso fiscal
tax relief *n* desgravación *f* fiscal
tax return *n* declaración *f* de la renta
tax shelter *n* protección *f* fiscal
tax year *n* año fiscal
TB *n abbr* = **tuberculosis**
tbc *abbr* (= *to be confirmed*) por confirmar
TD *n abbr* (*US*) = **Treasury Department**; (*: Football*) = **touchdown**
tea [tiː] *n* té *m*; (*Brit: snack*) ≈ merienda; **high ~** (*Brit*) ≈ merienda-cena
tea bag *n* bolsita de té
tea break *n* (*Brit*) descanso para el té
teacake ['tiːkeɪk] *n* bollito, queque *m* (*LAm*)
teach (*pt, pp* **taught**) [tiːtʃ, tɔːt] *vt*: **to ~ sb sth, ~ sth to sb** enseñar algo a algn ■ *vi* enseñar; (*be a teacher*) ser profesor(a); **it taught him a lesson** (eso) le sirvió de escarmiento
teacher ['tiːtʃəʳ] *n* (*in secondary school*) profesor(a) *m(f)*; (*in primary school*) maestro(-a); **Spanish ~** profesor(a) *m(f)* de español
teacher training college *n* (*for primary schools*) escuela normal; (*for secondary schools*) centro de formación del profesorado
teach-in ['tiːtʃɪn] *n* seminario
teaching ['tiːtʃɪŋ] *n* enseñanza
teaching aids *npl* materiales *mpl* pedagógicos
teaching hospital *n* hospital universitario
tea cosy *n* cubretetera *m*
teacup ['tiːkʌp] *n* taza de té
teak [tiːk] *n* (madera de) teca
tea leaves *npl* hojas *fpl* de té
team [tiːm] *n* equipo; (*of animals*) pareja
▸ **team up** *vi* asociarse
team spirit *n* espíritu *m* de equipo
teamwork ['tiːmwəːk] *n* trabajo en equipo
tea party *n* té *m*
teapot ['tiːpɔt] *n* tetera
tear [tɛəʳ] (*pt* **tore**, *pp* **torn**) *n* rasgón *m*, desgarrón *m* [tɪəʳ] lágrima ■ *vb* [tɛəʳ] ■ *vt* romper, rasgar ■ *vi* rasgarse; **in tears** llorando; **to burst into tears** deshacerse en lágrimas; **to ~ to pieces** *or* **to bits** *or* **to shreds** (*also fig*) hacer pedazos, destrozar
▸ **tear along** *vi* (*rush*) precipitarse
▸ **tear apart** *vt* (*also fig*) hacer pedazos
▸ **tear away** *vt*: **to ~ o.s. away (from sth)** alejarse (de algo)
▸ **tear out** *vt* (*sheet of paper, cheque*) arrancar
▸ **tear up** *vt* (*sheet of paper etc*) romper
tearaway ['tɛərəweɪ] *n* (*col*) gamberro(-a)
teardrop ['tɪədrɔp] *n* lágrima
tearful ['tɪəful] *adj* lloroso

tear gas *n* gas *m* lacrimógeno
tearing ['tɛərɪŋ] *adj*: **to be in a ~ hurry** tener muchísima prisa
tearoom ['ti:ru:m] *n* salón *m* de té
tease [ti:z] *n* bromista *m/f* ■ *vt* tomar el pelo a
tea set *n* servicio de té
teashop ['ti:ʃɔp] *n* café *m*, cafetería
Teasmaid® ['ti:zmeɪd] *n* tetera automática
teaspoon ['ti:spu:n] *n* cucharita; (*also*: **teaspoonful**: *as measurement*) cucharadita
tea strainer *n* colador *m* de té
teat [ti:t] *n* (*of bottle*) boquilla, tetilla
teatime ['ti:taɪm] *n* hora del té
tea towel *n* (*Brit*) paño de cocina
tea urn *n* tetera grande
tech [tɛk] *n abbr* (*col*) = **technology**; **technical college**
technical ['tɛknɪkl] *adj* técnico
technical college *n* centro de formación profesional
technicality [tɛknɪ'kælɪtɪ] *n* detalle *m* técnico; **on a legal ~** por una cuestión formal
technically ['tɛknɪklɪ] *adv* técnicamente
technician [tɛk'nɪʃn] *n* técnico(-a)
technique [tɛk'ni:k] *n* técnica
techno ['tɛknəu] *n* (*Mus*) (música) tecno
technocrat ['tɛknəkræt] *n* tecnócrata *m/f*
technological [tɛknə'lɔdʒɪkl] *adj* tecnológico
technologist [tɛk'nɔlədʒɪst] *n* tecnólogo(-a)
technology [tɛk'nɔlədʒɪ] *n* tecnología
teddy ['tɛdɪ], **teddy bear** *n* osito de peluche
tedious ['ti:dɪəs] *adj* pesado, aburrido
tedium ['ti:dɪəm] *n* tedio
tee [ti:] *n* (*Golf*) tee *m*
teem [ti:m] *vi*: **to ~ with** rebosar de; **it is teeming (with rain)** llueve a mares
teenage ['ti:neɪdʒ] *adj* (*fashions etc*) juvenil
teenager ['ti:neɪdʒə^r] *n* adolescente *m/f*, quinceañero(-a)
teens [ti:nz] *npl*: **to be in one's ~** ser adolescente
tee-shirt ['ti:ʃə:t] *n* = **T-shirt**
teeter ['ti:tə^r] *vi* balancearse
teeth [ti:θ] *npl of* **tooth**
teethe [ti:ð] *vi* echar los dientes
teething ring ['ti:ðɪŋ-] *n* mordedor *m*
teething troubles ['ti:ðɪŋ-] *npl* (*fig*) dificultades *fpl* iniciales
teetotal ['ti:'təutl] *adj* (*person*) abstemio
teetotaller, teetotaler (*US*) ['ti:'təutlə^r] *n* (*person*) abstemio(-a)
TEFL ['tɛfl] *n abbr* (= *Teaching of English as a Foreign Language, TEFL qualification*) *título para la enseñanza del inglés como lengua extranjera*
Teflon® ['tɛflɔn] *n* teflón® *m*
Teheran [tɛə'rɑ:n] *n* Teherán *m*
tel. *abbr* (= *telephone*) tel
Tel Aviv ['tɛlə'vi:v] *n* Tel Aviv *m*
telecast ['tɛlɪkɑ:st] *vt, vi* transmitir por televisión
telecommunications ['tɛlɪkəmju:nɪ] *n* telecomunicaciones *fpl*
teleconferencing ['tɛlɪkɒnfərənsɪŋ] *n* teleconferencias *fpl*
telefax ['tɛlɪfæks] *n* telefax *m*
telegram ['tɛlɪgræm] *n* telegrama *m*
telegraph ['tɛlɪgrɑ:f] *n* telégrafo
telegraphic [tɛlɪ'græfɪk] *adj* telegráfico
telegraph pole *n* poste *m* telegráfico
telegraph wire *n* hilo telegráfico
telepathic [tɛlɪ'pæθɪk] *adj* telepático
telepathy [tə'lɛpəθɪ] *n* telepatía
telephone ['tɛlɪfəun] *n* teléfono ■ *vt* llamar por teléfono, telefonear; **to be on the ~** (*subscriber*) tener teléfono; (*be speaking*) estar hablando por teléfono
telephone booth, (*Brit*) **telephone box** *n* cabina telefónica
telephone call *n* llamada telefónica
telephone directory *n* guía telefónica
telephone exchange *n* central *f* telefónica
telephone number *n* número de teléfono
telephonist [tə'lɛfənɪst] *n* (*Brit*) telefonista *m/f*
telephoto ['tɛlɪ'fəutəu] *adj*: **~ lens** teleobjetivo
teleprinter ['tɛlɪprɪntə^r] *n* teletipo, teleimpresora
teleprompter® ['tɛlɪprɔmptə^r] *n* teleapuntador *m*
telesales ['tɛlɪseɪlz] *npl* televentas *fpl*
telescope ['tɛlɪskəup] *n* telescopio
telescopic [tɛlɪ'skɔpɪk] *adj* telescópico; (*umbrella*) plegable
Teletext® ['tɛlɪtɛkst] *n* teletexto *m*
telethon ['tɛlɪθɔn] *n* telemaratón *m*, maratón *m* televisivo (*con fines benéficos*)
televise ['tɛlɪvaɪz] *vt* televisar
television ['tɛlɪvɪʒən] *n* televisión *f*; **to watch ~** mirar *or* ver la televisión
television licence *n* impuesto por uso de televisor
television set *n* televisor *m*
teleworking ['tɛlɪwɜ:kɪŋ] *n* teletrabajo
telex ['tɛlɛks] *n* télex *m* ■ *vt* (*message*) enviar por télex; (*person*) enviar un télex a ■ *vi* enviar un télex
tell (*pt, pp* **told**) [tɛl, təuld] *vt* decir; (*relate*: *story*) contar; (*distinguish*): **to ~ sth from** distinguir algo de ■ *vi* (*talk*): **to ~ (of)** contar; (*have effect*) tener efecto; **to ~ sb to do sth** decir a algn que haga algo; **to ~ sb about**

sth contar algo a algn; **to ~ the time** dar *or* decir la hora; **can you ~ me the time?** ¿me puedes decir la hora?; **(I) ~ you what ...** fíjate ...; **I couldn't ~ them apart** no podía distinguirlos
▸ **tell off** *vt*: **to ~ sb off** regañar a algn
▸ **tell on** *vt fus*: **to ~ on sb** chivarse de algn
teller ['tɛlər] *n* (*in bank*) cajero(-a)
telling ['tɛlɪŋ] *adj* (*remark, detail*) revelador(a)
telltale ['tɛlteɪl] *adj* (*sign*) indicador(a)
telly ['tɛlɪ] *n* (*Brit col*) tele *f*
temerity [tə'mɛrɪtɪ] *n* temeridad *f*
temp [tɛmp] *n abbr* (*Brit*: = *temporary office worker*) empleado(-a) eventual ■ *vi* trabajar como empleado(-a) eventual
temper ['tɛmpər] *n* (*mood*) humor *m*; (*bad temper*) (mal) genio; (*fit of anger*) ira; (*of child*) rabieta ■ *vt* (*moderate*) moderar; **to be in a ~** estar furioso; **to lose one's ~** enfadarse, enojarse (*LAm*); **to keep one's ~** contenerse, no alterarse
temperament ['tɛmprəmənt] *n* (*nature*) temperamento
temperamental [tɛmprə'mɛntl] *adj* temperamental
temperance ['tɛmpərns] *n* moderación *f*; (*in drinking*) sobriedad *f*
temperate ['tɛmprət] *adj* moderado; (*climate*) templado
temperature ['tɛmprətʃər] *n* temperatura; **to have** *or* **run a ~** tener fiebre
tempered ['tɛmpəd] *adj* (*steel*) templado
tempest ['tɛmpɪst] *n* tempestad *f*
tempestuous [tɛm'pɛstjuəs] *adj* (*relationship, meeting*) tempestuoso
tempi ['tɛmpi:] *npl of* **tempo**
template ['tɛmplɪt] *n* plantilla
temple ['tɛmpl] *n* (*building*) templo; (*Anat*) sien *f*
templet ['tɛmplɪt] *n* = **template**
tempo (*pl* **tempos** *or* **tempi**) ['tɛmpəu, 'tɛmpi:] *n* tempo; (*fig: of life etc*) ritmo
temporal ['tɛmpərl] *adj* temporal
temporarily ['tɛmpərərɪlɪ] *adv* temporalmente
temporary ['tɛmpərərɪ] *adj* provisional, temporal; (*passing*) transitorio; (*worker*) eventual; **~ teacher** maestro(-a) interino(-a)
tempt [tɛmpt] *vt* tentar; **to ~ sb into doing sth** tentar *or* inducir a algn a hacer algo; **to be tempted to do sth** (*person*) sentirse tentado de hacer algo
temptation [tɛmp'teɪʃən] *n* tentación *f*
tempting ['tɛmptɪŋ] *adj* tentador(a)
ten [tɛn] *num* diez; **tens of thousands** decenas *fpl* de miles
tenable ['tɛnəbl] *adj* sostenible
tenacious [tə'neɪʃəs] *adj* tenaz
tenaciously [tə'neɪʃəslɪ] *adv* tenazmente
tenacity [tə'næsɪtɪ] *n* tenacidad *f*
tenancy ['tɛnənsɪ] *n* alquiler *m*
tenant ['tɛnənt] *n* (*rent-payer*) inquilino(-a); (*occupant*) habitante *m/f*
tend [tɛnd] *vt* (*sick etc*) cuidar, atender; (*cattle, machine*) vigilar, cuidar ■ *vi*: **to ~ to do sth** tener tendencia a hacer algo
tendency ['tɛndənsɪ] *n* tendencia
tender ['tɛndər] *adj* tierno, blando; (*delicate*) delicado; (*sore*) sensible; (*affectionate*) tierno, cariñoso ■ *n* (*Comm: offer*) oferta; (*money*): **legal ~** moneda de curso legal ■ *vt* ofrecer; **to put in a ~ (for)** hacer una oferta (para); **to put work out to ~** ofrecer un trabajo a contrata; **to ~ one's resignation** presentar la dimisión
tenderize ['tɛndəraɪz] *vt* (*Culin*) ablandar
tenderly ['tɛndəlɪ] *adv* tiernamente
tenderness ['tɛndənɪs] *n* ternura; (*of meat*) blandura
tendon ['tɛndən] *n* tendón *m*
tendril ['tɛndrɪl] *n* zarcillo
tenement ['tɛnəmənt] *n* casa *or* bloque *m* de pisos *or* vecinos (*LAm*)
Tenerife [tɛnə'ri:f] *n* Tenerife *m*
tenet ['tɛnət] *n* principio
Tenn. *abbr* (*US*) = **Tennessee**
tenner ['tɛnər] *n* (billete *m* de) diez libras *fpl*
tennis ['tɛnɪs] *n* tenis *m*
tennis ball *n* pelota de tenis
tennis club *n* club *m* de tenis
tennis court *n* cancha de tenis
tennis elbow *n* (*Med*) sinovitis *f* del codo
tennis match *n* partido de tenis
tennis player *n* tenista *m/f*
tennis racket *n* raqueta de tenis
tennis shoes *npl* zapatillas *fpl* de tenis
tenor ['tɛnər] *n* (*Mus*) tenor *m*
tenpin bowling ['tɛnpɪn-] *n* bolos *mpl*
tense [tɛns] *adj* tenso; (*stretched*) tirante; (*stiff*) rígido, tieso; (*person*) nervioso ■ *n* (*Ling*) tiempo ■ *vt* (*tighten: muscles*) tensar
tensely ['tɛnslɪ] *adv*: **they waited ~** esperaban tensos
tenseness ['tɛnsnɪs] *n* tirantez *f*, tensión *f*
tension ['tɛnʃən] *n* tensión *f*
tent [tɛnt] *n* tienda (de campaña), carpa (*LAm*)
tentacle ['tɛntəkl] *n* tentáculo
tentative ['tɛntətɪv] *adj* (*person*) indeciso; (*provisional*) provisional
tentatively ['tɛntətɪvlɪ] *adv* con indecisión; (*provisionally*) provisionalmente
tenterhooks ['tɛntəhuks] *npl*: **on ~** sobre ascuas

tenth [tɛnθ] *adj* décimo
tent peg *n* clavija, estaca
tent pole *n* mástil *m*
tenuous ['tɛnjuəs] *adj* tenue
tenure ['tɛnjuəʳ] *n* posesión *f*, tenencia; **to have** ~ tener posesión *or* título de propiedad
tepid ['tɛpɪd] *adj* tibio
Ter. *abbr* = **terrace**
term [tə:m] *n* (*limit*) límite *m*; (*Comm*) plazo; (*word*) término; (*period*) período; (*Scol*) trimestre *m* ■ *vt* llamar, calificar de; **terms** *npl* (*conditions*) condiciones *fpl*; (*Comm*) precio, tarifa; **in the short/long** ~ a corto/largo plazo; **during his ~ of office** bajo su mandato; **to be on good terms with sb** llevarse bien con algn; **to come to terms with** (*problem*) aceptar; **in terms of ...** en cuanto a ..., en términos de ...
terminal ['tə:mɪnl] *adj* terminal ■ *n* (*Elec*) borne *m*; (*Comput*) terminal *m*; (*also*: **air terminal**) terminal *f*; (*Brit*: *also*: **coach terminal**) (estación *f*) terminal *f*
terminate ['tə:mɪneɪt] *vt* poner término a; (*pregnancy*) interrumpir ■ *vi*: **to ~ in** acabar en
termination [tə:mɪ'neɪʃən] *n* fin *m*; (*of contract*) terminación *f*; **~ of pregnancy** interrupción *f* del embarazo
termini ['tə:mɪnaɪ] *npl of* **terminus**
terminology [tə:mɪ'nɔlədʒɪ] *n* terminología
terminus (*pl* **termini**) ['tə:mɪnəs, 'tə:mɪnaɪ] *n* término, (estación *f*) terminal *f*
termite ['tə:maɪt] *n* termita, comején *m*
term paper *n* (*US Univ*) trabajo escrito trimestral *or* semestral
Terr. *abbr* = **terrace**
terrace ['tɛrəs] *n* terraza; (*Brit*: *row of houses*) hilera de casas adosadas; **the terraces** (*Brit Sport*) las gradas *fpl*
terraced ['tɛrəst] *adj* (*garden*) escalonado; (*house*) adosado
terracotta ['tɛrə'kɔtə] *n* terracota
terrain [tɛ'reɪn] *n* terreno
terrible ['tɛrɪbl] *adj* terrible, horrible; (*fam*) malísimo
terribly ['tɛrɪblɪ] *adv* terriblemente; (*very badly*) malísimamente
terrier ['tɛrɪəʳ] *n* terrier *m*
terrific [tə'rɪfɪk] *adj* fantástico, fenomenal, macanudo (*LAm*); (*wonderful*) maravilloso
terrify ['tɛrɪfaɪ] *vt* aterrorizar; **to be terrified** estar aterrado *or* aterrorizado
terrifying ['tɛrɪfaɪɪŋ] *adj* aterrador(a)
territorial [tɛrɪ'tɔ:rɪəl] *adj* territorial
territorial waters *npl* aguas *fpl* jurisdiccionales
territory ['tɛrɪtərɪ] *n* territorio
terror ['tɛrəʳ] *n* terror *m*
terror attack *n* atentado (terrorista)
terrorism ['tɛrərɪzəm] *n* terrorismo
terrorist ['tɛrərɪst] *n* terrorista *m/f*
terrorize ['tɛrəraɪz] *vt* aterrorizar
terse [tə:s] *adj* (*style*) conciso; (*reply*) brusco
tertiary ['tə:ʃərɪ] *adj* terciario; **~ education** enseñanza superior
Terylene® ['tɛrəli:n] *n* (*Brit*) terylene® *m*
TESL [tɛsl] *n abbr* = **Teaching of English as a Second Language**
TESSA ['tɛsə] *n abbr* (*Brit*: = *Tax Exempt Special Savings Account*) *plan de ahorro por el que se invierte a largo plazo a cambio de intereses libres de impuestos*
test [tɛst] *n* (*trial, check*) prueba, ensayo; (: *of goods in factory*) control *m*; (*of courage etc*) prueba; (*Chem, Med*) prueba; (*of blood, urine*) análisis *m inv*; (*exam*) examen *m*, test *m*; (*also*: **driving test**) examen *m* de conducir ■ *vt* probar, poner a prueba; (*Med*) examinar; (: *blood*) analizar; **to put sth to the ~** someter algo a prueba; **to ~ sth for sth** analizar algo en busca de algo
testament ['tɛstəmənt] *n* testamento; **the Old/New T~** el Antiguo/Nuevo Testamento
test ban *n* (*also*: **nuclear test ban**) suspensión *f* de pruebas nucleares
test card *n* (*TV*) carta de ajuste
test case *n* juicio que sienta precedente
testes ['tɛsti:z] *npl* testes *mpl*
test flight *n* vuelo de ensayo
testicle ['tɛstɪkl] *n* testículo
testify ['tɛstɪfaɪ] *vi* (*Law*) prestar declaración; **to ~ to sth** atestiguar algo
testimonial [tɛstɪ'məunɪəl] *n* (*of character*) (carta de) recomendación *f*
testimony ['tɛstɪmənɪ] *n* (*Law*) testimonio, declaración *f*
testing ['tɛstɪŋ] *adj* (*difficult*: *time*) duro
test match *n* partido internacional
testosterone [tɛs'tɔstərəun] *n* testosterona
test paper *n* examen *m*, test *m*
test pilot *n* piloto *m/f* de pruebas
test tube *n* probeta
test-tube baby *n* bebé *m* probeta *inv*
testy ['tɛstɪ] *adj* irritable
tetanus ['tɛtənəs] *n* tétano
tetchy ['tɛtʃɪ] *adj* irritable
tether ['tɛðəʳ] *vt* atar ■ *n*: **to be at the end of one's ~** no aguantar más
Tex. *abbr* (*US*) = **Texas**
text [tɛkst] *n* text ■ *vt*: **to ~ sb** enviar un mensaje (de texto) a algn
textbook ['tɛkstbuk] *n* libro de texto
textiles ['tɛkstaɪlz] *npl* tejidos *mpl*
text message *n* mensaje *m* de texto
text messaging [-'mɛsɪdʒɪŋ] *n* (envío de) mensajes *mpl* de texto

textual ['tɛkstjuəl] *adj* del texto, textual
texture ['tɛkstʃəʳ] *n* textura
TGIF *abbr (col)* = **thank God it's Friday**
TGWU *n abbr (Brit: = Transport and General Workers' Union) sindicato de transportistas*
Thai [taɪ] *adj, n* tailandés(-esa) *m(f)*
Thailand ['taɪlænd] *n* Tailandia
thalidomide® [θə'lɪdəmaɪd] *n* talidomida®
Thames [tɛmz] *n*: **the ~** el (río) Támesis
than [ðæn, ðən] *conj* que; (*with numerals*): **more ~ 10/once** más de 10/una vez; **I have more/less ~ you** tengo más/menos que tú; **it is better to phone ~ to write** es mejor llamar por teléfono que escribir; **no sooner did he leave ~ the phone rang** en cuanto se marchó, sonó el teléfono
thank [θæŋk] *vt* dar las gracias a, agradecer; **~ you (very much)** muchas gracias; **~ heavens, ~ God!** ¡gracias a Dios!, ¡menos mal!
thankful ['θæŋkful] *adj*: **~ for** agradecido (por)
thankfully ['θæŋkfəlɪ] *adv (gratefully)* con agradecimiento; (*with relief*) por suerte; **~ there were few victims** afortunadamente hubo pocas víctimas
thankless ['θæŋklɪs] *adj* ingrato
thanks [θæŋks] *npl* gracias *fpl* ■ *excl* ¡gracias!; **~ to** *prep* gracias a
Thanksgiving ['θæŋksgɪvɪŋ], **Thanksgiving Day** *n* día *m* de Acción de Gracias; *ver nota*

THANKSGIVING DAY

En Estados Unidos el cuarto jueves de noviembre es *Thanksgiving Day*, fiesta oficial en la que se conmemora la celebración que tuvieron los primeros colonos norteamericanos ("Pilgrims" o "Pilgrim Fathers") tras la estupenda cosecha de 1621, por la que se dan gracias a Dios. En Canadá se celebra una fiesta semejante el segundo lunes de octubre, aunque no está relacionada con dicha fecha histórica.

KEYWORD

that [ðæt] (*pl* **those**) *adj (demonstrative)* ese(-a), esos(-as) *pl*; (*more remote*) aquel/aquella *m/f*, aquellos(-as) *m(f)pl*; **leave those books on the table** deja esos libros sobre la mesa; **that one** ése/ésa; (*more remote*) aquél/aquélla; **that one over there** ése/ésa de ahí; aquél/aquélla de allí
■ *pron* **1** (*demonstrative*) ése(-a), ésos(-as) *pl*; (*neuter*) eso; (*more remote*) aquél/aquélla *m/f*, aquéllos(-as) *m(f)pl*, aquello *neuter*; **what's that?** ¿qué es eso (*or* aquello)?; **who's that?** ¿quién es?; (*pointing etc*) ¿quién es ése/a?; **is that you?** ¿eres tú?; **will you eat all that?** ¿vas a comer todo eso?; **that's my house** ésa es mi casa; **that's what he said** eso es lo que dijo; **that is (to say)** es decir; **at** *or* **with that she ...** en eso, ella ...; **do it like that** hazlo así
2 (*relative: subject, object*) que; (*with preposition*) (el/la) que, el/la cual; **the book (that) I read** el libro que leí; **the books that are in the library** los libros que están en la biblioteca; **all (that) I have** todo lo que tengo; **the box (that) I put it in** la caja en la que *or* donde lo puse; **the people (that) I spoke to** la gente con la que hablé; **not that I know of** que yo sepa, no
3 (*relative: of time*) que; **the day (that) he came** el día (en) que vino
■ *conj* que; **he thought that I was ill** creyó que yo estaba enfermo
■ *adv (demonstrative)*: **I can't work that much** no puedo trabajar tanto; **I didn't realize it was that bad** no creí que fuera tan malo; **that high** así de alto

thatched [θætʃt] *adj (roof)* de paja; **~ cottage** casita con tejado de paja
Thatcherism ['θætʃərɪzəm] *n* thatcherismo
thaw [θɔː] *n* deshielo ■ *vi (ice)* derretirse; (*food*) descongelarse ■ *vt* descongelar

KEYWORD

the [ðiː, ðə] *def art* **1** (*gen*) el, la *f*, los *pl*, las *fpl* (*NB =el immediately before feminine noun beginning with stressed (h)a; a+el = al; de + el = del*): **the boy/girl** el chico/la chica; **the books/flowers** los libros/las flores; **to the postman/from the drawer** al cartero/del cajón; **I haven't the time/money** no tengo tiempo/dinero; **1.10 euros to the dollar** 1,10 euros por dólar; **paid by the hour** pagado por hora
2 (*+adj to form noun*) los; lo; **the rich and the poor** los ricos y los pobres; **to attempt the impossible** intentar lo imposible
3 (*in titles, surnames*): **Elizabeth the First** Isabel Primera; **Peter the Great** Pedro el Grande; **do you know the Smiths?** ¿conoce a los Smith?
4 (*in comparisons*): **the more he works the more he earns** cuanto más trabaja más gana

theatre, theater (US) ['θɪətəʳ] *n* teatro
theatre-goer, theater-goer (US) ['θɪətəgəuəʳ] *n* aficionado(-a) al teatro

theatrical [θɪ'ætrɪkl] *adj* teatral
theft [θɛft] *n* robo
their [ðɛəʳ] *adj* su
theirs [ðɛəz] *pron* (el) suyo/(la) suya *etc*; *see also* **my**; **mine**
them [ðɛm, ðəm] *pron* (*direct*) los/las; (*indirect*) les; (*stressed, after prep*) ellos/ellas; **I see ~** los veo; **both of ~** ambos(-as), los/las dos; **give me a few of ~** dame algunos(-as); *see also* **me**
theme [θi:m] *n* tema *m*
theme park *n* parque *m* temático
theme song *n* tema *m* (musical)
themselves [ðəm'sɛlvz] *pl pron* (*subject*) ellos mismos/ellas mismas; (*complement*) se; (*after prep*) sí (mismos(-as)); *see also* **oneself**
then [ðɛn] *adv* (*at that time*) entonces; (*next*) pues; (*later*) luego, después; (*and also*) además ■ *conj* (*therefore*) en ese caso, entonces ■ *adj*: **the ~ president** el entonces presidente; **from ~ on** desde entonces; **until ~** hasta entonces; **and ~ what?** y luego, ¿qué?; **what do you want me to do, ~?** ¿entonces, qué quiere que haga?
theologian [θɪə'ləudʒən] *n* teólogo(-a)
theological [θɪə'lɔdʒɪkl] *adj* teológico
theology [θɪ'ɔlədʒɪ] *n* teología
theorem ['θɪərəm] *n* teorema *m*
theoretical [θɪə'rɛtɪkl] *adj* teórico
theoretically [θɪə'rɛtɪklɪ] *adv* teóricamente, en teoría
theorize ['θɪəraɪz] *vi* teorizar
theory ['θɪərɪ] *n* teoría
therapeutic [θɛrə'pju:tɪk], **therapeutical** [θɛrə'pju:tɪkl] *adj* terapéutico
therapist ['θɛrəpɪst] *n* terapeuta *m/f*
therapy ['θɛrəpɪ] *n* terapia

KEYWORD

there ['ðɛəʳ] *adv* **1**: **there is, there are** hay; **there is no-one here** no hay nadie aquí; **there is no bread left** no queda pan; **there has been an accident** ha habido un accidente
2 (*referring to place*) ahí; (*distant*) allí; **it's there** está ahí; **put it in/on/up/down there** ponlo ahí dentro/encima/arriba/abajo; **I want that book there** quiero ese libro de ahí; **there he is!** ¡ahí está!; **there's the bus** ahí *or* ya viene el autobús; **back/down there** allí atrás/abajo; **over there, through there** por allí
3: **there, there** (*esp to child*) ¡venga, venga!

thereabouts ['ðɛərə'bauts] *adv* por ahí
thereafter [ðɛər'ɑ:ftəʳ] *adv* después
thereby ['ðɛəbaɪ] *adv* así, de ese modo
therefore ['ðɛəfɔ:ʳ] *adv* por lo tanto
there's [ðɛəz] = **there is; there has**
thereupon [ðɛərə'pɔn] *adv* (*at that point*) en eso, en seguida
thermal ['θə:ml] *adj* termal
thermal paper *n* papel *m* térmico
thermal printer *n* termoimpresora
thermodynamics ['θə:mədaɪnæmɪks] *n* termodinámica
thermometer [θə'mɔmɪtəʳ] *n* termómetro
thermonuclear [θə:məu'nju:klɪəʳ] *adj* termonuclear
Thermos® ['θə:məs] *n* (*also*: **Thermos flask**) termo
thermostat ['θə:məustæt] *n* termostato
thesaurus [θɪ'sɔ:rəs] *n* tesoro, diccionario de sinónimos
these [ði:z] *pl adj* estos(-as) ■ *pl pron* éstos(-as)
thesis (*pl* **theses**) ['θi:sɪs, -si:z] *n* tesis *f inv*; *see also* **doctorate**
they [ðeɪ] *pl pron* ellos/ellas; **~ say that ...** (*it is said that*) se dice que ...
they'd [ðeɪd] = **they had; they would**
they'll [ðeɪl] = **they shall; they will**
they're [ðɛəʳ] = **they are**
they've [ðeɪv] = **they have**
thick [θɪk] *adj* (*wall, slice*) grueso; (*dense: liquid, smoke etc*) espeso; (*vegetation, beard*) tupido; (*stupid*) torpe ■ *n*: **in the ~ of the battle** en lo más reñido de la batalla; **it's 20 cm ~** tiene 20 cm de espesor
thicken ['θɪkn] *vi* espesarse ■ *vt* (*sauce etc*) espesar
thicket ['θɪkɪt] *n* espesura
thickly ['θɪklɪ] *adv* (*spread*) en capa espesa; (*cut*) en rebanada gruesa; (*populated*) densamente
thickness ['θɪknɪs] *n* espesor *m*, grueso
thickset [θɪk'sɛt] *adj* fornido
thickskinned [θɪk'skɪnd] *adj* (*fig*) insensible
thief (*pl* **thieves**) [θi:f, θi:vz] *n* ladrón(-ona) *m(f)*
thieving ['θi:vɪŋ] *n* robo, hurto ■ *adj* ladrón(-ona)
thigh [θaɪ] *n* muslo
thighbone ['θaɪbəun] *n* fémur *m*
thimble ['θɪmbl] *n* dedal *m*
thin [θɪn] *adj* delgado; (*wall, layer*) fino; (*watery*) aguado; (*light*) tenue; (*hair*) escaso; (*fog*) ligero; (*crowd*) disperso ■ *vt*: **to ~ (down)** (*sauce, paint*) diluir ■ *vi* (*fog*) aclararse; (*also*: **thin out**: *crowd*) dispersarse; **his hair is thinning** se está quedando calvo
thing [θɪŋ] *n* cosa; (*object*) objeto, artículo; (*contraption*) chisme *m*; (*mania*) manía; **things** *npl* (*belongings*) cosas *fpl*; **the best ~ would**

be to ... lo mejor sería ...; **the main ~ is ...** lo principal es ...; **first ~ (in the morning)** a primera hora (de la mañana); **last ~ (at night)** a última hora (de la noche); **the ~ is ...** lo que pasa es que ...; **how are things?** ¿qué tal van las cosas?; **she's got a ~ about mice** le dan no sé qué los ratones; **poor ~!** ¡pobre! *m/f*, ¡pobrecito(-a)!

think (*pl* **thought**) [θɪŋk, θɔːt] *vi* pensar ■ *vt* pensar, creer; (*imagine*) imaginar; **what did you ~ of it?** ¿qué te parece?; **what did you ~ of them?** ¿qué te parecieron?; **to ~ about sth/sb** pensar en algo/uno; **I'll ~ about it** lo pensaré; **to ~ of doing sth** pensar en hacer algo; **I ~ so/not** creo que sí/no; **~ again!** ¡piénsalo bien!; **to ~ aloud** pensar en voz alta; **to ~ well of sb** tener buen concepto de algn
▸ **think out** *vt* (*plan*) elaborar, tramar; (*solution*) encontrar
▸ **think over** *vt* reflexionar sobre, meditar; **I'd like to ~ things over** me gustaría pensármelo
▸ **think through** *vt* pensar bien
▸ **think up** *vt* imaginar

thinking ['θɪŋkɪŋ] *n*: **to my (way of) ~** a mi parecer

think tank *n* grupo de expertos

thinly ['θɪnlɪ] *adv* (*cut*) en lonchas finas; (*spread*) en una capa fina

thinness ['θɪnnɪs] *n* delgadez *f*

third [θəːd] *adj* (*before nmsg*) tercer; tercero ■ *n* tercero(-a); (*fraction*) tercio; (*Brit Scol: degree*) *título universitario de tercera clase*

third degree *adj* (*burns*) de tercer grado

thirdly ['θəːdlɪ] *adv* en tercer lugar

third party insurance *n* (*Brit*) seguro a terceros

third-rate ['θəːd'reɪt] *adj* de poca calidad

Third World *n*: **the ~** el Tercer Mundo ■ *cpd* tercermundista

thirst [θəːst] *n* sed *f*

thirsty ['θəːstɪ] *adj* (*person*) sediento; **to be ~** tener sed

thirteen [θəː'tiːn] *num* trece

thirteenth [θəː'tiːnθ] *adj* decimotercero ■ *n* (*in series*) decimotercero(-a); (*fraction*) decimotercio

thirtieth ['θəːtɪəθ] *adj* trigésimo ■ *n* (*in series*) trigésimo(-a); (*fraction*) treintavo

thirty ['θəːtɪ] *num* treinta

KEYWORD

this [ðɪs] (*pl* **these**) *adj* (*demonstrative*) este(-a), estos(-as) *pl*, esto *neuter*; **this man/woman** este hombre/esta mujer; **these children/flowers** estos chicos/estas flores; **this way** por aquí; **this time last year** hoy hace un año; **this one (here)** éste(-a), esto (de aquí)
■ *pron* (*demonstrative*) éste(-a), éstos(-as) *pl*, esto *neuter*; **who is this?** ¿quién es éste/ésta?; **what is this?** ¿qué es esto?; **this is where I live** aquí vivo; **this is what he said** esto es lo que dijo; **this is Mr Brown** (*in introductions*) le presento al Sr. Brown; (*photo*) éste es el Sr. Brown; (*on telephone*) habla el Sr. Brown; **they were talking of this and that** hablaban de esto y lo otro
■ *adv* (*demonstrative*): **this high/long** así de alto/largo; **this far** hasta aquí

thistle ['θɪsl] *n* cardo

thong [θɔŋ] *n* correa

thorn [θɔːn] *n* espina

thorny ['θɔːnɪ] *adj* espinoso

thorough ['θʌrə] *adj* (*search*) minucioso; (*knowledge*) profundo; (*research*) a fondo

thoroughbred ['θʌrəbrɛd] *adj* (*horse*) de pura sangre

thoroughfare ['θʌrəfɛəʳ] *n* calle *f*; **"no ~"** "prohibido el paso"

thoroughgoing ['θʌrəgəuɪŋ] *adj* a fondo

thoroughly ['θʌrəlɪ] *adv* minuciosamente; a fondo

thoroughness ['θʌrənɪs] *n* minuciosidad *f*

those [ðəuz] *pl pron* ésos/ésas; (*more remote*) aquéllos(-as) ■ *pl adj* esos/esas; aquellos(-as)

though [ðəu] *conj* aunque ■ *adv* sin embargo, aún así; **even ~** aunque; **it's not so easy, ~** sin embargo no es tan fácil

thought [θɔːt] *pt, pp of* **think** ■ *n* pensamiento; (*opinion*) opinión *f*; (*intention*) intención *f*; **to give sth some ~** pensar algo detenidamente; **after much ~** después de pensarlo bien; **I've just had a ~** se me acaba de ocurrir una idea

thoughtful ['θɔːtful] *adj* pensativo; (*considerate*) atento

thoughtfully ['θɔːtfəlɪ] *adv* pensativamente; atentamente

thoughtless ['θɔːtlɪs] *adj* desconsiderado

thoughtlessly ['θɔːtlɪslɪ] *adv* insensatamente

thought-provoking ['θɔːtprəvəukɪŋ] *adj* estimulante

thousand ['θauzənd] *num* mil; **two ~** dos mil; **thousands of** miles de

thousandth ['θauzəntθ] *num* milésimo

thrash [θræʃ] *vt* dar una paliza a
▸ **thrash about** *vi* revolverse
▸ **thrash out** *vt* discutir a fondo

thrashing ['θræʃɪŋ] *n*: **to give sb a ~** dar una paliza a algn

thread [θrɛd] *n* hilo; (*of screw*) rosca ■ *vt* (*needle*) enhebrar
threadbare ['θrɛdbɛəʳ] *adj* raído
threat [θrɛt] *n* amenaza; **to be under ~ of** estar amenazado de
threaten ['θrɛtn] *vi* amenazar ■ *vt*: **to ~ sb with sth/to do** amenazar a algn con algo/con hacer
threatening ['θrɛtnɪŋ] *adj* amenazador(a), amenazante
three [θri:] *num* tres
three-dimensional [θri:dɪ'mɛnʃənl] *adj* tridimensional
threefold ['θri:fəuld] *adv*: **to increase ~** triplicar
three-piece ['θri:pi:s]: **~ suit** *n* traje *m* de tres piezas
three-piece suite *n* tresillo
three-ply [θri:'plaɪ] *adj* (*wood*) de tres capas; (*wool*) triple
three-quarter [θri:'kwɔ:təʳ] *adj*: **~ length sleeves** mangas *fpl* tres cuartos
three-quarters [θri:'kwɔ:təz] *npl* tres cuartas partes; **~ full** tres cuartas partes lleno
three-wheeler [θri:'wi:ləʳ] *n* (*car*) coche *m* cabina
thresh [θrɛʃ] *vt* (*Agr*) trillar
threshing machine ['θrɛʃɪŋ-] *n* trilladora
threshold ['θrɛʃhəuld] *n* umbral *m*; **to be on the ~ of** (*fig*) estar al borde de
threshold agreement *n* convenio de nivel crítico
threw [θru:] *pt of* **throw**
thrift [θrɪft] *n* economía
thrifty ['θrɪftɪ] *adj* económico
thrill [θrɪl] *n* (*excitement*) emoción *f* ■ *vt* emocionar; **to be thrilled** (*with gift etc*) estar encantado
thriller ['θrɪləʳ] *n* película/novela de suspense
thrilling ['θrɪlɪŋ] *adj* emocionante
thrive (*pt* **thrived, throve**, *pp* **thrived, thriven**) [θraɪv, θrəuv, 'θrɪvn] *vi* (*grow*) crecer; (*do well*) prosperar
thriving ['θraɪvɪŋ] *adj* próspero
throat [θrəut] *n* garganta; **I have a sore ~** me duele la garganta
throb [θrɔb] *n* (*of heart*) latido; (*of engine*) vibración *f* ■ *vi* latir; vibrar; (*with pain*) dar punzadas; **my head is throbbing** la cabeza me da punzadas
throes [θrəuz] *npl*: **in the ~ of** en medio de
thrombosis [θrɔm'bəusɪs] *n* trombosis *f*
throne [θrəun] *n* trono
throng [θrɔŋ] *n* multitud *f*, muchedumbre *f* ■ *vt, vi* apiñarse, agolparse
throttle ['θrɔtl] *n* (*Aut*) acelerador *m* ■ *vt* estrangular
through [θru:] *prep* por, a través de; (*time*) durante; (*by means of*) por medio de, mediante; (*owing to*) gracias a ■ *adj* (*ticket, train*) directo ■ *adv* completamente, de parte a parte; de principio a fin; **(from) Monday ~ Friday** (*US*) de lunes a viernes; **to go ~ sb's papers** mirar entre los papeles de algn; **I am halfway ~ the book** voy por la mitad del libro; **the soldiers didn't let us ~** los soldados no nos dejaron pasar; **to put sb ~ to sb** (*Tel*) poner *or* pasar a algn con algn; **to be ~** (*Tel*) tener comunicación; (*have finished*) haber terminado; **"no ~ road"** (*Brit*) "calle sin salida"
throughout [θru:'aut] *prep* (*place*) por todas partes de, por todo; (*time*) durante todo ■ *adv* por *or* en todas partes
throughput ['θru:put] *n* (*of goods, materials*) producción *f*; (*Comput*) capacidad *f* de procesamiento
throve [θrəuv] *pt of* **thrive**
throw [θrəu] *n* tiro; (*Sport*) lanzamiento ■ *vt* (*pt* **threw**, *pp* **thrown**) [θru:, θrəun] tirar, echar, botar (*LAm*); (*Sport*) lanzar; (*rider*) derribar; (*fig*) desconcertar; **to ~ a party** dar una fiesta
▸ **throw about, throw around** *vt* (*litter etc*) tirar, esparcir
▸ **throw away** *vt* tirar
▸ **throw off** *vt* deshacerse de
▸ **throw open** *vt* (*doors, windows*) abrir de par en par; (*house, gardens etc*) abrir al público; (*competition, race*) abrir a todos
▸ **throw out** *vt* tirar, botar (*LAm*)
▸ **throw together** *vt* (*clothes*) amontonar; (*meal*) preparar a la carrera; (*essay*) hacer sin cuidado
▸ **throw up** *vi* vomitar, devolver
throwaway ['θrəuəweɪ] *adj* para tirar, desechable
throwback ['θrəubæk] *n*: **it's a ~ to** (*fig*) eso nos lleva de nuevo a
throw-in ['θrəuɪn] *n* (*Sport*) saque *m* de banda
thrown [θrəun] *pp of* **throw**
thru [θru:] (*US*) = **through**
thrush [θrʌʃ] *n* zorzal *m*, tordo; (*Med*) candiasis *f*
thrust [θrʌst] *n* (*Tech*) empuje *m* ■ *vt* (*pt, pp* **thrust**) empujar; (*push in*) introducir
thrusting ['θrʌstɪŋ] *adj* (*person*) dinámico, con empuje
thud [θʌd] *n* golpe *m* sordo
thug [θʌg] *n* gamberro(-a)
thumb [θʌm] *n* (*Anat*) pulgar *m* ■ *vt*: **to ~ a lift** hacer dedo; **to give sth/sb the thumbs up/down** aprobar/desaprobar algo/a algn
▸ **thumb through** *vt fus* (*book*) hojear

thumb index *n* uñero, índice *m* recortado
thumbnail ['θʌmneɪl] *n* uña del pulgar
thumbnail sketch *n* esbozo
thumbtack ['θʌmtæk] *n* (*US*) chincheta, chinche *f*
thump [θʌmp] *n* golpe *m*; (*sound*) ruido seco *or* sordo ■ *vt, vi* golpear
thumping ['θʌmpɪŋ] *adj* (*col*: *huge*) descomunal
thunder ['θʌndəʳ] *n* trueno; (*of applause etc*) estruendo ■ *vi* tronar; (*train etc*): **to ~ past** pasar como un trueno
thunderbolt ['θʌndəbəult] *n* rayo
thunderclap ['θʌndəklæp] *n* trueno
thunderous ['θʌndərəs] *adj* ensordecedor(a), estruendoso
thunderstorm ['θʌndəstɔːm] *n* tormenta
thunderstruck ['θʌndəstrʌk] *adj* pasmado
thundery ['θʌndərɪ] *adj* tormentoso
Thur., Thurs. *abbr* (= *Thursday*) juev
Thursday ['θəːzdɪ] *n* jueves *m inv*; *see also* **Tuesday**
thus [ðʌs] *adv* así, de este modo
thwart [θwɔːt] *vt* frustrar
thyme [taɪm] *n* tomillo
thyroid ['θaɪrɔɪd] *n* tiroides *m inv*
tiara [tɪ'ɑːrə] *n* tiara, diadema
Tiber ['taɪbəʳ] *n* Tíber *m*
Tibet [tɪ'bɛt] *n* el Tibet
Tibetan [tɪ'bɛtən] *adj* tibetano ■ *n* tibetano(-a); (*Ling*) tibetano
tibia ['tɪbɪə] *n* tibia
tic [tɪk] *n* tic *m*
tick [tɪk] *n* (*sound*: *of clock*) tictac *m*; (*mark*) señal *f* (de visto bueno), palomita (*LAm*); (*Zool*) garrapata; (*Brit col*): **in a ~** en un instante; (*Brit col*: *credit*): **to buy sth on ~** comprar algo a crédito ■ *vi* hacer tictac ■ *vt* marcar, señalar; **to put a ~ against sth** poner una señal en algo
▸ **tick off** *vt* marcar; (*person*) reñir
▸ **tick over** *vi* (*Brit*: *engine*) girar en marcha lenta; (: *fig*) ir tirando
ticker tape ['tɪkə-] *n* cinta perforada
ticket ['tɪkɪt] *n* billete *m*, tíquet *m*, boleto (*LAm*); (*for cinema etc*) entrada, boleto (*LAm*); (*in shop*: *on goods*) etiqueta; (*for library*) tarjeta; (*US Pol*) lista (de candidatos); **to get a parking ~** (*Aut*) ser multado por estacionamiento ilegal
ticket agency *n* (*Theat*) agencia de venta de entradas
ticket collector *n* revisor(a) *m(f)*
ticket holder *n* poseedor(a) *m(f)* de billete *or* entrada
ticket inspector *n* revisor(a) *m(f)*, inspector(a) *m(f)* de boletos (*LAm*)
ticket office *n* (*Theat*) taquilla, boletería (*LAm*); (*Rail*) despacho de billetes *or* boletos (*LAm*)
ticking-off ['tɪkɪŋ'ɔf] *n* (*col*): **to give sb a ~** echarle una bronca a algn
tickle ['tɪkl] *n*: **to give sb a ~** hacer cosquillas a algn ■ *vt* hacer cosquillas a
ticklish ['tɪklɪʃ] *adj* (*which tickles*: *blanket*) que pica; (: *cough*) irritante; **to be ~** tener cosquillas
tidal ['taɪdl] *adj* de marea
tidal wave *n* maremoto
tidbit ['tɪdbɪt] (*US*) = **titbit**
tiddlywinks ['tɪdlɪwɪŋks] *n* juego de la pulga
tide [taɪd] *n* marea; (*fig*: *of events*) curso, marcha ■ *vt*: **to ~ sb over** *or* **through (until)** sacar a algn del apuro (hasta); **high/low ~** marea alta/baja; **the ~ of public opinion** la tendencia de la opinión pública
tidily ['taɪdɪlɪ] *adv* bien, ordenadamente; **to arrange ~** ordenar; **to dress ~** vestir bien
tidiness ['taɪdɪnɪs] *n* (*order*) orden *m*; (*cleanliness*) aseo
tidy ['taɪdɪ] *adj* (*room*) ordenado; (*drawing, work*) limpio; (*person*) (bien) arreglado; (: *in character*) metódico; (*mind*) claro, metódico ■ *vt* (*also*: **tidy up**) ordenar, poner en orden
tie [taɪ] *n* (*string etc*) atadura; (*Brit*: *necktie*) corbata; (*fig*: *link*) vínculo, lazo; (*Sport*: *draw*) empate *m* ■ *vt* atar ■ *vi* (*Sport*) empatar; **family ties** obligaciones *fpl* familiares; **cup ~** (*Sport*: *match*) partido de copa; **to ~ in a bow** hacer un lazo; **to ~ a knot in sth** hacer un nudo en algo
▸ **tie down** *vt* atar; (*fig*): **to ~ sb down to** obligar a algn a
▸ **tie in** *vi*: **to ~ in (with)** (*correspond*) concordar (con)
▸ **tie on** *vt* (*Brit*: *label etc*) atar
▸ **tie up** *vt* (*parcel*) envolver; (*dog*) atar; (*boat*) amarrar; (*arrangements*) concluir; **to be tied up** (*busy*) estar ocupado
tie-break ['taɪbreɪk], **tie-breaker** ['taɪbreɪkəʳ] *n* (*Tennis*) tiebreak *m*, muerte *f* súbita; (*in quiz*) punto decisivo
tie-on ['taɪɔn] *adj* (*Brit*: *label*) para atar
tie-pin ['taɪpɪn] *n* (*Brit*) alfiler *m* de corbata
tier [tɪəʳ] *n* grada; (*of cake*) piso
tie tack *n* (*US*) alfiler *m* de corbata
tiff [tɪf] *n* (*col*) pelea, riña
tiger ['taɪgəʳ] *n* tigre *m*
tight [taɪt] *adj* (*rope*) tirante; (*money*) escaso; (*clothes, budget*) ajustado; (*programme*) apretado; (*col*: *drunk*) borracho ■ *adv* (*squeeze*) muy fuerte; (*shut*) herméticamente; **to be packed ~** (*suitcase*) estar completamente lleno; (*people*) estar apretados; **everybody hold ~!** ¡agárense bien!

tighten ['taɪtn] *vt* (*rope*) tensar, estirar; (*screw*) apretar ■ *vi* estirarse; apretarse
tight-fisted [taɪt'fɪstɪd] *adj* tacaño
tight-lipped ['taɪt'lɪpt] *adj*: **to be ~** (*silent*) rehusar hablar; (*angry*) apretar los labios
tightly ['taɪtlɪ] *adv* (*grasp*) muy fuerte
tightness ['taɪtnɪs] *n* (*of rope*) tirantez *f*; (*of clothes*) estrechez *f*; (*of budget*) lo ajustado
tightrope ['taɪtrəup] *n* cuerda floja
tightrope walker *n* equilibrista *m/f*, funambulista *m/f*
tights [taɪts] *npl* (*Brit*) medias *fpl*, panties *mpl*
tigress ['taɪgrɪs] *n* tigresa
tilde ['tɪldə] *n* tilde *f*
tile [taɪl] *n* (*on roof*) teja; (*on floor*) baldosa; (*on wall*) azulejo ■ *vt* (*floor*) poner baldosas en; (*wall*) alicatar
tiled [taɪld] *adj* (*floor*) embaldosado; (*wall, bathroom*) alicatado; (*roof*) con tejas
till [tɪl] *n* caja (registradora) ■ *vt* (*land*) cultivar ■ *prep, conj* = **until**
tiller ['tɪlər] *n* (*Naut*) caña del timón
tilt [tɪlt] *vt* inclinar ■ *vi* inclinarse ■ *n* (*slope*) inclinación *f*; **to wear one's hat at a ~** llevar el sombrero echado a un lado *or* terciado; **(at) full ~** a toda velocidad *or* carrera
timber [tɪmbər] *n* (*material*) madera; (*trees*) árboles *mpl*
time [taɪm] *n* tiempo; (*epoch: often pl*) época; (*by clock*) hora; (*moment*) momento; (*occasion*) vez *f*; (*Mus*) compás *m* ■ *vt* calcular *or* medir el tiempo de; (*race*) cronometrar; (*remark etc*) elegir el momento para; **a long ~** mucho tiempo; **four at a ~** cuarto a la vez; **for the ~ being** de momento, por ahora; **at times** a veces, a ratos; **~ after ~, ~ and again** repetidas veces, una y otra vez; **from ~ to ~** de vez en cuando; **in ~** (*soon enough*) a tiempo; (*after some time*) con el tiempo; (*Mus*) al compás; **in a week's ~** dentro de una semana; **in no ~** en un abrir y cerrar de ojos; **any ~** cuando sea; **on ~** a la hora; **to be 30 minutes behind/ahead of ~** llevar media hora de retraso/adelanto; **to take one's ~** tomárselo con calma; **he'll do it in his own ~** (*without being hurried*) lo hará sin prisa; (*out of working hours*) lo hará en su tiempo libre; **by the ~ he arrived** cuando llegó; **5 times 5** 5 por 5; **what ~ is it?** ¿qué hora es?; **what ~ do you make it?** ¿qué hora es *or* tiene?; **to be behind the times** estar atrasado; **to carry three boxes at a ~** llevar tres cajas a la vez; **to keep ~** llevar el ritmo *or* el compás; **to have a good ~** pasarlo bien, divertirse; **to ~ sth well/badly** elegir un buen/mal momento para algo; **the bomb was timed to explode five minutes later** la bomba estaba programada para explotar cinco minutos más tarde
time-and-motion expert ['taɪmənd'məuʃən-] *n* experto(-a) en la ciencia de la producción
time-and-motion study ['taɪmənd'məuʃən-] *n* estudio de desplazamientos y tiempos
time bomb *n* bomba de relojería
time card *n* tarjeta de registro horario
time clock *n* reloj *m* registrador
time-consuming ['taɪmkənsju:mɪŋ] *adj* que requiere mucho tiempo
time frame *n* plazo
time-honoured, time-honored (*US*) ['taɪmɔnəd] *adj* consagrado
timekeeper ['taɪmki:pər] *n* (*Sport*) cronómetro
time lag *n* desfase *m*
timeless ['taɪmlɪs] *adj* eterno
time limit *n* (*gen*) límite *m* de tiempo; (*Comm*) plazo
timely ['taɪmlɪ] *adj* oportuno
time off *n* tiempo libre
timer ['taɪmər] *n* (*also:* **timer switch**) interruptor *m*; (*in kitchen*) temporizador *m*; (*Tech*) temporizador *m*
time-saving ['taɪmseɪvɪŋ] *adj* que ahorra tiempo
time scale *n* escala de tiempo
time sharing *n* (*Comput*) tiempo compartido
time sheet *n* = **time card**
time signal *n* señal *f* horaria
time switch *n* (*Brit*) interruptor *m* (horario)
timetable ['taɪmteɪbl] *n* horario; (*programme of events etc*) programa *m*
time zone *n* huso horario
timid ['tɪmɪd] *adj* tímido
timidity [tɪ'mɪdɪtɪ] *n* timidez *f*
timidly ['tɪmɪdlɪ] *adv* tímidamente
timing ['taɪmɪŋ] *n* (*Sport*) cronometraje *m*; **the ~ of his resignation** el momento que eligió para dimitir
timpani ['tɪmpənɪ] *npl* tímpanos *mpl*
tin [tɪn] *n* estaño; (*also:* **tin plate**) hojalata; (*Brit: can*) lata
tinfoil ['tɪnfɔɪl] *n* papel *m* de estaño
tinge [tɪndʒ] *n* matiz *m* ■ *vt*: **tinged with** teñido de
tingle ['tɪŋgl] *n* hormigueo ■ *vi* (*cheeks, skin: from cold*) sentir comezón; (*: from bad circulation*) sentir hormigueo
tinker ['tɪŋkər] *n* calderero(-a); (*gipsy*) gitano(-a)
▸ **tinker with** *vt fus* jugar con, tocar
tinkle ['tɪŋkl] *vi* tintinear
tin mine *n* mina de estaño

tinned [tɪnd] *adj* (*Brit: food*) en lata, en conserva
tinnitus ['tɪnɪtəs] *n* (*Med*) acufeno
tinny ['tɪnɪ] *adj* (*sound, taste*) metálico; (*pej: car*) poco sólido, de pacotilla
tin opener [-əupnəʳ] *n* (*Brit*) abrelatas *m inv*
tinsel ['tɪnsl] *n* oropel *m*
tint [tɪnt] *n* matiz *m*; (*for hair*) tinte *m* ■ *vt* (*hair*) teñir
tinted ['tɪntɪd] *adj* (*hair*) teñido; (*glass, spectacles*) ahumado
tiny ['taɪnɪ] *adj* minúsculo, pequeñito
tip [tɪp] *n* (*end*) punta; (*gratuity*) propina; (*Brit: for rubbish*) vertedero; (*advice*) consejo ■ *vt* (*waiter*) dar una propina a; (*tilt*) inclinar; (*empty: also:* **tip out**) vaciar, echar; (*predict: winner*) pronosticar; (*: horse*) recomendar; **he tipped out the contents of the box** volcó el contenido de la caja
▸ **tip off** *vt* avisar, poner sobre aviso a
▸ **tip over** *vt* volcar ■ *vi* volcarse
tip-off ['tɪpɔf] *n* (*hint*) advertencia
tipped [tɪpt] *adj* (*Brit: cigarette*) con filtro
Tipp-Ex® ['tɪpɛks] *n* Tipp-Ex® *m*
tipple ['tɪpl] *n* (*Brit*): **his ~ is Cointreau** bebe Cointreau
tipster ['tɪpstəʳ] *n* (*Racing*) pronosticador(a) *m(f)*
tipsy ['tɪpsɪ] *adj* alegre, achispado
tiptoe ['tɪptəu] *n* (*Brit*): **on ~** de puntillas
tiptop ['tɪptɔp] *adj*: **in ~ condition** en perfectas condiciones
tirade [taɪ'reɪd] *n* diatriba
tire ['taɪəʳ] *n* (*US*) = **tyre** ■ *vt* cansar ■ *vi* (*gen*) cansarse; (*become bored*) aburrirse
▸ **tire out** *vt* agotar, rendir
tired ['taɪəd] *adj* cansado; **to be ~ of sth** estar harto de algo; **to be/feel/look ~** estar/sentirse/parecer cansado
tiredness ['taɪədnɪs] *n* cansancio
tireless ['taɪəlɪs] *adj* incansable
tirelessly ['taɪəlɪslɪ] *adv* incansablemente
tiresome ['taɪəsəm] *adj* aburrido
tiring ['taɪrɪŋ] *adj* cansado
tissue ['tɪʃuː] *n* tejido; (*paper handkerchief*) pañuelo de papel, kleenex® *m*
tissue paper *n* papel *m* de seda
tit [tɪt] *n* (*bird*) herrerillo común; **to give ~ for tat** dar ojo por ojo
titbit ['tɪtbɪt], **tidbit** (*US*) ['tɪdbɪt] *n* (*food*) golosina; (*news*) pedazo
titillate ['tɪtɪleɪt] *vt* estimular, excitar
titillation [tɪtɪ'leɪʃən] *n* estimulación *f*, excitación *f*
titivate ['tɪtɪveɪt] *vt* emperejilar
title ['taɪtl] *n* título; (*Law: right*): **~ (to)** derecho (a)
title deed *n* (*Law*) título de propiedad
title page *n* portada
title role *n* papel *m* principal
titter ['tɪtəʳ] *vi* reírse entre dientes
tittle-tattle ['tɪtltætl] *n* chismes *mpl*
titular ['tɪtjuləʳ] *adj* (*in name only*) nominal
T-junction ['tiːdʒʌŋkʃən] *n* cruce *m* en T
TM *abbr* (*= trademark*) marca de fábrica; = **transcendental meditation**
TN *abbr* (*US*) = **Tennessee**
TNT *n abbr* (*= trinitrotoluene*) TNT *m*

KEYWORD

to [tuː, tə] *prep* **1** (*direction*) a; **to go to France/London/school/the station** ir a Francia/Londres/al colegio/a la estación; **to go to Claude's/the doctor's** ir a casa de Claude/al médico; **the road to Edinburgh** la carretera de Edimburgo; **to the left/right** a la izquierda/derecha
2 (*as far as*) hasta, a; **from here to London** de aquí a *or* hasta Londres; **to count to 10** contar hasta 10; **from 40 to 50 people** entre 40 y 50 personas
3 (*with expressions of time*): **a quarter/twenty to five** las cuarto menos cuarto/veinte
4 (*for, of*): **the key to the front door** la llave de la puerta principal; **she is secretary to the director** es la secretaria del director; **a letter to his wife** una carta a *or* para su mujer
5 (*expressing indirect object*) a; **to give sth to sb** darle algo a algn; **give it to me** dámelo; **to talk to sb** hablar con algn; **to be a danger to sb** ser un peligro para algn; **to carry out repairs to sth** hacer reparaciones en algo
6 (*in relation to*): **3 goals to 2** 3 goles a 2; **30 miles to the gallon** ≈ 9,4 litros a los cien (kilómetros); **8 apples to the kilo** 8 manzanas por kilo
7 (*purpose, result*): **to come to sb's aid** venir en auxilio *or* ayuda de algn; **to sentence sb to death** condenar a algn a muerte; **to my great surprise** con gran sorpresa mía
■ *infin particle* **1** (*simple infin*): **to go/eat** ir/comer
2 (*following another vb; see also relevant vb*): **to want/try/start to do** querer/intentar/empezar a hacer
3 (*with vb omitted*): **I don't want to** no quiero
4 (*purpose, result*) para; **I did it to help you** lo hice para ayudarte; **he came to see you** vino a verte
5 (*equivalent to relative clause*): **I have things to do** tengo cosas que hacer; **the main thing is to try** lo principal es intentarlo

6 (*after adj etc*): **ready to go** listo para irse; **too old to ...** demasiado viejo (como) para ... ■ *adv*: **pull/push the door to** tirar de/empujar la puerta; **to go to and fro** ir y venir

toad [təud] *n* sapo
toadstool ['təudstu:l] *n* seta venenosa
toady ['təudı] *n* pelota *m/f* ■ *vi*: **to ~ to sb** hacer la pelota *or* dar coba a algn
toast [təust] *n* (*Culin*: *also*: **piece of toast**) tostada; (*drink, speech*) brindis *m inv* ■ *vt* (*Culin*) tostar; (*drink to*) brindar
toaster ['təustəʳ] *n* tostador *m*
toastmaster ['təustmɑ:stəʳ] *n persona que propone brindis y anuncia a los oradores en un banquete*
toast rack *n* rejilla para tostadas
tobacco [tə'bækəu] *n* tabaco; **pipe ~** tabaco de pipa
tobacconist [tə'bækənıst] *n* estanquero(-a), tabaquero(-a) (*LAm*); **~'s (shop)** (*Brit*) estanco, tabaquería (*LAm*)
tobacco plantation *n* plantación *f* de tabaco, tabacal *m*
Tobago [tə'beıgəu] *n see* **Trinidad and Tobago**
toboggan [tə'bɔgən] *n* tobogán *m*
today [tə'deı] *adv, n* (*also fig*) hoy *m*; **what day is it ~?** ¿qué día es hoy?; **what date is it ~?** ¿a qué fecha estamos hoy?; **~ is the 4th of March** hoy es el 4 de marzo; **~'s paper** el periódico de hoy; **a fortnight ~** de hoy en 15 días, dentro de 15 días
toddle ['tɔdl] *vi* empezar a andar, dar los primeros pasos
toddler ['tɔdləʳ] *n* niño(-a) (que empieza a andar)
toddy ['tɔdı] *n* ponche *m*
to-do [tə'du:] *n* (*fuss*) lío
toe [təu] *n* dedo (del pie); (*of shoe*) punta ■ *vt*: **to ~ the line** (*fig*) acatar las normas; **big/little ~** dedo gordo/pequeño del pie
TOEFL ['təufl] *n abbr* = **Test(ing) of English as a Foreign Language**
toehold ['təuhəuld] *n* punto de apoyo (para el pie)
toenail ['təuneıl] *n* uña del pie
toffee ['tɔfı] *n* caramelo
toffee apple *n* (*Brit*) manzana de caramelo
tofu ['təufu:] *n* tofu *m*
toga ['təugə] *n* toga
together [tə'gɛðəʳ] *adv* juntos; (*at same time*) al mismo tiempo, a la vez; **~ with** junto con
togetherness [tə'gɛðənıs] *n* compañerismo
toggle switch ['tɔgl-] *n* (*Comput*) conmutador *m* de palanca
Togo ['təugəu] *n* Togo
togs [tɔgz] *npl* (*col*: *clothes*) atuendo, ropa
toil [tɔıl] *n* trabajo duro, labor *f* ■ *vi* esforzarse
toilet ['tɔılət] *n* (*Brit*: *lavatory*) servicios *mpl*, wáter *m* ■ *cpd* (*bag, soap etc*) de aseo; **to go to the ~** ir al baño; *see also* **toilets**
toilet bag *n* neceser *m*, bolsa de aseo
toilet bowl *n* taza (de retrete)
toilet paper *n* papel *m* higiénico
toiletries ['tɔılətrız] *npl* artículos *mpl* de aseo; (*make-up etc*) artículos *mpl* de tocador
toilet roll *n* rollo de papel higiénico
toilets ['tɔıləts] *npl* (*Brit*) servicios *mpl*
toilet soap *n* jabón *m* de tocador
toilet water *n* (agua de) colonia
to-ing and fro-ing ['tuıŋən'frəuıŋ] *n* vaivén *m*
token ['təukən] *n* (*sign*) señal *f*, muestra; (*souvenir*) recuerdo; (*voucher*) vale *m*; (*disc*) ficha ■ *cpd* (*fee, strike*) nominal, simbólico; **book/record ~** (*Brit*) vale *m* para comprar libros/discos; **by the same ~** (*fig*) por la misma razón
tokenism ['təukənızəm] *n* (*Pol*) política simbólica *or* de fachada
Tokyo ['təukjəu] *n* Tokio, Tokío
told [təuld] *pt, pp of* **tell**
tolerable ['tɔlərəbl] *adj* (*bearable*) soportable; (*fairly good*) pasable
tolerably ['tɔlərəblı] *adv* (*good, comfortable*) medianamente
tolerance ['tɔlərns] *n* (*also Tech*) tolerancia
tolerant ['tɔlərnt] *adj*: **~ of** tolerante con
tolerantly ['tɔlərntlı] *adv* con tolerancia
tolerate ['tɔləreıt] *vt* tolerar
toleration [tɔlə'reıʃən] *n* tolerancia
toll [təul] *n* (*of casualties*) número de víctimas; (*tax, charge*) peaje *m* ■ *vi* (*bell*) doblar
toll bridge *n* puente *m* de peaje
toll call *n* (*US Telec*) conferencia, llamada interurbana
toll-free *adj, adv* (*US*) gratis
toll road *n* carretera de peaje
tomato (*pl* **tomatoes**) [tə'mɑ:təu] *n* tomate *m*
tomato puree *n* puré *m* de tomate
tomb [tu:m] *n* tumba
tombola [tɔm'bəulə] *n* tómbola
tomboy ['tɔmbɔı] *n* marimacho
tombstone ['tu:mstəun] *n* lápida
tomcat ['tɔmkæt] *n* gato
tomorrow [tə'mɔrəu] *adv, n* (*also fig*) mañana; **the day after ~** pasado mañana; **~ morning** mañana por la mañana; **a week ~** de mañana en ocho (días)
ton [tʌn] *n* tonelada; **tons of** (*col*) montones de
tonal ['təunl] *adj* tonal

tone [təun] *n* tono ■ *vi* armonizar; **dialling ~** (*Tel*) señal *f* para marcar
▸ **tone down** *vt* (*criticism*) suavizar; (*colour*) atenuar
▸ **tone up** *vt* (*muscles*) tonificar
tone-deaf [təun'dɛf] *adj* sin oído musical
toner ['təunəʳ] *n* (*for photocopier*) virador *m*
Tonga ['tɔŋə] *n* Islas *fpl* Tonga
tongs [tɔŋz] *npl* (*for coal*) tenazas *fpl*; (*for hair*) tenacillas *fpl*
tongue [tʌŋ] *n* lengua; **~ in cheek** *adv* en plan de broma
tongue-tied ['tʌŋtaɪd] *adj* (*fig*) mudo
tongue-twister ['tʌŋtwɪstəʳ] *n* trabalenguas *m inv*
tonic ['tɔnɪk] *n* (*Med*) tónico; (*Mus*) tónica; (*also*: **tonic water**) (agua) tónica
tonight [tə'naɪt] *adv, n* esta noche; **I'll see you ~** nos vemos esta noche
tonnage ['tʌnɪdʒ] *n* (*Naut*) tonelaje *m*
tonsil ['tɔnsl] *n* amígdala; **to have one's tonsils out** sacarse las amígdalas *or* anginas
tonsillitis [tɔnsɪ'laɪtɪs] *n* amigdalitis *f*
too [tu:] *adv* (*excessively*) demasiado; (*very*) muy; (*also*) también; (*also*: **it's too sweet**) está demasiado dulce; **I'm not ~ sure about that** no estoy muy seguro de eso; **I went ~** yo también fui; **~ much** *adv, adj* demasiado; **~ many** *adj* demasiados(-as); **~ bad!** ¡mala suerte!
took [tuk] *pt of* **take**
tool [tu:l] *n* herramienta; (*fig: person*) instrumento
toolbar ['tu:lbɑ:ʳ] *n* barra de herramientas
tool box *n* caja de herramientas
tool kit *n* juego de herramientas
tool shed *n* cobertizo (para herramientas)
toot [tu:t] *n* (*of horn*) bocinazo; (*of whistle*) silbido ■ *vi* (*with car horn*) tocar la bocina
tooth (*pl* **teeth**) [tu:θ, ti:θ] *n* (*Anat, Tech*) diente *m*; (*molar*) muela; **to clean one's teeth** lavarse los dientes; **to have a ~ out** sacarse una muela; **by the skin of one's teeth** por un pelo
toothache ['tu:θeɪk] *n* dolor *m* de muelas
toothbrush ['tu:θbrʌʃ] *n* cepillo de dientes
toothpaste ['tu:θpeɪst] *n* pasta de dientes
toothpick ['tu:θpɪk] *n* palillo
tooth powder *n* polvos *mpl* dentífricos
top [tɔp] *n* (*of mountain*) cumbre *f*, cima; (*of head*) coronilla; (*of ladder*) (lo) alto; (*of cupboard, table*) superficie *f*; (*lid: of box, jar*) tapa; (*: of bottle*) tapón *m*; (*of list, table, queue, page*) cabeza; (*toy*) peonza; (*Dress: blouse*) blusa; (*: T-shirt*) camiseta; (*: of pyjamas*) chaqueta ■ *adj* de arriba; (*in rank*) principal, primero; (*best*) mejor ■ *vt* (*exceed*) exceder; (*be first in*) encabezar; **on ~ of** sobre, encima de; **from ~ to bottom** de pies a cabeza; **the ~ of the milk** la nata; **at the ~ of the stairs** en lo alto de la escalera; **at the ~ of the street** al final de la calle; **at the ~ of one's voice** (*fig*) a voz en grito; **at ~ speed** a máxima velocidad; **a ~ surgeon** un cirujano eminente; **over the ~** (*col*) excesivo, desmesurado; **to go over the ~** pasarse
▸ **top up**, (*US*) **top off** *vt* volver a llenar
topaz ['təupæz] *n* topacio
top-class ['tɔp'klɑ:s] *adj* de primera clase
topcoat ['tɔpkəut] *n* sobretodo, abrigo
topflight ['tɔpflaɪt] *adj* de primera (categoría *or* clase)
top floor *n* último piso
top hat *n* sombrero de copa
top-heavy [tɔp'hɛvɪ] *adj* (*object*) con más peso en la parte superior
topic ['tɔpɪk] *n* tema *m*
topical ['tɔpɪkl] *adj* actual
topless ['tɔplɪs] *adj* (*bather etc*) topless
top-level ['tɔplɛvl] *adj* (*talks*) al más alto nivel
topmost ['tɔpməust] *adj* más alto
top-notch ['tɔp'nɔtʃ] *adj* (*col*) de primerísima categoría
topography [tə'pɔgrəfɪ] *n* topografía
topping ['tɔpɪŋ] *n* (*Culin*): **with a ~ of cream** con nata por encima
topple ['tɔpl] *vt* volcar, derribar ■ *vi* caerse
top-ranking ['tɔpræŋkɪŋ] *adj* de alto rango
top-secret [tɔp'si:krɪt] *adj* de alto secreto
top-security ['tɔpsɪ'kjuərɪtɪ] *adj* (*Brit*) de máxima seguridad
topsy-turvy ['tɔpsɪ'tə:vɪ] *adj, adv* patas arriba
top-up ['tɔpʌp] *n*: **would you like a ~?** ¿quiere que se lo vuelva a llenar?
top-up loan *n* (*Brit*) préstamo complementario
torch [tɔ:tʃ] *n* antorcha; (*Brit: electric*) linterna
tore [tɔ:ʳ] *pt of* **tear**
torment *n* ['tɔ:mɛnt] tormento ■ *vt* [tɔ:'mɛnt] atormentar; (*fig: annoy*) fastidiar
torn [tɔ:n] *pp of* **tear**
tornado (*pl* **tornadoes**) [tɔ:'neɪdəu] *n* tornado
torpedo (*pl* **torpedoes**) [tɔ:'pi:dəu] *n* torpedo
torpedo boat *n* torpedero, lancha torpedera
torpor ['tɔ:pəʳ] *n* letargo
torrent ['tɔrnt] *n* torrente *m*
torrential [tɔ'rɛnʃl] *adj* torrencial
torrid ['tɔrɪd] *adj* tórrido; (*fig*) apasionado
torso ['tɔ:səu] *n* torso
tortoise ['tɔ:təs] *n* tortuga
tortoiseshell ['tɔ:təʃɛl] *adj* de carey
tortuous ['tɔ:tjuəs] *adj* tortuoso
torture ['tɔ:tʃəʳ] *n* tortura ■ *vt* torturar; (*fig*) atormentar

torturer ['tɔːtʃərəʳ] *n* torturador(a) *m(f)*
Tory ['tɔːrɪ] *adj, n* (*Brit Pol*) conservador(a) *m(f)*
toss [tɔs] *vt* tirar, echar; (*head*) sacudir ■ *n* (*movement: of head etc*) sacudida; (*of coin*) tirada, echada (*LAm*); **to ~ a coin** echar a cara o cruz; **to ~ up for sth** jugar algo a cara o cruz; **to ~ and turn** (*in bed*) dar vueltas (en la cama); **to win/lose the ~** (*also Sport*) ganar/perder (a cara o cruz)
tot [tɔt] *n* (*Brit: drink*) copita; (*child*) nene(-a) *m(f)*
▸**tot up** *vt* sumar
total ['təutl] *adj* total, entero ■ *n* total *m*, suma ■ *vt* (*add up*) sumar; (*amount to*) ascender a; **grand ~** cantidad *f* total; (*cost*) importe *m* total; **in ~** en total, en suma
totalitarian [təutælɪ'tɛərɪən] *adj* totalitario
totality [təu'tælɪtɪ] *n* totalidad *f*
total loss *n* siniestra total
totally ['təutəlɪ] *adv* totalmente
tote [təut] *vt* (*col*) acarrear, cargar con
tote bag *n* bolsa
totem pole ['təutəm-] *n* poste *m* totémico
totter ['tɔtəʳ] *vi* tambalearse
touch [tʌtʃ] *n* (*sense*) tacto; (*contact*) contacto; (*Football*) fuera de juego ■ *vt* tocar; (*emotionally*) conmover; **a ~ of** (*fig*) una pizca *or* un poquito de; **to get in ~ with sb** ponerse en contacto con algn; **I'll be in ~** le llamaré/escribiré; **to lose ~** (*friends*) perder contacto; **to be out of ~ with events** no estar al corriente (de los acontecimientos); **the personal ~** el toque personal; **to put the finishing touches to sth** dar el último toque a algo; **no artist in the country can ~ him** no hay artista en todo el país que le iguale
▸**touch on** *vt fus* (*topic*) aludir (brevemente) a
▸**touch up** *vt* (*paint*) retocar
touch-and-go ['tʌtʃən'gəu] *adj* arriesgado
touchdown ['tʌtʃdaun] *n* aterrizaje *m*; (*US Football*) ensayo
touched [tʌtʃt] *adj* conmovido; (*col*) chiflado
touchiness ['tʌtʃɪnɪs] *n* susceptibilidad *f*
touching ['tʌtʃɪŋ] *adj* conmovedor(a)
touchline ['tʌtʃlaɪn] *n* (*Sport*) línea de banda
touch-sensitive ['tʌtʃsɛnsɪtɪv] *adj* sensible al tacto
touch-type ['tʌtʃtaɪp] *vi* mecanografiar al tacto
touchy ['tʌtʃɪ] *adj* (*person*) quisquilloso
tough [tʌf] *adj* (*meat*) duro; (*journey*) penoso; (*task, problem, situation*) difícil; (*resistant*) resistente; (*person*) fuerte; (*: pej*) bruto ■ *n* (*gangster etc*) gorila *m*; **they got ~ with the workers** se pusieron muy duros con los trabajadores
toughen ['tʌfn] *vt* endurecer
toughness ['tʌfnɪs] *n* dureza; (*resistance*) resistencia; (*strictness*) inflexibilidad *f*
toupée ['tuːpeɪ] *n* peluquín *m*
tour ['tuəʳ] *n* viaje *m*; (*also*: **package tour**) viaje *m* con todo incluido; (*of town, museum*) visita ■ *vt* viajar por; **to go on a ~ of** (*region, country*) ir de viaje por; (*museum, castle*) visitar; **to go on ~** partir *or* ir de gira
touring ['tuərɪŋ] *n* viajes *mpl* turísticos, turismo
tourism ['tuərɪzm] *n* turismo
tourist ['tuərɪst] *n* turista *m/f* ■ *cpd* turístico; **the ~ trade** el turismo
tourist class *n* (*Aviat*) clase *f* turista
tourist office *n* oficina de turismo
tournament ['tuənəmənt] *n* torneo
tourniquet ['tuənɪkeɪ] *n* (*Med*) torniquete *m*
tour operator *n* touroperador(a) *m(f)*, operador(a) *m(f)* turístico(-a)
tousled ['tauzld] *adj* (*hair*) despeinado
tout [taut] *vi*: **to ~ for business** solicitar clientes ■ *n*: **ticket ~** revendedor(a) *m(f)*
tow [təu] *n*: **to give sb a ~** (*Aut*) remolcar a algn ■ *vt* remolcar; **"on** *or* (*US*) **in ~"** (*Aut*) "a remolque"
toward [tə'wɔːd], **towards** [tə'wɔːdz] *prep* hacia; (*of attitude*) respecto a, con; (*of purpose*) para; **~(s) noon** alrededor de mediodía; **~(s) the end of the year** hacia finales de año; **to feel friendly ~(s) sb** sentir amistad hacia algn
towel ['tauəl] *n* toalla; **to throw in the ~** (*fig*) darse por vencido, renunciar
towelling ['tauəlɪŋ] *n* (*fabric*) felpa
towel rail, towel rack (*US*) *n* toallero
tower ['tauəʳ] *n* torre *f* ■ *vi* (*building, mountain*) elevarse; **to ~ above** *or* **over sth/sb** dominar algo/destacarse sobre algn
tower block *n* (*Brit*) bloque *m* de pisos
towering ['tauərɪŋ] *adj* muy alto, imponente
town [taun] *n* ciudad *f*; **to go to ~** ir a la ciudad; (*fig*) tirar la casa por la ventana; **in the ~** en la ciudad; **to be out of ~** estar fuera de la ciudad
town centre *n* centro de la ciudad
town clerk *n* secretario(-a) del Ayuntamiento
town council *n* Ayuntamiento, consejo municipal
town crier [-kraɪəʳ] *n* (*Brit*) pregonero
town hall *n* ayuntamiento
townie ['taunɪ] *n* (*Brit col*) persona de la ciudad
town plan *n* plano de la ciudad
town planner *n* urbanista *m/f*
town planning *n* urbanismo

township ['taunʃɪp] *n municipio habitado sólo por negros en Sudáfrica*
townspeople ['taunzpi:pl] *npl* gente *f* de ciudad
towpath ['təupɑ:θ] *n* camino de sirga
towrope ['təurəup] *n* cable *m* de remolque
tow truck *n* (*US*) camión *m* grúa
toxic ['tɔksɪk] *adj* tóxico
toxin ['tɔksɪn] *n* toxina
toy [tɔɪ] *n* juguete *m*
▸ **toy with** *vt fus* jugar con; (*idea*) acariciar
toyshop ['tɔɪʃɔp] *n* juguetería
toy train *n* tren *m* de juguete
trace [treɪs] *n* rastro ■ *vt* (*draw*) trazar, delinear; (*locate*) encontrar; **there was no ~ of it** no había ningún indicio de ello
trace element *n* oligoelemento
trachea [trə'kɪə] *n* (*Anat*) tráquea
tracing paper ['treɪsɪŋ-] *n* papel *m* de calco
track [træk] *n* (*mark*) huella, pista; (*path: gen*) camino, senda; (*: of bullet etc*) trayectoria; (*: of suspect, animal*) pista, rastro; (*Rail*) vía; (*Comput, Sport*) pista; (*on record*) canción *f* ■ *vt* seguir la pista de; **to keep ~ of** mantenerse al tanto de, seguir; **a four-~ tape** una cinta de cuarto pistas; **the first ~ on the record/tape** la primera canción en el disco/la cinta; **to be on the right ~** (*fig*) ir por buen camino
▸ **track down** *vt* (*person*) localizar; (*sth lost*) encontrar
tracker dog ['trækəʳ-] *n* (*Brit*) perro rastreador
track events *npl* (*Sport*) pruebas *fpl* en pista
tracking station ['trækɪŋ-] *n* (*Space*) estación *f* de seguimiento
track meet *n* (*US*) concurso de carreras y saltos
track record *n*: **to have a good ~** (*fig*) tener un buen historial
tracksuit ['træksu:t] *n* chandal *m*
tract [trækt] *n* (*Geo*) región *f*; (*pamphlet*) folleto
traction ['trækʃən] *n* (*Aut: power*) tracción *f*; **in ~** (*Med*) en tracción
traction engine *n* locomotora de tracción
tractor ['træktəʳ] *n* tractor *m*
trade [treɪd] *n* comercio, negocio; (*skill, job*) oficio, empleo; (*industry*) industria ■ *vi* negociar, comerciar; **foreign ~** comercio exterior
▸ **trade in** *vt* (*old car etc*) ofrecer como parte del pago
trade barrier *n* barrera comercial
trade deficit *n* déficit *m* comercial
Trade Descriptions Act *n* (*Brit*) *ley sobre descripciones comerciales*
trade discount *n* descuento comercial
trade fair *n* feria de muestras
trade-in ['treɪdɪn] *adj*: **~ price/value** *precio/valor de un artículo usado que se descuenta del precio de otro nuevo*
trademark ['treɪdmɑ:k] *n* marca de fábrica
trade mission *n* misión *f* comercial
trade name *n* marca registrada
trade-off *n*: **a ~ (between)** un equilibrio (entre)
trade price *n* precio al detallista
trader ['treɪdəʳ] *n* comerciante *m/f*
trade reference *n* referencia comercial
trade secret *n* secreto profesional
tradesman ['treɪdzmən] *n* (*shopkeeper*) comerciante *m/f*
trade union *n* sindicato
trade unionist [-'ju:njənɪst] *n* sindicalista *m/f*
trade wind *n* viento alisio
trading ['treɪdɪŋ] *n* comercio
trading account *n* cuenta de compraventa
trading estate *n* (*Brit*) polígono industrial
trading stamp *n* cupón *m*, sello de prima
tradition [trə'dɪʃən] *n* tradición *f*
traditional [trə'dɪʃənl] *adj* tradicional
traditionally [trə'dɪʃənlɪ] *adv* tradicionalmente
traffic ['træfɪk] *n* tráfico, circulación *f*, tránsito ■ *vi*: **to ~ in** (*pej: liquor, drugs*) traficar en; **air ~** tráfico aéreo
traffic calming [-'kɑ:mɪŋ] *n* reducción *f* de la velocidad de la circulación
traffic circle *n* (*US*) glorieta de tráfico
traffic island *n* refugio, isleta
traffic jam *n* embotellamiento, atasco
trafficker ['træfɪkəʳ] *n* traficante *m/f*
traffic lights *npl* semáforo *sg*
traffic offence, traffic violation (*US*) *n* infracción *f* de tráfico
traffic warden *n* guardia *m/f* de tráfico
tragedy ['trædʒədɪ] *n* tragedia
tragic ['trædʒɪk] *adj* trágico
tragically ['trædʒɪkəlɪ] *adv* trágicamente
trail [treɪl] *n* (*tracks*) rastro, pista; (*path*) camino, sendero; (*dust, smoke*) estela ■ *vt* (*drag*) arrastrar; (*follow*) seguir la pista de; (*follow closely*) vigilar ■ *vi* arrastrarse; **to be on sb's ~** seguir la pista de algn
▸ **trail away, trail off** *vi* (*sound*) desvanecerse; (*interest, voice*) desaparecer
▸ **trail behind** *vi* quedar a la zaga
trailer ['treɪləʳ] *n* (*Aut*) remolque *m*; (*caravan*) caravana; (*Cine*) trailer *m*, avance *m*
trail truck *n* (*US*) trailer *m*
train [treɪn] *n* tren *m*; (*of dress*) cola; (*series*): **~ of events** curso de los acontecimientos ■ *vt* (*educate*) formar; (*teach skills to*) adiestrar;

(*sportsman*) entrenar; (*dog*) amaestrar; (*point: gun etc*): **to ~ on** apuntar a ■ *vi* (*Sport*) entrenarse; (*be educated, learn a skill*) formarse; **to go by ~** ir en tren; **one's ~ of thought** el razonamiento de algn; **to ~ sb to do sth** enseñar a algn a hacer algo
train attendant *n* (*US Rail*) empleado(-a) de coches-cama
trained [treɪnd] *adj* (*worker*) cualificado; (*animal*) amaestrado
trainee [treɪ'niː] *n* trabajador(a) *m(f)* en prácticas ■ *cpd*: **he's a ~ teacher** (*primary*) es estudiante de magisterio; (*secondary*) está haciendo las prácticas del I.C.E.
trainer ['treɪnə^r] *n* (*Sport*) entrenador(a) *m(f)*; (*of animals*) domador(a) *m(f)*; **trainers** *npl* (*shoes*) zapatillas *fpl* (de deporte)
training ['treɪnɪŋ] *n* formación *f*; entrenamiento; **to be in ~** (*Sport*) estar entrenando; (*: fit*) estar en forma
training college *n* (*gen*) colegio de formación profesional; (*for teachers*) escuela normal
training course *n* curso de formación
traipse [treɪps] *vi* andar penosamente
trait [treɪt] *n* rasgo
traitor ['treɪtə^r] *n* traidor(a) *m(f)*
trajectory [trə'dʒɛktərɪ] *n* trayectoria, curso
tram [træm] *n* (*Brit: also*: **tramcar**) tranvía *m*
tramline ['træmlaɪn] *n* carril *m* de tranvía
tramp [træmp] *n* (*person*) vagabundo(-a); (*col: offensive: woman*) puta ■ *vi* andar con pasos pesados
trample ['træmpl] *vt*: **to ~ (underfoot)** pisotear
trampoline ['træmpəliːn] *n* trampolín *m*
trance [trɑːns] *n* trance *m*; **to go into a ~** entrar en trance
tranquil ['træŋkwɪl] *adj* tranquilo
tranquillity, tranquility (*US*) [træŋ'kwɪlɪtɪ] *n* tranquilidad *f*
tranquillizer, tranquilizer (*US*) ['træŋkwɪlaɪzə^r] *n* (*Med*) tranquilizante *m*
trans- [trænz] *pref* trans-, tras-
transact [træn'zækt] *vt* (*business*) tramitar
transaction [træn'zækʃən] *n* transacción *f*, operación *f*; **cash transactions** transacciones al contado
transatlantic ['trænzət'læntɪk] *adj* transatlántico
transcend [træn'sɛnd] *vt* rebasar
transcendent [træn'sɛndənt] *adj* trascendente
transcendental [trænsɛn'dɛntl] *adj*: **~ meditation** meditación *f* transcendental
transcribe [træn'skraɪb] *vt* transcribir, copiar
transcript ['trænskrɪpt] *n* copia
transcription [træn'skrɪpʃən] *n* transcripción *f*
transept ['trænsɛpt] *n* crucero
transfer *n* ['trænsfə^r] transferencia; (*Sport*) traspaso; (*picture, design*) calcomanía ■ *vt* [træns'fəː^r] trasladar, pasar; **to ~ the charges** (*Brit Tel*) llamar a cobro revertido; **by bank ~** por transferencia bancaria *or* giro bancario; **to ~ money from one account to another** transferir dinero de una cuenta a otra; **to ~ sth to sb's name** transferir algo al nombre de algn
transferable [træns'fəːrəbl] *adj*: **not ~** intransferible
transfix [træns'fɪks] *vt* traspasar; (*fig*): **transfixed with fear** paralizado por el miedo
transform [træns'fɔːm] *vt* transformar
transformation [trænsfə'meɪʃən] *n* transformación *f*
transformer [træns'fɔːmə^r] *n* (*Elec*) transformador *m*
transfusion [træns'fjuːʒən] *n* transfusión *f*
transgress [træns'grɛs] *vt* (*go beyond*) traspasar; (*violate*) violar, infringir
tranship [træn'ʃɪp] *vt* trasbordar
transient ['trænzɪənt] *adj* transitorio
transistor [træn'zɪstə^r] *n* (*Elec*) transistor *m*
transistorized [træn'zɪstəraɪzd] *adj* (*circuit*) transistorizado
transistor radio *n* transistor *m*
transit ['trænzɪt] *n*: **in ~** en tránsito
transit camp *n* campamento de tránsito
transition [træn'zɪʃən] *n* transición *f*
transitional [træn'zɪʃənl] *adj* transitorio
transition period *n* período de transición
transitive ['trænzɪtɪv] *adj* (*Ling*) transitivo
transitively ['trænzɪtɪvlɪ] *adv* transitivamente
transitory ['trænzɪtərɪ] *adj* transitorio
transit visa *n* visado de tránsito
translate [trænz'leɪt] *vt*: **to ~ (from/into)** traducir (de/a)
translation [trænz'leɪʃən] *n* traducción *f*
translator [trænz'leɪtə^r] *n* traductor(a) *m(f)*
translucent [trænz'luːsnt] *adj* traslúcido
transmission [trænz'mɪʃən] *n* transmisión *f*
transmit [trænz'mɪt] *vt* transmitir
transmitter [trænz'mɪtə^r] *n* transmisor *m*; (*station*) emisora
transparency [træns'pɛərnsɪ] *n* (*Brit Phot*) diapositiva
transparent [træns'pærnt] *adj* transparente
transpire [træns'paɪə^r] *vi* (*turn out*) resultar (ser); (*happen*) ocurrir, suceder; (*become known*): **it finally transpired that ...** por fin se supo que ...

transplant *vt* [træns'plɑːnt] transplantar ■ *n* ['trænsplɑːnt] (*Med*) transplante *m*; **to have a heart ~** hacerse un transplante de corazón
transport *n* ['trænspɔːt] transporte *m* ■ *vt* [træns'pɔːt] transportar; **public ~** transporte *m* público
transportable [træns'pɔːtəbl] *adj* transportable
transportation [trænspɔː'teɪʃən] *n* transporte *m*; (*of prisoners*) deportación *f*
transport café *n* (*Brit*) bar-restaurante *m* de carretera
transpose [træns'pəuz] *vt* transponer
transsexual [trænz'sɛksjuəl] *adj, n* transexual *m/f*
transverse ['trænzvəːs] *adj* transverso, transversal
transvestite [trænz'vɛstaɪt] *n* travesti *m/f*
trap [træp] *n* (*snare, trick*) trampa; (*carriage*) cabriolé *m* ■ *vt* coger (*SP*) *or* agarrar (*LAm*) en una trampa; (*immobilize*) bloquear; (*jam*) atascar; **to set** *or* **lay a ~ (for sb)** poner(le) una trampa (a algn); **to ~ one's finger in the door** pillarse el dedo en la puerta
trap door *n* escotilla
trapeze [trə'piːz] *n* trapecio
trapper ['træpəʳ] *n* trampero, cazador *m*
trappings ['træpɪŋz] *npl* adornos *mpl*
trash [træʃ] *n* basura; (*nonsense*) tonterías *fpl*
trash can *n* (*US*) cubo, balde *m* (*LAm*) *or* bote *m* (*LAm*) de la basura
trash can liner *n* (*US*) bolsa de basura
trashy ['træʃɪ] *adj* (*col*) chungo
trauma ['trɔːmə] *n* trauma *m*
traumatic [trɔː'mætɪk] *adj* traumático
travel ['trævl] *n* viaje *m* ■ *vi* viajar ■ *vt* (*distance*) recorrer; **this wine doesn't ~ well** este vino pierde con los viajes
travel agency *n* agencia de viajes
travel agent *n* agente *m/f* de viajes
travel brochure *n* folleto turístico
traveller, traveler (*US*) ['trævləʳ] *n* viajero(-a); (*Comm*) viajante *m/f*
traveller's cheque, traveler's check (*US*) *n* cheque *m* de viaje
travelling, traveling (*US*) ['trævlɪŋ] *n* los viajes, el viajar ■ *adj* (*circus, exhibition*) ambulante ■ *cpd* (*bag, clock*) de viaje
travelling expenses, traveling expenses (*US*) *npl* dietas *fpl*
travelling salesman, traveling salesman (*US*) *n* viajante *m*
travelogue ['trævəlɔg] *n* (*book*) relación *f* de viajes; (*film*) documental *m* de viajes; (*talk*) recuento de viajes
travel sickness *n* mareo
traverse ['trævəs] *vt* atravesar
travesty ['trævəstɪ] *n* parodia
trawler ['trɔːləʳ] *n* pesquero de arrastre
tray [treɪ] *n* (*for carrying*) bandeja; (*on desk*) cajón *m*
treacherous ['trɛtʃərəs] *adj* traidor(a); **road conditions are ~** el estado de las carreteras es peligroso
treachery ['trɛtʃərɪ] *n* traición *f*
treacle ['triːkl] *n* (*Brit*) melaza
tread [trɛd] *n* paso, pisada; (*of tyre*) banda de rodadura ■ *vi* (*pt* **trod**, *pp* **trodden**) [trɔd, 'trɔdn] pisar
▸ **tread on** *vt fus* pisar
treas. *abbr* = **treasurer**
treason ['triːzn] *n* traición *f*
treasure ['trɛʒəʳ] *n* tesoro ■ *vt* (*value*) apreciar, valorar
treasure hunt *n* caza del tesoro
treasurer ['trɛʒərəʳ] *n* tesorero(-a)
treasury ['trɛʒərɪ] *n*: **the T~**, (*US*) **the T~ Department** ≈ el Ministerio de Economía y de Hacienda
treasury bill *n* bono del Tesoro
treat [triːt] *n* (*present*) regalo; (*pleasure*) placer *m* ■ *vt* tratar; (*consider*) considerar; **to give sb a ~** hacer un regalo a algn; **to ~ sb to sth** invitar a algn a algo; **to ~ sth as a joke** tomar algo a broma
treatise ['triːtɪz] *n* tratado
treatment ['triːtmənt] *n* tratamiento; **to have ~ for sth** recibir tratamiento por algo
treaty ['triːtɪ] *n* tratado
treble ['trɛbl] *adj* triple ■ *vt* triplicar ■ *vi* triplicarse
treble clef *n* (*Mus*) clave *f* de sol
tree [triː] *n* árbol *m*
tree-lined ['triːlaɪnd] *adj* bordeado de árboles
tree trunk *n* tronco de árbol
trek [trɛk] *n* (*long journey*) expedición *f*; (*tiring walk*) caminata
trellis ['trɛlɪs] *n* enrejado
tremble ['trɛmbl] *vi* temblar
trembling ['trɛmblɪŋ] *n* temblor *m* ■ *adj* tembloroso
tremendous [trɪ'mɛndəs] *adj* tremendo; (*enormous*) enorme; (*excellent*) estupendo
tremendously [trɪ'mɛndəslɪ] *adv* enormemente, sobremanera; **he enjoyed it ~** lo disfrutó de lo lindo
tremor ['trɛməʳ] *n* temblor *m*; (*also*: **earth tremor**) temblor *m* de tierra
trench [trɛntʃ] *n* zanja; (*Mil*) trinchera
trench coat *n* trinchera
trench warfare *n* guerra de trincheras
trend [trɛnd] *n* (*tendency*) tendencia; (*of events*) curso; (*fashion*) moda; **~ towards/away from**

sth tendencia hacia/en contra de algo; **to set the ~** marcar la pauta
trendy ['trɛndɪ] *adj* de moda
trepidation [trɛpɪ'deɪʃən] *n* inquietud *f*
trespass ['trɛspəs] *vi*: **to ~ on** entrar sin permiso en; **"no trespassing"** "prohibido el paso"
trespasser ['trɛspəsəʳ] *n* intruso(-a) *m(f)*; **"trespassers will be prosecuted"** "se procesará a los intrusos"
tress [trɛs] *n* guedeja
trestle ['trɛsl] *n* caballete *m*
trestle table *n* mesa de caballete
tri- [traɪ] *pref* tri-
trial ['traɪəl] *n* (*Law*) juicio, proceso; (*test: of machine etc*) prueba; (*hardship*) desgracia; **trials** *npl* (*Athletics*) pruebas *fpl*; (*of horses*) pruebas *fpl*; **to bring sb to ~ (for a crime)** llevar a algn a juicio (por un delito); **~ by jury** juicio ante jurado; **to be sent for ~** ser remitido al tribunal; **by ~ and error** a fuerza de probar
trial balance *n* balance *m* de comprobación
trial basis *n*: **on a ~** a modo de prueba
trial offer *n* oferta de prueba
trial run *n* prueba
triangle ['traɪæŋgl] *n* (*Math, Mus*) triángulo
triangular [traɪ'æŋgjuləʳ] *adj* triangular
triathlon [traɪ'æθlən] *n* triatlón *m*
tribal ['traɪbəl] *adj* tribal
tribe [traɪb] *n* tribu *f*
tribesman ['traɪbzmən] *n* miembro de una tribu
tribulation [trɪbju'leɪʃən] *n* tribulación *f*
tribunal [traɪ'bju:nl] *n* tribunal *m*
tributary ['trɪbju:tərɪ] *n* (*river*) afluente *m*
tribute ['trɪbju:t] *n* homenaje *m*, tributo; **to pay ~ to** rendir homenaje a
trice [traɪs] *n*: **in a ~** en un santiamén
trick [trɪk] *n* trampa; (*conjuring trick, deceit*) truco; (*joke*) broma; (*Cards*) baza ■ *vt* engañar; **it's a ~ of the light** es una ilusión óptica; **to play a ~ on sb** gastar una broma a algn; **that should do the ~** eso servirá; **to ~ sb out of sth** quitarle algo a algn con engaños; **to ~ sb into doing sth** hacer que algn haga algo con engaños
trickery ['trɪkərɪ] *n* engaño
trickle ['trɪkl] *n* (*of water etc*) hilo ■ *vi* gotear
trick question *n* pregunta capciosa
trickster ['trɪkstəʳ] *n* estafador(a) *m(f)*
tricky ['trɪkɪ] *adj* difícil; (*problem*) delicado
tricycle ['traɪsɪkl] *n* triciclo
tried [traɪd] *adj* probado
trifle ['traɪfl] *n* bagatela; (*Culin*) *dulce de bizcocho, gelatina, fruta y natillas* ■ *adv*: **a ~ long** un pelín largo ■ *vi*: **to ~ with** jugar con
trifling ['traɪflɪŋ] *adj* insignificante
trigger ['trɪgəʳ] *n* (*of gun*) gatillo
▸**trigger off** *vt* desencadenar
trigonometry [trɪgə'nɔmətrɪ] *n* trigonometría
trilby ['trɪlbɪ] *n* (*also*: **trilby hat**) sombrero flexible *or* tirolés
trill [trɪl] *n* (*of bird*) gorjeo; (*Mus*) trino
trilogy ['trɪlədʒɪ] *n* trilogía
trim [trɪm] *adj* (*elegant*) aseado; (*house, garden*) en buen estado; (*figure*): **to be ~** tener buen talle ■ *n* (*haircut etc*) recorte *m* ■ *vt* (*neaten*) arreglar; (*cut*) recortar; (*decorate*) adornar; (*Naut: a sail*) orientar; **to keep in (good) ~** mantener en buen estado
trimmings ['trɪmɪŋz] *npl* (*extras*) accesorios *mpl*; (*cuttings*) recortes *mpl*
Trinidad and Tobago ['trɪnɪdæd-] *n* Trinidad *f* y Tobago
Trinity ['trɪnɪtɪ] *n*: **the ~** la Trinidad
trinket ['trɪŋkɪt] *n* chuchería, baratija
trio ['tri:əu] *n* trío
trip [trɪp] *n* viaje *m*; (*excursion*) excursión *f*; (*stumble*) traspié *m* ■ *vi* (*stumble*) tropezar; (*go lightly*) andar a paso ligero; **on a ~** de viaje
▸**trip over** *vt fus* tropezar con
▸**trip up** *vi* tropezar, caerse ■ *vt* hacer tropezar *or* caer
tripartite [traɪ'pɑ:taɪt] *adj* (*agreement, talks*) tripartito
tripe [traɪp] *n* (*Culin*) callos *mpl*; (*pej: rubbish*) bobadas *fpl*
triple ['trɪpl] *adj* triple ■ *adv*: **~ the distance/the speed** 3 veces la distancia/la velocidad
triple jump *n* triple salto
triplets ['trɪplɪts] *npl* trillizos(-as) *m(f)pl*
triplicate ['trɪplɪkət] *n*: **in ~** por triplicado
tripod ['traɪpɔd] *n* trípode *m*
Tripoli ['trɪpəlɪ] *n* Trípoli *m*
tripper ['trɪpəʳ] *n* turista *m/f*, excursionista *m/f*
tripwire ['trɪpwaɪəʳ] *n* cable *m* de trampa
trite [traɪt] *adj* trillado
triumph ['traɪʌmf] *n* triunfo ■ *vi*: **to ~ (over)** vencer
triumphal [traɪ'ʌmfl] *adj* triunfal
triumphant [traɪ'ʌmfənt] *adj* triunfante
triumphantly [traɪ'ʌmfəntlɪ] *adv* triunfalmente, en tono triunfal
trivia ['trɪvɪə] *npl* trivialidades *fpl*
trivial ['trɪvɪəl] *adj* insignificante, trivial
triviality [trɪvɪ'ælɪtɪ] *n* insignificancia, trivialidad *f*
trivialize ['trɪvɪəlaɪz] *vt* trivializar
trod [trɔd] *pt of* **tread**
trodden ['trɔdn] *pp of* **tread**
trolley ['trɔlɪ] *n* carrito; (*in hospital*) camilla

trolley bus *n* trolebús *m*
trombone [trɔm'bəun] *n* trombón *m*
troop [tru:p] *n* grupo, banda; *see also* **troops**
▸ **troop in** *vi* entrar en tropel
▸ **troop out** *vi* salir en tropel
troop carrier *n* (*plane*) transporte *m* (militar); (*Naut*: *also*: **troopship**) (buque *m* de) transporte *m*
trooper ['tru:pə^r] *n* (*Mil*) soldado (de caballería); (*US*: *policeman*) policía *m/f* montado(-a)
trooping the colour ['tru:pɪŋ-] *n* (*ceremony*) presentación *f* de la bandera
troopship ['tru:pʃɪp] *n* (buque *m* de) transporte *m*
trophy ['trəufɪ] *n* trofeo
tropic ['trɔpɪk] *n* trópico; **the tropics** los trópicos, la zona tropical; **T~ of Cancer/Capricorn** trópico de Cáncer/Capricornio
tropical ['trɔpɪkl] *adj* tropical
trot [trɔt] *n* trote *m* ■ *vi* trotar; **on the ~** (*Brit fig*) seguidos(-as)
▸ **trot out** *vt* (*excuse, reason*) volver a usar; (*names, facts*) sacar a relucir
trouble ['trʌbl] *n* problema *m*, dificultad *f*; (*worry*) preocupación *f*; (*bother, effort*) molestia, esfuerzo; (*unrest*) inquietud *f*; (*with machine etc*) fallo, avería; (*Med*): **stomach ~** problemas *mpl* gástricos ■ *vt* molestar; (*worry*) preocupar, inquietar ■ *vi*: **to ~ to do sth** molestarse en hacer algo; **troubles** *npl* (*Pol etc*) conflictos *mpl*; **to be in ~** estar en un apuro; (*for doing wrong*) tener problemas; **to have ~ doing sth** tener dificultad en *or* para hacer algo; **to go to the ~ of doing sth** tomarse la molestia de hacer algo; **what's the ~?** ¿qué pasa?; **the ~ is ...** el problema es ..., lo que pasa es ...; **please don't ~ yourself** por favor no se moleste
troubled ['trʌbld] *adj* (*person*) preocupado; (*epoch, life*) agitado
trouble-free ['trʌblfri:] *adj* sin problemas *or* dificultades
troublemaker ['trʌblmeɪkə^r] *n* agitador(a) *m(f)*
troubleshooter ['trʌblʃu:tə^r] *n* (*in conflict*) mediador(a) *m(f)*
troublesome ['trʌblsəm] *adj* molesto, inoportuno
trouble spot *n* centro de fricción, punto caliente
troubling ['trʌblɪŋ] *adj* (*thought*) preocupante; **these are ~ times** son malos tiempos
trough [trɔf] *n* (*also*: **drinking trough**) abrevadero; (*also*: **feeding trough**) comedero; (*channel*) canal *m*
trounce [trauns] *vt* dar una paliza a
troupe [tru:p] *n* grupo
trouser press *n* prensa para pantalones
trousers ['trauzəz] *npl* pantalones *mpl*; **short ~** pantalones *mpl* cortos
trouser suit *n* traje *m* de chaqueta y pantalón
trousseau (*pl* **trousseaux** *or* **trousseaus**) ['tru:səu, -z] *n* ajuar *m*
trout [traut] *n* (*pl inv*) trucha
trowel ['trauəl] *n* paleta
truant ['truənt] *n*: **to play ~** (*Brit*) hacer novillos
truce [tru:s] *n* tregua
truck [trʌk] *n* (*US*) camión *m*; (*Rail*) vagón *m*
truck driver *n* camionero(-a)
trucker ['trʌkə^r] *n* (*esp US*) camionero(-a)
truck farm *n* (*US*) huerto de hortalizas
trucking ['trʌkɪŋ] *n* (*esp US*) transporte *m* en camión
trucking company *n* (*US*) compañía de transporte por carretera
truckload ['trʌkləud] *n* camión *m* lleno
truculent ['trʌkjulənt] *adj* agresivo
trudge [trʌdʒ] *vi* caminar penosamente
true [tru:] *adj* verdadero; (*accurate*) exacto; (*genuine*) auténtico; (*faithful*) fiel; (*wheel*) centrado; (*wall*) a plomo; (*beam*) alineado; **~ to life** verídico; **to come ~** realizarse, cumplirse
truffle ['trʌfl] *n* trufa
truly ['tru:lɪ] *adv* realmente; (*faithfully*) fielmente; **yours ~** (*in letter-writing*) atentamente
trump [trʌmp] *n* (*Cards*) triunfo; **to turn up trumps** (*fig*) salir *or* resultar bien
trump card *n* triunfo; (*fig*) baza
trumped-up ['trʌmptʌp] *adj* inventado
trumpet ['trʌmpɪt] *n* trompeta
truncated [trʌŋ'keɪtɪd] *adj* truncado
truncheon ['trʌntʃən] *n* (*Brit*) porra
trundle ['trʌndl] *vt, vi*: **to ~ along** rodar haciendo ruido
trunk [trʌŋk] *n* (*of tree, person*) tronco; (*of elephant*) trompa; (*case*) baúl *m*; (*US Aut*) maletero, baúl *m* (*LAm*); *see also* **trunks**
trunk call *n* (*Brit Tel*) llamada interurbana
trunk road *n* carretera principal
trunks [trʌŋks] *npl* (*also*: **swimming trunks**) bañador *m*
truss [trʌs] *n* (*Med*) braguero ■ *vt*: **to ~ (up)** atar
trust [trʌst] *n* confianza; (*Comm*) trust *m*; (*Law*) fideicomiso ■ *vt* (*rely on*) tener confianza en; (*entrust*): **to ~ sth to sb** confiar algo a algn; (*hope*): **to ~ (that)** esperar (que); **in ~** en fideicomiso; **you'll have to take it on ~** tienes que aceptarlo a ojos cerrados
trust company *n* banco fideicomisario

trusted ['trʌstɪd] *adj* de confianza, fiable, de fiar
trustee [trʌs'ti:] *n* (*Law*) fideicomisario
trustful ['trʌstful] *adj* confiado
trust fund *n* fondo fiduciario *or* de fideicomiso
trusting ['trʌstɪŋ] *adj* confiado
trustworthy ['trʌstwə:ðɪ] *adj* digno de confianza, fiable, de fiar
trusty ['trʌstɪ] *adj* fiel
truth, truths [tru:θ, tru:ðz] *n* verdad *f*
truthful ['tru:θfəl] *adj* (*person*) sincero; (*account*) fidedigno
truthfully ['tru:θfulɪ] *adv* (*answer*) con sinceridad
truthfulness ['tru:θfulnɪs] *n* (*of account*) verdad *f*; (*of person*) sinceridad *f*
try [traɪ] *n* tentativa, intento; (*Rugby*) ensayo ■ *vt* (*Law*) juzgar, procesar; (*test: sth new*) probar, someter a prueba; (*attempt*) intentar; (*strain: patience*) hacer perder ■ *vi* probar; **to give sth a ~** intentar hacer algo; **to ~ one's (very) best** *or* **hardest** poner todo su empeño, esmerarse; **to ~ to do sth** intentar hacer algo
▸**try on** *vt* (*clothes*) probarse
▸**try out** *vt* probar, poner a prueba
trying ['traɪɪŋ] *adj* cansado; (*person*) pesado
tsar [zɑ:ʳ] *n* zar *m*
T-shirt ['ti:ʃə:t] *n* camiseta
TSO *n abbr* (*Brit*) = **The Stationery Office**
T-square ['ti:skwɛəʳ] *n* regla en T
tsunami [tsʊ'nɑ:mɪ] *n* tsunami *m*
TT *adj abbr* (*Brit col*) = **teetotal** ■ *abbr* (*US*) = **Trust Territory**
tub [tʌb] *n* cubo (*SP*), balde *m* (*LAm*); (*bath*) bañera, tina (*LAm*)
tuba ['tju:bə] *n* tuba
tubby ['tʌbɪ] *adj* regordete
tube [tju:b] *n* tubo; (*Brit: underground*) metro; (*US col: television*) tele *f*
tubeless ['tju:blɪs] *adj* (*tyre*) sin cámara
tuber ['tju:bəʳ] *n* (*Bot*) tubérculo
tuberculosis [tjubə:kju'ləusɪs] *n* tuberculosis *f inv*
tube station *n* (*Brit*) estación *f* de metro
tubing ['tju:bɪŋ] *n* tubería (*SP*), cañería; **a piece of ~** un trozo de tubo
tubular ['tju:bjuləʳ] *adj* tubular
TUC *n abbr* (*Brit: = Trades Union Congress*) *federación nacional de sindicatos*
tuck [tʌk] *n* (*Sewing*) pliegue *m* ■ *vt* (*put*) poner
▸**tuck away** *vt* esconder
▸**tuck in** *vt* meter; (*child*) arropar ■ *vi* (*eat*) comer con apetito
▸**tuck up** *vt* (*child*) arropar
tuck shop *n* (*Scol*) tienda de golosinas
Tue., Tues. *abbr* (= *Tuesday*) mart
Tuesday ['tju:zdɪ] *n* martes *m inv*; **on ~** el martes; **on Tuesdays** los martes; **every ~** todos los martes; **every other ~** cada dos martes, un martes sí y otro no; **last/next ~** el martes pasado/próximo; **a week/fortnight on ~, ~ week/fortnight** del martes en 8/15 días, del martes en una semana/dos semanas
tuft [tʌft] *n* mechón *m*; (*of grass etc*) manojo
tug [tʌg] *n* (*ship*) remolcador *m* ■ *vt* remolcar
tug-of-love [tʌgəv'lʌv] *n*: **~ children** *hijos envueltos en el litigio de los padres por su custodia*
tug-of-war [tʌgəv'wɔ:ʳ] *n* juego de la cuerda
tuition [tju:'ɪʃən] *n* (*Brit*) enseñanza; (*: private tuition*) clases *fpl* particulares; (*US: school fees*) matrícula
tulip ['tju:lɪp] *n* tulipán *m*
tumble ['tʌmbl] *n* (*fall*) caída ■ *vi* caerse, tropezar; **to ~ to sth** (*col*) caer en la cuenta de algo
tumbledown ['tʌmbldaun] *adj* ruinoso
tumble dryer *n* (*Brit*) secadora
tumbler ['tʌmbləʳ] *n* vaso
tummy ['tʌmɪ] *n* (*col*) barriga, vientre *m*
tumour, tumor (*US*) ['tju:məʳ] *n* tumor *m*
tumult ['tju:mʌlt] *n* tumulto
tumultuous [tju:'mʌltjuəs] *adj* tumultuoso
tuna ['tju:nə] *n* (*pl inv: also:* **tuna fish**) atún *m*
tundra ['tʌndrə] *n* tundra
tune [tju:n] *n* (*melody*) melodía ■ *vt* (*Mus*) afinar; (*Radio, TV, Aut*) sintonizar; **to be in/out of ~** (*instrument*) estar afinado/desafinado; (*singer*) afinar/desafinar; **to be in/out of ~ with** (*fig*) armonizar/desentonar con; **to the ~ of** (*fig: amount*) por (la) cantidad de
▸**tune in** *vi* (*Radio, TV*): **to ~ in (to)** sintonizar (con)
▸**tune up** *vi* (*musician*) afinar (su instrumento)
tuneful ['tju:nful] *adj* melodioso
tuner ['tju:nəʳ] *n* (*radio set*) sintonizador *m*; **piano ~** afinador(a) *m(f)* de pianos
tungsten ['tʌŋstn] *n* tungsteno
tunic ['tju:nɪk] *n* túnica
tuning ['tju:nɪŋ] *n* sintonización *f*; (*Mus*) afinación *f*
tuning fork *n* diapasón *m*
Tunis ['tju:nɪs] *n* Túnez *m*
Tunisia [tju:'nɪzɪə] *n* Túnez *m*
Tunisian [tju:'nɪzɪən] *adj, n* tunecino(-a) *m(f)*
tunnel ['tʌnl] *n* túnel *m*; (*in mine*) galería ■ *vi* construir un túnel/una galería
tunnel vision *n* (*Med*) visión *f* periférica restringida; (*fig*) estrechez *f* de miras

tunny ['tʌnɪ] *n* atún *m*
turban ['tə:bən] *n* turbante *m*
turbid ['tə:bɪd] *adj* turbio
turbine ['tə:baɪn] *n* turbina
turbo ['tə:bəu] *n* turbo
turboprop ['tə:bəuprɔp] *n* turbohélice *m*
turbot ['tə:bət] *n* (*pl inv*) rodaballo
turbulence ['tə:bjuləns] *n* (*Aviat*) turbulencia
turbulent ['tə:bjulənt] *adj* turbulento
tureen [tə'ri:n] *n* sopera
turf [tə:f] *n* césped *m*; (*clod*) tepe *m* ■ *vt* cubrir con césped
▸ **turf out** *vt* (*col*) echar a la calle
turf accountant *n* corredor(a) *m(f)* de apuestas
turgid ['tə:dʒɪd] *adj* (*prose*) pesado
Turin [tjuə'rɪn] *n* Turín *m*
Turk [tə:k] *n* turco(-a)
Turkey ['tə:kɪ] *n* Turquía
turkey ['tə:kɪ] *n* pavo
Turkish ['tə:kɪʃ] *adj* turco ■ *n* (*Ling*) turco
Turkish bath *n* baño turco
turmeric ['tə:mərɪk] *n* cúrcuma
turmoil ['tə:mɔɪl] *n* desorden *m*, alboroto
turn [tə:n] *n* turno; (*in road*) curva; (*Theat*) número; (*Med*) ataque *m* ■ *vt* girar, volver, voltear (*LAm*); (*collar, steak*) dar la vuelta a; (*shape: wood, metal*) tornear; (*change*): **to ~ sth into** convertir algo en ■ *vi* volver, voltearse (*LAm*); (*person: look back*) volverse; (*reverse direction*) dar la vuelta, voltear (*LAm*); (*milk*) cortarse; (*change*) cambiar; (*become*): **to ~ into sth** convertirse *or* transformarse en algo; **a good ~** un favor; **it gave me quite a ~** me dio un susto; **"no left ~"** (*Aut*) "prohibido girar a la izquierda"; **it's your ~** te toca a ti; **in ~** por turnos; **to take turns** turnarse; **at the ~ of the year/century** a fin de año/a finales de siglo; **to take a ~ for the worse** (*situation, patient*) empeorar; **they turned him against us** le pusieron en contra nuestra; **the car turned the corner** el coche dobló la esquina; **to ~ left** (*Aut*) torcer *or* girar a la izquierda; **she has no-one to ~ to** no tiene a quién recurrir
▸ **turn away** *vi* apartar la vista ■ *vt* (*reject: person, business*) rechazar
▸ **turn back** *vi* volverse atrás
▸ **turn down** *vt* (*refuse*) rechazar; (*reduce*) bajar; (*fold*) doblar
▸ **turn in** *vi* (*col: go to bed*) acostarse ■ *vt* (*fold*) doblar hacia dentro
▸ **turn off** *vi* (*from road*) desviarse ■ *vt* (*light, radio etc*) apagar; (*engine*) parar
▸ **turn on** *vt* (*light, radio etc*) encender, prender (*LAm*); (*engine*) poner en marcha
▸ **turn out** *vt* (*light, gas*) apagar; (*produce: goods, novel etc*) producir ■ *vi* (*attend: troops*) presentarse; (*: doctor*) atender; **to ~ out to be ...** resultar ser ...
▸ **turn over** *vi* (*person*) volverse ■ *vt* (*mattress, card*) dar la vuelta a; (*page*) volver
▸ **turn round** *vi* volverse; (*rotate*) girar
▸ **turn to** *vt fus*: **to ~ to sb** acudir a algn
▸ **turn up** *vi* (*person*) llegar, presentarse; (*lost object*) aparecer ■ *vt* (*radio*) subir, poner más alto; (*heat, gas*) poner más fuerte
turnabout ['tə:nəbaut], **turnaround** ['tə:nəraund] *n* (*fig*) giro total
turncoat ['tə:nkəut] *n* renegado(-a)
turned-up ['tə:ndʌp] *adj* (*nose*) respingón(-ona)
turning ['tə:nɪŋ] *n* (*side road*) bocacalle *f*; (*bend*) curva; **the first ~ on the right** la primera bocacalle a la derecha
turning point *n* (*fig*) momento decisivo
turnip ['tə:nɪp] *n* nabo
turnkey system ['tə:nki:-] *n* (*Comput*) sistema *m* de seguridad
turnout ['tə:naut] *n* asistencia, número de asistentes, público
turnover ['tə:nəuvə^r] *n* (*Comm: amount of money*) facturación *f*; (*of goods*) movimiento; **there is a rapid ~ in staff** hay mucho movimiento de personal
turnpike ['tə:npaɪk] *n* (*US*) autopista de peaje
turnstile ['tə:nstaɪl] *n* torniquete *m*
turntable ['tə:nteɪbl] *n* plato
turn-up ['tə:nʌp] *n* (*Brit: on trousers*) vuelta
turpentine ['tə:pəntaɪn] *n* (*also*: **turps**) trementina
turquoise ['tə:kwɔɪz] *n* (*stone*) turquesa ■ *adj* color turquesa
turret ['tʌrɪt] *n* torreón *m*
turtle ['tə:tl] *n* tortuga (marina)
turtleneck ['tə:tlnɛk], **turtleneck sweater** *n* (jersey *m* de) cuello cisne
Tuscany ['tʌskənɪ] *n* Toscana
tusk [tʌsk] *n* colmillo
tussle ['tʌsl] *n* lucha, pelea
tutor ['tju:tə^r] *n* profesor(a) *m(f)*
tutorial [tju:'tɔ:rɪəl] *n* (*Scol*) seminario
tuxedo [tʌk'si:dəu] *n* (*US*) smóking *m*, esmoquin *m*
TV [ti:'vi:] *n abbr* (= *television*) televisión *f*
TV dinner *n* cena precocinada
TV licence *n licencia que se paga por el uso del televisor, destinada a financiar la BBC*
twaddle ['twɔdl] *n* (*col*) tonterías *fpl*
twang [twæŋ] *n* (*of instrument*) tañido; (*of voice*) timbre *m* nasal
tweak [twi:k] *vt* (*nose, ear*) pellizcar; (*hair*) tirar
tweed [twi:d] *n* tweed *m*
tweezers ['twi:zəz] *npl* pinzas *fpl* (de depilar)

twelfth [twɛlfθ] *num* duodécimo
Twelfth Night *n* (Día *m* de) Reyes *mpl*
twelve [twɛlv] *num* doce; **at ~ o'clock** (*midday*) a mediodía; (*midnight*) a medianoche
twentieth ['twɛntɪɪθ] *num* vigésimo
twenty ['twɛntɪ] *num* veinte
twerp [twəːp] *n* (*col*) idiota *m/f*
twice [twaɪs] *adv* dos veces; **~ as much** dos veces más, el doble; **she is ~ your age** ella te dobla edad; **~ a week** dos veces a la *or* por semana
twiddle ['twɪdl] *vt, vi*: **to ~ (with) sth** dar vueltas a algo; **to ~ one's thumbs** (*fig*) estar de brazos cruzados
twig [twɪg] *n* ramita ■ *vi* (*col*) caer en la cuenta
twilight ['twaɪlaɪt] *n* crepúsculo; (*morning*) madrugada; **in the ~** en la media luz
twill [twɪl] *n* sarga, estameña
twin [twɪn] *adj, n* gemelo(-a) *m(f)* ■ *vt* hermanar
twin-bedded room ['twɪn'bɛdɪd-] *n* = **twin room**
twin beds *npl* camas *fpl* gemelas
twin-carburettor ['twɪnkɑːbju'rɛtəʳ] *adj* de dos carburadores
twine [twaɪn] *n* bramante *m* ■ *vi* (*plant*) enroscarse
twin-engined [twɪn'ɛndʒɪnd] *adj* bimotor; **~ aircraft** avión *m* bimotor
twinge [twɪndʒ] *n* (*of pain*) punzada; (*of conscience*) remordimiento
twinkle ['twɪŋkl] *n* centelleo ■ *vi* centellear; (*eyes*) parpadear
twin room *n* habitación *f* con dos camas
twin town *n* ciudad *f* hermanada *or* gemela
twirl [twəːl] *n* giro ■ *vt* dar vueltas a ■ *vi* piruetear
twist [twɪst] *n* (*action*) torsión *f*; (*in road, coil*) vuelta; (*in wire, flex*) doblez *f*; (*in story*) giro ■ *vt* torcer, retorcer; (*roll around*) enrollar; (*fig*) deformar ■ *vi* serpentear; **to ~ one's ankle/wrist** (*Med*) torcerse el tobillo/la muñeca
twisted ['twɪstɪd] *adj* (*wire, rope*) trenzado, enroscado; (*ankle, wrist*) torcido; (*fig: logic, mind*) retorcido
twit [twɪt] *n* (*col*) tonto
twitch [twɪtʃ] *n* sacudida; (*nervous*) tic *m* nervioso ■ *vi* moverse nerviosamente
two [tuː] *num* dos; **~ by ~, in twos** de dos en dos; **to put ~ and ~ together** (*fig*) atar cabos
two-bit [tuː'bɪt] *adj* (*esp US: col, pej*) de poca monta, de tres al cuarto
two-door [tuː'dɔːʳ] *adj* (*Aut*) de dos puertas
two-faced [tuː'feɪst] *adj* (*pej: person*) falso, hipócrita
twofold ['tuːfəuld] *adv*: **to increase ~** duplicarse ■ *adj* (*increase*) doble; (*reply*) en dos partes
two-piece [tuː'piːs] *n* (*also*: **two-piece suit**) traje *m* de dos piezas; (*also*: **two-piece swimsuit**) dos piezas *m inv*, bikini *m*
two-seater [tuː'siːtəʳ] *n* (*plane, car*) avión *m*/coche *m* de dos plazas, biplaza *m*
twosome ['tuːsəm] *n* (*people*) pareja
two-stroke ['tuːstrəuk] *n* (*also*: **two-stroke engine**) motor *m* de dos tiempos ■ *adj* de dos tiempos
two-tone ['tuː'təun] *adj* (*colour*) bicolor, de dos tonos
two-way ['tuːweɪ] *adj*: **~ traffic** circulación *f* de dos sentidos; **~ radio** radio *f* emisora y receptora
TX *abbr* (*US*) = **Texas**
tycoon [taɪ'kuːn] *n*: **(business) ~** magnate *m/f*
type [taɪp] *n* (*category*) tipo, género; (*model*) modelo; (*Typ*) tipo, letra ■ *vt* (*letter etc*) escribir a máquina; **what ~ do you want?** ¿qué tipo quieres?; **in bold/italic ~** en negrita/cursiva
type-cast ['taɪpkɑːst] *adj* (*actor*) encasillado
typeface ['taɪpfeɪs] *n* tipo de letra
typescript ['taɪpskrɪpt] *n* texto mecanografiado
typeset ['taɪpsɛt] *vt* (*irreg: like* **set**) componer
typesetter ['taɪpsɛtəʳ] *n* cajista *m/f*
typewriter ['taɪpraɪtəʳ] *n* máquina de escribir
typewritten ['taɪprɪtn] *adj* mecanografiado
typhoid ['taɪfɔɪd] *n* (fiebre *f*) tifoidea
typhoon [taɪ'fuːn] *n* tifón *m*
typhus ['taɪfəs] *n* tifus *m*
typical ['tɪpɪkl] *adj* típico
typically ['tɪpɪklɪ] *adv* típicamente
typify ['tɪpɪfaɪ] *vt* tipificar
typing ['taɪpɪŋ] *n* mecanografía
typing pool *n* (*Brit*) servicio de mecanógrafos
typist ['taɪpɪst] *n* mecanógrafo(-a)
typography [taɪ'pɔgrəfɪ] *n* tipografía
tyranny ['tɪrənɪ] *n* tiranía
tyrant ['taɪərənt] *n* tirano(-a)
tyre, tire (*US*) ['taɪəʳ] *n* neumático, llanta (*LAm*)
tyre pressure *n* presión *f* de los neumáticos
Tyrol [tɪ'rəul] *n* Tirol *m*
Tyrolean [tɪrə'lɪən], **Tyrolese** [tɪrə'liːz] *adj* tirolés(-esa)
Tyrrhenian Sea [tɪ'riːnɪən-] *n* Mar *m* Tirreno
tzar [zɑːʳ] *n* = **tsar**

Uu

U, u [juː] *n* (*letter*) U, u *f*; **U for Uncle** U de Uruguay
U *n abbr* (*Brit Cine*: = *universal*) todos los públicos
UAW *n abbr* (*US*) = **United Automobile Workers**
UB40 *n abbr* (*Brit*: = *unemployment benefit form 40*) *número de referencia en la solicitud de inscripción en la lista de parados por extensión, la tarjeta del paro o su beneficiario*
U-bend ['juːbɛnd] *n* recodo
ubiquitous [juː'bɪkwɪtəs] *adj* omnipresente, ubicuo
UCAS ['juːkæs] *n abbr* (*Brit*) = **Universities and Colleges Admissions Service**
UDA *n abbr* (*Brit*: = *Ulster Defence Association*) *organización paramilitar protestante de Irlanda del Norte*
UDC *n abbr* (*Brit*) = **Urban District Council**
udder ['ʌdə^r] *n* ubre *f*
UDI *n abbr* (*Brit Pol*) = **unilateral declaration of independence**
UDR *n abbr* (*Brit*: = *Ulster Defence Regiment*) *fuerza de seguridad de Irlanda del Norte*
UEFA [juː'eɪfə] *n abbr* (= *Union of European Football Associations*) U.E.F.A. *f*
UFO ['juːfəu] *n abbr* (= *unidentified flying object*) OVNI *m*
Uganda [juː'gændə] *n* Uganda
Ugandan [juː'gændən] *adj* de Uganda
UGC *n abbr* (*Brit*: = *University Grants Committee*) *entidad gubernamental que controla las finanzas de las universidades*
ugh [əːh] *excl* ¡uf!
ugliness ['ʌglɪnɪs] *n* fealdad *f*
ugly ['ʌglɪ] *adj* feo; (*dangerous*) peligroso
UHF *abbr* (= *ultra-high frequency*) UHF *f*
UHT *adj abbr* (= *ultra heat treated*): **~ milk** leche *f* uperizada
UK *n abbr* (= *United Kingdom*) Reino Unido, R.U.
Ukraine [juː'kreɪn] *n* Ucrania
Ukrainian [juː'kreɪnɪən] *adj* ucraniano ■ *n* ucraniano(-a); (*Ling*) ucraniano
ulcer ['ʌlsə^r] *n* úlcera; **mouth ~** úlcera bucal
Ulster ['ʌlstə^r] *n* Ulster *m*
ulterior [ʌl'tɪərɪə^r] *adj* ulterior; **~ motive** segundas intenciones *fpl*
ultimate ['ʌltɪmət] *adj* último, final; (*greatest*) mayor ■ *n*: **the ~ in luxury** el colmo del lujo
ultimately ['ʌltɪmətlɪ] *adv* (*in the end*) por último, al final; (*fundamentally*) a fin de cuentas
ultimatum (*pl* **ultimatums** *or* **ultimata**) [ʌltɪ'meɪtəm, -tə] *n* ultimátum *m*
ultra- ['ʌltrə] *pref* ultra-
ultrasonic [ʌltrə'sɔnɪk] *adj* ultrasónico
ultrasound ['ʌltrəsaund] *n* (*Med*) ultrasonido
ultraviolet ['ʌltrə'vaɪəlɪt] *adj* ultravioleta
um [ʌm] *interj* (*col*: *in hesitation*) esto, este (*LAm*)
umbilical cord [ʌmbɪ'laɪkl-] *n* cordón *m* umbilical
umbrage ['ʌmbrɪdʒ] *n*: **to take ~ (at)** ofenderse (por)
umbrella [ʌm'brɛlə] *n* paraguas *m inv*; **under the ~ of** (*fig*) bajo la protección de
umlaut ['umlaut] *n* diéresis *f inv*
umpire ['ʌmpaɪə^r] *n* árbitro ■ *vt* arbitrar
umpteen [ʌmp'tiːn] *num* enésimos(-as); **for the umpteenth time** por enésima vez
UMW *n abbr* (= *United Mineworkers of America*) *sindicato de mineros*
UN *n abbr* (= *United Nations*) ONU *f*
un- [ʌn] *pref* in-; des-; no …; (*XX*) poco …; nada …
unabashed [ʌnə'bæʃt] *adj* nada avergonzado
unabated [ʌnə'beɪtɪd] *adj*: **to continue ~** seguir con la misma intensidad
unable [ʌn'eɪbl] *adj*: **to be ~ to do sth** no poder hacer algo; (*not know how to*) ser incapaz de hacer algo, no saber hacer algo
unabridged [ʌnə'brɪdʒd] *adj* íntegro
unacceptable [ʌnək'sɛptəbl] *adj* (*proposal, behaviour, price*) inaceptable; **it's ~ that** no se puede aceptar que
unaccompanied [ʌnə'kʌmpənɪd] *adj* no acompañado; (*singing, song*) sin acompañamiento

unaccountably [ʌnəˈkauntəblɪ] *adv* inexplicablemente
unaccounted [ʌnəˈkauntɪd] *adj*: **two passengers are ~ for** faltan dos pasajeros
unaccustomed [ʌnəˈkʌstəmd] *adj*: **to be ~ to** no estar acostumbrado a
unacquainted [ʌnəˈkweɪntɪd] *adj*: **to be ~ with** *(facts)* desconocer, ignorar
unadulterated [ʌnəˈdʌltəreɪtɪd] *adj (gen)* puro; *(wine)* sin mezcla
unaffected [ʌnəˈfɛktɪd] *adj (person, behaviour)* sin afectación, sencillo; *(emotionally)*: **to be ~ by** no estar afectado por
unafraid [ʌnəˈfreɪd] *adj*: **to be ~** no tener miedo
unaided [ʌnˈeɪdɪd] *adj* sin ayuda, por sí solo
unanimity [juːnəˈnɪmɪtɪ] *n* unanimidad *f*
unanimous [juːˈnænɪməs] *adj* unánime
unanimously [juːˈnænɪməslɪ] *adv* unánimemente
unanswered [ʌnˈɑːnsəd] *adj (question, letter)* sin contestar; *(criticism)* incontestado
unappetizing [ʌnˈæpɪtaɪzɪŋ] *adj* poco apetitoso
unappreciative [ʌnəˈpriːʃɪətɪv] *adj* desagradecido
unarmed [ʌnˈɑːmd] *adj (person)* desarmado; *(combat)* sin armas
unashamed [ʌnəˈʃeɪmd] *adj* desvergonzado
unassisted [ʌnəˈsɪstɪd] *adj, adv* sin ayuda
unassuming [ʌnəˈsjuːmɪŋ] *adj* modesto, sin pretensiones
unattached [ʌnəˈtætʃt] *adj (person)* soltero; *(part etc)* suelto
unattended [ʌnəˈtɛndɪd] *adj (car, luggage)* sin atender
unattractive [ʌnəˈtræktɪv] *adj* poco atractivo
unauthorized [ʌnˈɔːθəraɪzd] *adj* no autorizado
unavailable [ʌnəˈveɪləbl] *adj (article, room, book)* no disponible; *(person)* ocupado
unavoidable [ʌnəˈvɔɪdəbl] *adj* inevitable
unavoidably [ʌnəˈvɔɪdəblɪ] *adv (detained)* por causas ajenas a su voluntad
unaware [ʌnəˈwɛəʳ] *adj*: **to be ~ of** ignorar
unawares [ʌnəˈwɛəz] *adv* de improviso
unbalanced [ʌnˈbælənst] *adj* desequilibrado; *(mentally)* trastornado
unbearable [ʌnˈbɛərəbl] *adj* insoportable
unbeatable [ʌnˈbiːtəbl] *adj (gen)* invencible; *(price)* inmejorable
unbeaten [ʌnˈbiːtn] *adj (team)* imbatido; *(army)* invicto; *(record)* no batido
unbecoming [ʌnbɪˈkʌmɪŋ] *adj (unseemly: language, behaviour)* indecoroso, impropio; *(unflattering: garment)* poco favorecedor(a)
unbeknown [ʌnbɪˈnəun], **unbeknownst** [ʌnbɪˈnəunst] *adv*: **~(st) to me** sin saberlo yo
unbelief [ʌnbɪˈliːf] *n* incredulidad *f*
unbelievable [ʌnbɪˈliːvəbl] *adj* increíble
unbelievingly [ʌnbɪˈliːvɪŋlɪ] *adv* sin creer
unbend [ʌnˈbɛnd] *(irreg: like* **bend***) vi (fig: person)* relajarse ■ *vt (wire)* enderezar
unbending [ʌnˈbɛndɪŋ] *adj (fig)* inflexible
unbiased, unbiassed [ʌnˈbaɪəst] *adj* imparcial
unblemished [ʌnˈblɛmɪʃt] *adj* sin mancha
unblock [ʌnˈblɔk] *vt (pipe)* desatascar; *(road)* despejar
unborn [ʌnˈbɔːn] *adj* que va a nacer
unbounded [ʌnˈbaundɪd] *adj* ilimitado, sin límite
unbreakable [ʌnˈbreɪkəbl] *adj* irrompible
unbridled [ʌnˈbraɪdld] *adj (fig)* desenfrenado
unbroken [ʌnˈbrəukən] *adj (seal)* intacto; *(series)* continuo, ininterrumpido; *(record)* no batido; *(spirit)* indómito
unbuckle [ʌnˈbʌkl] *vt* desabrochar
unburden [ʌnˈbəːdn] *vt*: **to ~ o.s.** desahogarse
unbusinesslike [ʌnˈbɪznɪslaɪk] *adj (trader)* poco profesional; *(transaction)* incorrecto; *(fig: person)* poco práctico; *(: without method)* desorganizado
unbutton [ʌnˈbʌtn] *vt* desabrochar
uncalled-for [ʌnˈkɔːldfɔːʳ] *adj* gratuito, inmerecido
uncanny [ʌnˈkænɪ] *adj* extraño, extraordinario
unceasing [ʌnˈsiːsɪŋ] *adj* incesante
unceremonious [ˈʌnsɛrɪˈməunɪəs] *adj (abrupt, rude)* brusco, hosco
uncertain [ʌnˈsəːtn] *adj* incierto; *(indecisive)* indeciso; **it's ~ whether** no se sabe si; **in no ~ terms** sin dejar lugar a dudas
uncertainty [ʌnˈsəːtntɪ] *n* incertidumbre *f*
unchallenged [ʌnˈtʃælɪndʒd] *adj (Law etc)* incontestado; **to go ~** no encontrar respuesta
unchanged [ʌnˈtʃeɪndʒd] *adj* sin cambiar *or* alterar
uncharitable [ʌnˈtʃærɪtəbl] *adj (remark, behaviour)* demasiado duro
uncharted [ʌnˈtʃɑːtɪd] *adj* inexplorado
unchecked [ʌnˈtʃɛkt] *adj* desenfrenado
uncivil [ʌnˈsɪvɪl] *adj* descortés, grosero
uncivilized [ʌnˈsɪvɪlaɪzd] *adj (gen)* inculto, poco civilizado; *(fig: behaviour etc)* bárbaro
uncle [ˈʌŋkl] *n* tío
unclear [ʌnˈklɪəʳ] *adj* poco claro; **I'm still ~ about what I'm supposed to do** todavía no tengo muy claro lo que tengo que hacer
uncoil [ʌnˈkɔɪl] *vt* desenrollar ■ *vi* desenrollarse

uncomfortable [ʌnˈkʌmfətəbl] *adj* incómodo; (*uneasy*) inquieto
uncomfortably [ʌnˈkʌmfətəblɪ] *adv* (*uneasily: say*) con inquietud; (*: think*) con remordimiento *or* nerviosismo
uncommitted [ʌnkəˈmɪtɪd] *adj* (*attitude, country*) no comprometido; **to remain ~ to** (*policy, party*) no comprometerse a
uncommon [ʌnˈkɔmən] *adj* poco común, raro
uncommunicative [ʌnkəˈmjuːnɪkətɪv] *adj* poco comunicativo, reservado
uncomplicated [ʌnˈkɔmplɪkeɪtɪd] *adj* sin complicaciones
uncompromising [ʌnˈkɔmprəmaɪzɪŋ] *adj* intransigente
unconcerned [ʌnkənˈsəːnd] *adj* indiferente; **to be ~ about** ser indiferente a, no preocuparse de
unconditional [ʌnkənˈdɪʃənl] *adj* incondicional
uncongenial [ʌnkənˈdʒiːnɪəl] *adj* desagradable
unconnected [ʌnkəˈnɛktɪd] *adj* (*unrelated*): **to be ~ with** no estar relacionado con
unconscious [ʌnˈkɔnʃəs] *adj* sin sentido; (*unaware*) inconsciente ■ *n*: **the ~** el inconsciente; **to knock sb ~** dejar a algn sin sentido
unconsciously [ʌnˈkɔnʃəslɪ] *adv* inconscientemente
unconsciousness [ʌnˈkɔnʃəsnɪs] *n* inconsciencia
unconstitutional [ʌnkɔnstɪˈtjuːʃənl] *adj* anticonstitucional
uncontested [ʌnkənˈtɛstɪd] *adj* (*champion*) incontestado; (*Parliament: seat*) ganado sin oposición
uncontrollable [ʌnkənˈtrəuləbl] *adj* (*temper*) indomable; (*laughter*) incontenible
uncontrolled [ʌnkənˈtrəuld] *adj* (*child, dog, emotion*) incontrolado; (*inflation, price rises*) desenfrenado
unconventional [ʌnkənˈvɛnʃənl] *adj* poco convencional
unconvinced [ʌnkənˈvɪnst] *adj*: **to be** *or* **remain ~** seguir sin convencerse
unconvincing [ʌnkənˈvɪnsɪŋ] *adj* poco convincente
uncork [ʌnˈkɔːk] *vt* descorchar
uncorroborated [ʌnkəˈrɔbəreɪtɪd] *adj* no confirmado
uncouth [ʌnˈkuːθ] *adj* grosero, inculto
uncover [ʌnˈkʌvəʳ] *vt* (*gen*) descubrir; (*take lid off*) destapar
undamaged [ʌnˈdæmɪdʒd] *adj* (*goods*) en buen estado; (*fig: reputation*) intacto
undaunted [ʌnˈdɔːntɪd] *adj*: **~ by** sin dejarse desanimar por
undecided [ʌndɪˈsaɪdɪd] *adj* (*person*) indeciso; (*question*) no resuelto, pendiente
undelivered [ʌndɪˈlɪvəd] *adj* no entregado al destinatario; **if ~ return to sender** en caso de no llegar a su destino devolver al, remitente
undeniable [ʌndɪˈnaɪəbl] *adj* innegable
undeniably [ʌndɪˈnaɪəblɪ] *adv* innegablemente
under [ˈʌndəʳ] *prep* debajo de; (*less than*) menos de; (*according to*) según, de acuerdo con ■ *adv* debajo, abajo; **~ there** ahí debajo; **~ construction** en construcción; en obras; **~ the circumstances** dadas las circunstancias; **in ~ 2 hours** en menos de dos horas; **~ anaesthetic** bajo los efectos de la anestesia; **~ discussion** en discusión, sobre el tapete
under... [ʌndəʳ] *pref* sub...
under-age [ʌndərˈeɪdʒ] *adj* menor de edad
underarm [ˈʌndərɑːm] *n* axila, sobaco ■ *cpd*: **~ deodorant** desodorante *m* corporal
undercapitalised [ʌndəˈkæpɪtəlaɪzd] *adj* descapitalizado
undercarriage [ˈʌndəkærɪdʒ] *n* (*Brit Aviat*) tren *m* de aterrizaje
undercharge [ʌndəˈtʃɑːdʒ] *vt* cobrar de menos
underclass [ˈʌndəklɑːs] *n* clase *f* marginada
underclothes [ˈʌndəkləuðz] *npl* ropa *sg* interior *or* íntima (*LAm*)
undercoat [ˈʌndəkəut] *n* (*paint*) primera mano
undercover [ʌndəˈkʌvəʳ] *adj* clandestino
undercurrent [ˈʌndəkʌrnt] *n* corriente *f* submarina; (*fig*) tendencia oculta
undercut [ˈʌndəkʌt] *vt* (*irreg: like* **cut**) vender más barato que; fijar un precio más barato que
underdeveloped [ʌndədɪˈvɛləpt] *adj* subdesarrollado
underdog [ˈʌndədɔg] *n* desvalido(-a)
underdone [ʌndəˈdʌn] *adj* (*Culin*) poco hecho
underemployment [ʌndərɪmˈplɔɪmənt] *n* subempleo
underestimate [ʌndərˈɛstɪmeɪt] *vt* subestimar
underexposed [ʌndərɪksˈpəuzd] *adj* (*Phot*) subexpuesto
underfed [ʌndəˈfɛd] *adj* subalimentado
underfoot [ʌndəˈfut] *adv*: **it's wet ~** el suelo está mojado
underfunded [ʌndəˈfʌndɪd] *adj* infradotado (económicamente)
undergo [ʌndəˈgəu] *vt* (*irreg: like* **go**) sufrir;

(treatment) recibir, someterse a; **the car is undergoing repairs** están reparando el coche
undergraduate ['ʌndə'grædjuət] *n* estudiante *m/f* ▪ *cpd*: **~ courses** cursos *mpl* de licenciatura
underground ['ʌndəgraund] *n* *(Brit: railway)* metro; *(Pol)* movimiento clandestino ▪ *adj* subterráneo
undergrowth ['ʌndəgrəuθ] *n* maleza
underhand [ʌndə'hænd], **underhanded** [ʌndə'hændɪd] *adj (fig)* poco limpio
underinsured [ʌndərɪn'ʃuəd] *adj* insuficientemente asegurado
underlie [ʌndə'laɪ] *vt (irreg: like* **lie***)* *(fig)* ser la razón fundamental de; **the underlying cause** la causa fundamental
underline [ʌndə'laɪn] *vt* subrayar
underling ['ʌndəlɪŋ] *n (pej)* subalterno(-a)
undermanning [ʌndə'mænɪŋ] *n* falta de personal
undermentioned [ʌndə'mɛnʃənd] *adj* abajo citado
undermine [ʌndə'maɪn] *vt* socavar, minar
underneath [ʌndə'ni:θ] *adv* debajo ▪ *prep* debajo de, bajo
undernourished [ʌndə'nʌrɪʃt] *adj* desnutrido
underpaid [ʌndə'peɪd] *adj* mal pagado
underpants ['ʌndəpænts] *npl* calzoncillos *mpl*
underpass ['ʌndəpɑ:s] *n (Brit)* paso subterráneo
underpin [ʌndə'pɪn] *vt (argument, case)* secundar, sostener
underplay [ʌndə'pleɪ] *vt (Brit)* minimizar
underpopulated [ʌndə'pɔpjuleɪtɪd] *adj* poco poblado
underprice [ʌndə'praɪs] *vt* vender demasiado barato
underpriced [ʌndə'praɪst] *adj* con precio demasiado bajo
underprivileged [ʌndə'prɪvɪlɪdʒd] *adj* desvalido
underrate [ʌndə'reɪt] *vt* infravalorar, subestimar
underscore ['ʌndəskɔ:ʳ] *vt* subrayar, sostener
underseal [ʌndə'si:l] *vt (Aut)* proteger contra la corrosión
undersecretary [ʌndə'sɛkrətrɪ] *n* subsecretario(-a)
undersell [ʌndə'sɛl] *vt (competitors)* vender más barato que
undershirt ['ʌndəʃə:t] *n (US)* camiseta
undershorts ['ʌndəʃɔ:ts] *npl (US)* calzoncillos *mpl*
underside ['ʌndəsaɪd] *n* parte *f* inferior, revés *m*
undersigned ['ʌndəsaɪnd] *adj, n*: **the ~** el/la *etc* abajo firmante
underskirt ['ʌndəskə:t] *n (Brit)* enaguas *fpl*
understaffed [ʌndə'stɑ:ft] *adj* falto de personal
understand [ʌndə'stænd] *(irreg: like* **stand***)* *vt, vi* entender, comprender; *(assume)* tener entendido; **to make o.s. understood** hacerse entender; **I ~ you have been absent** tengo entendido que (usted) ha estado ausente
understandable [ʌndə'stændəbl] *adj* comprensible
understanding [ʌndə'stændɪŋ] *adj* comprensivo ▪ *n* comprensión *f*, entendimiento; *(agreement)* acuerdo; **to come to an ~ with sb** llegar a un acuerdo con algn; **on the ~ that** a condición de que *+ subjun*
understate [ʌndə'steɪt] *vt* minimizar
understatement [ʌndə'steɪtmənt] *n* subestimación *f*; *(modesty)* modestia (excesiva); **to say it was good is quite an ~** decir que estuvo bien es quedarse corto
understood [ʌndə'stud] *pt, pp of* **understand** ▪ *adj* entendido; *(implied)*: **it is ~ that** se sobreentiende que
understudy ['ʌndəstʌdɪ] *n* suplente *m/f*
undertake [ʌndə'teɪk] *vt (irreg: like* **take***)* emprender; **to ~ to do sth** comprometerse a hacer algo
undertaker ['ʌndəteɪkəʳ] *n* director(a) *m(f)* de pompas fúnebres
undertaking ['ʌndəteɪkɪŋ] *n* empresa; *(promise)* promesa
undertone ['ʌndətəun] *n (of criticism)* connotación *f*; *(low voice)*: **in an ~** en voz baja
undervalue [ʌndə'vælju:] *vt (fig)* subestimar, infravalorar; *(Comm etc)* valorizar por debajo de su precio
underwater [ʌndə'wɔ:təʳ] *adv* bajo el agua ▪ *adj* submarino
underwear ['ʌndəwɛəʳ] *n* ropa interior *or* íntima *(LAm)*
underweight [ʌndə'weɪt] *adj* de peso insuficiente; *(person)* demasiado delgado
underworld ['ʌndəwə:ld] *n (of crime)* hampa, inframundo
underwrite [ʌndə'raɪt] *vt (irreg: like* **write***)* *(Comm)* suscribir; *(Insurance)* asegurar *(contra riesgos)*
underwriter ['ʌndəraɪtəʳ] *n (Insurance)* asegurador(a) *m(f)*
undeserving [ʌndɪ'zə:vɪŋ] *adj*: **to be ~ of** no ser digno de
undesirable [ʌndɪ'zaɪərəbl] *adj* indeseable
undeveloped [ʌndɪ'vɛləpt] *adj (land, resources)* sin explotar

undies ['ʌndɪz] *npl* (*col*) paños *mpl* menores
undiluted [ʌndaɪ'lu:tɪd] *adj* (*concentrate*) concentrado
undiplomatic [ʌndɪplə'mætɪk] *adj* poco diplomático
undischarged [ʌndɪs'tʃɑ:dʒd] *adj*: ~ **bankrupt** quebrado(-a) no rehabilitado(-a)
undisciplined [ʌn'dɪsɪplɪnd] *adj* indisciplinado
undiscovered [ʌndɪs'kʌvəd] *adj* no descubierto; (*unknown*) desconocido
undisguised [ʌndɪs'gaɪzd] *adj* franco, abierto
undisputed [ʌndɪ'spju:tɪd] *adj* incontestable
undistinguished [ʌndɪs'tɪŋgwɪʃt] *adj* mediocre
undisturbed [ʌndɪs'tə:bd] *adj* (*sleep*) ininterrumpido; **to leave sth ~** dejar algo tranquilo *or* como está
undivided [ʌndɪ'vaɪdɪd] *adj*: **I want your ~ attention** quiero su completa atención
undo [ʌn'du:] *vt* (*irreg: like* **do**) deshacer
undoing [ʌn'du:ɪŋ] *n* ruina, perdición *f*
undone [ʌn'dʌn] *pp of* **undo** ■ *adj*: **to come ~** (*clothes*) desabrocharse; (*parcel*) desatarse
undoubted [ʌn'dautɪd] *adj* indudable
undoubtedly [ʌn'dautɪdlɪ] *adv* indudablemente, sin duda
undress [ʌn'drɛs] *vi* desnudarse, desvestirse (*esp LAm*)
undrinkable [ʌn'drɪŋkəbl] *adj* (*unpalatable*) imbebible; (*poisonous*) no potable
undue [ʌn'dju:] *adj* indebido, excesivo
undulating ['ʌndjuleɪtɪŋ] *adj* ondulante
unduly [ʌn'dju:lɪ] *adv* excesivamente, demasiado
undying [ʌn'daɪɪŋ] *adj* eterno
unearned [ʌn'ə:nd] *adj* (*praise, respect*) inmerecido; ~ **income** ingresos *mpl* no ganados, renta no ganada *or* salarial
unearth [ʌn'ə:θ] *vt* desenterrar
unearthly [ʌn'ə:θlɪ] *adj*: ~ **hour** (*col*) hora intempestiva
unease [ʌn'i:z] *n* malestar *m*
uneasy [ʌn'i:zɪ] *adj* intranquilo; (*worried*) preocupado; **to feel ~ about doing sth** sentirse incómodo con la idea de hacer algo
uneconomic ['ʌni:kə'nɔmɪk], **uneconomical** ['ʌni:kə'nɔmɪkl] *adj* no económico
uneducated [ʌn'ɛdjukeɪtɪd] *adj* ignorante, inculto
unemployed [ʌnɪm'plɔɪd] *adj* parado, sin trabajo ■ *n*: **the** ~ los parados
unemployment [ʌnɪm'plɔɪmənt] *n* paro, desempleo, cesantía (*LAm*)
unemployment benefit *n* (*Brit*) subsidio de desempleo *or* paro
unending [ʌn'ɛndɪŋ] *adj* interminable
unenviable [ʌn'ɛnvɪəbl] *adj* poco envidiable
unequal [ʌn'i:kwəl] *adj* (*length, objects etc*) desigual; (*amounts*) distinto; (*division of labour*) poco justo
unequalled, unequaled (*US*) [ʌn'i:kwəld] *adj* inigualado, sin par
unequivocal [ʌnɪ'kwɪvəkəl] *adj* (*answer*) inequívoco, claro; (*person*) claro
unerring [ʌn'ə:rɪŋ] *adj* infalible
UNESCO [ju:'nɛskəu] *n abbr* (= *United Nations Educational, Scientific and Cultural Organization*) UNESCO *f*
unethical [ʌn'ɛθɪkəl] *adj* (*methods*) inmoral; (*doctor's behaviour*) que infringe la ética profesional
uneven [ʌn'i:vn] *adj* desigual; (*road etc*) con baches
uneventful [ʌnɪ'vɛntful] *adj* sin incidentes
unexceptional [ʌnɪk'sɛpʃənl] *adj* sin nada de extraordinario, corriente
unexciting [ʌnɪk'saɪtɪŋ] *adj* (*news*) sin interés; (*film, evening*) aburrido
unexpected [ʌnɪk'spɛktɪd] *adj* inesperado
unexpectedly [ʌnɪk'spɛktɪdlɪ] *adv* inesperadamente
unexplained [ʌnɪks'pleɪnd] *adj* inexplicado
unexploded [ʌnɪks'pləudɪd] *adj* sin explotar
unfailing [ʌn'feɪlɪŋ] *adj* (*support*) indefectible; (*energy*) inagotable
unfair [ʌn'fɛə^r] *adj*: ~ **(to sb)** injusto (con algn); **it's ~ that ...** es injusto que ..., no es justo que ...
unfair dismissal *n* despido improcedente
unfairly [ʌn'fɛəlɪ] *adv* injustamente
unfaithful [ʌn'feɪθful] *adj* infiel
unfamiliar [ʌnfə'mɪlɪə^r] *adj* extraño, desconocido; **to be ~ with sth** desconocer *or* ignorar algo
unfashionable [ʌn'fæʃnəbl] *adj* (*clothes*) pasado *or* fuera de moda; (*district*) poco elegante
unfasten [ʌn'fɑ:sn] *vt* desatar
unfathomable [ʌn'fæðəməbl] *adj* insondable
unfavourable, unfavorable (*US*) [ʌn'feɪvərəbl] *adj* desfavorable
unfavourably, unfavorably (*US*) [ʌn'feɪvrəblɪ] *adv*: **to look ~ upon** ser adverso a
unfeeling [ʌn'fi:lɪŋ] *adj* insensible
unfinished [ʌn'fɪnɪʃt] *adj* inacabado, sin terminar
unfit [ʌn'fɪt] *adj* en baja forma; (*incompetent*) incapaz; ~ **for work** no apto para trabajar
unflagging [ʌn'flægɪŋ] *adj* incansable
unflappable [ʌn'flæpəbl] *adj* imperturbable
unflattering [ʌn'flætərɪŋ] *adj* (*dress, hairstyle*) poco favorecedor

unflinching [ʌn'flɪntʃɪŋ] *adj* impávido
unfold [ʌn'fəuld] *vt* desdoblar; (*fig*) revelar ■ *vi* abrirse; revelarse
unforeseeable [ʌnfɔː'siːəbl] *adj* imprevisible
unforeseen ['ʌnfɔː'siːn] *adj* imprevisto
unforgettable [ʌnfə'gɛtəbl] *adj* inolvidable
unforgivable [ʌnfə'gɪvəbl] *adj* imperdonable
unformatted [ʌn'fɔːmætɪd] *adj* (*disk, text*) sin formatear
unfortunate [ʌn'fɔːtʃnət] *adj* desgraciado; (*event, remark*) inoportuno
unfortunately [ʌn'fɔːtʃnətlɪ] *adv* desgraciadamente, por desgracia
unfounded [ʌn'faundɪd] *adj* infundado
unfriendly [ʌn'frɛndlɪ] *adj* antipático
unfulfilled [ʌnful'fɪld] *adj* (*ambition*) sin realizar; (*prophecy, promise, terms of contract*) incumplido; (*desire, person*) insatisfecho
unfurl [ʌn'fəːl] *vt* desplegar
unfurnished [ʌn'fəːnɪʃt] *adj* sin amueblar
ungainly [ʌn'geɪnlɪ] *adj* (*walk*) desgarbado
ungodly [ʌn'gɔdlɪ] *adj*: **at an ~ hour** a una hora intempestiva
ungrateful [ʌn'greɪtful] *adj* ingrato
unguarded [ʌn'gɑːdɪd] *adj* (*moment*) de descuido
unhappily [ʌn'hæpɪlɪ] *adv* (*unfortunately*) desgraciadamente
unhappiness [ʌn'hæpɪnɪs] *n* tristeza
unhappy [ʌn'haepɪ] *adj* (*sad*) triste; (*unfortunate*) desgraciado; (*childhood*) infeliz; **~ with** (*arrangements etc*) poco contento con, descontento de
unharmed [ʌn'hɑːmd] *adj* (*person*) ileso
UNHCR *n abbr* (= *United Nations High Commission for Refugees*) ACNUR *m*
unhealthy [ʌn'hɛlθɪ] *adj* (*gen*) malsano, insalubre; (*person*) enfermizo; (*interest*) morboso
unheard-of [ʌn'həːdɔv] *adj* inaudito, sin precedente
unhelpful [ʌn'hɛlpful] *adj* (*person*) poco servicial; (*advice*) inútil
unhesitating [ʌn'hɛzɪteɪtɪŋ] *adj* (*loyalty*) automático; (*reply, offer*) inmediato; (*person*) resuelto
unholy [ʌn'həulɪ] *adj*: **an ~ alliance** una alianza nefasta; **he returned at an ~ hour** volvió a una hora intempestiva
unhook [ʌn'huk] *vt* desenganchar; (*from wall*) descolgar; (*undo*) desabrochar
unhurt [ʌn'həːt] *adj* ileso
unhygienic [ʌnhaɪ'dʒiːnɪk] *adj* antihigiénico
UNICEF ['juːnɪsɛf] *n abbr* (= *United Nations International Children's Emergency Fund*) UNICEF *f*
unidentified [ʌnaɪ'dɛntɪfaɪd] *adj* no identificado; **~ flying object (UFO)** objeto volante no identificado
unification [juːnɪfɪ'keɪʃən] *n* unificación *f*
uniform ['juːnɪfɔːm] *n* uniforme *m* ■ *adj* uniforme
uniformity [juːnɪ'fɔːmɪtɪ] *n* uniformidad *f*
unify ['juːnɪfaɪ] *vt* unificar, unir
unilateral [juːnɪ'lætərəl] *adj* unilateral
unimaginable [ʌnɪ'mædʒɪnəbl] *adj* inconcebible, inimaginable
unimaginative [ʌnɪ'mædʒɪnətɪv] *adj* falto de imaginación
unimpaired [ʌnɪm'pɛəd] *adj* (*unharmed*) intacto; (*not lessened*) no disminuido; (*unaltered*) inalterado
unimportant [ʌnɪm'pɔːtənt] *adj* sin importancia
unimpressed [ʌnɪm'prɛst] *adj* poco impresionado
uninhabited [ʌnɪn'hæbɪtɪd] *adj* desierto; (*country*) despoblado; (*house*) deshabitado, desocupado
uninhibited [ʌnɪn'hɪbɪtɪd] *adj* nada cohibido, desinhibido
uninjured [ʌn'ɪndʒəd] *adj* (*person*) ileso
uninspiring [ʌnɪn'spaɪərɪŋ] *adj* anodino
unintelligent [ʌnɪn'tɛlɪdʒənt] *adj* poco inteligente
unintentional [ʌnɪn'tɛnʃənəl] *adj* involuntario
unintentionally [ʌnɪn'tɛnʃnəlɪ] *adv* sin querer
uninvited [ʌnɪn'vaɪtɪd] *adj* (*guest*) sin invitación
uninviting [ʌnɪn'vaɪtɪŋ] *adj* (*place, offer*) poco atractivo; (*food*) poco apetecible
union ['juːnjən] *n* unión *f*; (*also*: **trade union**) sindicato ■ *cpd* sindical; **the U~** (*US*) la Unión
union card *n* carnet *m* de sindicato
unionize ['juːnjənaɪz] *vt* sindicalizar
Union Jack *n* bandera del Reino Unido
Union of Soviet Socialist Republics *n* Unión *f* de Repúblicas Socialistas Soviéticas
union shop *n* (*US*) *empresa de afiliación sindical obligatoria*
unique [juː'niːk] *adj* único
unisex ['juːnɪsɛks] *adj* unisex
Unison ['juːnɪsn] *n* (*trade union*) *gran sindicato de funcionarios*
unison ['juːnɪsn] *n*: **in ~** en armonía
unissued capital [ʌn'ɪʃuːd-] *n* capital *m* no emitido
unit ['juːnɪt] *n* unidad *f*; (*team, squad*) grupo; **kitchen ~** módulo de cocina; **production ~** taller *m* de fabricación; **sink ~** fregadero
unit cost *n* costo unitario
unite [juː'naɪt] *vt* unir ■ *vi* unirse
united [juː'naɪtɪd] *adj* unido

United Arab Emirates *npl* Emiratos *mpl* Árabes Unidos
United Kingdom *n* Reino Unido
United Nations, United Nations Organization *n* Naciones Unidas *fpl*
United States, United States of America *n* Estados Unidos *mpl* (de América)
unit price *n* precio unitario
unit trust *n* (*Brit*) bono fiduciario
unity ['ju:nɪtɪ] *n* unidad *f*
Univ. *abbr* = **university**
universal [ju:nɪ'və:sl] *adj* universal
universally [ju:nɪ'və:səlɪ] *adv* universalmente
universe ['ju:nɪvə:s] *n* universo
university [ju:nɪ'və:sɪtɪ] *n* universidad *f* ▪ *cpd* (*student, professor, education, degree*) universitario; (*year*) académico; **to be at/go to ~** estudiar en/ir a la universidad
unjust [ʌn'dʒʌst] *adj* injusto
unjustifiable [ʌndʒʌstɪ'faɪəbl] *adj* injustificable
unjustified [ʌn'dʒʌstɪfaɪd] *adj* (*text*) no alineado *or* justificado
unkempt [ʌn'kɛmpt] *adj* descuidado; (*hair*) despeinado
unkind [ʌn'kaɪnd] *adj* poco amable; (*comment etc*) cruel
unkindly [ʌn'kaɪndlɪ] *adv* (*speak*) severamente; (*treat*) cruelmente, mal
unknown [ʌn'nəun] *adj* desconocido ▪ *adv*: **~ to me** sin saberlo yo; **~ quantity** incógnita
unladen [ʌn'leɪdən] *adj* (*weight*) vacío, sin cargamento
unlawful [ʌn'lɔ:ful] *adj* ilegal, ilícito
unleaded [ʌn'lɛdɪd] *n* (*also*: **unleaded petrol**) gasolina sin plomo
unleash [ʌn'li:ʃ] *vt* desatar
unleavened [ʌn'lɛvənd] *adj* ácimo, sin levadura
unless [ʌn'lɛs] *conj* a menos que; **~ he comes** a menos que venga; **~ otherwise stated** salvo indicación contraria; **~ I am mistaken** si no mi equivoco
unlicensed [ʌn'laɪsənst] *adj* (*Brit: to sell alcohol*) no autorizado
unlike [ʌn'laɪk] *adj* distinto ▪ *prep* a diferencia de
unlikelihood [ʌn'laɪklɪhud] *n* improbabilidad *f*
unlikely [ʌn'laɪklɪ] *adj* improbable
unlimited [ʌn'lɪmɪtɪd] *adj* ilimitado; **~ liability** responsabilidad *f* ilimitada
unlisted [ʌn'lɪstɪd] *adj* (*US Tel*) que no figura en la guía; **~ company** empresa sin cotización en bolsa
unlit [ʌn'lɪt] *adj* (*room*) oscuro, sin luz
unload [ʌn'ləud] *vt* descargar
unlock [ʌn'lɔk] *vt* abrir (con llave)
unlucky [ʌn'lʌkɪ] *adj* desgraciado; (*object, number*) que da mala suerte; **to be ~** (*person*) tener mala suerte
unmanageable [ʌn'mænɪdʒəbl] *adj* (*unwieldy: tool, vehicle*) difícil de manejar; (*situation*) incontrolable
unmanned [ʌn'mænd] *adj* (*spacecraft*) sin tripulación
unmannerly [ʌn'mænəlɪ] *adj* mal educado, descortés
unmarked [ʌn'mɑ:kt] *adj* (*unstained*) sin mancha; **~ police car** vehículo policial camuflado
unmarried [ʌn'mærɪd] *adj* soltero
unmask [ʌn'mɑ:sk] *vt* desenmascarar
unmatched [ʌn'mætʃt] *adj* incomparable
unmentionable [ʌn'mɛnʃnəbl] *adj* (*topic, vice*) indecible; (*word*) que no se debe decir
unmerciful [ʌn'mə:sɪful] *adj* despiadado
unmistakable [ʌnmɪs'teɪkəbl] *adj* inconfundible
unmistakably [ʌnmɪs'teɪkəblɪ] *adv* de modo inconfundible
unmitigated [ʌn'mɪtɪgeɪtɪd] *adj* rematado, absoluto
unnamed [ʌn'neɪmd] *adj* (*nameless*) sin nombre; (*anonymous*) anónimo
unnatural [ʌn'nætʃrəl] *adj* (*gen*) antinatural; (*manner*) afectado; (*habit*) perverso
unnecessary [ʌn'nɛsəsərɪ] *adj* innecesario, inútil
unnerve [ʌn'nə:v] *vt* (*accident*) poner nervioso; (*hostile attitude*) acobardar; (*long wait, interview*) intimidar
unnoticed [ʌn'nəutɪst] *adj*: **to go** *or* **pass ~** pasar desapercibido
UNO ['ju:nəu] *n abbr* (= *United Nations Organization*) ONU *f*
unobservant [ʌnəb'zə:vnt] *adj*: **to be ~** ser poco observador, ser distraído
unobtainable [ʌnəb'teɪnəbl] *adj* inasequible; (*Tel*) inexistente
unobtrusive [ʌnəb'tru:sɪv] *adj* discreto
unoccupied [ʌn'ɔkjupaɪd] *adj* (*house etc*) libre, desocupado
unofficial [ʌnə'fɪʃl] *adj* no oficial; **~ strike** huelga no oficial
unopened [ʌn'əupənd] *adj* (*letter, present*) sin abrir
unopposed [ʌnə'pəuzd] *adv* (*enter, be elected*) sin oposición
unorthodox [ʌn'ɔ:θədɔks] *adj* poco ortodoxo
unpack [ʌn'pæk] *vi* deshacer las maletas, desempacar (*LAm*)
unpaid [ʌn'peɪd] *adj* (*bill, debt*) sin pagar,

impagado; (*Comm*) pendiente; (*holiday*) sin sueldo; (*work*) sin pago, voluntario
unpalatable [ʌn'pælətəbl] *adj* (*truth*) desagradable
unparalleled [ʌn'pærəlɛld] *adj* (*unequalled*) sin par; (*unique*) sin precedentes
unpatriotic [ʌnpætrɪ'ɔtɪk] *adj* (*person*) poco patriota; (*speech, attitude*) antipatriótico
unplanned [ʌn'plænd] *adj* (*visit*) imprevisto; (*baby*) no planeado
unpleasant [ʌn'plɛznt] *adj* (*disagreeable*) desagradable; (*person, manner*) antipático
unplug [ʌn'plʌg] *vt* desenchufar, desconectar
unpolluted [ʌnpə'lu:tɪd] *adj* impoluto, no contaminado
unpopular [ʌn'pɔpjulə^r] *adj* poco popular; **to be ~ with sb** (*person, law*) no ser popular con algn; **to make o.s. ~ (with)** hacerse impopular (con)
unprecedented [ʌn'prɛsɪdəntɪd] *adj* sin precedentes
unpredictable [ʌnprɪ'dɪktəbl] *adj* imprevisible
unprejudiced [ʌn'prɛdʒudɪst] *adj* (*not biased*) imparcial; (*having no prejudices*) sin prejuicio
unprepared [ʌnprɪ'pɛəd] *adj* (*person*) desprevenido; (*speech*) improvisado
unprepossessing [ʌnpri:pə'zɛsɪŋ] *adj* poco atractivo
unprincipled [ʌn'prɪnsɪpld] *adj* sin escrúpulos
unproductive [ʌnprə'dʌktɪv] *adj* improductivo; (*discussion*) infructuoso
unprofessional [ʌnprə'fɛʃənl] *adj* poco profesional; **~ conduct** negligencia
unprofitable [ʌn'prɔfɪtəbl] *adj* poco provechoso, no rentable
UNPROFOR *n abbr* (= *United Nations Protection Force*) FORPRONU *f*, Unprofor *f*
unprotected ['ʌnprə'tɛktɪd] *adj* (*sex*) sin protección
unprovoked [ʌnprə'vəukt] *adj* no provocado
unpunished [ʌn'pʌnɪʃt] *adj*: **to go ~** quedar sin castigo, salir impune
unqualified [ʌn'kwɔlɪfaɪd] *adj* sin título, no cualificado; (*success*) total, incondicional
unquestionably [ʌn'kwɛstʃənəblɪ] *adv* indiscutiblemente
unquestioning [ʌn'kwɛstʃənɪŋ] *adj* (*obedience, acceptance*) incondicional
unravel [ʌn'rævl] *vt* desenmarañar
unreal [ʌn'rɪəl] *adj* irreal
unrealistic [ʌnrɪə'lɪstɪk] *adj* poco realista
unreasonable [ʌn'ri:znəbl] *adj* irrazonable; **to make ~ demands on sb** hacer demandas excesivas a algn
unrecognizable [ʌn'rɛkəgnaɪzəbl] *adj* irreconocible
unrecognized [ʌn'rɛkəgnaɪzd] *adj* (*talent, genius*) ignorado; (*Pol: regime*) no reconocido
unrecorded [ʌnrɪ'kɔ:dɪd] *adj* no registrado
unrefined [ʌnrɪ'faɪnd] *adj* (*sugar, petroleum*) sin refinar
unrehearsed [ʌnrɪ'hə:st] *adj* (*Theat etc*) improvisado; (*spontaneous*) espontáneo
unrelated [ʌnrɪ'leɪtɪd] *adj* sin relación; (*family*) no emparentado
unrelenting [ʌnrɪ'lɛntɪŋ] *adj* implacable
unreliable [ʌnrɪ'laɪəbl] *adj* (*person*) informal; (*machine*) poco fiable
unrelieved [ʌnrɪ'li:vd] *adj* (*monotony*) constante
unremitting [ʌnrɪ'mɪtɪŋ] *adj* incesante
unrepeatable [ʌnrɪ'pi:təbl] *adj* irrepetible
unrepentant [ʌnrɪ'pɛntənt] *adj* (*smoker, sinner*) impenitente; **to be ~ about sth** no arrepentirse de algo
unrepresentative [ʌnrɛprɪ'zɛntətɪv] *adj* (*untypical*) poco representativo
unreserved [ʌnrɪ'zə:vd] *adj* (*seat*) no reservado; (*approval, admiration*) total
unreservedly [ʌnrɪ'zə:vɪdlɪ] *adv* sin reserva
unresponsive [ʌnrɪ'spɔnsɪv] *adj* insensible
unrest [ʌn'rɛst] *n* inquietud *f*, malestar *m*; (*Pol*) disturbios *mpl*
unrestricted [ʌnrɪ'strɪktɪd] *adj* (*power, time*) sin restricción; (*access*) libre
unrewarded [ʌnrɪ'wɔ:dɪd] *adj* sin recompensa
unripe [ʌn'raɪp] *adj* verde, inmaduro
unrivalled, unrivaled (*US*) [ʌn'raɪvəld] *adj* incomparable, sin par
unroll [ʌn'rəul] *vt* desenrollar
unruffled [ʌn'rʌfld] *adj* (*person*) imperturbable; (*hair*) liso
unruly [ʌn'ru:lɪ] *adj* indisciplinado
unsafe [ʌn'seɪf] *adj* (*journey*) peligroso; (*car etc*) inseguro; (*method*) arriesgado; **~ to drink/ eat** no apto para el consumo humano
unsaid [ʌn'sɛd] *adj*: **to leave sth ~** dejar algo sin decir
unsaleable, unsalable (*US*) [ʌn'seɪləbl] *adj* invendible
unsatisfactory ['ʌnsætɪs'fæktərɪ] *adj* poco satisfactorio
unsatisfied [ʌn'sætɪsfaɪd] *adj* (*desire, need etc*) insatisfecho
unsavoury, unsavory (*US*) [ʌn'seɪvərɪ] *adj* (*fig*) repugnante
unscathed [ʌn'skeɪðd] *adj* ileso
unscientific [ʌnsaɪən'tɪfɪk] *adj* poco científico
unscrew [ʌn'skru:] *vt* destornillar
unscrupulous [ʌn'skru:pjuləs] *adj* sin escrúpulos

unseat [ʌn'si:t] *vt* (*rider*) hacer caerse de la silla a; (*fig: official*) hacer perder su escaño a
unsecured [ʌnsɪ'kjuəd] *adj*: **~ creditor** acreedor(a) *m(f)* común
unseeded [ʌn'si:dɪd] *adj* (*Sport*) no preseleccionado
unseen [ʌn'si:n] *adj* (*person, danger*) oculto
unselfish [ʌn'sɛlfɪʃ] *adj* generoso, poco egoísta; (*act*) desinteresado
unsettled [ʌn'sɛtld] *adj* inquieto; (*situation*) inestable; (*weather*) variable
unsettling [ʌn'sɛtlɪŋ] *adj* perturbador(a), inquietante
unshakable, unshakeable [ʌn'ʃeɪkəbl] *adj* inquebrantable
unshaven [ʌn'ʃeɪvn] *adj* sin afeitar
unsightly [ʌn'saɪtlɪ] *adj* desagradable
unskilled [ʌn'skɪld] *adj*: **~ workers** mano *f* de obra no cualificada
unsociable [ʌn'səuʃəbl] *adj* insociable
unsocial [ʌn'səuʃl] *adj*: **~ hours** horario nocturno
unsold [ʌn'səuld] *adj* sin vender
unsolicited [ʌnsə'lɪsɪtɪd] *adj* no solicitado
unsophisticated [ʌnsə'fɪstɪkeɪtɪd] *adj* (*person*) sencillo, ingenuo; (*method*) poco sofisticado
unsound [ʌn'saund] *adj* (*health*) malo; (*in construction: floor, foundations*) defectuoso; (*policy, advice, judgment*) erróneo; (*investment*) poco seguro
unspeakable [ʌn'spi:kəbl] *adj* indecible; (*awful*) incalificable
unspoken [ʌn'spəukn] *adj* (*words*) sobreentendido; (*agreement, approval*) tácito
unstable [ʌn'steɪbl] *adj* inestable
unsteady [ʌn'stɛdɪ] *adj* inestable
unstinting [ʌn'stɪntɪŋ] *adj* (*support etc*) pródigo
unstuck [ʌn'stʌk] *adj*: **to come ~** despegarse; (*fig*) fracasar
unsubscribe [ʌnsəb'skraɪb] *vt* (*Internet*) borrarse
unsubstantiated [ʌnsəb'stænʃɪeɪtɪd] *adj* (*rumour, accusation*) no comprobado
unsuccessful [ʌnsək'sɛsful] *adj* (*attempt*) infructuoso; (*writer, proposal*) sin éxito; **to be ~** (*in attempting sth*) no tener éxito, fracasar
unsuccessfully [ʌnsək'sɛsfulɪ] *adv* en vano, sin éxito
unsuitable [ʌn'su:təbl] *adj* inconveniente, inapropiado; (*time*) inoportuno
unsuited [ʌn'su:tɪd] *adj*: **to be ~ for** *or* **to** no ser apropiado para
unsung ['ʌnsʌŋ] *adj*: **an ~ hero** un héroe desconocido
unsupported [ʌnsə'pɔ:tɪd] *adj* (*claim*) sin fundamento; (*theory*) sin base firme
unsure [ʌn'ʃuəʳ] *adj* inseguro, poco seguro; **to be ~ of o.s.** estar poco seguro de sí mismo
unsuspecting [ʌnsə'spɛktɪŋ] *adj* confiado
unsweetened [ʌn'swi:tnd] *adj* sin azúcar
unsympathetic [ʌnsɪmpə'θɛtɪk] *adj* (*attitude*) poco comprensivo; (*person*) sin compasión; **~ (to)** indiferente (a)
untangle [ʌn'tæŋgl] *vt* desenredar
untapped [ʌn'tæpt] *adj* (*resources*) sin explotar
untaxed [ʌn'tækst] *adj* (*goods*) libre de impuestos; (*income*) antes de impuestos
unthinkable [ʌn'θɪŋkəbl] *adj* inconcebible, impensable
unthinkingly [ʌn'θɪŋkɪŋlɪ] *adv* irreflexivamente
untidy [ʌn'taɪdɪ] *adj* (*room*) desordenado, en desorden; (*appearance*) desaliñado
untie [ʌn'taɪ] *vt* desatar
until [ən'tɪl] *prep* hasta ■ *conj* hasta que; **~ he comes** hasta que venga; **~ now** hasta ahora; **~ then** hasta entonces; **from morning ~ night** de la mañana a la noche
untimely [ʌn'taɪmlɪ] *adj* inoportuno; (*death*) prematuro
untold [ʌn'təuld] *adj* (*story*) nunca contado; (*suffering*) indecible; (*wealth*) incalculable
untouched [ʌn'tʌtʃt] *adj* (*not used etc*) intacto, sin tocar; (*safe: person*) indemne, ileso; (*unaffected*): **~ by** insensible a
untoward [ʌntə'wɔ:d] *adj* (*behaviour*) impropio; (*event*) adverso
untrained [ʌn'treɪnd] *adj* (*worker*) sin formación; (*troops*) no entrenado; **to the ~ eye** para los no entendidos
untrammelled, untrammeled (*US*) [ʌn'træməld] *adj* ilimitado
untranslatable [ʌntrænz'leɪtəbl] *adj* intraducible
untried [ʌn'traɪd] *adj* (*plan*) no probado
untrue [ʌn'tru:] *adj* (*statement*) falso
untrustworthy [ʌn'trʌstwə:ðɪ] *adj* (*person*) poco fiable
unusable [ʌn'ju:zəbl] *adj* inservible
unused [ʌn'ju:zd] *adj* sin usar, nuevo; **to be ~ to (doing) sth** no estar acostumbrado a (hacer) algo
unusual [ʌn'ju:ʒuəl] *adj* insólito, poco común
unusually [ʌn'ju:ʒuəlɪ] *adv*: **he arrived ~ early** llegó más temprano que de costumbre
unveil [ʌn'veɪl] *vt* (*statue*) descubrir
unwanted [ʌn'wɔntɪd] *adj* (*person, effect*) no deseado
unwarranted [ʌn'wɔrəntɪd] *adj* injustificado
unwary [ʌn'wɛərɪ] *adj* imprudente, incauto
unwavering [ʌn'weɪvərɪŋ] *adj* inquebrantable

unwelcome [ʌn'wɛlkəm] *adj* (*at a bad time*) inoportuno, molesto; **to feel ~** sentirse incómodo
unwell [ʌn'wɛl] *adj*: **to feel ~** estar indispuesto, sentirse mal
unwieldy [ʌn'wi:ldɪ] *adj* difícil de manejar
unwilling [ʌn'wɪlɪŋ] *adj*: **to be ~ to do sth** estar poco dispuesto a hacer algo
unwillingly [ʌn'wɪlɪŋlɪ] *adv* de mala gana
unwind [ʌn'waɪnd] (*irreg: like* **wind**) *vt* desenvolver ■ *vi* (*relax*) relajarse
unwise [ʌn'waɪz] *adj* imprudente
unwitting [ʌn'wɪtɪŋ] *adj* inconsciente
unworkable [ʌn'wə:kəbl] *adj* (*plan*) impracticable
unworthy [ʌn'wə:ðɪ] *adj* indigno; **to be ~ of sth/to do sth** ser indigno de algo/de hacer algo
unwrap [ʌn'ræp] *vt* deshacer
unwritten [ʌn'rɪtn] *adj* (*agreement*) tácito; (*rules, law*) no escrito
unzip [ʌn'zɪp] *vt* abrir la cremallera de; (*Comput*) descomprimir

KEYWORD

up [ʌp] *prep*: **to go/be up sth** subir/estar subido en algo; **he went up the stairs/the hill** subió las escaleras/la colina; **we walked/climbed up the hill** subimos la colina; **they live further up the street** viven más arriba en la calle; **go up that road and turn left** sigue por esa calle y gira a la izquierda
■ *adv* **1** (*upwards, higher*) más arriba; **up in the mountains** en lo alto (de la montaña); **put it a bit higher up** ponlo un poco más arriba *or* alto; **to stop halfway up** pararse a la mitad del camino *or* de la subida; **up there** ahí *or* allí arriba; **up above** en lo alto, por encima, arriba; **"this side up"** "este lado hacia arriba"; **to live/go up North** vivir en el norte/ir al norte
2: **to be up** (*out of bed*) estar levantado; (*prices, level*) haber subido; (*building*) estar construido; (*tent*) estar montado; (*curtains, paper etc*) estar puesto; **time's up** se acabó el tiempo; **when the year was up** al terminarse el año; **he's well up in** *or* **on politics** (*Brit: knowledgeable*) está muy al día en política; **what's up?** (*wrong*) ¿qué pasa?; **what's up with him?** ¿qué le pasa?; **prices are up on last year** los precios han subido desde el año pasado
3: **up to** (*as far as*) hasta; **up to now** hasta ahora *or* la fecha
4: **to be up to** (*depending on*): **it's up to you** depende de ti; **he's not up to it** (*job, task etc*) no es capaz de hacerlo; **I don't feel up to it** no me encuentro con ánimos para ello; **his work is not up to the required standard** su trabajo no da la talla; (*col: be doing*): **what is he up to?** ¿qué estará tramando?
■ *vi* (*col*): **she upped and left** se levantó y se marchó
■ *vt* (*col: price*) subir
■ *n*: **ups and downs** altibajos *mpl*

up-and-coming [ʌpənd'kʌmɪŋ] *adj* prometedor(a)
upbeat ['ʌpbi:t] *n* (*Mus*) tiempo no acentuado; (*in economy, prosperity*) aumento ■ *adj* (*col*) optimista, animado
upbraid [ʌp'breɪd] *vt* censurar, reprender
upbringing ['ʌpbrɪŋɪŋ] *n* educación *f*
upcoming ['ʌpkʌmɪŋ] *adj* próximo
update [ʌp'deɪt] *vt* poner al día
upend [ʌp'ɛnd] *vt* poner vertical
upfront [ʌp'frʌnt] *adj* claro, directo ■ *adv* a las claras; (*pay*) por adelantado; **to be ~ about sth** admitir algo claramente
upgrade [ʌp'greɪd] *vt* ascender; (*Comput*) modernizar
upheaval [ʌp'hi:vl] *n* trastornos *mpl*; (*Pol*) agitación *f*
uphill [ʌp'hɪl] *adj* cuesta arriba; (*fig: task*) penoso, difícil ■ *adv*: **to go ~** ir cuesta arriba
uphold [ʌp'həuld] *vt* (*irreg: like* **hold**) sostener
upholstery [ʌp'həulstərɪ] *n* tapicería
upkeep ['ʌpki:p] *n* mantenimiento
upmarket [ʌp'mɑ:kɪt] *adj* (*product*) de categoría
upon [ə'pɔn] *prep* sobre
upper ['ʌpə^r] *adj* superior, de arriba ■ *n* (*of shoe: also:* **uppers**) pala
upper case *n* (*Typ*) mayúsculas *fpl*
upper-class [ʌpə'klɑ:s] *adj* (*district, people, accent*) de clase alta; (*attitude*) altivo
uppercut ['ʌpəkʌt] *n* uppercut *m*, gancho a la cara
upper hand *n*: **to have the ~** tener la sartén por el mango
Upper House *n* (*Pol*): **the ~** la Cámara alta
uppermost ['ʌpəməust] *adj* el más alto; **what was ~ in my mind** lo que me preocupaba más
Upper Volta [-'vəultə] *n* Alto Volta *m*
upright ['ʌpraɪt] *adj* vertical; (*fig*) honrado
uprising ['ʌpraɪzɪŋ] *n* sublevación *f*
uproar ['ʌprɔ:^r] *n* tumulto, escándalo
uproarious [ʌp'rɔ:rɪəs] *adj* escandaloso; (*hilarious*) graciosísimo
uproot [ʌp'ru:t] *vt* desarraigar
upset *n* ['ʌpsɛt] (*to plan etc*) revés *m*,

contratiempo; (*Med*) trastorno ■ *vt* [ʌp'sɛt] (*irreg: like* **set**) (*glass etc*) volcar; (*spill*) derramar; (*plan*) alterar; (*person*) molestar, perturbar ■ *adj* [ʌp'sɛt] preocupado, perturbado; (*stomach*) revuelto; **to have a stomach** ~ (*Brit*) tener el estómago revuelto; **to get** ~ molestarse, llevarse un disgusto
upset price *n* (*US, Scottish*) precio mínimo *or* de reserva
upsetting [ʌp'sɛtɪŋ] *adj* (*worrying*) inquietante; (*offending*) ofensivo; (*annoying*) molesto
upshot ['ʌpʃɔt] *n* resultado
upside-down ['ʌpsaɪd'daun] *adv* al revés
upstage ['ʌp'steɪdʒ] *vt* robar protagonismo a
upstairs [ʌp'stɛəz] *adv* arriba ■ *adj* (*room*) de arriba ■ *n* el piso superior
upstart ['ʌpstɑ:t] *n* advenedizo
upstream [ʌp'stri:m] *adv* río arriba
upsurge ['ʌpsə:dʒ] *n* (*of enthusiasm etc*) arrebato
uptake ['ʌpteɪk] *n*: **he is quick/slow on the ~** es muy listo/torpe
uptight [ʌp'taɪt] *adj* tenso, nervioso
up-to-date ['ʌptə'deɪt] *adj* moderno, actual; **to bring sb ~ (on sth)** poner a algn al corriente/tanto (de algo)
upturn ['ʌptə:n] *n* (*in luck*) mejora; (*Comm: in market*) resurgimiento económico; (*: in value of currency*) aumento
upturned ['ʌptə:nd] *adj*: **~ nose** nariz *f* respingona
upward ['ʌpwəd] *adj* ascendente ■ *adv* hacia arriba
upwardly-mobile ['ʌpwədlɪ'məubaɪl] *adj*: **to be** ~ mejorar socialmente
upwards ['ʌpwədz] *adv* hacia arriba
URA *n abbr* (*US*) = **Urban Renewal Administration**
Ural Mountains ['juərəl-] *npl*: **the** ~ (*also*: **the Urals**) los Montes Urales
uranium [juə'reɪnɪəm] *n* uranio
Uranus [juə'reɪnəs] *n* (*Astro*) Urano
urban ['ə:bən] *adj* urbano
urbane [ə:'beɪn] *adj* cortés, urbano
urbanization ['ə:bənaɪ'zeɪʃən] *n* urbanización *f*
urchin ['ə:tʃɪn] *n* pilluelo, golfillo
Urdu ['uədu:] *n* urdu *m*
urge [ə:dʒ] *n* (*force*) impulso; (*desire*) deseo ■ *vt*: **to ~ sb to do sth** animar a algn a hacer algo
▸ **urge on** *vt* animar
urgency ['ə:dʒənsɪ] *n* urgencia
urgent ['ə:dʒənt] *adj* (*earnest, persistent: plea*) insistente; (*: tone*) urgente
urgently ['ə:dʒəntlɪ] *adv* con urgencia, urgentemente
urinal ['juərɪnl] *n* (*building*) urinario; (*vessel*) orinal *m*
urinate ['juərɪneɪt] *vi* orinar
urine ['juərɪn] *n* orina
urn [ə:n] *n* urna; (*also*: **tea urn**) tetera (grande)
Uruguay ['juerəgwaɪ] *n* el Uruguay
Uruguayan [juərə'gwaɪən] *adj, n* uruguayo(-a) *m(f)*
US *n abbr* (= *United States*) EE.UU.
us [ʌs] *pron* nos; (*after prep*) nosotros(-as); (*col: me*): **give us a kiss** dame un beso; *see also* **me**
USA *n abbr* = **United States of America**; (*Mil*) = **United States Army**
usable ['ju:zəbl] *adj* utilizable
USAF *n abbr* = **United States Air Force**
usage ['ju:zɪdʒ] *n* (*Ling*) uso; (*utilization*) utilización *f*
USB key *n* llave *f* USB, memoria *f* USB
USCG *n abbr* = **United States Coast Guard**
USDA *n abbr* = **United States Department of Agriculture**
USDAW ['ʌzdɔ:] *n abbr* (*Brit: = Union of Shop, Distributive, and Allied Workers*) *sindicato de empleados de comercio*
USDI *n abbr* = **United States Department of the Interior**
use *n* [ju:s] uso, empleo; (*usefulness*) utilidad *f* ■ *vt* [ju:z] usar, emplear; **in** ~ en uso; **out of** ~ en desuso; **to be of** ~ servir; **ready for** ~ listo (para usar); **to make ~ of sth** aprovecharse *or* servirse de algo; **it's no** ~ (*pointless*) es inútil; (*not useful*) no sirve; **what's this used for?** ¿para qué sirve esto?; **to be used to** estar acostumbrado a (*SP*), acostumbrar; **to get used to** acostumbrarse a; **she used to do it** (ella) solía *or* acostumbraba hacerlo
▸ **use up** *vt* agotar
used [ju:zd] *adj* (*car*) usado
useful ['ju:sful] *adj* útil; **to come in** ~ ser útil
usefulness ['ju:sfəlnɪs] *n* utilidad *f*
useless ['ju:slɪs] *adj* inútil; (*unusable: object*) inservible
uselessly ['ju:slɪslɪ] *adv* inútilmente, en vano
uselessness ['ju:slɪsnɪs] *n* inutilidad *f*
user ['ju:zə^r] *n* usuario(-a); (*of petrol, gas etc*) consumidor(a) *m(f)*
user-friendly ['ju:zə'frɛndlɪ] *adj* (*Comput*) fácil de utilizar
USES *n abbr* = **United States Employment Service**
usher ['ʌʃə^r] *n* (*at wedding*) ujier *m*; (*in cinema etc*) acomodador *m* ■ *vt*: **to ~ sb in** (*into room*) hacer pasar a algn; **it ushered in a new era** (*fig*) inició una nueva era
usherette [ʌʃə'rɛt] *n* (*in cinema*) acomodadora

USIA *n abbr* = **United States Information Agency**
USM *n abbr* = **United States Mail; United States Mint**
USN *n abbr* = **United States Navy**
USP *n abbr* = **unique selling point** *or* **proposition**
USPHS *n abbr* = **United States Public Health Service**
USPO *n abbr* = **United States Post Office**
USS *abbr* = **United States Ship (***or* **Steamer)**
USSR *n abbr* (*History*): **the (former) ~** la (antigua) U.R.S.S.; *see* **Union of Soviet Socialist Republics**
usu. *abbr* = **usually**
usual ['juːʒuəl] *adj* normal, corriente; **as ~** como de costumbre, como siempre
usually ['juːʒuəlɪ] *adv* normalmente
usurer ['juːʒərəʳ] *n* usurero
usurp [juː'zəːp] *vt* usurpar
usury ['juːʒərɪ] *n* usura
UT *abbr* (*US*) = **Utah**
utensil [juː'tɛnsl] *n* utensilio; **kitchen utensils** batería de cocina
uterus ['juːtərəs] *n* útero
utilitarian [juːtɪlɪ'tɛərɪən] *adj* utilitario
utility [juː'tɪlɪtɪ] *n* utilidad *f*
utility room *n* trascocina
utilization [juːtɪlaɪ'zeɪʃən] *n* utilización *f*
utilize ['juːtɪlaɪz] *vt* utilizar
utmost ['ʌtməust] *adj* mayor ■ *n*: **to do one's ~** hacer todo lo posible; **it is of the ~ importance that ...** es de la mayor importancia que ...
utter ['ʌtəʳ] *adj* total, completo ■ *vt* pronunciar, proferir
utterance ['ʌtərns] *n* palabras *fpl*, declaración *f*
utterly ['ʌtəlɪ] *adv* completamente, totalmente
U-turn ['juː'təːn] *n* cambio de sentido; (*fig*) giro de 180 grados
Uzbekistan [ʌzbɛkɪ'stɑːn] *n* Uzbekistán *m*

Vv

V, v [viː] *n* (*letter*) V, v *f*; **V for Victor** V de Valencia
v. *abbr* (= *verse*) vers.º; (= *vide: see*) V, vid., vide; (= *versus*) vs.; = **volt**
VA, Va. *abbr* (*US*) = **Virginia**
vac [væk] *n abbr* (*Brit col*) = **vacation**
vacancy ['veɪkənsɪ] *n* (*Brit: job*) vacante *f*; (*room*) cuarto libro; **have you any vacancies?** ¿tiene *or* hay alguna habitación *or* algún cuarto libre?
vacant ['veɪkənt] *adj* desocupado, libre; (*expression*) distraído
vacant lot *n* (*US*) solar *m*
vacate [və'keɪt] *vt* (*house*) desocupar; (*job*) dejar (vacante)
vacation [və'keɪʃən] *n* vacaciones *fpl*; **on ~** de vacaciones; **to take a ~** (*esp US*) tomarse unas vacaciones
vacation course *n* curso de vacaciones
vacationer [və'keɪʃənəʳ], **vacationist** [və'keɪʃənɪst] *n* (*US*) turista *m/f*
vaccinate ['væksɪneɪt] *vt* vacunar
vaccination [væksɪ'neɪʃən] *n* vacunación *f*
vaccine ['væksiːn] *n* vacuna
vacuum ['vækjum] *n* vacío
vacuum bottle *n* (*US*) = **vacuum flask**
vacuum cleaner *n* aspiradora
vacuum flask *n* (*Brit*) termo
vacuum-packed [vækjum'pækt] *adj* envasado al vacío
vagabond ['vægəbɔnd] *n* vagabundo(-a)
vagary ['veɪgərɪ] *n* capricho
vagina [və'dʒaɪnə] *n* vagina
vagrancy ['veɪgrənsɪ] *n* vagabundeo
vagrant ['veɪgrənt] *n* vagabundo(-a)
vague [veɪg] *adj* vago; (*blurred: memory*) borroso; (*uncertain*) incierto, impreciso; (*person*) distraído; **I haven't the vaguest idea** no tengo la más remota idea
vaguely ['veɪglɪ] *adv* vagamente
vagueness ['veɪgnɪs] *n* vaguedad *f*; imprecisión *f*; (*absent-mindedness*) despiste *m*
vain [veɪn] *adj* (*conceited*) presumido; (*useless*) vano, inútil; **in ~** en vano
vainly ['veɪnlɪ] *adv* (*to no effect*) en vano; (*conceitedly*) vanidosamente
valance ['væləns] *n* (*for bed*) *volante alrededor de la colcha o sábana que cuelga hasta el suelo*
valedictory [vælɪ'dɪktərɪ] *adj* de despedida
valentine ['væləntaɪn] *n* (*also*: **valentine card**) tarjeta del Día de los Enamorados
valet ['væleɪ] *n* ayuda *m* de cámara
valet service *n* (*for clothes*) planchado
valiant ['væljənt] *adj* valiente
valiantly ['væljəntlɪ] *adv* valientemente, con valor
valid ['vælɪd] *adj* válido; (*ticket*) valedero; (*law*) vigente
validate ['vælɪdeɪt] *vt* (*contract, document*) convalidar; (*argument, claim*) dar validez a
validity [və'lɪdɪtɪ] *n* validez *f*; vigencia
valise [və'liːz] *n* maletín *m*
valley ['vælɪ] *n* valle *m*
valour, valor (*US*) ['væləʳ] *n* valor *m*, valentía
valuable ['væljuəbl] *adj* (*jewel*) de valor; (*time*) valioso; **valuables** *npl* objetos *mpl* de valor
valuation [vælju'eɪʃən] *n* tasación *f*, valuación *f*
value ['væljuː] *n* valor *m*; (*importance*) importancia ■ *vt* (*fix price of*) tasar, valorar; (*esteem*) apreciar; **values** *npl* (*moral*) valores *mpl* morales; **to lose (in) ~** (*currency*) bajar; (*property*) desvalorizarse; **to gain (in) ~** (*currency*) subir; (*property*) revalorizarse; **you get good ~ (for money) in that shop** la relación calidad-precio es muy buena en esa tienda; **to be of great ~ to sb** ser de gran valor para algn; **it is valued at £8** está valorado en ocho libras
value added tax *n* (*Brit*) impuesto sobre el valor añadido *or* agregado (*LAm*)
valued ['væljuːd] *adj* (*appreciated*) apreciado
valueless ['væljuːlɪs] *adj* sin valor
valuer ['væljuːəʳ] *n* tasador(a) *m(f)*
valve [vælv] *n* (*Anat, Tech*) válvula
vampire ['væmpaɪəʳ] *n* vampiro

van [væn] *n* (*Aut*) furgoneta, camioneta (*LAm*); (*Brit Rail*) furgón *m* (de equipajes)
V and A *n abbr* (*Brit*) = **Victoria and Albert Museum**
vandal ['vændl] *n* vándalo(-a)
vandalism ['vændəlɪzəm] *n* vandalismo
vandalize ['vændəlaɪz] *vt* dañar, destruir, destrozar
vanguard ['vængɑːd] *n* vanguardia
vanilla [və'nɪlə] *n* vainilla
vanish ['vænɪʃ] *vi* desaparecer, esfumarse
vanity ['vænɪtɪ] *n* vanidad *f*
vanity case *n* neceser *m*
vantage point ['vɑːntɪdʒ-] *n* posición *f* ventajosa
vaporize ['veɪpəraɪz] *vt* vaporizar ■ *vi* vaporizarse
vapour, vapor (*US*) ['veɪpə^r] *n* vapor *m*; (*on breath, window*) vaho
vapour trail, vapor trail (*US*) *n* (*Aviat*) estela
variable ['vɛərɪəbl] *adj* variable ■ *n* variable *f*
variance ['vɛərɪəns] *n*: **to be at ~ (with)** estar en desacuerdo (con), no cuadrar (con)
variant ['vɛərɪənt] *n* variante *f*
variation [vɛərɪ'eɪʃən] *n* variación *f*
varicose ['værɪkəus] *adj*: **~ veins** varices *fpl*
varied ['vɛərɪd] *adj* variado
variety [və'raɪətɪ] *n* variedad *f*, diversidad *f*; (*quantity*) surtido; **for a ~ of reasons** por varias *or* diversas razones
variety show *n* espectáculo de variedades
various ['vɛərɪəs] *adj* varios(-as), diversos(-as); **at ~ times** (*different*) en distintos momentos; (*several*) varias veces
varnish ['vɑːnɪʃ] *n* (*gen*) barniz *m*; (*also*: **nail varnish**) esmalte *m* ■ *vt* (*gen*) barnizar; (*nails*) pintar (con esmalte)
vary ['vɛərɪ] *vt* variar; (*change*) cambiar ■ *vi* variar; (*disagree*) discrepar; **to ~ with** *or* **according to** variar según *or* de acuerdo con
varying ['vɛərɪɪŋ] *adj* diversos(-as)
vase [vɑːz] *n* florero
vasectomy [və'sɛktəmɪ] *n* vasectomía
Vaseline® ['væsɪliːn] *n* vaselina®
vast [vɑːst] *adj* enorme; (*success*) abrumador(a), arrollador(a)
vastly ['vɑːstlɪ] *adv* enormemente
vastness ['vɑːstnɪs] *n* inmensidad *f*
VAT [væt] *n abbr* (*Brit*: = *value added tax*) IVA *m*
vat [væt] *n* tina, tinaja
Vatican ['vætɪkən] *n*: **the ~** el Vaticano
vatman ['vætmæn] *n* (*Brit col*) inspector *m or* recaudador *m* del IVA; **"how to avoid the ~"** "cómo evitar pagar el IVA"
vaudeville ['vəudəvɪl] *n* (*US*) vodevil *m*
vault [vɔːlt] *n* (*of roof*) bóveda; (*tomb*) tumba; (*in bank*) cámara acorazada ■ *vt* (*also*: **vault over**) saltar (por encima de)
vaunted ['vɔːntɪd] *adj*: **much ~** cacareado
VC *n abbr* = **vice-chairman**; **vice-chancellor**; (*Brit*: = *Victoria Cross*) *condecoración militar*
VCR *n abbr* = **video cassette recorder**
VD *n abbr see* **venereal disease**
VDU *n abbr see* **visual display unit**
veal [viːl] *n* ternera
veer [vɪə^r] *vi* (*ship*) virar
veg. [vɛdʒ] *n abbr* (*Brit col*) = **vegetable(s)**
vegan ['viːgən] *n* vegetariano(-a) estricto(-a)
vegeburger, veggieburger ['vɛdʒɪbəːgə^r] *n* hamburguesa vegetal
vegetable ['vɛdʒtəbl] *n* (*Bot*) vegetal *m*; (*edible plant*) legumbre *f*, hortaliza ■ *adj* vegetal; **vegetables** *npl* (*cooked*) verduras *fpl*
vegetable garden *n* huerta, huerto
vegetarian [vɛdʒɪ'tɛərɪən] *adj, n* vegetariano(-a) *m(f)*
vegetate ['vɛdʒɪteɪt] *vi* vegetar
vegetation [vɛdʒɪ'teɪʃən] *n* vegetación *f*
vegetative ['vɛdʒɪtətɪv] *adj* vegetativo; (*Bot*) vegetal
vehemence ['viːɪməns] *n* vehemencia; violencia
vehement ['viːɪmənt] *adj* vehemente, apasionado; (*dislike, hatred*) violento
vehicle ['viːɪkl] *n* vehículo; (*fig*) vehículo, medio
vehicular [vɪ'hɪkjulə^r] *adj*: **~ traffic** circulación *f* rodada
veil [veɪl] *n* velo ■ *vt* velar; **under a ~ of secrecy** (*fig*) en el mayor secreto
veiled [veɪld] *adj* (*also fig*) disimulado, velado
vein [veɪn] *n* vena; (*of ore etc*) veta
Velcro® ['vɛlkrəu] *n* velcro® *m*
vellum ['vɛləm] *n* (*writing paper*) papel *m* vitela
velocity [vɪ'lɔsɪtɪ] *n* velocidad *f*
velour [və'luə^r] *n* terciopelo
velvet ['vɛlvɪt] *n* terciopelo ■ *adj* aterciopelado
vendetta [vɛn'dɛtə] *n* vendetta
vending machine ['vɛndɪŋ-] *n* máquina expendedora, expendedor *m*
vendor ['vɛndə^r] *n* vendedor(a) *m(f)*; **street ~** vendedor(a) *m(f)* callejero(-a)
veneer [və'nɪə^r] *n* chapa, enchapado; (*fig*) barniz *m*
venereal [vɪ'nɪərɪəl] *adj*: **~ disease (VD)** enfermedad *f* venérea
Venetian blind [vɪ'niːʃən-] *n* persiana
Venezuela [vɛnɛ'zweɪlə] *n* Venezuela
Venezuelan [vɛnɛ'zweɪlən] *adj, n* venezolano(-a) *m(f)*
vengeance ['vɛndʒəns] *n* venganza; **with a ~** (*fig*) con creces

vengeful ['vɛndʒful] *adj* vengativo
Venice ['vɛnɪs] *n* Venecia
venison ['vɛnɪsn] *n* carne *f* de venado
venom ['vɛnəm] *n* veneno
venomous ['vɛnəməs] *adj* venenoso
venomously ['vɛnəməslɪ] *adv* con odio
vent [vɛnt] *n* (*opening*) abertura; (*air-hole*) respiradero; (*in wall*) rejilla (de ventilación) ■ *vt* (*fig: feelings*) desahogar
ventilate ['vɛntɪleɪt] *vt* ventilar
ventilation [vɛntɪ'leɪʃən] *n* ventilación *f*
ventilation shaft *n* pozo de ventilación
ventilator ['vɛntɪleɪtəʳ] *n* ventilador *m*
ventriloquist [vɛn'trɪləkwɪst] *n* ventrílocuo(-a)
venture ['vɛntʃəʳ] *n* empresa ■ *vt* arriesgar; (*opinion*) ofrecer ■ *vi* arriesgarse, lanzarse; **a business ~** una empresa comercial; **to ~ to do sth** aventurarse a hacer algo
venture capital *n* capital *m* arriesgado
venue ['vɛnju:] *n* (*meeting place*) lugar *m* de reunión; (*for concert*) local *m*
Venus ['vi:nəs] *n* (*Astro*) Venus *m*
veracity [və'ræsɪtɪ] *n* veracidad *f*
veranda, verandah [və'rændə] *n* terraza; (*with glass*) galería
verb [və:b] *n* verbo
verbal ['və:bl] *adj* verbal
verbally ['və:bəlɪ] *adv* verbalmente, de palabra
verbatim [və:'beɪtɪm] *adj, adv* al pie de la letra, palabra por palabra
verbose [və:'bəus] *adj* prolijo
verdict ['və:dɪkt] *n* veredicto, fallo; (*fig: opinion*) opinión *f*, juicio; **~ of guilty/not guilty** veredicto de culpabilidad/inocencia
verge [və:dʒ] *n* (*Brit*) borde *m*; **to be on the ~ of doing sth** estar a punto de hacer algo
▸ **verge on** *vt fus* rayar en
verger ['və:dʒəʳ] *n* sacristán *m*
verification [vɛrɪfɪ'keɪʃən] *n* comprobación *f*, verificación *f*
verify ['vɛrɪfaɪ] *vt* comprobar, verificar; (*prove the truth of*) confirmar
veritable ['vɛrɪtəbl] *adj* verdadero, auténtico
vermin ['və:mɪn] *npl* (*animals*) bichos *mpl*; (*insects*) sabandijas *fpl*; (*fig*) sabandijas *fpl*
vermouth ['və:məθ] *n* vermut *m*
vernacular [və'nækjuləʳ] *n* lengua vernácula
versatile ['və:sətaɪl] *adj* (*person*) polifacético; (*machine, tool etc*) versátil
versatility [və:sə'tɪlɪtɪ] *n* versatilidad *f*
verse [və:s] *n* versos *mpl*, poesía; (*stanza*) estrofa; (*in bible*) versículo; **in ~** en verso
versed [və:st] *adj*: **(well-)~ in** versado en
version ['və:ʃən] *n* versión *f*
versus ['və:səs] *prep* contra
vertebra (*pl* **vertebrae**) ['və:tɪbrə, bri:] *n* vértebra
vertebrate ['və:tɪbrɪt] *n* vertebrado
vertical ['və:tɪkl] *adj* vertical
vertically ['və:tɪkəlɪ] *adv* verticalmente
vertigo ['və:tɪgəu] *n* vértigo; **to suffer from ~** tener vértigo
verve [və:v] *n* brío
very ['vɛrɪ] *adv* muy ■ *adj*: **the ~ book which** el mismo libro que; **the ~ last** el último (de todos); **at the ~ least** al menos; **~ much** muchísimo; **~ well/little** muy bien/poco; **~ high frequency** (*Radio*) frecuencia muy alta; **it's ~ cold** hace mucho frío; **the ~ thought (of it) alarms me** con sólo pensarlo me entra miedo
vespers ['vɛspəz] *npl* vísperas *fpl*
vessel ['vɛsl] *n* (*Anat*) vaso; (*ship*) barco; (*container*) vasija
vest [vɛst] *n* (*Brit*) camiseta; (*US: waistcoat*) chaleco
vested interests ['vɛstɪd-] *npl* (*Comm*) intereses *mpl* creados
vestibule ['vɛstɪbju:l] *n* vestíbulo
vestige ['vɛstɪdʒ] *n* vestigio, rastro
vestry ['vɛstrɪ] *n* sacristía
Vesuvius [vɪ'su:vɪəs] *n* Vesubio
vet [vɛt] *n abbr* = **veterinary surgeon**; (*US: col*) = **veteran** ■ *vt* revisar; **to ~ sb for a job** someter a investigación a algn para un trabajo
veteran ['vɛtərn] *n* veterano(-a) ■ *adj*: **she is a ~ campaigner for ...** es una veterana de la campaña de ...
veteran car *n* coche *m* antiguo
veterinarian [vɛtrɪ'nɛərɪən] *n* (*US*) = **veterinary surgeon**
veterinary ['vɛtrɪnərɪ] *adj* veterinario
veterinary surgeon *n* (*Brit*) veterinario(-a)
veto ['vi:təu] *n* (*pl* **vetoes**) veto ■ *vt* prohibir, vedar; **to put a ~ on** vetar
vetting ['vɛtɪŋ] *n*: **positive ~** *investigación gubernamental de los futuros altos cargos de la Administración*
vex [vɛks] *vt* (*irritate*) fastidiar; (*make impatient*) impacientar
vexed [vɛkst] *adj* (*question*) controvertido
vexing ['vɛksɪŋ] *adj* molesto, engorroso
VFD *n abbr* (*US*) = **voluntary fire department**
VG *n abbr* (*Brit Scol etc: = very good*) S (*= sobresaliente*)
VHF *abbr* (*= very high frequency*) VHF *f*
VI *abbr* (*US*) = **Virgin Islands**
via ['vaɪə] *prep* por, por vía de
viability [vaɪə'bɪlɪtɪ] *n* viabilidad *f*
viable ['vaɪəbl] *adj* viable
viaduct ['vaɪədʌkt] *n* viaducto

vial ['vaɪəl] *n* frasco pequeño
vibes [vaɪbz] *npl (col)*: **I got good/bad ~** me dio buen/mal rollo
vibrant ['vaɪbrənt] *adj (lively, bright)* vivo; *(full of emotion: voice)* vibrante; *(colour)* fuerte
vibraphone ['vaɪbrəfəun] *n* vibráfono
vibrate [vaɪ'breɪt] *vi* vibrar
vibration [vaɪ'breɪʃən] *n* vibración *f*
vibrator [vaɪ'breɪtəʳ] *n* vibrador *m*
vicar ['vɪkəʳ] *n* párroco
vicarage ['vɪkərɪdʒ] *n* parroquia
vicarious [vɪ'kɛərɪəs] *adj* indirecto; *(responsibility)* delegado
vice [vaɪs] *n (evil)* vicio; *(Tech)* torno de banco
vice- [vaɪs] *pref* vice...
vice-chairman ['vaɪs'tʃɛəmən] *n* vicepresidente *m*
vice-chancellor [vaɪs'tʃɑ:nsələʳ] *n (Brit Univ)* rector(a) *m(f)*
vice-president [vaɪs'prɛzɪdənt] *n* vicepresidente(-a) *m(f)*
viceroy ['vaɪsrɔɪ] *n* virrey *m*
vice versa ['vaɪsɪ'və:sə] *adv* viceversa
vicinity [vɪ'sɪnɪtɪ] *n (area)* vecindad *f*; *(nearness)* proximidad *f*; **in the ~ (of)** cercano (a)
vicious ['vɪʃəs] *adj (remark)* malicioso; *(blow)* brutal; **a ~ circle** un círculo vicioso
viciousness ['vɪʃəsnɪs] *n* brutalidad *f*
vicissitudes [vɪ'sɪsɪtju:dz] *npl* vicisitudes *fpl*, peripecias *fpl*
victim ['vɪktɪm] *n* víctima; **to be the ~ of** ser víctima de
victimization [vɪktɪmaɪ'zeɪʃən] *n* persecución *f*; *(of striker etc)* represalias *fpl*
victimize ['vɪktɪmaɪz] *vt (strikers etc)* tomar represalias contra
victor ['vɪktəʳ] *n* vencedor(a) *m(f)*
Victorian [vɪk'tɔ:rɪən] *adj* victoriano
victorious [vɪk'tɔ:rɪəs] *adj* vencedor(a)
victory ['vɪktərɪ] *n* victoria; **to win a ~ over sb** obtener una victoria sobre algn
video ['vɪdɪəu] *cpd* de vídeo ■ *n* vídeo ■ *vt* grabar (en vídeo)
video call *n* llamada de vídeo
video camera *n* videocámara, cámara de vídeo
video cassette *n* videocassette *f*
video cassette recorder *n* = **video recorder**
videodisk ['vɪdɪəudɪsk] *n* videodisco
video game *n* videojuego
video nasty *n* vídeo de violencia y/o porno duro
videophone ['vɪdɪəufəun] *n* videoteléfono, videófono
video recorder *n* vídeo, videocassette *f*
video recording *n* videograbación *f*
video tape *n* cinta de vídeo
vie [vaɪ] *vi*: **to ~ with** competir con
Vienna [vɪ'ɛnə] *n* Viena
Viennese [vɪə'ni:z] *adj, n* vienés(-esa) *m(f)*
Vietnam, Viet Nam [vjɛt'næm] *n* Vietnam *m*
Vietnamese [vjɛtnə'mi:z] *adj* vietnamita ■ *n (pl inv)* vietnamita *m/f*; *(Ling)* vietnamita *m*
view [vju:] *n* vista; *(landscape)* paisaje *m*; *(opinion)* opinión *f*, criterio ■ *vt (look at)* mirar; *(examine)* examinar; **on ~** *(in museum etc)* expuesto; **in full ~ of sb** a la vista de algn; **to be within ~ (of sth)** estar a la vista (de algo); **an overall ~ of the situation** una visión de conjunto de la situación; **in ~ of the fact that** en vista de que; **to take** *or* **hold the ~ that ...** opinar *or* pensar que ...; **with a ~ to doing sth** con miras *or* vistas a hacer algo
viewdata ['vju:deɪtə] *n (Brit)* videodatos *mpl*
viewer ['vju:əʳ] *n (small projector)* visionadora; *(TV)* televidente *m/f*, telespectador(a) *m(f)*
viewfinder ['vju:faɪndəʳ] *n* visor *m* de imagen
viewpoint ['vju:pɔɪnt] *n* punto de vista
vigil ['vɪdʒɪl] *n* vigilia; **to keep ~** velar
vigilance ['vɪdʒɪləns] *n* vigilancia
vigilance committee *n (US)* comité *m* de autodefensa
vigilant ['vɪdʒɪlənt] *adj* vigilante
vigilante [vɪdʒɪ'læntɪ] *n vecino/a que se toma la justicia por su mano*
vigorous ['vɪgərəs] *adj* enérgico, vigoroso
vigorously ['vɪgərəslɪ] *adv* enérgicamente, vigorosamente
vigour, vigor *(US)* ['vɪgəʳ] *n* energía, vigor *m*
vile [vaɪl] *adj (action)* vil, infame; *(smell)* repugnante
vilify ['vɪlɪfaɪ] *vt* denigrar, vilipendiar
villa ['vɪlə] *n (country house)* casa de campo; *(suburban house)* chalet *m*
village ['vɪlɪdʒ] *n* aldea
villager ['vɪlɪdʒəʳ] *n* aldeano(-a)
villain ['vɪlən] *n (scoundrel)* malvado(-a); *(criminal)* maleante *m/f*; *see also* **pantomime**
VIN *n abbr (US)* = **vehicle identification number**
vinaigrette [vɪneɪ'grɛt] *n* vinagreta
vindicate ['vɪndɪkeɪt] *vt* vindicar, justificar
vindication [vɪndɪ'keɪʃən] *n*: **in ~ of** en justificación de
vindictive [vɪn'dɪktɪv] *adj* vengativo
vine [vaɪn] *n* vid *f*
vinegar ['vɪnɪgəʳ] *n* vinagre *m*
vine-growing ['vaɪngrəuɪŋ] *adj (region)* viticultor(a)
vineyard ['vɪnjɑ:d] *n* viña, viñedo
vintage ['vɪntɪdʒ] *n (year)* vendimia, cosecha; **the 1970 ~** la cosecha de 1970
vintage car *n* coche *m* antiguo *or* de época

vintage wine *n* vino añejo
vintage year *n*: **it's been a ~ for plays** ha sido un año destacado en lo que a teatro se refiere
vinyl ['vaɪnl] *n* vinilo
viola [vɪ'əulə] *n* (*Mus*) viola
violate ['vaɪəleɪt] *vt* violar
violation [vaɪə'leɪʃən] *n* violación *f*; **in ~ of sth** en violación de algo
violence ['vaɪələns] *n* violencia; **acts of ~** actos *mpl* de violencia
violent ['vaɪələnt] *adj* (*gen*) violento; (*pain*) intenso; **a ~ dislike of sb/sth** una profunda antipatía *or* manía a algn/algo
violently ['vaɪələntlɪ] *adv* (*severely: ill, angry*) muy
violet ['vaɪələt] *adj* violado, violeta ■ *n* (*plant*) violeta
violin [vaɪə'lɪn] *n* violín *m*
violinist [vaɪə'lɪnɪst] *n* violinista *m/f*
VIP *n abbr* (= *very important person*) VIP *m*
viper ['vaɪpəʳ] *n* víbora
viral ['vaɪərəl] *adj* vírico
virgin ['və:dʒɪn] *n* virgen *m/f* ■ *adj* virgen; **the Blessed V~** la Santísima Virgen
virginity [və:'dʒɪnɪtɪ] *n* virginidad *f*
Virgo ['və:gəu] *n* Virgo
virile ['vɪraɪl] *adj* viril
virility [vɪ'rɪlɪtɪ] *n* virilidad *f*
virtual ['və:tjuəl] *adj* (*also COMPUT, PHYS*) virtual
virtually ['və:tjuəlɪ] *adv* (*almost*) prácticamente, virtualmente; **it is ~ impossible** es prácticamente imposible
virtual reality *n* (*Comput*) realidad *f* virtual
virtue ['və:tju:] *n* virtud *f*; **by ~ of** en virtud de
virtuosity [və:tju'ɔsɪtɪ] *n* virtuosismo
virtuoso [və:tju'əusəu] *n* virtuoso
virtuous ['və:tjuəs] *adj* virtuoso
virulence ['vɪruləns] *n* virulencia
virulent ['vɪrulənt] *adj* virulento, violento
virus ['vaɪərəs] *n* virus *m inv*
visa ['vi:zə] *n* visado, visa (*LAm*)
vis-à-vis [vi:zə'vi:] *prep* con respecto a
viscount ['vaɪkaunt] *n* vizconde *m*
viscous ['vɪskəs] *adj* viscoso
vise [vaɪs] *n* (*US Tech*) = **vice**
visibility [vɪzɪ'bɪlɪtɪ] *n* visibilidad *f*
visible ['vɪzəbl] *adj* visible; **~ exports/imports** exportaciones *fpl*/importaciones *fpl* visibles
visibly ['vɪzɪblɪ] *adv* visiblemente
vision ['vɪʒən] *n* (*sight*) vista; (*foresight: in dream*) visión *f*
visionary ['vɪʒənrɪ] *n* visionario(-a)
visit ['vɪzɪt] *n* visita ■ *vt* (*person*) visitar, hacer una visita a; (*place*) ir a, (ir a) conocer; **to pay a ~ to** (*person*) visitar a; **on a private/official ~** en visita privada/oficial
visiting ['vɪzɪtɪŋ] *adj* (*speaker, professor*) invitado; (*team*) visitante
visiting card *n* tarjeta de visita
visiting hours *npl* (*in hospital etc*) horas *fpl* de visita
visitor *n* (*gen*) visitante *m/f*; (*to one's house*) visita; (*tourist*) turista *m/f*; (*tripper*) excursionista *m/f*; **to have visitors** (*at home*) tener visita
visitors' book *n* libro de visitas
visor ['vaɪzəʳ] *n* visera
VISTA ['vɪstə] *n abbr* (= *Volunteers In Service to America*) *programa de ayuda voluntaria a los necesitados*
vista ['vɪstə] *n* vista, panorama
visual ['vɪzjuəl] *adj* visual
visual aid *n* medio visual
visual arts *npl* artes *fpl* plásticas
visual display unit *n* unidad *f* de despliegue visual, monitor *m*
visualize ['vɪzjuəlaɪz] *vt* imaginarse; (*foresee*) prever
visually ['vɪzjuəlɪ] *adv*: **~ handicapped** con visión deficiente
vital ['vaɪtl] *adj* (*essential*) esencial, imprescindible; (*crucial*) crítico; (*person*) enérgico, vivo; (*of life*) vital; **of ~ importance (to sb/sth)** de suma importancia (para algn/algo)
vitality [vaɪ'tælɪtɪ] *n* energía, vitalidad *f*
vitally ['vaɪtəlɪ] *adv*: **~ important** de suma importancia
vital statistics *npl* (*of population*) estadísticas *fpl* demográficas; (*col: of woman*) medidas *fpl* (corporales)
vitamin ['vɪtəmɪn] *n* vitamina
vitamin pill *n* pastilla de vitaminas
vitreous ['vɪtrɪəs] *adj* (*china, enamel*) vítreo
vitriolic [vɪtrɪ'ɔlɪk] *adj* mordaz
viva ['vaɪvə] *n* (*also*: **viva voce**) examen *m* oral
vivacious [vɪ'veɪʃəs] *adj* vivaz, alegre
vivacity [vɪ'væsɪtɪ] *n* vivacidad *f*
vivid ['vɪvɪd] *adj* (*account*) gráfico; (*light*) intenso; (*imagination*) vivo
vividly ['vɪvɪdlɪ] *adv* (*describe*) gráficamente; (*remember*) como si fuera hoy
vivisection [vɪvɪ'sɛkʃən] *n* vivisección *f*
vixen ['vɪksn] *n* (*Zool*) zorra, raposa; (*pej: woman*) arpía, bruja
viz *abbr* (= *vide licet: namely*) v.gr.
VLF *abbr* = **very low frequency**
V-neck ['vi:nɛk] *n* cuello de pico
VOA *n abbr* (= *Voice of America*) Voz *f* de América
vocabulary [vəu'kæbjulərɪ] *n* vocabulario
vocal ['vəukl] *adj* vocal; (*articulate*) elocuente

vocal cords *npl* cuerdas *fpl* vocales
vocalist ['vəukəlɪst] *n* cantante *m/f*
vocation [vəu'keɪʃən] *n* vocación *f*
vocational [vəu'keɪʃənl] *adj* vocacional; **~ guidance** orientación *f* profesional; **~ training** formación *f* profesional
vociferous [və'sɪfərəs] *adj* vociferante
vociferously [və'sɪfərəslɪ] *adv* a gritos
vodka ['vɔdkə] *n* vodka *m*
vogue [vəug] *n* boga, moda; **to be in ~, be the ~** estar de moda *or* en boga
voice [vɔɪs] *n* voz *f* ■ *vt* (*opinion*) expresar; **in a loud/soft ~** en voz alta/baja; **to give ~ to** expresar
voice mail *n* (*Tel*) fonobuzón *m*
voice-over ['vɔɪsəuvə[r]] *n* voz *f* en off
void [vɔɪd] *n* vacío; (*hole*) hueco ■ *adj* (*invalid*) nulo, inválido; (*empty*): **~ of** carente *or* desprovisto de
voile [vɔɪl] *n* gasa
vol. *abbr* (= *volume*) t
volatile ['vɔlətaɪl] *adj* volátil; (*Comput: memory*) no permanente
volcanic [vɔl'kænɪk] *adj* volcánico
volcano (*pl* **volcanoes**) [vɔl'keɪnəu] *n* volcán *m*
volition [və'lɪʃən] *n*: **of one's own ~** por su propia voluntad
volley ['vɔlɪ] *n* (*of gunfire*) descarga; (*of stones etc*) lluvia; (*Tennis etc*) volea
volleyball *n* voleibol *m*, balonvolea *m*
volt [vəult] *n* voltio
voltage ['vəultɪdʒ] *n* voltaje *m*; **high/low ~** alto/bajo voltaje, alta/baja tensión
volte-face ['vɔlt'fɑ:s] *n* viraje *m*
voluble ['vɔljubl] *adj* locuaz, hablador(a)
volume ['vɔlju:m] *n* (*of tank*) volumen *m*; (*book*) tomo; **~ one/two** (*of book*) tomo primero/segundo; **volumes** *npl* (*great quantities*) cantidad *fsg*; **his expression spoke volumes** su expresión (lo) decía todo
volume control *n* (*Radio, TV*) (botón *m* del) volumen *m*
volume discount *n* (*Comm*) descuento por volumen de compras
voluminous [və'lu:mɪnəs] *adj* (*large*) voluminoso; (*prolific*) prolífico
voluntarily ['vɔləntrɪlɪ] *adv* libremente, voluntariamente
voluntary ['vɔləntərɪ] *adj* voluntario, espontáneo
voluntary liquidation *n* (*Comm*) liquidación *f* voluntaria
voluntary redundancy *n* (*Brit*) despido voluntario
volunteer [vɔlən'tɪə[r]] *n* voluntario(-a) ■ *vi* ofrecerse (de voluntario); **to ~ to do** ofrecerse a hacer
voluptuous [və'lʌptjuəs] *adj* voluptuoso
vomit ['vɔmɪt] *n* vómito ■ *vt, vi* vomitar
voracious [və'reɪʃəs] *adj* voraz; (*reader*) ávido
vote [vəut] *n* voto; (*votes cast*) votación *f*; (*right to vote*) derecho a votar; (*franchise*) sufragio ■ *vt* (*chairman*) elegir ■ *vi* votar, ir a votar; **~ of thanks** voto de gracias; **to put sth to the ~, to take a ~ on sth** someter algo a votación; **~ for** *or* **in favour of/against** voto a favor de/en contra de; **to ~ to do sth** votar por hacer algo; **he was voted secretary** fue elegido secretario por votación; **to pass a ~ of confidence/no confidence** aprobar un voto de confianza/de censura
voter ['vəutə[r]] *n* votante *m/f*
voting ['vəutɪŋ] *n* votación *f*
voting paper *n* (*Brit*) papeleta de votación
voting right *n* derecho a voto
vouch [vautʃ]: **to ~ for** *vt fus* garantizar, responder de
voucher ['vautʃə[r]] *n* (*for meal, petrol*) vale *m*; **luncheon/travel ~** vale *m* de comida/de viaje
vow [vau] *n* voto ■ *vi* hacer voto; **to take** *or* **make a ~ to do sth** jurar hacer algo, comprometerse a hacer algo
vowel ['vauəl] *n* vocal *f*
voyage ['vɔɪɪdʒ] *n* (*journey*) viaje *m*; (*crossing*) travesía
voyeur [vwɑ:'jə:[r]] *n* voyeur *m/f*, mirón(-ona) *m(f)*
VP *n abbr* (= *vice-president*) V.P.
vs *abbr* (= *versus*) vs
VSO *n abbr* (*Brit*: = *Voluntary Service Overseas*) *organización que envía jóvenes voluntarios a trabajar y enseñar en los países del Tercer Mundo*
VT, Vt. *abbr* (*US*) = **Vermont**
vulgar ['vʌlgə[r]] *adj* (*rude*) ordinario, grosero; (*in bad taste*) de mal gusto
vulgarity [vʌl'gærɪtɪ] *n* grosería; mal gusto
vulnerability [vʌlnərə'bɪlɪtɪ] *n* vulnerabilidad *f*
vulnerable ['vʌlnərəbl] *adj* vulnerable
vulture ['vʌltʃə[r]] *n* buitre *m*, gallinazo (*LAm*)

Ww

W, w ['dʌblju:] *n* (*letter*) W, w *f*; **W for William** W de Washington
W *abbr* (= *west*) O; (*Elec*: = *watt*) v
WA *abbr* (*US*) = **Washington**
wad [wɔd] *n* (*of cotton wool, paper*) bolita; (*of banknotes etc*) fajo
wadding ['wɔdɪŋ] *n* relleno
waddle ['wɔdl] *vi* andar como un pato
wade [weɪd] *vi*: **to ~ through** caminar por el agua; (*fig: a book*) leer con dificultad
wading pool ['weɪdɪŋ-] *n* (*US*) piscina para niños
wafer ['weɪfəʳ] *n* (*biscuit*) barquillo; (*Rel*) oblea; (: *consecrated*) hostia; (*Comput*) oblea, microplaqueta
wafer-thin ['weɪfə'θɪn] *adj* finísimo
waffle ['wɔfl] *n* (*Culin*) gofre *m* ■ *vi* meter el rollo
waffle iron *n* molde *m* para hacer gofres
waft [wɔft] *vt* llevar por el aire ■ *vi* flotar
wag [wæg] *vt* menear, agitar ■ *vi* moverse, menearse; **the dog wagged its tail** el perro meneó la cola
wage [weɪdʒ] *n* (*also*: **wages**) sueldo, salario ■ *vt*: **to ~ war** hacer la guerra; **a day's ~** el sueldo de un día
wage claim *n* reivindicación *f* salarial
wage differential *n* diferencia salarial
wage earner *n* asalariado(-a)
wage freeze *n* congelación *f* de salarios
wage packet *n* sobre *m* de la paga
wager ['weɪdʒəʳ] *n* apuesta ■ *vt* apostar
waggle ['wægl] *vt* menear, mover
wagon, waggon ['wægən] *n* (*horse-drawn*) carro; (*Brit Rail*) vagón *m*
wail [weɪl] *n* gemido ■ *vi* gemir
waist [weɪst] *n* cintura, talle *m*
waistcoat ['weɪstkəut] *n* (*Brit*) chaleco
waistline ['weɪstlaɪn] *n* talle *m*
wait [weɪt] *n* espera; (*interval*) pausa ■ *vi* esperar; **to lie in ~ for** acechar a; **I can't ~ to** (*fig*) estoy deseando; **to ~ for** esperar (a); **to keep sb waiting** hacer esperar a algn; **~ a moment!** ¡un momento!, ¡un momentito!; **"repairs while you ~"** "reparaciones en el acto"
▸ **wait behind** *vi* quedarse
▸ **wait on** *vt fus* servir a
▸ **wait up** *vi* esperar levantado
waiter ['weɪtəʳ] *n* camarero
waiting ['weɪtɪŋ] *n*: **"no ~"** (*Brit Aut*) "prohibido estacionarse"
waiting list *n* lista de espera
waiting room *n* sala de espera
waitress ['weɪtrɪs] *n* camarera
waive [weɪv] *vt* suspender
waiver ['weɪvəʳ] *n* renuncia
wake [weɪk] (*pt* **woke** *or* **waked**, *pp* **woken** *or* **waked**) *vt* (*also*: **wake up**) despertar ■ *vi* (*also*: **wake up**) despertarse ■ *n* (*for dead person*) velatorio; (*Naut*) estela; **to ~ up to sth** (*fig*) darse cuenta de algo; **in the ~ of** tras, después de; **to follow in sb's ~** (*fig*) seguir las huellas de algn
waken ['weɪkn] *vt, vi* = **wake**
Wales [weɪlz] *n* País *m* de Gales
walk [wɔ:k] *n* (*stroll*) paseo; (*hike*) excursión *f* a pie, caminata; (*gait*) paso, andar *m*; (*in park etc*) paseo ■ *vi* andar, caminar; (*for pleasure, exercise*) pasearse ■ *vt* (*distance*) recorrer a pie, andar; (*dog*) (sacar a) pasear; **to go for a ~** ir a dar un paseo; **10 minutes' ~ from here** a 10 minutos de aquí andando; **people from all walks of life** gente de todas las esferas; **to ~ in one's sleep** ser sonámbulo(-a); **I'll ~ you home** te acompañaré a casa
▸ **walk out** *vi* (*go out*) salir; (*as protest*) marcharse, salirse; (*strike*) declararse en huelga; **to ~ out on sb** abandonar a algn
walkabout ['wɔ:kəbaut] *n*: **to go (on a) ~** darse un baño de multitudes
walker ['wɔ:kəʳ] *n* (*person*) paseante *m/f*, caminante *m/f*
walkie-talkie ['wɔ:kɪ'tɔ:kɪ] *n* walkie-talkie *m*
walking ['wɔ:kɪŋ] *n* (el) andar; **it's within ~ distance** se puede ir andando *or* a pie

walking stick *n* bastón *m*
Walkman® ['wɔːkmən] *n* walkman® *m*
walk-on ['wɔːkɔn] *adj* (*Theat: part*) de comparsa
walkout ['wɔːkaut] *n* (*of workers*) huelga
walkover ['wɔːkəuvəʳ] *n* (*col*) pan *m* comido
walkway ['wɔːkweɪ] *n* paseo
wall [wɔːl] *n* pared *f*; (*exterior*) muro; (*city wall etc*) muralla; **to go to the ~** (*fig: firm etc*) quebrar, ir a la bancarrota
▸ **wall in** *vt* (*garden etc*) cercar con una tapia
walled [wɔːld] *adj* (*city*) amurallado; (*garden*) con tapia
wallet ['wɔlɪt] *n* cartera, billetera (*esp LAm*)
wallflower ['wɔːlflauəʳ] *n* alhelí *m*; **to be a ~** (*fig*) comer pavo
wall hanging *n* tapiz *m*
wallop ['wɔləp] *vt* (*col*) zurrar
wallow ['wɔləu] *vi* revolcarse; **to ~ in one's grief** sumirse en su pena
wallpaper ['wɔːlpeɪpəʳ] *n* (*for walls*) papel *m* pintado; (*Comput*) fondo de escritorio
wall-to-wall ['wɔːltə'wɔːl] *adj*: **~ carpeting** moqueta
wally ['wɔlɪ] *n* (*col*) majadero(-a)
walnut ['wɔːlnʌt] *n* nuez *f*; (*tree*) nogal *m*
walrus (*pl* **~** *or* **walruses**) ['wɔːlrəs] *n* morsa
waltz [wɔːlts] *n* vals *m* ■ *vi* bailar el vals
wan [wɔn] *adj* pálido
wand [wɔnd] *n* (*also*: **magic wand**) varita (mágica)
wander ['wɔndəʳ] *vi* (*person*) vagar; deambular; (*thoughts*) divagar; (*get lost*) extraviarse ■ *vt* recorrer, vagar por
wanderer ['wɔndərəʳ] *n* vagabundo(-a)
wandering ['wɔndərɪŋ] *adj* (*tribe*) nómada; (*minstrel, actor*) ambulante; (*path, river*) sinuoso; (*glance, mind*) distraído
wane [weɪn] *vi* menguar
wangle ['wæŋgl] (*Brit col*) *vt*: **to ~ sth** agenciarse *or* conseguir algo ■ *n* chanchullo
wanker ['wæŋkəʳ] *n* (*col!*) pajero(-a) (*!*); (*as insult*) mamón(-ona) (*!*) *m/f*
want [wɔnt] *vt* (*wish for*) querer, desear; (*need*) necesitar; (*lack*) carecer de ■ *n* (*poverty*) pobreza; **for ~ of** por falta de; **wants** *npl* (*needs*) necesidades *fpl*; **to ~ to do** querer hacer; **to ~ sb to do sth** querer que algn haga algo; **you're wanted on the phone** te llaman al teléfono; **to be in ~** estar necesitado; **"cook wanted"** "se necesita cocinero(-a)"
want ads *npl* (*US*) anuncios *mpl* por palabras
wanting ['wɔntɪŋ] *adj*: **to be ~ (in)** estar falto (de); **to be found ~** no estar a la altura de las circunstancias
wanton ['wɔntn] *adj* (*licentious*) lascivo
WAP [wæp] *n abbr* (*= wireless application protocol*) WAP *f*
WAP phone *n* teléfono WAP
war [wɔːʳ] *n* guerra; **to make ~** hacer la guerra; **the First/Second World W~** la primera/segunda guerra mundial
warble ['wɔːbl] *n* (*of bird*) trino, gorjeo ■ *vi* (*bird*) trinar
war cry *n* grito de guerra
ward [wɔːd] *n* (*in hospital*) sala; (*Pol*) distrito electoral; (*Law: child*) pupilo(-a)
▸ **ward off** *vt* desviar, parar; (*attack*) rechazar
warden ['wɔːdn] *n* (*Brit: of institution*) director(a) *m(f)*; (*of park, game reserve*) guardián(-ana) *m(f)*; (*Brit: also*: **traffic warden**) guardia *m/f*
warder ['wɔːdəʳ] *n* (*Brit*) guardián(-ana) *m(f)*, carcelero(-a) *m(f)*
wardrobe ['wɔːdrəub] *n* armario, guardarropa, ropero, clóset/closet *m* (*LAm*)
warehouse ['wɛəhaus] *n* almacén *m*, depósito
wares [wɛəz] *npl* mercancías *fpl*
warfare ['wɔːfɛəʳ] *n* guerra
war game *n* juego de estrategia militar
warhead ['wɔːhɛd] *n* cabeza armada; **nuclear warheads** cabezas *fpl* nucleares
warily ['wɛərɪlɪ] *adv* con cautela, cautelosamente
warlike ['wɔːlaɪk] *adj* guerrero
warm [wɔːm] *adj* caliente; (*person, greeting, heart*) afectuoso, cariñoso; (*supporter*) entusiasta; (*thanks, congratulations, apologies*) efusivo; (*clothes etc*) que abriga; (*welcome, day*) caluroso; **it's ~** hace calor; **I'm ~** tengo calor; **to keep sth ~** mantener algo caliente
▸ **warm up** *vi* (*room*) calentarse; (*person*) entrar en calor; (*athlete*) hacer ejercicios de calentamiento; (*discussion*) acalorarse ■ *vt* calentar
warm-blooded ['wɔːm'blʌdɪd] *adj* de sangre caliente
war memorial *n* monumento a los caídos
warm-hearted [wɔːm'hɑːtɪd] *adj* afectuoso
warmly ['wɔːmlɪ] *adv* afectuosamente
warmonger ['wɔːmʌŋgəʳ] *n* belicista *m/f*
warmongering ['wɔːmʌŋgrɪŋ] *n* belicismo
warmth [wɔːmθ] *n* calor *m*
warm-up ['wɔːmʌp] *n* (*Sport*) ejercicios *mpl* de calentamiento
warn [wɔːn] *vt* avisar, advertir; **to ~ sb not to do sth** *or* **against doing sth** aconsejar a algn que no haga algo
warning ['wɔːnɪŋ] *n* aviso, advertencia; **gale ~** (*Meteorology*) aviso de vendaval; **without (any) ~** sin aviso *or* avisar
warning light *n* luz *f* de advertencia

warning triangle *n* (*Aut*) triángulo señalizador
warp [wɔːp] *vi* (*wood*) combarse
warpath ['wɔːpɑːθ] *n*: **to be on the ~** (*fig*) estar en pie de guerra
warped [wɔːpt] *adj* (*wood*) alabeado; (*fig: character, sense of humour etc*) pervertido
warrant ['wɔrnt] *n* (*Law: to arrest*) orden *f* de detención; (*: to search*) mandamiento de registro ■ *vt* (*justify, merit*) merecer
warrant officer *n* (*Mil*) brigada *m*; (*Naut*) contramaestre *m*
warranty ['wɔrəntɪ] *n* garantía; **under ~** (*Comm*) bajo garantía
warren ['wɔrən] *n* (*of rabbits*) madriguera; (*fig*) laberinto
warring ['wɔːrɪŋ] *adj* (*interests etc*) opuesto; (*nations*) en guerra
warrior ['wɔrɪəʳ] *n* guerrero(-a)
Warsaw ['wɔːsɔː] *n* Varsovia
warship ['wɔːʃɪp] *n* buque *m or* barco de guerra
wart [wɔːt] *n* verruga
wartime ['wɔːtaɪm] *n*: **in ~** en tiempos de guerra, en la guerra
wary ['wɛərɪ] *adj* cauteloso; **to be ~ about** *or* **of doing sth** tener cuidado con hacer algo
was [wɔz] *pt of* **be**
wash [wɔʃ] *vt* lavar; (*sweep, carry: sea etc*) llevar ■ *vi* lavarse ■ *n* (*clothes etc*) lavado; (*bath*) baño; (*of ship*) estela; **he was washed overboard** fue arrastrado del barco por las olas; **to have a ~** lavarse
▸ **wash away** *vt* (*stain*) quitar lavando; (*river etc*) llevarse; (*fig*) limpiar
▸ **wash down** *vt* lavar
▸ **wash off** *vt* quitar lavando
▸ **wash up** *vi* (*Brit*) fregar los platos; (*US: have a wash*) lavarse
Wash. *abbr* (*US*) = **Washington**
washable ['wɔʃəbl] *adj* lavable
washbasin ['wɔʃbeɪsn], **washbowl** (*US*) ['wɔʃbəul] *n* lavabo
washcloth ['wɔʃklɔθ] *n* (*US*) manopla
washer ['wɔʃəʳ] *n* (*Tech*) arandela
washing ['wɔʃɪŋ] *n* (*dirty*) ropa sucia; (*clean*) colada
washing line *n* cuerda de (colgar) la ropa
washing machine *n* lavadora
washing powder *n* (*Brit*) detergente *m* (en polvo)
Washington ['wɔʃɪŋtən] *n* (*city, state*) Washington *m*
washing-up [wɔʃɪŋ'ʌp] *n* fregado; (*dishes*) platos *mpl* (para fregar); **to do the ~** fregar los platos
washing-up liquid *n* lavavajillas *m inv*
wash leather *n* gamuza
wash-out ['wɔʃaut] *n* (*col*) fracaso
washroom ['wɔʃrum] *n* servicios *mpl*
wasn't ['wɔznt] = **was not**
WASP, Wasp [wɔsp] *n abbr* (*US col: = White Anglo-Saxon Protestant*) *sobrenombre, en general peyorativo, que se da a los americanos de origen anglosajón, acomodados y de tendencia conservadora*
wasp [wɔsp] *n* avispa
waspish ['wɔspɪʃ] *adj* (*character*) irascible; (*comment*) mordaz, punzante
wastage ['weɪstɪdʒ] *n* desgaste *m*; (*loss*) pérdida; **natural ~** desgaste natural
waste [weɪst] *n* derroche *m*, despilfarro; (*misuse*) desgaste *m*; (*of time*) pérdida; (*food*) sobras *fpl*; (*rubbish*) basura, desperdicios *mpl* ■ *adj* (*material*) de desecho; (*left over*) sobrante; (*energy, heat*) desperdiciado; (*land, ground: in city*) sin construir; (*: in country*) baldío ■ *vt* (*squander*) malgastar, derrochar; (*time*) perder; (*opportunity*) desperdiciar; **wastes** *npl* (*area of land*) tierras *fpl* baldías; **to lay ~** devastar, arrasar; **it's a ~ of money** es tirar el dinero; **to go to ~** desperdiciarse
▸ **waste away** *vi* consumirse
wastebasket ['weɪstbɑːskɪt] *n* (*esp US*) = **wastepaper basket**
waste disposal, waste disposal unit *n* (*Brit*) triturador *m* de basura
wasteful ['weɪstful] *adj* derrochador(a); (*process*) antieconómico
wastefully ['weɪstfulɪ] *adv*: **to spend money ~** derrochar dinero
waste ground *n* (*Brit*) terreno baldío
wasteland ['weɪstlənd] *n* (*urban*) descampados *mpl*
wastepaper basket ['weɪstpeɪpə-] *n* papelera; (*Comput*) papelera de reciclaje
waste pipe *n* tubo de desagüe
waste products *npl* (*Industry*) residuos *mpl*
waster ['weɪstəʳ] *n* (*col*) gandul *m/f*
watch [wɔtʃ] *n* reloj *m*; (*vigil*) vigilia; (*vigilance*) vigilancia; (*Mil: guard*) centinela *m*; (*Naut: spell of duty*) guardia ■ *vt* (*look at*) mirar, observar; (*: match, programme*) ver; (*spy on, guard*) vigilar; (*be careful of*) cuidar, tener cuidado de ■ *vi* ver, mirar; (*keep guard*) montar guardia; **to keep a close ~ on sth/sb** vigilar algo/a algn de cerca; **~ how you drive/what you're doing** ten cuidado al conducir/con lo que haces
▸ **watch out** *vi* cuidarse, tener cuidado
watch band *n* (*US*) pulsera (de reloj)
watchdog ['wɔtʃdɔg] *n* perro guardián; (*fig*) organismo de control
watchful ['wɔtʃful] *adj* vigilante, sobre aviso
watchfully ['wɔtʃfulɪ] *adv*: **to stand ~** permanecer vigilante

watchmaker ['wɔtʃmeɪkəʳ] *n* relojero(-a)
watchman *n* guardián *m*; (*also:* **night watchman**) sereno, vigilante *m*; (*in factory*) vigilante *m* nocturno
watch stem *n* (*US*) cuerda
watch strap *n* pulsera (de reloj)
watchword ['wɔtʃwəːd] *n* consigna, contraseña
water ['wɔːtəʳ] *n* agua ■ *vt* (*plant*) regar ■ *vi* (*eyes*) llorar; **I'd like a drink of ~** quisiera un vaso de agua; **in British waters** en aguas británicas; **to pass ~** orinar; **his mouth watered** se le hizo la boca agua
▸ **water down** *vt* (*milk etc*) aguar
water closet *n* wáter *m*
watercolour, watercolor (*US*) ['wɔːtəkʌləʳ] *n* acuarela
water-cooled ['wɔːtəkuːld] *adj* refrigerado (por agua)
watercress ['wɔːtəkrɛs] *n* berro
waterfall ['wɔːtəfɔːl] *n* cascada, salto de agua
waterfront ['wɔːtəfrʌnt] *n* (*seafront*) parte *f* que da al mar; (*at docks*) muelles *mpl*
water heater *n* calentador *m* de agua
water hole *n* abrevadero
watering can ['wɔːtərɪŋ-] *n* regadera
water level *n* nivel *m* del agua
water lily *n* nenúfar *m*
waterline ['wɔːtəlaɪn] *n* (*Naut*) línea de flotación
waterlogged ['wɔːtəlɔgd] *adj* (*boat*) anegado; (*ground*) inundado
water main *n* cañería del agua
watermark ['wɔːtəmɑːk] *n* (*on paper*) filigrana
watermelon ['wɔːtəmɛlən] *n* sandía
water polo *n* waterpolo, polo acuático
waterproof ['wɔːtəpruːf] *adj* impermeable
water-repellent ['wɔːtərɪ'pɛlənt] *adj* hidrófugo
watershed ['wɔːtəʃɛd] *n* (*Geo*) cuenca; (*fig*) momento crítico
water-skiing ['wɔːtəskiːɪŋ] *n* esquí *m* acuático
water softener *n* ablandador *m* de agua
water tank *n* depósito de agua
watertight ['wɔːtətaɪt] *adj* hermético
water vapour, water vapor (*US*) *n* vapor *m* de agua
waterway ['wɔːtəweɪ] *n* vía fluvial *or* navegable
waterworks ['wɔːtəwəːks] *npl* central *fsg* depuradora
watery ['wɔːtərɪ] *adj* (*colour*) desvaído; (*coffee*) aguado; (*eyes*) lloroso
watt [wɔt] *n* vatio
wattage ['wɔtɪdʒ] *n* potencia en vatios
wattle ['wɔtl] *n* zarzo
wave [weɪv] *n* ola; (*of hand*) señal *f* con la mano; (*Radio*) onda; (*in hair*) onda; (*fig: of enthusiasm, strikes*) oleada ■ *vi* agitar la mano; (*flag*) ondear ■ *vt* (*handkerchief, gun*) agitar; **short/medium/long ~** (*Radio*) onda corta/media/larga; **the new ~** (*Cine, Mus*) la nueva ola; **to ~ goodbye to sb** decir adiós a algn con la mano; **he waved us over to his table** nos hizo señas (con la mano) para que nos acercásemos a su mesa
▸ **wave aside, wave away** *vt* (*person*): **to ~ sb aside** apartar a algn con la mano; (*fig: suggestion, objection*) rechazar; (*doubts*) desechar
waveband ['weɪvbænd] *n* banda de ondas
wavelength ['weɪvlɛŋθ] *n* longitud *f* de onda
waver ['weɪvəʳ] *vi* oscilar; (*confidence*) disminuir; (*faith*) flaquear
wavy ['weɪvɪ] *adj* ondulado
wax [wæks] *n* cera ■ *vt* encerar ■ *vi* (*moon*) crecer
waxen ['wæksn] *adj* (*fig: pale*) blanco como la cera
waxworks ['wækswəːks] *npl* museo *sg* de cera
way [weɪ] *n* camino; (*distance*) trayecto, recorrido; (*direction*) dirección *f*, sentido; (*manner*) modo, manera; (*habit*) costumbre *f*; **which ~? — this ~** ¿por dónde? *or* ¿en qué dirección? — por aquí; **on the ~** (*en route*) en (el) camino; (*expected*) en camino; **to be on one's ~** estar en camino; **you pass it on your ~ home** está de camino a tu casa; **to be in the ~** bloquear el camino; (*fig*) estorbar; **to keep out of sb's ~** esquivar a algn; **to make ~ (for sb/sth)** dejar paso (a algn/algo); (*fig*) abrir camino (a algn/algo); **to go out of one's ~ to do sth** desvivirse por hacer algo; **to lose one's ~** perderse, extraviarse; **to be the wrong ~ round** estar del *or* al revés; **in a ~** en cierto modo *or* sentido; **by the ~** a propósito; **by ~ of** (*via*) pasando por; (*as a sort of*) como, a modo de; **"~ in"** (*Brit*) "entrada"; **"~ out"** (*Brit*) "salida"; **the ~ back** el camino de vuelta; **the village is rather out of the ~** el pueblo está un poco apartado *or* retirado; **it's a long ~ away** está muy lejos; **to get one's own ~** salirse con la suya; **"give ~"** (*Brit Aut*) "ceda el paso"; **no ~!** (*col*) ¡ni pensarlo!; **put it the right ~ up** ponlo boca arriba; **he's in a bad ~** está grave; **to be under ~** (*work, project*) estar en marcha
waybill ['weɪbɪl] *n* (*Comm*) hoja de ruta, carta de porte
waylay [weɪ'leɪ] *vt* (*irreg: like* **lay**) atacar
wayside ['weɪsaɪd] *n* borde *m* del camino; **to fall by the ~** (*fig*) fracasar

way station *n* (*US Rail*) apeadero
wayward ['weɪwəd] *adj* díscolo, caprichoso
WC ['dʌblju'si:] *n abbr* (*Brit*: = *water closet*) wáter *m*
WCC *n abbr* = **World Council of Churches**
we [wi:] *pl pron* nosotros(-as); **we understand** (nosotros) entendemos; **here we are** aquí estamos
weak [wi:k] *adj* débil, flojo; (*tea, coffee*) flojo, aguado; **to grow ~(er)** debilitarse
weaken ['wi:kən] *vi* debilitarse; (*give way*) ceder ■ *vt* debilitar
weak-kneed [wi:k'ni:d] *adj* (*fig*) sin voluntad *or* carácter
weakling ['wi:klɪŋ] *n* debilucho(-a)
weakly ['wi:klɪ] *adj* enfermizo, débil ■ *adv* débilmente
weakness ['wi:knɪs] *n* debilidad *f*; (*fault*) punto débil
wealth [wɛlθ] *n* (*money, resources*) riqueza; (*of details*) abundancia
wealth tax *n* impuesto sobre el patrimonio
wealthy ['wɛlθɪ] *adj* rico
wean [wi:n] *vt* destetar
weapon ['wɛpən] *n* arma; **weapons of mass destruction** armas de destrucción masiva
wear [wɛəʳ] (*pt* **wore**, *pp* **worn**) *n* (*use*) uso; (*deterioration through use*) desgaste *m*; (*clothing*): **sports/babywear** ropa de deportes/de niños ■ *vt* (*clothes, beard*) llevar; (*shoes*) calzar; (*look, smile*) tener; (*damage: through use*) gastar, usar ■ *vi* (*last*) durar; (*rub through etc*) desgastarse; **evening ~** (*man's*) traje *m* de etiqueta; (*woman's*) traje *m* de noche; **to ~ a hole in sth** hacer un agujero en algo
▸ **wear away** *vt* gastar ■ *vi* desgastarse
▸ **wear down** *vt* gastar; (*strength*) agotar
▸ **wear off** *vi* (*pain, excitement etc*) pasar, desaparecer
▸ **wear out** *vt* desgastar; (*person, strength*) agotar
wearable ['wɛərəbl] *adj* que se puede llevar, ponible
wear and tear *n* desgaste *m*
wearer ['wɛərəʳ] *n*: **the ~ of this jacket** el/la que lleva puesta esta chaqueta
wearily ['wɪərɪlɪ] *adv* con cansancio
weariness ['wɪərɪnɪs] *n* cansancio; abatimiento
wearisome ['wɪərɪsəm] *adj* (*tiring*) cansado, pesado; (*boring*) aburrido
weary ['wɪərɪ] *adj* (*tired*) cansado; (*dispirited*) abatido ■ *vt* cansar ■ *vi*: **to ~ of** cansarse de, aburrirse de
weasel ['wi:zl] *n* (*Zool*) comadreja
weather ['wɛðəʳ] *n* tiempo ■ *vt* (*storm, crisis*) hacer frente a; **under the ~** (*fig: ill*) mal, pachucho; **what's the ~ like?** ¿qué tiempo hace?, ¿cómo hace?
weather-beaten ['wɛðəbi:tn] *adj* curtido
weathercock ['wɛðəkɔk] *n* veleta
weather forecast *n* boletín *m* meteorológico
weatherman ['wɛðəmæn] *n* hombre *m* del tiempo
weatherproof ['wɛðəpru:f] *adj* (*garment*) impermeable
weather report *n* parte *m* meteorológico
weather vane *n* = **weathercock**
weave (*pt* **wove**, *pp* **woven**) [wi:v, wəuv, 'wəuvn] *vt* (*cloth*) tejer; (*fig*) entretejer ■ *vi* (*fig*) (*pt, pp* **weaved**) (*move in and out*) zigzaguear
weaver ['wi:vəʳ] *n* tejedor(a) *m(f)*
weaving ['wi:vɪŋ] *n* tejeduría
web [wɛb] *n* (*of spider*) telaraña; (*on foot*) membrana; (*Comput: network*) red *f*; **the (World Wide) W~** el *or* la Web
web address *n* dirección *f* de página web
webbed [wɛbd] *adj* (*foot*) palmeado
webbing ['wɛbɪŋ] *n* (*on chair*) cinchas *fpl*
webcam ['wɛbkæm] *n* webcam *f*
weblog ['wɛblɔg] *n* weblog *m*
web page *n* página web
website ['wɛbsaɪt] *n* sitio web
wed [wɛd] *vt* (*pt, pp* **wedded**) casar ■ *n*: **the newly-weds** los recién casados
Wed. *abbr* (= *Wednesday*) miérc
we'd [wi:d] = **we had; we would**
wedded ['wɛdɪd] *pt, pp of* **wed**
wedding ['wɛdɪŋ] *n* boda, casamiento
wedding anniversary *n* aniversario de boda; **silver/golden ~** bodas *fpl* de plata/de oro
wedding day *n* día *m* de la boda
wedding dress *n* traje *m* de novia
wedding present *n* regalo de boda
wedding ring *n* alianza
wedge [wɛdʒ] *n* (*of wood etc*) cuña; (*of cake*) trozo ■ *vt* acuñar; (*push*) apretar
wedge-heeled ['wɛdʒ'hi:ld] *adj* con suela de cuña
wedlock ['wɛdlɔk] *n* matrimonio
Wednesday ['wɛdnzdɪ] *n* miércoles *m inv*; *see also* **Tuesday**
wee [wi:] *adj* (*Scottish*) pequeñito
weed [wi:d] *n* mala hierba, maleza ■ *vt* escardar, desherbar
▸ **weed out** *vt* eliminar
weedkiller ['wi:dkɪləʳ] *n* herbicida *m*
weedy ['wi:dɪ] *adj* (*person*) debilucho
week [wi:k] *n* semana; **a ~ today** de hoy en ocho días; **Tuesday ~, a ~ on Tuesday** del martes en una semana; **once/twice a ~** una vez/dos veces a la semana; **this ~** esta semana; **in two weeks' time** dentro de dos semanas; **every other ~** cada dos semanas

weekday ['wi:kdeɪ] *n* día *m* laborable; **on weekdays** entre semana, en días laborables
weekend [wi:k'ɛnd] *n* fin *m* de semana
weekend case *n* neceser *m*
weekly ['wi:klɪ] *adv* semanalmente, cada semana ■ *adj* semanal ■ *n* semanario; ~ **newspaper** semanario
weep (*pt, pp* **wept**) [wi:p, wɛpt] *vi, vt* llorar; (*Med: wound etc*) supurar
weeping willow ['wi:pɪŋ-] *n* sauce *m* llorón
weepy ['wi:pɪ] *n* (*col: film*) película lacrimógena; (*: story*) historia lacrimógena
weft [wɛft] *n* (*Textiles*) trama
weigh [weɪ] *vt, vi* pesar; **to ~ anchor** levar anclas; **to ~ the pros and cons** pesar los pros y los contras
▸ **weigh down** *vt* sobrecargar; (*fig: with worry*) agobiar
▸ **weigh out** *vt* (*goods*) pesar
▸ **weigh up** *vt* pesar
weighbridge ['weɪbrɪdʒ] *n* báscula para camiones
weighing machine ['weɪɪŋ-] *n* báscula, peso
weight [weɪt] *n* peso; (*on scale*) pesa; **to lose/put on ~** adelgazar/engordar; **weights and measures** pesas y medidas
weighting ['weɪtɪŋ] *n* (*allowance*): **(London) ~** *dietas (por residir en Londres)*
weightlessness ['weɪtlɪsnɪs] *n* ingravidez *f*
weight lifter *n* levantador(a) *m(f)* de pesas
weight limit *n* límite *m* de peso
weight training *n* musculación *f* (con pesas)
weighty ['weɪtɪ] *adj* pesado
weir [wɪəʳ] *n* presa
weird [wɪəd] *adj* raro, extraño
weirdo ['wɪədəu] *n* (*col*) tio(-a) raro(-a)
welcome ['wɛlkəm] *adj* bienvenido ■ *n* bienvenida ■ *vt* dar la bienvenida a; (*be glad of*) alegrarse de; **to make sb ~** recibir *or* acoger bien a algn; **thank you — you're ~** gracias — de nada; **you're ~ to try** puede intentar cuando quiera; **we ~ this step** celebramos esta medida
weld [wɛld] *n* soldadura ■ *vt* soldar
welding ['wɛldɪŋ] *n* soldadura
welfare ['wɛlfɛəʳ] *n* bienestar *m*; (*social aid*) asistencia social; **W~** (*US*) subsidio de paro; **to look after sb's ~** cuidar del bienestar de algn
welfare state *n* estado del bienestar
welfare work *n* asistencia social
well [wɛl] *n* pozo ■ *adv* bien ■ *adj*: **to be ~** estar bien (de salud) ■ *excl* ¡vaya!, ¡bueno!; **as ~** (*in addition*) además, también; **as ~ as** además de; **you might as ~ tell me** más vale que me lo digas; **it would be as ~ to ask** más valdría preguntar; **~ done!** ¡bien hecho!; **get ~ soon!** ¡que te mejores pronto!; **to do ~** (*business*) ir bien; **I did ~ in my exams** me han salido bien los exámenes; **they are doing ~ now** les va bien ahora; **to think ~ of sb** pensar bien de algn; **I don't feel ~** no me encuentro *or* siento bien; **~, as I was saying ...** bueno, como decía ...
▸ **well up** *vi* brotar
we'll [wi:l] = **we will; we shall**
well-behaved ['wɛlbɪ'heɪvd] *adj*: **to be ~** portarse bien
well-being ['wɛl'bi:ɪŋ] *n* bienestar *m*
well-bred ['wɛl'brɛd] *adj* bien educado
well-built ['wɛl'bɪlt] *adj* (*person*) fornido
well-chosen ['wɛl'tʃəuzn] *adj* (*remarks, words*) acertado
well-deserved ['wɛldɪ'zə:vd] *adj* merecido
well-developed ['wɛldɪ'vɛləpt] *adj* (*arm, muscle etc*) bien desarrollado; (*sense*) agudo, fino
well-disposed ['wɛldɪs'pəuzd] *adj*: **~ to(wards)** bien dispuesto a
well-dressed ['wɛl'drɛst] *adj* bien vestido
well-earned ['wɛl'ə:nd] *adj* (*rest*) merecido
well-groomed ['wɛl'gru:md] *adj* de apariencia cuidada
well-heeled ['wɛl'hi:ld] *adj* (*col: wealthy*) rico
well-informed ['wɛlɪn'fɔ:md] *adj* (*having knowledge of sth*) enterado, al corriente
Wellington ['wɛlɪŋtən] *n* Wellington *m*
wellingtons ['wɛlɪŋtənz] *npl* (*also:* **Wellington boots**) botas *fpl* de goma
well-kept ['wɛl'kɛpt] *adj* (*secret*) bien guardado; (*hair, hands, house, grounds*) bien cuidado
well-known ['wɛl'nəun] *adj* (*person*) conocido
well-mannered ['wɛl'mænəd] *adj* educado
well-meaning ['wɛl'mi:nɪŋ] *adj* bienintencionado
well-nigh ['wɛl'naɪ] *adv*: **~ impossible** casi imposible
well-off ['wɛl'ɔf] *adj* acomodado
well-read ['wɛl'rɛd] *adj* culto
well-spoken ['wɛl'spəukən] *adj* bienhablado
well-stocked ['wɛl'stɔkt] *adj* (*shop, larder*) bien surtido
well-timed ['wɛl'taɪmd] *adj* oportuno
well-to-do ['wɛltə'du:] *adj* acomodado
well-wisher ['wɛlwɪʃəʳ] *n* admirador(a) *m(f)*
well-woman clinic ['wɛlwumən-] *n* *centro de prevención médica para mujeres*
Welsh [wɛlʃ] *adj* galés(-esa) ■ *n* (*Ling*) galés *m*; **the Welsh** *npl* los galeses; **the ~ Assembly** el Parlamento galés
Welshman ['wɛlʃmən] *n* galés *m*
Welsh rarebit [-'rɛəbɪt] *n* pan *m* con queso tostado

Welshwoman ['wɛlʃwumən] *n* galesa
welter ['wɛltəʳ] *n* mescolanza, revoltijo
went [wɛnt] *pt of* **go**
wept [wɛpt] *pt, pp of* **weep**
were [wəːʳ] *pt of* **be**
we're [wɪəʳ] = **we are**
weren't [wəːnt] = **were not**
werewolf (*pl* **werewolves**) ['wɪəwulf, -wulvz] *n* hombre *m* lobo
west [wɛst] *n* oeste *m* ■ *adj* occidental, del oeste ■ *adv* al *or* hacia el oeste; **the W~** Occidente *m*
westbound ['wɛstbaund] *adj* (*traffic, carriageway*) con rumbo al oeste
West Country *n*: **the ~** el suroeste de Inglaterra
westerly ['wɛstəlɪ] *adj* (*wind*) del oeste
western ['wɛstən] *adj* occidental ■ *n* (*Cine*) película del oeste
westerner ['wɛstənəʳ] *n* (*Pol*) occidental *m/f*
westernized ['wɛstənaɪzd] *adj* occidentalizado
West German (*formerly*) *adj* de Alemania Occidental ■ *n* alemán(-ana) *m(f)* (de Alemania Occidental)
West Germany *n* (*formerly*) Alemania Occidental
West Indian *adj, n* antillano(-a) *m(f)*
West Indies [-'ɪndɪz] *npl*: **the ~** las Antillas
Westminster ['wɛstmɪnstəʳ] *n el parlamento británico*, Westminster *m*
westward ['wɛstwəd], **westwards** ['wɛstwədz] *adv* hacia el oeste
wet [wɛt] *adj* (*damp*) húmedo; (*wet through*) mojado; (*rainy*) lluvioso ■ *vt*: **to ~ one's pants** *or* **o.s.** mearse; **to get ~** mojarse; **"~ paint"** "recién pintado"
wet blanket *n*: **to be a ~** (*fig*) ser un/una aguafiestas
wetness ['wɛtnɪs] *n* humedad *f*
wet rot *n* putrefacción *f* por humedad
wet suit *n* traje *m* de buzo
we've [wiːv] = **we have**
whack [wæk] *vt* dar un buen golpe a
whale [weɪl] *n* (*Zool*) ballena
whaler ['weɪləʳ] *n* (*ship*) ballenero
whaling ['weɪlɪŋ] *n* pesca de ballenas
wharf (*pl* **wharves**) [wɔːf, wɔːvz] *n* muelle *m*

KEYWORD

what [wɔt] *adj* **1** (*in direct/indirect questions*) qué; **what size is he?** ¿qué talla usa?; **what colour/shape is it?** ¿de qué color/forma es?; **what books do you need?** ¿qué libros necesitas?
2 (*in exclamations*): **what a mess!** ¡qué desastre!; **what a fool I am!** ¡qué tonto soy!
■ *pron* **1** (*interrogative*) qué; **what are you doing?** ¿qué haces *or* estás haciendo?; **what is happening?** ¿qué pasa *or* está pasando?; **what is it called?** ¿cómo se llama?; **what about me?** ¿y yo qué?; **what about doing ...?** ¿qué tal si hacemos ...?; **what is his address?** ¿cuáles son sus señas?; **what will it cost?** ¿cuánto costará?
2 (*relative*) lo que; **I saw what you did/was on the table** vi lo que hiciste/había en la mesa; **what I want is a cup of tea** lo que quiero es una taza de té; **I don't know what to do** no sé qué hacer; **tell me what you're thinking about** dime en qué estás pensando
3 (*reported questions*): **she asked me what I wanted** me preguntó qué quería
■ *excl* (*disbelieving*) ¡cómo!; **what, no coffee!** ¡que no hay café!

whatever [wɔt'ɛvəʳ] *adj*: **~ book you choose** cualquier libro que elijas ■ *pron*: **do ~ is necessary** haga lo que sea necesario; **no reason ~** ninguna razón en absoluto; **nothing ~** nada en absoluto; **~ it costs** cueste lo que cueste
wheat [wiːt] *n* trigo
wheatgerm ['wiːtdʒəːm] *n* germen *m* de trigo
wheatmeal ['wiːtmiːl] *n* harina de trigo
wheedle ['wiːdl] *vt*: **to ~ sb into doing sth** engatusar a algn para que haga algo; **to ~ sth out of sb** sonsacar algo a algn
wheel [wiːl] *n* rueda; (*Aut*: *also*: **steering wheel**) volante *m*; (*Naut*) timón *m* ■ *vt* (*pram etc*) empujar ■ *vi* (*also*: **wheel round**) dar la vuelta, girar; **four-~ drive** tracción *f* en las cuatro ruedas; **front-/rear-~ drive** tracción *f* delantera/trasera
wheelbarrow ['wiːlbærəu] *n* carretilla
wheelbase ['wiːlbeɪs] *n* batalla
wheelchair ['wiːltʃɛəʳ] *n* silla de ruedas
wheel clamp *n* (*Aut*) cepo
wheeler-dealer ['wiːlə'diːləʳ] *n* chanchullero(-a)
wheelie-bin ['wiːlɪbɪn] *n* (*Brit*) contenedor *m* de basura
wheeling ['wiːlɪŋ] *n*: **~ and dealing** (*col*) chanchullos *mpl*
wheeze [wiːz] *vi* resollar
wheezy ['wiːzɪ] *adj* silbante

KEYWORD

when [wɛn] *adv* cuando; **when did it happen?** ¿cuándo ocurrió?; **I know when it happened** sé cuándo ocurrió

■ *conj* **1** (*at, during, after the time that*) cuando; **be careful when you cross the road** ten cuidado al cruzar la calle; **that was when I needed you** entonces era cuando te necesitaba; **I'll buy you a car when you're 18** te compraré un coche cuando cumplas 18 años **2** (*on, at which*): **on the day when I met him** el día en qué le conocí **3** (*whereas*) cuando; **you said I was wrong when in fact I was right** dijiste que no tenía razón, cuando en realidad sí la tenía

whenever [wɛn'ɛvəʳ] *conj* cuando; (*every time*) cada vez que; **I go ~ I can** voy siempre *or* todas las veces que puedo
where [wɛəʳ] *adv* dónde ■ *conj* donde; **this is ~** aquí es donde; **~ possible** donde sea posible; **~ are you from?** ¿de dónde es usted?
whereabouts ['wɛərəbauts] *adv* dónde ■ *n*: **nobody knows his ~** nadie conoce su paradero
whereas [wɛər'æz] *conj* mientras
whereby [wɛə'baɪ] *adv* mediante el/la cual *etc*
whereupon [wɛərə'pɔn] *conj* con lo cual, después de lo cual
wherever [wɛər'ɛvəʳ] *adv* dondequiera que; (*interrogative*) dónde; **sit ~ you like** siéntese donde quiera
wherewithal ['wɛəwɪðɔːl] *n* recursos *mpl*; **the ~ (to do sth)** los medios económicos (para hacer algo)
whet [wɛt] *vt* estimular; (*appetite*) abrir
whether ['wɛðəʳ] *conj* si; **I don't know ~ to accept or not** no sé si aceptar o no; **~ you go or not** vayas o no vayas
whey [weɪ] *n* suero

KEYWORD

which [wɪtʃ] *adj* **1** (*interrogative: direct, indirect*) qué; **which picture(s) do you want?** ¿qué cuadro(s) quieres?; **which one?** ¿cuál?; **which one of you?** ¿cuál de vosotros?; **tell me which one you want** dime cuál (es el que) quieres
2: **in which case** en cuyo caso; **we got there at eight pm, by which time the cinema was full** llegamos allí a las ocho, cuando el cine estaba lleno
■ *pron* (*interrogative*) cual; **I don't mind which** el(-la) que sea; **which do you want?** ¿cuál quieres?
3 (*relative: replacing noun*) que; (*: replacing clause*) lo que; (*: after preposition*) (el(-la)) que, el(-la) cual; **the apple which you ate/which is on the table** la manzana que comiste/que está en la mesa; **the chair on which you are sitting** la silla en la que estás sentado; **he didn't believe it, which upset me** no se lo creyó, lo cual *or* lo que me disgustó; **after which** después de lo cual

whichever [wɪtʃ'ɛvəʳ] *adj*: **take ~ book you prefer** coja el libro que prefiera; **~ book you take** cualquier libro que coja
whiff [wɪf] *n* bocanada; **to catch a ~ of sth** oler algo
while [waɪl] *n* rato, momento ■ *conj* durante; (*whereas*) mientras; (*although*) aunque ■ *vt*: **to ~ away the time** pasar el rato; **for a ~** durante algún tiempo; **in a ~** dentro de poco; **all the ~** todo el tiempo; **we'll make it worth your ~** te compensaremos generosamente
whilst [waɪlst] *conj* = **while**
whim [wɪm] *n* capricho
whimper ['wɪmpəʳ] *n* (*weeping*) lloriqueo; (*moan*) quejido ■ *vi* lloriquear; quejarse
whimsical ['wɪmzɪkl] *adj* (*person*) caprichoso
whine [waɪn] *n* (*of pain*) gemido; (*of engine*) zumbido ■ *vi* gemir; zumbar
whip [wɪp] *n* látigo; (*Brit: Pol*) *diputado encargado de la disciplina del partido en el parlamento* ■ *vt* azotar; (*snatch*) arrebatar; (*US Culin*) batir
▸ **whip up** *vt* (*cream etc*) batir (rápidamente); (*col: meal*) preparar rápidamente; (*: stir up: support, feeling*) avivar; *ver nota*

WHIP

En el Parlamento británico la disciplina de partido (en concreto de voto y de asistencia a la Cámara de los Comunes) está a cargo de un grupo de parlamentarios llamados *whips*, encabezados por el "Chief Whip". Por lo general todos ellos tienen también altos cargos en la Administración del Estado si pertenecen al partido en el poder.

whiplash ['wɪplæʃ] *n* (*Med: also:* **whiplash injury**) latigazo
whipped cream [wɪpt-] *n* nata montada
whipping boy ['wɪpɪŋ-] *n* (*fig*) cabeza de turco
whip-round ['wɪpraund] *n* (*Brit*) colecta
whirl [wəːl] *n* remolino ■ *vt* hacer girar, dar vueltas a ■ *vi* (*dancers*) girar, dar vueltas; (*leaves, dust, water etc*) arremolinarse
whirlpool ['wəːlpuːl] *n* remolino
whirlwind ['wəːlwɪnd] *n* torbellino
whirr [wəːʳ] *vi* zumbar
whisk [wɪsk] *n* (*Brit Culin*) batidor *m* ■ *vt* (*Brit Culin*) batir; **to ~ sb away** *or* **off** llevarse volando a algn

whiskers [wɪskəz] *npl* (*of animal*) bigotes *mpl*; (*of man*) patillas *fpl*
whisky, whiskey (*US, Ireland*) ['wɪskɪ] *n* whisky *m*
whisper ['wɪspəʳ] *n* cuchicheo; (*rumour*) rumor *m*; (*fig*) susurro, murmullo ■ *vi* cuchichear, hablar bajo; (*fig*) susurrar ■ *vt* decir en voz muy baja; **to ~ sth to sb** decirle algo al oído a algn
whispering ['wɪspərɪŋ] *n* cuchicheo
whist [wɪst] *n* (*Brit*) whist *m*
whistle ['wɪsl] *n* (*sound*) silbido; (*object*) silbato ■ *vi* silbar; **to ~ a tune** silbar una melodía
whistle-stop ['wɪslstɔp] *adj*: **~ tour** (*US Pol*) gira electoral rápida; (*fig*) recorrido rápido
Whit [wɪt] *n* Pentecostés *m*
white [waɪt] *adj* blanco; (*pale*) pálido ■ *n* blanco; (*of egg*) clara; **to turn** *or* **go ~** (*person*) palidecer, ponerse blanco; (*hair*) encanecer; **the whites** (*washing*) la ropa blanca; **tennis whites** ropa *f* de tenis
whitebait ['waɪtbeɪt] *n* chanquetes *mpl*
whiteboard ['waɪtbɔːd] *n* pizarra blanca; **interactive ~** pizarra interactiva
white coffee *n* (*Brit*) café *m* con leche
white-collar worker ['waɪtkɔlə-] *n* oficinista *m/f*
white elephant *n* (*fig*) maula
white goods *npl* (*appliances*) electrodomésticos *mpl* de línea blanca; (*linen etc*) ropa blanca
white-hot [waɪt'hɔt] *adj* (*metal*) candente, calentado al (rojo) blanco
white lie *n* mentirijilla
whiteness ['waɪtnɪs] *n* blancura
white noise *n* sonido blanco
whiteout ['waɪtaut] *n* resplandor *m* sin sombras; (*fig*) masa confusa
white paper *n* (*Pol*) libro blanco
whitewash ['waɪtwɔʃ] *n* (*paint*) cal *f*, jalbegue *m* ■ *vt* encalar, blanquear; (*fig*) encubrir
whiting ['waɪtɪŋ] *n* (*pl inv: fish*) pescadilla
Whit Monday *n* lunes *m* de Pentecostés
Whitsun ['wɪtsn] *n* (*Brit*) Pentecostés *m*
whittle ['wɪtl] *vt*: **to ~ away**: **whittle down** ir reduciendo
whizz [wɪz] *vi*: **to ~ past** *or* **by** pasar a toda velocidad
whizz kid *n* (*col*) prodigio(-a)
WHO *n abbr* (= *World Health Organization*) OMS *f*

KEYWORD

who [huː] *pron* **1** (*interrogative*) quién; **who is it?, who's there?** ¿quién es?; **who are you looking for?** ¿a quién buscas?; **I told her who I was** le dije quién era yo
2 (*relative*) que; **the man/woman who spoke to me** el hombre/la mujer que habló conmigo; **those who can swim** los que saben *or* sepan nadar

whodunit, whodunnit [huː'dʌnɪt] *n* (*col*) novela policíaca
whoever [huː'ɛvəʳ] *pron*: **~ finds it** cualquiera *or* quienquiera que lo encuentre; **ask ~ you like** pregunta a quien quieras; **~ he marries** se case con quien se case
whole [həul] *adj* (*complete*) todo, entero; (*not broken*) intacto ■ *n* (*total*) total *m*; (*sum*) conjunto; **~ villages were destroyed** pueblos enteros fueron destruídos; **the ~ of the town** toda la ciudad, la ciudad entera; **on the ~, as a ~** en general
wholehearted [həul'hɑːtɪd] *adj* (*support, approval*) total; (*sympathy*) todo
wholeheartedly [həul'hɑːtɪdlɪ] *adv* con entusiasmo
wholemeal ['həulmiːl] *adj* (*Brit: flour, bread*) integral
wholesale ['həulseɪl] *n* venta al por mayor ■ *adj* al por mayor; (*destruction*) sistemático
wholesaler ['həulseɪləʳ] *n* mayorista *m/f*
wholesome ['həulsəm] *adj* sano
wholewheat ['həulwiːt] *adj* = **wholemeal**
wholly ['həulɪ] *adv* totalmente, enteramente

KEYWORD

whom [huːm] *pron* **1** (*interrogative*): **whom did you see?** ¿a quién viste?; **to whom did you give it?** ¿a quién se lo diste?; **tell me from whom you received it** dígame de quién lo recibiste
2 (*relative*) que; **to whom** a quien(es); **of whom** de quien(es), del/de la que; **the man whom I saw** el hombre qui vi; **the man to whom I wrote** el hombre a quien escribí; **the lady about whom I was talking** la señora de (la) que hablaba; **the lady with whom I was talking** la señora con quien *or* (la) que hablaba

whooping cough ['huːpɪŋ-] *n* tos *f* ferina
whoops [wuːps] *excl* (*also*: **whoops-a-daisy!**) ¡huy!
whoosh [wuʃ] *n*: **it came out with a ~** (*sauce etc*) salió todo de repente; (*air*) salió con mucho ruido
whopper ['wɔpəʳ] *n* (*col: lie*) embuste *m*; (*: large thing*): **a ~** uno(-a) enorme
whopping ['wɔpɪŋ] *adj* (*col*) enorme
whore [hɔːʳ] *n* (*col: pej*) puta

KEYWORD

whose [hu:z] *adj* **1** (*possessive: interrogative*) de quién; **whose book is this?, whose is this book?** ¿de quién es este libro?; **whose pencil have you taken?** ¿de quién es el lápiz que has cogido?; **whose daughter are you?** ¿de quién eres hija?
2 (*possessive: relative*) cuyo(-a) *m(f)*, cuyos(-as) *m(f)pl*; **the man whose son they rescued** el hombre cuyo hijo rescataron; **the girl whose sister he was speaking to** la chica con cuya hermana estaba hablando; **those whose passports I have** aquellas personas cuyos pasaportes tengo; **the woman whose car was stolen** la mujer a quien le robaron el coche
■ *pron* de quién; **whose is this?** ¿de quién es esto?; **I know whose it is** sé de quién es

KEYWORD

why [waɪ] *adv* por qué; **why not?** ¿por qué no?; **why not do it now?** ¿por qué no lo haces (*or* hacemos ahora?
■ *conj*: **I wonder why he said that** me pregunto por qué dijo eso; **that's not why I'm here** no es por eso (por lo) que estoy aquí; **the reason why** la razón por la que
■ *excl* (*expressing surprise, shock, annoyance*) ¡hombre!, ¡vaya!; (*explaining*): **why, it's you!** ¡hombre, eres tú!; **why, that's impossible** ¡pero si eso es imposible!

whyever [waɪ'ɛvəʳ] *adv* por qué
WI *n abbr* (*Brit: = Women's Institute*) *asociación de amas de casa* ■ *abbr* (*Geo*) = **West Indies**; (*US*) = **Wisconsin**
wick [wɪk] *n* mecha
wicked ['wɪkɪd] *adj* malvado, cruel
wickedness ['wɪkɪdnɪs] *n* maldad *f*, crueldad *f*
wicker ['wɪkəʳ] *n* mimbre *m*
wickerwork ['wɪkəwə:k] *n* artículos *mpl* de mimbre
wicket ['wɪkɪt] *n* (*Cricket*) palos *mpl*
wicket keeper *n* guardameta *m*
wide [waɪd] *adj* ancho; (*area, knowledge*) vasto, grande; (*choice*) grande ■ *adv*: **to open ~** abrir de par en par; **to shoot ~** errar el tiro; **it is three metres ~** tiene tres metros de ancho
wide-angle lens ['waɪdæŋgl-] *n* (objetivo) gran angular *m*
wide-awake [waɪdə'weɪk] *adj* bien despierto
wide-eyed [waɪd'aɪd] *adj* con los ojos muy abiertos; (*fig*) ingenuo
widely ['waɪdlɪ] *adv* (*differing*) muy; **it is ~ believed that …** existe la creencia generalizada de que …; **to be ~ read** (*author*) ser muy leído; (*reader*) haber leído mucho
widen ['waɪdn] *vt* ensanchar
wideness ['waɪdnɪs] *n* anchura; amplitud *f*
wide open *adj* abierto de par en par
wide-ranging [waɪd'reɪndʒɪŋ] *adj* (*survey, report*) de gran alcance; (*interests*) muy diversos
widespread ['waɪdsprɛd] *adj* (*belief etc*) extendido, general
widow ['wɪdəu] *n* viuda
widowed ['wɪdəud] *adj* viudo
widower ['wɪdəuəʳ] *n* viudo
width [wɪdθ] *n* anchura; (*of cloth*) ancho; **it's seven metres in ~** tiene siete metros de ancho
widthways ['wɪdθweɪz] *adv* a lo ancho
wield [wi:ld] *vt* (*sword*) manejar; (*power*) ejercer
wife (*pl* **wives**) [waɪf, waɪvz] *n* mujer *f*, esposa
WiFi ['waɪfaɪ] *n abbr* (*= wireless fidelity*) wi-fi *m* ■ *adj* (*hot spot, network etc*) wi-fi
wig [wɪg] *n* peluca
wigging ['wɪgɪŋ] *n* (*Brit col*) rapapolvo, bronca
wiggle ['wɪgl] *vt* menear ■ *vi* menearse
wiggly ['wɪglɪ] *adj* (*line*) ondulado
wigwam ['wɪgwæm] *n* tipi *m*, tienda india
wild [waɪld] *adj* (*animal*) salvaje; (*plant*) silvestre; (*rough*) furioso, violento; (*idea*) descabellado; (*col: angry*) furioso ■ *n*: **the ~** la naturaleza; **wilds** *npl* regiones *fpl* salvajes, tierras *fpl* vírgenes; **to be ~ about** (*enthusiastic*) estar *or* andar loco por; **in its ~ state** en estado salvaje
wild card *n* (*Comput*) comodín *m*
wildcat ['waɪldkæt] *n* gato montés
wildcat strike *n* huelga salvaje
wilderness ['wɪldənɪs] *n* desierto; (*jungle*) jungla
wildfire ['waɪldfaɪəʳ] *n*: **to spread like ~** correr como un reguero de pólvora
wild-goose chase [waɪld'gu:s-] *n* (*fig*) búsqueda inútil
wildlife ['waɪldlaɪf] *n* fauna
wildly ['waɪldlɪ] *adv* (*roughly*) violentamente; (*foolishly*) locamente; (*rashly*) descabelladamente
wiles [waɪlz] *npl* artimañas *fpl*, ardides *mpl*
wilful, willful (*US*) ['wɪlful] *adj* (*action*) deliberado; (*obstinate*) testarudo

KEYWORD

will [wɪl] *aux vb* **1** (*forming future tense*): **I will finish it tomorrow** lo terminaré *or* voy a terminar mañana; **I will have finished it by tomorrow** lo habré terminado para mañana; **will you do it? — yes I will/no I**

won't ¿lo harás? — sí/no; **you won't lose it, will you?** no lo vayas a perder *or* no lo perderás ¿verdad?
2 (*in conjectures, predictions*): **he will** *or* **he'll be there by now** ya habrá llegado, ya debe (de) haber llegado; **that will be the postman** será el cartero, debe ser el cartero
3 (*in commands, requests, offers*): **will you be quiet!** ¿quieres callarte?; **will you help me?** ¿quieres ayudarme?; **will you have a cup of tea?** ¿te apetece un té?; **I won't put up with it!** ¡no lo soporto!
4 (*habits, persistence*): **the car won't start** el coche no arranca; **accidents will happen** son cosas que pasan
■ *vt* (*pt, pp* **willed**); **to will sb to do sth** desear que algn haga algo; **he willed himself to go on** con gran fuerza de voluntad, continuó
■ *n* **1** (*desire*) voluntad *f*; **against sb's will** contra la voluntad de algn; **he did it of his own free will** lo hizo por su propia voluntad
2 (*Law*) testamento; **to make a** *or* **one's will** hacer su testamento

willful ['wɪful] *adj* (*US*) = **wilful**
willing ['wɪlɪŋ] *adj* (*with goodwill*) de buena voluntad; complaciente; **he's ~ to do it** está dispuesto a hacerlo; **to show ~** mostrarse dispuesto
willingly ['wɪlɪŋlɪ] *adv* con mucho gusto
willingness ['wɪlɪŋnɪs] *n* buena voluntad
will-o'-the-wisp ['wɪləðə'wɪsp] *n* fuego fatuo; (*fig*) quimera
willow ['wɪləu] *n* sauce *m*
willpower ['wɪlpauəʳ] *n* fuerza de voluntad
willy-nilly [wɪlɪ'nɪlɪ] *adv* quiérase o no
wilt [wɪlt] *vi* marchitarse
Wilts *abbr* (*Brit*) = **Wiltshire**
wily ['waɪlɪ] *adj* astuto
wimp [wɪmp] *n* (*col*) enclenque *m/f*; (*character*) calzonazos *m inv*
win [wɪn] (*pt, pp* **won**) *n* (*in sports etc*) victoria, triunfo ■ *vt* ganar; (*obtain: contract etc*) conseguir, lograr ■ *vi* ganar
▸ **win over, win round** (*Brit*) *vt* convencer a
wince [wɪns] *vi* encogerse
winch [wɪntʃ] *n* torno
Winchester disk® ['wɪntʃɪstə-] *n* (*Comput*) disco Winchester®
wind [*n* wɪnd, *vb* waɪnd] (*pt, pp* **wound**) *n* viento; (*Med*) gases *mpl*; (*breath*) aliento ■ *vt* enrollar; (*wrap*) envolver; (*clock, toy*) dar cuerda a [wɪnd] (*take breath away from*) dejar sin aliento a ■ *vi* (*road, river*) serpentear; **into** *or* **against the ~** contra el viento; **to get ~ of sth** enterarse de algo; **to break ~** ventosear
▸ **wind down** *vt* (*car window*) bajar; (*fig: production, business*) disminuir
▸ **wind up** *vt* (*clock*) dar cuerda a; (*debate*) concluir, terminar
windbreak ['wɪndbreɪk] *n* barrera contra el viento
windcheater ['wɪndtʃiːtəʳ], **windbreaker** (*US*) ['wɪndbreɪkəʳ] *n* cazadora
winder ['waɪndəʳ] *n* (*on watch*) cuerda
wind erosion *n* erosión *f* del viento
windfall ['wɪndfɔːl] *n* golpe *m* de suerte
winding ['waɪndɪŋ] *adj* (*road*) tortuoso
wind instrument *n* (*Mus*) instrumento de viento
windmill ['wɪndmɪl] *n* molino de viento
window ['wɪndəu] *n* ventana; (*in car, train*) ventana; (*in shop etc*) escaparate *m*, vitrina (*LAm*), vidriera (*LAm*); (*Comput*) ventana
window box *n* jardinera (de ventana)
window cleaner *n* (*person*) limpiacristales *m inv*
window dressing *n* decoración *f* de escaparates
window envelope *n* sobre *m* de ventanilla
window frame *n* marco de ventana
window ledge *n* alféizar *m*, repisa
window pane *n* cristal *m*
window-shopping [wɪndəu'ʃɔpɪŋ] *n*: **to go ~** ir a ver *or* mirar escaparates
windowsill ['wɪndəusɪl] *n* alféizar *m*, repisa
windpipe ['wɪndpaɪp] *n* tráquea
wind power *n* energía eólica
windscreen ['wɪndskriːn], **windshield** (*US*) ['wɪndʃiːld] *n* parabrisas *m inv*
windscreen washer, windshield washer (*US*) *n* lavaparabrisas *m inv*
windscreen wiper, windshield wiper (*US*) *n* limpiaparabrisas *m inv*
windsurfing ['wɪndsəːfɪŋ] *n* windsurf *m*
windswept ['wɪndswɛpt] *adj* azotado por el viento
wind tunnel *n* túnel *m* aerodinámico
windy ['wɪndɪ] *adj* de mucho viento; **it's ~** hace viento
wine [waɪn] *n* vino ■ *vt*: **to ~ and dine sb** agasajar *or* festejar a algn
wine bar *n* *bar especializado en vinos*
wine cellar *n* bodega
wine glass *n* copa (de *or* para vino)
wine-growing ['waɪngrəuɪŋ] *adj* viticultor(a)
wine list *n* lista de vinos
wine merchant *n* vinatero
wine tasting *n* degustación *f* de vinos
wine waiter *n* escanciador *m*
wing [wɪŋ] *n* ala; (*Brit Aut*) aleta; **wings** *npl* (*Theat*) bastidores *mpl*
winger ['wɪŋəʳ] *n* (*Sport*) extremo
wing mirror *n* (espejo) retrovisor *m*

wing nut *n* tuerca (de) mariposa
wingspan ['wɪŋspaen], **wingspread** ['wɪŋsprɛd] *n* envergadura
wink [wɪŋk] *n* guiño; (*blink*) pestañeo ■ *vi* guiñar; (*blink*) pestañear; (*light etc*) parpadear
winkle ['wɪŋkl] *n* bígaro, bigarro
winner ['wɪnəʳ] *n* ganador(a) *m(f)*
winning ['wɪnɪŋ] *adj* (*team*) ganador(a); (*goal*) decisivo; (*charming*) encantador(a)
winning post *n* meta
winnings ['wɪnɪŋz] *npl* ganancias *fpl*
winter ['wɪntəʳ] *n* invierno ■ *vi* invernar
winter sports *npl* deportes *mpl* de invierno
wintry ['wɪntrɪ] *adj* invernal
wipe [waɪp] *n*: **to give sth a ~** pasar un trapo sobre algo ■ *vt* limpiar; **to ~ one's nose** limpiarse la nariz
▸ **wipe off** *vt* limpiar con un trapo
▸ **wipe out** *vt* (*debt*) liquidar; (*memory*) borrar; (*destroy*) destruir
▸ **wipe up** *vt* limpiar
wire ['waɪəʳ] *n* alambre *m*; (*Elec*) cable *m* (eléctrico); (*Tel*) telegrama *m* ■ *vt* (*house*) poner la instalación eléctrica en; (*also*: **wire up**) conectar
wire cutters *npl* cortaalambres *msg inv*
wireless ['waɪəlɪs] *n* (*Brit*) radio *f* ■ *adj* inalámbrico
wireless technology *n* tecnología inalámbrico
wire mesh, wire netting *n* tela metálica
wire service *n* (*US*) agencia de noticias
wire-tapping ['waɪə'tæpɪŋ] *n* intervención *f* telefónica
wiring ['waɪərɪŋ] *n* instalación *f* eléctrica
wiry ['waɪərɪ] *adj* enjuto y fuerte
Wis., Wisc. *abbr* (*US*) = **Wisconsin**
wisdom ['wɪzdəm] *n* sabiduría, saber *m*; (*good sense*) cordura
wisdom tooth *n* muela del juicio
wise [waɪz] *adj* sabio; (*sensible*) juicioso; **I'm none the wiser** sigo sin entender
▸ **wise up** *vi* (*col*): **to ~ up (to sth)** enterarse (de algo)
...wise [waɪz] *suff*: **timewise** en cuanto a *or* respecto al tiempo
wisecrack ['waɪzkræk] *n* broma
wish [wɪʃ] *n* (*desire*) deseo ■ *vt* desear; (*want*) querer; **best wishes** (*on birthday etc*) felicidades *fpl*; **with best wishes** (*in letter*) saludos *mpl*, recuerdos *mpl*; **he wished me well** me deseó mucha suerte; **to ~ sth on sb** imponer algo a algn; **to ~ to do/sb to do sth** querer hacer/que algn haga algo; **to ~ for** desear
wishbone ['wɪʃbəun] *n* espoleta (*de la que tiran dos personas quien se quede con el hueso más largo pide un deseo*)
wishful ['wɪʃful] *adj*: **it's ~ thinking** eso es hacerse ilusiones
wishy-washy ['wɪʃɪwɔʃɪ] *adj* (*col: colour*) desvaído; (*: ideas, thinking*) flojo
wisp [wɪsp] *n* mechón *m*; (*of smoke*) voluta
wistful ['wɪstful] *adj* pensativo; (*nostalgic*) nostálgico
wit [wɪt] *n* (*wittiness*) ingenio, gracia; (*intelligence*: *also*: **wits**) inteligencia; (*person*) chistoso(-a); **to have** *or* **keep one's wits about one** no perder la cabeza
witch [wɪtʃ] *n* bruja
witchcraft ['wɪtʃkrɑːft] *n* brujería
witch doctor *n* hechicero
witch-hunt ['wɪtʃhʌnt] *n* (*Pol*) caza de brujas

KEYWORD

with [wɪð, wɪθ] *prep* **1** (*accompanying, in the company of*) con (*con +mí, ti, sí = conmigo, contigo, consigo*); **I was with him** estaba con él; **we stayed with friends** nos quedamos en casa de unos amigos
2 (*descriptive, indicating manner etc*) con; de; **a room with a view** una habitación con vistas; **the man with the grey hat/blue eyes** el hombre del sombrero gris/de los ojos azules; **red with anger** rojo de ira; **to shake with fear** temblar de miedo; **to fill sth with water** llenar algo de agua
3: **I'm with you/I'm not with you** (*understand*) ya te entiendo/no te entiendo; **I'm not really with it today** no doy pie con bola hoy

withdraw [wɪθ'drɔː] (*irreg*: *like* **draw**) *vt* retirar ■ *vi* retirarse; (*go back on promise*) retractarse; **to ~ money (from the bank)** retirar fondos (del banco); **to ~ into o.s.** ensimismarse
withdrawal [wɪθ'drɔːəl] *n* retirada
withdrawal symptoms *npl* síndrome *m* de abstinencia
withdrawn [wɪθ'drɔːn] *adj* (*person*) reservado, introvertido ■ *pp of* **withdraw**
wither ['wɪðəʳ] *vi* marchitarse
withered ['wɪðəd] *adj* marchito, seco
withhold [wɪθ'həuld] *vt* (*irreg*: *like* **hold**) (*money*) retener; (*decision*) aplazar; (*permission*) negar; (*information*) ocultar
within [wɪð'ɪn] *prep* dentro de ■ *adv* dentro; **~ reach** al alcance de la mano; **~ sight of** a la vista de; **~ the week** antes de que acabe la semana; **to be ~ the law** atenerse a la legalidad; **~ an hour from now** dentro de una hora

without [wɪð'aut] *prep* sin; **to go** *or* **do ~ sth** prescindir de algo; **~ anybody knowing** sin saberlo nadie
withstand [wɪθ'stænd] *vt* (*irreg: like* **stand**) resistir a
witness ['wɪtnɪs] *n* (*person*) testigo *m/f*; (*evidence*) testimonio ■ *vt* (*event*) presenciar, ser testigo de; (*document*) atestiguar la veracidad de; **~ for the prosecution/defence** testigo de cargo/descargo; **to ~ to (having seen) sth** dar testimonio de (haber visto) algo
witness box, witness stand (*US*) *n* tribuna de los testigos
witticism ['wɪtɪsɪzm] *n* dicho ingenioso
wittily ['wɪtɪlɪ] *adv* ingeniosamente
witty ['wɪtɪ] *adj* ingenioso
wives [waɪvz] *npl of* **wife**
wizard ['wɪzəd] *n* hechicero
wizened ['wɪznd] *adj* arrugado, marchito
wk *abbr* = **week**
Wm. *abbr* = **William**
WMD *n abbr see* **weapons of mass destruction**
WO *n abbr* = **warrant officer**
wobble ['wɔbl] *vi* tambalearse
wobbly ['wɔblɪ] *adj* (*hand, voice*) tembloroso; (*table, chair*) tambaleante, cojo
woe [wəu] *n* desgracia
woeful ['wəuful] *adj* (*bad*) lamentable; (*sad*) apesadumbrado
wok [wɔk] *n* wok *m*
woke [wəuk] *pt of* **wake**
woken ['wəukn] *pp of* **wake**
wolf (*pl* **wolves**) [wulf, wulvz] *n* lobo
woman (*pl* **women**) ['wumən, 'wɪmɪn] *n* mujer *f*; **young ~** (mujer *f*) joven *f*; **women's page** (*Press*) sección *f* de la mujer
woman doctor *n* doctora
woman friend *n* amiga
womanize ['wumənaɪz] *vi* ser un mujeriego
womanly ['wumənlɪ] *adj* femenino
womb [wu:m] *n* (*Anat*) matriz *f*, útero
women ['wɪmɪn] *npl of* **woman**
Women's Liberation Movement, Women's Movement *n* (*also*: **women's lib**) Movimiento de liberación de la mujer
won [wʌn] *pt, pp of* **win**
wonder ['wʌndə^r] *n* maravilla, prodigio; (*feeling*) asombro ■ *vi*: **to ~ whether** preguntarse si; **to ~ at** asombrarse de; **to ~ about** pensar sobre *or* en; **it's no ~ that** no es de extrañar que
wonderful ['wʌndəful] *adj* maravilloso
wonderfully ['wʌndəfəlɪ] *adv* maravillosamente, estupendamente
wonky ['wɔŋkɪ] *adj* (*Brit col: unsteady*) poco seguro, cojo; (*: broken down*) estropeado
wont [wɔnt] *n*: **as is his/her ~** como tiene por costumbre
won't [wəunt] = **will not**
woo [wu:] *vt* (*woman*) cortejar
wood [wud] *n* (*timber*) madera; (*forest*) bosque *m* ■ *cpd* de madera
wood alcohol *n* (*US*) alcohol *m* desnaturalizado
wood carving *n* tallado en madera
wooded ['wudɪd] *adj* arbolado
wooden ['wudn] *adj* de madera; (*fig*) inexpresivo
woodland ['wudlənd] *n* bosque *m*
woodpecker ['wudpɛkə^r] *n* pájaro carpintero
wood pigeon *n* paloma torcaz
woodwind ['wudwɪnd] *n* (*Mus*) instrumentos *mpl* de viento de madera
woodwork ['wudwə:k] *n* carpintería
woodworm ['wudwə:m] *n* carcoma
woof [wuf] *n* (*of dog*) ladrido ■ *vi* ladrar; **~, ~!** ¡guau, guau!
wool [wul] *n* lana; **knitting ~** lana (de hacer punto); **to pull the ~ over sb's eyes** (*fig*) dar a algn gato por liebre
woollen, woolen (*US*) ['wulən] *adj* de lana ■ *n*: **woollens** géneros *mpl* de lana
woolly, wooly (*US*) ['wulɪ] *adj* de lana; (*fig: ideas*) confuso
woozy ['wu:zɪ] *adj* (*col*) mareado
word [wə:d] *n* palabra; (*news*) noticia; (*promise*) palabra (de honor) ■ *vt* redactar; **~ for ~** palabra por palabra; **what's the ~ for "pen" in Spanish?** ¿cómo se dice "pen" en español?; **to put sth into words** expresar algo en palabras; **to have a ~ with sb** hablar (dos palabras) con algn; **in other words** en otras palabras; **to break/keep one's ~** faltar a la palabra/cumplir la promesa; **to leave ~ (with/for sb) that ...** dejar recado (con/para algn) de que ...; **to have words with sb** (*quarrel with*) discutir *or* reñir con algn
wording ['wə:dɪŋ] *n* redacción *f*
word-of-mouth [wə:dəv'mauθ] *n*: **by** *or* **through ~** de palabra, por el boca a boca
word-perfect ['wə:d'pə:fɪkt] *adj* (*speech etc*) sin faltas de expresión
word processing *n* procesamiento *or* tratamiento de textos
word processor [-'prəusɛsə^r] *n* procesador *m* de textos
wordwrap ['wə:dræp] *n* (*Comput*) salto de línea automático
wordy ['wə:dɪ] *adj* verboso, prolijo
wore [wɔ:^r] *pt of* **wear**
work [wə:k] *n* trabajo; (*job*) empleo, trabajo; (*Art, Lit*) obra ■ *vi* trabajar; (*mechanism*) funcionar, marchar; (*medicine*) ser eficaz,

surtir efecto ■ *vt* (*shape*) trabajar; (*stone etc*) tallar; (*mine etc*) explotar; (*machine*) manejar, hacer funcionar; (*cause*) producir; **to go to ~** ir a trabajar *or* al trabajo; **to be at ~ (on sth)** estar trabajando (en algo); **to set to ~, start ~** ponerse a trabajar; **to be out of ~** estar parado, no tener trabajo; **his life's ~** el trabajo de su vida; **to ~ hard** trabajar mucho *or* duro; **to ~ to rule** (*Industry*) hacer una huelga de celo; **to ~ loose** (*part*) desprenderse; (*knot*) aflojarse; *see also* **works**
▸ **work off** *vt*: **to ~ off one's feelings** desahogarse
▸ **work on** *vt fus* trabajar en, dedicarse a; (*principle*) basarse en; **he's working on the car** está reparando el coche
▸ **work out** *vi* (*plans etc*) salir bien, funcionar; (*Sport*) hacer ejercicios ■ *vt* (*problem*) resolver; (*plan*) elaborar; **it works out at £100** asciende a 100 libras
▸ **work up** *vt*: **he worked his way up in the company** ascendió en la compañía mediante sus propios esfuerzos

workable ['wəːkəbl] *adj* (*solution*) práctico, factible
workaholic [wəːkə'hɔlɪk] *n* adicto(-a) al trabajo
workbench ['wəːkbɛntʃ] *n* banco *or* mesa de trabajo
worked up [wəːkt-] *adj*: **to get ~** excitarse
worker ['wəːkəʳ] *n* trabajador(a) *m(f)*, obrero(-a) *m(f)*; **office ~** oficinista *m/f*
work force *n* mano *f* de obra
work-in ['wəːkɪn] *n* (*Brit*) ocupación *f* (de la empresa sin interrupción del trabajo)
working ['wəːkɪŋ] *adj* (*day, week*) laborable; (*tools, conditions, clothes*) de trabajo; (*wife*) que trabaja; (*partner*) activo
working capital *n* (*Comm*) capital *m* circulante
working class *n* clase *f* obrera ■ *adj*: **working-class** obrero
working knowledge *n* conocimientos *mpl* básicos
working man *n* obrero
working order *n*: **in ~** en funcionamiento
working party *n* comisión *f* de investigación, grupo de trabajo
working week *n* semana laboral
work-in-progress ['wəːkɪn'prəugrɛs] *n* (*Comm*) trabajo en curso
workload ['wəːkləud] *n* cantidad *f* de trabajo
workman ['wəːkmən] *n* obrero
workmanship ['wəːkmənʃɪp] *n* (*art*) hechura; (*skill*) habilidad *f*
workmate ['wəːkmeɪt] *n* compañero(-a) de trabajo
workout ['wəːkaut] *n* (*Sport*) sesión *f* de ejercicios
work permit *n* permiso de trabajo
works [wəːks] *nsg* (*Brit: factory*) fábrica ■ *npl* (*of clock, machine*) mecanismo; **road ~** obras *fpl*
works council *n* comité *m* de empresa
worksheet ['wəːkʃiːt] *n* (*Comput*) hoja de trabajo; (*Scol*) hoja de ejercicios
workshop ['wəːkʃɔp] *n* taller *m*
work station *n* estación *f* de trabajo
work study *n* estudio del trabajo
worktop ['wəːktɔp] *n* encimera
work-to-rule ['wəːktə'ruːl] *n* (*Brit*) huelga de celo
world [wəːld] *n* mundo ■ *cpd* (*champion*) del mundo; (*power, war*) mundial; **all over the ~** por todo el mundo, en el mundo entero; **the business ~** el mundo de los negocios; **what in the ~ is he doing?** ¿qué diablos está haciendo?; **to think the ~ of sb** (*fig*) tener un concepto muy alto de algn; **to do sb a ~ of good** sentar muy bien a algn; **W~ War One/Two** la primera/segunda Guerra Mundial
World Cup *n* (*Football*): **the ~** el Mundial, los Mundiales
world-famous [wəːld'feɪməs] *adj* de fama mundial, mundialmente famoso
worldly ['wəːldlɪ] *adj* mundano
world music *n* música étnica
World Series *n*: **the ~** (*US Baseball*) el campeonato nacional de béisbol de EEUU
World Service *n see* **BBC**
world-wide ['wəːldwaɪd] *adj* mundial, universal
worm [wəːm] *n* gusano; (*earthworm*) lombriz *f*
worn [wɔːn] *pp of* **wear** ■ *adj* usado
worn-out ['wɔːnaut] *adj* (*object*) gastado; (*person*) rendido, agotado
worried ['wʌrɪd] *adj* preocupado; **to be ~ about sth** estar preocupado por algo
worrisome ['wʌrɪsəm] *adj* preocupante, inquietante
worry ['wʌrɪ] *n* preocupación *f* ■ *vt* preocupar, inquietar ■ *vi* preocuparse; **to ~ about** *or* **over sth/sb** preocuparse por algo/algn
worrying ['wʌrɪɪŋ] *adj* inquietante
worse [wəːs] *adj, adv* peor ■ *n* el peor, lo peor; **a change for the ~** un empeoramiento; **so much the ~ for you** tanto peor para ti; **he is none the ~ for it** se ha quedado tan fresco *or* tan tranquilo; **to get ~, to grow ~** empeorar
worsen ['wəːsn] *vt, vi* empeorar
worse off *adj* (*fig*): **you'll be ~ this way** de esta forma estarás peor que antes
worship ['wəːʃɪp] *n* (*organized worship*) culto; (*act*) adoración *f* ■ *vt* adorar; **Your W~** (*Brit:*

to mayor) su Ilustrísima; (: *to judge*) su señoría
worshipper, worshiper (*US*) ['wəːʃɪpə^r] *n* devoto(-a)
worst [wəːst] *adj* (el/la) peor ■ *adv* peor ■ *n* lo peor; **at ~** en el peor de los casos; **to come off ~** llevar la peor parte; **if the ~ comes to the ~** en el peor de los casos
worst-case ['wəːstkeɪs] *adj*: **the ~ scenario** el peor de los casos
worsted ['wustɪd] *n*: **(wool) ~** estambre *m*
worth [wəːθ] *n* valor *m* ■ *adj*: **to be ~** valer; **how much is it ~?** ¿cuánto vale?; **it's ~ it** vale *or* merece la pena; **to be ~ one's while (to do)** merecer la pena (hacer); **it's not ~ the trouble** no vale *or* merece la pena
worthless ['wəːθlɪs] *adj* sin valor; (*useless*) inútil
worthwhile ['wəːθwaɪl] *adj* (*activity*) que merece la pena; (*cause*) loable
worthy ['wəːðɪ] *adj* (*person*) respetable; (*motive*) honesto; **~ of** digno de

KEYWORD

would [wud] *aux vb* **1** (*conditional tense*): **if you asked him he would do it** si se lo pidieras, lo haría; **if you had asked him he would have done it** si se lo hubieras pedido, lo habría *or* hubiera hecho
2 (*in offers, invitations, requests*): **would you like a biscuit?** ¿quieres una galleta?; (*formal*) ¿querría una galleta?; **would you ask him to come in?** ¿quiere hacerle pasar?; **would you open the window please?** ¿quiere *or* podría abrir la ventana, por favor?
3 (*in indirect speech*): **I said I would do it** dije que lo haría
4 (*emphatic*): **it WOULD have to snow today!** ¡tenía que nevar precisamente hoy!
5 (*insistence*): **she wouldn't behave** no quiso comportarse bien
6 (*conjecture*): **it would have been midnight** sería medianoche; **it would seem so** parece ser que sí
7 (*indicating habit*): **he would go there on Mondays** iba allí los lunes

would-be ['wudbiː] *adj* (*pej*) presunto
wouldn't ['wudnt] = **would not**
wound [*n* wuːnd, *vb* waund] *pt, pp of* **wind** ■ *n* herida ■ *vt* herir
wove [wəuv] *pt of* **weave**
woven ['wəuvən] *pp of* **weave**
WP *n abbr* = **word processing**; **word processor** ■ *abbr* (*Brit col*: = *weather permitting*) si lo permite el tiempo
WPC *n abbr* (*Brit*) = **woman police constable**
wpm *abbr* (= *words per minute*) p.p.m.
WRAC *n abbr* (*Brit*: = *Women's Royal Army Corps*) *cuerpo auxiliar femenino del ejército de tierra*
WRAF *n abbr* (*Brit*: = *Women's Royal Air Force*) *cuerpo auxiliar femenino del ejército del aire*
wrangle ['ræŋgl] *n* riña ■ *vi* reñir
wrap [ræp] *n* (*stole*) chal *m* ■ *vt* (*also*: **wrap up**) envolver; **under wraps** (*fig*: *plan, scheme*) oculto, tapado
wrapper ['ræpə^r] *n* (*Brit*: *of book*) sobrecubierta; (*on chocolate etc*) envoltura
wrapping paper ['ræpɪŋ-] *n* papel *m* de envolver
wrath [rɔθ] *n* cólera
wreak [riːk] *vt* (*destruction*) causar; **to ~ havoc (on)** hacer *or* causar estragos (en); **to ~ vengeance (on)** vengarse (en)
wreath (*pl* **wreaths**) [riːθ, riːðz] *n* (*also*: **funeral wreath**) corona; (*of flowers*) guirnalda
wreck [rɛk] *n* (*ship*: *destruction*) naufragio; (: *remains*) restos *mpl* del barco; (*pej*: *person*) ruina ■ *vt* destrozar; **to be wrecked** (*Naut*) naufragar
wreckage ['rɛkɪdʒ] *n* (*remains*) restos *mpl*; (*of building*) escombros *mpl*
wrecker ['rɛkə^r] *n* (*US*: *breakdown van*) camión-grúa *m*
WREN [rɛn] *n abbr* (*Brit*) *miembro del WRNS*
wren [rɛn] *n* (*Zool*) reyezuelo
wrench [rɛntʃ] *n* (*Tech*) llave *f* inglesa; (*tug*) tirón *m* ■ *vt* arrancar; **to ~ sth from sb** arrebatar algo violentamente a algn
wrest [rɛst] *vt*: **to ~ sth from sb** arrebatar *or* arrancar algo a algn
wrestle ['rɛsl] *vi*: **to ~ (with sb)** luchar (con *or* contra algn)
wrestler ['rɛslə^r] *n* luchador(a) *m(f)* (de lucha libre)
wrestling ['rɛslɪŋ] *n* lucha libre
wrestling match *n* combate *m* de lucha libre
wretch [rɛtʃ] *n* desgraciado(-a), miserable *m/f*; **little ~!** (*often humorous*) ¡granuja!
wretched ['rɛtʃɪd] *adj* miserable
wriggle ['rɪgl] *vi* serpentear
wring (*pt, pp* **wrung**) [rɪŋ, rʌŋ] *vt* torcer, retorcer; (*wet clothes*) escurrir; (*fig*): **to ~ sth out of sb** sacar algo por la fuerza a algn
wringer ['rɪŋə^r] *n* escurridor *m*
wringing ['rɪŋɪŋ] *adj* (*also*: **wringing wet**) empapado
wrinkle ['rɪŋkl] *n* arruga ■ *vt* arrugar ■ *vi* arrugarse
wrinkled ['rɪŋkld], **wrinkly** ['rɪŋklɪ] *adj* (*fabric, paper etc*) arrugado
wrist [rɪst] *n* muñeca
wristband ['rɪstbænd] *n* (*Brit*: *of shirt*) puño; (: *of watch*) correa

wrist watch *n* reloj *m* de pulsera
writ [rɪt] *n* mandato judicial; **to serve a ~ on sb** notificar un mandato judicial a algn
writable ['raɪtəbl] *adj* (*CD, DVD*) escribible
write (*pt* **wrote**, *pp* **written**) [raɪt, rəut, 'rɪtn] *vt, vi* escribir; **to ~ sb a letter** escribir una carta a algn
▸ **write away** *vi*: **to ~ away for** (*information, goods*) pedir por escrito *or* carta
▸ **write down** *vt* escribir; (*note*) apuntar
▸ **write off** *vt* (*debt*) borrar (como incobrable); (*fig*) desechar por inútil; (*smash up: car*) destrozar
▸ **write out** *vt* escribir
▸ **write up** *vt* redactar
write-off ['raɪtɔf] *n* siniestro total; **the car is a ~** el coche es pura chatarra
write-protect ['raɪtprə'tɛkt] *vt* (*Comput*) proteger contra escritura
writer ['raɪtə^r] *n* escritor(a) *m(f)*
write-up ['raɪtʌp] *n* (*review*) crítica, reseña
writhe [raɪð] *vi* retorcerse
writing ['raɪtɪŋ] *n* escritura; (*handwriting*) letra; (*of author*) obras *fpl*; **in ~** por escrito; **to put sth in ~** poner algo por escrito; **in my own ~** escrito por mí; *see also* **writings**
writing case *n* estuche *m* de papel de escribir
writing desk *n* escritorio
writing paper *n* papel *m* de escribir
writings *npl* obras *fpl*
written ['rɪtn] *pp of* **write**
WRNS *n abbr* (*Brit: = Women's Royal Naval Service*) *cuerpo auxiliar femenino de la armada*
wrong [rɔŋ] *adj* (*wicked*) malo; (*unfair*) injusto; (*incorrect*) equivocado, incorrecto; (*not suitable*) inoportuno, inconveniente ■ *adv* mal ■ *n* mal *m*; (*injustice*) injusticia ■ *vt* ser injusto con; (*hurt*) agraviar; **to be ~** (*answer*) estar equivocado; (*in doing, saying*) equivocarse; **it's ~ to steal, stealing is ~** es mal robar; **you are ~ to do it** haces mal en hacerlo; **you are ~ about that, you've got it ~** en eso estás equivocado; **to be in the ~** no tener razón; (*guilty*) tener la culpa; **what's ~?** ¿qué pasa?; **what's ~ with the car?** ¿qué le pasa al coche?; **there's nothing ~** no pasa nada; **you have the ~ number** (*Tel*) se ha equivocado de número; **to go ~** (*person*) equivocarse; (*plan*) salir mal; (*machine*) estropearse
wrongdoer ['rɔŋduə^r] *n* malhechor(a) *m(f)*
wrong-foot [rɔŋ'fut] *vt* (*Sport*) hacer perder el equilibrio a; (*fig*) poner en un aprieto a
wrongful ['rɔŋful] *adj* injusto; **~ dismissal** (*Industry*) despido improcedente
wrongly ['rɔŋlɪ] *adv* (*answer, do, count*) incorrectamente; (*treat*) injustamente
wrote [rəut] *pt of* **write**
wrought [rɔːt] *adj*: **~ iron** hierro forjado
wrung [rʌŋ] *pt, pp of* **wring**
WRVS *n abbr* (*Brit: = Women's Royal Voluntary Service*) *cuerpo de voluntarias al servicio de la comunidad*
wry [raɪ] *adj* irónico
wt. *abbr* = **weight**
WV, W. Va. *abbr* (*US*) = **West Virginia**
WWW *n abbr* (= *World Wide Web*) WWW *m or f*
WY, Wyo. *abbr* (*US*) = **Wyoming**
WYSIWYG ['wɪzɪwɪg] *abbr* (*Comput: = what you see is what you get*) *tipo de presentación en un procesador de textos*

Xx

X, x [eks] *n* (*letter*) X, x *f*; (*Brit Cine*: *formerly*) no apto para menores de 18 años; **X for Xmas** X de Xiquena; **if you earn X dollars a year** si ganas X dólares al año
X-certificate ['ɛkssə'tɪfɪkɪt] *adj* (*Brit*: *film*: *formerly*) no apto para menores de 18 años
Xerox® ['zɪərɔks] *n* (*also*: **Xerox machine**) fotocopiadora; (*photocopy*) fotocopia ■ *vt* fotocopiar
XL *abbr* = **extra large**
Xmas ['ɛksməs] *n abbr* = **Christmas**
X-rated ['eks'reɪtɪd] *adj* (*US*: *film*) no apto para menores de 18 años
X-ray [ɛks'reɪ] *n* radiografía; **X-rays** *npl* rayos *mpl* X ■ *vt* radiografiar
xylophone ['zaɪləfəun] *n* xilófono

Yy

Y, y [waɪ] *n* (*letter*) Y, y *f*; **Y for Yellow,** (*US*) **Y for Yoke** Y de Yegua
Y2K [ˌwaɪtuːˈkeɪ] *abbr* (= *Year 2000*): **the ~ problem** (*Comput*) el efecto 2000
yacht [jɔt] *n* yate *m*
yachting [ˈjɔtɪŋ] *n* (*sport*) balandrismo
yachtsman [ˈjɔtsmən] *n* balandrista *m*
yachtswoman [ˈjɔtswumən] *n* balandrista
yam [jæm] *n* ñame *m*; (*sweet potato*) batata, camote *m* (*LAm*)
Yank [jæŋk], **Yankee** [ˈjæŋkɪ] *n* (*pej*) yanqui *m/f*
yank [jæŋk] *vt* tirar de, jalar de (*LAm*) ■ *n* tirón *m*
yap [jæp] *vi* (*dog*) aullar
yard [jɑːd] *n* patio; (*US: garden*) jardín *m*; (*measure*) yarda; **builder's ~** almacén *m*
yardstick [ˈjɑːdstɪk] *n* (*fig*) criterio, norma
yarn [jɑːn] *n* hilo; (*tale*) cuento (chino), historia
yawn [jɔːn] *n* bostezo ■ *vi* bostezar
yawning [ˈjɔːnɪŋ] *adj* (*gap*) muy abierto
yd. *abbr* (= *yard*) yda
yeah [jɛə] *adv* (*col*) sí
year [jɪə^r] *n* año; (*Scol, Univ*) curso; **this ~** este año; **~ in, ~ out** año tras año; **a** *or* **per ~** al año; **to be eight years old** tener ocho años; **she's three years old** tiene tres años; **an eight-~-old child** un niño de ocho años (de edad)
yearbook [ˈjɪəbuk] *n* anuario
yearling [ˈjɪəlɪŋ] *n* (*racehorse*) potro de un año
yearly [ˈjɪəlɪ] *adj* anual ■ *adv* anualmente, cada año; **twice ~** dos veces al año
yearn [jəːn] *vi*: **to ~ for sth** añorar algo, suspirar por algo
yearning [ˈjəːnɪŋ] *n* ansia; (*longing*) añoranza
yeast [jiːst] *n* levadura
yell [jɛl] *n* grito, alarido ■ *vi* gritar
yellow [ˈjɛləu] *adj, n* amarillo
yellow fever *n* fiebre *f* amarilla
yellowish [ˈjɛləuɪʃ] *adj* amarillento
Yellow Pages® *npl* páginas *fpl* amarillas
Yellow Sea *n*: **the ~** el Mar Amarillo
yelp [jɛlp] *n* aullido ■ *vi* aullar
Yemen [ˈjɛmən] *n* Yemen *m*
Yemeni [ˈjɛmənɪ] *adj, n* yemení *m/f*, yemenita *m/f*
yen [jɛn] *n* (*currency*) yen *m*
yeoman [ˈjəumən] *n*: **Y~ of the Guard** *alabardero de la Casa Real*
yes [jɛs] *adv, n* sí *m*; **to say/answer ~** decir/contestar que sí; **to say ~ (to)** decir que sí (a), conformarse (con)
yes man *n* pelotillero
yesterday [ˈjɛstədɪ] *adv, n* ayer *m*; **~ morning/evening** ayer por la mañana/tarde; **all day ~** todo el día de ayer; **the day before ~** antes de ayer, anteayer
yet [jɛt] *adv* todavía ■ *conj* sin embargo, a pesar de todo; **~ again** de nuevo; **it is not finished ~** todavía no está acabado; **the best ~** el/la mejor hasta ahora; **as ~** hasta ahora, todavía
yew [juː] *n* tejo
Y-fronts® [ˈwaɪfrʌnts] *npl* (*Brit*) calzoncillos *mpl*, eslip *msg* tradicional
YHA *n abbr* (*Brit*: = *Youth Hostel Association*) ≈ Red *f* Española de Albergues Juveniles
Yiddish [ˈjɪdɪʃ] *n* yiddish *m*
yield [jiːld] *n* producción *f*; (*Agr*) cosecha; (*Comm*) rendimiento ■ *vt* producir, dar; (*profit*) rendir ■ *vi* rendirse, ceder; (*US Aut*) ceder el paso; **a ~ of 5%** un rédito del 5 por ciento
YMCA *n abbr* (= *Young Men's Christian Association*) Asociación *f* de Jóvenes Cristianos
yob [ˈjɔb], **yobbo** [ˈjɔbbəu] *n* (*Brit col*) gamberro
yodel [ˈjəudl] *vi* cantar a la tirolesa
yoga [ˈjəugə] *n* yoga *m*
yoghurt, yogurt [ˈjəugət] *n* yogur *m*
yoke [jəuk] *n* (*of oxen*) yunta; (*on shoulders*) balancín *m*; (*fig*) yugo ■ *vt* (*also*: **yoke together**: *oxen*) uncir
yolk [jəuk] *n* yema (de huevo)
yonder [ˈjɔndə^r] *adv* allá (a lo lejos)

yonks [jɔŋks] *npl* (*col*): **I haven't seen him for ~** hace siglos que no lo veo
Yorks [jɔːks] *abbr* (*Brit*) = **Yorkshire**

KEYWORD

you [juː] *pron* **1** (*subject: familiar*) tú, vosotros(-as) (*SP*) *pl*, ustedes (*LAm*); (*polite*) usted, ustedes *pl*; **you are very kind** eres/es *etc* muy amable; **you French enjoy your food** a vosotros (*or* ustedes) los franceses os (*or* les) gusta la comida; **you and I will go** iremos tú y yo
2 (*object: direct: familiar*) te, os *pl* (*SP*), les (*LAm*); (*polite*) lo *or* le; (*pl*) los *or* les; (*f*) la; (*pl*) las; **I know you** te/le *etc* conozco
3 (*object: indirect: familiar*) te, os *pl* (*SP*), les (*LAm*); (*polite*) le, les *pl*; **I gave the letter to you yesterday** te/os *etc* di la carta ayer
4 (*stressed*): **I told YOU to do it** te dije a ti que lo hicieras, es a ti a quien dije que lo hicieras; *see also* **3, 5**
5 (*after prep: NB: con +ti = contigo: familiar*) ti, vosotros(-as) *pl* (*SP*), ustedes *pl* (*LAm*); (*: polite*) usted, ustedes *pl*; **it's for you** es para ti/vosotros *etc*
6 (*comparisons: familiar*) tú, vosotros(-as) *pl* (*SP*), ustedes *pl* (*LAm*); (*: polite*) usted, ustedes *pl*; **she's younger than you** es más joven que tú/vosotros *etc*
7 (*impersonal: one*): **fresh air does you good** el aire puro (te) hace bien; **you never know** nunca se sabe; **you can't do that!** ¡eso no se hace!

you'd [juːd] = **you had; you would**
you'll [juːl] = **you will; you shall**
young [jʌŋ] *adj* joven ■ *npl* (*of animal*) cría; (*people*): **the ~** los jóvenes, la juventud; **a ~ man/lady** un(a) joven; **my younger brother** mi hermano menor *or* pequeño; **the younger generation** la nueva generación
youngster [ˈjʌŋstəʳ] *n* joven *m/f*
your [jɔːʳ] *adj* tu, vuestro *pl*; (*formal*) su; **~ house** tu *etc* casa; *see also* **my**
you're [juəʳ] = **you are**
yours [jɔːz] *pron* tuyo, vuestro *pl*; (*formal*) suyo; **a friend of ~** un amigo tuyo *etc*; *see also* **faithfully; mine; sincerely**
yourself [jɔːˈsɛlf] *pron* (*reflexive*) tú mismo; (*complement*) te; (*after prep*) ti (mismo); (*formal*) usted mismo; (*: complement*) se; (*: after prep*) sí (mismo); **you ~ told me** me lo dijiste tú mismo; **(all) by ~** sin ayuda de nadie, solo; *see also* **oneself**
yourselves [jɔːˈsɛlvz] *pl pron* vosotros mismos; (*after prep*) vosotros (mismos); (*formal*) ustedes (mismos); (*: complement*) se; (*: after prep*) sí mismos
youth [juːθ] *n* juventud *f*; (*young man*) (*pl* **youths**) [juːðz] joven *m*; **in my ~** en mi juventud
youth club *n* club *m* juvenil
youthful [ˈjuːθful] *adj* juvenil
youthfulness [ˈjuːθfəlnɪs] *n* juventud *f*
youth hostel *n* albergue *m* juvenil
youth movement *n* movimiento juvenil
you've [juːv] = **you have**
yowl [jaul] *n* (*of animal, person*) aullido ■ *vi* aullar
yr *abbr* (= *year*) a
YT *abbr* (*Canada*) = **Yukon Territory**
Yugoslav [ˈjuːgəuslɑːv] *adj, n* yugoslavo(-a) *m(f)*
Yugoslavia [juːgəuˈslɑːvɪə] *n* Yugoslavia
Yugoslavian [juːgəuˈslɑːvɪən] *adj* yugoslavo(-a)
yuppie [ˈjʌpɪ] (*col*) *adj, n* yuppie *m/f*
YWCA *n abbr* (= *Young Women's Christian Association*) Asociación *f* de Jóvenes Cristianas

Zz

Z, z [zɛd] (*US*) [zi:] *n* (*letter*) Z, z *f*; **Z for Zebra** Z de Zaragoza
Zaire [zɑ:'i:əʳ] *n* Zaire *m*
Zambia ['zæmbɪə] *n* Zambia
Zambian ['zæmbɪən] *adj, n* zambiano(-a) *m(f)*
zany ['zeɪnɪ] *adj* estrafalario
zap [zæp] *vt* (*Comput*) borrar
zeal [zi:l] *n* celo, entusiasmo
zealot ['zɛlət] *n* fanático(-a)
zealous ['zɛləs] *adj* celoso, entusiasta
zebra ['zi:brə] *n* cebra
zebra crossing *n* (*Brit*) paso de peatones
zenith ['zɛnɪθ] *n* (*Astro*) cénit *m*; (*fig*) apogeo
zero ['zɪərəu] *n* cero; **5 degrees below ~** 5 grados bajo cero
zero hour *n* hora cero
zero option *n* (*Pol*) opción *f* cero
zero-rated ['zɪərəureɪtɪd] *adj* (*Brit*) de tasa cero
zest [zɛst] *n* entusiasmo; **~ for living** brío
zigzag ['zɪgzæg] *n* zigzag *m* ▪ *vi* zigzaguear
Zimbabwe [zɪm'bɑ:bwɪ] *n* Zimbabwe *m*
Zimbabwean [zɪm'bɑ:bwɪən] *adj, n* zimbabuo(-a) *m(f)*
Zimmer® ['zɪməʳ] *n* (*also*: **Zimmer frame**) andador *m*, andaderas *fpl*
zinc [zɪŋk] *n* cinc *m*, zinc *m*
Zionism ['zaɪənɪzm] *n* sionismo
Zionist ['zaɪənɪst] *adj, n* sionista *m/f*
zip [zɪp] *n* (*also*: **zip fastener**: *US*: *also*: **zipper**) cremallera, cierre *m* relámpago (*LAm*); (*energy*) energía, vigor *m* ▪ *vt* (*Comput*) comprimir; (*also*: **zip up**) cerrar la cremallera de ▪ *vi*: **to ~ along to the shops** ir de compras volando
zip code *n* (*US*) código postal
zip file *n* (*Comput*) archivo *m* comprimido
zither ['zɪðəʳ] *n* cítara
zodiac ['zəudɪæk] *n* zodíaco
zombie ['zɔmbɪ] *n* zombi *m*
zone [zəun] *n* zona
zonked [zɔŋkt] *adj* (*col*) hecho polvo
zoo [zu:] *n* zoo, (parque *m*) zoológico
zoological [zu:ə'lɔdʒɪkəl] *adj* zoológico
zoologist [zu'ɔlədʒɪst] *n* zoólogo(-a)
zoology [zu:'ɔlədʒɪ] *n* zoología
zoom [zu:m] *vi*: **to ~ past** pasar zumbando; **to ~ in (on sth/sb)** (*Phot, Cine*) enfocar (algo/a algn) con el zoom
zoom lens *n* zoom *m*
zucchini [zu:'ki:nɪ] *n(pl)* (*US*) calabacín(ines) *m(pl)*

Grammar
Gramática

Using the grammar

The Grammar section deals systematically and comprehensively with all the information you will need in order to communicate accurately in Spanish. The user-friendly layout explains the grammar point on a left hand page, leaving the facing page free for illustrative examples. The circled numbers, → ① etc, direct you to the relevant example in every case. Another strong point of the Grammar section is its comprehensive treatment of verbs. Regular verbs are fully explained, and 80 major irregular verbs are conjugated in their simple tenses. The irregular verbs are given in alphabetical order and laid out in tables, making them easy and efficient to consult. In addition, a verb index lists every Spanish verb in this dictionary each cross-referred to the appropriate conjugation model.

The Grammar section also provides invaluable guidance on the danger of translating English structures by identical structures in Spanish. Use of Numbers and Punctuation are important areas covered towards the end of the section. Finally, the index lists the main words and grammatical terms in both English and Spanish.

Abbreviations

cond.	*conditional*
fem.	*feminine*
masc.	*masculine*
plur.	*plural*
sing.	*singular*
subj	*subjunctive*
algn	alguien
sb	somebody
sth	something

Contents

Simple Tenses: Formation

In Spanish the simple tenses are:

- Present → 1
- Imperfect → 2
- Future → 3
- Conditional → 4
- Preterite → 5
- Present Subjunctive → 6
- Imperfect Subjunctive → 7

They are formed by adding endings to a verb stem. The endings show the number and person of the subject of the verb → 8

The stem and endings of regular verbs are totally predictable. The following sections show all the patterns for regular verbs. For irregular verbs see page 80 onwards.

Regular Verbs

There are three regular verb patterns (called conjugations), each identifiable by the ending of the infinitive:

First conjugation verbs end in **-ar** e.g. **hablar** to speak.

Second conjugation verbs end in **-er** e.g. **comer** to eat.

Third conjugation verbs end in **-ir** e.g. **vivir** to live.

These three conjugations are treated in order on the following pages. The subject pronouns will appear in brackets because they are not always necessary in Spanish (see page 230).

Examples

❶ (yo) hablo	I speak I am speaking I do speak
❷ (yo) hablaba	I spoke I was speaking I used to speak
❸ (yo) hablaré	I shall speak I shall be speaking
❹ (yo) hablaría	I should/would speak I should/would be speaking
❺ (yo) hablé	I spoke
❻ (que) (yo) hable	(that) I speak
❼ (que) (yo) hablara *or* hablase	(that) I spoke
❽ (yo) hablo (nosotros) hablamos (yo) hablaría (nosotros) hablaríamos	I speak we speak I would speak we would speak

Simple Tenses: First Conjugation

The stem is formed as follows:

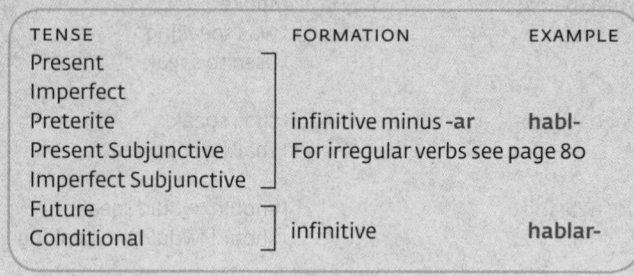

TENSE	FORMATION	EXAMPLE
Present Imperfect Preterite Present Subjunctive Imperfect Subjunctive	infinitive minus **-ar** For irregular verbs see page 80	**habl-**
Future Conditional	infinitive	**hablar-**

To the appropriate stem add the following endings:

		❶ PRESENT	❷ IMPERFECT	❸ PRETERITE
sing.	1st person	**-o**	**-aba**	**-é**
	2nd person	**-as**	**-abas**	**-aste**
	3rd person	**-a**	**-aba**	**-ó**
plur.	1st person	**-amos**	**-ábamos**	**-ames**
	2nd person	**-áis**	**-abais**	**-asteis**
	3rd person	**-an**	**-aban**	**-aron**

		❹ PRESENT SUBJUNCTIVE	❺ IMPERFECT SUBJUNCTIVE
sing.	1st person	**-e**	**-ara** *or* **-ase**
	2nd person	**-es**	**-aras** *or* **-ases**
	3rd person	**-e**	**-ara** *or* **-ase**
plur.	1st person	**-emos**	**-áramos** *or* **-ásemos**
	2nd person	**-éis**	**-arais** *or* **-aseis**
	3rd person	**-en**	**-aran** *or* **-asen**

		❻ FUTURE	❼ CONDITIONAL
sing.	1st person	**-é**	**-ía**
	2nd person	**-ás**	**-ías**
	3rd person	**-á**	**-ía**
plur.	1st person	**-emos**	**-íamos**
	2nd person	**-éis**	**-íais**
	3rd person	**-án**	**-ían**

Examples

❶ PRESENT

(yo)	habl**o**
(tú)	habl**as**
(él/ella/Vd)	habl**a**
(nosotros/as)	habl**amos**
(vosotros/as)	habl**áis**
(ellos/as/Vds)	habl**an**

❷ IMPERFECT

habl**aba**
habl**abas**
habl**aba**
habl**ábamos**
habl**abais**
habl**aban**

❸ PRETERITE

habl**é**
habl**aste**
habl**ó**
habl**amos**
habl**asteis**
habl**aron**

❹ PRESENT SUBJUNCTIVE

(yo)	habl**e**
(tú)	habl**es**
(él/ella/Vd)	habl**e**
(nosotros/as)	habl**emos**
(vosotros/as)	habl**éis**
(ellos/as/Vds)	habl**en**

❺ IMPERFECT SUBJUNCTIVE

habl**ara** *or* habl**ase**
habl**aras** *or* habl**ases**
habl**ara** *or* habl**ase**
habl**áramos** *or* habl**ásemos**
habl**arais** *or* habl**aseis**
habl**aran** *or* habl**asen**

❻ FUTURE

(yo)	hablar**é**
(tú)	hablar**ás**
(él/ella/Vd)	hablar**á**
(nosotros/as)	hablar**emos**
(vosotros/as)	hablar**éis**
(ellos/as/Vds)	hablar**án**

❼ CONDITIONAL

hablar**ía**
hablar**ías**
hablar**ía**
hablar**íamos**
hablar**íais**
hablar**ían**

Simple Tenses: Second Conjugation

The stem is formed as follows:

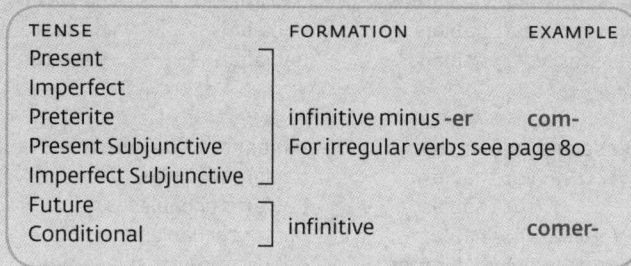

TENSE	FORMATION	EXAMPLE
Present Imperfect Preterite Present Subjunctive Imperfect Subjunctive	infinitive minus -er For irregular verbs see page 80	com-
Future Conditional	infinitive	comer-

To the appropriate stem add the following endings:

		① PRESENT	② IMPERFECT	③ PRETERITE
sing.	1st person	-o	-ía	-í
	2nd person	-es	-ías	-iste
	3rd person	-e	-ía	-ió
plur.	1st person	-emos	-íamos	-imos
	2nd person	-éis	-íais	-isteis
	3rd person	-en	-ían	-ieron

		④ PRESENT SUBJUNCTIVE	⑤ IMPERFECT SUBJUNCTIVE
sing.	1st person	-a	-iera *or* -iese
	2nd person	-as	-ieras *or* -ieses
	3rd person	-a	-iera *or* -iese
plur.	1st person	-amos	-iéramos *or* -iésemos
	2nd person	-áis	-ierais *or* -ieseis
	3rd person	-an	-ieran *or* -iesen

		⑥ FUTURE	⑦ CONDITIONAL
sing.	1st person	-é	-ía
	2nd person	-ás	-ías
	3rd person	-á	-ía
plur.	1st person	-emos	-íamos
	2nd person	-éis	-íais
	3rd person	-án	-ían

Examples

1 PRESENT | **2 IMPERFECT** | **3 PRETERITE**

	1 PRESENT	2 IMPERFECT	3 PRETERITE
(yo)	com**o**	com**ía**	com**í**
(tú)	com**es**	com**ías**	com**iste**
(él/ella/Vd)	com**e**	com**ía**	com**ió**
(nosotros/as)	com**emos**	com**íamos**	com**imos**
(vosotros/as)	com**éis**	com**íais**	com**isteis**
(ellos/as/Vds)	com**en**	com**ían**	com**ieron**

	4 PRESENT SUBJUNCTIVE	5 IMPERFECT SUBJUNCTIVE
(yo)	com**a**	com**iera** *or* com**iese**
(tú)	com**as**	com**ieras** *or* com**ieses**
(él/ella/Vd)	com**a**	com**iera** *or* com**iese**
(nosotros/as)	com**amos**	com**iéramos** *or* com**iésemos**
(vosotros/as)	com**áis**	com**ierais** *or* com**ieseis**
(ellos/as/Vds)	com**an**	com**ieran** *or* com**iesen**

	6 FUTURE	7 CONDITIONAL
(yo)	comer**é**	comer**ía**
(tú)	comer**ás**	comer**ías**
(él/ella/Vd)	comer**á**	comer**ía**
(nosotros/as)	comer**emos**	comer**íamos**
(vosotros/as)	comer**éis**	comer**íais**
(ellos/as/Vds)	comer**án**	comer**ían**

Simple Tenses: Third Conjugation

The stem is formed as follows:

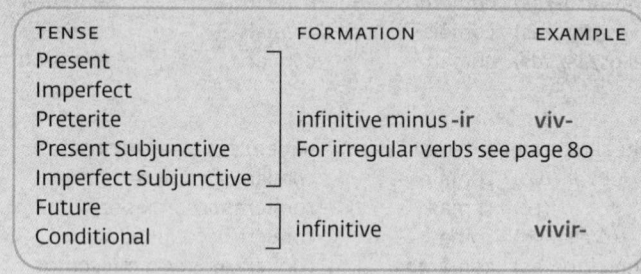

TENSE	FORMATION	EXAMPLE
Present Imperfect Preterite Present Subjunctive Imperfect Subjunctive	infinitive minus -ir For irregular verbs see page 80	**viv-**
Future Conditional	infinitive	**vivir-**

To the appropriate stem add the following endings:

		❶ PRESENT	❷ IMPERFECT	❸ PRETERITE
sing.	1st person	**-o**	**-ía**	**-í**
	2nd person	**-es**	**-ías**	**-iste**
	3rd person	**-e**	**-ía**	**-ió**
plur.	1st person	**-imos**	**-íamos**	**-imos**
	2nd person	**-ís**	**-íais**	**-isteis**
	3rd person	**-en**	**-ían**	**-ieron**

		❹ PRESENT SUBJUNCTIVE	❺ IMPERFECT SUBJUNCTIVE
sing.	1st person	**-a**	**-iera** *or* **-iese**
	2nd person	**-as**	**-ieras** *or* **-ieses**
	3rd person	**-a**	**-iera** *or* **-iese**
plur.	1st person	**-amos**	**-iéramos** *or* **-iésemos**
	2nd person	**-áis**	**-ierais** *or* **-ieseis**
	3rd person	**-an**	**-ieran** *or* **-iesen**

		❻ FUTURE	❼ CONDITIONAL
sing.	1st person	**-é**	**-ía**
	2nd person	**-ás**	**-ías**
	3rd person	**-á**	**-ía**
plur.	1st person	**-emos**	**-íamos**
	2nd person	**-éis**	**-íais**
	3rd person	**-án**	**-ían**

Examples

	❶ PRESENT	❷ IMPERFECT	❸ PRETERITE
(yo)	viv**o**	viv**ía**	viv**í**
(tú)	viv**es**	viv**ías**	viv**iste**
(él/ella/Vd)	viv**e**	viv**ía**	viv**ió**
(nosotros/as)	viv**imos**	viv**íamos**	viv**imos**
(vosotros/as)	viv**ís**	viv**íais**	viv**isteis**
(ellos/as/Vds)	viv**en**	viv**ían**	viv**ieron**

	❹ PRESENT SUBJUNCTIVE	❺ IMPERFECT SUBJUNCTIVE
(yo)	viv**a**	viv**iera** *or* viv**iese**
(tú)	viv**as**	viv**ieras** *or* viv**ieses**
(él/ella/Vd)	viv**a**	viv**iera** *or* viv**iese**
(nosotros/as)	viv**amos**	viv**iéramos** *or* viv**iésemos**
(vosotros/as)	viv**áis**	viv**ierais** *or* viv**ieseis**
(ellos/as/Vds)	viv**an**	viv**ieran** *or* viv**iesen**

	❻ FUTURE	❼ CONDITIONAL
(yo)	vivir**é**	vivir**ía**
(tú)	vivir**ás**	vivir**ías**
(él/ella/Vd)	vivir**á**	vivir**ía**
(nosotros/as)	vivir**emos**	vivir**íamos**
(vosotros/as)	vivir**éis**	vivir**íais**
(ellos/as/Vds)	vivir**án**	vivir**ían**

The Imperative

The imperative is the form of the verb used to give commands or orders. It can be used politely, as in English 'Shut the door, please'.

In *positive* commands, the imperative forms for **Vd**, **Vds** and **nosotros** are the same as the subjunctive. The other forms are as follows:

tú (same as 3rd person singular present indicative)
vosotros (final **-r** of infinitive changes to **-d**) → ❶

(tú)	**habla** speak	**come** eat	**vive** live
(Vd)	**hable** speak	**coma** eat	**viva** live
(nosotros)	**hablemos** let's speak	**comamos** let's eat	**vivamos** let's live
(vosotros)	**hablad** speak	**comed** eat	**vivid** live
(Vds)	**hablen** speak	**coman** eat	**vivan** live

In *negative* commands, all the imperative forms are exactly the same as the present subjunctive.

The imperative of irregular verbs is given in the verb tables, pages 82 to 160.

Position of object pronouns with the imperative:

- in *positive* commands: they follow the verb and are attached to it. An accent is needed to show the correct position for stress (see page 296) → ❷
- in *negative* commands: they precede the verb and are not attached to it → ❸

For the order of object pronouns, see page 236.

Examples

1	cantar	to sing
	cantad	sing
2	Perdóneme	Excuse me
	Enviémoselos	Let's send them to him/her/them
	Elíjanos	Choose us
	Explíquemelo	Explain it to me
	Esperémosla	Let's wait for her/it
	Devuélvaselo	Give it back to him/her/them
3	No me molestes	Don't disturb me
	No se la devolvamos	Let's not give it back to him/her/them
	No les castiguemos	Let's not punish them
	No me lo mandes	Don't send it to me
	No las conteste	Don't answer them
	No nos lo hagan	Don't do it to us

The Imperative *continued*

For reflexive verbs – e.g. **levantarse** to get up – the object pronoun is the reflexive pronoun. It should be noted that the imperative forms need an accent to show the correct position for stress (see page 296). The forms **nosotros** and **vosotros** also drop the final **-s** and **-d** respectively before the pronoun → 1

BUT: **idos (vosotros)** go

ⓘ Note: For general instructions, the infinitive is used instead of the imperative → 2, but when it is preceded by **vamos a** it often translates *let's* ... → 3

Examples

1 Levántate	Get up
No te levantes	Don't get up
Levántese (Vd)	Get up
No se levante (Vd)	Don't get up
Levantémonos	Let's get up
No nos levantemos	Let's not get up
Levantaos	Get up
No os levantéis	Don't get up
Levántense (Vds)	Get up
No se levanten (Vds)	Don't get up
2 Ver pág ...	See page
No pasar	Do not pass ...
3 Vamos a ver	Let's see
Vamos a empezar	Let's start

Compound Tenses: formation

In Spanish the compound tenses are:

Perfect → 1
Pluperfect → 2
Future Perfect → 3
Conditional Perfect → 4
Past Anterior → 5
Perfect Subjunctive → 6
Pluperfect Subjunctive → 7

They consist of the past participle of the verb together with the auxiliary verb **haber**.

Compound tenses are formed in exactly the same way for both regular and irregular verbs, the only difference being that irregular verbs may have an irregular past participle.

The Past Participle

For all compound tenses you need to know how to form the past participle of the verb. For regular verbs this is as follows:

First conjugation: replace the **-ar** of the infinitive by **-ado** → 8

Second conjugation: replace the **-er** of the infinitive by **-ido** → 9

Third conjugation: replace the **-ir** of the infinitive by **-ido** → 10

Examples

1. (yo) he hablado — I have spoken
2. (yo) había hablado — I had spoken
3. (yo) habré hablado — I shall have spoken
4. (yo) habría hablado — I should/would have spoken
5. (yo) hube hablado — I had spoken
6. (que) (yo) haya hablado — (that) I spoke, have spoken
7. (que) (yo) hubiera/hubiese hablado — (that) I had spoken
8. **cantar** to sing → **cantado** sung
9. **comer** to eat → **comido** eaten
10. **vivir** to live → **vivido** lived

Compound Tenses: formation *continued*

PERFECT TENSE
The present tense of **haber** plus the past participle → ①

PLUPERFECT TENSE
The imperfect tense of **haber** plus the past participle → ②

FUTURE PERFECT
The future tense of **haber** plus the past participle → ③

CONDITIONAL PERFECT
The conditional of **haber** plus the past participle → ④

Examples

❶ PERFECT

(yo)	**he** habl**ado**
(tú)	**has** habl**ado**
(él/ella/Vd)	**ha** habl**ado**
(nosotros/as)	**hemos** habl**ado**
(vosotros/as)	**habéis** habl**ado**
(ellos/as/Vds)	**han** habl**ado**

❷ PLUPERFECT

(yo)	**había** habl**ado**
(tú)	**habías** habl**ado**
(él/ella/Vd)	**había** habl**ado**
(nosotros/as)	**habíamos** habl**ado**
(vosotros/as)	**habíais** habl**ado**
(ellos/as/Vds)	**habían** habl**ado**

❸ FUTURE PERFECT

(yo)	**habré** habl**ado**
(tú)	**habrás** habl**ado**
(él/ella/Vd)	**habrá** habl**ado**
(nosotros/as)	**habremos** habl**ado**
(vosotros/as)	**habréis** habl**ado**
(ellos/as/Vds)	**habrán** habl**ado**

❹ CONDITIONAL PERFECT

(yo)	**habría** habl**ado**
(tú)	**habrías** habl**ado**
(él/ella/Vd)	**habría** habl**ado**
(nosotros/as)	**habríamos** habl**ado**
(vosotros/as)	**habríais** habl**ado**
(ellos/as/Vds)	**habrían** habl**ado**

Compound Tenses: Formation *continued*

PAST ANTERIOR
The preterite of **haber** plus the past participle → 1

PERFECT SUBJUNCTIVE
The present subjunctive of **haber** plus the past participle → 2

PLUPERFECT SUBJUNCTIVE
The imperfect subjunctive of **haber** plus the past participle → 3

For how to form the past participle of regular verbs see page 18.
The past participle of irregular verbs is given for each verb in the verb tables, pages 82 to 160.

Examples

1 PAST ANTERIOR

(yo)	**hube** habl**ado**
(tú)	**hubiste** habl**ado**
(él/ella/Vd)	**hubo** habl**ado**
(nosotros/as)	**hubimos** habl**ado**
(vosotros/as)	**hubisteis** habl**ado**
(ellos/as/Vds)	**hubieron** habl**ado**

2 PERFECT SUBJUNCTIVE

(yo)	**haya** habl**ado**
(tú)	**hayas** habl**ado**
(él/ella/Vd)	**haya** habl**ado**
(nosotros/as)	**hayamos** habl**ado**
(vosotros/as)	**hayáis** habl**ado**
(ellos/as/Vds)	**hayan** habl**ado**

3 PLUPERFECT SUBJUNCTIVE

(yo)	**hubiera** *or* **hubiese** habl**ado**
(tú)	**hubieras** *or* **hubieses** habl**ado**
(él/ella/Vd)	**hubiera** *or* **hubiese** habl**ado**
(nosotros/as)	**hubiéramos** *or* **hubiésemos** habl**ado**
(vosotros/as)	**hubierais** *or* **hubieseis** habl**ado**
(ellos/as/Vds)	**hubieran** *or* **hubiesen** habl**ado**

Reflexive Verbs

A reflexive verb is one accompanied by a reflexive pronoun. The infinitive of a reflexive verb ends with the pronoun **se**, which is added to the verb form e.g. **levantarse** to get up; **lavarse** to wash (oneself)
The reflexive pronouns are:

	SINGULAR	PLURAL
1st person	**me**	**nos**
2nd person	**te**	**os**
3rd person	**se**	**se**

The reflexive pronoun 'reflects back' to the subject, but it is not always translated in English → 1

The plural pronouns are sometimes translated as 'one another', 'each other' (the *reciprocal* meaning) → 2

The reciprocal meaning may be emphasized by **el uno al otro/ la una a la otra (los unos a los otros/las unas a las otras)** → 3

Both simple and compound tenses of reflexive verbs are conjugated in exactly the same way as those of non-reflexive verbs, except that the reflexive pronoun is always used.

The only irregularity is in the 1st and 2nd person plural of the affirmative imperative (see page 16). A sample reflexive verb is conjugated in full on pages 28 to 31.

Position of reflexive pronouns

Except with the infinitive, gerund and positive commands, the pronoun comes before the verb → 4

In the infinitive, gerund and positive commands, the pronoun follows the verb and is attached to it (but see also page 232) → 5

Examples

1	Me visto	I'm dressing (myself)
	Nos lavamos	We're washing (ourselves)
	Se levanta	He gets up
2	Nos queremos	We love each other
	Se parecen	They resemble one another
3	Se miraban el uno al otro	They were looking at each other
4	Me acuesto temprano	I go to bed early
	¿Cómo se llama Vd?	What is your name?
	No se ha despertado	He hasn't woken up
	No te levantes	Don't get up
5	Quiero irme	I want to go away
	Estoy levantándome	I am getting up
	Siéntense	Sit down
	Vámonos	Let's go

Reflexive Verbs *continued*

Some verbs have both a reflexive and non-reflexive form. When used reflexively, they have a different but closely related meaning, as shown in the following examples.

NON-REFLEXIVE	REFLEXIVE
acostar to put to bed	**acostarse** to go to bed
casar to marry (off)	**casarse** to get married
detener to stop	**detenerse** to come to a halt
dormir to sleep	**dormirse** to go to sleep
enfadar to annoy	**enfadarse** to get annoyed
hacer to make	**hacerse** to become
ir to go	**irse** to leave, go away
lavar to wash	**lavarse** to get washed
levantar to raise	**levantarse** to get up
llamar to call	**llamarse** to be called
poner to put	**ponerse** to put on (clothing), to become
sentir to feel (something)	**sentirse** to feel (sick, tired, *etc*)
vestir to dress (someone)	**vestirse** to get dressed
volver to return	**volverse** to turn round

Some other verbs exist only in the reflexive:

arrepentirse to repent
atreverse to dare
jactarse to boast
quejarse to complain

Some verbs acquire a different nuance when used reflexively:

caer to fall → 1
caerse to fall down (by accident) → 2

morir to die, be killed (by accident or on purpose) → 3
morirse to die (from natural causes) → 4

Often a reflexive verb can be used:

- to avoid the passive (see page 32) → 5
- in impersonal expressions (see page 40) → 6

Examples

1 El agua caía desde las rocas	Water fell from the rocks
2 Me caí y me rompí el brazo	I fell and broke my arm
3 Tres personas han muerto en un accidente/atentado terrorista	Three people were killed in an accident/a terrorist attack
4 Mi abuelo se murió a los ochenta años	My grandfather died at the age of eighty
5 Se perdió la batalla No se veían las casas	The battle was lost The houses could not be seen
6 Se dice que ... No se puede entrar No se permite	(It is said that) People say that ... You/One can't go in It is not allowed

Reflexive Verbs *continued*

Conjugation of: **lavarse** to wash oneself

1 SIMPLE TENSES

PRESENT

(yo)	**me** lav**o**
(tú)	**te** lav**as**
(él/ella/Vd)	**se** lav**a**
(nosotros/as)	**nos** lav**amos**
(vosotros/as)	**os** lav**áis**
(ellos/as/Vds)	**se** lav**an**

IMPERFECT

(yo)	**me** lav**aba**
(tú)	**te** lav**abas**
(él/ella/Vd)	**se** lav**aba**
(nosotros/as)	**nos** lav**ábamos**
(vosotros/as)	**os** lav**abais**
(ellos/as/Vds)	**se** lav**aban**

FUTURE

(yo)	**me** lavar**é**
(tú)	**te** lavar**ás**
(él/ella/Vd)	**se** lavar**á**
(nosotros/as)	**nos** lavar**emos**
(vosotros/as)	**os** lavar**éis**
(ellos/as/Vds)	**se** lavar**án**

CONDITIONAL

(yo)	**me** lavar**ía**
(tú)	**te** lavar**ías**
(él/ella/Vd)	**se** lavar**ía**
(nosotros/as)	**nos** lavar**íamos**
(vosotros/as)	**os** lavar**íais**
(ellos/as/Vds)	**se** lavar**ían**

Reflexive Verbs *continued*

Conjugation of: **lavarse** to wash oneself

1 SIMPLE TENSES

PRETERITE

(yo)	**me** lav**é**
(tú)	**te** lav**aste**
(él/ella/Vd)	**se** lav**ó**
(nosotros/as)	**nos** lav**amos**
(vosotros/as)	**os** lav**asteis**
(ellos/as/Vds)	**se** lav**aron**

PRESENT SUBJUNCTIVE

(yo)	**me** lav**e**
(tú)	**te** lav**es**
(él/ella/Vd)	**se** lav**e**
(nosotros/as)	**nos** lav**emos**
(vosotros/as)	**os** lav**éis**
(ellos/as/Vds)	**se** lav**en**

IMPERFECT SUBJUNCTIVE

(yo)	**me** lav**ara** *or* lav**ase**
(tú)	**te** lav**aras** *or* lav**ases**
(él/ella/Vd)	**se** lav**ara** *or* lav**ase**
(nosotros/as)	**nos** lav**áramos** *or* lav**ásemos**
(vosotros/as)	**os** lav**arais** *or* lav**aseis**
(ellos/as/Vds)	**se** lav**aran** *or* lav**asen**

Reflexive Verbs *continued*

Conjugation of: **lavarse** to wash oneself

2 COMPOUND TENSES

PERFECT

(yo)	**me he** lav**ado**
(tú)	**te has** lav**ado**
(él/ella/Vd)	**se ha** lav**ado**
(nosotros/as)	**nos hemos** lav**ado**
(vosotros/as)	**os habéis** lav**ado**
(ellos/as/Vds)	**se han** lav**ado**

PLUPERFECT

(yo)	**me había** lav**ado**
(tú)	**te habías** lav**ado**
(él/ella/Vd)	**se había** lav**ado**
(nosotros/as)	**nos habíamos** lav**ado**
(vosotros/as)	**os habíais** lav**ado**
(ellos/as/Vds)	**se habían** lav**ado**

FUTURE PERFECT

(yo)	**me habré** lav**ado**
(tú)	**te habrás** lav**ado**
(él/ella/Vd)	**se habrá** lav**ado**
(nosotros/as)	**nos habremos** lav**ado**
(vosotros/as)	**os habréis** lav**ado**
(ellos/as/Vds)	**se habrán** lav**ado**

Reflexive Verbs *continued*

Conjugation of: **lavarse** to wash oneself

2 COMPOUND TENSES

PAST ANTERIOR

(yo)	**me hube** lav**ado**
(tú)	**te hubiste** lav**ado**
(él/ella/Vd)	**se hubo** lav**ado**
(nosotros/as)	**nos hubimos** lav**ado**
(vosotros/as)	**os hubisteis** lav**ado**
(ellos/as/Vds)	**se hubieron** lav**ado**

PERFECT SUBJUNCTIVE

(yo)	**me haya** lav**ado**
(tú)	**te hayas** lav**ado**
(él/ella/Vd)	**se haya** lav**ado**
(nosotros/as)	**nos hayamos** lav**ado**
(vosotros/as)	**os hayáis** lav**ado**
(ellos/as/Vds)	**se hayan** lav**ado**

PLUPERFECT SUBJUNCTIVE

(yo)	**me hubiera** *or* **hubiese** lav**ado**
(tú)	**te hubieras** *or* **hubieses** lav**ado**
(él/ella/Vd)	**se hubiera** *or* **hubiese** lav**ado**
(nosotros/as)	**nos hubiéramos** *or* **hubiésemos** lav**ado**
(vosotros/as)	**os hubierais** *or* **hubieseis** lav**ado**
(ellos/as/Vds)	**se hubieran** *or* **hubiesen** lav**ado**

The Passive

In active sentences, the subject of a verb carries out the action of that verb, but in passive sentences the subject receives the action. Compare the following:

The car hit Jane (*subject*: the car)
Jane was hit by the car (*subject*: Jane)

English uses the verb 'to be' with the past participle to form passive sentences. Spanish forms them in the same way, i.e.:
a tense of **ser** + *past participle*.

The past participle agrees in number and gender with the subject → 1

A sample verb is conjugated in the passive voice on pages 36 to 39.

In English, the word 'by' usually introduces the agent through which the action of a passive sentence is performed. In Spanish this agent is preceded by **por** → 2

The passive voice is used much less frequently in Spanish than English. It is, however, often used in expressions where the identity of the agent is unknown or unimportant → 3

Examples

1	Pablo ha sido despedido	Paul has been sacked
	Su madre era muy admirada	His mother was greatly admired
	El palacio será vendido	The palace will be sold
	Las puertas habían sido cerradas	The doors had been closed
2	La casa fue diseñada por mi hermano	The house was designed by my brother
3	La ciudad fue conquistada tras un largo asedio	The city was conquered after a long siege
	Ha sido declarado el estado de excepción	A state of emergency has been declared

The Passive *continued*

In English the indirect object in an active sentence can become the subject of the related passive sentence, e.g.

'His mother gave him the book' (*indirect object*: him)
He was given the book by his mother

This is not possible in Spanish. The indirect object remains as such, while the object of the active sentence becomes the subject of the passive sentence → 1

Other ways to express a passive meaning

Since modern Spanish tends to avoid the passive, it uses various other constructions to replace it:

If the agent (person or object performing the action) is known, the active is often preferred where English might prefer the passive → 2

The 3rd person plural of the active voice can be used. The meaning is equivalent to 'they' + *verb* → 3

When the action of the sentence is performed on a person, the reflexive form of the verb can be used in the 3rd person singular, and the person becomes the object → 4

When the action is performed on a thing, this becomes the subject of the sentence and the verb is made reflexive, agreeing in number with the subject → 5

Examples

① Su madre le regaló el libro	His mother gave him the book
BECOMES:	
El libro le fue regalado por su madre	The book was given to him by his mother
② La policía interrogó al sospechoso	The police questioned the suspect
RATHER THAN:	
El sospechoso fue interrogado por la policía	
③ Usan demasiada publicidad en la televisión	Too much advertising is used on television
④ Últimamente no se le/les ha visto mucho en público	He has/they have not been seen much in public recently
⑤ Esta palabra ya no se usa	This word is no longer used
Todos los libros se han vendido	All the books have been sold

The Passive *continued*

Conjugation of: **ser amado** to be loved

PRESENT

(yo)	**soy** amado(a)
(tú)	**eres** amado(a)
(él/ella/Vd)	**es** amado(a)
(nosotros/as)	**somos** amado(a)s
(vosotros/as)	**sois** amado(a)s
(ellos/as/Vds)	**son** amado(a)s

IMPERFECT

(yo)	**era** amado(a)
(tú)	**eras** amado(a)
(él/ella/Vd)	**era** amado(a)
(nosotros/as)	**éramos** amado(a)s
(vosotros/as)	**erais** amado(a)s
(ellos/as/Vds)	**eran** amado(a)s

FUTURE

(yo)	**seré** amado(a)
(tú)	**serás** amado(a)
(él/ella/Vd)	**será** amado(a)
(nosotros/as)	**seremos** amado(a)s
(vosotros/as)	**seréis** amado(a)s
(ellos/as/Vds)	**serán** amado(a)s

CONDITIONAL

(yo)	**sería** amado(a)
(tú)	**serías** amado(a)
(él/ella/Vd)	**sería** amado(a)
(nosotros/as)	**seríamos** amado(a)s
(vosotros/as)	**seríais** amado(a)s
(ellos/as/Vds)	**serían** amado(a)s

The Passive *continued*

Conjugation of: **ser amado** to be loved

PRETERITE

(yo)	**fui** am**ado(a)**
(tú)	**fuiste** am**ado(a)**
(él/ella/Vd)	**fue** am**ado(a)**
(nosotros/as)	**fuimos** am**ado(a)s**
(vosotros/as)	**fuisteis** am**ado(a)s**
(ellos/as/Vds)	**fueron** am**ado(a)s**

PRESENT SUBJUNCTIVE

(yo)	**sea** am**ado(a)**
(tú)	**seas** am**ado(a)**
(él/ella/Vd)	**sea** am**ado(a)**
(nosotros/as)	**seamos** am**ado(a)s**
(vosotros/as)	**seáis** am**ado(a)s**
(ellos/as/Vds)	**sean** am**ado(a)s**

IMPERFECT SUBJUNCTIVE

(yo)	**fuera** *or* **fuese** am**ado(a)**
(tú)	**fueras** *or* **fueses** am**ado(a)**
(él/ella/Vd)	**fuera** *or* **fuese** am**ado(a)**
(nosotros/as)	**fuéramos** *or* **fuésemos** am**ado(a)s**
(vosotros/as)	**fuerais** *or* **fueseis** am**ado(a)s**
(ellos/as/Vds)	**fueran** *or* **fuesen** am**ado(a)s**

The Passive *continued*

Conjugation of: **ser amado** to be loved

PERFECT

(yo)	**he sido** am**ado(a)**
(tú)	**has sido** am**ado(a)**
(él/ella/Vd)	**ha sido** am**ado(a)**
(nosotros/as)	**hemos sido** am**ado(a)s**
(vosotros/as)	**habéis sido** am**ado(a)s**
(ellos/as/Vds)	**han sido** am**ado(a)s**

PLUPERFECT

(yo)	**había sido** am**ado(a)**
(tú)	**habías sido** am**ado(a)**
(él/ella/Vd)	**había sido** am**ado(a)**
(nosotros/as)	**habíamos sido** am**ado(a)s**
(vosotros/as)	**habíais sido** am**ado(a)s**
(ellos/as/Vds)	**habían sido** am**ado(a)s**

FUTURE PERFECT

(yo)	**habré sido** am**ado(a)**
(tú)	**habrás sido** am**ado(a)**
(él/ella/Vd)	**habrá sido** am**ado(a)**
(nosotros/as)	**habremos sido** am**ado(a)s**
(vosotros/as)	**habréis sido** am**ado(a)s**
(ellos/as/Vds)	**habrán sido** am**ado(a)s**

CONDITIONAL PERFECT

(yo)	**habría sido** am**ado(a)**
(tú)	**habrías sido** am**ado(a)**
(él/ella/Vd)	**habría sido** am**ado(a)**
(nosotros/as)	**habríamos sido** am**ado(a)s**
(vosotros/as)	**habríais sido** am**ado(a)s**
(ellos/as/Vds)	**habrían sido** am**ado(a)s**

The Passive *continued*

Conjugation of: **ser amado** to be loved

PAST ANTERIOR

(yo)	**hube sido** am**ado(a)**
(tú)	**hubiste sido** am**ado(a)**
(él/ella/Vd)	**hubo sido** am**ado(a)**
(nosotros/as)	**hubimos sido** am**ado(a)s**
(vosotros/as)	**hubisteis sido** am**ado(a)s**
(ellos/as/Vds)	**hubieron sido** am**ado(a)s**

PERFECT SUBJUNCTIVE

(yo)	**haya sido** am**ado(a)**
(tú)	**hayas sido** am**ado(a)**
(él/ella/Vd)	**haya sido** am**ado(a)**
(nosotros/as)	**hayamos sido** am**ado(a)s**
(vosotros/as)	**hayáis sido** am**ado(a)s**
(ellos/as/Vds)	**hayan sido** am**ado(a)s**

PLUPERFECT SUBJUNCTIVE

(yo)	**hubiera/-se sido** am**ado(a)**
(tú)	**hubieras/-ses sido** am**ado(a)**
(él/ella/Vd)	**hubiera/-se sido** am**ado(a)**
(nosotros/as)	**hubiéramos/-semos sido** am**ado(a)s**
(vosotros/as)	**hubierais/-seis sido** am**ado(a)s**
(ellos/as/Vds)	**hubieran/-sen sido** am**ado(a)s**

Impersonal Verbs

Impersonal verbs are used only in the infinitive, the gerund, and in the 3rd person (usually singular); unlike English, Spanish does not use the subject pronoun with impersonal verbs, e.g.

llueve it's raining
es fácil decir que ... it's easy to say that ...

The most common impersonal verbs are:

INFINITIVE	CONSTRUCTION
amanecer	amanece/está amaneciendo it's daybreak
anochecer	anochece/está anocheciendo it's getting dark
granizar	graniza/está granizando it's hailing
llover	llueve/está lloviendo it's raining → 1
lloviznar	llovizna/está lloviznando it's drizzling
nevar	nieva/está nevando it's snowing → 1
tronar	truena/está tronando it's thundering

Some reflexive verbs are also used impersonally.
The most common are:

INFINITIVE	CONSTRUCTION
creerse	se cree que* + *indicative* → 2 it is thought that; people think that
decirse	se dice que* + *indicative* → 3 it is said that; people say that

Examples

❶ Llovía a cántaros	It was raining cats and dogs
Estaba nevando cuando salieron	It was snowing when they left
❷ Se cree que llegarán mañana	It is thought they will arrive tomorrow
❸ Se dice que ha sido el peor invierno en 50 años	People say it's been the worst winter in 50 years

Impersonal Verbs *continued*

INFINITIVE	CONSTRUCTION
poderse	**se puede** + *infinitive* → 1 one/people can, it is possible to
tratarse de	**se trata de** + *noun* → 2 it's a question/matter of something it's about something
	se trata de + *infinitive* → 3 it's a question/matter of doing; somebody must do
venderse	**se vende*** + *noun* → 4 to be sold; for sale

* This impersonal construction conveys the same meaning as the 3rd person plural of these verbs; **creen que**, **dicen que**, **venden**

The following verbs are also commonly used in impersonal constructions:

INFINITIVE	CONSTRUCTION
bastar	**basta con** + *infinitive* → 5 it is enough to do **basta con** + *noun* → 6 something is enough, it only takes something
faltar	**falta** + *infinitive* → 7 we still have to/one still has to
haber	**hay** + *noun* → 8 there is/are **hay que** + *infinitive* → 9 one has to/we have to
hacer	**hace** + *noun/adjective depicting weather/dark/light etc* → 10 it is **hace** + *time expression* + **que** + *indicative* → 11 somebody has done *or* been doing something since ... **hace** + *time expression* + **que** + *negative indicative* → 12 it is ... since

Examples

1 Aquí se puede aparcar	One can park here
2 No se trata de dinero	It isn't a question/matter of money
3 Se trata de poner fin al asunto	We must put an end to the matter
4 Se vende coche	Car for sale
5 Basta con telefonear para reservar un asiento	You need only phone to reserve a seat
6 Basta con un error para que todo se estropee	One single error is enough to ruin everything
7 Aún falta cerrar las maletas	We/One still have/has to close the suitcases
8 Hay una habitación libre	There is one spare room
No había cartas esta mañana	There were no letters this morning
9 Hay que cerrar las puertas	We have/One has to shut the doors
10 Hace calor/viento/sol	It is hot/windy/sunny
Mañana hará bueno	It'll be nice (weather) tomorrow
11 Hace seis meses que vivo/vivimos aquí	I/We have lived *or* been living here for six months
12 Hace tres años que no le veo	It is three years since I last saw him

Impersonal Verbs *continued*

INFINITIVE	CONSTRUCTION
hacer falta	**hace falta** + *noun object (+ indirect object)* → ❶ (somebody) needs something; something is necessary (to somebody)
	hace falta + *infinitive* (+ *indirect object*) → ❷ it is necessary to do
	hace falta que + *subjunctive* → ❸ it is necessary to do, somebody must do
parecer	**parece que** (+ *indirect object*) + *indicative* → ❹ it seems/appears that
ser	**es/son** + *time expression* → ❺ it is
	es + de día/noche → ❻ it is
	es + *adjective* + *infinitive* → ❼ it is
ser mejor	**es mejor** + *infinitive* → ❽ it's better to do
	es mejor que + *subjunctive* → ❾ it's better if/that
valer más	**más vale** + *infinitive* → ❿ it's better to do
	más vale que + *subjunctive* → ⓫ it's better to do/that somebody does

Examples

1	Hace falta valor para hacer eso	One needs courage to do that/ Courage is needed to do that
	Me hace falta otro vaso más	I need an extra glass
2	Hace falta volver	It is necessary to return/ We/I/You must return*
	Me hacía falta volver	I had to return
3	Hace falta que Vd se vaya	You have to/must leave
4	(Me) parece que estás equivocado	It seems (to me) you are wrong
5	Son las tres y media	It is half past three
	Ya es primavera	It is spring now
6	Era de noche cuando llegamos	It was night when we arrived
7	Era inútil protestar	It was useless to complain
8	Es mejor no decir nada	It's better to keep quiet
9	Es mejor que lo pongas aquí	It's better if/that you put it here
10	Más vale prevenir que curar	Prevention is better than cure
11	Más valdría que no fuéramos	It would be better if we didn't go/ We'd better not go

*The translation here obviously depends on context

The Infinitive

The infinitive is the form of the verb found in dictionary entries meaning 'to ...', e.g. **hablar** to speak, **vivir** to live.

The infinitive is used in the following ways:

After a preposition → ❶

As a verbal noun → ❷
In this use the article may precede the infinitive, especially when the infinitive is the subject and begins the sentence → ❸

As a dependent infinitive, in the following verbal constructions:

- with no linking preposition → ❹
- with the linking preposition **a** → ❺ (see also page 66)
- with the linking preposition **de** → ❻ (see also page 66)
- with the linking preposition **en** → ❼ (see also page 66)
- with the linking preposition **con** → ❽ (see also page 66)
- with the linking preposition **por** → ❾ (see also page 66)

The following construction should also be noted:
indefinite pronoun + **que** + *infinitive* → ❿

The object pronouns generally follow the infinitive and are attached to it. For exceptions see page 232.

Examples

1 Después de acabar el desayuno, salió de casa	After finishing her breakfast she went out
Al enterarse de lo ocurrido se puso furiosa	When she found out what had happened she was furious
Me hizo daño sin saberlo	She hurt me without her knowing
2 Su deporte preferido es montar a caballo	Her favourite sport is horse riding
Ver es creer	Seeing is believing
3 El viajar tanto me resulta cansado	I find so much travelling tiring
4 ¿Quiere Vd esperar?	Would you like to wait?
5 Aprenderán pronto a nadar	They will soon learn to swim
6 Pronto dejará de llover	It'll stop raining soon
7 La comida tarda en hacerse	The meal is taking a long time to cook
8 Amenazó con denunciarles	He threatened to report them (to the police)
9 Comience Vd por decirme su nombre	Please start by giving me your name
10 Tengo algo que decirte	I have something to tell you

The Infinitive *continued*

The verbs set out below are followed by the infinitive with no linking preposition.

deber, **poder**, **saber**, **querer** and **tener que** (**hay que** in impersonal constructions) → ❶

valer más, **hacer falta**: see Impersonal Verbs, page 44.

verbs of seeing or hearing, e.g. **ver** to see, **oír** to hear → ❷

hacer → ❸

dejar to let, allow → ❸

The following common verbs:

- **aconsejar** to advise → ❹
- **conseguir** to manage to → ❺
- **decidir** to decide
- **desear** to wish, want → ❻
- **esperar** to hope → ❼
- **evitar** to avoid → ❽
- **impedir** to prevent → ❾
- **intentar** to try → ❿
- **lograr** to manage to → ❺
- **necesitar** to need → ⓫
- **odiar** to hate
- **olvidar** to forget → ⓬
- **pensar** to think → ⓭
- **preferir** to prefer → ⓮
- **procurar** to try → ❿
- **prohibir** to forbid → ⓯
- **prometer** to promise → ⓰
- **proponer** to propose → ⓱

Examples

1	¿Quiere Vd esperar? No puede venir	Would you like to wait? She can't come
2	Nos ha visto llegar Se les oye cantar	She saw us arriving You can hear them singing
3	No me hagas reír Déjeme pasar	Don't make me laugh Let me past
4	Le aconsejamos dejarlo para mañana	We advise you to leave it until tomorrow
5	Aún no he conseguido/logrado entenderlo	I still haven't managed to understand it
6	No desea tener más hijos	She doesn't want to have any more children
7	Esperamos ir de vacaciones este verano	We are hoping to go on holiday this summer
8	Evite beber cuando conduzca	Avoid drinking and driving
9	No pudo impedirle hablar	He couldn't prevent him from speaking
10	Intentamos/procuramos pasar desapercibidos	We tried not to be noticed
11	Necesitaba salir a la calle	I/he/she needed to go out
12	Olvidó dejar su dirección	He/she forgot to leave his/her address
13	¿Piensan venir por Navidad?	Are you thinking of coming for Christmas?
14	Preferiría elegirlo yo mismo	I'd rather choose it myself
15	Prohibió fumar a los alumnos	He forbade the pupils to smoke
16	Prometieron volver pronto	They promised to come back soon
17	Propongo salir cuanto antes	I propose to leave as soon as possible

The Infinitive: Set Expressions

The following are set in Spanish with the meaning shown:

dejar caer to drop → ❶
hacer entrar to show in → ❷
hacer saber to let know, make known → ❸
hacer salir to let out → ❹
hacer venir to send for → ❺
ir(se) a buscar to go for, go and get → ❻
mandar hacer to order → ❼
mandar llamar to send for → ❽
oír decir que to hear it said that → ❾
oír hablar de to hear of/about → ❿
querer decir to mean → ⓫

The Perfect Infinitive

The perfect infinitive is formed using the auxiliary verb **haber** with the past participle of the verb → ⓬

The perfect infinitive is found:

- following certain prepositions, especially **después de** after → ⓭
- following certain verbal constructions → ⓮

Examples

1	Al verlo, dejó caer lo que llevaba en las manos	When he saw him he dropped what he was carrying
2	Haz entrar a nuestros invitados	Show our guests in
3	Quiero hacerles saber que no serán bien recibidos	I want to let them know that they won't be welcome
4	Hágale salir, por favor	Please let him out
5	Le he hecho venir a Vd porque ...	I sent for you because ...
6	Vete a buscar los guantes	Go and get your gloves
7	Me he mandado hacer un traje	I have ordered a suit
8	Mandaron llamar al médico	They sent for the doctor
9	He oído decir que está enfermo	I've heard it said that he's ill
10	No he oído hablar más de él	I haven't heard anything more (said) of him
11	¿Qué quiere decir eso?	What does that mean?
12	haber terminado haberse vestido	to have finished to have got dressed
13	Después de haber comprado el regalo, volvió a casa Después de haber madrugado tanto, el taxi se retrasó	After buying/having bought the present, he went back home After she got up so early, the taxi arrived late
14	perdonar a alguien por haber hecho dar las gracias a alguien por haber hecho pedir perdón por haber hecho	to forgive somebody for doing/having done to thank somebody for doing/having done to be sorry for doing/having done

The Gerund

Formation

First conjugation:

- replace the **-ar** of the infinitive by **-ando** → ①

Second conjugation:

- replace the **-er** of the infinitive by **-iendo** → ②

Third conjugation:

- replace the **-ir** of the infinitive by **-iendo** → ③

For irregular gerunds, see irregular verbs, page 80 onwards.

Uses

After the verb **estar**, to form the continuous tenses → ④

After the verbs **seguir** and **continuar** *to continue*, and **ir** when meaning to *happen gradually* → ⑤

In time constructions, after **llevar** → ⑥

When the action in the main clause needs to be complemented by another action → ⑦

The position of object pronouns is the same as for the infinitive (see page 46).

The gerund is invariable and strictly verbal in sense.

The Present Participle

It is formed by replacing the **-ar** of the infinitive of 1st conjugation verbs by **-ante**, and the **-er** and **-ir** of the 2nd and 3rd conjugations by **-iente** → ⑧

A very limited number of verbs have a present participle used either as an adjective or a noun → ⑨/⑩

Examples

1 cantar to sing → cantando singing

2 temer to fear → temiendo fearing

3 partir to leave → partiendo leaving

4 Estoy escribiendo una carta	I am writing a letter
Estaban esperándonos	They were waiting for us
5 Sigue viniendo todos los días	He/she is still coming every day
Continuarán subiendo los precios	Prices will continue to go up
El ejército iba avanzando poco a poco	The army was gradually advancing
6 Lleva dos años estudiando inglés	He/she has been studying English for two years
7 Pasamos el día tomando el sol en la playa	We spent the day sunbathing on the beach
Iba cojeando	He/she/I was limping
Salieron corriendo	They ran out

8 cantar to sing → cantante singing/singer
pender to hang → pendiente hanging
seguir to follow → siguiente following

9 agua corriente	running water
10 un estudiante	a student

Use of Tenses

The Present

Unlike English, Spanish often uses the same verb form for the simple present (e.g. I smoke, he reads, we live) and the continuous present (e.g. I am smoking, he is reading, we are living) → ①

Normally, however, the continuous present is used to translate the Spanish:
estar haciendo to be doing → ②

Spanish uses the present tense where English uses the perfect in the following cases:

- with certain prepositions of time – notably **desde** for/since – when an action begun in the past is continued in the present → ③
  ⓘ Note: The perfect can be used as in English when the verb is negative → ④
- in the construction **acabar de hacer** to have just done → ⑤

Like English, Spanish often uses the present where a future action is implied → ⑥

The Future

The future is generally used as in English → ⑦, but note the following:

Immediate future time is often expressed by means of the present tense of **ir** + **a** + infinitive → ⑧

When 'will' or 'shall' mean 'wish to', 'are willing to', **querer** is used → ⑨

The Future Perfect

Used as in English shall/will have done → ⑩

It can also express conjecture, usually about things in the recent past → ⑪

Examples

1 Fumo I smoke *or* I am smoking
Lee He reads *or* He is reading
Vivimos We live *or* We are living

2 Está fumando	He is smoking
3 Linda estudia español desde hace seis meses	Linda's been learning Spanish for six months (and still is)
Estoy de pie desde las siete	I've been up since seven
¿Hace mucho que esperan?	Have you been waiting long?
Ya hace dos semanas que estamos aquí	That's two weeks we've been here (now)
4 No se han visto desde hace meses	They haven't seen each other for months
5 Isabel acaba de salir	Isabel has just left
6 Mañana voy a Madrid	I am going to Madrid tomorrow
7 Lo haré mañana	I'll do it tomorrow
8 Te vas a caer si no tienes cuidado	You'll fall if you're not careful
Va a perder el tren	He's going to miss the train
Va a llevar una media hora	It'll take about half an hour
9 ¿Me quieres esperar un momento, por favor?	Will you wait for me a second, please?
10 Lo habré acabado para mañana	I will have finished it for tomorrow
11 Ya habrán llegado a casa	They must have arrived home by now

Use of Tenses *continued*

The Imperfect

The imperfect describes:

- an action or state in the past without definite limits in time → 1
- habitual action(s) in the past (often expressed in English by means of would or used to) → 2

Spanish uses the imperfect tense where English uses the pluperfect in the following cases:

- with certain prepositions of time – notably **desde** for/since – when an action begun in the remoter past was continued in the more recent past → 3
  - ⓘ Note: The pluperfect is used as in English when the verb is negative or the action has been completed → 4
- in the construction **acabar de hacer** to have just done → 5

Both the continuous and simple forms in English can be translated by the Spanish simple imperfect, but the continuous imperfect is used when the emphasis is on the fact that an action was going on at a precise moment in the past → 6

The Perfect

The perfect is generally used as in English → 7

The Preterite

The preterite generally corresponds to the English simple past in both written and spoken Spanish → 8

However, while English can use the simple past to describe habitual actions or settings, Spanish uses the imperfect (see above) → 9

The Past Anterior

This tense is only ever used in written, literary Spanish, to replace the pluperfect in time clauses where the verb in the main clause is in the preterite → 10

Examples

1	Todos mirábamos en silencio	We were all watching in silence
	Nuestras habitaciones daban a la playa	Our rooms overlooked the beach
2	En su juventud se levantaba de madrugada	In his youth he got up at dawn
	Hablábamos sin parar durante horas	We would talk non-stop for hours on end
	Mi hermano siempre me tomaba el pelo	My brother always used to tease me
3	Hacía dos años que vivíamos en Irlanda	We had been living in Ireland for two years
	Estaba enfermo desde 1990	He had been ill since 1990
	Hacía mucho tiempo que salían juntos	They had been going out together for a long time
4	Hacía un año que no le había visto	I hadn't seen him for a year
	Hacía una hora que había llegado	She had arrived an hour before
5	Acababa de encontrármelos	I had just met them
6	Cuando llegué, todos estaban fumando	When I arrived, they were all smoking
7	Todavía no han salido	They haven't come out yet
8	Me desperté y salté de la cama	I woke up and jumped out of bed
9	Siempre iban en coche al trabajo	They always travelled to work by car
10	Apenas hubo acabado, se oyeron unos golpes en la puerta	She had scarcely finished when there was a knock at the door

The Subjunctive: when to use it

For how to form the subjunctive see page 6 onwards.

After verbs of:

- 'wishing'

querer que **desear que**	to wish that, want → 1

- 'emotion' (e.g. regret, surprise, shame, pleasure, etc)

sentir que	to be sorry that → 2
sorprender que	to be surprised that → 3
alegrarse de que	to be pleased that → 4

- 'asking' and 'advising'

pedir que	to ask that → 5
aconsejar que	to advise that → 6

In all the above constructions, when the subject of the verbs in the main and subordinate clause is the same, the infinitive is used, and the conjunction **que** omitted → 7

- 'ordering', 'forbidding', 'allowing'

mandar que* **ordenar que**	to order that → 8
permitir que* **dejar que***	to allow that → 9
prohibir que*	to forbid that → 10
impedir que*	to prevent that → 11

*With these verbs either the subjunctive or the infinitive is used when the object of the main verb is the subject of the subordinate verb → 12

Always after verbs expressing doubt or uncertainty, and verbs of opinion used negatively.

dudar que	to doubt that → 13
no creer que **no pensar que**	not to think that → 14

Examples

1	Queremos que esté contenta	We want her to be happy (*literally*: We want that she is happy)
	¿Desea Vd que lo haga yo?	Do you want me to do it?
2	Sentí mucho que no vinieran	I was very sorry that they didn't come
3	Nos sorprendió que no les vieran Vds	We were surprised you didn't see them
4	Me alegro de que te gusten	I'm pleased that you like them
5	Sólo les pedimos que tengan cuidado	We're only asking you to take care
6	Le aconsejé que no llegara tarde	I advised him not to be late
7	Quiero que lo termines pronto	I want you to finish it soon
	BUT:	
	Quiero terminarlo pronto	I want to finish it soon
8	Ha mandado que vuelvan	He has ordered them to come back
	Ordenó que fueran castigados	He ordered them to be punished
9	No permitas que te tomen el pelo	Don't let them pull your leg
	No me dejó que la llevara a casa	She didn't allow me to take her home
10	Te prohíbo que digas eso	I forbid you to say that
11	No les impido que vengan	I am not preventing them from coming
12	Les ordenó que salieran *or* Les ordenó salir	She ordered them to go out
13	Dudo que lo sepan hacer	I doubt they can do it
14	No creo que sean tan listos	I don't think they are as clever as that

The Subjunctive: when to use it *continued*

In impersonal constructions which express necessity, possibility, etc:

hace falta que / **es necesario que**	it is necessary that → 1
es posible que	it is possible that → 2
más vale que	it is better that → 3
es una lástima que	it is a pity that → 4

ⓘ Note: In impersonal constructions which state a fact or express certainty the indicative is used when the impersonal verb is affirmative. When it is negative, the subjunctive is used → 5

After certain conjunctions:

para que / **a fin de que***	so that → 6
como si	as if → 7
sin que*	without → 8
a condición de que* / **con tal (de) que*** / **siempre que**	provided that, on condition that → 9
a menos que / **a no ser que**	unless → 10
antes (de) que*	before → 11
no sea que	lest/in case → 12
mientras (que) / **siempre que**	as long as → 13
(el) que	the fact that → 14

*When the subject of both verbs is the same, the infinitive is used, and the final **que** is omitted → 8

Examples

1	¿Hace falta que vaya Jaime?	Does James have to go?
2	Es posible que tengan razón	It's possible that they are right
3	Más vale que se quede Vd en su casa	It's better that you stay at home
4	Es una lástima que haya perdido su perrito	It's a shame/pity that she has lost her puppy
5	Es verdad que va a venir	It's true that he's coming
	BUT:	
	No es verdad que vayan a hacerlo	It's not true that they are going to do it
6	Átalas bien para que no se caigan	Tie them up tightly so that they won't fall
7	Hablaba como si no creyera en sus propias palabras	He talked as if he didn't believe in his own words
8	Salimos sin que nos vieran	We left without them seeing us
	BUT:	
	Me fui sin esperarla	I went without waiting for her
9	Lo haré con tal de que me cuentes todo lo que pasó	I'll do it provided you tell me all that happened
10	Saldremos de paseo a menos que esté lloviendo	We'll go for a walk unless it's raining
11	Avísale antes de que sea demasiado tarde	Warn him before it's too late
12	Habla en voz baja, no sea que alguien nos oiga	Speak softly in case anyone hears us
13	Eso no pasará mientras yo sea el jefe aquí	That won't happen as long as I am the boss here
14	El que no me escribiera no me importaba demasiado	The fact that he didn't write didn't matter to me too much

The Subjunctive: when to use it *continued*

After the conjunctions:

de modo que
de forma que so that (*indicating a purpose*) → 1
de manera que

ⓘ Note: When these conjunctions introduce a result and not a purpose the subjunctive is not used → 2

In relative clauses with an antecedent which is:

- negative → 3
- indefinite → 4
- non-specific → 5

In main clauses, to express a wish or exhortation. The verb may be preceded by expressions like **ojalá** or **que** → 6

In the **si** clause of conditions where the English sentence contains a conditional tense → 7

In set expressions → 8

In the following constructions which translate however:

- **por** + *adjective* + *subjunctive* → 9
- **por** + *adverb* + *subjunctive* → 10
- **por** + **mucho** + *subjunctive* → 11

Examples

❶ Vuélvanse de manera que les vea bien	Turn round so that I can see you properly
❷ No quieren hacerlo, de manera que tendré que hacerlo yo	They won't do it, so I'll have to do it myself
❸ No he encontrado a nadie que la conociera	I haven't met anyone who knows her
No dijo nada que no supiéramos ya	He/she didn't say anything we didn't already know
❹ Necesito alguien que sepa conducir	I need someone who can drive
Busco algo que me distraiga	I'm looking for something to take my mind off it
❺ Busca una casa que tenga calefacción central	He/she's looking for a house which has central heating (*subjunctive used since such a house may or may not exist*)
El que lo haya visto tiene que decírmelo	Anyone who has seen it must tell me (*subjunctive used since it is not known who has seen it*)
❻ ¡Ojalá haga buen tiempo!	Let's hope the weather will be good!
¡Que te diviertas!	Have a good time!
❼ Si fuéramos en coche llegaríamos a tiempo	If we went by car we'd be there in time
❽ Diga lo que diga ...	Whatever he may say ...
Sea lo que sea ...	Be that as it may ...
Pase lo que pase ...	Come what may ...
Sea como sea ...	One way or another ...
❾ Por cansado que esté, seguirá trabajando	No matter how/however tired he may be, he'll go on working
❿ Por lejos que viva, iremos a buscarle	No matter how/however far away he lives, we'll go and look for him
⓫ Por mucho que lo intente, nunca lo conseguirá	No matter how/however hard he tries, he'll never succeed

The Subjunctive: when to use it *continued*

Clauses taking either a subjunctive or an indicative

In certain constructions, a subjunctive is needed when the action refers to future events or hypothetical situations, whereas an indicative is used when stating a fact or experience → 1

The commonest of these are:

The conjunctions:

cuando	when → 1
en cuanto / **tan pronto como**	as soon as → 2
después (de) que*	after → 3
hasta que	until → 4
mientras	while → 5
siempre que	whenever → 6
aunque	even though → 7

All conjunctions and pronouns ending in **-quiera** (*-ever*) → 8

* ⓘ Note: If the subject of both verbs is the same, the subjunctive introduced by **después (de) que** may be replaced by **después de** + *infinitive* → 9

Sequence of tenses in Subordinate Clauses

If the verb in the main clause is in the present, future or imperative, the verb in the dependent clause will be in the present or perfect subjunctive → 10

If the verb in the main clause is in the conditional or any past tense, the verb in the dependent clause will be in the imperfect or pluperfect subjunctive → 11

Examples

1 Le aconsejé que oyera música cuando estuviera nervioso	I advised him to listen to music when he felt nervous
Me gusta nadar cuando hace calor	I like to swim when it is warm
2 Te devolveré el libro tan pronto como lo haya leído	I'll give you back the book as soon as I have read it
3 Te lo diré después de que te hayas sentado	I'll tell you after you've sat down
4 Quédate aquí hasta que volvamos	Stay here until we come back
5 No hablen en voz alta mientras estén ellos aquí	Don't speak loudly while they are here
6 Vuelvan por aquí siempre que quieran	Come back whenever you wish to
7 No le creeré aunque diga la verdad	I won't believe him even if he tells the truth
8 La encontraré dondequiera que esté	I will find her wherever she might be
9 Después de cenar nos fuimos al cine	After dinner we went to the cinema
Quiero que lo hagas (*pres + pres subj*)	I want you to do it
Temo que no haya venido (*pres + perf subj*)	I fear he hasn't come (might not have come)
Iremos por aquí para que no nos vean (*future + pres subj*)	We'll go this way so that they won't see us
Me gustaría que llegaras temprano (*cond + imperf subj*)	I'd like you to arrive early
Les pedí que me esperaran (*preterite + imperf subj*)	I asked them to wait for me
Sentiría mucho que hubiese muerto (*cond + pluperf subj*)	I would be very sorry if he were dead

Verbs governing a, de, con, en, por and para

The following lists (pages 66 to 73) contain common verbal constructions using the prepositions **a**, **de**, **con**, **en**, **por** and **para**.

Note the following abbreviations:

infin.	*infinitive*
perf. infin.	*perfect infinitive**
algn	alguien
sb	somebody
sth	something

* For information see page 50.

aburrirse de + *infin.*	to get bored with doing → 1
acabar con algo/algn	to put an end to sth/finish with sb → 2
acabar de* + *infin.*	to have just done → 3
acabar por + *infin.*	to end up doing → 4
acercarse a algo/algn	to approach sth/sb
acordarse de algo/algn/de + *infin.*	to remember sth/sb/doing → 5
acostumbrarse a algo/algn/a + *infin.*	to get used to sth/sb/to doing → 6
acusar a algn de algo/de + *perf. infin*	to accuse sb of sth/of doing, having done. → 7
advertir a algn de algo	to notify, warn sb about sth → 8
aficionarse a algo/a + *infin.*	to grow fond of sth/of doing → 9
alegrarse de algo/de + *perf. infin.*	to be glad about sth/of doing, having done → 10
alejarse de algn/algo	to move away from sb/sth
amenazar a algn con algo/con + *infin.*	to threaten sb with sth/to do → 11
animar a algn a + *infin.*	to encourage sb to do
apresurarse a + *infin.*	to hurry to do → 12

* See also Use of Tenses, pages 54 and 56

Examples

1 Me aburría de no poder salir de casa	I used to get bored with not being able to leave the house
2 Quiso acabar con su vida	He wanted to put an end to his life
3 Acababan de llegar cuando ...	They had just arrived when ...
4 El acusado acabó por confesarlo todo	The accused ended up by confessing everything
5 Nos acordamos muy bien de aquellas vacaciones	We remember that holiday very well
6 Me he acostumbrado a levantarme temprano	I've got used to getting up early
7 Le acusó de haber mentido	She accused him of lying
8 Advertí a mi amigo del peligro que corría	I warned my friend about the danger he was in
9 Nos hemos aficionado a la música clásica	We've grown fond of classical music
10 Me alegro de haberle conocido	I'm glad I met him
11 Amenazó con denunciarles	He threatened to report them
12 Se apresuraron a coger sitio	They hurried to find a seat

Verbs governing a, de, con, en, por and para *continued*

aprender a + *infin.*	to learn to do → 1
aprovecharse de algo/algn	to take advantage of sth/sb
aproximarse a algn/algo	to approach sb/sth
asistir a algo	to attend sth, be at sth
asomarse a/por	to lean out of → 2
asombrarse de + *infin.*	to be surprised at doing → 3
atreverse a + *infin.*	to dare to do
avergonzarse de algo/algn/de + *perf. infin.*	to be ashamed of sth/sb/of doing, having done → 4
ayudar a algn a + *infin.*	to help sb to do → 5
bajarse de (+ *place/vehicle*)	to get off/out of → 6
burlarse de algn	to make fun of sb
cansarse de algo/algn/de + *infin.*	to tire of sth/sb/of doing
carecer de algo	to lack sth → 7
cargar de algo	to load with sth → 8
casarse con algn	to get married to sb → 9
cesar de + *infin.*	to stop doing
chocar con algo	to crash/bump into sth → 10
comenzar a + *infin.*	to begin to do
comparar con algn/algo	to compare with sb/sth
consentir en + *infin.*	to agree to do
consistir en + *infin.*	to consist of doing → 11
constar de algo	to consist of sth → 12
contar con algn/algo	to rely on sb/sth → 13
convenir en + *infin.*	to agree to do → 14
darse cuenta de algo	to realize sth
dejar de + *infin.*	to stop doing → 15
depender de algo/algn	to depend on sth/sb → 16
despedirse de algn	to say goodbye to sb
dirigirse a algn/+ place	to address sb/head for
disponerse a + *infin.*	to get ready to do
empezar a + *infin.*	to begin to do
empezar por + *infin.*	to begin by doing → 17

Examples

❶ Me gustaría aprender a nadar	I'd like to learn to swim
❷ No te asomes a la ventana	Don't lean out of the window
❸ Nos asombramos mucho de verles ahí	We were very surprised at seeing them there
❹ No me avergüenzo de haberlo hecho	I'm not ashamed of having done it
❺ Ayúdeme a llevar estas maletas	Help me to carry these cases
❻ Se bajó del coche	He got out of the car
❼ La casa carecía de jardín	The house lacked (did not have) a garden
❽ El carro iba cargado de paja	The cart was loaded with straw
❾ Se casó con Andrés	She married Andrew
❿ Enciende la luz, o chocarás con la puerta	Turn the light on, or you'll bump into the door
⓫ Mi plan consistía en vigilarles de cerca	My plan consisted of keeping a close eye on them
⓬ El examen consta de tres partes	The exam consists of three parts
⓭ Cuento contigo para que me ayudes a hacerlo	I rely on you to help me do it
⓮ Convinieron en reunirse al día siguiente	They agreed to meet the following day
⓯ ¿Quieres dejar de hablar?	Will you stop talking?
⓰ No depende de mí	It doesn't depend on me
⓱ Empieza por enterarte de lo que se trata	Begin by finding out what it is about

Verbs governing a, de, con, en, por and para *continued*

encontrarse con algn	to meet sb (by chance) → 1
enfadarse con algn	to get annoyed with sb
enseñar a algn a + *infin.*	to teach sb to → 2
enterarse de algo	to find out about sth → 3
entrar en (+ *place*)	to enter, go into
esperar a + *infin.*	to wait until → 4
estar de acuerdo con algn/algo	to agree with sb/sth
fiarse de algn/algo	to trust sb/sth
fijarse en algo/algn	to notice sth/sb → 5
hablar con algn	to talk to sb → 6
hacer caso a algn	to pay attention to sb
hartarse de algo/algn/de + *infin.*	to get fed up with sth/sb/with doing → 7
interesarse por algo/algn	to be interested in sth/sb → 8
invitar a algn a + *infin.*	to invite sb to do
jugar a (+ sports, games)	to play
luchar por algo/por + *infin.*	to fight, strive for/to do → 9
llegar a + *infin.*/(place)	to manage to do/to reach → 10
llenar de algo	to fill with sth
negarse a + *infin.*	to refuse to do → 11
obligar a algn a + *infin.*	to make sb do → 12
ocuparse de algn/algo	to take care of sb/attend to sth
oler a algo	to smell of sth → 13
olvidarse de algo/algn/de + *infin.*	to forget sth/sb/to do → 14
oponerse a algo/a + *infin.*	to be opposed to sth/to doing
parecerse a algn/algo	to resemble sb/sth
pensar en algo/algn/en + *infin.*	to think about sth/sb/about doing → 15
preguntar por algn	to ask for/about sb
preocuparse de *or* **por algo/algn**	to worry about sth/sb → 16

Examples

1 Me encontré con ella al entrar en el banco	I met her as I was entering the bank
2 Le estoy enseñando a nadar	I am teaching him to swim
3 ¿Te has enterado del sitio adonde hay que ir?	Have you found out where we have to go?
4 Espera a saber lo que quiere antes de comprar el regalo	Wait until you know what he wants before buying the present
5 Me fijé en él cuando subía a su coche	I noticed him when he was getting into his car
6 ¿Puedo hablar con Vd un momento?	May I talk to you for a moment?
7 Me he hartado de escribirle	I've got fed up with writing to him
8 Me interesaba mucho por la arqueología	I was very interested in archaeology
9 Hay que luchar por mantener la paz	One must strive to preserve peace
10 Lo intenté sin llegar a conseguirlo	I tried without managing to do it
11 Se negó a hacerlo	He refused to do it
12 Le obligó a sentarse	He made him sit down
13 Este perfume huele a jazmín	This perfume smells of jasmine
14 Siempre me olvido de cerrar la puerta	I always forget to shut the door
15 No quiero pensar en eso	I don't want to think about that
16 Se preocupa mucho de/por su apariencia	He worries a lot about his appearance

Verbs governing a, de, con, en, por and para *continued*

preparárse a + *infin.*	to prepare to do
probar a + *infin.*	to try to do
quedar en + *infin.*	to agree to do → 1
quedar por + *infin.*	to remain to be done → 2
quejarse de algo	to complain of sth
referirse a algo	to refer to sth
reírse de algo/algn	to laugh at sth/sb
rodear de	to surround with → 3
romper a + *infin.*	to (suddenly) start to do → 4
salir de (+ *place*)	to leave
sentarse a (+ *table etc*)	to sit down at
subir(se) a (+ *vehicle/place*)	to get on, into/to climb → 5
servir de algo a algn	to be useful to/serve sb as sth → 6
servir para algo/para + *infin.*	to be good as sth/for doing → 7
servirse de algo	to use sth → 8
soñar con algn/algo/con + *infin.*	to dream about/of sb/sth/of doing
sorprenderse de algo	to be surprised at sth
tardar en + *infin.*	to take time to do → 9
tener ganas de algo/de + *infin.*	to want sth/to do → 10
tener miedo de algo	to be afraid of sth → 11
tener miedo a algn	to be afraid of sb → 12
terminar por + *infin.*	to end by doing
tirar de algo/algn	to pull sth/sb
trabajar de (+ *occupation*)	to work as → 13
trabajar en (+ *place of work*)	to work at/in → 14
traducir a (+ *language*)	to translate into
tratar de + *infin.*	to try to do → 15
tratarse de algo/algn/de + *infin.*	to be a question of sth/about sb/ about doing → 16
vacilar en + *infin.*	to hesitate to do → 17
volver a + *infin.*	to do again → 18

Examples

1	Habíamos quedado en encontrarnos a las 8	We had agreed to meet at 8
2	Queda por averiguar dónde se ocultan	It remains to be discovered where they are hiding
3	Habían rodeado el jardín de un seto de cipreses	They had surrounded the garden with a hedge of cypress trees
4	Al apagarse la luz, el niño rompió a llorar	When the lights went out, the little boy suddenly started to cry
5	¡De prisa, sube al coche!	Get into the car, quick!
6	Esto me servirá de bastón	This will serve me as a walking stick
7	No sirvo para (ser) jardinero	I'm no good as a gardener
8	Se sirvió de un destornillador para abrirlo	She used a screwdriver to open it
9	Tardaron mucho en salir	They took a long time to come out
10	Tengo ganas de volver a España	I want to go back to Spain
11	Mi hija tiene miedo de la oscuridad	My daughter is afraid of the dark
12	Nunca tuvieron miedo a su padre	They were never afraid of their father
13	Pedro trabaja de camarero en Londres	Peter works as a waiter in London
14	Trabajaba en una oficina	I used to work in an office
15	No trates de engañarme	Don't try to fool me
16	Se trata de nuestro nuevo vecino	It's about our new neighbour
17	Nunca vacilaban en pedir dinero	They never hesitated to borrow money
18	No vuelvas a hacerlo nunca más	Don't ever do it again

Ser and Estar

Spanish has two verbs – **ser** and **estar** – for 'to be'.

They are not interchangeable and each one is used in defined contexts.

ser is used:

- with an adjective, to express a permanent or inherent quality → 1
- to express occupation or nationality → 2
- to express possession → 3
- to express origin or the material from which something is made → 4
- with a noun, pronoun or infinitive following the verb → 5
- to express the time and date → 6
- to form the passive, with the past participle (see page 32).

ⓘ Note: This use emphasizes the action of the verb. If, however, the resultant state or condition needs to be emphasized, **estar** is used. The past participle then functions as an adjective (see page 208) and has to agree in gender and in number with the noun → 7

estar is used:

- always, to indicate place or location → 8
- with an adjective or adjectival phrase, to express a quality or state seen by the speaker as subject to change or different from expected → 9
- when speaking of a person's state of health → 10
- to form the continuous tenses, used with the gerund (see page 52) → 11
- with **de** + *noun*, to indicate a temporary occupation → 12

Examples

1	Mi hermano es alto María es inteligente	My brother is tall Mary is intelligent
2	Javier es aviador Sus padres son italianos	Javier is an airman His parents are Italian
3	La casa es de Miguel	The house belongs to Michael
4	Mi hermana es de Granada Las paredes son de ladrillo	My sister is from Granada The walls are made of brick
5	Andrés es un niño travieso Soy yo, Enrique Todo es proponérselo	Andrew is a naughty boy It's me, Henry It's all a question of putting your mind to it
6	Son las tres y media Mañana es sábado	It's half past three Tomorrow is Saturday
7	Las puertas eran cerradas sigilosamente Las puertas estaban cerradas	The doors were being silently closed The doors were closed (resultant action)
8	La comida está en la mesa	The meal is on the table
9	Su amigo está enfermo El lavabo está ocupado Hoy estoy de mal humor Las tiendas están cerradas	Her friend is ill The toilet is engaged I'm in a bad mood today The shops are closed
10	¿Cómo están Vds? Estamos todos bien	How are you? We are all well
11	Estamos aprendiendo mucho	We are learning a great deal
12	Mi primo está de médico en un pueblo	My cousin works as a doctor in a village

Ser and Estar *continued*

With certain adjectives, both ser and estar can be used, although they are not interchangeable when used in this way:

- **ser** will express a permanent or inherent quality → 1
- **estar** will express a temporary state or quality → 2

Both **ser** and **estar** may also be used in set expressions.

The commonest of these are:

With **ser**

Sea como sea	Be that as it may
Es igual/Es lo mismo	It's all the same
llegar a ser	to become
¿Cómo fue eso?	How did that happen?
¿Qué ha sido de él?	What has become of him?
ser para (*with the idea of purpose*)	to be for → 3

With **estar**

estar de pie/de rodillas	to be standing/kneeling
estar de viaje	to be travelling
estar de vacaciones	to be on holiday
estar de vuelta	to be back
estar de moda	to be in fashion
Está bien	It's all right
estar para	to be about to do sth/to be in a mood for → 4
estar por	to be inclined to/to be (all) for → 5
estar a punto de	to be just about to do sth → 6

Examples

1	Su hermana es muy joven/vieja	His sister is very young/old
	Son muy ricos/pobres	They are very rich/poor
	Su amigo era un enfermo	His friend was an invalid
	Es un borracho	He is a drunkard
	Mi hijo es bueno/malo	My son is good/naughty
	Viajar es cansado	Travelling is tiring
2	Está muy joven/vieja con ese vestido	She looks very young/old in that dress
	Ahora están muy ricos/pobres	They have become very rich/poor lately
	Estaba enfermo	He was ill
	Está borracho	He is drunk
	Está bueno/malo	He is well/ill
	Hoy estoy cansada	I am tired today
3	Este paquete es para Vd	This parcel is for you
	Esta caja es para guardar semillas	This box is for keeping seeds in
4	Están para llegar	They're about to arrive
5	Estoy por irme a vivir a España	I'm inclined to go and live in Spain
6	Las rosas están a punto de salir	The roses are about to come out

Verbal Idioms

Special Intransitive Verbs

With the following verbs the Spanish construction is the opposite of the English. The subject in English becomes the indirect object of the Spanish verb, while the object in English becomes the subject of the Spanish verb. Compare the following:

I like that house (subject: I, object: that house)
Esa casa me gusta (subject: **esa casa**, indirect object: **me**)

The commonest of these verbs are:

gustar	to like → 1
gustar más	to prefer → 2
encantar	(colloquial) to love → 3
faltar	to need/to be short of/to have missing → 4
quedar	to be/have left → 5
doler	to have a pain in/to hurt, ache → 6
interesar	to be interested in → 7
importar	to mind → 8

Examples

1	Me gusta este vestido	I like this dress (This dress pleases me)
2	Me gustan más éstas	I prefer these
3	Nos encanta hacer deporte	We love sport
4	Me faltaban 100 euros Sólo le falta el toque final Le faltaban tres dientes	I was short of 100 euros It just needs the finishing touch He/she had three teeth missing
5	Sólo nos quedan dos kilómetros	We only have two kilometres (left) to go
6	Me duele la cabeza	I have a headache
7	Nos interesa mucho la política	We are very interested in politics
8	No me importa la lluvia	I don't mind the rain

Irregular Verbs

The verbs listed opposite and conjugated on pages 82 to 160 provide the main patterns for irregular verbs. The verbs are grouped opposite according to their infinitive ending and are shown in the following tables in alphabetical order.

In the tables, the most important irregular verbs are given in their most common simple tenses, together with the imperative and the gerund.

The past participle is also shown for each verb, to enable you to form all the compound tenses, as on pages 18 to 23.

The pronouns **ella** and **Vd** take the same verb endings as **él**, while **ellas** and **Vds** take the same endings as **ellos**.

> All the verbs included in the tables differ from the three conjugations set out on pages 8 to 13. Many – e.g. **contar** – serve as models for groups of verbs, while others – e.g. **ir** – are unique. On pages 161–190 you will find every verb in this dictionary listed alphabetically and cross-referred either to the relevant basic conjugation or to the appropriate model in the verb tables.

Imperfect Subjunctive of Irregular Verbs

For verbs with an irregular root form in the preterite tense – e.g. **andar** → **anduvieron** – the imperfect subjunctive is formed by using the root form of the 3rd person plural of the preterite tense, and adding the imperfect subjunctive endings **-iera/-iese** etc where the verb has an 'i' in the preterite ending – e.g. anduv**ieron** → anduv**iera/iese**. Where the verb has no 'i' in the preterite ending, add **-era/-ese** etc – e.g. produj**eron** → produj**era/ese**.

'-ar': actuar
almorzar
andar
aullar
avergonzar
averiguar
contar
cruzar
dar
empezar
enviar
errar
estar
jugar
negar
pagar
pensar
rehusar
rogar
sacar
volcar

'-er': caber
caer
cocer
coger
crecer
entender
haber
hacer
hay
leer
llover
mover
nacer
oler
poder
poner
querer
resolver
romper
saber
satisfacer
ser
tener
torcer
traer
valer
vencer
ver
volver

'-ir': abolir
abrir
adquirir
bendecir
conducir
construir
decir
dirigir
distinguir
dormir
elegir
erguir
escribir
freír
gruñir
ir
lucir
morir
oír
pedir
prohibir
reír
reñir
reunir
salir
seguir
sentir
venir
zurcir

abolir (to abolish)

	PRESENT*		IMPERFECT
nosotros	abol**imos**	yo	abol**ía**
vosotros	abol**ís**	tú	abol**ías**
		él	abol**ía**
		nosotros	abol**íamos**
		vosotros	abol**íais**
		ellos	abol**ían**

* Present tense only used in persons shown

	FUTURE		CONDITIONAL
yo	abolir**é**	yo	abolir**ía**
tú	abolir**ás**	tú	abolir**ías**
él	abolir**á**	él	abolir**ía**
nosotros	abolir**emos**	nosotros	abolir**íamos**
vosotros	abolir**éis**	vosotros	abolir**íais**
ellos	abolir**án**	ellos	abolir**ían**

	PRESENT SUBJUNCTIVE		PRETERITE
	not used	yo	abol**í**
		tú	abol**iste**
		él	abol**ió**
		nosotros	abol**imos**
		vosotros	abol**isteis**
		ellos	abol**ieron**

PAST PARTICIPLE
abol**ido**

IMPERATIVE
abol**id**

GERUND
abol**iendo**

abrir (to open)

	PRESENT
yo	abr**o**
tú	abr**es**
él	abr**e**
nosotros	abr**imos**
vosotros	abr**ís**
ellos	abr**en**

	IMPERFECT
yo	abr**ía**
tú	abr**ías**
él	abr**ía**
nosotros	abr**íamos**
vosotros	abr**íais**
ellos	abr**ían**

	FUTURE
yo	abrir**é**
tú	abrir**ás**
él	abrir**á**
nosotros	abrir**emos**
vosotros	abrir**éis**
ellos	abrir**án**

	CONDITIONAL
yo	abrir**ía**
tú	abrir**ías**
él	abrir**ía**
nosotros	abrir**íamos**
vosotros	abrir**íais**
ellos	abrir**ían**

	PRESENT SUBJUNCTIVE
yo	abr**a**
tú	abr**as**
él	abr**a**
nosotros	abr**amos**
vosotros	abr**áis**
ellos	abr**an**

	PRETERITE
yo	abr**í**
tú	abr**iste**
él	abr**ió**
nosotros	abr**imos**
vosotros	abr**isteis**
ellos	abr**ieron**

PAST PARTICIPLE

abierto

IMPERATIVE

abr**e**

abr**id**

GERUND

abr**iendo**

actuar (to act)

	PRESENT		IMPERFECT
yo	**actúo**	yo	actu**aba**
tú	**actúas**	tú	actu**abas**
él	**actúa**	él	actu**aba**
nosotros	actu**amos**	nosotros	actu**ábamos**
vosotros	actu**áis**	vosotros	actu**abais**
ellos	**actúan**	ellos	actu**aban**

	FUTURE		CONDITIONAL
yo	actuar**é**	yo	actuar**ía**
tú	actuar**ás**	tú	actuar**ías**
él	actuar**á**	él	actuar**ía**
nosotros	actuar**emos**	nosotros	actuar**íamos**
vosotros	actuar**éis**	vosotros	actuar**íais**
ellos	actuar**án**	ellos	actuar**ían**

	PRESENT SUBJUNCTIVE		PRETERITE
yo	**actúe**	yo	actu**é**
tú	**actúes**	tú	actu**aste**
él	**actúe**	él	actu**ó**
nosotros	actu**emos**	nosotros	actu**amos**
vosotros	actu**éis**	vosotros	actu**asteis**
ellos	**actúen**	ellos	actu**aron**

PAST PARTICIPLE
actu**ado**

IMPERATIVE
actúa
actua**d**

GERUND
actu**ando**

adquirir (to acquire)

	PRESENT		IMPERFECT
yo	**adquiero**	yo	adquir**ía**
tú	**adquieres**	tú	adquir**ías**
él	**adquiere**	él	adquir**ía**
nosotros	adquir**imos**	nosotros	adquir**íamos**
vosotros	adquir**ís**	vosotros	adquir**íais**
ellos	**adquieren**	ellos	adquir**ían**

	FUTURE		CONDITIONAL
yo	adquirir**é**	yo	adquirir**ía**
tú	adquirir**ás**	tú	adquirir**ías**
él	adquirir**á**	él	adquirir**ía**
nosotros	adquirir**emos**	nosotros	adquirir**íamos**
vosotros	adquirir**éis**	vosotros	adquirir**íais**
ellos	adquirir**án**	ellos	adquirir**ían**

	PRESENT SUBJUNCTIVE		PRETERITE
yo	**adquiera**	yo	adquir**í**
tú	**adquieras**	tú	adquir**iste**
él	**adquiera**	él	adquir**ió**
nosotros	adquir**amos**	nosotros	adquir**imos**
vosotros	adquir**áis**	vosotros	adquir**isteis**
ellos	**adquieran**	ellos	adquir**ieron**

PAST PARTICIPLE
adquir**ido**

IMPERATIVE
adquiere
adquiri**d**

GERUND
adquir**iendo**

almorzar (to have lunch)

	PRESENT		IMPERFECT
yo	**almuerzo**	yo	almorz**aba**
tú	**almuerzas**	tú	almorz**abas**
él	**almuerza**	él	almorz**aba**
nosotros	almorz**amos**	nosotros	almorz**ábamos**
vosotros	almorz**áis**	vosotros	almorz**abais**
ellos	**almuerzan**	ellos	almorz**aban**

	FUTURE		CONDITIONAL
yo	almorzar**é**	yo	almorzar**ía**
tú	almorzar**ás**	tú	almorzar**ías**
él	almorzar**á**	él	almorzar**ía**
nosotros	almorzar**emos**	nosotros	almorzar**íamos**
vosotros	almorzar**éis**	vosotros	almorzar**íais**
ellos	almorzar**án**	ellos	almorzar**ían**

	PRESENT SUBJUNCTIVE		PRETERITE
yo	**almuerce**	yo	**almorcé**
tú	**almuerces**	tú	almorz**aste**
él	**almuerce**	él	almorz**ó**
nosotros	**almorcemos**	nosotros	almorz**amos**
vosotros	**almorcéis**	vosotros	almorz**asteis**
ellos	**almuercen**	ellos	almorz**aron**

PAST PARTICIPLE
almorz**ado**

IMPERATIVE
almuerza
almorza**d**

GERUND
almorz**ando**

andar (to walk)

	PRESENT		IMPERFECT
yo	and**o**	yo	and**aba**
tú	and**as**	tú	and**abas**
él	and**a**	él	and**aba**
nosotros	and**amos**	nosotros	and**ábamos**
vosotros	and**áis**	vosotros	and**abais**
ellos	and**an**	ellos	and**aban**

	FUTURE		CONDITIONAL
yo	andar**é**	yo	andar**ía**
tú	andar**ás**	tú	andar**ías**
él	andar**á**	él	andar**ía**
nosotros	andar**emos**	nosotros	andar**íamos**
vosotros	andar**éis**	vosotros	andar**íais**
ellos	andar**án**	ellos	andar**ían**

	PRESENT SUBJUNCTIVE		PRETERITE
yo	and**e**	yo	**anduve**
tú	and**es**	tú	**anduviste**
él	and**e**	él	**anduvo**
nosotros	and**emos**	nosotros	**anduvimos**
vosotros	and**éis**	vosotros	**anduvisteis**
ellos	and**en**	ellos	**anduvieron**

PAST PARTICIPLE
and**ado**

IMPERATIVE
and**a**
anda**d**

GERUND
and**ando**

aullar (to howl)

	PRESENT		IMPERFECT
yo	**aúllo**	yo	aull**aba**
tú	**aúllas**	tú	aull**abas**
él	**aúlla**	él	aull**aba**
nosotros	aull**amos**	nosotros	aull**ábamos**
vosotros	aull**áis**	vosotros	aull**abais**
ellos	**aúllan**	ellos	aull**aban**

	FUTURE		CONDITIONAL
yo	aullar**é**	yo	aullar**ía**
tú	aullar**ás**	tú	aullar**ías**
él	aullar**á**	él	aullar**ía**
nosotros	aullar**emos**	nosotros	aullar**íamos**
vosotros	aullar**éis**	vosotros	aullar**íais**
ellos	aullar**án**	ellos	aullar**ían**

	PRESENT SUBJUNCTIVE		PRETERITE
yo	**aúlle**	yo	aull**é**
tú	**aúlles**	tú	aull**aste**
él	**aúlle**	él	aull**ó**
nosotros	aull**emos**	nosotros	aull**amos**
vosotros	aull**éis**	vosotros	aull**asteis**
ellos	**aúllen**	ellos	aull**aron**

PAST PARTICIPLE
aull**ado**

IMPERATIVE
aúlla
aull**ad**

GERUND
aull**ando**

avergonzar (to shame)

	PRESENT		IMPERFECT
yo	**avergüenzo**	yo	avergonz**aba**
tú	**avergüenzas**	tú	avergonz**abas**
él	**avergüenza**	él	avergonz**aba**
nosotros	avergonz**amos**	nosotros	avergonz**ábamos**
vosotros	avergonz**áis**	vosotros	avergonz**abais**
ellos	**avergüenzan**	ellos	avergonz**aban**

	FUTURE		CONDITIONAL
yo	avergonzar**é**	yo	avergonzar**ía**
tú	avergonzar**ás**	tú	avergonzar**ías**
él	avergonzar**á**	él	avergonzar**ía**
nosotros	avergonzar**emos**	nosotros	avergonzar**íamos**
vosotros	avergonzar**éis**	vosotros	avergonzar**íais**
ellos	avergonzar**án**	ellos	avergonzar**ían**

	PRESENT SUBJUNCTIVE		PRETERITE
yo	**avergüence**	yo	**avergoncé**
tú	**avergüences**	tú	avergonz**aste**
él	**avergüence**	él	avergonz**ó**
nosotros	**avergoncemos**	nosotros	avergonz**amos**
vosotros	**avergoncéis**	vosotros	avergonz**asteis**
ellos	**avergüencen**	ellos	avergonz**aron**

PAST PARTICIPLE
avergonz**ado**

IMPERATIVE
avergüenza
avergonza**d**

GERUND
avergonz**ando**

averiguar (to find out)

	PRESENT		IMPERFECT
yo	averigu**o**	yo	averigu**aba**
tú	averigu**as**	tú	averigu**abas**
él	averigu**a**	él	averigu**aba**
nosotros	averigu**amos**	nosotros	averigu**ábamos**
vosotros	averigu**áis**	vosotros	averigu**abais**
ellos	averigu**an**	ellos	averigu**aban**

	FUTURE		CONDITIONAL
yo	averiguar**é**	yo	averiguar**ía**
tú	averiguar**ás**	tú	averiguar**ías**
él	averiguar**á**	él	averiguar**ía**
nosotros	averiguar**emos**	nosotros	averiguar**íamos**
vosotros	averiguar**éis**	vosotros	averiguar**íais**
ellos	averiguar**án**	ellos	averiguar**ían**

	PRESENT SUBJUNCTIVE		PRETERITE
yo	**averigüe**	yo	**averigüé**
tú	**averigües**	tú	averigu**aste**
él	**averigüe**	él	averigu**ó**
nosotros	**averigüemos**	nosotros	averigu**amos**
vosotros	**averigüéis**	vosotros	averigu**asteis**
ellos	**averigüen**	ellos	averigu**aron**

PAST PARTICIPLE
averigu**ado**

IMPERATIVE
averigu**a**
averigu**ad**

GERUND
averigu**ando**

bendecir (to bless)

	PRESENT		IMPERFECT
yo	**bendigo**	yo	bendec**ía**
tú	**bendices**	tú	bendec**ías**
él	**bendice**	él	bendec**ía**
nosotros	bendec**imos**	nosotros	bendec**íamos**
vosotros	bendec**ís**	vosotros	bendec**íais**
ellos	**bendicen**	ellos	bendec**ían**

	FUTURE		CONDITIONAL
yo	bendecir**é**	yo	bendecir**ía**
tú	bendecir**ás**	tú	bendecir**ías**
él	bendecir**á**	él	bendecir**ía**
nosotros	bendecir**emos**	nosotros	bendecir**íamos**
vosotros	bendecir**éis**	vosotros	bendecir**íais**
ellos	bendecir**án**	ellos	bendecir**ían**

	PRESENT SUBJUNCTIVE		PRETERITE
yo	**bendiga**	yo	**bendije**
tú	**bendigas**	tú	**bendijiste**
él	**bendiga**	él	**bendijo**
nosotros	**bendigamos**	nosotros	**bendijimos**
vosotros	**bendigáis**	vosotros	**bendijisteis**
ellos	**bendigan**	ellos	**bendijeron**

PAST PARTICIPLE
bendec**ido**

IMPERATIVE
bendice
bendeci**d**

GERUND
bendiciendo

caber (to fit)

PRESENT

yo	**quepo**
tú	cab**es**
él	cab**e**
nosotros	cab**emos**
vosotros	cab**éis**
ellos	cab**en**

IMPERFECT

yo	cab**ía**
tú	cab**ías**
él	cab**ía**
nosotros	cab**íamos**
vosotros	cab**íais**
ellos	cab**ían**

FUTURE

yo	**cabré**
tú	**cabrás**
él	**cabrá**
nosotros	**cabremos**
vosotros	**cabréis**
ellos	**cabrán**

CONDITIONAL

yo	**cabría**
tú	**cabrías**
él	**cabría**
nosotros	**cabríamos**
vosotros	**cabríais**
ellos	**cabrían**

PRESENT SUBJUNCTIVE

yo	**quepa**
tú	**quepas**
él	**quepa**
nosotros	**quepamos**
vosotros	**quepáis**
ellos	**quepan**

PRETERITE

yo	**cupe**
tú	**cupiste**
él	**cupo**
nosotros	**cupimos**
vosotros	**cupisteis**
ellos	**cupieron**

PAST PARTICIPLE

cab**ido**

IMPERATIVE

cab**e**

cabe**d**

GERUND

cab**iendo**

caer (to fall)

	PRESENT		IMPERFECT
yo	**caigo**	yo	ca**ía**
tú	ca**es**	tú	ca**ías**
él	ca**e**	él	ca**ía**
nosotros	ca**emos**	nosotros	ca**íamos**
vosotros	ca**éis**	vosotros	ca**íais**
ellos	ca**en**	ellos	ca**ían**

	FUTURE		CONDITIONAL
yo	caer**é**	yo	caer**ía**
tú	caer**ás**	tú	caer**ías**
él	caer**á**	él	caer**ía**
nosotros	caer**emos**	nosotros	caer**íamos**
vosotros	caer**éis**	vosotros	caer**íais**
ellos	caer**án**	ellos	caer**ían**

	PRESENT SUBJUNCTIVE		PRETERITE
yo	**caiga**	yo	**caí**
tú	**caigas**	tú	**caíste**
él	**caiga**	él	**cayó**
nosotros	**caigamos**	nosotros	**caímos**
vosotros	**caigáis**	vosotros	**caísteis**
ellos	**caigan**	ellos	**cayeron**

PAST PARTICIPLE
caído

IMPERATIVE
ca**e**
cae**d**

GERUND
cayendo

cocer (to boil)

	PRESENT		IMPERFECT
yo	**cuezo**	yo	coc**ía**
tú	**cueces**	tú	coc**ías**
él	**cuece**	él	coc**ía**
nosotros	coc**emos**	nosotros	coc**íamos**
vosotros	coc**éis**	vosotros	coc**íais**
ellos	**cuecen**	ellos	coc**ían**

	FUTURE		CONDITIONAL
yo	cocer**é**	yo	coce**ría**
tú	cocer**ás**	tú	coce**rías**
él	cocer**á**	él	coce**ría**
nosotros	cocer**emos**	nosotros	coce**ríamos**
vosotros	cocer**éis**	vosotros	coce**ríais**
ellos	cocer**án**	ellos	coce**rían**

	PRESENT SUBJUNCTIVE		PRETERITE
yo	**cueza**	yo	coc**í**
tú	**cuezas**	tú	coc**iste**
él	**cueza**	él	coc**ió**
nosotros	**cozamos**	nosotros	coc**imos**
vosotros	**cozáis**	vosotros	coc**isteis**
ellos	**cuezan**	ellos	coc**ieron**

PAST PARTICIPLE
coc**ido**

IMPERATIVE
cuece
coce**d**

GERUND
coc**iendo**

coger (to take)

	PRESENT		IMPERFECT
yo	**cojo**	yo	cog**ía**
tú	cog**es**	tú	cog**ías**
él	cog**e**	él	cog**ía**
nosotros	cog**emos**	nosotros	cog**íamos**
vosotros	cog**éis**	vosotros	cog**íais**
ellos	cog**en**	ellos	cog**ían**

	FUTURE		CONDITIONAL
yo	coger**é**	yo	coger**ía**
tú	coger**ás**	tú	coger**ías**
él	coger**á**	él	coger**ía**
nosotros	coger**emos**	nosotros	coger**íamos**
vosotros	coger**éis**	vosotros	coger**íais**
ellos	coger**án**	ellos	coger**ían**

	PRESENT SUBJUNCTIVE		PRETERITE
yo	**coja**	yo	cog**í**
tú	**cojas**	tú	cog**iste**
él	**coja**	él	cog**ió**
nosotros	**cojamos**	nosotros	cog**imos**
vosotros	**cojáis**	vosotros	cog**isteis**
ellos	**cojan**	ellos	cog**ieron**

PAST PARTICIPLE
cog**ido**

IMPERATIVE
cog**e**
cog**ed**

GERUND
cog**iendo**

conducir (to drive, to lead)

	PRESENT		IMPERFECT
yo	**conduzco**	yo	conduc**ía**
tú	conduc**es**	tú	conduc**ías**
él	conduc**e**	él	conduc**ía**
nosotros	conduc**imos**	nosotros	conduc**íamos**
vosotros	conduc**ís**	vosotros	conduc**íais**
ellos	conduc**en**	ellos	conduc**ían**

	FUTURE		CONDITIONAL
yo	conducir**é**	yo	conducir**ía**
tú	conducir**ás**	tú	conducir**ías**
él	conducir**á**	él	conducir**ía**
nosotros	conducir**emos**	nosotros	conducir**íamos**
vosotros	conducir**éis**	vosotros	conducir**íais**
ellos	conducir**án**	ellos	conducir**ían**

	PRESENT SUBJUNCTIVE		PRETERITE
yo	**conduzca**	yo	**conduje**
tú	**conduzcas**	tú	**condujiste**
él	**conduzca**	él	**condujo**
nosotros	**conduzcamos**	nosotros	**condujimos**
vosotros	**conduzcáis**	vosotros	**condujisteis**
ellos	**conduzcan**	ellos	**condujeron**

PAST PARTICIPLE
conduc**ido**

IMPERATIVE
conduc**e**
conduc**id**

GERUND
conduc**iendo**

construir (to build)

	PRESENT		IMPERFECT
yo	**construyo**	yo	constru**ía**
tú	**construyes**	tú	constru**ías**
él	**construye**	él	constru**ía**
nosotros	constru**imos**	nosotros	constru**íamos**
vosotros	constru**ís**	vosotros	constru**íais**
ellos	**construyen**	ellos	constru**ían**

	FUTURE		CONDITIONAL
yo	construir**é**	yo	construir**ía**
tú	construir**ás**	tú	construir**ías**
él	construir**á**	él	construir**ía**
nosotros	construir**emos**	nosotros	construir**íamos**
vosotros	construir**éis**	vosotros	construir**íais**
ellos	construir**án**	ellos	construir**ían**

	PRESENT SUBJUNCTIVE		PRETERITE
yo	**construya**	yo	constru**í**
tú	**construyas**	tú	constru**íste**
él	**construya**	él	**construyó**
nosotros	**construyamos**	nosotros	constru**imos**
vosotros	**construyáis**	vosotros	constru**isteis**
ellos	**construyan**	ellos	**construyeron**

PAST PARTICIPLE
constru**ido**

IMPERATIVE
construye
construi**d**

GERUND
construyendo

contar (to tell, to count)

	PRESENT		IMPERFECT
yo	**cuento**	yo	cont**aba**
tú	**cuentas**	tú	cont**abas**
él	**cuenta**	él	cont**aba**
nosotros	cont**amos**	nosotros	cont**ábamos**
vosotros	cont**áis**	vosotros	cont**abais**
ellos	**cuentan**	ellos	cont**aban**

	FUTURE		CONDITIONAL
yo	contar**é**	yo	contar**ía**
tú	contar**ás**	tú	contar**ías**
él	contar**á**	él	contar**ía**
nosotros	contar**emos**	nosotros	contar**íamos**
vosotros	contar**éis**	vosotros	contar**íais**
ellos	contar**án**	ellos	contar**ían**

	PRESENT SUBJUNCTIVE		PRETERITE
yo	**cuente**	yo	cont**é**
tú	**cuentes**	tú	cont**aste**
él	**cuente**	él	cont**ó**
nosotros	cont**emos**	nosotros	cont**amos**
vosotros	cont**éis**	vosotros	cont**asteis**
ellos	**cuenten**	ellos	cont**aron**

PAST PARTICIPLE
cont**ado**

IMPERATIVE
cuenta
conta**d**

GERUND
cont**ando**

crecer (to grow)

	PRESENT		IMPERFECT
yo	**crezco**	yo	crec**ía**
tú	crec**es**	tú	crec**ías**
él	crec**e**	él	crec**ía**
nosotros	crec**emos**	nosotros	crec**íamos**
vosotros	crec**éis**	vosotros	crec**íais**
ellos	crec**en**	ellos	crec**ían**

	FUTURE		CONDITIONAL
yo	crecer**é**	yo	crecer**ía**
tú	crecer**ás**	tú	crecer**ías**
él	crecer**á**	él	crecer**ía**
nosotros	crecer**emos**	nosotros	crecer**íamos**
vosotros	crecer**éis**	vosotros	crecer**íais**
ellos	crecer**án**	ellos	crecer**ían**

	PRESENT SUBJUNCTIVE		PRETERITE
yo	**crezca**	yo	crec**í**
tú	**crezcas**	tú	crec**iste**
él	**crezca**	él	crec**ió**
nosotros	**crezcamos**	nosotros	crec**imos**
vosotros	**crezcáis**	vosotros	crec**isteis**
ellos	**crezcan**	ellos	crec**ieron**

PAST PARTICIPLE
crec**ido**

IMPERATIVE
crec**e**
crece**d**

GERUND
crec**iendo**

cruzar (to cross)

	PRESENT		IMPERFECT
yo	cruz**o**	yo	cruz**aba**
tú	cruz**as**	tú	cruz**abas**
él	cruz**a**	él	cruz**aba**
nosotros	cruz**amos**	nosotros	cruz**ábamos**
vosotros	cruz**áis**	vosotros	cruz**abais**
ellos	cruz**an**	ellos	cruz**aban**

	FUTURE		CONDITIONAL
yo	cruzar**é**	yo	cruzar**ía**
tú	cruzar**ás**	tú	cruzar**ías**
él	cruzar**á**	él	cruzar**ía**
nosotros	cruzar**emos**	nosotros	cruzar**íamos**
vosotros	cruzar**éis**	vosotros	cruzar**íais**
ellos	cruzar**án**	ellos	cruzar**ían**

	PRESENT SUBJUNCTIVE		PRETERITE
yo	**cruce**	yo	**crucé**
tú	**cruces**	tú	cruz**aste**
él	**cruce**	él	cruz**ó**
nosotros	**crucemos**	nosotros	cruz**amos**
vosotros	**crucéis**	vosotros	cruz**asteis**
ellos	**crucen**	ellos	cruz**aron**

PAST PARTICIPLE
cruz**ado**

IMPERATIVE
cruz**a**
cruz**ad**

GERUND
cruz**ando**

dar (to give)

	PRESENT
yo	**doy**
tú	d**as**
él	d**a**
nosotros	d**amos**
vosotros	d**ais**
ellos	d**an**

	IMPERFECT
yo	d**aba**
tú	d**abas**
él	d**aba**
nosotros	d**ábamos**
vosotros	d**abais**
ellos	d**aban**

	FUTURE
yo	dar**é**
tú	dar**ás**
él	dar**á**
nosotros	dar**emos**
vosotros	dar**éis**
ellos	dar**án**

	CONDITIONAL
yo	dar**ía**
tú	dar**ías**
él	dar**ía**
nosotros	dar**íamos**
vosotros	dar**íais**
ellos	dar**ían**

	PRESENT SUBJUNCTIVE
yo	**dé**
tú	d**es**
él	**dé**
nosotros	d**emos**
vosotros	d**eis**
ellos	d**en**

	PRETERITE
yo	**di**
tú	**diste**
él	**dio**
nosotros	**dimos**
vosotros	**disteis**
ellos	**dieron**

PAST PARTICIPLE

d**ado**

IMPERATIVE

d**a**

da**d**

GERUND

d**ando**

decir (to say)

	PRESENT
yo	**digo**
tú	**dices**
él	**dice**
nosotros	dec**imos**
vosotros	dec**ís**
ellos	**dicen**

	IMPERFECT
yo	dec**ía**
tú	dec**ías**
él	dec**ía**
nosotros	dec**íamos**
vosotros	dec**íais**
ellos	dec**ían**

	FUTURE
yo	**diré**
tú	**dirás**
él	**dirá**
nosotros	**diremos**
vosotros	**diréis**
ellos	**dirán**

	CONDITIONAL
yo	**diría**
tú	**dirías**
él	**diría**
nosotros	**diríamos**
vosotros	**diríais**
ellos	**dirían**

	PRESENT SUBJUNCTIVE
yo	**diga**
tú	**digas**
él	**diga**
nosotros	**digamos**
vosotros	**digáis**
ellos	**digan**

	PRETERITE
yo	**dije**
tú	**dijiste**
él	**dijo**
nosotros	**dijimos**
vosotros	**dijisteis**
ellos	**dijeron**

PAST PARTICIPLE
dicho

IMPERATIVE
di
deci**d**

GERUND
diciendo

dirigir (to direct)

	PRESENT		IMPERFECT
yo	**dirijo**	yo	dirig**ía**
tú	dirig**es**	tú	dirig**ías**
él	dirig**e**	él	dirig**ía**
nosotros	dirig**imos**	nosotros	dirig**íamos**
vosotros	dirig**ís**	vosotros	dirig**íais**
ellos	dirig**en**	ellos	dirig**ían**

	FUTURE		CONDITIONAL
yo	dirigir**é**	yo	dirigir**ía**
tú	dirigir**ás**	tú	dirigir**ías**
él	dirigir**á**	él	dirigir**ía**
nosotros	dirigir**emos**	nosotros	dirigir**íamos**
vosotros	dirigir**éis**	vosotros	dirigir**íais**
ellos	dirigir**án**	ellos	dirigir**ían**

	PRESENT SUBJUNCTIVE		PRETERITE
yo	**dirija**	yo	dirig**í**
tú	**dirijas**	tú	dirig**iste**
él	**dirija**	él	dirig**ió**
nosotros	**dirijamos**	nosotros	dirig**imos**
vosotros	**dirijáis**	vosotros	dirig**isteis**
ellos	**dirijan**	ellos	dirig**ieron**

PAST PARTICIPLE
dirig**ido**

IMPERATIVE
dirig**e**
dirig**id**

GERUND
dirig**iendo**

distinguir (to distinguish)

	PRESENT		IMPERFECT
yo	**distingo**	yo	distingu**ía**
tú	disting**ues**	tú	distingu**ías**
él	disting**ue**	él	distingu**ía**
nosotros	distingu**imos**	nosotros	distingu**íamos**
vosotros	distingu**ís**	vosotros	distingu**íais**
ellos	disting**uen**	ellos	distingu**ían**

	FUTURE		CONDITIONAL
yo	distingui**ré**	yo	distingui**ría**
tú	distingui**rás**	tú	distingui**rías**
él	distingui**rá**	él	distingui**ría**
nosotros	distingui**remos**	nosotros	distingui**ríamos**
vosotros	distingui**réis**	vosotros	distingui**ríais**
ellos	distingui**rán**	ellos	distingui**rían**

	PRESENT SUBJUNCTIVE		PRETERITE
yo	**distinga**	yo	distingu**í**
tú	**distingas**	tú	distingu**iste**
él	**distinga**	él	distingu**ió**
nosotros	**distingamos**	nosotros	distingu**imos**
vosotros	**distingáis**	vosotros	distingu**isteis**
ellos	**distingan**	ellos	distingu**ieron**

PAST PARTICIPLE

distingu**ido**

IMPERATIVE

disting**ue**

distingui**d**

GERUND

distingu**iendo**

dormir (to sleep)

	PRESENT		IMPERFECT
yo	**duermo**	yo	dorm**ía**
tú	**duermes**	tú	dorm**ías**
él	**duerme**	él	dorm**ía**
nosotros	dorm**imos**	nosotros	dorm**íamos**
vosotros	dorm**ís**	vosotros	dorm**íais**
ellos	**duermen**	ellos	dorm**ían**

	FUTURE		CONDITIONAL
yo	dormir**é**	yo	dormir**ía**
tú	dormir**ás**	tú	dormir**ías**
él	dormir**á**	él	dormir**ía**
nosotros	dormir**emos**	nosotros	dormir**íamos**
vosotros	dormir**éis**	vosotros	dormir**íais**
ellos	dormir**án**	ellos	dormir**ían**

	PRESENT SUBJUNCTIVE		PRETERITE
yo	**duerma**	yo	dorm**í**
tú	**duermas**	tú	dorm**iste**
él	**duerma**	él	**durmió**
nosotros	**durmamos**	nosotros	dorm**imos**
vosotros	**durmáis**	vosotros	dorm**isteis**
ellos	**duerman**	ellos	**durmieron**

PAST PARTICIPLE
dorm**ido**

IMPERATIVE
duerme
dormi**d**

GERUND
durmiendo

elegir (to choose)

	PRESENT		IMPERFECT
yo	**elijo**	yo	eleg**ía**
tú	**eliges**	tú	eleg**ías**
él	**elige**	él	eleg**ía**
nosotros	eleg**imos**	nosotros	eleg**íamos**
vosotros	eleg**ís**	vosotros	eleg**íais**
ellos	**eligen**	ellos	eleg**ían**

	FUTURE		CONDITIONAL
yo	elegir**é**	yo	elegir**ía**
tú	elegir**ás**	tú	elegir**ías**
él	elegir**á**	él	elegir**ía**
nosotros	elegir**emos**	nosotros	elegir**íamos**
vosotros	elegir**éis**	vosotros	elegir**íais**
ellos	elegir**án**	ellos	elegir**ían**

	PRESENT SUBJUNCTIVE		PRETERITE
yo	**elija**	yo	eleg**í**
tú	**elijas**	tú	eleg**iste**
él	**elija**	él	**eligió**
nosotros	**elijamos**	nosotros	eleg**imos**
vosotros	**elijáis**	vosotros	eleg**isteis**
ellos	**elijan**	ellos	**eligieron**

PAST PARTICIPLE
eleg**ido**

IMPERATIVE
elige
elegi**d**

GERUND
eligiendo

empezar (to begin)

	PRESENT		IMPERFECT
yo	**empiezo**	yo	empez**aba**
tú	**empiezas**	tú	empez**abas**
él	**empieza**	él	empez**aba**
nosotros	empez**amos**	nosotros	empez**ábamos**
vosotros	empez**áis**	vosotros	empez**abais**
ellos	**empiezan**	ellos	empez**aban**

	FUTURE		CONDITIONAL
yo	empezar**é**	yo	empezar**ía**
tú	empezar**ás**	tú	empezar**ías**
él	empezar**á**	él	empezar**ía**
nosotros	empezar**emos**	nosotros	empezar**íamos**
vosotros	empezar**éis**	vosotros	empezar**íais**
ellos	empezar**án**	ellos	empezar**ían**

	PRESENT SUBJUNCTIVE		PRETERITE
yo	**empiece**	yo	**empecé**
tú	**empieces**	tú	empez**aste**
él	**empiece**	él	empez**ó**
nosotros	**empecemos**	nosotros	empez**amos**
vosotros	**empecéis**	vosotros	empez**asteis**
ellos	**empiecen**	ellos	empez**aron**

PAST PARTICIPLE
empez**ado**

IMPERATIVE
empieza
empeza**d**

GERUND
empez**ando**

entender (to understand)

	PRESENT
yo	**entiendo**
tú	**entiendes**
él	**entiende**
nosotros	entend**emos**
vosotros	entend**éis**
ellos	**entienden**

	IMPERFECT
yo	entend**ía**
tú	entend**ías**
él	entend**ía**
nosotros	entend**íamos**
vosotros	entend**íais**
ellos	entend**ían**

	FUTURE
yo	entender**é**
tú	entender**ás**
él	entender**á**
nosotros	entender**emos**
vosotros	entender**éis**
ellos	entender**án**

	CONDITIONAL
yo	entender**ía**
tú	entender**ías**
él	entender**ía**
nosotros	entender**íamos**
vosotros	entender**íais**
ellos	entender**ían**

	PRESENT SUBJUNCTIVE
yo	**entienda**
tú	**entiendas**
él	**entienda**
nosotros	entend**amos**
vosotros	entend**áis**
ellos	**entiendan**

	PRETERITE
yo	entend**í**
tú	entend**iste**
él	entend**ió**
nosotros	entend**imos**
vosotros	entend**isteis**
ellos	entend**ieron**

PAST PARTICIPLE
entend**ido**

IMPERATIVE
entiende
entende**d**

GERUND
entend**iendo**

enviar (to send)

	PRESENT		IMPERFECT
yo	**envío**	yo	envi**aba**
tú	**envías**	tú	envi**abas**
él	**envía**	él	envi**aba**
nosotros	envi**amos**	nosotros	envi**ábamos**
vosotros	envi**áis**	vosotros	envi**abais**
ellos	**envían**	ellos	envi**aban**

	FUTURE		CONDITIONAL
yo	enviar**é**	yo	enviar**ía**
tú	enviar**ás**	tú	enviar**ías**
él	enviar**á**	él	enviar**ía**
nosotros	enviar**emos**	nosotros	enviar**íamos**
vosotros	enviar**éis**	vosotros	enviar**íais**
ellos	enviar**án**	ellos	enviar**ían**

	PRESENT SUBJUNCTIVE		PRETERITE
yo	**envíe**	yo	envi**é**
tú	**envíes**	tú	envi**aste**
él	**envíe**	él	envi**ó**
nosotros	envi**emos**	nosotros	envi**amos**
vosotros	envi**éis**	vosotros	envi**asteis**
ellos	**envíen**	ellos	envi**aron**

PAST PARTICIPLE
envi**ado**

IMPERATIVE
envía
envia**d**

GERUND
envi**ando**

erguir (to erect)

	PRESENT		IMPERFECT
yo	**yergo**	yo	ergu**ía**
tú	**yergues**	tú	ergu**ías**
él	**yergue**	él	ergu**ía**
nosotros	ergu**imos**	nosotros	ergu**íamos**
vosotros	ergu**ís**	vosotros	ergu**íais**
ellos	**yerguen**	ellos	ergu**ían**

	FUTURE		CONDITIONAL
yo	erguir**é**	yo	erguir**ía**
tú	erguir**ás**	tú	erguir**ías**
él	erguir**á**	él	erguir**ía**
nosotros	erguir**emos**	nosotros	erguir**íamos**
vosotros	erguir**éis**	vosotros	erguir**íais**
ellos	erguir**án**	ellos	erguir**ían**

	PRESENT SUBJUNCTIVE		PRETERITE
yo	**yerga**	yo	ergu**í**
tú	**yergas**	tú	ergu**iste**
él	**yerga**	él	**irguió**
nosotros	**irgamos**	nosotros	ergu**imos**
vosotros	**irgáis**	vosotros	ergu**isteis**
ellos	**yergan**	ellos	**irguieron**

PAST PARTICIPLE
ergu**ido**

IMPERATIVE
yergue
ergui**d**

GERUND
irguiendo

errar (to err)

	PRESENT		IMPERFECT
yo	**yerro**	yo	err**aba**
tú	**yerras**	tú	err**abas**
él	**yerra**	él	err**aba**
nosotros	err**amos**	nosotros	err**ábamos**
vosotros	err**áis**	vosotros	err**abais**
ellos	**yerran**	ellos	err**aban**

	FUTURE		CONDITIONAL
yo	errar**é**	yo	errar**ía**
tú	errar**ás**	tú	errar**ías**
él	errar**á**	él	errar**ía**
nosotros	errar**emos**	nosotros	errar**íamos**
vosotros	errar**éis**	vosotros	errar**íais**
ellos	errar**án**	ellos	errar**ían**

	PRESENT SUBJUNCTIVE		PRETERITE
yo	**yerre**	yo	err**é**
tú	**yerres**	tú	err**aste**
él	**yerre**	él	err**ó**
nosotros	err**emos**	nosotros	err**amos**
vosotros	err**éis**	vosotros	err**asteis**
ellos	**yerren**	ellos	err**aron**

PAST PARTICIPLE
err**ado**

IMPERATIVE
yerra
erra**d**

GERUND
err**ando**

escribir (to write)

	PRESENT		IMPERFECT
yo	escrib**o**	yo	escrib**ía**
tú	escrib**es**	tú	escrib**ías**
él	escrib**e**	él	escrib**ía**
nosotros	escrib**imos**	nosotros	escrib**íamos**
vosotros	escrib**ís**	vosotros	escrib**íais**
ellos	escrib**en**	ellos	escrib**ían**

	FUTURE		CONDITIONAL
yo	escribir**é**	yo	escribir**ía**
tú	escribir**ás**	tú	escribir**ías**
él	escribir**á**	él	escribir**ía**
nosotros	escribir**emos**	nosotros	escribir**íamos**
vosotros	escribir**éis**	vosotros	escribir**íais**
ellos	escribir**án**	ellos	escribir**ían**

	PRESENT SUBJUNCTIVE		PRETERITE
yo	escrib**a**	yo	escrib**í**
tú	escrib**as**	tú	escrib**iste**
él	escrib**a**	él	escrib**ió**
nosotros	escrib**amos**	nosotros	escrib**imos**
vosotros	escrib**áis**	vosotros	escrib**isteis**
ellos	escrib**an**	ellos	escrib**ieron**

PAST PARTICIPLE
escrito

IMPERATIVE
escrib**e**
escrib**id**

GERUND
escrib**iendo**

estar (to be)

PRESENT

yo	**estoy**
tú	**estás**
él	**está**
nosotros	est**amos**
vosotros	est**áis**
ellos	**están**

IMPERFECT

yo	est**aba**
tú	est**abas**
él	est**aba**
nosotros	est**ábamos**
vosotros	est**abais**
ellos	est**aban**

FUTURE

yo	estar**é**
tú	estar**ás**
él	estar**á**
nosotros	estar**emos**
vosotros	estar**éis**
ellos	estar**án**

CONDITIONAL

yo	estar**ía**
tú	estar**ías**
él	estar**ía**
nosotros	estar**íamos**
vosotros	estar**íais**
ellos	estar**ían**

PRESENT SUBJUNCTIVE

yo	**esté**
tú	**estés**
él	**esté**
nosotros	est**emos**
vosotros	est**éis**
ellos	**estén**

PRETERITE

yo	**estuve**
tú	**estuviste**
él	**estuvo**
nosotros	**estuvimos**
vosotros	**estuvisteis**
ellos	**estuvieron**

PAST PARTICIPLE

est**ado**

IMPERATIVE

está

esta**d**

GERUND

est**ando**

freír (to fry)

	PRESENT		IMPERFECT
yo	**frío**	yo	fre**ía**
tú	**fríes**	tú	fre**ías**
él	**fríe**	él	fre**ía**
nosotros	fre**ímos**	nosotros	fre**íamos**
vosotros	fre**ís**	vosotros	fre**íais**
ellos	**fríen**	ellos	fre**ían**

	FUTURE		CONDITIONAL
yo	freir**é**	yo	freir**ía**
tú	freir**ás**	tú	freir**ías**
él	freir**á**	él	freir**ía**
nosotros	freir**emos**	nosotros	freir**íamos**
vosotros	freir**éis**	vosotros	freir**íais**
ellos	freir**án**	ellos	freir**ían**

	PRESENT SUBJUNCTIVE		PRETERITE
yo	**fría**	yo	fre**í**
tú	**frías**	tú	fre**íste**
él	**fría**	él	**frió**
nosotros	**friamos**	nosotros	fre**ímos**
vosotros	**friáis**	vosotros	fre**ísteis**
ellos	**frían**	ellos	**frieron**

PAST PARTICIPLE
frito

IMPERATIVE
fríe
fre**íd**

GERUND
friendo

gruñir (to grunt)

	PRESENT		IMPERFECT
yo	gruñ**o**	yo	gruñ**ía**
tú	gruñ**es**	tú	gruñ**ías**
él	gruñ**e**	él	gruñ**ía**
nosotros	gruñ**imos**	nosotros	gruñ**íamos**
vosotros	gruñ**ís**	vosotros	gruñ**íais**
ellos	gruñ**en**	ellos	gruñ**ían**

	FUTURE		CONDITIONAL
yo	gruñir**é**	yo	gruñir**ía**
tú	gruñir**ás**	tú	gruñir**ías**
él	gruñir**á**	él	gruñir**ía**
nosotros	gruñir**emos**	nosotros	gruñir**íamos**
vosotros	gruñir**éis**	vosotros	gruñir**íais**
ellos	gruñir**án**	ellos	gruñir**ían**

	PRESENT SUBJUNCTIVE		PRETERITE
yo	gruñ**a**	yo	gruñ**í**
tú	gruñ**as**	tú	gruñ**íste**
él	gruñ**a**	él	**gruñó**
nosotros	gruñ**amos**	nosotros	gruñ**imos**
vosotros	gruñ**áis**	vosotros	gruñ**isteis**
ellos	gruñ**an**	ellos	**gruñeron**

PAST PARTICIPLE
gruñ**ido**

IMPERATIVE
gruñ**e**
gruñ**id**

GERUND
gruñendo

haber (to have, *auxiliary*)

	PRESENT		IMPERFECT
yo	**he**	yo	hab**ía**
tú	**has**	tú	hab**ías**
él	**ha**	él	hab**ía**
nosotros	**hemos**	nosotros	hab**íamos**
vosotros	hab**éis**	vosotros	hab**íais**
ellos	**han**	ellos	hab**ían**

	FUTURE		CONDITIONAL
yo	**habré**	yo	**habría**
tú	**habrás**	tú	**habrías**
él	**habrá**	él	**habría**
nosotros	**habremos**	nosotros	**habríamos**
vosotros	**habréis**	vosotros	**habríais**
ellos	**habrán**	ellos	**habrían**

	PRESENT SUBJUNCTIVE		PRETERITE
yo	**haya**	yo	**hube**
tú	**hayas**	tú	**hubiste**
él	**haya**	él	**hubo**
nosotros	**hayamos**	nosotros	**hubimos**
vosotros	**hayáis**	vosotros	**hubisteis**
ellos	**hayan**	ellos	**hubieron**

PAST PARTICIPLE
hab**ido**

IMPERATIVE
not used

GERUND
hab**iendo**

hacer (to do, to make)

	PRESENT		IMPERFECT
yo	**hago**	yo	hac**ía**
tú	hac**es**	tú	hac**ías**
él	hac**e**	él	hac**ía**
nosotros	hac**emos**	nosotros	hac**íamos**
vosotros	hac**éis**	vosotros	hac**íais**
ellos	hac**en**	ellos	hac**ían**

	FUTURE		CONDITIONAL
yo	**haré**	yo	**haría**
tú	**harás**	tú	**harías**
él	**hará**	él	**haría**
nosotros	**haremos**	nosotros	**haríamos**
vosotros	**haréis**	vosotros	**haríais**
ellos	**harán**	ellos	**harían**

	PRESENT SUBJUNCTIVE		PRETERITE
yo	**haga**	yo	**hice**
tú	**hagas**	tú	**hiciste**
él	**haga**	él	**hizo**
nosotros	**hagamos**	nosotros	**hicimos**
vosotros	**hagáis**	vosotros	**hicisteis**
ellos	**hagan**	ellos	**hicieron**

PAST PARTICIPLE
hecho

IMPERATIVE
haz
hace**d**

GERUND
hac**iendo**

hay (there is, there are)

PRESENT **hay**	**IMPERFECT** hab**ía**
FUTURE **habrá**	**CONDITIONAL** **habría**
PRESENT SUBJUNCTIVE **haya**	**PRETERITE** **hubo**
PAST PARTICIPLE hab**ido**	**IMPERATIVE** *not used*
GERUND hab**iendo**	

ir (to go)

	PRESENT		IMPERFECT
yo	**voy**	yo	**iba**
tú	**vas**	tú	**ibas**
él	**va**	él	**iba**
nosotros	**vamos**	nosotros	**íbamos**
vosotros	**vais**	vosotros	**ibais**
ellos	**van**	ellos	**iban**

	FUTURE		CONDITIONAL
yo	ir**é**	yo	ir**ía**
tú	ir**ás**	tú	ir**ías**
él	ir**á**	él	ir**ía**
nosotros	ir**emos**	nosotros	ir**íamos**
vosotros	ir**éis**	vosotros	ir**íais**
ellos	ir**án**	ellos	ir**ían**

	PRESENT SUBJUNCTIVE		PRETERITE
yo	**vaya**	yo	**fui**
tú	**vayas**	tú	**fuiste**
él	**vaya**	él	**fue**
nosotros	**vayamos**	nosotros	**fuimos**
vosotros	**vayáis**	vosotros	**fuisteis**
ellos	**vayan**	ellos	**fueron**

PAST PARTICIPLE

ido

IMPERATIVE

ve

id

GERUND

yendo

jugar (to play)

	PRESENT		IMPERFECT
yo	**juego**	yo	jug**aba**
tú	**juegas**	tú	jug**abas**
él	**juega**	él	jug**aba**
nosotros	jug**amos**	nosotros	jug**ábamos**
vosotros	jug**áis**	vosotros	jug**abais**
ellos	**juegan**	ellos	jug**aban**

	FUTURE		CONDITIONAL
yo	jugar**é**	yo	jugar**ía**
tú	jugar**ás**	tú	jugar**ías**
él	jugar**á**	él	jugar**ía**
nosotros	jugar**emos**	nosotros	jugar**íamos**
vosotros	jugar**éis**	vosotros	jugar**íais**
ellos	jugar**án**	ellos	jugar**ían**

	PRESENT SUBJUNCTIVE		PRETERITE
yo	**juegue**	yo	**jugué**
tú	**juegues**	tú	jug**aste**
él	**juegue**	él	jug**ó**
nosotros	**juguemos**	nosotros	jug**amos**
vosotros	**juguéis**	vosotros	jug**asteis**
ellos	**jueguen**	ellos	jug**aron**

PAST PARTICIPLE
jug**ado**

IMPERATIVE
juega
jug**ad**

GERUND
jug**ando**

leer (to read)

	PRESENT		IMPERFECT
yo	le**o**	yo	le**ía**
tú	le**es**	tú	le**ías**
él	le**e**	él	le**ía**
nosotros	le**emos**	nosotros	le**íamos**
vosotros	le**éis**	vosotros	le**íais**
ellos	le**en**	ellos	le**ían**

	FUTURE		CONDITIONAL
yo	leer**é**	yo	leer**ía**
tú	leer**ás**	tú	leer**ías**
él	leer**á**	él	leer**ía**
nosotros	leer**emos**	nosotros	leer**íamos**
vosotros	leer**éis**	vosotros	leer**íais**
ellos	leer**án**	ellos	leer**ían**

	PRESENT SUBJUNCTIVE		PRETERITE
yo	le**a**	yo	**leí**
tú	le**as**	tú	**leíste**
él	le**a**	él	**leyó**
nosotros	le**amos**	nosotros	**leímos**
vosotros	le**áis**	vosotros	**leísteis**
ellos	le**an**	ellos	**leyeron**

PAST PARTICIPLE
le**ído**

IMPERATIVE
le**e**
lee**d**

GERUND
leyendo

lucir (to shine)

	PRESENT		IMPERFECT
yo	**luzco**	yo	luc**ía**
tú	luc**es**	tú	luc**ías**
él	luc**e**	él	luc**ía**
nosotros	luc**imos**	nosotros	luc**íamos**
vosotros	luc**ís**	vosotros	luc**íais**
ellos	luc**en**	ellos	luc**ían**

	FUTURE		CONDITIONAL
yo	lucir**é**	yo	lucir**ía**
tú	lucir**ás**	tú	lucir**ías**
él	lucir**á**	él	lucir**ía**
nosotros	lucir**emos**	nosotros	lucir**íamos**
vosotros	lucir**éis**	vosotros	lucir**íais**
ellos	lucir**án**	ellos	lucir**ían**

	PRESENT SUBJUNCTIVE		PRETERITE
yo	**luzca**	yo	luc**í**
tú	**luzcas**	tú	luc**iste**
él	**luzca**	él	luc**ió**
nosotros	**luzcamos**	nosotros	luc**imos**
vosotros	**luzcáis**	vosotros	luc**isteis**
ellos	**luzcan**	ellos	luc**ieron**

PAST PARTICIPLE
luc**ido**

IMPERATIVE
luc**e**
luci**d**

GERUND
luc**iendo**

llover (to rain)

PRESENT
llueve

IMPERFECT
llov**ía**

FUTURE
llover**á**

CONDITIONAL
llover**ía**

PRESENT SUBJUNCTIVE
llueva

PRETERITE
llov**ió**

PAST PARTICIPLE
llov**ido**

IMPERATIVE
not used

GERUND
llov**iendo**

morir (to die)

	PRESENT		IMPERFECT
yo	**muero**	yo	mor**ía**
tú	**mueres**	tú	mor**ías**
él	**muere**	él	mor**ía**
nosotros	mor**imos**	nosotros	mor**íamos**
vosotros	mor**ís**	vosotros	mor**íais**
ellos	**mueren**	ellos	mor**ían**

	FUTURE		CONDITIONAL
yo	morir**é**	yo	morir**ía**
tú	morir**ás**	tú	morir**ías**
él	morir**á**	él	morir**ía**
nosotros	morir**emos**	nosotros	morir**íamos**
vosotros	morir**éis**	vosotros	morir**íais**
ellos	morir**án**	ellos	morir**ían**

	PRESENT SUBJUNCTIVE		PRETERITE
yo	**muera**	yo	mor**í**
tú	**mueras**	tú	mor**iste**
él	**muera**	él	**murió**
nosotros	**muramos**	nosotros	mor**imos**
vosotros	**muráis**	vosotros	mor**isteis**
ellos	**mueran**	ellos	**murieron**

PAST PARTICIPLE
muerto

IMPERATIVE
muere
mori**d**

GERUND
muriendo

mover (to move)

	PRESENT		IMPERFECT
yo	**muevo**	yo	mov**ía**
tú	**mueves**	tú	mov**ías**
él	**mueve**	él	mov**ía**
nosotros	mov**emos**	nosotros	mov**íamos**
vosotros	mov**éis**	vosotros	mov**íais**
ellos	**mueven**	ellos	mov**ían**

	FUTURE		CONDITIONAL
yo	mover**é**	yo	mover**ía**
tú	mover**ás**	tú	mover**ías**
él	mover**á**	él	mover**ía**
nosotros	mover**emos**	nosotros	mover**íamos**
vosotros	mover**éis**	vosotros	mover**íais**
ellos	mover**án**	ellos	mover**ían**

	PRESENT SUBJUNCTIVE		PRETERITE
yo	**mueva**	yo	mov**í**
tú	**muevas**	tú	mov**iste**
él	**mueva**	él	mov**ió**
nosotros	mov**amos**	nosotros	mov**imos**
vosotros	mov**áis**	vosotros	mov**isteis**
ellos	**muevan**	ellos	mov**ieron**

PAST PARTICIPLE
mov**ido**

IMPERATIVE
mueve
move**d**

GERUND
mov**iendo**

nacer (to be born)

	PRESENT		IMPERFECT
yo	**nazco**	yo	nac**ía**
tú	nac**es**	tú	nac**ías**
él	nac**e**	él	nac**ía**
nosotros	nac**emos**	nosotros	nac**íamos**
vosotros	nac**éis**	vosotros	nac**íais**
ellos	nac**en**	ellos	nac**ían**

	FUTURE		CONDITIONAL
yo	nacer**é**	yo	nacer**ía**
tú	nacer**ás**	tú	nacer**ías**
él	nacer**á**	él	nacer**ía**
nosotros	nacer**emos**	nosotros	nacer**íamos**
vosotros	nacer**éis**	vosotros	nacer**íais**
ellos	nacer**án**	ellos	nacer**ían**

	PRESENT SUBJUNCTIVE		PRETERITE
yo	**nazca**	yo	nac**í**
tú	**nazcas**	tú	nac**iste**
él	**nazca**	él	nac**ió**
nosotros	**nazcamos**	nosotros	nac**imos**
vosotros	**nazcáis**	vosotros	nac**isteis**
ellos	**nazcan**	ellos	nac**ieron**

PAST PARTICIPLE
nac**ido**

IMPERATIVE
nac**e**
nace**d**

GERUND
nac**iendo**

negar (to deny)

	PRESENT		IMPERFECT
yo	**niego**	yo	neg**aba**
tú	**niegas**	tú	neg**abas**
él	**niega**	él	neg**aba**
nosotros	neg**amos**	nosotros	neg**ábamos**
vosotros	neg**áis**	vosotros	neg**abais**
ellos	**niegan**	ellos	neg**aban**

	FUTURE		CONDITIONAL
yo	negar**é**	yo	negar**ía**
tú	negar**ás**	tú	negar**ías**
él	negar**á**	él	negar**ía**
nosotros	negar**emos**	nosotros	negar**íamos**
vosotros	negar**éis**	vosotros	negar**íais**
ellos	negar**án**	ellos	negar**ían**

	PRESENT SUBJUNCTIVE		PRETERITE
yo	**niegue**	yo	**negué**
tú	**niegues**	tú	neg**aste**
él	**niegue**	él	neg**ó**
nosotros	**nieguemos**	nosotros	neg**amos**
vosotros	**neguéis**	vosotros	neg**asteis**
ellos	**nieguen**	ellos	neg**aron**

PAST PARTICIPLE
neg**ado**

IMPERATIVE
niega
nega**d**

GERUND
neg**ando**

oír (to hear)

	PRESENT		IMPERFECT
yo	**oigo**	yo	oía
tú	**oyes**	tú	oías
él	**oye**	él	oía
nosotros	**oímos**	nosotros	oíamos
vosotros	oís	vosotros	oíais
ellos	**oyen**	ellos	oían

	FUTURE		CONDITIONAL
yo	**oiré**	yo	**oiría**
tú	**oirás**	tú	**oirías**
él	**oirá**	él	**oiría**
nosotros	**oiremos**	nosotros	**oiríamos**
vosotros	**oiréis**	vosotros	**oiríais**
ellos	**oirán**	ellos	**oirían**

	PRESENT SUBJUNCTIVE		PRETERITE
yo	**oiga**	yo	**oí**
tú	**oigas**	tú	**oíste**
él	**oiga**	él	**oyó**
nosotros	**oigamos**	nosotros	**oímos**
vosotros	**oigáis**	vosotros	**oísteis**
ellos	**oigan**	ellos	**oyeron**

PAST PARTICIPLE
oído

IMPERATIVE
oye
oíd

GERUND
oyendo

oler (to smell)

	PRESENT		IMPERFECT
yo	**huelo**	yo	ol**ía**
tú	**hueles**	tú	ol**ías**
él	**huele**	él	ol**ía**
nosotros	ol**emos**	nosotros	ol**íamos**
vosotros	ol**éis**	vosotros	ol**íais**
ellos	**huelen**	ellos	ol**ían**

	FUTURE		CONDITIONAL
yo	oler**é**	yo	oler**ía**
tú	oler**ás**	tú	oler**ías**
él	oler**á**	él	oler**ía**
nosotros	oler**emos**	nosotros	oler**íamos**
vosotros	oler**éis**	vosotros	oler**íais**
ellos	oler**án**	ellos	oler**ían**

	PRESENT SUBJUNCTIVE		PRETERITE
yo	**huela**	yo	ol**í**
tú	**huelas**	tú	ol**iste**
él	**huela**	él	ol**ió**
nosotros	ol**amos**	nosotros	ol**imos**
vosotros	ol**áis**	vosotros	ol**isteis**
ellos	**huelan**	ellos	ol**ieron**

PAST PARTICIPLE
ol**ido**

IMPERATIVE
huele
ole**d**

GERUND
ol**iendo**

pagar (to pay)

	PRESENT		IMPERFECT
yo	pag**o**	yo	pag**aba**
tú	pag**as**	tú	pag**abas**
él	pag**a**	él	pag**aba**
nosotros	pag**amos**	nosotros	pag**ábamos**
vosotros	pag**áis**	vosotros	pag**abais**
ellos	pag**an**	ellos	pag**aban**

	FUTURE		CONDITIONAL
yo	pagar**é**	yo	pagar**ía**
tú	pagar**ás**	tú	pagar**ías**
él	pagar**á**	él	pagar**ía**
nosotros	pagar**emos**	nosotros	pagar**íamos**
vosotros	pagar**éis**	vosotros	pagar**íais**
ellos	pagar**án**	ellos	pagar**ían**

	PRESENT SUBJUNCTIVE		PRETERITE
yo	**pague**	yo	**pagué**
tú	**pagues**	tú	pag**aste**
él	**pague**	él	pag**ó**
nosotros	**paguemos**	nosotros	pag**amos**
vosotros	**paguéis**	vosotros	pag**asteis**
ellos	**paguen**	ellos	pag**aron**

PAST PARTICIPLE
pag**ado**

IMPERATIVE
pag**a**
pag**ad**

GERUND
pag**ando**

pedir (to ask for)

	PRESENT		IMPERFECT
yo	**pido**	yo	ped**ía**
tú	**pides**	tú	ped**ías**
él	**pide**	él	ped**ía**
nosotros	ped**imos**	nosotros	ped**íamos**
vosotros	ped**ís**	vosotros	ped**íais**
ellos	**piden**	ellos	ped**ían**

	FUTURE		CONDITIONAL
yo	pedir**é**	yo	pedir**ía**
tú	pedir**ás**	tú	pedir**ías**
él	pedir**á**	él	pedir**ía**
nosotros	pedir**emos**	nosotros	pedir**íamos**
vosotros	pedir**éis**	vosotros	pedir**íais**
ellos	pedir**án**	ellos	pedir**ían**

	PRESENT SUBJUNCTIVE		PRETERITE
yo	**pida**	yo	ped**í**
tú	**pidas**	tú	ped**iste**
él	**pida**	él	**pidió**
nosotros	**pidamos**	nosotros	ped**imos**
vosotros	**pidáis**	vosotros	ped**isteis**
ellos	**pidan**	ellos	**pidieron**

PAST PARTICIPLE	IMPERATIVE
ped**ido**	**pide**
	ped**id**

GERUND

pidiendo

pensar (to think)

	PRESENT		IMPERFECT
yo	**pienso**	yo	pens**aba**
tú	**piensas**	tú	pens**abas**
él	**piensa**	él	pens**aba**
nosotros	pens**amos**	nosotros	pens**ábamos**
vosotros	pens**áis**	vosotros	pens**abais**
ellos	**piensan**	ellos	pens**aban**

	FUTURE		CONDITIONAL
yo	pensar**é**	yo	pensar**ía**
tú	pensar**ás**	tú	pensar**ías**
él	pensar**á**	él	pensar**ía**
nosotros	pensar**emos**	nosotros	pensar**íamos**
vosotros	pensar**éis**	vosotros	pensar**íais**
ellos	pensar**án**	ellos	pensar**ían**

	PRESENT SUBJUNCTIVE		PRETERITE
yo	**piense**	yo	pens**é**
tú	**pienses**	tú	pens**aste**
él	**piense**	él	pens**ó**
nosotros	pens**emos**	nosotros	pens**amos**
vosotros	pens**éis**	vosotros	pens**asteis**
ellos	**piensen**	ellos	pens**aron**

PAST PARTICIPLE
pens**ado**

IMPERATIVE
piensa
pensa**d**

GERUND
pens**ando**

poder (to be able)

	PRESENT
yo	**puedo**
tú	**puedes**
él	**puede**
nosotros	pod**emos**
vosotros	pod**éis**
ellos	**pueden**

	IMPERFECT
yo	pod**ía**
tú	pod**ías**
él	pod**ía**
nosotros	pod**íamos**
vosotros	pod**íais**
ellos	pod**ían**

	FUTURE
yo	**podré**
tú	**podrás**
él	**podrá**
nosotros	**podremos**
vosotros	**podréis**
ellos	**podrán**

	CONDITIONAL
yo	**podría**
tú	**podrías**
él	**podría**
nosotros	**podríamos**
vosotros	**podríais**
ellos	**podrían**

	PRESENT SUBJUNCTIVE
yo	**pueda**
tú	**puedas**
él	**pueda**
nosotros	pod**amos**
vosotros	pod**áis**
ellos	**puedan**

	PRETERITE
yo	**pude**
tú	**pudiste**
él	**pudo**
nosotros	**pudimos**
vosotros	**pudisteis**
ellos	**pudieron**

PAST PARTICIPLE

pod**ido**

IMPERATIVE

puede

pode**d**

GERUND

pudiendo

poner (to put)

	PRESENT		IMPERFECT
yo	**pongo**	yo	pon**ía**
tú	pon**es**	tú	pon**ías**
él	pon**e**	él	pon**ía**
nosotros	pon**emos**	nosotros	pon**íamos**
vosotros	pon**éis**	vosotros	pon**íais**
ellos	pon**en**	ellos	pon**ían**

	FUTURE		CONDITIONAL
yo	**pondré**	yo	**pondría**
tú	**pondrás**	tú	**pondrías**
él	**pondrá**	él	**pondría**
nosotros	**pondremos**	nosotros	**pondríamos**
vosotros	**pondréis**	vosotros	**pondríais**
ellos	**pondrán**	ellos	**pondrían**

	PRESENT SUBJUNCTIVE		PRETERITE
yo	**ponga**	yo	**puse**
tú	**pongas**	tú	**pusiste**
él	**ponga**	él	**puso**
nosotros	**pongamos**	nosotros	**pusimos**
vosotros	**pongáis**	vosotros	**pusisteis**
ellos	**pongan**	ellos	**pusieron**

PAST PARTICIPLE
puesto

IMPERATIVE
pon
pone**d**

GERUND
pon**iendo**

prohibir (to forbid)

PRESENT

yo	**prohíbo**
tú	**prohíbes**
él	**prohíbe**
nosotros	prohib**imos**
vosotros	prohib**ís**
ellos	**prohíben**

IMPERFECT

yo	prohib**ía**
tú	prohib**ías**
él	prohib**ía**
nosotros	prohib**íamos**
vosotros	prohib**íais**
ellos	prohib**ían**

FUTURE

yo	prohibir**é**
tú	prohibir**ás**
él	prohibir**á**
nosotros	prohibir**emos**
vosotros	prohibir**éis**
ellos	prohibir**án**

CONDITIONAL

yo	prohibir**ía**
tú	prohibir**ías**
él	prohibir**ía**
nosotros	prohibir**íamos**
vosotros	prohibir**íais**
ellos	prohibir**ían**

PRESENT SUBJUNCTIVE

yo	**prohíba**
tú	**prohíbas**
él	**prohíba**
nosotros	prohib**amos**
vosotros	prohib**áis**
ellos	**prohíban**

PRETERITE

yo	prohib**í**
tú	prohib**iste**
él	prohib**ió**
nosotros	prohib**imos**
vosotros	prohib**isteis**
ellos	prohib**ieron**

PAST PARTICIPLE

prohib**ido**

IMPERATIVE

prohíbe

prohibi**d**

GERUND

prohib**iendo**

querer (to want)

	PRESENT		IMPERFECT
yo	**quiero**	yo	quer**ía**
tú	**quieres**	tú	quer**ías**
él	**quiere**	él	quer**ía**
nosotros	quer**emos**	nosotros	quer**íamos**
vosotros	quer**éis**	vosotros	quer**íais**
ellos	**quieren**	ellos	quer**ían**

	FUTURE		CONDITIONAL
yo	**querré**	yo	**querría**
tú	**querrás**	tú	**querrías**
él	**querrá**	él	**querría**
nosotros	**querremos**	nosotros	**querríamos**
vosotros	**querréis**	vosotros	**querríais**
ellos	**querrán**	ellos	**querrían**

	PRESENT SUBJUNCTIVE		PRETERITE
yo	**quiera**	yo	**quise**
tú	**quieras**	tú	**quisiste**
él	**quiera**	él	**quiso**
nosotros	quer**amos**	nosotros	**quisimos**
vosotros	quer**áis**	vosotros	**quisisteis**
ellos	**quieran**	ellos	**quisieron**

PAST PARTICIPLE
quer**ido**

IMPERATIVE
quiere
quere**d**

GERUND
quer**iendo**

rehusar (to refuse)

	PRESENT		IMPERFECT
yo	**rehúso**	yo	rehus**aba**
tú	**rehúsas**	tú	rehus**abas**
él	**rehúsa**	él	rehus**aba**
nosotros	rehus**amos**	nosotros	rehus**ábamos**
vosotros	rehus**áis**	vosotros	rehus**abais**
ellos	**rehúsan**	ellos	rehus**aban**

	FUTURE		CONDITIONAL
yo	rehusar**é**	yo	rehusar**ía**
tú	rehusar**ás**	tú	rehusar**ías**
él	rehusar**á**	él	rehusar**ía**
nosotros	rehusar**emos**	nosotros	rehusar**íamos**
vosotros	rehusar**éis**	vosotros	rehusar**íais**
ellos	rehusar**án**	ellos	rehusar**ían**

	PRESENT SUBJUNCTIVE		PRETERITE
yo	**rehúse**	yo	rehus**é**
tú	**rehúses**	tú	rehus**aste**
él	**rehúse**	él	rehus**ó**
nosotros	rehus**emos**	nosotros	rehus**amos**
vosotros	rehus**éis**	vosotros	rehus**asteis**
ellos	**rehúsen**	ellos	rehus**aron**

PAST PARTICIPLE
rehus**ado**

IMPERATIVE
rehúsa
rehusa**d**

GERUND
rehus**ando**

reír (to laugh)

	PRESENT		IMPERFECT
yo	**río**	yo	re**ía**
tú	**ríes**	tú	re**ías**
él	**ríe**	él	re**ía**
nosotros	**reímos**	nosotros	re**íamos**
vosotros	**reís**	vosotros	re**íais**
ellos	**ríen**	ellos	re**ían**

	FUTURE		CONDITIONAL
yo	**reiré**	yo	**reiría**
tú	**reirás**	tú	**reirías**
él	**reirá**	él	**reiría**
nosotros	**reiremos**	nosotros	**reiríamos**
vosotros	**reiréis**	vosotros	**reiríais**
ellos	**reirán**	ellos	**reirían**

	PRESENT SUBJUNCTIVE		PRETERITE
yo	**ría**	yo	**reí**
tú	**rías**	tú	**reíste**
él	**ría**	él	**rió**
nosotros	**riamos**	nosotros	**reímos**
vosotros	**riáis**	vosotros	**reísteis**
ellos	**rían**	ellos	**rieron**

PAST PARTICIPLE
re**ído**

IMPERATIVE
ríe
reí**d**

GERUND
riendo

reñir (to scold)

	PRESENT		IMPERFECT
yo	**riño**	yo	reñ**ía**
tú	**riñes**	tú	reñ**ías**
él	**riñe**	él	reñ**ía**
nosotros	reñ**imos**	nosotros	reñ**íamos**
vosotros	reñ**ís**	vosotros	reñ**íais**
ellos	**riñen**	ellos	reñ**ían**

	FUTURE		CONDITIONAL
yo	reñir**é**	yo	reñir**ía**
tú	reñir**ás**	tú	reñir**ías**
él	reñir**á**	él	reñir**ía**
nosotros	reñir**emos**	nosotros	reñir**íamos**
vosotros	reñir**éis**	vosotros	reñir**íais**
ellos	reñir**án**	ellos	reñir**ían**

	PRESENT SUBJUNCTIVE		PRETERITE
yo	**riña**	yo	reñ**í**
tú	**riñas**	tú	reñ**iste**
él	**riña**	él	**riñó**
nosotros	**riñamos**	nosotros	reñ**imos**
vosotros	**riñáis**	vosotros	reñ**isteis**
ellos	**riñan**	ellos	**riñeron**

PAST PARTICIPLE
reñ**ido**

IMPERATIVE
ríñe
reñi**d**

GERUND
riñendo

resolver (to solve)

	PRESENT		IMPERFECT
yo	**resuelvo**	yo	resolv**ía**
tú	**resuelves**	tú	resolv**ías**
él	**resuelve**	él	resolv**ía**
nosotros	resolv**emos**	nosotros	resolv**íamos**
vosotros	resolv**éis**	vosotros	resolv**íais**
ellos	**resuelven**	ellos	resolv**ían**

	FUTURE		CONDITIONAL
yo	resolver**é**	yo	resolver**ía**
tú	resolver**ás**	tú	resolver**ías**
él	resolver**á**	él	resolver**ía**
nosotros	resolver**emos**	nosotros	resolver**íamos**
vosotros	resolver**éis**	vosotros	resolver**íais**
ellos	resolver**án**	ellos	resolver**ían**

	PRESENT SUBJUNCTIVE		PRETERITE
yo	**resuelva**	yo	resolv**í**
tú	**resuelvas**	tú	resolv**iste**
él	**resuelva**	él	resolv**ió**
nosotros	resolv**amos**	nosotros	resolv**imos**
vosotros	resolv**áis**	vosotros	resolv**isteis**
ellos	**resuelvan**	ellos	resolv**ieron**

PAST PARTICIPLE
resuelto

IMPERATIVE
resuelve
resolve**d**

GERUND
resolv**iendo**

reunir (to put together, to gather)

	PRESENT		IMPERFECT
yo	**reúno**	yo	reuní**a**
tú	**reúnes**	tú	reuní**as**
él	**reúne**	él	reuní**a**
nosotros	reun**imos**	nosotros	reuní**amos**
vosotros	reun**ís**	vosotros	reuní**ais**
ellos	**reúnen**	ellos	reuní**an**

	FUTURE		CONDITIONAL
yo	reunir**é**	yo	reunir**ía**
tú	reunir**ás**	tú	reunir**ías**
él	reunir**á**	él	reunir**ía**
nosotros	reunir**emos**	nosotros	reunir**íamos**
vosotros	reunir**éis**	vosotros	reunir**íais**
ellos	reunir**án**	ellos	reunir**ían**

	PRESENT SUBJUNCTIVE		PRETERITE
yo	**reúna**	yo	reun**í**
tú	**reúnas**	tú	reun**iste**
él	**reúna**	él	reun**ió**
nosotros	reun**amos**	nosotros	reun**imos**
vosotros	reun**áis**	vosotros	reun**isteis**
ellos	**reúnan**	ellos	reun**ieron**

PAST PARTICIPLE
reun**ido**

IMPERATIVE
reúne
reuni**d**

GERUND
reun**iendo**

rogar (to beg)

	PRESENT		IMPERFECT
yo	**ruego**	yo	rog**aba**
tú	**ruegas**	tú	rog**abas**
él	**ruega**	él	rog**aba**
nosotros	rog**amos**	nosotros	rog**ábamos**
vosotros	rog**áis**	vosotros	rog**abais**
ellos	**ruegan**	ellos	rog**aban**

	FUTURE		CONDITIONAL
yo	rogar**é**	yo	rogar**ía**
tú	rogar**ás**	tú	rogar**ías**
él	rogar**á**	él	rogar**ía**
nosotros	rogar**emos**	nosotros	rogar**íamos**
vosotros	rogar**éis**	vosotros	rogar**íais**
ellos	rogar**án**	ellos	rogar**ían**

	PRESENT SUBJUNCTIVE		PRETERITE
yo	**ruegue**	yo	**rogué**
tú	**ruegues**	tú	rog**aste**
él	**ruegue**	él	rog**ó**
nosotros	**roguemos**	nosotros	rog**amos**
vosotros	**roguéis**	vosotros	rog**asteis**
ellos	**rueguen**	ellos	rog**aron**

PAST PARTICIPLE

rog**ado**

IMPERATIVE

ruega

roga**d**

GERUND

rog**ando**

romper (to break)

	PRESENT		IMPERFECT
yo	romp**o**	yo	romp**ía**
tú	romp**es**	tú	romp**ías**
él	romp**e**	él	romp**ía**
nosotros	romp**emos**	nosotros	romp**íamos**
vosotros	romp**éis**	vosotros	romp**íais**
ellos	romp**en**	ellos	romp**ían**

	FUTURE		CONDITIONAL
yo	romper**é**	yo	romper**ía**
tú	romper**ás**	tú	romper**ías**
él	romper**á**	él	romper**ía**
nosotros	romper**emos**	nosotros	romper**íamos**
vosotros	romper**éis**	vosotros	romper**íais**
ellos	romper**án**	ellos	romper**ían**

	PRESENT SUBJUNCTIVE		PRETERITE
yo	romp**a**	yo	romp**í**
tú	romp**as**	tú	romp**iste**
él	romp**a**	él	romp**ió**
nosotros	romp**amos**	nosotros	romp**imos**
vosotros	romp**áis**	vosotros	romp**isteis**
ellos	romp**an**	ellos	romp**ieron**

PAST PARTICIPLE
roto

IMPERATIVE
romp**e**
romp**ed**

GERUND
romp**iendo**

saber (to know)

	PRESENT		IMPERFECT
yo	**sé**	yo	sab**ía**
tú	sab**es**	tú	sab**ías**
él	sab**e**	él	sab**ía**
nosotros	sab**emos**	nosotros	sab**íamos**
vosotros	sab**éis**	vosotros	sab**íais**
ellos	sab**en**	ellos	sab**ían**

	FUTURE		CONDITIONAL
yo	**sabré**	yo	**sabría**
tú	**sabrás**	tú	**sabrías**
él	**sabrá**	él	**sabría**
nosotros	**sabremos**	nosotros	**sabríamos**
vosotros	**sabréis**	vosotros	**sabríais**
ellos	**sabrán**	ellos	**sabrían**

	PRESENT SUBJUNCTIVE		PRETERITE
yo	**sepa**	yo	**supe**
tú	**sepas**	tú	**supiste**
él	**sepa**	él	**supo**
nosotros	**sepamos**	nosotros	**supimos**
vosotros	**sepáis**	vosotros	**supisteis**
ellos	**sepan**	ellos	**supieron**

PAST PARTICIPLE
sab**ido**

IMPERATIVE
sab**e**
sabe**d**

GERUND
sab**iendo**

sacar (to take out)

	PRESENT		IMPERFECT
yo	sac**o**	yo	sac**aba**
tú	sac**as**	tú	sac**abas**
él	sac**a**	él	sac**aba**
nosotros	sac**amos**	nosotros	sac**ábamos**
vosotros	sac**áis**	vosotros	sac**abais**
ellos	sac**an**	ellos	sac**aban**

	FUTURE		CONDITIONAL
yo	sacar**é**	yo	sacar**ía**
tú	sacar**ás**	tú	sacar**ías**
él	sacar**á**	él	sacar**ía**
nosotros	sacar**emos**	nosotros	sacar**íamos**
vosotros	sacar**éis**	vosotros	sacar**íais**
ellos	sacar**án**	ellos	sacar**ían**

	PRESENT SUBJUNCTIVE		PRETERITE
yo	**saque**	yo	**saqué**
tú	**saques**	tú	sac**aste**
él	**saque**	él	sac**ó**
nosotros	**saquemos**	nosotros	sac**amos**
vosotros	**saqueís**	vosotros	sac**asteis**
ellos	**saquen**	ellos	sac**aron**

PAST PARTICIPLE
sac**ado**

IMPERATIVE
sac**a**
saca**d**

GERUND
sac**ando**

salir (to go out)

	PRESENT
yo	**salgo**
tú	sal**es**
él	sal**e**
nosotros	sal**imos**
vosotros	sal**ís**
ellos	sal**en**

	IMPERFECT
yo	sal**ía**
tú	sal**ías**
él	sal**ía**
nosotros	sal**íamos**
vosotros	sal**íais**
ellos	sal**ían**

	FUTURE
yo	**saldré**
tú	**saldrás**
él	**saldrá**
nosotros	**saldremos**
vosotros	**saldréis**
ellos	**saldrán**

	CONDITIONAL
yo	**saldría**
tú	**saldrías**
él	**saldría**
nosotros	**saldríamos**
vosotros	**saldríais**
ellos	**saldrían**

	PRESENT SUBJUNCTIVE
yo	**salga**
tú	**salgas**
él	**salga**
nosotros	**salgamos**
vosotros	**salgáis**
ellos	**salgan**

	PRETERITE
yo	sal**í**
tú	sal**iste**
él	sal**ió**
nosotros	sal**imos**
vosotros	sal**isteis**
ellos	sal**ieron**

PAST PARTICIPLE

sal**ido**

IMPERATIVE

sal
sali**d**

GERUND

sal**iendo**

satisfacer (to satisfy)

	PRESENT		IMPERFECT
yo	**satisfago**	yo	satisfac**ía**
tú	satisfac**es**	tú	satisfac**ías**
él	satisfac**e**	él	satisfac**ía**
nosotros	satisfac**emos**	nosotros	satisfac**íamos**
vosotros	satisfac**éis**	vosotros	satisfac**íais**
ellos	satisfac**en**	ellos	satisfac**ían**

	FUTURE		CONDITIONAL
yo	**satisfaré**	yo	**satisfaría**
tú	**satisfarás**	tú	**satisfarías**
él	**satisfará**	él	**satisfaría**
nosotros	**satisfaremos**	nosotros	**satisfaríamos**
vosotros	**satisfaréis**	vosotros	**satisfaríais**
ellos	**satisfarán**	ellos	**satisfarían**

	PRESENT SUBJUNCTIVE		PRETERITE
yo	**satisfaga**	yo	**satisfice**
tú	**satisfagas**	tú	**satisficiste**
él	**satisfaga**	él	**satisfizo**
nosotros	**satisfagamos**	nosotros	**satisficimos**
vosotros	**satisfagáis**	vosotros	**satisficisteis**
ellos	**satisfagan**	ellos	**satisficieron**

PAST PARTICIPLE
satisfecho

IMPERATIVE
satisfaz/satisfac**e**
satisface**d**

GERUND
satisfac**iendo**

seguir (to follow)

	PRESENT		IMPERFECT
yo	**sigo**	yo	seg**uía**
tú	**sigues**	tú	seg**uías**
él	**sigue**	él	seg**uía**
nosotros	segu**imos**	nosotros	seg**uíamos**
vosotros	segu**ís**	vosotros	seg**uíais**
ellos	**siguen**	ellos	seg**uían**

	FUTURE		CONDITIONAL
yo	seguir**é**	yo	seguir**ía**
tú	seguir**ás**	tú	seguir**ías**
él	seguir**á**	él	seguir**ía**
nosotros	seguir**emos**	nosotros	seguir**íamos**
vosotros	seguir**éis**	vosotros	seguir**íais**
ellos	seguir**án**	ellos	seguir**ían**

	PRESENT SUBJUNCTIVE		PRETERITE
yo	**siga**	yo	segu**í**
tú	**sigas**	tú	segu**iste**
él	**siga**	él	**siguió**
nosotros	**sigamos**	nosotros	segu**imos**
vosotros	**sigáis**	vosotros	segu**isteis**
ellos	**sigan**	ellos	**siguieron**

PAST PARTICIPLE
segu**ido**

IMPERATIVE
sigue
segu**id**

GERUND
siguiendo

sentir (to feel)

	PRESENT		IMPERFECT
yo	**siento**	yo	sent**ía**
tú	**sientes**	tú	sent**ías**
él	**siente**	él	sent**ía**
nosotros	sent**imos**	nosotros	sent**íamos**
vosotros	sent**ís**	vosotros	sent**íais**
ellos	**sienten**	ellos	sent**ían**

	FUTURE		CONDITIONAL
yo	sentir**é**	yo	sentir**ía**
tú	sentir**ás**	tú	sentir**ías**
él	sentir**á**	él	sentir**ía**
nosotros	sentir**emos**	nosotros	sentir**íamos**
vosotros	sentir**éis**	vosotros	sentir**íais**
ellos	sentir**án**	ellos	sentir**ían**

	PRESENT SUBJUNCTIVE		PRETERITE
yo	**sienta**	yo	sent**í**
tú	**sientas**	tú	sent**iste**
él	**sienta**	él	**sintió**
nosotros	**sintamos**	nosotros	sent**imos**
vosotros	**sintáis**	vosotros	sent**isteis**
ellos	**sientan**	ellos	**sintieron**

PAST PARTICIPLE
sent**ido**

IMPERATIVE
siente
sent**id**

GERUND
sintiendo

ser (to be)

	PRESENT
yo	**soy**
tú	**eres**
él	**es**
nosotros	**somos**
vosotros	**sois**
ellos	**son**

	IMPERFECT
yo	**era**
tú	**eras**
él	**era**
nosotros	**éramos**
vosotros	**erais**
ellos	**eran**

	FUTURE
yo	ser**é**
tú	ser**ás**
él	ser**á**
nosotros	ser**emos**
vosotros	ser**éis**
ellos	ser**án**

	CONDITIONAL
yo	ser**ía**
tú	ser**ías**
él	ser**ía**
nosotros	ser**íamos**
vosotros	ser**íais**
ellos	ser**ían**

	PRESENT SUBJUNCTIVE
yo	**sea**
tú	**seas**
él	**sea**
nosotros	**seamos**
vosotros	**seáis**
ellos	**sean**

	PRETERITE
yo	**fui**
tú	**fuiste**
él	**fue**
nosotros	**fuimos**
vosotros	**fuisteis**
ellos	**fueron**

PAST PARTICIPLE

sido

IMPERATIVE

sé

se**d**

GERUND

siendo

tener (to have)

	PRESENT		IMPERFECT
yo	**tengo**	yo	ten**ía**
tú	**tienes**	tú	ten**ías**
él	**tiene**	él	ten**ía**
nosotros	ten**emos**	nosotros	ten**íamos**
vosotros	ten**éis**	vosotros	ten**íais**
ellos	**tienen**	ellos	ten**ían**

	FUTURE		CONDITIONAL
yo	**tendré**	yo	**tendría**
tú	**tendrás**	tú	**tendrías**
él	**tendrá**	él	**tendría**
nosotros	**tendremos**	nosotros	**tendríamos**
vosotros	**tendréis**	vosotros	**tendríais**
ellos	**tendrán**	ellos	**tendrían**

	PRESENT SUBJUNCTIVE		PRETERITE
yo	**tenga**	yo	**tuve**
tú	**tengas**	tú	**tuviste**
él	**tenga**	él	**tuvo**
nosotros	**tengamos**	nosotros	**tuvimos**
vosotros	**tengáis**	vosotros	**tuvisteis**
ellos	**tengan**	ellos	**tuvieron**

PAST PARTICIPLE

ten**ido**

IMPERATIVE

ten

tene**d**

GERUND

ten**iendo**

torcer (to twist)

	PRESENT		IMPERFECT
yo	**tuerzo**	yo	torc**ía**
tú	**tuerces**	tú	torc**ías**
él	**tuerce**	él	torc**ía**
nosotros	torc**emos**	nosotros	torc**íamos**
vosotros	toc**éis**	vosotros	torc**íais**
ellos	**tuercen**	ellos	torc**ían**

	FUTURE		CONDITIONAL
yo	torcer**é**	yo	torcer**ía**
tú	torcer**ás**	tú	torcer**ías**
él	torcer**á**	él	torcer**ía**
nosotros	torcer**emos**	nosotros	torcer**íamos**
vosotros	torcer**éis**	vosotros	torcer**íais**
ellos	torcer**án**	ellos	torcer**ían**

	PRESENT SUBJUNCTIVE		PRETERITE
yo	**tuerza**	yo	torc**í**
tú	**tuerzas**	tú	torc**iste**
él	**tuerza**	él	torc**ió**
nosotros	**tuerzamos**	nosotros	torc**imos**
vosotros	**tuerzáis**	vosotros	torc**isteis**
ellos	**tuerzan**	ellos	torc**ieron**

PAST PARTICIPLE
torc**ido**

IMPERATIVE
tuerce
torce**d**

GERUND
torc**iendo**

traer (to bring)

	PRESENT		IMPERFECT
yo	**traigo**	yo	tra**ía**
tú	tra**es**	tú	tra**ías**
él	tra**e**	él	tra**ía**
nosotros	tra**emos**	nosotros	tra**íamos**
vosotros	tra**éis**	vosotros	tra**íais**
ellos	tra**en**	ellos	tra**ían**

	FUTURE		CONDITIONAL
yo	traer**é**	yo	traer**ía**
tú	traer**ás**	tú	traer**ías**
él	traer**á**	él	traer**ía**
nosotros	traer**emos**	nosotros	traer**íamos**
vosotros	traer**éis**	vosotros	traer**íais**
ellos	traer**án**	ellos	traer**ían**

	PRESENT SUBJUNCTIVE		PRETERITE
yo	**traiga**	yo	**traje**
tú	**traigas**	tú	**trajiste**
él	**traiga**	él	**trajo**
nosotros	**traigamos**	nosotros	**trajimos**
vosotros	**traigáis**	vosotros	**trajisteis**
ellos	**traigan**	ellos	**trajeron**

PAST PARTICIPLE
traído

IMPERATIVE
trae
trae**d**

GERUND
trayendo

valer (to be worth)

	PRESENT		IMPERFECT
yo	val**go**	yo	val**ía**
tú	val**es**	tú	val**ías**
él	val**e**	él	val**ía**
nosotros	val**emos**	nosotros	val**íamos**
vosotros	val**éis**	vosotros	val**íais**
ellos	val**en**	ellos	val**ían**

	FUTURE		CONDITIONAL
yo	**valdré**	yo	**valdría**
tú	**valdrás**	tú	**valdrías**
él	**valdrá**	él	**valdría**
nosotros	**valdremos**	nosotros	**valdríamos**
vosotros	**valdréis**	vosotros	**valdríais**
ellos	**valdrán**	ellos	**valdrían**

	PRESENT SUBJUNCTIVE		PRETERITE
yo	**valga**	yo	val**í**
tú	**valgas**	tú	val**iste**
él	**valga**	él	val**ió**
nosotros	**valgamos**	nosotros	val**imos**
vosotros	**valgáis**	vosotros	val**isteis**
ellos	**valgan**	ellos	val**ieron**

PAST PARTICIPLE
val**ido**

IMPERATIVE
val**e**
val**ed**

GERUND
val**iendo**

vencer (to win)

	PRESENT		IMPERFECT
yo	**venzo**	yo	venc**ía**
tú	venc**es**	tú	venc**ías**
él	venc**e**	él	venc**ía**
nosotros	venc**emos**	nosotros	venc**íamos**
vosotros	venc**éis**	vosotros	venc**íais**
ellos	venc**en**	ellos	venc**ían**

	FUTURE		CONDITIONAL
yo	vencer**é**	yo	vencer**ía**
tú	vencer**ás**	tú	vencer**ías**
él	vencer**á**	él	vencer**ía**
nosotros	vencer**emos**	nosotros	vencer**íamos**
vosotros	vencer**éis**	vosotros	vencer**íais**
ellos	vencer**án**	ellos	vencer**ían**

	PRESENT SUBJUNCTIVE		PRETERITE
yo	**venza**	yo	venc**í**
tú	**venzas**	tú	venc**iste**
él	**venza**	él	venc**ió**
nosotros	**venzamos**	nosotros	venc**imos**
vosotros	**venzáis**	vosotros	venc**isteis**
ellos	**venzan**	ellos	venc**ieron**

PAST PARTICIPLE
venc**ido**

IMPERATIVE
venc**e**
vence**d**

GERUND
venc**iendo**

venir (to come)

PRESENT

yo	**vengo**
tú	**vienes**
él	**viene**
nosotros	ven**imos**
vosotros	ven**ís**
ellos	**vienen**

IMPERFECT

yo	ven**ía**
tú	ven**ías**
él	ven**ía**
nosotros	ven**íamos**
vosotros	ven**íais**
ellos	ven**ían**

FUTURE

yo	**vendré**
tú	**vendrás**
él	**vendrá**
nosotros	**vendremos**
vosotros	**vendréis**
ellos	**vendrán**

CONDITIONAL

yo	**vendría**
tú	**vendrías**
él	**vendría**
nosotros	**vendríamos**
vosotros	**vendríais**
ellos	**vendrían**

PRESENT SUBJUNCTIVE

yo	**venga**
tú	**vengas**
él	**venga**
nosotros	**vengamos**
vosotros	**vengáis**
ellos	**vengan**

PRETERITE

yo	**vine**
tú	**viniste**
él	**vino**
nosotros	**vinimos**
vosotros	**vinisteis**
ellos	**vinieron**

PAST PARTICIPLE

ven**ido**

IMPERATIVE

ven
veni**d**

GERUND

viniendo

ver (to see)

	PRESENT		IMPERFECT
yo	**veo**	yo	**veía**
tú	**ves**	tú	**veías**
él	**ve**	él	**veía**
nosotros	**vemos**	nosotros	**veíamos**
vosotros	**veis**	vosotros	**veíais**
ellos	**ven**	ellos	**veían**

	FUTURE		CONDITIONAL
yo	ver**é**	yo	ver**ía**
tú	ver**ás**	tú	ver**ías**
él	ver**á**	él	ver**ía**
nosotros	ver**emos**	nosotros	ver**íamos**
vosotros	ver**éis**	vosotros	ver**íais**
ellos	ver**án**	ellos	ver**ían**

	PRESENT SUBJUNCTIVE		PRETERITE
yo	**vea**	yo	v**i**
tú	**veas**	tú	v**iste**
él	**vea**	él	v**io**
nosotros	**veamos**	nosotros	v**imos**
vosotros	**veáis**	vosotros	v**isteis**
ellos	**vean**	ellos	v**ieron**

PAST PARTICIPLE
visto

IMPERATIVE
v**e**
ve**d**

GERUND
v**iendo**

volcar (to overturn)

	PRESENT		IMPERFECT
yo	**vuelco**	yo	volc**aba**
tú	**vuelcas**	tú	volc**abas**
él	**vuelca**	él	volc**aba**
nosotros	volc**amos**	nosotros	volc**ábamos**
vosotros	volc**áis**	vosotros	volc**abais**
ellos	**vuelcan**	ellos	volc**aban**

	FUTURE		CONDITIONAL
yo	volcar**é**	yo	volcar**ía**
tú	volcar**ás**	tú	volcar**ías**
él	volcar**á**	él	volcar**ía**
nosotros	volcar**emos**	nosotros	volcar**íamos**
vosotros	volcar**éis**	vosotros	volcar**íais**
ellos	volcar**án**	ellos	volcar**ían**

	PRESENT SUBJUNCTIVE		PRETERITE
yo	**vuelque**	yo	**volqué**
tú	**vuelques**	tú	volc**aste**
él	**vuelque**	él	volc**ó**
nosotros	**volquemos**	nosotros	volc**amos**
vosotros	**volquéis**	vosotros	volc**asteis**
ellos	**vuelquen**	ellos	volc**aron**

PAST PARTICIPLE
volc**ado**

IMPERATIVE
vuelca
volca**d**

GERUND
volc**ando**

volver (to return)

	PRESENT		IMPERFECT
yo	**vuelvo**	yo	volv**ía**
tú	**vuelves**	tú	volv**ías**
él	**vuelve**	él	volv**ía**
nosotros	volv**emos**	nosotros	volv**íamos**
vosotros	volv**éis**	vosotros	volv**íais**
ellos	**vuelven**	ellos	volv**ían**

	FUTURE		CONDITIONAL
yo	volver**é**	yo	volver**ía**
tú	volver**ás**	tú	volver**ías**
él	volver**á**	él	volver**ía**
nosotros	volver**emos**	nosotros	volver**íamos**
vosotros	volver**éis**	vosotros	volver**íais**
ellos	volver**án**	ellos	volver**ían**

	PRESENT SUBJUNCTIVE		PRETERITE
yo	**vuelva**	yo	volv**í**
tú	**vuelvas**	tú	volv**iste**
él	**vuelva**	él	volv**ió**
nosotros	volv**amos**	nosotros	volv**imos**
vosotros	volv**áis**	vosotros	volv**isteis**
ellos	**vuelvan**	ellos	volv**ieron**

PAST PARTICIPLE
vuelto

IMPERATIVE
vuelve
volve**d**

GERUND
volv**iendo**

zurcir (to darn)

	PRESENT		IMPERFECT
yo	**zurzo**	yo	zurc**ía**
tú	zurc**es**	tú	zurc**ías**
él	zurc**e**	él	zurc**ía**
nosotros	zurc**imos**	nosotros	zurc**íamos**
vosotros	zurc**ís**	vosotros	zurc**íais**
ellos	zurc**en**	ellos	zurc**ían**

	FUTURE		CONDITIONAL
yo	zurcir**é**	yo	zurcir**ía**
tú	zurcir**ás**	tú	zurcir**ías**
él	zurcir**á**	él	zurcir**ía**
nosotros	zurcir**emos**	nosotros	zurcir**íamos**
vosotros	zurcir**éis**	vosotros	zurcir**íais**
ellos	zurcir**án**	ellos	zurcir**ían**

	PRESENT SUBJUNCTIVE		PRETERITE
yo	**zurza**	yo	zurc**í**
tú	**zurzas**	tú	zurc**iste**
él	**zurza**	él	zurc**ió**
nosotros	**zurzamos**	nosotros	zurc**imos**
vosotros	**zurzáis**	vosotros	zurc**isteis**
ellos	**zurzan**	ellos	zurc**ieron**

PAST PARTICIPLE
zurc**ido**

IMPERATIVE
zurc**e**
zurci**d**

GERUND
zurc**iendo**

Verb Index

The following pages, 162 to 190, contain an index of all the Spanish verbs in this dictionary cross-referred to the appropriate conjugation model:

- Regular verbs belonging to the first, second and third conjugation are numbered 1, 2 and 3 respectively. For the regular conjugations see pages 6 to 13.

- Irregular verbs are numerically cross-referred to the appropriate model as conjugated on pages 82 to 160. Thus, **alzar** is cross-referred to page 100 where **cruzar**, the model for this verb group, is conjugated.

- Verbs which are most commonly used in the reflexive form – e.g. **amodorrarse** – have been cross-referred to the appropriate non-reflexive model. For the full conjugation of a reflexive verb, see pages 28 to 31.

- Verbs printed in **bold** – e.g. **abrir** – are themselves models.

- Superior numbers refer you to notes on page 191 which indicate how the verb differs from its model.

Verb Index

Notes

The notes below indicate special peculiarities of individual verbs. When only some forms of a given tense are affected, all these are shown. When all forms of the tense are affected, only the 1st and 2nd persons are shown, followed by *etc*.

1 Gerund 2 Past Participle 3 Present 4 Preterite 5 Present Subjunctive 6 Imperfect Subjunctive

1 **acaecer, acontecer, amanecer, anochecer, competer, deshelar, escampar, granizar, helar, nevar, nublar, relampaguear, tronar, verdear**: used almost exclusively in infinitive and 3rd person singular
2 **asir** 3 asgo 5 asga, asgar *etc*
3 **atañer, -tañer** 1 atañendo 4 atañó: see also 1 above
4 **balbucir** 3 balbuceo 5 balbucee, balbucees *etc*
5 **concernir** 3 concierne, conciernen 5 concierna, conciernan: only used in 3rd person
6 **degollar** 3 degüello, degüellas, degüella, degüellan 5 degüelle, degüelles, degüellen
7 **delinquir** 3 delinco 5 delinca, delincas *etc*
8 **desasir** 3 desasgo 5 desasga, desasgas *etc*
9 **discernir** 3 discierno, disciernes, discierne, disciernen 5 discierna, disciernas, disciernan
10 **enraizar** 3 enraízo, enraízas, enraíza, enraízan 5 enraíce, enraíces, enraícen
11 **pudrir** 2 podrido
12 **rehuir** 3 rehúyo, rehúyes, rehúye, rehúyen 5 rehúya, rehúyas, rehúyan
13 **roer** 4 royó, royeron 6 royera, royeras *etc*
14 **soler**: used only in present and imperfect indicative
15 **yacer** 3 yazgo *or* yazco *or* yago 5 yazga *etc* or yazca *etc or* yaga *etc*

The Gender of Nouns

In Spanish, all nouns are either masculine or feminine, whether denoting people, animals or things. Gender is largely unpredictable and has to be learnt for each noun. However, the following guidelines will help you determine the gender for certain types of nouns:

Nouns denoting male people and animals are usually – but not always – masculine, e.g.

un hombre a man
un toro a bull
un enfermero a (*male*) nurse
un semental a stallion

Nouns denoting female people and animals are usually – but not always – feminine, e.g.

una niña a girl
una vaca a cow
una enfermera a nurse
una yegua a mare

Some nouns are masculine *or* feminine depending on the sex of the person to whom they refer, e.g.

un camarada a (*male*) comrade
una camarada a (*female*) comrade
un belga a Belgian (*man*)
una belga a Belgian (*woman*)
un marroquí a Moroccan (*man*)
una marroquí a Moroccan (*woman*)

Other nouns referring to either men *or* women have only one gender which applies to both, e.g.

una persona a person
una visita a visitor
una víctima a victim
una estrella a star

Often the ending of a noun indicates its gender. Shown opposite are some of the most important to guide you.

Often the ending of the noun indicates its gender. Shown below are some of the most important to guide you:

Masculine endings

-o	**un clavo** a nail, **un plátano** a banana EXCEPTIONS: **mano** hand, **foto** photograph, **moto(cicleta)** motorbike
-l	**un tonel** a barrel, **un hotel** a hotel EXCEPTIONS: **cal** lime, **cárcel** prison, **catedral** cathedral, **col** cabbage, **miel** honey, **piel** skin, **sal** salt, **señal** sign
-r	**un tractor** a tractor, **el altar** the altar EXCEPTIONS: **coliflor** cauliflower, **flor** flower, **labor** task
-y	**el rey** the king, **un buey** an ox EXCEPTION: **ley** law

Feminine endings

-a	**un casa** a house, **la cara** the face EXCEPTIONS: **día** day, **mapa** map, **planeta** planet, **tranvía** tram, and most words ending in **-ma** (**tema** subject, **problema** problem, *etc*)
-ión	**una canción** a song, **una procesión** a procession EXCEPTIONS: most nouns not ending in **-ción** or **-sión**, e.g. **avión** aeroplane, **camión** lorry, **gorrión** sparrow
-dad, -tad, -tud	**una ciudad** a town, **la libertad** freedom, **una multitud** a crowd
-ed	**una pared** a wall, **la sed** thirst EXCEPTION: **césped** lawn
-itis	**una faringitis** pharyngitis, **la celulitis** cellulitis
-iz	**una perdiz** a partridge, **una matriz** a matri EXCEPTIONS: **lápiz** pencil, **maíz** corn, **tapiz** tapestry
-sis	**una tesis** a thesis, **una dosis** a dose EXCEPTIONS: **análysis** analysis, **énfasis** emphasis, **paréntesis** parenthesis
-umbre	**la podredumbre** rot, **la muchedrume** crowd

The Gender of Nouns *continued*

Some nouns change meaning according to gender. The most common are set out below:

	MASCULINE	FEMININE
capital	capital (*money*)	capital (*city*) → 1
clave	harpsichord	clue
cólera	cholera	anger → 2
cometa	comet	kite
corriente	current month	current
corte	cut	court (*royal*) → 3
coma	coma	comma → 4
cura	priest	cure → 5
frente	front (*in war*)	forehead → 6
guardia	guard(sman)	guard → 7
guía	guide (*person*)	guide(book) → 8
moral	mulberry tree	morals
orden	order (*arrangement*)	order (*command*) → 9
ordenanza	office boy	ordinance
papa	Pope	potato
parte	dispatch	part → 10
pendiente	earring	slope
pez	fish	pitch
policía	policeman	police
radio	radius, radium	radio

Examples

❶ Invirtieron mucho capital	They invested a lot of capital
La capital es muy fea	The capital city is very ugly
❷ Es difícil luchar contra el cólera	Cholera is difficult to combat
Montó en cólera	He got angry
❸ Me encanta tu corte de pelo	I love your haircut
Se trasladó la corte a Madrid	The court was moved to Madrid
❹ Entró en un coma profundo	He went into a deep coma
Aquí hace falta una coma	You need to put a comma here
❺ ¿Quién es? – El cura	Who is it? – The priest
No tiene cura	It's hopeless
❻ Han mandado a su hijo al frente	Her son has been sent to the front
Tiene la frente muy ancha	She has a very broad forehead
❼ Vino un guardia de tráfico	A traffic policeman came
Están relevando la guardia ahora	They're changing the guard now
❽ Nuestro guía nos hizo reír a carcajadas	Our guide had us falling about laughing
Busco una guía turística	I'm looking for a guidebook
❾ Están en orden alfabético	They're in alphabetical order
No hemos recibido la orden de pago	We haven't had the payment order
❿ Le mandó un parte al general	He sent a dispatch to the general
En alguna parte debe estar	It must be somewhere or other

Gender: the Formation of Feminines

As in English, male and female are sometimes differentiated by the use of two quite separate words, e.g.

mi marido my husband
mi mujer my wife
un toro a bull
una vaca a cow

There are, however, some words in Spanish which show this distinction by the form of their ending:

Nouns ending in **-o** change to **-a** to form the feminine → 1

If the masculine singular form already ends in **-a**, no further **-a** is added to the feminine → 2

If the last letter of the masculine singular form is a consonant, an **-a** is normally added in the feminine* → 3

Feminine forms to note

MASCULINE	FEMININE	
el abad	**la abadesa**	abbot/abbess
un actor	**una actriz**	actor/actress
el alcalde	**la alcaldesa**	mayor/mayoress
el conde	**la condesa**	count/countess
el duque	**la duquesa**	duke/duchess
el emperador	**la emperatriz**	emperor/empress
un poeta	**una poetisa**	poet/poetess
el príncipe	**la princesa**	prince/princess
el rey	**la reina**	king/queen
un sacerdote	**una sacerdotisa**	priest/priestess
un tigre	**una tigresa**	tiger/tigress
el zar	**la zarina**	tzar/tzarina

* If the last syllable has an accent, it disappears in the feminine (see page 296) → 4

Examples

❶ un amigo a (*male*) friend	una amiga a (*female*) friend
un empleado a (*male*) employee	una empleada a (*female*) employee
un gato a cat	una gata a (*female*) cat
❷ un deportista a sportsman	una deportista a sportswoman
un colega a (*male*) colleague	una colega a (*female*) colleague
un camarada a (*male*) comrade	una camarada a (*female*) comrade
❸ un español a Spaniard, a Spanish man	una española a Spanish woman
un vendedor a salesman	una vendedora a saleswoman
un jugador a (*male*) player	una jugadora a (*female*) player
❹ un lapón a Laplander (*man*)	una lapona a Laplander (*woman*)
un león a lion	una leona a lioness
un neocelandés a New Zealander (*man*)	una neocelandesa a New Zealander (*woman*)

The Formation of Plurals

Nouns ending in an unstressed vowel add **-s** to the singular form → 1

Nouns ending in a consonant or a stressed vowel add **-es** to the singular form → 2

ⓘ BUT: **café** coffee shop (*plural*: **cafés**)
mamá mummy (*plural*: **mamás**)
papá daddy (*plural*: **papás**)
pie foot (*plural*: **pies**)
sofá sofa (*plural*: **sofás**)
té tea (*plural*: **tes**)

and words of foreign origin ending in a consonant, e.g.:

coñac brandy (*plural*: **coñacs**)
jersey jumper (*plural*: **jerseys**)

ⓘ Note:

- nouns ending in **-n** or **-s** with an accent on the last syllable drop this accent in the plural (see page 296) → 3
- nouns ending in **-n** with the stress on the second-last syllable in the singular add an accent to that syllable in the plural in order to show the correct position for stress (see page 296) → 4
- nouns ending in **-z** change this to **c** in the plural → 5

Nouns with an unstressed final syllable ending in **-s** do not change in the plural → 6

Examples

❶ la casa the house	las casas the houses
el libro the book	los libros the books
❷ un rumor a rumour	unos rumores (some) rumours
un jabalí a boar	unos jabalíes (some) boars
❸ la canción the song	las canciones the songs
el autobús the bus	los autobuses the buses
❹ un examen an exam	unos exámenes (some) exams
un crimen a crime	unos crímenes (some) crimes
❺ la luz the light	las luces the lights
❻ un paraguas an umbrella	unos paraguas (some) umbrellas
la dosis the dose	las dosis the doses
el lunes Monday	los lunes Mondays

The Definite Article

	WITH MASC. NOUN	WITH FEM. NOUN	
SING.	**el**	**la**	the
PLUR.	**los**	**las**	the

The gender and number of the noun determine the form of the article → 1

> ⓘ Note: However, if the article comes directly before a feminine singular noun which starts with a stressed **a-** or **ha-**, the masculine form **el** is used instead of the feminine **la** → 2

For uses of the definite article see page 203.

a + **el** becomes **al** → 3

de + **el** becomes **del** → 4

Examples

1. el tren the train — la estación the station
   el actor the actor — la actriz the actress
   los hoteles the hotels — las escuelas the schools
   los profesores the teachers — las mujeres the women

② el agua	the water
BUT:	
la misma agua	the same water
el hacha	the axe
BUT:	
la mejor hacha	the best axe
③ al cine	to the cinema
al empleado	to the employee
al hospital	to the hospital
④ del departamento	from/of the department
del autor	from/of the author
del presidente	from/of the president

Uses of the Definite Article

While the definite article is used in much the same way in Spanish as it is in English, its use is more widespread in Spanish. Unlike English the definite article is also used:

with abstract nouns, except when following certain prepositions → ①

in generalizations, especially with plural or uncountable* nouns → ②

with parts of the body → ③
'Ownership' is often indicated by an indirect object pronoun or a reflexive pronoun → ④

with titles/ranks/professions followed by a proper name → ⑤
EXCEPTIONS: with **Don/Doña**, **San/Santo(a)** → ⑥

before nouns of official, academic and religious buildings, and names of meals and games → ⑦

The definite article is *not* used with nouns in apposition unless those nouns are individualized → ⑧

* An uncountable noun is one which cannot be used in the plural or with an indefinite article, e.g. **el acero** steel; **la leche** milk.

Examples

1 Los precios suben	Prices are rising
El tiempo es oro	Time is money
BUT:	
con pasión	with passion
sin esperanza	without hope
2 No me gusta el café	I don't like coffee
Los niños necesitan ser queridos	Children need to be loved
3 Vuelva la cabeza hacia la izquierda	Turn your head to the left
No puedo mover las piernas	I can't move my legs
4 La cabeza me da vueltas	My head is spinning
Lávate las manos	Wash your hands
5 El rey Jorge III	King George III
el capitán Menéndez	Captain Menéndez
el doctor Ochoa	Doctor Ochoa
el señor Ramírez	Mr Ramírez
6 Don Arturo Ruiz	Mr Arturo Ruiz
Santa Teresa	Saint Teresa
7 en la cárcel	in prison
en la universidad	at university
en la iglesia	at church
la cena	dinner
el tenis	tennis
el ajedrez	chess
8 Madrid, capital de España, es la ciudad que ...	Madrid, the capital of Spain, is the city which ...
BUT:	
Maria Callas, la famosa cantante de ópera ...	Maria Callas, the famous opera singer ...

The Indefinite Article

	WITH MASC. NOUN	WITH FEM. NOUN	
SING.	**un**	**una**	a
PLUR.	**unos**	**unas**	some

The indefinite article is used in Spanish largely as it is in English.

BUT:

There is no article when a person's profession is being stated → ❶

The article is used, however, when the profession is qualified by an adjective → ❷

The article is not used with the following words:

otro	another	→ ❸
cierto	certain	→ ❹
semejante	such (a)	→ ❺
tal	such (a)	→ ❻
cien	a hundred	→ ❼
mil	a thousand	→ ❽
sin	without	→ ❾
qué	what a	→ ❿

There is no article with a noun in apposition → ⓫. When an abstract noun is qualified by an adjective, the indefinite article is used, but is not translated in English → ⓬

Examples

① Es profesor Mi madre es enfermera	He's a teacher My mother is a nurse
② Es un buen médico Se hizo una escritora célebre	He's a good doctor She became a famous writer
③ otro libro	another book
④ cierta calle	a certain street
⑤ semejante ruido	such a noise
⑥ tal mentira	such a lie
⑦ cien soldados	a hundred soldiers
⑧ mil años	a thousand years
⑨ sin casa	without a house
⑩ ¡Qué sorpresa!	What a surprise!
⑪ Baroja, gran escritor de la Generación del 98	Baroja, a great writer of the 'Generación del 98'
⑫ con una gran sabiduría/un valor admirable Dieron pruebas de una sangre fría increíble una película de un mal gusto espantoso	with great wisdom/admirable courage They showed incredible coolness a film in appallingly bad taste

The Article 'lo'

This is never used with a noun. Instead, it is used in the following ways:

as an intensifier before an adjective or adverb in the construction

lo + adjective/adverb + **que** → 1

ⓘ Note: The adjective agrees with the noun it refers to → 2

With an adjective or participle to form an abstract noun → 3

In the phrase **lo de** to refer to a subject of which speaker and listener are already aware. It can often be translated as *the business/affair of/about ...* → 4

In set expressions, the commonest of which are:

a lo mejor	maybe, perhaps	→ 5
a lo lejos	in the distance	→ 6
a lo largo de	along, through	→ 7
por lo menos	at least	→ 8
por lo tanto	therefore, so	→ 9
por lo visto	apparently	→ 10

Examples

1 No sabíamos lo pequeña que era la casa	We didn't know how small the house was
Sé lo mucho que te gusta la música	I know how much you like music
2 No te imaginas lo simpáticos que son	You can't imagine how nice they are
Ya sabes lo buenas que son estas manzanas	You already know how good these apples are
3 Lo bueno de eso es que ...	The good thing about it is that ...
Sentimos mucho lo ocurrido	We are very sorry about what happened
4 Lo de ayer es mejor que lo olvides	It's better if you forget what happened yesterday
Lo de tu hermano me preocupa mucho	The business about your brother worries me very much
5 A lo mejor ha salido	Perhaps he's gone out
6 A lo lejos se veían unas casas	Some houses could be seen in the distance
7 A lo largo de su vida	Throughout his life
A lo largo de la carretera	Along the road
8 Hubo por lo menos cincuenta heridos	At least fifty people were injured
9 No hemos recibido ninguna instrucción al respecto, y por lo tanto no podemos ...	We have not received any instructions about it, therefore we cannot ...
10 Por lo visto, no viene	Apparently he's not coming *or*: He's not coming, it seems

Adjectives

Most adjectives agree in number and in gender with the noun or pronoun.

ⓘ Note that:

- if the adjective refers to two or more singular nouns of the same gender, a plural ending of that gender is required → 1
- if the adjective refers to two or more singular nouns of different genders, a masculine plural ending is required → 2

The formation of feminines

Adjectives ending in **-o** change to **-a** → 3

Some groups of adjectives add **-a**:
- adjectives of nationality or geographical origin → 4
- adjectives ending in **-or** (except irregular comparatives: see page 214), **-án**, **-ón**, **-ín** → 5

ⓘ Note: When there is an accent on the last syllable, it disappears in the feminine (see page 296).

Other adjectives do not change → 6

The formation of plurals

Adjectives ending in an unstressed vowel add **-s** → 7

Adjectives ending in a stressed vowel or a consonant add **-es** → 8

ⓘ Note:

- if there is an accent on the last syllable of a word ending in a consonant, it will disappear in the plural (see page 296) → 9
- if the last letter is a **z** it will become a **c** in the plural → 10

Examples

1 la lengua y la literatura españolas	(the) Spanish language and literature
2 Nunca había visto árboles y flores tan raros	I had never seen such strange trees and flowers
3 mi hermano pequeño	my little brother
mi hermana pequeña	my little sister
4 un chico español	a Spanish boy
una chica española	a Spanish girl
el equipo barcelonés	the team from Barcelona
la vida barcelonesa	the Barcelona way of life
5 un niño encantador	a charming little boy
una niña encantadora	a charming little girl
un hombre holgazán	an idle man
una mujer holgazana	an idle woman
un gesto burlón	a mocking gesture
una sonrisa burlona	a mocking smile
un chico cantarín	a boy fond of singing
una chica cantarina	a girl fond of singing
6 un final feliz	a happy ending
una infancia feliz	a happy childhood
mi amigo belga	my Belgian (*male*) friend
mi amiga belga	my Belgian (*female*) friend
el vestido verde	the green dress
la blusa verde	the green blouse
7 el último tren	the last train
los últimos trenes	the last trains
una casa vieja	an old house
unas casas viejas	(some) old houses
8 un médico iraní	an Iranian doctor
unos médicos iraníes	(some) Iranian doctors
un examen fácil	easy exam
unos exámenes fáciles	(some) easy exams
9 un río francés	a French river
unos ríos franceses	(some) French rivers
10 un día feliz	a happy day
unos días felices	(some) happy days

Invariable Adjectives

Some adjectives and other parts of speech when used adjectivally never change in the feminine or plural.

The commonest of these are:

- nouns denoting colour → 1
- compound adjectives → 2
- nouns used as adjectives → 3

Shortening of adjectives

The following drop the final **-o** before a masculine singular noun:

bueno good → 4
malo bad
alguno* some → 5
ninguno* none
uno one → 6
primero first → 7
tercero third
postrero last → 8

* ⓘ Note: An accent is required to show the correct position for stress.

Grande *big*, *great* is usually shortened to **gran** before a masculine *or* feminine singular noun → 9

Santo *Saint* changes to **San** except with saints' names beginning with **Do-** *or* **To-** → 10

Ciento *a hundred* is shortened to **cien** before a masculine *or* feminine plural noun → 11

Cualquiera drops the final **-a** before a masculine *or* feminine singular noun → 12

Examples

1	los vestidos naranja	the orange dresses
2	las chaquetas azul marino	the navy blue jackets
3	bebés probeta mujeres soldado	test-tube babies women soldiers
4	un buen libro	a good book
5	algún libro	some book
6	cuarenta y un años	forty-one years
7	el primer hijo	the first child
8	un postrer deseo	a last wish
9	un gran actor una gran decepción	a great actor a great disappointment
10	San Antonio Santo Tomás	Saint Anthony Saint Thomas
11	cien años cien millones	a hundred years a hundred million
12	cualquier día a cualquier hora	any day any time

Comparatives and Superlatives

Comparatives

These are formed using the following constructions:

más ... (que) more ... (than) → ➊
menos ... (que) less ... (than) → ➋
tanto ... como as ... as → ➌
tan ... como as ... as → ➍
tan ... que so ... that → ➎

demasiado ...		too ...	
bastante ...	**para**	enough ...	to → ➏
suficiente ...		enough ...	

'Than' followed by a clause is translated by **de lo que** → ➐

Superlatives

These are formed using the following constructions:

el/la/los/las más ... (que) the most ... (that) → ➑
el/la/los/las menos ... (que) the least ... (that) → ➒

After a superlative the preposition **de** is often translated as 'in' → ➓

The absolute superlative (*very, most, extremely + adjective*) is expressed in Spanish by **muy** + adjective, or by adding **-ísimo/a/os/as** to the adjective when it ends in a consonant, or to its stem (adjective minus final vowel) when it ends in a vowel → ⓫

ⓘ Note: It is sometimes necessary to change the spelling of the adjective when **-ísimo** is added, in order to maintain the same sound (see page 300) → ⓬

Examples

1	una razón más seria	a more serious reason
	Es más alto que mi hermano	He's taller than my brother
2	una película menos conocida	a less well known film
	Luis es menos tímido que tú	Luis is less shy than you
3	Pablo tenía tanto miedo como yo	Paul was as frightened as I was
4	No es tan grande como creía	It isn't as big as I thought
5	El examen era tan difícil que nadie aprobó	The exam was so difficult that nobody passed
6	No tengo suficiente dinero para comprarlo	I haven't got enough money to buy it
7	Está más cansada de lo que parece	She is more tired than she seems
8	el caballo más veloz	the fastest horse
	la casa más pequeña	the smallest house
	los días más lluviosos	the wettest days
	las manzanas más maduras	the ripest apples
9	el hombre menos simpático	the least likeable man
	la niña menos habladora	the least talkative girl
	los cuadros menos bonitos	the least attractive paintings
	las camisas menos viejas	the least old shirts
10	la estación más ruidosa de Londres	the noisiest station in London
11	Este libro es muy interesante	This book is very interesting
12	Tienen un coche rapidísimo	They have an extremely fast car
	Era facilísimo de hacer	It was very easy to make
	Mi tío era muy rico	My uncle was very rich
	Se hizo riquísimo	He became extremely rich
	un león muy feroz	a very ferocious lion
	un tigre ferocísimo	an extremely ferocious tiger

Comparatives and Superlatives *continued*

Adjectives with irregular comparatives/superlatives

ADJECTIVE	COMPARATIVE	SUPERLATIVE
bueno	**mejor**	**el mejor**
good	better	the best
malo	**peor**	**el peor**
bad	worse	the worst
grande	**mayor** *or* **más grande**	**el más grande**
big	bigger; older	the biggest; the oldest
pequeño	**menor** *or* **más pequeño**	**el más pequeño**
small	smaller; younger; lesser	the smallest; the youngest; the least

The irregular comparative and superlative forms of **grande** and **pequeño** are used mainly to express:

- age, in which case they come after the noun → 1
- abstract size and degrees of importance, in which case they come before the noun → 2

The regular forms are used mainly to express physical size → 3

Irregular comparatives and superlatives have one form for both masculine and feminine, but always agree in number with the noun → 1

Examples

❶ mis hermanos mayores	my older brothers
la hija menor	the youngest daughter
❷ el menor ruido	the slightest sound
las mayores dificultades	the biggest difficulties
❸ Este plato es más grande que aquél	This plate is bigger than that one
Mi casa es más pequeña que la tuya	My house is smaller than yours

Demonstrative Adjectives

	MASCULINE	FEMININE	
SING.	**este**	**esta**	this
	ese	**esa**	that
	aquel	**aquella**	that
PLUR.	**estos**	**estas**	these
	esos	**esas**	those
	aquellos	**aquellas**	those

Demonstrative adjectives normally precede the noun and always agree in number and in gender → 1

The forms **ese/a/os/as** are used:

- to indicate distance from the speaker but proximity to the person addressed → 2
- to indicate a not too remote distance → 3

The forms **aquel/la/los/las** are used to indicate distance, in space or time → 4

Examples

1	Este bolígrafo no escribe	This pen is not working
	Esa revista es muy mala	That is a very bad magazine
	Aquella montaña es muy alta	That mountain (over there) is very high
	¿Conoces a esos señores?	Do you know those gentlemen?
	Siga Vd hasta aquellos edificios	Carry on until you come to those buildings
	¿Ves aquellas personas?	Can you see those people (over there)?
2	Ese papel en donde escribes ...	That paper you are writing on ...
3	No me gustan esos cuadros	I don't like those pictures
4	Aquella calle parece muy ancha	That street (over there) looks very wide
	Aquellos años sí que fueron felices	Those were really happy years

Interrogative Adjectives

	MASCULINE	FEMININE	
SING.	¿qué?	¿qué?	what?, which?
	¿cuánto?	¿cuánta?	how much?, how many?
PLUR.	¿qué?	¿qué?	what?, which?
	¿cuántos?	¿cuántas?	how much?, how many?

Interrogative adjectives, when not invariable, agree in number and gender with the noun → 1

The forms shown above are also used in indirect questions → 2

Exclamatory Adjectives

	MASCULINE	FEMININE	
SING.	¡qué!	¡qué!	what (a)
	¡cuánto!	¡cuánta!	what (a lot of)
PLUR.	¡qué!	¡qué!	what
	¡cuántos!	¡cuántas!	what (a lot of)

Exclamatory adjectives, when not invariable, agree in number and gender with the noun → 3

Examples

❶ ¿Qué libro te gustó más?	Which book did you like most?
¿Qué clase de hombre es?	What type of man is he?
¿Qué instrumentos toca Vd?	What instruments do you play?
¿Qué ofertas ha recibido Vd?	What offers have you received?
¿Cuánto dinero te queda?	How much money have you got left?
¿Cuánta lluvia ha caído?	How much rain have we had?
¿Cuántos vestidos quieres comprar?	How many dresses do you want to buy?
¿Cuántas personas van a venir?	How many people are coming?
❷ No sé a qué hora llegó	I don't know at what time she arrived
Dígame cuántas postales quiere	Tell me how many postcards you'd like
❸ ¡Qué pena!	What a pity!
¡Qué tiempo tan/más malo!	What lousy weather!
¡Cuánto tiempo!	What a long time!
¡Cuánta pobreza!	What poverty!
¡Cuántos autobuses!	What a lot of buses!
¡Cuántas mentiras!	What a lot of lies!

Possessive Adjectives

Weak forms

WITH SING. NOUN		WITH PLUR. NOUN		
MASC.	FEM.	MASC.	FEM.	
mi	**mi**	**mis**	**mis**	my
tu	**tu**	**tus**	**tus**	your
su	**su**	**sus**	**sus**	his; her; its; your (of Vd)
nuestro	**nuestra**	**nuestros**	**nuestras**	our
vuestro	**vuestra**	**vuestros**	**vuestras**	your
su	**su**	**sus**	**sus**	their; your (of Vds)

All possessive adjectives agree in number and (when applicable) in gender with the noun, not with the owner → ❶
The weak forms always precede the noun → ❶

Since the form **su(s)** can mean his, her, your (of **Vd**, **Vds**) or their, clarification is often needed. This is done by adding **de él**, **de ella**, **de Vds** etc to the noun, and usually (but not always) changing the possessive to a definite article → ❷

Examples

❶ Pilar no ha traído nuestros libros	Pilar hasn't brought our books
Antonio irá a vuestra casa	Anthony will go to your house
¿Han vendido su coche tus vecinos?	Have your neighbours sold their car?
Mi hermano y tu primo no se llevan bien	My brother and your cousin don't get on
❷ su casa → la casa de él	his house
sus amigos → los amigos de Vd	your friends
sus coches → los coches de ellos	their cars
su abrigo → el abrigo de ella	her coat

Possessive Adjectives *continued*

Strong forms

WITH SING. NOUN		WITH PLUR. NOUN		
MASC.	FEM.	MASC.	FEM.	
mío	mía	míos	mías	my
tuyo	tuya	tuyos	tuyas	your
suyo	suya	suyos	suyas	his; her; its; your (of Vd)
nuestro	nuestra	nuestros	nuestras	our
vuestro	vuestra	vuestros	vuestras	your
suyo	suya	suyos	suyas	their; your (of Vds)

The strong forms agree in the same way as the weak forms (see page 220)

The strong forms always follow the noun, and they are used:

- to translate the English *of mine*, *of yours*, etc → 1
- to address people → 2

Examples

❶ Es un capricho suyo	It's a whim of hers
un amigo nuestro	a friend of ours
una revista tuya	a magazine of yours
❷ Muy señor mío (in letters)	Dear Sir
hija mía	my daughter
¡Dios mío!	My God!
Amor mío	Darling/My love

Indefinite Adjectives

alguno(a)s	some
ambos(as)	both
cada	each; every
cierto(a)s	certain; definite
cualquiera plural **culaesquiera**	some; any
los (las) demás	the others; the remainder
mismo(a)s	same; -self
mucho(a)s	many; much
ningún, ninguna plural **ningunos, ningunas**	any; no
otro(a)s	other; another
poco(a)s	few; little
tal(es)	such (a)
tanto(a)s	so much; so many
todo(a)s	all; every
varios(as)	several; various

Unless invariable, all indefinite adjectives agree in number and gender with the noun → ❶

alguno
Before a masculine singular noun, this drops the final **-o** and adds an accent to show the correct position for stress → ❷ (see also page 296)

ambos
This is usually only used in written Spanish. The spoken language prefers the form **los dos/las dos** → ❸

cierto and **mismo**
These change their meaning according to their position in relation to the noun (see also Position of Adjectives, page 228) → ❹

cualquiera
This drops the final **-a** before a masculine *or* feminine noun → ❺

Examples

❶ el mismo día	the same day
las mismas películas	the same films
mucha/poca gente	many/few people
mucho/poco dinero	much/little money
❷ algún día	some day
alguna razón	some reason
❸ Me gustan los dos cuadros	I like both pictures
¿Conoces a las dos enfermeras?	Do you know both nurses?
❹ cierto tiempo	a certain time
BUT:	
éxito cierto	sure success
el mismo color	the same colour
BUT:	
en la iglesia misma	in the church itself
❺ cualquier casa	any house
BUT:	
una revista cualquiera	any magazine

Indefinite Adjectives *continued*

ningún is only used in negative sentences or phrases → 1

otro is never preceded by an indefinite article → 2

tal is never followed by an indefinite article → 3

todo can be followed by a definite article, a demonstrative or possessive adjective or a place name → 4

EXCEPTIONS:
- when **todo** in the singular means any, every, or each → 5
- in some set expressions → 6

Examples

❶ No es ninguna tonta	She's no fool
¿No tienes parientes?	Haven't you any relatives?
— No, ninguno	— No, none
❷ ¿Me das otra manzana?	Will you give me another apple?
Prefiero estos otros zapatos	I prefer these other shoes
❸ Nunca dije tal cosa	I never said such a thing
❹ Estudian durante toda la noche	They study all night
Ha llovido toda esta semana	It has rained all this week
Pondré en orden todos mis libros	I'll sort out all my books
Lo sabe todo Madrid	All Madrid knows it
❺ Podrá entrar toda persona que lo desee	Any person who wishes to enter may do so
BUT:	
Vienen todos los días	They come every day
❻ de todos modos	anyway
a toda velocidad	at full/top speed
por todas partes por todos lados a/en todas partes a/en todos lados	everywhere

Position of Adjectives

Spanish adjectives usually follow the noun → 1, 2

Note that when used figuratively or to express a quality already inherent in the noun, adjectives can precede the noun → 3

As in English, demonstrative, possessive (weak forms), numerical, interrogative and exclamatory adjectives precede the noun → 4

Indefinite adjectives also usually precede the noun → 5

ⓘ Note: **alguno** *some* in negative expressions follows the noun → 6

Some adjectives can precede or follow the noun, but their meaning varies according to their position:

	BEFORE NOUN	AFTER NOUN
antiguo	former	old, ancient → 7
diferente	various	different → 8
grande	great	big → 9
medio	half	average → 10
mismo	same	-self, very/precisely → 11
nuevo	new, another, fresh	brand new → 12
pobre	poor (wretched)	poor (not rich) → 13
puro	sheer, mere	pure (clear) → 14
varios	several	various, different → 15
viejo	old (long known, etc)	old (aged) → 16

Adjectives following the noun are linked by **y** → 17

Examples

1	la página siguiente la hora exacta	the following page the right time
2	una corbata azul una palabra española	a blue tie a Spanish word
3	un dulce sueño un terrible desastre	a sweet dream a terrible disaster (*all disasters are terrible*)
4	este sombrero mi padre ¿qué hombre?	this hat my father what man?
5	cada día otra vez poco dinero	every day another time little money
6	sin duda alguna	without any doubt
7	un antiguo colega la historia antigua	a former colleague ancient history
8	diferentes capítulos personas diferentes	various chapters different people
9	un gran pintor una casa grande	a great painter a big house
10	medio melón velocidad media	half a melon average speed
11	la misma respuesta yo mismo eso mismo	the same answer myself precisely that
12	mi nuevo coche unos zapatos nuevos	my new car (some) brand new shoes
13	esa pobre mujer un país pobre	that poor woman a poor country
14	la pura verdad aire puro	the plain truth fresh air
15	varios caminos artículos varios	several ways/paths various items
16	un viejo amigo esas toallas viejas	an old friend those old towels
17	una acción cobarde y falsa	a cowardly, deceitful act

Personal Pronouns

SUBJECT PRONOUNS

	SINGULAR	PLURAL	
1st person	**yo** I	**nosotros** we	*(masc./masc. + fem.)*
		nosotras we	*(all fem.)*
2nd person	**tú** you	**vosotros** you	*(masc./masc. + fem.)*
		vosotras you	*(all fem.)*
3rd person	**él** he; it	**ellos** they	*(masc./masc. + fem.)*
	ella she; it	**ellas** they	*(all fem.)*
	usted (Vd) you	**ustedes (Vds)** you	

Subject pronouns have a limited usage in Spanish. Normally they are only used:

- for emphasis → 1
- for clarity → 2

BUT: **Vd** and **Vds** should always be used for politeness, whether they are otherwise needed or not → 3

It as subject and *they*, referring to things, are never translated into Spanish → 4

tú/usted
As a general rule, you should use **tú** (or **vosotros**, if plural) when addressing a friend, a child, a relative, someone you know well, or when invited to do so. In all other cases, use **usted** (or **ustedes**).

nosotros/as; vosotros/as; él/ella; ellos/ellas
All these forms reflect the number and gender of the noun(s) they replace. **Nosotros**, **vosotros** and **ellos** also replace a combination of masculine and feminine nouns.

Examples

1	Ellos sí que llegaron tarde	They really did arrive late
	Tú no tienes por qué venir	There is no reason for you to come
	Ella jamás creería eso	She would never believe that
2	Yo estudio español pero él estudia francés	I study Spanish but he studies French
	Ella era muy deportista pero él prefería jugar a las cartas	She was a sporty type but he preferred to play cards
	Vosotros saldréis primero y nosotros os seguiremos	You leave first and we will follow you
3	Pase Vd por aquí	Please come this way
	¿Habían estado Vds antes en esta ciudad?	Had you been to this town before?
4	¿Qué es? — Es una sorpresa	What is it? — It's a surprise
	¿Qué son? — Son abrelatas	What are they? — They are tin-openers

Personal Pronouns *continued*

	DIRECT OBJECT PRONOUNS	
	SINGULAR	PLURAL
1st person	**me** me	**nos** us
2nd person	**te** you	**os** you
3rd person (*masc.*)	**lo** him; it; you (of **Vd**)	**los** them; you (of **Vds**)
(*fem.*)	**la** her; it; you (of **Vd**)	**las** them; you (of **Vds**)

lo sometimes functions as a 'neuter' pronoun, referring to an idea or information contained in a previous statement or question. It is often not translated → 1

Position of direct object pronouns

In constructions other than the imperative affirmative, infinitive or gerund, the pronoun always comes before the verb → 2

In the imperative affirmative, infinitive and gerund, the pronoun follows the verb and is attached to it. An accent is needed in certain cases to show the correct position for stress (see also page 296) → 3

Where an infinitive or gerund depends on a previous verb, the pronoun may be used either after the infinitive or gerund, or before the main verb → 4

ⓘ Note: see how this applies to reflexive verbs → 4

For further information, see Order of Object Pronouns, page 236.

Reflexive Pronouns

These are dealt with under reflexive verbs, page 24.

Examples

1	¿Va a venir María? — No lo sé	Is Maria coming? — I don't know
	Hay que regar las plantas — Yo lo haré	The plants need watering — I'll do it
	Habían comido ya pero no nos lo dijeron	They had already eaten, but they didn't tell us
	Yo conduzco de prisa pero él lo hace despacio	I drive fast but he drives slowly
2	Te quiero	I love you
	¿Las ve Vd?	Can you see them?
	¿No me oyen Vds?	Can't you hear me?
	Tu hija no nos conoce	Your daughter doesn't know us
	No los toques	Don't touch them
3	Ayúdame	Help me
	Acompáñenos	Come with us
	Quiero decirte algo	I want to tell you something
	Estaban persiguiéndonos	They were coming after us
4	Lo está comiendo *or* Está comiéndolo	She is eating it
	Nos vienen a ver *or* Vienen a vernos	They are coming to see us
	No quería levantarse *or* No se quería levantar	He didn't want to get up
	Estoy afeitándome *or* Me estoy afeitando	I'm shaving

Personal Pronouns *continued*

	INDIRECT OBJECT PRONOUNS	
	SINGULAR	PLURAL
1st person	**me**	**nos**
2nd person	**te**	**os**
3rd person	**le**	**les**

The pronouns shown in the above table replace the preposition a + noun → 1

Position of indirect object pronouns

In constructions other than the imperative affirmative, the infinitive or the gerund, the pronoun comes before the verb → 2

In the imperative affirmative, infinitive and gerund, the pronoun follows the verb and is attached to it. An accent is needed in certain cases to show the correct position for stress (see also page 296) → 3

Where an infinitive or gerund depends on a previous verb, the pronoun may be used either after the infinitive or gerund, or before the main verb → 4

For further information, see Order of Object Pronouns, page 236.

Reflexive Pronouns

These are dealt with under reflexive verbs, page 24.

Examples

❶ Estoy escribiendo a Teresa	I am writing to Teresa
Le estoy escribiendo	I am writing to her
Da de comer al gato	Give the cat some food
Dale de comer	Give it some food
❷ Sofía os ha escrito	Sophie has written to you
¿Os ha escrito Sofía?	Has Sophie written to you?
Carlos no nos habla	Charles doesn't speak to us
¿Qué te pedían?	What were they asking you for?
No les haga caso Vd	Don't take any notice of them
❸ Respóndame Vd	Answer me
Díganos Vd la respuesta	Tell us the answer
No quería darte la noticia todavía	I didn't want to tell you the news yet
Llegaron diciéndome que ...	They came telling me that ...
❹ Estoy escribiéndole *or* Le estoy escribiendo	I am writing to him/her
Les voy a hablar *or* Voy a hablarles	I'm going to talk to them

Personal Pronouns *continued*

Order of object pronouns

When two object pronouns of different persons are combined, the order is: indirect before direct, i.e.

me **te** **nos** **os**	before	**lo** **la** **los** **las**	→ ❶

ⓘ Note: When two 3rd person object pronouns are combined, the first (i.e. the indirect object pronoun) becomes **se** → ❷

Points to note on object pronouns

As **le/les** can refer to either gender, and **se** to either gender, singular or plural, sometimes clarification is needed. This is done by adding **a él** *to him*, **a ella** *to her*, **a Vd** *to you* etc to the phrase, usually after the verb → ❸

When a noun object precedes the verb, the corresponding object pronoun must be used too → ❹

Indirect object pronouns are often used instead of possessive adjectives with parts of the body or clothing to indicate 'ownership', and also in certain common constructions involving reflexive verbs (see also The Indefinite Article, page 202) → ❺

Le and **les** are often used in Spanish instead of **lo** and **los** when referring to people. Equally **la** is sometimes used instead of **le** when referring to a feminine person or animal, although this usage is considered incorrect by some speakers of Spanish → ❻

Examples

1	Paloma os lo mandará mañana	Paloma is sending it to you tomorrow
	¿Te los ha enseñado mi hermana?	Has my sister shown them to you?
	No me lo digas	Don't tell me (that)
	Todos estaban pidiéndotelo	They were all asking you for it
	No quiere prestárnosla	He won't lend it to us
2	Se lo di ayer	I gave it to him/her/them yesterday
3	Le escriben mucho a ella	They write to her often
	Se lo van a mandar pronto a ellos	They will be sending it to them soon
4	A tu hermano lo conozco bien	I know your brother well
	A María la vemos algunas veces	We sometimes see Maria
5	La chaqueta le estaba ancha	His jacket was too loose
	Me duele el tobillo	My ankle is aching
	Se me ha perdido el bolígrafo	I have lost my pen
6	Le/lo encontraron en el cine	They met him at the cinema
	Les/los oímos llegar	We heard them coming
	Le/la escribimos una carta	We wrote a letter to her

Personal Pronouns *continued*

Pronouns after prepositions

These are the same as the subject pronouns, except for the forms **mí** me, **ti** you (*singular*), and the reflexive **sí** himself, herself, themselves, yourselves → 1

Con with combines with **mí**, **ti** and **sí** to form

conmigo	with me → 2
contigo	with you
consigo	with himself/herself *etc*

The following prepositions always take a subject pronoun:

entre	between, among → 3
hasta, **incluso**	even, including → 4
salvo, **menos**	except → 5
según	according to → 6

These pronouns are used for emphasis, especially where contrast is involved → 7

Ello it, that is used after a preposition when referring to an idea already mentioned, but never to a concrete noun → 7

A él, **de él** never contract → 9

Examples

1	Pienso en ti	I think about you
	¿Son para mí?	Are they for me?
	Es para ella	This is for her
	Iban hacia ellos	They were going towards them
	Volveréis sin nosotros	You'll come back without
	Volaban sobre vosotros	They were flying above you us
	Hablaba para si	He was talking to himself
2	Venid conmigo	Come with me
	Lo trajeron consigo	They brought it/him with them
	BUT:	
	¿Hablaron con vosotros?	Did they talk to you?
3	entre tú y ella	between you and her
4	Hasta yo puedo hacerlo	Even I can do it
5	todos menos yo	everybody except me
6	según tú	according to you
7	¿A ti no te escriben?	Don't they write to you?
	Me lo manda a mí, no a ti	She is sending it to me, not to you
8	Nunca pensaba en ello	He never thought about it
	Por todo ello me parece que ...	For all those reasons it seems to me that ...
9	A él no lo conozco	I don't know him
	No he sabido nada de él	I haven't heard from him

Indefinite Pronouns

algo	something, anything → 1
alguien	somebody, anybody → 2
alguno/a/os/as	some, a few → 3
cada uno/a	each (one) → 4 everybody
cualquiera	anybody; any → 5
los/las demás	the others the rest → 6
mucho/a/os/as	many; much → 7
nada	nothing → 8
nadie	nobody → 9
ninguno/a	none, not any → 10
poco/a/os/as	few; little → 11
tanto/a/os/as	so much; so many → 12
todo/a/os/as	all; everything → 13
uno ... (el) otro **una ... (la) otra**	(the) one ... the other → 14
unos ... (los) otros **unas ... (las) otras**	some ... (the) others → 14
varios/as	several → 15

algo, alguien, alguno

They can never be used after a negative. The appropriate negative pronouns are used instead: **nada**, **nadie**, **ninguno** (see also negatives, page 276) → 16

Examples

1	Tengo algo para ti ¿Viste algo?	I have something for you Did you see anything?
2	Alguien me lo ha dicho ¿Has visto a alguien?	Somebody said it to me Have you seen anybody?
3	Algunos de los niños ya sabían leer	Some of the children could read already
4	Le dió una manzana a cada uno !Cada uno a su casa!	She gave each of them an apple Everybody go home!
5	Cualquiera puede hacerlo Cualquiera de las explicaciones vale	Anybody can do it Any of the explanations is a valid one
6	Yo me fui, los demás se quedaron	I went, the others stayed
7	Muchas de las casas no tenían jardín	Many of the houses didn't have a garden
8	¿Qué tienes en la mano? — Nada	What have you got in your hand? — Nothing
9	¡A quién ves? — A nadie	Who can you see? — Nobody
10	¿Cuántas tienes? — Ninguna	How many have you got? — None
11	Había muchos cuadros, pero vi pocos que me gustaran	There were many pictures, but I saw few I liked
12	¿Se oía mucho ruido? — No tanto	Was it very noisy? — Not so very
13	Lo ha estropeado todo Todo va bien	He has spoiled everything All is going well
14	Unos cuestan 30 euros, los otros 40 euros	Some cost 30 euros, the others 40 euros
15	Varios de ellos me gustaron mucho	I liked several of them very much
16	Veo a alguien No veo a nadie Tengo algo que hacer No tengo nada que hacer	I can see somebody I can't see anybody I have something to do I don't have anything to do

Relative Pronouns

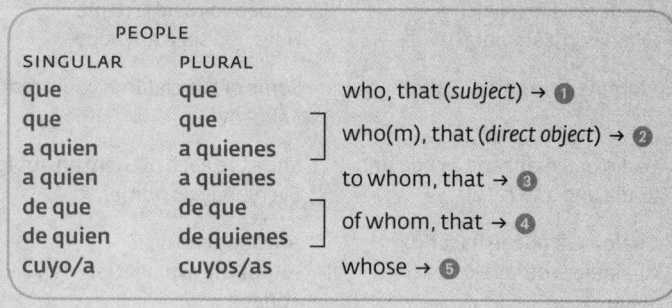

PEOPLE		
SINGULAR	PLURAL	
que	**que**	who, that (*subject*) → 1
que / **a quien**	**que** / **a quienes**	who(m), that (*direct object*) → 2
a quien	**a quienes**	to whom, that → 3
de que / **de quien**	**de que** / **de quienes**	of whom, that → 4
cuyo/a	**cuyos/as**	whose → 5

THINGS	
SINGULAR AND PLURAL	
que	which, that (*subject*) → 6
que	which, that (*direct object*) → 7
a que	to which, that → 8
de que	of which, that → 9
cuyo	whose → 10

ⓘ Note: These forms can also refer to people.

cuyo agrees with the noun it accompanies, not with the owner → 5/10

You cannot omit the relative pronoun in Spanish as you can in English → 2/7

Examples

❶ Mi hermano, que tiene veinte años, es el más joven	My brother, who is twenty, is the youngest
❷ Los amigos que más quiero son ...	The friends (that) I like best are ...
María, a quien Daniel admira tanto, es ...	Maria, whom Daniel admires so much, is ...
❸ Mis abogados, a quienes he escrito hace poco, están ...	My lawyers, to whom I wrote recently, are ...
❹ La chica de que te hablé llega mañana	The girl (that) I told you about is coming tomorrow
los niños de quienes se ocupa Vd	the children (that) you look after
❺ Vendrá la mujer cuyo hijo está enfermo	The woman whose son is ill will be coming
❻ Hay una escalera que lleva a la buhardilla	There's a staircase which leads to the loft
❼ La casa que hemos comprado tiene ...	The house (which) we've bought has ...
Este es el regalo que me ha mandado mi amiga	This is the present (that) my friend has sent to me
❽ la tienda a que siempre va	the shop (which) she always goes to
❾ las injusticias de que se quejan	the injustices (that) they're complaining about
❿ la ventana cuyas cortinas están corridas	the window whose curtains are drawn

Relative Pronouns *continued*

el cual, el que
These are used when the relative is separated from the word it refers to, or when it would otherwise be unclear which word it referred to. The pronouns always agree in number and gender with the noun → 1

> **El cual** may also be used when the verb in the relative clause is separated from the relative pronoun → 2

lo que, lo cual
The neuter form **lo** is normally used when referring to an idea, statement or abstract noun. In certain expressions, the form **lo cual** may also be used as the subject of the relative clause → 3

Relative pronouns after prepositions

Que and **quienes** are generally used after the prepositions:

a	to	→ 4
con	with	→ 5
de	from, about, of	→ 6
en	in, on, into	→ 7

It should be noted that **en que** can sometimes be translated by:
- *where*. In this case it can also be replaced by **en donde** or **donde** → 8
- *when*. Sometimes here it can be replaced by **cuando** → 9

El que or **el cual** are used after other prepositions, and they always agree → 10

Examples

1	El padre de Elena, el cual tiene mucho dinero, es ...	Elena's father, who has a lot of money, is ...
	(el cual *is used here since* que *or* quien *might equally refer to Elena*)	
	Su hermana, a la cual/la que hacía mucho que no veía, estaba también allí	His sister, whom I hadn't seen for a long time, was also there
2	Vieron a su tio, el cual, después de levantarse, salió	They saw their uncle, who, after having got up, went out
3	No sabe lo que hace	He doesn't know what he is doing
	Lo que dijiste fue una tontería	What you said was foolish
	Todo estaba en silencio, lo que (*or* lo cual) me pareció muy raro	All was silent; which I thought most odd
4	las tiendas a (las) que íbamos	the shops we used to go to
5	la chica con quien (or la que) sale	the girl he's going out with
6	el libro de(l) que te hablé	the book I told you about
7	el lío en (el) que te has metido	the trouble you've got yourself into
8	el sitio en que (en donde/donde) se escondía	the place where he/she was hiding
9	el año en que naciste	the year (when) you were born
10	el puente debajo del que/cual pasa el río	the bridge under which the river flows
	las obras por las cuales/que es famosa	the plays for which she is famous

Relative Pronouns *continued*

el que, la que; los que, las que
These mean *the one(s) who/which, those who* → 1

> ⓘ Note: **quien(es)** can replace **el que** *etc* when used in a general sense → 2

todos los que, todas las que
These mean *all who, all those/the ones which* → 3

todo lo que
This translates *all that, everything that* → 4

el de, la de; los de, las de
These can mean:
- *the one(s) of, that/those of* → 5
- *the one(s) with* → 6

Examples

1	Esa película es la que quiero ver	That film is the one I want to see
	¿Te acuerdas de ese amigo? El que te presenté ayer	Do you remember that friend? The one I introduced you to yesterday
	Los que quieran entrar tendrán que pagar	Those who want to go in will have to pay
2	Quien (*or* el que) llegue antes ganará el premio	He who arrives first will win the prize
3	Todos los que salían iban de negro	All those who were coming out were dressed in black
	¿Qué autobuses puedo tomar? – Todos los que pasen por aquí	Which buses can I take? – Any (All those) that come this way
4	Quiero saber todo lo que ha pasado	I want to know all that has happened
5	Trae la foto de tu novio y la de tu hermano	Bring the photo of your boyfriend and the one of your brother
	Viajamos en mi coche y en el de María	We travelled in my car and Maria's
	Te doy estos libros y también los de mi hermana	I'll give you these books and my sister's too
6	Tu amigo, el de las gafas, me lo contó	Your friend, the one with glasses, told me

Interrogative Pronouns

¿qué? what?; which?
¿cuál(es)? which?; what?
¿quién(es)? who?

qué

It always translates *what* → 1

ⓘ Note: **por** + **qué** is normally translated by *why* → 2

cuál

It normally implies a choice, and translates *which* → 3

ⓘ EXCEPT: when no choice is implied or more specific information is required → 4

ⓘ Note: Whilst the pronoun **qué** can also work as an adjective, **cuál** only works as a pronoun → 5

quién

SUBJECT *or* AFTER PREPOSITION	**quién(es)**	who → 6
OBJECT	**a quién(es)**	whom → 7
	de quién(es)	whose → 8

All the forms shown above are also used in indirect questions → 9

Examples

1	¿Qué estan haciendo?	What are they doing?
	¿Qué dices?	What are you saying?
	¿Para qué lo quieres?	What do you want it for?
2	¿Por qué no llegaron Vds antes?	Why didn't you arrive earlier?
3	¿Cuál de estos vestidos te gusta más?	Which of these dresses do you like best?
	¿Cuáles viste?	Which ones did you see?
4	¿Cuál es la capital de España?	What is the capital of Spain?
	¿Cuál es tu consejo?	What is your advice?
	¿Cuál es su fecha de nacimiento?	What is your date of birth?
5	¿Qué libro es más interesante?	Which book is more interesting?
	¿Cuál (de estos libros) es más interesante?	Which (of these books) is more interesting?
6	¿Quién ganó la carrera?	Who won the race?
	¿Con quiénes los viste?	Who did you see them with?
7	¿A quiénes ayudaste?	Who(m) did you help?
	¿A quién se lo diste?	Who did you give it to?
8	¿De quién es este libro?	Whose is this book?
9	Le pregunté para qué lo quería	I asked him/her what he/she wanted it for
	No me dijeron cuáles preferían	They didn't tell me which ones they preferred
	No sabía a quién acudir	I didn't know who to turn to

Possessive Pronouns

These are the same as the strong forms of the possessive adjectives, but they are always accompanied by the definite article.

Singular:

MASCULINE	FEMININE	
el mío	**la mía**	mine
el tuyo	**la tuya**	yours (of **tú**)
el suyo	**la suya**	his; hers; its; yours (of **Vd**)
el nuestro	**la nuestra**	ours
el vuestro	**la vuestra**	yours (of **vosotros**)
el suyo	**la suya**	theirs; yours (of **Vds**)

Plural:

MASCULINE	FEMININE	
los míos	**las mías**	mine
los tuyos	**las tuyas**	yours (of **tú**)
los suyos	**las suyas**	his; hers; its; yours (of **Vd**)
los nuestros	**las nuestras**	ours
los vuestros	**las vuestras**	yours (of **vosotros**)
los suyos	**las suyas**	theirs; yours (of **Vds**)

The pronoun agrees in number and gender with the noun it replaces, not with the owner → 1

Alternative translations are 'my own', 'your own' *etc* → 2

After the prepositions **a** and **de** the article **el** is contracted in the normal way (see page 200):

a + el mío → **al mío** → 3

de + el mío → **del mío** → 4

Examples

❶	Pregunta a Cristina si este bolígrafo es el suyo	Ask Christine if this pen is hers
	¿Qué equipo ha ganado, el suyo o el nuestro?	Which team won – theirs or ours?
	Mi perro es más joven que el tuyo	My dog is younger than yours
	Daniel pensó que esos libros eran los suyos	Daniel thought those books were his
	Si no tienes discos, te prestaré los míos	If you don't have any records, I'll lend you mine
	Las habitaciones son menos amplias que las vuestras	The rooms are smaller than yours
❷	¿Es su familia tan grande como la tuya?	Is his/her/their family as big as your own?
	Sus precios son más bajos que los nuestros	Their prices are lower than our own
❸	¿Por qué prefieres este sombrero al mío?	Why do you prefer this hat to mine?
	Su coche se parece al vuestro	His/her/their car looks like yours
❹	Mi libro está encima del tuyo	My book is on top of yours
	Su padre vive cerca del nuestro	His/her/their father lives near ours

Demonstrative Pronouns

	MASCULINE	FEMININE	NEUTER	
SING.	**éste**	**ésta**	**esto**	this
	ése	**ésa**	**eso**	that
	aquél	**aquélla**	**aquello**	that
PLUR.	**éstos**	**éstas**		these
	ésos	**ésas**		those
	aquéllos	**aquéllas**		those

The pronoun agrees in number and gender with the noun it replaces → 1

The difference in meaning between the forms **ése** and **aquél** is the same as between the corresponding adjectives (see page 216).

The masculine and feminine forms have an accent, which is the only thing that differentiates them from the corresponding adjectives.

The neuter forms always refer to an idea or a statement or to an object when we want to identify it, etc, but never to specified nouns → 2

An additional meaning of **aquél** is *the former*, and of **éste** *the latter* → 3

Examples

❶ ¿Qué abrigo te gusta más? — Éste de aquí	Which coat do you like best? — This one here
Aquella casa era más grande que ésta	That house was bigger than this one
estos libros y aquéllos	these books and those (over there)
Quiero estas sandalias y ésas	I'd like these sandals and those ones
❷ No puedo creer que esto me esté pasando a mí	I can't believe this is really happening to me
Eso de madrugar es algo que no le gusta	(This business of) getting up early is something she doesn't like
Aquello sí que me gustó	I really did like that
Esto es una bicicleta	This is a bicycle
❸ Hablaban Jaime y Andrés, éste a voces y aquél casi en un susurro	James and Andrew were talking, the latter in a loud voice and the former almost in a whisper

Adverbs

Formation

Most adverbs are formed by adding **-mente** to the feminine form of the adjective. Accents on the adjective are not affected since the suffix **-mente** is stressed independently → 1

ⓘ Note: **-mente** is omitted:

- in the first of two or more of these adverbs when joined by a conjunction → 2
- in **recientemente** *recently* when immediately preceding a past participle → 3
  An accent is then needed on the last syllable (see page 296)

The following adverbs are formed in an irregular way:

bueno	→	**bien**
good		well
malo	→	**mal**
bad		badly

Adjectives used as adverbs

Certain adjectives are used adverbially. These include:
alto, **bajo**, **barato**, **caro**, **claro**, **derecho**, **fuerte** and **rápido** → 4

ⓘ Note: Other adjectives used as adverbs agree with the subject, and can normally be replaced by the adverb ending in **-mente** or an adverbial phrase → 5

Position of adverbs

When the adverb accompanies a verb, it may either immediately follow it or precede it for emphasis → 6

ⓘ Note: The adverb can never be placed between **haber** and the past participle in compound tenses → 7

When the adverb accompanies an adjective or another adverb, it generally precedes the adjective or adverb → 8

Examples

1	FEM ADJECTIVE	ADVERB
	lenta slow	lentamente slowly
	franca frank	francamente frankly
	feliz happy	felizmente happily
	fácil easy	fácilmente easily
2	Lo hicieron lenta pero eficazmente	They did it slowly but efficiently
3	El pan estaba recién hecho	The bread had just been baked
4	hablar alto/bajo	to speak loudly/softly
	cortar derecho	to cut (in a) straight (line)
	costar barato/caro	to be cheap/expensive
	Habla muy fuerte	He talks very loudly
	ver claro	to see clearly
	correr rápido	to run fast
5	Esperaban impacientes (*or* impacientemente/ con impaciencia)	They were waiting impatiently
	Vivieron muy felices (*or* muy felizmente)	They lived very happily
6	No conocemos aún al nuevo médico	We still haven't met the new doctor
	Aún estoy esperando	I'm still waiting
	Han hablado muy bien	They have spoken very well
	Siempre le regalaban flores	They always gave her flowers
7	Lo he hecho ya	I've already done it
	No ha estado nunca en Italia	She's never been to Italy
8	un sombrero muy bonito	a very nice hat
	hablar demasiado alto	to talk too loud
	mañana temprano	early tomorrow
	hoy mismo	today

Comparatives and Superlatives

Comparatives

These are formed using the following constructions:

más ... (que) more ... (than) → 1
menos ... (que) less ... (than) → 2
tanto como as much as → 3
tan ... como as ... as → 4
tan ... que so ... that → 5
demasiado ... para too ... to → 6
(lo) bastante ... / **(lo) suficientemente ...** **para** enough to → 7
cada vez más/menos more and more/less and less → 8

Superlatives

These are formed by placing **más/menos** *the most/the least* before the adverb → 9

lo is added before a superlative which is qualified → 10

The absolute superlative (*very, most, extremely* + adverb) is formed by placing **muy** before the adverb. The form **-ísimo** (see also page 296) is also occasionally found → 11

Adverbs with irregular comparatives/superlatives

ADVERB	COMPARATIVE	SUPERLATIVE
bien well	**mejor*** better	**(lo) mejor** (the) best
mal badly	**peor** worse	**(lo) peor** (the) worst
mucho a lot	**más** more	**(lo) más** (the) most
poco little	**menos** less	**(lo) menos** (the) least

* **más bien** also exists, meaning *rather* → 12

Examples

1	más de prisa más abiertamente Mi hermana canta más fuerte que yo	more quickly more openly My sister sings louder than me
2	menos fácilmente menos a menudo Nos vemos menos frecuentemente que antes	less easily less often We see each other less frequently than before
3	Daniel no lee tanto como Andrés	Daniel doesn't read as much as Andrew
4	Hágalo tan rápido como le sea posible Ganan tan poco como nosotros	Do it as quickly as you can They earn as little as we do
5	Llegaron tan pronto que tuvieron que esperarnos	They arrived so early that they had to wait for us
6	Es demasiado tarde para ir al cine	It's too late to go to the cinema
7	Eres (lo) bastante grande para hacerlo solo	You're old enough to do it by yourself
8	Me gusta el campo cada vez más	I like the countryside more and more
9	María es la que corre más rápido El que llegó menos tarde fue Miguel	Maria is the one who runs fastest Miguel was the one to arrive the least late
10	Lo hice lo más de prisa que pude	I did it as quickly as I could
11	muy lentamente tempranísimo muchísimo	very slowly extremely early very much
12	Era un hombre más bien bajito Estaba más bien inquieta que impaciente	He was a rather short man I was restless rather than impatient

Common Adverbs and their Usage

Some common adverbs:

bastante	enough; quite → 1
bien	well → 2
cómo	how → 3
cuánto	how much → 4
demasiado	too much; too → 5
más	more → 6
menos	less → 7
mucho	a lot; much → 8
poco	little, not much; not very → 9
siempre	always → 10
también	also, too → 11
tan	as → 12
tanto	as much → 13
todavía/aún	still; yet; even → 14
ya	already → 15

bastante, **cuánto**, **demasiado**, **mucho**, **poco** and **tanto** are also used as adjectives that agree with the noun they qualify (see indefinite adjectives, page 224 and interrogative adjectives, page 218)

Examples

1	Es bastante tarde	It's quite late
2	¡Bien hecho!	Well done!
3	¡Cómo me ha gustado!	How I liked it!
4	¿Cuánto cuesta este libro?	How much is this book?
5	He comido demasiado Es demasiado caro	I've eaten too much It's too expensive
6	Mi hermano trabaja más ahora Es más tímida que Sofía	My brother works more now She is shyer than Sophie
7	Se debe beber menos Estoy menos sorprendida que tú	One must drink less I'm less surprised than you are
8	¿Lees mucho? ¿Está mucho más lejos?	Do you read a lot? Is it much further?
9	Comen poco María es poco decidida	They don't eat (very) much Maria is not very daring
10	Siempre dicen lo mismo	They always say the same (thing)
11	A mí también me gusta	I like it too
12	Ana es tan alta como yo	Ana is as tall as I am
13	Nos aburrimos tanto como vosotros	We got as bored as you did
14	Todavía/aún tengo dos Todavía/aún no han llegado Mejor aún/todavía	I've still got two They haven't arrived yet Even better
15	Ya lo he hecho	I've done it already

Prepositions

On the following pages you will find some of the most frequent uses of prepositions in Spanish. Particular attention is paid to cases where usage differs markedly from English. It is often difficult to give an English equivalent for Spanish prepositions, since usage *does* vary so much between the two languages. In the list below, the broad meaning of the preposition is given on the left, with examples of usage following. Prepositions are dealt with in alphabetical order, except **a**, **de**, **en** and **por** which are shown first.

a

at **echar algo a algn** to throw sth at sb
a 50 euros el kilo (at) 50 euros a kilo
a 100 km por hora at 100 km per hour
sentarse a la mesa to sit down at the table

in **al sol** in the sun
a la sombra in the shade

onto **cayeron al suelo** they fell onto the floor
pegar una foto al álbum to stick a photo into the album

to **ir al cine** to go to the cinema
dar algo a algn to give sth to sb
venir a hacer to come to do

from **quitarle algo a algn** to take sth from sb
robarle algo a algn to steal sth from sb
arrebatarle algo a algn to snatch sth from sb
comprarle algo a algn to buy sth from/for sb*
esconderle algo a algn to hide sth from sb

means **a mano** by hand
a caballo on horseback
(*but note other forms of transport used with* **en** *and* **por**)
a pie on foot

*The translation here obviously depends on the context.

manner	**a la inglesa** in the English manner **a pasos lentos** with slow steps **poco a poco** little by little **a ciegas** blindly
time, date: at, on	**a medianoche** at midnight **a las dos y cuarto** at quarter past two **a tiempo** on time **a final/fines de mes** at the end of the month **a veces** at times
distance	**a 8 km de aquí** (at a distance of) 8 kms from here **a dos pasos de mi casa** just a step from my house **a lo lejos** in the distance
with **el** + *infin.*	**al levantarse** on getting up **al abrir la puerta** on opening the door
after certain adjectives	**dispuesto a todo** ready for anything **parecido a esto** similar to this **obligado a ello** obliged to (do) that
after certain verbs	see page 66

Personal a

When the direct object of a verb is a person or pet animal, **a** must always be placed immediately before it.

EXAMPLES: **querían mucho a sus hijos**
they loved their children dearly
el niño miraba a su perro con asombro
the boy kept looking at his dog in astonishment

EXCEPTIONS: **tener**
to have
tienen dos hijos
they have two children

de

from	**venir de Londres** to come from London **un médico de Valencia** a doctor from Valencia **de la mañana a la noche** from morning till night **de 10 a 15** from 10 to 15
belonging to, of	**el sombrero de mi padre** my father's hat **las lluvias de abril** April showers
contents, composition, material	**una caja de cerillas** a box of matches **una taza de té** a cup of tea; a tea-cup **un vestido de seda** a silk dress
destined for	**una silla de cocina** a kitchen chair **un traje de noche** an evening dress
descriptive	**la mujer del sombrero verde** the woman with the green hat **el vecino de al lad/lado** the next door neighbour
manner	**de manera irregular** in an irregular way **de una puñalada** by stabbing
quality	**una mujer de edad** an aged lady **objetos de valor** valuable items
comparative + a number	**había más/menos de 100 personas** there were more/fewer than 100 people
in (*after superlatives*)	**la ciudad más/menos bonita del mundo** the most/least beautiful city in the world
after certain adjectives	**contento de ver** pleased to see **fácil/difícil de entender** easy/difficult to understand **capaz de hacer** capable of doing
after certain verbs	see page 66

Prepositions

en

in, at	**en el campo** in the country **en Londres** in London **en la cama** in bed **con un libro en la mano** with a book in his hand **en voz baja** in a low voice **en la escuela** in/at school
into	**entra en la casa** go into the house **metió la mano en su bolso** she put her hand into her handbag
on	**un cuadro en la pared** a picture on the wall **sentado en una silla** sitting on a chair **en la planta baja** on the ground floor
time, dates, months: at, in	**en este momento** at this moment **en 1994** in 1994 **en enero** in January
transport: by	**en coche** by car **en avión** by plane **en tren** by train (but see also **por**)
language	**en español** in Spanish
duration	**lo haré en una semana** I'll do it in one week
after certain adjectives	**es muy buena/mala en geografía** she is very good/bad at geography **fueron los primeros/últimos/únicos en** + *infin.* they were the first/last/only ones + *infin.*
after certain verbs	see page 66

por

motion: along, through, around	**vaya por ese camino** go along that path **por el túnel** through the tunnel **pasear por el campo** to walk around the countryside
vague location	**tiene que estar por aquí** it's got to be somewhere around here **le busqué por todas partes** I looked for him everywhere
vague time	**por la tarde** in the afternoon **por aquellos días** in those days
rate	**90 km por hora** 90 km per hour **un cinco por ciento** five per cent **ganaron por 3 a 0** they won by 3 to 0
by (*agent of passive*)	**descubierto por unos niños** discovered by some children **odiado por sus enemigos** hated by his enemies
by (*means of*)	**por barco** by boat **por tren** by train (freight) **por correo aéreo** by airmail **llamar por teléfono** to telephone
cause, reason: for, because	**¿por qué?** why?, for what reason? **por todo eso** because of all that **por lo que he oído** judging by what I've heard
+ *infinitive*: to	**libros por leer** books to be read **cuentas por pagar** bills to be paid
equivalence	**¿me tienes por tonto?** do you think I'm stupid?
+ *adjective*/+ *adverb* + **que**: however	**por buenos que sean** however good they are **por mucho que lo quieras** however much you want it

for	**¿cuanto me darán por este libro?** how much will they give me for this book?
	te lo cambio por éste I'll swap you this one for it
	no siento nada por ti I feel nothing for you
	si no fuera por ti if it weren't for you
	¡Por Dios! For God's sake!
for the benefit of	**lo hago por ellos** I do it for their benefit
on behalf of	**firma por mí** sign on my behalf

por also combines with other prepositions to form double prepositions usually conveying the idea of movement. The commonest of these are:

over	**saltó por encima de la mesa** she jumped over the table
under	**nadamos por debajo del puente** we swam under the bridge
past	**pasaron por delante de Correos** they went past the post office
behind	**por detrás de la puerta** behind the door
through	**la luz entraba por entre las cortinas** light was coming in through the curtains
+ donde	**¿por dónde has venido?** which way did you come?

ante

faced with, before	**lo hicieron ante mis propios ojos** they did it before my very eyes
	ante eso no se puede hacer nada one can't do anything when faced with that
preference	**la salud ante todo** health above all things

antes de

before (*time*)	**antes de las 5** before 5 o'clock

bajo/debajo de

These are usually equivalent, although **bajo** is used more frequently in a figurative sense and with temperatures.

under	**bajo/debajo de la cama** under the bed **bajo el dominio romano** under Roman rule
below	**un grado bajo cero** one degree below zero

con

with	**vino con su amigo** she came with her friend
after certain adjectives	**enfadado con ellos** angry with them **magnánimo con sus súbditos** magnanimous with his subjects

contra

against	**no tengo nada contra ti** I've nothing against you **apoyado contra la pared** leaning against the wall

delante de

in front of	**iba delante de mí** she was walking in front of me

desde

from	**desde aquí se puede ver** you can see it from here **llamaban desde España** they were phoning from Spain **desde otro punto de vista** from a different point of view **desde la 1 hasta las 6** from 1 till 6 **desde entonces** from then onwards
since	**desde que volvieron** since they returned

for	**viven en esa casa desde hace 3 años** they've been living in that house for 3 years (*note tense*)

detrás de

behind	**están detrás de la puerta** they are behind the door

durante

during	**durante la guerra** during the war
for	**anduvieron durante 3 días** they walked for 3 days

entre

between	**entre 8 y 10** between 8 and 10
among	**María y Elena, entre otras** Maria and Elena, among others
reciprocal	**ayudarse entre sí** to help each other

excepto

except (for)	**todos excepto tú** everybody except you

hacia

towards	**van hacia ese edificio** they're going towards that building
around (*time*)	**hacia las 3** at around 3 (o'clock) **hacia fines de enero** around the end of January

Hacia can also combine with some adverbs to convey a sense of motion in a particular direction:

hacia arriba upwards
hacia abajo downwards
hacia adelante forwards
hacia atrás backwards
hacia adentro inwards
hacia afuera outwards

hasta

until	**hasta la noche** until night
as far as	**viajaron hasta Sevilla** they travelled as far as Seville
up to	**conté hasta 300 ovejas** I counted up to 300 lambs **hasta ahora no los había visto** up to now I hadn't seen them
even	**hasta un tonto lo entendería** even an imbecile would understand that

para

for	**es para ti** it's for you **es para mañana** it's for tomorrow **una habitación para dos noches** a room for two nights **para ser un niño, lo hace muy bien** for a child he is very good at it **salen para Cádiz** they are leaving for Cádiz **se conserva muy bien para sus años** he keeps very well for his age
+ *infinitive*: (in order) to	**es demasiado torpe para comprenderlo** he's too stupid to understand
+ **sí**: to oneself	**hablar para sí** to talk to oneself **reír para sí** to laugh to oneself
with time	**todavía tengo para 1 hora** I'll be another hour (at it) yet

salvo

except (for)	**todos salvo él** all except him **salvo cuando llueve** except when it's raining
barring	**salvo imprevistos** barring the unexpected **salvo contraorden** unless you hear to the contrary

según

according to	**según su consejo** according to her advice **según lo que me dijiste** according to what you told me

sin

without	**sin agua/dinero** without water/money **sin mi marido** without my husband
+ *infinitive*	**sin contar a los otros** without counting the others

sobre

on	**sobre la cama** on the bed **sobre el armario** on (top of) the wardrobe
on (to)	**póngalo sobre la mesa** put it on the table
about, on	**un libro sobre Eva Perón** a book about Eva Perón
above, over	**volábamos sobre el mar** we were flying over the sea **la nube sobre aquella montaña** the cloud above that mountain
approximately	**vendré sobre las 4** I'll come about 4 o'clock
about	**Madrid tiene sobre 4 millones de habitantes** Madrid has about 4 million inhabitants

tras

behind	**está tras el asiento** it's behind the seat
after	**uno tras otro** one after another **día tras día** day after day **corríeron tras el ladrón** they ran after the thief

Conjunctions

There are conjunctions which introduce a main clause, such as **y** (*and*), **pero** (*but*), **si** (*if*), **o** (*or*) etc, and those which introduce subordinate clauses like **porque** (*because*), **mientras que** (*while*), **después de que** (*after*) etc. They are all used in much the same way as in English, but the following points are of note:

Some conjunctions in Spanish require a following subjunctive, see pages 60 to 63.

Some conjunctions are 'split' in Spanish like 'both ... and', 'either ... or' in English:

tanto ... como both ... and → ①
ni ... ni neither ... nor → ②
o (bien) ... o (bien) either ... or (else) → ③
sea ... sea either ... or, whether ... or → ④

y

- Before words beginning with **i-** or **hi-** + consonant it becomes **e** → ⑤

o

- Before words beginning with **o-** or **ho-** it becomes **u** → ⑥
- Between numerals it becomes **ó** → ⑦

que

- meaning *that* → ⑧
- in comparisons, meaning *than* → ⑨
- followed by the subjunctive, see page 58.

porque (Not to be confused with **por qué** *why*)

- como should be used instead at the beginning of a sentence → ⑩

pero, sino

- pero normally translates *but* → ⑪
- sino is used when there is a direct contrast after a negative → ⑫

Examples

1 Estas flores crecen tanto en verano como en invierno	These flowers grow in both summer and winter
2 Ni él ni ella vinieron No tengo ni dinero ni comida	Neither he nor she came I have neither money nor food
3 Debe de ser o ingenua o tonta	She must be either naïve or stupid
O bien me huyen o bien no me reconocen	Either they're avoiding me or else they don't recognize me
4 Sea en verano, sea en invierno, siempre me gusta andar	I always like walking, whether in summer or in winter
5 Diana e Isabel madre e hija BUT: árboles y hierba	Diana and Isabel mother and daughter trees and grass
6 diez u once minutos u horas	ten or eleven minutes or hours
7 37 ó 38	37 or 38
8 Dicen que te han visto ¿Sabías que estábamos allí?	They say (that) they've seen you Did you know that we were there?
9 Le gustan más que nunca María es menos guapa que su hermana	He likes them more than ever Maria is less attractive than her sister
10 Como estaba lloviendo no pudimos salir (*Compare with*: No pudimos salir porque estaba lloviendo)	Because/As it was raining we couldn't go out
11 Me gustaría ir, pero estoy muy cansada	I'd like to go, but I am very tired
12 No es escocesa sino irlandesa	She is not Scottish but Irish

Augmentative, Diminutive and Pejorative Suffixes

These can be used after nouns, adjectives and some adverbs. They are attached to the end of the word after any final vowel has been removed:

e.g. **puerta → puertita**
doctor → doctorcito

ⓘ Note: Further changes sometimes take place (see page 300).

Augmentatives

These are used mainly to imply largeness, but they can also suggest clumsiness, ugliness or grotesqueness. The commonest augmentatives are:

ón/ona → ❶
azo/a → ❷
ote/a → ❸

Diminutives

These are used mainly to suggest smallness or to express a feeling of affection. Occasionally they can be used to express ridicule or contempt. The commonest diminutives are:

ito/a → ❹
(e)cito/a → ❺
(ec)illo/a → ❻
(z)uelo/a → ❼

Pejoratives

These are used to convey the idea that something is unpleasant or to express contempt. The commonest suffixes are:

ucho/a → ❽
acho/a → ❾
uzo/a → ❿
uco/a → ⓫
astro/a → ⓬

Examples

	ORIGINAL WORD	DERIVED FORM
1	un hombre a man	un hombrón a big man
2	bueno good	buenazo (person) easily imposed on
	un perro a dog	un perrazo a really big dog
	gripe flu	un gripazo a really bad bout of flu
3	grande big	grandote huge
	palabra word	palabrota swear word
	amigo friend	amigote old pal
4	una casa a house	una casita a cottage
	un poco a little	un poquito a little bit
	un rato a while	un ratito a little while
	mi hija my daughter	mi hijita my dear sweet daughter
	despacio slowly	despacito nice and slowly
5	un viejo an old man	un viejecito a little old man
	un pueblo a village	un pueblecito a small village
	una voz a voice	una vocecita a sweet little voice
6	una ventana a window	una ventanilla a small window *(car, train etc)*
	un chico a boy	un chiquillo a small boy
	una campana a bell	una campanilla a small bell
	un palo a stick	un palillo a toothpick
	un médico a doctor	un mediquillo a quack (*doctor*)
7	los pollos the chickens	los polluelos the little chicks
	hoyos hollows	hoyuelos dimples
	un ladrón a thief	un ladronzuelo a petty thief
	una mujer a woman	una mujerzuela a whore
8	un animal an animal	un animalucho a wretched animal
	un cuarto a room	un cuartucho a poky little room
	una casa a house	una casucha a shack
9	rico rich	ricacho nouveau riche
10	gente people	gentuza scum
11	una ventana a window	un ventanuco a miserable little window
12	un político a politician	un politicastro a third-rate politician

Word Order

Word order in Spanish is much more flexible than in English. You can often find the subject placed after the verb or the object before the verb, either for emphasis or for stylistic reasons → ①

There are some cases, however, where the order is always different from English. Most of these have already been dealt with under the appropriate part of speech, but are summarized here along with other instances not covered elsewhere.

Object pronouns nearly always come before the verb → ②
For details, see pages 232 to 235.

Qualifying adjectives nearly always come after the noun → ③
For details, see page 228.

Following direct speech the subject always follows the verb → ④

For word order in negative sentences, see page 276.

For word order in interrogative sentences, see page 280 → ①

Examples

1 Ese libro te lo di yo	I gave you that book
No nos vio nadie	Nobody saw us
2 Ya los veo	I can see them now
Me lo dieron ayer	They gave it to me yesterday
3 Ya los veo	I can see them now
Me lo dieron ayer	They gave it to me yesterday
4 una ciudad española	a Spanish town
vino tinto	red wine
5 – Pienso que sí – dijo María	'I think so,' said Maria
– No importa – replicó Daniel	'It doesn't matter,' Daniel replied

Negatives

A sentence is made negative by adding **no** between the subject and the verb (and any preceding object pronouns) → 1

There are, however, some points to note:
- in phrases like *not her, not now*, etc the Spanish **no** usually comes after the word it qualifies → 2
- with verbs of saying, hoping, thinking etc *not* is translated by **que no** → 3

Double negatives

The following are the most common negative pairs:

no ... nada nothing (*not ... anything*)
no ... nadie nobody (*not ... anybody*)
no ... más no longer (*not ... any more*)
no ... nunca never (*not ... ever*)
no ... jamás never (stronger) (*not ... ever*)
no ... más que only (*not ... more than*)
no ... ningún(o)(a) no (*not any*)
no ... tampoco not ... either
no ... ni ... ni neither ... nor
no ... ni siquiera not even

Word order

No precedes the verb (and any object pronouns) in both simple and compound tenses, and the second element follows the verb → 4

Sometimes the above negatives are placed before the verb (with the exception of **más** and **más que**), and **no** is then dropped → 5

For use of **nada**, **nadie** and **ninguno** as pronouns, see page 240.

Examples

	AFFIRMATIVE		NEGATIVE
1	El coche es suyo	→	El coche no es suyo
	The car is his		The car is not his
	Yo me lo pondré	→	Yo no me lo pondré
	I will put it on		I will not put it on

2	¿Quién lo ha hecho? — Ella no	Who did it? — Not her
	¿Quieres un cigarrillo? — Ahora no	Do you want a cigarette? — Not now
	Dame ese libro, el que está a tu lado no, el otro	Give me that book, not the one near you, the other one
3	Opino que no	I think not
	Dijeron que no	They said not
4	No dicen nada	They don't say anything
	No han visto a nadie	They haven't seen anybody
	No me veréis más	You won't see me any more
	No te olvidaré nunca/jamás	I'll never forget you
	No habían recorrido más que 40 kms cuando ...	They hadn't travelled more than 40 kms when ...
	No se me ha ocurrido ninguna idea	I haven't had any ideas
	No les estaban esperando ni mi hijo ni mi hija	Neither my son nor my daughter were waiting for them
	No ha venido ni siquiera Juan	Even John hasn't come
5	Nadie ha venido hoy	Nobody came today
	Nunca me han gustado	I've never liked them
	Ni mi hermano ni mi hermana fuman	Neither my brother nor my sister smokes

Negatives *continued*

Negatives in short replies

No *no* is the usual negative response to a question → 1

ⓘ Note: It is often translated as 'not' → 2
(see also page 276)

Nearly all the other negatives listed on page 276 may be used without a verb in a short reply → 3

Combination of negatives

These are the most common combinations of negative particles:

no ... nunca más → 4
no ... nunca a nadie → 5
no ... nunca nada/nada nunca → 6
no ... nunca más que → 7
no ... ni ... nunca ... → 8

Examples

1 ¿Quieres venir con nosotros? — No	Do you want to come with us? — No
2 ¿Vienes o no?	Are you coming or not?
3 ¿Ha venido alguien? — ¡Nadie! ¿Has ido al Japón alguna vez? — Nunca	Has anyone come? — Nobody! Have you ever been to Japan? — Never
4 No lo haré nunca más	I'll never do it again
5 No se ve nunca a nadie por allí	You never see anybody around there
6 No cambiaron nada nunca	They never changed anything
7 No he hablado nunca más que con su mujer	I've only ever spoken to his wife
8 No me ha escrito ni llamado por teléfono nunca	He/she has never written to me or phoned me

Question Forms

Direct

There are two ways of forming direct questions in Spanish:

- by inverting the normal word order so that *subject + verb* → *verb + subject* → 1

- by maintaining the word order *subject + verb*, but by using a rising intonation at the end of the sentence → 2

  ⓘ Note: In compound tenses the auxiliary may never be separated from the past participle, as happens in English → 3

Indirect

An indirect question is one that is 'reported', e.g. he asked me 'what the time was', tell me 'which way to go'. Word order in indirect questions can adopt one of the two following patterns:

- *interrogative word + subject + verb* → 4

- *interrogative word + verb + subject* → 5

¿verdad?, ¿no?

These are used wherever English would use 'isn't it?', 'don't they?', 'weren't we?', 'is it?' etc tagged on to the end of a sentence → 6

sí

Sí is the word for 'yes' in answer to a question put either in the affirmative or in the negative → 7

Examples

1	¿Vendrá tu madre?	Will your mother come?
	¿Lo trajo Vd?	Did you bring it?
	¿Es posible eso?	Is it possible?
	¿Cuándo volverán Vds?	When will you come back?
2	El gato, ¿se bebió toda la leche?	Did the cat drink up all his milk?
	Andrés, ¿va a venir?	Is Andrew coming?
3	¿Lo ha terminado Vd?	Have you finished it?
	¿Había llegado tu amigo?	Had your friend arrived?
4	Dime qué autobuses pasan por aquí	Tell me which buses come this way
	No sé cuántas personas vendrán	I don't know how many people will turn up
5	Me preguntó dónde trabajaba mi hermano	He asked me where my brother worked
	No sabemos a qué hora empieza la película	We don't know what time the film starts
6	Hace calor, ¿verdad?	It's warm, isn't it?
	No se olvidará Vd, ¿verdad?	You won't forget, will you?
	Estaréis cansados, ¿no?	You will be tired, won't you?
	Te lo dijo María, ¿no?	Maria told you, didn't she?
7	¿Lo has hecho? — Sí	Have you done it? — Yes (I have)
	¿No lo has hecho? — Sí	Haven't you done it? — Yes (I have)

Beware of translating word by word. While on occasions this is possible, quite often it is not. The need for caution is illustrated by the following:

English phrasal verbs (i.e. verbs followed by a preposition), e.g. 'to run away', 'to fall down', are often translated by one word in Spanish → ❶

English verbal constructions often contain a preposition where none exists in Spanish, or vice versa → ❷

Two or more prepositions in English may have a single rendering in Spanish → ❸

A word which is singular in English may be plural in Spanish, or vice versa → ❹

Spanish has no equivalent of the possessive construction denoted by ...'s/...s' → ❺

Problems

-ing

This is translated in a variety of ways in Spanish:

'to be ... -ing' can sometimes be translated by a simple tense (see also pages 54 to 56) → ❻
But, when a physical position is denoted, a past participle is used → ❼

in the construction 'to see/hear sb ... -ing', use an infinitive → ❽
'-ing' can also be translated by:

- an infinitive, see page 46 → ❾
- a perfect infinitive, see page 50 → ❿
- a gerund, see page 52 → ⓫
- a noun → ⓬

Examples

1	huir	to run away
	caerse	to fall down
	ceder	to give in
2	pagar	to pay for
	mirar	to look at
	escuchar	to listen to
	encontrarse con	to meet
	fijarse en	to notice
	servirse de	to use
3	extrañarse de	to be surprised at
	harto de	fed up with
	soñar con	to dream of
	contar con	to count on
4	unas vacaciones	a holiday
	sus cabellos	his/her hair
	la gente	people
	mi pantalón	my trousers
5	el coche de mi hermano	my brother's car (*literally*: ... of my brother)
	el cuarto de las niñas	the children's bedroom (*literally*: ... of the children)
6	Se va mañana	He/she is leaving tomorrow
	¿Qué haces?	What are you doing?
7	Está sentado ahí	He is sitting over there
	Estaba tendida en el suelo	She was lying on the ground
8	Les veo venir	I can see them coming
	La he oído cantar	I've heard her singing
9	Me gusta ir al cine	I like going to the cinema
10	¡Deja de hablar!	Stop talking!
	En vez de contestar	Instead of answering
	Antes de salir	Before leaving
	Después de haber abierto la caja, María ...	After opening the box, Maria ...
11	Pasamos la tarde fumando y charlando	We spent the afternoon smoking and chatting
12	El esquí me mantiene en forma	Skiing keeps me fit

to be (*See also Verbal Idioms*, pages 74 to 76)

In set expressions, describing physical and emotional conditions, **tener** is used:

tener calor/frío to be warm/cold
tener hambre/sed to be hungry/thirsty
tener miedo to be afraid
tener razón to be right

Describing the weather, e.g. 'what's the weather like?', 'it's windy/sunny', use **hacer** → 1

For ages, e.g. 'he is 6', use **tener** (see also page 310) → 2

there is/there are

Both are translated by **hay** → 3

can, be able

Physical ability is expressed by **poder** → 4

If the meaning is 'to know how to', use **saber** → 5

'Can' + a 'verb of hearing or seeing etc' in English is not translated in Spanish → 6

to

Generally translated by **a** → 7

In time expressions, e.g. 10 to 6, use **menos** → 8

When the meaning is 'in order to', use **para** → 9

Following a verb, as in 'to try to do', 'to like to do', see pages 46 and 48.

'easy/difficult/impossible' etc 'to do' are translated by **fácil/difícil/imposible** etc **de hacer** → 10

Examples

1	¿Qué tiempo hace? Hace bueno/malo/viento	What's the weather like? It's lovely/miserable/windy
2	¿Cuántos años tienes? Tengo quince (años)	How old are you? I'm fifteen
3	Hay un señor en la puerta Hay cinco libros en la mesa	There's a gentleman at the door There are five books on the table
4	No puedo salir contigo	I can't go out with you
5	¿Sabes nadar?	Can you swim?
6	No veo nada ¿Es que no me oyes?	I can't see anything Can't you hear me?
7	Dale el libro a Isabel	Give the book to Isabel
8	las diez menos cinco a las siete menos cuarto	five to ten at a quarter to seven
9	Lo hice para ayudaros Se inclinó para atarse el cordón de zapato	I did it to help you He bent down to tie his shoe-lace
10	Este libro es fácil/difícil de leer	This book is easy/difficult to read

must

When *must* expresses an assumption, **deber de** is often used → 1

> ⓘ Note: This meaning is also often expressed by **deber** directly followed by the infinitive → 2

When it expresses obligation, there are three possible translations:

- **tener que** → 3
- **deber** → 4
- **hay que** (impersonal) → 5

may

If *may* expresses possibility, it can be translated by:

- **poder** → 6
- **puede (ser) que** + *subjunctive*

To express permission, use **poder** → 7

will

If *will* expresses willingness or desire rather than the future, the present tense of **querer** is used → 8

would

If *would* expresses willingness, use the preterite or imperfect of **querer** → 9

When a repeated or habitual action in the past is referred to, use

- the imperfect → 10
- the imperfect of **soler** + *infinitive* → 11

Examples

1	Ha debido de mentir Debe de gustarle	He must have lied She must like it
2	Debe estar por aquí cerca Debo haberlo dejado en el tren	It must be near here I must have left it on the train
3	Tenemos que salir temprano mañana Tengo que irme	We must leave early tomorrow I must go
4	Debo visitarles Debéis escuchar lo que se os dice	I must visit them You must listen to what is said to you
5	Hay que entrar por ese lado	One (We etc) must get in that way
6	Todavía puede cambiar de opinión Creo que puede llover esta tarde Puede (ser) que no lo sepa	He may still change his mind I think it may rain this afternoon She may not know
7	¿Puedo irme? Puede sentarse	May I go? You may sit down
8	Quiere Vd esperar un momento, por favor? No quiere ayudarme	Will you wait a moment, please? He won't help me
9	No quisieron venir	They wouldn't come
10	Las miraba hora tras hora	She would watch them for hours on end
11	Últimamente solía comer muy poco	Latterly he would eat very little

Pronunciation of Vowels

Spanish vowels are always clearly pronounced and not relaxed in unstressed syllables as happens in English.

	EXAMPLES	HINTS ON PRONUNCIATION
[a]	c**a**sa	Between English *a* as in *hat* and *u* as in *hut*
[e]	p**e**nsar	Similar to English *e* in *pet*
[i]	f**i**lo	Between English *i* as in *pin* and *ee* as in *been*
[o]	l**o**c**o**	Similar to English *o* in *hot*
[u]	l**u**na	Between English *ew* as in *few* and *u* as in *put*

Pronunciation of Diphthongs

All these diphthongs are shorter than similar English diphthongs.

[ai]	b**ai**le h**ay**	Like *i* in *side*
[au]	c**au**sa	Like *ou* in *sound*
[ei]	p**ei**ne r**ey**	Like *ey* in *grey*
[eu]	d**eu**da	Like the vowel sounds in English *may you*, but without the sound of the *y*
[oi]	b**oi**na v**oy**	Like *oy* in *boy*

Semi-consonants

[j]	hac**i**a **y**a t**i**ene **y**eso lab**i**o **y**o	**i** following a consonant and preceding a vowel, and **y** preceding a vowel are pronounced as *y* inEnglish *yet*
[w]	ag**u**a b**u**eno ard**u**o r**u**ido	**u** following a consonant and preceding a vowel is pronounced as *w* in English *walk*

EXCEPTIONS: **gue**, **gui** (see page 290)

Pronunciation of Consonants

Some consonants are pronounced almost exactly as in English: [l, m, n, f, k, and in some cases g].

Others, listed below, are similar to English, but differences should be noted.

	EXAMPLES	HINTS ON PRONUNCIATION
[p]	**p**adre	They are not aspirated, unlike English *p*ot, *c*ook and *t*en.
[k]	**c**o**c**o	
[t]	**t**an	
[t]	**t**odo **t**ú	Pronounced with the tip of the tongue touching the upper front teeth and not the roof of the mouth as in English.
[d]	**d**oy bal**d**e	

The following consonants are not heard in English:

[β]	la**b**io	This is pronounced between upper and lower lips, which do not touch, unlike English *b* as in *b*end.
[ɣ]	ha**g**a	Similar to English *g* as in *g*ate, but tongue does not touch the soft palate.
[ɲ]	a**ñ**o	Similar to *ni* in o*ni*on
[x]	**j**ota	Like the guttural *ch* in lo*ch*
[r]	pe**r**a	A single trill with the tip of the tongue against the teeth ridge.
[rr]	**r**ojo pe**rr**o	A multiple trill with the tip of the tongue against the teeth ridge.

From Spelling to Sounds

Note the pronunciation of the following (groups of) letters.

LETTER	PRONOUNCED	EXAMPLES
b,v	[b]	These letters have the same value. At the start of a breath group, and after written **m** and **n**, the sound is similar to English *boy* → 1
	[β]	in all other positions, the sound is unknown in English (see page 289) → 2
c	[k]	Before **a**, **o**, **u** or a consonant, like English *k*eep, but not aspirated → 3
	[θ/s]	Before **e**, **i** like English *th*in, or, in Latin America and parts of Spain, like English *s*ame → 4
ch	[tʃ]	Like English *ch*urch → 5
d	[d]	At the start of the breath group and after **l** or **n**, it is pronounced similar to English *d*eep (see page 289) → 6
	[ð]	Between vowels and after consonants (except **l** or **n**), it is pronounced very like English *th*ough → 7
	[(ð)]	At the end of words, and in the verb ending **-ado**, it is often not pronounced → 8
g	[x]	Before **e**, **i**, pronounced gutturally, similar to English lo*ch* → 9
	[g]	At the start of the breath group and after **n**, it is pronounced like English *g*et → 10
	[ɣ]	In other positions the sound is unknown in English → 11
gue	[ge/ɣe]	The **u** is silent → 12
gui	[gi/ɣi]	
güe	[gwe/ɣwe]	The **u** is pronounced like English
güi	[gwi/ɣwi]	*w*alk → 13

Examples

1	bomba ['bomba]	voy [boi]	vicio ['biθjo]
2	hubo ['uβo]	de veras [de 'βeras]	lavar [la'βar]
3	casa ['kasa]	coco ['koko]	cumbre ['kumbre]
4	cero ['θero/'sero]	cinco ['θiŋko/'siŋko]	
5	mucho ['mutʃo]	chuchería [tʃutʃe'ria]	
6	doy [doi]	balde ['balde]	bondad [bon'dað]
7	modo ['moðo]	ideal [iðe'al]	
8	Madrid [ma'ðri(ð)]	comprado [kom'pra(ð)o]	
9	gente ['xente]	giro ['xiro]	general [xene'ral]
10	ganar [ga'nar]	pongo ['poŋgo]	
11	agua ['aɣwa]	agrícola [a'ɣrikola]	
12	guija ['gixa]	guerra ['gerra]	pague ['paɣe]
13	agüero [a 'ɣwero]	argüir [ar'ɣwir]	

From Spelling to Sounds *continued*

LETTER	PRONOUNCED	EXAMPLES
h	[-]	This is always silent → 1
j	[x]	Like the guttural sound in English lo*ch*, but often aspirated at the end of a word → 2
ll	[ʎ]	Similar to English *-ll-* in mi*ll*ion → 3
	[j/ʒ]	In some parts of Spain and in Latin America, like English *y*et or plea*s*ure → 4
-nv-	[mb]	This combination of letters is pronounced as in English i*mb*ibe → 5
ñ	[ɲ]	As in English o*ni*on → 6
q	[k]	Always followed by silent letter **u**, and pronounced as in English *k*eep, but not aspirated → 7
s	[s]	Except where mentioned below, like English *s*ing → 8
	[z]	When followed by **b**, **d**, **g**, **l**, **m**, **n** like English *z*oo → 9
w	[w]	Like English *v*, *w* → 10
x	[ks]	Between vowels, often like English e*x*it → 11
	[s]	Before a consonant, and, increasingly, even between vowels, like English *s*end → 12
y	[j]	Like English *y*es → 13
	[ʒ]	In some parts of Latin America, like English lei*s*ure → 14
z	[θ]	Like English *th*in → 15
	[s]	In some parts of Spain and in Latin America, like English *s*end → 16

Examples

1	hombre ['ombre]	hoja ['oxa]	ahorrar [ao'rrar]
2	jota ['xota]	tejer [te'xer]	reloj [re'lo(h)]
3	calle ['kaʎe]	llamar [ʎa'mar]	
4	pillar [pi'jar/pi'ʒar]	olla ['oja/'oʒa]	
5	enviar [em'bjar]	sin valor ['sim ba'lor]	
6	uña ['uɲa]	bañar [ba'ɲar]	
7	aquel [a'kel]	querer [ke'rer]	
8	está [es'ta]	serio ['serjo]	
9	desde ['dezðe]	mismo ['mizmo]	asno ['azno]
10	wáter ['bater]	Walkman® [wak'man]	
11	éxito ['eksito]	máximo ['maksimo]	
12	extra ['estra]	sexto ['sesto]	
13	yo [jo]	yedra ['jeðra]	
14	yeso ['ʒeso]	yerno ['ʒerno]	
15	zapato [θa'pato]	zona ['θona]	luz [luθ]
16	zaguán [sa'ʎwan]	zueco ['sweko]	pez [pes]

Normal Word Stress

There are simple rules to establish which syllable in a Spanish word is stressed. When an exception to these rules occurs an acute accent (stress-mark) is needed (see page 296). These rules are as follows:

- words ending in a vowel or combination of vowels, or with the consonants **-s** or **-n** are stressed on the next to last syllable. The great majority of Spanish words fall into this category → 1
- words ending in a consonant other than **-s** or **-n** bear the stress on the last syllable → 2
- a minority of words bear the stress on the second to last syllable, and these always need an accent → 3
- some nouns change their stress from singular to plural → 4

Stress in Diphthongs

In the case of diphthongs there are rules to establish which of the vowels is stressed (see page 288 for pronunciation). These rules are as follows:

- diphthongs formed by the combination of a 'weak' vowel (**i**, **u**) and a 'strong' vowel (**a**, **e** or **o**) bear the stress on the strong vowel → 5
- diphthongs formed by the combination of two 'weak' vowels bear the stress on the second vowel → 6

ⓘ Note: Two 'strong' vowels don't form a diphthong but are pronounced as two separate vowels. In these cases stress follows the normal rules → 7

Examples

1. **ca**sa house — **ca**sas houses
   corre he runs — **co**rren they run
   pa**la**bra word — pa**la**bras words
   crisis crisis — **cri**sis crises

2. re**loj** watch
   ver**dad** truth
   bati**dor** beater

3. mur**cié**lago bat
   pájaro bird

4. car**á**cter character — carac**te**res characters
   régimen regime — re**gí**menes regimes

5. **bai**le dance
   boina beret
   peine comb
   causa cause
   reina queen

6. fu**i** I went
   vi**u**do widower

7. me ma**re**o I feel dizzy
   ca**er** to fall
   caos chaos
   co**rrea** leash

The Acute Accent (´)

This is used in writing to show that a word is stressed contrary to the normal rules for stress (see page 294) → 1

The following points should be noted:

The same syllable is stressed in the plural form of adjectives and nouns as in the singular. To show this, it is necessary to

- add an accent in the case of unaccented nouns and adjectives ending in **-n** → 2
- drop the accent from nouns and adjectives ending in **-n** or **-s** which have an accent on the last syllable → 3

The feminine form of accented nouns or adjectives does not have an accent → 4

When object pronouns are added to certain verb forms an accent is required to show that the syllable stressed in the verb form does not change. These verb forms are:

- the gerund → 5
- the infinitive, when followed by two pronouns → 6
- imperative forms, except for the 2nd person plural → 7

The absolute superlative forms of adjectives are always accented → 8

Accents on adjectives are not affected by the addition of the adverbial suffix **-mente** → 9

Examples

1	autobús		revolución
	bus		revolution
	relámpago		árboles
	lightning		trees
2	orden	→	órdenes
	order		orders
	examen	→	exámenes
	examination		examinations
	joven	→	jóvenes
	young		young
3	revolución	→	revoluciones
	revolution		revolutions
	autobús	→	autobuses
	bus		buses
	parlanchín	→	parlanchines
	chatty		chatty
4	marqués	→	marquesa
	marquis		marchioness
	francés	→	francesa
	French (*masc*)		French (*fem*)
5	comprando	→	comprándo(se)lo
	buying		buying it (for him/her/them)
6	vender	→	vendérselas
	to sell		to sell them to him/her/them
7	compra	→	cómpralo
	buy		buy it
	hagan	→	háganselo
	do		do it for him/her/them
8	viejo	→	viejísimo
	old		ancient
	caro	→	carísimo
	expensive		very expensive
9	fácil	→	fácilmente
	easy		easily

The Acute Accent *continued*

It is also used to distinguish between the written forms of words which are pronounced the same but have a different meaning or function. These are as follows:

Possessive adjectives/personal pronouns → ❶

Demonstrative adjectives/demonstrative pronouns → ❷

Interrogative and exclamatory forms of adverbs, pronouns and adjectives → ❸

ⓘ Note: The accent is used in indirect as well as direct questions and exclamations → ❹

The pronoun **él** and the article **el** → ❺

A small group of words which could otherwise be confused. These are:

de	of, from	**dé**	give (*pres. subj.*)
mas	but	**más**	more
si	if	**sí**	yes; himself etc → ❻
solo/a	alone	**sólo**	only → ❼
te	you	**té**	tea

The Dieresis (¨)

This is used only in the combinations **güi** or **güe** to show that the **u** is pronounced as a semi-consonant (see page 288) → ❽

Examples

1	Han robado mi coche	They've stolen my car
	A mí no me vio	He didn't see me
	¿Te gusta tu trabajo?	Do you like your job?
	Tú, ¿que opinas?	What do you think?
2	Me gusta esta casa	I like this house
	Me quedo con ésta	I'll take this one
	¿Ves aquellos edificios?	Can you see those buildings?
	Aquéllos son más bonitos	Those are prettier
3	El chico con quien viajé	The boy I travelled with
	¿Con quién viajaste?	Who did you travel with?
	Donde quieras	Wherever you want
	¿Dónde encontraste eso?	Where did you find that?
4	¿Cómo se abre?	How does it open?
	No sé cómo se abre	I don't know how it opens
5	El puerto queda cerca	The harbour's nearby
	Él no quiso hacerlo	*He* refused to do it
6	si no viene	if he doesn't come
	Sí que lo sabe	Yes he *does* know
7	Vino solo	He came by himself
	Sólo lo sabe él	Only he knows
8	¡Qué vergüenza!	How shocking!
	En seguida averigüé dónde estaba	I found out straight away where it was

Regular Spelling Changes

The consonants **c**, **g** and **z** are modified by the addition of certain verb or plural endings and by some suffixes. Most of the cases where this occurs have already been dealt with under the appropriate part of speech, but are summarized here along with other instances not covered elsewhere.

Verbs

The changes set out below occur so that the consonant of the verb stem is always pronounced the same as in the infinitive. For verbs affected by these changes see the list of verbs on page 81.

INFINITIVE	CHANGE			TENSES AFFECTED
-car	c + e	→	-que	Present subj, pret → 1
-cer, -cir	c + a, o	→	-za, -zo	Present, pres subj → 2
-gar	g + e, i	→	-gue	Present subj, pret → 3
-guar	gu + e	→	-güe	Present subj, pret → 4
-ger, -gir	g + a, o	→	-ja, -jo	Present, pres subj → 5
-guir	gu + a, o	→	-ga, -go	Present, pres subj → 6
-zar	z + e	→	-ce	Present subj, pret → 7

Noun and adjective plurals

SINGULAR		PLURAL
vowel + z	→	-ces → 8

Nouns and adjectives + suffixes

ENDING	SUFFIX	NEW ENDING
vowel + z +	-cito	-cecito → 9
-go, -ga +	-ito, -illo	-guito/a, -guillo/a → 10
-co, -ca +	-ito, -illo	-quito/a, -quillo/a → 11

Adjective absolute superlatives

ENDING	SUPERLATVE
-co	-quísimo → 12
-go	-guísimo → 13
vowel + z	-císimo → 14

Examples

1	Es inútil que lo busques aquí	It's no good looking for it here
	Saqué dos entradas	I got two tickets
2	Hace falta que venzas tu miedo	You must overcome your fear
3	No creo que lleguemos antes	I don't think we'll be there any sooner
	Ya le pagué	I've already paid her
4	Averigüé dónde estaba la casa	I found out where the house was
5	Cojo el autobús, es más barato	I take the bus, it's cheaper
6	¿Sigo?	Shall I go on?
7	No permiten que se cruce la frontera	They don't allow people to cross the border
	Nunca simpaticé mucho con él	I never got on very well with him

8	voz	→	voces	luz	→	luces
	voice		voices	light		lights
	veloz	→	veloces	capaz	→	capaces
	quick			capable		

9	luz	→	lucecita
	light		little light
10	amigo	→	amiguito
	friend		chum
11	chico	→	chiquillo
	boy		little boy
12	rico	→	riquísimo
	rich		extremely rich
13	largo	→	larguísimo
	long		very, very long
14	feroz	→	ferocísimo
	fierce		extremely fierce

The Alphabet

A, a [a]
B, b [be]
C, c [θe]
Ch, ch [tʃe]
D, d [de]
E, e [e]
F, f ['efe]
G, g [xe]
H, h ['atʃe]
I, i [i]
J, j ['xota]
K, k [ka]
L, l ['ele]
Ll, ll ['eʎe]
M, m ['eme]
N, n ['ene]
Ñ, ñ ['eɲe]
O, o [o]
P, p [pe]
Q, q [ku]
R, r ['erre]
S, s ['ese]
T, t [te]
U, u [u]
V, v ['uβe]
W, w ['uβe'doble]
X, x ['ekis]
Y, y [i'ɣrjeɣa]
Z, z ['θeta]

The letters are feminine and you therefore talk of **una a**, or **la a**.

Capital letters are used as in English except for the following:

adjectives of nationality:
e.g. **una ciudad alemana** a German town
un autor español a Spanish author

languages:
e.g. **¿Habla Vd inglés?** Do you speak English?
Hablan español e italiano They speak Spanish and Italian

days of the week:
lunes Monday
martes Tuesday
miércoles Wednesday
jueves Thursday
viernes Friday
sábado Saturday
domingo Sunday

months of the year:
enero January
febrero February
marzo March
abril April
mayo May
junio June
julio July
agosto August
se(p)tiembre September
octubre October
noviembre November
diciembre December

Punctuation

Spanish punctuation differs from English in the following ways:

Question marks

There are inverted question marks and exclamation marks at the beginning of a question or exclamation, as well as upright ones at the end.

Indications of dialogue

Dashes are used to indicate dialogue, and are equivalent to the English inverted commas:

– ¿Vendrás conmigo? – le preguntó María
'Will you come with me?' Maria asked him

ⓘ Note: When no expression of saying, replying etc follows, only one dash is used at the beginning:
– Sí. 'Yes.'

Letter headings

At the beginning of a letter, a colon is used instead of the English comma:
Querida Cristina: Dear Cristina, Muy Sr. mío: Dear Sir,

Punctuation terms in Spanish

.	**punto**	!	**se cierra admiración**
,	**coma**	" "	**comillas** (used as '...')
;	**punto y coma**	"	**se abren comillas**
:	**dos puntos**	"	**se cierran comillas**
...	**puntos suspensivos**	( )	**paréntesis**
¿ ?	**interrogación**	(	**se abre paréntesis**
¿	**se abre interrogación**	)	**se cierra paréntesis**
?	**se cierra interrogación**	–	**guión**
¡ !	**admiración**		
¡	**se abre admiración**	**punto y aparte**	new paragraph
		punto final	last full stop

Numbers

Cardinal (one, two, three *etc*)

cero	0	setenta	70
uno (un, una)	1	ochenta	80
dos	2	noventa	90
tres	3	cien (ciento)	100
cuatro	4	ciento uno(una)	101
cinco	5	ciento dos	102
seis	6	ciento diez	110
siete	7	ciento cuarenta y dos	142
ocho	8	doscientos(as)	200
nueve	9	doscientos(as) uno(una)	201
diez	10	doscientos(as) dos	202
once	11	trescientos(as)	300
doce	12	cuatrocientos(as)	400
trece	13	quinientos(as)	500
catorce	14	seiscientos(as)	600
quince	15	setecientos(as)	700
dieciséis	16	ochocientos(as)	800
diecisiete	17	novecientos(as)	900
dieciocho	18	mil	1.000
diecinueve	19	mil uno(una)	1.001
veinte	20	mil dos	1.002
veintiuno	21	mil doscientos veinte	1.220
veintidós	22	dos mil	2.000
treinta	30	cien mil	100.000
treinta y uno	31	doscientos(as) mil	200.000
cuarenta	40	un millón	1.000.000
cincuenta	50	dos millones	2.000.000
sesenta	60	un billón	1.000.000.000.000

Fractions		Others	
un medio; medio(a)	½	cero coma cinco	0,5
un tercio	⅓	uno coma tres	1,3
dos tercios	⅔	(el, un) diez por ciento	10%
un cuarto	¼	dos más/y dos	2 + 2
tres cuartos	¾	dos menos dos	2 − 2
un quinto	⅕	dos por dos	2 × 2
cinco y tres cuartos	5¾	dos dividido por dos	2 ÷ 2

Points to note on cardinals

uno drops the **o** before masculine nouns, and the same applies when in compound numerals:

- **un libro** 1 book, **treinta y un niños** 31 children

1, 21, 31 etc and 200, 300, 400 etc have feminine forms:

- **cuarenta y una euros** 41 euros, **quinientas libras** £500

ciento is used before numbers smaller than 100, otherwise **cien** is used:

- **ciento cuatro** 104 but **cien euros** 100 euros, **cien mil** 100,000 (see also page 210)

millón takes **de** before a noun:

- **un millón de personas** 1,000,000 people

mil is only found in the plural when meaning thousands of:

- **miles de solicitantes** thousands of applicants

cardinals normally precede ordinals:

- **los tres primeros pisos** the first three floors

ⓘ Note: The full stop is used with numbers over one thousand and the comma with decimals i.e. the opposite of English usage.

Ordinal Numbers (first, second, third *etc*)

primero (primer, primera)	$1^{o},1^{a}$	**undécimo(a)**	$11^{o},11^{a}$
segundo(a)	$2^{o},2^{a}$	**duodécimo(a)**	$12^{o},12^{a}$
tercero (tercer, tercera)	$3^{o},3^{a}$	**decimotercer(o)(a)**	$13^{o},13^{a}$
cuarto(a)	$4^{o},4^{a}$	**decimocuarto(a)**	$14^{o},14^{a}$
quinto(a)	$5^{o},5^{a}$	**decimoquinto(a)**	$15^{o},15^{a}$
sexto(a)	$6^{o},6^{a}$	**decimosexto(a)**	$16^{o},16^{a}$
séptimo(a)	$7^{o},7^{a}$	**decimoséptimo(a)**	$17^{o},17^{a}$
octavo(a)	$8^{o},8^{a}$	**decimoctavo(a)**	$18^{o},18^{a}$
noveno(a)	$9^{o},9^{a}$	**decimonoveno(a)**	$19^{o},19^{a}$
décimo(a)	$10^{o},10^{a}$	**vigésimo(a)**	$20^{o},20^{a}$

Points to note on ordinals

They agree in gender and in number with the noun, which they normally precede, except with royal titles:

la primera vez the first time
Felipe segundo Philip II

primero and **tercero** drop the **o** before a masculine singular noun:

el primer premio the first prize
el tercer día the third day

Beyond **décimo** ordinal numbers are rarely used, and they are replaced by the cardinal number placed immediately after the noun:

el siglo diecisiete the seventeenth century
Alfonso doce Alfonso XII
en el piso trece on the 13th floor

BUT: **vigésimo(a)** 20th
(but not with royal titles or centuries)
centésimo(a) 100th
milésimo(a) 1,000th
millonésimo(a) 1,000,000th

Other Uses

collective numbers:

un par	2, a couple
una decena (de personas)	about 10 (people)
una docena (de niños)	(about) a dozen (children)
una quincena (de hombres)	about fifteen (men)
una veintena* (de coches)	about twenty (cars)
un centenar, una centena (de casas)	about a hundred (houses)
cientos/centenares de personas	hundreds of people
un millar (de soldados)	about a thousand (soldiers)
miles/millares de moscas	thousands of flies

* 20, 30, 40, 50 can also be converted in the same way.

measurements:

veinte metros cuadrados 20 square metres
veinte metros cúbicos 20 cubic metres
un puente de cuarenta metros de largo/longitud a bridge 40 metres long

distance:

De aquí a Madrid hay 400 km Madrid is 400 km away
a siete km de aquí 7 km from here

Telephone numbers

Póngame con Madrid, el cuatro, cincuenta y ocho, veintidós, noventa y tres
I would like Madrid 458 22 93
Me da Valencia, el veinte, cincuenta y uno, setenta y tres
Could you get me Valencia 20 51 73
Extensión tres, tres, cinco/trescientos treinta y cinco
Extension number 335

ⓘ Note: In Spanish telephone numbers may be read out individually, but more frequently they are broken down into groups of two. They are written in groups of two or three numbers (never four).

The Time

¿Qué hora es? *What time is it?*

Es ... *(1 o'clock, midnight, noon)* Son las ... *(other times)*	It's ...
Es la una y cuarto	It's 1.15
Son las diez menos cinco	It's 9.55

00.00	**medianoche; las doce (de la noche)** midnight, twelve o'clock
00.10	**las doce y diez (de la noche)**
00.15	**las doce y cuarto**
00.30	**las doce y media**
00.45	**la una menos cuarto**
01.00	**la una (de la madrugada)** one a.m., one o'clock in the morning
01.10	**la una y diez (de la madrugada)**
02.45	**las tres menos cuarto**
07.00	**las siete (de la mañana)**
07.50	**las ocho menos diez**
12.00	**mediodía; las doce (de la mañana)** noon, twelve o'clock
13.00	**la una (de la tarde)** one p.m., one o'clock in the afternoon
19.00	**las siete (de la tarde)** seven p.m., seven o'clock in the evening
21.00	**las nueve (de la noche)** nine p.m., nine o'clock at night

ⓘ Note: When referring to a timetable, the 24 hour clock is used:

las dieciséis cuarenta y cinco	16.45
las veintiuna quince	21.15

Examples

¿A qué hora vas a venir? — A las siete	What time are you coming? — At seven o'clock
Las oficinas cierran de dos a cuatro	The offices are closed from two until four
Vendré a eso de/hacia las siete y media	I'll come at around 7.30
a las seis y pico	just after 6 o'clock
a las cinco en punto	at 5 o'clock sharp
entre las ocho y las nueve	between 8 and 9 o'clock
Son más de las tres y media	It's after half past three
Hay que estar allí lo más tarde a las diez	You have to be there by ten o'clock at the latest
Tiene para media hora	He'll be half an hour (at it)
Estuvo sin conocimiento durante un cuarto de hora	She was unconscious for a quarter of an hour
Les estoy esperando desde hace una hora/desde las dos	I've been waiting for them for an hour/since two o'clock
Se fueron hace unos minutos	They left a few minutes ago
Lo hice en veinte minutos	I did it in twenty minutes
El tren llega dentro de una hora	The train arrives in an hour('s time)
¿Cuánto (tiempo) dura la película?	How long does the film last?
por la mañana/tarde/noche	in the morning/afternoon or evening/at night
mañana por la mañana	tomorrow morning
ayer por la tarde	yesterday afternoon *or* evening
anoche	last night
anteayer	the day before yesterday
pasado mañana	the day after tomorrow

Dates

¿Qué día es hoy? ¿A qué día estamos?	What's the date today?
Es (el) ... Estamos a ...	It's the ...
uno/primero de mayo	1st of May
dos de mayo	2nd of May
veintiocho de mayo	28th of May
lunes tres de octubre	Monday the 3rd of October
Vienen el siete de marzo	They're coming on the 7th of March

ⓘ Note: Use cardinal numbers for dates. Only for the first of the month can the ordinal number sometimes be used.

Years

Nací en 1970	I was born in 1970
el veinte de enero de mil novecientos setenta	(on) 20th January 1970

Other expressions

en los años cincuenta	during the fifties
en el siglo veinte	in the twentieth century
en mayo	in May
lunes (quince)	Monday (the 15th)
el quince de marzo	on March the 15th
el/los lunes	on Monday/Mondays
dentro de diez días	in 10 days' time
hace diez días	10 days ago

Age

¿Qué edad tiene? ¿Cuántos años tiene?	How old is he/she?
Tiene 23 (años)	He/She is 23
Tiene unos 40 años	He/She is around 40
A los 21 años	At the age of 21

Index

The following index lists comprehensively both grammatical terms and key words in English and Spanish.